S. Pub.114-1

2015-2016

OFFICIAL
CONGRESSIONAL DIRECTORY
114TH CONGRESS

CONVENED JANUARY 6, 2015

JOINT COMMITTEE ON PRINTING
UNITED STATES CONGRESS

UNITED STATES GOVERNMENT PUBLISHING OFFICE
WASHINGTON, DC

Front Cover

Twilight view from the west front of the U.S. Capitol toward the National Mall. This photograph, offering an unusual perspective from one of the most recognized buildings in the world, evokes a sense of serenity and continuity at the end of a (typical) day in America's capital city.

Photo Credit: Architect of the Capitol.

U.S. GOVERNMENT OFFICIAL EDITION NOTICE

Use of ISBN Prefix

This is the Official U.S. Government edition of this publication and is herein identified to certify its authenticity. Use of the 0-16 ISBN prefix is for U.S. Government Publishing Office Official Editions only. The Superintendent of Documents of the U.S. Government Publishing Office requests that any reprinted edition clearly be labeled as a copy of the authentic work with a new ISBN.

For sale by the Superintendent of Documents, U.S. Government Publishing Office
Internet: bookstore.gpo.gov Phone: toll free (866) 512-1800; DC area (202) 512-1800
Fax: (202) 512-2250 Mail: Stop SSOP, Washington, DC 20402-0001

Paper Cover   ISBN-978-0-16-092997-7
Casebound   ISBN-978-0-16-092996-0

NOTES

Closing date for compilation of the Congressional Directory was February 12, 2016.

[Republicans in roman, Democrats in *italic*.]

The following changes have occurred in the membership of the 114th Congress since the election of November 4, 2014:

Name	Resigned, [Died] or (Interim Vacant Status)	Successor	Elected or [Appointed]	Sworn in
REPRESENTATIVES				
John A. Boehner, [1] 8th OH	Oct. 31, 2015	....	....	
Aaron Schock, 18th IL	Mar. 31, 2015	Darin LaHood	Sept. 10, 2015 ..	Sept. 17, 2015
Alan Nunnelee, 1st MS	[Feb. 6, 2015]	Trent Kelly	June 2, 2015	June 9, 2015
Michael G. Grimm, 11th NY	Jan. 5, 2015	Daniel M. Donovan, Jr.	May 5, 2015	May 12, 2015

[1] Honorable John A. Boehner served as the 53rd Speaker of the United States House of Representatives from 2011 to 2015. The Washington, DC, office and the district offices of former Representative John A. Boehner will continue to serve the people of the Eighth Congressional District of Ohio under the supervision of the Clerk of the House of Representatives. Representative Boehner resigned from Congress effective October 31, 2015.

SENATE

[Democrats in roman, Republicans in *italic*.]

REPRESENTATIVES

[Republicans in roman, Democrats in *italic*.]

The following changes have occurred in the membership of the 113th Congress since the election of November 6, 2012:

Name	Resigned, [Died] or [Term Ended]	Successor	Elected or [Appointed]	Sworn in
SENATOR				
John F. Kerry, MA [1]	Feb. 1, 2013	William M. Cowan	[Feb. 1, 2013] ..	Feb. 7, 2013
Frank R. Lautenberg, NJ	[June 3, 2013]	*Jeff Chiesa*	[June 6, 2013] ..	June 10, 2013
William M. Cowan, MA	[July 16, 2013]	Edward J. Markey	June 25, 2013 ..	July 16, 2013
Jeff Chiesa, NJ	[Oct. 31, 2013]	Cory A. Booker	Oct. 16, 2013 ...	Oct. 31, 2013
Max Baucus, MT [2]	Feb. 6, 2014	John E. Walsh	[Feb. 9, 2014] ..	Feb. 11, 2014
REPRESENTATIVES				
Jo Ann Emerson, 8th MO	Jan. 22, 2013	Jason Smith	June 4, 2013	June 5, 2013
Robin L. Kelly, 2d IL [3]	....	....	Apr. 9, 2013	Apr. 11, 2013
Mark Sanford, 1st SC [4]	....	....	May 7, 2013	May 15, 2013
Jo Bonner, 1st AL	Aug. 2, 2013	Bradley Byrne	Dec. 17, 2013 ..	Jan. 8, 2014
Rodney Alexander, 5th LA	Sept. 27, 2013	Vance M. McAllister ...	Nov. 16, 2013 ..	Nov. 21, 2013
C. W. Bill Young, 10th FL	[Oct. 18, 2013]	David W. Jolly	Mar. 11, 2014 ..	Mar. 13, 2014
Edward J. Markey, 5th MA	July 15, 2013 [5]	*Katherine M. Clark*	Dec. 10, 2013 ..	Dec. 12, 2013
Melvin L. Watt, 12th NC	Jan. 6, 2014	*Alma S. Adams*	Nov. 4, 2014	Nov. 12, 2014
Trey Radel, 19th FL	Jan. 27, 2014	Curt Clawson	June 24, 2014 ..	June 25, 2014
Robert E. Andrews, 1st NJ	Feb. 18, 2014	*Donald Norcross*	Nov. 4, 2014	Nov. 12, 2014
Eric Cantor, 7th VA	Aug. 18, 2014	Dave Brat	Nov. 4, 2014	Nov. 12, 2014

[1] Senator Kerry resigned to become Secretary of State.
[2] Senator Baucus resigned to become U.S. Ambassador to China.
[3] Representative Kelly elected to the 113th Congress, by special election, to fill the vacancy caused by the resignation of Representative Jesse L. Jackson, Jr., and took the oath of office on April 11, 2013.
[4] Representative Sanford elected to the 113th Congress, by special election, to fill the vacancy caused by the resignation of Representative Tim Scott, and took the oath of office on May 15, 2013.
[5] Representative Markey resigned following his election to the United States Senate.

FOREWORD

The *Congressional Directory* is one of the oldest working handbooks within the United States Government. While there were unofficial directories for Congress in one form or another beginning with the 1st Congress in 1789, the *Congressional Directory* published in 1847 for the 30th Congress is considered by scholars and historians to be the first official edition because it was the first to be ordered and paid for by Congress. With the addition of biographical sketches of legislators in 1867, the *Congressional Directory* attained its modern format.

The *Congressional Directory* is published by the United States Congress in partnership with the Government Publishing Office, at the direction of the Joint Committee on Printing under the authority of Title 44, Section 721 of the U.S. Code.

JOINT COMMITTEE ON PRINTING

Gregg Harper, Representative from Mississippi, *Chair*

Roy Blunt, Senator from Missouri, *Vice Chair*

House	**Senate**
Candice S. Miller, of Michigan.	Pat Roberts, of Kansas.
Rodney Davis, of Illinois.	John Boozman, of Arkansas.
Robert A. Brady, of Pennsylvania.	*Charles E. Schumer,* of New York.
Juan Vargas, of California.	*Tom Udall,* of New Mexico.

The 2015–2016 *Congressional Directory* was compiled by the Government Publishing Office, under the direction of the Joint Committee on Printing by:

Project Manager.—Margaret V. Ross Smith.

Editors: Michael Bush; Natoshka Faxio-Douglas; Regina G. Mitchell.

Typographer.—Michael E. Colbert.

Proofreader/Editor.—Rowena F. Dagang.

State District Maps.—Election Data Services, Inc.

Representatives' Zip Codes.—House Office of Mailing Services/U.S. Postal Service.

For sale by the Superintendent of Documents, U.S. Government Publishing Office

Internet: bookstore.gpo.gov; Phone: toll free (866) 512–1800; DC area (202) 512–1800

Fax: (202) 512–2250; Mail: Stop SSOP, Washington, DC 20402–0001

Paper Cover	ISBN–978–0–16–092997–7
Casebound	ISBN–978–0–16–092996–0

CONTENTS

Name Index on page 1141

Contents

Contents

Page

Page

Contents

114th Congress*

THE VICE PRESIDENT

JOSEPH R. BIDEN, JR., Democrat, of Wilmington, DE; born in Scranton, PA, November 20, 1942; education: St. Helena's School, Wilmington, DE; Archmere Academy, Claymont, DE; A.B., history and political science, University of Delaware; J.D., Syracuse University College of Law; married: Jill Tracy Biden; children: Robert Hunter Biden and Ashley Blazer Biden; admitted to the bar, December 1968, Wilmington, DE; engaged in private practice until 1972; served on New Castle County Council, 1970–72; elected to the U.S. Senate on November 7, 1972; reelected to each succeeding Senate term; served on committees: chair, Foreign Relations; Judiciary; elected as 47th Vice President of the United States on November 4, 2008; took the oath of office on January 20, 2009 and took the oath of office for a second time on January 20, 2013.

The Office of the Vice President is S–212 in the Capitol. The Vice President has offices in the Dirksen Senate Office Building, the Eisenhower Executive Office Building (EEOB) and the White House (West Wing).

Assistant to the President and Chief of Staff to the Vice President.—Steve Ricchetti, EEOB, room 272, 456–9951.
Deputy Assistant to the President and Chief of Staff to Dr. Jill Biden.—Sheila Nix, EEOB, room 201, 456–7458.
Deputy Assistant to the President and and Counselor to the Vice President.—Don Graves, EEOB, room 282, 456–2982.
Chief Economist and Economic Advisor to the Vice President.—Ben Harris, EEOB, room 289A, 456–1437.
Deputy Assistant to the President and National Security Advisor to the Vice President.— Colin Kahl, EEOB, room 208, 456–2744.
Special Assistant to the President and Senior Advisor to the Vice President.—Greg Schultz, EEOB, room 204, 456–3639.
Special Assistant to the President and Director of Intergovernmental Affairs to the Vice President.—Evan "Michael" Schrum, EEOB, room 202A, 456–1734.
Special Assistant to the President and Director of Public Engagement to the Vice President.— Carri Twigg, EEOB, room 202A, 456–6222.
Counsel to the Vice President.—Victoria Nourse, EEOB, room 270, 456–2734.
Press Secretary to the Vice President.—Kendra Barkoff, EEOB, room 284A, 456–4390.
Special Assistant to the Vice President and Director of Legislative Affairs.—Tonya Williams, EEOB, room 279A, 456–1540.
Director of:
  Administration and Associate Counsel for Fiscal Law.—Faisal Amin, EEOB, room 263A, 456–2599.
  Operations and Planning.—Chad Bolduc, EEOB, room 269A, 456–3878.
  Scheduling.—Virginia "Ginna" Lance, EEOB, room 265A, 456–6264.
Personal Aide and Advisor to the Vice President.—John Flynn, West Wing, 456–1715.
Assistants to the Vice President: Kathy Chung, 456–1715, West Wing; Anne Marie Muldoon, 456–1732, West Wing.

---

*Biographies are based on information furnished or authorized by the respective Senators and Representatives.

ALABAMA

(Population 2010, 4,779,736)

SENATORS

RICHARD C. SHELBY, Republican, of Tuscaloosa, AL; born in Birmingham, AL, May 6, 1934; education: attended the public schools; B.A., University of Alabama, 1957; LL.B., University of Alabama School of Law, 1963; professional: attorney; admitted to the Alabama bar in 1961 and commenced practice in Tuscaloosa; member, Alabama State Senate, 1970–78; law clerk, Supreme Court of Alabama, 1961–62; city prosecutor, Tuscaloosa, 1963–71; U.S. Magistrate, Northern District of Alabama, 1966–70; special assistant Attorney General, State of Alabama, 1969–71; chairman, legislative council of the Alabama Legislature, 1977–78; former president, Tuscaloosa County Mental Health Association; member of Alabama Code Revision Committee, 1971–75; member: Phi Alpha Delta legal fraternity, Tuscaloosa County; Alabama and American bar associations; First Presbyterian Church of Tuscaloosa; Exchange Club; American Judicature Society; Alabama Law Institute; married: the former Annette Nevin in 1960; children: Richard C., Jr., and Claude Nevin; committees: chair, Banking, Housing, and Urban Affairs; Appropriations; Rules and Administration; elected to the 96th Congress on November 7, 1978; reelected to the three succeeding Congresses; elected to the U.S. Senate on November 4, 1986; reelected to each succeeding Senate term.

Office Listings ·

http://shelby.senate.gov   twitter: @senshelby

304 Russell Senate Office Building, Washington, DC 20510	(202) 224–5744
Chief of Staff.—Alan Hanson.	FAX: 224–3416
Personal Secretary / Appointments.—Anne Caldwell.	
Communications Director.—Torrie Miller.	
The Federal Building, 1118 Greensboro Avenue, #240, Tuscaloosa, AL 35401	(205) 759–5047
Vance Federal Building, Room 321, 1800 5th Avenue North, Birmingham, AL 35203	(205) 731–1384
John A. Campbell Federal Courthouse, Suite 445, 113 St. Joseph Street, Mobile, AL 36602	(251) 694–4164
Frank M. Johnson Federal Courthouse, Suite 208, 15 Lee Street, Montgomery, AL 36104 ..	(334) 223–7303
Huntsville International Airport, 1000 Glenn Hearn Boulevard, Box 20127, Huntsville, AL 35824	(256) 772–0460

* * *

JEFF SESSIONS, Republican, of Mobile, AL; born in Selma, AL, December 24, 1946; education: graduated, Wilcox County High School, Camden, AL; B.A., Huntingdon College, Montgomery, AL, 1969; J.D., University of Alabama, Tuscaloosa, 1973; professional: U.S. Army Reserves, captain, 1973–86; attorney; admitted to the Alabama bar in 1973 and commenced practice for Guin, Bouldin and Porch in Russellville, 1973–75; Assistant U.S. Attorney, South District of Alabama, 1975–77; attorney for Stockman and Bedsole, 1977–81; U.S. Attorney, South District of Alabama, 1981–93; attorney for Stockman, Bedsole and Sessions, 1993–94; Attorney General, State of Alabama, 1994–96; member: Huntingdon College Board of Trustees; Samford University, Board of Overseers; delegate, General Conference, United Methodist Church; Montgomery Lions Club; Mobile United Methodist Inner City Mission; American Bar Association; Ashland Place United Methodist Church; married: the former Mary Blackshear, 1969; children: Ruth, Mary Abigail, and Samuel; International Narcotics Control Caucus; committees: Armed Services; Budget; Environment and Public Works; Judiciary; elected to the U.S. Senate on November 5, 1996; reelected to each succeeding Senate term.

Office Listings

http://sessions.senate.gov

326 Russell Senate Office Building, Washington, DC 20510	(202) 224–4124
Chief of Staff.—Rick Dearborn.	FAX: 224–3149
Scheduler.—Kate Hollis.	
Executive Assistant.—Peggi Hanrahan.	
Press Secretary.—Andrew Logan.	
341 Vance Federal Building, 1800 Fifth Avenue North, Birmingham, AL 35203	(205) 731–1500
Field Representative.—Virginia Amason.	
Colonial Bank Centre, Suite 2300–A, 41 West I–65 Service Road North, Mobile, AL 36608	(251) 414–3083
Field Representative.—Valerie Day.	
200 Clinton Avenue, NW., Suite 802, Huntsville, AL 35801	(256) 533–0979
Field Representative.—Lisa Montgomery.	
7550 Halcyon Summit Drive, Suite 150, Montgomery, AL 36117	(334) 244–7017

Office Listings—Continued

State Director.—Rick Dearborn.

REPRESENTATIVES

FIRST DISTRICT

BRADLEY BYRNE, Republican, of Fairhope, AL; born in Mobile, AL, February 16, 1955; education: B.A. in public policy and history, Duke University, 1977; J.D., the University of Alabama, 1980; professional: Alabama State Board of Education; Chancellor of two-year college system, Alabama State Senate/Organizations: Leadership Alabama, Alabama PTA, U.S. Supreme Court Bar, Alabama State Workforce Planning Council; chair/awards: Council for Leaders in Alabama Schools Legislative Leadership Award (2007); Alabama Wildlife Foundation Legislator of the Year Award (2005); South Alabama Literacy Champion Award (2006); religion: Episcopalian; wife: Rebecca; children: Patrick, Laura, Kathleen, and Colin; committees: Armed Services; Education and the Workforce; Rules; elected by special election to the 113th Congress on December 17, 2013, to fill the vacancy caused by the resignation of United States Representative Jo Bonner; reelected to the 114th Congress on November 4, 2014.

Office Listings
http://byrne.house.gov

119 Cannon House Office Building, Washington, DC 20515	(202) 225–4931
Chief of Staff.—Alex Schriver.	FAX: 225–0562
Legislative Director.—Matt Weinstein.	
Communications Director. Seth Morrow.	
Scheduler.—Errical Bryant.	
11 North Water Street, Suite 15290, Mobile, AL 36602	(251) 690 2811
502 West Lee Street, Summerdale, AL 26580	(251) 989–2664

Counties: BALDWIN, CLARKE (part), ESCAMBIA, MOBILE, MONROE, AND WASHINGTON. Population (2010), 687,841.

ZIP Codes: 36420, 36425–27, 36432, 36439, 36441, 36444–46, 36451, 36460–62, 36470–71, 36475, 36480–83, 36502–05, 36507, 36509, 36511–13, 36518, 36521–30, 36532–33, 36535–36, 36538–39, 36541–45, 36547–51, 36553, 36555–56, 6558–62, 36564, 36567–69, 36571–72, 36575–85, 36587, 36590, 36601–13, 36615–19, 36628, 36633, 36640, 36652, 36660, 36663, 36670–71, 36685, 36688–89, 36691, 36693, 36695, 36768–69

* * *

SECOND DISTRICT

MARTHA ROBY, Republican, of Montgomery, AL; born in Montgomery, July 26, 1976; education: B.M., New York University, New York, NY, 1998; J.D., Cumberland School of Law at Samford University, Birmingham, AL, 2001; professional: attorney, Copeland, Franco, Screws, and Gill, P.A.; Councilor, District Seven, City of Montgomery; awards: Alabama's Most Outstanding Minuteman (2014), Alabama Association of School Boards Legislative Award (2013), Running Start Women to Watch (2012); religion: Christian (Presbyterian); family: husband, Riley; children: Margaret and George; committees: Appropriations; Select Committee on Benghazi; elected to the 112th Congress on November 2, 2010; reelected to each succeeding Congress.

Office Listings
http://roby.house.gov   http://twitter.com/repmartharoby

442 Cannon House Office Building, Washington, DC 20515	(202) 225–2901
Chief of Staff.—Stephen Boyd.	FAX: 225–8913
Legislative Director.—Mike Albares.	
Communications Director.—Todd Stacy.	
Director of Scheduling.—Jessica Hamilton.	
401 Adams Avenue, Suite 160, Montgomery, AL 36104	(334) 277–9113
217 Graceland Drive, Suite 5, Dothan, AL 36303	(334) 794–9680
505 East Three Notch Street, Andalusia City Hall, Room 322, Andalusia, AL 36420	(334) 428–1129

Counties: AUTAUGA, BARBOUR, BULLOCK, BUTLER, COFFEE, CONECUH, COVINGTON, CRENSHAW, DALE, ELMORE, GENEVA, HENRY, HOUSTON, MONTGOMERY (part), PIKE. Population (2010), 673,887.

ZIP Codes: 35010, 36003, 36005–06, 36009–10, 36016–17, 36020, 36022, 36024–30, 36032–38, 36041–43, 36046–49, 36051–54, 36064, 36066–67, 36069, 36071, 36078–82, 36089, 36091–93, 36104–13, 36115–17, 36301, 36303, 36305,

36310–14, 36316–23, 36330, 36340, 36343–46, 36350–53, 36360, 36362, 36370–71, 36373–76, 36401, 36420–21, 36426, 36432, 36442, 36453–56, 36460, 36467, 36471, 36473–77, 36483, 36502, 36703, 36749, 36758, 36860

* * *

THIRD DISTRICT

MIKE ROGERS, Republican, of Saks, AL; born in Hammond, IN, July 16, 1958; education: B.A., Jacksonville State University, 1981; M.P.A., Jacksonville State University, 1984; J.D., Birmingham School of Law, 1991; professional: attorney; awards: Anniston Star Citizen of the Year, 1998; public service: Calhoun County Commissioner, 1987–91; Alabama House of Representatives, 1994–2002; family: married to Beth; children: Emily, Evan, and Elliot; committees: Agriculture; Armed Services; Homeland Security; elected to the 108th Congress on November 5, 2002; reelected to each succeeding Congress.

Office Listings

http://www/mikerogers.house.gov   twitter: @repmikerogersal

324 Cannon House Office Building, Washington, DC 20515 .... (202) 225–3261
    Chief of Staff.—Marshall Macomber.   FAX: 226–8485
    Deputy Chief of Staff.—Chris Brinson.
    Legislative Director.—Whitney Verett.
    Press Secretary.—Shea Snider.
    Scheduler.—Vincent Lynch.
1129 Noble Street, 104 Federal Building, Anniston, AL 36201 .... (256) 236–5655
    District Director.—Sheri Rollins.
1819 Pepperell Parkway, Suite 203, Opelika, AL 36801 .... (334) 745–6221
    Field Representative.—Cheryl Cunningham.

Counties: CALHOUN, CHAMBERS, CHEROKEE, CLAY, CLEBURNE, COOSA (part), LEE, MACON, MONTGOMERY (part), RANDOLPH, RUSSELL, ST. CLAIR, TALLADEGA, AND TALLAPOOSA. Population (2010), 682,819.

ZIP Codes: 30165, 31905, 35004, 35010, 35014, 35032, 35044, 35052, 35054, 35072, 35082, 35089, 35094, 35096, 35112, 35120–21, 35125, 35128, 35131, 35133, 35135, 35146, 35149–51, 35160, 35173, 35178, 35901, 35903, 35905, 35953, 35959–61, 35967, 35972–73, 35983, 35987, 36013, 36027, 36029, 36031, 36039, 36052, 36064, 36075, 36078, 36083, 36088–89, 36116–17, 36201, 36203, 36205–07, 36250–51, 36255–56, 36258, 36260, 36262–69, 36271–74, 36276–80, 36801, 36804, 36830, 36832, 36849–50, 36852–56, 36858–63, 36865–67, 36869–71, 36874–75, 36877, 36879

* * *

FOURTH DISTRICT

ROBERT B. ADERHOLT, Republican, of Haleyville, AL; born in Haleyville, July 22, 1965; education: graduate, Birmingham Southern University; J.D., Cumberland School of Law, Samford University; professional: attorney; assistant legal advisor to Governor Fob James, 1995–96; Haleyville municipal judge, 1992–96; George Bush delegate, Republican National Convention, 1992; Republican nominee for the 17th District, Alabama House of Representatives, 1990; married: Caroline McDonald; children: Mary Elliott and Robert Hayes; committees: Appropriations; elected to the 105th Congress; reelected to each succeeding Congress.

Office Listings

http://www.aderholt.house.gov   twitter: @robert_aderholt

235 Cannon House Office Building, Washington, DC 20515 .... (202) 225–4876
    Chief of Staff.—Brian Rell.   FAX: 225–5587
    Legislative Director.—Mark Dawson.
    Communications Director / Press Secretary.—Brian Rell, Carson Clark.
    Administrative Director.—Chris Lawson.
Carl Elliott Building, 1710 Alabama Avenue, Room 247, Jasper, AL 35501 .... (205) 221–2310
    District Field Director.—Paul Housel.
205 Fourth Avenue, Northeast, Suite 104, Cullman, AL 35055 .... (256) 734–6043
    Director of Constituent Services.—Jennifer Taylor.
107 Federal Building, 600 Broad Street, Gadsden, AL 35901 .... (256) 546–0201
    Field Representative.—Alex Mastin.
1011 George Wallace Boulevard, Suite 146, Tuscumbia, AL 35674 .... (256) 381–3450
    Field Representative.—Kreg Kennedy.

Counties: BLOUNT (part), CHEROKEE (part), COLBERT, CULLMAN, DEKALB, ETOWAH, FAYETTE, FRANKLIN, JACKSON (part), LAMAR, LAWRENCE, MARION, MARSHALL, TUSCALOOSA (part), WALKER, WINSTON. Population (2010), 682,029.

ZIP Codes: 35006, 35013, 35016, 35019, 35031, 35033, 35049, 35053, 35055, 35057–58, 35062–63, 35070, 35077, 35079, 35083, 35087, 35097–98, 35121, 35126, 35130, 35133, 35146, 35172, 35175, 35179–80, 35447, 35461, 35481, 35501,

35503–04, 35540–46, 35548–50, 35552–55, 35563–65, 35570–72, 35574–82, 35584–87, 35592–94, 35601, 35603, 35619, 35621–22, 35640, 35653–54, 35670, 35673, 35747, 35754–55, 35760, 35765, 35769, 35771, 35775–76, 35901, 35903–07, 35950–54, 35956–57, 35961–64, 35966–68, 35971–72, 35974–76, 35978–81, 35984, 35986–90, 36272

* * *

FIFTH DISTRICT

MO BROOKS, Republican, of Huntsville, AL; born in Charleston, SC, April 29, 1954; education: B.A., Duke University, Durham, NC, 1975; J.D., University of Alabama School of Law, Tuscaloosa, AL, 1978; professional: lawyer, private practice, partner in Leo and Brooks law firm; prosecutor, Office of the District Attorney, Tuscaloosa County, AL, 1978–80; clerk, Circuit Court Judge John Snodgrass, 1980–82; member of the Alabama State House of Representatives, 1983–91; district attorney, Office of the District Attorney, Madison County, AL, 1991–93; special assistant attorney general, state of Alabama, 1995–2002; commissioner, Madison County, AL, board of commissions, 1996–2010; religion: Christian; married: Martha; four children; committees: Armed Services; Foreign Affairs; Science, Space, and Technology; elected to the 112th Congress on November 2, 2010; reelected to each succeeding Congress.

Office Listings

http://brooks.house.gov   https://twitter.com/repmobrooks

1230 Longworth House Office Building, Washington, DC 20515 .... (202) 225–4801
    Chief of Staff/Legislative Director.—Mark Pettitt.   FAX: 225–4392
    Scheduler/Office Manager.—Kelly Zams.
2101 West Clinton Avenue, Suite 302, Huntsville, AL 35805 .... (256) 551–0190
    District Director.—Tiffany Noel.
    Field Representative.—Kathy Murray.
    Special Projects Coordinator and Caseworker.—Sandy Garvey.
    Caseworkers: Debi Echols, Timothy Jackson.
302 Lee Street, Room 86, Decatur, AL 35601 .... (256) 355–9400
    District Field Representative and Caseworker.—Johnny Turner.
102 South Court Street, Suite 310, Florence, AL 35630 .... (256) 718–5155
    District Field Representative and Caseworker.—Laura Smith.

Counties: JACKSON, LAUDERDALE, LIMESTONE, MADISON, MORGAN. Population (2010), 718,724.

ZIP Codes: 35652, 35648, 35645, 35630–34, 35677, 35617, 35610 15, 35620, 35647–49, 35671, 35741, 35748–52, 35756–63, 35767, 35773–76, 35801–16, 35824, 35893–94, 35601–03, 35609–15, 35619–21, 35622, 35640, 35670, 35673, 35699, 35754, 35775, 35740, 35744–46, 35751–52, 35755–69, 35771, 35772, 35774, 35776, 35958, 35966, 35979, 35016, 35739–42, 35896, 35898–99, 35958, 35966, 35978–79

* * *

SIXTH DISTRICT

GARY PLAMER, Republican, of Hoover AL; born in Hackleburg, AL, May 14, 1954; education: B.S., University of Alabama, Tuscaloosa, 1977; professional: president, Alabama Policy Institute; founding member, State Policy Network; member, Briarwood Presbyterian Church; spouse: Ann; children: Claire, Kathleen, and Rob; committees: Budget; Oversight and Government Reform; Science, Space, and Technology; elected to the 114th Congress on November 4, 2014.

Office Listings

https://palmer.house.gov   http://www.facebook.com/usrepresentativegarypalmer
twitter @usrepgarypalmer   http://www.youtube.com/channel/ucyzfp-cnivljy3acac9oppq

206 Cannon House Office Building, Washington, DC 20515 .... (202) 225 4921
    Chief of Staff.—William Smith.   FAX: 225–2082
    Press Secretary.—Cliff Smith.
    Legislative Director.—Cari Kelly.
    Scheduler.—Nonie Brown.
3535 Grandview Parkway, Suite 525, Birmingham, AL 35243 .... (205) 968–1290
703 Second Avenue North, P.O. Box 502, Clanton, AL 35046 .... (205) 280–6846
202 3rd Avenue, East Oneonta, AL 35121 .... (205) 274–2136

Counties: BIBB, BLOUNT (part), CHILTON, COOSA (part), JEFFERSON (part), SHELBY. CITIES AND TOWNSHIPS: Adamsville, Allgood, Altoona, Argo, Bessemer, Birmingham, Blountsville, Brantleyville, Brent, Brook Highland, Brookside, Calera, Cardiff, Center Point, Centreville, Chelsea, Clanton, Clay, Cleveland, Columbiana, Concord, County Line, Dunnavant, Forestdale, Fultondale, Gardendale, Garden City, Goodwatter, Graysville, Harpersville, Hayden, Helena, Highland Lake,

Hissop, Homewood, Hoover, Hueytown, Indian Springs Village, Irondale, Jemison, Kellyton, Kimberly, Leeds, Locust Fork, Maplesville, Maytown, McDonald Chapel, Meadowbrook, Montevallo, Morris, Mount Olive, Mountain Brook, Mulga, Nectar, North Johns, Oneonta, Pelham, Pinson, Pleasant Grove, Rock Creek, Rockford, Rosa, Shelby, Shoal Creek, Smoke Rise, Snead, Sterrett, Susan Moore, Sylvan Springs, Tarrant, Thorsby, Trafford, Trussville, Vance, Vandiver, Vestavia Hills, Vincent, Warrior, West Blocton, West Jefferson, Westover, Wilsonville, Wilton, and Woodstock. Population (2010), 682 ,819.

ZIP Codes: 35004–07, 35015, 35022–23, 35035, 35040, 35043, 35046, 35048, 35051–52, 35054, 35060, 35062–63, 35068, 35071, 35073–74, 35078–80, 35085, 35091, 35094, 35096, 35111–12, 35114–20, 35123–28, 35130–31, 35133, 35135, 35137, 35139, 35142–44, 35146–48, 35151, 35171–73, 35175–76, 35178, 35180–88, 35201–03, 35205–07, 35209–10, 35212–17, 35219, 35222–26, 35230, 35233, 35235–37, 35240, 35242–46, 35249, 35253–55, 35259–61, 35266, 35277–83, 35285, 35287–99, 35402–03, 35406–07, 35444, 35446, 35452, 35456–58, 35466, 35468, 35473, 35475–76, 35480, 35482, 35490, 35546, 35579, 35953, 35987, 36006, 36051, 36064, 36091, 36750, 36758, 36790, 36792–93

* * *

SEVENTH DISTRICT

TERRI A. SEWELL, Democrat, of Birmingham, AL; born in Selma, AL, January 1, 1965; education: graduated from Selma High School, Selma, AL; B.A., *cum laude,* Princeton University, Princeton, NJ, 1986; master's degree with first class honors from Oxford University, Oxford, UK, 1988; J.D., Harvard Law School, Cambridge, MA, 1992; professional: attorney; judicial law clerk to the Honorable Chief Judge U.W. Clemon, U.S. District Court, Northern District of Alabama, in Birmingham; memberships and boards: Treasurer of the Board and Chair of the Finance Committee; St. Vincent's Foundation; Girl Scouts of Cahaba Council; Community Advisory Board for the DAB Minority Health and Research Center; Governing Board of the Alabama Council on Economic Education; Corporate Partners Council for the Birmingham Art Museum; Alpha Kappa Alpha Sorority, Inc.; professional affiliations: American Bar Association; National Bar Association; Alabama Bar Association; religion: African Methodist; Chief Deputy Whip; committees: Financial Services; Permanent Select Committee on Intelligence; elected to the 112th Congress on November 2, 2010; reelected to each succeeding Congress.

Office Listings

http://sewell.house.gov   twitter: @repterrisewell
facebook: https://www.facebook.com/repsewell

1133 Longworth House Office Building, Washington, DC 20515	(202) 225–2665
Chief of Staff.—Shashrina Thomas.	FAX: 226–9567
Legislative Director.—Cachavious English.	
Communications Director.—Deshundra Jefferson.	
Legislative Assistant.—Hillary Beard.	
Legislative Correspondent.—Robert Nuttall.	
Executive Assistant.—Keri Hunigan.	
Two 20th Street North, Suite 1130, Birmingham, AL 35203	(205) 254–1960
District Director.—Chasseny Lewis.	FAX: 254–1974
Federal Building, 908 Alabama Avenue, Suite 112, Selma, AL 36701	(334) 877–4414
	FAX: 877–4489
2501 7th Street, Suite 300, Tuscaloosa, AL 35401	(205) 752–5380
	FAX: 752–5899
101 South Lawrence Street, Montgomery, AL 36104	(334) 262–1919
	FAX: 262–1921

Counties: CHOCTAW, CLARKE (part), DALLAS, GREENE, HALE, JEFFERSON (part), MARENGO, PERRY, PICKENS (part), SUMTER, TUSCALOOSA (part), AND WILCOX. Population (2010), 682,742.

ZIP Codes: 35005–06, 35020–23, 35034, 35036, 35041–42, 35061, 35064, 35068, 35071, 35073–74, 35079, 35111, 35117, 35126–27, 35173, 35175, 35184, 35188, 35203–15, 35217–18, 35221–22, 35224, 35228–29, 35233–35, 35238, 35243, 35401, 35404–06, 35440–44, 35446–49, 35452–53, 35456, 35459–60, 35462–64, 35466, 35469–71, 35473–78, 35480–81, 35485–87, 35490–91, 35546, 35601, 35603, 35640, 35754, 36030, 36032, 36040, 36064, 36105, 36435–36, 36451, 36482, 36524, 36540, 36545, 36558, 36701–03, 36720, 36722–23, 36726–28, 36732, 36736, 36738, 36740–42, 36744–45, 36748–54, 36756, 36758–59, 36761–69, 36773, 36775–76, 36782–86, 36790, 36792–93, 36901, 36904, 36906–08, 36910, 36912–13, 36915–16, 36919, 36921–22, 36925

ALASKA

(Population 2010, 710,231)

SENATORS

LISA MURKOWSKI, Republican, of Anchorage, AK; born in Ketchikan, AK, May 22, 1957; education: Willamette University, 1975–77; Georgetown University, 1978–80, B.A., economics; Willamette College of Law, 1982–85, J.D.; professional: attorney; private law practice; Alaska and Anchorage Bar Associations: public service: Anchorage Equal Rights Commission; Anchorage District Court Attorney, 1987–89; Task Force on the Homeless, 1990–91; Alaska State Representative, 1998–2002; family: married to Verne Martell; children: Nicholas and Matthew; committees: chair, Energy and Natural Resources; Appropriations; Health, Education, Labor, and Pensions; Indian Affairs; appointed to the U.S. Senate on December 20, 2002; elected to the 109th Congress for a full Senate term on November 2, 2004; reelected as a write-in candidate to the 112th Congress on November 2, 2010.

Office Listings

http://murkowski.senate.gov   https://www.facebook.com/senlisamurkowski
https://twitter.com/lisamurkowski

709 Hart Senate Office Building, Washington, DC 20510	(202) 224–6665
Chief of Staff.—Edward G. Hild.	FAX: 224–5301
Legislative Director.—Kate Williams.	
Scheduler.—Kristen Daimler-Nothdurft.	
510 L Street, Suite 550, Anchorage, AK 99501	(907) 271–3735
101 12th Avenue, Room 329, Fairbanks, AK 99701	(907) 456–0233
4079 Tongass Avenue, Suite 204, Ketchikan, AK 99901	(907) 225–6880
851 East Westpoint Drive, Wasilla, AK 99654	(907) 376–7665
805 Frontage Road, Suite 105, Kenai, AK 99611	(907) 283–5808
800 Glacier Avenue, Suite 101, Juneau, AK	(907) 586–7277

* * *

DAN SULLIVAN, Republican, of Anchorage, AK; born in Fairview Park, OH, November 13, 1964; education: B.A., Economics, Harvard University, 1987; Joint Masters of Science in Foreign Service and J.D., Georgetown University, 1993; military: United States Marine Corps 1993–97; United States Marine Corps Reserves 1997–present, attaining rank of lieutenant colonel; public service: Director, National Security Council Staff, 2002–04; U.S. Assistant Secretary of State for Economic, Energy and Business Affairs, 2006–09; Attorney General, State of Alaska, 2009–10; Commissioner, Alaska Department of Natural Resources, 2011–13; professional: attorney, private law practice,1997–2001; awards: National Security Council Outstanding Service Award; Defense Meritorious Service Medal; religion: Catholic; family: married to Julie Fate Sullivan; children: Meghan, Isabella, and Laurel; committees: Armed Services; Commerce, Science, and Transportation; Environment and Public Works; Veterans' Affairs; elected to the U.S. Senate on November 4, 2014.

Office Listings

http://sullivan.senate.gov

702 Hart Senate Office Building, Washington, DC 20510	(202) 224–3004
Chief of Staff.—Joe Balash.	FAX: 224–6501
Legislative Director.—Peter Henry.	
Scheduling Director.—DeLynn Henry.	
510 L Street, Suite 750, Anchorage, AK 99501	(907) 271–5915
101 12th Avenue, Room 328, Fairbanks, AK 99701	(907) 456–0261
851 East Westpoint Drive, Suite 309, Wasilla, AK 99654	(907) 357–9956
800 Glacier Avenue, Suite 101, Juneau, AK 99801	(907) 586–7277
805 Frontage Road, Suite 101, Kenai, AK 99611	(907) 283–4000
1900 First Avenue, Suite 225, Ketchikan, AK 99901	(907) 225–6880

REPRESENTATIVE

AT LARGE

DON YOUNG, Republican, of Fort Yukon, AK; born in Meridian, CA, June 9, 1933; education: A.A., Yuba Junior College; B.A., Chico State College, Chico, CA; Honorary Doctorate of Laws, University of Alaska, Fairbanks; State House of Representatives, 1966–70; U.S. Army, 41st Tank Battalion, 1955–957; elected member of the State Senate, 1970–73; served on the Fort Yukon City Council for six years, serving four years as mayor; educator for nine years; river boat captain; member: National Education Association, Elks, Lions, Jaycees; widowed: Lula Fredson of Fort Yukon; children: Joni and Dawn; committees: Natural Resources; Transportation and Infrastructure; elected to the 93rd Congress in a special election, March 6, 1973, to fill the vacancy created by the death of Congressman Nick Begich; reelected to each succeeding Congress.

Office Listings

http://www.donyoung.house.gov

2314 Rayburn House Office Building, Washington, DC 20515	(202) 225–5765
Chief of Staff.—Pamela Day.	FAX: 225–0425
Executive Assistant / Office Manager.—Paula Conru.	
Legislative Director.—Scott Leathard.	
4241 B Street, Suite 203, Anchorage, AK 99503	(907) 271–5978
	FAX: 271–5950
100 Cushman Street, Suite 307, Fairbanks, AK 99707	(907) 456–0210
	FAX: 456–0279

Population (2010), 710,231.

ZIP Codes: 99501–24, 99540, 99546–59, 99561, 99563–69, 99571–81, 99583–91, 99599, 99602–15, 99619–22, 99624–41, 99643–45, 99647–72, 99674–95, 99697, 99701–12, 99714, 99716, 99720–27, 99729–30, 99732–34, 99736–86, 99788–89, 99791, 99801–03, 99811, 99820–21, 99824–27, 99829–30, 99832–33, 99835–36, 99840–41, 99850

ARIZONA

(Population 2010, 6,392,017)

SENATORS

JOHN McCAIN, Republican, of Phoenix, AZ; born in the Panama Canal Zone, August 29, 1936; education: graduated, Episcopal High School, Alexandria, VA, 1954; graduated, U.S. Naval Academy, Annapolis, MD, 1958; National War College, Washington, DC, 1973; retired captain (pilot), U.S. Navy, 1958–81; military awards: Silver Star, Bronze Star, Legion of Merit, Purple Heart, and Distinguished Flying Cross; chair, International Republican Institute; married to the former Cindy Hensley; seven children: Doug, Andy, Sidney, Meghan, Jack, Jim, and Bridget; committees: chair, Armed Services; Homeland Security and Governmental Affairs; Indian Affairs; elected to the 98th Congress in November, 1982; reelected to the 99th Congress in November, 1984; elected to the U.S. Senate in November, 1986; reelected to each succeeding Senate term.

Office Listings

http://mccain.senate.gov   twitter: @senjohnmccain

218 Russell Senate Office Building, Washington, DC 20510	(202) 224–2235
Chief of Staff.—Pablo Carrillo.	TDD: 224–7132
Legislative Director.—Joseph Donoghue.	
Communications Director.—Brian Rogers.	
Scheduler.—Ellen Cahill.	
2201 East Camelback Road, Suite 115, Phoenix, AZ 85016	(602) 952–2410
	TDD: 952–0170
122 North Cortez Street, Suite 108, Prescott, AZ 86301	(928) 445–0833
407 West Congress Street, Suite 103, Tucson, AZ 85701	(602) 670–6334

* * *

JEFFRY "JEFF" FLAKE, Republican, of Mesa, AZ; born in Snowflake, AZ, December 31, 1962; education: B.A. degree in international relations, Brigham Young University, Provo, UT, 1986; M.A. degree, political science, Brigham Young University, Provo, UT, 1987; professional: executive director, Foundation for Democracy, Namibia 1989–90; director, Interface Public Affairs, Washington, DC, 1990–92; executive director, Goldwater Institute, Phoenix, AZ, 1992–99; member, United States House of Representatives, 2001–13; religion: Church of Jesus Christ of Latter-Day Saints; family: wife, Cheryl; children: Ryan, Alexis, Austin, Tanner, Dallin; grandchild: Aiden Jeffry; committees: Energy and Natural Resources; Foreign Relations; Judiciary; Special Committee on Aging; elected to the U.S. Senate on November 6, 2012.

Office Listings

http://flake.senate.gov   twitter: @jeffflake   www.facebook.com/senatorjeffflake

S–413 Russell Senate Office Building, Washington, DC 20510	(202) 224–4521
Chief of Staff.—Steve Voeller.	FAX: 228–0515
Legislative Director.—Chandler Morse.	
Administrative Director.—Celeste Gold.	
Scheduler.—Megan Runyan.	
2200 East Camelback Road, Suite 120, Phoenix, AZ 85016	(602) 840–1891
	FAX: 840–4848
6840 North Oracle Road, Suite 150, Tucson, AZ 85704	(520) 575–8633
	FAX: 797–3232

REPRESENTATIVES

FIRST DISTRICT

ANN KIRKPATRICK, Democrat, of Flagstaff, AZ; born in McNary, AZ, March 24, 1950; education: B.A., University of Arizona, Tucson, 1972; J.D., University of Arizona College of Law, Tucson, 1979; professional: Coconino Deputy County Attorney, 1980–81; Pima Deputy County Attorney, 1981–85; Sedona City Attorney, 1990–91; Partner, Kirkpatrick & Harris, Law Firm P.C., 1991–2008; Instructor, Business Law & Ethics, Coconino Community College, 2004; Representative, Arizona State House, District 2, 2005–07; Representative, 111th United States Congress, District 1, 2009–10; caucuses: Veterans' Jobs; Native American; General Aviation;

Small Brewers; United Solutions; Youth Drug Prevention; Anti-Bullying; Healthcare Innovation Task Force; Congressional Gaming; Congressional Diabetes; Mental Health; Small Business; Healthy Forests Caucus; P3 Caucus; Congressional Academic Medicine Caucus; High Performance Building Caucus; Congressional Tennis Caucus; Hidden Heroes; Afterschool; Tourism and Travel; Writers; Career and Technical Education; Academic Medicine; religion: Catholic; married: husband Roger Curley, two children; committees: Agriculture; Transportation and Infrastructure; elected to the 113th Congress on November 6, 2012; reelected to the 114th Congress on November 4, 2014.

Office Listings

http://kirkpatrick.house.gov   twitter.com/repkirkpatrick
facebook.com/repkirkpatrick   instagram.com/repkirkpartrick

201 Cannon House Office Building, Washington, DC 20515	(202) 225–3361
Chief of Staff.—Carmen Gallus.	FAX: 225–3462
Legislative Director.—Ken Montoya.	
Communications Director.—Jennifer Johnson.	
Scheduler.—Makenzie Mastrud.	
Legislative Assistants: Molly Brown, Christian Walker.	
405 North Beaver Street, Suite 6, Flagstaff, AZ 86001	(928) 213–9977
District Director.—Ron Lee.	
Casework Manager.—Judy Sulltrop.	
Youth Leadership Coordinator.—Astrid Price.	
Caseworker.—Steven Flanagan.	
211 North Florence Street, Suite 1, Casa Grande, AZ 85122	(520) 316–0839
Deputy Director / Community Outreach.—Blanca Varela.	
Caseworker.—Palmer Miller.	
Deputy Communications Director.—D.B. Mitchell.	
11555 West Civic Center Drive, Suite 104A, Marana, AZ 85653	(520) 382–2663
Caseworker.—Zak Royse.	
550 North 9th Place, Show Low, AZ 85901	(928) 537–5657
Community Outreach.—Sharon Adams.	
1400 East Ash, Globe, AZ 85501	(928) 402–4318
Community Outreach.—Cathy Melvin.	
Apache County District 1 South State Highway 191, Mile Post 477, P.O. Box 1952, Chinle, AZ 86503	(202) 247–0073
District Outreach Representative.—Stan Robbins.	
P.O. Box 948, Tuba City, AZ 86045	(202) 247–5903
District Outreach Representative.—Marie Nez.	

Counties: APACHE, COCONINO (part), GILA (part), GRAHAM, GREENLEE, MARICOPA (part), NAVAJO, PIMA (part), PINAL (part), and YAVAPAI (part). Population: (2010), 724,868.

ZIP Codes: 85122–23, 85128, 85130–32, 85135, 85137–39, 85141–42, 85145, 85172–73, 85191–94, 85226, 85248, 85339, 85501–02, 85530–36, 85539–40, 85542–43, 85545–46, 85548, 85550–52, 85618, 85623, 85631, 85643, 85652–54, 85658, 85704, 85718, 85737, 85739, 85741–43, 85755, 85901–02, 85911–12, 85920, 85922–42, 86001–04, 86011, 86015, 86017–18, 86020, 86022–25, 86028, 86030–33, 86035–36, 86038–40, 86042, 86044–47, 86052–54, 86322, 86325–26, 86335–36, 86339–42, 86351, 86434–35, 86502–08, 86510–12, 86514–15, 86520, 86535, 86538, 86540, 86544–45, 86547, 86556

* * *

SECOND DISTRICT

MARTHA McSALLY, Republican, of Tucson, AZ; born in Warwick, RI, March, 22, 1966; education: St. Mary Academy-Bay View, Riverside, RI, 1984; United States Air Force Academy, Colorado Springs, CO, 1988; Master of Public Policy, Harvard, Cambridge, MA, 1990; Master of Strategic Studies, U.S. Air War College, Montgomery, AL, 2007; professional: United States Air Force officer with various assignments, 1988–2010; T–37 Instructor Pilot, 1991–1994; A–10 pilot / Instructor Pilot, 1994–1999; Air Force Legislative Fellowship Program, 1999–2000; Director of Joint Search and Rescue Center, 2000–2001; Flight Commander / Operation Officer, 612th Combat Operations Squadron, 2002–2004; 354th Fighter Squadron Commander, 2004–2006; Chief of Current Operations, United States Africa Command, 2007–2010; Professor of National Security Studies, George C. Marshall European Center for Security Studies, 2010–2012; Leadership Development and Inspirational Speaker, 2012–2014; military: Bronze Star and 6 Air Medals; Defense Superior Service Medal; Defense and Air Force Meritorious Service Medal; Air Force Association David C. Schilling Award for the most outstanding contribution in the field of flight in 2006 (awarded to 354th Fighter Squadron under McSally's command); awards: Al Neuharth Free Spirit Award; Lifetime Achievement Award from the National Center on Women in Policing; Tucson YWCA Women on the Move Award; religion: Christian; committees: Armed Services, Homeland Security; elected to the 114th Congress on December 17, 2014.

Office Listings

https://mcsally.house.gov

1029 Longworth House Office Building, Washington, DC 20515 .... (202) 225–2542
Chief of Staff.—Justin Roth.   FAX: 225–0378
Scheduler.—Chase Kassel.
Legislative Director.—Vacant.
Communications Director.—Patrick Ptak.
4400 East Broadway Boulevard, Suite 510, Tucson, AZ 85711 .... (520) 881–3588
77 Calle Portal, Suite B–160, Sierra Vista, AZ 85635 .... (520) 459–3115

Counties: COCHISE, PIMA (part). Population (2010), 722,918.

ZIP Codes: 85602–03, 85605–10, 85613–17, 85619–20, 85622, 85625–27, 85629–30, 85632, 85635–36, 85638, 85641, 85643–45, 85650, 85655, 85670, 85704–08, 85710–19, 85722, 85728, 85730–33, 85738, 85740–45, 85747–52

* * *

THIRD DISTRICT

RAÚL M. GRIJALVA, Democrat, of Tucson, AZ; born in Tucson, February 19, 1948; education: Sunnyside High School, Tucson, AZ; B.A., University of Arizona; professional: former Assistant Dean for Hispanic Student Affairs, University of Arizona; former Director of the El Pueblo Neighborhood Center; public service: Tucson Unified School District Governing Board 1974–86; Pima County Board of Supervisors, 1989–2002; family: married to Ramona; three daughters; committees: ranking member, Natural Resources; Education and the Workforce; elected to the 108th Congress on November 5, 2002; reelected to each succeeding Congress.

Office Listings

http://www.grijalva.house.gov

1511 Longworth House Office Building, Washington, DC 20515 .... (202) 225–2435
Chief of Staff.—Amy Emerick.   FAX: 225–1541
Legislative Director.—Kelsey Mishkin.
Communications Director.—Dan Lindner.
Scheduler.—Cristina Villa.
738 North 5th Avenue, Suite 110, Tucson, AZ 85705 .... (520) 622–6788
146 North State Avenue, Somerton, AZ 85350 .... (928) 343–7933
13065 West McDowell Road, Suite C–113, Avondale, AZ 85392 .... (623) 536–3388

Counties: LA PAZ (part), MARICOPA (part), PIMA (part), PINAL (part), SANTA CRUZ (part), and YUMA. Population (2010), 710,224.

ZIP Codes: 85033 (part), 85037 (part), 85043 (part), 85123 (part), 85139 (part), 85193 (part), 85305 (part), 85307 (part), 85321–22, 85323 (part), 85326 (part), 85333 (part), 85336–337, 85338 (part), 85339 (part), 85340 (part), 85341, 85343, 85347 (part), 85349–50, 85353 (part), 85354 (part), 85364 (part), 85365 (part), 85392 (part), 85395 (part), 85396, 85601, 85611 (part), 85621, 85622 (part), 85624, 85629 (part), 85633–34, 85637 (part), 85640, 85645 (part), 85646, 85648, 85653 (part), 85701, 85705 (part), 85706 (part), 85713 (part), 85714 (part), 85719 (part), 85723–724, 85726, 85735–85736, 85743 (part), 85745 (part), 85746, 85756 (part), 85757

* * *

FOURTH DISTRICT

PAUL GOSAR, Republican, of Prescott, AZ; born in Rock Springs, WY, November 27, 1958; education: graduated, Pinedale High School, Pinedale, WY; B.S., Creighton University, Omaha, NE, 1981; D.D.S., Creighton University, Omaha, NE, 1985; religion: Catholic; family: wife, Maude; children: Elle, Gaston, and Isabelle; caucuses: GOP Doctor's Caucus; Immigration Reform Caucus; Coal Caucus; committees: Natural Resources; Oversight and Government Reform; elected to the 112th Congress on November 2, 2010; reelected to each succeeding Congress.

Office Listings

http://www.gosar.house.gov   twitter: @repgosar   https://www.facebook.com/repgosar
http://www.youtube.com/repgosar   http://www.flickr.com/photos/repgosar

504 Cannon House Office Building, Washington, DC 20515 .... (202) 225–2315

Office Listings—Continued

Chief of Staff.—Thomas Van Flein.
Legislative Director.—Jeff Small.
Press Secretary.—Steven Smith.
Scheduler/Office Manager.—Leslie Rath.
District Director.—Penny Pew.
6499 South Kings Ranch Road, #4, Gold Canyon, AZ 85118.

Counties: GILA, LA PAZ, MARICOPA, MOHAVE, PINAL, YAVAPAI, YUMA. CITIES AND TOWNSHIPS: Ak-Chin Village, Apache Junction, Arcosanti, Arizona City, Arizona Village, Ash Fork, Bagdad, Beaver Dam, Big Park, Black Canyon City, Blackwater, Bouse, Buckeye, Bullhead City, Central Heights-Midland City, Chino Valley, Chloride, Chuichu, Cibola, Clarkdale, Claypool, Colorado City, Cordes Lakes, Cornville, Cottonwood-Verde Village, Desert Hills, Dewey-Humboldt, Dolan Springs, Dudleyville, Ehrenberg, Eloy, Florence, Fort Mohave, Fortuna Foothills, Gadsden, Gisela, Globe, Gold Canyon, Golden Valley, Hackberry, Hayden, Hope, Jerome, Kaibab, Kearny, Kingman, Kohls Ranch, Lake Havasu City, Lake Montezuma, Litchfield Park, Littlefield, Mammoth, Marana, Maricopa, Mayer, Meadview, Mesquite Creek, Mohave Valley, Mojave Ranch Estates, New Kingman-Butler, Nothing, Oatman, Oracle, Parker, Parker Strip, Paulden, Payson, Peach Springs, Peeples Valley, Peoria, Pine, Poston, Prescott Valley, Quartzsite, Queen Creek, Queen Valley, Sacaton, Salome, San Luis, San Manuel, San Tan Valley, Santan, Scenic, Seligman, Somerton, Spring Valley, Stanfield, Star Valley, Superior, Surprise, Tacna, Topock, Top-of-the-World, Valentine, Wellton, Wendon, Wickenburg, Wikieup, Wilhoit, Williamson, Willow Valley, Winkelman, Yarnell, Young, Yucca, and Yuma. Population (2010), 707,750.

ZIP Codes: 85118, 85140, 85142–43, 85173, 85324–26, 85328, 85334, 85340, 85344, 85346, 85348, 85352, 85356–60, 85362, 85364–65, 85367, 85371, 85383, 85387, 85390, 85541, 85544, 85547, 85554, 86021–22, 86305, 86312, 86314–15, 86320–21, 86323–27, 86331–34, 86337, 86401–06, 86409, 86411–13, 86426, 86431–33, 86436–38, 86440–42, 86444–46

* * *

FIFTH DISTRICT

MATT SALMON, Republican, of Mesa, AZ; born in Salt Lake City, UT, January 21, 1958; education: B.A. in english, Arizona State University, Phoenix, AZ, 1981; M.P.A., Brigham Young University, Provo, UT 1986; professional: telecommunications executive; community affairs manager; member of the Arizona State Senate, 1991–95; assistant majority leader, 1993–95; religion: Church of Jesus Christ of Latter-Day Saints; family: Matt has spent the last 34 years married to Nancy; four children; six grandchildren; served in Congress from 1995–2000; committees: Education and the Work Force; Foreign Affairs; elected to the 113th Congress on November 6, 2012; reelected to the 114th Congress on November 4, 2014.

Office Listings

http://salmon.house.gov

2349 Rayburn House Office Building, Washington, DC 20515 .... (202) 226–2635
    Chief of Staff.—Adam Deguire.   FAX: 226–4386
    Scheduler.—Olivia Vickers.
    Communications Director.—Tristan Daedalus.
207 North Gilbert Road, Suite 209, Gilbert, AZ 85234 .... (480) 699–8239

Counties: MARICOPA (part), PINAL (part). CITIES AND TOWNSHIPS: Apache Junction, Chandler, Gilbert, Mesa, and Queen Creek. Population (2010), 710,224.

ZIP Codes: 85120–21, 85127, 85142, 85147, 85201, 85203–10, 85212–13, 85215–16, 85224–25, 85233–34, 85236, 85249, 85275, 85277, 85286, 85295–97

* * *

SIXTH DISTRICT

DAVID SCHWEIKERT, Republican, of Fountain Hills, AZ; born March 3, 1962; education: B.A., Arizona State University, Tempe, AZ, 1988; M.B.A., Arizona State University, Tempe, AZ, 2005; professional: business owner of a real estate company; realtor; financial consultant; member of the Arizona State House of Representatives, 1989–94; member of the Arizona State Board of Equalization, 1995–2003; former treasurer, Maricopa County, AZ, 2004–06; religion: Catholic; married: Joyce Schweikert; committees: Financial Services; Joint Economic; elected to 112th Congress on November 2, 2010; reelected to each succeeding Congress.

Office Listings

http://schweikert.house.gov   twitter: @repdavid

409 Cannon House Office Building, Washington, DC 20515 .... (202) 225–2190

Office Listings—Continued

Chief of Staff.—Oliver Schwab.　　　　　　　　　　　　　　　　FAX: 225–0096
Scheduler.—Kyle Souza.
Legislative Director / Deputy Chief of Staff.—Beau Brunson.
Communications Director.—Kyle Souza.
10603 North Hayden Road, Suite 108, Scottsdale, AZ 85260 .... (480) 946–2411
　　　　　　　　　　　　　　　　　　　　　　　　　　　　　　　　FAX: 946–2446

Counties: MARICOPA (part). CITIES AND TOWNSHIPS: Fountain Hills, Paradise Valley, Cave Creek, Carefree, Rio Verde, Scottsdale, Phoenix (part), Yavapai Nation, and Salt River Pima Maricopa Indian Community. Population (2010), 754,482.

ZIP Codes: 85020, 85022–24, 85027–29, 85032, 85050, 85054, 85201, 85250–51, 85253–56, 85258–60, 85264, 85268

* * *

SEVENTH DISTRICT

RUBEN GALLEGO, Democrat, of Phoenix, AZ; born in Chicago, IL, November 20 1979; education: A.B., Harvard, Cambridge MA, 2004; professional: Delegate, Democratic National Convention 2008; Chief of Staff to Phoenix Councilman Michael Nowakowski 2008–10; vice-chair, Arizona Democratic Party 2009; Member of the Arizona House of Representatives, 2011–14; Assistant Democratic Leader for the Arizona House of Representatives, 2013–2014; military: United States Marine Corps, 2000–06; awards: Combat Action Ribbon; religion: Catholic; married: Phoenix Councilwoman Kate Gallego; caucuses: Congressional Hispanic Caucus; Congressional Progressive Caucus; Congressional LGBT Equality Caucus; Post 9/11 Veterans Caucus; Quiet Skies Caucus, Medicaid Expansion Caucus; committees: Armed Services; Natural Resources; elected to the 114th Congress on November 4, 2014.

Office Listings

https://rubengallego.house.gov　　　twitter @reprubengallego　　　www.facebook.com/reprubengallego

1218 Longworth House Office Building, Washington, DC 20515 .... (202) 225–4065
Scheduler.—Rome Hall.
411 North Central Avenue, Suite 150, Phoenix, AZ 85004 .... (602) 256–0551
District Director.—Luis Heredia.

Counties: MARICOPA (part). Population (2010), 725,197.

ZIP Codes: 85001–10, 85012–19, 85021, 85025–26, 85030–31, 85033–38, 85040–44, 85048, 85051, 85061–64, 85066–67, 85072, 85074–75, 85079, 85082, 85098, 85282–83, 85301, 85303, 85305, 85311, 85318, 85323, 85339, 85353

* * *

EIGHTH DISTRICT

TRENT FRANKS, Republican, of Phoenix, AZ; born in Uravan, CO, June 19, 1957; education: attended Ottawa University; graduate of the Center for Constitutional Studies; professional: small business owner; oil field and drilling engineer; Executive Director, Arizona Family Research Institute; conservative writer, and former radio commentator, with Family Life Radio and NBC affiliate KTKP 1280 AM; public service: Arizona House of Representatives, 1985–87; appointed in 1987 to head the Arizona Governor's Office for Children; awards: True Blue Award, Family Research Council; Spirit of Enterprise Award, U.S. Chamber of Commerce; Taxpayer Hero, Council for Citizens Against Government Waste; Friend of Education Award, Education Freedom Coalition; religion: Baptist; member, North Phoenix Baptist Church; married: Josephine; children: Josh and Grace (twins); committees: Armed Services; Judiciary; elected to the 108th Congress on November 5, 2002; reelected to each succeeding Congress.

Office Listings

http://www.franks.house.gov

2435 Rayburn House Office Building, Washington, DC 20515 .... (202) 225–4576

Office Listings—Continued

Chief of Staff.—Jonathan Hayes.   FAX: 225–6328
Deputy Chief of Staff/Legislative Director.—Bobby Cornett.
Scheduler/Office Manager.—Chelsea Patterson.
Press Secretary.—Destiny Decker.
Press Assistant/Personal Assistant.—Jessica Cahill.
MLA.—Ari Zimmerman.
Legislative Assistants: Bethany Haley, Ellie Stern.
Legislative Correspondent.—Daniel Stefanski.
DoD Fellow.—Amy Glisson.
IAF Fellow.—David Daoud.
Religious Freedom Fellow.—Lena Smith.
7121 West Bell Road, Suite 200, Glendale, AZ 85308 .... (623) 776–7911
District Director.—Dan Hay.
Executive Assistant.—Lisa Teschler.
District Representatives: Lloyd Bostrom, Steve Montenegro, Doyle Scott, Daniel
    Stefanski.
Field Representative/Finance Director.—Shari Farrington.
Business/Commerce Liaison.—Michael Jameson.
Staff Assistant.—Terry Murray.

Counties: MARICOPA, NEW RIVER, SUN CITY, SUN CITY WEST, SURPRISE (part), NORTH GATEWAY, GLENDALE, NEW
    VILLAGE, PEORIA. Population (2014), 741,374.

ZIP Codes: 85083, 85085–87, 85301–10, 85312, 85318, 85331, 85335, 85338, 85340, 85345, 85351, 85361, 85363, 85372–
    76, 85378–83, 85385, 85387–88, 85395

* * *

NINTH DISTRICT

KYRSTEN SINEMA, Democrat, of Phoenix, AZ; born in Tucson, AZ, July 12, 1976; education: B.A., social work, Brigham Young University, Provo, UT, 1995; M.A., social work, Arizona State University, Tempe, AZ, 1999; J.D., Arizona State University, Tempe, AZ, 2004;
Ph.D., social justice, social inquiry, Arizona State University, Tempe, AZ, 2012; professional:
member of the Arizona House of Representatives, 2005–11; Aspen-Rodel Public Leadership
Fellow, 2008; assistant minority leader, Arizona House of Representatives, 2009–11; *Time* Magazine's Top 40 Under 40, 2010; member of the Arizona State Senate, 2011–12; TED Fellow,
2012; committees: Financial Services; elected to the 113th Congress on November 6, 2012; reelected to the 114th Congress on November 4, 2014.

Office Listings

http://sinema.house.gov   twitter: @repsinema

1530 Longworth House Office Building, Washington, DC 20515 .... (202) 225–9888
Chief of Staff.—Meg Joseph.   FAX: 225–9731
Legislative Director.—Michael Brownlie.
Communications Director.—Macey Matthews.
Scheduler.—Jessie Andrews.
2944 North 44th Street, Suite 150, Maricopa County, AZ 85018 .... (602) 956–2285
District Director.—Michelle Davidson.

Counties: MARICOPA COUNTY (part). CITIES: Ahwatukee, Chandler, Guadalupe, Mesa, Phoenix, Tempe. Population (2010),
    722,896.

ZIP Codes: 85008 (part), 85012 (part), 85013 (part), 85014 (part), 85016 (part), 85018 (part), 85020 (part), 85021 (part),
    85034 (part), 85040 (part), 85044 (part), 85045, 85048 (part), 85051 (part), 85201 (part), 85202, 85203 (part), 85204
    (part), 85210 (part), 85224 (part), 85225 (part), 85226 (part), 85233 (part), 85251 (part), 85253 (part), 85256 (part),
    85257 (part), 85281 (part), 85282 (part), 85283 (part), 85284

ARKANSAS

(Population 2010, 2,915,918)

SENATORS

JOHN NICHOLS BOOZMAN, Republican, of Rogers, AR; born in Shreveport, LA, December 10, 1950; education: Southern College of Optometry, Memphis, TN, 1977; also attended University of Arkansas, Fayetteville, AR; professional: doctor of optometry; business owner; rancher; religion: Southern Baptist; married: Mrs. Cathy Boozman; children: three daughters; committees: Agriculture, Nutrition, and Forestry; Appropriations; Environment and Public Works; Rules and Administration; Veterans' Affairs; Joint Committee on Printing; elected to the U.S. House of Representatives 2001–11; elected to the U.S. Senate on November 2, 2010.

Office Listings

http://boozman.senate.gov   facebook: johnboozman   twitter: @johnboozman

141 Hart Senate Office Building, Washington, DC 20510	(202) 224–4843
Chief of Staff.—Helen Tolar.	FAX: 228–1371

Deputy Chief of Staff / Counsel.—Susan Olson.
Legislative Director.—Toni-Marie Higgins.
Communications Director.—Sara Lasure.
Scheduler.—Lesley Parker.

* * *

TOM COTTON, Republican, of Dardanelle, AR; born in Dardanelle, AR, May 13, 1977; education: graduated Dardanelle High School; B.A., Harvard University, 1999; J.D., Harvard University, 2002; professional: attorney, management consultant; military service: United States Army Infantry Officer, 2005–09; awards: graduated Magna Cum Laude, Harvard University; Ranger Tab Recipient; Army Commendation Medal; Combat Infantryman Badge; Iraq Campaign Medal; Bronze Star Medal; committees: Armed Services; Banking, Housing, and Urban Affairs; Joint Economic Committee; Select Committee on Intelligence; Special Committee on Aging; elected to the 113th Congress on November 6, 2012; elected to the U.S. Senate on November 4, 2014.

Office Listings

http://cotton.senate.gov

124 Russell Senate Office Building, Washington, DC 20510	(202) 224–2353
Chief of Staff.—Doug Coutts.	FAX: 228–0908

Legislative Director.—Jonathan Hiler.
Communications Director.—Caroline Rabbitt.

11809 Hinson Road, Suite 100, Little Rock, AR 72212	(501) 223–9081
State Director.—Lesley Nelms.	
1108 South Old Missouri Road, Suite B, Springdale, AR 72764	(479) 751–0879
300 South Church, Suite 338, Jonesboro, AR 72401	(870) 933–6223
106 West Main Street, Suite 410, El Dorado, AR 71730	(870) 864–8582

REPRESENTATIVES

FIRST DISTRICT

RICK CRAWFORD, Republican, of Jonesboro, AR; born in Homestead AFB, FL, January 22, 1966; education: graduated, Alvirne High School; B.A., agricultural business and economics, Arkansas State University, 1996; professional: U.S. Army—Bomb Disposal Technician, 1985–89, Professional Rodeo Announcer; KAIT–TV Jonesboro—News Anchor; KFIN–FM—Farm Director; Delta Farm Roundup TV Show—Producer and Anchor; Agwatch—Owner and Operator; member: National Association of Farm Broadcasting; 4-H Foundation Board of Arkansas; recipient of the NAFB Newscast Award, 2006 and 2008; married: Stacy; children: Will and Delaney; Republican Study Committee; committees: Agriculture; Transportation and Infrastructure; elected to the 112th Congress on November 2, 2010; reelected to each succeeding Congress.

Office Listings

http://crawford.house.gov	twitter: @reprickcrawford
https://www.facebook.com/reprickcrawford?ref=brltf

1711 Longworth House Office Building, Washington, DC 20515 .... (202) 225–4076
  Chief of Staff.—Jonah Shumate.	FAX: 225–5602
  Press Secretary.—James Arnold.
  Legislative Director.—Chris Jones.
112 South First Street, Cabot, AR 72023 .... (501) 843–3043
2400 East Highland Drive, Suite 300, Jonesboro, AR 72401 .... (870) 203–0540
1001 Highway 62 East, Suite 9, Mountain Home, AR 72653 .... (870) 424–2075

Counties: ARKANSAS, BAXTER, CHICOT, CLAY, CLEBURNE, CRAIGHEAD, CRITTENDEN, CROSS, DESHA, FULTON, GREENE, INDEPENDENCE, IZARD, JACKSON, JEFFERSON (part), LAWRENCE, LEE, LINCOLN, LONOKE, MISSISSIPPI, MONROE, PHILLIPS, POINSETT, PRAIRIE, RANDOLPH, SAINT FRANCIS, SEARCY, SHARP, STONE, AND WOODRUFF. Population (2013), 729,510.

ZIP Codes: 72003, 72005–07, 72014, 72017, 72020–21, 72023–24, 72026, 72029, 72031, 72036–38, 72040–44, 72046, 72048, 72051, 72055, 72059–60, 72064, 72067, 72069, 72072–76, 72083, 72086, 72101–02, 72108, 72112, 72121, 72123, 72130–31, 72134, 72137, 72139–40, 72142–43, 72153, 72160, 72165–66, 72169–70, 72175–76, 72179, 72189, 72301, 72303, 72310–13, 72315–16, 72319–22, 72324–33, 72335–36, 72338–42, 72346–48, 72350–55, 72358–60, 72364–70, 72372–74, 72376–77, 72383–84, 72386–87, 72389–92, 72394–96, 72401–04, 72410–17, 72419, 72421–22, 72424–45, 72447, 72449–51, 72453–62, 72464–67, 72469–76, 72478–79, 72482, 72501, 72503, 72512–13, 72515, 72517, 72519–34, 72536–40, 72542–46, 72550, 72553–56, 72560–62, 72564–69, 72571–73, 72575–79, 72581, 72583–85, 72587, 72610, 72613, 72617, 72623, 72626, 72629, 72631, 72633, 72635–36, 72639, 72642, 72645, 72650–51, 72653–54, 72658, 72663, 72669, 72675, 72679–80, 72685–86

* * *

SECOND DISTRICT

J. FRENCH HILL, Republican, of Little Rock, AR; born in Little Rock, December 5, 1956; education: Bachelor of Science degree in Economics, Vanderbilt University, Nashville, TN, 1979, graduated *magna cum laude*; professional: Senior Financial Analyst, InterFirst Corporation, 1979–82; Legislative Assistant, Assistant to the Chairman, Subcommittee on Housing and Urban Development, The Honorable John Tower (R–TX), Senate Committee on Banking, Housing and Urban Affairs, 1982–84; Director, Mason Best Company, 1984–89; Deputy Assistant Secretary (Corporate Finance), U.S. Department of the Treasury, 1989–91; Special Assistant to the President, Executive Office of the White House, 1991–93; Executive Officer, Regions West, 1993–99; Chief Executive Officer, Delta Trust & Banking Corp., 1999–2014; Religion: Roman Catholic; married, two children; caucuses: Congressional Diabetes Caucus; Congressional Chicken Caucus; Bipartisan Congressional Arts Caucus; Congressional Prayer Caucus; Congressional Scouting Caucus; National Guard and Reserve Components Caucus (NGRCC); Congressional Army Caucus; Congressional Air Force Caucus; House Republican Israel Caucus; Congressional Missile Defense Caucus; Congressional Sportsmen's Caucus; Congressional Natural Gas Caucus; House Small Brewers Caucus; Congressional Caucus on Fitness; Congressional Kidney Caucus; Congressional Israel Allies Caucus; Congressional Boating Caucus; Congressional Caucus on Foster Youth; Congressional International Conservation Caucus; Congressional French Caucus; Congressional Wine Caucus; U.S.-Japan Caucus; Science, Technology, Engineering, and Math (STEM) Education Caucus; Congressional Caucus on India and Indian-Americans; Congressional Congenital Heart Caucus; Congressional Historic Preservation Caucus; committees: Financial Services; elected to the 114th Congress on November 4, 2014.

Office Listings

https://www.hill.house.gov
https://twitter.com/repfrenchhill	https://www.facebook.com/repfrenchhill
https://www.youtube.com/channel/uct8uwrojtkwsscjlvg0ikvq

1229 Longworth House Office Building, Washington, DC 20515 .... (202) 225–2506
  Chief of Staff.—A. Brooke Bennett.	FAX: 225–5903
  Communications Director.—Mike Siegel.
  Legislative Director.—Peter Comstock.
  Senior Advisor and Counsel.—Holli Heiles.
  Senior Legislative Assistant.—Dylan Frost.
  Legislative Correspondent.—Lesley Hill.
  Executive Assistant.—Toska Gamble.
  Staff Assistant.—Matt Karvelas.
1501 North University, Suite 150, Little Rock, AR 72207 .... (501) 324–5941
  Deputy District Director.—Jill Cox.	FAX: 324–6029
  District Representative.—Josh Mesker.
1105 Deer Street, Suite 12, Conway, AR 72032 .... (501) 358–3481
  Senior District Representative.—Tom McNabb.	FAX: 358–3481
  (Military / Veterans Affairs) District Representative.—Anushree Jumde.

Counties: CONWAY, FAULKNER, PERRY, PULASKI, SALINE, VAN BUREN, AND WHITE. Population (2010), 751,377.

ZIP Codes: 71772, 71909, 72001–02, 72010–13, 72015–18, 72020, 72022–23, 72025, 72027–28, 72030–35, 72039, 72045–47, 72052–53, 72057–61, 72063, 72065–68, 72070, 72076, 72078–82, 72085, 72087–89, 72099, 72102–04, 72106–08, 72110–11, 72113–22, 72124–27, 72131, 72135–37, 72139, 72141–43, 72145, 72149, 72153, 72156–57, 72164, 72167, 72173, 72178, 72180–81, 72183, 72190, 72199, 72201–07, 72209–12, 72214–17, 72219, 72221–23, 72225, 72227, 72231, 72260, 72295, 72419, 72568, 72629, 72645, 72679, 72823

* * *

THIRD DISTRICT

STEVE WOMACK, Republican, of Rogers, AR; born in Russellville, AR, February 18, 1957; education: Russellville High School, Russellville, AR; B.A., Arkansas Tech University, 1979; professional: radio station manager; financial consultant; mayor of Rogers, AR; military: retired colonel, National Guard; awards: Legion of Merit; Meritorious Service Medal; Army Commendation Medal; Army Achievement Medal; Global War on Terror Expeditionary and Service Medals; religion: Southern Baptist; family: married the former Terri Williams of DeWitt, AR; three sons; caucuses: Congressional Chicken Caucus; committees: Appropriations; Budget; elected to the 112th Congress on November 2, 2010; reelected to each succeeding Congress.

Office Listings

http://womack.house.gov

1119 Longworth House Office Building, Washington, DC 20515	(202) 225–4301
Chief of Staff.—Beau Walker.	FAX: 225–5713
Communications Director.—Claire Burghoff.	
Scheduler.—Meg Gazzini.	
Legislative Director.—Adrielle Churchill.	
Legislative Assistants: Benjamin Cantrell, Lauren M. Johnson.	
Legislative Correspondent.—Chelsea Taff.	
Military Fellow.—Ramses Cypress.	
Staff Assistant.—Amy Lawrence.	
3333 Pinnacle Hills, Suite 120, Rogers, AR 72758	(479) 464–0446
District Director.—Bootsie Ackerman.	FAX: 464–0063
Constituent Service Manager.—Janet Foster.	
Caseworker.—Gillie Brandolini.	
Field Representative.—Jeff Thacker.	
Projects Director.—Kyle Weaver.	
423 North 6th Street, Fort Smith, AR 72902	(479) 424–1146
Field Representative / Military and Veterans Advisor.—Janice Scaggs.	FAX: 424–2737
Caseworker.—Chris Bader.	
303 North Main Street, Suite 102, Harrison, AR 72601	(870) 741–6900
Field Representative.—Teri Garrett.	FAX: 741–7741

Counties: BENTON, BOONE, CARROLL, CRAWFORD, FRANKLIN, JOHNSON, MADISON, MARION, NEWTON, POPE, SEBASTIAN, WASHINGTON. Population (2010), 754,704.

ZIP Codes: 65729, 65733, 65761, 72063, 72080, 72601, 72611, 72616, 72619, 72624, 72630–34, 72638, 72640–41, 72644, 72648, 72653, 72655, 72660–62, 72668–69, 72672, 72675, 72677, 72679, 72682–83, 72685, 72687, 72701, 72703–04, 72712, 72714–15, 72717–19, 72722, 72727, 72729–30, 72732, 72734, 72736, 72738–40, 72744–45, 72747, 72749, 72751, 72753, 72756, 72758, 72761–62, 72764, 72768–69, 72773–74, 72801–02, 72823, 72837, 72839, 72843, 72846–47, 72856, 72858, 72901, 72903–04, 72908, 72916, 72921, 72923, 72927, 72932–34, 72936–37, 72940–41, 72945–46, 72948, 72952, 72955–56, 72959

* * *

FOURTH DISTRICT

BRUCE WESTERMAN, Republican, of Hot Springs, AR; born in Hot Springs, AR, November 18, 1967; education: graduated, Fountain Lake High School, 1986; B.S., University of Arkansas, 1990; M.F., Yale University, 2001; professional: professional engineer, forester; past elected office: Arkansas House of Representatives Majority Leader, 2013; Arkansas House of Representatives Minority Leader, 2012; Arkansas State Representative, 2011–15; Fountain Lake School Board President, 2009–10; Fountain Lake School Board, 2006–10; awards: University of Arkansas College of Engineering, Outstanding Young Alumni Award, 2005; University of Arkansas College of Engineering, Distinguished Alumni Award, 2012; Engineer of the Year by the Arkansas Society of Professional Engineers, 2013; committees: Budget; Natural Resources; Science, Space, and Technology; elected to the 114th Congress on November 4, 2014.

Office Listings
http://westerman.house.gov

130 Cannon House Office Building, Washington, DC 20515 .... (202) 225–3772
   Chief of Staff.—Vivian Moeglein.   FAX: 225–1314
   Legislative Director.—Jonathan Shuffield.
   Communications Director.—Ryan Saylor.
National Parks Service Headquarters, 101 Reserve Street, Suite 200, Hot Springs, AR
   71901 .... (501) 609–9796
   District Director.—Jason McGehee.
George Howard Jr. Federal Building, 100 East 8th Avenue, Room 2521, Pine Bluff, AR
   71601 .... (870) 536–8178
Franklin County Courthouse, 211 W Commercial St, Ozark, AR 72949 .... (501) 295–9752
Union County Courthouse, Suite 406, 101 North Washington Street, El Dorado, AR 71730 (870) 864–8946

Counties: ASHLEY, BRADLEY, CALHOUN, CLARK, CLEVELAND, COLUMBIA, CRAWFORD, DALLAS, DREW, FRANKLIN, GARLAND, GRANT, HEMPSTEAD, HOT SPRING, HOWARD, JEFFERSON, JOHNSON, LAFAYETTE, LITTLE RIVER, LOGAN, MADISON, MILLER, MONTGOMERY, NEVADA, NEWTON (part), OUACHITA, PIKE, POLK, SCOTT, SEBASTIAN, SEVIER, UNION, AND YELL. Population (2010), 717,926.

ZIP Codes: 71601–03, 71631, 71635, 71638, 71642, 71644, 71646–47, 71651–52, 71655, 71658–61, 71663, 71665, 71667, 71670–71, 71675–77, 71701, 71711, 71720, 71722, 71724–26, 71730, 71740, 71742–45, 71747, 71751–53, 71758–59, 71762–66, 71770, 71772, 71801, 71820, 71822–23, 71825–27, 71832–39, 71841–42, 71845–47, 71851–55, 71857–62, 71865–66, 71901, 71909, 71913, 71921–23, 71929, 71933, 71935, 71937, 71940–41, 71943–45, 71949–50, 71952–53, 71956–62, 71964–65, 71968–73, 71998–99, 72004, 72015, 72025, 72046, 72057, 72065, 72079, 72084, 72087, 72104, 72128–29, 72132, 72150, 72152, 72167–68, 72175, 72601, 72624, 72628, 72632, 72638, 72641, 72648, 72655, 72666, 72670, 72703, 72721, 72727, 72738, 72740, 72742, 72752, 72756, 72760, 72773, 72776, 72821, 72824, 72826–28, 72830, 72832–35, 72838–42, 72845–47, 72851–57, 72860, 72863, 72865, 72921, 72926–28, 72930, 72933–38, 72940–41, 72943–47, 72949–51, 72956, 72958–59

CALIFORNIA

(Population 2010, 37,253,956)

SENATORS

DIANNE FEINSTEIN, Democrat, of San Francisco, CA; born in San Francisco, June 22, 1933; education: B.A., Stanford University, 1955; elected to San Francisco Board of Supervisors, 1970–78; president of Board of Supervisors: 1970–71, 1974–75, 1978; mayor of San Francisco, 1978–88; candidate for governor of California, 1990; recipient: Distinguished Woman Award, *San Francisco Examiner*; Achievement Award, Business and Professional Women's Club, 1970; Golden Gate University, California, LL.D. (hon.), 1979; SCOPUS Award for Outstanding Public Service, American Friends of the Hebrew University of Jerusalem; University of Santa Clara, D.P.S. (hon.); University of Manila, D.P.A. (hon.), 1981; Antioch University, LL.D. (hon.), 1983; Los Angeles Anti-Defamation League of B'nai B'rith's Distinguished Service Award, 1984; French Legion d'Honneur from President Mitterand, 1984; Mills College, LL.D. (hon.), 1985; U.S. Army Commander's Award for Public Service, 1986; Brotherhood/ Sisterhood Award, National Conference of Christians and Jews, 1986; Paulist Fathers Award, 1987; Episcopal Church Award for Service, 1987; U.S. Navy Distinguished Civilian Award, 1987; Silver Spur Award for Outstanding Public Service, San Francisco Planning and Urban Renewal Association, 1987; All Pro Management Team Award for No. 1 Mayor, *City and State Magazine*, 1987; Community Service Award Honoree for Public Service, 1987; American Jewish Congress, 1987; President's Award, St. Ignatius High School, San Francisco, 1988; Coro Investment in Leadership Award, 1988; President's Medal, University of California at San Francisco, 1988; University of San Francisco, D.H.L. (hon.), 1988; member: Coro Foundation, Fellowship, 1955–56; California Women's Board of Terms and Parole, 1960–66, executive committee; U.S. Conference of Mayors, 1983–88; Mayor's Commission on Crime, San Francisco; Bank of California, director, 1988–89; San Francisco Education Fund's Permanent Fund, 1988–89; Japan Society of Northern California, 1988–89; Inter-American Dialogue, 1988–present; Publius Award from the Center for the Study of the Presidency and Congress, 2009; chair, U.S. Senate Caucus on International Narcotics Control; married: Dr. Bertram Feinstein (dec.); married on January 20, 1980, to Richard C. Blum; children: one child; three stepchildren; religion: Jewish; committees: vice chair, Select Committee on Intelligence; Appropriations; Judiciary; Rules and Administration; elected to the U.S. Senate, by special election, on November 3, 1992, to fill the vacancy caused by the resignation of Senator Pete Wilson; reelected to each succeeding Senate term.

Office Listings

http://feinstein.senate.gov　　　twitter: @senfeinstein

331 Hart Senate Office Building, Washington, DC 20510	(202) 224–3841
Chief of Staff.—Jennifer Duck.	FAX: 228–3954
Legislative Director.—John Watts.	
Director of Communications.—Tom Mentzer.	
880 Front Street, Suite 3296, San Diego, CA 92101	(619) 231–9712
2500 Tulare Street, Suite 4290, Fresno, CA 93721	(559) 485–7430
One Post Street, Suite 2450, San Francisco, CA 94104	(415) 393–0707
11111 Santa Monica Boulevard, Suite 915, Los Angeles, CA 90025	(310) 914–7300

* * *

BARBARA BOXER, Democrat, of Rancho Mirage, CA; born in Brooklyn, NY, November 11, 1940; education: B.A. in economics, Brooklyn College, 1962; professional: stockbroker and economic researcher with securities firms on Wall Street, 1962–65; journalist and associate editor, Pacific Sun newspaper, 1972–74; congressional aide, Fifth Congressional District, California, 1974–76; elected Marin County Board of Supervisors, 1976–82; first woman president, Marin County Board of Supervisors; awards: Human Rights for Vietnam Award, Vietnamese Community of Southern California, 1994; Legislator of the Year Award, Southern California Public Health Association, 1996; Lifetime Consumer Hero, Consumer Federation of America, 1997; Edgar Wayburn Award, Sierra Club, 1997; President's Award, California State Conference of the NAACP, 2001; Phillip Burton Wilderness Award, California Wilderness Coalition (CWC), 2003; Children's Champion Award, California Head Start Association, 2003; Circle of Courage Award, Afghan Women's Association International and the Women's 2003 Intercultural Network, 2003; National End Family Violence Achievement Award, Family Violence Law Center, 2003; Leadership Award, National Foundation for Women Legislators, 2005; Champion of Affordability Award, Housing Trust of Santa Clara County, 2005; Friend of the National Parenthood Action Council, 2005; Champion for Children Award, California Children's Hospital, 2006; Woman of the Year, Women's Image Network, 2006; Visionary Leadership Award, San Francisco Democratic Party, 2006; Award, Native American Heritage Association, 2007; Champion Award for Public Service, Endangered Species Coalition, 2007; Lifetime Achievement Award, City Year San Jose/Silicon Valley, 2008; Breakfast of Champions, Afterschool Alliance, 2008; Transportation Leader's Award, National Stone, Sand, and Gravel Association, 2008; John H. Chafee Congressional Environmental Award, Association of American Railroads, 2008; Legislative Leadership Award, National Association of Clean Water Agencies, 2008; Legislator of the Year Award, American Planning Association, 2008; Humane Champion, Humane Society of the United States, 2008; Legislator of the Year Award, Information and Technology Industry Council, 2008; Vera Shultz Visionary Leadership Award, Marin Women's Commission, 2009; 25th Annual Leadership Conference Award, Cyprus and Hellenic Leadership, 2009; Aviation Safety Award, National Air Traffic Controllers Association, 2009; Legislator of the Year Award, California Primary Care Association, 2009; Children's Champion Award, Global Action for Children, 2009; Award, Oxfam America, 2009; Legislator of the Year Award, Air Quality Management District, 2009; National Transportation Leadership Award for the 21st Century, American Association of State Highway and Transportation Officials, 2009; Defender of Children Award, First Focus Campaign for Children, 2010; Golden Triangle Award, National Farmers Union, 2010; Safety Leadership Award, Advocates for Highway and Auto Safety, 2010; Award, National Association of Community Health Centers, 2010; Safety Net Award, National Association of Public Hospitals and Health Systems, 2010; President's Leadership Award, American Burn Association, 2010; Phil Burton Badge of Courage Award, The Sierra Club-San Francisco Bay Chapter, 2010; Service Award, Entertainment Leadership Initiative/Grammy Foundation, 2010; Public Service Award, American College of Nurse-Midwives, 2010; All Rise Leadership Award, National Association of Drug Court Professionals, 2011; Friends of the National Parks Award, National Parks Conservation Association, 2011; Outstanding Leadership Recognition, American Water Works Association, California-Nevada Section, 2011; Recognition, East Bay Municipal Utility District, 2011; Champion for the National Parent Helpline Award, Parents Anonymous, 2011; Nightingale Award, Nurse Alliance, 2011; Legislative Leader Award, The Humane Society, 2011; Congressional Champion Award, The Corps Network, 2012; YMCA Congressional Champion, YMCA, 2012; Distinguished Community Health Defender Award, National Association of Community Health Centers, Inc., 2012; Fearless Trailblazer Award, Feminist Majority, 2012; Certificate of Recognition, Orange County Fire Authority, 2012; Certificate of Recognition, Treasure Island Jobs Corps, 2012; Congressional Champion, American Great Outdoors, 2012; Award, Associated Professional and Contractors of CA, Inc., 2012; Award, The City of West Hollywood, 2013; Congressional Champion Award, The Corps Network, 2013; Distinguished Community Health Advocate, National Association of Community Health Centers, 2013; married: Stewart Boxer, 1962; children: Doug and Nicole; committees: ranking member, Environment and Public Works; vice chair, Select Committee on Ethics; Foreign Relations; elected November 2, 1982, to the 98th Congress; reelected to the 99th–102nd Congresses; elected to the U.S. Senate on November 3, 1992; reelected to each succeeding Senate term.

Office Listings

http://boxer.senate.gov   twitter: @senatorboxer
facebook.com/senatorboxer

112 Hart Senate Office Building, Washington, DC 20510	(202) 224–3553
Chief of Staff.—Laura Schiller.	FAX: 228–2382
Legislative Director.—Sean Moore.	
Director of Scheduling.—Kelly Boyer.	
Communications Director.—Zachary Coile.	
70 Washington Street, Suite 203, Oakland, CA 94607	(510) 286–8537
312 North Spring Street, Suite 1748, Los Angeles, CA 90012	(213) 894–5000
501 I Street, Suite 7–600, Sacramento, CA 95814	(916) 448–2787
600 B Street, Suite 2240, San Diego, CA 92101	(619) 239–3884
2500 Tulare Street, Suite 5290, Fresno, CA 93721	(559) 497–5109
3403 10th Street, Suite 704, Riverside, CA 92501	(951) 684–4849

REPRESENTATIVES

FIRST DISTRICT

DOUG LaMALFA, Republican, of Richvale, CA; born in Oroville, CA, July 2, 1960; education: graduated from Oroville High School; B.S., California Polytechnic State University, San Luis Obispo, CA, 1982; rice farmer; California State Assemblyman, 2002–08; California State Senator, 2010–12; married: Jill; children: four; caucuses: Congressional Western Caucus, Republican Study Committee; Congressional Sportsmen's Caucus; Small Business Caucus; Rice

Caucus; PORTS Caucus; Natural Gas Caucus; Sikh Caucus; Congressional Wine Caucus; Prayer Caucus; Values Action Team; National Guard and Reserve Components Caucus; Cement Caucus; committees: Agriculture; Natural Resources; elected to the 113th Congress on November 6, 2012; reelected to the 114th Congress on November 4, 2014.

Office Listings

http://lamalfa.house.gov   twitter: @replamalfa

322 Cannon House Office Building, Washington, DC 20515 .... (202) 225–3076
 Chief of Staff.—Mark Spannagel.   FAX: 226–0852
 Scheduler.—Caitlin Dorman.
 Legislative Director.—Kevin Eastman.
 Communications Director.—Kevin Eastman.
1453 Downer Street, Suite A, Oroville, CA 95965 .... (530) 534–7100
                        FAX: 534–7800
2885 Churn Creek Road, Suite C, Redding, CA 96002 .... (530) 223–5898
                        FAX: 605–4342
2399 Rickenbacker Way, Auburn, CA 95602 .... (530) 878–5035
                        FAX: 878–5037

Counties: SISKIYOU, MODOC, SHASTA, LASSEN, TEHAMA, PLUMAS, GLENN, BUTTE, SIERRA, NEVADA, AND PLACER. Population (2010), 702,905.

ZIP Codes: 95568, 95602–03, 95712–13, 95728, 95910, 95914–17, 95923–24, 95926–30, 95934, 95936, 95938, 95940–42, 95944–49, 95954, 95956–60, 95965–66, 95968–69, 95971, 95973–78, 95980, 95983–84, 95986, 96001, 96006–09, 96011, 96013–17, 96019–23, 96025, 96027–29, 96031, 96032–35, 96037–40, 96044, 96047, 96050–51, 96054–59, 96061–62, 96064–65, 96067–71, 96073–75, 96078–80, 96084–90, 96092, 96094–97, 96101, 96104–06, 96108–19, 96121–30, 96132, 96134–37, 96161, 97635

* * *

SECOND DISTRICT

JARED W. HUFFMAN, Democrat, of San Rafael, California; born in Independence, MO, February 18, 1964; education: B.A., University of California, Santa Barbara, 1986; J.D., Boston College, 1990; professional: California Assembly, 2006–12; senior lawyer, Natural Resources Defense Council, 2001–06; board member, Marin Municipal Water District, 1994–2006; public interest attorney, 1990–2001; family: married, Susan Huffman; two children; caucuses: Congressional Progressive Caucus, co-chair, Wild Salmon Caucus, Sustainable Energy & Environment Coalition, Problem Solvers Caucus, National Marine Sanctuary Caucus, Congressional Wine Caucus, Congressional Labor and Working Families Caucus, Congressional Shellfish Caucus, Sensible Drug Policy Working Group, Bicameral Task Force on Climate Change, Congressional Rare Disease Caucus; committees: Natural Resources; Transportation and Infrastructure; elected to the 113th Congress on November 6, 2012; reelected to the 114th Congress on November 4, 2014.

Office Listings

http://huffman.house.gov   twitter: @rephuffman   https://www.facebook.com/rephuffman

1630 Longworth House Office Building, Washington, DC 20515 .... (202) 225–5161
 Chief of Staff.—Benjamin Miller.   FAX: 225–5163
 Executive Assistant / Scheduler.—Melissa Burnell.
999 Fifth Avenue, Suite 290, San Rafael, CA 94901 .... (415) 258–9657
 District Director.—Jeannine Callaway.
430 North Franklin Street, P.O. Box 2208, Fort Bragg, CA 95437 .... (707) 962–0933
 District Representative.—Heather Gurewitz.
317 Third Street, Suite 1, Eureka, CA 95501 .... (707) 407–3585
 District Representative.—John Driscoll.

Counties: HUMBOLDT, DEL NORTE, MARIN, MENDOCINO, SONOMA (part), TRINITY. CITIES AND TOWNSHIPS: ARCATA, CLOVERDALE, CRESCENT CITY, EUREKA, FORT BRAGG, GARBERVILLE, HEALDSBURG, MENDOCINO, NOVATO, PETALUMA, SAN RAFAEL, SEBASTOPOL, UKIAH, WINDSOR, AND WILLITS. Population (2010), 708,596.

ZIP Codes: 94946–50, 94952–54, 94956–57, 94960, 94963–66, 94970–79, 94998–99, 95401, 95403–4, 95410, 95412, 95415, 95417–18, 95420–21, 95425, 95427–30, 95432, 95436–37, 95441, 95444–46, 95448–51, 95454, 95456, 95459–60, 95462–63, 95465–66, 95468–73, 95480–82, 95486, 95488, 95490, 95492, 95494, 95497, 95501–03, 95511, 95514, 95518–19, 95521, 95524–28, 95531–32, 95534, 95536–38, 95540, 95542–43, 95545–52

* * *

THIRD DISTRICT

JOHN GARAMENDI, Democrat, of Walnut Grove, CA; born in Camp Blanding, FL, January 24, 1945; education: B.A., business, University of California-Berkeley, Berkeley, CA, 1966; M.B.A., Harvard University, Cambridge, MA, 1974; professional: small business owner; Peace Corps volunteer, 1966–68; California State Assembly member, 1974–76; member of the California State Senate, 1976–90; California Insurance Commissioner, 1991–94, and 2002–06; Deputy Secretary of the U.S. Interior Department, 1995–98; previously California Lieutenant Governor, 2007–09; regent, University of California; trustee, California State University; co-chair, Mobility Air Forces Caucus; co-chair, American Sikh Caucus; member of Make It In America Working Group; religion: Christian; family: married to Patricia Garamendi; six children; eleven grandchildren; Deputy Whip; committees: Armed Services; Transportation and Infrastructure; elected by special election on November 3, 2009, to fill the vacancy caused by the resignation of U.S. Representative Ellen Tauscher; elected to each succeeding Congress.

Office Listings

http://garamendi.house.gov

2438 Rayburn House Office Building, Washington, DC 20515	(202) 225–1880
Chief of Staff.—Emily Burns.	FAX: 225–5914
Scheduler.—Nicole McAllister.	
Communications Director.—Donald Lathbury.	
Legislative Director.—Emily Burns.	
795 Plumas Street, Yuba City, CA 95991	(530) 329–8865
	FAX: 763–4248
412 G Street, Davis, CA 95616	(530) 753–5301
	FAX: 753–5614
1261 Travis Boulevard, Suite 130, Fairfield, CA 94533	(707) 438–1822
	FAX: 438–0523

Counties: COLUSA, GLENN (part), LAKE (part), SACRAMENTO (part), SOLANO (part), SUTTER, YOLO (part), and YUBA. Population (2010), 712,075.

ZIP Codes: 94503, 94510, 94512, 94533–35, 94558, 94571, 94585, 94591, 95422–24, 95443, 95451, 95453, 95457–58, 95464, 95485, 95493, 95606–07, 95612, 95615–18, 95620, 95625–27, 95632, 95637, 95639, 95641, 95645, 95653–54, 95659–60, 95668, 95673–74, 95676, 95679–80, 95687–88, 95690–92, 95694–98, 95757–59, 95776, 95823, 95834–37, 95843, 95901, 95903, 95912–14, 95918–19, 95922, 95925, 95932, 95935, 95937, 95939, 95941, 95950–51, 95953, 95955, 95957, 95960–63, 95966, 95970, 95972, 95977, 95979, 95982, 95987–88, 95991–93

FOURTH DISTRICT

TOM McCLINTOCK, Republican, of Granite Bay, CA; born in Bronxville, NY, July 10, 1956; education: B.A., *cum laude,* political science, UCLA, Los Angeles, CA; 1978; professional: member, California State Assembly, 1982–92 and 1996–2000; member, California State Senate, 2000–08; director, Center for the California Taxpayer, National Tax Limitation Foundation, 1992–94; director, Economic and Regulatory Affairs, Claremont Institute, 1994–96; married: Lori; two children; committees: Budget; Natural Resources; elected to the 111th Congress on November 4, 2008; reelected to each succeeding Congress.

Office Listings

http://www.mcclintock.house.gov   twitter: @repmcclintock

2331 Rayburn House Office Building, Washington, DC 20515	(202) 225–2511
Chief of Staff.—Igor Birman.	FAX: 225–5444
Scheduler.—Rachel Long.	
Legislative Director.—Brittan Specht.	
Deputy Legislative Director.—Chris Tudor.	
Legislative Assistant.—Steven Koncar.	
Legislative Correspondent.—Brittany Madni.	
2200A Douglas Boulevard, Suite 240, Roseville, CA	(916) 786–5560
District Director.—Rocky Deal.	

Counties: ALPINE, AMADOR, CALAVERAS, EL DORADO, MARIPOSA, TUOLUMNE, FRESNO (part), MADERA (part), NEVADA (part), PLACER (part). Population (2010), 760,078.

ZIP Codes: 35251, 59223, 85252, 92532, 93601–02, 93604–05, 93610–11, 93614, 93619, 93621, 93623, 93626, 93628, 93633–34, 93636, 93638, 93641, 93643–45, 93649, 93651, 93653, 93657, 93664, 93667, 93669, 93675, 93701, 94248, 95147, 95221–26, 95228–30, 95232–33, 95236, 95245–49, 95251–52, 95254–57, 95256–57, 95305–06, 95309–11, 95318,

95321, 95325, 95327, 95329, 95333, 95335, 95338, 95345–47, 95364, 95369–70, 95372–73, 95379, 95383, 95389, 95601, 95603, 95613–14, 95619, 95623, 95626, 95629, 95631, 95633–36, 95640, 95642, 95644, 95646, 95648, 95650–51, 95656, 95658, 95661, 95663–69, 95672, 95675, 95678, 95681–82, 95684–85, 95689, 95699, 95709, 95713, 95715, 95720–21, 95724, 95726, 95728, 95735, 95746–47, 95762, 95765, 95945–46, 95949, 95959, 96120, 96140,. 96141–43, 96145–46, 96148, 96150, 96161–62

* * *

FIFTH DISTRICT

MIKE THOMPSON, Democrat, of Napa Valley, CA; born in St. Helena, CA, January 24, 1951; education: graduated, St. Helena High School, St. Helena, CA; U.S. Army, 1969–72; Purple Heart; B.A., Chico State University, 1982; M.A., Chico State University, 1996; teacher at San Francisco State University, and Chico State University; elected to the California State Senate, 2nd District, 1990–98; former chairman of the California State Senate Budget Committee; married to Janet; two children: Christopher and Jon; committees: Ways and Means; elected to the 106th Congress; reelected to each succeeding Congress.

Office Listings

http://mikethompson.house.gov   http://www.house.gov/writerep   twitter: @repthompson

231 Cannon House Office Building, Washington, DC 20515	(202) 225–3311
Chiefs of Staff: Melanie Rhinehart, Van Tassell.	FAX: 225–4335
Legislative Director.—Jennifer Goedke.	
Communications Director.—Austin Vevurka.	
2751 Napa Valley Corporate Drive, Building 2, Napa, CA 94558	(707) 226–9898
1985 Walnut Avenue, Vallejo, CA 94592	(707) 645–1888
2300 County Center Drive, Suite A100, Santa Rosa, CA 95403	(707) 542–7182

Counties: CONTRA COSTA. CITIES AND TOWNSHIPS: Christie, Crockett, Glen Frazer, Hercules, Martinez, Pinole, Port Costa, Rodeo, Selby, Tara Hills, Tormey, Vine Hill. LAKE COUNTY. CITIES AND TOWNSHIPS: Cobb, Kelseyville, Lakeport, Middletown. SONOMA COUNTY. CITIES AND TOWNSHIPS: Boyes Hot Springs, Cotati, El Verano, Eldridge, Fetters Hot Springs, Fulton, Glen Ellen, Kenwood, Mark West, Rohnert Park, Santa Rosa, Sonoma, Vineburg. NAPA COUNTY. CITIES AND TOWNSHIPS: American Canyon, Angwin, Aetna Springs, Calistoga, Deer Park, Oakville, Pope Valley, Rutherford, St. Helena. SOLANO COUNTY. CITIES AND TOWNSHIPS: Benicia, Tiara, Vallejo. Population (2011), 547,495.

ZIP Codes: 94508, 94510, 94515, 94525, 94547, 94553, 94558–59, 94562, 94564, 94567, 94569, 94572–74, 94576, 94581, 94587, 94589–92, 94599, 94806, 94926 28, 94931, 95401, 95409, 95416, 95426, 95431, 95433, 95435, 95439, 95442, 95451–53, 95461, 95476, 95492, 95621.

* * *

SIXTH DISTRICT

DORIS OKADA MATSUI, Democrat, of Sacramento, CA; born in Posten, AZ, September 25, 1944; education: B.A., University of California, Berkeley, CA, 1966; professional: staff, White House, 1992–98; private advocate; organizations: Meridian International Center Board of Trustees; Woodrow Wilson Center Board of Trustees; California Institute Board of Directors; married: Robert Matsui, 1966; children: Brian Robert; committees: Energy and Commerce; elected by special election on March 8, 2005 to the 109th Congress, to fill the vacancy caused by the death of her husband, Representative Robert Matsui; reelected to each succeeding Congress.

Office Listings

http://www.matsui.house.gov   https://twitter.com/dorismatsui

2311 Rayburn House Office Building, Washington, DC 20515	(202) 225–7163
Chief of Staff.—Julie Eddy.	FAX: 225–0566
Executive Assistant.—Clare Chmiel.	
Legislative Director.—Kyle Victor.	
Press Secretary.—Julie Eddy.	
501 I Street, 12–600, Sacramento, CA 95814	(916) 498–5600
District Director.—Nathan Dietrich.	

County: SACRAMENTO COUNTY (part), YOLO COUNTY (part). CITY: Sacramento and West Sacramento. Population (2010), 702,905.

ZIP Codes: 95605, 95618, 95620–21, 95652, 95660, 95673, 95691, 95758, 95811, 95814 26, 95828–29, 95831–35, 95837, 95838, 95841–43, 95864

* * *

SEVENTH DISTRICT

AMI BERA, Democrat of Elk Grove, CA; born in La Palma, CA, March 2, 1965; education: B.S., University of California, Irvine, CA; M.D., University of California, Irvine, CA, 1991; professional: military; awards: medical director for care management, Mercy Hospital, Sacramento, CA; chief medical officer, Sacramento, CA; associate dean of admissions for University of California, Davis Medical School, 2004–07; religion: Unitarian; married: Janine Bera (also a physician); children: Sydra; committees: Foreign Affairs; Science, Space, and Technology; elected to the 113th Congress on November 6, 2012.

Office Listings

http://bera.house.gov   htps://twitter.com/repbera

1535 Longworth House Office Building, Washington, DC 20515	(202) 225–5716
Chief of Staff.—Mini Timmaraju.	FAX: 226–1298
Director of Operations.—Erin Fyffe.	
Legislative Director.—Matt Horowitz.	
Communications Director.—Allison Teixeira.	
11070 White Rock Road, Suite 195, Rancho Cordova, CA 95670	(916) 635–0505
District Director.—Faith Whitmore.	

Counties: EASTERN HALF OF SACRAMENTO COUNTY. CITIES: Citrus Heights, Folsom, Rancho Cordova, and Elk Grove as well as the unincorporated communities of, Carmichael, Fair Oaks, Orangevale, Rosemont, La Riviera, Sloughhouse, Rancho Murieta, Vineyard, Florin, Vintage Park, Wilton, Herald and half of Arden Arcade. Population: (2010), 710,607.

ZIP Codes: 95608–11, 95621, 95624, 95628, 95630, 95632, 95638, 95655, 95662, 95670, 95678, 95683, 95693, 95741–42, 95757–58, 95763, 95821, 95823, 95825–30, 95841–42, 95864–66 (Some of these zips are only partially in the District)

* * *

EIGHTH DISTRICT

PAUL COOK, Republican, of Yucca Valley, CA, born in Meridien, CT, March 3, 1943; B.S., Southern Connecticut University, New Haven, CT, 1966; M.P.A., California State University San Bernardino, San Bernardino, CA, 1996; M.A., University of California Riverside, Riverside, CA, 2000; professional: United States Marine Corps, 1966–92; professor; member, Yucca Valley California Town Council, 1998–2006; California State Assemblyman, 2006–12; married: Jeanne; committees: Armed Services; Foreign Affairs; Natural Resources; elected to the 113th Congress on November 6, 2012; reelected to the 114th Congress on November 4, 2014.

Office Listings

http://cook.house.gov

1222 Longworth House Office Building, Washington, DC 20515	(202) 225–5861
Chief of Staff.—John Sobel.	FAX: 225–6498
14955 Dale Evans Parkway, Apple Valley, CA 92307	(760) 247–1815
District Director.—Matthew Knox.	

Counties: SAN BERNARDINO (part), MONO, INYO. CITIES AND TOWNSHIPS: Adelanto, Angelus Oaks, Apple Valley, Arrowbear, Arrowhead Farms, Baldy Mesa, Baker, Barstow, Bear Valley, Benton, Big Bear City, Big Bear Lake, Big Pine, Big River, Bishop, Bridgeport, Bums Canyon, Cartago, Cedar Glen, Cedar Pines Park, Coleville, Crestline, Daggett, Darwin, El Mirage, Erwin Lake, Fawnskin, Flamingo Heights, Forest Falls, Furnace Creek, Green Valley Lake, Helendale, Hesperia, Highland, Hinkley, Independence, Joshua Tree, June Lake, Lake Arrowhead, Keeler, Landers, Lenwood, Lee Vining, Lytle Creek, Mono City, Mount Baldy, Morongo Valley, Needles, Newberry Springs, Oak Glen, Oak Hills, Oro Grande, Paradise, Pioneertown, Pinon Hills, Phelan, Red Mountain, Rimrock, Running Springs, Skyforest, Sugarloaf, Topaz, Trona, Twentynine Palms, Twin Peaks, Victorville, Walker, Wrightwood, Yucca Valley, and Yucaipa. Population (2010) 708,578.

ZIP Codes: 91759, 92242, 92252, 92256, 92268, 92277–78, 92284–86, 92301, 92305, 92309–64, 92310–12, 92314–15, 92321–22, 92325, 92327–28, 92333, 92339–42, 92344–47, 92352, 92358, 92363, 92368, 92372, 92382, 92385–86, 92388–65, 92391–95, 92397–99, 92407, 93512–15, 93522, 93526, 93529–30, 93541, 93549, 93558, 93562–92, 95223, 95967, 95969, 96107, 96133

* * *

NINTH DISTRICT

JERRY McNERNEY, Democrat, of Stockton, CA; born in Albuquerque, NM, June 18, 1951; attended the U.S. Military Academy, West Point, NY, 1969–71; B.S., University of New Mexico, Albuquerque, NM, 1973; M.S., University of New Mexico, NM, 1975; Ph.D. in Mathematics, University of New Mexico, 1981; professional: wind engineer; entrepreneur; business owner; married: Mary; children: Michael, Windy, and Greg; committees: Energy and Commerce; Veterans' Affairs; elected to the 110th Congress on November 7, 2006; reelected to each succeeding Congress.

Office Listings

http://mcnerney.house.gov　　twitter: @repmcnerney

2265 Rayburn House Office Building, Washington, DC 20515	(202) 225–1947
Chief of Staff.—Nicole Damasco Alioto.	FAX: 225–4060
Scheduler.—Teresa Frison.	
Communications Director.—Mike Naple.	
Legislative Director.—Patrick Arness.	
District Director.—Alisa Alva.	
2222 Grand Canal Boulevard, #7, Stockton, CA 95207	(209) 476–8552
4703 Lone Tree Way, Antioch, CA 94531	(925) 754–0716

Counties: SAN JOAQUIN (part), CONTRA COSTA (part), SACRAMENTO (part). CITIES AND TOWNSHIPS: Stockton, Antioch, Lodi, Brentwood, Oakley, Galt, Lathrop, and Discovery Bay. Population (2010), 648,766.

ZIP Codes: 94505, 94509, 94511, 94513–14, 94531, 94548, 94561, 95201–15, 95219–20, 95227, 95230–31, 95234, 95236–37, 95240–42, 95253, 95258, 95267, 95269, 95296, 95304, 95320, 95330, 95336–37, 95361, 95366, 95391, 95632, 95686, 95690, 95757

* * *

TENTH DISTRICT

JEFF DENHAM, Republican, of Turlock, CA; born in Hawthorne, CA, July 29, 1967; education: A.A., Victor Valley Junior College, Victorville, CA, 1989; B.A., California Polytechnic State University, San Luis Obispo, CA, 1992; military: United States Air Force, 1984–88; United States Air Force Reserve, 1988–2000; professional: business owner; served in the California State Senate, 2002–10; religion: Christian; family: wife, Sonia; two children; committees: Agriculture; Natural Resources; Transportation and Infrastructure; elected to the 112th Congress on November 2, 2010; reelected to each succeeding Congress.

Office Listings

http://www.denham.house.gov　　twitter: @repjeffdenham　　https://facebook.com/repjeffdenham
https://www.youtube.com/repjeffdenham　　http://www.flickr.com/photos/59309318@No4/

1730 Longworth House Office Building, Washington, DC 20515	(202) 225–4540
Chief of Staff.—Jason Larrabee.	FAX: 225–3402
Scheduler.—Carol Kresse.	
4701 Sisk Road, Suite 202, Modesto, CA 95356	(209) 579–5458
District Director.—Bob Rucker.	

Counties: STANISLAUS COUNTY (part), SAN JOAQUIN COUNTY (part). CITIES AND TOWNSHIPS: Airport, Bret Harte, Bystrom, Ceres, Cowan, Cowan Landing, Del Rio, Denair, Diablo Grande, East Oakdale, Empire, Escalon, Grayson, Hickman, Hughson, Keyes, Manteca, Modesto, Monterey Park Tract, Newman, Oakdale, Parklawn, Patterson, Ripon, Riverbank, Riverdale Park, Rouse, Salida, Shackelford, Tracy, Turlock, Valley Home, Waterford, West Modesto, Woodbridge, Westley, and Westport. Population (2010), 714,750.

ZIP Codes: 94550, 95230, 95304, 95307, 95313, 95316, 95319–20, 95322–23, 95326, 95328–30, 95336–37, 95350–51, 95354–58, 95360–61, 95363, 95366–68, 95376–77, 95380, 95382, 95385–87

* * *

ELEVENTH DISTRICT

MARK DESAULNIER, Democrat, of Concord, CA; born in Lowell, MA, March 31, 1952; B.A., history, College of the Holy Cross, Worcester, MA, 1974; professional: deputy probation officer, 1970–74; hotel service employee, 1975–76; restaurant general manager, 1978; restaurant owner, 1978–2006; Concord mayor, 1993; Concord City Council, 1991–94; Contra Costa County Supervisor, 1994–2006; California Assembly, 2006–08; California Senate, 2008–15; religion: Catholic; children: Tristan and Tucker; committees: Education and the Workforce; Oversight and Government Reform; elected to the 114th Congress on November 4, 2014.

Office Listings

https://desaulnier.house.gov   twitter @repdesaulnier

327 Cannon House Office Building, Washington, DC 20515 .... (202) 225–2095
    Chief of Staff.—Betsy Arnold Marr.   FAX: 225–5609
    Executive Assistant / Scheduler.—Aimee Wall.
101 Ygnacio Valley Road, Suite 210, Walnut Creek, CA 94596 .... (925) 602–1880
    District Director.—Shanelle Scales Preston.
440 Civic Center Plaza, Second Floor, Richmond, CA 94804 .... (510) 262–6500
    Outreach Coordinator.—Christopher Whitmore.

Counties: CONTRA COSTA (part), SOLANO (part). CITIES AND TOWNSHIPS: Alomo, Antioch, Bay Point, Blackhawk, Clayton, Concord, El Cerrito, El Sobrante, Kensington, Lafayette, Martinez, Moraga, Orinda, Pittsburg, Pleasant Hil, Richmond, San Pablo, and Walnut Creek. Population (2014), 773,916.

ZIP Codes: 92526, 94506–07, 94509, 94517–24, 94527–30, 94549, 94553, 94556–57, 94563, 94565, 94595–98, 94708, 94801–08, 94820, 94850

* * *

TWELFTH DISTRICT

NANCY PELOSI, Democrat, of San Francisco, CA; born in Baltimore, MD, March 26, 1940; daughter of the late Representative Thomas D'Alesandro, Jr., of MD; education: graduated, Institute of Notre Dame High School, 1958; B.A., Trinity College, Washington, DC (major, political science; minor, history), 1962; northern chair, California Democratic Party, 1977–81; state chair, California Democratic Party, 1981–83; chair, 1984 Democratic National Convention Host Committee; finance chair, Democratic Senatorial Campaign Committee, 1985–86; member: Democratic National Committee; California Democratic Party Executive Committee; San Francisco Library Commission; Board of Trustees, LSB Leakey Foundation; married: Paul F. Pelosi, 1963; children: Nancy Corinne, Christine, Jacqueline, Paul, Jr., and Alexandra; 9 grandchildren; elected by special election, June 2, 1987, to the 100th Congress to fill the vacancy caused by the death of Representative Sala Burton; reelected to each succeeding Congress; elected Democratic Whip in the 107th Congress; Democratic Leader in the 108th and 109th Congresses; elected Speaker of the House in the 110th and 111th Congresses; elected Democratic Leader in the 112th, 113th, and 114th Congresses.

Office Listings

http://www.pelosi.house.gov   twitter: @nancypelosi

233 Cannon House Office Building, Washington, DC 20515 .... (202) 225–4965
    Chief of Staff.—Robert Edmondson (California).   FAX: 225–8259
90 7th Street, Suite 2–800, San Francisco, CA 94103 .... (415) 556–4862
    District Chief of Staff.—Dan Bernal.

County: SAN FRANCISCO COUNTY (part). CITY: San Francisco. Population (2010), 702,905.

ZIP Codes: 94014, 94102–05, 94107–12, 94114–18, 94121–24, 94127, 94129–34, 94158, 94164

* * *

THIRTEENTH DISTRICT

BARBARA LEE, Democrat, of Oakland, CA; born in El Paso, TX, July 16, 1946; education: graduated, San Fernando High School; B.A., Mills College, 1973; MSW, University of California, Berkeley, 1975; congressional aide and public servant; senior advisor and chief of staff to Congressman Ronald V. Dellums in Washington, DC, and Oakland, CA, 1975–87; California State Assembly, 1990–96; California State Senate, 1996–98; Assembly committees: Housing and Land Use; Appropriations; Business and Professions; Industrial Relations; Judiciary; Revenue and Taxation; board member, California State Coastal Conservancy, District Export Council, and California Defense Conversion Council; committees: Appropriations; Budget; elected to the 105th Congress on April 7, 1998, by special election, to fill the remaining term of retiring Representative Ronald V. Dellums; reelected to each succeeding Congress.

Office Listings

http://lee.house.gov   twitter: @repbarbaralee

2267 Rayburn House Office Building, Washington, DC 20515 .... (202) 225–2661
    Chief of Staff.—Julie Nickson.   FAX: 225–9817
    Scheduler.—Tatyana Kalinga.
    Communications Director.—James Lewis.
    Legislative Director.—Diala Jadallah.
1301 Clay Street, Suite 1000–N, Oakland, CA 94612 .... (510) 763–0370

Counties: ALAMEDA COUNTY. CITIES: Alameda, Albany, Berkeley, Emeryville, Oakland, Piedmont, San Leandro. Population (2010), 691,592.

ZIP Codes: 94501–02, 94577–79, 94601–15, 94617–94621, 94623–27, 94643, 94649, 94660–62, 94666, 94701–10, 94712, 94720

* * *

FOURTEENTH DISTRICT

JACKIE SPEIER, Democrat, of Hillsborough, CA; born in San Francisco, CA, May 14, 1950; education: B.A., University of California at Davis; J.D., University of California, Hastings College of the Law, 1976; legislative council, Congressman Leo J. Ryan; member, San Mateo County Board of Supervisors; member, California State Assembly; senator, California State Senate; married: Barry Dennis; two children: Jackson Sierra and Stephanie Sierra; committees: Armed Services; Permanent Select Committee on Intelligence; elected in a special election, April 8, 2008, to fill the vacancy caused by the death of Representative Thomas P. Lantos; elected to the 111th Congress on November 4, 2008; reelected to each succeeding Congress.

Office Listings

http://speier.house.gov   https://www.facebook.com/jackiespeier   twitter: @repspeier
http://www.youtube.com/user/jackiespeierCA12   Instagram: @jackiespeier

2465 Rayburn House Office Building, Washington, DC 20515 .... (202) 225–3531
    Chief of Staff.—Cookab Hashemi.   FAX: 226–4183
    Legislative Director.—Josh Connolly.
155 Bovet Road, Suite 780, San Mateo, CA 94402 .... (650) 342–0300
    District Representative.—Brian Perkins.   FAX: 375–8270

Counties: SAN MATEO COUNTY (part). CITIES: Belmont, Brisbane, Burlingame, Colma, Daly City, East Palo Alto, Foster City, Half Moon Bay, Hillsborough, Menlo Park, Millbrae, Montara, Moss Beach, Pacifica, Redwood City, San Bruno, San Carlos, San Gregorio, San Mateo, South San Francisco, and Woodside. SAN FRANCISCO COUNTY (part). CITIES: San Francisco. Population (2012), 726,938.

ZIP Codes: 94002, 94005, 94010–11, 94013–15, 94019, 94025, 94030, 94038, 94044, 94061–66, 94070, 94074, 94080, 94083, 94099, 94112, 94116–17, 94127–28, 94131–32, 94134, 94143, 94303, 94401–04, 94497

* * *

FIFTEENTH DISTRICT

ERIC SWALWELL, Democrat, of Dublin, CA; born in Sac City, IA, November 16, 1980; education: graduated, Dublin High School, Dublin, CA, 1999; B.A., University of Maryland, College Park, College Park, MD, 2003; J.D., University of Maryland School of Law, Baltimore, MD, 2006; professional: former city councilman at City of Dublin City Council; former Deputy District Attorney at Alameda County District Attorney's Office; Planning Commissioner at City of Dublin; Heritage & Cultural Arts Commissioner at City of Dublin; law clerk at Alameda County District Attorney's Office; commission: Tom Lantos Human Rights; caucuses: Pro-Choice; Ad Hoc Committee for Irish Affairs; Anti-Bullying; Congressional Asian Pacific America; Congressional Dyslexia; Cyber Security; Democratic Whip's Task Force on Poverty and Opportunity; Diabetes; Friends of Ireland; High Tech; India; International Religious Freedom; Internet; LGBT Equality; Ports; Science and Labs; Sikh; Soccer; Victims' Rights; Wine; committees: Science, Space, and Technology; Select Committee on Intelligence; elected to the 113th Congress on November 6, 2012; reelected to the 114th Congress on November 4, 2014.

Office Listings

http://www.swalwell.house.gov   twitter: @repswalwell

129 Cannon House Office Building, Washington, DC 20515	(202) 225–5065
Chief of Staff.—Ricky Le.	FAX: 226–3805
5075 Hopyard Road, Pleasanton, CA 94588	(925) 460–5100
1260 B Street, Suite 150, Hayward, CA 94541	(510) 370–3322

Counties: ALAMEDA COUNTY (part) AND CONTRA COSTA (part). CITIES AND TOWNSHIPS: San Leandro (part), San Lorenzo, Castro Valley, Union City, Fremont (part), Hayward, Pleasanton, San Ramon, Dublin, Sunol, Ashland, Danville (part), and Fairview. Population (2010), 732,515.

ZIP Codes: 94505–06, 94514, 94526, 94536, 94538–39, 94541–42, 94544–46, 94550–52, 94555, 94566, 94568, 94577–78

* * *

SIXTEENTH DISTRICT

JIM COSTA, Democrat, of Fresno, CA; born in Fresno, April 13, 1952; education: B.A., California State University, Fresno, CA, 1974; professional: special assistant, Congressman John Krebs, 1975–76; administrative assistant, California Assemblyman Richard Lehman, 1976–78; California State Assembly, 1978–94; California State Senate, 1994–2002; Chief Executive Officer, Costa Group, 2002–03; religion: Catholic; committees: Agriculture; Natural Resources; elected to the 109th Congress on November 2, 2004; reelected to each succeeding Congress.

Office Listings

http://www.costa.house.govt   https://twitter.com/repjimcosta
https://www.facebook.com/repjimcosta   https://www.youtube.com/user/repjimcostaca20

1314 Longworth House Office Building, Washington, DC 20515	(202) 225–3341
Chief of Staff.—Juan Lopez.	FAX: 225–9308
Legislative Director.—Scott Petersen.	
Communications Director.—Dianna Zamora Marroquin.	
Schedulers: Christy Bourdon (CA), Claudia Santiago (DC).	
District Director. Vacant.	
855 M Street, Suite 940, Fresno, CA 93721	(559) 495–1620
2222 M Street, Suite 305, Merced, CA 95340	(209) 384–1620

Counties: FRESNO (part), MADERA (part), MERCED. Population (2011), 714,214.

ZIP Codes: 93606, 93610 (part), 93620 (part), 93622 (part), 93626 (part), 93630 (part), 93635, 93636 (part), 93637, 93638 (part), 93639, 93661, 93665, 93701–03, 93704–06 (part), 93707–09, 93711 (part), 93712, 93714–18, 93721, 93722–23 (part), 93724, 93725–27 (part), 93728, 92741, 93744–45, 93747, 93750, 93755, 93760–61, 93764, 93771–79, 93786, 93790–94, 93844, 93888, 95301, 95303, 95312, 95315, 95316 (part), 95317, 95322 (part), 95324, 95333–34, 95340–41, 95343–44, 95348, 95356, 95360 (part), 95369 (part), 95374, 95380 (part), 95388

* * *

SEVENTEENTH DISTRICT

MICHAEL M. HONDA, Democrat, of San Jose, CA; born in Walnut Creek, CA, June 27, 1941; education: San Jose State University, received degrees in biological sciences and spanish, and a master's degree in education; awards: California Federation of Teachers Legislator of the Year; Outreach Paratransit Services Humanitarian Award; AEA Legislator of the Year; Service Employees International Union Home Care Champion Award; Asian Law Alliance Community Impact Award; AFL–CIO Distinguished Friend of Labor Award; chair emeritus, Congressional Asian Pacific American Caucus; chair, Ethiopia and Ethiopian American Caucus; chair, Congressional Anti-Bullying Caucus; public service: Peace Corps; San Jose Planning Commission; San Jose Unified School Board; Santa Clara County Board of Supervisors; California State Assemblyman; family: widower; children: Mark and Michelle; committees: Appropriations; Democratic Senior Whip; elected to the 107th Congress on November 7, 2000; reelected to each succeeding Congress.

Office Listings

http://honda.house.gov   http://twitter.com/repmikehonda
https://vine.co/u/1154920290497736704   http://facebook.com/repmikehonda
http://instagram.com/repmikehonda   http://plus.google.com/+mikehonda
http://youtube.com/repmikehonda   https://www.pinterest.com/repmikehonda/
http://repmikehonda.tumblr.com/   http://repmikehonda.eventbrite.com/
http://www.scribd.com/repmikehonda

1713 Longworth House Office Building, Washington, DC 20515 .... (202) 225–2631
    Chief of Staff.—Jennifer Van der Heide.   FAX: 225–2699
    Legislative Director.—Eric Werwa.
    Communications Director.—Lauren Smith.
900 Lafayette Street, Suite 206, Santa Clara, CA 95050 .... (408) 436–2720
    District Director.—Edwin Tan.

Counties: ALAMEDA COUNTY (part), Santa Clara County (part). CITIES AND TOWNSHIPS: Cupertino, Fremont, Milpitas, Newark, North San Jose, Santa Clara, and Sunnyvale. Population (2014), 724,244.

ZIP Codes: 94024, 94040, 94043, 94085–89, 94536, 94538–39, 94555, 94560, 95002, 95014–15, 95035–36, 95050–56, 95070, 95101, 95110, 95112, 95116–17, 95126–29, 95131–34, 95140

* * *

EIGHTEENTH DISTRICT

ANNA G. ESHOO, Democrat, of Menlo Park, CA; born in New Britain, CT, December 13, 1942; education: attended Cañada College; a graduate of the CORO Foundation and holds an Honorary Degree from Menlo College; San Mateo County Board of Supervisors, 1982–92; committees: Energy and Commerce; elected on November 3, 1992, to the 103rd Congress; reelected to each succeeding Congress.

Office Listings

http://www.eshoo.house.gov

241 Cannon House Office Building, Washington, DC 20515 .... (202) 225–8104
    Senior Advisor.—Jena Gross.   FAX: 225–8890
698 Emerson Street, Palo Alto, CA 94301 .... (650) 323–2984
    Chief of Staff.—Karen Chapman.

Counties: SAN MATEO, SANTA CLARA, SANTA CRUZ. CITIES AND TOWNSHIPS: Atherton, Ben Lomond, Boony Doon, Boulder Creek, Brookdale, Campbell, Cambrian Park, Davenport, Felton, Fruitdale, La Honda, Ladera, Lexington Hills, Loma Mar, Lompico, Los Altos, Los Altos Hills, Los Gatos, Menlo Park, Monte Sereno, Mountain View, Palo Alto, Pescadero, Portola Valley, Redwood City, San Jose, Saratoga, Scott's Valley, Stanford, Woodside, and Zayante. Population (2010), 702,906.

ZIP Codes: 94020–28, 94035, 94039–43, 94060–63, 94074, 94301 06, 94309, 95005–09, 95011, 95014, 95017–18, 95026, 95030–33, 95041–42, 95044, 95050, 95060, 95065–67, 95070–71, 95073, 95076, 95117–18, 95120, 95123–26, 95128–30, 95141, 95154, 95157–58, 95160, 95170

* * *

NINETEENTH DISTRICT

ZOE LOFGREN, Democrat, of San Jose, CA; born in San Mateo, CA, December 21, 1947; education: graduated, Gunn High School, 1966; B.A., Stanford University, Stanford, CA, 1970; J.D., Santa Clara Law School, Santa Clara, CA, 1975; admitted to the California Bar, 1975; District of Columbia Bar, 1981; Supreme Court, 1986; member: board of trustees, San Jose Evergreen Community College District, 1979–81; board of supervisors, Santa Clara County, CA, 1981–94; married: John Marshall Collins, 1978; children: Sheila and John; committees: House Administration; Judiciary; Science, Space, and Technology; Joint Committee on the Library; elected to the 104th Congress; reelected to each succeeding Congress.

Office Listings

http://www.lofgren.house.gov   twitter: @repzoelofgren

1401 Longworth House Office Building, Washington, DC 20515 .... (202) 225–3072
    Chief of Staff.—Stacey Leavandosky.   FAX: 225–3336
    Communications Director.—Peter Whippey.
    Executive Assistant / Scheduler.—Sabrina Kirkwood.
635 North First Street, Suite B, San Jose, CA 95112 .... (408) 271–8700

Office Listings—Continued

District Chief of Staff.—Sandra Soto.

Counties: SANTA CLARA (part). CITIES AND TOWNSHIPS: San Jose, San Martin, Gilroy and unincorporated portions of southern Santa Clara County. Population (2010), 702,904.

ZIP Codes: 94550, 95013, 95020, 95023, 95033, 95035, 95037–38, 95046, 95050, 95076, 95103, 95106, 95108–13, 95109–13, 95115–16, 95118–28, 95132–33, 95135–36, 95138–41, 95148, 95150–53, 95155–56, 95159, 95172–73, 95191–92, 95196

* * *

TWENTIETH DISTRICT

SAM FARR, Democrat, of Carmel, CA; born in San Francisco, CA, July 4, 1941; education: attended Carmel, CA, public schools; B.S., biology, Willamette University, Salem, OR; studied at the Monterey Institute of International Studies; served in the Peace Corps for two years in Colombia, South America; worked as a consultant and employee of the California Assembly; elected to the California Assembly, 1980–93; former member of California Assembly's Committees on Education, Insurance, and Natural Resources; married to Shary Baldwin; one daughter: Jessica; committees: Appropriations; elected on June 8, 1993, by special election, to fill the vacancy caused by the resignation of Representative Leon Panetta; reelected to each succeeding Congress.

Office Listings

http://www.farr.house.gov   twitter: @repsamfarr   http://www.facebook.com/repsamfarr

1126 Longworth House Office Building, Washington, DC 20515 .... (202) 225–2861
  Chief of Staff.—Rochelle Dornatt.
  Legislative Director.—Debbie Merrill.
  Press Secretary.—Adam Russell.
701 Ocean Avenue, Santa Cruz, CA 95060 .... (831) 429–1976
100 West Alisal Street, Salinas, CA 93901 .... (831) 424–2229

Counties: MONTEREY, SAN BENITO, SANTA CRUZ (southern half), SANTA CLARA (southern portion). Population (2010), 744,350.

ZIP Codes: 93426, 93450–51, 93901–02, 93905–08, 93912, 93915, 93920–28, 93930, 93932–33, 93940, 93942–44, 93950, 93953–55, 93960, 93962, 95001, 95003–04, 95010, 95012, 95019, 95020–21, 95023–24, 95039, 95043, 95045, 95060–65, 95073, 95075–77

* * *

TWENTY-FIRST DISTRICT

DAVID VALADAO, Republican, of Hanford, CA; born in Hanford, CA, April 14, 1977; education: graduated from Hanford High School; attended College of the Sequoias in Visalia, CA. professional: dairy farmer; leadership: the California Milk Advisory Board, Western States Dairy Trade Association; elected as Regional Leadership Council Chairman for Land O' Lakes Inc., a Fortune 200 company; member of the California State Assembly, 2010–12; religion: Catholic; married: Terra Valadao; three children, Connor, Madeline, and Lucas; committees: Appropriations; elected to the 113th Congress on November 6, 2012; reelected to the 114th Congress on November 4, 2014.

Office Listings

http://www.valadao.house.gov   https://www.facebook.com/congressmandavidvaladao
https://twitter.com/repdavidvaladao

1004 Longworth House Office Building, Washington, DC 20515 .... (202) 225–4695
  Chief of Staff.—Tal Eslick.   FAX: 225–3196
  Scheduler.—Molly Harris.
  Legislative Director.—Jessica Butler.
101 Irwin Street, Suite 110B, Hanford, CA 93230 .... (559) 582–5526
  District Director.—Justin Mendes.
2700 M Street, Suite 250B, Bakersfield, CA 93301 .... (661) 864–7736

Counties: KINGS, TULARE (part), KERN (part), FRESNO (part). Population (2010), 714,164.

ZIP Codes: 93201–04, 93206, 93210, 93212, 93215, 93218–19, 93227, 93230, 93234, 93237, 93239, 93241–43, 93245, 93249–51, 93256–57, 93261, 93263, 93266, 93270, 93272, 93274–75, 93278–80, 93290–91, 93304–07, 93311–12, 93314, 93607–09, 93616, 93620, 93622, 93624–25, 93627, 93631, 93640, 93648, 93652, 93654, 93656–57, 93660, 93662, 93668, 93706, 93723, 93725

* * *

TWENTY-SECOND DISTRICT

DEVIN NUNES, Republican, of Tulare, CA; born in Tulare County, CA, October 1, 1973; education: A.A., College of the Sequoias; B.S., Agricultural Business, and a Master's Degree in Agriculture, from California Polytechnic State University, San Luis Obispo; graduate, California Agriculture Leadership Fellowship Program; professional: farmer and businessman; elected, College of the Sequoias Board of Trustees, 1996; reelected, 2000; appointed by President George W. Bush to serve as California State Director of the U.S. Department of Agriculture Rural Development Office, 2001; religion: Catholic; married: the former Elizabeth Tamariz, 2003; three children; committees: Ways and Means; Permanent Select Committee on Intelligence; Joint Committee on Taxation; elected to the 108th Congress on November 5, 2002; reelected to each succeeding Congress.

Office Listings

http://www.nunes.house.gov

1013 Longworth House Office Building, Washington, DC 20515	(202) 225–2523
Chief of Staff.—Anthony Ratekin.	FAX: 225–3404
Deputy Chief of Staff.—Caitlin Shannon.	
Legislative Director.—Jilian Plank.	
Communications Director.—Jack Langer.	
Scheduler.—Jennifer Morrow.	
113 North Church Street, Suite 208, Visalia, CA 93291	(559) 733–3861
264 Clovis Avenue, Suite 206, Clovis, CA 93612	(559) 323–5235

Counties: TULARE, FRESNO (part). Population (2010), 702,904.

ZIP Codes: 93201, 93207–08, 93212, 93215, 93218–19, 93221, 93223, 93227, 93235, 93237, 93242, 93244, 93247, 93256–58, 93260–62, 93265, 93267, 93270–72, 93274–75, 93277–79, 93286, 93290–92, 93602–03, 93605, 93609, 93611–13, 93615–16, 93618, 93621, 93625–26, 93628, 93631, 93633–34, 93641–42, 93646–49, 93651, 93654, 93656–57, 93662, 93664, 93666–67, 93670, 93673, 93675, 93703, 93710, 93720, 93726–27, 93740, 93747

* * *

TWENTY-THIRD DISTRICT

KEVIN McCARTHY, Republican, of Bakersfield, CA; born in Bakersfield, January 26, 1965; education: graduated, Bakersfield High School, 1983; B.S., business administration, CSU-Bakersfield, 1989; M.B.A., CSU-Bakersfield, 1994; professional: intern, worked up to District Director for U.S. Congressman Bill Thomas, 1987–2002; served as Trustee, Kern Community College District, 2000–02; served in the California State Assembly, 2002–06; elected, California Assembly Republican Leader, 2003–06; married to the former Judy Wages, 1992; two children: Connor and Meghan; elected, House Majority Whip, 2011–14; elected, House Majority Leader, 2014–present; committees: Financial Services (on leave); elected to the 110th Congress on November 7, 2006; reelected to each succeeding Congress.

Office Listings

http://www.kevinmccarthy.house.gov   twitter: @GOPleader

2421 Rayburn House Office Building, Washington, DC 20515	(202) 225–2915
Chief of Staff.—James Min.	FAX: 225–2908
Scheduler.—Kristin Stipicevic.	
Legislative Director.—Kyle Lombardi.	
Press Secretary.—Matt Sparks.	
4100 Empire Drive, Suite 150, Bakersfield, CA 93309	(661) 327–3611
District Director.—Vincent Fong.	
District Administrator.—Robin Lake Foster.	

Counties: KERN COUNTY (part). CITIES AND TOWNSHIPS: Arvin, Bakersfield, Bodfish, Boron, Caliente, California City, Cantil, China Lake, Edison, Edwards, Fellows, Frazier Park, Glennville, Havilah, Inyokern, Keene, Kernville, Lake Isabella, Lebec, Maricopa, McKittrick, Mojave, Monolith, North Edwards, Onyx, Randsberg, Ridgecrest, Rosamond, Taft, Tehachapi, Tupman, Weldon, Willow Springs, Wofford Heights, Woody, TULARE COUNTY (part). CITIES AND

TOWNSHIPS: Badger, California Hot Springs, Exeter, Lemon Cove, Lindsay, Orosi, Porterville, Posey, Springville, Strathmore, Terra Bella, Three Rivers, Visalia, Woodlake. LOS ANGELES COUNTY (part). CITIES AND TOWNSHIPS: Lancaster. Population (2012) 707,345.

ZIP Codes: 93203, 93205, 93207–08, 93221–22, 93224–26, 93238, 93240, 93243–44, 93247, 93251–52, 93255, 93257, 93260, 93262, 93265, 93267–68, 93270–71, 93276, 93283, 93285–87, 93292, 93301, 93304–07, 93309, 93311–14, 93501, 93505, 93516, 93518–19, 93523, 93527–28, 93531, 93534, 93536, 93554–55, 93560–61, 93603, 93633, 93647

* * *

TWENTY-FOURTH DISTRICT

LOIS CAPPS, Democrat, of Santa Barbara, CA; born in Ladysmith, WI, January 10, 1938; education: graduated, Flathead County High School, Kalispell, MT, 1955; B.S. in Nursing, Pacific Lutheran University, 1959; M.A. in Religion, Yale University, 1964; M.A. in Education, University of California at Santa Barbara, 1990; professional: head nurse, Yale New Haven Hospital; staff nurse, Visiting Nurses Association, Hamden, CT; elementary district nurse, Santa Barbara School District; director, Teenage Pregnancy and Parenting Project, Santa Barbara County; director, Santa Barbara School District Parent and Child Education Center; instructor of early childhood education, Santa Barbara City College; board member: American Red Cross, American Heart Association, Family Service Agency, Santa Barbara Women's Political Committee; married: Walter Capps, 1960; children: Lisa, Todd, and Laura; committees: Energy and Commerce; Natural Resources; elected by special election on March 10, 1998, to the 105th Congress, to fill the vacancy caused by the death of her husband Representative Walter Capps; reelected to each succeeding Congress.

Office Listings

http://www.capps.house.gov　　　twitter: @reploiscapps

2231 Rayburn House Office Building, Washington, DC 20515	(202) 225–3601
Chief of Staff.—Sarah Rubinfield.	FAX: 225–5632
Executive Assistant.—Chantelle Tolliver.	
Deputy Chief of Staff/Legislative Director.—Adriane Casalotti.	
Press Secretary.—Chris Meagher.	
1411 Marsh Street, Suite 205, San Luis Obispo, CA 93401	(805) 546–8348
District Representatives: Greg Haas, Betsy Umhofer.	
301 East Carrillo Street, Suite A, Santa Barbara, CA 93101	(805) 730–1710
District Director: Mollie Culver.	
District Representatives: Wendy Motta, Erica Reyes.	
1101 South Broadway, Suite A, Santa Maria, CA 93454	(805) 349–3832
District Representatives.—Blanca Figueroa.	

Counties: SAN LUIS OBISPO COUNTY (All). CITIES AND TOWNSHIPS: Atascadero, Arroyo Grande, Baywood-Los Osos, Cambria, Cayucos, Grover Beach, Morro Bay, Nipomo, Oceano, Paso Robles, Pismo Beach, San Luis Obispo. SANTA BARBARA COUNTY (All). CITIES AND TOWNSHIPS: Carpinteria, Goleta, Guadalupe, Isla Vista, Mission Canyon, Montecito, Santa Barbara, Santa Maria, Summerland, Toro Canyon. VENTURA COUNTY (part). CITIES AND TOWNSHIPS: Ventura. Population (2010), 708,744.

ZIP Codes: 93001, 93013–14, 93067, 93101–21, 93130, 93140, 93150, 93160, 93190, 93199, 93254, 93401–12, 93420–24, 93427–30, 93432–37, 93440–49, 93451–58, 93460–61, 93463–65, 93475, 93483, 94338

* * *

TWENTY-FIFTH DISTRICT

STEVE KNIGHT, Republican, of Palmdale, CA; born at Edwards AFB, CA, December 17, 1966; professional: Veteran, U.S. Army; married: Lily; children: Christopher and Michael; caucuses: Alzheimer's Disease Task Force; Congressional Lupus Caucus; Congressional Military Family Caucus; 21st Century Agency Reform Task Force; committees: Armed Services; Science, Space and Technology; Small Business; elected to the 114th Congress on November 4, 2014.

Office Listings

https://knight.house.gov　　　twitter: @steveknight25

1023 Longworth House Office Building, Washington, DC 20515	(202) 225–1956
Chief of Staff.—David Orosco.	FAX: 226–0683
Scheduler.—Zac Wall.	
District Director.—Lisa Moulton.	
1008 West Avenue, M–14, Suite E, Palmdale, CA 93551	(661) 441–0320

Office Listings—Continued

1445 East Los Angeles Avenue, #206, Simi Valley, CA 93065 .... (805) 581–7130
26415 Carl Boyer Drive, Suite 220, Santa Clarita, CA 91350 .... (661) 255–5630

Counties: NORTHERN LOS ANGELES (part), VENTURA (part). CITIES: Santa Clarita, Simi Valley, Palmdale, Lancaster, and Northern San Fernando Valley (part). Population (2010), 702,904.

ZIP Codes: 91042, 91304, 91311, 91321, 91326, 91344, 91350–51, 91354–55, 91362, 91381, 91384, 91387, 91390, 93063–65, 93510, 93532, 93534–36, 93543–44, 93550–53, 93563, 93591

* * *

TWENTY-SIXTH DISTRICT

JULIA BROWNLEY, Democrat, of Westlake Village, CA; born in Aiken, SC, August 28, 1952; education: B.A., Mount Vernon College at George Washington University, 1975; M.B.A., American University, 1979; professional: product manager, Steelcase, 1984–92; sales manager, Pitney Bowes, 1981–84; sales manager, Burroughs Corporation, 1976–81; Santa Monica-Malibu School Board, 1994–2006; California State Assembly, 2007–12; chair of California State Assembly Committee on Education; children: Fred and Hannah; committees: Transportation and Infrastructure; Veterans' Affairs; elected to the 113th Congress on November 6, 2012; reelected to the 114th Congress on November 4, 2014.

Office Listings

http://juliabrownley.house.gov

1019 Longworth House Office Building, Washington, DC 20515 .... (202) 225–5811
    Chief of Staff.—Lenny Young.   FAX: 225–5811
    Legislative Director.—Sharon Wagener.
    Communications Director.—Eric Parker.
    Scheduler.—Jonathan Cousimano.
300 East Esplanade Drive, Suite 470, Oxnard, CA 93036 .... (805) 379–1779
    District Director.—Carina Armenta.   FAX: 379–1799
223 East Thousand Oaks Boulevard, Suite 411, Thousand Oaks, CA 91360 .... (805) 379–1779
                                                             FAX: 379–1799

Counties: LOS ANGELES (part) AND VENTURA (part). Population (2010), 702,905.

ZIP Codes: 91320, 91360–62, 91377, 93003–04, 93010, 93012, 93015, 93021–23, 93030, 93033, 93035–36, 93040–41, 93060, 93065–66

* * *

TWENTY-SEVENTH DISTRICT

JUDY M. CHU, Democrat, of Pasadena, CA; born in Los Angeles, CA, July 7, 1953; education: B.A. in math from UCLA, Los Angeles, CA, 1974; Ph.D. in psychology from the California School of Professional Psychology, 1979; professional: Garvey School District Board member, 1985–88; Monterey Park City Council and Mayor, 1988–2001; California State Assembly, 2001–06; California State Board of Equalization, 2006–09; first Chinese American woman elected to Congress; family: married to former Assemblymember Mike Eng in 1978; committees: Judiciary; Small Business; elected to the 111th Congress on July 14, 2009, by special election, to fill the vacancy caused by the resignation of United States Representative Hilda Solis; reelected to each succeeding Congress.

Office Listings

http://www.chu.house.gov   https://twitter.com/repjudychu

2423 Rayburn House Office Building, Washington, DC 20515 .... (202) 225–5464

Office Listings—Continued

Chief of Staff.—Linda Shim. FAX: 225–5467
Legislative Director.—Joleen Rivera.
Congressional Asian Pacific American Caucus (CAPAC) Executive Director.—Krystal Ka'ai.
Congressional Asian Pacific American Caucus (CAPAC) Policy Advisor.—Diana Lim.
Legislative Assistants: Sonali Desai, Liliana Rocha.
Legislative Correspondent / Legislative Aide.—Ellen Hamilton.
Press Secretary.—Ben Suarato.
Scheduler.—Mina Kato.
Staff Assistant.—Laura Driscoll.
527 South Lake Avenue, Suite 106, Pasadena, CA 91101 .... (626) 304–0110
District Director.—Becky Cheng. FAX: 304–0132
Field Representative / Case Workers: Anthony Duarte, Matt Hovsepian, Enrique Robles, Viola Van.
District Scheduler.—Lindsay Plake.
Staff Assistant.—Vacant.

Counties: Los Angeles County (part). Cities: Alhambra, Altadena (unincorporated), Arcadia, Bradbury, Claremont, Glendora, Monterey Park, Monrovia, Pasadena, Rosemead, South Pasadena, San Gabriel, San Marino, Sierra Madre, Temple City, Upland, San Antonio Heights (unincorporated), East Pasadena (unincorporated), South San Gabriel (unincorporated). Population (2010), 684,496.

ZIP Codes: 91001, 91003, 91006–07, 91010, 91711, 91016–17, 91024–25, 91030–31, 91066–77, 91101–10, 91108, 91114–18, 91118, 91121, 91123–26, 91129, 91131, 91175, 91182, 91184–89, 91191, 91740–41, 91754–56, 91770, 91770–72, 91775–76, 91778, 91780, 91784–86, 91801–04, 91841, 91896, 91899

* * *

TWENTY-EIGHTH DISTRICT

ADAM B. SCHIFF, Democrat, of Burbank, CA; born in Framingham, MA, June 20, 1960; education: B.A., Stanford University, 1982; J.D., Harvard University, 1985; professional: attorney; U.S. Attorney's Office, served as a criminal prosecutor; chosen by the Department of Justice to assist the Czechoslovakian Government in reforming their criminal justice system; public service: elected to the California State Senate, 1996; involved in numerous community service activities; awards: Department of Justice Special Achievement Award; Council of State Governments Toll Fellowship; California League of High Schools Legislator of the Year; family: married: Eve; children: Alexa and Elijah; committees: Appropriations; Permanent Select Committee on Intelligence; Select Committee on Benghazi; elected to the 107th Congress on November 7, 2000; reelected to each succeeding Congress.

Office Listings

http://www.schiff.house.gov   twitter: @repadamschiff

2411 Rayburn House Office Building, Washington, DC 20515 .... (202) 225–4176
Chief of Staff.—Jeff Lowenstein. FAX: 225–5828
Communications Director.—Patrick Boland.
Executive Assistant.—Christopher Hoven.
245 East Olive Avenue, Burbank, CA 91502 .... (626) 304–2727
District Director.—Ann Peifer.

Counties: Los Angeles (part). Cities: Burbank, Glendale, Hollywood, La Canada-Flintridge, La Crescenta, Los Feliz, Pasadena, Sunland, and Tujunga. Population (2010), 702,904.

ZIP Codes: 9004, 90026–29, 90031, 90036, 90038–39, 90046, 90048, 90068–69, 91011, 91020, 91040, 91042–43, 91103, 91105, 91201–08, 91214, 91352, 91501–02, 91504–06

* * *

TWENTY-NINTH DISTRICT

ANTONIO CÁRDENAS, Democrat, of San Fernando Valley, CA; born in Pacoima, CA, March 31, 1963; education: B.A., University of California at Santa Barbara, 1986; professional: businessman; public service: California State Assembly, 1996–2002; Los Angeles City Council, 2002–13; religion: Christian; family: married to Norma Sanchez; children: Andres, Alina, Vanessa, Cristian; committees: Energy and Commerce; elected to the 113th Congress on November 6, 2012; reelected to the 114th Congress on November 4, 2014.

Office Listings

http://www.cárdenas.house.gov   twitter: @repcárdenas

1510 Longworth House Office Building, Washington, DC 20515 .... (202) 225–6131
  Chief of Staff.—Sam Jammal.   FAX: 225–0819
  Legislative Director.—Miguel Franco.
8134 Van Nuys Boulevard, Suite 206, Panorama City, CA 91402 .... (818) 781–7407

Counties: Los Angeles. Population (2010), 680,661.

ZIP Codes: 91040, 91321, 91331, 91340, 91342–45, 91352, 91387, 91401–02, 91405–06, 91411, 91504–05, 91601–02, 91605–07

* * *

THIRTIETH DISTRICT

BRAD SHERMAN, Democrat, of Sherman Oaks, CA; born in Los Angeles, CA, October 24, 1954; education: B.A., *summa cum laude,* UCLA, 1974; J.D., *magna cum laude,* Harvard Law School, 1979; professional: admitted to the California Bar in 1979 and began practice in Los Angeles; attorney, CPA, certified tax law specialist; elected to the California State Board of Equalization, 1990, serving as chairman, 1991–95; committees: Financial Services; Foreign Affairs; elected to the 105th Congress; reelected to each succeeding Congress.

Office Listings

twitter: @bradsherman   facebook: congessmanbradsherman

2242 Rayburn House Office Building, Washington, DC 20515 .... (202) 225–5911
  Chief of Staff.—Don MacDonald.   FAX: 225–5879
5000 Van Nuys Boulevard, Suite 420, Sherman Oaks, CA 91403 .... (818) 501–9200
  District Director.—Scott Abrams.

Counties: Los Angeles (part). Population (2013), 744,617.

ZIP Codes: 90046, 90049, 90068, 90077, 90210, 91302–04, 91306–07, 91311, 91316, 91324–26, 91330, 91335, 91342–44, 91356, 91364, 91367, 91371, 91401, 91403, 91406, 91411, 91423, 91436, 91505–06, 91601–02, 91604, 91607–08, 93064

* * *

THIRTY-FIRST DISTRICT

PETE AGUILAR, Democrat, of Redlands, CA; born in Fontana, San Bernadino County, CA, June 19, 1979; education: B.S., University of Redlands, Redlands, CA, 2001; professional: business owner; Interim Director and Deputy Director, Inland Empire Regional Office of the Governor of California, 2001; member of the Redlands, California City Council, 2006–14; mayor of Redlands, California, 2010–14; married: Alisha; children: Evan and Palmer; committees: Agriculture; Armed Services; elected to the 114th Congress on November 4, 2014.

Office Listings

https://aguilar.house.gov   @reppeteaguilar

1223 Longworth House Office Building, Washington, DC 20515 .... (202) 225–3201
  Chief of Staff.—Boris Medzhibovsky.   FAX: 226–6962
  Legislative Director.—Becky Cornell.
  Communications Director.—Sarah Weinstein.
685 E. Carnegie Drive, Suite 100, San Bernardino, CA 92408 .... (909) 890–4445
  Director of Constituent Services.—Teresa Valdez.   FAX: 890–9643

Counties: San Bernardino (part). Cities and Townships: Upland, Rancho Cucamonga, Fontana, Rialto, Colton, Grand Terrace, Loma Linda, San Bernardino, and Redlands. Population: (2011) 727,523.

ZIP Codes: 91701, 91730, 91737, 91739, 91786, 92313, 92316, 92324, 92335–36, 92346, 92350, 92354, 92357, 92359, 92373–74, 92376–77, 92399, 92401, 92404–05, 92407–08, 92410–11, 92509

* * *

THIRTY-SECOND DISTRICT

GRACE F. NAPOLITANO, Democrat, of Los Angeles, CA; born in Brownsville, TX, December 4, 1936; education: Brownsville High School, Brownsville, TX; Cerritos College, Norwalk, CA; Texas Southmost College, Brownsville, TX; professional: Transportation Coordinator, Ford Motor Company; elected to Norwalk, CA, City Council, 1986; became mayor of Norwalk, CA, 1989; elected to the California Assembly, 58th District, 1992–98; organizations: Norwalk Lions Club; Veterans of Foreign Wars (auxiliary); American Legion (auxiliary); Soroptimist International; past director, Cerritos College Foundation; director, Community Family Guidance Center; League of United Latin American Citizens; director, Los Angeles County Sanitation District; director, Los Angeles County Vector Control (Southeast District); director, Southeast Los Angeles Private Industry Council; director, Los Angeles County Sheriff's Authority; National Women's Political Caucus; past national board secretary, United States-Mexico Sister Cities Association; member, Congressional Hispanic Caucus; co-chair, Congressional Mental Health Caucus; maiden name: Flores; married: Frank Napolitano; children: Yolanda Louwers (deceased), Fred Musquiz, Edward Musquiz, Michael Musquiz, and Cynthia Dowling; committees: Natural Resources; Transportation and Infrastructure; elected to the 106th Congress; reelected to each succeeding Congress.

Office Listings

http://www.napolitano.house.gov   www.facebook.com/repgracenapolitano
http://www.youtube.com/repgracenapolitano   http://www.twitter.com/gracenapolitano

1610 Longworth House Office Building, Washington, DC 20515	(202) 225–5256
Chief of Staff.—Daniel Chao.	FAX: 225–0027
Legislative Director.—Joe Sheehy.	
Press Secretary.—Jerry O'Donnell.	
Scheduler.—Joseph Ciccone.	
4401 Santa Anita Avenue, Suite 201, El Monte, CA 91731	(626) 350–0150
District Director.—Perla Hernandez.	

Counties: LOS ANGELES (part). Population (2010), 702,905.

ZIP Codes: 91009–10, 91016–17, 91702, 91706, 91714–16, 91722–24, 91731–32, 91734–35, 91744, 91746–47, 91749–50, 91773, 91790–93, 91797

* * *

THIRTY-THIRD DISTRICT

TED LIEU, Democrat, of Torrance, CA; born in Taipei, Taiwan, March 29, 1969; education: B.A., political science, Stanford University, 1991; B.S., computer science, Stanford University, CA, 1991; J.D., Georgetown University Law Center, 1994; admitted to the California State Bar 1994; United States Air Force, 1995-1999; United States Air War College, 2012; United States Air Force Reserve, 2000–present; Air Force Humanitarian Service Medal; Air Force Commendation Medal; Air Force Meritorious Service Medal; Torrance City Council member, 2002–05; California State Assemblyman, 2005–10; California State Senator, 2011–14; married to Betty Chim; children: Brennan and Austin; elected as President of the Democratic Freshman class; committees: Budget; Oversight and Government Reform; elected to the 114th Congress on November 4, 2014.

Office Listings

https://lieu.house.gov   facebook: rep.tedlieu   twitter: @reptedlieu

415 Cannon House Office Building, Washington, DC 20515	(202) 225–3976
Chief of Staff.—Marc Cevasco.	
5055 Wilshire Boulevard, Suite 310, Los Angeles, CA 90036	(323) 651–1040
1600 Rosecrans Avenue, 4th Floor, Manhattan Beach, CA 90266	(310) 321–7664
District Director.—Lisa Pina.	

Counties: LOS ANGELES COUNTY (part). CITIES AND TOWNSHIPS: Agoura Hills, Bel-Air, Beverly Hills, Brentwood, Calabasas, El Segundo, Hermosa Beach, Malibu, Manhattan Beach, Marina Del Rey, Pacific Palisades, Palos Verdes Estates, Rancho Palos Verdes, Redondo Beach, Rolling Hills, Rolling Hills Estates, Santa Monica, Topanga, Venice, and Vista Del Mar. The 33rd Congressional District also includes a portion of the communities of Hancock Park, Harbor City, San Pedro, Torrance, West Los Angeles, and Westwood. Population (2010), 707,854.

ZIP Codes: 90004 (part), 90020 (part), 90024 (part), 90036, 90048–49, 90073, 90077, 90095, 90209, 90211–13, 90245, 90254, 90263–67, 90272, 90274–75, 90277–78, 90290–95, 90401–08 (part), 90409–11, 90503 (part), 90505 (part),

90710 (part), 90731 (part), 90732 (part), 90744 (part), 91301–02, 91376, 90254, 90263–67, 90272, 90274–75, 90277–78, 90290–95, 90401–090710 (part), 90731 (part), 90732 (part), 90744 (part), 91301–02, 91376

* * *

THIRTY-FOURTH DISTRICT

XAVIER BECERRA, Democrat, of Los Angeles, CA; born in Sacramento, CA, January 26, 1958; education: graduated, McClatchy High School, Sacramento, 1976; B.A., Stanford University, 1980; J.D., Stanford Law School, 1984; admitted to California bar, 1985; attended Universidad de Salamanca, 1978–79; staff attorney, "Reggie Fellow," Legal Assistance Corporation of Central Massachusetts, 1984–85; administrative assistant for State Senator Art Torres, California State Legislature, 1986; Deputy Attorney General, Office of the Attorney General, State of California, 1987–90; Assemblyman, California State Legislature, 1990–92; member: Mexican American State Legislators Policy Institute; Mexican American Bar Association; chairperson, Hispanic Employee Advisory Committee to the State Attorney General, 1989; honorary member, Association of California State Attorneys and Administrative Law Judges; former member, steering committee, Greater Eastside Voter Registration Project; Construction and General Laborers Union, Local 185 (Sacramento); Pitzer College Board of Trustees; National Association of Latino's Electoral and appointed to the Official Board of Directors; vice-chair, Democratic Caucus of the 111th Congress; reelected vice-chair, Democratic Caucus of the 112th Congress; married to Dr. Carolina Reyes; children: Clarisa, Olivia, Natalia; committees: Ways and Means; elected to the 103rd Congress on November 3, 1992; reelected to each succeeding Congress.

Office Listings

http://www.becerra.house.gov   twitter: @repbecerra

1226 Longworth House Office Building, Washington, DC 20515	(202) 225–6235
Chief of Staff.—Sean McCluskie	FAX: 225–2202
Legislative Director.—Esther Oh.	
Scheduler.—Cynthia Palafox.	
350 South Bixel Street, Suite 120, Los Angeles, CA 90017	(213) 481–1425
District Director.—Liz Saldivar.	

Counties: LOS ANGELES COUNTY (part). CITIES: Los Angeles. Population (2010), 698,741.

ZIP Codes: 90004–07, 90010, 90012–15, 90017–23, 90026, 90030–33, 90030–33, 90038, 90041–42, 90053, 90057, 90063, 90065, 90071, 90079, 90086, 90090

* * *

THIRTY-FIFTH DISTRICT

NORMA TORRES, Democrat, of Pomona, CA; born in Escuintla, Guatemala, April 1965; education: B.A., labor studies, National Labor College, Silver Spring, MD, 2012; professional: 9-1-1 dispatcher; Pomona City Council, 2001–06; mayor of Pomona, 2006–08; member of the California State Assembly, 2008–13; member of the California State Senate, 2013–14; married: Louis; 3 children, 1 grandchild; caucuses: Congressional Hispanic Caucus; Women's Caucus; PORTS Caucus; 9-1-1 Caucus; Job Corps Caucus; Manufacturing Caucus; Mayors Caucus; Tom Lantos Human Rights Commission; committees: Homeland Security; Natural Resources; elected to the 114th Congress on November 4, 2014.

Office Listings

https://torres.house.gov   twitter @normajtorres   https://www.facebook.com/repnormatorres

516 Cannon House Office Building, Washington, DC 20515	(202) 225–6161
Chief of Staff.—Dara Postar.	FAX: 225–8671
Legislative Director.—Grant Kerr.	
Communications Director.—Anna Gonzalez.	
Scheduler.—Bambi Yingst.	
Legislative Assistant.—Ben Ward.	
3200 Inland Empire Boulevard, Suite 200B, Ontario, CA 91764	(909) 481–6474
District Director.—Veronica Zendejas.	FAX: 941–1362

Counties: SAN BERNARDINO COUNTY (part). CITIES: Chino, Fontana, Montclair, Ontario, Rialto, Bloomington. LOS ANGELES COUNTY (part). CITIES: Pomona. Population (2014), 728,298.

ZIP Codes: 91708–11, 91730, 91739, 91743, 91750, 91752, 91758, 91761–69, 91786, 91789, 92316, 92324, 92331, 92334–37, 92509, 92880

* * *

THIRTY-SIXTH DISTRICT

RAUL RUIZ, M.D., Democrat, of Palm Springs, CA; born in Coachella, CA, August 25, 1972; education: B.S., University of California, Los Angeles, 1994; M.D., Harvard University, 2001; M.P.P., Harvard University, 2001; M.P.H., Harvard University, 2007; professional: emergency physician, Eisenhower Medical Center; founder, Coachella Valley Healthcare Initiative, 2010; senior associate dean, School of Medicine at University of California Riverside, 2011; caucuses: Seniors Task Force; Native American Caucus; No Labels-Problem Solvers; Veterans Job Caucus; Law Enforcement Caucus; LGBT Caucus; Renewable Energy Caucus; Government Efficiency Caucus; Small Business Caucus; Specialty Crop Caucus; Friends of Canada Caucus; committees: Natural Resources; Veterans' Affairs; elected to the 113th Congress on November 6, 2012; reelected to the 114th Congress on November 4, 2014.

Office Listings

http://ruiz.house.gov

1319 Longworth House Office Building, Washington, DC 20515	(202) 225–5330
Chief of Staff.—Reed Adamson.	FAX: 225–1238
Legislative Director.—Erin Doty.	
Communications Director.—Michael Ford.	
Scheduler.—Sadie Hansen.	
43875 Washington Street, Suite F, Palm Desert, CA 92211	(760) 424–8888
District Director.—Jamie Patton.	

Counties: RIVERSIDE COUNTY. CITIES: Palm Springs, Palm Desert, Indio, Coachella, Rancho Mirage, Desert Hot Springs, Indian Wells, and Cathedral City. Population (2010), 714,975.

ZIP Codes: 92201–03, 92210–11, 92220, 92230, 92234, 92236, 92240–41, 92253–54, 92258, 92260, 92262, 92264, 92270, 92276, 92282, 92539, 92549, 92561, 92583

* * *

THIRTY-SEVENTH DISTRICT

KAREN R. BASS, Democrat, of Los Angeles, CA; born in Los Angeles, October 3, 1953; education: B.S., health sciences, California State University, Dominguez Hills, CA, 1990; Master of Social Work, USC, 2015; P.A., University of Southern California School of Medicine, Los Angeles; professional: elected first Democratic woman Speaker of the California Assembly; founded and served as Executive Director of the non-profit organization Community Coalition, Los Angeles; physician assistant, Los Angeles County General Hospital; religion: Baptist; family: daughter Emilia Bass-Lechuga, son-in-law Michael Wright; step children: Scythia, Omar, Yvette, and Jesse Lechuga; awards: JFK Profile in Courage Award; Congressional Black Caucus Phoenix Award; committees: Foreign Affairs; Judiciary; elected to the 112th Congress on November 2, 2010; reelected to each succeeding Congress.

Office Listings

http://www.bass.house.gov   twitter: @repkarenbass

408 Cannon House Office Building, Washington, DC 20515	(202) 225–7084
Chief of Staff.—Carrie Kohns.	FAX: 225–2422
Senior Legislative Assistant.—Sara Nitz.	
Scheduler / Executive Assistant.—Allison Fialkov.	
Communications Director.—Dan Roth.	
4929 Wilshire Boulevard, Suite 650, Los Angeles, CA 90010	(323) 965–1422
District Director.—Maral Karaccusian.	

Counties: LOS ANGELES (part). CITIES: Culver and Los Angeles. COMMUNITIES OF: Ladera Heights and View Park-Windsor Hills. Population (2010), 702,904.

ZIP Codes: 90004–08, 90010–11, 90016, 90018–20, 90022, 90026–29, 90033–39, 90043–45, 90047–48, 90053, 90056–58, 90062–64, 90066, 90068, 90070, 90078, 90083, 90093, 90099, 90103, 90230–33

* * *

THIRTY-EIGHTH DISTRICT

LINDA T. SÁNCHEZ, Democrat, of Lakewood, CA; born in Orange, CA, January 28, 1969; education: B.A., University of California, Berkeley; J.D., U.C.L.A. Law School; passed bar exam in 1995; professional: attorney; has practiced in the areas of appellate, civil rights, and employment law; International Brotherhood of Electrical Workers Local 441; National Electrical Contractors Association; Orange County Central Labor Council Executive Secretary, AFL–CIO; organizations: chair, Congressional Hispanic Caucus; National Women's Political Caucus; Women in Leadership; religion: Catholic; committees: ranking member, Ethics; Ways and Means; elected to the 108th Congress on November 5, 2002; reelected to each succeeding Congress.

Office Listings

http://www.lindasanchez.house.gov   twitter: @replindasanchez

2329 Rayburn House Office Building, Washington, DC 20515 .... (202) 225–6676
Chief of Staff.—Lea Sulkala.   FAX: 226–1012
Legislative Director.—Melissa Kiedrowicz.
Communications Director.—Alex Nguyen.
17906 Crusader Avenue, Suite 100, Cerritos, CA 90703 .... (562) 860–5050
District Director.—Yvette Shahinian.

Counties: LOS ANGELES (part). Population (2010), 715,745,

ZIP Codes: 90601–06, 90623, 90638, 90701, 90703, 90706, 90716, 90712–13, 90715, 90640, 90650, 90660, 90670, 91733

* * *

THIRTY-NINTH DISTRICT

EDWARD R. ROYCE, Republican, of Fullerton, CA; born in Los Angeles, CA, October 12, 1951; education: B.A., California State University, Fullerton, 1977; professional: small business owner; controller; corporate tax manager; California State Senate, 1982–92; member: Fullerton Chamber of Commerce; board member, Literacy Volunteers of America; California Inter-scholastic Athletic Foundation board of advisers; married: Marie Therese Porter, 1985; commit tees: chair, Foreign Affairs; Financial Services; elected on November 3, 1992 to the 103rd Congress; reelected to each succeeding Congress.

Office Listings

http://www.royce.house.gov   twitter: @repedroyce

2310 Rayburn House Office Building, Washington, DC 20515 .... (202) 225–4111
Chief of Staff.—Amy Porter.   FAX: 226–0335
Deputy Chief of Staff/Legislative Director.—Peter Freeman.
Communications Director.—Saat Alety.
Scheduler.—Kate Barlow.
210 West Birch Street, Suite 201, Brea, CA 92821 .... (714) 255–0101
FAX: 225–0109
1380 South Fullerton Road, Suite 205, Rowland Heights, CA 91748 .... (626) 964–5123
District Director.—Sara Catalan.   FAX: 810–3891

Counties: California's 39th district encompasses cities in northern ORANGE COUNTY, eastern LOS ANGELES COUNTY, and southwestern SAN BERNARDINO COUNTY. The cities include Brea, Buena Park, Chino Hills, Diamond Bar, Fullerton, Hacienda Heights, La Habra, Placentia, Rosemead, Rowland Heights, Walnut, and Yorba Linda. Population (2013), 721,014.

ZIP Codes: 90603, 90620–22, 90624, 90631–33, 90638, 91709–10, 91745–46, 91748–49, 91765–66, 91768, 91788–89, 92801, 92806–07, 92811, 92817, 92821–23, 92831–38, 92865, 92867, 92870–71, 92885–87, 92899

* * *

FORTIETH DISTRICT

LUCILLE ROYBAL-ALLARD, Democrat, of Los Angeles, CA; born in Los Angeles, June 12, 1941; education: B.A., California State University, Los Angeles, 1965; served in the California State Assembly, 1987–92; the first woman to serve as the chair of the California Democratic Congressional Delegation in the 105th Congress; in the 106th Congress, she became the first woman to chair the Congressional Hispanic Caucus, and the first Latina in history to be appointed to the House Appropriations Committee; married: Edward T. Allard III; two children: Lisa Marie and Ricardo; two stepchildren: Angela and Guy Mark; committees: Appropriations; the first Mexican-American woman elected to Congress on November 3, 1992 to the 103rd Congress; reelected to each succeeding Congress.

Office Listings

http://www.roybal-allard.house.gov   https://twitter.com/reproybalallard
https://www.facebook.com/reproybalallard

2330 Rayburn House Office Building, Washington, DC 20515–0534 .... (202) 225–1766
  Chief of Staff.—Victor G. Castillo.   FAX: 226–0350
  Legislative Director.—Karen De Los Santos.
  Executive Assistant.—Christine C. Ochoa.
500 Citadel Drive, Suite 320, Commerce, CA 90040–1572 .... (323) 721–8790
  District Director.—Ana Figueroa.   FAX: 721–8789

Counties: LOS ANGELES COUNTY (part). CITIES: Bill, Bell Gardens, Bellflower, Commerce, Cudahy, Downey, East Los Angeles, Florence-Graham, Huntington Park, Maywood, Paramount, South Los Angeles, Vernon, and Walnut Park. Population (2010), 694,514.

ZIP Codes: 90001, 90003, 90007, 90011, 90015, 90021–23, 90037, 90040, 90052, 90058–59, 90063, 90082, 90091, 90201–02, 90239–42, 90255, 90270, 90280, 90640, 90650, 90660, 90706, 90723, 91754

* * *

FORTY-FIRST DISTRICT

MARK TAKANO, Democrat, of Riverside, CA; born in Riverside, December 10, 1960; education: B.A. in government, Harvard College, 1983; M.A. in fine arts, University of California Riverside, 2010; professional: Public School Teacher; Riverside Community College District Board Trustee; awards: Chairman of the Asian Pacific Islander Caucus of the California Democratic Party; charter member of the Association of Latino Community College Trustees; member of the Association of California Asian American Trustees; member of Asian Pacific Americans in Higher Education; recipient of Martin Luther King Visionaries Award; religion: Methodist; committees: Education and the Workforce; Science, Space, and Technology; Veterans' Affairs; elected to the 113th Congress on November 6, 2012; reelected to the 114th Congress on November 4, 2014.

Office Listings

http://takano.house.gov   http://twitter.com/repmarktakano

1507 Longworth House Office Building, Washington, DC 20515 .... (202) 225–2305
  Chief of Staff.—Richard Kirk McPike.   FAX: 225–7018
  Deputy Chief of Staff / Legislative Director.—Yuri Beckelman.
3403 10th Street, Suite 610, Riverside, CA 92501 .... (951) 222–0203
  District Director.—Rafael Elizalde.

Counties: RIVERSIDE (part). CITIES: Jurupa Valley, Moreno Valley, Perris, and Riverside. Population (2010), 797,133.

ZIP Codes: 91572, 92324, 92373, 92501, 92503–09, 92518, 92551, 92553, 92555, 92557, 92570–71, 92880

* * *

FORTY-SECOND DISTRICT

KEN CALVERT, Republican, of Corona, CA; born in Corona, June 8, 1953; education: A.A., Chaffey College, CA, 1973; B.A. in economics, San Diego State University, 1975; professional: congressional aide to Representative Victor V. Veysey, CA; general manager, Jolly Fox Restaurant, Corona, 1975–79; Marcus W. Meairs Co., Corona, 1979–81; president and general manager, Ken Calvert Real Properties, 1981–92; County Youth Chairman, Representative Veysey's District, 1970–72; Corona / Norco Youth Chairman for Nixon, 1968 and 1972; Reagan-Bush campaign worker, 1980; co-chairman, Wilson for Senate Campaign, 1982; chairman, Riverside Republican Party, 1984–88; co-chairman, George Deukmejian election, 1978, 1982 and 1986;

co-chairman, George Bush election, 1988; co-chairman, Pete Wilson Senate elections, 1982 and 1988; co-chairman, Pete Wilson for Governor election, 1990; chairman and charter member, Lincoln Club of Riverside County, 1986–90; past president, Corona Rotary Club; Corona Elks; Navy League of Corona/Norco; Corona Chamber of Commerce; past chairman, Norco Chamber of Commerce; County of Riverside Asset Leasing; past chairman, Corona/Norco Board of Realtors; Monday Morning Group; Corona Group; executive board, Economic Development Partnership; charter member, Corona Community Hospital Corporate 200 Club; Silver Eagles (March AFB Support Group); Corona Airport Advisory Commission; committees: Appropriations; elected on November 3, 1992 to the 103rd Congress; reelected to each succeeding Congress.

Office Listings

http://www.calvert.house.gov   twitter: @kencalvert

2205 Rayburn House Office Building, Washington, DC 20515 ....:.. (202) 225–1986
Chief of Staff.—Dave Ramey. FAX: 225–2004
Legislative Director.—Rebecca Keightley.
4160 Temescal Canyon Road, Suite 214, Corona, CA 92883 .... (951) 277–0042
District Director.—Jolyn Murphy.
Press Secretary.—Jason Gagnon.

Counties: RIVERSIDE COUNTY. CITIES AND TOWNSHIPS: Canyon Lake, Corona, Eastvale, Lake Elsinore, Menifee, Murrieta, Norco, a portion of Temecula, and Wildomar. Population (2010), 710,617.

ZIP Codes: 91752, 92028, 92223, 92503–04, 92506–08, 92530–32, 92536, 92544–45, 92548, 92555, 92562–63, 92567, 92570–71, 92582, 92584–87, 92590–92, 92595–96, 92860, 92877–83

* * *

FORTY-THIRD DISTRICT

MAXINE WATERS, Democrat, of Los Angeles, CA; born in St. Louis, MO, August 15, 1938; education: B.A., California State University; honorary degrees: Harris-Stowe State College, St. Louis, MO, and Central State University, Wilberforce, OH, Spelman College, Atlanta, GA, North Carolina A&T State University, Howard University, Central State University, Bishop College, Morgan State University; elected to California State Assembly, 1976; reelected every two years thereafter; member: Assembly Democratic Caucus, Board of TransAfrica Foundation, National Women's Political Caucus; chair, Democratic Caucus Special Committee on Election Reform; chair, Ways and Means Subcommittee on State Administration; chair, Joint Committee on Public Pension Fund Investments; founding member, National Commission for Economic Conversion and Disarmament; member of the board, Center for National Policy; Clara Elizabeth Jackson Carter Foundation (Spelman College); Minority AIDS Project; married to Sidney Williams, former U.S. Ambassador to the Commonwealth of the Bahamas; two children: Karen and Edward; committees: ranking member, Financial Services; elected to the 102nd Congress on November 6, 1990; reelected to each succeeding Congress.

Office Listings

http://www.waters.house.gov   twitter: @maxinewaters

2221 Rayburn House Office Building, Washington, DC 20515 .... (202) 225–2201
Chief of Staff.—Twaun Samuel. FAX: 225–7854
Legislative Director.—Deanne Millison.
10124 South Broadway, Suite 1, Los Angeles, CA 90003 .... (323) 757–8900
District Director.—Blanca Jimenez.

Counties: LOS ANGELES COUNTY (part). CITIES: Gardena, Hawthorne, Inglewood, Lawndale, Los Angeles, Playa Del Ray, Lomita, and Torrance. Population (2010), 702,983.

ZIP Codes: 90007, 90009, 90044–45, 90047, 90052, 90056, 90059, 90061, 90066, 90082, 90094, 90189, 90247–51, 90260–61, 90293, 90301–13, 90397–98, 90504, 90506, 90717

* * *

FORTY-FOURTH DISTRICT

JANICE HAHN, Democrat, of San Pedro, CA; born in Los Angeles, CA, March 30, 1952; education: B.S. in education, Abilene Christian University, Abilene, TX, 1974; professional:

teacher, Good News Academy, 1974–78; stay-at-home mother, 1978–88; Director of Marketing, Alexander Haagan Company, 1988–90; Director of Community Outreach, Western Waste Industries, 1990–92; Vice President of Public Finance, Prudential Securities, 1993–95; Public Affairs Regional Manager, Southern California Edison Co., 1995–2000; elected to the Charter Reform Commission, 1997–99; Los Angeles City Council, 15th District, 2001–11; family: children, Danny, Mark, and Katy; grandchildren, McKenna, Brooklyn, Isabela, Josiah, and Luke; committees: Small Business; Transportation and Infrastructure; elected to the 112th Congress by special election, July 12, 2011, to fill the vacancy caused by the resignation of United States Representative Jane Harman, and took the oath of office July 19, 2011; elected to a full term in the 113th Congress on November 6, 2012; reelected to each succeeding Congress.

Office Listings

http://www.hahn.house.gov   twitter: twitter: @repljanicehahn

404 Cannon House Office Building, Washington, DC 20515	(202) 225–8220
Chief of Staff.—Laurie Saroff.	FAX: 226–7290
Legislative Director.—Justin Vogt.	
Scheduler.—Mckinley Krongaus.	
140 West 6th Street, San Pedro, CA 90731 ....:	(310) 831–1799
544 North Avalon Boulevard, Suite 307, Wilmington, CA 90744	(310) 549–8282
205 South Willowbrook Avenue, Compton, CA 90220 ....:	(310) 605–5520

Counties: LOS ANGELES (part). CITIES: Carson, Compton, Los Angeles, Lynwood, Port of Los Angeles, San Pedro, Southgate, Watts, and Wilmington. Population (2010), 702,904.

ZIP Codes: 90001 (part), 90002 (part), 90003 (part), 90004 (part), 90005 (part), 90007 (part), 90011 (part), 90015 (part), 90018 (part), 90020 (part), 90021 (part), 90022 (part), 90023 (part), 90025 (part), 90026 (part), 90031 (part), 90037 (part), 90038 (part), 90058 (part), 90059 (part), 90061 (part), 90063 (part), 90064 (part), 90089 (part), 90220, 90221 (part), 90222, 90223 (part), 90230 (part), 90248 (part), 90255 (part), 90262 (part), 90280, 90291 (part), 90292 (part), 90302 (part), 90405 (part), 90503 (part), 90504 (part), 90505 (part), 90631 (part), 90640 (part), 90706 (part), 90710 (part), 90712 (part), 90717 (part), 90731 (part), 90732 (part), 90733–34, 90744 (part), 90745–49, 90802 (part), 90805 (part), 90810 (part), 90811 (part), 90895, 91016 (part), 91030 (part), 91103 (part), 91105 (part), 91124 (part), 91321 (part), 91344 (part), 91505 (part), 91702 (part), 91711 (part), 91724 (part), 91731 (part), 91732 (part), 91740 (part), 91745 (part), 91754 (part), 91768 (part), 91770 (part), 91773 (part), 91789 (part), 93550 (part), 93551 (part)

* * *

FORTY-FIFTH DISTRICT

MIMI WALTERS, Republican, of Irvine, CA; born in Pasadena, CA, May 14, 1962; education: B.A., University of California, Los Angeles, CA; professional: member of Laguna Niguel City Council; member of the California State Assembly; member of the California State Senate; married: David; children: two daughters; two sons; committees: Judiciary; Transportation and Infrastructure; elected to the 114th Congress on November 4, 2014.

Office Listings

https://walters.house.gov   twitter: @repmimiwalters

236 Cannon House Office Building, Washington, DC 20515	(202) 225–5611
Chief of Staff.—David Bowser.	FAX: 225–9177
Office Manager.—Gabriela Sterling.	
Legislative Director.—Yvette Wissmann.	
Communications Director.—Christine Hardman.	
3333 Michelson Drive Suite 230, Irvine, CA, 92612	(949) 263–8703

Counties: ORANGE COUNTY (part). CITIES: Irvine, Tustin, North Tustin, Villa Park, Anaheim Hills, Laguna Hills, Lake Forest, Rancho Santa Margarita, and Mission Viejo.

ZIP Codes: 922530, 92602–04, 92606, 92609–10, 92612, 92614, 92617–18, 92620, 92630, 92637, 92653, 92656, 92660, 92676–79, 92688, 92691–92, 92701, 92705, 92780, 92782, 92807–08, 92861, 92865, 92867, 92869, 92887

* * *

FORTY-SIXTH DISTRICT

LORETTA SANCHEZ, Democrat, of Anaheim, CA; born in Lynwood, CA, January 7, 1960; education: graduate of Chapman University; M.B.A., American University; specializes in assisting public agencies with finance matters; member, Blue Dog Coalition; California Democratic Congressional Delegation; Congressional Caucus on Competitiveness in Entertainment

Technology; Congressional Caucus on Entertainment Industries; Congressional Caucus on Innovation and Entrepreneurship; Congressional Caucus on Korea; Congressional Caucus on Vietnam; Congressional Caucus on Women in the Military; Congressional Cyber-Security Caucus; Congressional Human Rights Caucus; Congressional Labor and Working Families Caucus; Congressional LGBT Equality Caucus; Congressional Mental Health Caucus; Congressional Military Families Caucus; New Democrat Coalition; committees: Armed Services; Homeland Security; elected to the 105th Congress; reelected to each succeeding Congress.

Office Listings

http://lorettasanchez.house.gov   twitter: @lorettasanchez
facebook: www.facebook.com/lorettasanchez

1211 Longworth House Office Building, Washington, DC 20515 .... (202) 225–2965
Chief of Staff.—Jennifer Alvarez Warburton.   FAX: 225–5859
Deputy Chief of Staff.—Eduardo Lerma.
Scheduler.—Shane Moore.
Legislative Director.—Eduardo Lerma.
Senior Defense and Foreign Affairs Advisor.—Annie Yea.
Legislative Assistant: Jacquelyn Gonzalez.
Communications Director: Vacant.
Legislative Correspondent / Staff Assistant: Lorenzo Rubalcava.
12397 Lewis Street, Suite 101, Garden Grove, CA 92840 .... (714) 621–0102
District Director.—Carlos Urquiza.

Counties: ORANGE COUNTY (part). CITIES: Anaheim, Garden Grove, Orange, and Santa Ana. Population (2010), 648,663.

ZIP Codes: 90620–21, 92606, 92614, 92701, 92703–07, 92780, 92801–07, 92840, 92843, 92865–68, 92870

* * *

FORTY-SEVENTH DISTRICT

ALAN LOWENTHAL, Democrat, of Long Beach, CA; born in Manhattan, New York County, NY, March 8, 1941; Baldwin High School, Baldwin, NY, 1958; B.A., Hobart College, Geneva, NY, 1962; M.A., Ohio State University, Columbus, OH, 1965; Ph.D., Ohio State University, Columbus, OH, 1967; psychology professor, California State University, Long Beach, 1969–1998; president, Long Beach Area Citizens Involved 1989–1992; member of the Long Beach, Calif., City Council, 1992–1998; member of the California State Assembly, 1998–2004; member of the California State Senate, 2004–2012; caucuses: chair, Congressional Safe Climate Caucus; chair, Green Schools Caucus; vice-chair, House LGBT Equality Caucus; vice-chair, Sustainable Energy and Environment Coalition; committees: Foreign Affairs; Natural Resources; elected to the 113th Congress on November 6, 2012; reelected to the 114th Congress on November 4, 2014.

Office Listings

http://www.lowenthal.house.gov   twitter: @replowenthal   facebook: replowenthal

108 Cannon House Office Building, Washington, DC 20515 .... (202) 225–7924
Chief of Staff.—Tim Hysom.   FAX: 225–7926
Legislative Director.—Devin Helfrich.
Communications Director.—Keith Higginbotham.
Scheduler.— Emily Strombom.
100 West Broadway Street, West Tower, Suite 600, Long Beach, CA 90802 .... (562) 436–3828
District Director.—Mark Pulido.

Counties: LOS ANGELES COUNTY (part). CITIES: Avalon, Lakewood, Long Beach, Signal Hill. ORANGE COUNTY (part). CITIES: Buena Park, Cypress, Garden Grove, Los Alamitos, Midway City, Rossmoor, Stanton, and Westminster. Population (2013), 719,805.

ZIP Codes: 90620, 90623, 90630, 90680, 90704, 90712, 90713, 90716, 90720–21, 90731, 90740, 90744, 90755, 90801–10, 90813–15, 90831–35, 90840, 90842, 90844, 90846–48, 90853, 92647, 92655, 92683–85, 92703, 92801, 92802, 92804, 92840–46

* * *

FORTY-EIGHTH DISTRICT

DANA T. ROHRABACHER, Republican, of Costa Mesa, CA; born in Coronado, CA, June 21, 1947; education: graduated, Palos Verdes High School, CA, 1965; attended Los Angeles

Harbor College, Wilmington, CA, 1965–67; B.A., Long Beach State College, CA, 1969; M.A., University of Southern California, Los Angeles, 1975; professional: writer/journalist; speechwriter and special assistant to the President, The White House, Washington, DC, 1981–88; assistant press secretary, Reagan/Bush Committee, 1980; reporter, City News Service/Radio News West, and editorial writer, *Orange County Register,* 1972–80; family: wife and triplets; committees: Foreign Affairs; Science, Space, and Technology; elected on November 8, 1988, to the 101st Congress; reelected to each succeeding Congress.

Office Listings

http://www.rohrabacher.house.gov

2300 Rayburn House Office Building, Washington, DC 20515 .... (202) 225–2415
    Chief of Staff.—Rick Dykema.   FAX: 225–0145
    Legislative Director.—Jeff Vanderslice.
    Communications Director.—Ken Grubbs.
    Senior Policy Advisor.—Tony DeTora.
    Legislative Assistant.—Brian Alesi.
    Executive Assistant/Scheduler.—Justin Ahn.
101 Main Street, Suite 380, Huntington Beach, CA 92648 .... (714) 960–6483
    District Director.—Kathleen Staunton.
    Deputy District Director.—Tony Capitelli.

Counties: ORANGE COUNTY (part). COMMUNITIES OF ALISO VIEJO, CORONA DEL MAR, COSTA MESA, FOUNTAIN VALLEY, GARDEN GROVE (part), HUNTINGTON BEACH, LAGUNA BEACH, LAGUNA NIGUEL, MIDWAY CITY (part), NEWPORT BEACH, SANTA ANA (part), SEAL BEACH, SUNSET BEACH, SURFSIDE, AND WESTMINSTER (part). Population (2010), 702,905.

ZIP Codes: 90740, 90742–043, 92625–27, 92646–49, 92651, 92655 (part), 92656–57, 92660–63, 92677, 92683 (part), 92703–04 (part), 92708, 92843–44 (part).

* * *

FORTY-NINTH DISTRICT

DARRELL E. ISSA, Republican, of Vista, CA; born in Cleveland, OH, November 1, 1953; education: Siena Heights College; military service: Captain U.S. Army; attended college on an ROTC scholarship; professional: businessman; founder and CEO of Directed Electronics, Inc.; past chairman, Consumer Electronics Association; previously on Board of Directors, Electronics Industry Association; public service: co-chairman of the campaign to pass the California Civil Rights Initiative (Proposition 209); chairman of the Volunteer Committee for the 1996 Republican National Convention; chairman of the San Diego County Lincoln Club; candidate for the U.S. Senate in 1998; architect of 2003 California recall campaign of former Governor Gray Davis; married: Kathy; children: William; committees: Foreign Affairs; Judiciary; elected to the 107th Congress on November 7, 2000; reelected to each succeeding Congress.

Office Listings

http://issa.house.gov   twitter: @darrellissa

2269 Rayburn House Office Building, Washington, DC 20515 .... (202) 225–3906
    Chief of Staff.—Dale Neugebauer.   FAX: 225–3303
    Deputy Chief of Staff.—Veronica Wong.
    Deputy Staff Director for Communication and Strategy.—Ben Carnes.
    Scheduler.—Katie Weiss.
1800 Thibodo Road, Suite 310, Vista, CA 92081 .... (760) 599–5000

Counties: ORANGE (part), SAN DIEGO (part). Population (2010), 702,906.

ZIP Codes: 92003, 92007–14, 92018, 92023–24, 92028–29, 92037, 92049, 92051–52, 92054–58, 92067–69, 92075, 92078, 92081, 92083–85, 92091–93, 92121, 92127, 92130, 92624, 92629, 92672–75, 92677, 92688, 92690–94

* * *

FIFTIETH DISTRICT

DUNCAN HUNTER, Republican, of Lakeside, CA; born in San Diego, CA, December 7, 1976; education: graduated, Granite Hills High School; B.S., Business Administration, San Diego State University, San Diego, CA, 2001; professional: business analyst; military: captain, United States Marine Corps, 2002–05; United States Marine Corps Reserves, 2005–08; religion: Protestant; married: Margaret; children: Duncan, Elizabeth, and Sarah; committees: Armed Services; Education and the Workforce; Transportation and Infrastructure; elected to the 111th Congress on November 4, 2008; reelected to each succeeding Congress.

Office Listings

http://www.hunter.house.gov

2429 Rayburn House Office Building, Washington, DC 20515 .... (202) 225–5672
    Chief of Staff.—Joe Kasper.   FAX: 225–0235
    Deputy Chief of Staff / Communications Director.—Joe Kasper.
    Legislative Director.—Reed Linsk.
    Scheduler / Office Manager.—Liz Argo.
    Military Legislative Assistant.—Peter Davidson.
    Legislative Assistant.—Tim Carlton.
    Legislative Correspondent.—Cassie Roper.
    Staff Assistant.—Meghan Badame.
    Military Fellow.—Peter Boby.
1611 North Magnolia Avenue, Suite 310, El Cajon, CA 92020 .... (619) 448–5201
41000 Main Street, Temecula, CA 92590 .... (951) 216–2111

Counties: SAN DIEGO COUNTY (part). CITIES AND TOWNSHIPS: Alpine, Barona I.R., Borrego Springs, Bonsall, Boulevard, Descanso, El Cajon, Escondido, Fallbrook, Guatay, Jamul, Julian, Lakeside, La Mesa, Mount Laguna, Pala, Palamar Mountain, Pauma Valley, Pine Valley, Potrero, Poway, Ramona, Ranchita, San Marcos, Santa Ysabel, Santee, Spring Valley, Temecula, Valley Center, Vista, and Warner Springs. Population (2010), 724,472.

ZIP Codes: 91901, 91903, 91916, 91931, 91935, 91941, 91948, 91962, 91978, 92003–04, 92019–21, 92025–30, 92033, 92036, 92040, 92046, 92059–61, 92064–66, 92069–72, 92078–79, 92082, 92084, 92086, 92088, 92589–93

* * *

FIFTY-FIRST DISTRICT

JUAN VARGAS, Democrat, of San Diego, CA; born in National City, CA, March 7, 1961; education: B.A., University of San Diego, San Diego, CA, 1983; M.A., Fordham University, New York, NY, 1987; J.D., Harvard University, Cambridge, MA, 1991; professional: lawyer; business executive; member of the San Diego, CA, city council, 1993–2000; member of the California State Assembly, 2000–06; member of the California State Senate, 2010–12; religion: Roman Catholic; spouse: Adrienne Vargas; children: Rosa Celina Vargas and Helena Jeanne Vargas; committees: Financial Services; House Administration; elected to the 113th Congress on November 6, 2012; reelected to the 114th Congress on November 4, 2014.

Office Listings

http://vargas.house.gov   https://twitter.com/repjuanvargas

1605 Longworth House Office Building, Washington, DC 20515 .... (202) 225–8045
    Chief of Staff.—Tim Walsh.   FAX: 225–2772
    Scheduler/Executive Assistant.—Christina Reyes.
    Legislative Director.—Scott Hinkle.
333 F Street, Suite A, Chula Vista, CA 91910 .... (619) 422–5963
    District Director.—Janine Pairis.   FAX: 422–7290
380 North 8th Street, Suite 14, El Centro, CA 92243 .... (760) 355–8800
    Senior Field Representative.—Rebecca Terrazas-Baxter.   FAX: 312–9664

Counties: COUNTIES: SAN DIEGO (part), AND IMPERIAL COUNTY. CITIES: Bombay Beach, Bonita, Boulevard, Brawley, Calexico, Calipatria, Campo, Chula Vista, Desert Shores, Dulzura, El Centro, Heber, Holtville, Imperial, Imperial Beach, Jacumba, National City, Niland, Ocotillo, Palo Verde, Potrero, Salton City, Salton City Beach, San Diego, Seeley, Westmorland, and Winterhaven. Population (2010), 702,906.

ZIP Codes: 91901–02, 91905–06, 91909–12, 91915, 91917, 91932–35, 91945, 91950–51, 91962–63, 91980, 91987, 92019, 92101–02, 92104–05, 92113–15, 92136, 92139, 92143, 92153–54, 92158, 92165, 92170, 92173–74, 92179, 92222, 92225, 92227, 92231–33, 92243–44, 92249–51, 92257, 92259, 92266, 92273–74, 92281, 92283

* * *

FIFTY-SECOND DISTRICT

SCOTT PETERS, Democrat, of La Jolla, CA; born in Springfield, OH, June 17, 1958; education: *magna cum laude*, Phi Beta Kappa, Duke University; New York University School of Law, professional: Environmental lawyer; City Council President; San Diego Port Commissioner; religion: Lutheran; Wife, Lynn; 2 children; committees: Armed Services; Judiciary; elected to the 113th Congress on November 6, 2012; reelected to the 114th Congress on November 4, 2014.

Office Listings

http://scottpeters.house.gov   twitter: @repscottpeters

1122 Longworth House Office Building, Washington, DC 20515 .... (202) 225–0508
    Chief of Staff.—Michelle Dorothy.
    Scheduler/Deputy Chief of Staff.—Anne Moriarity.
    Legislative Director.—Dan Zawitoski.
    Press Secretary.—Michael Campbell.
    Director of New Media.—Amanda Sherman.
4350 Executive Drive, Suite 105, San Diego, CA 92121 .... (858) 455–5550
    District Director.—MaryAnne Pintar.

Counties: SAN DIEGO COUNTY (part). CITIES AND TOWNSHIPS: Carmel Valley, La Jolla, Point Loma, Downtown San Diego, Coronado and Poway. Population (2010), 704,565.

ZIP Codes: 91901, 91905–06, 91916–17, 91931, 91935, 91941–42, 91945, 91948, 91962, 91977–78, 92004, 92019, 92021, 92025, 92029, 92036, 92040, 92064–66, 92071, 92108, 92111, 92115, 92117, 92119–20, 92123–24, 92126, 92128–29, 92131, 92145

* * *

FIFTY-THIRD DISTRICT

SUSAN A. DAVIS, Democrat, of San Diego, CA; born in Cambridge, MA, April 13, 1944; education: B.S., University of California at Berkeley; M.A., University of North Carolina; public service: served three terms in the California State Assembly; served nine years on the San Diego City School Board; former President of the League of Women Voters of San Diego; awards: California School Boards Association Legislator of the Year; League of Middle Schools Legislator of the Year; family: married to Steve; children: Jeffrey and Benjamin; grandsons: Henry and Theo; granddaughter: Jane; committees: Armed Services; Education and the Workforce; elected to the 107th Congress on November 7, 2000; reelected to each succeeding Congress.

Office Listings

http://www.susandavis.house.gov

1214 Longworth House Office Building, Washington, DC 20515 .... (202) 225–2040
    Chief of Staff.—Lisa Sherman.   FAX: 225–2948
    Press Secretary.—Aaron Hunter.
    Scheduler.—Cynthia Patton.
2700 Adams Avenue, Suite 102, San Diego, CA 92116 .... (619) 280–5353
    District Director.—Jessica Poole.   FAX: 280–5311

Counties: SAN DIEGO COUNTY (part). Population (2010), 639,008.

ZIP Codes: 91902, 91908, 91910–11, 91913–15, 91921, 91941–46, 91976–79, 92019–22, 92101–05, 92108, 92110–11, 92114–16, 92119–20, 92123–24, 92134, 92139, 92149, 92154, 92160, 92163–64, 92168, 92171, 92175–76, 92182, 92190, 92193, 92195

COLORADO

(Population 2010, 5,029,196)

SENATORS

* * *

MICHAEL F. BENNET, Democrat, of Denver, CO; born in New Delhi, India, November 28, 1964; education: B.A., Wesleyan University, 1987; J.D., Yale Law School, 1993; editor-in-chief of the *Yale Law Journal;* counsel to U.S. Deputy Attorney General, 1995–97; special assistant, U.S. Attorney, CT, 1997; managing director, Anschutz Investment Co., 1997–2003; chief of staff to mayor of Denver, CO, 2003–05; superintendent, Denver Public Schools, 2005–09; married: Susan D. Dagget; children: Caroline, Halina, and Anne; committees: Agriculture, Nutrition, and Forestry; Finance; Health, Education, Labor, and Pensions; appointed January 21, 2009, to the 111th United States Senate for the term ending January 3, 2011; elected to the 112th Congress for a full Senate term on November 2, 2010.

Office Listings

http://bennet.senate.gov   www.facebook.com/senatorbennet   twitter: @senbennetco

261 Russell Senate Office Building, Washington, DC 20510–0606	(202) 224–5852
Chief of Staff.—Jonathan Davidson.	FAX: 228–5036
Legislative Director.—Brian Appel.	
Communications Director.—Adam Bozzi.	
Scheduler.—Kristin Mollet.	
1127 Sherman Street, Suite 150, Denver, CO 80203	(303) 455–7600
	FAX: 455–8851
129 West B Street, Pueblo, CO 81003	(719) 542–7550
	FAX: 542–7555
609 Main Street, Suite 110, Alamosa, CO 81101	(719) 587–0096
	FAX: 587 0098
409 North Tejon, Suite 107, Colorado Springs, CO 80903	(719) 328–1100
	FAX: 328–1129
1200 South College Avenue, Suite 211, Fort Collins, CO 80524	(970) 224–2200
	FAX: 224–2205
225 North 5th Street, Suite 511, Grand Junction, CO 81501	(970) 241–6631
	FAX: 241–8313
835 East 2nd Avenue, Suite 203, Durango, CO 81301	(970) 259–1710
	FAX: 259–9789

* * *

CORY GARDNER, Republican, of Yuma, CO; born in Yuma, CO, August 22, 1976; education: B.A., political science, Colorado State University, Fort Collins, CO, 1997; J.D., University of Colorado, Boulder, CO, 2001; professional: agricultural advocate; staff, United States Senator Wayne Allard of Colorado, 2002–05; member of the Colorado State House of Representatives, 2005–10; member of the U.S. House of Representatives, 2011–2014; committees: Commerce, Science, and Transportation; Energy and Natural Resources; Foreign Relations; Small Business and Entrepreneurship; elected to the U.S. Senate on November 4, 2014.

Office Listings

http://gardner.senate.gov   http://facebook.com/sencorygardner
http://twitter.com/sencorygardner

354 Russell Senate Office Building, Washington, DC 20510	(202) 224–5941
Chief of Staff.—Chris Hansen.	
Deputy Chief of Staff.—Natalie Farr.	
Legislative Director.—Curtis Swager.	
Communications Director.—Alex Siciliano.	
Director of Scheduling.—Amy Barrera.	
999 18th Street, Suite 1525, Denver, CO 80202	(303) 391–5777
400 Rood Avenue, Suite 220, Grand Junction, CO 81501	(970) 245–9553
801 8th Street, Suite 140A, Greeley, CO 80631	(970) 352–5546
529 North Albany Street, Suite 1220, Yuma, CO 80759	(970) 848–3095

REPRESENTATIVES

FIRST DISTRICT

DIANA DeGETTE, Democrat, of Denver, CO; born in Tachikowa, Japan, July 29, 1957; education: B.A., political science, *magna cum laude*, The Colorado College, 1979; J.D., New York University School of Law, 1982 (Root Tilden Scholar); professional: attorney with McDermott, Hansen, and Reilly; Colorado Deputy State Public Defender, Appellate Division, 1982–84; Colorado House of Representatives, 1992–96; board of directors, Planned Parenthood, Rocky Mountain Chapter; member and formerly on board of governors, Colorado Bar Association; member, Colorado Women's Bar Association; past memberships: board of trustees, The Colorado College; Denver Women's Commission; board of directors, Colorado Trial Lawyers Association; former editor, *Trial Talk* magazine; listed in 1994–96 edition of *Who's Who in America*; Chief Deputy Whip; committees: Energy and Commerce; elected to the 105th Congress; reelected to each succeeding Congress.

Office Listings

http://degette.house.gov

2368 Rayburn House Office Building, Washington, DC 20515	(202) 225–4431
Chief of Staff.—Lisa B. Cohen.	FAX: 225–5657
Scheduler.—Diana Gambrel.	
Communications Director.—Matt Inzeo.	
600 Grant Street, Suite 202, Denver, CO 80203	(303) 844–4988
District Director.—Morris Price.	

Counties: ARAPAHOE (part), DENVER, AND JEFFERSON (part). Population (2010), 718,457.

ZIP Codes: 80012, 80014, 80110–11, 80113, 80120–21, 80123, 80127–28, 80202–07, 80209–12, 80214–16, 80218–24, 80226–27, 80230–32, 80235–39, 80246–47, 80249, 80264, 80290, 80293–94

* * *

SECOND DISTRICT

JARED POLIS, Democrat, of Boulder, CO; born in Boulder, CO, May 12, 1975; education: B.A., political science, Princeton University, Princeton, NJ, 1996; professional: Internet entrepreneur; founder of New America Schools; chair, Colorado State Board of Education; House Democratic Steering and Policy Committee; religion: Jewish; committees: Education and the Workforce; Natural Resources; Rules; elected to the 111th Congress on November 4, 2008; reelected to each succeeding Congress.

Office Listings

http://www.polis.house.gov

1433 Longworth House Office Building, Washington, DC 20515	(202) 225–2161
Chief of Staff.—Eve Lieberman.	
Legislative Director.—Mike Berman.	
1644 Walnut Street, Boulder, CO 80302	(303) 484–9596
Communications Director.—Kristin Lynch.	
P.O. Box 1453, Frisco, CO 80443	(970) 409–7301
1220 S. College Avenue, Fort Collins, CO 80525	(970) 226–1239

Counties: BOULDER (part), BROOMFIELD, CLEAR CREEK, EAGLE (part), GILPIN, GRAND, JEFFERSON, LARIMER, PARK (part), AND SUMMIT. Population (2010), 732,658.

ZIP Codes: 80007, 80020–21, 80023, 80025–28, 80135, 80228, 80234, 80301–05, 80310, 80401, 80403, 80419, 80421, 80422–25, 80427, 80433, 80435–36, 80438–39, 80442–44, 80446–48, 80451–55, 80457, 80459, 80465–66, 80468, 80470–71, 80475–76, 80478, 80481–82, 80497–98, 80503–04, 80510–13, 80515–17, 80521, 80524–26, 80528, 80532, 80534–38, 80540, 80544–45, 80547, 80549–50, 80612, 81620, 81632, 81645, 81649, 81655, 81657, 82063

* * *

THIRD DISTRICT

SCOTT TIPTON, Republican, of Cortez, CO; born in Espanola, NM, November 9, 1956; education: graduated, B.S., political science, Ft. Lewis College, Durango, CO, 1978; professional: Owner/President of Mesa Verde Pottery, Cortez, CO; public service: elected to Colorado House of Representatives, 2008–10; religion: Anglican; married: Jean Tipton; children: Liesl (married to Chris Ross) and Elizabeth (married to Jace Weber); caucuses: chair, Small Business Caucus; Coal; Natural Gas; Western; Sportsmen's; Israel; Beef; Dairy; committees: Financial Services; elected to the 112th Congress on November 2, 2010; reelected to each succeeding Congress.

Office Listings
http://tipton.house.gov

218 Cannon House Office Building, Washington, DC 20515 .... (202) 225–4761
Chief of Staff.—Nicholas Zupancic.   FAX: 226–9669
Legislative Director.—Dustin Sherer.
Executive Assistant.—Agustina Andisco.
225 North 5th Street, Suite 702, Grand Junction, CO 81501 .... (970) 241–2499
District Director.—Joshua Green.
609 Main Street, Suite 105, Box 11, Alamosa, CO 81101 .... (719) 587–5105
503 North Main Street, Suite 658, Pueblo, CO 81003 .... (719) 542–1073
835 East Second Avenue, Suite 230, Durango, CO 81301 .... (970) 259–1490

Counties: ALAMOSA, ARCHULETA, CONEJOS, COSTILLA, CUSTER, DELTA, DOLORES, EAGLE (part), GARFIELD, GUNNISON, HINSDALE, HUERFANO, JACKSON, LA PLATA, LAKE, MESA, MINERAL, MOFFAT, MONTEZUMA, MONTROSE, OURAY, PITKIN, PUEBLO, RIO BLANCO, RIO GRANDE, ROUTT, SAGUACHE, SAN JUAN, AND SAN MIGUEL. Population (2010), 718,457.

ZIP Codes: 80423, 80426, 80428, 80434, 80461, 80463, 80467, 80469, 80473, 80477, 80479–80, 80483, 80487–88, 81001, 81003–08, 81019, 81022–23, 81025, 81039–40, 81055, 81069, 81089, 81101, 81120–26, 81128–33, 81136–38, 81140–41, 81143–44, 81146–49, 81151–52, 81154–55, 81210, 81220, 81224–25, 81230–31, 81235, 81237, 81239, 81241, 81243, 81248, 81251–53, 81301, 81303, 81320–21, 81323–28, 81330–32, 81334–35, 81401, 81403, 81410–11, 81413, 81415–16, 81418–19, 81422–35, 81501, 81503–07, 81520–27, 81601, 81610–12, 81615, 81620–21, 81623–25, 81630–33, 81635, 81637–43, 81645–50, 81652–56

* * *

FOURTH DISTRICT

KEN BUCK, Republican, of Windsor, CO; born February 16, 1959; education: undergraduate, Princeton University, Princeton, NJ, 1980, J.D., University of Wyoming, Laramie, WY, 1983; professional: prosecutor; U.S. Department of Justice, Washington, DC, 1985–1995; U.S. Attorney's Office, Colorado, 1995–2000; District Attorney, Weld County, Colorado, 2004–14; Corporate Counsel, Hansel Phelps Construction, 2002–04; committees: Judiciary; Oversight and Government Reform; elected to the 114th Congress on November 4, 2014.

Office Listings
http://www.buck.house.gov

416 Cannon House Office Building, Washington, DC 20515 .... (202) 225–4676
Chief of Staff.—Greg Brophy.
Legislative Director.—Ritika Rodrigues.
Communications Director.—Katherine Rosario.
Scheduling / Office Administrator.—Sheryl Fernandez.
1122 9th Street, Unit 204, Greeley, CO 80631 .... (970) 702–2136
900 Castleton Road, Meadows Crossing, Suite 112, Castle Rock, CO 80109 .... (720) 639–9165
302 North 3rd Street, Sterling, CO 80751 .... (970) 762–0109

Counties: ADAMS (part), ARAPAHOE (part), BACA, BOULDER (part), BENT, CHEYENNE, CROWLEY, DOUGLAS (part), ELBERT, KIOWA, KIT CARSON, LAS ANIMAS, LINCOLN, LOGAN, MORGAN, OTERO, PHILLIPS, PROWERS, SEDGWICK, WASHINGTON, WELD, AND YUMA.

ZIP Codes: 80101–09, 80112, 80116–18, 80124–27, 80130–31, 80134–38, 80501–04, 80514, 80520, 80530, 80534, 80542–43, 80546, 80550–51, 80603, 80610–12, 80615, 80620–24, 80631–34, 80638–39, 80642–46, 80648–54, 80701, 80705, 80720–23, 80726–29, 80731–37, 80740–47, 80749–51, 80754–55, 80757–59, 80801–02, 80804–05, 80807, 80810, 80812, 80815, 80818, 80821–26, 80828, 80830, 80832–36, 80861–62, 81020–21, 81024, 81027, 81029–30, 81033–34, 81036, 81038–39, 81041, 81043–47, 81049–50, 81052, 81054, 81057–59, 81062–64, 81067, 81071, 81073, 81076–77, 81084, 81087, 81090–92

* * *

FIFTH DISTRICT

DOUG LAMBORN, Republican, of Colorado Springs, CO; born in Leavenworth, KS, May 24, 1954; education: B.S., University of Kansas, Lawrence, 1978; J.D., University of Kansas,

Lawrence, 1985; professional: lawyer, private practice (business and real estate); Colorado State House of Representatives, 1995–98; Colorado State Senate, 1998–2006; married: Jeanie; five children; committees: Armed Services; Natural Resources; Veterans' Affairs; elected to the 110th Congress on November 7, 2006; reelected to each succeeding Congress.

Office Listings

http://www.lamborn.house.gov　　　https://www.facebook.com/congressmandouglamborn

2402 Rayburn House Office Building, Washington, DC 20515 .... (202) 225–4422
Chief of Staff.—Adam Magary.　　　　　　　　　　　　　　　　　　　　　　　　　FAX: 226–2638
Legislative Director.—James Thomas.
Director of Communications.—Jarred Rego.
Scheduler / Executive Assistant.—Chelsea Tessier.
1125 Kelly Johnson Boulevard, Suite 330, Colorado Springs, CO 80920 .... (719) 520–0055

Counties: CHAFFEE, EL PASO, FREMONT, PARK (part), AND TELLER. Population (2010), 718,457.

ZIP Codes: 80106, 80132–33, 80420–21, 80432, 80440, 80448–49, 80456, 80808–09, 80813–14, 80816–17, 80819–20, 80827, 80829, 80831–33, 80840, 80860, 80863–64, 80902–11, 80913–30, 80938–39, 80951, 81008, 81201, 81211–12, 81221–23, 81226–27, 81232–33, 81236, 81240, 81242, 81244, 81253

* * *

SIXTH DISTRICT

MIKE COFFMAN, Republican, of Aurora, CO; born in Fort Leonard Wood, MO, March 19, 1955; education: attended, Aurora Central High School; B.A., University of Colorado, Boulder, CO, 1979; military: United States Army, 1972–74; United States Army Reserve, 1975–78; United States Marine Corps, 1979–82; United States Marine Corps Reserve, 1983–94, and 2005–06; professional: business owner; elected to the Colorado State House of Representatives, 1989–94; elected to the Colorado State Senate, 1994–98; Colorado State Treasurer, 1999–2007; Colorado Secretary of State, 2007–08; religion: Methodist; married: Cynthia; committees: Armed Services; Veterans' Affairs; elected to the 111th Congress on November 4, 2008; reelected to each succeeding Congress.

Office Listings

http://www.coffman.house.gov

2443 Rayburn House Office Building, Washington, DC 20515 .... (202) 225–7882
Chief of Staff.—Ben Stein.　　　　　　　　　　　　　　　　　　　　　　　　　　FAX: 226–4623
Scheduler.—Michelle Patrick.
3300 South Parker Road, Suite 305, Aurora, CO 80014 .... (720) 748–7514

Counties: ADAMS (part), ARAPAHOE (part), DOUGLAS (part). Population (2010), 718,456.

ZIP Codes: 80013–19, 80040–42, 80044–46, 80102, 80111–12, 80120–80126, 80128–30, 80137–38, 80160–61, 80163, 80165–66, 80231, 80247

* * *

SEVENTH DISTRICT

ED PERLMUTTER, Democrat, of Golden, CO; born in Denver, CO, May 1, 1953; education: B.A., University of Colorado, 1975; J.D., University of Colorado, 1978; professional: former partner at the law firm Berenbaum Weinshienk specializing in bankruptcy law. Served as a member of the Board of Governors of the Colorado Bar Association; served on the Board of Trustees and Judicial Performance Commission for the First Judicial District; Trustee, Midwest Research Institute, the primary operator of the National Renewable Energy Laboratory; board member, National Jewish Medical and Research Center; elected to two 4-year terms to represent central Jefferson County as a Colorado State Senator, 1995–2003; served on numerous committees in the State Senate, including Water, Finance, Judiciary, Child Welfare, Telecommunication, Transportation, Legal Services, and Oil and Gas; also served as chair of the Public Policy and Planning Committee, chair of the Bi-Partisan Renewable Energy Caucus, and President Pro Tem (2001–02 session); married to Nancy Perlmutter; between them they have six adult children; committees: Financial Services; Science, Space, and Technology; elected to the 110th Congress on November 7, 2006; reelected to each succeeding Congress.

Office Listings

http://perlmutter.house.gov

1410 Longworth House Office Building, Washington, DC 20515 .... (202) 225–2645
    Chief of Staff.—Danielle Radovich Piper.   FAX: 225–5278
    Legislative Director.—Noah Marine.
    Chief of Operations/Scheduler.—Alison Inderfurth.
    Staff Assistant.—Eddie Wytkind.
12600 West Colfax Avenue, Suite B400, Lakewood, CO 80215 .... (303) 274–7944

Counties: ADAMS (part), JEFFERSON (part). CITIES AND TOWNSHIPS: Arvada, Commerce City, Edgewater, Golden, Lakewood, Wheat Ridge, Westminster, Thornton and Northglenn. Population (2010), 718,456.

ZIP Codes: 80001, 80002 (part), 80003–07, 80020 (part), 80021 (part), 80022 (part), 80023 (part), 80024, 80030–31,80033 (part), 80034–37, 80123 (part), 80212 (part), 80214 (part), 80215, 80216 (part), 80221 (part), 80225, 80226 (part), 80227 (part), 80228–29, 80232 (part), 80233, 80234 (part), 80235 (part), 80239 (part), 80241 (part), 80260, 80303 (part), 80401 (part), 80402, 80403 (part), 80419, 80465 (part), 80601 (part), 80602 (part), 80603 (part), 80614, 80640 (part), 80260, 80303 (part), 80614, 80640 (part)

CONNECTICUT

(Population 2010, 3,574,097)

SENATORS

RICHARD BLUMENTHAL, Democrat, of Greenwich, CT; born in Brooklyn, NY, February 13, 1946; son of Martin and Jane Rosenstock Blumenthal; education: graduated, Riverdale Country School, Riverdale, NY, 1963; B.A., government, Harvard College, Cambridge, MA, 1967; J.D., Yale Law School, New Haven, CT, 1973; admitted to Connecticut Bar, 1976; admitted to District of Columbia Bar, 1977; appointed United States Attorney for the District of Connecticut, 1977–81; Connecticut State House of Representatives, 1984–87; Connecticut State Senate, 1987–90; elected Attorney General for the State of Connecticut, 1990, reelected in 1994, 1998, 2002, and 2006; military: served in the United States Marine Corps Reserves, 1970–76, honorably discharged as Sergeant; married: Cynthia M. Blumenthal; four children: Matthew, Michael, David, and Claire; committees: ranking member, Veterans' Affairs; Armed Services; Commerce, Science, and Transportation; Judiciary; Special Committee on Aging; elected to the U.S. Senate on November 2, 2010.

Office Listings

http://blumenthal.senate.gov

706 Hart Senate Office Building, Washington, DC 20510	(202) 224–2823
Chief of Staff.—Laurie Rubiner.	FAX: 224–9673
Legislative Director.—Ethan Saxon.	
Scheduling Director.—Dana Sandman.	
Communications Director.—Josh Zembik.	
90 State House Square, 10th Floor, Hartford, CT 06103	(860) 258–6940
	FAX: 258–6958
915 Lafayette Boulevard, Room 330, Bridgeport, CT 06604	(203) 330–0598
	FAX: 330–0608

* * *

CHRISTOPHER S. MURPHY, Democrat, of Cheshire, CT; born in White Plains, West-chester County, NY, August 3, 1973; education: attended Exeter College, Oxford, England, 1994–95; graduated with honors with double majors in history and political science, Williams College, Williamstown, MA, 1996; J.D., University of Connecticut, Hartford, CT, 2002; profes-sional: lawyer, private practice; Southington, Connecticut; planning and zoning commission, 1997–99; practiced real estate and banking law from 2002–06, with the firm of Ruben, Johnson & Morgan in Hartford; member of the Connecticut State House of Representatives, 1999–2003; member of the Connecticut State Senate, 2003–06; married: Cathy Holahan, a legal aid attorney who represents children in need in New Britain and Waterbury; children: Chris, Cathy, and their sons Owen and Rider; elected as a Democrat to the 110th and to the two succeeding Con-gresses, January 3, 2007–January 3, 2013; committees: Appropriations; Foreign Relations; Health, Education, Labor, and Pensions; elected to the U.S. Senate on November 6, 2012.

Office Listings

http://www.chrismurphy.house.gov

136 Hart Senate Office Building, Washington, DC 20510	(202) 224–4041
Chief of Staff.—Allison Herwitt.	FAX: 224–9750
Executive Assistant.—Maya Ashwal.	
Legislative Director.—David Bonine.	
One Constitution Plaza, 7th Floor, Hartford, CT 06103	(860) 549–8463
State Director.—Kenny Curran.	

REPRESENTATIVES

FIRST DISTRICT

JOHN B. LARSON, Democrat, of East Hartford, CT; born in Hartford, CT, July 22, 1948; education: Mayberry Elementary School, East Hartford, CT; East Hartford High School; B.A., Central Connecticut State University; Senior Fellow, Yale University, Bush Center for Child Development and Social Policy; professional: high school teacher, 1972–77; insurance broker,

1978–98; president, Larson and Lyork; public service: Connecticut State Senate, 12 years, President Pro Tempore, 8 years; married: Leslie Larson; children: Carolyn, Laura, and Raymond; committees: Ethics; Ways and Means; elected to the 106th Congress; reelected to each succeeding Congress.

Office Listings

http://www.larson.house.gov

1501 Longworth House Office Building, Washington, DC 20515	(202) 225–2265
Chief of Staff.—Lee Slater.	FAX: 225–1031
Deputy Chief of Staff.—Geraldine de Puy.	
Legislative Director.—David Sitcovsky.	
221 Main Street, Hartford, CT 06106–1864	(860) 278–8888
District Director.—Kevin Brown.	
Press Secretary.—Amanda Schoen.	

Counties: HARTFORD (part), LITCHFIELD (part), MIDDLESEX (part). Population (2010), 714,820.

ZIP Codes: 06002, 06010, 06013, 06016, 06021, 06023, 06026–27, 06033, 06035, 06037, 06040, 06042, 06052, 06057–63, 06065, 06067, 06073–74, 06088, 06090–91, 06095–96, 06098, 06103, 06105–12, 06114, 06117–20, 06160, 06416, 06444, 06451, 06457, 06467, 06479–80, 06489, 06759, 06790

* * *

SECOND DISTRICT

JOE COURTNEY, Democrat, of Vernon, CT; born in Hartford, CT, April 6, 1953; education: B.A., Tufts University, 1971–75; University of Connecticut Law School, 1975–78; public service: Connecticut State Representative, 1987–94; Vernon Town Attorney, 2003–06; professional: attorney, Courtney, Boyan, and Foran, LLC, 1978–2006; religion: Roman Catholic; married: Audrey Courtney; children: Robert and Elizabeth; committees: Armed Services; Education and the Workforce; elected to the 110th Congress on November 7, 2006; reelected to each succeeding Congress.

Office Listings

http://www.courtney.house.gov　　　https://www.facebook.com/joecourtney
https://twitter.com/repjoecourtney

2348 Rayburn House Office Building, Washington, DC 20515	(202) 225–2076
Chief of Staff.—Jason Gross.	FAX: 225–4977
Communications Director.—Elizabeth Donovan.	
Scheduler.—Maria Costigan.	
Legislative Director.—Neil McKiernan.	
55 Main Street, Suite 250, Norwich, CT 06360	(860) 886–0139
District Director.—Ayanti Grant.	FAX: 886–2974
77 Hazard Avenue, Unit J, Enfield, CT 06082	(860) 741–6011
	FAX: 741–6036

Counties: HARTFORD (part), MIDDLESEX (part), NEW HAVEN (part), NEW LONDON, TOLLAND, AND WINDHAM. Population (2010), 714,819.

ZIP Codes: 06029, 06033, 06043, 06066, 06071, 06076, 06078, 06082, 06084, 06093, 06226, 06231–32, 06234–35, 06237–39, 06241–43, 06247–50, 06254–56, 06259–60, 06262–64, 06266, 06268–69, 06277–82, 06320, 06330–36, 06339–40, 06350–51, 06353–55, 06357, 06359–60, 06365, 06370–71, 06373–80, 06382, 06384–85, 06387, 06389, 06409, 06412–15, 06417, 06419–20, 06423–24, 06426, 06438, 06441–43, 06447, 06456, 06469, 06475

* * *

THIRD DISTRICT

ROSA L. DeLAURO, Democrat, of New Haven, CT; born in New Haven, March 2, 1943; education: graduated, Lauralton Hall High School; attended London School of Economics, Queen Mary College, London, 1962–63; B.A., *cum laude*, history and political science, Marymount College, NY, 1964; M.A., international politics, Columbia University, NY, 1966; professional: executive assistant to Mayor Frank Logue, city of New Haven, 1976–77; executive assistant/development administrator, city of New Haven, 1977–78; chief of staff, Senator Christopher Dodd, 1980–87; executive director, Countdown '87, 1987–88; executive director, Emily's List, 1989–90; religion: Catholic; family: married, Stanley Greenberg; children: Anna,

Kathryn, and Jonathan; co-chair, Democratic Steering and Policy Committee; committees: Appropriations; elected to the 102nd Congress on November 6, 1990; reelected to each succeeding Congress.

Office Listings

http://www.delauro.house.gov

2413 Rayburn House Office Building, Washington, DC 20515 .... (202) 225–3661
    Chief of Staff.—Beverly Pheto. FAX: 225–4890
    Scheduler.—Ryann Kinney.
59 Elm Street, New Haven, CT 06510 .... (203) 562–3718
    District Director.—Jennifer Lamb.

Counties: FAIRFIELD (part), MIDDLESEX (part), NEW HAVEN (part). CITIES AND TOWNSHIPS: Ansonia, Beacon Falls, Bethany, Branford, Derby, Durham, East Haven, Guilford, Hamden, Middlefield, Middletown (part), Milford, Naugatuck, New Haven, North Branford, North Haven, Orange, Prospect, Seymour, Shelton (part), Stratford, Wallingford, Waterbury (part), West Haven, and Woodbridge. Population (2011), 718,549.

ZIP Codes: 06401, 06403, 06405, 06410, 06418, 06422, 06437, 06450, 06455, 06457, 06460, 06471–73, 06477, 06481, 06483–84, 06492–94, 06501–21, 06524–25, 06530–38, 06540, 06607, 06614–15, 06706, 06708, 06712, 06762, 06770

* * *

FOURTH DISTRICT

JAMES A. HIMES, Democrat, of Cos Cob, CT; born in Lima, Peru to American parents, July 5, 1966; education: B.A., Harvard University, Cambridge, MA, 1988; M.Phil, Oxford University, Oxford, England, 1990; professional: vice president, Goldman Sachs & Co., 1990–2002; vice president, Enterprise Community Partners, 2002–07; Commissioner, Greenwich Housing Authority; chair, Greenwich Democratic Town Committee; religion: Presbyterian; married: Mary Himes, 1994; children: Emma and Linley; committees: Financial Services; Permanent Select Committee on Intelligence; elected to the 111th Congress on November 4, 2008; reelected to each succeeding Congress.

Office Listings

http://www.himes.house.gov

1227 Longworth House Office Building, Washington, DC 20515 .... (202) 225–5541
    Chief of Staff.—Mark Henson. FAX: 225–9629
    Executive Aide.—Cara Pavlock.
888 Washington Boulevard, Stamford, CT 06901–2927 .... (866) 453–0028
211 State Street, 2nd Floor, Bridgeport, CT 06604–4223 .... (866) 453–0028
    District Director.—Tyrone McClain.

Counties: FAIRFIELD (part), NEW HAVEN (part). CITIES AND TOWNSHIPS: Bridgeport, Darien, Easton, Fairfield, Greenwich, Monroe, New Canaan, Norwalk, Oxford, Redding, Ridgefield, Shelton, Stamford, Trumbull Weston, Westport, and Wilton. Population (2010), 714,819.

ZIP Codes: 06468, 06478, 06604–08, 06610–12, 06807, 06820, 06824–25, 06830–31, 06840, 06850–51, 06853–56, 06870, 06877–78, 06880, 06883, 06890, 06896–97, 06901–03, 06905–07

* * *

FIFTH DISTRICT

ELIZABETH H. ESTY, Democrat, of Cheshire, CT; born August 25, 1959; education: graduated, A.B., Harvard College, Cambridge, MA, 1981; graduated, J.D., Yale University, New Haven, CT, 1985; professional: law clerk for a federal judge; a Supreme Court lawyer at Sidley Austin LLP in Washington, DC; professor at American University; former member, Cheshire Town Council, CT, 2005–08; member of the Connecticut State House of Representatives, 2008–10; caucuses: serves on Gun Violence Prevention Task Force; committees: Science, Space, and Technology; Transportation and Infrastructure; elected to 113th Congress on November 6, 2012; reelected to the 114th Congress on November 4, 2014.

Office Listings

http://esty.house.gov

405 Cannon House Office Building, Washington, DC 20515 .... (202) 225–4476
    Chief of Staff.—Tony Baker.   FAX: (860) 223–8412
    Communications Director.—Laura Maloney.
    Scheduler.—Kelley Anne Carney.
114 West Main Street, Suite 206, New Britain, CT 06053 .... (860) 223–8412
    District Director.—Stephanie Podewell.

Counties: FAIRFIELD (part), HARTFORD (part), LITCHFIELD, NEW HAVEN (part). CITIES: Danbury, Meriden, New Britain, Torrington, and Waterbury. Population (2010), 714,820.

ZIP Codes: 06001, 06013, 06018–20, 06022, 06024, 06030–32, 06034, 06039, 06050–53, 06058–59, 06062, 06068–70, 06079, 06081, 06085, 06087, 06089, 06092, 06107, 06404, 06408, 06410–11, 06440, 06450–51, 06454, 06470, 06482, 06487–88, 06701–06, 06708, 06710, 06716, 06720–26, 06749–59, 06762–63, 06776–79, 06781–87, 06790–91, 06793–96, 06798, 06801, 06804, 06810–14, 06816–17

DELAWARE

(Population 2010, 897,934)

SENATORS

THOMAS R. CARPER, Democrat, of Wilmington, DE; born in Beckley, WV, January 23, 1947; education: B.A., Ohio State University, 1968; M.B.A., University of Delaware, 1975; military service: U.S. Navy, served during Vietnam War; public service: Delaware State Treasurer, 1977–83; U.S. House of Representatives, 1983–93; Governor of Delaware, 1993–2001; organizations: Third Way; New Democrat Network; former National Governors' Association chair; religion: Presbyterian; family: married to the former Martha Ann Stacy; children: Ben and Christopher; committees: ranking member, Homeland Security and Governmental Affairs; Environment and Public Works; Finance; elected to the U.S. Senate on November 7, 2000; re-elected to each succeeding Senate term.

Office Listings

http://carper.senate.gov   www.facebook.com/tomcarper   twitter: @senatorcarper

513 Hart Senate Office Building, Washington, DC 20510	(202) 224–2441
Chief of Staff.—Bill Ghent.	FAX: 228–2190
Legislative Director.—Emily Spain.	
Administrative Director.—Madge Farooq.	
500 West Loockerman Street, Suite 470, Dover, DE 19904	(302) 674–3308
301 North Walnut Street, Suite 102 L–1, Wilmington, DE 19801	(302) 573–6291
12 The Circle, Georgetown, DE 19947	(302) 856–7690

* * *

CHRISTOPHER A. COONS, Democrat, of Wilmington, DE; born in Greenwich, CT, September 9, 1963; education: B.A., Amherst College, 1985; M.A.R., Yale University, 1992; J.D., Yale University, 1992; professional: associate (legal counsel), W.L. Gore & Associates, 1996–2004; president of New Castle County Council, 2000–04; county executive, New Castle County, 2005–10; religion: Presbyterian; married: Annie; children: Michael, Jack, and Maggie; committees: Appropriations; Ethics; Foreign Relations; Judiciary; Small Business; elected on November 2, 2010 to the United States Senate to fill the remainder of the vacancy caused by the unfinished term of Joseph R. Biden, Jr. and took the oath of office on November 15, 2010.

Office Listings

http://coons.senate.gov   http://www.facebook.com/senatorchriscoons
http://www.twitter.com/sencoonsoffice

127A Russell Senate Office Building, Washington, DC 20510	(202) 224–5042
Chief of Staff.—Todd Webster.	FAX: 228–3075
Legislative Director.—Jonathan Stahler.	
Communications Director.—Sean Coit.	
Administrative Director.—Trinity Hall.	
1105 North Market Street, Suite 100, Wilmington, DE 19801–1233	(302) 573–6345
State Director.—Jim Paoli.	
500 West Loockerman Street, Suite 450, Dover, DE 19904	(302) 736–5601

REPRESENTATIVE

AT LARGE

JOHN CARNEY, JR., Democrat, of Wilmington, DE; born in Wilmington, May 20, 1956; education: B.A., english, Dartmouth College, Hanover, NH, 1978; M.P.A., University of Delaware, Newark, DE, 1987; professional: staff assistant, United States Senator Joseph Biden, Jr., Delaware, 1986–89; deputy chief administrative officer, New Castle County Executive Dennis Greenhouse, Delaware, 1989–94; deputy chief of staff, Governor Tom Carper, 1994–97; secretary of finance, Delaware, 1997–2000; lieutenant governor, Delaware, 2001–2009; awards: Order of the First State; Outstanding Alumni, University of Delaware; Recipient of the Outstanding Public Service Award, National Association of Community Health Centers, 2004; Recipient of the James Ewing Layman Award, Society of Surgical Oncology, 2008; City of Wilmington Public Service Award; religion: Roman Catholic; family: wife, Tracey, two sons;

caucuses: New Democrats Caucus; National Guard Caucus; committees: Financial Services; elected to the 112th Congress on November 2, 2010; reelected to each succeeding Congress.

Office Listings
http://www.johncarney.house.gov

1406 Longworth House Office Building, Washington, DC 20515 .... (202) 225–4165
Chief of Staff.—Sheila Grant. FAX: 225–2291
Legislative Director.—Craig Radcliffe.
DC Scheduler.—Kristy Huxhold.
233 North King Street, Suite 200, Wilmington, DE 19801 .... (302) 428–1902
State Director.—Molly Magarik. FAX: 428–1905
DE Scheduler.—Kristy Huxhold.

Counties: KENT, NEW CASTLE, SUSSEX. CITIES AND TOWNSHIPS: Bethany Beach, Bethel, Bellefonte, Blades, Bowers, Bridgeville, Camden, Cheswold, Dagsboro, Delmar, Delaware City, Dewey Beach, Dover, Ellendale, Elsmere, Farmington, Felton, Fenwick Island, Frankford, Frederica, Georgetown, Greenwood, Harrington, Hartly, Henlopen Acres, Houston, Kenton, Laurel, Lewes, Little Creek, Leipsic, Magnolia, Middletown, Milford, Millsboro, Millville, Milton, New Castle, Newark, Newport, Ocean View, Odessa, Rehoboth Beach, Seaford, Selbyville, Slaughter Beach, South Bethany, Smyrna, Townsend, Viola, Wilmington, Woodside, and Wyoming. Population (2010), 897,934.

ZIP Codes: 19701–03, 19706–18, 19720–21, 19725–26, 19730–36, 19801–10, 19850, 19880, 19884–87, 19890–99, 19901–06, 19930–31, 19933–34, 19936, 19938–41, 19943–47, 19950–56, 19958, 19960–64, 19966 71, 19973, 19975, 19977, 19979–80

FLORIDA

(Population 2010, 18,801,310)

SENATORS

BILL NELSON, Democrat, of Orlando, FL; born in Miami, FL, September 29, 1942; education: Melbourne High School, 1960; B.A., Yale University, 1965; J.D., University of Virginia School of Law, 1968; professional: attorney; admitted to the Florida Bar, 1968; captain, U.S. Army Reserve, 1965–71; active duty, 1968–70; public service: Florida State House of Representatives, 1973–79; U.S. House of Representatives, 1979–91; Florida Treasurer, Insurance Commissioner, and State Fire Marshal, 1995–2001; Astronaut: payload specialist on the space shuttle *Columbia,* January, 1986; married: the former Grace Cavert; children: Bill Jr. and Nan Ellen; committees: ranking member, Commerce, Science, and Transportation; Armed Services; Finance; Special Committee on Aging; elected to the U.S. Senate on November 7, 2000; reelected to each succeeding Senate term.

Office Listings

http://billnelson.senate.gov   twitter: @senbillnelson

716 Hart Senate Office Building, Washington, DC 20510	(202) 224–5274
Chief of Staff.—Pete Mitchell.	FAX: 228–2183
Deputy Chief of Staff, Communications.—Dan McLaughlin.	
Deputy Chief of Staff, Administration.—Brenda Strickland.	
Deputy Chief of Staff, Policy.—Susie Perez Quinn.	
U.S. Courthouse Annex, 111 North Adams Street, Tallahassee, FL 32301	(850) 942–8415
Chief of Staff.—Pete Mitchell.	
801 North Florida Avenue, 4th Floor, Tampa, FL 33602	(813) 225–7040
2555 Ponce De Leon Boulevard, Suite 610, Coral Gables, FL 33134	(305) 536–5999
3416 University Drive, Ft. Lauderdale, FL 33328	(954) 693–4851
413 Clematis Street, Suite 210, West Palm Beach, FL 33401	(561) 514–0189
225 East Robinson Street, Suite 410, Orlando, FL 32801	(407) 872–7161
1301 Riverplace Boulevard, Suite 2010, Jacksonville, FL 32207	(904) 346–4500
2000 Main Street, Suite 801, Ft. Myers, FL 33901	(239) 334–7760

* * *

MARCO A. RUBIO, Republican, of West Miami, FL; born in Miami, FL, May 28, 1971; education: South Miami Senior High School, 1989; B.S., political science, University of Florida, 1993; J.D., *cum laude,* University of Miami, 1996; professional: Florida House of Representatives, 2000–08; served as majority whip, majority leader and speaker of the house; attorney, Broad and Cassel; Marco Rubio, P.A.; lecturer at Florida International University's Metropolitan Center, 2009–10; Bob Dole for President, 1996, Miami-Dade County Director; religion: Roman Catholic; married: Jeanette; children: Amanda, Daniella, Anthony, and Dominick; committees: Commerce, Science, and Transportation; Foreign Relations; Small Business and Entrepreneurship; Select Committee on Intelligence; elected to the U.S. Senate on November 2, 2010.

Office Listings

http://rubio.senate.gov   twitter: @marcorubio

SR–284 Russell Building, Washington, DC 20510	(202) 224–3041
Chief of Staff.—Alberto Martinez.	FAX: 228–0285
Legislative Director.—Sara Decker.	
201 South Orange Avenue, Suite 350, Orlando, FL 32801	(407) 254–2573
1650 Prudential Drive, Suite 220, Jacksonville, FL 32207	(904) 398–8586
1 North Palafox Street, Suite 159, Pensacola, FL 32502	(850) 433–2603
5201 West Kennedy Boulevard, Suite 530, Tampa, FL 33609	(813) 287–5035
8669 Northwest 36th Street, Suite 110, Miami, FL 33166	(305) 418–8553
3299 East Tamiami Trail, Suite 106, Naples, FL 34112	(239) 213–1521
402 South Monroe Street, Suite 2105E, Tallahassee, FL 32399	(850) 599–9100
4580 PGA Boulevard, Suite 201, Palm Beach Gardens, FL 33418	(561) 775–3360

REPRESENTATIVES

FIRST DISTRICT

JEFF MILLER, Republican, of Chumuckla, FL; born in Pinellas County, June 27, 1959; education: B.A., University of Florida, 1984; professional: real estate broker; public service: Executive Assistant to the Commissioner of Agriculture, 1984–88; Environmental Land Management Study Commission, 1992; Santa Rosa County Planning Board Vice Chairman, 1996–98; elected to the Florida House of Representatives in 1998, reelected in 2000; served as House Majority Whip; organizations: Kiwanis Club of Milton; Florida Historical Society; Santa Rosa County United Way; Milton Pregnancy Resource Center Advisory Board; Gulf Coast Council of Boy Scouts; Florida FFA Foundation; religion: Methodist, married: Vicki Griswold; children: Scott and Clint; committees: chair, Veterans' Affairs; Armed Services; Permanent Select Committee on Intelligence; elected to the 107th Congress, by special election, on October 16, 2001; reelected to each succeeding Congress.

Office Listings

http://jeffmiller.house.gov

336 Cannon House Office Building, Washington, DC 20515 .... (202) 225–4136
Chief of Staff.—Dan McFaul.   FAX: 225–3414
Legislative Director.—Diane Cihota.
Scheduler.—Jessica Turner.
4300 Bayou Boulevard, Suite 13, Pensacola, FL 32503 .... (850) 479–1183
District Director.—Sheilah Bowman.
348 Southwest Miracle Strip Parkway, Unit 24, Ft. Walton Beach, FL 32548 .... (850) 664–1266

Counties: ESCAMBIA, HOLMES (part), OKALOOSA, SANTA ROSA, WALTON. CITIES AND TOWNSHIPS: Pensacola, Pace, Milton, Cantonment, Jay, Gulf Breeze, Fort Walton Beach, Santa Rosa Beach, DeFuniak Springs, Laurel Hill, Crestview, Destin, Ferrypass, Navarre, Valparaiso, Miramar Beach, Chumuckla, Century, Walnut Hill, Seaside. Population (2010), 687,856.

ZIP Codes: 32422, 32427, 32433–35, 32439, 32454, 32459, 32501–09, 32511–14, 32516, 32520–24, 32526, 32530, 32531, 32533–42, 32544, 32547–49, 32559–83, 32588

* * *

SECOND DISTRICT

GWEN GRAHAM, Democrat, of Tallahassee, FL; born in Miami Lakes, FL, January 31, 1963; education: graduated, Leon High School, Tallahassee, FL, 1980; B.A., University of North Carolina at Chapel Hill, 1984; J.D., Washington College of Law, 1988; professional: attorney at Andrews & Kurth, attorney at Leon County Public Schools; religion: Episcopal; married: yes; children: three; committees: Agriculture; Armed Services; elected to the 114th Congress on November 4, 2014.

Office Listings

http://graham.house.gov   twitter: https://twitter.com/repgwengraham
facebook: https://www.facebook.com/repgwengraham

1213 Longworth House Office Building, Washington, DC 20515 .... (202) 225–5235
Chief of Staff.—Julia Woodward.
Operations Director.—Brendan Olsen.
Communications Director.—Matt Harringer.
Legislative Director.—Hill Thomas.
Legislative Assistant.—Jessie Andrews.
Legislative Correspondent.—Todd Smith-Schoenwalder.
Scheduler.—Eva Gavrish.
300 South Adams Street, Suite A–3, Tallahassee, FL 32301 .... (850) 891–8610
District Director.—Mary Lee Kiracofe.
840 West 11th Street, Suite 2250, Panama City, FL 32401 .... (850) 785–0812

Counties: BAY, CALHOUN, FRANKLIN, GADSDEN, GULF, HOLMES (part), JACKSON, JEFFERSON, LEON, LIBERTY, MADISON (part), TAYLOR, WAKULLA, AND WASHINGTON. Population (2010), 737,519.

ZIP Codes: 32008, 32013, 32024, 32038, 32055, 32060, 32062, 32064, 32066, 32071, 32094, 32096, 32126, 32140, 32170, 32175, 32267, 32301–18, 32320–24, 32326–34, 32336, 32343–44, 32346–48, 32351–53, 32355–62, 32395, 32399, 32401–13, 32417, 32420–21, 32423–24, 32426, 32428, 32430–32, 32437–38, 32440, 32442–49, 32454, 32456–57, 32459–61, 32465–66, 32541, 32550, 32578, 32628, 32648, 32680, 32692

* * *

THIRD DISTRICT

TED S. YOHO, DVM, Republican, of Gainesville, FL; born in Minneapolis, MN, April 13, 1955; education: graduated from Deerfield Beach High School, Deerfield Beach, FL, 1973; attended Florence State University (University of North Alabama), Florence, AL; A.A., Broward Community College, Fort Lauderdale, FL, 1977; B.S.A., University of Florida, Gainesville, FL, 1979; D.V.M., University of Florida, Gainesville, FL, 1983; professional: large animal veterinarian; religion: Christian; married: the former Carolyn Sue Marlin, children: Katie, Tyler, and Lauren; caucuses: Veterinary Medicine Caucus; Congressional Sportsmen's Caucus; Republican Study Committee; Florida Ports Caucus; House Liberty Caucus; Freshman Regulatory Reform Working Group; Congressional Cystic Fibrosis Caucus; committees: Agriculture; Foreign Affairs; elected to the 113th Congress on November 6, 2012; reelected to the 114th Congress on November 4, 2014.

Office Listings

http://yoho.house.gov   www.facebook.com/congressmantedyoho   instagram: @reptedyoho

511 Cannon House Office Building, Washington, DC 20515 .... (202) 225–5744
    Chief of Staff.—Omar Raschid.   FAX: 225–3973
    Scheduler.—Lexi Pursley.
    Legislative Director.—Larry Calhoun.
    Communications Director.—Brian Kaveney.
5000 Northwest 27th Court, Suite E, Gainesville, FL 32606 .... (352) 505–0838
    Deputy Chief of staff.—Kat Cammack.
    District Director.—Clay Martin.
35–1 Knight Boxx Road, Orange Park, FL 32065 .... (904) 276–9626
    Constituent Advocacy Manager.—Greg Rawson.

Counties: ALACHUA, BRADFORD, CLAY, COLUMBIA, DIXIE, GILCHRIST, HAMILTON, LAFAYETTE, LEVY, MARION, SUWANEE, AND UNION. Population (2010), 696,000.

ZIP Codes: 32003, 32006, 32008, 32013, 32024–26, 32030, 32038, 32042–44, 32050, 32052–56, 32058–62, 32064–68, 32071, 32073, 32079, 32083, 32087, 32091, 32094, 32096, 32140, 32160, 32234, 32340–41, 32348, 32350, 32601, 32603–12, 32614–16, 32618–19, 32621–22, 32625–26, 32628, 32631, 32633–35, 32639–41, 32643–44, 32648, 32653, 32655–56, 32658, 32666–69, 32680, 32683, 32686, 32692–94, 32696–97, 34430–32, 34449, 34474, 34476, 34481–82, 34498

* * *

FOURTH DISTRICT

ANDER CRENSHAW, Republican, of Jacksonville, FL; born in Jacksonville, September 1, 1944; education: B.A., University of Georgia, 1966; J.D., University of Florida, 1969; professional: investment banker; religion: Episcopal; public service: former member of the Florida House of Representatives and the Florida State Senate; served as President of the Florida State Senate; married: Kitty; children: Sarah and Alex; member of House Republican Leadership Whip team serving as Deputy Majority Whip; committees: Appropriations; elected to the 107th Congress on November 7, 2000; reelected to each succeeding Congress.

Office Listings

http://www.crenshaw.house.gov   https://twitter.com/andercrenshaw

2161 Rayburn House Office Building, Washington, DC 20515 .... (202) 225–2501
    Chief of Staff.—Erica Striebel.
    Legislative Director.—Jennifer Debes.
    Communications Director.—Barbara Riley.
1061 Riverside Avenue, Suite 100, Jacksonville, FL 32204 .... (904) 598–0481
    District Director.—Jacqueline Smith.

Counties: BAKER, DUVAL, NASSAU. CITIES AND TOWNSHIPS: Jacksonville, Jacksonville Beach, Macclenny, and Yulee. Population (2010), 696,345.

ZIP Codes: 32009, 32011, 32034–35, 32040–41, 32046, 32063, 32072, 32082, 32087, 32097, 32099, 32204–05, 32207, 32210–12, 32214, 32216–29, 32233–34, 32237, 32239–41, 32244–46, 32250, 32254–59, 32266, 32277

* * *

FIFTH DISTRICT

CORRINE BROWN, Democrat, of Jacksonville, FL; born in Jacksonville, November 11, 1946; education: B.S., Florida A&M University, 1969; master's degree, Florida A&M University, 1971; education specialist degree, University of Florida; honorary doctor of law, Edward

Waters College; faculty member: Florida Community College in Jacksonville; University of Florida; Edward Waters College; served in the Florida House of Representatives for 10 years; first woman elected chairperson of the Duval County Legislative Delegation; served as a consultant to the Governor's Committee on Aging; member: Congressional Black Caucus; Women's Caucus; Progressive Caucus; Human Rights Caucus; Missing and Exploited Children's Caucus; Diabetes Caucus; Duma Study Group; Community College Caucus; Older Americans Caucus; one child: Shantrel; committees: Transportation and Infrastructure; Veterans' Affairs; elected on November 3, 1992 to the 103rd Congress; reelected to each succeeding Congress.

Office Listings

http://www.corrinebrown.house.gov   https://twitter.com/repcorrinebrown
https://www.facebook.com/congresswomanbrown

2111 Rayburn House Office Building, Washington, DC 20515	(202) 225–0123
Chief of Staff.—E. Ronnie Simmons.	FAX: 225–2256
Executive Assistant / Scheduler.—Cathy Gass.	
Legislative Director.—Nick Martinelli.	
Communications Director.—David Simon.	
101 East Union Street, Suite 202, Jacksonville, FL 32202	(904) 354–1652
455 North Garland Avenue, Suite 414, Orlando, FL 32801	(407) 872–2208

Counties: ALACHUA (part), CLAY (part), DUVAL (part), LAKE (part), MARION (part), ORANGE (part), PUTNAM (part), AND SEMINOLE (part). Population (2010), 696,345.

ZIP Codes: 32003, 32043, 32073, 32102, 32113, 32134, 32140, 32148, 32177, 32202, 32204 12, 32216, 32218–22, 32224, 32244, 32254, 32277, 32601, 32609, 32631, 32640–41, 32664, 32666–67, 32681, 32686, 32702–03, 32712, 32720, 32736, 32746, 32751, 32757, 32767, 32771, 32773, 32776, 32784, 32798, 32801, 32804–06, 32808–11, 32818–19, 32835, 32839, 34734, 34761

* * *

SIXTH DISTRICT

RONALD "RON" DeSANTIS, Republican, of Ponte Vedra Beach, FL; born in Jacksonville, FL, September 14, 1978; education: *magna cum laude* with a B.A. in history, Yale University, New Haven, CT, 2001; J.D., Harvard Law School, Cambridge University, MA, 2005; sworn into the Judge Advocate General Corps of the U.S. Navy, while still a student at the Harvard Law School; completing U.S. Naval Justice School in 2005; professional: served in the Trial Service Office Command South East at the Naval Station Mayport, Florida as a military prosecutor; promoted to Lieutenant (O–3) and worked for the Joint Task Force-Guantanamo Commander (JTF–GTMO), at the Guantanamo Bay Joint Detention Facility, 2006; assigned to SEAL Team One and deployed to Iraq with the troop surge as the Legal Advisor to the SEAL Commander, Special Operations Task Force-West in Fallujah, 2007; earned an appointment with the U.S. Department of Justice to serve as a federal prosecutor at the U.S. Attorney's Office in the Middle District of Florida, 2008; concurrently accepted a Reserve commission as a Lieutenant, Judge Advocate General Corps, in the U.S. Navy Reserve; currently a Lieutenant Commander; awards: Bronze Star Medal and Iraq Campaign Medal Award; authored a book entitled *Dreams From Our Founding Fathers: First Principles in the Age of Obama*, which was published in 2011; religion: Roman Catholic; married: Casey Black DeSantis; committees: Foreign Affairs; Judiciary; Oversight and Government Reform; elected to the 113th Congress on November 6, 2012; reelected to the 114th Congress on November 4, 2014.

Office Listings

http://desantis.house.gov   https://www.facebook.com/repdesantis
https://twitter.com/repdesantis

308 Cannon House Office Building, Washington, DC 20515	(202) 225–2706
Chief of Staff.—Dustin Carmack.	FAX: 226–6299
Deputy Chief of Staff / Scheduler.—Shira Gladstone.	
Legislative Director.—Jordan Kaye.	
Communications Director.—Elizabeth Dillon.	
1000 City Center Circle, 2nd Floor, Port Orange, FL 32129	(386) 756–9798
3940 Lewis Speedway, Suite 2104, St. Augustine, FL 32084	(904) 827–1114

Counties: ST. JOHNS, FLAGLER, PUTNAM (part), AND VOLUSIA (part). CITIES: St. Augustine and Daytona Beach. Population (2010) 696,345.

ZIP Codes: 32033, 32080–82, 32084, 32086, 32092, 32095, 32110, 32112, 32114, 32117–19, 32124, 32127–32, 32136, 32139, 32141, 32145, 32147, 32157, 32164, 32167, 32169, 32174, 32176, 32180–81, 32187, 32189, 32190, 32193, 32259, 32759

* * *

SEVENTH DISTRICT

JOHN L. MICA, Republican, of Winter Park, FL; born in Binghamton, NY, January 27, 1943; education: graduated, Miami-Edison High School, Miami, FL; B.A., University of Florida, 1967; professional: president, MK Development; managing general partner, Cellular Communications; former government affairs consultant, Mica, Dudinsky and Associates; executive director, Local Government Study Commissions, Palm Beach County, 1970–72; executive director, Orange County Local Government Study Commission, 1972–74; Florida State House of Representatives, 1976–80; administrative assistant, U.S. Senator Paula Hawkins, 1980–85; Florida State Good Government Award, 1973; one of five Florida Jaycees Outstanding Young Men of America, 1978; member: Kiwanis; U.S. Capitol Preservation Commission; Tiger Bay Club; co-chairman, Speaker's Task Force for a Drug Free America; Florida Blue Key; U.S. Capitol Preservation Commission; brother of former Congressman Daniel A. Mica; married: the former Patricia Szymanek, 1972; children: D'Anne Leigh and John Clark; committees: Oversight and Government Reform; Transportation and Infrastructure; elected on November 3, 1992 to the 103rd Congress; reelected to each succeeding Congress.

Office Listings

http://www.mica.house.gov

2187 Rayburn House Office Building, Washington, DC 20515	(202) 225–4035
Chief of Staff.—Wiley Deck.	FAX: 226–0821
Deputy Chief of Staff.—Sean McMaster.	
Legislative Director.—Brian Waldrip.	
Scheduler.—Chelsey Neuhaus.	
100 East Sybelia Avenue, Suite 340, Maitland, FL 32751	(407) 657–8080
840 Deltona Boulevard, Suite G, Deltona, FL 32725	(386) 860–1499
95 East Mitchell Hammock Boulevard, Suite 202, Oviedo, FL 32765	(407) 366–0833

Counties: ORANGE COUNTY (part). CITIES AND TOWNSHIPS: Apopka, Maitland, Winter Park. SEMINOLE COUNTY (part). CITIES AND TOWNSHIPS: Altamonte Springs, Casselberry, Heathrow, Lake Mary, Longwood, Oviedo, Sanford, and Winter Springs. VOLUSIA COUNTY (part). CITIES AND TOWNSHIPS: Deltona, Debary, and Orange City. Population, (2010), 702,203.

ZIP Codes: 32701, 32703, 32706–08, 32712–16, 32718–19, 32724–25, 32728, 32730, 32732–33, 32738–39, 32744–46, 32750–54, 32762–66, 32771, 32773–74, 32779, 32789–91, 32793–95, 32799, 32803–04, 32807, 32810, 32814, 32816–17, 32820, 32826, 32833, 32867

* * *

EIGHTH DISTRICT

BILL POSEY, Republican, of Rockledge, FL; born in Washington, DC, December 18, 1947; education: graduated, Cocoa High School, 1966; A.A., Brevard Community College, Cocoa, FL; National Legislator of the Year by the American Legislative Exchange Council; married: Katie Posey; children: Pamela and Catherine; member, House Aerospace Caucus; Military Veterans Caucus; Congressional Autism Caucus; Republican Study Committee; committees: Financial Services; Science, Space, and Technology; elected to the 111th Congress on November 4, 2008; reelected to each succeeding Congress.

Office Listings

http://www.posey.house.gov   https://twitter.com/congbillposey
https://www.facebook.com/bill.posey15

120 Cannon House Office Building, Washington, DC 20515	(202) 225–3671
Chief of Staff.—Marcus Brubaker.	FAX: 225–3516
Legislative Director.—Patrick Deitz.	
Communications Director.—George Cecala.	
Scheduler.—Kyra Thomas.	
2725 Judge Fran Jamieson Way Building C, Melbourne, FL 32940	(321) 632–1776
Indian River County	(772) 226–1701

Office Listings—Continued

Titusville .... (321) 383–6090
    Directors of Community Relations: Patrick Gavin, Pam Gillespie, David Jackson, Rob
    Medina.

Counties: BREVARD, INDIAN RIVER, AND ORANGE (part). Population (2010), 696,344.

ZIP Codes: 32903–05, 32907–09, 32920, 32922, 32925–27, 32931, 32934–35, 32937, 32940, 32948–53, 32955, 32958, 32960, 32962–63, 32966–68, 32970, 32976, 32780, 32796, 32831, 32833

* * *

NINTH DISTRICT

ALAN GRAYSON, Democrat, of Orlando, FL; born in New York, NY, March 13, 1958; education: B.A., economics, Harvard College, Cambridge, MA, 1978; J.D., Harvard Law, Cambridge, MA, 1983; M.P.P., Harvard Kennedy School, Cambridge, MA, 1978; professional: co-founder and former President of IDT Corporation; founder of Grayson & Kubli, P.C.; separated; children: Skye, Star, Storm, Stone, Sage; committees: Foreign Affairs; Science, Space, and Technology; elected to the 111th Congress on November 4, 2008; reelected to each succeeding Congress.

Office Listings

http://www.grayson.house.gov

303 Cannon House Office Building, Washington, DC 20515 .... (202) 225–9889
    Chief of Staff.—Julie Tagen.   FAX: 225–9742
    Legislative Director.—David Bagby.
    Communications Director.—Vacant.
    Legislative Aides.—Shilpa Deshpande Finnerty, Mike Nichola.
    Scheduler/Office Manager.—Carla Coleman.
    Staff Assistant.—David Holladay.
5842 South Semoran Boulevard, Orlando, FL 32822 .... (407) 615–8889
    District Director.—Susannah Randolph.   FAX: 615–8890
    Press Secretary.—David Damron.
    Deputy District Director.—Juan R. Lopez-Sanchez.
    Outreach Director.—Clint Diamond.
    Director of Operations.—Jose Rodriguez.
    Constituent Advocate.—Justin Taylor.
101 North Church Street, Suite 550, Kissimmee, FL 34741 .... (407) 518–4983
    Director of Constituent Services.—Lizy H. Price.   FAX: 846–2087

Counties: ORANGE (part), OSCEOLA, POLK (part). Population (2010), 753,549.

ZIP Codes: 32792, 32803, 32806–07, 32809, 32812, 32817, 32821–22, 32824–32, 32837, 32857, 32862, 32872, 32877–78, 32885, 33836–38, 33844–45, 33848, 33851, 33858, 33896–97, 34739, 34741–47, 34758–59, 34769–73, 34972

* * *

TENTH DISTRICT

DANIEL WEBSTER, Republican, of Winter Garden, FL; born in Charleston, WV, April 27, 1949; education: graduated from Evans High School, Orlando, FL; B.S., Georgia Institute of Technology, Atlanta, GA, 1971; professional: owner, Webster Air Conditioning & Heating, Inc., Orlando, FL; Florida House of Representatives, 1980–98; Speaker, Florida House of Representatives, 1996–98; Florida Senate, 1998–2008; Senate Majority Leader, Florida Senate, 2006–08; married: Sandy Jordan; father of six children and grandfather of eleven; committees: Transportation and Infrastructure; elected to the 112th Congress on November 2, 2010; reelected to each succeeding Congress.

Office Listings

http://www.webster.house.gov   twitter: @repwebster   facebook.com/repwebster

1039 Longworth House Office Building, Washington, DC 20515 .... (202) 225–2176

Office Listings—Continued

Chief of Staff.—Frank Walker. FAX: 225–0999
Legislative Director.—Garrett Bess.
Legislative Assistants: Evan Lee, Andrew Tyrrell.
Legislative Aide.—Christa Pearson.
Staff Assistant.—Laura Murtha.
300 West Plant Street, Winter Garden, FL 34787 .... (407) 654–5705
Deputy Chief of Staff/Communications Director.—Elizabeth Tyrrell. FAX: 654–5814
Scheduler.—Melissa Rogers.
Community Relations Manager.—Cindy Brown.
Community Relations Representative.—Pam Jones.
Constituent Services Director/Office Manager.—Abigail Tyrrell.
Constituent Services Representative.—Debbie Warren.
122 East Main Street, Tavares, FL 32778 .... (352) 383–3552
686 West Montrose Street, Clermont, FL 34711 .... (352) 383–3552
Constituent Services Representative.—Ann Drawdy.
451 Third Street Northwest, Winter Haven, FL 33881 .... (863) 453–0273
Community Relations Representative.—Natali Knight.

Counties: ORANGE (part), LAKE (part), and POLK (part). CITIES AND TOWNSHIPS: Auburndale, Astatula, Azalea, Bay Hill, Bay Lake, Belle Isle, Belleview, Conway, Doctor Phillips, Eustis, Fairview Shores, Fruitland Park, Groveland, Howey-in-the-Hills, Holden Heights, Lake Alfred, Leesburg, Meadow Wood, Mascotte, Mid Florida Lakes, Minneola, Montverde, Mount Dora, Oakland, Ocoee, Orlando, Polk City, Tavares, Umatilla, Union Park, Williamsburg, Windermere, and Winter Haven. Population (2010), 696,345.

ZIP Codes: 32159, 32702–03, 32726, 32735–36, 32757, 32776, 32778, 32784, 32801, 32803–07, 32809, 32811–12, 32818–19, 32821–22, 32830, 32835–37, 32839, 33805, 33809, 33823, 33837, 33844, 33850, 33868, 33880–81, 33884, 33896–97, 34705, 34711, 34714–15, 34731, 34734, 34736–37, 34747–48, 34753, 34756, 34760–62, 34786–88, 34797

* * *

ELEVENTH DISTRICT

RICHARD NUGENT, Republican, of Spring Hill, FL; born in Evergreen Park, IL, May 26, 1951; education: B.A. in criminology, Saint Leo College, Saint Leo, FL, 1990; FBI National Academy graduate, FBI Academy, Quantico, VA, 1991; M.P.A., public administration, Troy State University, MacDill Air Force Base, FL, 1995; executive leadership training, National Sheriff's Institute, Longmount, CO, 2002; professional: Illinois Air National Guard, 1969–75; 38+ years in law enforcement; Deputy County Sheriff, Hernando County, FL; elected Sheriff, Hernando County, FL, 2001–10; military: law enforcement; family: wife, Wendy; children: three sons; committees: Armed Services; House Administration; elected to the 112th Congress on November 2, 2010; reelected to the 113th Congress on November 6, 2012.

Office Listings

http://nugent.house.gov

1727 Longworth House Office Building, Washington, DC 20515 .... (202) 225–1002
Chief of Staff.—Justin Grabelle. FAX: 226–6559
Deputy Chief of Staff/Legislative and Communications Director.—Harrison Lewis.
Scheduler.—Lindsay Reidenbach.
11035 Spring Hill Drive, Spring Hill, FL 34608 .... (352) 684–4446
FAX: 684–4484

Counties: CITRUS, HERNANDO, LAKE (part), MARION (part), PASCO (part), SUMTER. CITIES AND TOWNSHIPS: Brooksville, Ocala, and The Villages. Population (2010), 696,345.

ZIP Codes: 32113, 32133, 32159, 32162, 32179, 32195, 32617, 32686, 32702, 32784, 33513–14, 33521, 33523, 33538, 33585, 33597, 34420, 34428–29, 34432–34, 34436, 34442, 34445–46, 34448–50, 34452–53, 34461, 34465, 34470–76, 34479–82, 34484, 34488, 34491, 34601–02, 34604, 34606–07, 34609, 34613–14, 34661, 34731, 34785

* * *

TWELFTH DISTRICT

GUS M. BILIRAKIS, Republican, of Palm Harbor, FL; born in Gainesville, FL, February 8, 1963; raised in Tarpon Springs, FL; education: B.A., University of Florida, 1986; J.D., Stetson University, 1989; son of former Representative Michael Bilirakis (1983–2006); volunteered on his father's congressional campaigns; interned for President Ronald Reagan and the National Republican Congressional Committee; worked for former Representative Don Sundquist (R–TN); ran the Bilirakis Law Group in Holiday, FL; taught government classes at St. Petersburg College; member of the Florida House of Representatives, 1998–2006; chaired several prominent panels in the State House, including Crime Prevention, Public Safety Appropriations, and the Economic Development, Trade, and Banking Committee; married: Eva; children: Michael, Teddy, Manuel, and Nicholas; committees: vice chair, Veterans' Affairs; Energy and Commerce; elected to the 110th Congress on November 7, 2006; reelected to each succeeding Congress.

Office Listings

http://bilirakis.house.gov   https://twitter.com/repgusbilirakis
https://www.facebook.com/gusbilirakis

2112 Rayburn House Office Building, Washington, DC 20515	(202) 225–5755
Chief of Staff.—Elizabeth Hittos.	FAX: 225–4085
Legislative Director.—Thomas Power.	
Communications Director.—Ian Martorana.	
Executive Assistant.—Hannah Anderson.	
7132 Little Road, New Port Richey, FL 34654	(727) 232–2921
District Director.—Summer Robertson.	FAX: 232–2923
5901 Argerian Drive, Suite 102, Wesley Chapel, FL 33545	(813) 501–4942
	FAX: 501–4944
600 Klosterman Road, Room BB–038, Tarpon Springs, FL 34689	(727) 940–5860
	FAX: 940–5861

Counties: PASCO, HILLSBOROUGH (part), AND PINELLAS (part). CITIES AND TOWNSHIPS: Dade City, New Port Richey, Port Richey, San Antonio, St Leo, Zephyrhills, Aripeka, Bayonet Point, Beacon Square, Connerton, Crystal Springs, Dade City North, Elfers, Heritage Pines, Holiday, Hudson, Jasmine Esastes, Key Vista, Lacoochee, Land O'Lakes, Meadow Oaks, Moon Lake, New Port Richey East, Odessa, Pasadena Hills, Quail Ridge, River Ridge, Shady Hills, Trinity, Tilby, Wesley Chapel, Zephyrhills North, Zephyrhills South, Zephyrhills West, Tarpon Springs, Palm Harbor, East Lake, Oldsmar, Keystone, Lutz, Cheval, North Dale, Citrus Park, Westchase, Lake Magdalene, and Carrollwood Population (2010), 696,344

ZIP Codes: 33252–24, 33526, 33537, 33539–45, 33548–49, 33558–59, 33574, 33576, 33593, 34610, 33612–13, 33618, 33624–26, 34637–39, 34652–56, 34667–69, 34674, 33677, 34679–81, 34683–85, 34688–92

* * *

THIRTEENTH DISTRICT

DAVID W. JOLLY, Republican, of Indian Shores, FL; born in Dunedin, FL, October 31, 1972; education: graduated, Pasco High School, Dade City, FL; B.A., Emory University, 1994; J.D., George Mason University School of Law, 2001; professional: former Vice President, Boston Finance Group; former President, Three Bridges Advisors; former General Counsel, U.S. Representative C.W. Bill Young; married: the former Laura Donahoe, 2015; committees: Appropriations; Veterans' Affairs; elected on March 11, 2014 to the 113th Congress, by special election, to fill a vacancy caused by the death of Representative Charles William "Bill" Young; elected to the 114th Congress on November 4, 2014.

Office Listings

http://jolly.house.gov

1728 Longworth House Office Building, Washington, DC 20515	(202) 225–5961
Deputy Chief of Staff.—Nick Catroppo.	
Legislative Director.—Jenifer Nawrocki.	
Senior Policy Advisor.—Ian Manzano.	
Legislative Assistant.—Tim Mederios.	
Legislative Correspondents: Alex Goodman, Brittany Roberts.	
Staff Assistant.—Doug deWysocki.	
9210 113th Street, Seminole, FL 33772	(727) 392–4100
Chief of Staff.—John David White.	
Communications Director.—Preston Rudie.	
Constituent Services Supervisor.—Nicole Smith.	
Constituent Services Representative.—Natalee Campagnola.	
425 22nd Avenue North, Suite C, St. Petersburg, FL 33704	(727) 823–8900
Scheduler.—Reggie Paros.	
Constituent Services Representatives: Stephani Lavely, Paul Matthews.	
29275 U.S. Highway 19 North Clearwater, FL 33761	(727) 781–4400
Constituent Services Representatives: Brenda Frantz, Sandy Hutton.	

Counties: PINELLAS COUNTY (part). Population (2010), 696,345.

ZIP Codes: 33701–11, 33713–16, 33744, 33755–56, 33759–67, 33770–74, 33776–78, 33781–82, 33785–86, 34677, 34683–84, 34695, 34698

* * *

FOURTEENTH DISTRICT

KATHY CASTOR, Democrat, of Tampa, FL; born in Miami, FL, August 20, 1966; education: B.A., political science, Emory University, 1988; J.D., Florida State University, 1991; professional: Assistant General Counsel, State of Florida, Department of Community Affairs, 1991–94; attorney, Icard Merrill, 1994–95; partner, Broad and Cassel, 1995–2000; ran for Florida State Senate, 2000; Hillsborough County Commissioner, 2002–06; religion: member of Palma Ceia Presbyterian Church; married: William Lewis; children: two; committees: Budget; Energy and Commerce; elected to the 110th Congress on November 7, 2006; reelected to each succeeding Congress.

Office Listings

http://castor.house.gov

205 Cannon House Office Building, Washington, DC 20515	(202) 225–3376
Chief of Staff.—Clay Phillips.	FAX: 225–5652
Legislative Director.—Elizabeth Brown.	
Scheduler.—Lara Hopkins.	
4144 North Armenia Avenue, Suite 300, Tampa, FL 33607	(813) 871–2817
District Director.—Chloe Coney.	
Press Secretary.—Marcia Mejia.	
511 Second Street South, St. Petersburg, FL 33701	(727) 873–2817

Counties: HILLSBOROUGH (part), PINELLAS (part). CITIES: Apollo Beach, Brandon, Carrollwood, Carrollwood Village, Citrus Park, Gibsonton, Riverview, Ruskin, St. Petersburg, Tampa, Temple Terrace, and Town 'N' Country, Ybor City. Population (2010), 696,345.

ZIP Codes: 33508–11, 33534, 33549, 33570, 33572, 33575, 33578, 33586, 33601–19, 33621–26, 33629–31, 33633–35, 33637, 33646, 33650, 33655, 33660–64, 33672–75, 33677, 33679–82, 33684–86, 33689, 33694, 33701, 33704–05, 33707, 33710–13, 33730–31, 33733, 33747, 33784, 34677

* * *

FIFTEENTH DISTRICT

DENNIS A. ROSS, Republican, of Lakeland, FL; born in Lakeland, October 18, 1959; education: Lakeland Senior High School; B.S., organizational management, Auburn University, Auburn, AL, 1981; J.D., Cumberland School of Law at Samford University, Birmingham, AL, 1987; professional: attorney, Holland and Knight; attorney, Walt Disney World; founder and attorney, Ross Vecchio, PA, 1989–2010; awards: Workers Compensation Section, Appreciation Award, 2001; Florida Building Material Association, Legislator of the Year Award, 2001 and 2003; Florida Workers Advocate, Outstanding Freshman Representative Award, 2001; The Trust for Public Land, Legislative Leadership Award, 2001; Polk Community College, Outstanding Legislator, 2001; Florida Crane Owners Council, Representative of the Year, 2003; Florida Association of Roofing Professionals, Legislative Achievement Award, 2003; Florida Automotive Dealer Association, Legislator of the Year, 2003; Florida Retail Federation, Legislator of the Year, 2003; Florida Bankers Association, Outstanding Leadership Award, 2004; ARC Florida, Representative of the Year, 2004; YMCA of Florida, Outstanding Leadership Award, 2005; Florida League of Cities, Legislative Appreciation Award, 2005, 2006 and 2007; Florida Insurance Council, Harry G. Landrum Outstanding Legislative Leadership, 2005 and 2008; Florida Association of Counties, Champion Award, 2005; Florida Trucking Association, Legislator of the Year, 2005 and 2006; Associated Industries of Florida, Champion for Business Award, 2005; Florida Association of Insurance and Financial Advisors, Representative of the Year, 2005; Florida Association of Mortgage Brokers, Grateful Recognition Award, 2005; Florida Association of Insurance Agents, Legislator of the Year, 2006; Florida Chamber, Most Valuable Legislator, 2008; Governor's Hurricane Conference, Legislative Award, 2008; Associated Industries of Florida Financial Securities Council, Legislator of the Year, 2008; Florida Chamber Honor Roll 2001, 2002, 2003, 2004, 2005, 2007 and 2008; religion: member, First Presbyterian Church, Lakeland; married: Cindy; children: Shane and Travis; committees: Financial Services; elected to the 112th Congress on November 2, 2010; reelected to each succeeding Congress.

Office Listings

http://www.dennisross.house.gov   twitter: @repdennisross

229 Cannon House Office Building, Washington, DC 20515	(202) 225–1252

Office Listings—Continued

Chief of Staff.—Anthony Foti.   FAX: 226–0585
Deputy Chief of Staff.—Kyle Glenn.
DC Scheduler.—Sara Budsock.
170 Fitzgerald Road, Suite 1, Lakeland, FL 33813 .... (863) 644–8215
                                                                                 FAX: 648–0749
110 West Reynolds Street, Suite 101, Plant City, FL 33563 .... (813) 752–4790
Director of Administration and Scheduling.—Shelee Meeker.
Field Representative.—Stephen Gately.

Counties: HILLSBOROUGH (part), POLK (part). CITIES AND TOWNSHIPS: Auburndale, Bartow, Brandon, Dover, Durant, Eaton Park, Highland City, Kathleen, Lakeland, Lithia, Lutz, Mulberry, Plant City, Riverview, Ruskin, Seffner, Tampa, Temple Terrace, Thonotosassa, Valrico, Winter Haven, and Zephyrhills. Population (2010), 813,570.

ZIP Codes: 33510–11, 33527, 33530, 33540, 33547–49, 33559, 33563, 33565–67, 33569, 33578, 33584, 33592, 33594, 33596, 33610, 33612–13, 33617–18, 33620, 33637, 33647, 33801, 33803, 33805, 33809–13, 33815, 33823, 33830, 33840, 33846–47, 33849, 33860, 33863, 33880

* * *

SIXTEENTH DISTRICT

VERN BUCHANAN, Republican, of Longboat Key, FL; born in Detroit, MI, May 8, 1951; education: B.B.A., business administration, Cleary University; M.B.A., University of Detroit; honorary degree: Doctorate of Science in Business Administration, Cleary University; professional: founder and chairman, Buchanan Enterprises; founder and chairman, Buchanan Automotive Group, 1992; operations include Sarasota Ford and 18 auto franchises in the southeastern United States; experience in real estate including home building and property development and management; awards: One of America's Ten Outstanding Young Men, U.S. Jaycees; Entrepreneur of the Year, *Inc.* Magazine and Arthur Young; Entrepreneur of the Year, Harvard Business School, Club of Detroit; One of Michigan's Five Outstanding Young Men, Michigan Jaycees; President's Award, Ford Motor Company; Certified Retailer Award, J.D. Power and Associates; Outstanding Citizen Award, United Negro College Fund; Outstanding Philanthropic Corporation Award, National Society of Fund Raising Executives; Freedom Award for Business and Industry, NAACP; The American Jewish Committee Civic Achievement Award; Tampa Bay Business Hall of Fame Award; married: Sandy Buchanan; children: James and Matt; committee: Budget; Ways and Means; elected to the 110th Congress on November 7, 2006; reelected to each succeeding Congress.

Office Listings

http://www.buchanan.house.gov   twitter: @vernbuchanan
https://www.facebook.com/congressmanbuchanan

2104 Cannon House Office Building, Washington, DC 20515 .... (202) 225–5015
Chief of Staff.—Dave Karvelas.   FAX: 226–0828
Deputy Chief of Staff.—Max Goodman.
Legislative Director.—Katie Wise.
Communications Director.—Vacant.
Scheduler.—Hobart Richey.
111 South Orange Avenue, Suite 200W, Sarasota, FL 34236 .... (941) 951–6643
District Director.—Sally Tibbetts.
Scheduler.—Sydney Gruters.
151 Manatee Avenue West, Suite 205, Bradenton, FL 34205 .... (941) 747–9081

Counties: MANATEE, SARASOTA. Population (2010), 639,345.

ZIP Codes: 33834, 34211–12, 34219, 34221, 34223, 34240–41, 34251, 34287–88, 34292–93

* * *

SEVENTEENTH DISTRICT

THOMAS J. ROONEY, Republican, of Tequesta, FL; born in Philadelphia, PA, November 21, 1970; education: B.A., Washington and Jefferson, Washington, PA; M.A., University of Florida, Gainesville, FL; J.D., University of Miami, Coral Gables, FL; member, Roman Catholic Church; married: Tara; children: Tommy, Sean, and Seamus; committees: Appropriations; Permanent Select Committee on Intelligence; elected to the 111th Congress on November 4, 2008; reelected to each succeeding Congress.

Office Listings

http://www.rooney.house.gov https://www.facebook.com/reptomrooney?ref=mf
https://twitter.com/tomrooney http://www.youtube.com/user/congressmanrooney

2160 Rayburn House Office Building, Washington, DC 20515 .... (202) 225–5792
Chief of Staff.—Pete Giambastiani. FAX: 225–3132
Communications Director.—Michael Mahaffey.
226 Taylor Street, Suite 230, Punta Gorda, FL 33950 .... (941) 575–9101
10008 Park Place Avenue, Riverview, FL 33578 .... (813) 677–8646
4507 George Boulevard, Sebring, FL 33875 .... (863) 402–9082

Counties: CHARLOTTE, DESOTO, GLADES, HARDEE, HIGHLANDS, HILLSBOROUGH, LEE, MANATEE, OKEECHOBEE, AND POLK. Population (2010), 696,344.

ZIP Codes: 33471, 33503, 33511, 33534, 33547, 33569–70, 33573, 33578–79, 33596, 33598, 33825, 33827, 33830, 33834, 33838–39, 33841, 33843–44, 33847, 33852–57, 33859–60, 33865, 33867, 33870, 33872–73, 33875–77, 33880–81, 33884, 33890, 33898, 33903, 33905, 33917, 33920–21, 33935–36, 33944, 33946–48, 33950, 33952–55, 33960, 33971–72, 33974, 33980–83, 34219, 34223–24, 34251, 34266, 34268–69, 34972, 34974

* * *

EIGHTEENTH DISTRICT

PATRICK E. MURPHY, Democrat, of Jupiter, FL; born in Miami, FL, March 30, 1983; education: B.S. in business administration from the University of Miami, 2006; professional: CPA, Deloitte and Touche; Vice President, Coastal Environmental Services; religion: Roman Catholic; caucuses: co-founder and co-chair of the United Solutions Caucus, co-chair of the No Labels' Problem Solvers Group; member, New Democrat Coalition, Congressional Arts Caucus, Congressional Boating Caucus, Congressional Caucus on Access to Capital and Credit, Congressional SPA and Accountants Caucus, Congressional Everglades Caucus, Congressional Human Trafficking Caucus, Congressional Small Business Caucus, Congressional Veterans Jobs Caucus, Florida PORTS Caucus, PORTS Caucus; co-chair of the Congressional Citrus Caucus and the Disaster Relief Caucus; committees: Financial Services; Permanent Select Committee on Intelligence; elected to the 113th Congress on November 6, 2012; reelected to the 114th Congress on November 4, 2014.

Office Listings

http://www.patrickmurphy.house.gov twitter: @repmurphyfl
instagram: @patrickmurphyfl https://www.facebook.com/congressmanpatrickmurphy

211 Cannon House Office Building, Washington, DC 20515 .... (202) 225–3026
Chief of Staff.—Eric Johnson. FAX: 225–8398
Deputy Chief of Staff (Operations).—Anthony Kusich.
Deputy Chief of Staff (Policy).—Christopher Fisher.
Deputy Legislative Director.—Morgan Cashwell.
Press Secretary.—Richard Carbo.
Scheduler.—Angie Toro.
2000 PGA Boulevard, Suite A3220, Palm Beach Gardens, FL 33408 .... (561) 253–8433
District Director.—Michael Kenny. FAX: 253–8436
Executive Assistant.—Sherlean Purvis.
Constituent Services Representative.—John Foster.
171 Southwest Flagler Avenue, Stuart, FL 34994 .... (772) 781–3266
Constituent Services Representative.—Kaylene Rowles. FAX: 781–3267
121 Southwest Port St. Lucie Boulevard, Room 187, Port St. Lucie, FL 34984 .... (772) 336–2877
Constituent Services Representative.—Candace Walls. FAX: 336–2899

Counties: MARTIN, ST. LUCIE, AND PALM BEACH (NORTHERN PART). Cities: Fort Pierce, Port St. Lucie, Tradition, Lakewood Park, Eden, Indian River Estates, Stuart, Palm City, Hutchinson Island, Hobe Sound, Indiantown, Jensen Beach, Port Salerno, Jupiter Island, Sewall's Point, Jupiter, Palm Beach Gardens, West Palm Beach (part), Riviera Beach, Singer Island (part), Jupiter Inlet Colony, Juno Beach, Loxahatchee, Palm Beach Shores, North Palm Beach, Royal Palm Beach, Tequesta, and Juno Beach. Population (2010), 696,345.

ZIP Codes: 33403–04, 33407–12, 33417–18, 33420, 33422, 33438, 33455, 33458, 33468–70, 33475, 33477–78, 34945–54, 34956–58, 34972, 34974, 34979, 34981–88, 34990–92, 34994–97

* * *

NINETEENTH DISTRICT

CURT CLAWSON, Republican, of Bonita Springs, FL; born in Tacoma, WA, September 28, 1959; committees: Foreign Affairs; Homeland Security; elected to the 113th Congress on June

24, 2014, by special election to fill the vacancy caused by the resignation of United States Representative Trey Radel; elected to a full term in the 114th Congress on November 4, 2014.

Office Listings

http://clawson.house.gov

228 Cannon House Office Building, Washington, DC 20515 .... (202) 225–2536
    Chief of Staff.—Pat Cauley.
    Legislative Director.—Mark Brebberman.
    Communications Director.—David James.
    Scheduler.—Rochelle Colburn.
3299 Tamiami Trail, Suite 105, Naples, FL 34112 .... (239) 252–6225
804 Nicholas Parkway East, Suite 1, Cape Coral, FL 33990 .... (239) 573–5837

Counties: LEE AND COLLIER. Population (2010), 696,345.

ZIP Codes: 33901–16, 33919, 33921–22, 33924, 33928–29, 33931–32, 33936, 33945, 33955–57, 33965–67, 33970–71, 33973–74, 33976, 33990–91, 33993–94, 34101–10, 34112–14, 34119, 34133–34, 34136, 34140, 34142, 34145–46

* * *

TWENTIETH DISTRICT

ALCEE L. HASTINGS, Democrat, of Miramar, FL; born in Altamonte Springs, FL, September 5, 1936; education: graduated, Crooms Academy, Sanford, FL, 1954; B.A., Fisk University, Nashville, TN, 1958; Howard University, Washington, DC; J.D., Florida A&M University, Tallahassee, 1963; attorney; admitted to the Florida bar, 1963; circuit judge, U.S. District Court for the Southern District of Florida; member: African Methodist Episcopal Church, NAACP, Miami-Dade Chamber of Commerce, Family Christian Association, ACLU, Southern Poverty Law Center, National Organization for Women, Planned Parenthood, Women and Children First, Inc., Sierra Club, Cousteau Society, Broward County Democratic Executive Committee, Dade County Democratic Executive Committee, Lauderhill Democratic Club, Hollywood Hills Democratic Club, Pembroke Pines Democratic Club, Urban League, National Bar Association, Florida Chapter of the National Bar Association, T.J. Reddick Bar Association, National Conference of Black Lawyers, Simon Wiesenthal Center, The Furtivist Society; Progressive Black Police Officers Club, International Black Firefighters Association; co-chair, Florida Delegation; ranking Democratic member, Helsinki Commission; three children: Alcee Lamar II, Chelsea, and Leigh; Senior Democratic Whip; committees: Rules; elected on November 3, 1992, to the 103rd Congress; reelected to each succeeding Congress.

Office Listings

http://www.alceehastings.house.gov

2353 Rayburn House Office Building, Washington, DC 20515 .... (202) 225–1313
    Chief of Staff / Press Secretary.—Lale Morrison.   FAX: 225–1171
    Counsels: Tom Carnes, Jennifer Kaufmann.
    Legislative Assistant.—David Opong-Waddee.
    Policy Advisor.—Clarey Walker.
    Executive Administrator.—DeBorah Posey.
2701 West Oakland Park Boulevard, Suite 200, Ft. Lauderdale, FL 33311 .... (954) 733–2800
    Chief of Staff.—Arthur W. Kennedy.
Palm Beach County Office, Town of Mangonia Park Municipal Center, 1755 East Tiffany
    Drive, Mangonia Park, FL 33407 .... (561) 469–7048

Counties: BROWARD (part), AND PALM BEACH (part). Population (2013), 728,883.

ZIP Codes: 33068, 33313, 33319, 33321, 33351, 33430, 33476, 33493

* * *

TWENTY-FIRST DISTRICT

THEODORE DEUTCH, Democrat, of Boca Raton, FL; born in Bethlehem, PA, May 7, 1966; education: graduate of Liberty High School; B.A., University of Michigan, Ann Arbor, MI, 1988; J.D., University of Michigan Law School, Ann Arbor, MI, 1990; admitted to the Florida Bar, 1991; professional: attorney; Florida State Senator, 2006–10; member: Florida Bar Association; Jewish Federation of South Palm Beach County; League of Women Voters; married to the former Jill Weinstock, three children; committees: Ethics; Foreign Affairs; Judiciary; elected to the 111th Congress on April 13, 2010, by special election, to fill the vacancy caused by the resignation of United States Representative Robert Wexler; reelected to each succeeding Congress.

Office Listings

http://deutch.house.gov   twitter: @repteddeutch
instagram: @repteddeutch   www.facebook.com/congressmanteddeutch

2447 Rayburn House Office Building, Washington, DC 20515	(202) 225–3001
Chief of Staff.—Joshua Rogin.	FAX: 225–5974
Deputy Chief of Staff.—Ellen McLaren.	
Communications Director.—Ashley Mushnick.	
7900 Glades Road, Suite 250, Boca Raton, FL 33434	(561) 470–5440
District Director.—Wendi Lipsich.	FAX: 470–5446

Counties: BROWARD (part), PALM BEACH (part). CITIES AND TOWNSHIPS: Boynton Beach (part), Boca Raton (part), Delray Beach (part), Greenacres, Coral Springs, Parkland, Coconut Creek, Margate (part), Pompano Beach (part), Deerfield Beach (part), and Wellington. Population (2010), 738,875.

ZIP Codes: 33063–67, 33069, 33071, 33073, 33076, 33406, 33411, 33413–15, 33428, 33433–24, 22436–37, 33441–42, 33446, 33449, 33461, 33463, 33467, 33470, 33472–73, 33484, 33496, 33498

* * *

TWENTY-SECOND DISTRICT

LOIS FRANKEL, Democrat, of West Palm Beach, FL; born in New York City, NY, May 17, 1948; education: B.A., Boston University, Boston, MA, 1970; J.D., Georgetown University Law Center, Washington, DC, 1973; professional: elected State Representative in the 83rd district of the Florida House of Representatives, 1986; first female Florida House Minority Leader from 1995–2003; elected Mayor of West Palm Beach from 2003–11; religion: Jewish; caucuses: member of the Congressional Progressive Caucus; Congressional Everglades Caucus; Congressional Ports Caucus; Florida Ports Caucus; Congressional Pro-Choice Caucus; Congressional Caucus for Women's Issues; Democratic Israel Working Group; Democratic Steering and Policy Committee; committees: Foreign Affairs; Transportation and Infrastructure; elected to the 113th Congress on November 6, 2012; reelected to the 114th Congress on November 4, 2014.

Office Listings

http://frankel.house.gov   https://www.facebook.com/reploisfrankel
https://twitter.com/reploisfrankel

1037 Longworth House Office Building, Washington, DC 20515	(202) 225–9890
Chief of Staff.—Jonathon Bray.	FAX: 225–1224
Legislative Director.—Jim Cho.	
Legislative Assistants: Josh Cohen, Grant Dubler, Kelsey Moran.	
Communications Director.—Erin Moffet Hale.	
Scheduler.—Kate Regan.	
Staff Assistant.—Bradley Solyan.	
2500 North Military Trail, Suite 490, Boca Raton, FL 33431	(561) 998–9045
District Director.—Felicia Goldstein.	FAX: 998–9048

Counties: BROWARD (part), PALM BEACH (part). CITIES: Pompano Beach, West Palm Beach, Oakland Park, Delray Beach, Palm Springs, Boca Raton, Fort Lauderdale, Plantation, Ocean Ridge, Lantana, Boynton Beach, Highland Beach, Wilton Manors, and Lighthouse Point. Population (2010), 696,345.

ZIP Codes: 33060, 33062, 33064, 33069, 33301, 33304–06, 33308–09, 33311–12, 33315–17, 33322–25, 33334, 33401, 33404–07, 33415, 33431–36, 33441, 33444–45, 33461–63, 33480, 33483–84, 33486–87, 33496

* * *

TWENTY-THIRD DISTRICT

DEBBIE WASSERMAN SCHULTZ, Democrat, of Weston, FL; born in Forest Hills, Queens County, NY, September 27, 1966; education: B.A., University of Florida, Gainesville, FL, 1988; M.A., University of Florida, FL, 1990; professional: Public Policy Curriculum Specialist, Nova Southeastern University; Adjunct Instructor, Political Science, Broward Community College; aide to United States Representative Peter Deutsch, 1989–92; member, Florida State House of

Representatives, 1992–2000; member, Florida State Senate, 2000–04; organizations: Board of Trustees, Westside Regional Medical Center; Outstanding Freshman Legislator, Florida Women's Political Caucus; Secretary; Board of Directors, American Jewish Congress; Member, Broward National Organization for Women; Board of Directors, National Safety Council, South Florida Chapter; religion: Jewish; married: Steve; children: Rebecca, Jake, Shelby; Chief Democratic Whip; elected chair, Democratic National Committee, 2011; committees: Appropriations; elected to the 109th Congress on November 2, 2004; reelected to each succeeding Congress.

Office Listings

http://wassermanschultz.house.gov   twitter: @repdwstweet

1114 Longworth House Office Building, Washington, DC 20515	(202) 225–7931
Chief of Staff.—Tracie Pough.	FAX: 226–2052
Communications Director.—Sean Bartlett.	
Legislative Director / General Counsel.—Coby Dolan.	
Executive Assistant.—Ana Stolitzka.	
10100 Pines Boulevard, Pembroke Pines, FL 33026	(954) 437–3936
19200 West Country Club Drive, Third Floor, Aventura, FL 33180	(305) 936–5724

Counties: BROWARD COUNTY (part). CITIES: Cooper City, Dania Beach, Davie, Fort Lauderdale, Hallandale Beach, Hollywood, Hollywood Hills, Pembroke Pines, Plantation, Sunrise, Southwest Ranches, and Weston. MIAMI-DADE COUNTY (part). CITIES: Aventura, Bal Harbour, Bay Harbor Islands, Golden Beach, Miami Beach, and North Bay Village. Population (2010), 703,594.

ZIP Codes: 33004, 33009, 33019–21, 33023–24, 33026–28, 33139–41, 33154, 33160, 33180, 33312, 33314–16, 33324–28, 33330–32

* * *

TWENTY-FOURTH DISTRICT

FREDERICA S. WILSON, Democrat, of Miami, FL; born in Miami, November 5; education: B.S., Fisk University; M.S., University of Miami; Florida Memorial University, Honorary Doctorate of Humane Letters; professional: executive director, Office of Alternative Education and Dropout Prevention, Miami-Dade County Schools; member, Miami-Dade County School Board, 1992–98; Minority Whip, Florida State House of Representatives, 1998–2002; Democratic Whip, Florida State Senate, 2002–04; Minority Leader Pro Tempore, Florida State Senate, 2002–10; Minority Whip, Florida State Senate, 2008–10; members: regional director, Alpha Kappa Alpha Sorority, Inc., 1986–present; founder / member, 5000 Role Models of Excellence, Inc., 1993–present; member, National Association of Black School Educators, present; member, the Links, Inc., present; founder, Stop Day Enough is Enough, 1996–present; Miami Delegate, President's Summit for America's Future, 1997; State of Florida "STOP DAY", Enough is Enough, founder, 1996; President's Summit for America's Future, Philadelphia, Pennsylvania, Miami Delegate, 1997; founder, Miami-Dade County "Keep Me Safe" summit, march, and candlelight vigil board member, Women's Action for New Directions Educational Fund, 2004; honors and awards: Southern Living, Outstanding Southerner, May 1993; Macedonia Missionary Baptist Church, Image Maker, 1993; South Florida Association of Black Journalists, Kuumba Award, 1994; St. Petersburg Junior College, In Recognition, 1996; American Red Cross, Spectrum Award, 1998; African-American Achiever Award for Education, 1998; Peace Education Foundation, Peacemaker of the Year, 1998; Youth Crime Watch / Citizens Crime Watch, A Champion for All Poor and Minority Students, 1998; Imperial Daughters of Isis Miami Beach, Florida Hall of Fame, 1999; NAACP, Florida Chapter, Morris Milton Memorial Award, 2001; Zeta Phi Beta Sorority, Inc., Leadership Award, 2001; Florida A&M University, National Alumni Association Expresses Gratitude, 2001; The Florida HIV-AIDS Ministries, Inc., Honors State Representative Frederica S. Wilson, 2001; Florida AIDS Action, Outstanding Leadership and Support for HIV / AIDS and Health Care, 2002; Alpha Kappa Alpha Sorority, Inc., In Appreciation, 2002; Western Union, L'Union Fait la Force Award, 2003; Community Action Agency, Citizen of the Year Award, 2004; American Cancer Society, Florida Chapter, Legislative Leadership Award, 2004; Florida Education Association, Educator of the Year, 2004; Association of Black Health-System Pharmacists, Legislator Achievement Award, 2004; Easter Seals of Miami-Dade, Legislator of the Year Award, 2004; Northside Seventh Day Adventist Church (Miami), Distinguished Community Leader Award, 2004; The Black Archives, History and Research Foundation of South Florida, Inc., Chairman's Award, 2004; Sierra Club, Florida Chapter, Legislative Recognition Award, 2004; Network Miami Magazine, One of Miami's 50 Most Influential Black Business Professionals, 2004; Millennium Movers, Inc., Shaker Award, 2004; Alpha Kappa Alpha Sorority, Ft. Pierce, Florida Chapter, Soror of the Year, 2005; Alpha Kappa Alpha Sorority, Ft. Walton Beach, Florida Chapter, Soror of the Year, 2005; Alpha Kappa Alpha Sorority, Thomasville, GA Chapter, Soror of the Year, 2005; Carrie P. Meek Education

Leadership Achievement Award, 2005; Miami Gardens Jaycees, Distinguished Service Award, 2005; Alpha Kappa Alpha, Inc., Emerald Service Award, 2005; The Links, Inc., Links of Gold Award, 2005; Belafonte TACOLCY Center, Inc., U.S. Department of Justice/Drug Enforcement Administration in Recognition of State Senator Frederica S. Wilson, 2005; SEIU Florida Healthcare Union, Legislative Hero Award, 2006; Barry University, SGA Acknowledgement of Florida's Residents Access Grant Award, 2006; City of Miami, Women Builders of Community Dreams Award, 2006; Florida Memorial University, SGA Leadership Character and Service Award, 2006; Holy Faith Missionary Baptist Church, Participation Award, 2006; Miami-Dade Police Department, Appreciation Award, 2006; The Historic St. Agnes Episcopal Church, 108th Anniversary Appreciation Award, 2006; FAU, Small Business Development Appreciation Award, 2006; Day of the Child, Mentoring Award, 2006; Project H.O.P.E., Katrina Humanitarian Award, 2006; South Florida Chapter of the Coalition of Black Trade Unionists, Audrey McCollum Scholarship Award, 2006; CEO Magazine, Legislative Action Recognition, 2006; Community Action Agency, Youth Leadership Award, 2006; I.B.P.O.E. of W., Antlers Temple #39, Legislative Excellence Award, 2006; Community Health of South Dade, Inc., Health Hero Award, 2006; Health Council of South Florida, Inc., Health Leadership Award, 2006; National Coalition of 100 Black Women, Inc., Greater Miami Chapter, Candace Award, 2006; Kiwanis Club of Miami Shores, North Dade Exemplary Service Award, 2006; Academy of Florida Trial Lawyers, Rosemary Barkett Award, 2006; National Pan Hellenic Council, Inc., Celebration of Excellence, 2006; NAACP Milton Morris Award, 2007; Jessie C. Trice Humanitarian Award, 2007; Liberty City's Community Action Agency, Community Service Award, 2007; Miami Dade College, Pathway to Opportunity Appreciation Award, 2007; Florida Association of School Administrators, Legislator of the Year, 2007; Florida Association of Women Lawyers, Legislative Recognition Award, 2007; Florida Health Center, Jessie C. Trice Humanitarian Award, 2007; Miami Dade Community Action Agency, Liberty City Advisor Committee in Recognition of State Senator Frederica S. Wilson June 2007; The National Medical Association, Scroll of Merit for Public Education Advocacy, 2008; American School Health Association, Legislator of the Year, 2008; Alpha Kappa Alpha Sorority International, Rosa Parks Coretta Scott King Award, 2008; Florida Association of Counties (FAC), County Partner Award, 2008; Florida Cable Telecommunications Association, Leaders in Learning Award, 2008; AKA Educational Advancement Foundation, The Green Diamond Award, 2008; Bethune-Cookman University, In Tribute, 2009; Alpha Kappa Alpha Sorority, Inc., With Appreciation, 2009; The Links, Inc., In Appreciation, 2010 Alpha Kappa Alpha Sorority, Inc., Timeless Service to Mankind, 2011; Miami Dade Chamber of Commerce, H.T. Smith Lifetime Achievement Award, 2011; ICABA, Salutes South Florida's 100 Accomplished Caribbean Americans, 2012; TheGrio.com, The Grio's 100, 2012; Louie Bing Scholarship Fund, Inc., Award of Excellence, 2012; National Voices for Equality Education and Enlightenment Voices of Leadership Award, Congresswoman Wilson, April 2012; First Focus Campaign for Children, Defender of Children, 2012; Youth Power Movement, First Annual Humanitarian Award, 2012; I Am Empowered for Jobs Award, National Urban League, 2013; Broward Black Elected Officials Inaugural Lifetime Achievement Community Service Award; The Links, Inc., Services to Youth Award, 2013; City of North Miami, In Recognition, 2013; committees: Education and the Workforce; elected to the 112th Congress on November 2, 2010; reelected to each succeeding Congress.

Office Listings

http://wilson.house.gov   twitter.com/repwilson   https://www.facebook.com/repwilson

208 Cannon House Office Building, Washington, DC 20515 .... (202) 225–4506
    Chief of Staff.—Kim Bowman.   FAX: 226–0777
    Deputy Chief of Staff.—Keenan Austin.
    Legislative Director.—Vacant.
    Legislative Assistant/Scheduler.—Corey Solow.
    Legislative Correspondent.—Jean Roseme.
    Staff Assistant.—Jon Engel.
18425 Northwest, 2nd Avenue, Suite 355, Miami, FL 33169 .... (305) 690–5905
    District Chief of Staff.—Alexis Snyder.
    District Office Director.—Joyce Postell.
    South Florida Communications Director.—Gwen Belton.
    Director of Special Community Relations.—Greg King.
    Director of Special Operations.—Vacant.
    Director of International Relations.—Vacant.
    Director of Field Operations.—Shirlee Moreau-Lafleur.
    District Policy Director.—Vacant.
    Congressional Aides: Jessica Lopez, Walta Tolbert.
10100 Pines Boulevard, 3rd Floor, Building B, Pembroke Pines, FL 33026 .... (954) 450–6767
    Director of International Relations.—Vacant.
West Park City Hall, 1965 South State Road 7, West Park, FL 33023 .... (954) 989–2688
    Congressional Aide.—Walta Tolbert.
Miramar City Hall, 2300 Civic Center Place, Miramar, FL 33025 .... (954) 883–6165
    Congressional Aide.—Walta Tolbert.

Counties: DADE (part), BROWARD (part). Population (2010), 693,086.

ZIP Codes: 33054–56, 33083, 33101, 33127, 33142, 33147, 33150–51, 33164, 33167–69, 33179–81, 33238, 33242, 33261

* * *

TWENTY-FIFTH DISTRICT

MARIO DIAZ-BALART, Republican, of Miami, FL; born in Ft. Lauderdale, FL, September 25, 1961; education: University of South Florida; professional: president, Gordon Diaz-Balart and Partners (public relations and marketing business); religion: Catholic; public service: administrative assistant to the Mayor of Miami, 1985–88; Florida House of Representatives, 1988–92, and 2000–02; Florida State Senate, 1992–2000; committees: Appropriations; Budget; elected to the 25th District in the 108th Congress on November 5, 2002; reelected to each succeeding Congress; ran unopposed and was elected to the 21st District in the 112th Congress on November 2, 2010; elected to the 25th District in the 113th Congress on November 6, 2012; reelected to the 114th Congress on November 4, 2014.

Office Listings

http://www.mariodiaz-balart.house.gov   https://www.facebook.com/mdiazbalart
https://twitter.com/mariodb   https://www.youtube.com/user/mariodiazbalart
http://instagram.com/repmariodb

440 Cannon House Office Building, Washington, DC 20515	(202) 225–4211
Chief of Staff.—Cesar A. Gonzalez.	FAX: 226–8576
Legislative Director.—Miguel Mendoza.	
8669 Northwest 36th Street, Suite 100, Doral, FL 33166	(305) 470–8555
District Director.—Miguel Otero.	FAX: 470–8575
Deputy District Director.—Gloria Amor.	
4715 Golden Gate Parkway, Suite 1, Naples, FL 34116	(239) 348–1620
Congressional Aide.—Enrique Padron.	FAX: 348–3569

Counties: BROWARD COUNTY (part), COLLIER (part), HENDRY (part), MIAMI-DADE COUNTY (part). CITIES AND TOWNSHIPS: Ave Maria, Doral, Everglades City, Fontainebleau, Golden Gate, Golden Gate Estates, Hialeah, Immokalee, LaBelle, Medley, Miami Lakes, Miami Springs, Miramar, Pembroke Pines, and Sweetwater. Population (2010), 723,113.

ZIP Codes: 33002, 33010, 33012–18, 33027, 33029, 33054–55, 33102, 33112, 33122, 33126, 33135, 33147, 33152, 33166–67, 33172, 33174, 33178, 33182, 33184–85, 33194, 33199, 33222, 33331–32, 33440, 33928, 33930, 33935–36, 33972, 33975, 34104–05, 34109, 34112–14, 34116–17, 34119–20, 34135, 34137–43

* * *

TWENTY-SIXTH DISTRICT

CARLOS CURBELO, Republican, of Miami, FL; born in Miami, March 1, 1980; education: B.A., Business Administration, University of Miami; M.P.A., University of Miami, 2011; professional: founder of Capitol Gains; State Director for U.S. Senator George LeMieux, 2009; member of Miami Dade County School Board, 2010; appointed to Miami-Dade Metropolitan Planning Organization (MPO), 2010; co-founder of Centre Court Charities; Governor's Education Transition Team; religion: Catholic; married with two children; committees: Education and the Workforce; Small Business; Transportation and Infrastructure; elected to the 114th Congress on November 4, 2014.

Office Listings

http://www.curbelo.house.gov   twitter: @repcurbelo

1429 Longworth House Office Building, Washington, DC 20515	(202) 225–2778
Chief of Staff.—Roy Schultheis.	FAX: 226–0346
Legislative Director.—Adam Wolf.	
Legislative Assistants: Ashley Rose, Hector Arguello.	
Communications Assistant.—Brittany Martinez.	
Scheduler.—Alex Cisneros.	
12851 Southwest 42 Street, Suite 131, Miami, FL 33175	(305) 222–0160
District Director.—Chris Miles.	FAX: 228–9397
Legislative Correspondent / Staff Assistant.—Charles Castagna.	
404 West Palm Drive, Florida City, FL 33034	(305) 247–1234
1100 Simonton Street, Suite 1–213, Key West, FL 33040	(305) 292–4485
Monroe County Director.—Nicole Rapanos.	

Counties: DADE (part), MONROE. Population (2014), 728,285.

ZIP Codes: 33001, 33030–37, 33040, 33042–43, 33050–51, 33070, 33141, 33157, 33165, 33170, 33173–77, 33183–87, 33189, 33193–94, 33196, 34141

* * *

TWENTY-SEVENTH DISTRICT

ILEANA ROS-LEHTINEN, Republican, of Miami, FL; born in Havana, Cuba, July 15, 1952; education: B.A., English, Florida International University; M.S., educational leadership, Florida International University; Ed.D., University of Miami, 2004; certified Florida school teacher; founder and former owner, Eastern Academy; elected to the Florida House of Representatives, 1982; elected to the Florida State Senate, 1986; former president, Bilingual Private School Association; regular contributor to leading Spanish-language newspaper; during House tenure, married then-State Representative Dexter Lehtinen; two children and two step-children; committees: chairman emeritus, Foreign Affairs; Permanent Select Committee on Intelligence; elected on August 29, 1989 to the 101st Congress; reelected to each succeeding Congress.

Office Listings

http://ros-lehtinen.house gov   http://twitter: @roslehtinen

2206 Rayburn House Office Building, Washington, DC	(202) 225–3931
Chief of Staff.—Arthur Estopinan.	FAX: 225–5620
Deputy Director.—Christine del Portillo.	
Legislative Director.—Joshua H. Salpeter.	
Press Secretary.—Alex Cruz.	
4960 Southwest 72nd Avenue, Suite 208, Miani, FL 33155	(305) 668–2285

Counties: DADE (part). CITIES AND TOWNSHIPS: Coral Gables, Cutler Bay, Hialeah, Key Biscayne, Little Havana, Miami, Pinecrest, South Miami, and Westchester. Population (2010), 696,345.

ZIP Codes: 33010, 33012–13, 33030, 33032–33, 33035, 33039, 33109, 33122, 33125–26, 33128–31, 33133–36, 33142–47, 33149, 33155–58, 33165–66, 33170, 33173–74, 33176, 33189–90

GEORGIA

(Population 2010, 9,687,653)

SENATORS

JOHNNY ISAKSON, Republican, of Marietta, GA; born in Fulton County, GA, December 28, 1944; education: University of Georgia; professional: real estate executive; president, Northside Realty; public service: Georgia State House of Representatives, 1977–90; Georgia State Senate, 1993–96; appointed chairman of the Georgia Board of Education, 1997–99; awards: Republican National Committee "Best Legislator in America," 1989; organizations: past board of directors, Metro Atlanta and Georgia Chambers of Commerce; past president, Cobb Chamber of Commerce; past executive committee, National Association of Realtors; past president, Realty Alliance; married: Dianne; children: John, Kevin, and Julie; religion: Methodist; elected to the 106th Congress on February 23, 1999, by special election; reelected to each succeeding Congress; committees: chair, Veterans' Affairs; chair, Select Committee on Ethics; Finance; Foreign Relations; Health, Education, Labor, and Pensions; elected to the U.S. Senate on November 2, 2004; reelected to the U.S. Senate on November 2, 2010.

Office Listings

http://isakson.senate.gov   facebook: johnnyisakson   twitter: @senatorisakson

131 Russell Senate Office Building, Washington, DC 20510 .... (202) 224–3643
    Chief of Staff.—Joan Kirchner.   FAX: 228–0724
    Deputy Chief of Staff.—Edward Tate.
    Scheduler.—Stefanie Mohler.
One Overton Park, 3625 Cumberland Boulevard, Suite 970, Atlanta, GA 30339 .... (770) 661–0999

* * *

DAVID PERDUE, Republican, of Glynn County, GA; born in Macon, GA, December 10, 1949; education: graduated, Northside High School, Warner Robins, GA, 1968; bachelor's degree in industrial engineering, Georgia Institute of Technology, 1972; master's degree in operations research, Georgia Institute of Technology, 1975; professional: senior vice president of operations for Sara Lee Corporation, 1992–94; senior vice president of Haggar Corporation, 1994–98; CEO of Reebok, 2001–02; CEO of Pillowtex, 2002–03; CEO of Dollar General, 2003–07; religion: United Methodist; married: the former Bonnie Dunn, 1972; children: David A. Perdue III and Blake Perdue; committees: Agriculture, Nutrition and Forestry; Budget; Foreign Relations; Judiciary; Special Committee on Aging; elected to the U.S. Senate on November 4, 2014.

Office Listings

http://perdue.senate.gov

383 Russell Senate Office Building, Washington, DC 20510 .... (202) 224–3521
    Chief of Staff.—Derrick Dickey.   FAX: 228–1031
    Director of Operations.—Caleb Moore.
    Legislative Director.—PJ Waldrop.
    Communications Director.—Megan Whittemore.
191 Peachtree Street, NE., Suite 3250, Atlanta, GA 30303 .... (770) 661–0999
    State Director.—Joyce White.   FAX: 661–0768

REPRESENTATIVES

FIRST DISTRICT

EARL L. "BUDDY" CARTER, Republican, of Pooler, GA; born in Port Wentworth, GA, September, 6, 1957; education: Young Harris College, 1977; University of Georgia, 1980; professional: pharmacist; small business owner; Mayor of Pooler, GA, 1996–2004; Georgia State Legislature, 2006–14; married: Amy Carter, 1979; children: Joel, Barrett, and Travis; committees: Education and the Workforce; Homeland Security; Oversight and Government Reform; elected on the 114th Congress on November 4, 2014.

Office Listings

http://www.buddycarter.house.gov

432 Cannon House Office Building, Washington, DC 20515 .... (202) 225–5831

Office Listings—Continued

Chief of Staff.—Chris Crawford. FAX: 226–2269
Legislative Director.—Chase Cannon.
Legislative Assistants: Caralee Conklin, Nick Schemmel.
Legislative Correspondent.—Zellie Duvall.
Communications Director.—Mary Carpenter.
Scheduler.—Phillip Fordham.
Staff Assistant.—Hart Thompson.
6602 Abercorn Street, Suite 105–B, Savannah, GA 31405 .... (912) 352–0101
Casework Manager.—Trish DePriest.
Caseworker.—Bruce Bazemore.
Staff Assistant.—Elizabeth Gooch.
Field Representative.—Brooke Childers.
1510 Newcastle Street, Suite 200, Brunswick, GA 31520 .... (912) 265–9010
District Director.—Jud Seymour.
Field Representative.—Emmitt Nolan.

Counties: BACON, BRANTLEY, BRYAN, CAMDEN, CHARLTON, CHATHAM, CLINCH, ECHOLS, EFFINGHAM (part), GLYNN, LIBERTY, LONG, LOWNDES (part), MCINTOSH, PIERCE, WARE, AND WAYNE. Population (2014), 703,020.

ZIP Codes: 30427–28, 31300–01, 31305, 31308–09, 31313–16, 31319–21, 31323–24, 31327–28, 31331–33, 31401–12, 31414–16, 31418–21, 31501–03, 31520–21, 31523–25, 31542, 31553, 31605–24, 31630–32, 31634–36

* * *

SECOND DISTRICT

SANFORD D. BISHOP, JR., Democrat, of Albany, GA; born in Mobile, AL, February 4, 1947; education: attended Mobile County public schools; B.A., Morehouse College, 1968; J.D., Emory University, 1971; professional: attorney; admitted to the Georgia and Alabama Bars; Georgia House of Representatives, 1977–91; Georgia Senate, 1991–93; former member: Executive Board, Boy Scouts of America; YMCA; Sigma Pi Phi Fraternity; Kappa Alpha Psi Fraternity; 32nd Degree Mason, Shriner; member: Mt. Zion Baptist Church, Albany, GA; married: Vivian Creighton Bishop; child: Aeysha Reese; committees: Appropriations; elected to the 103rd Congress; reelected to each succeeding Congress.

Office Listings

http://www.bishop.house.gov

2407 Rayburn House Office Building, Washington, DC 20515 .... (202) 225–3631
Chief of Staff.—Michael Reed. FAX: 225–2203
Staff Assistant / Scheduler.—Haley Fulford.
Legislative Director.—Jonathan Halpern.
Legislative Assistant / Press Assistant.—Adilene Rosales.
Legislative Assistant / Office Manager.—Julian Johnson.
Communications Director.—Maxwell Gigle.
Albany Towers, 235 West Roosevelt Avenue, Suite 114, Albany, GA 31701 .... (229) 439–8067
District Director / Ag Advisor.—Kenneth Cutts.
Constituent Services Director.—Sharon Richter.
Office Manager / Constituent Services.—Toni Pickel.
Staff Assistant.—Tameka Wimbush.
18 Ninth Street, Suite 201, Columbus, GA 31901 .... (706) 320–9477
Office Manager / Constituent Services.—Harry Crawford.
Field Representative.—Elaine Gillispie.
Staff Assistant.—Peggy Sagul.
682 Cherry Street, Suite 302, Macon, GA 31201 .... (478) 803–2361
Constituent Services.—Vanessa Mills.
Field Representative.—Michelle Sands.

Counties: BAKER, CALHOUN, CHATTAHOOCHEE, CLAY, CRAWFORD, CRISP, DECATUR, DOOLY, DOUGHERTY, EARLY, GRADY, LEE, MACON, MARION, MILLER, MITCHELL, MUSCOGEE, PEACH, QUITMAN, RANDOLPH, SCHLEY, SEMINOLE, STEWART, SUMTER, TALBOT, TAYLOR, TERRELL, AND WEBSTER. Population (2010), 631,973.

ZIP Codes: 31010, 31015, 31039, 31068–69, 31072, 31092, 31201, 31204, 31211, 31217, 31701–12, 31714, 31716, 31719–22, 31730, 31735, 31743–44, 31763–65, 31787–96, 31803, 31805, 31814–15, 31821, 31824–25, 31832, 31901–07, 31995, 31997–99, 39813, 39815, 39817–19, 39823–29, 39832, 39834, 39836–37, 39840–42, 39845–46, 39851–52, 39854, 39859, 39861–62, 39866–67, 39870, 39877, 39885–86, 39897

* * *

THIRD DISTRICT

LYNN A. WESTMORELAND, Republican, of Grantville, GA; born in Atlanta, GA, April 2, 1950; education: graduated from Therrell High School, Atlanta, GA; attended Georgia State University, Atlanta, GA, 1969–71; professional: real estate developer; public service: Minority Leader, Georgia State House, 2000–04; Representative, Georgia State House, 1992–2004; religion: Baptist; organizations: National Rifle Association; married: Joan; children: Heather, Marcy, and Trae; committees: Financial Services; Permanent Select Committee on Intelligence; elected to the 109th Congress on November 2, 2004; reelected to each succeeding Congress.

Office Listings

http://www.westmoreland.house.gov

2202 Rayburn House Office Building, Washington, DC 20515	(202) 225–5901
Chief of Staff.—Brad Bohannon.	FAX: 225–2515
Communications Director.—Leigh Claffey.	
Legislative Director / Deputy Chief of Staff.—Jason Lawrence.	
Office Manager.—Claire Ouimet.	
Scheduler.—Cason Hightower.	
1601–B East Highway 34, Suite 3, Newnan, GA 30265	(770) 683–2033

Counties: CARROLL. CITIES AND TOWNSHIPS: Bowdon, Carrollton, Mount Zion, Roopville, Temple, Villa Rica, and Whitesburg. COWETA (part). CITIES AND TOWNSHIPS: Grantville, Haralson, Lone Oak, Meriwether, Luthersville, Moreland, Newnan, Palmetto, Senoia, Sharpsburg, and Turin. FAYETTE Cities and Townships: Brooks, Fayetteville, Peachtree City, Tyrone, and Woolsey. HARRIS. CITIES AND TOWNSHIPS: Cataula, Ellerslie, Fortson, Hamilton, Midland, Pine Mountain, Pine Mountain Valley, Shiloh, Waverly Hall, and West Point. HENRY (part). CITIES AND TOWNSHIPS: Hampton, Locust Grove, McDonough, and Stockbridge. LAMAR. Cities and Townships: Aldora, Barnesville, Milner. MUSCOGEE (part). CITIES AND TOWNSHIPS: Columbus. PIKE. CITIES AND TOWNSHIPS: Concord, Meansville, Molena, Williamson, and Zebulon. SPALDING. CITIES AND TOWNSHIPS: Griffin, Orchard Hill, and Sunny Side. TROUP. CITIES AND TOWNSHIPS: Hogansville, and LaGrange. UPSON. CITIES AND TOWNSHIPS: Thomaston, and Yatesville. Population (2010), 757,344.

ZIP Codes: 30257–59, 30263, 30265, 30268–69, 30275–77, 30285–86, 30290, 30292–93, 30295, 31016, 31029, 31066, 31097, 31800, 31804, 31807–08, 31811, 31816, 31820, 31822–23, 31826, 31829–31, 31833, 31901, 31904, 31906, 31909

* * *

FOURTH DISTRICT

HENRY C. "HANK" JOHNSON, JR., Democrat, of Lithonia, GA; born in Washington, DC, October 2, 1954; B.A., Clark College (Clark Atlanta University), Atlanta, GA, 1976; J.D., Thurgood Marshall School of Law, Texas Southern University, Houston, TX, 1979; professional: partner, Johnson & Johnson Law Group LLC, 1980–2007; judge, Magistrate Court, 1989–2001; DeKalb County Commissioner, 2001–06; married: Mereda, 1979; two children: Randi and Alex; committees: Armed Services; Judiciary; elected to the 110th Congress on November 7, 2006; reelected to each succeeding Congress.

Office Listings

http://www.hankjohnson.house.gov

2240 Rayburn House Office Building, Washington, DC 20515	(202) 225–1605
Chief of Staff.—Arthur D. Sidney.	FAX: 226–0691
Legislative Director.—Scott Goldstein.	
Office Manager / Scheduler.—Glenn Miles.	
5700 Hillandale Drive, Suite 120, Lithonia, GA 30058	(770) 987–2291
District Director.—Kathy Register.	

Counties: DEKALB (part), GWINNETT (part), ROCKDALE, NEWTON (part). CITIES: Atlanta (part), Avondale Estates (part), Clarkston, Conyers, Covington, Decatur (part), Lilburn (part), Lithonia, Norcross, Pine Lake, Snellville, Stone Mountain and Tucker (part). Population (2010), 691,976.

ZIP Codes: 30002–03, 30012–17, 30021, 30030–39, 30047, 30052, 30058, 30070, 30072, 30074, 30078–79, 30083–84, 30086–88, 30252, 30281, 30294, 30329, 30340, 30345, 30359

* * *

FIFTH DISTRICT

JOHN LEWIS, Democrat, of Atlanta, GA; born in Pike County, AL, February 21, 1940; education: graduated, Pike County Training School, Brundidge, AL, 1957; B.A., American Baptist Theological Seminary, Nashville, TN, 1961; B.A., Fisk University, Nashville, TN, 1963; civil rights leader; Atlanta City Council, 1982–86; member: Martin Luther King Center for Social Change; African American Institute; Robert F. Kennedy Memorial; married the former Lillian Miles in 1968; one child, John Miles Lewis; appointed Senior Chief Deputy Democratic Whip for the 109th Congress; committees: Ways and Means; elected to the 100th Congress on November 4, 1986; reelected to each succeeding Congress.

Office Listings

http://www.johnlewis.house.gov   www.facebook.com/repjohnlewis   twitter: @repjohnlewis

343 Cannon House Office Building, Washington, DC 20515 .... (202) 225–3801
    Chief of Staff.—Michael Collins.   FAX: 225–0351
    Officer Manager / Scheduler.—David Bowan.
    Director of Communications.—Brenda Jones.
    Legislative Director.—Jamila Thompson.
100 Peachtree Street, NW., Suite 1920, Atlanta, GA 30303 .... (404) 659–0116
    District Director.—Aaron Ward.

Counties: CLAYTON (part), DeKALB (part), AND FULTON (part). Population (2012), 691,975.

ZIP Codes: 30030 (part), 30032 (part), 30034 (part), 30236 (part), 30260 (part), 30273–74 (part), 30281 (part), 30288, 30294 (part), 30296–97 (part), 30303, 30305 (part), 30306–19 (part), 30322, 30324 (part), 30326–27 (part), 30331–32, 30334, 30336, 30337 (part), 30342 (part), 30344 (part), 30349 (part), 30354, 30363

* * *

SIXTH DISTRICT

TOM PRICE, Republican, of Roswell, GA; born in Lansing, MI, October 8, 1954; education: B.A., University of Michigan, 1976; M.D., University of Michigan, 1979; professional: physician; member of the Georgia State Senate, 1997–2004; member: Cobb Chamber of Commerce; Civil Air Patrol; Advisory Board, Georgia Partnership for Excellence in Education; religion: Presbyterian; married: Elizabeth; one child, Robert; committees: chair, Budget; Ways and Means; elected to the 109th Congress on November 2, 2004; reelected to each succeeding Congress.

Office Listings

http://www.tomprice.house.gov

100 Cannon House Office Building, Washington, DC 20515 .... (202) 225–4501
    Chief of Staff.—Kris Skrzycki.   FAX: 225–4656
    District Director.—Kyle McGowan.
85–C Mill Street, Suite 300, Roswell, GA 30075 .... (770) 998–0049

Counties: COBB (part), FULTON (part), AND DeKALB (part). CITIES AND TOWNSHIPS: Roswell, Johns Creek, Tucker, Alpharetta, Sandy Springs, Brookhaven, Chamblee, Doraville, and Dunwoody. Population (2010), 699,103.

ZIP Codes: 30004–07, 30009, 30022–24, 30033, 30062, 30065–68, 30075–77, 30084–85, 30092–93, 30097–98, 30102, 30144, 30188, 30319, 30324, 30326, 30328–29, 30338–42, 30345–46, 30350, 30356, 30358, 30360, 30362, 30366, 31119, 31141, 31145–46, 31150, 31156

* * *

SEVENTH DISTRICT

W. ROBERT WOODALL, Republican, of Lawrenceville, GA; born in Athens, GA, February 11, 1970; education: undergraduate, B.A., Furman University, Greenville, SC, 1992; graduate, J.D., University of Georgia, Athens, GA, 1997; awards: co-author of the New York Times bestsellling book *Fair Tax: The Truth;* religion: Methodist; committees: Budget; Transportation and Infrastructure; Rules; elected to the 112th Congress on November 2, 2010; reelected to each succeeding Congress.

Office Listings

http://woodall.house.gov

1724 Longworth House Office Building, Washington, DC 20515 .... (202) 225–4272
  Chief of Staff.—Derick Corbett.   FAX: 225–4696
  Legislative Director.—Janet Rossi.
  District Director.—Debra Poirot.
75 Langley Drive, Lawrenceville, GA 30046 .... (770) 232–3005
(No Mail Accepted At This Address)   FAX: 232–2909

Counties: FORSYTH (part), AND GWINNETT (part). Population (2010), 691,975.

ZIP Codes: 30004–05, 30017, 30019, 30040–41, 30043–49, 30052, 30078, 30091–93, 30095–97, 30099, 30340, 30360, 30518–19

* * *

EIGHTH DISTRICT

AUSTIN SCOTT, Republican, of Tifton, GA; born in Augusta, GA, December 10, 1969; B.B.A., University of Georgia, 1993; professional: business owner; member of the Georgia State House of Representatives, 1997–2010; religion: Southern Baptist; married: wife, Vivien; son, Wells; daughter, Carmen Gabriela; member, National Association of Insurance and Financial Advisors; Coastal Plains Chapter of the American Red Cross; awards: American Cancer Society's Outstanding Legislative Leadership Award, 2003 and 2004; Georgia Association of Emergency Medical Services Star of Life Legislative Award, 2007 and 2008; Republican Freshman Class President; committees: Agriculture; Armed Services; elected to the 112th Congress on November 2, 2010; reelected to each succeeding Congress.

Office Listings

http://austinscott.house.gov   twitter: @austinscottga08
www.youtube.com/user/repaustinscott   www.facebook.com/repaustinscott

2417 Rayburn House Office Building, Washington, DC 20515 .... (202) 225–6531
  Chief of Staff.—John Young.   FAX: 225–3013
  Legislative Director and Military Legislative Assistant.—Matt Hodge.
  Legislative Correspondent.—Craig Anderson.
  Communications Director.—Ryann DuRant.
  Legislative Assistant.—Mary Dee Beal.
  Scheduler.—Haley Dorval.
127–B North Central Avenue, Tifton, GA 31794 .... (229) 396–5175
                                                                                                FAX: 396–5179
230 Margie Drive, Suite 500, Warner Robins, GA 31088   .... (478) 971–1776
                                                                                                FAX: 971–1778

Counties: ATKINSON, BEN HILL, BERRIEN, BIBB (part), BLECKLEY, BROOKS, COLQUITT, COOK, DODGE, HOUSTON, IRWIN, JONES, LANIER, LOWNDES (part), MONROE, PULASKI, TELFAIR, THOMAS, TIFT, TURNER, TWIGGS, WILCOX, WILKINSON, AND WORTH. Population (2011), 693,640

ZIP Codes: 30233, 31001, 31033–35, 31008, 31011–17, 31020–21, 31023, 31035, 31028–33, 31036–38, 31042, 31044, 31046–47, 31054–55, 31060–61, 31065–66, 31069, 31071–72, 31077, 31079, 31083–84, 31086, 31088, 31090–93, 31095, 31098–99, 31204, 31209, 31210–11, 31217, 31220–21, 31297, 31512, 31544, 31549, 31601–66, 31620, 31622, 31624–27, 31629, 31632, 31635–39, 31641–45, 31647, 31649, 31650, 31698, 31705, 31712, 31714, 31720, 31722, 31727, 31733, 31738, 31744, 31747, 31749–50, 31753, 31756–58, 31760, 31765, 31768–69, 31771–79, 31781, 31783–84, 31788–96, 31798–99

* * *

NINTH DISTRICT

DOUGLAS COLLINS, Republican, of Gainesville, GA; born in Gainesville, August 16, 1966; education: B.A., political science, criminal law, North Georgia College and State University, Dahlonega, GA, 1988; Master of Divinity, New Orleans Baptist Theological Seminary, New Orleans, LA, 1996; Juris Doctorate, John Marshall Law School, Atlanta, GA, 2007; professional: preacher; business owner; soldier; lawyer; Georgia State House of Representatives, 2006–12; religion: Baptist; married: Lisa Collins; children: Jordan, Copelan, and Cameron; committees: Foreign Affairs; Judiciary; Oversight and Government Reform; elected by regular election to the 113th Congress on November 6, 2012 to fill the vacancy caused by the redistricting of District 9; reelected to the 114th Congress on November 4, 2014.

Office Listings

http://www.dougcollins.house.gov

1504 Longworth House Office Building, Washington, DC 20515 .... (202) 225–9893
    Chief of Staff.—Brendan Belair.   FAX: 226–1224
    Communications Director.—Brendan Thomas.
    Legislative Director.—Jennifer Choudhry.
    Scheduler.—Erin Wall.
    Senior Legislative Aide.—Sally Rose Larson.
    Legislative Aide.—Vernon Robinson.
    Legislative Aide / Legislative Correspondent.—Kathryn Evans.
    Staff Assistant.—Harrison Payne.
210 Washington Street Northwest, Suite 202, Gainesville, GA 30501 .... (770) 297–3388

Counties: BANKS, CLARKE (part), DAWSON, ELBERT, FANNIN, FORSYTH (part), FRANKLIN, GILMER, HABERSHAM, HALL, HART, JACKSON, LUMPKIN, MADISON, PICKENS (part), RABUN, STEPHENS, TOWNS, UNION, WHITE. CITIES AND TOWNSHIPS: Homer, Gillsville, Dawsonville, Elberton, Bowman, Blue Ridge, McCaysville, Morganton, Cumming, Canon, Carnesville, Franklin Springs, Lavonia, Royston, Elijay, Alto, Baldwin, Clarkesville, Cornelia, Demorest, Mount Airy, Tallulah Falls, Clermont, Flowery Branch, Gainesville, Lula, Oakwood, Bowersville, Hartwell, Arcade, Braselton, Commerce, Hoschton, Jefferson, Nicholson, Pendergrass, Talmo, Dahlonega, Carlton, Colbert, Comer, Danielsville, Hull, Ila, Jasper, Nelson, Talking Rock, Clayton, Dillard, Mountain City, Sky Valley, Martin, Toccoa, Hiawassee, Young Harris, Blairsville, Cleveland, and Helen. Population (2010), 691,975.

ZIP Codes: 30028, 30040–41, 30143, 30151, 30175, 30501–04, 30506–07, 30510–13, 30516–17, 30520–23, 30525, 30527–31, 30533–37, 30540, 30542–49, 30553–55, 30557, 30560, 30562, 30565–67, 30573, 30575, 30577, 30582, 30597, 30599, 30624, 30627–29, 30633, 30635, 30639, 30643, 30646–47, 30662

* * *

TENTH DISTRICT

JODY B. HICE, Republican of Monroe, GA; grew up in Tucker, GA, born on April 22, 1960; education: B.A., Ministry, Asbury University, Wilmore KY; professional: pastor; religion; Southern Baptist; married: Dee Dee Crocker Hice; children: Anna, Sara; grandchildren: Peter, Margaret, Aylssa; committees: Natural Resources; Oversight and Government Reform: elected to the 114th Congress on November 4, 2014.

Office Listings

http://www.hice.house.gov

1516 Longworth House Office Building, Washington, DC 20515 .... (202) 225–4101
    Chief of Staff.—David Sours.
    Office Manager / Scheduler.—Taylor Ford.

Counties: BALDWIN, BARROW, BUTTS, COLUMBIA (part), CLARKE (part), GLASCOCK, GREENE, GWINNETT (part), HANCOCK, HENRY, JASPER, JEFFERSON, JOHNSON, LINCOLN, MCDUFFIE, MORGAN, NEWTON (part), OCONEE, OGLETHORPE, PUTNAM, TALIAFERRO, WALTON, WARREN, WASHINGTON, AND WILKES. POPULATION (2010), 691,976.

ZIP Codes: 30011–12, 30014, 30016, 30019, 30025, 30043, 30045, 30052, 30054–56, 30216, 30233–34, 30248, 30252–53, 30413, 30434, 30477, 30517, 30519, 30548, 30601–02, 30605–07, 30609, 30619–23, 30625, 30627–31, 30641–42, 30648, 30650, 30655–56, 30660, 30663–69, 30773, 30677–78, 30680, 30683, 30802–03, 30807–10, 30814, 30816–18, 30820–21, 30823–24, 30828, 30833, 31002, 31018, 31024, 31029, 31031, 31033, 31035, 31038, 31045, 31049, 31061–62, 31064, 31067, 31082, 31085, 31087, 31089, 31094, 31096

* * *

ELEVENTH DISTRICT

BARRY LOUDERMILK, Republican, of Cassville, GA; born in Riverdale, GA, December 22, 1963; education: A.A. in Telecommunications Technology, Community College of the Air Force, Maxwell AFB, AL, 1987; B.S. in Occupational Education and Information Systems Technology, Wayland Baptist University, Plainview, TX, 1992; professional: former small business owner, Innovative Network Systems, Inc. and Freedom Flight Center; founded non-profit, Firm Reliance, in 2011; served in Georgia State House, 2005–10; Georgia State Senate, 2011–13; member, NRA; Aircraft Owners and Pilots Association; American Legion; served in the U.S. Air Force, 1984–92; Civil Air Patrol member, official auxiliary of the U.S. Air Force, 2005–present; religion: Protestant; married to Desiree since 1983; children: Travis, Christiana, and Michael; committees: Homeland Security; Science, Space, and Technology; elected to the 114th Congress on November 4, 2014.

Office Listings

http://www.loudermilk.house.gov   twitter: https://twitter.com/reploudermilk

238 Cannon House Office Building, Washington, DC 20515 .... (202) 225–2931
  Chief of Staff.—Robert Adkerson.   FAX: 225–2944
  Legislative Director / Deputy Chief of Staff.—Easton Randall.
  District Director.—Caric Martin.
9898 Highway 92, Suite 100, Woodstock, GA 30188 .... (770) 429–1776
135 West Cherokee Avenue, Suite 122, Cartersville, GA 30120 .... (770) 429–1776

Counties: BARTOW, CHEROKEE, COBB (part), FULTON (part). Population (2010) 794,969.

ZIP Codes: 30004, 30008, 30040, 30060, 30062, 30064, 30066–68, 30075, 30080, 30082, 30101–04, 30107, 30114–15,
   30120–21, 30127, 30132, 30137, 30139, 30143–45, 30152–53, 30157, 30161, 30171, 30178, 30183–84, 30188–89,
   30305, 30318–19, 30326–27, 30339, 30342

* * *

TWELFTH DISTRICT

RICK W. ALLEN, Republican, of Augusta, GA; born in Augusta, November 7, 1951; education: graduated, Evans High School, Evans, GA, 1969; B.S., in Building Construction, Auburn University, Auburn, AL, 1973; professional: founder and owner of R.W. Allen & Associates construction company, Augusta, GA and Athens, GA, founded in 1976; awards: Augusta Metro Chamber of Commerce Small Business Person of the Year, 2008; CSRA Business Hall of Fame Inductee, 2011; religion: Methodist; married: wife, Robin; children: Jennifer Allen Green, Andy Allen, Molly Allen Hargather, and Robin Anne Allen Wills; grandchildren: Hadley Green, Wyche Green, Hutton Green, Collier Green, Hammond Hargather, Delle Hargather, Riley Kate Wills, and Ellis Wills; committees: Agriculture; Education and the Workforce; elected to the 114th Congress on November 4, 2014.

Office Listings

http://www.allen.house.gov

513 Cannon House Office Building, Washington, DC 20515 .... (202) 225–2823
  Chief of Staff.—Tim Baker.   FAX: 225–3377
  Deputy Chief of Staff.—Lauren Swing.
  Legislative Director.—Cameron Bishop.
  Communications Director.—Virginia Dent.
2743 Perimeter Parkway, Bldg. 200, Suite 225, Augusta, GA 30909 .... (706) 228–1980
Statesboro City Hall, 50 East Main Street, Statesboro, GA 30458 .... (912) 243–9452
101 North Jefferson Street, Dublin, GA 31021 .... (478) 272–4030
Vidalia Community Center, 107 Old Airport Road, Suite A, Vidalia, GA 30475 .... (912) 403–3311

Counties: APPLING, BULLOCH, BURKE, CANDLER, COFFEE, COLUMBIA (part), EFFINGHAM (part), EMANUEL, EVANS, JEFF
   DAVIS, JENKINS, LAURENS, MONTGOMERY, RICHMOND, SCREVEN, TATTNALL, TOOMBS, TREUTLEN, AND WHEELER. POPU-
   LATION (2010), 701,142.

ZIP Codes: 30401, 30410–12, 30415, 30417, 30420–21, 30423, 30425–29, 30434, 30436, 30438–39, 30441–42, 30445–
   46, 30448–58, 30460–61, 30464, 30467, 30470–71, 30473–75, 30802, 30805, 30809, 30812 16, 30822, 30830, 30901,
   30903–07, 30909, 30912, 31002, 31009, 31019, 31021 23, 31027, 31037, 31049, 31065, 31075, 31083, 31303, 31308,
   31312, 31321, 31326, 31329, 31510, 31512–13, 31518 19, 31532–33, 31535, 31539, 31549, 31552, 31554–55, 31563,
   31567, 31624, 31650, 31798

* * *

THIRTEENTH DISTRICT

DAVID SCOTT, Democrat, of Atlanta, GA; born in Aynor, SC, June 27, 1945; education: Florida A&M University, graduated with honors, 1967; M.B.A., graduated with honors, University of Pennsylvania Wharton School of Finance, 1969; professional: businessman; owner and CEO, Dayn-Mark Advertising; public service: Georgia House of Representatives, 1974–82; Georgia State Senate, 1983–2002; married: Alfredia Aaron, 1969; children: Dayna and Marcye; committees: Agriculture; Financial Services; elected to the 108th Congress on November 5, 2002; reelected to each succeeding Congress.

Office Listings

http://davidscott.house.gov   facebook: repdavidscott   twitter: @repdavidscott

225 Cannon House Office Building, Washington, DC 20515 .... (202) 225–2939

Office Listings—Continued

Chief of Staff.—Michael Andel.   FAX: 225–4628
Scheduler and Executive Assistant.—Chinmayee Tambe.
Legislative Director.—Lauren Lattany.
173 North Main Street, Jonesboro, GA 30236 .... (770) 210–5073
888 Concord Road, Suite 100, Smyra, GA 30080 .... (770) 432–5405

Counties: CLAYTON, COBB, DOUGLAS, FAYETTE, FULTON, AND HENRY. Population (2010), 707,070.

ZIP Codes: 30252–53, 30260, 30268, 30273–74, 30281, 30290–91, 30294, 30296–97, 30331, 30337, 30344, 30349

* * *

FOURTEENTH DISTRICT

TOM GRAVES, Republican, of Ranger, GA; born in St. Petersburg, FL, February 3, 1970; education: B.A.A., finance, University of Georgia, Athens, GA, 1993; professional: business owner; Georgia State House of Representatives, 2003–10; religion: Baptist: married: Julie Howard Graves; children: JoAnn, John, and Janey; committees: Appropriations; Joint Committee on the Library; elected to the 111th Congress on June 8, 2010, by special election, to fill the vacancy caused by the resignation of United States Representative John Nathan Deal; elected to the 112th Congress on November 2, 2010; reelected to each succeeding Congress.

Office Listings

http://www.tomgraves.house.gov

2442 Rayburn House Office Building, Washington, DC 20515 .... (202) 225–5211
Chief of Staff.—John Donnelly.   FAX: 225–8272
Legislative Director.—Bo Butler.
Communications Director.—Garrett Hawkins.
Scheduler.—Morgan Jocye.
702 South Thornton Avenue, Dalton, GA 30720 .... (706) 226–5320
                                                                                                         FAX: 278–0840
600 East First Street, Suite 301, Rome, GA 30161 .... (706) 290–1776
                                                                                                         FAX: 232–7864

Counties: CATOOSA, CHATTOOGA, DADE, FLOYD, GORDON, HARALSON, MURRAY, PAULDING, PICKENS (part), POLK, WALKER, AND WHITFIELD. Population (2010), 619,974.

ZIP Codes: 30101, 30103–05, 30110, 30113, 30120, 30124–25, 30127, 30129, 30132, 30134, 30138–41, 30143

HAWAII

(Population 2010, 1,360,301)

SENATORS

BRIAN SCHATZ, Democrat, of Hawaii; born in Ann Arbor, MI, October 20, 1972; education: graduated from Punahou School, Honolulu, HI, 1990; B.A., Pomona College, Claremont, CA, 1994; professional: chairman, Democratic Party of Hawaii, 2008–10; CEO, Helping Hands Hawaii, 2002–10; Hawaii House of Representatives, 1998–2006; Lieutenant Governor of Hawaii, 2010–12; married: Linda Schatz; committees: Appropriations; Commerce, Science, and Transportation; Indian Affairs; Select Committee on Ethics; appointed to the United States Senate on December 26, 2012, and took the oath of office on December 27, 2012.

Office Listings

http://www.schatz.senate.gov   twitter: @senbrianschatz
https://www.facebook.com/senbrianschatz

722 Hart Senate Office Building, Washington, DC 20510	(202) 224–3934
Chief of Staff.—Andrew Winer.	FAX: 228–1153
Scheduler.—Diane Miyasato.	
Legislative Director.—Arun Revana.	
Communications Director.—Karen Lightfoot.	
300 Ala Moana Boulevard, Room 7–212, Honolulu, HI 96850	(808) 523–2061
	FAX: 523–2065

* * *

MAZIE HIRONO, Democrat, of Hawaii; born in Fukushima, Japan, November 3, 1947; graduated from Kaimuki High School, Honolulu, HI; B.A., University of Hawaii, Manoa, HI, 1970; J.D., Georgetown University, Washington, DC, 1978; professional: lawyer, private practice; member of the Hawaii State House of Representatives, 1981–94; Hawaii Lieutenant Governor, 1994–2002; elected to the United States House of Representatives as a Democrat to the 110th, 111th, and 112th Congresses; was not a candidate for reelection to the United States House of Representatives for the 113th Congress; committees: Armed Services; Energy and Natural Resources; Small Business; Veterans' Affairs; Select Committee on Intelligence; elected to the United States Senate on November 6, 2012.

Office Listings

http://www.hirono.senate.gov   twitter: @maziehirono

330 Hart Senate Office Building, Washington, DC 20510	(202) 224–6361
Chief of Staff.—Betsy Lin.	FAX: 224–2126
Prince Kuhio Federal Building, 300 Ala Moana Boulevard, Room 3–106, Honolulu, HI	
96850	(808) 522–8970
District Director.—Alan Yamamoto.	

REPRESENTATIVES

FIRST DISTRICT

MARK TAKAI, Democrat, of Hawaii; born in Honolulu, HI, July 1, 1967; education: graduated from Pearl City High School, Pearl City, HI, 1985; B.A., University of Hawaii, Honolulu, HI, 1990; M.P.H., University of Hawaii, Honolulu, HI, 1993; professional: small business owner, 2002–14; Hawaii State House of Representatives, 1994–2014; Vice Speaker of the House, 2005–06; military: Hawaii Army National Guard, 1999–present; religion: Christian; married: Sami Takai; committees, Armed Services; Small Business; elected to the 114th Congress on November 4, 2014.

Office Listings

http://www.takai.house.gov

422 Cannon House Office Building, Washington, DC 20515	(202) 225–2726

Office Listings—Continued

Chief of Staff.—Rod Tanonaka.   FAX: 225–0688
Deputy Chief of Staff.—Sean Callahan.
Legislative Director.—Sean Callahan.
Communications Director.—Alex Hetherington.
300 Ala Moana Boulevard, Room 4–104, Honolulu, HI 96850 .... (808) 541–2570
District Director.—Rod Tanonaka.

Counties: HONOLULU (part). CITIES AND TOWNSHIPS: Aiea, Pearl City, Ewa Beach, Honolulu, Mililani, and Waipahu. Population (2010), 680,496.

ZIP Codes: 96701, 96706–07, 96782, 96789, 96797, 96813–19, 96821–22, 96825–26, 96850, 96853, 96859–60

* * *

SECOND DISTRICT

TULSI GABBARD, Democrat, of Hawaii; born in Leloaloa, American Samoa, April 12, 1981; education: Hawaii Pacific University, Officer Candidate School, Army; professional: member of the Hawaii House of Representatives from the 42nd District, 2002–04; member of the Honolulu City Council from the Sixth District, 2011–12; member of the U.S. House of Representatives from Hawaii's 2nd District, 2013–present; member of the Army National Guard, 2003–present; committees: Armed Services; Foreign Affairs; elected to the 113th Congress on November 6, 2012; reelected to the 114th Congress on November 4, 2014.

Office Listings

http://gabbard.house.gov

1609 Longworth House Office Building, Washington, DC 20515 .... (202) 603–3809
Chief of Staff.—Kainoa Penaroza.   FAX: 225–4987
300 Ala Moana Boulevard, 5–104 Prince Kuhio Federal Building, Honolulu, HI 96850 .... (808) 541–1986
District Director.—Col. (Ret.) Walt Kaneakua.

Counties: HAWAI'I. CITIES: Hawi, Hilo, Honoka'a, Kailua-Kona, Na'alehu, Kealakekua, Pahoa, Ocean View, Volcano, Waimea, and Waikoloa. HONOLULU COUNTY (part). CITIES: Hale'iwa, Honolulu, Kailua, Kane'ohe, Kapolei, La'ie, Makakilo, Nanakuli, Wahiawa, Waialua, Wai'anae, Waimanalo. KALAWAO COUNTY. CITY: Kalaupapa. KAUA'I COUNTY. CITIES: Hanalei, Hanapepe, Kalaheo, Kapa'a, Kekaha, Kilauea, Koloa, Lihue, Waimea. MAUI COUNTY. CITIES: Hana, Kahului, Kaunakakai, Lahaina, Lana'i City, Makawao, Wailuku. NORTHWESTERN HAWAIIAN ISLANDS. ISLANDS OF: Becker, French Frigate Shoals, Gardener Pinnacles, Hermes and Kure Atolls, Laysan, Lisianski, Maro Reef, Nihoa, and Pearl. Population (2010), 679,805.

ZIP Codes: 96703–05, 96707–08, 96710, 96712–14, 96716–17, 96719–20, 96722, 96725–32, 96734, 96737–38, 96740–44, 96746–57, 96759–66, 96768–74, 96776–81, 96783, 96785–86, 96789–93, 96795–97, 96825, 96857, 96863

IDAHO

(Population 2010, 1,567,582)

SENATORS

MIKE CRAPO, Republican, of Idaho Falls, ID; born in Idaho Falls, May 20, 1951; education: graduated, Idaho Falls High School, 1969; B.A., Brigham Young University, Provo, UT, 1973; J.D., Harvard University Law School, Cambridge, MA, 1977; professional: attorney; admitted to the California Bar, 1977; admitted to the Idaho Bar, 1979; law clerk, Hon. James M. Carter, Judge of the U.S. Court of Appeals for the Ninth Circuit, San Diego, CA, 1977–78; associate attorney, Gibson, Dunn, and Crutcher, San Diego, 1978–79; attorney, Holden, Kidwell, Hahn and Crapo, 1979–92; partner, 1983–92; Idaho State Senate, 1984–92, assistant majority leader, 1987–89, president pro tempore, 1989–92; member: American Bar Association, Boy Scouts of America, Idaho Falls Rotary Club, 1984–88; married: the former Susan Diane Hasleton, 1974; children: Michelle, Brian, Stephanie, Lara, and Paul; co-chair, Western Water Caucus; Sportsman Caucus; co-chair, COPD Caucus; Majority Chief Deputy Whip; committees: Banking, Housing, and Urban Affairs; Budget; Environment and Public Works; Finance; Indian Affairs; elected on November 3, 1992, to the 103rd Congress; reelected to each succeeding Congress; elected to the U.S. Senate on November 3, 1998; reelected to each succeeding Senate term.

Office Listings

http://www.crapo.senate.gov   https://www.facebook.com/mikecrapo
twitter: @mikecrapo

239 Dirksen Senate Office Building, Washington, DC 20510	(202) 224–6142
Chief of Staff.—Susan Wheeler.	FAX: 228–1375
Legislative Director.—Ken Flanz.	
251 East Front Street, Suite 205, Boise, ID 83702	(208) 334–1776
Chief of Staff.—John Hoehne.	
Communications Director.—Lindsay Nothern.	
610 Hubbard Street, Suite 209, Coeur d'Alene, ID 83814	(208) 664–5490
Director.—Karen Roetter.	
313 D Street, Suite 105, Lewiston, ID 83501	(208) 743–1492
Director.—Tony Snodderly.	
275 South 5th Avenue, Suite 225, Pocatello, ID 83201	(208) 236–9635
Director.—Farhanna Hibbert.	
410 Memorial Drive, Suite 204, Idaho Falls, ID 83402	(208) 522–9779
Director.—Kathryn Hitch.	
202 Falls Avenue, Suite 2, Twin Falls, ID 83301	(208) 734–2515
Director.—Vacant.	

* * *

JAMES E. RISCH, Republican, of Boise, ID; born in Milwaukee, WI, May 3, 1943; education: St. Johns Cathedral High School, Milwaukee, WI; B.S., forestry, University of Idaho, Moscow, ID, 1965; J.D., University of Idaho, Moscow, ID, 1968, Law Review, College of Law Advisory Committee; professional: Ada County Prosecuting Attorney, 1970–74; president, Idaho Prosecuting Attorneys Association, 1973; Idaho State Senate, 1974–88, 1995–2003; Assistant Majority Leader, 1996; Majority Leader, 1976–82, 1997–2002; President Pro Tempore, 1983–1988; Lieutenant Governor of Idaho, 2003–06, 2007–09; Governor of Idaho, 2006; small business owner; ranch/farmer; former partner Risch, Goss, Insinger, Gustavel law firm; member, National Cattle Association; Idaho Cattle Association; American, Idaho and Boise Valley Angus Associations; National Rifle Association; Ducks Unlimited; Rocky Mountain Elk Foundation; married: Vicki; children: James, Jason, and Jordan, 3 daughters-in-law; 8 grandchildren; Congressional Youth Leadership Council; Impact Aid Coalition; Senate Rural Health Caucus; Rural Education Caucus; WMD/ Terrorism Caucus; National Guard Caucus; Western Caucus, Sportsmen's Caucus, Recycling Caucus, Republican High Tech Task Force; committees: Energy and Natural Resources; Foreign Relations; Small Business and Entrepreneurship; Select Committee on Ethics; Select Committee on Intelligence; elected to the U.S. Senate on November 4, 2008; reelected to the U.S. Senate on November 4, 2014.

Office Listings

http://risch.senate.gov   twitter: @senatorrisch

483 Russell Senate Office Building, Washington, DC 20510	(202) 224–2752

Office Listings—Continued

Chief of Staff.—John Sandy. FAX: 224–2573
Communications Director.—Brad Hoaglun.
Executive Assistant / Scheduler.—Suzanne Wrasse.
Legislative Director.—Chris Socha.
350 North Ninth Street, Suite 302, Boise, ID 83702 .... (208) 342–7985

REPRESENTATIVES

FIRST DISTRICT

RAÚL R. LABRADOR, Republican, of Eagle, ID; born in Carolina, PR, December 8, 1967; education: B.A., Brigham Young University, Provo, UT, 1992, J.D., University of Washington, Seattle, WA, 1995; professional: attorney; religion: The Church of Jesus Christ of Latter-Day Saints; married: Becca Labrador; five children; committees: Judiciary; Natural Resources; elected to the 112th Congress on November 2, 2010; reelected to each succeeding Congress.

Office Listings

http://labrador.house.gov

1523 Longworth House Office Building, Washington, DC 20515 .... (202) 225–6611
Chief of Staff.—Mike Cunnington. FAX: 225–3029
Legislative Director.—Aaron Calkins.
Scheduler.—Jocelyn Jaszkowiak.
33 East Broadway Avenue, Suite 251, Meridian, ID 83642 .... (208) 888–3188
1250 Ironwood Drive, Suite 241, Coeur d'Alene, ID 83814 .... (208) 667–0127
313 D Street, Suite 107, Lewiston, ID 83501 .... (208) 743–1388

Counties: ADA (part), ADAMS, BENEWAH, BOISE, BONNER, BOUNDARY, CANYON, CLEARWATER, GEM, IDAHO, KOOTENAI, LATAH, LEWIS, NEZ PERCE, OWYHEE, PAYETTE, SHOSHONE, VALLEY, WASHINGTON. Population (2010), 784,132.

ZIP Codes: 59847, 83302, 83316, 83501, 83520, 83522–26, 83530, 83533, 83535–37, 83539–49, 83552–55, 83602, 83604–05, 83607, 83610–12, 83615–17, 83619, 83622, 83624, 83626–29, 83631–32, 83634, 83636–39, 83641–46, 83650–51, 83654–57, 83660–61, 83666, 83669–72, 83676–77, 83686–87, 83702, 83705, 83709, 83713–14, 83716, 83801–06, 83808–15, 83821–27, 83830, 83832–37, 83839–52, 83854–58, 83860–61, 83864, 83866–74, 83876, 89832, 97910, 97913, 99128

* * *

SECOND DISTRICT

MICHAEL K. SIMPSON, Republican, of Blackfoot, ID; born in Burley, ID, September 8, 1950; education: graduated, Blackfoot High School, 1968; Utah State University, 1972; Washington University School of Dental Medicine, 1977; professional: dentist, private practice; Blackfoot, ID, City Council, 1981–85; Idaho State Legislature, 1985–98; Idaho Speaker of the House, 1992–98; married: Kathy Simpson; committees: Appropriations; elected to the 106th Congress; reelected to each succeeding Congress.

Office Listings

http://simpson.house.gov

2312 Rayburn House Office Building, Washington, DC 20515 .... (202) 225–5531
Chief of Staff.—Lindsay Slater. FAX: 225–8216
Scheduler.—Emilee Henshaw.
Legislative Director.—Nathan Greene.
Communications Director.—Nikki Wallace.
802 West Bannock, Suite 600, Boise, ID 83702 .... (208) 334–1953
1341 Fillmore, #202, Twin Falls, ID 83301 .... (208) 734–7219
410 Memorial Drive, Suite 203, Idaho Falls, ID 83402 .... (208) 523–6701
275 South Fifth Avenue, #275, Pocatello, ID 83201 .... (208) 233–2222

Counties: ADA (Part), BANNOCK, BEAR LAKE, BINGHAM, BLAINE, BONNEVILLE, BUTTE, CAMAS, CARIBOU, CASSIA, CLARK, CUSTER, ELMORE, FRANKLIN, FREMONT, GOODING, JEFFERSON, JEROME, LEMHI, LINCOLN, MADISON, MINIDOKA, ONEIDA, POWER, TETON, AND TWIN FALLS. Population (2010), 793,109.

ZIP Codes: 83201–06, 83209–15, 83217–18, 83220–21, 83223, 83226–30, 83232–39, 83241, 83243–46, 83250–56, 83261–63, 83271–72, 83274, 83276–78, 83281, 83283, 83285–87, 83301–03, 83311–14, 83316, 83318, 83320–25, 83327–

28, 83330, 83332–38, 83340–44, 83346–50, 83352–55, 83401–06, 83415, 83420–25, 83427–29, 83431, 83433–36, 83438, 83440–46, 83448–52, 83454–55, 83460, 83462–69, 83601–02, 83604, 83623–24, 83627, 83633–34, 83647–48, 83701–09, 83712, 83714–17, 83720–33, 83735, 83744, 83756

ILLINOIS

(Population, 2010 12,830,632)

SENATORS

RICHARD DURBIN, Democrat, of Springfield, IL; born in East St. Louis, IL, November 21, 1944; son of William and Ann Durbin; education: graduated, Assumption High School, East St. Louis; B.S., foreign service and economics, Georgetown University, Washington, DC, 1966; J.D., Georgetown University Law Center, 1969; professional: attorney, admitted to the Illinois Bar in 1969; began practice in Springfield; legal counsel to Lieutenant Governor Paul Simon, 1969–72; legal counsel to Illinois Senate Judiciary Committee, 1972–82; parliamentarian, Illinois Senate, 1969–82; president, New Members Democratic Caucus, 98th Congress; associate professor of medical humanities, Southern Illinois University School of Medicine; elected as Assistant Democratic Leader, 2004; elected as Assistant Majority Leader, 2006; married: the former Loretta Schaefer, 1967; children: Christine, Paul, and Jennifer; committees: Appropriations; Judiciary; Rules and Administration; elected to the 98th Congress, November 2, 1982; reelected to each succeeding Congress; elected to the U.S. Senate on November 5, 1996; reelected to each succeeding Senate term.

Office Listings

http://durbin.senate.gov   facebook.com/senatordurbin   twitter.com/senatordurbin

711 Hart Senate Office Building, Washington, DC 20510	(202) 224–2152
Chief of Staff.—Patrick Souders.	
Legislative Director.—Dena Morris.	TTY: 224–8180
Communications Director.—Ben Marter.	TTY: 228–5244
Director of Scheduling.—Claire Reuschel.	
230 South Dearborn, Kluczynski Building, 38th Floor, Chicago, IL 60604	(312) 353–4952
Chicago Director.—Clarisol Duque.	
525 South Eighth Street, Springfield, IL 62703	(217) 492–4062
State Director.—Bill Houlihan.	
1504 Third Avenue, Suite 227, Rock Island, IL 61201	(309) 786–5173
250 West Cherry Street, Suite 115D, Carbondale, IL 62901	(618) 351–1122

* * *

MARK KIRK, Republican, of Highland Park, IL; born in Champaign, IL, September 15, 1959; education: B.A., Cornell University, Ithaca, NY, 1981; M.S., London School of Economics, London, UK, 1982; J.D., Georgetown University, Washington, DC, 1992; professional: United States Naval Reserve, 1989–2013; staff member, U.S. Representative John Porter, 1984–90; served, World Bank, 1990–91; special assistant, U.S. State Department, 1991–93; attorney, Baker & McKenzie, 1993–95; counsel, House International Relations Committee, 1995–99, elected to the U.S. House of Representatives, 2001–10; awards: Navy and Marine Corps Commendation Medal; Navy Achievement Medal; National Defense Service Medal; Global War on Terror Service Medal; and other various decorations; married: no; children: none; committees: Appropriations; Banking, Housing, and Urban Affairs; Health, Education, Labor, and Pensions; Special Committee on Aging; elected in a special election on November 2, 2010 and sworn-in on November 29, 2010 to the United States Senate to serve the remainder of former Senator Barack Obama's unexpired term; concurrently elected in a general election on November 2, 2010 to the United States Senate for a full six-year term.

Office Listings

http://kirk.senate.gov

524 Hart Senate Office Building, Washington, DC 20510	(202) 224–2854
Chief of Staff.—Kate Dickens.	FAX: 228–4611
Deputy Chief of Staff.—Alissa McCurley.	
Legislative Director.—Jeannette Windon.	
Deputy Scheduler.—Rebecca Glawe.	
230 South Dearborn Street, Suite 3900, Chicago, IL 60604	(312) 886–3506
607 East Adams Street, Suite 1520, Springfield, IL 62701	(217) 492–5089

REPRESENTATIVES

FIRST DISTRICT

BOBBY L. RUSH, Democrat, of Chicago, IL; born in Albany, GA; November 23, 1946; education: attended Marshall High School, Marshall, IL; B.A., Roosevelt University, Chicago, IL, 1974; M.A., University of Illinois, Chicago, IL, 1994; M.A., McCormick Theological Seminary, Chicago, IL, 1998; professional: United States Army, 1963–68; insurance agent; alderman, Chicago, Illinois, city council, 1983–93; deputy chairman, Illinois Democratic Party, 1990; unsuccessful candidate for mayor of Chicago, IL, 1999; minister; married: Carolyn; five children; committees: Energy and Commerce; elected on November 3, 1992 to the 103rd Congress; reelected to each succeeding Congress.

Office Listings

http://www.rush.house.gov

2188 Rayburn House Office Building, Washington, DC 20515	(202) 225–4372
Chief of Staff.—Rev. Stanley Watkins.	FAX: 226–0333
Senior Policy Counsel / Legislative Director.—Yardly Pollas.	
Director of Administration and Operations.—N. Lenette Myers.	
Communications Director.—Debra Johnson.	
700–706 East 79th Street, Chicago, IL 60619	(773) 224–6500
District Director.—Robyn Wheeler Grange.	
3235 West 147th Street, Midlothian, IL 60445	(708) 385–9550
Deputy District Director.—Younus Suleman.	FAX: 385–3860

Counties: COOK COUNTY (part), WILL COUNTY (part). CITIES AND TOWNSHIPS: Bremen Township, Calumet Township, Orland Township, Palos Township, Rich Township, Thornton Township, Worth Township, Will County, Frankfort Township, Green Garden Township, Jackson Township, Manhattan Township, New Lenox Township, Alsip, Blue Island, Calumet Park, Chicago Country, Club Hills, Crestwood, Dixmoor, Elwood, Evergreen Park, Frankfort, Frankfort Square, Harvey, Manhattan, Markham, Merrionette Park, Midlothian, Mokena, New Lenox, Oak Forest, Oak Lawn, Orland Hills, Orland Park, Palos Heights, Posen, Riverdale, Robbins, Tinley Park, and Worth. Population (2012), 711,982.

ZIP Codes: 60406, 60421, 60423, 60426, 60428, 60442, 60445, 60448–49, 60451–53, 60462–64, 60467–69, 60472, 60477–78, 60482, 60487, 60609, 60615–17, 60619–21, 60628–29, 60636–37, 60643, 60649, 60652–53, 60655, 60803, 60805, 60827

* * *

SECOND DISTRICT

ROBIN L. KELLY, Democrat, of Matteson, IL; born in New York, NY, April 30, 1956; education: B.A. in psychology, Bradley University, IL, 1977; M.A., counseling, Bradley University, 1982; Ph.D., political science, Northern Illinois University, IL, 2004; professional: counselor; community affairs director, Matteson, IL, 1992–2006; member, Illinois State House of Representatives, 2003–07; chief of staff, Illinois State Treasurer, 2007–10; chief administrative officer, Cook County, IL, 2010–12; caucuses: member, Congressional Black Caucus; married: Dr. Nathaniel Horn; two children; committees: Foreign Affairs; Oversight and Government Reform; elected to the 113th Congress on April 9, 2013, by special election, to fill the vacancy caused by the resignation of United States Representative Jesse L. Jackson, Jr.; elected to the 114th Congress on November 4, 2014.

Office Listings

http://www.robinkelly.house.gov   www.facebook.com/reprobinkelly
https://twitter.com/reprobinkelly

1239 Longworth House Office Building, Washington, DC 20515	(202) 225–0773
Chief of Staff.—Brandon Garrett.	FAX: 225–4583
Legislative Director.—Brandon Webb.	
Legislative Assistant.—Zachary Ostro.	
Legislative Correspondent.—Jay Cho.	
Director of Advance / Scheduler.—Tony Presta.	
600 Holiday Plaza Drive, Suite 505, Matteson, IL 60443	(708) 679–0078
District Director.—Audra Wilson.	

Counties: COOK (part), KANKAKEE, WILL (part). CITIES AND TOWNSHIPS: Beecher, Blue Island, Bonfield, Bourbonnais, Bradley, Buckingham, Cabery, Calumet City, Chebanse, Chicago, Chicago Heights, Country Club Hills, Crete, Custer Park, Dixmoor, Dolton, Essex, Flossmoor, Ford Heights, Frankfort, Gardner, Glenwood, Grant Park, Harvey, Hazel Crest, Herscher, Homewood, Hopkins Park, Kankakee, Lansing, Lynwood, Manhattan, Manteno, Markham, Matteson, Momence, Monee, Olympia Fields, Park Forest, Pembroke Township, Peotone, Phoenix, Reddick, Richton Park, Riverdale, Saint Anne, Sauk Village, South Chicago Heights, South Holland, Steger, Tinley Park, Thornton, Union Hill, University Park, and Wilmington. Population (2010), 718,507.

ZIP Codes: 60401, 60406, 60409, 60411–12, 60417, 60419, 60422–23, 60425–26, 60428–30, 60438, 60443, 60449, 60461, 60466, 60468, 60471, 60473, 60475–78, 60481, 60484, 60615, 60617, 60628, 60633, 60637, 60649, 60827, 60901, 60913–15, 60917, 60919, 60922, 60935, 60940–42, 60944, 60950, 60954, 60958, 60961, 60964, 60969

* * *

THIRD DISTRICT

DANIEL LIPINSKI, Democrat, of Chicago, IL; born in Chicago, July 15, 1966; son of former Congressman William Lipinski, 1983–2004; education: B.S., mechanical engineering, *magna cum laude*, Northwestern University, 1988; M.S., engineering-economic systems, Stanford University, 1989; Ph.D., political science, Duke University, 1998; professional: aide to United States Representative George Sangmeister, 1993–94; aide to United States Representative Jerry Costello, 1995–96; aide to United States Representative Rod Blagojevich, 1999–2000; professor, James Madison University Washington Program, Washington, DC, 2000; professor, University of Notre Dame, South Bend, IN, 2000–01; professor, University of Tennessee, Knoxville, TN, 2001–04; married: Judy; committees: Science, Space, and Technology; Transportation and Infrastructure; elected to the 109th Congress on November 2, 2004; reelected to each succeeding Congress.

Office Listings

http://www.lipinski.house.gov

2346 Rayburn House Office Building, Washington, DC 20515	(202) 225–5701
Chief of Staff.—Eric Lausten.	FAX: 225–1012
Office Administrative.—Jennifer Sypolt.	
Legislative Director.—Jason Day.	
6245 South Archer Avenue, Chicago, IL 60638	(312) 886–0481
District Chief of Staff.—Jerry Hurckes.	
222 East 9th Street, Suite 109, Lockport, IL 60441	(815) 838–1990
Communications Director.—Isaac Sanchken.	
5309 West 95th Street, Oak Lawn, IL 60453	(708) 424–0853
14700 Ravinia Avenue, 1st Floor, Orland Park, IL 60462	(708) 403–4379

Counties: COOK (part), WILL (PART), DUPAGE (part). CITIES AND TOWNSHIPS: Alsip, Bedford Park, Berwyn, Bridgeview, Brookfield, Burbank, Burr Ridge, Chicago, Chicago Ridge, Cicero, Countryside, Crest Hill, Forest Park, Forest View, Hickory Hills, Hillside, Hinsdale, Homer Glen, Hometown, Hodgkins, Indian Head Park, Justice Burbank, LaGrange, Lemont, Lockport, Lyons, McCook, Merrionette Park, North Riverside, Oak Lawn, Oak Park, Palos Heights, Palos Hills, Palos Park, Proviso, Riverside, Romeoville, Stickney, Summit Brookfield, Western Springs, Willow Springs, and Worth. Population (2012), 704,438.

ZIP Codes: 60402 (part), 60406, 60415, 60432 (part), 60435 (part), 60439 (part), 60441 (part), 60446 (part), 60448 (part), 60451 (part), 60463 (part), 60455, 60456, 60457–58, 60459 (part), 60462 (part), 60463 (part), 60464 (part), 60465, 60467 (part), 60477 (part), 60480 (part), 60482 (part), 60501, 60513 (part), 60521 (part), 60425 (part), 60526 (part), 60534 (part), 60544 (part), 60546 (part), 60558 (part), 60561 (part), 60608 (part), 60609 (part), 60616 (part), 60620 (part), 60629 (part), 60632 (part), 60636 (part), 60638 (part), 60643 (part), 60652 (part), 60655 (part), 60803 (part), 60804 (part), 60805 (part)

* * *

FOURTH DISTRICT

LUIS V. GUTIÉRREZ, Democrat, of Chicago, IL; born in Chicago, December 10, 1953; education: B.A., Northeastern Illinois University, DeKalb, IL, 1974; professional: teacher; social worker, Illinois; state department of children and family services; administrative assistant, Chicago, IL, mayor's office subcommittee on infrastructure, 1984–85; co-founder, West Town-26th Ward Independent Political Organization, 1985; alderman, Chicago, IL, city council, 1986–93, president pro tem, 1989–92; Democratic National Committee, 1984; married: Soraida Arocho; children: Omaira and Jessica; committees: Judiciary; Permanent Select Committee on Intelligence; elected on November 3, 1992, to the 103rd Congress; reelected to each succeeding Congress.

Office Listings

http://www.gutierrez.house.gov

2408 Rayburn House Office Building, Washington, DC 20515	(202) 225–8203
Chief of Staff.—Susan Collins.	FAX: 225–7810
Communications Director.—Douglas Rivlin.	
3210 West North Avenue, Chicago, IL 60647	(773) 342–0774
	FAX: 342–0776

Counties: COOK COUNTY (part). CITIES. Berkeley, Berwyn, Brookfield, Chicago, Cicero, Elmwood Park, Forest Park, Hillside, La Grange Park, Lyons, Maywood, Melrose Park, Northlake, North Riverside, Oak Park, Riverside, Stickney, Stone Park, and Westchester. Population (2012), 724,644.

ZIP Codes: 60126, 60154, 60160, 60162–64, 60304–05, 60402, 60513, 60546, 60608–09, 60616, 60618, 60622–23, 60625, 60629–30, 60632, 60634, 60639, 60641, 60647, 60651, 60707, 60804

* * *

FIFTH DISTRICT

MIKE QUIGLEY, Democrat, of Chicago, IL; born in Indianapolis, October 17, 1958; education: B.A., political science, Roosevelt University, 1981; M.P.P., University of Chicago, 1985; J.D., Loyola University, 1989; professional: Chicago aldermanic aide, 1983–89; practicing attorney, 1990–2009; Cook County Commissioner, 1998–2009; adjunct professor, Roosevelt University, 2006–07; adjunct professor, Loyola University, 2002–09; married: Barbara; children: Meghan and Alyson; committees: Appropriations; Permanent Select Committee on Intelligence; elected to the 111th Congress on April 7, 2009, by special election, to fill the vacancy caused by the resignation of United States Representative Rahm Emanuel; reelected to the 112th Congress on November 2, 2010; reelected to each succeeding Congress.

Office Listings

http://www.quigley.house.gov

2458 Rayburn House Office Building, Washington, DC 20515	(202) 225–4061
Chief of Staff.— Juan Hinojosa.	FAX: 225–5603
Communications Director.—Katie Lewallen.	
Scheduler.—Blaine Nolan.	
Legislative Director.— Joseph Bushong.	
3742 West Irving Park Road, Chicago, IL 60618	(773) 267–5926
	FAX: 267–6583
3223 North Sheffield Avenue, Chicago, IL 60657	(773) 267–5926

Counties: COOK COUNTY (part). Population (2010), 648,610.

ZIP Codes: 60018, 60106, 60126, 60131, 60154, 60160, 60162, 60164, 60171, 60176, 60181, 60191, 60521, 60523, 60525–26, 60559, 60610, 60612–14, 60618, 60622, 60625, 60630–31, 60634, 60640–42, 60645–47, 60656 57, 60659, 60706–07, 60714

* * *

SIXTH DISTRICT

PETER J. ROSKAM, Republican, of Wheaton, IL; born in Hinsdale, IL, September 13, 1961; education: B.A., University of Illinois, Urbana-Champaign, IL, 1983; J.D., Illinois Institute of Technology Chicago-Kent College of Law, Chicago, IL, 1989; professional: lawyer, private practice; staff, United States Representative Tom DeLay of Texas, 1985–86; United States Representative Henry Hyde of Illinois, 1986–87; teacher; businessman; member, Illinois House of Representatives, 1993–99; member, Illinois Senate, 2000–06; married: Elizabeth; children: four; committees: Ways and Means; Select Committee on Benghazi; elected to the 110th Congress on November 7, 2006; reelected to each succeeding Congress.

Office Listings

http://roskam.house.gov

2246 Cannon House Office Building, Washington, DC 20515	(202) 225–4561
Chief of Staff.—David Mork.	FAX: 225–1166
Scheduler.—Amanda Scherb.	
Legislative Director.– David Mork.	
Press Secretary.—Michael Shapiro.	
2700 International Drive, Suite 304, West Chicago, IL 60185	(630) 232–0006

Counties: COOK (part), DUPAGE (part), MCHENRY (part), LAKE (part). CITIES AND TOWNSHIPS: Algonquin, Barrington, Barrington Hills, Bartlett, Carol Stream, Carpentersville, Cary, Clarendon Hills, Crystal Lake, Darien, Deer Park, Downers Grove, Dundee, East Dundee, Elgin, Fox River Grove, Gilberts, Glen Ellyn, Hanover Park, Hawthorne Woods, Hinsdale, Hoffman Estates, Huntley, Inverness, Kildeer, Lake In The Hills, Lakewood, Lake Barrington, Lake Zurich, Lisle, Lombard, Long Grove, Naperville, North Barrington, Oak Brook, Oakwood Hills, Oakbrook Terrace, Palatine, Port Barrington, Rolling Meadows, Saint Charles, Schaumburg, Sleepy Hollow, South Barrington, South Elgin, Tower Lakes, Trout Valley, Warrenville, Wayne, West Chicago, West Dundee, Westmont, Wheaton, Willowbrook, and Winfield. Population (2010) 712,813.

ZIP Codes: 60008, 60010, 60011, 60013, 60014, 60021, 60039, 60047, 60055, 60060, 60067, 60074, 60078, 60094, 60102–03, 60107, 60110, 60118, 60120, 60122–24, 60133, 60136–39, 60142, 60148, 60156, 60169, 60173–75, 60177, 60179, 60181, 60184–85, 60187–90, 60192, 60195, 60197, 60199, 60514–16, 60521, 60523, 60527, 60532, 60540, 60555, 60559, 60561, 60563–65

* * *

SEVENTH DISTRICT

DANNY K. DAVIS, Democrat, of Chicago, IL; born in Parkdale, AR, September 6, 1941; education: B.A., Arkansas AM&N College, 1961; M.A., Chicago State University; Ph.D., Union Institute, Cincinnati, OH; educator and health planner-administrator; board of directors, National Housing Partnership; Cook County Board of Commissioners, 1990–96; former alderman of the Chicago City Council's 29th Ward, receiving the Independent Voters of Illinois "Best Alderman Award" for 1980–81, 1981–82, and 1989–90; co-chair, Clinton-Gore-Braun '92; founder and past president, Westside Association for Community Action; past president, National Association of Community Health Centers; 1987 recipient of the Leon M. Despres Award; married to Vera G. Davis; two sons: Jonathan and Stacey; committees: Ways and Means; elected to the 105th Congress; reelected to each succeeding Congress.

Office Listings

http://www.davis.house.gov

2159 Rayburn House Office Building, Washington, DC 20515 .... (202) 225–5006
Chief of Staff.—Yul Edwards.   FAX: 225–5641
Deputy Chief of Staff.—Jill Hunter-Williams.
Director of Issues and Communications.—Ira Cohen.
2746 West Madison Street, Chicago, IL 60612 .... (773) 533–7520

Counties: COOK. CITIES AND TOWNSHIPS: Berwyn, Chicago, Oak Park, Proviso, River Forest and Riverside. Population (2010), 712,812.

ZIP Codes: 60104, 60130, 60141, 60153–55, 60160, 60162–63, 60301–12, 60614–16, 60621–24, 60629, 60632, 60636–37, 60639, 60642, 60644, 60651, 60653–54, 60661, 60707, 60804

* * *

EIGHTH DISTRICT

TAMMY DUCKWORTH, Democrat, of Hoffman Estates, IL, born in Bangkok; education: B.A., political science, University of Hawaii, 1989; M.A., George Washington University, DC, 1992; Ph.D., in Human Services at Capella University, 2014; professional: Rotary International; Illinois Department of Veterans Affairs; U.S. Department of Veterans Affairs; military: Lt. Colonel, Illinois National Guard; Combat Veteran, Operation Iraqi Freedom; married: Bryan Bowlsbey; committees: Armed Services; Oversight and Government Reform; Select Committee on Benghazi; elected to the 113th Congress on November 6, 2012; reelected to the 114th Congress on November 4, 2014.

Office Listings

http://Duckworth.house.gov   https://twitter.com/repduckworth
https://www.facebook.com/congresswomantammyduckworth
https://flickr.com/photos/tammyduckworth/show
https://youtube.com/user/repduckworth   https://instagram.com/repduckworth

104 Cannon House Office Building, Washington, DC 20515 .... (202) 225–3711
Chief of Staff.—Kalina Bakalov.   FAX: 225–7830
1701 East Woodfield Road, Suite 704, Schaumburg, IL 60173 .... (847) 413–1959
District Director.—Sendy Soto.   FAX: 413–1965

Counties: COOK COUNTY (part). TOWNSHIPS: Arlington Heights, Barrington Hills, Buffalo Grove, Chicago (part), Des Plaines, Elk Grove, Hoffman Estates, Mount Prospect, Palatine, Rolling Meadows, Rosemont, Schaumburg, Streamwood, and Wheeling. DUPAGE COUNTY (part). TOWNSHIPS: Addison, Bartlett, Bensenville, Bloomingdale, Carol Stream, Elmhurst, Glen Ellyn, Glendale, Hanover Park, Itasca, Lombard, Oak Brook, Oakbrook Terrace, Roselle, Villa Park, and Wheaton. KANE COUNTY (part). TOWNSHIPS: Algonquin, Carpentersville, East Dundee, and Elgin. Population (2010), 726,418.

ZIP Codes: 60004–05, 60007–10, 60016, 60018, 60038, 60056, 60067, 60074, 60089–90, 60101–103, 60106–108, 60110, 60116–118, 60120–21, 60123–24, 60126, 60131–33, 60137, 60139, 60143, 60148, 60157, 60168–70, 60172–173, 60177, 60179, 60181, 60187–188, 60191–195, 60399, 60523

* * *

NINTH DISTRICT

JANICE D. SCHAKOWSKY, Democrat, of Evanston, IL; born in Chicago, IL, May 26, 1944; education: B.A., University of Illinois, 1965; consumer advocate; program director, Illinois Public Action; executive director, Illinois State Council of Senior Citizens, 1985–90; State Representative, 18th District, Illinois General Assembly, 1991–99; served on Labor and Commerce, Human Service Appropriations, Health Care, and Electric Deregulation Committees; religion: Jewish; married: Robert Creamer; children: Ian, Mary, and Lauren; committees: Energy and Commerce; elected to the 106th Congress; reelected to each succeeding Congress.

Office Listings

http://www.schakowsky.house.gov

2367 Rayburn House Office Building, Washington, DC 20515	(202) 225–2111
Chief of Staff.—Cathy Hurwit.	FAX: 226–6890
Communications Director.—Lee Whack.	
Legislative Director.—Brian Laughlin.	
Appointments Secretary.—Kim Muzeroll.	
5533 Broadway, Chicago, IL 60640	(773) 506–7100
District Director.—Leslie Combs.	
1852 Johns Drive, Glenview, IL 60025	(847) 328–3409

Counties: COOK COUNTY (part). CITIES: Arlington Heights, Chicago, Des Plaines, Evanston, Glenview, Golf, Kenilworth, Lincolnwood, Morton Grove, Mount Prospect, Niles, Northbrook, Northfield, Park Ridge, Prospect Heights, Skokie, Wheeling, Wilmette, and Winnetka. Population (2010), 712,813.

ZIP Codes: 60004–05, 60016, 60018–19, 60025–26, 60029, 60043, 60053, 60056, 60062, 60068, 60070, 60076–77, 60090–91, 60093, 60176, 60201–03, 60613, 60626, 60630, 60640, 60645–46, 60656–57, 60659–60, 60706, 60712, 60714

* * *

TENTH DISTRICT

ROBERT J. DOLD, Republican, of Kenilworth, IL; born in Evanston, IL, June 23, 1969; education: New Trier High School, Winnetka, IL, 1987; B.A., Denison University, Granville, Ohio, 1991; J.D., Indiana University, Bloomington, IN, 1996; M.B.A., Kellogg School of Management, Evanston, IL, 2000; professional: business owner; staff, United States Vice President James Danforth Quayle, 1991–93; staff, United States House of Representatives Committee on Reform and Oversight, 1997–99; elected to represent the 10th District of Illinois in the 112th Congress; unsuccessful candidate for reelection to the 113th Congress in 2012; family: wife, Danielle; children: Harper, Bobby, and Honor; committees: Ways and Means; elected to the 114th Congress on November 4, 2014.

Office Listings

http://dold.house.gov

221 Cannon House Office Building, Washington, DC 20515	(202) 225–4835
Chief of Staff.—James Slepian.	FAX: 225–0837
300 Village Green, Suite 335, Lincolnshire, IL 60069	(847) 793 8400
442 North Cedar Lake Road, Round Lake, IL 60073	(847) 309–6627
District Director.—Philippe Melin.	FAX: 793–8449

Counties: COOK (part), LAKE (part). Population (2010), 709,209.

ZIP Codes: 60004, 60015–16, 60020, 60022, 60025–26, 60030–31, 60035, 60037, 60040–41, 60044–48, 60050–51, 60053, 60056, 60060–62, 60064, 60068–70, 60073, 60081, 60083, 60085, 60087–90, 60093, 60096, 60099, 60714

* * *

ELEVENTH DISTRICT

BILL FOSTER, Democrat, of Naperville, IL; born in Madison, WI, October 7, 1955; education: B.S., University of Wisconsin-Madison, 1976; Ph.D., Harvard University, 1983; professional: small business owner, physicist; committees: Financial Services; Science, Space, and

Technology; elected to the 113th Congress on November 6, 2012; reelected to the 114th Congress on November 4, 2014.

Office Listings

http://www.foster.house.gov   https://twitter.com/repbillfoster
https://www.facebook.com/congressmanbillfoster?ref=hl

1224 Longworth House Office Building, Washington, DC 20515	(202) 225–3515
Chief of Staff.—Adam Elias.	FAX: 225–9420
2711 East New York Street, Suite 204, Aurora, IL 60502	(630) 585–7672
195 Springfield Avenue, Suite 102, Joliet, IL 60435	(815) 280–5876
District Director.—Carole Cheney.	

Counties: COOK (part), DUPAGE (part), KANE (part), KENDALL (part), AND WILL (part). Population (2010), 722,173.

ZIP Codes: 60403–04, 60410, 60421, 60431–36, 60439–42, 60446–48, 60451, 60480, 60490, 60502–06, 60512, 60515–17, 60519, 60525, 60527, 60532, 60538, 60540, 60542–44, 60559–65, 60586

* * *

TWELFTH DISTRICT

MIKE BOST, Republican, of Murphysboro, IL; born in Murphysboro, IL, December 30, 1960; education: University of Illinois Certified Firefighter II Academy; professional: state representative, small business owner, firefighter; military: United States Marine Corps, 1979–82; religion: Christian, Non-Denominational; married: Tracy Stanton, 1980; children: Steven, Kasey, and Kaitlin; committees: Agriculture, Transportation and Infrastructure; Veterans' Affairs; elected to the 114th Congress on November 4, 2014.

Office Listings

http://www.bost.house.gov   http://www.twitter.com/repbost   http://www.facebook.com/repbost

1440 Longworth House Office Building, Washington, DC 20515	(202) 225–5661
Chief of Staff.—Matt McCullough.	FAX: 225–0285
Scheduler.—Kimberly Powell.	
Legislative Director.—Mark Ratto.	
Communications Director.—Jim Forbes.	
District Director.—Matt Rice.	
23 Public Square, Suite 404, Belleville, IL 62220	(618) 233–8026
	FAX: 233–8765
300 East Main Street, Suite 4, Carbondale, IL 62901	(618) 457–5787
	FAX: 457–2990
1100 Main Street, Mt. Vernon, IL 62864	618) 826–3043

Counties: ALEXANDER, FRANKLIN, JACKSON, JEFFERSON, MADISON (part), MONROE, PERRY, PULASKI, RANDOLPH, ST. CLAIR, UNION, AND WILLIAMSON. Population (2010), 712,813.

ZIP Codes: 62002, 62010, 62018, 62024–25, 62035, 62040, 62048, 62059–60, 62067, 62084, 62087, 62090, 62095, 62201, 62203–08, 62217, 62220–21, 62223, 62225–26, 62232–34, 62236–44, 62248, 62254–55, 62257–58, 62260–61, 62263–65, 62268–69, 62272, 62274, 62277–80, 62282, 62285–86, 62288–89, 62292–95, 62297–98, 62801, 62808, 62810, 62812, 62814, 62816, 62819, 62822, 62825, 62830–32, 62836, 62841, 62846, 62851, 62856, 62860, 62864–65, 62872, 62874, 62877, 62883–84, 62888–91, 62893–94, 62896–98, 62901–03, 62905–07, 62912, 62914–18, 62920–24, 62926–27, 62932–33, 62939–42, 62948–52, 62956–59, 62961–64, 62966, 62969–70, 62974–76, 62983, 62987–88, 62990, 62992, 62994, 62996–99

* * *

THIRTEENTH DISTRICT

RODNEY DAVIS, Republican, of Taylorville, IL; born in Des Moines, IA, January 5, 1970; education: graduated from Taylorville High School, 1988; B.A., Millikin University, IL, 1992; professional: congressional aide, 1999–2012; has served on numerous local civic and community organizations and groups; religion: Catholic; married: Shannon R. Davis; children: Toryn, Clark, and Griffin; committees: Agriculture; House Administration; Transportation and Infrastructure; elected to the 113th Congress on November 6, 2012; reelected to the 114th Congress on November 4, 2014.

Office Listings

http://www.rodneydavis.house.gov   https://www.facebook.com/reprodneydavis
twitter.com/rodneydavis

1740 Longworth House Office Building, Washington, DC 20515	(202) 225–2371
Chief of Staff.—Jen Daulby.	
Legislative Director.—Bobby Frederick.	
Scheduler.—Brittany Randall.	
Communications Director.—Ashley Phelps.	
243 South Water Street, Suite 100, Decatur, IL 62523	(217) 791–6224
District Director.—Helen Albert.	
2004 Fox Drive, Champaign, IL 61820	(217) 403–4690
2833 South Grand Avenue East, Springfield, IL 62703	(217) 791–6224
104 West North Street, Normal, IL 61761	(309) 252–8834
108 East Market Street, Taylorville, IL 62568	(217) 824–5117
9 Junction Drive, Suite 9, Glen Carbon, IL 62034	(618) 205–8660

Counties: BOND (part), CALHOUN, CHAMPAIGN (part), CHRISTIAN, DEWITT, GREENE, JERSEY, MACON, MACOUPIN, MADISON (part), MCLEAN (part), MONTGOMERY, PIATT, SANGAMON (part). Population (2010), 710,784.

ZIP Codes: 60481, 61252, 61701–02, 61704–05, 61709–10, 61727, 61735, 61745, 61749, 61756, 61761, 61772, 61777–78, 61790–91, 61799, 61801–03, 61813, 61815, 61818, 61820–22, 61824, 61826, 61830, 61839, 61842, 61854–56, 61864, 61872, 61874, 61880, 61882, 61884, 61913, 61929, 61936, 62002, 62006, 62009, 62013–17, 61719, 61721–23, 61725–28, 62031–37, 62044–45, 62049–54, 62056, 62058, 62060, 62062–63, 62065, 62069–70, 62074–77, 62079, 62081–83, 62086, 62088–89, 62091–94, 62097, 62234, 62262, 62355, 62501, 62510, 62513, 62517, 62521–26, 62531, 62533, 62535, 62538, 62540, 62544–47, 62549–51, 62554–58, 62560, 62563, 62567–68, 62570, 62572–73, 62626, 62629–30, 62640, 62649, 62667, 62670, 62672, 62674, 62685–86, 62690, 62701–04, 62707, 62711–12

* * *

FOURTEENTH DISTRICT

RANDY HULTGREN, Republican, of Plano, IL; born in Park Ridge, IL, March 1, 1966; education: graduated, B.A., Bethel College, 1988; J.D., Chicago-Kent College of Law, 1993; professional: elected to the DuPage County Board and county Forest Preserve Board, 1994; elected to the Illinois House of Representatives, 1999, elected to the Illinois State Senate, 2007; married: wife, Christy; four children; committees: Financial Services; Science, Space, and Technology; elected to the 112th Congress on November 2, 2010; reelected to each succeeding Congress.

Office Listings

http://hultgren.house.gov   facebook.com/rephultgren   twitter: @rephultgren

2455 Rayburn House Office Building, Washington, DC 20515	(202) 225–2976
Chief of Staff.—Katherine McGuire.	FAX: 225–0697
Deputy Chief of Staff,—Doug Thomas.	
Communications Director.—Jameson Cunningham.	
Special Projects / Office Manager.—Brandon McKee.	
Legislative Assistants: Andrew Mooney, Elise Tollefson.	
Legislative Aide.—Gina Gregolunas.	
Executive Assistant / Scheduler.—Katie Hunt.	
40W310 Lafox Road, Suite F2, Campton Hills, IL 60175	(630) 584–2734
District Director.—David Carlin.	FAX: 584–2746
Deputy District Director.—Beth Goncher.	
Coalitions Director.—Susan Russell.	
Senior Field Representative.—Nick Provenzano.	
Constituent Services: Carol Berger, Ruth Richardson.	
Staff Assistant.—Austin Frank.	

Counties: DEKALB (part), DUPAGE (part), KANE (part), KENDALL (part), LAKE (part), MCHENRY (part), AND WILL (part). CITIES AND TOWNSHIPS: Alden, Algonquin, Antioch, Aurora, Batavia, Beach Park, Big Grove, Big Rock, Blackberry, Bolingbrook, Boulder Hill, Bristol, Bull Valley, Burlington, Burton, Campton, Campton Hills, Channahon, Channel Lake, Chemung, Coral, Cortland, Crystal Lake, DeKalb, Dorr, Dunham, Elburn, Elgin, Fox, Fox Lake Hills, Fox Lake, Fremont, Geneva, Grafton, Grandwood Park, Greenwood, Gurnee, Hampshire, Hartland, Harvard, Hawthorn Woods, Hebron, Hinckley, Holiday Hills, Huntley, Island Lake, Johnsburg, Joliet, Kaneville, Kendall, Lake Barrington, Lake Catherine, Lake in the Hills, Lake Villa, Lakemoor, Lakewood, Lily Lake, Lindenhurst, Lisbon, Little Rock, Maple Park, Marengo, McCullom Lake, McHenry, Millbrook, Millington, Minooka, Montgomery, Mundelein, Na-Au-Say, Naperville, Newark, Newport, North Aurora, North Barrington, Nunda, Oakwood Hills, Old Mill Creek, Oswego, Pierce, Pingree Grove, Pistakee Highlands, Pittsfield, Plainfield, Plano, Plato, Plattville, Port Barrington, Prairie Grove, Prestbury, Richmond, Riley, Ringwood, Romeoville, Rutland, Sandwich, Seneca, Seward, Shorewood, Somonauk, Spring Grove, Squaw Grove, St. Charles, Sugar Grove, Sycamore, Troy, Union, Virgil, Volo, Wadsworth, Warren, Warrenville, Wauconda, Waukegan, West Chicago, Wheatland, Winfield, Wonder Lake, Woodstock, and Yorkville. Population (2010), 721,774.

ZIP Codes: 60001–02, 60010, 60012–14, 60020, 60030–31, 60033–34, 60042, 60046–48, 60050–51, 60060, 60071–73, 60075, 60081, 60083–84, 60087, 60097–99, 60102, 60109, 60112, 60115, 60119, 60124, 60134–36, 60140, 60142,

60144, 60147, 60151–52, 60156, 60174–75, 60178, 60180, 60183, 60185–86, 60189–90, 60404, 60410, 60431, 60447, 60450, 60490, 60502–03, 60506, 60510–12, 60520, 60536–39, 60541–45, 60548, 60552, 60554–56, 60560, 60563– 65, 60585, 61012, 61038

* * *

FIFTEENTH DISTRICT

JOHN SHIMKUS, Republican, of Collinsville, IL; born in Collinsville, February 21, 1958; education: graduated from Collinsville High School; B.S., United States Military Academy, West Point, NY, 1980; teaching certificate, Christ College, Irvine, CA, 1990; M.B.A., Southern Illinois University, Edwardsville, 1997; U.S. Army, 1980–85; Reserves, 1985–2008; government and history teacher, Metro East Lutheran High School, Edwardsville, IL; Collinsville township trustee, 1989; Madison county treasurer, 1990–96; married: the former Karen Muth, 1987; children: David, Daniel, and Joshua; committees: Energy and Commerce; elected to the 105th Congress; reelected to each succeeding Congress.

Office Listings

http://www.shimkus.house.gov   https://www.facebook.com/repshimkus
https://twitter.com/repshimkus

2217 Rayburn House Office Building, Washington, DC 20515	(202) 225–5271
Chief of Staff.—Craig Roberts.	FAX: 225–5880
Legislative Director / Deputy Chief of Staff.—Greta Joynes.	
15 Professional Park Drive, Maryville, IL 62062	(217) 492–5090
District Director.—Deb Detmers.	
101 North 4th Street, Suite 303, Effingham, IL 62401	(618) 532–9676
201 North Vermillion Street, Suite 218, Danville, IL 61832	(217) 446–0664
110 East Locust Street, Room 12, Harrisburg, IL 62946	(618) 252–8271

Counties: BOND, CHAMPAIGN, CLARK, CLAY, COLES, CRAWFORD, CUMBERLAND, DOUGLAS (part), EDGAR, EDWARDS, EFFINGHAM, FAYETTE, FORD, GALLATIN, HAMILTON, HARDIN, JASPER, JOHNSON, LAWRENCE, MADISON (part), MARION, MASSAC, MOULTRIE, POPE, RICHLAND, SALINE (part), SHELBY, VERMILLION, WABASH, WASHINGTON, WAYNE, AND WHITE. Population (2010), 712,813.

ZIP Codes: 60932–33, 60936 (part), 60942 (part), 60949, 60957, 60960, 60963, 61802 (part), 61810–11, 61814, 61816– 17, 61822 (part), 61832–34, 61840–41, 61843–44, 61845 (part), 61846–50, 61852, 61853 (part), 61857–59, 61863 (part), 61864 (part), 61865–66, 61870–73, 61875 (part), 61876–78, 61880 (part), 61883, 61910–12, 61913 (part), 61914 (part), 61917, 61919–20, 61924, 61925 (part), 61928, 61929 (part), 61930–33, 61937 (part), 61938, 61940–44, 61949, 61951, 61953, 61955–57, 62001 (part), 62002, 62011–12, 62025 (part), 62032 (part), 62034 (part), 62035, 62040, 62046, 62061–62, 62074 (part), 62075 (part), 62080 (part), 62086 (part), 62097 (part), 62214, 62231–32, 62234 (part), 62237 (part), 62246 (part), 62249, 62253, 62255 (part), 62257 (part), 62262 (part), 62263, 62265 (part), 62266, 62268 (part), 62271, 62273, 62275, 62281 (part), 62284 (part), 62292, 62293 (part), 62294 (part), 62401, 62410–11, 62414, 62417–22, 62424, 62426–28, 62431–33, 62435–36, 62439–43, 62445–52, 62454, 62458–68, 62471, 62473–76, 62479– 81, 62510 (part), 62534, 62544 (part), 62550 (part), 62553 (part), 62557 (part), 62565, 62571, 62801 (part), 62803, 62806–07, 62808 (part), 62809, 62810 (part), 62811, 62814 (part), 62815, 62817–18, 62820–21, 62823–24, 62827– 28, 62830 (part), 62831 (part), 62835, 62836 (part), 62837–39, 62842–44, 62848–50, 62851 (part), 62852–54, 62858– 59, 62860 (part), 62861–63, 62875–76, 62877 (part), 62879–82, 62886–87, 62889 (part), 62890 (part), 62892, 62893 (part), 62895, 62899 (part), 62908, 62910 (part), 62912 (part), 62917 (part), 62919, 62922 (part), 62923 (part), 62928, 62930–31, 62934–35, 62938, 62939 (part), 62941 (part), 62946, 62953–54, 62956 (part), 62960, 62965, 62967, 62977, 62979, 62982, 62984–85, 62987 (part), 62995

* * *

SIXTEENTH DISTRICT

ADAM KINZINGER, Republican, of Channahon, IL; born in Kankakee, IL, February 27, 1978; education: graduated, Normal Community West High School, 1996; B.S., Illinois State University, 2000; professional: McLean County Board, 1998–2003; Sales Representative, STL Technologies, 2000–03; United States Air National Guard, 2003–present, current rank: Major; religion: Protestant; single; Deputy Republican Whip; committees: Energy and Commerce; elected to the 112th Congress on November 2, 2010; reelected to each succeeding Congress.

Office Listings

http://www.kinzinger.house.gov

1221 Longworth House Office Building, Washington, DC 20515	(202) 225–3635
Chief of Staff.—Austin Weatherford.	
628 Columbus Street, Suite 507, Ottawa, IL 61350	(815) 431–9271
District Director.—Bonnie Walsh.	
Deputy District Director.—Reed Wilson.	
Legislative Director.—Jash Baggett.	
Communications Director.—Catherine Gatewood.	

Counties: BOONE, BUREAU, DEKALB (part), FORD (part), GRUNDY, IROQUOIS, LASALLE, LEE, LIVINGSTON, OGLE, PUTNAM, STARK (part), WILL (part), AND WINNEBAGO (part). Population (2010), 712,813.

ZIP Codes: 60033, 60111, 60113, 60115, 60129, 60135, 60140, 60145–46, 60150, 60152, 60178, 60407–08, 60410, 60416, 60420–21, 60424, 60437, 60444, 60447, 60450, 60460, 60470, 60474, 60479, 60481, 60518, 60530–31, 60537, 60541, 60548–53, 60556–57, 60911–12, 60917–22, 60924, 60926–31, 60934–36, 60938–39, 60941–42, 60945–46, 60948, 60950–53, 60955–56, 60958–62, 60964, 60966–68, 60970, 60973–74, 61006–08, 61010–12, 61015–16, 61019–21, 61024, 61030–31, 61038–39, 61042–43, 61047, 61049, 61051–52, 61054, 61057, 61061, 61063–65, 61068, 61071–73, 61078–81, 61084, 61088, 61091, 61101–04, 61107–09, 61111–12, 61114–15, 61126, 61130–32, 61243, 61283, 61301, 61310–38, 61340–42, 61344–46, 61348–50, 61353–54, 61356, 61358–64, 61367–68, 61370–74, 61376–79, 61421, 61443, 61560, 61726, 61731, 61739–41, 61743–44, 61764, 61769, 61773, 61775, 61845

* * *

SEVENTEENTH DISTRICT

CHERI BUSTOS, Democrat, of East Moline, IL; born in Springfield, IL, October 17, 1960; education: graduated B.A., University of Maryland, College Park, MD, 1983; M.A., University of Illinois at Springfield, 1985; religion: Roman Catholic; married: Gerry; children: Tony, Nick, and Joseph; committees: Agriculture; Transportation and Infrastructure; elected to the 113th Congress on November 6, 2012; reelected to the 114th Congress on November 4, 2014.

Office Listings

http://bustos.house.gov   twitter: @repcheri
facebook: rep.cheribustos

1009 Longworth House Office Building, Washington, DC 20515	(202) 225–5905

Chief of Staff.—Jon Pyatt.
Legislative Director.—Todd Wolf
Communications Director.—Colin Milligan.
Scheduler.—Vacant.
Legislative Assistants: Lyron Blum-Evitts, Alex Hadley, Jonathan Tauberg.
Legislative Correspondent.—Steffanie Bezruki.
Staff Assistant.—Kyle Morse.

2401 4th Avenue, Rock Island, IL 61201	(309) 786–3406

District Director.—Chris Shallow.
Constituent Advocates: Miranda French, Laura Glessing, Lucie VanHecke.
Events Coordinator.—Kerry Myers.

3100 North Knoxville Avenue, Suite 205, Peoria, IL 61603	(309) 966–1813

Constituent Advocates: Andrew Colgan, Laura Glessing.

119 North Church Street, Suites 207 and 208, Rockford, IL 61101	(815) 968–8011

Outreach Director.—Alexander Finke.
Constituent Advocate.—Catherine Gray.

Counties: CARROLL, FULTON, HENDERSON, HENRY, JO DAVIESS, KNOX, MERCER, PEORIA (part), ROCK ISLAND, STEPHENSON, TAZEWELL (part), WARREN, WHITESIDE, AND WINNEBAGO (part). Population (2010), 712,813.

ZIP Codes: 61001, 61007, 61013–14, 61018–20, 61025, 61027–28, 61032, 61036–37, 61039, 61041, 61044, 61046–48, 61050–51, 61053, 61059–60, 61062–64, 61067, 61070 71, 61074–75, 61077–78, 61081, 61084–85, 61087–89, 61101–10, 61125, 61201, 61204, 61230–44, 61250–52, 61254, 61256–66, 61270, 61272–79, 61281–85, 61299, 61344, 61361, 61401–02, 61410, 61412–15, 61417–19, 61422–23, 61425, 61427–28, 61430–37, 61439, 61441–43, 61447–50, 61453–54, 61458–60, 61462, 61465–78, 61480, 61482, 61484–86, 61488–90, 61501, 61519–20, 61524, 61529, 61531, 61533–34, 61536, 61539, 61542–47, 61553–55, 61558, 61563–64, 61569, 61572, 61601–07, 61610–11, 61613–16, 61625, 61629–30, 61633–34, 61636–37, 61641, 61650–56, 62330, 62644

* * *

EIGHTEENTH DISTRICT

DARIN LAHOOD, Republican, of Peoria, IL; born in Peoria, July 5, 1968; B.A. Loras College, Dubuque, IA, 1990; Juris Doctorate, John Marshall Law School, 1997; professional: Illinois State Senate, 2011–15; Miller, Hall, & Triggs, 2006–15; Assistant United States Attorney, 2001–06; religion: Roman Catholic; married: Kristen; children: McKay, Lucas, Teddy; committees: Natural Resources; Science, Space, and Technology; elected by special election to the 114th Congress on September 10, 2015, to fill the vacancy caused by the resignation of United States Representative Aaron Schock.

Office Listings

http://www.lahood.house.gov   http://www.facebook.com/replahood
http://www.twitter.com/replahood

2464 Rayburn House Office Building, Washington, DC 20515	(202) 225–6201

Chief of Staff.—Steven Pfrang.   FAX: 225–9249
Legislative Director.—Ashley Antoskiewicz.
Scheduler.—Jonathan Skarzynski.
Legislative Assistant.—Mary Ellen Richardson.
Legislative Correspondent.—Keelin McGee.
Staff Assistant.—Samantha Dybas.
100 Northeast Monroe Street, Peoria, IL 61602 .... (309) 271–7027
District Director.—Brad Stotler.
Communications Director.—JD Dalfonso.
Office Manager.—Sheila Sader.
Military Affairs Advisor.—Michael Gilmore.
Constituent Service Representatives: Lester Davis, Autum Greeson.
Staff Assistant.—Tanner Schutte.
201 West Morgan Street, Jacksonville, IL 62650 .... (309) 245–1431
Constituent Service Representative.—Barb Baker.
235 South 6th Street, Springfield, IL 62701 .... (217) 670–1653

INDIANA

(Population 2010, 6,483,802)

SENATORS

DANIEL COATS, Republican, of Indianapolis, IN; born in Jackson, MI, May 16, 1943; education: B.A., Wheaton College, Wheaton, IL, 1965; J.D., Indiana University, Indianapolis, IN, 1971; professional: served in the United States Army, 1966–68; U.S. House of Representatives, 1981–89; U.S. Senate, 1989–98; U.S. Ambassador to the Federal Republic of Germany, 2001–05; religion: Presbyterian (P.C.A.); married: Marsha Crawford, 1965; three children; ten grandchildren; committees: Finance; Joint Economic Committee; Select Committee on Intelligence; elected to the U.S. Senate on November 2, 2010.

Office Listings

http://coats.senate.gov   twitter: @sendancoats

493 Russell Senate Office Building, Washington, DC 20510	(202) 224–5623
Chief of Staff.—Dean Hingson.	FAX: 228–1820
Legislative Director.—Viraj Mirani.	
Communications Director.—Matt Lahr.	
Scheduler.—Stephanie Eastman.	
11035 Broadway, Suite A, Crown Point, IN 46307	(219) 663–2595
	FAX: 663–4586
101 Martin Luther King, Jr. Boulevard, Evansville, IN 47708	(812) 465–6500
	FAX: 465–6503
1300 South Harrison Street, Suite 3161, Ft. Wayne, IN 46802	(260) 426–3151
	FAX: 420–0060
1650 Market Tower, 10 West Market Street, Indianapolis, IN 46204	(317) 554–0750
	FAX: 554–0760
2 East McClain Avenue, Suite 2–A, Scottsburg, IN 47170	(812) 754–0520
	FAX: 754–0539

* * *

JOSEPH S. DONNELLY, Democrat, of Granger, IN; born in Queens, NY, September 29, 1955; education: graduated, B.A., University of Notre Dame, Notre Dame, IN, 1977; J.D., University of Notre Dame, Notre Dame, IN, 1981; religion: Roman Catholic; married: Jill Truitt, 1979; two children; committees: Agriculture, Nutrition and Forestry; Armed Services; Banking, Housing, and Urban Affairs; Special Committee on Aging; elected to the U.S. Senate on November 6, 2012.

Office Listings

http://www.donnelly.senate.gov   https://www.facebook.com/senatordonnelly
twitter.com/sendonnelly

720 Hart Senate Office Building, Washington, DC 20510	(202) 224–4814
Chief of Staff.—Joel Elliott.	FAX: 224–5011
Scheduler.—Lynn Demos.	
Legislative Director.—Andrew Lattanner.	
Communications Director.—Elizabeth Shappell.	
115 North Pennsylvania Street, Suite 100, Indianapolis, IN 46204	(317) 226–5555
205 West Colfax Avenue, South Bend, IN 46601	(574) 288–2780
5400 Federal Plaza, Suite 3200, Hammond, IN 46320	(219) 852–0089
123 Northwest 4th Street, Suite 417, Evansville, IN 47708	(812) 425–5862
702 North Shore Drive, Suite LL–101, Jeffersonville, IN 47130	(812) 284–2027
203 East Berry Street, Suite 702B, Fort Wayne, IN 46802	(260) 420–4955

REPRESENTATIVES

FIRST DISTRICT

PETER J. VISCLOSKY, Democrat, of Merrillville, IN; born in Gary, IN, August 13, 1949; education: graduated, Andrean High School, Merrillville, 1967; B.S., accounting, Indiana University Northwest, Gary, 1970; J.D., University of Notre Dame Law School, Notre Dame, IN, 1973; LL.M., international and comparative law, Georgetown University Law Center, Washington, DC, 1982; professional: attorney; admitted to the Indiana State Bar, 1974, the

District of Columbia Bar, 1978, and the U.S. Supreme Court Bar, 1980; associate staff, U.S. House of Representatives, Committee on Appropriations, 1977–80, Committee on the Budget, 1980–82; practicing attorney, Merrillville law firm, 1983–84; wife: Joanne Royce; children: John Daniel and Timothy Patrick; committees: Appropriations; elected to the 99th Congress on November 6, 1984; reelected to each succeeding Congress.

Office Listings

http://www.visclosky.house.gov   twitter: @repvisclosky

2328 Rayburn House Office Building, Washington, DC 20515 .... (202) 225–2461
    Chief of Staff.—Mark Lopez.   FAX: 225–2493
    Deputy Chief of Staff.—Joe DeVooght.
    Executive Assistant.—Korry Baack.
    Communications Director.—Celina Weatherwax.
7895 Broadway, Suite A, Merrillville, IN 46410 .... (219) 795–1844
    District Directors: Gregory Gulvas, Elizabeth Johnson.   FAX: 795–1850
                                                              (888) 423–7383

Counties: LAKE, LAPORTE (part), PORTER. Population (2010), 720,422.

ZIP Codes: 46301–04, 46307–08, 46310–12, 46319–25, 46327, 46341–42, 46345, 46347–49, 46350, 46355–56, 46360, 46368, 46373, 46375–77, 46379–85, 46390, 46392–94, 46401–11

* * *

SECOND DISTRICT

JACKIE WALORSKI, Republican, of Elkhart, IN; born in South Bend, IN, August 17, 1963; education: B.A., major: communications, Taylor University, Upland, IN, 1985; professional: served in the Indiana General Assembly from 2005–10; religion: Christian; married: Dean; committees: Agriculture; Armed Services; Veterans' Affairs; elected to the 113th Congress on November 6, 2012; reelected to the 114th Congress on November 4, 2014.

Office Listings

http://walorksi.house.gov   https://www.facebook.com/repjackiewalorski
https://twitter.com/repwalorski

419 Cannon House Office Building, Washington, DC 20515 .... (202) 225–3915
    Chief of Staff.—Brendon DelToro.   FAX: 225–6798
    Legislative Director.—Stephen Davis.
    Scheduler.—Emily Daniels.
    Communications Director.—Lindsay Jancek.
202 Lincolnway East, Sutie 101, Mishawaka, IN 46544 .... (574) 204–2645
709 Main Street, Rochester, IN 46975 .... (574) 780–1330

Counties: ELKHART, FULTON, KOSCIUSKO (part), LAPORTE (part), MARSHALL, MIAMI, PULASKI, ST. JOSEPH, STARKE, AND WABASH. CITIES: Elkhart, Goshen, Knox, La Porte, Mishawaka, Peru, Plymouth, Rochester, South Bend, Syracuse, Wabash and Winamac. Population (2010), 718,237.

ZIP Codes: 46340, 46345–46, 46348, 46350, 46352, 46365–66, 46374, 46382, 46501–02, 46504, 46506–08, 46510–11, 46513–17, 46524, 46526–28, 46530–32, 46534, 46536–39, 46540, 46542–46, 46550, 46552–56, 46561, 46563, 46565, 46567, 46570, 46572–74, 46580, 46582, 46595, 46601, 46613–17, 46619, 46624, 46626, 46628, 46634–35, 46637, 46660, 46680, 46702, 46732, 46750, 46767, 46787, 46901, 46910–12, 46914, 46919, 46921–22, 46926, 46931–32, 46939, 46940–41, 46943, 46945–46, 46950–51, 46958–59, 46960, 46962, 46968, 46970–71, 46974–75, 46978, 46980, 46982, 46984–85, 46988, 46990, 46992, 46996, 47946, 47957, 47959, 47960

* * *

THIRD DISTRICT

MARLIN A. STUTZMAN, Republican, of Howe, IN; born in Sturgis, MI, August 31, 1976; education: graduated from Lake Area Christian High School, 1994; studied business at Glen Oaks Community College, Centreville, MI, and Trine State University, Angola, IN; professional: co-owner of family's 3,000-acre farm in northeast Indiana; elected to the Indiana House as the youngest member of the Legislature, 2002–08; elected to the State Senate, 2008–10; assistant Republican Whip; caucus and member: Indiana Senate Conservative Caucus, 2009; served on the Commerce, Public Policy and Interstate Cooperation Committee; Pensions and Labor Committee; Natural Resources Committee; ranking member, Utilities and Technology

Committee; Association for Retarded Children (ARC); Howe Community Association; Indiana Farm Bureau; LaGrange County Farm Bureau; National Federation for Independent Businesses (NFIB); National Rifle Association (NRA); Young Republicans of LaGrange County; religion: Southern Baptist; married: the former Christy Chavers, 2000; children: Payton and Preston; committees: Financial Services; elected to the 111th Congress, by special election and simultaneously elected to the 112th Congress on November 2, 2010; reelected to each succeeding Congress.

Office Listings

http://stutzman.house.gov   https://twitter.com/repstutzman

2418 Rayburn House Office Building, Washington, DC 20515	(202) 225–4436
Chief of Staff.—John R. Hammond IV.	
Legislative Director.—William Young.	
Scheduler.—Mary Wells.	
1300 South Harrison, Room 3105, Fort Wayne, IN 46802	(260) 424–3041
District Director.—Carlin Yoder.	
Communications Director.—Vacant.	
700 Park Avenue, Suite D, Winona Lake, IN 46590	(574) 269–1940
118 South Johnson Street, Bluffton, IN 46714	(260) 824–1900

Counties: ALLEN, DEKALB, KOSCIUSKO (portions), LAGRANGE, NOBLE, STEUBEN, WHITLEY. HUNTINGTON, ADAMS, WELLS, JAY, BLACKFORD (portions). Population (2010), 723,633.

ZIP Codes: 46538, 46555, 46562, 46565, 46571, 46580, 46582, 46590, 46701–03, 46705–06, 46710–11, 46714, 46721, 46723, 46725, 46730–33, 46737–38, 46740–43, 46745–48, 46750, 46755, 46759, 46760, 46762–67, 46770, 46772–74, 46776–77, 46779, 46781, 46783–85, 46787–88, 46791–95, 46797–98, 46802–09, 46814–16, 46818–19, 46825, 46835, 46845, 47326, 47359, 47369, 47371, 47373, 47381

* * *

FOURTH DISTRICT

TODD ROKITA, Republican, of Indianapolis, IN; born in Munster, IN, February 9, 1970; education: graduated with a B.A., Wabash College, Crawfordsville, IN, 1992; J.D., Indiana University School of Law, Indianapolis, IN, 1995; professional: practicing attorney, 1995–97; general counsel at the Indiana Secretary of State's office, 1997–2000; deputy Secretary of State, 2000–2002; Secretary of State, 2002–2010; President of the Association of Secretaries of State (NASS), 2007–08; awards: Indianapolis Choice Award, by the Indianapolis Chapter of the Association of Women Business Owners, 2008; "Award of Merit", by the International Association of Commercial Administrators (IACA), 2008 and 2010; Friend of Foreign Service Medal, by the Taiwanese Government, 2010; religion: Roman Catholic; married: Kathy Rokita, children: Teddy and Ryan; committees: vice-chair, Budget; Education and the Workforce; Transportation and Infrastructure; elected to the 112th Congress on November 2, 2010; reelected to each succeeding Congress.

Office Listings

http://www.rokita.house.gov   twitter: @toddrokita

1717 Longworth House Office Building, Washington, DC 20515	(202) 225–5037
Chief of Staff.—Renee Hudson.	FAX: 226–0544
Legislative Director.—Tom Borck.	
Communications Director.—Vacant.	
Scheduler.—Jessica Williams.	
355 South Washington Street, Danville, IN 46122	(317) 718–0404
District Director.—Matt Steward.	
337 Columbia Street, Lafayette, IN 47901	(765) 838–3930

Counties: BOONE, CLINTON, FOUNTAIN (part), HENDRICKS, JOHNSON (part), LAWRENCE, MARION (part), MONROE (part) MONTGOMERY, MORGAN, TIPPECANOE, AND WHITE (part). Population (2010), 774,798.

ZIP Codes: 46035, 46039, 46041, 46049–50, 46052, 46057–58, 46065, 46069, 46071, 46075, 46077, 46105, 46112–13, 46118, 46120–23, 46128, 46135, 46147, 46149, 46151, 46157–58, 46165–68, 46171–72, 46175, 46180, 46231, 46234, 46278, 46310, 46341, 46349, 46374, 46392, 46901–02, 46913, 46917, 46920, 46923, 46926, 46929, 46932, 46947, 46950, 46970, 46978–79, 46985, 46988, 46994, 47456, 47868, 47901, 47904–07

* * *

FIFTH DISTRICT

SUSAN W. BROOKS, Republican, of Carmel, IN; born in Fort Wayne, IN, August 25, 1960; education: graduated, Homestead High School, 1978; Miami University, Oxford, OH 1982; J.D. from the Indiana University Robert H. McKinney School of Law, 1985; professional: criminal defense attorney, 1985–97; Deputy Mayor of Indianapolis, 1998–99; Ice Miller Government Affairs, 1999–2001; U.S. Attorney for the Southern District of Indiana, 2001–07; Ivy Tech Community College Senior Vice President and General Counsel, 2007–11; married: David; children: Jessica and Conner; committees: Energy and Commerce; Ethics; Select Committee on Benghazi; elected to the 113th Congress on November 6, 2012; reelected to the 114th Congress on November 4, 2014.

Office Listings

http://www.susanwbrooks.house.gov

1505 Longworth House Office Building, Washington, DC 20515	(202) 225–2276
Chief of Staff.—Megan Savage.	FAX: 225–0016
Legislative Director.—Paul Mandelson.	
Communications Director.—Alex Damron.	
Scheduler / Executive Assistant.—Oliver Wise.	
District Director.—Karen Glaser.	
11611 North Meridian Street, Suite 415, Carmel, IN 46032	(317) 848–0201
120 East 8th Street, Anderson, IN 46016	(765) 640–5115

Counties: BLACKFORD, BOONE, GRANT, HAMILTON, HOWARD, MADISON, MARION, AND TIPTON. Population (2010), 720,423.

ZIP Codes: 46001, 46011–13, 46016–17, 46030–34, 46036–38, 46040, 46044–45, 46047–52, 46055–56, 46060, 46062–64, 46068–70, 46072, 46074–77, 46112, 46205, 46208, 46216, 46220, 46226, 46228, 46234–36, 46240, 46250, 46254, 46256, 46260, 46268, 46278, 46280, 46290–02, 46919, 46928, 46930, 46933, 46936, 46938, 46940, 46952–53, 46957, 46986–87, 46989, 46991, 47336, 47348, 47356

* * *

SIXTH DISTRICT

LUKE MESSER, Republican, of Greensburg, IN; born in Evansville, IN, February 27, 1969; education: B.A., Wabash College, Crawfordsville, IN, 1991; J.D., Vanderbilt University, Nashville, TN, 1994; professional: attorney; religion: Presbyterian; wife, Jennifer Messer; children, Emma, Ava and Hudson; committees: Financial Services; Education and the Workforce; chair, Republican Policy Committee; elected to the 113th Congress on November 6, 2012; reelected to the 114th Congress on November 4, 2014.

Office Listings

http://www.messer.house.gov   www.policy.house.gov   twitter: @replukemesser
www.facebook.com/replukemesser   www.youtube.com/user/replukemesser

508 Cannon House Office Building, Washington, DC 20515	(202) 225–3021
Chief of Staff.—Doug Menorca.	FAX: 225–3382
Legislative Director.—Jake Vreeburg.	
Communications Director.—Liz Hill.	
Scheduler/Office Manager.—Amy Burke.	
2 Public Square, Shelbyville, IN 46176	(317) 421–0704
Deputy Chief of Staff for Indiana.—Marissa Lynch.	FAX: 421–0739
Director of Constituent Services.—John Hatter.	
107 West Charles Street, Muncie, IN 47305	(765) 747–5566
50 North 5th Street, Richmond, IN 47374	(765) 962–2883

Counties: BARTHOLOMEW, DEARBORN, DECATUR, DELAWARE, FAYETTE, FRANKLIN, HANCOCK, HENRY, JEFFERSON, JENNINGS, OHIO, RANDOLPH, RIPLEY, RUSH, SCOTT (part), SHELBY, SWITZERLAND, UNION, AND WAYNE. Population (2010), 720,422.

ZIP Codes: 45003, 45030, 45053, 45056, 45347, 45390, 46001, 46012, 46017, 46040, 46055–56, 46064, 46070, 46104, 46110, 46115, 46117, 46124, 46126–27, 46130–31, 46133, 46140, 46144, 46146, 46148, 46150, 46154–56, 46161–63, 46173, 46176, 46182, 46186, 46229, 46235–36, 46239, 46259, 46725, 46989, 46994, 47001, 47003, 47006, 47010–12, 47016–18, 47020, 47022–25, 47030–32, 47034–38, 47040–43, 47060, 47102, 47138, 47141, 47147, 47170, 47177, 47201–03, 47223–27, 47229–32, 47234, 47236, 47240, 47243–47, 47250, 47261, 47263, 47265, 47270, 47272–74, 47280, 47282–83, 47302–05, 47307–08, 47320, 47322, 47324–25, 47327, 47330–31, 47334–42, 47344–46, 47351–58, 47360–62, 47366–68, 47370, 47373–75, 47380, 47382–88, 47390, 47392–94, 47396, 47448, 47546

* * *

SEVENTH DISTRICT

ANDRÉ CARSON, Democrat, of Indianapolis, IN; born in Indianapolis, October 16, 1974; graduated, Arsenal Technical High School, Indianapolis, IN; education: B.A. in Criminal Justice Management, Concordia University Wisconsin, Mequon, WI; M.B.A, Indiana Wesleyan University, Marion, IN; professional: Investigative Officer for the Indiana State Excise Police, 1997–2006; Indiana Department of Homeland Security's Intelligence Fusion Center, 2006; City County Councilor, Marion County, 2007; religion: Muslim; married: Mariama; children: Salimah; caucuses: Whip, Congressional Black Caucus; Progressive Caucus; New Democrat Coalition; committees: Permanent Select Committee on Intelligence; Transportation and Infrastructure; elected to the 110th Congress on March 11, 2008, by special election, to fill the vacancy caused by the death of United States Representative Julia Carson; reelected to each succeeding Congress.

Office Listings

http://www.carson.house.gov   https://twitter.com/repandrecarson
www.facebook.com/congressmanandrecarson

2453 Rayburn House Office Building, Washington, DC 20515	(202) 225–4011
Chief of Staff.—Kim Rudolph.	FAX: 225–5633
Legislative Director.—Nathan Bennett.	
Legislative Assistants: Andrea Martin, Erica Powell.	
Scheduler.—Sarah Paulos.	
300 East Fall Creek Parkway North Drive, Suite 300, Indianapolis, IN 46205	(317) 283–6516
District Director.—Megan Sims.	FAX: 283–6567
Communications Director.—Jessica Gail.	
Staff Assistant/Legislative Correspondent.—Omair Mirza.	

Counties: MARION. City of Indianapolis, township of Center, parts of the townships of Decatur, Lawrence, Perry, Pike, Warren, Washington, and Wayne, included are the cities of Beech Grove and Lawrence. Population (2010), 676,351.

ZIP Codes: 46107, 46160, 46201–09, 46211, 46214, 46216–22, 46224–31, 46234–35, 46237, 46239–42, 46244, 46247, 46249, 46251, 46253–55, 46260, 46266, 46268, 46274–75, 46277–78, 46282–83, 46285, 46291, 46295–96, 46298

* * *

EIGHTH DISTRICT

LARRY BUCSHON, Republican, of Newburgh, IN; born in Kincaid, IL, May 31, 1962; graduated from South Fork High School, Kincaid, IL, 1980; B.S., with a concentration in chemistry, University of Illinois, Urbana-Champaign, IL, 1984; M.D., University of Illinois, Chicago, 1988; residency, Medical College of Wisconsin in Milwaukee, 1988–95; cardiothoracic surgeon, 1995–2010; commissioned lieutenant, U.S. Navy Reserves, 1989; promoted, lieutenant commander, 1994; honorable discharge, 1998; married: Kathryn; children: Luke, Alec, Blair, and Zoe; committees: Energy and Commerce; elected to the 112th Congress on November 2, 2010; reelected to each succeeding Congress.

Office Listings

http://www.bucshon.house.gov   twitter: @replarrybucshon

1005 Longworth House Office Building, Washington, DC 20515	(202) 225–4636
Chief of Staff.—Jon Causey.	FAX: 225–3284
Press Secretary.—Nick McGee.	
Legislative Director.—Teresa Buckley.	
Executive Assistant.—Susey Davis.	
420 Main Street, Suite 1402, Evansville, IN 47708	(812) 465–6484
District Director.—Matthew Huckleby.	
901 Wabash Avenue, Suite 140, Terre Haute, IN 47807	(812) 232–0523

Counties: CLAY, CRAWFORD (part), DAVIESS, DUBOIS, GIBSON, GREENE, KNOX, MARTIN, OWEN, PARKE, PERRY, PIKE, POSEY, SPENCER, SULLIVAN, VANDERBURGH, VERMILLION, VIGO, AND WARRICK. Population (2010), 694,398.

ZIP Codes: 46105, 46120–21, 46128, 46135, 46165–66, 46170–72, 46175, 47403–04, 47424, 47427, 47429, 47431–33, 47438–39, 47441, 47443, 47445–46, 47449, 47453, 47455–57, 47459–60, 47462, 47465, 47469–71, 47501, 47512, 47516, 47519, 47522–24, 47527–29, 47535, 47537, 47541–42, 47553, 47557–58, 47561–62, 47564, 47567–68, 47573, 47578, 47581, 47584–85, 47590–91, 47596–98, 47601, 47610–14, 47616, 47618–20, 47629–31, 47633, 47637–40, 47647–

49, 47654, 47660, 47665–66, 47670, 47683, 47701–06, 47708, 47710–16, 47719–22, 47724–25, 47727–28, 47730–37, 47739–41, 47744, 47747, 47750, 47801–05, 47807–09, 47811–12, 47830–34, 47836–38, 47840–42, 47845–66, 47868–72, 47874–76, 47878–82, 47884–85, 47917–18, 47921, 47928, 47932, 47952, 47966, 47969–70, 47974–75, 47982, 47987, 47989, 47991–93

* * *

NINTH DISTRICT

TODD C. YOUNG, Republican, of Bloomington, IN; born in Indianapolis, IN, August 24, 1972; education: B.S., political science, United States Naval Academy, Annapolis, MD, 1995; M.B.A., University of Chicago, Chicago, IL, 2000; M.A., american history, School of Advanced Study, University of London, UK, 2001; J.D., Indiana University, Bloomington, IN, 2005; professional: legislative assistant, United States Senate, 2002–03; management consultant, Crowe Chizek, 2003–05; attorney, Tucker and Tucker, PC in Paoli, IN, 2005–09; military: United States Navy, 1990–95; United States Marine Corps, 1995–2000; member: Sherwood Oaks Christian Church, Bloomington, IN; married: Jennifer Tucker Hill; children: Tucker, Annalise, Abigal, and Ava; committees: Ways and Means; elected to the 112th Congress on November 2, 2010; reelected to each succeeding Congress.

Office Listings

http://toddyoung.house.gov   twitter: @reptoddyoung

1007 Longworth House Office Building, Washington, DC 20515	(202) 225–5315
Chief of Staff.—John Connell.	FAX: 226–6866
Legislative Director.—Jacob Triolo.	
Communications Director.—Trevor Foughty.	
Scheduler.—Clay Helton.	
279 Quartermaster Drive, Jeffersonville, IN 47130	(812) 288–3999
320 West 8th Street, Suite 114, Bloomington, IN 47404	(812) 335–3355

Counties: BROWN, CLARK, CRAWFORD (part), FLOYD, HARRISON, JACKSON, JOHNSON, LAWRENCE, MONROE, MORGAN (part), ORANGE, SCOTT (part), and Washington. Population (2010), 726,570.

ZIP Codes: 46106, 46110–11, 46113, 46124, 46131, 46140, 46142–43, 46151, 46158, 46160, 46162, 46164, 46166, 56181, 46184, 46229, 46259, 47019, 47021, 47033, 47039, 47102, 47104, 47106–08, 47110–12, 47114–20, 47122–26, 47129–38, 47140–47, 47150–51, 47160–67, 47170, 47172, 47175, 47177, 47190, 47199, 47201, 47220, 47228–29, 47235, 47249, 47260, 47264, 47274, 47281, 47401–08, 47420–21, 47426, 47429, 47432–37, 47446, 47448, 47451–52, 47454, 47458, 47460, 47462–64, 47467–70

IOWA

(Population 2010, 3,046,355)

SENATORS

CHUCK GRASSLEY, Republican, of New Hartford, IA; born in New Hartford, IA, September 17, 1933; education: graduated, New Hartford Community High School, 1951; B.A., University of Northern Iowa, 1955; M.A., University of Northern Iowa, 1956; doctoral studies, University of Iowa, 1957–58; professional: farmer; member: Iowa State Legislature, 1959–74; Farm Bureau; State and County Historical Society; Masons; Baptist Church; and International Association of Machinists, 1962–71; co-chair, International Narcotics Control Caucus; married: the former Barbara Ann Speicher, 1954; children: Lee, Wendy, Robin Lynn, Michele Marie; committees: chair, Judiciary; Agriculture, Nutrition, and Forestry; Budget; Finance; Joint Committee on Taxation; elected to the 94th Congress, November 5, 1974; reelected to the 95th and 96th Congresses; elected to the U.S. Senate, November 4, 1980; reelected to each succeeding Senate term.

Office Listings

http://grassley.senate.gov   https://www.facebook.com/grassley
https://twitter.com/chuckgrassley

135 Hart Senate Office Building, Washington, DC 20510	(202) 224–3744
Chief of Staff.—Jill Kozeny.	FAX: 224–6020
Legislative Director.—Kolan Davis.	
721 Federal Building, 210 Walnut Street, Des Moines, IA 50309	(515) 288–1145
State Administrator.—Robert Renaud.	
111 7th Avenue, Southeast, Suite 6800, Cedar Rapids, IA 52404	(319) 363–6832
120 Federal Courthouse Building, 320 Sixth Street, Sioux City, IA 51101	(712) 233–1860
210 Waterloo Building, 531 Commercial Street, Waterloo, IA 50701	(319) 232–6657
201 West 2nd Street, Suite 720, Davenport, IA 52801	(563) 322–4331
307 Federal Building, 8 South Sixth Street, Council Bluffs, IA 51501	(712) 322–7103

* * *

JONI ERNST, Republican of Red Oak, IA; born in Red Oak, July 1, 1970; education: graduated Stanton High School, Stanton, IA; B.S., Iowa State University, Ames, 1992; M.P.A. Columbus State University, 1995; military service: U.S. Army Reserves, 1993–2001; Iowa Army National Guard, 1992 to present; auditor of Montgomery County, IA, 2005–11; member of the Iowa State Senate, 2011–14; married: Gail Ernst; children: Regina, Jennifer, and Elizabeth; committees: Agriculture, Nutrition, and Forestry; Armed Services; Homeland Security and Governmental Affairs; Small Business and Entrepreneurship; elected to the U.S. Senate on November 4, 2014.

Office Listings

http://ernst.senate.gov

111 Russell Hart Senate Office Building, Washington, DC 20510	(202) 224 3254
Chief of Staff.—Lisa Goeas.	FAX: 224 9369
Communications Director. Brook Hougesen.	
733 Federal Building, 210 Walnut Street, Des Moines, IA 50309	(515) 284–4574
111 7th Avenue Southeast, Suite 480, Cedar Rapids, IA 52401	(319) 365–4504
1606 Brady Street, Suite 323, Davenport, IA 52803	(563) 322–0677
194 Federal Building, 320 Sixth Street, Room 110, Sioux City, IA 51101	(712) 252–1550

REPRESENTATIVES

FIRST DISTRICT

ROD BLUM, Republican, of Dubuque, IA; born in Dubuque, April 26, 1955; education: B.A., Loras College, 1977; M.B.A., University of Dubuque, 1989; professional: CyCare Systems Inc., 1978–88; Eagle Point Software Inc., chairman and CEO, 1989–2000; Digital Canal Inc., chairman and CEO, 2000–present; Salto de Fede, 2006–present; former Iowa Entrepreneur of the Year; student pilot; basketball coach; Dubuque Senior High School chair; married: Karen; five children; caucuses: chair, Czech and Slovak Caucus; chair, Congressional Term Limits Caucus; committees: Budget; Oversight and Government Reform; elected to the 114th Congress on November 4, 2014.

Office Listings

http://www.blum.house.gov

213 Cannon House Office Building, Washington, DC 20515	(202) 225–2911
Chief of Staff.—Paul Smith.	
1050 Main Street, Dubuque, IA 52001	(563) 557–7789
District Director.—John Ferland.	
515 Main Street, Suite D, Cedar Falls, IA 50613	(319) 266–6925
310 3rd Street, Southeast, Cedar Rapids, IA 52401	(319) 364–2288

Counties: ALLAMAKEE, BENTON, BLACK HAWK, BREMER, BUCHANAN, CLAYTON, DELAWARE, DUBUQUE, FAYETTE, HOWARD, IOWA, JACKSON, JONES, LINN, MARSHALL, MITCHELL, POWESHIEK, TAMA, WINNESHIEK, AND WORTH. Population (2010), 761,548.

ZIP Codes: 50005, 50027, 50051, 50078, 50106, 50112, 50120, 50136, 50141–42, 50148, 50153, 50157–58, 50162, 50171, 50173, 50206–07, 50234, 50239, 50242, 50247, 50258, 50434, 50440, 50444, 50446, 50448, 50450, 50454–56, 50458– 61, 50464, 50466, 50471–72, 50476, 50603, 50606–07, 50609, 50612–13, 50621–22, 50626, 50628–30, 50632, 50634– 35, 50641, 50643–45, 50647–48, 50650–52, 50654–55, 50662, 50664, 50666–71, 50674–77, 50681–82, 50701–03, 50707, 52001–03, 52030–33, 52035, 52037–50, 52052–54, 52057, 52060, 52064–66, 52068–70, 52072–74, 52076–79, 52101, 52132–36, 52140–42, 52144, 52146–47, 52151, 52154–66, 52168–72, 52175, 52201–03, 52205–25, 52227–29, 52232– 33, 52236–37, 52249, 52251, 52253, 52257, 52301–02, 52305–16, 52318, 52320–21, 52323–26, 52328–30, 52332, 52334, 52336, 52338–39, 52341–42, 52345–49, 52351–52, 52354–56, 52361–62, 52401–05, 52411, 52731

* * *

SECOND DISTRICT

DAVID LOEBSACK, Democrat, of Iowa City, IA; born in Sioux City, IA, December 23, 1952; education: graduated, East High School, 1970; B.A., Iowa State University, 1974; M.A., Iowa State University, 1976; Ph.D., political science, University of California, Davis, 1985; professional: professor, political science, Cornell College, 1982–2006; married: Teresa Loebsack; four children; committees: Energy and Commerce; elected to the 110th Congress on November 7, 2006; reelected to each succeeding Congress.

Office Listings

http://www.loebsack.house.gov

1527 Longworth House Office Building, Washington, DC 20515	(202) 225–6576
Chief of Staff.—Eric Witte.	
Office Manager / Scheduler.—Brad Wilson.	
209 West 4th Street, Suite 104, Davenport, IA 52801	(563) 323–5988
District Director.—Rob Sueppel.	FAX: 323–5231
125 South Dubuque Street, Iowa City, IA 52240–4003	(319) 351–0789
	(866) 914–4692

Counties: APPANOOSE, CLARKE, CEDAR, CLINTON, DECATUR, DES MOINES, DAVIS, HENRY, JASPER, JOHNSON, JEFFERSON, KEOKUK, LOUISA, LEE, LUCAS, MUSCATINE, MAHASKA, MONROE, MARION, SCOTT, VAN BUREN, WASHINGTON, WAYNE, AND WAPELLO. Population (2010), 761,624.

ZIP Codes: 50008, 50027–28, 50044, 50049, 50052, 50054, 50057, 50060, 50062, 50065, 50067–68, 50103–04, 50108, 50116, 50119, 50123, 50127, 50135–38, 50140, 50143–44, 50147, 50150–51, 50153, 50163, 50165, 50168, 50170, 50174, 50207–08, 50213–14, 50219, 50225, 50228, 50232, 50238, 50251–52, 50255–56, 50262, 50264, 50268, 50272, 50275, 52037, 52201, 52216, 52231, 52235, 52240, 52241, 52242–48, 52254–55, 52306, 52317, 52319, 52322, 52327, 52333, 52335, 52337–38, 52340, 52353, 52355–56, 52358–59, 52531, 52533–35, 52537–38, 52540, 52542–44, 52549– 52, 52555–57, 52560–63, 52565, 52567–74, 52576–77, 52580–81, 52583–86, 52588, 52590–91, 52593–95, 52601, 52619– 21, 52623–27, 52630–32, 52635, 52637–42, 52644–60, 52701, 52720–22, 52726–34, 52736–39, 52742, 52745–61, 52765– 69, 52771–74, 52776–78, 52801–09

* * *

THIRD DISTRICT

DAVID YOUNG, Republican, of Van Meter, IA, May 11, 1968; education: graduated Johnston High School, 1986; attended Buena Vista College; bachelor of arts degree in English; Drake University, 1991; professional: manager loan trainee, Norwest Financial, 1992; legislative aide, U.S. Senator Hank Brown, 1993; legislative director, chief of staff, campaign manager, Senator Jim Bunning, 1998; chief of staff, Senator Chuck Grassley, 2006; committees: Appropriations; elected to the 114th Congress on November 4, 2014.

Office Listings

http://www.davidyoung.house.gov

515 Cannon House Office Building, Washington, DC 20515	(202) 225–5476

Office Listings—Continued

Chief of Staff.—James D. Carstensen.
601 East Locust Street, Suite 204, Des Moines, IA 50309 .... (515) 282–1909
District Manager.—Sherill Whisenand.
208 West Taylor Street, Creston, IA 50801 .... (641) 782–2495
Office Manager.—Laura Hartman.
501 5th Avenue, Council Bluffs, IA 51503 .... (712) 325–1404
Office Manager.—Charlie Johnson.

Counties: ADAIR, ADAMS, CASS, DALLAS, FREMONT, GUTHRIE, MADISON, MILLS, MONTGOMERY, PAGE, POLK, POTTAWATTAMIE, RINGGOLD, TAYLOR, UNION, AND WARREN. Population (2010), 761,612.

ZIP Codes: 50001–03, 50007, 50009, 50020–23, 50026, 50029, 50032–33, 50035, 50038–39, 50047–48, 50061, 50063, 50066, 50069–70, 50072–74, 50109, 50111, 50115, 50118, 50125, 50128, 50131, 50133, 50139, 50145–46, 50149, 50155, 50160, 50164, 50166–67, 50169, 50210–11, 50216, 50218, 50220, 50222, 50226, 50229, 50233, 50237, 50240– 41, 50243, 50250, 50254, 50257, 50261, 50263, 50265–66, 50273–74, 50276–77, 50301–25, 50327–36, 50339–40, 50359–64, 50367–69, 50380–81, 50391–96, 50398, 50801, 50830–31, 50833, 50835–37, 50839–43, 50845–49, 50851, 50853–54, 50857–64, 50936, 50940, 50947, 50950, 50980–83, 51501–03, 51510, 51521, 51525–26, 51532–36, 51540– 42, 51544, 51548–49, 51551–54, 51559–61, 51566, 51571, 51573, 51575–77, 51591, 51601, 51603, 51630–32, 51636– 40, 51645–54, 51656

* * *

FOURTH DISTRICT

STEVE KING, Republican, of Kiron, IA; born in Storm Lake, IA, May 28, 1949; education: graduated, Denison Community High School; attended Northwest Missouri State University, Maryville, MO, 1967–70; professional: agri-businessman; owner and operator of King Construction Company; public service: Iowa State Senate, 1996–2002; religion: Catholic; family: married to Marilyn; children: David, Michael, and Jeff; committees: Agriculture; Judiciary; Small Business; elected to the 108th Congress on November 5, 2002; reelected to each succeeding Congress.

Office Listings

http://www.steveking.house.gov

2210 Rayburn House Office Building, Washington, DC 20515 .... (202) 225–4426
                                     FAX: 225–3193
Chief of Staff.—Sarah Stevens.
Legislative Director.—Jared Culver.
Scheduler.—Molly Leif.
Communications Director.—Sarah Stevens.
526 Nebraska Street, Sioux City, IA 51101 .... (712) 224–4692
202 1st Street, SE., Suite 126, Mason City, IA 50401 .... (641) 201–1624
723 Central Avenue, Fort Dodge, IA 50501 .... (515) 573–2738
306 North Grand Avenue, Spencer, IA 51301 .... (712) 580–7754
1421 South Bell Avenue, Suite 102, Ames, IA 50010 .... (515) 232–2885

Counties: AUDUBON, BOONE, BUENA VISTA, BUTLER, CALHOUN, CARROLL, CERRO GORDO, CHEROKEE, CHICKASAW, CLAY, CRAWFORD, DICKINSON, EMMET, FLOYD, FRANKLIN, GREENE, GRUNDY, HAMILTON, HANCOCK, HARDIN, HARRISON, HUMBOLDT, IDA, KOSSUTH, LYON, MONONA, O'BRIEN, OSCEOLA, PALO ALTO, PLYMOUTH, POCAHONTAS, SAC, SHELBY, SIOUX, STORY, WEBSTER, WINNEBAGO, WOODBURY, AND WRIGHT. Population (2010), 761,571.

ZIP Codes: 50006, 50010–12, 50014, 50020, 50022, 50025–26, 50029, 50034, 50036, 50040–42, 50046, 50050, 50055– 56, 50058, 50064, 50071, 50075–76, 50101–02, 50105, 50107, 50117, 50122, 50124, 50126, 50128–30, 50132, 50134, 50154, 50156, 50161, 50201, 50206, 50212, 50217, 50220, 50223, 50227, 50230–31, 50235–36, 50243–44, 50246– 49, 50258, 50269, 50271, 50276, 50278, 50401, 50420–21, 50423–24, 50428, 50430–36, 50438–39, 50441, 50444, 50446, 50449–53, 50457–58, 50460–61, 50464–65, 50467–71, 50473, 50475, 50477–80, 50482–84, 50501, 50510– 11, 50514–25, 50527–33, 50535–36, 50538–46, 50548, 50551, 50554, 50556–63, 50565–71, 50573–79, 50581–83, 50585– 86, 50588, 50590–95, 50597–99, 50601–05, 50609, 50611, 50613, 50616, 50619–21, 50624–25, 50627, 50630, 50633, 50636, 50638, 50642–43, 50645, 50653, 50657–60, 50665–66, 50669–70, 50672–74, 50680, 51001–12, 51014, 51016, 51018–20, 51022–31, 51033–41, 51044–56, 51058, 51060–63, 51101, 51103–06, 51108–09, 51111, 51201, 51230– 32, 51234–35, 51237–50, 51301, 51331, 51333–34, 51338, 51340–43, 51345–47, 51350–51, 51354–55, 51357–58, 51360, 51363–66, 51401, 51430–31, 51433, 51436, 51439–55, 51458–59, 51460–63, 51465–67, 51520–21, 51523, 51527– 31, 51537, 51543, 51545–46, 51550, 51552, 51555–59, 51562–65, 51570, 51572, 51577–79, 52154, 52171

KANSAS

(Population 2010, 2,853,118)

SENATORS

PAT ROBERTS, Republican, of Dodge City, KS; born in Topeka, KS, April 20, 1936; education: graduated, Holton High School, Holton, KS, 1954; B.S., journalism, Kansas State University, Manhattan, KS, 1958; professional: captain, U.S. Marine Corps, 1958–62; editor and reporter, Arizona newspapers, 1962–67; aide to Senator Frank Carlson, 1967–68; aide to Representative Keith Sebelius, 1969–80; U.S. House of Representatives, 1980–96; married: the former Franki Fann, 1969; children: David, Ashleigh, and Anne-Wesley; committees: chair, Agriculture, Nutrition, and Forestry; Finance; Health, Education, Labor, and Pensions; Rules and Administration; Joint Committee on the Library; Joint Committee on Printing; Select Committee on Ethics; elected to the U.S. Senate in November, 1996; reelected to each succeeding Senate term.

Office Listings

http://roberts.senate.gov   www.facebook.com/senpatroberts
twitter: @senpatroberts

109 Hart Senate Office Building, Washington, DC 20510	(202) 224–4774
Chief of Staff.—Jackie Cottrell.	FAX: 224–3514
Legislative Director.—Amber Kirchhoefer.	
Scheduler.—Jensine Moyer.	
Communications Director.—Sarah Little.	
100 Military Plaza, P.O. Box 550, Dodge City, KS 67801	(620) 227–2244
District Director.—Martha Ruiz-Martinez.	
155 North Market Street, Suite 120, Wichita, KS 67202	(316) 263–0416
District Director.—Tamara Woods.	
Frank Carlson Federal Building, 444 SE Quincy, Room 392, Topeka, KS 66683	(785) 295–2745
District Director.—Gilda Lintz.	
11900 College Boulevard, Suite 203, Overland Park, KS 66210	(913) 451–9343
State Director.—Chad Tenpenny.	

* * *

JERRY MORAN, Republican, of Hays, KS; born in Plainville, KS, May 29, 1954; education: B.S., University of Kansas, Lawrence, KS, 1976; J.D., University of Kansas School of Law, Lawrence, KS, 1981; M.B.A., candidate, Fort Hays State University, Hays, KS; professional: bank officer; instructor; U.S. House of Representatives, 1997–2010; Kansas State Senate, 1989–97, serving as vice president, 1993–95, majority leader, 1995–97; Kansas State Special Assistant Attorney General, 1982–85; deputy attorney, Rooks County, KS, 1987–95; University of Kansas School of Law Board of Governors, served as vice president, 1993–94, president, 1994–95; Board of Directors, Kansas Chamber of Commerce and Industry, 1996–97; religion: Christian; family: married Robba; two daughters, Kelsey and Alex; caucuses: the Senate Hunger Caucus, the Senate Western Caucus, Senate Rural Health Caucus, co-chair of Community Pharmacy Caucus; committees: Appropriations; Banking, Housing, and Urban Affairs; Commerce, Science, and Transportation; Indian Affairs; Veterans' Affairs; elected to the U.S. Senate on November 2, 2010.

Office Listings

http://moran.senate.gov

521 Dirksen Senate Office Building, Washington, DC 20510	(202) 224–6521
Chief of Staff.—Todd Novascone.	FAX: 228–6966
Legislative Director.—Alex Richard.	
Scheduler.—Emily Whitfield.	
Communications Director.—Garrette Silverman.	
1200 Main Street, Suite 402, Hays, KS 67601	(785) 628–6401
State Casework Director.—Rachel Robben.	
Constituent Services Representative.—Chelsey Gillogly.	
23600 College Boulevard, Suite 201, Olathe, KS 66061	(913) 393–0711
Kansas State Scheduler.—Lisa Dethloff.	
306 North Broadway, Suite 125, P.O. Box 1372, Pittsburg, KS 66762	(620) 232–2286
	FAX: 232–2284
923 Westport Place, Suite 210, P.O. Box 067, Manhattan, KS 66502	(785) 539–8973
	FAX: 587–0789
3450 North Rock Road, Building 200, Suite 209, P.O. Box 781753, Wichita, KS 67226	(316) 631–1410

Office Listings—Continued

State Director.—Brennen Britton.   FAX: 631–1297
Deputy State Director.—Mike Zamrzia.

REPRESENTATIVES

FIRST DISTRICT

TIM HUELSKAMP, Republican, of Fowler, KS; born in Fowler, November 11, 1968; education: attended seminary in Santa Fe, NM; B.S., social science, College of Santa Fe, Santa Fe, NM, 1991; Ph.D., political science, American University, Washington, DC, 1995; professional: farmer; rancher; budget and legislative analyst for the State of New Mexico; served in the Kansas State Senate, 1996–2010; married: Angela Huelskamp; children: Natasha, Rebecca, Athan, and Alexander; committees: Small Business; Veterans' Affairs; elected to the 112th Congress on November 2, 2010; reelected to each succeeding Congress.

Office Listings

http://huelskamp.house.gov

1110 Longworth House Office Building, Washington, DC 20515 .... (202) 225–2715
Chief of Staff.—Mark Kelly.
Legislative Director.—Juliana Heerschap.
Communications Assistants: Jon Meadows, Jennifer Pett.
Office Manager.—Naysa Woomer.
100 Military Avenue, Suite 205, Dodge City, KS 67801–0249 .... (620) 225–0172
One North Main, Suite 525, P.O. Box 1128, Hutchinson, KS 67504 .... (620) 665–6138
200 South Santa Fe, Suite 6, Salina, KS 67401 .... (785) 309–0572
727 Poyntz Avenue, Suite 10, Manhattan, KS 66502 .... (785) 309–0572

Counties: BARBER, BARTON, CHASE, CHEYENNE, CLARK, CLAY, CLOUD, COMANCHE, DECATUR, DICKINSON, EDWARDS, ELLIS, ELLSWORTH, FINNEY, FORD, GEARY (part), GOVE, GRAHAM, GRANT, GRAY, GREELEY, GREENWOOD (part), HAMILTON, HASKELL, HODGEMAN, JEWELL, KEARNY, KIOWA, LANE, LINCOLN, LOGAN, LYON, MCPHERSON, MARION (part), MARSHALL, MEADE, MITCHELL, MORRIS, MORTON, NEMAHA (part), NESS, NORTON, OSBORNE, OTTAWA, PAWNEE, PHILLIPS, PRATT, RAWLINS, RENO, REPUBLIC, RICE, ROOKS, RUSH, RUSSELL, SALINE, SCOTT, SEWARD, SHERIDAN, SHERMAN, SMITH, STAFFORD, STANTON, STEVENS, THOMAS, TREGO, WABAUNSEE, WALLACE, WASHINGTON, AND WICHITA. Population (2010), 713,278.

ZIP Codes: 66401, 66403–04, 66406–08, 66411–13, 66423, 66427, 66431, 66438, 66441, 66501–02, 66507–08, 66514, 66518, 66523, 66526, 66534, 66536, 66538, 66541, 66544, 66547–48, 66610, 66614–15, 66801, 66830, 66833–35, 66838, 66840, 66843, 66845–46, 66849–51, 66853–54, 66858–62, 66864–66, 66868–70, 66872–73, 66901, 66930, 66932–33, 66935–46, 66948–49, 66951–53, 66955–56, 66958–64, 66966–68, 66970, 67009, 67020–21, 67028–29, 67035, 67053–54, 67057, 67059, 67061–63, 67065–66, 67068, 67070, 67073, 67104, 67107–09, 67112, 67124, 67127, 67134, 67138, 67143, 67151, 67155, 67335, 67401–02, 67410, 67416–18, 67420, 67422–23, 67425, 67427–28, 67430–32, 67436–39, 67441–52, 67454–60, 67464, 67466–68, 67470, 7473–76, 67478, 67480–85, 67487, 67490–92, 67501–02, 67504–05, 67510–16, 67518–26, 67529–30, 67543–48, 67550, 67552–54, 67556–57, 67559–61, 67563–68, 67570, 67572–76, 67578–79, 67581, 67583–85, 67601, 67621–23, 67625–29, 67631–32, 67634–35, 67637–40, 67642–51, 67653–61, 67663–65, 67667, 67669, 67671–75, 67701, 67730–41, 67743–45, 67748–49, 67751–53, 67756–58, 67761–62, 67764, 67801, 67831, 67834–42, 67844, 67846, 67849–51, 67853–55, 67857, 67859–65, 67867, 67869–71, 67876–80, 67882, 67901, 67905, 67950–54

* * *

SECOND DISTRICT

LYNN JENKINS, Republican, of Topeka, KS; born in Topeka, KS, June 10, 1963; education: A.A., Kansas State University, Manhattan, KS, 1985; B.S., accounting / economics, Weber State College, Ogden, UT, 1985; professional: certified public accountant; accountant, Braunsdorf, Carson, and Clinkinbeard; accountant, Baird, Kurtz and Dobson; certified public accountant, Public Accounting / Specialty Taxation, 1985–present; Representative, Kansas State House of Representatives, 1999–2000; Senator, Kansas State Senate, 2001–02; Treasurer, State of Kansas, 2003–08; children: Hayley and Hayden; caucuses: House Hunger Caucus; Defense Communities Caucus; Impact Aid Caucus; No Labels Problem Solvers Caucus, Community Pharmacy Caucus; Financial and Economic Literacy Caucus; House Army Caucus; Military Veterans Caucus; Nursing Caucus; Cystic Fibrosis Caucus; Down Syndrome Caucus, Yellow Pages Caucus; committees: Ways and Means; elected to the 111th Congress on November 4, 2008; reelected to each succeeding Congress.

Office Listings

http://lynnjenkins.house.gov

1526 Longworth House Office Building, Washington, DC 20515 .... (202) 225–6601
Chief of Staff.—Pat Leopold.   FAX: 225–7986
Legislative Director.—Eric Schmutz.
Scheduler.—Lauren Hoover.
Press Aide.—Thomas Brandt.
3550 SW 5th St., Topeka, KS 66606 .... (785) 234–5966
1001 North Broadway, Suite C, Pittsburg, KS 66762 .... (620) 231–5966

Counties: ALLEN, ANDERSON, ATCHISON, BOURBON, BROWN, CHEROKEE, COFFEY, CRAWFORD, DONIPHAN, DOUGLAS, FRANK-
LIN, JACKSON, JEFFERSON, LABETTE, LEAVENWORTH, LINN, MARSHALL (part), MIAMI (part), MONTGOMERY, NEMAHA,
NEOSHO, OSAGE, SHAWNEE, WILSON, AND WOODSON. Population (2010), 713,272.

ZIP Codes: 66002, 66006–08, 66010, 66012, 66014–17, 66020–21, 66023–27, 66032–33, 66035, 66039–50, 66052–54,
66056, 66058, 66060, 66064, 66066–67, 66070–73, 66075–76, 66078–80, 66083, 66086–88, 66090–95, 66097, 66109,
66402–04, 66406, 66408–09, 66411–19, 66422, 66424–25, 66427–29, 66431–32, 66434, 66436, 66438–40, 66451, 66508–
10, 66512, 66515–16, 66521–24, 66527–28, 66532–34, 66536–44, 66546, 66548, 66550, 66552, 66603–12, 66614–
19, 66621–22, 66701, 66710–14, 66716–17, 66720, 66724–25, 66728, 66732–36, 66738–41, 66743, 66746, 66748–
49, 66751, 66753–58, 66760–63, 66767, 66769–73, 66775–83, 66839, 66852, 66854, 66856–57, 66864, 66868, 66871,
67047, 67301, 67330, 67332–33, 67335–37, 67340–42, 67344, 67347, 67351, 67354, 67356–57, 67363–64

* * *

THIRD DISTRICT

KEVIN YODER, Republican, of Overland Park; born in Hutchison, KS, January 8, 1976;
education: B.A., University of Kansas, Lawrence, KS, 1999; J.D., University of Kansas College
of Law, Lawrence, KS, 2002; professional: attorney; admitted to the Kansas Bar, 2002; State
Representative, Kansas House of Representatives, 20th District; 2003–11; chairman, House
Appropriations Committee; chairman, General Government Budget Committee; serves on the
Board of Directors of the Johnson County Bar Association; married: Brooke Robinson Yoder;
member: Kansas Sentencing Commission; Kansas City Chamber's Congressional Forum; Overland Park Rotary Club; Johnson County Bar Association; Greater Kansas City Area University
of Kansas Alumni Association Board of Directors; Overland Park Republican Precinct Com-
mitteeman; committees: Appropriations; elected to the 112th Congress on November 2, 2010;
reelected to each succeeding Congress.

Office Listings

http://www.yoder.house.gov

215 Cannon House Office Building, Washington, DC 20515 .... (202) 225–2865
Chief of Staff.—Dave Natonski.
Legislative Director.—Vacant.
Scheduler.—Cate Duerst.
Communications Director.—CJ Grover.
7325 West 79th Terrace, Overland Park, KS 66204 .... (913) 621–0832
District Director.—Molly Haase.   FAX: 621–1533
Constituent Services Director.—Cheyne Worley.

Counties: JOHNSON, MIAMI (part), and WYANDOTTE. Population (2010), 713,272.

ZIP Codes: 66012–13, 66018–19, 66021, 66025, 66030–31, 66053, 66061–62, 66071, 66083, 66085, 66101–06, 66109,
66111–12, 66115, 66118, 66202–21, 66223–24, 66226–27

* * *

FOURTH DISTRICT

MIKE POMPEO, Republican, of Wichita, KS; born in Orange, CA, December 30, 1963;
education: B.S., mechanical engineering, United States Military Academy at West Point, NY,
1986, graduated first in his class; J.D., Harvard Law School, Cambridge, MA, 1994; professional: owned / founder, Thayer Aerospace; president, Sentry International; editor of *Harvard
Law Review*; religion: Presbyterian; married: Susan Pompeo of Wichita, KS; children: Nick;
caucus: Republican Study Committee; committees: Energy and Commerce; Permanent Select
Committee on Intelligence; Select Committee on Benghazi; elected to the 112th Congress on
November 2, 2010; reelected to each succeeding Congress.

Office Listings

http://www.pompeo.house.gov

436 Cannon House Office Building, Washington, DC 20515 .... (202) 225–6216
    Chief of Staff.—Jim Richardson.   FAX: 225–3489
    Legislative Director.—Aaron Ringel.
    Senior Policy Advisor.—Blake Hollander.
    Legislative Aide.—Mike Netherton.
    Scheduler / Office Manager.—Rebekah Bear.
    Staff Assistant.—Kalli Wheeler.
7701 East Kellogg, Suite 510, Wichita, KS 67207 .... (316) 262–8992
    District Director.—Sarah Metz.
    Communications Director.—Heather Denker.

Counties: BARBER, BUTLER, CHAUTAUQUA, COMANCHE, COWLEY, EDWARDS, ELK, GREENWOOD, HARPER, HARVEY, KINGMAN, KIOWA, PAWNEE (part), Pratt, Sedgwick, Stafford, and Sumner. Population (2010), 715,456.

ZIP Codes: 66759, 66853, 66855, 66860, 66863, 66870, 67001–05, 67008–10, 67012–13, 67016–26, 67028–31, 67035–39, 67041–42, 67045, 67047, 67049–52, 67054–62, 67065–68, 67070–72, 67074, 67101–06, 67108–12, 67114, 67117–20, 67122–24, 67127, 67131–35, 67137–38, 67140, 67142–44, 67146–47, 67149–52, 67154–56, 67159, 67201–21, 67223, 67226–28, 67230, 67232, 67235, 67260, 67275–78, 67334–46, 67349, 67352–53, 67355, 67360–61, 67511, 67519, 67523, 67529, 67547, 67550, 67552, 67563, 67574

KENTUCKY

(Population 2010, 4,339,367)

SENATORS

MITCH McCONNELL, Republican, of Louisville, KY; born in Colbert County, AL, February 20, 1942; education: graduated, Manual High School, Louisville, 1960, president of the student body; B.A. with honors, University of Louisville, 1964, president of the student council, president of the student body of the College of Arts and Sciences; J.D., University of Kentucky Law School, 1967, president of student bar association, outstanding oral advocate; professional: attorney, admitted to the Kentucky Bar, 1967; chief legislative assistant to U.S. Senator Marlow Cook, 1968–70; Deputy Assistant U.S. Attorney General, 1974–75; Judge/Executive of Jefferson County, KY, 1978–84; chairman, National Republican Senatorial Committee, 1997–2000; chairman, Joint Congressional Committee on Inaugural Ceremonies, 1999–2001; Senate Majority Whip, 2002–06; Senate Republican Leader, 2007–14, Senate Majority Leader, 2015–present; married to Elaine Chao on February 6, 1993; children: Elly, Claire and Porter; committees: Agriculture, Nutrition, and Forestry; Appropriations; Rules and Administration; elected to the U.S. Senate on November 6, 1984; reelected to each succeeding Senate term.

Office Listings

http://mcconnell.senate.gov   https://twitter.com/mcconnellpress
https://www.facebook.com/mitchmcconnell

317 Russell Senate Office Building, Washington, DC 20510	(202) 224–2541
Chief of Staff.—Brian McGuire.	FAX: 224–2499
Scheduler.—Laura Vincent.	
Legislative Director.—Jennifer Kuskowski.	
Communications Director.—Robert Steurer.	
601 West Broadway, Suite 630, Louisville, KY 40202	(502) 582–6304
State Director.—Terry Carmack.	
1885 Dixie Highway, Suite 345, Fort Wright, KY 41011	(606) 578–0188
300 South Main Street, Suite 310, London, KY 40741	(606) 864–2026
Professional Arts Building, Suite 100, 2320 Broadway, Paducah, KY 42001	(270) 442–4554
771 Corporate Drive, Suite 108, Lexington, KY 40503	(606) 224–8286
Federal Building, Room 102, 241 Main Street, Bowling Green, KY 42101	(270) 781–1673

* * *

RAND PAUL, Republican, of Bowling Green, KY; born in Pittsburgh, PA, January 7, 1963; education: undergraduate, Baylor University, Waco, Texas, 1981–84; M.D., Duke University School of Medicine, 1988; religion: Methodist; family: married to the former Kelley Ashby; three sons, William, Duncan, and Robert; committees: Foreign Relations; Health, Education, Labor, and Pensions; Homeland Security and Governmental Affairs; Small Business and Entrepreneurship; elected to the U.S. Senate on November 2, 2010.

Office Listings

http://paul.senate.gov   https://www.facebook.com/senatorrandpaul   twitter: @senrandpaul

167 Russell Senate Office Building, Washington, DC 20510	(202) 224–4343
Chief of Staff.—William Henderson.	FAX: 228–6917
Legislative Director.—Kathee Facchiano.	
Press Secretaries: Jillian Lane, Eleanor May.	
Scheduler.—Jessica Jelgerhuis.	
600 Dr. Martin Luther King, Jr. Place, Suite 1072B, Louisville, KY 40202	(502) 582–5341
State Director.—Jim Milliman.	
1029 State Street, Bowling Green, KY 42101	(270) 782–8303
1100 South Main Street, Suite 12, Hopkinsville, KY 42240	(270) 885–1212
423 Frederica Street, Room 305, Owensboro, KY 42301	(270) 689–9085
541 Buttermilk Pike, Suite 102, Crescent Springs, KY 41017	(859) 426–0165
771 Corporate Drive, Suite 105, Lexington, KY 40503	(859) 219–2269

REPRESENTATIVES

FIRST DISTRICT

ED WHITFIELD, Republican, of Hopkinsville, KY; born in Hopkinsville, May 25, 1943; education: graduated, Madisonville High School, Madisonville, KY; B.S., University of Kentucky, Lexington, 1965; J.D., University of Kentucky, 1969; attended American University's Wesley Theological Seminary, Washington, DC; military service: first lieutenant, U.S. Army Reserves, 1967–73; professional: attorney, private practice, 1970–79; vice president, CSX Corporation, 1979–90; admitted to bar: Kentucky, 1970, and Florida, 1993; began practice in 1970 in Hopkinsville, KY; member, Kentucky House, 1973, one term; married: Constance Harriman Whitfield; children: Kate; committees: Energy and Commerce; elected to the 104th Congress; reelected to each succeeding Congress.

Office Listings

http://www.whitfield.house.gov   http://twitter.com/repedwhitfield

2184 Rayburn House Office Building, Washington, DC 20515	(202) 225–3115
Chief of Staff.—Taylor Booth.	FAX: 225–3547
Scheduler / Office Manager.—Meaghan Dowdy.	
Legislative Director.—Melissa Buchanan.	
1403 South Main Street, Hopkinsville, KY 42240	(270) 885–8079
District Director.—Michael Pape.	
200 North Main, Suite F, Tompkinsville, KY 42167	(270) 487–9509
Field Representative.—Sandy Simpson.	
222 First Street, Suite 224, Henderson, KY 42420	(270) 826–4180
Field Representative.—Ed West.	
100 Fountain Avenue, Room 104, Paducah, KY 42001	(270) 442–6901
Field Representative.—Janece Everett.	

Counties: ADAIR, ALLEN, BALLARD, CALDWELL, CALLOWAY, CARLISLE, CASEY, CHRISTIAN, CLINTON, CRITTENDEN, CUMBERLAND, FULTON, GRAVES, HENDERSON, HICKMAN, HOPKINS, LIVINGSTON, LOGAN, LYON, MARION, MARSHALL, MCCRACKEN, MCLEAN, METCALF, MONROE, MUHLENBERG, OHIO, RUSSELL, SIMPSON, TAYLOR, TODD, TRIGG, UNION, WASHINGTON, AND WEBSTER. Population (2010), 725,929.

ZIP Codes: 40009, 40033, 40037, 40040, 40049, 40052, 40060–63, 40069, 40078, 40119, 40328, 40330, 40437, 40442, 40448, 40464, 40468, 40484, 40489, 42001–03, 42020–25, 42027–29, 42031–33, 42035–41, 42044–45, 42047–51, 42053–56, 42058, 42060–61, 42063–64, 42066, 42069–71, 42076, 42078–79, 42081–88, 42101, 42104, 42120, 42122–24, 42129, 42133–35, 42140–41, 42150–51, 42153–54, 42164, 42166–67, 42170, 42201–04, 42206, 42209–211, 42214–17, 42219–21, 42223, 42232, 42234, 42236, 42240–41, 42251–52, 42254, 42256, 42262, 42265–67, 42274, 42276, 42280, 42283, 42286–88, 42301, 42320–28, 42330, 42332–34, 42337, 42338, 42344–45, 42347, 42349–50, 42352, 42354, 42356, 42361, 42367–69, 42370, 42371–72, 42374–76, 42378, 42402–04, 42406, 42408–11, 42413,42419–20, 42431, 42436–37, 42440–42, 42444–45, 42450–53, 42455–64, 42516, 42528, 42539, 42541, 42544, 42565–67, 42602–03, 42629, 42642, 42711, 42715–16, 42718–20, 42728, 42731, 42733, 42735, 42740–43, 42746, 42749, 42753, 42758, 42759, 42786

* * *

SECOND DISTRICT

BRETT GUTHRIE, Republican, of Bowling Green, KY; born in Florence, AL, February 18, 1964; education: B.S., United States Military Academy, West Point, NY, 1987; M.P.M., Yale University, New Haven, CT, 1997; military service: U.S. Army, Field Artillery Office, 101st Airborne Division, 1987–90; professional: Vice President, Trace Die Cast, 1991–2009; member: Kentucky Senate, 1998–2009; married: Beth; children: Caroline, Robby, and Elizabeth; committees: Education and the Workforce; Energy and Commerce; elected to the 111th Congress on November 4, 2008; reelected to each succeeding Congress.

Office Listings

http://www.guthrie.house.gov

2434 Rayburn House Office Building, Washington, DC 20515	(202) 225–3501
Chief of Staff.—Eric Bergren.	
Legislative Director.—Megan Jackson.	
Communications Director.—Jennifer Sherman.	
Scheduler.—Jennifer Beil.	
996 Wilkinson Trace, Suite B2, Bowling Green, KY 42103	(270) 842–9896
District Director.—Mark Lord.	

Counties: BARREN, WARREN, BRECKINRIDGE, DAVIESS, HANCOCK, GRAYSON, BUTLER, HARDIN, GREEN, BULLITT, SPENCER (part), WASHINGTON (part), GARRARD, BOYLE, MERCER, JESSAMINE (part), HARDIN, LARUE, MEADE, NELSON, EDMONSON, AND HART. Population (2010), 723,137.

ZIP Codes: 40004, 40008, 40012–13, 40020, 40037 (part), 40040, 40046 (part), 40047–48, 40051, 40052 (part), 40069 (part), 40071 (part), 40078, 40104, 40107–11, 40115, 40117, 40119 (part), 40121, 40140, 40142–46, 40150, 40152, 40155, 40157, 40160–62, 40165, 40170–71, 40175–76, 40177 (part), 40178, 40229 (part), 40272 (part), 40299, 40310, 40328 (part), 40330, 40339, 40356 (part), 40372 (part), 40383 (part), 40390 (part), 40403 (part), 40419 (part), 40422 (part), 40440 (part), 40444 (part), 40461 (part), 40464 (part), 40468 (part), 40484 (part), 42101–03, 42104 (part),

42122 (part), 42123, 42127, 42130, 42133 (part), 42141, 42154 (part), 42156, 42159–60, 42163, 42166 (part), 42170 (part), 42171, 42206 (part), 42207, 42210, 42214 (part), 42256 (part), 42259, 42261, 42273, 42274 (part), 42275, 42285, 42301 (part), 42303, 42320 (part), 42327 (part), 42333 (part), 42339 (part), 42343 (part), 42348, 42349 (part), 42351, 42355–56, 42361 (part), 42366 (part), 42368 (part), 42376 (part), 42378 (part), 42701, 42712–13, 42716 (part), 42718 (part), 42721–22, 42724, 42726, 42729, 42732, 42740, 42743 (part), 42746 (part), 42748, 42749 (part), 42754, 42757, 42762, 42764–65, 42776, 42782, 42784, 42788

* * *

THIRD DISTRICT

JOHN A. YARMUTH, Democrat, of Louisville, KY; born in Louisville, November 4, 1947; education: graduated, Atherton High School, Louisville, 1965; graduated, Yale University, New Haven, CT, 1969; professional: Legislative Aide for Kentucky Senator Marlow Cook, 1971–74; publisher, *Louisville Today Magazine*, 1976–82; Associate Vice President of University Relations at the University of Louisville, 1983–86; Vice President of a local healthcare firm 1986–90; founder, editor and writer *LEO Newsweekly*, 1990–2005; Television host and commentator, 2003–05; awards: 2007 Spirit of Enterprise Award; Louisville Alzheimer's Association Person of the Year; named Outstanding New Member of Congress by the Committee for Education and Funding; 16 Metro Louisville Journalism Awards for editorial and column writing; married: Cathy Yarmuth, 1981; child: Aaron; committees: Budget; Energy and Commerce; elected to the 110th Congress on November 7, 2006; reelected to each succeeding Congress.

Office Listings

http://www.yarmuth.house.gov

403 Cannon House Office Building, Washington, DC 20515	(202) 225–5401
Chief of Staff.—Julie Carr.	FAX: 225–5776
Legislative Director.—Zack Marshall.	
Press Secretary.—Christopher Schuler.	
Scheduler.—Erica DiCio.	
600 Martin Luther King, Jr. Place, Suite 216, Louisville, KY 40202	(502) 582–5129
District Director.—Carolyn Tandy.	

Counties: JEFFERSON. Population (2010), 741,096.

ZIP Codes: 40025, 40027, 40041, 40047, 40059 (part), 40118, 40177 (part), 40201–22, 40223 (part), 40224–25, 40228, 40229 (part), 40231–33, 40241 (part), 40242–43, 40245 (part), 40250–53, 40255–59, 40261, 40266, 40268–70, 40272 (part), 40280–83, 40285, 40289–90, 40291 (part), 40292–93, 40295, 40297–98, 40299 (part)

* * *

FOURTH DISTRICT

THOMAS MASSIE, Republican, of Garrison, KY; born in Huntington, WV, January 13, 1971; education: graduated from Lewis County High School; B.S., electrical engineering/economics, Massachusetts Institute of Technology, 1993; M.S., mechanical engineering, Massachusetts Institute of Technology, 1996; professional: inventor/engineer; founder of SensAble Devices, Inc.; farmer; Lewis County Judge Executive; married: Rhonda; four children; committees: Oversight and Government Reform; Science, Space, and Technology; Transportation and Infrastructure; elected simultaneously to the 112th and 113th Congresses on November 6, 2012, by special election to fill the vacancy caused by the resignation of United States Representative Geoffrey C. (Geoff) Davis; reelected to the 114th Congress on November 4, 2014.

Office Listings

http://massie.house.gov

314 Cannon House Office Building, Washington, DC 20515	(202) 225–3465
Chief of Staff.—Hans Hoeg.	FAX: 225–0003
Legislative Director/Deputy Chief of Staff.—Seana Cranston.	
Legislative Correspondent.—Ryan Falk.	
Press Secretary.—Lorenz Isidro.	
Scheduler.—Lauren Wills.	
Staff Assistant.—Jonathan Tkachuk.	
541 Buttermilk Pike, Suite 208, Crescent Springs, KY 41017	(859) 426–0080
District Director.—Chris McCane.	FAX: 426–0061
1700 Greenup Avenue, R–505, Ashland, KY 41101	(606) 324–9898
Eastern District Field Representative.—J.R. Reed.	
108 West Jefferson Street, LaGrange, KY 40031	(502) 265–9119

Office Listings—Continued

Western District Field Representative.—Stacie Rockaway.   FAX: 265–9126

Counties: BOYD, BOONE, BRACKEN, CARROLL, CAMPBELL, GREENUP, GALLATIN, GRANT, HENRY, HARRISON, JEFFERSON, KENTON, LEWIS, MASON, OLDHAM, OWEN, PENDLETON, SHELBY, SPENCER, AND TRIMBLE. Population (2010), 723,450.

ZIP Codes: 40003 (part), 40006–07, 40010–11, 40014, 40019, 40022–23, 40026, 40031, 40036, 40045, 40046 (part), 40050, 40055–58, 40059 (part), 40065, 40067–68, 40070, 40071 (part), 40075, 40076 (part), 40077, 40241 (part), 40245 (part), 40291 (part), 40299 (part), 40359, 40363, 40370 (part), 40379 (part), 40601 (part), 41001–03, 41004 (part), 41005–08, 41010 (part), 41011, 41014–18, 41030, 41031 (part), 41033–35, 41040, 41042–43, 41044 (part), 41045–46, 41048, 41051–52, 41055 (part), 41056, 41059, 41062–63, 41064 (part), 41071, 41073–76, 41080, 41083, 41085–86, 41091–92, 41093 (part), 41094–95, 41097–99, 41101, 41102 (part), 41121, 41129 (part), 41135, 41139, 41141, 41143 (part), 41144, 41164 (part), 41166, 41169, 41174–75, 41179, 41183, 41189

* * *

FIFTH DISTRICT

HAROLD ROGERS, Republican, of Somerset, KY; born in Barrier, KY, December 31, 1937; education: graduated, Wayne County High School, 1955; attended Western Kentucky University, 1956–57; A.B., University of Kentucky, 1962; LL.B., University of Kentucky Law School, 1964; professional: lawyer, admitted to the Kentucky State Bar, 1964; commenced practice in Somerset; member, North Carolina and Kentucky National Guard, 1957–64; associate, Smith and Blackburn, 1964–67; private practice, 1967–69; Commonwealth Attorney, Pulaski and Rockcastle Counties, KY, 1969–80; delegate, Republican National Convention, 1972, 1976, 1980, 1984, and 1988; Republican nominee for Lieutenant Governor, KY, 1979; past president, Kentucky Commonwealth Attorneys Association; member and past president, Somerset-Pulaski County Chamber of Commerce and Pulaski County Industrial Foundation; founder, Southern Kentucky Economic Development Council, 1986; member, Chowder and Marching Society, 1981–present; member, Republican Steering Committee; married the former Shirley McDowell, 1957; three children: Anthony, Allison, and John Marshall; committees: chair, Appropriations; elected to the 97th Congress, November 4, 1980; reelected to each succeeding Congress.

Office Listings

http://halrogers.house.gov

2406 Rayburn House Office Building, Washington, DC 20515	(202) 225–4601
Chief of Staff.—Megan O'Donnell Bell.	FAX: 225–0940
Office Manager.—Chelsea Whalen.	
Legislative Correspondent.—Alex Pinson.	
Staff Assistant.—Kathryn Kennedy.	
Legislative Assistants: Ashley Nichols, Shannon Rickett.	
District Director.—Karen Kelly.	FAX: 439–4647
551 Clifty Street, Somerset, KY 42503	(606) 679–8346
48 South Kentucky Highway 15, Hazard, KY 41701	(606) 439–0794
110 Resource Court, Suite A, Prestonsburg, KY 41653–1842	(606) 886–0844
	FAX: 889–0371

Counties: BELL, BOYD, BREATHITT, CARTER, CLAY, ELLIOTT, FLOYD, HARLAN, JACKSON, JOHNSON, KNOTT, KNOX, LAUREL, LAWRENCE, LEE, LESLIE, LETCHER, LINCOLN, MAGOFFIN, MARTIN, MORGAN, OWSLEY, PERRY, PIKE, PULASKI, ROCKCASTLE, ROWAN, WAYNE, AND WHITLEY.Population (2010), 723,228.

ZIP Codes: 40313, 40351, 40393, 40402, 40409, 40434, 40445, 40447, 40447–48, 40456, 40460, 40481, 40486, 40701, 40729, 40734, 40737, 40740–41, 40743–44, 40759, 40763, 40769, 40771, 40801, 40806–08, 40813, 40815–16, 40818–20, 40823–24, 40826–31, 40840, 40843–45, 40847, 40849, 40854–56, 40862–63, 40865, 40868, 40870, 40873–74, 40902–03, 40906, 40913–15, 40921, 40923, 40927, 40935, 40940–41, 40943, 40946, 40949, 40953, 40958, 40962, 40964–65, 40972, 40977, 40979, 40982–83, 40988, 40995, 40997, 41124, 41132, 41142, 41146, 41149, 41159, 41168, 41171, 41180, 41201, 41203–04, 41214, 41216, 41219, 41222, 41224, 41226, 41230–32, 41234, 41238, 41240, 41250, 41254–57, 41260, 41262–65, 41267–68, 41271, 41274, 41311, 41314, 41317, 41339, 41348, 41352, 41366–67, 41385, 41390, 41397, 41408, 41421, 41425, 41464–65, 41472, 41501, 41503, 41512–14, 41517, 41519, 41522, 41526, 41527–28, 41531, 41534–35, 41537–40, 41544, 41547–48, 41553–55, 41557–60, 41562–64, 41566–68, 41571, 41601–07, 41612, 41615–16, 41619, 41621–22, 41630–32, 41635–36, 41640, 41642–43, 41645, 41647, 41649–50, 41653, 41659, 41663, 41666–67, 41669, 41701, 41712–14, 41719, 41721–23, 41725, 41727, 41729, 41731, 41735, 41739–40, 41745–46, 41749, 41751, 41754, 41759–60, 41762–64, 41766, 41772–77, 41804, 41810, 41815, 41817, 41819, 41822, 41824–26, 41828, 41831–37, 41840, 41843–45, 41847–49, 41855, 41858, 41861–62, 42501, 42503, 42518–19, 42533, 42567, 42631, 42634–35, 42638, 42649, 42653

* * *

SIXTH DISTRICT

ANDY BARR, Republican, of Lexington, KY; born in Lexington, July 24, 1973; education: B.A. degree in government and philosophy from the University of Virginia in Charlottesville,

VA, 1996, graduating with *magna cum laude* and *Phi Beta Kappa* honors; J.D., from the University of Kentucky College of Law, in Lexington, KY, 2001; religion: Episcopal; married to the former Eleanor Carol Leavell of Georgetown, Kentucky; together, they are the proud parents of two daughters; caucus: Bi-Partisan Prescription Drug Caucus; Congressional Arthritis Caucus; Congressional Automotive Caucus; Congressional Bourbon Caucus; Congressional Coal Caucus; Congressional Diabetes Caucus; Congressional Down Syndrome Caucus; chair of Congressional Horse Caucus; Congressional Natural Gas Caucus; Congressional Prayer Caucus; Congressional Recycling Caucus; Congressional Sportsmen's Caucus; Congressional United Solutions Caucus; Congressional Veterans Job Caucus; German-American Caucus; Historic Preservation Caucus; House Manufacturing Caucus; National Guard and Reserves Components Caucus; National Guard Youth Challenge Caucus; Pro-Life Caucus; USO Congressional Caucus; US-Japan Caucus; Can Caucus; Republican Study Committee; committees: Financial Services; elected to the 113th Congress on November 6, 2012; reelected to the 114th Congress on November 4, 2014.

Office Listings

http://www.barr.house.gov   www.facebook.com/repandybarr
www.twitter.com/repandybarr   www.youtube.com/repandybarr

1432 Longworth House Office Building, Washington, DC 20515 .... (202) 225-4706
    Chief of Staff.—Mary Rosado.   FAX: 225-2122
    Legislative Director.—Travis Cone.
    Communications Director.—Rick VanMeter.
    Scheduler.—Holly Lewis.
2709 Old Rosebud Road, Lexington, KY 40509 .... (859) 219-1366

Counties: ANDERSON, BATH, BOURBON, CLARK, ESTILL, FAYETTE, FLEMING, FRANKLIN, HARRISON (part), JESSAMINE (part), MADISON, MENIFEE, MONTGOMERY, NICHOLAS, POWELL, ROBERTSON, SCOTT, WOLFE, AND WOODFORD. Population (2010), 723,203.

ZIP Codes: 40003, 40046, 40076, 40311–13, 40316, 40322, 40324, 40334, 40336–37, 40340, 40342, 40346–48, 40350, 40353, 40356, 40358, 40360–61, 40370–72, 40374, 40376, 40379–80, 40383, 40385, 40387, 40390–91, 40403–04, 40461, 40472, 40475, 40502–11, 40513–17, 40601, 40604, 41004, 41010, 41031, 41039, 41041, 41044, 41049, 41055, 41064, 41093, 41301, 41332, 41360, 41365

LOUISIANA

(Population 2010, 4,553,762)

SENATORS

DAVID VITTER, Republican, of Metairie, LA; born in Metairie, May 3, 1961; education: Harvard University; Oxford University Rhodes Scholar; Tulane University School of Law; professional: attorney; adjunct law professor, Tulane and Loyola Universities; religion: Catholic; public service: Louisiana House of Representatives, 1992–99; U.S. House of Representatives, 1999–2005; awards: Alliance for Good Government "Legislator of the Year"; Victims and Citizens Against Crime "Outstanding Legislator" and "Lifetime Achievement Award"; married: Wendy Baldwin Vitter; children: Sophie, Lise, Airey, and Jack; caucuses: chairman of the Border Security and Enforcement First Immigration Caucus; committees: chair, Small Business and Entrepreneurship; Banking, Housing, and Urban Affairs; Environment and Public Works; Judiciary; elected to the U.S. Senate on November 2, 2004; reelected to the U.S. Senate on November 2, 2010.

Office Listings

http://vitter.senate.gov

516 Hart Senate Office Building, Washington, DC 20510	(202) 224–4623
Chief of Staff.—Kyle Ruckert.	FAX: 228–5061
2800 Veterans Boulevard, Suite 201, Metairie, LA 70002	(504) 589–2753
858 Convention Street, Baton Rouge, LA 70801	(225) 383–0331
1651 Louisville Avenue, Suite 148, Monroe, LA 71201	(318) 325–8120
6501 Coliseum Boulevard, Suite 700 A, Alexandria, LA 71303	(318) 448–0169
920 Pierremont Road, Suite 113, Shreveport, LA 71106	(318) 861–0437
1424 Ryan Street, Suite A, Lake Charles, LA 70601	(337) 436–0453
2201 Kaliste Saloom, Suite 201, Lafayette, LA 70508	(337) 993–6502

* * *

BILL CASSIDY, Republican, of Baton Rouge, LA; born in Highland Park, IL, September 28, 1957; education: graduated, Tara High School; B.S., Louisiana State University, Baton Rouge, LA, 1979; M.D., Louisiana State University medical school, New Orleans, LA, 1983; professional: Baton Rouge; medical doctor, Associate Professor of Medicine with LSU Health Sciences Center; member of the Louisiana State Senate; married: Laura Layden Cassidy, M.D.; children: Will, Meg, and Kate; committees: Appropriations; Energy and Natural Resources; Health, Education, Labor, and Pensions; Veterans' Affairs; Joint Economic; elected to the 111th Congress, reelected to the 112th and 113th Congresses; won the runoff election to the U.S. Senate on December 6, 2014.

Office Listings

http//:www.cassidy.senate.gov

703 Hart Senate Office Building, Washington, DC 20510	(202) 224–5824
Chief of Staff.—James Quinn.	FAX: 224–9735
Communications Director.—John Cummins.	
Executive Assistant/Director of Scheduling.—Allison Kapsner.	
5555 Hilton Avenue, Suite 100, Baton Rouge, LA 70808	(225) 929–7711
3421 North Causeway Boulevard, Suite 204, Metairie, LA 70002	(504) 838–0130
101 La Rue France, Suite 505, Lafayette, LA 70508	(337) 261–1400
1651 Louisville Avenue, Suite 123, Monroe, LA 70201.	

REPRESENTATIVES

FIRST DISTRICT

STEVE SCALISE, Republican, of Jefferson, LA; born in New Orleans, LA, October 6, 1965; education: B.S., Louisiana State University, Baton Rouge, LA, 1983; professional: Computer Programmer for technology company; Louisiana House of Representatives, 1995–2007; Louisiana Senate, 2007–08; awards: Spirit of Enterprise, U.S. Chamber of Commerce; religion: Catholic; married: former Jennifer LeTulle; children: Madison and Harrison; committees: Energy and Commerce; elected to 110th Congress on May 4, 2008 in special election; reelected to each succeeding Congress.

Office Listings

http://www.scalise.house.gov   www.facebok.com/repstevescalise
https://twitter.com/stevescalise

2338 Rayburn House Office Building, Washington, DC 20515	(202) 225–3015
Chiefs of Staff: Charles Henry, Lynnel Ruckert.	FAX: 226–0386
Legislative Director.—Darren Achord.	
Scheduler.—Megan Becker.	
Communications Director.—Vacant.	
110 Veterans Memorial Boulevard, Suite 500, Metaire, LA 70005	(504) 837–1259
21454 Koop Drive, Suite 1E, Mandeville, LA 70471	(985) 893–9064
112 South Cypress Street, Hammond, LA 70403	(985) 340–2185
8026 Main Street, Suite 700, Houma, LA 70360	(985) 879–2300

Parishes: all or parts of: JEFFERSON, ORLEANS, ST. TAMMANY, TANGIPAHOA, ST. BERNARD, PLAQUEMINES, TERREBONNE, LAFOURCHE. Population (2010), 758,994.

ZIP Codes: 70001–06, 70009–11, 70033, 70038, 70041, 70055–56, 70060, 70062, 70064–65, 70083, 70091, 70115, 70118–19, 70121–24, 70160, 70181, 70183–84, 70343–45, 70353–54, 70357–58, 70360–61, 70363–64, 70373–74, 70377, 70401–04, 70420, 70427, 70431, 70433–38, 70445, 70447–48, 70452, 70454–67, 70469–71, 70764–65

* * *

SECOND DISTRICT

CEDRIC L. RICHMOND, Democrat, of New Orleans, LA; born in New Orleans, September 13, 1973; education: B.A., Morehouse College, Atlanta, GA, 1995; J.D., Tulane School of Law, New Orleans, LA, 1998; Harvard University Executive Education Program at the John F. Kennedy School of Government, Cambridge, MA; professional: member of the Louisiana State House of Representatives, 1999–2010; awards: _Time_ Magazine's 2010 40 Under 40, Innocence Project Legislative Champion Award; religion: Baptist; commissions, caucuses: New Democrat Coalition; Congressional Black Caucus; Gulf Coast Caucus; committees: Homeland Security; Judiciary; elected to the 112th Congress on November 2, 2010; reelected to each succeeding Congress.

Office Listings

http://www.richmond.house.gov   twitter: @reprichmond
www.facebook.com/reprichmond

240 Cannon House Office Building, Washington, DC 20515	(202) 225–6636
Chief of Staff.—Virgil Miller.	FAX: 225–1988
Executive Assistant.—Kemah Dennis-Morial.	
Legislative Director.—Ross Nodurft.	
Press Secretary.—Brandon Gassaway.	
2021 Lakeshore Drive, Suite 309, New Orleans, LA 70122	(504) 288–3777
District Director.—Enix Smith.	
200 Derbigny Street, Suite 3200, Gretna, LA 70053	(504) 365–0390
1520 Thomas H. Delpit Drive, Suite 126, Baton Rouge, LA 70802	(225) 636–5600

Parishes: ASCENSION (part), ASSUMPTION (part), EAST BATON ROUGE (part), IBERVILLE (part), JEFFERSON (part), ORLEANS (part), ST. CHARLES (part), ST. JAMES, ST. JOHN THE BAPTIST (part), WEST BATON ROUGE (part). Population (2010), 755,538.

ZIP Codes: 70001, 70003, 70030, 70031, 70039, 70047, 70049, 70051–53, 70056–58, 70062, 70065, 70068, 70070–72, 70076, 70080, 70084, 70086, 70087, 70090, 70094, 70112–19, 70121–31, 70139, 70163, 70301, 70341, 70346, 70372, 70390, 70391, 70393, 70710, 70714, 70719, 70721, 70723, 70725, 70734, 70737, 70743, 70763, 70764, 70767, 70776, 70780, 70788, 70791, 70802, 70805–07, 70811, 70812, 70814, 70815

* * *

THIRD DISTRICT

CHARLES W. BOUSTANY, JR., Republican, of Lafayette, LA; born in New Orleans, LA, February 21, 1956; education: graduated, Cathedral Carmel High School, Lafayette, LA; B.S., University of Southwestern Louisiana, Lafayette, LA, 1978; M.D., Louisiana State University School of Medicine, New Orleans, LA, 1982; professional: cardiothoracic surgeon; public service: served on the Louisiana Organ Procurement Agency Tissue Advisory Board; board of directors for the Greater Lafayette Chamber of Commerce, 2001; Chamber of Commerce as Vice President for Government Affairs, 2002; president of the Lafayette Parish Medical Society; chaired the American Heart Association's Gala; Healthcare Division of the UL-Lafayette Centennial Fundraiser, which provided $75 million of university endowed chairs, professorships and scholarships; member of Leadership Lafayette Class of 2002; member, Lafayette Parish Republican Executive Committee, 1996–2001; Republican Policy Committee; vice-chairman of the Bush/Cheney Victory 2000 Campaign for Lafayette Parish; board of directors for Lafayette General Medical Center; married: the former Bridget Edwards; children: Erik and Ashley; committees: Ways and Means; elected to the 109th Congress on December 4, 2004; reelected to each succeeding Congress.

Office Listings

http://www.boustany.house.gov

1431 Longworth House Office Building, Washington, DC 20515	(202) 225–2031
Chief of Staff.—Terri Fish.	FAX: 225–5724
Legislative Director.—Kaitlin Sighinolfi.	
Scheduler.—Rebecca Hobbs.	
800 Lafayette Street, Suite 1400, Lafayette, LA 70501	(337) 235–6322
One Lakeshore Drive, Suite 1775, Lake Charles, LA 70629	(337) 433–1747

Parishes: ACADIA, CALCASIEU, CAMERON, EVANGELINE, IBERIA, JEFFERSON DAVIS, LAFAYETTE, ST. LANDRY, ST. MARTIN, ST. MARY VERMILION. Population (2010), 760,696.

ZIP Codes: 70380, 70342, 70392, 70501–12, 70515–18, 70520, 70524–29, 70531–35, 70537, 70538, 70541–43, 70544, 70546, 70548–51, 70552, 70554–56, 70558–59, 70560, 70563, 70570–71, 70575, 70577–78, 70580–81, 70582, 70583–84, 70586, 70589, 70591–92, 70596, 70598, 70601–02, 70605–07, 70609, 70611–12, 70615–16, 70630–33, 70640, 70643, 70645–48, 70650, 70655, 70658, 70661, 70663–65, 70668–69, 70750, 71322, 71345, 71353, 71356, 71358, 71362

* * *

FOURTH DISTRICT

JOHN FLEMING, Republican, of Minden, LA; born in Meridian, MS, July 5, 1951; education: B.S., University of Mississippi, Oxford, MS, 1973; M.D., University of Mississippi, Oxford, MS, 1976; professional: family physician and businessman; military: Lieutenant Commander, U.S. Navy; awards: Louisiana Family Doctor of the Year, 2007; religion: Southern Baptist; married: Cindy; four children; committees: Armed Services; Natural Resources; elected to the 111th Congress on November 4, 2008; reelected to each succeeding Congress.

Office Listings

http://www.fleming.house.gov

2182 Rayburn House Office Building, Washington, DC 20515	(202) 225–2777
Chief of Staff.—Dana Gartzke.	FAX: 225–8039
Legislative Director.—Garth Van Meter.	
Scheduler.—Marilyn Rothfus.	
Communications Director.—Sarah Kuziomko.	
6425 Youree Drive, Suite 350, Shreveport, LA 71105	(318) 798–2254
District Director.—John Barr.	
103 North Third Street, Leesville, LA 71446	(337) 238–0778
Southern District Director.—Lee Turner.	
700 Benton Road, Bossier City, LA 71111	(318) 549–1712

Parishes: ALLEN, BEAUREGARD, BIENVILLE, BOSSIER, CADDO, CLAIBORNE, DESOTO, EVANGELINE, NATCHITOCHES, RED RIVER, SABINE, ST. LANDRY, UNION, VERNON, AND WEBSTER. Population (2010), 667,109.

ZIP Codes: 70515, 70524, 70535, 70541, 70570, 70576, 70584–86, 70589, 70634, 70637–39, 70644, 70648, 70651–60, 70662, 71001–09, 71016, 71018–19, 71021, 71023–24, 71027–34, 71037–40, 71043–52, 71055, 71058, 71060–61, 71063–73, 71075, 71078–80, 71082, 71101–13, 71115, 71118–20, 71129–30, 71133–38, 71148, 71156, 71161, 71163–66, 71171–72, 71222, 71234, 71241, 71256, 71260, 71277, 71403, 71406, 71411, 71414, 71416, 71419, 71426, 71429, 71434, 71438–39, 71443, 71446–47, 71449–50, 71456–63, 71468–69, 71474–75, 71486, 71496–97, 71526

* * *

FIFTH DISTRICT

RALPH LEE ABRAHAM, Republican, of Alto, LA; born in Monroe, LA, September 16, 1954; education: studied biochemistry as an undergraduate at Louisiana State University, Baton Rouge, LA, 1972–76; D.V.M., Louisiana State University School of Veterinary Medicine, Baton Rouge, LA, 1980; M.D., Louisiana State University School of Medicine, Shreveport, LA, 1994;

professional: general family practitioner; military: Army National Guard; religion: Baptist; married: Dianne; three children, eight grandchildren; committees: Agriculture; Veterans' Affairs; elected to the 114th Congress on December 6, 2014 in a run-off election.

Office Listings

https://abraham.house.gov

417 Cannon House Office Building, Washington, DC 20515	(202) 225–8490
Chief of Staff.—Luke Letlow.	FAX: 225–5639
Communications Director.—Cole Avery.	
Scheduler.—Ann Pierce.	
Legislative Director.—Ted Verrill.	
426 DeSiard Street, Monroe, LA 71201	(318) 322–3500
1434 Dorchester Drive, Suite E, Alexandria, LA 71301	(318) 445–0818
Southeast Louisiana Field Operations	(985) 516–5858

Parishes: AVOYELLES, CALDWELL, CATAHOULA, CONCORDIA, EAST CARROLL, EAST FELICIANA (part), FRANKLIN, JACKSON, LASALLE, LINCOLN, MADISON, MOREHOUSE, OUACHITA, RAPIDES, RICHLAND, ST. LANDRY (part), ST. HELENA (part), TANGIPAHOA (part), TENSAS, WASHINGTON, WEST CARROLL, WEST FELICIANA, AND WINN. Population (2010), 758,851.

ZIP Codes: 70401, 70422, 70426–27, 70431, 70435–38, 70441–44, 70446, 70450–51, 70455–56, 70465–66, 70512, 70570, 70577, 70589, 70656, 70712, 70722, 70730, 70748, 70750, 70761, 70775, 70782, 70787, 70789, 71001, 71031, 71201–03, 71209, 71219–20, 71223, 71225–27, 71229, 71232–35, 71237, 71238, 71243, 71245, 71247, 71250–51, 71253–54, 71259, 71261, 71263–64, 71266, 71268–70, 71272, 71275–76, 71279–80, 71282, 71286, 71291–92, 71295, 71301–03, 71316, 71322–23, 71325–28, 71331, 71333–34, 71336, 71339–43, 71345–46, 71350–51, 71353–58, 71360, 71362, 71366–69, 71371, 71373, 71375, 71377–78, 71401, 71404–05, 71407, 71409–10, 71417, 71418, 71422–25, 71427, 71430, 71432–33, 71435, 71438, 71441, 71447, 71454–55, 71457, 71463, 71465–67, 71472–73, 71479–80, 71483, 71485

* * *

SIXTH DISTRICT

GARRET GRAVES, Republican, of Baton Rouge, LA; born in Baton Rouge, LA, January 31, 1972; education: graduated, Catholic High School; studied at Louisiana Tech, University of Alabama, and The American University; professional: Coastal Preservation; served as an aide for the United States Senate Committee on Commerce, Science, and Transportation; staff director for the United States Senate Subcommittee on Climate Change and Impacts; chief legislative aide to the U.S. Senate Committee on Environment and Public Works; served as the head of the Louisiana Coastal Protection and Restoration Authority; married: Carissa Vanderleest Graves; children: Ralston, Calla, and Kulshan; committees: Natural Resources; Transportation and Infrastructure; elected to the 114th Congress in a runoff election on December 6, 2014.

Office Listings

https://garretgraves.house.gov

204 Cannon House Office Building, Washington, DC 20515	(202) 225–3901
Chief of Staff.—Paul Sawyer.	FAX: 225–7313
Press Secretary.—Kevin Roig.	
2351 Energy Drive Suite 1200, Baton Rouge, LA 70808	(225) 442–1731
29261 Frost Road, Livingston, LA 70753	(225) 686–4413
908 East 1st Street NSU, Candies Hall, Suite 405, Thibodaux, LA 70301	(985) 448–4103

Parishes: ASCENSION, ASSUMPTION, EAST BATON ROUGE, EAST FELICIANA, IBERVILLE, LAFOURCHE, LIVINGSTON, POINTE COUPEE, ST. CHARLES, ST. HELENA, ST. JOHN THE BAPTIST, TERREBONNE, AND WEST BATON ROUGE. Population (2010), 755,607.

ZIP Codes: 70030, 70047, 70068–69, 70079, 70087, 70301–02, 70339, 70341, 70352, 70356, 70359–61, 70364, 70371–72, 70375, 70380, 70390, 70394–95, 70403, 70422, 70436, 70441, 70443, 70449, 70453, 70456, 70462, 70466, 70704, 70706–07, 70710–11, 70714–15, 70718–19, 70722, 70725–30, 70732–34, 70736–37, 70739–40, 70744, 70747–49, 70752–57, 70759–60, 70762, 70764–65, 70767, 70769–70, 70772–74, 70777–78, 70783, 70785–86, 70788, 70791, 70801–02, 70806–11, 70814–21, 70825–27, 70831, 70835–37, 70874, 70879, 70884, 70893–96, 70898

MAINE

(Population, 2010 1,328,361)

SENATORS

SUSAN M. COLLINS, Republican, of Bangor, ME; born in Caribou, ME, December 7, 1952; education: graduated, Caribou High School, 1971; B.A., *magna cum laude,* Phi Beta Kappa, St. Lawrence University, Canton, NY; Outstanding Alumni Award, St. Lawrence University, 1992; staff director, Senate Subcommittee on the Oversight of Government Management, 1981–87; for 12 years, principal advisor on business issues to former Senator William S. Cohen; Commissioner of Professional and Financial Regulation for Maine Governor John R. McKernan, Jr., 1987; New England administrator, Small Business Administration, 1992–93; appointed Deputy Treasurer of Massachusetts, 1993; executive director, Husson College Center for Family Business, 1994–96; committees: chair, Special Committee on Aging; Appropriations; Health, Education, Labor, and Pensions; Select Committee on Intelligence; elected to the U.S. Senate on November 5, 1996; reelected to each succeeding Senate term.

Office Listings

http://collins.senate.gov   www.facebook.com/susancollins   twitter: @senatorcollins

413 Dirksen Senate Office Building, Washington, DC 20510	(202) 224–2523
Chief of Staff.—Steve Abbott.	FAX: 224–2693
Communications Director.—Alleigh Marre.	
Legislative Director.—Elizabeth McDonnell.	
202 Harlow Street, Suite 20100, Bangor, ME 04401	(207) 945–0417
State Representative.—Carol Woodcock.	
68 Sewall Street, Room 507, Augusta, ME 04330	(207) 622–8414
State Representative.—Vacant.	
160 Main Street, Biddeford, ME 04005	(207) 283–1101
State Representative.—Cathy Goodwin.	
55 Lisbon Street, Suite 1100, Lewiston, ME 04240	(207) 784–6969
State Representative.—Carlene Tremblay.	
25 Sweden Street, Suite A, Caribou, ME 04736	(207) 493–7873
State Representative.—Philip Bosse.	
One Canal Plaza, Suite 802, Portland, ME 04101	(207) 780–3575
State Representative.—Kate Norfleet.	

* * *

ANGUS S. KING, JR., Independent, of Brunswick, ME; born in Alexandria, VA, March 31, 1944; education: graduated, Dartmouth College, 1966; University of Virginia Law School, 1969; chief counsel to U.S. Senate Subcommittee on Alcoholism and Narcotics for former Maine Senator William Hathaway; founded Northeast Energy Management, Inc., 1989; elected Maine's 71st Governor, 1994, reelected 1998 by one of the largest margins in Maine's history; Maine's first independent U.S. Senator; committees: Armed Services; Budget; Energy and Natural Resources; Rules and Administration; Select Committee on Intelligence; elected to the U.S. Senate on November 6, 2012.

Office Listings

http://king.senate.gov   twitter: @senangusking
https://www.facebook.com/senatorangusskingjr

133 Hart Senate Office Building, Washington, DC 20510	(202) 224–5344
Chief of Staff.—Kay Rand.	FAX: 224–1946
Executive Assistant.—Jacob "Izzy" Rosen.	
Communications Director.—Kathleen Connery Dawe.	
DC Scheduler.—Matt Liscovitz.	
Legislative Director.—Chad Metzler.	
Senior Policy Advisor.—Marge Kilkelly.	
Administrative Director.—Patrick Doak.	
4 Gabriel Drive, Suite F1, Augusta, ME 04330	(207) 622–8292
169 Academy Street, Suite A, Presque Isle, ME 04769	(207) 764–5124
383 U.S. Route 1, Suite 1C, Scarborough, ME 04074	(207) 883–1588
State Director.—Edie Smith.	
Regional Representatives: Sharon Campbell, Travis Kennedy, Gail Kezer, Elizabeth Schneider MacTaggart, Bonnie Pothier, Chris Rector, Ben Tucker.	

REPRESENTATIVES

FIRST DISTRICT

CHELLIE PINGREE, Democrat, of North Haven, ME; born in Minneapolis, MN, April 2, 1955; education: B.A., College of the Atlantic, Bar Harbor, ME, 1979; professional: farmer; businesswoman; religion: Lutheran; married: three children; House Oceans Caucus; Progressive Caucus; Women's Caucus; Sustainable Energy and Environment Coalition; National Guard and Reserve Component Caucus; Humanities Caucus; Bicycle Caucus; Philanthropy Caucus; House Trade Working Group; committees: Appropriations; elected to the 111th Congress on November 4, 2008; reelected to each succeeding Congress.

Office Listings

http://pingree.house.gov

2162 Rayburn House Office Building, Washington, DC 20515	(202) 225–6116
Chief of Staff.—Jesse Connolly.	FAX: 225–5590
Scheduler.—Karen Sudbay.	
2 Portland Fish Pier, Suite 304, Portland, ME 04101	(207) 774–5019

Counties: CUMBERLAND, KENNEBEC (part), KNOX, LINCOLN, SAGADAHOC, YORK. Population (2010), 668,515.

ZIP Codes: 03901–11, 04001–11, 04013–15, 04017, 04019–21, 04024, 04027–30, 04032–34, 04038–40, 04042–43, 04046–50, 04053–57, 04061–64, 04066, 04069–79, 04082–87, 04090–98, 04101–10, 04112, 04116, 04122–24, 04259–60, 04265, 04284, 04287, 04330, 04332–33, 04336, 04338, 04341–55, 04357–60, 04363–64, 04530, 04541, 04543–44, 04547–48, 04551, 04553–56, 04558, 04562–65, 04567–68, 04570–76, 04578–79, 04841, 04843, 04846–56, 04858–65, 04901, 04910, 04917–18, 04922, 04926–27, 04935, 04937, 04941, 04949, 04952, 04962–63

* * *

SECOND DISTRICT

BRUCE POLIQUIN, Republican, of Maine; born in Waterville, Kennebec County, ME, November 1, 1953; graduated from Phillips Exeter Academy, Exeter, New Hampshire, 1972; A.B., Harvard University, Cambridge, Massachusetts, 1976; professional: businessman; State Treasurer of Maine, 2010–12; committees: Financial Services; elected to the 114th Congress on November 4, 2014.

Office Listings

https://poliquin.house.gov

426 Cannon House Office Building, Washington, DC 20515	(202) 225–6306
Chief of Staff.—Matt Hutson.	
Deputy Chief of Staff.—Julie Mulvee.	
Legislative Director.—Philip Swatzfager.	
Press Secretary.—Michael Byerly.	
6 State Street, Suite 101, Bangor, ME 04401	(207) 942–0583
179 Lisbon Street, Ground Floor, Lewiston, ME 04240	(207) 784–0768
631 Main Street, Suite 2, Presque Isle, ME 04769	(207) 764–1968

Counties: ANDROSCOGGIN, AROOSTOOK, FRANKLIN, HANCOCK, KENNEBEC (part), OXFORD, PENOBSCOT, PISCATAQUIS, SOMERSET, WALDO, AND WASHINGTON. Population (2010), 664,180.

ZIP Codes: 04010, 04016, 04022, 04037, 04041, 04051, 04068, 04088, 04210–12, 04216–17, 04219–28, 04230–31, 04234, 04236–41, 04243, 04250, 04252–58, 04261–63, 04266–68, 04270–71, 04274–76, 04278, 04280–83, 04285–86, 04288–92, 04294, 04354, 04401–02, 04406, 04408, 04410–24, 04426–31, 04434–35, 04438, 04441–44, 04448–51, 04453–57, 04459–64, 04467–69, 04471–76, 04478–79, 04481, 04485, 04487–93, 04495–97, 04549, 04605–07, 04609, 04611–17, 04619, 04622–31, 04634–35, 04637, 04640, 04642–46, 04648–50, 04652–58, 04660, 04662, 04664, 04666–69, 04671–77, 04679–81, 04683–86, 04691, 04693–94, 04730, 04732–47, 04750–51, 04756–66, 04768–70, 04772–77, 04779–81, 04783, 04785–88, 04848–51, 04857, 04903, 04911–12, 04915, 04920–25, 04928–30, 04932–33, 04936–45, 04947, 04949–58, 04961, 04964–67, 04969–76, 04978–79, 04981–88, 04992

MARYLAND

(Population 2010, 5,773,552)

SENATORS

BARBARA A. MIKULSKI, Democrat, of Baltimore, MD; born in Baltimore, July 20, 1936; education: B.A., Mount St. Agnes College, 1958; M.S.W., University of Maryland School of Social Work, 1965; former social worker for Catholic Charities and city of Baltimore; former adjunct professor, Department of Sociology, Loyola College; elected to the Baltimore City Council in 1971; Democratic nominee for the U.S. Senate in 1974; elected to the U.S. House of Representatives in November, 1976; first woman appointed to the Energy and Commerce Committee; also served on the Merchant Marine and Fisheries Committee; became the first Democratic woman to be elected to a Senate seat not previously held by her husband, and the first Democratic woman ever to serve in both houses of Congress; first woman to be elected to a leadership post; Secretary of the Democratic Conference; first woman to serve as Chair of the Senate Appropriations Committee; committees: vice chair, Appropriations; Health, Education, Labor, and Pensions; Select Committee on Intelligence; elected to the U.S. Senate in November, 1986; reelected to each succeeding Senate term.

Office Listings

http://mikulski.senate.gov   http://twitter.com/senatorbarb
https://www.facebook.com/senatormikulski

503 Hart Senate Office Building, Washington, DC 20510	(202) 224–4654
Chief of Staff.—Shannon Kula.	FAX: 224–8858
Legislative Director.—Jean Doyle.	
901 South Bond Street, Suite 310, Baltimore, MD 21231	(410) 962–4510
60 West Street, Suite 202, Annapolis, MD 21401	(410) 263–1805
6404 Ivy Lane, Suite 406, Greenbelt, MD 20770	(301) 345–5517
32 West Washington Street, Suite 203, Hagerstown, MD 21740	(301) 797–2826
The Gallery Plaza Building, 212 Main Street, Suite 200, Salisbury, MD 21801	(410) 546–7711

* * *

BENJAMIN L. "BEN" CARDIN, Democrat, of Baltimore, MD; born in Baltimore, October 5, 1943; education: graduated, City College High School, 1961; B.A., cum laude, University of Pittsburgh, 1964; L.L.B., 1st in class, University of Maryland School of Law, 1967; professional: attorney, Rosen and Esterson, 1967–78; elected to Maryland House of Delegates in November 1966, served from 1967–87; Speaker of the House of Delegates, youngest Speaker at the time, 1979–87; elected to U.S. House of Representatives in November 1986, Maryland 3rd Congressional District, served from 1987–2007; member: Associated Jewish Charities and Welfare Fund, 1985–89; Trustee, Baltimore Council on Foreign Affairs, 1999–2007 Trustee, Goucher College, 1999–2008; St. Mary's College, 1988–99; Lifetime Member, NAACP, since 1990; Board of Visitors, University of Maryland Law School, 1998–present; President's Board of Visitors, UMBC, 1993–present; Johns Hopkins University Institute for Policy Studies' National Advisory Board, 2003–present; Board of Visitors, U.S. Naval Academy, 2007–present; Board of Trustees, The James Madison Memorial Fellowship, 2010–present; awards: Congressional Award, Small Business Council of America, 1993, 1999, 2005; Public Sector Distinguished Award, Tax Foundation, 2003; Congressional Voice for Children Award, National PTA, 2009; Congressional Leadership Award, American College of Emergency Physicians, 2010; Whitney M. Young Award, Baltimore Urban League, 2011; Chesapeake Conservation Hero, Chesapeake Conservancy, 2012; Commissioner, Commission for Security and Cooperation in Europe (CSCE), since 1993; co-chair, CSCE, 2007–08; chair, CSCE, 2009–10; co-chair, CSCE, 2011–13; chair, CSCE, 2013–14; Vice President, Organization for Security and Cooperation in Europe (OSCE) Parliamentary Assembly, 2006–14; Special Representative on Anti-Semitism, Racism, and Intolerance for the OSCE Parliamentary Assembly (2014–present); religion: Jewish; married: Myrna Edelman of Baltimore, 1964; two children, (one deceased); two grandchildren; committees: ranking member, Foreign Relations; Environment and Public Works; Finance; Small Business and Entrepreneurship; elected to the U.S. Senate on November 7, 2006; reelected to the U.S. Senate on November 6, 2012.

Office Listings

http://cardin.senate.gov   www.facebook.com/senatorbencardin
twitter: @senatorcardin

509 Hart Senate Office Building, Washington, DC 20510	(202) 224–4524

Office Listings—Continued

Chief of Staff.—Chris Lynch.	FAX: 224–1651
Floor Director.—Gray Maxwell.	
Scheduler.—Debbie Yamada.	
Communications Director.—Sue Walitsky.	
100 South Charles Street, Tower I, Suite 1710, Baltimore, MD 21201	(410) 962–4436
State Director.—Carleton Atkinson.	FAX: 962–4256
10201 Martin Luther King, Jr. Highway, Suite 210, Bowie, MD 20720	(301) 860–0414
451 Hungerford Drive, Suite 230, Rockville, MD 20850	(301) 762–2974
212 West Main Street, Suite 301C, P.O. Box 11, Salisbury, MD 21801	(410) 546–4250
13 Canal Street, Room 305, Cumberland, MD 21502	(301) 777–2957

REPRESENTATIVES

FIRST DISTRICT

ANDY HARRIS, Republican, of Cockeysville, MD; born in Brooklyn, NY, January 25, 1957; education: B.S., Johns Hopkins University, Baltimore, MD, 1977; M.D., Johns Hopkins University, Baltimore, 1980; M.H.S., Johns Hopkins University, Baltimore, 1995; professional: anesthesiologist, as an Associate Professor of Anesthesiology and Critical Care Medicine; member of the Maryland State Senate, 1998–2010; minority whip, Maryland State Senate; military: Commander, Johns Hopkins Medical Naval Reserve Primus Unit P0605C; religion: Catholic; widowed; five children; three grandchildren; committees: Appropriations; elected to the 112th Congress on November 2, 2010; reelected to each succeeding Congress.

Office Listings

http://harris.house.gov

1533 Longworth House Office Building, Washington, DC 20515	(202) 225–5311
Chief of Staff.—Chris Meekins.	FAX: 225–0254
Legislative Director.—John Dutton.	
Press Secretary.—Shelby Hodgkins.	
Scheduler.—Charlotte Heyworth.	
100 Olde Point Village, Suite 101, Chester, MD 21619	(410) 643–5425
15 Churchville Road, Suite 102B, Bel Air, MD 21014	(410) 588–5670
212 West Main Street, Suite 204B, Salisbury, MD 21801	(443) 944–8624

Counties: COUNTIES: BALTIMORE (part), CAROLINE, CARROLL (part), CECIL, DORCHESTER, KENT, HARFORD (part), QUEEN ANNE'S, SOMERSET, TALBOT, WICOMICO, AND WORCESTER. Population (2010), 721,529.

ZIP Codes: 21001, 21009, 21013–15, 21018, 21023, 21028, 21030–32, 21034, 21040, 21047–48, 21050–51, 21053, 21057, 21074, 21078, 21082, 21084–85, 21087–88, 21102, 21111, 21120, 21128, 21131–32, 21136, 21154–57, 21160–62, 21234, 21236, 21286, 21601, 21606–07, 21609–10, 21612–13, 21617, 21619–20, 21622–29, 21631–32, 21634–36, 21638–41, 21643–45, 21647–73, 21675–79, 21681–85, 21687, 21690, 21757, 21784, 21787, 21791, 21801–04, 21810–11, 21813–14, 21817, 21821–22, 21824, 21826, 21829–30, 21835–38, 21840–43, 21849–53, 21856–57, 21861–67, 21869, 21871–72, 21874–75, 21890, 21901–04, 21911–22, 21930

* * *

SECOND DISTRICT

C. A. DUTCH RUPPERSBERGER, Democrat, of Cockeysville, MD; born in Baltimore, MD, January 31, 1946; education: Baltimore City College; University of Maryland, College Park; J.D., University of Baltimore Law School, 1970; professional: attorney; partner, Ruppersberger, Clark, and Mister (law firm); public service: Baltimore County Assistant State's Attorney; Baltimore County Council; Baltimore County Executive, 1994–2002; married: the former Kay Murphy; children: Cory and Jill; committees: Appropriations; elected to the 108th Congress on November 5, 2002; reelected to each succeeding Congress.

Office Listings

http://dutch.house.gov   twitter.com/call__me__dutch
https://www.facebook.com/dutchruppersberger

2416 Rayburn House Office Building, Washington, DC 20515	(202) 225–3061
Chief of Staff.—Tara Oursler.	FAX: 225–3094
Deputy Chief of Staff.—Cori Duggins.	
Communications Director.—Jaime Lennon.	
Senior Policy Advisor.—Walter Gonzales.	
The Atrium, 375 West Padonia Road, Suite 200, Timonium, MD 21093	(410) 628–2701

Office Listings—Continued

District Director.—Jennifer Riggs.   FAX: 628–2708
Scheduler.—Elliott Phaup.

Counties: ANNE ARUNDEL (part), BALTIMORE CITY (part), BALTIMORE COUNTY (part), HARFORD (part), HOWARD (part).
Population (2010), 721,529.

ZIP Codes: 20701, 20723–24, 20755, 20794, 21001, 21005, 21009–10, 21015, 21017, 21022, 21027, 21030–31, 21034, 21040, 21043, 21052, 21057, 21062–63, 21065, 21071, 21075–78, 21085, 21090, 21093, 21113, 21117, 21128–30, 21133, 21136, 21144, 21162–63, 21204, 21206, 21208, 21212–14, 21219–22, 21224–27, 21230–31, 21234, 21236–37, 21239, 21240, 21244, 21252, 21286

* * *

THIRD DISTRICT

JOHN P. SARBANES, Democrat, of Baltimore, MD; born in Baltimore, May 22, 1962; education: A.B., *cum laude*, Woodrow Wilson School of Public and International Affairs, Princeton University, 1984; Fulbright Scholar, Greece, 1985; J.D., Harvard University School of Law, 1988; professional: law clerk to Judge J. Frederick Motz, U.S. District Court for the District of Maryland, 1988–89; admitted to Maryland Bar, 1988; member: American Bar Association; Maryland State Bar Association; attorney, Venable, LLP, 1989–2006 (chair, health care practice); founding member, Board of Trustees, Dunbar Project, 1990–94; Board of Directors, Public Justice Center, 1991–2006 (president, 1994–97); Institute for Christian and Jewish Studies, 1991–present (past chair, membership committee); Special Assistant to State Superintendent of Schools, State Department of Education, 1998–2005; awards: Unsung Hero Award, Maryland Chapter of the Association of Fundraising Professionals, 2006; Arthur W. Machen, Jr. Award, Maryland Legal Services Corp., 2006; married to Dina Sarbanes; three children; committees: Energy and Commerce; elected to the 110th Congress on November 7, 2006; reelected to each succeeding Congress.

Office Listings

http://www.sarbanes.house.gov

2444 Rayburn House Office Building, Washington, DC 20510 .... (202) 225–4016
    Chief of Staff.—Jason Gleason.   FAX: 225–9219
    Deputy Chief of Staff.—Dvora Lovinger.
    Legislative Director.—Raymond O'Mara.
    Scheduler.—Kate Gieron.
    Legislative Assistant.—Anna Killius.
    Legislative Correspondent.—Peter Gelman.
    Communications Director.—Daniel Jacobs.
600 Baltimore Avenue, Suite 303, Towson, MD 21204 .... (410) 832–8890
44 Calvert Street, Suite 349, Annapolis, MD 21401 .... (410) 295 1679

Counties: ANNE ARUNDEL (part), BALTIMORE (part), BALTIMORE CITY (part), HOWARD (part), AND MONTGOMERY (part).
Population (2010), 720,094.

ZIP Codes: 20705, 20707, 20723–24, 20759, 20777, 20783, 20832–33, 20853, 20855, 20860–62, 20866, 20868, 20882, 20901, 20903–06, 21012, 21022, 21029, 21037, 21043–46, 21054, 21056, 21060–61, 21075–77, 21090, 21093, 21108, 21113, 21117, 21122, 21128, 21136, 21139, 21144, 21153, 21201–15, 21218, 21223–27, 21229–31, 21234, 21236–37, 21239, 21252, 21281–82, 21285–86, 21401–03, 21409, 21412, 21797

* * *

FOURTH DISTRICT

DONNA F. EDWARDS, Democrat, of Fort Washington, MD; born in Yanceyville, NC, June 28, 1959; education: B.A., Wake Forest University, Winston-Salem, NC, 1980; J.D., Franklin Pierce Law Center, Concord, NH, 1989; professional: executive director, Arca Foundation, 2000–08; founder and executive director, National Network to End Domestic Violence, 1996–99; executive director, Center for New Democracy, 1994–96; member: board of directors, National Network to End Domestic Violence; Citizens for Responsibility and Ethics in Washington; League of Conservation Voters, Common Cause; Tom Lantos Human Rights Commission; committees: Science, Space, and Technology; Transportation and Infrastructure; elected by special election on June 17, 2008, to fill the vacancy caused by the resignation of U.S. Representative Albert Russell Wynn; elected to a full term in the 111th Congress on November 4, 2008; reelected to each succeeding Congress.

Office Listings

http://www.donnaedwards.house.gov   https://twitter.com/repdonnaedwards
https://www.facebook.com/pages/congresswoman-donna-f-edwards/107297211756

2445 Rayburn House Office Building, Washington, DC 20515 .... (202) 225–8699
Chief of Staff.—Adrienne Christian.   FAX: 225–8714
Legislative Director.—Chris Schloesser.
Communications Director.—Dan Weber.
5001 Silver Hill Road, Suite 106, Suitland, MD 20746 .... (301) 516–7601
877 Baltimore Annapolis Boulevard, #101, Severna Park, MD 21146 .... (410) 421–8061

Counties: ANNE ARUNDEL (part), PRINCE GEORGE'S (part). CITIES AND TOWNSHIPS: Andrews Air Force Base, Annapolis, Arnold, Beltsville, Bladensburg, Bowie, Brentwood, Capitol Heights, Clinton, College Park, Crofton, Crownsville, Davidsonville, District Heights, Edgewater, Fort Washington, Gambrills, Glen Burnie, Glenn Dale, Hyattsville, Lanham, Laurel, Millersville, Mount Rainier, Odenton, Oxon Hill, Pasadena, Riva, Riverdale, Severn, Severna Park, Sherwood Forest, Silver Spring, Suitland, Takoma Park, Temple Hills, and Upper Marlboro. Population (2010) 720,065.

ZIP Codes: 20705–08, 20710, 20712, 20720–22, 20724, 20735, 20737, 20740, 20743–48, 20762, 20769, 20772, 20774, 20781–85, 20903–04, 20912, 21012, 21032, 21035, 21037, 21054, 21061, 21108, 21113–14, 21122, 21140, 21144, 21146, 21401, 21405, 21409

* * *

FIFTH DISTRICT

STENY H. HOYER, Democrat, of Mechanicsville, MD; born in New York, NY, June 14, 1939; education: graduated, Suitland High School; B.S., University of Maryland, 1963; J.D., Georgetown University Law Center, 1966; Honorary Doctor of Public Service, University of Maryland, 1988; admitted to the Maryland Bar Association, 1966; professional: practicing attorney, 1966–90; Maryland State Senate, 1967–79; vice chairman, Prince George's County, MD, Senate delegation, 1967–69; chairman, Prince George's County, MD, Senate delegation, 1969–75; president, Maryland State Senate, 1975–79; member, State Board for Higher Education, 1978–81; married: Judith Pickett, deceased, February 6, 1997; children: Susan, Stefany, and Anne; Democratic Steering Committee; Democratic Whip, 108th and 109th Congresses; House Majority Leader, 110th and 111th Congresses; Democratic Whip, 112th, 113th, and 114th Congresses; elected to the 97th Congress on May 19, 1981, by special election; reelected to each succeeding Congress.

Office Listings

http://www.hoyer.house.gov   www.facebook.com/whiphoyer   twitter: @whiphoyer

1705 Longworth House Office Building, Washington, DC 20515 .... (202) 225–4131
Chief of Staff.—Alexis Covey-Brandt.   FAX: 226–0663
Senior Advisor / Personal Office Director.—Jim Notter.
U.S. Federal Courthouse, Suite 310, 6500 Cherrywood Lane, Greenbelt, MD 20770 .... (301) 474–0119
401 Post Office Road, Suite 202, Waldorf, MD 20602 .... (301) 843–1577

Counties: ANNE ARUNDEL (part), CALVERT, CHARLES, PRINCE GEORGE'S (part), ST. MARY'S. Population (2012), 721,529.

ZIP Codes: 20601–03, 20606–09, 20611–13, 20615–26, 20628–30, 20632, 20634, 20636–37, 20639–40, 20645–46, 20650, 20653, 20657–60, 20662, 20664, 20667, 20670, 20674–76, 20678, 20680, 20684–90, 20692–93, 20695, 20705–08, 20711, 20714–16, 20720–21, 20732–33, 20735–37, 20740, 20742, 20744, 20746, 20748, 20751, 20754, 20758, 20762, 20764–65, 20769–70, 20772, 20774, 20776, 20778–79, 20781–84, 21035, 21037, 21054, 21113–14

* * *

SIXTH DISTRICT

JOHN K. DELANEY, Democrat of Potomac, MD; born in Wood-Ridge, NJ, April 16, 1963; education: B.A., Columbia University, 1985; J.D., Georgetown University Law School, 1988; professional: former practicing attorney, Shaw, Pittman, Potts & Trowbridge; co-founder, chair, and chief executive officer, Health Care Financial Partners, Inc., 1993–99; co-founder and executive chair, Capital Source, 2000–12; awards: Ernst & Young Entrepreneur of the Year, 2005; married: April; children: Summer, Brooke, Lily, Grace; committees: Financial Services; Joint Economic Committee; elected to the 113th Congress on November 6, 2012; reelected to the 114th Congress on November 4, 2014.

Office Listings

http://www.delaney.house.gov   https://www.facebook.com/congressmanjohndelaney
https://twitter.com/repjohndelaney

1632 Longworth House Office Building, Washington, DC 20515 .... (202) 225–2721
Chief of Staff.—Justin Schall.
Legislative Director.—Xan Fishman.
Scheduler.—Jeri Sparling.
9801 Washingtonian Boulevard, Suite 330, Gaithersburg, MD 20878 .... (301) 926–0300
38 South Potomac Street, Suite 205, Hagerstown, MD 21740 .... (301) 733–2900

Counties: ALLEGANY, FREDERICK (part), GARRETT, MONTGOMERY (part), WASHINGTON. CITIES AND TOWNSHIPS: Bethesda, Boonsboro, Boyds, Clarksburg, Cumberland, Darnestown, Frederick, Frostburg, Funkstown, Gaithersburg, Germantown, Hagerstown, Hancock, Montgomery Village, Oakland, Olney, Poolesville, Potomac, Rockville, Sharpsburg, Smithburg, Urbana, Williamsport, Woodsboro. Also includes Antietam National Battlefield and Camp David. Population (2010), 728,400.

ZIP Codes: 20817, 20827, 20837–39, 20841–42, 20850, 20852–55, 20859, 20871–72, 20874–80, 20882, 20884–86, 20898–99, 20906, 21501–05, 21520–24, 21528–30, 21531–32, 21536, 21538–43, 21545, 21550, 21555–57, 21560–62, 21701–05, 21709–11, 21713, 21715–17, 21719–22, 21733–34, 21740–42, 21746–50, 21754–56, 21758, 21766–67, 21769, 21774, 21777, 21779–83, 21790, 21795

* * *

SEVENTH DISTRICT

ELIJAH E. CUMMINGS, Democrat, of Baltimore City, Baltimore County and Howard County, MD; born in Baltimore, January 18, 1951; education: graduated, Baltimore City College High School, 1969; B.S., political science, Phi Beta Kappa, Howard University, Washington, DC, 1973; J.D., University of Maryland Law School, 1976; professional: attorney; admitted to the Maryland Bar in 1976; delegate, Maryland State Legislature, 1982–96; chairman, Maryland Legislative Black Caucus, 1984; speaker pro tempore, Maryland General Assembly, 1995–96; vice chairman, Constitutional and Administrative Law Committee; vice chairman, Economic Matters Committee; active in civic affairs, and recipient of numerous community awards; member, U.S. Naval Academy Board of Visitors, Morgan State University Board of Regents, University of Maryland Law School Board of Advisors; member, New Psalmist Baptist Church, Baltimore, MD; married: Dr. Maya Rockeymoore; committees: ranking member, Oversight and Government Reform; ranking member, Select Committee on Benghazi; Transportation and Infrastructure; elected to the 104th Congress by special election in April, 1996; reelected to each succeeding Congress.

Office Listings

http://www.cummings.house.gov   https://www.facebook.com/elijahcummings
https://twitter.com/elijahecummings

2230 Rayburn House Office Building, Washington, DC 20515 .... (202) 225–4741
Chief of Staff.—Vernon Simms.   FAX: 225–3178
Legislative Director.—Suzanne Owen.
Legislative Assistants: Jimmy Fremgen, Karen Kudelko, Brandon Reavis.
Communications Director.—Trudy Perkins.
1010 Park Avenue, Suite 105, Baltimore, MD 21201 .... (410) 685–9199
754 Frederick Road, Catonsville, MD 21228 .... (410) 719–8777
8267 Main Street, Room 102, Ellicott City, MD 21043 .... (410) 465–8259

Counties: BALTIMORE (part), HOWARD (part), BALTIMORE CITY (part). Population (2010), 660,523.

ZIP Codes: 21036, 21042, 21051, 21111, 21152, 21207, 21216–17, 21228, 21235, 21245, 21250–51, 21287, 21723, 21737–38, 21794, 20777, 20833, 21013, 21029–31, 21043–45, 21047, 21057, 21074–75, 21082, 21087, 21093, 21102, 21104, 21117, 21120, 21131, 21133, 21136, 21155, 21161

* * *

EIGHTH DISTRICT

CHRIS VAN HOLLEN, Democrat, of Kensington, MD; born in Karachi, Pakistan, January 10, 1959; education: B.A., Swarthmore College, 1982; master's in public policy, Harvard University, 1985; J.D., Georgetown University, 1990; professional: attorney; legislative assistant to former Maryland U.S. Senator Charles McC. Mathias, Jr.; staff member, U.S. Senate Committee on Foreign Relations; senior legislative advisor to former Maryland Governor William Donald

Schaefer; public service: elected, Maryland House of Delegates, 1990; elected, Maryland State Senate, 1994; married: Katherine; children: Anna, Nicholas, and Alexander; committees: ranking member, Budget; elected to the 108th Congress on November 5, 2002; reelected to each succeeding Congress.

Office Listings

http://www.vanhollen.house.gov

1707 Longworth House Office Building, Washington, DC 20515	(202) 225–5341
Chief of Staff.—Bill Parsons.	FAX: 225–0375
Legislative Director.—Sarah Schenning.	
Legislative Assistants: Matt Kretman, Cornelius Queen.	
Communications Director.—Bridgett Frey.	
51 Monroe Street, Suite 507, Rockville, MD 20850	(301) 424–3501
205 Center Street, Suite 206, Mount Airy, MD 21771	(301) 829–2181
District Director.—Joan Kleinman.	

Counties: MONTGOMERY (part), FREDERICK (part), CARROLL (part). Population (2010), 721,528.

ZIP Codes: 20811–18, 20824–25, 20847–55, 20857, 20872, 20882, 20889, 20891–92, 20894–96, 20901–08, 20910–16, 20918, 21104, 21157–58, 21701–04, 21714, 21718, 21727, 21754–55, 21757, 21759, 21762, 21765, 21769–71, 21773–76, 21778, 21780, 21783–84, 21787–21788, 21791–93, 21797–98

MASSACHUSETTS

(Population 2010, 6,547,629)

SENATORS

ELIZABETH WARREN, Democrat, of Cambridge, MA; born in Oklahoma City, OK, June 22, 1949; education: B.A., University of Houston, Houston, TX, 1970; J.D., Rutgers Law School, Newark, NJ, 1976; professional: Leo Gottlieb Professor of Law, Harvard Law School, 1995–2012; Chief Advisor, National Bankruptcy Review Commission, 1995–97; chair, Congressional Oversight Panel, 2008–10; Assistant to the President and Special Advisor to the Secretary of the Treasury for the Consumer Financial Protection Bureau, 2010–11; married: Bruce Mann; two children, three grandchildren; committees: Banking, Housing, and Urban Affairs; Energy and Natural Resources; Health, Education, Labor, and Pensions; Special Committee on Aging; elected to the U.S. Senate on November 6, 2012.

Office Listings

http://warren.senate.gov   facebook.com/senatorelizabethwarren
twitter: @senwarren

317 Hart Senate Office Building, Washington, DC 20510	(202) 224–4543

Chief of Staff.—Mindy Myers.
Deputy Chief of Staff.—Bruno Freitas.
Legislative Director.—Jon Donenberg.

2400 JFK Federal Building, 15 New Sudbury Street, Boston, MA 02203	(617) 565–3170

State Director.—Roger Lau.

1550 Main Street, Suite 406, Springfield, MA 01103	(413) 788–2690

* * *

EDWARD J. MARKEY, Democrat, of Malden, MA; born in Malden, MA, July 11, 1946; education: B.A., Boston College, Boston, MA, 1968; J.D., Boston College, Boston, MA, 1972; U.S. Army Reserve (1968–73); professional: member, Massachusetts House of Representatives (1973–76); U.S. House of Representatives (1976–2013); ranking member, Natural Resources Committee (2011–13); chair, Select Committee on Energy Independence and Global Warming (2007–11); chair, Subcommittee on Energy and the Environment (2009–11); chair, subcommittee on Telecommunications and the Internet (2007–09); married: Dr. Susan Blumenthal; committees: Commerce, Science, and Transportation; Environment and Public Works; Foreign Relations; Small Business and Entrepreneurship; elected to the U.S. Senate in a special election on June 25, 2013, to fill the vacancy caused by the resignation of John F. Kerry to become Secretary of State.

Office Listings

http://www.markey.senate.gov   twitter: @senmarkey
https://www.facebook.com/edjmarkey

255 Dirksen Senate Office Building, Washington, DC 20510	(202) 224–2742

Chief of Staff.—Mark Bayer.
Scheduler.—Sarah Butler.
Communications Director.—Giselle Barry.

JFK Federal Building, Suite 975, 15 New Sudbury Street, Boston, MA 02203	(617) 565–8519
222 Milliken Boulevard, Suite 312, Fall River, MA 02721	(508) 677–0523
1550 Main Street, 4th Floor, Springfield, MA 01101	(413) 785–4610

REPRESENTATIVES

FIRST DISTRICT

RICHARD E. NEAL, Democrat, of Springfield, MA; born in Springfield, February 14, 1949; education: graduated, Springfield Technical High School, 1968; B.A., American International College, Springfield, 1972; M.A., University of Hartford Barney School of Business and Public Administration, West Hartford, CT, 1976; instructor and lecturer; assistant to mayor of Springfield, 1973–78; Springfield City Council, 1978–84; mayor, City of Springfield, 1983–89; member: Massachusetts Mayors Association; Adult Education Council; American International College Alumni Association; Boys Club Alumni Association; Emily Bill Athletic Association;

Cancer Crusade; John Boyle O'Reilly Club; United States Conference of Mayors; Valley Press Club; Solid Waste Advisory Committee for the State of Massachusetts; Committee on Leadership and Government; Mass Jobs Council; trustee: Springfield Libraries and Museums Association, Springfield Red Cross, Springfield YMCA; married: Maureen; four children: Rory Christopher, Brendan Conway, Maura Katherine, and Sean Richard; committees: Ways and Means; elected on November 8, 1988 to the 101st Congress; reelected to each succeeding Congress.

Office Listings

http://www.neal.house.gov

341 Cannon House Office Building, Washington, DC 20515 .... (202) 225–5601
    Administrative Assistant.—Ann Jablon.   FAX: 225–8112
    Executive Assistant.—Tim Ranstrom.
    Press Secretary.—William Tranghese.
300 State Street, Suite 200, Springfield, MA 01105 .... (413) 785–0325
    District Manager.—Vacant.
78 Center Street, Pittsfield, MA 01201 .... (508) 634–8198
    Office Manager.—Cynthia Clark.

Counties: BERKSHIRE, FRANKLIN (part), HAMPDEN (part), HAMPSHIRE (part), and WORCESTER (part). Population (2010), 727,515.

ZIP Codes: 01001, 01008–13, 01020–22, 01026–30, 01032–34, 01036, 01039, 01040, 01050, 01056–57, 01069–71, 01073, 01075, 01077, 01079–81, 01083–86, 01089, 01092, 01095–98, 01103–09, 01118–19, 01128–29, 01151, 01199, 01201, 01220, 01222–26, 01229, 01230, 01235–38, 01240, 01242–45, 01247, 01253–60, 01262, 01264, 01266–67, 01270, 01301, 01330, 01337–41, 01343, 01346, 01350, 01367, 01370, 01506–07, 01515, 01518, 01521, 01550, 01566, 01571, 01585

* * *

SECOND DISTRICT

JAMES P. McGOVERN, Democrat, of Worcester, MA; born in Worcester, November 20, 1959; education: B.A., M.P.A., American University; legislative director and senior aide to Congressman Joe Moakley (D–South Boston); led the 1989 investigation into the murders of six Jesuit priests and two lay women in El Salvador; managed George McGovern's (D–SD) 1984 presidential campaign in Massachusetts and delivered his nomination speech at the Democratic National Convention; board of directors, Jesuit International Volunteers; former volunteer, Mt. Carmel House, an emergency shelter for battered and abused women; married: Lisa Murray McGovern; committees: Agriculture; Rules; elected to the 105th Congress; reelected to each succeeding Congress.

Office Listings

http://www.mcgovern.house.gov

438 Cannon House Office Building, Washington, DC 20515 .... (202) 225–6101
    Legislative Director.—Cindy Buhl.   FAX: 225–5759
    Press Secretary.—Abraham White.
12 East Worcester Street, Suite 1, Worcester, MA 01604 .... (508) 831–7356
    District Director.—Kathleen Polanowicz.
24 Church Street, Suite 29, Leominster, MA 01543 .... (978) 466–3552
    District Representative.—Eladia Romero.
94 Pleasant Street, Northampton, MA 01060 .... (413) 341–8700
    District Representative.—Natalie Blais.

Counties: FRANKLIN (part), HAMPDEN (part), HAMPSHIRE (part), NORFOLK (part), AND WORCESTER (part). CITIES AND TOWNSHIPS: Amherst, Athol, Auburn, Barre, Belchertown, Bellingham, Blackstone, Boylston, Deerfield, Douglas, Erving, Gill, Grafton, Greenfield, Hadley, Hardwick, Hatfield, Holden, Hubbardston, Leicester, Leominster, Leverett, Mendon, Millbury, Millville, Montague, New Braintree, New Salem, North Brookfield, Northampton, Northborough, Northbridge, Northfield, Oakham, Orange, Oxford, Palmer, Paxton, Pelham, Petersham, Phillipston, Princeton, Royalston, Rutland, Shrewsbury, Shutesbury, Spencer, Sterling, Sunderland, Sutton, Templeton, Upton, Uxbridge, Ware, Warwick, Webster, Wendell, West Boylston, West Brookfield, Westborough, Whately, Winchendon, and Worcester. Population (2010), 727,514.

ZIP Codes: 01002–03, 01005, 01007, 01031, 01035, 01037–39, 01053–54, 01060, 01062–63, 01066, 01068–69, 01072, 01074, 01082, 01088, 01093–94, 01301, 01331, 01342, 01344, 01347, 01349, 01351, 01354–55, 01360, 01364, 01366, 01368, 01370, 01373, 01375–76, 01378–79, 01420, 01436, 01438, 01440, 01452–53, 01468, 01475, 01501, 01504–05, 01516, 01519–20, 01522, 01524–25, 01527, 01529, 01531–32, 01534–37, 01540–43, 01545, 01560, 01562, 01564, 01568–70, 01581, 01583, 01585, 01588, 01590, 01602–12, 01756–57, 02019

* * *

THIRD DISTRICT

NIKI TSONGAS, Democrat, of Lowell, MA; born in Chico, CA, April 26, 1946; graduated from Narimasu American High School, Japan, 1964; B.A., Smith College, Northampton, MA, 1968; J.D., Boston University, Boston, MA, 1988; professional: social worker; lawyer, Middlesex Community College's dean of external affairs; widowed: Paul Tsongas; children: Ashley Tsongas, Katina Tsongas, and Molly Tsongas; committees: Armed Services; Natural Resources; elected to the 110th Congress, by special election, to fill the vacancy caused by the resignation of Representative Martin Meehan; elected to the 111th Congress on November 4, 2008; reelected to each succeeding Congress.

Office Listings

http://www.tsongas.house.gov

1714 Longworth House Office Building, Washington, DC 20515	(202) 225–3411
Chief of Staff.—Katie Enos.	FAX: 226–0771
Washington Director.—Sara Outterson.	
Scheduler.—George Eng.	
126 John Street, Suite 12, Lowell, MA 01852	(978) 459–0101
District Director.—Chris Mullin.	

Counties: ESSEX COUNTY, MIDDLESEX COUNTY, WORCESTER COUNTY. Population (2010), 732,090.

ZIP Codes: 01432, 01450–51, 01460, 01464, 01503, 01523, 01718–20, 01740–42, 01749, 01754, 01775–76, 01778, 01810, 01821, 01824, 01826–27, 01830, 01840–44, 01850–54, 01862–63, 01876, 01879, 01886

* * *

FOURTH DISTRICT

JOSEPH P. KENNEDY III, Democrat, of Brookline, MA; born in Brighton, MA, October 4, 1980; education: graduated, Buckingham, Browne & Nichols, 1999; B.S., Stanford College, 2003; J.D., Harvard University, 2009; professional: Peace Corps, 2004–06; assistant district attorney, Cape and Islands Office, 2009–11; assistant district attorney, Middlesex Office, 2011–2012; committees: Energy and Commerce; elected to the 113th Congress on November 6, 2012; reelected to the 114th Congress on November 4, 2014.

Office Listings

http://kennedy.house.gov

306 Cannon House Office Building, Washington, DC 20515	(202) 225–5931
Chief of Staff.—Greg Mecher.	FAX: 225–0182
Deputy Chief of Staff / Legislative Director.—Sarah Curtis.	
Scheduler.—Andrew Greenough.	
8 North Main Street, Suite 200, Attleboro, MA 02703	(508) 431–1110
29 Crafts Street, Suite 375, Newton, MA 02458	(617) 332–3333
District Director.—Nick Clemons.	
Communications Director.—Emily Browne.	

Counties: BRISTOL (part), MIDDLESEX (part), NORFOLK (part), PLYMOUTH (part), WORCESTER (part). CITIES AND TOWNSHIPS: Attleboro, Bellingham, Berkley, Brookline, Dighton, Dover, Easton, Fall River, Foxboro, Franklin, Freetown, Hopedale, Hopkinton, Lakeville, Mansfield, Medfield, Medway, Milford, Millis, Needham, Newton, Norfolk, North Attleborough, Norton, Plainville, Raynham, Rehoboth, Seekonk, Sharon, Somerset, Swansea, Taunton, Wellesley, and Wrentham. Population (2010), 727,514.

ZIP Codes: 01747–48, 01757, 02019, 02030–31, 02035, 02038, 02048, 02052–54, 02056, 02067, 02070, 02093, 02171, 02334, 02347–48, 02356–57, 02375, 02445–47, 02456–62, 02464–68, 02481–82, 02492, 02494–95, 02702–03, 02712, 02715, 02718, 02725–26, 02760–63, 02766–69, 02771, 02777, 02779–80

* * *

FIFTH DISTRICT

KATHERINE M. CLARK, Democrat, of Melrose, MA; born in New Haven, CT, July, 17 1963; education: B.A., Saint Lawrence University, 1985; J.D., Cornell School of Law, 1989; M.P.A., Harvard University, 1997; professional: admitted to the Massachusetts Bar, 1997; served as general counsel for the Massachusetts Office of Child Care Services; Chief of the

Policy Division for the Massachusetts Attorney General and prosecutor; elected in March 2008 to the Massachusetts House of Representatives; elected to the Massachusetts State Senate in November 2010; religion: Protestant; married: Rodney Dowell; children: Addison, Jared, and Nathaniel; Democratic Steering and Policy Committee; committees: Education and the Workforce; Science, Space, and Technology; elected to the 113th Congress, by special election, on December 10, 2013; reelected to the 114th Congress on November 4, 2014.

Office Listings

http://www.katherineclark.house.gov

1721 Longworth House Office Building, Washington, DC 20515 .... (202) 225–2836
Chief of Staff.—Brooke Scannell.   FAX: 226–0092
Deputy Chief of Staff / Legislative Director.—David Bond.
5 High Street, Suite 101, Medford, MA 02155 .... (781) 396–2900
District Director.—Christian Lobue.

Counties: MIDDLESEX (part), SUFFOLK (part), AND WORCESTER (part). CITIES AND TOWNSHIPS: Arlington, Ashland, Belmont, Cambridge, Framingham, Holliston, Lexington, Lincoln, Malden, Medford, Melrose, Natick, Revere, Sherborn, Southborough, Stoneham, Sudbury, Waltham, Watertown, Wayland, Weston, Winchester, Winthrop, and Woburn. Population (2010), 727,515.

ZIP Codes: 01701–05, 01721, 01746, 01760, 01770, 01772–73, 01776, 01778, 01890, 02138–42, 02148, 02151–53, 02155, 02176, 02180, 02238, 02420–21, 02451–54, 02471–72, 02474, 02476–78, 02493

* * *

SIXTH DISTRICT

SETH MOULTON, Democrat, of Salem, MA; born in Salem, October 24, 1978; education: Phillips Academy Andover, 1997; A.B., Harvard College, 2001; M.B.A., Harvard Business School, 2011; M.P.A., Harvard Kennedy School of Government, 2011; professional: United States Marine Corps, 2002–08; business manager; Committees: Armed Services, Budget, Small Business; elected to the 114th Congress on November 4, 2014.

Office Listings

https://moulton.house.gov

1408 Longworth House Office Building, Washington, DC 20515 .... (202) 225–8020
Chief of Staff.—Roger Dean Huffstetler.
Deputy Chief of Staff.—Andy Flick.
Legislative Assistant.—Eric Kanter.
Legislative Aide.—Margo Brown.
Staff Assistant.—Meaghan Doherty.
Scheduler.—Brendan O'Bryan.
17 Peabody Square, Peabody, MA 01960 .... (978) 531–1669
District Director.—Rick Jakious.
Communications Director.—Carrie Rankin.
District Scheduler.—Dylan O'Sullivan.
District Representatives: Morgan Bell, Blake Hansen, Jennifer Migliore, Lucas Santos.

Counties: ESSEX, MIDDLESEX. CITIES AND TOWNSHIPS: Amesbury, Bedford, Beverly, Billerica, Boxford, Burlington, Danvers, Essex, Georgetown, Gloucester, Groveland, Hamilton, Ipswich, Lynn, Lynnfield, Manchester by the Sea, Marblehead, Merrimac, Middletown, Nahant, Newbury, Newburyport, Andover, North Andover, North Reading, Peabody, Reading, Rockport, Rowley, Salem, Salisbury, Saugus, Swampscott, Tewksbury, Topsfield, Wenham, West Newbury, Wakefield, and Wilmington. Population (2010), 731,681.

ZIP Codes: 01730–31, 01801, 01803, 01805, 01810, 01821–22, 01833–34, 01845, 01860, 01864, 01867, 01876, 01880, 01885, 01887, 01889, 01901–08, 01910, 01913, 01915, 01921–23, 01929–31, 01936–38, 01940, 01944–45, 01949–52, 01960–61, 01965–66, 01969–71, 01982–85

* * *

SEVENTH DISTRICT

MICHAEL E. CAPUANO, Democrat, of Somerville, MA; born in Somerville, January 9, 1952; education: graduated, Somerville High School, 1969; B.A., Dartmouth College, 1973; J.D., Boston College Law School, 1977; professional: admitted to the Massachusetts Bar, 1977; Alderman in Somerville, MA, 1977–79; Alderman-at-Large, 1985–89; elected Mayor for five terms, 1990 to January, 1999, when he resigned to be sworn in as a U.S. Representative; Democratic Caucus; married: Barbara Teebagy of Somerville, MA, in 1974; children: Michael and Joseph; committees: Ethics; Financial Services; Transportation and Infrastructure; elected to the 106th Congress; reelected to each succeeding Congress.

Office Listings

http://www.capuano.house.gov

1414 Longworth House Office Building, Washington, DC 20515	(202) 225–5111
Chief of Staff.—Robert Primus.	FAX: 225–9322
Office Manager / Scheduler.—Mary Doherty.	
Legislative Counsel.—Gira Bose.	
110 First Street, Cambridge, MA 02141	(617) 621–6208
District Director.—Jon Lenicheck.	

Counties: MIDDLESEX (part), NORFOLK (part), SUFFOLK (part). CITIES AND TOWNSHIPS: Boston (part), Cambridge (part), Chelsea, Everett, Milton (part), Randolph, and Somerville. Population (2010), 727,514.

ZIP Codes: 02111, 02115–26, 02128–32, 02134–36, 02138–45, 02149–50, 02163, 02186, 02199, 02368

* * *

EIGHTH DISTRICT

STEPHEN F. LYNCH, Democrat, of South Boston, MA; born in South Boston, March 31, 1955; education: South Boston High School, 1973; B.S., Wentworth Institute of Technology, J.D., Boston College Law School; master in public administration, JFK School of Government, Harvard University; professional: attorney; former President of Ironworkers Local #7; organizations: South Boston Boys and Girls Club; Colonel Daniel Marr Boys and Girls Club; Friends for Children; public service: elected to the Massachusetts House of Representatives in 1994, and the State Senate in 1996; family: married to Margaret; one child: Victoria; committees: Financial Services; Oversight and Government Reform; elected to the 107th Congress, by special election, on October 16, 2001; reelected to each succeeding Congress.

Office Listings

http://lynch.house.gov

2369 Rayburn House Office Building, Washington, DC 20515	(202) 225–8273
Chief of Staff.—Kevin Ryan.	FAX: 225–3984
Legislative Director.—Bruce Fernandez.	
Scheduler.—Megan Hollingshead.	
1 Harbor Place, Suite 304, Boston, MA 02210	(617) 428–2000
Plymouth County Registry Building, 155 West Elm Street, Brockton, MA 02401	(508) 586–5555
1245 Hancock Street, Suite 16, Quincy, MA 02169	(617) 657–6305

Counties: BRISTOL (part), NORFOLK (part), PLYMOUTH (part), SUFFOLK (part). Population (2010), 732,884.

ZIP Codes: 02021, 02025–26, 02032, 02043, 02045, 02047, 02050, 02062, 02066, 02071–72, 02081, 02090, 02108–10, 02113–14, 02118, 02122, 02124–25, 02127, 02130–32, 02136, 02169–71, 02184, 02186, 02188–91, 02203, 02210, 02301–02, 02322, 02324, 02333, 02343, 02351, 02368, 02379, 02382, 02467, 02767

* * *

NINTH DISTRICT

WILLIAM "BILL" KEATING, Democrat, of Bourne, MA; born in Norwood, MA, September 6, 1952; education: B.A., Boston College, MA, 1974; M.B.A., Boston College, MA, 1982; J.D., Suffolk University Law School, MA, 1985; professional: admitted to the Massachusetts Bar in 1985 and began practice in Stoughton, MA; Massachusetts House of Representatives, 1977–84; vice chairman, Committee on Criminal Justice; Committee on Election Laws; Massachusetts State Senate, 1985–98; chairman, Judiciary Committee; Committee on Taxation; Committee on Public Safety; Steering and Policy Committee; Norfolk County District Attorney, 1999–2011; religion: Roman Catholic; family: wife, Tevis; two children, Kristen and Patrick; committees: Foreign Affairs; Homeland Security; elected to the 112th Congress on November 2, 2010; reelected to each succeeding Congress.

Office Listings

http://www.keating.house.gov

315 Cannon House Office Building, Washington, DC 20515	(202) 225–3111

Office Listings—Continued

Chief of Staff.—Garrett Donovan. FAX: 225–5658
2 Court Street, Plymouth, MA 02360 .... (508) 746–9000
District Director.—Michael Jackman.
297 North Street, Suite 312, Hyannis, MA 02061 .... (508) 771–0666
558 Pleasant Street, Suite 309, New Bedford, MA 02740 .... (508) 999–6462

Counties: BARNSTABLE, BRISTOL (part), DUKES, NANTUCKET, AND PLYMOUTH. Population (2010), 727,514.

ZIP Codes: 02050, 02061, 02330, 02332, 02338–39, 02341, 02344–46, 02349, 02359–60, 02364, 02367, 02370, 02532, 02534–40, 02542–43, 02553–54, 02556–59, 02561–63, 02568, 02571, 02574–76, 02601, 02631, 02633, 02635–39, 02641–53, 02655, 02657, 02659–64, 02666–73, 02675, 02713–14, 02719–24, 02738–48, 02770, 02790

MICHIGAN

(Population 2010, 9,883,640)

SENATORS

DEBBIE STABENOW, Democrat, of Lansing, MI; born in Gladwin, MI, April 29, 1950; education: Clare High School; B.A., Michigan State University, 1972; M.S.W., Michigan State University, 1975; public service: Ingham County, MI, Commissioner, 1975–78, chairperson for two years; Michigan State House of Representatives, 1979–90; Michigan State Senate, 1991–94; religion: Methodist; children: Todd and Michelle; committees: ranking member, Agriculture, Nutrition, and Forestry; Budget; Finance; Energy and Natural Resources; elected to the U.S. House of Representatives in 1996 and 1998; elected to the U.S. Senate on November 7, 2000; reelected to each succeeding Senate term.

Office Listings

http://stabenow.senate.gov

731 Hart Senate Office Building, Washington, DC 20510	(202) 224–4822
Chief of Staff.—Bill Sweeney.	FAX: 228–0325
Legislative Director.—Matt VanKuiken.	
Scheduler.—Anne Stanski.	
221 West Lake Lansing Road, Suite 100, East Lansing, MI 48823	(517) 203–1760
719 Griswold Street, Suite 700 Detroit, MI 48226	(313) 961–4330
432 North Saginaw, Suite 301, Flint, MI 48502	(810) 720–4172
3335 South Airport Road West, Suite 6B, Traverse City, MI 49684	(231) 929–1031
3280 Beltline Court, Suite 400, Grand Rapids, MI 49525	(616) 975–0052
1901 West Ridge, Suite 7, Marquette, MI 49855	(906) 228–8756

* * *

GARY C. PETERS, Democrat, of Bloomfield Township, MI; born in Pontiac, MI, December 1, 1958; education: B.A., Alma College, Alma, MI, 1980; M.B.A. in Finance, University of Detroit, Detroit, MI, 1984; J.D., Wayne State University Law School, Detroit, MI, 1989; M.A. in Philosophy, Michigan State University, East Lansing, MI, 2007; professional: Assistant Vice President, Merrill Lynch, 1980–89; Vice President, UBS/Paine Webber, 1989–2003; former arbitrator, Financial Industry Regulatory Authority; At-Large City Councilman, Rochester Hills, MI, 1991–93; Lieutenant Commander, Seabee Combat Warfare Specialist, U.S. Navy Reserve, 1993–2000, 2001–05; Michigan State Senator, 1995–2002; Chief Administrative Officer for the Bureau of Investments, State of Michigan, 2003; Lottery Commissioner, State of Michigan, 2003–07; former instructor, Oakland University and Wayne State University; Griffin Endowed Chair in American Government, Central Michigan University, 2007–08; member, Michigan Bar Association; religion: Episcopalian; married: Colleen Ochoa Peters; three children: Gary Jr., Madeleine, and Alana; committees: Commerce, Science, and Transportation; Homeland Security and Governmental Affairs; Small Business and Entrepreneurship; Joint Economic Committee; elected to the U.S. House of Representatives in 2008, 2010 and 2012; elected to the U.S. Senate on November 4, 2014.

Office Listings

http://www.peters.senate.gov   https://www.facebook.com/senatorgarypeters
twitter: @sengarypeters   instagram: @sengarypeters

724 Hart Senate Office Building, Washington, DC 20510	(202) 224–6221
Chief of Staff.—Eric Feldman.	FAX: 224–7387
Legislative Director.—David Weinberg.	
Communications Director.—Amber Moon.	
477 Michigan Avenue, Suite 1860, Detroit MI 48226	(313) 226–6020
State Director.—Elise Lancaster.	

REPRESENTATIVES

FIRST DISTRICT

DAN BENISHEK, Republican, of Crystal Falls, MI; born in Iron Mountain, MI, April 20, 1952; education: graduated from West Iron County High School, 1970; B.S., biology, University of Michigan, 1974; M.D., Wayne State Medical School, Detroit, MI, 1978; completed, family practice internship in Flint at St. Joseph's Hospital; completed, general surgery residency at Wayne State in Detroit; professional: served as a general surgeon in Michigan's Upper Peninsula in a private practice since 1983; worked part-time at Oscar G. Johnson VA Medical Center in Iron Mountain for twenty years; married: wife Judy; five children and two grandchildren; Dr. Benishek, avid hunter and fisherman; proud member of the National Rifle Association (NRA) and Gun Owners of America (GOA); committees: Agriculture; Natural Resources; Veterans' Affairs; elected to the 112th Congress on November 2, 2010; reelected to each succeeding Congress.

Office Listings

http://www.benishek.house.gov

514 Cannon House Office Building, Washington, DC 20515	(202) 225–4735
Chief of Staff.—John Billings.	FAX: 225–4710
Press Secretary.—Kyle Bonini.	
Legislative Director.—Michelle Lane.	
Scheduler / Executive Assistant.—Summer Fields.	
District Director.—Traci Jahnke.	
3301 Veterans Drive, Suite 106, Traverse City, MI 49684	(231) 421–5599
500 South Stephenson Avenue, Suite 500, Iron Mountain, MI 49801	(906) 828–2114
307 South Front Street, Suite 120, Marquette, MI 49855	(906) 273–2074
454 West Baldwin Street, Alpena, MI 49707	(989) 340–1634

Counties: ALCONA, ALGER, ALPENA, ANTRIM, BARAGA, BENZIE, CHARLEVOIX, CHEBOYGAN, CHIPPEWA, CRAWFORD, DELTA, DICKINSON, EMMET, GRAND TRAVERSE, HOUGHTON, IRON, KALKASKA, KEWEENAW, LEELANAU, LUCE, MACKINAC, MANISTEE, MARQUETTE, MASON (part), MENOMINEE, MONTMORENCY, ONTONAGON, OSCODA, OTSEGO, PRESQUE ISLE, AND SCHOOLCRAFT. Population (2010), 650,222.

ZIP Codes: 48621, 48636, 48705, 48721, 48740, 48742, 49402, 49405, 49410–11, 49431, 49610–11, 49614–15, 49617, 49619, 49621–22, 49626, 49627–29, 49634–37, 49645–46, 49648, 49650, 49653–54, 49660, 49664, 49666, 49670, 49673–75, 49680, 49682, 49685–86, 49696, 49705, 49709–11, 49715, 49717, 49719, 49722–26, 49728, 49734–37, 49739–40, 49743–45, 49748–49, 49752–53, 49757, 49759–62, 49764, 49766, 49768, 49775, 49779, 49781–86, 49788, 49791–93, 49796–97, 49799, 49802, 49805–06, 49808, 49812, 49814–16, 49819–21, 49826–27, 49829, 49833–35, 49837–41, 49845, 49847–49, 49852, 49858, 49862–66, 49868, 49870–72, 49874, 49876–77, 49881, 49886–87, 49891, 49893–94, 49896, 49901–03, 49905, 49908, 49910–12, 49915–19, 49921–22, 49925, 49927, 49929–31, 49934–35, 49938, 49942, 49946, 49948, 49950, 49952–53, 49955, 49959–64, 49968–71

* * *

SECOND DISTRICT

BILL HUIZENGA, Republican, of Zeeland, MI; born in Zeeland, January 31, 1969; education: graduated, Holland Christian High School; B.A., Calvin College, Grand Rapids, MI, 1987; professional: co-owner, Huizenga Gravel Company, Jenison, MI; formerly licensed realtor and developer; married: the former Natalie Tiesma; children: Garrett, Adrian, Alexandra, Willam, and Sieger; committees: Financial Services; elected to the 112th Congress on November 2, 2010; reelected to each succeeding Congress.

Office Listings

http://huizenga.house.gov

1217 Longworth House Office Building, Washington, DC 20515	(202) 225–4401
Chief of Staff.—Jon DeWitte.	FAX: 226–0779
Legislative Director.—Marliss McManus.	
Communications Director.—Brian Patrick.	
Scheduler / Executive Assistant.—Alicia Orzechowski.	
District Director of Policy.—Greg Van Woerkom.	
4555 Wilson Avenue Southwest, Suite 3, Grandville, MI 49418	(616) 570–0917
1 South Harbor Avenue, Suite 6B, Grand Haven, MI 49417	(616) 414–5516

Counties: ALLEGAN (part), KENT (part), LAKE, MASON, MUSKEGON, NEWAYGO, OCEANA, OTTAWA. Population (2010), 705,975.

ZIP Codes: 49303–04, 49307, 49309, 49312, 49315–16, 49318, 49321, 49323, 49327, 49329–30, 49337–38, 49343, 49345, 49349, 49401–05, 49409–10, 49412–13, 49415, 49417–18, 49420–31, 49434–37, 49440–46, 49448–49, 49451–52, 49454–61, 49463–64, 49504, 49508–09, 49512, 49519, 49534, 49544, 49546, 49548, 49601, 49623, 49642, 49644, 49655–56, 49677, 49688

* * *

THIRD DISTRICT

JUSTIN A. AMASH, Republican, of Cascade, MI; born in Grand Rapids, MI, April 18, 1980; education: attended Kelloggsville Christian School and Grand Rapids Christian High School; B.A., economics, *magna cum laude,* University of Michigan, Ann Arbor, MI, 2002; J.D., University of Michigan Law School, Ann Arbor, MI, 2005; professional: small business owner; attorney; member, State Bar of Michigan, Grand Rapids Bar Association; State Representative, Michigan's 72nd district, 2009–10; religion: member, St. Nicholas Antiochian Orthodox Christian Church; married: Kara; three children: Alexander, Anwen, and Evelyn; committees: Oversight and Government Reform; Joint Economic Committee; elected to the 112th Congress on November 2, 2010; reelected to each succeeding Congress.

Office Listings

http://amash.house.gov   facebook.com/repjustinamash

114 Cannon House Office Building, Washington, DC 20515 .... (202) 225–3831
Chief of Staff.—Poppy Nelson.   FAX: 225–5144
Senior Advisor.—Ben Vanderveen.
Executive Assistant / Scheduler.—Lindsey Gardner.
110 Michigan Street, NW., Suite 460, Grand Rapids, MI 49503 .... (616) 451–8383
District Director.—Jordan Bush.
70 West Michigan Avenue, Suite 212, Battle Creek, MI 49017 .... (269) 205–3823

Counties: BARRY, CALHOUN, IONIA, KENT (part), MONTCALM (part). CITIES: Albion, Battle Creek, Belding, Cedar Springs, East Grand Rapids, Grand Rapids, Hastings, Ionia, Lowell, Marshall, Portland, Rockford, and Springfield. Population (2010), 707,975.

ZIP Codes: 48809, 48815, 48838, 48845-46, 48849, 48851, 48860, 48865, 48870, 48873, 48875, 48881, 48887, 48897, 49011, 49014-18, 49020, 49029, 49033, 49035, 49037, 49046, 49050-51, 49058, 49060, 49068-69, 49073, 49092, 49224, 49245, 49301-02, 49306, 49315-17, 49319, 49321, 49325-26, 49331, 49333, 49341, 49343, 49345, 49351, 49355-57, 49501, 49503-10, 49512, 49514-16, 49518, 49523, 49525, 49528, 49534, 49544, 49546, 49548, 49550, 49555, 49560, 49599

* * *

FOURTH DISTRICT

JOHN MOOLENAAR, Republican, of Midland, MI; born in Midland, May 8, 1961; graduated from Herbert Henry Dow High School, Midland, MI; B.S., Hope College, Holland, MI, 1983; M.P.A., Harvard University, Cambridge, MA, 1989; professional: chemist; businessman; school administrator; member of the Midland, MI city council, 1997–2000; member of the Michigan House of Representatives, 2003–08; member of the Michigan State Senate, 2011–14; committees: Agriculture; Budget; Science, Space, and Technology; elected to the 114th Congress on November 4, 2014.

Office Listings

http://www.moolenaar.house.gov   twitter: @repmoolenaar
facebook: facebook.com/repmoolenaar

117 Cannon House Office Building, Washington, DC 20515 .... (202) 225–3561
Chief of Staff.—Ryan Tarrant.   FAX: 225–9679
Press Secretary.—David Russell.
Legislative Director.—Mike Telliga.
Scheduler.—Eva Vrana.
200 East Main Street, Suite 230, Midland, MI 48640 .... (989) 631–2552
District Director.—Ashton Bortz.

Counties: CLARE COUNTY. CITIES: Clare, Farwell, Harrison, Lake, Lake George. CLINTON COUNTY. CITIES: Dewitt, East Lansing (part), Grand Ledge (part), St. Johns. GLADWIN COUNTY. CITIES: Beaverton, Gladwin. GRATIOT COUNTY. CITIES: Alma, Ashley, Bannister, Breckenridge, Elm Hall, Elwell, Ithaca, Middleton, North Star, Perrinton, Pompeii, Riverdale, Sumner, St. Louis, Wheeler. ISABELLA COUNTY. CITIES: Blanchard, Millbrook, Mt. Pleasant, Rosebush, Shepherd, Weidman, Winn. MECOSTA COUNTY. CITIES: Barryton, Big Rapids, Canadian Lakes, Chippewa Lakes, Mecosta, Morley, Paris, Remus, Stanwood. MIDLAND COUNTY. CITIES: Coleman, Edenville, Hope, Laporte, Midland, North Bradley, Poseyville, Sanford. MISSAUKEE COUNTY. CITIES: Falmouth, Lake City, McBain, Merritt, Moorestown. MONTCALM COUNTY. CITIES: Alger, Butternut, Carson City, Cedar Lake, Coral, Crystal, Edmore, Entrican, Fenwick, Gowen, Greenville, Howard City, Lakeview, Langston, Maple Hill, McBride, Pierson, Sand Lake, Sheridan, Sidney, Six Lakes, Stanton, Trufant, Vestaburg, Vickeryville. OGEMAW COUNTY. CITIES: Rose City, West Branch. OSCEOLA COUNTY. CITIES: Evart, Hersey, LeRoy, Marion, Reed City, Sears, Tustin. ROSCOMMON COUNTY. CITIES: Higgins Lake, Houghton Lake, Houghton Lake Heights, Prudenville, Roscommon, St. Helen. SAGINAW COUNTY (part). CITIES: Birch Run, Brant,

Burt, Carrollton, Chesaning, Frankenmuth, Freeland, Fremont, Hemlock, Merrill, Oakley, St. Charles, University Center. SHIAWASSEE COUNTY. CITIES: Bancroft, Caledonia, Chapin, Corunna, Durand, Henderson, Laingsburg, Morrice, New Haven, New Lothrup, Owosso, Perry, Shaftsburg, Venice, and Vernon. WEXFORD COUNTY. CITIES: Cadillac, Manton. Population (2010), 705,974.

ZIP Codes: 48048, 48050, 48264, 48414–15, 48417–18, 48429, 48449, 48460, 48476, 48601, 48609–10, 48612, 48614–18, 48620, 48622–23, 48625–30, 48632–33, 48637, 48642, 48648–49, 48651, 48653–57, 48661–63, 48670, 48674, 48686, 48710, 48722, 48724, 48734, 48756, 48801, 48804, 48806–07, 48811–12, 48817–18, 48820, 48822, 48829–32, 48834–35, 48838, 48841, 48847–48, 48850, 48852, 48856–59, 48862, 48866–67, 48871–72, 48874, 48877–80, 48882–86, 48888–89, 48891, 48893–94, 48896, 49083, 49305, 49307, 49310, 49316, 49320, 49322, 49326, 49329, 49332, 49334, 49336, 49338–40, 49343, 49346–47, 49412–13, 49601, 49620, 49631–32, 49638–40, 49651, 49653, 49655, 49657, 49665, 49667–68, 49677, 49679, 49688, 49886

* * *

FIFTH DISTRICT

DANIEL T. KILDEE, Democrat, of Flint Township, MI; born in Flint, MI, August 11, 1958; education: graduated, Northern High School, 1976; B.S., administration, Central Michigan University, 2011; married: Jennifer, 1988; children: Ryan, Kenneth, and Katy; two grandchildren, Caitlin and Colin; Senior Whip; Democratic Policy and Communications Committee; committees: Financial Services; elected to the 113th Congress, November 6, 2012; reelected to the 114th Congress on November 4, 2014.

Office Listings

http://www.dankildee.house.gov

227 Cannon House Office Building, Washington, DC 20515	(202) 225–3611
Chief of Staff.—Jennifer Cox.	FAX: 225–6393
Legislative Director.—Alison Share.	
Deputy Chief of Staff / Communications Director.—Mitchell Rivard.	
Scheduler / Executive Assistant.—Nathaniel Brunner.	
111 East Court Street, #3B, Flint, MI 48502	(810) 238–8627
District Chief of Staff.—Amy Hovey.	FAX: 238–8658

Counties: ARENAC, BAY, GENESEE, IOSCO, SAGINAW (part), TUSCOLA (part). Population (2010), 705,975.

ZIP Codes: 48411, 48415, 48418, 48420–21, 48423, 48429–30, 48433, 48436–39, 48442, 48449, 48451, 48457–58, 48462–64, 48473, 48480, 48501–07, 48509, 48519, 48529, 48531–32, 48550–57, 48601–08, 48610–11, 48613, 48623, 48631, 48634, 48638, 48642, 48650, 48652, 48658–59, 48663, 48703, 48706–08, 48710, 48722, 48724, 48730, 48732–34, 48737–39, 48743, 48745–50

* * *

SIXTH DISTRICT

FRED UPTON, Republican, of St. Joseph, MI; born in St. Joseph, April 23, 1953; education: graduated, Shattuck School, Fairbault, MN, 1971; B.A., journalism, University of Michigan, Ann Arbor, 1975; professional: field manager, Dave Stockman Campaign, 1976; staff member, Congressman Dave Stockman, 1976–80; legislative assistant, Office of Management and Budget, 1981–83; deputy director of Legislative Affairs, 1983–84; director of Legislative Affairs, 1984–85; member: First Congregational Church, Emil Verbin Society; married: the former Amey Rulon-Miller; committees: chair, Energy and Commerce; elected to the 100th Congress on November 4, 1986; reelected to each succeeding Congress.

Office Listings

http://www.upton.house.gov

2183 Rayburn House Office Building, Washington, DC 20515	(202) 225–3761
Chief of Staff.—Joan Hillebrands.	FAX: 225–4986
Senior Advisor / Executive Assistant.—Bits Thomas.	
800 Centre, Suite 106, 800 Ship Street, St. Joseph, MI 49085	(269) 982–1986
157 South Kalamazoo Mall, Suite 180, Kalamazoo, MI 49007	(269) 385–0039

Counties: ALLEGAN (part), BERRIEN, CASS, KALAMAZOO, ST. JOSEPH, VAN BUREN. CITIES AND TOWNSHIPS: Allegan, Augusta, Bangor, Baroda, Benton Harbor, Berrien Springs, Berrien Center, Bloomingdale, Breedsville, Bridgman, Buchanan, Burr Oak, Cassopolis, Centreville, Climax, Coloma, Colon, Comstock, Constantine, Covert, Decatur, Delton, Douglas, Dowagiac, Eau Claire, Edwardsburg, Fulton, Galesburg, Galien, Gobles, Grand Junction, Hagar Shores, Harbert, Hartford, Hickory Corners, Holland, Jones, Kalamazoo, Lakeside, Lawrence, Lawton, Leonidas, Marcellus, Mattawan,

Mendon, Nazareth, New Troy, New Buffalo, Niles, Nottawa, Oshtemo, Otsego, Paw Paw, Plainwell, Portage, Pullman, Richland, Riverside, Saugatuck, Sawyer, Schoolcraft, Scotts, Sodus, South Haven, St. Joseph, Stevensville, Sturgis, Three Oaks, Three Rivers, Union Pier, Union, Vandalia, Vicksburg, Watervliet, and White Pigeon. Population (2010), 705,974.

ZIP Codes: 49001–49013, 49015, 49019, 49022–24, 49026–27, 49030–32, 49034, 49038–43, 49045, 49047–48, 49052–53, 49055–57, 49060–67, 49070–72, 49074–75, 49077–81, 49083–85, 49087–88, 49090–91, 49093, 49095, 49097–99, 49101–04, 49106–07, 49111–13, 49115–17, 49119–20, 49125–30, 49311, 49314–16, 49323, 49328, 49333, 49335, 49344, 49348, 49406, 49408, 49416, 49419, 49423, 49426, 49450, 49453, 49464

* * *

SEVENTH DISTRICT

TIMOTHY L. WALBERG, Republican, of Tipton, MI; born in Chicago, IL, April 12, 1951; education: studied forestry at Western Illinois University, Macomb, IL; graduated from Moody Bible Institute, Chicago, IL; B.A., religious education, Fort Wayne Bible College, 1975; M.A., communications, Wheaton College Graduate School, Wheaton, IL, 1978; professional: minister, New Haven Baptist Church, 1973–77; minister, Union Grace Gospel Church, 1978–82; member of the Michigan House of Representatives, 1983–98; president, Warren Reuther Center for Education and Community Impact; division manager, Moody Bible Institute; elected to the U.S. House of Representatives for the 110th Congress, 2007–09; married: Susan; three children; committees: Education and the Workforce; Oversight and Government Reform; elected to the 112th Congress on November 2, 2010; reelected to each succeeding Congress.

Office Listings

http://www.walberg.house.gov

2436 Rayburn House Office Building, Washington, DC 20515	(202) 225–6276
Chief of Staff.—R.J. Laukitis.	FAX: 225–6281
Legislative Director.—Jonathan Hirte.	
Press Secretary.—Dan Kotman.	
110 1st Street, Suite 2, Jackson, MI 49201	(517) 780–9075

Counties: BRANCH, EATON, HILLSDALE, JACKSON, LENAWEE, MONROE, WASHTENAW (part). Population (2010), 705,974.

ZIP Codes: 48103, 48105, 48108, 48111, 48117–18, 48130–31, 48133–34, 48137, 48140, 48144–45, 48157–62, 48164, 48166–70, 48176–79, 48182, 48189–91, 48197, 48813, 48821, 48827, 48837, 48849, 48861, 48876, 48890, 48897, 48906, 48911, 48917, 49011, 49021, 49028, 49030, 49036, 49040, 49073, 49076, 49082, 49089, 49092, 49094, 49096, 49201–03, 49220–21, 49224, 49227–30, 49232–38, 49240–42, 49245–56, 49259, 49261–72, 49274, 49276–77, 49279, 49282–89

* * *

EIGHTH DISTRICT

MIKE BISHOP, Republican, of Rochester, MI; born in Almont, MI, March 18, 1967; education: Bachelor of Arts, University of Michigan, Ann Arbor, MI, 1989; Juris Doctor, Michigan State University, East Lansing, MI, 1993; professional: private practice attorney, State Representative, 1999–2002; State Senator, 2003–10; State Senate Majority Leader, 2007–10; Chief Legal Officer at International Bancard Corporation; religion: Protestant; family: wife, Cristina; children: ages 15, 13, 9; House Republican Steering Committee; committees: Education and the Workforce; Judiciary; elected to the 114th Congress on November 4, 2014.

Office Listings

http://www.mikebishop.house.gov

428 Cannon House Office Building, Washington, DC 20515	(202) 225–4872
Chief of Staff.—Allan Filip.	FAX: 225–5820
Legislative Director.—Kyle Kizzier.	
Communications Director.—Kelli Ford.	
Scheduler.—Susan Larson.	
711 East Grand River Avenue, Suite A, Brighton, MI 48116	(810) 227–8600

Counties: INGHAM, LIVINGSTON, OAKLAND (part). CITIES AND TOWNSHIPS: Addison Township, Brandon Township, Brighton, Cohoctah, Dansville, East Lansing, Fenton, Fowlerville, Gregory, Groveland Township, Hamburg, Hartland, Haslett, Hell, Holly Township, Holt, Howell, Independence Township, Lakeland, Lansing, Leslie, Mason, Meridian Township, Oak Grove, Oakland Township, Okemos, Onondaga, Orion Township, Oxford Township, Pinckney, Rochester, Rochester Hills (part), Rose Township, Springfield Township, Stockbridge, Unadilla, Village of Clarkston, Webberville, and Williamston. Population, (2010), 705,974.

ZIP Codes: 48114, 48116, 48139, 48143, 48306–07, 48309, 48346, 48350, 48359–60, 48362–63, 48366–67, 48370–71, 48430, 48442, 48462, 48805, 48816, 48819, 48824–26, 48842–44, 48854–55, 48864, 48895, 48901, 48909–10, 48912– 13, 48915–16, 48918–19, 48921–22, 48924, 48929–30, 48933, 48937, 48951, 48956, 48980, 49251

* * *

NINTH DISTRICT

SANDER M. LEVIN, Democrat, of Royal Oak, MI; born in Detroit, MI, September 6, 1931; education: graduated, Central High School, Detroit, 1949; B.A., University of Chicago, 1952; M.A., Columbia University, New York, NY, 1954; LL.B., Harvard University, Cambridge, MA, 1957; professional: attorney, admitted to the Michigan Bar in 1958 and commenced practice in Detroit, MI; member: Oakland Board of Supervisors, 1961–64; Michigan Senate, 1965–70; Democratic floor leader in State Senate; served on the Advisory Committee on the Education of Handicapped Children in the Department of Health, Education, and Welfare, 1965–68; chairman, Michigan Democratic Party, 1968–69; Democratic candidate for Governor, 1970 and 1974; fellow, Kennedy School of Government, Institute of Politics, Harvard University, 1975; assistant administrator, Agency for International Development, 1977–81; married: Dr. Pamela Cole; children (with the late Victoria Levin): Jennifer, Andrew, Madeleine, and Matthew; committees: Ways and Means; Joint Committee on Taxation; elected on November 2, 1982, to the 98th Congress; reelected to each succeeding Congress.

Office Listings

http://www.levin.house.gov   http://www.facebook.com/repsandylevin
http://twitter.com/#!/repsandylevin

1236 Longworth Office House Building, Washington, DC 20515	(202) 225–4961
Chief of Staff.—Hilarie Chambers.	FAX: 226–1033
Scheduler.—Alexis Gipson.	
27085 Gratiot Avenue, Roseville, MI 48066	(586) 498–7122

Counties: MACOMB (part), OAKLAND (part). CITIES: Berkley, Beverly Hills, Bingham Farms, Bloomfield Township, Clawson (part), Center Line, Clinton Township, Eastpointe, Ferndale, Franklin, Fraser, Lake Township, Hazel Park, Huntington Woods, Madison Heights, Mount Clemens, Pleasant Ridge, Roseville, Royal Oak, Southfield Township, St. Clair Shores, Sterling Heights (part), and Warren. Population (2010), 705,975.

ZIP Codes: 48009, 48015, 48017, 48021, 48025–26, 48030, 48034–36, 48038, 48043, 48046, 48066–73, 48080–82, 48088– 93, 48220, 48236, 48301–02, 48304, 48310, 48312–14, 48320, 48323

* * *

TENTH DISTRICT

CANDICE S. MILLER, Republican, of Harrison Township, MI; born in St. Clair Shores, MI, May 7, 1954; education: attended Macomb Community College and Northwood University; public service: Harrison Township Board of Trustees, 1979; Harrison Township Supervisor, 1980–92; Macomb County Treasurer, 1992–94; Michigan Secretary of State, 1994–2002; professional: worked in a family-owned marina business before she became involved in public service; religion: Presbyterian; married: Macomb County Circuit Court Judge Donald Miller; children: Wendy; committees: chair, House Administration; Homeland Security; Transportation and Infrastructure; Joint Committee on the Library; Joint Committee on Printing; elected to the 108th Congress on November 5, 2002; reelected to each succeeding Congress.

Office Listings

http://candicemiller.house.gov

320 Cannon House Office Building, Washington, DC 20515	(202) 225–2106
Chief of Staff / Communications Director.—Salley Wood.	FAX: 226–1169
Deputy Chief of Staff / Legislative Director.—Dena Kozanas.	
Scheduler.—Kristen Lebryk.	
48701 Van Dyke Avenue, Shelby Township, MI 48317	(586) 997–5010

Counties: HURON, LAPEER, MACOMB (part), SAINT CLAIR, SANILAC. TUSCOLA (part). Population (2010), 719,712.

ZIP Codes: 48001–03, 48005–06, 48014, 48022–23, 48027–28, 48032, 48035, 48039–42, 48044–45, 48047–51, 48054, 48059–60, 48062–65, 48074, 48079, 48094–97, 48306, 48312–17, 48367, 48371, 48401, 48412–13, 48416, 48419, 48421–23, 48426–28, 48432, 48435, 48438, 48441, 48444–46, 48450, 48453–56, 48461–72, 48475, 48720, 48725– 27, 48729, 48731, 48735, 48759–60, 48767

* * *

ELEVENTH DISTRICT

DAVID A. TROTT, Republican, of Birmingham, MI; born in Birmingham, October 16, 1960; education: B.A. from University of Michigan, 1981; J.D. from Duke University, 1985; professional: business owner; attorney; community service: teaching American government, served on University of Michigan Advisory Board, Detroit Country Day School Board of Trustees; Community House Board; Karmanos Cancer Center Board; Michigan State Building Authority Board of Trustees; Michigan Chamber of Commerce Board of Trustees; religion: Roman Catholic; married: Kappy; children: Duke, Taylor, and Courtney; committees: Foreign Affairs; Judiciary; elected to the 114th Congress on November 4, 2014.

Office Listings

http://www.trott.house.gov

1722 Longworth House Office Building, Washington, DC 20515 .... (202) 225–8171
    Chief of Staff.—Jennifer Gorski.
    Scheduler.—Marla Rondo.
    Legislative Director.—Anna Leieritz.
    Communications Director.—Kyle Bonini.
625 East Big Beaver Road, Suite 204, Troy, MI 48083 .... (248) 528–0711

Counties: WAYNE COUNTY. CITIES: Caton Township, Livonia, Northville, Northville Township, Plymouth, Plymouth Township. OAKLAND COUNTY. CITIES: Auburn Hills, Birmingham, Bloomfield Hills, Clawson, Commerce Township, Farmington, Highland, Lake Angelus, Lyon Township, Milford, Novi, Rochester Hills, South Lyon, Troy, Walled Lake, Waterford, West Bloomfield, White Lake, Wixom, and Wolverine Lake. Population (2010), 705,974.

ZIP Codes: 48007, 48009, 48012, 48017, 48073, 48083–85, 48098–99, 48111, 48150–65, 48167–68, 48170, 48178, 48184–85, 48187–88, 48240, 48301, 48304, 48307, 48309, 48321, 48326–32, 48335–36, 48346, 48350, 48353, 48356–57, 48359, 48374–78, 48380–83, 48386–87, 48390–91, 48393, 48442

* * *

TWELFTH DISTRICT

DEBBIE DINGELL, Democrat, of Dearborn, MI; born in Detroit, MI, November 23, 1953; education: B.S., Georgetown University, 1975; M.S., Georgetown University, 1998; professional: president, General Motors Foundation; executive director of Global Community Relations and Government Relations, GM; president, D2 Strategies; electoral: Wayne State University Board of Governors; married: former Congressman John D. Dingell; committees: Budget; Natural Resources; elected to the 114th Congress on November 4, 2014.

Office Listings

http://www.debbiedingell.house.gov

116 Cannon House Office Building, Washington, DC 20515 .... (202) 225–4071
    Chief of Staff.—Karen Defilippi.
    Legislative Director.—Greg Sunstrum.
    Scheduler.—Sarah Shepson
    Communications Director.—Hannah Smith.
19855 West Outer Drive, Suite 103–E, Dearborn, MI 48124 .... (313) 278–2936
    District Administrator.—Kevin Hrit.
301 West Michigan Avenue, Ypsilanti, MI 48197 .... (734) 481–1100
    Office Manager.—Jelani McGadney.

Counties: WAYNE COUNTY (part). CITIES AND TOWNSHIPS: Allen Park, Belleville, Brownstown, Brownstone Township, Dearborn, Dearborn Heights (part), Flat Rock, Gibraltar, Grosse Ile Township, Huron Township, Lincoln Park, Riverview, Rockwood, Southgate, Sumpter Township, Taylor, Trenton, Van Buren Township, Woodhaven, and Wyandotte. WASHTENAW COUNTY (part). CITIES AND TOWNSHIPS: Ann Arbor, Ann Arbor Township, Pittsfield Township, Scio Township, Ypsilanti, Ypsilanti Township. Population (from Census.gov), 711,313.

ZIP Codes: 48101, 48103–05, 48108–09, 48111, 48114, 48120, 48122, 48124–28, 48130, 48134, 48139, 48146, 48164, 48173–74, 48176, 48180, 48183–84, 48188, 48192–93, 48195, 48197–98, 48127, 48229

* * *

THIRTEENTH DISTRICT

JOHN CONYERS, JR., Democrat, of Detroit, MI; born in Detroit, May 16, 1929; son of John and Lucille Conyers; education: B.A., Wayne State University, 1957; LL.B., Wayne State Law

School, June 1958; served as officer in the U.S. Army Corps of Engineers, one year in Korea; awarded combat and merit citations; engaged in many civil rights and labor activities; legislative assistant to Congressman John D. Dingell, December 1958 to May 1961; appointed Referee for the Workmen's Compensation Department, State of Michigan, by Governor John B. Swainson in October 1961; former vice chairman of Americans for Democratic Action; vice chairman of the National Advisory Council of the ACLU; member: Kappa Alpha Psi; Wolverine Bar; NAACP; Tuskegee Airmen, Inc.; organizations: Congressional Black Caucus; Progressive Caucus; married: Monica Conyers; children: John III, and Carl; committees: ranking member, Judiciary; elected to the 89th Congress on November 3, 1964; reelected to each succeeding Congress. In the 114th Congress, he became the first black dean of Congress.

Office Listings

http://www.conyers.house.gov

2426 Rayburn House Office Building, Washington, DC 20515 .... (202) 225–5126
  Chief of Staff.—Cynthia Martin.   FAX: 225–0072
  Scheduler.—Rinia Shelby.
Federal Courthouse, Suite 669, 231 West Lafayette, Detroit, MI 48226 .... (313) 961–5670
  District Director.—Yolanda Lipsey.
33300 Warren Road, Suite 13, Westland, MI 48185 .... (734) 675–4084
                                                                                                FAX: 675–4218

Counties: WAYNE COUNTY (part). CITIES AND TOWNSHIPS: Detroit, Dearborn Heights, Ecorse, Garden City, Highland Park, Inkster, Melvindale, Redford, River Rouge, Romulus, Wayne, and Westland. Population (2010), 699,214.

ZIP Codes: 48125, 48203, 48207, 48210–16, 48221, 481226–27, 48235, 48238

* * *

FOURTEENTH DISTRICT

BRENDA L. LAWRENCE, Democrat, of Bloomfield, MI; born in Detroit, MI, October 18, 1954; education: attended University of Detroit; B.S., Public Administration, Central Michigan University; professional: United States Postal Service, Letter Carrier to Human Relations Executive, 1978–2008; Mayor of Southfield, 2001–15; Southfield City Council, 1996–2000; South Field City Council President, 1999; Southfield Public School Board of Education, President, Vice President, Secretary, 1992–96; religion: Christian, non-denominational; married: M. McArthur Lawrence; children: Michael and Michelle; granddaughter, Aysa; caucuses: Congressional Black Caucus; Congressional Progressive Caucus; Skilled Workforce Caucus; Former Mayors Caucus; committees: Oversight and Government Reform; Small Business; elected to the 114th Congress on November 4, 2014.

Office Listings

http://www.lawrence.house.gov

1237 Longworth House Office Building, Washington, DC 20515 .... (202) 225–5802
  Chief of Staff.—Duron Marshall.   FAX: 226–2356
  Legislative Director.—Christina McWilson Thomas.
  Communications Director.—Tracy Manzer.
26700 Lahser Road, Suite 330, Southfield, MI 48033 .... (248) 356–2052
  District Office Director.—Christine Jensen.

Counties: OAKLAND (part) WAYNE (part). CITIES AND TOWNSHIPS: Detroit, Farmington Hills, Grosse Pointe, Grosse Pointe Farms, Grosse Pointe Park, Grosse Pointe Woods, Hamtramck, Harper Woods, Keego Harbor, Lathrup Village, Oak Park, Orchard Lake, Pointe Shores, Pontiac, Royal Oak Township, Southfield, Sylvan Lake, Village of Grosse Pointe Shores, and West Bloomfield. Population (2010), 706, 429.

ZIP Codes: 48033–34, 48075–76, 48203, 48205, 48207 48209, 48212, 48214, 48216, 48221, 48224–26, 48230, 48233–34, 48234–35, 48237, 48243, 48322, 48325, 48331, 48334, 48336, 48343, 48320–23, 48340–42

MINNESOTA

(Population 2010, 5,303,925)

SENATORS

AMY KLOBUCHAR, Democrat, of Minneapolis, MN; born in Plymouth, MN, May 25, 1960; education: B.A., *magna cum laude*, Yale University, 1982; J.D., *magna cum laude*, University of Chicago Law School, 1985; professional: Attorney at law firm Dorsey & Whitney, 1985–93, Partner in 1993; Partner at law firm Gray, Plant, Mooty, Mooty & Bennett, 1993–98; religion: Congregationalist; public service: City of Minneapolis prosecutor, 1988; elected Hennepin County Attorney, 1998, reelected, 2002; married: John; child: Abigail; committees: Agriculture, Nutrition, and Forestry; Commerce, Science, and Transportation; Judiciary; Rules and Administration; Joint Economic Committee; elected to the U.S. Senate on November 7, 2006; reelected to the U.S. Senate on November 6, 2012.

Office Listings

http://klobuchar.senate.gov

302 Hart Senate Office Building, Washington, DC 20510	(202) 224–3244
Chief of Staff.—Elizabeth Peluso.	
Legislative Director.—Travis Talvitie.	
Deputy Chief of Staff.—Vacant.	
Communications Director.—Julia Krahe.	
Scheduler.—Asal Sayas.	
1200 Washington Avenue South, Suite 250, Minneapolis, MN 55415	(612) 727–5220
State Director.—Ben Hill.	
1130½ 7th Street Northwest, Suite 212, Rochester, MN 55901	(507) 288–5321
121 4th Street South, Moorhead, MN 56560	(218) 287–2219
Olcott Plaza, 820 9th Street North, Suite 105, Virginia, MN 55792	(218) 741–9690

* * *

AL FRANKEN, Democrat, of St. Louis Park, MN; raised in St. Louis Park, MN, born May 21, 1951; education: Harvard, Cambridge, MA, 1973; professional: comedy writer, author, and radio talk show host; has taken part in seven USO tours, visiting our troops overseas in Germany, Bosnia, Kosovo and Uzbekistan—as well as visiting Iraq, Afghanistan, and Kuwait four times; married: Franni Franken for 39 years; two children; one grandchild; committees: Energy and Natural Resources; Health, Education, Labor, and Pensions; Indian Affairs; Judiciary; elected to the 111th U.S. Senate on November 4, 2008, the election was contested; following a June 30, 2009, decision in his favor by the Minnesota State Supreme Court, he took the oath of office and began service on July 7, 2009; reelected November 4, 2014.

Office Listings

www.franken.senate.gov

309 Hart Senate Office Building, Washington, DC 20510	(202) 224–5641
Chief of Staff.—Casey Aden-Wansbury.	FAX: 224–0044
State Director.—Alana Petersen.	
Legislative Director.—Jeff Lomonaco.	
Scheduler.—Tara Mazer.	
Communications Director.—Ed Shelleby.	
Press Secretary.—Michael Dale-Stein.	
60 East Plato Boulevard, Suite 220, St. Paul, MN 55107	(651) 221–1016
	FAX: 221–1078
1202 1/2 Seventh Street, NW, Suite 213, Rochester, MN 55901	(507) 288–2003
	FAX: 288–2217
515 West First Street, Suite 104, Duluth, MN 55802	(218) 722–2390
	FAX: 722–4131

REPRESENTATIVES

FIRST DISTRICT

TIMOTHY J. WALZ, Democrat, of Mankato, MN; born in West Point, NE, April 6, 1964; education: B.S., Chadron State College, Chadron, NE; M.S., St. Mary's University, Winona,

MN; professional: high school teacher; military: Command Sergeant Major, Minnesota's 1st/34th Division of the Army National Guard, 1981–2005; awards: 2002 Minnesota Ethics in Education award winner, 2003 Mankato Teacher of the Year, and the 2003 Minnesota Teacher of Excellence; married: Gwen Whipple Walz, 1994; children: Hope and Gus; committees: Agriculture; Armed Services; Veterans' Affairs; elected to the 110th Congress on November 7, 2006; reelected to each succeeding Congress.

Office Listings

http://www.walz.house.gov

1034 Longworth House Office Building, Washington, DC 20515 .... (202) 225–2472
  Chief of Staff.—Josh Syrjamaki.   FAX: 225–3433
  Legislative Director.—Timothy Bertocci.
  Scheduler.—Denise Fleming.
527½ South Front Street, Mankato, MN 56001 .... (507) 388–2149
1202½ Seventh Street, NW., Suite 211, Rochester, MN 55901 .... (507) 388–2149

Counties: BLUE EARTH COUNTY. CITIES: Amboy, Eagle Lake, Garden City, Good Thunder, Lake Crystal, Madison Lake, Mankato, Mapleton, Pemberton, St. Clair, Vernon Center. BROWN COUNTY. CITIES: Comfrey, Hanska, New Ulm, Sleepy Eye, Springfield. COTTONWOOD COUNTY. CITIES: Mountain Lake, Storeden, Westbrook. DODGE COUNTY. CITIES: Claremont, Dodge Center, Hayfield, Kasson, Mantorville, West Concord, Windom. FARIBAULT COUNTY. CITIES: Blue Earth, Bricelyn, Delavan, Easton, Elmore, Frost, Huntley, Kiester, Minnesota Lake, Walters, Wells, Winnebago. FILLMORE COUNTY. CITIES: Canton, Chatfield, Fountain, Harmony, Lanesboro, Mabel, Ostrander, Peterson, Preston, Rushford, Spring Valley, Whalan, Wykoff. FREEBORN COUNTY. CITIES: Albert Lea, Alden, Clarks Grove, Conger, Emmons, Freeborn, Geneva, Glenville, Hartland, Hayward, Hollandale, London, Manchester, Myrtle, Oakland, Twin Lakes. HOUSTON COUNTY. CITIES: Brownsville, Caledonia, Eitzen, Hokah, Houston, La Crescent, Spring Grove. JACKSON COUNTY. CITIES: Heron, Jackson, Lake Field. LE SUEUR COUNTY. CITIES: Cleveland, Elysian, Heidelberg, Kasota, Kilkenny, Le Center, Le Sueur, Montgomery, New Prague, Waterville. MARTIN COUNTY. CITY: Fairmount. MOWER COUNTY. CITIES: Adams, Austin, Brownsdale, Dexter, Elkton, Grand Meadow, Lansing, LeRoy, Lyle, Rose Creek, Sargeant, Taopi, Waltham. NICOLLET COUNTY. CITIES: North Mankato, St. Peter. NOLES COUNTY. CITIES: Adrian, Worthington. OLMSTED COUNTY. CITIES: Byron, Dover, Eyota, Oronoco, Rochester, Stewartville, Viola. RICE COUNTY. CITIES: Webster, Wheatland, Warsaw, Walcott, Morristown, Shieldsville, Faribault. ROCK COUNTY. CITIES: Lurverne. STEELE COUNTY. CITIES: Blooming Prairie, Ellendale, Hope, Medford, Meriden, Owatonna. WASECA COUNTY. CITIES: Janesville, New Richland, Otisco, Waldorf, Waseca. WATONWAN COUNTY. CITIES: Madelia, St. James. WINONA COUNTY. CITIES: Altura, Dakota, Goodview, Homer, Lewiston, Minnesota City, Rollingstone, St. Charles, Stockton, Utica, and Winona. Population (2010), 644,787.

ZIP Codes: 55019, 55021, 55046, 55049, 55052, 55057, 55060, 55087–88, 55332–35, 55901–02, 55904, 55906, 55909–10, 55912, 55917–27, 55929, 55931–36, 55939–41, 55943–44, 55947, 55949–56, 55959–65, 55967, 55969–77, 55979, 55982, 55985, 55987, 55990–01, 56001, 56003, 56007, 56009–11, 56013–14, 56016–17, 56019–29, 56031–37, 56039, 56041–48, 56050–52, 56054–58, 56060, 56062–63, 56065, 56068–69, 56071–75, 56078, 56080–83, 56085, 56087–91, 56093, 56096–98, 56101, 56110–11, 56116–22, 56127–29, 56131, 56134, 56137–38, 56141, 56143–47, 56150, 56153, 56155–56, 56158–62, 56165, 56167–68, 56171, 56173, 56176, 56181, 56185, 56187, 56266

* * *

SECOND DISTRICT

JOHN KLINE, Republican, of Lakeville, MN; born in Allentown, PA, September 6, 1947; education: B.A., Rice University, 1969; M.P.A., Shippensburg University, 1988; military service: U.S. Marine Corps, 1969–94; retired at the rank of Colonel; organizations: Boy Scouts of America; Marine Corps League; Veterans of Foreign Wars; Marine Corps Association; American Legion; Retired Officers Association; past president, Marine Corps Coordinating Council of Minnesota; religion: Methodist; family: married to Vicky; children: Kathy and Dan; committees: chair, Education and the Workforce; Armed Services; elected to the 108th Congress on November 5, 2002; reelected to each succeeding Congress.

Office Listings

http://www.kline.house.gov

2439 Rayburn House Office Building, Washington, DC 20515 .... (202) 225–2271
  Chief of Staff.—Jean Hinz.   FAX: 225–2595
  Communications Director.—Troy Young.
  Scheduler.—Meg Boland.
350 West Burnsville Parkway, Suite 135, Burnsville, MN 55337 .... (952) 808–1213
  District Director.—Brooke Schaeffer.

Counties: DAKOTA COUNTY. CITIES: Apple Valley, Burnsville, Eagan, Farmington, Hastings, Inver Grove Heights, Lakeville, Rosemount, South St. Paul, West St. Paul. GOODHUE COUNTY. CITIES: Cannon Falls, Pine Island, Red Wing, Zumbrota. RICE COUNTY (part). CITIES: Northfield. SCOTT COUNTY. CITIES: Shakopee, Savage, Prior Lake, New Prague, Jordan, Belle Plaine. WASHINGTON COUNTY (part). CITIES: Cottage Grove, St. Paul Park. Population (2010), 668,891.

ZIP Codes: 55009, 55010 (part), 55016 (part), 55018 (part), 55019 (part), 55020 (part), 55021 (part), 55024, 55026–27, 55031, 55033, 55041, 55044, 55049 (part), 55053 (part), 55054 (part), 55057 (part), 55065–66, 55068 (part), 55071 (part),

55075 (part), 55076 (part), 55077, 55085, 55088 (part), 55089 (part), 55118 (part), 55120–24, 55150 (part), 55306, 55337, 55352, 55372, 55378, 55379 (part), 55910 (part), 55932 (part), 55945, 55946 (part), 55956 (part), 55957, 55960 (part), 55963 (part), 55964 (part), 55968, 55981, 55983 (part), 55985 (part), 55991, 55992 (part), 56071 (part), 56011 (part), 56044 (part), 56071 (part)

* * *

THIRD DISTRICT

ERIK PAULSEN, Republican, of Eden Prairie, MN; born in Bakersfield, CA, May 14, 1965; education: B.A., St. Olaf College, Northfield, MN, 1987; caucuses: co-chair, Medical Technology Caucus; co-chair, Charter Schools Caucus; co-chair, Congressional Wellness Caucus; co-chair, Friends of Norway Caucus; Civility Caucus; National Parks Caucus; Land Conservation Caucus; Zoo Caucus; Diabetes Caucus; Rare Disease Caucus; National Guard Caucus; General Aviation Caucus; Law Enforcement Caucus; Financial Literacy Caucus; Sportsmen's Caucus; Nuclear Issues Working Group; U.S.-China Working Group; Renewable Energy Caucus; India Caucus; Bike Caucus; religion: Lutheran; married: Kelly; children: four daughters; committees: Ways and Means; Joint Economic Committee; elected to the 111th Congress on November 4, 2008; reelected to each succeeding Congress.

Office Listings

http://www.paulsen.house.gov   facebook: congressmanerikpaulsen   twitter: @reperikpaulsen

127 Cannon House Office Building, Washington, DC 20515 .... (202) 225–2871
    Chief of Staff.—Laurie Esau.   FAX: 225–6351
    Legislative Director.—Mike Stober.
    Press Secretary.—Drew Griffin.
    Scheduler. Kate Paul.
250 Prairie Center Drive, Suite 230, Eden Prairie, MN 55344 .... (952) 405–8510
                                          FAX: 405–8514

Counties: ANOKA (part), CARVER (part), HENNEPIN (part). CITIES AND TOWNSHIPS: Bloomington, Brooklyn Park, Champlin, Chanhassen, Chaska, Coon Rapids, Corcoran, Dahlgren, Dayton, Deephaven, Excelsior, Eden Prairie, Edina, Greenfield, Greenwood, Independence, Laketown, Long Lake, Loretto, Maple Grove, Maple Plain, Medina, Medicine Lake, Minnetonka, Minnetonka Beach, Minnetrista, Mound, Orono, Osseo, Plymouth, Rogers, Shorewood, Spring Park, St. Bonifacius, Tonka Bay, Victoria, Wayzata, and Woodland. Population (2010), 650,185.

ZIP Codes: 55305, 55311, 55316–18, 55327–28, 55331, 55340, 55343–47, 55356–57, 55359, 55364, 55369, 55373–75, 55384, 55386–88, 55391, 55420, 55425, 55428–31, 55433, 55435–39, 55441–48

* * *

FOURTH DISTRICT

BETTY McCOLLUM, Democrat-Farmer-Labor, of St. Paul, MN; born in Minneapolis, MN, July 12, 1954; education: A.A., Inver Hills Community College; B.S., College of St. Catherine; professional: teacher and sales manager; public service: North St. Paul City Council, 1986–92; Minnesota House of Representatives, 1992–2000; organizations: Girl Scouts of America; VFW Ladies Auxiliary; American Legion Ladies Auxiliary; awards: Friend of the National Parks Award, National Parks Conservation Association, 2013; Congressional Leadership Award, National Council of Urban Indian Health, 2013; Groundwater Protector Award, National Ground Water Association, 2012; Bruce Vento Hope-Builder Award, Mesothelioma Applied Research Foundation, 2014; founder, Congressional Global Health Caucus; co-chair, Congressional Native American Caucus; appointments: National Council on the Arts; single; children: Sean and Katie; committees: Appropriations; elected to the 107th Congress on November 7, 2000; reelected to each succeeding Congress.

Office Listings

http://www.mccollum.house.gov

2256 Rayburn House Office Building, Washington, DC 20515 .... (202) 225–6631
    Chief of Staff.—Bill Harper.   FAX: 225–1968
    Legislative Director.—Jenn Holcomb.
    Office Director.—Meredith Raimondi.
    Communications Director.—Sam McCullough.
165 Western Avenue North, Suite 17, St. Paul, MN 55102 .... (651) 224–9191
    District Director.—Joshua Straka.

Counties: RAMSEY, WASHINGTON (part). Population (2010), 614,624.

ZIP Codes: 55001, 55003, 55016, 55042–43, 55055, 55082, 55090, 55101–30, 55133, 55144–46, 55155, 55164–66, 55168, 55170–72, 55175, 55187–88, 55449

* * *

FIFTH DISTRICT

KEITH ELLISON, Democrat-Farmer-Labor, of Minneapolis, MN; born in Detroit, MI, August 4, 1963; education: University of Detroit Jesuit High School and Academy, 1981; Wayne State University, 1987; University of Minnesota Law School, 1990; professional: The Law Office of Lindquist & Vennum, 1990–93; Executive Director of the nonprofit Legal Rights Center in Minneapolis, 1993–98; Hassan & Reed Ltd., 1998–2001; Ellison Law Offices, 2003–06; served in Minnesota State Legislature District 58B, 2003–06; four children; commissions: Center for Strategic and International Studies; Commission on Global Health; House Democracy Assistance Commission; Tom Lantos Human Rights Commission; caucuses: founder, Consumer Justice Caucus; co-chair, Progressive Caucus; Out of Iraq Caucus; Children's Environmental Health Caucus; Congressional Human Rights Caucus; Congressional Labor and Working Families Caucus; Congressional Anti-Terrorism Caucus; Congressional Caucus of India and Indian Americans; Congressional Arts Caucus; Law Enforcement Caucus; Congressional Caucus to Fight and Control Methamphetamine; Financial and Economic Literacy Caucus; Bicameral Congressional Caucus on Parkinson's Disease; Congressional Diabetes Caucus; Congressional E9-1-1 (Emergency Responders) Caucus; Congressional Adoption Caucus; Congressional Wildlife Caucus; Congressional Black Caucus; Populist Caucus; Pro-Choice Caucus; Credit Caucus; Green Jobs Caucus; Hunger Caucus; Full Employment Caucus; committees: Financial Services; elected to the 110th Congress on November 7, 2006; reelected to each succeeding Congress.

Office Listings

http://ellison.house.gov

2263 Rayburn House Office Building, Washington, DC 20515 .... (202) 225–4755
    Chief of Staff.—Kari Moe.
    Legislative Director.—Carol Wayman.
    Communications Director.—Mike Casca.
2100 Plymouth Avenue, Minneapolis, MN 55411 .... (612) 522–1212
    District Director.—Jamie Long.

Counties: ANOKA (part), HENNEPIN (part), RAMSEY (part). CITIES: Minneapolis and the surrounding suburbs of Brooklyn Center, Columbia Heights, Crystal, Edina, Fridley, Fort Snelling, Golden Valley, Hilltop, Hopkins, Richfield, Robbinsdale, Spring Lake Park, St. Anthony, and St. Louis Park. Population (2010), 677,196.

ZIP Codes: 55111–12, 55305, 55343, 55401–30, 55432–33, 55440–41, 55450, 55454–55, 55458–60, 55470, 55472, 55474, 55479–80, 55483–88

* * *

SIXTH DISTRICT

TOM EMMER, Republican of Delano, MN; born in South Bend, IN, March 3, 1961; education: B.A. in Political Science from the University of Alaska-Fairbanks, Fairbanks, AK, 1984; J.D. from William Mitchell College of Law, St. Paul, MN, 1988; professional: practiced insurance, banking and equity law through his own practice; served in the Minnesota House of Representatives from 2004–08; became a radio host on Twin Cities News Talk AM 1130; married: Jacquie; children: Thomas Earl III "Tripp", Jack, Bobby, Joey, Billy, and Johnny (sons), and Katie (daughter); committees: Financial Services; elected to the 114th Congress on November 4, 2014.

Office Listings

http://www.emmer.house.gov

503 Cannon House Office Building, Washington, DC 20515 .... (202) 225–2331
    Chief of Staff.—David FitzSimmons.   FAX: 225–6475
    Deputy Chief of Staff.—Robert Boland.
    Legislative Director.—Jason Frye.
    Communications Director.—Becky Alery.
9201 Quaday Avenue Northeast, Otsego, MN 55330 .... (763) 241–6848

Counties: ANOKA, BENTON, CARVER, HENNEPIN (part), SHERBURNE, STEARNS, WASHINGTON (part), WRIGHT. POPULATION (2010), 662,990.

ZIP Codes: 55005, 55011, 55014, 55025, 55038, 55047, 55070, 55073, 55079, 55082, 55092, 55110, 55126, 55301–04, 55308–09, 55313, 55315, 55318–22, 55327–30, 55339, 55341, 55349, 55353, 55357–58, 55360, 55362–63, 55367–68, 55371, 55373–76, 55382, 55387–90, 55395, 55397–98, 55434, 55449, 56011, 56301, 56303–04, 56307, 56310, 56314, 56320–21, 56329–30, 56340, 56357, 56362, 56367–69, 56373–75, 56377, 56379, 56387

* * *

SEVENTH DISTRICT

COLLIN C. PETERSON, Democrat, of Detroit Lakes, MN; born in Fargo, ND, June 29, 1944; education: graduated from Glyndon (MN) High School, 1962; B.A. in business administration and accounting, Moorhead State University, 1966; U.S. Army National Guard, 1963–69; CPA, owner and partner; Minnesota State Senator, 1976–86; member: AOPA, Safari Club, Ducks Unlimited, American Legion, Sea Plane Pilots Association, Pheasants Forever, Benevolent Protective Order of Elks, Cormorant Lakes Sportsman's Club; three children: Sean, Jason, and Elliott; committees: ranking member, Agriculture; elected to the 102nd Congress, November 6, 1990; reelected to each succeeding Congress.

Office Listings

http://collinpeterson.house.gov

2204 Rayburn House Office Building, Washington, DC 20515	(202) 225–2165
Chief of Staff.—Allison Myhre.	FAX: 225–1593
Deputy Chief of Staff/Legislative Director.—Adam Durand.	
Assistants: Chris Iacaruso, Richard Lee, Zach Martin, Rebekah Solem, Natalie Winters.	
Lake Avenue Plaza Building, Suite 107, 714 Lake Avenue, Detroit Lakes, MN 56501	(218) 847–5056
Minnesota Wheat Growers Building, 2603 Wheat Drive, Red Lake, MN 56750	(218) 253–4356
324 3rd Street, SW., Suite 4, Willmar, MN 56201	(320) 235–1061

Counties: BECKER, BELTRAMI (part), BIG STONE, CHIPPEWA, CLAY, CLEARWATER, COTTONWOOD (part), DOUGLAS, GRANT, KANDIYOHI, KITTSON, LAC QUI PARLE, LAKE OF THE WOODS, LINCOLN, LYON, MAHNOMEN, MARSHALL, MCLEOD, MEEKER, MURRAY, NORMAN, OTTER, PIPESTONE, TAIL, PENNINGTON, POLK, POPE, RED LAKE, REDWOOD, RENVILLE, ROSEAU, SIBLEY, STEARNS (part), STEVENS, SWIFT, TODD, TRAVERSE, WILKIN, AND YELLOW MEDICINE. Population (2010), 662,991.

ZIP Codes: 55307, 55310, 55312, 55314, 55321, 55324–25, 55329, 55332–36, 55338–39, 55342, 55350, 55353–55, 55366, 55368, 55370, 55381–82, 55385, 55389, 55395–96, 55409, 55970, 56011, 56044, 56054, 56058, 56083, 56085, 56087, 56113, 56115, 56129, 56132, 56136, 56142, 56149, 56152, 56157, 56164, 56166, 56169–70, 56175, 56178, 56180, 56201, 56207–12, 56214–16, 56218–32, 56235–37, 56239–41, 56242–45, 56248–49, 56251–53, 56255–58, 56260, 56262–67, 56270–71, 56273–74, 56276–85, 56287–89, 56291–97, 56301–04, 56307–12, 56314–16, 56318–21, 56323–24, 56326–27, 56329, 56331–32, 56334, 56336, 56339–40, 56343, 56345, 56347, 56349, 56352, 56354–55, 56360–62, 56368, 56372–74, 56377–79, 56381–82, 56385, 56387, 56393, 56395–99, 56433–34, 56436–38, 56440, 56443, 56446, 56452, 56458, 56461, 56464, 56466–67, 56470, 56473, 56477–79, 56481–82, 56501–02, 56510–11, 56514–25, 56527–29, 56531, 56534–48, 56556–57, 56560–63, 56565–81, 56583–94, 56601, 56619, 56621, 56623, 56633–34, 56644, 56646–47, 56650–52, 56661, 56663, 56666–67, 56670–71, 56673, 56676, 56678, 56682–87, 56701, 56710–11, 56713–16, 56720–29, 56731–38, 56740–42, 56744, 56748, 56750–51, 56754–63

* * *

EIGHTH DISTRICT

RICHARD M. NOLAN, Democrat-Farmer-Labor, of Crosby, MN; born in Brainerd, MN, December 17, 1943; education: attended St. John's University, Collegeville, MN, 1962; B.A., University of Minnesota, Minneapolis, MN, 1966; post-graduate work at the University of Maryland, College Park, MD, St. Cloud State, St. Cloud, MN, and Central Lakes Community College, Brainerd, MN; professional: High School Social Studies Teacher; Head Start Program Director; Curriculum Coordinator; Fingerhut Corporation Assistant to the President; Minnesota State Representative; U.S. Congressman; U.S. Export Corporation President; Minnesota World Trade Center President; International Business Consultant; Emily Forest Products CEO; religion: Roman Catholic; married: Mary Nolan; four children; ten grandchildren; committees: Agriculture; Transportation and Infrastructure; elected to the 94th Congress and did not seek reelection after serving three terms; elected to the 113th Congress on November 6, 2012; reelected to the 114th Congress on November 4, 2014.

Office Listings

http://www.nolan.house.gov

2366 Rayburn House Office Building, Washington, DC 20515	(202) 225–6211

Office Listings—Continued

Chief of Staff.—Jodie Torkelson.
Legislative Director.—Jim Swiderski.
Communications Director.—Steve Johnson.
Scheduler.—Taryn Brown.
Duluth Technology Village, 11 East Superior Street, Suite 125, Duluth, MN 55802 .... (218) 464–5095
    District Director.—Jeff Anderson.　　　　　　　　　　　　　　　　　　　　　　FAX: 464–5098
Brainerd City Hall, 501 Laurel Street, Brainerd, MN 56401 .... (218) 454–4078
　　　　　　　　　　　　　　　　　　　　　　　　　　　　　　　　　　　　FAX: 454–4096
Chisago County Government Center, 313 North Main Street, Room 103, Center City, MN
  55012 .... (218) 491–3131
Chisholm City Hall, 316 West Lake Street, Room 7, Chisholm, MN 55719 .... (218) 491–3114

Counties: AITKIN, BELTRAMI (part), CARLTON, CASS, CHISAGO, COOK, CROW WING, HUBBARD, ISANTI, ITASCA, KANABEC, KOOCHICHING, LAKE, MILLE LACS, MORRISON, PINE, ST. LOUIS, WADENA. CITIES: Baxter, Brainerd, Cambridge, Chisago City, Chisholm, Cloquet, Duluth, Ely, Eveleth, Grand Rapids, Hermantown, Hibbing, International Falls, Isanti, Lindstrom, Little Falls, Mora, North Branch, Park Rapids, Pine City, Princeton, Proctor, Rush City, Two Harbors, Virginia, Wadena, and Wyoming. Population (2010), 660,347.

ZIP Codes: 55005–08, 55012–13, 55017, 55025, 55029–30, 55032, 55036–37, 55040, 55045, 55051, 55056, 55063, 55069–70, 55072–74, 55079–80, 55084, 55092, 55371, 55398, 55601–07, 55609, 55612–16, 55702–13, 55716–26, 55731–36, 55738, 55741–42, 55744, 55746, 55748–53, 55756–58, 55760, 55763–69, 55771–72, 55775, 55779–87, 55790, 55792–93, 55795–98, 55802–08, 55810–12, 56307, 56313–14, 56317–18, 56328–31, 56336, 56338, 56340, 56342, 56344–45, 56347, 56350, 56353, 56357–59, 56363–64, 56367, 56373, 56382, 56384, 56386, 56401, 56425, 56431, 56433–36, 56441–44, 56447–50, 56452, 56455, 56458, 56461, 56464–70, 56472–75, 56477, 56479, 56481–82, 56484, 56601, 56623, 56626–31, 56633, 56636–37, 56639–41, 56647, 56649–50, 56653–55, 56657–63, 56667–69, 56672, 56678–81, 56683, 56688

MISSISSIPPI

(Population 2010, 2,967,297)

SENATORS

THAD COCHRAN, Republican, of Oxford, MS; born in Pontotoc, MS, December 7, 1937; education: B.A., University of Mississippi, 1959; J.D., University of Mississippi Law School, 1965; received a Rotary Foundation Fellowship and studied international law and jurisprudence at Trinity College, University of Dublin, Ireland, 1963–64; military service: served in the U.S. Navy, 1959–61; professional: admitted to Mississippi Bar in 1965; board of directors, Jackson Rotary Club, 1970–71; Outstanding Young Man of the Year Award, Junior Chamber of Commerce in Mississippi, 1971; president, young lawyers section of Mississippi State Bar, 1972–73; married: the former Rose Clayton of New Albany, MS, 1964; widowed: 2014; two children and three grandchildren; committees: chairman, Appropriations; Agriculture, Nutrition, and Forestry; Rules and Administration; elected to the 93rd Congress, November 7, 1972; reelected to 94th and 95th Congresses; chairman of the Senate Republican Conference, 1990–96; elected to the U.S. Senate, November 7, 1978, for the six-year term beginning January 3, 1979; subsequently appointed by the Governor, December 27, 1978, to fill the vacancy caused by the resignation of Senator James O. Eastland; reelected to each succeeding Senate term.

Office Listings

http://cochran.senate.gov

113 Dirksen Senate Office Building, Washington, DC 20510	(202) 224–5054
Chief of Staff.—Keith Heard.	
Legislative Director.—Adam Telle.	
Press Secretary.—Chris Gallegos.	
Scheduler.—Doris Wagley.	
190 East Capitol Street, Suite 550, Jackson, MS 39201	(601) 965–4459
911 East Jackson Avenue, Suite 249, Oxford, MS 38655	(662) 236–1018
2012 15th Street, Suite 451, Gulfport, MS 39501	(228) 867–9710

* * *

ROGER F. WICKER, Republican, of Tupelo, MS; born in Pontotoc, MS, July 5, 1951; education: graduated, Pontotoc High School; University of Mississippi: B.A., 1973; J.D., 1975; president, Associated Student Body, 1972–73; *Mississippi Law Journal*, 1973–75; Air Force ROTC; U.S. Air Force, 1976–80; U.S. Air Force Reserve, 1980–2004 (retired with rank of lieutenant colonel); U.S. House of Representatives Rules Committee staff for Representative Trent Lott, 1980–82; private law practice, 1982–94; Lee County Public Defender, 1984–87; Tupelo City Judge pro tempore, 1986–87; Mississippi State Senate, 1988–94, chairman: Elections Committee (1992), Public Health and Welfare Committee (1993–94); member: Lions Club, University of Mississippi Hall of Fame, Sigma Nu Fraternity Hall of Fame, Omicron Delta Kappa, Phi Delta Phi; religion: Southern Baptist, deacon, adult choir of First Baptist Church, Tupelo, MS; married: Gayle Long Wicker; children: Margaret (Manning) McPhillips, Caroline (Kirk) Sims, and McDaniel (Kellee) Wicker; grandchildren: Caroline McPhillips; Henry McPhillips; Maury McPhillips, Evelyn Sims; Commission on Security and Cooperation in Europe; committees: Armed Services; Budget; Commerce, Science, and Transportation; Environment and Public Works; Rules and Administration; elected to the 104th Congress, November 8, 1994; president, Republican freshman class, 1995; reelected to each succeeding Congress; appointed by the governor, December 31, 2007, to fill the vacancy caused by the resignation of Senator Trent Lott; elected to the U.S. Senate on November 4, 2008; reelected to the U.S. Senate on November 6, 2012.

Office Listings

http://wicker.senate.gov　　　http://facebook.com/senatorwicker　　　twitter: @senatorwicker

555 Dirksen Senate Office Building, Washington, DC 20510	(202) 224–6253
	FAX: 228–0378
Chief of Staff.—Michelle Barlow Richardson.	
Legislative Director.—Bob Foster.	
Communications Director.—Ryan Taylor.	
Scheduler.—Hall Carter.	
U.S. Federal Courthouse, 501 East Court Street, Suite 3.500, Jackson, MS 39201	(601) 965–4644
	FAX: 695–4007

Office Listings—Continued

2909 13th Street, Suite 303, Gulfport, MS 39501	(228) 871–7017
	FAX: 896–4359
330 West Jefferson Street, Suite B, Tupelo, MS 33804	(662) 844–5010
321 Losher Street, Hernando, MS	(662) 429–1002
	FAX: 429–6002

REPRESENTATIVES

FIRST DISTRICT

TRENT KELLY, Republican, of Saltillo, MS; born in Union, MS, March 1, 1966; education: Union High School, Union, MS, 1984; Associate of Arts, East Central Community College, Decatur, MS, 1986; Bachelor of Business Administration, marketing, University of Mississippi, Oxford, MS, 1989; Juris Doctor, University of Mississippi, Oxford, MS, 1994; Master's in Strategic Studies, United States Army War College, Carlisle, Pennsylvania, 2010; professional: private law practice, Saltillo, MS, 1995–99; City Prosecutor, Tupelo, MS, 1999–2011; Forfeiture Attorney, North Mississippi Narcotics Unit, 2000–11; District Attorney for Lee, Pontotoc, Alcorn, Monroe, Itawamba, Prentiss and Tishomingo Counties, 2012–June 2015; military: 29 years in the Mississippi Army National Guard as an Engineer; currently a Colonel; Mobilized for Desert Storm as an Engineer Second Lieutenant, 1990; deployed as a Major to Iraq with the 155th Brigade as the Operations Officer of the 150th Engineer Battalion, 2005; deployed as a Lieutenant Colonel to Iraq as the Battalion Commander of Task Force Knight of the 155th Brigade Combat Team and commanded over 670 troops from Mississippi, Ohio, and Kentucky, 2009–10; awards: two Bronze Stars; Combat Action Badge; DeFleury Medal, and numerous other federal and state awards; religion: Methodist; married: Sheila Stephens Kelly; children: John Forrest, Morgan, and Jackson; committees: Agriculture; Small Business; elected to the 114th Congress on June 2, 2015, by special election, to fill the vacancy caused by the death of United States Representative Alan S. Nunnelee.

Office Listings

http://trentkelly.house.gov   www.facebook.com/reptrentkelly   twitter: @reptrentkelly

1427 Longworth House Office Building, Washington, DC 20515	(202) 225–4306
Chief of Staff.—Ted Maness.	FAX: 225–3549
Deputy Chief of Staff.—Elizabeth Parks.	
District Director / Scheduler.—Mabel Murphree.	
431 West Main Street, Suite 450, Tupelo, MS 38804	(662) 841–8808
	FAX: 841–8845
318 Seventh Street North, Suite D, Columbus, MS 39701	(662) 327–0748
Mailing: P.O. Box 1012, Columbus, MS 39703	FAX: 328–5982
2565 Caffey Street, #200, Hernando, MS 38632	(662) 449–3090
Mailing: P.O. Box 218, Hernando, MS 38632	FAX: 449–4836

Counties: ALCORN, BENTON, CALHOUN, CHICKASAW, CHOCTAW, CLAY, DESOTO, ITAWAMBA, LAFAYETTE, LEE, LOWNDES, MARSHALL, MONROE, PONTOTOC, PRENTISS, TATE, TIPPAH, TISHOMINGO, UNION, WEBSTER, WINSTON, AND OKTIBBEHA (part). Population (2013), 756,459.

ZIP Codes: 38601, 38603, 38606 (part), 38610–11, 38618, 38619 (part), 38625, 38627, 38629, 38632–33, 38635, 38637, 38641–42, 38647, 38650–52, 38654–55, 38659, 38661, 38663, 38665, 38668, 38671–74, 38677, 38680, 38683, 38685, 38801, 38804, 38821, 38824, 38826–29, 38833–34, 38838, 38841, 38843–44, 38846–52, 38855–60, 38862–66, 38868–71, 38873, 38876, 38878–79, 38913–16, 38929 (part), 38949, 38951, 39108 (part), 39339, 39346 (part), 39354 (part), 39701–02, 39705, 39730, 39735–37, 39740–41, 39743 (part), 39744, 39745 (part), 39746, 39750 (part), 39751–52, 39755 (part), 39756, 39766–67, 39769 (part), 39771, 39772 (part), 39773, 39776

* * *

SECOND DISTRICT

BENNIE G. THOMPSON, Democrat, of Bolton, MS; born in Bolton, January 28, 1948; education: graduated, Hinds County Agriculture High School; B.A., Tougaloo College, 1968; M.S., Jackson State University, 1972; professional: teacher; Bolton Board of Aldermen, 1969–73; mayor of Bolton, 1973–79; Hinds County Board of Supervisors, 1980–93; Congressional Black Caucus; Congressional Gaming Caucus; Congressional Sportsmen's Caucus; House Education Caucus; Rural Caucus; Progressive Caucus; Housing Assistance Council; NAACP 100 Black Men of Jackson, MS; Southern Regional Council; Kappa Alpha Psi Fraternity; married to the former London Johnson, Ph.D.; one daughter: BendaLonne; committees: ranking member, Homeland Security; elected to the 103rd Congress in a special election; reelected to each succeeding Congress.

Office Listings

http://www.benniethompson.house.gov

2466 Rayburn House Office Building, Washington, DC 20515	(202) 225–5876
Chief of Staff.—Lanier Avant.	FAX: 225–5898
Legislative Director.—Cory Horton.	
Press Secretary/Legislative Assistant.—LeMia Jenkins.	
Legislative Assistant.—John "Trey" Baker.	
Scheduler.—Andrea Lee.	
Staff Assistant.—Daphene Brooks.	
107 West Madison Street, P.O. Box 610, Bolton, MS 39041–0610	(601) 866–9003
District Director.—Vacant.	
3607 Medgar Evers Boulevard, Jackson, MS 39213	(601) 982–8582
263 East Main Street, Marks, MS 38646	(662) 326–9003
Mound Bayou City Hall, Room 134, 106 West Green Street, Mound Bayou, MS 38762	(662) 741–9003
509 Highway 82 West, Greenwood, MS 38930	(662) 455–9003
910 Courthouse Lane, Greenville, MS 38701	(662) 335–9003

Counties: ATTALA, BOLIVAR, CARROLL, CLAIBORNE, COAHOMA, COPIAH, GRENADA, HINDS (part), HOLMES, HUMPHREYS, ISSAQUENA, JEFFERSON, LEAKE, LEFLORE, MADISON (part), MONTGOMERY, PANOLA, QUITMAN, SHARKEY, SUNFLOWER, TALLAHATCHIE, TUNICA, WARREN, WASHINGTON, YALOBUSHA, AND YAZOO. Population (2010), 741,862.

ZIP Codes: 38606, 38614, 38617, 38619–23, 38626, 38630–31, 38639, 38643–46, 38658, 38664–66, 38670, 38676, 38701–04, 38720–23, 38725–26, 38730–32, 38736–38, 38740, 38744–46, 38748–49, 38751, 38753–54, 38756, 38759–62, 38764–65, 38767–69, 38771–74, 38778, 38781, 38901, 38914, 38917, 38920–25, 38927–30, 38940–41, 38943–48, 38950, 38952–54, 38957–58, 38961–67, 39038–41, 39045–46, 39051, 39054, 39056, 39059, 39061, 39063, 39066–67, 39069, 39071, 39078–79, 39083, 39086, 39088, 39090, 39094–97, 39108, 39110, 39113, 39115, 39120, 39144, 39146, 39150, 39154, 39156–57, 39159–60, 39162, 39166, 39169–70, 39174–77, 39179–80, 39183, 39189, 39191–92, 39194, 39201–04, 39206, 39209, 39211–13, 39216–17, 39272, 39365, 39653, 39668, 39745, 39747, 39767

* * *

THIRD DISTRICT

GREGG HARPER, Republican, of Pearl, MS; born in Jackson, MS, June 1, 1956; education: graduated from Pearl High School, Pearl, MS, 1974; B.S., Mississippi College, Clinton, MS, 1978; J.D., University of Mississippi, Oxford, MS, 1981; professional: private practice attorney and prosecuting attorney; member, Pearl Chamber of Commerce, Rankin County Chamber of Commerce; religion: Southern Baptist; married: the former Sidney Carol Hancock; children: Livingston and Maggie; committees: chair, Joint Committee on Printing, vice-chair, Joint Committee on the Library; Energy and Commerce; House Administration; elected to the 111th Congress on November 4, 2008; reelected to each succeeding Congress.

Office Listings

http://www.harper.house.gov

307 Cannon House Office Building, Washington, DC 20515	(202) 225–5031
Chief of Staff.—Michael Cravens.	FAX: 225–5797
Policy Director.—Scot Malvaney.	
Communications Director.—Jordan See.	
2507–A Old Brandon Road, Pearl, MS 39208	(601) 932–2410
District Director.—Chip Reynolds.	
Scheduler.—Debra Boutwell.	
1901 Front Street, Suite A, Meridian, MS 39301	(601) 693–6681
Special Assistant.—Frances White.	
1 Research Boulevard, Suite 206, Starkville, MS 39759	(662) 324–0007
Special Assistant.—Henry Moseley.	
Senior Field Representative.—Kyle Jordan.	

Counties: ADAMS, AMITE, CLARK (part), COVINGTON, FRANKLIN, HINDS (part), JASPER, JEFFERSON DAVIS, KEMPER, LAUDERDALE, LAWRENCE, LINCOLN, MADISON (part), NESHOBA, NEWTON, NOXUBEE, OKTIBBEHA (part), PIKE, RANKIN, SCOTT, SIMPSON, SMITH, WALTHALL, AND WILKINSON. Population (2014), 711,115.

ZIP Codes: 39042, 39044, 39046–07, 39501, 39057, 39062, 39071, 39073–74, 39082, 39092, 39094, 39110–11, 39114, 39116–17, 39119–20, 39410, 39145, 39149, 39152–53, 39157, 39167–68, 39189, 39191, 39193, 39201, 39203–04, 39206, 39208–09, 39211–13, 39216, 39218, 39232, 39269, 39301, 39305, 39307, 39309, 39320, 39323, 39325–28, 39330, 39332, 39335–38, 39341–42, 39345–48, 39350, 39352, 39354–56, 39358–61, 39363–66, 39401–02, 39421–22, 39428–29, 39439, 39443, 39474, 39478–83, 39601, 39629–31, 39633, 39635, 39638, 39641, 39643, 39645, 39647–48, 39652–54, 39657, 39661–63, 39666–69, 39743, 39750, 39759–60, 39762, 39769

* * *

FOURTH DISTRICT

STEVEN M. PALAZZO, Republican, of Biloxi, MS; born in Gulfport, MS, February 21, 1970; education: B.S., University of Southern Mississippi, Hattiesburg, MS, 1994; M.P.A., University of Southern Mississippi, Hattiesburg, 1996; professional: accountant; military: United States Marine Corps Reserve, 1988–96; Mississippi Army National Guard, 2007–present; member of Mississippi State House of Representatives, 2007–10; commissions and caucuses: Congressional Sportsmen's Caucus; Gulf Coast Caucus; Home Protection Caucus; National Guard Caucus; Shipbuilding Caucus; family: spouse, Lisa; children: Barrett, Aubrey, and Bennett; committees: Appropriations; Science, Space, and Technology; elected to the 112th Congress on November 2, 2010; reelected to each succeeding Congress.

Office Listings

http://www.palazzo.house.gov   www.facebook.com/stevenpalazzo   twitter.com/congpalazzo

331 Cannon House Office Building, Washington, DC 20515	(202) 225–5772
Chief of Staff.—Casey Street.	FAX: 225–7074
Legislative Director.—Patrick Large.	
Scheduler.—Leslie Churchwell.	
1325 25th Avenue, Gulfport, MS 39501	(228) 864–7670
Deputy Chief of Staff.—Hunter Lipscomb.	
641 Main Street, Suite 215, Hattiesburg, MS 39401	(601) 582–3246
3118 Pascagoula Street, Suite 181, Pascagoula, MS 39567	(228) 202–8104
	FAX: 202–8105
72 Technology Boulevard, Suite 216, Ellisville, MS 39437	(601) 428–9711

Counties: CLARKE (part), FORREST, GEORGE, GREENE, HANCOCK, HARRISON, JACKSON, JONES, LAMAR, MARION, PEARL RIVER, PERRY, STONE, AND WAYNE. CITIES AND TOWNSHIPS: Biloxi, Gulfport, Hattiesburg, Laurel, and Pascagoula. Population (2010), 741,776.

ZIP Codes: 39301, 39307, 39322, 39324, 39330, 39332, 39347–48, 39355–56, 39360, 39362–63, 39366–67, 39401–04, 39406, 39422–23, 39425–26, 39429, 39436–37, 39439–43, 39451–52, 39455–57, 39459, 39461–66, 39470, 39475–78, 39480–82, 39501–03, 39505–07, 39520–22, 39525, 39529–35, 39540, 39552–53, 39555–56, 39558, 39560–69, 39571–74, 39576–77, 39581, 39595

MISSOURI

(Population 2010, 5,988,927)

SENATORS

CLAIRE McCASKILL, Democrat, of Kirkwood, MO; born in Rolla, MO, July 24, 1953; raised in Lebanon, MO and Columbia, MO; education: B.A., University of Missouri-Columbia, 1975; J.D., University of Missouri-Columbia School of Law, 1978; professional: clerk with the Missouri Court of Appeals, Western District in Kansas City, 1978; assistant prosecutor, Jackson County prosecutor's office, 1979–83; Missouri State Representative, 1983–88; practiced law in Kansas City, MO, 1983–92; Jackson County Legislator-At-Large, 1991–93; Jackson County Prosecutor, 1993–99; Missouri State Auditor, 1999–2006; married: Joseph Shephard, 2002; together, they have seven children: Benjamin, Carl, Marilyn, Michael, Austin, Maddie, Lily; appointed deputy whip for the majority, 2007; committees: ranking member, Special Committee on Aging; Armed Services; Commerce, Science, and Transportation; Homeland Security and Governmental Affairs; elected to the U.S. Senate of the 110th Congress on November 7, 2006; reelected to the U.S. Senate on November 6, 2012.

Office Listings

http://mccaskill.senate.gov   https://www.facebook.com/senatormccaskill
https://twitter.com/mccaskilloffice

730 Hart Senate Office Building, Washington, DC 20510	(202) 224–6154
Chief of Staff.—Julie Dwyer.	FAX: 228–6326
Deputy Chief of Staff.—Tod Martin.	
Legislative Director.—Anna Laitin.	
Communications Director.—John LaBombard.	
5850 Delmar Boulevard, Suite A, St. Louis, MO 63112	(314) 367–1364
Regional Director.—Joeana Middleton.	
4141 Pennsylvania Avenue, Suite 101, Kansas City, MO 64111	(816) 421–1639
Regional Director.—Corey Dillon.	
555 Independence Avenue, Room 1600, Cape Girardeau, MO 63703	(573) 651–0964
District Director.—Christy Mercer.	
28 North 8th Street, Suite 500, Columbia, MO 65201	(573) 442–7130
Regional Director.—Cindy Hall.	
324 Park Central West, Suite 101, Springfield, MO 65806	(417) 868–8745
District Director.—David Stokely.	

* * *

ROY BLUNT, Republican, of Springfield, MO; born in Niangua, MO, January 10, 1950; education: B.A., Southwest Baptist University, 1970; M.A., Missouri State University, 1972; professional: county clerk and chief election official of Greene County, 1972–84; Secretary of State of Missouri, 1984–92; president of Southwest Baptist University, 1993–96; U.S. House of Representatives for Missouri's 7th District, 1996–2010; married: Abigail Blunt; children: Governor Matthew Blunt, Amy Blunt, Andrew Blunt, Alexander Charles Blunt; committees: chair, Rules and Administration; chair, Joint Committee on the Library; vice chair, Joint Committee on Printing; Appropriations; Commerce, Science, and Transportation; Select Committee on Intelligence; elected to the U.S. Senate on November 2, 2010.

Office Listings

http://blunt.senate.gov

260 Russell Senate Office Building, Washington, DC 20510	(202) 224–5721
Chief of Staff.—Glen Chambers.	FAX: 224–8149
Deputy Chief of Staff.—Burson Snyder.	
Legislative Director.—Tracy Henke.	
Communications Director.—Brian Hart.	
Director of Scheduling.—Richard Eddings.	
2740B East Sunshine, Springfield, MO 65804	(417) 877–7814
1000 Walnut Street, Suite 1560, Kansas City, MO 64106	(816) 471–7141
State Director.—Matt Haase.	
7700 Bonhomme, Suite 315, Clayton, MO 63105	(314) 725–4484
1001 Cherry Street, Suite 104, Columbia, MO 65201	(573) 442–8151
2502 Tanner Drive, Suite 208, Cape Girardeau, MO 63703	(573) 334–7044

REPRESENTATIVES

FIRST DISTRICT

WM. LACY CLAY, Democrat, of St. Louis, MO; born in St. Louis, July 27, 1956; education: Springbrook High School, Silver Spring, MD, 1974; B.A., University of Maryland, College Park, MD, 1983; public service: Missouri House of Representatives, 1983–91; Missouri State Senate, 1991–2000; nonprofit organizations: St. Louis Gateway Classic Sports Foundation; Mary Ryder Homes; William L. Clay Scholarship and Research Fund; religion: Catholic; divorced; children: Carol and William III; committees: Financial Services; Oversight and Government Reform; elected to the 107th Congress on November 7, 2000; reelected to each succeeding Congress.

Office Listings

http://www.lacyclay.house.gov

2428 Rayburn House Office Building, Washington, DC 20515	(202) 225–2406
Chief of Staff.—Yvette P. Cravins.	FAX: 226–3717
Scheduler.—Karyn Long.	
Legislative Assistants: Pauline Jamry, Richard Pecantte.	
Thomas F. Eagleton U.S. Courthouse, 111 South 10th Street, Suite 24–344, St. Louis, MO 63102	(314) 367–1970
	FAX: 367–1341
6830 Gravois, St. Louis, MO 63116	(314) 669–9393
	FAX: 669–9398

Counties: ST. LOUIS (part). Population (2010), 748,616.

ZIP Codes: 63031, 63033–34, 63042–45, 63074, 63101–25, 63130, 63132–41, 63143–44, 63146–47, 63155

* * *

SECOND DISTRICT

ANN L. WAGNER, Republican, of Ballwin, MO; born in St. Louis, MO, September 13, 1962; education: B.A.B.S., University of Missouri, Columbia, 1984; professional: businesswoman; Hallmark Cards; Ralston Purina; public service: Committeewoman for Lafayette Township; chair of Missouri Republican Party, 1999–2005; co-chair of the Republican National Committee, 2001–05; U.S. Ambassador to Luxembourg, 2005–09; family: married to Raymond Jr.; children: Raymond III, Stephen, Mary Ruth; committees: Financial Services; elected to the 113th Congress on November 6, 2012; reelected to the 114th Congress on November 4, 2014.

Office Listings

http://wagner.house.gov https://twitter.com/repannwagner
https://www.facebook.com/repannwagner

435 Cannon House Office Building, Washington, DC 20515	(202) 225–1621
Chief of Staff.—Christian Morgan.	
Scheduler.—Courtney Ellis.	
301 Sovereign Court, Suite 201, St. Louis, MO 63011	(636) 779–5449
District Director.—Miriam Stonebraker.	

Counties: JEFFERSON (part), CHARLES (part), ST. LOUIS (part). Population (2010), 706,622.

ZIP Codes: 63005, 63010–11, 63017, 63021, 63025–26, 63038, 63040, 63043–44, 63049, 63069, 63074, 63088, 63105, 63114, 63117, 63119, 63122–32, 63141, 63144, 63146, 63301, 63303–04, 63341, 63366, 63368, 63376

* * *

THIRD DISTRICT

BLAINE LUETKEMEYER, Republican, of St. Elizabeth, MO; born in Jefferson City, MO, May 7, 1952; education: graduate of Lincoln University, Jefferson City, MO, 1974, where he earned a degree with distinction in political science and a minor in business administration, 1999–2005; professional: served as Missouri State Representative and after leaving office was appointed by the Governor to serve as the Director of the Missouri Division of Tourism; lifelong member of St. Elizabeth Catholic Church; married: Jackie, three children; committees: vice-chair, Small Business; Financial Services; elected to the 111th Congress on November 4, 2008; reelected to each succeeding Congress.

Office Listings

http://luetkemeyer.house.gov

2440 Rayburn House Office Building, Washington, DC 20515 .... (202) 225–2956
 Chief of Staff.—Seth Appleton.   FAX: 225–5712
 Legislative Director.—Kristina Weger.
 Communications Director.—Kristina Weger.
 Legislative Assistants: Trey McKenzie, Meghan Sanguinette.
 Legislative Aide.—Lucas West.
 Staff Assistant.—Claire Torkey.
 Director of Scheduling.—Lauren Orndorff.
2117 Missouri Boulevard, Jefferson City, MO 65109 .... (573) 635–7232
 District Office Director.—Jeremy Ketterer.   FAX: 635–8346
 Director of Constituent Affairs.—Keri Stuart.
 Caseworker.—Lori Boykin.
 Office Manager.—Laura Hardecke.
516 Jefferson Street, Washington, MO 63090 .... (636) 239–2276
 District Office Director.—Jim McNichols.   FAX: 239–0478
 Field Representative.—Mary Tinsley.
113 East Pearce, Wentzville, MO 63385 .... (573) 327–7055
 District Office Director.—Tanner Smith.

Counties: CALLAWAY, CAMDEN (part), COLE, FRANKLIN, GASCONADE, JEFFERSON (part), LINCOLN, MARIES, MILLER, MONT-GOMERY, OSAGE, ST. CHARLES (part) and WARREN. Population (2010), 748,615.

ZIP Codes: 63005 (part), 63010 (part), 63012 (part), 63013–63014, 63015 (part), 63016 (part), 63019 (part), 63023 (part), 63025 (part), 63026 (part), 63028 (part), 63037, 63039, 63041 (part), 63048, 63049 (part), 63050 (part), 63051–53, 63055, 63057, 63060–61, 63068, 63069 (part), 63070 (part), 63072 (part), 63073, 63077, 63079, 63080 (part), 63084, 63089–91, 63301 (part), 63302, 63303 (part), 63332–33, 63334 (part), 63341 (part), 63342 (part), 63343 (part), 63344 (part), 63346–51, 63352 (part), 63357, 63359 (part), 63361–63, 63365, 63366 (part), 63367, 63368 (part), 63369–70, 63373, 63376 (part), 63377–79, 63381, 63383, 63384 (part)

* * *

FOURTH DISTRICT

VICKY HARTZLER, Republican, of Harrisonville, MO; born in Archie, MO, October 13, 1960; education: B.S., in education, *summa cum laude*, University of Missouri-Columbia, Columbia, MO, 1983; M.S., in education, Central Missouri State University (now University of Central Missouri), Warrensburg, MO, 1992; professional: served as State spokesperson for the Coalition to Protect Marriage, 2004; member of the Missouri State House of Representatives, 124th District, 1995–2001; appointed chair, Missouri Women's Council, 2005; teacher of family and consumer sciences for 11 years in Lebanon and Belton, MO; religion: Evangelical Christian; family: married Lowell Hartzler; one child: Tiffany, caucuses: Pro-Life Caucus; Israel Allies Caucus; International Religious Freedom Caucus; Republican Study Committee; Long-Range Strike Caucus; Congressional Coalition on Adoption; Army Caucus; Air Force Caucus; China Caucus; Missile Defense Caucus; EMP Caucus; Human Trafficking Caucus; Small Business Caucus; Prayer Caucus; Military Family Caucus; Job Creators' Caucus; Rural Caucus; Taiwan Caucus; General Aviation Caucus; committees: Agriculture; Armed Services; Budget; elected to the 112th Congress on November 2, 2010; reelected to each succeeding Congress.

Office Listings

http://www.hartzler.house.gov

2235 Rayburn House Office Building, Washington, DC 20515 .... (202) 225–2876
 Chief of Staff.—Eric Bohl.   FAX: 225–0148
 Legislative Director.—Daniel Burgess.
 Communications Director.—Kyle Buckles.
 Scheduler.—Adrienne Cornelius.
2415 Carter Lane, Suite 4, Columbia, MO 65201 .... (573) 442–9311
1909 North Commercial Street, Harrisonville, MO 64701 .... (816) 884–3411
219 North Adams Street, Lebanon, MO 65536 .... (417) 532–5582

Counties: AUDRAIN (part), BARTON, BATES, BENTON, BOONE, CAMDEN, CASS, CEDAR, COOPER, DADE, DALLAS, HENRY, HICKORY, HOWARD, JOHNSON, LACLEDE, MONITEAU, MORGAN, PULASKI, RANDOLPH, ST. CLAIR, VERNON, AND WEBSTER (part). Population (2010), 748,616.

ZIP Codes: 63352, 64011–12, 64019–20, 64030, 64034, 64037, 64040, 64061, 64070–71, 64076, 64078, 64080, 64082–83, 64090, 64093, 64147, 64149, 64701, 64720, 64722–26, 64728, 64730, 64733–35, 64738–48, 64750, 64752, 64755–56, 64759, 64761–63, 64765–67, 64769–72, 64776, 64778–81, 64783–84, 64788, 64790, 64832, 64855, 65010–11, 65018, 65020, 65023, 65025–26, 65034, 65037–39, 65042, 65046, 65050, 65055, 65064, 65068, 65072, 65074, 65078–79, 65081, 65084, 65201–03, 65205, 65211–12, 65215–18, 65230–33, 65237, 65239–40, 65243–44, 65247–48, 65250, 65254–57, 65259–60, 65264–65, 65270, 65274, 65276, 65278–80, 65284–85, 65287, 65299, 65301–02, 65305, 65322–26, 65329, 65332–38, 65340, 65345, 65347–48, 65350–51, 65354–55, 65360, 65452, 65457, 65459, 65461, 65463, 65470, 65473, 65534, 65536, 65543, 65550, 65552, 65556, 65567, 65583–84, 65590–91, 65603–04, 65607, 65622, 65632, 65634–36, 65644, 65646, 65648–50, 65652, 65661–62, 65668, 65674, 65682, 65685, 65706, 65713, 65722, 65724, 65732, 65735, 65742, 65746, 65752, 65757, 65764, 65767, 65770, 65774, 65779, 65783, 65785–87

* * *

FIFTH DISTRICT

EMANUEL CLEAVER II, Democrat, of Kansas City, MO; born in Waxahachie, TX, October 26, 1944; education: M. Div., Saint Paul School of Theology, MO, 1974; B.S., Prairie View A&M University, TX, 1972; professional: Senior Pastor, St. James United Methodist Church, 1973–2009; City Councilman, Kansas City, MO, 5th District, 1979–91; founder, Harmony in a World of Difference, 1991; founder, Southern Christian Leadership Conference, Kansas City Chapter; Mayor of Kansas City, MO, 1991–99; member, President-elect Bill Clinton's Transitional Team, 1992; host, Under the Clock, KCUR radio, 1999–2004; chairman of the Congressional Black Caucus, 2010–12; member, National Co-Chair of President Barack Obama Campaign Committee, 2012; married: Dianne; four children; four grandchildren; committees: Financial Services; elected to the 109th Congress on November 2, 2004; reelected to each succeeding Congress.

Office Listings

http://www.cleaver.house.gov

2335 Rayburn House Office Building, Washington, DC 20515	(202) 225–4535
Legislative Director.—Jennifer Shapiro.	FAX: 225–4403
Scheduler.—Justin Thaxton.	
101 West 31st Street, Kansas City, MO 64108	(816) 842–4545
Chief of Staff.—John Jones.	
Communications Director.—John Jones.	
211 Maple Avenue, Independence, MO 64050	(816) 833–4545

Counties: CLAY COUNTY (part), JACKSON COUNTY (part), LAFAYETTE, RAY, AND SALINE COUNTIES. CITIES AND TOWNSHIPS: Kansas City, Independence, Lee's Summit, Raytown, Grandview, Sugar Creek, Blue Springs, Grain Valley, Oak Grove, North Kansas City, Gladstone, Claycomo, Lawson, Richmond, Concordia, Higginsville, Lexington, Odessa, Marshall, Sweet Springs, and Slater. Population (2010), 747,573.

ZIP Codes: 64001, 64011, 64017, 64020–22, 64024, 64029, 64035–37, 64062, 64067, 64071, 64074–77, 64084–85, 64096–97, 64747–48, 65320, 65327, 65330, 65339–40, 65344, 65347, 65349, 65351

* * *

SIXTH DISTRICT

SAM GRAVES, Republican, of Tarkio, MO; born in Fairfax, MO, November 7, 1963; education: B.S., University of Missouri-Columbia, 1986; professional: farmer; organizations: Missouri Farm Bureau; Northwest Missouri State University Agriculture Advisory Committee; University Extension Council; Rotary Club; awards: Associated Industries Voice of Missouri Business Award; Tom Henderson Award; Tarkio Community Betterment Award; Missouri Physical Therapy Association Award; Outstanding Young Farmer Award, 1997; Hero of the Taxpayer Award; NFIB Guardian of Small Business Award; public service: elected to the Missouri House of Representatives, 1992; elected to the Missouri State Senate, 1994; religion: Baptist; committees: Armed Services; Transportation and Infrastructure; elected to the 107th Congress on November 7, 2000; reelected to each succeeding Congress.

Office Listings

http://www.graves.house.gov

1415 Longworth House Office Building, Washington, DC 20515	(202) 225–7041
Chief of Staff.—Paul J. Sass.	FAX: 225–8221
Legislative Director.—Jack Ruddy.	
Communications Director.—Sean Brown.	
Scheduler.—Kylie Mills.	
411 Jules Street, Suite 111, St. Joseph, MO 64501	(816) 233–9818

Office Listings—Continued

11724 Northwest Plaza Circle, Suite 900, Kansas City, MO 64153 .... (816) 792-3976
906 Broadway, P.O. Box 364, Hannibal, MO 63401 .... (573) 221-3400

Counties: ADAIR, ANDREW, ATCHISON, AUDRAIN (PART), BUCHANAN, CALDWELL, CARROLL, CHARITON, CLARK, CLAY (PART), CLINTON, DAVIESS, DEKALB, GENTRY, GRUNDY, HARRISON, HOLT, JACKSON (PART), KNOX, LEWIS, LINN, LIVINGSTON, MACON, MARION, MERCER, MONROE, NODAWAY, PIKE, PLATTE, PUTNAM, RALLS, SCHUYLER, SCOTLAND, SHELBY, SULLIVAN, AND WORTH. Population (2010), 748,616.

ZIP Codes: 63119, 63330, 63334, 63336, 63339, 63343–45, 63352–53, 63359, 63382, 63384, 63401, 63430–43, 63445–48, 63450–54, 63456–69, 63471–74, 63501, 63530–41, 63543–49, 63551–52, 63555–61, 63563, 63565–67, 64013–16, 64018, 64024, 64028–30, 64048, 64051, 64055–58, 64060, 64062–64, 64066, 64068–69, 64072, 64074–75, 64077, 64079, 64085–86, 64088–89, 64092, 64098, 64106, 64112, 64116, 64118–19, 64134, 64150–58, 64163–68, 64188, 64190, 64195, 64401–02, 64420–24, 64426–34, 64436–46, 64448–49, 64451, 64453–59, 64461, 64463, 64465–71, 64473–77, 64479–87, 64489–94, 64496–99, 64501–08, 64601, 64620, 64622–25, 64628, 64630–33, 64635–61, 64664, 64667–68, 64670–74, 64676, 64679, 64681–83, 64686, 64688–89, 64701, 65065, 65202, 65205, 65230, 65232, 65236, 65240, 65243–44, 65246–47, 65254–55, 65258, 65260–61, 65263–65, 65270, 65275, 65280–83, 65286

* * *

SEVENTH DISTRICT

BILLY LONG, Republican, of Springfield, MO; born in Springfield, MO, August 11, 1955; education: attended University of Missouri, Columbia, MO, 1973–74; Missouri Auction School, Kansas City, MO, 1979; Certified Auctioneer Institute designation, University of Indiana, Bloomington, IN, 1983; professional: owner, Billy Long Auctions, LLC; radio talk show host, KWTO AM 560, 1999–2006; former president, Missouri Professional Auctioneers Association; past board member, National Auctioneers Association; past member, Southeast Rotary Club, Springfield; awards: Missouri Professional Auctioneers' Hall of Fame; Outstanding Young Alumni Award, Greenwood Lab School; religion: Presbyterian; family: wife, Barbara Long; two daughters; caucuses: Republican Conference, 2011–present; committees: Energy and Commerce; elected to the 112th Congress on November 2, 2010; reelected to each succeeding Congress.

Office Listings

http://long.house.gov

1541 Longworth House Office Building, Washington, DC 20515 .... (202) 225-6536
    Chief of Staff.—Joe Lillis.   FAX: 225-5604
    Legislative Director.—Peter Stehouwer.
    Scheduler.—Ben Elleson.
    Communications Director.—Cole Karr.
3232 East Ridgeview Street, Springfield, MO 65804 .... (417) 889-1899
     FAX: 889-4915
2727 East 32nd Street, Suite 2, Joplin, MO 64804 .... (417) 781-1041
     FAX: 781-2832

Counties: BARRY, CHRISTIAN, GREENE, JASPER, LAWRENCE, MCDONALD, NEWTON, POLK, STONE, TANEY, AND WEBSTER (part). Population (2010), 721,754.

ZIP Codes: 64748, 64755–56, 64766, 64769, 64801–04, 64830–36, 64840–44, 64847–50, 64853–59, 64861–70, 64873–74, 65603–05, 65608–20, 65622–27, 65629–31, 65633, 65635, 65637–38, 65640–41, 65645–50, 65652–58, 65661, 65663–64, 65666, 65669, 65672–76, 65679–82, 65686, 65702, 65705, 65707–08, 65710, 65712, 65714–15, 65720–21, 65723, 65725–30, 65733–34, 65737–42, 65744–45, 65747, 65752–57, 65759–62, 65765–73, 65781, 65784–85, 65801–10, 65814, 65817, 65890, 65898–99

* * *

EIGHTH DISTRICT

JASON T. SMITH, Republican, of Salem, MO; born in St. Louis, MO, June 16, 1980; education: graduate of Salem High School, received B.S. degrees, agricultural economics and business administration with an emphasis in finance, University of Missouri, Columbia; earned law degree from Oklahoma City University School of Law; Trinity College, Cambridge, England; professional: attorney; real estate agent; small business owner and fourth generation owner of the family farm; religion: Assemblies of God; NRA; Missouri Farm Bureau; former president, current member of the Salem FFA Alumni Association; holds an American FFA degree; elected to the Missouri State House of Representatives, 2005 (special election), 2006, 2008; leadership: served as Majority Whip in 96th General Assembly; youngest Speaker Pro Tem in 97th General Assembly; committees: Ways and Means; elected by special election on June 4, 2013 to the

113th Congress, to fill the vacancy caused by the resignation of United States Representative Jo Ann Emerson; reelected to the 114th Congress on November 4, 2014.

Office Listings

http://jasonsmith.house.gov   http://www.facebook.com/repjasonsmith
http://twitter.com/repjasonsmith

1118 Longworth House Office Building, Washington, DC 20515	(202) 225–4404
Chief of Staff.—Josh Haynes.	FAX: 226–0326
Executive Assistant / Scheduler.—Estephania Gongora.	
2502 Tanner Drive, Suite 205, Cape Girardeau, MO 63703	(573) 335–0101
830A South Bishop, Rolla, MO 65401	(573) 364–2455
22 East Columbia, Farmington, MO 63640	(573) 756–9755
35 Court Square, Suite 300, West Plains, MO 65775	(417) 255–1515
2911 North Westwood Boulevard, Suite C, Poplar Bluff, MO 63907.	

Counties: BOLLINGER, BUTLER, CAPE GIRARDEAU, CARTER, CRAWFORD, DENT, DOUGLAS, DUNKLIN, HOWELL, IRON, JEFFERSON (part), MADISON, MISSISSIPPI, NEW MADRID, OREGON, OZARK, PEMISCOT, PERRY, PHELPS, REYNOLDS, RIPLEY, SCOTT, SHANNON, ST. FRANCOIS, STE. GENEVIEVE, STODDARD, TEXAS, WASHINGTON, WAYNE AND WRIGHT. Population (2010), 748,616.

ZIP Codes: 63036, 63071, 63601, 63620–26, 63628–33, 63636–38, 63640, 63648, 63650–51, 63653–56, 63660, 63662–66, 63674–75, 63701–03, 63730, 63732, 63735–40, 63742–48, 63750–52, 63755, 63758, 63760, 63763–64, 63766–67, 63769–72, 63774–76, 63779–85, 63787, 63801, 63820–30, 63833–34, 63837, 63839–41, 63845–53, 63855, 63857, 63860, 63862–63, 63866–70, 63873–82, 63901–02, 63931–45, 63950–57, 63960–67, 65401–02, 65409, 65436, 65438–41, 65444, 65446, 65449, 65453, 65456, 65459, 65461–62, 65464, 65466, 65468, 65479, 65483–84, 65501, 65529, 65532, 65541–42, 65546, 65548, 65550, 65552, 65555, 65557, 65564–66, 65570–71, 65586, 65588–89, 65606, 65608–09, 65614, 65616, 65618, 65620, 65626–27, 65629, 65637–38, 65652–53, 65655, 65660, 65662, 65666–67, 65676, 65679–80, 65688–90, 65692, 65701–02, 65704, 65711, 65713, 65715, 65717, 65720, 65729, 65731, 65733, 65740–41, 65744, 65746, 65753, 65755, 65759–62, 65766, 65768, 65773, 65775, 65777–78, 65784, 65788–91, 65793

MONTANA

(Population 2010, 989,415)

SENATORS

JON TESTER, Democrat, of Big Sandy, MT; born in Havre, MT, August 21, 1956; education: graduated, Big Sandy High School, 1974; B.S. in music, University of Great Falls, 1978; professional: farmer, T-Bone Farms, Big Sandy, 1978–present; teacher, Big Sandy School District, 1978–80; member, Big Sandy Soil Conservation Service Committee, 1980–83; chairman, Big Sandy School Board of Trustees, 1983–92; Past Master, Treasure Lodge #95 of the Masons; member, Choutcau County Agricultural Stabilization and Conservation Service Committee, 1990–95; member, Organic Crop Improvement Association, 1996–97; served in Montana Senate, 1999–2007; Montana Senate Democratic Whip, 2001–03; Montana Senate Democratic Leader, 2003–05; Montana Senate President, 2005–07; vice chair, Congressional Sportsmen's Caucus; married: Sharla Tester; two children: Christine and Shon; committees: vice chair, Indian Affairs; Appropriations; Banking, Housing, and Urban Affairs; Homeland Security and Governmental Affairs; Veterans' Affairs; elected to the U.S. Senate on November 7, 2006; reelected to the U.S. Senate on November 6, 2012.

Office Listings

http://tester.senate.gov   http://www.facebook.com/senatortester   twitter: @senatortester

311 Hart Senate Office Building, Washington, DC 20510	(202) 224–2644
Chief of Staff.—James Wise.	FAX: 224–8594
Legislative Director.—Dylan Laslovich.	
Communications Director.—Marnee Banks.	
Director of Scheduling.—Trecia McEvoy.	
State Director.—Dayna Swanson.	
222 North 32nd Street, Suite 101, Billings, MT 59101	(406) 252–0550
1 East Main Street, Suite 202, Bozeman, MT 59715	(406) 586–4450
125 West Granite, Suite 200, Butte, MT 59701	(406) 723–3277
122 West Towne, Glendive, MT 59330	(406) 452–9585
119 First Avenue North, Suite 102, Great Falls, MT 59401	(406) 452–9585
208 North Montana Avenue, Suite 202, Helena, MT 59601	(406) 449–5401
14 Third Street East, Suite 230, Kalispell, MT 59901	(406) 257–3360
130 West Front Street, Missoula, MT 59801	(406) 728–3003

* * *

STEVE DAINES, Republican, of Bozeman, MT; born in Van Nuys, CA, August 20, 1962; education: B.S., Montana State University, Bozeman, MT, 1984; professional: businessman; public service: U.S. Representative, 2013–15; Republican National Convention delegate, 1984; married: Cindy; children: David, Annie, Michael, and Caroline; committees: Appropriations; Commerce, Science, and Transportation; Energy and Natural Resources; Indian Affairs; elected to the 113th Congress on November 6, 2012; elected to the 114th Congress as U.S. Senator for Montana on November 4, 2014.

Office Listings

http://daines.senate.gov   www.facebook.com/stevedainesmt
www.twitter.com/stevedaines

320 Hart Senate Office Building, Washington, DC 20510	(202) 224–2651
Chief of Staff.—Jason Thielman.	
Deputy Chief of Staff.—Wally Hsueh.	
Legislative Director.—Darin Thacker.	
Communications Director.—Alee Lockman.	
Scheduler.—Jesika Whittle.	
30 West 14th Street, Helena, MT 59601	(406) 443–3189
State Director.—Charles Robison.	
222 North 32nd Street, Suite 100, Billings, MT 59101	(406) 245–6822
220 West Lamme Street, Suite 1D, Bozeman, MT 59715	(406) 587–3446
280 East Front Street, Suite 100, Missoula, MT 59802	(406) 549–8198
113 3rd Street North, Great Falls, MT 59401	(406) 453–0148

REPRESENTATIVE

AT LARGE

RYAN ZINKE, Republican, of Whitefish, MT; born in Bozeman, MT, November 1, 1961; education: B.S., University of Oregon, Eugene, OR, 1984; M.B.A., National University, San Diego, CA, 1991; M.S., University of San Diego, San Diego, CA, 2004; professional: Navy SEAL; public service: Montana State Senator, 2009–11; married: Lolita; children: Jennifer, Wolfgang, and Konrad; committees: Armed Services; Natural Resources; elected to the 114th Congress on November 4, 2014.

Office Listings

https://zinke.house.gov   twitter: @repryanzinke

113 Cannon House Office Building, Washington, DC 20515	(202) 225–3211
Chief of Staff.—Scott Hommel.	FAX: 225–5687
Communications Director.—Heather Swift.	
222 North 32nd Street, Suite 900, Billings, MT 59101	(406) 969–1736
District Director.—Randy Vogel.	
910 North Last Chance Gulch, Suite B, Helena, MT 59601	(406) 502–1435
1008 South Avenue, Suite 2, Missoula, MT 59802	(406) 540–4370
710 Central Avenue, Great Falls, MT 59401	(406) 952–1210

Counties: BEAVERHEAD, BIG HORN, BLAINE, BROADWATER, CARBON, CARTER, CASCADE, CHOUTEAU, CUSTER, DANIELS, DAWSON, DEER LODGE, FALLON, FERGUS, FLATHEAD, GALLATIN, GARFIELD, GLACIER, GOLDEN VALLEY, GRANITE, HILL, JEFFERSON, JUDITH BASIN, LAKE, LEWIS AND CLARK, LIBERTY, LINCOLN, MADISON, MCCONE, MEAGHER, MINERAL, MISSOULA, MUSSELLSHELL, PARK, PETROLEUM, PHILLIPS, PONDERA, POWDER RIVER, POWELL, PRAIRIE, RAVALLI, RICH-LAND, ROOSEVELT, ROSEBUD, SANDERS, SHERIDAN, SILVER BOW, STILLWATER, SWEET GRASS, TETON, TOOLE, TREASURE, VALLEY, WHEATLAND, WIBAUX, AND YELLOWSTONE. Population (2010), 989,415.

ZIP Codes: 59001–04, 59006–08, 59010–16, 59018–20, 59022, 59024–39, 59041, 59043–44, 59046–47, 59050, 59052–55, 59057–59, 59061–72, 59074–79, 59081–89, 59101–08, 59201, 59211–15, 59217–19, 59221–23, 59225–26, 59230–31, 59240–44, 59247–48, 59250, 59252–63, 59270, 59273–76, 59301, 59311–19, 59322–24, 59326–27, 59330,59332–33, 59336–39, 59341, 59343–45, 59347, 59349, 59351, 59353–54, 59401–06, 59410–12, 59414, 59416–22, 59424–25, 59427, 59430, 59432–36, 59440–48, 59450–54, 59456–57, 59460–69, 59471–72, 59474, 59477, 59479–80, 59482–87, 59489, 59501, 59520–32, 59535, 59537–38, 59540, 59542, 59544–47, 59601–02, 59604, 59620, 59623–24, 59626, 59631–36, 59638–45, 59647–48, 59701–03, 59710–11, 59713–22, 59724–25, 59727–33, 59735–36, 59739–41, 59743, 59745–52, 59754–56, 59758–62, 59771–73, 59801–04, 59806–08, 59812, 59820–21, 59823–35, 59837, 59840–48, 59851, 59853–56, 59858–60, 59863–68, 59870–75, 59901, 59903–04, 59910–23, 59925–37

NEBRASKA

(Population 2010, 1,826,341)

SENATORS

DEB FISCHER, Republican, of Valentine, NE; born in Lincoln, NE, March 1, 1951; education: B.S., University of Nebraska-Lincoln, Lincoln, NE, 1988; professional: rancher; Senator in the Nebraska Unicameral, 2005–13; President of the Nebraska Association of School Boards; Commissioner on the Coordinating Commission for Post-Secondary Education; Valentine Rural High School Board of Education; awards: BILLD Fellow, Midwest Council of State Governments Bowhay Institute for Legislative Leadership, 2005; NRD Farm and Ranch Conservation Award, 1999; Nebraska Association of School Boards Lifetime Achievement Award, 1999; Nebraska Rural Community Schools Association Outstanding Board Member Award, 1998–99; Nebraska Cattlemen Environmental Stewardship Award, 1995; Rangeman's Award, Nebraska Section Society for Range Management, 1994; NRD State Grasslands Conservation Award, 1993; Kellogg Fellow, National Center for Food and Policy Research, Resources for the Future, Washington, DC, 1991; LEAD VIII Fellow, Nebraska Leadership Program, 1988–90; religion: Presbyterian; married: Bruce Fischer; three children, three grandchildren; caucuses: vice chair, Sportsmen's Caucus; Senate Western Caucus; Senate Rural Health Caucus; General Aviation Caucus; Republican High-Tech Task Force; National Guard Caucus; committees: Armed Services; Commerce, Science, and Transportation; Environment and Public Works; Small Business and Entrepreneurship; elected to the U.S. Senate on November 6, 2012.

Office Listings

http://fischer.senate.gov

454 Russell Senate Office Building, Washington, DC 20510	(202) 224–6551
Chief of Staff.—Joe Hack.	FAX: 228–1325
Legislative Director.—Stephen Higgins.	
Communications Director.—Thomas Doheny.	
Administrative Director.—Sherri Hupart.	
11819 Miracle Hills Drive, Suite 205, Omaha, NE 68154	(402) 391–3411
State Director.—Dusty Vaughan.	FAX: 391–4725
440 North 8th Street, Suite 120, Lincoln, NE 68508	(402) 441–4600
	FAX: 476–8753
1110 Circle Drive, Suite 400, Scottsbluff, NE 69361	(308) 636–6344
20 West 23rd Street, Kearney, NE 68847	(308) 234–2361
	FAX: 234–3684
P.O. Box 1021, Norfolk, NE 68702	(402) 200–8816

* * *

BEN SASSE, Republican, of Fremont, NE; born in Plainview, NE, February 22, 1972; education: B.A., Harvard University, Cambridge, MA, 1994; M.A., St. John's College, Annapolis, MD, 1998; M.A., M.Phil., and Ph.D., Yale University, New Haven, CT, 2004; professional: management strategist; policy strategist; historian; college president; religion: evangelical; married: Melissa McLeod Sasse; three children: Elizabeth, Katherine, and Augustine; committees: Agriculture, Nutrition and Forestry; Banking, Housing, and Urban Affairs; Homeland Security and Governmental Affairs; Joint Economic Committee; Special Committee on Aging; elected to the U.S. Senate on November 4, 2014.

Office Listings

http://sasse.senate.gov   https://www.facebook.com/senatorsasse
https://twitter.com/sensasse

386A Russell Senate Office Building, Washington, DC 20510	(202) 224–4224
Chief of Staff.—Derrick Morgan.	
Deputy Chiefs of Staff: Shelly Blake, Tyler Grassmeyer.	
Legislative Director.—Patrick Lehman.	
1128 Lincoln Mall, Lincoln, NE 68508	(402) 476–1400
4111 Fourth Avenue, Suite 26, Kearney, NE 68845	(308) 233–3677
115 Railway Street, Suite C102, Scottsbluff, NE 69361	(308) 632–6032
304 North 168th Circle, Suite 213, Omaha, NE 68118.	

REPRESENTATIVES

FIRST DISTRICT

JEFF FORTENBERRY, Republican, of Lincoln, NE; born in Baton Rouge, LA, December 27, 1960; education: B.A., Louisiana State University, 1982; M.P.P., Georgetown University, Washington, DC, 1986; M. Div., Franciscan University, Steubenville, Ohio, 1996; professional: Lincoln City Council, 1997–2001; publishing executive; worked as economist; managed a public relations firm; congressional aide for the Senate Subcommittee on Intergovernmental Relations; family: married to Celeste Gregory; children: five; committees: Appropriations; elected to the 109th Congress on November 2, 2004; reelected to each succeeding Congress.

Office Listings

http://www.fortenberry.house.gov   twitter: @jefffortenberry
https://www.facebook.com/jefffortenberry

1514 Longworth House Office Building, Washington, DC 20515	(202) 225–4806
Chief of Staff.—Margaux Matter.	FAX: 225–5686
Legislative Director.—Alan Feyerherm.	
Communications Director.—Jennifer Allen.	
Executive Assistant.—Christine Capobianco.	
301 South 13th Street, Suite 100, Lincoln, NE 68508	(402) 438–1598
641 North Broad Street, Fremont, NE 68026	(402) 727–0888
125 South 4th Street, Suite 101, Norfolk, NE 68701	(402) 379–2064

Counties: BURT, BUTLER, CASS, COLFAX, CUMING, DODGE, LANCASTER, MADISON, OTOE, PLATTE, POLK, SARPY, SAUNDERS, SEWARD, STANTON, THURSTON, AND WASHINGTON. Population (2010), 608,780.

ZIP Codes: 68001–05, 68007–09, 68014–20, 68023, 68025–26, 68029, 68031, 68033–34, 68036–42, 68044–45, 68047–48, 68050, 68055–58, 68061–68, 68070–73, 68112–13, 68122–23, 68133, 68142, 68147, 68152, 68157, 68301, 68304, 68307, 68313–14, 68317, 68320, 68324, 68329–31, 68333, 68336, 68339, 68343–44, 68346–47, 68349, 68358–60, 68364, 68366–68, 68372, 68379, 68382, 68402–05, 68407, 68409–10, 68413, 68417–19, 68421, 68423, 68428, 68430, 68434, 68438–39, 68443, 68446, 68448, 68454–56, 68460–63, 68465, 68501–10, 68512, 68514, 68516–17, 68520–24, 68526–29, 68531–32, 68542, 68583, 68588, 68601–02, 68621, 68624, 68626, 68629, 68631–35, 68640–44, 68647–49, 68651, 68653–54, 68658–59, 68661–62, 68664, 68666–67, 68669, 68701–02, 68715–16, 68733, 68748, 68752, 68758, 68768, 68779, 68781, 68784, 68788, 68791

* * *

SECOND DISTRICT

BRAD ASHFORD, Democrat, of Omaha, NE; born in Omaha, November 10, 1949; education: B.A., Colgate University, 1971; J.D., Creighton University School of Law, 1974; attorney; elected to the Nebraska Unicameral 1987–94 (District 6); elected to the Nebraska Unicameral 2007–14 (District 20), served as Chairman of the Judiciary Committee; religion: Christian; married: Ann Ferlic Ashford; children: John, Ellie, and Tom; committees: Agriculture; Armed Services; elected to the 114th Congress November 4, 2014.

Office Listings

https://ashford.house.gov   twitter: @repbradashford

107 Cannon House Office Building, Washington, DC 20515	(202) 225–4155
Chief of Staff.—Jeremy Nordquist.	FAX: 226–5452
Policy Director.—Joel Bailey.	
Executive Assistant.—Willa Prescott.	
Communications Director.—Joe Jordan.	
7126 Pacific Street, Omaha, NE 68106	(402) 916–5678
District Director.—Amanda McGill.	

Counties: DOUGLAS, SARPY (part). CITIES: Bennington, Boys Town, Elkhorn, Gretna, La Vista, Omaha, Papillion, Ralston, Springfield, Valley, and Waterloo. Population (2010), 608,781.

ZIP Codes: 68010, 68022, 68028, 68046, 68059, 68069, 68102, 68104–06, 68108, 68110–11, 68114, 68116–18, 68124, 68127–28, 68130–32, 68134–38, 68144, 68154, 68164, 68178

* * *

THIRD DISTRICT

ADRIAN SMITH, Republican, of Gering, NE; born in Scotts Bluff, NE, December 19, 1970; education: graduated from Gering High School, Gering, NE, 1989; attended Liberty University,

Lynchburg, VA; 1989–90; B.S., University of Nebraska, 1993; professional: business owner; teacher; Gering, NE, city council, 1994–98; member of the Nebraska state legislature, 1999– 2007; married: Andrea McDaniel Smith; committees: Ways and Means; elected to the 110th Congress on November 7, 2006; reelected to each succeeding Congress.

Office Listings

http://adriansmith.house.gov   twitter: @repadriansmith

2241 Rayburn House Office Building, Washington, DC 20515 .... (202) 225–6435
Chief of Staff.—Monica Jirik.   FAX: 225–0207
Legislative Director.—Josh Jackson.
Communications Director.—Emily Miller.
Director of Outreach and Strategic Planning (NE Schedule).—Jena Hoehne.
Scheduler.—Jill Sims.
416 Valley View Drive, Suite 600, Scottsbluff, NE 69361 .... (308) 633–6333
1811 West Second Street, Suite 275, Grand Island, NE 68803 .... (308) 384–3900

Counties: ADAMS, ANTELOPE, ARTHUR, BANNER, BLAINE, BOONE, BOX BUTTE, BOYD, BROWN, BUFFALO, CEDAR, CHASE, CHERRY, CHEYENNE, CLAY, CUSTER, DAKOTA, DAWES, DAWSON, DEUEL, DIXON, DUNDY, FILLMORE, FRANKLIN, FRONTIER, FURNAS, GAGE, GARDEN, GARFIELD, GOSPER, GRANT, GREELEY, HALL, HAMILTON, HARLAN, HAYES, HITCHCOCK, HOLT, HOOKER, HOWARD, JEFFERSON, JOHNSON, KEARNEY, KEITH, KEYA PAHA, KIMBALL, KNOX, LINCOLN, LOGAN, LOUP, MCPHERSON, MERRICK, MORRILL, NANCE, NEMAHA, NUCKOLLS, PAWNEE, PERKINS, PHELPS, PIERCE, RED WILLOW, RICHARDSON, ROCK, SALINE, SCOTTSBLUFF, SHERIDAN, SHERMAN, SIOUX, THAYER, THOMAS, VALLEY, WAYNE, WEBSTER, WHEELER, AND YORK. Population (2010), 608,438.

ZIP Codes: 60902, 68030, 68305, 68309–10, 68315, 68318, 68320–21, 68326, 68328, 68330, 68337, 68340, 68350, 68352, 68355, 68361–62, 68375, 68377, 68380, 68401, 68406, 68414–15, 68422, 68429, 68431, 68433, 68440, 68444–45, 68450, 68457, 68467, 68620, 68622, 68710–11, 68713, 68717–18, 68720, 68722–24, 68727–28, 68731, 68736, 68738, 68741–43, 68749, 68751, 68753, 68756, 68760–61, 68763, 68765–66, 68774, 68776, 68778, 68780, 68783, 68787, 68789–90, 68802, 68810, 68812, 68814, 68816, 68818, 68820–22, 68824–27, 68837–38, 68841–44, 68846–50, 68852– 54, 68861–62, 68865, 68870–71, 68873, 68879, 68881, 68901, 68920, 68923, 68925–26, 68929, 68932–33, 68939– 40, 68946, 68950, 68952, 68954, 68956, 68959, 68961, 68966, 68969–71, 68973, 68975–76, 69020–21, 69023, 69032, 69034, 69036–37, 69041–42, 69046, 69103, 69121, 69123, 69125, 69131–33, 69140–44, 69150–52, 69154, 69160, 69162, 69170, 69171, 69190, 69211, 69218–21, 69331, 69339, 69345–46, 69354, 69361, 69363, 69366–67, 69855

NEVADA

(Population 2010, 2,700,551)

SENATORS

HARRY REID, Democrat, of Searchlight, NV; born in Searchlight, December 2, 1939; education: graduated, Basic High School, Henderson, NV, 1957; associate degree, College of Southern Utah (now Southern Utah State College), 1959; B.S., Utah State University, Phi Kappa Phi, 1961; J.D., George Washington School of Law, Washington, DC, 1964; admitted to the Nevada State Bar in 1963, a year before graduating from law school; while attending law school, worked as a U.S. Capitol police officer; city attorney, Henderson, 1964–66; member and chairman, South Nevada Memorial Hospital Board of Trustees, 1967–69; elected: Nevada State Assembly, 1969–70; Lieutenant Governor, State of Nevada, 1970–74; served, executive committee, National Conference of Lieutenant Governors; chairman, Nevada Gaming Commission, 1977–81; member: Nevada State, Clark County and American Bar Associations; married the former Landra Gould in 1959; five children: Lana, Rory, Leif, Josh, and Key; elected to the 98th Congress on November 2, 1982, and reelected to the 99th Congress; Assistant Democratic Leader, 1998–2004; elected Democratic leader for the 109th Congress, and Majority leader for the 110th, 111th, 112th and 113th Congress; elected to the U.S. Senate on November 4, 1986; reelected to each succeeding Senate term.

Office Listings

http://reid.senate.gov

522 Hart Senate Office Building, Washington, DC 20510	(202) 224–3542
Chief of Staff.—David Krone.	FAX: 224–7327
Deputy Chief of Staff.—David McCallum.	
Deputy Chief of Staff for Policy.—Bill Dauster.	
Executive Assistant.—Adelle Cruz.	
Legislative Director.—Jason Unger.	
600 East Williams Street, Room 302, Carson City, NV 89701	(775) 882–7343
State Director.—Mary Conelly.	
333 Las Vegas Boulevard South, Suite 8016, Las Vegas, NV 89101	(702) 388–5020
Southern Nevada Director.—Shannon Raborn.	
400 South Virginia Street, Suite 902, Reno, NV 89501	(775) 686–5750
State Director.—Mary Conelly.	

* * *

DEAN HELLER, Republican, of Carson City, NV; born in Castro Valley, CA, May 10, 1960; education: B.B.A., specializing in finance and securities analysis, University of Southern California, 1985; professional: institutional stockbroker and broker/trader on the Pacific Stock Exchange; Chief Deputy State Treasurer, Public Funds Representative; Nevada State Assemblyman, 1990–94; Secretary of State, 1994–2002; founding member of the Boys and Girls Club of Western Nevada Community College Foundation; married: Lynne Heller; children: Hillary, Harris, Drew, and Emmy; committees: Banking, Housing, and Urban Affairs; Commerce, Science, and Transportation; Finance; Veterans' Affairs; Special Committee on Aging; elected to the 110th Congress on November 7, 2006, reelected to two succeeding Congresses, when he resigned to become a U.S. Senator; appointed May 3, 2011, to the U.S. Senate for the term ending January 3, 2013, to fill the vacancy caused by the resignation of John E. Ensign; took the oath of office on May 9, 2011; elected to a full term in the U.S. Senate on November 6, 2012.

Office Listings

http://heller.senate.gov

324 Hart Senate Office Building, Washington, DC 20510	(202) 224–6244
Chief of Staff.—Mac Abrams.	FAX: 228–6753
Legislative Director.—Sarah Timoney Paul.	
Communications Director.—Neal Patel.	
Deputy Communications Director.—Michawn Rich.	
Scheduler.—Corinne Zakzeski.	
8930 West Sunset Road, Suite 230, Las Vegas, NV 89148	(702) 388–6605
	FAX: 388–6501
Bruce Thompson Federal Building, 400 South Virginia Street, Suite 738, Reno, NV 89501	(775) 686–5770
	FAX: 686–5729
3290 Idaho Street, Suite 2A, Elko, NV 89801	(775) 738–2001
	FAX: 738–2004

REPRESENTATIVES

FIRST DISTRICT

DINA TITUS, Democrat, of Las Vegas, NV; born in Thomasville, Thomas County, GA, May 23, 1950; education: B.A., College of William and Mary, Williamsburg, VA, 1970; M.A., University of Georgia, Athens, GA, 1973; Ph.D., Florida State University, Tallahassee, FL, 1976; professor, University of Nevada, Las Vegas, NV, 1977–2011; member of Nevada State Senate, 1989–2008; minority leader of Nevada State Senate, 1993–2008; married: Dr. Thomas Wright; committees: Transportation and Infrastructure; Veterans' Affairs; elected to the 111th Congress; reelected to each succeeding Congress.

Office Listings

http://www.titus.house.gov

401 Cannon House Office Building, Washington, DC 20515 .... (202) 225–5965
    Chief of Staff.—Jay Gertsema.   FAX: 225–3119
    Legislative Director.—David Rosenbaum.
    Communications Director.—Caitlin Teare.
    Scheduler.—Elizabeth Shepherd.
550 East Charleston Boulevard, Las Vegas, NV 89104 .... (702) 220–9823
    District Director.—Mike Naft.   FAX: 220–9841

Counties: CLARK COUNTY (part). CITIES: Las Vegas, and North Las Vegas. Population (2010), 659,962.

ZIP Codes: 88901, 88905, 89002, 89004–06, 89009, 89011–12, 89014–16, 89019, 89028–29, 89039, 89044, 89046, 89052–54, 89074, 89077, 89105, 89113, 89117, 89118 20, 89122 23, 89134 35, 89137 41, 89144 45, 89147 48, 89157, 89159, 89161, 89163, 89178–79, 89183, 89195, 89199

✦ ✦ ✦

SECOND DISTRICT

MARK E. AMODEI, Republican, of Carson City, NV; born in Carson City, June 12, 1958; education: B.A., University of Nevada, Reno, NV, 1980; J.D., University of Pacific, McGeorge School of Law, Sacramento, CA, 1983; professional: lawyer, Allison, MacKenzie et al., 1987 present; lawyer, United States Army Judge Advocate General Corps, 1983–87; Nevada State Assembly, 1996–98; Senator, Nevada State Senate, 1998–2010; President Pro Tempore, Nevada State Senate, 2003–08; member of Carson City Master Plan Advisory Committee; member of Education Commission of the States; vice chair of Governor's Task Force on Access to Public Health Care; member of Nevada Supreme Court's Committee on Court Funding; member of Tahoe Regional Planning Agency Legislative Oversight Committee; committees: Appropriations; elected by special election to the 112th Congress on September 13, 2011; reelected to each succeeding Congress.

Office Listings

http://www.amodei.house.gov   twitter: @markamodeinv2
https://www.facebook.com/markamodeinv2

332 Cannon House Office Building, Washington, DC 20515 .... (202) 225–6155
    Chief of Staff.—Rick Goddard.   FAX: 225–5679
905 Railroad Street, Suite 104 D, Elko, NV 89801 .... (775) 777–7705
                                                                       FAX: 753–9984
5310 Kietzke Lane, Suite 103, Reno, NV 89511.

Counties: CARSON CITY, CHURCHILL, DOUGLAS, ELKO, HUMBOLDT, LANDER, LYON (part), PERSHING, STOREY, AND WASHOE. Population (2010), 679,147.

ZIP Codes: 89310, 89316, 89402–06, 89408, 89410–14, 89418–19, 89421, 89423–26, 89428–29, 89431, 89433–34, 89436, 89438–42, 89444–51, 89460, 89501–03, 89506, 89508–12, 89519, 89521, 89523, 89701–06, 89801, 89815, 89820–23, 89825–26, 89828, 89830–35, 89883

* * *

THIRD DISTRICT

JOSEPH HECK, Republican, of Henderson, NV; born in Queens, NY, October 30, 1961; education: B.A., Penn State University, 1984; D.O., Philadelphia College of Osteopathic Medicine, 1988; M.S.S., United States Army War College, Carlisle, PA, 2006; professional: Brigadier General, U.S. Army Reserve; emergency room physician; president of emergency management consulting firm; Nevada State Senate 2004–05; religion: Roman Catholic; married: Lisa Heck; committees: Armed Services; Education and the Workforce; Permanent Select Committee on Intelligence; elected to the 112th Congress on November 2, 2010; reelected to each succeeding Congress.

Office Listings
http://www.heck.house.gov

132 Cannon House Office Building, Washington, DC 20515 .... (202) 225–3252
Chief of Staff.—Greg Facchiano.   FAX: 225–2185
Executive Assistant.—Caitlin Callahan.
Legislative Director.—James Langenderfer.
Communications Director.—Greg Lemon.
8485 West Sunset Road, Suite 300, Las Vegas, NV 89113 .... (702) 387–4941
District Director.—Keith Hughes.

Counties: CLARK COUNTY (part). Population (2010), 675,138.

ZIP Codes: 88901, 88905, 89002, 89004–06, 89009, 89011–12, 89014–16, 89019, 89028–29, 89039, 89044, 89046, 89052–54, 89074, 89077, 89105, 89113, 89117–20, 89122–23, 89134–35, 89137–41, 89144–45, 89147

* * *

FOURTH DISTRICT

CRESENT HARDY, Republican, of Mesquite, NV; born in St. George, UT, June 23, 1957; education: high school, attended Dixie State College; professional: general construction contractor and former owner, Legacy Construction and Development; member of the Nevada State Assembly, 2011–14; assistant minority leader, Nevada State Assembly, 2013–14; vice-chair, Clark County Regional Flood Control District, 1997–2002; member, Mesquite City Council, 1997–2002; member, Regional Transportation Commission of Southern Nevada, 1997–2002; Board of Directors, Virgin Valley Water District, 1990–1996; Director of Public Works, City of Mesquite, 1986–93; religion: Church of Jesus Christ of Latter-Day Saints; married: Peri Hardy; caucuses: Congressional Western Caucus; Congressional Air Force Caucus; Congressional Sportsmen's Caucus; I–11 Caucus; committees: Natural Resources; Small Business; Transportation and Infrastructure; elected to the 114th Congress on November 4, 2014.

Office Listings
https://hardy.house.gov   twitter: @rephardy
www.fb.com/repcresenthardy   www.youtube.com/c/rephardy

430 Cannon House Office Building, Washington, DC 20515 .... (202) 225–9894
Chief of Staff.—Alan Tennille.   FAX: 225–9783
Legislative Director.—Rob Yavor.
Communications Director.—Scott Knuteson.
Scheduler.—Deborah Hansen.
2250 North Las Vegas Boulevard, Suite 500, North Las Vegas, NV 89030 .... (702) 912–1634
District Director.—Sonia Joya.

Counties: CLARK COUNTY (most of the northern part), ESMERALDA, LINCOLN, LYON (part), MINERAL, NYE, AND WHITE PINE. Population (2010), 680,935.

ZIP Codes: 89001, 89003, 89007–08, 89010, 89013–14, 89017–18, 89020–23, 89025, 89027, 89030–32, 89034, 89040–43, 89045, 89047–49, 89060–61, 89081, 89084–86, 89101, 89103, 89106–10, 89115, 89124, 89128–31, 89134–35, 89142–43, 89149, 89156, 89158, 89161, 89166, 89191, 89301, 89310–11, 89314–19, 89409, 89415, 89420, 89422, 89427, 89430, 89444, 89447, 89833, 89883, 89142–43, 89149, 89156, 89158, 89161, 89427, 89430, 89444, 89447

NEW HAMPSHIRE

(Population 2010, 1,316,470)

SENATORS

JEANNE SHAHEEN, Democrat, of Madbury, NH; born in Saint Charles, MO, January 28, 1947; education: graduated, Selinsgrove Area High School, Selinsgrove, PA, 1965; B.A., Shippensburg University, Shippensburg, PA, 1969; M.S.S., University of Mississippi, 1973; professional: high school teacher; co-owner of a small retail business; consultant; New Hampshire State Senator; Governor of New Hampshire; Director of Harvard's Institute of Politics; married: William Shaheen; three children: Stefany, Stacey, and Molly; Commission on Security and Cooperation in Europe; committees: ranking member, Small Business and Entrepreneurship; Appropriations; Armed Services; Foreign Relations; elected to the 111th U.S. Senate on November 4, 2008; reelected to the U.S. Senate on November 4, 2014.

Office Listings

http://shaheen.senate.gov   https://www.facebook.com/senatorshaheen
https://twitter.com/senatorshaheen

506 Hart Senate Office Building, Washington, DC 20510	(202) 224–2841

Chief of Staff.—Maura Keefe.
Deputy Chief of Staff.—Justin Burkhardt.
Legislative Director.—Brian McKeon.
Communications Director.—Ryan Nickel.
Press Secretary.—Vivek Kembaiyan
Scheduler.—Jennifer MacLellan.

1589 Elm Street, Suite 3, Manchester, NH 03101	(603) 647–7500
60 Main Street, Nashua, NH 03060	(603) 883–0196
340 Central Avenue, Suite 205, Dover, NH 03820	(603) 750–3004
50 Opera House Square, Claremont, NH 03743	(603) 542–4872
961 Main Street, Berlin, NH 03570	(603) 752–6300
12 Gilbo Avenue, Suite C, Keene, NH 03431	(603) 358–6604

* * *

KELLY AYOTTE, Republican, of Nashua, NH; born in Nashua, NH, June 27, 1968; education: graduated, Nashua High School, 1986; B.A., Pennsylvania State University, University Park, PA, 1990; J.D., Villanova University School of Law, Villanova, PA, 1993; professional: lawyer; married: Lt. Col. Joseph Daley (Ret.); two children; committees: Armed Services; Budget; Commerce, Science, and Transportation; Homeland Security and Governmental Affairs; Small Business and Entrepreneurship; elected to the 112th U.S. Senate on November 2, 2010.

Office Listings

http://ayotte.senate.gov

144 Russell Senate Office Building, Washington, DC 20510	(202) 224–3324
	FAX: 224–4952

Chief of Staff.—Rick Murphy.
Administrative Director.—Christin Ballou.
Legislative Director.—Adam Hechavarria.
Communications Director.—Liz Johnson.
Scheduler.—Lauren Spivey.

1200 Elm Street, Suite 2, Manchester, NH 03101	(603) 622–7979
	FAX: 622–0422
144 Main Street, Nashua, NH 03060	(603) 880–3335
14 Manchester Square, Suite 140, Portsmouth, NH 03801	(603) 436–7161
19 Pleasant Street, Suite 13B, Berlin, NH 03570	(603) 752–7702

REPRESENTATIVES

FIRST DISTRICT

FRANK GUINTA, Republican, of Manchester, NH; born in Edison, NJ, September 26, 1970; education: philosophy and political science, Assumption College in Worcester, Massachusetts; attended Franklin Pierce Law Center in Concord with Master's Degree in Intellectual Property; professional: businessman; Mayor of Manchester, 2006–10; religion: Catholic; family: wife,

Morgan, two children; committees: Financial Services; elected to the 114th Congress on November 4, 2014.

Office Listings

http://guinta.house.gov

326 Cannon House Office Building, Washington, DC 20515 .... (202) 225–5456
    Chief of Staff.—Jay Ruais.   FAX: 225–5822
    Legislative Director.—Michelle Jelnicky.
    Communications Director.—Danielle Adams.
    Scheduler.—Karon Karami.
33 Lowell Street, Manchester, NH 03101 .... (603) 641–9536

Counties: BELKNAP (part), CARROLL, ROCKINGHAM (part), STAFFORD. CITIES: Bedford, Campton, Goffstown, Hooksett, Manchester, and Merrimack. Population (2012), 657,984.

ZIP Codes: 03031–32, 03034, 03036, 03038, 03042, 03044–45, 03053–54, 03077, 03101–06, 03109–10, 03218, 03220, 03223, 03225–27, 03237, 03246, 03249, 03253–54, 03256, 03259, 03261, 03269, 03276, 03291, 03801, 03809–20, 03823–27, 03830, 03832–33, 03835–42, 03844–62, 03864–65, 03867–75, 03878, 03882–87, 03890, 03894

* * *

SECOND DISTRICT

ANN McLANE KUSTER, Democrat, of Hopkinton, NH; born in Concord, NH, September 5, 1956; education: B.A., Dartmouth College, Hanover, NH, 1978; J.D., Georgetown University Law Center, Washington, DC, 1984; professional: consultant and owner Newfound Strategies LLC, lawyer and partner Rath, Young and Pignatelli; married: Brad Kuster; children: Zach and Travis; committees: Agriculture; Veterans' Affairs; elected to the 113th Congress on November 6, 2012; reelected to the 114th Congress on November 4, 2014.

Office Listings

http://kuster.house.gov

137 Cannon Building, Washington, DC 20515 .... (202) 225–5206
    Chief of Staff.—Abby Curran Horrell.   FAX: 225–2946
    Legislative Director.—Blake Anderson.
    Scheduler.—Corey Garry.
    Press Secretary.—Rosie Hilmer.
18 North Main Street, Concord, NH 03301 .... (603) 226–1002
    District Director.—Jake Berry   FAX: 226–1010
70 East Pearl Street, Nashua, NH 03060 .... (603) 595–2006
     FAX: 595–2016
33 Main Street, Littleton, NH 03561 .... (603) 444–7700

Counties: BELKNAP (part), CHESHIRE, COOS, GRAFTON (part), HILLSBOROUGH (part), MERRIMACK (part), ROCKINGHAM (part), SULLIVAN. Population (2013), 658,237.

ZIP Codes: 03031, 03033–34, 03037–38, 03043, 03045–49, 03051–52, 03054–55, 03057, 03060–64, 03070–71, 03073, 03076, 03079, 03082, 03084, 03086–87, 03110, 03215–17, 03220–24, 03226, 03229–31, 03233–35, 03237–38, 03240–45, 03251, 03253, 03255–58, 03260–64, 03266, 03268, 03272–73, 03275–76, 03278–82, 03284–85, 03287, 03293, 03301–05, 03307, 03431, 03435, 03440–52, 03455–58, 03461–62, 03464–70, 03561, 03570, 03574–76, 03579–86, 03588–90, 03592–93, 03595, 03597–98, 03601–05, 03607–09, 03740–41, 03743, 03745–46, 03748–56, 03765–66, 03768–71, 03773–74, 03777, 03779–82, 03784–85, 03811, 03825, 03841

NEW JERSEY

(Population 2010 8,791,894)

SENATORS

ROBERT MENENDEZ, Democrat, of Paramus, NJ; born in New York City, NY, January 1, 1954; children: Alicia and Robert; education: graduated, Union Hill High School, 1972; B.A., St. Peter's College, Jersey City, NJ, 1976; J.D., Rutgers Law School, Newark, NJ, 1979; professional: attorney; elected to the Union City Board of Education, 1974–78; admitted to the New Jersey Bar, 1980; mayor of Union City, 1986–92; member: New Jersey Assembly, 1987–91; New Jersey State Senate, Alliance Civic Association; U.S. House of Representatives 1993–2006; vice chair, Democratic Caucus, 1998–99; chair, Democratic Caucus, 2003–06; chair, Democratic Senatorial Campaign Committee, 2009–10; chairman, Senate Committee on Foreign Relations, 2013–15; committees: Banking, Housing and Urban Affairs; Finance; Foreign Relations; elected on November 3, 1992 to the 103rd Congress; reelected to each succeeding Congress; appointed to the U.S. Senate on January 17, 2006 by Governor Jon S. Corzine; elected to the 110th Congress for a full Senate term on November 7, 2006; reelected to the 114th Congress on November 6, 2012.

Office Listings

http://menendez.senate.gov   https://www.facebook.com/senatormenendez
https://twitter.com/SenatorMenendez

528 Hart Senate Office Building, Washington, DC 20510	(202) 224–4744
Chief of Staff.—Fred L. Turner.	FAX: 228–2197
Deputy Chief of Staff.—Tim Del Monico.	
Administrative Director —Robert Kelly	
One Gateway Center, 11th Floor, Newark, NJ 07102	(973) 645–3030
208 Whitehorse Pike, Suite 18, Barrington, NJ 08007	(856) 757–5353

* * *

CORY A. BOOKER, Democrat, of Newark, NJ; born in Washington, DC, April 27, 1969; education: graduated, Northern Valley Regional High School at Old Tappan, 1987; B.A., political science, Stanford University, 1991; M.A., sociology, Stanford University, 1992; Oxford University Rhodes Scholar, 1994; J.D., Yale Law School, 1997; professional: staff attorney, Urban Justice Center, New York, NY, 1997; member, Newark City Council, 1998–2002; partner, Booker, Rabinowitz, Trenk, Lubetkin, Tully, DiPasquale & Webster, P.C., 2002-2006; mayor, City of Newark, 2006–13; religion: Baptist; committees: Commerce, Science, and Transportation; Environment and Public Works; Homeland Security and Governmental Affairs; Small Business and Entrepreneurship; elected to the U.S. Senate on October 16, 2013 to fill the vacancy caused by the death of Frank R. Lautenberg; reelected to a full six-year term on November 4, 2014.

Office Listings

http://www.booker.senate.gov   twitter: @senbookerofc

359 Dirksen Senate Office Building, Washington, DC 20510	(202) 224–3224
Chief of Staff.—Matt Klapper.	FAX: 224–8378
Scheduler.—Unjin Lee.	
Communications Director.—Jeff Giertz.	
Gateway One, 11–43 Raymond Plaza West, Suite 2300, Newark, NJ 07102	(973) 639–8700
One Port Center, 2 Riverside Drive, Suite 505, Camden, NJ 08101	(856) 338–8922

REPRESENTATIVES

FIRST DISTRICT

DONALD NORCROSS, Democrat, of Camden, NJ; born in Camden, NJ, December 13, 1958; education: graduated, Pennsauken High School, Pennsauken, NJ, 1977; Associate's Degree, Criminal Justice, Camden County College, Blackwood, NJ, 1979; professional: vice president of United Building Trades Council of Southern New Jersey, 2004–2013; electrician at IBEW Local 351, 1979–93; United Way Board Member, 1992–2014; Union Organization for Social Service, president and CEO, 1993–98; business agent/assistant business manager of

IBEW Local 351, 1998–2014; president of the Southern New Jersey AFL-CIO Central Labor Council, 1995–2011; New Jersey General Assembly, 2010; New Jersey State Senate, 2010–14; married: Andrea Doran; children: Donald Jr., Corey, and Greg; committees: Armed Services; Budget; elected simultaneously to the 113th and 114th Congress on November 4, 2014, by special election, to fill the vacancy caused by the resignation of U.S. Representative Robert Andrews.

Office Listings

http://www.norcross.house.gov

1531 Longworth House Office Building, Washington, DC 20515 .... (202) 225–6501
    Legislative Director.—Morgan Jones.
    Chief of Staff.—Michael J. Maitland.
    Press Secretary.—Fran Tagmire.
10 Melrose Avenue, Suite 210, Cherry Hill, NJ 08003 .... (856) 427–7000
    District/Communications Director.—Karl Parker.

Counties: BURLINGTON COUNTY. CITIES AND TOWNSHIPS: Maple Shade Township, Palmyra. CAMDEN COUNTY. CITIES AND TOWNSHIPS: Audubon, Audubon Park, Barrington, Bellmawr, Berlin, Berlin Township, Brooklawn, Camden, Chesilhurst, Clementon, Collingswood, Gibbsboro, Gloucester City, Gloucester Township, Haddon Heights, Haddon Township, Hi–Nella, Laurel Springs, Lawnside, Lindenwold, Magnolia, Merchantville, Mt. Ephraim, Oaklyn, Pennsauken Township, Pine Hill, Pine Valley, Runnemede, Somerdale, Stratford, Tavistock, Voorhees Township, Winslow Township, Cherry Hill, Woodlynne. GLOUCESTER COUNTY. CITIES AND TOWNSHIPS: Deptford, East Greenwich, Greenwich, Logan Township, Monroe, National Park, Paulsboro, Washington Township, Wenonah, West Deptford Township, Westville, Woodbury Heights, and Woodbury. Population (2015), 727,496

ZIP Codes: 08002–04, 08007, 08009, 08012, 08014, 08020–21, 08026–33, 08037, 08043, 08045, 08049, 08051–52, 08056, 08059, 08061–63, 08065–66, 08077–78, 08080–81, 08083–86, 08089–91, 08093–94, 08096–97, 08099, 08101–05, 08107–10

* * *

SECOND DISTRICT

FRANK A. LoBIONDO, Republican, of Ventnor, NJ; born in Bridgeton, NJ, May 12, 1946; education: graduated, B.S., St. Joseph's University, Philadelphia, PA, 1968; professional: operations manager, LoBiondo Brothers Motor Express, 1968–94; Cumberland County Freeholder, 1985–87; New Jersey General Assembly, 1988–94; awards and honors: honorary Coast Guard Chief Petty Officer; Taxpayer Hero Award; Watchdog of the Treasury Award; Veterans Foreign Wars "Outstanding Federal Legislator of the Year" Award; Humane Society of the United States, Humane Champion Award; National Association of Community Health Centers, Distinguished Community Health Superhero; Super Friend of Seniors Award; two-time winner of the Friend of the National Parks Award; March of Dimes FDR Award for community service; 2001 President's Award, Literacy Volunteers of America, NJ, Inc.; committees: Armed Services; Transportation and Infrastructure; Permanent Select Committee on Intelligence; elected to the 104th Congress; reelected to each succeeding Congress.

Office Listings

http://www.lobiondo.house.gov

2427 Rayburn House Office Building, Washington, DC 20515 .... (202) 225–6572
    Chief of Staff.—Mary Annie Harper.   FAX: 225–3318
    Executive Assistant.—Mehgan Perez-Acosta.
5914 Main Street, Mays Landing, NJ 08330 .... (609) 625–5008
    District Director.—Linda Hinckley.

Counties: BURLINGTON (part). CITIES AND TOWNSHIPS: Bass River Washington. Camden County (part). ATLANTIC COUNTY. CITIES AND TOWNSHIPS: Absecon, Atlantic City, Brigantine, Buena, Cardiff, Collings Lake, Cologne, Corbin City, Dorothy, Egg Harbor, Estell Manor, Galloway, Hammonton, Landisville, Leeds Point, Linwood, Longport, Margate, Mays Landing, Milmay, Minotola, Mizpah, Newtonville, Northfield, Oceanville, Pleasantville, Pomona, Port Republic, Richland, Somers Point, Ventnor. CAPE MAY COUNTY. CITIES AND TOWNSHIPS: Avalon, Bargaintown, Beesley's, Belleplain, Burleigh, Cape May, Cape May C.H., Cape May Point, Cold Springs, Del Haven, Dennisville, Dias Creek, Eldora, Erma, Fishing Creek, Goshen, Green Creek, Marmora, Ocean City, Ocean View, Rio Grande, Sea Isle, South Dennis, South Seaville, Stone Harbor, Strathmere, Tuckahoe, Villas, Whitesboro, Wildwood, Woodbine. CUMBERLAND COUNTY. CITIES AND TOWNSHIPS: Bridgeton, Cedarville, Deerfield, Delmont, Dividing Creek, Dorchester, Fairton, Fortescue, Greenwich, Heislerville, Hopewell, Leesburg, Mauricetown, Millville, Newport, Port Elizabeth, Port Norris, Rosenhayn, Shiloh, Vineland. GLOUCESTER COUNTY (part). CITIES AND TOWNSHIPS: Clayton, East Greenwich Ewan, Franklinville, Harrisonville, Malaga, Mantua, Mickleton, Mullica Hill, Newfield, Pitman, Richwood, Swedesboro, Williamstown. OCEAN COUNTY (part). CITIES AND TOWNSHIPS: Barnegat Light, Harvey Cedars, Stafford Twp, Eagleswood, Tuckerton, Little Egg Harbor, Loveladies, Surf City, Ship Bottom, Long Beach Twp, Beach Haven. SALEM COUNTY. CITIES AND TOWNSHIPS: Alloway, Carney's Point, Daretown, Deepwater, Elmer, Elsinboro, Hancocks Bridge, Monroeville, Norma, Pedricktown, Penns Grove, Pennsville, Quinton, Salem, and Woodstown. Population (2010), 736,397.

ZIP Codes: 08001, 08004, 08006–09, 08019–20, 08023, 08025, 08028, 08037–39, 08050–51, 08056, 08061–62, 08067, 08069–72, 08074, 08079–80, 08085, 08087–89, 08092, 08094, 08098, 08201–05, 08210, 08212–15, 08217–21, 08223–26, 08230–32, 08234, 08240–48, 08250–52, 08260, 08270, 08302, 08310–24, 08326–30, 08332, 08340–50, 08352–53, 08360–62, 08401–04, 08406

* * *

THIRD DISTRICT

THOMAS MACARTHUR, Republican, of Toms River, NJ; born in Hebron, CT, October 16, 1960; education: graduated from RHAM High School, Hebron, CT; attended Hofstra University, Hempstead, NY, 1978–82; professional: insurance services industry chief executive officer; married: Debbie; committees: Armed Services, Natural Resources; elected to the 114th Congress on November 4, 2014.

Office Listings

https://macarthur.house.gov

506 Cannon House Office Building, Washington, DC 20515	(202) 225–4765
Chief of Staff.—Ryan Carney.	FAX: 225–0778
Gibson House Community Center, 535 East Main Street, Marlton, NJ 08053	(856) 267–5182
New Jersey Chief of Staff.—Frank Luna.	FAX: 574–4697
Township of Toms River Town Hall, 33 Washington Street, Toms River, NJ 08753	(732) 569–6495
	FAX: 998–8137

Counties: BURLINGTON (part), OCEAN (part). Population (2010), 732,658.

ZIP Codes: 08005–06, 08008, 08010–11, 08015–16, 08019, 08022, 08036, 08041–42, 08046, 08048, 08050, 08052–55, 08057, 08060, 08064–65, 08068, 08073, 08075, 08077, 08087–88, 08092, 08501, 08505, 08511, 08515, 08518, 08554, 08562, 08610, 08620, 08640–41, 08701, 08721–24, 08731–32, 08734–35, 08738, 08740–42, 08751–53, 08755, 08757–59

* * *

FOURTH DISTRICT

CHRISTOPHER H. SMITH, Republican, of Robbinsville, NJ; born in Rahway, NJ, March 4, 1953; attended Worcester College, England, 1974; B.A., Trenton State College, 1975; businessman; executive director, New Jersey Right to Life Committee, Inc., 1976–78; religion: Catholic; married to the former Marie Hahn, 1977; four adult children; three grandchildren; caucuses: chair, Commission on Security and Cooperation in Europe; co-chair, Congressional Pro-Life Caucus; Congressional Human Trafficking Caucus; Bipartisan; Bicameral Congressional Task Force on Alzheimer's Disease; Coalition on Autism Research and Education (CARE); Lyme Disease Caucus; Bi-Partisan Coalition for Combating Anti-Semitism; former chair, House Veterans' Affairs Committee; co-chair, Congressional-Executive Commission on China; committees: Foreign Affairs; elected to the 97th Congress, November 4, 1980; reelected to each succeeding Congress.

Office Listings

http://www.chrissmith.house.gov   https://twitter.com/repchrissmith
https://www.facebook.com/repchrissmith

2373 Rayburn House Office Building, Washington, DC 20515	(202) 225–3765
Chief of Staff.—Mary McDermott Noonan.	FAX: 225–7768
112 Village Center Drive, 2nd Floor, Freehold, NJ 07728	(732) 780–3035
4573 South Broad Street, First Floor, Hamilton, NJ 08619	(609) 585–7878
405 Route 539, Plumsted, NJ 08514	(609) 286–2571

Counties: MERCER. MUNICIPALITIES: Hamilton and Robbinsville. MONMOUTH. MUNICIPALITIES: Allentown, Avon-by-the-Sea, Belmar, Bradley Beach, Brielle, Colts Neck, Eatontown, Englishtown, Fair Haven, Farmingdale, Freehold Borough, Freehold Twp, Homdel, Howell, Lake Como, Little Silver, Manalapan, Manasquan, Middletown (part), Millstone, Neptune City, Neptune Twp, Ocean Twp, Red Bank, Roosevelt, Rumson, Sea Girt, Shrewsbury Twp, Shrewsbury Borough, Spring Lake, Spring Lake Heights, Tinton Falls, Upper Freehold, and Wall. OCEAN. MUNICIPALITIES: Bay Head, Jackson, Lakehurst, Lakewood, Manchester, Plumsted, Pt. Pleasant (part), and Pt. Pleasant Beach. Population (2010), 732,657.

ZIP Codes: 07701–04, 07717, 07719–20, 07722, 07724, 07726–28, 07731, 07733, 07739, 07748, 07753, 07755, 07760, 07762, 08501, 08510, 08514, 08527, 08533, 08555, 08690–91, 08701, 08730, 08733, 08736, 08742, 08750, 08759, 08844

* * *

FIFTH DISTRICT

SCOTT GARRETT, Republican, of Wantage Township, NJ; born in Englewood, NJ, July 7, 1959; education: High Point Regional High School, 1977; B.A., Montclair State University, 1981; J.D., Rutgers University Law School, 1984; professional: attorney; counsel attorney with law firm of Sellar Richardson; organizations: Big Brothers, Big Sisters; Sussex County Chamber of Commerce; Sussex County Board of Agriculture; New Jersey State Assemblyman, 1990–2002; family: married to Mary Ellen; children: Jennifer and Brittany; committees: Budget; Financial Services; elected to the 108th Congress on November 5, 2002; reelected to each succeeding Congress.

Office Listings

http://www.garrett.house.gov　　twitter: @repgarrett　　https://www.facebook.com/repscottgarrett

2232 Russell House Office Building, Washington, DC 20515	(202) 225–4465
Chief of Staff.—Amy Smith.	FAX: 225–9048
Legislative Director.—John Maniscalco.	
Communications Director.—Chris Carofine.	
266 Harristown Road, Suite 104, Glen Rock, NJ 07452	(201) 444–5454
District Director.—Rob Pettet.	
83 Spring Street, Suite 302A, Newton, NJ 07860	(973) 300–2000

Counties: BERGEN (part), PASSAIC (part), SUSSEX (part), WARREN (part). Population (2010), 731,055.

ZIP Codes: 07401, 07410, 07416–19, 07422–23, 07428, 07430, 07432, 07436, 07446, 07450–52, 07456, 07458, 07461–63, 07466, 07480–81, 07495, 07508, 07601–04, 07607, 07620–22, 07624, 07626–28, 07630–31, 07640–49, 07652–53, 07656, 07660–61, 07663, 07666, 07675–77, 07820–23, 07825–27, 07832–33, 07838–39, 07844, 07846, 07848, 07851, 07855, 07860, 07863, 07865, 07874–75, 07877, 07879–80, 07882, 07890

* * *

SIXTH DISTRICT

FRANK PALLONE, JR., Democrat, of Long Branch, NJ; born in Long Branch, October 30, 1951; education: B.A., Middlebury College, Middlebury, VT, 1973; M.A., Fletcher School of Law and Diplomacy, 1974; J.D., Rutgers University School of Law, 1978; member of the bar: Florida, New York, Pennsylvania, and New Jersey; attorney, Marine Advisory Service; assistant professor, Cook College, Rutgers University Sea Grant Extension Program; counsel, Monmouth County, NJ, Protective Services for the Elderly; instructor, Monmouth College; Long Branch City Council, 1982–88; New Jersey State Senate, 1983–88; married the former Sarah Hospodor, 1992; committees: ranking member, Energy and Commerce; elected to the 100th Congress, by special election, on November 8, 1988, to fill the vacancy caused by the death of James J. Howard; reelected to each succeeding Congress.

Office Listings

http://www.pallone.house.gov　　www.facebook.com/repfrankpallone　　twitter: @frankpallone

237 Cannon House Office Building, Washington, DC 20515	(202) 225–4671
Chief of Staff.—Janice Fuller.	FAX: 225–9665
Legislative Director.—Tuley Wright.	
Communications Director.—Daniel van Hoogstraten.	
504 Broadway, Long Branch, NJ 07740	(732) 571–1140
67/69 Church Street, Kilmer Square, New Brunswick, NJ 08901–1242	(732) 249–8892

Counties: MIDDLESEX COUNTY. CITIES AND TOWNSHIPS: Avenel, Carteret, Colonia, Edison, Fords, Highland Park, Hopelawn, Iselin, Keasbey, Menlo Park Terrace, Metuchen, New Brunswick, Old Bridge, Perth Amboy, Piscataway, Port Reading, Sayreville, Sewaren, South Amboy, South Plainfield, and Woodbridge. MONMOUTH COUNTY. CITIES AND TOWNSHIPS: Aberdeen, Allenhurst, Asbury Park, Atlantic Highlands, Deal, Hazlet, Highlands, Interlaken, Keansburg, Keyport, Loch Arbor, Long Branch, Marlboro, Matawan, Middletown, Monmouth Beach, Oceanport, Sea Bright, Union Beach, and West Long Branch. Population (2010), 732,657.

ZIP Codes: 07001, 07008, 07060, 07064–65, 07067, 07077, 07080, 07095, 07701, 07703, 07711–12, 07716, 07718, 07721–23, 07726, 07728, 07730, 07732–35, 07737, 07740, 07746–48, 07750–53, 07755, 07757–58, 07760, 07764–65, 08812, 08817–18, 08820, 08830, 08832, 08837, 08840, 08846, 08854–55, 08857, 08859, 08861–63, 08871–73, 08879, 08899, 08901–04, 08906, 08933, 08989

* * *

SEVENTH DISTRICT

LEONARD LANCE, Republican, of Clinton Township, NJ; born in Easton, PA, June 25, 1952; education: B.A., Lehigh University, Bethlehem, PA, 1974; J.D., Vanderbilt University Law School, Memphis, TN, 1977; M.P.A., Woodrow Wilson School of Public and International Affairs at Princeton University, Princeton, NJ, 1982; professional: judicial clerk; lawyer, private practice; member, New Jersey State Assembly, 1991–2002; member, New Jersey State Senate, 2002–09; minority leader, New Jersey State Senate, 2004–08; Congressional Diabetes Caucus; Congressional Wildlife Caucus; co-chair, House Republican Israel Caucus; House Cancer Care Working Group; Passenger Rail Caucus; religion: Roman Catholic; committees: Energy and Commerce; elected to the 111th Congress on November 4, 2008; reelected to each succeeding Congress.

Office Listings

http://www.lance.house.gov

2352 Rayburn House Office Building, Washington, DC 20515	(202) 225–5361
Chief of Staff.—Todd Mitchell.	FAX: 225–9460
Deputy Chief of Staff/Communications Director.—John Byers.	
Scheduler.—Anna Pellecchia.	
425 North Avenue East, Westfield, NJ 07090	(908) 518–7733
361 Route 31, Unit 1400, Flemington, NJ 08822	(908) 789–6900
District Director.—Amanda Woloshen.	

Counties: UNION COUNTY. MUNICIPALITIES: Berkeley Heights, Clark, Cranford, Garwood, Kenilworth, Linden, Mountainside, New Providence, Springfield, Summit, Union, Westfield, Winfield. HUNTERDON COUNTY. MUNICIPALITIES: Alexandria, Bethlehem, Bloomsbury, Califon, Clinton Township, Clinton, Delaware Township, East Amwell, Flemington, Frenchtown, Glen Gardner, Hampton, High Bridge, Holland, Kingwood, Lambertville, Lebanon, Lebanon Township, Milford, Oldwick, Raritan, Readington, Whitehouse Station, Stockton, Tewksbury, Union, West Amwell. SOMERSET COUNTY. MUNICIPALITIES: Bedminster, Bernards, Bernardsville, Branchburg, Bridgewater, Far Hills, Green Brook, Hillsborough, Montgomery Township, Millstone, North Plainfield, Peapack-Gladstone, Raritan, Rocky Hill, Somerville, Warren, and Watchung. MORRIS COUNTY. MUNICIPALITIES: Chester, Dover, Long Hill, Mine Hill, Mount Arlington, Mount Olive, Netcong, Roxbury, Washington, Wharton. WARREN COUNTY. MUNICIPALITIES: Alpha, Franklin, Greenwich, Harmony, Lopatcong, and Phillipsburg. ESSEX COUNTY. MUNICIPALITIES: Millburn. Population (2010), 733,961.

ZIP Codes: 07016, 07027, 07033, 07036, 07041, 07059–60, 07066, 07069, 07081, 07083, 07090, 07092, 07416, 07676, 07801–03, 07806, 07828, 07830, 07836, 07856–57, 07869, 07885, 07901, 07920–22, 07930–31, 07933–34, 07974, 07977–78, 08323, 08502, 08504, 08530, 08540, 08551, 08553, 08557–59, 08801–04, 08807, 08809, 08812, 08821–22, 08825–27, 08829, 08833, 08836, 08844, 08848, 08853, 08858, 08865, 08867, 08869–70, 08876, 08889

* * *

EIGHTH DISTRICT

ALBIO SIRES, Democrat, of West New York, NJ; born in Bejucal, Provincia de la Habana, Cuba, January 26, 1951; education: graduated, Memorial High School; B.A., St. Peter's College, 1974; M.A., Middlebury College, Middlebury, VT, 1985; studied Spanish in Madrid, Spain; professional: businessman; teacher; part-owner, A.M. Title Agency, Union Township; mayor, West New York, NJ, 1995–2006; member, New Jersey General Assembly, 1999–2006; speaker, New Jersey General Assembly, 2002–2005; family: wife, Adrienne; stepdaughter, Tara Kole; committees: Foreign Affairs; Transportation and Infrastructure; elected to the 109th Congress, by special election, to fill the vacancy caused by the resignation of Robert Menendez; elected to the 110th Congress; reelected to each succeeding Congress.

Office Listings

http://www.sires.house.gov

2342 Rayburn House Office Building, Washington, DC 20515	(202) 225–7919
Chief of Staff.—Gene Martorony.	FAX: 226–0792
Administrative Director/Scheduler.—Judi Wolford.	
Legislative Director.—Kaylan Koszela.	
121 Newark Avenue, Suite 200, Jersey City, NJ 07302	(201) 309–0301
Communications Director.—Erica Daughtrey.	FAX: 309–0384
5500 Palisades Avenue, Suite A, West New York, NJ 07093	(201) 558–0800
800 Anna Street, Elizabeth, NJ 07201	(908) 820–0692
	FAX: 820–0694

Counties: ESSEX (part), BERGEN (PART), HUDSON (part), UNION (part). CITIES AND TOWNSHIPS: Bayonne, Belleville, East Newark, Elizabeth, Fairview, Guttenberg, Harrison, Hoboken, Jersey City, Kearny, Newark, North Bergen, Union City, Weehawken, West New York. Population (2010), 732,658.

ZIP Codes: 07002, 07022, 07029–30, 07032, 07036, 07047 (part), 07086–87, 07093, 07097, 07099, 07101–02, 07104–05, 07107, 07109, 07114, 07184, 07188–89, 07191–93, 07195, 07198–99, 07201–02, 07206–08, 07302–08, 07310–11, 07399

* * *

NINTH DISTRICT

BILL PASCRELL, JR., Democrat, of Paterson, NJ; born in Paterson, January 25, 1937; education: B.A., journalism, and M.A., philosophy, Fordham University; veteran, U.S. Army and Army Reserves; professional: educator; elected Minority Leader Pro Tempore, New Jersey General Assembly, 1988–96; Mayor of Paterson, 1990–96; named Mayor of the Year by bipartisan NJ Conference of Mayors, 1996; started Paterson's first Economic Development Corporation; married the former Elsie Marie Botto; three children: William III, Glenn, and David; committees: Budget; Ways and Means; elected to the 105th Congress; reelected to each succeeding Congress.

Office Listings

http://www.pascrell.house.gov   https://www.facebook.com/pascrell
twitter: @billpascrell

2370 Rayburn House Office Building, Washington, DC 20515	(202) 225–5751
Chief of Staff.—Ben Rich.	FAX: 225–5782
Legislative Director.—Alyssa Penna.	
Economic Policy Advisor.—Elaina Houser.	
200 Federal Plaza, Suite 500, Paterson, NJ 07505	(973) 523–5152
Deputy Chief of Staff.—Assad Akhter.	
Communications Director.—Thomas A. Pietrykoski.	
2–10 North Van Brunt Street, Englewood, NJ 07631	(201) 935–2248
367 Valley Brook Avenue, Lyndhurst, NJ 07071	(201) 935–2248
330 Passaic Street, Passaic, NJ 07055	(973) 472–4510

Counties: BERGEN COUNTY. CITIES: Carlstadt, Cliffside Park, Cresskill, East Rutherford, Edgewater, Elmwood Park, Englewood, Englewood Cliffs, Fort Lee, Garfield, Hasbrouck Heights, Leonia, Little Ferry, Lyndhurst, Moonachie, North Arlington, Palisades Park, Ridgefield, Ridgefield Park, Rutherford, Saddle Brook, South Hackensack, Teaneck (part), Tenafly, Teterboro, Wallington, Wood-Ridge. HUDSON COUNTY, CITIES: Kearny (part), Secaucus. PASSAIC COUNTY, CITIES: Clifton, Haledon, Hawthorne, Passaic, Paterson, Prospect Park. Population (2010), 742,508.

ZIP Codes: 07010–15, 07020, 07024, 07026, 07031–32, 07055, 07057, 07070–75, 07094, 07096, 07099, 07407, 07501–14, 07522, 07524, 07533, 07538, 07543–44, 07604–06, 07608, 07626, 07631–32, 07643, 07650, 07657, 07660, 07663, 07666, 07670

* * *

TENTH DISTRICT

DONALD M. PAYNE, JR., Democrat, of Newark, NJ; born in Newark, December 17, 1958; education: graduated from Hillside High School; attended Kean College (now Kean University), Union, NJ; professional: elected to Newark Municipal Council (President), 2006–12; elected to Essex County Board of Chosen Freeholders, 2006–12; director of Student Transportation for the Essex County Educational Services Commission; married: wife, Beatrice; three children: Jack, Yvonne, and Donald III (triplets); caucuses: Addiction, Treatment, and Recovery Caucus; Congressional Animal Protection Caucus; Congressional Black Caucus; Congressional Caucus on Sudan and South Sudan; Congressional Diabetes Caucus; Congressional Down Syndrome Caucus; Congressional Full Employment Caucus; Congressional LGBT Equality Caucus; Congressional Library of Congress Caucus; Congressional Men's Health Caucus; Congressional Small Business Caucus; Congressional Taiwan Caucus; Congressional TRIO Caucus; Democratic Whip Task Force on Poverty, Income Equality, and Opportunity; Fire Services Caucus; Foster Care Youth Caucus; Homeland Security Task Force; House Medical Technology Caucus; Indian and American Indian Caucus; Ports, Opportunity, Renewable, Trade, and Security (PORTS) Caucus; United States Senate International Conservation Caucus; United States Senate Oceans Caucus; committees: Homeland Security, Small Business; elected simultaneously to the 112th and 113th Congresses on November 6, 2012, by special election, to fill the vacancy caused by the death of United States Representative Donald Milford Payne; reelected to the 114th Congress on November 4, 2014.

Office Listings

http://payne.house.gov   twitter: @repdonaldpayne

103 Cannon House Office Building, Washington, DC 20515 .... (202) 225–3436

Office Listings—Continued

Chief of Staff.—LaVerne Alexander.   FAX: 225–4160
Communications Director.—Michael Burns.
60 Nelson Place, 14th Floor, Newark, NJ 07102 .... (973) 645–3213
253 Martin Luther King Drive, Jersey City, NJ 07305 .... (201) 369–0392
1455 Liberty Avenue, Hillside, NJ 07205.

Counties: ESSEX, HUDSON, UNION. CITIES AND TOWNSHIPS: Bayonne, East Orange, Hillside, Irvington, Jersey City, Linden, Maplewood, Montclair, Newark, Orange, Rahway, Roselle, Roselle Park, South Orange, Union, and West Orange. Population (2010), 732,658.

ZIP Codes: 07002–03, 07017–19, 07028, 07033, 07036, 07040, 07042–44, 07050–52, 07065–67, 07079, 07083, 07088, 07102–09, 07111–12, 07114, 07175, 07202–05, 07208, 07302–06

* * *

ELEVENTH DISTRICT

RODNEY P. FRELINGHUYSEN, Republican, of Morristown, NJ; born in New York, NY, April 29, 1946; education: graduated, Hobart College, NY, 1969; attended graduate school in Connecticut; served, U.S. Army, 93rd Engineer Construction Battalion; honorably discharged, 1971; Morris County State and Federal Aid Coordinator and Administrative Assistant, 1972; member, Morris County Board of Chosen Freeholders, 1974–83 (director, 1980); served on: Welfare and Mental Health boards; Human Services and Private Industry Councils; New Jersey General Assembly, 1983–94; chairman, Assembly Appropriations Committee, 1988–89 and 1992–94; member: American Legion and Veterans of Foreign Wars; named Legislator of the Year by the Veterans of Foreign Wars, the New Jersey Association of Mental Health Agencies, and the New Jersey Association of Retarded Citizens; honored by numerous organizations; married: Virginia Frelinghuysen; children: two daughters; committees: Appropriations; elected to the 104th Congress on November 8, 1994; reelected to each succeeding Congress.

Office Listings

http://www.frelinghuysen.house.gov

2306 Rayburn House Office Building, Washington, DC 20515 .... (202) 225–5034
Chief of Staff.—Nancy Fox.   FAX: 225–3186
Press Secretary.—Steve Wilson.
Legislative Director.—Kathleen Hazlett.
Scheduler.—Steve Silvestri.
30 Schuyler Place, 2nd Floor, Morristown, NJ 07960 .... (973) 984–0711

Counties: ESSEX COUNTY. CITIES AND TOWNSHIPS: Bloomfield, Caldwell, Cedar Grove, Essex Fells, Fairfield Township, Livingston, Montclair, North Caldwell, Nutley, Roseland, Verona, West Caldwell, and West Orange. MORRIS COUNTY. CITIES AND TOWNSHIPS: Municipalities of Boonton Town, Boonton Township, Brookside, Budd Lake, Butler, Cedar Knolls, Chatham Borough, Chatham Township, Convent Station, Denville, East Hanover, Florham Park, Green Pond, Green Village, Hanover, Harding, Hibernia, Jefferson, Kinnelon, Lake Hiawatha, Lake Hopatcong, Lincoln Park, Madison, Mendham Borough, Mendham Township, Montville, Morris Plains, Morris Township, Morristown, Mountain Lakes, Mount Tabor, Newfoundland, New Vernon, Oak Ridge, Parsippany-Troy Hills, Pequannock, Picatinny, Pine Brook, Randolph, Riverdale, Rockaway Borough, Rockaway Township, Stanhope, Towaco, Victory Gardens, and Whippany. PASSAIC COUNTY. CITIES: Bloomingdale, Haskell, Little Falls, North Haledon, Pompton Lakes, Totowa, Wanaque, Wayne and Woodland Park. SUSSEX COUNTY. CITIES AND TOWNSHIPS: Byram, Hopatcong, Ogdensburg, Sparta, and Stanhope. Population (2010), 724,761.

ZIP Codes: 07003–07, 07009, 07021, 07028, 07034–39, 07042–46, 07052, 07054, 07058, 07068, 07082, 07110, 07403, 07405, 07420, 07424, 07435, 07438–40, 07442, 07444, 07457, 07465, 07470, 07474, 07508, 07512, 07806, 07821, 07828, 07834, 07837, 07842–43, 07845, 7848–49, 07866, 07869, 07871, 07874, 07878, 07920, 07926–28, 07932, 07935–36, 07930, 07940, 07945, 07950, 07960–63, 07976, 07980, 07999

* * *

TWELFTH DISTRICT

BONNIE WATSON COLEMAN, Democrat, of Ewing Township, NJ; born in Camden, NJ, February 6, 1945; first African American woman ever elected to Congress from New Jersey; education: B.A., Thomas Edison State College; professional: former Assistant Commissioner, New Jersey Department of Community Affairs; former Bureau Chief, New Jersey Division on Civil Rights; eight-term member of the New Jersey General Assembly; First African American woman to serve as Majority Leader of the New Jersey General Assembly; First African American woman to chair the New Jersey Democratic State Committee; religion: Baptist; married:

Rev. William E. Coleman; children: William, Jared, and Troy; two grandchildren: Kamryn and William; committees: Homeland Security; Oversight and Government Reform; elected to the 114th Congress on November 4, 2014.

Office Listings

http://watsoncoleman.house.gov   twitter: @repbwcoleman
https://www.facebook.com/repbonniewatsoncoleman

126 Cannon House Office Building, Washington, DC 20515 .... (202) 225–5801
    Chief of Staff.—James Gee.   FAX: 225–6025
    Legislative Director.—Michael Reed.
    Communications Director.—Courtney Cochran.
    Scheduler.—Jaimee Gilmartin.
850 Bear Tavern Road, Ewing, NJ 08628 .... (609) 883–0026
    District Director.—Kari Osmond.

Counties: Mercer County. Cities and Townships: East Windsor, Ewing, Hightstown, Hopewell Borough, Hopewell Township, Lawrence, Pennington, Princeton, Trenton, and West Windsor. MIDDLESEX COUNTY. CITIES AND TOWNSHIPS: Cranbury, Dunellen, East Brunswick, Helmetta, Jamesburg, Middlesex, Milltown, Monroe, North Brunswick, Old Bridge, Plainsboro, South Brunswick, South River, and Spotswood. SOMERSET COUNTY. CITIES AND TOWNSHIPS: Bound Brook, Franklin, Manville, and South Bound Brook. UNION COUNTY. CITIES AND TOWNSHIPS: Fanwood, Plainfield, Scotch Plains. Population (2010), 732,658.

ZIP Codes: 07023, 07060–63, 07076, 07747, 08512, 08520, 08525, 08528, 08530, 08534, 08536, 08540–44, 08550, 08560, 08608–11, 08618–19, 08628–29, 08638, 08648, 08691, 08805, 08810, 08812, 08816, 08823–24, 08828, 08831, 08835, 08846, 08850, 08852, 08857, 08859, 08873, 08875, 08880, 08882, 08884, 08890, 08902

NEW MEXICO

(Population 2010, 2,059,179)

SENATORS

TOM UDALL, Democrat, of Santa Fe, NM; born in Tucson, AZ, May 18, 1948; education: graduate of McLean High School, 1966; B.A., Prescott College, Prescott, AZ, 1970; LL.B., Cambridge University, Cambridge, England, 1975; J.D., University of New Mexico, Albuquerque, NM, 1977; professional: admitted to New Mexico Bar, 1978; served as New Mexico Attorney General, 1990–98; served as U.S. Representative for New Mexico's Third Congressional District, 1998–2008; married: Jill Z. Cooper; children: Amanda; member of the Commission on Security and Cooperation in Europe; committees: Appropriations; Commerce, Science, and Transportation; Foreign Relations; Indian Affairs; Rules and Administration; Joint Committee on Printing; elected to the U.S. Senate on November 4, 2008; reelected to the U.S. Senate on November 4, 2014.

Office Listings

http://tomudall.senate.gov

531 Hart Senate Office Building, Washington, DC 20510	(202) 224–6621
Chief of Staff.—Michael Collins.	FAX: 228–3261
Legislative Director.—Andrew Wallace.	
Communications Director.—Jennifer Talhelm.	
Executive Assistant.—Donda Morgan.	
219 Central Avenue, NW., Suite 210, Albuquerque, NM 87102	(505) 346–6791
201 North Church Street, Suite 201B, Las Cruces, NM 88001	(575) 526–5475
120 South Federal Place, Suite 302, Santa Fe, NM 87501	(505) 988–6511
102 West Hagerman, Suite A, Carlsbad, NM 88220	(575) 234–0366
100 South Avenue A, Suite 113, Portales, NM 88130	(505) 356–6811

* * *

MARTIN HEINRICH, Democrat, of Albuquerque, NM; born in Fallon, NV, October 17, 1971; education: B.S., mechanical engineering, University of Missouri, Columbia, MO, 1995; professional: Executive Director of the Cottonwood Gulch Foundation, 1996–2001; Albuquerque City Council, 2003–07; State of New Mexico Natural Resources Trustee, 2006–07; served as U.S. Representative for New Mexico's First Congressional District, 2009–12; married: Julie Heinrich; children: Carter Heinrich and Micah Heinrich; caucuses: Senate Climate Action Task Force; Congressional Sportsmen's Caucus; Congressional Dietary Supplement Caucus; committees: Armed Services; Energy and Natural Resources; Joint Economic Committee; Select Committee on Intelligence; elected to the U.S. Senate on November 6, 2012.

Office Listings

http://heinrich.senate.gov   www.facebook.com/martinheinrich   twitter: @martinheinrich

303 Hart Senate Office Building, Washington, DC 20510	(202) 224–5521
Chief of Staff.—Steve Haro.	FAX: 228–2841
Legislative Director.—Jude McCartin.	
Communications Director.—Whitney Potter.	
Director of Scheduling.—Catherine Melsheimer.	
400 Gold Avenue Southwest, Suite 1080, Albuquerque, NM 87102	(505) 346–6601
7450 East Main Street, Suite A, Farmington, NM 87402	(505) 325–5030
505 South Main Street, Suite 148, Las Cruces, NM 88001	(575) 523–6561
200 East 4th Street, Suite 300, Roswell, NM 88201	(575) 622–7113
123 East Marcy Street, Suite 103, Santa Fe, NM 87501	(505) 988–6647

REPRESENTATIVES

FIRST DISTRICT

MICHELLE LUJAN GRISHAM, Democrat, of Albuquerque, NM; born in Los Alamos, NM, October 24, 1959; education: B.U.S., University of New Mexico, 1981; J.D., University of New Mexico, 1987; professional: Director, New Mexico State Agency on Aging (1991–2002); Secretary, New Mexico Department of Aging and Long-Term Services (2002–04); Secretary, New Mexico Department of Health (2004–07); Bernalillo County Commissioner (2010–12); children:

Taylor Stewart and Erin Grisham; committees: Agriculture; Budget; Oversight and Government Reform; elected to the 113th Congress on November 6, 2012; reelected to the 114th Congress on November 4, 2014.

Office Listings

http://www.lujangrisham.house.gov   twitter: @replujangrisham
http://www.facebook.com/replujangrisham

214 Cannon House Office Building, Washington, DC 20515 .... (202) 225–6316
    Chief of Staff.—Dominic Gabello.
    Legislative Director.—Courtney Weaver.
    Executive Assistant.—Natalie Armijo.
400 Gold Avenue, Southwest, Suite 680, Albuquerque, NM 87102 .... (505) 346–6781

Counties: BERNALILLO (part), SANDOVAL (part), SANTA FE (part), TORRANCE, AND VALENCIA (part). CITIES AND TOWNSHIPS: Albuquerque, Bernalillo, Edgewood, Estancia, Moriarty, Mountainair, Rio Rancho, and South Valley. Population (2010), 693,772.

ZIP Codes: 87004, 87008, 87015, 87026, 87035–36, 87047–48, 87059, 87063, 87067, 87102, 87104–14, 87116–17, 87120–24, 87131, 87144, 88321

* * *

SECOND DISTRICT

STEVAN PEARCE, Republican, of Hobbs, NM; born in Lamesa, TX, August 24, 1947; education: M.B.A., Eastern New Mexico, Las Cruces, NM, 1970; B.B.A., New Mexico State University, Portales, NM, 1991; professional: owner, oil well services company; served in Vietnam as a pilot for the U.S. Air Force; member of the New Mexico State House of Representatives, 1997–2000; elected as a Republican to the 108th, 109th, 110th, 112th, and 113th Congresses; religion: Baptist; married: Cynthia; caucuses: chairman emeritus of Western Caucus; member of Sportsmen's Caucus; Prayer Caucus; Republican Study Committee; committees: Financial Services; elected to the 112th Congress on November 2, 2010; reelected to each succeeding Congress.

Office Listings

http://www.pearce.house.gov   twitter: @repstevepearce   facebook:repstevepearce

2432 Rayburn House Office Building, Washington, DC 20515 .... (202) 225–2365
    Chief of Staff.—Todd Willens.   FAX: 225–9599
    Communications Director.—Tom Intorcio.
    Legislative Director.—Patrick Cuff.
    Scheduler.—Kristine Nichols.
    Legislative Correspondent/Communications Assistant.—Bridget Condon.
    Legislative Correspondent.—Andrew Aragon.
    Legislative Assistants: Jacci Guy, Rob MacGregor.
570 North Telshor Boulevard, Las Cruces, NM 88011 .... (575) 522–0771
1717 West 2nd Street, Suite 110, Roswell, NM 88201 .... (575) 622–6200
111 School of Mines Road, Socorro, NM 87801 .... (575) 855–8979
200 East Broadway, Suite 200, Hobbs, NM 88240 .... (575) 393–6995

Counties: BERNALILLO (part), CATRON, CHAVES, CIBOLA, DEBACA, DONA ANA, EDDY, GRANT, GUADALUPE, HIDALGO, LEA, LINCOLN, LUNA, MCKINLEY (part), OTERO, ROOSEVELT, SIERRA, SOCORRO, AND VALENCIA (part). Population (2010), 686,393.

ZIP Codes: 79821, 79835, 79922, 79932, 79934, 85534, 87002, 87005–07, 87011, 87014, 87020–23, 87026, 87028, 87031, 87034, 87038, 87040, 87045, 87049, 87051, 87062, 87068, 87105, 87121, 88024–34, 88036, 88038–49, 88051–56, 88058, 88061–63, 88065, 88072, 88081, 88113–6, 88118–9, 88123–26, 88130, 88132, 88134, 88136, 88201–03, 88210–11, 88213 88220–21, 88230–32, 88240–42, 88250, 88252–56, 88260, 88262–65, 88267–68, 88301, 88310–12, 88314, 88316–18, 88323–25, 88330, 88336–55, 88417, 88431, 88435

* * *

THIRD DISTRICT

BEN RAY LUJÁN, Democrat, of Santa Fe, NM; born in Nambe, NM; June 7, 1972; education: New Mexico Highland University; business administration, Highlands University, Las Vegas, NM; professional: elected to the New Mexico Public Regulation Commission, 2005–08; co-chair of the Nuclear Cleanup Caucus; co-chair of the Technology Transfer Caucus; co-chair of the Science and National Labs Caucus; member of the Hispanic Caucus; Native American Caucus; committees: Energy and Commerce; elected to the 111th Congress on November 4, 2008; reelected to each succeeding Congress.

Office Listings

http://www.lujan.house.gov   facebook.com/repbenraylujan   www.twitter.com/repbenraylujan

2446 Rayburn House Office Building, Washington, DC 20515 .... (202) 225–6190
    Chief of Staff.—Angela Ramirez.   FAX: 226–1528
    Deputy Chief of Staff/Communications Director.—Andrew Stoddard.
    Legislative Director.—Graham Mason.
    Executive Assistant/Scheduler.—Chris Garcia.
1611 Calle Lorca, Suite A, Santa Fe, NM 87505 .... (505) 984–8950
    District Director.—Jennifer Catechis.
800 Municipal Drive, Farmington, NM 87401 .... (505) 324–1005
    Constituent Services Representative/Veterans Liaison.—Pete Valencia.
110 West Aztec, Suite 102, Gallup, NM 87301 .... (505) 863–0582
    Field Representative and Navajo Nation Liaison.—Brian Lee.
903 University Avenue, P.O. Box 1368, Las Vegas, NM 87701 .... (505) 454–3038
    Constituent Liaison.—Stephen Salas.
404 West Route 66 Boulevard, Tucumcari, NM 88401 .... (575) 461–3029
    Field Representative.—Ron Wilmot.
3200 Civic Center Circle, NE., Suite 330, Rio Rancho, NM 87144 .... (505) 994–0499
    Scheduler and Constituent Liaison.—Jeffery Bustamante.

Counties: BERNALILLO (part), NAVAJO NATION, COLFAX, CURRY, HARDING, LOS ALAMOS, MCKINLEY (part), MORA, QUAY, RIO ARRIBA, ROOSEVELT (part), SANDOVAL (part), SAN JUAN, SAN MIGUEL, SANTA FE, TAOS, UNION. Population (2010), 686,393.

ZIP Codes: 87001, 87004, 87010, 87012–13, 87015, 87017–18, 87024–25, 87027, 87029, 87037, 87041, 87044–48, 87052–53, 87056, 87064, 87072, 87083, 87114, 87120, 87123–24, 87144, 87174, 87301–02, 87305, 87310–13, 87316–17, 87319–23, 87325–26, 87328, 87347, 87364–65, 87375, 87401–02, 87410, 87412–13, 87413–21, 87455, 87461, 87499, 87501–25, 87527–33, 87535, 87537–40, 87543–45, 87548–49, 87551–54, 87556–58, 87560, 87562, 87564–67, 87569, 87571, 87573–83, 87592, 87594, 87701, 87710, 87712–15, 87718, 87722–23, 87728–36, 87740, 87742–43, 87745–47, 87749–50, 87752–53, 88101–03, 88112–13, 88115–16, 88118, 88120–26, 88130, 88132–35, 88401, 88410–11, 88414–16, 88418–19, 88421–22, 88424, 88426–27, 88430, 88433–34, 88436–37, 88439

NEW YORK

(Population 2010, 19,378,102)

SENATORS

CHARLES E. SCHUMER, Democrat, of Brooklyn and Queens, NY; born in Brooklyn, November 23, 1950; education: graduated valedictorian, Madison High School; Harvard University, magna cum laude, 1971; J.D. with honors, Harvard Law School, 1974; professional: admitted to the New York State Bar in 1975; elected to the New York State Assembly, 1974; served on Judiciary, Health, Education, and Cities committees; chairman, subcommittee on City Management and Governance, 1977; chairman, Committee on Oversight and Investigation, 1979; re-elected to each succeeding legislative session until December 1980; married: Iris Weinshall, 1980; children: Jessica Emily and Alison Emma; committees: ranking member, Rules and Administration; ranking member, Joint Committee on Printing; Banking, Housing, and Urban Affairs; Finance; Judiciary; Joint Committee on the Library; elected to the 97th Congress on November 4, 1980; reelected to each succeeding Congress; elected to the U.S. Senate on November 3, 1998; reelected to each succeeding Senate term.

Office Listings

http://schumer.senate.gov

322 Hart Senate Office Building, Washington, DC 20510	(202) 224–6542
Chief of Staff.—Mike Lynch.	FAX: 228–3027
Communications Director.—Matt House.	
Executive Assistant.—Dana Gansman.	
780 Third Avenue, Suite 2301, New York, NY 10017	(212) 486–4430
Leo O'Brien Building, 1 Clinton Square, Room 420, Albany, NY 12207	(518) 431–4070
130 South Elmwood Avenue, #660, Buffalo, NY 14202	(716) 846–4111
100 State Street, Room 3040, Rochester, NY 14614	(585) 263–5866
100 South Clinton, Room 841, Syracuse, NY 13261–7318	(315) 423–5471
Federal Office Building, 15 Henry Street, #100A–F Binghamton, NY 13901	(607) 772–6792
Two Greenway Plaza, 145 Pine Lawn Road, #300N, Melville, NY 11747	(631) 753–0978
One Park Place, Suite 100, Peekskill, NY 10566	(914) 734–1532

* * *

KIRSTEN E. GILLIBRAND, Democrat, of Brunswick, NY; born in Albany, NY, December 9, 1966; education: B.A., Dartmouth College, Hanover, NH, 1988; J.D., UCLA, Los Angeles, CA, 1991; professional: attorney; Special Counsel to the U.S. Secretary of Housing and Urban Development Andrew Cuomo; private legal practice; religion: Catholic; married: Jonathan Gillibrand 2001; two sons: Theodore 2004, Henry 2008; committees: Agriculture, Nutrition, and Forestry; Armed Services; Environment and Public Works; Special Committee on Aging; appointed to the 111th Congress on January 23, 2009, to fill the vacancy caused by the resignation of Hillary Clinton, subsequently elected on November 2, 2010, for the remaining two years of the unexpired term; reelected to full Senate term on November 6, 2012.

Office Listings

http://gillibrand.senate.gov

478 Russell Senate Office Building, Washington, DC 20510	(202) 224–4451
Chief of Staff.—Jess Fassler.	FAX: 228–0282
Legislative Director.—Brooke Jamison.	
Communications Director.—Lauren Passalacqua.	
Scheduler.—Jason Rubin.	
780 Third Avenue, Suite 2601, New York, NY 10017	(212) 688–6262
Federal Office Building, 1 Clinton Square, Room 821, Albany, NY 12207	(518) 431–0120
Larkin at Exchange, 726 Exchange Street, Suite 511, Buffalo, NY 14210	(716) 854–9725
155 Pinelawn Road, Suite 250 North, Melville, NY 11747	(631) 249–2825
P.O. Box 273, Lowville, NY 13367	(315) 376–6118
Federal Office Building, 100 State Street, Room 4195, Rochester, NY 14614	(585) 263–6250
Federal Office Building, 100 South Clinton Street, Room 1470, P.O. Box 7378, Syracuse, NY 13261	(315) 448–0470
Lower Hudson Valley Office, P.O. Box 893, Mahopac, NY 10541	(845) 875–4585
Westchester County Office	(914) 725–9294

REPRESENTATIVES

FIRST DISTRICT

LEE M. ZELDIN, Republican, of Shirley, NY; education: William Floyd High School; University at Albany, SUNY; Albany Law School; religion: Jewish; married: Diana Zeldin; children: Mikayla and Arianna; committees: Foreign Affairs; Transportation and Infrastructure; Veterans' Affairs; elected to the 114th Congress on November 4, 2014.

Office Listings

https://zeldin.house.gov

1517 Longworth House Office Building, Washington, DC 20515 .... (202) 225–3826
Chief of Staff.—Eric Amidon.
Deputy Chief of Staff / Legislative Director.—Scott Shiller.
Communications Director.—Jennifer DiSiena.
Scheduler / Legislative Correspondent.—Nicole Paciello.
31 Oak Street, Suite 20, Patchogue, NY 11772 .... (631) 289–1097
District Director.—Mark Woolley.

Counties: SUFFOLK COUNTY (part). TOWNS: Brookhaven, Smithtown, Southampton, Islip, Riverhead, East Hampton, Southold, and Shelter Island. Population (2000), 654,360.

ZIP Codes: 00501, 00544, 11713, 11715, 11719–20, 11727, 11733, 11738, 11741–42, 11745, 11754–55, 11763–64, 11766–68, 11772, 11776–80, 11784, 11786–90, 11792, 11794, 11901, 11930–35, 11937, 11939–42, 11944, 11946–65, 11967–73, 11975–78, 11980

* * *

SECOND DISTRICT

PETER T. KING, Republican, of Seaford, NY; born in Manhattan, NY, April 5, 1944; education: B.A., St. Francis College, NY, 1965; J.D., University of Notre Dame Law School, IN, 1968; military service: served, U.S. Army Reserve National Guard, specialist 5, 1968 73; admitted to New York Bar, 1968; professional: attorney; Deputy Nassau County Attorney, 1972–74; executive assistant to the Nassau County Executive, 1974–76; general counsel, Nassau Off-Track Betting Corporation, 1977; Hempstead Town Councilman, 1978–81; Nassau County Comptroller, 1981–92; member: Ancient Order of Hibernians; Long Island Committee for Soviet Jewry; Sons of Italy; Knights of Columbus; 69th Infantry Veterans Corps; American Legion; married: Rosemary Wiedl King, 1967; children: Sean and Erin; grandson, Jack; committees: Financial Services; Homeland Security; Permanent Select Committee on Intelligence; elected on November 3, 1992 to the 103rd Congress; reelected to each succeeding Congress.

Office Listings

http://www.peteking.house.gov

339 Cannon House Office Building, Washington, DC 20515 .... (202) 225–7896
Chief of Staff / Press Secretary.—Kevin Fogarty.   FAX: 226–2279
Legislative Director.—Jamie Tricarico.
1003 Park Boulevard, Massapequa Park, NY 11762 .... (516) 541–4225
District Director.—Anne Rosenfeld.
Suffolk County .... (631) 541–4225

Counties: NASSAU (part), SUFFOLK (part). CITIES AND TOWNSHIPS: Amityville, Babylon, Bayport, Bay Shore, Bethpage, Bohemia, Brentwood, Brightwaters, Copiague, Central Islip, East Islip, Deer Park, Farmingdale, Holbrook, Great River, Islip, Islip Terrace, Levittown, Lindenhurst, Massapequa, Massapequa Park, North Babylon, North Lindenhurst, Oakdale, Patemogue, Seaford, Wantagh, West Babylon, West Islip, and Wyandanch. Population (2010), 724,053.

ZIP Codes: 11701–06, 11714, 11716–18, 11722, 11726, 11730, 11735, 11739, 11741, 11751–53, 11756–58, 11756–58, 11762, 11769, 11772, 11779, 11782, 11793, 11795, 11798

* * *

THIRD DISTRICT

STEVE ISRAEL, Democrat, of Huntington, NY; born in Brooklyn, NY, May 30, 1958; education: B.A., George Washington University, 1982; professional: public relations and marketing executive; public service: legislative assistant for Rep. Richard Ottinger (D–NY),

1980–83; Suffolk County Executive for Intergovernmental Relations, 1988–91; elected to the Huntington Town Board, 1993; reelected two times; organizations: Institute on the Holocaust; Touro Law Center; Nature Conservancy; Audubon Society; awards: Child Care Council of Suffolk Leadership Award; Anti-Defamation League and Sons of Italy Purple Aster Award; committees: Appropriations; elected to the 107th Congress on November 7, 2000; reelected to each succeeding Congress.

Office Listings

http://www.israel.house.gov

2457 Rayburn House Office Building, Washington, DC 20515 .... (202) 225–3335
    Chief of Staff.—Tricia Russell.   FAX: 225–4669
    Communications Director.—Caitlin Girouard.
    Legislative Director.—Jessica Schwartz.
534 Broad Hollow Road, Suite 302, Melville, NY 11747 .... (631) 777–7391
    District Director.—Seema Bhansali .... (516) 505–1448

Nassau County (part), SUFFOLK COUNTY (part). CITIES: Asharoken, Bay Shore, Bayport, Bayside, Bayville, Centerport, Cold Springs Harbor, Commack, Deer Park, Dix Hills, Douglaston, East Hills, East Williston, East Northport, Eaton's Neck, Elwood, Farmingdale, Flushing, Fort Salonga, Glen Cove, Great Neck, Greenlawn, Greenvale, Halesite, Hauppauge, Herricks, Hicksville, Huntington, Huntington Station, Jericho, King's Park, Kings Point, Lake Success, Little Neck, Lloyd Harbor, Manhasset, Melville, Mill Neck, Mineola, Muttontown, North Hills, Northport, Old Bethpage, Old Brookville, Old Westbury, Oyster Bay, Plandome, Plainview, Port Washington, Queens Village, Roslyn, Roslyn Harbor, Roslyn Heights, Saddle Rock, Sands Point, Sea Cliff, Smithtown, South Huntington, Syosset, West Hills, Whitestone, Williston Park, Woodbury and Wyandanch. Population (2013), 724,490.

ZIP Codes: 11101, 11004–05, 11020–21, 11023–24, 11030, 11040, 11042, 11050, 11357–63, 11426–28, 11507, 11542, 11545, 11547–48, 11560, 11577, 11579, 11590, 11596, 11709, 11714, 11721, 11724–25, 11729, 11731–32, 11739, 11743, 11746–47, 11753–54, 11756, 11765, 11768, 11771, 11787–88, 11791, 11797, 11801, 11803–04

* * *

FOURTH DISTRICT

KATHLEEN M. RICE, Democrat, of Garden City, NY; born in New York City, NY, February 15, 1965; education: graduated, Garden City High School, 1983; B.A., The Catholic University of America, Washington, DC, 1987; J.D., Touro Law Center, Long Island, NY, 1991; professional: Assistant District Attorney, Kings County, NY (Brooklyn), 1992–99; Assistant U.S. Attorney, U.S. Department of Justice, Philadelphia, PA, 1999–2005; elected District Attorney of Nassau County, NY, 2006–2014; President, District Attorneys Association of the State of New York, 2013–2014; awards: Mothers Against Drunk Driving (MADD) Lifetime Achievement Award; Governors Highway Safety Association (GHSA) James J. Howard Highway Safety Trailblazer Award; U.S. Inspector General's Integrity Award; U.S. Attorney General's Director's Award for Superior Performance as an Assistant U.S. Attorney; religion: Catholic; caucuses: Bipartisan Taskforce for Combating Anti-Semitism; Bipartisan Working Group; Congressional Caucus for Women's Issues; Congressional Coalition on Autism Research and Education; Congressional Diabetes Caucus; Congressional Long Island Sound Caucus; Congressional Pro-Choice Caucus; Congressional Stop DUI Caucus; Congressional Taiwan Caucus; Congressional Tourette Caucus; Democracy Task Force; Democratic Israel Working Group; New Democrat Coalition; NY Defense Working Group; Quiet Skies Caucus; U.S.-Philippines Friendship Caucus; Congressional Fire Services Caucus; committees: Homeland Security; Veterans' Affairs; elected to the 114th Congress on November 4, 2014.

Office Listings

http://kathleenrice.house.gov

1508 Longworth House Office Building, Washington, DC 20515 .... (202) 225–5516
    Chief of Staff.—Nell Reilly.   FAX: 225–5758
    District Director.—Cheryl Rice.
    Executive Assistant.—Amanda Walsh.
    Communications Director.—Coleman Lamb.
300 Garden City Plaza, Suite 200, Garden City, NY 11530 .... (516) 739–3008

Counties: NASSAU (part). Cities and Townships: Atlantic Beach, Baldwin, Bellerose, Carle Place, Cedarhurst, East Meadow, East Rockaway, East Williston, Elmont, Floral Park, Franklin Square, Freeport, Garden City, Garden City Park, Hempstead, Hewlett, Inwood, Lakeview, Lawrence, Lynbrook, Malverne, Merrick, Mineola, New Cassel, New Hyde Park, North Bellmore, North New Hyde Park, Oceanside, Rockville Centre, Roosevelt, Salisbury, Stewart Manor, South Floral Park, South Valley Stream, Uniondale, Valley Stream, West Hempstead, Westbury, Williston Park, Woodmere, and Woodsburgh. Population (2010) 717,708.

ZIP Codes: 11003, 11010, 11040, 11096, 11501, 11509, 11510, 11514, 11516, 11518, 11520, 11530, 11549, 11550, 11552–54, 11556–59, 11561, 11563, 11565–66, 11569, 11570, 11572, 11575, 11580–81, 11590, 11596, 11598, 11710, 11793, 11801

* * *

FIFTH DISTRICT

GREGORY W. MEEKS, Democrat, of Southern Queens, NY; born in Harlem, NY, September 25, 1953; education: P.S. 183; Robert F. Wagner Junior High School; Julia Richman High School, New York, NY; B.A., Adelphi University, 1971–75; J.D., Howard University School of Law, 1975–78; professional: lawyer, admitted to bar, 1979; Queens District Attorney's Office, 1978–83, Assistant Specialist Narcotic Prosecutor, 1981–83; Assistant Counsel to State Investigation Commission, 1983–85; serving as Assistant District Attorney; Supervising Judge, New York State Workers' Compensation Board; public service: New York State Assemblyman, 1992–97; organizations: Alpha Phi Alpha Fraternity; National Bar Association; caucuses: co-chair of the Congressional Services Caucus; co-chair of the Organizations of American States; active member of the Congressional Black Caucus; married: Simone-Marie Meeks, 1997; children: Aja, Ebony, and Nia-Ayana; committees: Financial Services; Foreign Affairs; elected to the 105th Congress on February 3, 1998; reelected to each succeeding Congress.

Office Listings

http://www.meeks.house.gov

2234 Rayburn House Office Building, Washington, DC 20515	(202) 225–3461
Chief of Staff.—Sophia Lafargue.	FAX: 226–4169
Legislative Director.—Gabriel Bitol.	
Office Manager / Scheduler.—Kim Fuller.	
153–01 Jamaica Avenue, Jamaica, NY 11432	(718) 725–6000
Chief of Staff.—Robert Simmons.	
6712 Rockaway Beach Boulevard, Arverne, NY 11692	(347) 230–4032
Community Liaison.—Jermaine Huell.	

Counties: QUEENS COUNTY (part). CITIES AND TOWNSHIPS: Belmont, Cambria Heights, Elmont, Floral Park, Glen Oaks, Hollis, Howard Beach, Jamaica, Jamaica Estates, Kew Gardens, Laurelton, New Hyde Park, Ozone Park, Queens Village, Richmond Hill, the Rockaway Peninsula, Rosedale, St. Albans, South Jamaica, South Ozone Park, Springfield Gardens, Valley Stream (North & South), and Woodhaven. Population (2010), 717,708.

ZIP Codes: 11001, 11004, 11040, 11405, 11411–20, 11422–23, 11425–36, 11439, 11451, 11484, 11690–93

* * *

SIXTH DISTRICT

GRACE MENG, Democrat, of Queens, NY; born in Corona, NY, October 1, 1975; education: Stuyvesant High School; B.A, University of Michigan, 1997; J.D., Yeshiva University's Benjamin Cardozo School of Law, 2002; professional: practicing lawyer / pro bono attorney, 2003–08; New York State Assembly, 2008–12; religion: Christian; husband, Wayne Kye; children, Brandon and Tyler; caucuses: Congressional Kids Safety Caucus; Congressional Quiet Skies Caucus; Congressional Asian Pacific American Caucus; Congressional Caucus on India and Indian Americans; Congressional Bangladesh Caucus; Congressional Caucus on Sikh Americans; United Solutions Caucus; Congressional Hellenic Caucus; Congressional Caucus on Korea; Congressional Equality Caucus; Congressional Creative Rights Caucus; Congressional Pro-Choice Caucus; Congressional Caucus for Women's Issues; Congressional Oral Health Caucus; Congressional Hellenic-Israel Caucus; Congressional Taiwan Caucus; U.S.-Philippines Friendship Caucus; Gun Violence Prevention Task Force; Women's Working Group on Immigration Reform; committees: Foreign Affairs; Small Business; elected to the 113th Congress on November 6, 2012; reelected to the 114th Congress on November 4, 2014.

Office Listings

http://meng.house.gov   https://twitter.com/repgracemeng
https://www.facebook.com/repgracemeng

1317 Longworth House Office Building, Washington, DC 20515	(202) 225–2601
Chief of Staff.—Justin Oswald.	FAX: 225–1589
Executive Assistant / Scheduler.—Brenda Connolly.	
40–13 159 Street, Flushing, NY 11358	(718) 358–6364
	FAX: 445–7868
118–15 Queens Boulevard, 17th Floor, Forest Hills, NY 11375	(718) 358–6364

Office Listings—Continued

District Director.—Anthony Lemma.
Communications Director.—Jordan Goldes.

Counties: QUEENS COUNTY (part), CITIES AND TOWNSHIPS: Auburndale, Bayside, Elmhurst, Electchester-Pomonok, Flushing, Forest Hills, Fresh Meadows, Glendale, Jamaica, Kew Gardens, Maspeth, Middle Village, Rego Park, Ridgewood, and Woodside. Population (2010), 724,352.

ZIP Codes: 11352, 11354–55, 11357–58, 11360–61, 11364–67, 11373–75, 11377–81, 11385, 11415, 11418, 11421, 11423–24, 11427, 11432, 11435

* * *

SEVENTH DISTRICT

NYDIA M. VELÁZQUEZ, Democrat, of New York, NY; born in Yabucoa, Puerto Rico, March 28, 1953; education: B.A. in political science, University of Puerto Rico, 1974; M.A. in political science, New York University, 1976; professional: faculty member, University of Puerto Rico, 1976–81; adjunct professor, Hunter College of the City University of New York, 1981–83; special assistant to Congressman Ed Towns, 1983; member, City Council of New York, 1984–86; national director of Migration Division Office, Department of Labor and Human Resources of Puerto Rico, 1986–89; director, Department of Puerto Rican Community Affairs in the United States, 1989–92; committees: Financial Services; Small Business; elected on November 3, 1992, to the 103rd Congress; reelected to each succeeding Congress.

Office Listings

http://www.velazquez.house.gov

2302 Rayburn House Office Building, Washington, DC 20515	(202) 225–2361
Chief of Staff.—Michael Day.	FAX: 226–0327
Communications Director.—Alex Haurek.	
Scheduler.—Jocelyn Garay.	
Legislative Director.—Clarinda Landeros.	
266 Broadway, Suite 201, Brooklyn, NY 11211	(718) 599–3658
16 Court Street, Suite 1006, Brooklyn, NY 11241	(718) 222–5819
500 Pearl Street, Suite 973, New York, NY 10007	(212) 619–2606

Counties: KINGS (part), NEW YORK (part), AND QUEENS (part). Population (2010), 717,708.

ZIP Codes: 10002, 10004, 10007, 10009, 10012–13, 10038, 11201, 11205–08, 11211, 11215, 11217–21, 11231–32, 11237, 11378–79, 11385, 11416–18, 11421

* * *

EIGHTH DISTRICT

HAKEEM S. JEFFRIES, Democrat of New York, NY; born in Brooklyn, NY, August 4, 1970; education: graduated from Midwood High School, 1988; B.A., State University of New York at Binghamton, 1992; M.P.P., Georgetown University, 1994; J.D., New York University Law School, 1997; professional: member, New York State Assembly, 2007–13; religion: Baptist; married; two children; committees: Education and the Workforce; Judiciary; elected to the 113th Congress on November 6, 2012; reelected to the 114th Congress on November 4, 2014.

Office Listings

http://www.jeffries.house.gov   twitter: @repjeffries   facebook.com/rephakeemjeffries

1607 Longworth House Office Building, Washington, DC 20515	(202) 225–5936
Chief of Staff.—Cedric Grant.	FAX: 225–1018
Scheduler.—Katey McCutcheon.	
Legislative Director.—Kirsten Donaldson.	
Communications Director.—Michael Hardaway.	
District Director.—Tasia Jackson.	
55 Hanson Place, Suite 603, Brooklyn, NY 11217	(718) 237–2211
445 Neptune Avenue, 1st Floor, Brooklyn, NY 11224	(718) 373–0033

Counties: KINGS (part), QUEENS (part). Population (2010), 713,512.

ZIP Codes: 11201, 11205–08, 11210, 11212–13, 11216–17, 11221, 11224, 11233–36, 11238–39, 11414, 11416–17

* * *

NINTH DISTRICT

YVETTE D. CLARKE, Democrat, of Brooklyn, NY; born in Brooklyn, November 21, 1964; education: attended Edward R. Murrow High School; attended Oberlin College; professional: legislative aide to New York State Senator Velmanette Montgomery; executive assistant to New York Assemblywoman Barbara Clark; staff assistant, New York State Workers' Compensation Board Chair Barbara Patton; Director of Youth Programs, Hospital League/Local 1199 Training and Upgrading Fund; Director of Business Development for the Bronx Empowerment Zone (BOEDC); member of City Council of New York, 2001–06; committees: Energy and Commerce; Ethics; Small Business; elected to the 110th Congress on November 7, 2006; reelected to each succeeding Congress.

Office Listings

http://www.clarke.house.gov   twitter: @yvetteclarke
https://www.facebook.com/repyvettedclarke

2351 Rayburn House Office Building, Washington, DC 20515	(202) 225–6231
Chief of Staff.—Shelley Davis.	FAX: 226–0112
Legislative Director.—Asi Ofosu.	
123 Linden Boulevard, 4th Floor, Brooklyn, NY 11226	(718) 287–1142

Counties: KINGS (part). Population (2010), 717,708.

ZIP Codes: 11203, 11210, 11212–13, 11216–18, 11225–26, 11229–30, 11233–36, 11238

* * *

TENTH DISTRICT

JERROLD NADLER, Democrat, of New York, NY; born in Brooklyn, NY, June 13, 1947; education: graduated from Stuyvesant High School, 1965; B.A., Columbia University, 1970; J.D., Fordham University, 1978; professional: New York State Assembly, 1977–92; member: ACLU; NARAL Pro-Choice America; AIPAC; National Organization for Women; Assistant Whip; married: 1976; one child; committees: Judiciary; Transportation and Infrastructure; elected to the 102nd Congress on November 3, 1992, to fill the vacancy caused by the death of Representative Ted Weiss; at the same time elected to the 103rd Congress; reelected to each succeeding Congress.

Office Listings

http://www.nadler.house.gov

2109 Rayburn House Office Building, Washington, DC 20515	(202) 225–5635
Director.—John Doty.	FAX: 225–6923
201 Varick Street, Suite 669, New York, NY 10014	(212) 367–7350
Chief of Staff.—Amy Rutkin.	
6605 Fort Hamilton Parkway, NY 11229	(718) 373–3198

Counties: KINGS (part), NEW YORK (part). Population (2010), 716,172.

ZIP Codes: 10001, 10003–08, 10011–14, 10018–19, 10021, 10023–25, 10027–28, 10036, 10038, 10041, 10043, 10045, 10048, 10060, 10065, 10069, 10075, 10080–81, 10087, 10090, 10101–02, 10104–09, 10115–18, 10121–23, 10125, 10129–30, 10132–33, 10138, 10166, 10175–76, 10178, 10199, 10203, 10212–13, 10242, 10249, 10256–61, 10265, 10268–75, 10277–82, 10285–86, 11102, 11202, 11204, 11214, 11218–20, 11223, 11228, 11230–32, 11245, 11247

* * *

ELEVENTH DISTRICT

DANIEL M. DONOVAN, JR., Republican, of Staten Island, NY; born in Staten Island, November 6, 1956; education: B.S., St. John's University, Staten Island, NY; J.D., Fordham University School of Law, 1988; professional: Assistant District Attorney, Manhattan DA; Chief of Staff and Deputy Borough President, Office of the Staten Island Borough President; District Attorney, Richmond County, NY; religion: Roman Catholic; committees: Foreign Affairs; Homeland Security; elected to the 114th Congress on May 5, 2015, by special election, to fill the vacancy caused by the resignation of U.S. Representative Michael G. Grimm.

Office Listings

http://www.donovan.house.gov

1725 Longworth House Office Building, Washington, DC 20515	(202) 225–3371
Chief of Staff.—Ronald Carara.	FAX: 226–1272
Deputy Chief of Staff.—Blaire Bartlett.	
Staff Assistant.—Joseph Kalmin.	
265 New Dorp Lane, 2nd Floor, Staten Island, NY 10306	(718) 351–1062
District Director.—Brendan Lantry.	
7308 13th Avenue, Brooklyn, NY 11228	(718) 630–5277
Brooklyn Manager.—Fran Vella-Marrone.	

Counties: KINGS (part), RICHMOND. POPULATION (2010), 717,707.

ZIP Codes: 10301–10, 10312–14, 11204, 11209, 11214, 11219–20, 11223, 11228, 11252

* * *

TWELFTH DISTRICT

CAROLYN B. MALONEY, Democrat, of New York City, NY; born in Greensboro, NC, February 19, 1946; education: B.A., Greensboro College, Greensboro, NC, 1968; professional: various positions, New York City Board of Education, 1970–77; legislative aide, New York State Assembly, senior program analyst, 1977–79; executive director of advisory council, 1979–82; director of special projects, New York State Senate Office of the Minority Leader; New York City council member, 1982–93; chairperson, New York City Council Committee on Contracts; member: Council Committee on Aging, National Organization of Women, Common Cause, Sierra Club, Americans for Democratic Action, New York City Council Committee on Housing and Buildings, Citizens Union, Grand Central Business Improvement District, Harlem Urban Development Corporation (1982–91), Commission on Early Childhood Development Programs, Council of Senior Citizen Centers of New York City (1982–87); widowed (Clifton H.W. Maloney); children: Virginia Marshall Maloney and Christina Paul Maloney; committees: Financial Services; Oversight and Government Reform; Joint Economic Committee; elected on November 3, 1992, to the 103rd Congress; reelected to each succeeding Congress.

Office Listings

http://www.maloney.house.gov   twitter: @repmaloney

2308 Rayburn House Office Building, Washington, DC 20515	(202) 225–7944
Chief of Staff.—Michael Iger.	FAX: 225–4709
Legislative Director.—Elizabeth Darnall.	
Executive Assistant.—Rebecca Tulloch.	
1651 Third Avenue, Suite 311, New York, NY 10128	(212) 860–0606
31–19 Newtown Avenue, Astoria, NY 11102	(718) 932–1804
619 Lorimer Street, Brooklyn, NY 11211	(718) 349–5972

Counties: KINGS (part), New York (part), QUEENS (part). CITIES AND NEIGHBORHOODS: Astoria, Brooklyn, Greenpoint, Long Island City, Manhattan, Queens, Roosevelt Island, and Williamsburg. Population (2010), 712,053.

ZIP Codes: 10001–03, 10009, 10010–12, 10016–19, 10020–22, 10028–29, 10035–36, 10044, 10055, 10065, 10075, 10087, 10103–07, 10110–13, 10118–19, 10120–21, 10123–24, 10128, 10130–31, 10150–56, 10158–59, 10162–69, 10170–79, 10199, 10259, 10261, 10276, 11101–13, 11106, 11109, 11206, 11211, 11222, 11249, 11377–78

* * *

THIRTEENTH DISTRICT

CHARLES B. RANGEL, Democrat-Liberal, of New York, NY; born in Harlem, NY, June 11, 1930; attended DeWitt Clinton High School; served in the U.S. Army, 1948–52; awarded the Purple Heart, Bronze Star for Valor, U.S. and Korean presidential citations, and three battle stars while serving in combat with the Second Infantry Division in Korea; honorably discharged with rank of staff sergeant; after military duty, completed high school, 1953; graduated from New York University School of Commerce, student under the G.I. bill; 1957 dean's list; graduated from St. John's University School of Law, dean's list student under a full three-year scholarship, 1960; lawyer; admitted to practice in the courts of the State of New York, U.S. Federal Court, Southern District of New York, and U.S. Customs Court; appointed assistant U.S. attorney, Southern District of New York, 1961; legal counsel, New York City Housing and Redevelopment Board, Neighborhood Conservation Bureau; general counsel, National Advisory Commission on Selective Service, 1966; served two terms in the New York State Assembly, 1966–70; active in 369th Veterans Association; Community Education Program; Martin Luther King, Jr. Democratic Club; married: Alma Carter; two children: Steven and Alicia; committees: Ways and Means; Joint Committee on Taxation; elected to the 92nd Congress, November 3, 1970; reelected to each succeeding Congress.

Office Listings

http://www.rangel.house.gov   http://www.twitter.com/cbrangel
http://www.facebook.com/cbrangel

2354 Rayburn House Office Building, Washington, DC 20515	(202) 225–4365
Counsel/Chief of Staff.—Vacant.	FAX: 225–0816
163 West 125th Street, Room 507, New York, NY 10027	(212) 663–3900
District Director.—Geoffrey Eaton.	

Counties: BRONX (part), NEW YORK (part). Population (2012), 738,943.

ZIP Codes: 10025 (part), 10026–27, 10029–35, 10037, 10039–40, 10453, 10458, 10463, 10467–68

* * *

FOURTEENTH DISTRICT

JOSEPH CROWLEY, Democrat, of Elmhurst, Queens, NY; born in Woodside, NY, March 16, 1962; education: graduated, Power Memorial High School, 1981; B.A., political science and communications, Queens College (City University of New York), Flushing, NY, 1985; professional: elected to the New York State Assembly, 1986–98; religion: Roman Catholic; married: Kasey Nilson; three children; founder and current chair of the Bangladesh Caucus; two-time co-chair of Congressional Caucus on India and Indian Americans; co-chair of the Ad Hoc Committee on Irish Affairs; serving in elected leadership of the U.S. House of Representatives as vice-chair of the House Democratic Caucus; committees: Ways and Means; elected to the 106th Congress; reelected to each succeeding Congress.

Office Listings

http://crowley.house.gov   twitter: @repjoecrowley   www.facebook.com/repjoecrowley

1436 Longworth House Office Building, Washington, DC 20510	(202) 225–3965
Chief of Staff.—Kate Keating.	FAX: 225–1909
Deputy Chief of Staff.—Jeremy Woodrum.	
Legislative Director.—Nicole Cohen.	
82–11 37th Avenue, Suite 402, Jackson Heights, NY 11372	(718) 779–1400
2800 Bruckner Boulevard, Suite 301, Bronx, NY 10465	(718) 931–1400

Counties: BRONX (part), QUEENS (part). Population (2010), 717,708.

ZIP Codes: 10458, 10460–62, 10464–67, 10469, 10475, 11101–05, 11354, 11356–58, 11368–73, 11375, 11377

* * *

FIFTEENTH DISTRICT

JOSÉ E. SERRANO, Democrat, of Bronx, NY; born in Mayagüez, PR, October 24, 1943; education: Dodge Vocational High School, Bronx, NY; attended Lehman College, City University of New York, NY; served with the U.S. Army Medical Corps, 1964–66; employed by the Manufacturers Hanover Bank, 1961–69; Community School District 7, 1969–74; New York State Assemblyman, 1974–90; chairman, Consumer Affairs Committee, 1979–83; chairman, Education Committee, 1983–90; religion: Roman Catholic; five children: Lisa, José Marco, Justine, Jonathan, and Benjamin; committees: Appropriations; elected to the 101st Congress, by special election, March 28, 1990, to fill the vacancy caused by the resignation of Robert Garcia; reelected to each succeeding Congress.

Office Listings

http://serrano.house.gov   http://www.facebook.com/repjoseserrano
https://instagram.com/repjoseserrano   http://www.youtube.com/user/congressmanserrano
http://twitter.com/repjoseserrano

2227 Rayburn House Office Building, Washington, DC 20515 .... (202) 225–4361
     Chief Administrator.—Idalia Domínguez de Marty.   FAX: 225–6001
     Chief of Staff.—Matthew Alpert.
     Scheduler.—Frederick Vélez.
     Communications Director.—Paola Amador.
     Legislative Counsel.—Angel Nigaglioni.
     Legislative Assistant.—Lukogho Kasomo.
1231 Lafayette Street, 4th Floor, Bronx, NY 10474 .... (718) 620–0084
     District Director.—Amanda Septimo.

Counties: BRONX COUNTY (part). CITIES AND TOWNSHIPS: Bronx. Population (2013), 747,271.

ZIP Codes: 10451–60, 10462, 10468, 10472–74

* * *

SIXTEENTH DISTRICT

ELIOT L. ENGEL, Democrat, of Bronx, NY; born in Bronx, February 18, 1947; education: B.A., Hunter-Lehman College, 1969; M.A., City University of New York, 1973; J.D., New York Law School, 1987; professional: teacher and counselor in the New York City public school system, 1969–77; elected to the New York legislature, 1977–88; chaired the Assembly Committee on Alcoholism and Substance Abuse and Subcommittee on Mitchell-Lama Housing (twelve years prior to his election to Congress); member: co-chairman, Albanian Issues Caucus; board member, Congressional Ad Hoc Committee on Irish Affairs; Congressional Human Rights Caucus; Long Island Sound Caucus; Oil and National Security Caucus; EU Caucus; Fragile X Caucus; Tuberculosis Elimination Caucus; Allergy and Asthma Caucus; New Democrat Coalition; Animal Protection Caucus; Renewable and Energy Efficiency Caucus; Pro-Choice Caucus; Task Force on Anti-Semitism; HIV / AIDS Caucus; Arts Caucus; Diabetes Caucus; married: Patricia Ennis, 1980; three children; committees: ranking member, Foreign Affairs; Energy and Commerce; elected on November 8, 1988 to the 101st Congress; reelected to each succeeding Congress.

Office Listings

http://www.engel.house.gov

2462 Rayburn House Office Building, Washington, DC 20515 .... (202) 225–2464
     Administrative Assistant.—E.H. "Ned" Michalek.   FAX: 225–5513
     Office Manager.—Heather Beckman.
     Legislative Director.—Brian Skretny.
3655 Johnson Avenue, Bronx, NY 10463 .... (718) 796–9700
                                                  FAX: 796–5134
     Chief of Staff.—William F. Weitz.
6 Gramatan Avenue, Suite 205, Mt. Vernon, NY 10550 .... (914) 699–4100
                                                  FAX: 699–3646
177 Dreiser Loop, Room 3, Bronx, NY 10475 .... (718) 320–2314
                                                  FAX: 320–2047

Counties: BRONX (part), WESTCHESTER (part). CITIES AND TOWNSHIPS: Parts of Bronx, Eastchester, Greenburgh, Mamaroneck, Mount Vernon, New Rochelle, Pelham, Rye, Scarsdale, and Yonkers. Population (2010), 717,707.

ZIP Codes: 10463, 10466–67, 10469–71, 10475, 10502, 10528, 10530, 10538, 10543, 10550–53, 10557–58, 10580, 10583, 10701–05, 10707–10, 10801–02, 10804–05

* * *

SEVENTEENTH DISTRICT

NITA M. LOWEY, Democrat, of Harrison, NY; born in New York, NY, July 5, 1937; education: graduated, Bronx High School of Science, 1955; B.A., Mount Holyoke College, 1959; assistant to the Secretary of State for Economic Development and Neighborhood Preservation, and deputy director, Division of Economic Opportunity, 1975–85; Assistant Secretary of State, 1985–87; member: boards of directors, Close-Up Foundation; Effective Parenting Information for Children; Windward School, Downstate (New York Region); Westchester

Jewish Conference; Westchester Opportunity Program; National Committee of the Police Corps; Women's Network of the YWCA; Legal Awareness for Women; National Women's Political Caucus of Westchester; American Jewish Committee of Westchester; married: Stephen Lowey, 1961; children: Dana, Jacqueline, and Douglas; committees: Appropriations; elected on November 8, 1988 to the 101st Congress; reelected to each succeeding Congress.

Office Listings

http://www.lowey.house.gov   twitter.com/nitalowey   www.facebook.com/replowey

2365 Rayburn House Office Building, Washington, DC 20515 .... (202) 225–6506
    Chief of Staff.—Elizabeth Stanley.   FAX: 225–0546
    Executive Assistant.—Kelly Healton.
    Legislative Director.—Chris Bigelow.
    Press Secretary.—Matt Wojtkun.
222 Mamaroneck Avenue, Suite 312, White Plains, NY 10605 .... (914) 428–1707
67 North Main Street, Suite 101, New City, NY 10956 .... (845) 639–3485
    District Director.—Patricia Keegan.

Counties: ROCKLAND (all), WESTCHESTER (part). CITIES AND TOWNSHIPS: Briarcliff Manor; Buchanan; Chappaqua, Cortlandt, Cortlandt Manor, Crompond, Croton-on-Hudson, Dobbs Ferry, Elmsford, East Irvington, Fairview, Harrison, Hartsdale, Haverstraw, Hawthorne, Irvington, Jefferson Valley, Millwood, Mohegan Lake, Mount Kisco, Mount Pleasant, New City, North White Plains, Ossining, Peekskill, Pleasantville, Pocantico Hills, Port Chester, Purchase, Rye Brook, Scarborough, Sleepy Hollow, Tarrytown, Thornwood, Valhalla, Verplanck, West Harrison, West Haverstraw, White Plains, and Yorktown Heights. Population (2010), 717,708.

ZIP Codes: 10510–11, 10514, 10517, 10520, 10522–23, 10528, 10530, 10532–33, 10535, 10546–49, 10562, 10566–67, 10570, 10573, 10577, 10580, 10588, 10591, 10594–96, 10598, 10601, 10603–07, 10901, 10913, 10920, 10923, 10927, 10931, 10952, 10954, 10956, 10960, 10964–65, 10968, 10970, 10974, 10976–77, 10980, 10982–84, 10986, 10989, 10993–94

* * *

EIGHTEENTH DISTRICT

SEAN PATRICK MALONEY, Democrat, of Cold Spring, NY; born in Sherbrooke, Quebec, July 30, 1966; education: graduated, Hanover High School, Hanover, NH, 1984; B.A., University of Virginia, 1988; J.D., University of Virginia, 1992; professional: Deputy White House Staff Secretary, 1997–99; White House Staff Secretary and Assistant to the President of the United States, 1999–2000; Chief Operating Officer, Kiodex, Inc., 2000–03; first deputy secretary to the Governor of New York, 2007–08; corporate partner, Kirkland & Ellis LLP, 2009–11; partner, Orrick, Herrington & Sutcliffe LLP; husband, Randy Florke, 1992–present; children: Jesus, Daley, and Essie; committees: Agriculture; Transportation and Infrastructure; elected to the 113th Congress on November 6, 2012; reelected to the 114th Congress on November 4, 2014.

Office Listings

http://seanmaloney.house.gov

1529 Longworth House Office Building, Washington, DC 20515 .... (202) 225–5441
    Chief of Staff.—Timothy Persico.   FAX: 225–3289
    Executive Assistant.—Molly Carey.
    Legislative Director.—Jennifer Steel.
    Communications Director.—Alexandra Miller.
123 Grand Street, 2nd Floor, Newburgh, NY 12550 .... (845) 561–1259
    District Director.—Mike Limperopulos.   FAX: 561–2890

Counties: NORTHERN WESTCHESTER (part), ORANGE, PUTNAM, SOUTHERN DUTCHESS (part). CITIES AND TOWNSHIPS: Arlington, Balmville, Beacon, Beaver Dam Lake, Bedford, Bedford Hills, Brewster Hill, Brewster, Brinckerhoff, Carmel Hamlet, Chester, Cold Spring, Cornwall-on-Hudson, Crown Heights, Fairview, Firthcliffe, Fishkill, Florida, Fort Montgomery, Gardnertown, Golden's Bridge, Goshen, Greenwood Lake, Harriman, Heritage Hills, Highland Falls, Hillside Lake, Hopewell Junction, Katonah, Kiryas Joel, Lake Carmel, Lincolndale, Mahopac, Maybrook, Mechanicstown, Merritt Park, Middletown, Monroe, Montgomery, Mountain Lodge Park, Myers Corner, Nelsonville, New Windsor, Newburgh, Orange Lake, Otisville, Peach Lake, Pine Bush, Port Jervis, Poughkeepsie, Putnam Lake, Red Oaks Mill, Salisbury Mills, Scotchtown, Scotts Corners, Shenorock, South Blooming Grove, Spackenkill, Titusville, Tuxedo Park, Vails Gate, Walden, Walton Park, Wappingers Falls, Warwick, Washington Heights, Washingtonville, West Point, and Woodbury. Population (2010), 717,707.

ZIP Codes: 10501, 10504–07, 10509, 10512, 10516, 10518–19, 10524, 10526–27, 10536–37, 10540–42, 10549, 10560, 10562, 10576, 10578–79, 10587, 10589–90, 10597–98, 10910, 10912, 10914–19, 10921–22, 10924–26, 10928, 10930, 10932–33, 10940–41, 10949–50, 10953, 10958–59, 10963, 10969, 10973–75, 10979, 10981, 10985, 10987–88, 12508, 12511–12, 12518, 12520, 12524, 12527, 12531, 12533, 12537–38, 12540, 12542–43, 12549–53, 12555, 12563–64, 12566, 12569, 12575, 12577, 12582, 12584, 12586, 12589–90, 12601–04, 12721, 12729, 12746, 12771, 12780, 12785

* * *

NINETEENTH DISTRICT

CHRISTOPHER GIBSON, Republican, Kinderhook, NY; born in Rockville Centre, NY, May 13, 1964; education: B.A., history, *magna cum laude,* ROTC Commission, Siena College, Loudonville, NY, 1986; M.P.A., government, Cornell University, Ithaca, NY, 1995; Ph.D., government, Cornell University, Ithaca, 1998; professional: military, colonel, U.S. Army; Hoover National Security Affairs Fellowship, Stanford University; Congressional Fellow; awards: 2 Legions of Merit, 4 Bronze Star Medals; Purple Heart; Combat Infantryman's Badge with Star; Master Parachutist Badge, Ranger Tab; book: *Securing the State*; religion: Roman Catholic; married: Mary Jo; children: Katie, Maggie, and Connor; committees: Agriculture; Armed Services; Small Business; elected to the 112th Congress on November 2, 2010; reelected to each succeeding Congress.

Office Listings

http://www.gibson.house.gov

1708 Longworth House Office Building, Washington, DC 20515	(202) 225–5614
Chief of Staff.—Stephanie Valle.	FAX: 225–1168
Deputy Chief of Staff.—Vacant.	
District Director.—Steve Bulger.	
Legislative Director.—Rebecca Shaw.	
Scheduler / Executive Assistant.—Megan Paulsen.	
25 Chestnut Street, Cooperstown, NY 13326	(607) 282–4002
2 Hudson Street, Kinderhook, NY 12106	(518) 610–8133
4254 Albany Post Road, Route 9, Hyde Park, NY 12538	(845) 698–0132
111 Main Street, Delhi, NY 13753	(607) 746–9537
721 Broadway, Kingston, NY 12401	(845) 514–2322
92 Sullivan Avenue, Liberty, NY 12754	(845) 747–9261

Counties: OTSEGO, DELAWARE, SULLIVAN, ULSTER, COLUMBIA, GREENE, SCHOHARIE, MONTGOMERY (part), RENSSELAER (part), DUTCHESS (part), and BROOME (part). Population (2010), 717,708.

ZIP Codes: 12015, 12017, 12022–24, 12029, 12031, 12033, 12035–37, 12042–43, 12050–53, 12057–58, 12060–63, 12110, 12115–16, 12118, 12121, 12153–57, 12160, 12165–68, 12172–76, 12180–82, 12184–85, 12187, 12189, 12192, 12194–98, 12401, 12404–05, 12407, 12409–21, 12435–36, 12438, 12451–61, 12463–75, 12481–82, 12485–87, 12489–96, 12498, 12501–04, 12506–07, 12561, 12563–65, 12592, 12594, 12601, 12603, 12701, 12719–27, 12732–34, 12736–38, 12740–45, 12747, 12749–52, 12754, 12758–60, 12762–64, 12766–67, 12776–79, 12781, 12783–92, 12816, 13315, 13317, 13459, 13468, 13475, 13482, 13485, 13755–57, 13774, 13786, 13788, 13796, 13804, 13806–10

* * *

TWENTIETH DISTRICT

PAUL D. TONKO, Democrat, of Amsterdam, NY; born in Amsterdam, NY, June 18, 1949; education: graduated, Amsterdam High School, Amsterdam, NY, 1967; B.S. degree, mechanical and industrial engineering, Clarkson University, Potsdam, NY, 1971; professional: engineer, NYS Department of Transportation; engineer, NYS Department of Public Service; Montgomery County Board of Supervisors, 1976–83; chairman, Montgomery County Board of Supervisors, 1981–83; NYS Assembly, 1983–2007; chairman, NYS Assembly Standing Committee on Energy, 1992–2007; President & CEO, NYS Energy Research and Development Authority, 2007–08; caucuses: co-chair, Sustainable Energy and Environment Coalition, co-chair, Congressional Horse Caucus; committees: Energy and Commerce; Science, Space, and Technology; elected to the 111th Congress on November 4, 2008; reelected to each succeeding Congress.

Office Listings

http://www.tonko.house.gov   twitter: @reppaultonko
https://www.facebook.com/reppaultonko

2463 Rayburn House Office Building, Washington, DC 20515	(202) 225–5076
Chief of Staff.—Clinton Britt.	FAX: 225–5077
Communications Director.—Sean Magers.	
Legislative Director.—Jean Fruci.	
Director of Operations.—David Mastrangelo.	
Legislative Assistants: Emily Duhovny, Brendan Larkin, Jeff Morgan.	
Legislative Correspondent.—James Johnson.	
61 Columbia Street, 4th Floor, Albany, NY 12210	(518) 465–0700
105 Jay Street (Schenectady City Hall), Room 15, Schenectady, NY 12305	(518) 374–4547

Office Listings—Continued

61 Church Street (Amsterdam City Hall), Room 309, Amsterdam, NY 12010 .... (518) 843–3400

Counties: ALBANY, MONTGOMERY (part), RENSSELAER (part), SARATOGA (part), and SCHENECTADY. Population (2010), 720,133.

ZIP Codes: 12007–10, 12016, 12019–20, 12023, 12027, 12033, 12041, 12045–47, 12053–56, 12059, 12061, 12065–70, 12072, 12074, 12077, 12083–87, 12095, 12107, 12110, 12118, 12120, 12122–23, 12128, 12137, 12141, 12143–44, 12147–48, 12150–51, 12157–61, 12166, 12170, 12177, 12180–83, 12186, 12188–89, 12193, 12196, 12198, 12201–12, 12220, 12222–24, 12226–50, 12252, 12255–57, 12260–61, 12288, 12301–09, 12325, 12345, 12460, 12469, 12866

* * *

TWENTY–FIRST DISTRICT

ELISE M. STEFANIK, Republican, of Willsboro, NY; born in Albany, NY, July 2, 1984; graduated from Albany Academy for Girls, Albany, NY, 2002; B.A., Harvard University, Cambridge, MA, 2006; professional: staff, President George W. Bush Administration, 2006–09; campaign aide; businesswoman; committees: Armed Services; Education and the Workforce; elected to the 114th Congress on November 4, 2014.

Office Listings

https://stefanik.house.gov

512 Cannon House Office Building, Washington, DC 20515 .... (202) 225–4611
Chief of Staff.—Lindley Kratovil.
Communications Director.—Tom Flanagin.
Legislative Director.—Chris Perry.
136 Glen Street, Glens Falls, NY 12801 .... (518) 743–0964
District Director.—Anthony Pileggi.
23 Durkee Street, Suite C, Plattsburgh, NY 12901 .... (518) 561–2324
120 Washington Street, Suite 200, Watertown, NY 13601 .... (315) 782–3150

Counties: CLINTON, ESSEX, FRANKLIN, FULTON, HAMILTON, HERKIMER, JEFFERSON, LEWIS, SARATOGA, ST. LAWRENCE, WARREN, AND WASHINGTON. Population (2013), 716,340.

Zip Codes: 12010 (part), 12020 (part), 12025, 12028 (part), 12032, 12057 (part), 12068 (part), 12070 (part), 12074 (part), 12078, 12086 (part), 12094 (part), 12095 (part), 12108, 12117, 12118 (part), 12134, 12139, 12154 (part), 12164, 12170 (part), 12185 (part), 12190, 12801, 12803–04, 12808–12, 12814–17, 12819, 12821–24, 12827–28, 12831–32, 12833 (part), 12834–39, 12841–47, 12849–53, 12855–65, 12866 (part), 12870–74, 12878, 12883–87, 12901, 12903, 12910–14, 12916–24, 12926–30, 12932–37, 12939, 12941–46, 12950, 12952–53, 12955–62, 12964–67, 12969–70, 12972–81, 12983, 12985–87, 12989, 12992–93, 12996–98, 13305, 13312, 13316, 13324 (part), 13325, 13327, 13329, 13331, 13338 (part), 13339 (part), 13343, 13345, 13353, 13360, 13367–68, 13404, 13420, 13431 (part), 13433, 13436–38, 13452 (part), 13454, 13470, 13471, 13472–73, 13489 (part), 13601–03, 13605–08, 13612–26, 13628, 13630, 13633–43, 13646–48, 13650–52, 13654–56, 13658–62, 13664–70, 13672–82, 13684–85, 13687, 13690–97

* * *

TWENTY–SECOND DISTRICT

RICHARD L. HANNA, Republican, of Barneveld, NY; born in Utica, January 25, 1951; education: graduated from Whitesboro High School, 1969; B.A., economics and political science with honors, Reed College, Portland, OR, 1976; professional: owner and president of Hanna Construction; married: two children; committees: Small Business; Transportation and Infrastructure; Joint Economic Committee; elected to the 112th Congress on November 2, 2010; reelected to each succeeding Congress.

Office Listings

http://www.hanna.house.gov   twitter: @reprichardhanna
https://www.facebook.com/reprichardhanna

319 Cannon House Office Building, Washington, DC 20515 .... (202) 225–3665
Chief of Staff.—Justin Stokes.   FAX: 225–1891
Executive Assistant.—Jaclyn Schwinghamer.
Senior Advisor.—Renee Gamela.
Deputy Chief of Staff.—Andrew Brady.
District Director.—Patricia Vail Dellonte.
258 Genesee Street, First Floor, Utica, NY 13502 .... (315) 724–9740
                                                                                                          FAX: 724–9746
49 Court Street, Metro Center, Suite 230, Binghamton, NY 13901 .... (607) 723–0212

Office Listings—Continued

FAX: 723–0215

Counties: BROOME (part), CHENANGO, CORTLAND, HERKIMER, MADISON, ONEIDA, OSWEGO (part), TIOGA (part), TOMPKINS (part). CITIES, TOWNS AND VILLAGES: Binghamton, Camden, Cortland, Cortlandville, Forestport, Little Falls, New Berlin, Mexico, Norwich, Oneida, Sandy Creek, Sherrill, Sullivan, Utica, Vestal, and Windsor. Population (2010), 717,708.

ZIP Codes: 13028, 13030, 13032, 13035–37, 13040, 13042, 13044–45, 13052–54, 13061, 13072, 13076–77, 13082–83, 13087, 13101, 13103–04, 13114, 13122–24, 13126, 13131–32, 13134, 13136, 13141–42, 13144–45, 13155, 13157–59, 13162–63, 13167, 13301–04, 13308–10, 13313–14, 13316, 13318–19, 13321–24, 13328, 13332, 13334, 13338–41, 13346, 13350, 13352, 13354–55, 13357, 13361–65, 13402–03, 13406–09, 13411, 13413, 13416–18, 13421, 13424–25, 13431, 13435, 13437–41, 13456, 13460–61, 13464, 13469, 13471, 13475–78, 13480, 13483–86, 13489–95, 13501–02, 13661, 13730, 13732–33, 13736, 13744, 13746, 13748, 13760, 13777–78, 13780, 13784, 13787, 13790, 13794–95, 13797, 13801–03, 13809, 13811–13, 13815, 13826–27, 13830, 13832–33, 13835, 13841, 13843–44, 13850, 13862–63, 13865, 13901–05

* * *

TWENTY-THIRD DISTRICT

TOM REED, Republican, of Corning, NY; born in Joliet, IL, November 18, 1971; education: graduated, B.A., Alfred University, Alfred, NY, 1993; J.D., Ohio Northern University College of Law, Ada, OH, 1996; professional: lawyer, private practice, Law Office of Thomas W. Reed II; business owner; mayor of Corning, NY, 2008–09; religion: Catholic; married: wife, Jean, and two children; committees: Ways and Means; elected November 2, 2010, to the 111th Congress by special election to fill the vacancy caused by the resignation of United States Representative Eric J.J. Massa; subsequently elected to a full term in the 112th Congress on November 2, 2010; reelected to each succeeding Congress.

Office Listings

http://www.reed.house.gov

2437 Rayburn House Office Building, Washington, DC 20515	(202) 225–3161
Chief of Staff.—Tim Kolpien.	FAX: 226–6599
Deputy Chief of Staff.—Steve Pfrang.	
Legislative Director.—Drew Wayne.	
Communications Director.—Brandy Brown.	
District Director.—Joe Sempolinski.	
89 West Market Street, Corning, NY 14830	(607) 654–7566
433 Exchange Street, Geneva, NY 14456	(315) 759–5229
401 East State Street, Suite 304–1, Ithaca, NY 14850	(607) 222–2027
2 East 2nd Street, Suite 300, Jamestown, NY 14701	(716) 708–6369
One Bluebird Square, Olean, NY 14760	(716) 379–8434

Counties: ALLEGANY, CATTARAUGUS, CHAUTAUQUA, CHEMUNG, ONTARIO (part), SCHUYLER, SENECA, STEUBEN, TIOGA (part), TOMPKINS, YATES. Population (2010), 717,707.

ZIP Codes: 13053, 13062, 13068, 13073, 13102, 13734, 13736, 13743, 13811–12, 13827, 13835, 13840, 13845, 13864, 14029, 14041–42, 14048, 14060, 14062–63, 14065, 14070, 14081, 14101, 14129, 14133, 14135–36, 14168, 14171, 14173, 14415, 14418, 14424, 14432, 14441, 14453, 14456, 14461, 14463, 14478, 14504, 14507, 14512, 14518, 14527, 14529, 14532, 14537, 14544, 14547–48, 14561, 14572, 14701–02, 14706–24, 14726–45, 14747–48, 14750–58, 14760, 14766–67, 14769–70, 14772, 14774–75, 14777–79, 14781–88, 14801–10, 14812–27, 14830, 14837–43, 14845, 14850, 14854–59, 14861, 14863–65, 14867, 14869–74, 14876–87, 14889, 14891–95, 14897–98, 14901–05, 14925

* * *

TWENTY-FOURTH DISTRICT

JOHN KATKO, Republican, of Camillus, NY; education: graduated from Bishop Ludden High School; B.A., Niagara University, *cum laude*; J.D., Syracuse University College of Law, *cum laude*; Federal Prosecutor (most recently as an Assistant U.S. Attorney with the Northern District of New York) for over twenty years; married: wife of over 27 years, Robin; three sons; committees: Homeland Security; Transportation and Infrastructure; elected to the 114th Congress on November 4, 2014.

Office Listings

https://katko.house.gov

1123 Longworth House Office Building, Washington, DC 20515	(202) 225–3701

Office Listings—Continued

Chief of Staff.—Brad Gentile.
Executive Assistant.—Jordan Lane.
440 South Warren Street, 7th Floor Suite 711, Syracuse, NY 13202 .... (315) 423–5657
    FAX: 423–5604
71 Genesee Street, Auburn, NY 13021 .... (315) 253–4068
    FAX: 253–2435
7376 State Route 31, Lyons, NY 14489 (open Wednesdays 10 a.m. until 4 p.m.).
13 West Oneida Street, 2nd Floor, Oswego, NY 13126 (open Wednesdays 10 a.m. until 3
p.m.).

Counties: ONONDAGA, CAYUGA, WAYNE, OSWEGO (part). Population (2010) 717,707.

ZIP Codes: 13020–21, 13024, 13026–31, 13033–37, 13039, 13041, 13045, 13051–52, 13057, 13060, 13063–64, 13066, 13069, 113071, 13073–74, 13077–78, 138080–84, 13088, 13090, 13092, 13102, 13104, 13108, 13110–18, 13120, 13122, 13126, 13131–13132, 13135, 13138, 13140–41, 13143, 13146–47, 13152–53, 13156, 13158–60, 13164, 13166, 13202–12, 13214–15, 13219, 13224, 13290, 14433, 14450, 14489, 14502, 14505, 14551, 14555, 14568, 14580, 14589, 14590

* * *

TWENTY-FIFTH DISTRICT

LOUISE McINTOSH SLAUGHTER, Democrat, of Fairport, NY; born in Harlan County, KY, August 14, 1929; education: B.S. in microbiology (1951) and M.S. in public health (1953), University of Kentucky; elected to Monroe County Legislature, two terms, 1976–79; elected to New York State Assembly, two terms, 1982–86; Distinguished Public Health Legislation Award, American Public Health Association, 1998; widowed: Robert Slaughter; three daughters; seven grandchildren; committees: ranking member, Rules; elected to the 100th Congress on November 4, 1986; reelected to each succeeding Congress.

Office Listings

http://www.louise.house.gov   https://twitter.com/louiseslaughter
https://www.facebook.com/replouiseslaughter

2469 Rayburn House Office Building, Washington, DC 20515 .... (202) 225–3615
    Chief of Staff.—Liam Fitzsimmons.   FAX: 225–7822
    Legislative Director.—Cheri Hoffman.
    Press Assistant.—Katie Condello.
    Scheduler.—Yodit Tewelde
3120 Federal Building, 100 State Street, Rochester, NY 14614 .... (585) 232–4850
    FAX: 232–1954

Counties: MONROE (majority). CITIES AND TOWNSHIPS: Brighton, Brockport, Chili, Churchville, Clarkson, East Rochester, Fairport, Gates, Greece, Hamlin, Henrietta, Hilton, Irondequoit, Ogden, Parma, Penfield, Perinton, Pittsford, Riga, Rochester, Rush, Scottsville, Spencerport, Sweden, and Webster. Population (2013), 724,587.

ZIP Codes: 14416, 14420, 14428, 14445, 14450, 14464, 14467–68, 14502, 14514, 14519, 14526, 14534, 14543, 14546, 14559, 14564, 14580, 14586, 14604–10, 14612–13, 14615–18, 14620–26

* * *

TWENTY-SIXTH DISTRICT

BRIAN HIGGINS, Democrat, of Buffalo, NY; born in Buffalo, October 6, 1959; education: B.A., Buffalo State College, NY, 1984; M.P.A., Harvard University, Cambridge, MA, 1996; professional: lecturer, Buffalo State College; member of the Buffalo Common Council, 1988–93; member of the New York State Assembly, 1999–2004; married: Mary Jane Hannon; two children: John and Maeve; committees: Foreign Affairs; Homeland Security; elected to the 109th Congress on November 2, 2004; reelected to each succeeding Congress.

Office Listings

http://www.higgins.house.gov   twittter: @repbrianhiggins
www.facebook.com/repbrianhiggins

2459 Rayburn House Office Building, Washington, DC 20515 .... (202) 225–3306
    Chief of Staff.—Chuck Eaton.   FAX: 226–0347
    Chief of Staff/DC and Legislative Director.—Andy Tantillo.
    Communications Director.—Theresa Kennedy.
Larkin at Exchange, 726 Exchange Street, Suite 601, Buffalo, NY 14210 .... (716) 852–3501

Office Listings—Continued

640 Park Place, Niagara Falls, NY 14301 .... (716) 282–1274

Counties: ERIE (part), NIAGARA (part). CITIES AND TOWNSHIPS: Amherst (part), Buffalo, Cheektowaga, Grand Island, Lackawanna, Niagara Falls (part), North Tonawanda, Tonawanda (city), Tonawanda (township), and West Seneca. Population (2010), 717,707.

ZIP Codes: 14026, 14043, 14051, 14068, 14072, 14120, 14127, 14150–51, 14201–28, 14260, 14301–05

* * *

TWENTY-SEVENTH DISTRICT

CHRIS COLLINS, Republican of Clarence, NY; born in Schenectady, NY, May 20, 1950; graduated, Hendersonville High School, Hendersonville, NC, 1968; B.S.M.E., mechanical engineering, NC State University, Raleigh, NC, 1972; M.B.A., University of Alabama at Birmingham, Birmingham, AL, 1975; professional: businessman; elected as Erie County Executive of Erie County, NY, 2007; married to Mary Collins; children: Caitlin and Cameron; caucuses: Auto Industry Pension Task Force; Automotive Performance and Motorsports Caucus; Canada-U.S. Caucus; Dairy Farmers Caucus; Diabetes Caucus; Fire Services Caucus; General Aviation Caucus; House Manufacturing Caucus; International Conservation Caucus; House Small Brewers Caucus; Job Creators Caucus; Law Enforcement Caucus; Mitochondrial Disease Caucus; Morocco Caucus; National Guard and Reserve Components Caucus; Natural Gas Caucus; New York Defense Working Group; Northern Border Caucus; Pilot Caucus; Propane Caucus; Republican Israel Caucus; Republican Study Committee; Scouting Caucus; Small Business Caucus; Small Business Information Technology Caucus; Specialty Crop Caucus; STEM Education Caucus; Technology Transfer Caucus; Toy Caucus; committees: Energy and Commerce; elected to the 113th Congress on November 6, 2012; reelected to the 114th Congress on November 4, 2014.

Office Listings

http://www.chriscollins.house.gov

1117 Longworth House Office Building, Washington, DC 20515 .... (202) 225–5265
    Chief of Staff.—Christopher Grant.   FAX: 225–5910
    Executive Assistant.—Samantha Zager.
    Legislative Director.—Jeffrey Freeland.
    Communications Director.—Michael McAdams.
2813 Wehrle Drive, Suite 13, Williamsville, NY 14221 .... (716) 634–2324
    District Director.—Michael Kracker.
75 Main Street, Suite C, Geneseo, NY 14454 .... (585) 519–4002

Counties: ERIE (part), NIAGARA (part), ORLEANS (part), GENESEE, WYOMING, LIVINGSTON, ONTARIO, MONROE (part). Population (2010) 717,707.

ZIP Codes: 14001, 14004–06, 14008–13, 14020–21, 14024–28, 14030–40, 14043, 14047, 14051–52, 14054–59, 14061, 14066–67, 14069–70, 14075, 14080–83, 14085–86, 14091–92, 14094–95, 14098, 14102–05, 14107–13, 14120, 14125–27, 14130–32, 14134, 14139–41, 14143–45, 14167, 14169–70, 14172, 14174, 14218–19, 14221, 14224, 14228, 14270, 14304–05, 14411, 14414, 14416, 14420, 14422–25, 14427–29, 14435, 14437, 14443, 14452–54, 14462, 14464, 14466–72, 14475–77, 14479–82, 14485–88, 14506, 14508, 14510–12, 14517, 14522, 14525, 14530, 14533–34, 14536, 14539, 14543, 14545–46, 14548–50, 14556–58, 14560, 14564, 14569, 14571–72, 14585–86, 14591–92, 14735, 14822, 14836, 14846, 14884

NORTH CAROLINA

(Population 2010, 9,535,483)

SENATORS

RICHARD BURR, Republican, of Winston-Salem, NC; born in Charlottesville, VA, November 30, 1955; education: R.J. Reynolds High School, Winston-Salem, NC, 1974; B.A., communications, Wake Forest University, Winston-Salem, NC, 1978; professional: sales manager, Carswell Distributing; member: Reynolds Rotary Club; board member, Brenner Children's Hospital; public service: U.S. House of Representatives, 1995–2005; served as vice-chairman of the Energy and Commerce Committee; married: Brooke Fauth, 1984; children: two sons; committees: chair, Select Committee on Intelligence; Finance; Health, Education, Labor, and Pensions; elected to the U.S. Senate on November 2, 2004; reelected to the U.S. Senate on November 2, 2010.

Office Listings

http://burr.senate.gov

217 Russell Senate Office Building, Washington, DC 20510	(202) 224–3154
Deputy Chief of Staff.—Polly Walker.	FAX: 228–2981
Legislative Director.—Natasha Hickman.	
2000 West First Street, Suite 508, Winston-Salem, NC 27104	(336) 631–5125
Chief of Staff.—Dean Myers.	
100 Coast Line Street, Room 210, Rocky Mount, NC 27804	(252) 977–9522
201 North Front Street, Suite 809, Wilmington, NC 28401	(910) 251 1058

* * *

THOM TILLIS, Republican, of Huntersville, NC; born in Jacksonville, FL, August 30, 1960; education: B.S., University of Maryland University College, 1997; professional: partner, IBM Global Business Services, 2002–09; partner, PricewaterhouseCoopers 1990–2002; public service: North Carolina State House Speaker, 2011–15, North Carolina State House, 2009–15; religion: Catholic; married: Susan Tillis; children: one daughter, one son; committees: Agriculture, Nutrition, and Forestry; Armed Services; Judiciary, Veterans' Affairs; Special Committee on Aging; elected to the U.S. Senate on November 4, 2014.

Office Listings

http://tillis.senate.gov　　　facebook: senatorthomtillis
twitter: @senthomtillis

185 Dirksen Senate Office Building, Washington, DC 20510	(202) 224–6342
Chief of Staff.—John Mashburn.	
Deputy Chief of Staff.—Chris Hayes.	
Communications Director.—Daniel Keylin.	
State Director.—Jordan Shaw.	
301 South Evans Street, Suite 102, Greenville, NC 27858	(252) 329–0371
310 New Bern Avenue, Suite 122, Raleigh, NC 27601	(919) 856–4630
1520 South Boulevard, Charlotte, NC 28203	(704) 334–2448

REPRESENTATIVES

FIRST DISTRICT

G. K. BUTTERFIELD, Democrat, of Wilson County, NC; born, April 27, 1947; education: North Carolina Central University, graduated in 1971, with degrees in sociology and political science; North Carolina Central University School of Law, graduated in 1974, with a Juris Doctor degree; military service: U.S. Army, 1968–1970; served as a Personnel Specialist; discharged with the rank of Specialist E–4; professional: attorney; private practice, 1974–1988; public service: elected to the North Carolina Superior Court bench in November, 1988; appointed on February 8, 2001, by Governor Michael F. Easley to the North Carolina Supreme Court; after leaving the Supreme Court, following the 2002 election, Governor Easley appointed Justice Butterfield as a Special Superior Court Judge; served until his retirement on May 7, 2004; organizations: North Carolina Bar Association; North Carolina Association of Black Lawyers; Wilson Opportunities Industrialization Center; religion: Baptist; appointed Chief Deputy

Whip, 110th Congress; chair, Congressional Black Caucus; committees: Energy and Commerce; elected to the 108th Congress, by special election, on July 20, 2004; elected to the 109th Congress on November 2, 2004; reelected to each succeeding Congress.

Office Listings

http://www.butterfield.house.gov

2305 Rayburn House Office Building, Washington, DC 20515 .... (202) 225–3101
    Chief of Staff.—Troy Clair.
    Communications Director.—Kim Atterbury.
    Scheduler.—Lindsey Bowen.
216 Northeast Nash Street, Suite B, Wilson, NC 27893 .... (252) 237–9816
411 West Chapel Hill Street, Suite 905, Durham, NC 27701.

Counties: BEAUFORT (part), BERTIE, CHOWAN (part), CRAVEN (part), DURHAM (part), EDGECOMBE (part), FRANKLIN (part), GATES (part), GRANVILLE, GREENE (part), HALIFAX, HERTFORD, LENOIR (part), MARTIN (part), NASH (part), NORTHAMPTON, PASQUOTANK (part), PERQUIMANS (part), PITT (part), VANCE (part), WARREN, WASHINGTON (part), WAYNE (part), WILSON (part). Population (2014), 724,668.

ZIP Codes: 27507, 27509, 27522, 27525, 27530–34, 27536–37, 27544, 27549, 27551, 27553, 27556, 27560, 27563, 27565, 27570, 27572, 27581, 27584, 27586, 27589, 27594, 27596, 27701–05, 27707–08, 27712–13, 27801–05, 27809, 27812, 27816, 27818–20, 27822–23, 27827–29, 27831–35, 27837, 27839–47, 27849–50, 27852–53, 27855–58, 27860–63, 27866–67, 27869–77, 27881–83, 27886–95, 27897, 27906–07, 27909–10, 27922, 27924, 27926, 27930, 27932, 27937–38, 27942, 27944, 27957, 27962, 27967, 27970, 27979–80, 27983, 27985–86, 28333, 28365, 28501–04, 28523, 28526, 28537, 28551, 28560, 28562, 28578, 28580, 28586, 28590

* * *

SECOND DISTRICT

RENEE ELLMERS, Republican, of Dunn, NC; born in Ironwood, MI, February 9, 1964; education: B.S., nursing, Oakland University, Auburn Hills, MI, 1990; professional: registered nurse; president elect/vice president, Community Development for the Chamber of Commerce; member of the Betsy Johnson Hospital Foundation, member of the Dunn Planning Board, NC, 2006–10; chair, Dunn Planning Board, NC, 2008–10; member of the Harnett County Nursing Home Committee; religion: Roman Catholic; married: Dr. Brent Ellmers; one child: Ben; committees: Energy and Commerce; elected to the 112th Congress on November 2, 2010; reelected to each succeeding Congress.

Office Listings

http://www.ellmers.house.gov

1210 Longworth House Office Building, Washington, DC 20515 .... (202) 225–4531
    Chief of Staff.—Al Lytton.
    Press Secretary.—Blair Ellis.
    Scheduler.—Anna Helms.
406 West Broad Street, Dunn, NC 28334 .... (910) 230–1910
222 Sunset Avenue, #101, Asheboro, NC 27203 .... (336) 626–3060

Counties: ALAMANCE (part), CHATHAM (part), CUMBERLAND (part), HARNETT (part), HOKE (part), LEE, MOORE, RANDOLPH (part), WAKE (part). Population (2010), 744,671.

ZIP Codes: 27207–08, 27213, 27237, 27252, 27256, 27298, 27312, 27325, 27330–32, 27344, 27349, 27355, 27405, 27501, 27504–06, 27508, 27520–21, 27524–26, 27529, 27536–37, 27540, 27542–44, 27546, 27549, 27552, 27555, 27557, 27559, 27562, 27564, 27568–70, 27576–77, 27589, 27591–93, 27596–97, 27601–03, 27605–07, 27610, 27614, 27625, 27698, 27801–04, 27807, 27809, 27816, 27822, 27829, 27850, 27856, 27863, 27878, 27880, 27882, 27891, 27893–94, 27896, 28301, 28303, 28307–08, 28310–11, 28314, 28323, 28326, 28328, 28334–35, 28339, 28341, 28355–56, 28365–66, 28368, 28382, 28385, 28390, 28393, 28441, 28444, 28447, 28453, 28458, 28466, 28478

* * *

THIRD DISTRICT

WALTER B. JONES, Republican, of Farmville, NC; born in Farmville, February 10, 1943; education: graduated, Hargrave Military Academy, Chatham, VA, 1961; B.A., Atlantic Christian College, Wilson, NC, 1966; served in North Carolina National Guard; self-employed, sales; member: North Carolina House of Representatives, 1983–92; married: Joe Anne Whitehurst Jones; one child, Ashley Elizabeth Jones; committees: Armed Services; elected to the 104th Congress; reelected to each succeeding Congress.

Office Listings

http://www.jones.house.gov   twitter: @repwalterjones
https://www.facebook.com/pages/walter-jones/15083070102

2333 Rayburn House Office Building, Washington, DC 20515 .... (202) 225–3415
Chief of Staff.—Glen Downs.   FAX: 225–3286
Office Manager.—Maggie Ayrea.
Communications Director.—Maria Jeffrey.
1105–C Corporate Drive, Greenville, NC 27858 .... (252) 931–1003
District Constituent Outreach Director.—Catherine Jordan.

Counties: BEAUFORT (part), CAMDEN, CHAOWAN, CARTERET, CRAVEN (part), CURRITUCK, DARE, GATES, GREENE, HYDE, JONES (part), LENOIR (part), MARTIN (part), NEW HANOVER, ONSLOW (part), PAMLICO, PENDER (part), PITT (part), TYRRELL, WASHINGTON, WAYNE, PASQUOTANK, PERQUIMANS (part). CITIES: Atlantic Beach, Ayden, Beaufort, Belhaven, Burgaw, Clinton, Emerald Isle, Fremont, Greenville, Havelock, Jacksonville, Kill Devil Hills, Kinston, Kitty Hawk, Morehead City, Mount Olive, Nags Head, New Bern, Newport, River Bend, Trent Woods, Wallace, Washington, Wilmington, and Winterville. Population (2010), 749,823.

ZIP Codes: 27806, 27808, 27810–12, 27814, 27817, 27821, 27824, 27826, 27828, 27834, 27836–37, 27846, 27858, 27860, 27865, 27871, 27875, 27879, 27884–85, 27888–89, 27892, 27909, 27915–17, 27919–21, 27923, 27925–30, 27932, 27935–39, 27941, 27943–44, 27946–50, 27953–54, 27956, 27958–60, 27962, 27964–66, 27968–70, 27972–74, 27976, 27978–82, 28401–03, 28405, 28407, 28412, 28421, 28425, 28429, 28435, 28445, 28447–48, 28454, 28457, 28460, 28466, 28478, 28501, 28509–13, 28515–16, 28518–24, 28526–33, 28537–47, 28552–57, 28560, 28562, 28564, 28570–75, 28577, 28579–87, 28589 90, 28594

* * *

FOURTH DISTRICT

DAVID E. PRICE, Democrat, of Chapel Hill, NC; born in Erwin, TN, August 17, 1940; education: B.A., Morehead Scholar, University of North Carolina; Bachelor of Divinity, 1964, and Ph.D., political science, 1969, Yale University; professional: professor of political science and public policy, Duke University; past chairman and executive director, North Carolina Democratic Party; author of four books and numerous book chapters, essays, and scholarly articles on Congress and the American political system; leadership roles: ranking member, House Democracy Partnership; co-chair, Democratic Budget Group; Assistant Democratic Whip; legislative accomplishments: Home Equity Loan Consumer Protection Act (100th Congress); Scientific and Technical Education Act (102nd Congress); Education Affordability Act (105th Congress); Stand By Your Ad Act (107th Congress); Teaching Fellows Act (110th Congress); Credit Card Minimum Payment Warning Act (111th Congress); selected awards: Hubert Humphrey Public Service Award, American Political Science Association, 1990; Champion of Science Award, The Science Coalition, 2002; Charles Dick Medal of Merit, North Carolina National Guard, 2002; William Sloane Coffin Award for Peace and Justice, Yale Divinity School, 2006; Legislator of the Year, Biotechnology Industry Association, 2011; John Tyler Caldwell Award for the Humanities, North Carolina Humanities Council, 2011; past chairman of the board and Sunday School teacher, Binkley Memorial Baptist Church; married: Lisa Price; children: Karen and Michael; committees: Appropriations; elected to the 100th–103rd Congresses; elected to the 105th Congress; reelected to each succeeding Congress.

Office Listings

http://www.price.house.gov

2108 Rayburn House Office Building, Washington, DC 20515 .... (202) 225–1784
Chief of Staff.—Jean-Louise Beard.   FAX: 225–2014
Legislative Director.—Justin Wein.
Executive Assistant.—Kate Throneburg.
Systems Manager.—Nora Blalock.
436 North Harrington Street, Suite 100, Raleigh, NC 27603 .... (919) 859–5999
District Director.—Asher Hildebrand.
1777 Fordham Boulevard, Suite 204, Chapel Hill, NC 27514 .... (919) 967–7924
301 Green Street, Suite 315, Fayetteville, NC 28301 .... (910) 323–0260

Counties: ALAMANCE (part), CHATHAM (part), CUMBERLAND (part), DURHAM (part), HARNETT (part), ORANGE (part), and WAKE (part). Population (2010), 733,498.

ZIP Codes: 27215 (part), 27216, 27217 (part), 27228, 27231 (part), 27243 (part), 27253 (part), 27258 (part), 27278 (part), 27302 (part), 27312 (part), 27330 (part), 27332 (part), 27505 (part), 27510, 27511 (part), 27513 (part), 27514 (part), 27515–16, 27517 (part), 27518 (part), 27523 (part), 27529 (part), 27540 (part), 27546 (part), 27552, 27559 (part), 27560 (part), 27562 (part), 27599, 27601–02, 27603 (part), 27604 (part), 27605 (part), 27606 (part), 27607 (part), 27608 (part), 27609 (part), 27610 (part), 27611, 27612 (part), 27613 (part), 27615 (part), 27616 (part), 27617 (part), 27619–20, 27622, 27625–27, 27629, 27634–36, 27640, 27650, 27658, 27661, 27695, 27698, 27699, 27703 (part), 27705 (part), 27707 (part), 27709, 27711, 27713 (part), 27717, 28301 (part), 28302, 28303 (part), 28304 (part), 28305 (part), 28306 (part), 28309, 28311 (part), 28312 (part), 28314 (part), 28323 (part), 28339 (part), 28356 (part), 28377 (part), 28395 (part), 28445 (part)

* * *

FIFTH DISTRICT

VIRGINIA FOXX, Republican, of Banner Elk, NC; born in New York, NY, June 29, 1943; education: A.B., University of North Carolina, Chapel Hill, NC, 1968; M.A.C.T., University of North Carolina, Chapel Hill, NC, 1972; Ed.D., University of North Carolina, Greensboro, NC, 1985; professional: instructor, Caldwell Community College, Hudson, NC; instructor, Appalachian State University, Boone, NC; Assistant Dean, Appalachian State University, Boone, NC; president, Mayland Community College, Spruce Pine, NC, 1987–94; nursery operator; deputy secretary for management, North Carolina Department of Administration; organizations: member, Watauga County Board of Education, 1967–88; member, North Carolina State Senate, 1994–2004; Executive Committee of North Carolina Citizens for Business and Industry; Z. Smith Reynolds Foundation Advisory Panel; National Advisory Council for Women's Educational Programs; Board of Directors of the NC Center for Public Research; UNC-Chapel Hill Board of Visitors; National Conference of State Legislatures' Blue Ribbon Advisory Panel on Child Care; Foscoe-Grandfather Community Center Board; family: married to Tom Foxx; one daughter; elected House GOP Conference Secretary in the 113th and 114th Congresses; committees: vice chair, Rules; Education and the Workforce; elected to the 109th Congress on November 2, 2004; reelected to each succeeding Congress.

Office Listings

http://www.foxx.house.gov

2350 Rayburn House Office Building, Washington, DC 20515	(202) 225–2071
Chief of Staff.—Brandon Renz.	FAX: 225–2995
Legislative Director.—Cyrus Artz.	
Communications Director.—Sheridan Watson.	
240 Shadowline Drive, Suite 205, Boone, NC 28607	(828) 265–0240
	FAX: 265–0390
3540 Clemmons Road, Suite 125, Clemmons, NC 27012	(336) 778–0211
	FAX: 778–2290

Counties: ALEXANDER, ALLEGHANY, ASHE, AVERY, CATAWBA, DAVIDSON, DAVIE, FORSYTH, IREDELL, ROWAN, WATAUGA, WILKES, AND YADKIN. CITIES: Advance, Banner Elk, Barber, Belews Creek, Blowing Rock, Boomer, Boone, Boonville, Clemmons, Cleveland, Creston, Crumpler, Deep Gap, Dobson, East Bend, Elk Park, Elkin, Ennice, Ferguson, Fleetwood, Germanton, Glade Valley, Glendale Springs, Granite Falls, Grassy Creek, Hamptonville, Harmony, Hays, Hickory, Hiddenite, High Point, Jefferson, Jonesville, Kernersville, King, Lansing, Laurel Springs, Lenoir, Lewisville, Lexington, Linwood, McGrady, Millers Creek, Mocksville, Mooresville, Moravian Falls, Mount Ulla, North Wilkesboro, Olin, Pfafftown, Piney Creek, Purlear, Roaring Gap, Roaring River, Ronda, Rural Hall, Salisbury, Sparta, State Road, Statesville, Stokesdale, Stony Point, Sugar Grove, Taylorsville, Thomasville, Thurmond, Tobaccoville, Todd, Traphill, Troutman, Union Grove, Vilas, Walkertown, Walnut Cove, Warrensville, West Jefferson, Wilkesboro, Winston Salem, Woodleaf, Yadkinville, and Zionville. Population (2010), 741,095.

ZIP Codes: 27006, 27009–14, 27017–21, 27023, 27028, 27040, 27045, 27050–52, 27054–55, 27094, 27098–99, 27101, 27103–09, 27113–14, 27116, 27127, 27130, 27157, 27262, 27265, 27284–85, 27292, 27294–95, 27299, 27357, 27360, 27374, 28115, 28125, 28144, 28147, 28166, 28601–08, 28615, 28617–18, 28621–27, 28629–31, 28634–36, 28640, 28642–45, 28649, 28651, 28654–56, 28659–60, 28663, 28665, 28668–70, 28672, 28675–79, 28681, 28683–85, 28687, 28689, 28691–94, 28697–98

* * *

SIXTH DISTRICT

MARK WALKER, Republican, of Greensboro, NC; born in Dothan, Houston County, AL, May 20, 1969; education: attended Trinity Baptist College, Jacksonville, FL, 1987–1988; B.A., Piedmont International University, Winston-Salem, NC, 1999; professional: businessman; minister; committees: House Administration; Homeland Security; Oversight and Government Reform; elected to the 114th Congress on November 4, 2014.

Office Listings

https://walker.house.gov   twitter: @repmarkwalker
facebook.com/repmarkwalker   instagram.com/repmarkwalker

312 Cannon House Office Building, Washington, DC 20515	(202) 225–3065
Chief of Staff.—Scott Luginbill.	FAX: 225–8611
Scheduler.—Katie Sessoms.	
Legislative Director.—Dwayne Carson.	
Communications Director.—Kate Disbrow.	
809 Green Valley Road, Suite 104, Greensboro, NC 27408	(336) 333–5005

Office Listings—Continued

District Director.—Julie Emmons.
219 B. West Elm Street, P.O. Box 812, Graham, NC 27253 .... (336) 229–0159
   District Representative.—Janine Osborne.   FAX: 350–9514

Counties: ALAMANCE (part), CASWELL, DURHAM (part), GRANVILLE (part), GUILFORD (part), ORANGE (part), PERSON, ROCKINGHAM, STOKES, AND SURRY. POPULATION (2010) 760,762.

ZIP Codes: 27007, 27009, 27016–17, 27019, 27021–22, 27024–25, 27027, 27030, 27041–49, 27050, 27052–53, 27201–02, 27212, 27214–15, 27217, 27229, 27231, 27233, 27235, 27243–44, 27249, 27253, 27258, 27260, 27262–63, 27265, 27278, 27282–84, 27288–89, 27291, 27295, 27298, 27301–02, 27305, 27310–15, 27317, 27320, 27323, 27326, 27340, 27342–43, 27349, 27357–59, 27377, 27379, 27401, 27403–13, 27438, 27455, 27503, 27507, 27514, 27516, 27541, 27565, 27572–74, 27582–83, 27705, 27712, 27722, 28621, 28676, 28683

* * *

SEVENTH DISTRICT

DAVID ROUZER, Republican, of McGee's Crossroads, NC; born at Landstuhl Army Medical Center in Landstuhl, Germany, February 16, 1972; education: B.S. in Agriculture Business Management, Agricultural Economics; B.A. in Chemistry; professional: Legislative Assistant, Office of U.S. Senator Jesse Helms; Senior Policy Advisor, U.S. Senator Jesse Helms; Assistant to the Dean and Director of Commodity Relations, College of Agriculture and Life Sciences, NC State University; Senior Advisor, U.S. Senator Elizabeth Dole; Associate Administrator, Rural Business-Cooperative Programs/Director; Legislative and Public Affairs, U.S. Department of Agriculture; Principal, The Rouzer Company; committees: Agriculture; Transportation and Infrastructure; elected to the 114th Congress on November 4, 2014.

Office Listings

https://rouzer.house.gov   www.facebook.com/reprouzer

424 Cannon House Office Building, Washington, DC 20515 .... (202) 225–2731
   Chief of Staff.—Melissa Murphy.   FAX: 225–5773
   Deputy Chief of Staff and Communications Director.—Tyler Foote.
   Legislative Director.—Allison Cooke.
   District Director.—Dwight Williams.
230 Government Center Drive, Suite 113, Wilmington, NC 28403 .... (910) 395–0202
310 Government Center Drive, Unit 1, Bolivia, NC 28422 .... (910) 253–6111
2736 North Carolina Highway 210, Smithfield, NC 27577 .... (919) 938–3040

Counties: BLADEN, BRUNSWICK, COLUMBUS, CUMBERLAND (part), DUPLIN, HOKE (part), JOHNSTON, LENOIR (part), NEW HANOVER (part), PENDER (part), ROBESON (part), AND SAMPSON. Population (2013), 762,540.

ZIP Codes: 27501, 27504, 27520, 27524, 27527, 27529, 27542, 27555, 27557, 27568–69, 27576–77, 27591–92, 27597, 27603, 28306, 28312, 28318, 28320, 28325, 28328, 28332, 28334, 28337, 28341, 28344, 28348–49, 28357, 28364–66, 28371, 28376, 28337, 28382, 28384–86, 28391–93, 28399, 28401, 28403, 28405, 28409, 28411–12, 28420, 28422–24, 28428–34, 28436, 28438–39, 28441–45, 28447–53, 28455–58, 28461–70, 28472, 28478–501, 28504, 28508, 28518, 28521, 28525, 28551, 28572, 28574, 28578, 28580

* * *

EIGHTH DISTRICT

RICHARD HUDSON, Republican, of Concord, NC; born in Franklin, VA, November 4, 1971; education: B.A. in history and political science, University of North Carolina at Charlotte, 1996; professional: served as District Director for Eighth District Congressman Robin Hayes; served as Chief of Staff for Congresswoman Virginia Foxx, Congressman John Carter and Congressman Mike Conaway; religion: Christian; married: Renee; caucuses: Atlantic Offshore Energy Caucus; Agriculture and Rural America Task Force; House Manufacturing Caucus; Congressional Textile Caucus; Agriculture Policy Group; House National Guard and Reserve Components Caucus; Congressional Sportsmen's Caucus; Congressional Prayer Caucus; committees: Energy and Commerce; elected to the 113th Congress on November 6, 2012; reelected to the 114th Congress on November 4, 2014.

Office Listings

http://www.hudson.house.gov

429 Cannon House Office Building, Washington, DC 20515 .... (202) 225–3715

Office Listings—Continued

Chief of Staff.—Pepper Natonski.   FAX: 225–4036
Press Secretary.—Tatum Gibson.
Legislative Director.—Curtis Rhyne.
Scheduler.—Regi Simpson.
325 McGill Avenue, Suite 500, Concord, NC 28027 .... (704) 786–1612
Deputy Chief of Staff.—Chris Carter.
1015 Fayetteville Road, Rockingham, NC 28379 .... (910) 997–2070

Counties: ANSON, CABARRUS (Part), DAVIDSON (part), MECKLENBURG (part), MONTGOMERY, RANDOLPH (part), RICHMOND,
ROBESON (part), ROWAN (part), SCOTLAND, STANLY, AND UNION (part). Population (2010), 701,000.

ZIP Codes: 27205, 27209, 27229, 27239, 27247, 27262, 27281, 27292, 27299, 27306, 27341, 27351, 27356, 27360,
27370–71, 28001–02, 28007, 28009, 28023, 28025–27, 28041, 28071–72, 28075, 28079, 28081–83, 28088, 28091,
28097, 28102–04, 28107, 28109–12, 28115, 28119, 28124, 28127–29, 28133, 28135, 28137–38, 28144, 28146–47,
28163, 28170, 28174, 28213, 28215, 28227, 28262, 28319, 28330, 28338, 28340, 28343, 28345, 28347, 28351–53,
28357–60, 28362–64, 28367, 28369, 28371–72, 28375, 28377, 28379–80, 28383–84, 28386, 28396

* * *

NINTH DISTRICT

ROBERT M. PITTENGER, Republican, of Charlotte, NC; born in Dallas, Texas, August 15,
1948; education: psychology and political science, University of Texas, Austin, TX, 1970;
professional: former Assistant to the President of Campus Crusade for Christ; founder of
Pittenger Land Investments; North Carolina State Senate, 2002–08; former board member of
the Presbyterian Hospital Foundation, Jesse Helms Educational Foundation, and Central Piedmont Community College Foundation; religion: Christian; family: wife: Suzanne Pittenger, four
children and seven grandchildren; commissions: Congressional-Executive Commission on China;
caucuses: co-chairman of the United Solutions Caucus; committees: Financial Services; elected
to the 113th Congress on November 6, 2012; reelected to the 114th Congress on November
4, 2014.

Office Listings

http://pittenger.house.gov   twitter: @reppittenger
www.facebook.com/congressmanpittenger

224 Cannon House Office Building, Washington, DC 20515 .... (202) 225–1976
Chief of Staff.—Brad Jones.   FAX: 225–3389
Deputy Chief of Staff and Legislative Director.—Stephen Billy.
Legislative Assistants: Caroline Barbee, Charles Thomas.
Legislative Correspondent.—Caroline Barbee.
Executive Assistant.—Blair Belk.
Staff Assistant.—John Caison.
2701 Coltsgate Road, Suite 105, Charlotte, NC 28211 .... (704) 362–1060
District Director and Veterans Specialist.—Robert Becker.   FAX: 365–6384
Communications Director.—Jamie Bowers.
Constituent Services Director.—Graham Long.
Constituent Liaisons: Linda Ferster, Chris Sullivan.
Staff Assistant and Case Worker.—Anna Coyle.
116 Morlake Drive, Suite 101A, Mooresville, NC 28117 .... (704) 861–1976
Regional District Director.—Preston Curtis.   FAX: 696–8190

Counties: IREDELL (part), MECKLENBURG (part), UNION (part). Population (2010), 733,498.

ZIP Codes: 27013, 28031, 28036, 28078–79, 28104–05, 28107–08, 28110, 28112, 28115, 28117, 28125, 28134, 28166,
28173, 28202–05, 28207–12, 28214–17, 28226–27, 28262, 28269–70, 28273, 28277–78, 28625, 28636, 28660,
28677–78

* * *

TENTH DISTRICT

PATRICK T. McHENRY, Republican, of Denver, NC; born in Gastonia, NC, October 22,
1975; education: graduated Ashbrook High School, Gastonia, NC; attended North Carolina State
University, Raleigh, NC; B.A., Belmont Abbey College, Belmont, NC, 1999; professional: realtor; media executive; appointed special assistant to the U.S. Secretary of Labor by President
George W. Bush in 2001; member, North Carolina House of Representatives, 2002–04; married:

Giulia, 2010; daughter Cecelia born in 2014; organizations: Gaston Chamber of Commerce, Gastonia Rotary Club, the National Rifle Association, Saint Michael Church; board of directors, United Way's Success by Six Youth Program; selected as Chief Deputy Whip on June 26, 2014; committees: vice chair, Financial Services; elected to the 109th Congress on November 2, 2004; reelected to each succeeding Congress.

Office Listings

http://mchenry.house.gov   ww.facebook.com/congressmanmchenry
twitter: @patrickmchenry

2334 Rayburn House Office Building, Washington, DC 20515	(202) 225–2576
Chief of Staff.—Austen Jensen.	FAX: 225–0316
Legislative Director.—Matt Mulder.	
Press Secretary.—Jeff Butler.	
Scheduler.—Lindsey Shackelford.	
87 Fourth Street, NW., Suite A, P.O. Box 1830, Hickory, NC 28603	(828) 327–6100

Counties: BUNCOMBE (part), CATAWBA (part), CLEVELAND, GASTON, LINCOLN, POLK, AND RUTHERFORD. CITIES AND TOWN-SHIPS: Hickory, Lenoir, Morganton, Shelby, and Mooresville. Population (2010), 733,499.

ZIP Codes: 28006, 28012, 28016–21, 28032–34, 28037, 28040, 28043, 28052, 28054, 28056, 28073, 28076–77, 28080, 28086, 28089–90, 28092, 28098, 28101, 28114, 28120, 28139, 28150, 28152, 28160, 28164, 28167–69, 28601–02, 28609–10, 28612–13, 28658, 28673, 28682, 28704, 28709, 28711, 28720, 28722, 28730, 28732, 28746, 28756–57, 28773, 28778, 28782, 28787, 28792, 28801, 28803–06

* * *

ELEVENTH DISTRICT

MARK R. MEADOWS, Republican, of Cashiers, NC; born in Maginot Barracks (Army), Verdun, France, July 28, 1959; education: graduated from the University of South Florida, Tampa, FL, 1980; professional: real estate developer, restaurateur; energy company customer relations director; Macon County Republican Party chairman, 2001–02; serves as a congressional liaison to the United Nations; religion: Christian; married: Debbie Meadows; two children; caucuses: appointed to the Congressional-Executive Commission on China; committees: Foreign Affairs; Oversight and Government Reform; Transportation and Infrastructure; elected to the 113th Congress on November 6, 2012; reelected to the 114th Congress on November 4, 2014.

Office Listings

http://www.meadows.house.gov

1024 Longworth House Office Building, Washington, DC 20515	(202) 225–6401
Chief of Staff.—Vacant.	FAX: 226–6422
Legislative Director.—Ansley Rhyne.	
Communications Director.—Alyssa Farah.	
Scheduler.—Eliza Thurston.	
Legislative Assistants: Patrick Fleming, Martha Van Lieshout.	
Legislative Research Assistant.—Zachary Enos.	
Legislative Correspondent.—Ben Williamson.	
200 North Grove Street, Suite 90, Hendersonville, NC 28792	(828) 693–5660

Counties: AVERY, BUNCOMBE (part), BURKE, CALDWELL, CHEROKEE, CLAY, GRAHAM, HAYWOOD, HENDERSON, JACKSON, MACON, MADISON, MCDOWELL, MITCHELL, SWAIN, TRANSYLVANIA, AND YANCEY. CITIES AND TOWNSHIPS: Hayesville, Hendersonville, Lenoir, Morganton, and Waynesville. Population (2010), 619,178.

ZIP Codes: 28604, 28645, 28655, 28657, 28701–02, 28704–05, 28707–08, 28712–13, 28715, 28717–19, 28721, 28723, 28730, 28734, 28736, 28739–43, 28747, 28751–54, 28759, 28763, 28771, 28774–75, 28779, 28781, 28783, 28765, 28786–87, 28789–91, 28901–02, 28904–06, 28909

* * *

TWELFTH DISTRICT

ALMA S. ADAMS, Democrat, of Greensboro, NC; born in High Point, North Carolina, May 27, 1946; education: art education, North Carolina A&T State University, Greensboro, NC, 1968; master's degree in Art Education, North Carolina A&T State University, Greensboro, NC, 1972; Ph.D. in Art Education and Multicultural Education from The Ohio State University in

Columbus, Ohio, 1981; professional: Greensboro City School Board, 1984–86; Greensboro City Council, 1987–94; Bennett College Art Professor, Curator and Administrator; North Carolina State House, 1994–2014; family: two children, Linda Jeanelle Lindsay, and Billy Eugene; Adams II, and 4 grandchildren; caucuses: Founder of the Congressional Bipartisan HBCU Caucus; Women's Caucus, Congressional Progress Caucus, Diabetes Caucus, Congressional Black Caucus, Historic Preservation Caucus; AIDS/HIV Caucus; Hunger Caucus; Art Caucus; committees: Agriculture; Education and the Workforce; Small Business; Joint Economic Committee; won the 2014 special election to fill the vacancy caused by the resignation of U.S. Representative Mel Watt, while simultaneously elected to the 114th Congress on November 4, 2014, to serve a full two-year term.

Office Listings

http://www.adams.house.gov

222 Cannon House Office Building, Washington, DC 20515	(202) 225–1510
Chief of Staff.—Rhonda Foxx.	FAX: 225–1512
Legislative Director.—Shaniqua McClendon.	
Communications Director.—Shadawn Reddick-Smith.	
Director of Operations.—Ivana Brancaccio.	
321 West 11th Street, Suites 100 & 200, Charlotte, NC 28202	(704) 344–9950
District Director.—Keith Kelly.	
1600 East Wendover Avenue, Suite I, Greensboro, NC 27405	(336) 275–9950

Counties: CABARRUS (part), DAVIDSON (part), FORSYTH (part), GUILFORD (part), MECKLENBURG (part), ROWAN (part). Population (2014), 773,617.

ZIP Codes: 27101, 27105–07, 27110, 27127, 27214, 27260, 27262, 27265, 27282, 27284, 27292, 27295, 27299, 27301, 27360, 27401, 27403, 27405–07, 27409–10, 27455, 28023, 28027, 28036, 28039, 28078, 28081, 28105, 28115, 28125, 28134, 28144, 28146–47, 28159, 28202–06, 28208–17, 28227, 28244, 28262, 28269–28270, 28273, 28280, 28282

* * *

THIRTEENTH DISTRICT

GEORGE HOLDING, Republican, of Raleigh, NC; born in Raleigh, April 17, 1968; education: B.A., classics, Wake Forest University, Winston-Salem, NC, 1991; J.D., Wake Forest University Law School, Winston-Salem, NC, 1996; professional: law clerk for U.S. District Judge Terrence Boyle; practiced law in Raleigh with Kilpatrick Stockton; served as legislative counsel to U.S. Senator Jessie Helms, 1998–2002; joined the U.S. Attorney's office for the Eastern District of North Carolina, 2002–06; confirmed by U.S. Senate as the U.S. Attorney for Eastern North Carolina, 2006–11; religion: Baptist; committees: Foreign Affairs; Judiciary; elected to the 113th Congress on November 6, 2012; reelected to the 114th Congress on November 4, 2014.

Office Listings

http://www.holding.house.gov

507 Cannon House Office Building, Washington, DC 20515	(202) 225–3032
Chief of Staff.—Tucker Knott.	FAX: 225–0181
Legislative Director.—Kris Denzel.	
Press Secretary.—Emily Wrenn.	
Scheduler.—Katie Lawrence.	
3725 National Drive, Suite 101, Raleigh, NC 27605	(919) 782–4400
120 Main Street, Fremont, NC 27830	(919) 440–5247

Counties: DURHAM (part), EDGECOMBE (part), FRANKLIN (part), GRANVILLE (part), NASH (part), WAKE (part), WAYNE (part), WILSON (part), and VANCE (part). Population (2010), 732,434.

ZIP Codes: 27501–02, 27508, 27511, 27513, 27518–20, 27522–26, 27529–31, 27534, 27537, 27539–40, 27542, 27544–45, 27549, 27557, 27560, 27565, 27569, 27571, 27581, 27587, 27591–92, 27596–97, 27603–10, 27612–17, 27703–04, 27801, 27803–04, 27807–09, 27813, 27816, 27822, 27829, 27830, 27851–52, 27856, 27863–64, 27878, 27880, 27882–83, 27886, 27893, 27896, 28333, 28365, 28551, 28578

NORTH DAKOTA

(Population 2010, 675,591)

SENATORS

JOHN HOEVEN, Republican, of Bismarck, ND; born in Bismarck, March 13, 1957; education: B.A., Dartmouth College, Hanover, NH, 1979; M.B.A., Northwestern University, Chicago, IL, 1981; professional: executive vice president, First Western Bank, Minot, 1986–93; president and CEO, Bank of North Dakota, 1993–2000; Governor of North Dakota, 2000–10; religion: Catholic; family: married to Mikey; two children; caucuses: Air Force Caucus; Congressional Sportsmen's Caucus; Senate Western Caucus; Norway Caucus; Rural Education Caucus; National Guard Caucus; E–911 Caucus; Rural Health Caucus; General Aviation Caucus; Impact Aid Coalition; Senate Republican High-Tech Task Force; Senate Veterans Jobs Caucus; Unmanned Aerial Systems Caucus; Hydrogen Fuel Cell Caucus; ICBM Coalition; Port-to-Plains Caucus; UAS Integration Working Group; committees: Agriculture, Nutrition, and Forestry; Appropriations; Energy and Natural Resources; Indian Affairs; elected to the U.S. Senate on November 2, 2010.

Office Listings

http://hoeven.senate.gov   www.facebook.com/senatorjohnhoeven
https://twitter.com/senjohnhoeven

338 Russell Senate Office Building, Washington, DC 20510	(202) 224–2551
Chiefs of Staff: Ryan Bernstein, Don Larson	FAX: 224–7999
Legislative Director.—Tony Eberhard.	
Communications Director.—Don Canton.	
U.S. Federal Building, 220 East Rosser Avenue, Room 312, Bismarck, ND 58501	(701) 250–4618
State Director.—Don Larson.	FAX: 239–5112
1802 32nd Avenue South, Suite B, Fargo, ND 58103	(701) 239–5389
Federal Building, 102 North Fourth Street, Room 108, Grand Forks, ND 58203	(701) 746–8972
100 1st Street SouthWest, Suite 107, Minot, ND 58701	(701) 838–1361
Williston, ND	(701) 580–4535

* * *

HEIDI HEITKAMP, Democrat, of Mandan, ND; born in Breckenridge, MN, October 30, 1955; education: B.A., University of North Dakota, ND, 1977; J.D., Lewis and Clark Law School, 1980; professional: attorney, United States Environmental Protection Agency, 1980–81; attorney, Office of the North Dakota State Tax Commissioner, 1981–86; Tax Commissioner, State of North Dakota, 1986–92; Attorney General, State of North Dakota, 1992–2000; Director, Dakota Gasification Company, 2001–12; religion: Catholic; family: married to Dr. Darwin Lange; two children; caucuses: Afterschool Caucus; Bicameral Congressional Arthritis Caucus; Bipartisan Task Force on Tribal Colleges and Universities; Career and Technical Education Caucus; Congressional Caucus on Foster Youth; Congressional Coalition on Adoption; Congressional Diabetes Caucus; Congressional ICBM Coalition; Congressional Next Generation 9-1-1 Caucus; Congressional Sportsmen's Caucus; Congressional Veterans Jobs Caucus; Deadly Cancers Caucus; Defense Communities Caucus; General Aviation Caucus; Impact Aid Coalition; Law Enforcement Caucus; National Guard Caucus; Nursing Caucus; Ports to Plains Caucus; Rural Health Caucus; Senate Cultural Caucus; Social Work Caucus; committees: Agriculture, Nutrition, and Forestry; Banking, Housing and Urban Affairs; Homeland Security and Governmental Affairs; Indian Affairs; Small Business and Entrepreneurship; elected to the U.S. Senate on November 6, 2012.

Office Listings

http://heitkamp.senate.gov   https://twitter.com/senatorheitkamp
www.facebook.com/senatorheidiheitkamp

110 Hart Senate Office Building, Washington, DC 20510	(202) 224–2043
Chief of Staff.—Tessa Gould.	FAX: 224–7776
Legislative Director.—Tracee Sutton.	
220 East Rosser Avenue, Room 228, Bismarck, ND 58501	(701) 258–4648
657 Second Avenue North, Room 306, Fargo, ND 58102	(701) 232–8030
State Director.—Ryan Nagle.	
33 South 3rd Street, Suite B, Grand Forks, ND 58201	(701) 775–9601
100 First Street, SW., Room 105, Minot, ND 58701	(701) 852–0703
40 First Avenue West, Suite 202, Dickinson, ND 58601	(701) 225–0974

REPRESENTATIVE

AT LARGE

KEVIN CRAMER, Republican, of Bismarck, ND; born in Rolette, ND, January 21, 1961; education: B.A., social work, Concordia College, Moorhead, MN, 1983; M.A., management, University of Mary, Bismarck, ND, 2003; professional: chairman, North Dakota Republican Party, 1991–93; North Dakota Tourism Director, 1993–97; State Economic Development and Finance Director, 1997–2000; Executive Director, Harold Schafer Leadership Foundation, 2000–03; North Dakota Public Service Commissioner, 2003–12; married: Kris Cramer; children: Ian, Isaac, Rachel (Cale) Wegner, Annie (Nick) Senne, and Abel; grandchildren: Lila and Beau; committees: Energy and Commerce; elected to the 113th Congress on November 6, 2012; reelected to the 114th Congress on November 4, 2014.

Office Listings

http://cramer.house.gov   facebook.com/congressmankevincramer   twitter.com/repkevincramer

1032 Longworth House Office Building, Washington, DC 20515	(202) 225–2611
Chief of Staff.—Mark Gruman.	FAX: 226–0893
Legislative Director.—Chris Marohl.	
Communications Director.—Jason Stverak.	
Federal Building, 220 East Rosser Avenue, Room 328, Bismarck, ND 58501	(701) 224–0355
3217 Fiechtner Drive South, Suite D, Fargo, ND 58103	(701) 356–2216
315 Main Street South, Suite 203, Minot, ND 58701	(701) 839–0255
4200 James Ray Drive, Office 600, Grand Forks, ND 58202	(701) 738–4880
State Director.—Lisa Gibbens.	

Population (2010), 672,591.

ZIP Codes: 58001–02, 58004–09, 58011–13, 58015–18, 58021, 58027, 58029, 58030–33, 58035–36, 58038, 58040–43, 58045–49, 58051–54, 58056–65, 58067–69, 58071–72, 58074–79, 58081, 58102–09, 58121–22, 58124–26, 58201–06, 58208, 58210, 58212, 58214, 58216, 58218–20, 58222–25, 58227–31, 58233, 58235–41, 58243–44, 58249–51, 58254–62, 58265–67, 58269–78, 58281–82, 58301, 58310–11, 58313, 58316–19, 58321, 58323–25, 58327, 58329–32, 58335, 58338–39, 58341, 58343–46, 58348, 58351–53, 58355–57, 58359, 58361–63, 58365–70, 58372, 58374, 58377, 58379–82, 58384–86, 58401–02, 58405, 58413, 58415–16, 58418, 58420–26, 58428–31, 58433, 58436, 58438–45, 58448, 58451–52, 58454–56, 58458, 58460–61, 58463–64, 58466–67, 58472, 58474–84, 58486–88, 58490, 58492, 58494–97, 58501–07, 58520–21, 58523–24, 58528–33, 58535, 58538, 58540–42, 58544–45, 58549, 58552, 58554, 58558–66, 58568–73, 58575–77, 58579–81, 58601–02, 58620–23, 58625–27, 58630–32, 58634, 58636, 58638–47, 58649–56, 58701–05, 58707, 58710–13, 58716, 58718, 58721–23, 58725, 58727, 58730–31, 58733–37, 58740–41, 58744, 58746–48, 58750, 58752, 58755–63, 58765, 58768–73, 58775–76, 58778–79, 58781–85, 58787–90, 58792–95, 58801–02, 58830–31, 58833, 58835, 58838, 58843–45, 58847, 58849, 58852–54, 58856

OHIO

(Population 2010, 11,536,504)

SENATORS

SHERROD BROWN, Democrat, of Cleveland, OH; born in Mansfield, OH, November 9, 1952; education: B.A., Yale University, New Haven, CT, 1974; M.A., education, Ohio State University, Columbus, OH, 1979; M.A., public administration, Ohio State University, Columbus, OH, 1981; professional: Ohio House of Representatives, 1975–83; Ohio Secretary of State, 1983–91; U.S. House of Representatives, 1992–2006; member: Eagle Scouts of America; married: Connie Schultz; children: Emily, Elizabeth, Andrew and Caitlin; committees: ranking member, Banking, Housing, and Urban Affairs; Agriculture, Nutrition, and Forestry; Finance; Veterans' Affairs; elected to the 103rd Congress on November 3, 1992; reelected to each succeeding Congress; elected to the U.S. Senate on November 7, 2006; reelected to the U.S. Senate on November 6, 2012.

Office Listings

http://brown.senate.gov

713 Hart Senate Office Building, Washington, DC 20510	(202) 224–2315
Chief of Staff.—Sarah Benzing.	FAX: 228–6321
Legislative Director.—Jeremy Hekhuis.	
Communications Director.—Meghan Dubyak.	
Press Secretaries: Lauren Kulik, Rachel Petri, Tamika Turner.	
801 West Superior Avenue, Suite 1400, Cleveland, OH 44113	(216) 522–7272
State Director.—John Ryan.	
Deputy State Director.—Beth Thames.	
425 Walnut Street, Suite 2310, Cincinnati, OH 45202	(513) 684–1021
200 North High Street, Room 614, Columbus, OH 43215	(614) 469–2083
200 West Erie Avenue, Suite 312, Lorain, OH 44052	(440) 242–4100

* * *

ROBERT J. PORTMAN, Republican, of Terrace Park, OH; born in Cincinnati, OH, December 19, 1955; education: B.A., Dartmouth College, Hanover, NH, 1979; J.D., University of Michigan Law School, Ann Arbor, MI, 1984; professional: associate counsel to George H.W. Bush, 1989; deputy assistant and director, White House Office of Legislative Affairs, 1989–91;
member of the U.S. House of Representatives, 1993–2005; U.S. Trade Representative, 2005–06; Director of the Office of Management and Budget, 2006–07; religion: Methodist; married: Jane Portman; three children: Jed, Will, and Sally; committees: Budget; Energy and Natural Resources; Finance; Homeland Security and Governmental Affairs; elected to the U.S. Senate on November 2, 2010.

Office Listings

http://portman.senate.gov

448 Russell Senate Office Building, Washington, DC 20510	(202) 224–3353
Chief of Staff.—Mark Isakowitz.	
Communications Director.—Caitlin Conant.	
Legislative Director.—Pam Thiessen.	
Scheduler.—Jeannie Etchart.	
37 West Broad Street, Suite 300, Columbus, OH 43215	(614) 469–6774
State Director.—Teri Geiger.	
District Director.—Steve White.	
District Representative.—Vacant.	
312 Walnut Street, Suite 3075, Cincinnati, OH 45202	(513) 684–3265
District Director.—Connie Laug.	
District Representative.—Vacant.	
1240 East 9th Street, Room 3061, Cleveland, OH 44199	(216) 522–7095
District Director.—Caryn Candisky.	
District Representative.—George Brown.	
420 Madison Avenue, Room 1210, Toledo, OH 43604	(419) 259–3895
District Representative.—Wes Fahrbach.	

REPRESENTATIVES

FIRST DISTRICT

STEVE CHABOT, Republican, of Cincinnati, OH; born in Cincinnati, January 22, 1953; education: graduated from LaSalle High School in Cincinnati; B.A., College of William and Mary, Williamsburg, VA, 1975; J.D., Salmon P. Chase College of Law, Highland Heights, KY, 1978; professional: teacher, 1975–76; member of the city council, Cincinnati, OH, 1985–90; commissioner, Hamilton County, OH, 1990–94; elected as a Republican to the 104th–110th Congresses, January 3, 1995–January 3, 2009; served as ranking member on the Committee on Small Business, 110th Congress; family: wife, Donna; two children: Erica and Randy; committees: chair, Small Business; Foreign Affairs; Judiciary; elected to the 112th Congress on November 2, 2010; reelected to each succeeding Congress.

Office Listings

http://chabot.house.gov   facebook: repstevechabot   twitter: @repstevechabot

2371 Rayburn House Office Building, Washington, DC 20515	(202) 225–2216
Chief of Staff.—Mark Wellman.	FAX: 225–3012
Legislative Director.—Priscilla Koepke.	
Washington Administrative Director / Scheduling.—Katie Moore.	
Carew Tower, 441 Vine Street, Room 3003, Cincinnati, OH 45202	(513) 684–2723
District Director.—Mike Cantwell.	FAX: 421–8722
Communications Director.—Brian Griffith.	
11 South Broadway Street, Third Floor, Lebanon, OH 45036	(513) 421–8704

Counties: HAMILTON (part), WARREN. Population (2010), 721,032.

ZIP Codes: 45001–02, 45005, 45030, 45033–34, 45036, 45039–40, 45052, 45054, 45065–66, 45068, 45111, 45140, 45152, 45162, 45202–07, 45210–11, 45214–17, 45219–21, 45223–25, 45229, 45232–33, 45237–43, 45246–49, 45251–52

* * *

SECOND DISTRICT

BRAD WENSTRUP, Republican, of Cincinnati, OH; born in Cincinnati, June 17, 1958; education: B.A., University of Cincinnati, 1980; B.S. and D.P.M., William M. Scholl College of Podiatric Medicine, Chicago, IL, 1985; professional: private practice physician/surgeon, 1986–2012; United States Army Reserve, 1998–present; religion: Catholic; married: Monica; children: Brad R. Wenstrup, Jr.; committees: Armed Services; Permanent Select Committee on Intelligence; Veterans' Affairs; elected to the 113th Congress on November 6, 2012; reelected to the 114th Congress on November 4, 2014.

Office Listings

http://wenstrup.house.gov   https://www.facebook.com/repbradwenstrup   twitter:@repbradwenstrup

1318 Longworth House Office Building, Washington, DC 20515	(202) 225–3164
Chief of Staff.—Derek Harley.	FAX: 225–1992
Legislative Director.—Lisa Collins.	
Communications Director.—Greg Brooks.	
Scheduler.—April Lyman.	
7954 Beechmont Avenue, Suite 200, Cincinnati, OH 45255	(513) 474–7777
District Director.—Jeff Groenke.	
170 North Main Street, Peebles, OH 45660	(513) 605–1380
4350 Aicholtz Road, Cincinnati, OH 45245	(513) 605–1389

Counties: ADAMS, BROWN, CLERMONT, HAMILTON (part), HIGHLAND, PIKE, SCIOTO (part), AND ROSS (part). CITIES AND TOWNSHIPS: Anderson TWP, Batavia, Blue Ash, Cincinnati (part), Chillicothe, Georgetown, Hillsboro, Loveland, Manchester, Milford, Mount Orab, New Richmond, Norwood, Peebles, Piketon, Portsmouth, Ripley, Sardinia, and Union TWP. Population (2010), 721,031.

ZIP Codes: 45101–03, 45106–07, 45112, 45115, 45118, 45120–22, 45130–31, 45133, 45140, 45142, 45144, 45150, 45153–54, 45156–57, 45160, 45162, 45167–68, 45171, 45174, 45176, 45202, 45206, 45208–09, 45212–13, 45226–27, 45230, 45236, 45241–46, 45255, 45601, 45612–13, 45616, 45624, 45642, 45646, 45648, 45650, 45652, 45657, 45660–63, 45671, 45679, 45684, 45690, 45693, 45697

* * *

THIRD DISTRICT

JOYCE BEATTY, Democrat, of Blacklick, OH; born in Dayton, OH, March 12, 1950; education: B.A., Central State University, Wilberforce, OH, 1972; M.S., Wright State University, Fairborn, OH, 1974; attended University of Cincinnati, Cincinnati, OH; professional: executive director, Montgomery County, OH; human services, professor; businesswoman; member, Ohio State House of Representatives, 1999–2008, Minority Leader, 2006–08; senior vice-president, The Ohio State University, 2008–12; member: House Human Trafficking Caucus; Financial Literacy Caucus; Women's Caucus; Heart and Stroke Coalition; Brain Injury Taskforce; Tom Lantos Human Rights Commission; CBC Taskforce on Economic Development and Wealth Creation; Delta Sigma Theta Sorority, Inc. (life member) and The Links, Inc.; House Region 10 Whip; named one of the 150 most powerful African Americans, *Ebony Magazine*, 2008; recipient, YWCA Women of Achievement Award, 2002; NAACP Freedom Award; United Way Key Club Community Leadership Award, 2014; married: Otto; stepchildren: Laurel and Otto; committees: Financial Services; elected to the 113th Congress on November 6, 2012; reelected to the 114th Congress on November 4, 2014.

Office Listings

http://www.beatty.house.gov

133 Cannon House Office Building, Washington, DC 20515	(202) 225–4324
Chief of Staff.—Kimberly Ross.	FAX: 225–1984
Legislative Director.—Jennifer Storipan.	
Scheduler/Executive Assistant.—Ashley-Dior Thomas.	
Communications Director.—Galen Alexander.	
471 East Broad Street, Suite 1100, Columbus, OH 43215	(614) 220–0003
District Director.—Matthew Woods-Koppitch.	FAX: 220–5640

Counties: FRANKLIN (part). Population (2010), 732,258.

ZIP Codes: 43004, 43026, 43054, 43068, 43081, 43085, 43109–10, 43119, 43123, 43125, 43137, 43201–07, 43209–15, 43217, 43219, 43221–24, 43227–32

* * *

FOURTH DISTRICT

JAMES D. "JIM" JORDAN, Republican, of Urbana, OH; born in Troy, OH, February 17, 1964; education: graduated, Graham High School, St. Paris, OH, 1982; B.S. in economics, University of Wisconsin, Madison, WI, 1986; M.A. in education, The Ohio State University, Columbus, OH, 1991; J.D., Capital University School of Law, Columbus, OH, 2001; professional: assistant wrestling coach, The Ohio State University, 1987–95; State Representative, Ohio House of Representatives, 85th District, 1995–2001; State Senator, Ohio State Senate, 12th District, 2001–07; awards: four-time high school wrestling champion (Ohio), 1979–82; two-time NCAA Division I National Wrestling Champion, 1985–86; three-time All American, 1984–86; Wisconsin Badgers Hall of Fame; third place, Olympic Trials in Wrestling, 1988; Friend of the Taxpayer, Americans for Tax Reform, 1997, Leadership In Government Award from the Ohio Roundtable and Freedom Forum, 2001; awards from the United Conservatives of Ohio: Outstanding Freshman Legislator Award, 1996; Watchdog of the Treasury, 1996, 2000, 2004; Pro-Life Legislator of the Year, 1998; Outstanding Legislator Award, 2004; Hero of the Taxpayer, Americans for Tax Reform, 2007; National Legislator of the Year, Coalitions for America, 2012; Freedom Fighter Award, Freedom Works, 2012; activities: Grace Bible Church, Springfield; Local and National Right to Life organizations; Champaign County Republican Executive Committee; married: Polly (Stickley) Jordan; parents: John and Shirley Jordan; children: Rachel, Benjamin, Jessie, and Issac; committees: Judiciary; Oversight and Government Reform; Select Committee on Benghazi; elected to the 110th Congress on November 7, 2006; reelected to each succeeding Congress.

Office Listings

http://www.jordan.house.gov   https://www.facebook.com/repjimjordan
twitter.com/jim__jordan

1524 Longworth House Office Building, Washington, DC 20515	(202) 225–2676
Chief of Staff.—Ray Yonkura.	FAX: 226–0577
Legislative Director.—Jared Dilley.	
Executive Assistant/Scheduler.—Melissa Wade.	
3121 West Elm Plaza, Lima, OH 45805–2516	(419) 999–6455

Office Listings—Continued

13B East Main Street, Norwalk, OH 44857 .... (419) 663–1426
District Director.—Cameron Warner.

Counties: ALLEN, AUGLAIZE, CHAMPAIGN, CRAWFORD, ERIE (part), HURON (part), LOGAN (part), MARION (part), MERCER (part), SANDUSKY, SENECA, SHELBY, AND UNION. Population (2010), 721,032.

ZIP Codes: 43009, 43036, 43044–45, 43047, 43060, 43067, 43070, 43072, 43077, 43084, 43310–11, 43314–26, 43330–38, 43340–51, 43356–60, 43407, 43410, 43420, 43431, 43435, 43442, 44049, 44802, 44809, 44814–16, 44818, 44820, 44828, 44836, 44841, 44846, 44849, 44853–54, 44856, 44861, 44864–65, 44867, 44875, 44881, 44883, 44887, 45302, 45306, 45312, 45317, 45326, 45333–34, 45336, 45340, 45344, 45353, 45356, 45360, 45363, 45365, 45380, 45388–89, 45502, 45801–02, 45804–10, 45812, 45819–20, 45822, 45830, 45833, 45845, 45850, 45854, 45865–66, 45969–71, 45877, 45884–85, 45887–88, 45894–96

* * *

FIFTH DISTRICT

ROBERT E. "BOB" LATTA, Republican, of Bowling Green, OH; born in Bluffton, OH, April 18, 1956; graduated, Bowling Green High School, Bowling Green, OH, 1974; Bowling Green State University, Bowling Green, OH, 1978; B.A., history, University of Toledo School of Law, Toledo, OH, 1981; J.D., legislator, lawyer; awards: Ohio Farm Bureau "Friend of Farm Bureau" Award; the United States Chamber of Commerce "Spirit of Enterprise" Award; American Conservative Union "ACU Conservative" Award; United Conservatives of Ohio "Watchdog of the Treasury"; the U.S. Sportsmen's Alliance, "Patriot Award"; Ohio National Guard "Major General Charles Dick Award for Legislative Excellence", "President's Award"; National Federation of Independent Business's (NFIB) Guardian of Small Business Award; National Association of Manufacturer's Manufacturing Legislative Excellence Award; Prism Propane Award; National Grocer's Association Spirit of America Award; Family Research Council's True Blue Award; National Retail Federation's Hero of Main Street Award; Healthcare Distribution Management Association's (HDMA) Rx Safety and Leadership Award (Rx Award); Safari Club Internationals Federal Legislator of the Year; the National Shooting Sports Foundation's Legislator of the Year; religion: Roman Catholic; family: wife, Marcia "Sloan" Latta; daughters, Elizabeth and Maria Latta; member, Bowling Green Noon Kiwanis, Bowling Green Chamber of Commerce; Wood County Farm Bureau; serves as Deputy Whip; caucuses: co-chair of the Republican New Media Caucus; co-chair of the Congressional French Caucus; committees: Energy and Commerce; elected to the 111th Congress on November 4, 2008; reelected to each succeeding Congress.

Office Listings

http://latta.house.gov

2448 Rayburn House Office Building, Washington, DC 20515 .... (202) 225–6405
Chief of Staff.—Ryan Walker. FAX: 225–1985
Deputy Chief/Legislative Director.—Allison Witt.
Scheduler.—Erin Partee.
1045 North Main Street, Suite 6, Bowling Green, OH 43402 .... (419) 354–8700
101 Clinton Street, Suite 1200, Defiance, OH 43512 .... (419) 782–1996
318 Dorney Plaza, Room 302, Findlay, OH 45840 .... (419) 422–7791

Counties: DEFIANCE, FULTON, HANCOCK, HARDIN, HENRY, LUCAS (part), MERCER (part), OTTAWA, PAULDING, PUTNAM, VAN WERT, WILLIAMS, WOOD, AND WYANDOT. Population (2010), 726,090.

ZIP Codes: 43310, 43316, 43323, 43326, 43330–32, 43337, 43340, 43345, 43347, 43351, 43359, 43402–03, 43406, 43408, 43412–13, 43416, 43430, 43432, 43443, 43445, 43447, 43449–52, 43457–58, 43460, 43462–63, 43465–69, 43501–02, 43504–06, 43511–12, 43515–19, 43521–29, 43531–37, 43540–43, 43545, 43547–49, 43551, 43553–58, 43560, 43565–67, 43569–71, 43605–06, 43613–15, 43617, 43619, 43623, 44802, 44804, 44817, 44830, 44844, 44849, 44882, 45810, 45812–14, 45816–17, 45821–22, 45827–28, 45830, 45831–33, 45835–36, 45838, 45840–41, 45843–44, 45846, 45849–51, 45853, 45855–56, 45858–59, 45861–64, 45867–68, 45872–77, 45879–82, 45886–87, 45889–91, 45894, 45896–99

* * *

SIXTH DISTRICT

WILLIAM L. "BILL" JOHNSON, Republican, of Marietta, OH; born in Roseboro, NC, November 10, 1954; raised in Roseboro, NC; education: B.A., graduated *summa cum laude* at Troy University, Troy, AL, 1979; M.A., computer sciences, Georgia Tech, Atlanta, GA, 1984; professional: co-founder of Johnson-Schley Management Group, Inc.; founder of J2 Business Solutions, Inc.; chief information officer of a global manufacturer of highly electronic components for the transportation industry; military: retired as Lieutenant Colonel, distinguished graduate from the Air Force Reserve Officer Training Corps, Squadron Officers School, and Air Command and Staff College; religion: Protestant; family: married to LeeAnn Johnson; children: Nathan, Joshua, Julie, and Jessica; awards: recipient of Air Force Meritorious Service Medal; Air Force Commendation Medal; National Defense Service Medal; caucuses: Air Force Caucus; Aluminum Caucus; Army Aviation Caucus; Automotive Caucus; Baseball Caucus; China Caucus; Cybersecurity Caucus; Diabetes Caucus; Dyslexia Caucus; E-Learning Caucus; Ethnic and Religious Freedom in Sri Lanka Caucus; Fire Services Caucus; General Aviation Caucus; Hellenic Issues Caucus; House Law Enforcement Caucus; Invisible Wounds Caucus; Israel Allies Caucus; Joint Strike Fighter Caucus; Military Sexual Assault Prevention Caucus; Military Veterans Caucus; Mobility Air Forces Caucus; Natural Gas Caucus; Ohio River Basin Congressional Caucus; Prayer Caucus; Problem Solvers Caucus; Pro-Israel Caucus; Republican Israel Caucus; Rock and Roll Caucus; Sportsmen's Caucus; Steel Caucus; U.S.-Turkish Relations and Turkish Americans Caucus; USO Congressional Caucus; Veterans Jobs Caucus; Congressional Vision Caucus; committees: Energy and Commerce; Science, Space, and Technology; elected to the 112th Congress on November 2, 2010; reelected to each succeeding Congress.

Office Listings

http://billjohnson.house.gov

1710 Longworth House Office Building, Washington, DC 20515	(202) 225–5705

Chief of Staff.—Mike Smullen.
Legislative Director.—Elise Conner.
Communications Director.—Ben Keeler.
Scheduler / Office Manager.—Lisl Davis.

246 Front Street, Marietta, OH 45750	(740) 376–0868
192 East State Street, Salem, OH 44460	(330) 337–6951
202 Park Avenue, Suite C, Ironton, OH 45638	(740) 534–9431
116 Southgate Parkway, Cambridge, OH 43725	(740) 432 2366

Counties: ATHENS (part), BELMONT, CARROLL, COLUMBIANA, GALLIA, GUERNSEY, HARRISON, JACKSON, JEFFERSON, LAWRENCE, MAHONING (part), MEIGS, MONROE, MUSKINGUM (part), NOBLE, SCIOTO (part), TUSCARAWAS (part), AND WASHINGTON. Population (2010), 721,032.

ZIP Codes: 43701, 43711, 43713, 43716–19, 43722–25, 43732–33, 43736, 43747, 43749–50, 43754–55, 43759, 43762, 43767–68, 43772–73, 43778–80, 43786–88, 43793, 43802, 43812, 43821–22, 43830, 43832, 43837, 43842, 43901–08, 43910, 43912–15, 43917, 43920, 43925–28, 43930–35, 43938–40, 43942–48, 43950–53, 43961–64, 43967–68, 43970–74, 43976–77, 43983, 43985–86, 43988, 44401, 44406, 44408, 44413, 44423, 44427, 44431–32, 44441–45, 44449, 44451–52, 44454–55, 44460, 44493, 44514, 44601, 44607, 44609, 44615, 44620–21, 44625, 44629, 44634, 44643–44, 44651, 44653, 44656–57, 44663, 44672, 44675, 44682–83, 44688, 44693, 44695, 44699, 44730, 45601, 45613–14, 45619–21, 45623, 45629, 45631, 45634, 45636, 45638, 45640, 45645, 45648, 45650, 45652, 45653, 45656, 45658–59, 45662–63, 45669, 45672, 45674, 45678, 45680, 45682, 45685–86, 45688, 45692, 45694, 45696, 45701, 45710–11, 45714–15, 45721, 45723–24, 45727, 45729, 45734–35, 45741–46, 45750, 45760, 45767–73, 45775–76, 45779, 45784, 45786–89.

* * *

SEVENTH DISTRICT

ROBERT B. GIBBS, Republican, of Lakeville, OH; born in Peru, IN, June 14, 1954; education: graduated from Bay Village Senior High School, Bay Village, OH; A.A.S., Ohio State University Agricultural Technical Institute, Wooster, OH, 1974; professional: technician; farmer; business owner; president, Ohio Farm Bureau Federation; member of the Ohio State House of Representatives, 2003–09; member of the Ohio State Senate, 2009–10; married: Jody Gibbs; children: Adam, Amy, and Andrew; committees: Agriculture; Transportation and Infrastructure; elected to the 112th Congress on November 2, 2010; reelected to each succeeding Congress.

Office Listings

http://www.gibbs.house.gov

329 Cannon House Office Building, Washington, DC 20515	(202) 225–6265
	FAX: 225–3394

Chief of Staff.—Jonathan Gormley.
Scheduler.—Meghan Keivel.
Legislative Director.—Meredith Gourash.
Legislative Aides: Bill Davis, Hillary Gross.
Communications Director.—Dallas Gerber.

110 Cottage Street, Ashland, OH 44805	(419) 207–0650
	FAX: 207–0655

District Director.—Darrell Kick.

Counties: HURON (part), MEDINA (part), RICHLAND (part), KNOX, HOLMES, ASHLAND, COSHOCTON (part), TUSCARAWAS (part), STARK (part), LORAIN (part). Population (2010), 726,076.

ZIP Codes: 43005–06, 43011, 43014, 43019, 43022, 43028, 43037, 43050, 43080, 43749, 43804, 43811–12, 43821–22, 43824, 43832, 43836, 43843–44, 43845, 44011, 44028, 44035, 44039, 44044, 44050, 44090, 44149, 44212, 44214–15, 44235, 44253–54, 44256, 44273, 44275, 44280, 44287, 44601, 44608, 44610–13, 44618, 44624, 44626–28, 44632–34, 44637–38, 44641, 44643, 44646–47, 44652, 44654, 44657, 44661–62, 44666, 44669–70, 44676, 44681, 44685, 44687–90, 44702–10, 44714, 44718, 44720–21, 44805, 44807, 44811, 44813, 44822, 44826–27, 44833, 44837–38, 44840, 44842–43, 44847–48, 44850–51, 44855, 44857, 44859, 44864–66, 44874–75, 44878, 44880–90, 44903, 44905–07

* * *

EIGHTH DISTRICT

Formerly the Office of Representative John A. Boehner

Office Listings

1011 Longworth House Office Building, Washington, DC 20515 .... (202) 225–6205
    Chief of Staff.—Ryan Day.
    Press Secretary.—Olivia Hnat.
7969 Cincinnati-Dayton Road, Suite B, West Chester, OH 45069 .... (513) 779–5400
12 South Plum Street, Troy, Ohio 45373 .... (937) 339–1524
76 East High Street, 3rd Floor, Springfield, OH 45502 .... (937) 322–1120

Counties: COUNTIES: BUTLER, CLARK, DARKE, MIAMI, PREBLE, MERCER (part). Population (2010), 721,032.

ZIP Codes: 43010, 43044, 43153, 45003–04, 45011–15, 45018, 45042, 45044, 45050, 45053, 45055–56, 45061–64, 45067, 45069–71, 45241, 45246, 45303–04, 45308, 45310–12, 45317–26, 45328, 45330–32, 45337–39, 45341, 45344, 45346–49, 45361–62, 45368–69, 45371–74, 45378, 45380–83, 45387–88, 45390, 45501–06, 45822, 45826, 45828, 45846, 45860, 45862, 45866, 45869, 45882–83, 45894, 45898

* * *

NINTH DISTRICT

MARCY KAPTUR, Democrat, of Toledo, OH; born in Toledo, June 17, 1946; education: graduated, St. Ursula Academy, Toledo, 1964; B.A., University of Wisconsin, Madison, 1968; Master of Urban Planning, University of Michigan, Ann Arbor, 1974; attended University of Manchester, England, 1974; professional: urban planner; assistant director for urban affairs, domestic policy staff, White House, 1977–79; American Planning Association and American Institute of Certified Planners Fellow; member: National Center for Urban Ethnic Affairs Advisory Committee; University of Michigan Urban Planning Alumni Association; NAACP Urban League; Polish Museum; Polish American Historical Association; Lucas County Democratic Party Executive Committee; Democratic Women's Campaign Association; Little Flower Parish Church; religion: Roman Catholic; caucuses: co-chair, House Auto Parts Task Force; co-chair, House Automotive Caucus; co-chair, House Great Lakes Caucus; Hungarian, Ukrainian and 4-H Caucuses; committees: Appropriations; elected on November 2, 1982, to the 98th Congress; reelected to each succeeding Congress.

Office Listings

http://www.kaptur.house.gov

2186 Rayburn House Office Building, Washington, DC 20515 .... (202) 225–4146
    Chief of Staff.—Steve Katich.
    Office Manager / Scheduler.—Shawn Ferguson.
    Legislative Director.—Jenny Perrino.
One Maritime Plaza, Suite 600, Toledo, OH 43604 .... (419) 259–7500
16024 Madison Street, Suite 3, Lakewood, OH 44107 .... (216) 767–5933
    FAX: (419) 255–9623
5592 Broadview Road, Room 101, Parma, OH 44134 .... (440) 799–8499
    FAX: (419) 225–9623

Counties: ERIE COUNTY. CITIES AND TOWNSHIPS: Bellevue, Berlin Heights, Berlinville, Birmingham, Bloomingville, Bronson, Castalia, Chatham, Clarksfield, Collins, East Townsend, Fitchville, Hartland, Huron, Kimball, Litchfield, Milan, Mitiwanga, Monroeville, New London, Norwalk, Nova, Olena, Ridgefield, River Corners, Ruggles, Ruggles Beach, Sandusky, Shinrock, Spencer, Steuben, Sullivan, Wakeman, West Clarksfield. LORAIN COUNTY. CITIES AND TOWNSHIPS: Amherst,

Beaver Park, Belden, Beulah Beach, Brownhelm, Columbia Station, Elyria, Grafton, Henrietta, Kipton, Lagrange, Linwood Park, Lorain, North Eaton, Oberlin, Ridgeville, Rochester, South Amherst, Vermilion, Wellington. LUCAS COUNTY (part). CITIES AND TOWNSHIPS: Berkey, Curtice, Gypsum, Harbor View, Holland, Maumee, Monclova, Northwood, Oregon, Swanton, Sylvania, Toledo, Waterville, Whitehouse, Woodville. OTTAWA COUNTY. CITIES AND TOWNSHIPS: Bay Shore, Bono, Catawba Island, Clay Center, Danbury, Eagle Beach, Elliston, Elmore, Gem Beach, Genoa, Graytown, Hessville, Isle St. George, Kelleys Island, Lacarne, Lakeside, Lindsey, Marblehead, Martin, Oak Harbor, Port Clinton, Portage, Put-in-Bay, Rocky Ridge, Springbrook, Vickery, Washington, Wayne, Whites Landing, and Williston. Population (2010), 721,032.

ZIP Codes: 43408, 43412, 43416, 43430, 43432–34, 43436, 43438–40, 43442, 43445–47, 43449, 43452, 43456, 43458, 43464, 43468–69, 43504, 43528, 43537, 43542, 43558, 43560, 43566, 43571, 43601–18, 43620, 43623–24, 43635, 43652, 43656–57, 43659–61, 43666–67, 43681–82, 43697, 43699, 44001, 44028, 44035, 44044, 44049–50, 44053, 44074, 44089–90, 44253, 44256, 44275, 44280, 44811, 44814, 44816, 44824, 44826, 44839, 44846–47, 44851, 44857, 44859, 44870–71, 44880, 44889

* * *

TENTH DISTRICT

MICHAEL R. TURNER, Republican, of Dayton, OH; born in Dayton, January 11, 1960; education: B.A., Ohio Northern University, 1982; J.D., Case Western Reserve University Law School, 1985; M.B.A., University of Dayton, 1992; professional: attorney; Ohio Bar Association; California Bar Association; Bar of the Supreme Court of the United States; public service: Mayor of Dayton, 1994–2002; children: Jessica and Carolyn; committees: Armed Services; Oversight and Government Reform; Permanent Select Committee on Intelligence; elected to the 108th Congress on November 5, 2002; reelected to each succeeding Congress.

Office Listings

http://www.turner.house.gov

2239 Rayburn House Office Building, Washington, DC 20515	(202) 225–6465
Chief of Staff.—Adam Howard.	FAX: 225 6754
Legislative Director.—Vincent Erte.	
Scheduler.—Kate Pietkiewicz.	
120 West Third Street, Suite 305, Dayton, OH 45402	(937) 225–2843
District Director.—Kelly Geers.	

Counties: MONTGOMERY, GREENE, AND FAYETTE (northern part). Population (2010), 721,032.

ZIP Codes: 43106, 43128, 43142–43, 43145, 43153, 43160, 45005, 45066, 45068–69, 45301, 45305, 45307, 45309, 45314–16, 45322, 45324, 45327, 45335, 45342, 45344–45, 45354, 45368, 45370 71, 45381, 45384–85, 45387, 45402–06, 45409–10, 45414 20, 45424, 45426, 45428–34, 45439–40, 45449, 45458–59

* * *

ELEVENTH DISTRICT

MARCIA L. FUDGE, Democrat, of Warrensville Heights, OH; born in Cleveland, OH, October 29, 1952; B.S., Ohio State University, 1975; J.D., Cleveland Marshall College of Law, 1983; professional: Director of Budget and Finance, Cuyahoga County Prosecutor's Office; Chief Administrator for Cuyahoga County Prosecutor; Mayor of Warrensville Heights, OH; committees: Agriculture; Education and the Workforce; elected to the 110th Congress, by special election, to fill the vacancy caused by the death of United States Representative Stephanie Tubbs Jones; elected to the 111th Congress on November 4, 2008; reelected to each succeeding Congress.

Office Listings

http://www.fudge.house.gov

2344 Rayburn House Office Building, Washington, DC 20515	(202) 225–7032
Chief of Staff.—Veleter Mazyck.	
Legislative Director.—Kellie Adesina.	
Press Secretary.—Lauren Williams.	
Scheduler/Office Manager.—Lewis Myers.	
4834 Richmond Road, Suite 150, Warrensville Heights, OH 44128	(216) 522–4900
District Director.—John Hairston.	
Scheduler/Office Manager.—Linda Matthews.	
1225 Lawton Street, Akron, OH 44320	(330) 835–4758
Outreach Coordinator.—Ginger Baylor.	

Counties: CUYAHOGA COUNTY (part), SUMMIT COUNTY (part). CITIES: Akron, Bath Township, Beachwood, Bedford, Bedford Heights, Bratenahl, Broadview Heights, Brooklyn Heights, Cleveland, Cleveland Heights, Cuyahoga Heights, East Cleveland, Euclid, Fairlawn, Garfield Heights, Glenwillow, Highland Hills, Maple Heights, Newburg Heights, North Randall, Oakwood Village, Orange, Pepper Pike, Richfield Township, Richfield Village, Richmond Heights, Seven Hills, Shaker Heights, South Euclid, University Heights, Warrensville Heights, and Woodmere. Population (2010), 705,659.

ZIP Codes: 44022, 44101–15, 44117–44125, 44127–28, 44131–33, 44137, 44139, 44141, 44143, 44146–47, 44256, 44264, 44286, 44301–08, 44310–14, 44319–21, 44333

* * *

TWELFTH DISTRICT

PATRICK J. TIBERI, Republican, of Columbus, OH; born in Columbus, October 21, 1962; education: B.A., Ohio State University, 1985; professional: real estate agent; assistant to U.S. Representative John Kasich (R–OH); public service: served as Majority Leader, Ohio House of Representatives, 1992–2000; organizations: Westerville Chamber of Commerce; Columbus Board of Realtors; Military Veterans and Community Service Commission; Sons of Italy; awards: Fraternal Order of Police Outstanding Legislator; Watchdog of the Treasury Award; American Red Cross Volunteer Service Award; married: Denice; committees: vice chair, Joint Economic Committee; Ways and Means; elected to the 107th Congress on November 7, 2000; reelected to each succeeding Congress.

Office Listings

http://www.tiberi.house.gov   https://twitter.com/pattiberi
https://www.facebook.com/reppattiberi   https://www.instagram.com/pattiberi

1203 Longworth House Office Building, Washington, DC 20515 .... (202) 225–5355
    Chief of Staff.—Kelli Briggs.   FAX: 226–4523
    Legislative Director.—Whitney Daffner.
    Communications Director.—Breann Gonzalez.
250 East Wilson Bridge Road, Suite 100, Worthington, OH 43085 .... (614) 523–2555
    District Director.—Mark Bell.

Counties: DELAWARE, FRANKLIN (part), LICKING, MARION (part), MORROW, MUSKINGUM (part), and RICHLAND (part). Population (2010), 728,420.

ZIP Codes: 43001–04, 43011, 43013, 43015–17, 43023, 43025–26, 43031–33, 43035, 43040, 43046, 43054–55, 43061– 62, 43065–66, 43068, 43071, 43074, 43082, 43085, 43147, 43201, 43229–30, 43235, 43240, 43334, 43342, 43344, 43356

* * *

THIRTEENTH DISTRICT

TIM RYAN, Democrat, of Howland, OH; born in Niles, July 16, 1973; education: B.S., Bowling Green University, 1995; J.D., University of New Hampshire School of Law (formerly Franklin Pierce Law Center), 2000; professional: legislative aide, Washington, DC; married: Andrea Ryan; committees: Appropriations; Budget; elected to the 108th Congress on November 5, 2002; reelected to each succeeding Congress.

Office Listings

http://timryan.house.gov   twitter: @reptimryan   facebook: congressmantimryan

1421 Longworth House Office Building, Washington, DC 20515 .... (202) 225–5261
    Chief of Staff.—Ron Grimes.   FAX: 225–3719
    Scheduler.—Erin Isenberg.
    Legislative Director.—Anne Sokolov.
197 West Market Street, Warren, OH 44481 .... (330) 373–0074
241 Federal Plaza West, Youngstown, OH 44503 .... (330) 740–0193
1030 East Tallmadge Avenue, Akron, OH 44310 .... (330) 630–7311

Counties: MAHONING (part), PORTAGE (part), STARK, SUMMIT (part), TRUMBULL (part). Population (2010), 723,713.

ZIP Codes: 44141, 44201, 44203, 44221, 44223–24, 44231, 44236, 44240, 44241, 44243, 44255, 44260, 44262, 44264, 44266, 44272, 44278, 44285, 44288, 44301–08, 44310–14, 44319–20, 44333, 44401–06, 44410–12, 44418, 44420, 44425, 44429–30, 44436–38, 44440, 44444, 44446, 44449, 44451, 44470–71, 44473, 44481, 44483–85, 44491, 44502– 07, 44509–12, 44514–15, 44601, 44640

* * *

FOURTEENTH DISTRICT

DAVID JOYCE, Republican, of Geauga, OH; born in Cleveland, OH, March 17, 1957; education: B.S., the University of Dayton, Dayton, OH, 1979; J.D., the University of Dayton, 1982; professional: prosecuting attorney, Geauga County, 1988–2012; married: Kelly Joyce; children: Trenton, KK, and Bridey; committees: Appropriations; elected to the 113th Congress on November 6, 2012; reelected to the 114th Congress on November 4, 2014.

Office Listings

http://joyce.house.gov

1124 Longworth House Office Building, Washington, DC 20515	(202) 225–5731
Chief of Staff.—Dino DiSanto.	FAX: 225–3307
Scheduler.—Maura Jochum.	
Legislative Director.—John Miceli.	
Communications Director.—Kevin Benacci.	
1 Victoria Place, Suite 320, Painesville, OH 44077	(440) 352–3939
	FAX: 352–3622
10075 Ravenna Road, Twinsburg, OH 44087	(330) 425–9291
	FAX: 425–7071

Counties: SUMMIT (part), CUYAHOGA (part), PORTAGE (part), TRUMBULL (part), LAKE, GEAUGA, AND ASHTABULA. Population (2010), 721,032.

ZIP Codes: 44003–04, 44010, 44021–24, 44026, 44030, 44032, 44040–41, 44045–48, 44056–57, 44060, 44062, 44064– 65, 44067, 44072, 44076–77, 44080–82, 44084–87, 44092–95, 44099, 44122, 44124–25, 44131, 44139, 44141, 44143, 44146–47, 44202, 44221, 44223–24, 44231, 44234, 44236, 44240–41, 44255, 44262, 44264, 44266, 44278, 44313, 44402, 44404, 44410, 44417–18, 44428, 44439, 44450, 44473, 44481, 44491

* * *

FIFTEENTH DISTRICT

STEVE STIVERS, Republican, of Columbus, OH; born in Cincinnati, OH, March 24, 1965; education: B.A., Ohio State University, Columbus, OH, 1989; M.B.A., Ohio State University, 1996; M.A., U.S. Army War College; professional: military; colonel, Ohio Army National Guard, 1988–present; Ohio Company and Bank One; member of the Ohio State Senate, 2003–08; married: Karen Stivers; children: Sarah and Samuel; committees: Financial Services; elected to the 112th Congress on November 2, 2010; reelected to each succeeding Congress.

Office Listings

http://www.stivers.house.gov

1022 Longworth House Office Building, Washington, DC 20515	(202) 225–2015
Chief of Staff.—Courtney Whetstone.	FAX: 225–3529
Scheduler.—Sara Donlon.	
Legislative Director.—Jesse Walls.	
Communications Director.—Vacant.	
3790 Municipal Way, Hilliard, OH 43026	(614) 771–4968
	FAX: 771–3990
Fairfield County District Office, 123 South Broad Street, Suite 235, Lancaster, OH 43130 ..	(740) 654–2654
	FAX: 654–2482
Clinton County District Office, 69 North South Street, Wilimington, OH 45177	(937) 283–7049
	FAX: 283–7052

Counties: ATHENS (part), CLINTON, FAIRFIELD, FAYETTE (part), FRANKLIN (part), Hocking, Madison, Morgan, Perry, Pickaway, Ross (part), and Vinton. Population (2010) 721,031.

ZIP Codes: 43002, 43016–17, 43026, 43029, 43044, 43046, 43062, 43064, 43068, 43076, 43101–03, 43105, 43107, 43110– 13, 43115–17, 43119, 43123, 43125–27, 43130, 43135–38, 43140, 43143–58, 43160, 43162, 43164, 43201, 43204, 43206–07, 43210, 43212, 43215, 43217, 43220–23, 43228, 43235, 43724, 43728, 43730–31, 43739, 43748, 43756, 43758, 43760–61, 43764, 43766, 43777, 43782–83, 43787, 45068, 45107, 45113, 45123, 45135, 45142, 45146, 45148, 45159, 45164, 45166, 45169, 45177, 45335, 45369, 45601, 45622, 45628, 45634, 45644, 45647, 45651, 45654, 45672, 45681, 45686, 45695, 45698, 45701, 45710–11, 45715–16, 45719, 45723, 45732, 45735, 45740, 45761, 45764, 45766, 45776, 45778, 45780, 45782

* * *

SIXTEENTH DISTRICT

JIM RENACCI, Republican, of Wadsworth, OH; born in Monongahela, PA, December 3, 1958; education: B.S., Indiana University of Pennsylvania, 1980; professional: certified public accountant (CPA); owner, nursing home facility; executive, professional arena football team; Wadsworth Board of Zoning Appeals, 1994–95; president, Wadsworth City Council, 1999– 2003; mayor of Wadsworth, 2004–2008; business management consultant; religion: Roman Catholic; married: Tina Renacci; 3 children; caucuses: Congressional Coal; Congressional Steel; Northeast-Midwest Coalition; Congressional CPA; General Aviation; Hydrogen and Fuel Cell; committees: Budget; Ways and Means; elected to the 112th Congress on November 2, 2010; reelected to each succeeding Congress.

Office Listings

http://www.renacci.house.gov

328 Cannon House Office Building, Washington, DC 20515 .... (202) 225–3876
    Chief of Staff.—Surya Gunasekara.   FAX: 225–3059
    Communications Director.—Megan Taylor.
    Director of Operations.—Michelle Runk.
    Legislative Director.—Patrick Velliky.
1 Park Center Drive, Suite 302, Wadsworth, OH 44281 .... (330) 334–0040
    Constituent Service Director.—Heidi Matthews.   FAX: 493–9265

Counties: WAYNE, STARK (part), MEDINA (part), PORTAGE (part), SUMMIT (part), CUYAHOGA (part). Population (2010), 724,108.

ZIP Codes: 44017, 44070, 44107, 44116, 44126, 44129–30, 44133–34, 44136, 44138, 44142, 44145, 44147, 44149, 44201, 44203, 44212, 44214–17, 44230, 44233, 44240, 44250–51, 44254, 44256, 44260, 44265–66, 44270, 44272–74, 44276, 44278, 44281, 44287, 44306, 44312, 44319–21, 44333, 44606, 44611, 44614, 44618, 44624, 44627, 44632, 44638, 44645–47, 44659, 44662, 44666–67, 44676–77, 44685, 44691, 44706, 44708–10, 44718, 44720–21, 44840

OKLAHOMA

(Population 2010, 3,751,351)

SENATORS

JAMES M. INHOFE, Republican, of Tulsa, OK; born in Des Moines, IA, November 17, 1934; education: graduated, Central High School, Tulsa, OK, 1953; B.A., University of Tulsa, OK, 1959; military service: served in the U.S. Army, private first class, 1957–58; professional: businessman; active pilot; president, Quaker Life Insurance Company; Oklahoma House of Representatives, 1967–69; Oklahoma State Senate, 1969–77; Mayor of Tulsa, OK, 1978–84; religion: member, First Presbyterian Church of Tulsa; married: Kay Kirkpatrick; children: Jim, Perry, Molly, and Katy; twelve grandchildren; committees: chair, Environment and Public Works; Armed Services; elected to the 100th Congress on November 4, 1986; reelected to each succeeding Congress; elected to the U.S. Senate on November 8, 1994, finishing the unexpired term of Senator David Boren; reelected to each succeeding Senate term.

Office Listings

http://inhofe.senate.gov

205 Russell Senate Office Building, Washington, DC 20510	(202) 224–4721
Chief of Staff.—Ryan Jackson.	FAX: 228–0380
Legislative Director.—Luke Holland.	
Communications Director.—Donelle Harder.	
Scheduler.—Wendi Price.	
1924 South Utica, Suite 530, Tulsa, OK 74104–6511	(918) 748–5111
1900 Northwest Expressway, Suite 1210, Oklahoma City, OK 73118	(405) 608–4381
302 North Independence, Suite 104, Enid, OK 73701	(580) 234–5105
215 East Choctaw, Suite 106, McAlester, OK 74501	(918) 426–0933

* * *

JAMES LANKFORD, Republican, of Oklahoma City, OK; born in Dallas, TX, March 4, 1968; education: B.S. Secondary Education, University of Texas, 1990; Master of Divinity, Southwestern Baptist Theological Seminary, 1994; professional: Baptist General Convention of Oklahoma Youth Ministry Specialist and Director of the Falls Creek Youth Camp, 1995–2009; public service: U.S. House of Representatives, 2011–14; elected House Republican Policy Committee Chair 2012–14; married: Cindy, 1992; children: Hannah and Jordan; religion: Christian; committees: Appropriations; Homeland Security and Governmental Affairs; Indian Affairs; Select Committee on Intelligence; elected to the U.S. Senate on November 4, 2014, to complete the unexpired term of Dr. Tom Coburn.

Office Listings

http://lankford.senate.gov　　　https://www.facebook.com/senatorlankford
https://www.flickr.com/photos/senatorlankford　　　https://instagram.com/senatorlankford
https://twitter.com/SenatorLankford

316 Hart Senate Office Building, Washington, DC 20510	(202) 225–5754
Chief of Staff.—Greg Slavonic.	
Legislative Director.—Michelle Altman.	
Scheduler.—Rachel King.	
Communications Director.—Darrell "DJ" Jordan.	
State Director.—Mona Taylor.	
1015 North Broadway Avenue, Suite 310, Oklahoma City, OK 73102	(405) 231–4941
5810 East Skelly Drive (Remington Tower), Tulsa, OK 74135	(918) 581–7651

REPRESENTATIVES

FIRST DISTRICT

JIM BRIDENSTINE, Republican, of Tulsa, OK; born in Ann Arbor, MI, June 15, 1975; education: B.A., Rice University, Texas, 1998; M.B.A., Cornell University, New York, 2009; professional: military awards: Eagle Scout, Air Medal; Navy Commendation Medal with Combat "V"; Navy and Marine Corps Achievement Medal x 2; National Defense Service Medal; Armed Forces Expeditionary Medal; Iraq Campaign Medal; Global War on Terrorism Expeditionary Medal; Navy Sea Service Deployment Ribbon; Expert Pistol Medal; Battle Efficiency

Ribbon; religion: Baptist; family: wife, Michelle; children: Walker, Sarah, and Grant; caucuses: Border Security; Cybersecurity; GOP Israel; House Freedom; F–35 Joint Strike Fighter; Missile Defense; National Guard and Reserve Component; Pilots; Pro-Life; Refinery; committees: Armed Services; Science, Space, and Technology; elected to the 113th Congress on November 6, 2012; reelected to the 114th Congress on November 4, 2014.

Office Listings

http://bridenstine.house.gov

216 Cannon House Office Building, Washington, DC 20510 ....   (202) 225–2211
    Chief of Staff.—Joseph Kaufman.   FAX: 225–9187
    Legislative Director.—James Mazol.
    Senior Legislative Assistant.—Christopher Ingraham.
    Legislative Assistant.—Mark Piland.
    Communications Director.—Sheryl Kaufman.
    Scheduler.—Megan Wenrich.
    Office Manager / Administrative Assistant.—Karen Schmitt.
2448 East 81st Street, Suite 5150, Tulsa, OK 74137 ....   (918) 935–3222
    District Director.—Gabe Sherman.
    Deputy District Director.—G. Erik Zoellner, Ed.D.
    Deputy Director of Communications.—Matt Rydin.
    Constituent Services Case Workers: Emily Helms, Sandy Minardi.
    Senior Field Representative.—Brian O'Hara.
    Field Representative.—Joe Newhouse.
    Office Manager.—Samantha Jones.

Counties: CREEK (part), ROGERS (part), TULSA, WAGONER, AND WASHINGTON. Population (2010), 750,270.

ZIP Codes: 74003, 74006, 74008, 74011–12, 74014–15, 74021–22, 74029, 74033, 74036–37, 74041, 74047, 74050–51, 74055, 74061, 74063, 74066, 74070, 74073, 74080, 74082–83, 74103–08, 74110, 74112, 74114–17, 74119–20, 74126–37, 74145–46, 74337, 74352, 74403, 74429, 74434, 74436, 74446, 74454, 74458, 74467, 74477

* * *

SECOND DISTRICT

MARKWAYNE MULLIN, Republican, of Westville, OK; born in Tulsa, OK, July 26, 1977; education: attended Missouri Valley College, Marshall, MO, 1996; A.A.S., Oklahoma State University Institute of Technology, Okmulgee, OK, 2010; professional: business owner; plumber; rancher; married on June 14, 1997; children: father of five; committees: Energy and Commerce; elected to the 113th Congress on November 6, 2012; reelected to the 114th Congress on November 4, 2014.

Office Listings

http://mullin.house.gov

1113 Longworth House Office Building, Washington, DC 20515 ....   (202) 225–2701
    Chief of Staff.—Karl Ahlgren.
    Deputy Chief of Staff.—Adam Buckalew.
    Legislative Director.—Michael Stwarka.
    Communications Director.—Liz Ritonia.
    Executive Assistant / Scheduler.—Kayla Priehs.
3109 Azalea Park Drive, Muskogee, OK 74401 ....   (918) 687–2533
1 East Choctaw, Suite 175, McAlester, OK 74501 ....   (918) 423–5951

Counties: ADAIR, ATOKA, BRYAN, CHEROKEE, CHOCTAW, COAL, CRAIG, DELAWARE, HASKELL, HUGHES, JOHNSTON, LATIMER, LEFLORE, MARSHALL, MAYES, MCCURTAIN, MCINTOSH, MUSKOGEE, NOWATA, OKFUSKEE, OKMULGEE, OTTAWA, PITTSBURGH, PUSHMATAHA, ROGERS, SEQUOYAH. Population (2010), 750,270.

ZIP Codes: 73432, 73439–40, 73446–47, 73449–50, 73455, 73460–61, 74016–19, 74027, 74042, 74048, 74053, 74072, 74301, 74330–33, 74338–40, 74342–44, 74346–47, 74349–50, 74354, 74358–63, 74364–67, 74368–70, 74401, 74421–23, 74425–28, 74430–32, 74435, 74437–38, 74441–42, 74445, 74447, 74450–52, 74455–57, 74459–60, 74462–64, 74468–70, 74471–72, 74501, 74521–23, 74525, 74528, 74530–31, 74533–36, 74538, 74540, 74543, 74546–47, 74549, 74552–53, 74556, 74560–63, 74565, 74569–72, 74576, 74578, 74701, 74720, 74723, 74726–30, 74733, 74735–36, 74740–41, 74743, 74745, 74747–48, 74750, 74756, 74759, 74764, 74766, 74829, 74833, 74839, 74845, 74848, 74850, 74856, 74859–60, 74880, 74883, 74885, 74901–02, 74930, 74932, 74935–37, 74940–42, 74944–46, 74948, 74951, 74953–56, 74959–60, 74962, 74964–66

* * *

THIRD DISTRICT

FRANK D. LUCAS, Republican, of Cheyenne, OK; born in Cheyenne, January 6, 1960; education: B.S., agricultural economics, Oklahoma State University, 1982; professional: rancher and farmer; served in Oklahoma State House of Representatives, 1989–94; secretary, Oklahoma House Republican Caucus, 1991–94; member: Oklahoma Farm Bureau, Oklahoma Cattlemen's Association, and Oklahoma Shorthorn Association; married: Lynda Bradshaw Lucas; children: Jessica, Ashlea, and Grant; committees: Agriculture; Financial Services; Science, Space, and Technology; elected to the 103rd Congress, by special election, in May 1994; reelected to each succeeding Congress.

Office Listings

http://www.lucas.house.gov

2405 Rayburn House Office Building, Washington, DC 20515	(202) 225–5565
Legislative Director.—Courtney Lincoln.	FAX: 225–8698
Communications Director.—Andrew Witmer.	
Scheduler / Office Manager.—Leslie Coppler.	
Legislative Assistants: Christian Dibblee, Jason Grassie, Brad Morris.	
10952 Northwest Expressway, Suite B, Yukon, OK 73099	(405) 373–1958
Chief of Staff.—Stacey Glasscock.	

Counties: ALFALFA, BEAVER, BECKHAM, BLAINE, CADDO, CANADIAN (part), CIMARRON, CREEK (part), CUSTER, DEWEY, ELLIS, GARFIELD, GRANT, GREER, HARMON, HARPER, JACKSON, KINGFISHER, KAY, KIOWA, LINCOLN, LOGAN, MAJOR, NOBLE, OSAGE, PAWNEE, PAYNE, ROGER MILLS, TEXAS, WASHITA, WOODS, AND WOODWARD. CITIES: Altus, Clinton, El Reno, Elk City, Enid, Guthrie, Guymon, Oklahoma City, Perry, Ponce City, Sapulpa, Stillwater, Tulsa, Weatherford, Woodward and Yukon. Population (2010), 745,941.

ZIP Codes: 73001, 73005–07, 73009, 73014–17, 73021–22, 73024, 73027–29, 73033–34, 73036, 73038, 73040–45, 73047–48, 73050, 73053–54, 73056, 73058–59, 73061–64, 73073, 73077–79, 73085, 73090, 73096–97, 73099, 73127, 73521–23, 73526, 73532, 73537, 73539, 73544, 73547, 73549–50, 73554, 73556, 73559–60, 73564, 73566, 73571, 73601, 73620, 73622, 73624–28, 73632, 73638–39, 73641–42, 73644–48, 73650–51, 73654–55, 73658–64, 73666–69, 73673, 73701–03, 73705–06, 73716–20, 73722, 73724, 73726–31, 73733–39, 73741–44, 73746–47, 73749–50, 73753–64, 73766, 73768, 73770–73, 73801–02, 73832, 73834–35, 73838, 73840–44, 73848, 73851–53, 73855, 73857–60, 73901, 73931–33, 73937–39, 73942, 73944–47, 73949–51, 74001–03, 74010, 74020, 74023, 74026, 74028, 74030, 74032, 74034–35, 74038–39, 74044–47, 74051–52, 74054, 74056, 74058–60, 74062–63, 74066–68, 74070–71, 74073–79, 74081, 74084–85, 74106, 74126–27, 74131–32, 74601–02, 74604, 74630–33, 74636–37, 74640–41, 74643–44, 74646–47, 74650–53, 74824, 74832, 74834, 74851, 74855, 74864, 74869, 74875, 74881

* * *

FOURTH DISTRICT

TOM COLE, Republican, of Moore, OK; born in Shreveport, LA, April 28, 1949; education: B.A., Grinnell College, 1971; M.A., Yale University, 1974; Ph.D., University of Oklahoma, 1984; Watson Fellow, 1971–72; Fulbright Fellow, 1977–78; professional: former college professor of history and politics; President, Cole Hargrave Snodgrass & Associates (political consulting firm); public service: Oklahoma State Senate, 1988–91; Oklahoma Secretary of State, 1995–99; has served as Chairman, and Executive Director, of the Oklahoma Republican Party; former Chairman of the National Republican Congressional Committee; and Chief of Staff of the Republican National Committee; family: married to Ellen; one child: Mason; religion: United Methodist; committees: Appropriations; Budget; Rules; elected to the 108th Congress on November 5, 2002; reelected to each succeeding Congress.

Office Listings

http://www.cole.house.gov

2467 Rayburn House Office Building, Washington, DC 20515	(202) 225–6165
Chief of Staff.—Sean Murphy.	FAX: 225–3512
Deputy Chief of Staff / Legislative Director.—Maria Bowie.	
Press Secretary.—Sarah Corley.	
Scheduler.—Sabrina Parker.	
2424 Springer Drive, Suite 201, Norman, OK 73069	(405) 329–6500
711 Southwest, D Avenue, Suite 201, Lawton, OK 73501	(580) 357–2131
Sugg Clinic Office Building, 100 East 13th Street, Suite 213, Ada, OK 74820	(580) 436–5375

Counties: CANADIAN (part), CARTER, CLEVELAND, COMANCHE, COTTON, GARVIN, GRADY, JEFFERSON, LOVE, MCCLAIN, MURRAY, OKLAHOMA (part), PONTOTOC, STEPHENS, AND TILLMAN. Population (2010), 750,270.

ZIP Codes: 73002, 73004, 73006, 73010–11, 73017–20, 73026, 73030, 73032, 73051–52, 73055, 73057, 73059, 73064–69, 73071–72, 73074–75, 73079–80, 73082, 73086, 73089, 73092–93, 73095, 73098, 73110, 73130, 73135, 73139, 73141, 73145, 73149–50, 73159–60, 73165, 73169–70, 73173, 73401, 73425, 73430, 73433–34, 73437–38, 73441–44, 73448, 73453, 73456, 73458–59, 73463, 73481, 73487, 73491, 73501, 73503, 73505, 73507, 73520, 73527–31, 73533, 73538, 73540–43, 73546, 73548, 73551–53, 73555, 73557, 73559, 73562, 73564–70, 73572–73, 74572, 74820, 74825, 74831, 74842–44, 74852, 74856–57, 74865, 74871–72, 74878

* * *

FIFTH DISTRICT

STEVE RUSSELL, Republican, of Choctaw, OK; born May 25, 1963, Oklahoma City, OK; education: graduated from Del City High School,1981; B.A., in public speaking, Ouachita Baptist University; M.M.A.S., Fort Leavenworth, KS, 1998; professional: owner and founder of Two Rivers Arms; U.S. Army, 1985–2006; author; member of the Oklahoma State Senate, 2008–12; married: Cindy; awards: Meritorious Service Medal, 6 x awards; Joint Forces Commendation Medal; Army Commendation Medal, 3 x awards; Army Achievement Medal, 4 x awards; National Defense Service Medal, 2 x awards; National Defense Service Medal, 2 x awards; Armed Forces Expeditionary Medal; Kosovo Campaign Medal; Afghanistan Campaign Medal; Iraq Campaign Medal; Global War on Terrorism Expeditionary Medal; Global War on Terrorism Service Medal; Outstanding Volunteer Service Medal; NATO Medal; member of the Military Order of the Loyal Legion of the United States; Ranger Tab; Combat Infantryman Badge; U.S. Army and Korean Parachutists Badge; member of the House Steering Committee; committees: Armed Services; Education and the Workforce; Oversight and Government Reform; elected to the 114th Congress on November 4, 2014.

Office Listings

http://www.russell.house.gov   facebook: reprussell   twitter: @reprussell

128 Cannon House Office Building, Washington, DC 20515	(202) 225–2132
Chief of Staff.—Dean Fisher.	FAX: 226–1463
Deputy Chief of Staff/Legislative Director.—Alex Hutkin.	
Scheduler.—Savannah Jolly.	
Communications Director.—Daniel Susskind.	
4600 Southeast 29th, Suite 400, Del City, OK 73115	(405) 602–3074

Counties: OKLAHOMA (part), POTTAWATOMIE, AND SEMINOLE. CITIES: Arcadia, Asher, Aydelotte, Bethany, Bethel Acres, Bowlegs, Brooksville, Choctaw, Cromwell, Del City, Earlsboro, Edmond, Forest Park, Harrah, Johnson, Jones, Konawa, Lake Aluma, Lima, Luther, Macomb, Maud, McLoud, Midwest City, Newalla, Nichols Hills, Nicoma Park, Oklahoma City, Pink, Prague, Sasakwa, Seminole, Shawnee, Smith Village, Spencer, St. Louis, Tecumesh, The Village, Tribbey, Valley Brook, Wanette, Warr Acres, Wewoka, and Woodlawn Park. Population (2010), 750,271.

ZIP Codes: 73003, 73007–08, 73013, 73020, 73034, 73045, 73049, 73054, 73066, 73083–84, 73101–32, 73134–37, 73139, 73141–49, 73151–52, 73154–57, 73159–60, 73162, 73164, 73169, 73172–73, 73178–79, 73184–85, 73190, 73194–96, 73198, 74587, 74801–02, 74804, 74818, 74826, 74830, 74837, 74840, 74849, 74851–52, 74854, 74857, 74866–68, 74873, 74878, 74884

OREGON

(Population 2010, 3,831,074)

SENATORS

RON WYDEN, Democrat, of Portland, OR; born in Wichita, KS, May 3, 1949; education: graduated from Palo Alto High School, 1967; B.A. in political science, with distinction, Stanford University, 1971; J.D., University of Oregon Law School, 1974; professional: attorney; member, American Bar Association; former director, Oregon Legal Services for the Elderly; former public member, Oregon State Board of Examiners of Nursing Home Administrators; cofounder and codirector, Oregon Gray Panthers, 1974–80; married: Nancy Bass Wyden; children: Adam David, Lilly Anne, Ava Rose, William Peter, and Scarlett Willa; committees: ranking member, Finance; Budget; Energy and Natural Resources; Joint Committee on Taxation; Select Committee on Intelligence; elected to the 97th Congress, November 4, 1980; reelected to each succeeding Congress; elected to the U.S. Senate on February 6, 1996, to fill the unexpired term of Senator Bob Packwood; reelected to each succeeding Senate term.

Office Listings

http://wyden.senate.gov

221 Dirksen Senate Office Building, Washington, DC 20510	(202) 224–5244
Chief of Staff.—Jeff Michels.	FAX: 228–2717
Legislative Director.—Sarah Bittleman.	
Director of Scheduling.—Wayne Binkley.	
911 Northeast 11th Avenue, Suite 630, Portland, OR 97232	(503) 326–7525
405 East Eighth Avenue, Suite 2020, Eugene, OR 97401	(541) 431–0229
The Federal Courthouse, 310 West Sixth Street, Room 118, Medford, OR 97501	(541) 858–5122
The Jamison Building, 131 Northwest Hawthorne Avenue, Suite 107, Bend, OR 97701	(541) 330–9142
SAC Annex Building, 105 Fir Street, Suite 201, LaGrande, OR 97850	(541) 962–7691
707 Thirteenth Street, SE., Suite 285, Salem, OR 97310	(503) 589–4555

* * *

JEFF MERKLEY, Democrat, of Portland, OR; born in Myrtle Creek, OR; October 24, 1956; education: graduated from David Douglas High School; B.A., international relations, Stanford University, 1979; M.P.P., Woodrow Wilson School Princeton University, 1982; professional: Presidential Fellow at the Office of the Secretary of Defense, 1982–85; Policy Analyst at the Congressional Budget Office, 1985–89; Executive Director of Portland Habitat for Humanity, 1991–94; Director of Housing Development at Human Solutions, 1995–96; President of World Affairs Council of Oregon, 1996–2003; elected to Oregon House of Representatives, 1999; Democratic Leader of the Oregon House of Representatives, 2003; elected Speaker of the Oregon House of Representatives, 2007; married: Mary Sorteberg; children: Brynne and Jonathan; committees: Appropriations; Banking, Housing, and Urban Affairs; Budget; Environment and Public Works; elected to the U.S. Senate on November 4, 2008; reelected to the U.S. Senate on November 4, 2014.

Office Listings

http://merkley.senate.gov

313 Hart Senate Office Building, Washington, DC 20510	(202) 224–3753
Chief of Staff.—Michael Zamore.	FAX: 228–3997
Legislative Director.—Jeremiah Baumann.	
Deputy Chief of Staff of Operations.—Jennifer Piorkowski.	
Communications Director.—Matt McNally.	
1400 One World Trade Center, 121 Southwest Salmon, Portland, OR 97204	(503) 326–3386
Jamison Building, 131 Northwest Hawthorne, Suite 208, Bend, OR 97701	(541) 318–1298
Wayne Morse Federal Courthouse, 405 East 8th, Suite 2010, Eugene, OR 97401	(541) 465–6750
10 South Bartlett Street, Suite 201, Medford, OR 97501	(541) 608–9102
495 State Street, Suite 330, Salem, OR 97301	(503) 362–8102
310 Southeast Second Street, Suite 105, Pendleton, OR 97801	(541) 278–1129

REPRESENTATIVES

FIRST DISTRICT

SUZANNE MARIE BONAMICI, Democrat, of Beaverton, OR; born in Michigan, October 14, 1954; education: J.D., University of Oregon, Eugene, OR, 1983; B.A., journalism, Eugene,

OR, 1980; professional: served in the Oregon State House from 2007–08, served in the Oregon State Senate from 2008–11; married: husband, Michael Simon; children: son, Andrew Simon, daughter, Sara Simon; caucuses: co-founder and co-chair of the STEAM Caucus; committees: Education and the Workforce; Science, Space, and Technology; elected to the 112th Congress on January 31, 2012, in a special election; reelected to each succeeding Congress.

Office Listings
http://www.bonamici.house.gov

439 Cannon House Office Building, Washington DC, 20515	(202) 225–0855
Chief of Staff.—Rachael Bornstein.	FAX: 225–9497
Legislative Director.—Russ Kelley.	
Scheduler.—Kimberly Koops-Wrabek.	
Press Secretary.—Alex Gilliland.	
12725 SW Millikan Way, Suite 220, Beaverton, OR 97005	(503) 469–6010
District Director.—Vacant.	FAX: 469–6018
District Scheduler.—Barbara Allen.	

Counties: CLATSOP, COLUMBIA, MULTNOMAH (part), WASHINGTON, AND YAMHILL. Population (2010) 766,216.

ZIP Codes: 97005–08, 97016, 97018, 97048, 97051, 97053–54, 97056, 97064, 97103, 97106, 97109–11, 97113–17, 97119, 97121, 97123–25, 97127–28, 97133, 97138, 97144–46, 97148, 97208, 97223–24, 97229, 97231

* * *

SECOND DISTRICT

GREG WALDEN, Republican, of Hood River, OR; born in The Dalles, OR, January 10, 1957; education: B.S., journalism, University of Oregon, 1981; member: Associated Oregon Industries; Oregon Health Sciences Foundation; Hood River Rotary Club; Hood River Elk's Club; National Federation of Independent Business; Hood River Chamber of Commerce; Hood River Memorial Hospital; Columbia Bancorp; Oregon State House of Representatives, 1989–95, and majority leader, 1991–93; assistant majority leader, Oregon State. Senate, 1995–97; awards: Oregon Jaycees Outstanding Young Oregonian, 1991; National Republican Legislators Association Legislator of the Year, 1993; married: Mylene Walden; one child: Anthony David Walden; committees: Energy and Commerce; elected to the 106th Congress on November 3, 1998; reelected to each succeeding Congress.

Office Listings
http://www.walden.house.gov

2185 Rayburn House Office Building, Washington, DC 20515	(202) 225–6730
Chief of Staff.—Brian MacDonald.	FAX: 225–5774
Senior Policy Advisor.—Ray Baum.	
Scheduler.—Mary Beth Spencer.	
Communications Director.—Andrew Malcolm.	
14 North Central Avenue, Suite 112, Medford, OR 97504	(541) 776–4646
1211 Washington Avenue, LaGrande, OR 97850	(541) 624–2400
	FAX: 624–2402
1051 Northwest Bond Street, Suite 400, Bend, OR 97701	(541) 389–4408
	FAX: 389–4452

Counties: BAKER, CROOK, DESCHUTES, GILLIAM, GRANT, HARNEY, HOOD RIVER, JACKSON, JEFFERSON, JOSEPHINE (part), KLAMATH, LAKE, MALHEUR, MORROW, SHERMAN, UMATILLA, UNION, WALLOWA, WASCO, AND WHEELER. Population (2010), 766,215.

ZIP Codes: 89421, 97001, 97014, 97021, 97029, 97031, 97033, 97037, 97039–41, 97050, 97057–58, 97063, 97065, 97497, 97501–04, 97520, 97522, 97524–27, 97530, 97535–37, 97539–41, 97601, 97603–04, 97620–27, 97630, 97632–41, 97701–02, 97707, 97710–12, 97720–22, 97730–39, 97741, 97750–56, 97758–61, 97801, 97810, 97812–14, 97817–20, 97823–28, 97830, 97833–46, 97848, 97850, 97856–57, 97859, 97862, 97864–65, 97867–70, 97873–77, 97880, 97882–86, 97901, 97903–11, 97913–14, 97918, 97920, 99362

* * *

THIRD DISTRICT

EARL BLUMENAUER, Democrat, of Portland, OR; born in Portland, August 16, 1948; education: graduated from Centennial High School; B.A., Lewis and Clark College; J.D.,

Northwestern School of Law; professional: assistant to the president, Portland State University; served in Oregon State Legislature 1973–78; chaired Revenue and School Finance Committee; Multnomah County Commissioner, 1978–85; Portland City Commissioner 1986–96; served on Governor's Commission on Higher Education; National League of Cities Transportation Committee; National Civic League Board of Directors; Oregon Environmental Council; Oregon Public Broadcasting; married: Margaret Kirkpatrick; children: Jon and Anne; committees: Ways and Means; elected to the U.S. House of Representatives on May 21, 1996, to fill the vacancy created by Representative Ron Wyden's election to the U.S. Senate; reelected to each succeeding Congress.

Office Listings

http://blumenauer.house.gov

1111 Longworth House Office Building, Washington, DC 20515 .... (202) 225–4811
    Chief of Staff.—Julia Pomeroy.   FAX: 225–8941
    Deputy Chief of Staff.—David Skillman.
    Scheduler.—Corine Weiler.
    Communications Director.—Nicole L'Esperance.
    Legislative Director.—Michael Harold.
911 Northeast 11th Avenue, Suite 200, Portland, OR 97232 .... (503) 231–2300
    District Director.—Willie Smith.

Counties: MULTNOMAH (part), CLACKAMAS (part). Population (2010), 766,215.

ZIP Codes: 97004, 97009, 97011, 97014–15, 97017, 97019, 97022–24, 97028, 97030, 97035, 97045, 97049, 97055, 97060, 97067, 97080, 97124, 97133, 97202–03, 97206, 97210–18, 97220, 97222, 97227, 97229–33, 97236, 97238, 97242, 97256, 97266–67, 97269, 97282–83, 97286, 97290, 97292–94, 97299

* * *

FOURTH DISTRICT

PETER A. DeFAZIO, Democrat, of Springfield, OR; born in Needham, MA, May 27, 1947; B.A., Tufts University, 1969; M.S., University of Oregon, 1977; professional: aide to Representative Jim Weaver, 1977–82; commissioner, Lane County, 1983–86; married: Myrnie Daut; committees: ranking member, Transportation and Infrastructure; elected to the 100th Congress, November 4, 1986; reelected to each succeeding Congress.

Office Listings

http://www.defazio.house.gov

2134 Rayburn House Office Building, Washington, DC 20515 .... (202) 225–6416
    Chief of Staff.—Kristie Greco.
    Legislative Director.—Kris Pratt.
    Scheduler.—Brittany Lundberg.
405 East Eighth Avenue, Suite 2030, Eugene, OR 97401 .... (541) 465–6732
    District Director.—Nick Batz.
125 Central Avenue, Room 350, Coos Bay, OR 97420 .... (541) 269–2609
612 Southeast Jackson Street, Room 9, Roseburg, OR 97470 .... (541) 440–3523

Counties: BENTON (part), COOS, CURRY, DOUGLAS, JOSEPHINE (part), LANE, AND LINN. CITIES: Eugene, Roseburg, and Coos Bay. Population (2010), 766,214.

ZIP Codes: 97321–22, 97324, 97326–27, 97329–31, 97333, 97345–46, 97348, 97350, 97352, 97355, 97358, 97360–61, 97370, 97374, 97377, 97383, 97386, 97389–90, 97401–06, 97408, 97410–17, 97419–20, 97423–24, 97426, 97429–31, 97434–39, 97446–59, 97461–63, 97465–67, 97469–71, 97476–81, 97484, 97486–90, 97492–99, 97523, 97526–27, 97531–32, 97534, 97538, 97543–44, 97731, 97759

* * *

FIFTH DISTRICT

KURT SCHRADER, Democrat, of Canby, OR; born in Bridgeport, CT, October 19, 1951; education; B.A., Cornell University, 1973; D.V.M., University of Illinois, 1977; professional: small business owner; veterinarian; farmer; past member: Oregon State Senate; Oregon House of Representatives; Canby Planning Commission; religion: Episcopalian; children: Clare, Maren, Steven, Travis, and R.J.; committees: Energy and Commerce; elected to the 111th Congress on November 4, 2008; reelected to each succeeding Congress.

Office Listings

http://schrader.house.gov   www.facebook.com/repschrader   twitter: @repschrader

2431 Rayburn House Office Building, Washington, DC 20515 .... (202) 225–5711
    Chief of Staff.—Paul Gage.   FAX: 225–5699
    Deputy Chief of Staff.—Chris Huckleberry.
    Executive Assistant / Scheduler.—Julia Stafford.
544 Ferry Street, Suite 2, Salem, OR 97301 .... (503) 588–9100
621 High Street, Oregon City, OR 97045 .... (503) 557–1324
    District Director.—Suzanne Kunse.

Counties: BENTON (part), CLACKAMAS (part), LINCOLN, MARION, MULTNOMAH (part), POLK, AND TILLAMOOK. CITIES: Lincoln City, Lake Oswego, Oregon City, Salem, and Tillamook. Population (2010), 766,214.

ZIP Codes: 97002, 97013, 97015, 97017, 97020, 97023, 97026–27, 97032, 97034–36, 97038, 97042, 97045, 97062, 97068, 97070–71, 97086, 97101, 97107–08, 97112, 97118, 97122, 97130–32, 97135–37, 97140–41, 97143, 97147, 97149, 97201–02, 97206, 97219, 97222, 97236, 97239, 97266–69, 97301–12, 97314, 97317, 97321, 97324–26, 97338, 97341–44, 97346–47, 97350–52, 97357–58, 97360–62, 97364–71, 97373, 97375–76, 97378, 97380–81, 97383–85, 97388, 97390–92, 97394, 97396, 97498

PENNSYLVANIA

(Population 2010, 12,702,379)

SENATORS

ROBERT P. CASEY, JR., Democrat, of Scranton, PA; born in Scranton, April 13, 1960; education: A.B., english, College of the Holy Cross, 1982; J.D., Catholic University of America, 1988; professional: lawyer; Pennsylvania State Auditor General, 1997–2005; Pennsylvania State Treasurer, 2005–07; married: Terese; four daughters: Elyse, Caroline, Julia, and Marena; committees: Agriculture, Nutrition, and Forestry; Finance; Health, Education, Labor, and Pensions; Joint Economic Committee; Special Committee on Aging; elected to the U.S. Senate on November 7, 2006; reelected to the U.S. Senate on November 6, 2012.

Office Listings

http://casey.senate.gov   http://www.facebook.com/senatorbobcasey
http://twitter.com/senbobcasey   http://youtube.com/senatorbobcasey

393 Russell Senate Office Building, Washington, DC 20510	(202) 224–6324
	(866) 802–2833
Chief of Staff.—James W. Brown.	FAX: 228–0604
Deputy Chief of Staff.—Kristen Gentile.	
Deputy Chief of Staff.—April Mellody.	
Legislative Director.—Derek Miller.	
Communications Director.—John Rizzo.	
22 South Third Street, Suite 6A, Harrisburg, PA 17101	(717) 231 7540
	(866) 461–9159
	FAX: 231–7542
2000 Market Street. Suite 1870, Philadelphia, PA 19103	(215) 405 9660
	FAX: 405–9669
Grant Building, 310 Grant Street, Suite 2415, Pittsburgh, PA 15219	(412) 803–7370
	FAX: 803–7379
409 Lackawanna Avenue, Suite 301, Scranton, PA 18503	(570) 941–0930
	FAX: 941–0937
817 East Bishop Street, Suite C, Bellefonte, PA 16823	(814) 357–0314
	FAX: 375–0318
17 South Park Row, Suite B–150, Erie, PA 16501	(814) 874–5080
	FAX: 874–5084
840 Hamilton Street, Suite 301, Allentown, PA 18101	(610) 782–9470
	FAX: 782–9474

* * *

PAT TOOMEY, Republican, of Zionsville, PA; born in East Providence, RI, November 17, 1961; education: graduated from La Salle Academy as valedictorian in 1980; B.A., political science, cum laude, Harvard University, Cambridge, MA, 1984; professional: worked for Chemical Bank and Morgan Grenfell in New York City; he has deep experience in the financial services sector, culminating with building a community bank from the ground up; founded several restaurants in Allentown, PA, with his two brothers, Steve and Michael Toomey, 1990–97; married: Kris Duncan, 1997; children: Bridget, Patrick, and Duncan; member of the Allentown Government Study Commission, 1994; elected to the U.S. House of Representatives in 1998, winning two reelections, 2000–02; president, Club for Growth, 2005; co-chairman of the Board of Directors of Team Capital Bank, 2005–09; committees: Banking, Housing, and Urban Affairs; Budget; Finance; elected to the U.S. Senate on November 2, 2010.

Office Listings

http://toomey.senate.gov   facebook:senatorpattoomey   twitter: @sentoomey

248 Rayburn Senate Office Building, Washington, DC 20510	(202) 224–4254
Chief of Staff.—Christopher Gahan.	FAX: 228–0284
Legislative Director.—Dan Brandt.	
Director of Operations.—Laurel Edmondson.	
1628 John F. Kennedy Boulevard, 8 Penn Center, Suite 1702, Philadelphia, PA 19103	(215) 241–1090
The Landmarks Building, 100 West Station Square Drive, Suite 225, Pittsburgh, PA 15219	(412) 803–3501
Federal Building, 17 South Park Row, Suite B–120, Erie, PA 16501	(814) 453–3010
Federal Building, 228 Walnut Street, Room 1104, Harrisburg, PA 17101	(717) 782–3951
1150 South Cedar Crest Boulevard, Suite 101, Allentown, PA 18103	(610) 434–1444
538 Spruce Street, Suite 302, Scranton, PA 18503	(570) 941–3540
Richland Square III, Suite 302, 1397 Eisenhower Boulevard, Johnstown, PA 15904	(814) 266–5970

REPRESENTATIVES

FIRST DISTRICT

ROBERT A. BRADY, Democrat, of Philadelphia, PA; born in Philadelphia, April 7, 1945; education: graduated from St. Thomas More High School; professional: carpenter; union official; assistant Sergeant-At-Arms, Philadelphia City Council, 1975–83; Deputy Mayor for Labor, W. Wilson Goode Administration; consultant to Pennsylvania State Senate; Pennsylvania Turnpike Commissioner; board of directors, Philadelphia Redevelopment Authority; Democratic Party Executive; ward leader; chairman, Philadelphia Democratic Party; member of Pennsylvania Democratic State Committee, and Democratic National Committee; religion: Catholic; married: Debra Brady; children: Robert and Kimberly; committees: ranking member, House Administration; Armed Services; Joint Committee on the Library; Joint Committee on Printing; elected to the 105th Congress on May 21, 1998, to fill the unexpired term of Representative Tom Foglietta; reelected to each succeeding Congress.

Office Listings

http://brady.house.gov

102 Cannon House Office Building, Washington, DC 20515	(202) 225–4731
Chief of Staff.—Stan White.	FAX: 225–0088
Appointments.—Colleen Carlos.	
Press Secretary.—Karen Warrington.	
1909 South Broad Street, Philadelphia, PA 19148	(215) 389–4627
1350 Edgemont Avenue, Suite 2575, Chester, PA 19103	(610) 874–7094
2637 East Clearfield Street, Philadelphia, PA 19134	(267) 519–2252
2630 Memphis Street, Philadelphia, PA 19121	(215) 426–4616

Counties: PHILADELPHIA (part), DELAWARE (part). CITIES AND TOWNSHIPS: Chester City, Chester Township, Collingdale Borough, Colwyn Borough, Darby Township, East Lansdowne Borough, Eddystone Borough, Folcroft Borough, Glenolden Borough, Lansdowne Borough, Millbourne Borough, Nether Providence Township, Philadelphia City, Ridley Township, Rose Valley Borough, Sharon Hill Borough, Swarthmore Borough, Tinicum Township, Upland Borough, Upper Darby Township and Yeadon Borough. Population (2010), 705,688.

ZIP Codes: 19013–16, 19018, 19020, 19022–23, 19026, 19029, 19032, 19036, 19050, 19063–64, 19066, 19074, 19078–79, 19081–82, 19086, 19094, 19096, 19102, 19105–09, 19112–14, 19121–25, 19130–31, 19133–37, 19139–40, 19142–43, 19145–49, 19151–53, 19171–72, 19175–77, 19181–82, 19185, 19188

* * *

SECOND DISTRICT

CHAKA FATTAH, Democrat, of Philadelphia, PA; born in Philadelphia, November 21, 1956; education: attended Overbrook High School, Community College of Philadelphia, M.A., University of Pennsylvania's Fels School of State and Local Government, 1986; completed Senior Executive Program for State Officials at Harvard University's John F. Kennedy School of Government; Pennsylvania State House of Representatives, 1983–88; Pennsylvania State Senate, 1988–94; author, *Gaining Early Awareness and Readiness for Undergraduate Programs* (GEAR-UP), enacted in 1998 offering college readiness preparation and scholarships for low-income students; founded Graduate Opportunity Initiative Conference, 1987; founded Philadelphia College Opportunity Resources for Education (CORE Philly) scholarship program; Chief sponsor of the American Opportunity Tax Credit Act; leading advocate for the Energy Efficiency and Conservation Block Grants; Emergency Homeowners' Relief Fund; authored the White House Conference on Children and Youth Act of 2010; architect of the Fattah Neuroscience Initiative; co-creator of the Equity and Excellence Commission; former trustee, Temple University, Pennsylvania State University, Lincoln University and Community College of Philadelphia; past chair, Executive Board, Pennsylvania Higher Education Assistance Agency; named one of the 50 most promising leaders in *Time* magazine, and in *Ebony* magazine as one of 50 Future Leaders; member, Mt. Carmel Baptist Church; chair, Congressional Urban Caucus; co-chair, Congressional Task Force on Alzheimer's Disease; co-chair, House Science and National Labs Caucus; married: the former Renee Chenault; four children; committees: Appropriations; elected to the 104th Congress on November 8, 1994; reelected to each succeeding Congress.

Office Listings

http://www.fattah.house.gov

2301 Rayburn House Office Building, Washington, DC 20515	(202) 225–4001

Office Listings—Continued

Chief of Staff.—Roger Jackson.   FAX: 225–5392
Legislative Director.—Brenden Chainey.
Deputy Chief of Staff.—Debra Anderson.
Communications Director.—Allyson Freeman.
2401 North 54th Street, Philadelphia, PA 19131 .... (215) 871–4455

Counties: MONTGOMERY (part), PHILADELPHIA. Population (2010), 705,688.

ZIP Codes: 19003–04, 19010, 19035, 19038, 19041, 19066, 19072, 19083, 19085, 19087, 19092–93, 19095–96, 19101–
    04, 19110, 19118–22, 19126–33, 19138–41, 19143–46, 19150–51, 19161–62, 19170–72, 19175, 19178, 19182, 19187–
    88, 19190–92, 19195–97, 19428, 19444

* * *

THIRD DISTRICT

MIKE KELLY, Republican, of Butler, PA; born in Pittsburgh, PA, May 10, 1948; education:
B.A., sociology with a minor in philosophy and theology, University of Notre Dame, South
Bend, IN, 1970; professional: owner and operator of Kelly Automotive Cadillac, Chevrolet,
Hyundai, and Kia car dealership; married 42 years: Vicki Kelly; four children; committees:
Ways and Means; elected to the 112th Congress on November 2, 2010; reelected to each suc-
ceeding Congress.

Office Listings

http://www.kelly.house.gov

1519 Longworth House Office Building, Washington, DC 20515 .... (202) 225–5406
Chief of Staff.—Matthew Stroia.   FAX: 225–3103
Policy Director/Tax Counsel.—Lori Prater.
Legislative Counsel.—Isaac Fong.
Director of Communications.—Tom Qualtere.
Director of Administration.—Tim Butler.
Senior Legislative Assistant.—Jeff Rein.
Legislative Correspondents: Brendan Fulmer, Robert Smith.
Staff Assistant.—Michael Walter.
208 East Bayfront Parkway, Suite 102, Erie, PA 16507 .... (814) 456–8190
District Director.—Brad Moore.
101 East Diamond Street, Suite 218, Butler, PA 16001 .... (724) 282–2557
                                                                       FAX: 282–3682
33 Chestnut Avenue, Sharon, PA 16146 .... (724) 885–1113
                                                                       FAX: 885–1114
908 Diamond Park, Meadville, PA 16335 .... (814) 454–8190
    Office Hours: By appointment on Wednesdays from 9 a.m. to 4 p.m.   FAX: 454–8197
300 South McKean Street, Kittanning, PA 16201.
    Office Hours: By appointment on Thursdays from 9 a.m. to 4 p.m.
430 Court Street, New Castle, PA 16101.
    Office Hours: Friday from 9 a.m. to 4 p.m.

Counties: ARMSTRONG, BUTLER (part), CLARION (part), CRAWFORD (part), ERIE (part), LAWRENCE, AND MERCER. Population:
    (2010), 705,688.

ZIP Codes: 16001–03, 16016–18, 16020, 16022–23, 16025, 16027–30, 16033–35, 16037–41, 16045–46, 16048–53, 16055–
    57, 16059, 16061, 16110–11, 16113–14, 16124–25, 16127, 16130–31, 16133–34, 16137, 16142–43, 16145–46, 16148,
    16150–51, 16153–54, 16156, 16159, 16201, 16210, 16218, 16222–24, 16226, 16229, 16232, 16242, 16244–45, 16249–
    50, 16253, 16259, 16261–63, 16311–12, 16314, 16316–17, 16327, 16335, 16342, 16354, 16360, 16362, 16388, 16401–
    07, 16410–12, 16415, 16417, 16420–23, 16430, 16433–35, 16438, 16440–43, 16475, 16501–12, 16514–15, 16522,
    16530–34, 16538, 16541, 16544, 16546, 16550, 16553–54

* * *

FOURTH DISTRICT

SCOTT PERRY, Republican, of York County, PA; born in San Diego, May 27, 1962; education: Northern York High School, 1980; B.S in business administration management, Pennsylvania State University, 1991; M.S. in strategic studies, U.S. Army War College, 2012; professional: small business owner at Hydrotech Mechanical Services; military: active Colonel (Pro-
motable), Pennsylvania Army National Guard; organizations: former President of Pennsylvania
Young Republicans; former Regional Director for Pennsylvania Chapter of Jaycees; Dillsburg
Legion Post #2; Dillsburg VFW Post #6771; public service: Pennsylvania House of Representatives, 2006–12; married: Christy; children: Ryenn and Mattea; committees: Foreign Affairs;

Homeland Security; Transportation and Infrastructure; elected to the 113th Congress on November 6, 2012; reelected to the 114th Congress on November 4, 2014.

Office Listings

http://perry.house.gov   twitter: @repscottperry

1207 Longworth House Office Building, Washington, DC 20515	(202) 225–5836
Chief of Staff.—Lauren Muglia.	FAX: 226–1000
Legislative Director.—John Drzewicki.	
Communications Director.—Ryan Nawrocki.	
Deputy Legislative Director.—George O'Conner.	
Legislative Assistant: Kelsey Griswold.	
Legislative Correspondent.—Lindsey Miller.	
Staff Assistant: Patrick Schilling.	
22 Chambersburg Street, Gettysburg, PA 17325	(717) 338–1919
Field Representative.—Holly Sutphin.	
2209 East Market Street, York, PA 17402	(717) 600–1919
Deputy Chief of Staff.—Bob Reilly.	
Scheduler.—Carol Wiest.	
Legislative Assistants: Donna Austin, Nicole McCleary, Ben Turner.	
Staff Assistant.—Vacant.	
730 North Front Street, Wormleysburg, PA 17043	(717) 635–9504
Director of Constituent Services.—Tyra Wallace.	

Counties: ADAMS, CUMBERLAND, DAUPHIN, AND YORK. CITIES AND TOWNSHIPS: Abbottstown, Arendtsville, Bendersville, Berwick, Biglerville, Bonneauville, Butler, Camp Hill, Carroll Valley, Carroll, Chanceford, Codorus, Conewago, Cross Roads, Cumberland, Dallastown, Delta, Dillsburg, Dover, Dover, East Berlin, East Hopewell, East Manchester, East Pennsboro, East Prospect, Fairfield, Fairview, Fawn Grove, Fawn, Felton, Franklin, Franklintown, Freedom, Germany, Gettysburg, Glen Rock, Goldsboro, Hallam, Hamilton, Hamiltonban, Hampden, Hanover, Harrisburg, Heidelberg, Hellam, Highland, Hopewell, Huntington, Jackson, Jacobus, Jefferson, Latimore, Lemoyne, Lewisberry, Liberty, Littlestown, Loganville, Lower Allen, Lower Chanceford, Lower Windsor, Manchester, Manchester, Manheim, McSherrystown, Mechanicsburg, Menallen, Monaghan, Mount Joy, Mount Pleasant, Mount Wolf, New Cumberland, New Freedom, New Oxford, New Salem, Newberry, North Codorus, North Hopewell, North York, Oxford, Paradise, Peach Bottom, Penn, Railroad, Reading, Red Lion, Seven Valleys, Shiremanstown, Shrewsbury, Shrewsbury, Silver Spring, Spring Garden, Spring Grove, Springettsbury, Springfield, Stewartstown, Straban, Susquehanna, Tyrone, Union, Upper Allen, Warrington, Washington, Wellsville, West Manchester, West Manheim, West York, Windsor, Windsor, Winterstown, Wormleysburg, Wrightsville, Yoe, York Haven, York Springs, York, York, and Yorkana. Population (2010), 705,687.

ZIP Codes: 17070, 17072, 17093, 17101–04, 17109–11, 17120, 17301–02, 17304, 17306–07, 17309, 17311, 17313–22, 17324–25, 17327, 17329, 17331, 17339–40, 17343–45, 17347, 17349–50, 17352–53, 17355–56, 17360–66, 17368, 17370–72, 17401–04, 17406–08

* * *

FIFTH DISTRICT

GLENN "GT" THOMPSON, Republican, of Howard Township, PA; born in Bellefonte, PA, July 27, 1959; education: B.S., therapeutic recreation, Pennsylvania State University, 1981; M.Ed., health science/therapeutic recreation, Temple University, 1998; NHA/L, Nursing Home Administrator, Marywood University, 2006; professional: Rehabilitation Services Manager for Susquehanna Health Services, Adjunct Faculty for Cambria County Community College; Chief, Recreational Therapist for the Williamsport Hospital; Residential Services Aid for Hope Enterprises, Orderly for Centre Crest Nursing Home; organization/awards: Past President/Fire Fighter/EMT/Rescue Technician for Howard VFD; former, Howard Boy Scout Master; former, President and Senior VP for Juniata Valley Boy Scout Council; International Advisory Council Member for the Accreditation of Rehabilitation Facilities Commission; board member/vice chair of Private Industry Council of Central Corridors; political career: Centre County Republican chair, Pennsylvania Republican State Committee, alternate delegate for the Republican National Convention; candidate for the Pennsylvania House of Representatives, 1998 and 2000; member, Bald Eagle Area School District Board of Education; religion: Protestant; married to Penny Ammerman-Thompson; three sons, Parker, Logan and Kale; committees: Agriculture; Education and the Workforce; Natural Resources; elected to the 111th Congress on November 4, 2008; reelected to each succeeding Congress.

Office Listings

http://thompson.house.gov

124 Cannon House Office Building, Washington, DC 20515	(202) 225–5121
Chief of Staff.—Matthew Brennan.	FAX: 225–5796
Legislative Director.—John Busovsky.	
Scheduler.—Erin Wilson.	
Communications Director.—Bailey Hall.	
127 West Spring Street, Suite C, Titusville, PA 16354	(814) 827–3985

Office Listings—Continued

District Director.—Peter Winkler.
3555 Benner Pike, Suite 101, Bellefonte, PA 16823 .... (814) 353–0215

Counties: CAMERON, CENTRE, CLARION (part), CLEARFIELD, CLINTON, CRAWFORD (part), ELK, ERIE (part), FOREST, HUNTINGDON (part), JEFFERSON, McKEAN, POTTER, TIOGA (part), VENANGO AND WARREN. Population (2010), 705,688.

ZIP Codes: 15711, 15715, 15721, 15724, 15730, 15733, 15742, 15744, 15753, 15757, 15764, 15767, 15770, 15776, 15778, 15780–81, 15784, 15801, 15821, 15823–25, 15827–29, 15832, 15834, 15840–41, 15845–49, 15851, 15853, 15856–57, 15860–61, 15863–66, 15868, 15870, 16036, 16038, 16054, 16127, 16153, 16214, 16217, 16222, 16224, 16232–33, 16235, 16239–40, 16242, 16254–55, 16258, 16260, 16301, 16311–14, 16317, 16319, 16321–23, 16326, 16329, 16331–34, 16340–47, 16350–54, 16361–62, 16364–65, 16370–74, 16402–03, 16405, 16407, 16410, 16412, 16415–17, 16420–21, 16426–28, 16434, 16436, 16438, 16441–42, 16444, 16504, 16506, 16509–11, 16563, 16611, 16616, 16620, 16622, 16627, 16639, 16645–47, 16651–52, 16656–57, 16661, 16666, 16669, 16671, 16677, 16680, 16683, 16686, 16692, 16701, 16720, 16724–35, 16738, 16740, 16743–46, 16748–50, 16801–03, 16820–23, 16825–30, 16832–41, 16843–45, 16847–49, 16851–55, 16858–61, 16863, 16865–66, 16868, 16870–72, 16874–79, 16881–82, 16901, 16915, 16921–23, 16927–28, 16935, 16937–38, 16941, 16943, 16948, 16950, 17002, 17052, 17060, 17066, 17243, 17260, 17721, 17729, 17740, 17745, 17747–48, 17750–51, 17760, 17764, 17767, 17778–79

* * *

SIXTH DISTRICT

RYAN A. COSTELLO, Republican, of West Chester, PA; born in Phoenixville, PA, September 7, 1976; education: B.A., Ursinus College, 1999; J.D., Villanova School of Law, 2002; professional: attorney in the law firm of O'Donnell, Weiss & Mattei, P.C.; public service: chairman, East Vincent Township Board of Supervisors, 2002–08; Chester County Recorder of Deeds, 2008–11; Chairman, Chester County Board of Commissioners, 2011–14; children: Ryan Jr.; committees: Transportation and Infrastructure; Veterans' Affairs; elected to the 114th Congress on November 4, 2014.

Office Listings

http://www.costello.house.gov   twitter: www.twitter.com/repryancostello
www.facebook.com/congressmanryancostello

427 Cannon House Office Building, Washington, DC 20515 .... (202) 225–4315
    Chief of Staff.—Lauryn Bernier Schothorst.   FAX: 225–8440
    Legislative Director.—Dante Cutrona.
    Communications Director.—Johanna Persing.
21 West Market Street, Suite 105, West Chester, PA 19382 .... (610) 696–2982
840 North Park Road, Wyomissing, PA 19610 .... (610) 376–7630

Counties: BERKS (part), CHESTER (part), LEBANON (part), MONTGOMERY (part). Population (2010), 720,487.

ZIP Codes: 17016, 17039, 17042, 17046, 17064, 17067, 17073, 17083, 17087–88, 17545, 17569, 18011, 18041, 18054, 18056, 18062, 18070, 18073–74, 18076, 18092, 19073, 19087, 19301, 19312, 19319, 19333, 19335, 19341–43, 19345, 19355, 19372, 19380, 19382–83, 19403, 19425–26, 19435, 19442, 19453, 19456–57, 19460, 19464–65, 19468, 19472–73, 19475, 19503–06, 19508, 19510, 19512, 19518, 19520, 19522, 19525–26, 19530, 19533, 19535, 19539, 19541, 19545, 19547, 19551, 19555, 19560, 19564–65, 19567, 19601–02, 19604–10

* * *

SEVENTH DISTRICT

PATRICK MEEHAN, Republican, of Delaware County, PA; born in Cheltenham, PA, October 20, 1955; education: B.S., Bowdoin College, Brunswick, ME, 1978; J.D., Temple University, Philadelphia, PA, 1985; professional: district attorney for Delaware County, 1996–2001; United States Attorney for the Eastern District of Pennsylvania, 2001–08; religion: Roman Catholic; married: Carolyn Meehan; children: Jack, Patrick, and Colin; caucuses: American Sikh, Youth Sports, Hockey, Brazil, Autism; committees: Ethics; Ways and Means; elected to the 112th Congress on November 2, 2010; reelected to each succeeding Congress.

Office Listings

http://meehan.house.gov

434 Cannon House Office Building, Washington, DC 20515 .... (202) 225–2011
    Chief of Staff.—Brian Schubert.   FAX: 226–0280
940 Sproul Road, Springfield, PA 19064 .... (610) 690–7323
    District Director.—Caitlin Ganley.   FAX: 690–7329

Counties: BERKS (part), CHESTER (part), DELAWARE (part), LANCASTER (part), AND MONTGOMERY (part). Population (2010), 692,866.

ZIP Codes: 17503, 17505, 17509, 17527, 17529, 17534–36, 17555, 17557, 17562, 17566, 17569, 17572, 17579, 18964, 19002–04, 19008, 19010, 19013–15, 19017–18, 19022, 19025–26, 19028–29, 19031, 19033–34, 19036–39, 19041, 19043–44, 19050, 19052, 19060–61, 19063–64, 19070, 19073–76, 19078, 19081–83, 19085, 19087, 19094, 19096, 19310–11, 19316–17, 19319–20, 19330–31, 19333, 19335, 19342–44, 19346–48, 19350–54, 19357, 19363, 19365–67, 19369, 19371–76, 19380–83, 19390, 19395, 19401, 19403–04, 19406, 19409, 19422–23, 19426, 19428, 19430, 19436–19438, 19440, 19444, 19446, 19454, 19462, 19465, 19470, 19473–74, 19477, 19484, 19486, 19490, 19501, 19508, 19512, 19518–20, 19523, 19535, 19540, 19542–43, 19547–48, 19606–09.

* * *

EIGHTH DISTRICT

MICHAEL FITZPATRICK, Republican, of Levittown, PA; born in Philadelphia, PA, June 28, 1963; education: B.S., St. Thomas University, Miami Gardens, FL, 1985; J.D., Dickinson School of Law, Carlisle, PA, 1988; professional: Bucks County Board of Commissioners; practiced law at Begley Carlin and Mandio; religion: Roman Catholic; married: Kathleen; three daughters, Katie, Maggie, and Molly; three sons, Jimmy, Mick, and Tommy; committees: Financial Services; elected to the 109th Congress on November 2, 2004; elected to the 112th Congress on November 2, 2010; reelected to each succeeding Congress.

Office Listings

http://www.fitzpatrick.house.gov

2400 Rayburn House Office Building, Washington, DC 20515	(202) 225–4276
Chief of Staff.—Kyle Whatley.	FAX: 225–9511
Legislative Director.—Justin Rusk.	
1717 Langhorne Newtown Road, Suite 400, Langhorne, PA 19047	(215) 579–8102
District Director.—Stacey Mulholland.	FAX: 579–8109

Counties: BUCKS, AND MONTGOMERY (part). Population (2010), 705,688.

ZIP Codes: 18036, 18042, 18054–55, 18073–74, 18076–77, 18081, 18902, 18907, 18912–15, 18917, 18920, 18923, 18925, 18929–30, 18932, 18935, 18938, 18940, 18942, 18944, 18947, 18950–51, 18954–55, 18960, 18962, 18964, 18966, 18969–70, 18972, 18974, 18976–77, 18980, 19006–07, 19021, 19030, 19040, 19047, 19053–57, 19067, 19438, 19440, 19446, 19473, 19492, 19504.

* * *

NINTH DISTRICT

BILL SHUSTER, Republican, of Hollidaysburg, PA; born in McKeesport, PA, January 10, 1961; education: Everett High School, Bedford County, PA; B.A., Dickinson College; M.B.A., American University; professional: businessman; Goodyear Tire & Rubber Corp.; Bandag, Inc.; President and General Manager, Shuster Chrysler; organizations: member, Zion Lutheran Church; National Federation of Independent Business; National Rifle Association; YMCA; Precious Life, Inc.; Rotary Club; Board of Directors, Pennsylvania Automotive Association; Board of Trustees, Homewood Home Retirement Community; Sigma Chi Fraternity; committees: chair, Transportation and Infrastructure; Armed Services; elected to the 107th Congress, by special election, on May 15, 2001; reelected to each succeeding Congress.

Office Listings

http://www.shuster.house.gov

2268 Rayburn House Office Building, Washington, DC 20515	(202) 225–2431
Chief of Staff.—Eric Burgeson.	FAX: 225–2486
Legislative Director.—Sean Joyce.	
Executive Assistant.—Brittany Smith.	
310 Penn Street, Suite 200, Hollidaysburg, PA 16648	(814) 696–6318
100 Lincoln Way East, Suite B, Chambersburg, PA 17201	(717) 264–8308
827 Water Street, Suite 3, Indiana, PA 15701	(724) 463–0516
Western Representative, Fayette County, PA	(724) 994–6220

Counties: BEDFORD, BLAIR, CAMBRIA (part), FAYETTE, FRANKLIN, FULTON, GREENE (part), HUNTINGDON (part), INDIANA, SOMERSET (part), WASHINGTON (part), and WESTMORELAND (part). Population (2010), 664,701.

ZIP Codes: 15012, 15022, 15033, 15062, 15067, 15314–15, 15320, 15322, 15325, 15327, 15332–34, 15338, 15344, 15346, 15348–49, 15351, 15357–58, 15366, 15368, 15370, 15401, 15410–13, 15415–17, 15419–25, 15427–40, 15442–47, 15449–

51, 15454–56, 15458–70, 15472–78, 15480, 15482–86, 15488–92, 15501, 15510, 15521–22, 15530, 15532–42, 15545, 15550, 15552–54, 15557–60, 15562–65, 15610, 15618, 15622, 15631, 15666, 15681, 15683, 15701, 15705, 15710, 15712–14, 15716–17, 15720, 15722–25, 15727–29, 15731–31, 15734, 15737–39, 15741–43, 15745–48, 15750, 15752, 15754, 15756–59, 15761–63, 15765, 15767, 15771–75, 15777, 15783, 15920, 15924, 15926, 15929, 15931, 15938, 15940, 15944, 15946, 15949, 15954, 15957, 15961, 16211, 16222, 16246, 16256, 16601–03, 16611, 16613, 16617, 16619, 16621–25, 16627, 16629–31, 16633–41, 16644, 16646–48, 16650, 16655, 16657, 16659, 16662, 16664–65, 16667–68, 16670, 16672–75, 16678–79, 16682, 16684–86, 16689, 16691, 16693–95, 17002, 17013, 18015, 17024, 17040, 17052–53, 17060, 17066, 17068, 17201–02, 17210–15, 17217, 17219–25, 17228–29, 17231–33, 17235–41, 17243–44, 17246–47, 17249–57, 17261–65, 17267–72, 17324

* * *

TENTH DISTRICT

TOM A. MARINO, Republican, of Cogan Station, PA; born in Williamsport, PA, August 13, 1952; education: American Institute of Baking, 1982; A.A., general studies, Williamsport Area Community College, 1983; B.A., political science/education, Lycoming College, 1985; J.D., Dickinson School of Law, 1987; United States Army War College, 2005; professional: manufacturing manager; lawyer, private practice; served as a Lycoming County District Attorney, PA, 1992–2002; U.S. Attorney for the Middle District of Pennsylvania, 1992–2002; married: Edith, 1974; two children: Chloe, Victor; committees: Foreign Affairs; Homeland Security; Judiciary; elected to the 112th Congress on November 2, 2010; reelected to each succeeding Congress.

Office Listings

http://www.marino.house.gov   https://twitter.com/reptommarino
https://www.facebook.com/congressmanmarino

410 Cannon House Office Building, Washington, DC 20515	(202) 225–3731
Chief of Staff.—Bill Tighe.	FAX: 225–9594

Legislative Director/Counsel.—Jaclyn Louis.
Senior Counsel.—Jeff Wieand.
Deputy Chief of Staff /Scheduler.—Sara Rogers.
Press Secretary.—Ryan Shucard.
Legislative Assistant.—Matthew Powell.
Legislative Assistant/Legislative Correspondent.—Judd Smith.
Staff Assistant.—Gavin McGovern.

1020 Commerce Park Drive, Suite 1A, Williamsport, PA 17701 .... (570) 322–3961
    Constituent Services Manager.—Jacqueline Bell.
District Representative: Matt Hutchinson.
Senior Advisor: Ryan Barton.

543 Easton Turnpike, Suite 101, Lake Ariel, PA 18436 .... (570) 689–6024
    District Director.—Dave Weber.
District Representatives: Tom Cahill, Cathy Romaniello.

713 Bridge Street, Room 29, Selinsgrove, PA 17870 .... (570) 374–9469
    District Representatives.—Mike Knouse, Amiee Snyder.

Counties: BRADFORD, JUNIATA, LACKAWANNA (part), LYCOMING, MIFFLIN, MONROE (part), NORTHUMBERLAND (part), PERRY, PIKE, SNYDER, SULLIVAN, SUSQUEHANNA, TIOGA, UNION, AND WAYNE. Population (2010), 669,257.

ZIP Codes: 16911–12, 16914, 16917, 16920, 16925–26, 16929–30, 16932–33, 16936, 16939–40, 16942, 16946–47, 17004, 17006, 17009, 17029, 17035, 17037, 17044–45, 17047, 17049, 17051, 17056, 17058–59, 17062–63, 17069, 17071, 17075–76, 17082, 17084, 17086, 17094, 17099, 17701–02, 17723–24, 17727–28, 17730–31, 17737, 17739, 17742, 17744, 17749, 17752, 17754, 17758, 17762–63, 17765, 17768, 17771, 17776, 17810, 17812–13, 17827, 17829, 17835, 17837, 17841–42, 17844–45, 17850, 17853, 17855–57, 17861–62, 17864–65, 17870, 17876, 17880, 17885–87, 17889, 18323, 18325, 18328, 18332, 18336–37, 18340, 18342, 18349, 18352, 18357, 18370–72, 18405, 18413, 18415, 18417, 18420–21, 18425–28, 18430–31, 18435–39, 18441, 18443, 18445, 18451, 18453–65, 18469–73, 18616, 18619, 18626, 18628, 18632, 18653, 18801, 18810, 18812, 18814, 18816–18, 18821–26, 18828–34, 18837, 18840, 18842–43, 18848, 18850–51, 18853–54

* * *

ELEVENTH DISTRICT

LOU BARLETTA, Republican, of Hazleton, PA; born in Hazleton, January 28, 1956; education: attended Bloomsburg University, Bloomsburg, PA; professional: business owner; member of city council in Hazleton, PA, 1998–2000; mayor of Hazleton, PA, 2000–10; married: Mary Grace; four daughters; committees: Education and the Workforce; Homeland Security; Transportation and Infrastructure; elected to the 112th Congress on November 2, 2010; reelected to each succeeding Congress.

Office Listings

http://www.barletta.house.gov

115 Cannon House Office Building, Washington, DC 20515	(202) 225–6511
Chief of Staff.—Andrea Niethold Waldock.	FAX: 226–6250
Legislative Director.—Mira Lezell.	
Executive Assistant.—Cherie Homa.	
Press Secretary.—Tim Murtaugh.	
1 South Church Street, Hazleton, PA 18201–5283	(570) 751–0050
59 West Louther Street, Carlisle, PA 17013	(717) 249–0190
4813 Jonestown Road, Suite 101, Harrisburg, PA 17109	(717) 525–7002
106 Arch Street, Sunbury, PA 17801	(570) 988–7801

Counties: CARBON (part), COLUMBIA, CUMBERLAND (part), DAUPHIN (part), LUZERNE (part), MONTOUR, NORTHUMBERLAND (part), PERRY (part), and Wyoming. Population (2010), 702,158.

ZIP Codes: 17005, 17007, 17013, 17015, 17017–20, 17023–24, 17030, 17032, 17034, 17036, 17040, 17048, 17050, 17053, 17055, 17057, 17061, 17065, 17068, 17074, 17080–81, 17090, 17094, 17097, 17103–04, 17109–13, 17240–41, 17257, 17266, 17307, 17324, 17756, 17772, 17774, 17777, 17801, 17814–15, 17822–24, 17829–30, 17832, 17834, 17836, 17840, 17846–47, 17851, 17859–60, 17866–68, 17872, 17878, 17881, 17884, 17888, 17920–21, 17941, 17945, 17964, 17980, 17985, 18201–02, 18210, 18221–25, 18229–30, 18234–35, 18237, 18239, 18241, 18244, 18246, 18249, 18251, 18254–56, 18414, 18417, 18424, 18446, 18602–03, 18610, 18612, 18614–15, 18617–18, 18621–25, 18629–31, 18634–36, 18643–44, 18651, 18655–57, 18660–61, 18702, 18704, 18706–09, 18844

* * *

TWELFTH DISTRICT

KEITH J. ROTHFUS, Republican, of Sewickley, PA; born in Endicott, NY, April 25, 1962; education: B.S., information systems, State University of New York College at Buffalo, Buffalo, NY, 1984; J.D., University of Notre Dame Law School, Notre Dame, IN, 1990; profession: lawyer; religion: Roman Catholic; family: Elsie, wife; six children; caucuses: Congressional Diabetes Caucus; Congressional Cybersecurity Caucus; Congressional Down Syndrome Caucus; National Guard and Reserve Components Caucus; Congressional Steel Caucus; Congressional Multiple Sclerosis Caucus; Congressional Coal Caucus; Congressional Pro-Life Caucus; Congressional Wire and Wire Producers Caucus; Ohio River Basin Congressional Caucus; Republican Policy Committee; committees: Financial Services; elected to the 113th Congress on November 6, 2012; reelected to the 114th Congress on November 4, 2014.

Office Listings

http://www.rothfus.house.gov   https://www.facebook.com/keithrothfus
https://twitter.com/keithrothfus

1205 Longworth House Office Building, Washington, DC 20515	(202) 225–2065
Chief of Staff.—Alex Shively.	FAX: (202) 225–5709
Office Manager / Schedule Coordinator.—Twinkle Patel.	
Legislative Director.—Danielle Janowski.	
Communications Director.—Lauren Beebe.	
Armed Services Staff.—Brian Ryckman.	
Small Business Staff.—Danielle Janowski.	
6000 Babcock Boulevard, Suite 104, Pittsburgh, PA 15237	(412) 837–1361
District Director.—Alex Brunory.	FAX: (412) 593–2022
Deputy District Director.—Allison Beresnyak.	
Military and Veterans' Affairs Representative.—Joshua Galiyas.	
650 Corporation Street, Suite 304, Beaver, PA 15009	(724) 359–1626
Field Representative.—Jeremy Honhold.	FAX: (412) 593–2022
Constituent Advocate.—Shannon Smith.	
110 Franklin Street, Suite 150, Johnstown, PA 15901	(814) 619–3659
Constituent Advocate.—Jose Luis Otero.	FAX: (412) 593–2022

Counties: ALLEGHENY COUNTY (part). CITIES AND TOWNSHIPS: Allison Park, Aspinwall, Bairdford, Bakerstown, Bell Acres, Bradford Woods, Curtisville, Fawn Harrison, Fox Chapel, Franklin Park, Frazer, Hampton, Haysville, Gibsonia, Glen Osborne, Glenshaw, Indiana, Kilbuck, Marshall, McCandless, O'Hara, Ohio, Pine, Richland, Ross, Russellton, Sewickley, Sewickley Heights, Sewickley Hills, Shaler, West Deer, West View. BEAVER. CITIES AND TOWNSHIPS: Aliquippa, Ambridge, Baden, Beaver, Big Beaver, Beaver Falls, Bridgewater, Brighton Township, Center, Chippewa, Conway, Darlington, Daugherty, East Rochester, Eastvale, Economy, Fallston, Frankfort Springs, Franklin, Freedom, Georgetown, Glasgow, Greene Township, Hanover, Harmony, Homewood, Hookstown, Hopewell, Independence, Industry, Koppel, Marion, Midland, Monaca, New Brighton, New Galilee, New Sewickley, North Sewickley, Ohioville, Patterson, Patterson Heights, Potter, Pulaski, Raccoon, Rochester, Shippingport, South Beaver, South Heights, Vanport, West Mayfield, White Township. CAMBRIA (part). CITIES AND TOWNSHIPS: Barr, Beaverdale, Belmont, Blacklick, Brownstown, Cambria, Carrolltown, Cassandra, Colver, Conemaugh, Croyle, Daisytown, Dale, Dunlo, East Carroll, East Conemaugh, East Taylor, Ehrenfeld, Geistown, Ebensburg, Elim, Ferndale, Johnstown, Jackson, Lilly, Lorain, Lower Yoder, Middle Taylor, Mundy's Corner, Nanty-Glo, Portagem, Revloc, Riverside, Salix, Scalp Level, Sidman, South Fork, Spring Hill, St. Michael, Stonycreek, Summerhill, Upper Yoder, Vinco, Vintonsale, Washington, West Taylor, Westmont, Wilmore.

LAWRENCE (part). CITIES AND TOWNSHIPS: Ellport, Ellwood City, Enon Valley, Little Beaver, Perry, Wampum, Wayne. SOMERSET (part). CITIES AND TOWNSHIPS: Benson, Black, Boswell, Cairnbrook, Casselman, Central City, Conemaugh, Davidsville, Edie, Friedens, Hooversville, Jefferson, Jenner, Jennersown, Jerome, Lincoln, Middle Creek, New Centerville, Ogle, Paint, Quemahoning, Rockwood, Somerset, Shade, Stoystown, Upper Turkeyfoot, Windber. WESTMORELAND (part). CITIES AND TOWNSHIPS: Allegheny, Avonmore, Bell, Bolivar, Bradenville, Delmont, Derry, East Vandergrift, Fairfield, Hyde Park, Lower Burrell, Loyalhanna, Millwood, Monroeville, Murrysville, New Alexandria, New Florence, Oklahoma, Plum, Salem, Seward, Slickville, St. Clair, Upper Burrell, Vandergrift, Washington, and West Leechburg. Population (2010), 700,573.

ZIP Codes: 15001, 15003, 15005–07, 15009–10, 15015, 15024, 15026–27, 15030, 15042–44, 15050–52, 15059, 15061, 15065–66, 15068, 15074–77, 15081, 15084, 15086, 15090, 15101, 15116, 15139, 15143, 15146–47, 15202, 15209, 15212, 15214–15, 15223, 15229, 15235, 15237–39, 15424–25, 15501–02, 15510, 15520, 15530–31, 15540–42, 15544, 15546–47, 15551, 15555, 15557, 15561, 15563, 15601, 15613, 15618, 15620, 15622, 15624, 15626–27, 15629, 15632–33, 15641, 15644, 15650, 15656, 15658, 15661, 15668, 15670–71, 15680–81, 15684, 15690, 15714, 15717, 15722, 15760, 15762, 15775, 15779, 15901–02, 15904–06, 15909, 15921–28, 15930–31, 15934–38, 15940, 15942–46, 15948, 15951–58, 15960–63, 16037, 16046, 16051, 16055, 16059, 16063, 16101, 16115, 16117, 16120, 16123, 16136, 16141, 16157, 16229

* * *

THIRTEENTH DISTRICT

BRENDAN F. BOYLE, Democrat, of Philadelphia, PA; born in the Olney section of Philadelphia, PA, February 6, 1977; education: graduated from the Cardinal Dougherty High School in Philadelphia, PA, 1995; B.A., University of Notre Dame, South Bend, IN, 1999; M.P.P., John F. Kennedy School of Government, Harvard University, Cambridge, MA, 2005; professional: Representative, Pennsylvania House of Representatives, 170th District, 2009–15; United States House of Representatives, 2015–present; married: Jennifer Boyle; children: Abigail; committees: Foreign Affairs, Government and Oversight; elected to the 114th Congress on November 4, 2014.

Office Listings

http://www.boyle.house.gov

118 Cannon House Office Building, Washington, DC 20515	(202) 225–6111
Chief of Staff.—Daniel A. Lodise.	FAX: 226–0611
Legislative Director.—Helena Mastrogianis.	
Communications Director.—Tasha Jamerson.	
115 East Glenside Avenue, Suite 1, Glenside, PA 19038	(215) 517–6572
District Office Directors: Scott Heppard, Anthony Luker.	
2375 Woodward Street, Philadelphia, PA 19115	(215) 335–3355
District Office Director.—James Kennedy.	
5675 North Front Street, Suite 180, Philadelphia, PA 19120	(267) 335–5643
District Office Director.—Nicholas Himebaugh.	

County: PHILADELPHIA COUNTY. CITY OF: Philadelphia. MONTGOMERY COUNTIES, CITIES AND TOWNSHIPS: Abington, Ambler, Blue Bell, Bridgeport, Bryn Athyn, Cheltenham, Conshohocken, Dresher, Elkins Park, Fort Washington, Glenside, Gwynedd, Hatboro, Horsham, HuntinGdon Valley, Jenkintown, King of Prussia, Lansdale, Meadowbrook, Montgomeryville, Norristown, North Wales, Philadelphia, Plymouth Meeting, Rockledge, Roslyn, Rydal, and Willow Grove. Population (2010), 705,687.

ZIP Codes: 18915 (part), 18936, 19001, 19002 (part), 19006 (part), 19009, 19012, 19025 (part), 19027, 19031 (part), 19034 (part), 19035 (part), 19038 (part), 19040 (part), 19044 (part), 19046, 19075 (part), 19087 (part), 19090, 19095, 19111, 19114 (part), 19115–16, 19118 (part), 19120 (part), 19124 (part), 19126 (part), 19136 (part), 19137 (part), 19140 (part), 19149 (part), 19150 (part), 19152, 19154, 19401 (part), 19403 (part), 19405, 19406 (part), 19422 (part), 19428 (part), 19436, 19437 (part), 19444 (part), 19446 (part), 19454 (part), 19462 (part)

* * *

FOURTEENTH DISTRICT

MIKE DOYLE, Democrat, of Forest Hills, PA; born in Swissvale, PA, August 5, 1953; graduated, Swissvale Area High School, 1971; B.S., Pennsylvania State University, 1975; co-owner, Eastgate Insurance Agency, Inc., 1983; elected and served as finance and recreation chairman, Swissvale Borough Council, 1977–81; member: Leadership Pittsburgh Alumni Association, Lions Club, Ancient Order of the Hibernians, Italian Sons and Daughters of America, and Penn State Alumni Association; member: Democratic Caucus, Democratic Study Group, Pennsylvania Democratic Delegation, Congressional Steel Caucus, Travel and Tourism CMO, Ad Hoc Committee on Irish Affairs, and National Italian-American Foundation; married Susan Beth Doyle, 1975; four children: Michael, David, Kevin, and Alexandra; committees: Energy and Commerce; elected to the 104th Congress, November 8, 1994; reelected to each succeeding Congress.

Office Listings
http://doyle.house.gov

239 Cannon House Office Building, Washington, DC 20515 .... (202) 225–2135
 Chief of Staff.—David Lucas.   FAX: 225–3084
 Legislative Director.—Phil Murphy.
 Office Manager / Scheduler.—Ellen Young.
2637 East Carson Street, Pittsburgh, PA 15203 .... (412) 390–1499
 District Director.—Paul D'Alesandro.
11 Duff Road, Penn Hills, PA 15235 .... (412) 241–6055
627 Lysle Boulevard, McKeesport, PA 15132 .... (412) 664–4049

Counties: ALLEGHENY AND WESTMORELAND. CITIES AND TOWNSHIPS: Arnold (Westmoreland) Avalon, Baldwin Borough, Baldwin Township, Bellevue, Ben Avon, Ben Avon Heights, Blawnox, Brackenridge, Braddock, Braddock Hills, Brentwood, Chalfant, Cheswick, Churchill, Clairton, Coraopolis, Crafton, Dormont, Duquesne, Dravosburg, East Deer, East McKeesport, East Pittsburgh, Edgewood, Emsworth, Etna, Forest Hills, Glassport, Glenfield, Greentree, Harmar, Harrison (Ward 1, District 1; Ward 2; Ward 5-District 1), Homestead, Ingram, Kennedy, Liberty, Lincoln, McKees Rocks, McKeesport, Millvale, Monroeville (Ward 1; Ward 2, District 2; Ward 3, District 3; Ward 5, District 1, 2, 4; Ward 6; Ward 7), Mt. Oliver, Munhall, Neville, New Kensington (Westmoreland), North Braddock, North Versailles, Oakmont, Penn Hills, Pitcairn, Pittsburgh, Port Vue, Rankin, Robinson (Districts 3 and 5), Sharpsburg, Springdale Borough, Springdale Township, Stowe, Swissvale, Tarentum, Trafford (Allegheny), Turtle Creek, Verona, Versailles, Wall, West Homestead, West Mifflin, Whitaker, White Oak, Whitehall (Part District 1; Districts 2–16), Wilkins, Wilkinsburg, and Wilmerding. Population (2010), 705,688.

ZIP Codes: 15014, 15024–25, 15030, 15034–35, 15037, 15045, 15049, 15065, 15068, 15084–85, 15104, 15106, 15108, 15110, 15112, 15120, 15122, 15131–33, 15135–37, 15139–40, 15143–48, 15201–28, 15232–36, 15238, 15260, 15290, 15642

* * *

FIFTEENTH DISTRICT

CHARLES W. DENT, Republican, of Allentown, PA, born in Allentown, May 24, 1960; education: B.A., foreign service and international politics, Pennsylvania State University, 1982; M.A., public administration, Lehigh University, 1993; professional: Legislator Development Officer, Lehigh University, 1986–90; sales representative, P.A. Peters, Inc.; Pennsylvania State House, District 132, 1991–98; Representative, Pennsylvania State Senate, 1998–2004; religion: First Presbyterian Church; married: Pamela Jane Serfass; children: Kathryn Elizabeth, William Reed, and Charles John (Jack); committees: chair, Ethics; Appropriations; elected to the 109th Congress on November 2, 2004; reelected to each succeeding Congress.

Office Listings
http://www.dent.house.gov   https://www.facebook.com/congressmandent
https://twitter.com/dentpressshop

2211 Rayburn House Office Building, Washington, DC 20515 .... (202) 225–6411
 Chief of Staff.—Drew Kent.   FAX: 226–0778
 Legislative Director.—Andrea Uckele.
3900 Hamilton Boulevard, Suite 207, Allentown, PA 18103 .... (610) 770–3490
61 North 3rd Street, Hamburg, PA 19526 .... (610) 562–4281
342 F West Main Street, Annville, PA 17003 .... (717) 867–1026
250 West Chocolate Avenue, Hershey, PA 17033 .... (717) 533–3959

Counties: BERKS (part), DAUPHIN (part), LEBANON (part), LEHIGH, AND NORTHAMPTON (part). Population (2010), 705,687.

ZIP Codes: 17003, 17010, 17022, 17026, 17028, 17033, 17036, 17038, 17041–42, 17046, 17057, 17064, 17067, 17077–78, 17087, 1711–12, 17545, 17963, 18011, 18014–18, 18020, 18031–32, 18034–38, 18040–42, 18045–46, 18049, 18051–53, 18055, 18059, 18062, 18064, 18066–69, 18072, 18077–80, 18086–88, 18091–92, 18101–06, 18109, 18195, 18951, 19504–07, 19511, 19526, 19529–30, 19533–34, 19536, 19538–39, 19541, 19544, 19550, 19554–55, 19559, 19562, 19567

* * *

SIXTEENTH DISTRICT

JOSEPH R. PITTS, Republican, of Kennett Square, PA; born in Lexington, KY, October 10, 1939; education: B.A., philosophy and religion, Asbury College, KY; military service: served in U.S. Air Force, 1963–69, rising from second lieutenant to captain; professional: nursery business owner and operator; math and science teacher, Great Valley High School, Malvern, PA, 1969–72; teacher, Mortonsville Elementary School, Versailles, KY; member: Pennsylvania House of Representatives, 1972–96, serving as chairman of Appropriations Committee,

1989-96, and of Labor Relations Committee, 1981–88; married: the former Virginia M. Pratt in 1961; children: Karen, Carol, and Daniel; committees: Energy and Commerce; elected to the 105th Congress; reelected to each succeeding Congress.

Office Listings

http://www.pitts.house.gov   twitter.com/repjoepitts
https://www.facebook.com/pages/congressman-joe-pitts/94156528752?ref=ts

420 Cannon House Office Building, Washington, DC 20515	(202) 225-2411
Chief of Staff.—Monica Volante.	FAX: 225-2013
Legislative Director.—Carson Middleton.	
Press Secretary.—Steven Stafford.	
P.O. Box 837, Unionville, PA 19375	(610) 444-4581
150 North Queen Street, Suite 716, Lancaster, PA 17603	(717) 393-0667

Counties: LANCASTER COUNTY. CITY: Lancaster. TOWNSHIPS: Brecknock, Caernarvon, Clay, Conestoga, Conoy, Drumore, Earl, East Cocalico, East Donegal, East Drumore, East Earl, East Hempfield, East Lampeter, Eden, Elizabeth, Ephrata, Fulton, Lancaster, Little Britain, Manheim, Manor, Martic, Mount Joy, Penn, Pequea, Providence, Rapho, Strasburg, Upper Leacock, Warwick, West Cocalico, West Donegal, West Earl, West Hempfield, and West Lampeter. BOROUGHS OF: Adamstown, Akron, Columbia, Denver, East Petersburg, Elizabethtown, Ephrata, Lititz, Manheim, Marietta, Millersville, Mount Joy, Mountville, New Holland, Quarryville, Strasburg, and Terre Hill. BERKS COUNTY. CITY: Reading. TOWNSHIPS: Cumru (District 1 only), Lower Alsace (District 1 only), Muhlenberg (Districts 1 and 4), Spring (Districts 2, 3, 4, 9, 10, 12). BOROUGHS OF: Laureldale (Districts 1 and 2), Mount Penn, Sinking Spring, West Reading, Wyomissing (District 3). CHESTER COUNTY. CITY: Coatesville. TOWNSHIPS: Caln (District 2), East Fallowfield, East Marlborough, East Nottingham, Elk, Franklin, Kennett (District 2 and 3), London Grove, Lower Oxford, New London, Pennsbury (North District), Sadsbury (South District), Valley, West Marlborough, West Nottingham. BOROUGHS OF: Avondale, Kennett, Square, Modena, Oxford, Parkesburg, South Coatesville, and West Grove. Population (2010), 705,688.

ZIP Codes: 17022, 17073, 17501–02, 17505, 17507–08, 17512, 17516–20, 17522, 17529, 17532, 17536, 17538, 17540, 17543, 17545, 17547, 17550–52, 17554–55, 17557, 17560, 17562–63, 17565–66, 17569–70, 17572, 17576, 17578– 79, 17581–82, 17584, 17601–03, 17606, 19311, 19317, 19320, 19330, 19344, 19348, 19350, 19352, 19358, 19362– 63, 19365, 19367, 19375, 19382, 19390, 19501, 19540, 19543, 19551, 19560–02, 19604–11

* * *

SEVENTEENTH DISTRICT

MATT CARTWRIGHT, Democrat, of Moosic, PA; born in Erie, PA, May 1, 1961; education: B.A., history, Hamilton College, Clinton, NY, 1983; J.D., University of Pennsylvania, Philadelphia, PA, 1986; professional: attorney, Munley, Munley and Cartwright, 1987– 2012; religion: Roman Catholic; family: wife, Marion; two sons, Jack and Matt; caucuses: Academic Medicine Caucus; Ad-Hoc Committee for Irish Affairs; Admadiyya Muslim Caucus; Adult Literacy Caucus; Aluminum Caucus; Animal Protection Caucus; Autism Caucus; Battlefield Caucus; Baseball Caucus; Bike Caucus; Bipartisan Congressional Watchdog Caucus; Bipartisan Disaster Relief Caucus; Bipartisan Peace Corps Caucus; Bipartisan Taskforce for Combating Anti-Semitism; Brain Injury Task Force; Caucus on Parkinson's Disease; Caucus on Travel and Tourism; Cement Caucus; Childhood Cancer Caucus; Clean Water Caucus; Coal Caucus, Cybersecurity Caucus; Cystic Fibrosis Caucus; Defense Communities Caucus; Democratic Caucus; Diabetes Caucus; Energy Savings Performance Caucus; Financial and Economic Literacy Caucus; Fire Services Caucus; Foster Youth Caucus; Friends of Ireland Caucus; Friends of Thailand Caucus; Full Employment Caucus; Free File Caucus; General Aviation Caucus; German-American Caucus; Hazards Caucus; Hearing Health Caucus; Historic Preservation Caucus; History Caucus; House Manufacturing Caucus; House Renewable Energy and Energy Efficiency Caucus; International Conservation Caucus; Iran Human Rights and Democracy Caucus; Kidney Caucus; LGBT Equality Caucus; Maker Caucus; Men's Health Caucus; Military Depot Caucus; Military Families Caucus; Military Mental Health Caucus; Military Sexual Assault Prevention Caucus; Military Veterans, Motorsports Caucus; National Parks Caucus; Nursing Caucus; Organ and Tissue Donation Awareness Caucus; P3 Caucus; Philanthropy Caucus; Poland Caucus; Pollinator Protection Caucus; Prescription Drug Abuse Caucus; Progressive Caucus; Public Broadcasting Caucus; Public Service Caucus; Public Transportation Caucus; Recycling Caucus; Safe Climate Caucus; Savings and Ownership Caucus; School Health & Safety Caucus; Scouting Caucus; Seniors Task Force; Ski and Snowboard Caucus; Skin Cancer Caucus; Small Brewers Caucus; Small Business Caucus; Soils Caucus; STEAM Caucus; Steel Caucus; Structured Settlements Caucus; Submarine Caucus; Sustainable Energy and Environment Coalition (SEEC); Taiwan Caucus; Tourette Syndrome Caucus; Ukrainian Caucus; USO Caucus; Veterans Job Caucus; Wildlife Refuge Caucus; Whip's Task Force on Poverty and Opportunity; Writers Caucus; committees: Natural Resources; Oversight and Government Reform; elected to the 113th Congress on November 6, 2012; reelected to the 114th Congress on November 4, 2014.

Office Listings

http://cartwright.house.gov   www.facebook.com/repmattcartwright
www.twitter.com/repcartwright

1419 Longworth House Office Building, Washington, DC 20515	202) 225–5546
Chief of Staff.—Hunter Ridgway.	FAX: 226–0996
Deputy Chief of Staff / Legislative Director.—Jeremy Marcus.	
Deputy Chief of Staff / Communications Director.—Shane Seaver.	
Scheduler.—Kate Huffman.	
226 Wyoming Avenue, Scranton, PA 18503	(570) 341–1050
20 North Pennsylvania Avenue, Suite 201, Wilkes-Barre, PA 18711	(570) 371–0317
400 Northampton Street, Suite 307, Easton, PA 18042	(484) 546–0776
121 Progress Avenue, Suite 310, Pottsville, PA 17901	(570) 624–0140

Counties: CARBON (part), LACKAWANNA (part), LUZERNE (part). MONROE (part), NORTHAMPTON (part), and SCHUYLKILL. Population: (2010), 705,687.

ZIP Codes: 17830, 17901, 17921–23, 17925, 17929–36. 17938, 17941, 17943–46, 17948–49, 17952–54, 17957, 17959–61, 17963–68, 17970, 17972, 17974, 17976, 17978–83, 17985, 18012–13, 18015, 18017, 18020, 18030, 18040, 18042–45, 18053, 18058, 18063–64, 18071–72, 18083, 18085, 18091, 18202, 18210–12, 18214, 18218, 18220, 18229, 18231–32, 18235, 18237, 18240–42, 18244–45, 18248–50, 18252, 18301–02, 18320–22, 18327, 18330–31, 18333–34, 18343–44, 18346–48, 18350–51, 18353–56, 18360, 18403, 18407, 18421, 18424, 18433–34, 18444, 18447–48, 18452, 18466, 18501–05, 18507–10, 18512, 18515, 18517–19, 18610, 18640–44, 18701–06, 18710–11, 18762, 18764, 18766–67, 18769, 18773, 19549

* * *

EIGHTEENTH DISTRICT

TIM MURPHY, Republican, of Upper St. Clair, PA; born in Cleveland, OH, September 11, 1952; education: B.S., Wheeling Jesuit University, 1974; M.A., Cleveland State University, 1976; Ph.D., University of Pittsburgh, 1979; professional: psychologist; holds two adjunct faculty positions at the University of Pittsburgh; Associate Professor in the Department of Public Health, and in the Department of Pediatrics; public service: Pennsylvania State Senate, 1996–2002; military: Lieutenant Commander, Medical Service Corps, United States Navy Reserve; religion: Catholic; family: married to Nan Missig; children: Bevin; grandchild: Thomasina; caucuses: chair, Congressional Steel Caucus; co-chair, Congressional Mental Health Caucus; Ad Hoc Congressional Committee for Irish Affairs / Friends of Ireland Caucus; Bipartisan Congressional Pro-Life Caucus; Congressional Manufacturing Caucus; Congressional Natural Gas Caucus; Congressional Coal Caucus; Congressional Sportsmen's Caucus; National Guard and Reserve Component Caucus; GOP Doctors Caucus; Military Veteran Caucus; USO Congressional Caucus; committees: Energy and Commerce; elected to the 108th Congress on November 5, 2002; reelected to each succeeding Congress.

Office Listings

http://murphy.house.gov   https://www.facebook.com/reptimmurphy
https://twitter.com/reptimmurphy

2332 Rayburn House Office Building, Washington, DC 20515	(202) 225–2301
Chief of Staff.—Susan Mosychuk.	
Legislative Director.—Scott Dziengelski.	
Scheduler.—Carmen Fuentes.	
Press Secretary.—Gretchen Andersen.	
504 Washington Road, Pittsburgh, PA 15228	(412) 344–5583
2040 Frederickson Place, Greensburg, PA 15601	(724) 850–7312

Counties: ALLEGHENY (part), GREENE (part), WASHINGTON (part), WESTMORELAND (part). CITIES AND TOWNSHIPS: Greensburg, Upper St. Clair, and Washington. Population (2010), 705,688.

ZIP Codes: 15003–04, 15012, 15017–21, 15025–26, 15028, 15031, 15037–38, 15046–47, 15053–57, 15060, 15062–64, 15067, 15071–72, 15078, 15082–83, 15085, 15087–89, 15102, 15108, 15122, 15126, 15129, 15131, 15135–37, 15143, 15146, 15205, 15216, 15220, 15226–28, 15234, 15236, 15241, 15243, 15301, 15310–14, 15316–17, 15321–24, 15329–33, 15337, 15340–42, 15344–45, 15347, 15349–50, 15352–53, 15359–64, 15367, 15370, 15376–80, 15417, 15423, 15427, 15448, 15479, 15501, 15531, 15610–12, 15615–17, 15621–25, 15628, 15632–40, 15642, 15644, 15646–47, 15650, 15655, 15658, 15660, 15662–63, 15665–66, 15670, 15672, 15675–80, 15683, 15687–89, 15691–93, 15695–98

RHODE ISLAND

(Population 2010, 1,052,567)

SENATORS

JACK REED, Democrat, of Jamestown, RI; born in Providence, RI, November 12, 1949; graduated, La Salle Academy, Providence, RI, 1967; B.S., U.S. Military Academy, West Point, NY, 1971; M.P.P., Kennedy School of Government, Harvard University, 1973; J.D., Harvard Law School, 1982; professional: served in the U.S. Army, 1967–79; platoon leader, company commander, battalion staff officer, 1973–77; associate professor, Department of Social Sciences, U.S. Military Academy, West Point, NY, 1978–79; 2nd BN (Abn) 504th Infantry, 82nd Airborne Division, Fort Bragg, NC; lawyer, admitted to the Washington, DC Bar, 1983; military awards: Army commendation medal with Oak Leaf Cluster, ranger, senior parachutist, jumpmaster, expert infantryman's badge; elected to the Rhode Island State Senate, 1985–90; ex-officio member of the Select Committee on Intelligence; committees: ranking member, Armed Services; Appropriations; Banking, Housing, and Urban Affairs; elected to the 102nd Congress on November 6, 1990; served three terms in the U.S. House of Representatives; elected to the U.S. Senate, November 5, 1996; reelected to each succeeding Senate term.

Office Listings

http://reed.senate.gov

728 Hart Senate Office Building, Washington, DC 20510	(202) 224–4642
Chief of Staff.—Neil Campbell.	FAX: 224–4680
Deputy Chief of Staff.—Cathy Nagle.	
Press Secretary.—Chip Unruh.	
1000 Chapel View Boulevard, Suite 290, Cranston, RI 02920	(401) 943–3100
Chief of Staff.—Raymond Simone.	
U.S. District Courthouse, One Exchange Terrace, Suite 408, Providence, RI 02903	(401) 528–5200

* * *

SHELDON WHITEHOUSE, Democrat, of Newport, RI; born in New York City, NY, October 20, 1955; education: B.A., Yale University, New Haven, CT, 1978; J.D., University of Virginia, Charlottesville, VA, 1982; director, Rhode Island Department of Business Regulation, 1992–94; United States Attorney, 1994–98; Attorney General, Rhode Island State, 1999–2003; committees: Budget; Environment and Public Works; Health, Education, Labor, and Pensions; Judiciary; Special Committee on Aging; elected to the U.S. Senate on November 7, 2006; reelected to the U.S. Senate on November 6, 2012.

Office Listings

http://whitehouse.senate.gov

530 Hart Senate Office Building, Washington, DC 20510	(202) 224–2921
Chief of Staff.—Sam Goodstein.	FAX: 228–6362
Legislative Director.—Joe Gaeta.	
Communications Director.—Seth Larson.	
170 Westminster Street, Suite 1100, Providence, RI 02903	(401) 453–5294
State Director.—George Carvalho.	

REPRESENTATIVES

FIRST DISTRICT

DAVID N. CICILLINE, Democrat, of Providence, RI; born in Providence, RI, July 15, 1961; education: graduated, Narragansett High School, Narragansett, RI; B.A., Brown University, Providence, RI, 1983; J.D., Georgetown University Law Center, Washington, DC, 1986; professional: public defender, Washington, DC, 1986–87; lawyer, private practice; lawyer, American Civil Liberties Union; faculty, Roger Williams Law School, Bristol, RI; member of the Rhode Island State House of Representatives, 1995–2003; mayor of Providence, RI, 2002–10; committees: Foreign Affairs; Judiciary; elected to the 112th Congress on November 2, 2010; reelected to each succeeding Congress.

Office Listings

http://www.cicilline.house.gov　　https://twitter.com/repcicilline
https://www.facebook.com/congressmandavidcicilline

2244 Rayburn House Office Building, Washington, DC 20515 .... (202) 225–4911
Chief of Staff.—Peter Karafotas.　　　　　　　　　　　　　　　　　　　　FAX: 225–3290
Legislative Director.—Sarah Trister.
Executive Assistant / Scheduler.—Katie Spoerer.
Communications Director.—Richard Luchette.
1070 Main Street, Suite 300, Pawtucket, RI 02860 .... (401) 729–5600

Counties: BRISTOL, NEWPORT, PROVIDENCE (part). CITIES AND TOWNSHIPS: Barrington, Bristol, Burrillville, Central Falls, Cumberland, East Providence, Jamestown, Lincoln, Little Compton, Middleton, Newport, North Providence, North Smithfield, Providence, Pawtucket, Portsmouth, Smithfield, Tiverton, Warren, and Woonsocket. Population (2010), 526,283.

ZIP Codes: 02802, 02806, 02809, 02828, 02835, 02837, 02838, 02840–42, 02860–61, 02863–65, 02871–72, 02876, 02878, 02885, 02895–96, 02903–12, 02914–17, 02919

* * *

SECOND DISTRICT

JAMES R. LANGEVIN, Democrat, of Warwick, RI; born in Providence, RI, April 22, 1964; education: B.A., political science / public administration, Rhode Island College, 1990; M.P.A., Harvard University, 1994; community service: American Red Cross; March of Dimes; Lions Club of Warwick; PARI Independent Living Center; Knights of Columbus; public service: secretary, Rhode Island Constitutional Convention, 1986; Rhode Island State Representative, 1989–95; Rhode Island Secretary of State, 1995–2000; committees: Armed Services; Homeland Security; elected to the 107th Congress; reelected to each succeeding Congress.

Office Listings

http://www.langevin.house.gov　　twitter: @jimlangevin
https://www.facebook.com/congressmanjimlangevin

109 Cannon House Office Building, Washington, DC 20515 .... (202) 225–2735
Chief of Staff.—Kristin Nicholson.　　　　　　　　　　　　　　　　　　　FAX: 225–5976
Legislative Director.—Todd Adams.
Office Manager.—Stu Rose.
The Summit South, 300 Centerville Road, Suite 200, Warwick, RI 02886 .... (401) 732–9400
District Director.—Seth Klaiman.

Counties: KENT, PROVIDENCE (part), WASHINGTON. CITIES AND TOWNSHIPS: Charleston, Coventry, Cranston, Exeter, Foster, Glocester, Greenwich (East and West), Hopkinton, Johnston, Kingstown (North and South), Narragansett, New Shoreham, Providence, Richmond, Scituate, Warwick, West Warwick, and Westerly. Population (2010), 516,587.

ZIP Codes: 02804, 02807–08, 02812–18, 02822–23, 02825, 02827–29, 02831–33, 02836, 02852, 02857, 02873–75, 02877, 02879–83, 02886–89, 02891–94, 02898, 02901–05, 02907–11, 02917, 02919–21

SOUTH CAROLINA

(Population 2010, 4,625,364)

SENATORS

LINDSEY GRAHAM, Republican, of Seneca, SC; born in Seneca, July 9, 1955; education: graduated, Daniel High School, Central, SC; B.A., University of South Carolina, 1977; awarded J.D., 1981; military service: joined the U.S. Air Force, 1982; Base Legal Office and Area Defense Counsel, Rhein Main Air Force Base, Germany, 1984; circuit trial counsel, U.S. Air Force; Base Staff Judge Advocate, McEntire Air National Guard Base, SC, 1989–94; presently a Colonel and Senior Individual Mobilization Augmentee to The Judge Advocate General, Air Force Reserves; award: Meritorious Service Medal for Outstanding Service; Meritorious Service Medal for Active Duty Tour in Europe; professional: established private law practice, 1988; former member, South Carolina House of Representatives; Assistant County Attorney for Oconee County, 1988–92; City Attorney for Central, SC, 1990–94; member: Walhalla Rotary; American Legion Post 120; appointed to the Judicial Arbitration Commission by the Chief Justice of the Supreme Court; religion: attends Corinth Baptist Church; committees: Appropriations; Armed Services; Budget; Judiciary; elected to the 104th Congress on November 8, 1994; reelected to each succeeding Congress; elected to the U.S. Senate on November 5, 2002, reelected to each succeeding Senate term.

Office Listings

http://lgraham.senate.gov

290 Russell Senate Office Building, Washington, DC 20510	(202) 224–5972
Chief of Staff.—Richard Perry.	FAX: 224–3808
Legislative Director.—Mathew Rimkunas.	
Scheduler / Press Secretary.—Alice James.	
Deputy Communications Director.—Lorcan Connick.	
130 South Main Street, Suite 700, Greenville, SC 29601	(864) 250–1417
State Director.—Van Cato.	
Upstate Regional Director.—Laura Bauld.	
Communications Director.—Kevin Bishop.	
530 Johnnie Dodds Boulevard, Suite 202, Mt. Pleasant, SC 29464	(843) 849–3887
Low Country Regional Director.—Mason Sullivan.	
508 Hampton Street, Suite 202, Columbia, SC 29201	(803) 933–0112
Midlands Regional Director.—Yvette Rowland.	
John L. McMillan Federal Building, 401 West Evans Street, Suite 111, Florence, SC 29501	(843) 669–1505
Pee Dee Regional Director.—Celia Urquhart.	
235 East Main Street, Suite 100, Rock Hill, SC 29730	(803) 366–2828
Piedmont Regional Outreach Director.—Theresa Thomas.	
124 Exchange Street, Suite A, Pendleton, SC 29670	(864) 646–4090
Senior Advisor.—Denise Bauld.	

*   *   *

TIM SCOTT, Republican, of North Charleston, SC; born in North Charleston, September 19, 1965; education: R.B. Stall High School; B.S., Charleston Southern University, Charleston, SC, 1988; professional: former owner of Tim Scott Allstate and partner of Pathway Real Estate Group; served on Charleston County Council, 1995–2008; four terms as chair of the Charleston County Council; member of the South Carolina State House of Representatives, 2009–10; member of the U.S. House of Representatives 2010–12; committees: Banking, Housing, and Urban Affairs; Finance; Health, Education, Labor, and Pensions; Small Business and Entrepreneurship; Special Committee on Aging; appointed by the Governor, January 2, 2013, to fill the vacancy caused by the resignation of Senator James DeMint; appointment took effect upon his resignation from the House of Representatives on January 2, 2013; took the oath of office on January 3, 2013; Senator Scott ran in a special election on November 4, 2014, for the final two years of Senator DeMint's second term, and won the seat.

Office Listings

http://scott.senate.gov

520 Hart Senate Office Building, Washington, DC 20510	(202) 224–6121
Chief of Staff.—Jennifer DeCasper.	FAX: 228–5143
Legislative Director.—Chuck Cogar.	
Communications Director.—Sean Smith.	
Scheduler.—John Don.	
2500 City Hall Lane, 3rd Floor Suite, North Charleston, SC 29406	(843) 727–4525

Office Listings—Continued

State Director.—Joe McKeown.
40 West Broad Street, Suite 320, Greenville, SC 29601 ....
1301 Gervais Street, Suite 825, Columbia, SC 29201 ....

FAX: (855) 802–9355
(861) 233–5366
(803) 771–6112

REPRESENTATIVES

FIRST DISTRICT

MARK SANFORD, Republican, of Mount Pleasant, SC; born in Ft. Lauderdale, FL, May 28, 1960; education: B.A., Furman University, Greenville, SC, 1983; M.B.A., Darden School of Business, University of Virginia, Charlottesville, VA, 1988; prior congressional service, 104th–106th Congresses; Governor of South Carolina: 2003–11; religion: Episcopalian; family: son of Margaret (Peg) Sanford and the late Dr. Marshall Sanford, Sr.; children: Marshall III, Landon, Bolton, and Blake; committees: Budget; Transportation and Infrastructure; elected to the 113th Congress, by special election, on May 7, 2013, to fill the vacancy caused by the appointment of United States Representative Tim Scott to the United States Senate; reelected to the 114th Congress on November 4, 2014.

Office Listings

http://www.sanford.house.gov   fb.com/repsanfordsc   youtube.com/repsanfordsc
twitter: @repsanfordsc

2201 Rayburn House Office Building, Washington, DC 20515–4001 ....
Chief of Staff.—Scott D. English.
530 Johnnie Dodds Bouvelard, Suite 201, Mount Pleasant, SC 29464–3083 ....
Deputy Chief of Staff.—Matthew Taylor.
Director of Constituent Services.—April Paris Derr.
710 Boundary Street, Suite 1D, P.O. Box 1538, Beaufort, SC 29902 ....

(202) 225–3176
FAX: 225–3407
(843) 352–7572
FAX: 352–7620

(843) 521–2530
FAX: 521–2535

Counties: BEAUFORT (part), BERKELEY (part), CHARLESTON (part), COLLETON (part), AND DORCHESTER (part). Population (2010), 660,766.

ZIP Codes: 29401–03, 29405–07, 29410, 29412, 29414, 29417–18, 29420, 29422, 29424–25, 29429, 29430–31, 29438–39, 29445, 29450, 29453, 29455–58, 29461, 29464–66, 29469–70, 29472, 29479, 29482–85, 29487, 29492, 29901–07, 29909, 29910, 29915, 29920, 29925–26, 29928, 29935–36, 29938

* * *

SECOND DISTRICT

JOE WILSON, Republican, of Springdale, SC; born in Charleston, SC, July 31, 1947; education: graduated, B.A., Washington & Lee University, Lexington, VA; J.D., University of South Carolina School of Law; professional: attorney; Kirkland, Wilson, Moore, Taylor; former Deputy General Counsel, U.S. Department of Energy; former Judge of the town of Springdale, SC; military service: U.S. Army Reserves, 1972–75; retired Colonel in the South Carolina Army National Guard as a Staff Judge Advocate for the 218th Mechanized Infantry Brigade, 1975–2003; organizations: Cayce-West Columbia Rotary Club; Sheriff's Department Law Enforcement Advisory Council; Reserve Officers Association; Lexington County Historical Society; Columbia Home Builders Association; County Community and Resource Development Committee; American Heart Association; Mid-Carolina Mental Health Association; Cayce-West Columbia Jaycees; Kidney Foundation; South Carolina Lung Association; Alston-Wilkes Society; Cayce-West Metro Chamber of Commerce; Columbia World Affairs Council; Fellowship of Christian Athletes, Sinclair Lodge 154; Jamil Temple; Woodmen of the World; Sons of Confederate Veterans; Military Order of the World Wars; Lexington, Greater Irmo, Chapin, Columbia, West Metro, and Batesburg-Leesville Chambers of Commerce; West Metro and Dutch Fork Women's Republican Clubs; Executive Council of the Indian Waters Council, Boy Scouts of America; awards: U.S. Chamber of Commerce Spirit of Enterprise Award; Americans for Tax Reform Friend of the Taxpayer Award; National Taxpayers' Union, Taxpayers' Friend Award; Americans for Prosperity, Friend of the American Motorist Award; public service: South Carolina State Senate, 1984–2001; family: married to Roxanne Dusenbury McCrory; four sons; Assistant GOP Whip; member, Republican Policy Committee; committees: Armed Services; Education and the Workforce; Foreign Affairs; elected to the 107th Congress, by special election, on December 18, 2001; reelected to each succeeding Congress.

Office Listings

http://joewilson.house.gov   https://www.facebook.com/joewilson
twitter: @repjoewilson

2229 Rayburn House Office Building, Washington, DC 20515 .... (202) 225–2452
Chief of Staff.—Jonathan Day.   FAX: 225–2455
Communications Director.—Leacy Burke.
Legislative Director.—Taylor Andreae.
1930 University Parkway, Suite 1600, Aiken, SC 29801 .... (803) 642–6416
1700 Sunset Boulevard (U.S. 378), Suite 1, West Columbia, SC 29169 .... (803) 939–0041

Counties: AIKEN, BARNWELL, LEXINGTON, ORANGEBURG (part), AND RICHLAND (part). CITIES AND TOWNSHIPS: Aiken, Arcadia Lakes, Ballentine, Barnwell, Batesburg-Leesville (part), Bath, Beech Island, Belvedere, Blackville, Blythewood, Bowman, Boyden Arbor, Branchville, Burnettown, Capitol View, Cayce, Chapin, Clearwater, Columbia (part), Cope, Cordova, Dentsville, Eastover, Eau Claire, Elko, Fairwood Acres, Gadsden, Gaston, Gilbert, Gloverville, Graniteville, Harbison, Hilda, Hilton, Hopkins, Horrell Hill, Irmo (part), Jackson, Killian, Kingville, Kline, Lake Murray, Langley, Lexington (county seat), Livingston, Lykes, Monetta, Montmorenci, Mountain Brook, Neeses, New Ellenton, North, North Augusta, Norway, Oak Grove, Pelion, Perry, Pine Ridge, Pontiac, Red Bank, Ridge Spring, Rowesville, Salley, Santee, Seven Oaks, Snelling, South Congaree, Springdale, Springfield, St. Andrews, State Park, Summit, Swansea, Vance, Vaucluse, Wagener, Warrenville, Wateree, West Columbia, Williston, Windsor, Windsor Estates, White Rock, and Woodford. Population (2010), 670,436.

ZIP Codes: 29002, 29006, 29016, 29033, 29036, 29038–39, 29044–45, 29053–54, 29061, 29063, 29070–73, 29075, 29078, 29105, 29107, 29112–13, 29115, 29123, 29129–30, 29137, 29146, 29160, 29164, 29169–72, 29177, 29180, 29203–07, 29209–10, 29212, 29219, 29223, 29229, 29260, 29801–05, 29808–09, 29812–13, 29816–17, 29822, 29826, 29898, 29829, 29831–32, 29834, 29836, 29839, 29841–43, 29847, 29849–51, 29853, 29856, 29860–61

* * *

THIRD DISTRICT

JEFF DUNCAN, Republican, of Laurens, SC; born in Greenville, SC, January 7, 1966; education: B.A., political science, Clemson University, 1988; professional: small business owner; public service: South Carolina House of Representatives, 2002–10; religion: Southern Baptist, attends Clinton First Baptist Church; married: Melody; children: Graham, John Philip, and Parker; committees: Foreign Affairs; Homeland Security; Natural Resources; elected to the 112th Congress on November 2, 2010; reelected to each succeeding Congress.

Office Listings

http://jeffduncan.house.gov

106 Cannon House Office Building, Washington, DC 20515 .... (202) 225–5301
Chief of Staff.—Lance Williams.   FAX: 225–3216
Deputy Chief of Staff.—Allen Klump
Legislative Director.—Joshua Gross.
303 West Beltline Boulevard, Anderson, SC 29625 .... (864) 224–7401
Deputy Chief of Staff.—Rick Adkins.
200 Courthouse Public Square, P.O. Box 471, Laurens, SC 29360 .... (864) 681–1028

Counties: ABBEVILLE, ANDERSON, EDGEFIELD, GREENWOOD, LAURENS, McCORMICK, OCONEE, PICKENS, SALUDA, NEWBERRY (part), GREENVILLE (part). Population (2010), 660,767.

ZIP Codes: 29006, 29037, 29070, 29105, 29108, 29127, 29129, 29138, 29145, 29166, 29178, 29325, 29332, 29335, 29351, 29355, 29360, 29370, 29384, 29388, 29605, 29611, 29620–21, 29624–28, 29630–35, 29638–46, 29649, 29653–59, 29661, 29664–67, 29669–73, 29675–78, 29680, 29682, 29684–86, 29689, 29691–93, 29695–97, 29801, 29803, 29805, 29808, 29819, 29821–22, 29824, 29832, 29835, 29838, 29840, 29844–45, 29847–48, 29853, 29860, 29899

* * *

FOURTH DISTRICT

TREY GOWDY, Republican, of Spartanburg, SC; born in Greenville, SC, August 22, 1964; native of Spartanburg, SC; education: Spartanburg High School, Spartanburg, SC, 1982; B.A., Baylor University, Waco, TX, 1986; J.D., University of South Carolina Law School, Columbia, SC, 1989; professional: Nelson, Mullins, Riley & Scarborough (law firm), 1992–94; United States Attorney, 1994–2000; South Carolina Solicitor, 7th Circuit, 2001–10; religion: Baptist; member, First Baptist Church of Spartanburg; married: the former Terri Dillard, 1989; two children; committees: Ethics; Judiciary; Oversight and Government Reform; Select Committee on Benghazi; elected to the 112th Congress on November 2, 2010; reelected to each succeeding Congress.

Office Listings

http://www.gowdy.house.gov

1404 Longworth House Office Building, Washington, DC 20515 .... (202) 225–6030
Chief of Staff.—Cindy Crick.   FAX: 226–1177
Legislative Director.—Ann Bartlett.
Legislative Assistants: Patrick Manion, Nick Spencer.
Executive Assistants: Robert DiBenedetto, Mary-Langston Willis.
Communications Director.—Amanda Duvall.
104 South Main Street, Greenville, SC 29601 .... (864) 241–0175
Chief of Staff.—Cindy Crick.
Constituent Liaison.—Belle Mercado.
101 West St. John Street, Spartanburg, SC 29306 .... (864) 583–3264
Administrative Coordinator.—Missy House.
Constituent Liaison.—Emily Davis.

Counties: GREENVILLE (part), SPARTANBURG (part). Population (2010), 660,766.

ZIP Codes: 29301–07, 29316, 29329–31, 29333–36, 29346, 29356, 29372–79, 29385–86, 29388, 29601–17, 29635–36, 29650–52, 29661–62, 29673, 29680–81, 29683, 29687–88, 29690

* * *

FIFTH DISTRICT

MICK MULVANEY, Republican, of Indian Land, SC; born in Alexandria, VA, July 21, 1967; education: graduated, Charlotte Catholic High School, 1985; B.S.F.S., international economics, commerce, and finance, Georgetown University, Washington, DC, 1989; J.D., University of North Carolina, Chapel Hill, NC, 1992; professional: Owners and Presidents Management Program, Harvard University Business School, Cambridge, MA, 2006; lawyer, private practice; real estate developer; member of the South Carolina State House of Representatives, 2007–09; member of the South Carolina State Senate, 2009–10; religion: Roman Catholic; committees: Financial Services; Oversight and Government Reform; elected to the 112th Congress on November 2, 2010; reelected to each succeeding Congress.

Office Listings

http://www.mulvaney.house.gov   facebook: rep.mickmulvaney   twitter: @repmickmulvaney

2419 Rayburn House Office Building, Washington, DC 20515 .... (202) 225–5501
Chief of Staff.—Al Simpson.   FAX: 225–0464
Communications Director.—Stephanie Faile.
1456 Ebenezer Road, Rock Hill, SC 29731 .... (803) 327–1114
District Director.—Jeffery Sligh.

Counties: CHEROKEE, CHESTER, FAIRFIELD, KERSHAW, LANCASTER, LEE, NEWBERRY (part), SPARTANBURG, SUMTER (part), YORK, AND UNION. Population (2013), 675,124.

ZIP Codes: 29009–10, 29014–16, 29020, 29031–32, 29036–37, 29040, 29045, 29055, 29058, 29065, 29067, 29069, 29074–75, 29078–79, 29101–02, 29104, 29106, 29108, 29122, 29126–28, 29130, 29132, 29145, 29150–54, 29161, 29163, 29175–76, 29178, 29180, 29203, 29218, 29307, 29323, 29330, 29332, 29340–42, 29355, 29372, 29501, 29506, 29512, 29516, 29520, 29525, 29532, 29536, 29540, 29543, 29547, 29550–51, 29563, 29565, 29567, 29570, 29573–74, 29581, 29584, 29592–94, 29596, 29654, 29702–04, 29706, 29708–10, 29712, 29714–18, 29720–22, 29724, 29726–32, 29734, 29741–45

* * *

SIXTH DISTRICT

JAMES E. CLYBURN, Democrat, of Columbia, SC; born in Sumter, SC, July 21, 1940; education: graduated, Mather Academy, Camden, SC, 1957; B.S., South Carolina State University, Orangeburg, 1962; attended University of South Carolina Law School, Columbia, 1972–74; professional: South Carolina State Human Affairs Commissioner; assistant to the Governor for Human Resource Development; executive director, South Carolina Commission for Farm Workers, Inc.; director, Neighborhood Youth Corps and New Careers; counselor, South Carolina Employment Security Commission; member: lifetime member, NAACP; Southern Regional Council; Omega Psi Phi Fraternity, Inc.; Arabian Temple, No. 139; Nemiah Lodge No. 51 F&AM; married: the former Emily England; children: Mignon, Jennifer and Angela; elected vice chair, Democratic Caucus, 2002; chair, Democratic Caucus, 2006; Majority Whip; Assistant Democratic Leader, 2010 and 2012; elected on November 3, 1992, to the 103rd Congress; reelected to each succeeding Congress.

Office Listings

http://www.clyburn.house.gov

242 Cannon House Office Building, Washington, DC 20515 .... (202) 225–3315
    Chief of Staff.—Yelberton Watkins.   FAX: 225–2313
    Deputy Chief of Staff.—Vacant.
    Scheduler.—Lindy Birch Kelly.
1225 Lady Street, Suite 200, Columbia, SC 29201 .... (803) 799–1100
    District Director.—Robert Nance.
    District Scheduler.—Melissa Lindler.
130 West Main Street, Kingstree, SC 29556 .... (843) 355–1211
176 Brooks Boulevard, Santee, SC 29142 .... (803) 854–4700

Counties: ALLENDALE COUNTY. CITIES AND TOWNS: Allendale, Appleton, Barton, Cave, Fairfax, Martin, Millett, Ulmer, and Sycamore. BAMBERG COUNTY. CITIES AND TOWNSHIPS: Bamberg, Denmark, Erhardt, and Olar. BEAUFORT COUNTY. CITIES AND TOWNS: Corner, Dale, Gardens, Lobeco, Sheldon, and Yemasee. BERKELEY COUNTY (part). CITIES AND TOWNSHIPS: Bethera, Cross, Daniel Island, Huger, Jamestown, Pineville, Russellville, Saint Stephen, and Wando. CALHOUN COUNTY (part). CITY OF: Cameron, Creston, Fort Motte, and St. Matthews. CHARLESTON COUNTY (part). CITIES AND TOWNSHIPS: Adams Run, Charleston, Edisto Island, Hollywood, Johns Island, Ravenel, and Wadmalaw Island. CLARENDON COUNTY. CITIES AND TOWNSHIPS: Alcolu, Davis Station, Gable, Manning, New Zion, Rimini, Summerton, and Turbeville. COLLETON COUNTY. CITIES AND TOWNSHIPS: Ashton, Cottageville, Green Pond, Hendersonville, Islandton, Jacksonboro, Lodge, Ritter, Round O, Smoaks, Walterboro, and Williams. DORCHESTER COUNTY (part). CITIES AND TOWNSHIPS: Dorchester, Harleyville, Reevesville, Ridgeville, Rosinville, and Saint George. HAMPTON COUNTY. CITIES AND TOWNS: Brunson, Crockettvillle, Cummings, Early Branch, Estill, Furman, Garnett, Gifford, Hampton, Luray, Miley, Scotia, Varnville, and Yemasee. JASPER COUNTY. CITIES AND TOWNS: Coosawhatchie, Gillisonville, Grays, Hardeeville, Pineland, Pocotaligo, Ridgeland, Robertville, Switzerland, Tarboro, and Tillman. ORANGEBURG COUNTY (part). CITIES AND TOWNSHIPS: Bowman, Branchville, Elloree, Eutawville, Holly Hill, Norway, Orangeburg, Rowesville, Santee, and Vance. RICHLAND COUNTY (part). CITIES AND TOWNSHIPS: Blythewood, Columbia, Eastover, Gadsden, and Hopkins. SUMTER COUNTY (part). CITIES AND TOWNSHIPS: Mayesville, and Sumter. WILLIAMSBURG COUNTY. CITIES AND TOWNSHIPS: Cades, Greeleyville, Hemingway, Kingstree, Lane, Nesmith, Salters, and Trio. Population (2010), 660,766.

ZIP Codes: 29001, 29003, 29016, 29018, 29030, 29039, 29042, 29044, 29047–48, 29051–53, 29056, 29059, 29061, 29078, 29080–82, 29102, 29104, 29107, 29111–12, 29114–15, 29117–18, 29125, 29133, 29135, 29142, 29147–148, 29150, 29153, 29160, 9162–63, 29201–06, 29208–10, 29212, 29223, 29225, 29229, 29401, 29403–06, 29409–10, 29418, 29420, 29426, 29431–32, 29434–37, 29445–46, 29448–50, 29452–53, 29456, 29461, 29464, 29468–72, 29474 75, 29477, 29479, 29481, 29483, 29487–88, 29492–93, 29510, 29518, 29530, 29554–56, 29560, 29564, 29580, 29583, 29590–91, 29810, 29812, 29817, 29827, 29836, 29843, 29849, 29906–07, 29909, 29911–12, 29916, 29918, 29921–24, 29927, 29929, 29932, 29934, 29936, 29939, 29940–41, 29943–45

* * *

SEVENTH DISTRICT

TOM RICE, Republican, of South Carolina, born in Charleston County, SC, August 4, 1957; education: attended high school in Myrtle Beach, SC; B.S., University of South Carolina, Columbia, SC, 1979; M.A., University of South Carolina, 1982; J.D., University of South Carolina, 1982; professional: lawyer, private practice; accountant; chairman of the Horry County Council, 2010–12; committees: Ways and Means; elected to the 113th Congress on November 6, 2012; reelected to the 114th Congress on November 4, 2014.

Office Listings

http://rice.house.gov

223 Cannon House Office Building, Washington, DC .... (202) 225–9895
    Chief of Staff.—Jennifer Watson.   FAX: 225–9690
    Legislative Director.—Courtney Titus Brooks.
2411 North Oak Street, Suite 405, Myrtle Beach, SC 29577 .... (843) 445–6459
1831 West Evans Street, Suite 300, Florence, SC 29501 .... (843) 679–9781

Counties: CHESTERFIELD, DARLINGTON, DILLON, FLORENCE (part), GEORGETOWN, HORRY, MARION, AND MARLBORO. Population (2010), 660,767.

ZIP Codes: 28112, 29009, 29069, 29101, 29114, 29161, 29440, 29442, 29501, 29505–06, 29510–12, 29516, 29519–20, 29525–27, 29530, 29532, 29536, 29540–41, 29543–47, 29550, 29554–55, 29560, 29563, 29565–72, 29574–77, 29579, 29581–85, 29588–89, 29591–94, 29596, 29709, 29718, 29727 28, 29741

SOUTH DAKOTA

(Population 2010, 814,180)

SENATORS

JOHN THUNE, Republican, of Murdo, SD; born in Pierre, SD, January 7, 1961; education: Jones County High School, 1979; B.S., business administration, Biola University, CA; M.B.A., University of South Dakota, 1984; professional: executive director, South Dakota Municipal League; board of directors, National League of Cities; executive director, South Dakota Republican Party, 1989–91; appointed, State Railroad Director, 1991; former congressional legislative assistant, and deputy staff director; elected, U.S. House of Representatives, 1997–2003; married: Kimberly Weems, 1984; children: Brittany and Larissa; committees: Agriculture, Nutrition, and Forestry; Commerce, Science, and Transportation; Finance; elected to the U.S. Senate on November 2, 2004; reelected to each succeeding Senate term.

Office Listings

http://thune.senate.gov

511 Dirksen Senate Office Building, Washington, DC 20510	(202) 224–2321
Chief of Staff.—Ryan Nelson.	FAX: 228–5429
Deputy Chief of Staff.—Brendon Plack.	
Legislative Director.—Jane Lucas.	
Communications Director.—Rachel Millard.	
5015 South Bur Oak, Sioux Falls, SD 57108	(605) 334–9596
246 Founders Park Drive, Suite 102, Rapid City, SD 57701	(605) 348–7551
320 South First Street, Suite 101, Aberdeen, SD 57401	(605) 225–8823

* * *

MIKE ROUNDS, Republican, of Fort Pierre, SD, born in Huron, SD, October 24, 1954; education: South Dakota State University, B.S., political science, 1977. Elected to South Dakota Senate in 1990 and reelected in 1992, 1994, 1996 and 1998; committees: Commerce, Education, Legislative Procedure, Local Government, Retirement, State Affairs and Taxation; became Senate Minority Whip in 1993. Selected as Senate Majority Leader in 1995; elected as Governor of South Dakota in 2002; reelected in 2006; religion: Roman Catholic. married: Jean Vedvei, 1978; children: Christopher, Brian, Carrie and John; committees: Armed Services; Banking, Housing, and Urban Affairs; Environment and Public Works; Veterans' Affairs; elected to the U.S. Senate in 2014.

Office Listings

http://rounds.senate.gov   https://www.facebook.com/senatormikerounds
https://twitter.com/senatorrounds

502 Hart Senate Office Building, Washington, DC 20510	(202) 224–5842
Chief of Staff.—Rob Skjonsberg.	
Deputy Chief of Staff.—Jonathan Kobes.	
Legislative Director.—Gregg Rickman.	
Communications Director.—Natalie Krings.	
320 North, Main Street, Suite A, Sioux Falls, SD 57104	(605) 336–0486
1312 West, Main Street, Rapid City, SD 57701	(605) 343–5035
111 West, Capitol Avenue, Suite 210, P.O. Box 309, Pierre, SD 57501	(605) 244–1450
514 South Main Street, Suite 100, Aberdeen, SD 57401	(605) 936–0992

REPRESENTATIVE

AT LARGE

KRISTI NOEM, Republican, of Castlewood, SD; born in Watertown, SD, November 30, 1971; professional: farmer; rancher; member of South Dakota State House of Representatives, 2007–10; committees: Ways & Means; elected to the 112th Congress on November 2, 2010; reelected to each succeeding Congress.

Office Listings

http://www.noem.house.gov

2422 Rayburn House Office Building, Washington, DC 20515	(202) 225–2801

Office Listings—Continued

Chief of Staff.—Jordan Stoick. FAX: 225–5823
Legislative Director.—Andrew Christianson.
Communications Director.—Brittany Comins.
Scheduler.—Christiana Frazee.
300 N. Dakota Avenue, Suite 314, Sioux Falls, SD 57104 .... (605) 275–2868
Southeast Director.—Andrew Curley.
343 Quincy Street, Rapid City, SD 57701 .... (605) 791–4673
West River Director.—Brad Otten.
415 South Main Street, Suite 203, Aberdeen, SD 57401 .... (605) 262–2862
818 S. Broadway Suite 113, Watertown, SD 57201 .... (605) 878–2868
State Director.—Beth Hollatz.

Population (2010), 814,180.

ZIP Codes: 57001–07, 57010, 57012–18, 57020–22, 57024–59, 57061–73, 57075–79, 57101, 57103–10, 57117–18, 57186, 57188–89, 57192–98, 57201, 57212–14, 57216–21, 57223–27, 57231–39, 57241–43, 57245–49, 57251–53, 57255–66, 57268–74, 57276, 57278–79, 57301, 57311–15, 57317, 57319, 57321–26, 57328–32, 57334–35, 57337, 57339–42, 57344–46, 57348–50, 57353–56, 57358–59, 57361–71, 57373–76, 57379–86, 57399, 57401–02, 57420–22, 57424, 57426–30, 57432–42, 57445–46, 57448–52, 57454–57, 57460–61, 57465–77, 57479, 57481, 57501, 57520–23, 57528–29, 57531–34, 57536–38, 57540–44, 57547–48, 57551–53, 57555, 57559–60, 57562–64, 57566–72, 57574, 57576–77, 57579–80, 57584–85, 57601, 57620–23, 57625–26, 57630–34, 57636, 57638–42, 57644–46, 57648–52, 57656–61, 57701–03, 57706, 57709, 57714, 57716–20, 57722, 57724–25, 57730, 57732, 57735, 57737–38, 57741, 57744–45, 57747–48, 57750–52, 57754–56, 57758–64, 57766–67, 57769–70, 57772–73, 57775–77, 57779–80, 57782–83, 57785, 57787–88, 57790–94, 57799

TENNESSEE

(Population 2010, 6,346,105)

SENATORS

LAMAR ALEXANDER, Republican, of Maryville, TN; born in Maryville, TN, July 3, 1940; education: graduated with honors in Latin American history, Phi Beta Kappa, Vanderbilt University; New York University Law School; served as *Law Review* editor; professional: clerk to Judge John Minor Wisdom, U.S. Court of Appeals in New Orleans; legislative assistant to Senator Howard Baker (R–TN), 1967; executive assistant to Bryce Harlow, counselor to President Nixon, 1969; President, University of Tennessee, 1988–91; co-director, Empower America, 1994–95; helped found a company that is now the nation's largest provider of worksite day care, Bright Horizons; public service: Republican nominee for Governor of Tennessee, 1974; Governor of Tennessee, 1979–87; U.S. Secretary of Education, 1991–93; community service: chairman, Salvation Army Red Shield Family Initiative; Museum of Appalachia in Norris, TN; received Tennessee Conservation League Conservationist of the Year Award; family: married to Honey Alexander; four children; eight grandchildren; chair, Senate Republican Conference, 2007–12; committees: chair, Health, Education, Labor, and Pensions; Appropriations; Energy and Natural Resources; Rules and Administration; elected to the U.S. Senate on November 5, 2002; reelected to each succeeding Senate term.

Office Listings

http://alexander.senate.gov   https://twitter.com/senalexander   handle: @senalexander
www.facebook.com/senatorlamaralexander

455 Dirksen Senate Office Building, Washington, DC 20510	(202) 224–4944
Chief of Staff.—David Cleary.	FAX: 228–3398
Legislative Director / Counsel.—Allison Martin.	
Communications Director.—Jim Jeffries.	
Executive Assistant / Scheduler.—Sarah Fairchild.	
3322 West End Avenue, Suite 120, Nashville, TN 37203	(615) 736–5129
Howard H. Baker, Jr. U.S. Courthouse, 800 Market Street, Suite 112, Knoxville, TN 37902	(865) 545–4253
Federal Building, 167 North Main Street, Suite 1068, Memphis, TN 38103	(901) 544–4224
111 Murray Guard Drive, Suite D, Jackson, TN 38305	(731) 664–0289
Joel E. Solomon Federal Building, 900 Georgia Avenue, Suite 260, Chattanooga, TN 37402	(423) 752–5337
Tri-Cities Regional Airport, Terminal Building, P.O. Box 1113, 2525 Highway 75, Suite 101, Blountville, TN 37617	(423) 325–6240

* * *

BOB CORKER, Republican, of Chattanooga, TN; born in Orangeburg, SC, August 24, 1952; education: B.S., Industrial Management, University of Tennessee, Knoxville, TN, 1974; professional: founder of Bencor Corporation, a construction company specializing in retail properties which operated in 18 states, 1978–90; founder of the Corker Group, acquisition, development, and operation of commercial real estate, 1982–2006; honors: named to the University of Tennessee at Chattanooga's "Entrepreneurial Hall of Fame," 2005; community service: founding chair, Chattanooga Neighborhood Enterprise, Inc., a non-profit organization that has helped over 10,000 families secure decent, fit and affordable housing, 1986–92; public service: commissioner, State of Tennessee Department of Finance and Administration, 1995–96; mayor, City of Chattanooga, 2001–05; married: Elizabeth Corker, 1987; two children: Julia and Emily; committees: chair, Foreign Relations; Banking, Housing, and Urban Affairs; Budget; Special Committee on Aging; elected to the U.S. Senate on November 7, 2006; reelected to the U.S. Senate on November 6, 2012.

Office Listings

http://corker.senate.gov

425 Dirksen Senate Office Building, Washington, DC 20510	(202) 224–3344
Chief of Staff.—Todd Womack.	FAX: 228–0566
Legislative Director.—Rob Strayer.	
Executive Assistant / Scheduler.—Hallie Williams.	
Communications Director.—Tara DiJulio.	
3322 West End Avenue, Suite 610, Nashville, TN 37203	(615) 279–8125
100 Peabody Place, Suite 1125, Memphis, TN 38103	(901) 683–1910
Howard Baker Federal Building, 800 Market Street, Suite 121, Knoxville, TN 37902	(865) 637–4180
1105 East Jackson Boulevard, Suite 4, Jonesborough, TN 37659	(423) 753–2263

Office Listings—Continued

10 West Martin Luther King Boulevard, Sixth Floor, Chattanooga, TN 37402 .... (423) 756–2757
91 Stonebridge Boulevard, Suite 103, Jackson, TN 38305 .... (731) 664–2294

REPRESENTATIVES

FIRST DISTRICT

DAVID "PHIL" ROE, Republican, of Johnson City, TN; born in Clarksville, TN; July 21, 1945; education: B.S., Austin Peay State University, Clarksville, TN, 1967; M.D., University of Tennessee, Knoxville, TN, 1970; professional: United States Army Medical Corps, 1970–72; Vice Mayor of Johnson City, 2003–07; Mayor of Johnson City, 2007–09; Doctors Caucus; Academic Medicine Caucus; religion: member of Munsey United Methodist Church; widowed: Pam; children: David C. Roe, John Roe, and Whitney Larkin: committees: Education and the Workforce; Veterans' Affairs; elected to the 111th Congress; reelected to each succeeding Congress.

Office Listings

http://www.roe.house.gov   https://www.facebook.com/drphilroe   https://twitter.com/drphilroe

407 Cannon House Office Building, Washington, DC 20515 .... (202) 225–6356
    Chief of Staff.—Matt Meyer.   FAX: 225–5714
    Communications Director.—Tiffany Haverly.
    Scheduler.—Catherine Bartley.
    Legislative Director.—John Martin.
    Legislative Staff: Alex Large, John Witherspoon.
    Staff Assistant.—Kyle Jacobs.
205 Revere Street, Kingsport, TN 37660 .... (423) 247–8161
                                                FAX: 247–0119
Higher Education Building, P.O. Box 1728, Kingsport, TN 37662.
    District Director.—Bill Snodgrass.
    Administrative Assistant.—Sheila Houser.
    Caseworkers: Carolyn Ferguson, Tracie O'Hara, Fran Woods.
1609 College Park Drive, Suite 4, Morristown, TN 37813 .... (423) 254–1400
    District Representative.—Bill Darden.   FAX: 254–1403
    Caseworkers: Cheryl Bennett, Angie Jarnagin.

Counties: CARTER, COCKE, GREENE, HAMBLEN, HANCOCK, HAWKINS, JEFFERSON, JOHNSON, SEVIER, SULLIVAN, UNICOI, AND WASHINGTON. Population (2010), 705,123.

ZIP Codes: 37601, 37604, 37614–18, 37620, 37640–43, 37645, 37650, 37656–60, 37663–65, 37681–83, 37686–88, 37690–92, 37694, 37711, 37713, 37722, 37725, 37727, 37731, 37738, 37743, 37745, 37748, 37753, 37760, 37764–65, 37809–11, 37813–14, 37818, 37821, 37843, 37857, 37860, 37862–63, 37865, 37869, 37871, 37873, 37876–77, 37879, 37881, 37890, 37891

* * *

SECOND DISTRICT

JOHN J. DUNCAN, JR., Republican, of Knoxville, TN; born in Lebanon, TN, July 21, 1947; education: B.S. in journalism, University of Tennessee, 1969; J.D., National Law Center, George Washington University, 1973; served in both the Army National Guard and the U.S. Army Reserves, retiring with the rank of captain; private law practice, Knoxville, 1973–81; appointed State Trial Judge by Governor Lamar Alexander in 1981 and elected to a full 8-year term in 1982 without opposition, receiving the highest number of votes of any candidate on the ballot that year; member: American Legion 40 and 8; Elks; Sertoma Club; Masons; Scottish Rite and Shrine; present or past board member: Red Cross; Girl's Club; YWCA; Sunshine Center for the Mentally Retarded; Beck Black Heritage Center; Knoxville Union Rescue Mission; Senior Citizens Home Aid Service; religion: active elder at Eastminster Presbyterian Church; married: the former Lynn Hawkins; children: Tara, Whitney, John J. III, and Zane; committees: Oversight and Government Reform; Transportation and Infrastructure; elected to both the 100th Congress (special election) and the 101st Congress in separate elections held on November 8, 1988; reelected to each succeeding Congress.

Office Listings

http://www.duncan.house.gov

2207 Rayburn House Office Building, Washington, DC 20515 .... (202) 225–5435

Office Listings—Continued

Chief of Staff.—Bob Griffitts.   FAX: 225–6440
Deputy Chief of Staff.—Don Walker.
Press Secretary.—Patrick Newton.
800 Market Street, Suite 100, Knoxville, TN 37902 .... (865) 523–3772
District Director.—Bob Griffitts.
331 Court Street, Blount County Courthouse, Maryville, TN 37804 .... (865) 984–5464

Counties: BLOUNT, CAMPBELL, CLAIBORNE, GRAINGER, JEFFERSON, KNOX, LOUDON. CITIES AND TOWNSHIPS: Alcoa, Farragut, Halls (Knox Co.), Harrogate, Jefferson City, Jellico, Knoxville, Lenoir City, Loudon, Maryville, Powell, and Seymour. Population (2010), 714,622.

ZIP Codes: 37303, 37309, 37311–12, 37314, 37322–23, 37325, 37329, 37331, 37353–54, 37369–71, 37385, 37701, 37709, 37721, 37725, 37737, 37742, 37754, 37764, 37771–72, 37774, 37777, 37779, 37801–04, 37806–07, 37820, 37826, 37830, 37846, 37849, 37853, 37865, 37871, 37874, 37876, 37878, 37880, 37882, 37885–86, 37901–02, 37909, 37912, 37914–24, 37927–33, 37938–40, 37950, 37990, 37995–98

* * *

THIRD DISTRICT

CHUCK FLEISCHMANN, Republican, of Ooltewah, TN; born in New York City, NY, October 11, 1962; graduated from Elk Grove High School, Elk Grove Village, IL, 1980; B.A., political science, University of Illinois, Urbana-Champaign, IL, 1983; J.D., University of Tennessee College of Law, Knoxville, TN, 1986; professional: attorney; small business owner; former president of the Chattanooga Bar Association, 1996; former chairman of the Chattanooga Lawyers Pro Bono Committee; religion: Catholic; married: Brenda Fleischmann; three children; committees: Appropriations; elected to the 112th Congress on November 2, 2010; reelected to each succeeding Congress.

Office Listings

http://www.fleischmann.house.gov   http://www.facebook.com/repchuck
https://twitter.com/repchuck

230 Cannon House Office Building, Washington, DC 20515 .... (202) 225–3271
Chief of Staff.—Jim Hippe.   FAX: 225–3494
Legislative Director.—Alek Vey.
Communications Director.—Tyler Threadgill.
Scheduler.—Carole Anne Spohn.
900 Georgia Avenue, Suite 126, Chattanooga, TN 37402 .... (423) 756–2342
District Director.—Bob White.
200 Administration Road, Suite 100, Oak Ridge, TN 37830 .... (865) 576–1976
6 East Madison Avenue, Athens, TN 37303 .... (423) 745–4671

Counties: ANDERSON, BRADLEY (part), CAMPBELL (part), HAMILTON, MCMINN, MONROE, MORGAN, POLK, ROANE, SCOTT, AND UNION. Population (2010), 711,391.

ZIP Codes: 37302–03, 37307–11, 37315, 37317, 37322–23, 37325–26, 37329, 37331, 37333, 37336, 37338, 37341, 37343, 37350–51, 37353–54, 37361–63, 37369–70, 37373, 37377, 37379, 37385, 37391, 37402–12, 37415, 37419, 37421, 37705, 37710, 37714, 37716, 37719, 37721, 37729, 37732–33, 37754–57, 37763, 37766, 37769, 37770–71, 37774, 37779, 37801, 37807, 37825–26, 37828–30, 37840–41, 37845–49, 37852, 37854, 37866, 37870, 37872, 37874, 37880, 37885, 37887–88, 37892, 37931, 38504

* * *

FOURTH DISTRICT

SCOTT DESJARLAIS, Republican, of South Pittsburg, TN; born in Sturgis, SD, February 21, 1964; education: B.S., chemistry and psychology, University of South Dakota, 1987; M.D., University of South Dakota School of Medicine, Vermillion, 1991; professional: general practitioner, Grand View Medical Center, Jasper, TN; religion: member, Epiphany Episcopalian Church, Sherwood, TN; married: Amy; children: Tyler, Ryan, and Maggie; committees: Agriculture; Foreign Affairs; Oversight and Government Reform; elected to the 112th Congress on November 2, 2010; reelected to each succeeding Congress.

Office Listings

http://www.desjarlais.house.gov

413 Cannon House Office Building, Washington, DC 20515 .... (202) 225–6831

Office Listings—Continued

Chief of Staff.—Richard Vaughn.   FAX: 226–5172
Legislative Director.—Vacant.
Communications Director.—Robert Jameson.
301 Keith Street, Suite 212, Cleveland, TN 37311 .... (423) 472–7500
711 North Gardeb Street, Columbia, TN 38401 .... (931) 381–9920
212 First Avenue Southeast, Winchester, TN 37398 .... (931) 962–3180
305 West Main Street, Murfreesboro, TN 37130 .... (931) 962–3180

Counties: BEDFORD, BLEDSOE, BRADLEY (part), FRANKLIN, GRUNDY, LINCOLN, MARION, MARSHALL, MAURY (part), MOORE, RHEA, RUTHERFORD, SEQUATCHIE, VAN BUREN (part), AND WARREN. Population (2010), 705,123.

ZIP Codes: 37014, 37018–20, 37025, 37034, 37037, 37046–47, 37060, 37063–64, 37085–86, 37090–91, 37110–11, 37118, 37122, 37127–30, 37132, 37135, 37144, 37149, 37153, 37160, 37166–67, 37174, 37180, 37183, 37190, 37301, 37305–06, 37308–13, 37318, 37321–24, 37327–28, 37330, 37332, 37334–40, 37345, 37347–49, 37352–53, 37356–57, 37359–60, 37365–67, 37373–83, 37387–89, 37394, 37396–98, 37405, 37419, 37773, 37778, 37826, 37880, 38402, 38449, 38451, 38453, 38459, 38472, 38474, 38483, 38488, 38550, 38555, 38557, 38559, 38572, 38581, 38583, 38585, 39401

* * *

FIFTH DISTRICT

JIM COOPER, Democrat, of Nashville, TN; born in Nashville, June 19, 1954; education: B.A., history and economics, University of North Carolina at Chapel Hill, 1975; Rhodes Scholar, Oxford University, 1977; J.D., Harvard Law School, 1980; admitted to Tennessee Bar, 1980; professional: attorney; Waller, Lansden, Dortch, and Davis (law firm), 1980–82; Managing Director, Equitable Securities, 1995–99; Adjunct Professor, Vanderbilt University Owen School of Management, 1995–2002 and 2006–present; partner, Brentwood Capital Advisors LLC, 1999–2002; married: Martha Hays; three children; caucuses: Blue Dog Coalition; New Democrat Coalition; committees: Armed Services, Oversight and Government Reform; elected to the U.S. House of Representatives, 1982–95; elected to the 108th Congress on November 5, 2002; reelected to each succeeding Congress.

Office Listings

http://www.cooper.house.gov   https://www.facebook.com/jimcooper
https://twitter.com/repjimcooper

1536 Longworth House Office Building, Washington, DC 20515 .... (202) 225–4311
Chief of Staff.—Lisa Quigley.   FAX: 226–1035
Legislative Director / Deputy Chief of Staff.—Jason Lumia.
605 Church Street, Nashville, TN 37219 .... (615) 736–5295

Counties: CHEATHAM (part), DAVIDSON, AND DICKSON. Population (2010), 713,990.

ZIP Codes: 37011, 37013, 37015, 37024–25, 37027, 37029, 37032, 37035–36, 37043, 37051–52, 37055–56, 37062, 37064, 37070, 37072–73, 37076, 37080, 37082, 37086, 37101, 37115–16, 37122, 37135, 37138, 37143, 37146, 37165, 37171, 37181, 37187, 37189, 37201–22, 37224, 37227–30, 37232, 37234–36, 37238, 37240–44, 37246, 37250

* * *

SIXTH DISTRICT

DIANE BLACK, Republican, of Gallatin, TN; born in Baltimore, MD, January 16, 1951; education: A.S.N., Arundel Community College, Baltimore, MD, 1971; B.S.N., Belmont University, Nashville, TN, 1991; professional: nurse; nonprofit community organization fundraiser; member of the Tennessee State House of Representatives, 1999–2005; member of the Tennessee State Senate, 2005–10; religion: attends Community Church of Hendersonville; married: Dr. David Black; three children; six grandchildren; caucuses: co-chair of the Congressional Range and Testing Center Caucus, co-chair of the Congressional Caucus on Foster Youth, vice chair of the GOP Doctors Caucus, member of the Pro Life Caucus; Congressional Military Families Caucus; Republican Study Committee; committees: Budget; Ways and Means; elected to the 112th Congress on November 2, 2010; reelected to each succeeding Congress.

Office Listings

http://www.black.house.gov

1131 Longworth House Office Building, Washington, DC 20515 .... (202) 225–4231

Office Listings—Continued

Chief of Staff.—Teresa Koeberlein. FAX: 225–6887
Scheduler.—Greg Dowell.
321 East Spring Street, Suite 301, Cookeville, TN 38501 .... (931) 854–0069
355 North Belvedere Drive, Suite 308, Gallatin, TN 37066 .... (615) 206–8204
District Director.—Charles Schneider.

Counties: CANNON, CLAY, COFFEE, CUMBERLAND, DEKALB, FENTRESS, JACKSON, MACON, OVERTON, PICKETT, PUTNAM, ROBERTSON, SMITH, SUMNER, TROUSDALE, WHITE, WILSON, CHEATHAM (part), and VAN BURDEN. CITIES AND TOWN- SHIPS: Byrdstown, Carthage, Celina, Cookeville, Crossville, Gainesboro, Gallatin, Grimsley, Hartsville, Hillsboro, Lafayette, Lebanon, Livingston, Mt. Juliet, Pleasant Hill, Sparta, Smithville, Springfield, Watertown, and Woodbury. Population (2010), 705,123.

ZIP Codes: 37010, 37012, 37015–16, 37018, 37022, 37030–32, 37034–36, 37048–49, 37059, 37066, 37072–75, 37077, 37080, 37082–83, 37085, 37087, 37090, 37095, 37143, 37155, 37118–19, 37122, 37141, 37146, 37150, 37152, 37166, 37172, 37183–84, 37186–88, 37190, 37337, 37342, 37355, 37357, 37360, 37388, 37723, 37726, 37854, 38501–06, 38543–44, 38547–49, 38551, 38553, 38555–56, 38558–59, 38562, 38565, 38570–74, 38577, 38579, 38581, 38583, 38585, 38587, 38589

* * *

SEVENTH DISTRICT

MARSHA BLACKBURN, Republican, of Franklin, TN; born in Laurel, MS, June 6, 1952; education: B.S., Mississippi State University, 1973; professional: retail marketing; public serv- ice: American Council of Young Political Leaders; Executive Director, Tennessee Film, Enter- tainment, and Music Commission; Chairman, Governor's Prayer Breakfast; Tennessee State Senate, 1998–2002; minority whip; community service: Rotary Club; Chamber of Commerce; Arthritis Foundation; Nashville Symphony Guild Board; Tennessee Biotechnology Association; March of Dimes; American Lung Association; awards: Chi Omega Alumnae Greek Woman of the Year, 1999; Middle Tennessee 100 Most Powerful People, 1999–2002; More Magazine *Women Run The World* Honoree, April 2013; married: Chuck; children: Mary Morgan Ketchel and Chad; founding member of the Republican Women's Policy Committee; committees: vice chair, Energy and Commerce; Budget; elected to the 108th Congress on November 5, 2002; reelected to each succeeding Congress.

Office Listings

http://blackburn.house.gov   www.facebook.com/marshablackburn
twitter: @marshablackburn

2266 Rayburn House Office Building, Washington, DC 20515 .... (202) 225–2811
Chief of Staff.—Mike Platt. FAX: 225–3004
Legislative Director.—Chuck Flint.
Executive Assistant.—Grace Burch.
305 Public Square, Suite 212, Franklin, TN 37064 .... (615) 591–5161
128 North 2nd Street, Suite 202, Clarksville, TN 37040 .... (931) 503–0391

Counties: BENTON (part), CHESTER, DECATUR, GILES, HARDEMAN, HARDIN, HENDERSON, HICKMAN, HOUSTON, HUMPHREYS, LAWRENCE, LEWIS, MAURY (part), McNairy, Montgomery, Perry, Stewart, Wayne, and Williamson. Population (2010), 705,192.

ZIP Codes: 37010, 37014–15, 37023, 37025, 37027–28, 37032, 37037, 37040, 37042–43, 37046–47, 37050–52, 37055, 37059–62, 37067, 37078–79, 37096–98, 37101, 37134–35, 37137, 37140, 37142, 37144, 37171, 37174–79, 37181, 37185, 37191, 37214–15, 37220, 38008, 38039, 38042, 38044, 38052, 38061, 38067, 38075, 38221, 38310, 38463– 64, 38468–69, 38471–78, 38481–83, 38485–87, 42223

* * *

EIGHTH DISTRICT

STEPHEN FINCHER, Republican, of Frog Jump, TN; born in Memphis, TN, February 7, 1973; education: Crockett County High School, 1990; professional: managing partner in Fincher Farms; public service: "The Fincher Family" singing ministry; president of Alamo Dixie Youth Baseball and Crockett County Dixie Youth Baseball; chairman of the board of the PPR Com- mittee at Archer's Chapel United Methodist Church; president of United Methodist Men; reli- gion: Archer's Chapel United Methodist Church; married: Lynn; children: John Austin, Noah, and Sarah; committees: Financial Services; elected to the 112th Congress on November 2, 2010; reelected to each succeeding Congress.

Office Listings

http://www.fincher.house.gov   www.twitter.com/repfinchertn08
www.facebook.com/repfinchertn08

2452 Rayburn House Office Building, Washington, DC 20515 .... (202) 225–4714
Chief of Staff.—Jessica Carter.   FAX: 225–1765
Communications Director.—Logan Ramsey.
Legislative Director.—Brett Quick.
Scheduler.—Molly Jacob.
Staff Assistant.—Kirby Richard.
Legislative Assistants: Kathleen Carlson, Corey Schrodt.
Legislative Correspondent.—Andrew Palmer.
12015 Walker Street, Arlington, TN 38002 .... (901) 581–4718
100 South Main Street, Suite 1, Dyersburg, TN 38024 .... (731) 285–0910
117 North Liberty Street, Jackson, TN 38301 .... (731) 423–4848
406 Lindell Street South, Suite C, Martin, TN 38237 .... (731) 588–5190
5384 Poplar Avenue, Memphis, TN 38119 .... (901) 682–4422

Counties: BENTON, CARROLL, CROCKETT, DYER, FAYETTE, GIBSON, HAYWOOD, HENRY, LAKE, LAUDERDALE, MADISON, OBION, SHELBY (part), TIPTON, AND WEAKLEY. Population (2010), 705,122.

ZIP Codes: 38001–02, 38004, 38006–07, 38011–12, 38015–19, 38021, 38023–24, 38028–30, 38034, 38036–37, 38039–42, 38046–47, 38049–50, 38053–54, 38057–60, 38063, 38066, 38068–70, 38075–77, 38079–80, 38111, 38117, 38119–20, 38125, 38128, 38133–35, 38138–39, 38141, 38152, 38201, 38220–22, 38224–26, 38229–33, 38235, 38237, 38240–42, 38251, 38253–61, 38301, 38305, 38313, 38316–18, 38326, 38330, 38337, 38341–44, 38348, 38351, 38355–56, 38358, 38362, 38366, 38369, 38382, 38387, 38390–92, 38401

* * *

NINTH DISTRICT

STEPHEN IRA "STEVE" COHEN, Democrat, of Memphis, TN; born in Memphis, May 24, 1949 of Dr. Morris D. Cohen and Genevieve Cohen; B.A., Vanderbilt University in Nashville, TN, 1971; J.D., Cecil C. Humphreys School of Law of Memphis State University (renamed University of Memphis), 1973; legal advisor for the Memphis Police Department, 1974–77; Delegate to and Vice President of Tennessee Constitutional Convention, 1977; Commissioner on the Shelby County Commission, 1978–80; Tennessee State Senator for District 30, 1982–2006; Delegate at the 1980 and 1992 Democratic National Conventions; Commission on Security and Cooperation in Europe; committees: Judiciary; Transportation and Infrastructure; elected to the 110th Congress on November 7, 2006; reelected to each succeeding Congress.

Office Listings

http://www.cohen.house.gov   https://twitter.com/repcohen
https://www.facebook.com/congressmanstevecohen

2404 Rayburn House Office Building, Washington, DC 20515 .... (202) 225–3265
Chief of Staff.—Marilyn Dillihay.   FAX: 225–5663
Scheduler.—Patrick Cassidy.
Legislative Director.—Matt Weisman.
Communications Director.—Ben Garmisa.
167 North Main Street, Suite 369, Memphis, TN 38103 .... (901) 544–4131
FAX: 544–4329

County: SHELBY COUNTY (part). CITY OF: Memphis. Population (2010), 705,123.

ZIP Codes: 37501, 38016, 38018, 38053, 38101, 38103–109, 38111–20, 38122–28, 38130–36, 38138, 38141, 38146, 38148, 38151–52, 38159, 38167–68, 38173–75, 38181–82, 38186, 38188, 38190, 38193–94

TEXAS

(Population 2010, 25,145,561)

SENATORS

JOHN CORNYN, Republican, of Austin, TX; born in Houston, TX, February 2, 1952; education: graduated, Trinity University, and St. Mary's School of Law, San Antonio, TX; Master of Laws, University of Virginia, Charlottesville, VA; professional: attorney; Bexar County District Court Judge; Presiding Judge, Fourth Administrative Judicial Region; Texas Supreme Court, 1990–97; Texas Attorney General, 1999–2002; community service: Salvation Army Adult Rehabilitation Council; World Affairs Council of San Antonio; Lutheran General Hospital Board; chair, National Republican Senatorial Committee 2009–13; committees: Finance; Judiciary; elected to the U.S. Senate on November 5, 2002, for the term beginning January 3, 2003; appointed to the Senate on December 2, 2002, to fill the vacancy caused by the resignation of Senator Phil Gramm; reelected to each succeeding Senate term.

Office Listings

http://cornyn.senate.gov   https://www.facebook.com/sen.johncornyn

517 Hart Senate Office Building, Washington, DC 20510	(202) 224–2934
Republican Whip Office, S–208 Capitol Building, Washington, DC 20510	(202) 224–2708
Chief of Staff.—Beth Jafari.	FAX: 224–5220
Legislative Director.—Jerr Rosenbaum.	
5300 Memorial Drive, Suite 980, Houston, TX 77007	(713) 572–3337
Providence Tower, 5001 Spring Valley Road, #1125E, Dallas, TX 75244	(972) 239–1310
100 East Ferguson Street, Suite 1004, Tyler, TX 75702	(903) 593–0902
221 West Sixth Street, Suite 1530, Austin, TX 78701	(512) 469–6034
Wells Fargo Center, 1500 Broadway, #1230, Lubbock, TX 79401	(806) 472–7533
222 East Van Buren, Suite 404, Harlingen, TX 78550	(956) 423–0162
600 Navarro Street, Suite 210, San Antonio, TX 78205	(210) 224–7485

* * *

TED CRUZ, Republican, of Houston, TX; born in Calgary, Alberta, Canada, December 22, 1970; raised in Houston, TX; education: graduated *cum laude* from Princeton University with a B.A. from the Woodrow Wilson School of Public and International Affairs in 1992 and *magna cum laude* from Harvard Law School with a J.D. in 1995; Domestic Policy Advisor on the 2000 Bush-Cheney campaign; director of the Office of Policy Planning at the Federal Trade Commission; Associate Deputy Attorney General at the U.S. Department of Justice; Adjunct Professor of Law at the University of Texas School of Law; Solicitor General of the State of Texas; Partner at Morgan, Lewis & Bockius LLP; religion: Southern Baptist; married: Heidi Cruz; committees: Armed Services; Commerce, Science, and Transportation; Judiciary; Rules and Administration; Joint Economic Committee; elected to the U.S. Senate on November 6, 2012.

Office Listings

http://cruz.senate.gov   https://www.facebook.com/senatortedcruz
https://twitter.com/sentedcruz

404 Russell Senate Office Building, Washington, DC 20510	(202) 224–5922
Chief of Staff.—Paul Teller.	FAX: 228–0755
Legislative Director.—Jeff Murray.	
300 East 8th Street, Suite 961, Austin, TX 78701	(512) 916–5834
808 Travis Street, Suite 1420, Houston, TX 77002	(713) 718–3057
Lee Park Tower II, 3626 North Hall Street, Suite 410, Dallas, TX 75219	(214) 599–8749
9901 IH–10 West, Suite 950, San Antonio, TX 78230	(210) 340–2885
305 South Broadway Avenue, Suite 501, Tyler, TX 75702	(903) 593–5130
200 South 10th Street, Suite 1603, McAllen, TX 78501	(956) 686–7339

REPRESENTATIVES

FIRST DISTRICT

LOUIE GOHMERT, Republican, of Tyler, TX; born in Pittsburg, TX, August 18, 1953; education: B.A., Texas A&M University, 1975; J.D., Baylor University, Waco, TX, 1977; professional: United States Army, 1978–82; district judge, Smith County, 1992–2002; appointed by Governor Rick Perry to complete an unexpired term as Chief Justice of the 12th Court of Appeals, 2002–03; Brigade Commander of the Corps of Cadets, Texas A&M; organizations: president of the South Tyler Rotary Club; Boy Scout District Board of Directors; religion: deacon at Green Acres Baptist Church; director of Leadership Tyler; director of Centrepoint Ministries; married: Kathy; children: Katy, Caroline, Sarah; committees: Judiciary; Natural Resources; elected to the 109th Congress on November 2, 2004; reelected to each succeeding Congress.

Office Listings

http://www.gohmert.house.gov   twitter: @replouiegohmert

2243 Rayburn House Office Building, Washington, DC 20515	(202) 225–3035
Chief of Staff.—Connie Hair.	FAX: 226–1230
Legislative Director.—Austin Smithson.	
Communications Director.—Kimberly Willingham.	
1121 East Southeast Loop 323, Suite 206, Tyler, TX 75701	(903) 561–6349

Counties: ANGELINA, GREGG, HARRISON, NACOGDOCHES, PANOLA, RUSK, SABINE, SAN AUGUSTINE, SHELBY, SMITH, WOOD (part), AND UPSHUR (part). Population (2010), 710,704.

ZIP Codes: 75551, 75555, 75562, 75564–65, 75601–08, 75615, 75631, 75633, 75637, 75639–45, 75647, 75650–54, 75657–63, 75666–67, 75669–72, 75680, 75682–85, 75687–89, 75691–94, 75701–13, 75750, 75755, 75757, 75760, 75762, 75771, 75788–89, 75791–92, 75797–99, 75901–04, 75915, 75929–31, 75935, 75937, 75941, 75943–44, 75946–49, 75954, 75958–59, 75961–65, 75968–69, 75972–75, 75978, 75980

* * *

SECOND DISTRICT

TED POE, Republican, of Humble, TX; born in Temple, TX, September 10, 1948; education: B.A., political science, Abilene Christian University, Abilene, TX, 1970; J.D., University of Houston, TX, 1973; professional: United States Air Force, 1970–1976; Felony Court Judge, 1981–2003; Trainer, Federal Bureau of Investigations National Academy; Chief Felony Prosecutor, District Attorney, Harris County, TX; United States Air Force Reserves Instructor, University of Houston; organizations: Congressional PORTS Caucus; Congressional Victim's Rights Caucus; committees: Foreign Affairs; Judiciary; elected to the 109th Congress on November 2, 2004; reelected to each succeeding Congress.

Office Listings

http://www.poe.house.gov

2412 Rayburn House Office Building, Washington, DC 20515	(202) 225–6565
Chief of Staff.—Gina Santucci.	FAX: 225–5547
Press Secretary.—Shaylyn Hynes.	
Scheduler.—Jessica Carlton.	
1801 Kingwood Drive, Suite 240, Kingwood, TX 77339	(866) 447 0242
710 North Post Oak, Suite 510, Houston, TX 77024	(866) 447 0242

Counties: HARRIS. Population (2010), 698,488.

ZIP Codes: 77002, 77004–08, 77018–19, 77024–25, 77030, 77040–41, 77043–44, 77055, 77064–66, 77069–70, 77079–80, 77084, 77086, 77088, 77092, 77095, 77098, 77336, 77338–39, 77345–46, 77357, 77365, 77373, 77375, 77377, 77379, 77388, 77396, 77429, 77532

* * *

THIRD DISTRICT

SAM JOHNSON, Republican, of Dallas, TX; born in San Antonio, TX, October 11, 1930; education: B.S., business administration, Southern Methodist University, Dallas, TX, 1951; M.A., international affairs, George Washington University, Washington, DC, 1974; military service: served in the U.S. Air Force, 29 years; Korea and Vietnam (POW in Vietnam, 6 years, 10 months); director, Air Force Fighter Weapons School; flew with Air Force Thunderbirds Precision Flying Demonstration Team; graduate of Armed Services Staff College and National War College; military awards: two Silver Stars, two Legions of Merit, Distinguished Flying Cross, one Bronze Star with Valor, two Purple Hearts, four Air Medals, and three Outstanding Unit awards; ended career with rank of colonel and Air Division commander; retired, 1979;

professional: opened homebuilding company, 1979; served 7 years in Texas House of Representatives; Smithsonian Board of Regents; U.S./Russian Joint Commission on POW/MIA; Texas State Society; Congressional Medal of Honor Society; National Patriot Award Recipient, 2009; caucus and award: co-chair, Air Force Caucus; Living Legends of Aviation "Freedom of Flight" Award recipient, 2011; Rotary International, Paul Harris Fellow; founder, Republican Study Committee (formerly Conservative Action Team); chairman of the Board of Directors, Institute of Basic Life Principles; Deputy Whip; married the former Shirley L. Melton, 1950; three children: Dr. James Robert Johnson, Shirley Virginia (Gini) Mulligan, and Beverly Briney; committees: Ways and Means; Joint Committee on Taxation; elected to the 102nd Congress by special election on May 18, 1991, to fill the vacancy caused by the resignation of Steve Bartlett; reelected to each succeeding Congress.

Office Listings

http://www.samjohnson.house.gov   https://twitter.com/samspressshop
https://www.facebook.com/repsamjohnson

2304 Rayburn House Office Building, Washington, DC 20515	(202) 225–4201
Chief of Staff.—Dave Heil.	FAX: 225–1485
Legislative Director.—David Eiselberg.	
Executive Assistant.—Amanda Hamilton.	
1255 West 15th Street, Suite 170, Plano, TX 75075	(469) 304–0382

Counties: The Third District of Texas encompasses the majority of COLLIN COUNTY including all or part of the CITIES of Allen, Anna, Blue Ridge, Dallas. (COLLIN COUNTY), Fairview, Frisco, Lavon, Lowry Crossing, Lucas, McKinney, Melissa, Murphy, New Hope. Parker, Plano, Princeton, Prosper, Richardson, St. Paul, Wylie, and portions of unincorporated land in COLLIN COUNTY. Population (2010), 747,284.

ZIP Codes: 75002, 75007, 75009, 75013, 75023–26, 75030, 75034–35, 75040–42, 75044–48, 75069–71, 75074–75, 75078, 75080–82, 75085–86, 75088–89, 75093–94, 75098, 75228, 75238, 75245, 75248, 75252, 75287, 75355, 75367, 75370, 75378. 75382, 75409, 75424, 75442, 75454, 78243

* * *

FOURTH DISTRICT

JOHN RATCLIFFE, Republican, of Heath, TX; born in Mt. Prospect, IL, October 20, 1965; education: attended the University of Notre Dame, 1987; J.D., Southern Methodist University Law School, 1989; professional: chief of Anti–Terrorism and National Security for the Eastern District of Texas, 2004–07; U.S. Attorney for the Eastern District of Texas, 2007–08; lawyer, The Ashcroft Law Firm, 2008–14, TX; religion: member, Our Lady of the Lake Catholic Church; wife: Michele Ratcliffe; children: Darby and Riley; committees: Homeland Security; Judiciary; elected to the 114th Congress on November 4, 2014.

Office Listings

https://ratcliffe.house.gov   https://www.facebook.com/repratcliffe
http://twitter.com/repratcliffe   https://www.youtube.com/channel/uco37ersrga4fuyijda6j6oa

325 Cannon House Office Building, Washington, DC 20515	(202) 225–6673
Chief of Staff.—Daniel Kroese.	FAX: 225–3332
Legislative Director and Counsel.—Emily Leviner.	
Communications Director.—Shayne Martin.	
6531 Horizon Road, Suite A, Rockwall, TX 75032	(972) 771–0100
District Director.—Jason Ross.	FAX: 771–1222
2600 North Robison Road, Texarkana, TX 75505	(903) 823–3173
	FAX: 823–3232
100 West Houston Street, 1st Floor, Sherman, TX 75090	(903) 813–5270
	FAX: 868–8613

Counties: BOWIE COUNTY. CITIES AND TOWNSHIPS: DeKalb, Hooks, Leary, Maud, Nash, New Boston, Red Lick, Redwater, Texarkana, Wake Village. CAMP COUNTY. CITIES AND TOWNSHIPS: Pittsburg, Rocky Mound. CASS COUNTY. CITIES AND TOWNSHIPS: Atlanta, Avinger, Bloomburg, Domino, Douglassville, Hughes Springs, Linden, Marietta, Queen City. COLLIN COUNTY. CITIES AND TOWNSHIPS: Anna, Blue Ridge, Celina, Farmersville, Josephine, Lavon, Nevada, Royse City, Van Alstyne, Westminster, Weston, Wylie. DELTA COUNTY. CITIES AND TOWNSHIPS: Cooper, Pecan Gap. FANNIN COUNTY. CITIES AND TOWNSHIPS: Bailey, Bonham, Dodd City, Ector, Honey Grove, Ladonia, Leonard, Pecan Gap, Ravenna, Savoy, Trenton, Whitewright, Windom. FRANKLIN COUNTY. CITIES AND TOWNSHIPS: Mount Vernon, Winnsboro. GRAYSON COUNTY. CITIES AND TOWNSHIPS: Bells, Collinsville, Denison, Dorchester, Gunter, Howe, Knollwood, Pottsboro, Sadler, Sherman, Southmayd, Tioga, Tom Bean, Van Alstyne, Whitesboro, Whitewright. HOPKINS COUNTY. CITIES AND TOWNSHIPS: Como, Cumby, Sulphur Springs, Tira. HUNT COUNTY. CITIES AND TOWNSHIPS: Caddo Mills, Campbell, Celeste, Commerce, Greenville, Hawk Cove, Josephine, Lone Oak, Neylandville, Quinlan, West Tawakoni, Wolfe City. LAMAR COUNTY. CITIES AND TOWNSHIPS: Blossom, Deport, Paris, Reno, Roxton, Sun Valley, Toco. MARION COUNTY. CITIES AND TOWNSHIPS: Jefferson City, Pine Harbor. MORRIS COUNTY. CITIES AND TOWNSHIPS: Daingerfield, Hughes Springs, Lone Star, Naples, Omaha. RAINS COUNTY. CITIES AND TOWNSHIPS: Alba, East Tawakoni, Emory, Point.

RED RIVER COUNTY. CITIES AND TOWNSHIPS: Annona, Avery, Bogata, Clarksville, Deport, Detroit. ROCKWALL COUNTY. CITIES AND TOWNSHIPS: Fate, Garland, Heath, Mclendon–Chisholm, Mobile City, Rockwall, Rowlett, Royse City, Wylie. TITUS COUNTY. CITIES AND TOWNSHIPS: Miller's Cove, Mount Pleasant, Talco. UPSHUR COUNTY. CITIES AND TOWNSHIPS: Clarksville City, East Mountain, Gilmer, Gladewater, Ore City, Union Grove, and Warren City. Population (2010), 705,523.

ZIP Codes: 75002, 75009, 75013, 75019, 75030, 75032, 75034–35, 75040–41, 75058, 75069, 75071, 75074, 75076, 75078, 75087–88, 75090, 75094, 75097–98, 75132, 75135, 75164, 75166, 75173, 75189, 75407, 75409, 75413–14, 75416–18, 75422–24, 75426, 75428–29, 75431–33, 75435–36, 75438–40, 75442, 75446, 75449, 75452–55, 75457, 75459, 75460, 75462, 75469, 75472–73, 75474, 75476, 75477, 75479, 75482, 75486–87, 75683, 75489, 75490–95, 75501, 75550–51, 75554, 75556, 75559–61, 75563, 75566–73, 75572, 75630, 75638, 75644–47, 75656, 75657, 75668, 75686, 75855, 76233, 76264, 76268, 76271, 76273

*   *   *

FIFTH DISTRICT

JEB HENSARLING, Republican, of Dallas, TX; born in Stephenville, TX, May 29, 1957; education: B.A., economics, Texas A&M University, 1979; J.D., University of Texas School of Law, 1982; professional: businessman; vice president, Maverick Capital, 1993–96; owner, San Jacinto Ventures, 1996–2002; vice president, Green Mountain Energy Co., 1999–2001; community service: American Cancer Society for the Dallas Metro Area; Children's Education Fund; Habitat for Humanity; religion: Christian; married: Melissa; children: Claire and Travis; committees: chair, Financial Services; elected to the 108th Congress on November 5, 2002; reelected to each succeeding Congress.

Office Listings

http://www.hensarling.house.gov   twitter: @rephensarling
https://www.facebook.com/rephensarling

2228 Rayburn House Office Building, Washington, DC 20515	(202) 225–3484
Chief of Staff.—Andrew Duke.	FAX: 226–4888
Legislative Director.—Kyle Jackson.	
Press Secretary.—Sarah Rozier.	
6510 Abrams Road, Suite 243, Dallas, TX 75238	(214) 349–9996
810 East Corsicana Street, Suite C, Athens, TX 77571	(903) 675–8288

Counties: ANDERSON, CHEROKEE, DALLAS (part), HENDERSON, KAUFMAN, VAN ZANDT, AND WOOD. Population (2010), 698,498.

ZIP Codes: 75041–43, 75103, 75114, 75117–18, 75124, 75126–27, 75140, 75142–43, 75147–50, 75156–61, 75163, 75169, 75180–82, 75185, 75187, 75214, 75217–18, 75227–28, 75231, 75238, 75243, 75253, 75336, 75355, 75382, 75389, 75410, 75431, 75440, 75444, 75474, 75494, 75497, 75751–52, 75754, 75756–59, 75763–64, 75766, 75770, 75772–73, 75778–80, 75782–85, 75789–90, 75801–03, 75832, 75839, 75844, 75853, 75861, 75880, 75882, 75884, 75886, 75925, 75976

*   *   *

SIXTH DISTRICT

JOE BARTON, Republican, of Ennis, TX; born in Waco, TX, September 15, 1949; education: graduated, Waco High School, 1968; B.S., industrial engineering, Texas A&M University, College Station, 1972; M.S., industrial administration, Purdue University, West Lafayette, IN, 1973; professional: plant manager, and assistant to the vice president, Ennis Business Forms, Inc., 1973–81; awarded White House Fellowship, 1981–82; served as aide to James B. Edwards, Secretary, Department of Energy; member, Natural Gas Decontrol Task Force in the Office of Planning, Policy and Analysis; worked with the Department of Energy task force in support of the President's Private Sector Survey on Cost Control; natural gas decontrol and project cost control consultant, Atlantic Richfield Company; cofounder, Houston County Volunteer Ambulance Service, 1976; vice president, Houston County Industrial Development Authority, 1980; chairman, Crockett Parks and Recreation Board, 1979–80; vice president, Houston County Chamber of Commerce, 1977–80; member, Dallas Energy Forum; religion: Methodist; son, Jack; children: Brad, Alison and Kristin; committees: chair emeritus, Energy and Commerce; elected to the 99th Congress on November 6, 1984; reelected to each succeeding Congress.

Office Listings

http://www.joebarton.house.gov

2107 Rayburn House Office Building, Washington, DC 20515 .... (202) 225–2002

Office Listings—Continued

Chief of Staff.—Ryan Thompson.   FAX: 225–3052
Communications Director.—Sean Brown.
Legislative Director.—Krista Rosenthall.
Senior Legislative Assistant.—Emmanual Guillory.
Legislative Assistants: Amy Murphy, Nina Shelat.
Special Assistant.—Daniel Rhea.
Staff Assistant.—Gable Brady.
6001 West Ronald Reagan Memorial Highway, Suite 200, Arlington, TX 76017 .... (817) 543–1000
Constituent Liaison.—Deborah Rollins.   FAX: 548–7029
Special Projects Director.—Jodi Saegesser.
Casework Director.—Christi Townsend.
2106A West Ennis Avenue, Ennis, TX 75119 (direct phone) .... (972) 875–8488
Deputy Chief of Staff.—Linda Gillespie.   FAX: 875–1907
District Assistant.—Hunter Thedford.

Counties: ELLIS, NAVARRO, AND TARRANT. CITIES AND TOWNSHIPS: Alma, Angus, Arlington, Bardwell, Barry, Blooming
    Grove, Burleson, Cedar Hill, Corsicana, Crowley, Dawson, Emhouse, Ennis, Eureka, Ferris, Fort Worth, Frost, Garrett,
    Glenn Heights, Goodlow, Grand Prairie, Italy, Kennedale, Kerens, Mansfield, Maypearl, Midlothian, Milford, Mustang,
    Navarro, Oak Leaf, Oak Valley, Ovilla, Palmer, Pecan Hill, Powell, Red Oak, Rendon, Retreat, Rice, Richland, Venus,
    and Waxahachie. Population (2010), 720,861.

ZIP Codes: 75050, 75052, 75054, 75101–02, 75104–06, 75109–10, 75119–20, 75125, 75144, 75146, 75151–55, 75165,
    75167–68, 75859, 76001–04, 76006, 76010–19, 76028, 76036, 76041, 76050, 76060, 76094, 76096, 76119–20, 76123,
    76133–34, 76140, 76623, 76626, 76639, 76641, 76651, 76670, 76679, 76681

* * *

SEVENTH DISTRICT

JOHN ABNEY CULBERSON, Republican, of Harris County, TX; born in Houston, TX,
August 24, 1956; education: B.A., Southern Methodist University; J.D., South Texas College
of Law; professional: attorney; awards: Citizens for a Sound Economy Friend of the Tax
payer Award; Texas Eagle Forum Freedom and Family Award; Houston Jaycees Outstanding
Young Houstonian Award; Champion of Border Security; Ancient Coin Collectors Guild; Friend
of Numismatics; Club for Growth's Defender of Economic Freedom; Congressional Management Foundation's Silver Mouse Award; Family Research Council True Blue Award; Water
Advocate "Friend of the Shareholder" Recognition; U.S. Chamber of Commerce; Spirit of
Enterprise Guardian of Small Business by NFIB; Recognition from the 60 Plus Association;
NumbersUSA "A" for Consistently Voting for American Workers and the Environment
through Immigration Reduction; public service: Texas House of Representatives, 1987–2000;
married: Belinda Burney, 1989; child: Caroline; committees: Appropriations; elected to the
107th Congress on November 7, 2000; reelected to each succeeding Congress.

Office Listings

http://www.culberson.house.gov

2372 Rayburn House Office Building, Washington, DC 20515 .... (202) 225–2571
Chief of Staff.—Jamie Gahun.   FAX: 225–4381
Legislative Director.—Catherine Knowles.
10000 Memorial Drive, Suite 620, Houston, TX 77024–3490 .... (713) 682–8828
District Director.—Cynthia Dannenbrink.

County: HARRIS (part). Population (2010), 717,354.

ZIP Codes: 77005, 77019, 77024–25, 77027, 77035–36, 77040–42, 77046, 77055–57, 77063–65, 77074, 77077, 77079,
    77080–82, 77084, 77094–96, 77098, 77215, 77218, 77224, 77227, 77242, 77244, 77256, 77257, 77265, 77274, 77277,
    77279, 77282, 77401–02, 77429, 77433, 77449, 77450

* * *

EIGHTH DISTRICT

KEVIN BRADY, Republican, of The Woodlands, TX; born in Vermillion, SD, April 11,
1955; education: B.S., business, University of South Dakota; professional: served in Texas
House of Representatives, 1991–96, the second Republican to capture the 8th District seat since
the district's creation; chair, Council of Chambers of Greater Houston; president, East Texas
Chamber Executive Association; president, South Montgomery County Woodlands Chamber of

Commerce, 1985–present; director, Texas Chamber of Commerce Executives; Rotarian; awards: Achievement Award, Texas Conservative Coalition; Outstanding Young Texan (one of five), Texas Jaycees; Ten Best Legislators for Families and Children, State Bar of Texas; Legislative Standout, Dallas Morning News; Scholars Achievement Award for Excellence in Public Service, North Harris Montgomery Community College District; Victims Rights Equalizer Award, Texans for Equal Justice Center; Support for Family Issues Award, Texas Extension Homemakers Association; religion: attends Saints Simon and Jude Catholic Church; married: Cathy Brady; committees: chair, Ways and Means; Joint Committee on Taxation; elected to the 105th Congress; reelected to each succeeding Congress.

Office Listings

http://www.kevinbrady.house.gov   https://www.facebook.com/kevinbrady
https://twitter.com/repkevinbrady

301 Cannon House Office Building, Washington, DC 20515	(202) 225–4901
Chief of Staff.—Lori Harju.	FAX: 225–5524
Legislative Director.—Aindriu Colgan.	
Communications Director.—Tracee Evans.	
Press Secretary.—David O'Brien.	
200 River Pointe Drive, Suite 304, Conroe, TX 77304	(936) 441–5700
District Director.—Todd Stephens.	
1300 11th Street, Suite 400, Huntsville, TX 77340	(936) 439–9532

Counties: GRIMES, HARRIS (part), HOUSTON, LEON, MADISON, MONTGOMERY, SAN JACINTO, TRINITY, AND WALKER. CITIES AND TOWNSHIPS: Anderson, Augusta, Bedias, Centerville, Conroe, Crockett, Decker Prairie, Grapeland, Groveton, Huntsville, Madisonville, Magnolia, Maynard, Midway, Montgomery, Navasota, New Caney, Normangee, Pinehurst, Plantersville, Point Blank, Porter Springs, Roans Prairie, Shepherd, Splendora, Spring, The Woodlands, Todd Mission, Tomball, Trinity, Weches, Willis, and Woodlake. Population (2010), 743,782.

ZIP Codes: 77371–73, 77365, 77379, 77353–59, 77375, 77377, 77070, 77340–42, 75844, 75852, 75862, 77328, 75849–51, 77365, 77830–31, 77393, 77447, 77380–89, 75835, 75856, 75858, 75926, 77316, 77318, 77320, 77331, 77333–34, 77367, 77378, 75845, 75847, 77855, 77861, 77864, 77876, 77301–06, 77354, 77447, 77868, 75833, 77328

* * *

NINTH DISTRICT

AL GREEN, Democrat, of Houston, TX; born in New Orleans, LA, September 1, 1947; raised in Florida; education: Florida A&M University, Tallahassee, FL, 1966–71; attended Tuskegee University, Tuskegee, AL; J.D., Texas Southern University, Houston, TX, 1974; professional: co-founded and co-managed the law firm of Green, Wilson, Dewberry and Fitch; Justice of the Peace, Precinct 7, Position 2, 1977–2004; organizations: former president of the Houston NAACP; Houston Citizens Chamber of Commerce; awards: Memorial Foundation's Leader of Democracy Award, 2014; VetsFirst Congressional Bronze Star; Texas Association of Realtors' Legacy Award, 2011; Texas Black Democrats' Profiles of Courage Award, 2007; AFL-CIO MLK Drum Major Award for Service, 2007; *Ebony* magazine's 100 Most Influential Black People, 2006; NAACP Mickey Leland Humanitarian Award, from the Houston branch as well as the Fort Bend branch of the NAACP; committees: Financial Services; elected to the 109th Congress on November 2, 2004; reelected to each succeeding Congress.

Office Listings

http://www.algreen.house.gov

2347 Rayburn House Office Building, Washington, DC 20515	(202) 225–7508
Chief of Staff.—Jacqueline Ellis.	FAX: 225–2947
Legislative Director / Deputy Chief of Staff.—Gregg Orton.	
Communications Director.—Michael Mouton.	
3003 South Loop West, Suite 460, Houston, TX 77054	(713) 383–9234
District Office Policy Manager / Deputy Chief of Staff.—Kevin Dancy.	FAX: 383–9202
District Office Administrative Manager.—Crystal Webster.	

Counties: FORT BEND (part), HARRIS (part). Population (2010), 698,488.

ZIP Codes: 77004, 77025, 77030–31, 77033, 77035–36, 77042, 77045, 77047–48, 77051, 77053–54, 77061, 77063, 77071–72, 77074, 77077, 77082–83, 77085, 77087, 77096, 77099, 77407, 77459, 77477, 77489, 77498, 77545

* * *

TENTH DISTRICT

MICHAEL T. McCAUL, Republican, of Austin, TX; born in Dallas, TX, January 14, 1962; education: B.S., Trinity University, San Antonio, TX, 1984; J.D., St. Mary's University, San Antonio, TX, 1987; professional: lawyer, private practice; deputy attorney general, office of Texas State Attorney General; committees: chair, Homeland Security; Foreign Affairs; Science, Space, and Technology; elected to the 109th Congress on November 2, 2004; reelected to each succeeding Congress.

Office Listings

http://www.mccaul.house.gov

131 Cannon House Office Building, Washington, DC 20515	(202) 225–2401
Chief of Staff.—Jessica Nalepa.	FAX: 226–1395
Legislative Director.—Andy Taylor.	
Scheduler/Office Manager.—Kelly Cotner.	
9009 Mountain Ridge Drive, Suite 230, Austin, TX 78731	(512) 473–2357
Communications Director.—Walter Zaykowski.	
Rosewood Professional Building, 990 Village Square, Suite B, Tomball, TX 77375	(281) 255–8372
1773 Westborough Drive, Suite 223, Katy, TX 77084	(281) 398–1247
2000 South Market Street, Suite 303, Brenham, TX 77833	(979) 830–8497

Counties: AUSTIN, BASTROP, COLORADO, FAYETTE, HARRIS, LEE, TRAVIS, WALLER, AND WASHINGTON. Population (2010), 698,487.

ZIP Codes: 77070, 77355, 77363, 77375, 77377, 77389, 77412, 77418, 77423, 77426, 77428–29, 77433–35, 77442, 77445–47, 77449–50, 77460, 77466, 77470, 77473–75, 77484–85, 77493–94, 77833, 77835, 77868, 77880, 77964, 78602, 78612–13, 78621, 78641, 78645, 78650, 78653, 78703, 78705, 78723–24, 78726, 78730–32, 78746, 78751–54, 8756–59, 78931–35, 78938, 78940–51, 78954, 78956–57, 78959, 78962–63

* * *

ELEVENTH DISTRICT

K. MICHAEL CONAWAY, Republican, of Midland, TX; born in Borger, TX, June 11, 1948; education: B.B.A., Texas A&M-Commerce, 1970; professional: Spec 5 United States Army, 1970–72; tax manager, Price Waterhouse & Company, 1972–80; Chief Financial Officer, Keith D. Graham & Lantern Petroleum Company, 1980–81; Chief Financial Officer, Bush Exploration Company, 1982–84; Chief Financial Officer, Spectrum 7 Energy Corporation, 1984–86; Senior Vice President/Chief Financial Officer, United Bank, 1987–90; Senior Vice President, Texas Commerce Bank, 1990–92; owner, K. Conaway CPA, 1993–present; Deputy Republican Whip; religion: Baptist; married: Suzanne; children: Brian, Erin, Kara, and Stephanie; committees: chair, Agriculture; Armed Services; Permanent Select Committee on Intelligence; elected to the 109th Congress on November 2, 2004; reelected to each succeeding Congress.

Office Listings

http://www.conaway.house.gov

2430 Rayburn House Office Building, Washington, DC 20515	(202) 225–3605
Chief of Staff.—Mark Williams.	FAX: 225–1783
Legislative Director.—Matthew Russell.	
Scheduler.—Emily Keener.	
6 Desta Drive, Suite 2000, Midland, TX 79705	(432) 687–2390
Regional Director.—Evan Thomas.	

Counties: ANDREWS, BROWN, CALLAHAN, COKE, COLEMAN, COMANCHE, CONCHO, DAWSON, EASTLAND, ECTOR, ERATH, GLASSCOCK, HOOD, IRION, KIMBLE, LLANO, MARTIN, MASON, McCULLOCH, MENARD, MIDLAND, MILLS, MITCHELL, PALO PINTO, RUNNELS, SAN SABA, STEPHENS, STERLING, AND TOM GREEN. Population (2010), 698,488.

ZIP Codes: 76033, 76035, 76048–49, 76066–67, 76087, 76401, 76424, 76429, 76432–33, 76435–37, 76442–46, 76448–50, 76452–55, 76462–64, 76466, 76469–72, 76474–76, 76484, 76486, 76801–02, 76820–21, 76823, 76825, 76827–28, 76831–32, 76834, 76836–37, 76841–42, 76844–45, 76848–49, 76852, 76854, 76856–59, 76861–62, 76864–66, 76869–73, 76875, 76877–78, 76882, 76884–85, 76887–88, 76890, 76901, 76903–05, 76908, 76930, 76933–35, 76937, 76939–41, 76945, 76949, 76951, 76953, 76955, 76957–58, 78607, 78609, 78639, 78643, 78657, 78672, 79331, 79351, 79377, 79504, 79506, 79510, 79512, 79519, 79532, 79538, 79565–67, 79601–02, 79701, 79703, 79705–07, 79713–14, 79720, 79739, 79741, 79749, 79758–59, 79761–66, 79782–83

* * *

TWELFTH DISTRICT

KAY GRANGER, Republican, of Fort Worth, TX; born in Greenville, TX, January 18, 1943; education: B.S., *magna cum laude*, 1965, and Honorary Doctorate of Humane Letters, 1992, Texas Wesleyan University; professional: owner, Kay Granger Insurance Agency, Inc.; former public school teacher; elected mayor of Fort Worth, 1991, serving three terms; during her tenure, Fort Worth received All-America City Award from the National Civic League; former Fort Worth Councilwoman; past chair, Fort Worth Zoning Commission; past board member: Dallas-Fort Worth International Airport; North Texas Commission; Fort Worth Convention and Visitors Bureau; U.S. Conference of Mayors Advisory Board; Business and Professional Women's Woman of the Year, 1989; three grown children: J.D., Brandon, and Chelsea; first woman Republican to represent Texas in the U.S. House of Representatives; Republican Whip; committees: Appropriations; elected to the 105th Congress; reelected to each succeeding Congress.

Office Listings

http://www.granger.house.gov

1026 Longworth House Office Building, Washington, DC 20515	(202) 225–5071
Chief of Staff.—Shannon Meade.	FAX: 225–5683
Legislative Director.—Jonathan Blyth.	
Staff Assistant.—Suzi Plasencia.	
Scheduler.—Brenan Tjelmeland.	
1701 River Run Road, Suite 407, Fort Worth, TX 76107	(817) 338–0909
District Director.—Kristin Vandergiff.	FAX: 335–5852

Counties: PARKER, TARRANT (part), and WISE. Population (2010), 698,488.

ZIP Codes: 76008, 76020, 76023, 76035–36, 76049, 76052, 76066–68, 76071, 76073, 76078, 76082, 76085–88, 76098, 76101–02, 76104, 76106–11, 76113–18, 76121–23, 76126–27, 76129–37, 76147–48, 76161–64, 76177, 76179–82, 76185, 76191–93, 76195–99, 76225, 76234, 76244, 76246, 76248, 76262, 76267, 76270, 76299, 76426, 76431, 76439, 76462, 76485–87, 76490

* * *

THIRTEENTH DISTRICT

MAC THORNBERRY, Republican, of Clarendon, TX; born in Clarendon, July 15, 1958; education: graduate, Clarendon High School; B.A., Texas Tech University; law degree, University of Texas; professional: rancher; attorney; admitted to the Texas Bar, 1983; member: Joint Forces Command Transformation; Republican Study Committee; married: Sally Adams, 1986; children: Will and Mary Kemp; committees: chair, Armed Services; elected to the 104th Congress; reelected to each succeeding Congress.

Office Listings

http://www.thornberry.house.gov	https://www.facebook.com/repmacthornberry
https://twitter.com/mactxpress	http://www.youtube.com/repmacthornberry

2208 Rayburn House Office Building, Washington, DC 20515	(202) 225–3706
Administrative Assistant.—Lauren Hensarling.	FAX: 225–3486
Office Managers: Lauren Hensarling, Jayla Lackey.	
620 South Taylor Street, Suite 200, Amarillo, TX 79101	(806) 371–8844
Chief of Staff.—Josh Martin.	
2525 Kell Boulevard, Suite 406, Wichita Falls, TX 76308	(940) 692–1700

Counties: ARCHER, ARMSTRONG, BAYLOR, BRISCOE, CARSON, CHILDRESS, CLAY, COLLINGSWORTH, COOKE, COTTLE, DALLAM, DEAF SMITH, DICKENS, DONLEY, FLOYD, FOARD, GRAY, HALL, HANSFORD, HARDEMAN, HARTLEY, HEMPHILL, HUTCHINSON, JACK, KING, KNOX, LIPSCOMB, MONTAGUE, MOORE, MOTLEY, OCHILTREE, OLDHAM, POTTER, RANDALL, ROBERTS, SHERMAN, SWISHER, WHEELER, WICHITA, WILBARGER, AND WISE (part). Population (2010), 703,835.

ZIP Codes: 73448, 73539, 73562, 73848–49, 76023, 76073, 76078, 76082, 76225, 76228, 76230, 76233–34, 76238–40, 76250–52, 76255, 76259, 76261, 76263, 76265–66, 76270–73, 76301–02, 76305–06, 76308–11, 76351, 76354, 76357, 76360, 76363–67, 76371, 76373–74, 76377, 76379–80, 76384, 76389, 76426–27, 76431, 76458–59, 76486–87, 79001, 79005, 79007, 79011, 79014–16, 79018–19, 79022, 79029, 79034, 79036, 79039–40, 79042, 79044–46, 79052, 79056–59, 79061–62, 79065, 79068, 79070, 79079–81, 79083–84, 79086–88, 79092, 79094–98, 79101–04, 79106–11, 79118–19, 79121, 79124, 79178, 79201, 79220, 79225–27, 79229–30, 79234–35, 79237, 79239–41, 79243–45, 79247–48, 79251–52, 79255–57, 79259, 79261, 79370, 79529

* * *

FOURTEENTH DISTRICT

RANDY WEBER, Republican, of Friendswood, TX; born in Pearland, TX, July 2, 1953; education: B.S., University of Houston, Clear Lake, 1977; professional: owner, Weber's Air and Heat, 1981–present; married: 1976; children: Kristin, Keith, and Kyle; grandchildren: seven; committees: Foreign Affairs; Science, Space, and Technology; elected to the 113th Congress on November 6, 2012; reelected to the 114th Congress on November 4, 2014.

Office Listings

http://weber.house.gov   https://www.facebook.com/txrandy14
https://twitter.com/txrandy14

510 Cannon House Office Building, Washington, DC 20515	(202) 225–2831
Chief of Staff.—Chara McMichael.	FAX: 225–0271
Legislative Director.—Artur Suchorzewski.	
Communications Director.—Courtney Weaver.	
505 Orleans Street, Suite 103, Beaumont, TX 77701	(409) 835–0108
122 West Way Street, Suite 301, Lake Jackson, TX 77566	(979) 285–0231
174 Calder Road, Suite 150, League City, TX 77573	(281) 316–0231

Counties: BRAZORIA, GALVESTON, AND JEFFERSON. Population (2010), 705,051.

ZIP Codes: 77510, 77517–18, 77539, 77546, 77549–55, 77563, 77565, 77568, 77573–74, 77590–92, 77617, 77623, 77650

* * *

FIFTEENTH DISTRICT

RUBÉN E. HINOJOSA, Democrat, of Mercedes, TX; born in Edcouch, August 20, 1940; education: B.B.A., 1962, and M.B.A., 1980, University of Texas; professional: president and chief financial officer, H&H Foods, Inc.; elected member, Texas State Board of Education, 1975–84; board of directors, National Livestock and Meat Board and Texas Beef Industry Council, 1989–93; past president and chair of the board of directors, Southwestern Meat Packers Association; chair and member, board of trustees, South Texas Community College, 1993–96; past public member, Texas State Bar Board of Directors; former adjunct professor, Pan American University School of Business; past director, Rio Grande Valley Chamber of Commerce; Knapp Memorial Hospital Board of Trustees; Our Lady of Mercy Church Board of Catholic Advisors; past member, board of trustees, Mercedes Independent School District; former U.S. Jaycee Ambassador to Colombia and Ecuador; married: Martha; children: Ruben, Jr., Laura, Iliana, Kaitlin, and Karén; chairman of the Congressional Hispanic Caucus, 2012–14; co-chair of the Financial Literacy Caucus; named one of the 100 most influential Hispanics in America by Hispanic Business Magazine, 2012; recipient of the Hispanic Heritage Award; committees: Education and the Workforce; Financial Services; elected to the 105th Congress; reelected to each succeeding Congress.

Office Listings

http://www.hinojosa.house.gov   https://www.facebook.com/congressmanrubenhinojosa
https://twitter.com/usreprhinojosa

2262 Rayburn House Office Building, Washington, DC 20515	(202) 225–2531
Chief of Staff.—Connie Humphrey.	FAX: 225–5688
Policy Advisor.—Ed Hill.	
Legislative Counsel.—Roberto Haddad.	
Communications Director.—Patricia Guillermo.	
2864 West Trenton Road, Edinburg, TX 78539	(956) 682–5545
District Director.—Cindy Garza.	
North District	(956) 682–5545
North District Director.—Mark Gonzales.	

Counties: BROOKS, DUVALL, GUADALUPE, HIDALGO (part), JIM HOGG, KARNES, WILSON, LIVE OAK, AND REFUGIO. CITIES AND TOWNSHIPS: Alamo, Alice, Donna, Edcouch, Edinburg, Elsa, Goliad, Harlingen, LaVilla, Las Milpas, Lopezville, Lull, Mathis, McAllen, Mercedes, Mission, Odem, Pharr, San Juan, Sinton, Taft, Three Rivers, Weslaco and Whitsett. Population (2011), 722,529.

ZIP Codes: 78022, 78060, 78071, 78075, 78108, 78111, 78113, 78116–17, 78119, 78121, 78123–24, 78130, 78140–41, 78144, 78151, 78155, 78341, 78349–50, 78353, 78355, 78357, 78360–61, 78376, 78383–84, 78501–02, 78504–05,

78516, 78537–43, 78549, 78557–58, 78560, 78562–63, 78565, 78570, 78572–74, 78576–77, 78579, 78589, 78595–96, 78599, 78638, 78648, 78655, 78666

* * *

SIXTEENTH DISTRICT

BETO O'ROURKE, Democrat, of TX; born in El Paso, El Paso County, TX, September 26, 1972; education: B.A., Columbia University, New York, NY, 1995; professional: business owner; member of the El Paso, Texas City Council, 2005–11; committees: Armed Services; Veterans' Affairs; elected to the 113th Congress on November 6, 2012; reelected to the 114th Congress on November 4, 2014.

Office Listings

http://www.orourke.house.gov

1330 Longworth House Office Building, Washington, DC 20515	(202) 225–4831
Chief of Staff.—David Wysong.	
Scheduler / Office Manager.—Diana Ramos.	
Legislative Director.—Aaron Woolf.	
303 North Oregon Street, Suite 210, El Paso, TX 79901	(915) 541–1400

Counties: EL PASO (part). Population (2010), 698,488.

ZIP Codes: 79901–06, 79908, 79911–12, 79915–16, 79920, 79922, 79924–25, 79930, 79932, 79934–36

* * *

SEVENTEENTH DISTRICT

WILLIAM H. "BILL" FLORES, Republican, of Bryan, TX; born at Warren Air Force Base, Cheyenne, WY, February 25, 1954; education: graduated, Stratford High School, Stratford, TX, 1972; B.B.A., *cum laude,* Texas A&M University, College Station, TX, 1976; M.B.A., Houston Baptist University, Houston, TX, 1985; Texas Certified Public Accountant (CPA), 1978–present; commissioner, Texas Real Estate Commission (appointed by Governor Perry), 2004–09; CEO and president, Phoenix Exploration Company, 2006–09; Texas A&M University Distinguished Alumnus, 2010; Houston Baptist University Distinguished Alumnus, 2013; married: the former Gina Bass; children: Will and John; daughter-in-law, Aimee; granddaughters, Britain and Charlie; committees: Energy and Commerce; elected to the 112th Congress on November 2, 2010; reelected to each succeeding Congress.

Office Listings

http://flores.house.gov

1030 Longworth House Office Building, Washington, DC 20515	(202) 225–6105
Chief of Staff.—Jeff Morehouse.	FAX: 225–0350
Press Secretary.—Andre Castro.	
400 Austin Avenue, Suite 302, Waco, TX 76701	(254) 732–0748
District Director.—Vacant.	
14205 Burnet Road, Suite 230, Austin, TX 78728	(512) 373–3378
3000 Briarcrest Drive, Suite 406, Bryan, TX 77802	(979) 703–4037
	FAX: 691–8939

Counties: BRAZOS, BURLESON, FALLS, FREESTONE, LEE, LEON, LIMESTONE, MCLENNAN, MILAM, ROBERTSON, AND TRAVIS, (part). Population (2010), 710,793.

ZIP Codes: 75833, 75840, 75848, 75850, 75860, 76518, 76520, 76523, 76632, 76635, 76638, 76640, 76643, 76654, 76656, 76661, 76678, 76680, 76684, 76686, 76701–05, 76707–08, 76710–12, 76714–16, 76797–99, 77801–03, 77805–06, 77837–38, 77840–45, 77850, 77852–53, 77855–57, 77862–63, 77865–67, 77870, 77878–79, 77881–82, 78660, 78691, 78727–28, 78753, 78948

* * *

EIGHTEENTH DISTRICT

SHEILA JACKSON LEE, Democrat, of Houston, TX; born in Queens, NY, January 12, 1950; education: graduated, Jamaica High School; B.A., Yale University, New Haven, CT,

1972; J.D., University of Virginia Law School, 1975; professional: practicing attorney for twelve years; AKA Sorority; Houston Area Urban League; American Bar Association; staff counsel, U.S. House Select Committee on Assassinations, 1977–78; admitted to the Texas Bar, 1975; city council (at large), Houston, 1990–94; Houston Municipal Judge, 1987–90; married Dr. Elwyn Cornelius Lee, 1973; two children: Erica Shelwyn and Jason Cornelius Bennett; committees: Homeland Security; Judiciary; elected to the 104th Congress; reelected to each succeeding Congress.

Office Listings

http://www.jacksonlee.house.gov

2252 Rayburn House Office Building, Washington, DC 20515 .... (202) 225–3816
    Chief of Staff.—Glenn Rushing.   FAX: 225–3317
    Chief Counsel.—Gregory Berry.
    Communications Director.—Mike McQuerry.
    Scheduler.—Alem Tewoldeberhan.
    Executive / Staff Assistant.—Sharef Al Najjar.
1919 Smith Street, Suite 1180, Houston, TX 77002 .... (713) 655–0050
    District Director.—Angel Tate-Moore.
    Senior Field Representative / Caseworker.—Daniel Espinoza.
    Executive Assistant.—Janice Weaver.
    Caseworkers: Ivan Sanchez, Tonya Williams.
    Account and Finance.—Michelle Donches.
420 West 19th Street, Houston, TX 77008 .... (713) 861–4070
6719 West Montgomery, Suite 204, Houston, Texas 77091 .... (713) 691–4882

Counties: HARRIS COUNTY (part). CITY OF: Houston. Population (2010), 698,488.

ZIP Codes: 77001–10, 77013, 77016, 77018–24, 77026, 77028–30, 77033, 77035, 77038, 77040–41, 77045, 77047–48, 77051–52, 77054–55, 77064, 77066–67, 77076, 77078, 77080, 77086–88, 77091–93, 77097–98, 77201–06, 77208, 77210, 77212, 77216, 77219, 77221, 77226, 77230, 77233, 77238, 77240–41, 77251–53, 77255, 77265–66, 77277, 77288, 77291–93, 77297–99

* * *

NINETEENTH DISTRICT

RANDY NEUGEBAUER, Republican, of Lubbock, TX; born in St. Louis, MO, December 24, 1949; education: Texas Tech University, 1972; professional: small businessman (home building industry); organizations: West Texas Home Builders Association; Land Use and Developers Council; Texas Association of Builders; National Association of Home Builders; Campus Crusade for Christ; public service: Lubbock City Council, 1992–98; served as Mayor Pro Tempore, 1994–96; leader, coalition to create the Ports-to-Plains Trade Corridor; awards: Lubbock Chamber of Commerce Distinguished Service Award; Reese Air Force Base Friend of Reese Award; religion: Baptist; married: Dana; two children; committees: Agriculture; Financial Services; Science, Space, and Technology; elected to the 108th Congress, by special election, on June 3, 2003; reelected to each succeeding Congress.

Office Listings

http://www.randy.house.gov   https://www.facebook.com/re.randy.neugebauer?ref=hl
https://twitter.com/randyneugebauer

1424 Longworth House Office Building, Washington, DC 20515 .... (202) 225–4005
    Chief of Staff.—Jeanette Whitener.   FAX: 225–9615
    Communications Director.—Adam Rice.
    Legislative Director.—Kelli McMorrow.
    Senior Legislative Assistant.—Coleman Garrison.
    Office Manager / Scheduler.—Melissa James.
    Legislative Correspondent.—Tara McGee.
    Staff Assistant.—Dana Hulin.
Federal Building, 611 University Avenue, Suite 220, Lubbock, TX 79401 .... (806) 763–1611
    District Director of Operations.—Mary Whistler.
    District Director of Constituent Services.—Jay Ibarra.

Counties: BAILEY, BORDEN, CASTRO, COCHRAN, CROSBY, FISHER, FLOYD (part), GAINES, GARZA, HALE, HASKELL, HOCKLEY, HOWARD, JONES, KENT, LAMB, LUBBOCK, LYNN, NOLAN, PARMER, SCURRY, SHACKELFORD, STEPHENS (part), STONEWALL, TAYLOR, TERRY, THROCKMORTON, YOAKUM, AND YOUNG. Population (2010), 707,772.

ZIP Codes: 76372, 76374 (part), 76388, 76424 (part), 76429 (part), 76430, 76450 (part), 76460, 76464 (part), 76481, 76483, 76491, 79009, 79021, 79027, 79031–32, 79035 (part), 79041, 79042 (part), 79043, 79045 (part), 79052 (part),

79053, 79063–64, 79072 (part), 79082, 79085, 79088 (part), 79231, 79235 (part), 79241 (part), 79250, 79311 14, 79316, 79322–26, 79329, 79330, 79331 (part), 79336, 79339, 79342–47, 79350, 79351 (part), 79353, 79355–60, 79363–64, 79366–67, 79369, 79370 (part), 79371–73, 79376, 79378–82, 79401, 79403–04, 79406–07, 79410–16, 79423–24, 79501–03, 79504 (part), 79506 (part), 79508, 79511, 79512 (part), 79517–18, 79520–21, 79525–28, 79529 (part), 79530, 79532 (part), 79533–37, 79539, 79540, 79541 (part), 79543–49, 79553, 79556, 79560–63, 79566 (part), 79567 (part), 79601 (part), 79602 (part), 79603, 79605–07, 79699, 79713 (part), 79720 (part), 79733, 79738, 79748 (part)

* * *

TWENTIETH DISTRICT

JOAQUIN CASTRO, Democrat, of San Antonio, TX; born in San Antonio, September 16, 1974; education: Thomas Jefferson High School, 1992; B.A., Stanford University, CA, 1996; J.D., Harvard University, Cambridge, MA, 2000; professional: attorney; law instructor; religion: Catholic; family: wife, Anna Flores; caucuses: Congressional Hispanic Caucus; New Democrat Coalition; committees: Armed Services; Foreign Affairs; elected to the 113th Congress on November 6, 2012.

Office Listings

http://castro.house.gov   https://www.facebook.com/joaquincastrotx
twitter: @joaquincastrotx

212 Cannon House Office Building, Washington, DC 20515	(202) 225–3236
Chief of Staff.—Carlos Sanchez.	FAX: 225–1915

Scheduler.—Hannah Katz.
Legislative Director.—Claudia Urrabazo.
Senior Legislative Assistant.—Ben Thomas.
Legislative Assistant.—Sandra Alcala.
Deputy Chief of Staff/Senior Foreign Policy Advisor.—Danny Meza.
Staff Assistant.—Jacqueline Sanchez.
Press Secretary.—Erin Hatch.

727 East Cesar E. Chavez Boulevard, Suite B–128, San Antonio, TX 78206 .... (210) 348–8216

Counties: BEXAR (part). CITIES: Alamo Heights, Balcones Heights, Lackland AFB, Helotes, Leon Valley, and San Antonio. Population (2010), 716,759.

ZIP Codes: 78023, 78073, 78201, 78204, 78207, 78209, 78211–14, 78216, 78221, 78224–31, 78236–38, 78240, 78242, 78245, 78249–57

* * *

TWENTY-FIRST DISTRICT

LAMAR S. SMITH, Republican, of San Antonio, TX; born in San Antonio, November 19, 1947; education: graduated, Texas Military Institute, San Antonio, 1965; B.A., Yale University, New Haven, CT, 1969; intern, Small Business Administration, Washington, DC, 1969–70; business and financial writer, *The Christian Science Monitor*, Boston, MA, 1970–72; J.D., Southern Methodist University School of Law, Dallas, TX, 1975, admitted to the State Bar of Texas, 1975, and commenced practice in San Antonio with the firm of Maebius and Duncan, Inc.; elected chairman of the Republican Party of Bexar County, TX, 1978 and 1980; elected District 57–F State Representative, 1981; elected Precinct 3 Commissioner of Bexar County, 1982 and 1984; partner, Lamar Seeligson Ranch, Jim Wells County, TX; married: Beth Schaefer; children: Nell and Tobin; committees: chair, Science, Space, and Technology; Judiciary; Homeland Security; elected to the 100th Congress on November 4, 1986; reelected to each succeeding Congress.

Office Listings

http://lamarsmith.house.gov

2409 Rayburn House Office Building, Washington, DC 20515	(202) 225–4236
Chief of Staff.—Jennifer Brown.	FAX: 225–8628

Legislative Director.—Abby Gunderson-Schwarz
Scheduler.—Christa Danford.

The Tetco Center, 1100 North East Loop 410, Suite 640, San Antonio, TX 78207 .... (210) 821–5024
District Director.—Mike Asmus.
2211 IH 35 South, Suite 106, Austin, TX 78741 .... (512) 912–7508
301 Junction Highway, Suite 346C, Kerrville, TX 78028 .... (830) 896–0154

Counties: BANDERA, BEXAR (part), BLANCO, COMAL (part), KENDALL, KERR, REAL, TRAVIS (part), GILLESPIE, AND HAYS (part). Population (2010), 698,488.

ZIP Codes: 78003, 78006, 78010, 78013, 78015, 78024–25, 78027–29, 78055, 78058, 78063, 78070, 78130–33, 78135, 78148, 78163, 78209, 78212–13, 78216–18, 78230–33, 78239, 78241, 78247, 78258–59, 78261, 78265–66, 78270, 78606, 78610, 78618–20, 78623–24, 78631, 78635–36, 78641, 78645, 78652, 78663, 78666, 78669, 78675–76, 78726, 78730–39, 78741, 78746, 78748–50, 78759, 78883, 78885

* * *

TWENTY-SECOND DISTRICT

PETE OLSON, Republican, of Sugar Land, TX; born in Fort Lewis, WA, December 9, 1962; education: B.A., Rice University, Houston, TX, 1985; Law Degree, University of Texas, Austin, TX, 1988; United States Navy, 1988–98; United States Senate, 1998–2007; Naval Aviator wings, 1991; Naval Liaison United States Senate; religion: United Methodist; married: Nancy Olson; children: Kate and Grant; committees: Energy and Commerce; elected to the 111th Congress on November 4, 2008; reelected to each succeeding Congress.

Office Listings

http://olson.house.gov

2133 Rayburn House Office Building, Washington, DC 20515	(202) 225–5951
Chief of Staff.—Tyler Nelson.	FAX: 225–5241
Legislative Director.—Sarah Whiting.	
Communications Director.—Melissa Kelly.	
Scheduler.—Victoria Ellington.	
1650 Highway 6, Suite 150, Sugarland, TX 77478	(281) 494–2690
District Director.—Robert Quarles.	
6302 West Broadway Street, Suite 220, Pearland, TX 77581	(281) 485–4855

Counties: BRAZORIA, FORT BEND, AND HARRIS (part). CITIES OF: Alvin, Arcola, Beasley, Brookside Village, Friendswood, Fulshear, Katy, Meadows Place, Missouri City, Manvel, Needville, Orchard, Pleak, Pearland, Richmond, Rosenberg, Sugar Land, Simonton, Stafford, Villages of Fairchild, Webster and Weston Lakes. Population (2010), 698,504.

ZIP Codes: 77511–12, 77545, 77583, 77417, 77581, 77441, 77450, 77493, 77494, 77546, 77477, 774589, 77578, 77464, 77469, 77581, 77584, 77588, 77406, 77407, 77469, 77471, 7747–79, 77487, 77476, 7461, 77469, 77598

* * *

TWENTY-THIRD DISTRICT

WILL HURD, Republican, of San Antonio, TX; born in San Antonio, August 19, 1977; education: attended public schools in San Antonio, TX; B.S., Computer Science, Texas A&M University, College Station, TX, 1999; professional: Cybersecurity Consultant; CIA Officer; religion: Christian; committees: Homeland Security; Oversight and Government Reform; elected to the 114th Congress on November 4, 2014.

Office Listings

https://hurd.house.gov   https://twitter.com/hurdonthehill
https://www.facebook.com/hurdonthehill

317 Cannon House Office Building, Washington, DC 20515	(202) 225–4511
Chief of Staff.—Stoney Burke.	FAX: 225–2237
Legislative Director.—Matthew Haskins.	
Executive Assistant.—Nancy Pack.	
Communications Director.—Shana Teehan.	
Legislative Assistant.—Madison Smith.	
Legislative Correspondent / Press Assistant.—Rachel Holland.	
17721 Rogers Ranch Parkway, Suite 120, San Antonio, TX 78258	(210) 921–3130
	FAX: 927–4903
One University Drive, Patriot's Casa, Suites C212 E&F, San Antonio, TX 78224	(210) 784–5023
124 South Horizon Boulevard, Socorro, TX 79927	(915) 235–6421
1104 West 10th, Del Rio, TX 78840	(210) 238–4296
100 Monroe Street, Eagle Pass, TX 78852	(210) 238–4296

Counties: Bexar (part), BREWSTER, CRANE, CROCKETT, CULBERSON, DIMMIT, EDWARDS, EL PASO (part), FRIO, HUDSPETH, JEFF DAVIS, KINNEY, LA SALLE (part), LOVING, MAVERICK, MEDINA, PECOS, PRESIDIO, REAGAN, REEVES, SCHLEICHER, SUTTON, TERRELL, UPTON, UVALDE, VAL VERDE, WARD, WINKLER, AND ZAVALA. POPULATION (2014), 725,874.

ZIP Codes: 76841, 76932, 76935–36, 76943, 76950, 78001–03, 78005–06, 78009, 78014–17, 78019, 78021, 78023, 78039, 78052, 78056–57, 78059, 78061, 78066, 78069, 78073, 78112, 78211, 78214, 78220–24, 78227, 78230–32, 78236,

78245, 78248–49, 78251–58, 78260, 78264, 78801–02, 78827–30, 78832–34, 78836–40, 78843, 78850–52, 78860 61, 78870–73, 78877, 78879–81, 78884, 78886, 79718–19, 79730–31, 79734–35, 79739, 79742–45, 79752, 79754– 56, 79766, 79770, 79772, 79777–78, 79780–81, 79785, 79788–89, 79830–31, 79834, 79836–39, 79842–43, 79845– 49, 79851–55, 79907, 79927–28, 79938, 79942, 88220

* * *

TWENTY-FOURTH DISTRICT

KENNY MARCHANT, Republican, of Coppell, TX; born in Bonham, TX, February 23, 1951; education: B.A., Southern Nazarene University, Bethany, OK, 1974; attended Nazarene Theological Seminary, Kansas City, MO, 1975–76; professional: real estate developer; member of the Carrollton, TX, city council, 1980–84; mayor of Carrollton, TX, 1984–87; member of the Texas State House of Representatives, 1987–2004; member, Advisory Board of Children's Medical Center; married: Donna; four children; committees: Ethics; Ways and Means; elected to the 109th Congress on November 2, 2004; reelected to each succeeding Congress.

Office Listings

http://www.marchant.house.gov   https://www.facebook.com/repkennymarchant
https://twitter.com/repkenmarchant

2313 Rayburn House Office Building, Washington, DC 20515 .... (202) 225–6605
Chief of Staff.—Brian Thomas.   FAX: 225–0074
Deputy Chief of Staff, Washington.—Scott Cunningham.
Legislative Director.—James J. Williams.
Communications Director.—Shane McDonald.
Legislative Assistant.—John Deoudes.
Legislative Assistant / Scheduler.—Robert Vega.
Staff Assistants: Chris Scoular, Nicholas Smith.
9901 East Valley Ranch Parkway, Suite 2060, Irving, TX 75063 .... (972) 556–0162
Deputy Chief of Staff, District.—Susie Miller.
Military and Veterans Liaison.—John Hayes.
Director of District Affairs.—Todd Martin.
District Operations Director.—Matt Jack.
Constituent Services Representative.—Chelsey Payne.
Staff Assistant.—Joy Carlet.

Counties: DALLAS (part), DENTON (part), TARRANT (part). CITIES AND TOWNSHIPS: Addison, Bedford, Carrollton, Colleyville, Coppell, Dallas (part), Euless, Farmer's Branch, Fort Worth (part), Grapevine, Hurst, Irving (part), Lewisville (part), Plano (part), Southlake, and The Colony. Population (2010), 698,488.

ZIP Codes: 75001, 75006–07, 75010–11, 75014, 75016, 75019, 75022, 75024, 75028, 75038–39, 75056, 75061–63, 75067, 75093, 75099, 75209, 75220, 75229–30, 75234, 75240, 75244, 75248, 75252, 75254, 75261, 75287, 75354, 75368, 75379–81, 75391, 76021–22, 76034, 76039–40, 76051, 76053–54, 76092, 76095, 76099, 76118, 76120, 76155, 76180, 76182, 76248, 76262

* * *

TWENTY-FIFTH DISTRICT

ROGER WILLIAMS, Republican, of Austin, TX; born in Evanston, IL, September 13, 1949; education: graduated, Arlington Heights High School; B.S., Texas Christian University, Fort Worth, 1972; professional: drafted by the Atlanta Braves Organization; owner Roger Williams Car Dealerships; 105th Secretary of State of Texas, 2004–07; regional finance chair for Governor Bush, 1994, 1998; North Texas chairman for the Bush/Cheney 2000 campaign; North Texas finance chairman and national grassroots fundraising chairman for Bush/Cheney 2004, Inc.; appointed chairman of the Republican National Finance Committee's Eagles program by President George W. Bush, 2001; state finance chair for John Cornyn for U.S. Senate, Inc., 2002; chief liaison for Texas Border and Mexican Affairs, 2005; chair of the Texas Base Realignment and Closure Response Strike Force; boards: Texas Christian University Board of Trustees; National Football Foundation; College Football Hall of Fame; religion: member, University Christian Church; married: Patty Williams; children: Sabrina and Jaclyn; committees: Financial Services; elected to the 113th Congress on November 6, 2012; reelected to the 114th Congress on November 4, 2014.

Office Listings

http://www.williams.house.gov

1323 Longworth House Office Building, Washington, DC 20515 .... (202) 225–9896

Office Listings—Continued

Chief of Staff.—Colby Hale.   FAX: 225–9692
Deputy Chief.—Spencer Freebairn.
Legislative Director.—Sean Dillon.
Legislative Aide.—Ross Gage.
Legislative Correspondent.—Nicole Lansford.
Staff Assistant.—Hayden Jewett.
Press Secretary.—Vince Zito.
Scheduler.—Vera Minter.
1005 Congress Avenue, Suite 925, Austin, TX 78701 .... (512) 473–8910
   District Director.—John Etue.   FAX: 473–8946
1 Walnut Street, Suite 145, Cleburne, TX 76033 .... (817) 774–2575
   Case Worker.—Robert Camacho.   FAX: 774–2577

Counties: BELL (part), BOSQUE, BURNET, CORYELL, ERATH (part), HAMILTON, HAYS (part), HILL, JOHNSON, LAMPASAS, SOMERVELL, TARRANT (part), AND TRAVIS (part). Population (2010), 698,478.

ZIP Codes: 76009, 76028, 76031, 76033, 76035–36, 76043–44, 76048–49, 76050, 76055, 76058–59, 76063, 76070, 76077, 76084, 76093, 76401–02, 76433, 76436, 76446, 76457, 76522, 76525, 76526–28, 76531, 76538–39, 76544, 76549–50, 76557, 76561, 76565–66, 76621–22, 76627, 76631, 76633–34, 76636–38, 76645, 76648–49, 76652, 76657, 76660, 76665–66, 76671, 76673, 76676, 76689–90, 76692, 76853, 76877, 76880, 78605, 78608, 78610–11, 78613, 78619–20, 78623, 78639, 78641–42, 78645, 78652, 78654, 78657, 78666, 78669, 78676, 78701–03, 78705, 78712, 78721–25, 78730–34, 78736–39, 78745–46, 78749–50

* * *

TWENTY-SIXTH DISTRICT

MICHAEL C. BURGESS, Republican, of Denton County, TX; born, December 23, 1950; education: B.A., biology, North Texas State University; M.S., physiology, North Texas State University; M.D., University of Texas Medical School, Houston; M.S. medical management, University of Texas, Dallas; completed medical residency programs, Parkland Hospital in Dallas; professional: founder, Private Practice Specialty Group for Obstetrics and Gynecology; former Chief of Staff and Chief of Obstetrics, Lewisville Medical Center; organizations: former president, Denton County Medical Society; Denton County delegate, Texas Medical Association; alternate delegate, American Medical Association; married: Laura; three children; committees: Energy and Commerce; Rules; elected to the 108th Congress on November 5, 2002; reelected to each succeeding Congress.

Office Listings

http://www.burgess.house.gov   http://www.facebok.com/michaelcburgess
twitter: @michaelcburgess

2336 Rayburn House Office Building, Washington, DC 20515 .... (202) 225–7772
   Chief of Staff.—Kelle Strickland.   FAX: 225–2919
   Legislative Director.—James Decker.
   Press Secretary.—Cameron Harley.
   Scheduler.—Amanda Stevens.
2000 South Stemmons Freeway, Suite 200, Lake Dallas, TX 75065 .... (940) 497–5031

Counties: DALLAS (part), DENTON (part), TARRANT (part). Population (2010) 698,488.

ZIP Codes: 75009, 75019, 75022, 75027–29, 75033–34, 75056–57, 75065, 75067–68, 75077–78, 76034, 76052, 76065, 76078, 76092, 76117, 76137, 76148, 76177, 76180, 76182, 76201–10, 76226–27, 76234, 76244, 76247–49, 76258–59, 76262

* * *

TWENTY-SEVENTH DISTRICT

BLAKE FARENTHOLD, Republican, of Corpus Christi, TX; born in Corpus Christi, December 12, 1961; education: B.S., radio television, and film, University of Texas, Austin, TX, 1985; J.D., St. Mary's University of Law School, San Antonio, TX, 1989; professional: lawyer, private practice; business owner; committees: Judiciary; Oversight and Government Reform; Transportation and Infrastructure; elected to the 112th Congress on November 2, 2010; reelected to each succeeding Congress.

Office Listings

http://www.farenthold.house.gov

1027 Longworth House Office Building, Washington, DC 20515 .... (202) 225–7742

Office Listings—Continued

Chief of Staff.—Bob Haueter. FAX: 226–1134
Executive Assistant / Scheduling.—Emily Wilkes.
Legislative Director.—Blake Adami.
Communications Director.—Michael Rekola.
101 North Shoreline Boulevard, Suite 300, Corpus Christi, TX 78401 .... (361) 884–2222
5606 North Navarro Street, Suite 203, Victoria, TX 77904 .... (361) 894–6446

Counties: ARANSAS, BASTROP, CALDWELL, CALHOUN, GONZALES, LAVACA, WHARTON, MATAGORDA, JACKSON, VICTORIA, REFUGIO, NUECES, AND SAN PATRICIO. Population (2010), 702,804.

ZIP Codes: 77404, 77414–15, 77419–20, 77428, 77432, 77435–37, 77440, 77443, 77448, 77453–58, 77465, 77467–68, 77482–83, 77488, 77901–05, 77950–51, 77957, 77961–62, 77964, 77968–71, 77973, 77975–79, 77982–84, 77986–88, 77990–91, 77995, 78330, 78335–36, 78339–40, 78343, 78347, 78351–52, 78358–59, 78362, 78368, 78370, 78373–74, 78377, 78380–82, 78387, 78390, 78393, 78401–19, 78426–27, 78460, 78463, 78465–69, 78472, 78480, 78602, 78612, 78614, 78616, 78629, 78632, 78648, 78655–56, 78658, 78661–62, 78953, 78957

* * *

TWENTY-EIGHTH DISTRICT

HENRY CUELLAR, Democrat, of Laredo, TX; born in Laredo, September 19, 1955; education: Associate's Degree from Laredo Community College, Laredo, TX, 1976 (then known as Laredo Junior College); B.S., *cum laude*, foreign service from the Edmund A. Walsh School of Foreign Service at Georgetown University, Washington, DC, 1978; J.D., University of Texas, Austin, TX, 1981; M.B.A., international trade, Texas A&M University, Laredo, TX, 1982; Ph.D., government, University of Texas, Austin, TX, 1998; with a total of five advanced degrees, Congressman Cuellar is the most degreed member of Congress; professional: lawyer, private practice; attorney, Law Office of Henry Cuellar, 1981–present; instructor, Department of Government, Laredo Community College, Laredo, TX, 1982–86; Licensed United States Customs Broker, 1983–present; adjunct professor, International Commercial Law, Texas A&M International, 1984–86; Representative, Texas State House of Representatives, 1986–2001; Secretary of State, State of Texas, 2001; public and civic organizations: board of directors, Kiwanis Club of Laredo, TX, 1982–83; co-founder / president, Laredo Volunteers Lawyers Program, Inc., 1982–83; board of directors, United Way, 1982–83; co-founder / treasurer, Stop Child Abuse and Neglect, 1982–83, and advisory board member, 1984; president, board of directors, Laredo Legal Aid Society, Inc., 1982–84; president, board of directors, Laredo Young Lawyers Association, 1983–84; sustaining member, Texas Democratic Party, 1984; legal advisor, American GI, local chapter, 1986–87; International Trade Association, Laredo State University, 1988; Texas Delegate, National Democratic Convention, 1992; president, board of directors, International Good Neighbor Council; member, The College of the State Bar of Texas, 1994; Texas Lyceum, 1997; policy board of advisors, Texas Hispanic Journal of Law, University of Texas Law School, 2002; member: American Bar Association; Inter-American Bar Association; Texas Bar Association; Webb / Laredo Bar Association; recipient of various awards; vice chairman of the Steering and Policy Committee; Congressional Unmanned Systems Caucus, Senior Whip; member of the Blue Dog Coalition; religion: Catholic; married: wife, Imelda; two daughters, Christina Alexandra and Catherine Ann; committees: Appropriations; elected to the 109th Congress on November 2, 2004; reelected to each succeeding Congress.

Office Listings

http://www.cuellar.house.gov   twitter: @repcuellar
https://www.facebook.com/pages/us-congressman-henry-cuellar-tx-28/152569121550

2209 Rayburn House Office Building, Washington, DC 20515 .... (202) 225–1640
Chief of Staff.—Cynthia Gaona. FAX: 225–1641
Legislative Director.—Ryan Rhly.
Scheduler.—Yijiao Zhuang.
615 East Houston Street, Suite 451, San Antonio, TX 78205 .... (210) 271–2851
602 East Calton Road, Suite 2, Laredo, TX 78041 .... (956) 725–0639
FAX: 725–2647
117 East Tom Landry, Mission, TX 78572 .... (956) 424–3942
FAX: 424–3936
100 North F.M. 3167, Rio Grande City, Texas 78582 .... (956) 487–5603
FAX: 488–0952
615 East Houston Street, Suite 563, San Antonio, TX 78205 .... (210) 271–2851
FAX: 277–6671

Counties: ATASCOSA, BEXAR (part), HIDALGO (part), LA SALLE (part), McMULLEN, STARR, WEBB, WILSON (part), AND ZAPATA. Population (2010), 698,488.

ZIP Codes: 78005, 78007, 78011–12, 78019, 78021, 78026, 78040–41, 78043, 78045–46, 78050, 78062, 78064–65, 78067, 78072, 78076, 78108, 78112–14, 78121, 78147, 78150, 78152, 78154, 78161, 78263, 78344, 78360–61, 78369, 78371, 78545, 78548, 78557, 78560, 78565, 78572–74, 78576, 78582, 78584–85, 78591, 78595

* * *

TWENTY-NINTH DISTRICT

GENE GREEN, Democrat, of Houston, TX; born in Houston, October 17, 1947; education: B.A., University of Houston, 1971; J.D., University of Houston Bates College of Law, 1977; admitted, Texas Bar, 1977; professional: business manager; attorney; Texas State Representative, 1973–85; Texas State Senator, 1985–92; member: Houston Bar Association; Texas Bar Association; American Bar Association; Communications Workers of America; Aldine Optimist Club; Gulf Coast Conservation Association; Lindale Lions Club; Texas Historical Society; Texas State Society; caucuses: co-chair, Democratic Israel Working Group; co-chair, Natural Gas Caucus; co-chair, Tuberculosis Elimination Caucus; co-chair, Sportsmen's Caucus; co-chair, Vision Caucus; Traumatic Brain Injury Task Force; Congressional Steel Caucus; National Marine Sanctuary Caucus; Urban Caucus; Victim's Rights Caucus; Diabetes Caucus; Caucus to Cure Blood Cancers and Other Blood Disorders; Pro-Choice Caucus; Nursing Caucus; House Cancer Caucus; Rare Disease Congressional Caucus; State Medicaid Expansion Caucus; Grid Reliability Caucus; Public Health Caucus; Autism Caucus; Azerbaijani Caucus; PORTS Caucus; Unmanned Systems Caucus; Financial and Economic Literacy Caucus; Friends of Job Corps Caucus; Aerospace Caucus; Guard and Reserve Caucus; Manufacturing Caucus; Wire and Wire Product Caucus; India Caucus; Israel Allies Caucus; Seniors Task Force; Democratic Senior Whip; married: Helen Albers, January 23, 1970; children: Angela and Christopher; committees: Energy and Commerce; elected on November 3, 1992 to the 103rd Congress; reelected to each succeeding Congress.

Office Listings

http://www.green.house.gov   Twitter: @repgenegreen   https://www.facebook.com/repgenegreen

2470 Rayburn House Office Building, Washington, DC 20515	(202) 225–1688
Legislative Director.—Sergio Espinosa.	FAX: 225–9903
Press Secretary.—Sharlett Mena.	
Legislative Assistants: Justin Ackley, Ben Jackson, Kristen O'Neill.	
Scheduler.—Sharlett Mena.	
256 North Sam Houston Parkway East, Suite 29, Houston, TX 77060	(281) 999–5879
Chief of Staff / Administrative Assistant.—Rhonda Jackson.	
11811 Interstate East, Suite 430, Houston, TX 77029	(713) 330–0761

Counties: HARRIS (part). CITIES AND TOWNSHIPS: Channelview, Galena Park, Houston, Humble, Jacinto City, Pasadena, and South Houston. Population (2013), 729,827.

ZIP Codes: 77003, 77009, 77011–13, 77015–17, 77020, 77022–23, 77026, 77029, 77032, 77034, 77037, 77039, 77044, 77049–50, 77060–61, 77075–76, 77087, 77089, 77091, 77093, 77396, 77502–06, 77530, 77536, 77547, 77587

* * *

THIRTIETH DISTRICT

EDDIE BERNICE JOHNSON, Democrat, of Dallas, TX; born in Waco, TX, December 3, 1935; education: nursing diploma, St. Mary's at Notre Dame, 1955; B.S., nursing, Texas Christian, 1967; M.P.A., Southern Methodist, 1976; proprietor, Eddie Bernice Johnson and Associates consulting and airport concession management; Texas House of Representatives, 1972–77; Carter Administration appointee, 1977–81; Texas State Senate, 1986–92; NABTP Mickey Leland Award for Excellence in Diversity, 2000; National Association of School Nurses, Inc., Legislative Award, 2000; the State of Texas Honorary Texan issued by the Governor of Texas, 2000; Links, Inc., Co-Founders Award, 2000; 100 Black Men of America, Inc., Woman of the Year, 2001; National Black Caucus of State Legislators Image Award, 2001; National Conference of Black Mayors, Inc. President's Award, 2001; Alpha Kappa Alpha Trailblazer, 2002; Thurgood Marshall Scholarship Community Leader, 2002; Phi Beta Sigma Fraternity Woman of the Year, 2002; CBCF Outstanding Leadership, 2002; congressional caucuses: Asian-Pacific; Airpower; Army; Arts; Biomedical Research; chair (107th Congress), Congressional Black Caucus; Children's Working Group; co-chair, Task Force on International HIV / AIDS; Fire Services; Human Rights Caucus; Korean Caucus; Livable Communities Task Force; Medical Technology; Oil & Gas Educational Forum; Singapore Caucus; Study Group on Japan; TX–21 Transportation Caucus; Urban; Womens' Caucus; Women's Issues; member: St. John Baptist Church, Dallas; children: Dawrence Kirk; grandchildren: Kirk, Jr., David and James; committees: ranking member, Science, Space, and Technology; Transportation and Infrastructure; elected on November 3, 1992 to the 103rd Congress; reelected to each succeeding Congress.

Office Listings

http://www.ebjohnson.house.gov

2468 Rayburn House Office Building, Washington, DC 20515 .... (202) 225–8885
    Chief of Staff/Legislative Director.—Murat Gokcigdem.   FAX: 226–1477
    Communications Director.—Yinka Robinson.
    Legislative Assistants: Don Andres, Justin Clayton, Carrie Palmer.
    Staff Assistant.—Nawaid Ladak.
3102 Maple Avenue, Suite 600, Dallas, TX 75201 .... (214) 922–8885
    District Director.—Trudy Lewis.

Counties: DALLAS (part). CITIES AND TOWNSHIPS: Downtown Dallas, Fair Park, Kessler Park, Old East Dallas, Pleasant Grove, South Dallas & South Oak Cliff; all of Cedar Hill, DeSoto, Duncanville, Hutchins, Lancaster & Wilmer and parts of Ferris, Glenn Heights, South Grand Prairie, Oak Lawn, Ovilla, Uptown/Victory Park and West Dallas. Population (2010), 698,487.

ZIP Codes: 75051–52, 75054, 75115–16, 75125, 75134, 75137, 75141, 75146, 75149–50, 75154, 75159, 75172, 75180, 75201–04, 75207–12, 75214–20, 75223–28, 75232–33, 75235–37, 75241, 75246–47, 75249, 75253, 75270

* * *

THIRTY-FIRST DISTRICT

JOHN R. CARTER, Republican, of Round Rock, TX; born in Houston, TX, November 6, 1941; education: Texas Tech University, 1964; University of Texas Law School, 1969; professional: attorney; private law practice; public service: appointed and elected a Texas District Court Judge, 1981–2001; awards: recipient and namesake of the Williamson County "John R. Carter Lifetime Achievement Award"; family: married to Erika Carter; children: Gilianne, John, Theodore, and Danielle; committees: Appropriations; elected to the 108th Congress on November 5, 2002; reelected to each succeeding Congress.

Office Listings

http://www.carter.house.gov

2110 Rayburn House Office Building, Washington, DC 20515 .... (202) 225–3864
    Chief of Staff.—Jonas Miller.   FAX: 225–5886
    Deputy Chief of Staff.—William Zito.
    Communications Director.—Corry Schiemeyer.
    Scheduler.—Carol Richmond.
1717 North IH 35, Suite 303, Round Rock, TX 78664 .... (512) 246–1600
6544B South General Bruce Drive, Temple, TX 76502 .... (254) 933–1392

Counties: BELL AND WILLIAMSON. Population (2010), 739,975.

ZIP Codes: 76501, 76504, 76511, 76513, 76527, 76530, 76534, 76537, 76542–43, 76548–49, 76557, 76559, 76569, 76571, 76574, 76578, 76613, 78615, 78621, 78628, 78633–34, 78641–42, 78664–65, 78681, 78717, 78728–29

* * *

THIRTY-SECOND DISTRICT

PETE SESSIONS, Republican, of Dallas, TX; born in Waco, TX, March 22, 1955; education: B.S., in social sciences, political science, Southwestern University, Georgetown, TX, 1978; professional: worked for Southwestern Bell, and Bell Communications Research (formerly Bell Labs), 1978–94; vice president for public policy, National Center for Policy Analysis, 1994–95; board member, White Rock YMCA; trustee, Southwestern University; member, National Eagle Scout Association's national committee; advisor to president, Special Olympics Texas; past chairman, East Dallas Chamber of Commerce; awards: Honorary Doctorate, Dallas Baptist University; National Distinguished Eagle Scout Award; Boy Scouts of America; Leadership Award, American College of Emergency Physicians; Spirit of Enterprise Award, U.S. Chamber of Commerce; Best and Brightest, American Conservative Union; Guardian of Small Business Award, National Federation of Independent Business; Taxpayers' Friend Award, National Taxpayers Union; National Leadership Award, National Down Syndrome Society; Champion of

Healthcare Innovation Award, Healthcare Leadership Council; Wireless Industry Achievement Award, Cellular Telecommunications and Internet Association; religion: Methodist; married: Karen Sessions; two sons: Bill and Alex; three stepsons: Conor, Liam and Nicholas; chairman, House Committee on Rules; former chairman, National Republican Congressional Committee; co-chair, Congressional Down Syndrome Caucus; co-chair, Congressional Missile Defense Caucus; committees: Rules; elected on November 5, 1996, to the 105th Congress; reelected to each succeeding Congress.

Office Listings

http://sessions.house.gov   http://www.flickr.com/photos/petesessions
https://www.facebook.com/petesessions   https://twitter.com/petesessions
https://instagram.com/congressmanpetesessions

2233 Rayburn House Office Building, Washington, DC 20515 .... (202) 225–2231
    Chief of Staff.—W. Kirk Bell.   FAX: 225–5878
    Communications Director.—Caroline Boothe.
    Legislative Director.—Kevin Hubbard.
Park Central VII, 12750 Merit Drive, Suite 1434, Dallas, TX 75251 .... (972) 392–0505
    Chief of Staff.—Matt Garcia.

County: DALLAS (part) AND COLLIN (part). CITIES AND TOWNSHIPS: DALLAS, RICHARDSON, UNIVERSITY PARK, HIGHLAND PARK, MESQUITE, GARLAND, SACHSE, ROWLETT AND WYLIE. Population (2010), 698,488.

ZIP Codes: 75002, 75040–44, 75048, 75080–82, 75088–89, 75094, 75098, 75150, 75166, 75182, 75201, 75204–06, 75209, 75214, 75218–19, 75223, 75225–26, 75229–31, 75235, 75238, 75243–46, 75248, 75251–52

* * *

THIRTY-THIRD DISTRICT

MARC VEASEY, Democrat, of Fort Worth, TX; born in Fort Worth, January 3, 1971; education: B.S., Texas Wesleyan University, Fort Worth, TX, 1995; professional: journalist; staff, U.S. Representative J. Martin Frost of Texas; real estate broker; Texas State Representative, 2004–12; religion: Christian; married: Tonya Veasey; children: Adam Veasey; commissions, caucuses: Congressional Black Caucus; LGBT Equality Caucus; committees: Armed Services; Science, Space, and Technology; elected to the 113th Congress on November 6, 2012; reelected to the 114th Congress on November 4, 2014.

Office Listings

http://www.veasey.house.gov   www.facebook.com/congressmanmarcveasey
twitter: @repveasey

414 Cannon House Office Building, Washington, DC 20515 .... (202) 225–9897
    Chief of Staff.—Jane Hamilton.   FAX: 225–9702
    Legislative Director.—Chris Kelley.
    Communications Director.—Nelly Decker.
    Executive Assistant / Scheduler.—Jane Phipps.
    Legislative Assistant.—Ashley Baker.
    Legislative Correspondent.—Paloma Perez.
    Staff Assistant.—Palak Gosar.
4200 South Freeway, Suite 412, Fort Worth, TX 76115 .... (817) 920–9086
    District Director.—Anne Hagan.
1881 Sylvan Avenue, Suite 108, Dallas, TX 75208 .... (214) 741–1387

Counties: DALLAS (part) AND TARRANT (part). CITIES AND TOWNSHIPS: Everman; Cockrell Hill; parts of Dallas, Irving, Grand Prairie, Arlington, Forest Hill, Fort Worth, Haltom City, Saginaw, and Sansom Park. Population: (2010), 698,488.

ZIP Codes: 75050–52, 75060–62, 75203, 75208, 75211–12, 75216, 75220, 75224, 75229, 75233–36, 75247, 76006, 76010– 12, 76014, 76103–07, 76109–12, 76114–15, 76117–20, 76133–34, 76137, 76140, 76155, 76164, 76179

* * *

THIRTY-FOURTH DISTRICT

FILEMON VELA, Democrat, of Brownsville, TX, born in Harlingen, TX, February 13, 1963; education: B.A., Georgetown University, 1985; J.D., University of Texas at Austin School of Law, 1987; professional: attorney; admitted, Texas Bar and U.S. District Court, Western and

Southern Districts of Texas, 1988; married: Rose Rivera, February 3, 1990; caucus: co-chair, Border Caucus; New Democrat Network; co-chair, Congressional LNG Export Caucus; Community Health Center Caucus; Diabetes Caucus; Disaster Relief Caucus; General Aviation Caucus; Texas Caucus on Shale Oil & Gas; TX–21 Transportation Congressional Caucus; Texas Maritime Caucus; Democratic Whip Fiscal Working Group; Democratic National Security Working Group; Democratic Whip Task Force on Poverty and Opportunity; Congressional Hispanic Caucus; Blue Dogs; Community College Caucus; I–69 Caucus; Friends of Job Corps Congressional Caucus; committees: Agriculture; Homeland Security; elected to the 113th Congress on November 6, 2012; reelected to the 114th Congress on November 4, 2014.

Office Listings

http://www.vela.house.gov

437 Cannon House Office Building, Washington, DC 20515 .... (202) 225–9901
    Chief of Staff.—Perry Brody.
    Scheduler.—Liza Lynch.
    Legislative Director.—Julie Merberg.
    Press Director.—Jose Borjon.
    Legislative Assistants: Jasey Cardenas, Mickeala Carter.
    Staff.—Greg Talamantez.
333 Ebony Avenue, Brownsville, TX 78520 .... (956) 544–8352
    District Director.—Marisela Cortez.
    Senior Caseworker.—Maria Barrera Jaross.
    Caseworker.—Laura Garza.
500 East Main Street, Alice, TX 78332 .... (361) 230–9776
    District Director.—Jose Pereida.
1390 West Expressway 83, San Benito, TX 78586 .... (956) 276–4497
    Office Manager / Caseworker.—Sally Lara.
    Press Secretary / Caseworker.—Brenda Lopez.
500 South Kansas Avenue, Weslaco, TX 78596 .... (956) 520–8273
    District Director.—Humberto Garza.
    Caseworker.—Anissa Guajardo.

Counties: BEE, CAMERON, DEWITT, GOLIAD, GONZALES, HIDALGO, JIM WELLS, KENEDY, KLEBERG, SAN PATRICIO, WILLACY. Population (2010), 716,416.

ZIP Codes: 77954, 77960, 77963, 77993–94, 78104, 78107, 78122, 78125, 78142, 78145–46, 78159, 78162, 78164, 78338, 78342, 78363, 78375, 78379, 78385, 78389, 78391, 78520–21, 78526, 78535, 78550, 78552, 78559, 78561, 78566 67, 78575, 78578 80, 78583, 78586, 78590, 78592–94, 78597–98, 78614, 78677

* * *

THIRTY-FIFTH DISTRICT

LLOYD DOGGETT, Democrat, of Austin, TX; born in Austin, October 6, 1946; education: graduated, Austin High School; B.B.A., University of Texas, Austin, 1967; J.D., University of Texas, 1970; president, University of Texas Student Body; associate editor, *Texas Law Review;* Outstanding Young Lawyer, Austin Association of Young Lawyers; president, Texas Consumer Association; religion: member, First United Methodist Church; admitted to the Texas State Bar, 1971; Texas State Senate, 1973–85, elected at age 26; Senate author of 124 state laws and Senate sponsor of 63 House bills enacted into law; elected president pro tempore of Texas Senate; served as acting governor; named Outstanding Young Texan by Texas Jaycees; Arthur B. DeWitty Award for outstanding achievement in human rights, Austin NAACP; honored for work by Austin Rape Crisis Center, Planned Parenthood of Austin; Austin Chapter, American Institute of Architects; Austin Council on Alcoholism; Disabled American Veterans; Save the Children Congressional Champion for Real and Lasting Change; AARP Legislative Achievement Award; justice on Texas Supreme Court, 1989-94; chairman, Supreme Court Task Force on Judicial Ethics, 1992–94; Outstanding Judge (Mexican-American Bar of Texas), 1993; adjunct professor, University of Texas School of Law, 1989-94; James Madison Award, Texas Freedom of Information Foundation, 1990; First Amendment Award, National Society of Professional Journalists, 1990; Congressional Task Force on Tobacco and Health; Democratic Caucus Task Force on Child Care; married: Libby Belk Doggett, 1969; children: Lisa and Cathy; committees: Ways and Means, elected to the 104th Congress; reelected to each succeeding Congress.

Office Listings

http://www.doggett.house.gov   https://twitter.com/replloyddoggett
https://www.facebook.com/lloyddoggett

2307 Rayburn House Office Building, Washington, DC 20515 .... (202) 225–4865

Office Listings—Continued

Chief of Staff.—Michael J. Mucchetti.   FAX: 225–3073
Press Secretary.—Leslie Tisdale.
Staff Assistant / Scheduler.—Bryan Botello.
217 West Travis, San Antonio, TX 78205 .... (210) 704–1080
District Director.—MaryEllen Veliz.
300 East 8th Street, Suite 763, Austin, TX 78701 .... (512) 916–5921
District Director.—Lee Ann Calaway.

Counties: BEXAR, COMAL, GUADALUPE, CALDWELL, HAYS, AND TRAVIS. Population (2010), 698,488.

ZIP Codes: 78108, 78130, 78132, 78154, 78201–05, 78207–08, 78210, 78212, 78214–15, 78217–20, 78222–23, 78228, 78233–35, 78239, 78244, 78247, 78266, 78610, 78612, 78617, 78622, 78640, 78644, 78653, 78655–56, 78666, 78702, 78704, 78719, 78721, 78725, 78741–42, 78744–45, 78747–48, 78753–54, 78758

* * *

THIRTY-SIXTH DISTRICT

BRIAN BABIN, Republican, of ·Woodville, TX; born in Port Arthur, TX, March 23, 1948; education: B.S., Lamar University; D.D.S., University of Texas; professional: dentist; Mayor of Woodville 1982–84; Woodville City Councilman 1984–1989; Woodville Independent School Board 1992–95; Director of Tyler County Chamber of Commerce; President of Texas State Board of Dental Examiners 1981–87; Deep East Texas Council of Governments Member 1982–84; Texas Historical Commission 1989–1995; Appointee to Lower Neches Valley Authority 1999–2014; caucuses: Republican Study Committee; Air Force Caucus; Boating Caucus; Ports Caucus; Pro Life Caucus; Foster Youth Caucus; Congressional Sportsmen's Caucus; Israel Allies Caucus; Refinery Caucus; Congressional Aerospace Caucus; GOP Doctors Caucus; Military Veterans Caucus; Autism Caucus; Border Security Caucus; House Republican Israel Caucus; Oral Health Caucus; Diabetes Caucus; committees: Science, Space, and Technology; Transportation and Infrastructure; elected to the 114th Congress November 4, 2014.

Office Listings

http://babin.house.gov   https://twitter.com/repbrianbabin   https://facebook.com/repbrianbabin

316 Cannon House Office Building, Washington, DC 20515 .... (202) 225–1555
Chief of Staff.—Stuart Burns.   FAX: 226–0396
Legislative Director.—Ben Couhig.
Press Secretary.—Jimmy Milstead.
Legislative Staff: Mary Moody, Rachel Tristan, Jessica Vittorio, Jack Wilson.
Scheduler.—Kathryn Whitehurst. ·
203 Ivy Avenue, Suite 600, Deer Park, TX 77536 .... (832) 780–0966
420 Green Avenue, Orange, TX 77630 .... (409) 883–8075
100 West Bluff Drive, Woodville, TX 75979 .... (844) 303–8934

Counties: CHAMBERS, HARDIN, JASPER, LIBERTY, NEWTON, ORANGE, POLK, TYLER, AND HARRIS (part). Population (2010), 714,368.

ZIP Codes: 75326–27, 75335, 75350, 75360, 75368, 75928, 75932–39, 75942, 75951, 75956, 75960, 75966, 75977, 75979, 77369, 77374, 77376, 77505, 77507, 77514, 77519, 77520–21, 77523, 77533, 77535, 77538, 77560–62, 77564, 77571, 77575, 77580, 77585–86, 77597, 77611–12, 77614–16, 77624–25, 77630, 77632, 77656–57, 77659–64

UTAH

(Population 2010, 2,763,885)

SENATORS

ORRIN G. HATCH, Republican, of Salt Lake City, UT; born in Pittsburgh, PA, March 22, 1934; education: B.S., Brigham Young University, Provo, UT, 1959; J.D., University of Pittsburgh, 1962; practiced law in Salt Lake City, UT, and Pittsburgh, PA; senior partner, Hatch and Plumb law firm, Salt Lake City; worked his way through high school, college, and law school at the metal lathing building trade; holds "AV" rating in Martindale-Hubbell Law Directory; member: AFL–CIO; Salt Lake County Bar Association; Utah Bar Association; American Bar Association; Pennsylvania Bar Association; Allegheny County Bar Association and numerous other professional and fraternal organizations; honorary doctorate, University of Maryland; honorary doctor of laws: Pepperdine University; Southern Utah University; Widener University; University of Pittsburgh; honorary national ski patroller and other honorary degrees; Senate Republican High Tech Task Force; Congressional International Anti-Privacy Caucus; author of numerous national publications; member, Church of Jesus Christ of Latter-Day Saints; married: Elaine Hansen of Newton, UT; children: Brent, Marcia, Scott, Kimberly, Alysa, and Jess; President Pro Tempore; committees: chair, Finance; Health, Education, Labor, and Pensions; Judiciary; Joint Committee on Taxation; Special Committee on Aging; elected to the U.S. Senate on November 2, 1976; reelected to each succeeding Senate term.

Office Listings

http://hatch.senate.gov   https://www.facebook.com/senatororrinhatch
https://twitter.com/senorrinhatch

104 Hart Senate Office Building, Washington, DC 20510	(202) 224–5251
Chief of Staff.—Robert Porter.	FAX: 224–6331
Legislative Director.—Jay Khosla.	
Communications Director.—JP Freire.	
Scheduler.—Ruthie Montoya.	
Federal Building, Suite 8402, 125 South State Street, Salt Lake City, UT 84138	(801) 524–4380
State Director.—Melanie Bowen.	
Federal Building, 324 25th Street, Suite 1006, Ogden, UT 84401	(801) 625–5672
51 South University Avenue, Suite 320, Provo, UT 84601	(801) 375–7881
196 East Tabernacle, Suite 14, St. George, UT 84770	(435) 634–1795
77 North Main Street, Suite 112, Cedar City, UT 84720	(435) 586–8435

* * *

MICHAEL S. LEE, Republican, of Alpine, UT; Mesa, AZ, June 4, 1971; education: B.S., Brigham Young University, Provo, UT, 1994; J.D., Brigham Young University, 1997; professional: law clerk to Judge Dee Benson of the U.S. District Court for the District of Utah; law clerk to Judge Samuel A. Alito, Jr. on the U.S. Court of Appeals for the Third Circuit Court; attorney with the law firm Sidley & Austin; Assistant U.S. Attorney in Salt Lake City; general counsel to the Governor of Utah; law clerk to Supreme Court Justice Samuel A. Alito; partner at Howrey law firm; religion: Church of Jesus Christ of Latter-Day Saints; married: Sharon Burr of Provo, UT; children: James, John, and Eliza; committees: Armed Services; Energy and Natural Resources; Judiciary; Joint Economic Committee; elected to the U.S. Senate on November 2, 2010.

Office Listings

http://lee.senate.gov   http://youtube.com/senatormikelee
http://facebook.com/senatormikelee   http://twitter.com/senmikelee

361A Russell Senate Office Building, Washington, DC 20510	(202) 224–5444
Chief of Staff.—Boyd Matheson.	FAX: 228–1168
Legislative Director.—Wendy Baig.	
Administrative Director.—Allyson Bell.	
Communications Director.—Conn Carroll.	
Press Secretary.—Emily Long.	
Federal Building, 125 South State, Suite 4425, Salt Lake City, UT 84138	(801) 524–5933
State Director.—Derek Brown.	
285 West Tabernacle Street, Suite 200, St. George, UT 84770	(435) 628–5514

REPRESENTATIVES

FIRST DISTRICT

ROB BISHOP, Republican, of Brigham City, UT; born in Kaysville, UT, July 13, 1951; education: B.A., political science, *magna cum laude*, University of Utah, 1974; professional: high school teacher; public service: Utah House of Representatives, 1979–94, Speaker of the House his last two years; elected, chair, Utah Republican Party, 1997 (served two terms); religion: Church of Jesus Christ of Latter-Day Saints; family: married to Jeralynn Hansen; children: Shule, Jarom, Zenock, Maren, and Jashon; committees: chair, Natural Resources; Armed Services; elected to the 108th Congress on November 5, 2002; reelected to each succeeding Congress.

Office Listings

http://www.robbishop.house.gov

123 Cannon House Office Building, Washington, DC 20515	(202) 225–0453
Chief of Staff.—Scott Parker.	FAX: 225–5857
Legislative Assistants: Steve Petersen, Casey Snider, Adam Stewart.	
Scheduler.—Jessica Sanford.	
6 North Main Street, Brigham City, UT 84302	(435) 734–2270
	FAX: 734–2290
324 25th Street, 1017 Federal Building, Ogden, UT 94401	(801) 625–0107

Counties: BOX ELDER, CACHE, DAVIS (part), DAGGETT, DUCHESNE, MORGAN, RICH, SUMMIT, UINTAH, AND WEBER. Population (2010), 690,971.

ZIP Codes: 82930, 83312, 83342, 84001–02, 84007, 84015, 84017–18, 84021, 84023–28, 84031, 84033, 84035–41, 84046, 84050–53, 84055–56, 84060–61, 84063–64, 84066–67, 84072–73, 84075–76, 84078, 84083, 84085–86, 84098, 84301–02, 84304–21, 84324–41, 84401, 84403–05, 84414, 84526, 84540

* * *

SECOND DISTRICT

CHRIS STEWART, Republican, of Farmington, UT; born in Logan, UT, July 15, 1960; education: B.S., economics, Utah State University; professional: President and CEO, Shipley Group; independent author; military: pilot, United States Air Force; religion: Church of Jesus Christ of Latter-Day Saints; married: Evie; children: Sean, Dane, Lance, Kayla, Bryce, and Megan; committees: Appropriations; Permanent Select Committee on Intelligence; elected to the 113th Congress on November 6, 2012; reelected to the 114th Congress on November 4, 2014.

Office Listings

http://stewart.house.gov   facebook.com/repchrisstewart
twitter.com/repchrisstewart   instagram.com/repchrisstewart   youtube.com/repchrisstewart

323 Cannon House Office Building, Washington, DC 20515	(202) 225–9730
Chief of Staff.—Brian Steed.	FAX: 225–9627
Executive Assistant.—Nathaniel Johnson.	
Press Secretary.—Allison Barker.	
420 East South Temple, #390, Salt Lake City, UT 84111	(801) 364–5550
District Director.—Dell Smith.	FAX: 364–5551
253 West St. George Boulevard, Suite 100, St. George, UT 84770	(435) 627–1500
Southern Utah Director.—Gary Webster.	FAX: 627–1911

Counties: BEAVER, DAVIS (part), GARFIELD, IRON, JUAB (part), KANE, MILLARD, PIUTE, SALT LAKE (part), SANPETE (part), SEVIER, TOOELE, WASHINGTON, AND WAYNE. CITIES: Alton Town, Annabella Town, Antimony Town, Apple Valley Town, Aurora City, Beaver City, Beryl Junction, Bicknell Town, Big Water Town, Boulder Town, Bountiful City, Brian Head Town, Bryce Canyon, Cannonville Town, Cedar City, Centerfield Town, Centerville City, Central, Central Valley Town, Circleville Town, Dammeron Valley, Delta City, Deseret, Dugway, Elsinore Town, Emigration Canyon, Enoch City, Enterprise City, Ephraim City, Erda, Escalante City, Eureka City, Farmington City (part), Fayette Town, Fillmore City, Fremont, Fruit Heights City (part), Glendale Town, Glenwood Town, Grantsville City, Gunnison City, Hanksville Town, Hatch Town, Henrieville Town, Hildale City, Hinckley Town, Holden Town, Hurricane City, Ivins City, Joseph Town, Junction Town, Kanab City, Kanarraville Town, Kanosh Town, Kaysville City (part), Kearns (part), Kingston Town, Koosharem Town, La Verkin City, Leamington Town, Leeds Town, Loa Town, Lyman Town, Lynndyl Town, Magna, Manti City, Marysvale Town, Mayfield Town, Meadow Town, Milford City, Minersville Town, Monroe City, New Harmony Town, Newcastle, North Salt Lake City, Oak City Town, Oasis, Ophir Town, Orderville Town, Panguitch City, Paragonah Town, Parowan City, Pine Valley, Redmond Town, Richfield City, Rockville Town, Rush Valley Town, Salina City, Salt Lake City (part), Santa Clara City, Scipio Town, Sigurd Town, Springdale Town, St. George City, Stansbury Park, Sterling Town, Stockton Town, Summit, Sutherland, Teasdale, Tooele City, Toquerville Town, Torrey Town, Tropic Town, Vernon Town, Veyo, Virgin Town, Washington City, Wendover City, West Bountiful City, West Valley City (part), and Woods Cross City. Population (2010), 690,971.

* * *

THIRD DISTRICT

JASON CHAFFETZ, Republican, of Alpine, UT; born in Los Gatos, CA; March 26, 1967; education: B.A., communications, Brigham Young University, Provo, UT, 1989; professional: business executive; chief of staff, Utah Governor John Huntsman, 2004; President, Maxtera Utah, 2005–present; trustee, Utah Valley Board of Trustees; chair, Utah National Guard Adjutant General Review; Commissioner, Highland City Planning Commission; President, BYU Utah County Cougar Club; Cougar Club (BYU) Board of Directors; awards: starting placekicker, BYU Football Team, 1988–89; Best Run Campaign, General Election, Utah 2004, Huntsman for Governor; Western Athletic Conference Champions, 1989; Cougar Club Academic Athlete Award, 1988–89; Academic All-WAC Football Team, 1989; National All-Bowl Football Team, 1988; religion: Church of Jesus Christ of Latter-Day Saints; married: Julie, in 1991; children: Max, Ellis, and Kate; committees: chair, Oversight and Government Reform; Judiciary; elected to the 111th Congress on November 4, 2008; reelected to each succeeding Congress.

Office Listings

http://chaffetz.house.gov

2236 Rayburn House Office Building, Washington, DC 20515	(202) 225–7751
Chief of Staff.—Fred Ferguson.	FAX: 225–5629
Legislative Director.—Amber Talley.	
Scheduler / Office Manager.—Danielle Suber.	
Media Manager / Legislative Aide.—MJ Henshaw.	
Legislative Assistant (Judiciary issues).—Chris Esparza.	
Senior Legislative Assistant.—Colton Miles.	
51 South University Avenue, Suite 318, Provo, UT 84601	(801) 851–2500
District Director.—Wade Garrett.	FAX: 851–2509

Counties: CARBON, EMERY, GRAND, SALT LAKE (part), SAN JUAN, UTAH (part), WASATCH. Population (2010), 708,809.

* * *

FOURTH DISTRICT

MIA B. LOVE, Republican, of Saratoga Springs, UT; born in Brooklyn, NY, December 6, 1975; education: B.A., University of Hartford; professional / politician: mayor of Saratoga Springs, UT; Saratoga Springs, Utah City council member; flight attendant; religion: Church of Jesus Christ of Latter-Day Saints; married: Jason; children: Alessa, Abigail, and Peyton; committees: Financial Services; elected to the 114th Congress on November 4, 2014.

Office Listings

https://love.house.gov

217 Cannon House Office Building, Washington, DC 20515	(202) 225–3011
Chief of Staff.—Muffy Day.	FAX: 225–5638
Scheduler.—Emilee Gorham.	
9067 South 1300 West, Suite 101, West Jordan, UT 84115	(801) 996–8729
District Director.—Laurel Price.	

Counties: SALT LAKE (part), UTAH (part), JUAB (part), SAN PETE (part). Population (2010), 690,971.

VERMONT

(Population 2010, 625,741)

SENATORS

PATRICK J. LEAHY, President Pro Tempore Emeritus; Democrat, of Middlesex, VT; born in Montpelier, VT, March 31, 1940, son of Howard and Alba Leahy; education: graduate of St. Michael's High School, Montpelier, 1957; B.A., St. Michael's College, 1961; J.D., Georgetown University, 1964; professional: attorney, admitted to the Vermont Bar, 1964; admitted to the District of Columbia Bar, 1979; admitted to practice before: the Vermont Supreme Court, 1964; the Federal District Court of Vermont, 1965; the Second Circuit Court of Appeals in New York, 1966; and the U.S. Supreme Court, 1968; State's Attorney, Chittenden County, 1966–74; vice president, National District Attorneys Association, 1971–74; married: the former Marcelle Pomerleau, 1962; children: Kevin, Alicia, and Mark; first Democrat and youngest person in Vermont to be elected to the U.S. Senate; member, Smithsonian Board of Regents committees: ranking member, Judiciary; Agriculture, Nutrition, and Forestry; Appropriations; Rules and Administration; Joint Committee on the Library; elected to the Senate on November 5, 1974; reelected to each succeeding Senate term.

Office Listings

http://leahy.senate.gov   instagram: @senatorleahy
facebook: senatorpartickleahy   twitter: @senatorleahy

437 Russell Senate Office Building, Washington, DC 20515	(202) 224–4242
Chief of Staff.—John P. Dowd.	FAX: 224–3479
Administrative Director.—Ann Berry.	
Legislative Director.—Erica Chabot.	
Communications Director.—David Carle.	
Federal Building, Room 338, Montpelier, VT 05602	(802) 229–0569
199 Main Street, Courthouse Plaza, Burlington, VT 05401	(802) 863–2525

* * *

BERNARD SANDERS, Independent, of Burlington, VT; born in Brooklyn, NY, September 8, 1941; education: graduated, Madison High School, Brooklyn; B.S., political science, University of Chicago, 1964; professional: carpenter; writer; college professor; Mayor of Burlington, VT, 1981–89; married: the former Jane O'Meara, 1988; children: Levi, Heather, Carina and David; committees: ranking member, Budget; Energy and Natural Resources; Environment and Public Works; Health, Education, Labor, and Pensions; Veterans' Affairs; elected to the 102nd Congress on November 6, 1990; reelected to each succeeding Congress; elected to the U.S. Senate on November 7, 2006; reelected to the U.S. Senate on November 6, 2012.

Office Listings

http://sanders.senate.gov   facebook.com/senatorsanders   twitter.com/sensanders

332 Dirksen Senate Office Building, Washington, DC 20510	(202) 224–5141
Chief of Staff.—Michaeleen Crowell.	FAX: 228–0776
Legislative Director.—Caryn Compton.	
Communications Director.—Michael Briggs.	
1 Church Street, Second Floor, Burlington, VT 05401	(800) 339–9834

REPRESENTATIVE

AT LARGE

PETER WELCH, Democrat, of Hartland, VT; born in Springfield, MA, May 2, 1947; education: Cathedral High School, Springfield, MA, 1969; B.A., *magna cum laude*, College of the Holy Cross, 1969; J.D., University of California at Berkeley, 1973; professional: attorney, admitted to Vermont Bar, 1974; founding partner, Welch, Graham & Manby; served in Vermont State Senate, 1981–89, 2001–07; Minority Leader, 1983–85; President pro tempore, 1985–89, 2003–07; family: wife, Joan Smith (deceased), currently married to Margaret Cheney; five children: Beth, Mary, Bill, John and Michael; three stepchildren; committees: Energy and Commerce; Oversight and Government Reform; elected to the 110th Congress on November 7, 2006; reelected to each succeeding Congress.

Office Listings

http://www.welch.house.gov   twitter: @peterwelch   https://www.facebook.com/peterwelch

2303 Rayburn House Office Building, Washington, DC 20515 .... (202) 225–4115
 Chief of Staff.—Bob Rogan.
 Scheduler / Executive Assistant.—John Goodwin.
 Legislative Director.—Patrick Satalin.
 Communications Director.—Kristen Hartman.
128 Lakeside Avenue, Suite 235, Burlington, VT 05401 .... (802) 652–2450
 State Director.—George Twigg.

Population (2014), 626,562.

ZIP Codes: 05001, 05009, 05030–43, 05045–56, 05058–62, 05065, 05067–77, 05079, 05081, 05083–86, 05088–89, 05091, 05101, 05141–43, 05146, 05148–56, 05158–59, 05161, 05201, 05250–55, 05257, 05260–62, 05301–04, 05340–46, 05350–63, 05401–07, 05439–66, 05468–74, 05476–79, 05481–83, 05485–92, 05494–95, 05601–04, 05609, 05620, 05633, 05640–41, 05647–58, 05660 67, 05669–82, 05701–02, 05730–48, 05750–51, 05753, 05757–70, 05772–78, 05819–30, 05832–33, 05836–43, 05845–51, 05853, 05855, 05857–63, 05866–68, 05871–75, 05901–07

VIRGINIA

(Population 2010, 8,001,024)

SENATORS

MARK R. WARNER, Democrat, of Alexandria, VA; born in Indianapolis, IN, December 15, 1954; son of Robert and Marge Warner of Vernon, CT; education: B.A., political science, George Washington University, 1977; J.D., Harvard Law School, 1980; Governor, Commonwealth of Virginia, 2002–06; chairman of the National Governor's Association, 2004–05; religion: Presbyterian; wife: Lisa Collis; children: Madison, Gillian, Eliza; committees: Banking, Housing, and Urban Affairs; Budget; Finance; Rules and Administration; Select Committee on Intelligence; elected to the U.S. Senate on November 4, 2008; reelected to the U.S. Senate on November 4, 2014.

Office Listings

http://warner.senate.gov

475 Russell Senate Office Building, Washington, DC 20510	(202) 224–2023
Chief of Staff.—David Hallock.	
Communications Director.—Kevin Hall.	
Press Secretary.—Rachel Cohen.	
Scheduler.—Carrig Balderston.	
Deputy Chief of Staff.—Kristin Sharp.	
Legislative Director.—Elizabeth Falcone.	
8000 Towers Crescent Drive, Suite 200, Vienna, VA 22182	(703) 442–0670
	FAX: 442–0408
180 West Main Street, Abingdon, VA 24210	(276) 628–8158
	FAX: 628–1036
101 West Main Street, Suite 4900, Norfolk, VA 23510	(757) 441–3079
	FAX: 441–6250
919 East Main Street, Richmond, VA 23219	(804) 775–2314
	FAX: 775–2319
129B Salem Avenue, Southwest, Roanoke, VA 24011	(540) 857–2676
	FAX: 857–2800

* * *

TIM KAINE, Democrat, of Richmond, VA; born in St. Paul, MN, February 26, 1958; education: graduated with a B.A., University of Missouri, 1979; graduated with a J.D., Harvard University, 1983; professional: work with the Jesuit order as a Catholic missionary in Honduras, 1980–81; civil rights lawyer; professor, University of Richmond, 1987–present; Richmond City Council, 1994–98; mayor of Richmond, VA, 1998–2001; lieutenant governor of Virginia, 2002–06; Governor of Virginia, 2006–10; married: Anne Holton, who currently serves as Virginia Secretary of Education; one of the Senate's few members who speak fluent Spanish; 51st chair of the Democratic National Committee, 2009–11; caucuses: chair, Senate Career and Technical Education (CTE) Caucus; committees: Armed Services; Budget; Foreign Relations; Special Committee on Aging; elected to the U.S. Senate on November 6, 2012.

Office Listings

http://kaine.senate.gov   https://twitter.com/@senkaineoffice
https://www.facebook.com/senatorkaine

231 Russell Senate Office Building, Washington, DC 20510	(202) 224–4024
Chief of Staff.—Mike Henry.	FAX: 228–6363
Communications Director.—Amy Dudley.	
Legislative Director.—Mary Naylor.	
Scheduler.—Kate McCarroll.	
State Director.—John Knapp.	
222 Central Park Avenue, Suite 120, Virginia Beach, VA 23462	(757) 518–1674
919 East Main Street, Suite 970, Richmond, VA 23219	(804) 771–2221
611 South Jefferson, Suite 5B, Roanoke, VA 24011	(540) 682–5693
121 Russell Road, Suite 2, Abingdon, VA 24210	(276) 525–4790
9408 Grant Avenue, Suite 202, Manassas, VA 20110	(703) 361–3192
308 Craghead Street, Suite 102A, Danville, VA 24541	(434) 792–0976

REPRESENTATIVES

FIRST DISTRICT

ROBERT J. WITTMAN, Republican, of Montross, VA; born in Washington, DC, February 2, 1959; B.S., biology, Virginia Polytechnic Institute and State University, 1981; M.P.H., health policy and administration, University of North Carolina at Chapel Hill, 1989; Ph.D., Virginia Commonwealth University, Richmond, VA, 2002; professional: field director for the Virginia Health Department's Division of Shellfish Sanitation; public service: Montross Town Council, 1986–96; public policy and administration, 1992; mayor of Montross, 1992–96; Westmoreland County Board of Supervisors, 1995–2003 and chairman, 2003–05; Virginia House of Delegates, 2005–07; religion: Episcopalian; married: Kathryn Wittman; children: Devon and Joshua; committees: Armed Services; Natural Resources; elected to the 110th Congress on December 11, 2007 in a special election; elected to the 111th Congress; reelected to each succeeding Congress.

Office Listings

http://www.wittman.house.gov

2454 Rayburn House Office Building, Washington, DC 20515	(202) 225–4261
Chief of Staff.—Jamie Miller.	FAX: 225–4382
Legislative Director.—Brent Robinson.	
Communications Director.—Gordon Neal.	
Scheduler / Office Manager.—Stacy Whitehouse.	
401 Main Street, P.O. Box 494, Yorktown, VA 23690	(757) 874–6687
District Director.—Joe Schumacher.	
95 Dunn Drive, Suite 201, Stafford, VA 22554	(540) 659–2734
508 Church Lane, Tappahannock, VA 22560	(804) 443–0668

Counties: ALL OF CAROLINE, ESSEX, GLOUCESTER, KING AND QUEEN, KING GEORGE, KING WILLIAM, LANCASTER, MATHEWS, MIDDLESEX, NORTHUMBERLAND, RICHMOND, STAFFORD, WESTMORELAND, AND YORK COUNTIES; ALL OF THE CITIES of Fredericksburg, Poquoson, and Williamsburg; PART OF FAUQUIER COUNTY COMPRISED OF THE BEALETON (303), CATLETT (102), LOIS (104), AND MORRISVILLE (301) PRECINCTS AND PART OF THE REMINGTON (302) PRECINCT; PART OF JAMES CITY COUNTY COMPRISED OF THE BERKELEY A PART 1 (101), BERKELEY A PART 2 (1012), BERKELEY B PART 1 (1021), BERKELEY B PART 2 (1022), BERKELEY C (103), JAMESTOWN A (201), JAMESTOWN B (202), POWHATAN A (301), POWHATAN B (302), POWHATAN C (303), POWHATAN D (304), ROBERTS A PART 1 (5011), ROBERTS A PART 2 (5012), ROBERTS C PART 1 (5031), ROBERTS C PART 2 (5032), STONEHOUSE A (401), STONEHOUSE B (402), AND STONEHOUSE C (403) PRECINCTS AND PART OF THE ROBERTS B (502) PRECINCT; PART OF PRINCE WILLIAM COUNTY COMPRISED OF THE ASHLAND (309), BENNETT (102), BENTON (203), BRENTSVILLE (101), BRISTOW RUN (111), CEDAR POINT (112), ELLIS (106), FOREST PARK (310), GLENKIRK (408), HENDERSON (307), LAKE RIDGE (501), LIMESTONE (113), LINDGE (207), MARSHALL (202), MARSTELLER (107), McCOART (204), MONTCLAIR (308), MULLEN (411), NOKESVILLE (104), PARK (109), PATTIE (305), PENN (210), POWELL (211), QUANTICO (304), SINCLAIR (404), STONEWALL (405), SUDLEY NORTH (409), VICTORY (108), WASHINGTON REID (306), WESTGATE (407), WESTRIDGE (208), AND WOODBINE (209) PRECINCTS AND PART OF THE BUCKLAND MILLS (110) PRECINCT; PART OF SPOTSYLVANIA COUNTY COMPRISED OF THE BATTLEFIELD (701), BRENT'S MILL (702), GRANGE HALL (202), HAZEL RUN (302), PLANK ROAD (801), AND SUMMIT (401) PRECINCTS AND PART OF THE LEE HILL (403) PRECINCT. AND PART OF THE CITY OF NEWPORT NEWS COMPRISED OF THE GREENWOOD (110) PRECINCT. Population (2010), 727,366.

ZIP Codes: 20109–12, 20119, 20136, 20155–56, 20181–82, 20187, 22025, 22134–35, 22172, 22192–93, 22401–08, 22412, 22427–28, 22430, 22432, 22435–38, 22442–43, 22446, 22448, 22451, 22454, 22456, 22460, 22463, 22469, 22471–73, 22476, 22480–82, 22485, 22488, 22501, 22503–04, 22507, 22509, 22511, 22512–14, 22617, 22520, 22523–24, 22526, 22520–30, 22533, 22538–39, 22544–48, 22552, 22554–56, 22558, 22560, 22570, 22572, 22576–81, 22712, 22720, 22728, 22734, 22739, 22742, 23001, 23003, 23009, 23015, 23018, 23021, 23023, 23025, 23031–32, 23035, 23043, 23045, 23047, 23050, 23056, 23061–62, 23064, 23066, 23068–72, 23076, 23079, 23081, 23085–86, 23089–92, 23106–10, 23115, 23119, 23125–28, 23130–31, 23138, 23148–49, 23154–56, 23161, 23163, 23168–69, 23175–78, 23180–81, 23183–88, 23190, 23602–03, 23608, 23662, 23665, 23690–94, 23696

* * *

SECOND DISTRICT

E. SCOTT RIGELL, Republican, of Virginia Beach, VA; born in Titusville, FL, May 28, 1960; education: A.A., Brevard Community College, Cocoa, FL, 1981; B.B.A., Mercer University, Macon, GA, 1983; M.B.A., Regent University, Virginia Beach, VA, 1990; professional: founder and chairman of Freedom Automotive; United States Marine Corps Reserve, 1978–84; married: Teri; children: Lindsey, Mallory, Justus, and Shannon; committees: Appropriations; elected to the 112th Congress on November 2, 2010; reelected to each succeeding Congress.

Office Listings

http://www.rigell.house.gov

418 Cannon House Office Building, Washington, DC 20515	(202) 225–4215

Office Listings—Continued

Chief of Staff.—Chris Connelly.   FAX: 225–4218
Communications Director.—Kim Mosser Knapp.
Legislative Director.—John Thomas.
4772 Euclid Road, Suite E, Virginia Beach, VA 23462 .... (757) 687–8290
District Director.—Shannon Kendrick.
36312 Lankford Highway, Suite 5, Belle Haven, VA 23306 .... (757) 442–4790

Counties: ACCOMACK, NORTHAMPTON. CITIES: Hampton, Newport News, Norfolk, and Virginia Beach. Population (2010), 721,969.

ZIP Codes: 23301–03, 23306–08, 23310, 23313, 23316, 23336–37, 23341, 23345, 23347, 23350, 23354, 23356–59, 23389, 23395, 23398–99, 23401, 23404–05, 23407–10, 23412–23, 23426–27, 23429, 23440–43, 23450–67, 23471, 23479–80, 23482–83, 23486, 23488, 23502–03, 23505–06, 23508–09, 23511, 23513, 23518–19, 23529, 23541, 23601–02, 23605, 23608–09, 23651, 23661, 23663–66, 23669

* * *

THIRD DISTRICT

ROBERT C. "BOBBY" SCOTT, Democrat, of Newport News, VA; born in Washington, DC, April 30, 1947; education: graduated, Groton High School; B.A., Harvard University; J.D., Boston College Law School; professional: served in the Massachusetts National Guard; attorney; admitted to the Virginia Bar; Virginia House of Delegates, 1978–83; Senate of Virginia, 1983–92; member: Alpha Phi Alpha Fraternity; NAACP; Sigma Pi Phi Fraternity; committees: ranking member, Education and the Workforce; elected on November 3, 1992 to the 103rd Congress; reelected to each succeeding Congress.

Office Listings

http://www.bobbyscott.house.gov   www.facebook.com/congressmanbobbyscott
twitter.com/repbobbyscott

1201 Longworth House Office Building, Washington, DC 20515 .... (202) 225–8351
Chief of Staff.—Joni L. Ivey.   FAX: 225–8354
Senior Advisor.—Randi Petty.
Legislative Director.—David Dailey.
2600 Washington Avenue, Suite 1010, Newport News, VA 23607 .... (757) 380–1000
District Director.—Vacant.
400 North 8th Street, Suite 430, Richmond, VA 23219 .... (804) 644–4845
Richmond Regional Director.—Nkechi George-Winkler.

Counties: CHARLES CITY, HENRICO (part), PRINCE GEORGE, SURRY. CITIES: Hampton (part), Newport News (part), Norfolk (part), Petersburg, Portsmouth, and Richmond (part). Population (2012), 751,694.

ZIP Codes: 23030, 23075, 23140, 23147, 23150, 23185, 23218–25, 23227, 23230–32, 23234, 23241, 23249–50, 23260–61, 23269, 23274, 23276, 23278, 23282, 23284–86, 23289–93, 23298, 23501–05, 23507–11, 23513–15, 23517, 23523, 23551, 23601–05, 23607–09, 23628, 23630, 23661, 23663–64, 23666–70, 23701–05, 23707–09, 23801, 23803–05, 23839, 23842, 23846, 23860, 23875, 23881, 23883, 23888, 23890, 23899

* * *

FOURTH DISTRICT

J. RANDY FORBES, Republican, of Chesapeake, VA; born in Chesapeake, February 17, 1952; education: B.A., Randolph-Macon College; J.D., University of Virginia School of Law; professional: attorney; religion: Baptist; public service: Virginia House of Delegates, 1990–97; Virginia State Senate, 1997–2001; Republican House Floor Leader, 1994–97; Republican Senate Floor Leader, 1998–2001; Chairman of the Republican Party of Virginia, 1996–2000; married: Shirley; children: Neil, Jamie, Jordan, and Justin; committees: Armed Services; Judiciary; elected to the 107th Congress, by special election, on June 19, 2001; reelected to each succeeding Congress.

Office Listings

http://forbes.house.gov

2135 Rayburn House Office Building, Washington, DC 20515 .... (202) 225–6365

Office Listings—Continued

Chief of Staff.—Dee Gilmore.   FAX: 226–1170
DC Chief of Staff.—Christy Grubbs.
Director of Operations.—Carolyn King.
Communications Director.—Hailey Sadler.
District Director.—Curtis Byrd.
505 Independence Parkway, Suite 104, Chesapeake, VA 23320 .... (757) 382–0080
District Director.—Ronald White.
9401 Courthouse Road, Suite 202, Chesterfield, VA 23832 .... (804) 318–1363
Director of Constituent Services.—Joan Fallon.

Counties: AMELIA, CHESTERFIELD (part), DINWIDDIE, GREENSVILLE, ISLE OF WIGHT (part), NOTTOWAY, POWHATAN, PRINCE GEORGE (part), SOUTHAMPTON, SUSSEX, CHESAPEAKE, COLONIAL HEIGHTS, EMPORIA, FRANKLIN, HOPEWELL, AND SUFFOLK. Population (2010), 881,217.

ZIP Codes: 23002, 23083, 23101, 23105, 23112–14, 23120, 23139, 23234, 23236–37, 23304, 23314–15, 23320–28, 23397, 23424, 23430–39, 23487, 23501, 23801, 23803–06, 23821, 23824, 23827–34, 23836–38, 23840–42, 23844–45, 23847, 23850–51, 23856–57, 23860, 23866–67, 23872–76, 23878–79, 23882, 23884–85, 23887–91, 23894, 23897–98, 23920, 23922, 23930, 23938, 23950, 23955

* * *

FIFTH DISTRICT

ROBERT HURT, Republican, of Chatham, VA; born in New York, NY, June 16, 1969; raised in Chatham, VA; education: B.S., Hampden-Sydney College, Hampden-Sydney, VA, 1991; J.D., Mississippi College School of Law, Clinton, MS, 1995; professional: attorney, Chatham Town Council, 2000–01; member of Virginia State House of Delegates, 2002–08; member of Virginia State Senate, 2008–10; committees: Financial Services; elected to the 112th Congress on November 2, 2010; reelected to each succeeding Congress.

Office Listings

http://www.hurt.house.gov

125 Cannon House Office Building, Washington, DC 20515 .... (202) 225–4711
Chief of Staff.—Kelly Simpson.   FAX: 225–5681
Scheduler.—Jeanna Buck.
Press Secretary.—Abigail Sigler.
Legislative Director.—John Lange.
308 Craghead Street, Suite 102–D, Danville, VA 24541 .... (434) 791–2596
District Director.—Linda Green.
686 Berkmar Circle, Charlottesville, VA 22901 .... (434) 973–9631
515 South Main Street, P.O. Box 0, Farmville, VA 23901 .... (434) 395–0120

Counties: ALBEMARLE. CITIES AND TOWNSHIPS: Barboursville, Charlotteville, Batesville, Covesville, Crozet, Earlysville, Esmont, Free Union, Greenwood, Hatton, Ivy, Keene, Keswick, North Garden, Scottsville. APPOMATTOX. CITIES AND TOWNSHIPS: Appomattox, Evergreen, Pamplin, Spout Spring. BEDFORD. CITIES AND TOWNSHIPS: Bedford, Big Island, Coleman Falls, Forest, Goode, Goodview, Hardy, Huddleston, Lowry, Moneta, Thaxton. BRUNSWICK. CITIES AND TOWNSHIPS: Alberta, Brodnax, Lawrenceville, Gasburg, White Plains. BUCKINGHAM. CITIES AND TOWNSHIPS: Andersonville, Arvonia, Buckingham, Dillwyn, Buckingham, New Canton. CAMPBELL. CITIES AND TOWNSHIPS: Altavista, Brookneal, Concord, Evington, Gladys, Long Island, Lynch Station, Naruna, Rustburg. CHARLOTTE. CITIES AND TOWNSHIPS: Barnesville, Charlotte Court House, Cullen, Drakes Branch, Keysville, Phenix, Randolph, Red House, Red Oak, Saxe, Wylliesburg. CHARLOTTESVILLE CITY: Charlottesville. CUMBERLAND. CITIES AND TOWNSHIPS: Carterville, Cumberland, Tamworth. DANVILLE CITY: Danville. FAUQUIER. CITIES AND TOWNSHIPS: Airlie, Bealeton, Belle Meade, Belvoir, Broad Run, Calverton, Casanova, Delaplane, Germantown, Halfway, Hume, Linden, Markham, Marshall, Midland, Morrisville, New Baltimore, Old Tavern, Opal, Orlean, Paris, Rectortown, Remington, The Plains, Upperville, Warrenton. FLUVANNA. CITIES AND TOWNSHIPS: Bremo Bluff, Bybee, Carysbrook, Columbia, Fork Union, Kents Store, Palmyra, Troy. FRANKLIN. CITIES AND TOWNSHIPS: Boones Mill, Callaway, Ferrum, Glade Hill, Henry, Redwood, Penhook, Rocky Mount, Union Hall, Waidsboro, Wirtz. GREENE. CITIES AND TOWNSHIPS: Amicus, Barnes, Burtonville, Dawsonville, Dyke, Geer, Haneytown, Lydia, McMullen, Midway, Newton, Pirkey, Quinque, Ruckersville, Stanardsville, St. George, Shady Grove, Simmons Gap, Twin Lakes, Upper Pocosin, Williams Fork. HALIFAX. CITIES AND TOWNSHIPS: Alton, Clover, Cluster Springs, Crystal Hall, Denniston, Halifax, Ingram, Lennig, Mayo, Nathalie, Republican Grove, Scottsburg, Turbeville, Vernon Hill, Virgilin. HENRY. CITIES AND TOWNSHIPS: Axton, Chatmoss, Ridgeway. LUNENBURG. CITIES AND TOWNSHIPS: Tamworth, Dundas, Fort Mitchell, Kenbridge, Lunenburg, Rehoboth, Victoria. MADISON. CITIES AND TOWNSHIPS: Achash, Aroda, Aylor, Banco, Beaver Park, Big Meadows, Burnt Tree, Criglersville, Decapolis, Duet, Elly, Etlan, Five Forks, Fletcher, Fordsville, Graves Mill, Haywood, Hood, Kinderhook, Leon, Locust Dale, Madison, Madison Mills, Nethers, Novum, O'Neal, Oakpark, Oldrag, Pratts, Radiant, Repton Mills, Rochelle, Ruth, Shelby, Shifflet Corner, Syria, Tanners, Tryme, Twyman's Mill, Uno, Wolftown, Zeus. MECKLENBURG. CITIES AND TOWNSHIPS: Baskerville, Blackridge, Boydton, Bracey, Chase City, Clarksville, Forksville, LaCross, Palmer Springs, Skipwith, South Hill, Union Level Buffalo Junction, Nelson. NELSON. CITIES AND TOWNSHIPS: Afton, Arrington, Faber, Lovingston, Massies Mill, Nellysford, Montebello, Gladstone, Norwood, Piney River, Roseland, Schuyler, Shipman, Tye River, Tyro, Wingina. PITTSYLVANIA. CITIES AND TOWNSHIPS: Blairs, Callands, Cascade, Chatham, Pittsville, Sandy Level, Dry Fork, Gretna, Hurt, Java, Keeling, Ringgold, Sutherlin. PRINCE EDWARD. CITIES AND TOWNSHIPS: Farmville, Darlington Heights, Green Bay, Hampden-Sydney, Meherrin, Prospect, Rice. RAPPAHANNOCK. CITIES AND TOWNSHIPS: Amissville, Castleton, Chester Gap, Flint Hill, Huntly, Laurel Mills, Massies Corner, Peola Mills, Revercombs Corner, Sperryville, Wakefield Manor, Washington, and Woodville. Population (2010), 727,365.

ZIP Codes: 20106, 20115–17, 20119, 20128, 20130, 20137–40, 20144, 20169, 20181, 20184–89, 20198, 22623, 22627, 22630, 22639, 22640, 22642, 22643, 22701, 22709, 22711–13, 22715, 22716, 22719, 22722–23, 22725, 22727–28, 22730–32, 22734–35, 22738, 22740, 22743, 22747–49, 22901–06, 22908–11, 22920, 22922–24, 22931–32, 22935– 38, 22940, 22942–43, 22945–49, 22958–60, 22963–69, 22971, 22973–74, 22976, 22987, 22989, 23004, 23022, 23027, 23038, 23040, 23055, 23084, 23093, 23123, 23139, 23821, 23824, 23843, 23845, 23847, 23856, 23857, 23868, 23873, 23876, 23887, 23889, 23893, 23901, 23909, 23915, 23917, 23919–24, 23927, 23934, 23936–39, 23941–44, 23947, 23950, 23952, 23954, 23958–60, 23962–64, 23966–68, 23970, 23974, 23976, 24054–55, 24059, 24064–65, 24067, 24069, 24079, 24088, 24091–92, 24095, 24101–02, 24104, 24112, 24137, 24139, 24148, 24151, 24161, 24174, 24176, 24179, 24184, 24464, 24483, 24501–02, 24504, 24517, 24520–23, 24527–31, 24534–35, 24538–41, 24543, 24549– 51, 24553–54, 24556–58, 24562–63, 24565–66, 24569–71, 24576–77, 24580–81, 24586, 24588–90, 24592–94, 24597

* * *

SIXTH DISTRICT

BOB GOODLATTE, Republican, of Roanoke, VA; born in Holyoke, MA, September 22, 1952; education: B.A., Bates College, Lewiston, ME, 1974; J.D., Washington and Lee University, 1977; Massachusetts Bar, 1977; Virginia Bar, 1978; professional: began practice in Roanoke, VA, 1979; district director for Congressman M. Caldwell Butler, 1977–79; attorney, sole practitioner, 1979–81; partner, 1981–92; chairman of the sixth district Virginia Republican Committee, 1983–88; member: Civitan Club of Roanoke (president, 1989–90); former member, Building Better Boards Advisory Council; married: Maryellen Flaherty, 1974; children: Jennifer and Robert; Deputy Republican Whip; committees: chair, Judiciary; Agriculture; elected on November 3, 1992, to the 103rd Congress; reelected to each succeeding Congress.

Office Listings

http://www.goodlatte.house.gov   twitter: @repgoodlatte
facebook.com/bobgoodlatte

2309 Rayburn House Office Building, Washington, DC 20515	(202) 225–5431
Chief of Staff.—Pete Larkin.	FAX: 225–9681
DC Chief of Staff.—Charlie Keller.	
Legislative Director.—Karen Williams.	
Communications Director.—Beth Breeding.	
10 Franklin Road, SE., Suite 540, Roanoke, VA 24011	(540) 857–2672
916 Main Street, Suite 300, Lynchburg, VA 24504	(434) 845–8306
117 South Lewis Street, Suite 215, Staunton, VA 24401	(540) 885–3861
District Director.—Debbie Garrett.	
70 North Mason Street, Harrisonburg, VA 22802	(540) 432–2391

Counties: AMHERST, AUGUSTA, BATH, BEDFORD (part), BOTETOURT, HIGHLAND, PAGE, ROANOKE (part), ROCKBRIDGE, ROCKINGHAM, SHENANDOAH, AND WARREN. CITIES: Buena Vista, Harrisonburg, Lexington, Lynchburg, Roanoke, Staunton, and Waynesboro. Population (2010), 737,755.

ZIP Codes: 22610, 22626, 22630, 22641, 22644–45, 22649–50, 22652, 22654, 22657, 22660, 22664, 22801–03, 22807, 22810–12, 22815, 22820–21, 22824, 22827, 22830–35, 22840–48, 22850–51, 22853, 22920, 22922, 22939, 22952, 22967, 22980, 24001–20, 24022–38, 24040, 24042–44, 24048, 24053, 24059, 24064–66, 24070, 24077, 24079, 24083, 24085, 24087, 24090, 24101, 24121–22, 24130, 24156, 24174–75, 24178–79, 24401–02, 24411–13, 24415–16, 24421– 22, 24430–33, 24435, 24437–42, 24445, 24450, 24458–60, 24463, 24465, 24467–69, 24471–73, 24476–77, 24479, 24482–87, 24501–06, 24512–15, 24521, 24523, 24526, 24533, 24536, 24550–51, 24553, 24555–56, 24572, 24574, 24578–79, 24595

* * *

SEVENTH DISTRICT

DAVE BRAT, Republican, of Glen Allen, Virginia; born in Detroit, Michigan, June 6, 1963; education: B.A., Hope College, Holland, MI, 1986; M. Div., Princeton Theological Seminary, Princeton, NJ, 1990; Ph.D., in economics, American University, Washington, DC, 1995; family: wife, Laura; children: Jonathan and Sophia; committees: Budget; Education and the Workforce; Small Business; elected to the 114th Congress on November 4, 2014.

Office Listings

http://www.brat.house.gov   facebook: representativedavebrat   twitter: @repdavebrat

330 Cannon House Office Building, Washington, DC 20515	(202) 225–2815
Chief of Staff.—Erin Siefring.	FAX: 225–0011
Scheduler.—Alexa Walker.	
Legislative Director.—Kurt Couchman.	
Press Secretary.—Julia Hahn.	
4201 Dominion Boulevard, Suite 110, Glen Allen, VA 23060	(804) 747–4073

Office Listings—Continued

9104 Courthouse Road, Room 249, Spotsylvania, VA 22553 ....   (540) 507–7216

Counties: CAROLINE (part), CHESTERFIELD (part), CULPEPER, GOOCHLAND, HANOVER, HENRICO (part), LOUISA, MADISON, ORANGE, RAPPAHANNOCK, SPOTSYLVANIA (part). CITIES: Richmond. Population (2010), 727,366.

ZIP Codes: 20106, 20186, 22407–08, 22433, 22508, 22534, 22542, 22546, 22551, 22553, 22565, 22567, 22580, 22701, 22713–14, 22716, 22718, 22724, 22726, 22729, 22733–37, 22740–41, 22923, 22942, 22947, 22957, 22960, 22972, 22974, 23005, 23015, 23024, 23038–39, 23047, 23058–60, 23063, 23065, 23067, 23069, 23084, 23093, 23102–03, 23111–14, 23116–17, 23120, 23124, 23129, 23146, 23153, 23160, 23162, 23170, 23173, 23192, 23221, 23224–30, 23233–36, 23238, 23242, 23255, 23273, 23294, 23832

* * *

EIGHTH DISTRICT

DONALD S. BEYER JR., Democrat, of Alexandria, VA; born in the Free Territory of Trieste, June 20, 1950; education: B.A., Williams College, Massachusetts, 1972; professional: Ambassador to Switzerland and Liechtenstein 2009–13; 36th Lieutenant Governor of Virginia, 1990–98; co-founder of the Northern Virginia Technology Council; former chair of Jobs for Virginia Graduates; served on Board of the D.C. Campaign to Prevent Teen Pregnancy; former chair of the Virginia Economic Recovery Commission; spouse: Megan; children: Don, Stephanie, Clara, Grace; caucuses: New Democrat Coalition, Congressional Progressive Caucus; committees: Natural Resources; Science, Space, and Technology; Joint Economic Committee; elected to the 114th Congress on November 4, 2014.

Office Listings

http://beyer.house.gov   https://twitter.com/repdonbeyer   https://www.facebook.com/repdonbeyer

431 Cannon House Office Building, Washington, DC 20515 ....   (202) 225–4376
   Chief of Staff.—Ann O'Hanlon.   FAX: 225–0017
   Legislative Director.—Zach Cafritz.
5285 Shawnee Road, Alexandria, VA 22312 ....   (703) 971–4700
   District Director.—Susie Warner.

Counties: ARLINGTON, FAIRFAX (part). CITIES: Alexandria, and Falls Church. Population (2010), 767,596.

ZIP Codes: 22003, 22037, 22040–44, 22046, 22060, 22079, 22101–02, 22107–08, 22121–22, 22150–51, 22153, 22199, 22201–07, 22209–17, 22219, 22225–27, 22230, 22240–45, 22301–15, 22320, 22331–34, 22350

* * *

NINTH DISTRICT

H. MORGAN GRIFFITH, Republican, of Salem, VA; born March 15, 1958; education: graduated, Andrew Lewis High School, 1976; B.A., Emory and Henry College, 1980; J.D., Washington and Lee University School of Law, 1983; professional: attorney, private practice, 1983–2011; partner, Albo & Oblon, L.L.P., 2008–11; Virginia House of Delegates, 1994–2011; majority leader, Virginia House of Delegates, 2001–11; married Hilary; children: Abby, Davis, and Starke; committees: Energy and Commerce; elected to the 112th Congress on November 2, 2010; reelected to each succeeding Congress.

Office Listings

http://www.morgangriffith.house.gov   twitter: @repmgriffith
https://www.facebook.com/repmorgangriffith

1108 Longworth House Office Building, Washington, DC 20515 ....   (202) 225–3861
   Chief of Staff.—Kelly Lungren McCollum.   FAX: 225–0076
   Legislative Director.—Adam Harbison.
   Communications Director.—Andie Pivarunas.
323 West Main Street, Abingdon, VA 24210 ....   (276) 525–1405
   District Director.—Michelle Jenkins.
17 West Main Street, Christiansburg, VA 24073 ....   (540) 381–5671

Counties: ALLEGHANY, BLAND, BUCHANAN, CARROLL, CRAIG, DICKENSON, FLOYD, GILES, GRAYSON, HENRY (part), LEE, MONTGOMERY, PATRICK, PULASKI, ROANOKE (part), RUSSELL, SCOTT, SMYTH, TAZEWELL, WASHINGTON, WISE, AND WYTHE. CITIES: Bristol, Covington, Galax, Martinsville, Norton, Radford and Salem. Population (2010), 727,366.

ZIP Codes: 24017, 24019, 24053, 24055, 24058–63, 24068, 24070, 24072–73, 24076, 24078, 24079, 24082, 24084, 24086–89, 24091, 24093, 24105, 24111–15, 24120, 24124, 24216–19, 24131–34, 24136, 24138, 24141–43, 24147–50, 24153,

24162, 24165, 24167–68, 24171, 24174–75, 24177, 24185, 24201–03, 24209–12, 24216–21, 24224–26, 24228, 24230, 24236–37, 24239, 24243–46, 24248, 24250–51, 24256, 24258, 24260, 24263, 24265–66, 24269–73, 24277, 24279–83, 24290, 24292–93, 24301, 24311–19, 24322–28, 24330, 24333, 24340, 24343, 24347–48, 24350–54, 24360–61, 24363, 24366, 24368, 24370, 24374–75, 24377–78, 24380–82, 24422, 24426, 24445, 24448, 24457, 24474, 24601–09, 24612–14, 24619–22, 24624, 24627–28, 24630–31, 24634–35, 24637, 24639–41, 24646–47, 24649, 24651, 24656–58

* * *

TENTH DISTRICT

BARBARA COMSTOCK, Republican, of McLean, VA; born in Springfield, MA, June 30, 1959; education: B.A., political science, Middlebury College, Middlebury, VT 1981; J.D., Georgetown University Law Center, Washington, DC, 1986; professional: senior aide to Congressman Frank Wolf, 1991–95; chief investigative counsel for the U.S. House of Representatives Committee on Government Reform, 1995–99; director of the Office of Public Affairs for the Justice Department, 2002–03; small business owner; elected to represent Virginia's 10th Congressional District; Virginia House of Delegates, 2010–15; chairwoman of the Science and Technology Committee of the Virginia House of Delegates; religion: member, St. Luke's Catholic Church in McLean; married: Elwyn Charles Comstock; children: Dan, Caity, and Peter; three grandchildren; committees: House Administration; Science, Space, and Technology; Transportation and Infrastructure; elected to the 114th Congress on November 4, 2014.

Office Listings

https://comstock.house.gov

226 Cannon House Office Building, Washington, DC 20515	(202) 225–5136
Chief of Staff.—Susan Falconer.	FAX: 225–0437
Legislative Director.—Michael Mansour.	
21430 Cedar Drive, Suite 218, Sterling, VA 20164	(703) 404–6903
District Director.—Lucy Norment.	
117 East Piccadilly Street, #100–D, Winchester, VA 22601	(540) 773–3600

Counties: CLARKE, FAIRFAX (part), FREDERICK, LOUDOUN, AND PRINCE WILLIAM (part). CITIES: Manassas, Manassas Park, and Winchester. Population (2010), 758,321.

ZIP Codes: 20105, 20107, 20109–11, 20117, 20120–21, 20124, 20129–30, 20132, 20135, 20137, 20141, 20143, 20147–48, 20151–52, 20155, 20158, 20164–66, 20169–71, 20175–76, 20180, 20184, 20187, 20197, 22015, 22030, 22033, 22039, 22066, 22079, 22101–02, 22124, 22151, 22153, 22182, 22601–03, 22611, 22620, 22624–25, 22630, 22637, 22645–46,22654–56, 22663

* * *

ELEVENTH DISTRICT

GERALD E. CONNOLLY, Democrat, of Fairfax, VA; born in Boston, MA, March 30, 1950; education: B.A., Maryknoll College; M.A., public administration, Harvard University, 1979; professional: member, Fairfax County Board of Supervisors, 1995–2003, chairman, 2003–07; religion: Roman Catholic; married: Cathy; children: Caitlin; committees: Foreign Affairs; Oversight and Government Reform; elected to the 111th Congress on November 4, 2008; reelected to each succeeding Congress.

Office Listings

http://www.geraldconnolly.house.gov

2238 Rayburn House Office Building, Washington, DC 20515	(202) 225–1492
Chief of Staff.—James Walkinshaw.	FAX: 225–3071
Legislative Director.—Dominic Bonaiuto.	
Communications Director.—George Burke.	
4115 Annandale Road, Annandale, VA 22003	(703) 256–3071
District Director.—Sharon Stark.	
2241–D Tackett's Mill Drive, Woodbridge, VA 22192	(703) 670–4989
Prince William Director.—Brianna Sewell.	

Counties: FAIRFAX (part), PRINCE WILLIAM (part). CITIES: Annandale, Burke, Centreville, Dale City, Fairfax, Fairfax Station, Herndon, Lorton, Manassas, Oakton, Occoquan, Reston, Springfield, Vienna, and Woodbridge. Population (2010), 770,944.

ZIP Codes: 20112, 20120–21, 20124, 20170–71, 20190–91, 20194, 22003, 22015, 22026–27, 22030–33, 22039, 22041–42, 22044, 22079, 22102, 22124–25, 22150–53, 22172, 22180–82, 22191–93

WASHINGTON

(Population 2010, 6,724,540)

SENATORS

PATTY MURRAY, Democrat, of Seattle, WA; born in Seattle, October 11, 1950; education: B.A., Washington State University, 1972; professional: teacher; Shoreline Community College; citizen lobbyist for environmental and educational issues, 1983–88; parent education instructor for Crystal Springs, 1984–87; school board member, 1985–89; elected Board of Directors, Shoreline School District, 1985–89; Washington State Senate, 1988–92; Democratic Whip, 1990–92; State Senate committees: Education; Ways and Means; Commerce and Labor; Domestic Timber Processing Select Committee; Open Government Select Committee; chair, School Transportation Safety Task Force; award: Washington State Legislator of the Year, 1990; married: Rob Murray; children: Randy and Sara; committees: ranking member, Health, Education, Labor, and Pensions; Appropriations; Budget; Veterans' Affairs; elected to the U.S. Senate on November 3, 1992; reelected to each succeeding Senate term.

Office Listings

http://murray.senate.gov

154 Russell Senate Office Building, Washington, DC 20510	(202) 224–2621
Chief of Staff.—Mike Spahn.	FAX: 224–0238
Legislative Director.—Shawn Bills.	TDD: 224–4430
Communications Director.—Eli Zupnick.	
2988 Jackson Federal Building, 915 Second Avenue, Seattle, WA 98174	(206) 553 5545
State Director.—Mindi Linquist.	
The Marshall House, 1323 Officer's Row, Vancouver, WA 98661	(360) 696–7797
District Director.—David Hodges.	
10 North Post Road, Suite 600, Spokane, WA 99201	(509) 624–9515
District Director.—John Culton.	
2930 Wetmore Avenue, Suite 903, Everett, WA 98201	(425) 259–6515
District Director.—Ann Seabott.	
402 East Yakima Avenue, Suite 390, Yakima, WA 98901	(509) 453–7462
District Director.—Rebecca Thornton.	
950 Pacific Avenue, Room 650, Tacoma, WA 98402	(253) 572–3636
District Director.—Kierra Phifer.	

* * *

MARIA CANTWELL, Democrat, of Edmonds, WA; born in Indianapolis, IN, October 13, 1958; education: B.A., Miami University, Miami, OH, 1980; professional: businesswoman; RealNetworks, Inc.; organizations: South Snohomish County Chamber of Commerce; Alderwood Rotary; Mountlake Terrace Friends of the Library; public service: Washington State House of Representatives, 1987–92; U.S. House of Representatives, 1992–94; religion: Roman Catholic; committees: ranking member, Energy and Natural Resources; Small Business and Entrepreneurship; Commerce, Science, and Transportation; Finance; Indian Affairs; elected to the U.S. Senate on November 7, 2000; reelected to each succeeding Senate term.

Office Listings

http://cantwell.senate.gov　　　twitter: @senatorcantwell

511 Hart Senate Office Building, Washington, DC 20510	(202) 224–3441
Chief of Staff.—James Fleet.	FAX: 228–0514
Legislative Director.—Pete Modaff.	
Administrative Director.—Nancy Hadley.	
915 Second Avenue, Suite 3206, Seattle, WA 98174	(206) 220–6400
The Marshall House, 1313 Officers Row, Vancouver, WA 98661	(360) 696–7838
950 Pacific Avenue, Suite 615, Tacoma, WA 98402	(253) 572–2281
U.S. Federal Courthouse, West 920 Riverside, Suite 697, Spokane, WA 99201	(509) 353–2507
825 Jadwin Avenue, 204/204A, Richland, WA 99352	(509) 946–8106
2930 Wetmore Avenue, Suite 9B, Everett, WA 98201	(425) 303–0114

REPRESENTATIVES

FIRST DISTRICT

SUZAN K. DELBENE, Democrat, of Medina, WA; born in Selma, Dallas County, AL, February 17, 1962; education: B.A., Reed College, Portland, OR, 1983; M.B.A., University of

Washington, Seattle, WA, 1990; business executive; unsuccessful candidate for election to the United States House of Representatives in 2010; director, Washington State Department of Revenue, 2010–12; married: Kurt; two children: Becca and Zach; committees: Agriculture; Judiciary; elected simultaneously as a Democrat to the 112th Congress and 113th Congress, by special election to fill the vacancy caused by the resignation of U.S. Representative Jay Inslee; reelected to the 114th Congress on November 4, 2014.

Office Listings

http://delbene.house.gov

318 Cannon House Office Building, Washington, DC 20515 .... (202) 225–6311
    Chief of Staff.—Aaron Schmidt.   FAX: 226–1606
    Legislative Director.—Ben Barasky.
    Communications Director.—Ramsey Cox.
    Scheduler.—Melissa Plummer.
Canyon Park Business Center, 22121 17th Avenue Southeast, Suite 220, Bothell, WA 98021 .... (425) 485–0085
204 West Montgomery Street, Mount Vernon, WA 98273 .... (360) 417–7879
    District Director.—Julien Loh.

Counties: KING (part), SKAGIT (part), SNOHOMISH (part), WHATCOM (part). CITIES AND TOWNSHIPS: Blaine, Bothell, Carnation, Concrete, Darrington, Duvall, Everson, Ferndale, Gold Bar, Granite Falls, Hamilton, Hunts Point, Index, Kenmore, Kirkland, Lake Stevens, Lyman, Lynden, Medina, Mill Creek, Monroe, Mount Vernon, Nooksack, Point Roberts, Redmond, Skykomish, Snohomish, Sultan, Sumas, Woodinville, and Yarrow Point. Population (2010) 691,738.

ZIP Codes: 98004 (part), 98007 (part), 98008 (part), 98011, 98012 (part), 98014, 98019, 98021 (part), 98024 (part), 98028, 98033, 98034, 98036 (part), 98039, 98041, 98045 (part), 98052 (part), 98053, 98065 (part), 98072–73, 98074 (part), 98077, 98082–83, 98155 (part), 98201 (part), 98208 (part), 98220, 98223 (part), 98224, 98225 (part), 98226 (part), 98230–31, 98233 (part), 98235, 98237, 98240–41, 98244, 98247–48, 98251–52, 98255–56, 98258 (part), 98262–64, 98266–67, 98270 (part), 98272, 98273 (part). 98274 (part), 98276, 98281, 98283, 98284 (part), 98288, 98290–91, 98293–96

* * *

SECOND DISTRICT

RICK LARSEN, Democrat, of Everett, WA; born in Arlington, WA, June 15, 1965; education: B.A., Pacific Lutheran University; M.P.A., University of Minnesota; professional: economic development official at the Port of Everett; Director of Public Affairs for a health provider association; public service: Snohomish County Council; religion: Methodist; married: Tiia Karlen; children: Robert and Per; committees: Armed Services; Transportation and Infrastructure; elected to the 107th Congress on November 7, 2000; reelected to each succeeding Congress.

Office Listings

http:/www.larsen.house.gov

2113 Rayburn House Office Building, Washington, DC 20515 .... (202) 225–2605
    Chief of Staff.—Kimberly Johnston.   FAX: 225–4420
    Legislative Director.—Terra Sabag.
    Communications Director.—Ingrid Stegemoeller.
2930 Wetmore Avenue, Suite 9F, Everett, WA 98201 .... (425) 252–3188
119 North Commercial Street, Suite 1350, Bellingham, WA 98225 .... (360) 733–5144

Counties: ISLAND, SAN JUAN, SKAGIT (part), SNOHOMISH (part), WHATCOM (part). CITIES AND TOWNSHIPS: Anacortes, Arlington, Bellingham, Blakely Island, Bow, Burlington, Clinton, Conway, Coupeville, Deer Harbor, East Sound, Everett, Freeland, Friday Harbor, Greenbank, Langley, Lopez Island, Lynnwood, Marysville, Mountlake Terrace, Mukilteo, Oak Harbor, Olga, Orcas, Shaw Island, Silvana, Stanwood, Tulalip, and Waldron. Population (2010), 672,454.

ZIP Codes: 98012, 98021, 98026, 98036–37, 98043, 98207, 98221–22, 98225–29, 98232–33, 98236, 98238–39, 98243, 98245, 98249–50, 98253, 98257, 98260–61, 98270–71, 98273, 98275, 98277–80, 98284, 98286–87, 98292, 98297

* * *

THIRD DISTRICT

JAIME HERRERA BEUTLER, Republican, of Camas, WA; born in Glendale, CA, November 3, 1978; education: communications, University of Washington, Seattle, WA, 2004; religion: Christian; family: married to Daniel Beutler; committees: Appropriations; elected to the 112th Congress on November 2, 2010; reelected to each succeeding Congress.

Office Listings

http://www.herrerabeutler.house.gov

1130 Longworth House Office Building, Washington, DC 20515 .... (202) 225–3536
    Chief of Staff.—Casey Bowman.   FAX: 225–3478
    Legislative Director.—Chad Ramey.
    Legislative Assistants: Jordan Evich, Jessica Wixson.
    Press Secretary.—Amy Pennington.
    Executive Assistant / Scheduler.—Terassa Wren.
    Legislative Correspondent.—Caroline Ehret.
    Staff Assistant.—Courtney Webb.
750 Anderson Street, Suite B, Vancouver, WA 98661 .... (360) 695–6292
    District Director.—Ryan Hart.
    Deputy District Director.—Shari Hildreth.
    Outreach Director.—Pam Peiper.
    Caseworkers: Ashley Lara, Dale Lewis, Jordan Meade.
    District Staff Assistant.—Jonathan Egan.

Counties: CLARK, COWLITZ, KLICKITAT, LEWIS, PACIFIC, SKAMANIA, THURSTON (part), WAHKIAKUM. Population (2010), 672,448.

ZIP Codes: 98304 (part), 98330 (part), 98336, 98355–56, 98361, 98377, 98522, 98527, 98530–33, 98537 (part), 98538–39, 98542, 98544, 98547 (part), 98554, 98561, 98564–65, 98568 (part), 98570, 98572, 98576 (part), 98577, 98579 (part), 98581–82, 98585–86, 98589 (part), 98590–91, 98593, 98596, 98597 (part), 98601–07, 98609–14, 98616–17, 98619–26, 98628–29, 98631–32, 98635, 98637–45, 98647–51, 98660–66, 98668, 98670–75, 98682–87, 98935 (part), 99322 (part), 99350 (part), 99356

* * *

FOURTH DISTRICT

DAN NEWHOUSE, Republican, of Sunnyside, WA; born in Sunnyside, WA, July 10, 1955; education: graduated, Sunnyside High School, 1973; B.S., Washington State University, 1977; graduated, Washington Agriculture and Forestry Leadership Program, 1981; member: Washington State House of Representatives, 2003–09; Assistant Whip; Assistant Floor Leader; Floor Leader; Water Caucus; Drought Committee Chairman; CSG Leadership Academy; director, Washington State Department of Agriculture, 2009–13; married: Carol Hammond, 1982; children: Jensena and Devon; committees: Agriculture; Natural Resources; Rules; Science, Space, and Technology; elected to 114th Congress on November 4, 2014.

Office Listings

http://www.newhouse.house.gov   twitter: @repnewhouse
https://www.facebook.com/repnewhouse

1641 Longworth House Office Building, Washington, DC 20515 .... (202) 225–5816
    Chief of Staff. Carrie Meadows.
    Scheduler / Office Manager.—Amy Harris.
    Communications Director.—Will Boyington.
3100 George Washington Way, #135, Richland, WA 99354 .... (509) 713–7374
402 East Yakima Avenue, Suite 445, WA 98901 .... (509) 452–3243

Counties: ADAMS COUNTY. CITIES: Othello, Ritzville. BENTON COUNTY. CITIES AND TOWNSHIPS: Benton City, Kennewick, Paterson, Plymouth, Prosser, Richland, West Richland. DOUGLAS COUNTY. CITIES AND TOWNSHIPS: Bridgeport, East Wenatchee, Leahy, Mansfield, Orondo, Pallsades, Rock Island, Waterville.T4Franklin County. Cities and Townships: Basin City, Connell, Eltopia, Kahlotus, Mesa, Pasco, Windust. GRANT COUNTY. CITIES AND TOWNSHIPS: Beverly, Coulee City, Desert Aire, Electric City, Ephrata, George, Grand Coulee, Hartline, Marlin, Mattawa, Moses Lake, Quincy, Royal City, Soap Lake, Stratford, Warden, Wilson Creek. OKANOGAN COUNTY. CITIES: Brewster, Nespelem, Okanogan, Omak, Oroville, Tonasket, and Twisp. WALLA WALLA COUNTY (part). CITIES: BURBANK. YAKIMA COUNTY. CITIES AND TOWNSHIPS: Brownstown, Buena, Carson, Cowiche, Grandview, Granger, Harrah, Mabton, Moxee, Naches, Outlook, Parker, Selah, Sunnyside, Tieton, Toppenish, Underwood, Wapato, White Swan, Yakima, and Zillah. Population (2010), 695,040.

ZIP Codes: 98068, 98602, 98605, 98610, 98613, 98617, 98619–20, 98623, 98628, 98635, 98648, 98650–51, 98670, 98672–73, 98801–02, 98807, 98811–13, 98815–17, 98819, 98821–24, 98826, 98828–32, 98834, 98836–37, 98840–44, 98843, 98845, 98847–48, 98850–53, 98855–56, 98857–58, 98860, 98901–04, 98907–09, 98920–23, 98925–26, 98929–30, 98932–44, 98946–48, 98950–53, 99103, 99115–16, 99123–24, 99133, 99135, 99155, 99169, 99301–02, 99320–22, 99323, 99326, 99330, 99335–38, 99343–46, 99349–50, 99352–54, 99356–57

* * *

FIFTH DISTRICT

CATHY McMORRIS RODGERS, Republican, of Spokane, WA; born in Salem, OR, May 22, 1969; education: B.A., Pensacola Christian College, Pensacola, FL, 1990; M.B.A., University of Washington, Seattle, WA, 2002; professional: fruit orchard worker; member, Washington State House of Representatives, 1994–2004; minority leader, 2002–03; organizations: member, Grace Evangelical Free Church; married: Brian Rodgers; children: Cole; chair, House Republican Conference; committees: Energy and Commerce; elected to the 109th Congress on November 2, 2004; reelected to each succeeding Congress.

Office Listings

http://www.mcmorris.house.gov https://twitter.com/cathymcmorris
https://www.facebook.com/#!/mcmorrisrodgers

203 Cannon House Office Building, Washington, DC 20515	(202) 225–2006
Chief of Staff.—Dave Peluso.	FAX: 225–3392
Executive Assistant.—Jessica Sunday.	
Staff Assistant.—Jared Powell.	
Legislative Director.—Melanie Steele.	
Press Secretary.—Ian Field.	
Legislative Correspondent.—Andrew Neill.	
10 North Post Street, 6th Floor, Spokane, WA 99210	(509) 353–2374
District Director.—Chud Wendle.	FAX: 225–9379
Deputy District Director.—Louise Fendrich.	
Constituent Relations Liaison.—Kristy Sauer.	
Executive Assistant.—Jesse Laughery.	
555 South Main Street, Suite C, Colville, WA 99114	(509) 684–3481
Deputy District Director.—Sheila Stalp.	FAX: 684–3482
Regional Representative.—Karen Dodson.	
29 South Palouse Street, Walla Walla, WA 99362	(509) 529–9358
Deputy District Director.—Cathy Schaeffer.	FAX: 529–9379

Counties: ASOTIN, COLUMBIA, FERRY, GARFIELD, PEND OREILLE, LINCOLN, SPOKANE, STEVENS, WALLA WALLA, AND WHITMAN. Population (2010), 672,455.

ZIP Codes: 98812, 98814, 98819, 98827, 98829, 98832–34, 98840–41, 98844, 98846, 98849, 98855–57, 98859, 98862, 99001, 99003–06, 99008–09, 99011–14, 99016–23, 99025–27, 99029–34, 99036–37, 99039–40, 99101–05, 99107, 99109–11, 99113–14, 99116–19, 99121–22, 99125–26, 99128–31, 99133–41, 99143–44, 99146–61, 99163–67, 99169–71, 99173–74, 99176, 99179–81, 99185, 99201–20, 99223–24, 99228, 99251–52, 99256, 99258, 99260, 99302, 99323–24, 99326, 99328–29, 99333, 99335, 99341, 99344, 99347–48, 99356, 99359–63, 99371, 99401–03

* * *

SIXTH DISTRICT

DEREK KILMER, Democrat, of Gig Harbor, WA; born in Port Angeles, January 1, 1974; education: graduated, Port Angeles High School, 1992; B.A., public affairs, Princeton University, 1996; Ph.D., University of Oxford, 1999; professional: worked as a consultant with McKinsey & Company from 1999–2002; worked for the Economic Development Board for Tacoma-Pierce County; elected to be a Washington State Representative in 2004; served in the Washington State Senate from 2007–12, caucuses: member, Democrat Caucus; New Democrats; co-chair of the Puget Sound Recovery Caucus; Rotary; married: the former Jennifer Saunders, children: Sophie and Tess; committees: Appropriations; elected to the 113th Congress on November 6, 2012; reelected to the 114th Congress on November 4, 2014.

Office Listings

http://kilmer.house.gov https://twitter: @repderekkilmer
https//www.facebook.com/derek.kilmer

1520 Longworth House Office Building, Washington, DC 20515	(202) 225–5916
Chief of Staff.—Jonathan Smith.	FAX: 226–3575
Press Secretary.—Jason Phelps.	
Legislative Director.—Kevin Warnke.	
Scheduler.—Andrea Friedhoff.	
950 Pacific Avenue, Suite 1320, Tacoma, WA 98402	(253) 272–3515
District Director.—Joe Dacca.	
345 Sixth Street, Suite 500, Bremerton, WA 98337	(360) 373–9725
322 East Fifth Street, Port Angeles, WA 98362	(360) 797–3623

Counties: CLALLAM. CITIES AND TOWNSHIPS: Blyn, Forks, Joyce, LaPush, Neah Bay, Port Angeles, Sequim, and Sieku. GRAYS HARBOR. CITIES AND TOWNSHIPS: Aberdeen, Amanda Park, Cosmopolis, Elma, Hoquiam, McCleary, MoClips, Montesano, Oakville, Ocean City, Ocean Shores, Quinault, Seabrook, Taholah, and Westport. JEFFERSON. CITIES AND TOWNSHIPS: Chimicum, Nordland, Port Hadlock, Port Ludlow, Port Townsend, and Quilcene. KITSAP. CITIES AND TOWNSHIPS: Bainbridge Island, Bremerton, Hansville, Indianola, Kingston, Manchester, Olalla, Port Orchard, Poulsbo, Seabeck, Silverdale, and Southworth. MASON (part). CITIES AND TOWNSHIPS: Allyn, Belfair, Grapeview, Harstine Island,

Shelton, Skokomish, and Union. PIERCE (part). CITIES AND TOWNSHIPS: Fox Island, Gig Harbor, Key Center, Lakebay, Longbranch, Purdy, Tacoma, Vaughn, and Wauna. Population: (2010), 687,387.

ZIP Codes: 98061, 98110, 98305, 98310–12, 98315, 98320, 98322, 98324–98326, 98329, 98331–33, 98335, 98337, 98339–40, 98342–43, 98345–46, 98349–51, 98353, 98357–59, 98362–68, 98370, 98376, 98378, 98380–84, 98386, 98392–95, 98401–98403, 98405–09, 98411–13, 98415, 98417–919, 98421, 98444, 98465–67, 98471, 98499, 98502, 98520, 98524, 98526, 98528, 98535 98537, 98541, 98546–48, 98550, 98552, 98555, 98557, 98559–60, 98562–63, 98566, 98568–69, 98571, 98575, 98583–84, 98587–88, 98592, 98595

* * *

SEVENTH DISTRICT

JIM McDERMOTT, Democrat, of Seattle, WA; born in Chicago, IL, December 28, 1936; education: B.S., Wheaton College, Wheaton, IL, 1958; M.D., University of Illinois Medical School, Chicago, 1963; residency in adult psychiatry, University of Illinois Hospitals, 1964–66; residency in child psychiatry, University of Washington Hospitals, Seattle, 1966–68; served, U.S. Navy Medical Corps, lieutenant commander, 1968–70; psychiatrist; Washington State House of Representatives, 1971–72; Washington State Senate, 1975–87; Democratic nominee for governor, 1980; regional medical officer, Sub-Saharan Africa, U.S. Foreign Service, 1987–88; practicing psychiatrist and assistant clinical professor of psychiatry, University of Washington, 1970–83; member: Washington State Medical Association; King County Medical Society; American Psychiatric Association; religion: St. Mark's Episcopal Church, Seattle; grown children: Katherine and James; grandchildren; committees: Budget; Ways and Means; elected on November 8, 1988 to the 101st Congress; reelected to each succeeding Congress.

Office Listings

http://www.mcdermott.house.gov   facebook.com/congressmanjimmcdermott
twitter.com/repjimmcdermott

1035 Longworth House Office Building, Washington, DC 20515	(202) 225–3106
Chief of Staff.—Diane Shust.	FAX: 225–6197
Scheduler.—Lona Watts.	
Communications Director.—Daniel Rubin.	
1809 Seventh Avenue, Suite 409, Seattle, WA 98101–1313	(206) 553–7170
District Administrator.—Tera Beach.	

Counties: KING COUNTY. CITIES AND TOWNSHIPS: Included in the district (in whole or in part): Burien, Des Moines, Edmonds, Lake Forest Park, Normandy Park, Seattle, Shoreline, Vashon, and Woodway. Population (2010), 672,455.

ZIP Codes: 98013, 98020, 98026, 98037, 98043, 98070, 98101–09, 98111–13, 98115–17, 98119, 98121–22, 98125–27, 98129, 98133–34, 98136, 98139, 98141, 98146–46, 98154–55, 98161, 98164–66, 98168, 98174–75, 98177, 98181, 98185, 98191, 98194–95, 98198–99

* * *

EIGHTH DISTRICT

DAVID G. REICHERT, Republican, of Auburn, WA; born in Detroit Lakes, MI, August 29, 1950; education: graduated, Kent Meridian High School, Renton, WA, 1968; A.A., Concordia Lutheran College, Portland, OR, 1970; professional: U.S. Air Force Reserve, 1971–76; U.S. Air Force, 1976; police officer, King County, WA, 1972–97; sheriff, King County, WA, 1997–2004; member: president, Washington State Sheriff's Association; executive board member, Washington Association of Sheriffs and Police Chiefs; co-chair, Washington State Partners in Crisis; awards: recipient of the 2004 National Sheriff's Association's "Sheriff of the Year"; two-time Medal of Valor Award recipient from the King County Sheriff's Office; Washington Policy Center's Champion of Freedom Award; Families Northwest Public Policy Award; married: Julie; children: Angela, Tabitha, and Daniel; committees: Ways and Means; elected to the 109th Congress on November 2, 2004; reelected to each succeeding Congress.

Office Listings

http://www.reichert.house.gov   https://www.facebook.com/repdavereichert
twitter: @davereichert

1127 Longworth House Office Building, Washington, DC 20515	(202) 225–7761
Chief of Staff.—Jeff Harvey.	FAX: 225–4282
Legislative Director.—Lindsay Manson.	
Executive Assistant / Scheduler.—Nichole Robison.	
22605 Southeast 56th Street, Suite 130, Issaquah, WA 98029	(425) 677–7414

Office Listings—Continued

District Director.—Sue Foy.
200 Palouse Street, Suite 201–1, Wenatchee, WA 98801 .... (509) 885–6615

Counties: KING COUNTY (part). CITIES AND TOWNSHIPS: Sammamish, Issaquah, Snoqualmie, North Bend, Covington, Auburn, Federal Way, Bonney Lake, Enumclaw, Issaquah, Black Diamond. CHELAN COUNTY. CITIES AND TOWNSHIPS: Wenatchee, Chelan, Cashmere, Leavenworth. KITTITAS. CITIES AND TOWNSHIPS: Cle Elum, Easton, Ellensburg, Kittitas, Snoqualmie Pass, Roslyn, Thorp. DOUGLAS. CITIES AND TOWHSHIPS: East Wenatchee. PIERCE COUNTY (part). CITIES AND TOWNSHIPS: Ashfort, Bonney Lake, Buckley, Eatonville, Graham, Orting, and Sumner. Population (2010), 690,250.

ZIP Codes: 98001–03, 98010, 98022, 98024, 98027, 98029–32, 98038, 98042, 98045, 98047, 98050–51, 98058–59, 98065, 98068, 98074–75, 98092, 98304, 98321, 98323, 98328, 98330, 98338, 98354, 98360, 98372, 98374–75, 98385, 98387, 98390–91, 98396, 98424, 98558, 98580, 98801–02, 98811, 98815–17, 98821–22, 98826, 98828, 98831, 98836, 98847, 98852, 98901, 98922, 98925–26, 98934, 98937, 98940–41, 98943, 98946, 98950

* * *

NINTH DISTRICT

ADAM SMITH, Democrat, of Tacoma, WA; born in Washington, DC, June 15, 1965; education: graduated, Tyee High School, 1983; graduated, Fordham University, NY, 1987; law degree, University of Washington, 1990; admitted to the Washington Bar in 1991; professional: prosecutor for the city of Seattle; Washington State Senate, 1990–96; member: Kent Drinking Driver Task Force; board member, Judson Park Retirement Home; married: Sara Smith, 1993; committees: ranking member, Armed Services; elected to the 105th Congress; reelected to each succeeding Congress.

Office Listings

http://www.adamsmith.house.gov

2264 Rayburn House Office Building, Washington, DC 20515 .... (202) 225–8901
　　Chief of Staff.—Shana Chandler.　　　　　　　　　　　　　　　　　　　　　　　　FAX: 225–5893
　　Communications Director.—Benjamin Halle.
101 Evergreen Building, 15 South Grady Way, Renton, WA 98057 .... (253) 593–6600
　　District Director.—Matt Perry.
　　Office Manager.—Christine Choe.

Counties: KING (part), PIERCE (part), THURSTON (part). CITIES: Bellevue, Burien, Des Moines, Federal Way, Kent, Mercer Island, Newcastle, Renton, SeaTac, Seattle, Tacoma, and Tukwila. Population (2010), 672,460.

ZIP Codes: 98001, 98003–09, 98015, 98023, 98027, 98030–32, 98040, 98042, 98055–59, 98063, 98089, 98093, 98104, 98108, 98112, 98114, 98118, 98122, 98131, 98134, 98138, 98141, 98144, 98148, 98158, 98161, 98168, 98178, 98188–89, 98198, 98402, 98421, 98422, 98424

* * *

TENTH DISTRICT

DENNY HECK, Democrat, of Olympia, WA; born in Vancouver, WA, July 29, 1952; education: graduated, Columbia River High School, WA, 1970; graduated, The Evergreen State College, WA, 1973; professional: small business owner; President and co-founder of TVW, Washington's statewide public affairs cable channel, 1993–2003; chief of staff to Governor Booth Gardner, 1989–93; elected to five consecutive terms in the Washington State House of Representatives starting in 1976; religion: member, The Lutheran Church of The Good Shepherd; former trustee, Washington State Historical Society; former trustee, The Evergreen State College; married: Paula Heck, 1976; committees: Financial Services; elected to the 113th Congress on November 6, 2012; reelected to the 114th Congress on November 4, 2014.

Office Listings

http://www.dennyheck.house.gov　　　www.facebook.com/congressmandennyheck
twitter: www.twitter.com/repdennyheck

425 Cannon House Office Building, Washington, DC 20515 .... (202) 225–9740
　　Chief of Staff.—Hart Edmonson.　　　　　　　　　　　　　　　　　　　　　　　　FAX: 225–0129
　　Legislative Director.—Jami Burgess.
　　Communications Director.—Kati Rutherford.
420 College Street Southeast, Suite 3000, Lacey, WA 98503 .... (360) 459–8514
1423 E 29th Street, Suite 203, Tacoma, WA 98404 .... (253) 722–5860

Office Listings—Continued

District Director.—LaTasha Wortham.

Counties: MASON (part), PIERCE (part), THURSTON (part). CITIES: Chehalis Indian Reservation (part), DuPont, Edgewood, Fife, Fircrest, Joint Base Lewis McChord, Lacey, Lakewood, Nisqually Indian Reservation, Olympia, Puyallup, Puyallup Indian Reservation (part), Rainier, Roy, Shelton, Squaxin Island Indian Reservation (part), Steilacoom, Sumner, Tacoma (part), Tenino, Tumwater, University Place, and Yelm. Population (2010), 672,455.

ZIP Codes: 98047, 98303, 98327, 98338, 98354, 98371–75, 98387–88, 98390–91, 98404, 98408, 98418, 98421, 98424, 98430, 98433, 98438–39, 98443–47, 98466–67, 98498–99, 98501–03, 98506, 98512–13, 98516, 98558, 98576, 98579–80, 98584, 98589, 98597

WEST VIRGINIA

(Population 2010, 1,852,994)

SENATORS

JOE MANCHIN III, Democrat, of Fairmont, WV; born in Farmington, August 24, 1947; education: graduated, Farmington High School, Farmington, 1965; B.A., West Virginia University, WV, 1970; businessman; member of the West Virginia House of Delegates, 1982–86; member of the West Virginia State Senate, 1986–96; Secretary of State, West Virginia, 2000–04; elected governor of West Virginia in 2004 and reelected in 2008; chairman of the National Governors Association, 2010; religion: Catholic; married: Gayle Conelly; three children, Heather, Joseph IV, and Brooke; seven grandchildren; committees: Armed Services; Commerce, Science, and Transportation; Energy and Natural Resources; Veterans' Affairs; elected to the 111th U.S. Senate in the November 2, 2010, special election to the term ending January 3, 2013, a seat previously held by Senator Carte Goodwin, and took the oath of office on November 15, 2010.

Office Listings

http://manchin.senate.gov　　https://www.facebook.com/joemanchinIII
https://twitter.com/sen_joemanchin

306 Hart Senate Office Building, Washington, DC 20510	(202) 224–3954
Chief of Staff.—Hayden Rogers.	FAX: 228–0002
Legislative Director.—Kirtan Mehta.	
Communications Director.—Jonathan Kott.	
900 Pennsylvania Avenue, Suite 629, Charleston, WV 25302	(304) 342–5855
State Director.—Mara Boggs.	
261 Aikens Center, Suite 305, Martinsburg, WV 25404	(304) 264–4626
48 Donley Street, Suite 504, Morgantown, WV 26501	(304) 284–8663
	FAX: 284–8681

* * *

SHELLEY MOORE CAPITO, Republican, of Charleston, WV; born in Glen Dale, WV, November 26, 1953; education: B.S., Duke University; M.Ed., University of Virginia; professional: career counselor, West Virginia State College; West Virginia Board of Regents; organizations: Community Council of Kanawha Valley; YWCA; West Virginia Interagency Council for Early Intervention; Habitat for Humanity; public service: elected to the West Virginia House of Delegates, 1996; reelected in 1998; awards: Coalition for a Tobacco-Free West Virginia Legislator of the Year; elected to the 107th Congress on November 7, 2000; served in the U.S. House of Representatives from 2001–14; religion: Presbyterian; married: Charles L. Capito, Jr.; three children; three grandchildren; first woman elected to the U.S. Senate from West Virginia; committees: Appropriations; Environment and Public Works; Energy and Natural Resources; Rules and Administration; Joint Committee on the Library; elected to the U.S. Senate on November 4, 2014.

Office Listings

http://www.capito.senate.gov　　https://www.facebook.com/senshelley
https://twitter.com/sencapito

172 Russell Senate Office Building, Washington, DC 20510	(202) 224–6472
Chief of Staff.—Joel Brubaker.	FAX: 224–7665
Office Manager.—Jim Durrett.	
Legislative Director.—Adam Tomlinson.	
Communications Director.—Ashley Berrang.	
405 Capitol Street, Charleston, WV 25301	(304) 347–5372
State Director.—Mary Elizabeth Eckerson.	
217 West King Street, Suite 307, Martinsburg, WV 24501	(304) 262–9285

REPRESENTATIVES

FIRST DISTRICT

DAVID B. McKINLEY, P.E., Republican, of Wheeling, WV; born in Wheeling, March 28, 1947; education: B.S.C.E., civil engineering, Purdue University, West Lafayette, IN, 1969; professional: engineer (started McKinley and Associates with offices in Wheeling and Charleston,

WV and Washington, PA); member of West Virginia State House of Representatives, 1981–94; chairman, West Virginia Republican Party, 1990–94; religion: Episcopalian; married: Mary McKinley; children: David, Amy, Elizabeth, and Bennett; committees: Energy and Commerce; elected to the 112th Congress on November 2, 2010; reelected to each succeeding Congress.

Office Listings

http://mckinley.house.gov

412 Cannon House Office Building, Washington, DC 20515	(202) 225–4172
Chief of Staff.—Mike Hamilton.	FAX: 225–7564
Executive Assistant.—Lou Hrkman.	
Legislative Director.—Devon Seibert.	
Communications Director.—Greg Dolan.	
709 Beechurst Avenue, Suite 14B, Morgantown, WV 26505	(304) 284–8506
Horne Building, 1100 Main Street, Suite 101, Wheeling, WV 26003	(304) 232–3801
Federal Building, 425 Juliana Street, Suite 1004, Parkersburg, WV 26101	(304) 422–5972

Counties: BARBOUR, BROOKE, DODDRIDGE, GILMER, GRANT, HANCOCK, HARRISON, MARION, MARSHALL, MINERAL, MONONGALIA, OHIO, PLEASANTS, PRESTON, RITCHIE, TAYLOR, TUCKER, TYLER, WETZEL, AND WOOD. CITIES AND TOWNSHIPS: Albright, Alma, Alvy, Anmoore, Arthur, Arthurdale, Auburn, Aurora, Baldwin, Barrackville, Baxter, Bayard, Beech Bottom, Belington, Belleville, Bellview, Belmont, Bens Run, Benwood, Berea, Bethany, Big Run, Blacksville, Blandville, Booth, Brandonville, Bretz, Bridgeport, Bristol, Brownton, Bruceton Mills, Burlington, Burnt House, Burton, Cabins, Cairo, Cameron, Carolina, Cassville, Cedarville, Center Point, Central Station, Century, Chester, Clarksburg, Coburn, Colfax, Colliers, Core, Corinth, Cove, Coxs Mills, Cuzzart, Dallas, Davis, Davisville, Dawmont, Dellslow, Dorcas, Eglon, Elk Garden, Ellenboro, Elm Grove, Enterprise, Eureka, Everettville, Fairmont, Fairview, Farmington, Flemington, Flower, Follansbee, Folsom, Fort Ashby, Fort Neal, Four States, Friendly, Galloway, Gilmer, Glen Dale, Glen Easton, Glenville, Goffs, Gormania, Grafton, Grant Town, Granville, Greenwood, Gypsy, Hambleton, Harrisville, Hastings, Haywood, Hazelton, Hebron, Hendricks, Hepzibah, Highland, Hundred, Idamay, Independence, Industrial, Jacksonburg, Jere, Jordan, Junior, Keyser, Kingmont, Kingwood, Knob Fork, Lahmansville, Letter Gap, Lima, Linn, Littleton, Lockney, Lost Creek, Lumberport, MacFarlan, Mahone, Maidsville, Mannington, Masontown, Maysville, McMechen, McWhorter, Meadowbrook, Medley, Metz, Middlebourne, Mineralwells, Moatsville, Monongah, Montana Mines, Morgantown, Moundsville, Mount Clare, Mount Storm, Mountain, New Creek, New Cumberland, New England, New Manchester, New Martinsville, New Milton, Newberne, Newburg, Newell, Normantown, North Parkersburg, Nutter Fort, Osage, Owings, Paden City, Parkersburg, Parsons, Pennsboro, Pentress, Perkins, Petersburg, Petroleum, Philippi, Piedmont, Pine Grove, Porters Falls, Proctor, Pullman, Pursglove, Rachel, Reader, Red Creek, Reedsville, Reynoldsville, Riegeley, Rivesville, Rocket Center, Rockport, Rosedale, Rosemont, Rowlesburg, Saint George, Saint Marys, Salem, Sand Fork, Shinnston, Shirley, Shocks, Short Creek, Simpson, Sistersville, Smithburg, Smithfield, Smithville, Spelter, Stonewood, Stouts Mill, Stumptown, Tanner, Terra Alta, Thomas, Thornton, Toll Gate, Troy, Triadelphia, Tunnelton, Valley Grove, Vienna, Volga, Wadestown, Walker, Wallace, Wana, Warwood, Washington, Watson, Waverly, Weirton, Wellsburg, Wendel, West Liberty, West Milford, West Union, Westover, Wheeling, Wick, Wilbur, Wiley Ford, Wileyville, Williamstown, Wilson, Wilsonburg, Windsor Heights, Wolf Summit, Worthington, and Wyatt. Population (2010), 615,991.

ZIP Codes: 25267, 26003, 26030–41, 26047, 26050, 26055–56, 26059–60, 26062, 26070, 26074–75, 26101, 26104–05, 26133–34, 26136–37, 26142–43, 26146, 26148–50, 26155, 26159, 26161, 26164, 26167, 26169–70, 26175, 26178, 26180–81, 26184, 26187, 26201, 26238, 26250, 26260, 26263, 26267, 26269, 26271, 26275–76, 26283, 26287, 26292, 26301, 26320, 26323, 26325, 26327, 26330, 26335, 26337, 26339, 26342, 26346–49, 26351, 26354, 26361, 62, 26366, 26369, 26374, 26377–78, 26384–86, 26404–05, 26408, 26410–12, 26415–16, 26419, 26421–22, 26424–26, 26430–31, 26435–38, 26440, 26443–44, 26448, 26451, 26456, 26501, 26505, 26508, 26519–21, 26525, 26534, 26537, 26541–43, 26547, 26554, 26559–60, 26562–63, 26568, 26570–72, 26574–76, 26581–82, 26585–88, 26590–91, 26611, 26636, 26638, 26705, 26707, 26710, 26716–17, 26719–20, 26726, 26731, 26739, 26743, 26750, 26753, 26763–64, 26767, 26833, 26847, 26855

*   *   *

SECOND DISTRICT

ALEXANDER X. MOONEY, Republican, of Charles Town, WV; born in Washington, DC, June 7, 1971; education: B.A., philosophy, Dartmouth College, 1993; professional: owner, AXM Consulting, LLC; executive director, The National Journalism Center (a program of Young America's Foundation), 2005–12; State Senator, Maryland State Senate, 1999–2010; religion: Roman Catholic; married: Dr. Grace Gonzalez Mooney, Ph.D., M.D.; three children; committees: Budget; Natural Resources; elected to the 114th Congress on November 4, 2014.

Office Listings

http://www.mooney.house.gov

1232 Longworth House Office Building, Washington, DC 20515	(202) 225–2711
Chief of Staff.—Brian Chatwin.	FAX: 225–7856
Office Manager.—Stephanie Cooper.	
Legislative Director.—Nick Butterfield.	
405 Capitol Street, Suite 514, Charleston, WV 25301	(304) 925–5964
300 Foxcroft Avenue, Suite 102, Martinsburg, WV 25401	(304) 264–8810

Counties: BERKELEY, BRAXTON, CALHOUN, CLAY, HAMPSHIRE, HARDY, JACKSON, JEFFERSON, KANAWHA, LEWIS, MORGAN, PENDLETON, PUTNAM, RANDOLPH, ROANE, UPSHUR, AND WIRT. Population (2010), 654,275.

ZIP Codes: 25002–03, 25005, 25011, 25015, 25019, 25025–26, 25030, 25033, 25035, 25039, 25043, 25045–46, 25054, 25059, 25061, 25063–64, 25067, 25070–71, 25075, 25079, 25081–83, 25085–86, 25088, 25102–03, 25106–07, 25109– 13, 25123–26, 25132–34, 25136, 25139, 25141, 25143, 25147, 25150, 25156, 25159–60, 25162, 25164, 25168, 25177, 25187, 25201–02, 25211, 25213–14, 25231, 25234–35, 25239, 25241, 25243–45, 25247–48, 25251–53, 25259–62, 25264– 68, 25270–71, 25275–76, 25279, 25281, 25285–87, 25301–06, 25309, 25311–15, 25317, 25320–39, 25350, 25356– 58, 25360–62, 25364–65, 25375, 25392, 25396, 25401–02, 25410–11, 25413–14, 25419–23, 25425, 25427–32, 25434, 25437–38, 25440–44, 25446, 25502–03, 25510, 25515, 25520, 25523, 25526, 25541, 25550, 25560, 25569, 26133, 26136–38, 26141, 26143, 26147, 26151–52, 26160–61, 26164, 26173, 26180, 26201–02, 26205, 26210, 26215, 26218, 26224, 26228–30, 26234, 26236–38, 26241, 26253–54, 26257, 26259, 26261, 26263, 26267–68, 26270, 26273, 26276, 26278, 26280, 26282–83, 26285, 26293–94, 26296, 26321, 26335, 26338, 26342–43, 26351, 26372, 26376, 26378, 26384–85, 26412, 26430, 26443, 26447, 26452, 26546, 26590, 26601, 26610–11, 26615, 26617, 26619, 26621, 26623– 24, 26627, 26629, 26631, 26636, 26638–39, 26641, 26651, 26656, 26660, 26662, 26667, 26671, 26675–76, 26678– 79, 26681, 26684, 26690–91, 26704–05, 26707, 26710–11, 26714, 26717, 26722, 26731, 26739, 26743, 26750, 26755, 26757, 26761, 26763–64, 26801–02, 26804, 26807–08, 26810, 26812, 26814–15, 26817–18, 26823–24, 26836, 26838, 26845, 26847, 26851–52, 26865–66, 26884, 26886

* * *

THIRD DISTRICT

EVAN H. JENKINS, Republican, of Huntington, WV; born in Huntington, September 12, 1960; graduated from Virginia Episcopal School in 1979; Bachelor of Science in business administration, University of Florida, Gainesville, FL, 1983; J.D., Cumberland School of Law at Samford University, Birmingham, AL, 1987; professional: associate attorney, Jenkins Fenstermaker, P.L.L.C, 1987–92; general counsel, West Virginia State Chamber of Commerce, 1992–99; executive director, West Virginia State Medical Association, 1999–2014; member, West Virginia House of Delegates, 1995–2001; member, West Virginia Senate, 2003–2015; religion: First Presbyterian Church in Huntington; married: Elizabeth; children: Evan Jr. "Hollin", Charles, and Olivia; caucuses: Congressional Steel Caucus; Ohio River Basin Congressional Caucus; House General Aviation Caucus; Congressional Caucus on Prescription Drug Abuse; Congressional Arts Caucus; Congressional Humanities Caucus; Congressional Historic Preservation Caucus; Congressional TRiO Caucus; Congressional Career and Technical Education Caucus; committees: Appropriations; elected to the 114th Congress on November 4, 2014.

Office Listings

http://www.evanjenkins.house.gov   twitter: @repevanjenkins

502 Cannon House Office Building, Washington, DC 20515		(202) 225–3452
Chief of Staff.—Patrick Howell.		FAX: 225–9061
Legislative Director.—Brian Barnard.		
Scheduler.—Lanier Savage.		
Communications Director.—Rebecca Neal.		
845 Fifth Avenue, Room 314, Huntington, WV 25701		(304) 522–2201
223 Prince Street, Beckley, WV 25801		(304) 250–6177
601 Federal Street, Room 1003, Bluefield, WV 24701		(304) 325–6800

Counties: BOONE, CABELL, FAYETTE, GREENBRIER, LINCOLN, LOGAN, MCDOWELL, MASON, MERCER, MINGO, MONROE, NICHOLAS, POCAHONTAS, RALEIGH, SUMMERS, WAYNE, WEBSTER, AND WYOMING. Population (2010), 613,376.

ZIP Codes: 24701, 24712, 24714–16, 24719, 24724, 24726, 24729, 24731–33, 24736–40, 24747, 24751, 24801, 24808, 24811, 24813, 24815–18, 24820–31, 24834, 24836, 24839, 24842–57, 24859–62, 24866–74, 24878–82, 24884, 24887– 88, 24892, 24894–99, 24901–02, 24910, 24915–18, 24920, 24924–25, 24927, 24931, 24934–36, 24938, 24941, 24943– 46, 24950–51, 24954, 24957, 24961–63, 24966, 24970, 24974, 24976–77, 24981, 24983–86, 24991, 24993, 25002– 04, 25007–10, 25021–22, 25024, 25028, 25031, 25036, 25040, 25043–44, 25047–49, 25051, 25053, 25057, 25059– 60, 25062, 25076, 25081, 25083, 25085, 25090, 25093, 25108, 25114–15, 25118–19, 25121, 25130, 25136, 25139– 40, 25142, 25148–49, 25152, 25154, 25161, 25165, 25169, 25173–74, 25180–81, 25183, 25185–86, 25193, 25202– 06, 25208–09, 25213, 25247, 25265, 25082, 25106, 25123, 25239, 25241, 25253, 25260, 25264, 25287, 25502–03, 25525, 25520, 25541, 25550–01, 25504–08, 25510–12, 25514, 25517, 25520–21, 25523–24, 25526, 25529–30, 25534– 35, 25537, 25540–41, 25544–45, 25547, 25555, 25557, 25559, 25562, 25564–65, 25567, 25570–73, 25601, 25606– 08, 25611–12, 25614, 25617, 25621, 25624–25, 25628, 25630, 25632, 25634–39, 25644, 25646–47, 25649–54, 25661, 25665–67, 25669–72, 25674, 25676, 25678, 25682, 25685–88, 25690–92, 25694, 25696, 25699, 25701–29, 25755, 25770–79, 25801–02, 25810–13, 25816–18, 25820, 25823, 25825–27, 25831–33, 25836–37, 25839–41, 25843–49, 25851, 25853–57, 25859–60, 25862, 25864–66, 25868, 25870–71, 25873, 25875–76, 25878–80, 25882, 25901–02, 25904, 25906– 09, 25911, 25913–22, 25927–28, 25931–32, 25934, 25936, 25938, 25942–43, 25951, 25958, 25961–62, 25965–67, 25969, 25971–72, 25976–79, 25981, 25984–86, 25989, 26202–03, 26205–06, 26208–09, 26217, 26222, 26230, 26234, 26261, 26264, 26266, 26288, 26291, 26294, 26298, 26610, 26617, 26639, 26651, 26656, 26660, 26662, 26674, 26676, 26678–81, 26684, 26690–91

WISCONSIN

(Population 2010, 5,686,986)

SENATORS

RONALD H. JOHNSON, Republican, of Oshkosh, WI; born in Mankato, MN, April 18, 1955; education: B.A., business administration, University of Minnesota, Twin Cities, MN, 1977; professional: CEO Pacur, LLC.; married: wife, Jane; three children: daughters, Carey and Jenna; son, Ben; committees: chair, Homeland Security and Governmental Affairs; Budget; Commerce, Science, and Transportation; Foreign Relations; elected to the U.S. Senate on November 2, 2010.

Office Listings

http://ronjohnson.senate.gov

328 Hart Senate Office Building, Washington, DC 20510	(202) 224–5323
Chief of Staff.—Tony Blando.	FAX: 228–6965
Legislative Director.—Lydia Westlake.	
Communications Director.—Melinda Schnell.	
517 East Wisconsin Avenue, Room 408, Milwaukee, WI 53202	(414) 276–7282
219 Washington Avenue, Suite 100, Oshkosh, WI 54901	(920) 230–7250
Deputy Chief of Staff.—Julie Leschke.	

* * *

TAMMY BALDWIN, Democrat, of Madison, WI; born in Madison, February 11, 1962; education: graduated, Madison West High School, Madison, 1980; A.B., Smith College, Northampton, MA, 1984; J.D., University of Wisconsin Law School, Madison, 1989; elected to Madison Common Council, Madison, 1986; elected to Dane County Board of Supervisors, Madison, served 1986–94; elected to the Wisconsin State Assembly, Madison, served 1992–98; elected to the U.S. House of Representatives, served 1998–2012; committees: Appropriations; Budget; Health, Education, Labor and Pensions; Homeland Security and Governmental Affairs; elected to the U.S. Senate on November 6, 2012.

Office Listings

http://baldwin.senate.gov   facebook.com/senatortammybaldwin   twitter: @senatorbaldwin

717 Hart Senate Office Building, Washington, DC 20510	(202) 224–5653
Chief of Staff.—Bill Murat.	
Legislative Director.—Dan McCarthy.	
Communications Director.—John Kraus.	
Executive Assistant.—Carolyn Walser	
30 West Mifflin Street, Suite 700, Madison, WI 53703	(608) 264–5338
State Director.—Janet Piraino.	
633 West Wisconsin Avenue, Suite 1920, Milwaukee, WI 53203	(414) 297–4451
From Wisconsin Only: (800) 247–5645	
205 5th Avenue South, Room 216, La Crosse, WI 54601	(608) 796–0045
2100 Stewart Avenue, Suite 250B, Wausau, WI 54401	(715) 261–2611
1039 West Mason Street, Suite 119, Green Bay, WI 54303	(920) 498–2668
402 Gorham Avenue, Eau Claire, WI 54701	(715) 832–8424

REPRESENTATIVES

FIRST DISTRICT

PAUL D. RYAN, Republican, of Janesville, WI; born in Janesville, January 29, 1970; education: Joseph A. Craig High School; economic and political science degrees, Miami University, Ohio; professional: marketing consultant, Ryan Inc., Central (construction firm); aide to former U.S. Senator Bob Kasten (R–WI); advisor to former Vice Presidential candidate Jack Kemp, and U.S. Drug Czar Bill Bennett; legislative director, U.S. Senate; Republican Vice Presidential candidate, 2012; organizations: Janesville Bowmen, Inc.; Ducks Unlimited; married: Janna Ryan; three children: daughter, Liza; sons, Charlie and Sam; elected to the 106th Congress; reelected to each succeeding Congress; elected Speaker of the U.S. House of Representatives on October 29, 2015.

Office Listings

http://paulryan.house.gov

1233 Longworth House Office Building, Washington, DC 20515 .... (202) 225–3031
　DC Chief of Staff.—Danyell Tremmel.　　　　　　　　　　　　　　　　　FAX: 225–3393
　Deputy Chief of Staff.—Allison Steil.
　Legislative Director.—Katie Donnell.
　Scheduler.—Tory Wickiser.
20 South Main Street, Suite 10, Janesville, WI 53545 .... (608) 752–4050
5031 Seventh Avenue, Kenosha, WI 53140 .... (262) 654–1901
216 Sixth Street, Racine, WI 53403 .... (262) 637–0510

Counties: KENOSHA, MILWAUKEE (part), RACINE, ROCK (part), WALWORTH (part), AND WAUKESHA (part). Population (2010), 728,042.

ZIP Codes: 53103–05, 53108, 53114–15, 53118–21, 53125–26, 53128–30, 53132, 53139–40, 53142–44, 53146–47, 53149–51, 53153–54, 53158, 53167–68, 53170, 53177, 53179, 53181–82, 53184–85, 53189–92, 53195, 53219–21, 53227–28, 53402–06, 53505, 53511, 53525, 53534, 53538, 53545–46, 53548, 53563

* * *

SECOND DISTRICT

MARK POCAN, Democrat, of Madison, WI; born in Kenosha, August 14, 1964; education: graduated from Bradford High School, 1982; journalism, University of Wisconsin, 1986; professional: small business owner, 1986–present; elected to the Dane County Board of Supervisors, 1991–96; elected to the State Assembly from the 78th district, 1999–2013; committees: Budget; Education and the Workforce; elected to the 113th Congress on November 6, 2012; reelected to the 114th Congress on November 4, 2014.

Office Listings

http://pocan.house.gov

313 Cannon House Office Building, Washington, DC 20515 .... (202) 225–2906
　Chief of Staff.—Glenn Wavrunek.　　　　　　　　　　　　　　　　　　FAX: 225–6942
　Legislative Director.—Alicia Molt.
　Scheduler.—Brian Walsh.
　Communications Director.—Alex Nguyen.
10 East Doty Street, Suite 405, Madison, WI 53703 .... (608) 258–9800
　District Director.—Dane Varese.
100 State Street, 3rd Floor, Beloit, WI 53511 .... (608) 365–8001

Counties: DANE, GREEN, IOWA, LAFAYETTE, RICHLAND (part), ROCK (part), and SAUK. Population (2010), 729,417.

ZIP Codes: 53501–02, 53503–04, 53506–08, 53510–12, 53515–17, 53520–23, 53526–37, 53541–46, 53548, 53553–56, 53558–63, 53565–56, 53569–73, 53574–78, 53580–83, 53586, 53588–89, 53593–99, 53701–08, 53711, 53713–19, 53725, 53744, 53777–79, 53782–94, 53803, 53807, 53811, 53818, 53911, 53913, 53924–25, 53937, 53940–44, 53951, 53958–61, 53965, 53968

* * *

THIRD DISTRICT

RON KIND, Democrat, of La Crosse, WI; born in La Crosse, March 16, 1963; education: B.A., Harvard University, 1985; M.A., London School of Economics, 1986; J.D., University of Minnesota Law School, 1990; admitted to the Wisconsin Bar, 1990; state prosecutor, La Crosse County District Attorney's Office; board of directors, La Crosse Boys and Girls Club; Coulee Council on Alcohol and Drug Abuse; Wisconsin Harvard Club; Wisconsin Bar Association; La Crosse County Bar Association; married: Tawni Zappa in 1994; two sons: Jonathan and Matthew; committees: Ways and Means; elected to the 105th Congress; reelected to each succeeding Congress.

Office Listings

http://www.kind.house.gov

1502 Longworth House Office Building, Washington, DC 20515 .... (202) 225–5506
　Chief of Staff.—Mike Goodman.　　　　　　　　　　　　　　　　　　FAX: 225–5739
　Press Secretary.—Amanda Sherman.
　Legislative Director.—Elizabeth Stower.
　Scheduler.—Wade Balkonis.
205 Fifth Avenue South, Suite 400, La Crosse, WI 54601 .... (608) 782–2558

Office Listings—Continued

District Director.—Loren Kannenberg.
131 South Barstow Street, Suite 301, Eau Claire, WI 54701 .... (715) 831-9214
Congressional Aide.—Mark Aumann.

Counties: ADAMS, BUFFALO, CHIPPEWA, CRAWFORD, DUNN, EAU CLAIRE, GRANT, JACKSON, JUNEAU, LA CROSSE, MONROE, PEPIN, PIERCE, PORTAGE, RICHLAND, TREMPEALEAU, VERNON, AND WOOD. Population (2010), 710,873.

ZIP Codes: 53518, 53543, 53554, 53556, 53569, 53573, 53581, 53801-02, 53804, 53805-11, 53813, 53816-18, 53820-21, 53825-27, 53910, 53920, 53924, 53929, 53934, 53936-37, 53941, 53944, 53948, 53950, 53952, 53964-65, 53968, 54003, 54005, 54010-11, 54013-14, 54021-22, 54406-07, 54410, 54412-13, 54423, 54443, 54454-55, 54457-58, 54466-67, 54469, 54473, 54475, 54481-82, 54489, 54494-95, 54499, 54601, 54603, 54610-16, 54618-19, 54621-32, 54634-39, 54642-45, 54648, 54650-61, 54664-67, 54669-70, 54701, 54703, 54720-27, 54729-30, 54734, 54736-42, 54747, 54749-51, 54754-63, 54765, 54767-70, 54772-73, 54909, 54921, 54930, 54943, 54945, 54966, 54977, 54981, 54984

*   *   *

FOURTH DISTRICT

GWENDOLYNNE S. "GWEN" MOORE, Democrat, of Milwaukee, WI; born in Racine, WI, April 18, 1951; education: graduated, Northern Division High School, Milwaukee, WI, 1969; B.A., Marquette University, Milwaukee, WI, 1978; professional: housing officer, Wisconsin Housing and Development Authority; member: Wisconsin State Assembly, 1989-92; Wisconsin State Senate, 1993-2004; president pro tempore, 1997-98; three children; committees: Budget; Financial Services; elected to the 109th Congress on November 2, 2004; reelected to each succeeding Congress.

Office Listings

http://gwenmoore.house.gov

2245 Rayburn House Office Building, Washington, DC 20515 .... (202) 225-4572
Chief of Staff.—Minh Ta.
316 North Milwaukee Street, Suite 406, Milwaukee, WI 53202 .... (414) 297-1140
District Administrator.—Shirley Ellis.   FAX: 297-1086

Counties: MILWAUKEE (part), WAUKESHA (part). CITIES AND TOWNSHIPS: Milwaukee, Cudahy, South Milwaukee, St. Francis, West Allis, and West Milwaukee. Population (2010), 710,873.

ZIP Codes: 53007, 53051, 53110, 53154, 53172, 53201-28, 53233, 53235, 53295

*   *   *

FIFTH DISTRICT

F. JAMES SENSENBRENNER, JR., Republican, of Menomonee Falls, WI; born in Chicago, IL, June 14, 1943; education: graduated, Milwaukee Country Day School, 1961; A.B., Stanford University, 1965; J.D., University of Wisconsin Law School, 1968; admitted to the Wisconsin Bar, 1968; commenced practice in Cedarburg, WI; admitted to practice before the U.S. Supreme Court in 1972; professional: attorney; staff member of former U.S. Congressman J. Arthur Younger of California, 1965; elected to the Wisconsin Assembly, 1968, reelected in 1970, 1972, and 1974; elected to Wisconsin Senate in a special election, 1975, reelected in 1976 (assistant minority leader); member: Waukesha County Republican Party; Wisconsin Bar Association; Friends of Museums; American Philatelic Society; married: the former Cheryl Warren, 1977; children: Frank James III and Robert Alan; committees: Judiciary; Science, Space, and Technology; elected to the 96th Congress, November 7, 1978; reelected to each succeeding Congress.

Office Listings

http://www.sensenbrenner.house.gov

2449 Rayburn House Office Building, Washington, DC 20515 .... (202) 225-5101
Chief of Staff.—Bart Forsyth.
Legislative Director.—Amy Bos.
Communications Director.—Ben Miller.
Scheduler/Office Manager.—Jake Peterson.
120 Bishops Way, Room 154, Brookfield, WI 53005 .... (262) 784-1111
Deputy Chief of Staff.—Loni Hagerup.

Counties: JEFFERSON, MILWAUKEE (part), DODGE (part), WASHINGTON, WAUKESHA (part). Population (2010), 716,218.

ZIP Codes: 53005, 53007, 53018, 53022, 53029, 53032, 53035, 53036–40, 53045–46, 53051–52, 53056, 53058, 53066, 53072, 53076, 53078, 53089, 53090, 53094–95, 53098, 53122, 53137, 53146, 53151, 53156, 53178, 53186, 53188–90, 53210, 53213–14, 53219, 53220–21, 53226–28, 53538, 53549, 53551, 53579, 53594

* * *

SIXTH DISTRICT

GLENN GROTHMAN, Republican, of Glenbeulah, WI; Born in Milwaukee, WI, July 3, 1955; education: graduated, Homestead High School, 1973; B.B.A., University of Wisconsin, 1978; J.D., University of Wisconsin, 1983; professional: admitted to the Wisconsin State Bar Association; lawyer, Schloemer Law Firm; elected to Wisconsin State Assembly, 1993; elected to the Wisconsin State Senate, 2004; served until 2015; committees: Budget; Education and the Workforce; Oversight and Government Reform; Joint Economic Committee; elected to the 114th Congress on November 4, 2014.

Office Listings

http://www.grothman.house.gov

501 Cannon House Office Building, Washington, DC 20515	(202) 225–2476

Chief of Staff.—Tyler Houlton.
Deputy Chief of Staff and Policy Director.—Rachel Ver Velde.
Legislative Director.—Kyle Roskam.
Press Secretary.—Brittni Palke.
Executive Assistant.—Hillary Lassiter.
District Director.—Jackie Trudell.

1020 South Main Street, Suite B, Fond du Lac, WI 54935	(920) 907–0624

Counties: COLUMBIA, DODGE (part), FOND DU LAC, GREEN LAKE, MANITOWOC, OZAUKEE, MILWAUKEE (part), SHEBOYGAN, WAUSHARA, AND WINNEBAGO (part). Population (2010), 709,482.

ZIP Codes: 53001, 53004, 53006, 53010–11, 53012–15, 53019–21, 53023–24, 53031–32, 53035, 53040, 53042, 53044, 53048–50, 53057, 53061–63, 53065, 53070, 53073–75, 53079–85, 53090–93, 53095, 53097, 53217, 53532, 53555, 53561, 53578, 53583, 53901, 53911–23, 53925–28, 53930–33, 53935, 53939, 53946–47, 53949, 53952–56, 53960, 53963–65, 53969, 54110, 54126, 54207–08, 54214, 54220–28, 54230–32, 54241–47, 54619, 54638, 54901–09, 54914–15, 54923, 54930, 54932, 54934–41, 54943, 54947, 54952–60, 54963–74, 54979–86

* * *

SEVENTH DISTRICT

SEAN P. DUFFY, Republican, of Wausau, WI; born in Hayward, WI, October 3, 1971; education: B.A., marketing, St. Mary's University, Winona, MN, 1994; J.D., William Mitchell College of Law, St. Paul, MN, 1999; professional: lawyer, private practice; prosecutor, Ashland County, WI; district attorney, Ashland County, WI, 2002–10; religion: Roman Catholic; married: wife, Rachel Campos-Duffy; seven children; committees: Financial Services; elected to the 112th Congress on November 2, 2010; reelected to each succeeding Congress.

Office Listings

http://duffy.house.gov

1208 Longworth House Office Building, Washington, DC 20515	(202) 225–3365
	FAX: 225–3240

Chief of Staff.—Pete Meachum.
Communications Director.—Cassie Smedile. (855) 585–4251
Scheduler.—Alana Wilson.

208 Grand Avenue, Wausau, WI 54403	(715) 298–9344
	FAX: 298–9348

District Director.—Jesse Garza.
District Scheduler.—Maggie Cronin.
Director of Constituent Services.—Johnathan Lanctin.

823 Belknap Street, Suite 102, Superior, WI 54880	(715) 392–3984
502 Second Street, Suite 202, Hudson, WI 54016	(715) 808–8160

Counties: ASHLAND, BARRON, BAYFIELD, BURNETT, CHIPPEWA (part), CLARK, DOUGLAS, FLORENCE, FOREST, IRON, JACKSON (part), JUNEAU (part), LANGLADE, LINCOLN, MARATHON, MONROE (part), ONEIDA, POLK, PRICE, RUSK, SAWYER, ST. CROIX, TAYLOR, VILAS, WASHBURN, AND WOOD (part). Population (2010), 710,873.

ZIP Codes: 53950, 54001–02, 54004–07, 54009, 54013, 54015–17, 54020, 54022–28, 54082, 54103–04, 54120–21, 54125, 54151, 54175, 54401, 54403, 54405, 54408–14, 54417–18, 54420–22, 54424–28, 54430, 54433, 54435–37, 54440–

43, 54446–49, 54451–52, 54454–57, 54459–60, 54462–63, 54465–66, 54470–71, 54473–74, 54476, 54479–80, 54484–85, 54487–91, 54493, 54495, 54498–99, 54501, 54511–15, 54517, 54519–21, 54524–27, 54529–31, 54534, 54536–42, 54545–48, 54550, 54552, 54554–66, 54568, 54611, 54615–16, 54618, 54635, 54641, 54646, 54660, 54666, 54724, 54726–34, 54741, 54745–46, 54748–49, 54754, 54757, 54762–63, 54765–68, 54771, 54801, 54805–06, 54810, 54812–14, 54817, 54819–22, 54824, 54826–30, 54832, 54835–50, 54853–59, 54861–62, 54864–65, 54867–68, 54870–76, 54880, 54888–89, 54891, 54893, 54895–96

* * *

EIGHTH DISTRICT

REID RIBBLE, Republican, of Appleton, WI; born in Neenah, WI, April 5, 1956; education: Appleton East High School, WI, 1974; Grand Rapids School of Bible and Music, MI; professional: business owner; married: DeaNa; committees: Foreign Affairs; Transportation and Infrastructure; elected to the 112th Congress on November 2, 2010; reelected to each succeeding Congress.

Office Listings

http://www.ribble.house.gov

1513 Longworth House Office Building, Washington, DC 20515	(202) 225–5665
Chief of Staff.—McKay Daniels.	FAX: 225–5729
Legislative Director.—Paul Bleiberg.	
Scheduler.—Teri Dorn.	
Communications Director.—Katherine Mize.	
333 West College Avenue, Appleton, WI 54911	(920) 380–0061
District Director.—Rick Sense.	
550 North Military Avenue, Suite 4B, Green Bay, WI 54303	(920) 471–1950

Counties: BROWN, CALUMET, DOOR, KEWAUNEE, MARINETTE, MENOMINEE, OCONTO, OUTAGAMIE (part), SHAWANO, WAUPACA, WINNEBAGO (part). Population (2010), 706,840.

ZIP Codes: 54101–04, 54106–07, 54110–15, 54119–21, 54124–28, 54130–31, 54135, 54137–41, 54143, 54149–57, 54159, 54161–62, 54165–66, 54169–71, 54173–75, 54177, 54180, 54182, 54201–02, 54204–05, 54208–13, 54216–17, 54226–27, 54229–30, 54234–35, 54241, 54246, 54301–08, 54311, 54313, 54324, 54344, 54408–09, 54414, 54416, 54418, 54424, 54427–28, 54430, 54435, 54450, 54452, 54462–65, 54485–87, 54491, 54499, 54501, 54511–12, 54519–21, 54529, 54531, 54538–43, 54545, 54548, 54554, 54557–58, 54560–62, 54564, 54566, 54568, 54911–15, 54919, 54922, 54926, 54928–29, 54931, 54933, 54940, 54942, 54944–50

WYOMING

(Population 2010, 563,626)

SENATORS

MICHAEL B. ENZI, Republican, of Gillette, WY; born in Bremerton, WA, February 1, 1944; education: B.A., accounting, George Washington University, 1966; M.B.A., Denver University, 1968; professional: served in Wyoming National Guard, 1967–73; accounting manager and computer programmer, Dunbar Well Service, 1985–97; director, Black Hills Corporation, a New York Stock Exchange company, 1992–96; member, founding board of directors, First Wyoming Bank of Gillette, 1978–88; owner, with wife, of NZ Shoes; served in Wyoming House of Representatives, 1987–91, and in Wyoming State Senate, 1991–96; Mayor of Gillette, 1975–82; commissioner, Western Interstate Commission for Higher Education, 1995–96; served on the Education Commission of the States, 1989–93; president, Wyoming Association of Municipalities, 1980–82; president, Wyoming Jaycees, 1973–74; member: Lions Club; elder, Presbyterian Church; Eagle Scout; married: Diana Buckley, 1969; children: Amy, Brad, and Emily; committees: chair, Budget; Finance; Health, Education, Labor, and Pensions; Homeland Security and Governmental Affairs; Small Business and Entrepreneurship; elected to the U.S. Senate in November, 1996; reelected to each succeeding Senate term.

Office Listings

http://enzi.senate.gov   https://www.facebook.com/mikeenzi
https://twitter.com/senatorenzi

379–A Russell Senate Office Building, Washington, DC 20510	(202) 224–3424
Chief of Staff.—Flip McConnaughey.	FAX: 228–0359
Legislative Director.—Tara Shaw.	
Press Secretary.—Max D'Onofrio.	
Office Manager.—Christen Thompson.	
Federal Center, Suite 2007, 2120 Capitol Avenue, Cheyenne, WY 82001.	(307) 772–2477
400 South Kendrick, Suite 303, Gillette, WY 82716	(307) 682–6268
100 East B Street, Room 3201, P.O. Box 33201, Casper, WY 82602	(307) 261–6572
P.O. Box 12470, Jackson, WY 83002	(307) 739–9507
1285 Sheridan Avenue, Suite 210, Cody, WY 82414	(307) 527–9444

* * *

JOHN BARRASSO, Republican, of Casper, WY; born in Reading, PA, July 21, 1952; education: B.S., Georgetown University, Washington, DC, 1974; M.D., Georgetown University, Washington, DC, 1978; professional: Casper Orthopaedic Associates, 1983–2007; Chief of Staff, Wyoming Medical Center, 2003–05; President, Wyoming Medical Society; President, National Association of Physician Broadcasters, 1988–89; member, Wyoming State Senate, 2002–06; wife: Bobbi; children: Peter, Emma and Hadley; committees: chair, Indian Affairs; Energy and Natural Resources; Environment and Public Works; Foreign Relations; appointed to the United States Senate on June 22, 2007, sworn in by Vice President Cheney on June 25, 2007 to the 110th Congress to fill the vacancy caused by the death of Senator Craig Thomas; elected to the U.S. Senate on November 4, 2008; reelected to the 113th Congress for a full Senate term on November 6, 2012.

Office Listings

http://barrasso.senate.gov   www.facebook.com/johnbarrasso   www.twitter.com/senjohnbarrasso

307 Dirksen Senate Office Building, Washington, DC 20510	(202) 224–6441
Chief of Staff.—Dan Kunsman.	FAX: 224–1724
Legislative Director.—Bryn Stewart.	
Communications Director.—Emily Lawrimore.	
Office Manager.—Amber Moyerman.	
100 East B Street, Suite 2201, Casper, WY 82602	(307) 261–6413
	FAX: 265–6706
2120 Capitol Avenue, Suite 2013, Cheyenne, WY 82001	(307) 772–2451
	FAX: 638–3512
324 East Washington Avenue, Riverton, WY 82501	(307) 856–6642
	FAX: 856–5901
1575 Dewar Drive, Suite 218, Rock Springs, WY 82901	(307) 362–5012
	FAX: 362–5129
2 North Main Street, Suite 206, Sheridan, WY 82801	(307) 672–6456
	FAX: 672–8227

REPRESENTATIVE

AT LARGE

CYNTHIA M. LUMMIS, Republican, of Cheyenne, WY; born in Cheyenne, September 10, 1954; education: graduated, B.S., animal science, University of Wyoming, 1976; B.S., biology, University of Wyoming, 1978; J.D., University of Wyoming, 1985; professional: Attorney at Law, 1986–present; rancher, 1976–present; Representative, Wyoming State House of Representatives, 1979–82; clerk, Wyoming Supreme Court, 1985; Representative, Wyoming State House of Representatives, 1985–93; Senator, Wyoming State Legislature, 1993–94; Interim Director of State Lands, State of Wyoming, 1997–98; General Counsel, Office of the Governor, 1995–97; State Treasurer, State of Wyoming, 1998–2006; chair, Western State Treasurer's Association; Advisory Board, Center for the Rocky Mountain West at the University of Montana; Board Member, American Women's Financial Education Foundation; Director, Cheyenne Frontier Days; member, Cheyenne's Vision 2020; member, Laramie Foundation and its Wyoming Women's History House; member, Leadership Wyoming Board; Advisory Board, Ruckelshaus Institute for Environment and Natural Resources at the University of Wyoming; member, Trinity Lutheran Church; member, Wyoming Business Alliance; member, Wyoming Stock Growers Agricultural Land Trust; married: Al Wiederspahn; children: Annaliese; committees: Natural Resources; Oversight and Government Reform; elected to the 111th Congress on November 4, 2008; reelected to each succeeding Congress.

Office Listings

http://lummis.house.gov　　　https://twitter.com/cynthialummis
https://www.facebook.com/pages/cynthia-lummis/152754318103332

2433 Rayburn House Office Building, Washington, DC 20515	(202) 225–2311
Chief of Staff.—Tom Wiblemo.	FAX: 225–3057
Legislative Director.—Landon Stropko.	
Press Secretary.—Joe Spiering.	
100 East B Street, Suite 4003, Casper, WY 82602	(307) 261–6595
District Representative.—Jackie King.	
8005 Capitol Avenue, Suite 2015, Cheyenne, WY 82001	(307) 772–2595
Chief of Staff.—Tucker Fagan.	FAX: 772–2597
Scheduler.—Christie Clark.	
District Representative.—Nancy Prosser.	
45 East Loucks, Suite 300F, Sheridan, WY 82801	(307) 673–4608
District Representative.—Matt Jones.	FAX: 673–4982

Population (2010), 563,626.

ZIP Codes: 82001, 82003, 82005–10, 82050–55, 82058–61, 82063, 82070–73, 82081–84, 82190, 82201, 82210, 82212–15, 82217–19, 82221–25, 82227, 82229, 82240, 82242–44, 82301, 82310, 82321–25, 82327, 82329, 82331–32, 82334–36, 82401, 82410–12, 82414, 82420–23, 82426, 82428, 82430–35, 82440–43, 82450, 82501, 82510, 82512–16, 82520, 82523–24, 82601–02, 82604–05, 82609, 82615, 82620, 82630, 82633, 82635–40, 82642–44, 82646, 82648–49, 82701, 82710–12, 82714–18, 82720–21, 82723, 82725, 82727, 82729–32, 82801, 82831–40, 82842, 82844–45, 82901–02, 82922–23, 82925, 82929–39, 82941–45, 83001–02, 83011–14, 83025, 83101, 83110–16, 83118–24, 83126–28

AMERICAN SAMOA

(Population 2010, 67,380)

DELEGATE

AUMUA AMATA COLEMAN RADEWAGEN, Republican, of Pago Pago, AS; born in Washington, DC, December 29, 1947; holds the orator (talking chief) title of Aumua from the village of Pago Pago, AS; education: graduate of Sacred Hearts High School in Hawaii; B.A., from University of Guam; professional: executive assistant to the first Delegate-at-Large to Washington from American Samoa; scheduling director for U.S. House of Representatives Majority Leadership for eight years; scheduling director to U.S. Representative Philip Crane of Illinois; appointed by President George W. Bush in 2001 as a White House Commissioner for Asian Americans and Pacific Islanders (AAPI), chairman of the Community Security Committee; member: American Council of Young Political Leaders, 1986; ACYPL Alumni Council in 1987; Business and Professional Women and board member of Goodwill Industries; Field House 100 American Samoa, a non-profit organization devoted to finding athletic scholarships for high school athletes in American Samoa; spokesperson for the Samoan Women's Health Project; liaison to the National Breast Cancer Coalition since 1993; married: Fred Radewagen; three children and two grandchildren; committees: Natural Resources; Small Business; Veterans' Affairs; elected to the 114th Congress on November 4, 2014.

Office Listings

https://radewagen.house.gov   https://twitter.com/repamata
https://www.facebook.com/congresswomanaumuaamata

1339 Longworth House Office building, Washington, DC 20515	(202) 225-8577
Chief of Staff.—Leafaina O. Yahn.	FAX: 225-8757
Scheduler / Office Manager.—Angie Borja.	
Legislative Director.—Casey Brinck.	
P.O. 5859, Pago Pago, AS 96799	(684) 633-3601

ZIP Codes: 96799

* * *

DISTRICT OF COLUMBIA

(Population 2010, 601,723)

DELEGATE

ELEANOR HOLMES NORTON, Democrat, of Washington, DC; born in Washington, DC, June 13, 1937; education: graduated, Dunbar High School, 1955; B.A., Antioch College, 1960; M.A., Yale Graduate School, 1963; J.D., Yale Law School, 1964; honorary degrees: Cedar Crest College, 1969; Bard College, 1971; Princeton University, 1973; Marymount College, 1974; City College of New York, 1975; Georgetown University, 1977; New York University, 1978; Howard University, 1978; Brown University, 1978; Wilberforce University, 1978; Wayne State University, 1980; Gallaudet College, 1980; Denison University, 1980; Syracuse University, 1981; Yeshiva University, 1981; Lawrence University, 1981; Emanuel College, 1981; Spelman College, 1982; University of Massachusetts, 1983; Smith College, 1983; Medical College of Pennsylvania, 1983; Tufts University, 1984; Bowdoin College, 1985; Antioch College, 1985; Haverford College, 1986; Lesley College, 1986; New Haven University, 1986; University of San Diego, 1986; Sojourner-Douglas College, 1987; Salem State College, 1987; Rutgers University, 1988; St. Joseph's College, 1988; University of Lowell, 1988; Colgate University, 1989; Drury College, 1989; Florida International University, 1989; St. Lawrence University, 1989; University of Wisconsin, 1989; University of Hartford, 1990; Ohio Wesleyan University, 1990; Wake Forest University, 1990; Fisk University, 1991; Tougalvo University, 1992; University of Southern Connecticut, 1992; professional: professor of law, Georgetown University, 1982–90; past / present member: chair, New York Commission on Human Rights, 1970–76; chair, Equal Employment Opportunity Commission, 1977–81; Community Foundation of Greater Washington, board; Yale Corporation, 1982–88; trustee, Rockefeller Foundation, 1982–90; executive assistant to the mayor of New York City (concurrent appointment); law clerk, Judge A. Leon Higginbotham, Federal District Court, 3rd Circuit; attorney, admitted to practice by examination in the District of Columbia, Pennsylvania and in the U.S. Supreme Court; Council on

Foreign Relations; Overseas Development Council; U.S. Committee to Monitor the Helsinki Accords; Carter Center, Atlanta, Georgia; boards of Martin Luther King, Jr. Center for Social Change and Environmental Law Institute; Workplace Health Fund; honors awards: Harper Fellow, Yale Law School, 1976, (for "a person . . . who has made a distinguished contribution to the public life of the nation . . ."); Yale Law School Association Citation of Merit Medal to the Outstanding Alumnus of the Law School, 1980; Chancellor's Distinguished Lecturer, University of California Law School (Boalt Hall), Berkeley, 1981; Visiting Fellow, Harvard University, John F. Kennedy School of Government, spring 1984; Visiting Phi Beta Kappa Scholar, 1985; Distinguished Public Service Award, Center for National Policy, 1985; Ralph E. Shikes Bicentennial Fellow, Harvard Law School, 1987; One Hundred Most Important Women (*Ladies Home Journal*, 1988); One Hundred Most Powerful Women in Washington (The *Washingtonian* magazine, September 1989); divorced; two children: John and Katherine; committees: Oversight and Government Reform; Transportation and Infrastructure; elected to the 102nd Congress on November 6, 1990; reelected to each succeeding Congress.

Office Listings

http://www.norton.house.gov   https://twitter.com/eleanornorton
https://www.facebook.com/congresswomannorton

2136 Rayburn House Office Building, Washington, DC 20515 .... (202) 225–8050
    Chief of Staff.—Raven Reeder.   FAX: 225–3002
    Legislative Director.—Bradley Truding.
    Communications Director.—Benjamin Fritsch.

ZIP Codes: 20001–13, 20015–20, 20024, 20026–27, 20029–30, 20032–33, 20035 45, 20047, 20049–53, 20055–71, 20073 77, 20080, 20088, 20090–91, 20099, 20201–04, 20206–08, 20210–13, 20215–24, 20226–33, 20235, 20237, 20239–42, 20244–45, 20250, 20254, 20260, 20268, 20270, 20277, 20289, 20301, 20303, 20306–07, 20310, 20314–15, 20317–19, 20330, 20340, 20350, 20370, 20372–76, 20380, 20388–95, 20398, 20401–16, 20418–29, 20431, 20433–37, 20439–42, 20444, 20447, 20451, 20453, 20456, 20460, 20463, 20469, 20472, 20500, 20503–10, 20515, 20520–27, 20530–36, 20538–44, 20546–49, 20551–55, 20557, 20559–60, 20565–66, 20570 73, 20575–77, 20579–81, 20585–86, 20590 91, 20593–94, 20597, 20599

* * *

GUAM

(Population 2010, 159,358)

DELEGATE

MADELEINE Z. BORDALLO, Democrat, of Tamuning, Guam, born on May 31, 1933; education: associate degree in music, St. Catherine's College, St. Paul, MN, 1953; professional: First Lady of Guam, 1975–78, and 1983–86; Guam Senator, 1981–82, and 1987–94 (five terms); Lt. Governor of Guam, 1995–2002 (two terms); National Committee Chair for the National Democratic Party, 1964–2004; family: Ricardo J. Bordallo (deceased); daughter, Deborah; granddaughter, Nicole; committees: Armed Services; Natural Resources; elected to the 108th Congress on November 5, 2002; reelected to each succeeding Congress.

Office Listings

http://www.bordallo.house.gov   https://www.facebook.com/madeleine.bordallo

2441 Rayburn House Office Building, Washington, DC 20515 .... (202) 225–1188
    Chief of Staff.—John Whitt.   FAX: 226–0341
    Legislative Director.—Matthew Herrmann.
    Communications Director.—Adam Carbullido.
    Scheduler.—Rosanne Meno.
120 Father Duenas Avenue, Suite 107, Hagåtña, GU 96910 .... (671) 477–4272

ZIP Codes: 96910, 96912–13, 96915–17, 96919, 96921, 96923, 96926, 96928–29, 96931–32

NORTHERN MARIANA ISLANDS

(Population 2010, 53,883)

DELEGATE

GREGORIO KILILI CAMACHO SABLAN, Independent, of Saipan, MP; born in Saipan, MP, January 19, 1955; education: University of Hawaii, Manoa Honolulu, HI; 1989–90; professional: member, Northern Mariana Islands Commonwealth Legislature, 1982–86 (2 terms); special assistant to Senator Daniel Inouye; special assistant to Northern Mariana Islands Governor Pedro P. Tenorio; Executive Director of the Commonwealth Election Commission; family: married Andrea C. Sablan, son Jesse, daughters Sharlene, Barbara Jean, Diane, Patricia and Madonna; caucuses: Congressional Asian Pacific American Caucus; Congressional Hispanic Caucus; American Citizens Abroad Caucus; Bi-Partisan Disabilities Caucus; Democratic Caucus; Community College Caucus; National Marine Sanctuary Caucus; Friends of New Zealand Caucus; International Conservation Caucus; committees: Education and the Workforce; Natural Resources; elected to the 111th Congress on November 4, 2008; reelected to each succeeding Congress.

Office Listings

http://www.sablan.house.gov
https://www.facebook.com/pages/gregorio-kilili-camacho-sablan/153423912663

423 Cannon House Office Building, Washington, DC 20515	(202) 225–2646
Chief of Staff.—Robert J. Schwalbach.	FAX: 226–4249
Scheduler.—Agnes Cornibert.	
JCT II Building, Susupe, P.O. Box 504879, Saipan, MP 96950	(670) 323–2647
Dolores Plaza Building, Songsong, P.O. Box 1361, Rota, MP 96951	(670) 532–2647
Villagomez Ent. Building, San Jose, P.O. Box 520394, Tinian, MP 96952	(670) 433–2647
District Officer Director.—Mike Tenorio.	FAX: 323–2649

ZIP Codes: 96950–52

* * *

PUERTO RICO

(Population 2010, 3,725,789)

RESIDENT COMMISSIONER

PEDRO R. PIERLUISI, Democrat, of Guaynabo, PR; born in San Juan, PR, April 26, 1959; education: contemporary U.S. history, Tulane University, New Orleans, LA, 1981; Juris Doctor, George Washington University, Washington, DC, 1984; professional: Verner & Lipfert Assoc., Washington, DC, 1984–85; Cole, Corette & Abrutyn, Washington, DC, 1985–88; Pierluisi & Pierluisi, San Juan, PR, 1990–92; Attorney General of Puerto Rico, 1993–96; O'Neill & Borges, San Juan, PR, 1997–2007; religion: Catholic; married: Maria Elena Carrión; family: four children; committees: Judiciary; Natural Resources; elected to the 111th Congress on November 4, 2008; reelected to each succeeding Congress.

Office Listings

http://www.pierluisi.house.gov

2410 Rayburn House Office Building, Washington, DC 20515	(202) 225–2615
Chief of Staff.—Carmen M. Feliciano.	FAX: 225–2154
Communications Director.—Dennise Pérez.	
Scheduler.—Frances Agosto.	
Legislative Director.—John Laufer.	
Senior Legislative Adviser.—Jed Bullock.	
Legislative Assistant.—George Laws.	
Staff Assistant.—Natalia Gandía.	
157 Avenida de la Constitución Antiguo Edificio de Medicina Tropical, Ala de la Enfermería 2ndo Piso, San Juan, PR 00901	(787) 723–6333

Office Listings—Continued

District Office Director.—Rosemarie "Maí" Vizcarrondo.   FAX: 729–7738
Deputy District Office Director.—Maria Cristina Figueroa.
Office Manager.—Aimée Irlanda.
Constituent Liaison.—Rosario Toro.
Press Aides: Marlena Riccio, Mariana Rodríguez.
Staff Assistant.—Michelle Manzano.
Senior Case Worker.—Luis Ortiz.
Social Security Case Worker.—Cristina Sierra.
Veteran's Case Worker.—Jorge Mas.
Field Representative.—Eduardo Hilera.

ZIP Codes: 00601–06, 00610–14, 00616–17, 00622–24, 00627, 00631, 00636–38, 00641, 00646–47, 00650, 00652–53, 00656, 00659–60, 00662, 00664, 00667, 00669–70, 00674, 00676–78, 00680–83, 00685, 00687–88, 00690, 00692, 00693–94, 00698, 00703–05, 00707, 00714–21, 00723, 00725–42, 00744–45, 00751, 00754, 00757, 00765–67, 00769, 00771–73, 00775, 00777–78, 00780, 00782–86, 00791–92, 00794–95, 00901–02, 00906–31, 00933–37, 00939–40, 00949–63, 00965–66, 00968–71, 00975–79, 00981–88

* * *

VIRGIN ISLANDS

(Population 2010, 106,405)

DELEGATE

STACEY PLASKETT, Democrat, of St. Croix, VI; born in New York, NY, May 13, 1966; B.S.F.S, Georgetown University, Washington, DC, 1988; J.D., American University School of Law, Washington, DC, 1994; professional: Bronx Assistant District Attorney, Counsel on U.S. House of Representatives' Committee on Ethics, Senior Counsel to the Deputy Attorney General at U.S. Justice Department, Deputy General Counsel at United Health Group; General Counsel Virgin Islands Economic Development Authority; family: spouse, Jonathan Buckney-Small; children: Jeremiah, Christian, Ariel, Israel Duffy, and Taliah Buckney-Small; caucuses: Congressional Black Caucus; Congressional Women's Caucus; Congressional Caribbean Caucus; Congressional Caucus on Public-Private Partnerships; Congressional Coastal Communities Caucus; Congressional Historically Black Colleges and Universities (HBCU) Caucus; Congressional Liquefied Natural Gas (LNG) Export Caucus; House National Guard and Reserve Components Caucus; committees: Agriculture; Oversight and Government Reform; elected to the 114th Congress on November 4, 2014.

Office Listings

https://plaskett.house.gov

509 Canon House Office Building, Washington, DC 20515 .... (202) 225–1790
    Chief of Staff.—Delmin Jerry Garcia.   FAX: 225–5517
    Executive Assistant / Scheduler.—Dorene Browne Louis.
    District Director.—Elizabeth Centeno.
60 King Street, Frederiksted, St. Croix, VI 00840 .... (340) 778–5900
    Case Worker / Field Representative.—Cletis Clendenin.
9100 Port of Sale, St. Thomas, VI 00803 .... (340) 774–4408

ZIP Codes: 00801–05, 00820–24, 00830–31, 00840–41, 00850–51

STATE DELEGATIONS

Number before names designates Congressional district. Senate and House Republicans in roman; Senate and House Democrats in *italic*; Independents in SMALL CAPS; Resident Commissioner and Delegates in **boldface**.

ALABAMA

SENATORS
Richard C. Shelby
Jeff Sessions

REPRESENTATIVES
[Republicans 6, Democrat 1]
1. Bradley Byrne
2. Martha Roby
3. Mike Rogers
4. Robert B. Aderholt
5. Mo Brooks
6. Gary J. Palmer
7. *Terri A. Sewell*

ALASKA

SENATORS
Lisa Murkowski
Dan Sullivan

REPRESENTATIVE
[Republican 1]
At Large - Don Young

ARIZONA

SENATORS
John McCain
Jeff Flake

REPRESENTATIVES
[Republicans 5, Democrats 4]
1. *Ann Kirkpatrick*
2. Martha McSally
3. *Raúl M. Grijalva*
4. Paul A. Gosar
5. Matt Salmon
6. David Schweikert
7. *Ruben Gallego*
8. Trent Franks
9. *Kyrsten Sinema*

ARKANSAS

SENATORS
John Boozman
Tom Cotton

REPRESENTATIVES
[Republicans 4]
1. Eric A. "Rick" Crawford
2. J. French Hill
3. Steve Womack
4. Bruce Westerman

CALIFORNIA

SENATORS
Dianne Feinstein
Barbara Boxer

REPRESENTATIVES
[Republicans 14, Democrats 39]
1. Doug LaMalfa
2. *Jared Huffman*
3. *John Garamendi*
4. Tom McClintock
5. *Mike Thompson*

6. *Doris O. Matsui*
7. *Ami Bera*
8. Paul Cook
9. *Jerry McNerney*
10. Jeff Denham
11. *Mark DeSaulnier*
12. *Nancy Pelosi*
13. *Barbara Lee*
14. *Jackie Speier*
15. *Eric Swalwell*
16. *Jim Costa*
17. *Michael M. Honda*
18. *Anna G. Eshoo*
19. *Zoe Lofgren*
20. *Sam Farr*
21. David G. Valadao
22. Devin Nunes
23. Kevin McCarthy
24. *Lois Capps*
25. Stephen Knight
26. *Julia Brownley*
27. *Judy Chu*
28. *Adam B. Schiff*
29. *Tony Cárdenas*

30. *Brad Sherman*
31. *Pete Aguilar*
32. *Grace F. Napolitano*
33. *Ted Lieu*
34. *Xavier Becerra*
35. *Norma J. Torres*
36. *Raul Ruiz*
37. *Karen Bass*
38. *Linda T. Sánchez*
39. Edward R. Royce
40. *Lucille Roybal-Allard*
41. *Mark Takano*
42. Ken Calvert
43. *Maxine Waters*
44. *Janice Hahn*
45. Mimi Walters
46. *Loretta Sanchez*
47. *Alan S. Lowenthal*
48. Dana Rohrabacher
49. Darrell E. Issa
50. Duncan Hunter
51. *Juan Vargas*
52. *Scott H. Peters*
53. *Susan A. Davis*

COLORADO

SENATORS
Michael F. Bennet
Cory Gardner

REPRESENTATIVES
[Republicans 4, Democrats 3]
1. *Diana DeGette*

2. *Jared Polis*
3. Scott R. Tipton
4. Ken Buck
5. Doug Lamborn
6. Mike Coffman
7. *Ed Perlmutter*

CONNECTICUT

SENATORS
Richard Blumenthal
Christopher Murphy

REPRESENTATIVES
[Democrats 5]
1. *John B. Larson*

2. *Joe Courtney*
3. *Rosa L. DeLauro*
4. *James A. Himes*
5. *Elizabeth H. Esty*

DELAWARE

SENATORS
Thomas R. Carper
Christopher A. Coons

REPRESENTATIVE
[Democrat 1]
At Large - *John C. Carney, Jr.*

FLORIDA

SENATORS
Bill Nelson
Marco Rubio

REPRESENTATIVES
[Republicans 17, Democrats 10]
1. Jeff Miller
2. *Gwen Graham*
3. Ted S. Yoho

4. Ander Crenshaw
5. *Corrine Brown*
6. Ron DeSantis
7. John L. Mica
8. Bill Posey
9. *Alan Grayson*
10. Daniel Webster
11. Richard B. Nugent
12. Gus M. Bilirakis

13. David W. Jolly
14. *Kathy Castor*
15. Dennis A. Ross
16. Vern Buchanan
17. Thomas J. Rooney
18. *Patrick Murphy*
19. Curt Clawson
20. *Alcee L. Hastings*

21. *Theodore E. Deutch*
22. *Lois Frankel*
23. *Debbie Wasserman Schultz*
24. *Frederica S. Wilson*
25. Mario Diaz-Balart
26. Carlos Curbelo
27. Ileana Ros-Lehtinen

GEORGIA

SENATORS
Johnny Isakson
David Perdue

REPRESENTATIVES
[Republicans 10, Democrats 4]
1. Earl L. "Buddy" Carter
2. *Sanford D. Bishop, Jr.*
3. Lynn A. Westmoreland
4. *Henry C. "Hank" Johnson, Jr.*

5. *John Lewis*
6. Tom Price
7. Rob Woodall
8. Austin Scott
9. Doug Collins
10. Jody B. Hice
11. Barry Loudermilk
12. Rick W. Allen
13. *David Scott*
14. Tom Graves

HAWAII

SENATORS
Brian Schatz
Mazie K. Hirono

REPRESENTATIVES
[Democrats 2]

1. *Mark Takai*
2. *Tulsi Gabbard*

IDAHO

SENATORS
Mike Crapo
James E. Risch

REPRESENTATIVES
[Republicans 2]

1. Raúl R. Labrador
2. Michael K. Simpson

ILLINOIS

SENATORS
Richard J. Durbin
Mark Kirk

REPRESENTATIVES
[Republicans 7, Democrats 11]

1. *Bobby L. Rush*
2. *Robin L. Kelly*
3. *Daniel Lipinski*
4. *Luis V. Gutiérrez*
5. *Mike Quigley*
6. Peter J. Roskam
7. *Danny K. Davis*

8. *Tammy Duckworth*
9. *Janice D. Schakowsky*
10. Robert J. Dold
11. *Bill Foster*
12. *Mike Bost*
13. Rodney Davis
14. Randy Hultgren
15. John Shimkus
16. Adam Kinzinger
17. *Cheri Bustos*
18. Darin LaHood

INDIANA

SENATORS
Daniel Coats
Joe Donnelly

REPRESENTATIVES
[Republicans 7, Democrats 2]

1. *Peter J. Visclosky*
2. Jackie Walorski

3. Marlin A. Stutzman
4. Todd Rokita
5. Susan W. Brooks
6. Luke Messer
7. *André Carson*
8. Larry Bucshon
9. Todd C. Young

IOWA

SENATORS
Chuck Grassley
Joni Ernst

REPRESENTATIVES
[Republicans 3, Democrat 1]
1. *Rod Blum*
2. *David Loebsack*
3. David Young
4. Steve King

KANSAS

SENATORS
Pat Roberts
Jerry Moran

REPRESENTATIVES
[Republicans 4]
1. Tim Huelskamp
2. Lynn Jenkins
3. Kevin Yoder
4. Mike Pompeo

KENTUCKY

SENATORS
Mitch McConnell
Rand Paul

REPRESENTATIVES
[Republicans 5, Democrat 1]
1. Ed Whitfield

2. Brett Guthrie
3. *John A. Yarmuth*
4. Thomas Massie
5. Harold Rogers
6. Andy Barr

LOUISIANA

SENATORS
David Vitter
Bill Cassidy

REPRESENTATIVES
[Republicans 5, Democrat 1]
1. Steve Scalise

2. *Cedric L. Richmond*
3. Charles W. Boustany, Jr.
4. John Fleming
5. Ralph Lee Abraham
6. Garret Graves

MAINE

SENATORS
Susan M. Collins
ANGUS S. KING, JR.*

REPRESENTATIVES
[Republican 1, Democrat 1]
1. *Chellie Pingree*
2. Bruce Poliquin

MARYLAND

SENATORS
Barbara A. Mikulski
Benjamin L. Cardin

REPRESENTATIVES
[Republican 1, Democrats 7]
1. Andy Harris
2. *C. A. Dutch Ruppersberger*

3. *John P. Sarbanes*
4. *Donna F. Edwards*
5. *Steny H. Hoyer*
6. *John K. Delaney*
7. *Elijah E. Cummings*
8. *Chris Van Hollen*

MASSACHUSETTS

SENATORS
Elizabeth Warren
Edward J. Markey

REPRESENTATIVES
[Democrats 9]
1. *Richard E. Neal*
2. *James P. McGovern*
3. *Niki Tsongas*
4. *Joseph P. Kennedy III*
5. *Katherine M. Clark*
6. *Seth Moulton*
7. *Michael E. Capuano*
8. *Stephen F. Lynch*
9. *William R. Keating*

MICHIGAN

SENATORS
Debbie Stabenow
Gary C. Peters

REPRESENTATIVES
[Republicans 9, Democrats 5]
1. Dan Benishek
2. Bill Huizenga
3. Justin Amash
4. John R. Moolenaar
5. *Daniel T. Kildee*
6. Fred Upton
7. Tim Walberg
8. Mike Bishop
9. *Sander M. Levin*
10. Candice S. Miller
11. David A. Trott
12. *Debbie Dingell*
13. *John Conyers, Jr.*
14. *Brenda L. Lawrence*

MINNESOTA

SENATORS
Amy Klobuchar
Al Franken

REPRESENTATIVES
[Republicans 3, Democrats 5]
1. *Timothy J. Walz*
2. John Kline
3. Erik Paulsen
4. *Betty McCollum*
5. *Keith Ellison*
6. Tom Emmer
7. *Collin C. Peterson*
8. *Richard M. Nolan*

MISSISSIPPI

SENATORS
Thad Cochran
Roger F. Wicker

REPRESENTATIVES
[Republicans 3, Democrat 1]
1. Trent Kelly
2. *Bennie G. Thompson*
3. Gregg Harper
4. Steven M. Palazzo

MISSOURI

SENATORS
Claire McCaskill
Roy Blunt

REPRESENTATIVES
[Republicans 6, Democrats 2]
1. *Wm. Lacy Clay*
2. Ann Wagner
3. Blaine Luetkemeyer
4. Vicky Hartzler
5. *Emanuel Cleaver*
6. Sam Graves
7. Billy Long
8. Jason Smith

MONTANA

SENATORS
Jon Tester
Steve Daines

REPRESENTATIVE
[Republican 1]
At Large - Ryan K. Zinke

NEBRASKA

SENATORS
Deb Fischer
Ben Sasse

REPRESENTATIVES
[Republicans 2, Democrat 1]
1. Jeff Fortenberry
2. *Brad Ashford*
3. Adrian Smith

NEVADA

SENATORS
Harry Reid
Dean Heller

REPRESENTATIVES
[Republicans 3, Democrat 1]
1. *Dina Titus*
2. Mark E. Amodei
3. Joseph J. Heck
4. Cresent Hardy

NEW HAMPSHIRE

SENATORS
Jeanne Shaheen
Kelly Ayotte

REPRESENTATIVES
[Republican 1, Democrat 1]
1. Frank C. Guinta
2. *Ann M. Kuster*

NEW JERSEY

SENATORS
Robert Menendez
Cory A. Booker

REPRESENTATIVES
[Republicans 6, Democrats 6]
1. *Donald Norcross*
2. Frank A. LoBiondo
3. Thomas MacArthur
4. Christopher H. Smith
5. Scott Garrett

6. *Frank Pallone, Jr.*
7. Leonard Lance
8. *Albio Sires*
9. *Bill Pascrell, Jr.*
10. *Donald M. Payne, Jr.*
11. Rodney P. Frelinghuysen
12. *Bonnie Watson Coleman*

NEW MEXICO

SENATORS
Tom Udall
Martin Heinrich

REPRESENTATIVES
[Republican 1, Democrats 2]
1. *Michelle Lujan Grisham*
2. Stevan Pearce
3. *Ben Ray Luján*

NEW YORK

SENATORS
Charles E. Schumer
Kirsten E. Gillibrand

REPRESENTATIVES
[Republicans 9, Democrats 18]
1. Lee M. Zeldin
2. Peter T. King

3. *Steve Israel*
4. *Kathleen M. Rice*
5. *Gregory W. Meeks*
6. *Grace Meng*
7. *Nydia M. Velázquez*
8. *Hakeem S. Jeffries*
9. *Yvette D. Clarke*
10. *Jerrold Nadler*

11. Daniel M. Donovan, Jr.
12. *Carolyn B. Maloney*
13. *Charles B. Rangel*
14. *Joseph Crowley*
15. *José E. Serrano*
16. *Eliot L. Engel*
17. *Nita M. Lowey*
18. *Sean Patrick Maloney*
19. Christopher P. Gibson

20. *Paul Tonko*
21. Elise M. Stefanik
22. Richard L. Hanna
23. Tom Reed
24. John Katko
25. *Louise McIntosh Slaughter*
26. *Brian Higgins*
27. Chris Collins

NORTH CAROLINA

SENATORS
Richard Burr
Thom Tillis

REPRESENTATIVES
[Republicans 10, Democrats 3]
1. *G. K. Butterfield*
2. Renee L. Ellmers
3. Walter B. Jones
4. *David E. Price*

5. Virginia Foxx
6. Mark Walker
7. David Rouzer
8. Richard Hudson
9. Robert Pittenger
10. Patrick T. McHenry
11. Mark Meadows
12. *Alma S. Adams*
13. George Holding

NORTH DAKOTA

SENATORS
John Hoeven
Heidi Heitkamp

REPRESENTATIVE
[Republican 1]
At Large - Kevin Cramer

OHIO

SENATORS
Sherrod Brown
Rob Portman

REPRESENTATIVES
[Republicans 12, Democrats 4]
1. Steve Chabot
2. Brad R. Wenstrup
3. *Joyce Beatty*
4. Jim Jordan
5. Robert E. Latta
6. Bill Johnson

7. Bob Gibbs
8. ——[1]
9. *Marcy Kaptur*
10. Michael R. Turner
11. *Marcia L. Fudge*
12. Patrick J. Tiberi
13. *Tim Ryan*
14. David P. Joyce
15. Steve Stivers
16. James B. Renacci

OKLAHOMA

SENATORS
James M. Inhofe
James Lankford

REPRESENTATIVES
[Republicans 5]
1. Jim Bridenstine

2. Markwayne Mullin
3. Frank D. Lucas
4. Tom Cole
5. Steve Russell

OREGON

SENATORS
Ron Wyden
Jeff Merkley

REPRESENTATIVES
[Republican 1, Democrats 4]
1. *Suzanne Bonamici*

2. Greg Walden
3. *Earl Blumenauer*

4. *Peter A. DeFazio*
5. *Kurt Schrader*

PENNSYLVANIA

SENATORS
Robert P. Casey, Jr.
Patrick J. Toomey

REPRESENTATIVES
[Republicans 13, Democrats 5]
1. *Robert A. Brady*
2. *Chaka Fattah*
3. Mike Kelly
4. Scott Perry
5. Glenn Thompson
6. Ryan A. Costello
7. Patrick Meehan

8. Michael G. Fitzpatrick
9. Bill Shuster
10. Tom Marino
11. Lou Barletta
12. Keith J. Rothfus
13. *Brendan F. Boyle*
14. *Michael F. Doyle*
15. Charles W. Dent
16. Joseph R. Pitts
17. *Matt Cartwright*
18. Tim Murphy

RHODE ISLAND

SENATORS
Jack Reed
Sheldon Whitehouse

REPRESENTATIVES
[Democrats 2]
1. *David N. Cicilline*
2. *James R. Langevin*

SOUTH CAROLINA

SENATORS
Lindsey Graham
Tim Scott

REPRESENTATIVES
[Republicans 6, Democrat 1]
1. Mark Sanford

2. Joe Wilson
3. Jeff Duncan
4. Trey Gowdy
5. Mick Mulvaney
6. *James E. Clyburn*
7. Tom Rice

SOUTH DAKOTA

SENATORS
John Thune
Mike Rounds

REPRESENTATIVE
[Republican 1]
At Large - Kristi L. Noem

TENNESSEE

SENATORS
Lamar Alexander
Bob Corker

REPRESENTATIVES
[Republicans 7, Democrats 2]
1. David P. Roe
2. John J. Duncan, Jr.

3. Charles J. "Chuck" Fleischmann
4. Scott DesJarlais
5. *Jim Cooper*
6. Diane Black
7. Marsha Blackburn
8. Stephen Lee Fincher
9. *Steve Cohen*

TEXAS

SENATORS
John Cornyn
Ted Cruz

REPRESENTATIVES
[Republicans 25, Democrats 11]
1. Louie Gohmert
2. Ted Poe
3. Sam Johnson
4. John Ratcliffe
5. Jeb Hensarling
6. Joe Barton
7. John Abney Culberson
8. Kevin Brady
9. *Al Green*
10. Michael T. McCaul
11. K. Michael Conaway
12. Kay Granger
13. Mac Thornberry
14. Randy K. Weber, Sr.
15. *Rubén Hinojosa*

16. *Beto O'Rourke*
17. Bill Flores
18. *Sheila Jackson Lee*
19. Randy Neugebauer
20. *Joaquin Castro*
21. Lamar Smith
22. Pete Olson
23. Will Hurd
24. Kenny Marchant
25. Roger Williams
26. Michael C. Burgess
27. Blake Farenthold
28. *Henry Cuellar*
29. *Gene Green*
30. *Eddie Bernice Johnson*
31. John R. Carter
32. Pete Sessions
33. *Marc A. Veasey*
34. *Filemon Vela*
35. *Lloyd Doggett*
36. Brian Babin

UTAH

SENATORS
Orrin G Hatch
Mike Lee

REPRESENTATIVES
[Republicans 4]
1. Rob Bishop
2. Chris Stewart
3. Jason Chaffetz
4. Mia B. Love

VERMONT

SENATORS
Patrick J. Leahy
BERNARD SANDERS*

REPRESENTATIVE
[Democrat 1]
At Large - *Peter Welch*

VIRGINIA

SENATORS
Mark R. Warner
Tim Kaine

REPRESENTATIVES
[Republicans 8, Democrats 3]
1. Robert J. Wittman
2. E. Scott Rigell
3. *Robert C. "Bobby" Scott*

4 1 Randy Forbes
5. Robert Hurt
6. Bob Goodlatte
7. Dave Brat
8. *Donald S. Beyer, Jr.*
9. H. Morgan Griffith
10. Barbara Comstock
11. *Gerald E. Connolly*

WASHINGTON

SENATORS
Patty Murray
Maria Cantwell

REPRESENTATIVES
[Republicans 4, Democrats 6]
1. *Suzan K. DelBene*
2. *Rick Larsen*

3. Jaime Herrera Beutler
4. Dan Newhouse
5. Cathy McMorris Rodgers
6. *Derek Kilmer*
7. *Jim McDermott*
8. David G. Reichert
9. *Adam Smith*
10. *Denny Heck*

WEST VIRGINIA

SENATORS
Joe Manchin III
Shelley Moore Capito

REPRESENTATIVES
[Republicans 3]
1. David B. McKinley
2. Alexander X. Mooney
3. Evan H. Jenkins

WISCONSIN

SENATORS
Ron Johnson
Tammy Baldwin

REPRESENTATIVES
[Republicans 5, Democrats 3]
1. Paul D. Ryan

2. *Mark Pocan*
3. *Ron Kind*
4. *Gwen Moore*
5. F. James Sensenbrenner, Jr.
6. Glenn Grothman
7. Sean P. Duffy
8. Reid J. Ribble

WYOMING

SENATORS
Michael B. Enzi
John Barrasso

REPRESENTATIVE
[Republican 1]
At Large - Cynthia M. Lummis

AMERICAN SAMOA

DELEGATE
[Republican 1]

Aumua Amata Coleman Radewagen

DISTRICT OF COLUMBIA

DELEGATE
[Democrat 1]

Eleanor Holmes Norton

GUAM

DELEGATE
[Democrat 1]

Madeleine Z. Bordallo

NORTHERN MARIANA ISLANDS

DELEGATE
[Democrat 1]

Gregorio Kilili Camacho Sablan

PUERTO RICO

RESIDENT COMMISSIONER
[Democrat 1]

Pedro R. Pierluisi

VIRGIN ISLANDS

DELEGATE
[Democrat 1]

Stacey E. Plaskett

* Independent.
1 Vacancy due to the resignation of Speaker John Boehner, October 31, 2015.

ALPHABETICAL LIST
SENATORS

Alphabetical list of Senators, Representatives, Delegates, and Resident Commissioner. Republicans in roman (54); Democrats in *italic* (44); Independents in SMALL CAPS (2).

Alexander, Lamar, TN
Ayotte, Kelly, NH
Baldwin, Tammy, WI
Barrasso, John, WY
Bennet, Michael F., CO
Blumenthal, Richard, CT
Blunt, Roy, MO
Booker, Cory A., NJ
Boozman, John, AR
Boxer, Barbara, CA
Brown, Sherrod, OH
Burr, Richard, NC
Cantwell, Maria, WA
Capito, Shelley Moore, WV
Cardin, Benjamin L., MD
Carper, Thomas R., DE
Casey, Robert P., Jr., PA
Cassidy, Bill, LA
Coats, Daniel, IN
Cochran, Thad, MS
Collins, Susan M., ME
Coons, Christopher A., DE
Corker, Bob, TN
Cornyn, John, TX
Cotton, Tom, AR
Crapo, Mike, ID
Cruz, Ted, TX
Daines, Steve, MT
Donnelly, Joe, IN
Durbin, Richard J., IL
Enzi, Michael B., WY
Ernst, Joni, IA
Feinstein, Dianne, CA
Fischer, Deb, NE
Flake, Jeff, AR
Franken, Al, MN
Gardner, Cory, CO
Gillibrand, Kirsten E., NY
Graham, Lindsey, SC
Grassley, Chuck, IA
Hatch, Orrin G., UT
Heinrich, Martin, NM
Heitkamp, Heidi, ND
Heller, Dean, NV
Hirono, Mazie K., HI
Hoeven, John, ND
Inhofe, James M., OK
Isakson, Johnny, GA
Johnson, Ron, WI
Kaine, Tim, VA

KING, ANGUS S., JR., ME
Kirk, Mark, IL
Klobuchar, Amy, MN
Lankford, James, OK
Leahy, Patrick J., VT
Lee, Mike, UT
McCain, John, AZ
McCaskill, Claire, MO
McConnell, Mitch, KY
Manchin, Joe III, WV
Markey, Edward J., MA
Menendez, Robert, NJ
Merkley, Jeff, OR
Mikulski, Barbara A., MD
Moran, Jerry, KS
Murkowski, Lisa, AK
Murphy, Christopher, CT
Murray, Patty, WA
Nelson, Bill, FL
Paul, Rand, KY
Perdue, David, GA
Peters, Gary C., MI
Portman, Rob, OH
Reed, Jack, RI
Reid, Harry, NV
Risch, James E., ID
Roberts, Pat, KS
Rounds, Mike, SD
Rubio, Marco, FL
SANDERS, BERNARD, VT
Sasse, Ben, NE
Schatz, Brian, HI
Schumer, Charles E., NY
Scott, Tim, SC
Sessions, Jeff, AL
Shaheen, Jeanne, NH
Shelby, Richard C., AL
Stabenow, Debbie, MI
Sullivan, Dan, AK
Tester, Jon, MT
Thune, John, SD
Tillis, Thom, NC
Toomey, Patrick J., PA
Udall, Tom, NM
Vitter, David, LA
Warner, Mark R., VA
Warren, Elizabeth, MA
Whitehouse, Sheldon, RI
Wicker, Roger F., MS
Wyden, Ron, OR

315

REPRESENTATIVES, RESIDENT COMMISSIONER, AND DELEGATES

Republicans in roman (247); Democrats in *italic* (188); Resident Commissioner and Delegates in **boldface** (6); total, 441.

Abraham, Ralph Lee, LA (5th)
Adams, Alma S., NC (12th)
Aderholt, Robert B., AL (4th)
Aguilar, Pete, CA (31st)
Allen, Rick W., GA (12th)
Amash, Justin, MI (3d)
Amodei, Mark E., NV (2d)
Ashford, Brad, NE (2d)
Babin, Brian, TX (36th)
Barletta, Lou, PA (11th)
Barr, Andy, KY (6th)
Barton, Joe, TX (6th)
Bass, Karen, CA (37th)
Beatty, Joyce, OH (3d)
Becerra, Xavier, CA (34th)
Benishek, Dan, MI (1st)
Bera, Ami, CA (7th)
Beyer, Donald S., Jr., VA (8th)
Bilirakis, Gus M., FL (12th)
Bishop, Mike, MI (8th)
Bishop, Rob, UT (1st)
Bishop, Sanford D., Jr., GA (2d)
Black, Diane, TN (6th)
Blackburn, Marsha, TN (7th)
Blum, Rod, IA (1st)
Blumenauer, Earl, OR (3d)
Bonamici, Suzanne, OR (1st)
Bost, Mike, IL (12th)
Boustany, Charles W., Jr., LA (3d)
Boyle, Brendan F., PA (13th)
Brady, Kevin, TX (8th)
Brady, Robert A., PA (1st)
Brat, Dave, VA (7th)
Bridenstine, Jim, OK (1st)
Brooks, Mo, AL (5th)
Brooks, Susan W., IN (5th)
Brown, Corrine, FL (5th)
Brownley, Julia, CA (26th)
Buchanan, Vern, FL (16th)
Buck, Ken, CO (4th)
Bucshon, Larry, IN (8th)
Burgess, Michael C., TX (26th)
Bustos, Cheri, IL (17th)
Butterfield, G. K., NC (1st)
Byrne, Bradley, AL (1st)
Calvert, Ken, CA (42d)
Capps, Lois, CA (24th)
Capuano, Michael E., MA (7th)
Cárdenas, Tony, CA (29th)
Carney, John C., Jr., DE (At Large)
Carson, André, IN (7th)
Carter, Earl L. "Buddy", GA (1st)
Carter, John R., TX (31st)
Cartwright, Matt, PA (17th)
Castor, Kathy, FL (14th)
Castro, Joaquin, TX (20th)
Chabot, Steve, OH (1st)
Chaffetz, Jason, UT (3d)
Chu, Judy, CA (27th)

Cicilline, David N., RI (1st)
Clark, Katherine M., MA (5th)
Clarke, Yvette D., NY (9th)
Clawson, Curt, FL (19th)
Clay, Wm. Lacy, MO (1st)
Cleaver, Emanuel, MO (5th)
Clyburn, James E., SC (6th)
Coffman, Mike, CO (6th)
Cohen, Steve, TN (9th)
Cole, Tom, OK (4th)
Collins, Chris, NY (27th)
Collins, Doug, GA (9th)
Comstock, Barbara, VA (10th)
Conaway, K. Michael, TX (11th)
Connolly, Gerald E., VA (11th)
Conyers, John, Jr., MI (13th)
Cook, Paul, CA (8th)
Cooper, Jim, TN (5th)
Costa, Jim, CA (16th)
Costello, Ryan A., PA (6th)
Courtney, Joe, CT (2d)
Cramer, Kevin, ND (At Large)
Crawford, Eric A. "Rick", AR (1st)
Crenshaw, Ander, FL (4th)
Crowley, Joseph, NY (14th)
Cuellar, Henry, TX (28th)
Culberson, John Abney, TX (7th)
Cummings, Elijah E., MD (7th)
Curbelo, Carlos, FL (26th)
Davis, Danny K., IL (7th)
Davis, Rodney, IL (13th)
Davis, Susan A., CA (53d)
DeFazio, Peter A., OR (4th)
DeGette, Diana, CO (1st)
Delaney, John K., MD (6th)
DeLauro, Rosa L., CT (3d)
DelBene, Suzan K., WA (1st)
Denham, Jeff, CA (10th)
Dent, Charles W., PA (15th)
DeSantis, Ron, FL (6th)
DeSaulnier, Mark, CA (11th)
DesJarlais, Scott, TN (4th)
Deutch, Theodore E., FL (21st)
Diaz-Balart, Mario, FL (25th)
Dingell, Debbie, MI (12th)
Doggett, Lloyd, TX (35th)
Dold, Robert J., IL (10th)
Donovan, Daniel M., Jr., NY (11th)
Doyle, Michael F., PA (14th)
Duckworth, Tammy, IL (8th)
Duffy, Sean P., WI (7th)
Duncan, Jeff, SC (3d)
Duncan, John J., Jr., TN (2d)
Edwards, Donna F., MD (4th)
Ellison, Keith, MN (5th)
Ellmers, Renee L., NC (2d)
Emmer, Tom, MN (6th)
Engel, Eliot L., NY (16th)
Eshoo, Anna G., CA (18th)

Esty, Elizabeth H., CT (5th)
Farenthold, Blake, TX (27th)
Farr, Sam, CA (20th)
Fattah, Chaka, PA (2d)
Fincher, Stephen Lee, TN (8th)
Fitzpatrick, Michael G., PA (8th)
Fleischmann, Charles J. "Chuck", TN (3d)
Fleming, John, LA (4th)
Flores, Bill, TX (17th)
Forbes, J. Randy, VA (4th)
Fortenberry, Jeff, NE (1st)
Foster, Bill, IL (11th)
Foxx, Virginia, NC (5th)
Frankel, Lois, FL (22d)
Franks, Trent, AZ (8th)
Frelinghuysen, Rodney P., NJ (11th)
Fudge, Marcia L., OH (11th)
Gabbard, Tulsi, HI (2d)
Gallego, Ruben, AZ (7th)
Garamendi, John, CA (3d)
Garrett, Scott, NJ (5th)
Gibbs, Bob, OH (7th)
Gibson, Christopher P., NY (19th)
Gohmert, Louie, TX (1st)
Goodlatte, Bob, VA (6th)
Gosar, Paul A., AZ (4th)
Gowdy, Trey, SC (4th)
Graham, Gwen, FL (2d)
Granger, Kay, TX (12th)
Graves, Garret, LA (6th)
Graves, Sam, MO (6th)
Graves, Tom, GA (14th)
Grayson, Alan, FL (9th)
Green, Al, TX (9th)
Green, Gene, TX (29th)
Griffith, H. Morgan, VA (9th)
Grijalva, Raúl M., AZ (3d)
Grothman, Glenn, WI (6th)
Guinta, Frank C., NH (1st)
Guthrie, Brett, KY (2d)
Gutiérrez, Luis V., IL (4th)
Hahn, Janice, CA (44th)
Hanna, Richard L., NY (22d)
Hardy, Cresent, NV (4th)
Harper, Gregg, MS (3d)
Harris, Andy, MD (1st)
Hartzler, Vicky, MO (4th)
Hastings, Alcee L., FL (20th)
Heck, Denny, WA (10th)
Heck, Joseph J., NV (3d)
Hensarling, Jeb, TX (5th)
Herrera Beutler, Jaime, WA (3d)
Hice, Jody B., GA (10th)
Higgins, Brian, NY (26th)
Hill, J. French, AR (2d)
Himes, James A., CT (4th)
Hinojosa, Rubén, TX (15th)
Holding, George, NC (13th)
Honda, Michael M., CA (17th)
Hoyer, Steny H., MD (5th)
Hudson, Richard, NC (8th)
Huelskamp, Tim, KS (1st)
Huffman, Jared, CA (2d)
Huizenga, Bill, MI (2d)
Hultgren, Randy, IL (14th)
Hunter, Duncan, CA (50th)

Hurd, Will, TX (23d)
Hurt, Robert, VA (5th)
Israel, Steve, NY (3d)
Issa, Darrell E., CA (49th)
Jackson Lee, Sheila, TX (18th)
Jeffries, Hakeem S., NY (8th)
Jenkins, Evan H., WV (3d)
Jenkins, Lynn, KS (2d)
Johnson, Bill, OH (6th)
Johnson, Eddie Bernice, TX (30th)
Johnson, Henry C. "Hank", Jr., GA (4th)
Johnson, Sam, TX (3d)
Jolly, David W., FL (13th)
Jones, Walter B., NC (3d)
Jordan, Jim, OH (4th)
Joyce, David P., OH (14th)
Kaptur, Marcy, OH (9th)
Katko, John, NY (24th)
Keating, William R., MA (9th)
Kelly, Mike, PA (3d)
Kelly, Robin L., IL (2d)
Kelly, Trent, MS (1st)
Kennedy, Joseph P. III, MA (4th)
Kildee, Daniel T., MI (5th)
Kilmer, Derek, WA (6th)
Kind, Ron, WI (3d)
King, Peter T., NY (2d)
King, Steve, IA (4th)
Kinzinger, Adam, IL (16th)
Kirkpatrick, Ann, AZ (1st)
Kline, John, MN (2d)
Knight, Stephen, CA (25th)
Kuster, Ann M., NH (2d)
Labrador, Raúl R., ID (1st)
LaHood, Darin, IL (18th)
LaMalfa, Doug, CA (1st)
Lamborn, Doug, CO (5th)
Lance, Leonard, NJ (7th)
Langevin, James R., (RI) (2d)
Larsen, Rick, WA (2d)
Larson, John B., CT (1st)
Latta, Robert E., OH (5th)
Lawrence, Brenda L., MI (14th)
Lee, Barbara, CA (13th)
Levin, Sander M., MI (9th)
Lewis, John, GA (5th)
Lieu, Ted, CA (33d)
Lipinski, Daniel, IL (3d)
LoBiondo, Frank A., NJ (2d)
Loebsack, David, IA (2d)
Lofgren, Zoe, CA (19th)
Long, Billy, MO (7th)
Loudermilk, Barry, GA (11th)
Love, Mia B., UT (4th)
Lowenthal, Alan S., CA (47th)
Lowey, Nita M., NY (17th)
Lucas, Frank D., OK (3d)
Luetkemeyer, Blaine, MO (3d)
Luján, Ben Ray, NM (3d)
Lujan Grisham, Michelle, NM (1st)
Lummis, Cynthia M., WY (At Large)
Lynch, Stephen F., MA (8th)
MacArthur, Thomas, NJ (3d)
Maloney, Carolyn B., NY (12th)
Maloney, Sean Patrick, NY (18th)
Marchant, Kenny, TX (24th)

Marino, Tom, PA (10th)
Massie, Thomas, KY (4th)
Matsui, Doris O., CA (6th)
McCarthy, Kevin, CA (23d)
McCaul, Michael T., TX (10th)
McClintock, Tom, CA (4th)
McCollum, Betty, MN (4th)
McDermott, Jim, WA (7th)
McGovern, James P., MA (2d)
McHenry, Patrick T., NC (10th)
McKinley, David B., WV (1st)
McMorris Rodgers, Cathy, WA (5th)
McNerney, Jerry, CA (9th)
McSally, Martha, AZ (2d)
Meadows, Mark, NC (11th)
Meehan, Patrick, PA (7th)
Meeks, Gregory W., NY (5th)
Meng, Grace, NY (6th)
Messer, Luke, IN (6th)
Mica, John L., FL (7th)
Miller, Candice S., MI (10th)
Miller, Jeff, FL (1st)
Moolenaar, John R., MI (4th)
Mooney, Alexander X., WV (2d)
Moore, Gwen, WI (4th)
Moulton, Seth, MA (6th)
Mullin, Markwayne, OK (2d)
Mulvaney, Mick, SC (5th)
Murphy, Patrick, FL (18th)
Murphy, Tim, PA (18th)
Nadler, Jerrold, NY (10th)
Napolitano, Grace F., CA (32d)
Neal, Richard E., MA (1st)
Neugebauer, Randy, TX (19th)
Newhouse, Dan, WA (4th)
Noem, Kristi L., SD (At Large)
Nolan, Richard M., MN (8th)
Norcross, Donald, NJ (1st)
Nugent, Richard B., FL (11th)
Nunes, Devin, CA (22d)
Olson, Pete, TX (22d)
O'Rourke, Beto, TX (16th)
Palazzo, Steven M., MS (4th)
Pallone, Frank, Jr., NJ (6th)
Palmer, Gary J., AL (6th)
Pascrell, Bill, Jr., NJ (9th)
Paulsen, Erik, MN (3d)
Payne, Donald M., Jr., NJ (10th)
Pearce, Stevan, NM (2d)
Pelosi, Nancy, CA (12th)
Perlmutter, Ed, CO (7th)
Perry, Scott, PA (4th)
Peters, Scott H., CA (52d)
Peterson, Collin C., MN (7th)
Pingree, Chellie, ME (1st)
Pittenger, Robert, NC (9th)
Pitts, Joseph R., PA (16th)
Pocan, Mark, WI (2d)
Poe, Ted, TX (2d)
Poliquin, Bruce, ME (2d)
Polis, Jared, CO (2d)
Pompeo, Mike, KS (4th)
Posey, Bill, FL (8th)
Price, David E., NC (4th)
Price, Tom, GA (6th)
Quigley, Mike, IL (5th)

Rangel, Charles B., NY (13th)
Ratcliffe, John, TX (4th)
Reed, Tom, NY (23d)
Reichert, David G., WA (8th)
Renacci, James B., OH (16th)
Ribble, Reid J., WI (8th)
Rice, Kathleen M., NY (4th)
Rice, Tom, SC (7th)
Richmond, Cedric L., LA (2d)
Rigell, E. Scott, VA (2d)
Roby, Martha, AL (2d)
Roe, David P., TN (1st)
Rogers, Harold, KY (5th)
Rogers, Mike, AL (3d)
Rohrabacher, Dana, CA (48th)
Rokita, Todd, IN (4th)
Rooney, Thomas J., FL (17th)
Roskam, Peter J., IL (6th)
Ros-Lehtinen, Ileana, FL (27th)
Ross, Dennis A., FL (15th)
Rothfus, Keith J., PA (12th)
Rouzer, David, NC (7th)
Roybal-Allard, Lucille, CA (40th)
Royce, Edward R., CA (39th)
Ruiz, Raul, CA (36th)
Ruppersberger, C. A. Dutch, MD (2d)
Rush, Bobby L., IL (1st)
Russell, Steve, OK (5th)
Ryan, Paul D., WI (1st)
Ryan, Tim, OH (13th)
Salmon, Matt, AZ (5th)
Sánchez, Linda T., CA (38th)
Sanchez, Loretta, CA (46th)
Sanford, Mark, SC (1st)
Sarbanes, John P., MD (3d)
Scalise, Steve, LA (1st)
Schakowsky, Janice D., IL (9th)
Schiff, Adam B., CA (28th)
Schrader, Kurt, OR (5th)
Schweikert, David, AZ (6th)
Scott, Austin, GA (8th)
Scott, David, GA (13th)
Scott, Robert C. "Bobby", VA (3d)
Sensenbrenner, F. James, Jr., WI (5th)
Serrano, José E., NY (15th)
Sessions, Pete, TX (32d)
Sewell, Terri A., AL (7th)
Sherman, Brad, CA (30th)
Shimkus, John, IL (15th)
Shuster, Bill, PA (9th)
Simpson, Michael K. ID (2d)
Sinema, Kyrsten, AZ (9th)
Sires, Albio, NJ (8th)
Slaughter, Louise McIntosh, NY (25th)
Smith, Adam, WA (9th)
Smith, Adrian, NE (3d)
Smith, Christopher H., NJ (4th)
Smith, Jason, MO (8th)
Smith, Lamar, TX (21st)
Speier, Jackie, CA (14th)
Stefanik, Elise M., NY (21st)
Stewart, Chris, UT (2d)
Stivers, Steve, OH (15th)
Stutzman, Marlin A., IN (3d)
Swalwell, Eric, CA (15th)
Takai, Mark, HI (1st)

Takano, Mark, CA (41st)
Thompson, Bennie G., MS (2d)
Thompson, Glenn, PA (5th)
Thompson, Mike, CA (5th)
Thornberry, Mac, TX (13th)
Tiberi, Patrick J., OH (12th)
Tipton, Scott R., CO (3d)
Titus, Dina, NV (1st)
Tonko, Paul, NY (20th)
Torres, Norma J., CA (35th)
Trott, David A., MI (11th)
Tsongas, Niki, MA (3d)
Turner, Michael R., OH (10th)
Upton, Fred, MI (6th)
Valadao, David G., CA (21st)
Van Hollen, Chris, MD (8th)
Vargas, Juan, CA (51st)
Veasey, Marc A., TX (33d)
Vela, Filemon, TX (34th)
Velázquez, Nydia M., NY (7th)
Visclosky, Peter J., IN (1st)
Wagner, Ann, MO (2d)
Walberg, Tim, MI (7th)
Walden, Greg, OR (2d)
Walker, Mark, NC (6th)
Walorski, Jackie, IN (2d)
Walters, Mimi, CA (45th)
Walz, Timothy J., MN (1st)
Wasserman Schultz, Debbie, FL (23d)
Waters, Maxine, CA (43d)
Watson Coleman, Bonnie, NJ (12th)

Weber, Randy K., Sr., TX (14th)
Webster, Daniel, FL (10th)
Welch, Peter, VT (At Large)
Wenstrup, Brad R., OH (2d)
Westerman, Bruce, AR (4th)
Westmoreland, Lynn A., GA (3d)
Whitfield, Ed, KY (1st)
Williams, Roger, TX (25th)
Wilson, Frederica S., FL (24th)
Wilson, Joe, SC (2d)
Wittman, Robert J., VA (1st)
Womack, Steve, AR (3d)
Woodall, Rob, GA (7th)
Yarmuth, John A., KY (3d)
Yoder, Kevin, KS (3d)
Yoho, Ted S., FL (3d)
Young, David, IA (3d)
Young, Don, AK (At Large)
Young, Todd C., IN (9th)
Zeldin, Lee M., NY (1st)
Zinke, Ryan K., MT (At Large)

RESIDENT COMMISSIONER
Pierluisi, Pedro R., PR

DELEGATES
Radewagen, Aumua Amata Coleman, AS
Norton, Eleanor Holmes, DC
Bordallo, Madeleine Z., GU
Sablan, Gregorio Kilili Camacho, MP
Plaskett, Stacey E., VI

114th Congress
Nine-Digit Postal ZIP Codes

Senate Post Office (20510): The four-digit numbers in these tables were assigned by the Senate Committee on Rules and Administration. Mail to all Senate offices is delivered by the main Post Office in the Dirksen Senate Office Building.

Senate Committees

Committee on Agriculture, Nutrition, and Forestry	–6000	Committee on Health, Education, Labor and Pensions	–6300
Committee on Appropriations	–6025	Committee on Homeland Security and Governmental Affairs	–6250
Committee on Armed Services	–6050	Committee on Indian Affairs	–6450
Committee on Banking, Housing, and Urban Affairs	–6075	Committee on the Judiciary	–6275
Committee on the Budget	–6100	Committee on Rules and Administration	–6325
Committee on Commerce, Science, and Transportation	–6125	Committee on Small Business and Entrepreneurship	–6350
Committee on Energy and Natural Resources	–6150	Committee on Veterans' Affairs	–6375
Committee on Environment and Public Works	–6175	Committee on Aging (Special)	–6400
Committee on Finance	–6200	Committee on Ethics (Select)	–6425
Committee on Foreign Relations	–6225	Committee on Intelligence (Select)	–6475

Joint Committee Offices, Senate Side

Joint Economic Committee	–6602	Joint Committee on Printing	–6650
Joint Committee on the Library	–6625	Joint Committee on Taxation	–6675

Senate Leadership Offices

President Pro Tempore	–7000	Secretary for the Minority	–7024
Chaplain	–7002	Democratic Policy Committee	–7050
Majority Leader	–7010	Republican Conference	–7060
Assistant Majority Leader	–7012	Secretary to the Republican Conference	–7062
Secretary for the Majority	–7014	Republican Policy Committee	–7064
Minority Leader	–7020	Republican Steering Committee	–7066
Assistant Minority Leader	–7022	National Security Working Group	–7070

Senate Officers

Secretary of the Senate	–7100	Employee Assistance Program Office	–7211
Curator	–7102	Human Resources	–7212
Disbursing Office	–7104	Safety Program	–7212
Printing and Document Service	–7106	Health Promotion/Seminars	–7213
Historical Office	–7108	Placement Office	–7214
Human Resources	–7109	Workman's Compensation	–7214
Interparliamentary Services	–7110	Joint Office of Education and Training	–7215
Senate Library	–7112	Capitol Police	–7218
Office of Senate Security	–7114	Congressional Special Services Office	–7228
Office of Public Records	–7116	Office Support Services	–7230
Office of Official Reporters of Debates	–7117	Customer Support	–7231
Stationery Room	–7118	IT Request Processing	–7232
U.S. Capitol Preservation Commission	–7122	Chief Information Officer	–7233
Office of Conservation and Preservation	–7124	State Liaison	–7285
Information Systems	–7125	Periodical Press Gallery	–7234
Web Technology Office	–7126	Press Gallery	–7238
Legislative Systems	–7127	Press Photo Gallery	–7242
Senate Gift Shop	–7128	Radio and TV Gallery	–7246
Senate Legal Counsel	–7130	Webster Hall	–7248
Emergency Terror Response (COOP)	–7131	Office of Protective Services and Continuity (OPSAC)	–7249
Chief Counsel for Employment	–7132	Law Enforcement Support Office	–7249
Senate Sergeant at Arms	–7200	Intelligence & Protective Services	–7249
General Counsel	–7201	State Office Readiness Program	–7249
Finance Division	–7205	Police Operations Security Emergency Preparedness (POSEP)	–7249
Budget	–7205	Office of Continuity & Emergency Preparedness (CEPO)	–7249
Accounting	–7205		
Hair Care Services	–7206		
Procurement	–7207		
Capitol Guide Service	–7209		

Other Offices on the Senate Side

Senate Legal Counsel	–7250	Printing Graphics and Direct Mail—Capitol Hill	–7266
Central Operations—Administration	–7260	Facilities	–7204
Parking/ID	–7262	Furniture Shop	–7204
Printing Graphics and Direct Mail—PSQ	–7264	Framing Shop	–7204

Cabinet Shop	–7204	Inter/Intranet Services	–7296
Photo Studio	–7216	Architect of the Capitol	–8000
Post Office	–7220	Superintendent of Senate Buildings	–8002
Recording Studio	–7220	Restaurant	–8050
Senate Legislative Counsel	–7275	Amtrak Ticket Office	–9010
Program Management	–7276	Airlines Ticket Office (CATO)	–9014
IT Support Services—Administration	–7280	Child Care Center	–9022
Telecom Support	–7281	Credit Union	–9026
Equipment Services	–7282	Veterans' Liaison	–9054
Desktop/Lan Support	–7284	Social Security Liaison	–9064
IT Research/Deployment	–7292	Caucus of International Narcotics Control	–9070
Technology Development—Administration	–7290	Army Liaison	–9082
Systems Architecture	–7277	Air Force Liaison	–9083
Information Security	–7278	Coast Guard Liaison	–9084
Applications Development	–7291	Navy Liaison	–9085
Network Engineering and Management	–7293	Marine Liaison	–9087
Enterprise IT Systems	–7294		

House Post Office (20515): Mail to all House offices is delivered by the main Post Office in the Longworth House Office Building.

House Committees Leadership

U.S. House of Representatives	–0001	Committee on Homeland Security	–6480
Cannon House Office Building	–0002	Committee on House Administration	–6157
Rayburn House Office Building	–0003	Committee on the Judiciary	–6216
Longworth House Office Building	–0004	Committee on Natural Resources	–6201
Ford House Office Building	–0006	Committee on Oversight and Government Reform	–6143
The Capitol	–0007	Committee on Rules	–6269
Committee on Agriculture	–6001	Committee on Science, Space, and Technology	–6301
Committee on Appropriations	–6015	Committee on Small Business	–6315
Committee on Armed Services	–6035	Committee on Transportation and Infrastructure	–6256
Committee on the Budget	–6065	Committee on Veterans' Affairs	–6335
Committee on Education and the Workforce	–6100	Committee on Ways and Means	–6348
Committee on Energy and Commerce	–6115	Permanent Select Committee on Intelligence	–6415
Committee on Ethics	–6328	Select Committee on the Events Surrounding the	
Committee on Financial Services	–6050	2012 Terrorist Attack in Benghazi	–6090
Committee on Foreign Affairs	–6128		

Joint Committee Offices, House Side

Joint Economic Committee	–6432	Joint Committee on Printing	–6157
Joint Committee on the Library	–6157	Joint Committee on Taxation	–6453

House Leadership Offices

Office of the Speaker	–6501	Office of the Democratic Leader	–6537
Office of the Majority Leader	–6502	Office of the Democratic Whip	–6538
Office of the Majority Whip	–6503	House Republican Conference	–6544
Democratic Caucus	–6524	Republican Congressional Committee, National	–6547
Democratic Congressional Campaign Committee	–6525	Republican Policy Committee	–6549
Democratic Steering and Policy Committee	–6527	Republican Cloakroom	–6650
Democratic Cloakroom	–6528		

House Officers

Office of the Clerk	–6601	Office of Employee Assistance	–6619
Office of Art and Archives	–6612	ADA Services	–6860
Office of Employment and Counsel	–6622	Personnel and Benefits	–9980
Legislative Computer Systems	–6618	Child Care Center	–0001
Office of Legislative Operations	–6602	Payroll and Benefits	–6604
Legislative Resource Center	–6612	Financial Counseling	–6604
Official Reporters	–6615	Members' Services	–9970
Office of Communications	–6611	Office Supply Service	–6860
Office of Interparliamentary Affairs	–6579	House Gift Shop	–6860
Office of the Chaplain	–6655	Mail List/Processing	–6860
Office of the House Historian	–6701	Mailing Services	–6860
Office of the Parliamentarian	–6731	Contractor Management	–6860
Chief Administrative Officer	–6860	Photography	–6623
First Call	–6660	House Recording Studio	–6613
Administrative Counsel	–6660	Furniture Support Services	–6610
Periodical Press Gallery	–6624	House Office Service Center	–6860
Press Gallery	–6625	Budget	–6604
Radio/TV Correspondents' Gallery	–6627	Financial Counseling	–6604
HIR Call Center	–6165	Procurement Management	–9940
HIR Information Systems Security	–6165	Office of the Sergeant at Arms	–6634
Outplacement Services	–9920		

House Commissions and Offices

Congressional Executive Commission on China	–6481
Commission on Security and Cooperation in Europe	–6460
Commission on Congressional Mailing Standards	–6461
Office of the Law Revision Counsel	–6711
Office of Emergency Management	–6462

Office of the Legislative Counsel	–6721
General Counsel	–6532
Architect of the Capitol	–6906
Attending Physician	–6907
Congressional Budget Office	–6925

Liaison Offices

Air Force	–6854
Army	–6855
Coast Guard	–6856

Navy	–6857
Office of Personnel Management	–6858
Veterans' Administration	–6859

TERMS OF SERVICE

EXPIRATION OF THE TERMS OF SENATORS

CLASS III.—SENATORS WHOSE TERMS OF SERVICE EXPIRE IN 2017

[34 Senators in this group: Republicans, 24; Democrats, 10]

Name	Party	Residence
Ayotte, Kelly	R.	Nashua, NH.
Bennet, Michael F.[1]	D.	Denver, CO.
Blunt, Roy	R.	Springfield, MO.
Blumenthal, Richard	D.	Greenwich, CT.
Boozman, John	R.	Rogers, AR.
Boxer, Barbara	D.	Rancho Mirage, CA.
Burr, Richard	R.	Winston-Salem, NC.
Coats, Daniel	R.	Indianapolis, IN.
Crapo, Mike	R.	Idaho Falls, ID.
Grassley, Chuck	R.	New Hartford, IA.
Hoeven, John	R.	Bismarck, ND.
Isakson, Johnny	R.	Marietta, GA.
Johnson, Ron	R.	Oshkosh, WI.
Kirk, Mark[2]	R.	Highland Park, IL.
Lankford, James[3]	R.	Oklahoma City, OK.
Leahy, Patrick J.	D.	Middlesex, VT.
Lee, Mike	R.	Alpine, UT.
McCain, John	R.	Phoenix, AZ.
Mikulski, Barbara A.	D.	Baltimore, MD.
Moran, Jerry	R.	Hays, KS.
Murkowski, Lisa[4]	R.	Anchorage, AK.
Murray, Patty	D.	Seattle, WA.
Paul, Rand	R.	Bowling Green, KY.
Portman, Rob	R.	Terrace Park, OH.
Reid, Harry	D.	Searchlight, NV.
Rubio, Marco	R.	West Miami, FL.
Schatz, Brian[5]	D.	Honolulu, HI.
Schumer, Charles E.	D.	Brooklyn, NY.
Scott, Tim[6]	R.	North Charleston, SC.
Shelby, Richard C.[7]	R.	Tuscaloosa, AL.
Thune, John	R.	Murdo, SD.
Toomey, Patrick J.	R.	Zionsville, PA.
Vitter, David	R.	Metairie, LA.
Wyden, Ron[8]	D.	Portland, OR.

[1] Senator Bennet was appointed on January 21, 2009, to fill the vacancy caused by the resignation of Senator Kenneth L. Salazar and took the oath of office on January 22, 2009; elected to a full term on November 2, 2010.

[2] Senator Kirk won the special election on November 2, 2010, to fill the vacancy caused by the resignation of Senator Barack Obama, and at the same time was elected in the general election for the full term ending January 3, 2017 and took the oath of office on November 29, 2010, replacing appointed Senator Roland Burris.

[3] Senator Lankford won the special election on November 4, 2014, for the term ending January 3, 2017, to fill the vacancy caused by the resignation of Senator Tom Coburn, and took the oath of office on January 3, 2015.

[4] Senator Murkowski was appointed on December 20, 2002, to fill the vacancy caused by the resignation of her father, Senator Frank Murkowski; elected to a full term on November 2, 2004.

[5] Senator Schatz was appointed on December 26, 2012, to fill the vacancy caused by the death of Senator Daniel Inouye, and took the oath of office on December 27, 2012; won the special election on November 4, 2014, for the term ending January 3, 2017.

[6] Senator Scott was appointed on January 2, 2013, to fill the vacancy caused by the resignation of Senator James DeMint; took the oath of office on January 3, 2013; won the special election on November 4, 2014, for the term ending January 3, 2017.

[7] Senator Shelby changed party affiliation from Democrat to Republican on November 5, 1994.

[8] Senator Wyden won the special election on January 30, 1996, to fill the vacancy caused by the resignation of Senator Robert Packwood, and began service on February 6, 1996. He was elected to a full term on November 3, 1998.

CLASS I.—SENATORS WHOSE TERMS OF SERVICE EXPIRE IN 2019

[33 Senators in this group: Republicans, 8; Democrats, 23; Independents, 2]

Name	Party	Residence
Baldwin, Tammy	D.	Madison, WI.
Barrasso, John [1]	R.	Casper, WY.
Brown, Sherrod	D.	Cleveland, OH.
Cantwell, Maria	D.	Edmonds, WA.
Cardin, Benjamin L.	D.	Baltimore, MD.
Carper, Thomas R.	D.	Wilmington, DE.
Casey, Robert P., Jr.	D.	Scranton, PA.
Corker, Bob	R.	Chattanooga, TN.
Cruz, Ted	R.	Houston, TX.
Donnelly, Joe	D.	Granger, IN.
Feinstein, Dianne [2]	D.	San Francisco, CA.
Fischer, Deb	R.	Valentine, NE.
Flake, Jeff	R.	Mesa, AZ.
Gillibrand, Kirsten E.[3]	D.	Brunswick, NY.
Hatch, Orrin G.	R.	Salt Lake City, UT.
Heinrich, Martin	D.	Albuquerque, NM.
Heitkamp, Heidi	D.	Mandan, ND.
Heller, Dean [4]	R.	Carson City, NV.
Hirono, Mazie K.	D.	Honolulu, HI.
Kaine, Tim	D.	Richmond, VA.
King, Angus S., Jr.	I.	Brunswick, ME.
Klobuchar, Amy	D.	Minneapolis, MN.
Manchin, Joe III [5]	D.	Fairmont, WV.
McCaskill, Claire	D.	Kirkwood, MO.
Menendez, Robert [6]	D.	Paramus, NJ.
Murphy, Christopher	D.	Cheshire, CT.
Nelson, Bill	D.	Orlando, FL.
Sanders, Bernard	I.	Burlington, VT.
Stabenow, Debbie	D.	Lansing, MI.
Tester, Jon	D.	Big Sandy, MT.
Warren, Elizabeth	D.	Cambridge, MA.
Whitehouse, Sheldon	D.	Newport, RI.
Wicker, Roger F.[7]	R.	Tupelo, MS.

[1] Senator Barrasso was appointed on June 22, 2007, to fill the vacancy caused by the death of Senator Craig Thomas and took the oath of office on June 25, 2007; subsequently elected on November 4, 2008, for the term ending January 3, 2013; reelected to a full term on November 6, 2012.

[2] Senator Feinstein won the special election on November 3, 1992, to fill the vacancy caused by the resignation of Senator Pete Wilson and took the oath of office on November 10, 1992. She defeated Senator John Seymour who had been appointed on January 7, 1991. She was elected to a full term on November 8, 1994.

[3] Senator Gillibrand was appointed on January 23, 2009, to fill the vacancy caused by the resignation of Senator Hillary Rodham Clinton and took the oath of office on January 27, 2009. She was elected in a special election on November 2, 2010, and to a full term on November 6, 2012.

[4] Senator Heller was appointed on May 3, 2011, to fill the vacancy caused by the resignation of Senator John Ensign and took the oath of office on May 9, 2011; he was elected to a full term on November 6, 2012.

[5] Senator Manchin won a special election on November 2, 2010, to fill the vacancy caused by the death of Senator Robert C. Byrd and took the oath of office on November 15, 2010, replacing appointed Senator Carte P. Goodwin. He was elected to a full term.

[6] Senator Menendez was appointed on January 17, 2006, to fill the vacancy caused by the resignation of Senator Jon S. Corzine and took the oath of office on January 18, 2006; subsequently elected to a full term on November 7, 2006.

[7] Senator Wicker was appointed on December 31, 2007, to fill the vacancy caused by the resignation of Senator Trent Lott and took the oath of office on December 31, 2007; subsequently elected in a special election on November 4, 2008, and to a full term on November 6, 2012.

CLASS II.—SENATORS WHOSE TERMS OF SERVICE EXPIRE IN 2021

[33 Senators in this group: Republicans, 22; Democrats, 11]

Name	Party	Residence
Alexander, Lamar	R.	Maryville, TN.
Booker, Cory A.[1]	D.	Newark, NJ.
Capito, Shelley Moore	R.	Charleston, WV.
Cassidy, Bill	R.	Baton Rouge, LA.
Cochran, Thad	R.	Oxford, MS.
Collins, Susan M.	R.	Bangor, ME.
Coons, Christopher A.[2]	D.	Wilmington, DE.
Cornyn, John	R.	Austin, TX.
Cotton, Tom	R.	Dardanelle, AR.
Daines, Steve	R.	Bozeman, MT.
Durbin, Richard J.	D.	Springfield, IL.
Ernst, Joni	R.	Red Oak, IA.
Enzi, Michael B.	R.	Gillette, WY.
Franken, Al[3]	D.	St. Louis Park, MN.
Gardner, Cory	R.	Yuma, CO.
Graham, Lindsey	R.	Seneca, SC.
Inhofe, James M.[4]	R.	Tulsa, OK.
McConnell, Mitch	R.	Louisville, KY.
Markey, Edward J.[5]	D.	Malden, MA.
Merkley, Jeff	D.	Portland, OR.
Perdue, David	R.	Glynn County, GA.
Peters, Gary C.	D.	Bloomfield Township, MI.
Reed, Jack	D.	Jamestown, RI.
Risch, James E.	R.	Boise, ID.
Roberts, Pat	R.	Dodge City, KS.
Rounds, Mike	R.	Fort Pierre, SD.
Sasse, Ben	R.	Fremont, NE.
Sessions, Jeff	R.	Mobile, AL.
Shaheen, Jeanne	D.	Madbury, NH.
Sullivan, Dan	R.	Anchorage, AK.
Tillis, Thom	R.	Huntersville, NC.
Udall, Tom	D.	Santa Fe, NM.
Warner, Mark R.	D.	Alexandria, VA.

[1] Senator Booker won the special election on October 16, 2013, to fill the vacancy caused by the death of Senator Frank Lautenberg, and took the oath of office on October 31, 2013, replacing appointed Senator Jeffrey Chiesa; elected to a full term on November 4, 2014.

[2] Senator Coons won the special election on November 2, 2010, to fill the vacancy caused by the resignation of Senator Joseph R. Biden, Jr., and took the oath of office on November 15, 2010, replacing appointed Senator Ted Kaufman; elected to a full term on November 4, 2014.

[3] Contested election was resolved June 30, 2009; Senator Franken was sworn into office on July 7, 2009.

[4] Senator Inhofe won the special election on November 8, 1994, to fill the vacancy caused by the resignation of Senator David Boren, and took the oath of office on November 17, 1994; elected to a full term on November 5, 1996.

[5] Senator Markey won the special election on June 25, 2013, to fill the vacancy caused by the resignation of Senator John F. Kerry, and took the oath of office on July 16, 2013, replacing appointed Senator William Cowan; elected to a full term on November 4, 2014.

CONTINUOUS SERVICE OF SENATORS

[Republicans in roman (54); Democrats in *italic* (44); Independents in SMALL CAPS (2); total, 100]

Rank	Name	State	Beginning of present service
1	*Leahy, Patrick J.*	Vermont	Jan. 3, 1975.
2	Hatch, Orrin G.	Utah	Jan. 3, 1977.
3	Cochran, Thad † [1]	Mississippi	Dec. 27, 1978.
4	Grassley, Chuck †	Iowa	Jan. 3, 1981.
5	McConnell, Mitch	Kentucky	Jan. 3, 1985.
6	McCain, John †	Arizona	Jan. 3, 1987.
	Mikulski, Barbara A. †	Maryland	
	Reid, Harry †	Nevada	
	Shelby, Richard C.†	Alabama	
7	*Feinstein, Dianne* [2]	California	Nov. 10, 1992.‡
8	*Boxer, Barbara* †	California	Jan. 3, 1993.
	Murray, Patty	Washington	
9	Inhofe, James M. † [3]	Oklahoma	Nov. 17, 1994. ‡
10	*Wyden, Ron* † [4]	Oregon	Feb. 6, 1996. ‡
11	Collins, Susan M.	Maine	Jan. 3, 1997.
	Durbin, Richard J. †	Illinois	
	Enzi, Michael B.	Wyoming	
	Reed, Jack †	Rhode Island	
	Roberts, Pat †	Kansas	
	Sessions, Jeff	Alabama	
12	Crapo, Mike †	Idaho	Jan. 3, 1999.
	Schumer, Charles E. †	New York	
13	*Cantwell, Maria* †	Washington	Jan. 3, 2001.
	Carper, Thomas R. †	Delaware	
	Nelson, Bill †	Florida	
	Stabenow, Debbie †	Michigan	
14	Cornyn, John [5]	Texas	Dec. 2, 2002.
15	Murkowski, Lisa [6]	Alaska	Dec. 20, 2002.
16	Alexander, Lamar	Tennessee	Jan. 3, 2003.
	Graham, Lindsey †	South Carolina ...	
17	Burr, Richard †	North Carolina ...	Jan. 3, 2005.
	Isakson, Johnny †	Georgia	
	Thune, John †	South Dakota	
	Vitter, David †	Louisiana	
18	*Menendez, Robert* † [7]	New Jersey	Jan. 17, 2006.
19	*Brown, Sherrod* †	Ohio	Jan. 3, 2007.
	Cardin, Benjamin L. †	Maryland	
	Casey, Robert P., Jr.	Pennsylvania	
	Corker, Bob	Tennessee	
	Klobuchar, Amy	Minnesota	
	McCaskill, Claire	Missouri	
	SANDERS, BERNARD †	Vermont	
	Tester, Jon	Montana	
	Whitehouse, Sheldon	Rhode Island	
20	Barrasso, John [8]	Wyoming	June 22, 2007.
21	Wicker, Roger F. † [9]	Mississippi	Dec. 31, 2007.
22	*Merkley, Jeff*	Oregon	Jan. 3, 2009.
	Risch, James E.	Idaho	
	Shaheen, Jeanne	New Hampshire	
	Udall, Tom †	New Mexico	
	Warner, Mark R.	Virginia	
23	*Bennet, Michael F.* [10]	Colorado	Jan. 21, 2009.
24	*Gillibrand, Kirsten E.*† [11]	New York	Jan. 26, 2009.
25	*Franken, Al* [12]	Minnesota	July 7, 2009.

CONTINUOUS SERVICE OF SENATORS—CONTINUED

[Republicans in roman (54); Democrats in *italic* (44); Independents in SMALL CAPS (2); total, 100]

Rank	Name	State	Beginning of present service
26	*Coons, Christopher A.* [13]	Delaware	Nov. 15, 2010.
	Manchin, Joe III [14]	West Virginia	
27	Kirk, Mark † [15]	Illinois	Nov. 29, 2010. ‡
28	Ayotte, Kelly	New Hampshire	Jan. 3, 2011.
	Blumenthal, Richard	Connecticut	
	Blunt, Roy	Missouri	
	Boozman, John †	Arkansas	
	Coats, Daniel † [16]	Indiana	
	Hoeven, John	North Dakota	
	Johnson, Ron	Wisconsin	
	Lee, Mike	Utah	
	Moran, Jerry	Kansas	
	Paul, Rand	Kentucky	
	Portman, Rob	Ohio	
	Rubio, Marco	Florida	
	Toomey, Patrick J.	Pennsylvania	
29	Heller, Dean † [17]	Nevada	May 9, 2011.
30	*Schatz, Brian* [18]	Hawaii	Dec. 26, 2012.
31	Scott, Tim † [19]	South Carolina ...	Jan. 2, 2013.
32	*Baldwin, Tammy*	Wisconsin	Jan. 3, 2013.
	Cruz, Ted	Texas	
	Donnelly, Joe	Indiana	
	Fischer, Deb	Nebraska	
	Flake, Jeff	Arizona	
	Heinrich, Martin	New Mexico	
	Heitkamp, Heidi	North Dakota	
	Hirono, Mazie K.	Hawaii	
	Kaine, Tim	Virginia	
	KING, ANGUS S., JR.	Maine	
	Murphy, Christopher	Connecticut	
	Warren, Elizabeth	Massachusetts	
33	*Markey, Edward J.*† [20]	Massachusetts	July 16, 2013. ‡
34	*Booker, Cory A.* [21]	New Jersey	Oct. 31, 2013 †
35	Capito, Shelley Moore †	West Virginia	Jan. 3, 2015.
	Cassidy, Bill †	Louisiana	
	Cotton, Tom †	Arkansas	
	Daines, Steve †	Montana	
	Ernst, Joni	Iowa	
	Gardner, Cory †	Colorado	
	Lankford, James †	Oklahoma	
	Perdue, David	Georgia	
	Peters, Gary C. †	Michigan	
	Rounds, Mike	South Dakota	
	Sasse, Ben	Nebraska	
	Sulivan, Dan	Alaska	
	Tillis, Thom	North Carolina ...	

† Served in the House of Representatives previous to service in the Senate.
‡ Senators elected to complete unexpired terms typically begin their terms on the day following the election, but individual cases may vary.
[1] Senator Cochran was elected on November 6, 1978, for the 6-year term commencing January 3, 1979; subsequently appointed December 27, 1978, to fill the vacancy caused by the resignation of Senator James Eastland.
[2] Senator Feinstein won the special election on November 3, 1992, to fill the vacancy caused by the resignation of Senator Pete Wilson, and took the oath of office on November 10, 1992 replacing appointed Senator John Seymour. She was elected to a full term on November 8, 1994.
[3] Senator Inhofe won the special election on November 8, 1994, to fill the vacancy caused by the resignation of Senator David Boren, and took the oath of office on November 17, 1994. He was elected to a full term on November 5, 1996.

[4] Senator Wyden won the special election on January 30, 1996, to fill the vacancy caused by the resignation of Senator Robert Packwood and began service on February 6, 1996. He was elected to a full term on November 3, 1998.

[5] Senator Cornyn was elected on November 5, 2002, for the 6-year term commencing January 3, 2003; subsequently appointed on December 2, 2002, to fill the vacancy caused by the resignation of Senator Phil Gramm.

[6] Senator Murkowski was appointed on December 20, 2002, to fill the vacancy caused by the resignation of her father, Senator Frank Murkowski. She was elected to a full term on November 2, 2004.

[7] Senator Menendez was appointed on January 17, 2006, to fill the vacancy caused by the resignation of Senator Jon S. Corzine; elected to a full term on November 7, 2006.

[8] Senator Barrasso was appointed on June 22, 2007, to fill the vacancy caused by the death of Senator Craig Thomas, and took the oath of office on June 25, 2007. He won the special election on November 4, 2008, for term ending January 3, 2013; elected to a full term on November 6, 2012.

[9] Senator Wicker was appointed on December 31, 2007, to fill the vacancy caused by the resignation of Senator Trent Lott. He won the special election on November 4, 2008, for the term ending January 3, 2013; elected to full term on November 6, 2012.

[10] Senator Bennet was appointed on January 21, 2009, to fill the vacancy caused by the resignation of Senator Ken Salazar, and took the oath of office on January 22, 2009; elected to a full term on November 2, 2010.

[11] Senator Gillibrand was appointed on January 23, 2009, to fill the vacancy caused by the resignation of Senator Hillary Clinton, and took the oath of office on January 27, 2009. She won the special election on November 2, 2010, for the term ending January 3, 2013; elected to a full term on November 6, 2012.

[12] The contested election case between Senator Franken and former Senator Coleman was resolved by Minnesota's Supreme Court on June 30, 2009. Franken was sworn into office on July 7, 2009. The Senate seat had remained vacant from January 3 until July 6.

[13] Senator Coons won the special election on November 2, 2010, to fill the vacancy caused by the resignation of Senator Joseph Biden, Jr., and took the oath of office on November 15, 2010, replacing appointed Senator Edward E. Kaufman; elected to a full term on November 4, 2014.

[14] Senator Manchin won the special election on November 2, 2010, to fill the vacancy caused by the death of Senator Robert C. Byrd, and took the oath of office on November 15, 2010, replacing appointed Senator Carte P. Goodwin; elected to a full term on November 6, 2012.

[15] Senator Kirk won the special election to the term ending January 3, 2011 on November 2, 2010, to fill the vacancy caused by the resignation of Senator Barack Obama, and at the same time was elected in the general election for the 6-year term ending January 3, 2017; took the oath of office on November 29, 2010, replacing appointed Senator Roland Burris.

[16] Senator Coats previously served in the Senate from January 3, 1989, until January 3, 1999.

[17] Senator Heller was appointed on May 3, 2011, to fill the vacancy caused by the resignation of Senator John E. Ensign, and took the oath of office on May 9, 2011; elected to a full term on November 6, 2012.

[18] Senator Schatz was appointed on December 26, 2012, to fill the vacancy caused by the death of Senator Daniel Inouye, and took the oath of office on December 27, 2012; he won the special election on November 4, 2014, for the term ending January 3, 2017.

[19] Senator Scott was appointed on January 2, 2013, to fill the vacancy caused by the resignation of Senator James DeMint; appointment took effect upon his resignation from the House of Representatives on January 2, 2013; took the oath of office on January 3, 2013. He won the special election on November 4, 2014, for the term ending January 3, 2017.

[20] Senator Markey won the special election on June 25, 2013, to fill the vacancy caused by the resignation of Senator John F. Kerry, and took the oath of office on July 16, 2013, replacing appointed Senator William Cowan; elected to a full term on November 4, 2014.

[21] Senator Booker won the special election on October 16, 2013, to fill the vacancy caused by the death of Senator Frank Lautenberg, and took the oath of office on October 31, 2013, replacing appointed Senator Jeffrey Chiesa; elected to a full term on November 4, 2014.

CONGRESSES IN WHICH REPRESENTATIVES, RESIDENT COMMISSIONER, AND DELEGATES HAVE SERVED WITH BEGINNING OF PRESENT SERVICE

[* Elected to fill a vacancy; Republicans in roman (246); Democrats in *italic* (188); Vacancies (1); Resident Commissioner and Delegates in **boldface** (6); total, 441]

Name	State	Congresses (inclusive)	Beginning of present service
26 terms, consecutive			
Conyers, John, Jr.	MI	89th to 114th	Jan. 3, 1965
23 terms, consecutive			
Rangel, Charles B.	NY	92d to 114th	Jan. 3, 1971
22 terms, consecutive			
Young, Don	AK	*93d to 114th	Mar. 14, 1973
19 terms, consecutive			
Sensenbrenner, F. James, Jr.	WI	96th to 114th	Jan. 3, 1979
18 terms, consecutive			
Hoyer, Steny H.	MD	*97th to 114th	June 3, 1981
Rogers, Harold	KY	97th to 114th	Jan. 3, 1981
Smith, Christopher H.	NJ	97th to 114th	Jan. 3, 1981
17 terms, consecutive			
Kaptur, Marcy	OH	98th to 114th	Jan. 3, 1983
Levin, Sander M.	MI	98th to 114th	Jan. 3, 1983
16 terms, consecutive			
Barton, Joe	TX	99th to 114th	Jan. 3, 1985
Visclosky, Peter J.	IN	99th to 114th	Jan. 3, 1985
15 terms, consecutive			
DeFazio, Peter A.	OR	100th to 114th	Jan. 3, 1987
Duncan, John J., Jr.	TN	*100th to 114th	Jan. 3, 1989
Lewis, John	GA	100th to 114th	Jan. 3, 1987
Pelosi, Nancy	CA	*100th to 114th	June 2, 1987
Slaughter, Louise McIntosh	NY	100th to 114th	Jan. 3, 1987
Smith, Lamar	TX	100th to 114th	Jan. 3, 1987
Upton, Fred	MI	100th to 114th	Jan. 3, 1987
14 terms, consecutive			
Engel, Eliot L.	NY	101st to 114th	Jan. 3, 1989
Lowey, Nita M.	NY	101st to 114th	Jan. 3, 1989
McDermott, Jim	WA	101st to 114th	Jan. 3, 1989
Neal, Richard E.	MA	101st to 114th	Jan. 3, 1989
Rohrabacher, Dana	CA	101st to 114th	Jan. 3, 1989
Ros-Lehtinen, Ileana	FL	*101st to 114th	Aug. 29, 1989
Serrano, José E.	NY	*101st to 114th	Mar. 20, 1990
14 terms, not consecutive			
Price, David E.	NC	100th to 103d, 105th to 114th.	Jan 3. 1997
13 terms, consecutive			
DeLauro, Rosa L.	CT	102d to 114th	Jan. 3, 1991

CONGRESSES IN WHICH REPRESENTATIVES, RESIDENT COMMISSIONER,
AND DELEGATES HAVE SERVED WITH BEGINNING OF PRESENT
SERVICE—CONTINUED

[*Elected to fill a vacancy; Republicans in roman (246); Democrats in *italic* (188); Vacancies (1); Resident Commissioner and Delegates in **boldface** (6); total, 441]

Name	State	Congresses (inclusive)	Beginning of present service
Johnson, Sam	TX	*102d to 114th	May 8, 1991
Nadler, Jerrold	NY	*102d to 114th	Nov. 4, 1992
Peterson, Collin C.	MN	102d to 114th	Jan. 3, 1991
Waters, Maxine	CA	102d to 114th	Jan. 3, 1991
13 terms, not consecutive			
Cooper, Jim	TN	98th to 103d and 108th to 114th.	Jan. 3, 2003
12 terms, consecutive			
Becerra, Xavier	CA	103d to 114th	Jan. 3, 1993
Bishop, Sanford D., Jr.	GA	103d to 114th	Jan. 3, 1993
Brown, Corrine	FL	103d to 114th	Jan. 3, 1993
Calvert, Ken	CA	103d to 114th	Jan. 3, 1993
Clyburn, James E.	SC	103d to 114th	Jan. 3, 1993
Eshoo, Anna G.	CA	103d to 114th	Jan. 3, 1993
Farr, Sam	CA	*103d to 114th	June 16, 1993
Goodlatte, Bob	VA	103d to 114th	Jan. 3, 1993
Green, Gene	TX	103d to 114th	Jan. 3, 1993
Gutiérrez, Luis V.	IL	103d to 114th	Jan. 3, 1993
Hastings, Alcee L.	FL	103d to 114th	Jan. 3, 1993
Johnson, Eddie Bernice	TX	103d to 114th	Jan. 3, 1993
King, Peter T.	NY	103d to 114th	Jan. 3, 1993
Lucas, Frank D.	OK	*103d to 114th	May 17, 1994
Maloney, Carolyn B.	NY	103d to 114th	Jan. 3, 1993
Mica, John L.	FL	103d to 114th	Jan. 3, 1993
Roybal-Allard, Lucille	CA	103d to 114th	Jan. 3, 1993
Royce, Edward R.	CA	103d to 114th	Jan. 3, 1993
Rush, Bobby L.	IL	103d to 114th	Jan. 3, 1993
Scott, Robert C. "Bobby"	VA	103d to 114th	Jan. 3, 1993
Thompson, Bennie G.	MS	*103d to 114th	Apr. 20, 1993
Velázquez, Nydia M.	NY	103d to 114th	Jan. 3, 1993
11 terms, consecutive			
Blumenauer, Earl	OR	*104th to 114th	May 30, 1996
Cummings, Elijah E.	MD	*104th to 114th	Apr. 25, 1996
Doggett, Lloyd	TX	104th to 114th	Jan. 3, 1995
Doyle, Michael F.	PA	104th to 114th	Jan. 3, 1995
Fattah, Chaka	PA	104th to 114th	Jan. 3, 1995
Frelinghuysen, Rodney P.	NJ	104th to 114th	Jan. 3, 1995
Jackson Lee, Sheila	TX	104th to 114th	Jan. 3, 1995
Jones, Walter B.	NC	104th to 114th	Jan. 3, 1995
LoBiondo, Frank A.	NJ	104th to 114th	Jan. 3, 1995
Lofgren, Zoe	CA	104th to 114th	Jan. 3, 1995
Thornberry, Mac	TX	104th to 114th	Jan. 3, 1995
Whitfield, Ed	KY	104th to 114th	Jan. 3, 1995
10 terms, consecutive			
Aderholt, Robert B.	AL	105th to 114th	Jan. 3, 1997
Brady, Kevin	TX	105th to 114th	Jan. 3, 1997
Brady, Robert A.	PA	*105th to 114th	May 21, 1998

CONGRESSES IN WHICH REPRESENTATIVES, RESIDENT COMMISSIONER, AND DELEGATES HAVE SERVED WITH BEGINNING OF PRESENT SERVICE—CONTINUED

[* Elected to fill a vacancy; Republicans in roman (246); Democrats in *italic* (188); Vacancies (1); Resident Commissioner and Delegates in **boldface** (6); total, 441]

Name	State	Congresses (inclusive)	Beginning of present service
Capps, Lois	CA	*105th to 114th	Mar. 17, 1998
Davis, Danny K.	IL	105th to 114th	Jan. 3, 1997
DeGette, Diana	CO	105th to 114th	Jan. 3, 1997
Granger, Kay	TX	105th to 114th	Jan. 3, 1997
Hinojosa, Rubén	TX	105th to 114th	Jan. 3, 1997
Kind, Ron	WI	105th to 114th	Jan. 3, 1997
Lee, Barbara	CA	*105th to 114th	Apr. 21, 1998
McGovern, James P.	MA	105th to 114th	Jan. 3, 1997
Meeks, Gregory W.	NY	*105th to 114th	Feb. 5, 1998
Pascrell, Bill, Jr.	NJ	105th to 114th	Jan. 3, 1997
Pitts, Joseph R.	PA	105th to 114th	Jan. 3, 1997
Sanchez, Loretta	CA	105th to 114th	Jan. 3, 1997
Sessions, Pete	TX	105th to 114th	Jan. 3, 1997
Sherman, Brad	CA	105th to 114th	Jan. 3, 1997
Shimkus, John	IL	105th to 114th	Jan. 3, 1997
Smith, Adam	WA	105th to 114th	Jan. 3, 1997

10 terms, not consecutive

Chabot, Steve	OH	104th to 110th and 112th to 114th.	Jan. 3, 2011

9 terms, consecutive

Capuano, Michael E.	MA	106th to 114th	Jan. 3, 1999
Crowley, Joseph	NY	106th to 114th	Jan. 3, 1999
Larson, John B.	CT	106th to 114th	Jan. 3, 1999
Napolitano, Grace F.	CA	106th to 114th	Jan. 3, 1999
Ryan, Paul D.	WI	106th to 114th	Jan. 3, 1999
Schakowsky, Janice D.	IL	106th to 114th	Jan. 3, 1999
Simpson, Michael K.	ID	106th to 114th	Jan. 3, 1999
Thompson, Mike	CA	106th to 114th	Jan. 3, 1999
Walden, Greg	OR	106th to 114th	Jan. 3, 1999

8 terms, consecutive

Clay, Wm. Lacy	MO	107th to 114th	Jan. 3, 2001
Crenshaw, Ander	FL	107th to 114th	Jan. 3, 2001
Culberson, John Abney	TX	107th to 114th	Jan. 3, 2001
Davis, Susan A.	CA	107th to 114th	Jan. 3, 2001
Forbes, J. Randy	VA	*107th to 114th	June 26, 2001
Graves, Sam	MO	107th to 114th	Jan. 3, 2001
Honda, Michael M.	CA	107th to 114th	Jan. 3, 2001
Israel, Steve	NY	107th to 114th	Jan. 3, 2001
Issa, Darrell E.	CA	107th to 114th	Jan. 3, 2001
Langevin, James R.	RI	107th to 114th	Jan. 3, 2001
Larsen, Rick	WA	107th to 114th	Jan. 3, 2001
Lynch, Stephen F.	MA	*107th to 114th	Oct. 23, 2001
McCollum, Betty	MN	107th to 114th	Jan. 3, 2001
Miller, Jeff	FL	*107th to 114th	Oct. 23, 2001
Schiff, Adam B.	CA	107th to 114th	Jan. 3, 2001
Shuster, Bill	PA	*107th to 114th	May 17, 2001
Tiberi, Patrick J.	OH	107th to 114th	Jan. 3, 2001

CONGRESSES IN WHICH REPRESENTATIVES, RESIDENT COMMISSIONER, AND DELEGATES HAVE SERVED WITH BEGINNING OF PRESENT SERVICE—CONTINUED

[* Elected to fill a vacancy; Republicans in roman (246); Democrats in *italic* (188); Vacancies (1); Resident Commissioner and Delegates in **boldface** (6); total, 441]

Name	State	Congresses (inclusive)	Beginning of present service
Wilson, Joe	SC	*107th to 114th	Dec. 19, 2001
7 terms, consecutive			
Bishop, Rob	UT	108th to 114th	Jan. 3, 2003
Blackburn, Marsha	TN	108th to 114th	Jan. 3, 2003
Burgess, Michael C.	TX	108th to 114th	Jan. 3, 2003
Butterfield, G. K.	NC	* 108th to 114th	July 21, 2004
Carter, John R.	TX	108th to 114th	Jan. 3, 2003
Cole, Tom	OK	108th to 114th	Jan. 3, 2003
Diaz-Balart, Mario	FL	108th to 114th	Jan. 3, 2003
Franks, Trent	AZ	108th to 114th	Jan. 3, 2003
Garrett, Scott	NJ	108th to 114th	Jan. 3, 2003
Grijalva, Raúl M.	AZ	108th to 114th	Jan. 3, 2003
Hensarling, Jeb	TX	108th to 114th	Jan. 3, 2003
King, Steve	IA	108th to 114th	Jan. 3, 2003
Kline, John	MN	108th to 114th	Jan. 3, 2003
Miller, Candice S.	MI	108th to 114th	Jan. 3, 2003
Murphy, Tim	PA	108th to 114th	Jan. 3, 2003
Neugebauer, Randy	TX	*108th to 114th	June 5, 2003
Nunes, Devin	CA	108th to 114th	Jan. 3, 2003
Rogers, Mike	AL	108th to 114th	Jan. 3, 2003
Ruppersberger, C. A. Dutch	MD	108th to 114th	Jan. 3, 2003
Ryan, Tim	OH	108th to 114th	Jan. 3, 2003
Sánchez, Linda T.	CA	108th to 114th	Jan. 3, 2003
Scott, David	GA	108th to 114th	Jan. 3, 2003
Turner, Michael R.	OH	108th to 114th	Jan. 3, 2003
Van Hollen, Chris	MD	108th to 114th	Jan. 3, 2003
6 terms, consecutive			
Boustany, Charles W., Jr.	LA	109th to 114th	Jan. 3, 2005
Cleaver, Emanuel	MO	109th to 114th	Jan. 3, 2005
Conaway, K. Michael	TX	109th to 114th	Jan. 3, 2005
Costa, Jim	CA	109th to 114th	Jan. 3, 2005
Cuellar, Henry	TX	109th to 114th	Jan. 3, 2005
Dent, Charles W.	PA	109th to 114th	Jan. 3, 2005
Fortenberry, Jeff	NE	109th to 114th	Jan. 3, 2005
Foxx, Virginia	NC	109th to 114th	Jan. 3, 2005
Gohmert, Louie	TX	109th to 114th	Jan. 3, 2005
Green, Al	TX	109th to 114th	Jan. 3, 2005
Higgins, Brian	NY	109th to 114th	Jan. 3, 2005
Lipinski, Daniel	IL	109th to 114th	Jan. 3, 2005
Marchant, Kenny	TX	109th to 114th	Jan. 3, 2005
Matsui, Doris O.	CA	*109th to 114th	Mar. 10, 2005
McCaul, Michael T.	TX	109th to 114th	Jan. 3, 2005
McHenry, Patrick T.	NC	109th to 114th	Jan. 3, 2005
McMorris Rodgers, Cathy	WA	109th to 114th	Jan. 3, 2005
Moore, Gwen	WI	109th to 114th	Jan. 3, 2005
Poe, Ted	TX	109th to 114th	Jan. 3, 2005
Price, Tom	GA	109th to 114th	Jan. 3, 2005
Reichert, David G.	WA	109th to 114th	Jan. 3, 2005

CONGRESSES IN WHICH REPRESENTATIVES, RESIDENT COMMISSIONER, AND DELEGATES HAVE SERVED WITH BEGINNING OF PRESENT SERVICE—CONTINUED

[* Elected to fill a vacancy; Republicans in roman (246); Democrats in *italic* (188); Vacancies (1); Resident Commissioner and Delegates in **boldface** (6); total, 441]

Name	State	Congresses (inclusive)	Beginning of present service
Sires, Albio	NJ	*109th to 114th	Nov. 13, 2006
Wasserman Schultz, Debbie	FL	109th to 114th	Jan. 3, 2005
Westmoreland, Lynn A.	GA	109th to 114th	Jan. 3, 2005
6 terms, not consecutive			
Pearce, Stevan	NM	108th to 110th and 112th to 114th.	Jan. 3. 2011
5 terms, consecutive			
Bilirakis, Gus M.	FL	110th to 114th	Jan. 3, 2007
Buchanan, Vern	FL	110th to 114th	Jan. 3, 2007
Carson, André	IN	*110th to 114th	Mar. 13, 2008
Castor, Kathy	FL	110th to 114th	Jan. 3, 2007
Clarke, Yvette D.	NY	110th to 114th	Jan. 3, 2007
Cohen, Steve	TN	110th to 114th	Jan. 3, 2007
Courtney, Joe	CT	110th to 114th	Jan. 3, 2007
Edwards, Donna F.	MD	*110th to 114th	June 19, 2008
Ellison, Keith	MN	110th to 114th	Jan. 3, 2007
Fudge, Marcia L.	OH	*110th to 114th	Nov. 19, 2008
Johnson, Henry C. "Hank", Jr.	GA	110th to 114th	Jan. 3, 2007
Jordan, Jim	OH	110th to 114th	Jan. 3, 2007
Lamborn, Doug	CO	110th to 114th	Jan. 3, 2007
Latta, Robert E.	OH	*110th to 114th	Dec. 13, 2007
Loebsack, David	IA	110th to 114th	Jan. 3, 2007
McCarthy, Kevin	CA	110th to 114th	Jan. 3, 2007
McNerney, Jerry	CA	110th to 114th	Jan. 3, 2007
Perlmutter, Ed	CO	110th to 114th	Jan. 3, 2007
Roskam, Peter J.	IL	110th to 114th	Jan. 3, 2007
Sarbanes, John P.	MD	110th to 114th	Jan. 3, 2007
Scalise, Steve	LA	*110th to 114th	May 7, 2008
Smith, Adrian	NE	110th to 114th	Jan. 3, 2007
Speier, Jackie	CA	*110th to 114th	Apr. 10, 2008
Tsongas, Niki	MA	*110th to 114th	Oct. 18, 2007
Walz, Timothy J.	MN	110th to 114th	Jan. 3, 2007
Welch, Peter	VT	110th to 114th	Jan. 3, 2007
Wittman, Robert J.	VA	*110th to 114th	Dec. 13, 2007
Yarmuth, John A.	KY	110th to 114th	Jan. 3, 2007
5 terms, not consecutive			
Nolan, Richard M.	MN	94th to 96th and 113th to 114th.	Jan. 3, 2013
Salmon, Matt	AZ	104th to 106th and 113th to 114th.	Jan. 3, 2013
Sanford, Mark	SC	*104th to 106th and 113th to 114th.	May 7, 2013
4 terms, consecutive			
Chaffetz, Jason	UT	111th to 114th	Jan. 3, 2009
Chu, Judy	CA	*111th to 114th	July 16, 2009
Coffman, Mike	CO	111th to 114th	Jan. 3, 2009

CONGRESSES IN WHICH REPRESENTATIVES, RESIDENT COMMISSIONER, AND DELEGATES HAVE SERVED WITH BEGINNING OF PRESENT SERVICE—CONTINUED

[* Elected to fill a vacancy; Republicans in roman (246); Democrats in *italic* (188); Vacancies (1); Resident Commissioner and Delegates in **boldface** (6); total, 441]

Name	State	Congresses (inclusive)	Beginning of present service
Connolly, Gerald E.	VA	111th to 114th	Jan. 3, 2009
Deutch, Theodore E.	FL	*111th to 114th	Apr. 15, 2010
Fleming, John	LA	111th to 114th	Jan. 3, 2009
Garamendi, John	CA	*111th to 114th	Nov. 5, 2009
Graves, Tom	GA	*111th to 114th	June 14, 2010
Guthrie, Brett	KY	111th to 114th	Jan. 3, 2009
Harper, Gregg	MS	111th to 114th	Jan. 3, 2009
Himes, James A.	CT	111th to 114th	Jan. 3, 2009
Hunter, Duncan	CA	111th to 114th	Jan. 3, 2009
Jenkins, Lynn	KS	111th to 114th	Jan. 3, 2009
Lance, Leonard	NJ	111th to 114th	Jan. 3, 2009
Luetkemeyer, Blaine	MO	111th to 114th	Jan. 3, 2009
Luján, Ben Ray	NM	111th to 114th	Jan. 3, 2009
Lummis, Cynthia M.	WY	111th to 114th	Jan. 3, 2009
McClintock, Tom	CA	111th to 114th	Jan. 3, 2009
Olson, Pete	TX	111th to 114th	Jan. 3, 2009
Paulsen, Erik	MN	111th to 114th	Jan. 3, 2009
Pingree, Chellie	ME	111th to 114th	Jan. 3, 2009
Polis, Jared	CO	111th to 114th	Jan. 3, 2009
Posey, Bill	FL	111th to 114th	Jan. 3, 2009
Quigley, Mike	IL	*111th to 114th	Apr. 21, 2009
Reed, Tom	NY	*111th to 114th	Nov. 18, 2010
Roe, David P.	TN	111th to 114th	Jan. 3, 2009
Rooney, Thomas J.	FL	111th to 114th	Jan. 3, 2009
Schrader, Kurt	OR	111th to 114th	Jan. 3, 2009
Stutzman, Marlin A.	IN	*111th to 114th	Nov. 16, 2010
Thompson, Glenn	PA	111th to 114th	Jan. 3, 2009
Tonko, Paul	NY	111th to 114th	Jan. 3, 2009

4 terms, not consecutive

Name	State	Congresses (inclusive)	Beginning of present service
Fitzpatrick, Michael G.	PA	109th and 112th to 114th.	Jan. 3, 2011
Foster, Bill	IL	110th to 111th and 113th to 114.	Jan. 3, 2013
Walberg, Tim	MI	110th and 112th to 114th.	Jan. 3, 2011

3 terms, consecutive

Name	State	Congresses (inclusive)	Beginning of present service
Amash, Justin	MI	112th to 114th	Jan. 3, 2011
Amodei, Mark E.	NV	*112th to 114th	Sept. 15, 2011
Barletta, Lou	PA	112th to 114th	Jan. 3, 2011
Bass, Karen	CA	112th to 114th	Jan. 3, 2011
Benishek, Dan	MI	112th to 114th	Jan. 3, 2011
Black, Diane	TN	112th to 114th	Jan. 3, 2011
Bonamici, Suzanne	OR	*112th to 114th	Feb. 7, 2012
Brooks, Mo	AL	112th to 114th	Jan. 3, 2011
Bucshon, Larry	IN	112th to 114th	Jan. 3, 2011
Carney, John C., Jr.	DE	112th to 114th	Jan. 3, 2011
Cicilline, David N.	RI	112th to 114th	Jan. 3, 2011
Crawford, Eric A. "Rick"	AR	112th to 114th	Jan. 3, 2011

CONGRESSES IN WHICH REPRESENTATIVES, RESIDENT COMMISSIONER, AND DELEGATES HAVE SERVED WITH BEGINNING OF PRESENT SERVICE—CONTINUED

[* Elected to fill a vacancy; Republicans in roman (246); Democrats in *italic* (188); Vacancies (1); Resident Commissioner and Delegates in **boldface** (6); total, 441]

Name	State	Congresses (inclusive)	Beginning of present service
DelBene, Suzan K.	WA	*112th to 114th	Nov. 13, 2012
Denham, Jeff	CA	112th to 114th	Jan. 3, 2011
DesJarlais, Scott	TN	112th to 114th	Jan. 3, 2011
Duffy, Sean P.	WI	112th to 114th	Jan. 3, 2011
Duncan, Jeff	SC	112th to 114th	Jan. 3, 2011
Ellmers, Renee L.	NC	112th to 114th	Jan. 3, 2011
Farenthold, Blake	TX	112th to 114th	Jan. 3, 2011
Fincher, Stephen Lee	TN	112th to 114th	Jan. 3, 2011
Fleischmann, Charles J. "Chuck"	TN	112th to 114th	Jan. 3, 2011
Flores, Bill	TX	112th to 114th	Jan. 3, 2011
Gibbs, Bob	OH	112th to 114th	Jan. 3, 2011
Gibson, Christopher P.	NY	112th to 114th	Jan. 3, 2011
Gosar, Paul A.	AZ	112th to 114th	Jan. 3, 2011
Gowdy, Trey	SC	112th to 114th	Jan. 3, 2011
Griffith, H. Morgan	VA	112th to 114th	Jan. 3, 2011
Hahn, Janice	CA	*112th to 114th	July 19, 2011
Hanna, Richard L.	NY	112th to 114th	Jan. 3, 2011
Harris, Andy	MD	112th to 114th	Jan. 3, 2011
Hartzler, Vicky	MO	112th to 114th	Jan. 3, 2011
Heck, Joseph J.	NV	112th to 114th	Jan. 3, 2011
Herrera Beutler, Jaime	WA	112th to 114th	Jan. 3, 2011
Huelskamp, Tim	KS	112th to 114th	Jan. 3, 2011
Huizenga, Bill	MI	112th to 114th	Jan. 3, 2011
Hultgren, Randy	IL	112th to 114th	Jan. 3, 2011
Hurt, Robert	VA	112th to 114th	Jan. 3, 2011
Johnson, Bill	OH	112th to 114th	Jan. 3, 2011
Keating, William R.	MA	112th to 114th	Jan. 3, 2011
Kelly, Mike	PA	112th to 114th	Jan. 3, 2011
Kinzinger, Adam	IL	112th to 114th	Jan. 3, 2011
Labrador, Raúl R.	ID	112th to 114th	Jan. 3, 2011
Long, Billy	MO	112th to 114th	Jan. 3, 2011
Marino, Tom	PA	112th to 114th	Jan. 3, 2011
Massie, Thomas	KY	*112th to 114th	Nov. 13, 2012
McKinley, David B.	WV	112th to 114th	Jan. 3, 2011
Meehan, Patrick	PA	112th to 114th	Jan. 3, 2011
Mulvaney, Mick	SC	112th to 114th	Jan. 3, 2011
Noem, Kristi L.	SD	112th to 114th	Jan. 3, 2011
Nugent, Richard B.	FL	112th to 114th	Jan. 3, 2011
Payne, Donald M., Jr.	NJ	*112th to 114th	Nov. 15, 2012
Palazzo, Steven M.	MS	112th to 114th	Jan. 3, 2011
Pompeo, Mike	KS	112th to 114th	Jan. 3, 2011
Renacci, James B.	OH	112th to 114th	Jan. 3, 2011
Ribble, Reid J.	WI	112th to 114th	Jan. 3, 2011
Richmond, Cedric L.	LA	112th to 114th	Jan. 3, 2011
Rigell, E. Scott	VA	112th to 114th	Jan. 3, 2011
Roby, Martha	AL	112th to 114th	Jan. 3, 2011
Rokita, Todd	IN	112th to 114th	Jan. 3, 2011
Ross, Dennis A.	FL	112th to 114th	Jan. 3, 2011
Schweikert, David	AZ	112th to 114th	Jan. 3, 2011
Scott, Austin	GA	112th to 114th	Jan. 3, 2011
Sewell, Terri A.	AL	112th to 114th	Jan. 3, 2011

CONGRESSES IN WHICH REPRESENTATIVES, RESIDENT COMMISSIONER, AND DELEGATES HAVE SERVED WITH BEGINNING OF PRESENT SERVICE—CONTINUED

[* Elected to fill a vacancy; Republicans in roman (246); Democrats in *italic* (188); Vacancies (1); Resident Commissioner and Delegates in **boldface** (6); total, 441]

Name	State	Congresses (inclusive)	Beginning of present service
Stivers, Steve	OH	112th to 114th	Jan. 3, 2011
Tipton, Scott R.	CO	112th to 114th	Jan. 3, 2011
Webster, Daniel	FL	112th to 114th	Jan. 3, 2011
Wilson, Frederica S.	FL	112th to 114th	Jan. 3, 2011
Womack, Steve	AR	112th to 114th	Jan. 3, 2011
Woodall, Rob	GA	112th to 114th	Jan. 3, 2011
Yoder, Kevin	KS	112th to 114th	Jan. 3, 2011
Young, Todd C.	IN	112th to 114th	Jan. 3, 2011
3 terms, not consecutive			
Grayson, Alan	FL	111th and 113th to 114th.	Jan. 3, 2013
Kirkpatrick, Ann	AZ	111th and 113th to 114th.	Jan. 3, 2013
Titus, Dina	NV	111th and 113th to 114th.	Jan. 3, 2013
2 terms, consecutive			
Adams, Alma S.	NC	*113th and 114th	Nov. 12, 2014
Barr, Andy	KY	113th and 114th	Jan. 3, 2013
Beatty, Joyce	OH	113th and 114th	Jan. 3, 2013
Bera, Ami	CA	113th and 114th	Jan. 3, 2013
Brat, Dave	VA	*113th and 114th	Nov. 12, 2014
Bridenstine, Jim	OK	113th and 114th	Jan. 3, 2013
Brooks, Susan W.	IN	113th and 114th	Jan. 3, 2013
Brownley, Julia	CA	113th and 114th	Jan. 3, 2013
Bustos, Cheri	IL	113th and 114th	Jan. 3, 2013
Byrne, Bradley	AL	*113th and 114th	Jan. 8, 2014
Cárdenas, Tony	CA	113th and 114th	Jan. 3, 2013
Cartwright, Matt	PA	113th and 114th	Jan. 3, 2013
Castro, Joaquin	TX	113th and 114th	Jan. 3, 2013
Clark, Katherine M.	MA	*113th and 114th	Dec. 12, 2013
Clawson, Curt	FL	*113th and 114th	June 25, 2014
Collins, Chris	NY	113th and 114th	Jan. 3, 2013
Collins, Doug	GA	113th and 114th	Jan. 3, 2013
Cook, Paul	CA	113th and 114th	Jan. 3, 2013
Cramer, Kevin	ND	113th and 114th	Jan. 3, 2013
Davis, Rodney	IL	113th and 114th	Jan. 3, 2013
Delaney, John K.	MD	113th and 114th	Jan. 3, 2013
DeSantis, Ron	FL	113th and 114th	Jan. 3, 2013
Duckworth, Tammy	IL	113th and 114th	Jan. 3, 2013
Esty, Elizabeth H.	CT	113th and 114th	Jan. 3, 2013
Frankel, Lois	FL	113th and 114th	Jan. 3, 2013
Gabbard, Tulsi	HI	113th and 114th	Jan. 3, 2013
Heck, Denny	WA	113th and 114th	Jan. 3, 2013
Holding, George	NC	113th and 114th	Jan. 3, 2013
Hudson, Richard	NC	113th and 114th	Jan. 3, 2013
Huffman, Jared	CA	113th and 114th	Jan. 3, 2013
Jeffries, Hakeem S.	NY	113th and 114th	Jan. 3, 2013
Jolly, David W.	FL	*113th and 114th	Mar. 13, 2014

CONGRESSES IN WHICH REPRESENTATIVES, RESIDENT COMMISSIONER, AND DELEGATES HAVE SERVED WITH BEGINNING OF PRESENT SERVICE—CONTINUED

[* Elected to fill a vacancy; Republicans in roman (246); Democrats in *italic* (188); Vacancies (1); Resident Commissioner and Delegates in **boldface** (6); total, 441]

Name	State	Congresses (inclusive)	Beginning of present service
Joyce, David P.	OH	113th and 114th	Jan. 3, 2013
Kelly, Robin L.	IL	*113th and 114th ...	Apr. 11, 2013
Kennedy, Joseph P. III	MA	113th and 114th	Jan. 3, 2013
Kildee, Daniel T.	MI	113th and 114th	Jan. 3, 2013
Kilmer, Derek	WA	113th and 114th	Jan. 3, 2013
Kuster, Ann M.	NH	113th and 114th	Jan. 3, 2013
LaMalfa, Doug	CA	113th and 114th	Jan. 3, 2013
Lowenthal, Alan S.	CA	113th and 114th	Jan. 3, 2013
Lujan Grisham, Michelle	NM	113th and 114th	Jan. 3, 2013
Maloney, Sean Patrick	NY	113th and 114th	Jan. 3, 2013
Meadows, Mark	NC	113th and 114th	Jan. 3, 2013
Meng, Grace	NY	113th and 114th	Jan. 3, 2013
Messer, Luke	IN	113th and 114th	Jan. 3, 2013
Mullin, Markwayne	OK	113th and 114th	Jan. 3, 2013
Murphy, Patrick	FL	113th and 114th	Jan. 3, 2013
Norcross, Donald	NJ	*113th and 114th ...	Nov. 12, 2014
O'Rourke, Beto	TX	113th and 114th	Jan. 3, 2013
Perry, Scott	PA	113th and 114th	Jan. 3, 2013
Peters, Scott H.	CA	113th and 114th	Jan. 3, 2013
Pittenger, Robert	NC	113th and 114th	Jan. 3, 2013
Pocan, Mark	WI	113th and 114th	Jan. 3, 2013
Rice, Tom	SC	113th and 114th	Jan. 3, 2013
Rothfus, Keith J.	PA	113th and 114th	Jan. 3, 2013
Ruiz, Raul	CA	113th and 114th	Jan. 3, 2013
Sinema, Kyrsten	AZ	113th and 114th	Jan. 3, 2013
Smith, Jason T.	MO	*113th and 114th ...	June 5, 2013
Stewart, Chris	UT	113th and 114th	Jan. 3, 2013
Swalwell, Eric	CA	113th and 114th	Jan. 3, 2013
Takano, Mark	CA	113th and 114th	Jan. 3, 2013
Valadao, David G.	CA	113th and 114th	Jan. 3, 2013
Vargas, Juan	CA	113th and 114th	Jan. 3, 2013
Veasey, Marc A.	TX	113th and 114th	Jan. 3, 2013
Vela, Filemon	TX	113th and 114th	Jan. 3, 2013
Wagner, Ann	MO	113th and 114th	Jan. 3, 2013
Walorski, Jackie	IN	113th and 114th	Jan. 3, 2013
Weber, Randy K., Sr.	TX	113th and 114th	Jan. 3, 2013
Wenstrup, Brad R.	OH	113th and 114th	Jan. 3, 2013
Williams, Roger	TX	113th and 114th	Jan. 3, 2013
Yoho, Ted S.	FL	113th and 114th	Jan. 3, 2013
2 terms, not consecutive			
Dold, Robert J.	IL	112th and 114th	Jan. 3, 2015
Guinta, Frank C.	NH	112th and 114th	Jan. 3, 2015
1 term			
Abraham, Ralph Lee	LA	114th	Jan. 3, 2015
Aguilar, Pete	CA	114th	Jan. 3, 2015
Allen, Rick W.	GA	114th	Jan. 3, 2015
Ashford, Brad	NE	114th	Jan. 3, 2015
Babin, Brian	TX	114th	Jan. 3, 2015

CONGRESSES IN WHICH REPRESENTATIVES, RESIDENT COMMISSIONER, AND DELEGATES HAVE SERVED WITH BEGINNING OF PRESENT SERVICE—CONTINUED

[* Elected to fill a vacancy; Republicans in roman (246); Democrats in *italic* (188); Vacancies (1); Resident Commissioner and Delegates in **boldface** (6); total, 441]

Name	State	Congresses (inclusive)	Beginning of present service
Beyer, Donald S., Jr.	VA	114th	Jan. 3, 2015
Bishop, Mike	MI	114th	Jan. 3, 2015
Blum, Rod	IA	114th	Jan. 3, 2015
Bost, Mike	IL	114th	Jan. 3, 2015
Boyle, Brendan F.	PA	114th	Jan. 3, 2015
Buck, Ken	CO	114th	Jan. 3, 2015
Carter, Earl L. "Buddy"	GA	114th	Jan. 3, 2015
Comstock, Barbara	VA	114th	Jan. 3, 2015
Costello, Ryan A.	PA	114th	Jan. 3, 2015
Curbelo, Carlos	FL	114th	Jan. 3, 2015
DeSaulnier, Mark	CA	114th	Jan. 3, 2015
Dingell, Debbie	MI	114th	Jan. 3, 2015
Donovan, Daniel M., Jr.	NY	*114th	May 12, 2015
Emmer, Tom	MN	114th	Jan. 3, 2015
Gallego, Ruben	AZ	114th	Jan. 3, 2015
Graham, Gwen	FL	114th	Jan. 3, 2015
Graves, Garret	LA	114th	Jan. 3, 2015
Grothman, Glenn	WI	114th	Jan. 3, 2015
Hardy, Cresent	NV	114th	Jan. 3, 2015
Hice, Jody B.	GA	114th	Jan. 3, 2015
Hill, J. French	AR	114th	Jan. 3, 2015
Hurd, Will	TX	114th	Jan. 3, 2015
Jenkins, Evan H.	WV	114th	Jan. 3, 2015
Katko, John	NY	114th	Jan. 3, 2015
Kelly, Trent	MS	*114th	June 9, 2015
Knight, Stephen	CA	114th	Jan. 3, 2015
LaHood, Darin	IL	*114th	Sept. 17, 2015
Lawrence, Brenda L.	MI	114th	Jan. 3, 2015
Lieu, Ted	CA	114th	Jan. 3, 2015
Loudermilk, Barry	GA	114th	Jan. 3, 2015
Love, Mia B.	UT	114th	Jan. 3, 2015
MacArthur, Thomas	NJ	114th	Jan. 3, 2015
McSally, Martha	AZ	114th	Jan. 3, 2015
Moolenaar, John R.	MI	114th	Jan. 3, 2015
Mooney, Alexander X.	WV	114th	Jan. 3, 2015
Moulton, Seth	MA	114th	Jan. 3, 2015
Newhouse, Dan	WA	114th	Jan. 3, 2015
Palmer, Gary J.	AL	114th	Jan. 3, 2015
Poliquin, Bruce	ME	114th	Jan. 3, 2015
Ratcliffe, John	TX	114th	Jan. 3, 2015
Rice, Kathleen M.	NY	114th	Jan. 3, 2015
Rouzer, David	NC	114th	Jan. 3, 2015
Russell, Steve	OK	114th	Jan. 3, 2015
Stefanik, Elise M.	NY	114th	Jan. 3, 2015
Takai, Mark	HI	114th	Jan. 3, 2015
Torres, Norma J.	CA	114th	Jan. 3, 2015
Trott, David A.	MI	114th	Jan. 3, 2015
Walker, Mark	NC	114th	Jan. 3, 2015
Walters, Mimi	CA	114th	Jan. 3, 2015
Watson Coleman, Bonnie	NJ	114th	Jan. 3, 2015
Westerman, Bruce	AR	114th	Jan. 3, 2015

CONGRESSES IN WHICH REPRESENTATIVES, RESIDENT COMMISSIONER, AND DELEGATES HAVE SERVED WITH BEGINNING OF PRESENT SERVICE—CONTINUED

[* Elected to fill a vacancy; Republicans in roman (246); Democrats in *italic* (188); Vacancies (1); Resident Commissioner and Delegates in **boldface** (6); total, 441]

Name	State	Congresses (inclusive)	Beginning of present service
Young, David	IA	114th	Jan. 3, 2015
Zeldin, Lee M.	NY	114th	Jan. 3, 2015
Zinke, Ryan K.	MT	114th	Jan. 3, 2015
RESIDENT COMMISSIONER			
Pierluisi, Pedro R.	PR	111th to 114th	Jan. 3, 2009
DELEGATES			
Radewagen, Aumua Amata Coleman	AS	114th	Jan. 3, 2015
Norton, Eleanor Holmes	DC	102d to 114th	Jan. 3, 1991
Bordallo, Madeleine Z.	GU	108th to 114th	Jan. 3, 2003
Sablan, Gregorio Kilili Camacho ...	MP	111th to 114th	Jan. 3, 2009
Plaskett, Stacey E.	VI	114th	Jan. 3, 2015

NOTE: Members elected by special election are considered to begin service on the date that they were sworn in, except for those elected after a sine die adjournment. If elected after the Congress has adjourned for the session, Members are considered to begin their service on the day after the election.

STANDING COMMITTEES OF THE SENATE

Agriculture, Nutrition, and Forestry

328A Russell Senate Office Building 20510–6000

phone 224–2035, fax 228–2125, TTY/TDD 224–2587

http://agriculture.senate.gov

meets first and third Wednesdays of each month

Pat Roberts, of Kansas, *Chair*

Thad Cochran, of Mississippi.
Mitch McConnell, of Kentucky.
John Boozman, of Arkansas.
John Hoeven, of North Dakota.
David Perdue, of Georgia.
Joni Ernst, of Iowa.
Thom Tillis, of North Carolina.
Ben Sasse, of Nebraska.
Chuck Grassley, of Iowa.
John Thune, of South Dakota.

Debbie Stabenow, of Michigan.
Patrick J. Leahy, of Vermont.
Sherrod Brown, of Ohio.
Amy Klobuchar, of Minnesota.
Michael F. Bennet, of Colorado.
Kirsten E. Gillibrand, of New York.
Joe Donnelly, of Indiana.
Heidi Heitkamp, of North Dakota.
Robert P. Casey, Jr., of Pennsylvania.

SUBCOMMITTEES

[The chairman and ranking minority member are ex officio (non-voting) members of all subcommittees on which they do not serve.]

Commodities, Risk Management and Trade

John Boozman, of Arkansas, *Chair*

Thad Cochran, of Mississippi.
John Hoeven, of North Dakota.
David Perdue, of Georgia.
Chuck Grassley, of Iowa.
John Thune, of South Dakota.

Joe Donnelly, of Indiana.
Heidi Heitkamp, of North Dakota.
Sherrod Brown, of Ohio.
Kirsten E. Gillibrand, of New York.
Michael F. Bennet, of Colorado.

Conservation, Forestry and Natural Resources

David Perdue, of Georgia, *Chair*

Thad Cochran, of Mississippi.
Mitch McConnell, of Kentucky.
John Boozman, of Arkansas.
Ben Sasse, of Nebraska.
Chuck Grassley, of Iowa.

Michael F. Bennet, of Colorado.
Amy Klobuchar, of Minnesota.
Patrick J. Leahy, of Vermont.
Heidi Heitkamp, of North Dakota.
Robert P. Casey, Jr., of Pennsylvania.

Livestock, Marketing and Agriculture Security

Ben Sasse, of Nebraska, *Chair*

Mitch McConnell, of Kentucky.
Joni Ernst, of Iowa.
Thom Tillis, of North Carolina.
John Thune, of South Dakota.
Chuck Grassley, of Iowa.

Kirsten E. Gillibrand, of New York.
Patrick J. Leahy, of Vermont.
Amy Klobuchar, of Minnesota.
Joe Donnelly, of Indiana.
Robert P. Casey, Jr., of Pennsylvania.

Nutrition, Specialty Crops and Agricultural Research

John Hoeven, of North Dakota, *Chair*

Mitch McConnell, of Kentucky.
John Boozman, of Arkansas.
Joni Ernst, of Iowa.
Thom Tillis, of North Carolina.
Ben Sasse, of Nebraska.

Robert P. Casey, Jr., of Pennsylvania.
Patrick J. Leahy, of Vermont.
Sherrod Brown, of Ohio.
Kirsten E. Gillibrand, of New York.
Michael F. Bennet, of Colorado.

Rural Development and Energy

Joni Ernst, of Iowa, *Chair*

Thad Cochran, of Mississippi.
John Hoeven, of North Dakota.
David Perdue, of Georgia.
Thom Tillis, of North Carolina.
John Thune, of South Dakota.

Heidi Heitkamp, of North Dakota.
Sherrod Brown, of Ohio.
Amy Klobuchar, of Minnesota.
Michael F. Bennet, of Colorado.
Joe Donnelly, of Indiana.

STAFF

Committee on Agriculture, Nutrition, and Forestry (SR–328A), 224–2035, fax 228–2125.
Majority Staff:
Staff Director.—Joel Leftwich.
  Chief Counsel and Senior Advisor.—Anne Hazlett.
  Chief Economist.—Matthew Erickson.
  Executive Assistant.—Katherine Thomas.
  Investigative Counsel.—Andrew Rezendes.
  Press Secretary.—Meghan Cline.
  Senior Counsel.—DaNita Murray.
  Senior Policy Advisors: Julian Baer, James Glueck.
  Senior Professional Staff.—Janae Brady, Darin Guries, Chelsie Keys, Andrew Vlasaty.
  Professional Staff.—Wayne Stoskopf.
  Senior Professional Staff/Counsel.—Charlie Thornton.
  Staff Assistant/Legislative Correspondents: Maddy Connor, Anthony Seiler.
Minority Staff:
Staff Director.—Chris Adamo.
  Chief Counsel.—Jonathan Cordone.
  Chief Economist.—Joe Shultz.
  Executive Assistant/Legislative Correspondent.—Kyle Varner.
  Legal Fellow.—Mary Olive.
  Legislative Assistant/Policy Analyst.—Katie Naessens.
  Legislative Correspondent.—Katie Bergh.
  Policy Analyst.—Grant Colvin.
  Press Secretary.—Ben Famous.
  Senior Counsel.—Russ Behnam.
  Senior Professional Staff: Sean Babington, Ashley McKeon, Jacqlyn Schneider.
Non-Designated:
  Archivist.—Katie Salay.
  Chief Clerk.—Jessie Williams.
  Deputy Chief Clerk.—Cindy Qualley.
  Director of Printing and Binding.—Micah Wortham.
  System Administrator.—Bobby Mehta.

Appropriations

S–128 The Capitol 20510–6025, phone 224–7257

http://appropriations.senate.gov

meets upon call of the chair

Thad Cochran, of Mississippi, *Chair*

Mitch McConnell, of Kentucky.
Richard C. Shelby, of Alabama.
Lamar Alexander, of Tennessee.
Susan M. Collins, of Maine.
Lisa Murkowski, of Alaska.
Lindsey Graham, of South Carolina.
Mark Kirk, of Illinois.
Roy Blunt, of Missouri.
Jerry Moran, of Kansas.
John Hoeven, of North Dakota.
John Boozman, of Arkansas.
Shelley Moore Capito, of West Virginia.
Bill Cassidy, of Louisiana.
James Lankford, of Oklahoma.
Steve Daines, of Montana.

Barbara A. Mikulski, of Maryland.
Patrick J. Leahy, of Vermont.
Patty Murray, of Washington.
Dianne Feinstein, of California.
Richard J. Durbin, of Illinois.
Jack Reed, of Rhode Island.
Jon Tester, of Montana.
Tom Udall, of New Mexico.
Jeanne Shaheen, of New Hampshire.
Jeff Merkley, of Oregon.
Christopher A. Coons, of Delaware.
Brian Schatz, of Hawaii.
Tammy Baldwin, of Wisconsin.
Christopher Murphy, of Connecticut.

SUBCOMMITTEES

[The chairman and ranking minority member are ex officio members of all subcommittees on which they do not serve.]

Agriculture, Rural Development, Food and Drug Administration, and Related Agencies

Jerry Moran, of Kansas, *Chair*

Roy Blunt, of Missouri.
Thad Cochran, of Mississippi.
Mitch McConnell, of Kentucky.
Susan M. Collins, of Maine.
John Hoeven, of North Dakota.
Steve Daines, of Montana.

Jeff Merkley, of Oregon.
Dianne Feinstein, of California.
Jon Tester, of Montana.
Tom Udall, of New Mexico.
Patrick J. Leahy, of Vermont.
Tammy Baldwin, of Wisconsin.

Commerce, Justice, Science, and Related Agencies

Richard C. Shelby, of Alabama, *Chair*

Lamar Alexander, of Tennessee.
Lisa Murkowski, of Alaska.
Susan M. Collins, of Maine.
Lindsey Graham, of South Carolina.
Mark Kirk, of Illinois.
John Boozman, of Arkansas.
Shelley Moore Capito, of West Virginia.
James Lankford, of Oklahoma.

Barbara A. Mikulski, of Maryland.
Patrick J. Leahy, of Vermont.
Dianne Feinstein, of California.
Jack Reed, of Rhode Island.
Jeanne Shaheen, of New Hampshire.
Christopher A. Coons, of Delaware.
Tammy Baldwin, of Wisconsin.
Christopher Murphy, of Connecticut.

Defense

Thad Cochran, of Mississippi, *Chair*

Mitch McConnell, of Kentucky.
Richard C. Shelby, of Alabama.
Lamar Alexander, of Tennessee.
Susan M. Collins, of Maine.
Lisa Murkowski, of Alaska.
Lindsey Graham, of South Carolina.
Roy Blunt, of Missouri.
Steve Daines, of Montana.
Jerry Moran, of Kansas.

Richard J. Durbin, of Illinois.
Patrick J. Leahy, of Vermont.
Dianne Feinstein, of California.
Barbara A. Mikulski, of Maryland.
Patty Murray, of Washington.
Jack Reed, of Rhode Island.
Jon Tester, of Montana.
Tom Udall, of New Mexico.
Brian Schatz, of Hawaii.

Energy and Water Development

Lamar Alexander, of Tennessee, *Chair*

Thad Cochran, of Mississippi.
Mitch McConnell, of Kentucky.
Richard C. Shelby, of Alabama.
Susan M. Collins, of Maine.
Lisa Murkowski, of Alaska.
Lindsey Graham, of South Carolina.
John Hoeven, of North Dakota.
James Lankford, of Oklahoma.

Dianne Feinstein, of California.
Patty Murray, of Washington.
Jon Tester, of Montana.
Richard J. Durbin, of Illinois.
Tom Udall, of New Mexico.
Jeanne Shaheen, of New Hampshire.
Jeff Merkley, of Oregon.
Christopher A. Coons, of Delaware.

Financial Services and General Government

John Boozman, of Arkansas, *Chair*

Jerry Moran, of Kansas.
James Lankford, of Oklahoma.

Christopher A. Coons, of Delaware,
Richard J. Durbin, of Illinois.

Homeland Security

John Hoeven, of North Dakota, *Chair*

Thad Cochran, of Mississippi.
Richard C. Shelby, of Alabama.
Lisa Murkowski, of Alaska.
Lindsey Graham, of South Carolina.
Bill Cassidy, of Louisiana.

Jeanne Shaheen, of New Hampshire.
Patrick J. Leahy, of Vermont.
Patty Murray, of Washington.
Jon Tester, of Montana.
Tammy Baldwin, of Wisconsin.

Interior, Environment, and Related Agencies

Lisa Murkowski, of Alaska, *Chair*

Lamar Alexander, of Tennessee.
Thad Cochran, of Mississippi.
Roy Blunt, of Missouri.
John Hoeven, of North Dakota.
Mitch McConnell, of Kentucky.
Steve Daines, of Montana.
Bill Cassidy, of Louisiana.

Tom Udall, of New Mexico.
Dianne Feinstein, of California.
Patrick J. Leahy, of Vermont.
Jack Reed, of Rhode Island.
Jon Tester, of Montana.
Jeff Merkley, of Oregon.

Labor, Health and Human Services, Education, and Related Agencies

Roy Blunt, of Missouri, *Chair*

Jerry Moran, of Kansas.
Richard C. Shelby, of Alabama.
Thad Cochran, of Mississippi.
Lamar Alexander, of Tennessee.
Lindsey Graham, of South Carolina.
Mark Kirk, of Illinois.
Bill Cassidy, of Louisiana.
Shelley Moore Capito, of West Virginia.
James Lankford, of Oklahoma.

Patty Murray, of Washington.
Richard J. Durbin, of Illinois.
Jack Reed, of Rhode Island.
Barbara A. Mikulski, of Maryland.
Jeanne Shaheen, of New Hampshire.
Jeff Merkley, of Oregon.
Brian Schatz, of Hawaii.
Tammy Baldwin, of Wisconsin.

Legislative Branch

Shelley Moore Capito, of West Virginia, *Chair*

Mark Kirk, of Illinois.
Jerry Moran, of Kansas.

Brian Schatz, of Hawaii.
Christopher Murphy, of Connecticut.

Military Construction, Veterans Affairs, and Related Agencies

Mark Kirk, of Illinois, *Chair*

Mitch McConnell, of Kentucky.
Lisa Murkowski, of Alaska.
John Hoeven, of North Dakota.
Susan M. Collins, of Maine.
John Boozman, of Arkansas.
Shelley Moore Capito, of West Virginia.
Bill Cassidy, of Louisiana.

Jon Tester, of Montana.
Patty Murray, of Washington.
Jack Reed, of Rhode Island.
Tom Udall, of New Mexico.
Brian Schatz, of Hawaii.
Tammy Baldwin, of Wisconsin.
Christopher Murphy, of Connecticut.

State, Foreign Operations, and Related Programs

Lindsey Graham, of South Carolina, *Chair*

Mitch McConnell, of Kentucky.
Mark Kirk, of Illinois.
Roy Blunt, of Missouri.
John Boozman, of Arkansas.
Jerry Moran, of Kansas.
James Lankford, of Oklahoma.
Steve Daines, of Montana.

Patrick J. Leahy, of Vermont.
Barbara A. Mikulski, of Maryland.
Richard J. Durbin, of Illinois.
Jeanne Shaheen, of New Hampshire.
Christopher A. Coons, of Delaware.
Jeff Merkley, of Oregon.
Christopher Murphy, of Connecticut.

Transportation, Housing and Urban Development,

and Related Agencies

Susan M. Collins, of Maine, *Chair*

Richard C. Shelby, of Alabama.
Lamar Alexander, of Tennessee.
Mark Kirk, of Illinois.
Roy Blunt, of Missouri.
John Boozman, of Arkansas.
Shelley Moore Capito, of West Virginia.
Bill Cassidy, of Louisiana.
Steve Daines, of Montana.

Jack Reed, of Rhode Island.
Barbara A. Mikulski, of Maryland.
Patty Murray, of Washington.
Richard J. Durbin, of Illinois.
Dianne Feinstein, of California.
Christopher A. Coons, of Delaware.
Brian Schatz, of Hawaii.
Christopher Murphy, of Connecticut.

STAFF

Committee on Appropriations (S-128), 224-7257.
  Staff Director.—Bruce Evans (S-128).
  Chief Clerk.—Robert W. Putnam (SD-114).
  Communications Director.—Chris Gallegos (S-128).
  Deputy Communications Director.—Stephen Worley (S-128).
  Professional Staff: Ben Hammond (S-128); Colin MacDermott (SD-114); Rachelle
    Schroeder (S-128); Courtney Stevens (S-128).
  Technical Systems Manager.—Hong Nguyen (SD-114).
  Security Manager.—Debbie Chiarello (SD-118).
  Clerical Assistant.—George Castro (SD-120), 4-5433.
  Minority Staff Director.—Charles E. Kieffer (S-146A), 4-7363.
  Minority Deputy Staff Director.—Jean Toal Eisen (S-146A).
  Press Assistant.—Mara Stark-Alcala (S-146A).
  Senior Advisor.—Brigid Houton (S-146A).
  Professional Staff: Jessica McNiece (SD-134); Kali Matalon (S-146A); Melissa
    Zimmerman (SH-125).
  Executive Assistant.—Teri Curtin (SD-156).
Subcommittee on Agriculture, Rural Development, Food and Drug Administration, and Related
  Agencies (SD-127), 4-5270.
  Majority Clerk.—Carlisle Clarke (SD-127).
  Professional Staff.—Patrick Carroll (SD-127); Rachel Santos (SD-127).
  Minority Clerk.—Jessica Arden Schulken (SD-190), 4-8090.
  Professional Staff.—Dianne Nellor (SD-190).
  Staff Assistant.—Teri Curtin (SD-156).
Subcommittee on Commerce, Justice, Science, and Related Agencies (SD-142), 4-7277.
  Majority Clerk.—Jeremy Weirich (SD-142).
  Professional Staff: Hayley Alexander (SD-142); Allen Cutler (SD-142); Kolo Rathburn
    (SD-142); Steven Wall (SD-142).
  Minority Clerk.—Jean Toal Eisen (SH-125), 4-5202.
  Professional Staff: Jennifer Eskra (SH-125); Molly O'Rourke (SH-125).
Subcommittee on Defense (SD-122), 4-7255.
  Majority Clerk.—Brian Potts (SD-122).
  Professional Staff: Colleen Gaydos (SD-122); Katy Hagan (SD-122); Chris Hall (SD-
    122); Church Hutton (SD-122); Kate Kaufer (SD-122), Jacqui Russell (SD-122); Jen-
    nifer S. Santos (SD-122); Will Todd (SD-122).
  Staff Assistant.—Casey Stafford (SD-122).
  Minority Clerk.—Erik Raven (SD-117), 4-6688.
  Professional Staff: David C. Gillies (SD-115); Maria Hammond (SD-115); Teri Spoutz
    (SD-115); Andy Vanlandingham (SD-115).
Subcommittee on Energy and Water Development (SD-142), 4-7260.
  Majority Clerk.—Tyler Owens (SD-142).
  Professional Staff: Hayley Alexander (SD-142); Adam DeMella (SD-142); Meyer
    Seligman (SD-142).
  Minority Clerk.—Doug Clapp (SD-188), 4-8119.
  Professional Staff.—Chris Hanson (SD-188).
  Staff Assistant.—Samantha Nelson (SH-125).
Subcommittee on Financial Services and General Government (SD-133), 4-2104.
  Majority Clerk.—Dale Cabaniss (SD-133).
  Professional Staff: Andrew Newton (SD-133); Taylor Nicholas (SD-133); LaShawnda
    Smith (SD-131).
  Minority Clerk.—Marianne Upton (SH-125), 4-1133.
  Professional Staff: Diana Gourlay Hamilton (SH-125); Emily Sharp (SH-125).
  Staff Assistant.—Samantha Nelson (SH-125).
Subcommittee on Homeland Security (SD-131), 4-4319.
  Majority Clerk.—Kathy Kraninger (SD-131).
  Professional Staff: Peter Babb (SD-131); Tom Bishop (SD-131); Matt Cowles (SD-
    131); LaShawnda Smith (SD-131).
  Minority Clerk.—Stephanie Gupta (SD-128), 4-8244.
  Professional Staff: Drenan A. Dudley (SD-128); Scott Nance (SD-128); Chip Walgren
    (SD-128).
  Staff Assistant.—Samantha Nelson (SH-125).
Subcommittee on Interior, Environment, and Related Agencies (SD-131), 4-7233.
  Majority Clerk.—Leif Fonnesbeck (SD-131).
  Professional Staff: Emy Lesofski (SD-131); Nona McCoy (SD-131); Chris Tomassi (SD-
    131); LaShawnda Smith (SD-131).

Minority Clerk.—Rachael Taylor (SH–125), 8–0774.
　Professional Staff: Ryan Hunt (SH–125); Melissa Zimmerman (SH–125).
　Staff Assistant.—Teri Curtin (SD–156).
Subcommittee on Labor, Health and Human Services, Education, and Related Agencies (SD–135), 4–7230.
Majority Clerk. Laura A. Friedel (SD–135).
　Professional Staff: Michael Gentile (SD–135); Chol Pak SD–135); Adam Sullivan SD–135).
　Staff Assistant.—Rob Taggart (SD–135).
Minority Clerk.—Alex Keenan (SD–156), 4–9145.
　Professional Staff: Lisa Bernhardt (SD–156); Kelly Brown (SD–156); Mark Laisch (SD–156).
　Staff Assistant.—Teri Curtin (SD–156).
Subcommittee on Legislative Branch (S–128), 4–9747.
Majority Clerk.—Rachelle G. Schroeder (S–128).
　Professional Staff.—Courtney Stevens (S–128).
Minority Clerk.—Melissa Zimmerman (S–146A), 4–7256.
　Professional Staff.—Kali Matalon (S–146A).
Subcommittee on Military Construction, Veterans Affairs, and Related Agencies (SD–125), 4–5245.
Majority Clerk.—Bob Henke (SD–125).
　Professional Staff: D'Ann Lettieri (SD–125); Patrick Magnuson (SD–125); Hayley Alexander (SD–142).
Minority Clerk.—Christina Evans (SH–125), 4–8224.
　Professional Staff: Michael Bain (SH–125); Chad C. Schulken (SH–125).
　Staff Assistant.—Samantha Nelson (SH–125).
Subcommittee on State, Foreign Operations, and Related Programs (SD–127), 4–2104.
Majority Clerk.—Paul Grove (SD–127).
　Professional Staff: LaShawnda Smith (SD–131); Jason Wheelock (SD–127), Adam Yezerski (SD–127).
Minority Clerk.—Tim Rieser (SD–127), 4–7284.
　Professional Staff: Alex Carnes (SH–125); Maria Hammond (SD–115); Janet Stormes (SH–125).
Subcommittee on Transportation, Housing and Urban Development, and Related Agencies (SD–184), 4–5310.
Majority Clerk.—Heideh Shahmoradi (SD–184).
　Professional Staff: Ken Altman (SD–184); Rajat Mathur (SD–184); Jason Woolwine (SD–184).
　Staff Assistant.—Gus Maples (SD–184).
Minority Clerk.—Dabney Hegg (SH–125), 4–7281.
　Professional Staff.—Rachel Milberg (SH–125).
　Editorial and Printing (SD–126): Elmer Barnes (GPO), 4–7266; Valerie A. Hutton, 4–7267; Celina Inman (GPO), 4–7217, Penny Myles (GPO), 4–7265.

Armed Services

228 Russell Senate Office Building 20510–6050
phone 224–3871, http://www.armed-services.senate.gov

meets every Tuesday and Thursday

John McCain, of Arizona, *Chair*

James M. Inhofe, of Oklahoma.
Jeff Sessions, of Alabama.
Roger F. Wicker, of Mississippi.
Kelly Ayotte, of New Hampshire.
Deb Fischer, of Nebraska.
Tom Cotton, of Arkansas.
Mike Rounds, of South Dakota.
Joni Ernst, of Iowa.
Thom Tillis, of North Carolina.
Dan Sullivan, of Alaska.
Mike Lee, of Utah.
Lindsey Graham, of South Carolina.
Ted Cruz, of Texas.

Jack Reed, of Rhode Island.
Bill Nelson, of Florida.
Claire McCaskill, of Missouri.
Joe Manchin III, of West Virginia.
Jeanne Shaheen, of New Hampshire.
Kirsten E. Gillibrand, of New York.
Richard Blumenthal, of Connecticut.
Joe Donnelly, of Indiana.
Mazie K. Hirono, of Hawaii.
Tim Kaine, of Virginia.
ANGUS S. KING, JR., of Maine.
Martin Heinrich, of New Mexico.

SUBCOMMITTEES

[The chairman and the ranking minority member are ex officio (non-voting) members of all subcommittees on which they do not serve.]

Airland

Tom Cotton, of Arkansas, *Chair*

James M. Inhofe, of Oklahoma.
Jeff Sessions, of Alabama.
Roger F. Wicker, of Mississippi.
Mike Rounds, of South Dakota.
Joni Ernst, of Iowa.
Dan Sullivan, of Alaska.
Mike Lee, of Utah.

Joe Manchin III, of West Virginia.
Claire McCaskill, of Missouri.
Kirsten E. Gillibrand, of New York.
Richard Blumenthal, of Connecticut.
Joe Donnelly, of Indiana.
Mazie K. Hirono, of Hawaii.
Martin Heinrich, of New Mexico.

Emerging Threats and Capabilities

Deb Fischer, of Nebraska, *Chair*

Kelly Ayotte, of New Hampshire.
Tom Cotton, of Arkansas.
Joni Ernst, of Iowa.
Thom Tillis, of North Carolina.
Lindsey Graham, of South Carolina.
Ted Cruz, of Texas.

Bill Nelson, of Florida.
Joe Manchin III, of West Virginia.
Jeanne Shaheen, of New Hampshire.
Kirsten E. Gillibrand, of New York.
Joe Donnelly, of Indiana.
Tim Kaine, of Virginia.

Personnel

Lindsey Graham, of South Carolina, *Chair*

Roger F. Wicker, of Mississippi.
Tom Cotton, of Arkansas.
Thom Tillis, of North Carolina.
Dan Sullivan, of Alaska.

Kirsten E. Gillibrand, of New York.
Claire McCaskill, of Missouri.
Richard Blumenthal, of Connecticut.
ANGUS S. KING, JR., of Maine.

Readiness and Management Support

Kelly Ayotte, of New Hampshire, *Chair*

James M. Inhofe, of Oklahoma.
Deb Fischer, of Nebraska.
Mike Rounds, of South Dakota.
Joni Ernst, of Iowa.
Mike Lee, of Utah.

Tim Kaine, of Virginia.
Claire McCaskill, of Missouri.
Jeanne Shaheen, of New Hampshire.
Mazie K. Hirono, of Hawaii.
Martin Heinrich, of New Mexico.

Seapower

Roger F. Wicker, of Mississippi, *Chair*

Jeff Sessions, of Alabama.
Kelly Ayotte, of New Hampshire.
Mike Rounds, of South Dakota.
Thom Tillis, of North Carolina.
Dan Sullivan, of Alaska.
Ted Cruz, of Texas.

Mazie K. Hirono, of Hawaii.
Bill Nelson, of Florida.
Jeanne Shaheen, of New Hampshire.
Richard Blumenthal, of Connecticut.
Tim Kaine, of Virginia.
ANGUS S. KING, JR., of Maine.

Strategic Forces

Jeff Sessions, of Alabama, *Chair*

James M. Inhofe, of Oklahoma.
Deb Fischer, of Nebraska.
Mike Lee, of Utah.
Lindsey Graham, of South Carolina.
Ted Cruz, of Texas.

Joe Donnelly, of Indiana.
Bill Nelson, of Florida.
Joe Manchin III, of West Virginia.
ANGUS S. KING, JR., of Maine.
Martin Heinrich, of New Mexico.

STAFF

Committee on Armed Services (SR–228), 224–3871.
  Majority and Non-Designated Staff:
  Staff Director.—Chris Brose.
    Deputy Staff Director.—Cord Sterling.
    Policy Director and Counsel.—Katie Wheelbarger.
    General Counsel.—Steve Barney.
    Senior Military Advisor.—James Hickey.
    Chief Clerk.—Greg Lilly.
    Chief Investigator.—Kathryn Edelman.
    Counsel.—Samantha Clark.
    Communications Director.—Dustin Walker.
    Professional Staff Members: Adam Barker, Matt Donovan, Allen Edwards, Elizabeth Everett, Anish Goel, Tom Goffus, Bill Greenwalt, Jeremy Hayes, John Lehman, Daniel Lerner, Brad Patout, Jason Potter, Diem Salmon, Eric Sayers, Rob Soofer, Jennifer White.
    Nominations and Hearings Clerk.—Leah Brewer.
    Security Manager.—Barry Walker.
    Systems Administrator.—Gary Howard.
    Printing and Documents Clerk.—June Borawski.
    Special Assistant.—Jackie Kerber.
    Research Analysts: Lauren Davis, Natalie Nicolas, Will Quinn.
    Staff Assistants: Jon Rosenthal, Brendan Sawyer, Leah Scheunemann, Robert Waisanen.
  Subcommittee on Airland
    Lead.—James Hickey.
    Staff Assistant.—Robert Waisanen.
  Subcommittee on Emerging Threats and Capabilities
    Lead.—Tom Goffus.
    Research Analyst.—Natalie Nicolas.
  Subcommittee on Personnel
    Lead.—Allen Edwards.
    Staff Assistant.—Brendan Sawyer.

Subcommittee on Readiness and Management Support
　Lead.—Bill Greenwalt.
　Staff Assistant.—Leah Scheunemann.
Subcommittee on Seapower
　Lead.—Jason Potter.
　Research Analyst.—Will Quinn.
Subcommittee on Strategic Forces
　Lead.—Rob Soofer.
　Research Analyst.—Lauren Davis.
　Majority Staff Subject Areas
　　Acquisition Policy.—Bill Greenwalt.
　　Acquisition Workforce.—Bill Greenwalt.
　　Ammunition.—Brad Patout.
　　Arms Control.—Rob Soofer.
　　Authorized Use of Military Force.—Katie Wheelbarger.
　　Aviation Systems (Except Rotary).—Matt Donovan.
　　Base Realignment and Closure (BRAC).—Cord Sterling.
　　Budget.—Diem Salmon.
　　Chemical—Biological Defense.—Elizabeth Everett.
　　Chemical Demilitarization.—Elizabeth Everett.
　　Civilian Nominations.—Steve Barney.
　　Civilian Personnel Policy.—Samantha Clark.
　　Combatant commands/Regions
　　　AFRICOM.—Adam Barker.
　　　CENTCOM.—Tom Goffus.
　　　EUCOM.—Tom Goffus.
　　　NORTHCOM.—Adam Barker.
　　　PACOM.—Eric Sayers.
　　　SOCOM.—Adam Barker.
　　　SOUTHCOM.—Adam Barker.
　　　STRATCOM.—Rob Soofer.
　　　TRANSCOM.—Jeremy Hayes.
　　　CYBERCOM.—Daniel Lerner.
　　Combating Terrorism.—Katie Wheelbarger.
　　Competition Policy.—Bill Greenwalt.
　　Competitive Sourcing/A-76.—Bill Greenwalt.
　　Contracting (Including Service Contracts).—Bill Greenwalt.
　　Cooperative Threat Reduction Programs.—Rob Soofer.
　　Counterdrug Programs.—Adam Barker.
　　Cybersecurity.—Daniel Lerner.
　　Defense Laboratory Management.—Cord Sterling.
　　Defense Security Assistance.—Adam Barker.
　　Department of Energy Issues.—Rob Soofer.
　　Depot Maintenance Policy.—Brad Patout.
　　Detainee Policy.—Katie Wheelbarger.
　　Domestic Preparedness.—Adam Barker.
　　Environmental Issues.—Elizabeth Everett.
　　Financial Management.—Diem Salmon.
　　Foreign Policy
　　　Afghanistan, Pakistan, Central Asia.—Tom Goffus.
　　　Africa.—Adam Barker.
　　　Asia, Pacific.—Eric Sayers.
　　　Europe, Russia.—Tom Goffus.
　　　Iraq.—Tom Goffus.
　　　Middle East.—Tom Goffus.
　　　South and Central Americas.—Adam Barker.
　　Global Basing.—Cord Sterling.
　　Ground Systems.—James Hickey.
　　Homeland Defense/Security.—Adam Barker.
　　Housing Construction.—Cord Sterling.
　　Humanitarian, Disaster, and Civic Assistance.—Elizabeth Everett.
　　Industrial Base.—Bill Greenwalt.
　　Industrial Operations (Military).—Brad Patout.
　　Information Assurance.—Daniel Lerner.
　　Information Management.—Jeremy Hayes.
　　Information Operations.—Daniel Lerner.

Information Technology Systems
    IT Acquisition Policy.—Bill Greenwalt.
    Business Systems.—Jeremy Hayes.
    Tactical Systems.—James Hickey.
    Intelligence Issues.—Katie Wheelbarger.
    Interagency Reform: Steve Barney, Kathryn Edelman, James Hickey, Cord Sterling.
    International Defense Cooperation.—Katie Wheelbarger.
    Inventory Management.—Jeremy Hayes.
    Investigations: Kathryn Edelman, Brad Patout, Jennifer White.
    Land Use.—Cord Sterling.
    Logistics Policy.—Jeremy Hayes.
    Mergers and Acquisitions.—Bill Greenwalt.
    Military Construction.—Cord Sterling.
Military Personnel Issues
    Commissaries and Exchanges.—Allen Edwards.
    DOD Schools.—Samantha Clark.
    End Strength.—Samantha Clark.
    Military Family Policy.—Allen Edwards.
    Health Care.—Allen Edwards.
    Military Justice.—Steve Barney.
    Military Nominations.—Steve Barney.
    Morale, Welfare, and Recreation.—Allen Edwards.
    POW/MIA Issues.—Samantha Clark.
    Pay and Benefits.—Samantha Clark.
    Military Personnel Policy.—Steve Barney.
    National Guard and Reserves.—Samantha Clark.
    Sexual Harassment/Assault Policy.—Steve Barney.
    Suicide Prevention and Response.—Allen Edwards.
    Women in Service.—Samantha Clark.
    Wounded Warrior Issues.—Allen Edwards.
    Military Space.—Daniel Lerner.
    Military Strategy.—James Hickey.
    Missile Defense.—Rob Soofer.
    Missile/Weapons Procurement (Non-Strategic).—John Lehman.
    National Defense Stockpile.—Jeremy Hayes.
    Non-Proliferation.—Rob Soofer.
    Nuclear Weapons Stockpile.—Rob Soofer.
    Operations and Maintenance.—Brad Patout.
    Peacekeeping.—Elizabeth Everett.
    Quadrennial Defense Review.—Eric Sayers.
    Readiness.—Brad Patout.
    Reprogramming.—Diem Salmon.
    Rotary Systems.—James Hickey.
    Science and Technology.—Anish Goel.
    Shipbuilding Programs.—Jason Potter.
    Special Operations Forces.—Adam Barker.
    Strategic Programs.—Rob Soofer.
    Training.—Brad Patout.
    Transportation Policy.—Jeremy Hayes.
    Unmanned Aircraft Systems: Matt Donovan, James Hickey.
    War Powers.—Katie Wheelbarger.
    Working Capital Fund.—Brad Patout.
Minority Staff:
    Staff Director.—Elizabeth L. King.
    Clerk.—Mariah K. McNamara.
    General Counsel.—Gerald J. Leeling.
    Counsel.—William G.P. Monahan, Jonathan D. Clark, Ozge Guzelsu, Jonathan S. Epstein.
    Professional Staff Members: Jody L. Bennett, Carolyn A. Chuhta, Creighton Greene, Michael J. Kuiken, Thomas K. McConnell, Michael J. Noblet, John H. Quirk V, Arun A. Seraphin.
Subcommittee on Airland
    Minority Staff Members: Jody L. Bennett (lead), Creighton Greene.
Subcommittee on Emerging Threats and Capabilities
    Minority Staff Members: Michael J. Noblet (lead), Jonathan S. Epstein, Ozge Guzelsu, Michael J. Kuiken, Thomas K. McConnell, William G.P. Monahan, Arun Seraphin.
Subcommittee on Personnel
    Minority Staff Members: Gerald J. Leeling (lead), Jonathan D. Clark.

Subcommittee on Readiness and Management Support
 Minority Staff Members: John H. Quirk V (lead), Ozge Guzelsu, Michael J. Noblet, Arun Seraphin.
Subcommittee on Seapower
 Minority Staff Members: Creighton Greene (lead), Jody L. Bennett.
Subcommittee on Strategic Forces
 Minority Staff Members: Jonathan S. Epstein (lead), Carolyn A. Chuhta, Creighton Greene, Thomas K. McConnell.
Minority Staff Subject Areas
 Acquisition Policy.—Arun A. Seraphin.
 Acquisition Workforce.—Arun A. Seraphin.
 Alternative Energy.—John H. Quirk V, Arun A. Seraphin.
 Ammunition.—John H. Quirk V.
 Arms Control.—Jonathan S. Epstein.
 Aviation Systems: Jonathan S. Epstein, Creighton Greene.
 Base Realignment and Closure (BRAC).—Michael J. Noblet.
 Border Security.—Mariah K. McNamara.
 Building Partnership Capacity Programs: William G.P. Monahan, Michael J. Kuiken.
 Budget.—Jody L. Bennett.
 Buy America.—Arun A. Seraphin.
 Chemical-Biological Defense.—Jonathan S. Epstein.
 Chemical Demilitarization.—Jonathan S. Epstein.
Combatant Commands / Foreign Policy
 AFRICOM.—Michael J. Kuiken.
 CENTCOM: Michael J. Kuiken, William G.P. Monahan.
 Central Asia.—William G.P. Monahan.
 Iraq.—William G.P. Monahan.
 Middle East.—Michael J. Kuiken.
 CYBERCOM.—Thomas K. McConnell.
 EUCOM / NATO.—William G.P. Monahan.
 Israel.—Michael J. Kuiken.
 NORTHCOM.—Carolyn A. Chuhta.
 PACOM.—Ozge Guzelsu.
 SOCOM.—Michael J. Noblet.
 SOUTHCOM.—Michael J. Kuiken.
 STRATCOM.—Jonathan S. Epstein.
 TRANSCOM.—Creighton Greene.
 Counterterrorism Partnership Fund.—Michael J. Kuiken.
 Counterterrorism Policy: Ozge Guzelsu, Michael J. Kuiken, Thomas K. McConnell, William G.P. Monahan, Michael J. Noblet.
 Competition Policy.—Arun A. Seraphin.
 Competitive Sourcing / A–76.—Arun A. Seraphin.
 Contracting (Including Service Contracts).—Arun A. Seraphin.
 Cooperative Threat Reduction.—Jonathan S. Epstein.
 Counternarcotics Account and Programs.—Michael J. Kuiken.
 Cybersecurity: Creighton Greene, Thomas K. McConnell.
 Defense Energy Use: John H. Quirk V, Arun A. Seraphin.
 Defense Security Cooperation Agency.—Michael J. Kuiken.
 Defense Strategy Review.—Jody L. Bennett.
 Department of Energy Issues.—Jonathan S. Epstein.
 Depot Maintenance.—John H. Quirk V.
 Detainee Policy.—William G.P. Monahan.
 Domestic Preparedness.—Carolyn A. Chuhta.
 Embassy Security.—Michael J. Kuiken.
 Environmental Issues.—Ozge Guzelsu.
 Export Controls.—Ozge Guzelsu.
 Financial Management.—Arun A. Seraphin.
 Foreign Language Policy.—Creighton Greene.
 Global Basing.—Michael J. Noblet.
 Ground Systems.—Jody L. Bennett.
 Homeland Defense / Security: Carolyn A. Chuhta, Mariah K. McNamara.
 Housing Construction.—Michael J. Noblet.
 Overseas Humanitarian, Disaster, and Civic Aid (OHDACA) Account.—Michael J. Kuiken.
 Information Assurance: Creighton Greene, Thomas K. McConnell.
 Information Management: Creighton Greene, Arun A. Seraphin.
 Information Operations.—Michael J. Kuiken.

Information Technology Systems
 IT Acquisition Policy: Thomas K. McConnell, Arun A. Seraphin.
 Business Systems.—Arun A. Seraphin.
 Tactical Systems.—Creighton Greene.
 Intelligence Issues: Creighton Greene, Thomas K. McConnell.
 Interagency Reform: Michael J. Kuiken, Thomas K. McConnell, William G.P. Monahan.
 Inventory Management.—Arun A. Seraphin.
 Investigations.—Ozge Guzelsu.
 Insider Threat.—Thomas K. McConnell.
 Joint IED Defeat Fund (JIEDDF).—Michael J. Kuiken.
 Land Use.—Michael J. Noblet.
 Laboratory Management.—Arun A. Seraphin.
 Logistics Policy.—Creighton Greene.
 Mergers and Acquisitions.—Arun A. Seraphin.
 Military Construction.—Michael J. Noblet.
 Military Space.—Jonathan S. Epstein.
 Military Strategy.—Jody L. Bennett.
 Missile Defense.—Carolyn A. Chuhta.
 National Defense Stockpile.—John H. Quirk V.
 Nominations
  Civilian.—Gerald J. Leeling.
  Military.—Jonathan D. Clark.
 Non-Proliferation.—Jonathan S. Epstein.
 Nuclear Weapons Stockpile.—Jonathan S. Epstein.
 Operation and Maintenance.—John H Quirk V.
 Peacekeeping.—Michael J. Kuiken.
 Personnel Policy
  Civilian Personnel Policy.—Jonathan D. Clark.
  Commissaries and Exchanges.—Jonathan D. Clark.
  Education.—Jonathan D. Clark.
  End Strength.—Jonathan D. Clark.
  Health Care.—Gerald J. Leeling.
  Military Family Policy.—Gerald J. Leeling.
  Military Justice.—Gerald J. Leeling.
  Military Nominations.—Jonathan D. Clark.
  Military Personnel Policy.—Gerald J. Leeling.
  Morale, Welfare, and Recreation.—Jonathan D. Clark.
  National Guard and Reserves: Jonathan D. Clark, Gerald J. Leeling.
  Pay Benefits, and Retirement.—Jonathan D. Clark.
  POW/MIA Issues.—Jonathan D. Clark.
  Religious Accommodation.—Jonathan D. Clark.
  Sexual Conduct Policy.—Gerald J. Leeling.
  Suicide Prevention and Response.—Gerald J. Leeling.
  Women in Service—Jonathan D. Clark.
  Wounded Warrior Issues.—Gerald J. Leeling.
  Personnel Security.—Thomas K. McConnell.
 Personnel Protective Items.—John H. Quirk V.
 Readiness.—John H. Quirk V.
 Reprogramming.—Jody L. Bennett.
 Science and Technology.—Arun A. Seraphin.
 Security Assistance Programs: Ozge Guzelsu, Michael J. Kuiken, William G.P. Monahan.
 Shipbuilding Programs.—Creighton Greene.
 Small Business.—Arun A. Seraphin.
 Special Operations Forces.—Michael J. Noblet.
 Strategic Communications.—Michael J. Kuiken.
 Strategic Programs.—Jonathan S. Epstein.
 Test and Evaluation.—Arun A. Seraphin.
 Training.—John H. Quirk V.
 Transportation Policy.—Creighton Greene.
 Unified Command Plan.—Jody L. Bennett.
 Unmanned Aircraft Systems: Creighton Greene, Thomas K. McConnell.
 Working Capital Fund.—John H. Quirk V.

Banking, Housing, and Urban Affairs

534 Dirksen Senate Office Building 20510

phone 224–7391, http://banking.senate.gov

Richard C. Shelby, of Alabama, *Chair*

Mike Crapo, of Idaho.	*Sherrod Brown, of Ohio.*
Bob Corker, of Tennessee.	*Jack Reed, of Rhode Island.*
David Vitter, of Louisiana.	*Charles E. Schumer, of New York.*
Patrick J. Toomey, of Pennsylvania.	*Robert Menendez, of New Jersey.*
Mark Kirk, of Illinois.	*Jon Tester, of Montana.*
Dean Heller, of Nevada.	*Mark R. Warner, of Virginia.*
Tim Scott, of South Carolina.	*Jeff Merkley, of Oregon.*
Ben Sasse, of Nebraska.	*Elizabeth Warren, of Massachusetts.*
Tom Cotton, of Arkansas.	*Heidi Heitkamp, of North Dakota.*
Mike Rounds, of South Dakota.	*Joe Donnelly, of Indiana.*
Jerry Moran, of Kansas.	

SUBCOMMITTEES

[The chairman and ranking minority member are ex officio members of all subcommittees.]

Economic Policy

Dean Heller, of Nevada, *Chair*

Patrick J. Toomey, of Pennsylvania.	*Elizabeth Warren, of Massachusetts.*
Tom Cotton, of Arkansas.	*Jon Tester, of Montana.*
Mike Rounds, of South Dakota.	*Jeff Merkley, of Oregon.*
Ben Sasse, of Nebraska.	*Heidi Heitkamp, of North Dakota.*
Jerry Moran, of Kansas.	

Financial Institutions and Consumer Protection

Patrick J. Toomey, of Pennsylvania, *Chair*

Mike Crapo, of Idaho.	*Jeff Merkley, of Oregon.*
Dean Heller, of Nevada.	*Jack Reed, of Rhode Island.*
Mike Rounds, of South Dakota.	*Charles E. Schumer, of New York.*
Tim Scott, of South Carolina.	*Robert Menendez, of New Jersey.*
Bob Corker, of Tennessee.	*Mark R. Warner, of Virginia.*
David Vitter, of Louisiana.	*Elizabeth Warren, of Massachusetts.*
Mark Kirk, of Illinois.	*Joe Donnelly, of Indiana.*

Housing, Transportation, and Community Development

Tim Scott, of South Carolina, *Chair*

Mike Crapo, of Idaho.	*Robert Menendez, of New Jersey.*
Dean Heller, of Nevada.	*Jack Reed, of Rhode Island.*
Jerry Moran, of Kansas.	*Charles E. Schumer, of New York.*
Bob Corker, of Tennessee.	*Jon Tester, of Montana.*
Tom Cotton, of Arkansas.	*Jeff Merkley, of Oregon.*
Mike Rounds, of South Dakota.	*Heidi Heitkamp, of North Dakota.*
David Vitter, of Louisiana.	*Joe Donnelly, of Indiana.*

National Security and International Trade and Finance

Mark Kirk, of Illinois, *Chair*

Tom Cotton, of Arkansas.	*Heidi Heitkamp, of North Dakota.*
Ben Sasse, of Nebraska.	*Mark R. Warner, of Virginia.*

Securities, Insurance, and Investment

Mike Crapo, of Idaho, *Chair*

Bob Corker, of Tennessee.	*Mark R. Warner,* of Virginia.
David Vitter, of Louisiana.	*Jack Reed,* of Rhode Island.
Patrick J. Toomey, of Pennsylvania.	*Charles E. Schumer,* of New York.
Mark Kirk, of Illinois.	*Robert Menendez,* of New Jersey.
Tim Scott, of South Carolina.	*Jon Tester,* of Montana.
Ben Sasse, of Nebraska.	*Elizabeth Warren,* of Massachusetts.
Jerry Moran, of Kansas.	*Joe Donnelly,* of Indiana.

STAFF

Committee on Banking, Housing, and Urban Affairs (SD–534), 224–7391, fax 224–5137.
 Majority Staff Director and General Counsel.—Bill Duhnke.
  Deputy Staff Director.—Dana Wade.
  Communications Director.—Torrie Miller.
  Chief Counsel.—Jelena McWilliams.
  Chief Economist.—Thomas Hogan.
  Chief Investigative Counsel.—Christopher Ford.
  Senior Counsel.—Beth Zorc.
  Senior Counsel, Illicit Financing and National Security Policy.—John O'Hara.
  Senior Investigative Counsel.—Lucas Moskowitz.
  Securities Counsel.—Elad Roisman.
  Counsel.—Travis Hill.
  Investigative Counsel.—Brian Daner.
  Senior Professional Staff Members: Chad Davis, Shannon Hines.
  Professional Staff Members: Shelby Begany, Jen Deci, Jay Dunn.
 Minority Staff Director.—Mark Powden.
  Deputy Staff Director.—Laura Swanson.
  Chief Counsel.—Graham Steele.
  Policy Director.—Colin McGinnis.
  Press Secretary.—Greg Vadala.
  Counsel and Chief Investigator.—Bob Roach.
  Senior Counsels: Jeanette Quick, Elisha Tuku.
  Counsel.—Kristen Hutchens.
  Professional Staff Members: Erin Barry, Homer Carlisle, Beth Cooper.
  Legislative Assistants: Megan Cheney, Phil Rudd.
  Non-Designated Staff:
   Chief Clerk.—Dawn Ratliff.
   IT Director.—Shelvin Simmons.
   Editor.—Jim Crowell.
   GPO Detailees.—Sheryl Arrington, Jason Parker.
   Hearing Clerk/Staff Assistant.—Troy Cornell.
   Staff Assistant.—Pamela Streeter.
Subcommittee on Economic Policy
 Majority Staff Director.—Scott Riplinger.
 Minority Staff Director.—Bharat Ramamurti.
Subcommittee on Financial Institutions and Consumer Protection
 Staff Director.—Geoffrey Okamoto.
 Minority Staff Director.—Lauren Oppenheimer.
Subcommittee on Housing, Transportation, and Community Development
 Majority Staff Director.—Travis Norton.
 Minority Staff Director.—Brian Chernoff.
Subcommittee on National Security and International Trade and Finance
 Majority Staff Director.—Bryan Blom.
 Minority Staff Director.—Jillian Fitzpatrick.
Subcommittee on Securities, Insurance, and Investment
 Majority Staff Director.—Gregg Richard.
 Minority Staff Director.—Milan Dalal.

Budget

624 Dirksen Senate Office Building 20510–6100
phone 224–0642, http://budget.senate.gov

meets first Thursday of each month

Michael B. Enzi, of Wyoming, *Chair*

Chuck Grassley, of Iowa.
Jeff Sessions, of Alabama.
Mike Crapo, of Idaho.
Lindsey Graham, of South Carolina.
Rob Portman, of Ohio.
Patrick J. Toomey, of Pennsylvania.
Ron Johnson, of Wisconsin.
Kelly Ayotte, of New Hampshire.
Roger F. Wicker, of Mississippi.
Bob Corker, of Tennessee.
David Perdue, of Georgia.

BERNARD SANDERS, of Vermont.
Patty Murray, of Washington.
Ron Wyden, of Oregon.
Debbie Stabenow, of Michigan.
Sheldon Whitehouse, of Rhode Island.
Mark R. Warner, of Virginia.
Jeff Merkley, of Oregon.
Tammy Baldwin, of Wisconsin.
Tim Kaine, of Virginia.
ANGUS S. KING, JR., of Maine.

(No Subcommittees)

STAFF

Committee on the Budget (SD–624), 224–0642.
  Majority Staff Director.—Eric Ueland.
    Deputy Staff Director.—Dan Kowalski.
    Chief Counsel.—Greg Dean.
    Deputy Counsel.—Clint Brown.
    Chief Economist.—Bill Beach.
    Communications Director.—Joe Brenckle.
    Parliamentarian.—Tori Gorman.
    Director of Budget Review.—Matt Giroux.
    Senior Budget Analyst and Director of Oversight.—Peter Warren.
    Editor.—Elizabeth Keys.
    Senior Budget Analyst.—Steve Robinson.
    Budget Analysts: Chris Cook, Kaitlin Vogt.
    Professional Staff Member.—Greg D'Angelo.
    Executive Assistant.—Kim Proctor.
    Staff Assistant.—Katie Wachob.
    Appropriations Analyst.—David Ditch.
    Fellows: Susan Eckerly, David Hebert.
  Minority Staff Director.—Warren Gunnels.
    Deputy Staff Director.—Mike Jones.
    Chief Economist.—Robert Etter.
    Chief Counsel.—Stephanie Kelton.
    Counsel and Analyst for Transportation and Revenue.—Jill Harrelson.
    Director of Appropriations and Senior Education Analyst.—Robyn Hiestand.
    Senior Analyst for Social Security and Income Security.—Jeff Cruz.
    Senior Analyst for Energy and Environment.—Kusai Merchant.
    Press and Legislative Research Associate.—Josh Caplan.
    Senior Communications Advisor.—Vincent Morris.
    Budget Policy Director.—Josh Smith.
    Director of Health Care Policy.—Kathryn Van Haste.
    Senior Budget Analyst for National Defense.—Ethan Rosenkranz.
    Senior Tax Analyst.—Stephen Wamhoff.
    Senior Budget Analyst.—Josh Ryan.
    Senior Policy Advisor and Budget Analyst.—Matt Stoller.
    Budget Review Professional.—Bobby Kogan.
    Executive Assistant and Legislative Aide.—Billy Gendell.
    OMB Detailees: Claire Mahoney, Keri Rice.
    Staff Non-Designated:
      Archivist.—Kathy Smith.

Publications.—Letitia Fletcher.
Chief Clerk.—Adam Kamp.
Computer Systems Administrator.—George Woodall.
Staff Assistants: Eric Chalmers, Phillip Longbrake.

Commerce, Science, and Transportation

512 Dirksen Senate Office Building 20510–6125

phone 224–1251, TTY / TDD 224–8418, http://commerce.senate.gov

meets first and third Tuesdays of each month

John Thune, of South Dakota, *Chair*

Roger F. Wicker, of Mississippi.
Roy Blunt, of Missouri.
Marco Rubio, of Florida.
Kelly Ayotte, of New Hampshire.
Ted Cruz, of Texas.
Deb Fischer, of Nebraska.
Jerry Moran, of Kansas.
Dan Sullivan, of Alaska.
Ron Johnson, of Wisconsin.
Dean Heller, of Nevada.
Cory Gardner, of Colorado.
Steve Daines, of Montana.

Bill Nelson, of Florida.
Maria Cantwell, of Washington.
Claire McCaskill, of Missouri.
Amy Klobuchar, of Minnesota.
Richard Blumenthal, of Connecticut.
Brian Schatz, of Hawaii.
Edward J. Markey, of Massachusetts.
Cory A. Booker, of New Jersey
Tom Udall, of New Mexico.
Joe Manchin III, of West Virginia.
Gary C. Peters, of Michigan.

SUBCOMMITTEES

[The chairman and the ranking minority member are ex officio members of all subcommittees.]

Aviation Operations, Safety, and Security

Kelly Ayotte, of New Hampshire, *Chair*

Roger F. Wicker, of Mississippi.
Roy Blunt, of Missouri.
Marco Rubio, of Florida.
Ted Cruz, of Texas.
Deb Fischer, of Nebraska.
Jerry Moran, of Kansas.
Dan Sullivan, of Alaska.
Ron Johnson, of Wisconsin.
Dean Heller, of Nevada.
Cory Gardner, of Colorado.

Maria Cantwell, of Washington.
Amy Klobuchar, of Minnesota.
Richard Blumenthal, of Connecticut.
Brian Schatz, of Hawaii.
Edward J. Markey, of Massachusetts.
Cory A. Booker, of New Jersey
Tom Udall, of New Mexico.
Joe Manchin III, of West Virginia.
Gary C. Peters, of Michigan.

Communications, Technology, Innovation and the Internet

Roger F. Wicker, of Mississippi, *Chair*

Roy Blunt, of Missouri.
Marco Rubio, of Florida.
Kelly Ayotte, of New Hampshire.
Ted Cruz, of Texas.
Deb Fischer, of Nebraska.
Jerry Moran, of Kansas.
Dan Sullivan, of Alaska.
Ron Johnson, of Wisconsin.
Dean Heller, of Nevada.
Cory Gardner, of Colorado.
Steve Daines, of Montana.

Brian Schatz, of Hawaii.
Maria Cantwell, of Washington.
Claire McCaskill, of Missouri.
Amy Klobuchar, of Minnesota.
Richard Blumenthal, of Connecticut.
Edward J. Markey, of Massachusetts.
Cory A. Booker, of New Jersey
Tom Udall, of New Mexico.
Joe Manchin III, of West Virginia.
Gary C. Peters, of Michigan.

Consumer Protection, Product Safety, Insurance, and Data Security

Jerry Moran, of Kansas, *Chair*

Roy Blunt, of Missouri.
Ted Cruz, of Texas.
Deb Fischer, of Nebraska.
Dean Heller, of Nevada.
Cory Gardner, of Colorado.
Steve Daines, of Montana.

Richard Blumenthal, of Connecticut.
Claire McCaskill, of Missouri.
Amy Klobuchar, of Minnesota.
Edward J. Markey, of Massachusetts.
Cory A. Booker, of New Jersey
Tom Udall, of New Mexico.

Oceans, Atmosphere, Fisheries, and Coast Guard

Marco Rubio, of Florida, *Chair*

Roger F. Wicker, of Mississippi.
Kelly Ayotte, of New Hampshire.
Ted Cruz, of Texas.
Dan Sullivan, of Alaska.
Ron Johnson, of Wisconsin.

Cory A. Booker, of New Jersey.
Maria Cantwell, of Washington.
Richard Blumenthal, of Connecticut.
Edward J. Markey, of Massachusetts.
Brian Schatz, of Hawaii.
Gary C. Peters, of Michigan.

Space, Science, and Competitiveness

Ted Cruz, of Texas, *Chair*

Marco Rubio, of Florida.
Jerry Moran, of Kansas.
Dan Sullivan, of Alaska.
Cory Gardner, of Colorado.
Steve Daines, of Montana.

Gary C. Peters, of Michigan.
Edward J. Markey, of Massachusetts.
Cory A Booker, of New Jersey
Tom Udall, of New Mexico.
Brian Schatz, of Hawaii.

Surface Transportation and Merchant Marine Infrastructure, Safety, and Security

Deb Fischer, of Nebraska, *Chair*

Roger F. Wicker, of Mississippi.
Roy Blunt, of Missouri.
Kelly Ayotte, of New Hampshire.
Jerry Moran, of Kansas.
Dan Sullivan, of Alaska.
Ron Johnson, of Wisconsin.
Dean Heller, of Nevada.
Steve Daines, of Montana

Cory A. Booker, of New Jersey.
Maria Cantwell, of Washington.
Claire McCaskill, of Missouri.
Amy Klobuchar, of Minnesota.
Richard Blumenthal, of Connecticut.
Brian Schatz, of Hawaii.
Edward J. Markey, of Massachusetts.
Tom Udall, of New Mexico.

STAFF

Committee on Commerce, Science, and Transportation (SD–512), 224–1251.
Majority Staff Director.—David Schwietert.
Deputy Staff Director.—Nick Rossi.
General Counsel.—Rebecca Seidel.
Deputy General Counsel.—Jason Van Beek.
Communications Director.—Frederick Hill.
Press Secretary.—Lauren Hammond.
Majority Office Manager.—Theresa Eugene.
Staff Assistant.—Tyler Stenberg.
Oversight and Investigations Staff:
Chief Investigative Counsel.—Ashok Pinto.
Deputy General Counsel.—Jason Van Beek.
Professional Staff Member and Investigator.—Cheri Pascoe.
Counsel.—Chapin Gregor.
Research Assistant.—Andrew Timm.
Minority Staff Director.—Kim Lipsky.
Deputy Minority Staff Director.—Chris Day.
Minority General Counsel/Policy Director.—Clint Odom.
Communications Director.—Bryan Gulley.

Counsel.—Renae Black.
Special Assistant.—Maria Stratienko.
Minority Oversight Counsels: Meeran Ahn, Brad Torppey.
Aviation Operations, Safety, and Security Staff:
Majority Policy Director.—Bailey Edwards.
   Majority Professional Staff Members: Missye Brickell, Suzanne Gillen.
   Counsel.—Mike Reynolds.
   Research Assistant.—Jaclyn Keshian.
   FAA Detailee.—Michael Beavin.
   Minority Counsel.—Tom Chapman.
   Minority Senior Professional Staff.—Jenny Solomon.
   FAA Detailee.—Laura Ponto.
   GAO Detailee.—David Goldstein.
Communications, Technology, Innovation and the Internet Staff:
Policy Director for Communications and Technology.—David Quinalty.
   Deputy General Counsel.—Jason Van Beek.
   Counsels: Jeffrey Farrah, Greg Orlando.
   Professional Staff Member.—Hap Rigby.
   Research Assistant.—Matthew Plaster.
   FCC Detailee.—Jamie Susskind.
   Minority Chief Counsel.—John Branscome.
   Minority Counsel.—Shawn Bone.
   Legislative Assistant.—Simone Hall.
   FCC Detailee.—Kate Dumouchel.
Consumer Protection, Product Safety, Insurance, and Data Security Staff:
   Counsel.—Peter Feldman.
   Professional Staff Member.—Cheri Pascoe.
   Research Assistant.—Andrew Timm.
   FTC Detailee.—Katherine White.
   Minority Chief Counsel.—Christian Tamotsu Fjeld.
   Legislative Assistant.—Brian No.
   FTC Detailee.—Kandi Parsons.
Oceans, Atmosphere, Fisheries, and Coast Guard Staff:
Policy Director and Counsel.—Adrian Arnakis.
   Professional Staff Member.—Fern Gibbons.
   Research Assistant.—Ross Dietrich.
   NOAA Detailee.—Wendy Lewis.
   Coast Guard Detailee.—Robert Donnell.
   Sea Grant Fellow.—Alexis Rudd.
   MARAD Detailee.—Tony Padilla.
   Minority Counsels: Jeff Lewis, Sara Rothi-Gonzalez.
   Professional Staff Member.—Matt Williams.
   Sea Grant Fellow.—Yvonne Baker.
Space, Science, and Competitiveness Staff:
Majority Policy Director.—Bailey Edwards.
   Professional Staff Members: Missye Brickell, Suzanne Gillen.
   Research Assistant.—Jaclyn Keshian.
   Minority Staff Director for Science and Space.—Nick Cummings.
   Professional Staff Member.—Richard-Duane Chambers.
   NASA Detailee.—Josh Manning.
Surface Transportation and Merchant Marine Infrastructure, Safety and Security Staff:
Majority Policy Director and Counsel.—Adrian Arnakis.
   Professional Staff Members: Allison Cullin, Patrick Fuchs.
   Research Assistant.—Ross Dietrich.
   Minority Counsel.—Devon Barnhart.
   Professional Staff Member.—Matt Kelly.
   Legislative Assistant.—Brandon Kaufman.
   Bipartisan Staff:
      Chief Clerk.—Anne Willis Hill.
      Hearing Clerk.—Stephanie Gamache.
      Director, Information Technology.—Jonathan Bowen.
      Staff Editor.—Debra Miller.
      Archivist.—Matthew Stahl.
      GPO Detailee.—Jacqueline Washington.
      Staff Assistant.—Stephanie Lieu.

Bipartisan Staff, Legislative Counsel's Office:
  Legislative Counsel.—Jennifer Dorrer.
  Staff Assistant.—Rahul Chopra.

Energy and Natural Resources

304 Dirksen Senate Office Building 20510

phone 224–4971, fax 224–6163, http://energy.senate.gov

meets upon call of the chair

Lisa Murkowski, of Alaska, *Chair*

John Barrasso, of Wyoming.
James E. Risch, of Idaho.
Mike Lee, of Utah.
Jeff Flake, of Arizona.
Bill Cassidy, of Louisiana.
Cory Gardner, of Colorado.
Steve Daines, of Montana.
Rob Portman, of Ohio.
John Hoeven, of North Dakota.
Lamar Alexander, of Tennessee.
Shelley Moore Capito, of West Virginia.

Maria Cantwell, of Washington.
Ron Wyden, of Oregon.
BERNARD SANDERS, of Vermont.
Debbie Stabenow, of Michigan.
Al Franken, of Minnesota.
Joe Manchin III, of West Virginia.
Martin Heinrich, of New Mexico.
Mazie K. Hirono, of Hawaii.
ANGUS S. KING, JR., of Maine.
Elizabeth Warren, of Massachusetts.

SUBCOMMITTEES

[The chairwoman and the ranking minority member are ex officio members of all subcommittees.]

Energy

James E. Risch, of Idaho, *Chair*

Jeff Flake, of Arizona.
Steve Daines, of Montana.
Bill Cassidy, of Louisiana.
Cory Gardner, of Colorado.
John Hoeven, of North Dakota.
Lamar Alexander, of Tennessee.
Rob Portman, of Ohio.
Shelley Moore Capito, of West Virginia.

Joe Manchin III, of West Virginia.
BERNARD SANDERS, of Vermont.
Debbie Stabenow, of Michigan.
Al Franken, of Minnesota.
Martin Heinrich, of New Mexico.
Mazie K. Hirono, of Hawaii.
ANGUS S. KING, JR., of Maine.
Elizabeth Warren, of Massachusetts.

National Parks

Bill Cassidy, of Louisiana, *Chair*

Rob Portman, of Ohio.
John Barrasso, of Wyoming.
Lamar Alexander, of Tennessee.
Mike Lee, of Utah.
John Hoeven, of North Dakota.
Shelley Moore Capito, of West Virginia.

Martin Heinrich, of New Mexico.
Ron Wyden, of Oregon.
BERNARD SANDERS, of Vermont.
Debbie Stabenow, of Michigan.
ANGUS S. KING, JR., of Maine.
Elizabeth Warren, of Massachusetts.

Public Lands, Forests, and Mining

John Barrasso, of Wyoming, *Chair*

Shelley Moore Capito, of West Virginia.
James E. Risch, of Idaho.
Mike Lee, of Utah.
Steve Daines, of Montana.
Bill Cassidy, of Louisiana.
Cory Gardner, of Colorado.
John Hoeven, of North Dakota.
Jeff Flake, of Arizona.
Lamar Alexander, of Tennessee.

Ron Wyden, of Oregon.
Debbie Stabenow, of Michigan.
Al Franken, of Minnesota.
Joe Manchin III, of West Virginia.
Martin Heinrich, of New Mexico.
Mazie K. Hirono, of Hawaii.
Elizabeth Warren, of Massachusetts.

Water and Power

Mike Lee, of Utah, *Chair*

Jeff Flake, of Arizona.
John Barrasso, of Wyoming.
James E. Risch, of Idaho.
Steve Daines, of Montana.
Cory Gardner, of Colorado.
Rob Portman, of Ohio.

Mazie K. Hirono, of Hawaii.
Ron Wyden, of Oregon.
BERNARD SANDERS, of Vermont.
Al Franken, of Minnesota.
Joe Manchin III, of West Virginia.
ANGUS S. KING, JR., of Maine.

STAFF

Committee on Energy and Natural Resources (SD–304), 224–4971, fax 224–6163.
  Majority Staff Director.—Karen Billups.
    Deputy Staff Director.—Colin Hayes.
    Chief Counsel.—Patrick McCormick.
    Deputy Chief Counsel.—Kellie Donnelly.
    Senior Counsel.—Isaac Edwards.
    Senior Counsel and Natural Resources Policy Director.—Lucy Murfitt.
    Counsels: Heidi Hansen, Severin Randall.
    Communications Director.—Robert Dillon.
    Deputy Communications Directory.—Michael Tadeo.
    Director of Digital Media.—Mary Leschper.
    Budget Analyst and Senior Professional Staff Member.—Christopher Kearney.
    Professional Staff Members: Tristan Abbey, Chester Carson, Chuck Kleeschulte, Brianne
      Miller.
    Senior Writer and Policy Advisor.—Brian Hughes.
    Senior Policy Advisor.—Michael Pawlowski.
    Legislative and Executive Assistant.—Jason Huffnagle.
    Bevinetto Fellow.—Pamela Rice.
    Congressional Fellow.—Catherine Cahill.
    Non-Designated Staff:
      Chief Clerk.—Darla Ripchensky.
      Staff Assistant.—Samin Peirovi.
      Systems Administrator.—Dominic Taylor.
  Minority Staff Director.—Angela Becker-Dippmann.
    Chief Counsel.—Sam Fowler.
    General Counsel.—David Brooks.
    Senior Counsel.—David Gillers.
    Executive Assistant.—Sa'Rah Hamm.
    Press Secretary.—Rosemarie Calabro Tully.
    Press Assistant.—Aisha Johnson.
    Senior Professional Staff Members: John Davis, Bryan Petit, Allen Stayman.
    Professional Staff Members: Clayton Allen, Spencer Gray, Scott McKee, Melanie
      Stansbury, Nick Sutter.
    Legislative Aides: Faynisha Matthews, Samantha Siegler, Rory Stanley.

Environment and Public Works

410 Dirksen Senate Office Building 20510–6175

phone 224–6176, www.epw.senate.gov

meets first and third Thursdays of each month

James M. Inhofe, of Oklahoma, *Chair*

David Vitter, of Louisiana.
John Barrasso, of Wyoming.
Shelley Moore Capito, of West Virginia.
Mike Crapo, of Idaho.
John Boozman, of Arkansas.
Jeff Sessions, of Alabama.
Roger F. Wicker, of Mississippi.
Deb Fischer, of Nebraska.
Mike Rounds, of South Dakota.
Dan Sullivan, of Alaska.

Barbara Boxer, of California.
Thomas R. Carper, of Delaware.
Benjamin L. Cardin, of Maryland.
BERNARD SANDERS, of Vermont.
Sheldon Whitehouse, of Rhode Island.
Jeff Merkley, of Oregon.
Kirsten E. Gillibrand, of New York.
Cory A. Booker, of New Jersey
Edward J. Markey, of Massachusetts.

SUBCOMMITTEES

[The chairman and the ranking minority member are ex officio (non-voting) members of all subcommittees on which they do not serve.]

Clean Air and Nuclear Safety

Shelley Moore Capito, of West Virginia, *Chair*

David Vitter, of Louisiana.
John Barrasso, of Wyoming.
Mike Crapo, of Idaho.
Jeff Sessions, of Alabama.
Roger F. Wicker, of Mississippi.
Deb Fischer, of Nebraska.

Thomas R. Carper, of Delaware.
Benjamin L. Cardin, of Maryland.
BERNARD SANDERS, of Vermont.
Sheldon Whitehouse, of Rhode Island.
Jeff Merkley, of Oregon.
Edward J. Markey, of Massachusetts.

Fisheries, Water, and Wildlife

Dan Sullivan, of Alaska, *Chair*

John Barrasso, of Wyoming.
Shelley Moore Capito, of West Virginia.
John Boozman, of Arkansas.
Jeff Sessions, of Alabama.
Roger F. Wicker, of Mississippi.
Deb Fischer, of Nebraska.
Mike Rounds, of South Dakota.

Sheldon Whitehouse, of Rhode Island.
Thomas R. Carper, of Delaware.
Benjamin L. Cardin, of Maryland.
BERNARD SANDERS, of Vermont.
Kirsten E. Gillibrand, of New York.
Cory A. Booker, of New Jersey
Edward J. Markey, of Massachusetts.

Superfund, Waste Management, and Regulatory Oversight

Mike Rounds, of South Dakota, *Chair*

David Vitter, of Louisiana.
Mike Crapo, of Idaho.
John Boozman, of Arkansas.
Dan Sullivan, of Alaska.

Edward J. Markey, of Massachusetts.
Thomas R. Carper, of Delaware.
Jeff Merkley, of Oregon.
Cory A. Booker, of New Jersey

Transportation and Infrastructure

David Vitter, of Louisiana, *Chair*

John Barrasso, of Wyoming.
Shelley Moore Capito, of West Virginia.
Mike Crapo, of Idaho.
John Boozman, of Arkansas.
Jeff Sessions, of Alabama.
Roger F. Wicker, of Mississippi.
Deb Fischer, of Nebraska.

Barbara Boxer, of California.
Thomas R. Carper, of Delaware.
Benjamin L. Cardin, of Maryland.
BERNARD SANDERS, of Vermont.
Sheldon Whitehouse, of Rhode Island.
Jeff Merkley, of Oregon.
Kirsten E. Gillibrand, of New York.

STAFF

Committee on Environment and Public Works (SD–410), phone 224–6176; Majority fax (SD–410), 224–5167; (SH–508), 228–2322.
 Majority Staff Director.—Ryan Jackson.
  Deputy Staff Director.—Alex Herrgott.
  Majority Chief Counsel.—Susan Bodine.
  Majority Senior Counsels: Byron Brown, Shant Boyajian, Dimitri Karakitsos.
  Counsels: Laura Atcheson, Brittany Bolen, Mandy Gunasekara, Hilary Moffett.
  Majority Transportation Counsel.—Jennie Wright.
  Majority Climate Counsel.—Mandy Gunasekara.
  Majority Detailee.—Chaya Koffman.
  Majority Professional Staff Members: Anna Burhop, Annie Caputo, Lauren Sturgeon.
  Editorial Director.—Stephen Chapman.
  Chief Clerk.—Alicia Gordon.
  System Administrator.—Rae Ann Phipps.
  Majority Communications Director.—Donelle Harder.
  Majority Director of Operations.—Elizabeth Olsen.
  Press Secretary.—Kristina Baum.
  Majority Director of New Media.—Daisy Letendre.
  Senior Counsel for Oversight.—Byron Brown.
  Majority Research Assistants: Joe Brown, John Glennon, Andrew Neely.
Committee on Environment and Public Works (SD–456), phone 224–8832; Minority fax (SD–456), 224–1273; (SH–508), 228–0574.
 Minority Staff Director/Chief Counsel.—Bettina Poirier.
  Minority Senior Counsel.—Thomas Fox.
  Counsels: Ted Illston, Tyler Rushforth.
  Minority Senior Policy Advisor.—Jason Albritton.
  Minority Director, Infrastructure and Economic Oversight.—David Napoliello
  Minority Chief Climate Counsel.—Ann Mesnikott.
  Office Manager.—Carolyn Mack.
  Chief Clerk.—Alicia Gordon.
  System Administrator.—Rae Ann Phipps.
  Communications Director.—Mary Kerr.
  Professional Staff Member.—Andrew Dohrmann.
  Minority Press Assistants: Kathryn Dachei, Colin MacCarthy.
  Minority Deputy Communications Director/Press Secretary.—Kate Gilman.

Finance

219 Dirksen Senate Office Building 20510

phone 224–4515, fax 224–0554, http://finance.senate.gov

meets second and fourth Tuesdays of each month

Orrin G. Hatch, of Utah, *Chair*

Chuck Grassley, of Iowa.
Mike Crapo, of Idaho.
Pat Roberts, of Kansas.
Michael B. Enzi, of Wyoming.
John Cornyn, of Texas.
John Thune, of South Dakota.
Richard Burr, of North Carolina.
Johnny Isakson, of Georgia.
Rob Portman, of Ohio.
Patrick J. Toomey, of Pennsylvania.
Daniel Coats, of Indiana.
Dean Heller, of Nevada.
Tim Scott, of South Carolina.

Ron Wyden, of Oregon.
Charles E. Schumer, of New York.
Debbie Stabenow, of Michigan.
Maria Cantwell, of Washington.
Bill Nelson, of Florida.
Robert Menendez, of New Jersey.
Thomas R. Carper, of Delaware.
Benjamin L. Cardin, of Maryland.
Sherrod Brown, of Ohio.
Michael F. Bennet, of Colorado.
Robert P. Casey, Jr., of Pennsylvania.
Mark R. Warner, of Virginia.

SUBCOMMITTEES

[The chairman and the ranking minority member are ex officio (non-voting) members of all subcommittees on which they do not serve.]

Energy, Natural Resources, and Infrastructure

Daniel Coats, of Indiana, *Chair*

Chuck Grassley, of Iowa.
Mike Crapo, of Idaho.
Michael B. Enzi, of Wyoming.
John Cornyn, of Texas.
John Thune, of South Dakota.
Richard Burr, of North Carolina.

Michael F. Bennet, of Colorado.
Maria Cantwell, of Washington.
Bill Nelson, of Florida.
Thomas R. Carper, of Delaware.
Robert P. Casey, Jr., of Pennsylvania.

Fiscal Responsibility and Economic Growth

Rob Portman, of Ohio, *Chair*

Mike Crapo, of Idaho.
Richard Burr, of North Carolina.

Mark R. Warner, of Virginia.

Health Care

Patrick J. Toomey, of Pennsylvania, *Chair*

Chuck Grassley, of Iowa.
Pat Roberts, of Kansas.
Michael B. Enzi, of Wyoming.
Richard Burr, of North Carolina.
Daniel Coats, of Indiana.
Dean Heller, of Nevada.
Tim Scott, of South Carolina.

Debbie Stabenow, of Michigan.
Maria Cantwell, of Washington.
Robert Menendez, of New Jersey.
Benjamin L. Cardin, of Maryland.
Sherrod Brown, of Ohio.
Mark R. Warner, of Virginia.

International Trade, Customs, and Global Competitiveness

John Cornyn, of Texas, *Chair*

Chuck Grassley, of Iowa.
Pat Roberts, of Kansas.
John Thune, of South Dakota.
Johnny Isakson, of Georgia.
Rob Portman, of Ohio.

Ron Wyden, of Oregon.
Charles E. Schumer, of New York.
Debbie Stabenow, of Michigan.
Bill Nelson, of Florida.

Social Security, Pensions, and Family Policy

Dean Heller, of Nevada, *Chair*

Johnny Isakson, of Georgia.
Patrick J. Toomey, of Pennsylvania.
Tim Scott, of South Carolina.

Sherrod Brown, of Ohio.
Charles E. Schumer, of New York.

Taxation and IRS Oversight

Mike Crapo, of Idaho, *Chair*

Pat Roberts, of Kansas.
Michael B. Enzi, of Wyoming.
John Cornyn, of Texas.
John Thune, of South Dakota.
Johnny Isakson, of Georgia.
Rob Portman, of Ohio.
Patrick J. Toomey, of Pennsylvania.
Daniel Coats, of Indiana.
Dean Heller, of Nevada.
Tim Scott, of South Carolina.

Robert P. Casey, Jr., of Pennsylvania.
Charles E. Schumer, of New York.
Bill Nelson, of Florida.
Robert Menendez, of New Jersey.
Thomas R. Carper, of Delaware.
Benjamin L. Cardin, of Maryland.
Michael F. Bennet, of Colorado.
Mark R. Warner, of Virginia.

STAFF

Committee on Finance (SD–219), 224–4515, fax 228–0554.
  Majority Staff Director.—Chris Campbell.
    Deputy Staff Director/Chief Tax Counsel.—Mark Prater.
    Tax Counsels: Tony Coughlan, James Lyons, Preston Rutledge.
    Senior Tax Policy Advisor.—Christopher Hanna.
    Tax and Nomination Professional Staff.—Nick Wyatt.
    Senior Policy Advisor for Tax and Accounting.—Eric Oman.
    Professional Staff Member.—Samuel Beaver.
    Senior Counsel.—Bryan Hickman.
    Professional Staff Member.—Joshua Blume.
    Chief Healthcare Investigative Counsel.—Kim Brandt.
    Deputy Chief Oversight Counsel.—Christopher Armstrong.
    Chief Health Counsel and Policy Director.—Jay Khosla.
    Oversight Analyst.—Harrison Moore.
    Outreach Director.—Jeyben Castro.
    Health Policy Advisors: Erin Dempsey, Katie Simeon, Kristin Welsh.
    Health and Human Resource Policy Advisor.—Becky Shipp.
    Office Manager.—Jason Stegmaier.
    Chief International Trade Counsel.—Everett Eissenstat.
    International Trade Counsels: Douglas Petersen, Shane Warren.
    International Trade Analyst.—Rebecca Eubank.
    Chief Economist and Social Security Analyst.—Jeff Wrase.
    Communications Director.—Julia Lawless.
    Press Secretary.—Aaron Fobes.
    Deputy Press Secretary.—Amelia Breinig.
    Detailees: Christine Brudevold, John Carlo, Justin Coon, Marc Ness, Andrew Rollo, Kevin Rosenbaum, Jill Wright.
  Minority Staff Director.—Amber Cottle.
    Assistant to the Director.—Kristin Smith.
    General Counsel.—Mac Campbell.
    Senior Advisor.—John Angell.

Counsel and Senior Advisor for Indian Affairs.—Richard Litsey.
Professional Staff.—Karen Fischer.
Research Assistants: Sara Harshman, Scott Levy.
Chief Tax.—Lily Batchelder.
Tax Counsels: Ryan Abraham, Ann Cammack, Kara Getz, Jude Lemke, Holly Porter, Tiffany Smith.
Tax Policy Analyst.—Anderson Heiman.
Research Associate.—Christopher Arneson.
Chief Health Counsel.—David Schwartz.
Professional Staff: Tony Clapsis, Diedra Henry-Spires.
Health Advisor.—Matt Kazan.
Professional Staff: Chelsea Thomas, Kelly Whitener.
Chief International Trade Counsel.—Bruce Hirsch.
International Trade Counsels: Elissa Alben, Lisa Pearlman.
Nomination and International Trade Advisor.—Rory Murphy.
Investigator.—Christopher Law.
Professional Staff—Social Security.—Tom Klouda.
Communication Director.—Sean Neary.
Deputy Communication Director.—Meghan Smith.
Press Assistant.—Ryan Carey.
Staff Assistants: Brandon Mourich, Logan Smith.
IT Director.—Joe Carnucci.
Archivist.—Bryan Palmer.
Detailees: Ronald Dabrowski, Laurie Dempsey, Melanie Rainer, Sibyl Tilson.

Foreign Relations

423 Dirksen Senate Office Building 20510–6225

phone 224–4651, http://foreign.senate.gov

meets each Tuesday

Bob Corker, of Tennessee, *Chair*

James E. Risch, of Idaho.
Marco Rubio, of Florida.
Ron Johnson, of Wisconsin.
Jeff Flake, of Arizona.
Cory Gardner, of Colorado.
David Perdue, of Georgia.
Johnny Isakson, of Georgia.
Rand Paul, of Kentucky.
John Barrasso, of Wyoming.

Benjamin L. Cardin, of Maryland.
Barbara Boxer, of California.
Robert Menendez, of New Jersey.
Jeanne Shaheen, of New Hampshire.
Christopher A. Coons, of Delaware.
Tom Udall, of New Mexico.
Christopher Murphy, of Connecticut.
Tim Kaine, of Virginia.
Edward J. Markey, of Massachusetts.

SUBCOMMITTEES

[The chairman and ranking minority member are ex officio (non-voting) members of all subcommittees on which they do not serve.]

Africa and Global Health Policy

Jeff Flake, of Arizona, *Chair*

Johnny Isakson, of Georgia.
Rand Paul, of Kentucky.
John Barrasso, of Wyoming.
Marco Rubio, of Florida.

Edward J. Markey, of Massachusetts.
Christopher A. Coons, of Delaware.
Tom Udall, of New Mexico.
Benjamin L. Cardin, of Maryland.

East Asia, the Pacific, and International Cybersecurity Policy

Cory Gardner, of Colorado, *Chair*

Marco Rubio, of Florida.
Ron Johnson, of Wisconsin.
Johnny Isakson, of Georgia.
Jeff Flake, of Arizona.

Benjamin L. Cardin, of Maryland.
Barbara Boxer, of California.
Christopher A. Coons, of Delaware.
Tom Udall, of New Mexico.

Europe and Regional Security Cooperation

Ron Johnson, of Wisconsin, *Chair*

Rand Paul, of Kentucky.
James E. Risch, of Idaho.
Cory Gardner, of Colorado.
John Barrasso, of Wyoming.

Jeanne Shaheen, of New Hampshire.
Christopher Murphy, of Connecticut.
Tim Kaine, of Virginia.
Edward J. Markey, of Massachusetts.

Multilateral International Development, Multilateral Institutions, and International Economic, Energy, and Environmental Policy

John Barrasso, of Wyoming, *Chair*

David Perdue, of Georgia.
James E. Risch, of Idaho.
Jeff Flake, of Arizona.
Cory Gardner, of Colorado.

Tom Udall, of New Mexico.
Barbara Boxer, of California.
Jeanne Shaheen, of New Hampshire.
Edward J. Markey, of Massachusetts.

Near East, South Asia, Central Asia, and Counterterrorism

James E. Risch, of Idaho, *Chair*

David Perdue, of Georgia.
Rand Paul, of Kentucky.
Marco Rubio, of Florida.
Ron Johnson, of Wisconsin.

Christopher Murphy, of Connecticut.
Benjamin L. Cardin, of Maryland.
Jeanne Shaheen, of New Hampshire.
Tim Kaine, of Virginia.

State Department and USAID Management, International Operations, and Bilateral International Development

David Perdue, of Georgia, *Chair*

James E. Risch, of Idaho.
Johnny Isakson, of Georgia.
Ron Johnson, of Wisconsin.
Rand Paul, of Kentucky.

Tim Kaine, of Virginia.
Barbara Boxer, of California.
Christopher A. Coons, of Delaware.
Christopher Murphy, of Connecticut.

Western Hemisphere, Transnational Crime, Civilian Security, Democracy, Human Rights, and Global Women's Issues

Marco Rubio, of Florida, *Chair*

Jeff Flake, of Arizona.
Cory Gardner, of Colorado.
David Perdue, of Georgia.
Johnny Isakson, of Georgia.

Barbara Boxer, of California.
Tom Udall, of New Mexico.
Tim Kaine, of Virginia.
Edward J. Markey, of Massachusetts.

STAFF

Committee on Foreign Relations (SD–423), 224–4651.
  Majority Staff Director.—Lester Munson.
    Deputy Staff Director.—Kirsten Madison.
    Deputy Chief Counsel.—John Lipsey.
  Majority Staff:
    Policy Analysts: Sarah Downs, Christen Mogavero, Frank Polley, John Rader, Morgan Vina.
    Communications Director.—Tara DiJulio.
    Press Secretary.—Chuck Harper.
    Senior Professional Staff Members: Carolyn Leddy, Caleb McCarry, Michael Phelan.
    Professional Staff Members: Brooke Eisele, Trey Hicks, Stacie Oliver.
    Senior Advisor.—Andy Olson.
    Legislative Fellow.—Brandeanna Sanders.
    Director of Operations.—Abby Meadors.
    Staff Assistant.—Owen Mercer.
  Minority Staff:
  Staff Director.—Jodi Herman.
    Director of Operations.—Danny Ricchetti.
    Chief Counsel.—Margaret Taylor.
    Deputy Chief Counsel.—John Ryan.
    Policy Director.—Algene Sajery.
    Press Secretary.—Adam Sharon.
    Senior Advisor/Counselor.—Michael Schiffer.
    Research/Legislative Assistants: Chris Barr, Brittany Beaulieu, Francisco Bencosme, Nury Gambarrotti, Sanna Khan, Janelle Johnson, Jessica Moses, Jonathan Tsentas.
    Senior Professional Staff Members: David Fite, Heather Flynn, Jim Greene, Damian Murphy, Charlotte Oldham-Moore, Lowell Schwartz, Dana Stroul, Brandon Yoder.
    Non-Designated Staff:
      Chief Clerk.—John Dutton.
      Deputy Chief Clerk.—Samantha Hamilton.
      Hearing Clerk.—Bertie Bowman.
      Chief of Protocol/Foreign Travel.—Meg Murphy.
      Protocol Assistant.—Bridget Winstead.
      Staff Assistant.—Bess McWherter.
      Printing Clerks.—Elizabeth Acton, Michael Bennet.

Health, Education, Labor, and Pensions

428 Dirksen Senate Office Building 20510–6300

phone 224–5375, http://help.senate.gov

meets second and fourth Wednesdays of each month

Lamar Alexander, of Tennessee, *Chair*

Michael B. Enzi, of Wyoming.	*Patty Murray, of Washington.*
Richard Burr, of North Carolina.	*Barbara A. Mikulski, of Maryland.*
Johnny Isakson, of Georgia.	BERNARD SANDERS, of Vermont.
Rand Paul, of Kentucky.	*Robert P. Casey, Jr., of Pennsylvania.*
Susan M. Collins, of Maine.	*Al Franken, of Minnesota.*
Lisa Murkowski, of Alaska.	*Michael F. Bennet, of Colorado.*
Mark Kirk, of Illinois.	*Sheldon Whitehouse, of Rhode Island.*
Tim Scott, of South Carolina.	*Tammy Baldwin, of Wisconsin.*
Orrin G. Hatch, of Utah.	*Christopher Murphy, of Connecticut.*
Pat Roberts, of Kansas.	*Elizabeth Warren, of Massachusetts.*
Bill Cassidy, of Louisiana.	

SUBCOMMITTEES

[The chairman and ranking minority member are ex officio members of all subcommittees on which they do not serve.]

Children and Families

Rand Paul, of Kentucky, *Chair*

Lisa Murkowski, of Alaska.	*Robert P. Casey, Jr., of Pennsylvania.*
Richard Burr, of North Carolina.	*Barbara A. Mikulski, of Maryland.*
Mark Kirk, of Illinois.	BERNARD SANDERS, of Vermont.
Orrin G. Hatch, of Utah.	*Al Franken, of Minnesota.*
Pat Roberts, of Kansas.	*Michael F. Bennet, of Colorado.*
Bill Cassidy, of Louisiana.	

Employment and Workplace Safety

Johnny Isakson, of Georgia, *Chair*

Rand Paul, of Kentucky.	*Al Franken, of Minnesota.*
Tim Scott, of South Carolina.	*Robert P. Casey, Jr., of Pennsylvania.*
Mark Kirk, of Illinois.	*Sheldon Whitehouse, of Rhode Island.*
Pat Roberts, of Kansas.	*Tammy Baldwin, of Wisconsin.*
Bill Cassidy, of Louisiana.	

Primary Health and Retirement Security

Michael B. Enzi, of Wyoming, *Chair*

Richard Burr, of North Carolina.	BERNARD SANDERS, of Vermont.
Susan M. Collins, of Maine.	*Barbara A. Mikulski, of Maryland.*
Mark Kirk, of Illinois.	*Michael F. Bennet, of Colorado.*
Tim Scott, of South Carolina.	*Sheldon Whitehouse, of Rhode Island.*
Orrin G. Hatch, of Utah.	*Tammy Baldwin, of Wisconsin.*
Pat Roberts, of Kansas.	*Christopher Murphy, of Connecticut.*
Bill Cassidy, of Louisiana.	*Elizabeth Warren, of Massachusetts.*
Lisa Murkowski, of Alaska.	

STAFF

Committee on Health, Education, Labor, and Pensions (SH–835), 224–6770, fax 224–6510.
Staff Director.—David Cleary, SH–835, 4–6770.
Operations Director.—Misty Marshall, SH–835, 4–6770.
Senior Policy Advisor.—Lindsey Seidman, SH–132, 4–6770.
Counsel.—Bobby McMillin, SH–132, 4–6770.
Communications Office, SH–132, 4–6770.
Senior Communications Advisor and Speechwriter.—Liz Wolgemuth, SH–132, 4–6770.
Deputy Press Secretary.—Taylor Haulsee, SH–132, 4–6770.
Press Secretary.—Margaret Atkinson, SH–132, 4–6770
Oversight and Investigations Office, SH–622B, 4–6770.
Chief Counsel.—Stacy Amin, SH–833, 4–6770.
Oversight Counsel.—Greg Proseus, SH–833, 4–6770.
Professional Staff Member.—Virginia Heppner, SH–833, 4–6770.
Counsel.—Kristin Nelson, SH–833, 4–6770.
Oversight and Investigations Counsel.—Lowell Schiller, SH–833, 4–6770.
Health Policy Office, SH–725, 4–0623.
Health Policy Director.—Mary Sumpter Lapinski, SH–725, 4–0623.
Deputy Health Policy Director.—Sarah Arbes, SH–725, 4–0623.
Health Policy Advisors: Alicia Hennie, Melissa Pfaff, SH–725, 4–0623.
Professional Staff Members: Brett Meeks, Laura Pence, SH–725, 4–0623.
Senior Policy Advisor and Health Counsel.—Liz Wroe, SH–725, 4–0623.
Health Research Assistant.—Kara Townsend, SH–725, 4–0623.
FDA Policy Advisor.—Grace Stuntz, SH–404, 4–0623.
Health Policy Assistant.—Margaret Coulter, SH–404, 4–0623.
Staff Assistant.—Curtis Vann, SH–404, 4–0623.
Fellows: Anh Nguyen, SH–404, 4–0623; Sue No, SH–404, 4–0623.
Staff Assistant.—Jamie Garden, SH–725, 4–0623.
Education Office, SH–632, 4–8484.
Education Policy Director and Counsel.—Peter Oppenheim, SH–632, 4–8484.
Senior Education Policy Advisor.—Lindsay Fryer, SH–632, 4–8484.
Education Policy Advisors: Bill Knudsen, Andrew LaCasse, Lauren Davies, SH–828, 4–8484.
Deputy Education Policy Director.—Bob Moran, SH–632, 8–8484.
Education Professional Staff.—Jordan Hynes, SH–632, 8–8484.
Fellow.—Steve Townsend, SH–632, 8–8484.
Staff Assistant.—Jake Baker, SH–632, 8–8484.
Education Research Assistant.—Hillary Knudson, SH–632, 8–8484.
Labor Policy Office, SH–835, 8–6770.
Labor Policy Director.—Kyle Fortson, SH–835, 8–6770.
Labor and Pensions Counsel.—Molly Conway, SH–835, 8–6770.
Policy Advisor.—Sean Thurman, SH–835, 8–6770.
Staff Assistant.—Carolyn Gorman, SH–835, 8–6770.
Subcommittee on Children and Families, SH–440, 4–0121.
No Staff.
Subcommittee on Employment and Workplace Safety, SH–607, 4–5800.
Staff Director.—Tommy Nguyen, SH–607, 4–5800.
Subcommittee on Primary Health and Retirement Security, SH–828, 4–5406.
Staff Director.—Elizabeth Schwartz, SH–828, 4–5406.
Research Assistant.—Alec Hinojosa, SH–828, 4–5406.
Minority Staff:
Staff Director.—Evan Schatz, SD–644, 4–0767.
Deputy Staff Director.—John Righter, SD–644, 4–0767.
Senior Advisor.—Michael Linden, SD–644, 4–0767.
Special Assistant.—Sarah Cupp, SD–644, 4–0767.
Press Secretary.—Helen Hare, SD–644, 4–0767.
Deputy Press Secretary.—Jeff Crooks, SD–644, 4–0767.
Policy Communications Aide.—Mary Robbins, SD–644, 4–0767.
Health Policy Office, 4–7675.
Health Policy Director.—Nick Bath, SH–527, 4–7675.
Health Policy Advisors: Andi Fristedt, Colin Goldfinch, SH–527, 4–7675.
Senior Health Counsel.—Melanie Rainer, SH–527, 4–7675.
Senior FDA Counsel.—Wade Ackerman, SH–527, 4–7675.
Legislative Aide.—Madeleine Pannel, SH–527, 4–7675.
NIH Fellow.—Katherine Blizinksy, SH–527, 4–7675.

Detailee.—Kayla Auchincloss, SH–527, 4–7675.
Labor Policy Office, 4–5441.
Labor Policy Director.—Leticia Mederos, SH–622B, 4–5441.
  Senior Advisor.—Jake Cornett, SH–622B, 4–5441.
  Detailees: Emily ONeill, Shruti Shah, SH–622B, 4–5441.
  Senior Advisor Workforce and Business Development.—Scott Cheney, SH–440, 4–5441.
Education Policy Office, 4–5501.
  Legislative Aides: Ariel Evans, Leanne Hotek, SH–632, 4–5501.
  Staff Assistant.—Aissa Canchola, SH–632, 4–5501.
  Policy Advisor.—Allie Kimmel, SH–632, 4–5501.
  Education Policy Director.—Sarah Bolton, SH–632, 4–5501.
  Policy Advisor.—Bryce McKibben, SH–632, 4–5501.
  Detailee.—Leslie Clithero, SH–632, 4–5501.
  Education Counsel.—Amanda Beaumont, SH–632, 4–5501.
Oversight and Investigation Office, 4–6403.
  Oversight and Investigations Counsel.—Beth Stein, SD–424, 4–6403.
Subcommittee on Children and Families, 8–1455.
  Subcommittee Staff Director.—Larry Smar, SH–143, 8–1455.
Subcommittee on Employment and Workplace Safety, 4–9243.
  Subcommittee Staff Director.—Amanda Perez, SH–143, 4–1028.
  Senior Policy Advisor.—Michael Waske, SH–143, 4–2570.
Subcommittee on Primary Health and Retirement Security, 4–5480.
  Subcommittee Staff Director.—Sophie Kasimow, SH–143, 4–5480.
  Legislative Aide.—Michaela Yarnell, SH–143, 4–5480.

Homeland Security and Governmental Affairs

340 Dirksen Senate Office Building 20510

phone 224–4751, fax 224–9603, http://hsgac.senate.gov

Hearing Room—SD–342 Dirksen Senate Office Building

meets first Wednesday of each month

Ron Johnson, of Wisconsin, *Chair*

John McCain, of Arizona.
Rob Portman, of Ohio.
Rand Paul, of Kentucky.
James Lankford, of Oklahoma.
Kelly Ayotte, of New Hampshire.
Michael B. Enzi, of Wyoming.
Joni Ernst, of Iowa.
Ben Sasse, of Nebraska.

Thomas R. Carper, of Delaware.
Claire McCaskill, of Missouri.
Jon Tester, of Montana.
Tammy Baldwin, of Wisconsin.
Heidi Heitkamp, of North Dakota.
Cory A. Booker, of New Jersey
Gary C. Peters, of Michigan.

SUBCOMMITTEES

[The chairman and the ranking minority member are ex officio members of all subcommittees.]

Permanent Subcommittee on Investigations

Rob Portman, of Ohio, *Chair*

John McCain, of Arizona.
Rand Paul, of Kentucky.
James Lankford, of Oklahoma.
Kelly Ayotte, of New Hampshire.
Ben Sasse, of Nebraska.

Claire McCaskill, of Missouri.
Jon Tester, of Montana.
Tammy Baldwin, of Wisconsin.
Heidi Heitkamp, of North Dakota.

Federal Spending Oversight and Emergency Management

Rand Paul, of Kentucky, *Chair*

James Lankford, of Oklahoma.
Michael B. Enzi, of Wyoming.
Kelly Ayotte, of New Hampshire.
Joni Ernst, of Iowa.
Ben Sasse, of Nebraska.

Tammy Baldwin, of Wisconsin.
Claire McCaskill, of Missouri.
Cory A. Booker, of New Jersey
Gary C. Peters, of Michigan.

Regulatory Affairs and Federal Management

James Lankford, of Oklahoma, *Chair*

John McCain, of Arizona.
Rob Portman, of Ohio.
Michael B. Enzi, of Wyoming.
Joni Ernst, of Iowa.
Ben Sasse, of Nebraska.

Heidi Heitkamp, of North Dakota.
Jon Tester, of Montana.
Cory A. Booker, of New Jersey
Gary C. Peters, of Michigan.

STAFF

Committee on Homeland Security and Governmental Affairs (SD–340), 224–4751.
Majority Staff Director.—Keith Ashdown.
    Chief Counsel.—Chris Hixon.
    Chief Clerk.—Laura W. Kilbride.
    Director of Homeland Security.—David Luckey.
    Chief Counsel for Governmental Affairs.—Patrick Bailey.

Chief Counsel for Homeland Security.—William McKenna.
Chief Investigative Counsel.—David Brewer.
Deputy Chief Counsel for Governmental Affairs.—Gabrielle D'Adamo Singer.
Deputy Chief Counsel for Homeland Security.—Brooke Ericson.
Senior Policy Advisor.—Roland Foster.
Chief Economist.—Satya Thallam.
Senior Investigator: Brian Downey, Luke Rosiak.
Counsels: Courtney Allen, Kyle Brosnan, Caroline Ingram, Emily Martin.
Investigative Counsel.—Michael Lueptow.
Investigator.—Scott Wittmann.
Senior Professional Staff: Sean Casey, Gabe Sudduth.
Professional Staff: Joske Bautista, Josh McLeod, Elizabeth McWhorter, Rebecca Nuzzi, Katie Pointer, Jennifer Scheaffer.
Research Assistant.—Colleen Berny.
Staff Assistants: Drew Baney, Chris Boness.
GAO Detailee.—Jeffrey Fiore.
USCG Detailee.—Lexia Littlejohn.
USSS Detailee.—Cory Wilson.
Hearing Clerk.—Lauren Corcoran.
Publications Clerk.—Joyce Ward.
Administrative Director.—Claudette David.
Archivist.—Katie Delacenserie.
Systems Administrator.—Dan Muchow.
Deputy Systems Administrator.—Scott Langill.
Minority Staff Director.—Gabrielle Batkin (SH–442), 224–2627.
Deputy Staff Director.—John Kilvington.
Chief Counsel.—Mary Beth Schultz.
Chief Counsel for Governmental Affairs.—Troy Cribb.
Chief Counsel for Homeland Security.—Stephen Vina.
Chief Counsel for Investigations.—Jim Secreto.
Senior Governmental Affairs Advisor.—John Kane.
Senior Counsels: Holly Idelson, Kata Sybenga.
Counsels: Kevin Burris, Rebecca Maddox.
Senior Professional Staff Members: Harlan Geer, Matt Grote, Brian Turbyfill, Peter Tyler.
Professional Staff Members: Deirdre Armstrong, Robert Bradley, Brian Papp, Abby Shenkle.
Communications Director.—Jennie Westbrook.
Press Assistant.—Jill Farquharson.
Legislative Correspondent.—Richard Colley.
Staff Assistant.—Brendan McDermott.
CBP Detailee.—Jill Mueller.
DHS Detailee.—Susan Corbin.
ODNI Detailee.—Charles Carithers.
USAF Detailee.—Paul Babiarz.
USPS OIG Detailees: Alexander Fiske, Bruce Marsh.
Permanent Subcommittee on Investigations (PSI), (SR–199), 224–3721.
Majority Staff Director/General Counsel.—Brian Callanan.
Chief Clerk.—Kelsey Stroud.
Policy Director.—Brent Bombach.
Chief Counsel.—Matt Owen.
Senior Counsel.—Mark Angher.
Counsels: Phil Alito, Andrew Polesovsky, Rachael Tucker.
Investigator.—Will Dagusch.
Professional Staff Member.—Adam Henderson.
FEMA Detailee.—Peter Danjczek.
Minority Staff Director/Chief Counsel.—Margaret Daum (SR–199), 224–9505.
Counsels: Mel Beras, Jackson Eaton, Sarah Garcia, Brandon Reavis.
GAO Detailee.—Kyle Browning.
Subcommittee on Federal Spending Oversight and Emergency Management (FSO), (SH–439), 224–2254.
Majority Staff Director.—Brandon Brooker.
Subcommittee Clerk.—Kelsey Stroud.
Deputy Director of Oversight.—Greg McNeill.
Professional Staff Member.—Brett King.
Research Assistant.—Adam Salmon.
NGA Detailee.—Alex Zemek.
Minority Staff Director.—Dahlia Melendrez (SH–432), 224–7155.

Counsel.—Marianna Boyd.
Legislative Assistant.—Meghan Ladwig.
GAO Detailee.—Teague Lyons.
Subcommittee on Regulatory Affairs and Federal Management (RAFM), (SH–601), 224–4551.
  Majority Staff Director.—John Cuaderes.
    Subcommittee Clerk.—Rachel Nitsche.
    Counsels: Elizabeth Gorman, Nathan Kaczmarek.
    Professional Staff Member.—James Mann.
    Research Assistant.—Tara Schonhoff.
    Research Analyst.—Doug Murray.
    GAO Detailee.—Alexandra Edwards.
  Minority Staff Director.—Eric Bursch (SH–605), 224–3682.
    Counsel.—Ashley Poling.
    Senior Professional Staff Member.—Lauren McClain.
    Legislative Aide.—Anthony Papian.
    CBC Fellow.—Antrell Tyson.

Judiciary

224 Dirksen Senate Office Building 20510–6275

phone 224–5225, fax 224–9102, http://www.judiciary.senate.gov

meets upon call of the chair

Chuck Grassley, of Iowa, *Chair*

Orrin G. Hatch, of Utah.
Jeff Sessions, of Alabama.
Lindsey Graham, of South Carolina.
John Cornyn, of Texas.
Mike Lee, of Utah.
Ted Cruz, of Texas.
Jeff Flake, of Arizona.
David Vitter, of Louisiana.
David Perdue, of Georgia.
Thom Tillis, of North Carolina.

Patrick J. Leahy, of Vermont.
Dianne Feinstein, of California.
Charles E. Schumer, of New York.
Richard J. Durbin, of Illinois.
Sheldon Whitehouse, of Rhode Island.
Amy Klobuchar, of Minnesota.
Al Franken, of Minnesota.
Christopher A. Coons, of Delaware.
Richard Blumenthal, of Connecticut.

SUBCOMMITTEES

Antitrust, Competition Policy and Consumer Rights

Mike Lee, of Utah, *Chair*

David Perdue, of Georgia.
Thom Tillis, of North Carolina.
Chuck Grassley, of Iowa.
Orrin G. Hatch, of Utah.

Amy Klobuchar, of Minnesota.
Christopher A. Coons, of Delaware.
Al Franken, of Minnesota.
Richard Blumenthal, of Connecticut.

Constitution

John Cornyn, of Texas, *Chair*

Thom Tillis, of North Carolina.
Lindsey Graham, of South Carolina.
Ted Cruz, of Texas.
David Vitter, of Louisiana.

Richard J. Durbin, of Illinois.
Sheldon Whitehouse, of Rhode Island.
Christopher A. Coons, of Delaware.
Al Franken, of Minnesota.

Crime and Terrorism

Lindsey Graham, of South Carolina, *Chair*

David Vitter, of Louisiana.
Jeff Sessions, of Alabama.
John Cornyn, of Texas.
Jeff Flake, of Arizona.

Sheldon Whitehouse, of Rhode Island.
Charles E. Schumer, of New York.
Amy Klobuchar, of Minnesota.
Al Franken, of Minnesota.

Immigration and the National Interest

Jeff Sessions, of Alabama, *Chair*

David Vitter, of Louisiana.
David Perdue, of Georgia.
Chuck Grassley, of Iowa.
John Cornyn, of Texas.
Mike Lee, of Utah.
Ted Cruz, of Texas.
Thom Tillis, of North Carolina.

Charles E. Schumer, of New York.
Patrick J. Leahy, of Vermont.
Dianne Feinstein, of California.
Richard J. Durbin, of Illinois.
Amy Klobuchar, of Minnesota.
Al Franken, of Minnesota.
Richard Blumenthal, of Connecticut.

Oversight, Agency Action, Federal Rights and Federal Courts

Ted Cruz, of Texas, *Chair*

Chuck Grassley, of Iowa.
Orrin G. Hatch, of Utah.
Jeff Sessions, of Alabama.
Jeff Flake, of Arizona.
Lindsey Graham, of South Carolina.
Mike Lee, of Utah.
David Vitter, of Louisiana.

Christopher A. Coons, of Delaware.
Dianne Feinstein, of California.
Richard J. Durbin, of Illinois.
Charles E. Schumer, of New York.
Sheldon Whitehouse, of Rhode Island.
Amy Klobuchar, of Minnesota.
Richard Blumenthal, of Connecticut.

Privacy, Technology and the Law

Jeff Flake, of Arizona, *Chair*

Orrin G. Hatch, of Utah.
David Perdue, of Georgia.
Mike Lee, of Utah.
Thom Tillis, of North Carolina.
Lindsey Graham, of South Carolina.

Al Franken, of Minnesota.
Dianne Feinstein, of California.
Charles E. Schumer, of New York.
Sheldon Whitehouse, of Rhode Island.
Christopher A. Coons, of Delaware.

STAFF

Committee on the Judiciary (SD–224), 224–5225.
  Chief Clerk.—Roslyne Turner.
    Law Librarian.—Charles Papirmeister.
    Legislative Calendar Clerk.—Alberta Easter.
    Assistant Clerk.—Michelle Heller.
    Hearings Clerk.—Jason Covey.
  Majority Office (SD–224), 224–5225, fax 224–9102.
  Majority Staff Director and Chief Counsel.—Kolan Davis.
    Deputy Staff Director and Chief Civil Counsel.—Rita Lari Jochum.
    Chief Constitution and Senior Counsel.—Fred Ansell.
    Chief National Security and Senior Criminal Counsel.—Tim Kelly.
    Chief Counsel for Nominations.—Ted Lehman.
    Chief Investigative Counsel.—Jason Foster.
    Investigative Counsels: Patrick Davis, Josh Flynn-Brown, Paul Junge, DeLisa Lay, Jay
      Lim, Katherine Nikas.
    Senior Counsel.—Nathan Hallford.
    Counsels: Tristan Dunford, Evelyn Fortier, Lauren Mehler, Jonathan Nabavi.
    Associate Counsel.—Kyle McCollum.
    Professional Staff Members: Christopher Boden, Kathy Nuebel Kovarik, Barbara Ledeen,
      Kasey O'Connor, Zoe O'Herin.
    Director of Communications.—Beth Levine.
    Press Secretary.—Taylor Foy.
    Staff Assistants.—Theresa Bauman, Jacob Neilson.
    Archivist.—Stuart Paine.
    Director of Information Systems.—Steve Kirkland.
  Minority Office (SD–152), 224–7703, fax 224–9516.
  Minority Staff Director and Chief Counsel.—Kristine Lucius.
    General Counsel.—Chan Park.
    Deputy General Counsel.—Anya McMurray.
    Chief Counsel for Nominations.—Maggie Whitney.
    Chief Counsel for I.P.—Alexandra Givens.
    Senior Counsels: Chanda Betourney, Josh Hsu.
    Counsels: Hasan Ali, Garrett Levin, Emily Livingston, Nazneen Mehta, Olga Medina,
      David Pendle.
    Professional Staff Members: Patrick Sheahan, Scott Wilson, Adrienne Wojeciechowski.
    Press Secretary.—Jessica Brady.
    Legislative Staff Assistant to the Chief Counsel.—Logan Gregoire.
    Nominations Clerk.—Rebecca Cooper.
    Legislative Staff Assistants: Jonathan Hoadley, Dan Taylor.
    Staff Assistant.—Joel Park.
    Archivist.—Anu Kasarabada.
    Systems Administrator.—Brian Hockin.

Subcommittee on Antitrust, Competition Policy and Consumer Rights.
   Majority Chief Counsel.—Matt Owen.
   Minority Chief Counsel.—Kirstin Dunham.
Subcommittee on the Constitution.
   Majority Chief Counsel.—Noah Phillips.
   Minority Chief Counsel.—Joe Zogby.
Subcommittee on Crime and Terrorism.
   Majority Chief Counsel.—David Glaccum.
   Minority Chief Counsel.—Ayo Griffin.
Subcommittee on Immigration and the National Interest.
   Majority Chief Counsel.—Danielle Cutrona.
   Minority Chief Counsel.—Rebecca Kelly Slaughter.
Subcommittee on Oversight, Agency Action, Federal Rights and Federal Courts.
   Majority Chief Counsel.—Ryan Newman.
   Minority Chief Counsel.—Ted Schroeder.
Subcommittee on Privacy, Technology and the Law.
   Majority Chief Counsel.—Gary Barnett.
   Minority Counsel.—Leslie Hylton.
Senator Hatch Judiciary Staff:
   Chief Counsel.—Tom Jipping.
Senator Vitter Judiciary Staff:
   Chief Counsel.—James Holland.
Senator Perdue Judiciary Staff:
   Chief Counsel.—David Rybicki.
Senator Tillis Judiciary Staff:
   Chief Counsel.—Ray Starling.
Senator Feinstein Judiciary Staff:
   Chief Counsel.—Eric Haren.
Senator Blumenthal Judiciary Staff·
   Chief Counsel.—Sam Simon.

Rules and Administration

305 Russell Senate Office Building 20510–6325

phone 224–6352, http://rules.senate.gov

[Legislative Reorganization Act of 1946]

meets second and fourth Wednesday of each month

Roy Blunt, of Missouri, *Chair*

Lamar Alexander, of Tennessee.
Mitch McConnell, of Kentucky.
Thad Cochran, of Mississippi.
Pat Roberts, of Kansas.
Richard C. Shelby, of Alabama.
Ted Cruz, of Texas.
Shelley Moore Capito, of West Virginia.
John Boozman, of Arkansas.
Roger F. Wicker, of Mississippi.

Charles E. Schumer, of New York.
Dianne Feinstein, of California.
Richard J. Durbin, of Illinois.
Tom Udall, of New Mexico.
Mark R. Warner, of Virginia.
Patrick J. Leahy, of Vermont.
Amy Klobuchar, of Minnesota.
Angus S. King, Jr., of Maine.

(No Subcommittees)

STAFF

Committee on Rules and Administration (SR–305), 224–6352.
  *Majority Staff Director.—*Stacy M. McBride.
    *Deputy Staff Director.—*Shaun Parkin.
    *Chief Counsel.—*Paul Vinovich.
    *Counsel.—*David Adkins.
    *Senior Professional Staff.—*Trish Kent.
    *Professional Staff.—*Nichole Kotschwar.
  *Minority Staff Director.—*Kelly L. Fado.
    *Director of Operations Oversight.—*Jay McCarthy.
    *Chief Counsel.—*Stacy J. Ettinger.
    *Counsel.—*Benjamin Hovland.
    *Professional Staff/Legislative Assistant.—*Abbie Sorrendino.
    *Legislative Aide.—*Phillip Rumsey.
    *Special Assistant.—*Leigh Schisler.
    Non-Designated Staff:
      *Chief Clerk.—*Jeff Johnson.
      *Professional Staff.—*Matthew McGowan.
      *Director of Administration and Policy.—*Maria Keebler.
      *Chief Auditor.—*Leann Alwood.
      Staff Assistants: Brittany Donnellan, Hans Hansen.

Small Business and Entrepreneurship
428A Russell Senate Office Building 20510
phone 224–5175, fax 224–5619, http://sbc.senate.gov
[Created pursuant to S. Res. 58, 81st Congress]

meets first Thursday of each month

David Vitter, of Louisiana, *Chair*

James E. Risch, of Idaho.
Marco Rubio, of Florida.
Rand Paul, of Kentucky.
Tim Scott, of South Carolina.
Deb Fischer, of Nebraska.
Cory Gardner, of Colorado.
Joni Ernst, of Iowa.
Kelly Ayotte, of New Hampshire.
Michael B. Enzi, of Wyoming.

Jeanne Shaheen, of New Hampshire.
Maria Cantwell, of Washington.
Benjamin L. Cardin, of Maryland.
Heidi Heitkamp, of North Dakota.
Edward J. Markey, of Massachusetts.
Cory A. Booker, of New Jersey
Christopher A. Coons, of Delaware.
Mazie K. Hirono, of Hawaii.
Gary C. Peters, of Michigan.

(No Subcommittees)

STAFF

Committee on Small Business and Entrepreneurship (SR–428A), 224–5175, fax 224–5619.
Majority Staff Director.—Zak Baig.
Deputy Staff Director.—Luke Tomanelli.
Communications Director.—Cheyenne Klotz.
Policy Director.—Meredith West.
Health Care Policy Advisor.—Arne Owens.
Senior Policy Advisor.—Charles Brittingham.
Professional Staff: Ward Cormier, John Steitz.
Counsel.—Drew Feeley.
Research Assistants: Rachel Bourgeois, Stephen Newton, Sarah Veatch.
Staff Assistant.—Rachel Ledbetter.
Chief Clerk.—Kathryn Eden.
Systems Administrator.—Clermon Acklin.
Minority Committee Main Office (SR–471), phone 224–2809.
Minority Staff Director.—Robert Diznoff.
Deputy Staff Director.—Kevin Wheeler
General Counsel.—Ami Sanchez.
Senior Professional Staff.—Chris Neary.
Professional Staff.—Debbie Kobrin.
Legal Analyst.—Harry Anastopulos.
Legal Researcher.—Brandon Locke.
Staff Assistant.—DeMarcus Finnell.

Veterans' Affairs

SR–412 Russell Senate Office Building

phone 224–9126, http://veterans.senate.gov

meets first Wednesday of each month

Johnny Isakson, of Georgia, *Chair*

Jerry Moran, of Kansas.
John Boozman, of Arkansas.
Dean Heller, of Nevada.
Bill Cassidy, of Louisiana.
Mike Rounds, of South Dakota.
Thom Tillis, of North Carolina.
Dan Sullivan, of Alaska.

Richard Blumenthal, of Connecticut.
Patty Murray, of Washington.
BERNARD SANDERS, of Vermont.
Sherrod Brown, of Ohio.
Jon Tester, of Montana.
Mazie K. Hirono, of Hawaii.
Joe Manchin III, of West Virginia.

(No Subcommittees)

STAFF

Committee on Veterans' Affairs Majority Staff (SR–412), 224–9126, fax 224–9575.
Majority Staff Director.—Thomas Bowman.
Deputy Staff Director/General Counsel.—Amanda Meredith.
Senior Policy Advisor for Health.—Maureen O'Neill.
Senior Professional Staff: Leslie Campbell, Adam Reece.
Legislative Assistants: Gretchan Blum, David Shearman, Jillian Workman.
Press Assistant.—Lauren Gaydos.
Senior Staff Assistant/Correspondence Administrator.—Tucker Zrebiec.
Staff Assistants: Britton Burkett, Torie Ness.
Committee on Veterans' Affairs Minority Staff (825A Hart), 224–2074, fax 228–1852.
Minority Staff Director.—John Kruse.
General Counsel.—Vacant.
Counsels: Jorge Rueda, Laurel Sakai.
Senior Legislative Assistant.—Kathryn Monet.
Legislative Assistant.—Elizabeth Austin.
Staff Assistants: Sean Donnelly, Ryan Tomlinson.
Non-Designated (SR–412), 224–9126.
Chief Clerk.—Heather Vachon.

SELECT AND SPECIAL COMMITTEES OF THE SENATE

Committee on Indian Affairs

838 Hart Senate Office Building 20510–6450

phone 224–2251, http://indian.senate.gov

[Created pursuant to S. Res. 4, 95th Congress; amended by S. Res. 71, 103d Congress]

meets every Wednesday of each month

John Barrasso, of Wyoming, *Chair*

Jon Tester, of Montana, *Vice Chair*

John McCain, of Arizona.
Lisa Murkowski, of Alaska.
John Hoeven, of North Dakota.
James Lankford, of Oklahoma.
Steve Daines, of Montana.
Mike Crapo, of Idaho.
Jerry Moran, of Kansas.

Maria Cantwell, of Washington.
Tom Udall, of New Mexico.
Al Franken, of Minnesota.
Brian Schatz, of Hawaii.
Heidi Heitkamp, of North Dakota.

(No Subcommittees)

STAFF

Majority Staff Director/Chief Counsel.—Mike Andrews.
  Deputy Chief Counsel.—Rhonda Harjo.
  Senior Policy Advisor.—Brandon Ashley.
  Counsel.—Emily Newman.
  Press Secretary.—Mike Danylak.
  Legislative Assistant.—Jacqueline Bisille.
  Research Assistant.—Natasha John.
  Staff Assistant.—David Wise.
Minority Staff Director/Chief Counsel.—Anthony Walters.
  Senior Policy Advisor.—Sierra Howlett.
  Counsel.—Wendy Helgemo.
  Policy Director.—Kenneth Martin.
  Staff Assistant.—Gerald Kaquatosh.
  Administrative Director.—Jim Eismeier.
  Clerk.—Amanda Kelly.
  Systems Administrator.—David Stuart.
  Receptionist.—Sarah Overton.
  GPO Detailee.—Jack Fulmer.

Select Committee on Ethics

220 Hart Senate Office Building 20510, phone 224-2981, fax 224-7416

[Created pursuant to S. Res. 338, 88th Congress; amended by S. Res. 110, 95th Congress]

Johnny Isakson, of Georgia, *Chair*

Barbara Boxer, of California, *Vice Chair*

Pat Roberts, of Kansas.
James E. Risch, of Idaho.

Christopher A. Coons, of Delaware.
Brian Schatz, of Hawaii.

STAFF

Chief Counsel and Staff Director.—Deborah Sue Mayer.
  Deputy Staff Director.—Annette Gillis.
  Senior Counsel.—Tremayne Bunaugh, Lynn Tran.
    Counsels: Rochelle Ford, Anna Stolarz, Geoff Turley, Ray Wolcott.
    Director of IT.—Danny Remington.
    Financial Disclosure Specialist.—Philip Kibbey.
    Special Assistant for Financial Disclosure.—Alyssa Brockington.
  Senior Staff Assistant.—Ben Toribio.
    Staff Assistants: Emily Gershon, Addison Winger.

Select Committee on Intelligence

211 Hart Senate Office Building 20510-6475, phone 224-1700

http://www.senate.gov/~intelligence

[Created pursuant to S. Res. 400, 94th Congress]

Richard Burr, of North Carolina, *Chair*

Dianne Feinstein, of California, *Vice Chair*

James E. Risch, of Idaho.
Daniel Coats, of Indiana.
Marco Rubio, of Florida.
Susan M. Collins, of Maine.
Roy Blunt, of Missouri.
James Lankford, of Oklahoma.
Tom Cotton, of Arkansas.

Ron Wyden, of Oregon.
Barbara A. Mikulski, of Maryland.
Mark R. Warner, of Virginia.
Martin Heinrich, of New Mexico.
Angus S. King, Jr., of Maine.
Mazie K. Hirono, of Hawaii.

Ex Officio

Mitch McConnell, of Kentucky.
John McCain, of Arizona.

Harry Reid, of Nevada.
Jack Reed, of Rhode Island.

STAFF

Majority Staff Director.—Christopher Joyner.
Minority Staff Director.—David Grannis.
  Chief Clerk.—Desiree Thompson Sayle.

Special Committee on Aging

G–31 Dirksen Senate Office Building 20510, phone 224–5364

http://aging.senate.gov

[Reauthorized pursuant to S. Res. 4, 95th Congress]

Susan M. Collins, of Maine, *Chair*

Orrin G. Hatch, of Utah.	*Claire McCaskill, of Missouri.*
Mark Kirk, of Illinois.	*Bill Nelson, of Florida.*
Jeff Flake, of Arizona.	*Robert P. Casey, Jr., of Pennsylvania.*
Tim Scott, of South Carolina.	*Sheldon Whitehouse, of Rhode Island.*
Bob Corker, of Tennessee.	*Kirsten E. Gillibrand, of New York.*
Dean Heller, of Nevada.	*Richard Blumenthal, of Connecticut.*
Tom Cotton, of Arkansas.	*Joe Donnelly, of Indiana.*
David Perdue, of Georgia.	*Elizabeth Warren, of Massachusetts.*
Thom Tillis, of North Carolina.	*Tim Kaine, of Virginia.*
Ben Sasse, of Nebraska.	

STAFF

Majority Staff Director.—Priscilla Hanley.
  Deputy Staff Director/Communications Director.—Jen Burita.
  Chief Counsel.—Mark LeDuc.
  Chief Investigator.—Sam Dewey.
  Investigator.—Sharon Utz.
  Legislative Assistant.—Christopher Knight.
  Staff Assistant.—Tim Stretton.
  Chief Clerk/System Administrator.—Matt Lawrence.
Minority Staff (SH–628), 224–8710, Fax 224–9926
Staff Director.—Derron Parks.
  Deputy Staff Director.—Joel Eskovitz.
  Communications Director.—Drew Pusateri.
  Counsels: Caitlin Warner, Cathy Yu.
  Senior Policy Aide.—Hannah Berner.
  Staff Assistant/Policy Aide.—Emma Kenyon.

Democratic Senatorial Campaign Committee

120 Maryland Avenue, NE., 20002, phone 224–2447

Jon Tester, of Montana, *Chair*

Harry Reid, of Nevada, *Democratic Leader*

STAFF

Executive Director.—Tom Lopach.
  Deputy Executive Director.—Preston Elliot.
  Communications Director.—Justin Barasky.
  Political Director.—Simone Ward.
  Finance Director.—Valerie Friedman.
  Legal Counsel.—Mark Elias.

Democratic Policy and Communications Center

419 Hart Senate Office Building, phone 224–3232

Harry Reid, of Nevada, Democratic Leader

Charles E. Schumer, of New York, *Chair.*
Debbie Stabenow, of Michigan, *Vice Chair.*

STAFF

Staff Director.—Mike Lynch, Capitol/S–318, mike_lynch@dpcc.senate.gov (202) 224–2939.
Communications Director.—Matt House, Capitol/S–318, matt_house@dpcc.senate.gov, 224–2939.
Director of Hispanic Media.—Jose Parra, Capitol/S–318, jose_parra@reid.senate.gov, 224–2939.
Communication Director for NV/National Press Secretary.—Kristen Orthman, Capitol/S–318, kristen_orthman@reid.senate.gov, 224–2939.
Deputy Regional Press Secretary.—Carolyn Seuthe, S–112, carolyn_seuthe@dpcc.senate.gov, 224–2939.
Press Secretary for Hispanic Media.—Jorge Silva, S–112, jorge_silva@dpcc.senate.gov, 224–2939.
Press Assistant for Hispanic Media.—Reynaldo Benitez, Capitol/S–112, reynaldo_benitez @dpcc.senate.gov, 224–2939.
Press Assistants: Bianca Recto, Capitol/S–318, bianca_recto@dpcc.senate.gov; Dylan Lierd, S–318, dylan_lierd@dpcc.senate.gov, 224–2939.
Policy Director.—Ryan McConaghy, SH419, ryan_mcconaghy@dpcc.senate.gov, 224–2939.
Counsel/Policy Advisor.—Pat Collier, SH419, pat_collier@dpcc.senate.gov, 224–2939.
Policy Advisors: Julie Klein, SH419, julie_klein@dpcc.senate.gov, 224–3232; Charlie Ellsworth, SH419, charlie_ellsworth@dpcc.senate.gov, 224–3232; Matt House, S318, matt_house@dpcc.senate.gov, 224–2939; Laura Erickson Hatalsky, SH419, laura_ericksonhatalsky@dpcc.senate.gov, 224–3232.
Policy Assistant.—Karlee Tebbutt, SH419, karlee_tebbutt@dpcc.senate.gov, 224–3232.
Deputy Regional Press Secretary.—Bilal Ali, SH–112, bilal_ali@dpcc.senate.gov.
Senior Rapid Response Advisor.—Dan Yoken, dan_yoken@dpcc.senate.gov, 224–2939.
Publications Director and Senior Vote Analyst.—Doug Connolly, SH705, doug_connolly @dpcc.senate.gov, 224–2939.
Votes Director.—Michael Mozden, SH705, michael_mozden@dpcc.senate.gov, 224–2939.
Deputy Press Secretary.—Brian Ahern, brian_ahern@dpcc.senate.gov, 224–2939.
Deputy Press Secretary/Deputy Speech Writer.—Christopher Huntley, christopher_huntley @dpcc.senate.gov, 224–2939.
Senior Advisor for Digital Media.—Faiz Shakir, S318, faiz_shakir@reid.senate.gov, 224–2939.

Steering and Outreach Committee

712 Hart Senate Office Building, phone 224–9048

Amy Klobuchar, of Minnesota, *Chair*

Jeanne Shaheen, of New Hampshire, *Vice Chair*

Harry Reid, of Nevada, *Democratic Leader*

Richard J. Durbin, of Illinois, *Assistant Democratic Leader*

Christopher A. Coons, of Delaware, *Chairman of Business Outreach*

Robert Menendez, of New Jersey, *Chairman of the Hispanic Task Force*

Cory A. Booker, of New Jersey, *Chair of Metropolitan Outreach*

Patrick J. Leahy, of Vermont.
Barbara Boxer, of California,
Kirsten E. Gillibrand, of New York.
Bill Nelson, of Florida.
Robert P. Casey, Jr., of Pennsylvania.

Jon Tester, of Montana.
Brian Schatz, of Hawaii.
Tammy Baldwin, of Wisconsin.
Christopher Murphy, of Connecticut.

STAFF

Staff Director.—David McMaster.
Director of Outreach.—Eloy J. Martinez.
Associate Directors: Claire Badger, Rayshon Payton.
Staff Assistant.—Victoria Laxalt.

Senate Democratic Conference

154 Russell Senate Office Building, phone 224–2621, fax 224–0238

Secretary.—Patty Murray, of Washington State.
 Chief of Staff.—Mike Spahn.
 Senior Leadership Advisor and Floor Directors: Emma Fulkerson, Stacy Rich.

Senate Democratic Media Center

619 Hart Senate Office Building, phone 224–1430

Harry Reid, of Nevada, *Chair*

STAFF

Director of Broadcast Operations.—Brian Jones.
 Director of New Media.—Faiz Shakir.
 Editors: Hisham Abdelhamid, Don Jonathan Webb.
 Engineer.—Luis Mattos.
 Event Coordinator.—Ryan King.
 Graphic Design Specialist.—Perisha Gates.
 Senior Developer.—Judson Blewett.
 Multimedia Specialist.—Ian Shifrin.
 Press Assistant.—Isaiah Calvin.
 Videographers: Kevin Kelleher, Clare Palace.

National Republican Senatorial Committee

425 Second Street, NE., 20002, phone 675–6000, fax 675–6058

Roger F. Wicker, of Mississippi, *Chair*

STAFF

Executive Director.—Ward Baker.
 Director of:
  Communications.—Andrea Bozek.
  Finance.—Claire Holloway.
  Legal Counsel.—Matt Raymer.
  Political Director.—Sarah Morgan.
  Research.—Mark McLaughlin.

Senate Republican Policy Committee

347 Russell Senate Office Building, phone 224–2946
fax 224–1235, http://rpc.senate.gov

John Barrasso, of Wyoming, *Chair*

STAFF

Staff Director.—Dan Kunsman.
 Policy Director.—Arjun Mody.
 Communications Director.—Emily Schillinger.
 Administrative Director.—Craig Cheney.
 Analysts:
  Agriculture, Energy and Environment.—Matthew Leggett.
  Budget, Tax, Appropriations.—Spencer Wayne.
  Health Care.—Brian Blase.
  Commerce, Transportation, Trade.—Mitchell Kominsky.
  Education, Labor, Banking, Housing.—Dana Barbieri.
  Defense, Foreign Affairs, Intelligence, Veterans Affairs.—Michael Stransky.

Judiciary/Immigration.—Michael Thorpe.
Professional Staff:
  Editor.—John Mitchell.
  System Administrator/RVA Analyst.—Thomas Pulju.
  Station Manager/Special Projects.—Carolyn Laird.
  Station Operator/Project Assistant.—Taylor Holgate.
  Digital Director.—Libby Marinaccio.
  Deputy Digital Director.—Maeve McKenna.

Senate Republican Conference

405 Hart Senate Office Building, phone 224–2764
http://src.senate.gov

John Thune, of South Dakota, *Chair*

Roy Blunt, of Missouri, *Vice Chair*

STAFF

Conference of the Majority (SH–405), 224–2764.
  Staff Director.—Brendon Plack.
  Deputy Staff Director.—Ann Marie Hauser.
  Media Services Director.—Dave Hodgdon.
  Office Manager/Communications Assistant.—Shelley Backstrom.
  Communications Director.—Chandler Smith.
  Senior Writer.—Mary Katherine Ascik.
  Internal Communications Advisor.—Erin Callanan.
  Production Manager.—Cyrus Pearson.
  Videographer/Editor.—Lane Marshall.
  Digital Director.—Robert Myers.
  Senior Graphics Designers: Chris Angrisani, Laura Gill.
  Systems Engineer.—Nate Green.
  Floor Monitor.—Taylor Hayes.

OFFICERS AND OFFICIALS OF THE SENATE

Capitol Telephone Directory, 224–3121
Senate room prefixes:
Capitol—S, Russell Senate Office Building—SR
Dirksen Senate Office Building—SD, Hart Senate Office Building—SH

PRESIDENT OF THE SENATE

Vice President of the United States and President of the Senate.—Joseph R. Biden, Jr.

The Ceremonial Office of the Vice President is S–212 in the Capitol. The Vice President has offices in the Dirksen Senate Office Building, the Eisenhower Executive Office Building (EEOB) and the White House (West Wing).

Chief of Staff to the Vice President.—Steve Ricchetti, EEOB, room 272, 456–9951.
Domestic Policy and Counselor to the Vice President.—Don Graves, EEOB, room 282, 456–2982.
Press Secretary to the Vice President.—Kendra Barkoff, EEOB, room 284A, 456–4390.
Director of Legislative Affairs.—Tonya Williams, EEOB, room 279A, 456–1540.
National Security Advisor to the Vice President.—Colin Kahl, EEOB, room 208, 456–2744.
Assistants to the Vice President: Kathy Chung, 456–1715; Anne Marie Muldoon, 456–1732, West Wing.
Deputy Assistant to the Vice President and Chief of Staff to Dr. Jill Biden.—Sheila Nix, EEOB, room 201, 456–7458.
Director of Scheduling.—Virginia "Ginna" Lance, EEOB, room 265A, 456–6264.

PRESIDENT PRO TEMPORE
S–125 The Capitol, phone 224–9400

President Pro Tempore of the Senate.—Orrin G. Hatch.
Administrative Director.—Celeste Gold.
Chief Counsel.—William Castle.
Counsel.—Ryan Leavitt.
Chief of Staff.—Rob Porter.

MAJORITY LEADER
S–230 The Capitol, phone 224–3135, fax 228–1264

Majority Leader.—Mitch McConnell.
Chief of Staff.—Sharon Soderstrom.
Deputy Chief of Staff.—Don Stewart.
Director of Operations.—Stefanie Muchow.
Scheduler.—Laura Vincent.
Assistant Scheduler.—Katie Barnes.
Director of Administration.—Rebecca Fleeson.
Policy Advisors: Jonathan Burks, Neil Chatterjee, Brendan Dunn, Hazen Marshall, Scott Raab, Erica Suarez, Terry Van Doren.
Legal Counsels: John Abegg, Brian Lewis.
National Security Advisor.—Tom Hawkins.
Communications Director.—Michael Brumas.
Speechwriter.—Brian Forest.
Press Assistant.—Laura Hendrickson.

Systems Administrator.—Elmamoun Sulfab.
Staff Assistants: Suzanne Burton, Mallory Shoffner, Emily Costanzo.

REPUBLICAN COMMUNICATIONS CENTER
S–230 The Capitol, phone 228–6397

Communications Staff Director.—Antonia Ferrier.
Analyst.—Matt Kenney.
Communications Advisor, New Media.—David Hauptmann.
Communications Advisor.—Scott Sloofman.
Creative Advisor.—Hunter Hawkins.

OFFICE OF THE MAJORITY WHIP
S–208 The Capitol, phone 224–2708, fax 228–1507

Republican Whip.—John Cornyn.
Chief of Staff.—Monica Popp.
Whip Liaison.—Emily Kirlin.
Policy Advisors: Johnathan Chapuis, Jane Lee.
Staff Assistant.—Noah McCullough.

DEMOCRATIC LEADER
S–221 The Capitol, phone 224–2158, fax 224–7362

Democratic Leader.—Harry Reid.
Chief of Staff.—Andrew B. Willison.
Deputy Chief of Staff.—David McCallum.
Executive Assistant.—Adelle Cruz.
Scheduler.—Krysta Juris.
Assistant Scheduler.—Laura Pedro.
Deputy Chief of Staff for Policy.—Bill Dauster.
Legislative Director.—Jason Unger.
Communications Director.—Kristen Orthman.
Speechwriter.—Vaughn Bray.
Chief Counsel.—Ayesha Khanna.
Executive Assistant to the Chief of Staff.—Alexis Villanueva.
Staff Assistant and Events Coordinator.—Maria Criswell.

ASSISTANT DEMOCRATIC LEADER
S–321 The Capitol, phone 224–9447

Assistant Democratic Leader.—Richard J. Durbin.
Chief of Staff.—Pat Souders.
Director of Operations.—Sally Brown-Shaklee.
Director of Scheduling.—Claire Reuschel.
Deputy Scheduler.—Lauren Zdanowitz.
Communications Director.—Ben Marter.
Deputy Communications Director.—Christina Mulka.
Floor Director.—Reema Dodin.
Deputy Floor Director.—MJ Kenny.
Staff Assistant.—Daniel Palacios.
Speechwriter.—Molly Rowley.

OFFICE OF THE SECRETARY
S–312 The Capitol, phone 224–3622

JULIE E. ADAMS, Secretary of the Senate; elected and sworn in as the 33rd Secretary of the Senate on January 6, 2015; native of Iowa; bachelor's degree in political science from Luther College, Decorah, IA; master's degree in education from the University of Iowa; Director of Administration, Majority Leader Mitch McConnell; Spokesperson, First Lady Laura Bush; Deputy Communications Director, then-Senate Majority Whip Mitch McConnell.

Secretary of the Senate.—Julie E. Adams (S–312), 224–3622.
  Assistant Secretary of the Senate.—Mary Suit Jones (S–333), 224–3622.
  Capitol Offices Liaison.—Gerald Thompson (SB–36C), 224–1483.
  Chief of Staff.—Rachel Creviston (S–414C), 224–3895.
  Deputy Chief of Staff.—Sydney G. Butler (S–312), 224–9461.
  Executive Accounts Administrator.—Zoraida Torres (S–414B), 224–7099.
  Executive Staff Assistant.—Annalee Ashley (S–333), 224–9278.
  General Counsel.—Adam Bramwell (S–414D), 224–8789.

ADMINISTRATIVE SERVICES

Chief Counsel for Employment.—Claudia A. Kostel (SH–103), 224–5424.
  Conservation and Preservation.—Beverly Adams (S–416), 224–4550.
  Curator.—Melinda K. Smith (S–411), 224–2955.
  Gift Shop.—Neil Schwartz (SD–G42), 224–7308.
  Historian.—Betty K. Koed (SH–201), 224–6900.
  Human Resources.—John McIlveen (SH–231B), 224–3625.
  Information Systems.—Dan Kulnis (S–422), 224–4883.
  Interparliamentary Services.—Sally Walsh (SH–808), 224–3047.
  Joint Office of Education and Training.—Megan Daly (SD–180), 224–7588.
  Legislative Info Systems (LIS) Project.—Marsha Misenhimer (SD–B44A), 224–2500.
  Library.—Leona Faust (SR–B15), 224–7106.
  Page School.—Kathryn S. Weeden (Webster Hall), 224–3927.
  Printing and Document Services.—Karen Moore (SH–B04), 224–0205.
  Public Records.—Dana McCallum (SH–232), 224–0322.
  Senate Security.—Michael P. DiSilvestro (SVC–217), 224–5632.
  Stationery Room.—Terri Keller (SDB–42), 224–4771.
  Web Technology.—Arin Shapiro (PSQ 6960), 224–2020.

FINANCIAL SERVICES

Disbursing Office.—Ileana M. Garcia (SH–127), 224–3205.

LEGISLATIVE SERVICES

Bill Clerk.—Sara Schwartzman (S–123), 224–2120.
  Captioning Services.—JoEllen R. Dicken (SVC–111), 224–4321.
  Daily Digest, Editor.—Elizabeth Tratos (S–421), 224–2658.
  Enrolling Clerk.—Margarida Curtis (S–139), 224–8427.
  Executive Clerk.—Jennifer Gorham (S–138), 224–4341.
  Journal Clerk.—Scott M. Sanborn (S–135), 224–4650.
  Legislative Clerk.—John J. Merlino (S–134), 224–4350.
  Official Reporters of Debates.—Patrick Renzi (S–410A), 224–3152.
  Parliamentarian.—Elizabeth C. MacDonough (S–133), 224–6128.

OFFICE OF THE CHAPLAIN
S–332 The Capitol, phone 224–2510, fax 224–9686

BARRY C. BLACK, Chaplain, U.S. Senate; born in Baltimore, MD, on November 1, 1948; education: Bachelor of Arts, Theology, Oakwood College, 1970; Master of Divinity, Andrews Theological Seminary, 1973; Master of Arts, Counseling, North Carolina Central University, 1978; Doctor of Ministry, Theology, Eastern Baptist Seminary, 1982; Master of Arts, Management, Salve Regina University, 1989; Doctor of Philosophy, Psychology, United States International University, 1996; military service: U.S. Navy, 1976–2003; rising to the rank of Rear Admiral; Chief of Navy Chaplains, 2000–2003; awards: Navy Distinguished Service Medal; Legion of Merit Medal; Defense Meritorious Service Medal; Meritorious Service Medals (two awards); Navy and Marine Corps Commendation Medals (two awards); 1995 NAACP Renowned Service Award; family: married to Brenda; three children: Barry II, Brendan, and Bradford.

Chaplain of the Senate.—Barry C. Black.
Chief of Staff.—Lisa Schultz, 224–3849.
Communications Director.—Jody Spraggins-Scott, 224–2048.
Staff Scheduler / Executive Assistant.—Suzanne Chapuis, 224–7456.

OFFICE OF THE SERGEANT AT ARMS
S–151 The Capitol, phone 224–2341, fax 224–7690

FRANK J. LARKIN was sworn in on January 6, 2015, as the 40th United States Senate Sergeant at Arms, continuing a distinguished career in law enforcement, national security, intelligence, and cyber and physical security. Larkin earned both a B.A. in criminal justice and an M.S. degree in public administration from Villanova University; a veteran of the U.S. Navy, he has a significant military and law enforcement special operations background; Larkin served as special warfare operator in the Navy SEALs and went on to serve as a uniformed patrol officer with the Norristown (PA) Police Department, a homicide detective with the Montgomery County (PA) District Attorney's Office, and a Maryland State Trooper-Flight Paramedic; Larkin served for more than two decades in the United States Secret Service, beginning in 1984 as a Special Agent assigned to the Philadelphia Field Office; he was transferred to Washington, DC, and held positions in the Office of Training, the Washington Field Office, and the Presidential Protection Division; more recently Larkin was a member of the Senior Executive Service serving as both the Acting Director and the Vice Director of the Joint Improvised Explosive Device Defeat Organization (JIEDDO) within the Department of Defense; Larkin has substantial private sector experience as Director, Program Management and Leadership for the Raytheon Company and more recently with Lockheed Martin's Information Systems and Global Solutions—Defense and Intelligence Solutions providing operations and intelligence analysis support to the intelligence community; Larkin is married and resides with his wife in Annapolis.

Sergeant at Arms.—Frank J. Larkin.
Deputy Sergeant at Arms.—James W. Morhard.
Chief of Staff.—Michael Stenger.
Assistant Sergeant at Arms Office of Protective Services and Continuity.—Dick Attridge, SVC 305, 224–3691.
Assistant Sergeant at Arms for Operations.—Bret Swanson, SDG61, 224–7052.
Assistant Sergeant at Arms and Chief Information Officer.—Vicki Sinnett (Postal Square), 224–0459.
Assistant Sergeant at Arms for Capitol Operations.—Kevin Morison, SB–8, 224–2506.
Deputy Assistant SAA for Operations.—Laura Parker, SD–G61, 224–1082.

APPOINTMENT DESK

Appointment Desk Manager.—Christine Catucci, North Door Capitol Building, 1st Floor, 224–7620.

CAPITOL FACILITIES

Director of Capitol Facilities.—Grace Ridgeway, SC–5, 224–2343.

CENTRAL OPERATIONS

Director of Central Operations.—Mike Brown, SD–150, 224–4035.
Hair Care Manager.—Cindi Brown, SR–B70, 224–4560.
Parking and ID Branch Manager.—Sam Jacobs, SD–G61, 224–9927.
Parking Operations.—Shawn Fretz, 224–8888.
ID Office.—Chris Carpenter, 224–2338.
Photo Studio Manager.—Bill Allen, SD–G85, 224–6000.

DOORKEEPERS

Director of Doorkeepers.—Krista Beal, S–213, Reception Room, 224–1879.

EMPLOYEE ASSISTANCE PROGRAM

Employee Assistance Program Administrator.—Vacant, 6278 Hart, 224–3902.

FINANCIAL MANAGEMENT

Chief Financial Officer.—Christopher Dey (Postal Square), 224–6292.
Accounting Manager.—Mary Ann Sifford, 224–1035.
Accounts Payable Manager.—David Salem, 224–8844.
Budget Manager.—Jeanne Burcham, 228–5584.
Procurement Manager.—David Baker, 224–2547.

HUMAN RESOURCES

Director of Human Resources.—Patrick Murphy, SH–142, 224–2889.
SAA Safety Office Officer.—Taurus Moore, 228–0823.
Senate Placement Office Administrator.—Brian Bean, 224–9167.
Workers' Compensation Office Manager.—Catherine Brooks, 224–3796.

IT SUPPORT SERVICES

Director of IT Support Services.—Robert E. Harris (Postal Square), 228–3499.
Desktop/LAN Support Manager.—Tim Dean, 224–3564.
Equipment Services Manager.—Win Grayson, 224–8065.
Telecom Services Manager.—Kenneth Kaus, 228–3517.

MEDIA GALLERIES

Director of the Daily Press Gallery.—Laura Lytle, S–316, 224–0241.
Director of the Periodical Press Gallery.—Edward V. Pesce, S–320, 224–0265.
Director of the Press Photographers Gallery.—Jeff Kent, S–317, 224–6548.
Director of the Radio and Television Gallery.—Michael Mastrian, S–325, 224–6421.

OFFICE OF EDUCATION AND TRAINING

Director of the Office of Education and Training.—Megan Daly, H–121, 224–7952.

OFFICE OF INTERNAL COMMUNICATIONS

Director of the Office of Internal Communications.—Kristan Trugman (Postal Square), 228–9852.

OFFICE OF PROTECTIVE SERVICES AND CONTINUITY

Deputy Assistant Sergeant at Arms for OPSAC.—Brian McGinty, SVC–305, 228–9788.
Director for Security Policy and Planning.—Michael Chandler (Postal Square), 228–0635.

OFFICE SUPPORT SERVICES

Director of Office Support Services.—Welda Wagstaff, PSB 6705, 224–0821.
State Office Liaison.—David Vignolo, PSB 6445, 224–0995.

PAGE PROGRAM

Director of the Page Program.—Elizabeth Roach (Webster Hall), 228–1291.

PRINTING, GRAPHICS AND DIRECT MAIL

Printing, Graphics and Direct Mail.—Darryl McDonald, SD–G82, 224–4871.

PROCESS MANAGEMENT AND INNOVATION

Director of Process Management and Innovation.—Ed Jankus (Postal Square), 224–7780.
IT Research and Deployment Manager.—Steve Walker, 224–1768.
Program Management Manager.—Joe Eckert, 224–2982.

PROTOCOL OFFICE

Protocol Officer.—Becky Daugherty, S–151, 224–2341.

RECORDING STUDIO

Recording Studio General Manager.—Dave Bass, SVC–160, 224–4979.

SENATE POST OFFICE

Senate Postmaster.—Donnie Cook, SD–B23, 224–5675.

TECHNOLOGY DEVELOPMENT

Director of Technology Development.—Jay Moore (Postal Square), 224–0092.
Enterprise IT Operations Manager.—Joe LaPalme, 228–4451.
Information Technology Security Manager.—Linus Barloon, 224–6454.
Network Engineering and Management Manager.—Bill Hill, 224–9380.
Systems Development Services Manager.—Laura Robertson (acting), 224–1831.

OFFICE OF THE SECRETARY FOR THE MAJORITY
S–337 The Capitol, phone 224–3835, fax 224–2860

Secretary for the Majority.—Laura C. Dove (S–337).
  Assistant Secretary for the Majority.—Robert Duncan (S–335).
  Administrative Assistant.—Noelle Busk Ringel (S–337).
  Senior Floor Assistant.—Chris Tuck (S–335), 224–6191
    Floor Assistant.—Megan Mercer (S–335), 224–6191.

S–226 Majority Cloakroom, phone 224–6191

Senior Cloakroom Assistant.—Mary Elizabeth Taylor.
Cloakroom Assistants: Tony Hanagan, Mike Smith.

OFFICE OF THE SECRETARY FOR THE MINORITY
S–309 The Capitol, phone 224–3735

Secretary for the Minority.—Gary Myrick.
  Assistant Secretary for the Minority.—Tim Mitchell (S–118), 224–5551.
  Administrative Assistant to the Secretary.—Nancy Iacomini.
  Executive Assistant to the Secretary.—Amber Huus.

S–118 The Capitol, phone 224–5551

Senior Floor Assistant.—Tricia Engle.
  Floor Assistant.—Daniel Tinsley.
  Executive Assistant to the Floor Staff.—Terri Taylor.

S–225 Minority Cloakroom, phone 224–4691

Cloakroom Assistants: Nicole Catucci, Stephanie Paone, Danica Rodman, Brad Watt.

OFFICE OF THE LEGISLATIVE COUNSEL
668 Dirksen Senate Office Building, phone 224–6461, fax 224–0567

Legislative Counsel.—Gary L. Endicott.
Deputy Legislative Counsel.—William R. Baird.
Senior Counsels: Charles E. Armstrong, Ruth Ann Ernst, John A. Goetcheus, Elizabeth
  Aldridge King.

Assistant Counsels: Kimberly D. Albrecht-Taylor, John W. Baggaley, Margaret A. Bomba, Heather L. Burnham, Kevin M. Davis, Stephanie Easley, Vincent J. Gaiani, Amy E. Gaynor, Kathryne M. Grendon, John A. Henderson, Thomas B. Heywood, Christina N. Jacquet, Michelle L. Johnson-Weider, Heather A. Lowell, Philip B. Lynch, Matthew D. McGhie, Mark M. McGunagle, Christine E. Miranda, James L. Ollen-Smith, Allison M. Otto, Kristin K. Romero, Margaret A. Roth-Warren, Robert F. Silver, Kimberly A. Tamber, Kelly M. Thornburg.

Staff Attorneys: Maureen C. Contreni, Deanna E. Edwards, Evan H. Frank.

Systems Integrator.—Thomas E. Cole.

Office Manager.—Donna L. Pasqualino.

Senior Staff Assistants: Kimberly R. Bourne-Goldring, Rebekah J. Musgrove, Diane E. Nesmeyer, Patricia H. Olsavsky.

Staff Assistant.—Daniela A. Navia.

OFFICE OF SENATE LEGAL COUNSEL

642 Hart Senate Office Building, phone 224–4435, fax 224–3391

Senate Legal Counsel.—Patricia Mack Bryan.

Deputy Senate Legal Counsel.—Morgan J. Frankel.

Assistant Senate Legal Counsels: Thomas E. Caballero, Grant R. Vinik.

Systems Administrator/Legal Assistant.—Lauren Fournier.

Administrative Assistant.—Kathleen M. Parker.

STANDING COMMITTEES OF THE HOUSE

[Republicans in roman; Democrats in *italic*; Resident Commissioner and Delegates in **boldface**]

[Room numbers beginning with H are in the Capitol, with CHOB in the Cannon House Office Building, with LHOB in the Longworth House Office Building, with RHOB in the Rayburn House Office Building, with H1 in O'Neill House Office Building, and with H2 in the Ford House Office Building]

Agriculture

1301 Longworth House Office Building, phone 225-2171

http://agriculture.house.gov

K. Michael Conaway, of Texas, *Chair*

Randy Neugebauer, of Texas, *Vice Chair*

Bob Goodlatte, of Virginia.
Frank D. Lucas, of Oklahoma.
Steve King, of Iowa.
Mike Rogers, of Alabama.
Glenn Thompson, of Pennsylvania.
Bob Gibbs, of Ohio.
Austin Scott, of Georgia.
Eric A. "Rick" Crawford, of Arkansas.
Scott DesJarlais, of Tennessee.
Christopher P. Gibson, of New York.
Vicky Hartzler, of Missouri.
Dan Benishek, of Michigan.
Jeff Denham, of California.
Doug LaMalfa, of California.
Rodney Davis, of Illinois.
Ted S. Yoho, of Florida.
Jackie Walorski, of Indiana.
Rick W. Allen, of Georgia.
Mike Bost, of Illinois.
David Rouzer, of North Carolina.
Ralph Lee Abraham, of Louisiana.
John R. Moolenaar, of Michigan.
Dan Newhouse, of Washington.
Trent Kelly, of Mississippi.

Collin C. Peterson, of Minnesota.
David Scott, of Georgia.
Jim Costa, of California.
Timothy J. Walz, of Minnesota.
Marcia L. Fudge, of Ohio.
James P. McGovern, of Massachusetts.
Suzan K. DelBene, of Washington.
Filemon Vela, of Texas.
Michelle Lujan Grisham, of New Mexico.
Ann M. Kuster, of New Hampshire.
Richard M. Nolan, of Minnesota.
Cheri Bustos, of Illinois.
Sean Patrick Maloney, of New York.
Ann Kirkpatrick, of Arizona.
Pete Aguilar, of California.
Stacey E. Plaskett, of Virgin Islands.
Alma S. Adams, of North Carolina.
Gwen Graham, of Florida.
Brad Ashford, of Nebraska.

SUBCOMMITTEES

[The chairman and ranking minority member are ex officio (voting) members of all subcommittees on which they do not serve.]

Biotechnology, Horticulture, and Research
Rodney Davis, of Illinois, *Chair*

Glenn Thompson, of Pennsylvania.
Austin Scott, of Georgia.
Christopher P. Gibson, of New York.
Jeff Denham, of California.
Ted S. Yoho, of Florida.
John R. Moolenaar, of Michigan.
Dan Newhouse, of Washington.

Suzan K. DelBene, of Washington.
Marcia L. Fudge, of Ohio.
James P. McGovern, of Massachusetts.
Ann M. Kuster, of New Hampshire.
Gwen Graham, of Florida.

Commodity Exchanges, Energy, and Credit
Austin Scott, of Georgia, *Chair*

Bob Goodlatte, of Virginia.
Frank D. Lucas, of Oklahoma.
Randy Neugebauer, of Texas.
Mike Rogers, of Alabama.
Doug LaMalfa, of California.
Rodney Davis, of Illinois.
Trent Kelly, of Mississippi.

David Scott, of Georgia.
Filemon Vela, of Texas.
Sean Patrick Maloney, of New York.
Ann Kirkpatrick, of Arizona.
Pete Aguilar, of California.

Conservation and Forestry
Glenn Thompson, of Pennsylvania, *Chair*

Frank D. Lucas, of Oklahoma.
Steve King, of Iowa.
Scott DesJarlais, of Tennessee.
Christopher P. Gibson, of New York.
Dan Benishek, of Michigan.
Rick W. Allen, of Georgia.
Mike Bost, of Illinois.

Michelle Lujan Grisham, of New Mexico.
Ann M. Kuster, of New Hampshire.
Richard M. Nolan, of Minnesota.
Suzan K. DelBene, of Washington.
Ann Kirkpatrick, of Arizona.

General Farm Commodities and Risk Management
Eric A. "Rick" Crawford, of Arkansas, *Chair*

Frank D. Lucas, of Oklahoma.
Randy Neugebauer, of Texas.
Mike Rogers, of Alabama.
Bob Gibbs, of Ohio.
Austin Scott, of Georgia.
Jeff Denham, of California.
Doug LaMalfa, of California.
Jackie Walorski, of Indiana.
Rick W. Allen, of Georgia.
Mike Bost, of Illinois.
Ralph Lee Abraham, of Louisiana.

Timothy J. Walz, of Minnesota.
Cheri Bustos, of Illinois.
Gwen Graham, of Florida.
Brad Ashford, of Nebraska.
David Scott, of Georgia.
Jim Costa, of California.
Sean Patrick Maloney, of New York.
Ann Kirkpatrick, of Arizona.

Livestock and Foreign Agriculture
David Rouzer, of North Carolina, *Chair*

Bob Goodlatte, of Virginia.
Steve King, of Iowa.
Scott DesJarlais, of Tennessee.
Vicky Hartzler, of Missouri.
Ted S. Yoho, of Florida.
Dan Newhouse, of Washington.
Trent Kelly, of Mississippi.

Jim Costa, of California.
Stacey E. Plaskett, of Virgin Islands.
Filemon Vela, of Texas.
Richard M. Nolan, of Minnesota.
Cheri Bustos, of Illinois.

Nutrition

Jackie Walorski, of Indiana, *Chair*

Randy Neugebauer, of Texas.
Glenn Thompson, of Pennsylvania.
Bob Gibbs, of Ohio.
Eric A. "Rick" Crawford, of Arkansas.
Vicky Hartzler, of Missouri.
Dan Benishek, of Michigan.
Rodney Davis, of Illinois.
Ted S. Yoho, of Florida.
David Rouzer, of North Carolina.
Ralph Lee Abraham, of Louisiana.
John R. Moolenaar, of Michigan.

James P. McGovern, of Massachusetts.
Marcia L. Fudge, of Ohio.
Alma S. Adams, of North Carolina.
Michelle Lujan Grisham, of New Mexico.
Pete Aguilar, of California.
Stacey E. Plaskett, of Virgin Islands.
Brad Ashford, of Nebraska.
Suzan K. DelBene, of Washington.

STAFF

Committee on Agriculture (1301 LHOB), 225-2171.
Majority Staff:
  Staff Director.—Scott Graves.
  Policy Director.—Matt Schertz.
  Chief Counsel.—Jackie Barber.
  Deputy Chief Counsel.—Patricia Straughn.
  Deputy Chief Oversight Counsel.—Ashley Callen.
  Chief Economist.—Bart Fisher.
  Chief Clerk.—Nicole Scott.
  Director of Coalitions and Outreach.—Christine Heggem.
  Director of Committee Operations and Member Services.—Leah Christensen.
  Financial Administrator.—Dean Lester.
  Communications Director.—Vacant.
  Press Secretary.—Haley Graves.
  Deputy Press Secretary.—Mollie Wilken.
  Information Technology Director.—John Konya.
  Information Technology Assistant.—Faisal Siddiqui.
  Professional Staff: Paul Balzano, Anne DeCesaro, Josh Maxwell.
  Science Advisor.—John Goldberg.
  Counsel.—Jessica Carter.
  Deputy Economist.—Callie McAdams.
  Senior Legislative Assistant.—Mary Nowak.
  Legislative Assistants: Caleb Crosswhite, Skylar Sowder.
  Deputy Clerk.—Carly Reedholm.
  Staff Assistant.—Vacant.
Minority Staff (1305 LHOB), 225-0317.
  Staff Director.—Rob Larew.
  Chief Counsel.—Andy Baker.
  Senior Policy Advisor.—Anne Simmons.
  Professional Staff: Keith Jones, Evan Jurkovich, Mary Knigge, Lisa Shelton, Mike Stranz.
  Professional Staff/Counsel.—Matthew MacKenzie.
  Communications Director.—Liz Friedlander.
  Office Manager.—Faye Smith.
  Director of InformationTechnology.—Merrick Munday.

Appropriations

H–305 The Capitol, phone 225–2771
http://www.house.gov/appropriations

Harold Rogers, of Kentucky, *Chair*

Rodney P. Frelinghuysen, of New Jersey.
Robert B. Aderholt, of Alabama.
Kay Granger, of Texas.
Michael K. Simpson, of Idaho.
John Abney Culberson, of Texas.
Ander Crenshaw, of Florida.
John R. Carter, of Texas.
Ken Calvert, of California.
Tom Cole, of Oklahoma.
Mario Diaz-Balart, of Florida.
Charles W. Dent, of Pennsylvania.
Tom Graves, of Georgia.
Kevin Yoder, of Kansas.
Steve Womack, of Arkansas.
Jeff Fortenberry, of Nebraska.
Thomas J. Rooney, of Florida.
Charles J. "Chuck" Fleischmann, of Tennessee.
Jaime Herrera Beutler, of Washington.
David P. Joyce, of Ohio.
David G. Valadao, of California.
Andy Harris, of Maryland.
Martha Roby, of Alabama.
Mark E. Amodei, of Nevada.
Chris Stewart, of Utah.
E. Scott Rigell, of Virginia.
David W. Jolly, of Florida.
David Young, of Iowa.
Evan H. Jenkins, of West Virginia.
Steven M. Palazzo, of Mississippi.

Nita M. Lowey, of New York.
Marcy Kaptur, of Ohio.
Peter J. Visclosky, of Indiana.
José E. Serrano, of New York.
Rosa L. DeLauro, of Connecticut.
David E. Price, of North Carolina.
Lucille Roybal-Allard, of California.
Sam Farr, of California.
Chaka Fattah, of Pennsylvania.
Sanford D. Bishop, Jr., of Georgia.
Barbara Lee, of California.
Michael M. Honda, of California.
Betty McCollum, of Minnesota.
Steve Israel, of New York.
Tim Ryan, of Ohio.
C. A. Dutch Ruppersberger, of Maryland.
Debbie Wasserman Schultz, of Florida.
Henry Cuellar, of Texas.
Chellie Pingree, of Maine.
Mike Quigley, of Illinois.
Derek Kilmer, of Washington.

SUBCOMMITTEES

[The chairman and ranking minority member are ex officio (voting) members of all subcommittees on which they do not serve.]

Agriculture, Rural Development, Food and Drug Administration, and Related Agencies

Robert B. Aderholt, of Alabama, *Chair*

David G. Valadao, of California, *Vice Chair*

Kevin Yoder, of Kansas.
Thomas J. Rooney, of Florida.
Andy Harris, of Maryland.
David Young, of Iowa.
Steven M. Palazzo, of Mississippi.

Sam Farr, of California.
Rosa L. DeLauro, of Connecticut.
Sanford D. Bishop, Jr., of Georgia.
Chellie Pingree, of Maine.

Commerce, Justice, Science, and Related Agencies

John Abney Culberson, of Texas, *Chair*

Robert B. Aderholt, of Alabama, *Vice Chair*

John R. Carter, of Texas.
Jaime Herrera Beutler, of Washington.
Martha Roby, of Alabama.
David W. Jolly, of Florida.
Steven M. Palazzo, of Mississippi.

Chaka Fattah, of Pennsylvania.
Michael M. Honda, of California.
José E. Serrano, of New York.
Derek Kilmer, of Washington.

Defense

Rodney P. Frelinghuysen, of New Jersey, *Chair*

Kay Granger, of Texas, *Vice Chair*

Ander Crenshaw, of Florida.
Ken Calvert, of California.
Tom Cole, of Oklahoma.
Steve Womack, of Arkansas.
Robert B. Aderholt, of Alabama.
John R. Carter, of Texas.
Mario Diaz-Balart, of Florida.
Tom Graves, of Georgia.

Peter J. Visclosky, of Indiana.
Betty McCollum, of Minnesota.
Steve Israel, of New York.
Tim Ryan, of Ohio.
C. A. Dutch Ruppersberger, of Maryland.
Marcy Kaptur, of Ohio.

Energy and Water Development, and Related Agencies

Michael K. Simpson, of Idaho, *Chair*

Charles J. "Chuck" Fleischmann, of Tennessee, *Vice Chair*

Rodney P. Frelinghuysen, of New Jersey.
Ken Calvert, of California.
Jeff Fortenberry, of Nebraska.
Kay Granger, of Texas.
Jaime Herrera Beutler, of Washington.
David G. Valadao, of California.

Marcy Kaptur, of Ohio.
Peter J. Visclosky, of Indiana.
Michael M. Honda, of California.
Lucille Roybal-Allard, of California.

Financial Services and General Government

Ander Crenshaw, of Florida, *Chair*

Jaime Herrera Beutler, of Washington, *Vice Chair*

Tom Graves, of Georgia.
Kevin Yoder, of Kansas.
Steve Womack, of Arkansas.
Mark E. Amodei, of Nevada.
E. Scott Rigell, of Virginia.

José E. Serrano, of New York.
Mike Quigley, of Illinois.
Chaka Fattah, of Pennsylvania.
Sanford D. Bishop, Jr., of Georgia.

Homeland Security

John R. Carter, of Texas, *Chair*

Rodney P. Frelinghuysen, of New Jersey, *Vice Chair*

John Abney Culberson, of Texas.
Charles J. "Chuck" Fleischmann, of Tennessee.
Andy Harris, of Maryland.
Chris Stewart, of Utah.
David Young, of Iowa.

Lucille Roybal-Allard, of California.
David E. Price, of North Carolina.
Henry Cuellar, of Texas.
Marcy Kaptur, of Ohio.

Interior, Environment, and Related Agencies

Ken Calvert, of California, *Chair*

Michael K. Simpson, of Idaho, *Vice Chair*

Tom Cole, of Oklahoma.
David P. Joyce, of Ohio.
Chris Stewart, of Utah.
Mark E. Amodei, of Nevada.
Evan H. Jenkins, of West Virginia.

Betty McCollum, of Minnesota.
Chellie Pingree, of Maine.
Derek Kilmer, of Washington.
Steve Israel, of New York.

Labor, Health and Human Services, Education, and Related Agencies

Tom Cole, of Oklahoma, *Chair*

Steve Womack, of Arkansas, *Vice Chair*

Michael K. Simpson, of Idaho.
Charles J. "Chuck" Fleischmann, of Tennessee.
Andy Harris, of Maryland.
Martha Roby, of Alabama.
Charles W. Dent, of Pennsylvania.
E. Scott Rigell, of Virginia.

Rosa L. DeLauro, of Connecticut.
Lucille Roybal-Allard, of California.
Barbara Lee, of California.
Chaka Fattah, of Pennsylvania.

Legislative Branch

Tom Graves, of Georgia, *Chair*

Mark E. Amodei, of Nevada, *Vice Chair*

E. Scott Rigell, of Virginia.
Evan H. Jenkins, of West Virginia.
Steven M. Palazzo, of Mississippi.

Debbie Wasserman Schultz, of Florida.
Sam Farr, of California.
Betty McCollum, of Minnesota.

Military Construction, Veterans Affairs, and Related Agencies

Charles W. Dent, of Pennsylvania, *Chair*

Jeff Fortenberry, of Nebraska, *Vice Chair*

Thomas J. Rooney, of Florida.
Martha Roby, of Alabama.
David G. Valadao, of California.
David P. Joyce, of Ohio.
David W. Jolly, of Florida.

Sanford D. Bishop, Jr., of Georgia.
Sam Farr, of California.
David E. Price, of North Carolina.
Barbara Lee, of California.

State, Foreign Operations, and Related Programs

Kay Granger, of Texas, *Chair*

Charles W. Dent, of Pennsylvania, *Vice Chair*

Mario Diaz-Balart, of Florida.
Ander Crenshaw, of Florida.
Thomas J. Rooney, of Florida.
Jeff Fortenberry, of Nebraska.
Chris Stewart, of Utah.

Nita M. Lowey, of New York.
Barbara Lee, of California.
C. A. Dutch Ruppersberger, of Maryland.
Debbie Wasserman Schultz, of Florida.
José E. Serrano, of New York.

Transportation, Housing and Urban Development, and Related Agencies

Mario Diaz-Balart, of Florida, *Chair*

Kevin Yoder, of Kansas, *Vice Chair*

David P. Joyce, of Ohio.
John Abney Culberson, of Texas.
David W. Jolly, of Florida.
David Young, of Iowa.
Evan H. Jenkins, of West Virginia.

David E. Price, of North Carolina.
Mike Quigley, of Illinois.
Tim Ryan, of Ohio.
Henry Cuellar, of Texas.

STAFF

Committee on Appropriations (H–305), 225–2771.
Majority Clerk and Staff Director.—Will Smith.
Deputy Clerk and Staff Director.—Jim Kulikowski.
Staff Assistants: Dale Oak, Stephen Sepp.
Coalitions Director.—Vacant.
Communications Director.—Jennifer Hing.
Press Assistant.—Marta Dehmlow.
Administrative Assistant.—Tammy Hughes.

Assistant to the Chairman.—Kelicia Rice.
Executive Assistant.—Victoria Luck.
Administrative Assistant. —Kaitlyn Eisner-Poor.
Administrative Aide.—Brad Allen.
Editors: Larry Boarman, Cathy Edwards (B–301A RHOB), 5–2851.
Computer Operations: Eric Jackson, Lonnie Johnson, Cathy Little, Linda Muir, Jay Sivulich, Don McKinnon, Jennifer Wheelock (B–305 RHOB), 5–2718.
Minority Staff Director.—David Pomerantz (1016 LHOB), 5–3481.
Minority Deputy Staff Director.—Lesley Turner.
Minority Press Secretary.—Matt Dennis.
Administrative Aide.—Deborah Spriggs.
Subcommittee on Agriculture, Rural Development, Food and Drug Administration, and Related Agencies (2362–A RHOB), 5–2638.
Staff Assistants: Andrew Cooper, Pam Miller, Tom O'Brien.
Administrative Aide.—Elizabeth King.
Minority Staff Assistant.—Martha Foley (1016 LHOB), 5–3481.
Subcommittee on Commerce, Justice, Science and Related Agencies (H–310), 5–3351.
Staff Assistants: Leslie Albright, Jeff Ashford, John Martens, Aschley Schiller, Colin Samples.
Administrative Aide.—Taylor Kelly.
Minority Staff Assistants: Bob Bonner, Matt Smith (1016 LHOB), 5–3481.
Subcommittee on Defense (H–405), 5–2847.
Staff Assistants: Rob Blair, Brooke Boyer, Walter Hearne, Collin Lee, Megan Milam, Tim Prince, Adrienne Ramsay, Cornell Teague, Paul Terry, B.G. Wright.
Administrative Aide.—Sherry Young.
Minority Staff Assistants: Taunja Berquam, Rebecca Leggieri (1016 LHOB), 5–3481.
Subcommittee on Energy and Water Development, and Related Agencies (2362–B RHOB), 5–3421.
Staff Assistants: Angie Giancarlo, Loraine Heckenberg, Donna Shahbaz, Perry Yates.
Administrative Aide.—Matthew Anderson.
Minority Staff Assistant.—Taunja Berquam (1016 LHOB), 5–3481.
Subcommittee on Financial Services (B–300 RHOB), 5–7245.
Staff Assistants: Winnie Chang, Kelly Hitchcock, Ariana Sarar.
Administrative Aide.—Amy Cushing.
Minority Staff Assistants: Angela Ohm, Shalanda Young (1016 LHOB), 5–3481.
Subcommittee on Homeland Security (B–307 RHOB), 5–5834.
Staff Assistants: Valerie Baldwin, Laura Cylke, Kris Mallard, Christopher Romig.
Administrative Aide.—Anne Wake.
Minority Staff Assistant.—Darek Newby (1016 LHOB), 5–3481.
Subcommittee on Interior, Environment, and Related Agencies (B–308 RHOB), 5–3081.
Staff Assistants: Darren Benjamin, Betsy Bina, Jason Gray, Dave LesStrang.
Administrative Aide.—Kristin Richmond.
Minority Staff Assistants: Joe Carlile, Rita Culp, Rick Healy (1016 LHOB), 5–3481.
Subcommittee on Labor, Health and Human Services, Education, and Related Agencies (2358 RHOB), 5–3508.
Staff Assistants: John Bartrum, Jennifer Cama, Allison Deters, Justin Gibbons, Susan Ross.
Administrative Aide.—Lori Bias.
Minority Staff Assistants: Siobhan Hulihan, Robin Juliano, Stephen Steigleder (1016 LHOB), 5–3481.
Subcommittee on Legislative Branch (HT–2), 6–7252.
Staff Assistants: Liz Dawson, Jennifer Panone, Chuck Turner.
Minority Staff Assistant.—Shalanda Young.
Subcommittee on Military Construction, Veterans Affairs, and Related Agencies (HVC–227), 5–3047.
Staff Assistants: Maureen Holohan, Sue Quantius, Sarah Young.
Administrative Aide.—Tracey Russell.
Minority Staff Assistant.—Matt Washington (1016 LHOB), 5–3481.
Subcommittee on State and Foreign Operations (HT–2), 5–2401.
Staff Assistants: Susan Adams, David Bortnick, Anne Marie Chotvacs, Craig Higgins, Alice Hogans.
Administrative Aide.—Clelia Alvarado.
Minority Staff Assistants: Erin Kolodjeski, Steve Marchese (1016 LHOB), 5–3481.
Subcommittee on Transportation, HUD and Independent Agencies (2358A RHOB), 5–2141.
Staff Assistants: Dena Baron, Carl Barrick, Doug Disrud, Cheryle Tucker.
Administrative Aide.—Jennifer Hollrah.
Minority Staff Assistants: Joe Carlile, Kate Hallahan (1016 LHOB), 5–3481.

Armed Services

2216 Rayburn House Office Building, phone 225–4151, fax 225–9077

http://www.armedservices.house.gov

Mac Thornberry, of Texas, *Chair*

Walter B. Jones, of North Carolina.
J. Randy Forbes, of Virginia.
Jeff Miller, of Florida.
Joe Wilson, of South Carolina.
Frank A. LoBiondo, of New Jersey.
Rob Bishop, of Utah.
Michael R. Turner, of Ohio.
John Kline, of Minnesota.
Mike Rogers, of Alabama.
Trent Franks, of Arizona.
Bill Shuster, of Pennsylvania.
K. Michael Conaway, of Texas.
Doug Lamborn, of Colorado.
Robert J. Wittman, of Virginia.
Duncan Hunter, of California.
John Fleming, of Louisiana.
Mike Coffman, of Colorado.
Christopher P. Gibson, of New York.
Vicky Hartzler, of Missouri.
Joseph J. Heck, of Nevada.
Austin Scott, of Georgia.
Mo Brooks, of Alabama.
Richard B. Nugent, of Florida.
Paul Cook, of California.
Jim Bridenstine, of Oklahoma.
Brad R. Wenstrup, of Ohio.
Jackie Walorski, of Indiana.
Bradley Byrne, of Alabama.
Sam Graves, of Missouri.
Ryan K. Zinke, of Montana.
Elise M. Stefanik, of New York.
Martha McSally, of Arizona.
Stephen Knight, of California.
Thomas MacArthur, of New Jersey.
Steve Russell, of Oklahoma.

Adam Smith, of Washington.
Loretta Sanchez, of California.
Robert A. Brady, of Pennsylvania.
Susan A. Davis, of California.
James R. Langevin, of Rhode Island.
Rick Larsen, of Washington.
Jim Cooper, of Tennessee.
***Madeleine Z. Bordallo,** of Guam.*
Joe Courtney, of Connecticut.
Niki Tsongas, of Massachusetts.
John Garamendi, of California.
Henry C. "Hank" Johnson, Jr., of Georgia.
Jackie Speier, of California.
Joaquin Castro, of Texas.
Tammy Duckworth, of Illinois.
Scott H. Peters, of California.
Marc A. Veasey, of Texas.
Tulsi Gabbard, of Hawaii.
Timothy J. Walz, of Minnesota.
Beto O'Rourke, of Texas.
Donald Norcross, of New Jersey.
Ruben Gallego, of Arizona.
Mark Takai, of Hawaii.
Gwen Graham, of Florida.
Brad Ashford, of Nebraska.
Seth Moulton, of Massachusetts.
Pete Aguilar, of California.

SUBCOMMITTEES

Emerging Threats and Capabilities

Joe Wilson, of South Carolina, *Chair*

Trent Franks, of Arizona, *Vice Chair*

John Kline, of Minnesota.
Bill Shuster, of Pennsylvania.
Duncan Hunter, of California.
Richard B. Nugent, of Florida.
Ryan K. Zinke, of Montana.
Doug Lamborn, of Colorado.
Mo Brooks, of Alabama.
Bradley Byrne, of Alabama.
Elise M. Stefanik, of New York.

James R. Langevin, of Rhode Island.
Jim Cooper, of Tennessee.
John Garamendi, of California.
Joaquin Castro, of Texas.
Marc A. Veasey, of Texas.
Donald Norcross, of New Jersey.
Brad Ashford, of Nebraska.
Pete Aguilar, of California.

Military Personnel

Joseph J. Heck, of Nevada, *Chair*

Thomas MacArthur, of New Jersey, *Vice Chair*

Walter B. Jones, of North Carolina.
John Kline, of Minnesota.
Mike Coffman, of Colorado.
Elise M. Stefanik, of New York.
Paul Cook, of California.
Stephen Knight, of California.

Susan A. Davis, of California.
Robert A. Brady, of Pennsylvania.
Niki Tsongas, of Massachusetts.
Jackie Speier, of California.
Timothy J. Walz, of Minnesota.
Beto O'Rourke, of Texas.

Oversight and Investigations

Vicky Hartzler, of Missouri, *Chair*

Jeff Miller, of Florida.
K. Michael Conaway, of Texas.
Joseph J. Heck, of Nevada.
Austin Scott, of Georgia.
Martha McSally, of Arizona.

Jackie Speier, of California.
Jim Cooper, of Tennessee.
Henry C. "Hank" Johnson, Jr., of Georgia.
Gwen Graham, of Florida.

Readiness

Robert J. Wittman, of Virginia, *Chair*

Elise M. Stefanik, of New York, *Vice Chair*

Rob Bishop, of Utah.
Vicky Hartzler, of Missouri.
Austin Scott, of Georgia.
Frank A. LoBiondo, of New Jersey.
Mike Rogers, of Alabama.
Christopher P. Gibson, of New York.
Richard B. Nugent, of Florida.
Brad R. Wenstrup, of Ohio.
Sam Graves, of Missouri.
Steve Russell, of Oklahoma.

Madeleine Z. Bordallo, of Guam.
Susan A. Davis, of California.
Joe Courtney, of Connecticut.
Joaquin Castro, of Texas.
Tammy Duckworth, of Illinois.
Scott H. Peters, of California.
Tulsi Gabbard, of Hawaii.
Beto O'Rourke, of Texas.
Ruben Gallego, of Arizona.

Seapower and Projection Forces

J. Randy Forbes, of Virginia, *Chair*

Duncan Hunter, of California, *Vice Chair*

K. Michael Conaway, of Texas.
Bradley Byrne, of Alabama.
Robert J. Wittman, of Virginia.
Vicky Hartzler, of Missouri.
Paul Cook, of California.
Jim Bridenstine, of Oklahoma.
Jackie Walorski, of Indiana.
Ryan K. Zinke, of Montana.
Stephen Knight, of California.
Steve Russell, of Oklahoma.

Joe Courtney, of Connecticut.
James R. Langevin, of Rhode Island.
Rick Larsen, of Washington.
Madeleine Z. Bordallo, of Guam.
Henry C. "Hank" Johnson, Jr., of Georgia.
Scott H. Peters, of California.
Tulsi Gabbard, of Hawaii.
Gwen Graham, of Florida.
Seth Moulton, of Massachusetts.

Strategic Forces

Mike Rogers, of Alabama, *Chair*

Doug Lamborn, of Colorado, *Vice Chair*

Trent Franks, of Arizona.
Mike Coffman, of Colorado.
Mo Brooks, of Alabama.
Jim Bridenstine, of Oklahoma.
J. Randy Forbes, of Virginia.
Rob Bishop, of Utah.
Michael R. Turner, of Ohio.
John Fleming, of Louisiana.

Jim Cooper, of Tennessee.
Loretta Sanchez, of California.
Rick Larsen, of Washington.
John Garamendi, of California.
Mark Takai, of Hawaii.
Brad Ashford, of Nebraska.
Pete Aguilar, of California.

Tactical Air and Land Forces

Michael R. Turner, of Ohio, *Chair*

Paul Cook, of California, *Vice Chair*

Frank A. LoBiondo, of New Jersey.
John Fleming, of Louisiana.
Christopher P. Gibson, of New York.
Brad R. Wenstrup, of Ohio.
Jackie Walorski, of Indiana.
Sam Graves, of Missouri.
Martha McSally, of Arizona.
Stephen Knight, of California.
Thomas MacArthur, of New Jersey.
Walter B. Jones, of North Carolina.
Joe Wilson, of South Carolina.

Loretta Sanchez, of California.
Niki Tsongas, of Massachusetts.
Henry C. "Hank" Johnson, Jr., of Georgia.
Tammy Duckworth, of Illinois.
Marc A. Veasey, of Texas.
Timothy J. Walz, of Minnesota.
Donald Norcross, of New Jersey.
Ruben Gallego, of Arizona.
Mark Takai, of Hawaii.
Gwen Graham, of Florida.
Seth Moulton, of Massachusetts.

STAFF

Committee on Armed Services (2216 RHOB), 225–4151, fax 225–9077.
Staff Director.—Bob Simmons.
Deputy Staff Director.—Jenness Simler.
General Counsel.—Catherine McElroy.
Counsels: Scott Glabe, William S. Johnson, Timothy Morrison, Leonor Tomero.
Director, Legislative Operations.—Zach Steacy.
Professional Staff: Michael Amato, Paul Arcangeli, Kari Bingen, Heath R. Bope, Christopher J. Bright, Douglas Bush, Michael Casey, Jaime Cheshire, Everett Coleman, Craig Collier, Elizabeth Conrad, Ryan Crumpler, Alexander Gallo, Brian Garrett, Kevin Gates, David Giachetti, Craig Greene, Jeanette S. James, Bruce Johnson, Lindsay Kavanaugh, Steve Kitay, Phil MacNaughton, Mike Miller, Mark Morehouse, Vickie Plunkett, Rebecca A. Ross, Jack Schuler, Catherine Sendak, Dan Sennott, David Sienicki, John F. Sullivan, Jesse D. Tolleson, Jr., Peter Villano, Andrew T. Walter, John Wason, Joe Whited, Lynn M. Williams.
Communications Director.—Claude Chafin.
Spokesman and Director of Member Initiatives.—Alison Lynn.
Press Secretary.—Nick Mikula.
Security Manager.—Cyndi Howard.
Executive Assistants: Betty B. Gray, Candace Wagner.
Clerks: Colin Bosse, Abigail Gage, Julie Herbert, Katie Rember, Eric L. Smith, Michael Tehrani, Katie Thompson.
Staff Assistant.—John N. Johnson.

Budget

207 Cannon House Office Building 20515–6065, phone 226–7270, fax 226–7174
http://www.budget.house.gov

Tom Price, of Georgia, *Chair*
Todd Rokita, of Indiana, *Vice Chair*

Scott Garrett, of New Jersey.
Mario Diaz-Balart, of Florida.
Tom Cole, of Oklahoma.
Tom McClintock, of California.
Diane Black, of Tennessee.
Rob Woodall, of Georgia.
Marsha Blackburn, of Tennessee.
Vicky Hartzler, of Missouri.
Marlin A. Stutzman, of Indiana.
Vern Buchanan, of Florida.
Mark Sanford, of South Carolina.
Steve Womack, of Arkansas.
Dave Brat, of Virginia.
Rod Blum, of Iowa.
Alexander X. Mooney, of West Virginia.
Glenn Grothman, of Wisconsin.
Gary J. Palmer, of Alabama.
John R. Moolenaar, of Michigan.
Bruce Westerman, of Arkansas.
James B. Renacci, of Ohio.

Chris Van Hollen, of Maryland.
John A. Yarmuth, of Kentucky.
Bill Pascrell, Jr., of New Jersey.
Tim Ryan, of Ohio.
Gwen Moore, of Wisconsin.
Kathy Castor, of Florida.
Jim McDermott, of Washington.
Barbara Lee, of California.
Mark Pocan, of Wisconsin.
Michelle Lujan Grisham, of New Mexico.
Debbie Dingell, of Michigan.
Ted Lieu, of California.
Donald Norcross, of New Jersey.
Seth Moulton, of Massachusetts.

(No Subcommittees)

STAFF

Committee on Budget (207 CHOB), 226–7270, fax 226–7174.
  Majority Staff Director.—Rick May.
    Executive Assistant.—Eric Davis.
    Director of Budget Review.—Jim Herz.
    Chief Economist.—Andy Morton.
    Senior Economist.—Timothy Flynn.
    Counsel to the Chairman.—Paul Restuccia.
    Chief Counsel.—Jim Bates.
    Counsels: Mary Popadiuk, Jon Romito.
    Associate Policy Advisor.—Patrick Louis Knudsen.
    Policy Advisors: Justin Bogie, Alexandra Pryor Campau, Kyle Cormney, Emily Goff, Jenna Spealman, Amanda Street, Brad Watson.
    Communications Director.—Ryan Murphy.
    Press Secretary.—Will Allison.
    Digital and Social Media Coordinator.—Kelle Long.
    Coalitions and Member Services.—Ashley Palmer.
    Chief Administrator.—Alex Stoddard.
    Systems Administrator.—Jose Guillen.
    Staff Assistant and Intern Coordinator.—Benjamin Gardenhour.
  Minority Staff Director.—Tom Kahn (134 Cannon), 226–7200, fax 225–9905.
    Chief Counsel.—Karen Robb.
    Counsel.—Jocelyn Griffin.
    Senior Policy Coordinator.—Sarah Abernathy.
    Budget Review Director.—Kimberly Overbeek.
    Senior Budget Review Specialist.—Ellen J. Balis.
    Senior Budget Analyst.—Diana Meredith.
    Budget Analysts: Erika Appel, Ken Cummings, Scott R. Russell, Beth Stephenson, Ted E. Zegers.
    Tax Counsel.—Jonathan Goldman.
    Communications Director.—Bridgett Frey.
    Digital Director.—Najy Kamal.
    Office Manager.—Sheila A. McDowell.
    Minority Staff Assistant.—Cody Willming.

Education and the Workforce

2181 Rayburn House Office Building, phone 225–4527, fax 225–9571

http://edworkforce.house.gov

John Kline, of Minnesota, *Chair*

Joe Wilson, of South Carolina.
Virginia Foxx, of North Carolina.
Duncan Hunter, of California.
David P. Roe, of Tennessee.
Glenn Thompson, of Pennsylvania.
Tim Walberg, of Michigan.
Matt Salmon, of Arizona.
Brett Guthrie, of Kentucky.
Todd Rokita, of Indiana.
Lou Barletta, of Pennsylvania.
Joseph J. Heck, of Nevada.
Luke Messer, of Indiana.
Bradley Byrne, of Alabama.
Dave Brat, of Virginia.
Earl L. "Buddy" Carter, of Georgia.
Mike Bishop, of Michigan.
Glenn Grothman, of Wisconsin.
Steve Russell, of Oklahoma.
Carlos Curbelo, of Florida.
Elise M. Stefanik, of New York.
Rick W. Allen, of Georgia.

Robert C. "Bobby" Scott, of Virginia.
Rubén Hinojosa, of Texas.
Susan A. Davis, of California.
Raúl M. Grijalva, of Arizona.
Joe Courtney, of Connecticut.
Marcia L. Fudge, of Ohio.
Jared Polis, of Colorado.
Gregorio Kilili Camacho Sablan, of Northern
   Mariana Islands.
Frederica S. Wilson, of Florida.
Suzanne Bonamici, of Oregon.
Mark Pocan, of Wisconsin.
Mark Takano, of California.
Hakeem S. Jeffries, of New York.
Katherine M. Clark, of Massachusetts.
Alma S. Adams, of North Carolina.
Mark DeSaulnier, of California.

SUBCOMMITTEES

[The chairman and ranking minority member are ex officio (non-voting) members of all
subcommittees on which they do not serve.]

Early Childhood, Elementary, and Secondary Education

Todd Rokita, of Indiana, *Chair*

Duncan Hunter, of California.
Glenn Thompson, of Pennsylvania.
Dave Brat, of Virginia.
Earl L. "Buddy" Carter, of Georgia.
Mike Bishop, of Michigan.
Glenn Grothman, of Wisconsin.
Steve Russell, of Oklahoma.
Carlos Curbelo, of Florida.

Marcia L. Fudge, of Ohio.
Susan A. Davis, of California.
Raúl M. Grijalva, of Arizona.
Gregorio Kilili Camacho Sablan, of Northern
   Mariana Islands.
Suzanne Bonamici, of Oregon.
Mark Takano, of California.
Katherine M. Clark, of Massachusetts.

Health, Employment, Labor, and Pensions

David P. Roe, of Tennessee, *Chair*

Joe Wilson, of South Carolina.
Virginia Foxx, of North Carolina.
Tim Walberg, of Michigan.
Matt Salmon, of Arizona.
Brett Guthrie, of Kentucky.
Lou Barletta, of Pennsylvania.
Joseph J. Heck, of Nevada.
Luke Messer, of Indiana.
Bradley Byrne, of Alabama.
Earl L. "Buddy" Carter, of Georgia.
Glenn Grothman, of Wisconsin.
Rick W. Allen, of Georgia.

Jared Polis, of Colorado.
Joe Courtney, of Connecticut.
Mark Pocan, of Wisconsin.
Rubén Hinojosa, of Texas.
Gregorio Kilili Camacho Sablan, of Northern
   Mariana Islands.
Frederica S. Wilson, of Florida.
Suzanne Bonamici, of Oregon.
Mark Takano, of California.
Hakeem S. Jeffries, of New York.
Robert C. "Bobby" Scott, of Virginia.

Higher Education and Workforce Training

Virginia Foxx, of North Carolina, *Chair*

David P. Roe, of Tennessee.
Matt Salmon, of Arizona.
Brett Guthrie, of Kentucky.
Lou Barletta, of Pennsylvania.
Joseph J. Heck, of Nevada.
Luke Messer, of Indiana.
Bradley Byrne, of Alabama.
Carlos Curbelo, of Florida.
Elise M. Stefanik, of New York.
Rick W. Allen, of Georgia.

Rubén Hinojosa, of Texas.
Hakeem S. Jeffries, of New York.
Alma S. Adams, of North Carolina.
Mark DeSaulnier, of California.
Susan A. Davis, of California.
Raúl M. Grijalva, of Arizona.
Joe Courtney, of Connecticut.
Jared Polis, of Colorado.

Workforce Protections

Tim Walberg, of Michigan, *Chair*

Duncan Hunter, of California.
Glenn Thompson, of Pennsylvania.
Todd Rokita, of Indiana.
Dave Brat, of Virginia.
Mike Bishop, of Michigan.
Steve Russell, of Oklahoma.
Elise M. Stefanik, of New York.

Frederica S. Wilson, of Florida.
Mark Pocan, of Wisconsin.
Katherine M. Clark, of Massachusetts.
Alma S. Adams, of North Carolina.
Mark DeSaulnier, of California.
Marcia L. Fudge, of Ohio.

STAFF

Committee on Education and Labor (2181 RHOB), 225–4527.
   Majority Staff Director.—Juliane Sullivan.
     General Counsel.—Krisann Pearce.
     Director of Education and Human Services Policy.—Amy Jones.
     Director of Workforce Policy.—Ed Gilroy.
     Communications Director.—Brian Newell.
     Press Secretaries: Lauren Aronson, Tyler Hernandez.
     Deputy Press Secretary.—Lauren Reddington.
     Coalitions and Member Services Representative.—Janelle Belland.
     Deputy Director of Education and Human Services Policy.—Amanda Schaumburg.
     Senior Education Policy Advisor.—Brad Thomas.
     Professional Staff Members—Education: Kathlyn Ehl, James Forester, Brian Melnyk, Jenny Prescott, Emily Slack, James Redstone, Leslie Tatum.
     Legislative Assistants—Education: Matthew Frame, Alex Ricci.
     Deputy Director of Workforce Policy.—Molly Salmi.
     Senior Policy Advisor.—Loren Sweatt.
     Workforce Policy Counsel.—Marvin Kaplan.
     Professional Staff Members—Workforce: Andrew Banducci, Christie Herman, John Martin, Michelle Neblett, Joe Wheeler.
     Legislative Assistant—Workforce.—Alexa Turner.
     Chief Clerk.—Nancy Locke.
     Deputy Clerk.—Alissa Strawcutter.
     Financial Administrative Officer.—Dianna Ruskowsky.
     Administrative Director.—Elizabeth Podgorski.
     Staff Assistant.—Martha Davis.
     Staff Assistant—Education.—Sheariah Yousefi.
     Staff Assistant—Workforce.—Callie Harman.
   Minority Staff (2101 RHOB), 5–3725.
   Staff Director.—Denise Forte.
     General Counsel.—Brian Kennedy.
     Special Assistant to the Staff Director.—Liz Hollis.
     Clerk/Intern and Fellow Coordinator.—Tylease Alli.
     Staff Assistants: Austin Barbera, Christine Godinez.
     Communications Director.—Kiara Pesante.
     Press Secretary.—Arika Trim.
     Labor Policy Director.—Liz Watson.
     Senior Labor Policy Advisors: Carrie Hughes, Kevin McDermott, Richard D. Miller.

Labor Policy Advisor.—Amy Peake.
Labor Policy Associate.—Eunice Ikene.
Director of Education Policy/Associate General Counsel.—Tina Hone.
Senior Education Policy Advisor.—Jacque Chevalier.
Education Policy Counsels: Jared Bass, Christian Haines, Rayna Reid.
Civil Rights Counsel.—Veronique Pluviose.
Systems Administrator.—Sheila Havenner.

Energy and Commerce

2125 Rayburn House Office Building, phone 225-2927

http://www.energycommerce.house.gov

Fred Upton, of Michigan, *Chair*

Marsha Blackburn, of Tennessee, *Vice Chair*

Joe Barton, of Texas.
Ed Whitfield, of Kentucky.
John Shimkus, of Illinois.
Joseph R. Pitts, of Pennsylvania.
Greg Walden, of Oregon.
Tim Murphy, of Pennsylvania.
Michael C. Burgess, of Texas.
Steve Scalise, of Louisiana.
Robert E. Latta, of Ohio.
Cathy McMorris Rodgers, of Washington.
Gregg Harper, of Mississippi.
Leonard Lance, of New Jersey.
Brett Guthrie, of Kentucky.
Pete Olson, of Texas.
David B. McKinley, of West Virginia.
Mike Pompeo, of Kansas.
Adam Kinzinger, of Illinois.
H. Morgan Griffith, of Virginia.
Gus M. Bilirakis, of Florida.
Bill Johnson, of Ohio.
Billy Long, of Missouri.
Renee L. Ellmers, of North Carolina.
Larry Bucshon, of Indiana.
Bill Flores, of Texas.
Susan W. Brooks, of Indiana.
Markwayne Mullin, of Oklahoma.
Richard Hudson, of North Carolina.
Chris Collins, of New York.
Kevin Cramer, of North Dakota.

Frank Pallone, Jr., of New Jersey.
Bobby L. Rush, of Illinois.
Anna G. Eshoo, of California.
Eliot L. Engel, of New York.
Gene Green, of Texas.
Diana DeGette, of Colorado.
Lois Capps, of California.
Michael F. Doyle, of Pennsylvania.
Janice D. Schakowsky, of Illinois.
G. K. Butterfield, of North Carolina.
Doris O. Matsui, of California.
Kathy Castor, of Florida.
John P. Sarbanes, of Maryland.
Jerry McNerney, of California.
Peter Welch, of Vermont.
Ben Ray Luján, of New Mexico.
Paul Tonko, of New York.
John A. Yarmuth, of Kentucky.
Yvette D. Clarke, of New York.
David Loebsack, of Iowa.
Kurt Schrader, of Oregon.
Joseph P. Kennedy III, of Massachusetts.
Tony Cárdenas, of California.

SUBCOMMITTEES

[The chairman and ranking minority member are ex officio (voting) members of all subcommittees on which they do not serve.]

Commerce, Manufacturing, and Trade

Michael C. Burgess, of Texas, *Chair*

Leonard Lance, of New Jersey, *Vice Chair*

Marsha Blackburn, of Tennessee.
Gregg Harper, of Mississippi.
Brett Guthrie, of Kentucky.
Pete Olson, of Texas.
Mike Pompeo, of Kansas.
Adam Kinzinger, of Illinois.
Gus M. Bilirakis, of Florida.
Susan W. Brooks, of Indiana.
Markwayne Mullin, of Oklahoma.

Janice D. Schakowsky, of Illinois.
Yvette D. Clarke, of New York.
Joseph P. Kennedy III, of Massachusetts.
Tony Cárdenas, of California.
Bobby L. Rush, of Illinois.
G. K. Butterfield, of North Carolina.
Peter Welch, of Vermont.

Communications and Technology

Greg Walden, of Oregon, *Chair*

Robert E. Latta, of Ohio, *Vice Chair*

John Shimkus, of Illinois.
Marsha Blackburn, of Tennessee.
Steve Scalise, of Louisiana.
Leonard Lance, of New Jersey.
Brett Guthrie, of Kentucky.
Pete Olson, of Texas.
Mike Pompeo, of Kansas.
Adam Kinzinger, of Illinois.
Gus M. Bilirakis, of Florida.
Bill Johnson, of Ohio.
Billy Long, of Missouri.
Renee L. Ellmers, of North Carolina.
Chris Collins, of New York.
Kevin Cramer, of North Dakota.
Joe Barton, of Texas.

Anna G. Eshoo, of California.
Michael F. Doyle, of Pennsylvania.
Peter Welch, of Vermont.
John A. Yarmuth, of Kentucky.
Yvette D. Clarke, of New York.
David Loebsack, of Iowa.
Bobby L. Rush, of Illinois.
Diana DeGette, of Colorado.
G. K. Butterfield, of North Carolina.
Doris O. Matsui, of California.
Jerry McNerney, of California.
Ben Ray Luján, of New Mexico.

Energy and Power

Ed Whitfield, of Kentucky, *Chair*

Pete Olson, of Texas, *Vice Chair*

John Shimkus, of Illinois.
Joseph R. Pitts, of Pennsylvania.
Robert E. Latta, of Ohio.
Gregg Harper, of Mississippi.
David B. McKinley, of West Virginia.
Mike Pompeo, of Kansas.
Adam Kinzinger, of Illinois.
H. Morgan Griffith, of Virginia.
Bill Johnson, of Ohio.
Billy Long, of Missouri.
Renee L. Ellmers, of North Carolina.
Bill Flores, of Texas.
Markwayne Mullin, of Oklahoma.
Richard Hudson, of North Carolina.
Joe Barton, of Texas.

Bobby L. Rush, of Illinois.
Jerry McNerney, of California.
Paul Tonko, of New York.
Eliot L. Engel, of New York.
Gene Green, of Texas.
Lois Capps, of California.
Michael F. Doyle, of Pennsylvania.
Kathy Castor, of Florida.
John P. Sarbanes, of Maryland.
Peter Welch, of Vermont.
John A. Yarmuth, of Kentucky.
David Loebsack, of Iowa.

Environment and the Economy

John Shimkus, of Illinois, *Chair*

Gregg Harper, of Mississippi, *Vice Chair*

Ed Whitfield, of Kentucky.
Joseph R. Pitts, of Pennsylvania.
Tim Murphy, of Pennsylvania.
Robert E. Latta, of Ohio.
David B. McKinley, of West Virginia.
Bill Johnson, of Ohio.
Larry Bucshon, of Indiana.
Bill Flores, of Texas.
Richard Hudson, of North Carolina.
Kevin Cramer, of North Dakota.

Paul Tonko, of New York.
Kurt Schrader, of Oregon.
Gene Green, of Texas.
Diana DeGette, of Colorado.
Lois Capps, of California.
Michael F. Doyle, of Pennsylvania.
Jerry McNerney, of California.
Tony Cárdenas, of California.

Health

Joseph R. Pitts, of Pennsylvania, *Chair*
Brett Guthrie, of Kentucky, *Vice Chair*

Ed Whitfield, of Kentucky.
John Shimkus, of Illinois.
Tim Murphy, of Pennsylvania.
Michael C. Burgess, of Texas.
Marsha Blackburn, of Tennessee.
Cathy McMorris Rodgers, of Washington.
Leonard Lance, of New Jersey.
H. Morgan Griffith, of Virginia.
Gus M. Bilirakis, of Florida.
Billy Long, of Missouri.
Renee L. Ellmers, of North Carolina.
Larry Bucshon, of Indiana.
Susan W. Brooks, of Indiana.
Chris Collins, of New York.
Joe Barton, of Texas.

Gene Green, of Texas.
Eliot L. Engel, of New York.
Lois Capps, of California.
Janice D. Schakowsky, of Illinois.
G. K. Butterfield, of North Carolina.
Kathy Castor, of Florida.
John P. Sarbanes, of Maryland.
Doris O. Matsui, of California.
Ben Ray Luján, of New Mexico.
Kurt Schrader, of Oregon.
Joseph P. Kennedy III, of Massachusetts.
Tony Cárdenas, of California.

Oversight and Investigations

Tim Murphy, of Pennsylvania, *Chair*
David B. McKinley, of West Virginia, *Vice Chair*

Michael C. Burgess, of Texas.
Marsha Blackburn, of Tennessee.
H. Morgan Griffith, of Virginia.
Larry Bucshon, of Indiana.
Bill Flores, of Texas.
Susan W. Brooks, of Indiana.
Markwayne Mullin, of Oklahoma.
Richard Hudson, of North Carolina.
Chris Collins, of New York.
Kevin Cramer, of North Dakota.
Joe Barton, of Texas.

Diana DeGette, of Colorado.
Janice D. Schakowsky, of Illinois.
Kathy Castor, of Florida.
Paul Tonko, of New York.
John A. Yarmuth, of Kentucky.
Yvette D. Clarke, of New York.
Joseph P. Kennedy III, of Massachusetts.
Gene Green, of Texas.
Peter Welch, of Vermont.

STAFF

Committee on Energy and Commerce (2125 RHOB), 225-2927, fax 225-1919.
  Majority Staff Director.—Gary Andres.
    Deputy Staff Director.—Michael Bloomquist.
    General Counsel.—Karen Christian.
    Deputy General Counsel.—Peter Kielty.
    Director, Communications.—Sean Bonyun.
    Senior Advisor.—Joan Hillebrands.
    Chief Counsel, Commerce, Manufacturing, and Trade.—Paul Nagle.
    Chief Counsel, Communications and Technology.—David Redl.
    Chief Counsel, Energy and Power.—Thomas Hassenboehler.
    Chief Counsel, Environment and the Economy.—David McCarthy.
    Chief Counsel, Health.—Clay Alspach.
    Chief Counsel, Oversight and Investigations.—Charles Ingebretson.
    Senior Policy Advisor, Director of Coalitions.—Martin Dannenfelser.
    Senior Policy Advisor.—Ray Baum.
    Chief Investigative Counsel, Oversight.—Alan Slobodin.
    Senior Energy Counsels.—Patrick Currier, Mary Neumayr.
    Counsels: Jessica Donlon, Graham Dufault, Melissa Froelich, Kelsey Guyselman, Grace Koh, Ben Lieberman, Emily Martin, Tina Richards, Samuel Spector, John Stone.
    Professional Staff: Gerald Couri, Paul Edattel, Robert Horne, Carly McWilliams, Brandon Mooney, Katie Novaria, John Ohly, Timothy Pataki, Peter Spencer, Joshua Trent, Olivia Trusty, Andrew Zach.
    Communications Advisor.—Thomas Wilbur.
    Press Secretaries: Noelle Clemente, Andrew Duberstein, Dan Schneider.
    Deputy Press Secretaries: Leighton Brown, Macey Sevcik.
    Policy Coordinator.—Mark Ratner.

Policy Coordinator, Commerce, Manufacturing and Trade.—James Decker.
Policy Coordinator, Energy and Power.—Allison Busbee.
Policy Coordinator, Environment and the Economy.—Christopher Sarley.
Policy Coordinator, Health.—Heidi Stirrup.
Policy Coordinator, Oversight and Investigations.—Christopher Santini.
Counsel to Chairman Emeritus.—Krista Rosenthall.
Senior Advisor and Professional Staff.—Ann Johnston.
Legislative Associates: Nicholas Abraham, Adrianna Simonelli.
Oversight Associates: Brittany Havens, Jessica Wilkerson.
Legislative Clerks: William Batson, Brian Howard, Graham Pittman, Charlotte Savercool.
Director, Information Technology.—Jean Woodrow.
Deputy Director, Information Technology.—Timothy Torres.
Financial and Administrative Coordinator.—Sean Corcoran.
Human Resources and Office Administrator.—Theresa Gambo.
Staff Assistants: David Bell, Rebecca Card, Dylan Vorbach, Gregory Watson.
Minority Staff Director.—Jeff Carroll.
Deputy Committee Staff Director/Chief Health Advisor.—Tiffany Guarascio.
Chief Counsel, Energy and Environment.—Michael Goo.
Chief Counsel.—Timothy Robinson.
Chief Counsel, Communications and Technology.—David Goldman.
Chief Counsel, Commerce, Manufacturing, and Trade.—Michelle Ash.
Staff Director for Energy and Environment.—Rick Kessler.
Oversight Staff Director.—Chris Knauer.
Chief Oversight Counsel.—Una Lee.
Senior Counsel.—Jacqueline Cohen.
Health Counsel.—Arielle Woronoff.
Counsel.—Lisa Goldman.
Health Policy Advisors: Rachel Pryor, Kimberlee Trzeciak.
Chief Clerk.—Jennifer Berenholz.
Deputy Clerk.—Elizabeth Ertel.
Professional Staff: Waverly Gordon, Caitlin Haberman, Elizabeth Letter.
Director of Communications, Member Services and Outreach.—Ashley Jones.
Policy Analysts: Adam Lowenstein, Alexander Ratner, Samantha Satchell, Ryan Skukowski.
Policy Coordinator.—John Marshall.
Staff Assistant.—Debbie Letter.
Director of Technology.—Edward Walker.
Press Secretary.—Christine Brennan.
Press Assistant.—Matt Schumacher.

Ethics

1015 Longworth House Office Building, phone 225–7103, fax 225–7392

Charles W. Dent, of Pennsylvania, *Chair*

Patrick Meehan, of Pennsylvania.
Trey Gowdy, of South Carolina.
Susan W. Brooks, of Indiana.
Kenny Marchant, of Texas.

Linda T. Sánchez, of California.
Michael E. Capuano, of Massachusetts.
Yvette D. Clarke, of New York.
Theodore E. Deutch, of Florida.
John B. Larson, of Connecticut.

(No Subcommittees)

STAFF

Chief Counsel/Staff Director.—Tom Rust.
  Administrative Staff Director.—Joanne White.
  Counsel to the Chairman.—Clifford Stoddard, Jr.
  Counsel to the Ranking Member.—Dan Taylor.
  Director of Advice and Education.—Tonia Smith.
  Director of Investigations.—Patrick McMullen.
  Senior Counsels: Karena Dees, Tamar Nedzar, Christopher Tate.
  Counsels: David Arrojo, Robert Eskridge, Nadia Konstantinova, Sarah Myers-Mutschall, Tonya Sloans, Wendy Smith.
  Senior Financial Disclosure Advisor. Deborah Bethea.
  Systems Administrator.—Craig Barber.
  Investigative Clerk.—Molly McCarty.
  Advice and Education Clerk.—Vacant.
  Financial Disclosure Clerk.—Melanie Baucom.
  Staff Assistants: Brittany Dowell, Audrey Hickenlooper, Christian Hollowell, Michael Koren, Adam Wambold.

Financial Services

2129 Rayburn House Office Building, phone 225–7502

http://www.house.gov/financialservices

Jeb Hensarling, of Texas, *Chair*

Patrick T. McHenry, of North Carolina, *Vice Chair*

Peter T. King, of New York.
Edward R. Royce, of California.
Frank D. Lucas, of Oklahoma.
Scott Garrett, of New Jersey.
Randy Neugebauer, of Texas.
Stevan Pearce, of New Mexico.
Bill Posey, of Florida.
Michael G. Fitzpatrick, of Pennsylvania.
Lynn A. Westmoreland, of Georgia.
Blaine Luetkemeyer, of Missouri.
Bill Huizenga, of Michigan.
Sean P. Duffy, of Wisconsin.
Robert Hurt, of Virginia.
Steve Stivers, of Ohio.
Stephen Lee Fincher, of Tennessee.
Marlin A. Stutzman, of Indiana.
Mick Mulvaney, of South Carolina.
Randy Hultgren, of Illinois.
Dennis A. Ross, of Florida.
Robert Pittenger, of North Carolina.
Ann Wagner, of Missouri.
Andy Barr, of Kentucky.
Keith J. Rothfus, of Pennsylvania.
Luke Messer, of Indiana.
David Schweikert, of Arizona.
Frank C. Guinta, of New Hampshire.
Scott R. Tipton, of Colorado.
Roger Williams, of Texas.
Bruce Poliquin, of Maine.
Mia B. Love, of Utah.
J. French Hill, of Arkansas.
Tom Emmer, of Minnesota.

Maxine Waters, of California.
Carolyn B. Maloney, of New York.
Nydia M. Velázquez, of New York.
Brad Sherman, of California.
Gregory W. Meeks, of New York.
Michael E. Capuano, of Massachusetts.
Rubén Hinojosa, of Texas.
Wm. Lacy Clay, of Missouri.
Stephen F. Lynch, of Massachusetts.
David Scott, of Georgia.
Al Green, of Texas.
Emanuel Cleaver, of Missouri.
Gwen Moore, of Wisconsin.
Keith Ellison, of Minnesota.
Ed Perlmutter, of Colorado.
James A. Himes, of Connecticut.
John C. Carney, Jr., of Delaware.
Terri A. Sewell, of Alabama.
Bill Foster, of Illinois.
Daniel T. Kildee, of Michigan.
Patrick Murphy, of Florida.
John K. Delaney, of Maryland.
Kyrsten Sinema, of Arizona.
Joyce Beatty, of Ohio.
Denny Heck, of Washington.
Juan Vargas, of California.

SUBCOMMITTEES

[The chairman and ranking minority member are ex officio (voting) members of all subcommittees on which they do not serve.]

Capital Markets and Government Sponsored Enterprises

Scott Garrett, of New Jersey, *Chair*

Robert Hurt, of Virginia, *Vice Chair*

Peter T. King, of New York.	*Carolyn B. Maloney, of New York.*
Edward R. Royce, of California.	*Brad Sherman, of California.*
Randy Neugebauer, of Texas.	*Rubén Hinojosa, of Texas.*
Patrick T. McHenry, of North Carolina.	*Stephen F. Lynch, of Massachusetts.*
Bill Huizenga, of Michigan.	*Ed Perlmutter, of Colorado.*
Sean P. Duffy, of Wisconsin.	*David Scott, of Georgia.*
Steve Stivers, of Ohio.	*James A. Himes, of Connecticut.*
Stephen Lee Fincher, of Tennessee.	*Keith Ellison, of Minnesota.*
Randy Hultgren, of Illinois.	*Bill Foster, of Illinois.*
Dennis A. Ross, of Florida.	*Gregory W. Meeks, of New York.*
Ann Wagner, of Missouri.	*John C. Carney, Jr., of Delaware.*
Luke Messer, of Indiana.	*Terri A. Sewell, of Alabama.*
David Schweikert, of Arizona.	*Patrick Murphy, of Florida.*
Bruce Poliquin, of Maine.	
J. French Hill, of Arkansas.	

Financial Institutions and Consumer Credit

Randy Neugebauer, of Texas, *Chair*

Stevan Pearce, of New Mexico, *Vice Chair*

Frank D. Lucas, of Oklahoma.	*Wm. Lacy Clay, of Missouri.*
Bill Posey, of Florida.	*Gregory W. Meeks, of New York.*
Michael G. Fitzpatrick, of Pennsylvania.	*Rubén Hinojosa, of Texas.*
Lynn A. Westmoreland, of Georgia.	*David Scott, of Georgia.*
Blaine Luetkemeyer, of Missouri.	*Carolyn B. Maloney, of New York.*
Marlin A. Stutzman, of Indiana.	*Nydia M. Velázquez, of New York.*
Mick Mulvaney, of South Carolina.	*Brad Sherman, of California.*
Robert Pittenger, of North Carolina.	*Stephen F. Lynch, of Massachusetts.*
Andy Barr, of Kentucky.	*Michael E. Capuano, of Massachusetts.*
Keith J. Rothfus, of Pennsylvania.	*John K. Delaney, of Maryland.*
Frank C. Guinta, of New Hampshire.	*Denny Heck, of Washington.*
Scott R. Tipton, of Colorado.	*Kyrsten Sinema, of Arizona.*
Roger Williams, of Texas.	*Juan Vargas, of California.*
Mia B. Love, of Utah.	
Tom Emmer, of Minnesota.	

Housing and Insurance

Blaine Luetkemeyer, of Missouri, *Chair*

Lynn A. Westmoreland, of Georgia, *Vice Chair*

Edward R. Royce, of California.	*Emanuel Cleaver, of Missouri.*
Scott Garrett, of New Jersey.	*Nydia M. Velázquez, of New York.*
Stevan Pearce, of New Mexico.	*Michael E. Capuano, of Massachusetts.*
Bill Posey, of Florida.	*Wm. Lacy Clay, of Missouri.*
Robert Hurt, of Virginia.	*Al Green, of Texas.*
Steve Stivers, of Ohio.	*Gwen Moore, of Wisconsin.*
Dennis A. Ross, of Florida.	*Keith Ellison, of Minnesota.*
Andy Barr, of Kentucky.	*Joyce Beatty, of Ohio.*
Keith J. Rothfus, of Pennsylvania.	*Daniel T. Kildee, of Michigan.*
Roger Williams, of Texas.	

Monetary Policy and Trade
Bill Huizenga, of Michigan, *Chair*
Mick Mulvaney, of South Carolina, *Vice Chair*

Frank D. Lucas, of Oklahoma.
Stevan Pearce, of New Mexico.
Lynn A. Westmoreland, of Georgia.
Marlin A. Stutzman, of Indiana.
Robert Pittenger, of North Carolina.
Luke Messer, of Indiana.
David Schweikert, of Arizona.
Frank C. Guinta, of New Hampshire.
Mia B. Love, of Utah.
Tom Emmer, of Minnesota.

Gwen Moore, of Wisconsin.
Bill Foster, of Illinois.
Ed Perlmutter, of Colorado.
James A. Himes, of Connecticut.
John C. Carney, Jr., of Delaware.
Terri A. Sewell, of Alabama.
Patrick Murphy, of Florida.
Daniel T. Kildee, of Michigan.
Denny Heck, of Washington.

Oversight and Investigations
Sean P. Duffy, of Wisconsin, *Chair*
Michael G. Fitzpatrick, of Pennsylvania, *Vice Chair*

Peter T. King, of New York.
Patrick T. McHenry, of North Carolina.
Robert Hurt, of Virginia.
Stephen Lee Fincher, of Tennessee.
Mick Mulvaney, of South Carolina.
Randy Hultgren, of Illinois.
Ann Wagner, of Missouri.
Scott R. Tipton, of Colorado.
Bruce Poliquin, of Maine.
J. French Hill, of Arkansas.

Al Green, of Texas.
Michael E. Capuano, of Massachusetts.
Emanuel Cleaver, of Missouri.
Keith Ellison, of Minnesota.
John K. Delaney, of Maryland.
Joyce Beatty, of Ohio.
Denny Heck, of Washington.
Kyrsten Sinema, of Arizona.
Juan Vargas, of California.

Task Force to Investigate Terrorism Financing
Michael G. Fitzpatrick, of Pennsylvania, *Chair*
Robert Pittenger, of North Carolina, *Vice Chair*

Peter T. King, of New York.
Steve Stivers, of Ohio.
Dennis A. Ross, of Florida.
Ann Wagner, of Missouri.
Andy Barr, of Kentucky.
Keith J. Rothfus, of Pennsylvania.
David Schweikert, of Arizona.
Roger Williams, of Texas.
Bruce Poliquin, of Maine.
J. French Hill, of Arkansas.

Stephen F. Lynch, of Massachusetts.
Brad Sherman, of California.
Gregory W. Meeks, of New York.
Al Green, of Texas.
Keith Ellison, of Minnesota.
James A. Himes, of Connecticut.
Bill Foster, of Illinois.
Daniel T. Kildee, of Michigan.
Kyrsten Sinema, of Arizona.

STAFF

Committee on Financial Services (2129 RHOB), 225–7502.
Majority Staff:
Staff Director.—Shannon Flaherty McGahn.
 Deputy Staff Director.—Kirsten J. Mork.
 Chief Counsel.—James H. Clinger.
 Deputy Staff Director/Communications.—Jeffrey Wade Emerson.
 Policy Director.—Edward G. Skala.
 General Counsel and Parliamentarian.—Joseph R. Clark.
 Chief Oversight Counsel.—Uttam A. Dhillon.
 Chief Economist.—Dino D. Falaschetti.
 Communications Director.—David Michael Popp.
 Senior Counsels: Kevin R. Edgar, Clinton Columbus Jones III, Brian Johnson.
 Senior Counsel and Chief Advisor, Regulatory Policy.—Ronald L. Rubin.
 Senior Professional Staff: Anthony E. Chang, Tallman Johnson, Joe Pinder.
 Counsels: Brian R. Anderson, Joseph A. Gammello, Rebekah E. Goshorn, Elie S. Greenbaum, Brett A. Sisto.

Professional Staff: Jonathan M. Blum, Thomas Christian Brown, Katelyn E. Christ, Andrew Davidhizar, Rachel D. Goldberg, Marliss A. McManus, Matthew Kinley Mulder, Brian P. O'Shea, Jared Cody Sawyer, Bryan Alexander Wood.
Administrative Assistant.—Angela S. Gambo.
Chief Clerk.—Rosemary E. Keech.
Systems Administrator.—Kim Trimble.
Editor.—Terisa L. Allison.
Digital Director.—Scott A. Schmidt.
Legislative Assistant.—E. Chase Burgess.
Communications Assistant.—Maria S. Kim.
Member Services and Coalition Coordinator.—Ja'Ron K. Smith.
Scheduler.—Jennifer Swinchatt.
Staff Assistants: Catherine M. Costakos, Isaac Borden Hoskins, Peter J. Tezza.
Minority Staff:
Staff Director.—Charla Ouertatani.
   Deputy Staff Director.—Amanda Fischer.
   Chief Oversight Counsel.—Jason Lynch.
   Senior Counsels: Katelynn Bradley, Jarrod Loadholt.
   Counsels: Esther Kahng, Deanne Millison.
   Director of Legislative Operations.—Lisa Peto.
   Senior Policy Director.—Erika Jeffers.
   Systems Administrator.—Alfred J. Forman, Jr.
   Director of Housing Policy.—Theresa Dumais.
   Chief Administrative Officer.—Anita L. Johnson.
   Press Assistant.—Marcos F. Monosalvas.
   Senior Professional Staff: Kristofor S. Erickson, Corey S. Frayer, Daniel P. McGlinchey, Kirk Schwarzbach.
   Professional Staff.—Francis O. Williams.
   Press Secretary.—Nina Smith.

Foreign Affairs

2170 Rayburn House Office Building, phone 225–5021

http://www.foreignaffairs.house.gov

Edward R. Royce, of California, *Chair*

Christopher H. Smith, of New Jersey.
Ileana Ros-Lehtinen, of Florida.
Dana Rohrabacher, of California.
Steve Chabot, of Ohio.
Joe Wilson, of South Carolina.
Michael T. McCaul, of Texas.
Ted Poe, of Texas.
Matt Salmon, of Arizona.
Darrell E. Issa, of California.
Tom Marino, of Pennsylvania.
Jeff Duncan, of South Carolina.
Mo Brooks, of Alabama.
Paul Cook, of California.
Randy K. Weber, Sr., of Texas.
Scott Perry, of Pennsylvania.
Ron DeSantis, of Florida.
Mark Meadows, of North Carolina.
Ted S. Yoho, of Florida.
Curt Clawson, of Florida.
Scott DesJarlais, of Tennessee.
Reid J. Ribble, of Wisconsin.
David A. Trott, of Michigan.
Lee M. Zeldin, of New York.
Daniel M. Donovan, Jr., of New York.

Eliot L. Engel, of New York.
Brad Sherman, of California.
Gregory W. Meeks, of New York.
Albio Sires, of New Jersey.
Gerald E. Connolly, of Virginia.
Theodore E. Deutch, of Florida.
Brian Higgins, of New York.
Karen Bass, of California.
William R. Keating, of Massachusetts.
David N. Cicilline, of Rhode Island.
Alan Grayson, of Florida.
Ami Bera, of California.
Alan S. Lowenthal, of California.
Grace Meng, of New York.
Lois Frankel, of Florida.
Tulsi Gabbard, of Hawaii.
Joaquin Castro, of Texas.
Robin L. Kelly, of Illinois.
Brendan F. Boyle, of Pennsylvania.

SUBCOMMITTEES

[The chairman and ranking minority member are ex officio (non-voting) members of all subcommittees on which they do not serve.]

Africa, Global Health, Global Human Rights, and International Organizations

Christopher H. Smith, of New Jersey, *Chair*

Mark Meadows, of North Carolina.
Curt Clawson, of Florida.
Scott DesJarlais, of Tennessee.
Daniel M. Donovan, Jr., of New York.

Karen Bass, of California.
David N. Cicilline, of Rhode Island.
Ami Bera, of California.

Asia and the Pacific

Matt Salmon, of Arizona, *Chair*

Dana Rohrabacher, of California.
Steve Chabot, of Ohio.
Tom Marino, of Pennsylvania.
Jeff Duncan, of South Carolina.
Mo Brooks, of Alabama.
Scott Perry, of Pennsylvania.
Scott DesJarlais, of Tennessee.

Brad Sherman, of California.
Ami Bera, of California.
Tulsi Gabbard, of Hawaii.
Alan S. Lowenthal, of California.
Gerald E. Connolly, of Virginia.
Grace Meng, of New York.

Europe, Eurasia, and Emerging Threats

Dana Rohrabacher, of California, *Chair*

Ted Poe, of Texas.
Tom Marino, of Pennsylvania.
Mo Brooks, of Alabama.
Paul Cook, of California.
Randy K. Weber, Sr., of Texas.
Reid J. Ribble, of Wisconsin.
David A. Trott, of Michigan.

Gregory W. Meeks, of New York.
Albio Sires, of New Jersey.
Theodore E. Deutch, of Florida.
William R. Keating, of Massachusetts.
Lois Frankel, of Florida.
Tulsi Gabbard, of Hawaii.

The Middle East and North Africa

Ileana Ros-Lehtinen, of Florida, *Chair*

Steve Chabot, of Ohio.
Joe Wilson, of South Carolina.
Darrell E. Issa, of California.
Randy K. Weber, Sr., of Texas.
Ron DeSantis, of Florida.
Mark Meadows, of North Carolina.
Ted S. Yoho, of Florida.
Curt Clawson, of Florida.
David A. Trott, of Michigan.
Lee M. Zeldin, of New York.

Theodore E. Deutch, of Florida.
Gerald E. Connolly, of Virginia.
Brian Higgins, of New York.
David N. Cicilline, of Rhode Island.
Alan Grayson, of Florida.
Grace Meng, of New York.
Lois Frankel, of Florida.
Brendan F. Boyle, of Pennsylvania.

Terrorism, Nonproliferation, and Trade

Ted Poe, of Texas, *Chair*

Joe Wilson, of South Carolina.
Darrell E. Issa, of California.
Paul Cook, of California.
Scott Perry, of Pennsylvania.
Reid J. Ribble, of Wisconsin.
Lee M. Zeldin, of New York.

William R. Keating, of Massachusetts.
Brad Sherman, of California.
Brian Higgins, of New York.
Joaquin Castro, of Texas.
Robin L. Kelly, of Illinois.

The Western Hemisphere

Jeff Duncan, of South Carolina, *Chair*

Christopher H. Smith, of New Jersey.
Ileana Ros-Lehtinen, of Florida.
Michael T. McCaul, of Texas.
Matt Salmon, of Arizona.
Ron DeSantis, of Florida.
Ted S. Yoho, of Florida.
Daniel M. Donovan, Jr., of New York.

Albio Sires, of New Jersey.
Joaquin Castro, of Texas.
Robin L. Kelly, of Illinois.
Gregory W. Meeks, of New York.
Alan Grayson, of Florida.
Alan S. Lowenthal, of California.

STAFF

Committee on Foreign Affairs (2170 RHOB), 225–5021, fax 225–5394.
Majority Staff:
Chief of Staff.—Amy Porter.
 Majority Staff Director.—Thomas P. Sheehy.
 Deputy Staff Director.—Edward A. Burrier.
 General Counsel.—Doug Anderson.
 Chief Counsel for Oversight and Investigations.—Thomas Alexander.
 Counsel for Oversight and Investigations.—Ari Fridman.
 Communications Director / Counsel.—Shane Wolfe.
 Deputy Communications Director.—Audra McGeorge.
 Digital Director.—Russell Solomon.
 Senior Professional Staff Members: Joan Condon, Jamie McCormick, Doug Seay.
 Senior Advisors: Leah Campos, Nilmini Rubin.
 Professional Staff Members: Sarah Blocher, Worku Gachou, Thomas Hill, Kristen Marquardt, Shelley Su, Matthew Zweig.

Security Officer / Professional Staff Member.—George Ritchey.
Director of Outreach and Protocol.—Elizabeth Heng.
Director of Committee Operations.—Jean Marter.
Policy Analyst.—Hunter Strupp.
Counsel and Policy Coordinator.—Jessica Kelch.
Special Assistant.—Brady Howell.
Hearing Coordinator.—Marie Spear.
Staff Associates: Alyssa Feldstein, Lila Nieves-Lee.
Finance Administrator.—John Gleason.
Information Resource Manager.—Vlad Cerga.
Assistant Systems Administrator.—Danny Marca.
Printing Manager / Web Assistant.—Shirley Alexander.
Minority Staff (B–360 RHOB), 226–8467.
Minority Staff Director.—Jason Steinbaum.
  Deputy Staff Director.—Doug Campbell.
  Chief Counsel.—Janice Kaguyutan.
  Communications Director / Senior Professional Staff Member.—Tim Mulvey.
  Senior Professional Staff Members: Sajit Gandhi, Eric Jacobstein, Kyle Parker, Mira Resnick, Edmund Rice, Brian Skretny.
  Professional Staff Members: Catherine Barnao, Jennifer Hendrixson-White, Mark Iozzi.
  Staff Associate.—Jamie Geller.
Subcommittee on Africa, Global Health, Global Human Rights, and International Organizations (5210 O'Neill FOB), 226–7812.
Staff Director.—Gregory Simpkins.
  Counsel.—Piero Tozzi.
  Staff Associate.—Mark Kearney.
  Minority Professional Staff.—Travis Adkins.
Subcommittee on Asia and the Pacific (5190 O'Neill FOB), 226–7825.
Staff Director.—Amy Chang.
  Professional Staff Member.—Jonathan Sarager.
  Staff Associate.—Bryan Burack.
  Minority Professional Staff.—Kinsey Kiriakos.
Subcommittee on Europe, Eurasia, and Emerging Threats (5210 O'Neill FOB), 226–6434.
Staff Director.—Paul Behrends.
  Professional Staff Member.—Scott Cullinane.
  Staff Associate.—Jessica Roxburgh.
  Minority Professional Staff.—Philip Bednarczyk.
Subcommittee on the Middle East and North Africa (5220 O'Neill FOB), 225–3345.
Staff Director.—Eddy Acevedo.
  Professional Staff Members: Nathan Gately, Golan Rodgers.
  Staff Associate.—Andres Uzcategui.
  Minority Professional Staff.—Casey Kustin.
Subcommittee on Terrorism, Nonproliferation, and Trade (5100 O'Neill FOB), 226–1500.
Staff Director.—Luke Murry.
  Professional Staff Member.—Oren Adaki.
  Staff Associate.—Mary Jacobson.
  Minority Professional Staff.—Garrett Donovan.
Subcommittee on the Western Hemisphere (5100 O'Neill FOB), 226–9980.
Staff Director.—Sadaf Khan.
  Professional Staff Member.—Rebecca Ulrich.
  Staff Associate.—Ron Criscuolo.
  Minority Professional Staff.—Sadaf Khan.

Homeland Security

176 Ford House Office Building, phone 226–8417, fax 226–3399

Michael T. McCaul, of Texas, *Chair*

Candice S. Miller, of Michigan, *Vice Chair*

Lamar Smith, of Texas.
Peter T. King, of New York.
Mike Rogers, of Alabama.
Jeff Duncan, of South Carolina.
Tom Marino, of Pennsylvania.
Lou Barletta, of Pennsylvania.
Scott Perry, of Pennsylvania.
Curt Clawson, of Florida.
John Katko, of New York.
Will Hurd, of Texas.
Earl L. "Buddy" Carter, of Georgia.
Mark Walker, of North Carolina.
Barry Loudermilk, of Georgia.
Martha McSally, of Arizona.
John Ratcliffe, of Texas.
Daniel M. Donovan, Jr., of New York.

Bennie G. Thompson, of Mississippi.
Loretta Sanchez, of California.
Sheila Jackson Lee, of Texas.
James R. Langevin, of Rhode Island.
Brian Higgins, of New York.
Cedric L. Richmond, of Louisiana.
William R. Keating, of Massachusetts.
Donald M. Payne, Jr., of New Jersey.
Filemon Vela, of Texas.
Bonnie Watson Coleman, of New Jersey.
Kathleen M. Rice, of New York.
Norma J. Torres, of California.

SUBCOMMITTEES

[The chairman and ranking minority member are ex officio members of all subcommittees on which they do not serve.]

Border and Maritime Security

Candice S. Miller, of Michigan, *Chair*

Lamar Smith, of Texas.
Mike Rogers, of Alabama.
Jeff Duncan, of South Carolina.
Lou Barletta, of Pennsylvania.
Will Hurd, of Texas.
Martha McSally, of Arizona.

Filemon Vela, of Texas.
Loretta Sanchez, of California.
Sheila Jackson Lee, of Texas.
Brian Higgins, of New York.
Norma J. Torres, of California.

Counterterrorism and Intelligence

Peter T. King, of New York, *Chair*

Candice S. Miller, of Michigan.
Lou Barletta, of Pennsylvania.
John Katko, of New York.
Will Hurd, of Texas.

Brian Higgins, of New York.
William R. Keating, of Massachusetts.
Filemon Vela, of Texas.

Cybersecurity, Infrastructure Protection, and Security Technologies

John Ratcliffe, of Texas, *Chair*

Peter T. King, of New York.
Tom Marino, of Pennsylvania.
Scott Perry, of Pennsylvania.
Curt Clawson, of Florida.
Daniel M. Donovan, Jr., of New York.

Cedric L. Richmond, of Louisiana.
Loretta Sanchez, of California.
Sheila Jackson Lee, of Texas.
James R. Langevin, of Rhode Island.

Emergency Preparedness, Response, and Communications

Martha McSally, of Arizona, *Chair*

Tom Marino, of Pennsylvania.
Mark Walker, of North Carolina.
Barry Loudermilk, of Georgia.
Daniel M. Donovan, Jr., of New York.

Donald M. Payne, Jr., of New Jersey.
Bonnie Watson Coleman, of New Jersey.
Kathleen M. Rice, of New York.

Oversight and Management Efficiency

Scott Perry, of Pennsylvania, *Chair*

Jeff Duncan, of South Carolina.
Curt Clawson, of Florida.
Earl L. "Buddy" Carter, of Georgia.
Barry Loudermilk, of Georgia.

Bonnie Watson Coleman, of New Jersey.
Cedric L. Richmond, of Louisiana.
Norma J. Torres, of California.

Transportation Security

John Katko, of New York, *Chair*

Mike Rogers, of Alabama.
Earl L. "Buddy" Carter, of Georgia.
Mark Walker, of North Carolina.
John Ratcliffe, of Texas.

Kathleen M. Rice, of New York.
William R. Keating, of Massachusetts.
Donald M. Payne, Jr., of New Jersey.

STAFF

Committee on Homeland Security (H2–176 Ford House Office Building) phone 226–8417, fax 226–3399.
  Majority Staff Director.—Brendan P. Shields, FHOB / H2–176 (202) 226–8417.
  Deputy Staff Director.—Eric Heighberger, FHOB / H2–176 (202) 226–8417.
  General Counsel.—Joan O'Hara, FHOB / H2–176 (202) 226–8417.
  Staff Director, Subcommittee on Border and Maritime Security.—Paul Anstine, FHOB / H2–176 (202) 226–8417.
  Staff Director, Subcommittee on Counterterrorism and Intelligence.—Mandy Bowers, FHOB / H2–176 (202) 226–8417.
  Staff Director, Subcommittee on Cybersecurity, Infrastructure Protection, and Security Technologies.—Brett DeWitt, FHOB / H2–176 (202) 226–8417.
  Staff Director, Subcommittee on Emergency Preparedness, Response, and Communications.—Kerry Kinirons, FHOB / H2–176 (202) 226–8417.
  Staff Director, Subcommittee on Oversight and Management Efficiency.—Ryan Consaul, FHOB / H2–176 (202) 226–8417.
  Staff Director, Subcommittee on Transportation Security.—Krista P. Harvey, FHOB / H2–176 (202) 226–8417.
  Deputy General Counsel.—Katy Crooks Flynn, FHOB / H2–176 (202) 226–8417.
  Senior Advisor.—Laura Fullerton, FHOB / H2–176 (202) 226–8417.
  National Security Senior Advisor.—Andrea Thompson, FHOB / H2–176 (202) 226–8417.
  Director of Member Services and Senior Advisor.—James Murphy, FHOB / H2–176 (202) 226–8417.
  Counsels: Steven Giaier, Tyler Lowe, Dena Kozanas, FHOB / H2–176 (202) 226–8417.
  Chief Clerk.—Michael S. Twinchek, FHOB / H2–176 (202) 226–8417.
  Calendar Clerk.—John Dickhaus, FHOB / H2–176 (202) 226–8417.
  Subcommittee Clerks.—Deborah Jordan, Dennis Terry, FHOB / H2–176 (202) 226–8417.
  Communications Director.—Susan Phalen, FHOB / H2–176 (202) 226–8417.
  Deputy Communications Director.—Matthew Ballard, FHOB / H2–176 (202) 226–8417.
  Digital Director.—Claire Woolfe, FHOB / H2–176 (202) 226–8417.
  Deputy Press Secretary.—Margaret Anne Moore, FHOB / H2–176 (202) 226–8417.
  Senior Professional Staff.—Luke Burke, FHOB / H2–176 (202) 226–8417.
  Security Director.—Kyle McFarland, FHOB / H2–176 (202) 226–8417.
  Senior Professional Staff / Investigator.—Luke Burke, FHOB / H2–176 (202) 226–8417.
  Professional Staff / Investigators: Miles Taylor, Maseh Zarif, FHOB / H2–176 (202) 226–8417.
  Senior Professional Staff: Alan Carroll, Jason Miller, John Neal, FHOB / H2–176 (202) 226–8417.

Professional Staff: Diana Bergwin, Kate Bonvechiom, Chad Carlough, Erik Peterson, Kirsten Duncan, Kyle Klein, Natalie Matson, Jason Olin, FHOB/H2–176 (202) 226–8417.

Staff Assistants: Paige Davies, Nathan Wheat, FHOB/H2–176 (202) 226–8417.

Special Assistant to the Chief of Staff.—Margaret Anne Moore, FHOB/H2–176 (202) 226–8417.

GPO Detailee, Printer.—Heather Crowell, FHOB/H2–176 (202) 226–8417.

Minority Staff Director.—I. Lanier Avant, FHOB/H2–117 (202) 226–2616.

Chief Counsel for Legislation.—Rosaline Cohen, FHOB/H2–117 (202) 226–2616.

Subcommittee on Border and Maritime Security Director and Counsel.—Alison B. Northrop, FHOB/H2–117 (202) 226–2616.

Subcommittee on Counterterrorism and Intelligence Director and Counsel.—Hope Goins, FHOB/H2–117 (202) 226–2616.

Subcommittee on Emergency Preparedness, Response, and Communications.—Moira Bergin, FHOB/H2–117 (202) 226–2616.

Senior Professional Staff Member/Counsel.—Nicole Tisdale, FHOB/H2–117 (202) 226–2616.

Senior Professional Staff Member.—K. Christopher Schepis, FHOB/H2–117 (202) 226–2616.

Press Secretary.—Adam M. Comis, FHOB/H2–117 (202) 226–2616.

Professional Staff Members: Alexandria Carnes, Ashley Delgado, Cedric Haynes, Cory Horton, Deborah R. Mack, Ramzi Nemo, Lori Stith, FHOB/H2–117 (202) 226–2616.

Office Manager.—Nicole Wade Johnson, FHOB/H2–117 (202) 226–2616.

Executive Assistant.—Shante Gauthier, FHOB/H2–117 (202) 226–2616.

Legislative Assistant.—Claytrice Henderson, FHOB/H2–117 (202) 226–2616.

House Administration

1309 Longworth House Office Building, phone 225–8281, fax 225–9957

http://cha.house.gov/

Candice S. Miller, of Michigan, *Chair*

Gregg Harper, of Mississippi.
Richard B. Nugent, of Florida.
Rodney Davis, of Illinois.
Barbara Comstock, of Virginia.
Mark Walker, of North Carolina.

Robert A. Brady, of Pennsylvania.
Zoe Lofgren, of California.
Juan Vargas, of California.

(No Subcommittees)

STAFF

Committee on House Administration (1309 LHOB), 5–8281.
   Staff Director.—Sean Moran.
      Deputy Staff Director, Policy and Planning.—John Clocker.
      Deputy Staff Director, Outreach and Communications.—Katie Patru.
      Director of Administration and Operations.—Mary Sue Englund.
      Director of Member and Committee Services.—George Hadijski.
      Director of Technology Policy.—Reynold Schweickhardt.
      Communications Director.—Erin McCracken.
      Finance and Personnel Administrator.—Anne Binsted.
      General Counsel.—Bob Sensenbrenner.
      Counsels: Cole Felder, Nick Hawatmeh.
      Legislative Clerk.—C. Maggie Moore.
      Legislative Fellow.—Anita Bhat.
      Manager of Planning and Strategic Initiatives.—Katie Ryan.
      Professional Staff: Max Engling, Alyssa Hinman, Courtney Joseph, Ryan Kelly, Ed
         Puccerella, Brad Walvort.
      Staff Assistants: Amanda Anger, Molly Harrington, Tim Sullivan.
   Minority Staff:
   Staff Director.—Jamie Fleet (1307 LHOB), 5–2061.
      Deputy Staff Director/Deputy Chief Counsel.—Teri Morgan.
      Chief Counsel.—Michael Harrison.
      Chief Clerk.—Eddie Flaherty.
      Deputy Staff Director/Director of Legislative Operations.—Khalil Abboud.
      Senior Policy Adviser.—Matt Pinkus.
      Finance Director.—Kim Stevens.
      Staff Assistant.—Tommy Sandstrom.
      Director of Member and Committee Services.—Robert Henline.
      Professional Staff: Matthew DeFreitas, Kristie Muchnok, Aislan Sims.
      Shared Employee.—Richard Subbio.
Commission on Congressional Mailing Standards (1216 LHOB), 6–0647.
   Staff Director.—Richard Cappetto.

Judiciary

2138 Rayburn House Office Building, phone 225-3951

http://www.judiciary.house.gov

Bob Goodlatte, of Virginia, *Chair*

F. James Sensenbrenner, Jr., of Wisconsin.	*John Conyers, Jr., of Michigan.*
Lamar Smith, of Texas.	*Jerrold Nadler, of New York.*
Steve Chabot, of Ohio.	*Zoe Lofgren, of California.*
Darrell E. Issa, of California.	*Sheila Jackson Lee, of Texas.*
J. Randy Forbes, of Virginia.	*Steve Cohen, of Tennessee.*
Steve King, of Iowa.	*Henry C. "Hank" Johnson, Jr., of Georgia.*
Trent Franks, of Arizona.	***Pedro R. Pierluisi,** of Puerto Rico.*
Louie Gohmert, of Texas.	*Judy Chu, of California.*
Jim Jordan, of Ohio.	*Theodore E. Deutch, of Florida.*
Ted Poe, of Texas.	*Luis V. Gutiérrez, of Illinois.*
Jason Chaffetz, of Utah.	*Karen Bass, of California.*
Tom Marino, of Pennsylvania.	*Cedric L. Richmond, of Louisiana.*
Trey Gowdy, of South Carolina.	*Suzan K. DelBene, of Washington.*
Raúl R. Labrador, of Idaho.	*Hakeem S. Jeffries, of New York.*
Blake Farenthold, of Texas.	*David N. Cicilline, of Rhode Island.*
Doug Collins, of Georgia.	*Scott H. Peters, of California.*
Ron DeSantis, of Florida.	
Mimi Walters, of California.	
Ken Buck, of Colorado.	
John Ratcliffe, of Texas.	
David A. Trott, of Michigan.	
Mike Bishop, of Michigan.	

SUBCOMMITTEES

[The chairman and the ranking minority member are ex officio (non-voting) members of all subcommittees on which they do not serve.]

The Constitution and Civil Justice

Trent Franks, of Arizona, *Chair*

Ron DeSantis, of Florida, *Vice Chair*

Steve King, of Iowa.	*Steve Cohen, of Tennessee.*
Louie Gohmert, of Texas.	*Jerrold Nadler, of New York.*
Jim Jordan, of Ohio.	*Theodore E. Deutch, of Florida.*

Courts, Intellectual Property, and the Internet

Darrell E. Issa, of California, *Chair*

Doug Collins, of Georgia, *Vice Chair*

F. James Sensenbrenner, Jr., of Wisconsin.	*Jerrold Nadler, of New York.*
Lamar Smith, of Texas.	*Judy Chu, of California.*
Steve Chabot, of Ohio.	*Theodore E. Deutch, of Florida.*
J. Randy Forbes, of Virginia.	*Karen Bass, of California.*
Trent Franks, of Arizona.	*Cedric L. Richmond, of Louisiana.*
Jim Jordan, of Ohio.	*Suzan K. DelBene, of Washington.*
Ted Poe, of Texas.	*Hakeem S. Jeffries, of New York.*
Jason Chaffetz, of Utah.	*David N. Cicilline, of Rhode Island.*
Tom Marino, of Pennsylvania.	*Scott H. Peters, of California.*
Blake Farenthold, of Texas.	*Zoe Lofgren, of California.*
Ron DeSantis, of Florida.	*Steve Cohen, of Tennessee.*
Mimi Walters, of California.	*Henry C. "Hank" Johnson, Jr., of Georgia.*

Crime, Terrorism, Homeland Security, and Investigations

F. James Sensenbrenner, Jr., of Wisconsin, *Chair*
Louie Gohmert, of Texas, *Vice Chair*

Steve Chabot, of Ohio.
J. Randy Forbes, of Virginia.
Ted Poe, of Texas.
Jason Chaffetz, of Utah.
Trey Gowdy, of South Carolina.
Raúl R. Labrador, of Idaho.
Ken Buck, of Colorado.
Mike Bishop, of Michigan.

Sheila Jackson Lee, of Texas.
Pedro R. Pierluisi, of Puerto Rico.
Judy Chu, of California.
Luis V. Gutiérrez, of Illinois.
Karen Bass, of California.
Cedric L. Richmond, of Louisiana.

Immigration and Border Security

Trey Gowdy, of South Carolina, *Chair*
Raúl R. Labrador, of Idaho, *Vice Chair*

Lamar Smith, of Texas.
Steve King, of Iowa.
Ken Buck, of Colorado.
John Ratcliffe, of Texas.
David A. Trott, of Michigan.

Zoe Lofgren, of California.
Luis V. Gutiérrez, of Illinois.
Sheila Jackson Lee, of Texas.
Pedro R. Pierluisi, of Puerto Rico.

Regulatory Reform, Commercial and Antitrust Law

Tom Marino, of Pennsylvania, *Chair*
Blake Farenthold, of Texas, *Vice Chair*

Darrell E. Issa, of California.
Doug Collins, of Georgia.
Mimi Walters, of California.
John Ratcliffe, of Texas.
David A. Trott, of Michigan.
Mike Bishop, of Michigan.

Henry C. "Hank" Johnson, Jr., of Georgia.
Suzan K. DelBene, of Washington.
Hakeem S. Jeffries, of New York.
David N. Cicilline, of Rhode Island.
Scott H. Peters, of California.

STAFF

Committee on the Judiciary (2138 RHOB), 225–3951, fax 5–7680.
Chief of Staff and General Counsel.—Shelley Husband.
　Deputy Chief of Staff and Chief Counsel.—Branden Ritchie.
　Professional Staff.—John Manning.
　Parliamentarian and General Counsel.—Allison Halataei.
　Senior Legislative Clerk.—Kelsey Williams.
　Legislative Clerk.—Allen Jamerson.
　Senior Counsels: Jason Cervenak, Stephanie Gadbois.
　Communications Director.—Kathryn Rexrode.
　Deputy Communications Director.—Jessica Collins.
　Deputy Press Secretary.—Michael Woeste.
　Director of New Media.—Amanda Walker.
　Public Affairs Liaison.—Bryan Alphin.
　Coalitions Director.—Joe Russo.
　Staff Assistant.—Alley Adcock.
　Financial Administrator.—Patrick Baugh.
　Publications Specialist.—Tim Pearson.
Constitution and Civil Justice Subcommittee, H2–362 Ford, phone: 5–2825, fax: 5–4299.
　Chief Counsel.—Paul Taylor.
　　Counsels: John Coleman, Zachary Somers.
　　Clerk.—Tricia White.
Courts, Intellectual Property, and the Internet Subcommittee, 6310 O'Neill, phone: 5–5741, fax: 5–3673.
　Chief Counsel.—Joe Keeley.
　　Counsels: Vishal Amin, David Whitney.

Clerk.—Eric Bagwell.
Crime, Terrorism, Homeland Security, and Investigations Subcommittee, 6340 O'Neill, phone: 5-5727, fax: 5-3672.
  Chief Counsel.—Caroline Lynch.
  Counsels: Bobby Parmiter, Chris Grieco.
  Detailee.—Jason Herring.
  Clerk.—Scott Johnson.
Immigration and Border Security Subcommittee, 6320 O'Neill, phone: 5-3926, fax: 5-3737.
  Chief Counsel.—George Fishman.
  Counsel.—Andrea Loving.
  Clerk.—Graham Owens.
Regulatory Reform, Commercial and Antitrust Law Subcommittee, 6240 O'Neill, phone: 6-7680, fax: 5-3746.
  Chief Counsel.—Daniel Flores.
  Counsels: Anthony Grossi, Dan Huff.
  Clerk.—Andrea Lindsey.
  IT Office, 2451 Rayburn, fax: 5-1842.
  Director of Information Technology.—Tom Ullrich.
  Deputy Director of Information Technology.—Banyon Vassar.
Committee Printing 105 Cannon, fax: 6-2362.
  Committee Printer.—Doug Alexander.
Minority Staff Members:
  Minority Chief Counsel and Staff Director.—Perry Apelbaum, 2142 Rayburn, phone: 5-6504, fax: 5-7686.
  Professional Staff.—Maggie Lopatin.
Minority Offices, B-351 Rayburn, B-336 Rayburn, and H2-347 Ford, phone: 5-6906, fax: 5-7682.
  Minority Counsels: Danielle Brown, Jason Everett, Lillian German, Joe Graupensperger, David Greengrass, Aaron Hiller, Tom Jawetz, Susan Jensen, Keenan Keller, James Park, Norberto Salinas, Heather Sawyer, Maunica Sthanki.
  Press Secretary.—Stephanie Baez.
  Professional Staff: Veronica Eligan, Rosalind Jackson, Dwight Sullivan.

Natural Resources

1324 Longworth House Office Building, phone 225–2761

http://naturalresources.house.gov

Rob Bishop, of Utah, *Chair*

Don Young, of Alaska.
Louie Gohmert, of Texas.
Doug Lamborn, of Colorado.
Robert J. Wittman, of Virginia.
John Fleming, of Louisiana.
Tom McClintock, of California.
Glenn Thompson, of Pennsylvania.
Cynthia M. Lummis, of Wyoming.
Dan Benishek, of Michigan.
Jeff Duncan, of South Carolina.
Paul A. Gosar, of Arizona.
Raúl R. Labrador, of Idaho.
Doug LaMalfa, of California.
Jeff Denham, of California.
Paul Cook, of California.
Bruce Westerman, of Arkansas.
Garret Graves, of Louisiana.
Dan Newhouse, of Washington.
Ryan K. Zinke, Montana.
Jody B. Hice, of Georgia.
Aumua Amata Coleman Radewagen, of American Samoa.
Thomas MacArthur, of New Jersey.
Alexander X. Mooney, of West Virginia.
Cresent Hardy, of Nevada.

Raúl M. Grijalva, of Arizona.
Grace F. Napolitano, of California.
Madeleine Z. Bordallo, of Guam.
Jim Costa, of California.
Gregorio Kilili Camacho Sablan, of Northern Mariana Islands.
Niki Tsongas, of Massachusetts.
Pedro R. Pierluisi, of Puerto Rico.
Jared Huffman, of California.
Raul Ruiz, of California.
Alan S. Lowenthal, of California.
Matt Cartwright, of Pennsylvania.
Donald S. Beyer, Jr., of Virginia.
Norma J. Torres, of California.
Debbie Dingell, of Michigan.
Mark Takai, of Hawaii.
Ruben Gallego, of Arizona.
Lois Capps, of California.
Jared Polis, of Colorado.
Wm. Lacy Clay, of Missouri.

SUBCOMMITTEES

[The chairman and ranking minority member are ex officio (non-voting) members of all subcommittees on which they do not serve.]

Energy and Mineral Resources

Doug Lamborn, of Colorado, *Chair*

Louie Gohmert, of Texas.
Robert J. Wittman, of Virginia.
John Fleming, of Louisiana.
Glenn Thompson, of Pennsylvania.
Cynthia M. Lummis, of Wyoming.
Dan Benishek, of Michigan.
Jeff Duncan, of South Carolina.
Paul A. Gosar, of Arizona.
Raúl R. Labrador, of Idaho.
Paul Cook, of California.
Garret Graves, of Louisiana.
Ryan K. Zinke, Montana.
Jody B. Hice, of Georgia.
Alexander X. Mooney, of West Virginia.
Cresent Hardy, of Nevada.

Alan S. Lowenthal, of California.
Mark Takai, of Hawaii.
Jim Costa, of California.
Niki Tsongas, of Massachusetts.
Matt Cartwright, of Pennsylvania.
Donald S. Beyer, Jr., of Virginia.
Ruben Gallego, of Arizona.
Lois Capps, of California.
Jared Polis, of Colorado.

Federal Lands

Tom McClintock, of California, *Chair*

Don Young, of Alaska.
Louie Gohmert, of Texas.
Glenn Thompson, of Pennsylvania.
Cynthia M. Lummis, of Wyoming.
Raúl R. Labrador, of Idaho.
Doug LaMalfa, of California.
Bruce Westerman, of Arkansas.
Dan Newhouse, of Washington.
Ryan K. Zinke, Montana.
Jody B. Hice, of Georgia.
Thomas MacArthur, of New Jersey.
Cresent Hardy, of Nevada.

Niki Tsongas, of Massachusetts.
Matt Cartwright, of Pennsylvania.
Donald S. Beyer, Jr., of Virginia.
Pedro R. Pierluisi, of Puerto Rico.
Jared Huffman, of California.
Mark Takai, of Hawaii.
Alan S. Lowenthal, of California.
Debbie Dingell, of Michigan.
Lois Capps, of California.
Jared Polis, of Colorado.

Indian, Insular and Alaska Native Affairs

Don Young, of Alaska, *Chair*

Dan Benishek, of Michigan.
Paul A. Gosar, of Arizona.
Doug LaMalfa, of California.
Jeff Denham, of California.
Paul Cook, of California.
Aumua Amata Coleman Radewagen, of American Samoa.

Raul Ruiz, of California.
Madeleine Z. Bordallo, of Guam.
Gregorio Kilili Camacho Sablan, of Northern Mariana Islands.
Pedro R. Pierluisi, of Puerto Rico.
Norma J. Torres, of California.

Oversight and Investigations

Louie Gohmert, of Texas, *Chair*

Doug Lamborn, of Colorado.
Raúl R. Labrador, of Idaho.
Bruce Westerman, of Arkansas.
Jody B. Hice, of Georgia.
Aumua Amata Coleman Radewagen, of American Samoa.
Alexander X. Mooney, of West Virginia.

Debbie Dingell, of Michigan.
Jared Huffman, of California.
Ruben Gallego, of Arizona.
Jared Polis, of Colorado.

Water, Power and Oceans

John Fleming, of Louisiana, *Chair*

Don Young, of Alaska.
Robert J. Wittman, of Virginia.
Tom McClintock, of California.
Cynthia M. Lummis, of Wyoming.
Jeff Duncan, of South Carolina.
Paul A. Gosar, of Arizona.
Doug LaMalfa, of California.
Jeff Denham, of California.
Garret Graves, of Louisiana.
Dan Newhouse, of Washington.
Thomas MacArthur, of New Jersey.

Jared Huffman, of California.
Grace F. Napolitano, of California.
Jim Costa, of California.
Ruben Gallego, of Arizona.
Madeleine Z. Bordallo, of Guam.
Gregorio Kilili Camacho Sablan, of Northern Mariana Islands.
Raul Ruiz, of California.
Alan S. Lowenthal, of California.
Norma J. Torres, of California.
Debbie Dingell, of Michigan.

STAFF

Committee on Natural Resources (1324 LHOB), 5–2761.
Majority Staff Director.—Jason Knox.
Deputy Staff Director.—Todd Ungerecht.
Director of Operations.—Ilene Clauson.
Deputy Director of Operations.—Sophia Varnasidis.
Chief Counsel.—Lisa Pittman.
Deputy Chief Counsel.—Devin Wiser.

Counsel.—Mike Freeman.
Director of Coalitions.—Sam Scales.
Staff Assistants: Jack Lincoln, Brett Nelson.
Calendar Clerk.—Joycelyn Coleman.
Director, Information Technology.—Ed VanScoyoc.
IT Staff.—Merrick Munday.
GPO Detailee.—Darlene Davis.
Democratic Staff Director.—David Watkins (1329 LHOB), 5–6065.
Democratic Deputy Chief Counsel.—Sarah Parker (1329 LHOB), 5–6065.
Democratic Senior Policy Advisor.—Glenn Miller.
Democratic Professional Staff Member.—Emily Lande.
Chief Democratic Clerk.—Peter Gallagher.
Democratic Staff Assistant.—Daniel Torrez.
Manager of Operations.—Cristina Villa.
Communications (1328), Ext. 6–9109
Director of Communications.—Parish Braden.
Press Secretary.—Julia Bell.
Digital Media Coordinator.—Erica Arbetter.
Press Assistant.—Brandon Cockerham.
Democratic Communications Director.—Adam Sarvana (H2–186), 5–6065
Democratic Director of Public Engagement.—Bertha Guerrero.
Democratic Press Secretary.—Diane Padilla.
Subcommittee on Energy and Mineral Resources (1333 LHOB), Ext. 5–9297.
Majority Staff Director.—Bill Cooper.
Senior Professional Staff.—Kate MacGregor.
Professional Staff.—Kathy Benedetto.
Fellow, SMME.—Josh Hoffman.
Counsels: Sean Stewart, Andrew Vecera.
Clerk.—Matt Schafle.
Democratic Senior Energy Policy Advisor.—Steve Feldgus (H2–186), 5–6065.
AAAS Fellow.—Emily Lewis.
Subcommittee on Federal Lands (1332 LHOB), Ext. 6–7736.
Majority Staff Director.—Erica Rhoad.
Professional Staff: Brent Blevins, Spencer Kimball.
Research Assistant.—Terry Camp.
Detailee, Forest Service.—Gary Schiff.
Clerk.—Aniela Butler.
Democratic Professional Staff Member.—Brandon Bragato (H2–269), 5–6065.
NPS Bevinetto Fellow.—Brian Joyner.
Subcommittee on Indian, Insular and Alaska Native Affairs (4450 OFOB), Ext. 6–9725.
Majority Staff Director.—Chris Fluhr.
Professional Staff.—Ken Degenfelder.
Clerk.—Marc Alberts.
Democratic Professional Staff Member.—Chris Kaumo (H2–269), 5–6065.
Democratic Counsel, Insular Affairs.—Brian Modeste (H2–186), 5–6065.
Subcommittee on Oversight and Investigations (4170 OFOB), Ext. 5–7107.
Majority Staff Director.—Rob Gordon.
Senior Advisor.—Casey Hammond.
Research Assistant.—Matt Dermody.
Counsel.—Jessica Conrad.
Clerk.—Wesley Gwinn.
Democratic Director of Investigations.—Vic Edgerton (H2–186), 5–6065.
Subcommittee on Water, Power and Oceans (1522 LHOB), Ext. 5–8331.
Majority Staff Director.—Kiel Weaver.
Professional Staff.—William Ball.
Counsel.—Lawrence Raab.
Research Assistant.—Bryson Wong.
Clerk.—Alex Semanko.
Democratic Professional Staff Members: Matthew Muirragui-Villagomez, Matt Strickler.
Sea Grant Knauss Fellow.—Thomas Farrugia.

Oversight and Government Reform

2157 Rayburn House Office Building, phone 225–5074, fax 225–3974, TTY 225–6852
http://oversight.house.gov

Jason Chaffetz, of Utah, *Chair*

John L. Mica, of Florida.
Michael R. Turner, of Ohio.
John J. Duncan, Jr., of Tennessee.
Jim Jordan, of Ohio.
Tim Walberg, of Michigan.
Justin Amash, of Michigan.
Paul A. Gosar, of Arizona.
Scott DesJarlais, of Tennessee.
Trey Gowdy, of South Carolina.
Blake Farenthold, of Texas.
Cynthia M. Lummis, of Wyoming.
Thomas Massie, of Kentucky.
Mark Meadows, of North Carolina.
Ron DeSantis, of Florida.
Mick Mulvaney, of South Carolina.
Ken Buck, of Colorado.
Mark Walker, of North Carolina.
Rod Blum, of Iowa.
Jody B. Hice, of Georgia.
Steve Russell, of Oklahoma.
Earl L. "Buddy" Carter, of Georgia.
Glenn Grothman, of Wisconsin.
Will Hurd, of Texas.
Gary J. Palmer, of Alabama.

Elijah E. Cummings, of Maryland.
Carolyn B. Maloney, of New York.
Eleanor Holmes Norton, of District of
Columbia.
Wm. Lacy Clay, of Missouri.
Stephen F. Lynch, of Massachusetts.
Jim Cooper, of Tennessee.
Gerald E. Connolly, of Virginia.
Matt Cartwright, of Pennsylvania.
Tammy Duckworth, of Illinois.
Robin L. Kelly, of Illinois.
Brenda L. Lawrence, of Michigan.
Ted Lieu, of California.
Bonnie Watson Coleman, of New Jersey.
Stacey E. Plaskett, of Virgin Islands.
Mark DeSaulnier, of California.
Brendan F. Boyle, of Pennsylvania.
Peter Welch, of Vermont.
Michelle Lujan Grisham, of New Mexico.

SUBCOMMITTEES

[The chairman and ranking minority member are ex officio (voting) members of all subcommittees]

Government Operations

Mark Meadows, of North Carolina, *Chair*
Tim Walberg, of Michigan, *Vice Chair*

Jim Jordan, of Ohio.
Trey Gowdy, of South Carolina.
Thomas Massie, of Kentucky.
Mick Mulvaney, of South Carolina.
Ken Buck, of Colorado.
Earl L. "Buddy" Carter, of Georgia.
Glenn Grothman, of Wisconsin.

Gerald E. Connolly, of Virginia.
Carolyn B. Maloney, of New York.
Eleanor Holmes Norton, of District of
Columbia.
Wm. Lacy Clay, of Missouri.
Stacey E. Plaskett, of Virgin Islands.
Stephen F. Lynch, of Massachusetts.

Health Care, Benefits, and Administrative Rules

Jim Jordan, of Ohio, *Chair*
Mick Mulvaney, of South Carolina, *Vice Chair*

Tim Walberg, of Michigan.
Scott DesJarlais, of Tennessee.
Trey Gowdy, of South Carolina.
Cynthia M. Lummis, of Wyoming.
Mark Meadows, of North Carolina.
Ron DeSantis, of Florida.
Mark Walker, of North Carolina.
Jody B. Hice, of Georgia.
Earl L. "Buddy" Carter, of Georgia.

Matt Cartwright, of Pennsylvania.
Eleanor Holmes Norton, of District of
Columbia.
Bonnie Watson Coleman, of New Jersey.
Mark DeSaulnier, of California.
Brendan F. Boyle, of Pennsylvania.
Jim Cooper, of Tennessee.
Michelle Lujan Grisham, of New Mexico.

Information Technology

Will Hurd, of Texas, *Chair*

Blake Farenthold, of Texas, *Vice Chair*

Mark Walker, of North Carolina.
Rod Blum, of Iowa.
Paul A. Gosar, of Arizona.

Robin L. Kelly, of Illinois.
Gerald E. Connolly, of Virginia.
Tammy Duckworth, of Illinois.
Ted Lieu, of California.

Interior

Cynthia M. Lummis, of Wyoming, *Chair*

Ken Buck, of Colorado, *Vice Chair*

Paul A. Gosar, of Arizona.
Blake Farenthold, of Texas.
Steve Russell, of Oklahoma.
Gary J. Palmer, of Alabama.

Brenda L. Lawrence, of Michigan.
Matt Cartwright, of Pennsylvania.
Stacey E. Plaskett, of Virgin Islands.
Jim Cooper, of Tennessee.

National Security

Ron DeSantis, of Florida, *Chair*

Steve Russell, of Oklahoma, *Vice Chair*

John L. Mica, of Florida.
John J. Duncan, Jr., of Tennessee.
Jody B. Hice, of Georgia.
Will Hurd, of Texas.

Stephen F. Lynch, of Massachusetts.
Ted Lieu, of California.
Robin L. Kelly, of Illinois.
Brenda L. Lawrence, of Michigan.

Transportation and Public Assets

John L. Mica, of Florida, *Chair*

Glenn Grothman, of Wisconsin, *Vice Chair*

Michael R. Turner, of Ohio.
John J. Duncan, Jr., of Tennessee.
Justin Amash, of Michigan.
Thomas Massie, of Kentucky.

Tammy Duckworth, of Illinois.
Bonnie Watson Coleman, of New Jersey.
Mark DeSaulnier, of California.
Brendan F. Boyle, of Pennsylvania.

STAFF

Oversight and Government Reform (2157 RHOB), 202–225–5074.
  Majority Staff Director.—Sean McLaughlin.
    Deputy Staff Director.—Rachel Weaver.
    General Counsel.—Andrew Dockham.
    Deputy General Counsel.—Steve Castor.
    Operations Director.—Ryan Little.
    Parliamentarian.—Kathy Loden.
    Communications Director.—Rebecca Edgar.
    Press Secretary.—MJ Henshaw.
    Deputy Press Secretary.—Alex Miehls.
    Coalitions and Communication Coordinator.—Derrick Dockery.
    Press Assistant.—Alex Hirst.
    Digital Director.—Andrew Shult.
    Deputy Digital Director.—Jonathan McKinstry.
    Digital Assistant.—Ashton Bingham.
    Chief Clerk.—Laura Rush.
    Deputy Chief Clerk.—Sharon Casey.
    Clerks: Melissa Beaumont, Sarah Vance.
    Professional Staff Member.—Olivia Lee.
    Financial Administrator.—Robin Butler.
    Chief Information Officer.—Jeff Wease.
    Executive Team Assistant.—Jen Jett.

Staff Assistants: Donna Harkins, William Marx.
Oversight and Investigations Director.—Machalagh Carr.
Deputy Oversight and Investigations Director.—Henry Kerner.
Senior Counsels: Sean Brebbia, Jon Skladany.
Counsels: Jen Barblan, Mike Howell, Cordell Hull, Tristan Leavitt, Jack Thorlin.
Senior Professional Staff Members: Katie Bailey, Tyler Grimm.
Professional Staff Member.—Ari Wisch.
Government Operations Subcommittee Staff Director.—Jennifer Hemingway.
Deputy Staff Director.—Jeff Post.
Senior Counsel.—Julie Dunne.
Counsels: Howie Denis, Katy Rother.
Professional Staff Members: Alexa Armstrong, Christopher D'Angelo.
National Security Subcommittee Staff Director.—Art Arthur.
Deputy Counsel.—Dimple Shah.
Professional Staff Member.—Sang Yi.
Interior Subcommittee Staff Director.—Bill McGrath.
Professional Staff Member.—Ryan Hambleton.
Health Care, Benefits and Administrative Rules Subcommittee Staff Director.—Sean Hayes.
Counsel.—Christina Aizcorbe.
IT Subcommittee Staff Director.—Troy Stock.
Counsel.—Mike Flynn.
Transportation and Public Assets Subcommittee Staff Director.—James Robertson.
Professional Staff Member.—Michael Kiko.
2471 Rayburn House Office Building (2471 RHOB) phone 225–5051, fax 225–4784, TTY 225–6852, http://democrats.oversight.house.gov.
Minority Staff Director.—Dave Rapallo.
Chief Investigative Counsel.—Meghan Berroya.
Director of Legislation.—Mark Stephenson.
Deputy Director of Legislation/Counsel.—Krista Boyd.
Policy Director.—Lucinda Lessley.
Legislative Director.—Suzanne Owen.
Administrative Director.—Jaron Bourke.
Communications Director.—Jennifer Werner.
Deputy Communications Director.—Aryele Bradford.
Digital Director.—Jessica Levandowski.
Senior Investigator.—Chris Knauer.
Senior Counsel.—Tim Lynch.
Senior Policy Advisor.—Jimmy Fremgen.
Policy Advisor/Counsel.—Karen Kudelko.
Counsels: Lena Chang, Beverly Britton Fraser, Courtney French, Christy Gamble, Ali Golden, Brian Quinn, Valerie Shen, Cecelia Thomas.
Professional Staff Member.—Kevin Corbin.
Director of Operations.—Elisa LaNier.
Deputy Clerk.—Brett Cozzolino.
Professional Staff Member.—Michael Wilkins.
Research Assistant.—Katie Teleky.
Minority Technology Director.—Eddie Walker.
Minority GAO Detailee.—Sally Williamson.

Rules

H–312 The Capitol, phone 225–9191

http://www.rules.house.gov

Pete Sessions, of Texas, *Chair*

Virginia Foxx, of North Carolina.
Tom Cole, of Oklahoma.
Rob Woodall, of Georgia.
Michael C. Burgess, of Texas.
Steve Stivers, of Ohio.
Doug Collins, of Georgia.
Bradley Byrne, of Alabama.
Dan Newhouse, of Washington.

Louise McIntosh Slaughter, of New York.
James P. McGovern, of Massachusetts.
Alcee L. Hastings, of Florida.
Jared Polis, of Colorado.

SUBCOMMITTEES

Legislative and Budget Process

Rob Woodall, of Georgia, *Chair*

Virginia Foxx, of North Carolina.
Michael C. Burgess, of Texas.
Bradley Byrne, of Alabama.
Dan Newhouse, of Washington.

Alcee L. Hastings, of Florida.
Jared Polis, of Colorado.

Rules and Organization of the House

Steve Stivers, of Ohio, *Chair*

Doug Collins, of Georgia.
Bradley Byrne, of Alabama.
Dan Newhouse, of Washington.
Pete Sessions, of Texas.

Louise McIntosh Slaughter, of New York.
James P. McGovern, of Massachusetts.

STAFF

Committee on Rules (H–312 The Capitol), 225–9191.
  Majority Staff Director.—Hugh Halpern.
    Deputy Staff Director.—Stephen Cote.
    Policy Director.—Kevin Hubbard.
    Communications Director.—Jill Shatzen.
    Deputy Communications Director.—Sarah Minkel.
    Senior Professional Staff: Nathan Blake, Karas Pattison.
    Professional Staff: Monica Chinn, Alec Davis.
    Director of Information Technology.—Chris Erb.
    Staff Assistants: James Fitzella, Hannah Gill.
    Associate Staff: Cyrus Artz (2350 RHOB); Justin Barnes (1022 LHOB); Jennifer Choudhry (513 CHOB); James Decker (2336 RHOB); Jason Herbert (1641 LHOB); Lora Hobbs (2236 RHOB); Janet Rossi (1725 LHOB); Steve Waskiewicz (2467 RHOB).
  Minority Staff Director.—Miles Lackey.
    Deputy Staff Director and Counsel.—Adam Berg.
    Professional Staff: George Agurkis, David Vince.
    Staff Assistant.—Rose Laughlin.
    Director of Legislative Operations.—Natalie Nixon.
    Communications Director.—Jeff Gohringer.
    Speechwriter and Senior Advisor.—Carrie Adams.
Subcommittee on Legislative and Budget Process (1725 LHOB), 5–4272.
  Majority Staff Director.—Janet Rossi (Woodall).
  Minority Staff Director.—Lale Mamaux (Hastings).

Subcommittee on Rules and Organization of the House (1727 LHOB), 5–1002.
  Majority Staff Director.—Justin Barnes (Stivers).
  Minority Staff Director.—Cindy Buhl (McGovern).

Science, Space, and Technology

2321 Rayburn House Office Building, phone 225–6371, fax 226–0113

http://www.science.house.gov

Lamar Smith, of Texas, *Chair*

Frank D. Lucas, of Oklahoma, *Vice Chair*

F. James Sensenbrenner, Jr., of Wisconsin.
Dana Rohrabacher, of California.
Randy Neugebauer, of Texas.
Michael T. McCaul, of Texas.
Mo Brooks, of Alabama.
Randy Hultgren, of Illinois.
Bill Posey, of Florida.
Thomas Massie, of Kentucky.
Jim Bridenstine, of Oklahoma.
Randy K. Weber, Sr., of Texas.
Bill Johnson, of Ohio.
John R. Moolenaar, of Michigan.
Stephen Knight, of California.
Brian Babin, of Texas.
Bruce Westerman, of Arkansas.
Barbara Comstock, of Virginia.
Dan Newhouse, of Washington.
Gary J. Palmer, of Alabama.
Barry Loudermilk, of Georgia.
Ralph Lee Abraham, of Louisiana.

Eddie Bernice Johnson, of Texas.
Zoe Lofgren, of California.
Daniel Lipinski, of Illinois.
Donna F. Edwards, of Maryland.
Suzanne Bonamici, of Oregon.
Eric Swalwell, of California.
Alan Grayson, of Florida.
Ami Bera, of California.
Elizabeth H. Esty, of Connecticut.
Marc A. Veasey, of Texas.
Katherine M. Clark, of Massachusetts.
Donald S. Beyer, Jr., of Virginia.
Ed Perlmutter, of Colorado.
Paul Tonko, of New York.
Mark Takano, of California.
Bill Foster, of Illinois.

SUBCOMMITTEES

[The chairman and ranking minority member are ex officio (voting) members of all subcommittees on which they do not serve.]

Energy

Randy K. Weber, Sr., of Texas, *Chair*

Stephen Knight, of California, *Vice Chair*

Dana Rohrabacher, of California.
Randy Neugebauer, of Texas.
Mo Brooks, of Alabama.
Randy Hultgren, of Illinois.
Thomas Massie, of Kentucky.
Barbara Comstock, of Virginia.
Barry Loudermilk, of Georgia.

Alan Grayson, of Florida.
Eric Swalwell, of California.
Marc A. Veasey, of Texas.
Daniel Lipinski, of Illinois.
Katherine M. Clark, of Massachusetts.
Ed Perlmutter, of Colorado.

Environment

Jim Bridenstine, of Oklahoma, *Chair*

Bruce Westerman, of Arkansas, *Vice Chair*

F. James Sensenbrenner, Jr., of Wisconsin.
Randy Neugebauer, of Texas.
Randy K. Weber, Sr., of Texas.
John R. Moolenaar, of Michigan.
Brian Babin, of Texas.
Gary J. Palmer, of Alabama.
Ralph Lee Abraham, of Louisiana.

Suzanne Bonamici, of Oregon.
Donna F. Edwards, of Maryland.
Alan Grayson, of Florida.
Ami Bera, of California.
Mark Takano, of California.
Bill Foster, of Illinois.

Oversight

Barry Loudermilk, of Georgia, *Chair*

Bill Johnson, of Ohio, *Vice Chair*

F. James Sensenbrenner, Jr., of Wisconsin.
Bill Posey, of Florida.
Thomas Massie, of Kentucky.
Dan Newhouse, of Washington.

Donald S. Beyer, Jr., of Virginia.
Alan Grayson, of Florida.
Zoe Lofgren, of California.

Research and Technology

Barbara Comstock, of Virginia, *Chair*

John R. Moolenaar, of Michigan, *Vice Chair*

Frank D. Lucas, of Oklahoma.
Michael T. McCaul, of Texas.
Randy Hultgren, of Illinois.
Bruce Westerman, of Arkansas.
Dan Newhouse, of Washington.
Gary J. Palmer, of Alabama.
Ralph Lee Abraham, of Louisiana.

Daniel Lipinski, of Illinois.
Elizabeth H. Esty, of Connecticut.
Katherine M. Clark, of Massachusetts.
Paul Tonko, of New York.
Suzanne Bonamici, of Oregon.
Eric Swalwell, of California.

Space

Brian Babin, of Texas, *Chair*

Mo Brooks, of Alabama, *Vice Chair*

Dana Rohrabacher, of California.
Frank D. Lucas, of Oklahoma.
Michael T. McCaul, of Texas.
Bill Posey, of Florida.
Jim Bridenstine, of Oklahoma.
Bill Johnson, of Ohio.
Stephen Knight, of California.

Donna F. Edwards, of Maryland.
Ami Bera, of California.
Zoe Lofgren, of California.
Ed Perlmutter, of Colorado.
Marc A. Veasey, of Texas.
Donald S. Beyer, Jr., of Virginia.

STAFF

Committee on Science, Space, and Technology (2321 RHOB), 225–6371, fax 226–0113.
Majority Staff:
Chief of Staff.—Jennifer Brown.
Policy Director.—Chris Shank.
Legislative Director and Senior Advisor to the Chairman.—Chris Wydler.
Administrative Director and Senior Counsel to the Chairman.—Ashley Smith.
Operations Director.—Mark Marin.
Administration:
Chief Clerk.—Ashley Smith.
Financial Administrator.—John Ross.
Policy Assistant.—Brian Corcoran.
Executive Assistant.—Thea McDonald.
Printer.—Sangina Wright.
Communications:
Communications Director.—Zac Kurz.
Press Secretary.—Laura Crist.
Editor/Speechwriter.—James Danford.
Press Assistant.—Thea McDonald.
Counsel:
General Counsel.—Molly Boyl.
Legal Assistant.—James Danford.
Energy Subcommittee
Staff Director.—Mark Marin.
Professional Staff.—Emily Domenech.
Counsel.—Aaron Weston.
Policy Assistant.—Michelle Stoika.
Environment Subcommittee

Staff Director.—Mark Marin.
  Senior Counsel.—Joe Brazauskas.
  Professional Staff: Taylor Jordan, Richard Yamada.
  Policy Assistant.—Michelle Stoika.
Oversight Subcommittee
  Staff Director.—Tim Doyle.
  Professional Staff: Drew Colliatie, Sarah Grady.
  Counsel.—Lamar Echols.
  Policy Assistant.—Brian Corcoran.
Research and Technology Subcommittee
  Staff Director.—Cliff Shannon.
  Deputy Staff Director.—Raj Bharwani.
  Professional Staff.—Jenn Wickre.
  Policy Assistants: Alisa Carrigan, Christian Rice.
Space Subcommittee
  Staff Director.—Tom Hammond.
  Professional Staff.—Jared Stout.
  Counsel.—Mike Mineiro.
  Policy Assistant.—Christian Rice.
  Minority Staff:
  Chief of Staff.—Richard Obermann.
  Chief Counsel.—John Piazza.
  Deputy Chief Counsel.—Russell Norman.
  Administrative and Communications Director.—Kristin Kopshever.
  Staff and Press Assistant.—Joe Flarida.
Energy Subcommittee
  Staff Director.—Adam Rosenberg.
  Professional Staff.—Chris O'Leary.
Environment Subcommittee
  Staff Director.—Marcy Gallo.
  Professional Staff.—Pamitha Weerasinghe.
Oversight Subcommittee
  Staff Director.—Dan Pearson.
  Professional Staff.—Doug Pasternak.
Research and Technology Subcommittee
  Staff Director.—Dahlia Sokolov.
  Professional Staff: Brystol English, Kim Montgomery.
Space Subcommittee
  Professional Staff: Allen Li, Pam Whitney.

Small Business

2361 Rayburn House Office Building, phone 225–5821, fax 226–5276
http://www.smallbusiness.house.gov

Steve Chabot, of Ohio, *Chair*

Steve King, of Iowa.
Blaine Luetkemeyer, of Missouri.
Richard L. Hanna, of New York.
Tim Huelskamp, of Kansas.
Christopher P. Gibson, of New York.
Dave Brat, of Virginia.
Aumua Amata Coleman Radewagen, of American Samoa.
Stephen Knight, of California.
Carlos Curbelo, of Florida.
Cresent Hardy, of Nevada.
Trent Kelly, of Mississippi.

Nydia M. Velázquez, of New York.
Yvette D. Clarke, of New York.
Judy Chu, of California.
Janice Hahn, of California.
Donald M. Payne, Jr., of New Jersey.
Grace Meng, of New York.
Brenda L. Lawrence, of Michigan.
Alma S. Adams, of North Carolina.
Seth Moulton, of Massachusetts.
Mark Takai, of Hawaii.

SUBCOMMITTEES

[The chairman and ranking minority member are ex officio (non-voting) members of all subcommittees for purposes of any meeting or hearing.]

Agriculture, Energy and Trade

Carlos Curbelo, of Florida, *Chair*

Steve King, of Iowa.
Blaine Luetkemeyer, of Missouri.
Tim Huelskamp, of Kansas.
Christopher P. Gibson, of New York.
Dave Brat, of Virginia.

Grace Meng, of New York.

Contracting and Workforce

Richard L. Hanna, of New York, *Chair*

Steve King, of Iowa.
Christopher P. Gibson, of New York.
Stephen Knight, of California.
Cresent Hardy, of Nevada.

Mark Takai, of Hawaii.

Economic Growth, Tax and Capital Access

TBD, *Chair*

Richard L. Hanna, of New York.
Tim Huelskamp, of Kansas.
Dave Brat, of Virginia.
Aumua Amata Coleman Radewagen, of American Samoa.

Judy Chu, of California.

Health and Technology

Aumua Amata Coleman Radewagen, of American Samoa, *Chair*

Blaine Luetkemeyer, of Missouri.
Carlos Curbelo, of Florida.

Seth Moulton, of Massachusetts.

Investigations, Oversight and Regulations

Cresent Hardy, of Nevada, *Chair*

Stephen Knight, of California.

Alma S. Adams, of North Carolina.

STAFF

Committee on Small Business (2361 RHOB).
  Staff Director.—Kevin Fitzpatrick.
    Deputy Staff Directors: Steve Denis, Jan Oliver.
    Chief Counsel.—Barry Pineles.
    Senior Counsel.—Emily Murphy.
    Counsels: Corey Cooke, Viktoria Ziebarth.
    Professional Staff: James Burchfield, Joe Hartz.
    Clerk.—Susan Marshall.
    Staff Assistant.—Dan Brown.
    Executive Assistant.—Delia Barr.
  Democratic Staff:
  Staff Director.—Michael Day.
    Office Manager.—Mory García.
    Communications Director.—Alex Haurek.
    Tax Counsel.—Melissa Jung.
    Deputy Staff Director.—Adam Minehardt.
    Procurement Counsel.—Eminence Northcutt.
    Banking Counsel.—Justin Pelletier.

Transportation and Infrastructure

2165 Rayburn House Office Building, phone 225–9446

http://www.transportation.house.gov

Majority (202) 225–9446, room 2165 RHOB

Minority (202) 225–4472, room 2163 RHOB

Bill Shuster, of Pennsylvania, *Chair*

John J. Duncan, Jr., of Tennessee, *Vice Chair*

Don Young, of Alaska.
John L. Mica, of Florida.
Frank A. LoBiondo, of New Jersey.
Sam Graves, of Missouri.
Candice S. Miller, of Michigan.
Duncan Hunter, of California.
Eric A. "Rick" Crawford, of Arkansas.
Lou Barletta, of Pennsylvania.
Blake Farenthold, of Texas.
Bob Gibbs, of Ohio.
Richard L. Hanna, of New York.
Daniel Webster, of Florida.
Jeff Denham, of California.
Reid J. Ribble, of Wisconsin.
Thomas Massie, of Kentucky.
Mark Meadows, of North Carolina.
Scott Perry, of Pennsylvania.
Rodney Davis, of Illinois.
Mark Sanford, of South Carolina.
Rob Woodall, of Georgia.
Todd Rokita, of Indiana.
John Katko, of New York.
Brian Babin, of Texas.
Cresent Hardy, of Nevada.
Ryan A. Costello, of Pennsylvania.
Garret Graves, of Louisiana.
Mimi Walters, of California.
Barbara Comstock, of Virginia.
Carlos Curbelo, of Florida.
David Rouzer, of North Carolina.
Lee M. Zeldin, of New York.
Mike Bost, of Illinois.

Peter A. DeFazio, of Oregon.
Eleanor Holmes Norton, of District of Columbia.
Jerrold Nadler, of New York.
Corrine Brown, of Florida.
Eddie Bernice Johnson, of Texas.
Elijah E. Cummings, of Maryland.
Rick Larsen, of Washington.
Michael E. Capuano, of Massachusetts.
Grace F. Napolitano, of California.
Daniel Lipinski, of Illinois.
Steve Cohen, of Tennessee.
Albio Sires, of New Jersey.
Donna F. Edwards, of Maryland.
John Garamendi, of California.
André Carson, of Indiana.
Janice Hahn, of California.
Richard M. Nolan, of Minnesota.
Ann Kirkpatrick, of Arizona.
Dina Titus, of Nevada.
Sean Patrick Maloney, of New York.
Elizabeth H. Esty, of Connecticut.
Lois Frankel, of Florida.
Cheri Bustos, of Illinois.
Jared Huffman, of California.
Julia Brownley, of California.

SUBCOMMITTEES

[The chairman and ranking minority member are ex officio (voting) members of all subcommittees on which they do not serve.]

Aviation

Frank A. LoBiondo, of New Jersey, *Chair*

Don Young, of Alaska.
John J. Duncan, Jr., of Tennessee.
John L. Mica, of Florida.
Sam Graves, of Missouri.
Candice S. Miller, of Michigan.
Blake Farenthold, of Texas.
Richard L. Hanna, of New York.
Reid J. Ribble, of Wisconsin.
Mark Meadows, of North Carolina.
Rodney Davis, of Illinois.
Mark Sanford, of South Carolina.
Rob Woodall, of Georgia.
Todd Rokita, of Indiana.
Ryan A. Costello, of Pennsylvania.
Mimi Walters, of California.
Barbara Comstock, of Virginia.
Carlos Curbelo, of Florida.
Lee M. Zeldin, of New York.

Rick Larsen, of Washington.
Eleanor Holmes Norton, of District of Columbia.
Eddie Bernice Johnson, of Texas.
Daniel Lipinski, of Illinois.
André Carson, of Indiana.
Ann Kirkpatrick, of Arizona.
Dina Titus, of Nevada.
Sean Patrick Maloney, of New York.
Cheri Bustos, of Illinois.
Julia Brownley, of California.
Michael E. Capuano, of Massachusetts.
Steve Cohen, of Tennessee.
Richard M. Nolan, of Minnesota.
John Garamendi, of California.

Coast Guard and Maritime Transportation

Duncan Hunter, of California, *Chair*

Don Young, of Alaska.
Frank A. LoBiondo, of New Jersey.
Bob Gibbs, of Ohio.
Mark Sanford, of South Carolina.
Garret Graves, of Louisiana.
Carlos Curbelo, of Florida.
David Rouzer, of North Carolina.
Lee M. Zeldin, of New York.

John Garamendi, of California.
Elijah E. Cummings, of Maryland.
Corrine Brown, of Florida.
Janice Hahn, of California.
Lois Frankel, of Florida.
Julia Brownley, of California.

Economic Development, Public Buildings, and Emergency Management

Lou Barletta, of Pennsylvania, *Chair*

Eric A. "Rick" Crawford, of Arkansas.
Thomas Massie, of Kentucky.
Mark Meadows, of North Carolina.
Scott Perry, of Pennsylvania.
Ryan A. Costello, of Pennsylvania.
Barbara Comstock, of Virginia.
Carlos Curbelo, of Florida.
David Rouzer, of North Carolina.

André Carson, of Indiana.
Eleanor Holmes Norton, of District of Columbia.
Albio Sires, of New Jersey.
Donna F. Edwards, of Maryland.
Dina Titus, of Nevada.

Highways and Transit

Sam Graves, of Missouri, *Chair*

Don Young, of Alaska.
John J. Duncan, Jr., of Tennessee.
John L. Mica, of Florida.
Frank A. LoBiondo, of New Jersey.
Duncan Hunter, of California.
Eric A. "Rick" Crawford, of Arkansas.
Lou Barletta, of Pennsylvania.
Blake Farenthold, of Texas.
Bob Gibbs, of Ohio.
Richard L. Hanna, of New York.
Daniel Webster, of Florida.
Jeff Denham, of California.
Reid J. Ribble, of Wisconsin.
Thomas Massie, of Kentucky.
Mark Meadows, of North Carolina.
Scott Perry, of Pennsylvania.
Rodney Davis, of Illinois.
Rob Woodall, of Georgia.
John Katko, of New York.
Brian Babin, of Texas.
Cresent Hardy, of Nevada.
Ryan A. Costello, of Pennsylvania.
Garret Graves, of Louisiana.
Mimi Walters, of California.
Barbara Comstock, of Virginia.
Mike Bost, of Illinois.

Eleanor Holmes Norton, of District of
  Columbia.
Jerrold Nadler, of New York.
Eddie Bernice Johnson, of Texas.
Steve Cohen, of Tennessee.
Albio Sires, of New Jersey.
Donna F. Edwards, of Maryland.
Janice Hahn, of California.
Richard M. Nolan, of Minnesota.
Ann Kirkpatrick, of Arizona.
Dina Titus, of Nevada.
Sean Patrick Maloney, of New York.
Elizabeth H. Esty, of Connecticut.
Lois Frankel, of Florida.
Cheri Bustos, of Illinois.
Jared Huffman, of California.
Julia Brownley, of California.
Michael E. Capuano, of Massachusetts.
Grace F. Napolitano, of California.
Corrine Brown, of Florida.
Daniel Lipinski, of Illinois.

Railroads, Pipelines, and Hazardous Materials

Jeff Denham, of California, *Chair*

John J. Duncan, Jr., of Tennessee.
John L. Mica, of Florida.
Sam Graves, of Missouri.
Candice S. Miller, of Michigan.
Lou Barletta, of Pennsylvania.
Blake Farenthold, of Texas.
Richard L. Hanna, of New York.
Daniel Webster, of Florida.
Scott Perry, of Pennsylvania.
Todd Rokita, of Indiana.
John Katko, of New York.
Brian Babin, of Texas.
Cresent Hardy, of Nevada.
Mimi Walters, of California.
Lee M. Zeldin, of New York.
Mike Bost, of Illinois.

Michael E. Capuano, of Massachusetts.
Corrine Brown, of Florida.
Daniel Lipinski, of Illinois.
Jerrold Nadler, of New York.
Elijah E. Cummings, of Maryland.
Rick Larsen, of Washington.
Steve Cohen, of Tennessee.
Albio Sires, of New Jersey.
Richard M. Nolan, of Minnesota.
Elizabeth H. Esty, of Connecticut.
Grace F. Napolitano, of California.
Janice Hahn, of California.

Water Resources and Environment
Bob Gibbs, of Ohio, *Chair*

Candice S. Miller, of Michigan.
Duncan Hunter, of California.
Eric A. "Rick" Crawford, of Arkansas.
Daniel Webster, of Florida.
Jeff Denham, of California.
Reid J. Ribble, of Wisconsin.
Thomas Massie, of Kentucky.
Rodney Davis, of Illinois.
Mark Sanford, of South Carolina.
Todd Rokita, of Indiana.
John Katko, of New York.
Brian Babin, of Texas.
Cresent Hardy, of Nevada.
Garret Graves, of Louisiana.
David Rouzer, of North Carolina.
Mike Bost, of Illinois.

Grace F. Napolitano, of California.
Donna F. Edwards, of Maryland.
John Garamendi, of California.
Lois Frankel, of Florida.
Jared Huffman, of California.
Eddie Bernice Johnson, of Texas.
Ann Kirkpatrick, of Arizona.
Dina Titus, of Nevada.
Sean Patrick Maloney, of New York.
Elizabeth H. Esty, of Connecticut.
Eleanor Holmes Norton, of District of Columbia.
Richard M. Nolan, of Minnesota.

STAFF

Committee on Transportation and Infrastructure (2165 RHOB) 225–9446, fax 225–6782.
Majority Full Committee Staff:
*Staff Director.—*Christopher P. Bertram.
　*Deputy Staff Director and General Counsel.—*Jennifer Hall.
　*Deputy Staff Director.—*Matt Sturges.
　*Deputy General Counsel.—*Holly E. Woodruff Lyons.
　*Director of Budget and Program Analysis.—*Clare Doherty.
　*Member Services Coordinator.—*Collin McCune.
　*Director of Outreach and Coalitions.—*Beth Spivey.
　*Financial Administrator.—*April Blankenship.
　*Legislative Assistant.—*Mary Mitchell Todd.
　*Press Aide.—*Kristin Alcalde.
　*Director of Facilities and Operations.—*Mike Legg.
　*Staff Assistant.—*Hannah Matesic.
Minority Full Committee Staff:
*Staff Director.—*Katherine W. Dedrick.
　*Chief Counsel.—*Ward McCarragher.
　*Director of Administration.—*Jamie Harrell.
　*Director of Pacific Northwest Policy and Member Services.—*Travis Joseph.
　*Legislative Assistant.—*Luke Strimer.
Information Systems
Systems Administrators: Scott Putz, Larry Whittaker.
Majority Communications
*Communications Director.—*Jim Billimoria.
　*Communications Advisor.—*Justin Harclerode.
　*Digital Coordinator.—*Keith Hall.
Minority Communications
*Communications Director.—*Jen Gilbreath.
　*Digital Director.—*Ashley Guill.
Clerk's Office
*Clerk.—*Tracy G. Mosebey.
　*Printer.—*Jean Paffenback.
Oversight and Investigations
Majority Staff:
　*Professional Staff.—*Jason W. Rosa.
Subcommittee on Aviation
Majority Staff:
*Staff Director.—*Chris Brown.
　*Counsel.—*Naveen Rao.
　Professional Staff: Simone Perez, Hunter Presti, Dennis Wirtz.
　*Staff Assistant.—*Isabelle Beegle-Levin.
Minority Staff:
　Counsels: Alex Burkett, Rachel Carr.

Legislative Assistant.—Luke Strimer.
Subcommittee on Coast Guard and Maritime Transportation
  Majority Staff:
  Staff Director.—John Rayfield.
    Professional Staff. —Bonnie Bruce.
    Staff Assistant.—Kevin Rieg.
  Minority Staff:
  Staff Director.—Dave Jansen.
    Legislative Assistant.—Alexa Old Crow.
Subcommittee on Economic Development, Public Buildings, and Emergency Management
  Majority Staff:
  Staff Director.—Dan Mathews.
    Counsels: Johanna Hardy, Pamela S. Williams.
    Staff Assistant.—Adam Twardzik.
  Minority Staff:
    Counsels: Elliot Doomes, Janet Erickson.
    Legislative Assistant.—Alexa Old Crow.
Subcommittee on Highways and Transit
  Majority Staff:
  Staff Director.—Murphie Barrett.
    Senior Professional Staff: Geoff Gosselin, Mary Phillips.
    Professional Staff: Andrew Brady, Alex Etchen, Caryn Lund.
    Staff Assistant.—Nicole Christus.
  Minority Staff:
  Staff Director.—Helena Zyblikewycz.
    Professional Staff: Auke Mahar-Piersma, Andrew Okuyiga.
    Legislative Assistant.—Luke Strimer.
Subcommittee on Railroads, Pipelines, and Hazardous Materials
  Majority Staff:
  Staff Director.—Mike Friedberg.
    Counsel.—Fred Miller.
    Professional Staff.—David Connolly.
    Staff Assistant.—George Riccardo.
  Minority Staff:
  Staff Director. —Jennifer Esposito.
    Legislative Assistant.—Alexa Old Crow.
Subcommittee on Water Resources and Environment
  Majority Staff:
  Staff Director.—Geoff Bowman.
    Counsel.—Jonathan Pawlow.
    Professional Staff.—Elizabeth Fox.
    Research Assistant. —Tracy Zea.
    Staff Assistant.—Anna Oaks.
  Minority Staff:
  Staff Director and Counsel.—Ryan Seiger.
    Counsel.—Mike Brain.
    Legislative Assistant.—Alexa Old Crow.

Veterans' Affairs

335 Cannon House Office Building, phone 225–3527, fax 225–5486
http://www.veterans.house.gov

Jeff Miller, of Florida, *Chair*

Doug Lamborn, of Colorado.
Gus M. Bilirakis, of Florida.
David P. Roe, of Tennessee.
Dan Benishek, of Michigan.
Tim Huelskamp, of Kansas.
Mike Coffman, of Colorado.
Brad R. Wenstrup, of Ohio.
Jackie Walorski, of Indiana.
Ralph Lee Abraham, of Louisiana.
Lee M. Zeldin, of New York.
Ryan A. Costello, of Pennsylvania.
Aumua Amata Coleman Radewagen, of
American Samoa.
Mike Bost, of Illinois.

Corrine Brown, of Florida.
Mark Takano, of California.
Julia Brownley, of California.
Dina Titus, of Nevada.
Raul Ruiz, of California.
Ann M. Kuster, of New Hampshire.
Beto O'Rourke, of Texas.
Kathleen M. Rice, of New York.
Timothy J. Walz, of Minnesota.
Jerry McNerney, of California.

SUBCOMMITTEES

Disability Assistance and Memorial Affairs

Ralph Lee Abraham, of Louisiana, *Chair*

Doug Lamborn, of Colorado.
Lee M. Zeldin, of New York.
Ryan A. Costello, of Pennsylvania.
Mike Bost, of Illinois.

Dina Titus, of Nevada.
Julia Brownley, of California.
Raul Ruiz, of California.

Economic Opportunity

Brad R. Wenstrup, of Ohio, *Chair*

Lee M. Zeldin, of New York.
Aumua Amata Coleman Radewagen, of
American Samoa.
Ryan A. Costello, of Pennsylvania.
Mike Bost, of Illinois.

Mark Takano, of California.
Dina Titus, of Nevada.
Kathleen M. Rice, of New York.
Jerry McNerney, of California.

Health

Dan Benishek, of Michigan, *Chair*

Gus M. Bilirakis, of Florida.
David P. Roe, of Tennessee.
Tim Huelskamp, of Kansas.
Mike Coffman, of Colorado.
Brad R. Wenstrup, of Ohio.
Ralph Lee Abraham, of Louisiana.

Julia Brownley, of California.
Mark Takano, of California.
Raul Ruiz, of California.
Ann M. Kuster, of New Hampshire.
Beto O'Rourke, of Texas.

Oversight and Investigations

Mike Coffman, of Colorado, *Chair*

Doug Lamborn, of Colorado.
David P. Roe, of Tennessee.
Dan Benishek, of Michigan.
Tim Huelskamp, of Kansas.
Jackie Walorski, of Indiana.

Ann M. Kuster, of New Hampshire.
Beto O'Rourke, of Texas.
Kathleen M. Rice, of New York.
Timothy J. Walz, of Minnesota.

STAFF

Committee on Veterans' Affairs (335 CHOB), 225-3527, fax 225-5486.
Majority Staff Director.—Jon Towers.
  Deputy Staff Director.—Mike Brinck.
  Communications Director.—Vacant.
  Financial Administrator and Printing Clerk.—Bernadine Dotson.
  Chief Clerk and Office Manager and Legislative Coordinator.—Jessica Eggimann.
  Press Assistant.—Tim Mantegna.
  Staff Assistant.—Christina Mandreucci.
Minority Staff Director.—Don Phillips (333 CHOB), 225-9756, fax 225-2034.
  Deputy Staff Director and Chief Counsel.—David Tucker.
  Communications Director.—David Simon.
  Executive Assistant.—Megan Bland.
  Legislative Coordinator and Office Manager.—Carol Murray.
  Senior Legislative Assistant.—Carolyn Blaydes.
Subcommittee on Disability Assistance and Memorial Affairs (337 CHOB), 225-9164, fax 226-4691.
  Majority Subcommittee Staff Director and Counsel.—Maria Tripplaar.
    Research Assistant.—John Vick.
    Professional Staff Member and Counsel.—Cecilia Daly.
  Minority Staff Director and Counsel.—Justin Brown.
    Senior Legislative Assistant.—Saki Ververis.
Subcommittee on Economic Opportunity (335 CHOB), 226-5491, fax 225-5486.
  Majority Staff Director.—Jon Clark.
    Legislative Aide.—Kelsey Baron.
  Minority Staff Director and Counsel.—Erin Snow.
Subcommittee on Health (338 CHOB), 225-9154, fax 226-4536.
  Majority Staff Director.—Christine Hill.
    Professional Staff Member.—Samantha Gonzalez.
    Research Assistant.—Vacant.
    Healthcare Investigator.—Tamara Bonzanto.
  Minority Staff Director.—Cathy Wiblemo.
    Professional Staff Member.—Lee Footer.
Subcommittee on Oversight and Investigations (337A CHOB), 225-3569, fax 225-6392.
  Majority Staff Director.—Eric Hannel.
    Senior Investigative Counsel.—Harold Rees.
    Investigative Counsels: Amy Centanni, Jon Hodnette.
    Contract Investigator.—Bill Mallison.
  Minority Investigative Counsel.—Grace Rodden.

Ways and Means

1102 Longworth House Office Building, phone 225–3625

http://waysandmeans.house.gov

Kevin Brady, of Texas, *Chair*

Sam Johnson, of Texas.
Devin Nunes, of California.
Patrick J. Tiberi, of Ohio.
David G. Reichert, of Washington.
Charles W. Boustany, Jr., of Louisiana.
Peter J. Roskam, of Illinois.
Tom Price, of Georgia.
Vern Buchanan, of Florida.
Adrian Smith, of Nebraska.
Lynn Jenkins, of Kansas.
Erik Paulsen, of Minnesota.
Kenny Marchant, of Texas.
Diane Black, of Tennessee.
Tom Reed, of New York.
Todd C. Young, of Indiana.
Mike Kelly, of Pennsylvania.
James B. Renacci, of Ohio.
Patrick Meehan, of Pennsylvania.
Kristi L. Noem, of South Dakota.
George Holding, of North Carolina.
Jason Smith, of Missouri.
Robert J. Dold, of Illinois.
Tom Rice, of South Carolina.

Sander M. Levin, of Michigan.
Charles B. Rangel, of New York.
Jim McDermott, of Washington.
John Lewis, of Georgia.
Richard E. Neal, of Massachusetts.
Xavier Becerra, of California.
Lloyd Doggett, of Texas.
Mike Thompson, of California.
John B. Larson, of Connecticut.
Earl Blumenauer, of Oregon.
Ron Kind, of Wisconsin.
Bill Pascrell, Jr., of New Jersey.
Joseph Crowley, of New York.
Danny K. Davis, of Illinois.
Linda T. Sánchez, of California.

SUBCOMMITTEES

[The chairman and ranking minority member are ex officio (non-voting) members of all subcommittees.]

Health

Patrick J. Tiberi, of Ohio, *Chair*

Sam Johnson, of Texas.
Devin Nunes, of California.
Peter J. Roskam, of Illinois.
Tom Price, of Georgia.
Vern Buchanan, of Florida.
Adrian Smith, of Nebraska.
Lynn Jenkins, of Kansas.
Kenny Marchant, of Texas.
Diane Black, of Tennessee.
Erik Paulsen, of Minnesota.

Jim McDermott, of Washington.
Mike Thompson, of California.
Ron Kind, of Wisconsin.
Earl Blumenauer, of Oregon.
Bill Pascrell, Jr., of New Jersey.
Danny K. Davis, of Illinois.
John Lewis, of Georgia.

Human Resources

Vern Buchanan, of Florida, *Chair*

Kristi L. Noem, of South Dakota.
Jason Smith, of Missouri.
Robert J. Dold, of Illinois.
Tom Rice, of South Carolina.
Tom Reed, of New York.
David G. Reichert, of Washington.

Lloyd Doggett, of Texas.
John Lewis, of Georgia.
Joseph Crowley, of New York.
Danny K. Davis, of Illinois.

Oversight

Peter J. Roskam, of Illinois, *Chair*

Patrick Meehan, of Pennsylvania.
George Holding, of North Carolina.
Jason Smith, of Missouri.
Tom Reed, of New York.
Tom Rice, of South Carolina.
Kenny Marchant, of Texas.

John Lewis, of Georgia.
Joseph Crowley, of New York.
Charles B. Rangel, of New York.
Lloyd Doggett, of Texas.
Danny K. Davis, of Illinois.

Social Security

Sam Johnson, of Texas, *Chair*

Robert J. Dold, of Illinois.
Vern Buchanan, of Florida.
Adrian Smith, of Nebraska.
Mike Kelly, of Pennsylvania.
James B. Renacci, of South Carolina.
Tom Rice, of Texas.

Xavier Becerra, of California.
John B. Larson, of Connecticut.
Earl Blumenauer, of Oregon.
Jim McDermott, of Washington.

Tax Policy

Charles W. Boustany, Jr., of Louisiana, *Chair*

David G. Reichert, of Washington.
Patrick J. Tiberi, of Ohio.
Tom Reed, of New York.
Mike Kelly, of Pennsylvania.
James B. Renacci, of Ohio.
Kristi L. Noem, of South Dakota.
George Holding, of North Carolina.

Richard E. Neal, of Massachusetts.
John B. Larson, of Connecticut.
Linda T. Sánchez, of California.
Mike Thompson, of California.
Lloyd Doggett, of Texas.

Trade

David G. Reichert, of Washington, *Chair*

Devin Nunes, of California.
Adrian Smith, of Nebraska.
Lynn Jenkins, of Kansas.
Charles W. Boustany, Jr., of Louisiana.
Erik Paulsen, of Minnesota.
Kenny Marchant, of Texas.
Todd C. Young, of Indiana.
Mike Kelly, of Pennsylvania.
Patrick Meehan, of Pennsylvania.

Charles B. Rangel, of New York.
Richard E. Neal, of Massachusetts.
Earl Blumenauer, of Oregon.
Ron Kind, of Wisconsin.
Bill Pascrell, Jr., of New Jersey.
Lloyd Doggett, of Texas.

STAFF

Committee on Ways and Means (1102 LHOB), 225–3625, fax 225–2610.
  Staff Director.—David Stewart.
    Economist.—AJ McKeown, Donald Schneider.
    Financial Administrator.—April Blankenship.
    Senior Clerk.—Michael K. Baker.
    Document Clerk.—Reggie Greene.
    Systems Administrators: Edward Baird, Mary Ford.
    Committee Administrator.—Chris Stottmann.
    Executive Assistant.—Andrew Rocca.
    Staff Assistant.—Sarah Rusciano.
    Tax Counsels: Jennifer Acuna, Aharon Friedman, Harold Hancock, Mark Warren.
    Associate Tax Counsel.—John Sandell.
    Legislative Assistant, Tax and Oversight.—Carly McCallie.
    Oversight Counsels: Amanda Neely, Tegan Millspaw.
    Professional Staff, Health and Oversight.—Meinan Goto.
    Staff Director/Chief Trade Counsel.—Angela Ellard.
    Trade Counsels: Geoffrey Antell, Stephen Claeys, Nasim Deylami, Casey Higgins, Neena Shenai.

Legislative Assistant, Trade.—Paul Guaglianone.
Professional Staff, Health: Brett Baker, Lisa Grabert, Stephanie Parks.
Senior Legislative Assistant, Health.—Nick Uehlecke.
Professional Staff, Social Security: Margret Hostetler, Amy Shuart.
Legislative Assistant, Social Security.—Erich Hartman.
Staff Director, Human Resources.—Matt Weidinger.
Professional Staff, Human Resources: Rosemary Lahasky, Ryan Martin.
Legislative Assistant, Human Resources.—Levi Stoep.
Minority Chief Counsel and Staff Director.—Janice Mays.
Oversight Staff Director.—Drew Crouch.
Communications Director.—Caroline Behringer.
Office Manager.—Jennifer Gould.
Assistant to Chief Counsel.—Carrie Breidenbach.
Staff/Research Assistant.—Moyer McCoy.
IT Director.—Antoine Walker.
Press Secretary.—Kevin Parker.
Chief Tax Counsel.—Karen McAfee.
Select Revenue Measures Staff Director.—Aruna Kalyanam.
Tax Counsel.—Alan Lee, Ji Prichard.
Staff Director, Health.—Amy Hall.
Deputy Staff Director, Health.—Jennifer Friedman.
Professional Staff, Health.—Melanie Egorin, Sarah Levin.
Detailee (Health).—Jennifer Dupee.
Staff Director, Human Resources.—Morna Miller.
Staff Director, Social Security.—Kathryn Olson.
Professional Staff, Social Security.—Sirat Attapit.
Staff Director, Trade.—Jason Kearns.
Trade Counsels: Beth Baltzan, Keigan Mull, Katherine Tai.

SELECT AND SPECIAL COMMITTEES OF THE HOUSE

Permanent Select Committee on Intelligence

HVC–304 The Capitol, phone 225–4121

[Created pursuant to H. Res. 658, 95th Congress]

Devin Nunes, of California, *Chair*

Jeff Miller, of Florida.
K. Michael Conaway, of Texas.
Peter T. King, of New York.
Frank A. LoBiondo, of New Jersey.
Lynn A. Westmoreland, of Georgia.
Thomas J. Rooney, of Florida.
Joseph J. Heck, of Nevada.
Mike Pompeo, of Kansas.
Ileana Ros-Lehtinen, of Florida.
Brad R. Wenstrup, of Ohio.
Chris Stewart, of Utah.
Michael R. Turner, of Ohio.

Adam B. Schiff, of California.
Luis V. Gutiérrez, of Illinois.
James A. Himes, of Connecticut.
Terri A. Sewell, of Alabama.
André Carson, of Indiana.
Jackie Speier, of California.
Mike Quigley, of Illinois.
Eric Swalwell, of California
Patrick Murphy, of Florida.

SUBCOMMITTEES

[The Speaker and Minority Leader are ex officio (non-voting) members of the committee.]

Central Intelligence Agency

Frank A. LoBiondo, New Jersey, *Chair*

K. Michael Conaway, of Texas.
Peter T. King, of New York.
Lynn A. Westmoreland, of Georgia.
Thomas J. Rooney, of Florida.
Mike Pompeo, of Kansas.

Eric Swalwell, of California.
Luis V. Gutiérrez, of Illinois.
James A. Himes, of Connecticut.
André Carson, of Indiana.

Department of Defense Intelligence and Overhead Architecture

Joseph J. Heck, of Nevada, *Chair*

Jeff Miller, of Florida.
Ileana Ros-Lehtinen, of Florida.
Michael R. Turner, of Ohio.
Brad R. Wenstrup, of Ohio.
Chris Stewart, of Utah.

Terri A. Sewell, of Alabama.
Luis V. Gutiérrez, of Illinois.
Eric Swalwell, of California.
Patrick Murphy, of Florida.

Emerging Threats

Thomas J. Rooney, of Florida, *Chair*

Frank A. LoBiondo, of New Jersey.
Joseph J. Heck, of Nevada.
Michael R. Turner, of Ohio.
Brad R. Wenstrup, of Ohio.
Chris Stewart, of Utah.

Mike Quigley, of Illinois.
Terri A. Sewell, of Alabama.
André Carson, of Indiana.
Jackie Speier, of California.

National Security Agency and Cybersecurity

Lynn A. Westmoreland, of Georgia, *Chair*

Jeff Miller, of Florida.
K. Michael Conaway, of Texas.
Peter T. King, of New York.
Mike Pompeo, of Kansas.
Ileana Ros-Lehtinen, of Florida.

James A. Himes, of Connecticut.
Jackie Speier, of California.
Mike Quigley, of Illinois.
Patrick Murphy, of Florida.

STAFF

Majority Staff Director.—Jeff Shockey.
  Senior Advisor.—Damon Nelson.
  Chief Counsel.—Andrew Peterson.
  Deputy General Counsel and Policy Director.—Michael Ellis.
  Budget Director.—Shannon Stuart.
  Professional Staff: Chelsey Campbell, Jacob Crisp, Geof Kahn, Steve Keith, Lisa Major,
    William Flanigan, Andrew House, Doug Presley, Diane Rinaldo, Randy Smith.
  Staff Assistant.—Nick Ciarlante.
Minority Staff Director.—Michael Bahar.
  Deputy Minority Staff Director.—Timothy Bergreen.
  Policy Advisor.—Robert Minehart.
  Minority Budget Director.—Carly Blake.
  Professional Staff: Linda Cohen, Allison Getty, Amanda Rogers Thorpe, Rheanne Wirkkala.
  Associate Professional Staff Member.—Thomas Eager.
  Security Director.—Kristin Jepson.
  Systems Administrator.—Kevin Klein.
  Director of Information Technology.—Brandon Smith.

Select Committee on the Events Surrounding the 2012 Terrorist Attack in Benghazi

1036 Longworth House Office Building
phone 226–7100 (Majority), 225–7100 (Minority)
http://www.benghazi.house.gov

Trey Gowdy, of South Carolina, *Chair*
Elijah E. Cummings, of Maryland, *Ranking Member*

Lynn A. Westmoreland, of Georgia.
Jim Jordan, of Ohio.
Peter J. Roskam, of Illinois.
Mike Pompeo, of Kansas.
Martha Roby, of Alabama.
Susan W. Brooks, of Indiana.

Adam Smith, of Washington.
Adam B. Schiff, of California.
Linda T. Sánchez, of California.
Tammy Duckworth, of Illinois.

STAFF

Staff Director and General Counsel.—Philip G. Kiko.
  Deputy Staff Director.—Chris Donesa.
  Chief Counsel.—Dana Chipman.
    Deputy Chief Counsels: Sharon Jackson, Craig Missakian.
    Deputy General Counsel.—Mark Grider.
    Member Liaison and Counsel.—Kimberly Betz.
  Senior Counsel.—Carlton Davis.
  Senior Counsel and Security Manager.—John "Mac" Tolar.
  Counsel.—Sheria Clarke.
  Professional Staff.—Brien Beattie.
  Senior Advisor.—Sarah Adams.
  Investigator.—Sara Barrineau.
  Communications Director.—Jamal Ware.
    Deputy Communications Director.—Amanda Duvall.

Finance and Personnel Administrator.—Anne Binsted.
Executive Assistant.—Paige Oneto.
Documents Clerk.—Barbara McCaffrey.
Minority Staff Director/General Counsel.—Susanne Sachsman Grooms.
Chief Counsel.—Heather Sawyer.
Senior Counsels: Krista Boyd, Peter Kenny.
Counsels: Ronak Desai, Shannon Green.
Senior Professional Staff: Linda Cohen, Laura Rauch, Brent Woolfork.
Professional Staff.—Daniel Rebnord.
Press Secretary.—Paul Bell.
Detailees: Jennifer Hoffman, Dave Rapallo, Kendal Robinson, Mone Ross.

National Republican Congressional Committee

320 First Street, SE., 20003, phone 479–7000

Greg Walden, of Oregon, *Chair*

Chair of:
 Finance.—Ann Wagner, of Missouri.
 Recruitment.—Richard Hudson, of North Carolina.
 Patriots.—Steve Stivers, of Ohio
 Women's Engagement.—Diane Black, of Tennessee.
 Digital.—Jeff Denham, of California.
 Coalitions.—Tom Graves, of Georgia.

EXECUTIVE COMMITTEE MEMBERS

Joe Barton, of Texas.
Susan W. Brooks, of Indiana.
Jason Chaffetz, of Utah.
Tom Cole, of Oklahoma.
Andy Harris, of Maryland.
Jeb Hensarling, of Texas.
Randy Hultgren, of Illinois.
Cynthia M. Lummis, of Wyoming.
Patrick T. McHenry, of North Carolina.
Mick Mulvaney, of South Carolina.
Devin Nunes, California.

Tom Price, of Georgia.
Mike Rogers, of Alabama.
Todd Rokita, of Indiana.
Edward R. Royce, of California.
Mac Thornberry, of Texas.
David A. Trott, of Michigan.
Fred Upton, of Michigan.
Mimi Walters, of California.
Steve Womack, of Arkansas.
Kevin Yoder, of Kansas.

STAFF

Executive Director.—Rob Simms.
 Deputy Executive Director and General Counsel.—Jessica Furst Johnson.
 Political Director.—John Rogers.
 Communications Director.—Katie Martin.
 Finance Director.—Megan Cummings.
 Digital Director.—Tom Newhouse.
 Research Director.—Todd Johnson.

House Republican Policy Committee

202A Cannon House Office Building, phone 226–5539
http://policy.house.gov

meets at the call of the Chair or the Speaker

Luke Messer, of Indiana, *Chair*

Republican Leadership:
 Speaker of the House.—Paul D. Ryan, of Wisconsin.
 Majority Leader.—Kevin McCarthy, of California.

Conference Chair.—Cathy McMorris Rodgers, of Washington.
Conference Vice Chair.—Lynn Jenkins, of Kansas.
Conference Secretary.—Virginia Foxx, of North Carolina.
NRCC Chair.—Greg Walden, of Oregon.

Policy Committee Staff.—202A Cannon HOB, 226–5539.
Chief of Staff.—Randy Swanson.

House Republican Conference

202A Cannon House Office Building, phone 225–5107, fax 226–0154

Cathy McMorris Rodgers, of Washington, *Chair*

Lynn Jenkins, of Kansas, *Vice Chair*

Virginia Foxx, of North Carolina, *Secretary*

STAFF

Chief of Staff.—Jeremy Deutsch.
Deputy Chief of Staff.—Nate Hodson.
Staff Assistant.—Louisa Gilson.
Director of Member Services.—Sarah Rogers.
Member Services Coordinator.—Nick Crocker.
Policy Director.—Evan McMullin.
Senior Advisor.—Nick Magallanes, Rebecca Mark.
Policy Advisor.—David Smentek.
Director of Coalitions.—Mattie Duppler.
Director of Digital Media.—Maurice Lewis.
Creative Media Director.—Drake Springer.
Design Director.—Erin Karriker.
Director of Media Affairs.—Pam Stevens.
Press Secretary for Hispanic Media.—Daniel Bucheli.
Director of Coalitions.—Nick Muzin.
Speechwriter.—Mikayla Hall.

Democratic Congressional Campaign Committee

430 South Capitol Street, SE., 20003, phone (202) 863–1500

Executive Committee:
  Nancy Pelosi, of California, *Democratic Leader.*
  Ben Ray Luján, of New Mexico, *Chair.*
Chairs:
  James E. Clyburn, National Mobilization, Chair.
  Donald S. Beyer, Jr., National Finance, Chair.
  Jan Schakowsky, National Chair for Candidate Services.

STAFF

Executive Director.—Kelly Ward, 478–9485.
Deputy Executive Director for Outreach and Voter Contact.—Dan Sena, 485–3434.
Deputy Executive Director for Finance.—Missy Kurek, 485–3455.
Chief Operating Officer.—Hayley Dierker, 485–3425.
Chief Financial Officer.—Jackie Forte-Mackay, 485–3401.
Deputy Executive Director and Political Director.—Ian Russell, 485–3454.
Candidate Fundraising and Deputy Political Director.—Nicole Eynard, 485–3436.
Deputy Executive Director and Director of Strategic Messaging.—Ty Matsdorf, 741–1878.
Communications Director.—Matt Thornton, 485–3458.
Member Services Director.—Charles Benton, 485–3516.

Director of Research and Strategic Communications.—Matt Fuehrmeyer, 485–3523.
Deputy Executive Director Digital Communications and Fundraising.—Brandon English, 485–3534.
National Finance Director.—Stella Ross, 485–3412.
National Press Secretary.—Meredith Kelly, 741–1858.
National Director for Analytics and Battlefield Advisor to the Chairman.—Christina Coloroso, 485–3452.
National Field Director.—Steve Sisneros, 485–3517.
Policy Director.—Amanda Hurley, 485–3531.

Democratic Steering and Policy Committee

H–204 The Capitol, phone 225–0100

Steering and Policy Chair.—Nancy Pelosi, Democratic Leader (CA–12).
Steering Co-Chair.—Rosa L. DeLauro (CT–3).
  Policy Co-Chair.—Donna F. Edwards (MD–4).

DEMOCRATIC STEERING AND POLICY COMMITTEE STAFF

Steering: Michael Bloom, George Kundanis.
Policy: Michael Bloom, George Kundanis, Richard Meltzer.

Democratic Caucus

1420 Longworth House Office Building, phone 225–1400, fax 226–4412

www.dems.gov

Xavier Becerra, of California, *Chair*

Joseph Crowley, of New York, *Vice Chair*

STAFF

Chief of Staff.—Sean McCluskie.
  Executive Director.—Fabiola Rodriguez-Ciampoli.
  Operations and Event Coordinator.—Manuel Carrillo.
  Senior Advisor for Member Services.—Eric Delaney.
  Advisor for Member Services: Leti Davalos, Noel Perez.
  Staff Assistants: Emily Noriega, Tre'Shonda Sheffey.
  Policy Director.—Grisella Martinez.
  Senior Policy Counsel.—Sirat Attapit.
  Policy Advisor.—Moh Sharma.
  New Media Press Secretary.—Matthew Handverger.
  Press Secretaries: Sam Avery, Miranda Margowsky.
  Policy Director to the Vice Chair.—Kevin Casey.
  Events and Projects Assistant to the Vice Chair.—Andrew Sachse.

OFFICERS AND OFFICIALS OF THE HOUSE

OFFICE OF THE SPEAKER
H–232 The Capitol, phone 225–0600, fax 225–5117

Speaker of the House of Representatives.— Paul D. Ryan.
   Chief of Staff.—David Hoppe.
      Deputy Chief of Staff.—Joyce Meyer.
   Director of Administration.—Kristene Blake.
   Director of Scheduling.—Maureen Mitchell.
      Deputy Directory of Scheduling.—Tory Wickiser.
      Special Assistant to the Speaker.—Ben Jordon.
   Director of House Operations.—Kelly Craven.
   Press Secretaries: Doug Andres, AshLee Strong.
      Deputy Press Secretary.—Molly Edwards.
   Director of Media Affairs.—Sarah Swinehart.
   Communications Director.—Mike Ricci.
      Deputy Communications Director.—Julia Slingsby.
   Chief Communications Advisor.—Brendan Buck.
   Senior Communications Advisor.—Vanessa Day.
   Communications Advisor.—Michael Shapiro.
   Digital Communications Director.—Caleb Smith.
   Director of Special Events and Protocol.—Seton Easby-Smith.
   Special Events Staff Assistant.—Carah Goldoust.
   Member Services Coordinator.—Tom Andrews.
   Director Information Technology.—Billy Benjamin.
   Systems Administrator.—Mike Sager.
   General Counsel.—Mark Epley.
   Floor Director.—Anne Bradbury.
      Deputy Floor Director.—Lydia Strunk.
   Floor Operations Counsel.—Nicole Foltz.
   Floor Assistants: Alex Becker, Sarah Coyle, Annie Minkler.
   Policy Director.—Austin Smythe.
   Cloakroom Director.—Jared Eichhron.
   Assistants to the Speaker for Policy: Maryam Brown, Jonathan Burks, George Callas, Cindy Herrle, Casey Higgins, Matt Hoffman, Ted McCann.
   Director of Speechwriting.—Brian Bolduc.
   Senior Advisor.—Andy Speth.
   Senior Staff Assistant.—Chris Marroletti.
   Staff Assistants: Rebekah Geffert, David Planning, Katie Pointer.

OFFICE OF THE MAJORITY LEADER
H–107 The Capitol, phone 225–4000, fax 225–0781

Majority Leader.—Kevin McCarthy.
   Chief of Staff.—Tim Berry.
   Deputy Chief of Staff and Counsel.—James Min.
   Deputy Chief of Staff for Floor and Member Services.—John Stipicevic.
   Deputy Chief of Staff for Policy.—Barrett Karr.
   Director of Communications.—Mike Long.
   Director of:
      External Affairs.—Danielle Burr.
      Floor Operations.—Ben Howard.
      Legislative Operations.—Kelly Dixon.

461

Member Services.—Natalie Buchanan.
Oversight.—Rob Borden.
Senior Policy Advisors: Jeff Dressler, Roger Mahan, Wes McClelland, Emily Murry.
Senior Advisor.—Matt Lira.
Executive Assistant.—Kristin Stipicevic.
Press Secretary.—Matt Sparks.
Floor Assistant.—John Leganski.
Digital Coordinator.—Tess Glancey.
External Affairs and Member Services Coordinator.—Brittany Carey.
Communication Aide and Speechwriter.—Alec Torres.
Special Assistant.—Lawson Kluttz.
Staff Assistants: Chris Bien, Alex Gourdikian.

OFFICE OF THE MAJORITY WHIP
H–329 The Capitol, phone 225–0197

Majority Whip.—Steve Scalise.
Chief of Staff.—Brett Horton.
Chief Deputy Whip.—Patrick T. McHenry.
Chief of Staff to the Chief Deputy Whip.—Parker Poling.
Special Assistant to the Chief Deputy Whip.—Tanner Black.
Floor Director.—Matt Bravo.
Business Coalitions Coordinator.—Kelley Hudak.
Conservative Coalitions Coordinator.—Laura Trueman.
Policy Director.—Bill Hughes.
Legislative Counsel.—Marty Reiser.
Communications Director.—Chris Bond.
Member Services Director.—Eric Zulkosky.
Policy Advisors: Dan Sadlosky, Laura Trueman.
Scheduler.—Megan Becker.
Deputy Communications Director.—TJ Tatum.
Floor Assistant.—Chris Hodgson.
Assistant to the Chief of Staff.—Andrew Cavazos.
Director of Operations.—Bart Reising.
Staff Assistants: Conner Brace, John Woodard.
Special Assistant.—Brendan DeLuke.
Floor Assistant.—Ben Napier.

OFFICE OF THE DEMOCRATIC LEADER
H–204 The Capitol, phone 225–0100, fax 225–4188
www.democraticleader.gov

Office of the Democratic Leader.—Hon. Nancy Pelosi.
Chief of Staff.—Nadeam Elshami, H–204, The Capitol, 225–0100.
Assistant to the Chief of Staff.—Ethan McClelland, H–204, The Capitol, 225–0100.
Chief of Staff (CA08 Office).—Robert Edmonson, 235 CHOB, 225–4965.
Deputy Chiefs of Staff: Diane Dewhirst, George Kundanis, H–204, The Capitol, 225–0100.
Senior Advisor.—Michael Bloom, H–204, The Capitol, 225–0100.
Counsel to the Democratic Leader.—Bernie Raimo, H–204, The Capitol, 225–0100.
Special Assistants to the Democratic Leader: Emily Berret, Kate Knudson, Bina Surgeon, H–204, The Capitol, 225–0100.
Staff Assistant.—Amy Williams-Navarro, H–204, The Capitol, 225–0100.
Co-Directors of Correspondence: Robyn Lea, David Silverman, 421 Cannon, 225–0100.
Director of Scheduling.—Kelsey Smith, H–204, The Capitol, 225–0100.
Deputy Director of Scheduling.—Devan Cayea, H–204, The Capitol, 225–0100.
Policy Director.—Dick Meltzer, H–204, The Capitol, 225–0100.
Policy Advisor.—Michael Tecklenburg, H–204, The Capitol, 225–0100.
Senior Policy Advisors: Kenneth DeGraff, Wyndee Parker, Wendell Primus, H–204, The Capitol, 225–0100.
Senior Advance Policy and Communications: Margaret Capron, H–204, The Capitol.
Senior Advance and Director of Member Service.—Jaime Lizarraga, H–204, The Capitol, 225–0100.

Senior Advisor for Member Services.—Michael Long, H–204, The Capitol.
Member Services Associate.—Emma Kaplan, H–204.
Director of Protocol and Special Events.—Kate Knudson, H–204, The Capitol, 225–0100.
Director of Speechwriting.—Henry Connely, H–204, The Capitol, 225–0100.
Deputy Speechwriter.—Malaika Robinson, H–204, The Capitol, 225–0100.
IT Director.—Wil Haynes, HB–13, The Capitol, 225–0100.
Deputy IT Director.—Kamilah Keita, HB–13, The Capitol, 225–0100.
Director of Advance.—Kelsey Smith, H–204, The Capitol, 225–0100.
Advance Associate.—Sinead Doherty.
Director of Outreach.—Reva Price, H–204, The Capitol, 225–0100.

DEMOCRATIC LEADER'S PRESS OFFICE
H–204 The Capitol, phone 225–0100

Communications Director and Senior Advisor.—Drew Hammill.
Deputy Communications Director and Press Secretary.—Evangeline George.
Deputy Press Secretary.—Jorge Aguilar.
Press Advisor.—Stephanie Cherry.
Research Director.—April Greener.
Director of New Media.—Kat Skiles.
Senior Press Assistant.—Ned Adriance.
Press Assistant.—Taylor Griffin.

DEMOCRATIC LEADER'S FLOOR OFFICE
H–204 The Capitol, phone 225–0100

Director of Floor Operations.—Jerry Hartz.

OFFICE OF THE DEMOCRATIC WHIP
H–148 The Capitol, phone 225–3130, fax 226–0663

Democratic Whip.—Steny H. Hoyer.
Chief of Staff.—Alexis Covey-Brandt.
Whip Director and Senior Advisor.—Brian Romick.
Floor Director.—Shuwanza Goff.
Floor Assistant.—Danielle Aviles.
Director of Member Services.—Courtney Fry.
Deputy Director of Member Services and Outreach Advisor.—Javier Martinez.
Communications Director.—Katie Grant.
Press Secretary.—Mariel Saez.
Press and Research Assistant.—Tara Vales.
Speechwriter.—Adam Weissman.
Policy Director.—Tom Mahr.
Senior Policy Advisors: Keith Abouchar, James Leuschen, Char MacDonald, Mary Frances Repko, Daniel Silverberg.
Office Manager/Executive Assistant.—Lindsey Cobia.
Director of Scheduling and Special Events.—Michelle Mittler.
Special Assistant.—Ray Salazar.
Digital Director and Policy Advisor.—Steve Dwyer.
Staff Assistants: Joseph Cortina, Deborah Rowe.

OFFICE OF THE ASSISTANT DEMOCRATIC LEADER
132 The Capitol, phone 226–3210
http://assistantdemocraticleader.house.gov

Assistant Democratic Leader.—James E. Clyburn.
Chief of Staff.—Yelberton R. Watkins.
Director of Policy.—Ashli Palmer.
Communications Director.—Patrick Devlin.
Senior Advisor.—Amy Miller Pfeiffer.
Legislative Assistant.—Matthew Ellison.
Special Assistant to the Assistant Democratic Leader.—Tamika Day.

OFFICE OF THE CLERK

H–154 The Capitol, phone 225–7000

KAREN L. HAAS, Clerk of the House of Representatives; Karen Lehman Haas, a native of Catonsville, MD, was sworn in as Clerk of the House of Representatives on January 5, 2011. She is the 34th individual to serve as Clerk. This is Ms. Haas' second occupancy of this position—in 2005, Speaker J. Dennis Hastert appointed Ms. Haas as Clerk of the U.S. House of Representatives. As Clerk, Ms. Haas plays a central role in the daily operations and legislative activities of the House. Ms. Haas began her service on Capitol Hill in 1984, when she worked for then-Minority Leader Robert H. Michel. For nearly 11 years, she served as his Executive Legislative Assistant. Following a brief leave to work in the private sector, Ms. Haas returned to Capitol Hill in June 1999 to serve as Floor Assistant to Speaker Hastert. Following her first term as Clerk, she served as Staff Director of the House Republican Conference and Minority Staff Director for the House Small Business Committee. Ms. Haas attended public schools in Maryland and received a bachelor's degree from the University of Maryland, College Park, with a major in political science and a minor in economics.

Clerk.—Karen L. Haas.
  Deputy Clerk.—Robert F. Reeves.
  Senior Advisor.—Marjorie "Gigi" Kelaher.
  Chief of:
    Legislative Computer Systems.—Scott Kim, 2401 RHOB, 225–1182.
    Legislative Operations.—Frances Chiappardi, HT–13, 225–7925.
    Legislative Resource Center.—Ronald Dale Thomas, 135 CHOB, 226–5200.
    Art and Archives.—Farar Elliott, 5140 OFOB, 226–1300.
    Communications.—Catherine Cooke, 5120 OFOB, 225–1908.
    House Employment Counsel.—Gloria Lett, 4300 OFOB, 225–7075.
  Official Reporter.—Melinda Walker, HT–59, The Capitol, 225–5621.

CHIEF ADMINISTRATIVE OFFICER

HB–26 The Capitol, phone 225–5555

WILL PLASTER, Chief Administrative Officer of the House of Representatives, native of Alexandria, VA.

Chief Administrative Officer.—Will Plaster.
  Chief Financial Officer.—Traci Beaubian, 3140, OFB.
  Chief Human Resources Officer.—Darnell Lee (acting), H2–102, FHOB.
  Chief Information Officer.—Catherine Szpindor, H2–631, FHOB.
  Chief Logistics Officer.—Tom Coyne, WA–34, RHOB.
  Chief Procurement Officer.—Lisa Grant, 5110, OFB.
  Administrative Counsel.—Christopher Brewster, H2–217, FHOB.
  Director of Communications.—Dan Weiser, H2–217, FHOB.
  Director of Internal Controls.—Konah Terry, H2–217, FHOB.

CHAPLAIN

HB–25 The Capitol, phone 225–2509, fax 226–4928

PATRICK J. CONROY, S.J., Chaplain, House of Representatives, residence, Portland, OR; a Jesuit of the Oregon Province of the Society of Jesus, graduated from Claremont McKenna College in CA in 1972, attended Gonzaga University Law School for one year before entering the Jesuit Order in 1973. Earned an M.A. in philosophy from Gonzaga University, a J.D. from St. Louis University, an M.Div. from the Jesuit School of Theology at Berkeley (CA), and an STM from Regis College of the University of Toronto in missiology. Practiced law for the Colville Confederated Tribes in Omak, WA and the U.S. Conference of Catholic Bishops representing Salvadoran refugees in San Francisco. Ordained a priest in 1983. From 1984 to 1989, pastored four villages on the Colville and Spokane Indian Reservations. Worked for the national Jesuit Office of Social Ministries in Washington, DC, then began a career of university chaplaincy at Georgetown University and Seattle University. In 2003 transferred to Jesuit High School in Portland, OR, to teach freshman theology and coach the mighty JV II girls' softball team. Also served as the Oregon Province's Provincial Assistant for Formation and as superior of the Jesuit community at Jesuit High School in Portland. Sworn in as 60th House Chaplain on May 25, 2011.

Chaplain of the House.—Patrick J. Conroy, S.J.
  Assistant to the Chaplain.—Elisa Aglieco.
  Liaison to Staff.—Karen Bronson.

OFFICE OF THE HOUSE HISTORIAN

5150 O'Neill Office Building, phone 226–5525

http://history.house.gov; history@mail.house.gov; @UShousehistory

House Historian.—Matthew Wasniewski.
  Associate Historian.—Ken Kato.
  Director—Office of House Historian Staff.—Erin M. Hromada.
  Manager of Oral History.—Kathleen Johnson.

OFFICE OF INTERPARLIAMENTARY AFFAIRS

HC–4 Capitol, phone 226–1766

Director.—Janice Robinson.
  Assistant Director.—Michael Smith.

HOUSE INFORMATION RESOURCES

H2–631, phone: 226–9788

Deputy CIO (Chief Information Officer) for the House of Representatives.—Catherine Szpindor.

OFFICE OF ATTENDING PHYSICIAN

H–166 The Capitol, phone 225–5421

(After office hours, call Capitol Operator 224–?145)

Attending Physician.—Dr. Brian P. Monahan.
  Chief of Staff.—Keith Pray.

OFFICE OF INSPECTOR GENERAL

H2–386 Ford House Office Building, phone 226–1250

Inspector General.—Theresa M. Grafenstine.
  Deputy Inspector Generals: Debbie B. Hunter, Michael T. Ptasienski.
  Director of Support Services.—Terry Upshur.
  Assistant Director of:
    Finance and Administration.—Susan Kozubski.
    Quality Assurance and Contract Services.—Steven Johnson.
  Administrative Assistant.—Deborah E. Jones.
  Director, Performance and Financial Audits and Investigative Services.—Susan Simpson.
  Assistant Director of Financial Audits and Investigative Services.—Julie Poole.
  Auditors: Ronnette Bailey, Nicole Loutsenhizer, Alexander Stewart.
  Director, Information Systems Audit.—David Cole.
  Assistant Director, Information Systems Audit.—Michael Howard, Clifton Persaud.
  Auditors: Emmanuel Akowuah, Keith Sullenberger.
  Director, Management and Advisory Services.—Joseph C. Picolla.
  Assistant Directors: Gregory Roberts, Donna Wolfgang.
  Management Analysts: Kevin Cornell, Saad Patel.

OFFICE OF THE LAW REVISION COUNSEL
H2–308 Ford House Office Building, 20515–6711, phone 226–2411, fax 225–0010

Law Revision Counsel.—Ralph V. Seep.
  Deputy Counsel.—Robert M. Sukol.
  Senior Counsels: Kenneth I. Paretzky, Timothy D. Trushel.
  Assistant Counsels: Joseph Cohen, Michelle Evans, Katrina M. Hall, Katherine L. Lane, Brian Lindsey, Edward T. Mulligan, Michele K. Skarvelis, Lindsey Skouras, John F. Wagner, Jr.
  Staff Assistants: Sylvia Tahirkheli, Monica Thompson.
  Printing Editors: Robert E. Belcher, James Cahill.
  Senior Systems Engineer.—Eric Loach.
  Systems Engineer.—Ken Thomas.

OFFICE OF THE LEGISLATIVE COUNSEL
H2–337 Ford House Office Building, phone 225–6060

Legislative Counsel.—Sandra L. Strokoff.
  Deputy Legislative Counsel.—Edward G. Grossman.
  Senior Counsels: Wade Ballou, Douglass Bellis, Timothy Brown, Paul Callen, Sherry Chriss, Susan Fleishman, Rosemary Gallagher, James Grossman, Curt Haensel, Jean Harmann, Gregory M. Kostka, Hank Savage, Mark Synnes, Robert Weinhagen, Noah Wofsy.
  Assistant Counsels: Karen Anderson, Marshall Barksdale, Hallet Brazelton, Warren Burke, Thomas Cassidy, Megan Chasnoff, Henry Christrup, Kenneth Cox, Jesse Cross, Lisa Daly, Thomas Dillon, Mathew Eckstein, Brendan Gallagher, Lucy Wolfe Goss, Ryan Greenlaw, Justin Gross, Alison Hartwich, Fiona Heckscher, Kakuti Lin, Christopher Osborne, Scott Probst, Hadley Ross, Anthony Sciascia, Jessica Shapiro, Anna Shpak, Veena Srinivasa, Kathryn Swiss, Michelle Vanek, Sally Walker, Brady Young.
  Office Administrator.—Nancy McNeillie.
  Assistant Office Administrator.—Debra Birch.
  Director, Information Systems.—Willie Blount.
  Senior Systems Analyst.—Peter Szwec.
  Systems Administrator.—David Topper.
  Publications Coordinator.—Craig Sterkx.
  Paralegal.—Kristen Amarosa.
  Staff Assistants/Paralegals: Elonda Blount, Kelly Meryweather.
  Staff Assistants: Ashley Anderson, Joseph Birch, Tomas Contreras, Miekl Joyner, Matthew Loggie, Tom Meryweather, Angelina Patton.

OFFICE OF THE PARLIAMENTARIAN
H–209 The Capitol, phone 225–7373

Parliamentarian.—Thomas J. Wickham, Jr.
  Deputy Parliamentarian.—Ethan B. Lauer.
  Assistant Parliamentarians: Anne D. Gooch, Kyle T. Jones, Jason A. Smith.
  Clerk to the Parliamentarian.—Brian C. Cooper.
  Assistant Clerks to the Parliamentarian: Kristen B. Donahue, Lloyd A. Jenkins.
  Precedent Consultant.—Charles W. Johnson III.
  Precedent Editors: Catherine A. Moran, Andrew S. Neal, Max A. Spitzer.
  Information Technology Manager.—Bryan J. Feldblum.

OFFICE OF THE SERGEANT AT ARMS
H–124 The Capitol, phone 225–2456

PAUL D. IRVING, Sergeant at Arms of the U.S. House of Representatives; born August 21, 1957 in Tampa, FL; B.S., Justice, American University; J.D., Whittier Law School; career record: clerk, Federal Bureau of Investigation, Los Angeles Field Office, 1980; special agent, U.S. Secret Service, Los Angeles Field Office, 1983; Assistant Director for Government and Public Affairs, 2002; elected 36th Sergeant at Arms of the U.S. House of Representatives on January 17, 2012 for the 112th Congress.

Sergeant at Arms.—Paul D. Irving.

Deputy Sergeant at Arms.—Tim Blodgett.
  Assistant Sergeant at Arms, Administration.—Kathleen Joyce.
  Assistant Sergeant at Arms, Protocol and Chamber Operations.—Ted Daniel.
  Assistants to the Sergeant at Arms, Floor Security: Joyce Hamlett, Rick Villa.
  Assistant Sergeant at Arms, Emergency Management.—Bob Dohr.
  Assistant Sergeant at Arms, Interoffice Coordination.—Curt Coughlin.
Chief Information Officer.—Jim Kaelin.
Directors:
  Division of Garage and Parking Security.—Dorian Coward.
  Division of House Security.—William McFarland.
  Identification Services.—Jack Looney.
Managers:
  Appointments Desk.—Teresa Johnson.
  Chamber Support Services.—Andrew Burns.
Senior Advisor for Police Services/Law Enforcement.—Larry Thompson.
Assistant to the Sergeant at Arms, Operations.—Stefan J. Bieret.
Staff Assistant.—KaSandra Greenhow.

JOINT COMMITTEES

Joint Economic Committee

G01 Dirksen Senate Office Building 20510–6432, phone 224–5171

[Created pursuant to sec. 5(a) of Public Law 304, 79th Congress]

Daniel Coats, Senator from Indiana, *Chair*
Patrick J. Tiberi, Representative from Ohio, *Vice Chair*

SENATE

Mike Lee, of Utah.
Tom Cotton, of Arkansas.
Ben Sasse, of Nebraska.
Ted Cruz, of Texas.
Bill Cassidy, of Louisiana.

Amy Klobuchar, of Minnesota.
Robert P. Casey, Jr., of Pennsylvania.
Martin Heinrich, of New Mexico.
Gary C. Peters, of Michigan.

HOUSE

Justin Amash, of Michigan.
Erik Paulsen, of Minnesota.
Richard L. Hanna, of New York.
David Schweikert, of Arizona.
Glenn Grothman, of Wisconsin.

Carolyn B. Maloney, of New York.
John K. Delaney, of Maryland.
Alma S. Adams, of North Carolina.
Donald S. Beyer, Jr., of Virginia.

STAFF

Joint Economic Committee (G–01), 224–5171, fax 224–0240.
Republican Staff:
Executive Director.—Viraj Mirani.
  Deputy Staff Director and Counsel.—Karin Hope.
  Deputy Staff Director.—Brian Neale.
  Chief Counsel.—Corey Astill.
  Communications Director.—Kristine Michalson.
  Policy Analyst and Digital Media Coordinator.—Aaron Smith.
  Senior Economists: Christina King, David Logan.
  Senior Policy Advisor.—Sue Sweet.
  Professional Staff Member.—Paige Hanson.
  Research Assistants: Hank Butler, Matthew Sommer.
  Financial Director.—Colleen Healy.
  System Administrator.—Barry Dexter.
  Executive Assistant.—Connie Foster.
House Republicans:
Staff Director.—Robert O'Quinn.
  Senior Economist and Energy Policy Advisor.—Theodore Boll.
  Senior Advisor.—Jeff Schlagenhauf.
  Senior Policy Advisor.—Doug Branch.
  Communications Advisor.—Al Felzenberg.
  Director of Economic Policy.—Doug Centilli.
Democratic Staff:
Staff Director.—Harry Gural.
  Senior Advisor.—Barry Nolan.
  Senior Economist.—Cary Elliott.
  Economist.—Phoebe Wong.

Senior Policy Advisors: Jason Kanter, Brian Phillips, Annabelle Tamerjan, Jim Whitney.
*Senior Policy Advisor/Communications Director.—*Leslie Phillips.
Policy Analysts: Harry Krejsa, Regina Willensky.
*Projects Assistant.—*Thomas Nicholas.
*Staff Assistant.—*Stephanie Salomon.

Joint Committee on the Library of Congress
305 Russell Senate Office Building, 20510, phone 224–6352

Roy Blunt, Senator from Missouri, *Chair*
Gregg Harper, Representative from Mississippi, *Vice Chair*

SENATE

Pat Roberts, of Kansas.
Shelley Moore Capito, of West Virginia.

Charles E. Schumer, of New York.
Patrick J. Leahy, of Vermont.

HOUSE

Candice S. Miller, of Michigan.
Tom Graves, of Georgia.

Robert A. Brady, of Pennsylvania.
Zoe Lofgren, of California.

Joint Committee on Printing
1309 Longworth House Office Building, 20515, phone 225–8281
[Created by act of August 3, 1846 (9 Stat. 114); U.S. Code 44, Section 101]

Gregg Harper, Representative from Mississippi, *Chair*
Roy Blunt, Senator from Missouri, *Vice Chair*

HOUSE

Candice S. Miller, of Michigan.
Rodney Davis, of Illinois.

Robert A. Brady, of Pennsylvania.
Juan Vargas, of California.

SENATE

Pat Roberts, of Kansas.
John Boozman, of Arkansas.

Charles E. Schumer, of New York.
Tom Udall, of New Mexico.

Joint Committee on Taxation
H2–502 Ford House Office Building 20515, phone 225–3621
fax 225–0832, http://www.jct.gov
SD–G18, Senate Dirksen Office Building, 20510, phone 224–5561
fax 224–1785, http://www.jct.gov
[Created by Public Law 20, 69th Congress]

Kevin Brady, Representative from Texas, *Chair*
Orrin G. Hatch, Senator from Utah, *Vice Chair*

HOUSE

Sam Johnson, of Texas.
Devin Nunes, of California.

Sander M. Levin, of Michigan.
Charles B. Rangel, of New York.

SENATE

Chuck Grassley, of Iowa.
Mike Crapo, of Idaho.

Ron Wyden, of Oregon.
Debbie Stabenow, of Michigan

NON-DESIGNATED STAFF

Joint Committee on Taxation (H2–502 FHOB), 225–3621.
  Chief of Staff.—Thomas Barthold, H2–502 FHOB, 225–3621.
  Deputy Chief of Staff.—Bernard Schmitt, 596 FHOB, 226–7575.
  Executive Assistant to COS.—Pamela Williams, H2–502 FHOB, 225–3621.
  Administrative Specialist.—Frank Shima, H2–502 FHOB, 225–3621.
  Senior Legislation Counsels: Laurie Coady, H2–502 FHOB, 225–7377; Harold Hirsch, H2–502 FHOB, 225–7377; Deirdre James, H2–502 FHOB, 225–7377; Cecily Rock, H2–502 FHOB, 225–7377.
  Legislation Counsels: Jeffrey Arbeit, H2–502 FHOB, 225–7377; Gordon Clay, SD G–18, 224–5561; Adam Gropper, SD G–18, 224–5561; Andrew Grossman, H2–502 FHOB, 225–7377; Viva Hammer, H2–502 FHOB, 225–7377; Marjorie Hoffman, SD G–18, 9224–5561; David Lenter, H2–502 FHOB, 225–7377; Patricia McDermott, H2–502 FHOB, 225–7377; Kristine Roth, SD G–18, 224–5561; Kashi Way, H2–502 FHOB, 225–7377; Kristeen Witt, H2–502 FHOB, 225–7377.
  Senior Refund Counsel.—Norman Brand, 1111 (IRS), 317–4463.
  Refund Counsels: Chase Gibson, 1111 (IRS), 317–4463; Robert Gotwald, 1111 (IRS), 317–4463.
  Senior Economist.—Nicholas Bull, 596 FHOB, 226–7575; James Cilke, 596 FHOB, 226–7575; Tim Dowd, 596 FHOB, 226–7575; Chris Giosa, 596 FHOB, 226–7575; Robert Harvey, 596 FHOB, 226–7575; Thomas Holtmann, 596 FHOB, 226–7575; Pamela Moomau, 596 FHOB, 226–7575; John Navratil, H2–502 FHOB, 225–7377; Christopher Overend, 596 FHOB, 226–7575; Brent Trigg, 596 FHOB, 226–7575.
  Economist.—Aaron Butz, 596 FHOB, 225–7575; Paul Chen, H2–502 FHOB, 225–7377; Sally Kwak, SD G–18, 224–5561; Paul Landefeld, 596 FHOB, 226–7575; Joseph LeCates, 596 FHOB, 226–7575; James McGuire, 596 FHOB, 226–7575; Kathleen T. Mackie, 596 FHOB, 226–7575; Anne Moore, 596 FHOB, 226–7575; Rachel Moore, 596 FHOB, 226–7575; Brandon Pecoraro, 596 FHOB, 226–7575; Zachary Richards, 596 FHOB, 226–7575; Karl Russo, H2–502 FHOB, 225–7377; Heidi Schramm, 596 FHOB, 226–7575; David Splinter, 596 FHOB, 226–7575; Lori Stuntz, 596 FHOB, 226–7575.
  Chief Statistical Analyst.—Melani Houser, 596 FHOB, 226–7575.
  Statistical Analyst.—Tanya Butler, 596 FHOB, 226–7575.
  Legislation Tax Accountants: Benjamin Gross, H2–502 FHOB, 225–7377; Natalie Tucker, H2–502 FHOB, 225–7377.
  Director of Information Technology.—Damion Jedlicka, 596 FHOB, 226–7575.
  Information Technology Specialists: Mark High, 596 FHOB, 226–7575; Merrick Munday, 596 FHOB, 226–7575; Jonathan Newton, 596 FHOB, 226–7575.
  Executive Assistants: Jean Best, H2–502 FHOB, 225–7377; Jayne Northern, SD G–18, 224–5561; Lucia Rogers, 596 FHOB, 226–7575; Sharon Watts, 1111 (IRS), 317–4463.
  Legal Research Assistant.—Genevieve Cowan, SD G–18, 224–5561.
  Document Production Specialist.—Chris Simmons, H2–502 FHOB, 225–7377.
  Economic Research Analyst.—Andrew Whitten, H2–502 FHOB, 225–7377.
  Senior Staff Assistant.—Debra McMullen, H2–502 FHOB, 225–7377.
  Staff Assistants: Neval McMullen, H2–502 FHOB, 225–7377; Kristine Means, H2–502 FHOB, 225–7377.
  Tax Resource Specialist.—Melissa O'Brien, SD G–18, 224–0494.
  Visiting Counsel.—Robert Russell, H2–502 FHOB, 225–7377.

ASSIGNMENTS OF SENATORS TO COMMITTEES

[Republicans in roman (54); Democrats in *italic* (44); Independents in SMALL CAPS (2); total, 100]

Senator	Committees (Standing, Joint, Select, and Special)
Alexander	Health, Education, Labor, and Pensions, *chair.* Appropriations. Energy and Natural Resources. Rules and Administration.
Ayotte	Armed Services. Budget. Commerce, Science, and Transportation. Homeland Security and Governmental Affairs. Small Business and Entrepreneurship.
Baldwin	Appropriations. Budget. Health, Education, Labor, and Pensions. Homeland Security and Governmental Affairs.
Barrasso	Indian Affairs, *chair.* Energy and Natural Resources. Environment and Public Works. Foreign Relations.
Bennet	Agriculture, Nutrition, and Forestry. Finance. Health, Education, Labor, and Pensions.
Blumenthal	Armed Services. Commerce, Science, and Transportation. Judiciary. Special Committee on Aging. Veterans' Affairs.
Blunt	Rules and Administration, *chair.* Joint Committee on the Library, *chair.* Joint Committee on Printing, *vice chair.* Appropriations. Commerce, Science, and Transportation. Select Committee on Intelligence.
Booker	Commerce, Science, and Transportation. Environment and Public Works. Homeland Security and Governmental Affairs. Small Business and Entrepreneurship.
Boozman	Agriculture, Nutrition, and Forestry. Appropriations. Environment and Public Works. Rules and Administration. Veterans' Affairs. Joint Committee on Printing.
Boxer	Select Committee on Ethics, *vice chair.* Environment and Public Works. Foreign Relations.

Senator	Committees (Standing, Joint, Select, and Special)
Brown	Agriculture, Nutrition, and Forestry. Banking, Housing, and Urban Affairs. Finance. Veterans' Affairs.
Burr	Select Committee on Intelligence, *chair*. Finance. Health, Education, Labor, and Pensions.
Cantwell	Commerce, Science, and Transportation. Energy and Natural Resources. Finance. Indian Affairs. Small Business and Entrepreneurship.
Capito	Appropriations. Energy and Natural Resources. Environment and Public Works. Rules and Administration. Joint Committee on the Library.
Cardin	Environment and Public Works. Finance. Foreign Relations. Small Business and Entrepreneurship.
Carper	Environment and Public Works. Finance. Homeland Security and Governmental Affairs.
Casey	Agriculture, Nutrition, and Forestry. Finance. Health, Education, Labor, and Pensions. Joint Economic Committee. Special Committee on Aging.
Cassidy	Appropriations. Energy and Natural Resources. Health, Education, Labor, and Pensions. Veterans' Affairs. Joint Economic Committee.
Coats	Joint Economic Committee, *chair*. Finance. Select Committee on Intelligence.
Cochran	Appropriations, *chair*. Agriculture, Nutrition, and Forestry. Rules and Administration.
Collins	Special Committee on Aging, *chair*. Appropriations. Health, Education, Labor, and Pensions. Select Committee on Intelligence.
Coons	Appropriations. Foreign Relations. Judiciary. Small Business and Entrepreneurship. Select Committee on Ethics.
Corker	Foreign Relations, *chair*. Banking, Housing, and Urban Affairs. Budget. Special Committee on Aging.

Senator	Committees (Standing, Joint, Select, and Special)
Cornyn	Finance. Judiciary.
Cotton	Armed Services. Banking, Housing, and Urban Affairs. Joint Economic Committee. Select Committee on Intelligence. Special Committee on Aging.
Crapo	Banking, Housing, and Urban Affairs. Budget. Environment and Public Works. Finance. Indian Affairs. Joint Committee on Taxation.
Cruz	Armed Services. Commerce, Science, and Transportation. Judiciary. Rules and Administration. Joint Economic Committee.
Daines	Appropriations. Commerce, Science, and Transportation. Energy and Natural Resources. Indian Affairs.
Donnelly	Agriculture, Nutrition, and Forestry. Armed Services. Banking, Housing, and Urban Affairs. Special Committee on Aging.
Durbin	Appropriations. Judiciary. Rules and Administration.
Enzi	Budget, *chair.* Finance. Health, Education, Labor, and Pensions. Homeland Security and Governmental Affairs. Small Business and Entrepreneurship.
Ernst	Agriculture, Nutrition, and Forestry. Armed Services. Homeland Security and Governmental Affairs. Small Business and Entrepreneurship.
Feinstein	Select Committee on Intelligence, *vice chair.* Appropriations. Judiciary. Rules and Administration.
Fischer	Armed Services. Commerce, Science, and Transportation. Environment and Public Works. Small Business and Entrepreneurship.
Flake	Energy and Natural Resources. Foreign Relations. Judiciary. Special Committee on Aging.
Franken	Energy and Natural Resources. Health, Education, Labor, and Pensions. Indian Affairs. Judiciary.

Senator	Committees (Standing, Joint, Select, and Special)
Gardner	Commerce, Science, and Transportation. Energy and Natural Resources. Foreign Relations. Small Business and Entrepreneurship.
Gillibrand	Agriculture, Nutrition, and Forestry. Armed Services. Environment and Public Works. Special Committee on Aging.
Graham	Appropriations. Armed Services. Budget. Judiciary.
Grassley	Judiciary, *chair.* Agriculture, Nutrition, and Forestry. Budget. Finance. Joint Committee on Taxation.
Hatch	Finance, *chair.* Joint Committee on Taxation, *vice chair.* Health, Education, Labor, and Pensions. Judiciary. Special Committee on Aging.
Heinrich	Armed Services. Energy and Natural Resources. Joint Economic Committee. Select Committee on Intelligence.
Heitkamp	Agriculture, Nutrition, and Forestry. Banking, Housing, and Urban Affairs. Homeland Security and Governmental Affairs. Indian Affairs. Small Business and Entrepreneurship.
Heller	Banking, Housing, and Urban Affairs. Commerce, Science, and Transportation. Finance. Veterans' Affairs. Special Committee on Aging.
Hirono	Armed Services. Energy and Natural Resources. Small Business and Entrepreneurship. Veterans' Affairs. Select Committee on Intelligence.
Hoeven	Agriculture, Nutrition, and Forestry. Appropriations. Energy and Natural Resources. Indian Affairs.
Inhofe	Environment and Public Works, *chair.* Armed Services.
Isakson	Veterans' Affairs, *chair.* Select Committee on Ethics, *chair.* Finance. Foreign Relations. Health, Education, Labor, and Pensions.
Johnson	Homeland Security and Governmental Affairs, *chair.* Budget. Commerce, Science, and Transportation. Foreign Relations.

Senator	Committees (Standing, Joint, Select, and Special)
Kaine	Armed Services. Budget. Foreign Relations. Special Committee on Aging.
KING	Armed Services. Budget. Energy and Natural Resources. Rules and Administration. Select Committee on Intelligence.
Kirk	Appropriations. Banking, Housing, and Urban Affairs. Health, Education, Labor, and Pensions. Special Committee on Aging.
Klobuchar	Agriculture, Nutrition, and Forestry. Commerce, Science, and Transportation. Judiciary. Rules and Administration. Joint Economic Committee.
Lankford	Appropriations. Homeland Security and Governmental Affairs. Indian Affairs. Select Committee on Intelligence.
Leahy	Agriculture, Nutrition, and Forestry. Appropriations. Judiciary. Rules and Administration. Joint Committee on the Library.
Lee	Armed Services. Energy and Natural Resources. Judiciary. Joint Economic Committee.
Manchin	Armed Services. Commerce, Science, and Transportation. Energy and Natural Resources. Veterans' Affairs.
Markey	Commerce, Science, and Transportation. Environment and Public Works. Foreign Relations. Small Business and Entrepreneurship.
McCain	Armed Services, *chair*. Homeland Security and Governmental Affairs. Indian Affairs. Select Committee on Intelligence.
McCaskill	Armed Services. Commerce, Science, and Transportation. Homeland Security and Governmental Affairs. Special Committee on Aging.
McConnell	Agriculture, Nutrition, and Forestry. Appropriations. Rules and Administration. Select Committee on Intelligence.
Menendez	Banking, Housing, and Urban Affairs. Finance. Foreign Relations.

Senator	Committees (Standing, Joint, Select, and Special)
Merkley	Appropriations. Banking, Housing, and Urban Affairs. Budget. Environment and Public Works.
Mikulski	Appropriations, *vice chair.* Health, Education, Labor, and Pensions. Select Committee on Intelligence.
Moran	Appropriations. Banking, Housing, and Urban Affairs. Commerce, Science, and Transportation. Indian Affairs. Veterans' Affairs.
Murkowski	Energy and Natural Resources, *chair.* Appropriations. Health, Education, Labor, and Pensions. Indian Affairs.
Murphy	Appropriations. Foreign Relations. Health, Education, Labor, and Pensions.
Murray	Appropriations. Budget. Health, Education, Labor, and Pensions. Veterans' Affairs.
Nelson	Armed Services. Commerce, Science, and Transportation. Finance. Special Committee on Aging.
Paul	Foreign Relations. Health, Education, Labor, and Pensions. Homeland Security and Governmental Affairs. Small Business and Entrepreneurship.
Perdue	Agriculture, Nutrition, and Forestry. Budget. Foreign Relations. Judiciary. Special Committee on Aging.
Peters	Commerce, Science, and Transportation. Homeland Security and Governmental Affairs. Small Business and Entrepreneurship. Joint Economic Committee.
Portman	Budget. Energy and Natural Resources. Finance. Homeland Security and Governmental Affairs.
Reed	Appropriations. Armed Services. Banking, Housing, and Urban Affairs. Select Committee on Intelligence.
Reid	Select Committee on Intelligence.
Risch	Energy and Natural Resources. Foreign Relations. Small Business and Entrepreneurship. Select Committee on Ethics. Select Committee on Intelligence.

Senator	Committees (Standing, Joint, Select, and Special)
Roberts	Agriculture, Nutrition, and Forestry, *chair*. Finance. Health, Education, Labor, and Pensions. Rules and Administration. Joint Committee on the Library. Joint Committee on Printing. Select Committee on Ethics.
Rounds	Armed Services. Banking, Housing, and Urban Affairs. Environment and Public Works. Veterans' Affairs.
Rubio	Commerce, Science, and Transportation. Foreign Relations. Small Business and Entrepreneurship. Select Committee on Intelligence.
SANDERS	Budget. Energy and Natural Resources. Environment and Public Works. Health, Education, Labor, and Pensions. Veterans' Affairs.
Sasse	Agriculture, Nutrition, and Forestry. Banking, Housing, and Urban Affairs. Homeland Security and Governmental Affairs. Joint Economic Committee. Special Committee on Aging.
Schatz	Appropriations. Commerce, Science, and Transportation. Indian Affairs. Select Committee on Ethics.
Schumer	Banking, Housing, and Urban Affairs. Finance. Judiciary. Rules and Administration. Joint Committee on the Library. Joint Committee on Printing.
Scott	Banking, Housing, and Urban Affairs. Finance. Health, Education, Labor, and Pensions. Small Business and Entrepreneurship. Special Committee on Aging.
Sessions	Armed Services. Budget. Environment and Public Works. Judiciary.
Shaheen	Appropriations. Armed Services. Foreign Relations. Small Business and Entrepreneurship.
Shelby	Banking, Housing, and Urban Affairs, *chair*. Appropriations. Rules and Administration.
Stabenow	Agriculture, Nutrition, and Forestry. Budget. Energy and Natural Resources. Finance. Joint Committee on Taxation.

Senator	Committees (Standing, Joint, Select, and Special)
Sullivan	Armed Services. Commerce, Science, and Transportation. Environment and Public Works. Veterans' Affairs.
Tester	Indian Affairs, *vice chair.* Appropriations. Banking, Housing, and Urban Affairs. Homeland Security and Governmental Affairs. Veterans' Affairs.
Thune	Commerce, Science, and Transportation, *chair.* Agriculture, Nutrition, and Forestry. Finance.
Tillis	Agriculture, Nutrition, and Forestry. Armed Services. Judiciary. Veterans' Affairs. Special Committee on Aging.
Toomey	Banking, Housing, and Urban Affairs. Budget. Finance.
Udall	Appropriations. Commerce, Science, and Transportation. Foreign Relations. Indian Affairs. Rules and Administration. Joint Committee on Printing.
Vitter	Small Business and Entrepreneurship, *chair.* Banking, Housing, and Urban Affairs. Environment and Public Works. Judiciary.
Warner	Banking, Housing, and Urban Affairs. Budget. Finance. Rules and Administration. Select Committee on Intelligence.
Warren	Banking, Housing, and Urban Affairs. Energy and Natural Resources. Health, Education, Labor, and Pensions. Special Committee on Aging.
Whitehouse	Budget. Environment and Public Works. Health, Education, Labor, and Pensions. Judiciary. Special Committee on Aging.
Wicker	Armed Services. Budget. Commerce, Science, and Transportation. Environment and Public Works. Rules and Administration.
Wyden	Budget. Energy and Natural Resources. Finance. Joint Committee on Taxation. Select Committee on Intelligence.

ASSIGNMENTS OF REPRESENTATIVES, RESIDENT COMMISSIONER, AND DELEGATES TO COMMITTEES

[Republicans in roman (246); Democrats in *italic* (188); Vacancies (1); Resident Commissioner and Delegates in **boldface** (6); total, 441]

Representative	Committees (Standing, Joint, and Select)
Abraham	Agriculture. Science, Space, and Technology. Veterans' Affairs.
Adams	Agriculture. Education and the Workforce. Small Business. Joint Economic Committee.
Aderholt	Appropriations.
Aguilar	Agriculture. Armed Services.
Allen	Agriculture. Education and the Workforce.
Amash	Oversight and Government Reform. Joint Economic Committee.
Amodei	Appropriations.
Ashford	Agriculture. Armed Services.
Babin	Science, Space, and Technology. Transportation and Infrastructure.
Barletta	Education and the Workforce. Homeland Security. Transportation and Infrastructure.
Barr	Financial Services.
Barton	Energy and Commerce.
Bass	Foreign Affairs. Judiciary.
Beatty	Financial Services.
Becerra	Ways and Means.
Benishek	Agriculture. Natural Resources. Veterans' Affairs.
Bera	Foreign Affairs. Science, Space, and Technology.
Beyer	Natural Resources. Science, Space, and Technology. Joint Economic Committee.
Bilirakis	Energy and Commerce. Veterans' Affairs.
Bishop, Mike, of Michigan	Education and the Workforce. Judiciary.

481

Representative	Committees (Standing, Joint, and Select)
Bishop, Rob, of Utah	Natural Resources, *chair.* Armed Services.
Bishop, Sanford D., Jr., of Georgia	Appropriations.
Black	Budget. Ways and Means.
Blackburn	Budget. Energy and Commerce.
Blum	Budget. Oversight and Government Reform.
Blumenauer	Ways and Means.
Bonamici	Education and the Workforce. Science, Space, and Technology.
Bordallo	Armed Services. Natural Resources.
Bost	Agriculture. Transportation and Infrastructure. Veterans' Affairs.
Boustany	Ways and Means.
Boyle, Brendan F., of Pennsylvania	Foreign Affairs. Oversight and Government Reform.
Brady, Kevin, of Texas	Ways and Means, *chair.* Joint Committee on Taxation.
Brady, Robert A., of Pennsylvania	Armed Services. House Administration. Joint Committee on the Library. Joint Committee on Printing.
Brat	Budget. Education and the Workforce. Small Business.
Bridenstine	Armed Services. Science, Space, and Technology.
Brooks, Mo, of Alabama	Armed Services. Foreign Affairs. Science, Space, and Technology.
Brooks, Susan W., of Indiana	Energy and Commerce. Ethics. Select Committee on the Events Surrounding the 2012 Terrorist Attack in Benghazi.
Brown, Corrine, of Florida	Transportation and Infrastructure. Veterans' Affairs.
Brownley, Julia, of California	Transportation and Infrastructure. Veterans' Affairs.
Buchanan	Budget. Ways and Means.
Buck	Judiciary. Oversight and Government Reform.
Bucshon	Energy and Commerce.
Burgess	Energy and Commerce. Rules.

Representative	Committees (Standing, Joint, and Select)
Bustos	Agriculture. Transportation and Infrastructure.
Butterfield	Energy and Commerce.
Byrne	Armed Services. Education and the Workforce. Rules.
Calvert	Appropriations.
Capps	Energy and Commerce. Natural Resources.
Capuano	Ethics. Financial Services. Transportation and Infrastructure.
Cárdenas	Energy and Commerce.
Carney	Financial Services.
Carson, *André*, of Indiana	Transportation and Infrastructure. Permanent Select Committee on Intelligence.
Carter, Earl L. "Buddy", of Georgia	Education and the Workforce. Homeland Security. Oversight and Government Reform.
Carter, John R., of Texas	Appropriations.
Cartwright	Natural Resources. Oversight and Government Reform.
Castor, Kathy, of Florida	Budget. Energy and Commerce.
Castro, Joaquin, of Texas	Armed Services. Foreign Affairs.
Chabot	Small Business, *chair*. Foreign Affairs. Judiciary.
Chaffetz	Oversight and Government Reform, *chair*. Judiciary.
Chu, Judy, of California	Judiciary. Small Business.
Cicilline	Foreign Affairs. Judiciary.
Clark, Katherine M., of Massachusetts	Education and the Workforce. Science, Space, and Technology.
Clarke, Yvette D., of New York	Energy and Commerce. Ethics. Small Business.
Clawson, Curt, of Florida	Foreign Affairs. Homeland Security.
Clay	Financial Services. Natural Resources. Oversight and Government Reform.
Cleaver	Financial Services.
Clyburn	Assistant Democratic Leader.
Coffman	Armed Services. Veterans' Affairs.

Representative	Committees (Standing, Joint, and Select)
Cohen	Judiciary.
	Transportation and Infrastructure.
Cole	Appropriations.
	Budget.
	Rules.
Collins, Chris, of New York	Energy and Commerce.
Collins, Doug, of Georgia	Judiciary.
	Rules.
Comstock	House Administration.
	Science, Space, and Technology.
	Transportation and Infrastructure.
Conaway	Agriculture, *chair*.
	Armed Services.
	Permanent Select Committee on Intelligence.
Connolly	Foreign Affairs.
	Oversight and Government Reform.
Conyers	Judiciary.
Cook	Armed Services.
	Foreign Affairs.
	Natural Resources.
Cooper	Armed Services.
	Oversight and Government Reform.
Costa	Agriculture.
	Natural Resources.
Costello, Ryan A., of Pennsylvania	Transportation and Infrastructure.
	Veterans' Affairs.
Courtney	Armed Services.
	Education and the Workforce.
Cramer	Energy and Commerce.
Crawford	Agriculture.
	Transportation and Infrastructure.
Crenshaw	Appropriations.
Crowley	Ways and Means.
Cuellar	Appropriations.
Culberson	Appropriations.
Cummings	Oversight and Government Reform.
	Transportation and Infrastructure.
	Select Committee on the Events Surrounding the 2012 Terrorist Attack in Benghazi.
Curbelo, Carlos, of Florida	Education and the Workforce.
	Small Business.
	Transportation and Infrastructure.
Davis, Danny K., of Illinois	Ways and Means.
Davis, Rodney, of Illinois	Agriculture.
	House Administration.
	Transportation and Infrastructure.
	Joint Committee on Printing.
Davis, Susan A., of California	Armed Services.
	Education and the Workforce.
DeFazio	Transportation and Infrastructure.
DeGette	Energy and Commerce.

Representative	Committees (Standing, Joint, and Select)
Delaney	Financial Services. Joint Economic Committee.
DeLauro	Appropriations.
DelBene	Agriculture. Judiciary.
Denham	Agriculture. Natural Resources. Transportation and Infrastructure.
Dent	Ethics, *chair*. Appropriations.
DeSantis	Foreign Affairs. Judiciary. Oversight and Government Reform.
DeSaulnier	Education and the Workforce. Oversight and Government Reform.
DesJarlais	Agriculture. Foreign Affairs. Oversight and Government Reform.
Deutch	Ethics. Foreign Affairs. Judiciary.
Diaz-Balart	Appropriations. Budget.
Dingell	Budget. Natural Resources.
Doggett	Ways and Means.
Dold	Ways and Means.
Donovan	Foreign Affairs. Homeland Security.
Doyle, Michael F., of Pennsylvania	Energy and Commerce.
Duckworth	Armed Services. Oversight and Government Reform. Select Committee on the Events Surrounding the 2012 Terrorist Attack in Benghazi.
Duffy	Financial Services.
Duncan, Jeff, of South Carolina ...	Foreign Affairs. Homeland Security. Natural Resources.
Duncan, John J., Jr., of Tennessee	Oversight and Government Reform. Transportation and Infrastructure.
Edwards	Science, Space, and Technology. Transportation and Infrastructure.
Ellison	Financial Services.
Ellmers, Renee L., of North Carolina.	Energy and Commerce.
Emmer, Tom, of Minnesota	Financial Services.
Engel	Energy and Commerce. Foreign Affairs.
Eshoo	Energy and Commerce.
Esty	Science, Space, and Technology. Transportation and Infrastructure.

Representative	Committees (Standing, Joint, and Select)
Farenthold	Judiciary. Oversight and Government Reform. Transportation and Infrastructure.
Farr	Appropriations.
Fattah	Appropriations.
Fincher	Financial Services.
Fitzpatrick	Financial Services.
Fleischmann	Appropriations.
Fleming	Armed Services. Natural Resources.
Flores	Energy and Commerce.
Forbes	Armed Services. Judiciary.
Fortenberry	Appropriations.
Foster	Financial Services. Science, Space, and Technology.
Foxx	Education and the Workforce. Rules.
Frankel, Lois, of Florida	Foreign Affairs. Transportation and Infrastructure.
Franks, Trent, of Arizona	Armed Services. Judiciary.
Frelinghuysen	Appropriations.
Fudge	Agriculture. Education and the Workforce.
Gabbard	Armed Services. Foreign Affairs.
Gallego	Armed Services. Natural Resources.
Garamendi	Armed Services. Transportation and Infrastructure.
Garrett	Budget. Financial Services.
Gibbs	Agriculture. Transportation and Infrastructure.
Gibson	Agriculture. Armed Services. Small Business.
Gohmert	Judiciary. Natural Resources.
Goodlatte	Judiciary, *chair.* Agriculture.
Gosar	Natural Resources. Oversight and Government Reform.
Gowdy	Select Committee on the Events Surrounding the 2012 Terrorist Attack in Benghazi, *chair.* Ethics. Judiciary. Oversight and Government Reform.

Representative	Committees (Standing, Joint, and Select)
Graham	Agriculture. Armed Services.
Granger	Appropriations.
Graves, Garret, of Louisiana	Natural Resources. Transportation and Infrastructure.
Graves, Sam, of Missouri	Armed Services. Transportation and Infrastructure.
Graves, Tom, of Georgia	Appropriations. Joint Committee on the Library.
Grayson	Foreign Affairs. Science, Space, and Technology.
Green, Al, of Texas	Financial Services.
Green, Gene, of Texas	Energy and Commerce.
Griffith	Energy and Commerce.
Grijalva	Education and the Workforce. Natural Resources.
Grothman	Budget. Education and the Workforce. Oversight and Government Reform. Joint Economic Committee.
Guinta	Financial Services.
Guthrie	Education and the Workforce. Energy and Commerce.
Gutiérrez	Judiciary. Permanent Select Committee on Intelligence.
Hahn	Small Business. Transportation and Infrastructure.
Hanna	Small Business. Transportation and Infrastructure. Joint Economic Committee.
Hardy	Natural Resources. Small Business. Transportation and Infrastructure.
Harper	Joint Committee on Printing, *chair.* Joint Committee on the Library, *vice chair.* Energy and Commerce. House Administration.
Harris	Appropriations.
Hartzler	Agriculture. Armed Services. Budget.
Hastings	Rules.
Heck, Denny, of Washington	Financial Services.
Heck, Joseph J., of Nevada	Armed Services. Education and the Workforce. Permanent Select Committee on Intelligence.
Hensarling	Financial Services, *chair.*
Herrera Beutler	Appropriations.
Hice, Jody B., of Georgia	Natural Resources. Oversight and Government Reform.
Higgins	Foreign Affairs.

Representative	Committees (Standing, Joint, and Select)
	Homeland Security.
Hill	Financial Services.
Himes	Financial Services. Permanent Select Committee on Intelligence.
Hinojosa	Education and the Workforce. Financial Services.
Holding	Ways and Means.
Honda	Appropriations.
Hoyer	Democratic Whip.
Hudson	Energy and Commerce.
Huelskamp	Small Business. Veterans' Affairs.
Huffman	Natural Resources. Transportation and Infrastructure.
Huizenga, Bill, of Michigan	Financial Services.
Hultgren	Financial Services. Science, Space, and Technology.
Hunter	Armed Services. Education and the Workforce. Transportation and Infrastructure.
Hurd, Will, of Texas	Homeland Security. Oversight and Government Reform.
Hurt, Robert, of Virginia	Financial Services.
Israel	Appropriations.
Issa	Foreign Affairs. Judiciary.
Jackson Lee	Homeland Security. Judiciary.
Jeffries	Education and the Workforce. Judiciary.
Jenkins, Evan H., of West Virginia.	Appropriations.
Jenkins, Lynn, of Kansas	Ways and Means.
Johnson, Bill, of Ohio	Energy and Commerce. Science, Space, and Technology.
Johnson, Eddie Bernice, of Texas	Science, Space, and Technology. Transportation and Infrastructure.
Johnson, Henry C. "Hank", Jr., of Georgia	Armed Services. Judiciary.
Johnson, Sam, of Texas	Ways and Means. Joint Committee on Taxation.
Jolly	Apropriations.
Jones	Armed Services.
Jordan	Judiciary. Oversight and Government Reform.

Representative	Committees (Standing, Joint, and Select)
	Select Committee on the Events Surrounding the 2012 Terrorist Attack in Benghazi.
Joyce	Appropriations.
Kaptur	Appropriations.
Katko	Homeland Security. Transportation and Infrastructure.
Keating	Foreign Affairs. Homeland Security.
Kelly, Mike, of Pennsylvania	Ways and Means.
Kelly, Robin L., of Illinois	Foreign Affairs. Oversight and Government Reform.
Kelly, Trent, of Mississippi	Agriculture. Small Business.
Kennedy	Energy and Commerce.
Kildee	Financial Services.
Kilmer	Appropriations.
Kind	Ways and Means.
King, Peter T., of New York	Financial Services. Homeland Security. Permanent Select Committee on Intelligence.
King, Steve, of Iowa	Agriculture. Judiciary. Small Business.
Kinzinger, Adam, of Illinois	Energy and Commerce.
Kirkpatrick	Agriculture. Transportation and Infrastructure.
Kline	Education and the Workforce, *chair*. Armed Services.
Knight	Armed Services. Science, Space, and Technology. Small Business.
Kuster	Agriculture. Veterans' Affairs.
Labrador	Judiciary. Natural Resources.
LaHood	Natural Resources. Science, Space, and Technology.
LaMalfa	Agriculture. Natural Resources.
Lamborn	Armed Services. Natural Resources. Veterans' Affairs.
Lance	Energy and Commerce.
Langevin	Armed Services. Homeland Security.
Larsen, Rick, of Washington	Armed Services. Transportation and Infrastructure.
Larson, John B., of Connecticut ...	Ethics. Ways and Means.
Latta	Energy and Commerce.

Representative	Committees (Standing, Joint, and Select)
Lawrence	Oversight and Government Reform. Small Business.
Lee	Appropriations. Budget.
Levin	Ways and Means. Joint Committee on Taxation.
Lewis	Ways and Means.
Lieu, Ted, of California	Budget. Oversight and Government Reform.
Lipinski	Science, Space, and Technology. Transportation and Infrastructure.
LoBiondo	Armed Services. Transportation and Infrastructure. Permanent Select Committee on Intelligence.
Loebsack	Energy and Commerce.
Lofgren	House Administration. Judiciary. Science, Space, and Technology. Joint Committee on the Library.
Long	Energy and Commerce.
Loudermilk	Homeland Security. Science, Space, and Technology.
Love	Financial Services.
Lowenthal	Foreign Affairs. Natural Resources.
Lowey	Appropriations.
Lucas	Agriculture. Financial Services. Science, Space, and Technology.
Luetkemeyer	Financial Services. Small Business.
Luján, Ben Ray, of New Mexico ..	Energy and Commerce.
Lujan Grisham, Michelle, of New Mexico	Agriculture. Budget. Oversight and Government Reform.
Lummis	Natural Resources. Oversight and Government Reform.
Lynch	Financial Services. Oversight and Government Reform.
MacArthur	Armed Services. Natural Resources.
Maloney, Carolyn B., of New York	Financial Services. Oversight and Government Reform. Joint Economic Committee.
Maloney, Sean Patrick, of New York	Agriculture. Transportation and Infrastructure.
Marchant	Ehtics. Ways and Means.
Marino	Foreign Affairs. Homeland Security.

Representative	Committees (Standing, Joint, and Select)
	Judiciary.
Massie	Oversight and Government Reform. Science, Space, and Technology. Transportation and Infrastructure.
Matsui	Energy and Commerce.
McCarthy	Majority Leader.
McCaul	Homeland Security, *chair*. Foreign Affairs. Science, Space, and Technology.
McClintock	Budget. Natural Resources.
McCollum	Appropriations.
McDermott	Budget. Ways and Means.
McGovern	Agriculture. Rules.
McHenry	Financial Services.
McKinley	Energy and Commerce.
McMorris Rodgers	Energy and Commerce.
McNerney	Energy and Commerce. Veterans' Affairs.
McSally	Armed Services. Homeland Security.
Mcadows	Foreign Affairs. Oversight and Government Reform. Transportation and Infrastructure.
Meehan	Ethics. Ways and Means.
Meeks	Financial Services. Foreign Affairs.
Meng	Foreign Affairs. Small Business.
Messer	Education and the Workforce. Financial Services.
Mica	Oversight and Government Reform. Transportation and Infrastructure.
Miller, Candice S., of Michigan ...	House Administration, *chair*. Homeland Security. Transportation and Infrastructure. Joint Committee on the Library. Joint Committee on Printing.
Miller, Jeff, of Florida	Veterans' Affairs, *chair*. Armed Services. Permanent Select Committee on Intelligence.
Moolenaar	Agriculture. Budget. Science, Space, and Technology.
Mooney, Alexander X., of West Virginia	Budget. Natural Resources.

Representative	Committees (Standing, Joint, and Select)
Moore	Budget. Financial Services.
Moulton	Armed Services. Budget. Small Business.
Mullin	Energy and Commerce.
Mulvaney	Financial Services. Oversight and Government Reform.
Murphy, Patrick, of Florida	Financial Services. Permanent Select Committee on Intelligence.
Murphy, Tim, of Pennsylvania	Energy and Commerce.
Nadler	Judiciary. Transportation and Infrastructure.
Napolitano	Natural Resources. Transportation and Infrastructure.
Neal	Ways and Means.
Neugebauer	Agriculture. Financial Services. Science, Space, and Technology.
Newhouse	Agriculture. Natural Resources. Rules.
Noem	Ways and Means.
Nolan	Agriculture. Transportation and Infrastructure.
Norcross	Armed Services. Budget.
Norton	Oversight and Government Reform. Transportation and Infrastructure.
Nugent	Armed Services. House Administration.
Nunes	Permanent Select Committee on Intelligence, *chair*. Ways and Means.
Olson	Energy and Commerce.
O'Rourke	Armed Services. Veterans' Affairs.
Palazzo	Appropriations.
Pallone	Energy and Commerce.
Palmer	Budget. Oversight and Government Reform. Science, Space, and Technology.
Pascrell	Budget. Ways and Means.
Paulsen	Ways and Means. Joint Economic Committee.
Payne	Homeland Security. Small Business.
Pearce	Financial Services.
Pelosi	Democratic Leader.
Perlmutter	Financial Services.

Representative	Committees (Standing, Joint, and Select)
	Science, Space, and Technology.
Perry	Foreign Affairs. Homeland Security. Transportation and Infrastructure.
Peters	Armed Services. Judiciary.
Peterson	Agriculture.
Pierluisi	Judiciary. Natural Resources.
Pingree	Appropriations.
Pittenger	Financial Services.
Pitts	Energy and Commerce.
Plaskett	Agriculture. Oversight and Government Reform.
Pocan	Budget. Education and the Workforce.
Poe, Ted, of Texas	Foreign Affairs. Judiciary.
Poliquin	Financial Services.
Polis	Education and the Workforce. Natural Resources. Rules.
Pompeo	Energy and Commerce. Permanent Select Committee on Intelligence. Select Committee on the Events Surrounding the 2012 Terrorist Attack in Benghazi.
Posey	Financial Services. Science, Space, and Technology.
Price, David E., of North Carolina	Appropriations.
Price, Tom, of Georgia	Budget. Ways and Means.
Quigley	Appropriations. Permanent Select Committee on Intelligence.
Radewagen	Natural Resources. Small Business. Veterans' Affairs.
Rangel	Ways and Means. Joint Committee on Taxation.
Ratcliffe	Homeland Security. Judiciary.
Reed	Ways and Means.
Reichert	Ways and Means.
Renacci	Ways and Means. Budget.
Ribble	Foreign Affairs. Transportation and Infrastructure.
Rice, Kathleen M., of New York ..	Homeland Security. Veterans' Affairs.
Rice, Tom, of South Carolina	Ways and Means.

Representative	Committees (Standing, Joint, and Select)
Richmond	Homeland Security. Judiciary.
Rigell	Appropriations.
Roby	Appropriations. Select Committee on the Events Surrounding the 2012 Terrorist Attack in Benghazi.
Roe, David P., of Tennessee	Education and the Workforce. Veterans' Affairs.
Rogers, Harold, of Kentucky	Appropriations, *chair*.
Rogers, Mike, of Alabama	Agriculture. Armed Services. Homeland Security.
Rohrabacher	Foreign Affairs. Science, Space, and Technology.
Rokita	Budget. Education and the Workforce. Transportation and Infrastructure.
Rooney, Thomas J., of Florida	Appropriations. Permanent Select Committee on Intelligence.
Roskam	Ways and Means. Select Committee on the Events Surrounding the 2012 Terrorist Attack in Benghazi.
Ros-Lehtinen	Foreign Affairs. Permanent Select Committee on Intelligence.
Ross	Financial Services.
Rothfus	Financial Services.
Rouzer	Agriculture. Transportation and Infrastructure.
Roybal-Allard	Appropriations.
Royce	Foreign Affairs, *chair*. Financial Services.
Ruiz	Natural Resources. Veterans' Affairs.
Ruppersberger	Appropriations.
Rush	Energy and Commerce.
Russell	Armed Services. Education and the Workforce. Oversight and Government Reform.
Ryan, Paul D., of Wisconsin	The Speaker.
Ryan, Tim, of Ohio	Appropriations. Budget.
Sablan	Education and the Workforce. Natural Resources.
Salmon	Education and the Workforce. Foreign Affairs.
Sánchez, Linda T., of California	Ethics. Ways and Means. Select Committee on the Events Surrounding the 2012 Terrorist Attack in Benghazi.

Representative	Committees (Standing, Joint, and Select)
Sanchez, Loretta, of California	Armed Services. Homeland Security.
Sanford	Budget. Transportation and Infrastructure.
Sarbanes	Energy and Commerce.
Scalise	Majority Whip. Energy and Commerce.
Schakowsky	Energy and Commerce.
Schiff	Permanent Select Committee on Intelligence. Select Committee on the Events Surrounding the 2012 Terrorist Attack in Benghazi.
Schrader	Energy and Commerce.
Schweikert	Financial Services. Joint Economic Committee.
Scott, Austin, of Georgia	Agriculture. Armed Services.
Scott, David, of Georgia	Agriculture. Financial Services.
Scott, Robert C. "Bobby", of Virginia	Education and the Workforce.
Sensenbrenner	Judiciary. Science, Space, and Technology.
Serrano	Appropriations.
Sessions	Rules, chair.
Sewell, Terri A., of Alabama	Financial Services. Permanent Select Committee on Intelligence.
Sherman	Financial Services. Foreign Affairs.
Shimkus	Energy and Commerce.
Shuster	Transportation and Infrastructure, chair. Armed Services.
Simpson	Appropriations.
Sinema	Financial Services.
Sires	Foreign Affairs. Transportation and Infrastructure.
Slaughter	Rules.
Smith, Adam, of Washington	Armed Services. Select Committee on the Events Surrounding the 2012 Terrorist Attack in Benghazi.
Smith, Adrian, of Nebraska	Ways and Means.
Smith, Christopher H., of New Jersey	Foreign Affairs.
Smith, Jason, of Missouri	Ways and Means.
Smith, Lamar, of Texas	Science, Space, and Technology, chair. Homeland Security. Judiciary.
Speier	Armed Services.

Representative	Committees (Standing, Joint, and Select)
	Permanent Select Committee on Intelligence.
Stefanik	Armed Services. Education and the Workforce.
Stewart	Appropriations. Permanent Select Committee on Intelligence.
Stivers	Financial Services. Rules.
Stutzman	Budget. Financial Services.
Swalwell, Eric, of California	Science, Space, and Technology. Permanent Select Committee on Intelligence.
Takai	Armed Services. Small Business.
Takano	Education and the Workforce. Science, Space, and Technology. Veterans' Affairs.
Thompson, Bennie G., of Mississippi	Homeland Security.
Thompson, Glenn, of Pennsylvania	Agriculture. Education and the Workforce. Natural Resources.
Thompson, Mike, of California	Ways and Means.
Thornberry	Armed Services, *chair.*
Tiberi	Joint Economic Committee, *vice chair.* Ways and Means.
Tipton	Financial Services.
Titus	Transportation and Infrastructure. Veterans' Affairs.
Tonko	Energy and Commerce. Science, Space, and Technology.
Torres	Homeland Security. Natural Resources.
Trott	Foreign Affairs. Judiciary.
Tsongas	Armed Services. Natural Resources.
Turner	Armed Services. Oversight and Government Reform. Permanent Select Committee on Intelligence.
Upton	Energy and Commerce, *chair.*
Valadao	Appropriations.
Van Hollen	Budget.
Vargas	Financial Services. House Administration. Joint Committee on Printing.
Veasey	Armed Services. Science, Space, and Technology.
Vela	Agriculture. Homeland Security.

Representative	Committees (Standing, Joint, and Select)
Velázquez	Financial Services. Small Business.
Visclosky	Appropriations.
Wagner	Financial Services.
Walberg	Education and the Workforce. Oversight and Government Reform.
Walden	Energy and Commerce.
Walker	Homeland Security. House Administration. Oversight and Government Reform.
Walorski	Agriculture. Armed Services. Veterans' Affairs.
Walters, Mimi, of California	Judiciary. Transportation and Infrastructure.
Walz	Agriculture. Armed Services. Veterans' Affairs.
Wasserman Schultz	Appropriations.
Waters, Maxine, of California	Financial Services.
Watson Coleman	Homeland Security. Oversight and Government Reform.
Weber, Randy K., Sr., of Texas ...	Foreign Affairs. Science, Space, and Technology.
Webster, Daniel, of Florida	Transportation and Infrastructure.
Welch	Energy and Commerce. Oversight and Government Reform.
Wenstrup	Armed Services. Veterans' Affairs. Permanent Select Committee on Intelligence.
Westerman	Budget. Natural Resources. Science, Space, and Technology.
Westmoreland	Financial Services. Permanent Select Committee on Intelligence. Select Committee on the Events Surrounding the 2012 Terrorist Attack in Benghazi.
Whitfield	Energy and Commerce.
Williams	Financial Services.
Wilson, Frederica S., of Florida ...	Education and the Workforce.
Wilson, Joe, of South Carolina	Armed Services. Education and the Workforce. Foreign Affairs.
Wittman	Armed Services. Natural Resources.
Womack	Appropriations. Budget.
Woodall	Budget. Rules. Transportation and Infrastructure.

Representative	Committees (Standing, Joint, and Select)
Yarmuth	Budget. Energy and Commerce.
Yoder	Appropriations.
Yoho	Agriculture. Foreign Affairs.
Young, David, of Iowa	Appropriations.
Young, Don, of Alaska	Natural Resources. Transportation and Infrastructure.
Young, Todd C., of Indiana	Ways and Means.
Zeldin	Foreign Affairs. Transportation and Infrastructure. Veterans' Affairs.
Zinke	Armed Services. Natural Resources.

CONGRESSIONAL ADVISORY BOARDS, COMMISSIONS, AND GROUPS

UNITED STATES AIR FORCE ACADEMY BOARD OF VISITORS
[Title 10, U.S.C., Section 9355(a)]

Board Member	Year Appointed
Appointed by the President:	
Arlen Jameson (Vice Chair)	2010
Marcelite Harris	2010
Thomas L. McKiernan	2011
Fletcher Wiley	2011
Sue Hoppin	2013
Dr. Paula Thronhill	2013
Appointed by the Vice President or the Senate President Pro Tempore:	
Senator Lindsey Graham, of South Carolina	2011
Senator John Hoeven, of North Dakota	2011
Appointed by the Speaker of the House of Representatives:	
Alfredo Sandoval (Chair)	2010
Representative Doug Lamborn, of Colorado	2007
Representative *Jared Polis*, of Colorado	2009
Appointed by the Chairman, Senate Armed Services Committee:	
Senator *Michael F. Bennet*, of Colorado	2011
Appointed by the Chairman, House Armed Services Committee:	
Representative *Niki Tsongas*, of Massachusetts	2008

UNITED STATES MILITARY ACADEMY BOARD OF VISITORS
[Title 10, U.S.C., Section 4355(a)]

Members of Congress

Senate

Richard Burr, of North Carolina.
Joni Ernst, of Iowa.

Kirsten E. Gillibrand, of New York.
Christopher Murphy of Connecticut.

House

K. Michael Conaway, Representative of Texas.
Steve Womack, Representative of Arkansas, Vice Chair.
Mike Pompeo, Representative of Kansas.

Steve Israel, Representative of New York.
Loretta Sanchez, Representative of California.

Presidential Appointees:

Hon. Bob Archuleta, of California.
Brenda Sue Fulton, of New Jersey, Chair.
Elizabeth McNally, of New York.

Patrick Murphy, of Pennsylvania.
Ethan Epstein, of New Mexico.
Hon. Gerald McGowan, of Wasington, DC.

UNITED STATES NAVAL ACADEMY BOARD OF VISITORS
[Title 10, U.S.C., Section 6968(a)]

Appointed by the President:

(Vice Chairman) ADM John Nathman, USN (Ret.) Former Commander, U.S. Fleet Forces.
VADM Michelle Howard, USN, Vice Chief of Naval Operations.
RADM Veronica Froman, USN (Ret.) CEO and chair of REBOOT, Chairman of Monarch School BoD.
Judge Evan Wallach, U.S. Court of Appeals.
Robert Stein, President of The Regency Group, King Distribution and St. John's Utilitites, Kerrco Inc. board member.

Appointed by the Vice President:

Senator Mark Kirk, of Illinois.
Senator *Jeanne Shaheen,* of New Hampshire.
Senator *Benjamin L. Cardin,* of Maryland.

Designees of the Chairmen, SASC/HASC:

Senator Dan Sullivan, of Alaska.
(Chairman) Representative Robert J. Wittman, of Virginia.

Appointed by the Speaker of the House:

Representative Thomas J. Rooney, of Florida.
Representative Todd C. Young, of Indiana.
Representative *Elijah E. Cummings,* of Maryland.
Representative *C. A. Dutch Ruppersberger,* of Maryland.

UNITED STATES COAST GUARD ACADEMY BOARD OF VISITORS *
[Title 14 U.S.C., Section 194(a)]

Roger F. Wicker, of Mississippi.
Dan Sullivan, of Alaska.
Bill Shuster, of Pennsylvania.
Adrian Smith, of Nebraska.

Richard Blumenthal, of Connecticut.
Maria Cantwell, of Washington.

BRITISH-AMERICAN PARLIAMENTARY GROUP
Senate Hart Building, Room 808, phone 224–3047
[Created by Public Law 98–164]

Senate Delegation:
Chair.—Thad Cochran, Senator from Mississippi.
Vice Chair.—*Patrick J. Leahy,* Senator from Vermont.

CANADA-UNITED STATES INTERPARLIAMENTARY GROUP
Senate Hart Building, Room 808, 224–3047
[Created by Public Law 86–42, 22 U.S.C., 1928a–1928d, 276d–276g]

Senate Delegation:
Chair.—Mike Crapo, Senator from Idaho.
Vice Chair.—*Amy Klobuchar,* Senator from Minnesota.

---

* This list is incomplete; three Congressional seats remain vacant at time of press.

House Delegation:
  Chair.—Bill Huizenga, Representative of Michigan.
  Vice Chair.—Candice S. Miller, Representative of Michigan.

CHINA-UNITED STATES INTERPARLIAMENTARY GROUP
Senate Hart Building, Room 808, phone 224–3047
[Created by Public Law 108–199, Section 153]

Senate Delegation:
  Chair.—Vacant.
  Vice Chair.—Vacant.

KOREA-UNITED STATES INTERPARLIAMENTARY GROUP

House Delegation:
  Chair.—Edward R. Royce, Representative of California.

MEXICO-UNITED STATES INTERPARLIAMENTARY GROUP
Senate Hart Building, Room 808, phone 224–3047
[Created by Public Law 82–420, 22 U.S.C. 276h–276k]

Senate Delegation:
  Chair.—Vacant.
  Vice Chair.—*Tim Kaine,* Senator from Virginia.
House Delegation:
  Chair.—Michael T. McCaul, Representative of Texas.
  Vice Chair.—Sean P. Duffy, Representative of Wisconsin.

NATO PARLIAMENTARY ASSEMBLY
Headquarters: Place du Petit Sablon 3, B–1000 Brussels, Belgium
[Created by Public Law 84–689, 22 U.S.C., 1928z]

Senate Delegation:
  Chair.—Vacant.
  Vice Chair.—Vacant.
House Delegation:
  Chair.—Michael R. Turner, Representative of Ohio.
  Vice Chair.—Ted Poe, Representative of Texas

STAFF

Secretary, Senate Delegation.—Julia Hart Reed, Interparliamentary Services, SH–808, 224–3047.
Secretary, House Delegation.—Jeff Dressler.

COMMISSION ON CONGRESSIONAL MAILING STANDARDS
1216 Longworth House Office Building, phone 226–0647
[Created by Public Law 93–191]

Chairman.—Candice S. Miller, of Michigan.
  Robert E. Latta, of Ohio.
  Rodney Davis, of Illinois.
  Susan A. Davis, of California.
  Brad Sherman, of California.
  Cedric L. Richmond, of Louisiana.

STAFF

Majority Staff Director.—Richard Cappetto, 226–0647.
  Professional Staff: George Hadijski, Ryan Kelly, Max Engling.
  Staff Assistant.—Amanda Anger.
  Counsel.—Bob Sensenbrenner.
Minority Professional Staff: Matthew DeFreitas, Tommy Sandstrom, Kimberly Stevens, Aislan Sims, 225–9337.
  Minority Counsel.—Michael Harrison.

COMMISSION ON SECURITY AND COOPERATION IN EUROPE
234 Ford House Office Building, phone 225–1901, fax 226–4199
http://www.csce.gov

Christopher H. Smith, Representative of New Jersey, *Chair*
Roger F. Wicker, Senator from Mississippi, *Co-Chair*

LEGISLATIVE BRANCH COMMISSIONERS

House

Robert B. Aderholt, of Alabama.
Michael C. Burgess, of Texas.
Randy Hultgren, of Illinois.
Joseph R. Pitts, of Pennsylvania.

Alcee L. Hastings, of Florida.
Steve Cohen, of Tennessee.
Alan Grayson, of Florida.
Louise McIntosh Slaughter, of New York.

Senate

John Boozman, of Arkansas.
Richard Burr, of North Carolina.

Benjamin L. Cardin, of Maryland.
Jeanne Shaheen, of New Hampshire.
Tom Udall, of New Mexico.
Sheldon Whitehouse, of Rhode Island.

EXECUTIVE BRANCH COMMISSIONERS

Department of State.—Vacant.
Department of Commerce.—Vacant.
Department of Defense.—Vacant.

COMMISSION STAFF

Chief of Staff.—Mark S. Milosch.
  Senior Staff Representative.—Ambassador David T. Killion.
  Senior State Departmnet Advisor.—David J. Kostelancik.
  Policy Advisors: Orest Deychakiwsky, Shelly Han, Robert Hand, Janice Helwig, Alex T. Johnson, Mischa E. Thompson.
  Counsel.—Allison B. Hollabaugh.
  Director of Administration.—Daniel R. Redfield.
  Counsel for International Law.—Erika B. Schlager.
  Staff Associate.—A. Paul Massaro III.

CONGRESSIONAL AWARD FOUNDATION
379 Ford House Office Building, phone (202) 226–0130, fax 226–0131
[Created by Public Law 96–114]

Chair.—Paxton K. Baker, Washington Nationals Baseball.

Vice Chairs:
  Linda Mitchell, Mississippi State University Extension Service.
  Hon. Rodney E. Slater, Squire Patton Boggs, LLP.
Secretary.—Cheryl Maddox, Humana, Inc.
Treasurer.—Lee Klumpp, BDO.

Members:

  Cliff Akiyama, Philadelphia College of Osteopathic Medicine.
  Simeon Banister, Greater Rochester Martin Luther King Jr. Commission.
  Ed Blansitt, Montgomery County Inspector General Office.
  Romero Brown, Boys and Girls Clubs of America.
  Laurel Call, Texas.
  Nick Cannon, New York.
  Dan Cohen, Enteromedics, Inc.
  Edward Cohen, Lerner Enterprises.
  Kathy Didawick, BlueCross BlueShield Association.
  Dr. Wiley Dobbs, Idaho.
  Mitch Draizin, Longview Capital Advisors, Inc.
  David Falk, FAME.
  George B. Gould, Washington, DC.
  Dr. Lawrence Green, Maryland.
  J. Steven Hart, Esq., Williams and Jensen, P.C.
  Erica Wheelan Heyse, National Director.
  Jesse Hill, Edward Jones.
  Hon. Richard Hudson, United States House of Representatives.
  David W. Hunt, Esq., Nexant.
  Hon. Johnny Isakson, United States Senate.
  Hon. Sheila Jackson Lee, United States House of Representatives.
  Paul Kelly, The Federal Group, Inc.
  Boris Kodjoe, California.
  Lynn Lyons, Florida.
  Raul Magdaleno, Magdaleno Consulting Group.
  Hon. Joe Manchin III, United States Senate.
  Lance Mangum, FedEx Corporation.
  Patrick McLain, Sanofi, U.S.
  Marc Monyek, Illinois.
  Kim Norman, G2 Secure Staff, LLC.
  Mark Reese, Johnson & Johnson.
  Adam Ruiz, Kentucky.
  Beth Ann Ruoff, Ogilvy Public Relations.
  DeMaurice Smith, NFL Players Association.
  Jason Van Pelt, Novartis.
  Rita Vaswani, Nevada State Bank.
  Kathryn Weeden, United States Senate Page School.
  Shawn Whitman, FMC Corporation.
  Jon Wood, Jon Wood & Associates, LLC.
  Charmaine Yoest, Americans United for Life.

CONGRESSIONAL CLUB

2001 New Hampshire Avenue, NW., 20009, phone (202) 332–1155, fax 797–0698

Executive Board
President.—Vera G. Davis.
  Vice Presidents:
    (1st) Jennifer Messer.
    (2d) Helen Green.
    (3d) Judy Benishek.
    (4th) Patricia Garamendi.
    (5th) Billie Gingrey.
    (6th) April McClain Delaney.
  Treasurer.—Martha Brooks.
  Recording Secretary.—Sonya Horsford.
  Corresponding Secretary.—Simone Marie Meeks.
  Executive Director.—Lydia de La Vina de Foley.

CONGRESSIONAL EXECUTIVE COMMISSION ON CHINA

243 Ford House Office Building, phone 226–3766, fax 226–3804

[Created by Public Law 106–286]

Christopher H. Smith, Representative of New Jersey, *Chair.*

Marco Rubio, Senator from Florida, *Co-Chair.*

LEGISLATIVE BRANCH COMMISSIONERS

House

Robert Pittenger, Representative of North Carolina.
Trent Franks, Representative of Arizona.
Randy Hultgren, Representative of Illinois.

Timothy J. Walz, Representative of Minnesota.
Marcy Kaptur, Representative of Ohio.
Michael M. Honda, Representative of California.
Ted Lieu, Representative of California.

Senate

James Lankford, of Oklahoma.
Tom Cotton, of Arkansas.
Steve Daines, of Montana.
Ben Sasse, of Nebraska.

Sherrod Brown, of Ohio.
Dianne Feinstein, of California.
Jeff Merkley, of Oregon.
Gary C. Peters, of Michigan

EXECUTIVE BRANCH COMMISSIONERS

Christopher P. Lu, U.S. Department of Labor.
Sarah Sewall, U.S. Department of State.
Stefan M. Selig, U.S. Department of Commerce.
Daniel R. Russel, U.S. Department of State.
Tom Malinowski, U.S. Department of State.

COMMISSION STAFF

Staff Director.—Paul B. Protic.
　Deputy Staff Director.—Elyse Anderson.
　Director of Administration, Budget and Contracts.—Judy Wright.
　Senior Advisor and Prisoner Database Program Director.—Steve Marshall.
　Senior Advisor.—Anna Brettell.
　Counsel.—Steve Andrews.
　Research Associates: Mingzhi Chen, David Machinist, David Petrick.
　Research Associate and Manager of Annual Report Production.—Jen Salen.
　Printer and Outreach Associate.—Deidre Jackson.
　Director of Communications and Policy.—Scott Flipse.

HOUSE DEMOCRACY PARTNERSHIP

227 Cannon House Office Building, phone 225–4561, fax 225–1166

democracy@mail.house.gov, http://democracy.house.gov

[Created by H. Res. 5, 112th Congress]

Chair.—Peter J. Roskam, of Illinois.
Ranking Member.—David E. Price, of North Carolina.

COMMISSIONERS

Jeff Fortenberry, of Nebraska.
Charles W. Boustany, Jr., of Louisiana.
K. Michael Conaway, of Texas.
Vern Buchanan, of Florida.
Ander Crenshaw, of Florida.
Jackie Walorski, of Indiana.
Susan W. Brooks, of Indiana.
Lee M. Zeldin, of New York.
Diane Black, of Tennessee.
Reid J. Ribble, of Wisconsin.

Sam Farr, of California.
Lois Capps, of California.
Keith Ellison, of Minnesota.
Gwen Moore, of Wisconsin.
Susan A. Davis, of California.
Dina Titus, of Nevada.
Jim McDermott, of Washington.

Legislative Director for Representative (Roskam).—Jeff Billman.
Legislative Director for Representative (Price).—Justin Wein.

HOUSE OFFICE BUILDING COMMISSION

H–232 The Capitol, phone 225–0600

[Title 40, U.S.C. 175–176]

Chair.—Paul D. Ryan, Speaker of the House of Representatives.
Kevin McCarthy, House Majority Leader.
Nancy Pelosi, House Minority Leader.

JAPAN-UNITED STATES FRIENDSHIP COMMISSION

1201 15th Street, NW., Suite 330, phone (202) 653–9800, fax 653–9802

[Created by Public Law 94–118]

Chairman.—Harry A. Hill, President and CEO, Oaklawn Marketing, Inc.
   Vice-Chairman.—Dr. Sheila Smith, Senior Fellow for Japan Studies, Council on Foreign Relations (CFR).
   Executive Director.—Paige Cottingham-Streater.
   Assistant Executive Director—Niharika C. Joe.
   Assistant Executive Director, CULCON.—Pamela L. Fields.
   Executive Assistant.—Sylvia L. Dandridge.
Members:
   Hon. Daniel Russel, Assistant Secretary of State for East Asian and Pacific Affairs, U.S. Department of State.
   Hon. Evan Ryan, Assistant Secretary of State for Educational and Cultural Affairs, U.S. Department of State.
   Dr. Deanna Marcum, Managing Director, Ithaka.
   Dr. Patricia Maclachlan, Associate Professor of Government and Asian Studies, University of Texas.
   Dr. Edward Lincoln, Professorial Lecturer, George Washington University.
   David Sneider, Simpson Thacher & Bartlett, LLP.
   Hon. Jane Chu, Chairman, National Endowment for the Arts.
   William "Bro" Adams, Chairman, National Endowment for the Humanities.
   Hon. Jim McDermott, U.S. House of Representatives.
   Dr. Anne Nishimura Morse, Curator of Japanese Art, Museum of Fine Arts, Boston.
   Hon. Lisa Murkowski, U.S. Senate.
   Hon. Brenda Dann-Messier (acting) Assistant Secretary of Education for Post-Secondary Education, U.S. Department of Education.
   Dr. T.J. Pempel, Professor of Political Science, University of California, Berkeley.
   Vacant, U.S. House of Representatives.
   Dr. Leonard J. Schoppa, Jr., Director, Woodrow Wilson Department of Politics, The University of Virginia.
   Vacant, U.S. Senate.

MIGRATORY BIRD CONSERVATION COMMISSION

5275 Leesburg Pike, Falls Church, 22041

phone (703) 358–1716, fax (703) 358–2234

[Created by act of February 18, 1929, 16 U.S.C. 715a]

Chair.—Sally Jewell, Secretary of the Interior.
Thad Cochran, Senator from Mississippi.
Martin Heinrich, Senator from New Mexico.
Robert J. Wittman, Representative from Virginia.
Mike Thompson, Representative from California.
Tom Vilsack, Secretary of Agriculture.
Gina McCarthy, Administrator of Environmental Protection Agency.
Secretary.—A. Eric Alvarez.

PERMANENT COMMITTEE FOR THE OLIVER WENDELL HOLMES DEVISE FUND

Library of Congress, 20540, phone 707–1082

[Created by act of Congress approved Aug. 5, 1955 (Public Law 246, 84th Congress), to administer Oliver Wendell Holmes Devise Fund, established by same act]

Chairman ex officio.—James H. Billington.
Administrative Officer for the Devise.—James H. Hutson.

UNITED STATES-CHINA ECONOMIC AND SECURITY REVIEW COMMISSION

444 North Capitol Street, NW., Suite 602, phone 624–1407, fax 624–1406

[Created by Public Law 106–398, 114 STAT]

COMMISSIONERS

Chair.—Hon. William A. Reinsch.
Vice Chair.—Hon. Dennis C. Shea.

Members:
Carolyn Bartholomew.
Peter Brookes.
Robin Cleveland.
Jeffrey L. Fiedler.
Hon. Carte P. Goodwin.
Daniel M. Slane.
Hon. James M. Talent.
Hon. Katherine C. Tobin, Ph.D.
Michael R. Wessel.
Larry M. Wortzel, Ph.D.

COMMISSION STAFF

Executive Director.—Michael R. Danis.
Human Resources and Administrative Specialist.—Rickisha C. Berrien-Lopez.
Congressional Liaison and Communications Director.—Anthony DeMarino.
Management Analyst.—Christopher P. Fioravante.
Research Director and Policy Analyst, Economics and Trade.—Katherine Koleski.
Security and Foreign Affairs Analysts: Ethan S. Meick, Matthew O. Southerland.
Economics and Trade Analysts: Lauren Gloudeman, Matthew Snyder.
Senior Policy Analyst, Security and Foreign Affairs.—Kristien T. Bergerson.
Senior Policy Analyst, Economics and Trade.—Kevin Rosier.
Supervisory Senior Policy Analyst, Economics and Trade.—Nargiza Salidjanova.
Supervisory Senior Policy Analyst, Security and Foreign Affairs.—Caitlin Campbell.
Finance and Operations Director.—Kathleen Wilson.

SENATE NATIONAL SECURITY WORKING GROUP
311 Hart Senate Office Building, 20510, phone 228–6425

Administrative Co-Chair.—Marco Rubio, Senator from Florida.
Administrative Co-Chair.—Dianne Feinstein, Senator from California.
  Republican Leader.—Mitch McConnell, Senator from Kentucky.
  Democratic Leader.—Harry Reid, Senator from Nevada.
    Co-Chair.—Jack Reed, Senator from Rhode Island.
    Co-Chair.—Thad Cochran, Senator from Mississippi.
    Co-Chair.—Robert Menendez, Senator from New Jersey.
    Co-Chair.—Barbara A. Mikulski, Senator from Maryland.
    Co-Chair.—Lindsey Graham, Senator from South Carolina.

Members:

James M. Inhofe, Senator from Oklahoma.
Jeff Sessions, Senator from Alabama.
Bob Corker, Senator from Tennessee.
Roy Blunt, Senator from Missouri.
John McCain, Senator from Arizona.
James E. Risch, Senator from Idaho.

Richard J. Durbin, Senator from Illinois.
Robert P. Casey, Jr., Senator from Pennsylvania.
Bill Nelson, Senator from Florida.
Heidi Heitkamp, Senator from North Dakota.
Benjamin L. Cardin, Senator from Maryland.

STAFF

Democratic Staff Director.—Chris Gaspar, 224–3841.
Republican Staff Director.—Jamie Fly, 224–3041.

U.S. ASSOCIATION OF FORMER MEMBERS OF CONGRESS
1401 K Street, NW., Suite 503, 20005
phone (202) 222–0972, fax 222–0977

The nonpartisan United States Association of Former Members of Congress was founded in 1970 as a nonprofit, educational, research and social organization. It has been chartered by the United States Congress and has approximately 600 members who represented American citizens in both the U.S. Senate and the House of Representatives. The Association promotes improved public understanding of the role of Congress as a unique institution as well as the crucial importance of representative democracy as a system of government, both domestically and internationally.

President.—Barbara B. Kennelly, of Connecticut.
  Vice President.—Jim Walsh, of New York.
  Treasurer.—Mary Bono, of California.
  Secretary.—Martin Frost, of Texas.
  Immediate Past President.—Dennis Hertel, of Michigan.
  Honorary Co-Chair.—Constance A. "Connie" Morella, of Maryland.
  Chief Executive Officer.—Peter M. Weichlein.
  Counselors: Jack Buechner, of Missouri; Dan Glickman, of Kansas; Lee H. Hamilton, of Indiana; H. Martin Lancaster, of North Carolina; Matthew F. McHugh, of New York; Connie A. Morella, of Maryland; Richard T. Schulze, of Pennsylvania.

U.S. CAPITOL HISTORICAL SOCIETY
200 Maryland Avenue, NE., 20002, phone (202) 543–8919, fax (202) 544–8244
[Congressional Charter, October 20, 1978, Public Law 95–493, 95th Congress, 92 Stat. 1643]

Chairman of the Board.—Hon. E. Thomas Coleman.
  President.—Hon. Ron Sarasin.
  Treasurer.—L. Neale Cosby.
  Vice President of:
    Membership and Development.—Laura McCulty Stepp.
    Merchandising and Design.—Diana E. Wailes.

BOARD OF TRUSTEES

STAFF

Director of:
  Corporate Giving.—Marilyn Green.
  Finance and Administration.—Peter B. McGuire.
  Historical Programs.—Lauren Borchard.
  Scholarship and Education.—William diGiacomantonio.
Manager of:
  Accounting.—Sheri Williams.
  Development and Outreach.—Victoria Wolfe.
  Operations.—Vince Scott.
  Receiving.—Mike Lawson.
Development and Tour Coordinator.—Samantha Wolfe.
Merchandise Assistant.—Samantha Crawford.
Receptionist, Merchandise Clerk.—Tara Vilaychith.

U.S. CAPITOL PRESERVATION COMMISSION
[Created pursuant to Public Law 100–696]

Co-Chairs:
  Paul D. Ryan, Speaker of the House.
  Orrin G. Hatch, Senate President Pro Tempore.

Senate Members:	**House Members:**
Mitch McConnell, Majority Leader.	Kevin McCarthy, Majority Leader.
Harry Reid, Democratic Leader.	*Nancy Pelosi,* Democratic Leader.
Roy Blunt.	Candice S. Miller.
Charles E. Schumer.	*Robert A. Brady.*
John Hoeven.	Gregg Harper.
Richard J. Durbin.	*Marcy Kaptur.*
Vacant.	Vacant.
Vacant.	Vacant.

Ex-Officio Member-Architect of the Capitol.—Stephen T. Ayers, AIA, LEED AP.

U.S. HOUSE OF REPRESENTATIVES FINE ARTS BOARD
1309 Longworth House Office Building, phone 225–8281
[Created by Public Law 101–696]

Chair.—Candice S. Miller, of Michigan.

Members:
  Gregg Harper, of Mississippi.
  Tom Graves, of Georgia.
  Robert A. Brady, of Pennsylvania.
  Zoe Lofgren, of California.

U.S. SENATE COMMISSION ON ART
S–411 The Capitol, phone 224–2955
[Created by Public Law 100–696]

Chair.—Mitch McConnell, of Kentucky.
  Vice Chair.—Harry Reid, of Nevada.

Members:
  Orrin G. Hatch, of Utah.
  Roy Blunt, of Missouri.
  Charles E. Schumer, of New York.

STAFF

Executive Secretary.—Julie E. Adams.
  Curator.—Melinda K. Smith.
  Associate Curator.—Alexander "Sasha" Lourie.
  Administrator.—Scott M. Strong.
  Historic Preservation Officer.—Kelly Steele.
  Collections Manager.—Vacant.
  Assistant Curator.—Amy Elizabeth Burton.
  Registrar.—Courtney Morfeld.
  Collections Specialist.—Theresa Malanum.
  Museum Speciulist.—Richard L. Doerner.
  Executive Assistant.—Anum Mirza.

OTHER CONGRESSIONAL OFFICIALS AND SERVICES

ARCHITECT OF THE CAPITOL

ARCHITECT'S OFFICE

SB–15, U.S. Capitol, phone 228–1793, fax 228–1893, http://www.aoc.gov

Architect of the Capitol.—Stephen T. Ayers, FAIA, LEED AP, 228–1793.
  Assistant Architect of the Capitol.—Michael G. Turnbull, 228–1221.
  Chief Operating Officer.—Christine Merdon, P.E., CMM, 228–1793.
  Chief Executive Officer for Visitor Services.—Beth Plemmons, 593–1837.
  Inspector General.—Kevin Mulshine, 593–0260.
  Director of:
    Communications and Congressional Relations.—Mamie Bittner, 228–1701.
    Safety, Fire and Environmental Programs.—Susan Adams, 226–0630.
  Chief Administrative Officer.—David Ferguson, 226–1222.
  Chief Financial Officer.—Tom Carroll, 228–1793.
  Communications Officer.—Laura Condeluci, 228–1793.
  General Counsel.—Jason Baltimore, 228–1793.
  Executive Officer, U.S. Botanic Garden.—Ari Novy, 225–6670.
  Curator.—Barbara Wolanin, 228–1222.

U.S. CAPITOL

HT–42, Capitol Superintendent's Service Center, phone 228–8800, fax 225–1957

[The Capitol Superintendent's Service Center provides Facility Services for the Capitol and CVC.]

Superintendent.—Carlos Elias.
  Deputy Superintendent.—Kristy Long, 228–8800.
  Assistant Superintendent.—John Deubler, 228–8800.

U.S. CAPITOL VISITOR CENTER

U.S. Capitol Visitor Center, Room SVC–101, 20515, phone 593–1816

Recorded Information 226–8000, Special Services 224–4048, TTY 224–4049

CEO for Visitor Services.—Beth Plemmons.
  Director of:
    Communications and Marketing.—Tom Fontana.
    Exhibits and Education.—Carol Beebe.
    Gift Shops.—Susan Sisk.
    Restaurant/Special Events.—Miguel Lopez.
    Visitor Services.—Tina Pearson.
    Volunteer Coordinator.—Wayne Kehoe.

SENATE OFFICE BUILDINGS

G–45 Dirksen Senate Office Building, phone 224–3141, fax 224–0652

Superintendent.—Takis Tzamaras, 224–2021.
  Deputy Superintendent.—Lawrence Barr, 224–7002.

Assistant Superintendents: Jean Gilles, Paul Kirkpatrick, Michael Shirven, 224–8023; Eric Swanson, 228–5002.

HOUSE OFFICE BUILDINGS
B–341 Rayburn House Office Building, phone 225–4141, fax 225–3003

Superintendent.—William M. Weidemeyer, P.E., CFM, 225–7012.
Deputy Superintendent.—Mark Reed, P.E., CFM, 225–4142.
Assistant Superintendents: Barron Dill, Jason McIntyre, Daniel Murphy, William Wood, 225–4142.

CAPITOL TELEPHONE EXCHANGE
6110 Postal Square Building, phone 224–3121

Supervisors: Debra Morgan, Joan Sartori.

CHILD CARE CENTERS

HOUSE OF REPRESENTATIVES CHILD CARE CENTER
147 Ford House Office Building
Virginia Avenue and 3rd Street, SW., 20515
phone 226–9320, fax 225–6908

Director.—Monica Barnabae.
Program Director.—Paige Beatty.

SENATE EMPLOYEES' CHILD CARE CENTER
United States Senate, 20510
phone 224–1461, fax 228–3686

Director.—Shannon Mara.

COMBINED AIRLINES TICKET OFFICES (CATO)
344 Maple West, Suite 224, Vienna, VA 22180
phone (703) 522–8664, 1 (888) 205–4482

General Manager.—Susan Willis.

SENATE AND HOUSE
B–222 Longworth House Office Building
phone (703) 522–2286, fax (202) 226–5992

Manager.—Misty Conner.

CONGRESSIONAL RECORD DAILY DIGEST

HOUSE SECTION
HT–13 The Capitol, phone 225–2868 (committees), 225–1501 (chamber)

Editors for—
Committee Meetings.—Nichole Shuman.
Chamber Action.—Glennis Webb.

SENATE SECTION
S–421 The Capitol, phone 224–2658, fax 224–1220

Editor.—Elizabeth Tratos.
Assistant Editor.—Joseph Johnston.

CONGRESSIONAL RECORD INDEX OFFICE

U.S. Government Publishing Office, Room C–738

North Capitol and H Streets, NW., 20401, phone 512–0275

Chief.—Marcia Thompson, 512–2010, ext. 3–1975.
Manager.—Philip C. Hart, 512–2010, ext. 3–1973.
Historian of Bills.—Barbre A. Brunson, 512–2010, ext. 3–1957.
Editors: Grafton J. Daniels, Jason Parsons.
Indexers: Ytta B. Carr, Joel K. Church, Jennifer E. Jones, Jane M. Wallace.

OFFICE OF CONGRESSIONAL ACCESSIBILITY SERVICES

S–156 Crypt of the Capitol 20510, phone 224–4048, TTY 224–4049

Director.—David Hauck.

LIAISON OFFICES

AIR FORCE

B–322 Rayburn House Office Building

phone 225–6656, 685–4530, DSN 325–4530, fax 685–2592

Chief.—Col. Wesley Hallman.
Deputy Chief.—Lt. Col. Heather Marshall.
Liaison Officers: Maj. Walter McMillan, Maj. Michael Reilly, Lt. Col. Stacy Wharton.
Budget and Appropriations Liaison Officer.—Lt. Col. Laurie Lanpher.
Legislative Assistant.—MSgt Purvis "Alex" Alexander.
Civilian.—Kathy Reece.

182 Russell Senate Office Building, phone 224–2481, 685–2573, fax (703) 571–3233

Chief.—Col. John Allen, Jr.
Deputy Chief.—Lt. Col. Jacob Middleton.
Liaison Officers: Lt. Col. Caroline Jensen, Maj. AJ Ashby.
Appropriations Liaison Officer.—Lt. Col. Christopher Carroll.
Office Manager/Scheduler.—Charlotte "Charli" Kiley.

ARMY

B–325 Rayburn House Office Building, phone (202) 685–2676, fax 685–2674

Chief.—COL David Hamilton.
Deputy Chief.—Jodi Beauchamp.
Liaison Officers: MAJ Trent Colestock, MAJ Adrian Foster, MAJ Cameron Gallagher, MAJ Christopher L'Heureux, CPT Catalina Rosales, CPT Matt Schardt, CPT Bishop Sparks, SGM Tonia Walker, MAJ Bryan Whittier, CPT Brent Weece.

183 Russell Senate Office Building, phone 224–2881, fax (703) 693–4574

Chief.—COL Scott Jackson.
Deputy Chief.—Kenneth Davis.
Liaison Officers: LTC Ned Ash, MAJ Donna Buono, SGM Terry Dokey, MAJ David Hawkins, MAJ Adisa King, MAJ J. Kevin McKittrick, MAJ Lee Small III, MAJ Courtney Sugai.
Congressional Operations Analyst.—Nyaesha "Nikki" Barnes.

COAST GUARD
B–320 Rayburn House Office Building, phone 225–4775, fax 426–6081

Director, House Liaison Officer.—CDR JoAnn Burdian.
Deputy, House Liaison Officer.—LCDR Kent Reinhold.
Assistant House Liaison.—LT Brittany Panetta.

183 Russell Senate Office Building, phone 224–2913, fax 755–1695

Liaison Officer.—CDR Brian LeFebvre.
Liaison Assistant.—LCDR Paul Miller.

NAVY/MARINE CORPS
B–324 Rayburn House Office Building, phone: Navy 225–7126, Marine Corps 225–7124

Director USN.—CAPT Todd Flannery, USN.
Deputy Director USN.—LCDR Alex Baerg, USN.
USN Liaison Officers: LCDR Rex Burman, USN; LT Brick Christensen, USN; LT Victoria Marum, USN; LT Alex Smith, USN; LT Neil Szymczak, USN.
Director USMC.—Col. Daniel Greenwood, USMC.
Deputy Director USMC.—Maj. Angel Hooper, USMC.
USMC Liaison Officers: Maj. Anthony Garofano, USMC; Capt. Sam Howe, USMC.
Office Manager/Administrative Clerk.—MSgt. Lacorie Delaney, USMC; Sgt. Gabriela Torian.

182 Russell Senate Office Building, phone: Navy 685–6003, Marine Corps 685–6010

Director.—CAPT Cedric Pringle, USN.
Deputy Director.—CDR John Brabazon, USN.
USN Liaison Officers: LT Gaylan Greenawalt, USN; LT Mike Mullee, USN; LT Meredith Manuel, USN; LT Cory Pleasanton, USN.
Director, USMC.—COL Robert Jones, USMC.
USMC Liaison Officers.—Maj. Joseph Steinfels, USMC; Capt. James Holt, USMC.
Liaison Staff Non-Commissioned Officers: GySgt. Efren Casas, USMC; Sgt. Jovanka Jaimefranco, USMC.

GOVERNMENT ACCOUNTABILITY OFFICE
Room 7125, 441 G Street, 20548, phone 512–4400, fax 512–7919 or 512–4641

Managing Director, Congressional Relations.—Katherine Siggerud, 512–6570.
Executive Assistant.—Jane Lusby, 512–4378.
Legislative Advisers: Patrick Dibattista, 512–6787; Carlos Diz, 512–8256; Rosa Harris, 512–9492; Carolyn Kirby, 512–9843; David Lewis, 512–7176; Tim Minelli, 512–8443; Paul Thompson, 512–9867; Mary Frances Widner, 512–3804.
Associate Legislative Adviser.—Martene Rhed, 512–5414.
Congressional Information Systems Specialist.—Ellen Wedge, 512–6817.
Engagement and Administrative Operations Assistant.—Theodora Guardado-Gallegos, 512–6224.

OFFICE OF PERSONNEL MANAGEMENT
B–332 Rayburn House Office Building, phone 225–4955

Chief.—Kristen Soper.
Constituent Services Officers: Sean McKew, Carlos Tingle, Melony Witherspoon.

SOCIAL SECURITY ADMINISTRATION
G3, L1, Rayburn House Office Building, phone 225–3133, fax 225–3144

Director.—Robert Forrester.
Congressional Relations Liaisons: Sylvia Taylor-Mackey, Latrice Wingo.

STATE DEPARTMENT LIAISON OFFICES
B–330 Rayburn House Office Building, fax 226–4643

Director.—Kevin Vaillancourt, 226–4644.
Deputy Director.—Kem Anderson, 228–1603.
Consular Officer.—Terry West, 226–4641.

189 Russell Senate Office Building, fax 224–1400

Director.—John Cooper, 228–1602.
Deputy Director.—Kem Anderson, 228–1603.
Consular Officer.—Glen Keiser, 228–1605.

VETERANS' AFFAIRS
B–328 Rayburn House Office Building, phone 225–2280, fax 453–9988

Director.—Dr. Ron Maurer.
Assistant Director.—Annmarie Amaral.
Liaison Assistants: Jeremy Dillard, Frank Morgan.
Representatives: Tasha Adams, Richard Armstrong, Jr., Gloria Galloway.

189 Russell Senate Office Building, phone 224–5351, fax 273–9988

Assistant Director.—Annmarie Amaral.
Representative.—Stuart A. Weiner.
Outreach: Tim Embree, Elena Kim, Jennifer McCarthy.

UNITED STATES SENATE PAGE SCHOOL

United States Senate, Washington, DC. 20510–7248, fax 224–1838

Principal.—Kathryn S. Weeden, 224–3926.
Executive Assistant.—Nikita Thompson, 224–3927.
English.—Frances Owens, 228–1024.
Mathematics.—Joshua Dorsey, 228–1018.
Science.—John Malek, 228–1025.
Social Studies.—Michael Bowers, 228–1012.

U.S. CAPITOL POLICE
119 D Street, NE., 20510–7218
Office of the Chief 224–9806, Command Center 224–0908
Communications 224–5151, Emergency 224–0911

U.S. CAPITOL POLICE BOARD

Sergeant at Arms, U.S. House of Representatives.—Paul D. Irving.
Sergeant at Arms, U.S. Senate.—Frank J. Larkin.
Architect of the Capitol.—Stephen T. Ayers, FAIA, LEED AP.

OFFICE OF THE CHIEF

Chief of Police.—Kim C. Dine.
 Chief of Staff.—Dominic A. Storelli (acting).
 Office of:
  Diversity, Opportunity and Inclusiveness.—Vacant.
  General Counsel.—Gretchen DeMar.
  Professional Responsibility.—Insp. Patrick Herrle.
  Public Information.—Tasha Jamerson.

CHIEF OF OPERATIONS

Assistant Chief of Police.—Matthew R. Verderosa.
 Executive Officer.—Vacant.

MISSION ASSURANCE BUREAU

Bureau Commander.—Deputy Chief Yancey Garner.
 Command Center: Capt. Michael Spochart, Insp. Wesley Mahr.
 Communications.—Capt. Darrin Bloxson.
 Emergency Management Division.—Vacant.
 Special Events.—Capt. Jeanita Mitchell.

OPERATIONAL SERVICES BUREAU

Bureau Commander.—Deputy Chief Fredinal Rogers.
 Hazardous Incident Response Division.—Capt. Kathleen McBride.
 Patrol/Mobile Response Division.—Insp. Eric Belknap.

PROTECTIVE SERVICES BUREAU

Bureau Commander.—Deputy Chief Chad Thomas.
 Dignitary Protection Division.—Insp. Kimberlie Bolinger.
 Investigations Division.—Capt. Timothy Bowen.

SECURITY SERVICES BUREAU

Bureau Commander.—Robert Ford.

UNIFORMED SERVICES BUREAU

Bureau Commander.—Deputy Chief Richard Rudd.
 Capitol Division Commander.—Insp. Eric Waldow.
 House Division Commander.—Insp. Thomas Loyd.
 Library Division Commander.—Insp. Donald Rouiller.
 Senate Division Commander.—Insp. Jeffrey Pickett.

CHIEF ADMINISTRATIVE OFFICER

Chief Administrative Officer.—Richard L. Braddock.
 Deputy Chief Administrative Officer.—Jay Miller.
 Director, Office of:
  Employment Counsel.—Frederick Herrera.
  Facilities and Logistics.—Cathleen English.

Financial Management.—Cherry Clipper.
Human Resources.—Jacqueline Whitaker.
Information Systems.—Heath Anderson.
Policy and Management Systems.—Jerome Boerste.
Training Services Bureau.—Thomas J. Madigan (acting).
Task Force (Discipline Process Review).—Insp. Yogananda Pittman.

STATISTICAL INFORMATION

VOTES CAST FOR SENATORS IN 2010, 2012, and 2014

[Compiled from official statistics obtained by the Clerk of the House. Figures in the last column, for the 2014 election, may include totals for more candidates than the ones shown.]

State	Vote						Total vote cast in 2014
	2010		2012		2014		
	Democrat	Republican	Democrat	Republican	Republican	Democrat	
Alabama	515,619	968,181			795,606		818,090
Alaska	60,045	90,839			135,445	129,431	282,400
Arizona	592,011	1,005,615	1,036,542	1,104,457			
Arkansas	288,156	451,618			478,819	334,174	847,505
California	5,218,441	4,217,366	7,864,624	4,713,887			
Colorado	851,590	822,731			983,891	944,203	2,041,058
Connecticut	605,204	498,341	792,983	604,569			
Delaware	174,012	123,053	265,415	113,700	98,823	130,655	234,038
Florida	1,092,936	2,645,743	4,523,451	3,458,267			
Georgia	996,516	1,489,904			1,358,088	1,160,811	2,567,805
Hawaii	277,228	79,939	269,489	160,994	98,006	246,877	369,703
Idaho	112,057	319,953			285,596	151,574	437,170
Illinois	1,719,478	1,778,698			1,538,522	1,929,637	3,603,519
Indiana	697,775	952,116	1,281,181	1,133,621			
Iowa	371,686	718,215			588,575	494,370	1,129,700
Kansas	220,971	587,175			460,350		866,191
Kentucky	600,052	755,706			806,787	584,698	1,435,868
Louisiana	476,572	715,415			929,108(1)	581,041	1,523,183
Maine			92,900(2)	215,399	413,505	190,254	616,996
Maryland	1,140,531	655,666	1,474,028	693,291			
Massachusetts			1,696,346	1,458,048	791,950	1,289,944	2,186,789
Michigan			2,735,826	1,767,386	1,290,199	1,704,936	3,121,771
Minnesota			1,854,595	867,974	850,227	1,053,205	1,981,528
Mississippi			503,467	709,626	378,481	239,439	631,858
Missouri	789,736	1,054,160	1,494,125	1,066,159			
Montana			236,123	218,051	213,709	148,184	369,826
Nebraska			332,979	455,593	347,636	170,127	540,337
Nevada	362,785	321,361	446,080	457,656			
New Hampshire	167,545	273,218			235,347	251,184	488,159
New Jersey			1,987,680	1,329,534	791,297	1,043,866	1,869,535
New Mexico			395,717	351,260	229,097	286,409	515,506
New York	3,047,880	1,239,605	4,420,043	1,514,647			
North Carolina	1,145,074	1,458,046			1,423,259	1,377,651	2,915,281
North Dakota	52,955	181,689	161,337	158,401			
Ohio	1,503,297	2,168,742	2,762,690	2,435,712			
Oklahoma	265,814	718,482			1,115,168	472,230	1,641,623
Oregon	825,507	566,199			538,847	814,537	1,461,618
Pennsylvania	1,948,716	2,028,945	3,021,364	2,509,132			
Rhode Island			271,034	146,222	92,684	223,675	316,898
South Carolina	364,598	810,771			1,430,156	916,309	2,479,057
South Dakota			227,947		140,741	82,456	279,412
Tennessee			705,882	1,506,443	850,087	437,848	1,374,065
Texas			3,194,927	4,440,137	2,861,531	1,597,387	4,648,358
Utah	191,732	360,403	301,873	657,608			
Vermont	151,281	72,699	(3)	72,898			
Virginia			2,010,067	1,785,542	1,055,940	1,073,667	2,184,473
Washington	1,314,930	1,196,164	1,855,493	1,213,924			
West Virginia	283,358	230,013	399,898	240,787	281,820	156,360	453,689
Wisconsin	1,020,958	1,125,999	1,547,104	1,380,126			
Wyoming			53,019	185,250	121,554	29,377	171,153

[1] This vote count is from Louisiana's December 6, 2014, general (runoff) election, which was held because neither candidate received a majority of the vote in Louisiana's open (nonpartisan) primary on November 4, 2014. Bill Cassidy received 603,048 votes in the primary, and Mary L. Landrieu received 619,402.

[2] Independent Angus S. King, Jr. was elected on November 6, 2012 with 370,580 votes.

[3] Independent Bernard Sanders was elected on November 6, 2012 with 207,848 votes.

VOTES CAST FOR REPRESENTATIVES, RESIDENT COMMISSIONER, AND DELEGATES IN 2010, 2012, and 2014

[The figures, compiled from official statistics obtained by the Clerk of the House, show the votes for the Republican and Democratic nominees, except as otherwise indicated. Figures in the last column, for the 2014 election, may include totals for more candidates than the ones shown.]

State and district	Vote cast in 2010 Republican	Vote cast in 2010 Democrat	State and district	Vote cast in 2012 Republican	Vote cast in 2012 Democrat	State and district	Vote cast in 2014 Republican	Vote cast in 2014 Democrat	Total vote cast in 2014
AL:			**AL:**			**AL:**			
1st	129,063	....	1st	196,374	....	1st	103,758	48,278	152,234
2d	111,645	106,865	2d	180,591	103,092	2d	113,103	54,692	167,952
3d	117,736	80,204	3d	175,306	98,141	3d	103,558	52,816	156,620
4th	167,714	....	4th	199,071	69,706	4th	132,831	....	134,752
5th	131,109	95,192	5th	189,185	101,772	5th	115,338	....	154,974
6th	205,288	....	6th	219,262	88,267	6th	135,945	42,291	178,449
7th	51,890	136,696	7th	73,835	232,520	7th	....	133,687	135,899
AK:			**AK:**			**AK:**			
At large ..	175,384	77,606	At large ..	185,296	82,927	At large ..	142,572	114,602	279,741
AZ:			**AZ:**			**AZ:**			
1st	112,816	99,233	1st	113,594	122,774	1st	87,723	97,391	185,114
2d	173,173	82,891	2d	144,884	147,338	2d	109,704	109,543	219,351
3d	108,689	85,610	3d	62,663	98,468	3d	46,185	58,192	104,428
4th	25,300	61,524	4th	162,907	69,154	4th	122,560	45,179	175,179
5th	110,374	91,749	5th	183,470	89,589	5th	124,867	54,596	179,463
6th	165,649	72,615	6th	179,706	97,666	6th	129,578	70,198	199,776
7th	70,385	79,935	7th	....	104,489	7th	....	54,235	72,454
8th	134,124	138,280	8th	172,809	95,635	8th	128,710	....	169,776
			9th	111,630	121,881	9th	67,841	88,609	162,062
AR:			**AR:**			**AR:**			
1st	93,224	78,267	1st	138,800	96,601	1st	124,139	63,555	196,256
2d	122,091	80,687	2d	158,175	113,156	2d	123,073	103,477	237,330
3d	148,581	56,542	3d	186,467	....	3d	151,630	....	190,935
4th	71,526	102,479	4th	154,149	95,013	4th	110,789	87,742	206,131
CA:			**CA:**			**CA:**			
1st	72,803	147,307	1st	168,827	125,386	1st	132,052	84,320	216,372
2d	130,837	98,092	2d	91,310	226,216	2d	54,400	163,124	217,524
3d	131,169	113,128	3d	107,086	126,882	3d	71,036	79,224	150,260
4th	186,397	95,653	4th	197,803	125,885	4th	211,134	....	211,134
5th	43,577	124,220	5th	69,545	202,872	5th	....	129,613	171,148
6th	77,361	172,216	6th	53,406	160,667	6th	36,448	97,008	133,456
7th	56,764	122,435	7th	132,050	141,241	7th	91,066	92,521	183,587
8th	31,711	167,957	8th	179,644	....	8th	77,480	37,056	114,536
9th	23,054	180,400	9th	94,704	118,373	9th	57,729	63,475	121,204
10th	88,512	137,578	10th	110,265	98,934	10th	70,582	55,123	125,705
11th	112,703	115,361	11th	87,136	200,743	11th	57,160	117,502	174,662
12th	44,475	152,044	12th	44,478	253,709	12th	32,197	160,067	192,264
13th	45,575	118,278	13th	....	250,436	13th	21,940	168,491	190,431
14th	60,917	151,217	14th	54,455	203,828	14th	34,757	114,389	149,146
15th	60,468	126,147	15th	....	231,034	15th	43,150	99,756	142,906
16th	37,913	105,841	16th	62,801	84,649	16th	44,943	46,277	91,220
17th	53,176	118,734	17th	57,336	159,392	17th	....	134,408	134,408
18th	51,716	72,853	18th	89,103	212,831	18th	63,326	133,060	196,386
19th	128,394	69,912	19th	59,313	162,300	19th	....	127,788	127,788
20th	43,197	46,247	20th	60,566	172,996	20th	....	106,034	141,044
21st	135,979	....	21st	67,164	49,119	21st	45,907	33,470	79,377
22d	173,490	....	22d	132,386	81,555	22d	96,053	37,289	133,342
23d	72,744	111,768	23d	158,161	....	23d	100,317	33,726	134,043
24th	144,055	96,279	24th	127,746	156,749	24th	95,566	103,228	198,794
25th	118,308	73,028	25th	129,593	106,982	25th	114,072	....	114,072
26th	112,774	76,093	26th	124,863	139,072	26th	82,653	87,176	169,829
27th	55,056	102,927	27th	86,817	154,191	27th	51,852	75,728	127,580
28th	28,493	88,385	28th	58,008	188,703	28th	....	91,996	120,264
29th	51,534	104,374	29th	....	111,287	29th	17,045	50,096	67,141
30th	75,948	153,663	30th	....	247,851	30th	45,315	86,568	131,883
31st	14,740	76,363	31st	161,219	....	31st	48,162	51,622	99,784
32d	31,697	77,759	32d	65,208	124,903	32d	34,053	50,353	84,406
33d	21,342	131,990	33d	....	171,860	33d	74,700	108,331	183,031
34th	20,457	69,382	34th	20,223	120,367	34th	....	61,621	61,621
35th	25,561	98,131	35th	....	142,680	35th	....	62,255	62,255
36th	66,706	114,489	36th	97,953	110,189	36th	61,457	72,682	134,139
37th	29,159	85,799	37th	32,541	207,039	37th	18,051	96,787	114,838
38th	30,883	85,459	38th	69,807	145,280	38th	40,288	58,192	98,480
39th	42,037	81,590	39th	145,607	106,360	39th	91,319	41,906	133,225
40th	119,455	59,400	40th	....	125,553	40th	....	49,379	49,379
41st	127,857	74,394	41st	72,074	103,578	41st	35,936	46,948	82,884
42d	127,161	65,122	42d	130,245	84,702	42d	74,540	38,850	113,390
43d	36,890	70,026	43d	....	200,894	43d	28,521	69,681	98,202
44th	107,482	85,784	44th	....	165,898	44th	....	59,670	68,862
45th	106,472	87,141	45th	171,417	121,814	45th	106,083	56,819	162,902
46th	139,822	84,940	46th	54,121	95,694	46th	33,577	49,738	83,315
47th	37,679	50,832	47th	99,919	130,093	47th	54,309	69,091	123,400
48th	145,481	88,465	48th	177,144	113,358	48th	112,082	62,713	174,795
49th	119,088	59,714	49th	159,725	114,893	49th	98,161	64,981	163,142
50th	142,247	97,818	50th	174,838	83,455	50th	111,997	45,302	157,299

VOTES CAST FOR REPRESENTATIVES, RESIDENT COMMISSIONER, AND DELEGATES IN 2010, 2012, and 2014—CONTINUED

[The figures, compiled from official statistics obtained by the Clerk of the House, show the votes for the Republican and Democratic nominees, except as otherwise indicated. Figures in the last column, for the 2014 election, may include totals for more candidates than the ones shown.]

State and district	Vote cast in 2010 Republican	Vote cast in 2010 Democrat	State and district	Vote cast in 2012 Republican	Vote cast in 2012 Democrat	State and district	Vote cast in 2014 Republican	Vote cast in 2014 Democrat	Total vote cast in 2014
51st	57,488	86,423	51st	45,464	113,934	51st	25,577	56,373	81,950
52d	139,460	70,870	52d	144,459	151,451	52d	92,746	98,826	191,572
53d	57,230	104,800	53d	103,482	164,825	53d	60,940	87,104	148,044
CO:			CO:			CO:			
1st	59,747	140,073	1st	93,217	237,579	1st	80,682	183,281	278,494
2d	98,171	148,720	2d	162,639	234,758	2d	149,645	196,300	345,945
3d	129,257	118,048	3d	185,291	142,619	3d	163,011	100,364	281,141
4th	138,634	109,249	4th	200,006	125,800	4th	185,292	83,727	286,507
5th	152,829	68,039	5th	199,639	....	5th	157,182	105,673	262,855
6th	217,368	104,104	6th	163,938	156,937	6th	143,467	118,847	276,440
7th	88,026	112,667	7th	139,066	182,460	7th	120,918	148,225	269,143
CT:			CT:			CT:			
1st	84,076	130,538	1st	82,321	192,840	1st	78,609	127,430	217,881
2d	95,671	140,888	2d	88,103	189,444	2d	80,837	131,294	227,936
3d	74,107	134,544	3d	73,726	197,163	3d	69,454	130,009	209,939
4th	102,030	110,746	4th	117,503	167,320	4th	88,209	101,401	198,800
5th	102,092	118,231	5th	128,927	137,631	5th	92,404	106,256	213,301
DE:			DE:			DE:			
At large	125,442	173,543	At large	129,757	249,933	At large	85,146	137,251	231,617
FL:			FL:			FL:			
1st	170,821	....	1st	238,440	92,961	1st	165,086	54,976	235,343
2d	136,371	105,211	2d	175,856	157,634	2d	123,262	126,096	249,780
3d	50,932	94,744	3d	204,331	102,468	3d	148,691	73,910	228,809
4th	178,238	....	4th	239,988	....	4th	177,887	....	227,253
5th	208,815	100,858	5th	70,700	190,472	5th	59,237	112,340	171,577
6th	179,349	....	6th	195,962	146,489	6th	166,254	99,563	265,817
7th	185,470	83,206	7th	185,518	130,479	7th	144,474	73,011	227,164
8th	123,586	84,167	8th	205,432	130,870	8th	180,728	93,724	274,513
9th	165,433	66,158	9th	98,856	164,891	9th	74,963	93,850	173,878
10th	137,943	71,313	10th	164,649	153,574	10th	143,128	89,426	232,574
11th	61,817	91,328	11th	218,360	120,303	11th	181,508	90,786	272,294
12th	102,704	87,769	12th	209,604	108,770	12th	(¹)		(¹)
13th	183,811	83,123	13th	189,605	139,742	13th	168,172	....	223,576
14th	188,341	74,525	14th	83,480	197,121	14th	....	(¹)	(¹)
15th	157,079	85,595	15th	(¹)	....	15th	128,750	84,832	213,582
16th	162,285	80,327	16th	187,147	161,979	16th	169,126	105,483	274,829
17th	....	106,361	17th	165,488	116,766	17th	141,493	82,263	223,756
18th	102,360	46,235	18th	164,353	166,257	18th	101,896	151,478	253,374
19th	78,733	132,098	19th	189,833	109,746	19th	159,354	80,824	246,861
20th	63,845	100,787	20th	....	214,727	20th	28,968	128,498	157,466
21st	(¹)		21st	....	221,263	21st	....	153,395	153,970
22d	118,890	99,804	22d	142,050	171,021	22d	90,685	125,404	216,096
23d	28,414	100,066	23d	98,096	174,205	23d	61,519	103,269	164,788
24th	146,129	98,787	24th	....	(¹)	24th	15,239	129,192	149,918
25th	74,859	61,138	25th	151,466	....	25th	(¹)		(¹)
			26th	108,820	135,694	26th	83,031	78,306	161,337
			27th	138,488	85,020	27th	(¹)	....	(¹)
GA:			GA:			GA:			
1st	117,270	46,449	1st	157,181	92,399	1st	95,337	61,175	156,512
2d	81,673	86,520	2d	92,410	162,751	2d	66,537	96,363	162,900
3d	168,304	73,932	3d	232,380	....	3d	156,277	....	156,277
4th	44,707	131,760	4th	75,041	208,861	4th	....	161,211	161,320
5th	46,622	130,782	5th	43,335	234,330	5th	....	170,326	170,326
6th	198,100	....	6th	189,669	104,365	6th	139,018	71,486	210,504
7th	160,898	78,996	7th	156,689	95,377	7th	113,557	60,112	173,669
8th	102,770	92,250	8th	197,789	....	8th	129,938	....	130,057
9th	173,512	....	9th	192,101	60,052	9th	146,059	34,988	181,047
10th	138,062	66,905	10th	211,065	....	10th	130,703	65,777	196,480
11th	163,515	....	11th	196,968	90,353	11th	161,532	....	161,532
12th	70,938	92,459	12th	119,973	139,148	12th	91,336	75,478	166,814
13th	61,771	140,294	13th	79,550	201,988	13th	....	159,445	159,445
			14th	159,947	59,245	14th	118,782	....	118,782
HI:			HI:			HI:			
1st	82,723	94,140	1st	96,824	116,505	1st	86,454	93,390	182,268
2d	46,404	132,290	2d	40,707	168,503	2d	33,630	142,010	187,435
ID:			ID:			ID:			
1st	126,231	102,135	1st	199,402	97,450	1st	143,580	77,277	220,864
2d	137,468	48,749	2d	207,412	110,847	2d	131,492	82,801	214,293
IL:			IL:			IL:			
1st	29,253	148,170	1st	83,989	236,854	1st	59,749	162,268	222,017
2d	25,883	150,666	2d	69,115	188,303	2d	43,799	160,337	204,266
3d	40,479	116,120	3d	77,653	168,738	3d	64,091	116,764	180,855
4th	11,711	63,273	4th	27,219	133,226	4th	22,278	79,666	101,944
5th	38,935	108,360	5th	77,289	177,729	5th	56,350	116,364	184,019
6th	114,456	65,379	6th	193,138	132,991	6th	160,287	78,465	238,752

VOTES CAST FOR REPRESENTATIVES, RESIDENT COMMISSIONER, AND DELEGATES IN 2010, 2012, and 2014—CONTINUED

[The figures, compiled from official statistics obtained by the Clerk of the House, show the votes for the Republican and Democratic nominees, except as otherwise indicated. Figures in the last column, for the 2014 election, may include totals for more candidates than the ones shown.]

State and district	Vote cast in 2010 Republican	Vote cast in 2010 Democrat	State and district	Vote cast in 2012 Republican	Vote cast in 2012 Democrat	State and district	Vote cast in 2014 Republican	Vote cast in 2014 Democrat	Total vote cast in 2014
7th	29,575	149,846	7th	31,466	242,439	7th	27,168	155,110	182,278
8th	98,115	97,825	8th	101,860	123,206	8th	66,878	84,178	151,056
9th	55,182	117,553	9th	98,924	194,869	9th	72,384	141,000	213,450
10th	109,941	105,290	10th	130,564	133,890	10th	95,992	91,136	187,128
11th	129,108	96,019	11th	105,348	148,928	11th	81,335	93,436	174,772
12th	74,046	121,272	12th	129,902	157,000	12th	110,038	87,860	209,738
13th	152,132	86,281	13th	137,034	136,032	13th	123,337	86,935	210,272
14th	112,369	98,645	14th	177,603	124,351	14th	145,369	76,861	222,230
15th	136,915	75,948	15th	205,775	94,162	15th	166,274	55,652	221,926
16th	138,299	66,037	16th	181,789	112,301	16th	153,388	63,810	217,198
17th	104,583	85,454	17th	134,623	153,519	17th	88,785	110,560	199,361
18th	152,868	57,046	18th	244,467	85,164	18th	184,363	62,377	246,740
19th	166,166	67,132							
IN:			**IN:**			**IN:**			
1st	65,558	99,387	1st	91,291	187,743	1st	51,000	86,579	142,293
2d	88,803	91,341	2d	134,033	130,113	2d	85,583	55,590	145,200
3d	116,140	61,267	3d	187,872	92,363	3d	97,892	39,771	148,793
4th	138,732	53,167	4th	168,688	93,015	4th	94,998	47,056	142,054
5th	146,899	60,024	5th	194,570	125,347	5th	105,277	49,756	161,440
6th	126,027	56,647	6th	162,613	96,678	6th	102,187	45,509	155,071
7th	55,213	86,011	7th	95,828	162,122	7th	46,887	61,443	112,261
8th	117,259	76,265	8th	151,533	122,325	8th	103,344	61,384	171,315
9th	118,040	95,353	9th	165,332	132,848	9th	101,594	55,016	163,387
IA:			**IA:**			**IA:**			
1st	100,219	104,428	1st	162,465	222,422	1st	147,762	141,145	289,306
2d	104,319	115,839	2d	161,977	211,863	2d	129,455	143,431	273,329
3d	111,925	122,147	3d	202,000	168,632	3d	148,814	119,109	282,066
4th	152,588	74,300	4th	200,063	169,470	4th	169,834	105,504	275,633
5th	128,363	63,160							
KS:			**KS:**			**KS:**			
1st	142,281	44,068	1st	211,337	....	1st	138,764	65,397	204,161
2d	130,034	66,588	2d	167,463	113,735	2d	128,742	87,153	225,686
3d	136,246	90,193	3d	201,087	....	3d	134,493	89,584	224,077
4th	119,575	74,143	4th	161,094	81,770	4th	138,757	69,396	208,153
KY:			**KY:**			**KY:**			
1st	153,840	62,090	1st	199,956	87,199	1st	173,022	63,596	236,618
2d	155,906	73,749	2d	181,508	89,541	2d	156,936	69,898	226,834
3d	112,627	139,940	3d	111,452	206,385	3d	87,981	157,056	247,355
4th	151,813	66,694	4th	186,036	104,734	4th	150,464	71,694	222,158
5th	151,019	44,034	5th	195,408	55,447	5th	171,350	47,617	218,967
6th	119,164	119,812	6th	153,222	141,438	6th	147,404	98,290	245,694
LA:			**LA:**			**LA:**			
1st	157,182	38,416	1st	218,340	61,703	1st	189,250	46,047	244,004
2d	43,378	83,705	2d	50,146	230,417	2d	....	190,006	221,570
3d	108,963	61,914	3d	240,558	67,070	3d	207,926	....	236,268
4th	105,223	54,609	4th	187,894	....	4th	152,683	....	207,919
5th	122,033	....	5th	202,536	....	5th	247,211	75,006	326,073
6th	138,607	72,577	6th	243,553	....	6th	234,200	95,127	332,888
7th	(2)	....							
ME:			**ME:**			**ME:**			
1st	128,501	169,114	1st	128,440	236,363	1st	94,751	186,674	321,987
2d	119,669	147,042	2d	137,542	191,456	2d	133,320	118,568	295,009
MD:			**MD:**			**MD:**			
1st	155,118	120,400	1st	214,204	92,812	1st	176,342	73,843	250,418
2d	69,523	134,133	2d	92,071	194,088	2d	70,411	120,412	196,354
3d	86,947	147,448	3d	94,549	213,747	3d	87,029	128,594	215,946
4th	31,467	160,228	4th	64,560	240,385	4th	54,217	134,628	191,837
5th	83,575	155,110	5th	95,271	238,618	5th	80,752	144,725	226,040
6th	148,820	80,455	6th	117,313	181,921	6th	91,930	94,704	190,536
7th	46,375	152,669	7th	67,405	247,770	7th	55,860	144,639	206,809
8th	52,421	153,613	8th	113,033	217,531	8th	87,859	136,722	225,097
MA:			**MA:**			**MA:**			
1st	74,418	128,011	1st	....	261,936	1st	....	167,612	227,075
2d	91,209	122,751	2d	....	259,257	2d	....	169,640	235,813
3d	85,124	122,708	3d	109,372	212,119	3d	81,638	139,104	230,789
4th	101,517	126,194	4th	129,936	221,303	4th	....	184,158	255,297
5th	94,646	122,858	5th	82,944	257,490	5th	....	182,100	256,486
6th	107,930	142,732	6th	176,612	180,942	6th	111,989	149,638	278,919
7th	73,467	145,696	7th	....	210,794	7th	....	142,133	176,077
8th	....	134,974	8th	82,242	263,999	8th	....	200,644	261,781
9th	59,965	157,071	9th	116,531	212,754	9th	114,971	140,413	264,552
10th	120,029	132,743							
MI:			**MI:**			**MI:**			
1st	120,523	94,824	1st	167,060	165,179	1st	130,414	113,263	250,131
2d	148,864	72,118	2d	194,653	108,973	2d	135,568	70,851	213,072

VOTES CAST FOR REPRESENTATIVES, RESIDENT COMMISSIONER, AND DELEGATES IN 2010, 2012, and 2014—CONTINUED

[The figures, compiled from official statistics obtained by the Clerk of the House, show the votes for the Republican and Democratic nominees, except as otherwise indicated. Figures in the last column, for the 2014 election, may include totals for more candidates than the ones shown.]

State and district	Vote cast in 2010 Repub-lican	Demo-crat	State and district	Vote cast in 2012 Repub-lican	Demo-crat	State and district	Vote cast in 2014 Repub-lican	Demo-crat	Total vote cast in 2014
3d	133,714	83,953	3d	171,675	144,108	3d	125,754	84,720	217,165
4th	148,531	68,458	4th	197,386	104,996	4th	123,962	85,777	219,423
5th	89,680	107,286	5th	103,931	214,531	5th	69,222	148,182	222,138
6th	123,142	66,729	6th	174,955	136,563	6th	116,801	84,391	208,976
7th	113,185	102,402	7th	169,668	136,849	7th	119,564	92,083	223,685
8th	156,931	84,069	8th	202,217	128,657	8th	132,739	102,269	243,125
9th	119,325	125,730	9th	114,760	208,846	9th	81,470	136,342	225,757
10th	168,364	58,530	10th	226,075	97,734	10th	157,069	67,143	228,692
11th	141,224	91,710	11th	181,788	158,879	11th	140,435	101,681	251,238
12th	71,372	124,671	12th	92,472	216,884	12th	64,716	134,346	206,660
13th	23,462	100,885	13th	38,769	235,336	13th	27,234	132,710	166,947
14th	29,902	115,511	14th	51,395	270,450	14th	41,801	165,272	212,468
15th	83,488	118,336							
MN:			MN:			MN:			
1st	109,242	122,365	1st	142,164	193,211	1st	103,536	122,851	226,695
2d	181,341	104,809	2d	193,587	164,338	2d	137,778	95,565	245,848
3d	161,177	100,240	3d	222,335	159,937	3d	167,515	101,846	269,585
4th	80,141	136,746	4th	109,659	216,685	4th	79,492	147,857	241,637
5th	55,222	154,833	5th	88,753	262,102	5th	56,577	167,079	236,010
6th	159,476	120,846	6th	179,240	174,944	6th	133,328	90,926	236,846
7th	90,652	133,096	7th	114,151	197,791	7th	109,955	130,546	240,835
8th	133,490	129,091	8th	160,520	191,976	8th	125,358	129,090	266,083
MS:			MS:			MS:			
1st	121,074	89,388	1st	186,760	114,076	1st	102,622	43,713	151,111
2d	64,499	105,327	2d	99,160	214,978	2d	....	100,688	148,646
3d	132,393	60,737	3d	234,717	....	3d	117,771	47,744	170,946
4th	105,613	95,243	4th	182,998	82,344	4th	108,776	37,869	155,576
MO:			MO:			MO:			
1st	43,649	135,907	1st	60,832	267,927	1st	35,273	119,315	163,494
2d	180,481	77,467	2d	236,971	146,272	2d	148,191	75,384	231,117
3d	94,757	99,398	3d	214,843	111,189	3d	130,940	52,021	191,620
4th	113,489	101,532	4th	192,237	113,120	4th	120,014	46,464	176,286
5th	84,578	102,076	5th	122,149	200,290	5th	69,071	79,256	153,635
6th	154,103	67,762	6th	216,906	108,503	6th	124,616	55,157	186,970
7th	141,010	67,545	7th	203,565	98,498	7th	104,054	47,282	163,957
8th	128,499	56,377	8th	216,083	73,755	8th	106,124	38,721	159,224
9th	162,724	46,817							
MT:			MT:			MT:			
At large	217,696	121,954	At large	255,468	204,939	At large	203,871	148,690	367,963
NE:			NE:			NE:			
1st	116,871	47,106	1st	174,889	81,206	1st	123,219	55,838	179,057
2d	93,840	60,486	2d	133,964	129,767	2d	78,157	83,872	171,509
3d	117,275	29,932	3d	187,423	65,266	3d	139,440	45,524	184,964
NV:			NV:			NV:			
1st	58,995	103,246	1st	56,521	113,967	1st	30,413	45,643	80,299
2d	169,458	87,421	2d	162,213	102,019	2d	122,402	52,016	186,210
3d	128,916	127,168	3d	137,244	116,823	3d	88,528	52,644	145,719
			4th	101,261	120,501	4th	63,466	59,844	130,781
NH:			NH:			NH:			
1st	121,655	95,503	1st	158,659	171,650	1st	125,508	116,769	242,736
2d	108,610	105,060	2d	152,977	169,275	2d	106,871	130,700	238,184
NJ:			NJ:			NJ:			
1st	58,562	106,334	1st	92,459	210,470	1st	64,073	93,315	162,492
2d	109,460	51,690	2d	166,677	116,462	2d	108,875	66,026	177,148
3d	110,215	104,252	3d	174,253	145,506	3d	100,471	82,537	186,103
4th	129,752	52,118	4th	195,145	107,991	4th	118,826	54,415	174,849
5th	124,030	62,634	5th	167,501	130,100	5th	104,678	81,808	188,921
6th	65,413	81,933	6th	84,360	151,782	6th	46,891	72,190	120,457
7th	105,084	71,902	7th	175,662	123,057	7th	104,287	68,232	175,997
8th	51,023	88,478	8th	31,763	130,853	8th	15,141	61,510	79,518
9th	52,082	83,564	9th	55,091	162,822	9th	36,246	82,498	120,459
10th	14,357	95,299	10th	24,271	201,435	10th	14,154	95,734	112,123
11th	122,149	55,472	11th	182,237	123,897	11th	109,455	65,477	174,932
12th	93,634	108,214	12th	80,906	189,926	12th	54,168	90,430	148,366
13th	19,538	62,840							
NM:			NM:			NM:			
1st	104,215	112,010	1st	112,473	162,924	1st	74,558	105,474	180,032
2d	94,053	75,708	2d	133,180	92,162	2d	95,209	52,499	147,777
3d	90,617	120,048	3d	97,616	167,103	3d	70,775	113,249	184,076
NY:			NY:			NY:			
1st	78,300	98,316	1st	106,678	134,205	1st	77,062	68,387	176,719
2d	58,525	94,594	2d	....	93,375	2d	....	41,814	146,617
3d	131,674	51,346	3d	....	146,016	3d	63,219	80,393	171,163
4th	69,323	94,483	4th	84,982	152,590	4th	67,811	83,772	175,305
5th	36,861	72,239	5th	17,875	167,835	5th	....	75,712	94,400

VOTES CAST FOR REPRESENTATIVES, RESIDENT COMMISSIONER, AND DELEGATES IN 2010, 2012, and 2014—CONTINUED

[The figures, compiled from official statistics obtained by the Clerk of the House, show the votes for the Republican and Democratic nominees, except as otherwise indicated. Figures in the last column, for the 2014 election, may include totals for more candidates than the ones shown.]

State and district	Vote cast in 2010 Republican	Democrat	State and district	Vote cast in 2012 Republican	Democrat	State and district	Vote cast in 2014 Republican	Democrat	Total vote cast in 2014
6th	10,057	85,096	6th	45,992	107,505	6th	....	49,227	77,306
7th	13,751	71,247	7th	....	132,456	7th	5,713	47,142	68,522
8th	29,514	98,839	8th	15,841	178,687	8th	....	70,469	95,113
9th	37,750	67,011	9th	20,899	178,168	9th	....	70,997	101,606
10th	7,419	95,485	10th	35,440	155,908	10th	....	73,945	113,226
11th	9,119	104,297	11th	91,030	87,718	11th	48,291	41,429	110,999
12th	....	68,624	12th	41,969	184,864	12th	19,564	78,440	117,420
13th	55,821	60,773	13th	12,132	170,470	13th	....	63,437	91,834
14th	32,065	107,327	14th	19,191	116,117	14th	....	45,370	67,372
15th	10,678	91,225	15th	3,487	150,243	15th	....	53,128	61,268
16th	2,257	61,642	16th	53,935	173,885	16th	....	90,088	138,655
17th	29,792	95,346	17th	91,899	161,624	17th	63,549	89,295	181,674
18th	60,513	115,619	18th	113,386	132,456	18th	66,523	76,235	186,715
19th	88,734	98,766	19th	122,654	120,302	19th	102,118	60,533	210,351
20th	110,813	107,075	20th	79,102	181,092	20th	61,820	103,437	211,965
21st	70,211	124,889	21st	104,368	117,856	21st	79,615	53,140	181,558
22d	75,558	98,661	22d	145,042	102,080	22d	113,574	....	175,372
23d	73,646	82,232	23d	117,641	114,590	23d	94,375	60,233	190,554
24th	85,702	89,809	24th	105,584	133,908	24th	93,881	72,631	203,417
25th	81,380	103,954	25th	109,292	168,761	25th	75,990	87,264	196,516
26th	151,449	54,307	26th	57,368	195,234	26th	38,477	100,648	173,911
27th	63,015	119,085	27th	137,250	140,008	27th	109,171	50,939	215,147
28th	45,630	102,514							
29th	93,167	....							
NC:			**NC:**			**NC:**			
1st	70,867	103,294	1st	77,288	254,644	1st	55,990	154,333	210,323
2d	93,876	92,393	2d	174,066	128,973	2d	122,128	85,479	207,607
3d	143,225	51,317	3d	195,571	114,344	3d	139,415	66,182	205,597
4th	116,448	155,384	4th	88,951	259,534	4th	57,416	169,946	227,362
5th	140,525	72,762	5th	200,945	148,252	5th	139,279	88,973	228,252
6th	156,252	51,507	6th	222,116	142,467	6th	147,312	103,758	251,070
7th	98,328	113,957	7th	168,041	168,695	7th	134,431	84,054	226,504
8th	73,129	88,776	8th	160,695	137,139	8th	121,568	65,854	187,422
9th	158,790	71,450	9th	194,537	171,503	9th	163,080	....	173,668
10th	130,813	52,972	10th	190,826	144,023	10th	133,504	85,292	218,796
11th	110,246	131,225	11th	190,319	141,107	11th	144,682	85,342	230,024
12th	55,315	103,495	12th	63,317	247,591	12th	42,568	130,096	172,664
13th	93,099	116,103	13th	210,495	160,115	13th	153,991	114,718	268,709
ND:			**ND:**			**ND:**			
At large ..	129,802	106,542	At large ..	173,585	131,870	At large ..	138,100	95,678	248,670
OH:			**OH:**			**OH:**			
1st	103,770	92,672	1st	201,907	131,490	1st	124,779	72,604	197,383
2d	139,027	82,431	2d	194,296	137,077	2d	132,658	68,453	201,111
3d	152,629	71,455	3d	77,901	201,897	3d	51,475	91,769	143,261
4th	146,029	50,533	4th	182,643	114,214	4th	125,907	60,165	186,072
5th	140,703	54,919	5th	201,514	137,806	5th	134,449	58,507	202,300
6th	103,170	92,823	6th	164,536	144,444	6th	111,026	73,561	190,652
7th	135,721	70,400	7th	178,104	137,708	7th	143,959	....	143,959
8th	142,731	65,883	8th	246,378	....	8th	126,539	51,534	188,330
9th	83,423	121,819	9th	68,668	217,771	9th	51,704	108,870	160,715
10th	83,809	101,343	10th	208,201	131,097	10th	130,752	63,249	200,606
11th	28,754	139,693	11th	....	258,359	11th	35,461	137,105	172,566
12th	150,163	110,307	12th	233,869	134,605	12th	150,573	61,360	221,081
13th	94,367	118,806	13th	88,120	235,492	13th	55,233	120,230	175,549
14th	149,878	72,604	14th	183,657	131,637	14th	135,736	70,856	214,580
15th	119,471	91,077	15th	205,274	128,188	15th	128,496	66,125	194,621
16th	114,652	90,833	16th	185,165	170,600	16th	132,176	75,199	207,375
17th	57,352	102,758							
18th	107,426	80,756							
OK:			**OK:**			**OK:**			
1st	151,173	45,656	1st	181,084	91,421	1st	(3)	....	(3)
2d	83,226	108,203	2d	143,701	96,081	2d	110,925	38,964	158,407
3d	161,927	45,689	3d	201,744	53,472	3d	133,335	36,270	169,605
4th	(3)		4th	176,740	71,846	4th	117,721	40,998	166,268
5th	123,236	68,074	5th	153,603	97,504	5th	95,632	57,790	159,133
OR:			**OR:**			**OR:**			
1st	122,858	160,357	1st	109,699	197,845	1st	96,245	160,038	279,253
2d	206,245	72,173	2d	228,043	....	2d	202,374	73,785	287,425
3d	67,714	193,104	3d	70,325	264,979	3d	57,424	211,748	292,757
4th	129,877	162,416	4th	....	212,866	4th	116,534	181,624	310,179
5th	130,313	145,379	5th	139,223	177,229	5th	110,332	150,944	281,088
PA:			**PA:**			**PA:**			
1st	....	149,944	1st	41,708	235,394	1st	27,193	131,248	158,441
2d	21,907	182,800	2d	33,381	318,176	2d	25,397	181,141	206,538
3d	111,909	88,924	3d	165,826	123,933	3d	113,859	73,931	187,790

VOTES CAST FOR REPRESENTATIVES, RESIDENT COMMISSIONER, AND DELEGATES IN 2010, 2012, and 2014—CONTINUED

[The figures, compiled from official statistics obtained by the Clerk of the House, show the votes for the Republican and Democratic nominees, except as otherwise indicated. Figures in the last column, for the 2014 election, may include totals for more candidates than the ones shown.]

State and district	Vote cast in 2010 Republican	Vote cast in 2010 Democrat	State and district	Vote cast in 2012 Republican	Vote cast in 2012 Democrat	State and district	Vote cast in 2014 Republican	Vote cast in 2014 Democrat	Total vote cast in 2014
4th	116,958	120,827	4th	181,603	104,643	4th	147,090	50,250	197,340
5th	127,427	52,375	5th	177,740	104,725	5th	115,018	65,839	180,857
6th	133,770	100,493	6th	191,725	143,803	6th	119,643	92,901	212,544
7th	137,825	110,314	7th	209,942	143,509	7th	145,869	89,256	235,125
8th	130,759	113,547	8th	199,379	152,859	8th	137,731	84,767	222,498
9th	141,904	52,322	9th	169,177	105,128	9th	110,094	63,223	173,317
10th	110,599	89,846	10th	179,563	94,227	10th	112,851	44,737	180,322
11th	102,179	84,618	11th	166,967	118,231	11th	122,464	62,228	184,692
12th	91,170	94,056	12th	175,352	163,589	12th	127,993	87,928	215,921
13th	91,987	118,710	13th	93,918	209,901	13th	60,549	123,601	184,150
14th	49,997	122,073	14th	75,702	251,932	14th		148,351	148,351
15th	109,534	79,766	15th	168,960	128,764	15th	128,285		128,285
16th	134,113	70,994	16th	156,192	111,185	16th	101,722	74,513	176,235
17th	95,000	118,486	17th	106,208	161,393	17th	71,371	93,680	165,051
18th	161,888	78,558	18th	216,727	122,146	18th	166,076		166,076
19th	165,219	53,549							
RI:			**RI:**			**RI:**			
1st	71,542	81,269	1st	83,737	108,612	1st	58,877	87,060	146,353
2d	55,409	104,442	2d	78,189	124,067	2d	63,844	105,716	169,904
SC:			**SC:**			**SC:**			
1st	152,755	67,008	1st	179,908	98,154	1st	119,392		127,815
2d	138,861	113,625	2d	196,116		2d	121,649	68,719	194,808
3d	126,235	66,497	3d	169,512	84,735	3d	116,741	47,181	164,009
4th	137,586	62,438	4th	173,201	84,087	4th	126,452		149,049
5th	125,834	102,296	5th	154,324	113,904	5th	103,078	66,802	175,145
6th	72,661	125,459	6th		218,717	6th	44,311	125,747	173,432
			7th	153,068	114,594	7th	102,833	68,576	171,524
SD:			**SD:**			**SD:**			
At large	153,703	146,589	At large	207,640	153,789	At large	183,834	92,485	276,319
TN:			**TN:**			**TN:**			
1st	123,006	26,045	1st	182,252	47,663	1st	115,533		139,470
2d	141,796	25,400	2d	196,894	54,522	2d	120,883	37,612	166,751
3d	92,032	45,387	3d	157,830	91,094	3d	97,344	53,983	156,097
4th	103,969	70,254	4th	120,568	102,022	4th	84,815	51,357	145,418
5th	74,204	99,162	5th	86,240	171,621	5th	55,078	96,148	154,276
6th	128,517	56,145	6th	184,383		6th	115,231	37,232	162,097
7th	158,916	54,347	7th	182,730	61,679	7th	110,534	42,280	157,907
8th	98,759	64,960	8th	190,923	79,490	8th	122,255	42,433	172,595
9th	33,879	99,827	9th	59,742	188,422	9th	27,173	87,376	116,550
TX:			**TX:**			**TX:**			
1st	129,398		1st	178,322	67,222	1st	115,084	33,476	148,560
2d	130,020		2d	159,664	80,512	2d	101,936	44,462	150,026
3d	101,180	47,848	3d	187,180		3d	113,404		138,280
4th	136,338	40,975	4th	182,679	60,214	4th	115,085		115,085
5th	106,742	41,649	5th	134,091	69,178	5th	88,998		104,262
6th	107,140	50,717	6th	145,019	98,053	6th	92,334	55,027	150,996
7th	143,655		7th	142,793	85,553	7th	90,606	49,478	143,219
8th	161,417	34,694	8th	194,043	51,051	8th	125,066		140,013
9th	24,201	80,107	9th	36,139	144,075	9th		78,109	86,003
10th	144,980	74,086	10th	159,783	95,710	10th	109,726	60,243	176,460
11th	125,581	23,989	11th	177,742	41,970	11th	107,939		119,574
12th	109,882	38,434	12th	175,649	66,080	12th	113,186	41,757	158,730
13th	113,201		13th	187,775		13th	110,842	16,822	131,451
14th	140,623	44,431	14th	131,460	109,697	14th	90,116	52,545	145,698
15th	39,964	53,546	15th	54,056	89,296	15th	39,016	48,708	90,184
16th	31,051	49,301	16th	51,043	101,403	16th	21,324	49,338	73,105
17th	106,696	63,138	17th	143,284		17th	85,807	43,049	132,865
18th	33,067	85,108	18th	44,015	146,223	18th	26,249	76,097	106,010
19th	106,059	25,984	19th	163,239		19th	90,160	21,458	116,818
20th	31,757	58,645	20th	62,376	119,032	20th		66,554	87,964
21st	162,924	65,927	21st	187,015	109,326	21st	135,660		188,996
22d	140,537	62,082	22d	160,668	80,203	22d	100,861	47,844	151,566
23d	74,853	67,348	23d	87,547	96,676	23d	57,459	55,037	115,429
24th	100,078		24th	148,586	87,645	24th	93,712	46,548	144,073
25th	84,849	99,967	25th	154,245	98,827	25th	107,120	64,463	177,883
26th	120,984	55,385	26th	176,642	74,237	26th	116,944		141,470
27th	50,976	50,179	27th	120,684	83,395	27th	83,342	44,152	131,047
28th	46,740	62,773	28th	49,309	112,456	28th		62,508	76,136
29th	22,825	43,257	29th		86,053	29th		41,321	46,143
30th	24,668	86,322	30th	41,222	171,059	30th		93,041	105,793
31st	126,384		31st	145,348	82,977	31st	91,607	45,715	143,028
32d	79,433	44,258	32d	146,653	99,288	32d	96,495	55,325	156,096
			33d	30,252	85,114	33d		43,769	50,592
			34th	52,448	89,606	34th	30,811	47,503	79,877
			35th	52,894	105,626	35th	32,040	60,124	96,225

526 Congressional Directory

VOTES CAST FOR REPRESENTATIVES, RESIDENT COMMISSIONER, AND DELEGATES IN 2010, 2012, and 2014—CONTINUED

[The figures, compiled from official statistics obtained by the Clerk of the House, show the votes for the Republican and Democratic nominees, except as otherwise indicated. Figures in the last column, for the 2014 election, may include totals for more candidates than the ones shown.]

State and district	Vote cast in 2010		State and district	Vote cast in 2012		State and district	Vote cast in 2014		Total vote cast in 2014
	Republican	Democrat		Republican	Democrat		Republican	Democrat	
			36th	165,405	62,143	36th	101,663	29,543	133,842
UT:			UT:			UT:			
1st	135,247	46,765	1st	175,487	60,611	1st	84,231	36,422	130,034
2d	116,001	127,151	2d	154,523	83,176	2d	88,915	47,585	146,188
3d	139,721	44,320	3d	198,828	60,719	3d	102,952	32,059	142,580
			4th	119,035	119,803	4th	74,936	67,425	147,168
VT:			VT:			VT:			
At large	76,403	154,006	At large	67,543	208,600	At large	59,432	123,349	191,504
VA:			VA:			VA:			
1st	135,564	73,824	1st	200,845	147,036	1st	131,861	72,059	209,621
2d	88,340	70,591	2d	166,231	142,548	2d	101,558	71,178	173,060
3d	44,553	114,754	3d	58,931	259,199	3d		139,197	147,402
4th	123,659	74,298	4th	199,292	150,190	4th	120,684	75,270	200,638
5th	119,560	110,562	5th	193,009	149,214	5th	124,735	73,482	204,945
6th	127,487		6th	211,278	111,949	6th	133,898		179,708
7th	138,209	79,616	7th	222,983	158,012	7th	148,026	89,914	243,351
8th	71,145	116,404	8th	107,370	226,847	8th	63,810	128,102	203,076
9th	95,726	86,743	9th	184,882	116,400	9th	117,465		162,815
10th	131,116	72,604	10th	214,038	142,024	10th	125,914	89,957	222,910
11th	110,739	111,720	11th	117,902	202,606	11th	75,796	106,780	187,805
WA:			WA:			WA:			
1st	126,737	172,642	1st	151,187	177,025	1st	101,428	124,151	225,579
2d	148,722	155,241	2d	117,465	184,826	2d	79,518	122,173	201,691
3d	152,799	135,654	3d	177,446	116,438	3d	124,796	78,018	202,814
4th	156,726	74,973	4th	154,749	78,940	4th	153,079		153,079
5th	177,235	101,146	5th	191,066	117,512	5th	135,470	87,772	223,242
6th	109,800	151,873	6th	129,725	186,661	6th	83,025	141,265	224,290
7th		232,649	7th	76,212	298,368	7th	47,921	203,954	251,875
8th	161,296	148,581	8th	180,204	121,886	8th	125,741	73,003	198,744
9th	101,851	123,743	9th	76,105	192,034	9th	48,662	118,132	166,794
			10th	115,381	163,036	10th	82,213	99,279	181,492
WV:			WV:			WV:			
1st	90,660	89,220	1st	133,809	80,342	1st	92,491	52,109	144,737
2d	126,814	55,001	2d	158,206	68,560	2d	72,619	67,687	154,250
3d	65,611	83,636	3d	92,238	108,199	3d	77,713	62,688	140,401
WI:			WI:			WI:			
1st	179,819	79,363	1st	200,423	158,414	1st	182,316	105,552	288,170
2d	118,099	191,164	2d	124,683	265,422	2d	103,619	224,920	328,847
3d	116,838	126,380	3d	121,713	217,712	3d	119,540	155,368	275,161
4th	61,543	143,559	4th	80,787	235,257	4th	68,490	179,045	254,892
5th	229,642	90,634	5th	250,335	118,478	5th	231,160	101,190	332,826
6th	183,271	75,926	6th	223,460	135,921	6th	169,767	122,212	299,033
7th	132,551	113,018	7th	201,720	157,524	7th	169,891	112,949	286,603
8th	143,998	118,646	8th	198,874	156,287	8th	188,553	101,345	290,048
WY:			WY:			WY:			
At large	131,661	45,768	At large	166,452	57,573	At large	113,038	37,803	171,153

[Table continues on next page]

VOTES CAST FOR REPRESENTATIVES, RESIDENT COMMISSIONER, AND DELEGATES IN 2010, 2012, and 2014—CONTINUED

[The figures, compiled from official statistics obtained by the Clerk of the House, show the votes for the Republican and Democratic nominees, except as otherwise indicated. Figures in the last column, for the 2014 election, may include totals for more candidates than the ones shown.]

Commonwealth of Puerto Rico	Vote						Total vote cast in 2014
	2010		2012		2014		
	New Progressive	Popular Democrat	Popular Democrat	Democrat	Popular Democrat	Democrat	
Resident Commissioner (4-year term)	....	....	881,181	905,066	....	....	....

District of Columbia	Vote						Total vote cast in 2014
	2010		2012		2014		
	Republican	Democrat	Libertarian	Democrat	Republican	Democrat	
Delegate	8,109	117,990	16,524	246,664	11,673	143,923	171,893

Guam	Vote						Total vote cast in 2014
	2010		2012		2014		
	Write-in	Democrat	Republican	Democrat	Republican	Democrat	
Delegate	1,502	35,919	12,995	19,765	14,956	20,693	37,368

Virgin Islands	Vote						Total vote cast in 2014
	2010		2012		2014		
	Republican	Democrat	Republican	Democrat	Republican	Democrat	
Delegate	2,329	19,844	2,131	11,512	1,964	21,224	23,412

American Samoa	Vote						Total vote cast in 2014
	2010		2012		2014		
	Republican	Democrat	Conservative	Democrat	Republican	Democrat	
Delegate	4,422	6,182	4,420	7,221	4,306	3,157	10,246

Northern Mariana Islands	Vote						Total vote cast in 2014
	2010		2012		2014		
	Republican	Democrat	Republican	Democrat	Democrat	Democrat	
Delegate	2,049	4,852	2,503	9,829	8,549	4,547	13,096

[1] According to Florida law, the names of those with no opposition are not printed on the ballot.
[2] According to Louisiana law, the names of those with no opposition are not printed on the ballot.
[3] According to Oklahoma law, the names of those with no opposition are not printed on the ballot.

SESSIONS OF CONGRESS, 1st–114th CONGRESSES, 1789–2015

[Closing date for this table was December 18, 2015.]

MEETING DATES OF CONGRESS: Pursuant to a resolution of the Confederation Congress in 1788, the Constitution went into effect on March 4, 1789. From then until the 20th amendment took effect in January 1934, the term of each Congress began on March 4th of each odd-numbered year; however, Article I, section 4, of the Constitution provided that "The Congress shall assemble at least once in every Year, and such Meeting shall be on the first Monday in December, unless they shall by law appoint a different day." The Congress therefore convened regularly on the first Monday in December until the 20th amendment became effective, which changed the beginning of Congress's term as well as its convening date to January 3rd. So prior to 1934, a new Congress typically would not convene for regular business until 13 months after being elected. One effect of this was that the last session of each Congress was a "lame duck" session. After the 20th amendment, the time from the election to the beginning of Congress's term as well as when it convened was reduced to two months. Recognizing that the need might exist for Congress to meet at times other than the regularly scheduled convening date, Article II, section 3 of the Constitution provides that the President "may, on extraordinary occasions, convene both Houses, or either of them"; hence these sessions occur only if convened by Presidential proclamation. Except as noted, these are separately numbered sessions of a Congress, and are marked by an E in the session column of the table. Until the 20th amendment was adopted, there were also times when special sessions of the Senate were convened, principally for confirming Cabinet and other executive nominations, and occasionally for the ratification of treaties or other executive business. These Senate sessions were also called by Presidential proclamation (typically by the outgoing President, although on occasion by incumbents as well) and are marked by an S in the session column. MEETING PLACES OF CONGRESS: Congress met for the first and second sessions of the First Congress (1789 and 1790) in New York City. From the third session of the First Congress through the first session of the Sixth Congress (1790 to 1800), Philadelphia was the meeting place. Congress has convened in Washington since the second session of the Sixth Congress (1800).

Congress	Session	Convening Date	Adjournment Date	Length in days [1]	Recesses [2] Senate	Recesses [2] House of Representatives	President pro tempore of the Senate [3]	Speaker of the House of Representatives
1st	1	Mar. 4, 1789	Sept. 29, 1789	210			John Langdon, of New Hampshire	Frederick A.C. Muhlenberg, of Pennsylvania.
	2	Jan. 4, 1790	Aug. 12, 1790	221			do.	
	3	Dec. 6, 1790	Mar. 3, 1791	88			do.	
2d	S	Mar. 4, 1791	Mar. 4, 1791	1			Richard Henry Lee, of Virginia; John Langdon, of New Hampshire.	Jonathan Trumbull, of Connecticut.
	1	Oct. 24, 1791	May 8, 1792	197			do.	
	2	Nov. 5, 1792	Mar. 2, 1793	119				
3d	S	Mar. 4, 1793	Mar. 4, 1793	1			John Langdon, of New Hampshire; Ralph Izard, of South Carolina. Henry Tazewell, of Virginia.	Frederick A.C. Muhlenberg, of Pennsylvania.
	1	Dec. 2, 1793	June 9, 1794	190				
	2	Nov. 3, 1794	Mar. 3, 1795	121			do.	
4th	S	June 8, 1795	June 26, 1795	19			Henry Tazewell, of Virginia; Samuel Livermore, of New Hampshire.	Jonathan Dayton, of New Jersey.
	1	Dec. 7, 1795	June 1, 1796	177			William Bingham, of Pennsylvania.	
	2	Dec. 5, 1796	Mar. 3, 1797	89				
5th	S	Mar. 4, 1797	Mar. 4, 1797	1			William Bradford, of Rhode Island	Do.
	1–E	May 15, 1797	July 10, 1797	57				
	S	July 17, 1797	July 19, 1797	3			Jacob Read, of South Carolina; Theodore Sedgwick, of Massachusetts.	
	2	Nov. 13, 1797	July 16, 1798	246				
	3	Dec. 3, 1798	Mar. 3, 1799	91			John Laurance, of New York; James Ross, of Pennsylvania.	
6th	1	Dec. 2, 1799	May 14, 1800	164			Samuel Livermore, of New Hampshire; Uriah Tracy, of Connecticut.	Theodore Sedgwick, of Massachusetts.
	2	Nov. 17, 1800	Mar. 3, 1801	107	Dec. 23–Dec. 30, 1800	Dec. 24–Dec. 29, 1800	John E. Howard, of Maryland; James Hillhouse, of Connecticut.	
7th	S	Mar. 4, 1801	Mar. 5, 1801	2			Abraham Baldwin, of Georgia	Nathaniel Macon, of North Carolina.
	1	Dec. 7, 1801	May 3, 1802	148				

Congress	Session	Date of assembling	Date of adjournment	Length in days	Special session of Senate	President pro tempore of the Senate	Speaker of the House of Representatives
8th	2	Dec. 6, 1802	Mar. 3, 1803	88		Stephen R. Bradley, of Vermont.	Do.
	1-E	Oct. 17, 1803	Mar. 27, 1804	163		John Brown, of Kentucky; Jesse Franklin, of North Carolina.	
9th	2	Nov. 5, 1804	Mar. 3, 1805	119		Joseph Anderson, of Tennessee.	Do.
	1	Dec. 2, 1805	Apr. 21, 1806	141		Samuel Smith, of Maryland	
10th	2	Dec. 1, 1806	Mar. 3, 1807	93		.do.	Joseph B. Varnum, of Massachusetts.
	1-E	Oct. 26, 1807	Apr. 25, 1808	182		Stephen R. Bradley, of Vermont; John Milledge, of Georgia.	
	2	Nov. 7, 1808	Mar. 3, 1809	117			
11th	S	Mar. 4, 1809	Mar. 7, 1809	4		Andrew Gregg, of Pennsylvania	Do.
	1	May 22, 1809	June 28, 1809	38		John Gaillard, of South Carolina.	
	2	Nov. 27, 1809	May 1, 1810	156		John Pope, of Kentucky.	
	3	Dec. 3, 1810	Mar. 3, 1811	91		William H. Crawford, of Georgia	
12th	1-E	Nov. 4, 1811	July 6, 1812	245		.do.	Henry Clay, of Kentucky.
	2	Nov. 2, 1812	Mar. 3, 1813	122		.do.	
13th	1	May 24, 1813	Aug. 2, 1813	71		Joseph B. Varnum, of Massachusetts; John Gaillard, of South Carolina.	Do.[4] Langdon Cheves, of South Carolina.[4]
	2	Dec. 6, 1813	Apr. 18, 1814	134		John Gaillard, of South Carolina.	
14th	3-E	Sept. 19, 1814	Mar. 3, 1815	166		.do.	Henry Clay, of Kentucky.
	1	Dec. 4, 1815	Apr. 30, 1816	148		.do.	
	S	Dec. 2, 1816	Mar. 3, 1817	92		.do.	
15th	1	Mar. 4, 1817	Mar. 6, 1817	3		.do.	Do.
	1	Dec. 1, 1817	Apr. 20, 1818	141	Dec. 24–Dec. 29, 1817; Dec. 25–Dec. 28, 1817	James Barbour, of Virginia; John Gaillard, of South Carolina.	
	2	Nov. 16, 1818	Mar. 3, 1819	108		James Barbour, of Virginia.	
16th	1	Dec. 6, 1819	May 15, 1820	162		John Gaillard, of South Carolina.	Do.[5]
	2	Nov. 13, 1820	Mar. 3, 1821	111		.do.	
17th	1	Dec. 3, 1821	May 8, 1822	157		.do.	John W. Taylor, of New York.[5] Philip P. Barbour, of Virginia.
	2	Dec. 2, 1822	Mar. 3, 1823	92		.do.	
18th	1	Dec. 1, 1823	May 27, 1824	178		.do.	Henry Clay, of Kentucky.
	2	Dec. 6, 1824	Mar. 3, 1825	88		Nathaniel Macon, of North Carolina	
19th	S	Mar. 4, 1825	Mar. 9, 1825	6		.do.	John W. Taylor, of New York.
	1	Dec. 5, 1825	May 22, 1826	169		.do.	
	2	Dec. 3, 1826	Mar. 3, 1827	90		.do.	
20th	1	Dec. 3, 1827	May 26, 1828	175		Samuel Smith, of Maryland	Andrew Stevenson, of Virginia.
	2	Dec. 1, 1828	Mar. 3, 1829	93	Dec. 24–Dec. 29, 1828; Dec. 25–Dec. 28, 1828	.do.	
21st	S	Mar. 4, 1829	Mar. 17, 1829	14		.do.	Do.
	1	Dec. 7, 1829	May 31, 1830	176		.do.	
	2	Dec. 6, 1830	Mar. 3, 1831	88		.do.	
22d	1	Dec. 5, 1831	July 16, 1832	225		.do.	Do.
	2	Dec. 2, 1832	Mar. 2, 1833	91		Littleton Waller Tazewell, of Virginia	
23d	1	Dec. 2, 1833	June 30, 1834	211		Hugh Lawson White, of Tennessee.	Do.[6]
	2	Dec. 1, 1834	Mar. 3, 1835	93		Hugh Lawson White, of Tennessee; George Poindexter, of Mississippi.	
24th	1	Dec. 7, 1835	July 4, 1836	211		John Tyler, of Virginia.	John Bell, of Tennessee.[6] James K. Polk, of Tennessee.
	2	Dec. 5, 1836	Mar. 3, 1837	89		William R. King, of Alabama	
25th	S	Mar. 4, 1837	Mar. 10, 1837	7		.do.	Do.
	1	Sept. 4, 1837	Oct. 16, 1837	43		.do.	
	2	Dec. 4, 1837	July 9, 1838	218		.do.	
	3	Dec. 3, 1838	Mar. 3, 1839	91		.do.	
26th	1	Dec. 2, 1839	July 21, 1840	233		.do.	Robert M.T. Hunter, of Virginia.
	2	Dec. 7, 1840	Mar. 3, 1841	87		.do.	
27th	S	Mar. 4, 1841	Mar. 15, 1841	12		William R. King, of Alabama; Samuel L. Southard, of New Jersey.	Do.

SESSIONS OF CONGRESS, 1st–114th CONGRESSES, 1789–2015—CONTINUED

[Closing date for this table was December 18, 2015.]

MEETING DATES OF CONGRESS: Pursuant to a resolution of the Confederation Congress in 1788, the Constitution went into effect on March 4, 1789. From then until the 20th amendment took effect in January 1934, the term of each Congress began on March 4th of each odd-numbered year; however, Article I, section 4, of the Constitution provided that "The Congress shall assemble at least once in every Year, and such Meeting shall be on the first Monday in December, unless they shall by law appoint a different day." The Congress therefore convened regularly on the first Monday in December until the 20th amendment became effective, which changed the beginning of Congress's term as well as its convening date to January 3rd. So prior to 1934, a new Congress typically would not convene for regular business until 13 months after being elected. One effect of this was that the last session of each Congress was a "lame duck" session. After the 20th amendment, the time from the election to the beginning of Congress's term as well as when it convened was reduced to two months. Recognizing that the need might exist for Congress to meet at times other than the regularly scheduled convening date, Article II, section 3 of the Constitution provides that the President "may, on extraordinary occasions, convene both Houses, or either of them"; hence these sessions occur only if convened by Presidential proclamation. Except as noted, these are separately numbered sessions of a Congress, and are marked by an E in the session column of the table. Until the 20th amendment was adopted, there were also times when special sessions of the Senate were convened, principally for confirming Cabinet and other executive nominations, and occasionally for the ratification of treaties or other executive business. These Senate sessions were also called by Presidential proclamation (typically by the outgoing President, although on occasion by incumbents as well) and are marked by an S in the session column. MEETING PLACES OF CONGRESS: Congress met for the first and second sessions of the First Congress (1789 and 1790) in New York City. From the third session of the First Congress through the first session of the Sixth Congress (1790 to 1800), Philadelphia was the meeting place. Congress has convened in Washington since the second session of the Sixth Congress (1800).

Congress	Session	Convening Date	Adjournment Date	Length in days[1]	Recesses[2] Senate	Recesses[2] House of Representatives	President pro tempore of the Senate[3]	Speaker of the House of Representatives
	1–E	May 31, 1841	Sept. 13, 1841	106			Samuel L. Southard, of New Jersey	John White, of Kentucky.
	2	Dec. 6, 1841	Aug. 31, 1842	269			Willie P. Mangum, of North Carolina.	
	3	Dec. 5, 1842	Mar. 3, 1843	89			..do..	
28th	1	Dec. 4, 1843	June 17, 1844	196			..do	John W. Jones, of Virginia.
	2	Dec. 2, 1844	Mar. 3, 1845	92			..do	
29th	S	Mar. 4, 1845	Mar. 20, 1845	17				
	1	Dec. 1, 1845	Aug. 10, 1846	253			Ambrose H. Sevier; David R. Atchison, of Missouri.	John W. Davis, of Indiana.
	2	Dec. 7, 1846	Mar. 3, 1847	87			David R. Atchison, of Missouri.	
30th	1	Dec. 6, 1847	Aug. 14, 1848	254			..do	Robert C. Winthrop, of Massachusetts.
	2	Dec. 4, 1848	Mar. 3, 1849	90			..do	
31st	S	Mar. 5, 1849	Mar. 23, 1849	19			..do	
	1	Dec. 3, 1849	Sept. 30, 1850	302			William R. King, of Alabama.	Howell Cobb, of Georgia.
	2	Dec. 2, 1850	Mar. 3, 1851	92			..do	
32d	S	Mar. 4, 1851	Mar. 13, 1851	10				
	1	Dec. 1, 1851	Aug. 31, 1852	275			..do	Linn Boyd, of Kentucky.
	2	Dec. 6, 1852	Mar. 3, 1853	88			David R. Atchison, of Missouri.	
33d	S	Mar. 4, 1853	Apr. 11, 1853	39			..do	
	1	Dec. 5, 1853	Aug. 7, 1854	246			Lewis Cass, of Michigan; Jesse D. Bright, of Indiana.	Do.
	2	Dec. 4, 1854	Mar. 3, 1855	90			Charles E. Stuart, of Michigan; Jesse D. Bright, of Indiana.	
34th	1	Dec. 3, 1855	Aug. 18, 1856	260			Jesse D. Bright, of Indiana.	Nathaniel P. Banks, of Massachusetts.
	2–E	Aug. 21, 1856	Aug. 30, 1856	10			James M. Mason, of Virginia.	
	3	Dec. 1, 1856	Mar. 3, 1857	93			James M. Mason, of Virginia; Thomas J. Rusk, of Texas.	
35th	S	Mar. 4, 1857	Mar. 14, 1857	11				
	1	Dec. 7, 1857	June 14, 1858	189	Dec. 23, 1857–Jan. 4, 1858	Dec. 24, 1857–Jan. 3, 1858	Benjamin Fitzpatrick, of Alabama	James L. Orr, of South Carolina.

Congress	Sess.	Date of commencement	Date of adjournment	Length, days	Recess	Recess	President of Senate pro tempore	Speaker of the House
36th	S	June 15, 1858	June 16, 1858	2			...do.	William Pennington, of New Jersey.
	2	Dec. 6, 1858	Mar. 3, 1859	88	Dec. 23, 1858–Jan. 4, 1859	Dec. 24, 1858–Jan. 3, 1859	...do.	
	S	Mar. 4, 1859	Mar. 10, 1859	7			Benjamin Fitzpatrick, of Alabama; Jesse D. Bright, of Indiana.	
	1	Dec. 5, 1859	June 25, 1860	202			Benjamin Fitzpatrick, of Alabama.	
37th	S	June 26, 1860	June 28, 1860	3			Solomon Foot, of Vermont.	Galusha A. Grow, of Pennsylvania.
	2	Dec. 3, 1860	Mar. 3, 1861	93			...do.	
	S	Mar. 4, 1861	Mar. 28, 1861	25			...do.	
	1-E	July 4, 1861	Aug. 6, 1861	34			...do.	
38th		Dec. 2, 1861	July 17, 1862	228	Dec. 23, 1862–Jan. 5, 1863	Dec. 24, 1862–Jan. 4, 1863	Solomon Foot, of Vermont; Daniel Clark, of New Hampshire.	Schuyler Colfax, of Indiana.
	3	Dec. 1, 1862	Mar. 3, 1863	93			Daniel Clark, of New Hampshire.	
	1	Dec. 7, 1863	July 4, 1854	209	Dec. 23, 1863–Jan. 5, 1864	Dec. 24, 1863–Jan. 4, 1864		
39th	2	Mar. 3, 1865	Mar. 11, 1865	89	Dec. 22, 1864–Jan. 5, 1865	Dec. 22, 1864–Jan. 4, 1865	Lafayette S. Foster, of Connecticut.	Do.
	S	Mar. 4, 1865	July 28, 1866	8	Dec. 6–Dec. 11, 1865	Dec. 7–Dec. 10, 1865		
	1	Dec. 4, 1865		237	Dec. 21, 1865–Jan. 5, 1866	Dec. 23, 1865–Jan. 4, 1866		
40th	2	Dec. 3, 1866	Mar. 3, 1867	91	Dec. 20, 1866–Jan. 3, 1867	Dec. 20, 1866–Jan. 3, 1867	Benjamin F. Wade, of Ohio.	Do.[7]
	1	Mar. 4, 1867	Dec. 1, 1867	273	Mar. 30–July 3, 1867	Mar. 31–July 2, 1867	...do	
					July 20–Nov. 21, 1867	July 21–Nov. 20, 1867		
41st	S	Apr. 1, 1867	Apr. 20, 1867	20	Dec. 20, 1867–Jan. 5, 1868	Dec. 21, 1867–Jan. 5, 1868	Henry B. Anthony, of Rhode Island	Theodore M. Pomeroy, of New York.[7]
	2	Dec. 2, 1867	Nov. 10, 1868	345	July 27–Sept. 21, 1868	July 26–Sept. 20, 1868		James G. Blaine, of Maine.
					Sept. 21–Oct. 16, 1868	Sept. 22–Oct. 15, 1868		
42d	3	Dec. 7, 1868	Mar. 3, 1869	87	Dec. 21, 1868–Jan. 5, 1869	Dec. 22, 1868–Jan. 4, 1869	...do	Do.
	S	Mar. 4, 1869	Apr. 10, 1869	38			...do	
	2	Apr. 12, 1869	Apr. 22, 1869	11			...do	
	3	Dec. 6, 1869	July 15, 1870	222	Dec. 22, 1869–Jan. 10, 1870	Dec. 23, 1869–Jan. 9, 1870	...do	
43d	1	Dec. 5, 1870	Mar. 3, 1871	89	Dec. 23, 1870–Jan. 4, 1871	Dec. 23, 1870–Jan. 3, 1871	...do	Do.
	S	Mar. 4, 1871	Apr. 20, 1871	48			...do	
	2	May 10, 1871	May 27, 1871	18			Matthew H. Carpenter, of Wisconsin.	
	3	Dec. 4, 1871	June 10, 1872	190	Dec. 21, 1871–Jan. 8, 1872	Dec. 22, 1871–Jan. 7, 1872	Matthew H. Carpenter, of Wisconsin; Henry B. Anthony, of Rhode Island.	
44th	1	Dec. 2, 1872	Mar. 3, 1873	92	Dec. 21, 1872–Jan. 6, 1873	Dec. 21, 1872–Jan. 5, 1873	Thomas W. Ferry, of Michigan.	Michael C. Kerr, of Indiana.[8]
	2	Mar. 4, 1873	Mar. 26, 1873	23	Dec. 19, 1873–Jan. 5, 1874	Dec. 20, 1873–Jan. 4, 1874	...do	Samuel J. Randall, of Pennsylvania.[8]
		Dec. 1, 1873	June 23, 1874	204	Dec. 23, 1874–Jan. 5, 1875	Dec. 24, 1874–Jan. 4, 1875	...do	
45th	S	Dec. 7, 1874	Mar. 3, 1875	87			...do	Do.
	1	Mar. 5, 1875	Mar. 24, 1875	20	Dec. 20, 1875–Jan. 5, 1876	Dec. 21, 1875–Jan. 4, 1876	...do	
	2	Dec. 6, 1875	Aug. 15, 1876	254			...do	
	1-E	Mar. 4, 1876	Mar. 17, 1876	90			...do	
46th		Mar. 5, 1877	Mar. 17, 1877	13			Allen G. Thurman, of Ohio	Do.
		Oct. 15, 1877	Dec. 3, 1877	50	Dec. 15, 1877–Jan. 10, 1878	Dec. 16, 1877–Jan. 10, 1878	...do	
	1-E	Dec. 3, 1877	June 20, 1878	200	Dec. 20, 1878–Jan. 7, 1879	Dec. 21, 1878–Jan. 6, 1879	...do	
		Dec. 2, 1878	Mar. 3, 1879	92				
47th		Mar. 18, 1879	July 1, 1879	106	Dec. 19, 1879–Jan. 6, 1880	Dec. 20, 1879–Jan. 5, 1880	Thomas F. Bayard, of Delaware; David Davis, of Illinois.	J. Warren Keifer, of Ohio.
	2	Dec. 1, 1879	June 16, 1880	199	Dec. 23, 1880–Jan. 5, 1881	Dec. 23, 1880–Jan. 4, 1881	...do	
	3	Dec. 6, 1880	Mar. 3, 1881	88			...do	
	S	Mar. 4, 1881	May 20, 1881	78			David Davis, of Illinois	
	S	Oct. 10, 1881	Oct. 29, 1881	20				
	1	Dec. 5, 1881	Aug. 8, 1882	247	Dec. 22, 1881–Jan. 5, 1882	Dec. 22, 1881–Jan. 4, 1882		

SESSIONS OF CONGRESS, 1st–114th CONGRESSES, 1789–2015—CONTINUED

[Closing date for this table was December 18, 2015.]

MEETING DATES OF CONGRESS: Pursuant to a resolution of the Confederation Congress in 1788, the Constitution went into effect on March 4, 1789. From then until the 20th amendment took effect in January 1934, the term of each Congress began on March 4th of each odd-numbered year; however, Article I, section 4, of the Constitution provided that ''The Congress shall assemble at least once in every Year, and such Meeting shall be on the first Monday in December, unless they shall by law appoint a different day.'' The Congress therefore convened regularly on the first Monday in December until the 20th amendment became effective, which changed the beginning of Congress's term as well as its convening date to January 3rd. So prior to 1934, a new Congress typically would not convene for regular business until 13 months after being elected. One effect of this was that the last session of each Congress was a ''lame duck'' session. After the 20th amendment, the time from the election to the beginning of Congress's term as well as when it convened was reduced to two months. Recognizing that the need might exist for Congress to meet at times other than the regularly scheduled convening date, Article II, section 3 of the Constitution provides that the President ''may, on extraordinary occasions, convene both Houses, or either of them''; hence these sessions occur only if convened by Presidential proclamation. Except as noted, these are separately numbered sessions of a Congress, and are marked by an E in the session column of the table. Until the 20th amendment was adopted, there were also times when special sessions of the Senate were convened, principally for confirming Cabinet and other executive nominations, and occasionally for the ratification of treaties or other executive business. These Senate sessions were also called by Presidential proclamation (typically by the outgoing President, although on occasion by incumbents as well) and are marked by an S in the session column. MEETING PLACES OF CONGRESS: Congress met for the first and second sessions of the First Congress (1789 and 1790) in New York City. From the third session of the First Congress through the first session of the Sixth Congress (1790 to 1800), Philadelphia was the meeting place. Congress has convened in Washington since the second session of the Sixth Congress (1800).

Congress	Session	Convening Date	Adjournment Date	Length in days[1]	Recesses[2] — Senate	Recesses[2] — House of Representatives	President pro tempore of the Senate[3]	Speaker of the House of Representatives
	2	Dec. 4, 1882	Mar. 3, 1883	90			George F. Edmunds, of Vermont.	J. Warren Keifer, of Ohio.
48th	1	Dec. 3, 1883	July 7, 1884	218	Dec. 24, 1883–Jan. 7, 1884	Dec. 25, 1883–Jan. 6, 1884	..do.	John G. Carlisle, of Kentucky.
	2	Dec. 1, 1884	Mar. 3, 1885	93	Dec. 24, 1884–Jan. 5, 1885	Dec. 25, 1884–Jan. 4, 1885	..do.	
49th	S	Mar. 4, 1885	Apr. 2, 1885	30			John Sherman, of Ohio	Do.
	1	Dec. 7, 1885	Aug. 5, 1886	242	Dec. 21, 1885–Jan. 5, 1886	Dec. 22, 1885–Jan. 4, 1886	John J. Ingalls, of Kansas.	
	2	Dec. 6, 1886	Mar. 3, 1887	88	Dec. 22, 1886–Jan. 4, 1887	Dec. 23, 1886–Jan. 3, 1887	..do.	
50th	1	Dec. 5, 1887	Oct. 20, 1888	321	Dec. 22, 1887–Jan. 4, 1888	Dec. 23, 1887–Jan. 3, 1888	..do.	Do.
	2	Dec. 3, 1888	Mar. 3, 1889	91	Dec. 21, 1888–Jan. 2, 1889	Dec. 22, 1888–Jan. 1, 1889	..do.	
51st	S	Mar. 4, 1889	Apr. 2, 1889	30			Charles F. Manderson, of Nebraska.	Thomas B. Reed, of Maine.
	1	Dec. 2, 1889	Oct. 1, 1890	304	Dec. 21, 1889–Jan. 6, 1890	Dec. 22, 1889–Jan. 5, 1890	..do	
	2	Dec. 1, 1890	Mar. 3, 1891	93			..do.	
52d	1	Dec. 7, 1891	Aug. 5, 1892	251			Charles F. Manderson, of Nebraska; Isham G. Harris, of Tennessee.	Charles F. Crisp, of Georgia.
	2	Dec. 5, 1892	Mar. 3, 1893	89	Dec. 22, 1892–Jan. 4, 1893	Dec. 23, 1892–Jan. 3, 1893	Isham G. Harris, of Tennessee	
53d	S	Mar. 4, 1893	Apr. 15, 1893	43			..do.	Do.
	1-E	Aug. 7, 1893	Nov. 3, 1893	89			Matt W. Ransom, of North Carolina; Isham G. Harris, of Tennessee.	
	2	Dec. 4, 1893	Aug. 28, 1894	268		Dec. 22, 1893–Jan. 2, 1894	..do.	
	3	Dec. 3, 1894	Mar. 3, 1895	97		Dec. 23, 1894–Jan. 2, 1895	..do.	
54th	1	Dec. 2, 1895	June 11, 1896	193			William P. Frye, of Maine	Thomas B. Reed, of Maine.
	2	Dec. 7, 1896	Mar. 3, 1897	87	Dec. 22, 1896–Jan. 5, 1897	Dec. 23, 1896–Jan. 4, 1897	..do.	
55th	S	Mar. 4, 1897	Mar. 10, 1897	11			..do.	Do.
	1-E	Mar. 15, 1897	July 24, 1897	131			..do.	
	2	Dec. 6, 1897	July 8, 1898	215	Dec. 18, 1897–Jan. 5, 1898	Dec. 19, 1897–Jan. 4, 1898	..do.	
	3	Dec. 5, 1898	Mar. 3, 1899	89	Dec. 21, 1898–Jan. 3, 1899	Dec. 20, 1898–Jan. 3, 1899	..do.	
56th	1	Dec. 4, 1899	June 7, 1900	186	Dec. 20, 1899–Jan. 3, 1900	Dec. 21, 1899–Jan. 2, 1900	..do.	David B. Henderson, of Iowa.
	2	Dec. 3, 1900	Mar. 3, 1901	91	Dec. 20, 1900–Jan. 3, 1901	Dec. 22, 1900–Jan. 2, 1901	..do.	
57th	S	Mar. 4, 1901	Mar. 9, 1901	6			..do.	

Congress	Session	Assembled	Adjourned	Length in days	Senate holiday recess	House holiday recess	President pro tempore of the Senate	Speaker of the House of Representatives
57th	1	Dec. 2, 1901	July 1, 1902	212	Dec. 19, 1901–Jan. 6, 1902	Dec. 20, 1901–Jan. 5, 1902	do.	Do.
	2	Dec. 1, 1902	Mar. 3, 1903	93	Dec. 20, 1902–Jan. 5, 1903	Dec. 21, 1902–Jan. 4, 1903	do.	Do.
58th	Spl.	Mar. 5, 1903	Mar. 19, 1903	15			do.	Joseph G. Cannon, of Illinois.
	1	Nov. 9, 1903	Dec. 7, 1903	29			do.	
	2	Dec. 7, 1903	Apr. 28, 1904	144	Dec. 19, 1903–Jan. 4, 1904	Dec. 19, 1903–Jan. 4, 1904	do.	Do.
	3	Dec. 5, 1904	Mar. 3, 1905	89	Dec. 21, 1904–Jan. 4, 1905	Dec. 22, 1904–Jan. 3, 1905	do.	Do.
59th	Spl.	Mar. 4, 1905	Mar. 18, 1905	15			do.	Do.
	1	Dec. 4, 1905	June 30, 1906	209	Dec. 21, 1905–Jan. 4, 1906	Dec. 22, 1905–Jan. 3, 1906	do.	Do.
	2	Dec. 3, 1906	Mar. 3, 1907	91	Dec. 20, 1906–Jan. 3, 1907	Dec. 21, 1906–Jan. 2, 1907	do.	Do.
60th	1	Dec. 2, 1907	May 30, 1908	181	Dec. 21, 1907–Jan. 6, 1908	Dec. 22, 1907–Jan. 5, 1908	do.	Do.
	2	Dec. 7, 1908	Mar. 3, 1909	87	Dec. 19, 1908–Jan. 4, 1909	Dec. 20, 1908–Jan. 3, 1909	do.	Do.
61st	Spl.	Mar. 4, 1909	Mar. 6, 1909	3			do.	Do.
	1	Mar. 15, 1909	Aug. 5, 1909	144			do.	Do.
	2	Dec. 6, 1909	June 25, 1910	202	Dec. 21, 1909–Jan. 4, 1910	Dec. 22, 1909–Jan. 3, 1910	do.	Do.
	3	Dec. 5, 1910	Mar. 3, 1911	89	Dec. 21, 1910–Jan. 5, 1911	Dec. 22, 1910–Jan. 4, 1911	do.[9]	Do.
62d	1	Apr. 4, 1911	Aug. 22, 1911	141			Charles Curtis, of Kansas; Augustus O. Bacon, of Georgia; Jacob H. Gallinger, of New Hampshire; Henry Cabot Lodge, of Massachusetts; Frank B. Brandegee, of Connecticut.	Champ Clark, of Missouri.
	2	Dec. 4, 1911	Aug. 26, 1912	267	Dec. 21, 1911–Jan. 3, 1912	Dec. 22, 1911–Jan. 2, 1912	do.	Do.
	3	Dec. 2, 1912	Mar. 3, 1913	92	Dec. 19, 1912–Jan. 2, 1913	Dec. 20, 1912–Jan. 1, 1913	do.	Do.
63d	Spl.	Mar. 4, 1913	Mar. 17, 1913	14			Augustus O. Bacon, of Georgia; Jacob H. Gallinger, of New Hampshire. James P. Clarke, of Arkansas.	Do.
	1	Apr. 7, 1913	Dec. 1, 1913	239			do.	Do.
	2	Dec. 1, 1913	Oct. 24, 1914	328	Dec. 23, 1913–Jan. 12, 1914	Dec. 24, 1913–Jan. 11, 1914	do.	Do.
	3	Dec. 7, 1914	Mar. 3, 1915	87	Dec. 23–Dec. 28, 1914	Dec. 24–Dec. 28, 1914	do.	Do.
64th	1	Dec. 6, 1915	Sept. 8, 1916	278	Dec. 17, 1915–Jan. 3, 1916	Dec. 18, 1915–Jan. 3, 1916	do.	Do.
	2	Dec. 4, 1916	Mar. 3, 1917	90	Dec. 22, 1916–Jan. 2, 1917	Dec. 23, 1916–Jan. 1, 1917	do.	Do.
65th	Spl.	Mar. 5, 1917	Mar. 16, 1917	12			Willard Saulsbury, of Delaware [10]	Do.
	1	Apr. 2, 1917	Oct. 6, 1917	188			do.	Do.
	2	Dec. 3, 1917	Nov. 21, 1918	354	Dec. 18, 1917–Jan. 3, 1918	Dec. 19, 1917–Jan. 2, 1918	do.	Do.
	3	Dec. 2, 1918	Mar. 3, 1919	92			do.	Do.
66th	1	May 19, 1919	Nov. 19, 1919	185	July 1–July 8, 1919	July 2–July 7, 1919	Albert B. Cummins, of Iowa	Frederick H. Gillett, of Massachusetts.
	2	Dec. 1, 1919	June 5, 1920	188	Dec. 20, 1919–Jan. 5, 1920	Dec. 21, 1919–Jan. 4, 1920	do.	Do.
	3	Dec. 6, 1920	Mar. 3, 1921	88			do.	Do.
67th	Spl.	Mar. 4, 1921	Mar. 15, 1921	12			do.	Do.
	1	Apr. 11, 1921	Nov. 23, 1921	227	Aug. 24–Sept. 21, 1921	Aug. 25–Sept. 20, 1921	do.	Do.
	2	Dec. 5, 1921	Sept. 22, 1922	292	Dec. 22, 1921–Jan. 3, 1922	Dec. 23, 1921–Jan. 2, 1922; July 1–Aug. 14, 1922	do.	Do.
	3	Nov. 20, 1922	Dec. 4, 1922	15			do.	Do.
	4	Dec. 4, 1922	Mar. 3, 1923	90			do.	Do.
68th	1	Dec. 3, 1923	June 7, 1924	188	Dec. 20, 1923–Jan. 3, 1924	Dec. 21, 1923–Jan. 2, 1924	Albert B. Cummins, of Iowa; George H. Moses, of New Hampshire.	Do.
	2	Dec. 1, 1924	Mar. 3, 1925	93	Dec. 20–Dec. 29, 1924	Dec. 21–Dec. 28, 1924	do.	Do.
69th	Spl.	Mar. 4, 1925	Mar. 18, 1925	15			do.	Nicholas Longworth, of Ohio.
	1	Dec. 7, 1925	July 3, 1926	209	Dec. 22, 1925–Jan. 4, 1926	Dec. 23, 1925–Jan. 3, 1926	do.	Do.
	2	Dec. 6, 1926	Mar. 4, 1927	88	Dec. 22, 1926–Jan. 3, 1927	Dec. 23, 1926–Jan. 2, 1927	do.	Do.
70th	1	Dec. 5, 1927	May 29, 1928	177	Dec. 21, 1927–Jan. 4, 1928	Dec. 22, 1927–Jan. 3, 1928	do.	Do.
	2	Dec. 3, 1928	Mar. 3, 1929	91	Dec. 22, 1928–Jan. 3, 1929	Dec. 22, 1928–Jan. 2, 1929	do.	Do.
71st	Spl.	Mar. 4, 1929	Mar. 5, 1929	2			do.	Do.
	1	Apr. 15, 1929	Nov. 22, 1929	222	June 19–Aug. 19, 1929	June 20–Sept. 22, 1929	do.	Do.
	2	Dec. 2, 1929	July 3, 1930	214	Dec. 21, 1929–Jan. 6, 1930	Dec. 22, 1929–Jan. 6, 1930	do.	Do.

SESSIONS OF CONGRESS, 1st–114th CONGRESSES, 1789–2015—CONTINUED

[Closing date for this table was December 18, 2015.]

MEETING DATES OF CONGRESS: Pursuant to a resolution of the Confederation Congress in 1788, the Constitution went into effect on March 4, 1789. From then until the 20th amendment took effect in January 1934, the term of each Congress began on March 4th of each odd-numbered year; however, Article I, section 4, of the Constitution provided that "The Congress shall assemble at least once in every Year, and such Meeting shall be on the first Monday in December, unless they shall by law appoint a different day." The Congress therefore convened regularly on the first Monday in December until the 20th amendment became effective, which changed the beginning of Congress's term as well as its convening date to January 3rd. So prior to 1934, a new Congress typically would not convene for regular business until 13 months after being elected. One effect of this was that the last session of each Congress was a "lame duck" session. After the 20th amendment, the time from the election to the beginning of Congress's term as well as when it convened was reduced to two months. Recognizing that the need might exist for Congress to meet at times other than the regularly scheduled convening date, Article II, section 3 of the Constitution provides that the President "may, on extraordinary occasions, convene both Houses, or either of them"; hence these sessions occur only if convened by Presidential proclamation. Except as noted, these are separately numbered sessions of a Congress, and are marked by an E in the session column of the table. Until the 20th amendment was adopted, there were also times when special sessions of the Senate were convened, principally for confirming Cabinet and other executive nominations, and occasionally for the ratification of treaties or other executive business. These Senate sessions were also called by Presidential proclamation (typically by the outgoing President, although on occasion by incumbents as well) and are marked by an S in the session column. MEETING PLACES OF CONGRESS: Congress met for the first and second sessions of the First Congress (1789 and 1790) in New York City. From the third session of the First Congress through the first session of the Sixth Congress (1790 to 1800), Philadelphia was the meeting place. Congress has convened in Washington since the second session of the Sixth Congress (1800).

Congress	Session	Convening Date	Adjournment Date	Length in days[1]	Recesses[2] — Senate	Recesses[2] — House of Representatives	President pro tempore of the Senate[3]	Speaker of the House of Representatives
	S	July 7, 1930	July 21, 1930	15			...do.	Nicholas Longworth, of Ohio.
	3	Dec. 1, 1930	Mar. 3, 1931	93	Dec. 20, 1930–Jan. 5, 1931	Dec. 21, 1930–Jan. 4, 1931	George H. Moses, of New Hampshire	do.
72d	1	Dec. 7, 1931	July 16, 1932	223	Dec. 22, 1931–Jan. 4, 1932	Dec. 23, 1931–Jan. 3, 1932	do.	John N. Garner, of Texas.
	2	Dec. 5, 1932	Mar. 3, 1933	89			do.	
73d	S	Mar. 4, 1933	Mar. 6, 1933	3			do.	
	1-E	Mar. 9, 1933	June 15, 1933	99			Key Pittman, of Nevada	Henry T. Rainey, of Illinois.
	2	Jan. 3, 1934	June 18, 1934	167			do.	
74th	1	Jan. 3, 1935	Aug. 26, 1935	236			do.	Joseph W. Byrns, of Tennessee.[11]
	2	Jan. 3, 1936	June 20, 1936	170	June 8–June 15, 1936	June 9–June 14, 1936	do.	William B. Bankhead, of Alabama.[11]
75th	1	Jan. 5, 1937	Aug. 21, 1937	229			do.	Do.
	2-E	Nov. 15, 1937	Dec. 21, 1937	37			do.	
	3	Jan. 3, 1938	June 16, 1938	165			do.	
76th	1	Jan. 3, 1939	Aug. 5, 1939	215			do.	Do.[12]
	2-E	Sept. 21, 1939	Nov. 3, 1939	44			do.	
	3	Jan. 3, 1940	Jan. 3, 1941	366	July 11–July 22, 1940	June 23–June 30, 1940; July 12–July 21, 1940	Key Pittman, of Nevada;[13] William H. King, of Utah.[13]	
77th	1	Jan. 3, 1941	Jan. 2, 1942	365			Pat Harrison, of Mississippi;[14] Carter Glass, of Virginia.[14]	Sam Rayburn, of Texas.[12]
	2	Jan. 5, 1942	Dec. 16, 1942	346			Carter Glass, of Virginia.	
78th	1	Jan. 6, 1943	Dec. 21, 1943	350	July 8–Sept. 14, 1943	Apr. 23–May 2, 1943; July 8–Sept. 13, 1943	do.	Do.
	2	Jan. 10, 1944	Dec. 19, 1944	345	Apr. 1–Apr. 12, 1944; June 23–Aug. 1, 1944; Sept. 21–Nov. 14, 1944	Apr. 2–Apr. 11, 1944; June 24–Aug. 31, 1944; Sept. 22–Nov. 13, 1944	do.	
79th	1	Jan. 3, 1945	Dec. 21, 1945	353	Aug. 1–Sept. 5, 1945	July 22–Sept. 4, 1945	Kenneth McKellar, of Tennessee	Do.
	2	Jan. 14, 1946	Aug. 2, 1946	201			do.	
80th	1 [15]	Jan. 3, 1947	Dec. 19, 1947	351	July 27–Nov. 17, 1947	July 28–Nov. 16, 1947	Arthur H. Vandenberg, of Michigan	Joseph W. Martin, Jr., of Massachusetts.

Congress	Session	Date of convening	Date of adjournment	Length in days	Recess	Recess	President pro tempore of the Senate	Speaker of the House
	2[15]	Jan. 6, 1948	Dec. 31, 1948	361	June 20–July 26, 1948 Aug. 7–Dec. 31, 1948	June 21–July 25, 1948 Aug. 8–Dec. 30, 1948	...do.	Do.
81st	1	Jan. 3, 1949	Oct. 19, 1949	290	Apr. 15–May 2, 1949		Kenneth McKellar, of Tennessee	Sam Rayburn, of Texas.
	2	Jan. 3, 1950	Jan. 2, 1951	365		Apr. 6–Apr. 18, 1950 Sept. 23–Nov. 27, 1950	...do.	Do.
82d	1	Jan. 3, 1951	Oct. 20, 1951	291		Mar. 23–Apr. 1, 1951 Aug. 24–Sept. 1, 1951	...do.	Do.
	2	Jan. 8, 1952	July 7, 1952	182		Apr. 11–Apr. 21, 1952	...do.	Do.
83d	1	Jan. 3, 1953	Aug. 3, 1953	213		Apr. 3–Apr. 12, 1953	Styles Bridges, of New Hampshire	Joseph W. Martin, Jr., of Massachusetts.
	2	Jan. 6, 1954	Dec. 2, 1954	331	Aug. 20–Nov. 8, 1954 Nov. 18–Nov. 29, 1954	Apr. 16–Apr. 25, 1954 Adjourned sine die Aug. 20, 1954	...do.	Do.
84th	1	Jan. 5, 1955	Aug. 2, 1955	210	Apr. 4–Apr. 13, 1955	Apr. 5–Apr. 12, 1955	Walter F. George, of Georgia	Sam Rayburn, of Texas.
	2	Jan. 3, 1956	July 27, 1956	207	Mar. 29–Apr. 9, 1956	Mar. 30–Apr. 8, 1956	...do.	Do.
85th	1	Jan. 3, 1957	Aug. 30, 1957	239	Apr. 18–Apr. 29, 1957	Apr. 19–Apr. 28, 1957	Carl Hayden, of Arizona	Do.
	2	Jan. 7, 1958	Aug. 24, 1958	230	Apr. 3–Apr. 14, 1958	Apr. 4–Apr. 13, 1958	...do.	Do.
86th	1	Jan. 7, 1959	Sept. 15, 1959	252	Mar. 26–Apr. 7, 1959	Mar. 27–Apr. 6, 1959	...do.	Do.
	2	Jan. 6, 1960	Sept. 1, 1960	240	Apr. 14–Apr. 18, 1960 May 27–May 31, 1960 July 3–Aug. 8, 1960	July 4–Aug. 14, 1960	...do.	Do.
87th	1	Jan. 3, 1961	Sept. 27, 1961	268		Mar. 31–Apr. 9, 1961	...do.	Do.[16]
	2	Jan. 10, 1962	Oct. 13, 1962	277		Apr. 20–Apr. 29, 1962	...do.	John W. McCormack, of Massachusetts.[16]
88th	1	Jan. 9, 1963	Dec. 30, 1963	356		Apr. 11–Apr. 21, 1963	...do.	Do.
	2	Jan. 7, 1964	Oct. 3, 1964	270	July 10–July 20, 1964 Aug. 21–Aug. 31, 1964	Mar. 27–Apr. 5, 1964 July 3–July 19, 1964 Aug. 22–Aug. 30, 1964	...do.	Do.
89th	1	Jan. 4, 1965	Oct. 23, 1965	293			...do.	Do.
	2	Jan. 10, 1966	Oct. 22, 1966	286	Apr. 7–Apr. 13, 1966 June 30–July 11, 1966	Apr. 8–Apr. 17, 1966 June 1–June 10, 1966	...do.	Do.
90th	1	Jan. 10, 1967	Dec. 15, 1967	340	Mar. 23–Apr. 3, 1967 June 29–July 10, 1967 Aug. 31–Sept. 11, 1967 Nov. 22–Nov. 27, 1967	Mar. 24–Apr. 3, 1967 June 30–July 9, 1967 Sept. 1–Sept. 10, 1967 Nov. 23–Nov. 26, 1967	...do.	Do.
	2	Jan. 15, 1968	Oct. 14, 1968	274	Apr. 11–Apr. 17, 1968 May 29–June 3, 1968 June 3–July 8, 1968 Aug. 2–Sept. 4, 1968	Apr. 12–Apr. 21, 1968 May 30–June 2, 1968 July 4–July 7, 1968 Aug. 3–Sept. 3, 1968	...do.	Do.
91st	1	Jan. 3, 1969	Dec. 23, 1969	355	Feb. 7–Feb. 17, 1969 Apr. 3–Apr. 14, 1969 July 2–July 7, 1969 Aug. 13–Sept. 3, 1969 Nov. 26–Dec. 1, 1969	Feb. 8–Feb. 16, 1969 Apr. 4–Apr. 13, 1969 May 29–June 1, 1969 July 3–July 6, 1969 Aug. 14–Sept. 2, 1969 Nov. 7–Nov. 11, 1969 Nov. 27–Nov. 30, 1969	Richard B. Russell, of Georgia	Do.

SESSIONS OF CONGRESS, 1st–114th CONGRESSES, 1789–2015—CONTINUED

[Closing date for this table was December 18, 2015.]

MEETING DATES OF CONGRESS: Pursuant to a resolution of the Confederation Congress in 1788, the Constitution went into effect on March 4, 1789. From then until the 20th amendment took effect in January 1934, the term of each Congress began on March 4th of each odd-numbered year; however, Article I, section 4, of the Constitution provided that "The Congress shall assemble at least once in every Year, and such Meeting shall be on the first Monday in December, unless they shall by law appoint a different day." The Congress therefore convened regularly on the first Monday in December until the 20th amendment became effective, which changed the beginning of Congress's term as well as its convening date to January 3rd. So prior to 1934, a new Congress typically would not convene for regular business until 13 months after being elected. One effect of this was that the last session of each Congress was a "lame duck" session. After the 20th amendment, the time from the election to the beginning of Congress's term as well as when it convened was reduced to two months. Recognizing that the need might exist for Congress to meet at times other than the regularly scheduled convening date, Article II, section 3 of the Constitution provides that the President "may, on extraordinary occasions, convene both Houses, or either of them"; hence these sessions occur only if convened by Presidential proclamation. Except as noted, these are separately numbered sessions of a Congress, and are marked by an E in the session column of the table. Until the 20th amendment was adopted, there were also times when special sessions of the Senate were convened, principally for confirming Cabinet and other executive nominations, and occasionally for the ratification of treaties or other executive business. These Senate sessions were also called by Presidential proclamation (typically by the outgoing President, although on occasion by incumbents as well) and are marked by an S in the session column. MEETING PLACES OF CONGRESS: Congress met for the first and second sessions of the First Congress (1789 and 1790) in New York City. From the third session of the First Congress through the first session of the Sixth Congress (1790 to 1800), Philadelphia was the meeting place. Congress has convened in Washington since the second session of the Sixth Congress (1800).

Con-gress	Ses-sion	Convening Date	Adjournment Date	Length in days [1]	Recesses [2]		President pro tempore of the Senate [3]	Speaker of the House of Representatives
					Senate	House of Representatives		
	2	Jan. 19, 1970	Jan. 2, 1971	349	Feb. 10–Feb. 16, 1970 Mar. 26–Mar. 31, 1970 Sept. 2–Sept. 8, 1970 Oct. 14–Nov. 16, 1970 Nov. 25–Nov. 30, 1970 Dec. 22–Dec. 28, 1970	Feb. 11–Feb. 15, 1970 Mar. 27–Mar. 30, 1970 May 28–May 31, 1970 July 2–July 5, 1970 Aug. 15–Sept. 8, 1970 Oct. 15–Nov. 15, 1970 Nov. 26–Nov. 29, 1970 Dec. 23–Dec. 28, 1970	...do.	Carl B. Albert, of Oklahoma.
92d	1	Jan. 21, 1971	Dec. 17, 1971	331	Feb. 11–Feb. 17, 1971 Apr. 7–Apr. 14, 1971 May 26–June 1, 1971 June 30–July 6, 1971 Aug. 6–Sept. 8, 1971 Oct. 21–Oct. 26, 1971 Nov. 24–Nov. 29, 1971	Feb. 11–Feb. 16, 1971 Apr. 8–Apr. 18, 1971 May 28–May 31, 1971 July 2–July 5, 1971 Aug. 7–Sept. 7, 1971 Oct. 8–Oct. 11, 1971 Oct. 22–Oct. 25, 1971 Nov. 20–Nov. 28, 1971	Richard B. Russell, of Georgia; [17] Allen J. Ellender, of Louisiana. [17]	
	2	Jan. 18, 1972	Oct. 18, 1972	275	Feb. 9–Feb. 14, 1972 Mar. 30–Apr. 4, 1972 May 25–May 30, 1972 June 30–July 17, 1972 Aug. 18–Sept. 5, 1972	Feb. 10–Feb. 15, 1972 Mar. 30–Apr. 9, 1972 May 25–May 29, 1972 June 1–July 16, 1972 Aug. 19–Sept. 4, 1972	Allen J. Ellender, of Louisiana; [18] James O. Eastland, of Mississippi. [18]	

Congress	Session	Date of beginning	Date of adjournment	Length in days	Recesses	President pro tempore of the Senate	Recesses	Speaker of the House
93d	1	Jan. 3, 1973	Dec. 22, 1973	354	Feb. 8–Feb. 15, 1973 Apr. 18–Apr. 30, 1973 May 23–May 29, 1972 June 30–July 9, 1973 Aug. 3–Sept. 5, 1973 Oct. 18–Oct. 23, 1973 Nov. 21–Nov. 26, 1973	James O. Eastland, of Mississippi	Feb. 9–Feb. 18, 1973 Apr. 20–Apr. 29, 1973 May 25–May 28, 1973 July 1–July 9, 1973 Aug. 4–Sept. 4, 1973 Oct. 5–Oct. 8, 1973 Oct. 16–Nov. 25, 1973	Do.
	2	Jan. 21, 1974	Dec. 20, 1974	334	Feb. 3–Feb. 18, 1974 Mar. 13–Mar. 19, 1974 Apr. 11–Apr. 22, 1974 May 23–May 28, 1974 Aug. 22–Sept. 4, 1974 Oct. 17–Nov. 18, 1974 Nov. 26–Dec. 2, 1974	...do	Feb. 8–Feb. 12, 1974 Apr. 12–Apr. 21, 1974 May 24–May 27, 1974 July 4–July 8, 1974 Aug. 23–Sept. 10, 1974 Oct. 18–Nov. 17, 1974 Nov. 27–Dec. 2, 1974	
94th	1	Jan. 14, 1975	Dec. 19, 1975	340	Mar. 26–Apr. 7, 1975 May 22–June 2, 1975 June 27–July 7, 1975 Aug. 1–Sept. 3, 1975 Oct. 9–Oct. 20, 1975 Oct. 23–Oct. 28, 1975 Nov. 20–Dec. 1, 1975	...do	Mar. 27–Apr. 6, 1975 May 23–June 1, 1975 June 27–July 7, 1975 Aug. 2–Sept. 2, 1975 Oct. 10–Oct. 19, 1975 Oct. 24–Oct. 27, 1975 Nov. 21–Nov. 30, 1975	Do.
	2	Jan. 19, 1976	Oct. 1, 1976	257	Feb. 6–Feb. 16, 1976 Apr. 14–Apr. 26, 1976 May 28–June 2, 1976 July 2–July 19, 1976 Aug. 10–Aug. 23, 1976 Sept. 1–Sept. 7, 1976	...do	Feb. 12–Feb. 15, 1976 Apr. 15–Apr. 25, 1976 May 28–May 31, 1976 July 3–July 18, 1976 Aug. 11–Aug. 22, 1976 Sept. 3–Sept. 7, 1976	
95th	1	Jan. 4, 1977	Dec. 15, 1977	346	Feb. 1–Feb. 21, 1977 Apr. 7–Apr. 18, 1977 May 27–June 6, 1977 July 1–July 11, 1977 Aug. 5–Sept. 7, 1977	...do	Feb. 10–Feb. 15, 1977 Apr. 7–Apr. 17, 1977 May 27–May 31, 1977 July 1–July 10, 1977 Aug. 6–Sept. 6, 1977 Oct. 7–Oct. 10, 1977	Thomas P. O'Neill, Jr., of Massachusetts.
	2	Jan. 19, 1978	Oct. 15, 1978	270	Feb. 10–Feb. 20, 1978 Mar. 23–Apr. 3, 1978 May 26–June 5, 1978 June 29–July 10, 1978 Aug. 25–Sept. 6, 1978	...do	Feb. 10–Feb. 13, 1978 Mar. 23–Apr. 2, 1978 May 26–May 30, 1978 June 30–July 9, 1978 Aug. 18–Sept. 5, 1978	
96th	1	Jan. 15, 1979	Jan. 3, 1980	354	Feb. 9–Feb. 19, 1979 Apr. 10–Apr. 23, 1979 May 24–June 4, 1979 June 27–July 9, 1979 Aug. 3–Sept. 5, 1979 Nov. 20–Nov. 26, 1979 Adjourned sine die, Dec. 20, 1979	Warren G. Magnuson, of Washington	Feb. 9–Feb. 12, 1979 Apr. 11–Apr. 22, 1979 May 25–May 29, 1979 June 30–July 8, 1979 Aug. 3–Sept. 4, 1979 Nov. 21–Nov. 25, 1979	Do.

SESSIONS OF CONGRESS, 1st–114th CONGRESSES, 1789–2015—CONTINUED

[Closing date for this table was December 18, 2015.]

MEETING DATES OF CONGRESS: Pursuant to a resolution of the Confederation Congress in 1788, the Constitution went into effect on March 4, 1789. From then until the 20th amendment took effect in January 1934, the term of each Congress began on March 4th of each odd-numbered year; however, Article I, section 4, of the Constitution provided that "The Congress shall assemble at least once in every Year, and such Meeting shall be on the first Monday in December, unless they shall by law appoint a different day." The Congress therefore convened regularly on the first Monday in December until the 20th amendment became effective, which changed the beginning of Congress's term as well as its convening date to January 3rd. So prior to 1934, a new Congress typically would not convene for regular business until 13 months after being elected. One effect of this was that the last session of each Congress was a "lame duck" session. After the 20th amendment, the time from the election to the beginning of Congress's term as well as when it convened was reduced to two months. Recognizing that the need might exist for Congress to meet at times other than the regularly scheduled convening date, Article II, section 3 of the Constitution provides that the President "may, on extraordinary occasions, convene both Houses, or either of them"; hence these sessions occur only if convened by Presidential proclamation. Except as noted, these are separately numbered sessions of a Congress, and are marked by an E in the session column of the table. Until the 20th amendment was adopted, there were also times when special sessions of the Senate were convened, principally for confirming Cabinet and other executive nominations, and occasionally for the ratification of treaties or other executive business. These Senate sessions were also called by Presidential proclamation (typically by the outgoing President, although on occasion by incumbents as well) and are marked by an S in the session column. MEETING PLACES OF CONGRESS: Congress met for the first and second sessions of the First Congress (1789 and 1790) in New York City. From the third session of the First Congress through the first session of the Sixth Congress (1790 to 1800), Philadelphia was the meeting place. Congress has convened in Washington since the second session of the Sixth Congress (1800).

Congress	Session	Convening Date	Adjournment Date	Length in days[1]	Recesses[2]		President pro tempore of the Senate[3]	Speaker of the House of Representatives
					Senate	House of Representatives		
	2	Jan. 3, 1980	Dec. 16, 1980	349	Apr. 3–Apr. 15, 1980 May 22–May 28, 1980 July 2–July 21, 1980 Aug. 6–Aug. 18, 1980 Aug. 27–Sept. 3, 1980 Oct. 1–Nov. 12, 1980 Nov. 25–Dec. 1, 1980	Jan. 18–21, 1980 Feb. 14–Feb. 18, 1980 Apr. 3–Apr. 14, 1980 May 23–May 27, 1980 July 3–July 20, 1980 Aug. 2–Aug. 17, 1980 Aug. 29–Sept. 2, 1980 Oct. 3–Nov. 11, 1980 Nov. 22–Nov. 30, 1980	Warren G. Magnuson, of Washington; Milton Young, of North Dakota;[19] Warren G. Magnuson, of Washington.[19]	
97th	1	Jan. 5, 1981	Dec. 16, 1981	347	Feb. 6–Feb. 16, 1981 Apr. 10–Apr. 27, 1981 June 25–July 8, 1981 Aug. 3–Sept. 9, 1981 Oct. 7–Oct. 14, 1981 Nov. 24–Nov. 30, 1981	Feb. 7–Feb. 16, 1981 Apr. 11–Apr. 26, 1981 June 27–July 7, 1981 Aug. 5–Sept. 8, 1981 Oct. 8–Oct. 12, 1981 Nov. 24–Nov. 29, 1981	Strom Thurmond, of South Carolina	Do.
	2	Jan. 25, 1982	Dec. 23, 1982	333	Feb. 11–Feb. 22, 1982 Apr. 1–Apr. 13, 1982 May 27–June 1, 1982 July 1–July 12, 1982 Aug. 20–Sept. 8, 1982 Oct. 1–Nov. 29, 1982	Feb. 11–Feb. 21, 1982 Apr. 7–Apr. 19, 1982 May 29–June 1, 1982 July 2–July 11, 1982 Aug. 21–Sept. 7, 1982 Oct. 1–Jan. 7, 1983	...do	
98th	1	Jan. 3, 1983	Nov. 18, 1983	320	Jan. 3–Jan. 25, 1983 Feb. 3–Feb. 14, 1983 Mar. 24–Apr. 5, 1983 May 26–June 6, 1983 June 29–July 11, 1983 Aug. 4–Sept. 12, 1983 Oct. 7–Oct. 17, 1983	Jan. 7–Jan. 24, 1983 Feb. 18–Feb. 21, 1983 Mar. 25–Apr. 4, 1983 May 27–May 31, 1983 July 1–July 10, 1983 Aug. 5–Sept. 11, 1983 Oct. 7–Oct. 16, 1983	Strom Thurmond, of South Carolina	Thomas P. O'Neill, Jr., of Massachusetts.

Congress	Session	Date of beginning	Date of adjournment	Length in days	Recess	Recess	President of Senate pro tempore	Speaker of the House
99th	2	Jan. 23, 1984	Oct. 12, 1984	264	Feb. 9–Feb. 20, 1984 Apr. 12–Apr. 24, 1984 May 24–May 31, 1984 June 29–July 23, 1984 Aug. 10–Sept. 5, 1984	Feb. 10–Feb. 20, 1984 Apr. 13–Apr. 23, 1984 May 25–May 29, 1984 June 30–July 22, 1984 Aug. 11–Sept. 4, 1984	..do.	Do.
	1	Jan. 3, 1985	Dec. 20, 1985	352	Jan. 7–Jan. 21, 1985 Feb. 7–Feb. 18, 1985 Apr. 4–Apr. 15, 1985 May 9–May 14, 1985 May 24–June 3, 1985 June 27–July 8, 1985 Aug. 1–Sept. 9, 1985 Nov. 23–Dec. 2, 1985	Jan. 8–Jan. 21, 1985 Feb. 8–Feb. 18, 1985 Mar. 8–Mar. 18, 1985 Apr. 5–Apr. 4, 1985 May 24–June 2, 1985 June 28–July 7, 1985 Aug. 2–Sept. 3, 1985 Nov. 22–Dec. 1, 1985	do	
100th	2	Jan. 21, 1986	Oct. 18, 1986	278	Feb. 7–Feb. 17, 1986 Mar. 27–Apr. 8, 1986 May 21–June 2, 1986 June 26–July 7, 1986 Aug. 15–Sept. 8, 1986	Feb. 7–Feb. 17, 1986 Mar. 25–Apr. 7, 1986 May 23–June 2, 1986 June 27–July 13, 1986 Aug. 17–Sept. 7, 1986	...do.	James C. Wright, Jr. of Texas.
	1	Jan. 6, 1987	Dec. 22, 1987	351	Jan. 6–Jan. 12, 1987 Feb. 5–Feb. 16, 1987 Apr. 10–Apr. 21, 1987 May 21–May 27, 1987 July 1–July 7, 1987 Aug. 7–Sept. 9, 1987 Nov. 20–Nov. 30, 1987	Jan. 9–Jan. 19, 1987 Feb. 12–Feb. 17, 1987 Apr. 10–Apr. 20, 1987 May 22–May 26, 1987 July 2–July 6, 1987 July 16–July 19, 1987 Aug. 8–Sept. 9, 1987 Nov. 11–Nov. 15, 1987 Nov. 21–Nov. 29, 1987	John C. Stennis, of Mississippi	
101st	2	Jan. 25, 1988	Oct. 22, 1988	272	Feb. 4–Feb. 15, 1988 Mar. 4–Mar. 14, 1988 Mar. 31–Apr. 11, 1988 Apr. 29–May 9, 1988 May 27–June 6, 1988 June 29–July 6, 1988 July 14–July 25, 1988 Aug. 11–Sept. 7, 1988	Feb. 10–Feb. 15, 1988 Apr. 1–Apr. 10, 1988 May 27–May 31, 1988 July 1–July 5, 1988 July 15–July 25, 1988 Aug. 12–Sept. 6, 1988	..do.	
	1	Jan. 3, 1989	Nov. 22, 1989	324	Jan. 4–Jan. 20, 1989 Jan. 20–Jan. 25, 1989 Feb. 9–Feb. 21, 1989 Mar. 17–Apr. 4, 1989 Apr. 19–May 1, 1989 May 18–May 31, 1989 June 23–July 11, 1989 Aug. 4–Sept. 6, 1989	Jan. 5–Jan. 18, 1989 Feb. 10–Feb. 20, 1989 Apr. 24–Apr. 2, 1989 Apr. 19–Apr. 24, 1989 May 26–May 30, 1989 June 30–July 9, 1989 Aug. 6–Sept. 5, 1989	Robert C. Byrd, of West Virginia	James C. Wright, Jr., of Texas;[22] Thomas S. Foley, of Washington.[20]
	2	Jan. 23, 1990	Oct. 28, 1990	260	Feb. 8–Feb. 20, 1990 Mar. 9–Mar. 20, 1990 Apr. 5–Apr. 18, 1990 May 24–June 5, 1990 June 28–July 10, 1990 Aug. 4–Sept. 10, 1990	Feb. 8–Feb. 19, 1990 Apr. 5–Apr. 17, 1990 May 26–June 4, 1990 June 29–July 9, 1990 Aug. 5–Sept. 4, 1990	..do.	

SESSIONS OF CONGRESS, 1st–114th CONGRESSES, 1789–2015—CONTINUED

[Closing date for this table was December 18, 2015.]

MEETING DATES OF CONGRESS: Pursuant to a resolution of the Confederation Congress in 1788, the Constitution went into effect on March 4, 1789. From then until the 20th amendment took effect in January 1934, the term of each Congress began on March 4th of each odd-numbered year; however, Article I, section 4, of the Constitution provided that "The Congress shall assemble at least once in every Year, and such Meeting shall be on the first Monday in December, unless they shall by law appoint a different day." The Congress therefore convened regularly on the first Monday in December until the 20th amendment became effective, which changed the beginning of Congress's term as well as its convening date to January 3rd. So prior to 1934, a new Congress typically would not convene for regular business until 13 months after being elected. One effect of this was that the last session of each Congress was a "lame duck" session. After the 20th amendment, the time from the election to the beginning of Congress's term as well as when it convened was reduced to two months. Recognizing that the need might exist for Congress to meet at times other than the regularly scheduled convening date, Article II, section 3 of the Constitution provides that the President "may, on extraordinary occasions, convene both Houses, or either of them"; hence these sessions occur only if convened by Presidential proclamation. Except as noted, these are separately numbered sessions of a Congress, and are marked by an E in the session column of the table. Until the 20th amendment was adopted, there were also times when special sessions of the Senate were convened, principally for confirming Cabinet and other executive nominations, and occasionally for the ratification of treaties or other executive business. These Senate sessions were also called by Presidential proclamation (typically by the outgoing President, although on occasion by incumbents as well) and are marked by an S in the session column. MEETING PLACES OF CONGRESS: Congress met for the first and second sessions of the First Congress (1789 and 1790) in New York City. From the third session of the First Congress through the first session of the Sixth Congress (1790 to 1800), Philadelphia was the meeting place. Congress has convened in Washington since the second session of the Sixth Congress (1800).

| Congress | Session | Convening Date | Adjournment Date | Length in days [1] | Recesses [2] | | President pro tempore of the Senate [3] | Speaker of the House of Representatives |
					Senate	House of Representatives		
102d ...	1	Jan. 3, 1991	Jan. 3, 1992	366	Feb. 7–Feb. 19, 1991 Mar. 22–Apr. 9, 1991 Apr. 25–May 6, 1991 May 24–June 3, 1991 June 28–July 8, 1991 Aug. 2–Sept. 10, 1991 Nov. 27, 1991–Jan. 3, 1992	Feb. 7–Feb. 18, 1991 Mar. 23–Apr. 8, 1991 May 24–May 28, 1991 May 28–July 8, 1991 June 28–July 8, 1991 Aug. 3–Sept. 10, 1991 Nov. 28, 1991–Jan. 2, 1992	...do	Thomas S. Foley, of Washington.
	2	Jan. 3, 1992	Oct. 9, 1992	281	Jan. 3–Jan. 21, 1992 Apr. 10–Apr. 28, 1992 May 21–June 1, 1992 July 2–July 20, 1992 Aug. 12–Sept. 8, 1992	Jan. 4–Jan. 21, 1992 Apr. 11–Apr. 27, 1992 May 22–May 25, 1992 July 3–July 6, 1992 July 10–July 20, 1992 Aug. 13–Sept. 8, 1992	...do.	
103d ...	1	Jan. 5, 1993 ...	Nov. 26, 1993 ...	326	Jan. 7–Jan. 19, 1993 Feb. 4–Feb. 16, 1993 Apr. 7–Apr. 19, 1993 May 28–June 7, 1993 July 1–July 13, 1993 Aug. 7–Sept. 7, 1993 Oct. 7–Oct. 13, 1993 Nov. 11–Nov. 16, 1993	Jan. 7–Jan. 19, 1993 Jan. 28–Feb. 1, 1993 Feb. 5–Feb. 15, 1993 Apr. 8–Apr. 18, 1993 May 28–June 7, 1993 July 2–July 12, 1993 Aug. 7–Sept. 7, 1993 Sept. 16–Sept. 20, 1993 Oct. 8–Oct. 11, 1993 Nov. 11–Nov. 14, 1993	Robert C. Byrd, of West Virginia	Thomas S. Foley, of Washington.

Congress	Session	Date of convening	Date of adjournment	Length in days	Recesses	Recesses	President pro tempore of the Senate	Speaker of the House of Representatives
	2	Jan. 25, 1994	Dec. 1, 1994	311	Feb. 11–Feb. 22, 1994 Mar. 26–Apr. 11, 1994 May 2–June 7, 1994 July 1–July 11, 1994 Aug. 25–Sept. 12, 1994 Oct. 8–Nov. 30, 1994	Jan. 27–Jan. 31, 1994 Feb. 12–Feb. 21, 1994 Mar. 25–Apr. 11, 1994 May 27–June 7, 1994 July 1–July 11, 1994 Aug. 27–Sept. 11, 1994 Oct. 8–Nov. 28, 1994	...do.	Newt Gingrich, of Georgia.
104th.	1	Jan. 4, 1995	Jan. 3, 1996	365	Feb. 16–Feb. 22, 1995 Apr. 7–Apr. 24, 1995 May 26–June 5, 1995 June 30–July 10, 1995 Aug. 11–Sept. 5, 1995 Sept. 25–Oct. 10, 1995 Nov. 20–Nov. 27, 1995	Feb. 17–Feb. 20, 1995 Mar. 17–Mar. 20, 1995 Apr. 8–Apr. 30, 1995 May 4–May 8, 1995 May 26–June 5, 1995 July 1–July 9, 1995 Aug. 5–Sept. 5, 1995 Sept. 30–Oct. 5, 1995 Nov. 21–Nov. 27, 1995	Strom Thurmond, of South Carolina	
	2	Jan. 3, 1996	Oct. 4, 1996	276	Jan. 10–Jan. 22, 1996 Mar. 29–Apr. 15, 1996 May 24–June 3, 1996 June 28–July 8, 1996 Aug. 2–Sept. 3, 1996	Jan. 10–Jan. 21, 1996 Mar. 30–Apr. 14, 1996 May 24–May 28, 1996 June 29–July 7, 1996 Aug. 3–Sept. 3, 1996	...do.	
105th.	1	Jan. 7, 1997	Nov. 13, 1997	311	Jan. 9–Jan. 21, 1997 Feb. 13–Feb. 24, 1997 Mar. 21–Apr. 7, 1997 June 27–July 7, 1997 July 31–Aug. 31, 1997 Oct. 9–Oct. 20, 1997	Jan. 10–Jan. 19, 1997 Jan. 22–Feb. 3, 1997 Feb. 14–Feb. 24, 1997 Mar. 22–Apr. 7, 1997 June 27–July 7, 1997 Aug. 2–Sept. 2, 1997 Oct. 10–Oct. 20, 1997	...do	Do.
	2	Jan. 27, 1998	Dec. 19, 1998	327	Feb. 13–Feb. 23, 1998 Apr. 3–Apr. 20, 1998 May 22–June 1, 1998 June 26–July 6, 1998 July 31–Aug. 31, 1998 Adjourned sine die, Oct. 21, 1998.	Jan. 29–Feb. 2, 1998 Feb. 6–Feb. 10, 1998 Feb. 13–Feb. 23, 1998 Apr. 2–Apr. 20, 1998 May 23–June 2, 1998 June 25–July 13, 1998 Aug. 8–Sept. 8, 1998 Oct. 22–Dec. 16, 1998	...do.	
106th.	1	Jan. 6, 1999	Nov. 22, 1999	321	Feb. 12–Feb. 22, 1999 Mar. 25–Apr. 12, 1999 May 27–June 7, 1999 July 1–July 12, 1999 Aug. 5–Sept. 8, 1999	Jan. 7–Jan. 18, 1999 Jan. 20–Feb. 1, 1999 Feb. 13–Feb. 22, 1999 Mar. 26–Apr. 11, 1999 May 28–June 6, 1999 July 2–July 11, 1999 Aug. 7–Sept. 7, 1999	...do	J. Dennis Hastert, of Illinois.
	2	Jan. 24, 2000	Dec. 15, 2000	326	Feb. 10–Feb. 22, 2000 Mar. 9–Mar. 20, 2000 Apr. 13–Apr. 25, 2000 May 25–June 6, 2000 June 30–July 10, 2000 July 27–Sept. 5, 2000 Nov. 2–Nov. 14, 2000 Nov. 14–Dec. 5, 2000	Feb. 17–Feb. 28, 2000 Apr. 14–May 1, 2000 May 26–June 5, 2000 July 1–July 9, 2000 July 28–Sept. 5, 2000 Nov. 4–Nov. 12, 2000 Nov. 15–Dec. 3, 2000	...do.	

SESSIONS OF CONGRESS, 1st–114th CONGRESSES, 1789–2015—CONTINUED

[Closing date for this table was December 18, 2015.]

MEETING DATES OF CONGRESS: Pursuant to a resolution of the Confederation Congress in 1788, the Constitution went into effect on March 4, 1789. From then until the 20th amendment took effect in January 1934, the term of each Congress began on March 4th of each odd-numbered year; however, Article I, section 4, of the Constitution provided that "The Congress shall assemble at least once in every Year, and such Meeting shall be on the first Monday in December, unless they shall by law appoint a different day." The Congress therefore convened regularly on the first Monday in December until the 20th amendment became effective, which changed the beginning of Congress's term as well as its convening date to January 3rd. So prior to 1934, a new Congress typically would not convene for regular business until 13 months after being elected. One effect of this was that the last session of each Congress was a "lame duck" session. After the 20th amendment, the time from the election to the beginning of Congress's term as well as when it convened was reduced to two months. Recognizing that the need might exist for Congress to meet at times other than the regularly scheduled convening date, Article II, section 3 of the Constitution provides that the President "may, on extraordinary occasions, convene both Houses, or either of them"; hence these sessions occur only if convened by Presidential proclamation. Except as noted, these are separately numbered sessions of a Congress, and are marked by an E in the session column of the table. Until the 20th amendment was adopted, there were also times when special sessions of the Senate were convened, principally for confirming Cabinet and other executive nominations, and occasionally for the ratification of treaties or other executive business. These Senate sessions were also called by Presidential proclamation (typically by the outgoing President, although on occasion by incumbents as well) and are marked by an S in the session column. MEETING PLACES OF CONGRESS: Congress met for the first and second sessions of the First Congress (1789 and 1790) in New York City. From the third session of the First Congress through the first session of the Sixth Congress (1790 to 1800), Philadelphia was the meeting place. Congress has convened in Washington since the second session of the Sixth Congress (1800).

Congress	Session	Convening Date	Adjournment Date	Length in days [1]	Recesses [2]		President pro tempore of the Senate [3]	Speaker of the House of Representatives
					Senate	House of Representatives		
107th	1	Jan. 3, 2001	Dec. 20, 2001	352	Jan. 8–Jan. 20, 2001 Feb. 15–Feb. 26, 2001 Apr. 6–Apr. 23, 2001 May 26–June 5, 2001 June 29–July 9, 2001 Aug. 3–Sept. 4, 2001 Oct. 18–Oct. 23, 2001 Nov. 16–Nov. 27, 2001	Jan. 7–Jan. 19, 2001 Jan. 21–Jan 29, 2001 Feb. 1–Feb. 5, 2001 Feb. 15–Feb. 25, 2001 Apr. 5–Apr. 23, 2001 May 27–June 4, 2001 June 29–July 9, 2001 Aug. 3–Sept. 4, 2001 Nov. 20–Nov. 26, 2001	Robert C. Byrd, of West Virginia;[21] Strom Thurmond, of South Carolina;[21] Robert C. Byrd, of West Virginia.[21]	Do.
	2	Jan. 23, 2002	Nov. 22, 2002	304	Jan. 29–Feb. 4, 2002 Feb. 15–Feb. 25, 2002 Mar. 22–Apr. 8, 2002 May 23–June 3, 2002 June 28–July 8, 2002 Aug. 1–Sept. 3, 2002	Jan. 30–Feb. 3, 2002 Feb. 15–Feb. 25, 2002 Mar. 21–Apr. 8, 2002 May 25–June 3, 2002 June 29–July 7, 2002 July 28–Sept. 3, 2002	Robert C. Byrd, of West Virginia.	
108th	1	Jan. 7, 2003	Dec. 9, 2003	337	Feb. 14–Feb. 24, 2003 Apr. 11–Apr. 28, 2003 May 23–June 2, 2003 June 27–July 7, 2003 Aug. 1–Sept 2, 2003 Oct. 3–Oct. 14, 2003 Nov. 25–Dec. 9, 2003	Jan. 9–Jan. 26, 2003 Feb. 14–Feb. 24, 2003 Apr. 13–Apr. 28, 2003 May 24–June 1, 2003 June 28–July 6, 2003 July 30–Sept. 2, 2003 Nov. 26–Dec. 7, 2003	Ted Stevens, of Alaska	J. Dennis Hastert, of Illinois.

					Recess dates (A)	Recess dates (B)	President pro tempore	Speaker
109th.	2	Jan. 20, 2004	Dec. 8, 2004	324	Feb. 12–Feb. 23, 2004 Mar. 12–Mar. 22, 2004 Apr. 3–Apr. 19, 2004 May 21–June 1, 2004 June 9–June 14, 2004 June 25–July 6, 2004 July 22–Sept. 7, 2004 Oct. 11–Nov. 16, 2004 Nov. 24–Dec. 7, 2004	Feb. 12–Feb. 23, 2004 Apr. 3–Apr. 19, 2004 May 21–May 31, 2004 June 10–June 13, 2004 June 26–July 5, 2004 July 23–Sept. 5, 2004 Oct. 10–Nov. 15, 2004 Nov. 25–Dec. 5, 2004	...do	Do.
	1	Jan. 4, 2005	Dec. 22, 2005	353	Jan. 6–Jan. 20, 2005 Jan. 25–Jan. 31, 2005 Feb. 18–Feb. 28, 2005 Mar. 20–Apr. 4, 2005 Apr. 29–May 9, 2005 May 26–June 6, 2005 July 1–July 11, 2005 July 29–Sept. 1, 2005 Sept. 1–Sept. 6, 2005 Oct. 7–Oct. 17, 2005 Nov. 18–Dec. 12, 2005	Jan. 7–Jan. 19, 2005 Jan. 21–Jan. 24, 2005 Jan. 27–Jan. 3, 2005 Feb. 3–Feb. 7, 2005 Feb. 18–Feb. 28, 2005 Mar. 22–Apr. 4, 2005 May 27–June 6, 2005 July 1–July 8, 2005 July 30–Sept. 1, 2005 Oct. 8–Oct. 16, 2005 Nov. 19–Dec. 5, 2005	...do	Do.
	2	Jan. 3, 2006	Dec. 9, 2006	341	Jan. 3–Jan. 18, 2006 Feb. 17–Feb. 27, 2006 Mar. 15–Mar. 27, 2006 Apr. 7–Apr. 24, 2006 May 26–June 5, 2006 June 29–July 10, 2006 Aug. 4–Sept. 5, 2006 Sept. 30–Nov. 9, 2006 Nov. 16–Dec. 4, 2006	Jan. 4–Jan. 30, 2006 Feb. 2–Feb. 6, 2006 Feb. 9–Feb. 13, 2006 Feb. 17–Feb. 27, 2006 Mar. 17–Mar. 27, 2006 Apr. 7–Apr. 24, 2006 May 26–June 5, 2006 June 30–July 9, 2006 Aug. 3–Sept. 5, 2006 Oct. 1–Nov. 8, 2006 Nov. 16–Dec. 3, 2006	...do	
110th.	1	Jan. 4, 2007	Dec. 31, 2007	362	Feb. 17–Feb. 26, 2007 Mar. 25–Apr. 10, 2007 May 25–June 4, 2007 June 29–July 9, 2007 Aug. 3–Sept. 4, 2007 Oct. 5–Oct. 15, 2007	Jan. 25–Jan. 28, 2007 Feb. 1–Feb. 4, 2007 Feb. 17–Feb. 26, 2007 Mar. 31–Apr. 15, 2007 May 25–June 4, 2007 June 29–July 9, 2007 Aug. 6–Sept. 3, 2007 Nov. 16–Dec. 3, 2007	Robert C. Byrd, of West Virginia	Nancy Pelosi, of California.
	2	Jan. 3, 2008	Jan. 3, 2009	367	June 27–July 7, 2008	Jan. 4–Jan. 14, 2008 Jan. 24–Jan. 27, 2008 Jan. 30–Feb. 5, 2008 Mar. 15–Mar. 30, 2008 May 23–June 2, 2008 June 27–July 7, 2008 Aug. 2–Sept. 7, 2008 Oct. 4–Nov. 18, 2008 Nov. 21–Dec. 8, 2008 Dec. 11, 2008–Jan. 3, 2009	...do	

SESSIONS OF CONGRESS, 1st–114th CONGRESSES, 1789–2015—CONTINUED

[Closing date for this table was December 18, 2015.]

MEETING DATES OF CONGRESS: Pursuant to a resolution of the Confederation Congress in 1788, the Constitution went into effect on March 4, 1789. From then until the 20th amendment took effect in January 1934, the term of each Congress began on March 4th of each odd-numbered year; however, Article I, section 4, of the Constitution provided that "The Congress shall assemble at least once in every Year, and such Meeting shall be on the first Monday in December, unless they shall by law appoint a different day." The Congress therefore convened regularly on the first Monday in December until the 20th amendment became effective, which changed the beginning of Congress's term as well as its convening date to January 3rd. So prior to 1934, a new Congress typically would not convene for regular business until 13 months after being elected. One effect of this was that the last session of each Congress was a "lame duck" session. After the 20th amendment, the time from the election to the beginning of Congress's term as well as when it convened was reduced to two months. Recognizing that the need might exist for Congress to meet at times other than the regularly scheduled convening date, Article II, section 3 of the Constitution provides that the President "may, on extraordinary occasions, convene both Houses, or either of them"; hence these sessions occur only if convened by Presidential proclamation. Except as noted, these are separately numbered sessions of a Congress, and are marked by an E in the session column of the table. Until the 20th amendment was adopted, there were also times when special sessions of the Senate were convened, principally for confirming Cabinet and other executive nominations, and occasionally for the ratification of treaties or other executive business. These Senate sessions were also called by Presidential proclamation (typically by the outgoing President, although on occasion by incumbents as well) and are marked by an S in the session column. MEETING PLACES OF CONGRESS: Congress met for the first and second sessions of the First Congress (1789 and 1790) in New York City. From the third session of the First Congress through the first session of the Sixth Congress (1790 to 1800), Philadelphia was the meeting place. Congress has convened in Washington since the second session of the Sixth Congress (1800).

Congress	Session	Convening Date	Adjournment Date	Length in days [1]	Recesses [2]		President pro tempore of the Senate [3]	Speaker of the House of Representatives
					Senate	House of Representatives		
111th.	1	Jan. 6, 2009	Dec. 24, 2009	353	Apr. 2–Apr. 20, 2009 May 21–June 1, 2009 June 25–July 6, 2009 Nov. 10–Nov. 16, 2009 Nov. 21–Nov. 30, 2009	Jan. 29–Feb. 1, 2009 Feb. 5–Feb. 8, 2009 Feb. 14–Feb. 22, 2009 Apr. 3–Apr. 20, 2009 May 22–June 1, 2009 June 27–July 6, 2009 Aug. 1–Sept. 7, 2009 Nov. 8–Nov. 15, 2009 Nov. 20–Nov. 30, 2009	do	Do.
	2	Jan. 5, 2010	Dec. 22, 2010	352	Feb. 11–Feb. 23, 2010 Mar. 26–Apr. 12, 2010 May 28–June 7, 2010 June 30–July 12, 2010 Aug. 5–Aug. 12, 2010 Aug. 12–Sept. 13, 2010 Nov. 19–Nov. 29, 2010	Jan. 6–Jan. 11, 2010 Feb. 10–Feb. 21, 2010 Mar. 26–Apr. 12, 2010 May 29–June 7, 2010 July 2–July 12, 2010 July 31–Aug. 8, 2010 Aug. 11–Sept. 13, 2010 Oct. 1–Nov. 14, 2010 Nov. 19–Nov. 28, 2010	Robert C. Byrd, of West Virginia;[22] Daniel K. Inouye, of Hawaii.[22]	
112th.	1	Jan. 5, 2011	Dec. 30, 2011	360	Jan. 5–Jan. 25, 2011 Feb. 17–Feb. 28, 2011 Mar. 17–Mar. 28, 2011 Apr. 14–May 2, 2011	Jan. 13–Jan. 17, 2011 Jan. 27–Feb. 7, 2011 Feb. 20–Feb. 27, 2011 Mar. 18–Mar. 28, 2011 Apr. 16–May 1, 2011 May 14–May 22, 2011	Daniel K. Inouye, of Hawaii	John A. Boehner, of Ohio.

Congress	Session	Convening date	Adjournment date	Length in days	Recesses (1)	Recesses (2)	President pro tempore	Speaker
113th	2	Jan. 3, 2012	Jan. 3, 2013	367	Aug. 3–Sept. 10, 2012	Mar. 31–Apr. 15, 2012 Apr. 28–May 5, 2012 June 30–July 8, 2012 Aug. 8–Sept. 9, 2012 Nov. 17–Nov. 26, 2012	Daniel K. Inouye, of Hawaii;[23] Patrick J. Leahy, of Vermont.[23]	Do.
113th	1	Jan. 3, 2013	Dec. 24, 2013	356	Jan. 4–Jan. 22, 2013 Feb. 15–Feb. 25, 2013 Mar. 22–Apr. 8, 2013 May 23–June 3, 2013 June 28–July 8, 2013 Aug. 2–Aug. 12, 2013 Aug. 12–Sept. 6, 2013	Jan. 5–Jan. 13, 2013 Feb. 16–Feb. 24, 2013 Mar. 26–Apr. 8, 2013 May 25–June 2, 2013 June 29–July 7, 2013 Aug. 3–Sept. 5, 2013 Oct. 31–Nov. 11, 2013 Nov. 23–Dec. 1, 2013	Patrick J. Leahy, of Vermont	Do.
113th	2	Jan. 3, 2014	Jan. 2, 2015	365	Apr. 11–Apr. 28, 2014 Aug. 8–Sept. 8, 2014 Sept. 18–Oct. 15, 2014 Oct. 15–Nov. 12, 2014	Dec. 27, 2013–Jan. 2, 2014 Apr. 11–Apr. 27, 2014 Sept. 20–Nov. 11, 2014 Nov. 21–Nov. 30, 2014	do	do
114th	1	Jan. 6, 2015	Dec. 18, 2015	347	Mar. 26–Apr. 13, 2015 June 25–July 7, 2015 Aug. 6–Sept. 8, 2015 Nov. 19–Nov. 30, 2015	Dec. 17–Jan. 1, 2015 Mar. 27–Apr. 12, 2015 June 26–July 6, 2015 Aug. 5–Sept. 7, 2015 Nov. 6–Nov. 15, 2015 Nov. 20–Nov. 29, 2015	do	John A. Boehner, of Ohio[24] Paul D. Ryan, of Wisconsin.[24]

[1] For the purposes of this table, a session's "length in days" is defined as the total number of calendar days from the convening date to the adjournment date, inclusive. It does not mean the actual number of days that Congress met during that session.

[2] For the purposes of this table, a "recess" is defined as a break in House or Senate proceedings of three or more days, excluding Sundays. According to Article I, section 5 of the U.S. Constitution, neither house may adjourn for more than three days without the consent of the other.

[3] The election and role of the President pro tempore has evolved considerably over the Senate's history. "Pro tempore" is Latin for "for the time being"; thus, the post was conceived as a temporary presiding officer. In the eighteenth and nineteenth centuries, the Senate frequently elected several Presidents pro tempore during a single session. Since Vice Presidents presided routinely, the Senate thought it necessary to choose a President pro tempore only for the limited periods when the Vice Presidency might be ill or otherwise absent." Since no provision was in place (until the 25th amendment was adopted in 1967) for replacing the Vice President if he died or resigned from office, or if he assumed the Vice Presidency, the Presidents pro tempore would continue under such circumstances to fill the duties of the chair until the next Vice President was elected. Since Mar. 12, 1890, however, Presidents pro tempore have served until "the Senate otherwise ordered." Since 1949, while still elected, the position has gone to the most senior member of the majority party (see footnote 19 for a minority party exception). To gain a more complete understanding of this position, see Robert C. Byrd's *The Senate 1789–1989: Addresses on the History of the United States Senate*, vol. 2, ch. 6 "The President Pro Tempore," pp. 167–183, from which the quotes in this footnote are taken. Also, a complete listing of the dates of election of the Presidents pro tempore is in vol. 4 of the Byrd series (*The Senate 1789–1989; Historical Statistics, 1789–1992*), table 6–2, pp. 647–653.

[4] Henry Clay resigned as Speaker on Jan. 19, 1814. He was succeeded by Langdon Cheves who was elected on that same day.

[5] Henry Clay resigned as Speaker on Oct. 28, 1820, after the sine die adjournment of the first session of the 16th Congress. He was succeeded by John W. Taylor who was elected at the beginning of the second session.

[6] Andrew Stevenson resigned as Speaker on June 2, 1834. He was succeeded by John Bell who was elected on that same day.

[7] Speaker Schuyler Colfax resigned as Speaker on the last day of the 40th Congress, Mar. 3, 1869, in preparation for becoming Vice President of the United States on the following day. Theodore M. Pomeroy was elected Speaker on Mar. 3, and served for only that one day.

[8] Speaker Michael C. Kerr died on Aug. 19, 1876, after the sine die adjournment of the first session of the 44th Congress. Samuel J. Randall was elected Speaker at the beginning of the second session.

[9] William P. Frye resigned as President pro tempore on Apr. 27, 1911.

[10] President pro tempore James P. Clarke died on Oct. 1, 1916, after the sine die adjournment of the first session of the 64th Congress. Willard Saulsbury was elected President pro tempore during the second session.

[11] Speaker Joseph W. Byrns died on June 4, 1936. He was succeeded by William B. Bankhead who was elected Speaker on that same day.

[12] Speaker William B. Bankhead died on Sept. 15, 1940. He was succeeded by Sam Rayburn who was elected Speaker on that same day.

[13] President pro tempore Key Pittman died on Nov. 10, 1940. He was succeeded by William H. King who was elected President pro tempore on Nov. 19, 1940.

[14] President pro tempore Pat Harrison died on June 22, 1941. He was succeeded by Carter Glass who was elected President pro tempore on July 10, 1941.

[15] President Harry S. Truman called the Congress into extraordinary session twice, both times during the 80th Congress. Each time Congress had essentially wrapped up its business for the year, but for technical reasons had not adjourned sine die, so in each case the Congress is considered an extension of the regularly numbered session rather than a separately numbered one. The dates of these extraordinary sessions were Nov. 17 to Dec. 19, 1947, and July 26 to Aug. 7, 1948.

[16] Speaker Sam Rayburn died on Nov. 16, 1961, after the sine die adjournment of the first session of the 87th Congress. John W. McCormack was elected Speaker at the beginning of the second session.
[17] President pro tempore Richard B. Russell died on Jan. 21, 1971. He was succeeded by Allen J. Ellender who was elected to that position on Jan. 22, 1971.
[18] President pro tempore Allen J. Ellender died on July 27, 1972. He was succeeded by James O. Eastland who was elected President pro tempore on July 28, 1972.
[19] Milton Young was elected President pro tempore for one day, Dec. 5, 1980, which was at the end of his 36-year career in the Senate. He was a Republican, which was the minority party at that time. Warren G. Magnuson resumed the position of President pro tempore on Dec. 6, 1980.
[20] James C. Wright, Jr., resigned as Speaker on June 6, 1989. He was succeeded by Thomas S. Foley who was elected on that same day.
[21] The 2000 election resulted in an even split in the Senate between Republicans and Democrats. From the date the 107th Congress convened on Jan. 3, 2001, until Inauguration Day on Jan. 20, 2001, Vice President Albert Gore's tie breaking vote resulted in a Democratic majority, hence Robert C. Byrd served as President pro tempore during this brief period. When Vice President Richard B. Cheney took office on Jan. 20, the Republicans became the majority party, and Strom Thurmond was elected President pro tempore. On June 6, 2001, Republican Senator James Jeffords became an Independent, creating a Democratic majority, and Robert C. Byrd was elected President pro tempore on that day.
[22] President pro tempore Robert C. Byrd died on June 28, 2010. He was succeeded by Daniel K. Inouye who was elected President pro tempore on that same day.
[23] President pro tempore Daniel K. Inouye died on December 17, 2012. He was succeeded by Patrick J. Leahy who was elected President pro tempore on that same day.
[24] John A. Boehner, resigned as Speaker on Oct. 29, 2015. He was succeeded by Paul D. Ryan who was elected as Speaker on that same day.

CEREMONIAL MEETINGS OF CONGRESS

The following ceremonial meetings of Congress occurred on the following dates, at the designated locations, and for the reasons indicated. Please note that Congress was not in session on these occasions.

-July 16, 1987, 100th Congress, Philadelphia, Pennsylvania, Independence Hall and Congress Hall—In honor of the bicentennial of the Constitution, and in commemoration of the Great Compromise of the Constitutional Convention which was agreed to on July 16, 1787.

-September 6, 2002, 107th Congress, New York City, New York, Federal Hall—In remembrance of the victims and heroes of September 11, 2001, and in recognition of the courage and spirit of the City of New York.

JOINT SESSIONS AND MEETINGS, ADDRESSES TO THE SENATE OR THE HOUSE, AND INAUGURATIONS

1st–114th CONGRESSES, 1789–2015 [1]

The parliamentary difference between a joint session and a joint meeting has evolved over time. In recent years the distinctions have become clearer: a joint session is more formal, and occurs upon the adoption of a concurrent resolution; a joint meeting occurs when each body adopts a unanimous consent agreement to recess to meet with the other legislative body. Joint sessions typically are held to hear an address from the President of the United States or to count electoral votes. Joint meetings typically are held to hear an address from a foreign dignitary or visitors other than the President.

The Speaker of the House of Representatives usually presides over joint sessions and joint meetings; however, the President of the Senate does preside over joint sessions where the electoral votes are counted, as required by the Constitution.

In the earliest years of the Republic, 1789 and 1790, when the national legislature met in New York City, joint gatherings were held in the Senate Chamber in Federal Hall. In Philadelphia, when the legislature met in Congress Hall, such meetings were held in the Senate Chamber, 1790–1793, and in the Hall of the House of Representatives, 1794–1799. Once the Congress moved to the Capitol in Washington in 1800, the Senate Chamber again was used for joint gatherings through 1805. Since 1809, with few exceptions, joint sessions and joint meetings have occurred in the Hall of the House.

Presidential messages on the state of the Union were originally known as the "Annual Message," but since the 80th Congress, in 1947, have been called the "State of the Union Address." After President John Adams's Annual Message on November 22, 1800, these addresses were read by clerks to the individual bodies until President Woodrow Wilson resumed the practice of delivering them to joint sessions on December 2, 1913.

In some instances more than one joint gathering has occurred on the same day. For example, on January 6, 1941, Congress met in joint session to count electoral votes for President and Vice President, and then met again in joint session to receive President Franklin Delano Roosevelt's Annual Message.

Whereas in more recent decades, foreign dignitaries invited to speak before Congress have typically done so at joint meetings, in earlier times (and with several notable exceptions), such visitors were received by the Senate and the House separately, or by one or the other singly, a tradition begun with the visit of General Lafayette of France in 1824. At that time a joint committee decided that each body would honor Lafayette separately, establishing the precedent. (See footnote 7 for more details.) Not all such occasions included formal addresses by such dignitaries (e.g., Lafayette's reception by the Senate in their chamber, at which he did not speak before they adjourned to greet him), hence the "occasions" listed in the third column of the table include not only addresses, but also remarks (defined as brief greetings or off-the-cuff comments often requested of the visitor at the last minute) and receptions. Relatively few foreign dignitaries were received by Congress before World War I.

Congress has hosted inaugurations since the first occasion in 1789. They always have been formal joint gatherings, and sometimes they also were joint sessions. Inaugurations were joint sessions when both houses of Congress were in session, and they processed to the ceremony as part of the business of the day. In many cases, however, one or both houses were not in session or were in recess at the time of the ceremony. In this table, inaugurations that were not joint sessions are listed in the second column. Those that were joint sessions are so identified and described in the third column.

JOINT SESSIONS AND MEETINGS, ADDRESSES TO THE SENATE OR THE HOUSE, AND INAUGURATIONS

[See notes at end of table]

Congress and Date	Type	Occasion, topic, or inaugural location	Name and position of dignitary (where applicable)
		NEW YORK CITY	
1st CONGRESS			
Apr. 6, 1789	Joint session	Counting electoral votes	N.A.
Apr. 30, 1789	...do	Inauguration and church service [2]	President George Washington; Right Reverend Samuel Provoost, Senate-appointed Chaplain.
Jan. 8, 1790	...do	Annual Message	President George Washington.
		PHILADELPHIA	
Dec. 8, 1790	...do	...do	Do.
2d CONGRESS			
Oct. 25, 1791	...do	...do	Do.
Nov. 6, 1792	...do	...do	Do.
Feb. 13, 1793	...do	Counting electoral votes	N.A.
3d CONGRESS			
Mar. 4, 1793	Inauguration	Senate Chamber	President George Washington.
Dec. 3, 1793	Joint session	Annual Message	Do.
Nov. 19, 1794	...do	...do	Do.
4th CONGRESS			
Dec. 8, 1795	...do	...do	Do.
Dec. 7, 1796	...do	...do	Do.
Feb. 8, 1797	...do	Counting electoral votes	N.A.
5th CONGRESS			
Mar. 4, 1797	Inauguration	Hall of the House	President John Adams.
May 16, 1797	Joint session	Relations with France	Do.
Nov. 23, 1797	...do	Annual Message	Do.
Dec. 8, 1798	...do	...do	Do.
6th CONGRESS			
Dec. 3, 1799	...do	...do	Do.
Dec. 26, 1799	...do	Funeral procession and oration in memory of George Washington. [3]	Representative Henry Lee.
		WASHINGTON	
Nov. 22, 1800	...do	Annual Message	President John Adams.
Feb. 11, 1801	...do	Counting electoral votes [4]	N.A.
7th CONGRESS			
Mar. 4, 1801	Inauguration	Senate Chamber	President Thomas Jefferson.
8th CONGRESS			
Feb. 13, 1805	Joint session	Counting electoral votes	N.A.
9th CONGRESS			
Mar. 4, 1805	Inauguration	Senate Chamber	President Thomas Jefferson.
10th CONGRESS			
Feb. 8, 1809	Joint session	Counting electoral votes	N.A.
11th CONGRESS			
Mar. 4, 1809	Inauguration	Hall of the House	President James Madison.
12th CONGRESS			
Feb. 10, 1813	Joint session	Counting electoral votes	N.A.
13th CONGRESS			
Mar. 4, 1813	Inauguration	Hall of the House	President James Madison.
14th CONGRESS			
Feb. 12, 1817	Joint session	Counting electoral votes [5]	N.A.
15th CONGRESS			
Mar. 4, 1817	Inauguration	In front of Brick Capitol	President James Monroe.
16th CONGRESS			
Feb. 14, 1821	Joint session	Counting electoral votes [6]	N.A.
17th CONGRESS			
Mar. 5, 1821	Inauguration	Hall of the House	President James Monroe.
18th CONGRESS			
Dec. 9, 1824	Senate	Reception	General Gilbert du Motier, Marquis de Lafayette, of France.

JOINT SESSIONS AND MEETINGS, ADDRESSES TO THE SENATE OR THE HOUSE, AND INAUGURATIONS—CONTINUED

[See notes at end of table]

Congress and Date	Type	Occasion, topic, or inaugural location	Name and position of dignitary (where applicable)
Dec. 10, 1824	House [7]	Address	Speaker Henry Clay; General Gilbert du Motier, Marquis de Lafayette, of France.
Feb. 9, 1825	Joint session	Counting electoral votes [8]	N.A.
19th CONGRESS Mar. 4, 1825	Inauguration	Hall of the House	President John Quincy Adams.
20th CONGRESS Feb. 11, 1829	Joint session	Counting electoral votes	N.A.
21st CONGRESS Mar. 4, 1829	Inauguration	East Portico [9]	President Andrew Jackson.
22d CONGRESS Feb. 13, 1833	Joint session	Counting electoral votes	N.A.
23d CONGRESS Mar. 4, 1833 .... Dec. 31, 1834	Inauguration ...... Joint session	Hall of the House [10] .... Lafayette eulogy	President Andrew Jackson. Representative and former President John Quincy Adams; ceremony attended by President Andrew Jackson.
24th CONGRESS Feb. 8, 1837	...do	Counting electoral votes	N.A.
25th CONGRESS Mar. 4, 1837	Inauguration	East Portico	President Martin Van Buren.
26th CONGRESS Feb. 10, 1841	Joint session	Counting electoral votes	N.A.
27th CONGRESS Mar. 4, 1841	Inauguration	East Portico	President William Henry Harrison.
28th CONGRESS Feb. 12, 1845	Joint session	Counting electoral votes	N.A.
29th CONGRESS Mar. 4, 1845	Inauguration	East Portico	President James Knox Polk.
30th CONGRESS Feb. 14, 1849	Joint session	Counting electoral votes	N.A.
31st CONGRESS Mar. 5, 1849 .... July 10, 1850	Inauguration ...... Joint session	East Portico .... Oath of office to President Millard Fillmore. [11]	President Zachary Taylor. N.A.
32d CONGRESS Jan. 5, 1852	Senate	Reception	Louis Kossuth, exiled Governor of Hungary.
Jan. 7, 1852	House	Remarks and Reception	Do.
Feb. 9, 1853	Joint session	Counting electoral votes	N.A.
33d CONGRESS Mar. 4, 1853	Inauguration	East Portico	President Franklin Pierce.
34th CONGRESS Feb. 11, 1857	Joint session	Counting electoral votes	N.A.
35th CONGRESS Mar. 4, 1857	Inauguration	East Portico	President James Buchanan.
36th CONGRESS Feb. 13, 1861	Joint session	Counting electoral votes	N.A.
37th CONGRESS Mar. 4, 1861 .... Feb. 22, 1862	Inauguration ...... Joint session	East Portico .... Reading of Washington's farewell address.	President Abraham Lincoln. John W. Forney, Secretary of the Senate.
38th CONGRESS Feb. 8, 1865	...do	Counting electoral votes	N.A.
39th CONGRESS Mar. 4, 1865 .... Feb. 12, 1866	Inauguration ...... Joint session	East Portico .... Memorial to Abraham Lincoln	President Abraham Lincoln. George Bancroft, historian; ceremony attended by President Andrew Johnson.

JOINT SESSIONS AND MEETINGS, ADDRESSES TO THE SENATE OR THE HOUSE, AND INAUGURATIONS—CONTINUED

[See notes at end of table]

Congress and Date	Type	Occasion, topic, or inaugural location	Name and position of dignitary (where applicable)
40th CONGRESS			
June 9, 1868	House	Address	Anson Burlingame, Envoy to the U.S. from China, and former Representative.
Feb. 10, 1869	Joint session	Counting electoral votes	N.A.
41st CONGRESS			
Mar. 4, 1869	Inauguration	East Portico	President Ulysses S. Grant.
42d CONGRESS			
Mar. 6, 1872	House	Address	Tomomi Iwakura, Ambassador from Japan.
Feb. 12, 1873	Joint session	Counting electoral votes [12]	N.A.
43d CONGRESS			
Mar. 4, 1873	Inauguration	East Portico	President Ulysses S. Grant.
Dec. 18, 1874	Joint meeting	Reception and Remarks	Speaker James G. Blaine; David Kalakaua, King of the Hawaiian Islands.[13]
44th CONGRESS			
Feb. 1, 1877 .... Feb. 10, 1877 Feb. 12, 1877 Feb. 19, 1877 Feb. 20, 1877 Feb. 21, 1877 Feb. 24, 1877 Feb. 26, 1877 Feb. 28, 1877 Mar. 1, 1877 Mar. 2, 1877	Joint session	Counting electoral votes [14]	N.A.
45th CONGRESS			
Mar. 5, 1877	Inauguration	East Portico	President Rutherford B. Hayes.
46th CONGRESS			
Feb. 2, 1880	House	Address	Charles Stewart Parnell, member of Parliament from Ireland.
Feb. 9, 1881	Joint session	Counting electoral votes	N.A.
47th CONGRESS			
Mar. 4, 1881	Inauguration	East Portico	President James A. Garfield.
Feb. 27, 1882	Joint session	Memorial to James A. Garfield	James G. Blaine, former Speaker, Senator, and Secretary of State; ceremony attended by President Chester A. Arthur.
48th CONGRESS			
Feb. 11, 1885	...do	Counting electoral votes	N.A.
Feb. 21, 1885	...do	Completion of Washington Monument	Representative John D. Long; Representative-elect John W. Daniel,[15] ceremony attended by President Chester A. Arthur.
49th CONGRESS			
Mar. 4, 1885	Inauguration	East Portico	President Grover Cleveland.
50th CONGRESS			
Feb. 13, 1889	Joint session	Counting electoral votes	N.A.
51st CONGRESS			
Mar. 4, 1889	Inauguration	East Portico	President Benjamin Harrison.
Dec. 11, 1889	Joint session	Centennial of George Washington's first inauguration.	Melville W. Fuller, Chief Justice of the United States; ceremony attended by President Benjamin Harrison.
52d CONGRESS			
Feb. 8, 1893	...do	Counting electoral votes	N.A.
53d CONGRESS			
Mar. 4, 1893	Inauguration	East Portico	President Grover Cleveland.
54th CONGRESS			
Feb. 10, 1897	Joint session	Counting electoral votes	N.A.
55th CONGRESS			
Mar. 4, 1897	Inauguration	In front of original Senate Wing of Capitol.	President William McKinley.

JOINT SESSIONS AND MEETINGS, ADDRESSES TO THE SENATE OR THE HOUSE, AND INAUGURATIONS—CONTINUED

[See notes at end of table]

Congress and Date	Type	Occasion, topic, or inaugural location	Name and position of dignitary (where applicable)
56th CONGRESS			
Dec. 12, 1900	Joint meeting	Centennial of the Capital City	Representatives James D. Richardson and Sereno E. Payne, and Senator George F. Hoar; ceremony attended by President William McKinley.
Feb. 13, 1901	Joint session	Counting electoral votes	N.A.
57th CONGRESS			
Mar. 4, 1901	Inauguration	East Portico	President William McKinley.
Feb. 27, 1902	Joint session	Memorial to William McKinley	John Hay, Secretary of State; ceremony attended by President Theodore Roosevelt and Prince Henry of Prussia.
58th CONGRESS			
Feb. 8, 1905	...do	Counting electoral votes	N.A.
59th CONGRESS			
Mar. 4, 1905	Inauguration	East Portico	President Theodore Roosevelt.
60th CONGRESS			
Feb. 10, 1909	Joint session	Counting electoral votes	N.A.
61st CONGRESS			
Mar. 4, 1909	Inauguration	Senate Chamber [16]	President William Howard Taft.
Feb. 9, 1911	House	Address	Count Albert Apponyi, Minister of Education from Hungary.
62d CONGRESS			
Feb. 12, 1913	Joint session	Counting electoral votes	N.A.
Feb. 15, 1913	...do	Memorial for Vice President James S. Sherman. [17]	Senators Elihu Root, Thomas S. Martin, Jacob H. Gallinger, John R. Thornton, Henry Cabot Lodge, John W. Kern, Robert M. LaFollette, John Sharp Williams, Charles Curtis, Albert B. Cummins, George T. Oliver, James A. O'Gorman; Speaker Champ Clark; President William Howard Taft.
63d CONGRESS			
Mar. 4, 1913	Inauguration	East Portico	President Woodrow Wilson.
Apr. 8, 1913	Joint session	Tariff message	Do.
June 23, 1913	...do	Currency and bank reform message	Do.
Aug. 27, 1913	...do	Mexican affairs message	Do.
Dec. 2, 1913	...do	Annual Message	Do.
Jan. 20, 1914	...do	Trusts message	Do.
Mar. 5, 1914	...do	Panama Canal tolls	Do.
Apr. 20, 1914	...do	Mexico message	Do.
Sept. 4, 1914	...do	War tax message	Do.
Dec. 8, 1914	...do	Annual Message	Do.
64th CONGRESS			
Dec. 7, 1915	...do	...do	Do.
Aug. 29, 1916	...do	Railroad message (labor-management dispute).	Do.
Dec. 5, 1916	...do	Annual Message	Do.
Jan. 22, 1917	Senate	Planning ahead for peace	Do.
Feb. 3, 1917	Joint session	Severing diplomatic relations with Germany.	Do.
Feb. 14, 1917	...do	Counting electoral votes	N.A.
Feb. 26, 1917	...do	Arming of merchant ships	President Woodrow Wilson.
65th CONGRESS			
Mar. 5, 1917	Inauguration	East Portico	Do.
Apr. 2, 1917	Joint session	War with Germany	Do.
May 1, 1917	Senate	Address	René Raphaël Viviani, Minister of Justice from France; Jules Jusserand, Ambassador from France; address attended by Marshal Joseph Jacques Césaire Joffre, member of French Commission to U.S.
May 3, 1917	House	...do	Do.
May 5, 1917	...do	...do	Arthur James Balfour, British Secretary of State for Foreign Affairs.
May 8, 1917	Senate	...do	Do.
May 31, 1917	...do	...do	Ferdinando di'Savoia, Prince of Udine, Head of Italian Mission to U.S.
June 2, 1917	House	...do	Ferdinando di'Savoia, Prince of Udine, Head of Italian Mission to U.S.; Guglielmo Marconi, member of Italian Mission to U.S.

JOINT SESSIONS AND MEETINGS, ADDRESSES TO THE SENATE OR THE HOUSE, AND INAUGURATIONS—CONTINUED

[See notes at end of table]

Congress and Date	Type	Occasion, topic, or inaugural location	Name and position of dignitary (where applicable)
June 22, 1917	Senate	Address	Baron Moncheur, Chief of Political Bureau of Belgian Foreign Office at Havre.
June 23, 1917	House	...do	Boris Bakhmetieff, Ambassador from Russia.[18]
June 26, 1917	Senate	...do	Do.
June 27, 1917	House	...do	Baron Moncheur, Chief of Political Bureau of Belgian Foreign Office at Havre.
Aug. 30, 1917	Senate	...do	Kikujirō Ishii, Ambassador from Japan.
Sept. 5, 1917	House	...do	Do.
Dec. 4, 1917	Joint session	Annual Message/War with Austria-Hungary.	President Woodrow Wilson.
Jan. 4, 1918	...do	Federal operation of transportation systems.	Do.
Jan. 5, 1918	Senate	Address	Milenko Vesnic, Head of Serbian War Mission.
Jan. 8, 1918	House	...do	Do.
Do	Joint session	Program for world's peace	President Woodrow Wilson.
Feb. 11, 1918	...do	Peace message	Do.
May 27, 1918	...do	War finance message	Do.
Sept. 24, 1918	Senate	Address and Reception [19]	Jules Jusserand, Ambassador from France; Vice President Thomas R. Marshall.
Sept. 30 1918	...do	Support of woman suffrage	President Woodrow Wilson.
Nov. 11, 1918	Joint session	Terms of armistice signed by Germany	Do.
Dec. 2, 1918	...do	Annual Message	Do.
Feb. 9, 1919	...do	Memorial to Theodore Roosevelt	Senator Henry Cabot Lodge, Sr.; ceremony attended by former President William Howard Taft.
66th CONGRESS			
June 23, 1919	Senate	Address	Epitácio da Silva Pessoa, President-elect of Brazil.
July 10, 1919	...do	Versailles Treaty	President Woodrow Wilson.
Aug. 8, 1919	Joint session	Cost of living message	Do.
Sept. 18, 1919	...do	Address	President pro tempore Albert B. Cummins; Speaker Frederick H. Gillett; Representative and former Speaker Champ Clark; General John J. Pershing.
Oct. 28, 1919	Senate	...do	Albert I, King of the Belgians.
Do	House	...do	Do.
Feb. 9, 1921	Joint session	Counting electoral votes	N.A.
67th CONGRESS			
Mar. 4, 1921	Inauguration	East Portico	President Warren G. Harding.
Apr. 12, 1921	Joint session	Federal problem message	Do.
July 12, 1921	Senate	Adjusted compensation for veterans of the World War [20].	Do.
Dec. 6, 1921	Joint session	Annual Message	Do.
Feb. 28, 1922	...do	Maintenance of the merchant marine	Do.
Aug. 18, 1922	...do	Coal and railroad message	Do.
Nov. 21, 1922	...do	Promotion of the American merchant marine.	Do.
Dec. 8, 1922	...do	Annual Message [21]	Do.
Feb. 7, 1923	...do	British debt due to the United States	Do.
68th CONGRESS			
Dec. 6, 1923	...do	Annual Message	President Calvin Coolidge.
Feb. 27, 1924	...do	Memorial to Warren G. Harding	Charles Evans Hughes, Secretary of State; ceremony attended by President Calvin Coolidge.
Dec. 15, 1924	...do	Memorial to Woodrow Wilson	Dr. Edwin Anderson Alderman, President of the University of Virginia; ceremony attended by President Calvin Coolidge.
Feb. 11, 1925	...do	Counting electoral votes	N.A.
69th CONGRESS			
Mar. 4, 1925	Inauguration	East Portico	President Calvin Coolidge.
Feb. 22, 1927	Joint session	George Washington birthday message ..	Do.
70th CONGRESS			
Jan. 25, 1928	House	Reception and Address	William Thomas Cosgrave, President of Executive Council of Ireland.
Feb. 13, 1929	Joint session	Counting electoral votes	N.A.
71st CONGRESS			
Mar. 4, 1929	Inauguration	East Portico	President Herbert Hoover.

JOINT SESSIONS AND MEETINGS, ADDRESSES TO THE SENATE OR THE HOUSE, AND INAUGURATIONS—CONTINUED

[See notes at end of table]

Congress and Date	Type	Occasion, topic, or inaugural location	Name and position of dignitary (where applicable)
Oct. 7, 1929	Senate	Address	James Ramsay MacDonald, Prime Minister of the United Kingdom.
Jan. 13, 1930	...do	Reception	Jan Christiaan Smuts, former Prime Minister of South Africa.
72d CONGRESS			
Feb. 22, 1932	Joint session	Bicentennial of George Washington's birth.	President Herbert Hoover.
May 31, 1932	Senate	Emergency character of economic situation in U.S.	Do.
Feb. 6, 1933	Joint meeting	Memorial to Calvin Coolidge	Arthur Prentice Rugg, Chief Justice of the Supreme Judicial Court of Massachusetts; ceremony attended by President Herbert Hoover.
Feb. 8, 1933	Joint session	Counting electoral votes	N.A.
73d CONGRESS			
Mar. 4, 1933	Inauguration	East Portico	President Franklin Delano Roosevelt.
Jan. 3, 1934	Joint session	Annual Message	Do.
May 20, 1934	...do	100th anniversary, death of Lafayette ...	André de Laboulaye, Ambassador of France; President Franklin Delano Roosevelt; ceremony attended by Count de Chambrun, great-grandson of Lafayette.
74th CONGRESS			
Jan. 4, 1935	...do	Annual Message	President Franklin Delano Roosevelt.
May 22, 1935	...do	Veto message	Do.
Jan. 3, 1936	...do	Annual Message	Do.
75th CONGRESS			
Jan. 6, 1937	...do	Counting electoral votes	N.A.
Do	...do	Annual Message	President Franklin Delano Roosevelt.
Jan. 20, 1937	Inauguration ...	East Portico	President Franklin Delano Roosevelt; Vice President John Nance Garner.[22]
Apr. 1, 1937	Senate	Address	John Buchan, Lord Tweedsmuir, Governor General of Canada.
Do	House	...do	Do.
Jan. 3, 1938	Joint session	Annual Message	President Franklin Delano Roosevelt.
76th CONGRESS			
Jan. 4, 1939	...do	...do	Do.
Mar. 4, 1939	...do	Sesquicentennial of the 1st Congress	Do.
May 8, 1939	Senate	Address	Anastasio Somoza Garcia, President of Nicaragua.
Do	House	...do	Do.
June 9, 1939	Joint meeting ...	Reception [23]	George VI and Elizabeth, King and Queen of the United Kingdom.
Sept. 21, 1939	Joint session	Neutrality address	President Franklin Delano Roosevelt.
Jan. 3, 1940	...do	Annual Message	Do.
May 16, 1940	...do	National defense message	Do.
77th CONGRESS			
Jan. 6, 1941	...do	Counting electoral votes	N.A.
Do	...do	Annual Message	President Franklin Delano Roosevelt.
Jan. 20, 1941	...do	Inauguration, East Portico	President Franklin Delano Roosevelt; Vice President Henry A. Wallace.
Dec. 8, 1941	...do	War with Japan	President Franklin Delano Roosevelt.
Dec. 26, 1941	Joint meeting [24]	Address	Winston Churchill, Prime Minister of the United Kingdom.
Jan. 6, 1942	Joint session	Annual Message	President Franklin Delano Roosevelt.
May 11, 1942	Senate	Address	Manuel Prado, President of Peru.
Do	House	...do	Do.
June 2, 1942	...do	...do	Manuel Luis Quezon, President of the Philippines.[25]
June 4, 1942	Senate	...do	Do.
June 15, 1942	...do	...do	George II, King of Greece.[26]
Do	House	...do	Do.
June 25, 1942	Senate	...do	Peter II, King of Yugoslavia.[26]
Do	House	...do	Do.
Aug. 6, 1942	Senate [27]	...do	Wilhelmina, Queen of the Netherlands.[26]
Nov. 24, 1942	House	...do	Carlos Arroyo del Rio, President of Ecuador.
Nov. 25, 1942	Senate	...do	Do.
Dec. 10, 1942	House	...do	Fulgencio Batista, President of Cuba.
78th CONGRESS			
Jan. 7, 1943	Joint session	Annual Message	President Franklin Delano Roosevelt.
Feb. 18, 1943	Senate	Remarks	Madame Chiang Kai-shek, of China.
Do	House	Address	Do.

JOINT SESSIONS AND MEETINGS, ADDRESSES TO THE SENATE OR THE HOUSE, AND INAUGURATIONS—CONTINUED

[See notes at end of table]

Congress and Date	Type	Occasion, topic, or inaugural location	Name and position of dignitary (where applicable)
May 6, 1943	Senate	Address	Enrique Peñaranda, President of Bolivia.
Do	House	...do	Do.
May 13, 1943	Senate	...do	Edvard Beneš, President of Czechoslovakia.[26]
Do	House	...do	Do.
May 19, 1943	Joint meeting	...do	Winston Churchill, Prime Minister of the United Kingdom.
May 27, 1943	Senate	Remarks	Edwin Barclay, President of Liberia.
Do	House	Address	Do.
June 10, 1943	Senate	...do	President Hininio Moríñigo M., President of Paraguay.
Do	House	...do	Do.
Oct. 15, 1943	Senate	...do	Elie Lescot, President of Haiti.
Nov. 18, 1943	Joint meeting	Moscow Conference	Cordell Hull, Secretary of State.
Jan. 20, 1944	Senate	Address	Isaías Medina Angarita, President of Venezuela.
Do	House	...do	Do.
79th CONGRESS			
Jan. 6, 1945	Joint session	Counting electoral votes	N.A.
Do	...do	Annual Message	President Roosevelt was not present. His message was read before the Joint Session of Congress.
Jan. 20, 1945	Inauguration	South Portico, The White House[28]	President Franklin Delano Roosevelt; Vice President Harry S. Truman.
Mar. 1, 1945	Joint session	Yalta Conference	President Franklin Delano Roosevelt.
Apr. 16, 1945	...do	Prosecution of the War	President Harry S. Truman.
May 21, 1945	...do	Bestowal of Congressional Medal of Honor on Tech. Sgt. Jake William Lindsey.	General George C. Marshall, Chief of Staff, U.S. Army; President Harry S. Truman.
June 18, 1945	Joint meeting	Address	General Dwight D. Eisenhower, Supreme Commander, Allied Expeditionary Force.
July 2, 1945	Senate	United Nations Charter	President Harry S. Truman.
Oct. 5, 1945	Joint meeting	Address	Admiral Chester W. Nimitz, Commander-in-Chief, Pacific Fleet.
Oct. 23, 1945	Joint session	Universal military training message	President Harry S. Truman.
Nov. 13, 1945	Joint meeting	Address	Clement R. Attlee, Prime Minister of the United Kingdom.
May 25, 1946	Joint session	Railroad strike message	President Harry S. Truman.
July 1, 1946	...do	Memorial to Franklin Delano Roosevelt	John Winant, U.S. Representative on the Economic and Social Council of the United Nations; ceremony attended by President Harry S. Truman and Mrs. Franklin Delano Roosevelt.
80th CONGRESS			
Jan. 6, 1947	...do	State of the Union Address[29]	President Harry S. Truman.
Mar. 12, 1947	...do	Greek-Turkish aid policy	Do.
May 1, 1947	Joint meeting	Address	Miguel Alemán, President of Mexico.
Nov. 17, 1947	Joint session	Aid to Europe message	President Harry S. Truman.
Jan. 7, 1948	...do	State of the Union Address	Do.
Mar. 17, 1948	...do	National security and conditions in Europe.	Do.
Apr. 19, 1948	...do	50th anniversary, liberation of Cuba	President Harry S. Truman; Guillermo Belt, Ambassador of Cuba.
July 27, 1948	...do	Inflation, housing, and civil rights	President Harry S. Truman.
81st CONGRESS			
Jan. 5, 1949	...do	State of the Union Address	Do.
Jan. 6, 1949	...do	Counting electoral votes	N.A.
Jan. 20, 1949	...do	Inauguration, East Portico	President Harry S. Truman; Vice President Alben W. Barkley.
May 17, 1949	House	Reception	General Lucius D. Clay.
Do	Senate	Address	Do.
May 19, 1949	Joint meeting	...do	Eurico Gaspar Dutra, President of Brazil.
Aug. 9, 1949	House	...do	Elpidio Quirino, President of the Philippines.
Do	Senate	...do	Do.
Oct. 13, 1949	...do	...do	Jawaharlal Nehru, Prime Minister of India.
Do	House	...do	Do.
Jan. 4, 1950	Joint session	State of the Union Address	President Harry S. Truman.
Apr. 13, 1950	Senate	Address	Gabriel González-Videla, President of Chile.
May 4, 1950	...do	...do	Liaquat Ali Khan, Prime Minister of Pakistan.
Do	House	...do	Do.
May 31, 1950	Joint meeting	...do	Dean Acheson, Secretary of State.

JOINT SESSIONS AND MEETINGS, ADDRESSES TO THE SENATE OR THE HOUSE, AND INAUGURATIONS—CONTINUED

[See notes at end of table]

Congress and Date	Type	Occasion, topic, or inaugural location	Name and position of dignitary (where applicable)
July 28, 1950	Senate	Address	Chōjirō Kuriyama, member of Japanese Diet.
July 31, 1950	House	...do	Tokutarō Kitamura, member of Japanese Diet.
Aug. 1, 1950	...do	...do	Robert Gordon Menzies, Prime Minister of Australia.
Do	Senate	...do	Do.
82d CONGRESS			
Jan. 8, 1951	Joint session	State of the Union Address	President Harry S. Truman.
Feb. 1, 1951	Joint meeting [30]	North Atlantic Treaty Organization	General Dwight D. Eisenhower.
Apr. 2, 1951	...do	Address	Vincent Auriol, President of France.
Apr. 19, 1951	...do	Return from Pacific Command	General Douglas MacArthur.
June 21, 1951	...do	Address	Galo Plaza, President of Ecuador.
July 2, 1951	Senate	Addresses	Tadao Kuraishi, and Aisuke Okamoto, members of Japanese Diet.
Aug. 23, 1951	...do	Address	Zentarō Kosaka, member of Japanese Diet.
Sept. 24, 1951	Joint meeting	...do	Alcide de Gasperi, Prime Minister of Italy.
Jan. 9, 1952	Joint session	State of the Union Address	President Harry S. Truman.
Jan. 17, 1952	Joint meeting	Address	Winston Churchill, Prime Minister of the United Kingdom.
Apr. 3, 1952	...do	...do	Juliana, Queen of the Netherlands.
May 22, 1952	...do	Korea	General Matthew B. Ridgway.
June 10, 1952	Joint session	Steel industry dispute	President Harry S. Truman.
83d CONGRESS			
Jan. 6, 1953	...do	Counting electoral votes	N.A.
Jan. 20, 1953	...do	Inauguration, East Portico	President Dwight D. Eisenhower; Vice President Richard M. Nixon.
Feb. 2, 1953	...do	State of the Union Address	President Dwight D. Eisenhower.
Jan. 7, 1954	...do	...do	Do.
Jan. 29, 1954	Joint meeting	Address	Celal Bayar, President of Turkey.
May 4, 1954	...do	...do	Vincent Massey, Governor General of Canada.
May 28, 1954	...do	...do	Haile Selassie I, Emperor of Ethiopia.
July 28, 1954	...do	...do	Syngman Rhee, President of South Korea.
Nov. 12, 1954	Senate	Remarks	Shigeru Yoshida, Prime Minister of Japan.
Nov. 17, 1954	...do	Address [31]	Sarvepalli Radhakrishnan, Vice President of India.
Nov. 18, 1954	...do	Remarks	Pierre Mendès-France, Premier of France.
84th CONGRESS			
Jan. 6, 1955	Joint session	State of the Union Address	President Dwight D. Eisenhower.
Jan. 27, 1955	Joint meeting	Address	Paul E. Magloire, President of Haiti.
Mar. 16, 1955	Senate	...do	Robert Gordon Menzies, Prime Minister of Australia.
Do	House	...do	Do.
Mar. 30, 1955	Senate	...do	Mario Scelba, Prime Minister of Italy.
Do	House	...do	Do.
May 4, 1955	Senate	...do	P. Phibunsongkhram, Prime Minister of Thailand.
Do	House	...do	Do.
June 30, 1955	Senate	...do	U Nu, Prime Minister of Burma.
Do	House	...do	Do.
Jan. 5, 1956	Senate	...do	Juscelino Kubitschek de Oliveira, President-elect of Brazil.
Feb. 2, 1956	...do	...do	Anthony Eden, Prime Minister of the United Kingdom.
Do	House	...do	Do.
Feb. 29, 1956	Joint meeting	...do	Giovanni Gronchi, President of Italy.
Mar. 15, 1956	Senate	...do	John Aloysius Costello, Prime Minister of Ireland.
Do	House	...do	Do.
Apr. 30, 1956	Senate	...do	João Goulart, Vice President of Brazil.
May 17, 1956	Joint meeting	...do	Sukarno, President of Indonesia.
85th CONGRESS			
Jan. 5, 1957	Joint session	Middle East message	President Dwight D. Eisenhower.
Jan. 7, 1957	...do	Counting electoral votes	N.A.
Jan. 10, 1957	...do	State of the Union Address	President Dwight D. Eisenhower.
Jan. 21, 1957	...do	Inauguration, East Portico	President Dwight D. Eisenhower; Vice President Richard M. Nixon.
Feb. 27, 1957	House	Address	Guy Mollet, Premier of France.
Do	Senate	...do	Do.
May 9, 1957	Joint meeting	...do	Ngo Dinh Diem, President of Vietnam.

JOINT SESSIONS AND MEETINGS, ADDRESSES TO THE SENATE OR THE HOUSE, AND INAUGURATIONS—CONTINUED

[See notes at end of table]

Congress and Date	Type	Occasion, topic, or inaugural location	Name and position of dignitary (where applicable)
May 28, 1957	House	Address	Konrad Adenauer, Chancellor of West Germany.
Do	Senate	...do	Do.
June 20, 1957	...do	...do	Nobusuke Kishi, Prime Minister of Japan.
Do	House	...do	Do.
July 11, 1957	Senate	...do	Husseyn Shaheed Suhrawardy, Prime Minister of Pakistan.
Jan. 9, 1958	Joint session	State of the Union Address	President Dwight D. Eisenhower.
June 5, 1958	Joint meeting	Address	Theodor Heuss, President of West Germany.
June 10, 1958	Senate	...do	Harold Macmillan, Prime Minister of the United Kingdom.
June 18, 1958	Joint meeting	...do	Carlos F. Garcia, President of the Philippines.
June 25, 1958	House	...do	Muhammad Daoud Khan, Prime Minister of Afghanistan.
Do	Senate	...do	Do.
July 24, 1958	...do	...do	Kwame Nkrumah, Prime Minister of Ghana.
July 25, 1958	House	...do	Do.
July 29, 1958	Senate	...do	Amintore Fanfani, Prime Minister of Italy.
Do	House	...do	Do.
86th CONGRESS			
Jan. 9, 1959	Joint session	State of the Union Address	President Dwight D. Eisenhower.
Jan. 21, 1959	Joint meeting	Address	Arturo Frondizi, President of Argentina.
Feb. 12, 1959	Joint session	Sesquicentennial of Abraham Lincoln's birth.	Fredric March, actor; Carl Sandburg, poet.
Mar. 11, 1959	Joint meeting	Address	Jose Maria Lemus, President of El Salvador.
Mar. 18, 1959	...do	...do	Sean T. O'Kelly, President of Ireland.
May 12, 1959	...do	...do	Baudouin, King of the Belgians.
Jan. 7, 1960	Joint session	State of the Union Address	President Dwight D. Eisenhower.
Mar. 30, 1960	Senate	Address	Harold Macmillan, Prime Minister of the United Kingdom.
Apr. 6, 1960	Joint meeting	...do	Alberto Lleras-Camargo, President of Colombia.
Apr. 25, 1960	...do	...do	Charles de Gaulle, President of France.
Apr. 28, 1960	...do	...do	Mahendra, King of Nepal.
June 29, 1960	...do	...do	Bhumibol Adulyadej, King of Thailand.
87th CONGRESS			
Jan. 6, 1961	Joint session	Counting electoral votes	N.A.
Jan. 20, 1961	...do	Inauguration, East Portico	President John F. Kennedy; Vice President Lyndon B. Johnson.
Jan. 30, 1961	...do	State of the Union Address	President John F. Kennedy.
Apr. 13, 1961	Senate	Remarks	Konrad Adenauer, Chancellor of West Germany.
Apr. 18, 1961	House	Address	Constantine Karamanlis, Prime Minister of Greece.
May 4, 1961	Joint meeting	...do	Habib Bourguiba, President of Tunisia.
May 25, 1961	Joint session	Urgent national needs: foreign aid, defense, civil defense, and outer space.	President John F. Kennedy.
June 22, 1961	Senate	Remarks	Hayato Ikeda, Prime Minister of Japan.
Do	House	Address	Do.
July 12, 1961	Joint meeting	...do	Mohammad Ayub Khan, President of Pakistan.
July 26, 1961	House	...do	Abubakar Tafawa Balewa, Prime Minister of Nigeria.
Sept. 21, 1961	Joint meeting	...do	Manuel Prado, President of Peru.
Jan. 11, 1962	Joint session	State of the Union Address	President John F. Kennedy.
Feb. 26, 1962	Joint meeting	Friendship 7: 1st United States orbital space flight.	Lt. Col. John H. Glenn, Jr., USMC; Friendship 7 astronaut.
Apr. 4, 1962	...do	Address	João Goulart, President of Brazil.
Apr. 12, 1962	...do	...do	Mohammad Reza Shah Pahlavi, Shahanshah of Iran.
88th CONGRESS			
Jan. 14, 1963	Joint session	State of the Union Address	President John F. Kennedy.
May 21, 1963	Joint meeting	Flight of Faith 7 Spacecraft	Maj. Gordon L. Cooper, Jr., USAF, Faith 7 astronaut.
Oct. 2, 1963	Senate	Address	Haile Selassie I, Emperor of Ethiopia.
Nov. 27, 1963	Joint session	Assumption of office	President Lyndon B. Johnson.
Jan. 8, 1964	...do	State of the Union Address	Do.
Jan. 15, 1964	Joint meeting	Address	Antonio Segni, President of Italy.
May 28, 1964	...do	...do	Eamon de Valera, President of Ireland.
89th CONGRESS			
Jan. 4, 1965	Joint session	State of the Union Address	President Lyndon B. Johnson.

JOINT SESSIONS AND MEETINGS, ADDRESSES TO THE SENATE OR THE HOUSE, AND INAUGURATIONS—CONTINUED

[See notes at end of table]

Congress and Date	Type	Occasion, topic, or inaugural location	Name and position of dignitary (where applicable)
Jan. 6, 1965	Joint session	Counting electoral votes	N.A.
Jan. 20, 1965	...do [32]	Inauguration, East Portico	President Lyndon B. Johnson; Vice President Hubert H. Humphrey.
Mar. 15, 1965	...do	Voting rights	President Lyndon B. Johnson.
Sept. 14, 1965	Joint meeting	Flight of Gemini 5 Spacecraft	Lt. Col. Gordon L. Cooper, Jr., USAF; and Charles Conrad, Jr., USN; Gemini 5 astronauts.
Jan. 12, 1966	Joint session	State of the Union Address	President Lyndon B. Johnson.
Sept. 15, 1966	Joint meeting	Address	Ferdinand E. Marcos, President of the Philippines.
90th CONGRESS			
Jan. 10, 1967	Joint session	State of the Union Address	President Lyndon B. Johnson.
Apr. 28, 1967	Joint meeting	Vietnam policy	General William C. Westmoreland.
Aug. 16, 1967	Senate	Address	Kurt George Kiesinger, Chancellor of West Germany.
Oct. 27, 1967	Joint meeting	...do	Gustavo Diaz Ordaz, President of Mexico.
Jan. 17, 1968	Joint session	State of the Union Address	President Lyndon B. Johnson.
91st CONGRESS			
Jan. 6, 1969	...do	Counting electoral votes [33]	N.A.
Jan. 9, 1969	Joint meeting	Apollo 8: 1st flight around the moon	Col. Frank Borman, USAF; Capt. James A. Lowell, Jr., USN; Lt. Col. William A. Anders, USAF; Apollo 8 astronauts.
Jan. 14, 1969	Joint session	State of the Union Address	President Lyndon B. Johnson.
Jan. 20, 1969	...do [32]	Inauguration, East Portico	President Richard M. Nixon; Vice President Spiro T. Agnew.
Sept. 16, 1969	Joint meeting	Apollo 11: 1st lunar landing	Neil A. Armstrong, Col. Edwin E. Aldrin, Jr., USAF; and Lt. Col. Michael Collins, USAF; Apollo 11 astronauts.
Nov. 13, 1969	House	Executive-Legislative branch relations and Vietnam policy.	President Richard M. Nixon.
Do	Senate	...do	Do.
Jan. 22, 1970	Joint session	State of the Union Address	Do.
Feb. 25, 1970	Joint meeting	Address	Georges Pompidou, President of France.
June 3, 1970	...do	...do	Rafael Caldera, President of Venezuela.
Sept. 22, 1970	...do	Report on prisoners of war	Col. Frank Borman, Representative to the President on Prisoners of War.
92d CONGRESS			
Jan. 22, 1971	Joint session	State of the Union Address	President Richard M. Nixon.
Sept. 9, 1971	...do	Economic policy	Do.
Do	Joint meeting	Apollo 15: lunar mission	Col. David R. Scott, USAF; Col. James B. Irwin, USAF; and Lt. Col. Alfred M. Worden, USAF; Apollo 15 astronauts.
Jan. 20, 1972	Joint session	State of the Union Address	President Richard M. Nixon.
June 1, 1972	...do	European trip report	Do.
June 15, 1972	Joint meeting	Address	Luis Echeverria Alvarez, President of Mexico.
93d CONGRESS			
Jan. 6, 1973	Joint session	Counting electoral votes	N.A.
Jan. 20, 1973	Inauguration	East Portico	President Richard M. Nixon; Vice President Spiro T. Agnew.
Dec. 6, 1973	Joint meeting	Oath of office to, and Address by Vice President Gerald R. Ford.	Vice President Gerald R. Ford; ceremony attended by President Richard M. Nixon.
Do	Senate	Remarks and Reception	Vice President Gerald R. Ford.
Jan. 30, 1974	Joint session	State of the Union Address	President Richard M. Nixon.
Aug. 12, 1974	...do	Assumption of office	President Gerald R. Ford.
Oct. 8, 1974	...do	Economy	Do.
Dec. 19, 1974	Senate	Address [34]	Vice President Nelson A. Rockefeller.
94th CONGRESS			
Jan. 15, 1975	Joint session	State of the Union Address	President Gerald R. Ford.
Apr. 10, 1975	...do	State of the World message	Do.
June 17, 1975	Joint meeting	Address	Walter Scheel, President of West Germany.
Nov. 5, 1975	...do	...do	Anwar El Sadat, President of Egypt.
Jan. 19, 1976	Joint session	State of the Union Address	President Gerald R. Ford.
Jan. 28, 1976	Joint meeting	Address	Yitzhak Rabin, Prime Minister of Israel.
Mar. 17, 1976	...do	...do	Liam Cosgrave, Prime Minister of Ireland.
May 18, 1976	...do	...do	Valery Giscard d'Estaing, President of France.
June 2, 1976	...do	...do	Juan Carlos I, King of Spain.

JOINT SESSIONS AND MEETINGS, ADDRESSES TO THE SENATE OR THE HOUSE, AND INAUGURATIONS—CONTINUED

[See notes at end of table]

Congress and Date	Type	Occasion, topic, or inaugural location	Name and position of dignitary (where applicable)
Sept. 23, 1976	Joint meeting	Address	William R. Tolbert, Jr., President of Liberia.
95th CONGRESS			
Jan. 6, 1977	Joint session	Counting electoral votes	N.A.
Jan. 12, 1977	...do	State of the Union Address	President Gerald R. Ford.
Jan. 20, 1977	Inauguration	East Portico	President Jimmy Carter; Vice President Walter F. Mondale.
Feb. 17, 1977	House	Address	José López Portillo, President of Mexico.
Feb. 22, 1977	Joint meeting	...do	Pierre Elliot Trudeau, Prime Minister of Canada.
Apr. 20, 1977	Joint session	Energy	President Jimmy Carter.
Jan. 19, 1978	...do	State of the Union Address	Do.
Sept. 18, 1978	...do	Middle East Peace agreements	President Jimmy Carter; joint session attended by Anwar El Sadat, President of Egypt, and by Menachem Begin, Prime Minister of Israel.
96th CONGRESS			
Jan. 23, 1979	...do	State of the Union Address	Do.
June 18, 1979	...do	Salt II agreements	Do.
Jan. 23, 1980	...do	State of the Union Address	Do.
97th CONGRESS			
Jan. 6, 1981	...do	Counting electoral votes	N.A.
Jan. 20, 1981	...do [32]	Inauguration, West Front	President Ronald Reagan; Vice President George Bush.
Feb. 18, 1981	...do	Economic recovery	President Ronald Reagan.
Apr. 28, 1981	...do	Economic recovery—inflation	Do.
Jan. 26, 1982	...do	State of the Union Address	Do.
Jan. 28, 1982	Joint meeting	Centennial of birth of Franklin Delano Roosevelt.	Dr. Arthur Schlesinger, historian; Senator Jennings Randolph; Representative Claude Pepper; Averell Harriman, former Governor of New York [35]; former Representative James Roosevelt, son of President Roosevelt.
Apr. 21, 1982	...do	Address	Beatrix, Queen of the Netherlands.
98th CONGRESS			
Jan. 25, 1983	Joint session	State of the Union Address	President Ronald Reagan.
Apr. 27, 1983	...do	Central America	Do.
Oct. 5, 1983	Joint meeting	Address	Karl Carstens, President of West Germany.
Jan. 25, 1984	Joint session	State of the Union Address	President Ronald Reagan.
Mar. 15, 1984	Joint meeting	Address	Dr. Garett FitzGerald, Prime Minister of Ireland.
Mar. 22, 1984	...do	...do	François Mitterand, President of France.
May 8, 1984	...do	Centennial of birth of Harry S. Truman	Representatives Ike Skelton and Alan Wheat; former Senator Stuart Symington; Margaret Truman Daniel, daughter of President Truman; and Senator Mark Hatfield.
May 16, 1984	...do	Address	Miguel de la Madrid, President of Mexico.
99th CONGRESS			
Jan. 7, 1985	Joint session	Counting electoral votes	N.A.
Jan. 21, 1985	Inauguration	Rotunda [36]	President Ronald Reagan; Vice President George Bush.
Feb. 6, 1985	Joint session	State of the Union Address	President Ronald Reagan.
Feb. 20, 1985	Joint meeting	Address	Margaret Thatcher, Prime Minister of the United Kingdom.
Mar. 6, 1985	...do	...do	Bettino Craxi, President of the Council of Ministers of Italy.
Mar. 20, 1985	...do	...do	Raul Alfonsin, President of Argentina.
June 13, 1985	...do	...do	Rajiv Gandhi, Prime Minister of India.
Oct. 9, 1985	...do	...do	Lee Kuan Yew, Prime Minister of Singapore.
Nov. 21, 1985	Joint session	Geneva Summit	President Ronald Reagan.
Feb. 4, 1986	...do	State of the Union Address	Do.
Sept. 11, 1986	Joint meeting	Address	Jose Sarney, President of Brazil.
Sept. 18, 1986	...do	...do	Corazon C. Aquino, President of the Philippines.
100th CONGRESS			
Jan. 27, 1987	Joint session	State of the Union Address	President Ronald Reagan.
Nov. 10, 1987	Joint meeting	Address	Chaim Herzog, President of Israel.
Jan. 25, 1988	Joint session	State of the Union Address	President Ronald Reagan.
Apr. 27, 1988	Joint meeting	Address	Brian Mulroney, Prime Minister of Canada.

JOINT SESSIONS AND MEETINGS, ADDRESSES TO THE SENATE OR THE HOUSE, AND INAUGURATIONS—CONTINUED

[See notes at end of table]

Congress and Date	Type	Occasion, topic, or inaugural location	Name and position of dignitary (where applicable)
June 23, 1988	Joint meeting	Address	Robert Hawke, Prime Minister of Australia.
101st CONGRESS			
Jan. 4, 1989	Joint session	Counting electoral votes	N.A.
Jan. 20, 1989	Inauguration	West Front	President George Bush; Vice President Dan Quayle.
Feb. 9, 1989	Joint session	Building a Better America	President George Bush.
Mar. 2, 1989	Joint meeting	Bicentennial of the 1st Congress	President Pro Tempore Robert C. Byrd; Speaker James C. Wright, Jr.; Representatives Lindy Boggs, Thomas S. Foley, and Robert H. Michel; Senators George Mitchell and Robert Dole; Howard Nemerov, Poet Laureate of the United States; David McCullough, historian; Anthony M. Frank, Postmaster General; former Senator Nicholas Brady, Secretary of the Treasury.
Apr. 6, 1989	Senate [37]	Addresses on the 200th anniversary commemoration of Senate's first legislative session.	Former Senators Thomas F. Eagleton and Howard H. Baker, Jr.
June 7, 1989	Joint meeting	Address	Benazir Bhutto, Prime Minister of Pakistan.
Oct. 4, 1989	...do	...do	Carlos Salinas de Gortari, President of Mexico.
Oct. 18, 1989	...do	...do	Roh Tae Woo, President of South Korea.
Nov. 15, 1989	...do	...do	Lech Walesa, chairman of Solidarność labor union, Poland.
Jan. 31, 1990	Joint session	State of the Union Address	President George Bush.
Feb. 21, 1990	Joint meeting	Address	Vaclav Hável, President of Czechoslovakia.
Mar. 7, 1990	...do	...do	Giulio Andreotti, President of the Council of Ministers of Italy.
Mar. 27, 1990	...do	Centennial of birth of Dwight D. Eisenhower.	Senator Robert Dole; Walter Cronkite, television journalist; Winston S. Churchill, member of British Parliament and grandson of Prime Minister Churchill; Clark M. Clifford, former Secretary of Defense; James D. Robinson III, chairman of Eisenhower Centennial Foundation; Arnold Palmer, professional golfer; John S.D. Eisenhower, former Ambassador to Belgium and son of President Eisenhower; Representatives Beverly Byron, William F. Goodling, and Pat Roberts.
June 26, 1990	...do	Address	Nelson Mandela, Deputy President of the African National Congress, South Africa.
Sept. 11, 1990	Joint session	Invasion of Kuwait by Iraq	President George Bush.
102d CONGRESS			
Jan. 29, 1991	...do	State of the Union Address	Do.
Mar. 6, 1991	...do	Conclusion of Persian Gulf War	Do.
Apr. 16, 1991	Joint meeting	Address	Violeta B. de Chamorro, President of Nicaragua.
May 8, 1991	House [38]	...do	General H. Norman Schwarzkopf.
May 16, 1991	Joint meeting	...do	Elizabeth II, Queen of the United Kingdom; joint meeting also attended by Prince Philip.
Nov. 14, 1991	...do	...do	Carlos Saul Menem, President of Argentina.
Jan. 28, 1992	Joint session	State of the Union Address	President George Bush.
Apr. 30, 1992	Joint meeting	Address	Richard von Weizsäcker, President of Germany.
June 17, 1992	...do	...do	Boris Yeltsin, President of Russia.
103d CONGRESS			
Jan. 6, 1993	Joint session	Counting electoral votes	N.A.
Jan. 20, 1993	Inauguration	West Front	President William J. Clinton; Vice President Albert Gore.
Feb. 17, 1993	Joint session	Economic Address [39]	President William J. Clinton.
Sept. 22, 1993	...do	Health care reform	Do.
Jan. 25, 1994	...do	State of the Union Address	Do.
May 18, 1994	Joint meeting	Address	Narasimha Rao, Prime Minister of India.
July 26, 1994	...do	Addresses	Hussein I, King of Jordan; Yitzhak Rabin, Prime Minister of Israel.
Oct. 6, 1994	...do	Address	Nelson Mandela, President of South Africa.

JOINT SESSIONS AND MEETINGS, ADDRESSES TO THE SENATE OR THE HOUSE, AND INAUGURATIONS—CONTINUED

[See notes at end of table]

Congress and Date	Type	Occasion. topic, or inaugural location	Name and position of dignitary (where applicable)
104th CONGRESS			
Jan. 24, 1995	Joint session	State of the Union Address	President William J. Clinton.
July 26, 1995	Joint meeting	Address	Kim Yong-sam, President of South Korea.[40]
Oct. 11, 1995	...do	Close of the Commemoration of the 50th Anniversary of World War II.	Speaker Newt Gingrich; Vice President Albert Gore; President Pro Tempore Strom Thurmond; Representatives Henry J. Hyde and G.V. "Sonny" Montgomery; Senators Daniel K. Inouye and Robert Dole; former Representative Robert H. Michel; General Louis H. Wilson (ret.), former Commandant of the Marine Corps.
Dec. 12, 1995	...do	Address	Shimon Peres, Prime Minister of Israel.
Jan. 30, 1996	Joint session	State of the Union Address	President William J. Clinton.
Feb. 1, 1996	Joint meeting	Address	Jacques Chirac, President of France.
July 10, 1996	...do	...do	Binyamin Netanyahu, Prime Minister of Israel.
Sept. 11, 1996	...do	...do	John Bruton, Prime Minister of Ireland.
105th CONGRESS			
Jan. 9, 1997	Joint session	Counting electoral votes	N.A.
Jan. 20, 1997	Inauguration	West Front	President William J. Clinton; Vice President Albert Gore.
Feb. 4, 1997	Joint session	State of the Union Address [41]	President William J. Clinton.
Feb. 27, 1997	Joint meeting	Address	Eduardo Frei, President of Chile.
Jan. 27, 1998	Joint session	State of the Union Address	President William J. Clinton.
June 10, 1998	Joint meeting	Address	Kim Dae-jung, President of South Korea.
July 15, 1998	...do	...do	Emil Constantinescu, President of Romania.
106th CONGRESS			
Jan. 19, 1999	Joint session	State of the Union Address	President William J. Clinton.
Jan. 27, 2000	...do	...do	Do.
Sept. 14, 2000	Joint meeting	Address	Atal Bihari Vajpayee, Prime Minister of India.
107th CONGRESS			
Jan. 6, 2001	Joint session	Counting electoral votes	N.A.
Jan. 20, 2001	Inauguration	West Front	President George W. Bush; Vice President Richard B. Cheney.
Feb. 27, 2001	Joint session	Budget message [39]	President George W. Bush.
Sept. 6, 2001	Joint meeting	Address	Vicente Fox, President of Mexico.
Sept. 20, 2001	Joint session	War on terrorism	President George W. Bush; joint session attended by Tony Blair, Prime Minister of the United Kingdom, by Tom Ridge, Governor of Pennsylvania, by George Pataki, Governor of New York, and by Rudolph Giuliani, Mayor of New York City.
Jan. 29, 2002	...do	State of the Union Address	President George W. Bush; joint session attended by Hamid Karzai, Chairman of the Interim Authority of Afghanistan.
June 12, 2002	Joint meeting	Address [42]	John Howard, Prime Minister of Australia.
108th CONGRESS			
Jan. 28, 2003	Joint session	State of the Union Address	President George W. Bush.
July 17, 2003	Joint meeting	Address	Tony Blair, Prime Minister of the United Kingdom; joint meeting attended by Mrs. George W. Bush.
Jan. 20, 2004	Joint session	State of the Union Address	President George W. Bush.
Feb. 4, 2004	Joint meeting	Address	Jose Maria Aznar, President of the Government of Spain.
June 15, 2004	...do	...do	Hamid Karzai, President of Afghanistan.
Sept. 23, 2004	...do	...do	Ayad Allawi, Interim Prime Minister of Iraq.
109th CONGRESS			
Jan. 6, 2005	Joint session	Counting electoral votes [43]	N.A.
Jan. 20, 2005	Inauguration	West Front	President George W. Bush; Vice President Richard B. Cheney.
Feb. 2, 2005	Joint session	State of the Union Address	President George W. Bush.
Apr. 6, 2005	Joint meeting	Address	Viktor Yushchenko, President of Ukraine.
July 19, 2005	...do	...do	Dr. Manmohan Singh, Prime Minister of India.
Jan. 31, 2006	Joint session	State of the Union Address	President George W. Bush.
Mar. 1, 2006	Joint meeting	Address	Silvio Berlusconi, Prime Minister of Italy.

JOINT SESSIONS AND MEETINGS, ADDRESSES TO THE SENATE OR THE HOUSE, AND INAUGURATIONS—CONTINUED

[See notes at end of table]

Congress and Date	Type	Occasion, topic, or inaugural location	Name and position of dignitary (where applicable)
Mar. 15, 2006	Joint meeting	Address	Ellen Johnson Sirleaf, President of Liberia.
May 24, 2006	...do	...do	Ehud Olmert, Prime Minister of Israel.
June 7, 2006	...do	...do	Dr. Vaira Vike-Freiberga, President of Latvia.
July 26, 2006	...do	...do	Nouri Al-Maliki, Prime Minister of Iraq.
110th CONGRESS			
Jan. 23, 2007	Joint session	State of the Union Address	President George W. Bush.
Mar. 7, 2007	Joint meeting	Address	Abdullah II Ibn Al Hussein, King of Jordan.
Nov. 7, 2007	...do	...do	Nicolas Sarkozy, President of France.
Jan. 28, 2008	Joint session	State of the Union Address	President George W. Bush.
Apr. 30, 2008	Joint meeting	Address	Bertie Ahern, Prime Minister of Ireland.
111th CONGRESS			
Jan. 8, 2009	Joint session	Counting electoral votes	N.A.
Jan. 20, 2009	Inauguration	West Front	President Barack H. Obama; Vice President Joseph R. Biden, Jr.
Feb. 24, 2009	Joint session	Economic Address	President Barack H. Obama.
Mar. 4, 2009	Joint meeting	...do	Gordon Brown, Prime Minister of the United Kingdom.
Sept. 9, 2009	Joint session	Health care reform	President Barack H. Obama.
Nov. 2, 2009	Joint meeting	Address	Angela Merkel, Chancellor of Germany.
Jan. 27, 2010	Joint session	State of the Union Address	President Barack H. Obama.
May 20, 2010	Joint meeting	Address	Felipe Calderon Hinojosa, President of Mexico.
112th CONGRESS			
Jan. 25, 2011	Joint session	State of the Union Address	President Barack H. Obama.
Mar. 9, 2011	Joint meeting	Address	Julia Gillard, Prime Minister of Australia.
May 24, 2011	...do	...do	Binyamin Netanyahu, Prime Minister of Israel.
Sept. 8, 2011	Joint session	American Jobs Act	President Barack H. Obama.
Oct. 13, 2011	Joint meeting	Address	Lee Myung-bak, President of the Republic of Korea.
Jan. 24, 2012	Joint session	State of the Union Address	President Barack H. Obama.
113th CONGRESS			
Jan. 4, 2013	...do	Counting electoral votes	N.A.
Jan. 21, 2013	Inauguration	West Front	President Barack H. Obama; Vice President Joseph R. Biden, Jr.
Feb. 12, 2013	Joint session	State of the Union Address	President Barack H. Obama.
May 8, 2013	Joint meeting	Address	Park Geun-hye, President of the Republic of Korea.
Jan. 28, 2014	Joint session	State of the Union Address	President Barack H. Obama.
Sept. 18, 2014	Joint meeting	Address	Petro Poroshenko, President of Ukraine.
114th CONGRESS			
Jan. 20, 2015	Joint session	State of the Union Address	President Barack H. Obama.
Mar. 3, 2015	Joint meeting	Address	Binyamin Netanyahu, Prime Minister of Israel.
Mar. 25, 2015	...do	...do	Mohammad Ashraf Ghani, President of the Islamic Republic of Afghanistan.
Apr. 29, 2015	...do	...do	Shinzo Abe, Prime Minister of Japan.
Sept. 24, 2015	...do	...do	Pope Francis of the Holy See.
Jan. 12, 2016	Joint session	State of the Union Address	President Barack H. Obama.

[1] Closing date for this table was January 12, 2016.

[2] The oath of office was administered to George Washington outside on the gallery in front of the Senate Chamber, after which the Congress and the President returned to the chamber to hear the inaugural address. They then proceeded to St. Paul's Chapel for the "divine service" performed by the Chaplain of the Congress. Adjournment of the ceremony did not occur until the Congress returned to Federal Hall.

[3] Funeral oration was delivered at the German Lutheran Church in Philadelphia.

[4] Because of a tie in the electoral vote between Thomas Jefferson and Aaron Burr, the House of Representatives had to decide the election. Thirty-six ballots were required to break the deadlock, with Jefferson's election as President and Burr's as Vice President on February 17. The Twelfth Amendment was added to the Constitution to prevent the 1800 problem from recurring.

[5] During most of the period while the Capitol was being reconstructed following the fire of 1814, the Congress met in the "Brick Capitol," constructed on the site of the present Supreme Court building. This joint session took place in the Representatives' chamber on the 2d floor of the building.

[6] The joint session to count electoral votes was dissolved because the House and Senate disagreed on Missouri's status regarding statehood. The joint session was reconvened the same day and Missouri's votes were counted.

[7] While this occasion has historically been referred to as the first joint meeting of Congress, the Journals of the House and Senate indicate that Lafayette actually addressed the House of Representatives, with some of the Senators present as guests of the House (having been invited at the last minute to attend). Similar occasions, when members of the one body were invited as guests of the other, include the Senate address by Queen Wilhelmina of the Netherlands on Aug. 6, 1942, and the House address by General H. Norman Schwarzkopf on May 8, 1991.

[8] Although Andrew Jackson won the popular vote by a substantial amount and had the highest number of electoral votes from among the several candidates, he did not receive the required majority of the electoral votes. The responsibility for choosing the new President therefore devolved upon the House of Representatives. As soon as the Senators left the chamber, the balloting proceeded, and John Quincy Adams was elected on the first ballot.

[9] The ceremony was moved outside to accommodate the extraordinarily large crowd of people who had come to Washington to see the inauguration.

[10] The ceremony was moved inside because of cold weather.

[11] Following the death of President Zachary Taylor, Vice President Millard Fillmore took the Presidential oath of office in a special joint session in the Hall of the House.

[12] The joint session to count electoral votes was dissolved three times so that the House and Senate could resolve several electoral disputes.

[13] Because of a severe cold and hoarseness, the King could not deliver his speech, which was read by former Representative Elisha Hunt Allen, then serving as Chancellor and Chief Justice of the Hawaiian Islands.

[14] The contested election between Rutherford B. Hayes and Samuel J. Tilden created a constitutional crisis. Tilden won the popular vote by a close margin, but disputes concerning the electoral vote returns from four states deadlocked the proceedings of the joint session. Anticipating this development, the Congress had created a special commission of five Senators, five Representatives, and five Supreme Court Justices to resolve such disputes. The Commission met in the Supreme Court Chamber (the present Old Senate Chamber) as each problem arose. In each case, the Commission accepted the Hayes electors, securing his election by one electoral vote. The joint session was convened on 15 occasions, with the last on March 2, just three days before the inauguration.

[15] The speech was written by former Speaker and Senator Robert C. Winthrop, who could not attend the ceremony because of ill health.

[16] Because of a blizzard, the ceremony was moved inside, where it was held as part of the Senate's special session. President William Howard Taft took the oath of office and gave his inaugural address after Vice President James S. Sherman's inaugural address and the swearing-in of the new senators.

[17] Held in the Senate Chamber.

[18] Bakhmetieff represented the provisional government of Russia set up after the overthrow of the monarchy in March 1917 and recognized by the United States. The Bolsheviks took over in November 1917.

[19] The address and reception were in conjunction with the presentation to the Senate by France of two Sèvres vases in appreciation of the United States' involvement in World War I. The vases are today in the Senate lobby, just off the Senate floor. Two additional Sèvres vases were given without ceremony to the House of Representatives, which today are in the Rayburn Room, not far from the floor of the House.

[20] Senators later objected to President Harding's speech (given with no advance notice to most of the Senators) as an unconstitutional effort to interfere with the deliberations of the Senate, and Harding did not repeat visits of this kind.

[21] This was the first Annual Message broadcast live on radio.

[22] This was the first inauguration held pursuant to the Twentieth Amendment, which changed the date from March 4 to January 20. The Vice Presidential oath, which previously had been given earlier on the same day in the Senate Chamber, was added to the inaugural ceremony as well, but the Vice Presidential inaugural address was discontinued.

[23] A joint reception for the King and Queen of the United Kingdom was held in the Rotunda, authorized by Senate Concurrent Resolution 17, 76th Congress. Although the concurrent resolution was structured to establish a joint meeting, the Senate, in fact, adjourned rather than recessed as called for by the resolution.

[24] Held in the Senate Chamber.

[25] At this time, the Philippines was still a possession of the United States, although it had been made a self-governing commonwealth in 1935, in preparation for full independence in 1946. From 1909 to 1916, Quezon had served in the U.S. House of Representatives as the resident commissioner from the Philippines.

[26] In exile.

[27] For this Senate Address by Queen Wilhelmina, the members of the House of Representatives were invited as guests. This occasion has sometimes been mistakenly referred to as a joint meeting.

[28] The oaths of office were taken in simple ceremonies at the White House because the expense and festivity of a Capitol ceremony were thought inappropriate because of the war. The Joint Committee on Arrangements of the Congress was in charge, however, and both the Senate and the House of Representatives were present.

[29] This was the first time the term "State of the Union Address" was used for the President's Annual Message. Also, it was the first time the address was shown live on television.

[30] This was an informal meeting in the Coolidge Auditorium of the Library of Congress.

[31] Presentation of new ivory gavel to the Senate.

[32] According to the Congressional Record, the Senate adjourned prior to the inaugural ceremonies, even though the previously adopted resolution had stated the adjournment would come immediately following the inauguration. The Senate Journal records the adjournment as called for in the resolution, hence this listing as a joint session.

[33] The joint session to count electoral votes was dissolved so that the House and Senate could each resolve the dispute regarding a ballot from North Carolina. The joint session was reconvened the same day and the North Carolina vote was counted.

[34] Rockefeller was sworn in as Vice President by Chief Justice Warren E. Burger, after which, by unanimous consent, he was allowed to address the Senate.

[35] Because the Governor had laryngitis, his speech was read by his wife, Pamela.

[36] The ceremony was moved inside because of extremely cold weather.

[37] These commemorative addresses were given in the Old Senate Chamber during a regular legislative session.

[38] For this House Address by General Schwarzkopf, the members of the Senate were invited as guests.

[39] This speech was mislabeled in many sources as a State of the Union Address.

[40] President Kim Yong-sam was in Washington for the dedication of the Korean Veterans' Memorial, held the day after this joint meeting.

[41] This was the first State of the Union Address carried live on the Internet.

[42] Prime Minister Howard was originally scheduled to address a joint meeting on September 12, 2001, but because of the attack on the United States on September 11, 2001, the event was postponed until this occasion.

[43] The joint session to count electoral votes was dissolved so that the House and Senate could each discuss the dispute regarding the ballots from Ohio. The joint session was reconvened the same day and the Ohio votes were counted.

REPRESENTATIVES UNDER EACH APPORTIONMENT

The original apportionment of Representatives was assigned in 1787 in the Constitution and remained in effect for the 1st and 2d Congresses. Subsequent apportionments based on the censuses over the years have been figured using several different methods approved by Congress, all with the goal of dividing representation among the states as equally as possible. After each census up to and including the thirteenth in 1910, Congress would enact a law designating the specific changes in the actual number of Representatives as well as the increase in the ratio of persons-per-Representative. After having made no apportionment after the Fourteenth census in 1920, Congress by statute in 1929 fixed the total number of Representatives at 435 (the number attained with the apportionment after the 1910 census), and since that time, only the ratio of persons-per-Representative has continued to increase, in fact, significantly so. Since the total is now fixed, the specific number of Representatives per state is adjusted after each census to reflect its percentage of the entire population. Since the Sixteenth Census in 1940, the "equal proportions" method of apportioning Representatives within the 435 total has been employed. A detailed explanation of the entire apportionment process can be found in *The Historical Atlas of United States Congressional Districts, 1989–1983*. Kenneth C. Martis, The Free Press, New York, 1982.

State	Constitutional apportionment	First Census 1790	Second Census 1800	Third Census 1810	Fourth Census 1820	Fifth Census 1830	Sixth Census 1840	Seventh Census 1850	Eighth Census 1860	Ninth Census 1870	Tenth Census 1880	Eleventh Census 1890	Twelfth Census 1900	Thirteenth Census 1910	Fifteenth Census 1930	Sixteenth Census 1940	Seventeenth Census 1950	Eighteenth Census 1960	Nineteenth Census 1970	Twentieth Census 1980	Twenty-First Census 1990	Twenty-Second Census 2000
AL					3	5	7	7	6	8	8	9	9	10	9	9	9	8	7	7	7	7
AK																		1[2,3]	1	1	1	1
AZ														1[4]	1	2	2	3	4	5	6	8
AR							1	2	3	4	5	6	7	7	7	7	6	4	4	4	4	4
CA								2	3	4	6	7	8	11	20	23	30	38	43	45	52	53
CO											1	2	3	4	4	4	4	4	5	6	6	7
CT	5	7	7	7	6	6	4	4	4	4	4	4	5	5	6	6	6	6	6	6	6	5
DE	1	1	1	2	1	1	1	1	1	1	1	1	1	1	1	1	1	1	1	1	1	1
FL								1	1	2	2	2	3	4	5	6	8	12	15	19	23	25
GA	3	2	4	6	7	9	8	8	7	9	10	11	11	12	10	10	10	10	10	10	11	13
HI																		2[2,3]	2	2	2	2
ID												1	1	2	2	2	2	2	2	2	2	2
IL					1	3	7	9	14	19	20	22	25	27	27	26	25	24	24	22	20	19
IN					3	7	10	11	11	13	13	13	13	13	12	11	11	11	11	10	10	9
IA								2	6	9	11	11	11	11	9	8	8	7	6	6	5	5
KS									1[4]	3	7	8	8	8	7	6	6	5	5	5	4	4
KY		2[4]	6	10	12	13	10	10	9	10	11	11	11	11	9	9	8	7	7	7	6	6
LA					3	3	4	4	5	6	6	6	7	8	8	8	8	8	8	8	7	7
ME					7	8	7	6	5	5	4	4	4	4	3	3	3	2	2	2	2	2
MD	6	8	9	9	9	8	6	6	5	6	6	6	6	6	6	6	7	8	8	8	8	8
MA	8	14	17	20[5]	13	12	10	11	10	11	12	13	14	16	15	14	14	12	12	11	10	10
MI							3	4	6	9	11	12	12	13	17	17	18	19	19	18	16	15
MN									2	3	5	7	9	10	9	9	9	8	8	8	8	8
MS					1	2	4	5	5	6	7	7	8	8	7	7	6	5	5	5	5	4
MO					1[4]	2	5	7	9	13	14	15	16	16	13	13	11	10	10	9	9	9
MT												1	1	2	2	2	2	2	2	2	1	1
NE										1	3	6	6	6	5	4	4	3	3	3	3	3
NV										1	1	1	1	1	1	1	1	1	1	2	2	3
NH	3	4	5	6	6	5	4	3	3	3	2	2	2	2	2	2	2	2	2	2	2	2
NJ	4	5	6	6	6	6	5	5	5	7	7	8	10	12	14	14	14	15	15	14	13	13
NM														1[4]	1	2	2	2	2	3	3	3
NY	6	10	17	27	34	40	34	33	31	33	34	34	37	43	45	45	43	41	39	34	31	29
NC	5	10	12	13	13	13	9	8	7	8	9	9	10	10	11	12	12	11	11	11	12	13
ND												1	2	3	2	2	2	2	1	1	1	1
OH				6	14	19	21	21	19	20	21	21	21	22	24	23	23	24	23	21	19	18
OK														8	9	8	6	6	6	6	6	5
OR									1	1	1	2	2	3	3	4	4	4	4	5	5	5
PA	8	13	18	23	26	28	24	25	24	27	28	30	32	36	34	33	30	27	25	23	21	19
RI	1	2	2	2	2	2	2	2	2	2	2	2	2	3	2	2	2	2	2	2	2	2
SC	5	6	8	9	9	9	7	6	4	5	7	7	7	7	6	6	6	6	6	6	6	6
SD												2	2	3	2	2	2	2	2	1	1	1
TN			3	6	9	13	11	10	8	10	10	10	10	10	9	10	9	9	8	9	9	9
TX								2	4	6	11	13	16	18	21	21	22	23	24	27	30	32
UT													1	2	2	2	2	2	2	3	3	3
VT		2	4	6	5	5	4	3	3	3	2	2	2	2	1	1	1	1	1	1	1	1
VA	10	19	22	23	22	21	15	13	11[6]	9	10	10	10	10	9	9	10	10	10	10	11	11
WA												2	3	5	6	6	7	7	7	8	9	9
WV										3	4	4	5	6	6	6	6	5	4	4	3	3
WI								3	6	8	9	10	11	11	10	10	10	10	9	9	9	8
WY												1	1	1	1	1	1	1	1	1	1	1
Total	65	105	141	181	213	240	223	234	241	292	325	356	386	435	435	435	435	435	435	435	435	435

NOTE: Information for table obtained from the U.S. Census Bureau.

564

¹ No apportionment was made after the 1920 census.

² The following Representatives were added after the indicated apportionments when these states were admitted in the years listed. The number of these additional Representatives for each state remained in effect until the next census's apportionment (with the exceptions of California and New Mexico, as explained in footnote 4). They are not included in the total for each column. In reading this table, please remember that the apportionments made after each census took effect with the election two years after the census date. As a result, in the table footnote 2 is placed for several states under the decade preceding the one in which it entered the Union, since the previous decade's apportionment was still in effect at the time of statehood. *Constitutional:* Vermont (1791), 2; Kentucky (1792), 2; *First:* Tennessee (1796), 1; *Second:* Ohio (1803), 1; *Third:* Louisiana (1812), 1; Indiana (1816), 1; Mississippi (1817), 1; Illinois (1818), 1; Alabama (1819), 1; Missouri (1821), 1; *Fifth:* Arkansas (1836), 1; Michigan (1837), 1; *Sixth:* Florida (1845), 1; Texas (1845), 2; Iowa (1846), 2; Wisconsin (1848), 2; California (1850), 2; *Seventh:* Minnesota (1858), 2; Oregon (1859), 1; Kansas (1861), 1; *Eighth:* Nevada (1864), 1; Nebraska (1867), 1; *Ninth:* Colorado (1876), 1; *Tenth:* North Dakota (1889), 1; South Dakota (1889), 2; Montana (1889), 1; Washington (1889), 1; Idaho (1890), 1; Wyoming (1890), 1; *Eleventh:* Utah (1896), 1; *Twelth:* Oklahoma (1907), 5; New Mexico (1912), 2; Arizona (1912), 1; *Seventeenth:* Alaska (1959), 1; Hawaii (1959), 1.

³ When Alaska and then Hawaii joined the Union in 1959, the law was changed to allow the total membership of the House of Representatives to increase to 436 and then to 437, apportioning one new Representative for each of those states. The total returned to 435 in 1963, when the 1960 census apportionment took effect.

⁴ Even though the respective censuses were taken before the following states joined the Union, Representatives for them were apportioned either because of anticipation of statehood or because they had become states in the period between the census and the apportionment, hence they are included in the totals of the respective columns. *First:* Vermont (1791); Kentucky (1792); *Fourth:* Missouri (1821); *Seventh:* California (1850); *Eighth:* Kansas (1861); *Thirteenth:* New Mexico (1912); Arizona (1912). (Please note: These seven states are also included in footnote 2 because they became states while the previous decade's apportionment was still in effect for the House of Representatives.) California's situation was unusual. It was scheduled for inclusion in the figures for the 1850 census apportionment; however, when the apportionment law was passed in 1852, California's census returns were still incomplete so Congress made special provision that the state would retain "the number of Representatives [two] prescribed by the act of admission * * * into the Union until a new apportionment [i.e., after the 1860 census]" would be made. The number of Representatives from California actually increased before the next apportionment to three when Congress gave the state an extra Representative during part of the 37th Congress, from 1862 to 1863. Regarding New Mexico, the 1911 apportionment law, passed by the 62d Congress in response to the 1910 census and effective with the 63d Congress in 1913, stated that "if the Territor[y] of * * * New Mexico shall become [a State] in the Union before the apportionment of Representatives under the next decennial census [it] shall have one Representative * * *." When New Mexico became a state in 1912 during the 62d Congress, it was given two Representatives. The number was decreased to one beginning the next year in the 63d.

⁵ The "Maine District" of Massachusetts became a separate state during the term of the 16th Congress, in 1820. For the remainder of that Congress, Maine was assigned one "at large" Representative while Massachusetts continued to have 20 Representatives, the number apportioned to it after the 1810 census. For the 17th Congress (the last before the 1820 census apportionment took effect), seven of Massachusetts's Representatives were reassigned to Maine, leaving Massachusetts with 13.

⁶ Of the 11 Representatives apportioned to Virginia after the 1860 census, three were reassigned to West Virginia when that part of Virginia became a separate state in 1863. Since the Virginia seats in the House were vacant at that time because of the Civil War, all of the new Representatives from West Virginia were able to take their seats at once. When Representatives from Virginia reentered the House in 1870, only eight members represented it.

IMPEACHMENT PROCEEDINGS

The provisions of the United States Constitution which apply specifically to impeachments are as follows: Article I, section 2, clause 5; Article I, section 3, clauses 6 and 7; Article II, section 2, clause 1; Article II, section 4; and Article III, section 2, clause 3.

For the officials listed below, the date of impeachment by the House of Representatives is followed by the dates of the Senate trial, with the result of each listed at the end of the entry.

WILLIAM BLOUNT, a Senator of the United States from Tennessee; impeached July 7, 1797; tried Monday, December 17, 1798, to Monday, January 14, 1799; charges dismissed for want of jurisdiction.

JOHN PICKERING, judge of the United States District Court for the District of New Hampshire; impeached March 2, 1803; tried Thursday, March 3, 1803, to Monday, March 12, 1804; removed from office.

SAMUEL CHASE, Associate Justice of the Supreme Court of the United States; impeached March 12, 1804; tried Friday, November 30, 1804, to Friday, March 1, 1805; acquitted.

JAMES H. PECK, judge of the United States District Court for the District of Missouri; impeached April 24, 1830; tried Monday, April 26, 1830, to Monday, January 31, 1831; acquitted.

WEST H. HUMPHREYS, judge of the United States District Court for the Middle, Eastern, and Western Districts of Tennessee; impeached May 6, 1862; tried Wednesday, May 7, 1862, to Thursday, June 26, 1862; removed from office and disqualified from future office.

ANDREW JOHNSON, President of the United States; impeached February 24, 1868; tried Tuesday, February 25, 1868, to Tuesday, May 26, 1868; acquitted.

MARK DELAHAY, judge of the United States District Court of Kansas; impeached February 28, 1873; resigned office Friday, December 12, 1873, before the Senate trial was held, with no further action taken by the Senate.

WILLIAM W. BELKNAP, Secretary of War; impeached March 2, 1876; tried Friday, March 3, 1876, to Tuesday, August 1, 1876; acquitted.

CHARLES SWAYNE, judge of the United States District Court for the Northern District of Florida; impeached December 13, 1904; tried Wednesday, December 14, 1904, to Monday, February 27, 1905; acquitted.

ROBERT W. ARCHBALD, associate judge, United States Commerce Court; impeached July 11, 1912; tried Saturday, July 13, 1912, to Monday, January 13, 1913; removed from office and disqualified from future office.

GEORGE W. ENGLISH, judge of the United States District Court for the Eastern District of Illinois; impeached April 1, 1926; tried Friday, April 23, 1926, to Monday, December 13, 1926; resigned office Thursday, November 4, 1926; Court of Impeachment adjourned to December 13, 1926, when, on request of House managers, the proceedings were dismissed.

HAROLD LOUDERBACK, judge of the United States District Court for the Northern District of California; impeached February 24, 1933; tried Monday, May 15, 1933, to Wednesday, May 24, 1933; acquitted.

HALSTED L. RITTER, judge of the United States District Court for the Southern District of Florida; impeached March 2, 1936; tried Monday, April 6, 1936, to Friday, April 17, 1936; removed from office.

HARRY E. CLAIBORNE, judge of the United States District Court of Nevada; impeached July 22, 1986; tried Tuesday, October 7, 1986, to Thursday, October 9, 1986; removed from office.

ALCEE L. HASTINGS, judge of the United States District Court for the Southern District of Florida; impeached August 3, 1988; tried Wednesday, October 18, 1989, to Friday, October 20, 1989; removed from office.

WALTER L. NIXON, judge of the United States District Court for the Southern District of Mississippi; impeached May 10, 1989; tried Wednesday, November 1, 1989, to Friday, November 3, 1989; removed from office.

WILLIAM JEFFERSON CLINTON, President of the United States; impeached December 19, 1998; tried Thursday, January 7, 1999, to Friday, February 12, 1999; acquitted.

SAMUEL B. KENT, judge of the United States District Court for the Southern District of Texas; impeached June 19, 2009; resigned office effective Tuesday, June 30, 2009; Court of Impeachment convened on Wednesday, July 22, 2009, when, on request of House managers, proceedings were dismissed.

G. THOMAS PORTEOUS, JR., judge of the United States District Court for the Eastern District of Louisiana; impeached March 11, 2010; tried Tuesday, December 7, 2010, to Wednesday, December 8, 2010; removed from office and disqualified from future office.

REPRESENTATIVES, SENATORS, DELEGATES, AND RESIDENT COMMISSIONERS SERVING IN THE 1st–114th CONGRESSES *

Since the U.S. Congress convened on March 4, 1789, 12,177 individuals have served as Representatives, Senators, or in both capacities. There have been 10,214 Members who served only as Representatives, 1,294 Members who served only in the Senate, and 669 Members with service in both chambers. The total number of Representatives (including individuals serving in both bodies) is 10,883.

These numbers do not include statutory representatives: Resident Commissioners and Delegates. An additional 144 people have served only as Territorial Delegates in the House and 32 people have served only as Resident Commissioners from Puerto Rico or the Philippines.

State/Territory	Date Became a U.S. Territory	Date Entered the Union	Delegates (Only)	Resident Commissioners [1]	Representatives (Only) [2]	Representatives and Delegates	Senators (Only) [3]	Senators and Representatives [4]	Senators and Delegates	Senators, Representatives, and Delegates	Total House Members
Alabama	Mar. 3, 1817	Dec. 14, 1819 (22d)	0	0	168	1	27	13	0	0	182
Alaska	Aug. 24, 1912	Jan. 3, 1959 (49th)	7	0	4	0	7	0	1	0	12
American Samoa	Apr. 17, 1900		2	0	0	0	0	0	0	0	2
Arizona	Feb. 24, 1863	Feb. 14, 1912 (48th)	10	0	32	0	5	4	2	0	48
Arkansas	Mar. 2, 1819	June 15, 1836 (25th)	2	0	86	0	22	11	1	0	100
California		Sept. 9, 1850 (31st)	0	0	349	0	34	8	0	1	358
Colorado	Feb. 28, 1861	Aug. 1, 1876 (38th)	2	0	59	0	23	10	2	0	73
Connecticut		Jan. 9, 1788 (5th)	0	0	209	0	29	26	0	0	235
Delaware		Dec. 7, 1787 (1st)	0	0	62	0	37	14	0	0	76
District of Columbia	July 16, 1790		3	0	0	0	0	0	0	0	3
Florida	Mar. 20, 1822	Mar. 3, 1845 (27th)	4	0	127	0	27	6	1	0	138
Georgia		Jan. 2, 1788 (4th)	0	0	280	0	39	22	0	0	302
Guam	Apr. 11, 1899		4	0	0	0	0	0	0	0	4
Hawaii	June 14, 1900	Aug. 21, 1959 (50th)	10	0	9	0	3	4	0	0	23
Idaho	Mar. 3, 1863	July 3, 1890 (43d)	8	0	27	0	19	6	1	0	42
Illinois	Feb. 3, 1809	Dec. 3, 1818 (21st)	3	0	449	0	31	19	0	0	471
Indiana	May 7, 1800	Dec. 11, 1816 (19th)	2	0	301	1	27	18	0	0	322
Iowa	June 12, 1838	Dec. 28, 1846 (29th)	1	0	169	0	22	12	0	0	182
Kansas	May 30, 1854	Jan. 29, 1861 (34th)	2	0	108	0	24	8	1	0	119
Kentucky		June 1, 1792 (15th)	0	0	312	0	38	28	0	0	340
Louisiana [5]	Mar. 4, 1804	Apr. 30, 1812 (18th)	2	0	148	0	35	13	0	0	163
Maine		Mar. 15, 1820 (23d)	0	0	134	0	22	15	0	0	149
Mariana Islands	Apr. 11, 1899		1	0	0	0	0	0	0	0	1
Maryland		Apr. 28, 1788 (7th)	0	0	280	0	29	27	0	0	307
Massachusetts		Feb. 6, 1788 (6th)	0	0	403	0	24	29	0	0	432
Michigan	Jan. 11, 1805	Jan. 26, 1837 (26th)	5	0	256	0	23	14	1	0	276
Minnesota	Mar. 3, 1849	May 11, 1858 (32d)	2	0	121	0	28	11	0	0	134
Mississippi	Apr. 7, 1798	Dec. 10, 1817 (20th)	3	0	110	0	29	14	0	1	128
Missouri	June 4, 1812	Aug. 10, 1821 (24th)	2	0	293	1	35	10	0	0	306
Montana	May 26, 1864	Nov. 8, 1889 (41st)	5	0	26	0	15	5	0	1	37

Nebraska	May 30, 1854	Mar. 1, 1867 (37th)	5	0	86	0	31	6	1	0	98
Nevada	Mar. 2, 1861	Oct. 31, 1864 (36th)	2	0	30	0	19	6	0	0	38
New Hampshire		June 21, 1788 (9th)	0	0	136	0	37	26	0	0	162
New Jersey		Dec. 18, 1787 (3d)	0	0	321	0	51	15	0	0	336
New Mexico	Sept. 9, 1850	Jan. 6, 1912 (47th)	16	0	23	1	11	5	1	0	46
New York		July 26, 1788 (11th)	0	0	1,443	0	36	23	0	0	1,466
North Carolina		Nov. 21, 1789 (12th)	0	0	330	0	37	18	0	0	348
North Dakota[6]	Mar. 2, 1861	Nov. 2, 1889 (39th)	9	0	14	0	17	6	0	1	29
Ohio		Mar. 1, 1803 (17th)	2	0	632	0	36	19	0	0	654
Oklahoma	May 2, 1890	Nov. 16, 1907 (46th)	3	0	75	1	11	7	1	0	85
Oregon	Aug. 14, 1848	Feb. 14, 1859 (33d)	1	0	57	0	32	4	0	0	53
Pennsylvania		Dec. 12, 1787 (2d)	0	0	1,051	0	33	21	0	0	1,072
Philippines[7]	Apr. 11, 1899		0	13	0	0	0	0	0	0	13
Puerto Rico[7]	Apr. 11, 1899		0	19	0	0	0	0	0	0	19
Rhode Island		May 29, 1790 (13th)	0	0	78	0	38	10	0	0	88
South Carolina		May 23, 1788 (8th)	0	0	225	0	39	17	0	0	242
South Dakota[6]	Mar. 2, 1861	Nov. 2, 1889 (40th)	9	0	14	1	15	11	0	0	35
Tennessee		June 1, 1796 (16th)	1	0	246	0	40	18	0	0	265
Texas		Dec. 29, 1845 (28th)	0	0	247	0	23	9	0	0	256
Utah	Sept. 9, 1850	Jan. 4, 1896 (45th)	5	0	34	0	11	3	0	0	44
Vermont		Mar. 4, 1791 (14th)	0	0	80	0	24	16	2	0	96
Virgin Islands	Mar. 31, 1917		4	0	0	0	0	0	0	0	4
Virginia		June 25, 1788 (10th)	0	0	413	0	27	27	0	0	439
Washington	Mar. 2, 1853	Nov. 11, 1889 (42d)	12	0	72	0	12	10	1	0	95
West Virginia		June 20, 1863 (35th)	0	0	86	0	24	9	0	0	94
Wisconsin	Apr. 20, 1836	May 29, 1848 (30th)	4	0	171	1	19	8	1	0	185
Wyoming	July 25, 1868	July 10, 1890 (44th)	6	0	15	0	17	3	1	0	25

* State Representation March 4, 1789 to October 21, 2015.

[1] Includes 3 members who served as Representatives and 2 members who served as Senators from a different state.

[2] Includes 3 members who served as Delegates and 18 members who served as Senators from a different state.

[3] Includes 18 members who served as Representatives from a different state. One Senator served from two states and one Senator served from three states.

[4] Includes only those members who served as both a Representative and a Senator from the same state. Eighteen members served as a Senator from one state and a Representative from a different state.

[5] Designated Orleans Territory before attaining statehood in 1812.

[6] Dakota Territory became North and South Dakota in 1889. The nine Delegates from this territory are included in counts for both states. The two Delegates who became Representatives from South Dakota are included only in that state's count.

[7] Resident Commissioners served the Philippines (1902–1946) and continue to serve Puerto Rico (1900 to present). Floor and committee privileges granted to statutory representatives (Territorial Delegates and Resident Commissioners) have changed over time; however they have never been permitted to vote on the final passage of a bill. The Resident Commissioner's duties vary from that of a Delegate in that he has diplomatic privileges as well as most of those of a Member of Congress. The Puerto Rican Resident Commissioner has served a four-year term since 1917. For more information, see "Status of Delegates and Resident Commissioner," Deschler's Precedents, H.Doc. 94–661, Volume 2, Chapter 7, Section 3.

SOURCE: Biographical Directory of the United States Congress.

POLITICAL DIVISIONS OF THE SENATE AND HOUSE FROM 1855 TO 2015

[All Figures Reflect Immediate Results of Elections. Figures Supplied by the Clerk of the House]

Congress	Years	SENATE					HOUSE OF REPRESENTATIVES				
		No. of Senators	Demo-crats	Repub-licans	Other par-ties	Vacan-cies	No. of Represent-atives	Demo-crats	Repub-licans	Other par-ties	Vacan-cies
34th	1855–1857	62	42	15	5	....	234	83	108	43	....
35th	1857–1859	64	39	20	5	....	237	131	92	14	....
36th	1859–1861	66	38	26	2	....	237	101	113	23	....
37th	1861–1863	50	11	31	7	1	178	42	106	28	2
38th	1863–1865	51	12	39	....	....	183	80	103	....	....
39th	1865–1867	52	10	42	....	....	191	46	145	....	....
40th	1867–1869	53	11	42	....	....	193	49	143	....	1
41st	1869–1871	74	11	61	....	2	243	73	170	....	....
42d	1871–1873	74	17	57	....	....	243	104	139	....	....
43d	1873–1875	74	19	54	....	1	293	88	203	....	2
44th	1875–1877	76	29	46	....	1	293	181	107	3	2
45th	1877–1879	76	36	39	1	....	293	156	137	....	....
46th	1879–1881	76	43	33	....	....	293	150	128	14	1
47th	1881–1883	76	37	37	2	....	293	130	152	11	....
48th	1883–1885	76	36	40	....	....	325	200	119	6	....
49th	1885–1887	76	34	41	....	1	325	182	140	2	1
50th	1887–1889	76	37	39	....	....	325	170	151	4	....
51st	1889–1891	84	37	47	....	....	330	156	173	1	....
52d	1891–1893	88	39	47	2	....	333	231	88	14	....
53d	1893–1895	88	44	38	3	3	356	220	126	10	....
54th	1895–1897	88	39	44	5	....	357	104	246	7	....
55th	1897–1899	90	34	46	10	....	357	134	206	16	1
56th	1899–1901	90	26	53	11	....	357	163	185	9	....
57th	1901–1903	90	29	56	3	2	357	153	198	5	1
58th	1903–1905	90	32	58	....	....	386	178	207	....	1
59th	1905–1907	90	32	58	....	....	386	136	250	....	....
60th	1907–1909	92	29	61	....	2	386	164	222	....	....
61st	1909–1911	92	32	59	....	1	391	172	219	....	....
62d	1911–1913	92	42	49	....	1	391	228	162	1	....
63d	1913–1915	96	51	44	1	....	435	290	127	18	....
64th	1915–1917	96	56	39	1	....	435	231	193	8	3
65th	1917–1919	96	53	42	1	....	435	[1] 210	216	9	....
66th	1919–1921	96	47	48	1	....	435	191	237	7	....
67th	1921–1923	96	37	59	....	....	435	132	300	1	2
68th	1923–1925	96	43	51	2	....	435	207	225	3	....
69th	1925–1927	96	40	54	1	1	435	183	247	5	....
70th	1927–1929	96	47	48	1	....	435	195	237	3	....
71st	1929–1931	96	39	56	1	....	435	163	267	1	4
72d	1931–1933	96	47	48	1	....	435	[2] 216	218	1	....
73d	1933–1935	96	59	36	1	....	435	313	117	5	....
74th	1935–1937	96	69	25	2	....	435	322	103	10	....
75th	1937–1939	96	75	17	4	....	435	333	89	13	....
76th	1939–1941	96	69	23	4	....	435	262	169	4	....
77th	1941–1943	96	66	28	2	....	435	267	162	6	....
78th	1943–1945	96	57	38	1	....	435	222	209	4	....
79th	1945–1947	96	57	38	1	....	435	243	190	2	....
80th	1947–1949	96	45	51	....	....	435	188	246	1	....
81st	1949–1951	96	54	42	....	....	435	263	171	1	....
82d	1951–1953	96	48	47	1	....	435	234	199	2	....
83d	1953–1955	96	46	48	2	....	435	213	221	1	....
84th	1955–1957	96	48	47	1	....	435	232	203	....	....
85th	1957–1959	96	49	47	....	....	435	234	201	....	....
86th	1959–1961	98	64	34	....	....	[3] 436	283	153	....	....
87th	1961–1963	100	64	36	....	....	[4] 437	262	175	....	....
88th	1963–1965	100	67	33	....	....	435	258	176	....	1
89th	1965–1967	100	68	32	....	....	435	295	140	....	....
90th	1967–1969	100	64	36	....	....	435	248	187	....	....
91st	1969–1971	100	58	42	....	....	435	243	192	....	....
92d	1971–1973	100	54	44	2	....	435	255	180	....	....
93d	1973–1975	100	56	42	2	....	435	242	192	1	....
94th	1975–1977	100	61	37	2	....	435	291	144	....	....
95th	1977–1979	100	61	38	1	....	435	292	143	....	....
96th	1979–1981	100	58	41	1	....	435	277	158	....	....
97th	1981–1983	100	46	53	1	....	435	242	192	1	....
98th	1983–1985	100	46	54	....	....	435	269	166	....	....
99th	1985–1987	100	47	53	....	....	435	253	182	....	....
100th	1987–1989	100	55	45	....	....	435	258	177	....	....
101st	1989–1991	100	55	45	....	....	435	260	175	....	....
102d	1991–1993	100	56	44	....	....	435	267	167	1	....
103d	1993–1995	100	57	43	....	....	435	258	176	1	....
104th	1995–1997	100	48	52	....	....	435	204	230	1	....
105th	1997–1999	100	45	55	....	....	435	207	226	2	....
106th	1999–2001	100	45	55	....	....	435	211	223	1	....
107th	2001–2003	100	50	50	....	....	435	212	221	2	....
108th	2003–2005	100	48	51	1	....	435	204	229	1	1
109th	2005–2007	100	44	55	1	....	435	202	232	1	....
110th	2007–2009	100	49	49	2	....	435	233	202	....	....
111th	2009–2011	100	55	41	2	2	435	256	178	....	1
112th	2011–2013	100	51	47	2	....	435	193	242	....	....
113th	2013–2015	100	53	45	2	....	435	200	234	....	1
114th	2015–2017	100	44	54	2	....	435	188	246	....	1

[1] Democrats organized House with help of other parties.
[2] Democrats organized House due to Republican deaths.
[3] Proclamation declaring Alaska a State issued January 3, 1959.
[4] Proclamation declaring Hawaii a State issued August 21, 1959.

GOVERNORS OF THE STATES, COMMONWEALTH, AND TERRITORIES—2015

State, Commonwealth, or Territory	Capital	Governor	Party	Term of service	Expiration of term
STATE				*Years*	
Alabama	Montgomery	Robert Bentley	Republican	c 4	Jan. 2019
Alaska	Juneau	Bill Walker	Independent	f 4	Dec. 2018
Arizona	Phoenix	Doug Ducey	Republican	f 4	Jan. 2019
Arkansas	Little Rock	Asa Hutchinson	Republican	c 4	Jan. 2019
California	Sacramento	Jerry Brown	Democrat	c 4	Jan. 2019
Colorado	Denver	John Hickenlooper	Democrat	c 4	Jan. 2019
Connecticut	Hartford	Dan Malloy	Democrat	b 4	Jan. 2019
Delaware	Dover	Jack Markell	Democrat	c 4	Jan. 2017
Florida	Tallahassee	Rick Scott	Republican	f 4	Jan. 2019
Georgia	Atlanta	Nathan Deal	Republican	f 4	Jan. 2019
Hawaii	Honolulu	David Ige	Democrat	c 4	Dec. 2018
Idaho	Boise	C.L. "Butch" Otter	Republican	b 4	Jan. 2019
Illinois	Springfield	Bruce Rauner	Republican	b 4	Jan. 2019
Indiana	Indianapolis	Mike Pence	Republican	f 4	Jan. 2017
Iowa	Des Moines	Terry Branstad	Republican	b 4	Jan. 2019
Kansas	Topeka	Sam Brownback	Republican	c 4	Jan. 2019
Kentucky	Frankfort	Matt Bevin	Republican	c 4	Dec. 2019
Louisiana	Baton Rouge	Bobby Jindal	Republican	f 4	Jan. 2016
Maine	Augusta	Paul LePage	Republican	f 4	Jan. 2019
Maryland	Annapolis	Larry Hogan	Republican	f 4	Jan. 2019
Massachusetts	Boston	Charlie Baker	Republican	b 4	Jan. 2019
Michigan	Lansing	Rick Snyder	Republican	b 4	Jan. 2019
Minnesota	St. Paul	Mark Dayton	Democrat	b 4	Jan. 2019
Mississippi	Jackson	Phil Bryant	Republican	c 4	Jan. 2016
Missouri	Jefferson City	Jay Nixon	Democrat	c 4	Jan. 2017
Montana	Helena	Steve Bullock	Democrat	x 4	Jan. 2017
Nebraska	Lincoln	Pete Ricketts	Republican	c 4	Jan. 2019
Nevada	Carson City	Brian Sandoval	Republican	c 4	Jan. 2019
New Hampshire	Concord	Maggie Hassan	Democrat	b 2	Jan. 2017
New Jersey	Trenton	Chris Christie	Republican	c 4	Jan. 2018
New Mexico	Santa Fe	Susana Martinez	Republican	v 4	Jan. 2019
New York	Albany	Andrew Cuomo	Democrat	b 4	Jan. 2019
North Carolina	Raleigh	Pat McCrory	Republican	c 4	Jan. 2017
North Dakota	Bismarck	Jack Dalrymple	Republican	b 4	Dec. 2016
Ohio	Columbus	John Kasich	Republican	c 4	Jan. 2019
Oklahoma	Oklahoma City	Mary Fallin	Republican	c 4	Jan. 2019
Oregon	Salem	Kate Brown	Democrat	f 4	Jan. 2019
Pennsylvania	Harrisburg	Tom Wolf	Democrat	c 4	Jan. 2019
Rhode Island	Providence	Gina Raimondo	Democrat	c 4	Jan. 2019
South Carolina	Columbia	Nikki R. Haley	Republican	c 4	Jan. 2019
South Dakota	Pierre	Dennis Daugaard	Republican	c 4	Jan. 2019
Tennessee	Nashville	Bill Haslam	Republican	c 4	Jan. 2019
Texas	Austin	Greg Abbott	Republican	b 4	Jan. 2019
Utah	Salt Lake City	Gary R. Herbert	Republican	b 4	Jan. 2017
Vermont	Montpelier	Peter Shumlin	Democrat	b 2	Jan. 2017
Virginia	Richmond	Terry McAuliffe	Democrat	a 4	Jan. 2018
Washington	Olympia	Jay Inslee	Democrat	d 4	Jan. 2017
West Virginia	Charleston	Earl Ray Tomblin	Democrat	c 4	Jan. 2017
Wisconsin	Madison	Scott Walker	Republican	b 4	Jan. 2019
Wyoming	Cheyenne	Matthew Mead	Republican	c 4	Jan. 2019
COMMONWEALTH OF					
Puerto Rico	San Juan	Alejandro García Padilla	Popular Democrat.	b 4	Jan. 2017
TERRITORIES					
Guam	Agana	Eddie Calvo	Republican	c 4	Jan. 2019
Virgin Islands	Charlotte Amalie	Kenneth Mapp	Independent	c 4	Jan. 2019
American Samoa	Pago Pago	Lolo Matalasi Moliga	Independent	c 4	Jan. 2017
Northern Mariana Islands.	Saipan	Eloy S. Inos	Republican	h 5	Jan. 2019

a Cannot succeed himself. b No limit. c Can serve 2 consecutive terms. d Can serve 3 consecutive terms. e Can serve 4 consecutive terms. f Can serve no more than 8 years in a 12-year period. x Can serve no more than 8 years in a 16-year period. h Absolute two-term limitation.

NOTE: Information for table obtained from the National Governors Association.

PRESIDENTS AND VICE PRESIDENTS AND THE CONGRESSES COINCIDENT WITH THEIR TERMS [1]

President	Vice President	Service	Congresses
George Washington	John Adams	Apr. 30, 1789–Mar. 3, 1797	1, 2, 3, 4.
John Adams	Thomas Jefferson	Mar. 4, 1797–Mar. 3, 1801	5, 6.
Thomas Jefferson	Aaron Burr	Mar. 4, 1801–Mar. 3, 1805	7, 8.
Do	George Clinton	Mar. 4, 1805–Mar. 3, 1809	9, 10.
James Madison	...do.[2]	Mar. 4, 1809–Mar. 3, 1813	11, 12.
Do	Elbridge Gerry[3]	Mar. 4, 1813–Mar. 3, 1817	13, 14.
James Monroe	Daniel D. Tompkins	Mar. 4, 1817–Mar. 3, 1825	15, 16, 17, 18, 19.
John Quincy Adams	John C. Calhoun	Mar. 4, 1825–Mar. 3, 1829	19, 20.
Andrew Jackson	...do.[4]	Mar. 4, 1829–Mar. 3, 1833	21, 22.
Do	Martin Van Buren	Mar. 4, 1833–Mar. 3, 1837	23, 24.
Martin Van Buren	Richard M. Johnson	Mar. 4, 1837–Mar. 3, 1841	25, 26.
William Henry Harrison[5]	John Tyler	Mar. 4, 1841–Apr. 4, 1841	27.
John Tyler		Apr. 6, 1841 –Mar. 3, 1845	27, 28.
James K. Polk	George M. Dallas	Mar. 4, 1845–Mar. 3, 1849	29, 30.
Zachary Taylor[5]	Millard Fillmore	Mar. 5, 1849–July 9, 1850	31.
Millard Fillmore		July 10, 1850–Mar. 3, 1853	31, 32.
Franklin Pierce	William R. King[6]	Mar. 4, 1853–Mar. 3, 1857	33, 34.
James Buchanan	John C. Breckinridge	Mar. 4, 1857–Mar. 3, 1861	35, 36.
Abraham Lincoln	Hannibal Hamlin	Mar. 4, 1861–Mar. 3, 1865	37, 38.
Do.[5]	Andrew Johnson	Mar. 4, 1865–Apr. 15, 1865	39.
Andrew Johnson		Apr. 15, 1865–Mar. 3, 1869	39, 40.
Ulysses S. Grant	Schuyler Colfax	Mar. 4, 1869–Mar. 3, 1873	41, 42.
Do	Henry Wilson[7]	Mar. 4, 1873–Mar. 3, 1877	43, 44.
Rutherford B. Hayes	William A. Wheeler	Mar. 4, 1877–Mar. 3, 1881	45, 46.
James A. Garfield[5]	Chester A. Arthur	Mar. 4, 1881–Sept. 19, 1881	47.
Chester A. Arthur		Sept. 20, 1881–Mar. 3, 1885	47, 48.
Grover Cleveland	Thomas A. Hendricks[8]	Mar. 4, 1885–Mar. 3, 1889	49, 50.
Benjamin Harrison	Levi P. Morton	Mar. 4, 1889–Mar. 3, 1893	51, 52.
Grover Cleveland	Adlai E. Stevenson	Mar. 4, 1893–Mar. 3, 1897	53, 54.
William McKinley	Garret A. Hobart[9]	Mar. 4, 1897–Mar. 3, 1901	55, 56.
Do.[5]	Theodore Roosevelt	Mar. 4, 1901–Sept. 14, 1901	57.
Theodore Roosevelt		Sept. 14, 1901–Mar. 3, 1905	57, 58.
Do	Charles W. Fairbanks	Mar. 4, 1905–Mar. 3, 1909	59, 60.
William H. Taft	James S. Sherman[10]	Mar. 4, 1909–Mar. 3, 1913	61, 62.
Woodrow Wilson	Thomas R. Marshall	Mar. 4, 1913–Mar. 3, 1921	63, 64, 65, 66, 67.
Warren G. Harding[5]	Calvin Coolidge	Mar. 4, 1921–Aug. 2, 1923	67.
Calvin Coolidge		Aug. 3, 1923–Mar. 3, 1925	68.
Do	Charles G. Dawes	Mar. 4, 1925–Mar. 3, 1929	69, 70.
Herbert C. Hoover	Charles Curtis	Mar. 4, 1929–Mar. 3, 1933	71, 72.
Franklin D. Roosevelt	John N. Garner	Mar. 4, 1933–Jan. 20, 1941	73, 74, 75, 76, 77.
Do	Henry A. Wallace	Jan. 20, 1941–Jan. 20, 1945	77, 78, 79.
Do.[5]	Harry S. Truman	Jan. 20, 1945–Apr. 12, 1945	79.
Harry S. Truman		Apr. 12, 1945–Jan. 20, 1949	79, 80, 81.
Do	Alben W. Barkley	Jan. 20, 1949–Jan. 20, 1953	81, 82, 83.
Dwight D. Eisenhower	Richard M. Nixon	Jan. 20, 1953–Jan. 20, 1961	83, 84, 85, 86, 87.
John F. Kennedy[5]	Lyndon B. Johnson	Jan. 20, 1961–Nov. 22, 1963	87, 88, 89.
Lyndon B. Johnson		Nov. 22, 1963–Jan. 20, 1965	88, 89.
Do	Hubert H. Humphrey	Jan. 20, 1965–Jan. 20, 1969	89, 90, 91.
Richard M. Nixon	Spiro T. Agnew[11]	Jan. 20, 1969–Dec. 6, 1973	91, 92, 93.
Do.[13]	Gerald R. Ford[12]	Dec. 6, 1973–Aug. 9, 1974	93.
Gerald R. Ford		Aug. 9, 1974–Dec. 19, 1974	93.
Do	Nelson A. Rockefeller[14]	Dec. 19, 1974–Jan. 20, 1977	93, 94, 95.
James Earl "Jimmy" Carter	Walter F. Mondale	Jan. 20, 1977–Jan. 20, 1981	95, 96, 97.
Ronald Reagan	George Bush	Jan. 20, 1981–Jan. 20, 1989	97, 98, 99, 100, 101.
George Bush	Dan Quayle	Jan. 20, 1989–Jan. 20, 1993	101, 102, 103.
William J. Clinton	Albert Gore	Jan. 20, 1993–Jan. 20, 2001	103, 104, 105, 106, 107.
George W. Bush	Richard B. Cheney	Jan. 20, 2001–Jan. 20, 2009	107, 108, 109, 110, 111.
Barack H. Obama	Joseph R. Biden, Jr.	Jan. 20, 2009–	111, 112, 113, 114.

[1] From 1789 until 1933, the terms of the President and Vice President and the term of the Congress coincided, beginning on March 4 and ending on March 3. This changed when the 20th amendment to the Constitution was adopted in 1933. Beginning in 1934 the convening date for Congress became January 3, and beginning in 1937 the starting date for the Presidential term became January 20. Because of this change, the number of Congresses overlapping with a Presidential term increased from two to three, although the third only overlaps by a few weeks.

[2] Died Apr. 20, 1812.

[3] Died Nov. 23, 1814.

[4] Resigned Dec. 28, 1832, to become a United States Senator from South Carolina.

[5] Died in office.

[6] Died Apr. 18, 1853.

[7] Died Nov. 22, 1875.

[8] Died Nov. 25, 1885.

[9] Died Nov. 21, 1899.

[10] Died Oct. 30, 1912.

[11] Resigned Oct. 10, 1973.

[12] Nominated to be Vice President by President Richard M. Nixon on Oct. 12, 1973; confirmed by the Senate on Nov. 27, 1973; confirmed by the House of Representatives on Dec. 6, 1973; took the oath of office on Dec. 6, 1973 in the Hall of the House of Representatives. This was the first time a Vice President was nominated by the President and confirmed by the Congress pursuant to the 25th amendment to the Constitution.

[13] Resigned from office.

[14] Nominated to be Vice President by President Gerald R. Ford on Aug. 20, 1974; confirmed by the Senate on Dec. 10, 1974; confirmed by the House of Representatives on Dec. 19, 1974; took the oath of office on Dec. 19, 1974, in the Senate Chamber.

CAPITOL BUILDINGS AND GROUNDS

UNITED STATES CAPITOL

OVERVIEW OF THE BUILDING AND ITS FUNCTION

The United States Capitol is among the most architecturally impressive and symbolically important buildings in the world. It has housed the chambers of the Senate and the House of Representatives for more than two centuries. Begun in 1793, the Capitol has been built, burnt, rebuilt, extended, and restored; today, it stands as a monument not only to its builders but also to the American people and their government.

As the focal point of the government's legislative branch, the Capitol is the centerpiece of the Capitol complex, which includes the six principal congressional office buildings and three Library of Congress buildings constructed on Capitol Hill in the 19th and 20th centuries.

In addition to its active use by Congress, the Capitol is a museum of American art and history. Each year, it is visited by millions of people from around the world.

A fine example of 19th-century neoclassical architecture, the Capitol combines function with aesthetics. Its design was derived from ancient Greece and Rome and evokes the ideals that guided the nation's founders as they framed their new republic. As the building was expanded from its original design, harmony with the existing portions was carefully maintained.

Today, the Capitol covers a ground area of 175,170 square feet, or about 4 acres, and has a floor area of approximately 16½ acres. Its length, from north to south, is 751 feet 4 inches; its greatest width, including approaches, is 350 feet. Its height above the base line on the east front to the top of the Statue of Freedom is 288 feet; from the basement floor to the top of the dome is an ascent of 365 steps.

The building is divided into five levels. The first, or ground, floor is occupied chiefly by committee rooms and the spaces allocated to various congressional officers. The areas accessible to visitors on this level include the Hall of Columns, the restored Old Supreme Court Chamber, and the Crypt beneath the Rotunda.

The second floor holds the chambers of the House of Representatives (in the south wing) and the Senate (in the north wing). This floor also contains three major public areas. In the center under the dome is the Rotunda, a circular ceremonial space that also serves as a gallery of paintings and sculpture depicting significant people and events in the nation's history. The Rotunda is 96 feet in diameter and rises 180 feet 3 inches to the canopy. The semicircular chamber south of the Rotunda served as the Hall of the House until 1857; now designated National Statuary Hall, it houses part of the Capitol's collection of statues donated by the states in commemoration of notable citizens. The Old Senate Chamber northeast of the Rotunda, which was used by the Senate until 1859, has been returned to its mid-19th-century appearance.

The third floor allows access to the galleries from which visitors to the Capitol may watch the proceedings of the House and the Senate when Congress is in session. The rest of this floor is occupied by offices, committee rooms, and press galleries.

The fourth floor and the basement/terrace level of the Capitol are occupied by offices, machinery rooms, workshops, and other support areas.

Located beneath the East Front plaza, the newest addition to the Capitol is the Capitol Visitor Center (CVC). Preparatory construction activities began in 2002, and the CVC was opened to the public on December 2, 2008. This date was chosen for its significance in the Capitol's history: it was on December 2, 1863, that the Statue of Freedom was placed atop the Capitol. The CVC occupies 580,000 square feet of space on three levels and includes an Exhibition Hall, a restaurant, orientation theaters, gift shops, and other visitor amenities as well as meeting space for the House and Senate.

LOCATION OF THE CAPITOL

The Capitol is located at the eastern end of the Mall on a plateau 88 feet above the level of the Potomac River, commanding a westward view across the Capitol Reflecting

Pool to the Washington Monument 1.4 miles away and the Lincoln Memorial 2.2 miles away.

Before 1791, the Federal Government had no permanent site. The early Congresses met in eight different cities: Philadelphia, Baltimore, Lancaster, York, Princeton, Annapolis, Trenton, and New York City. The subject of a permanent capital for the Government of the United States was first raised by Congress in 1783; it was ultimately addressed in Article I, Section 8 of the Constitution (1787), which gave the Congress legislative authority over "such District (not exceeding ten Miles square) as may, by Cession of Particular States, and the Acceptance of Congress, become the Seat of the Government of the United States. . . ."

In 1788, the State of Maryland ceded to Congress "any district in this State, not exceeding ten miles square," and in 1789 the State of Virginia ceded an equivalent amount of land. In accordance with the "Residence Act" passed by Congress in 1790, President Washington in 1791 selected the area that is now the District of Columbia from the land ceded by Maryland (private landowners whose property fell within this area were compensated by a payment of £25 per acre); that ceded by Virginia was not used for the capital and was returned to Virginia in 1846. Also under the provisions of that Act, he selected three commissioners to survey the site and oversee the design and construction of the capital city and its government buildings. The commissioners, in turn, selected the French-American engineer Pierre Charles L'Enfant to plan the new city of Washington. L'Enfant's plan, which was influenced by the gardens at Versailles, arranged the city's streets and avenues in a grid overlaid with baroque diagonals; the result is a functional and aesthetic whole in which government buildings are balanced against public lawns, gardens, squares, and paths. The Capitol itself was located at the elevated east end of the Mall, on the brow of what was then called Jenkins' Hill. The site was, in L'Enfant's words, "a pedestal waiting for a monument."

SELECTION OF A PLAN

L'Enfant was expected to design the Capitol and to supervise its construction. However, he refused to produce any drawings for the building, claiming that he carried the design "in his head"; this fact and his refusal to consider himself subject to the commissioners' authority led to his dismissal in 1792. In March of that year the commissioners announced a competition, suggested by Secretary of State Thomas Jefferson, that would award $500 and a city lot to whoever produced "the most approved plan" for the Capitol by mid-July. None of the 17 plans submitted, however, was wholly satisfactory. In October, a letter arrived from Dr. William Thornton, a Scottish-trained physician living in Tortola, British West Indies, requesting an opportunity to present a plan even though the competition had closed. The commissioners granted this request.

Thornton's plan depicted a building composed of three sections. The central section, which was topped by a low dome, was to be flanked on the north and south by two rectangular wings (one for the Senate and one for the House of Representatives). President Washington commended the plan for its "grandeur, simplicity and convenience," and on April 5, 1793, it was accepted by the commissioners; Washington gave his formal approval on July 25.

BRIEF CONSTRUCTION HISTORY

1793–1829

The cornerstone was laid by President Washington in the building's southeast corner on September 18, 1793, with Masonic ceremonies. Work progressed under the direction of three architects in succession. Stephen H. Hallet (an entrant in the earlier competition) and George Hadfield were eventually dismissed by the commissioners because of inappropriate design changes that they tried to impose; James Hoban, the architect of the White House, saw the first phase of the project through to completion.

Construction was a laborious and time-consuming process: the sandstone used for the building had to be ferried on boats from the quarries at Aquia, Virginia; workers had to be induced to leave their homes to come to the relative wilderness of Capitol Hill; and funding was inadequate. By August 1796 the commissioners were forced to focus the entire work effort on the building's north wing so that it at least could be ready for government occupancy as scheduled. Even so, some third-floor rooms were still unfinished when the Congress, the Supreme Court, the Library of Congress, and the courts of the District of Columbia occupied the Capitol in late 1800.

In 1803, Congress allocated funds to resume construction. A year earlier, the office of the Commissioners had been abolished and replaced by a superintendent of the city of Washington. To oversee the renewed construction effort, Benjamin Henry Latrobe was appointed surveyor of public buildings. The first professional architect and engineer to work in America, Latrobe modified Thornton's plan for the south wing to include space for offices and committee rooms; he also introduced alterations to simplify the construction work. Latrobe began work by removing a squat, oval, temporary building known as "the Oven," which had been erected in 1801 as a meeting place for the House of Representatives. By 1807 construction on the south wing was sufficiently advanced that the House was able to occupy its new legislative chamber, and the wing was completed in 1811.

In 1808, as work on the south wing progressed, Latrobe began the rebuilding of the north wing, which had fallen into disrepair. Rather than simply repair the wing, he redesigned the interior of the building to increase its usefulness and durability; among his changes was the addition of a chamber for the Supreme Court. By 1811, he had completed the eastern half of this wing, but funding was being increasingly diverted to preparations for a second war with Great Britain. By 1813, Latrobe had no further work in Washington and so he departed, leaving the north and south wings of the Capitol connected only by a temporary wooden passageway.

The War of 1812 left the Capitol, in Latrobe's later words, "a most magnificent ruin": on August 24, 1814, British troops set fire to the building, and only a sudden rainstorm prevented its complete destruction. Immediately after the fire, Congress met for one session in Blodget's Hotel, which was at Seventh and E Streets, NW. From 1815 to 1819, Congress occupied a building erected for it on First Street, NE., on part of the site now occupied by the Supreme Court Building. This building later came to be known as the Old Brick Capitol.

Latrobe returned to Washington in 1815, when he was rehired to restore the Capitol. In addition to making repairs, he took advantage of this opportunity to make further changes in the building's interior design (for example, an enlargement of the Senate Chamber) and introduce new materials (for example, marble discovered along the upper Potomac). However, he came under increasing pressure because of construction delays (most of which were beyond his control) and cost overruns; finally, he resigned his post in November 1817.

On January 8, 1818, Charles Bulfinch, a prominent Boston architect, was hired to succeed Latrobe. Continuing the restoration of the north and south wings, he was able to make the chambers for the Supreme Court, the House, and the Senate ready for use by 1819. Bulfinch also redesigned and supervised the construction of the Capitol's central section. The copper-covered wooden dome that topped this section was made higher than Bulfinch considered appropriate to the building's size (at the direction of President James Monroe and Secretary of State John Quincy Adams). After completing the last part of the building in 1826, Bulfinch spent the next few years on the Capitol's decoration and landscaping. In 1829, his work was done and his position with the government was terminated. In the 38 years following Bulfinch's tenure, the Capitol was entrusted to the care of the commissioner of public buildings.

1830–1868

The Capitol was by this point already an impressive structure. At ground level, its length was 351 feet 7½ inches and its width was 282 feet 10½ inches. Up to the year 1827— records from later years being incomplete—the project cost was $2,432,851.34. Improvements to the building continued in the years to come (running water in 1832, gas lighting in the 1840s), but by 1850 its size could no longer accommodate the increasing numbers of Senators and Representatives from newly admitted states. The Senate therefore voted to hold another competition, offering a prize of $500 for the best plan to extend the Capitol. Several suitable plans were submitted, some proposing an eastward extension of the building and others proposing the addition of large north and south wings. However, Congress was unable to decide between these two approaches, and the prize money was divided among five architects. Thus, the tasks of selecting a plan and appointing an architect fell to President Millard Fillmore.

Fillmore's choice was Thomas U. Walter, a Philadelphia architect who had entered the competition. On July 4, 1851, in a ceremony whose principal oration was delivered by Secretary of State Daniel Webster, the president laid the cornerstone in the northeast corner of the House wing. Over the next 14 years, Walter supervised the construction of the extension, ensuring their compatibility with the architectural style of the existing building. However, because the Aquia Creek sandstone used earlier had deteriorated noticeably, he chose to use marble for the exterior. For the veneer, Walter selected marble quarried at Lee, Massachusetts, and for the columns he used marble from Cockeysville, Maryland.

Walter faced several significant challenges during the course of construction. Chief among these was the steady imposition by the government of additional tasks without additional pay. Aside from his work on the Capitol extension, Walter designed the wings of the Patent

Office building, extensions to the Treasury and Post Office buildings, and the Marine barracks in Pensacola and Brooklyn. When the Library of Congress in the Capitol's west central section was gutted by a fire in 1851, Walter was commissioned to restore it. He also encountered obstacles in his work on the Capitol extensions. His location of the legislative chambers was changed in 1853 at the direction of President Franklin Pierce, based on the suggestions of the newly appointed supervising engineer, Captain Montgomery C. Meigs. In general, however, the project progressed rapidly: the House of Representatives was able to meet in its new chamber on December 16, 1857, and the Senate first met in its present chamber on January 4, 1859. The old House chamber was later designated National Statuary Hall. In 1861 most construction was suspended because of the Civil War, and the Capitol was used briefly as a military barracks, hospital, and bakery. In 1862 work on the entire building was resumed.

As the new wings were constructed, more than doubling the length of the Capitol, it became apparent that the dome erected by Bulfinch no longer suited the building's proportions. In 1855 Congress voted for its replacement based on Walter's design for a new, fireproof cast-iron dome. The old dome was removed in 1856 and 5,000,000 pounds of new masonry was placed on the existing rotunda walls. Iron used in the dome construction had an aggregate weight of 8,909,200 pounds and was lifted into place by steam-powered derricks.

In 1859, Thomas Crawford's plaster model for the Statue of Freedom, designed for the top of the dome, arrived from the sculptor's studio in Rome. With a height of 19 feet 6 inches, the statue was almost 3 feet taller than specified, and Walter was compelled to make revisions to his design for the dome. When cast in bronze by Clark Mills at his foundry on the outskirts of Washington, it weighed 14,985 pounds. The statue was lifted into place atop the dome in 1863, its final section being installed on December 2 to the accompaniment of gun salutes from the forts around the city.

The work on the dome and the extension was completed under the direction of Edward Clark, who had served as Walter's assistant and was appointed Architect of the Capitol in 1865 after Walter's resignation. In 1866, the Italian-born artist Constantino Brumidi finished the canopy fresco, a monumental painting entitled *The Apotheosis of George Washington*. The Capitol extension was completed in 1868.

1869–1902

Clark continued to hold the post of Architect of the Capitol until his death in 1902. During his tenure, the Capitol underwent considerable modernization. Steam heat was gradually installed in the old Capitol. In 1874 the first elevator was installed, and in the 1880s electric lighting began to replace gas lights.

Between 1884 and 1891, the marble terraces on the north, west, and south sides of the Capitol were constructed. As part of the landscape plan devised by Frederick Law Olmsted, these terraces not only added over 100 rooms to the Capitol but also provided a broader, more substantial visual base for the building.

On November 6, 1898, a gas explosion and fire in the original north wing dramatically illustrated the need for fireproofing. The roofs over the Statuary Hall wing and the original north wing were reconstructed and fireproofed, the work being completed in 1902 by Clark's successor, Elliott Woods. In 1901, the space in the west central front vacated by the Library of Congress was converted to committee rooms.

1903–1970

During the remainder of Woods's service, which ended with his death in 1923, no major structural work was required on the Capitol. The activities performed in the building were limited chiefly to cleaning and refurbishing the interior. David Lynn, the Architect of the Capitol from 1923 until his retirement in 1954, continued these tasks. Between July 1949 and January 1951, the corroded roofs and skylights of both wings and the connecting corridors were replaced with new roofs of concrete and steel, covered with copper. The cast-iron and glass ceilings of the House and Senate chambers were replaced with ceilings of stainless steel and plaster, with a laylight of carved glass and bronze in the middle of each. The House and Senate chambers were completely redecorated, modern lighting was added, and acoustical problems were solved. During this renovation program, the House and Senate vacated their chambers on several occasions so that the work could progress.

The next significant modification made to the Capitol was the east front extension. This project was carried out under the supervision of Architect of the Capitol J. George Stewart, who served from 1954 until his death in 1970. Begun in 1958, it involved the construction of a new east front 32 feet 6 inches east of the old front, faithfully reproducing the sandstone structure in marble. The old sandstone walls were not destroyed; rather, they were left in place to become a part of the interior wall and are now buttressed by the addition. The marble columns of the connecting corridors were also moved and reused. Other elements of this project included repairing the dome, constructing a subway terminal under the Senate steps, reconstructing those steps, cleaning both wings, birdproofing the building, providing furniture and furnishings for 90 new rooms created by the extension, and improving the lighting throughout the building. The project was completed in 1962.

1971–PRESENT

During the nearly 25-year tenure (1971–1995) of Architect of the Capitol George M. White, FAIA, the building was both modernized and restored. Electronic voting equipment was installed in the House chamber in 1973; facilities were added to allow television coverage of the House and Senate debates in 1979 and 1986, respectively; and improved climate control, electronic surveillance systems, and new computer and communications facilities have been added to bring the Capitol up-to-date. The Old Senate Chamber, National Statuary Hall, and the Old Supreme Court Chamber, on the other hand, were restored to their mid-19th-century appearance in the 1970s.

In 1983, work began on the strengthening, renovation, and preservation of the west front of the Capitol. Structural problems had developed over the years because of defects in the original foundations, deterioration of the sandstone facing material, alterations to the basic building fabric (a fourth-floor addition and channeling of the walls to install interior utilities), and damage from the fires of 1814 and 1851 and the 1898 gas explosion.

To strengthen the structure, over 1,000 stainless steel tie rods were set into the building's masonry. More than 30 layers of paint were removed, and damaged stonework was repaired or replicated. Ultimately, 40 percent of the sandstone blocks were replaced with limestone. The walls were treated with a special consolidant and then painted to match the marble wings. The entire project was completed in 1987.

A related project, completed in January 1993, effected the repair of the Olmsted terraces, which had been subject to damage from settling, and converted the terrace courtyards into several thousand square feet of meeting space.

As the Capitol enters its third century, restoration and modernization work continues. Alan M. Hantman, FAIA, was appointed in February 1997 to a 10-year term as Architect of the Capitol. Projects under his direction included rehabilitation of the Capitol dome; conservation of murals; improvement of speech-reinforcement, electrical, and fire-protection systems in the Capitol and the Congressional office buildings; work on security improvements within the Capitol complex; restoration of the U.S. Botanic Garden Conservatory; the design and construction of the National Garden adjacent to the Botanic Garden Conservatory; renovation of the building systems in the Dirksen Senate Office Building; publication of the first comprehensive history of the Capitol to appear in a century; and construction of the Capitol Visitor Center. At the end of Mr. Hantman's term in February 2007, Mr. Stephen T. Ayers, FAIA, LEED AP, assumed the position of Acting Architect of the Capitol. On February 24, 2010, President Barack Obama nominated Mr. Ayers to serve as the 11th Architect of the Capitol. On May 12, 2010, the United States Senate, by unanimous consent, confirmed Mr. Ayers, and on May 13, 2010, the President officially appointed Mr. Ayers to a 10-year term as Architect of the Capitol.

HOUSE OFFICE BUILDINGS

CANNON HOUSE OFFICE BUILDING

An increased membership of the Senate and House resulted in a demand for additional rooms for the accommodations of the Senators and Representatives. On March 3, 1903, the Congress authorized the erection of a fireproofed office building for the use of the House. It was designed by the firm of Carrere & Hastings of New York City in the Beaux Arts style. The first brick was laid July 5, 1905, in square No. 690, and formal exercises were held at the laying of the cornerstone on April 14, 1906, in which President Theodore Roosevelt participated. The building was completed and occupied January 10, 1908. A subsequent change in the basis of congressional representation made necessary the building of an additional story in 1913–1914. The total cost of the building, including site, furnishings, equipment, and the subway connecting it with the U.S. Capitol, amounted to $4,860,155.

This office building contains about 500 rooms, and was considered at the time of its completion fully equipped for all the needs of a modern building for office purposes. A garage was added in the building's courtyard in the 1960s.

Pursuant to authority in the Second Supplemental Appropriations Act, 1955, and subsequent action of the House Office Building Commission, remodeling of the Cannon Building began in 1966. The estimated cost of this work was $5,200,000. Pursuant to the provisions of Public Law 87–453, approved May 21, 1962, the building was named in honor of Joseph G. Cannon of Illinois, who was Speaker at the time the building was constructed.

LONGWORTH HOUSE OFFICE BUILDING

Under legislation contained in the Authorization Act of January 10, 1929, and in the urgent deficiency bill of March 4, 1929, provisions were made for an additional House office building, to be located on the west side of New Jersey Avenue (opposite the first House office building). The building was designed by the Allied Architects of Washington in the Neoclassical Revival style.

The cornerstone was laid June 24, 1932, and the building was completed on April 20, 1933. It contains 251 two-room suites and 16 committee rooms. Each suite and committee room is provided with a storeroom. Eight floors are occupied by members. The basement and subbasement contain shops and mechanical areas needed for the maintenance of the building. A cafeteria was added in the building's courtyard in the 1960s. The cost of this building, including site, furnishings, and equipment, was $7,805,705. Pursuant to the provisions of Public Law 87–453, approved May 21, 1962, the building was named in honor of Nicholas Longworth of Ohio, who was Speaker when the second House office building was constructed.

RAYBURN HOUSE OFFICE BUILDING AND OTHER RELATED CHANGES AND IMPROVEMENTS

Under legislation contained in the Second Supplemental Appropriations Act, 1955, provision was made for construction of a fireproof office building for the House of Representatives.

All work was carried forward by the Architect of the Capitol under the direction of the House Office Building Commission at a cost totaling $135,279,000.

The Rayburn Building is connected to the Capitol by a subway. Designs for the building were prepared by the firm of Harbeson, Hough, Livingston & Larson of Philadelphia, Associate Architects. The building contains 169 congressional suites; full-committee hearing rooms for 9 standing committees, 16 subcommittee hearing rooms, committee staff rooms and other committee facilities; a large cafeteria and other restaurant facilities; an underground garage; and a variety of liaison offices, press and television facilities, maintenance and equipment shops or rooms, and storage areas. This building has nine stories and a penthouse for machinery.

The cornerstone was laid May 24, 1962, by John W. McCormack, Speaker of the House of Representatives. President John F. Kennedy participated in the cornerstone laying and delivered the address.

A portion of the basement floor was occupied beginning March 12, 1964, by House of Representatives personnel moved from the George Washington Inn property. Full occupancy of the Rayburn Building, under the room-filing regulations, was begun February 23, 1965, and completed April 2, 1965. Pursuant to the provisions of Public Law 87–453, approved May 21, 1962, the building was named in honor of Sam Rayburn of Texas.

House Office Building Annex No. 2, named the "Gerald R. Ford House of Representatives Office Building," was acquired in 1975 from the General Services Administration. The structure, located at Second and D Streets, SW., was built in 1939 for the Federal Bureau of Investigation as a fingerprint file archives. This building has approximately 432,000 square feet of space.

SENATE OFFICE BUILDINGS

RICHARD BREVARD RUSSELL SENATE OFFICE BUILDING

In 1891 the Senate provided itself with office space by the purchase of the Maltby Building, then located on the northwest corner of B Street (now Constitution Avenue) and New Jersey

Avenue, NW. When it was condemned as an unsafe structure, Senators needed safer and more commodious office space. Under authorization of the Act of April 28, 1904, square 686 on the northeast corner of Delaware Avenue and B Street, NE. was purchased as a site for the Senate Office Building. The plans for the House Office Building were adapted for the Senate Office Building by the firm of Carrere & Hastings, with the exception that the side of the building fronting on First Street, NE. was temporarily omitted. The cornerstone was laid without special exercises on July 31, 1906, and the building was occupied March 5, 1909. In 1931, the completion of the fourth side of the building was commenced. In 1933 it was completed, together with alterations to the C Street facade, and the construction of terraces, balustrades, and approaches. The cost of the completed building, including the site, furnishings, equipment and the subway connecting it with the United States Capitol, was $8,390,892.

The building was named the "Richard Brevard Russell Senate Office Building" by Senate Resolution 296, 92nd Congress, agreed to October 11, 1972, as amended by Senate Resolution 295, 96th Congress, agreed to December 3, 1979.

EVERETT MCKINLEY DIRKSEN SENATE OFFICE BUILDING

Under legislation contained in the Second Deficiency Appropriations Act, 1948, Public Law 80–785, provision was made for an additional office building for the United States Senate with limits of cost of $1,100,000 for acquisition of the site and $20,600,000 for constructing and equipping the building.

The construction cost limit was subsequently increased to $24,196,000. All work was carried forward by the Architect of the Capitol under the direction of the Senate Office Building Commission. The New York firm of Eggers & Higgins served as the consulting architect.

The site was acquired and cleared in 1948–49 at a total cost of $1,011,492.

A contract for excavation, concrete footings, and mats for the new building was awarded in January 1955, in the amount of $747,200. Groundbreaking ceremonies were held January 26, 1955.

A contract for the superstructure of the new building was awarded September 9, 1955, in the amount of $17,200,000. The cornerstone was laid July 13, 1956.

As a part of this project, a new underground subway system was installed from the Capitol to both the Old and New Senate Office Buildings.

An appropriation of $1,000,000 for furniture and furnishings for the new building was provided in 1958. The building was accepted for beneficial occupancy on October 15, 1958.

The building was named the "Everett McKinley Dirksen Senate Office Building" by Senate Resolution 296, 92nd Congress, agreed to October 11, 1972, and Senate Resolution 295, 96th Congress, agreed to December 3, 1979.

PHILIP A. HART SENATE OFFICE BUILDING

Construction as an extension to the Dirksen Senate Office Building was authorized on October 31, 1972; legislation enacted in subsequent years increased the scope of the project and established a total cost ceiling of $137,700,400. The firm of John Carl Warnecke & Associates served as Associate Architect for the project.

Senate Resolution 525, passed August 30, 1976, amended by Senate Resolution 295, 96th Congress, agreed to December 3, 1979, provided that upon completion of the extension it would be named the "Philip A. Hart Senate Office Building" to honor the Senator from Michigan.

The contract for clearing of the site, piping for utilities, excavation, and construction of foundation was awarded in December 1975. Groundbreaking took place January 5, 1976 The contract for furnishing and delivery of the exterior stone was awarded in Februar 1977, and the contract for the superstructure, which included wall and roof systems a the erection of all exterior stonework, was awarded in October 1977. The contract for first portion of the interior and related work was awarded in December 1978. A co' for interior finishing was awarded in July 1980. The first suite was occupied on Nov 22, 1982. Alexander Calder's mobile/stabile *Mountains and Clouds* was installed building's atrium in November 1986.

CAPITOL POWER PLANT

During the development of the plans for the Cannon and Russell Buildings, the question of heat, light, and power was considered. The Senate and House wings of the Capitol were heated by separate heating plants. The Library of Congress also had a heating plant for that building. It was determined that needs for heating and lighting and electrical power could be met by a central power plant.

A site was selected in Garfield Park. Since this park was a Government reservation, an appropriation was not required to secure title. The determining factors leading to the selection of this site were its proximity to the tracks of what is now the Penn Central Railroad and to the buildings to be served.

The dimensions of the Capitol Power Plant, which was authorized on April 28, 1904, and completed in 1910, were 244 feet 8 inches by 117 feet.

The buildings originally served by the Capitol Power Plant were connected to it by a reinforced-concrete steam tunnel.

In September 1951, when the demand for electrical energy was reaching the maximum capacity of the Capitol Power Plant, arrangements were made to purchase electrical service from the local public utility company and to discontinue electrical generation. The heating and cooling functions of the Capitol Power Plant were expanded in 1935, 1939, 1958, 1973, and 1980. A new refrigeration plant modernization and expansion project was completed in 2007.

U.S. CAPITOL GROUNDS

A Description of the Grounds

Originally a wooded wilderness, the U.S. Capitol Grounds today provide a park-like setting for the Nation's Capitol, offering a picturesque counterpoint to the building's formal architecture. The grounds immediately surrounding the Capitol are bordered by a stone wall and cover an area of 58.8 acres. Their boundaries are Independence Avenue on the south, Constitution Avenue on the north, First Street, NE./SE. on the east, and First Street, NW./SW. on the west. Over 100 varieties of trees and bushes are planted around the Capitol, and thousands of flowers are used in seasonal displays. In contrast to the building's straight, neoclassical lines, most of the walkways in the grounds are curved. Benches along the paths offer pleasant spots for visitors to appreciate the building, its landscape, and the surrounding areas, most notably the Mall to the west.

The grounds were designed by Frederick Law Olmsted (1822–1903), who planned the landscaping of the area that was performed from 1874 to 1892. Olmsted, who also designed New York's Central Park, is considered the greatest American landscape architect of his day. He was a pioneer in the development of public parks in America, and many of his designs were influenced by his studies of European parks, gardens, and estates. In describing his plan for the Capitol Grounds, Olmsted noted that, "The ground is in design part of the Capitol, but in all respects subsidiary to the central structure." Therefore, he was careful not to group trees or other landscape features in any way that would distract the viewer from the Capitol. The use of sculpture and other ornamentation has also been kept to a minimum.

Many of the trees on the Capitol Grounds have historic or memorial associations. Over 30 states have made symbolic gifts of their state trees to the Capitol Grounds. Many of the trees on the grounds bear plaques that identify their species and their historic significance.

At the East Capitol Street entrance to the Capitol plaza are two large rectangular stone fountains. Six massive red granite lamp piers topped with light fixtures in wrought-iron cages, and 16 smaller bronze light fixtures, line the paved plaza. Three sets of benches are enclosed with wrought-iron railings and grilles; the roofed bench was originally a shelter for streetcar passengers.

The northern part of the grounds offers a shaded walk among trees, flowers, and shrubbery. A small, hexagonal brick structure named the Summer House may be found in the northwest corner of the grounds. This structure contains shaded benches, a central ornamental fountain, and three public drinking fountains. In a small grotto on the eastern side of the Summer House, a stream of water flows and splashes over rocks to create a pleasing sound and cool the summer breezes.

The land on which the Capitol stands was first occupied by the Manahoacs and the Monacans, who were subtribes of the Algonquin Indians. Early settlers reported that these tribes occasionally held councils not far from the foot of the hill. This land eventually became a part of Cerne Abbey Manor, and at the time of its acquisition by the Federal Government it was owned by Daniel Carroll of Duddington.

The "Residence Act" of 1790 provided that the Federal Government should be established in a permanent location by the year 1800. In early March 1791, the commissioners of the city of Washington, who had been appointed by President George Washington, selected the French engineer Pierre Charles L'Enfant to plan the new federal city. L'Enfant decided to locate the Capitol at the elevated east end of the Mall (on what was then called Jenkins' Hill); he described the site as "a pedestal waiting for a monument."

At this time the site of the Capitol was a relative wilderness partly overgrown with scrub oak. Oliver Wolcott, a signer of the Declaration of Independence, described the soil as an "*exceedingly stiff*" clay, becoming dust in dry and mortar in rainy weather."

In 1825, a plan was devised for imposing order on the Capitol Grounds, and it was carried out for almost 15 years. The plan divided the area into flat, rectangular grassy areas bordered by trees, flower beds, and gravel walks. The growth of the trees, however, soon deprived the other plantings of nourishment, and the design became increasingly difficult to maintain in light of sporadic and small appropriations. John Foy, who had charge of the grounds during most of this period, was "superseded for political reasons," and the area was then maintained with little care or forethought. Many rapidly growing but short-lived trees were introduced and soon depleted the soil; a lack of proper pruning and thinning left the majority of the area's vegetation ill-grown, feeble, or dead. Virtually all was removed by the early 1870s, either to make way for building operations during Thomas U. Walter's enlargement of the Capitol or as required by changes in grading to accommodate the new work on the building or the alterations to surrounding streets.

THE OLMSTED PLAN

The mid-19th-century extension of the Capitol, in which the House and Senate wings and the new dome were added, also required that the Capitol Grounds be enlarged, and in 1874 Frederick Law Olmsted was commissioned to plan and oversee the project. As noted above, Olmsted was determined that the grounds should complement the building. In addition, he addressed an architectural problem that had persisted for some years: from the west (the growth of the city had nothing to do with the terraces)—the earthen terraces at the building's base made it seem inadequately supported at the top of the hill. The solution, Olmsted believed, was to construct marble terraces on the north, west, and south sides of the building, thereby causing it to "gain greatly in the supreme qualities of stability, endurance, and repose." He submitted his design for these features in 1875, and after extensive study it was approved.

Work on the grounds began in 1874, concentrating first on the east side and then progressing to the west, north, and south sides. First, the ground was reduced in elevation. Almost 300,000 cubic yards of earth and other material were eventually removed, and over 200 trees were removed. New sewer, gas, and water lines were installed. The soil was then enriched with fertilizers to provide a suitable growth medium for new plantings. Paths and roadways were graded and laid.

By 1876, gas and water service was completed for the entire grounds, and electrical lamp-lighting apparatuses had been installed. Stables and workshops had been removed from the northwest and southwest corners. A streetcar system north and south of the west grounds had been relocated farther from the Capitol, and ornamental shelters were in place at the north and south car-track termini. The granite and bronze lamp piers and ornamental bronze lamps for the east plaza area were completed.

Work accelerated in 1877. By this time, according to Olmsted's report, "altogether 7,837 plants and trees [had] been set out." However, not all had survived: hundreds were stolen or destroyed by vandals, and, as Olmsted explained, "a large number of cattle [had] been caught trespassing." Other work met with less difficulty. Foot-walks were laid with artificial stone, a mixture of cement and sand, and approaches were paved with concrete. An ornamental iron trellis had been installed on the northern east-side walk, and another was under way on the southern walk.

The 1878 appointment of watchmen to patrol the grounds was quite effective in preventing further vandalism, allowing the lawns to be completed and much shrubbery to be added. Also in that year, the roads throughout the grounds were paved.

Most of the work required on the east side of the grounds was completed by 1879, and effort thus shifted largely to the west side. The Pennsylvania Avenue approach was virtually finished, and work on the Maryland Avenue approach had begun. The stone walls on the west side of the grounds were almost finished, and the red granite lamp piers were placed at the eastward entrance from Pennsylvania Avenue.

In the years 1880–1882, many features of the grounds were completed. These included the walls and coping around the entire perimeter, the approaches and entrances, and the Summer House. Work on the terraces began in 1882, and most work from this point until 1892 was concentrated on these structures.

In 1885, Olmsted retired from superintendency of the terrace project; he continued to direct the work on the grounds until 1889. Landscaping work was performed to adapt the surrounding areas to the new construction, grading the ground and planting shrubs at the bases of the walls, as the progress of the masonry work allowed. Some trees and other types of vegetation were removed, either because they had decayed or as part of a careful thinning-out process.

In 1888, the wrought-iron lamp frames and railings were placed at the Maryland Avenue entrance, making it the last to be completed. In 1892, the streetcar track that had extended into grounds from Independence Avenue was removed.

THE GROUNDS AFTER OLMSTED

In the last years of the 19th century, work on the grounds consisted chiefly of maintenance and repairs as needed. Trees, lawns, and plantings were tended, pruned, and thinned to allow their best growth. This work was quite successful: by 1894, the grounds were so deeply shaded by trees and shrubs that Architect of the Capitol Edward Clark recommended an all-night patrol by watchmen to ensure public safety. A hurricane in September 1896 damaged or destroyed a number of trees, requiring extensive removals in the following year. Also in 1897, electric lighting replaced gas lighting in the grounds.

Between 1910 and 1935, 61.4 acres north of Constitution Avenue were added to the grounds. Approximately 100 acres was added in subsequent years, bringing the total area to 274 acres. Late in 2011, care for the Grant Memorial and the reflecting pool at the eastern end of the National Mall was transferred from the National Park Service to the Architect of the Capitol.

Since 1983, increased security measures have been put into effect, however, the area still functions in many ways as a public park, and visitors are welcome to use the walks to tour the grounds. Demonstrations and ceremonies are often held on the grounds. In the summer, a series of evening concerts by the bands of the Armed Forces is offered free of charge on the west front plaza. On various holidays, concerts by the National Symphony Orchestra are held on the west front lawn.

LEGISLATIVE BRANCH

CONGRESSIONAL BUDGET OFFICE

H2–405 Ford House Office Building, Second and D Streets, SW., 20515
phone (202) 226–2600, http://www.cbo.gov
[Created by Public Law 93–344]

Director.—Keith Hall, 6–2700.
  Deputy Director.—Robert A. Sunshine, 6–2700.
  General Counsel.—Mark P. Hadley, 6–2633.
  Assistant Director for—
    Budget Analysis.—Peter H. Fontaine, 6–2800.
    Health, Retirement, and Long-Term Analysis.—Linda Bilheimer, 6–2666.
    Macroeconomic Analysis.—Wendy Edelberg, 6–2750.
    Management, Business and Information Services.—Joseph E. Evans Jr., 6–2600.
    Microeconomic Studies.—Joseph Kile, 6–2940.
    National Security.—David E. Mosher, 6–2900.
    Tax Analysis.—David Weiner, 6–2680.

GOVERNMENT ACCOUNTABILITY OFFICE

441 G Street, NW., 20548, phone (202) 512–3000
http://www.gao.gov

Comptroller General of the United States.—Gene L. Dodaro, 512–5500, fax 512–5507.
  Chief Operating Officer.—Patricia Dalton, 512–5600.
  Chief Administrative Officer/Chief Financial Officer.—Karl Maschino, 512–5800.
  General Counsel.—Susan A. Poling, 512–5400.
  Deputy General Counsel and Ethics Counselor.—Thomas A. Armstrong, 512–5207.
  Deputy Ethics Counselor.—James Lager, 512–8170.

TEAMS

Acquisition and Sourcing Management.—Paul Francis, 512–2811.
Applied Research and Methods.—Nancy Kingsbury, 512–2700.
Defense Capabilities and Management.—Cathleen A. Berrick, 512–4300.
Education Workforce and Income Security.—Barbara D. Bovbjerg, 512–7215.
Financial Management and Assurance.—Steve Sebastian, 512–2600.
Financial Markets and Community Investments.—Orice Williams Brown, 512–8678.
Forensic Audits and Investigative Services.—Stephen M. Lord, 512–4379.
Health Care.—Cynthia A. Bascetta, 512–7207.
Homeland Security and Justice.—George A. Scott, 512–5932.
Information Technology.—Joel Willemssen, 512–6408.
International Affairs and Trade.—Loren Yager, 512–4347.
Natural Resources and Environment.—Mark Gaffigan, 512–3841.
Physical Infrastructure.—Phil Herr, 512–8509.
Strategic Issues.—J. Christopher Mihm, 512–6806.

SUPPORT FUNCTIONS

Congressional Relations.—Katherine Siggerud, 512–6570.
  Legislative Advisers: Carlos Diz, 512–8256; Rosa Harris, 512–9492; Carolyn Kirby, 512–9843; Anne Laffoon, 512–4199; David Lewis, 512–7176; Tim Minelli, 512–8443; Paul Thompson, 512–9867; Mary Frances Widner, 512–3804.

Associate Legislative Adviser.—Kisha Clark, 512–3208.
Field Operations.—Linda Calbom (206) 287–4809.
Inspector General.—Adam Trzeciak, 512–8110.
Opportunity and Inclusiveness.—Reginald E. Jones, 512–8401.
Personnel Appeals Board.—William Persina, 512–6137.
Public Affairs.—Charles "Chuck" Young, 512–3823.
Audit Policy and Quality Assurance.—Tim Bowling, 512–6100.
Strategic Planning and External Liaison.—James-Christian Blockwood, 512–2639.

MISSION SUPPORT OFFICES

Chief Information Officer.—Howard Williams, Jr., 512–5589.
Controller/Deputy Chief Financial Officer.—William Anderson, 512–2908.
Chief Human Capital Officer.—Carolyn Taylor, 512–2974.
Infrastructure Operations.—Terry Dorn, 512–6923.
Professional Development Program.—Dave Clark, 512–4126.

U.S. GOVERNMENT PUBLISHING OFFICE
732 North Capitol Street, NW., 20401
Phone (202) 512–0000, http://www.gpo.gov

Director.—Davita Vance-Cooks, 512–0014, dvance-cooks@gpo.gov.
Deputy Director.—Jim Bradley, 512–0111, jbradley@gpo.gov.
Chief of Staff.—Andrew M. Sherman, 512–1100, asherman@gpo.gov.
General Counsel.—Drew Spalding, 512–0033, dspalding@gpo.gov.
Managing Director, Equal Employment Opportunity.—Juanita M. Flores, 512–2014, jflores@gpo.gov.
Chief Financial Officer.—Steven T. Shedd, 512–2073, sshedd@gpo.gov.
Chief Administrative Officer.—Herbert H. Jackson, Jr., 512–0952, hjackson@gpo.gov.
Superintendent of Documents.—Mary Alice Baish, 512–1313, mabaish@gpo.gov.
Inspector General.—Michael A. Raponi, 512–0039, mraponi@gpo.gov.

CHIEF OF STAFF

Chief of Staff.—Andrew M. Sherman, 512–1100, asherman@gpo.gov.

COMMUNICATIONS

Director, Congressional Relations.—Andrew M. Sherman (acting), 512–1100, asherman@gpo.gov.
Manager, Media and Public Relations.—Gary G. Somerset, 512–1957, gsomerset@gpo.gov.
Specialist, Employee Communications.—Terri Ehrenfeld, 512–0129, tehrenfeld@gpo.gov.

PROGRAMS, STRATEGY, AND TECHNOLOGY

Chief Technology Officer.—Richard G. Davis, 512–1622, rdavis@gpo.gov.

GENERAL COUNSEL

General Counsel.—Drew Spalding, 512–0033, dspalding@gpo.gov.
Deputy General Counsel.—Kerry L. Miller, 512–0033, kmiller@gpo.gov.
Associate General Counsel, Labor Relations.—Melissa S. Hatfield, 512–0064, mhatfield@gpo.gov.

EQUAL EMPLOYMENT OPPORTUNITY

Managing Director, Equal Employment Opportunity.—Juanita M. Flores, 512–2014, jflores@gpo.gov.
Chief, Equal Employment Opportunity Program.—Mark A. "Tony" Paras, 512–2331, mparas@gpo.gov.

FINANCE

Chief Financial Officer.—Steven T. Shedd, 512–2073, sshedd@gpo.gov.
 Deputy Chief Financial Officer.—William L. Boesch, Jr., 512–2073, wboesch@gpo.gov.
 Controller, Plant Operations.—June Vance, 512–2073, jvance@gpo.gov.
 Controller, Information Dissemination.—William J. Grennon III, 512–2010, ext. 31271 wgrennon@gpo.gov.
 Chief of:
  Accounts Receivable and Collections.—Donald L. Bartolomei, 512–1078, dbartolomei @gpo.gov.
  Financial Planning Programs and Systems Chief.—Frank P. McCraw, 512–0832, fmccraw @gpo.gov.

CHIEF ADMINISTRATIVE OFFICER

Chief Administrative Officer.—Herbert H. Jackson, Jr., 512–0952, hjackson@gpo.gov.

HUMAN CAPITAL

Chief Human Capital Officer.—Ginger T. Thomas, 512–1182, gthomas@gpo.gov.
 Chief of:
  Human Capital Operations.—Vacant, 512–0000.
  Workforce Development, Education and Training.—Dan M. Mielke, 512–1144, dmielke @gpo.gov.
  Medical Officer.—Vacant, 512–2061.

INFORMATION TECHNOLOGY

Chief Information Officer.—Charles E. Riddle, Jr., 512–1040, criddle@gpo.gov.
 Deputy Chief Information Officer.—Tracee Boxley, 512–1394, tboxley@gpo.gov,
 Chief of:
  Applications Development and Management Division.—Ajay Budhraja, 512–1024, abudhraja@gpo.gov.
  Customer Support Division.—John E. Matthews, 512–1349, jmatthews@gpo.gov.
  Enterprise Architecture Division.—Layton F. Clay, 512–2001, lclay@gpo.gov.
  Information Technology Security Division.—John L. Hannan, 512–1021, jhannan@gpo.gov.
  Systems Integration Division.—Byron C. Blocker, 512–2198, bcblocker@gpo.gov.

SECURITY SERVICES

Chief Security Officer.—LaMont R. Vernon, 512–1103, lvernon@gpo.gov.
 Commander, Uniformed Police Branch.—Paul D. Epley, 512–0872, pepley@gpo.gov.
 Chief of:
  Physical Security.—Gresham Harkless, 512–0988, gharkless@gpo.gov.
  Product Security.—Jeffrey T. Dorn, Jr., 512–0708, jdorn@gpo.gov.

ACQUISITION SERVICES

Chief Acquisition Operations Officer.—Vacant, 512–0351.
 Chief of:
  Complex and Specialized Acquisitions.—Beverly J. Williams, 512–0937, bwilliams @gpo.gov.
  Paper and General Procurements.—Jonathan Todd, 512–0803, jtodd2@gpo.gov.

DEPUTY DIRECTOR OF THE GOVERNMENT PUBLISHING OFFICE

Deputy Director.—Jim Bradley, 512–0111, jbradley@gpo.gov.

OFFICIAL JOURNALS OF GOVERNMENT

Managing Director.—Lyle L. Green, 512–0224, llgreen@gpo.gov.
 Chief of:
  Congressional Publishing Services.—Vacant, 512–0224.
  Congressional Record Index Office.—Marcia Thompson, 512–0275, mthompson2 @gpo.gov.

Office of Federal Register Publishing Services Manager.—Jeffrey D. MacAfee, 512–2100, jmacafee@gpo.gov.

PLANT OPERATIONS

Managing Director.—John W. Crawford, 512–0707, jcrawford@gpo.gov.
Deputy Managing Director.—Gregory E. Estep, 512–0707, gestep@gpo.gov.
Chief, Engineering Services.—Katherine L. Taylor, 512–0593, ktaylor@gpo.gov.
Production Manager (shift 1).—Shelley N. Welcher, 512–1407, swelcher@gpo.gov.
Assistant Production Manager.—Ibrahim N. "Abe" Sussan, 512–0589, isussan@gpo.gov.
Production Manager (shift 3).—Edna G. Lanier, 512–0625, elanier@gpo.gov.
Manager of:
  Bindery Operations .—Walter H. "Butch" Wingo, Jr., 512–0593, wwingo@gpo.gov.
  Prepress Operations.—Francine R. "Renee" Rosa, 512–1651, frosa@gpo.gov.
  Production Engineering.—David J. Robare, 512–1370, drobare@gpo.gov.
  Press Operations.—Gary W. Evans, 512–0673, gevans@gpo.gov.
  Production Planning and Control.—Robert M. Martein, 512–1470, rmartein@gpo.gov.
  Quality Control and Inventory Management.—Michael P. Mooney, 512–0766, mmooney@gpo.gov.

SECURITY AND INTELLIGENT DOCUMENTS

Managing Director.—Stephen G. LeBlanc, 512–2285, sleblanc@gpo.gov.
Operations Manager.—David H. Ford, 512–1194, dford@gpo.gov.
Manager of:
  Business Development.—Gerald Egan, 512–2010, gegan@gpo.gov.
  New Product and Program Development.—Scott Stole, 512–0697, sstole@gpo.gov.
  Secure Production (DC).—Melinda Ford, 512–1485, mford@gpo.gov.
  Secure Production (Stennis).—David Spiers (228) 813–1716, dspiers@gpo.gov.

CUSTOMER SERVICES

Managing Director.—Bruce A. Seger, 512–2213, bseger@gpo.gov.
Deputy Managing Director.—Sandra K. MacAfee, 512–0320, smacafee@gpo.gov.
Chief of:
  DC Agency Procurement Services.—Julie A. Hasenfus, 512–0655, jhasenfus@gpo.gov.
  Regional Agency Procurement Services.—Teddy J. Priebe, 512–2015, tpriebe@gpo.gov.
  Sales and Publishing Support.—Kirk D. Knoll, 512–1147, kknoll@gpo.gov.
Manager, Creative and Digital Media Services.—Ronald J. Keeney, 512–2012, rkeeney@gpo.gov.

GPO REGIONAL PRINTING PROCUREMENT OFFICES

Atlanta.—Elizabeth A. Bluestein, Manager, 3715 Northside Parkway, Suite 4–305, Atlanta, GA 30327 (404) 605–9160, fax 605–9185, infoatlanta@gpo.gov.
Boston.—Debra L. Rozdzielski, Manager, John F. Kennedy Federal Building, 15 New Sudbury Street, E270, Boston, MA 02203–0002 (617) 565–1370, fax 565–1385, infoboston@gpo.gov.
Charleston Office.—Richard W. Gilbert, Manager, 2825 Noisette Boulevard, Charleston, SC 29405–1819 (843) 743–2036, fax 743–2068, infocharleston@gpo.gov.
Chicago.—Clint J. Mixon, Manager, 200 North LaSalle Street, Suite 810, Chicago, IL 60601–1055 (312) 353–3916, fax 886–3163, infochicago@gpo.gov.
Columbus.—Michael J. Sommer, Manager, 1335 Dublin Road, Suite 112–B, Columbus, OH 43215–7034 (614) 488–4616, fax 488–4577, infocolumbus@gpo.gov.
Dallas.—Kelle J. Chatham, Manager, Federal Office Building, 1100 Commerce Street, Room 731, Dallas, TX 75242–1027 (214) 767–0451, fax 767–4101, infodallas@gpo.gov.
Denver.—Diane L. Abeyta, Manager, 12345 West Alameda Parkway, Suite 208, Lakewood, CO 80228–2824 (303) 236–5292, fax 236–5304, infodenver@gpo.gov.
New York.—Debra L. Rozdzielski, Manager, 26 Federal Plaza, Room 2930, New York, NY 10278–0004 (212) 264–2252, fax 264–2413, infonewyork@gpo.gov.
Oklahoma City Office.—Diane L. Abeyta, Manager, 3420 D Avenue, Suite 100, Tinker AFB, OK 73145–9188 (405) 610–4146, fax 610–4125, infooklahomacity@gpo.gov.
Philadelphia.—Debra L. Rozdzielski, Manager, 928 Jaymore Road, Suite A190, Southampton, PA 18966–3820 (215) 364–6465, fax 364–6479, infophiladelphia@gpo.gov.

San Antonio Office.—Kelle J. Chatham, Manager, 1531 Connally Street, Suite 2, Lackland AFB, TX 78236–5515 (210) 675–1480, fax 675–2429, infosanantonio@gpo.gov.
San Diego Office.—Michael A. Barnes, Manager, 8880 Rio San Diego Drive, 8th Floor, San Diego, CA 92108–3609 (619) 209–6178, fax 209–6179, infosandiego@gpo.gov.
San Francisco.—Michael A. Barnes, Manager, 536 Stone Road, Suite 1, Benicia, CA 94510–1170 (707) 748–1970, fax 748–1980, infosanfran@gpo.gov.
Seattle.—David S. Goldberg, Manager, Federal Center South, 4735 East Marginal Way South, Seattle, WA 98134–2397 (206) 764–3726, fax 764–3301, infoseattle@gpo.gov.
Virginia Beach, VA.—Richard W. Gilbert, Manager, 291 Independence Boulevard, Suite 401, Virginia Beach, VA 23462 (757) 490–7940, fax 490–7950, infovirginiabeach@gpo.gov.

SUPERINTENDENT OF DOCUMENTS

Superintendent of Documents.—Mary Alice Baish, 512–1313, mabaish@gpo.gov.

LIBRARY SERVICES AND CONTENT MANAGEMENT

Managing Director.—Laurie Beyer Hall, 512–0185, lhall@gpo.gov.
  Chief of:
    LSCM Outreach and Support.—Robin L. Haun-Mohamed, 512–0052, rhaun-mohamad
      @gpo.gov.
    Projects and Systems.—Anthony Donovan Smith, 512–1431, adsmith@gpo.gov.
    Library Technical Services.—Vacant, 512–1114.

PUBLICATION AND INFORMATION SALES

Deputy Director.—Jim Bradley, 512–0111, jbradley@gpo.gov.
Chief Administrative Officer.—Herbert H. Jackson, Jr., 512–0952, hjackson@gpo.gov.
  Chief of:
    Content Acquisitions and Contact Center.—Esther R. Edmonds, 512–1694, eedmonds
      @gpo.gov.
    Distribution Services and Outreach.—Lisa L. Williams, 512–1065, llwilliams@gpo.gov.
    Publication Sales and Marketing.—Jeffrey Turner, 512–1055, jturner@gpo.gov.

GPO BOOKSTORE

Metropolitan Area: GPO Bookstore, 710 North Capitol Street, NW., Washington, DC 20401, 512–0132.

TO ORDER PUBLICATIONS

Phone toll free (866) 512–1800 for Subscriptions and Publications [DC area: (202) 512–1800, fax: (202) 512–2104, bookstore walk in: (202) 512–1032]. Mail orders to the Superintendent of Documents, P.O. Box 371954, Pittsburgh, PA 15250–7954, or order online from the U.S. Government Bookstore at *http://bookstore.gpo.gov.* GPO customer support: ContactCenter@gpo.gov.

LAUREL FACILITY

Operations Manager.—Robert E. Mitchell, 8660 Cherry Lane, Mail Stop: SSR, Room 236D1, Laurel, MD 20707–4982 (301) 953–9751, remitchell@gpo.gov.

CONGRESSMAN FRANK EVANS GOVERNMENT PUBLISHING OFFICE DISTRIBUTION CENTER

Distribution Services and Outreach Chief.—Lisa L. Williams, 512–1065, llwilliams@gpo.gov.
  Operations Manager.—Thomas Hunt, P.O. Box 4007, Pueblo, CO 81003 (719) 295–2678, fax 948–3315, thunt@gpo.gov.

LIBRARY OF CONGRESS
101 Independence Avenue, SE., 20540, phone (202) 707–5000
http://www.loc.gov

OFFICE OF THE LIBRARIAN, LM 608, 707–3568

The Librarian of Congress.—David S. Mao (acting), 707–5205.
Deputy Librarian of Congress.—Vacant.
Confidential Assistant to the Librarian.—Elizabeth C. Morrison, 707–4599.
Special Assistant to the Librarian.—Nicole L. Marcou, 707–7159.

OFFICE OF THE CHIEF OF STAFF, LM 608, 707–0351

Chief of Staff.—Robert R. Newlen, LM 608, 707–0351.
  Office Operations Assistant.—Terri Humphries, LM 608, 707–0351.
  Director, Office of:
    Communications.—Gayle Osterberg, LM 106, 707–2905.
      Editor, Calendar of Events.—Erin Allen Sanchez, 707–7302.
      Editor, the Gazette.—Mark Hartsell, 707–9194.
    Congressional Relations.—Kathleen G. Ott, LM 611, 707–6577.
    Development.—Susan Siegel, LM 605, 707–1447.
    General Counsel.—Elizabeth Pugh, LM 601, 707–6316.
    Opportunity, Inclusiveness and Compliance.—Evelio Rubiella (acting), LM 623, 707–3343.
  Senior Advisor, Organizational Performance.—Dianne Houghton, LM 608, 707–3096.

OFFICE OF THE CHIEF OPERATING OFFICER, LM 643, 707–2758

Chief Operating Officer.—Edward R. Jablonski, LM 643, 707–2758.
Chief Financial Officer.—Mary Klutts, LM 613, 707–2418.
Director, Office of:
  Contracts and Grants Management.—Ronald Backes, 707–0833.
  Human Resources Services.—Rachel Bouman (acting), LM 645, 707–7364.
  Integrated Support Services.—Robert "Adrian" Upshur, LM 327, 707–0591.
Security and Emergency Preparedness.—Kenneth Lopez, LM G03, 707–8708.
Chief Information Officer.—Bernard "Bud" Barton, LM 635, 707–3300.

CONGRESSIONAL RESEARCH SERVICE, LM 203, 707–5700

Director.—Mary B. Mazanec, LM 203, 707–5775.
Deputy Director.—Colleen Shogan, LM 203, 707–8231.
Chief Information Officer.—Lisa M. Hoppis, LM 413, 707–2559.
Counselor to the Director.—Lizanne D. Kelley, LM 203, 707–8833.
Associate Director, Office of:
  Congressional Information and Publishing.—Clifford T. Cohen, LM 223, 707–1858.
  Finance and Administration.—Francois A. DiFolco, LM 209, 707–2877.
  Workforce Management and Development.—Monica M. Woods, LM 208, 707–7654.
Assistant Director, Division of:
  American Law.—Karen J. Lewis, LM 227, 707–7460.
  Domestic Social Policy.—Laura B. Shrestha, LM 323, 707–7046.
  Foreign Affairs, Defense and Trade.—Michael L. Moodie, LM 315, 707–8470.
  Government and Finance.—John R. Haskell, LM 303, 707–2198.
  Knowledge Services Group.—Lillian W. Gassie, LM 215, 707–7573.
  Resources, Science and Industry.—John L. Moore, LM 423, 707–7232.

U.S. COPYRIGHT OFFICE, LM 403, 707–8350

U.S. Register of Copyrights and Director.—Maria A. Pallante, LM 403, 707–8052.
  Special Assistant.—Syreeta N. Swann, LM 403, 707–8052.
  General Counsel.—Jacqueline C. Charlesworth, LM 403, 707–8772.
  Director of:
    Policy and International Affairs.—Karyn Temple Claggett, LM 413, 707–6447.
    Registration Policy and Practice.—Robert J. Kasunic, LM 453, 707–0229.
  Chief of:
    Literary Division.—Ted Hirakawa, LM 443, 707–6181.

Performing Arts Division.—Laura Lee Fischer, LM 443, 707–5751.
Visual Arts Division.—John H. Ashley, LM 433, 707–8223.
Director, Public Information and Education.—William J. Roberts, LM 453, 707–8391.
Head of:
  Copyright Information Section.—Denise Garrett, LM 519, 707–1521.
  Publications Section.—Vacant.
Chief Information Officer.—Douglas P. Ament, LM 403, 707–5440.
Director, Copyright Technology Office.—Ricardo Farraj-Feijoo, LM 560, 707–0110.
Chief of Operations.—David J. Christopher, LM 403, 707–8825.
Chief of:
  Acquisitions Division.—Stephen D. Want, LM 526, 707–6781.
  Administrative Services Office.—Bruce J. McCubbin, LM 458, 707–8395.
  Licensing Division.—James B. Enzinna, LM 504, 707–6801.
  Receipt Analysis and Control Division.—Victor A. Holmes, LM 422, 707–8244.
Director, Public Records and Repositories.—Elizabeth R. Scheffler, LM 433, 707–6042.
Head of:
  Recordation Section.—Zarifa Madyun, LM 433, 707–1643.
  Records Management Section.—Vacant.
  Records Research and Certification Section.—Vacant.

LAW LIBRARY, OFFICE OF THE LAW LIBRARIAN, LM 240, 707–5065

Law Librarian.—Roberta Shaffer, LM 240, 707–9825.
Administrative Operations.—Donald Simon, LM 240, 707–4884.
Director of:
  Global Legal Collection.—Janice Hyde, LM 240, 707–9836.
  Global Legal Research.—Peter Roudik, LM 240, 707–9861.
Chief of:
  Collections Services.—Kurt Carroll, LM 232, 707–1494.
  Foreign, Comparative and International Law Division I.—Kelly Buchanan, LM 240, 707–1166.
  Foreign, Comparative and International Law Division II.—Luis Acosta, LM 240, 707–9131.
  Public Services.—Debbie Keysor, LM 201, 707–3164.

LIBRARY SERVICES, LM 642, 707–5325

Associate Librarian.—Mark Sweeney, LM 642, 707–5325.
Deputy Associate Librarian/Administrative Services and Operations.—Sandra Lawson, 707–3332.
Director for:
  Acquisitions and Bibliographic Access.—Beacher Wiggins, LM 642, 707–5137.
  American Folklife Center.—Elizabeth Peterson, LJ G49, 707–1745.
  Collection Development Office.—Joseph Puccio, LA 5181, 707–1413
  Veterans History Project.—Robert Patrick, LA 143, 707–7308.
Chief of:
  Acquisitions, Fiscal and Support Office.—Richard Yarnall (acting), LM B42/B46, 707–9474.
  African, Latin American and Western European Division.—Angela Kinney, LM 542, 707–5572.
  Asian and Middle Eastern Division.—Randall Barry, LM 541, 707–5118.
  Cooperative and Instructional Programs Division.—Judith Cannan, LA 140, 707–2031.
  Germanic and Slavic Division.—Zbigniew Kantorosinki, LM 527, 707–3093.
  Network Development and MARC Standards Office.—Sally H. McCallum, LA 309, 707–5119.
  Policy and Standards Division.—Beacher Wiggins (acting), LM 642, 707–5137.
  U.S./Anglo Division.—Linda Geisler, LM G35, 707–0116.
  U.S. and Arts, Sciences and Humanities Division.—Vera Clyburn, LM 515, 707–3943.
  U.S. Programs, Law and Literature Division.—Karl Debus-Lopez, LM 501, 707–6641.
Director, Collections and Services.—Helena Zinkham (acting), LM 339, 707–2922.
Chief of:
  African and Middle Eastern Division.—Mary Jane Deeb, LJ 220, 707–1221.
  Asian Division.—Dongfang Shao, LJ 149, 707–5919.
  Children's Literature Center.—Sybille A. Jagusch, LJ 100, 707–5535.
  Collections Access, Loan and Management.—Steven J. Herman, LJ G02, 707–7400.
  Digital Conversion Team.—Michael Neubert, LA 516, 707–3706.
  European Division.—Georgette M. Dorn (acting), LJ 250, 707–5414.

Geography and Map Division.—Ralph Ehrenberg, LM B02, 707–1992.
Hispanic Division.—Georgette M. Dorn (acting), LJ 240, 707–5400.
Humanities and Social Sciences Division.—Jane Sanchez, LJ 139A, 707–1955.
Manuscript Division.—James H. Hutson, LM 102, 707–5383.
Music Division.—Susan H. Vita, LM 113, 707–5503.
Packard Campus for Audio-Visual Conservation/Motion Picture, Broadcasting and Recorded Sound Division.—Gregory Lukow, PC 2013, 707–5709.
Prints and Photographs Division.—Helena Zinkham, LM 339, 707–2922.
Rare Book and Special Collections Division.—Mark G. Dimunation, LJ 230, 707–2025.
Science, Technology and Business Division.—Ronald S. Bluestone, LA 5203, 707–0948.
Serial and Government Publications Division.—Teresa V. Sierra, LM 133, 707–5277.
Director, Preservation.—Adrija Henley (acting), LM G05, 707–0788.
Chief of:
  Binding and Collections Care Division.—Jeanne Drewes, LM G21, 707–5330.
  Conservation Division.—Elmer Eusman, LM G38, 707–5838.
  Preservation Reformatting Division.—Adrija Henley, LM G05, 707–0788.
  Preservation Research and Testing Division.—Fenella France, LM G38, 707–5525.
Director, Technology Policy.—Beth Dulabahn, LM 641, 707–2369.
Chief of:
  Automation Planning and Liaison Office.—Robert Palian (acting), LM 532, 707–1576.
  Integrated Library System Program Office.—Ann Della Porta, LA 301, 707–4761.

NATIONAL AND INTERNATIONAL OUTREACH, LM 637, 707–3100

Director.—Jane McAuliffe, LM 637, 707–3100.
  Deputy Director.—Colleen Shogan (acting), LM 637, 707–8231.
  Director of Operations.—Larry Stafford, LM 637, 707–6343.
  Director of National Programs.—Betsy Peterson (acting), LJ G49, 707–1745.
    Center for the Book.—John Cole, LM 650, 707–5221.
    Head, Poetry and Literature Center.—Rob Casper, LJ A02, 707–1308.
    Head, Young Readers Center.—Karen Jaffe, LJ G29, 707–1951.
    National Digital Initiatives.—Vacant, LM 330, 707–3100.
    National Library Service for the Blind and Physically Handicapped.—Karen Keninger, 707–5104.
  Director of National Enterprises.—Blane Dessy, LM 637, 707–3032.
    Office of Business Enterprises.—Eugene Flanagan, LA 130, 707–8203.
    Federal Research Division.—Mukta Ohri, LA 5282, 707–3919.
    FEDLINK.—Meg Tulloch, LA 217, 707–4801.
    Publishing.—Peggy Wagner (acting), LM 602, 707–6068.
  Director of Scholarly and Educational Programs.—John Van Oudenaren, LA 300, 707–4543.
    Educational Outreach.—Lee Ann Potter, LM 629, 707–8735.
    Interpretive Programs.—Jason Yasner (acting), LA 230, 707–2255.
    Internships and Fellowships Programs.—George Coulbourne, LM 330, 707–7856.
    Kluge Center.—Robert Gallucci (interim), LJ 120, 707–3090.
    Special Events and Public Programs.—Nishelle Wingfield (acting), LM 612, 707–5218.
    Visitor Services.—Giulia Adelfio, LJ G59, 707–2153.
    World Digital Library.—John Van Oudenaren, LA 300, 707–4543.

OFFICE OF THE INSPECTOR GENERAL, LM 630, 707–6314

Inspector General.—Kurt Hyde, LM 630, 707–6314.

UNITED STATES BOTANIC GARDEN
245 First Street, SW., Washington, DC 20024
(202) 225–8333 (information); (202) 226–8333 (receptionist)
http://www.usbg.gov

Director.—Stephen T. Ayers (acting), Architect of the Capitol, 228–1204.
  Executive Director.—Ari E. Novy, Ph.D., 225–6670.
  Administrative Officer.—Tonda S. Cave, 225–5002.
  Public Programs Manager.—Susan K. Pell, Ph.D., 225–1269.
  Horticulture Division Manager.—James T. Kaufmann, 438–5175.
  Facility Manager.—Ian M. Donegan, 225–6646.

THE CABINET

Vice President of the United States	JOSEPH R. BIDEN, JR.
Secretary of State	JOHN F. KERRY.
Secretary of the Treasury	JACOB J. LEW.
Secretary of Defense	ASHTON B. CARTER.
Attorney General	LORETTA E. LYNCH.
Secretary of the Interior	SALLY JEWELL.
Secretary of Agriculture	THOMAS J. VILSACK.
Secretary of Commerce	PENNY PRITZKER.
Secretary of Labor	THOMAS E. PEREZ.
Secretary of Health and Human Services	SYLVIA MATHEWS BURWELL.
Secretary of Housing and Urban Development	JULIÁN CASTRO.
Secretary of Transportation	ANTHONY FOXX.
Secretary of Energy	ERNEST MONIZ.
Secretary of Education	ARNE DUNCAN.
Secretary of Veterans Affairs	ROBERT MCDONALD.
Secretary of Homeland Security	JEH CHARLES JOHNSON.
Chief of Staff	DENIS MCDONOUGH.
Administrator, Environmental Protection Agency	GINA MCCARTHY.
Director, Office of Management and Budget	SHAUN L.S. DONOVAN.
U.S. Trade Representative	MICHAEL FROMAN.
Ambassador, United States Mission to the United Nations	SAMANTHA POWER.
Chair, Council of Economic Advisers	JASON FURMAN.
Administrator, Small Business Administration	MARIA CONTRERAS-SWEET.

EXECUTIVE BRANCH

THE PRESIDENT

BARACK H. OBAMA, Senator from Illinois and 44th President of the United States; born in Honolulu, Hawaii, August 4, 1961; received a B.A. in 1983 from Columbia University, New York City; worked as a community organizer in Chicago, IL; studied law at Harvard University, where he became the first African American president of the *Harvard Law Review,* and received a J.D. in 1991; practiced law in Chicago, IL; lecturer on constitutional law, University of Chicago; member, Illinois State Senate, 1997–2004; elected as a Democrat to the U.S. Senate in 2004; and served from January 3, 2005, to November 16, 2008, when he resigned from office, having been elected President; family: married to Michelle; two children: Malia and Sasha; elected as President of the United States on November 4, 2008, and took the oath of office on January 20, 2009.

EXECUTIVE OFFICE OF THE PRESIDENT
1600 Pennsylvania Avenue, NW., 20500
Eisenhower Executive Office Building (EEOB), 17th Street and Pennsylvania Avenue, NW., 20500, phone (202) 456–1414, http://www.whitehouse.gov

The President of the United States.—Barack H. Obama.
    Special Assistant to the President and Personal Aide to the President.— Anita Decker Breckenridge.
    Director of Oval Office Operations.—Brian Mosteller.

OFFICE OF THE VICE PRESIDENT
phone (202) 456–1414

The Vice President.—Joseph R. Biden, Jr.
    Assistant to the President and Chief of Staff to the Vice President.—Steve Ricchetti, EEOB, room 272, 456–9951.
    Deputy Assistant to the President and Chief of Staff to Dr. Jill Biden.—Sheila Nix, EEOB, room 201, 456–7458.
    Deputy Assistant to the President and Counselor to the Vice President.—Don Graves, EEOB, room 282, 456–2982.
    Chief Economist and Economic Advisor to the Vice President.—Ben Harris, EEOB, room 289A, 456–1437.
    Deputy Assistant to the President and National Security Advisor to the Vice President.— Colin Kahl, EEOB, room 208, 456–2744.
    Special Assistant to the President and Senior Advisor to the Vice President.—Greg Schultz, EEOB, room 204, 456–3639.
    Special Assistant to the President and Director of Intergovernmental Affairs to the Vice President.—Evan "Michael" Schrum, EEOB, room 202A, 456–1734.
    Special Assistant to the President and Director of Public Engagement to the Vice President.— Carri Twigg, EEOB, room 202A, 456–6222.
    Counsel to the Vice President.—John McGrail, EEOB, room 270, 456–2734.
    Director of Communications.—Kate Bedingfield, EEOB, room 280, 456–2448.
    Special Assistant to the Vice President and Director of Legislative Affairs.—Tonya Williams, EEOB, room 279A, 456–1540.
    Director of Administration.—Dana Rosenzweig (acting), EEOB, room 267, 456–3794.
    Director of Scheduling.—Virginia "Ginna" Lance, EEOB, room 265A, 456–6264.
    Personal Aide and Advisor to the Vice President.—John Flynn, West Wing, 456–1715.
    Assistants to the Vice President: Kathy Chung, Anne Marie Muldoon, West Wing, 456–1715, 456–1732.

COUNCIL OF ECONOMIC ADVISERS

725 Seventeenth Street, NW., 20006, phone (202) 395–5084
http://www.whitehouse.gov/cea

Chair.—Jason Furman.
Chief of Staff.—Andrea Taverna.
Members: Sandra Black, Jay Shambaugh.

COUNCIL ON ENVIRONMENTAL QUALITY

730 Jackson Place, NW., 20503, phone (202) 456–6224
http://www.whitehouse.gov/ceq

Managing Director.—Christina "Christy" Goldfuss.
Special Assistant to the Managing Director.—McKenzie Huffman.
Chief of Staff.—Christopher "Chris" Adamo.
Deputy Chief of Staff.—Lowery Crook.
General Counsel.—Brenda Mallory.
Deputy General Counsel.—Manisha Patel.
Deputy Associate Director for—
  International Affairs.—Vacant.
  Regulatory Policy.—Vacant.
Attorney Advisor.—Brooke Dorner.
Operations Manager.—Angela Matos.
Administrative Services Specialist.—Essence Washington.
Administrative Assistants: Brenda Butler, Mary Green.
Deputy Chief Sustainability Officer, Office of Federal Sustainability.—Amy Porter.
Associate Chief Sustainability Officer.—Bernice "Dee" Siegel.
OFS Senior Program Manager for Federal Outreach.—Vacant.
OFS Senior Program Managers: Matthew Kittell, Marissa McInnis, Andrew Wishnia.
Associate Director for Energy and Climate Change.—Richard Duke.
  Special Assistant to the Associate Director for Energy and Climate Change.—Peter Hansel.
Deputy Associate Directors for Energy and Climate Change: Aaron Bergman, Sven Hodges,
  Nathan Hultman, Molly Ward, Tristram West, Rama Zakaria.
Associate Director for Climate Preparedness.—Jainey Bavishi.
Climate Change Preparedness Analyst.—Rachel Isacoff.
Senior Advisor for Policy and Strategic Planning.—Andrew "Drew" McConville.
Deputy Associate Director for—
  Conservation and Wildlife.—Tim Male.
  Land and Water Ecosystems.—Michael Degnan.
Special Assistant to the Associate Director for Land and Water Ecosystems.—Susie Rojas.
Deputy Associate Director for—
  America's Great Outdoors.—Michael Degnan.
  Ecosystems.—Alexis Segal.
  Lands.—Mariel Murray.
  Water.—Ellen Tarquinio.
National Ocean Council Director.—Beth Kerttula.
NOC Policy Analysts: Margaret "Meg" Larrea, Jerry Smith.
Associate Director for Communications.—Noreen Nielsen.
  Special Assistant to the Associate Director for Communications.—Vacant.
Associate Director for—
  Legislative Affairs.—Trent Bauserman.
  NEPA Oversight.—Horst Greczmiel.
Special Assistant to the Associate Director for Legislative Affairs: Nathaniel "Nate" Norris.
Associate Director for Public Engagement.—Angela Barranco.
  Special Assistant to the Associate Director for Public Engagement.—Thomas Elson.

PRESIDENT'S INTELLIGENCE ADVISORY BOARD

phone (202) 456–2352

Executive Director.—Stefanie Osburn.
General Counsel.—Nancy Fortenberry.

NATIONAL SECURITY COUNCIL
Eisenhower Executive Office Building, 20504
phone (202) 456–1414, http://www.whitehouse.gov/nsc

MEMBERS

The President.—Barack H. Obama.
  The Vice President.—Joseph R. Biden, Jr.
  The Secretary of State.—John F. Kerry.
  The Secretary of Defense.—Ashton B. Carter.

STATUTORY ADVISERS

Director of National Intelligence.—James R. Clapper, Jr.
  Chairman, Joint Chiefs of Staff.—Gen. Martin E. Dempsey, USA.

STANDING PARTICIPANTS

The Secretary of the Treasury.—Jacob J. Lew.
  Chief of Staff to the President.—Denis McDonough.
  Counsel to the President.—W. Neil Eggleston.
  National Security Adviser.—Susan E. Rice.
  Assistant to the President for Economic Policy.—Jeffrey Zients.

OFFICIALS

Assistant to the President for National Security Affairs.—Susan E. Rice.
  Assistant to the President for National Security Affairs and Deputy National Security Adviser.—Avril Haines.

OFFICE OF ADMINISTRATION
Eisenhower Executive Office Building, phone (202) 395–5555

Director of the Office of Administration. Cathy Solomon.
  Chief, Office of:
  Equal Employment Opportunity.—Clara Patterson.
  Finance.—Faisal Amin.
  General Counsel.—Hugh Brady.
  Logistics.—Stephen Pearson.

OFFICE OF MANAGEMENT AND BUDGET
Eisenhower Executive Office Building, phone (202) 395–4840

Director.—Shaun L.S. Donovan.
  Deputy Director.—Aviva Aron-Dine (acting).
  Deputy Director for Management.—David Mader (acting).
  Executive Associate Director.—Aviva Aron-Dine.
  Administrator, Office of:
  Federal Procurement Policy.—Anne Rung.
  Information and Regulatory Affairs.—Howard Shelanski.
  Assistant Director for—
  Budget.—Courtney Timberlake.
  Legislative Reference.—Matthew Vaeth.
  Associate Director for—
  Economic Policy.—Aviva Aron-Dine.
  Education, Income Maintenance and Labor Programs.—Sharon Parrott.
  General Government Programs.—Andrew Mayock.
  Health Programs.—Adaeze Akamigbo.
  Legislative Affairs.—Tamara Fucile.
  National Security Programs.—Jonathan Lachman.

Natural Resources, Energy and Science Programs.—Ali Zaidi.
Strategic Planning and Communications.—Shannon Buckingham.
General Counsel.—Heather Walsh (acting).

OFFICE OF NATIONAL DRUG CONTROL POLICY
750 17th Street, NW., phone (202) 395–6700, fax 395–6711

Director.—Michael P. Botticelli, room 810, 395–6700.
Chief of Staff.—Regina M. LaBelle, room 809, 395–5505.
Deputy Chief of Staff.—Jon E. Rice, room 805, 395–6791.
Deputy Director, Office of:
 Demand Reduction.—Vacant.
 State and Local Affairs.—Mary Lou Leary, room 661, 395–4693.
 Supply Reduction.—James C. Olson (acting), room 713, 395–5535.
General Counsel.—Jeffrey J. Teitz, room 518, 395–6601.
Associate Director, Office of:
 Intelligence.—Gerard Burns, room 755, 395–6764.
 Intergovernmental Public Liaison.—Dalen A. Harris, room 845, 395–6652.
 Legislative Affairs.—Kimberley N. Alton, room 825, 395–6912.
 Management and Administration.—Michele C. Marx, room 326, 395–6883.
 Public Affairs.—William D. Jenkins, room 846, 395–6649.
 Research/Data Analysis.—Terry W. Zobeck, room 836, 395–5503.

OFFICE OF SCIENCE AND TECHNOLOGY POLICY
Eisenhower Executive Office Building, phone (202) 456–4444, fax 456–6021
http://www.ostp.gov

Director.—John P. Holdren.
 Deputy Director for Technology and Innovation.—Thomas Kalil.
 U.S. Chief Technology Officer.—Megan Smith.
 Chief of Staff.—Cristin Dorgelo.
 Associate Director for—
 Energy and Environment.—Vacant.
 National Security and International Affairs.—Patricia Falcone.
 Science.—Vacant.
General Counsel.—Rachael Leonard.
Assistant Directors:
 Legislative Affairs.—Donna Pignatelli.
 Strategic Communications.—Kristin Lee.
Executive Director for President's Council of Advisors on Science and Technology (PCAST).—Marjory Blumenthal.
Executive Director for National Science and Technology Council (NSTC).—Afua Bruce.

OFFICE OF THE UNITED STATES TRADE REPRESENTATIVE
600 17th Street, NW., 20508, phone (202) 395–6890
http://www.ustr.gov

United States Trade Representative.—Michael Froman.
 Deputy United States Trade Representatives: Wendy Cutler (acting), Robert Holleyman.
 Deputy U.S. Trade Representative, Geneva.—Michael Punke.
 Chief Agricultural Negotiator.—Darci Vetter.
 General Counsel.—Timothy Reif.
Assistant U.S. Trade Representative for—
 Administration.—Fred Ames.
 Africa.—Florie Liser.
 Agricultural Affairs.—Sharon Bomer Lauritsen.
 Central and South Asia Affairs.—Mike Delaney.
 China Affairs.—Audrey Winter (acting).
 Congressional Affairs.—Mike Harney.
 Trade Policy and Economics.—Douglas Bell.
 Environment and Natural Resources.—Jennifer Prescott.
 Europe and the Middle East.—Dan Mullaney.

Intellectual Property and Innovation.—Probir Mehta (acting).
Intergovernmental Affairs and Public Engagement.—Omar Khan.
Interagency Trade Enforcement Center.—Bradford Ward.
Japan, Korea and APEC Affairs.—Bruce Hirsh.
Labor Affairs.—Lewis Karesh.
Monitoring and Enforcement.—Juan Millan (acting).
Private Sector Engagement.—Elizabeth Kelley.
Public/Media Affairs.—Matthew McAlvanah.
Services and Investment.—Christine Bliss.
Small Business, Market Access, and Industrial Competitiveness.—Jim Sanford.
Southeast Asia and the Pacific.—Barbara Weisel.
Textiles.—Gail Strickler.
Western Hemisphere.—John Melle.
World Trade Organization (WTO) and Multilateral Affairs.—Mark Linscott.

THE WHITE HOUSE OFFICE

CABINET AFFAIRS

Assistant to the President and Cabinet Secretary.—Broderick Johnson.
Deputy Assistant to the President and Deputy Cabinet Secretary.—Gaurab Bansal.

CHIEF OF STAFF

Assistant to the President and Chief of Staff.—Denis McDonough.
Assistant to the President and Deputy Chief of Staff for Operations.—Anita Breckenridge.
Assistant to the President and Deputy Chief of Staff for Implementation.—Kristie Canegallo.
Assistant to the President and Senior Advisors: Brian Deese, Shailagh Murray.

COMMUNICATIONS

Assistant to the President and Director of Communications.—Jennifer Psaki.
Assistant to the President and Director of Speechwriting.—Cody Keenan.
Assistant to the President and Press Secretary.—Joshua Earnest.

OFFICE OF DIGITAL STRATEGY

Deputy Assistant to the President and Chief Digital Officer.—Jason Goldman.

DOMESTIC POLICY COUNCIL

Assistant to the President and Director of the Domestic Policy Council.—Cecilia Muñoz.
Deputy Assistant to the President and Deputy Director of the Domestic Policy Council.—James Kvaal.
Deputy Assistant to the President for Health Policy.—Jeanne Lambrew.
Deputy Assistant to the President for Energy and Climate Change.—Dan Utech.
Deputy Assistant to the President for Urban Affairs, Justice, and Opportunity.—Roy L. Austin, Jr.
Special Assistant to the President for Education Policy.—Roberto Rodriguez.
Special Assistant to the President and Executive Director of the White House Office of Faith-Based and Neighborhood Partnerships.—Melissa Rogers.
Special Assistant to the President for Labor and Workforce Policy.—Benjamin Olinsky.
Special Assistant to the President and Chief of Staff of the Domestic Policy Council.—Katherine Kochman.
Director of the Office of National AIDS Policy.—Douglas Brooks.

OFFICE OF THE FIRST LADY

Assistant to the President and Chief of Staff to the First Lady.—Christina Tchen.

Deputy Assistant to the President and Senior Advisor to the First Lady.—Melissa Winter.
Special Assistant to the President and Director of Strategic Planning.—Mackenzie Smith.
Special Assistant to the President and Director of Communications for the First Lady.—
Caroline Adler.
Special Assistant to the President and White House Social Secretary.—Deesha Dyer.

OFFICE OF LEGISLATIVE AFFAIRS

Assistant to the President and Director, Office of Legislative Affairs.—Katherine Fallon.
Deputy Assistant to the President for Legislative Affairs and Senate Liaison.—Martin Paone.
Deputy Assistant to the President for Legislative Affairs.—Amy Rosenbaum.
Deputy Assistant to the President for Legislative Affairs and House Liaison.—Alejandro
Perez.

OFFICE OF MANAGEMENT AND ADMINISTRATION

Assistant to the President for Management and Administration.—Maju Varghese.
Deputy Assistant to the President for Management and Administration.—Katherine Dickerson.
Special Assistant to the President and Director of Visitors Office.—Ellie Schafer.

NATIONAL ECONOMIC COUNCIL

*Assistant to the President for Economic Policy and Director of the National Economic
Council.*—Jeffrey Zients.
Deputy Assistants to the President and Deputy Directors, National Economic Council.—
Adewale Adeyemo, Jacob Leibenluft, Jason Miller.
*Deputy Assistant to the President and Deputy National Security Advisor for International
Economics.*—Caroline Atkinson.

OFFICE OF THE NATIONAL SECURITY ADVISOR

Assistant to the President and National Security Advisor.—Susan Rice.
Assistant to the President and Deputy National Security Advisor.—Avril Haines.
*Assistant to the President for Homeland Security and Counterterrorism and Deputy National
Security Advisor.*—Lisa Monaco.
*Assistant to the President and Deputy National Security Advisor for Strategic Communica-
tions and Speechwriting.*—Benjamin Rhodes.

PRESIDENTIAL PERSONNEL OFFICE

Assistant to the President and Director of Presidential Personnel.—Valerie Green.
Deputy Assistant to the President for Presidential Personnel.—Margaret McLaughlin, David
Noble.

OFFICE OF PUBLIC ENGAGEMENT AND INTERGOVERNMENTAL AFFAIRS

*Senior Advisor and Assistant to the President for Intergovernmental Affairs and Public
Engagement.*—Valerie Jarrett.
Deputy Assistant to the President and Director of the Office of Public Engagement.—
Paulette Aniskoff.
Deputy Assistant to the President and Director of Intergovernmental Affairs.—Jerry
Abramson.

OFFICE OF SCHEDULING AND ADVANCE

Assistant to the President and Director of Scheduling and Advance.—Chase Cushman.
Deputy Assistant to the President and Director of Scheduling.—Gregory Lojuste.
Deputy Assistant to the President and Director of Advance and Operations.—Michael Brush.

Special Assistant to the President, Trip Director and Personal Aide to the President.— Marvin Nicholson.

OFFICE OF THE STAFF SECRETARY

Deputy Assistant to the President and Staff Secretary. Joan Walsh.
Special Assistant to the President and Director of Presidential Correspondence.— Fiona Reeves.

WHITE HOUSE COUNSEL

*Assistant to the President and Counsel to the President.—*Warren Eggleston.
Deputy Assistants to the President and Deputy Counsel to the President: Michael Bosworth, Brian Egan, Nicholas McQuaid.

PRESIDENT'S COMMISSION ON WHITE HOUSE FELLOWSHIPS

*Director.—*Jennifer Kaplan.

DEPARTMENT OF STATE

2201 C Street, NW., 20520, phone (202) 647–4000

JOHN F. KERRY, Secretary of State; born in Denver, CO, December 11, 1943; education: graduated, St. Paul's School, Concord, NH, 1962; B.A., Yale University, New Haven, CT, 1966; J.D., Boston College Law School, Boston, MA, 1976; served, U.S. Navy, discharged with rank of lieutenant; decorations: Silver Star, Bronze Star with Combat "V", three Purple Hearts, various theatre campaign decorations; attorney, admitted to Massachusetts Bar, 1976; appointed first assistant district attorney, Middlesex County, 1977; elected lieutenant governor, Massachusetts, 1982; married: Teresa Heinz; Senator from Massachusetts, 1985–2013; committees: chair, Foreign Relations; Commerce, Science, and Transportation; Finance; Small Business and Entrepreneurship; appointed to the Democratic Leadership for 104th and 105th Congresses; nominated by President Barack Obama to become the 68th Secretary of State, and was confirmed by the U.S. Senate on January 29, 2013.

OFFICE OF THE SECRETARY

Secretary of State.—John F. Kerry, room 7226, 647–9572.
 Deputy Secretary.—Antony J. "Tony" Blinken.
 Deputy Secretary for Management and Resources.—Heather Anne Higginbottom.
 Executive Assistant.—Lisa Kenna, 647–8102.
 Chief of Staff.—Jonathan Finer, 647–5548.

AMBASSADOR-AT-LARGE FOR WAR CRIMES ISSUES

Ambassador-at-Large.—Stephen J. Rapp, room 7419A, 647–6051.
 Deputy.—Jane Stromseth, 647–9880.

OFFICE OF THE CHIEF OF PROTOCOL

Chief of Protocol.—Amb. Peter Selfridge, room 1238, 647–4543.
 Deputy Chiefs: Natalie Jones, 647–1144; Mark Walsh, 647–4120.

OFFICE OF CIVIL RIGHTS

Director.—John M. Robinson, room 7428, 647–9295.
 Deputy Director.—Gregory D. Smith.

BUREAU OF COUNTERTERRORISM

Coordinator.—Tina Kaidaow (acting), room 2509, 647–9892.
 Principal Deputy Coordinator.—Justin Siberell, 647–5810.

BUREAU FOR CONFLICT AND STABILIZATION OPERATIONS

Assistant Secretary.—Dolores Brown (acting), room 7100 SA–3 (202) 663–0807.

EXECUTIVE SECRETARIAT

Special Assistant and Executive Secretary.—Joseph E. Macmanus, room 7224, 647–5301.
 Deputy Executive Secretaries: Marykay Carlson, 647–8448; Kelly Degnan, 647–5302; Vacant, 647–5302.

OFFICE OF THE INSPECTOR GENERAL
2121 Virginia Avenue, NW., 20037

Inspector General.—Steve Linick, room 8100, 663–0361.
Deputy Inspector General.—Emilia DiSanto, 663–0365.

BUREAU OF INTELLIGENCE AND RESEARCH

Assistant Secretary.—Daniel B. Smith, room 6468, 647–9177.
Principal Deputy Assistant Secretary.—Kathleen Fitzpatrick, 647–7826.
Deputy Assistant Secretaries: Catherine Brown, 647–7754; James Buchanan, 647–9633.

OFFICE OF LEGAL ADVISER

The Legal Adviser.—Vacant, room 6421, 647–9598.
Principal Deputy Legal Adviser.—Mary McLeod, 647–5036.
Deputy Legal Advisers: Newell Highsmith, 647–7942; Katherine McManus, 647–7976; Richard C. Visek, 647–7942.

BUREAU OF LEGISLATIVE AFFAIRS

Assistant Secretary.—Julia Frifield, room 7531, 647–4204.
Deputy Assistant Secretary (Global, Regional and Functional).—Rori Kramer, 647–2623.
Deputy Assistant Secretary (Senate).—Vacant, 647–8733.
Deputy Assistant Secretary (House).—Joel Rubin, 647–1656.

POLICY PLANNING STAFF

Director.—David McKean, room 7311, 647–2972.
Principal Deputy Director.—Siddharth Mohandas.

OFFICE OF THE U.S. GLOBAL AIDS COORDINATOR

Coordinator.—Dr. Deborah Birx, room SA–22, 663–2579.
Principal Deputy U.S. Global AIDS Coordinator.—Vacant, 663–2802.

UNDER SECRETARY FOR POLITICAL AFFAIRS

Under Secretary.—Wendy Sherman, room 7250, 647–2471.
Executive Assistant.—Kamala Lakhdhir, 647–1598.

AFRICAN AFFAIRS

Assistant Secretary.—Linda Thomas-Greenfield, room 6234A, 647–2530.
Principal Deputy Assistant Secretary.—Robert P. Jackson, 647–4485.

EAST ASIAN AND PACIFIC AFFAIRS

Assistant Secretary.—Daniel Russel, 647–9596.
Principal Deputy Assistant Secretary.—Scot Marciel, 647–6910.
Deputy Assistant Secretaries: Michael Fuchs, 647–4612; Kristie Kenney, 647–7234; Dennise Mathieu, 647–6595; Susan Thornton, 647–8929.

EUROPEAN AND EURASIAN AFFAIRS

Assistant Secretary.—Victoria Nuland, room 6226, 647–9626.
Principal Deputy Assistant Secretary.—Paul Jones, 647–5146.
Deputy Assistant Secretaries: John Heffern, 647–6233; Julieta Noyes, 647–9373; Eric S. Rubin, 647–5447; Amanda Sloats, 647–5174; Mark Toner, 647–6402; Hoyt Yee, 647–6415.

NEAR EASTERN AFFAIRS

Assistant Secretary.—Anne Patterson, room 6242, 647–7209.
Principal Deputy Assistant Secretary.—Gerald Feirstein, 647–7207.
Deputy Assistant Secretaries: John Desrocher, 647–7170; Elizabeth Richard, 647–1651; Larry Schwartz, 647–4199; Larry Silverman, 647–8769; Susan Ziadeh, 647–0554.

SOUTH AND CENTRAL ASIAN AFFAIRS

Assistant Secretary.—Nisha Biswal, room 6254, 736–4325.
Principal Deputy Assistant Secretary.—Richard Hoagland, 647–9505.
Deputy Assistant Secretaries: Atul Keshap, 736–4328; Eileen O'Connor, 736–4328; Daniel Rosenblum, 647–9505; Vacant, 736–4328.

WESTERN HEMISPHERE AFFAIRS

Assistant Secretary.—Roberta Jacobson, room 6262, 647–5780.
Principal Deputy Assistant Secretary.—John Feeley, 647–8387.
Deputy Assistant Secretaries: Gonzalo Gallegos, 647–1313; Edward Alec Lee, 647–8563; Francisco Palmieri, 647–7337; Sue Saarnio, 647–6755.

INTERNATIONAL NARCOTICS AND LAW ENFORCEMENT AFFAIRS

Assistant Secretary.—William Brownfield, room 7826, 647–8464.
Principal Deputy Assistant Secretary.—Luis Arreaga, 647–6642.
Deputy Assistant Secretaries: Alexander Arzizu, 647–6642; Jim DeHart (acting), 647–9822; James A. Walsh, 647–9822.

INTERNATIONAL ORGANIZATION AFFAIRS

Assistant Secretary.—Bathsheba Crocker, room 6323, 647–9600.
Principal Deputy Assistant Secretary.—Theodore Allegra, 647–9602.
Deputy Assistant Secretaries: Eric M. Barclay, 647–9431; Nerissa J. Cook, 647–5798; Victoria K. Holt, 647–9604.

UNDER SECRETARY FOR ECONOMIC GROWTH, ENERGY, AND THE ENVIRONMENT

Under Secretary.—Catherine Novelli, room 7256, 647–7575.
Executive Assistant.—William Heidt, 647–7674.

ECONOMIC, ENERGY AND BUSINESS AFFAIRS

Assistant Secretary.—Charles H. Rivkin, room 4932 / 4934, 647–7971.
Principal Deputy Assistant Secretary.—Kurt W. Tong, 647–9496.
Deputy Assistant Secretaries: William Craft, 647–5968; Thomas Engle, 647–4045.

UNDER SECRETARY FOR ARMS CONTROL AND INTERNATIONAL SECURITY

Under Secretary.—Rose E. Gottemoeller, room 7208, 647–1049.
Executive Assistant.—Maureen Tucker, 647–0302.

INTERNATIONAL SECURITY AND NONPROLIFERATION

Assistant Secretary.—Thomas Countryman, room 3932, 647–9612.
Principal Deputy Assistant Secretary.—Vann H. Van Diepen, room 3932, 647–5122.
Deputy Assistant Secretary.—Eliott Kang, room 3932, 647–5999.
Deputy Assistant Secretary for Nonproliferation Programs.—Simon Limage, 647–6977.

POLITICAL-MILITARY AFFAIRS

Assistant Secretary.—Puneet Talwar, room 6212, 647–9022.

Principal Deputy Assistant Secretary.—Todd Chapman, 647–9023.
Deputy Assistant Secretaries: Gregory Kausner (202) 736–4036; Samuel Perez, 647–9023.

ARMS CONTROL, VERIFICATION AND COMPLIANCE

Assistant Secretary.—Frank Rose, room 5950, 647–5315.
Principal Deputy Assistant Secretary.—Anita Friedt, 647–6830.
Deputy Assistant Secretaries: Greg Delawie, 647–5315; Mallory Stewart, 647–5315.

UNDER SECRETARY FOR PUBLIC DIPLOMACY AND PUBLIC AFFAIRS

Under Secretary.—Richard Stengel, room 5932, 647–9199.
Chief of Staff and Executive Assistant.—Susan Stevenson.

EDUCATIONAL AND CULTURAL AFFAIRS

Assistant Secretary.—Evan Ryan, 632–9940.
Principal Deputy Assistant Secretary.—Kelly Keiderling, 632–9444.
Deputy Assistant Secretaries: Meghann Curtis, 632–9327; Robin Lerner, 632–3206; Mara Tekach, 632–3346.

INTERNATIONAL INFORMATION PROGRAMS

Coordinator.—Macon Phillips, 632–9942.

PUBLIC AFFAIRS

Assistant Secretary.—Doug Frantz, room 6634, 647–6607.
Deputy Assistant Secretaries: David Duckenfield, Valerie Fowler.
Deputy Spokesman.—Marie Harf, 647–8406.

UNDER SECRETARY FOR MANAGEMENT

Under Secretary.—Patrick F. Kennedy, room 7207, 647–1500.
Executive Assistant.—Kathleen Austin-Ferguson, 647–1501.

ADMINISTRATION

Assistant Secretary.—Joyce Barr, room 6529 , 647–1492.
Deputy Assistant Secretaries: Catherine Ebert-Gray (703) 875–6956; Margaret Grafeld, 261–8300; Keith Miller, 647–3427.

CONSULAR AFFAIRS

Assistant Secretary.—Michelle Bond (acting), room 6826, 647–9576.
Principal Deputy Assistant Secretary.—Michelle Bond, 647–9576.
Deputy Assistant Secretaries: Karen Christensen, 647–9003; Edward Ramotowski, 647–9584; Brenda Sprague, 647–9584.

DIPLOMATIC SECURITY

Assistant Secretary.—Gregory Starr, room 6316, 647–6290.
Principal Deputy Assistant Secretary.—Bill Miller (571) 345–3815.
Deputy Assistant Secretaries: Doug Allison (571) 345–3492; Wayne Ashbery (571) 345–3836; John Eustace (571) 345–3785; Robert Hartung (571) 345–3809; Ricardo Colon (acting), (571) 226–9761; Christian Schurman (571) 345–3841.

DIRECTOR GENERAL OF THE FOREIGN SERVICE AND DIRECTOR OF HUMAN RESOURCES

Director General.—Arnold Chacon, room 6218, 647–9898.

Department of State

Principal Deputy Assistant Secretary.—Carol Perez, 647–5942.
Deputy Assistant Secretaries: Philippe Lussier, 647–5152; Linda Taglialatela, 647–5152; Bruce Williamson, 647–9438.

FOREIGN SERVICE INSTITUTE

Director.—Amb. Nancy McEldowney, room F2101 (703) 302–6703.
Deputy Director.—Marc Oestfield (703) 302–6707.

INFORMATION RESOURCE MANAGEMENT

Chief Information Officer.—Steven Taylor, 647–2889.
Chief Technology Officer of Operations.—Glen Johnson, 634–3683.
Chief Knowledge Officer of Business Management and Planning. Patricia Lacina, 634–3083.
Chief Information Security Officer of Information Assurance.—William Lay (703) 812–2339.

MEDICAL SERVICES

Medical Director.—Dr. Gary Penner, 663–1649.
Deputy Medical Director.—Dean Smith, 663–1641.

OVERSEAS BUILDINGS OPERATIONS

Director.—Lydia Munic (703) 875–7493.
Principal Deputy Director.—William Moser (703) 875–6361.
Executive Assistant.—John Pette (703) 875–5036.

UNDER SECRETARY OF STATE FOR CIVILIAN SECURITY, DEMOCRACY, AND HUMAN RIGHTS

Under Secretary.—Sarah Sewall, room 7261, 647–1189.
Executive Assistant.—Jessica LaPenn, 647–7818.

DEMOCRACY, HUMAN RIGHTS AND LABOR

Assistant Secretary.—Tomasz Malinowski, room 7827, 647–4604.
Principal Deputy Assistant Secretary.—Virginia Bennett, 647–3273.

OCEANS AND INTERNATIONAL ENVIRONMENTAL AND SCIENTIFIC AFFAIRS

Assistant Secretary.—Amb. Judith Garber (acting), room 3880, 647–6950.
Principal Deputy Assistant Secretary.—Anne Hall, 647–1554.
Deputy Assistant Secretaries: David A. Balton, 647–2396; Jonathan Margolis, 647–3584; Daniel Reifsnyder, 647–2232.

POPULATION, REFUGEES AND MIGRATION

Assistant Secretary.—Anne C. Richard, room 6825, 647–7360.
Principal Deputy Assistant Secretary.—Simon Henshaw, 647–5982.
Deputy Assistant Secretaries: Kelly Clements, 647–5822; Catherine Wiesner, 647–5822.

U.S. MISSION TO THE UNITED NATIONS

U.S. Permanent Representative.—Amb. Samantha Power, room 633 (212) 415–4404.
Deputy to the Ambassador.—Jeremy Weinstein.

OFFICE OF U.S. FOREIGN ASSISTANCE RESOURCES

Director.—Hari Sastry, room 5923, 647–2608.

Executive Assistant.—Lisa Greene, 647–3690.

UNITED STATES DIPLOMATIC OFFICES—FOREIGN SERVICE
(C = Consular Office, N = No Embassy or Consular Office)
http://usembassy.state.gov

LIST OF CHIEFS OF MISSION

AFGHANISTAN, ISLAMIC REPUBLIC
OF (Kabul).
Hon. P. Michael McKinley.
ALBANIA, REPUBLIC OF (Tirana).
Hon. Donald Lu.
ALGERIA, DEMOCRATIC AND
POPULAR REPUBLIC OF (Algiers).
Hon. Joan A. Polaschik.
ANDORRA (Andorra La Vella) (N)
Hon. James Costos (Also U.S.
Ambassador to Spain).
ANGOLA, REPUBLIC OF (Luanda).
Hon. Helen Meagher La Lime.
ARGENTINA (Buenos Aires).
Hon. Noah B. Mamet.
ARMENIA, REPUBLIC OF (Yerevan).
Hon. Richard M. Mills, Jr.
Association of Southeast Asian Nations
(Asean).
Hon. Nina Lucine Hachigian.
AUSTRALIA (Canberra).
Hon. Morrell John Berry.
AUSTRIA, REPUBLIC OF (Vienna).
Hon. Alexa Lange Wesner.
AZERBAIJAN, REPUBLIC OF (Baku).
Hon. Robert F. Cekuta.
BAHAMAS, THE COMMONWEALTH
OF THE (Nassau).
Vacant.
BAHRAIN, STATE OF (Manama).
Hon. William V. Roebuck.
BANGLADESH, PEOPLE'S REPUBLIC
OF (Dhaka).
Hon. Marcia Stephens Bloom Bernicat.
BARBADOS (Bridgetown).
Hon. Larry Leon Palmer.
BELARUS, REPUBLIC OF (Minsk).
Vacant.
BELGIUM (Brussels).
Hon. Denise Campbell Bauer.
BELIZE (Belmopan).
Hon. Carlos Roberto Moreno.
BENIN, REPUBLIC OF (Cotonou).
Hon. Michael Raynor.
BOLIVIA, REPUBLIC OF (La Paz).
Vacant.
BOSNIA—HERZEGOVINA (Sarajevo).
Hon. Maureen Cormack.
BOTSWANA, REPUBLIC OF
(Gaborone).
Hon. Earl Miller.
BRAZIL, FEDERATIVE REPUBLIC OF
(Brasilia).
Hon. Liliana Ayalde.
BRUNEI DARUSSALAM (Bandar Seri
Begawan).

Hon. Craig Allen.
BULGARIA, REPUBLIC OF (Sofia).
Hon. Marcie B. Ries.
BURKINA FASO (Ouagadougou).
Hon. Tulinabo Salama Mushingi.
BURMA, UNION OF (Rangoon).
Hon. Derek J. Mitchell.
BURUNDI, REPUBLIC OF (Bujumbura).
Hon. Dawn M. Liberi.
CABO VERDE.
Hon. Donald L. Heflin.
CAMBODIA, KINGDOM OF (Phnom
Penh).
Hon. William A. Heidt.
CAMEROON, REPUBLIC OF
(Yaounde).
Hon. Michael S. Hoza.
CANADA (Ottawa).
Hon. Bruce A. Heyman.
CENTRAL AFRICAN REPUBLIC
(Bangui).
Vacant.
CHAD, REPUBLIC OF (N'Djamena).
Hon. James Knight.
CHILE, REPUBLIC OF (Santiago).
Hon. Michael A. Hammer.
CHINA, PEOPLE'S REPUBLIC OF
(Beijing).
Hon. Max Sieben Baucus.
COLOMBIA, REPUBLIC OF (Bogota).
Hon. Kevin Whitaker.
COMOROS, UNION OF (Moroni) (N).
Hon. Robert T. Yamate (Also
Ambassador to the Republic of
Madagascar).
CONGO, DEMOCRATIC REPUBLIC
OF THE (Kinshasa).
Hon. James C. Swan.
CONGO, REPUBLIC OF THE
(Brazzaville).
Hon. Stephanie Sanders Sullivan.
COSTA RICA, REPUBLIC OF (San
Jose).
Hon. S. Fitzgerald Haney.
COTE D'IVOIRE, REPUBLIC OF
(Abidjan).
Hon. Terence Patrick McCulley.
CROATIA, REPUBLIC OF (Zagreb).
Hon. Kenneth Merten.
CUBA (Havana).
Hon. Jeffrey DeLaurentis.
CURACAO and ARUBA (Consul
General).
Hon. James R. Moore.
CYPRUS, REPUBLIC OF (Nicosia).
Vacant.

CZECH REPUBLIC (Prague).
Hon. Andrew H. Schapiro.
DENMARK (Copenhagen).
Hon. John Rufus Gifford.
DJIBOUTI, REPUBLIC OF (Djibouti).
Hon. Tom Kelly.
DOMINICAN REPUBLIC (Santo
Domingo).
Hon. James "Wally" Brewster, Jr.
ECUADOR, REPUBLIC OF (Quito).
Hon. Adam E. Namm.
EGYPT, ARAB REPUBLIC OF (Cairo).
Hon. R. Stephen Beecroft.
EL SALVADOR, REPUBLIC OF (San
Salvador).
Hon. Mari Carmen Aponte.
EQUATORIAL GUINEA, REPUBLIC
OF (Malabo) (N).
Hon. Mark L. Asquino.
ERITREA, STATE OF (Asmara).
Vacant.
ESTONIA.
Hon. Jeffrey D. Levine.
ETHIOPIA, FEDERAL DEMOCRATIC
REPUBLIC OF (Addis Ababa).
Hon. Patricia Marie Haslach.
European Union.
Hon. Anthony Luzzatto Gardner.
FIJI ISLANDS, REPUBLIC OF THE
(Suva).
Hon. Judith Beth Cefkin.
FINLAND, REPUBLIC OF (Helsinki).
Hon. Charles C. Adams, Jr.
FRANCE (Paris).
Hon. Jane T. Hartley.
GABONESE REPUBLIC (Libreville).
Hon. Cynthia Akuetteh (Also
Ambassador to the Democratic
Republic of Sao Tome and Principe).
GAMBIA, REPUBLIC OF THE (Banjul).
Hon. Marc London Shaw.
GEORGIA (Tbilisi).
Hon. Ian C. Kelly.
GERMANY, FEDERAL REPUBLIC OF
(Berlin).
Hon. John B. Emerson.
GHANA, REPUBLIC OF (Accra).
Hon. Gene Allan Cretz.
GREECE (Athens).
Hon. David D. Pearce.
GUATEMALA, REPUBLIC OF
(Guatemala).
Hon. Todd D. Robinson.
GUINEA, REPUBLIC OF (Conakry).
Hon. Alexander Mark Laskaris.
GUINEA-BISSAU, REPUBLIC OF
(Bissau) (N).
Hon. James P. Zumwalt (Also
Ambassador to the Republic of
Senegal).
GUYANA, CO-OPERATIVE REPUBLIC
OF (Georgetown).
Hon. Perry Holloway.
HAITI, REPUBLIC OF (Port-au-Prince).
Hon. Pamela A. White.
HOLY SEE (Vatican City).

Hon. Kenneth Francis Hackett.
HONDURAS, REPUBLIC OF
(Tegucigalpa).
Hon. James D. Nealon.
HONG KONG (Hong Kong) (C).
Hon. Stephen M. Young.
HUNGARY, REPUBLIC OF (Budapest).
Hon. Colleen Bradley Bell.
ICELAND, REPUBLIC OF (Reykjavik).
Hon. Robert Cushman Barber.
INDIA (New Delhi).
Hon. Richard R. Verma.
INDONESIA, REPUBLIC OF (Jakarta).
Hon. Robert O. Blake, Jr.
IRAN.
No Diplomatic Relations.
IRAQ, REPUBLIC OF (Baghdad).
Hon. Stuart E. Jones.
IRELAND (Dublin).
Hon. Kevin F. O'Malley.
ISRAEL, STATE OF (Tel Aviv).
Hon. Daniel Benjamin Shapiro.
ITALY (Rome).
Hon. John R. Phillips.
JAMAICA (Kingston).
Hon. Luis G. Moreno.
JAPAN (Tokyo).
Hon. Caroline Kennedy.
JERUSALEM (Consul General).
Hon. Donald Blome.
JORDAN, HASHEMITE KINGDOM OF
(Amman).
Hon. Alice G. Wells.
KAZAKHSTAN, REPUBLIC OF
(Almaty).
Hon. George A. Krol.
KENYA, REPUBLIC OF (Nairobi).
Hon. Robert F. Godec.
KOSOVO (Pristina).
Hon. Greg Delawie.
KUWAIT, STATE OF (Kuwait City).
Hon. Douglas A. Silliman.
KYRGYZ REPUBLIC (Bishkek).
Hon. Sheila Gwaltney.
LAO PEOPLE'S DEMOCRATIC
REPUBLIC (Vientiane).
Hon. Daniel A. Clune.
LATVIA, REPUBLIC OF (Riga).
Hon. Nancy Bikoff Pettit.
LEBANON, REPUBLIC OF (Beirut).
Hon. David Hale.
LESOTHO, KINGDOM OF (Maseru).
Hon. Matthew T. Harrington.
LIBERIA, REPUBLIC OF (Monrovia).
Hon. Deborah Ruth Malac.
LIBYA (Tripoli).
Hon. Deborah Kay Jones.
LIECHTENSTEIN, PRINCIPALITY OF
(Vaduz) (N).
Hon. Suzan G. LeVine (Also
Ambassador to the Swiss
Confederation).
LITHUANIA, REPUBLIC OF (Vilnius).
Hon. Deborah Ann McCarthy.
LUXEMBOURG, GRAND DUCHY OF
(Luxembourg).

Vacant.

MACEDONIA, REPUBLIC OF (Skopje).
Hon. Jess L. Baily.

MADAGASCAR, REPUBLIC OF
(Antananarivo).
Hon. Robert T. Yamate (Also
Ambassador to Union of Comoros).

MALAWI, REPUBLIC OF (Lilongwe).
Hon. Virginia E. Palmer.

MALAYSIA (Kuala Lumpur).
Hon. Joseph Y. Yun.

MALI, REPUBLIC OF (Bamako).
Hon. Paul A. Folmsbee.

MALTA, REPUBLIC OF (Valletta).
Hon. Gina K. Abercrombie-Winstanley.

MARSHALL ISLANDS, REPUBLIC OF
THE (Majuro).
Hon. Thomas Hart Armbruster.

MAURITANIA, ISLAMIC REPUBLIC
OF (Nouakchott).
Hon. Larry Andre, Jr.

MAURITIUS, REPUBLIC OF (Port
Louis).
Hon. Sharon English Woods Villarosa
(Also Ambassador to the Republic of
the Seychelles).

MEXICO (Mexico City).
Hon. Earl Anthony Wayne.

MICRONESIA, FEDERATED STATES
OF (Kolonia).
Hon. Dorothea-Maria Rosen.

MOLDOVA, REPUBLIC OF (Chisinau).
Hon. James D. Pettit.

MONACO (Monaco).
Hon. Jane T. Hartley (Also
Ambassador to the French Republic).
Hon. Douglas M. Griffiths.

MONGOLIA (Ulaanbaatar).
Hon. Piper Anne Wind Campbell.

MONTENEGRO, REPUBLIC OF
(Podgorica).
Hon. Margaret Ann Uyehara.

MOROCCO, KINGDOM OF (Rabat).
Hon. Dwight L. Bush, Sr.

MOZAMBIQUE, REPUBLIC OF
(Maputo).
Hon. Douglas M. Griffiths.

NAMIBIA, REPUBLIC OF (Windhoek).
Hon. Thomas F. Daughton.

NEPAL, KINGDOM OF (Kathmandu).
Hon. Peter William Bodde.

NETHERLANDS, KINGDOM OF THE
(The Hague).
Hon. Timothy M. Broas.

NEW ZEALAND (Wellington).
Hon. Mark Gilbert (Also Ambassador
to the State of Samoa).

NICARAGUA, REPUBLIC OF
(Managua).
Hon. Lara F. Dogu.

NIGER, REPUBLIC OF (Niamey).
Hon. Eunice S. Reddick.

NIGERIA, FEDERAL REPUBLIC OF
(Abuja).
Hon. James F. Entwistle.

North Atlantic Treaty Organization
(NATO).
Hon. Douglas Edward Lute.

North Korea.
No Diplomatic Relations.

NORWAY (Oslo).
Vacant.

OMAN, SULTANATE OF (Muscat).
Hon. Greta Christine Holtz.

Organization for Security and
Cooperation in Europe (OSCE)
Hon. Daniel Brooks Baer.

Organization of American States (OAS)
Hon. Carmen Lomellin.

PAKISTAN, ISLAMIC REPUBLIC OF
(Islamabad).
Hon. Richard G. Olson.

PALAU, REPUBLIC OF (Koror).
Hon. Amy J. Hyatt.

PANAMA, REPUBLIC OF (Panama).
Hon. Jonathan D. Farrar.

PAPUA NEW GUINEA (Port Moresby).
Hon. Walter E. North.

PARAGUAY, REPUBLIC OF
(Asuncion)
Hon. Leslie A. Bassett.

PERU, REPUBLIC OF (Lima).
Hon. Brian A. Nichols.

PHILIPPINES, REPUBLIC OF THE
(Manila).
Hon. Phillip S. Goldberg.

POLAND, REPUBLIC OF (Warsaw).
Hon. Paul W. Jones.

PORTUGAL, REPUBLIC OF (Lisbon).
Hon. Robert A. Sherman.

QATAR, STATE OF (Doha).
Hon. Dana Shell Smith.

ROMANIA (Bucharest).
Hon. Hans Klemm.

RUSSIAN FEDERATION (Moscow).
Hon. John F. Tefft.

RWANDA, REPUBLIC OF (Kigali).
Hon. Erica J. BarksRuggles.

SAN MARINO, REPUBLIC OF (San
Marino) (N).
Hon. John R. Phillips (Also
Ambassador to the Italian Republic).

SAO TOME AND PRINCIPE,
DEMOCRATIC REPUBLIC OF (Sao
Tome) (N).
Hon. Cynthia Akuetteh (Also
Ambassador to Gabonese Republic).

SAUDI ARABIA, KINGDOM OF
(Riyadh).
Hon. Joseph William Westphal.

SENEGAL, REPUBLIC OF (Dakar).
Hon. James P. Zumwalt (Also
Ambassador to the Republic of Guinea-
Bissau).

SERBIA (Belgrade)
Hon. Michael D. Kirby.

SEYCHELLES, REPUBLIC OF
(Victoria) (N).
Hon. Sharon English Woods Villarosa
(Also Ambassador to the Republic of
Mauritius).

SIERRA LEONE, REPUBLIC OF
(Freetown).
Hon. John Hoover.
SINGAPORE, REPUBLIC OF
(Singapore).
Hon. Kirk W.B. Wagar.
SLOVAK REPUBLIC (Bratislava).
Hon. Liam Wasley.
SLOVENIA, REPUBLIC OF (Ljubljana).
Hon. Mark W. Lippert.
SOLOMON ISLANDS (Honiara) (N).
Hon. Walter E. North (Also
Ambassador to Papua New Guinea and
Republic of Vanuatu).
SOMALIA.
Hon. U.S. Special Representative
James P. McAnulty.
SOUTH AFRICA, REPUBLIC OF
(Pretoria).
Hon. Patrick Hubert Gaspard.
SOUTH KOREA.
Hon. Mark W. Lippert.
SOUTH SUDAN, REPUBLIC OF (Juba).
Hon. Mary Catherine Phee.
SPAIN (Madrid).
Hon. James Costos (Also Ambassador
to the Principality of Andorra).
SRI LANKA, DEMOCRATIC
SOCIALIST REPUBLIC OF
(Colombo).
Hon. Atul Keshap (Also Ambassador
to the Republic of Maldives).
SUDAN, REPUBLIC OF THE
(Khartoum).
Vacant.
SURINAME, REPUBLIC OF
(Paramaribo).
Hon. Jay Nicholas Anania.
SWAZILAND, KINGDOM OF
(Mbabane).
Hon. Makila James.
SWEDEN (Stockholm).
Hon. Mark Francis Brzezinski.
SWITZERLAND (Bern).
Hon. Suzan G. LeVine (Also
Ambassador to the Principality of
Liechtenstein).
SYRIAN ARAB REPUBLIC (Damascus).
Hon. Michael Ratney, Special Envoy
for Syria.
TAJIKISTAN, REPUBLIC OF
(Dushanbe).
Hon. Susan Marsh Elliott.
TANZANIA, UNITED REPUBLIC OF
(Dar es Salaam).
Hon. Mark B. Childress.
THAILAND, KINGDOM OF (Bangkok).
Hon. Glyn T. Davies.
TIMOR.
Hon. Karen Stanton.
TOGO.

Hon. Robert E. Whitehead.
TRINIDAD AND TOBAGO, REPUBLIC
OF (Port of Spain).
Vacant.
TUNISIA, REPUBLIC OF (Tunis).
Hon. Jacob Walles.
TURKEY, REPUBLIC OF (Ankara).
Hon. John R. Bass.
TURKMENISTAN (Ashgabat).
Hon. Allan Phillip Mustard.
U.S. Mission to UNESCO.
Hon. Crystal Nix-Hines.
U.S. MISSION TO THE AFRICAN
UNION (AU).
Hon. Michael A. Battle, Sr.
UGANDA, REPUBLIC OF (Kampala).
Hon. Scott H. DeLisi.
UKRAINE (Kyiv).
Hon. Geoffrey R. Pyatt.
UNITED ARAB EMIRATES (Abu
Dhabi).
Hon. Barbara A. Leaf.
UNITED KINGDOM OF GREAT
BRITAIN AND NORTHERN
IRELAND (London).
Hon. Matthew Winthrop Barzun.
UNITED NATIONS HUMAN RIGHTS
COUNCIL.
Hon. Keith M. Harper.
UNITED NATIONS IN GENEVA.
Hon. Pamela Hamamoto.
UNITED NATIONS IN ROME.
Hon. David J. Lane.
UNITED NATIONS IN VIENNA
Vacant (Also International Atomic Energy
Agency (IAEA)).
UNITED NATIONS.
Hon. Samantha Power.
URUGUAY, ORIENTAL REPUBLIC OF
(Montevideo).
Hon. Julissa Reynoso.
UZBEKISTAN, REPUBLIC OF
(Tashkent).
Hon. Pamela L. Spratlen.
VANUATU, REPUBLIC OF (Port Vila)
(N).
Hon. Walter E. North (Also
Ambassasdor to Solomon Islands and
Papua New Guinea).
VENEZUELA, BOLIVARIAN
REPUBLIC OF (Caracas).
Vacant.
VIETNAM, SOCIALIST REPUBLIC OF
(Hanoi).
Hon. Ted Osius III.
YEMEN, REPUBLIC OF (Sanaa).
Hon. Matthew H. Tueller.
ZAMBIA, REPUBLIC OF (Lusaka).
Hon. Eric T. Schultz.
ZIMBABWE, REPUBLIC OF (Harare).
Hon. David Bruce Wharton.

UNITED STATES PERMANENT DIPLOMATIC MISSIONS
TO INTERNATIONAL ORGANIZATIONS

ASSOCIATION OF SOUTHEAST
ASIAN NATIONS (Jakarta).
Hon. Nina Lucine Hachigian.
AFRICAN UNION (Addis Ababa).
Hon. Earl Reuban Brigety II.
EUROPEAN UNION (Brussels).
Anthony Luzzatto Gardner.
NORTH ATLANTIC TREATY
ORGANIZATION (Brussels).
Hon. Douglas E. Llute.
ORGANIZATION FOR
ECONOMIC COOPERATION
AND DEVELOPMENT (Paris).
Daniel W. Yohannes.

ORGANIZATION FOR SECURITY AND
COOPERATION IN EUROPE (Vienna).
Hon. Daniel Bear.
ORGANIZATION OF AMERICAN
STATES (Washington, DC).
Hon. Carmen Lomellin.
UNITED NATIONS (Geneva).
Hon. Betty E. King.
UNITED NATIONS (New York).
Hon. Samantha Power.
UNITED NATIONS (Vienna).
Hon. Joseph E. Macmanus.

DEPARTMENT OF THE TREASURY

1500 Pennsylvania Avenue, NW., 20220, phone (202) 622–2000, http://www.ustreas.gov

JACOB J. LEW, Secretary of the Treasury; born in New York, NY, August 29, 1955; education: A.B., Harvard College, 1978; J.D., Georgetown University Law Center, 1983; professional: Deputy Director of Program Analysis, Office of Management and Budget, City of Boston, 1978–79; Deputy Director, U.S. House Democratic Steering and Policy Committee, 1979–85; Executive Director, U.S. House Democratic Steering and Policy Committee, 1985–87; Of Counsel, Van Ness, Feldman and Curtiss, 1987; Partner, Van Ness, Feldman and Curtiss, 1988–91; Campaign '88 Issues Director, Democratic National Committee, 1988; Executive Director, Center for Middle East Research, 1992–93; Special Assistant to the President, White House, 1993–94; Associate Director, Office of Management and Budget, 1994; Executive Associate Director, Office of Management and Budget, 1995; Deputy Director, Office of Management and Budget, 1995–98; Director, Office of Management and Budget, 1998–2001; Research Professor, Georgetown University Public Policy Institute, 2001; Executive Vice President and Clinical Professor of Public Policy, New York University, 2001–06; Managing Director and Chief Operating Officer of Global Wealth Management Division, Citigroup, 2006–07; Managing Director and Chief Operating Officer of Citi Alternative Investments Division, Citigroup, 2008–09; Deputy Secretary of State for Management and Resources, 2009–10; Director, Office of Management and Budget, 2010–12; White House Chief of Staff, 2012–13; married: Ruth; children: Shoshana and Isaac; nominated by President Barack Obama to become the 76th Secretary of the Treasury and confirmed by the U.S. Senate on February 27, 2013.

OFFICE OF THE SECRETARY

Secretary of the Treasury.—Jacob J. Lew, room 3330, 622–1100.
  Executive Assistant.—Shirley E. Gathers, 622–1100.
  Confidential Assistant.—Cheryl L. Matera, 622–1100.

OFFICE OF THE DEPUTY SECRETARY

Deputy Secretary.—Sarah Bloom Raskin, room 3326, 622–1080.
  Executive Assistants: Pat Griffin, room 3326, 622–7588; Justina Williamson, room 3326, 622–5607.

OFFICE OF THE CHIEF OF STAFF

Chief of Staff. Christian A. Weideman, room 3408, 622 1906.
  Deputy Chief of Staff.—Adewale Adeyemo, room 3410, 622–1906.
  Executive Secretary.—David G. Clunie, room 3414, 622–1967.
  White House Liaison.—Margaret Buford, room 3420, 622–3431.
  Review Analyst.—Anita Maria Hunt, room 3408, 622–0502.

OFFICE OF THE GENERAL COUNSEL

General Counsel.—Christopher Meade, room 3000 (202) 622–0283.
  Deputy General Counsels: Priya Aiyar, 622–1135; Roberto Gonzalez, 622–0283.
  Staff Assistants: Aloma A. Shaw, Kim Wilson, 622–0283.
  Senior Advisor to the General Counsel.—Vacant, room 3006.
  Assistant General Counsel for Banking and Finance.—Peter Bieger, room 2304, 622–1975.
  Deputy Assistant General Counsel for Banking and Finance.—Steve Laughton, room 2001, 622–8413.
  Banking and Finance (FSOC).—Eric Froman, room 3023, 622–1942.
  Assistant General Counsel for Enforcement and Intelligence.—Trisha Anderson, room 3014, 622–1143.

Deputy Assistant General Counsel for Enforcement and Intelligence.—Paul Ahern, room 3020, 622–3108.
Assistant General Counsel for General Law, Ethics and Regulation.—Rochelle Granat, room 2312, 622–6052.
Deputy Assistant General Counsel for General Law, Ethics and Regulation.—Brian Sonfield, room 2020, 622–9804.
Deputy Assistant General Counsel for General Law, Ethics and Regulation (Ethics).—Elizabeth "Beth" Horton, room 2221, 622–9794.
Assistant General Counsel for International Affairs.—Himamauli "Him" Das, room 2308, 622–1147.
Deputy Assistant General Counsel for International Affairs.—Jeffrey Klein, room 2306, 622–2122.
Chief Counsel, Foreign Assets Control.—Bradley Smith, Annex 3123, 622–6922.
Deputy Chief Counsel.—Matthew Tuchband, Annex 3121, 622–1654.

OFFICE OF THE INSPECTOR GENERAL

Inspector General.—Eric Thorson, room 4436 (202) 622–1090.
  Deputy Inspector General.—Vacant.
  Special Deputy Inspector General for SBLF.—Lisa Carter (acting), room 4436 (202) 927–6236.
  Counsel to the Inspector General.—Richard Delmar, suite 510, 927–0650.
  Assistant Inspector General for—
    Audit.—Marla Freedman, suite 600, 927–5400.
    Investigations.—John L. Phillips, 1425 New York Avenue, NW., suite 500, 927–5260.
    Management Services.—Patricia Hollis, suite 510, 927–5200.
  Deputy Assistant Inspector General for—
    Audit.—Robert Taylor, suite 600, 927–5400.
    Investigations (Senior Advisor).—Jason Metrick, 927–5260.
    Management.—Jeffrey Lawrence, suite 510, 927–5356.

OFFICE OF THE UNDER SECRETARY FOR DOMESTIC FINANCE

Under Secretary.—Vacant (202) 622–1703.

OFFICE OF THE ASSISTANT SECRETARY FOR FINANCIAL INSTITUTIONS

Assistant Secretary.—Amias Gerety (acting), (202) 622–2610.
  Deputy Assistant Secretary, Office of:
    Consumer Policy.—Melissa Koide.
    Financial Institutions Policy.—Anjan Mukherjee.
    Small Business, Community Development, and Housing Policy.—Jessica Milano.
  Director, Office of:
    Critical Infrastructure Protection and Compliance Policy.—Brian Peretti.
    Federal Insurance Office.—Michael McRaith.
    Financial Institutions Policy.—Patricia Kao.
    Financial Security (and Financial Education).—Louisa Quittman.
  Deputy Director, Financial Institutions Policy.—Moses Kim.
  Community Development Financial Institutions Fund.—Annie Donovan.
  Small Business, Community Development, and Housing Policy.—Vacant.
  Small Business Lending Fund.—Sally Phillips.
  State Small Business Credit Initiative.—Jeffrey Stout.
  Terrorism Risk Insurance Program.—Vacant.

OFFICE OF THE ASSISTANT SECRETARY FOR FINANCIAL MARKETS

Assistant Secretary.—Seth Carpenter (acting), (202) 622–1660.
  Deputy Assistant Secretary, Office of:
    Capital Markets.—Monique Rollins.
    Federal Finance.—James Clark.
    Public Finance.—Gary Grippo.
  Director, Office of:
    Capital Markets.—Jake Liebschutz.
    Debt Management.—Fred Pietrangeli.
    Federal Lending.—Gary Burner.

Federal Program Finance.—Vacant.
State Housing Finance Agency Initiative.—Preston Atkins.
State and Local Finance.—Kent Hiteshew.

OFFICE OF THE FISCAL ASSISTANT SECRETARY

Assistant Secretary.—Dave Lebryk (202) 622–0560.
 Deputy Assistant Secretary, Office of:
  Accounting Policy and Financial Transparency.—Christina Ho.
  Fiscal Operations and Policy.—Kristine Conrath.
 Director, Office of:
  Financial Agents.—Vacant.
  Fiscal Projections.—David Monroe.
  Grants and Asset Management.—Ted Kowalsky.
  Gulf Coast Restoration.—Laurie McGilvray.
  Housing and Energy.—Ellen Neubauer.

OFFICE OF THE ASSISTANT SECRETARY FOR FINANCIAL STABILITY

Assistant Secretary.—Vacant (202) 622–0897.
 Deputy Assistant Secretary.—Mark McArdle.
 Chief of Staff.—Carole Florman.
 Chief:
  Compliance Officer.—Joyce Philip.
  Counsel.—John Sturc.
  Finance and Operations Officer.—Lorenzo Rasetti.
  Homeownership Preservation Officer.—Danielle Johnson-Kutch (acting).
  Investment Officer.—Trevor Montano.

FINANCIAL STABILITY OVERSIGHT COUNCIL

Deputy Assistant Secretary.—Patrick Pinschmidt.
 Independent Member With Insurance Expertise.—Roy Woodall.

FINANCIAL MANAGEMENT SERVICE
401 14th Street, SW., 20227, phone (202) 874–6740, fax 874–7016

Commissioner.—David A. Lebryk.
 Deputy Commissioner.—Wanda Rogers.
 Assistant Commissioner for—
  Debt Management Services.—Jeffrey Schramek.
  Enterprise Business Information Security and Services (EBISS).—Kim McCoy.
  Federal Finance.—Kristine Conrath.
  Government-wide Accounting.—Christina Ho.
  Management (Chief Financial Officer).—Marty Greiner.
  Payments Management.—John Hill.
 Chief Counsel.—Margaret Marquette.
 Director for Legislative and Public Affairs.—Joyce Harris.

BUREAU OF THE FISCAL SERVICE
401 14th Street, SW., 20227, phone (202) 874–7000, fax (202) 874–6743
[Codified under U.S.C. 31, section 306]

Commissioner.—Sheryl Morrow (202) 874–7000.
 Chief Counsel.—Margaret Marquette (202) 874–6680.
 Deputy Commissioner/Finance and Administration.—Kim McCoy (202) 504–3500.
 Deputy Commissioner/Financial Services and Operations.—Wanda Rogers (202) 874–7000.
 Deputy Commissioner/Accounting and Shared Services.—Cynthia Springer (304) 480–7888.
 Executive Director for Government Securities Regulations Staff.—Lori Santamorena (202) 504–3632.
 Assistant Commissioner, Office of:
  Administrative Services.—Doug Anderson (304) 480–8760.
  CIO/Information and Security Services.—Steve Manning (202) 874–8000.

CFO/Management.—Marty Greiner (202) 874–7100.
Debt Management.—Jeff Schramek (205) 912–6112.
Financing.—Dara Seaman (202) 504–3550.
Government-Wide Accounting.—Kristine Chadwick (202) 874–8010.
Payment Management.—John Hill (202) 874–6790.
Public Debt Accounting.—Matthew Miller (304) 480–5101.
Retail Securities.—Dara Seaman (202) 504–3550.
Revenue Collections Management.—Corvelli McDaniel (202) 874–6720.
Director, Office of Legislative and Public Affairs.—Joyce Harris (202) 874–6760.

OFFICE OF THE UNDER SECRETARY FOR INTERNATIONAL AFFAIRS

Under Secretary.—D. Nathan Sheets, room 3436 MT (202) 622–1270.
Deputy Assistant Secretary for International Economics Analysis.—Bradley Setser, room 4464 MT, 662–1191.
Senior Advisors: Eric Woodhouse, room 3217, 622–1545; Carl Westphal, room 3432A MT, 622–0907.
Senior Advisor and Director, IA Business Operations.—Gordon McDonald, room 3224 MT; 662–6427.
Staff Assistant.—Karen DeLaBarre Chase, room 3432B, 622–0060.
Executive Secretary and Senior Coordinator for China and the Strategic and Economic Dialogue.—Christopher Adams, room 3209 MT, 622–6883.

OFFICE OF THE ASSISTANT SECRETARY FOR INTERNATIONAL AFFAIRS

Assistant Secretary for International Finance.—Ramin Toloui, room 4138A MT, 622–0656.
Deputy Assistant Secretary for—
  Africa and the Middle East.—Andy Baukol, room 3218A MT, 622–2159.
  Asian Nations.—Robert Dohner, room 3218B MT, 622–7222.
  Europe and Eurasia.—Daleep Singh, room 3213 MT, 622–3638.
  Western Hemisphere.—Michael Kaplan, room 3037 MT, 622–4262.
Senior Advisor.—Mary Svenstrup, room 4138C MT, 622–1151.
Staff Assistant.—Andres Chong-Qui, room 4138B MT, 622–5696.
Assistant Secretary for International Markets and Developments.—Marisa Lago, room 3428 MT, 622–0200.
Deputy Assistant Secretary for—
  Afghanistan and Technical Assistance Policy.—W. Larry McDonald, room 3037 MT, 622–5504.
  Environment and Energy.—Leonardo Martinez, room 3037 MT, 622–0173.
  International Development Policy.—Alexia Latortue, room 3204A MT, 622–8125.
  International Monetary and Financial Policy.—Mark Sobel, room 3034 MT, 622–0168.
  Investment Security.—Aimen Mir (acting), room 3203 MT, 622–0478.
  Trade and Investment Policy.—Himamauli Das (acting), room 2308 MT, 622–1147.
Senior Advisor.—Mary "Molly" Brennan, room 3041B MT, 622–1172.
Staff Assistant.—Kimberly Richards, room 3430B MT, 622–4826.
Director for International Affairs:
(part of South and Southeast Asia)
  Africa (INN).—Eric Meyer, room 1064C MT, 622–2156 .
  Development Results and Accountability (IDR).—Daniel Peters, room 5406A MT, 622–5280.
  East Asia (ISA).—Robert Kaproth, room 4462 MT, 622–0132.
  Environment and Energy Policy.—C. Alex Severens, room 1024B MT, 622–2956.
  Europe and Eurasia (ICN).—Evangelia "Lea" Bouzis, room 4138D MT, 622–9190; Matthew Malloy, room 4128B MT, 622–5795.
  Global Economics Group (IMG).—John Weeks, room 5428 MT, 622–9885.
  International Banking and Securities Markets (IMB).—Susan Baker, room 5310 MT, 622–1025.
  International Debt Policy (IDD).—John Hurley, room 5417B MT, 622–9124.
  International Monetary Policy (IMP).—Patricia Pollard, room 5326 MT, 622–0439.
  Investment Security (IFI).—Stephen Hanson, room 5211A MT, 622–0184.
  Markets Room (IMR).—John Fagan, room 1328G MT, 622–1746.
  Middle East and North Africa (INM).—Elizabeth Shortino, room 5008 MT, 622–9142.
  South and Southeast Asia (ISS).—Seth Bleiweis, room 4440M MT, 622–4262.
  Technical Assistance.—Jason Orlando (acting), 740 15th Street, NW., 622–5792.
  Trade Finance and Investment Negotiations (ITF).—Anthony Ieronimo, room 5419J MT, 622–1747.

Western Hemisphere (IWH).—Matthew Mohlenkamp, room 1446A MT, 622–1246.

U.S. BANKS

U.S. Executive Director of:
Inter-American Development Bank.—Vacant (202) 623–1075.
International Monetary Fund.—Matthew Haarsager (acting), 623–7760.
World Bank.—Vacant, 458–0115.

OVERSEAS

U.S. Executive Director of:
African Development Bank and Fund (Cote d'Ivoire).—Vacant, 011–216–71–102–010.
Asian Development Bank (Manila, Philippines).—Robert M. "Skipp" Orr, 011–632–632–6050.
European Bank for Reconstruction and Development (London, England).—Luyen Tran, Alternate USED, 011–44–20–7338–6420.

UNDER SECRETARY FOR TERRORISM AND FINANCIAL INTELLIGENCE

Under Secretary.—Adam J. Szubin (acting), MT room 4326 (202) 622–8260.

ASSISTANT SECRETARY FOR TERRORIST FINANCING

Assistant Secretary.—Daniel L. Glaser, room 4316, MT 622–1943.
Deputy Assistant Secretary for Terrorist Financing and Financial Crimes.—Jennifer Fowler (acting), MT room 4000, 622–1634.
Director, Office of:
Global Affairs.—Colleen Stack, MT room 4001, 622–3447.
Strategic Policy.—Chip Poncy, MT room 4308, 622–9761.

ASSISTANT SECRETARY FOR INTELLIGENCE AND ANALYSIS

Assistant Secretary.—S. Leslie Ireland, room 4332 (202) 622–1835.
Deputy Assistant Secretary.—A. Daniel McGlynn, room 2441, 622–1841.
Deputy Assistant Secretary for Security.—Charles Cavella, room 2523, 622–2585.
Director, Emergency Programs.—Michael Thomas, room 1020, 622–2195.

OFFICE OF FOREIGN ASSETS CONTROL

Director.—Adam J. Szubin, room 2240 (202) 622–2510.

EXECUTIVE OFFICE FOR ASSET FORFEITURE

1341 G Street, NW., Suite 900, 20005, phone (202) 622–9600

Director.—Eric E. Hampl.

FINANCIAL CRIMES ENFORCEMENT NETWORK (FINCEN)

P.O. Box 39, Vienna, VA 22183, phone (703) 905–3591

Director.—Jennifer Shasky Calvery (202) 354–6393.
Deputy Director.—Frederick Reynolds (202) 354–6392.

OFFICE OF THE ASSISTANT SECRETARY FOR ECONOMIC POLICY

Assistant Secretary.—Karen Dynan, room 3454 (202) 622–2200.
Senior Advisor to the Assistant Secretary.—Gauri Subramani, room 3127, 622–2020.
Deputy Assistant Secretary for Policy Coordination.—Elaine Buckberg, room 3449, 622–2220.
Deputy Assistant Secretary for Macroeconomic Analysis.—Gerald Cohen, room 3450, 622–2734.

Director, Office of Macroeconomic Analysis.—Rachel Cononi, room 2454, 622–0156.
Deputy Assistant Secretary for Microeconomic Analysis.—Jennifer Hunt, room 3445, 622–1513.
Director, Office of Microeconomic Analysis.—Jason Brown, room 4426, 622–1757.

OFFICE OF THE ASSISTANT SECRETARY FOR LEGISLATIVE AFFAIRS

Assistant Secretary for Legislative Affairs.—Randall DeValk (acting), room 3134, 622–1900.
Senior Advisor.—Patrick Maloney, room 3464, 622–1900.
  Special Assistant.—Jackson Spivey, room 3134, 622–1900.
  Administrative Specialist.—Linda L. Powell, room 3453–D, 622–0535.
  Legislative Research Analyst.—Gail Harris-Berry, room 3453–C, 622–4401.
Deputy Assistant Secretary (Banking and Finance).—Glen Sears, 3124–B, 622–1900.
  Special Assistant.—Faiza Khan, room 3128–B, 622–1900.
Deputy Assistant Secretary (Appropriations and Management).—Lisa L. Pena, room 3462, 622–1900.
Deputy Assistant Secretary (Tax and Budget).—Sandra Salstrom, room 3132, 622–1900.
  Special Assistant.—AJ Bhadelia, room 3128–D, 622–1900.
Deputy Assistant Secretary (International).—Patrick Grant, room 3127, 622–1900.
  Special Assistant.—Eric Love, room 3128–A, 622–1900.
Deputy Assistant Secretary (TFI).—Luke Ballman, room 3124–C, 622–1900.
  Special Assistant.—J. Drew Colbert, room 3128–C, 622–1900.

OFFICE OF THE ASSISTANT SECRETARY FOR MANAGEMENT/CHIEF FINANCIAL OFFICER

Assistant Secretary for Management.—Brodi Fontenot, room 2438, Main Treasury (202) 622–0410.
  Special Assistant.—Taylor O'Brien, 622–3450.
Senior Advisors: Mike Lewis, 622–3068; Kody Kinsley, 927–5639.
Deputy Assistant Secretary for Management and Budget.—Vacant.
Departmental Budget Director.—Robert Mahaffie, 622–1471.
Conference Events and Meeting Services.—Lucinda Gooch, room 1128, 622–2071.
Strategic Planning and Performance Improvement.—Katie Malague, 622–5515.
Director of the Office of Financial Management.—Saesha Carlile (acting), 622–8841.
Director of Departmental Offices Operations.—Dan Cain (acting), 622–0074.
  Environmental Safety and Health.—Vacant.
  Facilities Management.—Polly Dietz, room 1155, 622–7067.
Deputy Assistant Secretary for Information Systems and Chief Information Officer.—Sonny Bhagowalia, 927–0777.
Deputy Assistant Secretary for Human Resources and Chief Human Capital Officer.—Anita Blair, 1801 L Street, NW., 927–0341.
  Equal Opportunity and Diversity.—Mariam Harvey, 1801 L Street, NW., 622–1160.
Deputy Assistant Secretary for Privacy, Transparency and Records.—Helen Foster, 622–2477.
Deputy Chief Financial Officer.—Dorrice Roth, 622–1693.
Director of Accounting and Internal Control.—Carole Banks, room 6263, 927–5281.
Senior Procurement Executive.—Iris Cooper, 622–1039.
Accounting Officer.—David Legge, room 6070, Met Square, 622–1167.
Director, Office of:
  Emergency Programs.—Mike Thomas, 622–2195.
  Minority and Women Inclusion.—Lorraine Cole, 927–8181.

OFFICE OF THE ASSISTANT SECRETARY FOR PUBLIC AFFAIRS

Assistant Secretary.—Vacant, room 3438 MT (202) 622–2910.
  Deputy Assistant Secretary, Public Affairs.—Victoria Esser, room 3439 MT, 622–2910.
  Deputy Assistant Secretary, Public Affairs.—Vacant.
Senior Advisor, Public Affairs.—Casey Hernandez, room 2126 MT, 622–2307.
Deputy Assistant Secretary/Public Liaison.—Blair Reinarman, room 3108 MT, 622–9760.
Review Analyst and Scheduling Coordinator.—Carmen Alvarado, room 3442 MT, 622–7483.
Spokesperson for Domestic Finance.—Suzanne Elio, room 2124 MT, 622–2960.
Enforcement Specialist.—Hagar Chemali, room 2124 MT, 622–2960.

International Affairs.—Vacant.
MHA & HHF.—Maya Newman, 1801 L Street, room 817 MT, 927–7280.
OFS.—Adam Hodge, room 2124 MT, 622–2960.
Tax, Budget, Economic Policy.—Erin Donar, room 2124 MT, 622–2960.
Speechwriter to the Secretary.—Mark Cohen, room 3111 MT, 622–5176.
Media Coordinator.—Vacant.
Media Affairs Specialists: Betsy Bourassa, Dan Cruz, room 2124 MT, 622–2960.
Senior Advisor (Public Liaison).—Antonio White, room 3111 MT, 622–9760.
Special Assistant.—Sarah Logan, room 3111, 622–1131.
Press Assistant.—Stephanie Ma, room 2124 MT, 622–2960.

OFFICE OF THE ASSISTANT SECRETARY FOR TAX POLICY

Assistant Secretary.—Mark J. Mazur, room 3120 MT (202) 622–0050.
Deputy Assistant Secretary for—
  International Tax Affairs.—Robert Stack, room 3045 MT, 622–1317.
  Tax Analysis.—Adam Looney, room 3064 MT, 622–0992.
  Tax Policy.—Emily McMahon, room 3112 MT, 622–0140.
  Tax, Trade and Tariff Policy.—Timothy Skud, room 3104 MT, 622–0220.
  Retirement and Health Policy and Senior Advisor to the Secretary.—J. Mark Iwry, room 3063 MT, 622–7827.
Tax Legislative Counsel.—Thomas West, room 3040 MT, 622–6707.
Deputy Tax Legislative Counsels.—Vacant, room 4202 MT, 622–1335.
International Tax Counsel.—Danielle Rolfes, room 3045 MT, 622–0843.
Deputy International Tax Counsels: Henry Louis, room 5064 MT, 622–1791; Douglas Poms, room 5104C MT, 622–1754.
Benefits Tax Counsel.—George Bostick, room 3050 MT, 622–1341.
Deputy Benefits Tax Counsel.—Robert Neis, room 4224 MT, 622–5293.
Director, Office of Tax Analysis.—James Mackie, room 4116 MT, 622–1326.
Director, Division of:
  Business and International Taxation.—Vacant, room 4221 MT, 622–1782.
  Economic Modeling and Computer Applications.—Robert Gillette, room 4039 MT, 622–0852.
  Individual Taxation.—Janet McCubbin, room 4043 MT, 622–0589.
  Revenue and Receipts Forecasting/Business Revenue Division.—Curtis Carlson, room 4112 MT, 622–0130.
  Revenue and Receipts Forecasting/Individual Revenue Division.—Scott Jaquette, room 4064 MT, 622–1319.

BUREAU OF ENGRAVING AND PRINTING
14th and C Streets, SW., 20228, phone (202) 874–2000

[Created by act of July 11, 1862; codified under U.S.C. 31, section 303]

Director.—Leonard R. Olijar (acting), 874–2016.
  Deputy Director.—Leonard R. Olijar, 874–2016.
  Chief Counsel.—Sidney Rocke, 874–2306.
Associate Directors:
  Chief Financial Officer.—Debra Richardson, 874–2020.
  Chief Technology Officer.—Mike Wash, 874–2030.
  Management and Chief Information Officer.—Will Levy III, 874–2040.
  Manufacturing.—Charlene Williams (817) 847–3802.
  Quality.—Vic Henry, 874–3909.

OFFICE OF THE COMPTROLLER OF THE CURRENCY
400 7th Street, SW., 20219, phone (202) 649–6800

Comptroller.—Thomas Curry (202) 649–6400.
  Chief of Staff and Public Affairs.—Paul Nash, 649–6480.
  Senior Deputy Comptroller and Chief Counsel.—Amy Friend, 649–5276.
  Senior Deputy Comptrollers for—
    Bank Supervision Policy and Chief National Bank Examiner.—Jennifer Kelly, 649–6770.
    Economics.—David Nebhut, 649–5472.
    Large Bank Supervision.—Marty Pfingraff, 649–6395.

Management and Chief Financial Officer.—Kathy Murphy, 649–6993.
Midsize and Community Bank Supervision.—Toney Bland, 649–5420.
Director for Congressional Liaison.—Carrie Moore, 649–6737.
Senior Deputy Comptroller EG and Ombudsman.—Larry Hattix, 649–6857.
Chief Information Officer.—James Decoster (acting), 649–8661.

INTERNAL REVENUE SERVICE
1111 Constitution Avenue, NW., 20224, phone (202) 622–5000
[Created by act of July 1, 1862; codified under U.S.C. 26, section 7802]

Commissioner.—John Koskinen, 317–7070.
Chief of Staff.—Crystal Philcox, 317–7070.
Deputy Commissioner, Services and Enforcement.—John Dalrymple, 317–4263.
Commissioner of:
  Large Business and International Division.—Heather Maloy, 515–4400.
  Small Business/Self-Employed.—Karen Schiller, 317–6500.
  Tax Exempt and Government Entities.—Sunita Lough, 317–8400.
  Wage and Investment.—Debra Holland, 317–7060.
Chief, Criminal Investigation.—Richard Weber, 317–3200.
Directors:
  Office of Professional Responsibility.—Karen Hawkins, 317–4676.
  Whistleblower Office.—Steve Whitlock, 317–3500.
Deputy Commissioner, Operations Support.—Stuart Burns (acting), 317–3950.
Chief:
  Agency-Wide Shared Services.—Stuart Burns, 317–7500.
  Appeals.—Kirsten Wielobob, 317–8975.
  Communications and Liaison.—Terry Lemons, 317–6849.
  Equity, Diversity and Inclusion.—Monica Davy, 317–5400.
  Financial Officer.—Robin Canady, 317–6400.
  IRS Human Capital Officer.—Daniel Riordan, 317–7600.
  Office of Privacy, Information Protection and Data Security.—Mary Howard, 317–6449.
  Technology Officer.—Terence Milholland, 317–5000.
Chief Counsel.—William J. Wilkins, 317–3300.
National Taxpayer Advocate.—Nina E. Olson, 317–6100.
Director, Office of Research, Analysis and Statistics.—Rosemary Marcuss, 803–9700.
Office of Legislative Affairs.—Leonard Oursler, 317–4316.

INSPECTOR GENERAL FOR TAX ADMINISTRATION (TIGTA)
1401 H Street, NW., Suite 469, 20005
phone (202) 622–6500, fax 927–0001

Inspector General.—J. Russell George.
Principal Deputy Inspector General.—Michael R. Phillips (acting), 927–7085.
Congressional Liaison.—Matthew S. Sutphen, 927–7266.
Chief Counsel.—Gladys M. Hernandez, 622–3103.
Deputy Inspector General for Audit.—Michael E. McKenney, 622–5916.
Assistant Inspector General for Compliance and Enforcement Operations.—Matthew A. Weir, 622–3837.
Management Planning and Workforce Development.—Nancy A. LaManna (acting), 927–7076.
Management Services and Organizations.—Greg D. Kutz, 622–5089.
Returns Processing and Accounts Services.—Russ Martin (acting), (978) 809–0296.
Security and Information Technology.—Alan R. Duncan, 622–5894.
Deputy Inspector General for Investigations.—Timothy P. Camus, 927–7160.
Assistant Inspectors General for Investigations (HQ Ops).—Michael A. Delgado, 927–7183.
Assistant Inspectors General for Investigations (Field Ops).—Randy M. Silvis, 927–0150.
Deputy Assistant Inspectors General for Investigations: Gayle A. Hatheway, 927–7178; James S. Jackson, 927–0029.
Deputy Inspector General for Inspections and Evaluations.—Greg D. Kutz (acting), 927–7048.
Associate Inspector General for Mission Support.—Mervin Hyndman (acting), 622–7586.

OFFICE OF THE TREASURER OF THE UNITED STATES

Treasurer.—Rosie Rios (202) 622–0100.

Senior Advisor.—Kristin Ward.
Executive Assistant.—Cheryl Ashton (detail).
Director, Advanced Counterfeit Deterrence.—Vacant.

UNITED STATES MINT

801 9th Street, NW., 20002, phone (202) 354–7200, fax 756–6160

Principal Director.—M. Rhett Jeppson (202) 354–7200.
  Executive Assistant to the Director.—Arnetta Cain, 354–7200.
Deputy Director.—Richard Peterson, 354–7200.
  Executive Assistant to the Deputy Director.—Judy Dixon, 354–7200.
Chief Administrative Officer.—Beverly Ortega Babers, 354–7200.
Chief Counsel.—Jean A. Gentry (acting), 354–7200.
Director, Legislative and Intergovernmental Affairs.—William Norton, 354–6700.
Director, Public Affairs.—Tom Jurkowsky, 354–7720.
Associate Director for Protection.—Dennis O'Connor, 354–7300.
  Deputy Associate Director.—Bill R. Bailey, 354–7300.
Associate Director/Chief Information Officer.—Lauren Buschor, 354–7700.
  Deputy Associate Director.—DeAnna Wynn, 354–7700.
Associate Director/Chief Financial Officer.—Dave Motl, 354–7800.
  Deputy Associate Director.—Peggy Yauss, 354–7800.
Associate Director, Sales and Marketing.—Vacant, 354–7500.
  Deputy Associate Director.—Mary Lhotsky, 354–7800.
Associate Director, Manufacturing.—David Croft, 354–7400.
  Deputy Associate Director.—Tom Walkinshaw, 354–7400.

DEPARTMENT OF DEFENSE

The Pentagon 20301–1155, phone (703) 545–6700

fax 695–3362/693–2161, http://www.defenselink.mil

ASHTON B. CARTER, Secretary of Defense; born in Philadelphia, Pennsylvania, September 24, 1954; education: earned his bachelor's degrees in physics and in medieval history, summa cum laude, at Yale University, where he was also awarded Phi Beta Kappa; received his doctorate in theoretical physics from Oxford University, where he was a Rhodes Scholar. He was a physics instructor at Oxford, a postdoctoral fellow at Rockefeller University and the Massachusetts Institute of Technology, and an experimental research associate at Brookhaven and Fermilab National Laboratories. From 1993–1996, Secretary Carter served as Assistant Secretary of Defense for International Security Policy, responsible for—among other issues—strategic affairs, nuclear weapons policy, and the Nunn-Lugar program that removed nuclear weapons from Ukraine, Kazakhstan, and Belarus. Secretary Carter also served on the Defense Policy Board, the Defense Science Board, and the Secretary of State's International Security Advisory Board. From 2009 to 2011, he was Under Secretary of Defense for Acquisition, Technology and Logistics with responsibility for DoD's procurement reform and innovation agenda and successful completion of key procurements like the KC–46 tanker. In this capacity, Secretary Carter also led the development and production of thousands of mine-resistant ambush protected (MRAP) vehicles and other rapid acquisitions that saved countless service members' lives. Determined to get the most for both the warfighters and the taxpayer, Secretary Carter instituted "Better Buying Power" for the first time guiding the department acquisition workforce to smarter and leaner purchasing. Secretary Carter was Deputy Secretary of Defense from 2011 to 2013, serving as DoD's chief operating officer, overseeing the department's annual budget and its over three million civilian and military personnel, steering strategy and budget through the turmoil of sequester and ensuring the future of the force and institutional best practices. Outside of his government service, Secretary Carter was most recently a distinguished visiting fellow at Stanford University's Hoover Institution and a lecturer at Stanford's Freeman Spogli Institute for International Studies. He also was a Senior Executive at the Markle Foundation, helping its Economic Future Initiative advance technology strategies to enable Americans to flourish in a networked global economy. Previously, Secretary Carter served as a Senior Partner of Global Technology Partners focused on advising major investment firms in technology, and an advisor on global affairs to Goldman Sachs. At Harvard's Kennedy School, he was Professor of Science and International Affairs and Chair of the International and Global Affairs faculty. He served on the boards of the MITRE Corporation, Mitretek Systems, and Lincoln Laboratories at M.I.T. and as a member of the Draper Laboratory Corporation. He was elected a Fellow of the American Academy of Arts and Sciences and is a member of the Council on Foreign Relations and the Aspen Strategy Group. For his government service, Secretary Carter has been awarded the Department of Defense Distinguished Service Medal, DoD's highest, on five separate occasions. He received the Defense Intelligence Medal for his contributions to intelligence and the Joint Distinguished Service Medal from the Chairman and Joint Chiefs of Staff. Secretary Carter is author or co-author of 11 books and more than 100 articles on physics, technology, national security, and management. He is married to Stephanie Carter and has two grown children; nominated by President Barack Obama to become the 25th Secretary of Defense, and was confirmed by the U.S. Senate on February 12, 2015.

OFFICE OF THE SECRETARY

1000 Defense Pentagon, Room 3E880, 20301–1000

phone (703) 692–7100, fax (703) 571–8951

Secretary of Defense.—Ashton B. Carter.

OFFICE OF THE DEPUTY SECRETARY
1010 Defense Pentagon, Room 3E944, 20301–1010, phone (703) 692–7150

Deputy Secretary of Defense.—Robert O. Work.

EXECUTIVE SECRETARIAT
Pentagon, Room 3E880, 20301–1000, phone (703) 692–7120, fax 571–8951

Executive Secretary.—Michael Bruhn.

GENERAL COUNSEL
Pentagon, Room 3E788, 20301–1600, phone (703) 695–3341, fax 693–7278

General Counsel.—Stephen W. Preston.
 Principal Deputy.—Robert S. Taylor.

OPERATIONAL TEST AND EVALUATION
Pentagon, Room 3E1088, 20301–1700, phone (703) 697–3655, fax 614–9103

Director.—Dr. J. Michael Gilmore.

INSPECTOR GENERAL
4800 Mark Center Drive, Suite 15G27, Alexandria, VA 22350–1500
phone (703) 604–8300, fax 604–8310
hotline 1–800–424–9098, hotline fax (703) 604–8567

Inspector General.—Jon T. Rymer.
 Principal Deputy Inspector General.—Vacant.

UNDER SECRETARY OF DEFENSE FOR ACQUISITION, TECHNOLOGY AND LOGISTICS
Pentagon, Room 3E1010, phone (703) 697–7021

Under Secretary.—Frank Kendall.
 Principal Deputy Under Secretary.—Alan Estevez.
 Assistant Secretary for—
  Acquisition.—Katrina McFarland.
  Logistics and Materiel Readiness.—David Berteau.
  Energy, Installations and Environment.—John Conger (acting).
  Research and Engineering.—Alan Shaffer (acting).
  Nuclear, Chemical, and Biological Defense Programs.—Tom Hopkins (acting).
 Deputy Assistant Secretary for Manufacturing and Industrial Base Policy.—Andre Gudger (acting).
 Director, Office of Small Business Programs.—Kenyata Wesley.

JOINT STRIKE FIGHTER PROGRAM OFFICE
200 12th Street South, Suite 600, Arlington, VA 22202–5402, phone (703) 602–7640

Program Executive Officer.—Lt. Gen. Christopher Bogdan.

UNDER SECRETARY OF DEFENSE (COMPTROLLER) AND CHIEF FINANCIAL OFFICER
Pentagon, Room 3E770, 20301–1100, phone (703) 695–3237

Under Secretary/Chief Financial Officer.—Michael J. McCord.
 Principal Deputy Under Secretary.—John P. Roth (acting).

UNDER SECRETARY OF DEFENSE FOR PERSONNEL AND READINESS
Pentagon, Room 3E986, 20301–4000, phone (703) 695–5254

Under Secretary.—Brad Carson (acting).
Principal Deputy Under Secretary.—Dr. Laura J. Junor.
Military Deputy.—Lt. Gen. Michael S. Linnington.
Assistant Secretary for—
  Health Affairs.—Dr. Jonathan Woodson, 697–2111.
  Readiness and Force Management.—Stephanie A. Barner (703) 614–3240.
  Reserve Affairs (Principal Deputy).—Richard Wightman, 697–6631.

UNDER SECRETARY OF DEFENSE FOR POLICY
Pentagon, Room 3E806, 20301–2000, phone (703) 697–7200

Under Secretary.—Hon. Christine E. Wormuth.
Principal Deputy Under Secretary.—Hon. Brian P. McKeon.
Assistant Secretary of Defense for—
  Asian and Pacific Security Affairs.—Hon. David Shear.
  Homeland Defense and Global Security.—Eric Rosenbach.
  International Security Affairs.—Elissa Slotkin (acting).
  Special Operations/Low-Intensity Conflict and Interdependent Capabilities.—Hon.
    Michael Lumpkin.
  Strategy, Plans, and Capabilities.—Hon. Robert Scher.

DEPARTMENT OF DEFENSE CHIEF INFORMATION OFFICER (DoD CIO)
Pentagon, Room 3E1030, 20301–6000, phone (703) 695–0348

DoD CIO.—Terry A. Halvorsen.
Principal Deputy DoD CIO.—David L. DeVries (acting).

ASSISTANT SECRETARY FOR LEGISLATIVE AFFAIRS
Pentagon, Room 3E970, 20301–1300, phone (703) 697–6210, fax 695–5860

Assistant Secretary.—Vacant.
Principal Deputy.—Stephen Hedger.
Deputy Assistant (Senate Affairs).—Michael Stella.

ASSISTANT TO THE SECRETARY FOR PUBLIC AFFAIRS
Pentagon, Room 2E964, 20301–1400, phone (703) 697–9312, fax 695–4299
public inquiries, 571–3343

Assistant to the Secretary.—Brent Colburn.
Principal Deputy.—Bryan G. Whitman.

OFFICE OF THE DEPUTY CHIEF MANAGEMENT OFFICER
Pentagon, Room 3E146, 20301–9010, phone (703) 614–8888, fax 695–5395

Deputy Chief Management Officer.—Vacant.
Assistant Deputy Chief Management Officer.—David Tillotson III.

DEPARTMENT OF DEFENSE FIELD ACTIVITIES
DEFENSE MEDIA ACTIVITY
6700 Taylor Avenue, Fort George G. Meade, MD 20755
phone (301) 222–6700, http://www.dma.mil/

Director.—Ray B. Shepherd.
Deputy Director.—Col. Andrew Mutter, USA.

DEPARTMENT OF DEFENSE EDUCATION ACTIVITY
4800 Mark Center Drive, Arlington, VA 22350–1400
School Information (571) 372–0610

Director.—Thomas M. Brady, 372–0590.
Principal Deputy Director and Associate Director for Education.—Adrian Talley, 372–5832.
Associate Director for Finance and Business Operations.—Robert Brady, 372–1901.
General Counsel.—Edwin Daniel, 372–0976.

DEPARTMENT OF DEFENSE HUMAN RESOURCES ACTIVITY
4800 Mark Center Drive, Suite 06J25–01, Alexandria, VA 22350–4000

Director.—Pamela S. Mitchell.
Deputy Director.—Jeffrey Register.
Executive Assistant.—Michelle Watson.

OFFICE OF ECONOMIC ADJUSTMENT
2231 Crystal Drive, Suite 520, Arlington, VA 22202, phone (703) 697–2130

Director.—Patrick J. O'Brien.
Deputy Director.—Ronald Adkins, 697–2206.
Sacramento Western Regional Office Director.—Gary Kuwabara (916) 557–7365.

WASHINGTON HEADQUARTERS SERVICES
Pentagon, phone (703) 693–7906

Director.—Patricia M. Young.
Deputy Director.—Vacant.
Director for—
   Acquisition Directorate.—Tim Applegate (acting), (703) 545–0423.
   Enterprise Information Technology Services Directorate.—Lytwaive Hutchinson (703) 695–2865.
   Enterprise Management.—Sajeel Ahmed, 693–7995.
   Executive Services.—Darren Irvine (acting), 693–7965.
   Financial Management.—Marcia Case, 545–0019.
   Human Resources Directorate.—Susan Yarwood (571) 256–4504.
   OSD Chief Information Office.—Lytwaive Hutchinson, 695–2865.
   Raven Rock Mountain Complex.—Col. Ramona Plemmons (717) 878–3343.
   WHS General Counsel.—John Albanese (acting), 693–7374.

JOINT CHIEFS OF STAFF
OFFICE OF THE CHAIRMAN
Pentagon, Room 2E872, 20318–0001, phone (703) 697–9121

Chairman.—GEN Martin E. Dempsey, USA.
   Vice Chairman.—ADM James A. Winnefeld, USN, room 2E724, 614–8949.
   Assistant to the Chairman, Joint Chiefs of Staff.—VADM Kurt W. Tidd, USN, room 2E868, 695–4605.

JOINT STAFF

Director.—Lt. Gen. David L. Goldfein, USAF, room 2E936, 614–5221.
   Vice Director.—Maj. Gen. Jacqueline Van Ovost, USAF, room 2E936, 614–5223.
   Director for—
      Manpower and Personnel, J–1.—BG Margaret W. Burcham, USA, room 1E948, 697–6098.
      Joint Staff Intelligence, J–2.—RADM Paul Becker, USN, room 1E880, 697–9773.
      Operations, J–3.—LTG William C. Mayville, USA, room 2D874, 697–3702.
      Logistics, J–4.—Lt. Gen. Robert R. Ruark, USMC, room 2E828, 697–7000.
      Strategic Plans and Policy, J–5.—VADM Frank C. Pandolfe, USN, room 2E996, 695–5618.

Command, Control, Communications and Computer Systems, J–6.—LTG Mark S. Bowman, USA, room 2D860, 695–6478.
Operational Plans and Joint Force Development, J–7.—Lt. Gen. Thomas D. Waldhauser, USMC, room 2B865, 697–9031.
Force Structure, Resources, and Assessment, J–8.—Lt. Gen. Mark F. Ramsay, USAF, room 1E962, 697–8853.

DEFENSE AGENCIES

MISSILE DEFENSE AGENCY
5700 18th Street, Fort Belvoir, VA 22060–5573

Director.—VADM James D. Syring, USN (571) 231–8006.
Deputy Director.—Brig. Gen. Kenneth E. Todorov, USAF, 231–8055.
Director, Public Affairs.—Richard Lehner, 231–8212.
Director, Legislative Affairs.—Kimo Hollingsworth, 231–8105.

DEFENSE ADVANCED RESEARCH PROJECTS AGENCY
675 North Randolph Street, Arlington, VA 22203

Director.—Dr. Arati Prabhakar, 696–2400.
Deputy Director.—Dr. Steve Walker, 696–2402.

DEFENSE COMMISSARY AGENCY
1300 E Avenue, Fort Lee, VA 23801–1800, phone (804) 734–8720/8330

Director.—Joseph H. Jeu, 734–8720.
Chief Operating Officer.—Michael J. Dowling, 734–8330.

WASHINGTON OFFICE
4100 Defense Pentagon, Room 5D636, 20301–4100, phone (703) 571–7186/7184

Chief.—Thomas Owens.

DEFENSE CONTRACT AUDIT AGENCY
8725 John J. Kingman Road, Suite 2135, Fort Belvoir, VA 22060
phone (703) 767–3200

Director.—Patrick J. Fitzgerald, 767–3200.
Deputy Director.—Anita F. Bales.

DEFENSE FINANCE AND ACCOUNTING SERVICE
8899 East 56th Street, Indianapolis, IN 46249–0100
phone (317) 212–0714

Director.—Teresa A. McKay.
Principal Deputy Director.—Audrey Y. Davis.

DEFENSE HEALTH AGENCY
7700 Arlington Boulevard, Falls Church, VA 22042–5101, phone (703) 681–8707

Director.—Lt. Gen. Douglas J. Robb, DO, MPH.
Deputy Director.—Paul J. Hutter (acting).

DEFENSE INFORMATION SYSTEMS AGENCY
P.O. Box 549, Command Building, Fort Meade, Maryland 20755

Director.—Lt. Gen. Ronnie D. Hawkins, USAF (301) 225–6001.

Vice Director.—MG Alan R. Lynn, USA, 225–6010.
Chief of Staff.—COL Mark E. Rosenstein, USA, 225–6020.

DEFENSE INTELLIGENCE AGENCY
200 MacDill Boulevard, Washington, DC 20340, phone (202) 231–0800

Director.—Lt. Gen. Vincent R. Stewart, USMC.
Deputy Director.—Douglas H. Wise.

DEFENSE LEGAL SERVICES AGENCY
Pentagon, Room 3E788, 20301–1600, phone (703) 695–3341, fax 693–7278

Director/General Counsel.—Robert S. Taylor (acting).
Principal Deputy Director.—Robert S. Taylor, 697–7248.

DEFENSE LOGISTICS AGENCY
8725 John J. Kingman Road, Suite 2533, Ft. Belvoir, VA 22060
phone (703) 767–5264

Director.—Lt. Gen. Andrew E. Busch, USAF.
Vice Director.—Edward J. Case.

DEFENSE POW/MIA ACCOUNTING AGENCY
2300 Defense Pentagon, Washington, DC 20301–2300
phone (703) 699–1102, fax 602–1890

Director.—RADM Michael Franken, USN.

DEFENSE SECURITY COOPERATION AGENCY
201 12th Street South, Suite 203, Arlington, VA 22202–5408, phone (703) 604–6605

Director.—VADM Joseph W. Rixey, 604–6604.
Deputy Director.—Jennifer N. Zakriski, 604–6606.

DEFENSE SECURITY SERVICE
27130 Telegraph Road, Quantico, VA 22134, phone (703) 617–2352

Director.—Stanley L. Sims.

DEFENSE THREAT REDUCTION AGENCY
8725 John J. Kingman Road, Stop 6201, Ft. Belvoir, VA 22060–6201
phone (703) 767–7594

Director.—Kenneth A. Myers III.
Deputy Director.—Maj. Gen. John P. Horner, USAF.
Chief, Governmental and Public Affairs.—Chris Geeslin.

NATIONAL GEOSPATIAL-INTELLIGENCE AGENCY
7500 GEOINT Drive, Springfield, VA 22150, phone (571) 557–7300

Director.—Robert Cardillo.
Deputy Director.—Susan Gordon.

NATIONAL SECURITY AGENCY/CENTRAL SECURITY SERVICE
Ft. George G. Meade, MD 20755, phone (301) 688–6524

Director, NSA/Chief, CSS.—ADM Michael S. Rogers, USN.

Deputy Director, NSA.—Richard H. Ledgett, Jr.
Deputy Chief, CSS.—Brig. Gen. John Bansemer, USAF.

JOINT SERVICE SCHOOLS
9820 Belvoir Road, Ft. Belvoir, VA 22060, phone (800) 845-7606

DEFENSE ACQUISITION UNIVERSITY

President.—James P. Woolsey (703) 805-3360.
 Vice President.—Roy L. Wood (acting), 805-2828.
 Chief of Staff.—Joseph E. Johnson, 805-2828.

NATIONAL INTELLIGENCE UNIVERSITY

President.—David R. Ellison (202) 231-3344.

NATIONAL DEFENSE UNIVERSITY
Fort McNair, Building 62, 300 Fifth Avenue, 20319

phone (202) 685-3912

President.—Maj. Gen. Frederick Padilla, USMC, Building 62, room 307, 685-3936.
 Senior Vice President.—Amb. Wanda Nesbitt, Building 62, room 307A, 685-3923.
 Provost and Vice President for Academic Affairs.—Dr. John Yaeger, Building 62, room 309C, 685-0080.

CAPSTONE / PINNACLE / KEYSTONE

Director.—Dr. Ricky L. Waddell, Building 64, room 3510, 685-2330.

COLLEGE OF INTERNATIONAL SECURITY AFFAIRS

Chancellor.—Dr. Michael Bell, Building 64, room 2102 (202) 685-7209.

INFORMATION RESOURCES MANAGEMENT COLLEGE

Chancellor.—RADM Janice M. Hamby (Ret.), USN, Building 62, room 201G (202) 685-3886.

JOINT FORCES STAFF COLLEGE
7800 Hampton Boulevard, Norfolk, VA 23511-1702, phone (757) 443-6200

Commandant.—RADM John Smith, USN, room A202.

NATIONAL WAR COLLEGE

Commandant.—BG Tom Cosentino, USA, Building 61, room 124 (202) 685-4341.

DWIGHT D. EISENHOWER SCHOOL FOR NATIONAL SECURITY AND RESOURCE STRATEGY

Commandant.—Brig. Gen. Thomas A. Gorry, USMC, room 200 (202) 685-4337.

UNIFORMED SERVICES UNIVERSITY OF THE HEALTH SCIENCES
4301 Jones Bridge Road, Bethesda, MD 20814

President.—Charles L. Rice, M.D., room A1019 (301) 295-3013.

DEPARTMENT OF THE AIR FORCE

Pentagon, 1670 Air Force, Washington, DC 20330–1670
phone (703) 697–7376, fax 695–8809

SECRETARY OF THE AIR FORCE

Secretary of the Air Force.—Hon. Deborah Lee James, room 4E878.
Confidential Assistant.—Rudy Sheffer.
Senior Military Assistant.—Brig. Gen. Wayne Monteith.
Deputy Military Assistant.—Lt. Col. Michelle Carns.
Military Aid.—Maj. Jason Bast.
Executive Assistants: MSgt Samay Thaboun, TSgt Iris Moore.

SECAF/CSAF EXECUTIVE ACTION GROUP

Director.—Col. Randall Reed (703) 697–5540.
Deputy Chief.—Karen Pound.

UNDER SECRETARY OF THE AIR FORCE

Pentagon, 1670 Air Force, Room 4E858, 20330–1670, phone (703) 697–1361

Under Secretary.—Vacant.
Confidential Assistant.—Cathy Merritt.
Senior Military Assistant.—Col. Andrew Gebara.
Military Assistant.—Maj. Myron Chivis.
Executive Assistants: MSgt Taisha Ross, TSgt Monieka Stewart.

CHIEF OF STAFF

Pentagon, 1670 Air Force, Room 4E924, 20330
phone (703) 697–9225

Chief of Staff.—Gen. Mark A. Welsh III.
Confidential Assistant.—Terri Stern.
Special Assistant.—Jason Yaley, 5E980, 697–1930.
Executive Officer.—Col. Heather Pringle.
Vice Chief of Staff.—Gen. Larry Spencer, room 4E938, 695–7911.
Assistant Vice Chief of Staff.—Lt. Gen. Stephen Hoog, room 4E944, 695–7913.
Chief Master Sergeant of the Air Force.—CMSAF James A. Cody, room 4E941, 695–0498.

DEPUTY UNDER SECRETARY FOR INTERNATIONAL AFFAIRS

Pentagon, 1080 Air Force Pentagon, Room 4E192, 20330–1080

Deputy Under Secretary.—Heidi H. Grant (703) 695–7262.
Assistant Deputy.—Maj. Gen. Lawrence Martin, 695–7261.
Executive Officers: Lt. Col. Paul Porter, 693–1941; Maj. Sarah Santoro, 695–7261; Georgia Smothers, 695–7263.

Pentagon, 1080 Air Force Pentagon, Room 4C253, 20330–1080

Director of Policy.—Anthony P. Reardon, (571) 256–7491.
Executive Officer.—Lt. Col. John Smith, 256–7494.
Executive Assistant.—Michelle Polk, 256–7495.

Pentagon, 1080 Air Force Pentagon, Room 4C947, 20330–1080

Director of Regional Affairs.—Brig. Gen. David Nahom (703) 695–2022.

Executive Officer.—Maj. Linda Thierauf, 695–2077.
Executive Assistant.—Sanura Wade, 695–2080.

Pentagon, 1080 Air Force Pentagon, Room 4C253, 20330–1080

Director of Strategy, Resources, and Integration.—Maj. Gen. Brian Neal (ANG), (571) 256–9492.
Executive Assistant.—Patricia Green, 256–9491.

ASSISTANT SECRETARY FOR ACQUISITION
Pentagon, 1060 Air Force, 20330
1745 Jefferson Davis Highway, Suite 307, Arlington, VA 22202
110 Luke Avenue, Suite 200, Bolling AFB, DC 20032–6400

Assistant Secretary.—Dr. William LaPlante (703) 697–6361.
Senior Military Assistant.—Col. C.J. Johnson, 697–6990.
Military Assistant.—Lt. Col. William L. Ottati, 697–6362.
Principal Deputy.—Richard Lombardi, 697–9373.
Military Deputy.—Lt. Gen. Ellen Pawlikowski, 697–6363.
Executive Officer.—Maj. Gerald Ferdinand, 695–7311.

DEPUTY ASSISTANT SECRETARY FOR ACQUISITION INTEGRATION

Deputy Assistant Secretary.—Bobby Smart (571) 256–0355.
Associate Deputy Assistant Secretary.—John Miller, 256–0351.
Executive Officer.—Maj. JJ McAfee, 256–0356.

DEPUTY ASSISTANT SECRETARY FOR CONTRACTING

Deputy Assistant Secretary.—Brig. Gen. Casey Blake (571) 256–2397.
Associate Deputy Assistant Secretary.—John Lyle, 256–2397.
Executive Officer.—Capt. Jason Holman, 256–2397.

DEPUTY ASSISTANT SECRETARY FOR SCIENCE, TECHNOLOGY AND ENGINEERING

Deputy Assistant Secretary.—Dr. David Walker (571) 256–0303.
Associate Deputy Assistant Secretary.—Col. Charles Ormsby, 256–0303.
Executive Officer.—Maj. Brad Worden, 256–0294.

CAPABILITY DIRECTORATE FOR GLOBAL POWER PROGRAMS

Director.—Maj. Gen. Timothy Ray (571) 256–0191.
Deputy Director.—Col. Aaron Clark, 256–0192.
Executive Officer.—Maj. Yong Sim, 256–0196.

CAPABILITY DIRECTORATE FOR GLOBAL REACH PROGRAMS

Director.—Maj. Gen. Dwyer Dennis (571) 256–0489.
Deputy Director.—Col. Matthew Bonavita, 256–0497.
Executive Officer.—Lt. Col. Jerry Litzo, 256–0522.

CAPABILITY DIRECTORATE FOR INFORMATION DOMINANCE

Director.—Gail Forest (571) 256–0081.
Deputy Director.—Col. Daniel Moy, 256–0082.
Executive Officer.—Maj. Greg Barber, 256–0083.

CAPABILITY DIRECTORATE FOR SPACE PROGRAMS

Director.—Maj. Gen. Roger Teague (571) 695–3423.
Deputy Director.—Col. Christopher Warack, 695–3499.
Executive Officer.—Maj. AJ Ashby, 695–3435.

DIRECTORATE FOR SPECIAL PROGRAMS

Director.—Col. Stephen Russell (571) 767–3890.
Deputy Director.—Chris DiNenna, 256–0005.
Executive Assistant.—Alesia Clark (202) 767–3890.

DIRECTORATE FOR AIR FORCE RAPID CAPABILITIES

Director.—Randall Walden (202) 767–1800.
Deputy and Technical Director.—Vacant.
Executive Officer.—Maj. Andrew MacDonald, 767–3203.

ASSISTANT SECRETARY FOR FINANCIAL MANAGEMENT AND COMPTROLLER OF THE AIR FORCE (SAF/FM)

Pentagon, 1130 Air Force Pentagon, 20330–1130

Air Force Cost Analysis Agency, Jones Building

1500 West Perimeter Road, Joint Base Andrews-Naval Air Facility

Washington, MD 20762

Assistant Secretary.—Hon. Lisa S. Disbrow, room 4E978 (703) 695–0829.
Senior Military Assistant.—Lt. Col. Brian T. Kehl, 695–0829.
Chief, Enlisted Matters.—CMSgt John A. Writer, 614–5429.

PRINCIPAL DEPUTY ASSISTANT SECRETARY FOR FINANCIAL MANAGEMENT

Principal Deputy Assistant Secretary.—Douglas M. Bennett (703) 697–4464.
Military Assistant.—Maj. Stuart Churchill, 697–4464.

DEPUTY ASSISTANT SECRETARY FOR BUDGET (SAF/FMB)

Deputy Assistant Secretary.—Maj. Gen. James F. Martin, room 5D912 (703) 695–1876.
Executive Officer.—Lt. Col. Monroe Neal, 695–1876.
Deputy.—Caral Spangler, 697–1876.
Director of:
  Budget and Appropriations Liaison. Col. Sam Grable, room 5C949, 614–8114.
  Budget Investment.—Pamela Schwenke, room 5D912, 697–1220.
  Budget Operations and Personnel.—Col. James Peccia, room 5D912, 697–0627.
  Budget Programs.—Col. Michael Monson, room 5C950, 614–7883.

DEPUTY ASSISTANT SECRETARY FOR COST AND ECONOMICS (SAF/FMC)

Deputy Assistant Secretary.—Kathy L. Watern, room 5E975 (703) 697–5311.
Associate Deputy Assistant Secretary.—Grant McVicker, room 5E975, 697–5313.
Executive Officer.—Lt. Col. Anthony Kimbrough, room 3E975, 697–5312.
Technical Director for Cost and Economics.—Ranae Woods, suite 3500 (240) 612–5615.
Director, Economics and Business Management.—Stephen M. Connair, room 4C843 (703) 693–9347.
Director, Cost Analysis Division.—Lt. Col. Anthony Smith, room 4C943, 697–0288.

DEPUTY ASSISTANT SECRETARY FOR FINANCIAL OPERATIONS (SAF/FMF)

Deputy Assistant Secretary.—Thomas J. Murphy, room 5D739 (703) 614–4180.
Associate Deputy Assistant Secretary.—Stephen Herrera, 5D739, 614–4180.
Chief Information Officer and Technology.—Vacant, 5D739, 614–5437.
Military Assistant.—Lt. Col. Edward Marshall, 614–4180.
Director for—
  Accounting Policy and Reporting.—Fred Carr, Andrews AFB, MD (240) 612–5212.
  AF Financial Systems Organization.—Glena Gibson, Wright-Patterson AFB, OH (937) 257–2262.
  AFAFO.—Eric Cuebas, Denver, CO (720) 847–2200.

AF–IPPS.—Lt. Col. Daniel Huffman, Andrews AFB, MD (240) 612–5322.
DEAMS.—Shirley Reed, Wright-Patterson AFB, OH (937) 656–8554.
FIAR.—Lori Stacey, Andrews AFB, MD (240) 612–5281.
Financial Services.—Gregory Wilson, Ellsworth AFB, SD (605) 385–8682.
Information Systems and Technology.—John Koski, Andrews AFB, MD (240) 612–5283.

DEPUTY ASSISTANT SECRETARY FOR PROGRAMS (SAF/FMP)

Deputy Assistant Secretary.—Brig. Gen. Edward A. Fienga, room 5E857 (703) 695–3695.
Executive Officer.—Maj. Clarence F. McRae, 695–3695.
Deputy.—Judith B. Oliva, 695–3695.
Director of:
    Program Integration.—Col. James Jacobson, room 5C950, 614–7977.
    Program Panel.—Gregory Parker, room 5C950, 614–7970.

ASSISTANT SECRETARY FOR INSTALLATIONS, ENVIRONMENT AND LOGISTICS

Assistant Secretary.—Hon. Miranda A.A. Ballentine, room 4E996 (703) 697–4936.
Principal Deputy Assistant Secretary.—Kathleen Ferguson, 697–4936.
Executive Officer.—Lt. Col. Aaron Altwies, 697–4219.
Military Assistant.—Col. Stephanie Wilson, 697–5023.
Confidential Assistant.—Heather Pittman, 697–4936.

EXECUTIVE SERVICES AND SUPPORT

Executive Service Superintendent.—Vacant (571) 256–1809.
    Executive Services: TSgt Darren Hardy (Deployed); TSgt Shamika Horton (703) 697–4391; TSgt Ray Lance (703) 693–3254; TSgt Shawn Taylor (703) 614–6230.
    Budget Resources: Helen Griffith (703) 614–0012; Wellington Selden Jr., 614–0014.
    Chief, Strategic Resources.—Candy Jones (703) 695–6716.
    Legislative/Public Affairs.—Maj. Christina Meinster, (703) 697–1641; Frank Smolinsky, 697–1980.

DEPUTY ASSISTANT SECRETARY FOR INSTALLATIONS (SAF/IEI)

Deputy Assistant Secretary.—Mark Pohlmeier (acting), room 4B941 (703) 695–3592.
    Deputy for Installation Policy.—Michael McGhee (703) 697–1019.
    Administrative Support Specialist/Secretary.—Sheenia T. Williams, 695–3592.
    Executive Officer.—Maj. Rachel Hamlyn, 695–6456.
    Director, Planning and Programs.—Col. Jonathan Webb, 697–7003.
    Director, Encroachment Management.—Steve Zander (703) 571–5771.
    Strategic Basing Analyst.—Mark Pohlmeier (703) 692–7477.

INSTALLATION PLANNING (SAF/IEIP)

Director.—Col. Jonathan Webb (703) 697–7003.
    Deputy Director.—Andrew Mendoza (703) 693–8309.
    Information Management.—JJ Cook, 693–9339.
    Program Management: Tim Brennan, 695–5730; Ed McCarthy, 693–9339; Rick Rankin, 697–6492; Terry Tallent, 697–7244.
    Operational Support.—James Sample, 693–3349.
    NEPA Compliance Support.—Giannina Ienco (540) 898–1763.

AIR FORCE REAL PROPERTY AGENCY

2261 Hughes Avenue, Suite 121, San Antonio, TX 78236–9821

Director.—Robert Moriarty (210) 395–9501.
    Secretary to the Director.—Linda Cosper, 395–9503.
    Executive Officer.—Jim Yee, 395–9505.

DEPUTY ASSISTANT SECRETARY FOR ENVIRONMENT, SAFETY AND OCCUPATIONAL HEALTH (SAF/IEE)

Deputy Assistant Secretary.—Mark Correll, room 4B941 (703) 697–9297.
Deputy for Installation Policy.—James P. Holland (703) 614–6232.
Executive Secretary.—Sheenia Williams, 697–9297.
Executive Officer.—Gina Ghilardi, 697–9297.
Director for—
   Environment Policy.—Catherine Fairlie, 614–8458.
   Occupational Health Policy.—Maj. David Gilliam, 693–2055.
   Plans and Policy.—Col. Victor Caravello (571) 256–4397.
   Safety Policy.—Vance Lineberger, 693–7706.
Director, Infrastructure Management.—Lt. Col. Yvonne Spencer, 693–2047.
Air Force Real Property Agency Liaison.—Robert McCann, 692–9515.
Director, Air National Guard and Reserve Affairs.—Lt. Col. Bradley Waters, 697–0997.
Director, Asset Management.—Vacant, 693–9328.
ESOH.—Daniel Kowalczyk, 697–1198.
Environment Support.—Michelle Brown, 697–0989.

REO COORDINATOR

Richard Treviono (210) 395–8784.

REGIONAL ENVIRONMENTAL OFFICE (EAST)

Dave Glass, Ron Joy (404) 562–4201.

DEPUTY ASSISTANT SECRETARY FOR ENERGY (SAF/IEN)

Deputy Assistant Secretary.—Roberto Guerrero, room 5E1000, 256–4711.
Deputy for Energy Policy.—Dr. Pasquale Gambatese, 697–1207.
Executive Officer.—Esther Sandel, 697–6032.
Administration Support/Secretary.—Ann Belfield (571) 256–4711.
Senior Energy Facilities Engineer.—Douglas Tucker, 697–1113.
Logistics Energy Management Specialist.—Jennifer Riley, 697–1098.
Special Assistant.—Richard Ballard, 697–7301.
Congressional/OA Support.—Richard Brill, 697–1018.
Energy Aviation Ops: Maj. Marc Gildner, Jim McCann (703) 571–5773.
Energy Facilities Engineer.—Vacant, 571–3944.
Energy Acquisitions.—Vacant, 697–1113.
EATF.—Col. Chip Bulger (703) 614–8279.

ASSISTANT SECRETARY FOR MANPOWER AND RESERVE AFFAIRS
1660 Air Force Pentagon, Room 4E1010, 20330–1660

Assistant Secretary.—Vacant (703) 697–2302.
Principal Deputy Assistant Secretary.—Daniel R. Sitterly, 697–1258.
Mobilization Assistant.—Brig. Gen. Ondra Berry (775) 887–7236.
Confidential Assistant,—Lydia S. Bennett (703) 695–6677.
Military Assistant.—Col. Petra McGregor, 697–2303.
Executive Officer.—Lt. Col. Carolyn Ammons, 697–1258.
Superintendent.—William Coates (703) 614–5654.

DEPUTY ASSISTANT SECRETARY FOR FORCE MANAGEMENT INTEGRATION

Deputy Assistant Secretary.—Jeffrey Mayo (703) 614–4751.
Executive Secretary.—Alicia K. Bobbitt, 614–4751.
Assistant Deputy for—
   Force Management Integration.—SMSgt. Chris Parrott, 693–9575.
   Manpower Force Management.—Charles Denmark, 695–2459.
   Military Force Management.—Scott Brady, 693–9309.
   Officer Accessions and Programs.—Steven Beatty, 693–9333.
   Total Air Force Compensation and Civilian Personnel.—Norma Inabinet, 693–9764.

DEPUTY ASSISTANT SECRETARY FOR RESERVE AFFAIRS

Deputy Assistant Secretary, Reserve Affairs and Airman Readiness.—John A. Fedrigo, room 5D742 (703) 697–6376.
Executive Secretary.—Stephanie Parry, 697–6375.
Assistant Deputy, Auxiliary, Education and Development Programs—Thomas Shubert (571) 256–4044.
Air Force Reserve Matters.—Col. Michael Phan, 697–6431.
ANG Matters.—Col. Mark Sheehan (571) 256-4043.
Assistant Deputy, Force Support and Family Programs.—Kimberly Yates (703) 693–9511.
Assistant Deputy for Health Policy.—Martha Soper, 693–9512.
Senior Enlisted Advisor.—CMSgt. Jennifer Koenig, 693–9505.
Executive Director for Air Reserve Forces Policy Committee.—Vacant, 697–6430.
Assistant Force Support and Family Programs.—Lt. Col. Steven C. Combs, 693–9504.

DEPUTY ASSISTANT SECRETARY FOR STRATEGIC DIVERSITY INTEGRATION

Deputy Assistant Secretary.—Dr. Jarris L. Taylor, Jr., room 5E783 (703) 697–6586.
Assistant Deputy.—Vacant, 697–6583.
Executive Secretary.—Karen Sauls, 697–6586.

AIR FORCE REVIEW BOARDS AGENCY (SAF/MRB)

1500 West Perimeter Road, Suite 3700, Joint Base Andrews NAF–Washington, MD 20762

Director.—R. Philip Deavel (240) 612–5400.
Deputy Director.—Michael LoGrande, 612–5403.
Chief Information Officer.—Clifford D. Tompkins, 612–4393.
Director of Operations.—Thomas Kearney, 612–5342.
Legal Advisor.—Ralph Arnold, 612–5404.
Medical Advisor.—Dr. Horace Carson, 612–5405.
Senior Enlisted Advisor.—SMSgt Eric McCross, 612–4528.
Human Resources.—Donna Atchison, 612–5401.
Confidential Assistant.—Marilyn Redmond, 612–5400.

AIR FORCE BOARD FOR CORRECTION OF MILITARY RECORDS (AFBCMR) SAF/MRBC

Executive Director.—Michael LoGrande (240) 612–5403.
Deputy.—John Vallario, 612–5392.
Chief Examiners: Janet Hutson, 612–5373; Daryl Lawrence, 612–5381.
Chief, AFBCMR Administrative Operations.—Brenda Thomas, 612–5393.

AIR FORCE CIVILIAN APPELLATE REVIEW OFFICE (AFCARO), SAF/MRBA

Director.—Rita S. Looney (240) 612–5330.
Assistant Director.—Vacant, 612–5331.

SECRETARY OF THE AIR FORCE PERSONNEL COUNCIL (SAFPC), SAF/MRBP

Director.—Col. Andrew Weaver (240) 612–5369.
Deputy Director.—Col. Elizabeth Hill, 612–5365.
Senior Medical Advisor.—Col. Mary Dvorak, 612–5360.
Chief, Air Force Discharge Review Board.—Col. Martha Mann, 612–5355.
Chief, Awards/Decorations/Air Force Reserve Advisor.—Col. Christopher Bennett, 612–5402.
Executive Secretary/Attorney Advisor on Clemency/Parole Board.—Bruce Brown, 612–5364.
Executive Secretary, DoD Civilian/Military Service Review Board.—Bruce Brown, 612–5364.
President Remissions Board.—Bruce Brown, 612–5364.

AIR FORCE REVIEW BOARDS AGENCY LEGAL DIRECTORATE, SAF/MRBL

Director.—Col. Calvin Anderson (240) 612–4529.

AIR FORCE PERSONNEL SECURITY APPEAL BOARD (PSAB), SAF/MRBS

President.—Al Walker (240) 612–5380.
Deputy.—Joseph Schott, 612–5350.

DoD PHYSICAL DISABILITY BOARD OF REVIEW (PDBR), SAF/MRBD

President.—James Davis (240) 612–4390.
Deputy.—Clifford D. Tompkins, 612–4393.

CHIEF, INFORMATION DOMINANCE AND CHIEF INFORMATION OFFICER
1800 Air Force Pentagon, Room 4E1050, 20330

Chief, Information Dominance and Chief Information Officer.—Lt. Gen. William J. "Bill" Bender (703) 695–6829.
Deputy Chief, Information Dominance and Chief Information Officer.—Teresa M. Salazar, 695–6829.
Director of:
    Cyberspace Operations and Warfighting Integration.—Peter Kim (acting), room 1D857, 695–1835.
    Cyberspace Strategy and Policy.—Brig. Gen. Sarah Zabel, room 1D857, 614–2997.
    Cyberspace Capabilities and Compliance.—Michael Sorrento, room 1D857, 695–1839.

DEPUTY CHIEF OF STAFF FOR INTELLIGENCE, SURVEILLANCE AND RECONNAISSANCE (ISR)

Deputy Chief of Staff.—Lt. Gen. Robert Otto (703) 695–5613.
Assistant Deputy Chief of Staff.—Maj. Gen. Urrutia-Varhall.
Executive Officer.—Lt. Col. Tracy Ward.
Director of:
    ISR Capabilities.—Brig. Gen. John Rauch, 697–5818.
    ISR Innovations.—James Clark, 693–3377.
    ISR Resources.—Keith Holt, 697–4925.
    ISR Strategy, Plans, Doctrine and Force Development.—Kenneth Dumm, 614–3478.
    Special Programs.—Dean Yount, 693–5201.

DEPUTY CHIEF OF STAFF FOR LOGISTICS, INSTALLATIONS AND MISSION SUPPORT
Pentagon, 1030 Air Force, 20330

Deputy Chief of Staff.—Lt. Gen. Judith A. Fedder, room 4E154 (703) 695–5590.
Assistant Deputy.—Tim Bridges, Pentagon, room 4E154, 695–6236.
Director of:
    Civil Engineer.—Brig. Gen. Tim Green, Pentagon, room 4C1057, 693–4308.
    Logistics.—Brig. Gen. Kathryn Johnson, Pentagon, room 4C1065, 695–4900.
    Resources Integration.—Lorna Estep, Pentagon, room 4B1088, 697–2822.
    Security Forces.—Brig. Gen. Allen Jamerson, Pentagon, room 5E1040, 693–5401.

DEPUTY CHIEF OF STAFF FOR MANPOWER, PERSONNEL AND SERVICES
Pentagon, 1040 Air Force, Room 4E168, 20330

Deputy Chief of Staff.—Lt. Gen. Samuel D. Cox (703) 697–6088.
Assistant Deputy Chief of Staff.—Robert E. Corsi, Jr.
Chief, AF/A1 Action Group.—Lt. Col. Catherine Logan, room 4E169, 695–4212.
Director of:
    Air Force General Officer Management.—Col. Christopher Craige, room 4D1066, 697–1181.
    Services.—Brig. Gen. Patrick Doherty, room 4D1054 (571) 256–8598.

Force Development.—Russell Frasz, room 4D950, 695–2144.
Force Management Policy.—Brig. Gen. Brian Kelly, room 4D950A, 695–6770.
Manpower, Organization, and Resources.—Brig. Gen. Richard Murphy, room 5B349, 692–1601.
Plans and Integration.—Michelle LoweSolis, room 4D1054A, 697–5222.

DEPUTY CHIEF OF STAFF FOR OPERATIONS, PLANS AND REQUIREMENTS
Pentagon, 1630 Air Force, Room 4E1024, 20330

Deputy Chief of Staff.—Lt. Gen. Tod Wolters (703) 697–9991.
Assistant Deputy.—Maj. Gen. Jeffrey Harrigian, 697–9881.
Mobility Assistant.—Brig. Gen. Robert Polumbo, 697–3087.
Director of:
    Cyberspace Operations and Warfighting Integration.—Peter Kim, room 1D857, 614–2997.
    Operations and Readiness.—Brig. Gen. Giovanni Tuck, room 5C756, 695–7602.
    Resource Integration.—Denise Hampt, room 5E873, 697–7833.
    Space Operations.—Maj. Gen. Martin Whelan, room 5D756, 697–9500.

DEPUTY CHIEF OF STAFF FOR STRATEGIC PLANS AND REQUIREMENTS
Pentagon, 1070 Air Force, Room 4E1082, 20330–1070

Deputy Chief of Staff.—Lt. Gen. James M. Holmes (703) 697–4469.
Assistant Deputy Chief of Staff.—Richard Hartley (703) 692–9944.
Directorate of:
    Operational Capability Requirements.—Maj. Gen. Paul Johnson, room 5C889 (703) 695–3018.
    Plans.—Maj. Gen. Jerry Harris, room 5D1088 (703) 614–2863.
    Strategy, Concepts, and Assessments.—Maj. Gen. David Alvin, room 5D1050 (703) 697–3117.

DIRECTORATE OF STUDIES AND ANALYSIS AND ASSESSMENTS
Pentagon, 1570 Air Force, Room 4E214
Washington, DC 20330–1570

Director.—Kevin E. Williams, SES (571) 256–2015.
Principal Deputy Director.—Lynne E. Baldrighi, SES.
Military Deputy Director.—Col. James G. Sturgeon.
Senior Advisor.—Vacant.
Technical Director.—Dr. Mark A. Gallagher, Ph.D., SL.
Chief Analyst.—Col. Scott Williams.

STRATEGIC DETERRENCE AND NUCLEAR INTEGRATION (A10)
Pentagon, 1488 Air Force, Suite 4E240, 20330

Assistant Chief of Staff.—Maj. Gen. Garrett Harencak (703) 693–9747.
    Deputy Assistant Chief of Staff.—Michael Shoults, SES, 693–9747.
    Associate Assistant Chief of Staff.—Dr. Billy Mullins, Ph.D., SES, 693–9747.
HQE.—Dr. Jim Blackwell, Ph.D. (703) 695–1365.
MA.—Brig. Gen. Thomas Clark (703) 697–1545.
Director of Staff.—Darphaus Mitchell, 693–9747.
Senior Executive.—Maj. Chris Maroney, 693–9747.
Junior Executive.—Maj. Nate Osborne, 693–9747.
Administrative Assistant.—Rhonda Gill, 693–9747.
Division Chiefs:
    Assessments.—David O'Donnell (202) 767–7420.
    Capabilities.—Col. Carl Jones (202) 404–7938.
    Executive Services.—Wilbert Smith, 695–7810.
    Functional Authority.—Zannis Pappas, 697–6056.
    NC3.—Col. Eric Beene (202) 767–4259.
    Strategic Stability and CWMD Policy.—Col. Thomas Summers (703) 614–6009.
    Planning, Policy and Strategy.—Col. Frank Link, 697–4098.

ADMINISTRATIVE ASSISTANT TO THE SECRETARY
Pentagon, 1720 Air Force, 20330

Administrative Assistant.—Patricia J. Zarodkiewicz, room 4E824 (703) 695–9492.
Deputy Administrative Assistant.—Jeffery R. Shelton, 695–9492.
Director of Staff.—Lt. Col. Heather Meyer, 693–9503.
Executive Officer.—Maj. Mark Cipolla, 695–9492.
Confidential Assistant.—Ruby Hill, 695–9492.
Executive Administrators: TSgt. Jenny Collins, 614–5637; TSgt. Aimee Miller, 695–3151.
Director of:
  Executive Dining Facility.—Shad Glover, room 4D869, 697–1112.
  Information Management.—Kent Chadrick, 5E915, 697–6529.
  Operations.—Ralph F. Davis, room 5D855, 697–8225.
  Resources—Personnel.—Anne Graham, room 1E868, 692–9516.
  Resources—Finance.—Lt. Col. Mark Snow, room 4D845, 695–3148.
  Security, Counterintelligence and Special Programs Oversight Division.—Michael Janosov, room MD779, 693–2013.
  Sensitive Activities Office.—Russell Wyler (202) 404–1500.

AUDITOR GENERAL
Pentagon, 1120 Air Force, 20330
4170 Hebble Creek Road, Building 280, Door 1
Wright-Patterson AFB, OH 45433–5643 (WPAFB)
1500 West Perimeter Road, Suite 4700
Joint Base Andrews, MD 20762
470 I Street East, Randolph AFB, TX 78150–4332

Auditor General.—Daniel F. McMillin, room 4E204 (703) 614–5626.

AIR FORCE AUDIT AGENCY

Director of Operations.—Catherine M. Bromley, JBA Andrews (240) 612–5114.
Assistant Auditor General for—
  Acquisition, Logistics, and Financial Audits.—Valerie L. Muck, WPAFB (937) 257–6355.
  Field Activities Audits.—Sharon Puschmann, Pentagon (703) 614–5626.
  Operations and Support Audits.—Michael D. Petersen, Randolph AFB (210) 652–0035.

CHIEF OF CHAPLAINS
1380 AF Pentagon, Room 4E260, Washington, DC 20330

Chief.—Chaplain (Maj. Gen.) Howard D. Stendahl (571) 256–7729.
Deputy Chief.—Chaplain (Brig. Gen.) Bobby V. Page, 256–7729.

AIR FORCE CHIEF OF SAFETY
Pentagon, 1400 Air Force Pentagon, Room 4E252, 20330–1400

Chief of Air Force Safety/Commander, Air Force Safety Center.—Maj. Gen. Kurt Neubauer (703) 693–7281.
Deputy Chief of Air Force Safety/Executive Director, Air Force Safety Center.—James Rubeor (505) 846–2372.
Executive Officer.—Maj. Patrick Schuldt (703) 614–3389.
Director, Safety Issues Division.—Col. Jason Edelblute, 693–3333.

AIR FORCE GENERAL COUNSEL
Pentagon, 1740 Air Force Pentagon, Suite 4E836, 20330

General Counsel.—Hon. Gordon O. Tanner (703) 697–0941.
Principal Deputy.—Joseph M. McDade, 697–4406.

Military Assistant.—Lt. Col. Thomas L. Cluff, Jr. (703) 693–7304.
Executive Assistant.—Debra R. Swanson, 697–8418.
Deputy General Counsel for—
  Acquisition.—Richard B. Clifford, Jr., room 5B914, 693–7284.
  Contractor Responsibility and Conflict Resolution.—Rodney Grandon, Crystal City (703) 604–0423.
  Fiscal, Ethics and Administrative Law.—F. Andrew Turley, room 4C934, 693–9291.
  Intelligence, International and Military Affairs.—Craig A. Smith, room 4C756 (703) 695–5663.
  Installations, Energy and Environment.—Jennifer Miller, room 5E773 (571) 256–4809.

AIR FORCE HISTORIAN

1190 Air Force Pentagon, Room 4E1062, Washington, DC 20330–1190

Director.—Walter Grudzinskas, (703) 697–5603.
Executive Officer.—David Bragg 697–9119.
Director, Air Force Historical Research Agency, Maxwell AFB, AL.—Dr. Charles O'Connell (334) 953–5342.

INSPECTOR GENERAL

Pentagon, 1140 Air Force, Room 4E1040, 20330–1140

Inspector General.—Lt. Gen. Gregory A. Biscone (703) 697–6733.
Deputy Inspector General.—Maj. Gen. Craig N. Gourley, 697–4351.
Executive Officer.—Lt. Col. Zachary L. Smith, 697–4787.
Advisor for—
  Air National Guard Matters.—Col. Suzanne B. Lipcaman, room 4E1037, 697–0339.
  Reserve Matters.—Col. Kathleen R. Mikkelson, room 4E1037, 614–3863.
Director of:
  Complaints Resolution Directorate.—Col. John Payne, JBAB-Building 5863, room 150 (202) 404–5262.
  Inspections.—Col. William Reese, JBAB-Building 5863, room 350, 404–3263.
  Senior Officials Inquiries.—Col. Matthew Bartlett, room 5B937 (703) 693–3579.
  Special Investigations.—Col. Jeffrey Hurlbert, room 5B919, 697–0411.

JUDGE ADVOCATE GENERAL

Pentagon, 1420 Air Force, 20330

1501 West Perimeter Road, Joint Base Andrews Naval Air

Facility Washington, MD 20762

The Judge Advocate General.—Lt. Gen. Christopher F. Burne, room 4E180 (703) 614–5732.
Deputy Judge Advocate General.—Maj. Gen. Jeffrey A. Rockwell, room 4E180, 614–5732.
Senior Paralegal Manager to TJAG.—CMSgt Larry G. Tolliver, room 5D116, 614–9004.
Director for—
  Administrative Law.—Conrad Von Wald, room 5D116, 614–4075.
  Civil Law and Litigation.—Col. Peter R. Marksteiner, JBANAFW, suite 1530 (240) 612–4610.
  Civilian Career Development, Plans and Programs.—David Sprowls, room 5D116, 692–2828.
  Commercial Law and Litigation.—Col. Robert J. Preston, JBANAFW, suite 1780, 612–6620.
  Operations and International Law.—Col. Robert A. Ramey, room 5D116 (703) 695–9633.
  Professional Development.—Col. Charles L. Plummer, room 5D116, 614–3021.
  USAF Court of Criminal Appeals.—Col. Mark L. Allred, JBANAFW, suite 1900, 612–5070.
  USAF Judiciary.—Col. Charles C. Killion, JBANAFW, suite 1310, 612–4760.
  USAF Trial Judiciary.—Col. Vance H. Spath, JBANAFW, suite 1150, 612–4570.

LEGAL OPERATIONS

Commander, Air Force Legal Operations Agency.—Brig. Gen. Dixie A. Morrow, JB Andrews, suite 1320 (240) 612–4590.

Command Paralegal Manager, Air Force Legal Operations Agency.—CMSgt Patricia Granan, suite 1320 (240) 612–4594.

DIRECTORATE OF LEGISLATIVE LIAISON

Pentagon, 1160 Air Force, 20330

Rayburn House Office Building, Room B–322, 20515 (RHOB)

Russell Senate Office Building, Room SR–182, 20510 (RSOB)

Director.—Maj. Gen. Thomas W. Bergeson, room 4E812 (703) 697–4142.
Deputy Director.—Christy Nolta (703) 697–4142.
Director of Staff.—Col. Daniel A. Blake, 4B852, 693–0315.
Mobilization Assistant to the Director.—Col. Farris "Carlos" Hill, 697–4142.
Executive Officer to the Director.—Lt. Col. Heather C.D. Marshall, 697–4142.
Congressional Actions.—Stephen Frye, room 4B852, 695–0182.
Congressional Inquiry and Travel.—Col. Matthew H. Yetishefsky, room 4B852, 697–3786.
House Liaison Office.—Col. Wesley Hallman, RHOB (202) 685–4531.
Programs and Legislation.—Matt Ernest, room 4B852 (703) 693–9111.
Senate Liaison Office.—Brig. Gen. Billy D. Thompson, RSOB (202) 685–2573.
Weapons Systems.—Col. David Slaydon, room 4B852 (703) 697–3376.

NATIONAL GUARD BUREAU

1636 Defense Pentagon (1E169), Washington, DC 20301

Chief.—GEN Frank G. Grass, Pentagon, room 1E169 (703) 614–3087.
Vice Chief.—Lt. Gen. Joseph L. Lengyel, Pentagon, room 1E169, 614–3038.
Legislative Liaison.—Brig. Gen. James K. Vogel, Pentagon, room 1D157 (571) 256–7339.
Director for—
　　Air National Guard.—Lt. Gen. Stanley Clarke, Pentagon, room 4E126, 614–8033.
　　Army National Guard.—LTG Timothy J. Kadavy, Arlington Hall Readiness Center, 111 South George Mason Drive, Arlington, VA 22204 (703) 607–7005.

OFFICE OF PUBLIC AFFAIRS

Director.—Brig. Gen. Kathleen Cook (703) 697–6061.
Executive Officer.—Maj. Christina Sukach.
Chief of:
　　Current Operations.—Lt. Col. Brett Ashworth, 695–0640.
　　Engagement.—Wendy Varhegyi, 695–9664.
　　Requirements and Development.—Sherry Medders, 697–6701.
　　Strategy and Assessment.—Col. Sean Monogue, 697–6715.

AIR FORCE RESERVE

Pentagon, 1150 Air Force, Room 4E138, 20330

Chief, Air Force Reserve/Commander, Air Force Reserve Command.—Lt. Gen. James F. Jackson (703) 695–9225.
Deputy to Chief of Air Force Reserve.—Maj. Gen. Maryanne Miller, 695–5528.
Executive Officer.—Col. Melissa A. Coburn, 695–5528.
Assistant Executive Officer.—Lt. Col. Angela Gundersen, 695–5528.
Executive SNCO.—SMSgt Adele Ruiz, 614–7307.

SCIENTIFIC ADVISORY BOARD

1500 West Perimeter Road, Suite 3300, Joint Base Andrews, MD 20762

Chair.—Dr. Werner Dahm (240) 612–5513.
Vice Chair.—Dr. Iain Boyd, 612–5513.
Military Director.—Lt. Gen. Arnold Bunch (Pentagon 4E962), (703) 697–6363.
Executive Director.—Lt. Col. Chris Jenkins (Pentagon 5E815), (703) 695–4297.
Administration.—MSgt Michael Salopek, 612–5500.

AIR FORCE SCIENTIST

Pentagon, 1075 Air Force, Room 4E130, 20330

Chief Scientist.—Dr. Mica R. Endsley (703) 697–7842.
Military Assistant.—Col. Anne Clark.

AIR FORCE OFFICE OF SMALL BUSINESS PROGRAMS

1060 Air Force Pentagon, Room 4E268, Washington, DC 20330–1060

Director.—Mark S. Teskey.
Deputy Director.—Carol E. White.
Executive Assistant.—Nina M. Payne.

SURGEON GENERAL

Pentagon, 1780 Air Force, Room 4E114, 20330–1780

7700 Arlington Boulevard, Suite 5152, Falls Church, VA 22042–5152

Surgeon General.—Lt. Gen. Thomas Travis (703) 692–6800.
  Executive Officer.—Lt. Col. Terence Cunningham, 692–6990.
  Deputy Surgeon General.—Maj. Gen. Mark Ediger, 681–6994.
  Executive Officer.—Maj. Vanessa Wong, 681–6994.
  Director for—
    Congressional and Public Affairs.—Tony Joyner, 681–7921.
    Financial Management.—Col. Billy Cecil, 681–6933.
    Force Development.—Maj. Gen. Charles Potter, 681–8157.
    Medical Operations.—Brig. Gen. Dorothy Hogg, 681–7113.
    Modernization.—Brig. Gen. James Carroll, 681–8137.
    Strategic Plans and Programs.—Farah Sharshar, 681–5639.
  Corps Director for—
    Biomedical Sciences.—Col. Richard Mooney, 681–7616.
    Dental Corps.—Col. Michael Cunningham, 681–6993.
    Medical.—Col. Dominic Hootsman, 681–6993.
    Medical Services.—Col. Patrick Dawson, 681–6993.
    Nursing.—Col. Stephen Donaldson, 681–8157.

DIRECTORATE OF TEST AND EVALUATION

Pentagon, 1650 Air Force, Room 4E276, 20330

Director.—Devin L. Cate (703) 697–4774.
  Deputy Director.—Tanya M. Skeen.
  Executive Assistant.—Dawniel C. Conner.

ARMY AND AIR FORCE EXCHANGE SERVICE

3911 S. Walton Walker Boulevard, Dallas, TX 75236, phone 1–800–527–6790

Director/Chief Executive Officer.—Thomas C. Shull.
  Deputy Director.—Michael E. Immler.
  Chief Operating Officer.—Michael P. Howard.

WASHINGTON OFFICE/OFFICE OF THE BOARD OF DIRECTORS

2530 Crystal Drive, Suite 4158, 4th Floor

Arlington, VA 22202, phone (703) 602–3439

Director.—Gregg Cox.

DEPARTMENT OF THE ARMY

The Pentagon, Washington, DC 20310

phone (703) 695–2442

SECRETARY OF THE ARMY

101 Army Pentagon, Room 3E700, Washington, DC 20310–0101

phone (703) 695–1717, fax (703) 697–8036

Secretary of the Army.—Hon. John M. McHugh.
Executive Officer.—LTC (P) Michael G. Pratt.

UNDER SECRETARY OF THE ARMY

102 Army Pentagon, Room 3E700, Washington, DC 20310–0102

phone (703) 695–4311, fax (703) 697–8036

Under Secretary of the Army.—Hon. Brad R. Carson.
Executive Officer.—COL Andrea Thompson.

CHIEF OF STAFF OF THE ARMY (CSA)

200 Army Pentagon, Room 3E672, Washington, DC 20310–0200

phone (703) 697–0900, fax (703) 614–5268

Chief of Staff, Army.—GEN Raymond T. Odierno.
Executive Officer.—COL Andrew M. Rohling.
Vice Chief of Staff, Army.—GEN Daniel B. Allyn (703) 695–4371.
Executive Officer.—COL Mark H. Landes (703) 695–4371.
Director, CSA Staff Group.—COL Christopher Norrie, room 3D654 (703) 693–8371.
Director of the Army Staff.—LTG William T. Grisoli, room 3E663 (703) 693–7707.
Sergeant Major of the Army.—SMA Daniel A. Dailey, room 3E677 (703) 695–2150.
Directors:
 Army Protocol.—Heidi Hulst, room 3A532 (703) 692–6701.
 Executive Communications and Control.—Thea Harvell III, room 3D664 (703) 695–7552.
 Joint and Defense Affairs.—COL Kevin Dunlop, room 3D644 (703) 614–8217.

Direct Reporting Units
 Commanding General, U.S. Army Test and Evaluation Command.—MG Peter D. Utley
  (703) 681–9360 / (410) 306–3327.
 Superintendent, U.S. Military Academy.—LTG Robert L. Caslen, Jr. (845) 938–2610.
 Commanding General, U.S. Army Military District of Washington.—MG Jeffrey S. Buchanan
  (202) 685–2807.
 Commandant, U.S. Army War College.—MG William E. Rapp (717) 245–4400.

DEPUTY UNDER SECRETARY OF THE ARMY (DUSA)

101 Army Pentagon, Room 3E650, Washington, DC 20310–0001

phone (703) 697–5075, fax (703) 697–3145

Deputy Under Secretary.—Thomas E. Hawley.
Deputy.—Vacant.
Executive Officer.—Mark Von Heeringen, room 3A514 (703) 695–8375.
Executive Assistant.—Renee L. Hughes, room 3E650 (703) 697–5075.

ASSISTANT SECRETARY OF THE ARMY

(ACQUISITION, LOGISTICS AND TECHNOLOGY) (ASA(ALT))

103 Army Pentagon, Room 2E532, Washington, DC 20310–0103

phone (703) 693–6153, fax (703) 697–40034

Assistant Secretary.—Hon. Heidi Shyu.
  Principal Deputy.—Gabriel O. Camarillo, room 2E520 (703) 614–4372.
  Principal Military Deputy.—LTG Michael E. Williamson, room 2E532 (703) 697–0356.
  Chief of Staff.—COL Karen D. Saunders (703) 695–5749.
  Executive Officer.—LTC Scott Beall (703) 695–6742.
  Confidential Assistant.—Anita J. Odom (703) 695–6153.
  Executive Assistant to the Military Deputy.—Patty Laws (703) 693–3927.
  Deputy Assistant Secretary of the Army (DASA):
    Acquisition and Systems Management.—MG Paul A. Ostrowski (703) 695–3115.
    Acquisition, Policy and Logistics.—Steven Karl (acting), (703) 697–5050.
    Defense Exports and Cooperation.—Ann Castiglione-Cataldo (703) 614–3434.
    Plans, Programs and Resources.—Thomas E. Mullins (703) 697–0387.
    Procurement.—Harry P. Hallock (703) 695–2488.
    Research and Technology.—Mary J. Miller (703) 692–1830.

Direct Reporting Units
Director, U.S. Army Acquisition Support Center.—Craig Spisak (703) 805–1013.

ASSISTANT SECRETARY OF THE ARMY (CIVIL WORKS) (ASA(CW))

108 Army Pentagon, Room 3E446, Washington, DC 20310–0108

phone (703) 697–4672, fax (703) 697–7401

Assistant Secretary.—Hon. Jo-Ellen Darcy.
  Principal Deputy.—Marie Therese Dominguez (703) 695–1370.
  Executive Officer.—COL Reinhard W. Koenig (703) 697–9809.
  Military Assistant.—LTC Antoinette R. Gant (703) 695–0482.
  Executive Assistant.—Regena Townsend-Treleaven (703) 697–4672.
  Deputy Assistant Secretary of the Army (DASA):
    Management and Budget.—Eric V. Hansen, room 3E441 (703) 695–1376.
    Policy, Planning and Review.—Douglas W. Lamont, GAO–6S91 (202) 761–0016.

ASSISTANT SECRETARY OF THE ARMY

(FINANCIAL MANAGEMENT AND COMPTROLLER) (ASA(FM&C))

109 Army Pentagon, Room 3E320, Washington, DC 20310–0109

phone (703) 614–4356, fax (703) 693–7584

Assistant Secretary.—Hon. Robert M. Speer.
  Principal Deputy.—Vacant (703) 614–4337.
  Military Deputy for Budget.—LTG Karen E. Dyson (703) 614–4034.
  Executive Officer.—COL Arie J. McSherry (703) 614–4292.
  Military Assistant.—MAJ Carmen J. Iglesias (703) 614–4240.
  Executive Assistant.—Deborah Glembocki (703) 614–1506.
  Deputy Assistant Secretary of the Army:
    Cost and Economics.—Stephen G. Barth, room 3E352 (703) 614–7550.
    Financial Information Management.—COL John T. Vogel (acting), room 3A320 (703) 692–8529.
    Financial Operations.—Laura N. Jankovich, room 3A320A (703) 693–2758.
  Director, Army Budget.—MG Thomas A. Horlander, room 3E336, 614–1573.
  Director, U.S. Army Financial Management Command.—COL Darrell Brimberry (317) 212–3617.

ASSISTANT SECRETARY OF THE ARMY

(INSTALLATIONS, ENERGY AND ENVIRONMENT) (ASA(IE&E))

110 Army Pentagon, Room 3E464, Washington, DC 20310–0110

phone (703) 692–9800, fax (703) 692–9808

Assistant Secretary.—Hon. Katherine G. Hammack.
Principal Deputy.—J. Randall Robinson (703) 692–9802.
Executive Officer.—COL Andrew W. Backus (703) 692–9804.
Military Assistant.—LTC Stephen J. Kolouch (703) 692–9805.
Executive Assistant.—Michelle R. Soares (703) 692–9800.
Deputy Assistant Secretary of the Army:
  Energy and Sustainability.—Richard G. Kidd IV, room 3D453 (703) 692–9890.
  Environment, Safety and Occupational Health.—Hershel "Hew" E. Wolfe, room 3D453
    (703) 697–1913.
  Installations, Housing and Partnerships.—Paul D. Cramer, room 3E475 (703) 697–0867.
  Strategic Integration.—Mark D. Rocke, room 3D453 (703) 692–9817.

ASSISTANT SECRETARY OF THE ARMY

(MANPOWER AND RESERVE AFFAIRS) (ASA(M&RA))

111 Army Pentagon, Room 2E460, Washington, DC 20310–0111

phone (703) 697–9253, fax (703) 692–9000

Assistant Secretary.—Hon. Debra S. Wada.
Principal Deputy.—Karl F. Schneider (703) 692–1292.
Executive Officer.—COL Michael C. Miller (703) 614–2850.
Executive Assistant.—Wanda L. Artis (703) 697–9253.
Deputy Assistant Secretary of the Army:
  Army Review Boards/Director, Army Review Boards Agency.—Francine C. Blackmon
    (703) 545–5639.
  Deputy Director.—COL Matthew B. Coleman, Crystal City (703) 545–5637.
  Military Personnel Policy and Quality of Life.—Anthony J. Stamilio, room 2D484 (703)
    614–1648.
  Civilian Personnel/Director, Civilian Senior Leader Management Office.—Gwendolyn R.
    DeFilippi, room 2E485 (703) 614–8143.
  Diversity and Leadership.—Larry Stubblefield (703) 614–5284.
  Marketing/Director, Army Marketing and Research Group.—Mark S. Davis (703) 545–
    3439.
  Training, Readiness and Mobilization.—Raymond F. "Fred" Rees, room 2E482 (703)
    697–2631.

Direct Reporting Unit
  U.S. Army Accessions Support Brigade.—COL Brian M. Cavanaugh (502) 626–1751.

ARMY GENERAL COUNSEL (GC)

104 Army Pentagon, Room 2E724, Washington, DC 20310–0104

phone (703) 697–9235, fax (703) 693–9254

General Counsel.—Philip R. Park (senior official).
Principal Deputy General Counsel.—Philip R. Park (acting).
Executive Officer/Special Counsel.—COL John B. Wells III.
Executive Assistant.—Christopher J. McCombs (703) 692–9141.
Deputy General Counsels:
  Acquisition.—Levator Norsworthy, Jr. , room 3C546 (703) 697–5120.
  Ethics and Fiscal Law.—Susan D. Tigner, room 3C546 (703) 695–4296.
  Installations, Environment and Civil Works.—Craig R. Schmauder, room 3C546 (703)
    695–3024.
  Operations and Personnel.—Daniel F. McCallum, room 3C546 (703) 695–0562.

ADMINISTRATIVE ASSISTANT TO THE SECRETARY OF THE ARMY (AASA)

105 Army Pentagon, room 3E733, Washington, DC 20310–0105

phone (703) 695–2442, fax (703) 697–6194

Administrative Assistant to the Secretary of the Army.—Gerald B. O'Keefe.
  Deputy Administrative Assistant.—Mark F. Averill (703) 697–7741.
  Executive Officer.—COL Kevin L. Berry (703) 695–7444.
  Executive Assistant.—Vacant (703) 695–2442.
  Director, Civilian Aides to the Secretary of the Army (CASA).—Laura L. DeFrancisco, room 3D742 (703) 697–2639.
  Executive Directors:
    U.S. Army Center of Military History.—Dr. Richard W. Stewart (acting), Fort McNair, Building 35, room 147 (202) 685–2705.
    U.S. Army Headquarters Services.—Michael E. Reheuser, Fort Belvoir, Building 1458 (703) 545–4870.
    U.S. Army Information Technology Agency.—Gregory L. Garcia, room ME882 (571) 256–1660.
    U.S. Army Resources and Programs Agency.—Mark F. Averill, Fort Belvoir, Building 1458 (703) 545–9393.

ARMY AUDITOR GENERAL

6000 6th Street, Bldg 1464, Fort Belvoir, VA 22060–5609

phone (703) 545–5907, fax (703) 806–1199

Auditor General.—Randall L. Exley.
  Principal Deputy Auditor General.—Joseph P. Bentz (703) 545–5910.
  Executive Officer.—COL Sheila C. Denham (703) 545–5909.
  Executive Assistant.—Carolyn Selquist (703) 545–5907.
  General Counsel.—Michael Hoadley (703) 545–5879.
  Director, Policy and Operations Management.—Felix Strelsky (703) 545–5874.
  Deputy Auditors General:
    Acquisition, Logistics and Technology Audits.—Kathleen A. Nelson (703) 545–5903.
    Financial Management and Comptroller Audits.—Kevin F. Kelly (703) 545–5851.
    Installations, Energy and Environment Audits.—William Jenkins (703) 545–5853.
    Manpower, Reserve Affairs and Training Audits.—Joseph P. Bentz (acting), (703) 545–5877.

ARMY NATIONAL MILITARY CEMETERIES (ANMC)

phone (703) 614–0615, fax (571) 256–3366

Executive Director.—Patrick K. Hallinan.
  Chief of Staff.—COL Joseph Simonelli, Jr. (703) 614–4140.
  Executive Officer.—COL Joseph Simonelli, Jr.(703) 614–4140.
  Executive Assistant.—Christa Petry (703) 614–0615.

Direct Reporting Unit
  Executive Director, Arlington National Cemetery.—Patrick K. Hallinan.
  Superintendent, Arlington National Cemetery.—Jack E. Lechner, Jr.

ASSISTANT CHIEF OF STAFF FOR INSTALLATION MANAGEMENT (ACSIM)

600 Army Pentagon, Room 3E484, Washington, DC 20310–0600

phone (703) 693–3233, fax (703) 693–3507

Assistant Chief of Staff.—LTG David D. Halverson.
  Deputy Assistant Chief of Staff.—Diane M. Randon.
  Executive Officer.—COL John J. Strycula.
  Executive Assistant.—Patricia L. Weaver.
  Director, Army Installation Support Management.—Diane M. Randon.

Direct Reporting Unit
Commanding General, U.S. Army Installation Management Command.—LTG David D. Halverson.

CHIEF ARMY RESERVE (CAR)

2400 Army Pentagon, Room 3E562, Washington, DC 20310–2400

phone (703) 695–0031, fax (703) 697–1891

Chief.—LTG Jeffrey W. Talley.
Assistant Chief.—Barbara A. Sisson (703) 695–0047.
Executive Officer.—COL Martin Klein (703) 695–0042.
Executive Assistant.—Janet L. Pendergraph (703) 695–0031.
Congressional Affairs Communication Officer.—Dorothy G. Singletary (703) 806–7546.

CHIEF INFORMATION OFFICER, G–6 (CIO, G–6)

107 Army Pentagon, Room 3E608, Washington, DC 20310–0107

phone (703) 695–4366, fax (703) 695–3091

Chief Information Officer.—LTG Robert S. Ferrell.
Deputy Chief.—Gary Wang (703) 695–6604.
Executive Officer.—COL Dana S. Tankins (703) 697–5503.
Civilian Executive Officer.—Marilyn Al-Mansoor (703) 695–4366.

Direct Reporting Unit
Second Army.—LTG Edward C. Cardon (703) 706–1517.

CHIEF LEGISLATIVE LIAISON (CLL)

1600 Army Pentagon, Room 1E416, Washington, DC 20310–1600

phone (703) 697–6767, fax (703) 614–7599

Chief.—MG Laura J. Richardson.
Principal Deputy.—Bernard P. Ingold (703) 697–0278.
Deputy.—COL R. J. Lillibridge (703) 695–1235.
Executive Officer.—COL William B. Johnson (703) 695–3524.
Enlisted Aide.—SFC Natasha S. Williams (703) 217–1696.
Executive Assistant.—Dellar M. Burch (703) 697–6767.
Chief Congressional Inquiry.—Harry B. Williams, room 1E423 (703) 697–8381.
Chief House Liaison Division.—COL David Hamilton, room B325, Rayburn House Office Building, Washington, DC (202) 685–2675.
Chief Investigations and Legislative Division.—COL Joseph Berger, room 1E433 (703) 697–8218.
Chief Programs Division.—COL Scott Efflandt, room 1E385 (703) 693–8766.
Chief Senate Liaison Division.—COL Scott Jackson, room SR183, Senate Russell Office Building, Washington, DC (202) 224–2881.
ACoS Operations.—COL Tracy Farrell, room 1D437 (703) 697–3206.
Plans Officer.—MAJ Dennis J. Call, room 1D437 (703) 697–3206.
Chief, Management and Support Operations Division.—Kyle McClelland, room 1E423 (703) 692–4159.

CHIEF NATIONAL GUARD BUREAU (CNGB)

Pentagon, room 1E169, Washington, DC 20301–1636

phone (703) 614–3087, fax (703) 614–0274

Chief.—GEN Frank J. Grass.
Vice Chief.—Lt. Gen. Joseph L. Lengyel (703) 614–3038.
Executive Officer.—COL Jeffrey B. Cashman (703) 614–3087.
Executive Assistant.—Carol Lagasse (703) 614–3117.
Directors:
  Air National Guard.—Lt. Gen. Stanley E. Clarke III (703) 614–8033.
  Army National Guard.—LTG Timothy J. Kadavy, room 2A514B (703) 693–8464.

CHIEF OF CHAPLAINS (CCH)

2700 Army Pentagon, Room 3E524, Washington, DC 20310–2700

phone (703) 695–1133, fax (703) 695–9834

Chief of Chaplains.—(MG) Donald L. Rutherford.
  Deputy Chief of Chaplains.—(BG) Charles Ray Bailey (703) 695–1135.
  Executive Officer.—Chaplain (LTC) Brad Baumann (703) 695–1133.
  Executive Assistant.—Caridad Gelineau (703) 695–1135.

CHIEF OF ENGINEERS (CoE)

GAO Building, 441 G Street NW., 20314–0001

phone (202) 761–0000, fax (202) 761–4463

Chief of Engineers.—LTG Thomas P. Bostick.
  Deputy.—MG Richard L. Stevens (202) 761–0002.
  Director.—COL David C. Hill (703) 693–4407.

Direct Reporting Unit
  Commanding General, U.S. Army Corps of Engineers.—LTG Thomas P. Bostick.
  Deputy.—MG Richard L. Stevens (202) 761–0002.
  Chief of Staff.—COL Michael D. Peloquin (202) 761–0380.
  Executive Officer.—LTC John C. Becking (202) 761–0468.
  Executive Assistant.—Karen Huff (202) 761–0001.

CHIEF, PUBLIC AFFAIRS (CPA)

1500 Army Pentagon, Room 1E484, Washington, DC 20310–1500

phone (703) 695–5135, fax (703) 693–8362

Chief.—BG Malcolm Frost.
  Principal Deputy.—Michael P. Brady (703) 697–1747.
  Deputy.—COL Richard T. Patterson (703) 697–4482.
  Chief of Staff.—Vacant.
  Executive Officer.—LTC Michael C. Nicholson (703) 697–4200.
  Executive Assistant.—Nicole Ortega (703) 695–5135.
  Chief, Media Relations Division.—LTC Alayne P. Conway (703) 693–4723.
  Director, U.S. Army Public Affairs Center.—COL Richard J. McNorton (301) 677–7270.
  Director, U.S. Army Field Band.—Vacant.

DEPUTY CHIEF OF STAFF, G–1 (DCS, G–1) (PERSONNEL)

300 Army Pentagon, Room 2E446, Washington, DC 20310–0300

phone (703) 697–8060

Deputy Chief of Staff.—LTG James C. McConville.
  Assistant Deputy Chief of Staff.—Roy A. Wallace (703) 692–1585.
  Executive Officer.—COL Mark Rado (703) 697–2893.
  Military Assistant.—MAJ Adam Smith (703) 614–1862.
  Executive Assistant.—Deborah Van Heest (703) 697–8060.
  Director, Assistant G–1 for Civilian Personnel.—Jay Aronowitz (703) 695–5701.
  Director, Army Resiliency.—Sharyn Saunders (703) 571–7357.
  Director, Human Systems Integration.—Dr. Michael Drillings (703) 695–6761.
  Director, Military Personnel Management.—MG Thomas Seamands (703) 695–5871.
  Director, Plans and Resources.—Dr. Robert Steinrauf (703) 697–5263.
  Director, Sexual Harassment, Assault and Response Prevention.—Monique Ferrell (703) 695–5568.
  Director, Technology and Business Architecture Integration.—Jeanne Brooks (703) 614–5138.

Field Operating Agencies
  Commanding General, U.S. Army Human Resources Command.—MG Richard P. Mustion (502) 613–8844.
  Director, U.S. Army Civilian Human Resources Agency.—Rhonda K. Diaz (410) 306–1701.

DEPUTY CHIEF OF STAFF, G–2 (DCS, G–2) (INTELLIGENCE)
1000 Army Pentagon, Room 2E408, Washington, DC 20310–1000
phone (703) 695–3033, fax (703) 697–7605

Deputy Chief of Staff.—LTG Mary A. Legere.
Assistant Deputy Chief of Staff.—Jeffrey N. Rapp.
Military Deputy.—MG William F. Duffy.
Executive Officer.—COL Jim Lee.
Executive Assistant.—Anne H. Fesmire.

Direct Reporting Unit
Commanding General, U.S. Army Intelligence and Security Command.—MG George J. Franz III.

DEPUTY CHIEF OF STAFF, G–3 (DCS, G–3) (OPERATIONS)
400 Army Pentagon, Room 2E670, Washington, DC 20310–0400
phone (703) 695–2904, fax (703) 697–4660

Deputy Chief of Staff.—LTG James L. Huggins, Jr.
Assistant Deputy Chief.—Dr. David M. Markowitz (703) 692–7883.
Military Assistant Deputy Chief.—MG Gary H. Cheek (703) 697–5180.
Executive Officer.—COL Ryan J. Kuhn (703) 697–4521.
Executive Assistant.—LTC Christopher L. Smith (703) 695–3447.
Director, Capabilities and Integration.—Peter Bechtel (703) 614–9120.
Director, Operations, Readiness, and Mobilization.—BG Ryan F. Gonsalves (703) 695–0526.
Director, Strategy, Plans, and Policy.—MG William C. Hix (703) 692–8805.
Director, Training.—BG JP "Pete" Johnson.

Field Operating Agencies
Director, U.S. Army Force Management Support Agency.—BG Roger L. Cloutier (703) 693–3227.
Director, U.S. Army Command and Control Support Agency.—COL Kenneth A. Stevens (703) 697–1245
Director, U.S. Army Nuclear and Combating WMD Agency.—Daniel M. Klippstein (703) 614–2670.

DEPUTY CHIEF OF STAFF, G–4 (DCS, G–4) (LOGISTICS)
500 Army Pentagon, Room 1E394, Washington, DC 20310–0500
phone (703) 695–4104, fax (703) 692–0759

Deputy Chief of Staff.—LTG Gustave F. Perna.
Assistant Deputy Chief.—Kathleen S. Miller (703) 697–9138.
Assistant Deputy Chief/Operations.—MG Dwayne A. Gamble (703) 697–5032.
Executive Officer.—COL Charles Hamilton (703) 697–9039.
Executive Assistant.—Torwanna D. Herbert (703) 695–4102.
Director, Force Projection and Distribution.—COL David G. Touznsky, room 1E380 (703) 697–2281.
Director, Logistics Information Management.—Alexander B. Raulerson, room 1E391 (703) 695–6160.
Director, Operations and Logistics Readiness.—Carlos D. Morrison, room 1E367 (703) 697–8007.
Director, Maintenance Policy, Programs and Processes.—Christopher J. Lowman, room 1E360 (703) 693–1624.
Director, Resource Management.—John A. "Art" Hagler, room 1E380 (703) 693–1900.
Director, Strategy and Integration.—COL Christopher J. Sharpsten, room 1E369 (703) 692–5127.
Director, Supply Policy, Programs and Processes.—Michael B. Cervone, room 1E360 (703) 693–1584.

Field Operating Agency
Director, U.S. Army Logistics Innovation Agency.—Michael K. Williams (703) 805–5440.

DEPUTY CHIEF OF STAFF, G–8 (DCS, G–8) (PROGRAMS)
700 Army Pentagon, Room 3E406, Washington, DC 20310–0700
phone (703) 697–8232, fax (703) 697–8242

Deputy Chief of Staff.—LTG Anthony R. Ierardi.
Assistant Deputy Chief.—Donald C. Tison (703) 692–9099.
Executive Officer.—COL Neil E. Fitzpatrick (703) 697–8232.
Executive Assistant.—Jessica M. Collins (703) 697–8236.
Director, Force Development.—MG Robert M. Dyess, Jr. (703) 692–7707.
Director, Program Analysis and Evaluation.—MG John G. Ferrari (703) 697–1475.
Director, Quadrennial Defense Review.—BG Frank M. Muth (703) 695–8997.

Field Operating Agency
Director, U.S. Army Center for Army Analysis.—Dr. William F. Crain (703) 806-5510.

DIRECTOR OF THE ARMY STAFF (DAS)
202 Army Pentagon, room 3E663, Washington, DC 20310–0202
phone (703) 693–7710, fax (703) 695–6117

Director of the Army Staff.—LTG William T. Grisoli.
Vice Director.—Steven J. Redmann, room 3D644 (703) 695–0294.
Executive Officer.—COL Thomas C. Hawn (703) 693–7710.
Executive Assistant.—Jill D. Goetz (703) 695–6117.

Field Operating Agency
Commanding General, U.S. Army Combat Readiness/Safety Center.—BG Jeffrey A. Farnsworth (334) 255–9360.

PROVOST MARSHAL GENERAL (PMG)
2800 Army Pentagon, room 1E596, Washington, DC 203103–2800
phone (703) 692–6966, fax (703) 614–5628

Provost Marshal General.—MG Mark S. Inch.
Deputy.—COL Dan McElroy (703) 692–7290.
Executive Officer.—COL Eugenia K. Guilmartin (703) 692–6970.
Chief of Staff.—Herman "Tracy" Williams III (703) 692–6829.
Executive Assistant.—Meribeth M. Puckett (703) 695–4036.

Direct Reporting Unit
Commanding General, U.S. Army Criminal Investigation Command.—MG Mark S. Inch.

Field Operating Agencies
Commanding General, U.S. Army Corrections Command.—MG Mark S. Inch.
Director, Defense Forensics and Biometrics Agency.—Donald G. Salo, Jr. (703) 571-0507.

OFFICE OF SMALL BUSINESS PROGRAMS (OSBP)
106 Army Pentagon, Room 3B514, Washington, DC 20310–0106
phone (703) 697–2868, fax (703) 693–3898

Director.—Tommy L. Marks.
Deputy/Executive Officer.—James C. Lloyd (acting), (703) 693–6113.
Executive Assistant.—Veronica Atkinson (703) 697–2868.

THE INSPECTOR GENERAL (TIG)
1700 Army Pentagon, Room 3E588, Washington, DC 20310–1700
phone (703) 695–1500, fax (703) 614–5628

The Inspector General.—LTG David E. Quantock.

Deputy Inspector General.—MG James H. Dickinson (703) 695–1501.
Executive Officer.—COL Joe Tyler (703) 695–1502.
Executive Assistant.—MSG John Marshall (703) 695–1500.

Field Operating Agency
Commanding General, U.S. Army Inspector General Agency.—LTG David E. Quantock.

THE JUDGE ADVOCATE GENERAL (TJAG)

2200 Army Pentagon, Room 3E542, Washington, DC 20310–2200
phone (703) 697–5151, fax (703) 697–1059

The Judge Advocate General.—LTG Flora D. Darpino.
Deputy Judge Advocate General.—MG Thomas E. Ayres (703) 693–5112.
Executive Officer.—COL George R. Smawley (703) 695–3786.
Executive Assistant.—Cindy G. Mitchell (703) 697–5151.

Field Operating Agencies
Commander, U.S. Army Legal Services Agency.—BG Charles N. Pede (703) 693–1100.
Commander/Commandant, U.S. Army Judge Advocate General's Legal Center and School.—
BG Stuart W. Risch (434) 971–3301.

THE SURGEON GENERAL (TSG)

7700 Arlington Boulevard, Defense Health Headquarters (DHHQ)
Falls Church, VA 22042, phone (703) 681–3000, fax (703) 681–3167

The Surgeon General.—LTG Patricia D. Horoho.
Deputy.—MG Joseph Caravalho, Jr. (703) 681–3002.
Chief of Staff.—Uldric L. "Ric" Fiore, Jr. (703) 681–9514.
Executive Officer.—COL William Stubbs (703) 681–3004.
Executive Assistant.—LTC John E. White (703) 695–1647.
Command Sergeant Major.—CSM Gerald C. Ecker (703) 681–8046.
Operations Center.—Duty Officer-in-Charge (703) 681–8052.

Direct Reporting Unit
Commanding General, U.S. Army Medical Command.—LTG Patricia D. Horoho.

ARMY COMMANDS

U.S. ARMY FORCES COMMAND (FORSCOM)

4700 Knox Street, Fort Bragg, NC 28310–5000
phone (910) 570–5052, fax (910) 570–1971

Commanding General.—GEN Mark A. Milley.
Deputy Commanding General.—LTG Patrick J. Donahue (910) 570–5001.
Chief of Staff.—MG Jimmie Jaye Wells (910) 570–5002.
Executive Officer.—COL Matt McFarlane (910) 570–5053.
Command Sergeant Major.—CSM Scott C. Shroeder (910) 570–5045.
Secretary of the General Staff.—COL Vincent D. Thompson (910) 570–5004.
Operations Center.—COL Larry A. Jackson (910) 570–6765.
Staff Action Control Officers.—Greg W. Tegg (910) 570–5040; Annette Taiwo (910) 570–5041.
Liaison Office (Washington, DC): Jennifer Bhartiya (703) 697–2252; LTC Bryce D. Pringle. (703) 697–2591.

U.S. ARMY TRAINING AND DOCTRINE COMMAND (TRADOC)

950 Jefferson Avenue, Fort Eustis, VA 23604–5700

phone (757) 501–6469, fax (757) 501–6576

Commanding General.—GEN David G. Perkins.
Executive Officer.—COL Antonio A. Aguto, Jr. (757) 501–6472.
Deputy Commanding General/Chief of Staff.—LTG Kevin W. Mangum (757) 501–6478.
Executive Officer.—COL James A. Rupkalvis (757) 501–6466.
Deputy Chief of Staff.—MG Rex A. Spitler (757) 501–6495.
Executive Officer.—LTC Daniel L. Leex (757) 501–6485.
Command Sergeant Major.—CSM David S. Davenport, Sr. (acting), (757) 501–6464.
Secretary of the General Staff.—Radames Cornier, Jr. (757) 501–5204.
Director, G–33/Operations Center.—James G. Lynch (757) 501–5094.

U.S. ARMY MATERIEL COMMAND (AMC)

4400 Martin Road, Redstone Arsenal, AL 35898–5000

phone (256) 450–6000, fax (256) 450–8833

Commanding General.—GEN Dennis L. Via.
Deputy Commanding General.—LTG Patricia E. McQuistion (256) 450–6100.
Executive Deputy Commanding General.—John B. Nerger (256) 450–6200.
Chief of Staff.—BG Edward M. Daly (256) 450–7867.
Executive Officer.—COL David Wilson (256) 450–6005.
Command Sergeant Major.—CSM James K. Sims (256) 450–6300.
Secretary of the General Staff.—LTC Monica Y. Robinson (256) 450–6440.
Operations Center.—Duty Officer-in-Charge (256) 450–9496.

ARMY SERVICE COMPONENT COMMANDS

LIAISON OFFICES

Pentagon, Washington, DC 203100

U.S. Army Africa/Southern European Task Force (USARAF/SETAF).—COL Patrick T. Sullivan, room 3D513 (571) 256–1803.
U.S. Army Central (USARCENT): Hank Foresman, room 2B475A4 (703) 693–4033; Mark R. Seeger, room 2B485 (703) 693–4035.
U.S. Army Europe (USAREUR).—Timothy C. Touzinsky, room 1E1074 (703) 692–6886.
U.S. Army North (USARNORTH).—John D. Nelson, room 2B485 (703) 692–6893.
U.S. Army Pacific (USARPAC).—Robert Ralston, room 2B485 (703) 693–4082.
U.S. Army South (USARSO).—LTC Phil Johnson, room 2D337 (703) 692–8221.
U.S. Army Space and Missile Defense Command/Army Strategic Command (SMCD/ARSTRAT): Christine Kral (703) 614–9592, room 2D831; COL Clark H. Risner (703) 614–9593.
Military Surface Deployment and Distribution Command (SDDC): COL Riley Cheramie (703) 571–9708; Melissa Higginbotham (703) 571–9710, room 2B858.

JOINT FORCE HEADQUARTERS-NATIONAL CAPITAL REGION

AND MILITARY DISTRICT OF WASHINGTON (JFHQ–NCR / MDW)

102 3rd Avenue, Building 39, Fort Lesley J. McNair, 20319

phone (202) 685–2807, fax (202) 685–3481

Commanding General.—MG Jeffrey S. Buchanan.
Executive Officer.—LTC Aaron L. Freeman (202) 685–2817.
Aide de Camp.—CPT Travis N. Reinold (202) 685–2807.
Deputy Commander.—Egon F. Hawrylak (202) 685–1949.
JTF Deputy.—RDML Markham K. Rich (202) 433–2777.
Command Sergeant Major.—CSM David O. Turnbull (202) 685–2923.
Chief of Staff.—COL Mark Bertolini (202) 685–2812.
Secretary of the General Staff.—Corey R. Langenwalter (202) 685–0640.

U.S. ARMY SPECIAL OPERATIONS COMMAND
Fort Bragg, NC 28310–5200
phone (910) 432–3000, fax (910) 432–4243

Commanding General.—LTG Charles T. Cleveland.
  Deputy Commanding General.—MG Clarence K. Chinn (910) 432–6622.
  Chief of Staff.—COL Patrick B. Roberson (910) 432–9861.
  Command Sergeant Major.—George A. Bequer (910) 432–0946.
  Secretary of the General Staff.—Charles E. Pimble (910) 432–7001.

DEPARTMENT OF THE NAVY

Pentagon 20350–1000, phone (703) 695–3131

OFFICE OF THE SECRETARY OF THE NAVY

Pentagon, Room 4E686, phone (703) 695–3131

Secretary of the Navy.—Ray Mabus.
  Confidential Assistant.—J. Scarbrough.
  Executive Assistant.—CAPT L. Franchetti, USN.
  Special Assistant.—T. Oppel.
  Administrative Aide.—CDR V. Burks, USN, 695–5410.
  Marine Personal Aide.—MAJ J. Livingston, USMC, 614–3100.
  Navy Personal Aide.—LCDR K. Jones, USN, 614–6473.
  Special Assistant for Public Affairs.—CAPT P. Kunze, 697–7491.
  Senior Military Assistant.—COL K. Heckl, USMC.

OFFICE OF THE UNDER SECRETARY OF THE NAVY

Pentagon, Room 4E720, phone (703) 695–3141

Under Secretary of the Navy.—Vacant.
  Executive Assistant and Naval Aide.—Vacant.
  Executive Assistant and Marine Aide.—COL Ronald Jones.
  Special Assistant.—Vacant.
  Administrative Assistants: YN1 Granville Johns, SSgt Mauricio Tellez.

GENERAL COUNSEL

Pentagon, Room 4E782, phone (703) 614–1994

General Counsel.—Hon. Paul L. Oostburg Sanz.
  Principal Deputy General Counsel.—Anne Brennan, 614–8733.
  Executive Assistant and Special Counsel.—CAPT Gordon Modari, JAGC, USN.
  Associate General Counsel for—
    Litigation.—R. Borro, Washington Navy Yard, Building 36 (202) 685–6989.
    Deputy General Counsel.—Thomas Ledvina, room 4E791, 614–6870.
  Assistant General Counsel for—
    Ethics.—Joel Weger (acting), room 4D641, 614–7425.
    Manpower and Reserve Affairs.—R. Woods, room 4D548, 614–1377.
    Research, Development and Acquisition.—Tom Frankfurt, room 4C682, 614–6985.
  Military Assistant.—Lt. Col. Stephen Stewartl, USMC, room 4E782, 692–6164.
  Administrative Assistant.—LT John Erickson, USN, room 4E782, 693–7813.

NAVAL INSPECTOR GENERAL

Washington Navy Yard, 1254 9th Street, SE., Building 172, 20374, phone (202) 433–2000

Inspector General.—VADM James P. Wisecup.
  Deputy Naval Inspector General.—Andrea Brotherton.

U.S. NAVY OFFICE OF INFORMATION

1200 Navy Pentagon, Room 4B463, Phone (703) 697–7391

Duty (703) 850–1047

Chief of Information (CI).—RDML John F. Kirby.
  Vice Chief of Information (VCI).—RDML Vic M. Beck.
  Deputy, Chief of Information (DCI).—CAPT Dawn E. Cutler.
  Executive Assistant to Chief of Information (EA).—CDR Tamara D. Lawrence.
  Flag Aide to Chief of Information.—LT Rebecca Rebarich.

651

Senior Enlisted Advisor (SEA).—MCPO Jon McMillan.
Staff Senior Enlisted Leader (SEL).—CPO Cody Harmon.
Flag Writer-PO1.—Juan P. Cisneros.
Assistant Chief for—
  Administration and Resource Management (OI–1).—William Mason, 692–4747.
  Afloat Media Systems (OI–7).—Janet Quigley (202) 781–3313.
  Communication Integration and Strategy (OI–9).—CDR Elissa Smith, 692–4728.
  Community Outreach (OI–6).—Rob Newell, 614–1879.
  Defense Media Activity (DMA) Liaison (OI–4).—LCDR David Luckett (301) 222–6401.
  Media Operations (OI–3).—CDR Ryan Perry, 697–5342.
  Navy Media Content Services (OI–2).—Chris Madden, 614–9154.
  Requirements and Policy (OI–8).—Bruce Cole, 695–0911.

JUDGE ADVOCATE GENERAL

Pentagon, Room 4C 642

Washington Navy Yard, 1322 Patterson Avenue, Suite 3000, 20374–5066

phone (703) 614–7420, fax (703) 697–4610

Judge Advocate General.—VADM Nanette M. DeRenzi.
  Executive Assistant.—CAPT David Grogan.
  Deputy Judge Advocate General.—RADM James W. Crawford III.
  Executive Assistant to the Deputy Judge Advocate General.—CDR Laurin Eskridge.
Assistant Judge Advocate General for Civil Law.—CAPT Kirk R. Foster, Pentagon, room 4D640, 614–7415, fax 614–9400.
Deputy Assistant Judge Advocate General for—
  Administrative Law.—CAPT Scott Thompson, 614–7415.
  Admiralty.—CAPT Anne B. Fischer (202) 685–5075.
  Claims, Investigations and Tort Litigation.—Patricia A. Leonard (202) 685–4600, fax 685–5484.
  General Litigation.—Grant Lattin (202) 685–5450, fax 685–5472.
  International and Operational Law.—CAPT Stuart W. Belt, 697–5406.
  Legal Assistance.—CDR Andrew R. House (202) 685–4642, fax 685–5486.
  National Security Litigation and Intelligence Law.—CDR Andrew Levitz (202) 685–5464, fax 685–5467.
Assistant Judge Advocate General for Military Justice.—COL John Ewers, USMC, Building 58, 3rd Floor, Washington Navy Yard, 20374–1111 (202) 685–7053, fax 685–7084.
Deputy Assistant Judge Advocate General for Criminal Law.—CAPT Robert J. Crow, USN (202) 685–7056, fax 685–7687.
Assistant Judge Advocate General for Operations and Management.—CAPT John Hannink (202) 685–5190, fax 685–8510.
Deputy Assistant Judge Advocate General for—
  Military Personnel.—CAPT Mark F. Klein (202) 685–7254, fax 685–5489.
  Reserve and Retired Personnel Programs.—LCDR Kathleen A. Elkins (202) 685–5397, fax 685–8510.
  Technology, Operations and Plans.—CDR Melissa Powers (202) 685–5230, fax 685–5479.
Special Assistants to the Judge Advocate General—
  Command Master Chief.—LNCM Paul C. St. Sauver (202) 685–5194, fax 685–8510.
  Comptroller.—Dawn C. Rooney (202) 685–5274, fax 685–5455.
  Inspector General.—Vacant (202) 685–5192, fax 685–5461.

LEGISLATIVE AFFAIRS

Room 4C549, phone (703) 697–7146, fax 697–1009

Chief.—RADM Michael Franken.
  Deputy Chief.—CAPT Mark Davis.
  Executive Assistant.—LCDR Micah Murphy.
  Congressional Information and Public Affairs.—CDR Gary Ross, 695–0395.
  Congressional Operations.—Dee Wingfield, 693–5764.
  Director for—
    House Liaison.—CAPT Paul Gronemeyer (202) 225–7808.
      Assistant House Liaison.—LCDR Jason Grizzle (202) 225–3075.
    Legislation.—CDR Dom Flatt, 697–2851.

Naval Programs.—Tom Crowley, 693–2919.
Senate Liaison.—CAPT James Loeblein (202) 685–6006.
Assistant Senate Liaison.—CDR Mike Vitali (202) 685–6007.

ASSISTANT SECRETARY FOR FINANCIAL MANAGEMENT AND COMPTROLLER
Pentagon, Room 4E618, phone (703) 697–2325

Executive Assistant and Naval Aide.—CAPT Daniel H. Fillion, USN.
Military Assistant and Marine Aide.—MAJ Edna Rodriguez, USMC.
Director, Office of:
  Budget.—RADM Joseph R. Mulloy, USN, room 4E348, 697–7105.
  Financial Operations.—D. Taitano, WNY (202) 685–6701.

ASSISTANT SECRETARY FOR ENERGY, INSTALLATIONS AND ENVIRONMENT
Pentagon, Room 4E739, phone (703) 693–4530

Assistant Secretary.—Vacant.
  Executive Assistant and Naval Aide.—CAPT Yancy Lindsey.
  Confidential Assistant.—Sgt Karl Strong.
  Military Aide.—LCDR Ben Wainwright.
  Principal Deputy for Energy, Installations and Environment.—Roger Natsuhara, room 4E739, 693–4530.
  Assistant General Counsel.—Craig Jensen, 614–1098.
  Deputy of:
    Energy.—Tom Hicks (571) 256–7879.
    Environment.—D. Schregardus, 614–5493.
    Safety.—Paul Hanley, 614–5516.

ASSISTANT SECRETARY FOR MANPOWER AND RESERVE AFFAIRS
Pentagon, Room 4E598, phone (703) 695–4333

Assistant Secretary.—Hon. Juan M. Garcia, room 4E598, 695 4333.
  Principal Deputy.—Robert Cali, room 4E598, 692–6162.
  Executive Assistant and Naval Aide.—CAPT Michael Selby, room 4E598, 695–4537.
  Military Assistant and Marine Aide.—COL Samuel Mowery, room 4E598, 697–0975.
  Secretary.—Antonio Sturgis, room 4E598, 695–4333.
  Administrative Officer.—Michael Stokes, room 4E590, 697–2179.
  Administrative Chief.—YNC Tyrone Pierce, room 4E590, 695–6472.
  Administrative Assistant.—Sgt Peter Barko, room 4E590, 614–4439.
  Deputy Assistant Secretary of:
    Civilian Human Resources.—Patricia C. Adams, room 4D548, 695–2633.
    Manpower Personnel Policy.—Dr. Russell W. Beland, room 4D548, 693–1213.
    Reserve Affairs.—Dennis Biddick, room 4D548, 614–1327.

SECRETARY OF THE NAVY COUNCIL OF REVIEW BOARDS
Washington Navy Yard, 720 Kennon Street, SE., Room 309, 20374–5023
phone (202) 685–6408, fax 685–6610

Director.—Jeffrey Riehl.
  Counsel.—Roger R. Claussen.
  Office Administrator.—Reginald B. Clark.
  Physical Evaluation Board.—Robert Powers.
  Naval Clemency and Parole Board.—Randall Lamoureux.
  Naval Discharge Review Board.—John D. Reeser.
  Combat-Related Special Compensation Board.—Leif Larsen.
  Board of Decorations and Medals.—James Nierle.

ASSISTANT SECRETARY FOR RESEARCH, DEVELOPMENT AND ACQUISITION
Pentagon, Room 4E665, phone (703) 695–6315

Assistant Secretary.—Hon. Sean J. Stackley.

Special Assistant.—Candy R. Hearn.
Executive Assistant and Naval Aide.—CAPT Brian Eckerle, USN.
Military Assistant and Marine Aide.—LT COL Eldon Metzger, USMC.
Principal Military Deputy.—VADM Paul Grosklags, USN.
   Executive Assistant and Naval Aide.—CAPT Todd Siddall, USN.
Principal Civilian Deputy.—James Thomsen, 614–6430.
   Executive Assistant and Naval Aide.—CDR Dave Norley, USN.
Deputy Assistant Secretary of the Navy for—
   Acquisition and Logistics Management.—Elliott Branch, BF992, 614–9445.
   Air Programs.—Richard Gilpin, room 4C712, 614–7794.
   C4I and Space Programs.—Dr. John Zangardi, room BF963, 914–6589.
   Expeditionary Warfare Programs.—Tom Dee, room 4C712, 614–4794.
   International Programs.—RDML Jim Shannon, WNY (202) 433–5900.
   Management and Budget.—BJ White-Olson, room 4C656, 695–6370.
   Ship Programs.—Allison Stiller, room 4C712, 697–1710.

DEPARTMENT OF THE NAVY CHIEF INFORMATION OFFICER

Chief Information Officer.—Terry A. Halvorsen, Pentagon, room 4A268 (703) 695–1840.

CHIEF OF NAVAL OPERATIONS

Pentagon, Room 4E662, phone (703) 695–5664, fax 693–9408

Chief of Naval Operations.—ADM Jonathan Greenert.
   Vice Chief of Naval Operations.—ADM Michelle Howard.
   Judge Advocate General of the Navy.—VADM Nanette M. DeRenzi.
   Directors:
      Naval Criminal Investigative Service.—Andrew Traver.
      Naval Intelligence.—Lynn Wright.
      Naval Nuclear Propulsion Program.—ADM John Richardson.
      Navy Staff.—VADM James Caldwell, Jr.
   Chief of:
      Chaplains.—RADM Margaret Kibben.
      Information.—RDML Dawn Cutler.
      Legislative Affairs.—RADM Craig Faller.
      Navy Reserve.—VADM Robin Braun.
      Surgeon General of the Navy.—VADM Matthew Nathan.
      Oceanographer of the Navy.—RADM Jonathan White.
   Master Chief Petty Officer of the Navy.—MCPON Michael Stevens.
   President, Board of Inspection and Survey.—RADM Michael Smith.
   Commander, Naval Education and Training.—VADM William Moran.
   Commander, Naval Safety Center.—RDML Christopher Murray.
   Deputy Chief of Naval Operations for—
      Fleet Readiness and Logistics.—VADM Philip Cullom.
      Integration of Capabilities and Resources.—VADM Joseph Mulloy.
      Manpower, Personnel, Training, and Education.—VADM William Moran.
      Operations, Plans, and Strategy.—RADM Kevin Donegan.
      Warfare Systems.—VADM Joseph Aucoin.

BUREAU OF MEDICINE AND SURGERY

7700 Arlington Boulevard, Suite 5113, Arlington, VA 22042–5113

phone (703) 681–5200, fax 681–9527

Chief.—VADM Matthew L. Nathan, MC, USN.

MILITARY SEALIFT COMMAND

914 Charles Morris Court, SE., Washington Navy Yard, 20398–5540

phone (202) 685–5001, fax 685–5020

Commander.—RADM Thomas K. Shannon.

WALTER REED NATIONAL MILITARY MEDICAL CENTER
8901 Wisconsin Avenue, Bethesda, MD 20889–5600
phone (301) 295–5800 / 5802, fax 295–5336.

Commander.—GEN Jeffrey Clark.

NAVAL AIR SYSTEMS COMMAND
47123 Buse Road, Building 2272, Suite 540, Patuxent River, MD 20670
phone (301) 757–7825

Commander.—VADM David A. Dunaway.

NAVAL CRIMINAL INVESTIGATIVE SERVICE HEADQUARTERS
27130 Telegraph Road, Quantico, VA 22134, phone (571) 305–9000

Director.—Andrew Traver.

NAVAL DISTRICT OF WASHINGTON
1343 Dahlgren Avenue, SE., Building 1, 20374–5001, phone (202) 433–2777, fax 433–2207

Commandant.—RDML Markham K. Rich.
Chief of Staff.—CAPT Scott F. Adams.

NAVAL FACILITIES ENGINEERING COMMAND
1322 Patterson Avenue, SE., Washington Navy Yard, 20374–5065
phone (202) 685–9499, fax 685–1463

Commander.—RADM Katherine L. Gregory, CEC, USN.

OFFICE OF NAVAL INTELLIGENCE
4251 Suitland Road, SE., Washington, DC 20020, phone (301) 669–3001, fax 669–3509

Commander.—RADM Elizabeth Train.

NAVAL SEA SYSTEMS COMMAND
1333 Isaac Hull Avenue, SE., Stop 1010, Washington Navy Yard, 20376–1010
phone (202) 781–0100

Commander.—VADM William H. Hilarides.

NAVAL SUPPLY SYSTEMS COMMAND
5450 Carlisle Pike, Mechanicsburg, PA 17050, phone (717) 605–3433

Commander.—RADM Jon Yuen.

SPACE AND NAVAL WARFARE SYSTEMS COMMAND SPACE FIELD ACTIVITY
14675 Lee Road, Chantilly, VA 20151, phone (703) 808–6104, fax 808–8504

Commander.—CAPT Mark Rudesill.

U.S. NAVAL ACADEMY
121 Blake Road, Annapolis, MD 21402, phone (410) 293–1000

Superintendent.—VADM Walter E. "Ted" Carter, Jr.

U.S. MARINE CORPS HEADQUARTERS
Pentagon, Room 4E734, phone (703) 614–2500

Commandant.—Gen. J.F. Dunford.
  Assistant Commandant.—Gen. J.M. Paxton, 614–1201.
  Aide-de-Camp.—Lt. Col. D.R. Alonso.
  Chaplain.—RDML B.W. Scott, 614–4627.
  Dental Officer.—Capt. F.R. Leal.
  Fiscal Director of the Marine Corps.—SES A.C. McDermott.
  Inspector General of the Marine Corps.—Vacant, 614–1533.
  Judge Advocate.—Maj. Gen. J.A. Ewers, 614–8661.
  Legislative Assistant.—Brig. Gen. D.J. Furness, 614–1686.
  Medical Officer.—RDML D.A. Lane.
  Military Secretary.—Col. M.S. Cederholm.
  Sergeant Major of the Marine Corps.—Sgt. Maj. R.L. Green, 614–8762.
  Deputy Commandant of Marine Corps for—
    Aviation.—Lt. Gen. J.M. Davis, 614–1010.
    Installations and Logistics.—Lt. Gen. W.M. Faulkner, 695–8572.
    Manpower and Reserve Affairs.—Vacant, 695–1929.
    Plans, Policies, and Operations.—Lt. Gen. R.L. Bailey, 614–8521.
    Programs and Resources.—Lt. Gen. G.M. Walters, 614–3435.
    Public Affairs.—Col. D.A. Lapan, 614–8010.
  Director of:
    Intelligence.—Brig. Gen. M.S. Groen.
    Marine Corps History and Museums.—Dr. C.P. Neimeyer.

MARINE BARRACKS
Eighth and I Streets, SE., 20390, phone (202) 433–4094

Commanding Officer.—Col. B.T. Watson.

TRAINING AND EDUCATION COMMAND
3300 Russell Road, Quantico, VA 22134, phone (703) 784–3730, fax 784–3724

Commanding General.—Maj. Gen. J.W. Lukeman.

DEPARTMENT OF JUSTICE

Robert F. Kennedy Department of Justice Building

950 Pennsylvania Avenue, NW., 20530, phone (202) 514–2000

http://www.usdoj.gov

LORETTA E. LYNCH, Attorney General; born in Greensboro, NC, education: Harvard College, 1981; Harvard Law School, 1984; professional: Assistant United States Attorney, Eastern District of New York, 1990–1999; United States Attorney for the Eastern District of New York, 1999–2001, 2010–2015; partner with law firm of Hogan and Hartson L.L.P., 2002–2010; nominated by President Barack Obama to become the Attorney General of the United States on November 8, 2014 and was sworn in on April 27, 2015.

OFFICE OF THE ATTORNEY GENERAL
RFK Main Justice Building, Room 5111, phone (202) 514–2001

Attorney General.—Loretta E. Lynch.
Chief of Staff and Counselor to the Attorney General.—Sharon Werner, room 5115, 514–3892.
Deputy Chief of Staff and Counselor to the Attorney General.—Carolyn Pokorny, room 5112, 616–2372.
Counselors to the Attorney General: Denise Cheung, room 5116, 305–7378; Eric Feigin, room 5119, 514–9798; Paige Herwig, room 5214, 305–8674; Channing Phillips, room 5224, 514–4969.
White House Liaison and Counselor to the Attorney General.—Shirlethia Franklin, room 5110, 514–9665.
Director of Advance.—Meki Bracken, room 5131, 514–6333.
Special Assistant and Scheduler to the Attorney General.—Christina Sivret, room 5127, 514–4195.
Confidential Assistant.—Bessie Meadows, room 5111, 514–2001.

OFFICE OF THE DEPUTY ATTORNEY GENERAL
RFK Main Justice Building, Room 4111, phone (202) 514–2101

Deputy Attorney General. Sally Quillian Yates, room 4111.
Principal Associate Deputy Attorney General.—Matthew S. Axelrod, room 4208, 514–2105.
Chief of Staff and Counselor to the Deputy Attorney General.—Heather G. Childs, room 4210, 514–8699.
Chief, Professional Misconduct Review Unit.—James H. Dinan, room 4131, 514–0049.
Associate Deputy Attorneys General: Armando O. Bonilla, room 4313, 616–1621; Danielle Y. Conley, room 4129, 514–6753; Tashina Gauhar, room 4218, 514–3712; Daniel J. Grooms, room 4216, 305–4127; Samir C. Jain, room 4215, 514–7373; Iris Lan, room 4311, 514–6907; David Margolis, room 4113, 514–4945; Rafi Prober, room 4315, 305–9886; Carlos F. Uriarte, room 4121, 305–0091; Miriam Vogel, room 4135, 307–2090.
Associate Deputy Attorney General and National Criminal Discovery Coordinator.—Andrew D. Goldsmith, room 4214, 514–5705.
Associate Deputy Attorney General and Director, OCDETF.—Bruce G. Ohr, room 4115, 307–2510.
Senior Counsels to the Deputy Attorney General: Amin Aminfar, room 4226, 305–0071; Andrew J. Bruck, room 4116, 305–3481; R. Scott Ferber, room 4411, 514–3853; Nekia S. Hackworth, room 4303, 616–0663; G. Scott Hulsey, room 4220, 353–3030; Kiran Raj, room 4315, 305–9886; Brette L. Steele, room 4224–305–0180; Brian Tomney, room 4114, 305–8657; Rae Woods, room 4413, 514–4995.
Emergency Preparedness and Crisis Response Coordinator.—Mark E. Michalic, room 4112, 514–0438.
Special Assistant to the Deputy Attorney General.—Joshua L. Mogil, room 4111, 514–1904.
Chief Privacy and Civil Liberties Officer.—Erika Brown Lee, room 4222, 307–0697.
Associate Deputy Attorney General and Executive Director, Financial Fraud Enforcement Task Force.—Virginia C. Romano, room 4119, 305–7848.
National Coordinator for Child Exploitation Prevention and Interdiction.—Jill E. Steinberg, room 4317, 514–9340.

OFFICE OF THE ASSOCIATE ATTORNEY GENERAL
RFK Main Justice Building, Room 5706, phone (202) 514–9500

Associate Attorney General.—Stuart F. Delery (acting).
Principal Deputy Associate Attorney General.—Molly J. Moran.
Deputy Associate Attorneys General: Christopher Casey, room 5734, 353–9314; *Tammie Gregg, room 5728, 307–5803; *Chad Golder, room 5724, 305–1777; *Javier Guzman, room 5732, 616–2728; Julie McEvoy, room 5726, 514–0624.
Chief of Staff to the Acting Associate Attorney General.—James "Jay" Cox, room 5718, 353–9471.
Counsels to the Associate Attorney General: *John Elias, room 5736, 532–6866; *Amy Kurren, room 5730, 353–2811; *Joshua Wilkenfeld, room 5738, 514–8357.
Deputy Chief of Staff and Counsel to the Acting Associate Attorney General.—Rita Aguilar, room 5722, 616–0038.
Confidential Assistant.—Currie Gunn, room 5708, 305–2636.
Staff Assistant.—Vacant, room 5706, 616–0656.

Note: * Indicates detailed from other component within DOJ.

OFFICE OF THE SOLICITOR GENERAL
RFK Main Justice Building, Room 5143, phone (202) 514–2201
http://www.usdoj.gov/osg

Solicitor General.—Donald B. Virrelli, Jr., room 5143, 514–2201.
Principal Deputy Solicitor General.—Ian Gershengorn, room 5143, 514–2206.
Executive Officer.—Valerie Hall Yancey, room 5142, 514–3957.
Supervisory Case Management Specialist.—Charlene Goodwin, room 5608, 514–2218.
Chief, Research and Publications Section.—Mary Cornaby, room 6634, 514–4459.

ANTITRUST DIVISION
RFK Main Justice Building, 950 Pennsylvania Avenue, NW., 20530
Liberty Square Building, 450 5th Street, NW., 20530 (LSB)

Assistant Attorney General.—William J. Baer, room 3109 (202) 514–2401.
Deputy Assistant Attorneys General: Renata B. Hesse, room 3214, 353–1535; Sonia Pfaffenroth, room 3210, 307–1342; Nancy Rose, room 3121, 353–0163; Brent C.J. Snyder, room 3214, 514–3543.
Director of:
  Civil Enforcement.—Patricia A. Brink, room 3213, 514–2562.
  Criminal Enforcement.—Marvin N. Price, Jr., room 3214, 307–0719.
  Economics Enforcement.—W. Robert Majure, room 3416.
  Freedom of Information Act Officer.—SueAnn Slates (LSB), room 1040, 307–1398.
Executive Officer.—Scott Cohen (acting), (LSB), room 10150, 514–4005.
Section Chiefs:
  Appellate.—Kristen Limarzi, room 3222, 514–2413.
  Competition Policy.—W. Robert Majure, room 3416, 9400, 307–6341.
  Economic Litigation.—Norman Familant (LSB), room 9912, 307–6323.
  Economic Regulatory.—Beth Armington (LSB), room 3700, 307–6332.
  Foreign Commerce.—Edward T. Hand (LSB), room 11000, 514–2464.
  Legal Policy.—Robert A. Potter (LSB), room 11700, 514–2512.
  Litigation I.—Peter J. Mucchetti (LSB), room 4700, 307–0001.
  Litigation II.—Maribeth Petrizzi (LSB), room 8700, 307–0924.
  Litigation III.—David C. Kully (LSB), room 4004, 305–9969.
  National Criminal Enforcement.—Lisa M. Phelan (LSB), room 11400, 307–6694.
  Networks and Technology.—James Tierney (LSB), room 7700, 307–6640.
  Telecommunications and Media.—Scott A. Scheele (LSB), room 7000, 307–6132.
  Transportation, Energy, and Agriculture.—Kathleen S. O'Neil (LSB), room 8000, 307–2931.

FIELD OFFICES

California: Marc Siegel, 450 Golden Gate Avenue, Room 10–0101, Box 36046, San Francisco, CA 94102 (415) 436–6660.
Illinois: Frank J. Vondrak (acting), Rookery Building, 209 South LaSalle Street, Suite 600, Chicago, IL 60604 (312) 353–7530.

New York: Jeffrey Martino, 26 Federal Plaza, Room 3630, New York, NY 10278–1040 (212) 385–8019.

BUREAU OF ALCOHOL, TOBACCO, FIREARMS, AND EXPLOSIVES (ATF)
99 New York Avenue, NE., Suite 5S–100, 20226

OFFICE OF THE DIRECTOR

Director.—Thomas E. Brandon (acting), (202) 648–8700.
Deputy Director.—Ronald B. Turk (acting), 648–8710.
Chief of Staff.—Robyn L. Thiemann (acting), 648–7825.
Deputy Chief of Staff.—Cherie Knoblock, 648–9211.
Special Assistant to the Deputy Director.—Betty L. Coleman, 648–8710.
Confidential Projects Manager to the Acting Director.—Michelle A. Back, 648–8700.

OFFICE OF STRATEGIC MANAGEMENT

Chief.—Christopher A. Pellettiere, 648–7425.

OFFICE OF DIVERSITY AND INCLUSION (ODI)

Chief Diversity Officer.—Stacie Brockman, suite 2S–125, 648–8770.
Deputy Chief Officer.—Dora Silas, 648–8770.

OFFICE OF CHIEF COUNSEL

Chief Counsel.—Charles R. Gross, 648–7836.
Deputy Chief Counsel.—Joel J. Roessner, 648–7058.

OFFICE OF ENFORCEMENT PROGRAMS AND SERVICES

Assistant Director.—Marvin G. Richardson, 648–7080.
Deputy Assistant Director.—Curtis W. Gilbert, 648–7080.

OFFICE OF EQUAL OPPORTUNITY

Chief.—Patricia R. Cangemi (acting), EEO, 648–8760.
Deputy Chief.—Robynn Ferguson-Russ, 684–8760.

OFFICE OF FIELD OPERATIONS

Assistant Director.—Michael P. Gleysteen (202) 648–8324.
Deputy Assistant Director for—
　Central.—Marino F. Vidoli, 648–7979.
　East.—Wayne L. Dixie, 648–7442.
　West.—Luke Franey, 648–7201.
　Industry Operations.—Andrew R. Graham, 648–7254.

OFFICE OF MANAGEMENT

Assistant Director/CFO.—Vivian B. Michalic, 648–7800.
Deputy Assistant Director.—Joseph M. Riehl, 648–7800.

OFFICE OF OMBUDSPERSON

Ombudsperson.— Grace M. Reisling, 648–7351.

OFFICE OF PROFESSIONAL RESPONSIBILITY AND SECURITY OPERATIONS

Assistant Director.—Melvin D. King, Jr., 648–7500.
Deputy Assistant Director.—Daryl R. McCrary, 648–7500.

OFFICE OF PUBLIC AND GOVERNMENTAL AFFAIRS

Assistant Director.—Christopher C. Shaefer, 648–8520.
Deputy Assistant Director.—Frederick J. Milanowski, 648–8520.
Chief, Division of:
    Intergovernmental Affairs.—Ross Arends, 648–7722.
    Legislative Affairs.—Dean Kueter, 648–7191.
    Public Affairs.—Ginger L. Colbrun, 648–7938.

OFFICE OF SCIENCE AND TECHNOLOGY / CIO

Assistant Director / Chief Information Officer.—Roger Beasley (acting), 648–8390.
Deputy Assistant Director for IT Services.—Francis Frande (acting), 648–7968.
Deputy Assistant Director for Forensic Services.—Greg Czarnopys, 648–6001.

OFFICE OF STRATEGIC INTELLIGENCE AND INFORMATION

Assistant Director.—James E. McDermond, 648–7600.
Deputy Assistant Director.—Scott Sweetow, 648–7600.

OFFICE OF HUMAN RESOURCES AND PROFESSIONAL DEVELOPMENT

Assistant Director.—David L. McCain, 648–8416.
Deputy Assistant Director, Professional Development.—Stewart Lowery, 648–8416.
Deputy Assistant Director, Human Resources.—Peter Berkstrom, 648–8416.

CIVIL DIVISION

RFK Main Justice Building, 950 Pennsylvania Avenue, NW., 20530

20 Massachusetts Avenue, NW., 20530 (20MASS)

1100 L Street, NW., 20530 (L ST)

National Place Building, 1331 Pennsylvania Avenue, NW., 20530 (NPB)

1425 New York Avenue, NW., 20530 (NYA)

Patrick Henry Building, 601 D Street, NW., 20530 (PHB)

Liberty Square Building, 450 5th Street, NW., 20530

Principal Deputy Assistant Attorney General.—Benjamin C. Mizer, room 3601 (202) 514–3301.
Chief of Staff.—Nitin Shah, room 3605 (202) 353–2793.

APPELLATE STAFF

Deputy Assistant Attorney General.—Beth Brinkmann, room 3135, 353–8679.
Director.—Douglas Letter, room 7519, 514–3602.
Deputy Director.—Dana Martin, room 7517, 514–2541.

COMMERCIAL LITIGATION BRANCH

Deputy Assistant Attorney General.—Joyce Branda, room 3607, 307–0231.
    Directors: David M. Cohen (L ST), room 12124, 514–7300; John N. Fargo (L ST), room 11116, 514–7223; Vacant (L ST), room 10036, 514–7450.
    Office of Foreign Litigation.—Vacant (L ST), room 11006, 514–7455.
    Deputy Directors: Jeanne Davidson (L ST), room 12132, 307–0290; Michael Granston (PHB), room 9902, 305–0632.
    Legal Officer.—Donna C. Maizel, Esq., U.S. Department of Justice, Civil Division European Office, The American Embassy, London, England, PSC 801, Box 42, FPO AE, 09498–4042, 9+011–44–20–7894–0840.
    Attorney-in-Charge.—Barbara Williams, Suite 359, 26 Federal Plaza, New York, NY 10278, (212) 264–9240.

CONSUMER LITIGATION

Deputy Assistant Attorney General.—Jonathan F. Olin, room 3611, 307–6482.
Director.—Michael S. Blume (LSB), room 6254, 307–3009.

FEDERAL PROGRAMS BRANCH

Deputy Assistant Attorney General.—Vacant, room 3137, 514–2331.
Directors: John Griffiths (20MASS), room 7100, 514–4651; Joseph H. Hunt, room 7348, 514–1259; Jennifer D. Richetts (20MASS), room 6100, 514–3671.
Deputy Directors: Tony Coppolino (20MASS), room 6102, 514–4782; Sheila M. Lieber (20MASS), room 7102, 514–3786.

IMMIGRATION LITIGATION

Deputy Assistant Attorney General.—August Flentje (acting), room 3613, 514–3309.
Director.—Thomas W. Hussey (NPB), room 7026S, 616–4852.
Deputy Directors: Donald E. Keener (NPB), room 7022S, 616–4878; David M. McConnell (NPB), room 7260N, 616–4881; Vacant (NPB), room 7006N, 616–4856.

MANAGEMENT PROGRAMS

Director.—Kenneth L. Zwick, room 3140, 514–4552.
Director, Office of:
  Administration.—Donna Cornett (L ST), room 9018, 307–0261.
  Litigation Support.—Vacant (L ST), room 9126, 616–5014.
  Management Information.—Dorothy Bahr (L ST), room 8044, 616–8026.
  Planning, Budget, and Evaluation.—Frankie Free (L ST), room 9040, 307–0842.
  Policy and Management Operations.—Frankie Free (L ST), room 9040, 307–0842.

TORTS BRANCH

Deputy Assistant Attorney General.—Kali Bracey, room 3131, 353–9328.
Directors: Rupa Bhattacharyya (NYA), room 8122, 305–0008; J. Patrick Glynn (NPB), room 8028S, 616–4200; James Touhey (NPB), room 8064N, 616–4292.
Deputy Directors: JoAnn J. Bordeaux (NPB), room 8024S, 616–4204; Paul F. Figley (NPB), room 8096N, 616–4248.
Attorneys-in-Charge: Robert Underhill, 450 Golden Gate Avenue, 10/6610, Box 36028, San Francisco, CA 94102–3463, FTS: (415) 436–6630; Vacant, Suite 320, 26 Federal Plaza, New York, NY 10278–0140, FTS: (212) 264–0480.

CIVIL RIGHTS DIVISION

RFK Main Justice Building, 950 Pennsylvania Avenue, NW., 20530

1425 New York Avenue, NW., 20035 (NYAV)

601 D Street, NW., 20004 (PHB)

100 Indiana Avenue, NW., 20004 (NALC)

1800 G Street, NW., 20004 (NWB)

http://www.usdoj.gov/crt

Assistant Attorney General.—Vacant, room 5643 (202) 514–2151.
Principal Deputy Assistant Attorney General.—Vanita Gupta, room 5649 (202) 616–7334.
Deputy Assistant Attorneys General: Greg Friel, room 5744, 353–9418; Eve Hill, room 5748, 353–9390; Justin Levitt, room 5531, 514–0603; Robert Moossy, room 5541, 514–0621.
Counsels to the Assistant Attorney General: Chriaag Bains, room 5533, 353–1994; James Cadogan, room 5642, 353–9374; Becky Monroe, room 5535, 305–0864; Johnathan Smith, room 5529, 353–9013.
Chief of Staff.—Kathleen Toomey (acting), room 5646, 353–0283.
Section Chiefs:
  Appellate.—David K. Flynn, room 3704, 514–2195.

Criminal.—Paige Fitzgerald (acting), (PHB), room 5102, 514–3204.
Disability Rights.—Rebecca Bond (NYAV), room 4055, 307–2227.
Educational Opportunities.—Anurima Bhargava (PHB), room 4002, 514–4092.
Employment Litigation.—Delora Kenebrew (PHB), room 4040, 514–3831.
Housing and Civil Enforcement.—Steven Rosenbaum (NWB), room 7036, 514–4713.
Policy and Strategy Section.—Aaron Schuham (PHB), room 5006, 305–4151.
Special Litigation.—Judy Preston (acting), (PHB), room 5034, 514–5393.
Voting.—Chris Herren (NWB), room 7254, 307–2767.
Office Special Counsel.—Alberto Ruisanchez, room 9030, 616–5594.

OFFICE OF COMMUNITY ORIENTED POLICING SERVICES

145 N Street, NE., 20530

DIRECTOR'S OFFICE

Director.—Ronald L. Davis, 11th floor (202) 616–2888.
Chief of Staff.—Melanca Clark.
Deputy Director for Management.—Wayne Henry.

COMMUNICATIONS DIVISION

Assistant Director.—Shannon Long (acting), 11th floor, 514–9079.

COMMUNITY RELATIONS SERVICE

600 E Street, NW., Suite 6000, 20530, phone (202) 305–2935

fax 305–3003 (BICN)

Director.—Grande Lum.
Deputy Director.—Gilbert Moore.
General Counsel.—Antoinette Barksdale.
Media Affairs Officer.—Vacant.

REGIONAL DIRECTORS

New England.—Francis Amoroso, 408 Atlantic Avenue, Suite 222, Boston, MA 02110–1032 (617) 424–5715.
Northeast Region.—Ben Lieu (acting), 26 Federal Plaza, Suite 36–118, New York, NY 10278 (212) 264–0700.
Mid-Atlantic Region.—Harpreet Singh Mokha, 200 2nd and Chestnut Streets, Suite 208, Philadelphia, PA 19106 (215) 597–2344.
Southeast Region.—Thomas Battles, 61 Forsyth Street, SW., Suite 7B65, Atlanta, GA 30303 (404) 331–6883.
Midwest Region.—Mary Gorecki, 230 South Dearborn Street, Suite 2130, Chicago, IL 60604 (312) 353–4391.
Southwest Region.—Synthia Taylor, Hardwood Center Building, 1999 Bryan Street, Suite 2050, Dallas, TX 75201 (214) 655–8175.
Central Region.—Ben Lieu (acting), 601 East 12th Street, Suite 0802, Kansas City, MO 64106 (816) 426–7434.
Rocky Mountain Region.—Carol Russo, 1244 Speer Boulevard, Suite 650, Denver, CO 80204–3584 (303) 844–2973.
Western Region.—Ronald Wakabayashi, 888 South Figueroa Street, Suite 2010, Los Angeles, CA 90017 (213) 894–2941.
Northwest Region.—Carol Russo, 915 Second Avenue, Suite 1808, Seattle, WA 98174 (206) 220–6700.

CRIMINAL DIVISION

RFK Main Justice Building, 950 Pennsylvania Avenue, NW., 20530

phone (202) 514–2601

Bond Building, 1400 New York Avenue, NW., 20005 (Bond)

1331 F Street, NW., 20004 (F Street)

John C. Keeney Building, 1301 New York Avenue, NW., 20530 (1301 NY)

2CON Building, 2 Constitution Square, 145 N Street NE., 20530 (2Con)

Assistant Attorney General.—Leslie R. Caldwell, room 2107, 514–7200.
Chief of Staff and Principal Deputy Assistant Attorney General.—David M. Bitkower, room 2206, 353–0182.
Deputy Assistant Attorneys General: Kenneth A. Blanco, room 2113, 514–3027; Paul M. O'Brien, room 2115, 514–0169; Sung-Hee Suh, room 2214, 353–9467; Bruce C. Swartz, room 2212, 514–2333.
Deputy Chief of Staff.—James C. Mann (acting), room 2208, 305–4763.
Counselor to the Assistant Attorney General.—Jonathan Wroblewski, room 2218, 514–4730.
Counsels to the Assistant Attorney General: Jessica Aber, room 2224, 514–9997; Edgar Chen, room 2224, 616–4500; Nancy Sumption, room 2222, 307–0849; James Yoon, room 2116, 514–1115; Deborah Zerwitz, room 2114, 305–9208.
Executive Officer.—Tracy Melton (Bond), room 5100, 305–0534.
Section Chiefs / Office Directors:
Appellate.—Patty M. Stemler, room 1264, 514–2611.
Asset Forfeiture and Money Laundering.—M. Kendall Day (Bond), suite 10100, 353–2248.
Capital Case Unit.—Kevin Carwile (F Street), suite 6100, 514–3705.
Child Exploitation and Obscenity.—Damon King (acting), (Bond), suite 6000, 353–7304.
Computer Crime and Intellectual Property.—John Lynch (1301 NY), suite 600, 305–8732.
Enforcement Operations.—Monique Roth (1301 NY), suite 1200, 353–6200.
Fraud.—Andrew Weissman (Bond), room 4100, 353–8855.
Human Rights and Special Prosecution.—Teresa McHenry (1301 NY), room 112, 616–5731.
International Affairs.—Mary Rodriguez (acting) (1301 NY), suite 900, 514–0029.
International Criminal Investigative Training Assistant Program.—Richard Miller (acting), (F Street), suite 600, 616–1768.
Narcotics and Dangerous Drugs.—Arthur Wyatt (2CON), room 2E.200, 514–0917.
Organized Crime and Gangs.—James Trusty (1301 NY), suite 700, 307–0207.
Overseas Prosecutorial Development, Assistance and Training.—Faye Ehrenstamm (F Street), room 400, 514–1323.
Policy and Legislation.—Jonathan Wroblewski, room 7730, 514–4194.
Public Integrity.—Raymond Hulser (Bond), suite 12100, 616–0387.

OFFICE OF DISPUTE RESOLUTION

RFK Main Justice Building, Room 4531, phone (202) 616–9471 / 616–9472

http://www.usdoj.gov/odr

Director and Senior Counsel.—Joanna M. Jacobs, room 4529, 305–4439.

DRUG ENFORCEMENT ADMINISTRATION

Lincoln Place-1 (East), 600 Army-Navy Drive, Arlington, VA 22202 (LP–1)

Lincoln Place-2 (West), 700 Army-Navy Drive, Arlington, VA 22202 (LP–2)

Administrator.—Chuck Rosenberg (acting), room W–12060 (202) 307–8000.
Chief of Staff.—Michael R. Gill, room 12060 (202) 353–1573.
Deputy Administrator.—John "Jack" Riley (acting), room W–12058–F, 307–7345.
Equal Employment Opportunity Officer.—Oliver C. Allen, room E–11275, 307–8888.
Executive Assistants.—Vacant.
Chief, Congressional and Public Affairs.—Gary Owen (acting), room W–12228, 307–7363.
Chief, Executive Policy and Strategic Planning.—Eric Akers, room W–11100, 307–7420.

Section Chiefs:
Communications Section.—Gary Owen (acting), room W–12232, 307–6747.
Congressional Affairs.—Matthew Strait, room W–12104, 307–7423.
Demand Reduction.—Deborah Augustine (acting), room W–9049–E, 307–7936.
Public Affairs.—Michael Shavers, 307–2402.
Chief Counsel.—Wendy H. Goggin, room W–12142–C, 307–7322.
Deputy Chief Counsel.—Robert C. Gleason, room E–12375, 307–8020.
Chief, Office of Administrative Law Judges.—John Mulrooney, 307–8188.

FINANCIAL MANAGEMENT DIVISION

Chief Financial Officer.—Christinia K. Sisk (acting), room W–12138, 307–7330.
Deputy Assistant Administrator for—
  Acquisition Management.—Christinia K. Sisk, room W–5100, 307–7888.
  Finance.—Daniel Gillette, room E–7397, 307–7002.
  Resource Management.—Brian Horn, room E–5102, 307–4800.
Section Chiefs:
  Acquisition Management.—Eliana Zavala, room E–8281, 307–7812.
  Controls and Coordination.—Brian Parks, room E–5384, 307–5276.
  Financial Integrity.—Angela Ivy, room E–7331, 307–5459.
  Financial Operations.—Daanish Ahmed, room E–7165, 307–7270.
  Financial Reports.—Sherri Woodle, room E–7297, 307–7040.
  Financial Systems.—Andrew Kenny, room E–8001, 307–7215.
  Organization and Staffing Management.—Susan Mosser, room E–5284, 307–5052.
  Policy and Transportation.—Carol S. Burger, room E–8161, 307–4732.
  Program Liaison and Analysis.—Nisha Kumar, room E–5102 (202) 598–8083.
  Statistical Services.—Gamaliel Rose, room E–5332, 307–8276.

HUMAN RESOURCES DIVISION

Assistant Administrator.—Diane E. Filler, room W–12020, 307–4195.
Section Chiefs:
  Administrative Management.—Glenda A. Rollins, room W–6108, 307–4701.
  Recruitment and Placement.—Joyce Thomas, room W–3262, 307–4097.
Career Board Executive Secretary.—Michael Rothermund, room W–2270, (202) 353–1165.
Chairman, Board of Professional Conduct.—Christopher Quaglino, room E–9359, 307–7382.
Special Agent-in-Charge, Office of Training.—James R. Gregorius, 2500 Investigation Parkway, DEA Academy, Quantico, VA 22135 (703) 632–5010.
Assistant Special Agents-in-Charge:
  Domestic Training Section 1.—David Zon (703) 632–5110.
  Domestic Training Section 2.—Michael Blackwood (703) 632–5310.
  International Training Section.—James T. Farnsworth (703) 632–5330.

INSPECTIONS DIVISION

Chief Inspector.—Jon Ciarletta (acting), room W–12042A, 307–7358.
Deputy Chief Inspector, Office of:
  Inspections.—Michael Stanfill, room W–4348, 307–4866.
  Professional Responsibility.—Jon Ciarletta (acting), room W–4176, 307–8235.
  Security Programs.—Mark Mazzei (acting), room W–2340, 307–3465.

INTELLIGENCE DIVISION

Assistant Administrator.—Douglas W. Poole, room W–12036, 307–3607.
Director/Special Agent-in-Charge, El Paso Intelligence Center.—Tim Jennings, Building 11339, SSG Sims Street, El Paso, TX 79908–8098 (915) 760–2011.
Deputy Assistant Administrator, Office of Intelligence.—Vacant, room W–12020C, 307–3607.
Executive Assistant.—Cheryl Hooper (acting), 307–3607.
Deputy Assistant Administrator, Office of:
  Fusion Center.—Rich Denholm (acting), (703) 561–7875.
  National Security Intelligence.—Arthur A. Doty, 307–7923.
  Special Intelligence.—Willard B. (Bond) Wells, Jr., Merrifield, VA (703) 561–7100.

Section Chiefs:
  Data Management.—Cheryl Hooper (703) 561-7671.
  Intelligence Policy and Strategic Planning Section.—Pat Lowery, 307-8541.
  Intelligence Programs Section.—Benjamin C. Sanborn, 307-4358.
  Investigative Support.—Amy Sansbury (acting) (703) 488-4204.
  Operation Support Section.—Dale Wink (703) 561-7437.
  Program Management and Budget Section.—Mamaa Kufour (acting), 307-5076.
  Requirements and Collection Section.—Lynn Behears, 307-6621.
  Strategic Intelligence Section.—Kevin O'Brien (202) 353-9581.
  Technical Support Section.—Gisele Gatjanis, 561-7107.

OPERATIONS DIVISION

Chief of Operations.—James Soiles (acting), room W-12050, 307-7340.
  Chief of:
  Financial Operations.—Anthony C. Marotta, room W-5110, 307-6080.
  Foreign/Administrative Support.—Thomas A. Duncan.
  Global Enforcement.—Mark E. Skeffington (acting), room W-11166, 307-4446.
  Operations Management.—Michael T. DellaCorte, room W-11148, 353-1164.
  Special Projects.—Paul E. Knierim, room W-11024, 353-7858.
Deputy Assistant Administrator, Office of Diversion Control.—Louis Milione, room E-6295, 307-7165.
Special Agent-in-Charge, Aviation Division.—Jeffrey B. Stamm, Fort Worth, TX (817) 837-2186.
Special Agent-in-Charge, Special Operations Division.—Mark W. Hamlet, Chantilly, VA (703) 488-4205.

OPERATIONAL SUPPORT DIVISION

Assistant Administrator.—Preston Grubbs, room W-12142, 307-4730.
  Deputy Assistant Administrator, Office of:
  Administration.—Renaldo Prillman, room W-9088, 307-7708.
  Forensic Sciences.—Nelson Santos, room W-7342, 307-8866.
  Information Systems.—Dennis R. McCrary, room E-3105, 307-3653.
  Investigative Technology.—Fred Smith, Lorton, VA (703) 495-6500.
  Section Chiefs:
  Administrative Operations.—Vacant, room W-5104-A, 307-7866.
  Business Program Management.—Millie Tyler, room E-3007, 307-9895.
  Facilities and Finance.—Mike Barbour, room W-5244, 307-7792.
  Hazardous Waste Disposal.—Stephen Wasem, room W-7310, 307-7206.
  Integration and Management.—Venita Phillips, room E-4063, 307-9892.
  Laboratory Operations.—Lance Kvetko, room W-7312, 307-8880.
  Software Operations.—Carl Conner, room E-3285, 307-9896.
  Surveillance Support.—Richard Rosa, Lorton, VA (703) 495-6574.
  Technology Officer.—Mark Shafernich (703) 285-4456.
  Telecommunications/Intercept Support.—John Sinkovits, Lorton, VA (703) 495-6734.
Associate Deputy Assistant Administrator, Office of:
  Forensic Sciences.—Scott Oulton, room W-7344, 307-8866.
  Information Systems.—Michelle Bower, room E-3005, 307-5269.

FIELD OFFICES

Special Agents-in-Charge:
  Atlanta Division.—Daniel R. Salter, Room 800, 75 Spring Street, SW., Atlanta, GA 30303 (404) 893-7100.
  Caribbean Division.—Vito S. Guarino, Metro Office Park, Millennium Park Plaza #15, 2nd Street, Suite 710, Guaynabo, PR 00968 (787) 277-4700.
  Chicago Division.—Dennis A. Wichern, Suite 1200, John C. Kluczynski Federal Building, 230 South Dearborn Street, Chicago, IL 60604 (312) 353-7875.
  Dallas Division.—Craig M. Wiles, 10160 Technology Boulevard East, Dallas, TX 75220 (214) 366-6900.
  Denver Division.—Barbra M. Roach, 12154 East Easter Avenue, Centennial, CO 80112-6740 (720) 895-4040.
  Detroit Division.—Joseph P. Reagan, 431 Howard Street, Detroit, MI 48226 (313) 234-4000.
  El Paso Division.—William R. Glaspy, 660 Mesa Hills Drive, Suite 2000, El Paso, TX 79912 (915) 832-6000.

Houston Division.—Joseph M. Arabit, 1433 West Loop South, Suite 600, Houston, TX 77027–9506 (713) 693–3000.

Los Angeles Division.—Anthony D. Williams, 255 East Temple Street, 17th Floor, Los Angeles, CA 90012 (213) 621–6700.

Miami Division.—Adolphus P. Wright, 2100 N. Commerce Parkway, Weston, FL 33326 (954) 660–4500.

Newark Division.—John McCabe (acting), 80 Mulberry Street, 2nd Floor, Newark, NJ 07102–4206 (973) 776–1100.

New England Division.—Michael J. Ferguson, JFK Federal Building, 15 New Sudbury Street, Room E–400, Boston, MA 02203 (617) 557–2100.

New Orleans Division.—R. Keith Brown, 3838 North Causeway Boulevard, Suite 1800, 3 Lakeway Center, Metaire, LA 70002 (504) 840–1100.

New York Division.—James J. Hunt, 99 10th Avenue, New York, NY 10011 (212) 337–3900.

Philadelphia Division.—Gary Tuggle, William J. Green Federal Building, 600 Arch Street, Room 10224, Philadelphia, PA 19106 (215) 861–3474.

Phoenix Division.—Douglas W. Coleman, 3010 North Second Street, Suite 100, Phoenix, AZ 85012 (602) 664–5600.

San Diego Division.—William R. Sherman, 4560 Viewridge Avenue, San Diego, CA 92123–1672 (858) 616–4100.

San Francisco Division.—John J. Martin, 450 Golden Gate Avenue, 14th Floor, San Francisco, CA 94102 (415) 436–7900.

Seattle Division.—Keith R. Weis, 300 Fifth Avenue, Suite 1300, Seattle, WA 98104–2398 (206) 553–5443.

St. Louis Division.—James P. Shroba, 317 South 16th Street, St. Louis, MO 63103 (314) 538–4600.

Washington, DC Division.—Karl C. Colder, 800 K Street, NW., Suite 500, Washington, DC 20001 (202) 305–8500.

OTHER DEA OFFICES

Special Agents-in-Charge:
Timothy A. Jennings, El Paso Intelligence Center, Building 11339, SSG Sims Street, El Paso,TX 79908 (915) 760–2000.

Jeffrey B. Stamm, Aviation Operations Division, 2300 Horizon Drive, Fort Worth, TX 76177 (817) 837–2000.

Mark W. Hamlet, Special Operations Division, 14560 Avion Parkway, Chantilly, VA 20151 (703) 488–4200.

James R. Gregorius, Office of Training, P.O. Box 1475, Quantico, VA 22134 (703) 632–5000.

FOREIGN OFFICES

Ankara, Turkey: American Embassy Ankara, DEA/Justice, PSC 93, Box 5000, APO AE 09823–5000, 9–011–90–312–468–6136.

Asuncion, Paraguay: DEA/Justice, American Embassy Asuncion, Unit 4740, APO AA 34036, 9–011–595–21–210–738.

Athens, Greece: American Embassy Athens, DEA/Justice, PSC 108, Box 14, APO AE 09842, 9–011–30–210–643–4328.

Bangkok, Thailand: American Embassy, DEA/Justice, Box 49, APO AP 96546–0001, 9–011–662–205–4984.

Beijing, China: American Embassy Beijing, DEA/Justice, PSC 461, Box 50, FPO AP 96521–0002, 9–011–8610–8529–6880.

Belmopan, Belize: American Embassy Belmopan, DEA/Justice, PSC 120, Unit 7405, APO AA 34025, 301–985–9387.

Bern, Switzerland: Department of State, DEA/Justice, 5110 Bern Place, Washington, DC 20521–5110, 9–011–41–31–357–7367.

Bogota, Colombia: American Embassy Bogota, DEA/Justice, Unit 5116, APO AA 34038, 9–011–571–315–2121.

Brasilia, Brazil: DEA/Justice, American Embassy Brasilia, Unit 3500, APO AA 34030, 9–011–55–61–3312–7122.

Bridgetown, Barbados: American Embassy Bridgetown, CMR 1014, DEA/Justice, FPO AA 34055, 9–1–246–227–4171.

Brussels, Belgium: American Embassy Brussels, DEA/Justice, PSC 82, Box 137, APO AE 09710, 9–011–32–2–508–2420.

Buenos Aires, Argentina: DEA/Justice, American Embassy Buenos Aires, Unit 4309, APO AA 34034, 9–011–5411–5777–4696.

Cairo, Egypt: American Embassy Cairo, DEA/Justice, Unit 64900, Box 25, APO AE 09839–4900, 9–011–20–2–2797–2461.

Canberra, Australia: American Embassy Canberra, DEA/Justice, APO AP 96549, 9–011–61–2–6214–5903.

Caracas, Venezuela: American Embassy Caracas, DEA/Justice, Unit 4962, APO AA 34037, 9–011–582–212–975–8380/8443/8407.

Cartagena, Resident Office: American Embassy, DEA Cartagena, Unit 5141, APO AA 34038, 9–011–575–664–9369.

Chiang-Mai, Resident Office: American Embassy Chiang-Mai, Box C, APO AP 96546, 9–011–66–53–217–285.

Ciudad, Resident Office: U.S. Consulate/Ciudad Juarez Resident Office, P.O. Box 10545, El Paso, TX 79925, 9–011–52–656–611–1179.

Cochabamba, Resident Office: Unit 3220, Box 211, APO AA 34032, 9–011–591–4–429–3320.

Copenhagen, Denmark: American Embassy Copenhagen, DEA/Justice, PSC 73, APO AE 09716, 9–011–45–35–42–2680.

Curacao, Netherlands Antilles: American Consulate Curacao, DEA/Justice, Washington, DC 20521, 9–011–5999–461–6985.

Dubai, United Arab Emirates: U.S. Consulate General, DEA/Justice, 6020 Dubai Place, Dulles, VA 20189–6020, 9–011–971–4–311–6220.

Dushanbe, Tajikistan: American Embassy Dushanbe, DEA/Justice, Drug Enforcement Administration,7090 Dushanbe Place, Dulles, VA 20189–7090, 9–011–992–37–229–2807.

Frankfurt, Resident Office: American Consulate General Frankfurt, DEA/Justice, PSC 115, Box 1017, APO AE 09213–0115, 9–011–49–69–7535–3770.

Freeport, Bahamas Resident Office: GPS, c/o U.S. Embassy, DEA, 5115 Northwest 17th Terrace, Hanger #39A, Ft. Lauderdale, FL 33309, 9–1–242–352–5353/5354.

Guadalajara, Resident Office: DEA, Guadalajara Resident Office, P.O. Box 9001, Brownsville, TX 78520, 9–011–52–33–3268–2191.

Guatemala City, Guatemala: American Embassy Guatemala City, DEA/Justice, Unit 3311, APO AA 34024, 9–011–502–331–4389.

Guayaquil, Resident Office: DEA/Justice, American Embassy Guayaquil, Unit 5350, APO AA, 34039, 9–011–593–42–32–3715.

The Hague, Netherlands: American Embassy The Hague, DEA/Justice, Unit 6707, Box 8, APO AE 09715, 9–011–31–70–310–2327.

Hanoi, Vietnam: American Embassy Hanoi, DEA/Justice, PSC 461, Box 400, FPO AP 96521–0002, 9–011–844–850–5011.

Hermosillo, Resident Office: U.S. Consulate-Hermosillo, P.O. Box 1689, Nogales, AZ 85628–1689, 9–011–52–662–289–3550.

Hong Kong, Resident Office: U.S. Consulate General Hong Kong, DEA/Justice, PSC 461, Box 16, FPO AP 96521–0006, 9–011–852–2521–4536.

Islamabad, Pakistan Country Office: DEA/Justice, American Embassy Islamabad, DEA/Justice, Unit 62215, APO AE 09812–2215, 9–011–92–51–208–2918.

Istanbul, Turkey Resident Office: American Consulate General, DEA/Justice, PSC 97, Box 0002, APO AE 09827, 9–011–90–212–335–9179.

Kabul, Afghanistan Country Office: DEA/Justice, American Embassy Kabul, 8160 Kabul Place, Washington, DC 20521–6180, 301–490–1042.

Kingston, Jamaica Country Office: U.S. Embassy Kingston, 142 Old Hope Road, Kingston 6, Jamaica, 9–1–876–702–6004.

Kuala Lumpur, Malaysia Country Office: American Embassy Kuala Lumpur, DEA/Justice, APO AP 96535–8152, 9–011–603–2142–1779.

Lagos, Nigeria: Department of State, DEA/Justice, 8300 Lagos Place, Washington, DC 20521–8300, 9–011–234–1–261–9837.

La Paz, Bolivia: American Embassy La Paz, DEA/Justice, Unit 3220, DPO AA 34032, 9–011–591–2–216–8313.

Lima, Peru: American Embassy Lima, DEA/Justice, Unit 3810, APO AA 34031, 9–011–511–618–2475.

London, England: American Embassy London, DEA/Justice, Unit 8400, Box 0008, FPO AE 09498–4008, 9–011–44–207–894–0826.

Madrid, Spain: American Embassy Madrid, DEA/Justice, PSC 61, Box 0014, APO AE 09642, 9–011–34–91–587–2280.

Managua, Nicaragua: DEA, American Embassy Nicaragua, Unit 2700, Box 21, APO AA 34021, 9–011–505–252–7738.

Manila, Philippines: American Embassy Manila, DEA/Justice, PSC 500, Box 11, FPO AP 96515, 9–011–632–301–2084.

Matamoros, Mexico Resident Office: Matamoros DEA, P.O. Box 9004, Brownsville, TX 78501, 9–011–52–868–149–1285.
Mazatlan, Resident Office: DEA, Mazatlan Resident Office, P.O. Box 9006, Brownsville, TX 78520–0906, 9–011–669–982–1775.
Merida, Mexico: U.S. Consulate-Merida, P.O. Box 9003, Brownsville, TX 78520–0903, 9–011–52–999–942–5738.
Mexico City, Mexico: DEA/Justice, U.S. Embassy Mexico City, P.O. Box 9000, Brownsville, TX 78520, 9–011–52–55–5080–2600.
Milan, Resident Office: American Consulate Milan, DEA/Justice, PSC 833, Box 60–M, FPO AE 09624, 9–011–39–02–2903–5422.
Monterrey, Resident Office: U.S. Consulate General, Monterrey Resident Office, P.O. Box 9002, Brownsville, TX 78520–0902, 9–011–5281–8340–1299.
Moscow, Russia: American Embassy Moscow, DEA/Justice, PSC 77, APO AE 09721, 9–011–7–495–728–5218.
Nassau: Nassau Country Office, DEA/Justice, American Embassy Nassau, 3370 Nassau Place, Washington, DC 20520, 9–1–242–322–1700.
New Delhi, India: American Embassy New Delhi, Department of State, 9000 New Delhi Place, Washington, DC 20521, 9–011–91–11–2419–8495.
Nicosia, Cyprus: American Embassy Nicosia, DEA/Justice, PSC 815, Box 1, FPO AE 09836–0001, 9–011–357–22–393–302.
Nuevo Laredo, Mexico: DEA, Nuevo Laredo Resident Office, P.O. Box 3089, Laredo, TX 78044–3089, 9–011–52–867–714–0512.
Ottawa, Canada: American Embassy Ottawa, DEA/Justice, P.O. Box 35, Ogdensburg, New York 13669, 9–1–613–238–5633.
Panama City, Panama: American Embassy Panama, DEA/Justice, Unit 0945, APO AA 34002, 9–011–507–317–5541.
Paramaribo, Suriname: American Embassy Paramaribo, DEA/Justice, 3390 Paramaribo Place, Dulles, VA 20189–3390, 301–985–8693.
Paris, France: American Embassy Paris, DEA/Justice, PSC 116, Box A–224, APO AE 09777, 9–011–33–1–4312–2732.
Peshawar, Pakistan: American Consulate Peshawar, DEA/Justice, Unit 62217, APO AE 09812–2217, 9–011–92–91–584–0424/0425.
Port-au-Prince, Haiti: U.S. Department of State, 3400 Port-au-Prince, DEA, Washington, DC 20521, 9–011–509–2–229–8413.
Port of Spain, Trinidad and Tobago: Department of State, DEA/Justice, Port of Spain Country Office, 3410 Port of Spain Place, Washington, DC 20537, 9–1–868–628–8136.
Pretoria, South Africa: American Embassy Pretoria, Department of State, DEA/Justice, Washington, DC 20521–9300, 9–011–2712–362–5008.
Quito, Ecuador: DEA/Justice, American Embassy Quito, Unit 5338, APO AA 34039, 9–011–593–22–231–547.
Rangoon, Burma: American Embassy Rangoon, DEA/Justice, Box B, APO AP 96546, 9–011–95–1–536–509.
Rome, Italy: American Embassy Rome, DEA/Justice, PSC 833, Box 22, FPO AE 09624, 9–011–39–06–4674–2319.
San Jose, Costa Rica: American Embassy San Jose, DEA/Justice, Unit 3440, Box 376, APO AA 34020–0376, 9–011–506–22–20–2433.
San Salvador, El Salvador: American Embassy San Salvador, DEA/Justice, Unit 3130, APO AA 34023, 9–011–503–2278–6005.
Santa Cruz, Resident Office: DEA/Justice, American Embassy, Unit 3913 (Santa Cruz), APO AA 34032, 9–011–591–332–7153.
Santiago, Chile: DEA/Justice, American Embassy Santiago, Unit 3460, Box 136, APO AA34033–0136, 9–011–56–2–330–3401.
Santo Domingo, Dominican Republic: American Embassy Santo Domingo, DEA/Justice, Unit 3470, APO AA 34041, 9–1–809–687–3754.
Sao Paulo, Resident Office: DEA/Justice, American Embassy Sao Paulo, Unit 3502, APO AA 34030, 301–985–9364.
Seoul, Korea: American Embassy Seoul, DEA/Justice, Unit 15550, APO AP 96205–0001, 9–011–82–2–397–4260.
Singapore: American Embassy Singapore, Unit 4280, Box #30, FPO AP 96507–90030, 9–011–65–6476–9021.
Tashkent: Uzbekistan Country Office, DEA/Justice, 7110 Tashkent Place, Washington, DC 20521, 9–011–998–371–120–8924.
Tegucigalpa, Honduras: American Embassy Tegucigalpa, Tegucigalpa Country Office, Unit 3480, Box 212, APO AA 34022, 301–985–9321.
Tijuana, Resident Office: DEA, Tijuana Resident Office, P.O. 439039, San Diego, CA 92143–9039, 9–011–526–646–22–7452.

Tokyo, Japan: American Embassy Tokyo, DEA/Justice, Unit 45004, Box 224, APO AP 96337–5004, 9–011–81–3–3224–5452.
Trinidad, Bolivia Resident Office: American Embassy La Paz, DEA/Justice, Unit 3220 TRO, DPO AA 34032, 301–985–9398.
Udorn, Thailand Resident Office: American Embassy (Udorn), Box UD, APO AP 96546, 9–011–66–42–247–636.
Vancouver Resident Office: DEA Vancouver, 1574 Gulf Road, #1509, Point Roberts, WA 98281, 9–1–604–694–7710.
Vienna, Austria: Vienna Country Office, DEA/Justice, American Embassy, 9900 Vienna Place, Dulles, VA 20189–9900, 9–011–43–1–31339–7551.
Vientiane, Laos: American Embassy Vientiane, DEA/Justice, Unit 8165, Box V, APO AP 96546, 9–011–856–21–219–565.
Warsaw, Poland Country Office: DEA/Justice, American Embassy Warsaw, Unit 5010, Box 27, DPO AE 09730–5010, 9 011–48–22–504–2000.

ENVIRONMENT AND NATURAL RESOURCES DIVISION

RFK Main Justice Building, 950 Pennsylvania Avenue, NW., 20530

601 D Street, NW., 20004 (PHB)

Assistant Attorney General.—John C. Cruden, room 2143 (202) 514–2701.
Principal Deputy Assistant Attorney General.—Sam Hirsch, room 2603, 514–3370.
Deputy Assistant Attorneys General: Bruce Gelber, room 2131, 514–4624; Lisa Jones, room 2611, 514–0943; Jean Williams, room 2129 (202) 305–0228.
Executive Officer.—Andrew Collier (PHB), room 2038 (202) 616–3147.
Section Chiefs:
 Appellate.—James C. Kilbourne (PHB), room 2339, 514–2748.
 Environmental Crimes.—Deborah Harris (PHB), room 2102 (202) 305–0347.
 Environmental Defense.—Letitia J. Grishaw (PHB), room 8002, 514–2219.
 Environmental Enforcement.—Ben Fisherow (PHB), room 6108, 514–2750.
 Indian Resources.—Craig Alexander (PHB), room 3016, 514 9080.
 Land Acquisition.—Andrew Goldfrank (PHB), room 3638, 305–0316.
 Law and Policy.—Karen Wardzinski (RFK), room 2617, 514–0474.
 Natural Resources.—Lisa Russell (PHB), room 3102, 305–0438.
 Wildlife and Marine Resources.—Seth Barsky (PHB), room 3902, 305 0210.

EXECUTIVE OFFICE FOR IMMIGRATION REVIEW (EOIR)

5107 Leesburg Pike, Suite 2600, Falls Church, VA 22041

Director.—Juan P. Osuna, 2600 SKYT, (703) 305–0169.
Deputy Director.—Ana M. Kocur.
Counsels to the Director: Rena E. Cutlip-Mason, Barbara J. Leen.
Executive Secretariat.—Rhonda L. Caldwell.
General Counsel.—Jean C. King, 2600 SKYT, 305–0470.
Deputy General Counsel.—Vacant.
Assistant Director of Administration.—Edward F. Kelly (acting), 2300 SKYT (703) 605–1730.
Deputy Assistant Director of Administration.—Vacant.
Assistant Director of Management Programs.—James McDaniel (acting), 2600 SKYT, 305–0289.
Deputy Assistant Director of Management Programs.—Vacant.
Assistant Director of Planning, Analysis, and Statistics.—Vacant, 2600 SKYT, 605–0445.
Deputy Assistant Director of Planning, Analysis, and Statistics.—Brett Endres (acting).
Chairman, Board of Immigration Appeals.—David L. Neal, 2400 SKYT, 305–1194.
Vice Chairman, Board of Immigration Appeals.—Charles Adkins-Blanch.
Chief Judge, Office of the Chief Immigration Judge.—Robert P. "Print" Maggard (acting), 2500 SKYT, 305–1247.
Deputy Chief Immigration Judges: Edward F. Kelly, Michael C. McGoings, Christopher A. Santoro (acting).
Chief, Office of the Chief Administrative Hearing Officer.—Robin M. Stutman, 2500 SKYT, 305–0864.
Counsel to the Chief Administrative Hearing Officer.—Elizabeth Vayo.
Chief Information Officer, Information Technology.—Terryne Murphy, 2300 SKYT, 605–6933.
Telephone Directory Coordinator.—Annette Thomas, 2300 SKYT, 605–1336.

EXECUTIVE OFFICE FOR UNITED STATES ATTORNEYS (EOUSA)
RFK Main Justice Building, Room 2245, phone (202) 252–1300

Director.—Monty Wilkinson, room 2243.
Deputy Director and Counsel to the Director.—Norman Wong, room 2246.
Deputy Director for Legal Management.—Suzanne L. Bell, room 2242.
Administrative Officer.—Joy Smith, room 2006, BICN, 252–5553.
Executive Assistant/Attorney General's Advisory Committee Liaison.—Karen Winzenberg, room 2261, RFK, 252–1374.
Victims Rights Ombudsman.—Marie O'Rourke, room 2245, RFK Main Justice Building, 252–1317.
Director, Office of Legal Education.—Chammy Chandler, National Advocacy Center, 1620 Pendleton Street, Columbia, SC 29201 (803) 705–5100.
General Counsel.—Jay Macklin, room 5000, BICN (202) 252–1600.
Assistant Directors:
　Communication and Law Enforcement Coordinator Staff.—David Ausiello, room 2523, RFK, 252–5985.
　Data Analysis Staff.—Michelle Slusher, room 2000, BICN, 252–5571.
　Equal Employment Opportunity Staff.—Jason Osborne, room 5100, BICN, 252–1460.
　Evaluation and Review Staff.—Dayle Elieson, room 6800, BICN, 252–5917.
　FOIA and Privacy Act Staff.—Susan Gerson, room 7300, BICN, 252–6020.
Counsels for—
　Asset Recovery Staff.—Mark Redmiles, room 7600, 252–5877.
　Crisis Management and Resource.—Vacant.
　Indian Violent and Cyber Crimes Staff.—Gretchen C. Shappert, room 7622, BICN, 252–5841.
　Legal and Victim Programs.—Dan Villegas, room 7600, BICN, 252–5888.
　Legal Initiatives.—David Smith, room 2256, RFK, 252–1326.
　Legislative Counsel.—Scott Laragy, room 2509, 252–1435.
　Victim Witness Staff.—Kristina Neal, room 7600, BICN, 252–5833.
　White Collar and Civil Litigation Staff.—Tammy Reno, room 7600, 252–5493.
Chief Financial Officer.—Paul Suddes, room 2200, BICN, 252–5605.
Assistant Director of:
　Audit and Review.—Louisa McCarter Dadzie, room 2200, BICN, 252–5624.
　Budget Execution.—Tracy Hall, room 2200, BICN, 252–5627.
　Budget Formulation.—Vacant.
　Financial Systems Staff.—Jonathan Pelletier, room 2200, BICN, 252–5628.
Acquisitions Staff.—Stephanie Girard, room 5200, BICN, 252–5407.
Facilities/Support Services Staff.—Ana Indovina, room 5200, BICN, 252–5964.
Chief Information Officer.—Mark Fleshman, room 9078, BICN, 252–6246.
Assistant Director of:
　Case Management Staff.—Siobhan Sperin, room 9125, BICN, 252–6120.
　EVOIP Program Staff.—Joe Pfeifer, room 9012, BICN, 252–4468.
　Information Security Staff.—Gregory Hall, room 9074, BICN, 252–6090.
　Office Automation Staff.—Glenn Shrieves, room 9039, BICN, 252–6281.
　Records and Information Management Staff (RIM).—Bonnie Curtin, room 9080, BICN, 252–6488.
　Telecommunications and Technology Development Staff.—Denny Ko, room 9136, BICN, 252–6430.
Litigation Technology Service Center.—Marc Fulkert, ITEC, Columbia, SC (803) 705–5432.
Chief Human Resources Officer, Human Resources Staff.—Shawn Flinn, room 8509, BICN, 252–5310.
Assistant Director of:
　District Management and Assistance Program.—Mary Lapitino (919) 264–3618.
　Employee Assistance Staff.—Ed Neunlist, room 2400, BICN, 252–5455.
　HR Operations Staff.—Valerie Mulcahy, room 8430, BICN, 252–5357.
　HR Policy Staff.—Vacant.
　Pre-Employment Security.—Wayne Engram, room 2400, BICN, 252–5719.
　Security Programs Staff.—Tim George, room 2600, BICN, 252–5694.

EXECUTIVE OFFICE FOR UNITED STATES TRUSTEES
441 G Street, NW., 20530, phone (202) 307–1391
http://www.usdoj.gov/ust

Director.—Clifford J. White III, suite 6150.

Deputy Directors:
  Field Operations.—William T. Neary (acting).
  General Counsel.—Ramona D. Elliott, suite 6150, 307–1399.
  Management.—Monique K. Bourque (acting).
  Chief Information Officer.—Barbara A. Brown, 353–8754.
Assistant Director, Office of:
  Administration.—Monique K. Bourque, suite 6150, 353–3548.
  Oversight.—Doreen Solomon, suite 6150, 305–0222.
  Planning and Evaluation.—Thomas Kearns, suite 6150, 305–7827.

U.S. TRUSTEES

Region I:
  Suite 1000, 5 Post Office Square, Boston, MA 02109 (617) 788–0400.
  Suite 303, 537 Congress Street, Portland, ME 04101 (207) 780–3564.
  14th Floor, Sovereign Tower Bldg., 446 Main, Worcester, MA 01608 (508) 793–0555.
  Suite 605, 1000 Elm Street, Manchester, NH 03101 (603) 666–7908.
  Suite 431, One Exchange Terrace, Providence, RI 02903 (401) 528–5551.
Region II:
  Suite 1006, U.S. Federal Building, 201 Varick Street, New York, NY 10014 (212) 510–0500.
  Suite 200, 74 Chapel Street, Albany, NY 12207 (518) 434–4553.
  Suite 401, 300 Pearl Street, Buffalo, NY 14202 (716) 551–5541.
  Suite 560, Long Island Federal Courthouse, 560 Federal Plaza, Central Islip, NY 11722–4456 (631) 715–7800.
  Suite 302, 150 Court Street, New Haven, CT 06510 (203) 773–2210.
  Room 609, 100 State Street, Rochester, NY 14614 (585) 263–5812.
  Room 105, 10 Broad Street, Utica, NY 13501 (315) 793–8191.
Region III:
  Suite 500, 833 Chestnut Street, Philadelphia, PA 19107 (215) 597–4411.
  Suite 2100, One Newark Center, Newark, NJ 07102 (973) 645–3014.
  Suite 970, 1001 Liberty Avenue, Pittsburgh, PA 15222 (412) 644–4756.
  Suite 1190, 228 Walnut Street, Harrisburg, PA 17101 or P.O. Box 969, Harrisburg, PA 17108 (717) 221–4515.
  Suite 2207, 844 King Street, Wilmington, DE 19801 (302) 573–6491.
Region IV:
  Suite 953, 1835 Assembly Street, Columbia, SC 29201 (803) 765–5250.
  Room 210, 115 S. Union Street, Alexandria, VA 22314 (703) 557–7176.
  Room 625, 200 Granby Street, Norfolk, VA 23510 (757) 441–6012.
  Room 2025, 300 Virginia Street East, Charleston, WV 25301 (304) 347–3400.
  First Campbell Square Building, 210 First Street, SW., Suite 505, Roanoke, VA 24011 (540) 857–2806.
  Suite 4304, U.S. Courthouse, 701 East Broad Street, Richmond, VA 23219 (804) 771–2310.
  Suite 600, 6305 Ivy Lane, Greenbelt, MD 20770 (301) 344–6216.
  Suite 2625, 101 West Lombard Street, Baltimore, MD 21201 (410) 962–4300.
Region V:
  Suite 2110, 400 Poydras Street, New Orleans, LA 70130 (504) 589–4018.
  Suite 3196, 300 Fannin Street, Shreveport, LA 71101–3099 (318) 676–3456.
  Suite 6–430, 501 East Court Street, Jackson, MS 39201 (601) 965–5241.
Region VI:
  Room 976, 1100 Commerce Street, Dallas, TX 75242 (214) 767–8967.
  Room 300, 110 North College Avenue, Tyler, TX 75702 (903) 590–1450.
Region VII:
  Suite 3516, 515 Rusk Street, Houston, TX 77002 (713) 718–4650.
  Room 230, 903 San Jacinto, Austin, TX 78701 (512) 916–5328.
  Suite 533, 615 East Houston Street, San Antonio, TX 78205 (210) 472–4640.
  Suite 1107, 606 North Carancahua Street, Corpus Christi, TX 78476 (361) 888–3261.
Region VIII:
  Suite 400, 200 Jefferson Avenue, Memphis, TN 38103 (901) 544–3251.
  Suite 512, 601 West Broadway, Louisville, KY 40202 (502) 582–6000.
  Fourth Floor, 31 East 11th Street, Chattanooga, TN 37402 (423) 752–5153.
  Suite 318, 701 Broadway, Nashville, TN 37203 (615) 736–2254.
  Suite 500, 100 East Vine Street, Lexington, KY 40507 (859) 233–2822.

Region IX:

Suite 441, BP Building, 201 Superior Avenue East, Cleveland, OH 44114 (216) 522–7800.
Suite 200, Schaff Building, 170 North High Street, Columbus, OH 43215–2403 (614) 469–7411.
Suite 2030, 36 East Seventh Street, Cincinnati, OH 45202 (513) 684–6988.
Suite 700, 211 West Fort Street, Detroit, MI 48226 (313) 226–7999.
Suite 200R, 125 Ottawa Street, Grand Rapids, MI 49503 (616) 456–2002.

Region X:

Room 1000, 101 West Ohio Street, Indianapolis, IN 46204 (317) 226–6101.
Suite 1100, 401 Main Street, Peoria, IL 61602 (309) 671–7854.
Suite 555, 100 East Wayne Street, South Bend, IN 46601 (574) 236–8105.

Region XI:

Suite 873, 219 South Dearborn Street, Chicago, IL 60604 (312) 886–5785.
Suite 430, 517 East Wisconsin Avenue, Milwaukee, WI 53202 (414) 297–4499.
Suite 304, 780 Regent Street, Madison, WI 53715 (608) 264–5522.

Region XII:

Suite 2800, 111 Seventh Avenue, SE., Cedar Rapids, IA 52401 (319) 364–2211.
Suite 1015, U.S. Courthouse, 300 S. Fourth Street, Minneapolis, MN 55415 (612) 334–1350.
Room 793, 210 Walnut Street, Des Moines, IA 50309–2108 (515) 284–4982.
Suite 303, 314 South Main Avenue, Sioux Falls, SD 57104 (605) 330–4450.

Region XIII:

Suite 3440, 400 East 9th Street, Kansas City, MO 64106–1910 (816) 512–1940.
Suite 6353, 111 South 10th Street, St. Louis, MO 63102 (314) 539–2976.
Suite 1200, 200 West Capitol Avenue, Little Rock, AR 72201–3344 (501) 324–7357.
Suite 1148, 111 South 18th Plaza, Omaha, NE 68102 (402) 221–4300.

Region XIV:

Suite 204, 230 North First Avenue, Phoenix, AZ 85003 (602) 682–2600.

Region XV:

Suite 600, 402 West Broadway Street, San Diego, CA 92101–8511 (619) 557–5013.
Suite 602, 1132 Bishop Street, Honolulu, HI 96813–2836 (808) 522–8150.

Region XVI:

Suite 1850, 915 Wilshire Boulevard, Los Angeles, CA 90017 (213) 894–6811.
Suite 9041, 411 West Fourth Street, Santa Ana, CA 92701–8000 (714) 338–3400.
Suite 720, 3801 University Avenue, Riverside, CA 92501 (951) 276–6990.

Region XVII:

Suite 700, 235 Pine Street, San Francisco, CA 94104–3401 (415) 705–3300.
Suite 7–500, U.S. Courthouse, 501 I Street, Sacramento, CA 95814–2322 (916) 930–2100.
Suite 1401, 2500 Tulare Street, Fresno, CA 93721 (559) 487–5002.
Suite 690N, 1301 Clay Street, Oakland, CA 94612–5217 (510) 637–3200.
Room 4300, 300 Las Vegas Boulevard South, Las Vegas, NV 89101 (702) 388–6600.
Suite 3009, 300 Booth Street, Reno, NV 89509 (775) 784–5335.
Room 268, 280 South First Street, San Jose, CA 95113 (408) 535–5525.

Region XVIII:

Suite 5103, 700 Stewart Street, Seattle, WA 98101 (206) 553–2000.
Suite 213, 620 Southwest Main Street, Portland, OR 97205 (503) 326–4000.
Suite 220, 720 Park Boulevard, Boise, ID 83712 (208) 334–1300.
Room 593, 920 West Riverside, Spokane, WA 99201 (509) 353–2999.
Suite 204, 301 Central Avenue, Great Falls, MT 59401 (406) 761–8777.
Suite 203, 605 West Fourth Avenue, Anchorage, AK 99501 (206) 553–2000.
Suite 1100, 405 East Eighth Avenue, Eugene, OR 97401 (541) 465–6330.

Region XIX:

Suite 12–200, Byron G. Rogers Federal Building, 1961 Stout Street, Denver, CO 80294 (303) 312–7230.
Suite 203, 308 West 21st Street, Cheyenne, WY 82001 (307) 772–2790.
Suite 300, 405 South Main Street, Salt Lake City, UT 84111 (801) 524–5734.

Region XX:

Suite 1150, Epic Center, 301 North Main Street, Wichita, KS 67202 (316) 269–6637.
Suite 112, 421 Gold Street, SW., Albuquerque, NM 87102 (505) 248–6544.
Suite 408, 215 Northwest Dean A. McGee Avenue, Oklahoma City, OK 73102 (405) 231–5950.
Suite 225, 224 South Boulder Avenue, Tulsa, OK 74103 (918) 581–6670.

Region XXI:

Suite 362, 75 Spring Street, SW., Atlanta, GA 30303 (404) 331–4437.

Suite 301, Edificio Ochoa, 500 Tanca Street, San Juan, PR 00901 (787) 729–7444.
Suite 1204, 51 Southwest First Avenue, Miami, FL 33130 (305) 536–7285.
Suite 725, 2 East Bryan Street, Savannah, GA 31401 (912) 652–4112.
Suite 1200, 501 East Polk Street, Tampa, FL 33602 (813) 228–2000.
Suite 302, 440 Martin Luther King Boulevard, Macon, GA 31201 (478) 752–3544.
Suite 128, 110 East Park Avenue, Tallahassee, FL 32301 (850) 942–1660.
Suite 1101, George C. Young Federal Building and Courthouse, 400 West Washington Street, Orlando, FL 32801 (407) 648–6301.

FEDERAL BUREAU OF INVESTIGATION

J. Edgar Hoover Building, 935 Pennsylvania Avenue, NW., 20535–0001

phone (202) 324–3000, http://www.fbi.gov

Director.—James B. Comey, 324–3444.
 Deputy Director.—Mark Giuliano, 324–3315.
 Associate Deputy Director.—Andrew McCabe, 324–0308.
 Chief of Staff.—James Rybicki, 324–3444.

OFFICE OF THE DIRECTOR / DEPUTY DIRECTOR / ASSOCIATE DEPUTY DIRECTOR

Office of the General Counsel.—James A. Baker, 324–6829.
Office of Congressional Affairs.—Stephen Kelly, 324–5051.
Office of Equal Employment Opportunity Affairs.—Kevin M. Walker, 324–4128.
Office of the Ombudsman.—Monique Bookstein, 324–2156.
Office of Partner Engagement.—Kerry Sleeper, 324–7126.
Office of Professional Responsibility.—Candice M. Will, 324–8284.
Office of Public Affairs.—Michael Kortan, 324–5352.
Inspection Division.—Nancy McNamara, 324–2901.
Facilities and Logistics Services Division.—Richard Haley II, 324–4104.
Finance Division.—Richard Haley II, 324–4104.
Records Management Division.—Michelle Ann Jupina, 324–7141.

INFORMATION AND TECHNOLOGY BRANCH

Executive Assistant Director / Chief Information Officer.—Brian A. Truchon, 324–6165.
 Associate EAD and Deputy Chief Information Officer.—Dean E. Hall.
 Assistant Director of:
  Information Technology and Customer Relationship Division.—Jennifer Sanchez (703) 872–5050.
 IT Applications and Data Division.—John Kevin Reid, 324–2259.
 IT Infrastructure Division.—Brian Truchon, 324–6165.

CRIMINAL, CYBER, RESPONSE AND SERVICES BRANCH

Executive Assistant Director.—Robert Anderson, Jr., 324–4180.
 Assistant Director of:
  Criminal Investigative Division.—Joseph S. Campbell, 324–4260.
  Critical Incident Response Group.—James Yacone (703) 632–4100.
  Cyber Division.—James C. Trainor, Jr., 324–7770.
  International Operations Division.—John Boles, 324–5904.
  Office of Victim Assistance.—Kathryn M. Turman, 324–1433.

HUMAN RESOURCES BRANCH

Executive Assistant Director.—Valerie Parlave, 324–3000.
 Assistant Director of:
  Human Resources Division.—James L. Turgal, 324–3514.
  Training and Development Division.—Owen D. Harris (703) 632–1100.
  Security Division.—Clifford C. Holley, 203–1700.

NATIONAL SECURITY BRANCH

Executive Assistant Director.—John Giacalone, 324–7045.
Assistant Director of:
  Counterintelligence Division.—Randall Coleman, 324–4614.
  Counterterrorism Division.—Michael Steinbach, 324–2770.
  Weapons of Mass Destruction Directorate.—John G. Perren, 324–4965.

SCIENCE AND TECHNOLOGY BRANCH

Executive Assistant Director.—Amy Hess, 324–0805.
Assistant Director of:
  Criminal Justice Information Services Division.—Stephen L. Morris (304) 625–2700.
  Laboratory Division.—Christopher Todd Doss (703) 632–7001.
  Operational Technology Division.—Stephen E. Richardson, 632–6100.

INTELLIGENCE BRANCH

Executive Assistant Director.—Eric Velez-Villar, 324–7705.
Assistant Director of Directorate of Intelligence.—Rafael J. Garcia, Jr., 324–7605.

FIELD DIVISIONS

Albany: 200 McCarty Avenue, Albany, NY 12209 (518) 465–7551.
Albuquerque: 4200 Luecking Park Avenue, NE., Albuquerque, NM 87107 (505) 224–2000.
Anchorage: 101 East Sixth Avenue, Anchorage, AK 99501 (907) 258–5322.
Atlanta: 2635 Century Center Parkway, NE., Suite 400, Atlanta, GA 30345 (404) 679–9000.
Baltimore: 2600 Lord Baltimore Avenue, Baltimore, MD 21244 (410) 265–8080.
Birmingham: 1000 18th Street North, Birmingham, AL 35203 (205) 326–6166.
Boston: One Center Plaza, Suite 600, Boston, MA 02108 (617) 742–5533.
Buffalo: One FBI Plaza, Buffalo, NY 14202 (716) 856–7800.
Charlotte: Wachovia Building, 400 South Tryon Street, Suite 900, Charlotte, NC 28285 (704) 377–9200.
Chicago: 2111 West Roosevelt Road, Chicago, IL 60608–1128 (312) 431–1333.
Cincinnati: Federal Office Building, 550 Main Street, Room 9000, Cincinnati, OH 45202 (513) 421–4310.
Cleveland: 1501 Lakeside Avenue, Cleveland, OH 44114 (216) 522–1400.
Columbia: 151 Westpark Boulevard, Columbia, SC 29210 (803) 551–4200.
Dallas: J. Gordon Shanklin Building, One Justice Way, Dallas, TX 75220 (972) 559–5000.
Denver: Federal Office Building, 1961 Stout Street, Room 1823, Denver, CO 80294 (303) 629–7171.
Detroit: P.V. McNamara Federal Office Building, 477 Michigan Avenue, 26th Floor, Detroit, MI 48226 (313) 965–2323.
El Paso: 660 South Mesa Hills Drive, Suite 3000, El Paso, TX 79912 (915) 832–5000.
Honolulu: Kalanianaole Federal Office Building, 300 Ala Moana Boulevard, Room 4–230, Honolulu, HI 96850 (808) 566–4300.
Houston: 2500 East T.C. Jester, Suite 200, Houston, TX 77008 (713) 693–5000.
Indianapolis: Federal Office Building, 575 North Pennsylvania Street, Room 679, Indianapolis, IN 46204 (371) 639–3301.
Jackson: Federal Office Building, 100 West Capitol Street, Suite 1553, Jackson, MS 39269 (601) 948–5000.
Jacksonville: 7820 Arlington Expressway, Suite 200, Jacksonville, FL 32211 (904) 721–1211.
Kansas City: 1300 Summit, Kansas City, MO 64105 (816) 512–8200.
Knoxville: John J. Duncan Federal Office Building, 710 Locust Street, Room 600, Knoxville, TN 37902 (423) 544–0751.
Las Vegas: John Lawrence Bailey Building, 1787 West Lake Mead Boulevard, Las Vegas, NV 89106–2135 (702) 385–1281.
Little Rock: 24 Shackleford West Boulevard, Little Rock, AR 72211 (501) 221–9100.
Los Angeles: Federal Office Building, 11000 Wilshire Boulevard, Suite 1700, Los Angeles, CA 90024 (310) 477–6565.
Louisville: 600 Martin Luther King, Jr. Place, Room 500, Louisville, KY 40202 (502) 583–2941.
Memphis: Eagle Crest Building, 225 North Humphreys Boulevard, Suite 3000, Memphis, TN 38120 (901) 747–4300.

Miami: 16320 Northwest Second Avenue, Miami, FL 33169 (305) 944–9101.
Milwaukee: 330 East Kilbourn Avenue, Suite 600, Milwaukee, WI 53202 (414) 276–4684.
Minneapolis: 111 Washington Avenue South, Suite 100, Minneapolis, MN 55401 (612) 376–3200.
Mobile: 200 North Royal Street, Mobile, AL 36602 (334) 438–3674.
New Haven: 600 State Street, New Haven, CT 06511 (203) 777–6311.
New Orleans: 2901 Leon C. Simon Boulevard, New Orleans, LA 70126 (504) 816–3122.
New York: 26 Federal Plaza, 23rd Floor, New York, NY 10278 (212) 384–1000.
Newark: Claremont Tower Building, 11 Centre Place, Newark, NJ 07102 (973) 792–3000.
Norfolk: 150 Corporate Boulevard, Norfolk, VA 23502 (757) 455–0100.
Oklahoma City: 3301 West Memorial, Oklahoma City, OK 73134 (405) 290–7770.
Omaha: 10755 Burt Street, Omaha, NE 68114 (402) 493–8688.
Philadelphia: William J. Green, Jr., Federal Office Building, 600 Arch Street, Eighth Floor, Philadelphia, PA 19106 (215) 418–4000.
Phoenix: 201 East Indianola Avenue, Suite 400, Phoenix, AZ 85012 (602) 279–5511.
Pittsburgh: Martha Dixon Building, 3311 East Carson Street, Pittsburgh, PA 15203 (412) 432–4000.
Portland: Crown Plaza Building, 1500 Southwest First Avenue, Suite 401, Portland, OR 97201 (503) 224–4181.
Richmond: 1970 East Parham Road, Richmond, VA 23228 (804) 261–1044.
Sacramento: 4500 Orange Grove Avenue, Sacramento, CA 95841 (916) 481–9110.
Salt Lake City: 257 Towers Building, 257 East, 200 South, Suite 1200, Salt Lake City, UT 84111 (801) 579–1400.
San Antonio: 5740 University Heights Boulevard, San Antonio, TX 78249 (210) 225–6741.
San Diego: Federal Office Building, 9797 Aero Drive, San Diego, CA 92123 (858) 565–1255.
San Francisco: 450 Golden Gate Avenue, 13th Floor, San Francisco, CA 64102 (415) 553–7400.
San Juan: U.S. Federal Office Building, 150 Chardon Avenue, Room 526, Hato Rey, PR 900918 (787) 754–6000.
Seattle: 1110 Third Avenue, Seattle, WA 98101 (206) 622–0460.
Springfield: 900 East Linton Avenue, Springfield, IL 62703 (217) 522–9675.
St. Louis: 2222 Market Street, St. Louis, MO 63103 (314) 241–5357.
Tampa: 5525 West Gray Street, Tampa, FL 33609 (813) 273–4566.
Washington, DC: 601 Fourth Street, NW., Washington, DC 20535 (202) 278–3400.

FEDERAL BUREAU OF PRISONS (BOP)

320 First Street, NW., 20534

General Information Number (202) 307–3198

Director.—Charles E. Samuels, Jr., room 654, HOLC, 307–3250.
Deputy Director.—L. C. Eichenlaub, room 654, HOLC, 307–3250.
Director, National Institute of Corrections.—Jim Cosby, 2nd floor, 320 First Street, 514–4202.
Assistant Director of:
  Administration.—Bradley T. Gross, 9th floor, 500 FRST, 307–3230.
  Correctional Programs.—Angela P. Dunbar, room 554, HOLC, 307–3226.
  General Counsel.—Kathleen M. Kenney, room 958C, HOLC, 307–3062.
  Health Services.—Deborah G. Schult, Ph.D., room 1054, HOLC, 307–3055.
  Human Resources Management.—Dan Joslin, room 754, HOLC, 307–3082.
  Industries, Education, and Vocational Training.—Mary Mitchell, 8th floor, 400 FRST, 305–3501.
  Information, Policy and Public Affairs.—Judi Simon Garrett, room 641, HOLC, 514–6537.
  Program Review.—Steve Mora, room 1054, HOLC, 307–1076.
Regional Director for—
  Mid-Atlantic.—John Caraway (301) 317–3101.
  North Central.—Sara Revell (913) 551–1000.
  Northeast.—Joseph Norwood (215) 521–7300.
  South Central.—Jeffery Keller (972) 730–8800.
  Southeast.—Helen Marberry (678) 686–1200.
  Western.—Juan Castillo (209) 956–9700.
Telephone Directory Coordinator.—Marla Clayton, 307–3250.

FOREIGN CLAIMS SETTLEMENT COMMISSION
Bicentennial Building (BICN), 600 E Street, NW., Suite 6002, 20579
phone (202) 616–6975

Chairman.—Vacant.
Commissioners: Sylvia M. Becker, Anuj C. Desai.
Chief Counsel.—Brian M. Simkin.
Executive Officer.—Judith H. Lock.

OFFICE OF INFORMATION POLICY
1425 New York Avenue, NW., Suite 11050
Washington, DC 20530, phone (202) 514–3642

Director.—Melanie Ann Pustay.
Chief of Staff.—Carmen L. Mallon.

OFFICE OF THE INSPECTOR GENERAL
RFK Main Justice Building, Room 4706, phone (202) 514–3435
950 Pennsylvania Avenue, NW., 20530

Inspector General.—Michael E. Horowith.
Deputy Inspector General.—Robert P. Storch.
Chief of Staff/Senior Counsel.—Jay N. Lerner.
Senior Counsel.—James Mitzelfeld.
Counselors to the IG.—John S. Lavinsky.
General Counsel.—William Blier, RFK, Suite 4726, 616–0646.
Assistant Inspectors General:
    Audit.—Jason R. Malmstrom (NYAV), Suite 13000, 616–1697.
    Evaluations and Inspections.—Nina Pelletier (NYAV), Suite 6100, 616–4620.
    Investigations.—Eric Johnson (NYAV), Suite 7100, 616–4760.
    Management and Planning.—Gregory T. Peters (NYAV), Suite 7000, 616–4550.
    Oversight and Review.—Dan C. Beckhard (acting), (NYAV), Suite 13000, 616–0645.

REGIONAL AUDIT OFFICES

Atlanta: Ferris B. Polk, Suite 1130, 75 Spring Street, Atlanta, GA 30303 (404) 331–5928.
Chicago: Carol S. Taraszka, Suite 3510, Citicorp Center, 500 West Madison Street, Chicago, IL 60661 (312) 353–1203.
Dallas: Fletcher Couglas, Suite 410, Box 21, 2505 State Highway 360, Grand Prairie, TX 75050 (214) 655–5000.
Denver: David M. Sheeren, Suite 1500, Chancery Building, 1120 Lincoln Street, Denver, CO 80203 (303) 864–2000.
Philadelphia: Thomas O. Puerzer, Suite 201, 701 Market Street, Philadelphia, PA 19106 (215) 580–2111.
San Francisco: David J. Gaschke, Suite 201, 1200 Bayhill Drive, San Bruno, CA 94066 (650) 876–9220.
Washington: John Manning, 1300 North 17th Street, Suite 3400, Arlington, VA 22209 (202) 616–4688.
    Computer Security and Information Technology Audit Office: Reginald Allen, room 5000 (202) 616–3801.
    Financial Statement Audit Office: Mark L. Hayes, 1425 New York Avenue, NW., #13000, Washington, DC 20530 (202) 616–4660.

REGIONAL INVESTIGATIONS OFFICES

Atlanta: Eddie D. Davis, 60 Forsyth Street, SW., Room 8M45, Atlanta, GA 30303 (404) 562–1980.
Boston: Daniel Benedict, U.S. Courthouse, 1 Courthouse Way, Room 9200, Boston, MA 02210 (617) 748–3218.
Chicago: John F. Oleskowicz, P.O. Box 1802, Chicago, IL 60690 (312) 886–7050.

Denver: Norman K. Lau, Suite 1501, 1120 Lincoln Street, Denver, CO 80203 (303) 335–4201.
Dallas: Sandra Barnes, 2505 State Highway 360, Room 410, Grand Prairie, TX 75050 (817) 385–5200.
Detroit: Nicholas V. Candela, Suite 1402, 211 West Fort Street, Detroit, MI 48226 (313) 226–4005.
El Paso: Eric Benn, Suite 135, 4050 Rio Bravo, El Paso, TX 79902 (915) 577–0102.
Houston: Carlos Capano, P.O. Box 53509, Houston, TX 77052 (713) 718–4888.
Los Angeles: Angel De Vora Gunn, Suite 655, 330 North Brand Street, Glendale, CA 91203 (818) 543–1172.
Miami: Robert Allen Bourbon, Suite 200, 510 Shotgun Road, Sunrise, FL 33326 (954) 370–8300.
New York: Nicolas Fabregas, One Battery Park Plaza, 29th Floor, New York, NY 10004 (212) 824–3650.
New Jersey: Kenneth R. Connaughton, Jr., 361 Scotch Road, West Trenton, NJ 08628 (609) 883–5423.
San Francisco: Michael Barranti, Suite 220, 1200 Bayhill Drive, San Bruno, CA 94066 (650) 876–9058.
Seattle: Wayne Hawney, Suite 104, 620 Kirkland Way, Kirkland, WA 98033 (253) 852–0194.
Tucson: James Greer, 405 West Congress, Room 3600, Tucson, AZ 85701 (520) 620–7389.
Washington: Ronald Powell, 1425 New York Avenue, NW., Suite 7100, Washington, DC 20530 (202) 616–4760.
Fraud Detection Office.—Elise Chawaga, room 7100 (202) 353–2975.

INTERPOL-U.S. NATIONAL CENTRAL BUREAU
phone (202) 616–9000

Director.—Shawn A. Bray, 532–4239.
Deputy Director.—Geoffrey Shank, 532–4239.
General Counsel.—Kevin Smith, 616–4103.
Chief Financial Officer.—Kimberly Grunett, 616–0537.
Administrative Officer.—Deborah Allen, 305–8747.
Chief Information Officer.—Wayne Towson, 616–3855.
Information Systems Security Officer.—Nathree Turner, Jr., 305–8764.
Public and Congressional Affairs Officer.—LaTonya Turner, 616–8006.
Assistant Director, Division of:
  Alien / Fugitive.—Darrell White, 616–3552.
  Counterterrorism.—Robert Meadows, 616–0312.
  Drug.—Richard Joyce, 616–3379
  Economic Crimes.—Gerard Doret, 616–7675
  Human Trafficking and Child Protection.—Paul Layman (202) 307–1753.
  INTERPOL Operations and Command Center.—Royce Walters, 616–3459 (24/7 Command Center).
  State and Local Liaison.—Juan Muñoz-Torres, 532–6615.
  Violent Crimes.—Joseph Trigg, 532–4457.
Deputy Assistant Directors, Division of INTERPOL Operations and Command Center: Mary Ann Brewster, 616–8269; Edwin Quall, 616–7589 (24/7 Command Center).

JUSTICE MANAGEMENT DIVISION
RFK Main Justice Building, 950 Pennsylvania Avenue, NW., 20530
2CON—145 N Street, NE., 20530
LSB—Liberty Square Building, 450 5th Street, NW., 20530

Assistant Attorney General for Administration.—Lee J. Lofthus, room 1111 (202) 514–3101.
  Deputy Assistant Attorney General, Policy, Management and Planning.—Michael H. Allen, room 1113 (202) 514–3101.
  Staff Directors:
    Department Ethics Office.—Janice Rodgers (2CON), room 8E310 (202) 514–8196.
    Facilities and Administrative Services Staff.—Scott Snell (2CON), room 9E.204 (202) 616–2995.
    General Counsel Office.—Arthur Gary, General Counsel (2CON), room 8E528 (202) 514–3452.

Internal Review and Evaluation Office.—Neil Ryder (2CON), room 8W1419 (202) 616–5499.
Senior Procurement Executive.—Michael H. Allen, room 1113 (202) 514–3101.
Office of Small and Disadvantaged Business Utilization.—Robert Connolly (2CON), room 8E1009 (202) 616–0521.
Procurement Services Staff.—Mark Selweski, room 8E202 (202) 307–2000.
Records Management Policy Office.—Jeanette Plante (2CON), room 8W1401 (202) 514–3528.
Deputy Assistant Attorney General/Controller.—Jolene Lauria Sullens, room 1117 (202) 514–1843.
Staff Directors:
    Asset Forfeiture Management.—Robert Marca (acting), (2CON), room 5W725 (202) 616–8000.
    Budget Staff.—Karin O'Leary, room 7601 (202) 514–4082.
    Debt Collection Management.—Dennis Dauphin (acting), (2CON), room 5E103 (202) 514–5343.
    Finance.—Melinda Morgan (2CON), room 7E202 (202) 616–5800.
Deputy Assistant Attorney General, Human Resources and Administration.—Mari Santangelo, room 1112 (202) 514–5501.
Staff Directors:
    Attorney Recruitment and Management Office.—Jamilia Frone, Suite 10200, 450 5th Street, NW. (Liberty Square), (202) 514–3905.
    Consolidated Executive Office.—Cyntoria Carter, room 7113(202) 514–5537.
    DOJ Executive Secretariat.—Dana Paige, room 4412 (202) 514–2063.
    Equal Employment Opportunity.—Richard Toscano (2CON), room 1W102, 616–4800.
    Library.—Dennis Feldt, room 7535 (202) 514–2133.
    Human Resources Staff.—Terry Cook (2CON), room 9W102 (202) 514–6788.
    Security and Emergency Planning Staff.—James Dunlap, room 6217 (202) 514–2094.
Deputy Assistant Attorney General, Information Resources Management/CIO.—Joseph Klimavicz, room 1310–A, 514–0507.
Staff Directors:
    IT Security.—Melinda Rogers (2CON), room 4E1407 (202) 353–2421.
    Operation Services.—Victoria Gold, (RDC), room 203 (202) 307–6944.
    Policy and Planning.—Kevin Deeley (acting), (2CON), room 4E202 (202) 353–2421.
    Systems Engineering.—Jeff Johnson (2CON), room 3W701 (202) 353–2355.

OFFICE OF JUSTICE PROGRAMS (OJP)

810 7th Street, NW., 20531

OFFICE OF THE ASSISTANT ATTORNEY GENERAL

Assistant Attorney General.—Karol V. Mason (202) 307–5933.
Principal Deputy Assistant General.—Beth McGarry, 307–5933.
Deputy Assistant Attorney General.—Maureen Henneberg, 307–5933.
Manager, Equal Employment Opportunity.—Laura Colón-Marrero (202) 616–1998.

BUREAU OF JUSTICE ASSISTANCE

Director.—Denise E. O'Donnell, 616–6500.
Deputy Director of:
    Planning.—Eileen Garry, 616–6500.
    Policy.—Kristen Mahoney, 616–6500.
    Programs.—Tracey Trautman, 616–6500.

BUREAU OF JUSTICE STATISTICS

Director.—William Sabol, 307–0765.
Principal Deputy Director, Statistical Operations.—Vacant, 307–0765.
Deputy Director of:
    Statistical Collections Division.—Vacant, 307–0765.
    Statistical Programs Division.—Howard Snyder, 307–0765.
    Planning, Policy and Operations Division.—Gerard Ramker, 307–0765.

NATIONAL INSTITUTE OF JUSTICE

Director.—Nancy Rodriguez, 307–2942.
  Deputy Directors: Jennifer Scherer, 307–2942; Howard Spivak, 307–2942.
    Investigative and Forensic Sciences.—Gerald LaPorte, 307–2942.
    Research and Evaluation.—Seri Irazola, 307–2942.
    Science and Technology.—George Tillery, 307–2942.

OFFICE OF JUVENILE JUSTICE AND DELINQUENCY PREVENTION

Administrator.—Robert Listenbee, 307–5911.
  Deputy Administrator of:
    Policy.—Vacant.
    Programs.—Chyrl Y. Jones, 307–5911.

OFFICE FOR VICTIMS OF CRIME

Director.—Joye E. Frost, 307–5983.
  Deputy Directors: Marilyn Robert, 307–5983; Kristina Rose, 307–5983; Allison Turkel, 307–5983.

OFFICE OF ADMINISTRATION

Director.—Phillip K. Merkle, 307–0087.
  Deputy Director, Division of:
    Acquisition Management.—Nichele C. Robinson, 514–9497.
    Human Resources.—Jennifer McCarthy, 307–0730.
    Support Services.—Angela Gant, 305–8006.

OFFICE OF THE CHIEF FINANCIAL OFFICER

Chief Financial Officer.—Leigh Benda, 307–0623.
  Deputy Chief Financial Officer.—Mikki Atsatt, 307–0623.

OFFICE OF THE CHIEF INFORMATION OFFICER

Chief Information Officer.—Brian McGrath, 305–9071.
  Deputy Chief Information Officer.—Angel Santa, 305–9071.

OFFICE FOR CIVIL RIGHTS

Director.—Michael Alston, 307–0690.

OFFICE OF COMMUNICATIONS

Deputy Director.—Silas Darden (acting), 307–0703.
  Deputy Director for Public Affairs.—Chuck Wagner, 307–0703.

OFFICE OF THE GENERAL COUNSEL

General Counsel.—Rafael A. Madan, 307–6235.

OFFICE OF SEX OFFENDER SENTENCING, MONITORING, APPREHENDING, REGISTERING, AND TRACKING

Director.—Luis CdeBaca, 514–4689.
  Deputy Director.—Dawn Doran, 514–4689.

OFFICE OF LEGAL COUNSEL
RFK Main Justice Building, Room 5218, phone (202) 514–2051

Assistant Attorney General.—Vacant, room 5218, 514–2051.

Principal Deputy Assistant Attorney General.—Karl Thompson, room 5218, 514–4132.
Deputy Assistant Attorneys General: John Bies, room 5237, 305–8521; Brian Boynton, room 5235, 514–9700; Daniel Koffsky, room 5238, 514–2030; Troy McKenzie, room 5229, 514–9700.
Special Counsels: Paul P. Colborn, room 5240, 514–2048; Rosemary Hart, room 5242, 514–2027.
Senior Counsel.—Jeffrey Singdahlsen, room 5262, 514–4174.

OFFICE OF LEGAL POLICY

RFK Main Justice Building, Room 4234, phone (202) 514–4601

Assistant Attorney General.—Vacant, room 4230, 514–4601.
Principal Deputy Assistant Attorney General.—Elana Tyrangiel, room 4238, 514–5651.
Deputy Assistant Attorneys General: Kevin Jones, room 4248, 514–4604; Alexander Krulic, room 4240, 305–4870; Robyn Thiemann, room 4237, 514–8356; Michael Zubrensky, room 4229, 514–4606.
Chief of Staff.—Hannah Fried (acting), room 4228, 353–3069.
Executive Officer.—Matrina Matthews, room 4517, 616–0040.

OFFICE OF LEGISLATIVE AFFAIRS (OLA)

RFK Main Justice Building, Room 1145, phone (202) 514–2141

Assistant Attorney General.—Peter J. Kadzik.
Deputy Assistant Attorneys General: Eric P. Losick, Alicia O'Brien, Elliot Williams.
Special Counsel.—M. Faith Burton.

NATIONAL SECURITY DIVISION

RFK Main Justice Building, Room 7339, phone (202) 514–1057

Assistant Attorney General.—John P. Carlin.
Principal Deputy Assistant Attorney General.—Mary McCord.
Deputy Assistant Attorneys General: Luke Dembosky, Stuart Evans, George Toscas, Brad Wiegmann.
Chief of Staff.—Anita Singh.
Executive Officer.—Mark A. Jenkins.
Special Assistants to the Assistant Attorney General: Brianna Carbonneau, Stephanie Ore-Brooks.

COUNTERINTELLIGENCE AND EXPORT CONTROL SECTION

600 E Street, NW., Room 10100, phone (202) 233–0986

Chief.—David Laufman.

COUNTERTERRORISM SECTION

RFK Main Justice Building, Room 2643, phone (202) 514–0849

Chief.—Michael J. Mullaney.
Principal Deputy Chief.—Jennifer Smith (acting).
International Terrorism Unit I.—Anthony Asuncion.
International Terrorism Unit II.—Matthew Blue.
Terrorist Financing Unit.—Vacant.

FOREIGN INVESTMENT REVIEW STAFF

600 E Street, NW., Room 10000

Director.—Richard Sofield.

OFFICE OF INTELLIGENCE

RFK Main Justice Building, Room 6150, phone (202) 514 5600

Section Chief for—
Litigation.—Vacant.
Operations.—Gabrielle Sanz-Rexach.
Oversight.—Kevin O'Connor.

OFFICE OF JUSTICE FOR VICTIMS OF OVERSEAS TERRORISM

600 E Street, NW., Room 10102, phone (202) 233–0701

Director.—Heather Cartwright.

OFFICE OF THE PARDON ATTORNEY

145 N Street, NE., 20530, phone (202) 616–6070

Pardon Attorney.—Deborah Leff.
Deputy Pardon Attorney.—Lawrence Kupers.
Executive Officer.—Will Taylor.

OFFICE OF PROFESSIONAL RESPONSIBILITY

RFK Main Justice Building, Room 3266, phone (202) 514–3365

Counsel.—Robin C. Ashton.
Deputy Counsel.—G, Bradley Weinsheimer.
Senior Associate Counsel.—William J. Birney.
Associate Counsels: Raymond C. "Neil" Hurley, Margaret McCarty.
Senior Counsel.—Lyn Hardy.
Senior Assistant Counsels: Suzanne Drouet, Frederick Leiner, Mark Masling.
Assistant Counsels: Allison Barlotta, Sarah Cable, Paul Colby, Leonard Evans, Mark G. Fraase, John "Jack" Geise, Gregory Gonzalez, Albert Herring, John Sciortino, James Vargason, Barbara Ward.

PROFESSIONAL RESPONSIBILITY ADVISORY OFFICE

1425 New York Avenue, NW., 20530, phone (202) 514–0458

Director.—Vacant.
Deputy Director.—Stacy Ludwig.

OFFICE OF PUBLIC AFFAIRS

RFK Main Justice Building, Room 1220, phone (202) 514 2007

Director.—Melanic Newman.
Deputy Directors: Wyn Hornbuckle, Emily Pierce.

TAX DIVISION

RFK Main Justice Building, 950 Pennsylvania Avenue, NW., 20530

Judiciary Center Building, 555 Fourth Street, NW., 20001 (JCB)

Maxus Energy Tower, 7717 North Harwood Street, Suite 400, Dallas, TX 75242 (MAX)

Patrick Henry Building, 601 D Street, NW., 20004 (PHB)

Assistant Attorney General.—Caroline D. Ciraolo (acting/policy and planning), (Main), room 4141, (202) 514–2901.
Deputy Assistant Attorneys General: David A. Hubbert (Main), room 4137, 514–1958 (Civil Trial Matters); Diana L. Erbsen (Main), room 4607, 514–8381 (Appellate and Review); Larry Wszalek (acting) (Main), room 4611, 616–3866 (Criminal Matters).

Senior Legislative Counsel.—Eileen M. Shatz (Main), room 4134, 307–6419.
Civil Trial Section Chiefs:
  Central Region.—R. Scott Clarke (JCB), room 8921–B, 514–6508.
  Eastern Region.—Deborah S. Meland (JCB), room 6126, 307–6426.
  Northern Region.—D. Patrick Mullarkey (JCB), room 7804–A, 307–6533.
  Southern Region.—Michael Kearns (JCB), room 6243–A, 514–5905.
  Southwestern Region.—Grover Hartt (MAX), suite 400 (214) 880–9725.
  Western Region.—Richard R. Ward (JCB), room 7907–B, 307–5867.
Criminal Enforcement Section Chiefs:
  Northern Region.—Rosemary E. Paguni (PHB), room 7802, 514–2323.
  Southern Region.—Bruce Salad (PHB), room 7640, 514–5145.
  Western Region.—Melissa Schraibman (PHB), room 7034, 514–5384.
Section Chiefs:
  Appellate.—Gilbert S. Rothenberg (Main), room 4326, 514–3361.
  Court of Federal Claims.—David I. Pincus (JCB), room 8804–A, 307–6440.
  Criminal Appeals and Tax Enforcement Policy.—Frank Cihlar (PHB), room 7002, 514–
    2839.
  Office of Review.—Ann Carroll Reid (JCB), room 6846–D, 514–6636.
Executive Officer.—Robert Bruffy (PHB), room 10002 (202) 616–8412.

UNITED STATES MARSHALS SERVICE (USMS)
Washington, DC 20530–1000
Communications Center (202) 307–9100

Director.—David L. Harlow (acting), (202) 307–9001.
Deputy Director.—Vacant, 307–9001.
Chief of Staff.—Sophia Edwards, 307–9001.
Associate Director for Administration.—David Musel, 307–9001.
Associate Director for Operations.—William Snelson, 307–9001.
Chief, Office of Congressional and Public Affairs.—William Delaney, 307–9220.

OFFICE OF EQUAL EMPLOYMENT OPPORTUNITY

Equal Employment Opportunity Officer.—Marcus Williams.

OFFICE OF THE GENERAL COUNSEL

General Counsel.—Gerald M. Auerbach.

OFFICE OF PROFESSIONAL RESPONSIBILITY

Assistant Director.—Carl Caulk.
Deputy Assistant Director.—Blair Deem.

ASSET FORFEITURE DIVISION

Assistant Director.—Kim Beal.
Deputy Assistant Director.—Timothy Virtue.

FINANCIAL SERVICES DIVISION

Chief Financial Officer.—Holley O'Brien.
Deputy Assistant Director.—Mary Ellen Kline.

HUMAN RESOURCES DIVISION

Assistant Director.—Katherine Mohan.
Deputy Assistant Director.—Beth Brown-Ghee.

INFORMATION TECHNOLOGY DIVISION

Assistant Director.—Karl Mathias.
Deputy Assistant Director.—Jarrod Bruner.

MANAGEMENT SUPPORT DIVISION

Assistant Director.—Thomas Sgroi.
Deputy Assistant Director.—Michael Clay.

TRAINING DIVISION

Federal Law Enforcement Training Center, Building 20, Glynco, GA 31524

Assistant Director.—William Fallon.
Deputy Assistant Director.—David Anderson.

INVESTIGATIVE OPERATIONS DIVISION

Assistant Director.—Derrick Driscoll.
Deputy Assistant Director.—Donald O'Hearn.

JUSTICE PRISONER AND ALIEN TRANSPORTATION SYSTEM (JPATS)

1251 Northwest Briar Cliff Parkway, Suite 300, Kansas City, MO 64116

Assistant Director.—Shannon Brown.
Deputy Assistant Director.—Scott Flood.

JUDICIAL SECURITY DIVISION

Assistant Director.—Noelle Douglas.
Deputy Assistant Director, Judicial Operations.—Thomas Wight.
Deputy Assistant Director, Judicial Services.—Gary Insley (acting).

PRISONER OPERATIONS DIVISION

Assistant Director.—Eben Morales.
Deputy Assistant Director.—Bruce Vargo.

TACTICAL OPERATIONS DIVISION

Assistant Director.—Neil DeSousa.
Deputy Assistant Director.—Marti Stanley (acting).

WITNESS SECURITY DIVISION

Assistant Director.—Michael Prout.
Deputy Assistant Director.—Marcus Walker.

U.S. PAROLE COMMISSION

90 K Street, NE., 3rd Floor, 20530, phone (202) 346–7000, fax (202) 357–1085

Chairman.—J. Patricia Wilson Smoot.
Vice Chairman.—Patricia K. Cushwa.
Commissioners: Patricia K. Cushwa, Charles T. Massarone, J. Patricia Wilson Smoot.
Case Operations Administrator.—Stephen J. Husk.
Case Services Administrator.—Deirdre M. McDaniel.
General Counsel.—Helen H. Krapels.
Chief Information Officer.—Jonathan H. Pinkerton.
Executive Officer.—Zelia M. Carter.
Staff Assistant to the Chairman.—Jacquelyn E. Graham.

OFFICE ON VIOLENCE AGAINST WOMEN
145 N Street, NE., Suites 10W.121, 20530

Director.—Vacant.
Principal Deputy Director.—Bea Hanson (202) 307–6026.
Special Assistant to the Director.—Brenda Auterman, 532–4482.
Chief of Staff.—Allison Randal, 532–4548.
Deputy Director, Policy and Communications.—Rosie Hidalgo, 514–0391.
Senior Attorney—Advisor.—Jennifer Kaplan, 514–0052.
Deputy Director, Grants Development and Management.—Nadine Neufville, 305–2590.
Deputy Director, Tribal Affairs.—Lorraine Edmo, 514–8804.
Executive Officer.—Sybil Barksdale, 353–7378.
Chief Financial Officer.—Angela Wood, 353–3982.
Confidential Assistant to the Director.—Carla Bernal, 616–3255.

DEPARTMENT OF THE INTERIOR

Interior Building, 1849 C Street, NW., 20240, phone (202) 208–3100, http://www.doi.gov

SALLY JEWELL, Secretary of the Interior; born in England, UK, 1955; education: graduate of the University of Washington, Seattle; professional: served in the private sector, most recently as President and Chief Executive Officer of Recreation Equipment, Inc. (REI); joined REI as Chief Operating Officer in 2000 and was named CEO in 2005; before joining REI, spent 19 years as a commercial banker; first as an energy and natural resources expert and later working with a diverse array of businesses that drive our nation's economy; trained as a petroleum engineer, started her career with Mobil Oil Corp. in the oil and gas fields of Oklahoma and the exploration and production office in Denver, CO, where she was exposed to the remarkable diversity of our nation's oil and gas resources; nominated by President Barack Obama to become the 51st Secretary of the Interior, and was confirmed by the U.S. Senate on April 10, 2013.

OFFICE OF THE SECRETARY

Secretary of the Interior.—Sally Jewell, room 6612, 208–7351.
  Special Assistant to the Secretary.—Erin Walls, room 6615.
  Chief of Staff.—Tommy P. Beaudreau, room 6616.
  Deputy Chiefs of Staff: Nicole "Nikki" Buffa, room 6617; Benjamin Milakofsky, room 6620.
  Counselor to the Secretary.—Sarah Greenberger, room 6627.
  Senior Advisors to the Secretary: David Jayo, room 6624; Kate Kelly, room 6629.
  Director for Scheduling and Advance.—Francis Iacobucci, room 6643.
  Director of External and Intergovernmental Affairs.—John Blair, room 6211, 208–1923.
  Senior Advisor for Alaska Affairs.—Vacant, room 6243, 208–4177.

EXECUTIVE SECRETARIAT

Director.—Fay Iudicello, room 7314, 208–3181.

CONGRESSIONAL AND LEGISLATIVE AFFAIRS

Director.—Sarah Neimeyer, room 6258, 208–7264.
  Deputy Directors: Jeremy Bratt, room 6253; Stephenne Harding, room 6252.
  Legislative Counsel.—Chris Salotti, room 6259.

OFFICE OF COMMUNICATIONS

Director.—Blake Androff, room 6210, 208–6416.
  Deputy Director.—Vacant, room 6212.
  Press Secretary.—Jessica Kershaw, room 6216.
  Director of Digital Strategy.—Tim Fullerton.
  Information Officers: Joan Moody, Frank Quimby, Hugh Vickery.

OFFICE OF THE DEPUTY SECRETARY

Deputy Secretary.—Michael Connor, room 6657, 208–6291.
  Associate Deputy Secretary.—Elizabeth Klein, room 6653, 208–6291.
  Chief of Staff.—Elizabeth Washburn, room 6655, 208–6291.
  Counselor to Deputy Secretary.—Letty Belin, room 6650, 208–6291.
  Special Assistant to the Deputy Secretary.—Jordan Finegan, room 6649.

ASSISTANT SECRETARY FOR FISH AND WILDLIFE AND PARKS

Assistant Secretary.—Vacant, room 7256 (202) 208–5347.
Principal Deputy Assistant Secretary.—Michael J. Bean, room 7257, 208–4416.
Deputy Assistant Secretary.—Vacant.
Chief of Staff.—Israporn Pananon, room 7246, 208–5914.

U.S. FISH AND WILDLIFE SERVICE

Director.—Dan Ashe (202) 208–4717.
Deputy Directors: Steve Guertin, Jim Kurth, 208–4545.
Associate Director.—Robert Dreher.
Chief, Office of Law Enforcement.—William Woody, 208–3809.
Assistant Director for External Affairs.—Betsy Hildebrandt.
Chief, Division of:
  Congressional and Legislative Affairs.—Matt Huggler (703) 358–2243.
  Public Affairs.—Chris Tollefson (703) 358–2222.
Assistant Director for—
  Migratory Birds.—Jerome Ford, 208–1050.
  Budget, Planning, and Human Capital.—Denise Sheehan (703) 358–2400.
  Business Management and Operations.—Paul Rauch (703) 358–1822.
  Endangered Species.—Gary Frazer, 208–4646.
  Fisheries and Habitat Conservation.—David Hoskins, 208–6394.
  Information Resources and Technology Management.—Kenneth Taylor (703) 358–1729.
  International Affairs.—Bryan Arroyo, 208–6393.
  Wildlife and Sport Fish Restoration.—Hannibal Bolton, 208–7337.
Chief, National Wildlife Refuge System.—Cynthia Martinez (acting), 208–5333.

Regional Directors:
  Region 1.—Robyn Thorson, Eastside Federal Complex, 911 Northeast 11th Avenue, Portland, OR 97232 (503) 231–6118, fax 872–2716.
  Region 2.—Benjamin Tuggle, Room 1306, 500 Gold Avenue, SW., Albuquerque, NM 87103 (505) 248–6845, fax (503) 872–2716.
  Region 3.—Thomas Melius, Federal Building, Fort Snelling, Twin Cities, MN 55111 (612) 713–5301, fax 713–5284.
  Region 4.—Cynthia Dohner, 1875 Century Boulevard, Atlanta, GA 30345 (404) 679–4000, fax 679–4006.
  Region 5.—Wendi Weber, 300 Westgate Center Drive, Hadley, MA 01035 (413) 253–8300, fax 253–8308.
  Region 6.—Noreen Walsh, 134 Union Boulevard, #400, Lakewood, CO 80228 (303) 236–7920, fax 236–8295.
  Region 7.—Geoff Haskett, 1011 East Tudor Road, Anchorage, AK 99503 (907) 786–3542, fax 786–3306.
  Region 8.—Renne Lohoefener, 2800 Cottage Way, #W2606, Sacramento, CA 95825 (916) 414–6464, fax 414–6484.

NATIONAL PARK SERVICE

Director.—Jon Jarvis, room 2711 (202) 208–4621.
Deputy Director, Operations.—Peggy O'Dell, room 2212, 208–3818.
Deputy Director, Communications and Community Assistance.—Vacant.
Chief of Staff.—Maureen Foster, room 2715, 208–3818.
Associate Director for—
  Business Services.—Lena McDowall, room 2274, 208–5651.
  Cultural Resources.—Stephanie Toothman, room 2217, 208–7625.
  Information Resources.—Shane Compton, room 2226, 208–2431.
  Interpretation and Education.—Julia Washburn, room 2223, 208–4829.
  Natural Resource Stewardship and Science.—Ray Sauvajot, room 2221, 208–3884.
  Park Planning, Facilities, and Lands.—Victor Knox, room 2216, 208–3264.
  Visitor and Resource Protection.—Louis Rowe (acting), room 2220, 565–1020.
  Workforce Management.—Michael Reynolds, room 2227, 208–5587.
Comptroller.—Bruce Sheaffer, room 2280, 208–4566.
Assistant Director for—
  Communications.—Roberta D'Amico, room 3310, 208–3046.
  Legislative and Congressional Affairs.—Don Hellmann, room 3309, 208–5656.
  Partnerships and Civic Engagement.—Jeffrey Reinbold, room 2222, 208–2428.

Regional Directors:
Alaska.—Bert Frost, 240 West Fifth Avenue, Room 114, Anchorage, AK 99501 (907) 644–3510, fax 644–3816.
Intermountain.—Sue Masica, P.O. Box 25287, 12795 West Alameda Parkway, Denver, CO 80225 (303) 969–2500, fax 969–2785.
Midwest.—Cam Sholly, 601 Riverfront Drive, Omaha, NE 68102 (402) 661–1736, fax 661–1737.
National Capital.—Bob Vogel, 1100 Ohio Drive, SW., Washington, DC 20242 (202) 619–7000, fax 619–7220.
Northeast.—Mike Caldwell, U.S. Custom House, 200 Chestnut Street, Suite 306, Philadelphia, PA 19106 (215) 597–7013, fax 597–0815.
Southeast.—Stan Austin, 100 Alabama Street, NW., 1924 Building, Atlanta, GA 30303 (404) 562–3327, fax 562–3216.
Pacific West.—Christine Lehnertz, 333 Bush Street, Suite 500, San Francisco, CA 94104–2828, fax (415) 623–2101.

ASSISTANT SECRETARY FOR INDIAN AFFAIRS

Assistant Secretary.—Kevin K. Washburn, room 3600 (202) 208–7163.
Principal Deputy Assistant Secretary.—Lawrence Roberts, 208–7163.
Deputy Assistant Secretary for—
 Management.—Thomas Thompson, 208–3508.
 Policy and Economic Development.—Ann Marie Bledsoe Downes, 208–7163.
Chief of Staff.—Sarah E. Harris, 208–7163.
Director of:
 Congressional Affairs.—Darren Pete, 208–6160.
 Public Affairs.—Nedra Darling, 208–3710.

BUREAU OF INDIAN AFFAIRS

Director.—Mike Black (202) 208–5116.
Deputy Director of:
 Field Operations.—Michael Smith, 208–5116.
 Justice Services.—Darren Cruzan, 208–5787.
 Tribal Services.—Hankie Ortiz (202) 513–7640.
 Trust Services.—Helen Riggs, 208–5831.

BUREAU OF INDIAN EDUCATION

Director.—Charles "Monty" Roessel (202) 208–6123.
Deputy Bureau Directors:
 School Operations.—Vicki Forrest, 208–6123.
Chief of Staff.—Gregory Anderson, 208–5504.
Special Assistant.—Jacquelyn Cheek, 208–6983.
Associate Deputy Director of:
 BIE Operated Schools.—Jimmy Hastings (acting), (602) 265–1592.
 Division of Performance and Accountability.—Jeffrey Hamley (505) 563–5260.
 Navajo.—Emily Arviso (acting), (928) 871–5961.
 Tribally Controlled Schools.—Rose Marie Davis (acting), (952) 851–5424.

ASSISTANT SECRETARY FOR LAND AND MINERALS MANAGEMENT

Assistant Secretary.—Janice M. Schneider, room 6310 (202) 208–6734.
Deputy Assistant Secretaries: David Haines, room 6316; James Lyons, room 6311.

BUREAU OF LAND MANAGEMENT

Director.—Neil Kornze, room 5661 (202) 208–3801.
Deputy Director of:
 Operations.—Steve Ellis, room 5660, 208–3801.
 Programs and Policy.—Linda Lance, room 5650, 208–3801.
Division Chief, Legislative Affairs and Correspondence.—Patrick Wilkerson (202) 912–7429.
 Deputy Division Chief.—Andrea Nelson (202) 912–7431.

State Directors:
  Alaska.—Bud Cribley, 222 West Seventh Avenue, No. 13, Anchorage, AK 99513 (907) 271–5080, fax 271–4596.
  Arizona.—Ray Suazo, One North Central Avenue, Suite 800, Phoenix, AZ 85004 (602) 417–9500, fax 417–9398.
  California.—Jim Kenna, 2800 Cottage Way, Suite W1623, Sacramento, CA 95825 (916) 978–4600, fax 978–4699.
  Colorado.—Ruth Welch, 2850 Youngfield Street, Lakewood, CO 80215 (303) 239–3700, fax 239–3934.
  Eastern States.—John Ruhs, 20th M Street, Suite 950, Washington, DC 20003 (202) 912–7701, fax 440–1701.
  Idaho.—Tim Murphy, 1387 South Vinnell Way, Boise, ID 83709 (208) 373–4000, fax 373–3919.
  Montana.—Jamie Connell, 5001 Southgate Drive, Billings, MT 59101 (406) 896–5012, fax 896–5004.
  Nevada.—Amy Lueders, 1340 Financial Boulevard, Reno, NV 89502 (775) 861–6590, fax 861–6601.
  New Mexico.—Aden Seidlitz (acting), 1474 Rodeo Road, P.O. Box 27115, Sante Fe, NM 87505 (505) 954–2222, fax 438–7452.
  Oregon.—Jerome Perez, 333 Southwest 1st Avenue, P.O. Box 2965, Portland, OR 97204 (503) 808–6026, fax 808–6308.
  Utah.—Juan Palma, 440 West 200 South, Suite 500, P.O. Box 45155, Salt Lake City, UT 84101 (801) 539–4010, fax 539–4013.
  Wyoming.—MaryJo Rudwell (acting), 5353 Yellowstone Road, P.O. Box 1828, Cheyenne, WY 82003 (307) 775–6001, fax 775–6028.

BUREAU OF OCEAN ENERGY MANAGEMENT

Director.—Abigail Ross Hopper (202) 208–6300.
  Deputy Director/Chief Financial Officer.—Walter D. Cruickshank, 208–6300.
    Budget and Program Coordination.—James G. Anderson, 208–6264.
    Congressional Affairs.—Lee Tilton, 208–3502.
    Policy, Regulation and Analysis.—Deanna P. Meyer-Pietruszka, 208–6352.
    Public Affairs.—Caren W. Madsen, 208–6474.
  Environmental Programs.—William Y. Brown, 208–6249.
  Outer Continental Shelf Regional Directors:
    Alaska.—James J. Kendall, Jr., 3801 Centerpoint Drive, Anchorage, AK 99503 (907) 334–5200.
    Gulf of Mexico.—John L. Rodi, 1201 Elmwood Park Boulevard, New Orleans, LA 70123 (504) 736–2592.
    Pacific.—Ellen G. Aronson, 760 Paseo, Camarillo, CA 93010–6002 (805) 389–7502.
  Renewable Energy.—James F. Bennett (703) 787–1300.
  Strategic Resources Programs.—L. Renee Orr, 208–3515.

BUREAU OF SAFETY AND ENVIRONMENTAL ENFORCEMENT

Director.—Brian M. Salerno (202) 208–3500.
  Deputy Director.—Margaret N. Schneider.
  Chief of Administration.—Scott Mabry, 208–3220.
  Budget.—Eric Modrow (703) 787–1694.
  Offshore Regulatory Programs.—Doug Morris, 208–3974.
  Policy and Analysis.—Molly Madden (acting), (202) 219–7271.
  Congressional Affairs.—Julie Fleming, 208–3827.
  Outer Continental Shelf Regional Directors:
    Alaska.—Mark Fesmire, 3801 Centerpoint Drive, Suite 500, Anchorage, AK 99503 (907) 334–5300.
    Gulf of Mexico.—Lars T. Herbst, 1201 Elmwood Park Boulevard, New Orleans, LA 70123 (504) 736–2589.
    Pacific.—Jaron Ming, 770 Paseo Camarillo, Camarillo, CA 93010 (805) 389–7514.

OFFICE OF SURFACE MINING RECLAMATION AND ENFORCEMENT

Director.—Joseph G. Pizarchik, room 233 (202) 208–4006.
  Deputy Director.—Glenda Owens, 208–4006.
  Assistant Director for Finance and Administration.—Ted Woronka, 208–2546.

Congressional Contact.—Tom Bukaweski, 208–2838.
Regional Director for—
  Appalachian Region.—Thomas D. Shope, Three Parkway Center, Pittsburgh, PA 15220 (412) 937–2828, fax 937–2903.
  Mid-Continent Region.—Ervin Barchenger, 501 Belle Street, Room 216, Alton, IL 62002 (618) 463–6460, fax 463–6470.
  Western Region.—David Berry, 1999 Broadway, Suite 3320, Denver, CO 80202 (303) 293–5001, fax 293–5006.

ASSISTANT SECRETARY FOR POLICY, MANAGEMENT AND BUDGET

Assistant Secretary.—Vacant, room 7212 (202) 208–1927.
Principal Deputy Assistant Secretary.—Kristen J. Sarri, room 7212, 208–1927.
Deputy Assistant Secretary for—
  Budget, Finance, Performance and Acquisition.—Olivia Ferriter, 208–4775.
  Human Capital and Diversity.—Mary Pletcher, 208–1738.
  Natural Resources Revenue Management.—Paul Mussenden, 208–2842.
  Policy and International Affairs.—Lori Faeth, 208–4852.
  Public Safety, Resource Protection, and Emergency Services.—Kim Thorsen, 208–5773.
  Technology, Information and Business Services.—Elena Gonzales (acting) 208–7966.

ASSISTANT SECRETARY FOR WATER AND SCIENCE

Principal Deputy Assistant Secretary.—Jennifer Gimbel, room 6358 (202) 208–3186.
Deputy Assistant Secretaries:—Lori Caramanian, Tom Iseman.
Chief of Staff.—Kerry Rae, room 6353 (202) 513 0535.

U.S. GEOLOGICAL SURVEY

The National Center, 12201 Sunrise Valley Drive, Reston, VA 20192

phone (703) 648–7411, fax 648–4454

Director.—Suzette M. Kimball (acting), 648–7411.
Deputy Director.—Mark Sogge (acting), 648–7412.
Chief of Staff.—Judy Nowakowski, 648–4411.
Office of:
  Administration (Administrative Policy and Services/Budget and Performance.—Jose Aragon, 648–7200.
  Communications and Outreach.—Barbara Wainman, 648–5750.
  Congressional Liaison Officer.—Timothy J. West, 648–4300.
  Human Capital.—Jose Aragon, 648–7200.
  Public Affairs Officer.—Anne-Berry Wade, 648–4483.
Associate Director for—
  Climate and Land Use Change.—Douglas Beard (acting), 648–4212.
  Core Science Systems.—Kevin Gallagher, 648–5747.
  Ecosystems.—Anne Kinsinger, 648–4050.
  Energy and Minerals, and Environmental Health.—Daniel Hayba (acting), 648–6403.
  Natural Hazards.—David Applegate, 648–6600.
  Water Resources.—William Wekheiser, 648–4557.
Regional Director for—
  Northeast Area.—David Russ, 12201 Sunrise Valley Drive, Reston, VA 20192 (703) 648–6600.
  Southeast Area.—Jess Weaver, 1770 Corporate Drive, Suite 500, Norcross, GA 30093 (678) 924–6614.
  Midwest Area.—Leon Carl, 1451 Green Road, Anne Arbor, MI 48105 (734) 214–7201.
  Southwest Area.—Max Ethridge, P.O. Box 25046, Denver Federal Center, Building 810, Denver, CO 80225 (303) 236–5438.
  Northwest Area.—Frank Shipley (acting), Federal Office Building, 909 First Avenue, 8th Floor, Seattle, WA 98104 (206) 220–4600.
  Pacific Area.—Richard Ferrero (acting), Modoc Hall, 3020 State University Drive East, Sacramento, CA 95819 (206) 795–4527.
  Alaska.—Nancy Lee (acting), 4230 University Drive, Suite 201, Anchorage, AK 99508 (907) 786–7055.

BUREAU OF RECLAMATION

Commissioner.—Estevan López, room 7657 (202) 513–0501.
Deputy Commissioner for—
  External and Intergovernmental Affairs.—Dionne Thompson, room 7653, 513–0615.
  Operations.—Lowell Pimley, room 7645, 513–0615.
  Policy, Administration, and Budget.—Grayford Payne, room 7650, 513–0542.
Chief of Staff.—Robert Quint, room 7641.
Chief of:
  Congressional and Legislative Affairs.—Vacant, room 7643, 513–0570.
  Public Affairs.—Daniel J. DuBray, room 7644, 513–0574.
Regional Directors:
  Great Plains.—Michael J. Ryan, P.O. Box 36900, Billings, MT 59107 (406) 247–7795, fax 247–7793.
  Lower Colorado.—Terrance Fulp, P.O. Box 61470, Boulder City, NV 89006 (702) 293–8000, fax 293–8333.
  Mid-Pacific.—David Murillo, 2800 Cottage Way, Sacramento, CA 95825 (916) 978–5000, fax 978–5005.
  Pacific Northwest.—Lorri Lee, 1150 North Curtis Road, Suite 100, Boise, ID 83706 (208) 378–5012, fax 378–5019.
  Upper Colorado.—Vacant, 125 South State Street, room 6107, Salt Lake City, UT 84138 (801) 524–3600, fax 524–3855.

OFFICE OF INSPECTOR GENERAL

Inspector General.—Vacant, room 4411 (202) 208–5745.
Deputy Inspector General.—Mary Kendall, room 4411 (202) 208–5745.
Chief of Staff.—Stephen Hardgrove, room 4410 (202) 208–5745.
Associate Inspector General for Whistleblower Protection.—Laurie Larson-Jackson, room 4429.
Associate Inspector General for External Affairs.—Kris Kolesnik, room 4429.

OFFICE OF THE SOLICITOR

Solicitor.—Hilary C. Tompkins, room 6415 (202) 208–4423.
Principal Deputy Solicitor.—K. Jack Haugrud (acting).
Deputy Solicitor for—
  General Law.—Ed Keable.
  Indian Affairs.—Venus Prince.
  Land Resources.—Bret Birdsong.
  Mineral Resources.—K. Jack Haugrud.
  Parks and Wildlife.—Ted Boling.
  Water.—Ramsey Kropf.
Deputy Solicitor for—
  General Law.—Mike Berrigan.
  Indian Affairs.—Vacant.
  Land and Water.—Laura Brown.
  Mineral Resources.—Karen Hawbecker.
  Parks and Wildlife.—Barry Roth.
Administration.—Shayla Simmons.
Designated Agency Ethics Official.—Melinda Loftin, 208–5295.

OFFICE OF THE SPECIAL TRUSTEE FOR AMERICAN INDIANS

Principal Deputy Special Trustee.—Michele Singer (acting), (202) 208–3946.

DEPARTMENT OF AGRICULTURE

Jamie L. Whitten Building, 1400 Independence Avenue, SW., 20250
phone (202) 720–3631, http://www.usda.gov

TOM VILSACK, Secretary of Agriculture; education: B.A., Hamilton College; J.D., Albany Law School; professional: Governor, Iowa, 1999–2007; nominated by President Barack Obama to become the 30th Secretary of Agriculture, and was confirmed by the U.S. Senate on January 20, 2009.

OFFICE OF THE SECRETARY

Secretary of Agriculture.—Tom Vilsack, room 200–A (202) 720–3631.
  Deputy Secretary.—Michael Scuse (acting).
  Chief of Staff.—Krysta Harden.
  Deputy Chief of Staff for Operations.—Oscar Gonzales.
  Deputy Chief of Staff for Policy.—Anne MacMillan.

OFFICE OF THE ASSISTANT SECRETARY FOR ADMINISTRATION
Jamie L. Whitten Building, Room 240–W, phone (202) 720–3291

Assistant Secretary.—Dr. Gregory Parham, 720 3291.
  Deputy Assistant Secretary.—Malcom A. Shorter, 720–3291.
  Chief of Staff.—Jennifer Yezak, 260–8497.
  Special Assistant.—Janice Williams, 720–3291.
  Senior Advisors: Max Finberg, 720–1271; Elizabeth Reiter, 720–3874.

OFFICE OF ADMINISTRATIVE LAW JUDGES
South Agriculture Building, Room 1049–S, phone (202) 720–6383

Chief Administrative Law Judge.—Vacant.
  Executive Assistant to the Chief Administrative Law Judge.—Diane Green.
  Administrative Law Judges: Janice K. Bullard, Jill S. Clifton, 720–8161.
  Hearing Clerk.—Vacant, 720–4443.

OFFICE OF HUMAN RESOURCES MANAGEMENT
Jamie L. Whitten Building, Room 318–W, phone (202) 720–3585

Director and Chief Human Capital Officer.—William P. Milton, Jr.
  Executive Assistant.—Melanie Clemons.
  Deputy Director.—Bobbi Jeanquart.
  Chief of Staff.—Lynne Short, 690–3973.
  Directors:
    Employee and Labor Relations Division.—Bryan Knowles, 720–6784.
    HR Enterprise Systems Management Division.—Indu Garg, 720–4963.
    HR Policy Division.—Christine Jones, 720–5873.
    Recruitment, Diversity and WorkLife Division.—Dr. Zina Sutch, 720–5618.
    Strategic HR, Planning and Accountability Division.—Allen Hatcher, 720–0941.
  Virtual University.—Dr. Karlease Kelly, Provost, 720–0185.
  Executive Resources Management Division.—Paticia Moore, 720–8629.

OFFICE OF THE JUDICIAL OFFICER
South Agriculture Building, Room 1633–S, phone (202) 720–4764

Judicial Officer.—William G. Jenson.

Attorney.—Kathleen Bright.
Legal Technician.—Sherida Hardy.

OFFICE OF OPERATIONS
South Agriculture Building, Room 1456–S, phone (202) 720–3937

Director of Operations.—Curtis Wilburn.
Executive Services.—Camelnita Fossum, 720–3199.
Director, Office of:
  Facilities Management.—Thomas Hoffman, 720–8290.
  Mail and Reproduction Management.—Dennis Banks (acting), 720–8393.
  Materiel Management Service Center.—Carlos Casaus (301) 394–0413.
  Program, Policy and Support Staff.—Morris Tate, 720–4134.
  Protective Operations.—Gilbert Stokes, 720–6270.
  Safety, Sustainability and Emergency Operations.—Edward Hogberg, 205–8923.

OFFICE OF PROCUREMENT AND PROPERTY MANAGEMENT
Whitten Building, Room 335W, phone (202) 720–9448

Director.—Lisa Wilusz.
  Division Director for—
  Procurement Operations.—Richard Jiron (970) 295–5487.
  Procurement Policy.—Vacant, 690–1060.
  Procurement Systems.—Loretta Smith-Hawkins, 401–1023.
  Property Management.—Paul Walden, 720–7283.
  Safety and Health Management.—Theresa Ferguson, 702–0889.

OFFICE OF HOMELAND SECURITY

Director.—Todd Repass, room S–310 (202) 720–0272.
  Division Chief for—
  Continuity and Planning.—Scott Linsky, 260–0106.
  Personnel and Document Security.—Cody Allers, 720–7373.
  Physical Security.—Richard Holman, 720–3901.
Director, Office of:
  Emergency Programs.—Todd Barrett, 690–3191.
  Protective Operations.—Daniel Downy, 720–6270.

OFFICE OF SMALL AND DISADVANTAGED BUSINESS UTILIZATION
South Agriculture Building, Room 1085–S, phone (202) 720–7117

Director.—Carmen Jones.

ASSISTANT SECRETARY FOR CIVIL RIGHTS
Jamie L. Whitten Building, Room 212–A, phone (202) 720–3808

Assistant Secretary.—Joe Leonard, Jr., Ph.D.
Deputy Assistant Secretary.—Frederick Pfaeffle Arana.

OFFICE OF BUDGET AND PROGRAM ANALYSIS
Jamie L. Whitten Building, Room 101–A, phone (202) 720–3323

Director.—Michael L. Young.
Associate Director.—Don Bice, 720–5303.
Deputy Director for—
  Budget, Legislative and Regulatory Systems.—Diem-Linh Jones, room 102–E, 720–6667.
  Program Analysis.—Christopher Zehren, room 126–W, 720–3396.

OFFICE OF THE CHIEF ECONOMIST
Jamie L. Whitten Building, Room 112–A, phone (202) 720–4164

Chief Economist.—Vacant.

Deputy Chief Economist.—Robert Johansson, room 112–A, 720–4737.
Chairperson, World Agricultural Outlook Board.—Vacant, room 4419–S, 720–6030.
Chief Meteorologist.—Vacant, room 4441–S, 720–8651.
Global Change Program Office.—William Hohenstein, room 4407–S, 720–6698.
Office of:
   Energy Policy and New Uses.—Harry Baumes, room 4059–S, 401–0461.
   Risk Assessment and Cost Benefit Analysis.—Linda C. Abbott, room 4032–S, 720–8022.
   Sustainable Development.—Elise Golan, room 112–A, 720–2456.
Supervisory Meteorologist, National Weather Service.—Mark Brusberg, room 4443–S, 720–6030.

OFFICE OF THE CHIEF FINANCIAL OFFICER
Jamie L. Whitten Building, Room 143–W, phone (202) 720–5539

Chief Financial Officer.—Jon Holladay.
   Deputy Chief Financial Officer.—John Brewer, room 140–W, 720–9427.
   Associate Chief Financial Officers for—
      Financial Operations.—Vacant, room 3053–S.
      Financial Policy and Planning.—Lynn Moaney, room 3054–S, 720–0065.
      Financial Systems.—Michael Clanton, room 3057–S, 690–3068.
   Director, National Finance Center.—John White, P.O. Box 60000, New Orleans, LA 70160 (504) 426–0120.

OFFICE OF THE CHIEF INFORMATION OFFICER
Jamie L. Whitten Building, Room 414–W, phone (202) 720–8833

Chief Information Officer.—Joyce M. Hunter (acting).
   Deputy Chief Information Officers for
      Operations.—Nancy Reeves-Flores (acting) 720–8833.
      Policy and Planning.—Joyce M. Hunter.
   Associate Chief Information Officers for—
      Agriculture Security Operations Center (ASOC).—Christopher Lowe, 720–8281.
      Client Technology Services.—Nancy Reeves-Flores, 690–2252.
      Data Center Operations (National Information Technology Center).—Richard Coffee, 690–0048.
      Enterprise Network Services.—John Donovan (202) 205–4394.
      Resource Management.—Lisa Keeter, 720–4109.
   Director, Distance Learning Program.—Jerome Davin, 694–0006.

OFFICE OF COMMUNICATIONS
Jamie L. Whitten Building, Room 412–A, phone (202) 720–4623

Director.—Matt Herrick (acting).
   Deputy Director for—
      Creative Development.—David Black.
      Press Operations.—Matt Herrick.
   Press Secretary.—Cullen Schwarz.
   Director, Center for—
      Brand Review.—Carolyn O'Connor.
      Broadcast Media and Technology.—Garth Clark.
      Constituent Affairs: Kathryn Hill, Mocile Trotter.
      Information Technology.—Wayne Moore.
      Web Communication.—Peter Rhee.

OFFICE OF CONGRESSIONAL RELATIONS
Jamie L. Whitten Building, Room 219–A, phone (202) 720–7095

Assistant Secretary.—Todd A. Batta.
   Deputy Assistant Secretary.—Melinda Cep.
   Legislative Director.—Trevor Reuschel.
   Congressional Liaisons:
      FFAS.—Melinda Cep.

NRE.—Trevor Reuschel.
REE.—Jenny Devine.
MRP.—Jenny Devine.
RD.—Kevin Bailey.
Food Safety.—Hillary Caron.
FNCS.—Hillary Caron.

EXTERNAL AND INTERGOVERNMENTAL AFFAIRS

Room 216–A, phone (202) 720–6643

Director.—Sarah Scanlon (acting).
Deputy Director.—Sarah Scanlon.

OFFICE OF TRIBAL RELATIONS

Room 501–A, phone (202) 205–2249

Director.—Leslie Wheelock.

OFFICE OF THE EXECUTIVE SECRETARIAT

Jamie L. Whitten Building, Room 116–A, phone (202) 720–7100

Director.—Sally Liska.
Deputy Director.—Maureen Wood.

OFFICE OF THE GENERAL COUNSEL

Jamie L. Whitten Building, Room 107–W, phone (202) 720–3351

General Counsel.—Jeffrey M. Prieto (acting).
Principal Deputy General Counsel.—Jeffrey M. Prieto.
Deputy General Counsel.—Inga Bumbary-Langston.
Associate General Counsel for—
  Civil Rights, Labor and Employment Law.—Arlean Leland, 720–1760.
  International Affairs, Food Assistance, and Farm and Rural Programs.—David P. Grahn, 720–8063.
  General Law and Research.—Benjamin Young, 720–4814.
  Marketing, Regulatory and Food Safety Programs.—Carrie Ricci, 720–3155.
  Natural Resources and Environment.—Ralph Linden, 720–6883.
Assistant General Counsel, Division of:
  Civil Rights Litigation.—Steven Brammer, 720–4375.
  Civil Rights Policy, Compliance, and Counsel.—Tami Trost, 690–3993.
  General Law and Research.—Shawn McGruder, 720–5565.
  International Affairs, Food Assistance, and Farm and Rural Programs: Peter Bonner, 720–3569; Janet Safian, 720–2923.
  Marketing, Regulatory and Food Safety.—James Booth, 720–3461; Mai Dinh, 720–5935.
  Natural Resources and Environment.—Ronald Mulach, 720–2063.
Director, Administration and Resource Management.—Charlene Buckner, 720–6324.
Resource Management Specialist.—Robyn Davis, 720–4861.

OFFICE OF INSPECTOR GENERAL

Jamie L. Whitten Building, Room 117–W, phone (202) 720–8001, fax 690–1278

Inspector General.—Phyllis K. Fong.
Deputy Inspector General.—David Gray.
Assistant Inspector General for—
  Audit.—Gil Harden, room 403–E, 720–6945.
  Offfice of Investigations.—Ann Coffey (acting), room 146–W, 720–3965.
  Office of Management.—Lane Timm, room 5–E, 720–6979.

NATIONAL APPEALS DIVISION

3101 Park Center Drive, Suite 1100, Alexandria, VA 22302

Director.—Steven C. Silverman (703) 305–2708.

UNDER SECRETARY FOR NATURAL RESOURCES AND ENVIRONMENT

Jamie L. Whitten Building, Room 240–E, phone (202) 720–7173

Under Secretary.—Robert Bonnie.
Deputy Under Secretaries: Arthur "Butch" Blazer, Ann Mills.

FOREST SERVICE

Sydney R. Yates Building, 201 14th Street, SW., 20250, phone (202) 205–1661

Chief.—Thomas Tidwell.
Associate Chief.—Mary Wagner, 205–1779.
Director for—
    International Programs. Valdis E. Mezainis, 644–4621
    Law Enforcement and Investigations.—David Ferrell (703) 605–4690.
    Legislative Affairs.—Douglas Crandall, 205–1637.

BUSINESS OPERATIONS

Sydney R. Yates Building, Fourth Floor, phone (202) 205–1707

Deputy Chief.—J. Lenise Lago (202) 205–1707.
Associate Deputy Chiefs: Robert Velasco (703) 605–4726; Jane Cottrell (703) 605–4167; Vacant.
Chief of Staff.—Anna Briatico (202) 205–1707.
Senior Staff Assistants: Donna Drelick (202) 205–0914; Deedra Fogle (202) 205–1545.
Deputy Area Budget Coordinator.—Tracey Hanson (202) 403–8975.
Director for—
    Acquisition Management.—George Sears (703) 605–4744.
    Enterprise.—Laura Nance (acting), (909) 382–2613.
    Homeland Security.—Arthur Bryant (202) 205–0942.
    Human Resources Management.—Mary Beth Lepore (703) 605–4604.
    Information Resources Management.—Douglas Nash (505) 563–7978.
    Job Corps.—Tina Terrell (303) 236–9939.
    Regulatory and Management Services.—Andria Weeks (202) 205–5102.
    Safety and Occupational Health.—Steven Schlientz (703) 605–4482.
    Sustainable Operations.—Anna Jones Crabtree (acting), (406) 459–7447.
    Strategic Program and Budget Analysis.—Antoine Dixon (202) 205–1088.

NATIONAL FOREST SYSTEM

Sydney R. Yates Building, Fifth Floor, phone (202) 205–1523

Deputy Chief.—Leslie A.C. Weldon.
Associate Deputy Chiefs: Emilee P. Blount (acting), 205–0824; Mary Beth Borst (acting), 205–3171.
Staff Director of:
    Ecosystem Management Coordination.—Leanne Marten, 205–0830.
    Engineering Technology and Geo-Spatial Service.—Ed James (acting), (703) 605–4616.
    Forest Management.—Bryan C. Rice (202) 649–1713.
    Lands and Realty.—Greg Smith, 205–1769.
    Minerals and Geology Management.—Nicholas Douglas, 605–4785.
    National Partnership Office.—Steve Lohr, 205–1072.
    Rangeland Management Vegetation Ecology.—Ralph Giffen (acting), 205–1455.
    Recreation Heritage and Volunteer Resources.—Joe Meade, 205–1240.
    Watershed, Fish, Wildlife, Air and Rare Plants.—Robert Harper, 205–1671.
    Wilderness, Wild and Scenic Rivers.—Susan Spear (202) 644–4862.

RESEARCH AND DEVELOPMENT
Sydney R. Yates Building, Second Floor, Fax (202) 205–1530

Deputy Chief.—Dr. Jim Reaves, 205–1665.
 Associate Deputy Chiefs: Carlos Rodriguez-Franco, Cynthia West, 205–1702.
 Senior Staff Assistants: Steve Hart, 205–0844; Linda Jones, 205–1200.
 Deputy Budget Coordinator.—Felipe Sanchez, 205–0833.
 Staff Directors:
   Inventory, Monitoring, and Assessment Research.—Vacant (703) 605–4177.
   Knowlege Management and Communications.—Daina Dravnieks Apple, 205–1452.
   Landscape Restoration and Ecosystem Services Research.—Carl Lucero, 605–5137.
   Policy Analysis.—Bill Lange (202) 207–8306.
   Sustainable Forest Management Research.—Toral Patel-Weynand, 605–4188.

STATE AND PRIVATE FORESTRY
Sydney R. Yates Building, Third Floor, phone (202) 205–1657

Deputy Chief.—James E. Hubbard, 205–1606.
 Associate Deputy Chiefs: Vicki Christiansen, Patti Hirami.
 Chief of Staff.—Debbie Pressman.
 Director of:
   Conservation Education.—Michiko Martin, 205–1241.
   Cooperative Forestry.—Steve Koehn, 205–1389.
   Fire and Aviation Management.—Tom Harbour, 205–1483.
   Forest Health Protection.—Monica Lear (703) 605–5340.
   Office of Tribal Relations.—Fred Clark, 205–1514.

NATURAL RESOURCES CONSERVATION SERVICE
South Building, Room 5105–A, phone (202) 720–4525

Chief.—Jason Weller.
 Associate Chiefs: Thomas Christensen 720–5811; Leonard Jordan, 720–4531.
 Director, Division of:
   Civil Rights.—Selina Lee (301) 504–2181.
   Legislative.—Callie Eideberg (acting), 720–2771.
   Public Affairs.—Kaveh Sadeghzadeh, 720–3210.

DEPUTY CHIEF FOR FINANCIAL MANAGEMENT

Chief Financial Officer.—Stephen M. Kunze (202) 720–5904, 720–4251.
 Deputy Chief Financial Officer.—Ravenna Bohan (202) 690–0431.
 Directors:
   Budget Division.—Jeffrey Machelski (202) 205–1442.
   Corporate Accounting Division.—Selma Cowan, 205–0013.
   Quality Assurance Division.—Brenda Rodriguez (acting), 205–6143.
   Policy, Systems and Training Division.—Brenda Rodriguez, 205–6143.
 Team Leader, Office of Financial Analysis.—Selena Miller, 690–2010.

DEPUTY CHIEF FOR PROGRAMS

Deputy Chief.—Kim Berns (acting), (202) 720–4527.
 Director, Division of:
   Conservation Technical Assistance.—Ron Harris (acting), 720–1510.
   Easement.—Jessica Groves (acting), 720–1854.
   Financial Assistance Programs.—Mark Rose, 720–1845.
   Outreach and Advocacy.—Ron Harris, 720–6646.

DEPUTY CHIEF OF MANAGEMENT

Deputy Chief.—Gayle N. Barry (202) 720–7847.

Ethics Officer.—Erin Auger (202) 205–1826.
Director, Division of:
  Business Services.—Michael Mahoney (acting), 720–9034.
  Human Resources Management.—Tammie Edmunds, 720–2227.
  National Employee Development Center.—Jeffrey Dziedzic (817) 509–3241.
Supervisory Agency Representative.—Lauren Ruby (301) 504–2197.

DEPUTY CHIEF OF SCIENCE AND TECHNOLOGY

Deputy Chief.—C. Wayne Honeycutt (202) 720–4630.
Director, Division of:
  Conservation Engineering.—Noller Herbert, 720–2520.
  Ecological Sciences.—Terrell Erickson, 720–5992.
  Soil Health Division.—Bianca Moebius-Clune (202) 205–7712.

DEPUTY CHIEF OF SOIL SURVEY AND RESOURCE ASSESSMENT

Deputy Chief.—David Smith (301) 504–2302.
Director, Division of:
  International Programs.—Lillian Woods, 504–2271.
  National Geospatial Center of Excellence.—Javier Ruiz (acting), (817) 509–3420.
  Resources Assessment.—Daryl Lund (acting), 504–2302.
  Resources Inventory and Assessment.—Dan Good, 504–2305.
  Soil Survey.—Luis Hernandez (acting), (202) 260–9233.

DEPUTY CHIEF OF STRATEGIC PLANNING AND ACCOUNTABILITY

Deputy Chief.—Lesia Reed (301) 504–0056.
Director, Division of:
  Compliance.—Leon Brooks, 504–2190.
  Resource Economics, Analysis and Policy.—Janet Perry, 504–2362.
  Strategic and Performance Planning.—Machelle Simmons, 504–0023.

UNDER SECRETARY FOR FARM AND FOREIGN AGRICULTURAL SERVICES

Under Secretary.—Michael Scuse.
  Deputy Under Secretaries: Karis Gutter, Alexis Taylor (202) 720–7107.
  Chief of Staff.—Benjamin Thomas.
  Special Assistants: Jamal Habibi, Misty Jones.
  Executive Assistants: Debra Anderson, Moriah Toepper.

FARM SERVICE AGENCY
South Building, Room 3086–S, phone (202) 720–3467

Administrator.—Valente Dolcini.
  Associate Administrator for Operations and Management.—Chris Beyerhelm.
  Civil Rights.—Brian Garner.
  Economic and Policy Analysis Staff.—Joy Harwood, room 3741–S (202) 720–3451.
  Deputy Administrator for Farm Programs.—Mike Schmidt, room 3612–S, 720–3175.
    Assistant Deputy Administrator.—Vacant, 720–2070.
    Conservation and Environmental Programs Division.—Matt Ponish, room 4714–S, 720–6221.
    Price Support Division.—Raellen Ericson (acting), room 4095–S, 720–7901.
    Production, Emergencies and Compliance Division.—Dan McGlynn (acting), room 4754, 720–7641.
  Deputy Administrator for Farm Loan Programs.—Jim Radintz (acting), 720–4671.
    Program Development and Economic Enhancement Division.—Nancy New, room 4919–S, 720–3647.
    Loan Making Division.—Vacant, room 5438–S, 720–1632.
    Loan Servicing and Property Management Division.—Michael Hinton, room 5449–S, 720–4572.
  Deputy Administrator for Field Operations.—Greg Diephouse, room 3092, 690–2807.
    Assistant Deputy Administrator.—John W. Chott, Jr., room 8092, 690–2807.
    Operations Review and Analysis Staff.—Phillip Sharp, room 2720–S, 690–2532.

Deputy Administrator for Commodity Operations.—Sandra Wood, room 3080–S, 720–3217.
Kansas City Commodity Office.—Vacant (816) 926–6301.
Deputy Administrator for Management.—Mark A. Rucker, room 3095–S, 720–3438.
Budget Division.—Heidi Ware, room 4720–S.
Human Resources Division.—Vacant, room 5200 (L–St), 418–8950.
Information Technology Services Division.—Loretta Burns, room 5768–S, 720–5320.
Management Services Division.—Ezekiel Dennison, room 520–PRTL, 720–3438.

FOREIGN AGRICULTURAL SERVICE
South Building, Room 5071, phone (202) 720–3935, fax (202) 690–2159

Administrator.—Phil Karsting.
Associate Administrators: Janet Nuzum, 720–5174; Suzanne Palmieri, 690–8108.
Associate Administrator/COO.—Bryce Quick, 720–2706.
General Sales Manager.—Asif Chaudhry, 720–2781.
Chief of Staff.—Allison Thomas, 690–8064.
Confidential Assistant to the Administrator.—Yaesul Park, 690–2553.
Trade Policy Coordinator.—Jason Hafemeister, 720–9084.
Director of:
   Civil Rights Staff.—Stefanie Watson (acting), 720–7061.
   Legislative and Public Affairs.—Christopher Church, 720–6830.
   Public Affairs and Executive Correspondence.—Sally Klusaritz, 720–4064.

OFFICE OF ADMINISTRATIVE OPERATIONS

Assistant Deputy Administrator.—Robert McGary (202) 720–1738.
Senior Advisor.—Ronald Croushorn, 720–3038.
Director, Division of:
   Budget.—Thomas Bellamy, 690–4052.
   Information Technology.—Richard Young, 720–7741.
   International Travel.—Ted Goldammer, 690–1800.

OFFICE OF CAPACITY BUILDING AND DEVELOPMENT

Deputy Administrator.—Jocelyn Brown (202) 690–1779.
Assistant Deputy Administrator.—Roger Mireles (202) 720–1314.
Assistant Deputy Administrator.—Vacant.
Policy Coordination and Planning Staff.—Vacant.
Director, Division of:
   Development Resources and Disaster Assistance.—Vacant.
   Food Assistance.—Vacant.
   Trade and Scientific Capacity Building.—Emel Lyons, 720–1818.
   Trade and Scientific Exchanges.—Brian Guse, 690–2870.

OFFICE OF COUNTRY AND REGIONAL AFFAIRS

Deputy Administrator.—Bonnie Borris (202) 690–4062.
Assistant Deputy Administrator.—Sharynne Nenon, 690–3412.
Director, Division of:
   Africa and Middle East.—Vacant.
   Asia.—Michael Riedel (acting), 690–4851.
   Europe.—Vacant.
   Western Hemisphere.—John Passino, 720–5219.

OFFICE OF FOREIGN SERVICE OPERATIONS

Deputy Administrator.—Daryl Brehm (202) 720–3405.
Assistant Deputy Administrator.—Aian Hrapsky, 690–1791.
Director for—
   Africa and Middle East Area.—Frederick Giles, 690–4066.
   Europe Area.—Robert Hanson, 690–4057.
   Planning and Global Resources Staff.—Karen Darden, 720–1346.
   South Asia Area.—Susan Phillips, 690–4053.
   Western Hemisphere Area.—Lisa Anderson, 720–3223.

OFFICE OF GLOBAL ANALYSIS

Deputy Administrator.—Daniel Whitley (202) 720–6301.
  Assistant Deputy Administrator.—Patrick Packnett, 720–1590.
  Director, Division of:
    Global Commodities Analysis Division.—Vacant.
    Global Policy Analysis Division.—Paul Trupo, 720–1335.
    International Production Assessment Division.—Ronald Frantz, 720–4056.

OFFICE OF AGREEMENTS AND SCIENTIFIC AFFAIRS

Deputy Administrator.—Robert Macke, 720–4434.
  Assistant Deputy Administrator.—Vacant.
  Policy Formulation Staff:
    Senior Policy Advisors: Mark Manis, 720–1743; Bob Spitzer, 720–4825.
  Planning and Operations Group:
    Chief.— JonAnn Flemings, 720–1277.
  Animal Division:
    Division Director.—Paul Spencer, 690–2868.
  Multilateral Affairs:
    Division Director.—Michelle Moore, 720–1341.
  Bilateral Agreements and Enforcement Division:
    Division Director.—Charles Bertsch, 720–6278.
  International Regulations and Standards Division:
    Division Director.—Cathy McKinnell, 690–0929.
  New Technologies and Production Methods Division:
    Division Director.—Katherine Nishiura, 720–7457.
  Plant Division:
    Division Director.—Mark Rasmussen (acting), 720–0765.
  Processed Products and Technical Regulations Division:
    Division Director.—Marianne McElroy, 720–9408.

OFFICE OF TRADE PROGRAMS

Deputy Administrator.—Christian Foster (202) 401–0015.
  Assistant Deputy Administrator.—Mark Slupek, 401–0023.
  Director, Division of:
    Cooperator Programs Division.—Jeanne Bailey, 690–0159.
    Credit Programs.—Mark Rowse, 720–0624.
    Import Policies and Export Reporting Division.—Ronald Lord, 720–0638.
    Program Operations Division.—Vacant, 720–4327.

RISK MANAGEMENT AGENCY

South Building, Room 6092–S, phone (202) 690–2803

Administrator.—Brandon Willis.
  Associate Administrator and Deputy Manager, FCIC, Board of Directors.—Michael A. Alston.
  Associate Administrator.—Timothy J. Gannon.
  Deputy Administrator for—
    Compliance.—Heather Manzano, room 6603–S, 720–0642.
    Insurance Services.—Robert Ibarra, room 6709–S, 690–4494.
    Product Management.—Timothy Witt, Kansas City (816) 926–7394.

UNDER SECRETARY FOR RURAL DEVELOPMENT

Jamie L. Whitten Building, phone (202) 720–4581

Under Secretary.—Lisa Mensah.
  Deputy Under Secretary.—Vernita Dore (acting).
  Chief of Staff.—Andrews Given (acting).
  Deputy Chief of Staff.—Irene Lin.
  Director, Legislative and Public Affairs.—David Sandretti, 720–1019.

BUSINESS AND COOPERATIVE PROGRAMS
South Building, Room 5801–S, phone (202) 690–4730

Administrator.—Lillian Salerno.
  Chief of Staff.—Justin Hatmaker, 720–6165.
  Deputy Administrator.—Sam Rikkers, 720–6165.
  Oversight/Resource Coordination Staff (OCS).—Vacant, 690–4100.
  Deputy Administrator for Business Programs.—Tom Hannah, 720–0813.
  Assistant Deputy Administrator.—William "Bill" Smith, 720–0813.
  Director of:
    Business and Industry Division.—John Broussard, 690–4103.
    Specialty Lenders Division.—Kristi Kubista-Hovis (acting), 720–1400.
  Deputy Administrator for Cooperative Programs.—Chad Parker, 720–7558.
  Assistant Deputy Administrator.—Andy Jermolowizc, 720–8460.
  Director of:
    Cooperative Marketing Division.—David Sears, 690–0368.
    Cooperative Resources Management Division.—Bruce Reynolds (acting), 690–1374.
    Education and Research.—Claudette Fernandez (acting), 720–3350.
    Grants and Agreements.—Amy Cavanaugh, 690–1376.

RURAL HOUSING SERVICE
South Building, Room 5014–S, phone (202) 690–1533

Administrator.—Tony Hernandez.
  Director, Program Support Staff.—Ed Duval, 720–9619.
  Deputy Administrator for Single Family.—Joyce Allen, 205–4996.
  Deputy Administrator for Multi-Family Housing.—Bryan Hooper, 720–9739.
  Director of:
    Direct Loan and Grant Processing Division.—Joseph Ben-Israel, 720–1505.
    Family Housing Direct Loan Division.—Cathy Glover, 720–0343.
    Family Housing Guaranteed Loan Division.—Joaquin Tremols, 720–1465.
    Multi-Family Housing Portfolio Management Division, Direct Housing.—Stephanie White, 720–1615.
    Preservation and Direct Loan Division.—C.B. Alonso, 720–1624.

RURAL UTILITIES SERVICE
South Building, Room 5135, phone (202) 720–9540

Administrator.—Brandon McBride, room 5135–S, 720–9540.
  Deputy Administrator.—Vacant.
  Chief of Staff.—Michele Brooks, room 5162–S, 690–1078.
  Assistant Administrator for Electric Division.—Christopher McLean, room 5165, 720–9505.
  Deputy Assistant Administrator, Office of:
    Loan Origination and Approval.—Annie Holloway-Jones, room 0221–S, 720–0848.
    Operations.—James Elliott, room 5165–S, 720–9545.
    Policy, Outreach and Standards.—Joseph Badin, room 0243–S, 720–1420.
    Portfolio Management and Risk Assessment.—Victor T. Vu, room 0270–S, 720–6436.
  Policy Advisor.—Jon Claffey, room 5165–S, 720–9545.
  Assistant Administrator for Telecommunications.—Keith Adams, room 5151, 720–9554.
  Deputy Assistant Administrator.—Sami Zarour, room 5151, 720–9556.
  Deputy Assistant Administrator, Office of:
    Loan Origination and Approval.—Shawn Arner, room 2808–S, 720–0800.
    Policy and Outreach.—Ken Kuchno, room 2868–S, 690–4673.
    Portfolio Management and Risk Assessment.—Peter Aimable, room 2839–S, 720–1025.
  Water and Environmental Programs (WEP).—Jacqueline Ponti-Lazaruk, room 5145–S, 690–2670.
  Deputy Assistant Administrator, WEP.—Scott Barringer, room 5145–S, 690–2670.
  Director, Engineering and Environmental Staff.—Kellie McGuiness Kubena, room 2237–S, 720–1649.
  Director, Water Programs Division.—Kent Evans, room 2232–S, 720–2567.
  Chief, Program Operations Branch.—Cheryl Francis, 2236–S, 720–1937.
  Chief, Portfolio Management Branch.—Steve Saulnier, room 2231–S, 720–2526.
  Assistant Administrator, Program Accounting and Regulatory Analysis.—James Murray (acting), 5159–S, 720–9450.

Legislative and Public Affairs Staff.— Anne Mayberry, room 5144–S, 690–1756.
Senior Level Program and Policy Advisor, Policy Analysis and Regulatory Management.—
Gary A. Bojes, room 5150–S, 720–1256.

FOOD, NUTRITION, AND CONSUMER SERVICES
1400 Independence Avenue, SW., Room 216–E, Whitten Building, 20250

*Under Secretary.—*Kevin Concannon (202) 720–7711.
*Deputy Under Secretary.—*Katie Wilson.
*Chief of Staff.—*Kumar Chandran.

FOOD AND NUTRITION SERVICE
3101 Park Center Drive, Room 906, Alexandria, VA 22302 (703) 305–2060

OFFICE OF THE ADMINISTRATOR

*Administrator.—*Audrey Rowe (703) 305–2060.
*Executive Assistant.—*Angela Torres, 305–2060.
*Chief, Governmental Affairs.—*Scott Carter, 305–2313.

OFFICE OF POLICY SUPPORT

*Deputy Administrator.—*Rich Lucas, room 1014 (703) 305–2017.
*Assistant Deputy Administrator.—*Melissa Abelev, room 1010, 305–2209.
Director, Division of:
  *SNAP Research and Analysis.—*Kathryn Law, room 1025, 305–2138.
  Special Nutrition Research and Analysis.— Jay Hirschman, room 1007, 305–2117.

OFFICE OF THE CHIEF COMMUNICATIONS OFFICER (OCCO)

Communications Division:
  *Director.—*Bruce C. Alexander, room 926–A (703) 305–1615.
  Branch Chief:
  *Media.—*Johnathan Monroe, room 941, 605–3236.
  *Social Media.—*Carol Johnson, room 941, 605–4009.
External and Government Affairs Division:
  *Director.—*Katherine Fink, room 926B, 305–4372.
  Branch Chief:
  *Stakeholder Relations.—*Pam Phillip, room 941, 305–2298.
  *Governmental Affairs.—*Scott A. Carter, room 941, 305–2313.
*Special Assistant.—*Jessica Milteer, room 941, 305–2707.
*Controlled Correspondence Officer.—*Twanda Rodgers, room 941, 305–2066.

OFFICE OF MANAGEMENT TECHNOLOGY AND FINANCE

*Associate Administrator and Chief Operating Officer.—*Robin Bailey, room 906 (703) 305–2064.
*Director of Civil Rights.—*David Youngblood, room 1200, 305–2195.

MANAGEMENT

*Deputy Administrator.—*Telora Dean, room 1400 (703) 305–2030.
Director, Division of:
  *Contracts Management.—*Lance Petteway, room 220, 305–2251.
  *Human Resources.—*Cristina Chiappe (acting), room 404, 305–2326.
  *Logistics and Facility Management.—*Javier Inclan, room 222, 305–2220.

FINANCIAL MANAGEMENT

*Deputy Administrator (Chief Financial Officer).—*David Burr, room 712C (703) 305–2191.

Director, Division of:
  Accounting (Chief Accounting Officer).—Larry Blim, room 716, 305–1548.
  Budget (Chief Budget Officer).—Lisa Greenwood, room 708, 305–2172.
  Grants and Fiscal Policy.—Lael Lubing, room 732, 305–2161.
Director, Office of Internal Controls, Audits, and Investigations.—Mark Porter, room 733, 305–0901.

INFORMATION TECHNOLOGY

Deputy Administrator.—Kimberly R. Jackson, room 314 (703) 305–4370.
  Chief, Information Security Office.—Leo Wong, room 310 (703) 605–1181.
  Director, Division of:
  Portfolio Management.—Jacquie Butler, room 316, 305–2556.
  Technology.—Sonja Farrell, room 320, 305–2275.

REGIONAL OPERATIONS AND SUPPORT

Associate Administrator.—Yvette Jackson, room 906 (703) 305–2060.
  Director, Division of:
  Emergency Management.—Toni Abernathy, room 1134, 305–2041.
  Retailer Operations.—Neva Terry, room 1138 (703) 605–4315.
  State Systems.—Karen Painter-Jacquess, room 1146 (303) 844–6533.

OFFICE OF SUPPLEMENTAL NUTRITION ASSISTANCE PROGRAM

Associate Administrator.—Jessica Shahin, room 808 (703) 305–2026.
  Director, Division of:
  Benefit Redemption.—Andrea Gold, room 408, 305–2434.
  Program Accountability and Administration.—Ron Ward, room 816, 305–2523.
  Program Development.—Liz Beth Silbernan, room 814, 305–2494

OFFICE OF SPECIAL NUTRITION PROGRAMS

Deputy Administrator.—Diane M. Kriviski, room 628 (703) 305–2052.
  Director, Division of:
  Child Nutrition.—Cindy Long, room 640, 305–2590.
  Food Distribution.—Laura Castro, room 500, 305–2680.
  Supplemental Food Program.—Debra R. Whitford, room 520, 305–2746.

CENTER FOR NUTRITION POLICY AND PROMOTION

Executive Director.—Angela M. Tagtow, room 1034 (703) 305–7600.
  Deputy Director.—Jackie Haven, room 1034, 305–7600.
  Director, Division of:
  Office of Guidance and Analysis.—Colette Rihane, room 1034, 305–2403.
  Office of Marketing and Communication Division.—Shelley Maniscalco (703) 605–0220.
  Senior Policy Advisor.—Stephenie Fu, room 1034, 305–2217.

UNDER SECRETARY FOR FOOD SAFETY

Under Secretary.—Vacant (202) 720–0350.
  Deputy Under Secretaries: Alfred V. Almanza, 720–7025; Brian Ronholm, 720–0351.
  Chief of Staff.—Adam Tarr, 720–0351.

FOOD SAFETY AND INSPECTION SERVICE

Jamie L. Whitten Building, Room 331–E, phone (202) 720–7025, fax 690–0550

Administrator.—Alfred V. Almanza (acting).
  Deputy Administrator.—Phil Derfler, 692–4207.
  U.S. Manager for Codex.—Karen Stuck, room 4861–S, 720–2057.

OFFICE OF FIELD OPERATIONS (OFO)

Assistant Administrator.—William C. Smith, room 344–E (202) 720–8803.
Deputy Assistant Administrator.—Dr. Ronald Jones, 720–8804.
Executive Associates, Regulatory Operations: Dr. Keith Gilmore, Lawrence, Kansas (785) 766–9830; Hany Sidrak, room 3171–S, 205–4208; Dr. Armia Tawadrous, room 3161–S, 720–5714.
Director, Recall Management Staff.—Dr. Regina Tan, room 0205–S, 690–1975.

OFFICE OF DATA INTEGRATION AND FOOD PROTECTION (ODIFP)

Assistant Administrator.—Terri Nintemann, room 3130–S (202) 720–5643.
Deputy Assistant Administrator.—Soumaya Tohamy, Ph.D., room 3130–S, 720–5643.
Director of:
    Data Analysis Integration Staff.—Christopher Alvares, room 3126–S (202) 690–6418.
    Emergency Coordination Staff.—Mary K. Cutshall, PPIII, 9–140, 690–6523.
    Food Defense Assessment Staff.—Jessica Pulz, PPIII, 9–148 (202) 772–9115.

OFFICE OF INTERNATIONAL COORDINATION (OIC)

International Coordination Executive.—Jane H. Doherty, room 3143–S (202) 708–8769.
Senior Advisor.—Mary Stanley, room 3151–S, 720–0287.
International Program Specialist.—Shannon McMurtrey, room 3149–S, 720–9966.

OFFICE OF MANAGEMENT (OM)

Assistant Administrator.—Jacqueline Myers, room 347–E (202) 720–4432.
Deputy Assistant Administrator.—Gabrielle James, room 347–E, 720 4745
Program Evaluation and Improvement Staff.—Matthew Michael.

OFFICE OF POLICY AND PROGRAM DEVELOPMENT (OPPD)

Assistant Administrator.—Daniel Engeljohn, room 350–E, JLW Bldg. (202) 205–0495.
Deputy Assistant Administrator.—Rachel Edelstein, room 350–E, JLW Bldg., 205–0495.

OFFICE OF INVESTIGATION, ENFORCEMENT AND AUDIT (OIEA)

Assistant Administrator.—Carl A. Mayes, room 3133–S (202) 720–8609.
Deputy Assistant Administrator.—Peter E. Bridgeman, room 3133–S, 720–8609.
Director of:
    Compliance and Investigations Division.—Jerry Elliott, room 2149–S, 720–3781.
    Management Controls and Audit.—Vincent Fayne, room 2175–S (202) 690–5662.
    Resource Management Staff (Budget).—Michelle Long, room 2175–S (202) 708–8177.

OFFICE OF PUBLIC AFFAIRS AND CONSUMER EDUCATION (OPACE)

Assistant Administrator.—Carol Blake, room 339–E (202) 720–3884.
Deputy Assistant Administrator.—Aaron Lavallee, room 3137 S, 720–0460.
Director of:
    Congressional and Public Affairs Staff.—Alan Lang, room 1175–S, 720–5509 or 9113.
    Executive Correspondence and Issues Management Staff.—Eshael Johnson, room 1167–S, 690–3881.

OFFICE OF PUBLIC HEALTH SCIENCE (OPHS)

Assistant Administrator.—Dr. David Goldman, room 341–E (202) 720–2644.
Deputy Assistant Administrator.—Dr. Vivian Chen, room 341–E, 720–1281.

OFFICE OF OUTREACH, EMPLOYEE EDUCATION AND TRAINING (OOEET)

Assistant Administrator.—Michael G. Watts, room 4862–S, 205–0194.

UNDER SECRETARY FOR RESEARCH, EDUCATION, AND ECONOMICS

Under Secretary.—Dr. Catherine Woteki (202) 720–5923.
Deputy Under Secretary.—Dr. Ann Bartuska, 720–5923.
Chief of Staff.—Yeshimebet Abebe, 720–1542.
Communications Director.—Damon Thompson, 720–1375.
Director of Congressional Affairs.—Ven Neralla, 720–8187.
Senior Advisor.—Caren Wilcox, 720–6118.
Confidential Assistant.—Melvin Washington II (202) 260–8208.
Executive Assistants: Loureatha Gibson, 720–5953; Michele Simmons, 720–1542.

AGRICULTURAL RESEARCH SERVICE
Administration Building, Room 302–A, phone (202) 720–3656, fax 720–5427

Administrator.— Dr. Chavonda Jacobs-Young.
Associate Administrator for—
  Research Operations.—Dr. Simon Liu, 720–3658.
  Research Programs.—Dr. Steven R. Shafer (301) 504–5084.
Director of:
  Budget and Program Management Staff.—Michael Arnold, room 358–A, 720–4421.
  Legislative Affairs.—Gary Mayo (202) 260–9494.
  Information Staff.—Vacant (301) 504–1638.
Assistant Administrator, Research Operations and Management, Office of Technology Transfer.—Mojdeh Bahar (301) 504–6905.
Deputy Administrator, Administrative and Financial Management.—Joon Park (202) 690–2575.
National Agricultural Library.—Vacant (301) 504–5248.

AREA OFFICES

Director of:
  Midwest Area.—Robert Matteri, 1815 North University Street, Room 2004, Peoria, IL 61604–0000 (309) 681–6602.
  Northeast Area.—Dariusz Swietlik, Building 003, Room 223, BARC-West, Beltsville, MD 20705 (301) 504–6078.
  Pacific West Area.—Andrew Hammond, 800 Buchanan Street, Room 2030, Albany, CA 94710 (510) 559–6060.
  Plains Area.—Larry Chandler, 2150 Centre Avenue, Building D, Suite 300, Ft. Collins, CO 80525–8119, (970) 492–7057.
  Southeast Area.—Deborah Brennan, 141 Experiment Station Road, Stoneville, MS 38776 (662) 686–5265.

NATIONAL INSTITUTE OF FOOD AND AGRICULTURE
Jamie L. Whitten Building, Room 305–A, phone (202) 720–4423, fax 720–8987

Director.—Dr. Sonny Ramaswamy.
Associate Director of Programs.—Meryl Broussard, 720–7441.
Associate Director of Operation.—Dr. Robert Holland.
Assistant Administrators/Legislative Liaisons: Betty Lou Gilliland, room 305–A, 720–8187; Kimberly Whittet, room 305–A, 720–8291.
Director, Office of:
  Budget.—Paula Geiger, room 332–A, 720–2675.
  Communications.—Virgina Bueno, room 4231, 720–2677.
  Equal Opportunity Staff.—Curt DeVille, room 1230, 720–2700.
  Planning and Accountability.—Bart Hewitt, room 1315, 720–5623.
Deputy Administrator for—
  Bioenergy, Climate, Environment/Science and Education Resources Development.—Luis Tupas, room 4343, 720–7947.
  Grants and Financial Management.—Cynthia Montgomery, room 2256, 401–6021.
  Information Systems and Technology Management.—Michel Desbois, room 4122, 401–0117.
  Institute of Food/Production and Sustainability.—Parag Chitnis, room 2334, 401–5024.
  Youth Families Community.—Muquarrab Qureshi, room 3231, 401–4555.

ECONOMIC RESEARCH SERVICE
355 E Street, SW., 20024–3221, phone (202) 694–5000

Administrator.—Mary Bohman, room 7–197.
Associate Administrator.—Greg Pompelli, room 7–203.
Assistant Administrator.—Stephen Crutchfield, room 7–191.
Special Assistant to Administrator.—Gatlyn "Gunner" Hamlyn, room 7–189A.
Civil Rights Director.—Henry Norcom, room 5–268, 694–5162.
Director, Division of:
 Food Economics.—Jay Variyam, room 5–203, 694–5457.
 Information Services.—Tony Williams, room 4–197, 694–5101.
 Market Trade and Economics.—Gopinath "Gopi" Munisamy, room 5–197, 694–5201.
 Resource and Rural Economics.—Marca Weinberg, room 6–197, 694–5478.

NATIONAL AGRICULTURAL STATISTICS SERVICE
South Agriculture Building, Room 5041A–S, phone (202) 720–2707, fax 720–9013

Administrator.—Joseph T. Reilly, room 5041A, 720–4333.
Associate Administrator.—Renee Picanso, room 5041A, 720–2707.
Director for—
 Census and Survey.—Barbara Rater, room 6306, 720–4557.
 Eastern Field Operations.—Jay Johnson, room 5053, 720–3638.
 Information Technology.—Joseph Parsons, room 5847, 720–2984.
 Methodology.—James Mark Harris, room 5305, 690–8141.
 National Operations.—Joseph Prusacki (314) 595–9501 ext. 57501.
 Research and Development.—Dr. Linda Young, room 6035, 690–1401.
 Statistics.—Hubert Hamer, room 5431, 720–3896.
 Western Field Operations.—Kevin Barnes, room 5053, 720–8220.

UNDER SECRETARY FOR MARKETING AND REGULATORY PROGRAMS
Jamie L. Whitten Building, Room 228–W, phone (202) 720–4256, fax 720–5775

Under Secretary.—Edward Avalos.
Deputy Under Secretaries: Elvis Cordova, Gary Woodward.
Special Assistant to the Under Secretary.—Sanah Baig.
Chief of Staff.—David Howard.

AGRICULTURAL MARKETING SERVICE
South Agriculture Building, Room 3069–S, phone (202) 720–5115, fax 720–8477

Administrator.—Anne Alonzo.
Associate Administrator.—Rex Barnes, 720–5116.
Deputy Associate Administrator.—Erin Morris, 720–4024.
Deputy Administrator for—
 Compliance and Analysis Programs.—Sonia Jimenez, room 2095–S, 720–6766.
 Cotton and Tobacco Programs.—Darryl Earnest (901) 384–3060.
 Dairy Programs.—Dana Coale, room 2968–S, 720–4392.
 Fruit and Vegetable Programs.—Charles Parrott, room 2077–S, 720–4722.
 National Organic Program.—Miles McEvoy, room 2646, 720–3252.
 Poultry Programs.—Craig Morris, room 2902–S, 720–3215.
 Science and Technology.—Ruihong Guo, room 3543–S, 720–8556.
 Transportation and Marketing.—Arthur Neal, room 4543, 690–1300.
 Director, Legislative and Review Staff.—Bill Allen, room 3521–S, 720–2468.

ANIMAL AND PLANT HEALTH INSPECTION SERVICE (APHIS)
Jamie L. Whitten Building, Room 312–E, phone (202) 720–3668, fax 720–3054

OFFICE OF THE ADMINISTRATOR

Administrator.—Kevin Shea.

Associate Administrators: Jere Dick, Michael Gregoire.
Director of Civil Rights Enforcement and Compliance.—Ken Johnson, room 1137–S, 720–7012, fax 720–2365.

ANIMAL CARE

4700 River Road, Riverdale, MD 20737, phone (301) 851–3751, fax 734–4328

Deputy Administrator.—Chester Gipson.
Associate Deputy Administrator.—Andrea Morgan.

BIOTECHNOLOGY REGULATORY SERVICES

4700 River Road, Riverdale, MD 20737, phone (301) 851–3877, fax (301) 734–6352

Deputy Administrator.—Michael J. Firko (301) 851–3941.
Associate Deputy Administrator.—Janet L. Bucknall, 851–3938.
Assistant Deputy Administrator.—Sidney W. Abel, 851–3896.

INTERNATIONAL SERVICES

Jamie L. Whitten Building, Room 324–E, phone (202) 799–7132, fax 690–1484

Deputy Administrator.—Beverly J. Simmons.
Associate Deputy Administrators: Murali Bandla (301) 851–3802; Cheryle Blakely; Jessica Mahalingappa (202) 799–7127.
Division Director.—Mark Prescott (301) 851–3769.
Trade Support Team.—Eric Nichols, room 1128, (202) 799–7127.

LEGISLATIVE AND PUBLIC AFFAIRS

South Building, Room 1147–S, phone (202) 799–7031, fax 720–3982

Deputy Administrator.—Bethany Jones.
Associate Deputy Administrator.—James Ivy.
Director of:
  Executive Correspondence.—Christina Myers (301) 851–4111.
  Freedom of Information.—Tonya Woods, 851–4102.
  Public Affairs.—Ed Curlett, 851–4100.

MARKETING AND REGULATORY PROGRAMS BUSINESS SERVICES

Jamie L. Whitten Building, Room 308–E, phone (202) 799–7065, fax 690–0686

Deputy Administrator.—Marilyn Holland (202) 799–7066.
Associate Deputy Administrator.—Robert J. Huttenlocker, 799–7064.

PLANT PROTECTION AND QUARANTINE

Jamie L. Whitten Building, Room 302–E, phone (202) 799–7163, fax 690–0472

Deputy Administrator.—Osama El-Lissy.
Associate Deputy Administrator—
  Field Operations.—Rebeca Bech (919) 855–7300.
  Policy Management.—Mike Watson (202) 799–7163.
  Science and Technology.—Ron Sequeira (301) 851–2244.

POLICY AND PROGRAM DEVELOPMENT

4700 River Road, Riverdale, MD 20737, phone (301) 851–3098, fax (301) 734–6357

Deputy Administrator.—Christine Zakarka.
Associate Deputy Administrator.—Shannon Hamm.

Unit Chiefs:
  Budget and Program Analysis.—Michelle Wenberg, 851–3143.
  Environmental and Risk Analysis Service.—David Reinhold, 851–3885.
  Program Assessment and Accountability.—Erik Anderson (612) 336–3393.
  Planning, Evaluation and Decision Support.—Connie Williams, 851–3087.
  Policy Analysis and Development.—Parveen Setia, 851–3126.
  Regulatory Analysis and Development.—Stephen O'Neill, 851–3072.

VETERINARY SERVICES

Jamie L. Whitten Building, Room 317–E, phone (202) 799–7146, fax 690–4171

Deputy Administrator.—John Clifford.
  Administrative Assistant.—Paula Lee, 799–7146.
  Associate Deputy Administrator.—Jack Shere, 799–7146.
  Administrative Assistant.—David Zimmerman, 799–7146.
  Associate Deputy Administrator for—
    Export Services.—Mark Davidson (301) 851–3547.
    Surveillance, Preparedness and Response Services.—TJ Myers, 851–3576.
    Science, Technology and Analysis Services.—Beth Lautner (515) 337–6161.
    Program Support Services.—Kevin Richardson, 851–3603.

WILDLIFE SERVICES

South Building, Room 1624, phone (202) 799–7095, fax 690–0053

Deputy Administrator.—William H. Clay.
  Assistant Deputy Administrator.—Martin Mendoza, Jr.
  Director for Operational Support.—Joanne Garrett (301) 851–4009.

GRAIN INSPECTION, PACKERS AND STOCKYARDS ADMINISTRATION

South Building, Room 2055, phone (202) 720–0219, fax 205–9237

Administrator.—Larry Mitchell.
  Director of:
    Management and Budget Services.—Marianne Plaus, room 2049–S (202) 690–3460.
    Civil Rights.—Kevin Smith, room 2508–S, 690–3640.
    Deputy Administrator for Federal Grain Inspection Service.—Randall Jones, room 2063 S (202) 720–9170.
  Director of:
    Compliance.—Samantha Simon, room 2420–S, 690–3206.
    Departmental and International Affairs.—Byron Reilly, room 2409–S, 690–3368.
    Field Management Division.—Anthony Goodman, room 2409–S, 720–0228.
    Technical Services Division.—Mary Alonzo, Kansas City, MO (816) 891–0463.
  Deputy Administrator for Packers and Stockyards Programs.—Susan Keith, room 2055–S, 720–7051.
  Director, Litigation and Economic Analysis Division.—Brett Offutt, room 2505–S, 690–4355.
  Regional Directors:
    Atlanta, GA.—Elkin Parker (404) 562–5840.
    Aurora, CO.—Kraig J. Roesch (303) 375–4240.
    Des Moines, IA.—Stuart Frank (515) 323–2579.

DEPARTMENT OF COMMERCE

Herbert C. Hoover Building

14th Street between Pennsylvania and Constitution Avenues, NW., 20230

phone (202) 482–2000, http://www.doc.gov

PENNY PRITZKER, Secretary of Commerce; education: A.B., economics, Harvard University; J.D./M.B.A., Stanford University; professional: CEO of PSP Capital Partners; served on boards of: Hyatt Hotels, La Salle Bank, and the William Wrigley Jr. Company; Executive Chairwoman of Trans Union; married: Dr. Bryan Traubert; two children; nominated by President Barack Obama to become the 38th Secretary of Commerce, and was sworn in by Vice President Joe Biden on June 26, 2013.

OFFICE OF THE SECRETARY

Secretary of Commerce.—Penny Pritzker, room 5854 (202) 482–2112.
Deputy Secretary.—Bruce H. Andrews, room 5838, 482–8376.
Chief of Staff.—Jim Hock, room 5854, 482–4246.
Senior Advisor.—Kate McAdams, room 5862, 482 4246.
Deputy Chiefs of Staff: Theodore LeCompte, 482–3028; Stephanie Valencia, 482–2771.
Director, Office of:
   Business Liaison.—Theodore Johnston, room 5062, 482–1360.
   Executive Secretariat.—Madhura Valverde, room 5516, 482–3934.
   Policy and Strategic Planning.—John Ratliff, room 5865, 482–4127.
   Public Affairs.—Erin Weinstein (acting), room 5413, 482–4883.
   Scheduling and Advance.—Sally Cluthe, room 5883, 482–5129.
   White House Liaison.—Lauren Leonard (acting), room 5835, 482–4147.

GENERAL COUNSEL

General Counsel.—Kelly R. Welsh, room 5870 (202) 482–4772.
Deputy General Counsel.—Justin S. Antonipillai.

ASSISTANT SECRETARY FOR LEGISLATIVE
AND INTERGOVERNMENTAL AFFAIRS

Deputy Assistant Secretary.—Jim Stowers, room 5421 (202) 482–3663, fax 482–4420.
Director for—
   Intergovernmental Affairs. William Ramos, room 5422, 482–3663, fax 482–4420.
Associate Director for—
   EDA, MBDA and Senior Advisor for Native American Affairs.—Cisco Minthorn, room 5422, 482–4602.
   NOAA, ESA, Census, BEA.—Jen Costanza, room 5422, 482–1286.
   NTIA, NIST, NTIS, USPTO, BIS.—Jenilee Keefe Singer, room 5422, 482–7473.
   Oversight.—Vacant.
Director of Legislative Outreach.—Emma Poorman, room 5421, 482–4030.

CHIEF FINANCIAL OFFICER (CFO) AND
ASSISTANT SECRETARY FOR ADMINISTRATION

Chief Financial Officer and Assistant Secretary.—Ellen Herbst, room 5830 (202) 482–6269, fax 482–3592.
Deputy Assistant Secretary for Administration.—Fred Stephens, room 5830.
Deputy Chief Financial Officer/Director for Financial Management.—Lisa Casias, room 6827, 482–1207, fax 482–5070.
Director for—
   Acquisition Management.—Barry Berkowitz, room 6422, 482–4248, fax 482–1711.

Administrative Services.—Mary Pleffner, room 6316, 482–1200, fax 482–8890.
Budget.—Michael Phelps, room 7313, 482–4648, fax 482–3361.
Civil Rights.—Tinisha Agramonte, room 6058, 482–4535, fax 482–3364.
Human Resources Management.—Kevin Mahoney, room 5003, 482–4807, fax 482–0249.
Program Evaluation and Risk Management.—Vacant, room 5327, 482–3707, fax 482–1423.
Security.—Tom Predmore, room 1069, 482–4371, fax 501–6355.

CHIEF INFORMATION OFFICER

Chief Information Officer.—Steve Cooper, room 5029B (202) 482–4797.
Deputy Chief Information Officer.—Izella Dornell, room 5027.
Office of:
   IT Policy and Planning, Deputy Chief Information Officer and Chief Technology Officer.—Kirit Amin, room 6612, 482–4444.
   IT Security, Infrastructure and Technology, Chief Information Security Officer.—Rod Turk, room 6895, 482–4708.
   Networking and Telecommunications Operations.—Ricardo Farraj-Feijoo, room 6625, 482–4444.

INSPECTOR GENERAL

Inspector General.—Todd J. Zinser, room 7898C (202) 482–4661.
   Deputy Inspector General.—C. Morgan Kim, room 7898C, 482–4661.
   Counsel to the Inspector General.—Vacant, room 7896, 482–5992.
   Assistant Inspector General, Office of:
      Audit.—Andrew Katsaros, room 7886B, 482–7859.
      Economic and Statistical Program Assessment.—Carol Rice, room 7520, 482–6020.
      Investigations.—C. Morgan Kim, room 7898C, 482–0300.
      Intellectual Property and Special Program Audits.—Dave Smith, PTO (571) 272–5561.
      Program Audits.—Richard Bachman, PTO (571) 272–1131.
      Systems Acquisition and IT Security.—Allen Crawley, room 7884, 482–1855.
   Principal Assistant Inspector General Audit and Evaluation.—Andrew Katsaros, room 7886B, 482–7859.

ECONOMICS AND STATISTICS ADMINISTRATION
1401 Constitution Avenue, NW., 20230, phone (202) 482–6607

Under Secretary for Economic Affairs.—Mark E. Doms, room 4848 (202) 482–3727.
   Deputy Under Secretary for Economic Affairs.—Kenneth Arnold, room 4848, 482–2405.
   Chief Counsel.—Barry Robinson, room 4877, 482–5394.
   Chief Economist.—Sue Helper, room 4860, 482–3523.
   Deputy Chief Economist.—Rob Rubinovitz, room 4861, 482–4871.
   Chief Financial Officer.—Brad Burke, room 4843, 482–3038.
   Director of External Affairs.—Burton Reist, room 4838, 482–3331

BUREAU OF ECONOMIC ANALYSIS
1441 L Street, NW., 20230, phone (202) 606–9900

Director.—Brian Moyer, room 6006, 606–9600.
   Deputy Director.—Vacant, room 6005, 606–9602.
   Chief Economist.—David Johnson, room 6060, 606–9985.
   Chief Information Officer.—Brian Callahan, room 6052, 606–9906.
   Chief Statistician.—Dennis J. Fixler, room 6060, 606–9607.
   Associate Director for—
      Industry Economics.—Brian Moyer (acting), room 6004, 606–9612.
      International Economics.—Sally Thompson, room 6062, 606–9660.
      National Economic Accounts.—Brent R. Moulton, room 6064, 606–9606.
      Regional Economics.—Joel Platt, room 6065, 606–9606.
   Chief Administrative Officer.—Kathleen James, room 6027, 606–9325.
   Division Chiefs:
      Administrative Services.—C. Brian Grove, room 3003, 606–9624.
      Balance of Payments.—Robert Yuskavage, room 8024, 606–9672.

Communications.—H. Lucas Hitt, room 3029, 606–9223.
Direct Investment Division.—David Galler, room 7005, 606–9835.
Government.—Pamela Kelly, room 4067, 606–9781.
Industry Applications Division.—Erich Strassner, room 4006, 606–9539.
Industry Sector Division.—Nicole Mayerhauser, room 4028, 606–9742.
National Income and Wealth.—Carol E. Moylan, room 5006, 606–9711.
Regional Income Division.—Sharon C. Carnevale (acting), room 8065a, 606–9247.
Regional Product Division.—C. Ian Mead, room 9018, 606–9661.

THE BUREAU OF THE CENSUS
4600 Silver Hill Road, Suitland, MD 20746

Director.—Robert M. Groves, room 8H002 (301) 763–2135.
Deputy Director and Chief Operating Officer.—Thomas Mesenbourg, room 8H006, 763–2138.
Associate Director for—
Administration and Chief Financial Officer.—Ted A. Johnson, room 8H144, 763–3464.
Communications.—Steven Jost, room 8H138, 763–2512.
Comptroller.—Ted A. Johnson, room 8H144, 763–3464.
Decennial Census.—Arnold Jackson, room 8H122, 763–8626.
Demographic Programs.—Howard Hogan, room 8H134, 763–2160.
Economic Programs.—William G. Bostic, Jr., room 8K108, 763–8842.
Field Operations.—Marilia Matos, room 8H126, 763–2072.
Information Technology and CIO.—Brian McGrath, room 8H140, 763–2117.
Strategic Planning and Innovation.—Nancy M. Gordon, room 8H128, 763–2126.
Assistant Director for Communications.—Burton Reist, room 8H062, 763–3949.
Chief Technology Officer.—Avi Bender, room 5K030, 763–7807.
Assistant Director for—
Acquisition Division.—Michael L. Palensky, room 3J438, 763–1818.
Decennial (Census) Management and American Community Survey.—Daniel Weinberg, room 3H162, 763–5791.
Economic Programs.—Vacant, room 8K108, 763–2932.
Division and Office Chief for—
Administrative and Customer Services.—F. Grailand Hall, room 3J436, 763–1629.
Administrative and Management Systems Division.—James Aikman, room 3K138, 763–3149.
Advisory Committee Office.—Jeri Green, room 8H153, 763–6590.
American Community Survey Office.—James B. Treat, room 3K276, 763–3609.
Analysis and Executive Support.—Kathleen Styles, room 8H028, 763–3460.
Budget Division.—Carol Rose, room 2K122, 763–5818.
Census 2010 Publicity Office.—Stephen L. Buckner (acting), room 8H484, 763–3586.
Center for Economic Studies.—Ron Jarmin, room 2K124, 763–1858.
Company Statistics Division.—Jeffrey L. Mayer, room 6K064, 763–2905.
Computer Services Division.—Thomas J. Berti, Bowie 28, 763–4341.
Congressional Affairs Office.—Angela M. Manso, room 8H166, 763–6100.
Customer Liaison and Marketing Services Office.—Kendall B. Johnson (acting), room 8H180, 763–1911.
Decennial Automation Contract Management Office.—Vacant.
Decennial Management Division.—Frank Vitrano, room 3H174, 763–3691.
Decennial Statistical Studies Division.—David Whitford, room 4K276, 763–4035.
Decennial Systems and Contract Management Office.—Michael T. Thieme (acting), room 2H174, 763–9062.
Demographic Statistical Methods Division.—Ruth Ann Killion, room 7H162, 763–2048.
Demographic Surveys Division.—Cheryl Landman, room 7H128, 763–3773.
Economic Planning and Coordination Division.—Shirin A. Ahmed, room 8K122, 763–2558.
Economic Statistical Methods and Programming Division.—Samuel Jones, room 7K108, 763–7600.
Equal Employment Opportunity Office.—Roy P. Castro, room 3K106, 763–5120.
Field Division.—Brian Monaghan, room 5H128, 763–2011.
Finance Division.—Joan Simms, room 2K106, 763–6803.
Foreign Trade Division.—Nick Orsini, room 6K032, 763–2255.
Geography Division.—Timothy Trainor, room 4H174, 763–2131.
Governments Division.—Lisa Blumerman, room 5K156, 763–8050.
Housing and Household Economic Statistics.—David S. Johnson, room 7H174, 763–6443.

Human Resources Division.—Ted A. Johnson (acting), room 2J436, 763–3721.
Information Systems Support and Review Office.—John Leidich (acting), room 4K020, 763–5740.
Information Technology Security Office.—Timothy P. Ruland, room 5K124, 763–2869.
International Relations Office.—Carole Popoff, room 8H017, 763–3222.
Manufacturing and Construction.—Thomas Zabelsky, Jr., room 7K154, 763–4593.
National Processing Center.—David Hackbarth (812) 218–3344.
Population.—Enrique Lamas, room 5H174, 763–2071.
Privacy Office.—Mary Frazier, room 8H168, 763–2906.
Public Information Office.—Kenneth C. Meyer, room 8H160, 763–3100.
Security Office.—Harold L. Washington, Jr., room 2J438, 763–1716.
Service Sector Statistics.—Mark E. Wallace, room 2J438, 763–2683.
Statistical Research Division.—Tommy Wright, room 5K108, 763–1702.
Systems Support.—Nora Bea Parker, room 5K032, 763–2999.
Technologies Management Office.—Barbara M. LoPresti, room 5H160, 763–7765.
Telecommunications Office.—Scott Williams, room 4K032, 763–1793.

BUREAU OF INDUSTRY AND SECURITY

Under Secretary.—Eric L. Hirschhorn, room 3898B (202) 482–1455.
Deputy Under Secretary.—Daniel O. Hill, room 3894, 482–1427.
Chief Counsel.—John Masterson, room 3839, 482–2315.
Office of Congressional and Public Affairs.—Charles L. Kinney, room 3895, 482–0097.
Director, Office of Administration.—Vacant, room 6622, 482–1900.
Chief Information Officer.—Eddie Donnell (acting), room 6092, 482–4296.
Assistant Secretary for Export Administration.—Kevin Wolf, room 3886C, 482–5491.
Deputy Assistant Secretary.—Matthew Borman, room 3886C, 482–5711.
Operating Committee Chair.—Eric Longnecker (acting), room 3889, 482–5863/5864.
End-User Review Committee Chair.—Joseph Cristofaro, room 2625, 482–5991.
Office of:
    Exporter Services.—Karen Nies-Vogel, room 1093, 482–0436.
    National Security and Technology Transfer Controls.—Eileen M. Albanese, room 2616, 482–0092.
    Nonproliferation and Treaty Compliance.—Alexander Lopes, room 2627, 482–3825.
    Strategic Industries and Economic Security.—Michael Vaccaro, room 3878, 482–4506.
    Technology Evaluation.—Gerard Horner, room 1093, 482–2078.
Assistant Secretary for Export Enforcement.—David W. Mills, room 3723, 482–3618.
Deputy Assistant Secretary.—Richard Majauskas, room 3723, 482–3618.
Office of:
    Antiboycott Compliance.—Cathleen Ryan, room 6098, 482–2381.
    Enforcement Analysis.—Kevin Kurland, room 4065, 482–4255.
    Export Enforcement.—Douglas Hassebrock, room 4508, 482–5079.

ECONOMIC DEVELOPMENT ADMINISTRATION

Assistant Secretary.—Roy K.J. Williams, room 78006, (202) 482–5081.
Deputy Assistant Secretary for—
    EDA and Chief Operating Officer.—Matt Erskine, room 78006, 482–5081.
    Regional Affairs.—Thomas Guevara, room 71030, 482–5081.
Chief Counsel.—Stephen Kong, room 72023, 482–4687.
Chief Financial Officer and Chief Administrative Officer.—Andrew Baldus, room 70025, 482–5892.
Director, Office of:
    Budget and Finance Division.—Robert White, room 70023, 482–5892.
    External Affairs.—Angela Martinez, room 71004, 482–2900.
    Innovation and Entrepreneurship.—Julie Kirk, room 78018, 482–8001.
    Legislative Affairs.—Angela Ewell-Madison, room 71019, 482–2900.
    Public Affairs.—Breelyn Peete, room 71004, 482–4085.
    Performance and National Programs.—Bryan Borlik, room 71021, 482–4122.

INTERNATIONAL TRADE ADMINISTRATION

Under Secretary.—Stefan M. Selig, room 3850 (202) 482–2867.
Deputy Under Secretary.—Ken Hyatt, room 3842, 482–3917.
Chief of Staff.—Jannine Versi, room 3850, 482–2867.

Legislative and Intergovernmental Affairs.—Arun V, room 3424, 482–3015.
Public Affairs.—Mary Trupo, room 3416, 482–3809.
Chief Counsel for International Commerce.—John Cobau, room 5624, 482–0937.

ADMINISTRATION

Director and Chief Financial Officer.—Tim Rosado, room 3827 (202) 482–5855.
Deputy Chief Administrative Officer.—Kurt Bersani, room 41012, 482–8026.
Office of Financial Management and Administrative Oversight.—Anne McDonagh, room 41018, 482–2136.
Chief Information Officer.—Joe Paiva, room 4800, 482–3801.
Management and Operations.—Victor E. Powers, suite 40001R, 482–5436.
Strategic Resources.—Blanche Ziv, room 41017, 482–3302.
Office of Budget.—Michael House, room 41028, 482–5739.

GLOBAL MARKETS AND U.S. AND FOREIGN COMMERCIAL SERVICE

Assistant Secretary for Global Markets and Director General of the Commercial Service.—Arun Kumar, room 38006 (202) 482–5777.
Deputy Director General.—Judy Reinke, HCH 38006, 482–5777.
Deputy Assistant Secretary for Domestic Operations.—Antwaun Griffin, RRB STE 800–M, 482–4767.
Regional Director, Office of:
　Africa, Near East and South Asia.—Janice Corbett, HCH 200–A, 482–1209.
　East Asia and Pacific.—Dan Harris, HCH 31018, 482–0423.
　Europe.—Danny Devito, HCH 200–A, 482–5402.
　National Field.—Dan O'Brien, RRB STE 800–M, 482–2732.
　Western Hemisphere.—John Andersen, RMC 300, 482–3484.
Director, Office of:
　Advocacy Center.—Jennifer Pilat, HCH 3814–A, 482–3896.
　Budget.—Barbara Gilchrist, HCH 21010, 482–0823.
　Business Information Technology.—Stanley Ed Howard, 482–3861.
　Foreign Service Human Capital.—Joseph Jackson, HCH 1842, 482–4939.
　Office of Administrative Services.—Jerome Holloway, 482–1594.
　Global Knowledge Center.—Anand Basu, RRB STE 800–M, 482–1489.
　Trade Promotion Coordinating Committee.—Pat Kirwan, HCH 31027, 482–5455.
　SelectUSA.—Vinay Thummalapally, HCHB 1235, 482–1889.
　Strategic Planning and Resource Management.—Debra Delay, HCH 21022, 482–8003.

ASSISTANT SECRETARY FOR ENFORCEMENT AND COMPLIANCE

Assistant Secretary.—Paul Piquado, room 3099B (202) 482–1780.
Deputy Assistant Secretary.—Ronald Lorentzen, room 3705, 482–2104.
Chief Counsel.—John D. McInerney, room 3622, 482–5589.
Director for
　Office of Accounting.—Neal Halper, room 3087B, 482–2210.
　Office of Policy.—Carole Showers, room 3713, 482–4412.
Executive Secretary for Foreign Trade Zones Board.—Andrew McGilvray, room 21013, 482–2862.
Deputy Assistant Secretary for—
　Antidumping Countervailing Duty Operations.—Christian Marsh, room 3095, 482–5497.
　Antidumping Countervailing Duty Policy and Negotiations.—Lynn Fischer Fox, room 3089, 482–6199.
　Textiles and Apparel.—Josh Teitelbaum, room 30003, 482–3737.

ASSISTANT SECRETARY FOR INDUSTRY AND ANALYSIS

Assistant Secretary.—Marcus Jadotte, room 3832 (202) 482–1461.
Deputy Assistant Secretary.—Maureen Smith room 3832.
Deputy Assistant Secretary for Industry Analysis.—Praveen Dixit, room 21028, 482–3177.
Director, Office of:
　Advisory Committees.—Shannon Roche, room 4043 (202) 482–4501.
　Energy and Environmental Industries.—Adam O'Malley, room 4055, 482–4850.
　Manufacturing.—Chandra Brown, room 28004, 482–1872.

Planning, Coordination and Management.—J. Slade Broom, room 4324 (202) 482–4921.
Technology and Electronic Commerce.—Robin Roark (acting), room 28008R, 482–3090.
Trade and Economic Analysis.—Joseph Flynn, room 7025R, 482–1606.
Trade Industry Information.—Wassel Mashagbeh, room A211, 482–4691.
Trade Policy Analysis.—Jean Janicke, room C126, 482–5947.
Trade Programs and Strategic Partnerships.—Anne Grey (acting), 482–5927.
Director, National Travel and Tourism Office.—Kelly Craigshead, 482–4931.
Deputy Assistant Secretary for Services.—Ted Dean, room 1128, 482–5261.

PRESIDENT'S EXPORT COUNCIL

[Authorized by Executive Orders 12131, 12534, 12551, 12610, 12692, 12774, 12869, and
12974 (May through September 1995)]

Executive Director, Under Secretary of International Trade.—Francisco Sanchez, room 3850
(202) 482–1124.
Executive Secretary and Staff Director.—Tricia Van Orden, room 4043.

MINORITY BUSINESS DEVELOPMENT AGENCY

Director.—Alejandra Castillo, room 5053 (202) 482–2332.
National Deputy Director.—Albert Shen, room 5053, 482–2332.
Associate Director for—
  Business Development.—Efrain Gonzalez, room 5079, 482–6407.
  Legislative, Education, and Intergovernmental Affairs.—Kimberly R. Marcus, room 5061,
    482–6272.
  Management.—Edith McCloud, room 5053, 482–2332.
Chief Counsel.—Josephine Arnold, room 5093, 482–5461.
Public Affairs Supervisor.—Velicia Woods, room 5612, 482–0491.
Chief of Legislative, Educational and Intergovernmental Affairs.—Bridget Gonzales, room
  5069A, 482–3774.

NATIONAL OCEANIC AND ATMOSPHERIC ADMINISTRATION

Under Secretary of Commerce for Oceans and Atmosphere.—Kathryn D. Sullivan, Ph.D.,
  room 51030 (202) 482–3436.
Assistant Secretary for Conservation and Management/Deputy Administrator.—Holly
  Banford (acting), room 51027, 482–6255.
Assistant Secretary Environmental Observation and Prediction/Deputy Administrator.—
  Vacant.
Chief Scientist.—Dr. Richard Spinrad, room 51207, 482–5688.
Deputy Under Secretary for Operations.—VADM Michael S. Devany, room 7316, 482–
  4569.
Chief of Staff.—Rene Stone, room 51030, 482–3436.
Deputy Assistant Secretary for International Fisheries.—Russell Smith, room 61013,
  482–5682.
Senior Advisor for International Affairs.—Elizabeth McLanahan (acting), room A–301,
  482–6076.
Director, Office of:
  Communications and External Affairs.—Ciaran Clayton, room AA–121, 482–6090.
  Education.—Louisa Koch, room 6869, 482–3384.
  Federal Coordinator for Meteorology.—Dave McCarren, SSMC1, room 1500 (301)
    427–2002.
  General Counsel.—Lois Schiffer, room A–125, 482–4080.
  Legislative and Intergovernmental Affairs.—Amanda Hallberg Greenwell, room A–103,
    482–4981.
  Marine and Aviation Operations.—RADM David Score, 8403 Colesville Road, Suite
    500, Silver Spring, MD 20910 (301) 713–7600.
  Chief Financial Officer.—Mark Seller, room D200, 482–0917.
  Chief Administrative Officer.—Edward Horton, SSMC4, room 8431 (301) 713–0836, ext.
    105.
  Chief Information Officer/High Performance Computing and Communications.—
    Zachary Goldstein, SSMC3, room 9651 (301) 713–9600.
  Acquisition and Grants.—Mitchell Ross, SSMC1, room 6300 (301) 713–0325.

Decision Coordination and Executive Secretariat.—Kelly Quickle, room 48026, 482–2985.
Workforce Management.—Kimberlyn Bauhs, SSMC4, room 12520 (301) 713–6300.

NATIONAL MARINE FISHERIES SERVICE
1315 East-West Highway, Silver Spring, MD 20910

Assistant Administrator.—Eileen Sobeck, room 14636 (301) 427–8000.
Deputy Assistant Administrator for—
  Operations.—Paul Doremus, room 14743, 427–8000.
  Regulatory Programs.—Samuel Rauch, room 14657, 427–8000.
Director, Office of:
  Habitat Conservation.—Buck Sutter, room 14828, 427–8600.
  International Affairs and Seafood Inspection.—John Henderschedt, room 12659, 427–8350.
  Law Enforcement.—Matthew Brandt (acting), room 415, 427–2300.
  Management and Budget.—Brian Pawlak, room 14450, 427–8720.
  Protected Resources.—Donna Wieting, room 13821, 427–8400.
  Science and Technology.—Ned Cyr, Ph.D., room 12450, 427–8100.
  Scientific Programs and Chief Science Advisor.—Richard Merrick, room 14659, 427–8000.
  Sustainable Fisheries.—Alan Risenhoover, room 13362, 427–8500.
Chief Information Officer.—Larry Tyminski, room 3657, 427–8800.
Aquaculture Program.—Michael Rubino, room 13117, 427–8325.
Policy.—Jennifer Lukens, room 14451, 427–8004.

NATIONAL OCEAN SERVICE

Assistant Administrator.—Russell Callender (acting), room 13632 (301) 713–3074.
Deputy Assistant Administrator.—David Holst (acting), room 13635, 713–3074.
Director, Center for Operational Oceanographic Products and Services.—Richard Edwing, room 6650, 713–2981.
Deputy Director.—Ellen Clark, room 6633, 713–2981.
Management and Budget.—Christopher Cartwright, room 13442, 713–3056.
Director, Office of:
  Coast Survey.—RADM Gerd Glang, room 6147, 713–2770.
  Coastal Management.—Jeff Payne (acting), room 10413, 713–3155.
  National Centers for Coastal Ocean Science.—Mary C. Erickson, room 8211, 713–3020.
  National Geodetic Survey.—Juliana Blackwell, room 8657, 713–3222.
  National Marine Sanctuaries.—Daniel Basta, room 11523, 713–7235.
  Response and Restoration.—Dave Westerholm, room 10102, 713–2989.

NATIONAL ENVIRONMENTAL SATELLITE, DATA AND INFORMATION SERVICE
1335 East-West Highway, Silver Spring, MD 20910

Assistant Administrator.—Stephen M. Volz, room 8268 (301) 713–3578.
Deputy Assistant Administrator.—Mark Paese, room 8300, 713–2010.
Deputy Assistant Administrator, Systems.—Thomas Burns, room 8212, 713–2005.
Chief Information Officer.—Irene Parker, room 7103, 713–9200.
Chief Financial Officer.—Cherish Johnson, room 8338, 713–9476.
Deputy Chief Financial Officer.—James Donnellon, room 8340, 713–9228.
International and Interagency Affairs Chief.—D. Brent Smith, room 7315, 713–2024.
Office of System Architecture and Advanced Planning.—Vanessa Griffin (acting), room 5410, 713–7342.
Director, Office of:
  Commercial Remote Sensing Regulatory Affairs.—Tahara Dawkins, room 8260, 713–3385.
  GOES–R Program.—Gregory A. Mandt, NASA GSFC, room C100D, 286–1355.
  Joint Polar Satellite System.—Harry Cikanek, room 3301, 713–4782.
  National Center for Environmental Information.—Thomas R. Karl, room 557–C (828) 271–4476.
  Satellite and Product Operations.—Vanessa Griffin, NSOF, room 1605, 817–4000.
  Satellite Applications and Research.—Al Powell, room 701, 763–8127.
  Satellite Ground Services.—Steven Petersen, SS3 room 4117, 713–7111.
  Space Commercialization.—Mark Paese (acting), room 8300, 713–2010.
  Systems Development.—Suzanne Hilding, room 6234, 713–0100.

NATIONAL WEATHER SERVICE
1325 East-West Highway, Silver Spring, MD 20910

Assistant Administrator.—Louis W. Uccellini, room 18150 (301) 713–9095.
Deputy Assistant Administrator.—Laura K. Furgione, room 18130, 713–0711.
Chief Financial Officer.—John Potts, room 18176, 427–6911.
Deputy Chief Financial Officer.—Marie Lovern, room 18212, 427–6914.
Assistant Chief Information Officer for Weather.—Iftikhar Jamil, room 17424, 427–9018.
Director, Office of:
    Climate, Water and Weather Services.—Andrew Stern, room 14348, 427–9120.
    Hydrologic Development.—Donald Cline, room 8176, 427–9522.
    National Centers for Environmental Prediction.—William Lapenta, room 101 (301) 683–1315.
    Operational Systems.—Deirdre Jones, room 16212, 427–9183.
    Science and Technology.—John Murphy, room 15146, 427–9119.

OCEANIC AND ATMOSPHERIC RESEARCH
1315 East-West Highway, Silver Spring, MD 20910

Assistant Administrator.—Craig McLean (acting), (301) 713–2458.
Deputy Assistant Administrator for—
    Labs and Cooperative Institutes.—Steven Fine, Ph.D. (301) 734–1167.
    Programs and Administration.—Steven Fine, Ph.D. (acting), 734–1167.
Chief Science Advisor.—Alexander MacDonald, Ph.D. (303) 497–6005.
Director of:
    Air Resources Laboratory.—Richard Artz (acting), (301) 683–1366.
    Atlantic Oceanographic and Meteorological Laboratory.—Robert Atlas (305) 361–4300.
    Earth System Research Laboratory.—Alexander MacDonald, Ph.D. (303) 497–6005.
Division of:
    Chemical Sciences.—David Fahey, Ph.D. (acting), (303) 497–5277.
    Global Monitoring.—James Butler, Ph.D. (303) 497–6898.
    Global Systems.—Kevin Kelleher (303) 497–4104.
    Physical Science.—William Neff, Ph.D. (303) 497–6265.
Geophysical Fluid Dynamics Laboratory.—Ram Ramaswamy, Ph.D. (609) 452–6510.
Great Lakes Environmental Research Laboratory.—Deborah H. Lee (734) 741–2245.
National Severe Storms Laboratory.—Steve Koch, Ph.D. (405) 325–6800.
Pacific Marine Environmental Laboratory.—Chris Sabine (206) 526–6810.
Director, Office of:
    Climate Program.—Wayne Higgins (301) 427–1263.
    Ocean Acidification.—Libby Jewett, Ph.D. (301) 734–1075
    Oceanic Exploration and Research.—Alan Leonardi, Ph.D. (301) 734–1016.
National Sea Grant College Program.—Leon Cammen, room 11716 (301) 734–1088.
Weather and Air Quality.—John Cortinas, Ph.D. (301) 734–1198.

PROGRAM PLANNING AND INTEGRATION

Director.—Patricia Montanio, room 15628 (240) 533–9012.
Deputy Director.—Paul Hirschberg, room 15629, 533–9017.

UNITED STATES PATENT AND TRADEMARK OFFICE
P.O. Box 1450, 600 Dulany Street, Arlington, VA 22313–1450
Phone (571) 272–8600

Under Secretary of Commerce for Intellectual Property and Director of U.S. Patent and Trademark Office.—Michelle Lee.
Deputy Under Secretary of Commerce for Intellectual Property and Deputy Director of the U.S. Patent and Trademark Office.—Russell Slifer.
Chief of Staff.—Andrew Byrnes (571) 272–8600.
Deputy Chief of Staff.—Vikrum Aiyer, 272–8600
Chief Communications Officer.—Todd Elmer, 272–3500.
Chief Administrative Patent Judge, Board of Patent Appeals and Interferences.—James Donald Smith, 272–9797.
Deputy Chief Administrative Patent Judge.—Nate Kelly, 272–9797.

Chief Administrative Trademark Judge, Trademark Trial and Appeal Board.—Gerard Rogers, 272–8500.
Director, Office of Enrollment and Discipline.—William Covey, 272–4097.

COMMISSIONER FOR PATENTS

Commissioner.—Andrew Faile (acting), (571) 272–8800.
Deputy Commissioner for—
  International Patent Cooperation.—Mark Powell.
  Patent Administration.—Bruce Kisliuk.
  Patent Examination Policy.—Andrew Hirshfeld.
  Patent Operations.—Robert Oberleitner (acting).
  Patent Quality.—Valencia Martin Wallace.
Associate Commissioner for—
  Innovation Development.—Anthony Knight (acting).
  Patent Examination Policy.—Janet Gongola.
  Patent Information Management.—Deborah Stephens.
  Patent Resources and Planning.—Vacant.
Director, Office of:
  Patent Cooperation Treaty Legal Administration.—Charles A. Pearson, 272–3224.
  Patent Legal Administration.—Brian Hanlon, 272–7735.
Assistant Deputy Commissioner for Patent Operations:
  Chemical and Design Discipline.—Jacqueline Stone (TC 1600, 1700, and 2900).
  Electrical and Mechanical Discipline.—Remy Yucel (TC 2100 and 3700).
  Electrical Discipline and Patent Examination Support Services (OPESS).—Don Hajec
    (TC 2800 and Patent Examination Support Services (OPESS).
  Electrical Discipline and Central Re-Exam Unit (CRU).—Robert Oberleitner (TC 2400
    and Central Re-Exam Unit).
  Electrical and Mechanical Discipline.—Richard Seidel (TC 2600 and TC 3600).
Patent Examining Group Directors:
  Technology Center 1600 (biotechnology and organic chemistry): Jerry Lorengo, 272–
    0600; Wanda Walker, 272–0500, 272–7600.
  Technology Center 1700 (chemical and materials engineering): Yvonne Eyler, 272–1200;
    Karen Young, 272–1100; Gladys Corcoran, 272–1300.
  Technology Center 2100 (computer architecture and software): Wendy Garber, 272–
    1400 ; Seema Rao, 272–0800; David Talbott, 272–4150.
  Technology Center 2400 (networking, multiplexing, cable, and security): Timothy Callahan,
    272–4066; Nancy Le, 272–4056; Nestor Ramirez, 272–3174.
  Technology Center 2600 (communications): Derris Banks, 272–4750; Tariq Hafiz, 272–
    4550; John LeGuyader, 272–4650; David Wiley, 272–4750.
  *Technology Center 2800 (semiconductor, electrical mechanical and physics/optical sys-
    tems and components):* James Kramer, 272–1850; Jack Harvey, 272–1850; Joseph
    Thomas, 272–1550; Robyn Evans, 272–1850.
  Technology Center 2900 (Designs).—Robert Olszewski, 272–2200.
  *Technology Center 3600 (transportation, construction, electronic commerce, agriculture,
    national security, and license and review):* Greg Vidovich, 272–5350; Katherine
    Matecki, 272–5250; Edward Lefkowitz, 272–5150; Rada Rinaldi, 272–5050.
  Technology Center 3700 (mechanical engineering, manufacturing, and products): Dmitry
    Suhol (acting), 272–2975; Angela Sykes, 272–4390; Andrew Wang, 272–3750; Diego
    Gutierrez, 272–3680.
  Technology Center 3900 (Central Reexamination Unit).—Steve Stein (acting), 272–1544.
  Technology Center 4100 (Patent Training).—Gary Jones, 272–8320.
Director, Office of:
  Central Reexamination Unit.—Steve Stein (acting), 272–1544.
  Classification Quality and International Solutions.—Chris Kim, 272–7980.
  Classification Standards and Development.—John Salotto (acting),
  Data Management (PUBS).—Thomas Koontz (703) 756–1492.
  International Patent Business Solutions.—Don Levin, 272–3785(703) 756–1850.
  International Patent Legal Administration.—Charles Pearson, 272–3224.
  Patent Application Processing.—Kevin Little (703) 756–1489.
  Patent Financial Management.—John Buie, 272–6283.
  Patent Information Resources (OPIR).—Sandra Bigsby (703) 756–1489.
  Patent Legal Administration.—Brian Hanlon, 272–7735.
  Patent Quality Assurance.—Anthony Caputa, 272–5021.
  Patent Training Academy.—Gary Jones, 272–8320.
  Petitions.—John Cottingham (acting), 272–3282.

Work Sharing Planning and Implementation.—Dan Hunter (acting), 272–8050.
Director, Satellite Offices:
    Denver.—Robin Evans (acting), (303) 297–2026.
    Detroit.—Christal Sheppard, (313) 446–4886.
    Silicon Valley.—John Cabeca (571) 272–3100.

COMMISSIONER FOR TRADEMARKS

Commissioner.—Mary Boney Denison (571) 272–8901.
Deputy Commissioner for Trademark Operations.—Meryl Hershkowitz, 272–8901.
Group Director, Trademark Law Offices:
    Tomas Vleek (571) 272–8901
    Dan Vanonese (acting), 272–9288.
    Chris Doninger (acting), 272–9297.
Trademark Examination Law Office Managing Attorneys:
    Law Office 101.—Ron Sussman, 272–9696.
    Law Office 102.—Mitchell Front, 272–9382.
    Law Office 103.—Michael Hamilton, 272–9278.
    Law Office 104.—Dayna Brown (acting), 272–836.
    Law Office 105.—Susan Hayash, 272–9692.
    Law Office 106.—Mary Sparrow, 272–9332.
    Law Office 107.—Leslie Bishop, 272–9445.
    Law Office 108.—Andrew Lawrence, 272–9342.
    Law Office 109.—Michael Kazazian (acting), 272–9434.
    Law Office 110.—Chris Pedersen, 272–9371.
    Law Office 111.—Robert Lorenzo, 272–9387.
    Law Office 112.—Angela Wilson, 272–9443.
    Law Office 113.—Odette Bonnet, 272–9426.
    Law Office 114.—Margaret Le, 272–9456.
    Law Office 115.—John Lincoski, 272–9436.
    Law Office 116.—Christine Cooper, 272–9844.
    Law Office 117.—Hellen Bryan-Johnson, 272–9446.
Virtual Law Office—Pilot Sometime in January 2014:
    Law Office 118.—Tomas Howell, 272–9302.
    Law Office 119.—Brett Golden, 272–9257.
    Law Office 120.—Michael Baird, 272–9487.
Director, Office of Trademark Program Control.—Betty Andrews, 272–9666.
Deputy Commissioner for Trademark Examination Policy.—Sharon Marsh, 272–8901.
Director, Office of Trademark Quality Review.—Kevin Peska, 272–9658.

POLICY AND EXTERNAL AFFAIRS

Chief Policy Officer and Director for International Affairs.—Shira Perlmutter.
Deputy Chief Policy Officer for Operations.—George Elliott, 272–9300.
Director, Office of:
    Copyright.—Michael Shapiro, 272–9300.
    Enforcement.—Michael Smith, 272–9300.
    Governmental Affairs.—Dana Colarulli, 272–7300.
    International Trade.—Paul Salmon, 272–9300.
    Patents.—Chuck Eloshway, 272–9300.
    Trademarks.—Amy Cotton, 272–9300.
Director of Global Intellectual Property Academy.—Rachel Wallace, 272–1500.

CHIEF FINANCIAL OFFICER

Chief Financial Officer.—Anthony Scardino (571) 272–9200.
Deputy Chief Financial Officer.—Frank Murphy, 272–9200.
Senior Financial Manager.—Michelle Picard, 272–6354.
Director, Office of Planning and Budget.—Brendan Hourigan, 272–8966.
Finance.—Mark Krieger, 272–6339.
Financial Management Systems.—Gita Zoks, 272–6363.
Procurement.—Scott Palmer, 270–7149.

Department of Commerce 719

CHIEF PERFORMANCE IMPROVEMENT OFFICER

Chief Performance Improvement Officer.—Vacant (571) 272–9200.

CHIEF ADMINISTRATIVE OFFICER

Chief Administrative Officer.—Frederick Steckler (571) 272–9600.
Deputy Chief Administrative Officer.—Wynn Coggins, 272–9600.
Director of Administrative Services.—Lisle Hannah (acting), 272–6541.
Human Resources.—Karen Karlinchak, 272–6200.

DIRECTOR OF THE OFFICE OF EQUAL EMPLOYMENT OPPORTUNITY AND DIVERSITY

Director.—Bismarck Myrick (571) 272–6315.

OFFICE OF GENERAL COUNSEL

General Counsel.—Sarah Harris (571) 272–7000.
Deputy General Counsels for—
General Law.—James O. Payne Jr., 272–3000.
Intellectual Property Law and Solicitor.—Nathan Kelley, 272–9035.

CHIEF INFORMATION OFFICER

Chief Information Officer.—John B. Owens II (571) 272–9400.
Deputy Chief Information Officer.—Anthony "Tony" Chiles, 272–9410.
Chief of Staff.—John S. Williams, 272–5664.
Director of:
  Application Engineering and Development.—Pamela Isom, 272–0341.
  Budget and Finance.—Keith M. VanderBrink (571) 272–5662.
  Customer Information Services.—Vacant.
  Information Management Services.—Rhonda Foltz, 272–6147.
  Infrastructure Engineering and Operations.—Robert Cobert, 272–5481.
  Organizational Policy and Governance.—Kevin Smith, 272–3200.
  Program Administration Organization.—Toby Bennett, 272–6205.
  Quality Management.—Brian R. Jones, 272–1659.
  Systems Development and Maintenance.—Patsy Riley, 272–3925.
Manager, Office of:
  Customer Support Services.—Vacant.
  Electronic Information Products.—James Thompson (571) 756–1422.
  Enterprise Systems Services.—Carol R. Eakins, 272–5426.
  Network and Telecommunications.—Vacant.
  Public Information Services.—Ted L. Parr (703) 756–1267.
  Public Records Division.—Donna Cooper, 756–1893.

NATIONAL INSTITUTE OF STANDARDS AND TECHNOLOGY
100 Bureau Drive Gaithersburg, MD 20899 (301) 975–6478

Under Secretary of Standards and Technology and Acting Director.—Dr. Willie E. May (301) 975–2300.
Associate Director for Laboratory Programs.—Dr. Richard Cavanagh (acting), (301) 975–2300.
Chief Safety Officer.—Dr. Richard Kayser, 975–4502.
Baldrige Performance Excellence Program.—Dr. Robert Fangmeyer, 975–2360.
International and Academic Affairs.—Dr. Claire M. Saundry, 975–2386.
NIST/Boulder Laboratories.—Dr. Mike Kelley (acting), (303) 497–5285.
Chief of Staff.—Kevin Kimball, 975–3070.
  Congressional and Legislative Affairs.—Jim Schufreider, 975–5675.
  Program Coordination Office.—Dr. Jason Boehm, 975–8678.
  Public and Business Affairs.—Gail J. Porter, 975–3392.
Chief Financial Officer.—George Jenkins, 975–5080.
  Budget.—Eddie Rivera, 975–2670.

Business Systems.—Fred Lehnhoff, 975–2290.
Finance.—Marvin Washington, 975–6897.
Office of Acquisition and Agreements Management.—Cecelia Royster, 975–6336.
Acquisitions Management.—Lambert McCullough, 975–3601
Grants Management.—Robin Bunch, 975–8006.
Enterprise Risk Management.—Nahla Ivy, 975–5496.
Chief Human Capital Officer.—Susanne Porch, 975–2487.
  Human Resources Management.—Janet Hoffman, 975–3185.
  Management and Organization.—Catherine S. Fletcher, 975–4054.
  Safety, Health and Environment.—Jeffrey Good, 975–6114.
Civil Rights and Diversity Office.—Mirta-Marie M. Keys, 975–2042.
  Applications Systems.—L. Dale Little, 975–8982.
  Customer Access and Support.—Tim Halton, 975–8920.
  Enterprise Systems.—James E. Fowler, 975–6888.
  Information Technology Security and Networking.—Robert Glenn, 975–3667.
Chief Facilities Management Officer.—Stephen Salber, 975–8836.
  Emergency Services.—Dr. Benjamin Overbey, 975–8247.
  Engineering, Maintenance and Support Services.—Donald Archibald (301) 975–5680.
  Plant.—David Henry, 975–6901.
Associate Director for Management Resources.—Mary H. Saunders, 975–5000
  Research Support Information Services.—Mary-Deirdre Coraggio, 975–5158.
  Reference Materials.—Robert L. Watters, Jr., 975–4122.
  Standards Coordination Office.—George Arnold, 975–5627.
  Weights and Measures.—Carol Hockert, 975–5507.
Associate Director for Industry and Innovation Services.—Dr. Phillip Singerman, 975–2340.
Director, Technology Innovation Program.—Thomas Wiggins, 975–2162.
  Project Management Office.—Linda Beth Schilling, 975–2887.
  Selection Management Office.—Thomas Wiggins, 975–5416.
Director, Hollings Manufacturing Extension Partnership Program.—Dr. Phillip Singerman
  (acting), 975–4676.
  Program Development Office.—Alex Folk, 975–8089.
  Systems Operations Office.—Michael J. Simpson, 975–6147.
Director, Engineering Laboratory.—Dr. Howard Harary, 975–5900.
  Deputy Director.—Dr. Joannie Chin, 975–6815.
    Electromagnetics.—Dr. Perry Wilson (acting), (303) 497–3406.
    Quantum Electronics and Photonics.—Dr. Robert Hickernell (acting), (303) 497–3455.
    Semiconductor Electronics.—Dr. David G. Seiler, 975–2054.
Director, Center for Nanoscale Science and Technology.—Dr. Robert Celotta, 975–8001.
  Intelligent Systems.—Dr. Al Wavering, 975–3401.
  Fabrication Technology.—Mark E. Luce, 975–2159.
  Systems Integration.—Vijay Srinivasan, 975–3524.
  Semiconductor and Dimensional Metrology Division.—Dr. Michael Postek, 975–2299.
Chief, Chemical Science and Technology Laboratory.—Dr. Carlos Gonzalez, 975–2483.
  Deputy Chief.—Dr. Roger D. Van Zee, 975–8301.
Director, Material Measurement Laboratory.—Dr. Laurie E. Locascio, 975–3130.
  Greenhouse Gas and Climate Science Measurements.—Dr. James R. Whetstone, 975–
  2609.
  Materials Measurement Science.—Dr. John Small, 975–3900.
  Energy Research.—Dr. Daniel G. Friend (303) 497–5424.
Director, Physical Measurement Laboratory.—Dr. Joseph Dehmer, 975–4200.
  Deputy Director.—Dr. James Olthoff, 975–2220.
    Quantum Measurement.—Dr. Carl J. Williams, 975–3531.
    Radiation Physics.—Dr. Lisa R. Karam, 975–5561.
    Sensor Science.—Dr. Gerald Fraser, 975–3797.
    Quantum Physics.—Dr. Thomas O'Brian (303) 497–4570.
    Time and Frequency.—Dr. Thomas R. O'Brian (303) 497–4570.
    Applied Chemicals and Materials.—Dr. Stephanie Hooker (303) 497–4326.
    Materials Science and Engineering.—Dr. Frank W. Gayle, 975–6161.
Chief, Materials Science.—Dr. Eric Lin, 975–6743.
Director, NIST Center for Neutron Research.—Dr. Robert Dimeo, 975–6210.
Chief, Fire Research.—Dr. Anthony Hamins, 975–6598.
  Energy and Environment.—Dr. Hunter Fanney, 975–5864.
  Materials and Structural Systems.—Jason Averill (acting), 975–6051.
Director, Information Technology Laboratory.—Dr. Charles Romine, 975–2900.
  Deputy Director.—James A. St. Pierre, 975–2900.
    Advanced Network Technologies.—Dr. Abdelila Battou, 975–5247.
    Computer Security.—Donna Dodson, 975–3669.

Information Access.—Dr. Ashit Talukder, 975–3889.
Applied and Computational Mathematics.—Dr. Ronald F. Boisvert, 975–3800.
Software and Systems.—Dr. Ram Sriram, 975–3507.
Statistical Engineering.—Dr. Antonio Possolo (acting), 975–2853.

NATIONAL TECHNICAL INFORMATION SERVICE
5301 Shawnee Road, Alexandria, VA 22312

Director.—Bruce Borzino (703) 605–6405.

NATIONAL TELECOMMUNICATIONS AND INFORMATION ADMINISTRATION
1401 Constitution Avenue, NW., 20230

Assistant Secretary and Administrator.—Lawrence E. Stickling, room 4898 (202) 482–1840.
Deputy Assistant Secretary.—Angela Simpson, 482–1840.
Chief of Staff.—Glenn Reynolds, 482–1840.
Deputy Chief of Staff and Congressional Affairs Director.—James Wasilewski.
Senior Advisors: Jennifer Duane, Derek Khlopin.
Chief Counsel.—Kathy Smith.
Director, Office of:
    Institute for Telecommunication Sciences.—Brian D. Lane (acting), (303) 497–3500.
    International Affairs.—Fiona Alexander.
    Policy Analysis and Development.—John B. Morris, Jr.
    Public Affairs.—Heather Phillips.
    Public Safety Communications.—Stephen Fletcher.
    Spectrum Management.—Paige R. Atkins.
    Telecommunications and Information Applications.—Douglas Kinkoph.

DEPARTMENT OF LABOR

Frances Perkins Building, Third Street and Constitution Avenue, NW., 20210

phone (202) 693–5000, http://www.dol.gov

THOMAS E. PEREZ, Secretary of Labor; education: B.A., Brown University, 1983; J.D., Harvard Law School, 1987; M.P.P., Harvard University John F. Kennedy School of Government, 1987; professional: Law Clerk, U.S. District Court for the District of Colorado, 1987–89; Federal Prosecutor, Civil Rights Division, Department of Justice, 1989–95; Special Counsel, Senator Edward Kennedy, 1995–98; Deputy Assistant Attorney General for Civil Rights, Department of Justice, 1998–99; Director, Office for Civil Rights, Department of Health and Human Services, 1999–2001; Professor, University of Maryland School of Law, 2001–07; Secretary, Maryland Department of Labor, Licensing and Regulation, 2007–09; Assistant United States Attorney General for the Civil Rights Division, 2009–13; Member, Montgomery County (MD) Council, 2002–06; President, Montgomery County (MD) Council, 2004–05; married: Ann Marie Staudenmaier; nominated by President Barack Obama to become the 26th Secretary of Labor, and was confirmed by the U.S. Senate on July 18, 2013.

OFFICE OF THE SECRETARY

phone (202) 693–6000

Secretary of Labor.—Thomas E. Perez.
  Deputy Secretary.—Christopher P. Lu.
  Associate Deputy Secretaries: Nancy Rooney, Megan Uzzell.
  Executive Secretariat Director.—Elizabeth Way (acting).
  Chief of Staff.—Matthew Colangelo.
  Director of Advance and Scheduling.—C. Wayne Skinner.

OFFICE OF PUBLIC ENGAGEMENT

Director.—Allison Zelman (202) 693–6459.

ADMINISTRATIVE LAW JUDGES

Techworld, 800 K Street, NW., Suite 400–N, 20001–8002

Chief Administrative Law Judge.—Stephen R. Henley (acting), (202) 693–7424.
  Associate Chief Judge.—William S. Colwell.

ADMINISTRATIVE REVIEW BOARD

Chief and Chair.—Paul M. Igasaki, room N–5404 (202) 693–6200.
  Vice Chair.—E. Cooper Brown, room N–5404, 693–6200.

OFFICE OF THE ASSISTANT SECRETARY FOR ADMINISTRATION
AND MANAGEMENT (OASAM)

Assistant Secretary.—T. Michael Kerr, room S–2203 (202) 693–4040.
  Deputy Assistant Secretary for—
    Operations.—Edward C. Hugler, room S–2203, 693–4040.
    Policy.—Charlotte Hayes, room S–2203, 693–4040.
  Special Assistants: Braye Cloud, Carolina Rizzo, Douglas Robins, Traci Smith, 693–4040.
  Administrative Officer.—Christopher Yerxa, 693–4040.
  Staff Assistants: Vacant.

BUSINESS OPERATIONS CENTER

Director.—Al Stewart, room S–1524 (202) 693–4028.
Deputy Director.—Vacant.
Office of:
　Acquisition Management Services.—Carl V. Campbell, room S–1510–C, 693–7246.
　Administrative Services.—Phil Puckett, room S–1521, 693–6650.
　Asset and Resource Management.—Tanisha Bynum-Frazier, room S–1519B, 693–4546.
　Procurement Services.—Sandra Foster, room S–4307, 693–4570.
　Small and Disadvantaged Business Utilization.—Sonya Carrion, room N–6402, 693–7262.
　Worker Safety and Health Services.—Stephanie Semmer, room S–1321, 693–6678.

PERFORMANCE MANAGEMENT CENTER

Director.—Holly Donnelly, room S–3317 (202) 693–7125.
Deputy Director.—David Frederickson, room S–3317, 693–7123.

CIVIL RIGHTS CENTER

Director.—Naomi Barry-Perez, room N–4123 (202) 693–6500.
Staff Assistant.—Jean Gales, room N–4123, 693–6549.
Office of:
　Compliance Assistance and Planning.—Roger Ocampo, 693–6562.
　Enforcement/External.—Denise Sudell, 693–6519.
　Enforcement/Internal.—Samuel Rhames, 693–6500.
　Reasonable Accommodation Hotline.—Kim Borowicz, room N–4123, 693–6527.

DEPARTMENTAL BUDGET CENTER

Director.—Mark P. Wichlin (acting), room S–4020 (202) 693–4090.
Deputy Director.—Mark P. Wichlin, 693–4090.
Administrative Officer.—Patricia Smith, 693–4067.
Office of:
　Budget Programs.—James Martin, 693–4077.
　Budget Policy and Systems.—Vacant.

EMERGENCY MANAGEMENT CENTER

800 K Street, NW., Suite 450 North, 20001–8002

Director.—Greg Rize (202) 693–7514.
Deputy Director.—Mary Jo Hogan, 693–7504.

BENEFITS.GOV

Program Manager.—Al Sloane, room N–4309 (202) 693–8067.

HUMAN RESOURCES CENTER

Director.—Sydney Rose, room C–5526 (202) 693–7600.
Deputy Director.—Kim Sasajima, room C–5526, 693–7600.
Office of:
　Administration and Management Services.—Donna Childs Speight, room C–5517, 693–7773.
　Diversity and Inclusion.—Paul Plasencia, room S–4015, 693–5840.
　Employee and Labor Management Relations.—Shawn Hooper, room N–5476, 693–7612.
　Executive Resources.—Lucy Cunningham, room N–2453, 693–7800.
　HRWorks.—Roy Abreu, room S3314, 693–4324.
　Human Resources Consulting and Operations.—Kristin Siegfried, room C–5516, 693–7690.
　Human Resources Policy and Accountability.—Vacant.
　Human Resources Systems.—Roy Abreu, room S–3314, 693–4324.
　Training and Development.—Vacant.

Worklife, Leave, Benefits Policy and Programs.—Deborah Dudley, room N–5454, 693–7610.

OFFICE OF THE CHIEF INFORMATION OFFICER

Chief Information Officer.—Dawn Leaf, room N–1301 (202) 693–4200.
Associate Deputy CIO.—Vacant.
Office of:
  Advanced Technology.—Vacant.
  Applications and Platform as a Service.—Phil Sullivan (acting), N–1301, 693–4179; Tim Erskine (acting), N–1301, 693–8128.
  Customer Advocacy.—Duane Eldridge, room N–1301, 693–0326.
  Information Assurance.—Tonya Manning, room N–1301, 693–4431.
  Infrastructure Services.—Lou Charlier, room N–1301, 693–4147.
  IT Administration.—Cheryle Greenaugh (acting), room N–1301, 693–4158.
  IT Acquisitions.—Claire Ward (acting), room N–1301, 693–4556.
  IT Governance.—Pete Sullivan, room N–1301, 693–4211.
  IT Policies and Procedures.—Cheryle Greenaugh, room N–1301, 693–4158.
  Systems Engineering.—Phil Sullivan (acting), room N–1301, 693–4179; Fred Whiteside (acting), room N–4416, 693–0440.
  Enterprise Service Desk.—24/7, room N–1505 (855) 522–6748, or EnterpriseServiceDesk @dol.gov.

SECURITY CENTER

Director.—Kenneth McCreless, room S–1229G (202) 693–7994.
Deputy Director.—Stacey Thompson, 693–7210.
Staff Assistant.—Dianna Cornish, 693–7991.

ASSISTANT SECRETARY FOR POLICY

Assistant Secretary.—Vacant, room S–2312 (202) 693–5959.
Deputy Assistant Secretary.—Raj Nayak.
Career Deputy Assistant Secretary.—Stephanie Swirsky.
Chief of Staff.—Justin N. Allen.
Staff Assistant.—Djuna Y. Brizzi.
Director, Office of:
  Compliance Assistance Policy.—Vacant.
  Economic Policy and Analysis.—Vacant.
  Regulatory and Programmatic Policy.—Kathleen Franks, 693–5072.
Chief Evaluation Officer.—Demetra Nightingale, room S–2312, 693–5959.
Deputy Chief Evaluation Officer.—Jonathan Simonetta.

BENEFITS REVIEW BOARD

Chair.—Betty Jean Hall, room N5101 (202) 693–6300.

BUREAU OF LABOR STATISTICS
Postal Square Building, Suite 4040, 2 Massachusetts Avenue, NE., 20212
phone (202) 691–7800

Commissioner.—Erica L. Groshen.
Deputy Commissioner.—William Wiatrowski (acting), 691–7802.
Associate Commissioner, Office of:
  Administration.—Nancy Ruiz de Gamboa, suite 4060, 691–7777.
  Compensation and Working Conditions.—Philip Doyle (acting), suite 4130, 691–6300.
  Employment and Unemployment Statistics.—Michael Horrigan, suite 4945, 691–6400.
  Field Operations.—Jay Mousa, suite 2935, 691–5800.
  Prices and Living Conditions.—David Friedman, suite 3120, 691–6960.
  Productivity and Technology.—Vacant, suite 2150, 691–5600.
  Publications and Special Studies.—Michael Levi, suite 4110, 691–5900.
  Survey Methods Research.—John Eltinge, suite 1950, 691–7404.

Technology and Survey Processing.—Carol Mullins, suite 5025, 691–7600.
Assistant Commissioner, Office of:
 Compensation Levels and Trends.—Phil Doyle, suite 4130, 691–6200.
 Current Employment Analysis.—Vacant, suite 4675, 691–6378.
 Industrial Prices and Price Indexes.—Vacant, suite 4170, 691–7700.
 Industry Employment Statistics.—Kenneth W. Robertson, suite 4840, 691–6521.
 Occupational Statistics and Employment Projections.—Rebecca Rust, suite 2135, 691–5701.
Assistant Commissioner, Division of Consumer Prices and Price Indexes.—John Layng, suite 3130, 691–6955.
Director of:
 Survey Processing.—Rick Kryger, suite 5025, 691–6730.
 Directorate of Technology and Computing Services.—Wesley S. Chou, suite 5025, 691–7203.

BUREAU OF INTERNATIONAL LABOR AFFAIRS

Deputy Under Secretary.—Carol Pier, room S–2235 (202) 693–4770.
 Associate Deputy Under Secretaries: Eric Biel, room S–2235, 693–4770; Mark Mittelhauser, room S–2235, 693–4770.
 Chief of Staff.—Thomas Richards, room S–2235, 693–4770.
 Administrative Officer.—Vacant, room S–2235, 693–4770.
 Executive Assistant.—Diane Ward, room S–2235, 693–4770.
 Program Analyst.—Candice Streeter, room S–2235, 693–4770.

OFFICE OF CHILD LABOR, FORCED LABOR, AND HUMAN TRAFFICKING

Director.—Marcia Eugenio, room S–5317 (202) 693–4849.
 Deputy Director.—Kevin Willcutts, room S–5317, 693–4832.

OFFICE OF ECONOMIC AND LABOR RESEARCH

Director.—Gregory Schoepfle, room S–5303 (202) 693–4887.
 Deputy Director.—Kenneth Swinnerton, room S–5303, 693–4916.

OFFICE OF INTERNATIONAL RELATIONS

Director.—Robert B. Shepard, room S–5004 (202) 693–4808.
 Deputy Director.—Zhao Li, room S–5004, 693–4803.
 Chief, Division of Multilateral Issues.—Joan Barrett, room S–5004, 693–4857.

OFFICE OF TRADE AND LABOR AFFAIRS

Director.—Matthew Levin, room S–5303 (202) 693–5745.
 Deputy Director.—Sueryun Hahn, room S–5303, 693–4800.

OFFICE OF THE CHIEF FINANCIAL OFFICER

Chief Financial Officer.—Karen Tekleberhan (acting), room S–4030 (202) 693–6800.
 Deputy Chief Financial Officer.—Karen Tekleberhan.
 Administrative Officer.—Marella Turner.
 Business Process Improvement.—Robert Beckman, room S–4030.
 Client Financial Management Services.—Janice Blake-Green, room S–4030.
 Associate Deputy CFO for—
  Central Accounting Operations.—Sahra Torres-Rivera, room S–4502.
  Client Accounting Services.—Adrienne Young, room S–5526.
  Customer Support.—Madhuri Edwards, room N–2719.
  Financial Policy and Travel.—Cynthia Jones (acting), room S–4030.
  Financial Reporting and Compliance.—Robert Balin, room S–4030.
  Financial Systems.—Sahra Torres-Rivera, room N–2719.
  Fiscal Integrity.—Kevin Brown (acting), room S–4030.
  Operations Support.—Madhuri Edwards, room N–2719.
  Security and Technology.—Richard Westmark, room N–2719.

OFFICE OF CONGRESSIONAL AND INTERGOVERNMENTAL AFFAIRS

Assistant Secretary.—Adri Jayaratne (acting), room S–2006, (202) 693–4601.
  Chief of Staff.—Kate Ahlgren Garza, room S–2220, 693–4600.
  Deputy Assistant Secretary for Congressional and Intergovernmental Affairs.—Nikki McKinney, room S–2006, 693–4601.
  Director, Intergovernmental Affairs.—Carrianna Suiter Kuruvilla, S–2220, 693–6400.
  Deputy Director, Intergovernmental Affairs.—Roberto Soberanis, S–2220, 693–4600.
  Associate Director, Intergovernmental Affairs.—Eduardo Cisneros, room S–2220, 693–4600.
  Staff Assistant.—Glenda Manning, room S–2006, 693–4601.
  Administrative Officer.—Joycelyn Daniels, room S–1204, 693–4600.
  Senior Legislative Officer.—Andria Oliver.
  Deputy Assistant Secretary, Appropriations/Budget.—Julie Aaronson, room S–2220, 693–4600.
  Senior Legislative Assistant, Employee Benefits/COBRA.—Jenny Waits, room S–2220, 693–4600.
  Senior Legislative Officer, Employment and Training.—Dan Zeitlin, room S–2220, 693–4600.
  Senior Legislative Officer, Foreign Labor Certification/Wage and Hour Division.—Tony Zaffirini, room S–2220, 693–4600.
  Legislative Officer, International Affairs/Child Labor.—Carmen Torres, room S–2220, 693–4600.
  Senior Legislative Assistant, ILAB/Trade and Labor Affairs.—Claudia Montelongo, room S–2220, 693–4600.
  Deputy Assistant Secretary, Mine Safety and Health.—Julie Aaronson, room S–2220, 693–4600.
  Senior Legislative Assistant, Native American Affairs/LGBT.—Jeremy Bishop, room S–2220, 693–4600.
  Senior Legislative Officer.—Margaret Cantrell.
  Senior Legislative Assistant, Occupational Safety and Health/Labor Management Standards.—Elva Linares, room S–2220, 693–4600.
  Senior Legislative Counsel, Oversight/Investigation and Labor Management Standards.—Kate Ahlgren Garza, room S–2220, 693–4600.
  Senior Legislative Assistant, Women's Bureau.—Elva Linares, room S–2220, 693–4600.
  Senior Legislative Assistant, Veteran's Affairs.—Jenny Waits, room S–2220, 693–4600.

SECRETARY'S REPRESENTATIVES IN THE REGIONAL OFFICES

Region II, New York.—Robert Angelo: Connecticut, Delaware, District of Columbia, Georgia, Florida, Maine, Massachusetts, New Hampshire, New Jersey, New York, North Carolina, Pennsylvania, South Carolina, Vermont, Virginia, West Virginia.
Region V, Chicago.—Jen Mason: Illinois, Indiana, Iowa, Kentucky, Michigan, Minnesota, Missouri, Ohio, Tennessee, Wisconsin.
Region VIII, Denver.—Dusti Gurule: Colorado, Kansas, Louisiana, Mississippi, Oklahoma, Texas.
Region IX, San Francisco.—Elmy Bermejo: Arizona, California, Hawaii, New Mexico, Utah.
Region X, Seattle.—John Lund: Alaska, Idaho, Kansas, Montana, Nebraska, North Dakota, Oregon, South Dakota, Washington, Wyoming.

OFFICE OF DISABILITY EMPLOYMENT POLICY

Assistant Secretary.—Jennifer Sheehy (acting), room S–1303, (202) 693–7880, TTY 693–7881.
  Deputy Assistant Secretary.—Jennifer Sheehy.
  Chief of Staff.—Taryn Williams.
  Special Assistant.—Elena Brown.
  Director of Policy Development.—Vacant.

EMPLOYEE BENEFITS SECURITY ADMINISTRATION

Assistant Secretary.—Phyllis C. Borzi, room S–2524, (202) 693–8300.
  Deputy Assistant Secretary.—Judith Mares, 693–8300.
  Special Assistants: Chelsea McCue, Terri Thomas, 693–8300.
  Senior Advisor.—Jane Norman, 693–8300.
  Confidential Assistant.—Michelle S. Brown.

Deputy Assistant Secretary for Program Operations.—Timothy Hauser, room N–5677, 693–8315.
Executive Assistant.—Becki Marchand, 693–8315.
Director of:
  Enforcement.—Mable Capolongo, 122 C Street, suite 600, 693–8440.
  Exemption Determinations.—Lyssa Hall, room N–5649, 693–8540.
  Health Plan Standards and Compliance Assistance.—Amy Turner, room 5653, 693–8335.
  Participant Assistance.—Mark Connor, room N–5625, 693–8630.
  Policy and Research.—Joseph Piacentini, room N–5718, 693–8410.
  Program, Planning, Evaluation and Management.—Joel Lovelace, room N–5668, 693–8480.
  Regulations and Interpretations.—Joseph Canary, room N–5669, 693–8500.
  Technology and Information Services.—Diane Schweizer, room N–5459, 693–8600.
Chief Accountant.—Ian Dingwall, 122 C Street, suite 400, 693–8360.

EMPLOYEES' COMPENSATION APPEALS BOARD

Chairman.—Christopher James Godfrey, room N–5416, (202) 693–6374.

EMPLOYMENT AND TRAINING ADMINISTRATION

Assistant Secretary.—Portia Wu, room S–2307, (202) 693–2700.
  Deputy Assistant Secretaries: Gerri Fiala, Byron Zuidema, room S–2307, 693–2700.
Administrator, Office of:
  Apprenticeship.—John Ladd, room N–5311, 693–2796.
  Contracts Management.—Jeffrey Saylor (acting), room N–4702, 693–3404.
  Financial Administration.—Ron Sissel, room N–4702, 693–3132.
  Foreign Labor Certification.—William W. Thompson II, room C–4312, 693–2800.
  Job Corps.—Lenita Jacobs-Simmons, room N–4463, 693–3000.
  Management and Administrative Services.—Lisa L. Lahrman (acting), room N–4655, 693–2800.
  Policy Development and Research.—Adele Gagliardi, room N–5637, 693–3700.
  Trade Adjustment Assistance.—Norris Tyler (acting), room C–5321, 693–3560.
  Unemployment Insurance.—Gay Gilbert, room S–4231, 693–3029.
  Workforce Investment.—Amanda Ahlstrand, room S–4231, 693–3980.

DOL CENTER FOR FAITH-BASED AND NEIGHBORHOOD PARTNERSHIPS

Director.—Benjamin Seigel (acting), (202) 693–6032.

OFFICE OF THE INSPECTOR GENERAL

Inspector General.—Scott S. Dahl, room S–5502, (202) 693–5100.
  Deputy Inspector General.—Larry D. Turner, room S–5502, 693–5100.
Assistant Inspector General for—
  Audit.—Elliot P. Lewis, room S–5518, 693–5170.
  Labor Racketeering and Fraud Investigations.—Lester Fernandez, room S–5014, 693–7034.
  Legal Services.—Howard L. Shapiro, room S–5506, 693–5116.
  Management and Policy.—Thomas Williams, room S–5028, 693–5191.

MINE SAFETY AND HEALTH ADMINISTRATION

1100 Wilson Boulevard, Arlington, VA 22209–3939, phone (202) 693–9414

fax 693–9401, http://www.msha.gov

Assistant Secretary.—Joseph A. Main, room 2322, 693–9402.
  Deputy Assistant Secretary for Policy.—Vacant, room 2321, 693–9407.
  Deputy Assistant Secretary for Operations.—Patricia W. Silvey, room 2324, 693–9642.
Director, Office of:
  Assessments, Accountability, Special Enforcement and Investigations.—Vacant, room 2518, 693–9702.

Program Education and Outreach Services.—Vacant, room 2317, 693–9422.
Program Evaluation and Information Resources.—Syed Hafeez (acting), room 2300, 693–9750.
Standards, Regulations and Variances (OSRV).—Sheila McConnell (acting), room 2313, 693–9440.
Technical Support.—Vacant, room 2330, 693–9470.

COAL MINE SAFETY AND HEALTH

Administrator.—Kevin Stricklin, room 2424 (202) 693–9500.
Deputy Administrator.—Charles J. Thomas (acting), room 2426, 693–9503.

METAL AND NONMETAL MINE SAFETY AND HEALTH

Administrator.—Neal H. Merrifield, room 2436 (202) 693–9600.
Deputy Administrator for Metal and Nonmetal.—Marvin Lichtenfels, room 2437, 693–9645.

EDUCATIONAL POLICY AND DEVELOPMENT

Director.—Jeffrey A. Duncan, room 2148 (202) 693–9570.
Administration and Management (A&M).—Eugene F. Hubbard, room 2125, 693–9802.

OCCUPATIONAL SAFETY AND HEALTH ADMINISTRATION

Assistant Secretary.—David Michaels, room S–2315 (202) 693–2000.
Deputy Assistant Secretaries: Jordan Barab, Dorothy Dougherty, 693–2000.
Chief of Staff.—Kirk Sander, 693–2000.
Senior Policy Advisor.—Deborah Berkowitz, 693–2000.
Director of:
   Administrative Programs.—Kimberly A. Locey, 693–1600.
   Communications.—Frank Meilinger, 693–1999.
   Construction.—Jim Maddux, 693–2100.
   Cooperative and State Programs.—Doug Kalinowski, 693–2200.
   Enforcement Programs.—Thomas Galassi, 693–2100.
   Technology Support and Emergency Management.—Amanda Edens, 693–2300.
   Standards and Guidance.—Bill Perry, 693–1950.
   Whistleblower Protection Programs.—MaryAnn Garrahan, 693–2199.

OFFICE OF PUBLIC AFFAIRS

Senior Advisor for Communications and Public Affairs.—Carl Fillichio, room S–2514 (202) 693–4676.
Senior Managing Directors: G. Stephen Barr, Dori Henry (acting).

REGIONAL OFFICES

Region I.—Boston.
   Regional Director.—Ted Fitzgerald, JFK Federal Building, Government Center, 25 New Sudbury Street, Room 525–A, Boston, MA 02203 (617) 565–2075.
Region III.—Philadelphia.
   Regional Director.—Leni Uddyback-Fortson, Curtis Center, 170 South Independence Mall West, Suite 633 East, Philadelphia, PA 19106–3306 (215) 861–5102.
Region IV.—Atlanta.
   Regional Director.—Michael D'Aquino, Atlanta Federal Center, 61 Forsyth, SW., Suite 6B75, Atlanta, GA 30303 (678) 237–0630.
Region V.—Chicago.
   Regional Director.—Scott Allen, 230 South Dearborn Street, Room 3194, Chicago, IL 60604 (312) 353–4727.
Region VI.—Dallas.
   Regional Director.—Diana Petterson, 525 Griffin Street, Room 734, Dallas, TX 75202 (972) 850–4710.
Region IX.—California.
   Regional Director.—Leo Kay, 90 7th Street, Suite 2–650, San Francisco, CA 94103–1516 (415) 625–2630.

OFFICE OF SMALL AND DISADVANTAGED BUSINESS UTILIZATION

Director.—Sonya Carrion, N–6432 (202) 693–7299.

OFFICE OF THE SOLICITOR

Solicitor.—M. Patricia Smith, room S–2002 (202) 693–5260.
Deputy Solicitor.—Deborah Greenfield.
Deputy Solicitor for National Operations.—Susan Harthill, 693–5260.
Deputy Solicitor for Regional Enforcement.—Katherine Bissell, 693–5260.
Senior Advisors: Craig Hukill, Edward Sieger.
Special Assistant.—Kerry O'Brien.

DIVISION OF BLACK LUNG AND LONGSHORE LEGAL SERVICES

Associate Solicitor.—Rae Ellen James, room N–2117 (202) 693–5660.
Deputy Associate Solicitor.—Maia Fisher.
Counsel for Administrative Litigation and Legal Advice.—Michael J. Rutledge.
Appellate Litigation.—Gary K. Stearman.
Enforcement and Appellate Litigation.—Sean G. Bajkowski.
Longshore.—Mark A. Reinhalter.
Regulations and Legislation.—Patricia M. Nece.

DIVISION OF CIVIL RIGHTS AND LABOR-MANAGEMENT

Associate Solicitor.—Christopher B. Wilkinson, room N–2474 (202) 693–5740.
Deputy Associate Solicitor.—Beverly Dankowitz.
Counsel for Civil Rights and Appellate Litigation.—Radine Legum.
Interpretation and Advice.—Kier Bickerstaff.
Litigation and Regional Coordination.—Consuela Pinto.
LMRDA Advice.—Clinton Wolcott.
LMRDA Programs.—Sharon E. Hanley.

DIVISION OF EMPLOYMENT AND TRAINING LEGAL SERVICES

Associate Solicitor.—Jeffrey L. Nesvet, room N–2101 (202) 693–5710.
Deputy Associate Solicitor.—Jonathan H. Waxman, 693–5730.
Counsel for Employment and Training Advice.—Robert P. Hines.
Immigration Programs.—Nora Carroll.
International Affairs and USERRA.—Katy Mastman.
Litigation.—Harry L. Sheinfeld.

DIVISION OF FAIR LABOR STANDARDS

Associate Solicitor.—Jennifer S. Brand, room N–2716 (202) 693–5555.
Deputy Associate Solicitor.—William C. Lesser.
Counsel for Appellate Litigation.—Paul L. Frieden.
Contract Labor Standards.—Jonathan T. Rees.
Legal Advice.—Lynn McIntosh.
Trial Litigation.—Jonathan M. Kronheim.
Whistleblower Programs.—Megan E. Guenther.

DIVISION OF FEDERAL EMPLOYEE AND ENERGY WORKERS COMPENSATION

Associate Solicitor.—Thomas G. Giblin (acting), room S–4325 (202) 693–5320.
Deputy Associate Solicitor.—Alexandra Tsiros (acting).
Counsel for Claims and Compensation.—Catherine P. Carter.
Energy Employees Compensation.—Sheldon O. Turley, Jr.
FECA Subrogation.—Alexandra Tsiros.

DIVISION OF MANAGEMENT AND ADMINISTRATIVE LEGAL SERVICES

Associate Solicitor.—Rose Marie L. Audette, room N–2420 (202) 693–5405.

Deputy Associate Solicitors: Allen K. Goshi, Susan E. Howe.
Counsel for Appropriations.—Omyra Ramsingh.
Employment Law.—James V. Blair.
FOIA and Information Law.—Joseph J. Plick.
FOIA Appeals, Paperwork Reduction Act and Federal Records Act.—Ray Mitten, Jr.
Procurement and Contracts.—David Koeppel.
Chief, Human Resources Office.—Michael Parrish.
Chief, Financial Management Office.—Debra Daniels.
Chief, Legal Technology Unit.—Denise Hoffman.
Director, Office of Information Services.—Ramona Oliver.

DIVISION OF MINE SAFETY AND HEALTH

1100 Wilson Boulevard, 22nd Floor, Arlington, VA 22209

Associate Solicitor.—Heidi W. Strassler, room 2222 (202) 693–9333.
Deputy Associate Solicitor.—Thomas A. Paige.
Counsel for Appellate Litigation.—W. Christian Schumann.
Standards and Legal Advice.—April E. Nelson.
Trial Litigation: Derek Baxter, Jason Grover.

DIVISION OF OCCUPATIONAL SAFETY AND HEALTH

Associate Solicitor.—Ann S. Rosenthal, room S–4004 (202) 693–5452.
Deputy Associate Solicitor.—Ian Thomas Moar.
Counsel for Appellate Litigation: Charles F. James, Heather Phillips.
Health Standards.—Nathan Spiller.
Regional Litigation and Legal Advice. Orlando J. Pannocchia, Robert W. Swain.
Safety Standards.—Edmund Baird.
Special Litigation.—Vacant.

DIVISION OF PLAN BENEFITS SECURITY

Associate Solicitor.—William Scott, room N–4611 (202) 693–5600.
Deputy Associate Solicitor.—Joanne Roskey.
Counsel for Appellate and Special Litigation.—Elizabeth Hopkins.
Fiduciary Litigation.—Risa D. Sandler.
Financial Litigation.—Michael Schloss.
General Litigation.—Leslie Canfield Perlman.
Regulations.—William White Taylor.

OFFICE OF LEGAL COUNSEL

Associate Solicitor.—Robert A. Shapiro, room N–2700 (202) 693–5300.
Counsel for Ethics.—Robert M. Sadler.
Legislative Affairs.—Jill M. Otte.
Honors Program Director.—Susan Hutton.

VETERANS' EMPLOYMENT AND TRAINING SERVICE

Assistant Secretary.—Teresa W. Gerton (acting), room S–1325 (202) 693–4700.
Deputy Assistant Secretary for Policy.—Teresa W. Gerton, 693–4700.
Deputy Assistant Secretary for Operations and Management.—Ralph Charlip, 693–4700.
Chief of Staff.—Michael Bocchini, 693–4735.
Executive Assistant.—Ann Dubois, 693–4710.
Staff Assistant.—Linda Powe, 693–4748.
Senior Advisors: Gordon Burke, 693–4707; Stephen Shapiro, 693–4761.
Director, Office of:
    Agency Management and Budget.—Maria Temiquel, 693–4706.
    National Programs.—Ruth Samardick, 693–4749.
    Strategic Outreach.—Tim Green, 693–4723.

REGIONAL OFFICES

Administrators:
  Atlanta: Maurice Buchanan (404) 665–4340.
  Boston: Vacant (617) 565–2080.
  Chicago: Heather Higgins (312) 353–4932.
  Dallas: Robert Creel (972) 850–4718.
  Philadelphia: Timothy Crowley (215) 861–5385.
  San Francisco: Alfred Kwok (415) 625–7670.

WOMEN'S BUREAU

Director.—Latifa Lyles, room S–3002 (202) 693–6719.
  Deputy Directors: Joan Harrigan-Farrelly, room S–3002, 693–6712; Pronita Gupta, room S–3002, 693–6762.
  Chief, Office of:
    Information and Support Services.—Paris M. Mack, room S–3002, 693–6754.
    Policy and Programs.—Tiffany Boiman, room S–3002, 693–6753.

OFFICE OF WORKERS' COMPENSATION PROGRAMS

Director.—Leonard Howie, room S–3524 (202) 343–5580.
  Chief of Staff.—Donna Kramer, room S–3229, 343–5580.
  Deputy Director.—Gary Steinberg, room S–3524, 343–5580.
  Director, Division of Financial Administration.—Sam Shellenberger, room 3524, 343–5580.
  Deputy Director.—Zoya Kaplan, room S–3524, 343–5580.
  Director, Division of Administration and Operations.—Vincent Alvarez (acting), room S–3201 (202) 354–5580.
  Deputy Director.—Vincent Alvarez, room S–3201, 354–5580.
  Director, Division of Federal Employees' Compensation.—Douglas Fitzgerald, room S–3229 (202) 693–0040.
  Director, Division of Longshore and Harbor Workers' Compensation.—Antonio Rios, room C–4319, 693–0038.
  Director, Division of Coal Mine Workers' Compensation.—Michael Chance, room C–3520, 693–0046.
  Director, Division of Energy Employees Occupational Illness Compensation.—Rachel Leiton, room C–3317, 693–0081.
  Regional Directors:
    Mid-Atlantic Region.—John McKenna (267) 687–4160.
    Midwest Region.—Robert Sullivan (312) 789–2800.
    Pacific Region.—Sharon Tyler (415) 241–3300.
    Northeast Region.—Zev Sapir (212) 863–0800.
    Southeast Region.—Magdalena Fernandez (904) 366–0100.
    Southwest Region.—Dean Woodard (214) 749–2320.

OFFICE OF LABOR-MANAGEMENT STANDARDS

Director.—Michael J. Hayes, room N–5603 (202) 692–0202.
  Deputy Director.—Andrew Auerbach, room N–5603 (202) 693–1203.
  Director of Field Operations.—Stephen Willertz, room N–5119, 693–1182.
  Regional Directors:
    Central Region.—Daniel LaFond (414) 297–1504.
    Northeastern Region.—Peter Papinchak (215) 861–4822.
    Southern Region.—Daniel Cherry (504) 589–6174.
    Western Region.—Jena de Mers Raney (720) 264–3122.
  Division of:
    Enforcement.—Patricia Fox, room N–5119, 693–1204.
    Interpretations and Standards.—Andrew Davis, room N–5609, 693–1254.
    Planning, Management and Technology.—Deborah Becker, room N–5613, 693–0605.
    Reports, Disclosure and Audits.—Lorenzo Harrison, room N–5609, 693–1299.
    Statutory Programs.—Ann Comer, room N–5112, 693–1193.

WAGE AND HOUR DIVISION

Administrator.—David Weil, room S–3502 (202) 693–0051.

Deputy Administrator.—Laura A. Fortman, room S–3502, 693–0051.
Chief of Staff.—Tony Martinez, room S–3502, 693–0686.
Senior Advisors: Joe McNeamey, room S–3502, 693–1255; Becky Ogle, room S–3502, 693–1032.
Senior Policy Advisor.—Tanya Goldman, room S–3502, 693–1245.
Policy Advisor.—Laura Tatum, room S–3502, 693–1199.
Deputy Administrator for Program Operations.—Patricia Davidson, room S–3502, 693–0663.
Assistant Administrator, Office of:
  Government Contracts.—Michael Lazzeri, room S–3502, 693–1283.
  Planning, Performance, Evaluation and Communications.—Ann Lichter, room S–3502, 693–0621.
  Policy.—Vacant, room S 3502, 693–0597.

OFFICE OF FEDERAL CONTRACT COMPLIANCE PROGRAMS

Director.—Patricia A. Shiu, room C–3325 (202) 693–0101.
Deputy Directors: Thomas M. Dowd, Patrick O. Patterson, room C–3325, 693–0101.
Chief of Staff.—Claudia Gordon, room C–3325, 693–0101.
Senior Civil Rights Advisor.—Donna R. Lenhoff, room C–3325, 693–0101.
Senior Policy Advisor.—Marva James (404) 893–4545.
Special Assistant.—Lissette Geán, room C–3325, 693–0101.
Program Management Specialist.—Kimberly Brummett, room C–3325, 693–0101.
Director, Division of:
  Management and Administrative Programs.—Heidi M. Casta (acting), room C–3315, 693–0119.
  Policy and Program Development.—Debra A. Carr, room N–3422, 693–0105.
  Program Operations.—Marika Litras, room N–3408, 693–0106.

DEPARTMENT OF HEALTH AND HUMAN SERVICES

200 Independence Avenue, SW., 20201, http://www.hhs.gov

SYLVIA M. BURWELL, Secretary of Health and Human Services; born in Hinton, West Virginia; education: A.B. from Harvard University and a B.A. from Oxford University (Rhodes Scholar); Director of the Office of Management and Budget (OMB); President of the Walmart Foundation in Bentonville, Arkansas; President of the Global Development Program at the Bill & Melinda Gates Foundation in Seattle, Washington; Deputy Director of OMB; Deputy Chief of Staff to the President; Chief of Staff to the Secretary of the Treasury; Staff Director of the National Economic Council. Nominated by President Barack Obama to become the 21st Secretary of Health and Human Services, confirmed by the U.S. Senate on June 9, 2014.

OFFICE OF THE SECRETARY

Secretary of Health and Human Services.—Sylvia M. Burwell (202) 690–7000.
Executive Assistant to the Secretary.—Lynda M. Gyles.

OFFICE OF THE DEPUTY SECRETARY

Chief of Staff.—Alistair Fitzpayne (202) 690–8157.
Deputy Chief of Staff.—Dawn O'Connell, 690–8157.
Deputy Secretary.—Mary K. Wakefield (acting), 690–6133.
Executive Secretary.—Madhura Valverde, 690–5627.
Deputy Executive Secretary.—Oliver Potts, 690–5627.
Director, Intergovernmental Affairs.—Emily Barson (acting), 690–6060.
Chair, Departmental Appeals Board.—Constance Tobias (202) 565–0220.

ASSISTANT SECRETARY FOR ADMINISTRATION AND MANAGEMENT

Assistant Secretary.—E.J. Holland, Jr. (202) 690–7431.
Deputy Assistant Secretary for—
    Human Resources.*—John W Gill, 690–6191.
    Security and Strategic Information.*—Patricia Long, 690–5756.
    Chief Information Officer.*—Frank Baitman, 690–6162.
    Director, Office of Equal Employment Opportunity and Compliance Operations.*—Cynthia Richardson-Crooks (202) 619–1564.
    Director, Office of Budget Management and Transformation.*—Michael Yea, 690–7431.

PROGRAM SUPPORT CENTER

5600 Fishers Lane, Rockville, MD 20857; 7700 Wisconsin Avenue, Bethesda, MD 20852

Deputy Assistant Secretary.—Paul S. Bartley (301) 492–4600.
Administration Operations Portfolio.—Allen Sample (301) 443–2516.
Occupational Health Portfolio.—Dr. Michelle Smith-Jefferies (acting), (301) 492–5410.
Financial Management Portfolio.—William McCabe, 492–4950.
Procurement Management Portfolio.—William McCabe (acting), 492–4950.
Real Estate and Logistics Portfolio.—Genevieve Hanson (202) 401–1437.

ASSISTANT SECRETARY FOR LEGISLATION

Assistant Secretary.—Jim Esquea (202) 690–7627.
Deputy Assistant Secretary for—
    Congressional Liaison.*—Fatima Cuevas, 690–6786.
    Discretionary Health Programs.*—Sara Singleton, 690–7450.

Human Services Programs.—Sonja Nesbit, 690–6311.
Mandatory Health Programs.—Bridgett Taylor, 690–7450.

ASSISTANT SECRETARY FOR PLANNING AND EVALUATION

Assistant Secretary for Planning and Evaluation.—Richard Frank (202) 690–7858.
Principal Deputy Assistant Secretary.—Jennifer Cannistra, 690–7858.
Deputy Assistant Secretary for—
  Disability and Long Term Care.—Linda Elam, 690–6443.
  Health Policy.—Arnold Epstein, 690–6870.
  Human Services Policy.—Charles Homer, 690–7409.
  Science and Data Policy.—Jim Scanlon, 690–7100.

ASSISTANT SECRETARY FOR PUBLIC AFFAIRS

Assistant Secretary.—Kevin Griffis (202) 401–2281.
Principal Deputy Assistant Secretary.—Marissa Padilla (202) 205–4347.
Deputy Assistant Secretary for—
  Health Care.—Lauren Crawford, 690–7048, fax 690–6247.
  Human Services.—Mark Weber (202) 260–6412, fax 690–6247.
  Public Health.—Bill Hall (acting), 690–6344, fax 690–6247.
Executive Officer/Deputy Agency Chief FOIA Officer.—Catherine Teti (202) 205–3592.
Director, Division of Freedom of Information/Privacy.—Michael Marquis, 260–7100.

ASSISTANT SECRETARY FOR PREPAREDNESS AND RESPONSE

Assistant Secretary.—Dr. Nicole Lurie (202) 205–2882.
Principal Deputy Assistant Secretary.—Edward Gabriel, 205–2882.
Deputy Assistant Secretary and Director, Office of:
  Biomedical Advanced Research and Development Authority.—Dr. Robin Robinson, 260–1200.
  Emergency Management.—Don Boyce, 205–8387.
  Policy and Planning.—Dr. Lisa Kaplowitz, 260–1202.

ASSISTANT SECRETARY FOR FINANCIAL RESOURCES

Assistant Secretary.—Ellen G. Murray (202) 690–6396.
Principal Deputy Assistant Secretary.—Vacant, 690–6061.
Senior Advisor.—John Gentile, 690–7512.
Deputy Assistant Secretary for—
  Budget.—Norris Cochran, 690–7393.
  Finance.—Shelia Conley, 690–7084.
  Grants.—Amy Haseltine, 690–6377.

OFFICE FOR CIVIL RIGHTS

Director.—Jocelyn Samuels (202) 619–0403.
Chief of Staff and Senior Advisor.—AJ Pearlman, 619–0403.
Deputy Director for—
  Civil Rights Division.—Robinsue Frohboese, 619–0403.
  Operations and Resources Division.—Steve Novy, 619–0403.
  Health Information Privacy.—Christina Heide (acting), 619–0403.
Toll Free Voice Number (Nationwide).—1–800–368–1019.
Toll Free TDD Number (Nationwide).—1–800–527–7697.

OFFICE OF THE GENERAL COUNSEL
fax [Immediate Office] 690–7998

General Counsel.—William B. Schultz.
  Deputy General Counsels: Jeffrey Davis, Peggy Dotzel, David Horowitz, Gia Lee (202) 690–7741.
  Senior Advisors to the General Counsel: Gemma Flamberg, Elizabeth Gianturco, Laura Stuber, 690–7741.

Associate General Counsels for—
  Centers for Medicare and Medicaid Division.—Janice Hoffman, 619–0150.
  Children, Family and Aging Division.—Robert Keith, 690–8005.
  Civil Rights Division.—Edwin Woo, 619–2777.
  Ethics Division/Special Counsel for Ethics.—Elizabeth Fischmann (acting), 690–7258.
  Food and Drug Division.—Elizabeth Dickinson (301) 796–3978.
  General Law Division.—Dan Barry, 619–0150.
  Legislation Division.—Edith Blackwell, 690–7773.
  Public Health Division.—David Benor (301) 443–2644.

OFFICE OF GLOBAL HEALTH AFFAIRS

Director.—Jimmy Kolker (202) 690–6174.

OFFICE OF THE INSPECTOR GENERAL
330 Independence Avenue, SW., 20201

Principal Deputy Inspector General.—Joanne M. Chiedi (202) 619–3148.
  Chief Counsel to the Inspector General.—Gregory E. Demske, 619–0568.
  Deputy Inspector General for Audit Services.—Gloria L. Jarmon, 619–3155.
  Deputy Inspectors for—
  Evaluation and Inspections.—Suzanne Murrin, 619–0480.
  Investigations.—Gary L. Cantrell, 205–4081.
  Management and Policy.—Robert Owens, 205–9117.
  Director, External Affairs.—Christopher Seagle, 206–7006.

OFFICE OF MEDICARE HEARINGS AND APPEALS

Chief Administrative Law Judge.—Nancy J. Griswold (703) 235–0635.
  Deputy Chief Administrative Law Judge.—C. F. Moore, 235–0635.
  Director of Programs.—Eileen McDaniel, 235–0635.

OFFICE OF THE NATIONAL COORDINATOR FOR HEALTH
INFORMATION TECHNOLOGY

National Coordinator for Health Information Technology.—Karen B. DeSalvo, M.D., M.P.H., M.Sc. (202) 690–7151.

OFFICE OF THE ASSISTANT SECRETARY FOR HEALTH

Assistant Secretary for Health.—Vacant (202) 690–7694.
  Senior Executive Assistant to the Assistant Secretary for Health.—Dinah Bembo, 690–7694.
  Principal Deputy Assistant Secretary for Health.—Wanda K. Jones, DrPH, 401–8034.
  The Surgeon General.—VADM Vivek H. Murthy, M.D., MBA (301) 443–4000.
  Deputy Assistant Secretary, Office of.
    Disease Prevention and Health Promotion.—Don Wright, M.D., M.P.H. (240) 453–8280.
    HIV/AIDS and Infectious Disease Policy.—Ronald O. Valdiserri, M.D., M.P.H. (202) 690–5560.
    Minority Health.—J. Nadine Gracia, M.D. (240) 453–6179.
    National Vaccine Program.—Bruce Gellin, M.D., M.P.H. (202) 205–5294.
    Population Affairs.—Susan Moskosky (acting), (240) 453–2805.
    Science and Medicine.—Anand K. Parekh, M.D., M.P.H. (202) 260–2873.
    Women's Health.—Nancy C. Lee, M.D. (202) 690–7650.
  Director, Office of:
    Adolescent Health.—Evelyn Kappeler (240) 453–2837.
    Communications.—Jonathan Beeton (202) 205–0143.
    Human Research Protections.—Jerry Menikoff, M.D., J.D. (240) 453–6900.
    Research Integrity.—David Wright, M.D., M.P.H. (301) 443–3400.
  Executive Director of:
    President's Council on Fitness, Sports and Nutrition.—Shellie Pfohl (240) 276–9567.
    Presidential Commission for the Study of Bioethical Issues.—Dr. Lisa Lee (202) 233–3960.
  Regional Administrator for—
    Region I: CT, ME, MA, NH, RI, VT.—Betsy Rosenfeld, JD–C (617) 565–1505.

Region II: NJ, NY, PR, VI.—Michelle Davis, Ph.D. (212) 742–7036.
Region III: DE, DC, MD, PA, VA, WV.—Dalton G. Paxman, Ph.D. (215) 861–4631.
Region IV: AL, FL, GA, KY, MS, NC, SC, TN.—RADM Clara H. Cobb, M.S., R.N. (404) 562–7894.
Region V: IL, IN, MI, MN, OH, WI.—CAPT James Lando (312) 886–3880.
Region VI: AR, LA, NM, OK, TX.—RADM Epi Elizondo, Ph.D., PA–C (214) 767–3879.
Region VII: IA, KS, MO, NE.—CAPT Jose Belardo, JD, MSW (816) 426–3294.
Region VIII: CO, MT, ND, SD, UT, WY.—CAPT Zachery Taylor, M.D., M.S. (303) 844–7680.
Region IX: AZ, CA, HI, NV, Guam, American Samoa, CNMI, FSMI, RMI, Palau.—CAPT Nadine Simons, MS, RN (415) 437–8102.
Region X: AK, ID, OR, WA.—RADM Patrick O'Carroll, M.D., M.P.H., FACPM (206) 615–2469.

ADMINISTRATION FOR COMMUNITY LIVING

1 Massachusetts Avenue, NW., 20001

Assistant Secretary for Aging and Administrator, Administration for Community Living.—Kathy Greenlee (202) 401–4541.
Principal Deputy Administrator, Administration for Community Living.—Sharon Lewis (202) 401–4634.
Deputy Assistant Secretary for Aging.—Edwin L. Walker, 401–4634.
Commissioner, Administration on Disabilities.—Aaron Bishop, 401–4634.
Legislative Affairs.—Brian Lutz (202) 357–3530.
Chief of Staff.—Richard Nicholls, 357–3408.

ADMINISTRATION FOR CHILDREN AND FAMILIES

370 L'Enfant Promenade, SW., 20447 (202) 401–9200

Assistant Secretary.—Mark Greenberg (acting), (202) 401–5383.
Chief of Staff.—Jeff Hild, 401–5180.
Deputy Assistant Secretary and Inter-Departmental Liaison for Early Childhood Development.—Linda K. Smith, 401–9204.
Deputy Assistant Secretary for External Affairs.—Marianne McMullen, 401–9215.
Deputy Assistant Secretary for Administration.—Robert Noonan, 401–9238.
Commissioner for Administration on Children, Youth and Families.—Mark Greenberg (acting), 401–5383.
Commissioner, Administration for Native Americans.—Lillian Sparks, 690–5780.
Commissioner, Office of Child Support Enforcement.—Vicki Turetsky, 401–9369.
Associate Commissioner, Children's Bureau.—JooYeun Chang, 205–8626.
Associate Commissioner, Family and Youth Services Bureau.—William H. Bentley, 205–8102.
Associate Deputy Assistant Secretary for Early Childhood Development.—Shannon Rudisill, 401–9204.
Director, Regional Operations Staff.—James Murry (acting), 401–4802.
Senior Advisor to the Assistant Secretary.—Laura Irazarry, 401–6947.
Senior Advisor, Human Trafficking.—Katherine Chon, 401–9253.
Director, Office of:
  Child Care.—Rachel Schumacher, 690–6782.
  Community Services.—Jeannie Chaffin, 401–5039.
  Family Assistance.—Nisha Patel, 401–9283.
  Head Start.—Dr. Blanca Enriquez, 205–5782.
  Human Services Emergency Preparedness Response, U.S. Public Health Service Public Affairs.—CAPT Mary Riley, 401–4966.
  Legislative Affairs and Budget.—Matthew McKearn, 401–9223.
  Planning, Research and Evaluation.—Naomi Goldstein, 401–9220.
  Refugee Resettlement.—Bob Carey, 401–6945.

AGENCY FOR HEALTHCARE RESEARCH AND QUALITY (AHRQ)

Director.—Richard Kronick, Ph.D. (301) 427–1200.
Deputy Director.—Sharon B. Arnold, Ph.D., 427–1200.

AGENCY FOR TOXIC SUBSTANCES AND DISEASE REGISTRY
1600 Clifton Road, NE., Atlanta, GA 30333

Director.—Thomas R. Frieden, M.D., M.P.H. (404) 639–7000.
Principal Deputy Director.—Ileana Arias, Ph.D.

CENTER FOR DISEASE CONTROL AND PREVENTION
1600 Clifton Road, NE., Atlanta, GA 30333, phone (404) 639–7000

Director.—Thomas R. Frieden, M.D., M.P.H.
Principal Deputy Director.—Ileana Arias, Ph.D.
Chief Operating Officer.—Sherri A. Berger, M.S.P.H.
Chief of Staff.—Carmen Villar, M.S.W.
CDC Washington Director.—Karyn Richman, M.P.A. (acting), (202) 245–0600
Director, Office of:
 Equal Employment Opportunity.—Reginald R. Mebane, M.S.
 Minority Health and Health Equity.—Leandris Liburd, Ph.D., M.P.H., M.A.
 Program Performance and Evaluation.—Kathleen Ethier, Ph.D.
Associate Director for—
 Communication.—Katherine Lyon Daniel, Ph.D. (acting).
 Science.—Harold W. Jaffe, M.D., M.A.
 Policy.—John Auerbach, MBA (202) 245–0600.
Directors:
 Center for Global Health.—Thomas Kenyon, M.D., M.P.H. (404) 639–7420.
 National Institute for Occupational Safety and Health.—John Howard, M.D., M.P.H.,
  J.D. (202) 245–0625.
 Office of Public Health Preparedness and Response.—Stephen Redd, M.D. (RADM,
  USPHS), (404) 639–7405.
Deputy Director, Office of.
 Infectious Diseases.—Rima Khabbaz, M.D. (404) 639–2100.
 Non-Communicable Diseases, Injury and Environmental Health.—Robin Ikeda, M.D.,
  M.P.H. (RADM, USPHS), (770) 488–0608.
Directors:
 Center for Surveillance, Epidemiology and Laboratory Services.—Michael F. Iademarco,
  M.D. M.P.H. (CAPT, USPHS).
 National Center on Birth Defects and Developmental Disabilities.—Coleen Boyle, Ph.D.,
  M.S. (404) 498–3800.
Director, National Center for—
 Chronic Disease Prevention and Health Promotion.—Ursula Bauer, Ph.D., M.P.H. (770)
  488–5401.
 Emerging and Zoonotic Infectious Diseases.—Beth P. Bell, M.D., M.P.H. (404) 639–
  3967.
 Environmental Health/Agency for Toxic Substances and Disease Registry.—Pat Breysse,
  Ph.D. (770) 488–0604.
 Health Statistics.—Charles J. Rothwell, MBA, M.S.
 HIV/AIDS, Viral Hepatitis, STD, and TB Prevention.—Jonathan Mermin, M.D., M.P.H.,
  (404) 639–8000.
 Immunization and Respiratory Diseases.—Anne Schuchat, M.D. (RADM USPHS).
 Injury Prevention and Control.—Debra Houry, M.D., M.P.H. (770) 488–4696.
Deputy Director, Office of Public Health Scientific Services.—Chelsey Richards, M.D.,
 M.P.H., FACP (404) 498–6001.
Deputy Director, Office for State, Tribal, Local and Territorial Support.—Judith A. Monroe,
 M.D., FAAFP (404) 498–0300.

CENTER FOR FAITH-BASED AND NEIGHBORHOOD PARTNERSHIPS

Director.—Acacia Bamberg Salatti (202) 358–3595.

CENTERS FOR MEDICARE & MEDICAID SERVICES
200 Independence Avenue, SW., 20201, phone (202) 690–6726

Administrator.—Andrew M. Slavitt (acting).
Principal Deputy Administrator.—Patrick Conway (acting).
Chief Operating Officer.—Deborah Taylor (410) 786–3151.

Deputy Chief Operating Officer.—David Nelson, 786–3151.
Chief Actuary, Office of the Actuary.—Paul Spitalnic, 786–6374.
Deputy Administrator and Director, Center for—
　Consumer Information and Insurance Oversight.—Kevin Counihan (202) 260–6085.
　Medicaid and CHIP Services.—Victoria Wachino (202) 690–7428.
　Medicare.—Sean Cavanaugh (202) 205–5060.
　Program Integrity.—Shantanu Agrawal (410) 786–1795.
　Strategic Planning.—Deborah Taylor (acting), 786–3151.
Director, Center for Medicare and Medicaid Innovation.—Patrick Conway, 786–3151.
Director and CMS Chief Medical Officer, Center for Clinical Standards and Quality.—
　Patrick Conway, M.D., 786–3151.
Director and Chief Information Officer, Office of Information Services.—David Nelson,
　786–3151.
Director and Chief Administrative Officer, Office of Operations Management.—James Weber,
　786–1051.
Director, Office of:
　Acquisition and Grants Management.—Daniel Kane, 786–1391.
　Communications.—Lori Lodes (202) 205–9450.
　Enterprise Management.—Niall Brennan (202) 690–6627.
　Equal Opportunity and Civil Rights.—Arlene Austin (410) 786–5110.
　Federal Coordinated Health Care.—Tim Engelhardt (202) 260–1291.
　Financial Management.—Deborah Taylor, 786–5448.
　Legislation.—Megan O'Reilly, 690–5960.
　Minority Health.—Cara James, 786–2773.
　Public Engagement.—Vacant.
　Strategic Operations and Regulatory Affairs.—Kathleen Cantwell, 690–8390.
Consortium Administrator for—
　Financial Management and FFS Operations.—Nanette Foster Reilly (816) 426–5233.
　Medicaid and Children's Health Operations.—Jackie Garner (312) 886–6432.
　Medicare Health Plans Operations.—James T. Kerr (212) 616–2205.
　Quality Improvement and Survey and Certification Operations.—James R. Farris, M.D.
　　(214) 767–6427.

FOOD AND DRUG ADMINISTRATION
10903 New Hampshire Avenue, Silver Spring, MD 20993

Commissioner.—Stephen Ostroff, M.D. (acting), (301) 796–5000.
　Chief of Staff.—Thomas Kraus, J.D., 796–8583.
　The Executive Secretariat.—Martina Varnado, 796–8331.
　Counselor to the Commissioner.—Vacant.
Deputy Commissioner for—
　Foods and Veterinary Medicine.—Michael Taylor, J.D., 796–4500.
　Global Regulatory Operations and Policy.—Howard Sklamberg, J.D., 796–7460.
　Medical Products and Tobacco.—Robert Califf, M.D., 796–5017.
　Policy, Planning, and Legislation.—Jeremy Sharp, 796–8770.
Chiefs:
Counsel.—Liz Dickinson, J.D., 796–8540.
Information Officer.—Todd Simpson, 796–6700.
Scientist (Informatics).—Dr. Taha Kass-Hout, 796–4583.
Operating Officer.—Walter Harris, 796–4700.
Scientist.—Luciana Borio (acting), 796–4880.
Financial.—James Tyler, 796–4770.
Associate Commissioner for—
　External Affairs.—Lisa Turner, 796–3347.
　Foods and Veterinary Medicine.—Erik Mettler, 796–9254.
　International Programs.—Mary Lou Valdez, 796–8400.
　Legislation.—Dayle Cristinzio (acting), 796–8900.
　OGROP.—Dara Corrigan, 796–3363.
　Planning.—Malcolm Bertoni, 796–4850.
　Policy.—Leslie Kux, J.D., 796–4830.
　Public Health Strategy and Analysis.—Peter Lurie, M.D., M.P.H., 402–4431.
　Regulatory Affairs.—Melinda Plaisier, M.S.W., 796–8800.
　Special Medical Programs.—Jill Warner, J.D., 796–4810.
Director, Center for—
　Biologics Evaluation and Research.—Karen Midthun, M.D. (240) 402–8000.
　Center for Drug Evaluation and Research.—Janet Woodcock, M.D., 796–5400.

Devices and Radiological Health.—Jeffrey Shuren, M.D., J.D., 796–5900.
Food Safety and Applied Nutrition.—Susan Mayne, Ph.D. (240) 402–1600.
Office of Crisis Management.—Mark Russo (acting), 796–8250.
Office of Minority Health.—Jonca Bull, M.D., 796–4649.
Tobacco Products.—Mitch Zeller, J.D., 796–9200.
Veterinary Medicine.—Bernadette Dunham, D.V.M., Ph.D. (240) 276–9000.
Director, National Center for Toxicological Research.—William Slikker, Jr., Ph.D. (870) 543–7517.
Senior Advisor and Representative for Global Issues.—Murray M. Lumpkin, M.D., M.Sc., 796–4804.
Senior Advisor for Science, Innovation and Policy.—Vacant, 847–3530.
Senior Advisor to the Commissioner.—Bruce Kuhlik, 796–7064.

HEALTH RESOURCES AND SERVICES ADMINISTRATION
5600 Fishers Lane, Rockville, MD 20857

Administrator.—James Macrae (acting), (301) 443–2216.
Deputy Administrator.—Diana Espinosa, 443–2216.
Senior Advisor.—Vacant, 443–2216.
Senior Advisor for HIV/AIDS Policy.—Deborah Parham-Hopson, RN, RADM, USPHS, 443–2216.
Chief Public Health Officer.—Sarah Linde, M.D., RADM, USPHS, 443–2216.
Chief Operating Officer.—Wendy Ponton, 443–4244.
Federal Assistance Management.—Rick Goodman, 443–5877.
Health Workforce.—Rebecca Spitzgo, Ph.D., 443–5794.
Healthcare Systems.—Cheryl Dammons, 443–3300.
HIV/AIDS.—Laura Cheever, M.D. (acting), 443–1993.
Maternal and Child Health.—Michael Lu, M.D., 443–2170.
Primary Health Care.—Tonya Bowers, 594–4110.
Regional Operations.—Dennis Malcomson, 443–7070.
Rural Health Policy.—Tom Morris, 443–0835.
Director, Office of:
  Communications.—Martin Kramer, 443–3376.
  Equal Opportunity, Civil Rights and Diversity Management.—Anthony Archeval, 443–5636.
  Health Equity.—Michelle Allender-Smith, RN, 443–5323.
  Legislation.—Leslie Atkinson, 443–1890.
  Planning, Analysis and Evaluation.—Rebecca Slifkin, Ph.D., 443–3983.
  Women's Health.—Sabrina Matoff-Stepp, Ph.D., 443–8664.

INDIAN HEALTH SERVICE
801 Thompson Avenue, Rockville, MD 20852

Director.—Robert G. McSwain (acting), (301) 443–1083.
Deputy Director.—Vacant.
Deputy Director for—
  Field Operations.—Richie Grinnell.
  Intergovernmental Affairs.—Sandra Pattea.
  Management Operations.—Elizabeth Fowler.
Chief Medical Officer.—Susan V. Karol, M.D.
Senior Advisor.—Geoffrey Roth.
Director of:
  Clinical and Preventative Services.—Alec Thundercloud, M.D., 443–4644.
  Direct Service and Contracting Tribes.—Chris Buchanan, 443–1104.
  Environmental Health and Engineering.—Gary Hartz, 443–1247.
  Equal Employment Opportunity.—Sarah Nelson, 443–1108.
  Executive Secretariat.—Julie Czajkowski, 443–1011.
  Finance and Accounting.—Ann Church (acting), 443–1270.
  Information Technology.—Mark Rives, 443–0750.
  Legislative and Congressional Affairs.—June Tracy (acting), 443–7261.
  Management Services.—Terri Schmidt (acting), 443–6290.
  Public Affairs.—Theresa Eiseman, 443–3593.
  Public Health Support.—Francis Frazier (acting), 443–0222.
  Resource Access and Partnerships.—Carl Harper, 443–2694.

Tribal Self-Governance.—Benjamin Smith, 443–7821.
Urban Indian Health Programs.—Jennifer Cooper (acting), 443–4680.

NATIONAL INSTITUTES OF HEALTH
9000 Rockville Pike, Bethesda, MD 20892

Director.—Francis S. Collins, M.D., Ph.D. (301) 496–2433.
Deputy Director.—Lawrence Tabak, D.D.S., Ph.D., 496–7322.
Deputy Director for Science, Outreach, and Policy.—Kathy Hudson, Ph.D., 496–1455.
Director, Executive Secretariat.—Ann Brewer, RN, 496–1461.
Director, Office of Federal Advisory Committee Policy.—Jennifer Spaeth, 496–2123.
Executive Officer, Office of the Director.—LaVerne Y. Stringfield, 594–8231.
Chief Information Officer.—Andrea Norris, Ph.D., 496–5703.
Legal Advisor, Office of the General Counsel.—Barbara M. McGarey, J.D., 496–6043.
Deputy Director for—
  Extramural Research.—Sally J. Rockey, Ph.D., 496–1096.
  Intramural Research.—Michael M. Gottesman, M.D., 496–1921.
  Management.—Colleen Barros, 496–3271.
Director, Division of Program Coordination, Planning, and Strategic Initiatives.—James Anderson, M.D., Ph.D., 402–9852.
Director, Office of Acquisition and Logistics Management.—Diane Frasier, 496–4422.
AIDS Research.—Robert W. Eisinger, Ph.D. (acting), 496–0357.
Behavioral and Social Sciences Research.—Vacant.
Associate Director for Budget.—Neil Shapiro, 496–4477.
Associate Director of Communications and Public Liaison.—John T. Burklow, 496–4461.
Director, Office of:
  Disease Prevention.—David Murray, Ph.D., 496–1508.
  Research on Women's Health.—Janine Clayton, M.D., 402–1770.
  Research Services.—Alfred C. Johnson, Ph.D., 496–2215.
Associate Director of Science Policy.—Carrie Wolinetz, Ph.D. 496–2122.
Director, NIH Office of Ethics.—Holli Beckerman Jaffe, J.D., 402–6628.
Director, Office of:
  Equal Opportunity and Diversity Management.—Debra Chew, Esq., 496–6301.
  Financial Management.—Kenneth Stith, 402–8831.
  Human Resources.—Chris Major, 496–3592.
Associate Director for Legislative Policy and Analysis.—Adrienne Hallett, 496–3471.
Director, Office of:
  Management Assessment.—Glenda Conroy, 496–1873.
  Research Facilities Development and Operations.—Daniel Wheeland, 594–0999.
  Technology Transfer.—Vacant.
Directors:
  Eunice Kennedy Shriver National Institute of Child Health and Human Development.—Alan Guttmacher, M.D., 496–3454.
  Fogarty International Center.—Roger I. Glass, M.D., Ph.D., 496–1415.
  National Center for Advancing Translational Sciences.—Christopher Austin, M.D., 496–5793.
  National Center for Complementary and Integrative Health.—Josephine P. Briggs, M.D., 435-6826.
  National Institute on Minority Health and Health Disparities.—Vacant.
  National Library of Medicine.—Betsy Humphreys (acting) 496–6221.
  Warren Grant Magnuson Clinical Center.—John I. Gallin, M.D., 496–4114.
Director, Center for—
  Information Technology.—Andrea T. Norris, Ph.D., 496–5703.
  Scientific Review.—Richard Nakamura, Ph.D., 435–1114.
Director, National Institute on:
  Alcohol Abuse and Alcoholism.—George Koob, Ph.D., 443–3885.
  Aging.—Richard J. Hodes, M.D., 496–9265.
  Drug Abuse.—Nora D. Volkow, M.D., 443–6480.
Director, National Institute of:
  Allergy and Infectious Diseases.—Anthony S. Fauci, M.D., 496–2263.
  Arthritis and Musculoskeletal and Skin Diseases.—Stephen I. Katz, M.D., Ph.D., 496–4353.
  Biomedical Imaging and Bioengineering.—Roderic I. Pettigrew, Ph.D., M.D., 496–8859.
  Deafness and Other Communication Disorders.—James F. Battey, Jr., M.D., Ph.D., 402–0900.
  Dental and Craniofacial Research.—Martha Somerman, D.D.S., Ph.D., 496–3571.

Diabetes and Digestive and Kidney Diseases.—Griffin P. Rodgers, M.D., M.A.C.P., 496–5877.
Environmental Health Sciences.—Linda S. Birnbaum, Ph.D., D.A.B.T., A.T.S. (919) 541–3201.
Mental Health.—Thomas Insel, M.D., 443–3673.
Neurological Disorders and Stroke.—Walter Koroshetz, M.D., 496–9746.
Nursing Research.—Patricia A. Grady, Ph.D., RN, 496–8230.
Directors:
    National Cancer Institute.—Douglas Lowy, M.D. (acting), 496–5615.
    National Eye Institute.—Paul A. Sieving, M.D., Ph.D., 496–2234.
    National General Medical Sciences.—Jon Lorsch, Ph.D., 594–2172.
    National Heart, Lung and Blood Institute.—Gary Gibbons, M.D., 496–5166.
    National Human Genome Research Institute.—Eric Green, M.D., Ph.D., 496–0844.

SUBSTANCE ABUSE AND MENTAL HEALTH SERVICES ADMINISTRATION (SAMHSA)

1 Choke Cherry Road, Rockville, MD 20857

www.samhsa.gov

Administrator.—Pamela Hyde, room 8–1061 (240) 276–2000.
Principal Deputy Administrator.—Kana Enomoto, room 8–1059, 276–2000.
Director, Office of:
    Behavioral Health Equity.—Larke Huang, room 8–1051, 276–2014.
    Communications.—Marla Hendriksson, room 8–1033, 276–2130.
    Financial Resources.—Deepa Avula (acting), room 8–1083, 276–2200.
    Management, Technology, and Operations.—Mike Etzinger, room 7–1073, 276–1110.
    Policy, Planning, and Innovation.—Anne Herron (acting), room 8–1015, 276–2856.
Director, Center for—
    Behavioral Health Statistics and Quality.—Peter Delany, Ph.D., LCSW–C, room 2–1049, 276–1250.
    Mental Health Services.—Paolo del Vecchio, room 6–1057, 276–1310.
    Substance Abuse Prevention.—Frances M. Harding, room 4–1057, 276–2420.
    Substance Abuse Treatment.—Daryl Kade (acting), room 5–1015, 276–1660.

DEPARTMENT OF HOUSING AND URBAN DEVELOPMENT

Robert C. Weaver Federal Building, 451 Seventh Street, SW., 20410

phone (202) 708–1112, http://www.hud.gov

JULIÁN CASTRO, Democrat, of Washington, DC; born in San Antonio, TX, September 16, 1974; undergraduate degree from Stanford University in 1996; J.D. from Harvard Law School in 2000. Mayor of the City of San Antonio, TX; Member of the San Antonio City Council; Private Practice; Attorney at Akin, Gump, Strauss, Hauer & Feld. Married to Erica Lira Castro; daughter and son; nominated by President Barack Obama on May 22, 2014; confirmed by the U.S. Senate on July 9, 2014; sworn-in on July 28, 2014.

OFFICE OF THE SECRETARY

Secretary of Housing and Urban Development.—Julián Castro, room 10000 (202) 708–0417.
Chief of Staff.—Nealin Parker, 708–2713.
Deputies Chief of Staff: Jaime Castillo, 402–2613; Frances Gonzalez, 402–6801.
Executive Operations Officer.—Tawanna Preston, 708–3750.
Administrative Officer.—Frieda Epps, 708–3750.

OFFICE OF THE DEPUTY SECRETARY

Deputy Secretary.—Nani A. Coloretti, 708–0123, room 10100 (202) 708–0123.
Chief of Staff for the Deputy Secretary.—Vacant, room 10100, 708–0123.

ASSISTANT SECRETARY FOR COMMUNITY PLANNING AND DEVELOPMENT

Assistant Secretary.—Vacant.
General Deputy Assistant Secretary.—Clifford Taffet, room 7100 (202) 708–2690.
Deputy Assistant Secretary for—
　Economic Development.—Valerie Piper, room 7136, 708–2690.
　Grant Programs.—Marion McFadden, room 7204, 708–2111.
　Operations.—Frances Bush, room 7128, 402–7515.
　Special Needs.—Ann Oliva, room 7100, 708–2690.

ASSISTANT SECRETARY FOR CONGRESSIONAL AND INTERGOVERNMENTAL RELATIONS

Assistant Secretary.—Erika Mortisugu, room 10120 (202) 708–0005.
General Deputy Assistant Secretary.—Dominique McCoy, room 10120, 708–0005.
Deputy Assistant Secretary for—
　Congressional Relations.—Bernard Fulton, room 10120, 708–0005.
　Intergovernmental Relations.—Jennifer Leigh Szubrowski, room 10148, 708–0005.

ASSISTANT SECRETARY FOR FAIR HOUSING AND EQUAL OPPORTUNITY

Assistant Secretary.—Gustavo Velasquez, room 5100 (202) 708–4252.
General Deputy Assistant Secretary.—Bryan Greene, 708–4252.
Deputy Assistant Secretary for—
　Enforcement and Programs.—Sara Pratt (202) 619–8046.
　Operations and Management.—David Ziaya, 708–0768.
　Policy, Legislative Initiatives and Outreach.—George Williams, 708–1145.

ASSISTANT SECRETARY FOR HOUSING

Assistant Secretary/Federal Housing Commissioner.—Biniam Gebre (acting), room 9100 (202) 708–2601.
General Deputy Assistant Secretary.—Genger Charles (acting).
Associate General Deputy Assistant Secretary.—Laura Marin.
Deputy Assistant Secretary for—
  Finance and Budget.—John Rabil (202) 401–8800.
  Healthcare Programs.—Roger Miller, 708–0599.
  Housing Counseling.—Sarah Gerecke, 708–0317.
  Housing Operations.—Lori Michalski, 708–1104.
  Multifamily Housing Programs.—Benjamin Metcalf, 708–2495.
  Risk Management and Regulatory Affairs.—Frank Vetrano, 708–6401.
  Single Family Housing.—Kathleen Zadareky, 708–3175.

ASSISTANT SECRETARY FOR POLICY DEVELOPMENT AND RESEARCH

Assistant Secretary.—Katherine M. O'Regan, room 8100, 708–1600.
General Deputy Assistant Secretary.—Jean Lin Pao, room 8100, 708–1600.
Deputy Assistant Secretary for the Office of:
  Economic Affairs.—Kurt G. Usowski, room 8204, 708–3080.
  International and Philanthropic Innovation.—Salin Geevarghese, room 8138, 708–0770.
  Research, Evaluation, and Monitoring.—Calvin C. Johnson, room 8124, 708–4230.
Associate Deputy Assistant Secretary, Policy Development.—Todd Richardson, room 8106, 708–1537.

ASSISTANT SECRETARY FOR PUBLIC AFFAIRS

Assistant Secretary for Public Affairs.—Betsaida Alcantara (202) 708–0980.
General Deputy Assistant Secretary.—Brandon Friedman.
Deputy Assistant Secretary.—Jereon M. Brown.
Press Secretary.—Cameron French.

ASSISTANT SECRETARY FOR PUBLIC AND INDIAN HOUSING

Assistant Secretary.—Jemine A. Bryon (acting), room 4100 (202) 708–0950.
General Deputy Assistant Secretary.—Jemine A. Bryon, 708–0950.
Office of:
  Field Operations.—Unabyrd Wadhams, 708–4016.
  Native American Programs.—Roger J. Boyd (202) 401–7914.
  Policy, Planning and Legislative Initiatives.—Danielle Bastarache, 708–0713.
  Public Housing and Voucher Programs.—Milan Ozdinec, 708–1380.
  Public Housing Investments.—Dominique Blom (202) 402–8500.
  Real Estate Assessment Center.—Donald Lavoy (202) 475–7949.

OFFICE OF FIELD POLICY AND MANAGEMENT

Assistant Deputy Secretary.—Mary McBride, room 7108 (202) 708–2426.
Associate Assistant Deputy Secretary.—Nelson Bregon, room 7108 (202) 708–4415.
Office of Labor Standards and Enforcement.—J. David Reeves, James.D.Reeves@hud.gov (202) 402–6418.

GOVERNMENT NATIONAL MORTGAGE ASSOCIATION

President.—Theodore W. Tozer (202) 708–0926.
Executive Vice President.—Mary K. Kinney, 708–0926.
Senior Vice Presidents, Office of:
  Capital Markets.—John Getchis, 401–8970.
  Finance.—Thomas R. Weakland (acting), 708–2884.
  Issuer and Portfolio Management.—Michael Drayne, 708–4141.
  Securities Operations.—Thomas R. Weakland, 708–2884.
Senior Vice President and Chief Risk Officer.—Gregory A. Keith, 708–0926.
Enterprise Data and Technology Solutions.—Barbara Cooper-Jones, 708–0926.

CHIEF FINANCIAL OFFICER

Chief Financial Officer.—Brad Huther.
  Deputy Chief Financial Officer.—Joseph Hungate.
  Assistant Chief Financial Officers for—
    Accounting.—Nita Nigam.
    Budget.—Sarah Lyberg (acting).
    Financial Management.—Jerome A. Vaiana.
    Systems.—Jon Gant.

CHIEF INFORMATION OFFICER

Chief Information Officer.—Rafael C. Diaz, room 4160 (202) 708–0306.
  Deputy Chief Information Officer.—Kevin R. Cooke, Jr., room 4158, 708–0306.
  Deputy Chief Information Officer for IT Operations.—Carlos M. Segarra, Sr. (acting), room 4178 (202) 402–4407.
  Chief Information Security Officer.—Carlos M. Segarra, Sr., room 4178, 402–4407.

CHIEF PROCUREMENT OFFICER

Chief Procurement Officer.—Vacant, room 5280 (202) 708–0600.
  Deputy Chief Procurement Officer.—Keith Surber, room 5256, 708–1290.

GENERAL COUNSEL

General Counsel.—Helen Kanovsky, room 10110 (202) 708–2244.
  Principal Deputy General Counsel.—Tonya T. Robinson, room 10110, 708–2244.
  Deputy General Counsel for Housing Programs.—Elton Lester, room 10238 (202) 402–5280.
  Deputy General Counsel for Operations.—Linda M. Cruciani, room 10240 (202) 402–5108.
  Associate General Counsel for—
    Assisted Housing and Community Development.—Althea Forrester, room 8152, 708–0470.
    Ethics and Personnel Law.—Peter J. Constantine, room 3170, 708–2864.
    Fair Housing.—Jeanine Worden, room 10272, 708–2787.
    Finance and Administrative Law.—Kevin M. Simpson, room 8150, 708–2203.
    Insured Housing.—Millicent Potts, room 9226, 708–1274.
    Legislation and Regulations.—Camille E. Acevedo, room 10282, 708–1793.
    Litigation.—Nancy Christopher, room 10258, 708–0300.
    Program Enforcement.—Dane M. Narode, Portals Bldg. (202) 245–4141.
  Director, Departmental Enforcement Center.—Craig Clemmensen, Portals Bldg. (202) 245–4195.

INSPECTOR GENERAL

Inspector General.—David A. Montoya, room 8256 (202) 708–0430.
  Deputy Inspector General.—Helen Albert.
  Counsel to the Inspector General, Office of Legal Counsel.—Jeremy Kirkland, 708–1613.
  Assistant Inspector General, Office of:
    Audit.—Randy McGinnis, 708–0364.
    Investigation.—Joseph Clarke, 708–0390.
    Management and Technology.—Eddie Saffarinia, 708–0006.

OFFICE OF DEPARTMENTAL EQUAL EMPLOYMENT OPPORTUNITY

Director.—John P. Benison, room 2134 (202) 708–3362.

OFFICE OF THE CHIEF HUMAN CAPITAL OFFICER

Chief Human Capital Officer.—Towanda Brooks (acting), (202) 708–0940.
  Chief Performance Officer.—Joseph Smith (202) 402–2808.
  Office of:
    Executive Resources.—Juliette Middleton, 402–3058.
    Human Capital Services.—Felicia Purifoy, 402–2356.
  Chief Learning Officer.—Sheila Wright, 402–2355.

OFFICE OF LEAD HAZARD CONTROL AND HEALTHY HOMES

Director.—Matthew Ammon (202) 708–0310.
Deputy Director.—Michelle Miller.

SMALL AND DISADVANTAGED BUSINESS UTILIZATION

Director.—Vacant, room 2200 (202) 402–5477.

HUD REGIONAL ADMINISTRATORS

Region I.—Connecticut, Maine, Massachusetts, New Hampshire, Rhode Island, Vermont.
Regional Administrator.—Kristine Foye (acting), Federal Building, 10 Causeway Street, Room 301, Boston, MA 02222–1092 (617) 994–8223.
Region II.—New Jersey, New York.
Regional Administrator.—Holly Leicht, 26 Federal Plaza, Suite 3541, New York, NY 10278–0068 (212) 542–7109.
Region III.—Delaware, District of Columbia, Maryland, Pennsylvania, Virginia, West Virginia.
Regional Administrator.—Jane C.W. Vincent, The Wanamaker Building, 100 Penn Square East, Philadelphia, PA 19107–3380 (215) 656–0600.
Region IV.—Alabama, Florida, Georgia, Kentucky, Mississippi, North Carolina, Puerto Rico, South Carolina, Tennessee.
Regional Administrator.—Edward Jennings, Jr., Five Points Plaza, 40 Marietta Street, NW., 2nd Floor, Atlanta, GA 30303–2806 (687) 732–2008.
Region V.—Illinois, Indiana, Michigan, Minnesota, Ohio, Wisconsin.
Regional Administrator.—Antonio R. Riley, Ralph Metcalfe Federal Building, 77 West Jackson Boulevard, Chicago, IL 60604–3507 (312) 353–5680.
Region VI.—Arkansas, Louisiana, New Mexico, Oklahoma, Texas.
Regional Administrator.—Tammye H. Treviño, 801 Cherry Street, Fort Worth, TX 76113–2905 (817) 978–5965.
Region VII.—Iowa, Kansas, Missouri, Nebraska.
Regional Administrator.—Jennifer Tidwell, Gateway Tower II, 400 State Avenue, Room 507, Kansas City, KS 66101–2406 (913) 551–5440.
Region VIII.—Colorado, Montana, North Dakota, South Dakota, Utah, Wyoming.
Regional Administrator.—Rick M. Garcia, 1670 Broadway, Denver, CO 80202–4801 (303) 672–5440.
Region IX.—Arizona, California, Hawaii, Nevada.
Regional Administrator.—Ophelia Basgal, 600 Harrison Street, 3rd Floor, San Francisco, CA 94107–1300 (415) 489–6401.
Region X.—Alaska, Idaho, Oregon, Washington.
Regional Administrator.—William Block, Seattle Federal Office Building, 909 First Avenue, Suite 200, Seattle, WA 98104–1000 (206) 220–5101.

DEPARTMENT OF TRANSPORTATION

1200 New Jersey Avenue, SE., Washington, DC 20590

phone (202) 366–4000, http://www.dot.gov

ANTHONY R. FOXX, Secretary of Transportation; born in Charlotte, NC, April 30, 1971; education: J.D., New York University School of Law, B.A., Davidson College, Davidson, NC; professional: Mayor of Charlotte, NC from 2009–13; Deputy General Counsel, DesignLine, from 2009–13; Charlotte City Council At-Large Representative from 2005–09; Litigator, Hunton & Williams, from 2001–09; Staff Counsel to the U.S. House of Representatives Committee on the Judiciary from 1999–2001; Trial Attorney for the Civil Rights Division of the U.S. Department of Justice from 1997–99; Law Clerk for the U.S. Sixth Circuit Court of Appeals, 1997; family: married to Samara Foxx; two children: Hillary and Zachary; nominated by President Barack H. Obama to become the 17th Secretary of Transportation, and was confirmed by the U.S. Senate on June 27, 2013.

OFFICE OF THE SECRETARY

[Created by the act of October 15, 1966; codified under U.S.C. 49]

Secretary of Transportation.—Anthony Foxx, room W91–317 (202) 366–1111.
　Deputy Secretary.—Victor Mendez, 366–2222.
　Chief of Staff.—Dorval Carter (acting), 366–1103.
　　Deputy Chiefs of Staff: Dan Katz, 366–7209; Stephanie Jones, 366–6805.
　Under Secretary of Transportation for Policy.—Peter Rogoff, 366–4540.
　Director, Office of:
　　Civil Rights.—Stephanie Jones (acting), room W78–318, 366–4648.
　　Executive Secretariat.—Carol C. Darr, room W93–324, 366–4277.
　　Intelligence and Security.—Michael Lowder, room W56–302, 366–6525.
　　Small and Disadvantaged Business Utilization.—Brandon Neal, room W56–308, 366–1930.

ASSISTANT SECRETARY FOR ADMINISTRATION

Assistant Secretary.—Keith Washington (acting), room W80–322 (202) 366–2332.
　Deputy Assistant Secretary.—Keith Washington, W80–320, 366–2332.
　Director, Office of:
　　Facilities, Information and Asset Management.—Vacant, room W58–334, 366–9756.
　　Financial Management.—Marie Petrosino, room W81–306, 366–3967.
　　Hearings, Chief Administrative Law Judge.—Judge Ronnie A. Yoder, room E12–356, 366–2142.
　　Human Resource Management.—Cynthia Vaughan, room W81–302, 366–4088.
　　Security.—Louis Widawski, room W54–336, 366–4677.
　　Senior Procurement Executive.—Willie Smith, room W83–306, 366–4212.

ASSISTANT SECRETARY FOR AVIATION AND INTERNATIONAL AFFAIRS

Assistant Secretary.—Susan Kurland, room W88–314 (202) 366–8822.
　Deputy Assistant Secretaries: Brandon Belford, room W88–324; Susan McDermott, room W88–326, 366–4551.
　　Director, Office of:
　　　Aviation Analysis.—Todd Homan, room W86–481, 366–5903.
　　　International Aviation.—Paul Gretch, room W86–406, 366–2423.
　　　International Transportation and Trade.—Julie Abraham, room W88–306, 366–4398.

ASSISTANT SECRETARY FOR BUDGET AND PROGRAMS

Chief Financial Officer/Assistant Secretary.—Sylvia Garcia, room W95–330 (202) 366–9191.
Deputy Assistant Secretary.—Lana Hurdle, room W95–316, 366–9192.
Deputy Assistant Secretary for Finance and Budget.—Blair Anderson, room W93–302, 366–9191.
Deputy Chief Financial Officer.—David Rivait, room W95–320, 366–9192.
Director, Office of:
  Budget and Program Performance.—Laura Ziff, room W93–308, 366–4594.
  Financial Management.—Vacant, room W93–322, 366–1306.

ASSISTANT SECRETARY FOR GOVERNMENTAL AFFAIRS

Assistant Secretary.—Dana Gresham, room W85–326 (202) 366–4573.
Deputy Assistant Secretaries: Kevin Monroe, Patricia Readinger.
Associate Directors: Natalie Angelo, Michael Daley, Maria Elena Juarez, Danielle Owen.

OFFICE OF THE UNDER SECRETARY OF TRANSPORTATION FOR POLICY

Under Secretary of Transportation for Policy.—Peter Rogoff, room W80–308 (202) 366–4540.
Assistant Secretary for Policy.—Carlos Monje, room W82–306, 366–4544.
Deputy Assistant Secretaries for Policy: John Drake, room W82–312, 366–4005; Shoshana Lew, room W82–308, 366–1815.

GENERAL COUNSEL

General Counsel.—Kathryn Thomson, room W92–300, 366–4702.
Deputy General Counsels: Kristin Amerling, room W92–318, 366–4702; Judith Kaleta, room W92–312, 366–4713.
Associate General Counsel.—Vacant, room W92–320, 366–4702.
Assistant General Counsel for—
  Aviation Enforcement and Proceedings.—Blane A. Workie, room W96–322, 366–9345.
  General Law.—Terence Carlson, room W94–306, 366–9152.
  International Law.—Donald H. Horn, room W98–324, 366–2972.
  Legislation.—Thomas W. Herlihy, room W96–326, 366–4687.
  Litigation.—Paul M. Geier, room W94–310, 366–4731.
  Operations.—Ronald Jackson, room W96–304, 366–4710.
  Regulation and Enforcement.—Brett Jortland (acting), room W94–304, 366–9314.

INSPECTOR GENERAL

Inspector General.—Calvin L. Scovel III, room W70–300 (202) 366–1959.
Deputy Inspector General.—Ann Calvaresi Barr, 366–6767.
Principal Assistant Inspector General for—
  Auditing and Evaluation.—Lou Dixon, 366–8751.
  Investigations.—Michelle McVicker, 366–1967.
Deputy Principal Assistant Inspector General for—
  Audits.—Joseph Comé, 366–8751.
  Investigations.—William Owens, 366–1967.
Assistant Inspector General for—
  Acquisition and Procurement Audits.—Mary Kay Langan Feirson, 366–5225.
  Administration.—Eileen Ennis, 366–2704.
  Aviation Audits: Matthew Hampton, Charles Ward, 366–0500.
  Financial and Information Technology Audits.—Louis King, 366–1407.
  Legal, Legislative and External Affairs.—Brian A. Dettelbach, 366–1967.
  Surface Transportation Audits: Mitch Behm, Thomas Yatsco, 366–5630.

REGIONAL AUDIT OFFICES

Regional Program Directors:
  Tina Nysted, 61 Forsyth Street, SW., Suite 17T60, Atlanta, GA 30303 (404) 562–3770.
  Robin Koch, 61 Forsyth Street, SW., Suite 17T60, Atlanta, GA 30303 (404) 562–3770.

Scott Macey, 201 Mission Street, Suite 1750, San Francisco, CA 94105 (415) 744–3090.
Barry DeWeese, 201 Mission Street, Suite 1750, San Francisco, CA 94105 (415) 744–3090.
Darren Murphy, 915 Second Avenue, Room 644, Seattle, WA 98174 (206) 220–7754.
George Banks, 10 South Howard Street, Suite 4500, Baltimore, MD 21201 (410) 962–3612.
Kerry Barras, 819 Taylor Street, Room 13A42, Fort Worth, TX 76102 (817) 978–3545.

REGIONAL INVESTIGATIONS OFFICES

Special Agents-In-Charge:
Region I.—Todd Damiani, 55 Broadway, Room 1055, Cambridge, MA 02142 (617) 494–2701.
Region II.—Douglas Shoemaker, 201 Varick Street, Room 1161, New York, NY 10014 (212) 337–1250.
Region III.—Kathryn Jones, 409 3rd Street, SW., Room 301, Washington, DC 20024 (202) 366–7100.
Region IV.—Marlies Gonzalez, 510 Shotgun Road, Suite 220, Sunrise, FL 33326 (954) 382–6645.
Region V.—Tom Ullom (acting), 200 West Adams Street, Suite 300, Chicago, IL 60606 (312) 353–0106.
Region VI.—Max Smith, 819 Taylor Street, Room 13A42, Fort Worth, TX 76102 (817) 978–3236.
Region IX.—Bill Swallow, 17785 Center Court Drive, Suite 350, Cerritos, CA 90703 (562) 467–5360.

OFFICE OF PUBLIC AFFAIRS

Assistant to the Secretary and Director of Public Affairs.—Suzanne Emmerling, room W93–310 (202) 366–4312.
Deputy Director.—Susan Lagana, 366–1621.
Associate Director of Media Relations.—Vacant, 366–4570.
Director of Speechwriting and Research Division.—Vacant, room W93–319, 366–0679.

FEDERAL AVIATION ADMINISTRATION
800 Independence Avenue, SW., 20591 (202) 267–3484

Administrator.—Michael Huerta, 267–3111.
  Chief of Staff.—Vacant, 267–7416.
  Counselor to the Administrator.—Christopher Rocheleau, 267–3180.
  Senior Advisor to the Deputy Administrator.—Trish Fritz, 267–8208.
  Executive Assistant to the Administrator.—Sharon Harrison, 267–3111.
Deputy Administrator.—Michael Whitaker, 267–8111.
Assistant Administrator for Finance and Management.—Victoria Wassmer, 267–8627.
  Senior Advisor to Assistant Administrator for Finance and Management.—Paula Lewis, 267–4282.
  Acquisitions and Business Services.—Nathan Tash, 267–7222.
  Financial Services/CFO.—Mark House, 267–9105.
  Information Services/CIO.—Tina Amereihn, 493–4570.
  Regions and Center Operations.—Ray Towles, 267–9011
  Regional Administrators:
    Alaskan.—Kerry Long (907) 271–5645.
    Central.—Joseph N. Miniace (816) 329–3050.
    Eastern.—Carmine Gallo (718) 553–3000.
    Great Lakes.—Barry D. Cooper (847) 294–7294.
    New England.—Amy Lind Corbett (781) 238–7020.
    Northwest Mountain.—Kathryn Vernon (425) 227–2001.
    Southern.—Dennis Roberts (404) 305–5000.
    Southwest.—Kelvin Solco (817) 222–5001.
    Western-Pacific.—Glenn A. Martin (A), (310) 725–3550.
  Director, Aviation Logistics.—David Foley, 267–9011.
  Director, Mike Monroney Aeronautical Center.—Michelle Coppedge (405) 954–4521.
  Director of:
    Budget and Programs.—Carl Burrus, 267–8010.

Financial Analysis.—David Rickard, 267–7140.
Financial Operations.—Peter Basso, 267–8242.
Financial Reporting and Accountability.—Allison Ritman, 267–3018.
Investment Planning and Analysis.—Kristen Burnham, 493–5672.
Labor Analysis.—Rich McCormick, 267–5943.
Assistant Administrator for Civil Rights.—Mamie Mallory, 267–3254.
Deputy Assistant Administrator for Civil Rights.—Courtney Wilkerson, 267–3254.
Assistant Administrator for Policy, International Affairs and Environment.—Julie Oettinger, 267–3927.
Deputy Assistant Administrator.—Carl Burleson, 267–7924.
Executive Director of:
  Aviation Policy and Plans.—Nan Shellabarger, 267–3274.
  Environment and Energy.—Lourdes Maurice, 267–3576.
  International Affairs.—Carey Fagan, 385–8900.
Director of:
  Asia-Pacific.—Mark Reeves, 011–65–6575–9475.
  Europe, Africa, and Middle East.—Steve Creamer, 011–322–811–5159.
  Western Hemisphere.—Christopher Banks (acting), 385–8900.
Chief Counsel.—Marc Warren (acting), 267–3222.
Deputy Chief Counsel.—Marc Warren, 267–3773.
Director of Audit and Evaluation.—H. Clayton Foushee, 267–9440.
Assistant Administrator for Government and Industry Affairs.—Molly Harris (A), 267–3277.
Deputy Assistant Administrator.—Molly Harris, 267–8211.
Assistant Administrator for Human Resource Management.—Rickie Cannon, 267–3850.
Deputy Assistant Administrator.—Rickie Cannon, 267–3850.
Executive Director of:
  Accountability Board.—Maria Fernandez-Greczmiel, 267–3065.
  Employee and Labor Relations.—John McFall, 267–5403.
  Human Resources Management Programs and Policies.—Angela Wilson (A), 267–3850.
  Regional Human Resource (HR) Services.—Rickie Cannon, 267–4028.
Director, Talent Development and Chief Learning Officer.—Melissa King, 267–9041.
Assistant Administrator for Communications.—Jenny Rosenberg, 267–3883.
Deputy Assistant Administrator for Public Affairs.—Laura Brown, 267–3883.
Deputy Assistant Administrator for Corporate Communications.—Deborah Green, 267–8859.
Assistant Administrator for Security and Hazardous Material.—Claudio Manno, 267–7211.
Deputy Assistant Administrator.—Thomas D. Ryan, 267–7211.
Director Office of:
  Emergency Operations, Communications, and Investigations.—Angela Stubblefield, 267–7576.
  Executive and Center Operations.—Victor Kemens, 267–3538.
  Hazardous Materials Safety.—Chris Glasow, 385–4904.
Director of:
  Joint Security and Hazardous Material Safety, Central.—Mary Alford (817) 222–5700.
  Joint Security and Hazardous Material Safety, East.—Wilie Gripper (404) 305–6750.
  Joint Security and Hazardous Material Safety, West.—Patricia Pausch (425) 227–2705.
Office of Security.—Bruce Herron, 493–5405.
Chief Operating Officer for Air Traffic Organization.—J. David Grizzle, 493–5602.
Deputy Chief Operating Officer.—Teri Bristol, 267–7224.
Vice President for—
  En Route and Oceanic Services.—Gregory Burke, 385–8501.
  Management Services.—Michael McCormick, 267–5724.
  Mission Support.—Elizabeth Ray, 267–8261.
  Program Management.—Chris Metts, 385–8343.
  Safety and Technical Training.—Joseph Teixeira, 267–3341.
  System Operations.—Nancy Kalinowski, 385–8704.
  Technical Operations.—Vaughn Turner, 267–3366.
  Terminal.—Walt Cochran, 385–8802.
Assistant Administrator for NextGen.—Edward Bolton, 267–7111.
Deputy Assistant Administrator.—Pamela Whitley, 267–7111.
Office of the Chief Scientist.—Steve Bradford, 267–7111.
Office of the Chief Scientist for Software.—Natesh Manikoth, 267–3250.
Director of:
  Advanced Concepts and Technology Development.—Paul Fontaine, 267–9250.
  Engineering Services.—Michele Merkle, 267–2708.
  Management Services.—Jaime Figueroa, 267–3837.
  NAS Lifecycle Integration.—J.C. Johns, 385–6724.
Director of Interagency Planning.—Gisele Mohler, 267–4693.

Systems Analysis and Modeling.—Joseph Post, 267–2766.
William J. Hughes Technical Center.—Dennis Filler (609) 485–6641.
Associate Administrator for Airports.—Eduardo A. Angeles, 267–9471.
Deputy Associate Administrator.—Benito Deleon, 267–9590.
Director of:
  Airport Compliance and Management Analysis.—Randall Fiertz, 267–3085.
  Airport Planning and Programming.—Elliott Black, 267–8775.
  Airport Safety and Standards.—Michael J. O'Donnell, 267–3053.
Associate Administrator for Commercial Space Transportation.—Dr. George C. Nield, 267–7793.
Deputy Associate Administrator.—Shana Dale, 267–7848.
Associate Administrator for Aviation Safety.—Margaret Gilligan, 267–3131.
Deputy Associate Administrator.—John J. Hickey, 267–7804.
Federal Air Surgeon.—James R. Fraser, 267–3535.
Director of:
  Aircraft Certification Service.—Dorenda Baker, 267–8235.
  Flight Standards Service.—John Allen, 267–8237.
  Office of Air Traffic Oversight.—Anthony Ferrante, 267–5202.
  Quality, Integration and Executive Service.—Sunny Lee Fanning, 493–5717.
  Rulemaking.—Lirio Liu (A), 267–9677.

FEDERAL HIGHWAY ADMINISTRATION

Washington Headquarters, 1200 New Jersey Avenue, SE., 20590–9898

Turner-Fairbank Highway Research Center (TFHRC)

6300 Georgetown Pike, McLean, VA 22201

Administrator.—Vacant.
  Deputy Administrator.—Greg Nadeau, 366–0650.
Associate Administrator/Director of TFHRC.—Michael F. Trentacoste, 493–3259.
Associate Administrator for Administration.—Sarah J. Shores, 366–0604.
Executive Director.—Jeffrey F. Paniati, 366–2242.
Chief Counsel.—Tom Echikson, 366–0740.
Chief Financial Officer.—Elissa K. Konove, 366–0622.
Associate Administrator for—
  Civil Rights.—Warren S. Whitlock, 366–0693.
  Federal Lands.—Bob Arnold, 366–9472.
  Infrastructure.—Walter Waidelich, 366–0116.
  Operations.—Jeffrey A. Lindley, 366–9210.
  Planning, Environment, and Realty.—Gloria M. Shepherd, 366–0116.
  Policy.—David Kim, 366–8169.
  Public Affairs.—Jane Mellow, 366–0660.
  Safety.—Tony T. Furst, 366–2288.

FIELD SERVICES

Organizationally report to Executive Director (HOA–3), Washington, DC

Director of Technical Services.—Amy Lucero, 12300 West Dakota Avenue, Suite 340, Lakewood, CO 80228 (720) 963–3246.
Director of:
  Field Services-North.—Martin C. Knopp, 10 South Howard Street, Baltimore, MD 21201–2819 (410) 962–0739.
  Field Services-South.—Derrell Turner, 61 Forsyth Street, SW., Suite 17T26, Atlanta, GA 30303–3104 (404) 562–3571.
  Field Services-West.—Janice Brown, 2520 West 4700 South, Suite 9C, Salt Lake City, UT 84118–1847 (720) 963–3730.
  Field Services-Mid America.—John Rohlf, 4749 Lincoln Mall Drive, Suite 600, Matteson, IL 60443 (605) 776–1000.

FEDERAL MOTOR CARRIER SAFETY ADMINISTRATION

Administrator.—Vacant, room W60–308 (202) 366–1927.
  Deputy Administrator.—Daphne Y. Jefferson, 366–1927.

Chief Safety Officer.—John Van Steenburg, 366–1927.
Chief Counsel.—T.F. Scott Darling III, 366–0349.
Associate Administrator for Field Operation.—Anne L. Collins, 366–2027.
Director, Office of:
  Communications.—Vacant, 366–8810.
  Governmental Affairs.—Trevor Dean, 366–1927.

FIELD OFFICES

Eastern Service Center (CT, DC, DE, MA, MD, ME, NJ, NH, NY, PA, PR, RI, VA, VT, WV).—802 Cromwell Park Drive, Suite N, Glen Burnie, MD 21061 (443) 703–2240.
Midwestern Service Center (IA, IL, IN, KS, MI, MO, MN, NE, OH, WI).—4749 Lincoln Mall Drive, Suite 300A, Matteson, IL 60443 (708) 283–3577.
Southern Service Center (AL, AR, FL, GA, KY, LA, MS, NC, NM, OK, SC, TN).—1800 Century Boulevard, Suite 1700, Atlanta, GA 30345 (404) 327–7400.
Western Service Center (American Samoa, AK, AZ, CA, CO, Guam, HI, ID, Mariana Islands, MT, ND, NV, NM, OR, SD, TX, UT, WA, WY).—Golden Hills Office Centre, 12600 W. Colfax Avenue, Suite B–300, Lakewood, CO 80215 (303) 407–2350.

FEDERAL RAILROAD ADMINISTRATION
1200 New Jersey Avenue, SE., Washington, DC 20590
http://www.fra.dot.gov

Administrator.—Sarah E. Feinberg (acting), room W30–308, 493–6014.
Deputy Administrator.—Vacant, room W32–308, 493–6015.
Executive Director.—Stacy Cummings, room W30–310, 493–6194.
Associate Administrator for—
  Administration.—Tami Riggs, room W34–332, 493–6301.
  Chief Financial Officer.—Rebecca Pennington, room W36–306, 440–2870.
  Railroad Policy and Development.—Paul Nissenbaum, room W38–328, 493–6312.
  Safety.—Robert Lauby (acting), room W35–306, 493–6474.
Chief Counsel.—Melissa Porter, room W31–320, 493–6034.
Communications and Legislative Affairs.—Kevin Thompson, room W31–326, 366–1299.
Director of:
  Budget.—Erin McCartney, room W36–306, 493–6454.
  Civil Rights.—Calvin Gibson, room W33–316, 493–6010.
  Financial Management.—Tiwalade Bello, room W34–308, 493–6163.
  Public Engagement.—Timothy Barkley, room W33–320, 493–1305.

REGIONAL OFFICES (RAILROAD SAFETY)

Region 1 (Northeastern).—Connecticut, Maine, Massachusetts, New Hampshire, New Jersey, New York, Rhode Island, Vermont.
  Regional Administrator.—Les Fiorenzo, Room 1077, 55 Broadway, Cambridge, MA 02142 (617) 494–3484.
Region 2 (Eastern).—Delaware, District of Columbia, Maryland, Pennsylvania, Virginia, West Virginia, Ohio.
  Regional Administrator.—Brian Hontz, 1510 Chester Pike, Baldwin Tower, Suite 660, Crum Lynne, PA 19022 (610) 521–8200.
Region 3 (Southern).—Kentucky, Tennessee, Mississippi, North Carolina, South Carolina, Georgia, Alabama, Florida.
  Regional Administrator.—Carmen Patriarca, 61 Forsyth Street, NW., Suite 16T20, Atlanta, GA 30303 (404) 562–3809.
Region 4 (Central).—Minnesota, Illinois, Indiana, Michigan, Wisconsin.
  Regional Administrator.—Steve Illich, 200 W. Adams Street, Chicago, IL 60606 (312) 353–6203.
Region 5 (Southwestern).—Arkansas, Louisiana, New Mexico, Oklahoma, Texas.
  Regional Administrator.—Vence Haggard, 4100 International Plaza, Suite 450, Ft. Worth, TX 96109 (817) 862–2220.
Region 6 (Midwestern).—Iowa, Missouri, Kansas, Nebraska, Colorado.
  Regional Administrator.—Steven Fender, DOT Building, 901 Locust Street, Suite 464, Kansas City, MO 64106 (816) 329–3840.

Region 7 (Western).—Arizona, California, Nevada, Utah.
Regional Administrator.—James Jordan, 801 I Street, Suite 466, Sacramento, CA 95814 (916) 498–6547.
Region 8 (Northwestern).—Idaho, Oregon, Wyoming, Montana, North Dakota, South Dakota, Washington, Alaska.
Regional Administrator.—Mark Daniels, 500 Broadway, Murdock Executive Plaza, Suite 240, Vancouver, WA 98660 (360) 696–7536.

FEDERAL TRANSIT ADMINISTRATION

Administrator.—Therese McMillan (acting), 366–4040.
Special Assistant to the Administrator.—Carolyn Flowers, 366–4040.
Chief Counsel.—Dana Nifosi (acting), 366–4011.
Director, Office of Civil Rights.—Linda C. Ford (acting), 366–4018.
Planning and Environment.—Lucy Garliauskas, 366–4033.
Associate Administrator for –
　Administration.—Matt Crouch (acting), 366–4007.
　Budget and Policy.—Robert Tuccillo, 366–4050.
　Communications and Congressional Affairs.—Nathan Robinson, 366–8042.
　Program Management.—Henrika Buchanan-Smith, 366–4020.
　Research, Demonstration and Innovation.—Vincent Valdes, 366–3052.
　Safety and Oversight.—Thomas Littleton, 366–9239.

MARITIME ADMINISTRATION

Administrator and Chairman, Maritime Subsidy Board.—Paul N. Jaenichen, room W22–318 (202) 366–1719.
Deputy Administrator.—Michael J. Rodriguez, room W22–314, 366–5823.
Secretary, Maritime Administration and Maritime Subsidy Board.—Vacant, 366–5746.
Chief Counsel and Member, Maritime Subsidy Board.—Franklin Parker, room W24–310, 366–0709.
Director, Office of Congressional and Public Affairs.—Michael Novak, room W22–324, 366–9407.
Public Affairs Officer.—Kim Strong, room W22–324, 366–5067.
Executive Director.—Joel Szabat, room W28–316, 366–3907.
Director of:
　International Activities.—Lonnie T. Kishiyama, room W28–312, 366–5493.
　Policy and Plans.—Douglas McDonald, room W26–326, 366–2145.
Associate Administrator for Budget and Programs / Chief Financial Officer.—Lydia Moschkin, room W21–334, 366–3071.
Director, Office of:
　Accounting.—Inga Maik, room W25–333, 366–1947.
　Budget.—Alex J. Caine, room W26–310, 493–0362.
　National Security Program / Funds Control.—Inga Maik, room W25–333, 366–1947.
　Resources.—Vacant, room W26–309, 366–5110.
Associate Administrator for Administration.—Delia P. Davis, room W26–312, 366–2181.
Director, Office of:
　Acquisition.—Wayne Leong, room W26–324, 366–5620.
　Information Technology.—Robert Ellington, room W26–320, 366–2531.
　Management and Information Services.—Steve Snipes, room W26–302, 366–2811.
　Personnel.—James D. Bridges, Sr., room W26–319, 366–0619.
Associate Administrator for Environment and Compliance.—John Quinn, room W21–326, 366–1931.
Director, Office of:
　Environment.—Michael C. Carter, room W25–302, 366–9431.
　Safety.—Kevin Kohlman, room W25–302, 366–5126.
　Security.—Cameron Naron, room W28–340, 366–1883.
Associate Administrator for Intermodal System Development.—Lauren K. Brand, room W21–320, 366–7057.
Deputy.—Roger V. Bohnert, room W21–324, 366–0720.
Director, Office of:
　Deepwater Ports and Offshore Activities.—Yvette Fields, room W21–309, 366–0926.
　Gateway Offices.—William Paape, room W21–307, 366–5005.
　Infrastructure Development and Congestion Mitigation.—Robert Bouchard, room W21–308, 366–5076.

Marine Highways and Passenger Services.—Scott Davies, room W21–312, 366–0951.
Shipper and Carrier Outreach.—Vacant, room W21–310, 366–0704.
Associate Administrator for National Security.—Kevin M. Tokarski, room W25–330, 366–5400.
Director, Office of:
Emergency Preparedness.—Thomas M.P. Christensen, room W23–304, 366–5909.
Sealift Support.—Bill Kurfehs, room W25–318, 366–2318.
Ship Disposal.—Vacant, room W25–334, 366–6467.
Ship Operations.—William H. Cahill, room W25–336, 366–1875.
Associate Administrator for Business and Finance Development.—Owen Doherty, room W21–318, 366–9595.
Director, Office of:
Cargo Preference and Domestic Trade.—Dennis Brennan, room W23–316, 366–1029.
Financial Approvals and Marine Insurance.—Michael Yarrington, room W23–312, 366–1915.
Chief, Division of Business Finance.—Vacant, room W23–321, 366–1908.
Director, Office of:
Maritime Workforce Development.—Anne Wehde, room W23–314, 366–5469.
Shipyards and Marine Finance.—David Heller, room W23–324, 366–1850.

FIELD ACTIVITIES

Director for:
Great Lakes and Upper Inland Waterways Region.—Floyd Miras, Suite 185, 2860 South River Road, Des Plaines, IL 60018 (847) 905–0122.
North Atlantic Region.—Jeffrey Flumignan, 1 Bowling Green, Room 418, New York, NY 10004 (212) 668–2064.
Northern California/Hawaii Region.—John Hummer, Suite 2200, 201 Mission Street, San Francisco, CA 94105 (415) 744–3125.
South Atlantic Region.—Frances Bohnsack, Building 4D, Room 211, 7737 Hampton Boulevard, Norfolk, VA 23505 (757) 441–6393.

U.S. MERCHANT MARINE ACADEMY

Superintendent.—RADM James Helis, Kings Point, NY 11024 (516) 773–5000.
Deputy Superintendent for Academic Affairs (Academic Dean).—RDML Susan Dunlap.

NATIONAL HIGHWAY TRAFFIC SAFETY ADMINISTRATION

Administrator.—Mark Rosekind, room W42–302 (202) 366–1836.
Deputy Administrator.—Vacant, 366–1836.
Director, Communications.—Gordon Trowbridge.
Director, Governmental Affairs, Policy and Strategic Planning.—Alison Pascale, 366–1836.
Senior Associate Administrator for—
Policy and Operation.—Vacant, 366–2330.
Traffic Injury Control.—Vacant, 366–1755.
Vehicle Safety.—Vacant, 366–9700.
Associate Administrator for—
Communications and Consumer Information.—Susan Gorcowski, 366–9550.
Enforcement.—Frank Borris (acting), 366–2669.
National Center for Statistics and Analysis.—Terry Sheldon, 366–1503.
Planning, Administrative and Financial Management.—Rebecca Pennington, 366–2550.
Regional Operations and Program Delivery.—Maggi Gunnels, 366–2121.
Research and Program Development.—Michael Brown (acting), 366–1755.
Rulemaking.—Ryan Posten, 366–1810.
Vehicle Safety Research Program.—Nathaniel Beuse, 366–4862.
Chief Information Officer.—Colleen Coggins, 366–4878.
Director, Office of Civil Rights.—Philip Newby, 366–0972.
Chief Counsel.—Paul Hemmersbaugh, 366–9511.
Director, Executive Correspondence.—Gregory Walter, 366–2330.
Supervisor, Executive Correspondence.—Julie Korkor, 366–5470.

REGIONAL OFFICES

Region 1.—Connecticut, Maine, Massachusetts, New Hampshire, Rhode Island, Vermont.

Regional Administrator.—Philip J. Weiser, Volpe National Transportation Center, 55 Broadway, Kendall Square, Code RTV–8E, Cambridge, MA 02142 (617) 494–3427.

Region 2.—Pennsylvania, New York, New Jersey, Puerto Rico, Virgin Islands.

Regional Administrator.—Thomas M. Louizou, 222 Mamaroneck Avenue, Suite 204, White Plains, NY 10605 (914) 682–6162.

Region 3.—Delaware, District of Columbia, Maryland, Kentucky, North Carolina, Virginia, West Virginia.

Regional Administrator.—Elizabeth Baker, 10 South Howard Street, Suite 6700, Baltimore, MD 21201 (410) 962–0090.

Region 4.—Alabama, Florida, Georgia, South Carolina, Tennessee.

Regional Administrator.—Terrance D. Schiavone, Atlanta Federal Center, 61 Forsyth Street, SW., Suite 17T30, Atlanta, GA 30303–3106 (404) 562–3739.

Region 5.—Illinois, Indiana, Michigan, Minnesota, Ohio, Wisconsin.

Regional Administrator.—Michael Witter, 19900 Governors Drive, Suite 201, Olympia Fields, IL 60461 (708) 503–8892.

Region 6.—Louisiana, Mississippi, New Mexico, Oklahoma, Texas, Indian Nations.

Regional Administrator.—George S. Chakiris, 819 Taylor Street, Room 8A38, Fort Worth, TX 76102–6177 (817) 978–3653.

Region 7.—Arkansas, Iowa, Kansas, Missouri, Nebraska.

Regional Administrator.—Romell Cooks, 901 Locust Street, Room 466, Kansas City, MO 64106 (816) 329–3900.

Region 8.—Colorado, North Dakota, Nevada, South Dakota, Utah, Wyoming.

Regional Administrator.—Bill Watada, 12300 West Dakota Avenue, Suite 140, Lakewood, CO 80228–2583 (720) 963–3100.

Region 9.—American Samoa, Arizona, California, Guam, Mariana Islands, Hawaii.

Regional Administrator.—David Manning, 201 Mission Street, Suite 1600, San Francisco, CA 94105 (415) 744–3089.

Region 10.—Alaska, Idaho, Montana, Oregon, Washington.

Regional Administrator.—John Moffat, Federal Building, 915 Second Avenue, Suite 3140, Seattle, WA 98174 (206) 220–7640.

PIPELINE AND HAZARDOUS MATERIALS SAFETY ADMINISTRATION

Administrator.—Timothy Butters (acting), room E27–300 (202) 366–4433.

Deputy Administrator.—Timothy Butters, room E27–300, 366–4461.

Assistant Administrator / Chief Safety Officer.—Stephen Domotor.

Chief Counsel.—Vanessa Sutherland, room E26–320, 366–4400.

Director, Office of Civil Rights.—Rosanne Goodwill, room E27–334, 366–9638.

Chief Financial Officer.—Monica Summitt, room E32–330, 366–5608.

Associate Administrator for—

   Governmental, International and Public Affairs.—Vacant, room E27–300, 366–4831.

   Hazardous Materials Safety.—Dr. Magdy El-Sibaie, room E21–316, 366–0656.

   Management and Administration.—Scott Poyer, room E22–312, 366–5608.

   Pipeline Safety.—Jeffrey Wiese, room E22–321, 366–4595.

HAZARDOUS MATERIALS SAFETY OFFICES

Chief of:

   Eastern Region. Colleen D. Abbenhaus, 820 Bear Tavern Road, Suite 306, West Trenton, NJ 08628 (609) 989–2256.

   Central Region.—Kipton Wills, Suite 478, 2350 East Devon Avenue, Des Plaines, IL 60018 (847) 294–8580.

   Western Region.—Sean Lynum, 3401 Centre Lake Drive, Suite 550–B, Ontario, CA 91761 (909) 937–3279.

   Southern Region.—John Heneghan, 233 Peachtree Street, NE., Suite 602, Atlanta, GA 30303 (404) 832–1140.

   Southwest Region.—Vacant, 8701 South Gessner Road, Suite 1110, Houston, TX 77004 (713) 272–2820.

PIPELINE SAFETY OFFICES

Director of:

   Eastern Region.—Byron Coy, 820 Bear Tavern Road, Suite 103, West Trenton, NJ 08628 (609) 989–2171.

   Central Region.—Alan Beshore, 901 Locust Street, Room 462, Kansas City, MO 64106 (816) 329–3800.

Western Region.—Chris Hoidal, 12300 West Dakota Avenue, Suite 110, Lakewood, CO 80228 (720) 963–3160.
Southwest Region.—Rodrick M. Seeley, 8701 South Gessner, Suite 1110, Houston, TX 77074 (713) 272–2859.
Southern Region.—Wayne Lemoi, 233 Peachtree Street, NE., Suite 600, Atlanta, GA 30303 (404) 832–1140.

OFFICE OF THE ASSISTANT SECRETARY FOR RESEARCH AND TECHNOLOGY (OST–R)

http://www.rita.dot.gov

Assistant Secretary.—Gregory Winfree (202) 366–4412.
Deputy Assistant Secretary.—Ellen Partridge, room E35–326, 366–1580.
Executive Director.—Audrey Farley, room E33–302, 366–4112.
Public Affairs Contact, Bureau of Transportation Statistics.—David Smallen, room E36–328, 366–5568; OST–R.—Nancy Wilochka, room E36–331, 366–5128.
Director for—
  Intelligent Transportation Systems.—Kenneth M. Leonard, room E31–301, 366–9536.
  Office of Technology Policy and Outreach.—Timothy Klein (acting), room E36–332, 366–0075.
  Transportation Safety Institute.—Kevin Womack, 6500 South MacArthur Boulevard, MPB–343, Oklahoma City, OK 73169 (405) 954–7312.
  Volpe National Transportation Systems Center.—Robert Johns, room 1240, 55 Broadway, Kendall Square, Cambridge, MA 02142 (617) 494–2222.

SAINT LAWRENCE SEAWAY DEVELOPMENT CORPORATION-U.S. DOT

www.greatlakes-seaway.com/en

Administrator.—Betty S. Sutton (202) 366–0091, fax 366–7147.
Deputy Administrator.—Craig H. Middlebrook, 366–0105.
Senior Advisor to the Administrator.—Anita K. Blackman, 366–0107.
Director, Office of:
  Budget and Economic Development.—Kevin P. O'Malley.
  Congressional and Public Relations.—Nancy T. Alcalde.

SEAWAY OPERATIONS

180 Andrews Street, P.O. Box 520, Massena, NY 13662–0520

phone (315) 764–3200, fax 764–3235

Associate Administrator.—Salvatore Pisani.
Deputy Associate Administrator.—Vacant.
Chief Counsel.—Carrie Mann Lavigne.
Director, Office of:
  Engineering and Maintenance.—Thomas A. Lavigne.
  Financial Management and Administration and CFO.—Nancy C. Scott (acting).
  Lock Operations and Marine Services.—Lori K. Curran.

SURFACE TRANSPORTATION BOARD

395 E Street, SW., 20423–0001, phone (202) 245–0245

http://www.stb.dot.gov

Chairman.—Deb Miller (acting), 245–0210.
Vice Chairman.—Ann Begeman, 245–0203.
Office of the Managing Director.—Leland L. Gardner, 245–0291.
General Counsel.—Craig Keats, 245–0264.
Director, Office of:
  Proceedings.—Rachel D. Campbell, 245–0352.
  Public Assistance, Governmental Affairs, and Compliance.—Lucille Marvin, 245–0238.

DEPARTMENT OF ENERGY

James Forrestal Building, 1000 Independence Avenue, SW., 20585

phone (202) 586–5000, http://www.energy.gov

ERNEST MONIZ, Secretary of Energy; born on December 22, 1944, in Fall River MA; education: B.S., physics, Boston College, 1966; Ph.D., theorectical physics, Stanford University, 1972; honorary degrees from three universities; professional: Under Secretary, Department of Energy; Associate Director for Science, Office of Science and Technology Policy; professor, Massachusetts Institute of Technology; organizations: President Obama's Council of Advisors on Science and Technology; Department of Defense Threat Reduction Advisory Committee; Blue Ribbon Commission on America's Nuclear Future; Council on Foreign Relations; Fellow of the American Association for the Advancement of Science, the Humboldt Foundation, and the American Physical Society; and a member of numerous other civic and professional organizations; married: Dr. Naoimi; one child, two grandchildren; nominated by President Barack Obama to become the 13th Secretary of Energy, and confirmed by the U.S. Senate on May 16, 2013.

OFFICE OF THE SECRETARY

Secretary of Energy.—Ernest Moniz (202) 586–6210.
Deputy Secretary.—Elizabeth Sherwood-Randall, 586–5500.
Associate Deputy Secretary.—Bruce Held, 586–6210.
Chief of Staff.—Kevin Knobloch, 586–6210.
Inspector General.—Gregory H. Friedman, 586–4393.
Assistant Secretary for—
  Congressional and Intergovernmental Affairs.—Brad Crowell, 586–5450.
  Policy and International Affairs.—Jon Elkind, 586–5800.
General Counsel.—Steve Croley, 586–5281.
Chief Information Officer.—Donald Adcock (acting), 586–0166.
Chief Human Capital Officer.—Bob Gibbs, 586–1234.
Chief Financial Officer.—Joseph Hezir, 586–4171.
Chief Health Safety and Security Officer.—Glenn Podonsky, 586–9275.
Executive Director of the Loan Programs Office.—Peter Davidson (acting), 287–5854.
Director, Office of·
  Economic Impact and Diversity.—Dot Harris, 586–8383.
  Hearings and Appeals.—Poli Marmolejos, 287–1566.
  Intelligence and Counterintelligence.—Steve Black, 586–2610.
  Management.—Ingrid Kolb, 586–2550.
  Public Affairs.—Aoife McCarthy (acting), 586–4940.
Director for Advanced Research Projects Agency—Energy.—Ellen Williams, 287–1046.
Administrator for Energy Information Administration.—Adam Sieminski, 586–4361.

UNDER SECRETARY FOR MANAGEMENT AND PERFORMANCE

Under Secretary for Management and Performance.—Vacant.
Deputy Under Secretary for Management and Performance.—David Klaus.
Principal Deputy Assistant Secretary for Environmental Management.—Mark Whitney (202) 586–0742.
Chiefs:
  Health Safety and Security Officer.—Matthew Moury, 586–1285.
  Human Capital Officer.—Bob Gibbs, 586–1234.
  Information Officer.—Donald Adcock, 586–0166.
Director, Office of:
  Economic Impact and Diversity.—Dot Harris, 586–8383.
  Hearings and Appeals.—Poli Marmolejos, 287–1566.

759

Management.—Ingrid Kolb, 586–2550.
Legacy Management.—David Geiser, 586–7550.

UNDER SECRETARY FOR SCIENCE AND ENERGY

Under Secretary for Science and Energy.—Franklin M. Orr, Jr. (202) 586–0505.
Assistant Secretary for—
  Electricity Delivery and Energy Reliability.—Patricia Hoffman, 586–1411.
  Energy Efficiency and Renewable Energy.—David Danielson, 586–9220.
  Fossil Energy.—Christopher Smith, 586–6660.
  Nuclear Energy.—Peter Lyons, 586–6630.
Director, Office of:
  Indian Energy Policy and Programs.—David Conrad (acting), (202) 596–1198.
  Science.—Patricia Dehmer (acting), 586–5430.

NATIONAL NUCLEAR SECURITY ADMINISTRATION

Administrator for National Nuclear Security Administration/Under Secretary for Nuclear Security.—Lt. Gen. Frank G. Klotz, USAF (Ret.), (202) 586–5555.
Principal Deputy Administrator.—Madelyn Creedon, 586–5555.
Deputy Administrator for—
  Defense Programs.—Donald Cook, 586–2179.
  Defense Nuclear Nonproliferation.—Anne Harrington, 586–0645.
  Naval Reactors.—Admiral John M. Richardson, USN, 781–6174.
Deputy Under Secretary for Counterterrorism.—Dr. Steven Aoki, 586–1734.
Associate Administrator for—
  Defense Nuclear Security.—Jeffrey Johnson, 586–8900.
  Emergency Operations.—Deborah Wilber (acting), 586–9892.
  Safety, Infrastructure and Operations.—James McConnell (acting), 586–8246.

MAJOR FIELD ORGANIZATIONS

OPERATIONS OFFICES

Managers:
  Idaho.—Richard Provencher (208) 526–7300, fax 526–0542.
  Oak Ridge.—Larry Kelly (865) 576–4444, fax 576–0006.
  Richland.—Stacy Charboneau (509) 376–7395, fax 376–4789.
  Savannah River.—David Moody (803) 952–8725, fax 952–8144.

INTEGRATED SUPPORT/BUSINESS CENTERS

Managers:
  Chicago Office.—Roxanne E. Purucker (630) 252–2110.
  EM Consolidated Business Center.—Jack Craig (513) 246–0460.
  NNSA Service Center.—Geoffrey Beausoleil (505) 845–4392.

POWER MARKETING ADMINISTRATIONS

Administrator, Power Administration:
  Bonneville.—Elliott Mainzer (503) 230–5101, fax 230–4018.
  Southeastern Area.—Kenneth Legg (706) 213–3800, fax 213–3884.
  Southwestern Area.—Christopher M. Turner (918) 595–6601, fax 595–6755.
  Western Area.—Mark Gabriel (720) 962–7077, fax 962–7083.

PETROLEUM RESERVES

Deputy Assistant Secretary for Petroleum Reserves.—Robert Corbin (202) 586–9460.

FEDERAL ENERGY REGULATORY COMMISSION
888 First Street, NE., 20426

Chair.—Norman C. Bay (202) 502–8000.
Commissioners:
  Philip D. Moeller, 502–8852.
  Cheryl A. LaFleur, 502–8961.
  Tony Clark, 502–6501.
  Colette D. Honorable, 502–8798.
Chief Administrative Law Judge.—Curtis L. Wagner, Jr., 502–8500.
Executive Director.—Anton C. Porter, 502–8300.
General Counsel.—David L. Morenoff, 502–6000.
Secretary, Office of the Secretary.—Kimberly Bose, 502–8400.
Director, Office of:
  Administrative Litigation.—Ted Gerarden, 502–6100.
  Electric Reliability.—Michael Bardee, 502–8600.
  Energy Infrastructure Security.—Joseph McClelland, 502–8867.
  Energy Market Regulation.—Jamie L. Simler, 502–8934.
  Energy Policy and Innovation.—Arnie Quinn, 502–8693.
  Energy Projects.—Ann Miles, 502–8700.
  Enforcement.—Lawrence Gastiger (acting), 502–8100.
  External Affairs.—Leonard Tao, 502–8004.

DEPARTMENT OF EDUCATION

400 Maryland Avenue, SW., 20202

phone (202) 401–3000, fax 401–0596, http://www.ed.gov

ARNE DUNCAN, Secretary of Education; born in Chicago, IL, November 6, 1964; children: Clare and Ryan; education: B.A., Harvard University, *magna cum laude*, 1987; professional: professional basketball player in Australia, 1987–91; Director of Ariel Education Initiative, 1992–98; Deputy Chief of Staff to the Chief Executive Officer of the Chicago Public Schools, 1999–2001; Chief Executive Officer of the Chicago Public Schools, 2001–09; nominated by President Barack Obama to become the 9th Secretary of Education on December 16, 2008; confirmed on January 20, 2009.

OFFICE OF THE SECRETARY
Room 7W301, phone (202) 401–3000, fax 260–7867

Secretary of Education.—Arne Duncan.
  Chief of Staff.—Emma Vadehra.
  Deputy Chief of Staff.—Joy Silvern.

OFFICE OF THE DEPUTY SECRETARY
Room 7W308, phone (202) 401–1000

Deputy Secretary.—John King (acting).
  Chief of Staff.—Tyra Mariani (acting).

OFFICE OF THE UNDER SECRETARY
Room 7E307, phone (202) 401–0429

Under Secretary.—Ted Mitchell.
  Deputy Under Secretaries: Jeff Appel, Jamienne Studley.
  Chief of Staff.—Mushtaq Gunja.

OFFICE OF THE CHIEF FINANCIAL OFFICER
PCP 550 12th Street, SW., phone (202) 245–8144, fax 485–0160

Chief Financial Officer.—Thomas Skelly (acting), LBJ, 400 Maryland Avenue, SW., room 5W313, 401–0287.
  Deputy Chief Financial Officers: James Ropelewski, PCP, room 6095, 245–6221; Timothy Soltis, PCP, room 6124, 245–6555.
  Executive Officer.—Michael Holloway, PCP, room 6090, 245–8150.
  Director of:
    Contracts and Acquisitions Management.—James Hairfield, PCP, room 7153, 245–6219.
    Financial Improvement Operations.—Phillip Juengst, PCP, room 6056, 245–8030.
    Financial Management Operations.—Gary Wood, PCP, room 6089, 245–8118.

OFFICE OF THE CHIEF INFORMATION OFFICER
PCP 550 12th Street, SW., phone (202) 245–6400, fax 245–6621

Chief Information Officer.—Danny Harris, PCP, room 9112, 245–6252.
  Deputy Chief Information Officer.—Vacant, PCP, room 9149, 245–6338.

Executive Officer.—Michael Holloway, PCP, room 6090, 245–8150.
Director of:
　Financial Systems Services.—Greg Robison, PCP, room 9150, 245–7187.
　Information Assurance Services.—Steven Grewal, PCP, room 10057, 245–6316.
　Information Technology Program Services.—Ken Moore, PCP, room 9109, 245–6908.
　Information Technology Services.—Tony Wood, PCP, room 9151, 245–7214.

OFFICE OF MANAGEMENT

Room 2W301, phone (202) 401–5848, fax 260–3761

Assistant Secretary.—Andrew Jackson, room 7W206, 401–5848, fax 260–3761.
　Principal Deputy Assistant Secretary.—Denise L. Carter, room 2W311, 401–5848, fax 260–3761.
　Chief of Staff.—Richard Smith, room 2W309, 260–8987, fax 260–3761.
　Executive Officer.—Wanda Davis, room 2W227, 401–5931, fax 401–3513.
　Director, Alternative Dispute Resolution Center.—Frank J. Furey, L'Enfant Plaza–2134, 619–9701, fax 619–9706.
　Service Director of:
　　Equal Employment Opportunity Services.—Michael Chew, room 2W240, 401–0691, fax 205–5760.
　　Facilities Services.—Scott Taylor, room 2C102, 401–9496, fax 453–5579.
　　Human Capital and Client Services.—Cassandra Cuffee-Graves, room 2E314, 453–5588, fax 401–0520.
　　Management Services.—David Cogdill, room 2W119, 401–0695, fax 205–1866.
　　Office of Hearings and Appeals.—Frank J. Furey, L'Enfant Plaza–2134, 619–9701, fax 619–9726.
　　Privacy, Information and Records Management Services.—Kathleen Styles, room 2E315, 453–5587, fax 401–0920.
　　Security Services.—Ronald Luczak, room 2W314, 260–7727, fax 260–3761.

OFFICE FOR CIVIL RIGHTS

400 Maryland Avenue, SW., Room 4E319, 20202–1100, phone (202) 423–5900

fax 423–6010

Assistant Secretary.—Catherine Lhamon, room 4E313, 453–7240.
　Confidential Assistant.—Courtney Taylor, room 4E319, 453–7127.
　Chief of Staff.—Max Lesko, room 4E309 (202) 260–1115.
　Principal Deputy Assistant Secretary.—Seth Galanter, room 4E329, 453–6048.
　Deputy Assistant Secretary for—
　　Enforcement.—Sandra Battle, room 4E314, 453–5749.
　　Policy.—James Ferg-Cadima, room 4E348, 453–6797.
　　Strategic Operations and Outreach.—Robert Kim, offsite, 453–6053.
　Directors of Enforcement: Carol Ashley, room 4E312, 453–6790; Lisa Chang, room 4E330, 453–6849; Debbie Osgood, room 4E342 (312) 730–1598; Randolph Wills, room 4E332, 453–5956.
　Executive Officer and Director, Resource Management.—Lavern Jordan (acting), room 4E305, 453–5993.
　Senior Counsel: Jessie Brown, room 4E307, 453–6640; Sherrell Evans, room 4E334, 453–5938; Kristine Minami, room 4E340, 453–6626.
　Special Assistant.—Ollie Cantos, room 4E327, 453–6543.
　Confidential Assistant.—Erin Randall, room 4E317, 453–6613.

OFFICE OF CAREER, TECHNICAL, AND ADULT EDUCATION

550 12th Street, SW., 11th Floor, 20202, phone (202) 245–7700, fax 245–7171

Assistant Secretary.—Vacant.
　Chief of Staff.—George Smith, george.smith@ed.gov.
　Deputy Assistant Secretaries: Mark Mitsui, mark.mitsui@ed.gov; Johan Uvin, johan.uvin@ed.gov.
　Staff Assistants: Francine Sinclair, francine.sinclair@ed.gov; Isabel Soto, isabel.soto@ed.gov.

OFFICE OF COMMUNICATIONS AND OUTREACH
Information Resource Center
Room 5E233, phone (202) 453–7000, (202) 401–2000

Assistant Secretary.—Jonathan Schorr (acting), room 7W101, LBJ, 401–6359.
Press Secretary.—Dorie Nolt, room 7C115, 453–6544, LBJ, press@ed.gov.
Deputy Assistant Secretaries:
   Communication Development.—Vacant.
   National Engagement.—Karen Stratman-Krusemark (acting), room 316, LBJ, 401–2559.
   Operations.—Cynthia Dorfman, room 5E231, LBJ, 205–2604.

OFFICE OF ELEMENTARY AND SECONDARY EDUCATION
Room 3W300, phone (202) 401–0113, fax 205–0303

Assistant Secretary.—Deb Delisle, room 3W315, 401–0113.
Deputy Assistant Secretary for—
   Early Learning.—Libby Doggett, room 3W311, 205–2828.
   Management.—Alex Goniprow, room 3W314, 401–9090.
   Policy and Strategic Initiatives.—Scott Sargrad, room 3W307, 453–7254.
Chief of Staff.—Heather Rieman, room 3W313, 260–1700.
Program Director, Office of:
   Academic Improvement.—Sylvia Lyles, room 3E314, 260–8228, fax 260–8969.
   Impact Aid Programs.—Alfred Lott, room 3E105, 260–3858, fax 205–0088.
   Indian Education.—Joyce Silverthorne, room 3W203, 401–0767.
   Migrant Education/School Support and Rural Programs.—Lisa Ramirez, room 3E317,
      260–1127, fax 205–0089.
   School Support Programs.—Monique Chism, room 3W224, 260–0826.
   Safe and Healthy Students Programs.—David Esquith, room 3E328, 453–6722.

OFFICE OF ENGLISH LANGUAGE ACQUISITION
400 Maryland Avenue, SW., 5C–132, 20202, phone (202) 401–4300, fax 401–8452

Assistant Deputy Secretary and Director.—Dr. Libia S. Gil.
   Deputy Director.—Marianna Vinson.

OFFICE OF FEDERAL STUDENT AID
830 First Street, NE., 20202, phone (202) 377–3000, fax 275–5000

Chief Operating Officer.—James Runcie.
   Deputy Chief Operating Officer.—Matthew Sessa.
   Chief of Staff.—Colleen McGinnis, room 112E1, 377–4330.
   Ombudsman.—Joyce DeMoss, room 4111, 377–3992.
   Chief Business Operations Officer.—Bill Leith, room 11I11, 377–3676.
   Director, Communications.—Gabrielle Turner, room 22C7, 377–4003.
   Chiefs:
      Compliance Officer.—Robin Minor, room 81K2, 377–4273.
      Finance Officer.—Jay Hurt, room 54E1, 377–3453.
      Information Officer.—Jerry Williams, room 101G3, 377–3101.
   Director, Policy Liaison and Implementation Staff.—Jeff Baker, room 113C1, 377–4009.
   Chiefs:
      Administration Officer.—Irma Blanchett, room 21A5, 377–4165.
      Customer Experience Officer.—Brenda Wensil, room 114F1, 377–4671.

OFFICE OF THE GENERAL COUNSEL
Room 6E313, phone (202) 401–6000, fax 205–2689

General Counsel.—James Cole.
   Chief of Staff.—Aaron Ament.
   Deputy Chief of Staff.—Kyle Flood.

Senior Counsel: Ron Petracca, Robert Wexler.
Senior Counsel for Information and Technology.—"Bucky" Methfessel.
*Executive Officer.—*Paula Shipp (202) 205–5203.
Deputy General Counsel for—
  *Ethics, Legislative Counsel and Regulatory Service.—*Elizabeth McFadden.
  *Postsecondary and Business Administrative Law Service.—*Tracey Sasser.
  *Program Service.—*Philip H. Rosenfelt.

OFFICE OF INNOVATION AND IMPROVEMENT
phone (202) 205–4500

*Assistant Deputy Secretary.—*Nadya Chinoy Dabby, 401–8532.
  Associate Assistant Deputy Secretary for—
  *Innovation and Reform.—*Margo Anderson.
  *Special Projects.—*Ursula Wright.
*Chief of Staff.—*Ahnna Smith.

OFFICE OF INSPECTOR GENERAL
Potomac Center Plaza (PCP), 8th Floor, 20024, phone (202) 245–6900, fax 245–6993

*Inspector General.—*Kathleen Tighe.
  *Deputy Inspector General.—*Sandra D. Bruce.
  *Counsel to the Inspector General.—*Marta Erceg, 245–7015.
  Assistant Inspector General for—
  *Audit Services.—*Patrick Howard, 245–6949.
  *Investigations.—*Aaron Jordan, 245–6966.
  *IT Audit and Computer Crimes Investigations.—*Charles Coe, 245–7033.
  *Management Services.—*Wanda Scott, 245–6065.

INTERNATIONAL AFFAIRS OFFICE
Room 6W108, phone (202) 401–0430, fax 401–2508

*Senior Advisor to the Secretary and Director.—*Maureen McLaughlin.
  *Deputy Director.—*JoAnne Livingston.
  *International Visitors.—*Sambia Shivers-Barclay.
  Western Hemisphere and Oceania Affairs, Organization of American States (OAS).—
    Rafael Nevarez.
  International Affairs Specialists: Adriana de Kanter, Beckey Miller.
  *Staff Assistant.—*Vacant.

INSTITUTE OF EDUCATION SCIENCES
555 New Jersey Avenue, NW., Room 600, 20208, phone (202) 219–1385, fax 219–1466

*Director.—*Sue Betka (acting), 219–1385.
  Deputy Director for—
  *Administration and Policy.—*Sue Betka, 219–1385.
  *Science.—*Anne Riccuiti, 219–2247.
  National Center for—
  *Education Evaluation and Regional Assistance.—*Ruth C. Neild, 208–1200.
  *Education Research.—*Thomas W. Brock, 219–2006.
  *Education Statistics.—*Peggy Carr (acting), 502–7321.
  *Special Education Research.—*Joan McLaughlin (acting), 219–1309.

OFFICE OF LEGISLATION AND CONGRESSIONAL AFFAIRS
Room 6W301, phone (202) 401–0020, email: OLCAinquiries@ed.gov

*Assistant Secretary.—*Vacant.
  *Assistant Secretary.—*Lloyd Horwich (acting) 453–6530.
  *Deputy Assistant Secretary.—*Jodie Fingland, 401–1043.
  *Chief of Staff.—*Irma Diggs, 453–5781.

OFFICE OF PLANNING, EVALUATION AND POLICY DEVELOPMENT
Room 5E301, phone (202) 401–0831, fax (202) 260–7741

Assistant Secretary.—Amy McIntosh, Deputy Assistant Secretary, Delegated Duties of Assistant Secretary, room 5E313.
Executive Officer.—Brenda Long, room 7E201.
Director of:
  Budget Service.—Thomas Skelly, room 5W313.
  Policy and Program Studies Service.—Jenn Bell-Ellwanger, room 6W231.

OFFICE OF POSTSECONDARY EDUCATION
1990 K Street, NW., 20006, phone (202) 502–7750, fax 502–7677

Assistant Secretary.—Jamienne S. Studley (acting).
Chief of Staff.—Christine Mica.
Deputy Assistant Secretary for—
  Higher Education Programs.—James Minor, 219–7027.
  International and Foreign Language Education.—Mohamed Abdel-Kader, 502–7601.
  Policy, Planning and Innovation.—Lynn Mahaffie, 502–7903.

OFFICE OF SPECIAL EDUCATION AND REHABILITATIVE SERVICES
Potomac Center Plaza (PCP), 550 12th Street, SW., 5th Floor, 20202
phone (202) 245–7468, fax 245–7638

Assistant Secretary.—Sue Swenson (acting), room 5138, 245–6496.
Executive Administrator.—Andrew J. Pepin, room 5106, 245–7632.
Deputy Assistant Secretary.—Sue Swenson, room 5138, 245–8021.
Office of Special Education Programs.—Melody Musgrove, room 4109, 245–8020.
Commissioner of the Rehabilitation Services Administration.—Janet Labreck, room 5086, 245–7408.

DEPARTMENT OF VETERANS AFFAIRS

Mail should be addressed to 810 Vermont Avenue, NW., Washington, DC 20420

http://www.va.gov

ROBERT A. McDONALD, Secretary of Veterans Affairs; education: graduated, U.S. Military Academy, West Point, NY, 1975; graduated, University of Utah, MBA, 1978; military service: CPT, U.S. Army, 1975–80, 82nd Airborne Division; decorations, badges, and citations: Meritorious Service Medal, Ranger Tab, Expert Infantryman Badge, Senior Parachutist Wings; married: Diane; two children, two grandchildren; nominated by President Barack Obama to become the 8th Secretary of the Department of Veterans Affairs, and was confirmed by the U.S. Senate on July 29, 2014.

OFFICE OF THE SECRETARY

Secretary of Veterans Affairs.—Robert A. McDonald (202) 461–4800.
Deputy Secretary of Veterans Affairs.—Sloan Gibson, 461–4817.
Chief of Staff—Jose D. Riojas, 461–4808.
Deputy Chief of Staff.—Hughes Turner, 461–4813.
Senior Advisor to the Secretary.—John Spinelli, 461–4874.
Special Assistant for Veterans Service Organizations.—Matthew Stiner, 461–4838.
Executive Secretary.—Bonnie Miranda, 461–4869.
Director, Center for—
    Faith-Based Community Initiative.—Rev. E. Terri LaVelle, 461–7689.
    Minority Veterans.—Barbara Ward, 461–6191.
    Women Veterans.—Elisa Basnight, 461–6193.
Employment Discrimination and Complaint Adjudication.—Maxanne R. Witkin, 1575 I Street, NW., 461–4050.
Office of Survivors Assistance.—Wendy Yeldell (acting), 1717 H Street, NW. (202) 632–7702.
Small and Disadvantaged Business Utilization.—Tom Leney, 801 I Street, NW., 461–4300.

BOARD OF VETERANS' APPEALS

Executive in Charge / Chairman.—Laura H. Eskenazi, 425 I Street, NW. (202) 632–4603.
Principal Deputy Vice Chairman.—Bruce P. Gipe.

OFFICE OF GENERAL COUNSEL

General Counsel.—Leigh A. Bradley (202) 461–4995.
Principal Deputy General Counsel.—Tammy L. Kennedy.

OFFICE OF INSPECTOR GENERAL

Inspector General.—Vacant, 801 I Street, NW. (202) 461–4720.
Deputy Inspector General.—Richard J. Griffin.

OFFICE OF ACQUISITIONS, LOGISTICS, AND CONSTRUCTION

Principal Executive Director.—Glenn D. Haggstrom, 425 I Street, NW. (202) 632–4606.
Deputy Assistant Secretary, Office of Acquisition and Logistics.—Jan R. Frye, 810 Vermont Avenue, NW., 461–6920.
Executive Director, Office of Construction and Facilities Management.—Stella S. Fiotes, 425 I Street, NW. (202) 632–4607.

ASSISTANT SECRETARY FOR CONGRESSIONAL AND LEGISLATIVE AFFAIRS

Assistant Secretary.—Christopher E. O'Connor (interim), (202) 461–6456.
Deputy Assistant Secretary.—Vacant.
Associate Deputy Assistant Secretary.—Christopher E. O'Connor, 461–6456.
Director of Operations.—Lawrence Hinkin, 461–5914.
Legislative Advisor.—David Ballenger, 461–6492.
Deputy Assistant Secretary for Intergovernmental Affairs.—David Montoya, 461–7378.
Director for—
Health Team.—Vacant.
Benefits Team.—Vacant.
Congressional Liaison.—Ronald Maurer, 461–0398.
Corporate Enterprise Legislative Affairs Service.—Lesia Mandzia, 461–6177.

ASSISTANT SECRETARY FOR PUBLIC AND INTERGOVERNMENTAL AFFAIRS

Assistant Secretary.—Maura Sullivan (202) 461–7500.
Deputy Assistant Secretary for Public Affairs.—Joshua Taylor, 461–7700.

ASSISTANT SECRETARY FOR POLICY AND PLANNING

Assistant Secretary.—Dr. Linda Spoonster Schwartz, 461–5800.
Principal Deputy Assistant Secretary.—Dat Tran (acting), 461–5800.
Deputy Assistant Secretary for—
Data Governance and Analysis.—Dat Tran, 461–5800.
Policy.—Susan D. Sullivan, 461–5831.
Executive Director for—
Corporate Analysis and Evaluation.—Subhi Mehdi, 461–5752.
Enterprise Program Management Office.—Greg L. Giddens, 461–6986.
Office of Interagency Collaboration and Integration.—John Medve, 461–5626.

ASSISTANT SECRETARY FOR OPERATIONS, SECURITY AND PREPAREDNESS

Assistant Secretary.—Kevin T. Hanretta (202) 461–4980.
Deputy Assistant Secretary for Emergency Management.—Lewis Ratchford, Jr., 461–5930.
Director, Security and Law Enforcement.—Frederick R. Jackson, 461–5544.

ASSISTANT SECRETARY FOR MANAGEMENT

Assistant Secretary/Chief Financial Officer.—Helen Tierney (202) 461–6600.
Principal Deputy Assistant Secretary for Management/Deputy Chief Financial Officer.—
Edward Murray, 461–6681.
Deputy Assistant Secretary for—
Budget.—Maureen Walsh, 461–6654.
Finance.—Laurie Park, 461–6180.

ASSISTANT SECRETARY FOR INFORMATION AND TECHNOLOGY

Assistant Secretary.—Vacant (202) 461–6910.
Executive in Charge/Chief Information Officer.—Stephen W. Warren, 461–6910.

ASSISTANT SECRETARY FOR HUMAN RESOURCES AND ADMINISTRATION

Assistant Secretary.—Gina Farrisee (202) 461–7750.
Principal Deputy Assistant Secretary.—Samuel B. Retherford, 461–7750.
Deputy Assistant Secretary for—
Administration.—Roy Hurndon, 461–5000.
Diversity Management and Inclusion.—Georgia Coffey, 461–4131.
Human Resources Management.—Vacant, 461–7765.
Labor-Management Relations.—Kimberly D. Moseley, 461–4115.
Resolution Management.—Catherine Mitrano, 1575 I Street, NW., 501–2800.

NATIONAL CEMETERY ADMINISTRATION

Under Secretary for Memorial Affairs.—Ronald E. Walters (interim), (202) 461–6112.
Principal Deputy Under Secretary.—Ronald E. Walters, 461–6013.
Executive Assistant.—Tom Howard, 461–6215.
Deputy Under Secretary for—
  Field Programs.—Glenn Powers, 461–6071.
  Finance and Planning/CFO.—Matthew Sullivan, 461–7334.
  Management.—Thomas Muir, 461–6234.
Director of:
  Budget Service.—Joan Jefferies, 461–6742.
  Design and Construction.—Michael Roth, 632–4691.
  Field Programs.—Kimberly Wright, 461–6748.
  IT Business Requirements and Administrative Service.—Timothy Godlove, 400–5630.
  Management and Communications Service.—Patricia "Tish" Tyson, 461–6307.
  Memorial Programs Service.—Anita Hanson, 501–3060.
  Veterans Cemetery Grants Program.—George Eisenbach, 632–7369.

VETERANS BENEFITS ADMINISTRATION

Under Secretary.—Allison A. Hickey, 1800 G Street, NW. (202) 461–9300.
Principal Deputy Under Secretary.—Danny Pummill.
Chief of Staff.—Lois Mittelstaedt.
Deputy Under Secretary for—
  Disability Assistance.—Dave McLenachen (acting), 461–9320.
  Economic Opportunity.—Curtis Coy, 443–6080.
  Field Operations.—Beth McCoy, 461–9340.
Chief Financial Officer.—Jamie Manker, 461–9900.
Director of:
  Business Process Integration.—Brad Houston, 461–9797.
  Compensation.—Thomas Murphy, 461–9700.
  Education.—Robert Worley, 461–9800.
  Employee Development and Training.—Catherine Campbell, 461–9860.
  Insurance.—Vincent Markey (215) 381–3029.
  Loan Guaranty.—Michael Frueh (202) 632–8862.
  Management.—Vacant, 461–9412.
  Pension and Fiduciary.—David McLenachen, 632–8863.
  Performance Analysis and Integrity.—Mark Seastrom, 461–9040.
  Strategic Planning.—Richard Buchanan, 632–8652.
  Veterans Benefits Management System.—Dawn Bontempo, 632–8656.
  Veterans Relationship Management.—Maureen Ellenberger, 461–1423.
  Vocational Rehabilitation and Employment.—Jack Kammerer, 461–9600.

VETERANS HEALTH ADMINISTRATION

Under Secretary.—David J. Schulkin (202) 461–7000.
  Principal Deputy Under Secretary for Health.—James Tuchschmidt, M.D. (acting), 461–7008.
Deputy Under Secretary for Health for Operations and Management.—Janet P. Murphy, MBA (acting), 461–7026.
Chief of Staff.—Jill Draime, Psy.D. (acting), 461–7016.
  Deputy Chief of Staff.—Cassandra Law (acting), 461–7016.
Deputy Under Secretary for Health for Policy and Services.—Madhulika Agarwal, M.D., M.P.H., 461–7590.
Assistant Deputy Under Secretary for—
  Health for Clinical Operations and Management.—Thomas Lynch, M.D., 461–7046.
  Health for Policy and Planning.—Patricia Vandenberg, M.H.A., B.S.N., 461–7100.
  Health for Policy and Services.—Gerard R. Cox, M.D., M.H.A., 461–7590.
  Health for Quality, Safety and Value.—Robin Hemphill, M.D., M.P.H. (acting).
Medical Inspector.—Gerard R. Cox, M.D., M.H.A. (acting), 461–4094.
Chief Officers for—
  Academic Affiliations.—Robert L. Jesse, M.D., Ph.D., 461–9490.
  Business.—Stephanie Mardon, 461–1600.
  Communications.—Todd Livick (acting), 461–7371.
  Compliance and Business Integrity.—Robbi Watnick (acting), 900 K Street, NE., 632–8335.

Employee Education System.—Volney James "Jim" Warner, 461–4019.
Ethics in Health Care.—Kenneth A. Berkowitz, M.D., F.C.C.P. (acting), (212) 951–3385
Financial.—Kathleen Turco, 266–4513.
Health Information and Analytics.—Gail Graham, 461–5874.
Nursing.—Donna Gage, 461–6700.
Patient Care Services.—Maureen McCarthy (acting), 461–7590.
Patient Safety.—Robin Hemphill, M.D., M.P.H.
Procurement and Logistics.—Norbert Doyle, 632–7942.
Public Health and Environmental Hazards.—Richard Kaslow, M.D., M.P.H., 461–1000.
Quality and Performance.—Joseph Francis, M.D., M.P.H. (acting), 1717 H Street, NW., 266–4533.
Readjustment Counseling.—Tommy Stewart, M.S., RN, NP, 461–7139.
Research and Development.—Joel Kupersmith, M.D., 461–1700.
Research Oversight.—J. Thomas Puglisi, Ph.D., CIP, 1717 H Street, NW., 266–4577.

DEPARTMENT OF HOMELAND SECURITY

U.S. Naval Security Station, 3801 Nebraska Avenue, NW., 20016

Phone (202) 282–8000

JEH CHARLES JOHNSON, Secretary of Homeland Security was sworn in on December 23, 2013 as the fourth Secretary of Homeland Security. Prior to joining DHS, Secretary Johnson served as General Counsel for the Department of Defense, where he was part of the senior management team and led the more than 10,000 military and civilian lawyers across the Department. As General Counsel of the Defense Department, Secretary Johnson oversaw the development of the legal aspects of many of our nation's counterterrorism policies, spearheaded reforms to the military commissions system at Guantanamo Bay in 2009, and co-authored the 250-page report that paved the way for the repeal of "Don't Ask, Don't Tell" in 2010.

Secretary Johnson's overall career has included extensive service in national security, law enforcement, and as an attorney in private corporate law practice. Secretary Johnson was General Counsel of the Department of the Air Force in 1998 to 2001, and he served as an Assistant U.S. Attorney in the Southern District of New York in 1989 to 1991.

In private law practice, Secretary Johnson was a partner with the New York City-based law firm of Paul, Weiss, Rifkind, Wharton and Garrison, LLP. In 2004, Secretary Johnson was elected a Fellow in the prestigious American College of Trial Lawyers, and he is a member of the Council on Foreign Relations.

Secretary Johnson graduated from Morehouse College in 1979 and received his law degree from Columbia Law School in 1982.

OFFICE OF THE SECRETARY

Secretary of Homeland Security.—Jeh Charles Johnson.
Deputy Secretary of Homeland Security.—Alejandro N. Mayorkas.
Chief of Staff.—Christian Marrone.

CITIZENSHIP AND IMMIGRATION SERVICES OMBUDSMAN

Phone (202) 357–8100

Ombudsman.—Maria Odom.

CIVIL RIGHTS AND CIVIL LIBERTIES

Phone (202) 401–1474, Toll Free: 1–866–644–8360

Officer for Civil Rights and Civil Liberties.—Megan H. Mack.

EXECUTIVE SECRETARIAT

Phone (202) 282–8221

Executive Secretary.—Kimberly O'Connor.

OFFICE OF THE GENERAL COUNSEL

Phone (202) 282–9822

General Counsel.—Stevan Bunnell.

OFFICE OF INSPECTOR GENERAL

Phone (202) 254–4100

Inspector General.—John Roth.

Deputy Inspector General.—Vacant.
Counsel to the Inspector General.—Laurel Rimon.
Assistant Inspector General for—
    Audits.—Mark Bell.
    Emergency Management Oversight.—John V. Kelly.
    Information Technology Audits.—Sondra McCauley.
    Inspections.—Anne Richards.
    Integrity and Quality Oversight.—John McCoy.
    Investigations.—Andrew "Drew" Oosterbaan.
    Management.—Louise McGlathery.
Director, Office of Legislative Affairs.—Erica Paulson.
Chief of Staff.—Vacant.
Special Assistant to the Inspector General.—Dorothy Balaban.

OFFICE OF INTELLIGENCE AND ANALYSIS
Phone (202) 282–8353

Under Secretary and Chief Intelligence Officer.—Francis Taylor.
Principal Deputy Under Secretary.—Kurt Reuther (acting).
Chief of Staff.—Mary Peterson.
    Deputy Under Secretary for Intelligence Operations—Kurt Reuther.
    Associate Deputy Under Secretary for Analysis.—Michael Plotts.
    Executive Director for Plans, Integration, and Evaluation.—Glenn Krizay.

OFFICE OF INTERGOVERNMENTAL AFFAIRS
Phone (202) 282–9310

Assistant Secretary.—Philip A. McNamara.
Deputy Assistant Secretary.—Alaina Clark.

OFFICE OF LEGISLATIVE AFFAIRS
Phone (202) 447–5890

Assistant Secretary.—Vacant.
Deputy Assistant Secretaries: Sue Ramanathan (Senate), Alexandra Veitch (House).

MILITARY ADVISOR'S OFFICE
Phone (202) 282–8239

Military Advisor to the Secretary.—RDML Joanna Nunan.

PRIVACY OFFICE
Phone (703) 235–0780

Chief Privacy Officer.—Karen Neuman.

OFFICE OF PUBLIC AFFAIRS
Phone (202) 282–8069

Assistant Secretary.—Tanya Bradsher.

NATIONAL PROTECTION AND PROGRAMS DIRECTORATE
Phone (202) 282–8400

Under Secretary.—Suzanne E. Spaulding.
Deputy Under Secretary.—Ronald Clark.
Deputy Under Secretary for Cybersecurity.—Phyllis Schneck.
Chief of Staff.—David Hess.

Assistant Secretary for—
  Cybersecurity and Communications.—Andy Ozment.
  Infrastructure Protection.—Caitlin Durkovich.
Director of:
  Federal Protective Service.—L. Eric Patterson.
  Office of Biometric Identity Management.—Shonnie Lyon.

SCIENCE AND TECHNOLOGY DIRECTORATE

Phone (202) 254–6033

Under Secretary.—Ronald Brothers.
  Deputy Under Secretary.—Robert Griffin.
  Chief of Staff.—Christina Murata.
  Deputy Chief of Staff.—Tod Companion (acting).
  Director of:
    Acquisition Support and Operations Analysis.—Debra Durham.
    Finance and Budget.—Richard Williams.
    Homeland Security Advanced Research Projects Agency.—Adam Cox (acting).
    Research and Development Partnerships.—Keith Holtermann.
    Support to the Homeland Security Enterprise and First Responders.—Robert Griffin.

MANAGEMENT DIRECTORATE

Phone (202) 447–3400

Under Secretary.—Russell Deyo.
  Deputy Under Secretary.—Chip Fulghum.
  Chief of Staff.—Vince Micone.
  Chief Readiness Support Officer.—Jeffrey Orner.
  Chief Financial Officer.—Chip Fulghum.
  Chief Human Capital Officer.—Catherine Emerson.
  Chief Information Officer.—Luke McCormack.
  Chief Procurement Officer.—Soraya Correa.
  Chief Security Officer.—Gregory Marshall.
  Executive Director, Office of Program Accountability and Risk Management.—Gary Carter.

OFFICE OF POLICY

Phone (202) 282–9708

Assistant Secretary.—Vacant.
  Assistant Secretary/Chief Diplomatic Officer, Office of International Affairs.—Alan Bersin.
  Principal Deputy Assistant Secretary.—Brodi Kotila.
  Chief of Staff.—Holly Canevari.
  Deputy Chief of Staff.—Gail Kaufman.
  Assistant Secretary, Office of Border, Immigration and Trade Policy.—Vacant.
  Deputy Assistant Secretary for—
    Americas.—Vacant.
    Foreign Investment and Trade.—Vacant.
    Immigration Policy.—Mary Giovagnoli.
    Office of Cyber Policy.—Rosemary Wenchel.
    Office of International Engagement.—Mark Koumans.
  Assistant Secretary, Office of Strategy, Planning, Analysis, and Risk.—Thomas Smith (acting).
  Director, Immigration Statistics.—Vacant.
  Deputy Assistant Secretary for—
    Plans.—Christian Abbott (acting).
    Risk and Decision Analysis—Vacant.
    Strategy—Vacant.
    Unity of Effort.—Andrew Kuepper (acting).
  Assistant Secretary, Office of Threat Prevention and Security Policy.—Seth Stodder.
  Deputy Assistant Secretary for—
    Information Sharing Policy.—Robert Mocny (acting).
    Law Enforcement Policy.—Matthew King (acting).
    Screening Coordination.—Kelli Burriesci.

FEDERAL EMERGENCY MANAGEMENT AGENCY (FEMA) DIRECTORATE
500 C Street, SW., 20472, phone (202) 646–2500

Administrator.—W. Craig Fugate.
 Deputy Administrator.—Joseph Nimmich.
 Chief of Staff.—Michael Coen, Jr.
 Senior Law Enforcement Advisor to the Administrator.—Roberto L. Hylton.
 Director, Office of:
  Center of Faith-Based and Neighborhood Partnerships.—David L. Myers.
  Executive Secretariat.—Alyson Vert.
  National Advisory Council.—Charlotte Porter.
  National Capital Region Coordination.—Kim Kadesch.
  Regional Operations.—Elizabeth Edge.
 Office of Chief Counsel.—Adrian Sevier.
 Deputy Administrator, Protection and National Preparedness.—Timothy W. Manning.
 Assistant Administrators:
  Grant Programs.—Brian E. Kamoie.
  National Continuity Programs.—Damon Penn.
  National Preparedness.—Kathleen Fox.
 Administrator, U.S. Fire Administration.—Ernest Mitchell, Jr.
 Associate Administrator, Mission Support.—David Robinson.
 Chiefs:
  Administrative Officer, Mission Support.—Robert Waltemeyer.
  Component Human Capital Officer, Mission Support—Corey Coleman.
  Enterprise Business Unit, Mission Support.—Sandy Geiselman.
  Information Officer, Mission Support.—Adrian R. Gardner.
  Procurement Officer, Mission Support.—David Grant.
  Security Officer, Mission Support.—Dwight Williams.
 Associate Administrator, Response and Recovery.—Elizabeth Zimmerman.
  Deputy Associate Administrator, Response and Recovery.—Corey Gruber.
 Assistant Administrators:
  Logistics.—Jeffrey Dorko.
  Recovery.—Alex Amparo.
  Response.—James Kish (acting).
 Director, Office of:
  Federal Disaster Coordination.—Jonathan Hoyes.
  Readiness and Assessment.—Steve Saunders.
 Deputy Associate Administrator for Insurance and Mitigation, Federal Insurance and Mitigation Administration.—Roy E. Wright.
 Associate Administrator for Policy, Program Analysis and International Affairs.—David Bibo (acting).
 Chief Financial Officer.—Edward Johnson.
 Director, Office of:
  Disability Integration and Coordination.—Marcie Roth.
  Equal Rights.—Pauline Campbell.
  External Affairs.—Joshua Batkin.

OFFICE OF OPERATIONS COORDINATION
phone (202) 282–9580

Director.—Richard Chávez.
 Deputy Director.—Frank DiFalco.
 Chief of Staff.—Tod Heinz.

DOMESTIC NUCLEAR DETECTION OFFICE
phone (202) 254–7300

Director.—Huban A. Gowadia, Ph.D.
 Deputy Director.—Dr. Wayne L. Brasure.
 Chief of Staff.—Vacant.
 Assistant Director, Office of:
  Architecture and Plans.—John Zabko.
  National Technical Nuclear Forensics Center.—William Daitch.
  Operations Support.—Paul Ryan.

Product Acquisition and Deployment.—Clarence Johnson.
Red Team/Net Assessments.—Kevin McCarthy.
Systems Engineering and Evaluation.—Julian Hill.
Transformational Research and Development.—Joel Rynes.

TRANSPORTATION SECURITY ADMINISTRATION (TSA)
601 South 12th Street, Arlington, VA 20598–6001

Administrator/Assistant Secretary.—Peter Neffenger.
Deputy Administrator.—Mark Hatfield.
Chief of Staff.—Thomas C. McDaniels, Jr.

UNITED STATES CUSTOMS AND BORDER PROTECTION (CBP)
1300 Pennsylvania Avenue, NW., 20229

Commissioner.—R. Gil Kerlikowske (202) 344–1010/344–2001.
Deputy Commissioner.—Kevin McAleenan, 344–1010/2001.
Chief of Staff.—Timothy Quinn (acting), 344–1080/1001.
Deputy Chief of Staff.—Stephen Schorr, 344–2568.
Deputy Chief of Staff (Policy).—Rene Hanna, 344–2116.
Chief Counsel.—Scott Falk, 344–2990.
Assistant Commissioner, Office of:
  Administration.—Eugene H. Schied, 344–2300.
  Air and Marine.—Randolph Alles, 344–3950.
  Congressional Affairs.—Michael Yeager, 344–1760.
  Field Operations.—Todd Owen, 344–1620.
  Human Resources Management. Linda Jacksta, 863 6100.
  Information and Technology.—Charles R. Armstrong, 344–1680.
  Intelligence.—David Glawe, 344–1150.
  Internal Affairs.—Matthew Klein, 344–1800.
  International Affairs.—Charles Stallworth, 344–3000.
  International Trade.—Brenda Smith, 863–6000.
  Public Affairs.—Philip Lavelle, 344–1700.
  Technology Innovation and Acquisition.—Mark Borkowski, 344–2450.
  Training and Development.—Christopher Hall, 344–1130.
Chief, Office of Border Patrol.—Michael Fisher, 344–2050.
Executive Director, Office of:
  Diversity and Civil Rights.—Franklin C. Jones, 344–1610.
  Policy and Planning.—Lewis Roach (acting), 344–2700.
Director, State, Local and Tribal Governments.—Mary Hyland, 325–3914.
Director, Executive Secretariat.—Joseph E. Tezak, 344–1040.
Senior Advisor Trade Relations.—Maria Luisa Boyce, 325–4290.

UNITED STATES IMMIGRATION AND CUSTOMS ENFORCEMENT (ICE)

Director.—Sara Saldaña (202) 732–3000.
Deputy Director.—Daniel Ragsdale, 732–3000.
Chief of Staff.—Leonard Joseph, 732–3000.
Assistant Director of:
  Detention Policy and Planning.—Kevin Landy, 732–5500.
  Professional Responsibility.—Timothy Moynihan, 732–8300.
Principal Legal Advisor.—Gwen Keyes Fleming, 732–5001.
Assistant Director of:
  Congressional Relations.—Jason Yanussi, 732–6171.
  Public Affairs.—Pedro Ribeiro, 732–4242.
Executive Secretariat.—Cynthia O'Connor, 732–5580.
Executive Associate Director, Enforcement and Removal Operations.—Thomas Homan, 732–5545.
  Deputy Executive Associate Director, Enforcement and Removal Operations.—Philip T. Miller, 732–3941.
Assistant Director of:
  Custody Management.—Tae D. Johnson, 732–3110.
  Enforcement.—Matthew Albence, 732–5513.

Field Operations.—Jon Gurule, 732–6203.
ICE Health Service Corps.—Dr. John Krohmer, 732–3047.
Operational Support.—William C. Randolph, 732–3090.
Repatriation.—Marlen Piñeiro, 732–4511.
Deputy Assistant Director, Law Enforcement Systems and Analysis.—Marc Rapp, 732–3915.
Executive Associate Director, Homeland Security Investigations.—Peter T. Edge, 732–5100.
  Deputy Executive Associate Director, Homeland Security Investigations.—Derek N. Benner, 732–5100.
Assistant Director for—
  Domestic Operations.—Dennis Ulrich, 732–3907.
  Information Management.—Gary Hartwig (acting), 732–5753.
  Intelligence.—Patricia Cogswell, 732–3101.
  International Affairs.—Lev Kubiak, 732–3868.
  Mission Support.—Shane Folden (acting), 732–4116.
  National Intellectual Property Rights Coordination Center.—Bruce Foucart (acting), (703) 603–3900.
  National Security.—Craig Healy (703) 287–6870.
  Programs.—Marc Witzal, 732–5852.
Executive Associate Director, Management and Administration.—Tracey Bardorf (acting), 732–3000.
Director, Acquisition Management.—Bill Weinberg, 732–2481.
Assistant Director, Diversity Officer and Civil Rights.—Scott F. Lanum, 732–0125.
Director, Chief Financial Officer.—Jonathan Carver, 732–6208.
Chief Information Officer.—Steven Smith (acting), 732–2000.
Freedom of Information Act Officer.—Catrina Pavlik Keenan, 732–6259.
Human Capital Officer.—Staci A. Barrera (acting), 732–7770.
Assistant Director, Office of Firearms and Tactical Programs.—Humberto Medina, 732–3006.
Assistant Director, Office of Policy.—Margaret Rice (acting), 732–3904.
Privacy Officer.—Lyn Rahilly, 732–3301.
Training and Development.—Donato W. Coyer (acting), 732–1306.

FEDERAL LAW ENFORCEMENT TRAINING CENTER

1131 Chapel Crossing Road, Glynco, GA 31524

Director.—Connie L. Patrick (912) 267–2070.
Deputy Director.—D. Kenneth Keene, 267–2680.
Chief of Staff.—Pamela A. Jastal, 267–2070.
Assistant Director for—
  Mission Readiness and Support Directorate.—Marcus L. Hill, 267–2231.
  Washington Operations.—George E. Kovatch (202) 233–0260.
Assistant Director/Chief Financial Officer.—Donald R. Lewis, 267–2999.
Assistant Director/Innovation and Technology Directorate.—Sandy Peavy, 267–2014.
Assistant Director for—
  Centralized Training Management.—Bradley W. Smith, 267–2451.
  Glynco Training Directorate.—Michael S. Milner, 267–3373.
  Regional and International Training Directorate.—Dominic D. Braccio, 267–2040.
Chief for—
  Office of Organizational Health.—Brenda M. Lloyd, 267–2280.
  Protocol and Communications Office.—Dana O'Quinn, 267–2447.
Chief Counsel.—Dave Brunjes, 267–2851.

UNITED STATES CITIZENSHIP AND IMMIGRATION SERVICES

20 Massachusetts Avenue, NW., Washington, DC 20529, phone (202) 272–1000

Director.—Leon Rodriguez.
Deputy Director.—Lori Scialabba.
Chief of Staff.—Juliet Choi.
Chief Information Officer.—Mark Schwartz.
Associate Director for—
  Fraud Detection and National Security Directorate.—Matthew Emrich (acting).
  Refugee, Asylum and International Operations Directorate.—Joseph Langlois.
  Service Center Operations Directorate.—Donald Neufeld.

Chief, Office of:
  Administration.—Michael Gibbs.
  Administrative Appeals.—Ron Rosenberg (acting).
  Chief Counsel.—Ur Jaddou.
  Chief Financial Officer.—Joseph Moore.
  Citizenship.—Laura Patching.
  Communications.—Angie Alfonso-Royals.
  Legislative Affairs.—James McCament.
  Policy and Strategy.—Denise Vanison.

UNITED STATES COAST GUARD

2100 Second Street, SW., 20593, phone (202) 372–4400

Commandant.—ADM Paul F. Zukunft.
  Vice Commandant.—VADM Charles Michel.
  Deputy Commandant for—
    Mission Support.—VADM Sandra L. Stosz.
    Operations.—VADM Mark E. Butt (acting).
  Chief Administrative Law Judge.—Hon. Walter Brudzinski.
  Judge Advocate General/Chief Counsel.—RADM Steven D. Poulin.
    Deputy Judge Advocate General/Deputy Chief Counsel.—Calvin Lederer.
  Director of Governmental and Public Affairs.—Ellen Engleman Conners.
  Senior Military Advisor to the Secretary of Homeland Security.—RDML Joanna M. Nunan.

UNITED STATES SECRET SERVICE

245 Murray Drive, SW., Building 410, 20223

Director.—Joseph P. Clancy.
  Deputy Director.—Craig D. Magaw.
  Deputy Assistant Director, Congressional Affairs Program.—R. Christopher Stanley (202) 406–5676, fax 406–5740.

INDEPENDENT AGENCIES, COMMISSIONS, BOARDS

ADVISORY COUNCIL ON HISTORIC PRESERVATION
401 F Street, NW., Suite 308, 20001
phone (202) 517–0200, http://www.achp.gov
[Created by Public Law 89–665, as amended]

Chairman.—Milford Wayne Donaldson, Sacramento, California.
Vice Chairman.—Vacant.
Expert Members:
    Lynne Sebastian, Rio Rancho, New Mexico.
    Terry Guen-Murray, Chicago, Illinois.
    Dorothy Lippert, Washington, District of Columbia.
    Robert G. Stanton, Fairfax, Virginia.
Citizen Members:
    Bradford J. White, Evanston, Illinois.
    Teresa Isabel Leger, Santa Fe, New Mexico.
Native American Member.—Chairman Leonard A. Forsman, Suquamish, Washington.
Governor.—Vacant.
Mayor.—Hon. Joseph P. Riley, Jr., Charleston, South Carolina.
Architect of the Capitol.—Hon. Stephen T. Ayers, FAIA.
Secretary, Department of:
    Agriculture.—Hon. Thomas J. Vilsack.
    Commerce.—Rebecca M. Blank (acting).
    Defense.—Hon. Ashton B. Carter.
    Education.—Hon. Arne Duncan.
    Housing and Urban Development.—Hon. Julian Castro.
    Interior.—Hon. Sally Jewell.
    Transportation.—Hon. Anthony Foxx.
    Veterans Affairs.—Hon. Robert McDonald.
Administrator of General Services Administration.—Denise Turner Roth (acting).
National Conference of State Historic Preservation Officer.—Elizabeth A. Hughes, Crownsville, Maryland.
National Trust for Historic Preservation.—Marita Rivero, Washington, DC.
Executive Director.—John M. Fowler.
Director for:
    Office of Administration.—Ralston Cox.
    Office of Communications, Education, and Outreach.—Susan A. Glimcher.
    Office of Federal Agency Programs.—Reid J. Nelson.
    Office of Native American Affairs.—Valerie Hauser.
    Office of Preservation Initiatives.—Ronald D. Anzalone.

AMERICAN BATTLE MONUMENTS COMMISSION
Courthouse Plaza II, Suite 500, 2300 Clarendon Boulevard, Arlington, VA 22201–3367
phone (703) 696–6902
[Created by Public Law 105–225]

Chairman.—Merrill A. "Tony" McPeak appointed as of 6/3/11.
Commissioners:
    Hon. Cindy Campbell.
    Hon. Barbaralee Diamonstein-Spielvogel.
    Hon. Darrell Dorgan.
    Hon. Larry R. Ellis.
    Hon. John L. Estrada.

    Hon. Rolland Kidder.
    Hon. Richard L. Klass.
    Hon. Thomas R. Lamont.
    Hon. Constance Morella.

Secretary.—Hon. Max Cleland.
Deputy Secretaries: Robert J. Dalessandro, John Wessels.
Chief of Staff.—Mike Conley.
Chief Engineer.—Tom Sole.
Chief Financial Officer.—Christine Philpot.
Chief of:
  Human Resources.—John Brennan.
  Knowledge Management.—Monique Ceruti.
  Public Affairs.—Tim Nosal.

(Note: Public law changed to 105–225, August 1998; H.R. 1085.)

AMERICAN NATIONAL RED CROSS

National Headquarters, 430 17th Street, 20006, phone (202) 303–5000

Government Relations, phone (202) 303–4371

HONORARY OFFICERS

Honorary Chair.—Barack H. Obama, President of the United States.

CORPORATE OFFICERS

Chairman.—Bonnie McElveen-Hunter.
  President/CEO.—Gail J. McGovern.
  Chief Audit Executive.—Dale P. Bateman.
  General Counsel/Chief International Officer.—David Meltzer.
  Chief Financial Officer.—Brian Rhoa.

BOARD OF GOVERNORS

Ajay Banga
Afsaneh M. Beschloss
Richard K. Davis
Allan I. Goldberg, M.D.
James W. Keyes
Joseph E. Madison
Bonnie McElveen-Hunter
Gail J. McGovern
Suzanne Nora Johnson

Richard C. Patton
Laurence E. Paul, M.D.
Emilio Romano
Melanie R. Sabelhaus
H. Marshall Schwarz
David A. Thomas, Ph.D.
Carol Tome
Tina M. Tyler
Steven H. Wunning

EXECUTIVE LEADERSHIP

Chief Development Officer.—Neal Litvack.
Chief Diversity Officer.—Floyd Pitts.
Chief Human Resources Officer.—Melissa Hurst.
Chief Information Officer.—Ronnie Strickland.
Chief Marketing Officer.—Peggy Dyer.
Chief Public Affairs Officer.—Suzanne DeFrancis.
Corporate Ombudsman.—Kevin Jessar.
President Biomedical Services.—Shaun P. Gilmore.
President Humanitarian Services.—Cliff Holtz.
President Preparedness and Health and Safety Services.—Jack McMaster.

GOVERNMENTAL RELATIONS

Senior Vice President for Government Relations.—Cherae L. Bishop.
  Legislative Associate.—Jacqueline G. Bassermann.
  Legislative Assistant, State and Federal Relations.—Michaela Keller.
  Senior Director, Government Relations.—Dawn P. Latham.
  Manager, Government Relations.—Marvin Steele.

APPALACHIAN REGIONAL COMMISSION
1666 Connecticut Avenue, NW., 20009, phone (202) 884–7660, fax 884–7693

Federal Co-Chair.—Earl F. Gohl.
  Alternate Federal Co-Chair.—Vacant.
  States' Washington Representative.—Jim McCleskey.
  Executive Director.—Scott T. Hamilton.
  Chief of Staff.—Guy Land.

ARMED FORCES RETIREMENT HOME
3700 North Capitol Street, NW., Box 1303, Washington, DC 20011–8400
phone (202) 541–7532, fax 541–7506

Chief Operating Officer.—Steven G. McManus.
  Chief Financial Officer.—Vicki Marrs.
  Chief Information Officer.—Maurice Swinton.

ARMED FORCES RETIREMENT HOME—WASHINGTON
phone (202) 541–7536, fax 541–7588 or 7615

Administrator.—Shaun Servais.

ARMED FORCES RETIREMENT HOME—GULFPORT
1800 Beach Drive, Gulfport, MS 39507
phone (202) 897–4408, fax 897–4488

Administrator.—Charles Dickerson.

BOARD OF GOVERNORS OF THE FEDERAL RESERVE SYSTEM
Constitution Avenue and 20th Street, NW., 20551, phone (202) 452–3000

Chair.—Janet L. Yellen.
  Vice Chair.—Stanley Fischer.
  Members: Lael Brainard, Jerome H. Powell, Daniel K. Tarullo.
  Assistant to the Board and Division Director.—Michelle A. Smith.
  Assistants to the Board: Lucretia M. Boyer, Linda L. Robertson, David W. Skidmore.
  Senior Special Adviser to the Board.—William B. English.
  Special Assistant to the Board.—Jennifer C. Gallagher.
  Senior Adviser.—Winthrop P. Hambley.

DIVISION OF BANKING SUPERVISION AND REGULATION

Director.—Michael S. Gibson.
  Deputy Directors: Maryann F. Hunter, Mark E. Van Der Weide.
  Senior Associate Directors: Barbara J. Bouchard, Timothy P. Clark, Jack P. Jennings, Arthur W. Lindo, Peter J. Purcell, William G. Spaniel, Todd Vermilyea.
  Associate Directors: Kevin M. Bertsch, Sean Campbell, Nida Davis, Christopher Finger, Ann E. Misback, Richard A. Naylor II, Lisa H. Ryu, Michael J. Sexton, Michael D. Solomon, Thomas Sullivan.
  Deputy Associate Directors: Mary L. Aiken, Jeffrey W. Gunther, Anna Lee Hewko, Michael J. Hsu, Steven P. Merriett, Nancy J. Perkins, Tameika Pope, Richard C. Watkins.
  Assistant Directors: Robert T. Ashman, Constance M. Horsley, Michael J. Kraemer, Ryan P. Lordos, David K. Lynch, T. Kirk Odegard, Catherine A. Piche, Tameika Pope, Laurie Priest, Suzanne L. Williams, Sarkis D. Yoghourtdjian.
  Senior Advisers: Norah M. Barger, David S. Jones.
  Advisers: John Beebe, Fang Du, Keith Ligon, Molly E. Mahar, William F. Treacy.

DIVISION OF CONSUMER AND COMMUNITY AFFAIRS

Director.—Eric Belsky.

Senior Associate Directors: Anna Alvarez Boyd, Suzanne G. Killian.
Associate Directors: Allen J. Fishbein, James A. Michaels.
Deputy Associate Director.—Joseph Firschein.
Assistant Directors: David E. Buchholz, Carol A. Evans, Phyllis L. Harwell, Marisa A. Reid.

DIVISION OF FEDERAL RESERVE BANK OPERATIONS AND PAYMENT SYSTEMS

Director.—Louise L. Roseman.
Deputy Directors.—Matthew J. Eichner, Jeffrey C. Marquardt, David P. Sidari.
Senior Associate Directors: Gregory L. Evans, Susan V. Foley.
Associate Directors: Paul W. Bettge, Michael J. Lambert, Bajinder N. Paul.
Deputy Associate Directors: Lisa K. Hoskins, Jennifer A. Lucier, Lawrence Mize, Stuart E. Sperry.
Assistant Directors: Timothy W. Maas, Jeffrey D. Walker, David Mills, Lorelei Pagano, Shaun Ferrari.
Senior Adviser.—Kenneth Buckley.

DIVISION OF INFORMATION TECHNOLOGY

Director.—Sharon L. Mowry.
Deputy Director: Wayne A. Edmondson.
Associate Directors: Lisa M. Bell, Raymond Romero, Kofi A. Sapong.
Deputy Associate Directors: William K. Dennison, Glenn S. Eskow, Marietta Murphy, Kassandra A. Quimby, Sheryl L. Warren, Rajasekhar R. Yelisetty.
Assistant Directors: Tom Nguyen, Theresa C. Palya, Virginia M. Wall, Edgar Wang, Charles B. Young.
Adviser: Tillena G. Clark.

DIVISION OF INTERNATIONAL FINANCE

Director.—Steve B. Kamin.
Deputy Directors: Thomas A. Connors, Michael P. Leahy.
Senior Associate Director.—Christopher J. Erceg.
Associate Directors: David H. Bowman, Mark S. Carey, Charles P. Thomas, Beth Anne Wilson.
Deputy Associate Directors: Shagil Ahmed, Joseph W. Gruber.
Assistant Director.—James Dahl.
Senior Advisers: Mark S. Carey, Sally M. Davies, Brian M. Doyle, Jane T. Haltmaier, John H. Rogers.

DIVISION OF MONETARY AFFAIRS

Director.—Thomas Laubach.
Deputy Directors: James Clouse, Stephen A. Meyer, William R. Nelson, Janice Shack-Marquez.
Associate Directors: Fabio M. Natalucci, Gretchen C. Weinbach, Egon Zakrajsek.
Deputy Associate Directors: William F. Bassett, Margaret DeBoer, Jane E. Ihrig, J. David Lopez-Salido.
Assistant Directors: Elizabeth Klee, Matthew M. Luecke, Edward M. Nelson, Min Wei.
Senior Advisers: Ellen Meade, Joyce K. Zickler.
Advisers.—Burcu Duygan-Bump, Mary T. Hoffman, Robert Tetlow.

DIVISION OF RESEARCH AND STATISTICS

Director.—David Wilcox.
Deputy Directors: Daniel Covitz, Janice Shack-Marquez, William L. Wascher III.
Senior Associate Directors: Eric M. Engen, Diana Hancock, David E. Lebow, Michael G. Palumbo.
Associate Director: Joshua H. Gallin.
Deputy Associate Directors: Jeffrey C. Campione, Diana Hancock, Elizabeth K. Kiser, John J. Stevens, Stacey M. Tevlin.

Assistant Directors: Stephanie Aaronson, Glenn Follette, Erik Heitfield, Arthur Kennickell, John Roberts, Steven A. Sharpe, Shane Sherlund.
Senior Advisers: Glenn B. Canner, Michael S. Cringoli, Michael Kiley, S. Wayne Passmore, Robin Prager, Jeremy Rudd.
Advisers.—Eric Engstrom, Patrick McCabe, Karen M. Pence.

INSPECTOR GENERAL

Inspector General.—Mark Bialek.
Deputy Inspector General.—J. Anthony Ogden.
Associate Inspectors General: Jacqueline M. Becker, Elise M. Ennis, Melissa Heist, Andrew Patchan, Jr., Alberto Rivera-Fournier, Lawrence Valctt.

LEGAL DIVISION

General Counsel.—Scott G. Alvarez.
Deputy General Counsels: Richard M. Ashton, Kathleen M. O'Day.
Associate General Counsels: Stephanie Martin, Laurie S. Schaffer, Katherine H. Wheatley.
Assistant General Counsels: Jean C. Anderson, Alison M. Thro, Cary K. Williams.

MANAGEMENT DIVISION

Director.—Michell C. Clark.
Deputy Directors: David J. Capp, David J. Harmon.
Senior Associate Director: Marie S. Savoy.
Associate Director: Tara Tinsley Pelitere.
Assistant Directors: Keith F. Bates, Curtis Eldridge, Jeffrey Martin, Reginald V. Roach, Carol A. Sanders, Theresa A. Trimble.
Senior Adviser: Todd A. Glissman.

OFFICE OF THE SECRETARY

Secretary.—Robert deV. Frierson.
Deputy Secretary.—Margaret M. Shanks.
Associate Secretary.—Michael J. Lewandowski.

OFFICE OF FINANCIAL STABILITY POLICY AND RESEARCH

Director.—J. Nellie Liang.
Deputy Director.—Andreas W. Lehnert.
Assistant Director.—John Schindler.
Senior Associate Director.—Michael Kiley.
Deputy Associate Director.—Rochelle M. Edge.
Advisor. David Aikman.

OFFICE OF THE CHIEF OPERATING OFFICER

Chief Operating Officer.—Donald V. Hammond.
ODI Program Director.—Sheila Clark.

BROADCASTING BOARD OF GOVERNORS
330 Independence Avenue, SW., Suite 3300, 20237
phone (202) 203–4545, fax 203–4568

The Broadcasting Board of Governors oversees the operation of the IBB and provides yearly funding grants approved by Congress to three non-profit grantee corporations, Radio Free Europe/Radio Liberty, Radio Free Asia, and the Middle East Broadcasting Networks.
Chairman.—Jeffrey Shell.

INTERNATIONAL BROADCASTING BUREAU

[Created by Public Law 103–236]

The International Broadcasting Bureau (IBB) is composed of the Voice of America, and Radio and TV Marti.

Chief Executive Officer and Director of Broadcasting Board of Governors.—Andrew Lack, (202) 203–4545, fax 203–4568.
Director of:
  Cuba Broadcasting.—Carlos Garcia-Perez (305) 437–7012, fax 437–7016.
  Voice of America.—David B. Ensor (202) 203–4500, fax 203–4513.
President, Radio Free Asia.—Libby Liu (202) 530–4900, fax 530–7795.
President, Radio Free Europe.—Vacant (202) 457–6900, fax 457–6933.
President, Middle East Broadcasting Networks.—Brian Conniff (703) 852–9000, fax 991–1250.

GOVERNORS

Matthew Armstrong
Leon Aron
Ryan Crocker
Michael Kempner

Karen Kornbluh
Kenneth Weinstein
John F. Kerry (ex officio)

CENTRAL INTELLIGENCE AGENCY

phone (703) 482–1100

Director.—John O. Brennan.
  Deputy Director.—David S. Cohen.
  Associate Deputy Director.—Meroe S. Park.
  General Counsel.—Caroline D. Krass.
Director of:
  Intelligence.—Richard W. Hoch.
  Public Affairs.—R. Dean Boyd.
  Science and Technology.—Glenn Gaffney.
  Support.—Jeanne C. Tinsinger.
  Congressional Affairs.—Neal Higgins.

COMMISSION OF FINE ARTS

National Building Museum, 401 F Street, NW., Suite 312, 20001–2728

phone (202) 504–2200, fax 504–2195, http://www.cfa.gov

Commissioners:
Earl A. Powell III, Washington, DC, Chair.
Elizabeth Plater-Zyberk, Miami, FL,
  Vice Chair.
Philip Freelon, FAIA, Durham, NC.

Beth Meyer, Charlottesville, VA.
Alex Krieger, Boston, MA.
Mia Lehrer, Los Angeles, CA.
Liza Gilbert, Washington, DC.

Secretary.—Thomas Luebke, FAIA.
Assistant Secretary.—Frederick J. Lindstrom.

BOARD OF ARCHITECTURAL CONSULTANTS FOR THE OLD GEORGETOWN ACT

Stephen Muse, FAIA, Chair.
H. Alan Brangman, AIA.

Richard Williams, FAIA.

COMMITTEE FOR PURCHASE FROM PEOPLE WHO ARE BLIND
OR SEVERELY DISABLED
1421 Jefferson Davis Highway, Jefferson Plaza 2, Suite 715
Arlington, VA 22202–3259, phone (703) 603–7740, fax 603–0655
[Operating as U.S. AbilityOne Commission]

Chairperson.—J. Anthony "Tony" Poleo.
Vice Chairperson.—James M. Kesteloot.
Executive Director.—Tina Ballard.
Members:
Perry Edward "Ed" Anthony, Department of Education.
Jan R. Frye, Department of Veterans Affairs.
Harry P. Hallock, Department of the Army.
J. Anthony "Tony" Poleo, Department of Defense.
Thomas D. Robinson, Department of the Air Force.
William Sisk, General Services Administration.
Lisa M. Wilusz, Department of Agriculture.
Virna L. Winters, Department of Commerce.
Rear Adm. Jonathan A. Yuen, Department of the Navy.
James M. Kesteloot, Private Citizen (Obstacles to Employment of People Who Are Blind).
Anil Lewis, Private Citizen (Nonprofit Agency Employees Who Are Blind).
Karen J. McCulloh, Private Citizen (Nonprofit Agency Employees with Other Severe Disabilities).
Robert T. Kelly, Jr., Private Citizen (Obstacles to Employment of People with Other Severe Disabilities).
Vacant, Department of Justice.
Vacant, Department of Labor.

COMMODITY FUTURES TRADING COMMISSION
Three Lafayette Centre, 1155 21st Street, NW., 20581, phone (202) 418–5000
fax 418–5521, http://www.cftc.gov

Chairman.—Tim Massad, 418–5050, fax 418–5533.
Chief of Staff.—Clark Ogilvie, 418–5050.
Special Counsels: Jeffrey Bandman, Ward P. Griffin, Lawranne Stewart, 418–5050.
Executive Assistant.—Karen Brown, 418–5050.
Commissioners:
Sharon Y. Bowen, 418–5060, fax 418–5620.
J. Christopher Giancarlo, 418–5030, fax 418–5072.
Mark Wetjen, 418–5010, fax 418–5067.
Director, Division of:
Clearing and Intermediary Oversight.—Phyllis Dietz (acting), 418–5449, fax 418–5547.
Enforcement.—Aitan Goelman, 418–5000, fax 418–5523.
Market Oversight.—Vince A. McGonagle, 418–5387, fax 418–5527.
Executive Director.—Anthony C. Thompson, 418–5697, fax 418–5541.
Chief Economist.—Sayee Srinivasan, 418–5309, fax 418–5660.
General Counsel.—Jonathan L. Marcus, 418–5649, fax 418–5524.
Inspector General.—A. Roy Lavik, 418–5110, fax 418–5522.
Data and Technology Chief Information Officer.—John Rogers, 418–5240.
Director, Office of:
Diversity and Inclusion.—Lorena Carrasco, 418–5935, fax 418–5546.
International Affairs.—Sarah Josephson, 418–5645, fax 418–5548.
Legislative Affairs.—Cory Claussen, 418–5075, fax 418–5525.
Public Affairs.—Steven W. Adamske, 418–5080, fax 418–5525.
Office of the Secretariat, Secretary of the Commission.—Chris Kirkpatrick, 418–5100, fax 418–5521.

REGIONAL OFFICES

Central Region: 525 West Monroe Street, Suite 1100, Chicago, IL 60601 (312) 596–0700, fax 596–0716, TTY 596–0565.

Southwestern Region: 4900 Main Street, Suite 500, Kansas City, MO 64112 (816) 960–7700, fax 960–7750, TTY 960–7704.
Eastern Region: 140 Broadway, Nineteenth floor, New York, NY 10005 (646) 746–9700, fax 746–9938, TTY 746–9820.

CONSUMER PRODUCT SAFETY COMMISSION
4330 East West Highway, Bethesda, MD 20814, phone (301) 504–7923
fax 504–0124, http://www.cpsc.gov
[Created by Public Law 92–573]

Chairperson.—Elliot Kay (301) 504–7900.
  Commissioners:
    Robert "Bob" Adler, 504–7731.
    Marietta Robinson, 504–7253.
    Ann Marie Buerkle, 504–7878.
    Joseph Mohorovic, 504–7738.
  Executive Director.—Patricia Adkins, 504–7582.
  Deputy Executive Director for—
    Operations Support.—DeWane Ray, 504–7547.
    Safety Operations.—Robert J. Howell, 504–7621.
  Director, Office of:
    The Secretary.—Todd A. Stevenson, 504–7923.
    Congressional Relations.—Jason Levine, 504–7882.
  General Counsel.—Stephanie Tsacoumis, 504–7612.

CORPORATION FOR NATIONAL AND COMMUNITY SERVICE
1201 New York Avenue, NW., 20525, phone (202) 606–5000
http://www.cns.gov
[Executive Order 11603, June 30, 1971; codified in 42 U.S.C., section 4951]

Chief Executive Officer.—Wendy Spencer.
  Chief of Staff.—Asim Mishra.
  Chief Financial Officer.—Cyprian O. Ejiasa, 606–6694.
  Inspector General.—Deborah Jeffrey.
  Director of:
    AmeriCorps/National Civilian Community Corps.—Jose M. Phillips, 606–6706.
    AmeriCorps/State and National.—Bill Basl, 606–6790.
    AmeriCorps/VISTA.—Paul Monteiro, 606–6943.
    Senior Corps.—Erwin Tan, 606–3237.
    Office of Government Relations.—Kim Allman, 606–6707.
  General Counsel.—Jeremy Joseph, 606–6677.

DEFENSE NUCLEAR FACILITIES SAFETY BOARD
625 Indiana Avenue, NW., Suite 700, 20004, phone (202) 694–7000
fax 208–6518, http://www.dnfsb.gov

Chairman.—Vacant.
  Vice Chairman.—Jessie Hill-Roberson.
  Members: Daniel J. Santos, Sean Sullivan.
    General Counsel.—Richard Reback (acting).
    General Manager.—Mark Welch.
    Technical Director.—Steven Stokes.

DELAWARE RIVER BASIN COMMISSION
25 State Police Drive, P.O. Box 7360, West Trenton, NJ 08628–0360
phone (609) 883–9500, fax 883–9522, http://www.drbc.net
[Created by Public Law 87–328]

FEDERAL REPRESENTATIVES

Federal Commissioner.—BG Kent D. Savre, Commander, Division Engineer, U.S. Army Corps of Engineers, North Atlantic Division (347) 370–4500.

First Alternate.—LTC Michael A. Bliss, Philadelphia District Commander, U.S. Army Corps of Engineers, Philadelphia (215) 656–6501.
Second Alternate.—David J. Leach, Director of Programs, U.S. Army Corps of Engineers, North Atlantic Division (347) 370–4629.
Third Alternate.—Henry W. Gruber, Program Manager, U.S. Army Corps of Engineers, North Atlantic Division (347) 370–4566.

STAFF

Executive Director.—Steven J. Tambini, P.E., ext. 200.
  Deputy Executive Director.—Vacant.
  Commission Secretary/Assistant General Counsel.—Pamela M. Bush, J.D., M.R.P., ext. 203.
  Communications Manager.—Clarke Rupert, ext. 260.

DELAWARE REPRESENTATIVES

State Commissioner.—Jack A. Markell, Governor (302) 577–3210.
  First Alternate.—David Small, Secretary, Delaware Department of Natural Resources and Environmental Control (DNREC), (302) 739–9000.
  Second Alternate.—Bryan A. Ashby, Program Manager, Division of Water Resources (DNREC), (302) 739–9949.

NEW JERSEY REPRESENTATIVES

State Commissioner.—Chris Christie, Governor (609) 292–6000.
  First Alternate.—Bob Martin, Commissioner, New Jersey Department of Environmental Protection (NJDEP), (609) 292–2885.
  Second Alternate.—Daniel M. Kennedy, MCRP, PP/AICP, Assistant Commissioner, Water Resource Management (NJDEP), (609) 292–4543.
  Third Alternate.—Fred Sickels, Director, Division of Water Supply and Geoscience (NJDEP), (609) 292–2957.

NEW YORK REPRESENTATIVES

State Commissioner.—Andrew M. Cuomo, Governor (518) 474–8390.
  First Alternate.—Joe Martens, Commissioner, New York State Department of Environmental Conservation (NYSDEC), (518) 402–8545.
  Second Alternate.—Mark Klotz, P.E., Director, Division of Water (NYSDEC), (518) 402 8233.
  Third Alternate.—Tom Cullen, Assistant Director, Division of Water (NYSDEC), (518) 402–8233.
  Fourth Alternate.—Angus Eaton, Director, Bureau of Water Resource Management (NYSDEC), (518) 402–8132.

PENNSYLVANIA REPRESENTATIVES

State Commissioner.—Tom Wolf, Governor (717) 787–2500.
  First Alternate.—John Quigley (acting), Secretary, Pennsylvania Department of Environmental Protection (PADEP), (717) 787–2814.
  Second Alternate.—Kelly J. Heffner, Deputy Secretary for Water Management (PADEP), (717) 783–4693.
  Third Alternate.—Andrew Zemba, Director of Interstate Waters (PADEP), (717) 772–5633.
  Fourth Alternate.—Charles W. Kirkwood (570) 421–6513.
  Fifth Alternate.—Randal Adams, Executive Assistant (PADEP), (717) 783–7404.

ENVIRONMENTAL PROTECTION AGENCY
1200 Pennsylvania Avenue, NW., 20460, phone (202) 564–4700, http://www.epa.gov

Administrator.—Gina McCarthy.
  Deputy Administrator.—Stan Meiburg (acting), 564–4711.
  Chief of Staff.—Gwendolyn Keyes-Fleming, 564–6999.
  Deputy Chief of Staff.—John Reeder, 564–4715.
  Agriculture Counsel.—Ron Carlton, 564–7719.
  White House Liaison.—Esther Morales, 564–7960.
  Environmental Appeals Board: Annette Duncan, Lesley Fraser, Catherine McCabe, 233–0122.

Associate Administrator for—
    Congressional and Intergovernmental Relations.—Laura Vaught, 564–5200.
    Homeland Security.—Samuel Wiggins (acting), 564–6978.
    Policy, Economics, and Innovation.—Joel Beauvais, 564–4332.
    Public Affairs.—Tom Reynolds, 564–8368.
Director, Office of:
    Children's Health Protection.—Ruth Etzel, 564–2188.
    Civil Rights.—Velveta Golightly-Howell (acting), 564–7272.
    Cooperative Environmental Management.—Vacant, 233–0090.
    Executive Secretariat.—Eric Wachter, 564–7311.
    Executive Services.—Louise Kitamura, 564–0444.
    Science Advisory Board.—Christopher Zarba, 343–9999.
    Small and Disadvantaged Business Utilization.—Kimberly Patrick, 564–2075.
Director of Management, Office of Administrative Law Judges.—Susan Biro, 564–6255.

ADMINISTRATION AND RESOURCES MANAGEMENT

Assistant Administrator.—Nancy Gelb (acting), 564–4600.
Principal Deputy Assistant Administrator.—Donna Vizian (acting), 564–4600.

AIR AND RADIATION

Assistant Administrator.—Janet McCabe (acting), 564–7404.
Deputy Assistant Administrator.—Betsy Shaw, 564–7400.

ENFORCEMENT AND COMPLIANCE ASSURANCE

Assistant Administrator.—Cynthia Giles, 564–2440.
Principal Deputy Assistant Administrator.—Lawrence Starfield, 564–2440

OFFICE OF ENVIRONMENTAL INFORMATION

Assistant Administrator.—Renee Wynn (acting), 564–6665.
Principal Deputy Assistant Administrator.—Ron Borsellino (acting).

CHIEF FINANCIAL OFFICER

Chief Financial Officer.—David Bloom (acting), 564–1152.
Deputy Chief Financial Officer.—David Bloom (acting).

GENERAL COUNSEL

General Counsel.—Avi Garbow, 564–8064.
Principal Deputy General Counsel.—Kevin Minoli, 564–8064.
Deputy General Counsels: Stacey Mitchell, Ethan Shenkman, 564–8064.

INSPECTOR GENERAL

Inspector General.—Arthur Elkins, Jr., 566–0847.
Deputy Inspector General.—Charles Sheehan.

INTERNATIONAL AFFAIRS

Assistant Administrator.—Jane Nishida (acting), 564–6600.
Deputy Assistant Administrator.—Vacant.

CHEMICAL SAFETY AND POLLUTION PREVENTION

Assistant Administrator.—James Jones (acting), 564–2902.
Principal Deputy Assistant Administrator.—Louise Wise.

RESEARCH AND DEVELOPMENT

Assistant Administrator.—Lek Kadeli (acting), 564–6620.

Deputy Assistant Administrator of:
  Research and Development.—Thomas Burke.
  Science.—Robert Kavlock.

SOLID WASTE AND EMERGENCY RESPONSE

Assistant Administrator.—Mathy Stanislaus, 566–0200.
Principal Deputy Assistant Administrator.—Barry Breen.

WATER

Assistant Administrator.—Vacant, 564–5700.
Deputy Assistant Administrator.—Ken Kopocis.

REGIONAL ADMINISTRATION

Region I, Boston.—Connecticut, Maine, New Hampshire, Rhode Island, Vermont.
  Regional Administrator.—Curt Spalding, One Congress Street, Suite 1100, Boston, MA 02114 (617) 918–1010.
  Public Affairs.—Nancy Grantham.
Region II, New York City.—New Jersey, New York, Puerto Rico, Virgin Islands.
  Regional Administrator.—Judith Enck, 290 Broadway, New York, NY 10007 (212) 637–5000.
  Public Affairs.—Dawn Dearden (212) 637–3660.
Region III, Philadelphia.—Delaware, Washington, DC, Maryland, Pennsylvania, Virginia, West Virginia.
  Regional Administrator.—Shawn Garvin, 1650 Arch Street, Philadelphia, PA 19103–2029 (215) 814–2900.
  Public Affairs.—Terri White (215) 814–2900.
Region IV, Atlanta.—Alabama, Florida, Georgia, Kentucky, Mississippi, North Carolina, South Carolina, Tennessee.
  Regional Administrator.—Heather McTeer Toncy, 61 Forsyth Street, SW., Atlanta, GA 30303–8960 (404) 562–8357.
  Public Affairs.—Larry Lincoln (404) 562–8327.
Region V, Chicago.—Illinois, Indiana, Michigan, Minnesota, Ohio, Wisconsin.
  Regional Administrator.—Susan Hedman, 77 West Jackson Boulevard, Chicago, IL 60604–3507 (312) 886–3000.
  Public Affairs.—Anne Rowan.
Region VI, Dallas.—Arkansas, Louisiana, New Mexico, Oklahoma, Texas.
  Regional Administrator.—Ron Curry, Fountain Place, 1445 Ross Avenue, 12th Floor, Suite 1200, Dallas, TX 75202–2733 (214) 665–2100.
  Public Affairs.—David W. Gray.
Region VII, Kansas City.—Iowa, Kansas, Missouri, Nebraska.
  Regional Administrator.—Karl Brooks, 901 North 5th Street, Kansas City, MO 66101 (913) 551–7006.
  Public Affairs.—Curtis Carey (913) 551–7003.
Region VIII, Denver.—Colorado, Montana, North Dakota, South Dakota, Utah, Wyoming.
  Regional Administrator.—Shaun McGrath, 999 18th Street, Suite 300, Denver, CO 80202–2466 (303) 312–6308.
  Public Affairs.—Paula Smith (303) 312–6608.
Region IX, San Francisco.—Arizona, California, Hawaii, Nevada, American Samoa, Guam.
  Regional Administrator.—Jared Blumenfeld, 75 Hawthorne Street, San Francisco, CA 94105 (415) 947–8702.
  Public Affairs.—Kelly Zito.
Region X, Seattle.—Alaska, Idaho, Oregon, Washington.
  Regional Administrator.—Dennis McLerran, 1200 Sixth Avenue, Seattle, WA 98101 (206) 553–1234.
  Public Affairs.—Marianne Holsman (206) 553–1234.

EQUAL EMPLOYMENT OPPORTUNITY COMMISSION
131 M Street, NE., 20507, phone (202) 663–4900

Chairman.—Jenny R. Yang, suite 6NW08F, 663–4001, fax 663–4110.
  Chief Operating Officer.—Cynthia Pierre, suite 6NW08F.
  Deputy Chief Operating Officer.—Vacant.

Confidential Assistant.—Denise Campbell-Parson, suite 6NW08F, 663–4002.
Commissioners: Constance Barker, suite 6NE25F, 663–4027, fax 663–7121; Charlotte A. Burrows, suite 6NE37F, 663–4052, fax 663–4108; Chai Feldblum, suite 6NE07F, 663–4090, fax 663–7101; Victoria Lipnic, suite 6NE19F, 663–4099, fax 663–7086.
General Counsel.—P. David Lopez, 5th floor, 663–7034, fax 663–4196.
Legal Counsel.—Peggy Mastroianni, 5th floor, 663–4327, fax 663–4639.
Director, Office of:
  Chief Financial Officer.—Germaine Roseboro, 4th floor, 663–4200, fax 663–7068.
  Communications and Legislative Affairs.—Brett Brenner (acting), 6th floor, 663–4191, fax 663–4912.
  Equal Opportunity.—Matthew Murphy (acting), 6th floor, 663–7081, fax 663–7003.
  Executive Secretariat/Executive Secretary.—Bernadette Wilson (acting), 6th floor, 663–4070, fax 663–4114.
  Field Operations.—Carlton Hadden, 5th floor, 663–4599, fax 663–7022.
  Field Programs.—Nicholas Inzeo, 5th floor, 663–4801, fax 663–7190.
  Human Resources.—Lisa Williams, 4th floor, 663–4306, fax 663–4324.
  Information Technology.—Kimberly Hancher, 4th floor, 663–4447, fax 663–4451.
  Inspector General.—Milton Mayo, 6th floor, 663–4327, fax 663–7204.
  Research, Information and Planning.—Deidre Flippen, 4th floor, 663–4853, fax 663–4093.

EXPORT-IMPORT BANK OF THE UNITED STATES

811 Vermont Avenue, NW., 20571, phone (800) 565–EXIM, fax 565–3380

President and Chairman.—Fred Hochberg, 565–3500.
  First Vice President and Vice Chair.—Wanda Felton, 565–3546.
  Directors: Patricia Loui, 565–3520; Sean Mulvaney, 565–3530.
  Chief of Staff.—Scott Schloegel, 565–3502.
  Chief Risk Officer.—Charles J. Hall, 565–3509.
  General Counsel.—Angela Freyre, 565–3430.
  Chief Financial Officer.—David Sena, 565–3272.
  Chief Information Officer.—Howard Spira, 565–3844.
  Senior Vice President of:
    Communications.—Brad Carroll, 565–3201.
    Congressional Affairs.—Erin Gulick, 565–3232.
    Credit Risk Management.—Kenneth Tinsley, 565–3668.
    Export Finance and Chief Banking Officer.—Claudia Slacik, 565–3854.
    Policy and Planning.—James C. Cruse, 565–3761.
    Resource Management.—Michael Cushing, 565–3561.
    Small Business.—James Burrows, 565–3801.
  Vice President of:
    Business Credit.—Pamela Bowers, 565–3792.
    Business Processes.—Michelle Kuester, 565–3221.
    Business Product Development.—Robert Morin, 565–3453.
    Chief Human Capital Officer.—Natasha McCarthy, 565–3592.
    Communications.—Dolline Hatchett, 565–3322.
    Congressional Affairs.—Stephen Rubright, 565–3233.
    Controller.—Joseph Sorbera, 565–3241.
    Country Risk and Economic Analysis.—William Marsteller, 565–3739.
    Credit Review and Compliance.—Walter Hill, Jr., 565–3672.
    Credit Underwriting.—David Carter, 565–3667.
    Customer Experience.—Stephanie Thum, 565–3603.
    Engineering and Environment.—James Mahoney, 565–3573.
    Office of Industry Sector Development.—Michael Forgione, 565–3224.
    Operation and Data Quality.—Nicole Valtos, 565–3411.
    Policy Analysis.—Helene Walsh, 565–3768.
    Project and Corporate Portfolio Management.—Richard Park, 565–3631.
    Public Affairs.—Catrell Brown, 565–3203.
    Short-Term Trade Finance.—Walter Kosciow, 565–3649.
    Structured Finance.—Mike Whelan, 565–3880.
    Strategic Initiatives.—Raymond Ellis, 565–3674.
    Trade Finance.—Annette Maresh, 565–3665.
    Transportation.—Robert Roy, 565–3557.
    Transportation Portfolio Management.—Andrew Falk, 565–3447.
    Treasurer.—Nathalie Herman, 565–3881.

Director of:
  Contracting Services.—William Boyd, 565–3388.
  Inspector General.—Mike McCarthy, 565–3169.
  Intergovernmental Affairs.—Lee Stewart, 565 3773.
  Security.—Selma Hamilton, 565–3313.

FARM CREDIT ADMINISTRATION
1501 Farm Credit Drive, McLean, VA 22102–5090
phone (703) 883–4000, fax 734–5784
[Reorganization pursuant to Public Law 99–205, December 23, 1985]

Board Chair and Chief Executive Officer.—Kenneth A. Spearman.
Board Members:
  Dallas P. Tonsager.
  Jeffery S. Hall.
Secretary to the Board.—Dale L. Aultman, 883–4009, fax 790–5241.
Chief Operating Officer.—William J. Hoffman, 883–4340, fax 790–5241.
Director, Office of:
  Congressional and Public Affairs.—Michael A. Stokke, 883–4056, fax 790–3260.
  Examination.—S. Robert Coleman, 883–4160, fax 893–2978.
General Counsel.—Charles R. Rawls, 883–4020, fax 790–0052.
Inspector General.—Elizabeth M. Dean, 883–4030, fax 883–4059.
Management Services.—Stephen G. Smith, 883–4200, fax 883–4151.
Regulatory Policy.—Gary K. Van Meter, 883–4414, fax 883–4477.
Secondary Market Oversight.—Laurie Rea, 883–4280, fax 883–4478.
Chief Financial Officer.—Stephen G. Smith, 883–4200, fax 883–4151.
Chief Human Capital Officer.—Stephen G. Smith, 883–4200, fax 883–4151.
Chief Information Officer.—Stephen G. Smith, 883 4200, fax 883–4151.
Director, Equal Employment Opportunity and Inclusion.—Thais Burlew, 883–4290, fax 883–4351.

FEDERAL COMMUNICATIONS COMMISSION
445 12th Street, SW., 20554, phone (202) 418–0200, http://www.fcc.gov
FCC National Consumer Center: 1–888–225–5322 / 1–888–835–5322 (TTY)

Chairman.—Thomas Wheeler.
  Chief of Staff.—Ruth Milkman.
  Senior Counselor to the Chairman.—Philip Verveer.
  Special Counsel for External Affairs.—Gigi B. Sohn.
  Special Counsel.—Diane Cornell.*
  Legal Advisors: Daniel Alvarez, Renee Gregory,* Maria Kirby.*
  Confidential Assistant.—Emmaka Porchea-Veneszec.
  Special Assistant.—Sagar Doshi.
  Kim Mattos. *
  Tushu Kinney.
  Latoya Matthews.
  Alva Roane.
Commissioner.—Michael P. O'Rielly.
  Robin Colwell.
  Amy Bender. *
  Erin McGrath. *
  Susan Fisenne. *
  Robert Bukowski. *
Commissioner.—Mignon Clyburn.
  Adonis Hoffman.
  Louis Peraertz. *
  Rebekah Goodheart *
  Drema Johnson.
  DeeAnn Smith.
Commissioner.—Jessica Rosenworcel.
  David Goldman *
  Priscilla Argeris.
  Valery Galasso.

Marquita Boozer.
Jennifer Thompson.
Commissioner.—Ajit Pai.
Matthew Berry.
Nicholas Degani.
Brendan Carr.*
Lori Alexiou.*
Deanne Erwin.

* *On detail (temporary position).*

OFFICE OF ADMINISTRATIVE LAW JUDGES

Administrative Law Judge.—Richard L. Sippel, room 1–C768, 418–2280.

OFFICE OF COMMUNICATIONS BUSINESS OPPORTUNITIES

Director.—Thomas Reed, room 4–A760, 418–0531.

CONSUMER AND GOVERNMENTAL AFFAIRS BUREAU

Chief.—Kris Monteith (acting), room 5–C758, 418–1400.
Deputy Bureau Chiefs: Michael Carowitz room 5–C751A, 418–0026; Karen Peltz-Strauss, room 5–C755; Mark Stone, room 5–C754, 418–0816.
Chief of Staff.—Dwana Terry, room 5–C831, 418–0643.
Associate Bureau Chief.—Roger Goldblatt, room 5–A848, 418–1035.
Assistant Bureau Chief for Management.—Tamika Jackson, room 5–A847, 418–0159.
Chief, Division of:
   Consumer Affairs and Outreach.—Lyle Ishida, room 4–A525, 418–8240.
   Consumer Inquiries and Complaints.—Sharon Bowers (Gettysburg), (717) 338–2533.
   Consumer Policy.—Kurt Schroeder, room 5–A812, 418–0966.
   Web and Print Publishing.—Howard Parnell, room 4–C456, 418–7280.
Chief, Office of:
   Disability Rights.—Gregory Hlibok, room 3–C341, 559–5158.
   Intergovernmental Affairs.—Gregory Vadas, room 5–A660, 418–1798.
   Office of Native Affairs and Policy.—Geoffrey Blackwell, room 4–C763, 418–3629.
Reference Information Center.—Melissa Askew, room CY–C203D, 418–0292.

ENFORCEMENT BUREAU

Chief.—Travis LeBlanc, room 3–C252, 418–7450.
Deputy Bureau Chiefs: Paula Blizzard, room 3–C254, 418–7450; William Davenport, room 3–C255, 418–7450; Phillip Rosario, room 3–C250, 418–7450.
Associate Chief.—Eric Bash, room 3–C204, 418–2057.
Chief, Division of:
   Investigations and Hearings.—Jeffrey Gee, room 4–C322, 418–7479.
   Market Disputes Resolutions.—Christopher Killion, room 4–C342, 418–1711.
   Spectrum Enforcement.—Bruce Jacobs, room 3–C366, 418–2172.
   Telecommunications.—Richard Hindman, room 4–C224, 418–3613.
Director of:
   North East Region: Chicago, IL.—Michael Moffitt.
   South Central Region: Kansas City, MO.—Denny Carlton.
   Western Region: San Diego, CA.—Rebecca Dorch.

OFFICE OF ENGINEERING AND TECHNOLOGY

Chief.—Julius P. Knapp, room 7–C155, 418–2470.

OFFICE OF GENERAL COUNSEL

General Counsel.—Jonathan Sallet, room 8–C750, 418–2836.
Deputy General Counsels: Michele Ellison, room 8–C712, 418–1718; David Gossett, room 8–C758, 418–0980; Suzanne Tetreault, room 8–C755, 418–1769.

Associate General Counsels: Madeleine Findley, room 8–C860, 418–7390; Karen Onyeije, room 8–C758, 418–1757; Jennifer Tatel, room 8–C833, 418–1817; Stephanie Weiner, room 8–C830, 418–1752.

OFFICE OF INSPECTOR GENERAL

Inspector General.—David L. Hunt, room 2–C327, 418–0470.

INTERNATIONAL BUREAU

Chief.—Mindel De La Torre, room 6–C750, 418–0437.
　Deputy Chiefs: Nese Guendelsberger, room 6–C752, 418–0634; Troy Tanner, room 6–C475, 418–1475.
　Chief, Division of:
　　Policy.—Howard Griboff (acting), room 7–A662, 418–0657.
　　Satellite.—Jose Albuquerque, room 6–A665, 418–2288.
　　Strategic Analysis and Negotiations.—Olga Madruga-Forti, room 6–A763, 418–2489.

OFFICE OF LEGISLATIVE AFFAIRS

Director.—Sara Morris, room 8–C453, 418–0095.
　Deputy Directors: David Toomey, room 8–C464, 418–0729; Andrew Woelfling, room 8–C457, 418–1953.

OFFICE OF MANAGING DIRECTOR

Managing Director.—Jon Wilkins, room 1–C152, 418–1919.
　Deputy Managing Directors: Mindy Ginsburg, room 1–C154, 418–0983; Joseph Hall, room 1–C150, 216–4024; Dana Shaffer, room 1–C155, 418–0832.
　Secretary.—Marlene Dortch, room TW–B204, 418–0300.
　Chief Human Capital Office.—Tom Green, room 1–A100, 418–0293, TTY 481–0150 (employment verification).
　Associate Managing Directors:
　　Administrative Operations.—Wanda Sims, room 1–C402, 418–2990.
　　Financial Operations.—Mark Stephens, 418–0817.
　　Information Technology.—David Bray, room 1–C264, 418–2020.
　　Performance Evaluations and Records Management.—Walter Boswell, room 1–A105, 418–2178.
　Assistant Chief for Management.—Toni McGowan, room CY–C458, 418–2202.

MEDIA BUREAU

Chief.—William Lake, room 3–C740, 418–7200.
　Deputy Bureau Chiefs: Michelle Carey, room 3–C830, 418–7200; Sarah Whitesell, room 3–C742, 418–7200.
　Chief of Staff.—Thomas Horan, room 3–C478, 418–7200.
　Assistant Bureau Chief for Management.—India Malcolm, room 3–C838, 418–7200
　Chief, Division of:
　　Audio Division.—Peter Doyle, room 2–A360, 418–2700.
　　Engineering Division.—John Wong, room 4–C838, 418–7012.
　　Industry Analysis Division.—Hillary DeNigro, room 2–C360, 418–2330.
　　Policy Division.—Mary Beth Murphy, room 4–A766, 418–2120.
　　Video Division.—Barbara A. Kreisman, room 2–A666, 418–1600.

OFFICE OF MEDIA RELATIONS

Director.—Shannon Gilson, room CY–C314B, 418–0505.
　Deputy Director.—Mark Wigfield, room CY–C314C, 418–0253.

OFFICE OF STRATEGIC PLANNING AND POLICY ANALYSIS

Chief.—Jonathan Chambers, room 7–C450, 418–2007.

Deputy Chief.—Elizabeth Andrion, room 7–C450, 418–2034.
Chief Economist.—David Waterman, room 7–C410, 418–1699.
Chief Technologists: Scott Jordan, room 7–C252, 418–1592; Henning Schulzrinne, room 7–C360, 418–1544.
Chief of Incentive Auctions/Senior Advisor to the Chairman.—Gary Epstein, room 7–C357, 418–2033.

WIRELESS TELECOMMUNICATIONS BUREAU

Chief.—Roger Sherman, room 6411, 418–0600.
Deputy Bureau Chiefs: Jean Kiddoo, room 6409, 418–0600; John Leibovitz, room 6417, 418–0600; Jim Schlichting, room 6413, 418–0600.
Associate Bureau Chiefs: Chad Breckinridge, room 6405, 418–0600; Charles Mathias, room 6419, 418–0600.
Assistant Bureau Chief for Management.—Stephen Ebner, room 6422, 418–2147.
Chief, Division of:
 Action and Spectrum Access.—Margaret Wiener, room 6423, 418–0660.
 Broadband.—Blaise Scinto, room 3–C124, 418–BITS.
 Mobility.—Roger Noel, room 6411, 418–0620.
 Spectrum and Competition Policy.—Joel Taubenblatt, room 6327, 418–1513.
 Technology, Systems and Innovation.—Stephen Ebner (acting), room 6422, 418–2147

WIRELINE COMPETITION BUREAU

Chief.—Julie Veach, room 5–C354, 418–1500.
Deputy Bureau Chiefs: Matthew DelNero, room 5–C450, 418–1500; Lisa Gelb, room 5–C451, 418–1500; Carol Mattey, room 5–C356, 418–1500.
Associate Bureau Chiefs: Trent Harkrader, room 5–C330, 418–1500; Deena Shetler, room 5–C413, 418–1500.
Chief of Staff.—Kirk Burgee, room 5–C441, 418–1500.
Chief Economist.—Eric Ralph, room 5–C408, 418–1500.
Chief Data Officer.—Steven Rosenberg, room 5–C352, 418–1500.
Legal Advisors: Michael Jacobs, room 5–C453, 418–1500; Mark Walker (acting), room 5–C424, 418–1500.
Program Manager for USF.—Rachael Kazan, room 5–C434, 418–1500.

OFFICE WORKPLACE DIVERSITY

Director.—Thomas Wyatt, room 5–C750, 418–1799.

REGIONAL AND FIELD OFFICES

NORTHEAST REGION

Regional Director of:
 Chicago: G. Michael Moffitt, Park Ridge Office Center, Room 306, 1550 Northwest Highway, Park Ridge, IL 60068 (847) 813–4671.

FIELD OFFICES—NORTHEAST REGION

Director of:
 Boston: Dennis V. Loria, One Batterymarch Park, Quincy, MA 02169 (617) 786–1154.
 Columbia: James T. Higgins, 9200 Farm House Lane, Columbia, MD 21046 (301) 725–0019.
 Detroit: James A. Bridgewater, 24897 Hathaway Street, Farmington Hills, MI 48335 (248) 471–5661.
 New York: Dan Noel, 201 Varick Street, Room 1151, New York, NY 10014 (212) 337–1865.
 Philadelphia: Gene J. Stanbro, One Oxford Valley Office Building, Room 404, 2300 East Lincoln Highway, Langhorne, PA 19047 (215) 741–3022.

SOUTH CENTRAL REGION

Regional Director of:
Kansas City: Ronald Ramage, 520 NE Colbern Road, Second Floor, Lee's Summit, MO 64086 (816) 316–1243.

FIELD OFFICES—SOUTH CENTRAL REGION

Director of:
Atlanta: Doug Miller, Koger Center, 3575 Koger Boulevard, Suite 320, Duluth, GA 30096 (770) 935–3372.

Dallas: James D. Wells, 9330 LBJ Freeway, Room 1170, Dallas, TX 75243 (214) 575–6361.

Kansas City: Robert C. McKinney, 520 Northeast Colbern Road, Second Floor, Lee's Summit, MO 64086 (816) 316–1248.

New Orleans: Walter Gernon, 2424 Edenborn Avenue, Room 460, Metarie, LA 70001 (504) 219–8989.

Tampa: Ralph M. Barlow, 4010 W. Boy Scout Boulevard, Suite 425, Tampa, FL 33607 (813) 348–1741.

WESTERN REGION

Regional Director of:
Denver: Rebecca Dorch, 215 South Wadsworth Boulevard, Suite 303, Lakewood, CO 80226 (303) 407–8708.

FIELD OFFICES—WESTERN REGION

Director of:
Denver: Nikki Shears, 215 South Wadsworth Boulevard, Suite 303, Lakewood, CO 80226 (303) 231–5212.

Los Angeles: Nader Haghighat, Cerritos Corporate Towers, 18000 Studebaker Road, Room 660, Cerritos, CA 90701 (562) 865–0235.

San Diego: James Lyons, Interstate Office Park, 4542 Ruffner Street, Room 370, San Diego, CA 92111 (858) 496–5125.

San Francisco: Thomas N. Van Stavern, 5653 Stoneridge Drive, Suite 105, Pleasanton, CA 94588 (925) 416–9777.

Seattle: Kris McGowan, 11410 Northeast 122nd Way, Room 312, Kirkland, WA 98034 (425) 820–6271.

FEDERAL DEPOSIT INSURANCE CORPORATION

550 17th Street, NW., 20429

phone (877) 275–3342, http://www.fdic.gov

Chairman.—Martin J. Gruenberg, 898–3888.
　Deputy to the Chairman, Chief of Staff, and Chief Operating Officer.—Barbara Ryan, 898–3841.
　Deputy to the Chairman and Chief Financial Officer.—Steve App, 898–8732.
Vice Chairman.—Thomas M. Hoenig, 898–6616.
　Deputy to the Vice Chairman.—Kathy Kalser (acting) 898–6682.
Director.—Jeremiah O. Norton, 898–3964.
　Deputy to the Director.—Patty Colohan, 898–7283.
Director (OCC).—Thomas Curry, 874–4900.
　Deputy.—William Rowe, 898–6960.
Director (CFPB).—Richard Cordray, 435–9637.
　Deputy.—Stephanie Richo, 435–9307.
Director, Office of Legislative Affairs.—Eric Spitler, 898–7140, fax 898–3745.

FEDERAL ELECTION COMMISSION
999 E Street, NW., 20463
phone (202) 694–1000, Toll Free (800) 424–9530, fax 219–3880, http://www.fec.gov

Chair.—Ann M. Ravel, 694–1020.
Vice Chairman.—Matthew S. Petersen, 694–1011.
Commissioners:
  Caroline C. Hunter, 694–1045.
  Lee E. Goodman, 694–1050.
  Steven T. Walther, 694–1055.
  Ellen L. Weintraub, 694–1035.
Staff Director.—D. Alec Palmer, 694–1007, fax 219–2338.
Deputy Staff Director for—
  Compliance / Chief Compliance Officer.—Patricia C. Orrock, 694–1150.
  Information Technology / Chief Information Officer.—D. Alec Palmer, 694–1250.
  Management and Administration.—Edward W. Holder (acting), 694–1365.
Assistant Staff Director for—
  Disclosure.—Patricia Klein Young, 694–1120.
  Information Division.—Greg J. Scott, 694–1100.
Director for Congressional Affairs.—J. Duane Pugh, 694–1006.
Press Officer.—Judith Ingram, 694–1220.
Director Human Resources.—Roger Cotton, 694–1080.
Administrative Officer.—India K. Robinson, 694–1240.
EEO Director.—Kevin Salley, 694–1229.
General Counsel.—Vacant.
Deputy General Counsel for—
  Administration.—Gregory R. Baker, 694–1650.
  Law.—Lisa J. Stevenson, 694–1650.
Associate General Counsel for—
  Enforcement.—Daniel A. Petalas.
  Litigation.—Kevin Deeley (acting).
  Policy.—Adav Noti (acting).
Library Director (Law).—Leta L. Holley.
Chief Financial Officer.—Judy Berning (acting), 694–1217.
Deputy Chief Financial Officer / Budget Director.—Gilbert Ford, 694–1216.
Director of Accounting.—Judy Berning, 694–1230.
Inspector General.—Lynne A. McFarland, 694–1015.
Deputy Inspector General.—James C. Thurber.

FEDERAL HOUSING FINANCE AGENCY
400 7th Street, NW., 20024
phone (202) 649–3800, fax 649–1017, http://www.fhfa.gov

[Created by Housing and Economic Recovery Act of 2008, 122 Stat. 2654, Public Law 110–289—July 30, 2008]

Director.—Melvin L. Watt, 649–3001.
Deputy Director, Division of:
  Bank Regulation.—Fred Graham, 649–3500.
  Conservatorship.—Wanda DeLeo, 649–3400.
  Enterprise Regulation.—Nina Nichols, 649–3265.
  Housing, Mission and Goals.—Sandra Thompson, 649–3384.
General Counsel.—Alfred Pollard, 649–3050.
Senior Deputy General Counsel.—Christopher Curtis, 649–3051.

OFFICE OF CONGRESSIONAL AFFAIRS AND COMMUNICATIONS

Senior Associate Director.—Megan Moore (acting), 649–3018.
  Associate Director for Congressional Affairs.—Peter Brereton, 649–3022.
  Congressional Affairs Staff: Dallin Merrill, 649–3763; Jeannine Schroeder, 649–3029.
  Director of Communications.—Peter Garuccio, 649–3036.
  Public Affairs Staff: Stefanie Johnson, 649–3030; Corinne Russell, 649–3032.
  Executive Advisor for Consumer Communications.—Owen Highfill (acting), 649–3042.
  Ombudsman.—Mario Ugoletti (acting), 649–3004.

Associate Director for the Office of Minority and Women Inclusion.—Sharron Levine, 649–3496.
Chief Operating Officer.—Lawrence Stauffer (acting), 649–3402.
Chief Information Officer.—Kevin Winkler, 649–3600.
Inspector General.—Laura S. Wertheimer (800) 793–7724.

FEDERAL LABOR RELATIONS AUTHORITY
1400 K Street, NW., 20424–0001, phone (202) 218–7770, fax 482–6635

FLRA Agency Head.—Carol Waller Pope, 218–7900.
Executive Director.—Sarah Whittle Spooner, 218–7791.
Counsel for Regulatory and External Affairs.—Gina K. Grippando, 218–7776.
Solicitor.—Fred B. Jacob, 218–7906.
Inspector General.—Dana Rooney-Fisher, 218–7744.
Collaboration and Alternative Dispute Resolution Program.—Michael Wolf, 218–7933.
Foreign Service Impasse Disputes Panel.—Mary Jacksteit, 218–7790.
Foreign Service Labor Relations Board.—Carol Waller Pope, 218–7900.

AUTHORITY

Chairman.—Carol Waller Pope, 218–7900.
Chief Counsel.—David S. Eddy III (acting), 218–7900.
Member.—Ernest DuBester, 218–7920.
Chief Counsel.—William R. Tobey, 218–7920.
Member.—Patrick Pizzella, 218–7930.
Chief Counsel.—James T. Abbott, 218–7930.
Chief, Case Intake and Publication.—Gina K. Grippando, 218–7740.

GENERAL COUNSEL OF THE FLRA

General Counsel.—Julia A. Clark, 218–7910.
Deputy General Counsel.—Peter A. Sutton, 218–7910.
Assistant General Counsel for—
    Advice and Legal Policy.—Kurt Rumsfeld, 218–7910.
    Appeals.—Richard Zorn, 218–7910.

OFFICE OF ADMINISTRATIVE LAW JUDGES

Chief Judge.—Charles Center, 218–7950.

FEDERAL SERVICE IMPASSES PANEL (FSIP)

FSIP Chairman.—Mary Jacksteit, 218–7790.
Executive Director.—H. Joseph Schimansky, 218–7790.

REGIONAL OFFICES

Regional Directors:
    Atlanta.—Richard S. Jones, Marquis Two Tower, Suite 701, 285 Peachtree Center Avenue, Atlanta, GA 30303 (404) 331–5300, fax 331–5280.
    Boston.—Philip T. Roberts, 10 Causeway Street, Suite 472, Boston, MA 02222 (617) 565–5100, fax 565–6262.
    Chicago.—Sandra LeBold, 224 South Michigan Avenue, Suite 445, Chicago, IL 60604 (312) 886–3465, fax 886–5977.
    Dallas.—James E. Petrucci, 525 Griffin Street, Suite 926, LB 107, Dallas, TX 75202 (214) 767–6266, fax 767–0156.
    Denver.—Tim Sullivan (acting), 1244 Speer Boulevard, Suite 446, Denver, CO 80204 (303) 844–5224, fax 844–2774.
    San Francisco.—Jean Perata, 901 Market Street, Suite 470, San Francisco, CA 94103 (415) 356–5000, fax 356–5017.
    Washington, DC.—Barbara Kraft, 1400 K Street, NW., Suite 200, Washington, DC 20005 (202) 357–6029, fax 482–6724.

FEDERAL MARITIME COMMISSION
800 North Capitol Street, NW., 20573
phone (202) 523–5725, fax 523–0014

OFFICE OF THE CHAIRMAN

Chairman.—Mario Cordero, room 1000, 523–5911.
　Counsel.—Mary T. Hoang.
Commissioner.—Rebecca F. Dye, room 1038, 523–5715.
　Counsel.—Edward L. Lee, Jr.
Commissioner.—Richard A. Lidinsky, room 1032, 523–5721.
　Counsel.—Jewel Jennings-Wright.
Commissioner.—Michael A. Khouri, room 1044, 523–5712.
　Counsel.—John A. Moran.
Commissioner.—William P. Doyle, room 1026, 523–5723.
　Counsel.—David J. Tubman, Jr.

OFFICE OF THE SECRETARY

Secretary.—Karen V. Gregory, room 1046, 523–5725.
Assistant Secretary.—Rachel E. Dickon.
Library.—Vacant, room 1085, 523–5762.

OFFICE OF EQUAL EMPLOYMENT OPPORTUNITY

Director.—Keith I. Gilmore, room 1052, 523–5859.

OFFICE OF THE GENERAL COUNSEL

General Counsel.—Vacant, room 1018, 523–5740.
Deputy General Counsel.—Tyler J. Wood.

OFFICE OF CONSUMER AFFAIRS AND DISPUTE RESOLUTION

Director.—Rebecca A. Fenneman, room 932, 523–5807.
Deputy Director.—Jennifer M. Gartlan.

OFFICE OF ADMINISTRATIVE LAW JUDGES

Chief Judge.—Clay G. Guthridge, room 1088, 523–5750.
Administrative Law Judge.—Erin M. Wirth, room 1088, 523–5750.

OFFICE OF THE INSPECTOR GENERAL

Inspector General.—Jonathan Hatfield, room 1054, 523–5863.

OFFICE OF THE MANAGING DIRECTOR

Director.—Vern W. Hill, room 1082, 523–5800.
Assistant Managing Director for Administration.—James A. Nussbaumer.
Area Representatives:
　Houston.—Adam Sinko (281) 386–8211.
　Los Angeles: Nash D. Asandas, Oliver E. Clark (310) 514–4905.
　New Orleans.—Bruce N. Johnson, Sr. (504) 589–6662.
　New York: Matthew D. Forst (732) 283–2497; Ron Podlaskowich (732) 283–2496.
　Seattle.—Michael A. Moneck (253) 922–7622.
　South Florida.—Andrew Margolis (954) 963–5362; Eric O. Mintz (954) 963–5284.
Director, Office of:
　Budget and Finance.—Karon E. Douglass, room 916, 523–5770.
　Human Resources.—William T. Cole, room 924, 523–5773.

Information Technology.—Vacant, room 904, 523–5835.
Management Services.—Kristian Jovanovic, room 926, 523–5900.

BUREAU OF CERTIFICATION AND LICENSING

Director.—Sandra K. Kusumoto, room 970, 523–5787.
Deputy Director.—Vacant.
Director, Office of:
  Passenger Vessels and Information Processing.—Tajuanda L. Singletary, 523–5818.
  Transportation Intermediaries.—Jeremiah D. Hospital, 523–5843.

BUREAU OF ENFORCEMENT

Director.—Peter J. King, room 900, 523–5783 or 523–5860.
Deputy Director.—Brian L. Troiano.

BUREAU OF TRADE ANALYSIS

Director.—Florence A. Carr, room 940, 523–5796.
Deputy Director.—Tanga S. FitzGibbon.
Director, Office of:
  Agreements.—Jason W. Guthrie, 523–5793.
  Economics and Competition Analysis.—Roy J. Pearson, 523–5845.
  Service Contracts and Tariffs.—Gary G. Kardian, room 940, 523–5856.

FEDERAL MEDIATION AND CONCILIATION SERVICE
2100 K Street, NW., 20427, phone (202) 606–8100, fax 606–4251
[Codified under 29 U.S.C. 172]

Director.—Allison Beck (acting).
Deputy Director.—Scot L. Beckenbaugh.
Chief of Staff.—Fran L. Leonard, 606–3661.
General Counsel.—Dawn Starr, 606–8090.
Director for—
  ADR/International/FMCS Institute.—Lu-Ann Glaser, 606–2222.
  Arbitration Services.—Arthur Pearlstein, 606–5111.
  Budget and Finance.—Fran L. Leonard, 606–3661.
  Grants.—Linda Gray-Broughton, 606–8181.
  Human Resources.—Tammy Van Keuren, 606–5460.
  Information Systems.—Doug Jones, 606–5483.
Administrative Services.—Cynthia Washington, 606–5477.
Regional Director (Eastern/Western).—Vacant.

FEDERAL MINE SAFETY AND HEALTH REVIEW COMMISSION
1331 Pennsylvania Avenue, NW., Suite 520N, 20004
phone (202) 434–9900, fax 434–9944
[Created by Public Law 95–164]

Chairperson.—Patrick K. Nakamura (acting), room 541, 233–3885.
Commissioners: Robert Cohen, room 547, 434–9912; Althen William, room 545, 434–9951.
Executive Director.—Lisa M. Boyd, room 553, 434–9905.
Chief Administrative Law Judge.—Robert J. Lesnick, room 1414, 434–9958.
General Counsel.—Michael McCord, room 554, 434–9920.

FEDERAL RETIREMENT THRIFT INVESTMENT BOARD
77 K Street, NW., 20002, phone (202) 942–1600, fax 942–1676
[Authorized by 5 U.S.C. 8472]

Executive Director.—Gregory T. Long, 942–1601.

Office of Chief Operating Officer, Deputy Executive Director.—Mark Walther, 942–1440.
General Counsel.—James B. Petrick, 942–1660.
Director, Office of:
  Communications and Education.—Jim Courtney, 942–1450.
  Enterprise Planning.—Renee Wilder, 942–1630.
  Enterprise Risk Management.—Jay Ahuja, 942–1630.
  External Affairs.—Kimberly Weaver, 942–1640.
  Financial Management.—Susan Crowder, 942–1620.
  Investments.—Theresa Ray, 942–1630.
  Participant Operations and Policy.—Thomas K. Emswiler, 942–1460.
  Resource Management.—Gisile Goethe, 942–1630.
  Technology Services.—Scott Cragg, 942–1440.
Chairman.—Michael Kennedy, 942–1660.
Board Members:
  Dana K. Bilyeu.
  Ronald D. McCray.
  David A. Jones.
  William Jasien.

FEDERAL TRADE COMMISSION

600 Pennsylvania Avenue, NW., 20580

phone (202) 326–2222, http://www.ftc.gov

Chairman.—Edith Ramirez, room 444, 326–2856.
Staff Assistant.—Monica Carter, room 444, 326–2666.
Chief of Staff.—Heather Hippsley, room 444, 326–3285.
Commissioners: Julie Brill, room 328, 326–2626; Terrell McSweeny, room 526, 326–2606;
  Maureen Ohlhausen, room 538, 326–2150; Joshua Wright, room 528, 326–2229.
Director, Office of:
  Competition.—Richard A. Feinstein, room 370, 326–3630.
  Congressional Relations.—Jeanne Bumpus, room 408, 326–2195.
  Consumer Protection.—Jessica L. Rich, room 470, 326–2148.
  Economics.—Francine Lafontaine, room 270, 326–2553.
  Policy Planning.—Marina Lao, room 392, 326–2384.
  Public Affairs.—Justin Cole, room 421, 326–3330.
International Affairs.—Randolph W. Tritell, room 492, 326–3051.
Executive Director.—David B. Robbins, room 426, 326–3035.
General Counsel.—Jonathan E. Nuechterlein, room 570, 326–2868.
Secretary.—Donald S. Clark, room 172, 326–2514.
Inspector General.—Roslyn Mazer, room CC–5216A, 326–3295.
Chief Administrative Law Judge.—D. Michael Chappell, room 106, 326–3637.

REGIONAL DIRECTORS

East Central Region: Jonathan M. Steiger, Eaton Center, Suite 200, 1111 Superior Avenue,
Cleveland, OH 44114 (216) 263–3455.
Midwest Region: C. Steve Baker, 55 East Monroe Street, Suite 1825, Chicago, IL 60603
(312) 960–5634.
Northeast Region: William Efron, One Bowling Green, Suite 318, New York, NY 10004
(212) 607–2829.
Northwest Region: Charles Harwood, 915 Second Avenue, Suite 2896, Seattle, WA 98174
(206) 220–6350.
Southeast Region: Cindy A. Liebes, 225 Peachtree Street, NE., Suite 1500, Atlanta, GA
30303 (404) 656–1390.
Southwest Region: Dama J. Brown, 1999 Bryan Street, Suite 2150, Dallas, TX 75201 (214)
979–9350.
Western Region—Los Angeles: Tom Dahdouh, 18077 Wilshire Boulevard, Suite 700, Los
Angeles, CA 90024–3679 (310) 824–4343.
Western Region—San Francisco: Tom Dahdouh, 901 Market Street, Suite 570,
San Francisco, CA 94103 (415) 848–5100.

FOREIGN-TRADE ZONES BOARD
1401 Constitution Avenue, NW., Room 21013, 20230
phone (202) 482–2862, fax 482–0002

Chairman.—Penny Pritzker, Secretary of Commerce.
Member.—Jacob J. Lew, Secretary of the Treasury.
Executive Secretary.—Andrew McGilvray.

GENERAL SERVICES ADMINISTRATION
1800 F Street, NW., 20405 phone (202) 501–0800, http://www.gsa.gov

OFFICE OF THE ADMINISTRATOR

Administrator.—Denise Turner Roth (acting).
Deputy Administrator.—Adam Neufeld (acting).
Chief of Staff.—Christine Harada (acting).
Associate Administrator for Communications Marketing.—Mafara Hobson.
White House Liaison.—Reginald H. Cardozo, Jr.

OFFICE OF CONGRESSIONAL AND INTERGOVERNMENTAL AFFAIRS

Associate Administrator.—Lisa A. Austin (202) 501–0563.
Deputy Associate Administrator.—Brett Prather.
Senior Advisor for Appropriations.—Saul Japson.
Director of:
   Congressional Operations.—Erin Mewhirter.
   Congressional Support Services.—Michael Gurgo.

OFFICE OF THE CHIEF FINANCIAL OFFICER

Chief Financial Officer.—Gerard Badorrek (202) 501–1721.
   Director of:
   Budget.—Erica Navarro.
   Financial Operations.—Lisa Ziehmann.
   Financial Services Federal Acquisition.—Agnes Leung.
   Financial Services Public Buildings.—Kathy Hammer.

OFFICE OF GOVERNMENTWIDE POLICY

Associate Administrator.—Giancarlo Brizzi (acting), (202) 501–8880.
   Chief Acquisition Officer.—Christine Harada.
   Senior Procurement Executive.—Jeff Koses.
   Chief of Staff.—Jonathan Clinto.
   Executive Officer.—Teresa Tippins.
   Deputy Associate Administrator, Office of:
   Asset and Transportation.—Alexander Kurien.
   Acquisition Policy.—Jeff Koses.
   High Performance Green Buildings.—Kevin Kampschroer.
   Information, Integrity and Access.—Dominic Sale.

OFFICE OF THE GENERAL COUNSEL

General Counsel.—Kris Durmer (202) 501–2200.
   Deputy General Counsel.—Lennard S. Loewentritt.
   Associate General Counsel for—
   General Law.—Eugenia D. Ellison, 501–1460.
   Personal Property.—Janet Harney, 501–1156.
   Real Property.—Berry Segal, 501–0430.

OFFICE OF CITIZEN SERVICES AND INNOVATIVE TECHNOLOGIES (OCSIT)/18F

Associate Administrator.—Phaedra S. Chrousos (202) 501–0705.
   OCSIT Principal Deputy Associate Administrator.—Kathy Conrad.

OFFICE OF THE CHIEF INFORMATION OFFICER

Chief Information Officer.—David Shive (acting), (202) 501–1000.
Deputy Chief Information Officer.—David Shive.
Chief of Staff .—Lesley Briante.
Director, Office of:
　Enterprise Infrastructure.—Teresa Curtis (acting).
　Enterprise Management Service.—Daryle "Mike" Seckar.

OFFICE OF HUMAN RESOURCES MANAGEMENT

Chief Human Capital Officer.—Antonia T. Harris (202) 501–0398.
Chief of Staff.—Autumn Jones.

OFFICE OF CIVIL RIGHTS

Associate Administrator.—Madeline Caliendo (202) 501–0767.

OFFICE OF SMALL BUSINESS UTILIZATION

Associate Administrator.—Jerome Fletcher (202) 501–1021.
Chief of Staff.—Stephanie Wilson-Coleman.

OFFICE OF ADMINISTRATIVE SERVICES

Chief Administrative Services Officer.—Cynthia Metzler (202) 357–9697.
Deputy Chief Administrative Services Officer.—Erika Dinnie.

OFFICE OF THE INSPECTOR GENERAL

Inspector General.—Robert C. Erickson (acting), (202) 501–0450.
Deputy Inspector General.—Robert C. Erickson, Jr., 501–3105.
Director of Congressional Affairs.—Jennifer Riedinger (202) 219–1062.
Director, Office of Internal Evaluation and Analysis.—Patricia Sheenan (202) 273–4989.
Counsel to the Inspector General.—Richard Levi, 501–1932.
Assistant Inspector General for—
　Administration.—Larry Gregg, 219–1041.
　Auditing.—Theodore R. Stehney, 501–0374.
　Investigations.—Jeff Seherrngton, 501–0035.

CIVILIAN BOARD OF CONTRACT APPEALS

Chair.—Stephen M. Daniels (202) 606–8820.
Vice Chair.—Jeri K. Somers, 606–8831.
Chief Counsel.—J. Gregory Parks, 606–8787.
Clerk.—Cheryl L. Hilton, 606–8800.
Board Judges, 606–8820: Jerome M. Drummond, Allan H. Goodman, Catherine B. Hyatt,
　Harold C. "Chuck" Kullberg, Harold D. "Harv" Lester, Jr., R. Anthony McCann,
　Howard A. Pollack, Patricia J. Sheridan, Candida S. Steel, James L. Stern, Marian
　E. Sullivan, Joseph A. Vergilio, Richard C. Walters, Jonathan D. Zischkau.

NATIONAL SERVICES
FEDERAL ACQUISITION SERVICE

Commissioner.—Thomas A. Sharpe, Jr. (703) 605–5400.
Deputy Commissioner.—Kevin Youel Page.
Chief of Staff.—Sheri Meadema.
Assistant Commissioner, Office of:
　Acquisition Management.—Donna Jenkins.
　Assisted Acquisition Services.—Timothy E. Fleming.
　Customer Accounts and Research.—Houston Taylor.
　General Supplies and Services.—Marty Jennings.
　Integrated Award Environment.—Karen Kopf.

Integrated Technology Services.—Mary A. Davie.
Strategy Management .—Amanda Fredriksen.
Travel, Motor Vehicle and Card Services.—Bill Sisk.

PUBLIC BUILDING SERVICE

Commissioner.—Norman Dong (202) 501–1100.
Deputy Commissioner.—Michael Gelber.
Chief of Staff.—Chelsea Waliser.

REGIONAL OFFICES

National Capital Region (NCR 11): 17th and D Street, SW., Washington, DC 20407 (202) 708–9100.
Regional Administrator.—Julia E. Hudson.
Regional Commissioner for Federal Acquisition Service.—Alfonso Finley.
Regional Commissioner for Public Buildings Service.—Darren Blue.
New England Region I: Thomas P. O'Neill Federal Building, 10 Causeway Street, Boston, MA 02222 (617) 565–5860.
Regional Administrator.—Robert Zarnetske.
Regional Commissioner for Federal Acquisition Service.—Joe Nickerson (acting).
Regional Commissioner for Public Buildings Service.—Glenn Rotondo.
Northeast and Caribbean Region 2: 26 Federal Plaza, New York, NY 10278 (212) 264–2600.
Regional Administrator.—Denise L. Pease.
Regional Commissioner for Federal Acquisition Service.—Jeff Lau (acting).
Regional Commissioner for Public Building Service.—Joanna Rosato (acting).
Mid-Atlantic Region 3: The Strawbridge's Building, 20 North Eight Street, Philadelphia, PA 19107 (215) 446–4900.
Regional Administrator.—Sara Manzano-Diaz.
Regional Commissioner for Federal Acquisition Service.—Linda Chero.
Regional Commissioner for Public Buildings Service.—Joanna Rosato.
Southeast Sunbelt Region 4: 77 Forsyth Street, Suite 600, Atlanta, GA 30303 (404) 331–3200.
Regional Administrator.—Torre J. Jessup.
Regional Commissioner for Federal Acquisition Service.—Erville Koehler.
Regional Commissioner for Public Buildings Service.—Dale Anderson (acting).
Great Lakes Region 5: 230 South Dearborn, Chicago, IL 60604 (312) 353–5395.
Regional Administrator.—Ann P. Kalayil.
Regional Commissioner for Federal Acquisition Service.—Kim E. Brown.
Regional Commissioner for Public Buildings Service.—Allison Azevedo (acting).
Heartland Region 6: 1500 East Bannister Road, Kansas City, MO 64131 (816) 926–7201.
Regional Administrator.—Jason O. Klumb.
Regional Commissioner for Federal Acquisition Service.—Mary Ruwwe.
Regional Commissioner for Public Buildings Service.—Allison Azevedo.
Great Southwest Region 7: 819 Taylor Street, Fort Worth, TX 76102 (817) 978–2321.
Regional Administrator.—Sylvia Hernandez (acting).
Regional Commissioner for Federal Acquisition Service.—George Prochaska.
Regional Commissioner for Public Buildings Service.—Jim Weller.
Rocky Mountain Region 8: Building 41, Denver Federal Center, Denver, CO 80225 (303) 236–7329.
Regional Administrator.—Susan B. Damour.
Regional Commissioner for Federal Acquisition Service.—Timothy Horne.
Regional Commissioner for Public Buildings Service.—Paul Prouty.
Pacific Mountain Region 9: 450 Golden Gate Avenue, Room 5–2690, San Francisco, CA 94102 (415) 522–3001.
Regional Administrator.—Samuel J. "Chip" Morris (acting).
Regional Commissioner for Federal Acquisition Service.—Linda Allen.
Regional Commissioner for Public Buildings Service.—Dan Brown.
Northwest/Arctic Region 10: GSA Center, 400 15th Street, SW., Auburn, WA 98001 (253) 931–7000.
Regional Administrator.—George Northcroft.
Regional Commissioner for Federal Acquisition Service. Tiffany Hixson.
Regional Commissioner for Public Buildings Service.—Benjamin Chaun (acting).

HARRY S. TRUMAN SCHOLARSHIP FOUNDATION

712 Jackson Place, NW., 20006

phone (202) 395–4831, fax 395–6995

[Created by Public Law 93–642]

BOARD OF TRUSTEES

President.—Madeleine K. Albright.
Vice President.—Max Sherman.
Treasurer.—Frederick Slabach.
General Counsel.—Westbrook Murphy.
  Members:
    Javaid Anwar, CEO, Quality Care Consultants, LLC.
    Hon. Roy Blunt, Senator from Missouri.
    Steven H. Cohen, Attorney, Cohen Law Group.
    Hon. Laura Cordero, Associate Judge, DC Superior Court.
    Hon. Charles W. Dent, Representative of Pennsylvania.
    Hon. Theodore E. Deutch, Representative of Florida.
    Hon. Arne Duncan, Secretary of Education.
    Ingrid Gregg, President and Trustee, the Earhart Foundation.
    Michael W. Hail, Professor of Government, Morehead State University.
    Hon. James Henderson, Judge / County Executive, Simpson County, Kentucky.
    Hon. Claire McCaskill, Senator from Missouri.
    Westbrook Murphy, General Counsel, Harry S. Truman Scholarship Foundation.
    Andrew Rich, Executive Secretary, Harry S. Truman Scholarship Foundation.
    Hon. Max Sherman, Professor and Dean Emeritus, Lyndon B. Johnson School of
      Public Affairs, University of Texas.
    Hon. Frederick Slabach, President, Texas Wesleyan University.
Chief Information Officer.—Tonji Wade.
Deputy Executive Secretary.—Tara Yglesias.
Education Officer.—Ruth Keen.
Executive Secretary.—Andrew Rich.
Program Manager.—Andrew Kirk.

INTER-AMERICAN FOUNDATION

1331 Pennsylvania Avenue, NW., 1200 North, Washington, DC, phone (202) 360–4530

Chair, Board of Directors.—Eddy Arriola.
Vice Chair, Board of Directors.—Thomas J. Dodd.
President and Chief Executive Officer.—Robert N. Kaplan.
Chief Operating Officer.—Lesley Duncan.
General Counsel.—Paul Zimmerman.
Managing Director of:
  Evaluation and Audit.—Emilia Rodríguez-Stein.
  External and Government Affairs.—Manuel Nuñez.
  Grant-Making and Portfolio Management.—Marcy Kelley.
  Networks and Strategic Initiatives.—Stephen Cox.

JAMES MADISON MEMORIAL FELLOWSHIP FOUNDATION

1613 Duke Street, Alexandria, VA 22314

phone (571) 858–4200, fax (703) 838–2180

[Created by Public Law 99–591]

BOARD OF TRUSTEES

Members Appointed by the President of the United States:

John Cornyn, Senator from Texas, Chairman.
Catherine Allgor, Nadine Skotheim, Robert A. Skotheim, Director of Education Huntington
  Library, Art Collections, and Botanical Gardens.
Benjamin L. Cardin, Senator from Maryland.
Steven M. Colloton, U.S. Circuit Judge, U.S. Court of Appeals, 8th Circuit, Des Moines, Iowa.

John J. Faso, Attorney, Manatt, Phelps and Phillips, Albany, New York.
William Terrell Hodges, Senior U.S. District Judge, Middle District, Florida.
Pauline Maier, William R. Kenan, Jr., Professor of American History, Massachusetts Institute of Technology.
Drew R. McCoy, Department of History, Clark University.
Harvey M. Tettlebaum, Partner, Husch Blackwell LLP, Jefferson City, Missouri.
Arne Duncan, U.S. Secretary of Education (ex officio).

Foundation Staff:
President Emeritus.—Admiral Paul A. Yost, Jr.
President.—Lewis F. Larsen.
Academic Advisor to the President.—Herman Belz.
Director of Academics.—Dr. Jeffry Morrison.
Administrative Assistant.—Vacant.
Director of Special Programs.—Claire Griffin.
Support Services Specialist.—Jason McCray.
Special Assistant/Office Manager.—Vacant.
Academic Advisor.—Sheila Osbourne.
Management and Program Analysis Officer.—Elizabeth G. Ray.

THE JOHN F. KENNEDY CENTER FOR THE PERFORMING ARTS
2700 F Street, NW., 20566, phone (202) 416–8000, fax 416–8205

BOARD OF TRUSTEES

Honorary Chairs:

Mrs. Michelle Obama
Mrs. Laura Bush
Hon. Hillary Rodham Clinton

Mrs. George Bush
Mrs. Ronald Reagan
Mrs. Jimmy Carter

Officers:
Chairman.—David M. Rubenstein.
President.—Deborah F. Rutter.
Secretary.—Helen Lee Henderson.
Treasurer.—Michael F. Neidorff.
General Counsel.—Maria C. Kersten.
Assistant Secretary.—Kathy Kruse.
Members Appointed by the President of the United States:

Adrienne Arsht
David C. Bohnett
Gordon J. Davis
Fred Eychaner
Giselle Fernandez
Sakurako Fisher
Norma Lee Funger
John Goldman
Janet Hill
Frank F. Islam
Victoria Reggie Kennedy

Michael Lombardo
Andrés W. López
Bryan Lourd
Amalia Perea Mahoney
Barbara Goodman Manilow
Alyssa Mastromonaco
Cappy R. McGarr
Charles B. Ortner
Rebecca Pohlad
Shonda L. Rhimes
Laura Ricketts

David M. Rubenstein
Margaret Russell
Rose Kennedy Schlossberg
Susan S. Sher
Alexandra C. Stanton
Bryan Traubert
Walter F. Ulloa
Reginald Van Lee
Romesh Wadhwani
Anthony Welters
Elaine Wynn

Members Ex Officio Designated by Act of Congress
(Note: The names of Senators and Representatives appear in order of their years of service)
John F. Kerry, Secretary of State.
Sylvia Mathews Burwell, Secretary of Health and Human Services.
Arne Duncan, Secretary of Education.
Harry Reid, Senate Democratic Leader from Nevada.
Thad Cochran, Senator from Mississippi.
Mitch McConnell, Senate Majority Leader from Kentucky.
Barbara Boxer, Senator from California.
James M. Inhofe, Senator from Oklahoma.
Mark R. Warner, Senator from Virginia.
Nancy Pelosi, Democratic Leader of the House of Representatives from California.
Paul D. Ryan, Speaker of the House of Representatives from Wisconsin.
Rosa L. DeLauro, Representative from Connecticut.
Bill Shuster, Representative from Pennsylvania.
Peter A. DeFazio, Representative from Oregon.
Roy Blunt, Senator from Missouri.
Muriel Bowser, Mayor of the District of Columbia.

James H. Billington, Librarian of Congress.
Albert Horvath (acting), Secretary, Smithsonian Institution.
Jonathan Jarvis, Director, National Park Service.
Kaya Henderson, Chancellor, D.C. Public Schools.
Earl A. Powell III, Chairman of the Commission of Fine Arts.

Senior Counsel.—Robert Barnett.
Founding Chairman.—Roger L. Stevens.†
Chairmen Emeriti: James A. Johnson, Stephen A. Schwarzman, James D. Wolfensohn.
President Emeritus.—Michael M. Kaiser.

Honorary Trustees:

Buffy Cafritz	Alma Gildenhorn	Jean Kennedy Smith
Kenneth M. Duberstein	Melvin R. Laird	
James H. Evans	Leonard L. Silverstein	

†*Deceased*

LEGAL SERVICES CORPORATION

3333 K Street, NW., 3rd Floor, 20007–3522

phone (202) 295–1500, fax 337–6797

BOARD OF DIRECTORS

John G. Levi, Board *Chair*	Victor B. Maddox
Martha L. Minow, Board *Vice Chair*	Laurie I. Mikva
Robert J. Grey, Jr.	Rev. Joseph Pius Pietrzyk
Charles N.W. Keckler	Julie A. Reiskin
Harry Korrell	Gloria Valencia-Weber

President.—James J. Sandman.
Vice President, Legal Affairs, General Counsel and Corporate Secretary.—Ronald Flagg.
Vice President for Grants Management.—Lynn Jennnings.
Comptroller and Treasurer.—David L. Richardson.
Inspector General.—Jeffrey E. Schanz.
Director, Government Relations and Public Affairs.—Carol Bergman.
Director of Communications and Media Director.—Carl Rauscher.

NATIONAL AERONAUTICS AND SPACE ADMINISTRATION

300 E Street, SW., 20546, phone (202) 358–0000, http://www.nasa.gov

OFFICE OF THE ADMINISTRATOR

Code AA000, room 9F44, phone 358–1010

Administrator.—Charles F. Bolden, Jr.
  Executive Assistant.—Kathryn Manuel, 358–1010.
Deputy Administrator.—Vacant.
Associate Administrator.—Robert Lightfoot.
Chief of Staff.—Michael French, 358–1441.
Director for Office of Evaluation.—Vacant.
Director for Council Staff.—Vacant.
Associate Deputy Administrator.—Richard Keegan, 358–2810.
Senior Advisor to the Administrator for Policy and Strategy Implementation.—Thomas E. Cremins.
White House Liaison.—Jonathan Herczeg, 358–2198.
Chiefs:
  Financial Officer.—David Radzanowski, 358–0978.
  Information Officer.—Larry Sweet, 358–1824.
  Engineer.—Ralph Roe (757) 864–2400.
  Health and Medical Officer.—Dr. Richard S. Williams, 358–2390.
  Safety and Mission Assurance.—Terrence Wilcutt (281) 244–8715.
  Scientist.—Ellen Stofan, 358–1163.
  Technologist.—David Miller (617) 253–3288.

OFFICE OF THE GENERAL COUNSEL
Code MA000, room 9V39, phone 358–2450

General Counsel.—Sumara Thompson-King.

OFFICE OF INSPECTOR GENERAL
Code WAH10, room 8U79, phone 358–1220

Inspector General.—Paul K. Martin.
Deputy Inspector General.—Gail A. Robinson.

OFFICE OF COMMUNICATIONS
Code NA000, room 5S87, phone 358–1898

Associate Administrator.—David Weaver.
Deputy Associate Administrator.—Robert Jacobs, 358–1600.

OFFICE OF DIVERSITY AND EQUAL OPPORTUNITY PROGRAMS
Code YA000, room 6J81, phone 358–2167

Associate Administrator.—Brenda R. Manuel.

OFFICE OF EDUCATION
Code HA000, room 4V76, phone 358–0100

Associate Administrator.—Donald James.

OFFICE OF INTERNATIONAL AND INTERAGENCY RELATIONS
Code TA000, room 5V16, phone 358–0450

Associate Administrator.—Michael F. O'Brien.
Deputy Associate Administrator.—Al Condes.

OFFICE OF LEGISLATIVE AND INTERGOVERNMENTAL AFFAIRS
Code VA000, room 9K39, phone 358–1948

Associate Administrator.—Seth Statler.
Deputy Assistant Administrator.—Mary D. Kerwin.

OFFICE OF SMALL BUSINESS PROGRAMS
Code ZA000, room 4F22, phone 358–2088

Associate Administrator.—Glenn A. Delgado.

AERONAUTICS RESEARCH MISSION DIRECTORATE
Code EA000, room 6J39–A, phone 358–4700

Associate Administrator.—Jaiwon Shin.
Deputy Associate Administrator.—Thomas B. Irvine.

HUMAN EXPLORATION AND OPERATIONS MISSION DIRECTORATE
Code CA000, room 7K39, phone 358–2015

Associate Administrator.—William H. Gerstenmaier.

SCIENCE MISSION DIRECTORATE
Code DA000, room 3C34, phone 358–3889

Associate Administrator.—Dr. John Grunsfeld.

Deputy Associate Administrator.—Chuck Gay, 358–2165.

SPACE TECHNOLOGY MISSION DIRECTORATE

Associate Administrator.—Stephen Jurczyk, 358–1405.

MISSION SUPPORT DIRECTORATE
Code LA000, room 4K39, phone 358–1903

Associate Administrator.—Richard Keegan.
Executive Director Headquarters Operations.—Jay Henn.

OFFICE OF HUMAN CAPITAL MANAGEMENT
Code LE000, room 4V76, phone 358–0100

Assistant Administrator.—Jeri Buchholz.

OFFICE OF PROCUREMENT
Code LP010, room 5G70, phone 358–2090

Assistant Administrator.—Bill McNally.

OFFICE OF PROTECTIVE SERVICES
Code LP020, room 6T26, phone 358–3752

Assistant Administrator.—Joseph Mahaley.
Deputy Associate Administrator.—Charles Lombard.

OFFICE OF STRATEGIC INFRASTRUCTURE
Code LD000, room 2Z88, phone 358–2800

Assistant Administrator.—Calvin Williams.

NASA MANAGEMENT OFFICE
Code LA000, room 4K39, phone 358–3540

Director.—Marcus Watkins.

NASA NATIONAL OFFICES

Air Force Space Command / XPX (NASA): Peterson Air Force Base, CO 80914.
NASA Senior Representative.—B. Alvin Drew (719) 554–4900.
Ames Research Center: Moffett Field, CA 94035.
Director.—Dr. Simon P. Worden (650) 604–5000.
Armstrong Flight Research Center: P.O. Box 273, Edwards, CA 93523.
Director.—David McBride (661) 276–3101.
Glenn Research Center at Lewisfield: 21000 Brookpark Road, Cleveland, OH 44135.
Director.—Chris Free (216) 433–4000.
Goddard Institute for Space Studies: Goddard Space Flight Center, 2880 Broadway, New York, NY 10025.
Head.—Vacant (212) 678–5500.
Goddard Space Flight Center: 8800 Greenbelt Road, Greenbelt, MD 20771.
Director.—Christopher Scolese (301) 286–2000.
Jet Propulsion Laboratory: 4800 Oak Grove Drive, Pasadena, CA 91109.
Director.—Dr. Charles Elachi (818) 354–4321.
Lyndon B. Johnson Space Center: 2101 NASA Parkway Houston, TX 77058–3696.
Director.—Dr. Ellen Ochoa (281) 483–5000.
John F. Kennedy Space Center: Kennedy Space Center, FL 32899.
Director.—Robert Cabana (321) 867–5000.
Langley Research Center: Hampton, VA 23681.
Director.—Lesa Roe (757) 864–1000.

George C. Marshall Space Flight Center: Marshall Space Flight Center, AL 35812.
Director.—Patrick Scheuermann (256) 544–1910.
Michoud Assembly Facility: P.O. Box 29300, New Orleans, LA 70189.
Manager.—Stephen C. Doering (504) 257–3311.
NASA IV and V Facility: NASA Independent Verification and Validation Facility, 100 University Drive, Fairmont, WV 26554.
Director.—Gregory D. Blaney (304) 367–8200.
NASA Management Office: Jet Propulsion Laboratory, 4800 Oak Grove Drive, Pasadena, CA 91109.
Director.—Eugene Trinh (818) 354–5359.
John C. Stennis Space Center: Stennis Space Center, MS 39529.
Director.—Dr. Richard Gilbrech (228) 688–2121.
Vandenberg AFB: P.O. Box 425, Lompoc, CA 93438.
Manager.—Ted L. Oglesby (805) 866–5859.
Wallops Flight Facility: Goddard Space Flight Center, Wallops Island, VA 23337.
Director.—William Wrobel (757) 824–1000.
White Sands Test Facility: Johnson Space Center, P.O. Drawer MM, Las Cruces, NM 88004.
Manager.—Frank J. Benz (505) 524–5771.

NASA OVERSEAS REPRESENTATIVES

Europe: U.S. Embassy, Paris, Unit 9200, Box 1653, DPO, AE 09777, 011–33–1–4312–7070.
NASA Representative.—Gilbert Kirkham.
Japan: U.S. Embassy, Tokyo, 1–10–5 Akasaka, Minato-ku, Tokyo, Japan 107–8420 81–3–3224–5000.
NASA Representative.—Christopher Blackerby.
Russia: U.S. Embassy, Moscow, NASA, DPO AE 09721 (256) 961–6333.
NASA Representative.—Thomas Plumb.

NATIONAL ARCHIVES AND RECORDS ADMINISTRATION
700 Pennsylvania Avenue, NW., 20408–0001
8601 Adelphi Road, College Park, MD 20740–6001
http://www.archives.gov
[Created by Public Law 98–497]

Archivist of the United States.—David Ferriero (202) 357–5900, (301) 837–1600, fax (202) 357–5901.
Deputy Archivist of the United States.—Debra S. Wall (202) 357–5900, (301) 837–1600, fax (202) 357–5901.
Chief Officers:
    Financial.—Micah Cheatham (301) 837–2992, fax 837–3224.
    Human Capital.—Sean Clayton (301) 837–3710, fax 837–3195.
    Innovation.—Pamela Wright (301) 837–2029, fax 837–0312.
    Operating.—William J. Bosanko (301) 837–3604, fax 837–3217.
    Records.—Paul Wester (301) 837–3120, fax 837–3697.
    Strategy and Communications.—Donna Garland (202) 357–7464, fax 357–5901.
Executive for—
    Agency Services.—Jay Trainer (301) 837–3064.
    Business Support Services.—Charles Piercy (301) 837–1973, fax 837–3191.
    Information Services.—Swarnali Haldar (301) 837–1583.
    Legislative Archives, Presidential Libraries, and Museum Services.— Jim Gardner (202) 357–5472, fax 357–5939.
    Research Services.—William Mayer (301) 837–3110, fax 837–3633.
Director for—
    Federal Register.—Oliver A. Potts (202) 741–6100, fax 741–6012.
    Congressional Affairs.—John O. Hamilton (202) 357–5100, fax 357–5959.
    National Historical Publications and Records Commission.—Kathleen Williams (202) 357–5263, fax 357–5914.
    Equal Employment Opportunity and Diversity Office.—Ismael Martinez (301) 837–1849, fax 837–0869.
    Information Security Oversight Office.—John Fitzpatrick (202) 357–5205, fax 357–5907.

General Counsel.—Gary M. Stern (301) 837–3025, fax 837–0293.
Inspector General.—James Springs (acting), (301) 837–3000, fax 837–3197.
Presidential Libraries.—Susan K. Donius (301) 837–3250, fax 837–3199.
Director for—
  Herbert Hoover Library.—Thomas Schwartz, West Branch, IA 52358–0488 (319) 643–5301.
  Franklin D. Roosevelt Library.—Robert Clark (acting), Hyde Park, NY 12538–1999 (845) 486–7770.
  Harry S. Truman Library.—Amy Williams (acting), Independence, MO 64050–1798 (816) 268–8200.
  Dwight D. Eisenhower Library.—Karl Weissenbach, Abilene, KS 67410–2900 (785) 263–6700.
  John F. Kennedy Library.—Thomas Putnam, Boston, MA 02125–3398 (617) 514–1600.
  Lyndon Baines Johnson Library.—Mark Updegrove, Austin, TX 78705–5737 (512) 721–0200.
  Richard Nixon Library.—Michael Ellzey, Yorba Linda, CA 92886 (714) 983–9120.
  Gerald R. Ford Library.—Elaine K. Didier, Ann Arbor, MI 48109–2114 (734) 205–0555.
  Gerald R. Ford Museum.—Elaine K. Didier, Grand Rapids, MI 49504–5353 (616) 254–0400.
  Jimmy Carter Library.—Sam McClure (acting), Atlanta, GA 30307–1498 (404) 865–7100.
  Ronald Reagan Library.—R. Duke Blackwood, Simi Valley, CA 93065–0699 (800) 410–8354.
  George Bush Library.—Warren Finch, College Station, TX 77845 (979) 691–4000.
  William J. Clinton Library.—Terri Garner, Little Rock, AR 72201 (501) 374–4242.
  George W. Bush Library.—Alan Lowe, Dallas, TX 75205–2300 (214) 346–1650.

ADMINISTRATIVE COMMITTEE OF THE FEDERAL REGISTER

800 North Capitol Street, NW., Suite 700, 20001, phone (202) 741–6100

Mailing Address: 8601 Adelphi Road, College Park, MD 20740

Members:
David Ferriero, Archivist of the United States, *Chair.*
Davita Vance-Cooks, Director of the U.S. Government Publishing Office.
Rosemary Hart, Senior Counsel, Department of Justice.
    Secretary.—Oliver A. Potts, Director of the Federal Register, National Archives and Records Administration.

NATIONAL ARCHIVES TRUST FUND BOARD

phone (301) 837–3550, fax 837–3191

Members:
David Ferriero, Archivist of the United States, *Chair.*
Dr. William Adams, Chairman, National Endowment for the Humanities.
David Lebryk, Fiscal Assistant Secretary, Department of the Treasury.
    Secretary.—Lawrence Post.

NATIONAL HISTORICAL PUBLICATIONS AND RECORDS COMMISSION

700 Pennsylvania Avenue, NW., 20408

phone (202) 357–5010, fax 357–5914

http://www.archives.gov/nhprc

Members:
David Ferriero, Chairman, Archivist of the United States, National Archives and Records Administration.
Jeremy D. Fogel, Director, Federal Judicial Center, Judicial Branch.
Vacant, member of the U.S. Senate.
Hon. Andy Barr, member of the U.S. House of Representatives, Kentucky.
Naomi Nelson, Associate University Librarian, Duke University, Presidential Appointee.

Karen L. Jefferson, Woodruff Library, Atlanta University Center, Presidential Appointee.
Erin Mahan, Chief Historian, Office of the Secretary, Department of Defense.
Nicole Saylor, Head, American Folklife Center Archive, Library of Congress.
Stephen P. Randolph, Chief Historian, Office of the Historian, Department of State.
Raymond Smock, Director, Robert C. Byrd Center for Legislative Studies, Shepherd University, Association for Documentary Editing.
W. Eric Emerson, Director, South Carolina Department of Archives and History, American Association for State and Local History.
William G. Thomas III, Department of History, American Historical Association.
Kaye Lanning Minchew, Director, Troup County Archives (GA), National Association of Government Archives and Records Administrators.
George A. Miles, Curator of Western Americana, Bienecke Rare Book and Manuscript Library, Yale University, Organization of American Historians.
Peter Gottlieb, Society of American Archivists.
Executive Director.—Kathleen Williams (202) 357–5010.

NATIONAL CAPITAL PLANNING COMMISSION
401 9th Street, NW., North Lobby, Suite 500, 20004, phone (202) 482–7200
fax 482–7272, info@ncpc.gov, http://www.ncpc.gov

APPOINTIVE MEMBERS

Presidential Appointees:
L. Preston Bryant, Jr., *Chair.*
Elizabeth Ann White.
Vacant.
Mayoral Appointees:
Arrington Dixon.
Geoffrey Griffis.
Ex Officio Members:
Ashton Carter, Secretary of Defense.
  First Alternate.—Michael L. Rhodes.
  Second Alternate.—Sajeel S. Ahmed.
  Third Alternate.—Bradley Provancha
Sally Jewell, Secretary of the Interior.
  First Alternate.—Jonathan B. Jarvis.
  Second Alternate.—Lisa Mendelson.
  Third Alternate.—Peter May.
Denise Turner Roth (acting), Administrator of General Services.
  First Alternate.—Julia E. Hudson.
  Second Alternate.—Vacant.
  Third Alternate.—Mina Wright.
  Fourth Alternate.—Michael S. McGill.
Ron Johnson, Chairman, Senate Committee on Homeland Security and
  Governmental Affairs.
  Alternate.—Patrick Bailey.
  Alternate.—Gabby D'Adamo.
Jason Chaffetz, Chairman, House Committee on Oversight and Government Reform.
  First Alternate.—Jennifer Hemingway.
  Second Alternate.—Howard A. Denis.
  Third Alternate.—Christopher D'Angelo.
Muriel Bowser, Mayor of the District of Columbia.
  First Alternate.—Eric Shaw.
  Second Alternate.—Jennifer Steingasser.
Phil Mendelson, Chairman, Council of the District of Columbia.
  First Alternate.—Evan Cash.

EXECUTIVE STAFF

Executive Director.—Marcel C. Acosta, 482–7221.
  Chief Operating Officer.—Barry S. Socks, 482–7209.
  Secretariat.—Deborah B. Young, 482–7228.
  General Counsel.—Anne R. Schuyler, 482–7223.
  Director, Office of:
    Administration.—Deborah B. Young, 482–7228.

Physical Planning.—Elizabeth Miller, 482–7246.
Policy and Research.—Michael A. Sherman, 482–7254.
Public Engagement.—Julia A. Koster, 482–7211.
Urban Design and Plan Review.—David Levy, 482–7247.

NATIONAL COUNCIL ON DISABILITY

1331 F Street, NW., Suite 850, 20004, phone (202) 272–2004, TTY 272–2074

fax 272–2022

Chairman.—Jeff Rosen, Rockville, MD.
Co-Vice Chairs: Katherine Seelman, Pittsburgh, PA; Royal Walker, Jackson, MS.
Members:

Gary Blumenthal, Sudbury, MA.
Bob Brown, Las Vegas, NV.
Chester Finn, Albany, NY.
Capt. Jonathan F. Kuniholm, USMC
 (Ret.), Durham, NC.
Janice Lehrer-Stein, San Francisco, CA.
Kamilah Oni Martin-Proctor, Washington,
 DC.

Ari Ne'eman, Silver Spring, MD.
Benro T. Ogunyipe, Chicago, IL.
Neil Romano, New York, NY.
Lynnae Ruttledge, Salem, OR.
Clyde Terry, Concord, NH.
Alice Wong, San Francisco, CA.

NATIONAL CREDIT UNION ADMINISTRATION

1775 Duke Street, Alexandria, VA 22314–3428, phone (703) 518–6300, fax 518–6319

Chairman.—Debbie Matz.
 Vice Chairman.—Rick Metsger.
 Board Member.—J. Mark McWatters.
 Secretary to the Board.—Gerard Poliquin.
Executive Director.—Mark Treichel, 518–6320, fax 518–6661.
 Deputy Executive Director.—John Kutchey, 518–6320.
Inspector General.—Jim Hagen, 518–6350.
Chief Financial Officer.—Rendell Jones, 518–6570, fax 518–6664.
Chief Information Officer.—David Chow (acting), 518–6440, fax 518–6669.
National Examinations and Supervision.—Scott Hunt, 518–6640, fax 518–6665.
Minority and Women Inclusion.—Wendy Angus (acting), 518–1650.
Examination and Insurance.—Larry Fazio, 518–6360, fax 518–6666.
General Counsel.—Michael McKenna, 518–6540, fax 518–6667.
 Deputy General Counsel.—Lara Rodriguez.
Human Resources.—Cheryl Eyre, 518–6510, fax 518–6668.
Public and Congressional Affairs.—Todd M. Harper, 518–6330.
Small Credit Union Initiatives.—William Myers, 518–6610.

REGIONAL OFFICES

Director, Office of:
 Region I (Albany).—L.J. Blankenberger, 9 Washington Square, Washington Avenue Extension, Albany, NY 12205 (518) 862–7400, fax 862–7420.
 Region II (National Capital Region).—Jane A. Walters, 1900 Duke Street, Suite 300, Alexandria, VA 22314 (703) 519–4600, fax 519–4620.
 Region III (Atlanta).—Myra Toeppe, 7000 Central Parkway, Suite 1600, Atlanta, GA 30328 (678) 443–3000, fax 443–3020.
 Region IV (Austin).—Keith Morton, 4807 Spicewood Springs Road, Suite 5200, Austin, TX 78759–8490 (512) 342–5600, fax 342–5620.
 Region V (Tempe).—Elizabeth Whitehead, 1230 West Washington Street, Suite 301, Tempe, AZ 85281 (602) 302–6000, fax 302–6024.
President, Asset Management and Assistance Center (Austin).—Mike Barton, 4807 Spicewood Springs Road, Suite 5100, Austin, TX 78759–8490 (512) 231–7900, fax 231–7920.

NATIONAL FOUNDATION ON THE ARTS AND THE HUMANITIES
Old Post Office Building, 1100 Pennsylvania Avenue, NW., 20506

NATIONAL ENDOWMENT FOR THE ARTS
http://www.arts.gov

Chairman.—Jane Chu.
Senior Deputy Chairman.—Laura Callanan, 682–5415.
Deputy Chairman for Management and Budget.—Winona Varnon, 682–5534.
Chief of Staff.—Mike Griffin, 682–5773.
Congressional Liaison.—Laura de la Torre, 682–5477.
Senior Adviser for Program Innovation.—Bill O'Brien, 682–5550.
Director of Research and Analysis.—Sunil Iyengar, 682–5654.
General Counsel.—India Pinkney, 682–5418.
Inspector General.—Tonie Jones, 682–5774.

THE NATIONAL COUNCIL ON THE ARTS

Chairman.—Jane Chu.
Members:

Bruce Carter, Ph.D.
Aaron Dworkin
Lee Greenwood
Deepa Gupta
Paul Hodes
Joan Israelite

Maria Rosario Jackson, Ph.D.
Emil J. Kang
Charlotte Kessler
María López De León
Rick Lower

David "Mas" Masumoto
Irvin Mayfield
Barbara Ernst Prey
Ranee Ramaswamy
Olga Viso

Ex Officio Members:
Tammy Baldwin, Senator
Sheldon Whitehouse, Senator
Betty McCollum, Representative
Patrick J. Tiberi, Representative

NATIONAL ENDOWMENT FOR THE HUMANITIES
phone 1–800–NEH–1121, or (202) 606–8446, info@neh.gov, http://www.nch.gov

Chairman.—William Adams, 606–8310.
Deputy Chairman.—Margaret Plympton, 606–8310.
Director, Communications.—Theola DeBose, 606–8446.
Director, White House and Congressional Affairs.—Timothy Aiken, 606–8273.
General Counsel.—Michael McDonald, 606–8322.
Inspector General.—Laura M.H. Davis, 606–8574.
Public Information Officer.—Christopher Flynn, 606–8440.
Director, Planning and Budget.—Larry Myers, 606–8428.

NATIONAL COUNCIL ON THE HUMANITIES

Members:

Rolena K. Adorno
Adele L. Alexander
Camila A. Alire
Albert J. Beveridge III
Allison Blakely
Constance M. Carroll
Jamsheed K. Choksy
Cathy N. Davidson

Dawn H. Delbanco
Jane M. Doggett
Paula B. Duffy
Gerald L. Early
Gary D. Glenn
David M. Hertz
Dorothy M. Kosinski
Marvin Krislov

Robert S. Martin
Christopher Merrill
Daniel I. Okimoto
Ramón Saldívar
Bruce R. Sievers
Katherine H. Tachau
John M. Unsworth
Martha W. Weinberg

FEDERAL COUNCIL ON THE ARTS AND THE HUMANITIES

Federal Council Members:
Jane Chu, Chairman, National Endowment for the Arts.
William Adams, Chairman, National Endowment for the Humanities.

Arne Duncan, Secretary, Department of Education.
G. Wayne Clough, Secretary, Smithsonian Institution.
France A. Córdova, Director, National Science Foundation.
James H. Billington, Librarian of Congress, Library of Congress.
Earl A. Powell III, Director, National Gallery of Art, Chairman, Commission of Fine
    Arts.
David Ferriero, Archivist of the United States, National Archives and Records Administration.
Norman Dong, Commissioner, Public Buildings Service, General Services Administration.
Evan Ryan, Assistant Secretary of State, Bureau of Educational and Cultural Affairs, Depart-
    ment of State.
Julie E. Adams, Secretary, United States Senate.
Penny Pritzker, Secretary, Department of Commerce.
Anthony R. Foxx, Secretary, Department of Transportation.
Maura Marx (acting), Chairman, National Museum and Library Services Board; Director,
    Institute of Museum and Library Services.
Julián Castro, Secretary, Department of Housing and Urban Development.
Daniel M. Tangherlini, Administrator, General Services Administration.
Thomas E. Perez, Secretary, Department of Labor.
Robert McDonald, Secretary, Department of Veterans Affairs.
Josefina Carbonell, Assistant Secretary for Aging, Department of Health and Human Services.

INSTITUTE OF MUSEUM AND LIBRARY SERVICES

phone (202) 653–4657, fax 653–4625, http://www.imls.gov

[The Institute of Museum and Library Services was created by the Museum and Library
Services Act of 1996, Public Law 104–208]

Director.—Maura Marx (acting), 653–4711.
  Deputy Director for Library Services.—Maura Marx, 653–4774.
  Deputy Director for Museum Services.—Claudia French, 653–4717.
  Director, Office of:
    Communications and Government Affairs.—Claudia French (acting), 653–4757.
    Chief Operating Officer.—Michael Jerger, 653–4721.
    General Counsel.—Nancy Weiss, 653–4640.
    Planning, Research and Evaluation.—Carlos Manjarrez, 653–4671.
  Associate Deputy Director for—
    Library Services, Discretionary Programs.—Robert Horton, 653–4660.
    Library Services, State Programs.—Robin Dale, 653–4650.

NATIONAL MUSEUM AND LIBRARY SERVICES BOARD

Members:

Althemese Pemberton Barnes	Paula Gangopadhyay	Susana Torruella Leval
Charles Benton	William J. Hagenah	Mary Minow
Christie Pearson Brandau	Carla Hayden	Lawrence J. Pijeaux, Jr.
Bert Castro	Luis Herrera	Jacquelyn K. Sundstrand
John Coppola	Eric Jolly	Winston Tabb
Vishakha N. Desai	Tammie Kahn	Suzanne Thorin
	George Kerscher	Robert Wedgeworth

NATIONAL GALLERY OF ART

Sixth Street and Constitution Avenue, NW., 20565

phone (202) 737–4215, http://www.nga.gov

[Under the direction of the Board of Trustees of the National Gallery of Art]

The National Gallery of Art is governed by a nine-member board of trustees, composed
of five general trustees, who are appointed to staggered ten-year terms, and four *ex officio*
trustees.

BOARD OF TRUSTEES

General Trustees:
Sharon Percy Rockefeller, Chairman.
Frederick W. Beinecke, President.
Mitchell P. Rales.
Victoria P. Sant.
Andrew Saul.
Trustees Emeriti:
Julian Ganz, Jr.
Alexander M. Laughlin.
David O. Maxwell.
John Wilmerding.
Ex Officio Trustees:
John G. Roberts, Jr., Chief Justice of the United States.
John F. Kerry, Secretary of State.
Jacob J. Lew, Secretary of the Treasury.
G. Wayne Clough, Secretary of the Smithsonian Institution.

The board of trustees appoints the National Gallery of Art director and five executive officers,
who manage the day-to-day operations of the museum.

Executive Officers:
Director.—Earl A. Powell III.
Deputy Director.—Franklin Kelly.
Administrator.—Darrell Willson.
Treasurer.—William W. McClure.
Secretary and General Counsel.—Elizabeth A. Croog.
Dean, Center for Advanced Study in the Visual Arts.—Elizabeth Cropper.

NATIONAL LABOR RELATIONS BOARD
1099 14th Street, NW., 20570–0001
Personnel Locator (202) 273–1000

Chairman.—Mark Gaston Pearce, 273–1070, fax 273–4270. (Term expires August 27, 2018.)
Chief Counsel.—Ellen Dichner.
Deputy Chief Counsel.—Kathleen Nixon.
Members:
Board Member.—Kent Hirozawa, 273–1740.
Chief Counsel.—Peter D. Winkler.
Deputy Chief Counsel.—Lara Zick.
Board Member.—Harry I. Johnson III, 273–1770.
Chief Counsel.—James R. Murphy.
Deputy Chief Counsel.—David P. Martin.
Board Member.—Lauren McGarity McFerran, 273–1700.
Chief Counsel.—John F. Colwell.
Deputy Chief Counsel.—Andrew J. Krafts.
Board Member.—Philip A. Miscimarra, 273–1790.
Chief Counsel.—Peter J. Carlton.
Deputy Chief Counsel.—Robert F. Kane.
Executive Secretary.—Gary W. Shinners, 273–1940, fax 273–4270.
Deputy Executive Secretary.—Vacant.
Associate Executive Secretaries: Henry S. Breiteneicher, 273–2917; Farah Qureshi,
273–1949; Roxanne L. Rothschild, 273–1746.
Solicitor.—William B. Cowen, 273–2914, fax 273–1962.
Inspector General.—David P. Berry, 273–1960, fax 273–2344.
Director, Representation Appeals: Co-Director Beverly Oyama (acting), 273–1973;
Co-Director Marc Seidman (acting), 273–1976, fax 273–1962.
Office of Congressional and Public Affairs, Director.—Celine McNicholas, 273–1991, fax
273–1789.
Office of the Chief Information Officer, Chief Information Officer.—Bryan Burnett,
273–2555, fax 273–2850.

DIVISION OF JUDGES

Chief Administrative Law Judge.—Robert A. Giannasi, 501–8800, fax 501–8686.

Deputy Chief Administrative Law Judge.—Arthur Amchan, 501–8800.
Associate Chief Administrative Law Judge.—Vacant.
Associate Chief Administrative Law Judges: Joel P. Biblowitz, 120 West 45th Street, 11th
Floor, New York, NY 10036–5503 (212) 944–2941, fax 944–4904; William N. Cates,
401 West Peachtree Street, NW., Suite 1708, Atlanta, GA 30308–3510 (404) 331–6652,
fax 331–2061; Gerald M. Etchingham, 901 Market Street, Suite 300, San Francisco,
CA 94103–1779 (415) 356–5255, fax 356–5254.
General Counsel.—Richard F. Griffin, Jr., 273–3700, fax 273–4483.
Deputy General Counsel.—Jennifer A. Abruzzo.
Director, Division of Administration.—Caroline Krewson, 273–3887, fax 273–2928.
Office of the Chief Financial Officer, Chief Financial Officer.—Ronald E. Crupi,
273–3884, fax 273–2928.

DIVISION OF OPERATIONS MANAGEMENT

Associate General Counsel.—Anne G. Purcell, 273–2900, fax 273–4274.
Deputy Associate General Counsel.—Beth Tursel.
Assistant General Counsels: Yvette Hatfield, 273–3798; Aaron Karsh, 273–3828; Elizabeth
Kilpatrick, 273–0058; Dottie Wilson, 273–3781.

DIVISION OF ADVICE

Associate General Counsel.—Barry J. Kearney, 273–3800, fax 273–4275.
Deputy Associate General Counsel.—Jayme Sophir.
Assistant General Counsels:
 Injunction Litigation Branch.—Elinor Merberg, 273–3833.
 Regional Advice Branch.—Miriam Szapiro, 273–0998.

DIVISION OF ENFORCEMENT LITIGATION

Associate General Counsel.—John H. Ferguson, 273–2950, fax 273–4244.
Deputy Associate General Counsel.—Vacant.
Appellate and Supreme Court Litigation Branch:
 Deputy Associate General Counsel.—Linda J. Dreeben, 273–2960,
 Assistant General Counsel.—David Habenstreit, 273–0979.
 Deputy Assistant General Counsels: Ruth E. Burdick, 273–7958; Meredith Jason, 273–
 2945.
Contempt Litigation and Compliance Branch:
 Assistant General Counsel.—Barbara O'Neil, 273–3739, fax 273–4244.
 Deputy Assistant General Counsel.—Nancy Platt.

DIVISION OF LEGAL COUNSEL

Associate General Counsel.—Margery E. Lieber, 273–2940.
Deputy Associate General Counsel.—Richard A. Bock.
Ethics, Employment and Administrative Law Branch:
 Special Ethics Counsel.—Lori Ketcham, 273–2939.
Freedom of Information Act Branch:
 FOIA Officer/Assistant General Counsel.—Deirdre MacNeil, 273–3842.

NATIONAL MEDIATION BOARD

1301 K Street, NW., Suite 250 East, 20005, phone (202) 692–5000, fax 692–5080

Chairman.—Harry Hoglander, 692–5022.
 Board Members: Nicholas Geale, 692–5016; Linda Puchala, 692–5019.
 Assistant Chief of Staff, Office of Administration.—Samantha T. Williams, 692–5010.
 Chief of Staff, Office of the Chief of Staff.—Daniel Rainey, 692–5000.
 Director, Office of Arbitration Services.—Roland Watkins, 692–5055.
 General Counsel, Office of Legal Affairs.—Mary L. Johnson, 692–5040.
 Deputy Chief of Staff, Office of Mediation Services and ADR Services.—Michael Kelliher,
 692–5040.

NATIONAL RESEARCH COUNCIL—NATIONAL ACADEMY OF SCIENCES
NATIONAL ACADEMY OF ENGINEERING—INSTITUTE OF MEDICINE
2101 Constitution Avenue, NW., 20418, phone (202) 334–2000
(Mailing address: 500 Fifth Street, NW., 20001)

The National Research Council, National Academy of Sciences, National Academy of Engineering, and Institute of Medicine, serves as an independent adviser to the Federal Government on scientific and technical questions of national importance. Although operating under a congressional charter granted the National Academy of Sciences in 1863, the National Research Council and its three parent organizations are private organizations, not agencies of the Federal Government, and receive no appropriations from Congress.

NATIONAL RESEARCH COUNCIL

Chairman.—Ralph J. Cicerone, President, National Academy of Sciences, 334–2000.
Vice Chairman.—C.D. "Dan" Mote, Jr., President, National Academy of Engineering, 334–3200.
Executive Officer.—Bruce B. Darling, 334–3000.
Executive Director, Office of Congressional and Government Affairs.—James E. Jensen, 334–1601.

NATIONAL ACADEMY OF SCIENCES

President.—Ralph J. Cicerone, 334–2101.
Vice President.—Diane E. Griffin, Johns Hopkins Bloomberg School of Public Health.
Home Secretary.—Susan R. Wessler, University of California, Riverside.
Foreign Secretary.—John Hildebrand, University of Arizona.
Treasurer.—Jeremiah P. Ostriker, Princeton University.
Executive Officer.—Bruce B. Darling, 334–3000.

NATIONAL ACADEMY OF ENGINEERING

President.—C.D. "Dan" Mote, Jr., 334–3200.
Chairman.—Charles O. Holliday, Jr. (Ret.), Chairman and CEO of DuPont.
Vice President.—Corale L. Brierley, Principal, Brierley Consultancy LLC.
Home Secretary.—Thomas F. Budinger, Lawrence Berkeley National Laboratory.
Foreign Secretary.—Venkatesh Narayanamurti, Harvard University.
Executive Officer.—Lance Davis, 334–3677.
Treasurer.—Martin B. Sherwin (Ret.), W.R. Grace.

INSTITUTE OF MEDICINE

President.—Victor J. Dzau, M.D., 334–3300.
The Leonard D. Schaeffer Executive Officer.—Clyde Behney (acting).

NATIONAL SCIENCE FOUNDATION
4201 Wilson Boulevard, Suite 1245, Arlington, VA 22230
phone (703) 292–5111, http://www.nsf.gov

Director.—Dr. Cora Marrett (acting), 292–8000.
Deputy Director.—Vacant.
Inspector General.—Allison C. Lerner, 292–7100.
Equal Opportunity Programs.—Claudia Postell, 292–8020.
Director, Office of:
  General Counsel.—Lawrence Rudolph, 292–8060.
  International and Integrative Activities.—Dr. Wanda Ward, 292–8040.
  Legislative and Public Affairs.—Dana Toupousis (acting), 292–8070.
  Polar Programs.—Dr. Kelly Falkner, 292–8030.
Assistant Director for—
  Biological Sciences.—Dr. James L. Olds, 292–8400.
  Computer and Information Science and Engineering.—Dr. James F. Kurose, 292–8900.

Education and Human Resources.—Dr. Joan Ferrini-Mundy, 292–8300.
Engineering.—Dr. Pramod Khargonekar, 292–8300.
Geosciences.—Dr. Roger Wakimoto, 292–8500.
Mathematical and Physical Sciences.—Dr. F. Fleming Crim, 292–8800.
Social, Behavioral, and Economic Sciences.—Dr. Fay L. Cook, 292–8700.
Director, Office of:
  Budget, Finance, and Award Management.—Martha Rubenstein, 292–8200.
  Information and Resource Management.—Joanne B. Tornow, 292–8100.

NATIONAL SCIENCE BOARD

Chairman.—Dan E. Arizu (703) 292–7000.
Vice Chairman.—Kelvin K. Droegemier.
Executive Officer.—Dr. Michael Van Woert.

MEMBERS

Dr. John L. Anderson
Dr. Dan E. Arvizu
Dr. Deborah L. Ball
Dr. Roger Beachy
Dr. Arthur Bienenstock
Dr. Vinton G. Cerf
Dr. Vicki Chandler
Dr. Ruth David
Dr. Kelvin K. Droegemier

Dr. Inez Fung
Dr. Robert M. Groves
Dr. James S. Jackson
Dr. G. Peter LePage
Dr. Alan I. Leshner
Dr. W. Carl Lineberger
Dr. Steven L. Mayo
Dr. Sethuraman Panchanathan
Dr. G.P. Peterson

Dr. Geraldine Richmond
Dr. Douglas D. Randall
Dr. Annelia Sargent
Dr. Diane L. Souvaine
Dr. Robert J. Zimmer
Dr. Maria T. Zuber
Dr. France A. Cordova

NATIONAL TRANSPORTATION SAFETY BOARD

490 L'Enfant Plaza, SW., 20594, phone (202) 314–6000

Chairman.—Christopher Hart (acting), 314–6145.
  Member.—Robert L. Sumwalt III, 314–6021.
Deputy Managing Director.—Stephen Klejst, 314–6060.
General Counsel.—David Tochen, 314–6616.
Chief Administrative Law Judge.—Alfonso Montano, Jr., 314–6150.
Chief Financial Officer.—Edward Benthall, 314–6241.
Director, Office of:
  Aviation Safety.—John Delisi, 314–6302.
  Communications.—Thomas Zoeller, 314–6690.
  Government Affairs.—Jane Terry, 314–6218.
  Highway Safety.—Donald Karol, 314–6419.
  Marine Safety.—Tracy Muurell, 314–6450.
  Public Affairs.—Kelly Nantel, 314–6100.
  Railroad, Pipeline and Hazardous Materials Investigations.—Robert Hall, 314–6257.
  Research and Engineering.—Joseph Kolly, 314–6501.
  Safety Advocacy.—Vacant.
  Transportation Disaster Assistance.—Paul Sledzik, 314–6134.

NEIGHBORHOOD REINVESTMENT CORPORATION

(Doing business as NeighborWorks America)

999 North Capitol Street, NE., Suite 900, 20002, phone (202) 760–4000, fax 376–2600

BOARD OF DIRECTORS

Chair.—Hon. Thomas J. Curry, Comptroller of the Currency.
Members:
  Hon. Lael Brainard, Member, Board of Governors, Federal Reserve System.
  Hon. Helen Kanovsky, General Counsel, HUD.
  Hon. Richard Metsger, Vice Chairman, National Credit Union Administration.
  Hon. Jeremiah O. Norton, Member, Board of Directors, Federal Deposit Insurance Corporation.
Chief Executive Officer.—Paul Weech, 760–4020.
General Counsel/Secretary.—Jeffrey T. Bryson, 760–4101.

Chief Operating Officer.—Chuck Wehrwein, 760–4025.
Chief Financial Officer.—Thomas Bloom, 760–4028.
Director for—
　Development and Communications.—Phyllis Kim, 760–4038.
　Field Operations.—Tom Chabolla, 760–4070.
　Finance and Administration.—Steven Slepian, 760–4085.
　Internal Audit.—Frederick Udochi, 524–9937.
　Public Policy and Legislative Affairs.—Kirsten Johnson-Obey, 760–4139.
　Training.—John McCloskey, 760–4205.

NUCLEAR REGULATORY COMMISSION

Washington, DC 20555–0001, phone (301) 415–7000, http//www.nrc.gov

[Authorized by 42 U.S.C. 5801 and U.S.C. 1201]

OFFICE OF THE CHAIRMAN

Chairman.—Stephen G. Burns, 415–1820.
　Chief of Staff.—Jason Zorn, 415–1820.
　Administrative Assistant.—Kathleen Blake.

COMMISSIONERS

Kristine L. Svinicki, 415–1855.
　Chief of Staff.—Patrice Bubar, 415–1855.
　Administrative Assistant.—Janet L. Lepre.
William C. Ostendorff, 415–1759.
　Chief of Staff.—Eric Benner, 415–1800.
　Administrative Assistant.—Linda S. Herr.
Jeff Baran, 415–1839.
　Chief of Staff.—Amy Powell, 415–1839.
　Administrative Assistant.—Renee Taylor.

STAFF OFFICES OF THE COMMISSION

Secretary.—Annette L. Vietti-Cook, 415–1969, fax 415–1672.
Chief Financial Officer.—Maureen Wylie, 415–7322, fax 415–4236.
Commission Appellate Adjudication.—Brooke D. Poole, 415–2653, fax 415–3200.
Congressional Affairs.—Eugene Dacus, 415–1776, fax 415–8571.
General Counsel.—Margaret M. Doane, 415–1743, fax 415–3086.
Inspector General.—Hubert T. Bell, 415–5930, fax 415–5091.
International Programs.—Nader L. Mamish, 415–1780, fax 415–2400.
Public Affairs.—Eliot B. Brenner, 415–8200, fax 415–2234.

ADVISORY COMMITTEE ON MEDICAL USES OF ISOTOPES

Chairman.—Bruce R. Thomadsen, Ph.D.
　Committee Coordinator.—Sophie Holiday, 415–7865.

ADVISORY COMMITTEE ON REACTOR SAFEGUARDS

Executive Director.—John W. Stetkar, 415–7360, fax 415–5589.

ATOMIC SAFETY AND LICENSING BOARD PANEL

Chief Administrative Judge.—E. Roy Hawkens, 415–7454, fax 415–5599.

OFFICE OF THE EXECUTIVE DIRECTOR FOR OPERATIONS

Executive Director for Operations.—Mark A. Satorius, 415–1700, fax 415–2700.
　Deputy Executive Director for—

Corporate Management.—Darren Ash, 415–7443, fax 415–2700.
Materials, Waste, Research, State, Tribal and Compliance Programs.—Michael F. Weber, 415–1705, fax 415–2700.
Reactor and Preparedness Programs.—Michael R. Johnson, 415–1713, fax 415–2700.
Director, Office of:
  Administration.—Cynthia A. Carpenter, 415–8747, fax 415–5352.
  Enforcement.—Patricia Holahan, 415–2741, fax 415–3431.
  Human Resources.—Miriam L. Cohen, 287–0747, fax 287–9343.
  Information Services.—James P. Flanagan, 415–8700, fax 415–4246.
  Investigations.—Cheryl L. McCrary, 415–2373, fax 415–2370.
  New Reactors.—Glenn M. Tracy, 415–1897, fax 415–2700.
  Nuclear Material Safety and Safeguards.—Catherine Haney, 287–9243, fax 492–3360.
  Nuclear Reactor Regulation.—William Dean, 415–1270, fax 415–8333.
  Nuclear Regulatory Research.—Brian W. Sheron, 251–7400, fax 251–7426.
  Nuclear Security and Incident Response.—James Wiggins, 287–3734, fax 287–9351.
  Small Business and Civil Rights.—Vonna L. Ordaz, 415–7380, fax 415–5953.

REGIONAL OFFICES

Region I: Daniel Dorman, 2100 Renaissance Boulevard, Suite 100, King of Prussia, PA 19406 (610) 337–5299, fax 337–5241.
Region II: Victor McCree, 245 Peachtree Center Avenue, NE., Suite 1200, Atlanta, GA 30303 (404) 997–4411.
Region III: Cynthia Pederson, 2443 Warrenville Road, Suite 210, Lisle, IL 60532 (630) 829–9658, fax (630) 515–1096.
Region IV: Marc Dapas, 1600 East Lamar Boulevard, Arlington, TX 76011 (817) 200–1225, fax (817) 860–8122.

OCCUPATIONAL SAFETY AND HEALTH REVIEW COMMISSION

1120 20th Street, NW., 20036–3457, phone (202) 606–5100

[Created by Public Law 91–596]

Chairman.—Thomasina V. Rogers, 606–5370.
  Chief of Staff and Legal Counsel to the Chairman.—Richard L. Huberman, 606–5723.
  Confidential Assistant to the Chairman (Public Affairs Officer).—Safiya A. Hamit, 606–5370.
Commissioner.—Cynthia L. Attwood, 606–5377.
  Chief Counsel to the Commissioner.—Janice L. Glick, 606–5703.
Commissioner.—Heather L. MacDougall, 606–5375.
  Chief Counsel to the Commissioner.—Rick S. Kozell, 606–5711.
Administrative Law Judges:
  Patrick B. Augustine, U.S. Customs House, 721 19th Street, Room 407, Denver, CO 80202–2517.
  Peggy S. Ball, U.S. Customs House, 721 19th Street, Room 407, Denver, CO 80202–2517.
  Carol A. Baumerich, 1120 20th Street, NW., 9th Floor, Washington, DC 20036–3457.
  Keith E. Bell, 1120 20th Street, NW., 9th Floor, Washington, DC 20036–3457.
  Sharon D. Calhoun, 100 Alabama Street, SW., Building 1924, Room 2R90, Atlanta, GA 30303–3104.
  William S. Coleman, 1120 20th Street, NW., 9th Floor, Washington, DC 20036–3457.
  Brian A. Duncan, U.S. Customs House, 721 19th Street, Room 407, Denver, CO 80202–2517.
  John B. Gatto, 100 Alabama Street, SW., Building 1924, Room 2R90, Atlanta, GA 30303–3104.
  Heather A. Joys, 100 Alabama Street, SW., Building 1924, Room 2R90, Atlanta, GA 30303–3104.
  Dennis L. Phillips, 1120 20th Street, NW., 9th Floor, Washington, DC 20036–3457.
  Covette Rooney, 1120 20th Street, NW., 9th Floor, Washington, DC 20036–3457.
  John H. Schumacher, U.S. Customs House, 721 19th Street, Room 407, Denver, CO 80202–2517.
General Counsel.—Nadine N. Mancini.
Executive Secretary.—John X. Cerveny.
Executive Director.—Debra A. Hall.

OFFICE OF GOVERNMENT ETHICS
1201 New York Avenue, NW., Suite 500, 20005, phone (202) 482–9300, fax 482–9238
[Created by Act of October 1, 1989; codified in 5 U.S.C. app., section 401]

Director.—Walter M. Shaub, Jr.
  Confidential Assistant.—Matthew A. Marinec.
  Chief of Staff and Program Counsel.—Shelley K. Finlayson.
  General Counsel.—David J. Apol.
  Deputy Director for—
    Compliance.—Dale A. Christopher.
    Financial Disclosure.—Barbara A. Mullen-Roth.
  Chief for Internal Operations.—Emory A. Rounds (acting).

OFFICE OF PERSONNEL MANAGEMENT
Theodore Roosevelt Building, 1900 E Street, NW., 20415–0001
phone (202) 606–1800, http://www.opm.gov

OFFICE OF THE DIRECTOR

Director.—Beth Colbert (acting), 606–1000.
  Senior Executive Assistant.—Dave Marsh.
  Deputy Director.—Vacant.
  Senior Advisor.—Vacant.
  Chief of Staff.—Vacant.
  Executive Assistant.—Rene Ralston.
  Deputy Chief of Staff.—Sergio Gonzales.
  Counselor to the Director.—Michael A. Grant.
  Executive Assistant.—Torlanda Young.
  Chief Operating Officer.—Angela Bailey.
  Executive Assistant.—Ingrid Reed.
  Senior Advisor to the Director.—Chris Canning.
  CHCO Executive Director.—Justin Johnson.

OFFICE OF THE EXECUTIVE SECRETARIAT

Director.—Jozetta Robinson, 606–8004.
  Executive Correspondence.—Lula Williams, 606–1000.
  International Affairs.—Jill Feldman, 606–5099.
  Regulatory Affairs.—Stephen D. Hickman, 606–1941.

CHIEF FINANCIAL OFFICER

Chief Financial Officer.—Dennis D. Coleman, 606–1918.
  Deputy Chief Financial Officer.—Daniel K. Marella, 606–2638.
  Executive Officer/Resource Management.—Katina P. Cotton, 606–4725.
  OPM Projects and Initiatives.—Teresa F. Williams, 606–1414.
  Policy and Internal Control.—Vacant.
  Travel Operations.—Anthony Rainey (acting), 606–8460.
  Associate CFO:
    Budget and Performance.—Margaret P. Pearson, 606–1491.
    Financial Services.—Kim Farington, 606–1143.
    Financial Systems Management.—Rochelle S. Bayard, 606–4366.

COMMUNICATIONS AND PUBLIC LIAISON

Director.—Jackie Koszczuk, 606–2402.
  Deputy Director.—Mark Anthony Dingbaum.
  Social Media Director.—Samuel Schumach.
  Director, External Communications.—Edmund D. Byrnes.
  Web Content Manager.—LaShonne Williams.
  Creative Services.—Jay Porter.
  Speechwriting and Editorial.—Dena Bunis.
  Administrative Assistant.—Jean A. Smith.

CONGRESSIONAL, LEGISLATIVE AND INTERGOVERNMENTAL AFFAIRS

Director.—Jason Levine, 606–1300.
Executive Assistant.—Elizabeth Barrett.
Deputy Director.—Jennifer Tyree.
Congressional Relations Officer: Kevin Franklin.
Chief, Legislative Affairs.—Christopher Wallace, 606–1424.
Legislative Analysts: John Barone, Steven J. Driscoll, Janell Fitzhugh.
Chief, Constituent Services, Capitol Hill.—Kristen Soper, B332 Rayburn House Office Building, 225–4955, fax 225–4974.
Constituent Services Representatives: Sean McKew, Carlos E. Tingle.

FEDERAL INVESTIGATIVE SERVICES

Associate Director.—Merton Miller (724) 794–5612.
Deputy Associate Director.—Colleen Kelly.
Executive Assistant.—Jody L. Montgomery.
Deputy Associate Directors:
    External Affairs.—Lisa Loss, 606–7017.
    Management Services.—David Fitzgerald, 606–0948.
    Operations.—Mark P. Sherwin (acting), (724) 794–5612.
    Quality.—Jeffrey C. Flora (443) 698–9400.

MERIT SYSTEM AUDIT AND COMPLIANCE

Associate Director.—Mark W. Lambert, 606–2360.
Deputy Associate Director.—Ana Mazzi.
Directors:
    CFC Operations.—Keith Willingham, 606–2564.
    Internal Oversight and Compliance.—Janet L. Barnes, 606–3207.
Voting Rights and Resource Management.—Vacant.
Administrative Assistant.—Kimberlin C. Clark.

CHIEF INFORMATION OFFICER

Chief Information Officer.—Donna K. Seymour, 606–2150.
Associate CIO:
    Enterprise Infrastructure Solutions.—Joy Fairtile, 606–2150.
    Federal Business Solutions.—Paul Craven, 606–0183.
    IT Strategy and Policy.—David Vargas (202) 418–3236.
Management Assistant.—Wanda Paige, 606–2150.
CIO, Executive Officer.—Vesen Thompson, 606–1129.
Chief Technology Officer.—Vacant.

HUMAN RESOURCES SOLUTIONS

Associate Director.—Joseph S. Kennedy, 606–5181.
Principal Deputy Associate Director.—Kathleen McGettigan, 606–1594.
Executive Assistant.—Shirl Sibley, 606–0900.
Deputy Associate Directors:
    Center for Leadership Development, Assistant Director.—Maureen B. Higgins, 606–2855.
    Center for Leadership Development, Federal Executive Institute Director.—Suzanne G. Logan (434) 980–6220.
    Center for Management Services.—Reginald M. Brown, 606–1332.
    Federal Staffing Group.—Dianna Saxman (215) 362–3154.
    HR Strategy and Evaluation Solutions.—Leslie Pollack, 606–1426.
    Training and Management Assistance Program.—George Price, 606–0409.

RETIREMENT SERVICES

Associate Director.—Kenneth Zawodny, Jr., 606–3502.

Deputy Associate Director for Retirement Operations.—Nicholas Ashenden (724) 794–2005 ext. 3214.
Executive Assistant.—Bill Cramer.
Deputy Associate Director for Administrative Operations.—Linda Bradford, 606–4168.
Executive Assistant.—Arminta Thompson-Smith.

OFFICE OF THE GENERAL COUNSEL

General Counsel.—Kamala Vasagam, 606–1700.
Deputy General Counsels: Teresa Gonsalves, Kathie Ann Whipple.
Deputy General Counsel for Policy.—Vacant.
Senior Counsel and Advisor to the General Counsel.—Praveen Fernandes.
Associate General Counsel (Compensation, Benefits, Products and Services).—R. Alan Miller.
Assistant General Counsel (Merit Systems and Accountability).—Steven E. Abow.
Chief, Administration (Administrative Officer).—Vacant.

OFFICE OF THE INSPECTOR GENERAL

Inspector General.—Patrick E. McFarland, 606–1200.
Deputy Inspector General.—Norbert E. Vint.
Executive Assistant.—A. Paulette Berry.
Assistant Inspector General for Legal Affairs.—J. David Cope.
Counsel to the Inspector General.—Timothy C. Watkins, 606–2030.
Assistant Inspector General for Management.—Terri H. Fazio, 606–0846.
Deputy Assistant Inspector General for Management.—Joyce D. Price, 606–2156.
Assistant Inspector General for Audits.—Michael R. Esser, 606–1200.
Deputy Assistant Inspectors General for Audits: Melissa D. Brown, 606 4714; Lewis F. Parker, 606–4738.
Assistant Inspector General for Investigations.—Michelle B. Schmitz, 606–1200.

FACILITIES, SECURITY AND CONTRACTING

Director.—Dean Hunter, 606–3130.
Deputy Director.—Nina Ferraro, 606–4591.
Small and Disadvantaged Business Utilization and Policy.—Desmond Brown, 606–2862.
Contracting.—W. Neal Patterson, 606–1984.
Facilities Management.—Mariano S. Aquino, 606–4590.
Security Services.—Kevin McCombs (acting), 418–0201.
Personnel Security.—Melinda M. Davis (724) 794–7112.
Emergency Services.—Sandra L. Hawthorne, 606–5068.

EQUAL EMPLOYMENT OPPORTUNITY

Director.—LaShonn M. Woodland, 606–2460.
Lead EEO Specialist.—Yasmin A. Rosa.

DIVERSITY AND INCLUSION

Director.—Sharon Wong (acting), 606–7992.
Senior Diversity Program Managers: Bruce Stewart, Sharon Wong.

HEALTHCARE AND INSURANCE

Director.—John O'Brien, 606–2634.
Deputy Director.—Vacant.
Chief Medical Officer.—Christine Hunter, 606–4653.
Assistant Director for—
  Federal Employee Insurance Operations.—Alan Spielman, 606–4995.
  National Healthcare Operations.—Elizabeth Hadley, 606–2503.

PLANNING AND POLICY ANALYSIS

Director.—Jonathan Foley, 606–4794.
  Deputy Director.—Anne Easton, 606–2213.
  Deputy Performance Improvement Officer.—Bernie Kluger, 606–7482.

EMPLOYEE SERVICES

Associate Director and Chief Human Capital Officer.—Mark Reinhold, 606–1882.
  Principal Deputy Associate Director.—Veronica Villalobos.
  Deputy Associate Directors:
    Partnership and Labor Relations.—Tim F. Curry, 606–2584.
    Pay and Leave.—Brenda Roberts, 606–2507.
    Recruitment and Hiring.—Kimberly Holden, 418–3218.
    Senior Executive Service and Performance Management.—Stephen T. Shih, 606–1951.
    Strategic Workforce Planning.—Sydney Smith-Heimbrock, 606–2762.
    Veterans Services.—Hakeem Basheerud-Deen, 606–3602.
  Deputy Associate Director, OPM Human Resources and Deputy Chief Human Capital Officer.—Andrea Bright, 606–3590.
  Human Resources Deputy Director.—Vacant.

OFFICE OF THE SPECIAL COUNSEL
1730 M Street, NW., Suite 300, 20036–4505, phone (202) 254–2000
[Authorized by 5 U.S.C. 1101 and 5 U.S.C. 1211]

Special Counsel.—Carolyn Lerner.
  Principal Deputy Special Counsel.—Mark Cohen.
  Deputy Special Counsel, Policy and Congressional Affairs.—Adam Miles.

PEACE CORPS
1111 20th Street, NW., 20526, phone (202) 692–2000
Toll-Free Number (855) 855–1961, http://www.peacecorps.gov
[Created by Public Law 97–113]

OFFICE OF THE DIRECTOR
phone (202) 962–2100, fax 692–2101

Director.—Carolyn Hessler-Radelet.
  Deputy Director.—Laura M. Chambers (acting).
  Chief of Staff.—Laura M. Chambers.
  White House Liaison.—Lyzz Ogunwo.
  Senior Advisors: Maryann Minutillo, Carl Sosebee, Carlos Torres.
  Executive Secretary.—Melanie Wilhelm.
  Administrative Office.—Nina Basiliko.
  Chief Compliance Officer.—Anne Hughes (acting).

OFFICE OF VICTIM ADVOCACY

Director.—Jamie Friedman (acting).

OFFICE OF INNOVATION

Director.—Patrick Choquette.

OFFICE OF CIVIL RIGHTS AND DIVERSITY

Director.—David King.

OFFICE OF COMMUNICATIONS

Director.—Melissa Silverman.

Deputy Director.—Kevin Harris.
Director of Press Relations.—Erin Durney.

OFFICE OF CONGRESSIONAL RELATIONS

Director.—Jeremy Haldeman.
Deputy Director.—Christopher Austin.

OFFICE OF THE GENERAL COUNSEL

General Counsel.—Rodin Mehrbani.

OFFICE OF STRATEGIC PARTNERSHIPS

Associate Director.—Tonia Wellons.

OFFICE OF INTERGOVERNMENTAL AND EXTERNAL AFFAIRS

Director.—Teresa Chaurand.

OFFICE OF GIFTS AND GRANTS MANAGEMENT

Director.—Jennifer Chavez-Rubio.

OFFICE OF UNIVERSITY AND DOMESTIC PARTNERSHIPS

Director.—Clayton Kennedy.

OFFICE OF STRATEGIC INFORMATION RESEARCH AND PLANNING

Director.—Cathryn Thorup.
Deputy Director.—Jeff Kwiecinski.

OFFICE OF THIRD GOAL AND RETURNED VOLUNTEER SERVICES

Director.—BJ Whetstine.

OFFICE OF GLOBAL OPERATIONS

Associate Director.—Ken Yamashita.
Senior Advisors: Peter Redmond, Diana Schmidt.
Africa Region:
Regional Director.—Dick Day.
Chief of Operations.—Dee Hertzberg, Carl Swartz.
Europe/Mediterranean/Asia Region:
Regional Director.—Keri Lowry.
Chief of Operations.—Kristen Besch, Rita Mahoney.
Inter-America and Pacific Region:
Regional Director.—Brian Riley (acting).
Chief of Operations: Brian Riley, Emily Untermeyer.

OFFICE OF OVERSEAS PROGRAMMING AND TRAINING SUPPORT

Director.—Sonia Stines Derenoncourt.

PEACE CORPS RESPONSE

Director.—Kate Beale (acting).

OFFICE OF GLOBAL HEALTH AND HIV

Director—Marie McLeod.

OFFICE OF MANAGEMENT

Associate Director.—Alan Price.
    Chief of Administrative Services.—Timothy Kelly (acting).
    Chief of Transportation.—Joey O'Farrell.
    Office of Human Resource Management.—Robert White.
    FOIA/Privacy Act Officer.—Denora Miller.

OFFICE OF THE INSPECTOR GENERAL

Inspector General.—Kathy Buller.
    Deputy Inspector General.—Joaquin Ferrao.

OFFICE OF THE CHIEF FINANCIAL OFFICER

Chief Financial Officer.—Joe Hepp.
    Deputy Chief Financial Officer.—Paul Shea.

OFFICE OF THE CHIEF INFORMATION OFFICER

Chief Information Officer.—Francisco Reinoso.
    Deputy Chief Information Officer.—Vince Groh.

OFFICE OF VOLUNTEER RECRUITMENT AND SELECTION

Associate Director.—Sheila Crowley (acting).
    Chief of Operations.—Sheila Crowley.
    Chief Administrative Officer—Denise Cagley-Jefferson.
    Director of:
        Placement.—Lateefah Burgess.
        Staging and Staff Development.—Emily Vilorio (acting).
        Recruitment.—Tina Williams.

REGIONAL OFFICES

Northeast Region, NERO (Connecticut, Massachusetts, Maine, New Hampshire, New Jersey, New York, Pennsylvania, Rhode Island, Vermont): 201 Varick Street, Suite 1025, New York, NY 10014, T: (855) 855–1961, (212) 352–5440, F: 352–5441.
    Manager.—Elizabeth A. Chamberlain.
    Supervisory Public Affairs Specialist.—Vacant.
Southeast Region, SERO DC (District of Columbia, Delaware, Maryland, North Carolina, Virginia, West Virginia): 1111 20th Street, NW., Washington, DC 20526, T: (855) 855–1961, (202) 692–1040, F: 692–1065.
    Manager.—Eric Zdanowicz.
    Supervisory Public Affairs Specialist.—Bruno Veselic.
Midwest Region, MWRO (Iowa, Illinois, Indiana, Kentucky, Michigan, Minnesota, Missouri, North Dakota, Ohio, South Dakota, Wisconsin): 55 West Monroe Street, Suite 450, Chicago, IL 60603, T: (855) 855–1961, (312) 353–4990, F: 353–4192.
    Manager.—Brad Merryman.
    Supervisory Public Affairs Specialist.—Jessica Mayle.
Southeast Region, SERO ATL (Alabama, Florida, Georgia, Mississippi, Puerto Rico, South Carolina, Tennessee, Virgin Islands): 60 Forsyth Street, Suite 3M40, Atlanta, GA 30303, T: (855) 855–1961, (404) 562–3456, F: 562–3455.
    Manager.—Eric Zdanowicz.
    Supervisory Public Affairs Specialist.—Bruno Veselic.
Southwest Region, SWRO (Arkansas, Arizona, Colorado, Kansas, Louisiana, Nebraska, New Mexico, Oklahoma, Texas, Utah, Wyoming): 1100 Commerce Street, Suite 427, Dallas, TX 75242, T: (855) 855–1961, (214) 253–5400, F: 253–5401.

Manager.—Michael McKay.
Supervisory Public Affairs Specialist.—Kiiva Williams.
West Coast Region, WCRO Los Angeles Office (Southern California): 2361 Rosecrans Avenue, Suite 155 El Segundo, CA 90245, T: (855) 855–1961, (310) 356–1100, F: 356–1125.
San Francisco Office (Northern California, Hawaii, Nevada): 1301 Clay Street, Suite 620N, Oakland, CA 94612, T: (855) 855–1961, (510) 452–8444, F: 452–8441.
Seattle Office (Alaska, Idaho, Montana, Oregon, Washington): 300 Fifth Avenue, Suite 100, Seattle, WA 98104, T: (855) 855–1961, (206) 553–5490, F: 553–2343.
Manager.—Erin Carlson.
Supervisory Public Affairs Specialist.—David Reese.

OFFICE OF SAFETY AND SECURITY

Associate Director.—Shawn Bardwell.
Physical Security Specialist.—John McIntire.

OFFICE OF HEALTH SERVICES

Associate Director.—Paul Jung.
Director of:
  Counseling and Outreach .—Tim Lawler.
  Medical Services.—Barry Simon.

PENSION BENEFIT GUARANTY CORPORATION
1200 K Street, 20005–4026, (202) 326–4000

BOARD OF DIRECTORS

Chairman.—Thomas Perez, Secretary of Labor.
  Members:
  Jack Lew, Secretary of the Treasury.
  Penny Pritzker, Secretary of Commerce.

OFFICIALS

Director.—Alice Maroni (acting), 326–4010.
  Deputy Chief Policy Officer.—Michael Rae, 326–4010.
  Chief Officers for—
    Finance.—Patricia Kelly, 326–4170.
    Information Technology.—Deborah Herald, 326–4130.
    Management.—Edgar Bennett, 326–4000.
    Negotiations and Restructuring.—Sandy Rich, 326–4000.
  Department Director for—
    Benefits Administration and Payment.—Cathy Kronopolus, 326–4000.
    Budget.—Wayne Hobbs, 326–4120.
    Communications Outreach and Public Affairs.—Sanford McLaurin, 326–4343.
    Contracts and Controls Review.—Martin Boehm, 326–4161.
    Corporate Finance and Restructuring.—Dana Cann, 326 4070.
    Financial Operations.—Theodore Winter, 326–4060.
    General Counsel.—Judith Starr, 326–4020.
    Human Resources.—Arrie Etheridge, 326–4110.
    Information Technology Infrastructure Operations.—Joshua Kossoy, 326–4130.
    Information Technology and Business Modernization.—Srividhya Shyamsunder, 326–4130.
    Policy, Research and Analysis.—Christopher Bone, 326–4080.
    Workplace Solutions.—Alisa Cottone, 326–4150.

POSTAL REGULATORY COMMISSION
901 New York Avenue, NW., Suite 200, 20268–0001
phone (202) 789–6800, fax 789–6891

Chairman.—Robert Taub (acting), 789–6897.

Vice Chairman.—Tony Hammond, 789–6805.
Commissioners:
 Mark Acton, 789–6866.
 Ruth Goldway, 789–6810.
 Nanci Langley, 789–6887.
Chief Administrative Officer and Secretary.—Shoshana Grove, 789–6842.
Director, Public Affairs and Government Relations.—Ann Fisher, 789–6803.
General Counsel.—David Trissell, 789–6818.
Director, Office of Accountability and Compliance.—Margaret Cigno, 789–6855.

SECURITIES AND EXCHANGE COMMISSION
100 F Street, NE., 20549, phone (202) 551–7500
TTY Relay Service 1–800–877–8339 http://www.sec.gov

THE COMMISSION

Chairman.—Mary Jo White, 551–2100, fax 772–9200.
Chief of Staff.—Lona Nallengara.
Deputy Chiefs of Staff: Nathaniel Stankard, Erica Williams.
Chief Counsel.—Vacant.
Senior Advisors to the Chairman: Tamara Brightwell, David Dimitrious, Michael Liftik, Jennifer Porter, Ryan VanGrack.
Commissioners:
Luis A. Aguilar, 551–2500, fax 772–9335.
 Counsels to the Commissioner: Giles Cohen, Paul Gumagay, Neil Lombardo, Smeeta Ramarathnam.
Daniel M. Gallagher, 551–2600, fax 772–9345.
 Counsels to the Commissioner: Benjamin Brown, John Cook, Rebekah Goshorn, Dawn Jessen.
Michael S. Piwowar, 551–2700, fax 772–9330.
 Counsels to the Commissioner: Adam Glazer, Richard Grant, Jaime Klima, Mark Uyeda.
Kara M. Stein, 551–2800, fax 772–9340.
 Counsels to the Commissioner: Robert Peak, Caroline Crenshaw, Andrew Green, Allison Lee.

OFFICE OF THE SECRETARY

Secretary.—Brent J. Fields, 551–5400.
Deputy Secretaries: Lynn Powalski, 551–5400; Vacant.
Assistant Secretary.—Jill Peterson, 551–5400.

OFFICE OF LEGISLATIVE AND INTERGOVERNMENTAL AFFAIRS

Director.—Timothy Henseler, 551–2010, fax 772–9250.
Deputy Directors: Keith Cassidy, 551–2010; Anne-Marie Kelley, 551–2010.

OFFICE OF THE CHIEF OPERATING OFFICER

Chief Operating Officer.—Jeff Heslop, 551–2200.

OFFICE OF INVESTOR EDUCATION AND ADVOCACY

Director.—Lori J. Schock, 551–6500, fax 772–9295.
Deputy Director.—Mary S. Head, 551–6500.

OFFICE OF SUPPORT OPERATIONS

Director/Chief FOIA Officer.—Barry Walters, 551–8400.
 FOIA Officer.—John Livornese, 551–8300, fax 772–9336/9337.

OFFICE OF EQUAL EMPLOYMENT OPPORTUNITY

Director.—Alta Rodriguez, 551–6040, fax 772–9316.

OFFICE OF MINORITY AND WOMEN INCLUSION

Director.—Pamela Gibbs, 551–6046.
Deputy Director.—Laura Stomski, 551–6046.

OFFICE OF THE CHIEF ACCOUNTANT

Chief Accountant.—James Schnurr, 551–5300, fax 772–9253.
Chief Counsel.—Jeff Minton, 551–5300.

OFFICE OF COMPLIANCE INSPECTIONS AND EXAMINATIONS

Director.—Andrew Bowden, 551–6200, fax 772–9184.
Deputy Director.—Marc Wyatt, 551–6200.
Associate Director/Chief Counsel.—Robert Fisher, 551–6460
Associate Directors: Kevin Goodman (Broker/Dealer); Barbara Lorenzen (Clearance and Settlement); John Polise (Market Oversight); Jane Jarcho (Investment Adviser/Investment Company).

DIVISION OF RISK, STRATEGY, AND FINANCIAL INNOVATION

Director and Chief Economist.—Mark J. Flannery, 551–6600, fax 772–9290.
Deputy Directors.—Scott Bauguess, 551–6600; Jennifer Marietta-Westberg, 551–6600.

OFFICE OF THE GENERAL COUNSEL

General Counsel.—Ann K. Small, 551–5100, fax 772–9260.
Deputy General Counsels: Michael Conley, 551–5100; Meredith Mitchell, 551–5100; Jeffrey Rosenblum, 551–5100.
Associate General Counsel for Litigation and Adjudication.—Laura Jarsulic, 551–5150.
Solicitor, Appellate Litigation and Bankruptcy.—Jacob Stillman, 551–5100.
Deputy Solicitor.—John Avery, 551–5100.
Associate General Counsel for Legal Policy 1.—Vacant, 551–5120.
Associate General Counsel for Legal Policy 2.—Vacant, 551–5120.
Associate General Counsel for Litigation and Administrative Practice: Richard M. Humes, 551–5140; Samuel Forstein; Melinda Hardy.

OFFICE OF ETHICS COUNSEL

Ethics Counsel and Designated Ethics Officer.—Shira Minton, 551–5170

DIVISION OF INVESTMENT MANAGEMENT

Director.—David Grim 551–6720, fax 772–9234.
Deputy Director.—David Grim, 551–6720.
Associate Director, Chief Counsel.—Douglas J. Scheidt, 551–6720.
Enforcement Liaison.—Janet Grossnickle, 551–6785.
Chief Counsel.—Vacant, 551–6825.
Associate Director, Office of:
 Exemptive Application.—Vacant, 551–6821.
 Disclosure Review and Accounting.—Vacant, 551–6921.
 Insured Investments.—Vacant, 551–6795.
 Regulatory Policy and Investment Adviser Regulation.—Vacant.
 Rulemaking.—Vacant, 551–6702.
Chief Accountant.—Vacant, 551–6918.
EDGAR Filer Support.—Vacant, 551–6989.
Investment Advisor Regulation Office.—Vacant, 551–6999.
Risk and Examinations Office.—Vacant, 551–6972.
Investment Company Regulation Office.—Vacant, 551–6792.

DIVISION OF CORPORATION FINANCE

Director.—Keith Higgins, 551–3110.
Managing Executive.—Peter Uhlmann, 551–3130.

Deputy Director of Disclosure Operations.—Shelley E. Parratt, 551–3130.
Associate Director Legal.—Elizabeth Murphy, 551–3180.
Policy and Capital Markets.—Vacant.
Associate Director, Regulatory Policy.—Vacant.
Chief Accountant.—Mark Kronforst, 551–3400.
Disclosure Operations: James Daly, 551–3140; Karen Garnett, 551–3032; Cicely LaMothe, 551–3411; Kyle Moffatt, 551–3031; Barry Summer, 551–3160.
Chief Counsel.—David Fredrickson, 551–3500.

DIVISION OF ENFORCEMENT

Director.—Andrew Ceresney, 551–4500, fax 772–9279.
Deputy Director.—Stephanie Avakian, 551–4500.
Managing Executive.—Victor Valdez, 551–4500.
Associate Directors: Antonia Chion, Stephen Cohen, Scott Friestad, Gerald Hodgkins.
Chief, Market Surveillance.—Vincente Martinez, 551–4500.
Chief Counsel.—Joseph Brenner, 551–4500.
Deputy Chiefs Litigation Counsel: Charlotte Buford, 551–4500; Samuel Waldon, 551–4500.
Chief Accountant.—Michael Maloney, 551–4610.
Senior Associate Chief Accountants: Dwayne Brown, Kristen Dieter, David Estabrook, Peter Rosario, 551–4647.
Office of Collections: Gordon Brumback, 551–4500; Marsha Massey, 551–4500.
Office of Whistleblower, Chief.—Sean McKessey, 551–4790.
Trial Unit.—Vacant, 551–4900.

DIVISION OF TRADING AND MARKETS

Director.—Stephen Luparello, 551–5500.
Deputy Directors: Gary Barnett, Gary Goldsholle, 551–5500.
Associate Director, Chief Counsel.—Heather Seidel, 551–5554.
Associate Directors:
  Broker Dealer Finances.—Michael Macchiaroli, 551–5889.
  Clearance and Settlement.—Peter Curley, 551–5696.
  Trading Practices.—Brian Bussey, 551–5799.
Market Supervision.—David Shillman, 551–5600.

OFFICE OF CREDIT RATINGS

Director.—Tom Butler (212) 336–9080.

OFFICE OF MUNICIPAL SECURITIES

Director.—Vacant, 551–5680.

OFFICE OF ADMINISTRATIVE LAW JUDGES

Chief Administrative Law Judge.—Brenda Murray, 551–6030, fax 777–1031.
Administrative Law Judges: Cameron Elliot, Carol Fox Foelak, James Grimes, Jason S. Patil.

OFFICE OF INTERNATIONAL AFFAIRS

Director.—Paul A. Leder, 551–6690.
Deputy Director.—Elizabeth Jacobs, 551–6690.

OFFICE OF THE INVESTOR ADVOCATE

Investor Advocate.—Rick Fleming, 551–3302.

OFFICE OF THE INSPECTOR GENERAL

Inspector General.—Carl Hoecker, 551–6061, fax 772–9265.

Deputy Inspector General for Audits, Evaluations, and Special Projects.—Rebecca Sharek, 551–6061.
Deputy Inspector General for Management Support.—Mary Beth Harrell, 551–6061.
Assistant Inspector General in Investigations.—Vacant, 551–6069.

OFFICE OF PUBLIC AFFAIRS

Director.—John Nester, 551–4120, fax 777–1026.
Deputy Director.—Florence Harmon, 551–4120.

OFFICE OF FINANCIAL MANAGEMENT

Chief Financial Officer.—Kenneth Johnson, 551–7840, fax 756–0473.
Chief Accounting Officer.—Caryn Kauffman, 551–7840.

OFFICE OF INFORMATION TECHNOLOGY

Director/Chief Information Officer.—Pamela Dyson, 551–8800.
Deputy Director/Deputy Chief Information Officer.—Vacant.

OFFICE OF ADMINISTRATIVE SERVICES

Associate Executive Director.—Vance Cathrell, 551–8385, fax (703) 914–4459.

OFFICE OF HUMAN RESOURCES

Director/Chief Human Capital Officer.—Lacey Dingman, 551–7500, fax 777–1028.
Disability Office.—Vacant, 551–7500.
Employee and Labor Relations.—Vacant, 551–7770.
Recruitment, Retention, and Worklife.—Vacant, 551–4100.
SEC University.—Vacant, 551–7328.

REGIONAL OFFICES

Atlanta Regional Office: 950 East Paces Ferry Road, NE., Suite 900, Atlanta, GA 30326 (404) 842–7600, fax 842–7633.
Regional Director.—Walter Jospin.
Associate Regional Director, Enforcement.—William P. Hicks.
Boston Regional Office: 33 Arch Street, 23rd Floor, Boston, MA 02110 (617) 573–8900, fax 573–4590.
Regional Director.—Paul Levenson.
Associate District Director, Enforcement.—John Dugan.
Associate Regional Director, Examinations.—Michael Garrity.
Chicago Regional Office: 175 West Jackson Boulevard, Suite 900, Chicago, IL 60604 (312) 353–7390, fax 353–7398.
Regional Director.—David Glockner.
Associate Regional Director, Enforcement.—Timothy L. Warren.
Associate Regional Directors, Examinations: Steven Levine, Daniel Gregus.
Denver Regional Office: Byron G. Rogers Federal Building, 1961 Stout St., Suite 1700, Denver, CO 80294 (303) 844–1000, fax 844–1010.
Regional Director.—Julie K. Lutz.
Assistant Regional Director.—Christopher Friedman.
Associate Regional Director, Enforcement.—Thomas J. Krysa.
Fort Worth Regional Office: 801 Cherry Street, Unit #18, Fort Worth, TX 76102 (817) 978–3821, fax 978–4096.
Regional Director.—David Woodcock.
Associate Regional Director, Enforcement.—David Peavler.
Regional Trial Counsel.—David Reece.
Associate Regional Director, Examinations.—Marshall Gandy.
Los Angeles Regional Office: 444 South Flower Street, Suite 900, Los Angeles, CA 90071 (323) 965–3998, fax 443–1902.
Regional Director.—Michele Layne.

Associate Regional Directors:
    Enforcement: Lorraine Echavarria.
    Examinations.—Karol Pollock.
    Supervisory Regional Trial Counsel.—John W. Berry.
Miami Regional Office: 801 Brickell Avenue, Suite 1800, Miami, FL 33131 (305) 982–6300, fax 536–4120.
Regional Director.—Eric Bustillo.
Associate Regional Directors:
    Enforcement.—Glenn S. Gordon.
    Examination.—John C. Mattimore.
New York Regional Office: 200 Vesey Street, Suite 400, New York, NY 10281–1022, (212) 336–1100, fax 336–1323.
Regional Director.—Andrew Calamari.
Associate Regional Directors, Enforcement: Amelia A. Cottrell, David Rosenfeld, Sanjay Wadhwa.
Associate Regional Directors:
    Broker/Dealer.—Robert A. Sollazzo.
    Investment Management.—Ken Joseph.
Philadelphia Regional Office: One Penn Center, 1617 John F. Kennedy Blvd., Suite 520, Philadelphia, PA 19103 (215) 597–3100, fax 597–1036.
Regional Director.—Sharon B. Binger.
Associate Regional Directors:
    Enforcement.—G. Jeffrey Boujoukos.
    Examinations.—Joy G. Thompson.
Salt Lake Regional Office: 351 S. West Temple, Suite 6.100, Salt Lake City, UT 84101 (801) 524–5796, fax 524–3558.
Regional Director.—Karen L. Martinez.
San Francisco Regional Office: 44 Montgomery Street, Suite 2800, San Francisco, CA 94104 (415) 705–2500, fax 705–2501.
Regional Director.—Jina L. Choi.
Associate Regional Directors:
    Enforcement.—Erin Schneider.
    Examinations.—Kristin A. Snyder.

SELECTIVE SERVICE SYSTEM

1515 Wilson Boulevard, 5th Floor, Arlington, VA 22209–2425

phone (703) 605–4100, fax 605–4106, http://www.sss.gov

Director.—Lawrence G. Romo, 605–4010.
Inspector General.—Mariano Campos (acting), 605–4111.
Director for—
    Operations.—Mariano Campos, 605–4111.
    Public and Intergovernmental Affairs.—Richard S. Flahavan, 605–4017, fax 605–4106.
    Financial Management.—Roderick R. Hubbard, 605–4022.
Registration Information Office, P.O. Box 94638, Palatine, IL 60094–4638, phone (847) 688–6888, fax (847) 688–2860.

SMITHSONIAN INSTITUTION

Smithsonian Institution Building—The Castle (SIB), 1000 Jefferson Drive, SW., 20560

phone (202) 633–1000, http://www.si.edu

The Smithsonian Institution is an independent trust instrumentality created in accordance with the terms of the will of James Smithson of England who in 1826 bequeathed his property to the United States of America "to found at Washington under the name of the Smithsonian Institution an establishment for the increase and diffusion of knowledge among men." Congress pledged the faith of the United States to carry out the trust in 1836 (Act of July 1, 1836, C. 252, 5 Stat. 64), and established the Institution in its present form in 1846 (August 10, 1846, C. 178, 9 Stat. 102), entrusting the management of the institution to its independent Board of Regents.

THE BOARD OF REGENTS
ex officio

Chief Justice of the United States.—John G. Roberts, Jr., Chancellor.
Vice President of the United States.—Joseph R. Biden, Jr.

Appointed by the President of the Senate	*Appointed by the Speaker of the House*
Hon. Patrick J. Leahy	Hon. Sam Johnson
Vacant	Hon. Tom Cole
Vacant	Hon. Xavier Becerra

Appointed by Joint Resolution of Congress

John McCarter	Roger Sant	Risa J. Lavizzo-Mourey
Shirley Ann Jackson	Steve Case	Michael M. Lynton
Robert P. Kogod	Barbara Barrett	
David M. Rubenstein	John Fahey	

Chief of Staff to the Regents.—Porter Wilkinson, 633–8899.

OFFICE OF THE SECRETARY

Secretary.—Albert G. Horvath (acting), 633–1846.
　Chief of Staff.—Patricia Bartlett, 633–1869.
　Inspector General.—Cathy Helm, 633–7095.
　General Counsel.—Judith Leonard, 633–5099.
　Director of:
　　Communications and Public Affairs.—Evelyn Lieberman, 633–5190.
　　External Affairs.—Virginia Clark, 633–5021.
　　Government Relations.—Nell Payne, 633–5125.
Assistant Secretary for Education and Access.—Claudine Brown, 633–0077.
　Smithsonian Affiliations Program.—Harold Closter, 633–5321.
　Smithsonian Associates Program.—Frederica Adelman, 633–8628.
　Smithsonian Center for Learning and Digital Access.—Stephanie L. Norby, 633–5297.
　Smithsonian Institution Traveling Exhibition Service.—Interim Director Myriam Springuel, 633–3136.
　Smithsonian Science Education Center.—Thomas Emrick, 633–2972.

OFFICE OF THE UNDER SECRETARY FOR FINANCE AND ADMINISTRATION

Under Secretary and CFO.—Albert G. Horvath, 633–5240.
　Director of:
　　Accessibility Program.—Elizabeth Ziebarth, 633–2946.
　　Special Events and Protocol.—Karen Keller, 633–2020.
　Director, Office of:
　　Equal Employment and Minority Affairs.—Era Marshall, 633–6414.
　　Facilities Engineering and Operations.—Nancy Bechtol, 633–1873.
　　Human Resources.—James Douglas, 633–6301.
　　Information Technology and CIO.—Deron Burba, 633–4901.
　　Ombudsman.—Chandra Heilman, 633–2010.

OFFICE OF THE UNDER SECRETARY FOR HISTORY, ART, AND CULTURE

Under Secretary.—Richard Kurin, 633–5240.
　Director of:
　　Anacostia Community Museum.—Camille Akeju, 633–4839.
　　Archives of American Art.—Kate Haw, 633–7969.
　　Asian Pacific American Program.—Konrad Ng, 786–2963.
　　Center for Folklife and Cultural Heritage.—Michael Mason, 633–6440.
　　Cooper Hewitt, Smithsonian Design Museum.—Caroline Baumann (acting), (212) 849–8320.
　　Freer and Sackler Galleries.—Julian Raby, 633–0456.
　　Hirshhorn Museum and Sculpture Garden.—Melissa Chiu, 633–2824.
　　National Museum of African American History and Culture.—Lonnie Bunch, 633–4751.
　　National Museum of African Art.—Johnnetta Cole, 633–4610.

National Museum of American History.—John L. Gray, 633–3435.
National Museum of the American Indian.—Kevin Gover, 633–6700.
National Portrait Gallery.—Kim Sajet, 275–1740.
National Postal Museum.—Allen Kane, 633–5500.
Smithsonian American Art Museum.—Elizabeth Broun, 275–1515.
Smithsonian Latino Center.—Eduardo Diaz, 633–1240.
Smithsonian Institution Archives.—Anne Van Camp, 633–5908.
Smithsonian Institution Libraries.—Nancy Gwinn, 633–2240.

OFFICE OF THE UNDER SECRETARY FOR SCIENCE

Under Secretary.—John Kress (acting), 633–5127.
Director of:
   International Relations.—Molly Fannon, 633–4795.
   National Air and Space Museum.—Jack Dailey, 633–2350.
   National Museum of Natural History.—Kirk Johnson, 633–2664.
   National Zoological Park.—Dennis Kelly, 633–4442.
   Office of Sponsored Projects.—Tracey Fraser, 633–3763.
   Smithsonian Astrophysical Observatory.—Charles Alcock (617) 495–7100.
   Smithsonian Environmental Research Center.—Anson Hines (443) 482–2208.
   Smithsonian Museum Conservation Institute.—Robert Koestler (301) 238–1205.
   Smithsonian Tropical Research Institute.—Matt Larsen, 011–507–212–8110.

SMITHSONIAN ENTERPRISES

President.—Chris Liedel, 633–5169.
   Publisher, Smithsonian Magazine.—Lori Erdos (212) 916–1337.
   Editor, Smithsonian Magazine.—Michael Caruso, 633–6072.

SOCIAL SECURITY ADMINISTRATION

Altmeyer Building, 6401 Security Boulevard, Baltimore, MD 21235 (ALTMB)

Annex Building, 6401 Security Boulevard, Baltimore, MD 21235 (ANXB)

East High Rise Building, 6401 Security Boulevard, Baltimore, MD 21235 (EHRB)

International Trade Commission Building, 500 E Street, SW., Washington, DC 20024 (ITCB)

Meadows East Building, 6300 Security Boulevard, Baltimore, MD 21235 (MEB)

National Computer Center, 6201 Security Boulevard, Baltimore, MD 21235 (NCC)

Oak Meadows Building, 6340 Security Boulevard, Baltimore, MD 21235 (OMB)

One Skyline Tower, 5107 Leesburg Pike, Falls Church, VA 22041 (SKY)

Robert M. Ball Building, 6401 Security Boulevard, Baltimore, MD 21235 (RMBB)

Rolling Road Commerce Center, 2709 Rolling Road, Baltimore, MD 21244 (RRCC)

Security West Tower, 1500 Woodlawn Drive, Baltimore, MD 21241 (SWTB)

West High Rise Building, 6401 Security Boulevard, Baltimore, MD 21235 (WHRB)

West Low Rise Building, 6401 Security Boulevard, Baltimore, MD 21235 (WLRB)

http://www.socialsecurity.gov

OFFICE OF THE COMMISSIONER

Commissioner.—Carolyn W. Colvin (acting), ALTMB, suite 900 (410) 965–3120 or ITCB, room 850 (202) 358–6000.
   Deputy Commissioner.—Vacant.
   Chief of Staff.—Stacy L. Rodgers, ALTMB, suite 900 (410) 965–4681 or ITCB, room 858 (202) 358–6134.

Deputy Chief of Staff.—Vacant.
Executive Counselor to the Commissioner.—Frank Cristaudo.
Executive Secretary.—Nancy J. Martinez, ALTMB, suite 960 (410) 966–0607.
Chief Strategic Officer/Performance Improvement Officer.—Ruby D. Burrell, ALTMB, suite 960 (410) 965–1250.

OFFICE OF THE CHIEF ACTUARY

Chief Actuary.—Stephen C. Goss, ALTMB, room 700 (410) 965–3000.
Deputy Chief Actuary for—
Long Range.—Alice H. Wade, ALTMB, room 700 (410) 965–3002.
Short Range.—Eli N. Donkar, ALTMB, room 760 (410) 965–3004.

OFFICE OF THE CHIEF STRATEGIC OFFICER

Chief Strategic Officer/Performance Improvement Officer.—Ruby Burrell, ALTMB, suite 516 (410) 965–1250.
Deputy Chief Strategic Officer/Performance Improvement Officer.—Darlynda Bogle, ALTMB, suite 571 (410) 965–3609.
Director, Office of:
Performance Management and Business Analytics.—Avis Payne, ALTMB, suite 571 (410) 965–2518.
Strategic Planning and Innovation.—Paul Funk, ALTMB, suite 571 (410) 966–1876.
Executive Director, Office of Open Government.—Alan Lane, WHRB, suite 1126.

OFFICE OF COMMUNICATIONS

Deputy Commissioner.—Douglas K. Walker, ALTMB, room 460 (410) 966–2030.
Assistant Deputy Commissioner.—Philip A. Gambino, ALTMB, room 460 (410) 966–2030.
Associate Commissioner, Office of:
Communications Planning and Technology.—Laura N. Train, ANXB, room 3165 (410) 966–9223.
External Affairs.—J. Jioni Palmer, ANXB, room 3505 (410) 965–1804.
Public Inquiries.—Steven L. Patrick, WHRB, room 1100 (410) 965–0709.
Press Officer.—LaVenia J. LaVelle, ALTMB, room 446 (410) 965–1967.

OFFICE OF DISABILITY ADJUDICATION AND REVIEW

Deputy Commissioner.—Glenn E. Sklar, SKY, suite 1600 (703) 605–8200, or ALTMB, room 560 (410) 965–6006.
Assistant Deputy Commissioner.—James C. Borland, SKY, suite 1600 (703) 605–8200, or ALTMB, room 560 (410) 965–5200.
Executive Director, Office of Appellate Operations.—Patricia A. Jonas, SKY, suite 1400 (703) 605–7100.
Chief Administrative Law Judge.—Debra Bice, SKY, suite 1608 (703) 605 8500.
Associate Commissioner, Office of:
Budget, Facilities and Security.—Frank Biro, SKY, suite 1500 (703) 605–8989.
Electronic Services and Strategic Information.—Nancy Webb, SKY, suite 1509 (703) 605–8970.
Executive Operations and Human Resources.—James R. Julian, SKY, suite 1700 (703) 605–8700.
Regional Chief Administrative Law Judges:
Atlanta.—Ollie L. Garmon III, 61 Forsyth Street, SW., Suite 20T10, Atlanta, GA 30303 (404) 562–1182.
Boston.—Carol Sax, One Bowdoin Square, 10th Floor, Boston, MA 02114 (888) 870–7578.
Chicago.—Sherry Thompson, 200 West Adams Street, Suite 2901, Chicago, IL 60606 (877) 800–7576.
Dallas.—Joan Parks Saunders, 1301 Young Street, Suite 460, Dallas, TX 75202 (214) 767–9401.
Denver.—Nicholas J. LoBurgio, 1244 North Speer Boulevard, Suite 600, Denver, CO 80204 (888) 397–9803.
Kansas City.—Sherianne Laba, 1100 Main Street, Suite 1700, Kansas City, MO 64105 (888) 238–7975.

New York.—Monica LaPolt (acting), 26 Federal Plaza, Room 34–102, New York, NY 10278 (212) 264–4036.
Philadelphia.—Jasper J. Bede, 300 Spring Garden Street, 4th Floor, Philadelphia, PA 19123 (215) 597–9980.
San Francisco.—John Rolph (acting), 555 Battery Street, 5th Floor, San Francisco, CA 94111 (866) 964–7584.
Seattle.—Lyle Olson (acting), 701 5th Avenue, Suite 2900 M/S 904, Seattle, WA 98104 (206) 615–2236.

OFFICE OF RETIREMENT AND DISABILITY POLICY

Deputy Commissioner.—Virginia Reno, ALTMB, room 100 (410) 965–0100 (Main Line) or ITC 826 (202) 358–6029.
Assistant Deputy Commissioner.—Marianna LaCanfora, ALTMB, room 100 (410) 965–5514.
Associate Commissioner, Office of:
    Data Exchange and Policy Publications.—Stephen Evangelista, RRCC, room 1910 (410) 965–6522.
    Disability Programs.—Arthur R. Spencer, ANXB, room 4550 (410) 966–5766.
    Employment Support Programs.—Robert R. Williams, OPRB, room 2607 (410) 597–1352 or ITCB, room 830 (202) 358–6921.
    Income Security Programs.—Gina Clemons (acting), ALTMB, room 250 (410) 966–9897.
    International Programs.—Vance N. Teel, RMBB, room 3700 (410) 597–1649 or ITCB, room 869 (202) 358–6177.
    Medical and Vocational Expertise.—Vacant.
    Program Development and Research.—David A. Weaver, ITCB, room 822 (202) 358–6252.
    Research, Evaluation and Statistics.—Manuel de la Puente, ITCB, room 828 (202) 358–6020.
    Retirement Policy.—Natalie Lu, ALTB, room 118 (410) 965–3327.
Director, Office of Regulations and Reports Clearance.—Paul Kryglik, WHRB, room 4400 (410) 965–3735.

OFFICE OF BUDGET, FINANCE, QUALITY, AND MANAGEMENT

Deputy Commissioner.—Pete D. Spencer, ALTMB, room 800 (410) 965–2475.
Assistant Deputy Commissioner.—Elizabeth Reich, ALTMB, room 800 (410) 965–5288.
Associate Commissioner, Office of:
    Acquisition and Grants.—Seth P. Binstock, RMBB, room 1540, (410) 965–9538.
    Anti-Fraud Programs.—Michelle King, RMBB, room 1513 (410) 965–7748.
    Budget.—Bonnie Kind, WHRB, room 2126 (410) 965–3501.
    Facilities and Supply Management.—Chris Molander, RMBB, room 2710 (410) 965–7401.
    Financial Policy and Operations.—Carla A. Krabbe, EHRB, room 3A10 (410) 965–0759.
    Media Management.—Mark E. Graydon, AB, room 1408 (410) 965–4121.
    Quality Improvement.—Daryl Wise, EHRB, room 4138 (410) 965–4557.
    Quality Review.—Amy Thompson, EHRB, room 6145 (410) 966–0569.
    Security and Emergency Preparedness.—Jonas M. Garland, 6301 Security Boulevard, room 201 (410) 965–6660.
    Records Management and Audit Liaison Staff Director.—John Biles, ALTMB, room 834 (410) 965–3758.
    Systems Support Staff Director.—Jim Guidry, EHRB, room 5139 (410) 965–9794.

OFFICE OF THE GENERAL COUNSEL

General Counsel.—David F. Black, ALTMB, room 600 (410) 965–0600.
Deputy General Counsel.—Kristi Schmidt (acting), ALTMB, room 600 (410) 965–0495.
Associate General Counsel for—
    General Law.—Dan Callahan (acting), WHRB, room G300 (410) 965–0644.
    Program Law.—Jeffrey C. Blair, ALTMB, room 6224 (410) 965–3157.
Executive Director, Office of Privacy and Disclosure.—Kirsten J. Moncada, WHRB, G400–F (410) 965–0205.
Regional Chief Counsels for—
    Atlanta.—Mary Ann Sloan, Atlanta Federal Center, 61 Forsyth Street, SW., Suite 20T45, Atlanta, GA 30303 (404) 562–1010.

Boston.—Christopher Michaels (acting), JFK Federal Building, 15 New Sudbury Street, Room 625, Boston, MA 02203 (617) 565–4287.
Chicago.—Kathryn Caldwell (acting), 200 West Adams Street, 30th Floor, Chicago, IL 60606, (877) 800–7578, ext. 19110.
Dallas.—Mike McGaughran, 1301 Young Street, Room A–702, Dallas, TX 75202–5433 (214) 767–4660.
Denver.—John J. Lee, 1961 Stout Street, Suite 4169, Denver, CO 80294 (303) 844–0013.
Kansas City.—Rhonda Wheeler (acting), Richard Bolling Federal Building, 601 East 12th Street, Room 965, Federal Office Building, Kansas City, MO 64106 (816) 936–5779.
New York.—Stephen P. Conte, 26 Federal Plaza, Suite 3904, New York, NY 12078 (212) 264–2216.
Philadelphia.—Nora Koch (acting), 300 Spring Garden Street, 6th Floor, Philadelphia, PA 19123 (215) 597–1847.
San Francisco.—Donna Calvert, 160 Spear Street, Suite 800, San Francisco, CA 94105 (415) 977–8971.
Seattle.—David F. Morado, 701 Fifth Avenue, Columbia Tower, Suite 2900, M/S 221A, Seattle, WA 98104 (206) 615–2662.

OFFICE OF HUMAN RESOURCES

Deputy Commissioner.—Dr. Reginald F. Wells, ALTMB, room 200 (410) 965–1900.
Assistant Deputy Commissioner.—Dot Smallwood (acting), ALTMB, room 200 (410) 965–0925.
Associate Commissioner, Office of:
    Civil Rights and Equal Opportunity.—Kojuan L. Almond, WHRB, room 3350 (410) 965–4531.
    Labor Management and Employee Relations.—Thomas Funciello, ANXB, room 2170 (410) 965–0468.
    Learning.—Lydia C. Marshall, EHRB, room 100 (410) 966–9916.
    Personnel.—Kristen Medley-Proctor, ANXB, room 2570 (410) 965–1037.
Director, Executive and Special Services.—Bonnie L. Doyle, ANXB, room 2510 (410) 965–4463.

OFFICE OF THE INSPECTOR GENERAL

Inspector General.—Patrick P. O'Carroll, ALTMB, suite 300 (410) 966–8385.
Deputy Inspector General.—Gale Stallworth Stone, ALTMB, suite 300 (410) 966–8385.
Counsel to the Inspector General.—Helen L. Cooper (acting), MEB, room 3–ME–1 (410) 966–2323.
Assistant Inspector General for—
    Audit.—Steven L. Schaeffer, MEB, room 3–ME–2 (410) 965–9701.
    Investigations.—Michael D. Robinson, MEB, room 3–ME–3 (410) 966–2436.
    Office of Communications and Resource Management.—Kelly Bloyer, MEB, room 2–ME–4 (410) 965 4866.

OFFICE OF LEGISLATION AND CONGRESSIONAL AFFAIRS

Deputy Commissioner.—Judy Chesser, ITCB, room 816 (202) 358–6030, or ALTMB, room 500 (410) 966–8088.
Assistant Deputy Commissioner.—Thomas M. Parrott, ITCB, room 819 (202) 358–6013 or ALTMB, room 500 (410) 965–3737.
Associate Commissioner, Office of:
    Legislative Development and Operations.—Royce B. Min, WHRB, room 3103–B (410) 965–4511.
    Congressional Affairs.—Ken Mannella, ITC, room 818 (202) 358–6083.
Director for—
    Legislative and Constituent Relations.—Robert J. Forrester, WHRB, room 3105 (410) 966–6706.
    Disability Insurance.—John Brzostowski, WHRB, room 3109 (410) 965–1472.
    Immigration, Data Exchange and Enumeration.—Elizabeth Tino, WHRB, room 3104 (410) 965 2871.
    Retirement and Survivors Insurance Benefits.—Susan Bussman, WHRB, room 3102 (410) 965–3313.

Program Administration and Financing Staff.—Perry Cocke (acting), WHRB, room 3107 (410) 965–4725.
Regulations and Reports Clearance.—Faye Lipsky (acting), (410) 965–8783.

OFFICE OF OPERATIONS

Deputy Commissioner.—Nancy A. Berryhill (acting), WHRB, room 1204 (410) 965–3145.
Assistant Deputy Commissioners: Mike Kramer (acting), WHRB, room 1204 (410) 966–4565; Van Roland, WHRB, room 1204 (410) 966–1751.
Associate Commissioner, Office of:
  Electronic Services and Technology.—Robin Sabatino, ANXB, room 4705 (410) 965–9885.
  Central Operations.—Jan Foushee, SWTB, room 7000 (410) 966–7000.
  Disability Determinations.—Ann P. Robert, ANXB, room 3570 (410) 965–1170.
  Public Service and Operations Support.—Eric N.D. Jones, WHRB, room 1224 (410) 965–5514.
  Telephone Services.—Cynthia Bennett (acting), ANXB, room 4845 (410) 965–7507.
Regional Commissioner for—
  Atlanta.—Michael W. Grochowski, 61 Forsyth Street, Suite 23T30, Atlanta, GA 30303 (404) 562–5600.
  Boston.—Linda M. Dorn, JFK Federal Building, 15 New Sudbury Street, Room 1900, Boston, MA 02203 (617) 565–2870.
  Chicago.—Phyllis Smith (acting), Harold Washington Social Security Center, 600 West Madison Street, Chicago, IL 60661 (312) 575–5914.
  Dallas.—Sheila Everett, 1301 Young Street, Suite 130, Dallas, TX 75202–5433 (214) 767–4207.
  Denver.—Wanda Colon-Mollfulleda, Federal Office Building, 1961 Stout Street, Suite 07–115, Denver, CO 80294 (303) 844–2388.
  Kansas City.—W. Kenneth Powell, Federal Office Building, 601 East 12th Street, Room 1016, Kansas City, MO 64106 (816) 936–5700.
  New York.—Fred Maurin, 26 Federal Plaza, Room 40–102, New York, NY 10278 (212) 264–3915.
  Philadelphia.—Terry M. Stradtman, 300 Spring Garden Street, Philadelphia, PA 19123 (215) 597–5157.
  San Francisco.—Grace Kim, 1221 Nevin Avenue, Richmond, CA 94801 (510) 970–8400.
  Seattle.—Stanley C. Friendship, 701 5th Avenue, Seattle, Suite 2900, M/S 301, WA 98104–7075 (206) 615–2100.

OFFICE OF SYSTEMS / OFFICE OF THE CHIEF INFORMATION OFFICER

Deputy Commissioner and Chief Information Officer.—William Zielinski, ALTMB, room 400 (410) 965–4380.
Assistant Deputy Commissioner and Deputy Chief Information Officer.—Herb Strauss, ALTMB, room 400 (410) 965–0710.
Associate Commissioner, Office of:
  Applications and Supplemental Security Income Systems.—Frank Sotaski, RMBB, room 2100 (410) 965–6546.
  Disability Systems.—Rachel Dumser, RMBB, room 3606 (410) 965–6398.
  Earnings, Enumeration and Administrative Systems.—Sylviane Haldiman, RMBB, room 3103 (410) 965–8040.
  Enterprise Support, Architecture and Engineering.—Dan Parry (acting), RMBB, room 4100 (410) 966–0778.
  Information Security.—Marti A. Eckert (acting), ANXB, room 3100 (410) 965–0445.
  Retirement and Survivors Insurance Systems.—John Simermeyer, RMBB, room 4700 (410) 965–5789.
  Systems Electronic Services.—Diana E. Andrews, RMBB, room 3003 (410) 965–7641.
  Telecommunications and Systems Operations.—Thomas G. Grzymski, NCC, room 550 (410) 965–7626.

STATE JUSTICE INSTITUTE
11951 Freedom Drive, Suite 1020, Reston, VA 20190, phone (571) 313–8843
http://www.sji.gov

BOARD OF DIRECTORS

Chairman.—James R. Hannah.
Vice Chairman.—Daniel J. Becker.
Secretary.—Gayle A. Nachtigal.
Treasurer.—Hernan D. Vera.

Members:

Chase T. Rogers
Jonathan Lippman
David V. Brewer
Wilfredo Martinez

Marsha J. Rabiteau
John B. Nalbandian
Isabel Framer

Officer:
Executive Director.—Jonathan D. Mattiello.

SUSQUEHANNA RIVER BASIN COMMISSION
COMMISSIONERS AND ALTERNATES

Federal Government.—BG Kent D. Savre (Commissioner); COL J. Richard Jordan III (Alternate); David J. Leach (2nd Alternate); Amy M. Guise (3rd Alternate).
New York.—James M. Tierney (Commissioner); Kenneth P. Lynch (Alternate); Peter Freehafer (2nd Alternate).
Pennsylvania.—Vacant (Commissioner); Kelly J. Heffner (Alternate); Andrew C. Zemba (2nd Alternate).
Maryland.—Vacant (Commissioner); Saeid Kasraei (Alternate).

STAFF

4423 North Front Street, Harrisburg, PA 17110, phone (717) 238–0423

srbc@srbc.net, http://www.srbc.net

Executive Director.—Andrew D. Dehoff.
Deputy Executive Director.—Andrew G. Gavin.
Director of Administration and Finance.—Marcia E. Rynearson.
Secretary to the Commission.—Stephanie L. Richardson.

TENNESSEE VALLEY AUTHORITY
One Massachusetts Avenue, NW., 20444, Suite 300, phone (202) 898–2999
Knoxville, TN 37902, phone (865) 632–2101
Chattanooga, TN 37401, phone (423) 751–0011

BOARD OF DIRECTORS

Chairman.—Joseph H. Ritch (Knoxville).
Directors: Marilyn A. Brown (Knoxville), V. Lynn Evans (Knoxville), Richard C. Howorth (Knoxville), Virginia S. Lodge (Knoxville), Pete Mahurin (Knoxville), Michael R. McWherter (Knoxville), Ronald A. Walter (Knoxville).

EXECUTIVE OFFICERS

President and Chief Executive Officer.—William D. Johnson (865) 632–2366 (Knoxville).
Executive Vice Presidents:
  Chief External Relations Officer.—Van M. Wardlaw (423) 751–2555 (Chattanooga).
  Chief Financial Officer.—John M. Thomas III, 751–8919 (Chattanooga).
  Chief Nuclear Officer.—Joseph P. Grimes (423) 751–8682 (Chattanooga).
  Chief Operating Officer.—Charles G. Pardee (865) 632–4049 (Knoxville).
  General Counsel.—Sherry A. Quirk (865) 632–3127 (Knoxville).

Senior Vice Presidents:
  Human Resources and Communications.—Katherine J. Black (423) 751–4747 (Chattanooga).
  Nuclear Construction.—Michael D. Skaggs (423) 751–6506 (Chattanooga).
  Shared Services.—Ricardo G. Perez (423) 751–8840 (Chattanooga).

WASHINGTON OFFICE

Director, Federal Government Relations.—Nick Pearson (202) 898–2999, fax: 898–2998.

U.S. ADVISORY COMMISSION ON PUBLIC DIPLOMACY

301 4th Street, SW., SA–44, M–04, 20547

phone (202) 203–7386, fax 203–7886

[Created by Executive Order 12048 and Public Law 96–60]

Chair.—William J. Hybl.
  Members: Vice-Chairman, Sim Farar, Vice-Chairman, Amb. Lyndon Olson, Jr., Amb. Penne
  K. Peacock, Anne Terman Wedner, Lezlee Westine.
  Executive Director.—Katherine Brown.

U.S. AGENCY FOR INTERNATIONAL DEVELOPMENT

1300 Pennsylvania Avenue, NW., 20523, phone (202) 712–0000

http://www.usaid.gov

Administrator.—Alonso E. Lenhardt (acting), room 6.09, 712–4040, fax 216–3445.
Deputy Administrator.—Mark Feierstein (acting), room 6.09, 712–4040, fax 216–3445.
Counselor.—Susan Reichle, room 6.08, 712–5010.
Executive Secretary.—Mark Hannafin, room 6.08–032, 712–0700.
Assistant Administrator for—
  Africa.—Eric Postel, room 4.08–031, 712–0500.
  Asia.—Jonathan Stivers, room 4.09, 712–1573.
  Democracy, Conflict and Humanitarian Assistance.—Thomas Staal (acting), room 8.06–084, 712–0100.
  Economic Growth, Education and Environment.—Charles North, room 3.09–008, 712–0670.
  Europe and Eurasia.—Susan Fritz, room 5.06, 567–4001.
  Global Health.—Ariel Pablos-Mendez, room 3.06, 712–4120.
  Latin America and the Caribbean.—Mark Feierstein, room 5.09–012, 712–4800.
  Legislative and Public Affairs.—Chuck Cooper, room 6.10–107, 712–4300.
  Management.—Angelique Crumbly, room 6.08, 712–1200.
  Middle East.—Paige Alexander, room 4.09–005 (202) 567–4020.
Director, Office of:
  Security.—Mark Webb (acting), room 2.06, 712–0990.
  Small and Disadvantaged Business Utilization.—Mauricio Vera, room 848–E, 567–4735, SA–44.
  General Counsel.—Susan Pascocello (acting), room 6.06–125, 712–0900.
  Inspector General.—Vacant, room 6.06D, 712–1150.

U.S. COMMISSION ON CIVIL RIGHTS

1331 Pennsylvania Avenue, NW., Suite 1150, 20425

phone (202) 376–8591, fax 376–7672

(Codified in 42 U.S.C., section 1975)

Chairman.—Martin Castro.
  Vice Chair.—Patricia Timmons-Goodson.
  Commissioners: Roberta Achtenberg, Gail Heriot, Peter N. Kirsanow, David Kladney, Karen
  Narasaki, Michael Yaki.
  Staff Director.—Vacant.

U.S. ELECTION ASSISTANCE COMMISSION

1335 East West Highway, Suite 4300, Silver Spring, MD 20910

phone (301) 563–3919, (866) 747–1471, fax (301) 734–3108, http://www.eac.gov

[Created by Public Law 107–252]

Commissioner.—Thomas Hicks.
Commissioner.—Matthew Masterson.
Commissioner.—Christy McCormick.
Commissioner.—Vacant.

OFFICE OF THE EXECUTIVE DIRECTOR

Executive Director.—Alice P. Miller (acting), (301) 563–3919.
  Chief Operating Officer.—Alice P. Miller.
  Chief Financial Officer.—Annette Lafferty.

OFFICE OF COMMUNICATIONS AND CONGRESSIONAL AFFAIRS

Director of Communications and Clearinghouse.—Bryan Whitener (301) 563–3919.

OFFICE OF THE GENERAL COUNSEL

General Counsel.—Vacant.

OFFICE OF THE INSPECTOR GENERAL

Inspector General.—Curtis Crider (301) 734–3104.

U.S. HOLOCAUST MEMORIAL COUNCIL

The United States Holocaust Memorial Museum

100 Raoul Wallenberg Place, SW., 20024, phones (202) 488–0400, (202) 314–7881

fax 488–2690

Officials:
  Chair.—Tom A. Bernstein, New York, NY.
  Vice Chair.—Joshua B. Bolten, Washington, DC.
  Director.—Sara J. Bloomfield, Washington, DC.

Members:

Elliott Abrams, Great Falls, VA.
Matthew L. Adler, Miami Beach, FL.
Elisa Spungen Bildner, Montclair, NJ.
Lee T. Bycel, Kensington, CA.
Michael Chertoff, Potomac, MD.
Diana Shaw Clark, London, England.
William J. Danhof, Lansing, MI.
Shefali Razdan Duggal, San Francisco, CA.
Kitty Dukakis, Brookline, MA.
John Farahi, Reno, NV.
Todd A. Fisher, New York, NY.
Jonathan Safran Foer, Brooklyn, NY.
Amy R. Friedkin, San Francisco, CA.
K. Chaya Friedman, Baltimore, MD.
Nancy B. Gilbert, Palm Beach, FL.
Mark D. Goodman, Cambridge, MA.
Samuel N. Gordon, Wilmette, IL.
Sanford L. Gottesman, Austin, TX.
Joseph D. Gutman, Chicago, IL.

Cheryl F. Halpern, Livingston, NJ.
S. Fitzgerald Haney, New York, NY.
Beth Heifetz, Chevy Chase, MD.
J. David Heller, Cleveland, OH.
Allan M. Holt, Washington, DC.
Jane H. Jelenko, Los Angeles, CA.
Amy Kaslow, Potomac, MD.
Roman R. Kent, New York, NY.
Howard Konar, West Henrietta, NY.
Alan B. Lazowski, Hartford, CT.
Deborah E. Lipstadt, Atlanta, GA.
Susan E. Lowenberg, San Francisco, CA.
Leslie Meyers, New York, NY.
Michael B. Mukasey, New York, NY.
Deborah A. Oppenheimer, Los Angeles, CA.
Cheryl Peisach, Golden Beach, FL.
Dana Perlman, Beverly Hills, CA.
Richard S. Price, Chicago, IL.
Ronald Ratner, Cleveland, OH.

Daniel J. Rosen, New York, NY.
Greg A. Rosenbaum, Bethesda, MD.
Menachem Z. Rosensaft, New York, NY.
Michael P. Ross, Boston, MA.
Kirk A. Rudy, Austin, TX.
Elliot J. Schrage, Menlo Park, CA.
Maureen Schulman, Chicago, IL.
Daniel J. Silva, Boca Raton, FL.

Andrea Lavin Solow, Chicago, IL.
Marc R. Stanley, Dallas, TX.
Michael Ashley Stein, Cambridge, MA.
Michéle Taylor, Atlanta, GA.
Howard D. Unger, Briarcliff Manor, NY.
Clementine Wamariya, Kenilworth, IL.
Elie Wiesel, Boston, MA.

Former Chairs:
Fred S. Zeidman, 2002–2010.
Irving Greenberg, 2000–2002.
*Miles Lerman, 1993–2000.
Harvey M. Meyerhoff, 1987–1993.
Elie Wiesel, 1980–1986.

Fomer Vice Chairs:
Joel M. Geiderman, 2005–2010.
Ruth B. Mandel, 1993–2005.
*William J. Lowenberg, 1986–1993.
Mark E. Talisman, 1980–1986.

Congressional Members:

U.S. House of Representatives:
Steve Israel, from New York.
Patrick Meehan, from Pennsylvania.

U.S. Senate:
Al Franken, from Minnesota.
Orrin G. Hatch, from Utah.
BERNARD SANDERS, from Vermont.

Ex Officio Members:
U.S. Department of:
Education.—Philip H. Rosenfelt.
Interior.—Benjamin Milakofsky.
State.—Nicholas J. Dean.

Council Staff:
General Counsel.—Gerard Leval.
Secretary of the Council.—Jane M. Miller.

*Deceased

U.S. INSTITUTE OF PEACE

2301 Constitution Avenue, NW., 20037
phone (202) 457–1700, fax 429–6063

BOARD OF DIRECTORS

Public Members:
Chairman.—Stephen J. Hadley.
Vice Chairman.—George E. Moose.
Members:

Judith A. Ansley
Eric E. Edelman
Joseph T. Eldridge
Kerry Kennedy
Ikram U. Khan

Stephen D. Krasner
John A. Lancaster
Jeremy A. Rabkin
J. Robinson West
Nancy M. Zirkin

Ex Officio:
Department of Defense.—Secretary Ashton B. Carter (or his designee).
Department of State.—Secretary John F. Kerry (or his designee).
National Defense University.—Major General Frederick M. Padilla.
United States Institute of Peace.—President Nancy Lindborg (non-voting).
Officials:
President.—Nancy Lindborg.
Executive Vice President.—William B. Taylor (acting).
Vice President for External Relations.—Peter Loge.
Congressional Relations.—Laurie Schultz Heim.
Intergovernmental Affairs.—Linwood Ham, Jr.
Communications—Diane Zeleny.

U.S. INTERNATIONAL TRADE COMMISSION

500 E Street, SW., 20436
phone (202) 205–2000, fax 205–2798, http://www.usitc.gov

COMMISSIONERS

Chairman.—Meredith M. Broadbent.

Vice Chairman.—Dean A. Pinkert.
Commissioners:
Irving A. Williamson.
David S. Johanson.
F. Scott Kieff.
Rhonda K. Schmidtlein.
External Relations/Executive Liaison.—Lyn M. Schlitt, 205–3141.
Congressional Relations Officer.—Maureen McLaughlin, 205–3151.
Public Affairs Officer.—Margaret O'Laughlin.
General Counsel.—Dominic Bianchi.
Secretary to the Commission.—Lisa Barton.
Inspector General.—Philip M. Heneghan.
Director, Office of:
  Economics.—Keith Hall.
  Industries.—Mark Paulson (acting).
  Tariff Affairs and Trade Agreements.—James Holbein.

U.S. MERIT SYSTEMS PROTECTION BOARD

1615 M Street, NW., 20419

phone (202) 653–7200, toll-free (800) 209–8960, fax 653–7130

[Created by Public Law 95–454]

Chairman.—Susan Tsui Grundmann.
Vice Chairman.—Anne M. Wagner.
Member.—Mark A. Robbins.
Executive Director.—James M. Eisenmann.
General Counsel.—Bryan Polisuk.
Appeals Counsel.—Susan Swafford.
Legislative Counsel.—Rosalyn L. Coates, 653–7171.
Clerk of the Board.—William D. Spencer, 653–7200.

REGIONAL OFFICES

Regional Directors:
  Atlanta Regional Office: Covering Alabama, Florida, Georgia, Mississippi, South Carolina, Tennessee.—Thomas J. Lanphear, 10th Floor, 401 West Peachtree Street, NW., Atlanta, GA 30308–3519 (404) 730–2751, fax 730–2767.
  Central Regional Office: Covering Illinois, Iowa, Kansas City, Kansas, Kentucky, Indiana, Michigan, Minnesota, Missouri, Ohio, Wisconsin.—Michele Schroeder, 31st Floor, 230 South Dearborn Street, Chicago, IL 60604–1669 (312) 353–2923, fax 886–4231.
  Dallas Regional Office: Covering Arkansas, Louisiana, Oklahoma, Texas.—Laura Albornoz, Room 620, 1100 Commerce Street, Dallas, TX 75242–9979 (214) 767–0555, fax 767–0102.
  Northeastern Regional Office: Covering Connecticut, Delaware, Maine, Maryland (except Montgomery and Prince Georges counties), Massachusetts, New Hampshire, New Jersey (except the counties of Bergen, Essex, Hudson, and Union), Pennsylvania, Rhode Island, Vermont, West Virginia.—William L. Boulden, 1601 Market Street, Suite 1700, Philadelphia, PA 19103–2310 (215) 597–9960, fax 597–3456.
  Western Regional Office: Covering Alaska, California, Hawaii, Idaho, Nevada, Oregon, Washington, and Pacific Overseas.—Benjamin Gutman, 201 Mission Street, Suite 2310, San Francisco, CA 94105–1831 (415) 904–6772, fax 904–0580.
  Washington Regional Office: Covering Washington, DC, Maryland (counties of Montgomery and Prince Georges), North Carolina, Virginia, all overseas areas not otherwise covered.—Jeremiah Cassidy, 1811 Diagonal Road, Suite 205, Alexandria, VA 22314–2840 (703) 756–6250, fax 756–7112.
  New York Field Office: Covering New York, Puerto Rico, Virgin Islands, the following counties in New Jersey: Bergen, Essex, Hudson, Union.—Arthur Joseph, Chief Administrative Judge, Room 3137–A, 26 Federal Plaza, New York, NY 10278–0022 (212) 264–9372, fax 264–1417.
  Denver Field Office: Covering Arizona, Colorado, Kansas (except Kansas City), Montana, Nebraska, New Mexico, North Dakota, South Dakota, Utah, Wyoming.—Stephen Mish, Chief Administrative Judge, 165 South Union Boulevard, Suite 318, Lakewood, CO 80228–2211 (303) 969–5101, fax 969–5109.

U.S. OVERSEAS PRIVATE INVESTMENT CORPORATION
1100 New York Avenue, NW., 20527, phone (202) 336–8400

President and CEO.—Elizabeth L. Littlefield.
Executive Vice President.—Vacant.
Chief of Staff.—John Morton.
Vice President and General Counsel.—Kimberly Heimert.
Head of Investment Funds and Chief Investment Strategist.—Brooks Preston.
Vice President for Investment Policy.—Margaret Kuhlow.
Deputy Chief of Staff.—Dori Friedberg.
Vice President of:
 External Affairs.—Judith Pryor.
 Insurance.—John Moran.
 Small and Medium Enterprise Finance.—James Polan.
 Structured Finance.—Vacant.
Financial and Portfolio Management.—Mildred Callear.
Special Assistant for Congressional and Intergovernmental Affairs.—James W. Morrison.

BOARD OF DIRECTORS

Government Directors:
 Dr. Rajiv Shah, Administrator, U.S. Agency for International Development.
 Robert W. Holleyman II, Deputy U.S. Trade Representative.
 Elizabeth L. Littlefield, President and Chief Executive Officer, OPIC.
 Stefan Selig, Under Secretary for International Trade, U.S. Department of Commerce.
 Christopher P. Lu, Deputy Secretary, U.S. Department of Labor.
 Catherine A. Novelli, Under Secretary for Economic, Energy and Agricultural Affairs, U.S.
  Department of State.
 D. Nathan Sheets, Under Secretary for International Affairs, U.S. Department of the Treasury.
Private Sector Directors:
 Matthew Maxwell Taylor Kennedy, Director, Kennedy Enterprises.
 Michael J. Warren, Principal, Albright Stonebridge Group, LLC.
 Terry Lewis, Principal, LIA Advisors, LLC.
 James Demers, President, Demers and Blaisdell, Inc.
 James Torrey, Director, The Torrey Family Office.
 Roberto Herencia, President and CEO, BXM Holdings, Inc.
 Naomi Walker, Assistant to the President, AFL/CIO.

U.S. POSTAL SERVICE
475 L'Enfant Plaza, SW., 20260–0010, phone (202) 268–2000

BOARD OF GOVERNORS

Vice Chairman.—James H. Bilbray.
Postmaster General and Chief Executive Officer.—Megan J. Brennan.
Deputy Postmaster General and Chief Government Relations Officer.—Ronald A. Stroman.

MEMBERS

Louis J. Giuliano   Ellen C. Williams

OFFICERS OF THE BOARD OF GOVERNORS

Secretary to the Board of Governors.—Julie S. Moore.

OFFICERS OF THE POSTAL SERVICE

Postmaster General and Chief Executive Officer.—Megan J. Brennan, 268–2550.
 Deputy Postmaster General and Chief Government Relations Officer.—Ronald A. Stroman,
  268–2519.

Congressional Contact:
  Government Relations and Public Policy.—Sheila T. Meyers, 268–2505.
  Judicial Officer.—Hon. William A. Campbell (703) 812–1904, 2101 Wilson Boulevard, Suite 600, Arlington, VA 22201–3078.
Vice President of:
  Consumer and Industry Affairs.—James Nemec, 268–2415.
Chief Operating Officer and Executive Vice President.—David Williams, 268–4841.
Vice President of:
  Delivery Operations.—Edward F. Phelan, Jr., 268–4359.
  Facilities.—Tom A. Samra, 268–2729.
  Network Operations.—Linda Malone, 268–3250.
  Retail and Customer Service Operations.—Kelly Sigmon, 268–2871.
Chief Information Officer and Executive Vice President.—James Cochrane, 268–5710.
Chief Information Security Officer and Digital Solutions Vice President.—Randy Miskanic, 268–6164.
Vice President of:
  Engineering Systems.—Michael J. Amato (703) 280–7002, 8403 Lee Highway, 4th Floor, Merrifield, VA 22082–8101.
  Enterprise Analytics.—Robert Cintron, 268–7458.
  Information Technology.—John T. Edgar, 268–4851.
  Mail Entry and Payment Technology.—Pritha Mehra, 268–4816.
Chief Financial Officer and Executive Vice President.—Joseph Corbett, 268–2447.
Vice President of:
  Controller.—Maura McNerney, 268–4229.
  Finance and Planning.—Shaun Mossman, 268–5285.
  Supply Management.—Susan M. Brownell, 268–4041.
Chief Human Resources Officer and Executive Vice President.—Jeffrey Williamson, 268–4010.
Vice President of:
  Employee Resource Management.—John Godlewski, Jr. (acting), 268–3784.
  Labor Relations.—Douglas A. Tulino, 268–6202.
Chief Marketing and Sales Officer and Executive Vice President.—Nagisa Manabe, 268–3355.
Vice President of:
  Global Business.—Giselle E. Valera, 268–2178.
  New Products and Innovation.—Gary C. Reblin, 268–3177.
  Pricing.—Cynthia Sanchez-Hernandez, 268–8116.
  Sales.—Cliff Rucker, 268–5301.
General Counsel and Executive Vice President.—Thomas Marshall, 268–2951.
Chief Postal Inspector.—Guy J. Cottrell, 268–4264.
Vice President of:
  Corporate Communications.—Elizabeth Johnson (acting), 268–2145.

U.S. RAILROAD RETIREMENT BOARD

844 North Rush Street, Chicago, IL 60611, phone (312) 751–4777, fax 751–7154
Office of Legislative Affairs, 1310 G Street, NW., Suite 500, 20005
phone (202) 272–7742, fax 272–7728, e-mail: ola@rrb.gov
http://www.rrb.gov

Chairman.—Michael S. Schwartz (312) 751–4900, fax 751–7193.
  Assistant to the Chairman.—Nancy S. Pittman.
  Counsel to the Chairman.—Stephen W. Seiple.
Labor Member.—Walter A. Barrows, 751–4905, fax 751–7194.
  Assistants to the Labor Member: Geraldine L. Clark, Michael J. Collins, Brigitte A. Munoz.
  Counsel to the Labor Member.—Nancy V. Russell.
Management Member.—Steven J. Anthony, 751–4910, fax 751–7189.
  Assistants to the Management Member: Natasha L. Marx, Joseph M. Waechter.
  Counsel to the Management Member.—Robert M. Perbohner.
Inspector General.—Martin J. Dickman, 751–4690, fax 751–4342.
General Counsel.—Karl T. Blank, 751–4941, fax 751–7102.
  Assistant General Counsel.—Marguerite P. Dadabo, 751–4945, fax 751–7102.
Secretary to the Board.—Martha P. "Pat" Rico, 751–4920, fax 751–4923.
Director of:
  Disability Benefits.—John R. Coleman, 751–4740, fax 751–7167.
  Equal Opportunity.—Lynn E. Cousins, 751–4942, fax 751–7179.

Field Service.—Daniel J. Fadden, 751–4627, fax 751–3360.
Hearings and Appeals.—Rachel L. Simmons, 751–4946, fax 751–7159.
Human Resources.—Marguerite V. Daniels, 751–4384, fax 751–7164.
Legislative Affairs.—Margaret A. Lindsley (202) 272–7742, fax 272–7728.
Policy and Systems.—Vacant.
Program Evaluation and Management Services.—Janet M. Hallman, 751–4543, fax 751–7190.
Programs.—Michael A. Tyllas, 751–4515, fax 751–4333.
Public Affairs.—Michael P. Freeman, 751–4777, fax 751–7154.
Retirement and Survivor Benefits.—Valerie F. Allen, 751–3323, fax 751–7104.
Unemployment and Programs Support.—Micheal T. Pawlak, 751–4708, fax 751–7157.
Supervisor of:
  Congressional Inquiry.—Carl D. Mende, 751–4970, fax 751–7154.
Chief of:
  Acquisition Management.—Paul T. Ahern, 751–7130, fax 751–4923.
  Actuary.—Frank J. Buzzi, 751–4915, fax 751–7129.
  Benefit and Employment Analysis.—Marla L. Huddleston, 751–4779, fax 751–7129.
  Information.—Ram Murthy, 751–4851, fax 751–7169.
  Librarian.—Katherine Tsang, 751–4926, fax 751–4924.
  SEO/Finance.—George V. Govan, 751–4930, fax 751–4931.

U.S. SENTENCING COMMISSION

One Columbus Circle, NE., Suite 2–500, South Lobby, 20002–8002
phone (202) 502–4500, fax 502–4699

Chair.—Patti B. Saris.
Vice Chair.—Charles R. Breyer.
Commissioners: Rachel Barkow, Dabney L. Friedrich,William H. Pryor, Jr.
Commissioner ex officio.—Jonathan J. Wroblewski.
Staff Director.—Kenneth P. Cohen, 502–4510.
General Counsel.—Kathleen C. Grilli, 502–4520.
Director of Legislative and Governmental Affairs.—Noah Bookbinder, 502–4519.
Director of:
  Administration.—Susan Brazel, 502–4610.
  Research and Data Collection.—Glenn R. Schmitt, 502–4530.
Director and Chief Counsel of Office of Training.—Vacant.
Public Affairs Officer.—Jeanne Doherty, 502–4502.

U.S. SMALL BUSINESS ADMINISTRATION

409 Third Street, SW., 20416
phone (202) 205–6600, fax 205–7064, http://www.sba.gov

Administrator.—Maria Contreras-Sweet, 205–6605.
Deputy Administrator.—Vacant, 205–6605.
Chief of Staff.—Nicolas Maduros, 205–6605.
Director of Executive Secretariat.—Kim Bradley, 205–2410.
General Counsel.—Melvin F. Williams, Jr., 619–1848.
Chief Counsel for Advocacy.—Claudia Rodgers (A), 205–6804.
Inspector General.—Peg Gustafson, 205–6586.
Chief Financial Officer.—Tami Perriello, 205–7420.
Associate Administrator, Office of:
  Disaster Assistance.—James Rivera, 205–6734.
  Field Operations.—Robert Hill, 205–6411.
Assistant Administrator, Office of:
  Communications and Public Liaison.—Iris Argueta (A), 205–6948.
Associate Administrator, Office of:
  Congressional and Legislative Affairs.—Thaddeus Inge, 205–6634.
  Diversity, Inclusion and Civil Rights.—Tinisha Agramonte, 205–6750.
Assistant Administrator, Office of:
  Hearings and Appeals.—Delorice Ford (202) 401–8200.
Chief Operating Officer.—Matthew Varilek (A), 205–6340.
Chief Information Officer.—Renee Macklin, 205–6708.
Deputy Chief Operating Officer and Chief Human Capital Officer.—Bridget Bean, 205–6749.

Associate Administrator, Office of:
  Capital Access.—Ann Marie Mehlum, 205–6663.
Director of:
  Entrepreneurship Education.—Ellen Thrasher, 205–6817.
  Financial Assistance.—Linda Rusche, 205 6396.
Associate Administrator, Office of:
  Investment and Innovation.—Javier Saade, 205–6513.
Assistant Administrator, Office of:
  Technology.—Edsel Brown, 205–7343.
Director of:
  Credit Risk Management.—Brent Ciurlino, 205–6538.
Associate Administrator, Office of:
  Small Business Development Centers. Carroll A. Thomas, 205–6439.
Director of:
  Surety Guarantees.—Frank Lalumiere, 205–6540.
Associate Administrator, Office of:
  International Trade.—Eileen Sanchez, 205–6720.
  Veterans Business Development.—Vacant, 205–6773.
Assistant Administrator, Office of:
  Women's Business Ownership.—Erin Andrew, 205–6774.
Associate Administrator, Office of:
  Government Contracting.—John Shoraka, 205–6459.
  8(a) Business Development.—Jackie Robinson-Burnette, 205–7026.
Director of Government Contracting.—Sean Crean, 205–6933.
Office of Size Standards.—Khem Sharma, 205–7189.

U.S. TRADE AND DEVELOPMENT AGENCY
1000 Wilson Boulevard, Suite 1600, Arlington, VA 22209, phone (703) 875–4357

Director.—Leocadia I. Zak.
  Deputy Director.—Enoh T. Ebong.
  General Counsel.—Vacant.
  Chief of Staff.—Clark Jennings.
  Director for Congressional and Public Affairs.—Thomas R. Hardy.
  Chief of Acquisitions Management.—Garth Hibbert.
  Director of Finance.—Michelle Bivins (acting).
  Grants Administrator.—Patricia Daughetee.
  Program Director for—
    East Asia.—Carl B. Kress.
    Latin America and the Caribbean.—Nathan Younge.
    Middle East, North Africa, Europe and Eurasia.—Carl B. Kress.
    South and Southeast Asia.—Henry Steingass.
    Sub-Saharan Africa.—Lida Fitts (acting).
    Global Programs.—Andrea Lupo.
    Program Evaluations.—Diana Harbison.

WASHINGTON METROPOLITAN AREA TRANSIT AUTHORITY
600 Fifth Street, NW., 20001, phone (202) 637–1234

General Manager and Chief Executive Officer. Jack Requa (interim).
  General Counsel.—Mark Pohl (acting).
  Deputy General Manager, Administration / Chief Financial Officer.—Dennis Anosike.
  Assistant General Managers for—
    Bus Service.—Robert Potts (acting).
    Customer Service, Communications and Marketing.—Lynn Bowersox.
  Deputy General Manager, Operations.—Robert Troup.
  Chief Safety Officer.—James Dougherty.
  Managing Director, Office of Government Relations.—Regina Sullivan.
  Managing Director, Public Relations.—Dan Stessel.
  Chief, Metro Transit Police Department.—Ronald Pavlik.

WASHINGTON NATIONAL MONUMENT SOCIETY
[Organized 1833; chartered 1859; amended by Acts of August 2, 1876, October, 1888]

President Ex Officio.—Barack H. Obama, President of the United States.

First Vice President.—Outerbridge Horsey, AIA, 1632 32nd Street, NW., Washington, DC 20007 (202) 714–4826.
Treasurer.—Henry Ravenel, Jr.
Secretary.—Karen Cucurullo, Acting Superintendent, National Mall and Memorial Parks, 900 Ohio Drive, SW., Washington, DC 20024–2000 (202) 485–9875.

Members:

Christopher Addison
Neil C. Folger
James M. Goode
Gilbert M. Grosvenor
Outerbridge Horsey, AIA
Henry Ravenel, Jr.

Hon. James W. Symington
John A. Washington
Robert Vogel, Regional Director of the National Capital Region, National Park Service.

Member Emeritus:
Harry F. Byrd, Jr.

WOODROW WILSON INTERNATIONAL CENTER FOR SCHOLARS
One Woodrow Wilson Plaza, 1300 Pennsylvania Avenue, NW., 20004–3027
phone (202) 691–4000, fax 691–4001
[Under the direction of the Board of Trustees of
Woodrow Wilson International Center for Scholars]

Director/President/CEO.—Hon. Jane Harman, 691–4202.
Executive Vice President.—Andrew Selee, 691–4088.
Vice President for—
External Relations.—Caroline Scullin, 691–4122.
Programs.—Blair Ruble, 691–4239.
Scholar and Academic Relations.—Robert Litwak, 691–4179.
Chief Financial Officer.—Michael Forster, 691–4366.

Board of Trustees:
Chairman.—Thomas R. Nides, Vice Chairman, Morgan Stanley.

Private Members:
Peter Beshar, Executive Vice President and General Counsel, Marsh and McLennan Companies, Inc.
John T. Casteen III, University Professor and President Emeritus, University of Virginia.
Thelma Duggin, President, AnBryce Foundation.
Lt. Gen. Susan Helms, USAF (Ret.).
Barry S. Jackson, Managing Director, The Lindsey Group and Strategic Advisor, Brownstein Hyatt Farber Schreck.
Nathalie Rayes, U.S. National Public Relations Director, Grupo Salinas and Executive Director, Fundacion Azteca América.
Earl W. Stafford, Chief Executive Officer, The Wentworth Group, LLC.
Jane Watson Stetson, Chair of the Partners for Community Wellness at Dartmouth-Hitchcock Medical Center.

Public Members:
William Adams, Chairman, National Endowment for the Humanities.
James H. Billington, The Librarian of Congress.
Sylvia Mathews Burwell, Secretary, U.S. Department of Health and Human Services.
Albert Horvath, Acting Secretary, Smithsonian Institution.
Arne Duncan, Secretary, U.S. Department of Education.
David Ferriero, Archivist of the United States.
John F. Kerry, Secretary, U.S. Department of State.
Designated Appointee of the President of the United States from within the Federal Government:
Fred Hochberg, Chairman and President, Export-Import Bank of the United States.

JUDICIAL BRANCH

SUPREME COURT OF THE UNITED STATES

One First Street, NE., 20543, phone (202) 479-3000

JOHN G. ROBERTS, JR., Chief Justice of the United States, was born in Buffalo, NY, January 27, 1955. He married Jane Marie Sullivan in 1996 and they have two children, Josephine and Jack. He received an A.B. from Harvard College in 1976 and a J.D. from Harvard Law School in 1979. He served as a law clerk for Judge Henry J. Friendly of the United States Court of Appeals for the Second Circuit from 1979–80 and as a law clerk for then Associate Justice William H. Rehnquist of the Supreme Court of the United States during the 1980 term. He was Special Assistant to the Attorney General, U.S. Department of Justice from 1981–82, Associate Counsel to President Ronald Reagan, White House Counsel's Office from 1982–86, and Principal Deputy Solicitor General, U.S. Department of Justice from 1989–93. From 1986–89 and 1993–2003, he practiced law in Washington, DC. He was appointed to the United States Court of Appeals for the District of Columbia Circuit in 2003. President George W. Bush nominated him as Chief Justice of the United States, and he took his seat September 29, 2005.

ANTONIN SCALIA, Associate Justice, was born in Trenton, NJ, March 11, 1936. He married Maureen McCarthy and has nine children, Ann Forrest, Eugene, John Francis, Catherine Elisabeth, Mary Clare, Paul David, Matthew, Christopher James, and Margaret Jane. He received his A.B. from Georgetown University and the University of Fribourg, Switzerland, and his LL.B. from Harvard Law School, and was a Sheldon Fellow of Harvard University from 1960–61. He was in private practice in Cleveland, OH from 1961–67, a Professor of Law at the University of Virginia from 1967–71, and a Professor of Law at the University of Chicago from 1977–82, and a Visiting Professor of Law at Georgetown University and Stanford University. He was chairman of the American Bar Association's Section of Administrative Law, 1981–82, and its Conference of Section Chairmen, 1982–83. He served the Federal Government as General Counsel of the Office of Telecommunications Policy from 1971–72, Chairman of the Administrative Conference of the United States from 1972–74, and Assistant Attorney General for the Office of Legal Counsel from 1974–77. He was appointed Judge of the United States Court of Appeals for the District of Columbia Circuit in 1982. President Reagan nominated him as an Associate Justice of the Supreme Court, and he took his seat September 26, 1986.

ANTHONY M. KENNEDY, Associate Justice, was born in Sacramento, CA, July 23, 1936. He married Mary Davis and has three children. He received his B.A. from Stanford University and the London School of Economics, and his LL.B. from Harvard Law School. He was in private practice in San Francisco, CA from 1961–63, as well as in Sacramento, CA from 1963–75. From 1965 to 1988, he was a Professor of Constitutional Law at the McGeorge School of Law, University of the Pacific. He has served in numerous positions during his career, including a member of the California Army National Guard in 1961, the board of the Federal Judicial Center from 1987–88, and two committees of the Judicial Conference of the United States: the Advisory Panel on Financial Disclosure Reports and Judicial Activities, subsequently renamed the Advisory Committee on Codes of Conduct, from 1979–87, and the Committee on Pacific Territories from 1979–90, which he chaired from 1982–90. He was appointed to the United States Court of Appeals for the Ninth Circuit in 1975. President Reagan nominated him as an Associate Justice of the Supreme Court, and he took his seat February 18, 1988.

CLARENCE THOMAS, Associate Justice, was born in the Pin Point community near Savannah, Georgia on June 23, 1948. He attended Conception Seminary from 1967–68 and received an A.B., *cum laude*, from Holy Cross College in 1971 and a J.D. from Yale Law School in 1974. He was admitted to law practice in Missouri in 1974, and served

851

as an Assistant Attorney General of Missouri, 1974–77; an attorney with the Monsanto Company, 1977–79; and Legislative Assistant to Senator John Danforth, 1979–81. From 1981–82 he served as Assistant Secretary for Civil Rights, U.S. Department of Education, and as Chairman of the U.S. Equal Employment Opportunity Commission, 1982–90. From 1990–91, he served as a Judge on the United States Court of Appeals for the District of Columbia Circuit. President Bush nominated him as an Associate Justice of the Supreme Court and he took his seat October 23, 1991. He married Virginia Lamp on May 30, 1987 and has one child, Jamal Adeen by a previous marriage.

RUTH BADER GINSBURG, Associate Justice, was born in Brooklyn, NY, March 15, 1933. She married Martin D. Ginsburg in 1954, and has a daughter, Jane, and a son, James. She received her B.A. from Cornell University, attended Harvard Law School, and received her LL.B. from Columbia Law School. She served as a law clerk to the Honorable Edmund L. Palmieri, Judge of the United States District Court for the Southern District of New York, from 1959–61. From 1961–63, she was a research associate and then associate director of the Columbia Law School Project on International Procedure. She was a Professor of Law at Rutgers University School of Law from 1963–72, and Columbia Law School from 1972–80, and a fellow at the Center for Advanced Study in the Behavioral Sciences in Stanford, CA from 1977–78. In 1971, she was instrumental in launching the Women's Rights Project of the American Civil Liberties Union, and served as the ACLU's General Counsel from 1973–80, and on the National Board of Directors from 1974–80. She was appointed a Judge of the United States Court of Appeals for the District of Columbia Circuit in 1980. President Clinton nominated her as an Associate Justice of the Supreme Court, and she took her seat August 10, 1993.

STEPHEN G. BREYER, Associate Justice, was born in San Francisco, CA, August 15, 1938. He married Joanna Hare in 1967, and has three children, Chloe, Nell, and Michael. He received an A.B. from Stanford University, a B.A. from Magdalen College, Oxford, and an LL.B. from Harvard Law School. He served as a law clerk to Justice Arthur Goldberg of the Supreme Court of the United States during the 1964 term, as a Special Assistant to the Assistant U.S. Attorney General for Antitrust, 1965–67, as an Assistant Special Prosecutor of the Watergate Special Prosecution Force, 1973, as Special Counsel of the U.S. Senate Judiciary Committee, 1974–75, and as Chief Counsel of the committee, 1979–80. He was an Assistant Professor, Professor of Law, and Lecturer at Harvard Law School, 1967–94, a Professor at the Harvard University Kennedy School of Government, 1977–80, and a Visiting Professor at the College of Law, Sydney, Australia and at the University of Rome. From 1980–90, he served as a Judge of the United States Court of Appeals for the First Circuit, and as its Chief Judge, 1990–94. He also served as a member of the Judicial Conference of the United States, 1990–94, and of the United States Sentencing Commission, 1985–89. President Clinton nominated him as an Associate Justice of the Supreme Court, and he took his seat August 3, 1994.

SAMUEL ANTHONY ALITO, JR., Associate Justice, was born in Trenton, NJ, April 1, 1950. He married Martha-Ann Bomgardner in 1985, and has two children, Philip and Laura. He served as a law clerk for Leonard I. Garth of the United States Court of Appeals for the Third Circuit from 1976–77. He was Assistant U.S. Attorney, District of New Jersey, 1977–81, Assistant to the Solicitor General, U.S. Department of Justice, 1981–85, Deputy Assistant Attorney General, U.S. Department of Justice, 1985–87, and U.S. Attorney, District of New Jersey, 1987–90. He was appointed to the United States Court of Appeals for the Third Circuit in 1990. President George W. Bush nominated him as an Associate Justice of the Supreme Court, and he took his seat January 31, 2006.

SONIA SOTOMAYOR, Associate Justice, was born in Bronx, NY, June 25, 1954. She earned a B.A. in 1976 from Princeton University, graduating *summa cum laude* and receiving the university's highest academic honor. In 1979, she earned a J.D. from Yale Law School where she served as an editor of the *Yale Law Journal*. She served as Assistant District Attorney in the New York County District Attorney's Office from 1979–84. She then litigated international commercial matters in New York City at Pavia & Harcourt, where she served as an associate and then partner from 1984–92. In 1991, President George H.W. Bush nominated her to the U.S. District Court Southern District of New York, and she served in that role from 1992–98. She served as a judge on the United States Court of Appeals for the Second Circuit from 1998–2009. President Barack Obama nominated her as an Associate Justice of the Supreme Court on May 26, 2009, and she assumed this role August 8, 2009.

ELENA KAGAN, Associate Justice, was born in New York, New York, on April 28, 1960. She received an A.B. from Princeton in 1981, an M.Phil. from Oxford in 1983, and a J.D. from Harvard Law School in 1986. She clerked for Judge Abner Mikva of the U.S. Court of Appeals for the D.C. Circuit from 1986–87 and for Justice Thurgood Marshall of the U.S. Supreme Court during the 1987 Term. After briefly practicing law at a Washington, DC law firm, she became a law professor, first at the University of Chicago Law School and later at Harvard Law School. She also served for four years in the Clinton Administration, as Associate Counsel to the President and then as Deputy Assistant to the President for Domestic Policy. Between 2003 and 2009, she served as the Dean of Harvard Law School. In 2009, President Obama nominated her as the Solicitor General of the United States. A year later, the President nominated her as an Associate Justice of the Supreme Court on May 10, 2010. She took her seat on August 7, 2010.

RETIRED ASSOCIATE JUSTICE

SANDRA DAY O'CONNOR (Retired), Associate Justice, was born in El Paso, TX, March 26, 1930. She married John Jay O'Connor III in 1952 and has three sons, Scott, Brian, and Jay. She received her B.A. and LL.B. from Stanford University. She served as Deputy County Attorney of San Mateo County, CA from 1952–53 and as a civilian attorney for Quartermaster Market Center, Frankfurt, Germany from 1954–57. From 1958–60, she practiced law in Maryvale, AZ, and served as Assistant Attorney General of Arizona from 1965–69. She was appointed to the Arizona State Senate in 1969 and was subsequently reelected to two two-year terms. In 1975 she was elected Judge of the Maricopa County Superior Court and served until 1979, when she was appointed to the Arizona Court of Appeals. President Reagan nominated her as an Associate Justice of the Supreme Court, and she took her seat September 25, 1981. Justice O'Connor retired from the Supreme Court on January 31, 2006.

DAVID H. SOUTER (Retired), Associate Justice, was born in Melrose, MA, September 17, 1939. He graduated from Harvard College, from which he received his A.B. After two years as a Rhodes Scholar at Magdalen College, Oxford, he received an A.B. in Jurisprudence from Oxford University and an M.A. in 1989. After receiving an LL.B. from Harvard Law School, he was an associate at Orr and Reno in Concord, NH from 1966 to 1968, when he became an Assistant Attorney General of New Hampshire. In 1971 he became Deputy Attorney General and in 1976, Attorney General of New Hampshire. In 1978 he was named an Associate Justice of the Superior Court of New Hampshire, and was appointed to the Supreme Court of New Hampshire as an Associate Justice in 1983. He became a Judge of the United States Court of Appeals for the First Circuit on May 25, 1990. President Bush nominated him as an Associate Justice of the Supreme Court, and he took his seat October 9, 1990. Justice Souter retired from the Supreme Court on June 29, 2009.

JOHN PAUL STEVENS (Retired), Associate Justice, was born in Chicago, IL, April 20, 1920. He married Maryan Mulholland, and has four children, John Joseph (deceased), Kathryn, Elizabeth Jane, and Susan Roberta. He received an A.B. from the University of Chicago, and a J.D. from Northwestern University School of Law. He served in the United States Navy from 1942–45, and was a law clerk to Justice Wiley Rutledge of the Supreme Court of the United States during the 1947 term. He was admitted to law practice in Illinois in 1949. He was Associate Counsel to the Subcommittee on the Study of Monopoly Power of the Judiciary Committee of the U.S. House of Representatives, 1951 52, and a member of the Attorney General's National Committee to Study Antitrust Law, 1953–55. He was Second Vice President of the Chicago Bar Association in 1970. From 1970–75, he served as a Judge of the United States Court of Appeals for the Seventh Circuit. President Ford nominated him as an Associate Justice of the Supreme Court, and he took his seat December 19, 1975. Justice Stevens retired from the Supreme Court on June 29, 2010.

Officers of the Supreme Court

Counselor to the Chief Justice.—Jeffrey P. Minear.
Clerk.—Scott S. Harris.
Librarian.—Linda Maslow.
Marshal.—Pamela Talkin.
Reporter of Decisions.—Christine L. Fallon.
Court Counsel.—Ethan V. Torrey.
Curator.—Catherine E. Fitts. .
Director of Information Technology.—Robert J. Hawkins.
Public Information Officer.—Kathleen L. Arberg.

UNITED STATES COURTS OF APPEALS

First Judicial Circuit (Districts of Maine, Massachusetts, New Hampshire, Puerto Rico, and Rhode Island).—*Chief Judge:* Jeffrey R. Howard. *Circuit Judges:* Juan R. Torruella; Sandra L. Lynch; O. Rogeriee Thompson; William J. Kayatta, Jr.; David J. Barron. *Senior Circuit Judges:* Bruce M. Selya; Michael Boudin; Norman H. Stahl; Kermit V. Lipez. *Circuit Executive:* Susan J. Goldberg (617) 748–9614. *Clerk:* Margaret Carter (617) 748–9057, John Joseph Moakley U.S. Courthouse, One Courthouse Way, Suite 2500, Boston, MA 02210.

Second Judicial Circuit (Districts of Connecticut, New York, and Vermont).—*Chief Judge:* Robert A. Katzmann. *Circuit Judges:* José A. Cabranes; Susan L. Carney; Denny Chin; Christopher F. Droney; Peter W. Hall; Dennis Jacobs; Robert A. Katzmann; Debra A. Livingston; Raymond J. Lohier; Gerard E. Lynch; Rosemary S. Pooler; Reena Raggi; Richard C. Wesley. *Senior Judges:* Giudo Calabresi; Amalya L. Kearse; Pierre N. Leval; Jon O. Newman; Barrington D. Parker, Jr.; Robert D. Sack; Chester J. Straub; John M. Walker, Jr.; Ralph K. Winter. *Circuit Executive:* Karen Greve Milton. *Clerk:* Catherine O'Hagan Wolfe (212) 857–8700, Thurgood Marshall United States Courthouse, 40 Foley Square, New York, NY 10007–1581.

Third Judicial Circuit (Districts of Delaware, New Jersey, Pennsylvania, and Virgin Islands).— *Chief Judge:* Theodore A. McKee. *Circuit Judges:* Thomas L. Ambro; Julio M. Fuentes; D. Brooks Smith; D. Michael Fisher; Michael A. Chagares; Kent A. Jordan; Thomas M. Hardiman; Joseph A. Greenaway, Jr.; Thomas I. Vanaskie; Patty Shwartz; Cheryl Ann Krause. *Senior Circuit Judges:* Leonard I. Garth; Dolores K. Sloviter; Walter K. Stapleton; Morton I. Greenberg; Anthony J. Scirica; Robert E. Cowen; Richard L. Nygaard; Jane R. Roth; Marjorie O. Rendell; Maryanne Trump Barry; Franklin S. VanAntwerpen. *Circuit Executive:* Margaret A. Wiegand (215) 597–0718. *Clerk:* Marcia M. Waldron (215) 597–2995, U.S. Courthouse, 601 Market Street, Philadelphia, PA 19106.

Fourth Judicial Circuit (Districts of Maryland, North Carolina, South Carolina, Virginia, and West Virginia).—*Chief Judge:* William B. Traxler, Jr. *Circuit Judges:* J. Harvie Wilkinson III; Paul V. Niemeyer; Diana Gribbon Motz; Robert B. King; Roger L. Gregory; Dennis W. Shedd; Allyson K. Duncan; G. Steven Agee; Barbara Milano Keenan; James A. Wynn, Jr.; Albert Diaz; Henry F. Floyd; Stephanie D. Thacker; Pamela A. Harris. *Senior Circuit Judges:* Clyde H. Hamilton; Andre M. Davis. *Circuit Executive:* Samuel W. Phillips (804) 916–2184. *Clerk:* Patricia S. Connor (804) 916–2700, Lewis F. Powell, Jr. U.S. Courthouse Annex, 1100 E. Main Street, Richmond, VA 23219.

Fifth Judicial Circuit (Districts of Louisiana, Mississippi, and Texas).—*Chief Judge:* Carl E. Stewart. *Circuit Judges:* E. Grady Jolly, W. Eugene Davis; Edith H. Jones; Jerry E. Smith; James L. Dennis; Edith Brown Clement; Edward C. Prado; Priscilla R. Owen; Jennifer Walker Elrod; Leslie H. Southwick; Catharina Haynes; James E. Graves, Jr.; Stephen A. Higginson; Gregg J. Costa. *Senior Circuit Judges:* Thomas M. Reavley; Carolyn Dineen King, Patrick E. Higginbotham; John M. Duhé, Jr.; Jacques L. Wiener, Jr.; Rhesa H. Barksdale; Fortunato P. Benavides. *Circuit Executive:* Paul Benjamin Anderson, Jr. (504) 310–7777. *Clerk:* Lyle W. Cayce (504) 310–7700, John Minor Wisdom U.S. Court of Appeals Building, 600 Camp Street, New Orleans, LA 70130–3425.

Sixth Judicial Circuit (Districts of Kentucky, Michigan, Ohio, and Tennessee).—*Chief Judge:* R. Guy Cole, Jr. *Circuit Judges:* Danny J. Boggs; Alice M. Batchelder; Karen Nelson Moore; Eric Lee Clay; Julia Smith Gibbons; John M. Rogers; Jeffrey S. Sutton; Deborah L. Cook; David W. McKeague; Richard Allen Griffin; Raymond M. Kethledge; Helene N. White; Jane B. Stranch; Bernice Bouie Donald. *Senior Circuit Judges:* Damon J. Keith; Gilbert S. Merritt; Ralph B. Guy; Alan E. Norris; Richard F. Suhrheinrich; Eugene E. Siler, Jr.; Martha Craig Daughtrey; Ronald Lee Gilman. *Circuit Executive:* Clarence Maddox (513) 564–7200. *Clerk:* Deborah Hunt (513) 564–7000, Potter Stewart U.S. Courthouse, 100 E. Fifth Street, Cincinnati, OH 45202.

Seventh Judicial Circuit (Districts of Illinois, Indiana, and Wisconsin).—*Chief Judge:* Diane P. Wood. *Circuit Judges:* Richard A. Posner; Joel M. Flaum; Frank H. Easterbrook; Michael

S. Kanne; Ilana Diamond Rovner; Ann Claire Williams; Diane S. Sykes; David F. Hamilton. *Senior Circuit Judges:* William J. Bauer; Richard D. Cudahy; Kenneth F. Ripple; Daniel A. Manion. *Circuit Executive:* Collins T. Fitzpatrick (312) 435–5803. *Clerk:* Gino J. Agnello (312) 435–5850, 2722 U.S. Courthouse, 219 S. Dearborn Street, Chicago, IL 60604.

Eighth Judicial Circuit (Districts of Arkansas, Iowa, Minnesota, Missouri, Nebraska, North Dakota, and South Dakota).—*Chief Judge:* William Jay Riley. *Circuit Judges:* Roger L. Wollman; James B. Loken; Diana E. Murphy; Lavenski R. Smith; Steven M. Colloton; Raymond W. Gruender; Duane Benton; Bobby E. Shepherd; Jane L. Kelly. *Senior Circuit Judges:* Myron H. Bright; Pasco M. Bowman II; C. Arlen Beam; Morris S. Arnold; Kermit E. Bye; Michael J. Melloy. *Circuit Executive:* Millie Adams (314) 244–2600. *Clerk:* Michael E. Gans (314) 244–2400, 111 S. Tenth Street, Suite 24.329, St. Louis, MO 63102.

Ninth Judicial Circuit (Districts of Alaska, Arizona, Central California, Eastern California, Northern California, Southern California, Guam, Hawaii, Idaho, Montana, Nevada, Northern Mariana Islands, Oregon, Eastern Washington, Western Washington).—*Chief Judge:* Sidney R. Thomas. *Circuit Judges:* Harry Pregerson; Stephen R. Reinhardt; Alex Kozinski; Diarmuid F. O'Scannlain; Barry G. Silverman; Susan P. Graber; M. Margaret McKeown; Kim McLane Wardlaw; William A. Fletcher; Ronald M. Gould; Richard A. Paez; Marsha L. Berzon; Richard C. Tallman; Johnnie B. Rawlinson; Richard R. Clifton; Jay S. Bybee; Consuelo M. Callahan; Carlos T. Bea; Milan D. Smith, Jr.; Sandra S. Ikuta; N. Randy Smith; Mary H. Murguia; Morgan Christen; Jacqueline H. Nguyen; Paul J. Watford; Andrew D. Hurwitz; John B. Owens; Michelle T. Friedland. *Senior Circuit Judges:* Alfred T. Goodwin; J. Clifford Wallace; Procter R. Hug, Jr.; Mary M. Schroeder; J. Jerome Farris; Dorothy W. Nelson; William C. Canby, Jr.; John T. Noonan, Jr.; Edward Leavy; Stephen S. Trott; Ferdinand F. Fernandez; Andrew J. Kleinfeld; Michael D. Hawkins; A. Wallace Tashima; Raymond C. Fisher. *Circuit and Court of Appeals Executive:* Cathy A. Catterson (415) 355–8800, *Clerk:* Molly C. Dwyer (415) 355–8000, P.O. Box 193939, San Francisco, CA 94119–3939.

Tenth Judicial Circuit (Districts of Colorado, Kansas, New Mexico, Oklahoma, Utah, and Wyoming).—*Chief Judge:* Timothy M. Tymkovich. *Circuit Judges:* Paul J. Kelly, Jr.; Mary Beck Briscoe; Carlos F. Lucero; Harris L Hartz; Neil M. Gorsuch; Jerome A. Holmes; Scott M. Matheson, Jr.; Robert E. Bacharach; Gregory A. Phillips, Carolyn B. McHugh, Nancy L. Moritz. *Senior Circuit Judges:* Monroe G. McKay; Stephanie K. Seymour; John C. Porfilio; Bobby R. Baldock; David M. Ebel; Michael R. Murphy; Terrence L. O'Brien. *Circuit Executive:* David Tighe (303) 844–2067. *Clerk:* Betsy Shumaker (303) 844–3157, Byron White United States Courthouse, 1823 Stout Street, Denver, CO 80257.

Eleventh Judicial Circuit (Districts of Alabama, Florida, and Georgia).—*Chief Judge:* Ed Carnes. *Circuit Judges:* Gerald Bard Tjoflat; Frank M. Hull; Stanley Marcus; Charles R. Wilson; William H. Pryor, Jr.; Beverly B. Martin; Adalberto Jordán; Robin S. Rosenbaum; Julie E. Carnes; Jill A. Pryor. *Senior Circuit Judges:* James C. Hill; Peter T. Fay; Phyllis A. Kravitch; R. Lanier Anderson III; J. L. Edmondson; Emmett R. Cox; Joel F. Dubina; Susan H. Black. *Circuit Executive:* James P. Gerstenlauer (404) 335–6535. *Clerk:* Douglas J. Mincher (404) 335–6100, 56 Forsyth Street, NW., Atlanta, GA 30303.

UNITED STATES COURT OF APPEALS
FOR THE DISTRICT OF COLUMBIA CIRCUIT

333 Constitution Avenue, NW., 20001, phone (202) 216-7300

MERRICK BRIAN GARLAND, chief circuit judge; born in Chicago, IL, 1952; A.B., Harvard University, 1974, *summa cum laude*, Phi Beta Kappa, Paul Revere Frothingham Award and Richard Perkins Parker Award; J.D., Harvard Law School, 1977, *magna cum laude*, articles editor, *Harvard Law Review*; law clerk to Judge Henry J. Friendly, U.S. Court of Appeals for the 2d Circuit, 1977–78; law clerk to Justice William J. Brennan, Jr., U.S. Supreme Court, 1978–79; Special Assistant to the Attorney General, 1979–81; associate then partner, Arnold and Porter, Washington, DC, 1981–89; Assistant U.S. Attorney, Washington, DC, 1989–92; partner, Arnold and Porter, 1992–93; Deputy Assistant Attorney General, Criminal Division, U.S. Department of Justice, 1993–94; Principal Associate Deputy Attorney General, 1994–97; Lecturer on Law, Harvard Law School, 1985–86. Edmund J. Randolph Award, U.S. Department of Justice, 1997. Admitted to the bars of the District of Columbia; U.S. District Court; Court of Appeals, District of Columbia Circuit; U.S. Courts of Appeals for the 4th, 9th, and 10th Circuits; and U.S. Supreme Court. Author: Antitrust and State Action, 96 Yale Law Journal 486 (1987); Antitrust and Federalism, 96 Yale Law Journal 1291 (1987); *Deregulation and Judicial Review*, 98 Harvard Law Review 505 (1985); co-chair, Administrative Law Section, District of Columbia Bar, 1991–94; President, Board of Overseers, Harvard University, 2009–10, member, 2003–09; American Law Institute; U.S. Judicial Conference Executive Committee, 2013-present, Committee on Judicial Security, 2008–13, Committee on the Judicial Branch, 2001–05; appointed to the U.S. Court of Appeals for the District of Columbia Circuit on April 9, 1997.

KAREN LeCRAFT HENDERSON, circuit judge. [Biographical information not supplied, per Judge Henderson's request.]

JUDITH W. ROGERS, circuit judge; born in New York, NY; A.B. (with honors), Radcliffe College, 1961; Phi Beta Kappa honors member; LL.B., Harvard Law School, 1964; LL.M., University of Virginia School of Law, 1988; law clerk, D.C. Juvenile Court, 1964–65; assistant U.S. Attorney for the District of Columbia, 1965–68; trial attorney, San Francisco Neighborhood Legal Assistance Foundation, 1968–69; Attorney, U.S. Department of Justice, Office of the Associate Deputy Attorney General and Criminal Division, 1969–71; General Counsel, Congressional Commission on the Organization of the D.C. Government, 1971–72; legislative assistant to D.C. Mayor Walter E. Washington, 1972–79; Corporation Counsel for the District of Columbia, 1979–83; trustee, Radcliffe College, 1982–90, member of Visiting Committee to Harvard Law School, 1984–90 and 2006–11; appointed by President Reagan to the District of Columbia Court of Appeals as an Associate Judge on September 15, 1983; served as Chief Judge, November 1, 1988 to March 17, 1994; appointed by President Clinton to the U.S. Court of Appeals for the District of Columbia Circuit on March 18, 1994, and entered on duty March 21, 1994; member of Executive Committee, Conference of Chief Justices, 1993–94; member, U.S. Judicial Conference Committee on the Codes of Conduct, 1998–2004.

DAVID S. TATEL, circuit judge; born in Washington, DC, March 16, 1942; son of Molly and Dr. Howard Tatel (both deceased); married to the former Edith Bassichis, 1965; children: Rebecca, Stephanie, Joshua, and Emily; grandchildren: Olivia, Maya, Olin, Reuben, Rae, Cameron, Ozzie, and Daria; B.A., University of Michigan, 1963; J.D., University of Chicago Law School, 1966; instructor, University of Michigan Law School, 1966–67; associate, Sidley and Austin, 1967–69, 1970–72; director, Chicago Lawyers' Committee for Civil Rights Under Law, 1969–70; director, National Lawyers' Committee for Civil Rights Under Law, 1972–74; director, Office for Civil Rights, U.S. Department of Health, Education and Welfare, 1977–79; associate and partner, Hogan and Hartson, 1974–77, 1979–94; lecturer, Stanford University Law School, 1991–92; board of directors, Spencer Foundation, 1987–97 (chair, 1990–97); board of directors, National Board for Professional Teaching Standards, 1997–

857

2000; National Lawyers' Committee for Civil Rights Under Law, co-chair, 1989–91; board of directors, Carnegie Foundation for the Advancement of Teaching, (chair, 2005–09); member of the American Academy of Arts and Sciences, member of the American Philosophical Society, the National Academy of Education, and the National Academy of Sciences Committee on Science, Technology and Law; admitted to practice law in Illinois in 1966 and the District Columbia in 1970; appointed to the U.S. Court of Appeals for the District of Columbia Circuit by President Clinton on October 7, 1994, and entered on duty October 11, 1994.

JANICE ROGERS BROWN, circuit judge; born in Greenville, AL; B.A., California State University, 1974; J.D., University of California School of Law, 1977; LL.M., University of Virginia School of Law, 2004; Deputy Legislative Counsel, Legislative Counsel Bureau, 1977–79; Deputy Attorney General, California Department of Justice, 1979–87; Deputy Secretary and General Counsel, California Business, Transportation, and Housing Agency, 1987–90; Senior Associate, Nielsen, Merksamer, Parinello, Mueller and Naylor, 1990–91; Legal Affairs Secretary for Governor Pete Wilson, 1991–94; Associate Justice, California Court of Appeals for the Third District, 1994–96; Associate Justice, California Supreme Court, 1996–2005; appointed to the U.S. Court of Appeals for the District of Columbia Circuit by President George W. Bush on June 10, 2005 and sworn in on July 1, 2005.

THOMAS B. GRIFFITH, circuit judge; born in Yokohama, Japan, July 5, 1954; B.A., Brigham Young University, 1978; J.D., University of Virginia School of Law, 1985; editor, *Virginia Law Review*; associate, Robinson, Bradshaw and Hinson, Charlotte, NC, 1985–89; associate and then a partner, Wiley, Rein and Fielding, Washington, DC, 1989–95 and 1999–2000; Senate Legal Counsel of the United States, 1995–99; Assistant to the President and General Counsel, Brigham Young University, Provo, UT, 2000–05; member, Executive Committee of the American Bar Association's Central European and Eurasian Law Initiative; appointed to the United States Court of Appeals for the District of Columbia Circuit on June 14, 2005 and sworn in on June 29, 2005.

BRETT M. KAVANAUGH, circuit judge; born in Washington, DC, February 12, 1965; son of Edward and Martha Kavanaugh; married to Ashley Estes; two daughters; B.A., *cum laude*, Yale College, 1987; J.D., Yale Law School, 1990; law clerk to Judge Walter Stapleton of the U.S. Court of Appeals for the Third Circuit, 1990–91; law clerk for Judge Alex Kozinski of the U.S. Court of Appeals for the Ninth Circuit, 1991–92; attorney, Office of the Solicitor General of the United States, 1992–93; law clerk to Associate Justice Anthony Kennedy of the U.S. Supreme Court, 1993–94; Associate Counsel, Office of Independent Counsel, 1994–97; partner, Kirkland & Ellis LLP, 1997–98, 1999–2001; Associate Counsel and then Senior Associate Counsel to President George W. Bush, 2001–03; Assistant to the President and Staff Secretary to President Bush, 2003–06; Adjunct Professor of Law, Georgetown University Law Center, 2007; Lecturer on Law, Harvard Law School, 2008–14; appointed to the U.S. Court of Appeals for the District of Columbia Circuit on May 30, 2006.

SRI SRINIVASAN, circuit judge; born in Chandigarh, India, February 23, 1967; son of Saroja and T.P. Srinivasan; two children; B.A. Stanford University, 1989; J.D. Stanford Law School, 1995; M.B.A. Stanford Graduate School of Business, 1995; law clerk to Judge J. Harvie Wilkinson III of the U.S. Court of Appeals for the Fourth Circuit, 1995–96; Bristow Fellow, Office of the Solicitor General of the United States, 1996–97; law clerk to Associate Justice Sandra Day O'Connor of the U.S. Supreme Court, 1997–98; associate, O'Melveny & Myers LLP, 1998–2002; Assistant to the Solicitor General, 2002–07; partner, O'Melveny & Myers LLP, 2007–11; Lecturer on Law, Harvard Law School, 2009–10; Principal Deputy Solicitor General, 2011–13; appointed to the U.S. Court of Appeals for the District of Columbia Circuit on May 24, 2013.

PATRICIA A. MILLETT, circuit judge; born in Dexter, MA, 1963; B.A., *summa cum laude*, University of Illinois at Urbana-Champaign, 1985; Harvard Law School, 1988, *magna cum laude*; litigation associate, Miller and Chevalier, 1988–90; law clerk, Judge Thomas Tang, U.S. Court of Appeals for the 9th Circuit, 1990–92; appellate staff, U.S. Department of Justice Civil Division, 1992–96; Assistant U.S. Solicitor General, 1996–2007; partner, Akin Gump Strauss Hauer and Feld, 2007–13; appointed by President Obama to the United States Court of Appeals for the District of Columbia Circuit on December 10, 2013.

CORNELIA T.L. PILLARD, circuit judge; born in Cambridge, MA, 1961; B.A. Yale College, *magna cum laude*, with distinction in History; J.D., Harvard Law School, *magna cum laude*, Editor, *Harvard Women's Law Journal*, 1984–85; Book Review and Commentary Editor, *Harvard Law Review*; law clerk to Judge Louis H. Pollak, U.S. District Court for the Eastern District of Pennsylvania, 1987–88; Marvin M. Karpatkin Fellowship, American

Civil Liberties Union, 1988–89; member of the Bars of New York (1989), Massachusetts (1989), D.C. (1990); Assistant Counsel, NAACP Legal Defense and Education Fund, Inc., 1989–94; Assistant to the Solicitor General of the United States, 1994–97; Assistant Professor, then Professor, Georgetown University Law Center, 1997–2013; Deputy Assistant Attorney General, Office of Legal Counsel, 1998–2000; Chair, American Bar Association Scholars' Reading Group, Standing Committee on the Federal Judiciary, 2005–06; Visiting Scholar, Institute for Advanced Legal Studies (London, U.K.), 2006; Academic Co-Director and Professor, Center for Transnational Legal Studies (London, U.K.), 2008–09; Advisory Board (2003–11) and Faculty Co-Director (2011–13) Georgetown Law Supreme Court Institute; member, Board of Directors, American Arbitration Association, 2005–13; Fellow, Woodrow Wilson International Center for Scholars, 2012–13; member, American Law Institute; appointed to the United States Court of Appeals for the District of Columbia Circuit on December 2013.

ROBERT L. WILKINS, circuit judge; born in Muncie, IN, 1963, B.S., Rose-Hulman Institute of Technology, 1986, *cum laude*, Herman A. Moench Distinguished Senior Commendation; J.D., Harvard Law School, 1989, executive editor and comments editor of the *Civil Rights-Civil Liberties Law Review*; law clerk to Judge Earl B. Gilliam of the U.S. District Court for the Southern District of California, 1989–90; staff attorney, Public Defender Service for the District of Columbia, 1990–95; chief, Special Litigation and Programs Division of Public Defender Service for the District of Columbia, 1995–2000; president, National African American Museum and Cultural Complex, Inc., 2000–02; partner, Venable LLP, 2002–11; selected one of the "90 Greatest Washington Lawyers of the Last 30 Years" by the *Legal Times* in 2008; selected one of the "40 under 40 most successful young litigators in America" by the *National Law Journal* in 2002; named one of "Washington's Top Lawyers: Criminal Defense," 2004, *Washingtonian* magazine; named one of "Washington's Top Lawyers: Education," 2007, *Washingtonian* magazine; Honor Alumni Award, 2005, Rose-Hulman Institute of Technology; Henry W. Edgerton Civil Liberties Award, 2001, American Civil Liberties Union Fund of the National Capital Area; Pro Bono Attorney of the Year, 2001, American Civil Liberties Union of Maryland; "Practitioner of the Year" Award, 1999, University of Maryland Black Law Students Association; Nominee, "Roger Baldwin Medal of Liberty" Award, 1999, American Civil Liberties Union of Maryland; District of Columbia Access to Justice Commission (2005–08); Board of Trustees, Public Defender Service for the District of Columbia (2002–08); National Museum of African American History and Culture Plan for Action Presidential Commission (chairman of the Site and Building Committee) (2002–03); member, District of Columbia Advisory Commission on Sentencing (1998–2000); member, District of Columbia Truth-In-Sentencing Commission (1997–98); District of Columbia Juvenile Justice Advisory Group (1998–2000); *Federal Influence on Sentencing Policy in the District of Columbia: An Oppressive and Dangerous Experiment*, 11 Fed. Sent. Rptr. 143 148 (Nov./Dec. 1998); *The South African Legal System: Black Lawyer's Views*, 7 TransAfrica Forum 9 (Fall 1990); *Black Neighborhoods Becoming Black Cities: Group Empowerment, Local Control and the Implications of Being Darker than Brown*, 23 Harv. C.R.-C.L. L. Rev. 415 (1988) (co-author); admitted to the bars of the District of Columbia; Massachusetts; U.S. Supreme Court, U.S. Court of Appeals for the D.C. Circuit, U.S. Court of Appeals for the Federal Circuit, U.S. District Court for the District of Columbia, U.S. District Court for the District of Maryland, and U.S. District Court for the Eastern District of Wisconsin; member, Judicial Conference of the United States, Committee on Judicial Security, 2013-present; appointed to the U.S. District Court for the District of Columbia on December 27, 2010; appointed to the U.S. Court of Appeals for the District of Columbia Circuit on January 13, 2014.

SENIOR CIRCUIT JUDGES

HARRY T. EDWARDS, senior circuit judge; born in New York, NY, November 3, 1940; son of George H. Edwards and Arline (Ross) Lyle; married to Pamela Carrington-Edwards; children: Brent and Michelle; B.S., Cornell University, 1962; J.D. (with distinction), University of Michigan Law School, 1965; associate with Seyfarth, Shaw, Fairweather and Geraldson, 1965–70; professor of law, University of Michigan, 1970–75 and 1977–80; professor of law, Harvard University, 1975–77; visiting professor of law, Free University of Brussels, 1974; arbitrator of labor/management disputes, 1970–80; vice president, National Academy of Arbitrators, 1978–80; member (1977–79) and chairman (1979–80), National Railroad Passenger Corporation (Amtrak); Executive Committee of the Association of American Law Schools, 1979–80; public member of the Administrative Conference of the United States, 1976–80; International Women's Year Commission, 1976–77; American Bar Association Commission of Law and the Economy; co-author of five books: *Labor Relations Law in the Public Sector, The Lawyer as a Negotiator, Higher Education and the Law*, and *Collective Bargaining and Labor Arbitration*; and, most recently, Edwards, Ellliot, and Levy, *Federal Standards of Review* (2d ed. 2013), recipient of the Judge William B. Groat Alumni Award, 1978, given by Cornell University; the Society of American Law Teachers Award (for "distinguished contributions to teaching and public service"); the Whitney North Seymour Medal presented by the American Arbitration Association for outstanding contributions to the use of arbitration; Recipient of the 2004 Robert J. Kutak Award, presented by the American Bar Association Selection of Legal Education and Admission to the Bar "to a person who meets the highest standards of professional responsibility and demonstrates substantial achievement toward increased understanding between legal education and the active practice of law", and several Honorary Doctor of Laws degrees; Professor of Law at NYU School of Law (member of faculty since 1990); has also taught part-time at Duke, Georgetown, Michigan, Harvard Law, Pennsylvania, and University of California Irvine Schools of Law; co-chair of the Forensics Science Committee established by the National Academy of Sciences, 2006–09; member of the Committee on Science, Technology, and Law at the National Academy of Sciences; appointed to the U.S. Court of Appeals, February 20, 1980; served as chief judge September 15, 1994 to July 16, 2001.

LAURENCE HIRSCH SILBERMAN, senior circuit judge; recipient of the Presidential Medal of Freedom, June 19, 2008; born in York, PA, October 12, 1935; son of William Silberman and Anna (Hirsch); married to Rosalie G. Gaull on April 28, 1957 (deceased), married Patricia Winn on January 5, 2008; children: Robert Stephen Silberman, Katherine DeBoer Balaban, and Anne Gaull Otis; B.A., Dartmouth College, 1957; LL.B., Harvard Law School, 1961; admitted to Hawaii Bar, 1962; District of Columbia Bar, 1973; associate, Moore, Torkildson and Rice, 1961–64; partner (Moore, Silberman and Schulze), Honolulu, 1964–67; attorney, National Labor Relations Board, Office of General Counsel, Appellate Division, 1967–69; Solicitor, Department of Labor, 1969–70; Under Secretary of Labor, 1970–73; partner, Steptoe and Johnson, 1973–74; Deputy Attorney General of the United States, 1974–75; Ambassador to Yugoslavia, 1975–77; President's Special Envoy on ILO Affairs, 1976; senior fellow, American Enterprise Institute, 1977–78; visiting fellow, 1978–85; managing partner, Morrison and Foerster, 1978–79 and 1983–85; executive vice president, Crocker National Bank, 1979–83; lecturer, University of Hawaii, 1962–63; board of directors, Commission on Present Danger, 1978–85, Institute for Educational Affairs, New York, NY, 1981–85, member: General Advisory Committee on Arms Control and Disarmament, 1981–85; Defense Policy Board, 1981–85; vice chairman, State Department's Commission on Security and Economic Assistance, 1983–84; American Bar Association (Labor Law Committee, 1965–72, Corporations and Banking Committee, 1973, Law and National Security Advisory Committee, 1981–85); Hawaii Bar Association Ethics Committee, 1965–67; Council on Foreign Relations, 1977–present; Judicial Conference Committee on Court Administration and Case Management, 1994; member, U.S. Foreign Intelligence Surveillance Act Court of Review, 1996–2003; Adjunct Professor of Law (Administrative Law and Labor Law) Georgetown Law Center, 1987–94; 1997; Adjunct Professor of Law, New York University Law School, 1995–96; Distinguished Visitor from the Judiciary, Georgetown Law Center, 2003–present; co-chairman of the President's Commission on The Intelligence Capabilities of the United States Regarding Weapons of Mass Destruction, 2004–05; appointed to the U.S. Court of Appeals for the District of Columbia Circuit by President Reagan on October 28, 1985.

STEPHEN F. WILLIAMS, senior circuit judge; born in New York, NY, September 23, 1936; son of Charles Dickerman Williams and Virginia (Fain); married to Faith Morrow, 1966; children: Susan, Geoffrey, Sarah, Timothy, and Nicholas; B.A., Yale, 1958, J.D., Harvard Law School, 1961; U.S. Army Reserves, 1961–62; associate, Debevoise, Plimpton, Lyons and Gates, 1962–66; Assistant U.S. Attorney, Southern District of New York, 1966–69; associate professor and professor of law, University of Colorado School of Law, 1969–86; visiting professor of law, UCLA, 1975–76; visiting professor of law and fellow in law and economics, University Chicago Law School, 1979–80; visiting George W. Hutchison Professor of Energy Law, SMU, 1983–84; consultant to: Administrative Conference of the United States, 1974–76; Federal Trade Commission on energy-related issues, 1983–85; member, American Law Institute; appointed to the U.S. Court of Appeals for the District of Columbia Circuit by President Reagan, June 16, 1986.

DOUGLAS HOWARD GINSBURG, circuit judge; born in Chicago, IL, May 25, 1946; diploma, Latin School of Chicago, 1963; B.S., Cornell University, 1970 (Phi Kappa Phi, Ives Award); J.D., University of Chicago, 1973 (Mecham Prize Scholarship 1970–73, Casper Platt Award, 1973, Order of Coif, Articles and Book Rev. Ed., 40 U. Chi. L. Rev.); bar admissions: Illinois (1973), Massachusetts (1982), U.S. Supreme Court (1984), U.S. Court of Appeals for the Ninth Circuit (1986); member: Mont Pelerin Society, American Economic Association, American Law and Economics Association, Honor Society of Phi Kappa Phi, American Bar Association, Antitrust Section, Council, 1985–86 (ex officio), judicial liaison

(2000–03 and 2009–12); advisory boards: Competition Policy International; Harvard Journal of Law and Public Policy; *Journal of Competition Law and Economics*; Law and Economics Center, George Mason University School of Law; *Supreme Court Economic Review; University of Chicago Law Review*; Board of Directors: Foundation for Research in Economics and the Environment, 1991–2004; Rappahannock County Conservation Alliance, 1998–2004; Rappahannock Association for Arts and Community, 1997–99; Committees: Judicial Conference of the United States, 2002–08, Budget Committee, 1997–2001, Committee on Judicial Resources, 1987–96; Boston University Law School, Visiting Committee, 1994–97; University of Chicago Law School, Visiting Committee, 1985–88; law clerk to: Judge Carl McGowan, U.S. Court of Appeals for the District of Columbia Circuit, 1973–74; Associate Justice Thurgood Marshall, U.S. Supreme Court, 1974–75; previous positions: assistant professor, Harvard University Law School, 1975–81; Professor 1981–83; Deputy Assistant Attorney General, Antitrust Division, U.S. Department of Justice, 1983–84; Administrator for Information and Regulatory Affairs, Executive Office of the President, Office of Management and Budget, 1984–85; Assistant Attorney General, Antitrust Division, U.S. Department of Justice, 1985–86; lecturer in law, Columbia University, New York City, 1987–88, 2009–11; lecturer in law, Harvard University, Cambridge, MA, 1988–89; distinguished professor of law, George Mason University, Arlington, VA, 1988–present; senior lecturer, University of Chicago Law School, 1990–present; lecturer on law, New York Law School, 2005–09; Visiting Professor, Faculty of Laws, University College, London, 2010–15; appointed to U.S. Court of Appeals for the District of Columbia Circuit by President Reagan on October 14, 1986, taking the oath of office on November 10, 1986, Chief Judge, 2001–08.

DAVID BRYAN SENTELLE, circuit judge, born in Canton, NC, February 12, 1943; son of Horace and Maude Sentelle; married to Jane LaRue Oldham; three daughters and four granddaughters; B.A., University of North Carolina at Chapel Hill, 1965; J.D. with honors, University of North Carolina School of Law, 1968; associate, Uzzell and Dumont, Charlotte, 1968–79; Assistant U.S. Attorney, Charlotte, 1970–74; North Carolina State District Judge, 1974–77; partner, Tucker, Hicks, Sentelle, Moon and Hodge, Charlotte, 1977–85; U.S. District Judge for the Western District of North Carolina, 1985–87; appointed to the U.S. Court of Appeals by President Reagan in October 1987; Chief Judge, 2008–13; assumed senior status February 12, 2013.

A. RAYMOND RANDOLPH, senior circuit judge; born in Riverside, NJ, November 1, 1943; son of Arthur Raymond Randolph, Sr. and Marile (Kelly); two children: John Trevor and Cynthia Lee Randolph; married to Eileen Janette O'Connor, May 18, 1984. B.S., Drexel University, 1966; J.D., University of Pennsylvania Law School, 1969, *summa cum laude;* managing editor, *University of Pennsylvania Law Review*; Order of the Coif. Admitted to Supreme Court of the United States; Supreme Court of California; District of Columbia Court of Appeals; U.S. Courts of Appeals for the First, Second, Fourth, Fifth, Sixth, Seventh, Ninth, Eleventh, and District of Columbia Circuits. Memberships: American Law Institute. Law clerk to Judge Henry J. Friendly, U.S. Court of Appeals for the Second Circuit, 1969–70; Assistant to the Solicitor General, 1970–73; adjunct professor of law, Georgetown University Law Center, 1974–78; George Mason School of Law, 1992; Deputy Solicitor General, 1975–77; Special Counsel, Committee on Standards of Official Conduct, House of Representatives, 1979–80; special assistant attorney general, State of Montana (honorary), 1983–July 1990; special assistant attorney general, State of New Mexico, 1985–July 1990; special assistant attorney general, State of Utah, 1986–July 1990; advisory panel, Federal Courts Study Committee, 1989–July 1990; partner, Pepper, Hamilton and Scheetz, 1987–July 1990; chairman, Committee on Codes of Conduct, U.S. Judicial Conference, 1995–98; distinguished professor of law, George Mason Law School, 1999–present; recipient, Distinguished Alumnus Award, University of Pennsylvania Law School, 2002; appointed to the U.S. Court of Appeals for the District of Columbia Circuit by President George H.W. Bush on July 16, 1990, and took oath of office on July 20, 1990.

OFFICERS OF THE UNITED STATES COURT OF APPEALS

FOR THE DISTRICT OF COLUMBIA CIRCUIT

Circuit Executive.—Betsy Paret (202) 216–7340.
Clerk.—Mark J. Langer, 216–7300.
Chief Deputy Clerk.—Marilyn R. Sargent, 216–7300.
Chief, Legal Division.—Martha Tomich, 216–7500.

UNITED STATES COURT OF APPEALS FOR THE FEDERAL CIRCUIT

717 Madison Place, NW., 20439, phone (202) 275–8000

SHARON PROST, chief judge; was appointed by President George W. Bush in 2001. Prior to her appointment, Judge Prost served as Minority Chief Counsel, Deputy Chief Counsel, and Chief Counsel of the Committee on the Judiciary, United States Senate from 1993 to 2001. She also served as Chief Labor Counsel (Minority), Senate Committee on Labor and Human Resources from 1989 to 1993. She was Assistant Solicitor, Associate Solicitor, and Acting Solicitor of the National Labor Relations Board from 1984 to 1989. She was an Attorney at the Internal Revenue Service from 1983 to 1984, and Field Attorney at the Federal Labor Relations Authority from 1980 to 1983. Judge Prost also served as Labor Relations Specialist/Auditor at the United States General Accounting Office from 1976 to 1980 and Labor Relations Specialist at the United States Civil Service Commission from 1973 to 1976. Judge Prost received a B.S. from Cornell University in 1973, an M.B.A. from George Washington University in 1975, a J.D. from the Washington College of Law, American University in 1979, and an LL.M. from George Washington University School of Law in 1984.

PAULINE NEWMAN, circuit judge; was appointed by President Ronald Reagan in 1984. From 1982 to 1984, Judge Newman was Special Adviser to the United States Delegation to the Diplomatic Conference on the Revision of the Paris Convention for the Protection of Industrial Property. She served on the advisory committee to the Domestic Policy Review of Industrial Innovation from 1978 to 1979 and on the State Department Advisory Committee on International Intellectual Property from 1974 to 1984. From 1969 to 1984, Judge Newman served as director, Patent, Trademark and Licensing Department, FMC Corp. From 1961 to 1962 she worked for the United Nations Educational, Scientific and Cultural Organization as a science policy specialist in the Department of Natural Sciences. She served as patent attorney and house counsel of FMC Corp. from 1954 to 1969 and as research scientist, American Cyanamid Co. from 1951 to 1954. Judge Newman received a B.A. from Vassar College in 1947, an M.A. from Columbia University in 1948, a Ph.D. from Yale University in 1952 and an LL.B. from New York University School of Law in 1958.

ALAN D. LOURIE, circuit judge; was appointed to the United States Court of Appeals for the Federal Circuit on April 6, 1990, by President George H.W. Bush. He was formerly Vice President, Corporate Patents and Trademarks, and Associate General Counsel of SmithKline Beecham Corporation. Born in Boston, Massachusetts, on January 13, 1935, Judge Lourie received his Bachelor's degree from Harvard University (1956), his Master's degree in organic chemistry from the University of Wisconsin (1958), and his Ph.D. in chemistry from the University of Pennsylvania (1965). He received his J.D. degree from Temple University in 1970. Before being appointed to the court, Judge Lourie had been President of the Philadelphia Patent Law Association, a member of the Board of Directors of the American Intellectual Property Law Association (formerly American Patent Law Association), treasurer of the Association of Corporate Patent Counsel, and a member of the board of directors of the Intellectual Property Owners Association. He was also Vice Chairman of the Industry Functional Advisory Committee on Intellectual Property Rights for Trade Policy Matters (IFAC 3) for the Department of Commerce and the Office of the U.S. Trade Representative. He was a member of the U.S. delegation to the Diplomatic Conference on the Revision of the Paris Convention for the Protection of Industrial Property, held in Geneva in October and November 1982, and in March 1984. He was chairman of the Patent Committee of the Law Section of the Pharmaceutical Manufacturers Association from 1980 to 1985. Judge Lourie was awarded the Jefferson Medal of the New Jersey Intellectual Property Law Association for extraordinary contributions to the field of intellectual property law in 1998; was a recipient of the Intellectual Property Owners Education Foundation Distinguished Intellectual Property Professional Award for extraordinary leadership in the intellectual property community and a lifetime commitment to invention and innovation in 2008; was a recipient of the Philadelphia Intellectual Property Law Association's Award for outstanding IP achievement in 2010; was a recipient of the Boston Patent Law Association's Distinguished Public Service Award in 2011; was a recipient of a "lifetime achievement" award from The Sedona Conference in 2011; and recently was a recipient of NYIPLA's 10th Annual Outstanding Public Service Award in 2012. He was a member of the Judicial Conference Committee on Financial Disclosure from 1990 to 1998 and has been a member of the Committee on Codes of Conduct since 2005. He is a member of the American Intellectual Property Law Association, the American Chemical Society, the Cosmos Club, and the Harvard Club of Washington. Judge Lourie is married and has two daughters and four grandchildren.

TIMOTHY B. DYK, circuit judge; was appointed by President William J. Clinton in 2000. Prior to his appointment, Judge Dyk was Partner and Chair, Issues and Appeals Practice Area, at Jones, Day, Reavis and Pogue from 1990 to 2000. He was Adjunct Professor at Yale Law School from 1986 to 1987 and 1989, at the University of Virginia Law School in 1984 and 1985, and from 1987 to 1988, and at the Georgetown University Law Center in 1983, 1986, 1989 and 1991. Judge Dyk was Associate and Partner, Wilmer Cutler and Pickering from 1964 to 1990. From 1963 to 1964, Judge Dyk served as Special Assistant to Assistant Attorney General Louis F. Oberdorfer. He also served as Law Clerk to Chief Justice Warren from 1962 to 1963, and to Justices Reed and Burton (retired) from 1961 to 1962. Judge Dyk received an A.B. from Harvard College in 1958 and an LL.B. from Harvard Law School in 1961. He was First President of the Edward Coke Appellate Inn of Court from 2000 to 2001 and President of the Giles Sutherland Rich Inn of Court from 2006 to 2007. He was the recipient of the 2012 American Inns of Court Professionalism Award for the Federal Circuit. Judge Dyk is the co-author of the Chapter on Patents in the Third Edition of the treatise, Business and Commercial Litigation in Federal Courts.

KIMBERLY A. MOORE, circuit judge; was appointed by President George W. Bush in 2006. Prior to her appointment, Judge Moore was a Professor of Law from 2004–06 and Associate Professor of Law from 2000 to 2004 at the George Mason University School of Law. She was an Assistant Professor of Law at the University of Maryland School of Law from 1999 to 2000. She served both as an Assistant Professor of Law from 1997 to 1999 and the Associate Director of the Intellectual Property Law Program from 1998 to 1999 at the Chicago-Kent College of Law. Judge Moore clerked from 1995 to 1997 for the Honorable Glenn L. Archer, Jr., Chief Judge of the United States Court of Appeals for the Federal Circuit, and was an Associate at Kirkland and Ellis from 1994 to 1995. From 1988 to 1992, Judge Moore was employed in electrical engineering with the Naval Surface Warfare Center. Judge Moore received her B.S.E.E. in 1990, M.S. in 1991, both from the Massachusetts Institute of Technology, and her J.D., cum laude from the Georgetown University Law Center in 1994. Judge Moore has written and presented widely on patent litigation. She co-authored a legal casebook entitled Patent Litigation and Strategy and served as the Editor of The Federal Circuit Bar Journal from 1998 to 2006.

KATHLEEN M. O'MALLEY, circuit judge; was appointed to the United States Court of Appeals for the Federal Circuit by President Barack Obama in 2010. Prior to her elevation to the Federal Circuit, Judge O'Malley was appointed to the United States District Court for the Northern District of Ohio by President William J. Clinton on October 12, 1994. Judge O'Malley served as First Assistant Attorney General and Chief of Staff for Ohio Attorney General Lee Fisher from 1992–94, and Chief Counsel to Attorney General Fisher from 1991–92. From 1985–91, she worked for Porter, Wright, Morris and Arthur, where she became a partner. From 1983–84, she was an associate at Jones, Day, Reavis and Pogue. During her sixteen years on the district court bench, Judge O'Malley presided over in excess of 100 patent and trademark cases and sat by designation on the United States Circuit Court for the Federal Circuit. As an educator, Judge O'Malley has regularly taught a course on Patent Litigation at Case Western Reserve University Law School; she is a member of the faculty of the Berkeley Center for Law and Technology's program designed to educate Federal Judges regarding the handling of intellectual property cases. Judge O'Malley serves as a board member of the Sedona Conference; as the judicial liaison to the Local Patent Rules Committee for the Northern District of Ohio; and as an advisor to national organizations publishing treatises on patent litigation (Anatomy of a Patent Case, Complex Litigation Committee of the American College of Trial Lawyers; Patent Case Management Judicial Guide, Berkeley Center for Law and Technology). Judge O'Malley began her legal career as a law clerk to the Honorable Nathaniel R. Jones, Sixth Circuit Court of Appeals in 1982–83. She received her J.D. degree from Case Western Reserve University School of Law, Order of the Coif, in 1982, where she served on Law Review and was a member of the National Mock Trial Team. Judge O'Malley attended Kenyon College in Gambier, Ohio where she graduated *magna cum laude* and Phi Beta Kappa in 1979.

JIMMIE V. REYNA, circuit judge; was appointed to the United States Court of Appeals for the Federal Circuit by President Barack Obama in 2011. Prior to his appointment, Judge Reyna was an international trade attorney and shareholder at Williams Mullen, where, from 1998 to 2011, he directed the firm's Trade and Customs Practice Group and its Latin America Task Force, and served on its board of directors (2006–08, 2009–11). He was an associate and partner at the law firm of Stewart and Stewart (1986–98). From 1981 to 1986, Judge Reyna was a solo practitioner in Albuquerque, New Mexico and, prior to that, an associate at Shaffer, Butt, Thornton and Baehr, also in Albuquerque, New Mexico. Judge Reyna served on the U.S. roster of dispute settlement panelists for trade disputes under Chapter 19 of the North American Free Trade Agreement, and the U.S. Indicative List of Non-Governmental Panelists for the World Trade Organization, Dispute Settlement Mechanism, for both trade in goods and trade in services. Judge Reyna is the author of two books, Passport to North American Trade: Rules of Origin and Customs Procedures Under the NAFTA (Shepards 1995), and The GATT Uruguay Round, A Negotiating History: Services, 1986–92 (Kluwer 1993) and numerous articles on international trade and customs issues. He was the founder and Senior Co-Editor of the Hispanic National Bar Association *Journal of Law and Policy*. Judge Reyna is a recipient of the Ohtli Award (the highest honor bestowed by the Mexican Government for non-Mexican citizens). Other awards include: 100 Influentials, *Hispanic Business Magazine*, 2011; 101 Latino Leaders in America, *Latino Leaders Magazine*, 2011 and 2012; Minority Business Leader, *Washington Business Journal*; Extraordinary Leadership, Hispanic National Bar Association (HNBA); Lifetime Honorary Membership, Society of Hispanic Professional Engineers; Distinguished Citizen Award, Military Airlift Command, U.S. Air Force; Spirit of Excellence Award, Albuquerque Hispano Chamber of Commerce. Judge Reyna served over a decade of leadership in the HNBA, including as National President (2006–07). He served in various leadership positions in the ABA Sections on International Law and Dispute Settlement. He was a founder and member of the board of directors of the U.S. Mexico Law Institute, and the Community Services for Autistic Adults and Children Foundation. He currently serves on the Nationwide Hispanic Advisory Council of Big Brothers Big Sisters of America. He received a B.A. from the University of Rochester in 1975 and a J.D. from the University of New Mexico School of Law in 1978.

EVAN J. WALLACH, circuit judge; was appointed to the United States Court of Appeals for the Federal Circuit by President Barack Obama in 2011, confirmed by the Senate on November 9, 2011, and assumed the duties of his office on November 18, 2011. Prior to his appointment, he served for sixteen years as a judge of the United States Court of International Trade, having been appointed to that court by President William J. Clinton in 1995. Judge Wallach worked as a general litigation partner with an emphasis on media representation at the law firm of Lionel Sawyer and Collins in Las Vegas, Nevada from 1982 to 1995. He was an associate at the same firm from 1976 to 1982. While working with the firm, Judge Wallach took a leave of absence to serve as General Counsel and Public Policy Advisor to Senator Harry Reid from 1987 to 1988. From 1989 to 1995, he served in the Nevada National Guard as a Judge Advocate. In 1991, while on leave from his firm, he served as an Attorney/Advisor in the International Affairs Division of the Judge Advocate of the Army at the Pentagon. Judge Wallach, a recognized expert in the law of war, has taught at a number of law schools, including Brooklyn Law School, New York Law School, George Mason University School of Law, and the University of Müenster in Münster, Germany. Judge Wallach has received a number of awards, including: the ABA Liberty Bell Award in 1993; the Nevada Press Association President's Award in 1994; and the Clark County School Librarians Intellectual Freedom Award in 1995. Judge Wallach served on active duty in the Army of the United States from 1969 to 1971. During his military career, he was awarded the Bronze Star, the Air Medal, the Good Conduct Medal, the Meritorious Service Medal, the Nevada Medal of Merit, the Valorous Unit Citation, a Vietnam Campaign Medal, and the RVN Cross of Gallantry with Palm. Judge Wallach received his B.A. in Journalism from the University of Arizona in 1973, his J.D. from the University of California, Berkeley in 1976, and an LLB with honors in International Law from Cambridge University in 1981.

RICHARD G. TARANTO, circuit judge; was appointed to the United States Court of Appeals for the Federal Circuit by President Barack H. Obama, in 2013, confirmed by the Senate on March 11, 2013 and assumed the duties of his office on March 15, 2013. Judge Taranto practiced law with the firm of Farr and Taranto from 1989 to 2013, where he specialized in appellate litigation. From 1986 to 1989, he served as an Assistant to the Solicitor General, representing the United States in the Supreme Court. He was in private practice from 1984 to 1986 with the law firm of Onek, Klein and Farr. Judge Taranto served as a law clerk at all three levels of the federal court system. He clerked for Justice Sandra Day O'Connor of the Supreme Court of the United States from 1983 to 1984; for Judge Robert Bork of the United States Court of Appeals for the District of Columbia Circuit from 1982 to 1983; and for Judge Abraham Sofaer of the United States District Court for the Southern District of New York from 1981 to 1982. Judge Taranto received a J.D. from Yale Law School in 1981 and a B.A. from Pomona College in 1977.

RAYMOND T. CHEN, circuit judge; was appointed to the United States Court of Appeals for the Federal Circuit by President Barack H. Obama in 2013, confirmed by the Senate on August 1, 2013 and assumed his office on August 5, 2013. Judge Chen served as Deputy General Counsel for Intellectual Property Law and Solicitor at the United States Patent and Trademark Office from 2008 to 2013. He was an Associate Solicitor in that office from 1998 to 2008. From 1996 to 1998, Judge Chen served as a Technical Assistant at the United States Court of Appeals for the Federal Circuit. Before joining the court staff, Judge Chen was an associate with Knobbe, Martens, Olson and Bear from 1994 to 1996. Before entering law school, Judge Chen worked as a scientist at the law firm of Hecker and Harriman from 1989 to 1991. Judge Chen received his J.D. from the New York University School of Law in 1994 and his B.S. in Electrical Engineering from the University of California, Los Angeles in 1990.

TODD M. HUGHES, circuit judge; was appointed to the United States Court of Appeals for the Federal Circuit by President Barack H. Obama in 2013, confirmed by the Senate on September 24, 2013 and assumed the duties of his office on September 30, 2013. Judge Hughes served as Deputy Director of the Commercial Litigation Branch of the Civil Division of the United States Department of Justice from 2007 to 2013. He was the Assistant Director in that office from 1999 to 2007 and a Trial Attorney from 1994 to 1999. From 1992 to 1994, Judge Hughes served as a Law Clerk to Circuit Judge Robert Krupansky of the United States Court of Appeals for the Sixth Circuit. He was an Adjunct Lecturer in Law at Cleveland-Marshall College of Law during the Spring, 1994 semester. Judge Hughes received a J.D. from Duke Law School in 1992, an M.A. from Duke University in 1992, and an A.B. from Harvard College in 1989.

KARA FARNANDEZ STOLL, circuit judge; was appointed to the United States Court of Appeals for the Federal Circuit by President Barack H. Obama on November 12, 2014, was confirmed unanimously by the United States Senate on July 7, 2015, and assumed her duties on July 17, 2015. Judge Stoll practiced law with the firm of Finnegan, Henderson, Farabow, Garrett and Dunner from 1998 to 2015, and became a partner at the firm in 2006. While in private practice, Judge Stoll specialized in patent litigation with an emphasis on appeals. Judge Stoll was an adjunct professor at George Mason University Law School from 2008 to 2015 and at the Howard University School of Law from 2004 to 2008. From 1997 to 1998, Judge Stoll served as a law clerk to The Honorable Alvin A. Schall of the United States Court of Appeals for the Federal Circuit. Judge Stoll worked as a patent examiner at the United States Patent and Trademark Office from 1991 to 1997. Judge Stoll received a J.D. from the Georgetown University School of Law in 1997, where she received the Leon Robin Patent Award, and a B.S.E.E. from Michigan State University in 1991.

SENIOR CIRCUIT JUDGES

HALDANE ROBERT MAYER, circuit judge; has been a member of the court since 1987. He served as Chief Judge from 1997 to 2004. Born in Buffalo, Judge Mayer was educated in the public schools of Lockport, New York, before attending the United States Military Academy at West Point, from which he graduated with a Bachelor of Science degree in 1963. He earned a law degree in 1971 at the Marshall-Wythe School of Law of The College of William and Mary, where he was editor-in-chief of the *William and Mary Law Review* as well as a member of Omicron Delta Kappa National Leadership Society. He has served as a director of the William and Mary Law School Association. Judge Mayer served on active duty in the Army of the United States from 1963 until 1975 in the Infantry and the Judge Advocate General's Corps. He was awarded the Bronze Star Medal, the Meritorious Service Medal, the Army Commendation Medal with Oak Leaf Cluster, the Combat Infantryman Badge, Parachutist Badge, Ranger Tab, RVN Ranger Combat Badge, and several campaign and service ribbons. He resigned his Regular Army commission to take an Army Reserve commission, retiring in 1985 as a lieutenant colonel. In 1971, Judge Mayer served as a law clerk for Judge John D. Butzner, Jr., of the United States Court of Appeals for the Fourth Circuit in Richmond, VA. He practiced law in Charlottesville, VA, in the mid-1970's, simultaneously serving as an adjunct at the University of Virginia School of Law, as he did again in the 1990's. He has also been an adjunct at George Washington University National Law Center. From 1977 through 1980, Judge Mayer was the Special Assistant to the Chief Justice of the United States, Warren E. Burger, after which he returned to private law practice in Washington, DC, until he became Deputy and Acting Special Counsel (by designation of the President). President Ronald Reagan appointed Judge Mayer to what is now the United States Court of Federal Claims in 1982, and to the United States Court of Appeals for the Federal Circuit in 1987. He assumed senior status on June 30, 2010.

S. JAY PLAGER, circuit judge; was appointed Circuit Judge by President George H.W. Bush in 1989. Prior to his appointment, Judge Plager served in the Executive Office of the President from 1987 to 1989, as Associate Director of OMB and as Administrator, OIRA. He served as Counselor to the Under Secretary, Department of Health and Human Services from 1986 to 1987. Judge Plager was Dean and Professor, Indiana University School of Law from 1977 to 1984. He was Professor, Faculty of Law, University of Illinois from 1964 to 1977, and from 1958 to 1964 was Professor, Faculty of Law, University of Florida. Judge Plager was Visiting Scholar, Stanford University Law School from 1984 to 1985, Visiting Fellow, Trinity College, and Visiting Professor, Cambridge University in 1980, and Visiting Research Professor of Law, University of Wisconsin from 1967 to 1968. Judge Plager served on active duty in the United States Navy during the Korean Conflict. Judge Plager grew up in New Jersey, where he attended public schools. In 1952, he received an A.B. degree from the University of North Carolina, a J.D. in 1958 from the University of Florida, with high honors, where he was editor-in-chief of the *Florida Law Review*, and in 1961 an LL.M. from Columbia University. He has three children. Judge Plager assumed senior status in 2000.

RAYMOND C. CLEVENGER III, circuit judge; was appointed by President George H.W. Bush in 1990. Judge Clevenger received a B.A. from Yale University in 1959. As a Carnegie Teaching Fellow, he taught European History at Yale College in the 1959–60 academic year. From 1960 to 1963, he was employed by the Morgan Guaranty Trust Company in New York City. He received an LL.B. from Yale University in 1966. Judge Clevenger served as a law clerk to Mr. Justice White in October Term 1966. Judge Clevenger joined Wilmer, Cutler and Pickering in 1967, serving as a partner in the firm from 1974 until his appointment to the bench. Judge Clevenger assumed senior status on February 1, 2006.

ALVIN A. SCHALL, circuit judge; was appointed by President George H.W. Bush in 1992. Prior to his appointment, Judge Schall served as Assistant to the Attorney General of the United States from 1988 to 1992. He was a member of the Washington, DC law firm of Perlman and Partners from 1987 to 1988. He served as Trial Attorney and Senior Trial Counsel, Civil Division, United States Department of Justice, from 1978 to 1987. Judge Schall was an Assistant United States Attorney, Office of the United States Attorney for the Eastern District of New York, from 1973 to 1978, and served as Chief of the Appeals Division from 1977 to 1978. From 1969 to 1973, Judge Schall was in private practice with the New York City law firm of Shearman and Sterling. Judge Schall received a B.A. degree from Princeton University in 1966 and a J.D. degree from Tulane Law School in 1969. Judge Schall assumed senior status on October 5, 2009.

WILLIAM C. BRYSON, circuit judge; was appointed by President William J. Clinton in 1994. Prior to his appointment, Judge Bryson was with the United States Department of Justice from 1978 to 1994. During that period, he served as an Assistant to the Solicitor General [1978–79], Chief of the Appellate Section of the Criminal Division [1979–83], Counsel to the Organized Crime and Racketeering Section [1983–86], Deputy Solicitor General [1986–94], Acting Solicitor General [1989 and 1993], and Acting Associate Attorney General [1994]. He was an Associate at the Washington, DC law firm of Miller, Cassidy, Larroca and Lewin from 1975 to 1978. Judge Bryson served as Law Clerk to the Honorable Henry J. Friendly, United States Court of Appeals for the Second Circuit from 1973 to 1974, and as Law Clerk to the Honorable Thurgood Marshall, Supreme Court of the United States, from 1974 to 1975. Judge Bryson received an A.B. from Harvard College in 1969 and a J.D. from the University of Texas School of Law in 1973.

RICHARD LINN, circuit judge; was appointed by President William J. Clinton in 1999. Prior to his appointment, Judge Linn was a Partner and Practice Group Leader at the Washington, DC law firm of Foley and Lardner from 1997 to 1999. He was a Partner and head of the intellectual property department at Marks and Murase, L.L.P. from 1977 to

1997. Judge Linn served as Patent Advisor, United States Naval Air Systems Command from 1971 to 1972, was a Patent Agent at the United States Naval Research Laboratory from 1968 to 1969, and served as a Patent Examiner at the United States Patent Office from 1965 to 1968. He was a member of the founding Board of Governors of the Virginia Bar Section on Patent, Trademark, and Copyright Law and served as Chairman in 1975. In 2000, Judge Linn received the Rensselaer Alumni Association Fellows Award. He was honored in 2006 for dedication, service, and devotion to justice by the Austin Intellectual Property Law Association. Judge Linn was awarded the 2009 New York Intellectual Property Law Association Leadership Award. He also received the 2009 Jefferson Medal from the New Jersey Intellectual Property Law Association "in recognition of meritorious and outstanding contributions in support of the Constitution of the United States of America and furtherance of a fundamental principle thereof—'to promote the progress of Science and useful Arts.'" In 2010, Judge Linn received the Outstanding Public Service Award from the New York Intellectual Property Law Association. In 2011, he was awarded the inaugural Mark Banner Award by the American Bar Association for his contributions to intellectual property law and the A. Sherman Christensen Award by the American Inns of Court Foundation for distinguished, exceptional and significant leadership to the American Inns of Court movement. He served as an Adjunct Professor and Professorial Lecturer in Law at George Washington University Law School from 2001 to 2003, and currently serves on the Law School's Intellectual Property Advisory Board. Judge Linn is a past president of the Giles Sutherland Rich American Inn of Court, a member of the Richard Linn American Inn of Court, a visiting member of the Hon. William C. Conner American Inn of Court, and an honorary lifetime member of the Benjamin Franklin American Inn of Court. He received a B.E.E. from Rensselaer Polytechnic Institute in 1965, and a J.D. from Georgetown University Law Center in 1969.

OFFICERS OF THE UNITED STATES COURT OF APPEALS

FOR THE FEDERAL CIRCUIT

Circuit Executive and Clerk of Court.—Daniel E. O'Toole (202) 275–8020.
General Counsel.—J. Douglas Steere, 275–8080.
Chief Deputy Clerk and Director of Information Technology.—Mona Harrington, 275–8420.
Deputy Circuit Executive and Operations Officer.—Dale Bosley, 275–8141.
Circuit Librarian.—John Moore, 275–8403.

UNITED STATES DISTRICT COURT FOR THE DISTRICT OF COLUMBIA

E. Barrett Prettyman U.S. Courthouse, 333 Constitution Avenue, NW., 20001
room 2002, phone (202) 354–3320, fax 354–3412

RICHARD W. ROBERTS, chief judge; born in New York, NY; son of Beverly N. Roberts and Angeline T. Roberts; graduate of the High School of Music and Art, 1970; A.B. Vassar College, 1974; M.I.A. School for International Training, 1978; J.D., Columbia Law School, 1978; Honors Program Trial Attorney, Criminal Section, Civil Rights Division, U.S. Department of Justice, Washington, DC, 1978–82; Associate, Covington and Burling, Washington, DC, 1982–86; Assistant U.S. Attorney, Southern District of NY, 1986–88; Assistant U.S. Attorney, 1988–93, then Principal Assistant U.S. Attorney, District of Columbia, 1993–95; Chief, Criminal Section, Civil Rights Division, U.S. Department of Justice, Washington, DC, 1995–98; adjunct professor of trial practice, Georgetown University Law Center, Washington, DC, 1983–84; Guest faculty, Harvard Law School, Trial Advocacy Workshop, 1984–present; admitted to bars of NY (1979) and DC (1983); U.S. District Court for District of Columbia, 1983; U.S. Court of Appeals for the D.C. Circuit, 1984; U.S. Supreme Court, 1985; U.S. District Court for the Southern District of NY and U.S. Court of Appeals for the Second Circuit, 1986; past or present member or officer of National Black Prosecutors Association; Washington Bar Association; National Conference of Black Lawyers; Department of Justice Association of Black Attorneys; Department of Justice Association of Hispanic Employees for Advancement and Development; DC Bar, Committee on Professionalism and Public Understanding About the Law; American Bar Association Criminal Justice Section Committees on Continuing Legal Education, and Race and Racism in the Criminal Justice System; ABA Task Force on the Judiciary; DC Circuit Judicial Conference Arrangements Committee; DC Judicial Conference Planning Committee; Edward Bennett Williams Inn of Court, Washington, DC, master; board of directors, Alumnae and Alumni of Vassar College; African American Alumni of Vassar College; Vassar Club of Washington, DC; Concerned Black Men, Inc., Washington, DC Chapter; Sigma Pi Phi, Epsilon Boule; Council on Foreign Relations; DC Coalition Against Drugs and Violence; Murch Elementary School Restructuring Team; nominated as U.S. District Judge for the District of Columbia by President Clinton on January 27, 1998 and confirmed by the Senate on June 5, 1998; took oath of office on July 31, 1998.

EMMET G. SULLIVAN, judge; son of Emmet A. Sullivan and Eileen G. Sullivan; born in Washington, DC; graduated McKinley High School, 1964; B.A., Howard University, 1968; J.D., Howard University Law School, 1971; recipient of Reginald Heber Smith Fellowship, assigned to the Neighborhood Legal Services Program in Washington, DC, 1971–72; law clerk to Judge James A. Washington, Jr., 1972–73; joined the law firm of Houston and Gardner, 1973–80, became a partner; thereafter was a partner with Houston, Sullivan and Gardner; board of directors of the DC Law Students in Court Program; DC Judicial Conference Voluntary Arbitration Committee; Nominating Committee of the Bar Association of the District of Columbia; U.S. District Court Committee on Grievances; adjunct professor at Howard University School of Law; adjunct professor at American University, Washington College of Law; member: National Bar Association, Washington Bar Association, Bar Association of the District of Columbia; appointed by President Reagan to the Superior Court of the District of Columbia as an associate judge, 1984; deputy presiding judge and presiding judge of the probate and tax division; chairperson of the rules committees for the probate and tax divisions; member: Court Rules Committee and the Jury Plan Committee; appointed by President George H.W. Bush to serve as an associate judge of the District of Columbia Court of Appeals, 1991; chairperson for the nineteenth annual judicial conference of the District of Columbia, 1994 (the Conference theme was "Rejuvenating Juvenile Justice-Responses to the Problems of Juvenile Violence in the District of Columbia"); appointed by chief judge Wagner to chair the "Task Force on Families and Violence for the District of Columbia Courts"; nominated to the U.S. District Court by President Clinton on March 22, 1994; and confirmed by the U.S. Senate on June 15, 1994; appointed by Chief Justice Rehnquist to serve on the Judicial Conference of the U.S. Committee on Criminal Law,

1998–2005; District of Columbia Judicial Disabilities and Tenure Commission, 1996–2001; chair of the District of Columbia Judicial Nomination Commission since 2005; appointed by Chief Justice Roberts to serve on the Judicial Conference of the U.S. Committee on Space and Facilities, 2012, re-appointed by the Chief Justice in 2015; only person in the District of Columbia to have been appointed to three judicial positions by three different U.S. Presidents; recipient of the Ollie May Cooper Award awarded by the Washington Bar Association; the Thurgood Marshall Award of Excellence awarded by the Howard University Alumni Association; the Howard University Distinguished Alumni Award awarded by the President and Board of Trustees of Howard University; American Inns of Court Professionalism Award for the District of Columbia Circuit for 2015; founder and current director of the Frederick B. Abramson Scholarship Foundation.

COLLEEN KOLLAR-KOTELLY, judge; born in New York, NY; daughter of Konstantine and Irene Kollar; attended bilingual schools in Mexico, Ecuador and Venezuela, and Georgetown Visitation Preparatory School in Washington, DC; received B.A. degree in English at Catholic University (Delta Epsilon Honor Society); received J.D. at Catholic University's Columbus School of Law (Moot Court Board of Governors); law clerk to Hon. Catherine B. Kelly, District of Columbia Court of Appeals, 1968–69; attorney, United States Department of Justice, Criminal Division, Appellate Section, 1969–72; chief legal counsel, Saint Elizabeths Hospital, Department of Health and Human Services, 1972–84; received Saint Elizabeths Hospital Certificate of Appreciation, 1981; Meritorious Achievement Award from Alcohol, Drug Abuse and Mental Health Administration (ADAMHA), Department of Health and Human Services, 1981; appointed judge, Superior Court of the District of Columbia by President Reagan, October 3, 1984, took oath of office October 21, 1984; served as Deputy Presiding Judge, Criminal Division, January 1996–April 1997; received Achievement Recognition Award, Hispanic Heritage CORO Awards Celebration, 1996; appointed judge, U.S. District Court for the District of Columbia by President Clinton on March 26, 1997, took oath of office May 12, 1997; appointed by Chief Justice Rehnquist to serve on the Financial Disclosure Committee, 2000–02; presiding judge of the United States Foreign Intelligence Surveillance Court, 2002–09.

REGGIE B. WALTON, judge; born in Donora, PA, 1949; son of the late Theodore and Ruth (Garard) Walton; B.A., West Virginia State College, 1971; J.D., American University, Washington College of Law, 1974; admitted to the bars of the Supreme Court of Pennsylvania, 1974; United States District Court for the Eastern District of Pennsylvania, 1975; District of Columbia Court of Appeals, 1976; United States Court of Appeals for the District of Columbia Circuit, 1977; Supreme Court of the United States, 1980; United States District Court for the District of Columbia; Staff Attorney, Defender Association of Philadelphia, 1974–76; Assistant United States Attorney for the District of Columbia, 1976–80; Chief, Career Criminal Unit, Assistant United States Attorney for the District of Columbia, 1979–80; Executive Assistant United States Attorney for the District of Columbia, 1980–81; Associate Judge, Superior Court of the District of Columbia, 1981–89; deputy presiding judge of the Criminal Division, Superior Court of the District of Columbia, 1986–89; Associate Director, Office of National Drug Control Policy, Executive Office of the President, 1989–91; Senior White House Advisor for Crime, The White House, 1991; Associate Judge, Superior Court of the District of Columbia, 1991–2001; Presiding Judge of the Domestic Violence Unit, Superior Court of the District of Columbia, 2000; Presiding Judge of the Family Division, Superior Court of the District of Columbia, 2001; Instructor: National Judicial College, Reno, Nevada, 1999–present; Harvard University Law School, Trial Advocacy Workshop, 1994–present; National Institute of Trial Advocacy, Georgetown University Law School, 1983–present; Co-author, Pretrial Drug Testing—An Essential Component of the National Drug Control Strategy, Brigham Young University Law Journal of Public Law (1991); Distinguished Alumnus Award, American University, Washington College of Law (1991); The William H. Hastie Award, The Judicial Council of the National Bar Association (1993); Commissioned as a Kentucky Colonel by the Governor (1990, 1991); Governor's Proclamation declaring April 9, 1991, Judge Reggie B. Walton Day in the State of Louisiana; The West Virginia State College National Alumni Association James R. Waddy Meritorious Service Award (1990); Secretary's Award, United States Department of Veterans Affairs (1990); Outstanding Alumnus Award, Ringgold High School (1987); Director's Award for Superior Performance as an Assistant United States Attorney (1980); Profiled in book entitled "Black Judges on Justice: Prospectives From The Bench" by Linn Washington (1995); appointed district judge, United States District Court for the District of Columbia by President George W. Bush, September 24, 2001, and took oath of office October 29, 2001; appointed by President Bush in June of 2004 to serve as the Chairperson of the National Prison Rape Reduction Commission, a two-year commission created by the United States Congress that is tasked with the mission of identifying methods to curb the incidents of prison rape; member, United States Foreign Intelligence Surveillance Court, 2007–present; Presiding Judge, 2013–present.

RICHARD J. LEON, judge; born in South Natick, MA, 1949; son of Silvano B. Leon and Rita (O'Rorke) Leon; A.B., Holy Cross College, 1971, J.D., *cum laude*, Suffolk Law School, 1974; LL.M. Harvard Law School, 1981; Law Clerk to Chief Justice McLaughlin and the Associate Justices, Superior Court of Massachusetts, 1974–75; Law Clerk to Hon. Thomas F. Kelleher, Supreme Court of Rhode Island, 1975–76; admitted to bar, Rhode Island, 1975 and District of Columbia, 1991; Special Assistant U.S. Attorney, Southern District of New York, 1977–78; Assistant Professor of Law, St. John's Law School, New York, 1979–83; Senior Trial Attorney, Criminal Section, Tax Division, U.S. Department of Justice, 1983–87; Deputy Chief Minority Counsel, U.S. House Select "Iran-Contra" Committee, 1987–88; Deputy Assistant U.S. Attorney General, Environment Division, 1988–89; Partner, Baker and Hostetler, Washington, DC, 1989–99; Commissioner, The White House Fellows Commission, 1990–92; Chief Minority Counsel, U.S. House Foreign Affairs Committee "October Suprise" Task Force, 1992–93; Special Counsel, U.S. House Banking Committee "Whitewater" Investigation, 1994; Special Counsel, U.S. House Ethics Reform Task Force, 1997; Adjunct Professor, Georgetown University Law Center, 1997–present; Partner, Vorys, Sater, Seymour and Pease, Washington, DC, 1999–2002; Commissioner, Judicial Review Commission on Foreign Asset Control, 2000–01; Master, Edward Bennett Williams Inn of Court; appointed U.S. District Judge for the District of Columbia by President George W. Bush on February 19, 2002; took oath of office on March 20, 2002.

ROSEMARY M. COLLYER, judge; born in White Plains, NY, 1945; daughter of Thomas C. and Alice Henry Mayers; educated in parochial and public schools in Stamford, Connecticut; B.A., Trinity College, Washington, DC, 1968; J.D., University of Denver College of Law, 1977; practiced with Sherman and Howard, Denver, Colorado, 1977–81; Chairman, Federal Mine Safety and Health Review Commission, 1981–84 by appointment of President Reagan with Senate confirmation; General Counsel, National Labor Relations Board, 1984–89 by appointment of President Reagan with Senate confirmation; private practice with Crowell and Moring LLP, Washington, DC 1989–2003; member and chairman of the firm's Management Committee; appointed U.S. District Judge for the District of Columbia by President George W. Bush and took oath of office on January 2, 2003. Member, Foreign Intelligence Surveillance Court, 2013–present.

BERYL A. HOWELL, judge; born in Fort Benning, GA; daughter of Col. (Ret.) Leamon and Ruth Howell; Killeen High School, 1974; B.A. with honors in philosophy, Bryn Mawr College (President and Member, Honor Board, 1976–78); J.D., Columbia University School of Law, 1983 (Harlan Fiske Stone Scholar, 1981–82; International Fellows Program, 1982–83, *Transnational Law Journal*, Notes Editor); law clerk to Hon. Dickinson R. Debevoise, District of New Jersey, 1983–84; litigation associate, Schulte, Roth and Zabel, 1985–87; Assistant United States Attorney, United States District Court for the Eastern District of New York, 1987–93; Deputy Chief, Narcotics Section, 1987–93; Senior Counsel, U.S. Senate Committee on the Judiciary Subcommittee on Technology and the Law, 1993–94; Senior Counsel, U.S. Senate Committee on the Judiciary Subcommittee on Antitrust, Business Rights and Competition, 1995–96; General Counsel, U.S. Senate Committee on the Judiciary, 1997–2003; Executive Managing Director and General Counsel, Stroz Friedberg, 2003–09; Member, Commission on Cyber Security for the 44th Presidency, 2008; Adjunct Professor of Law, American University's Washington College of Law, 2010; Awards include U.S. Attorney's Special Achievement Award for Sustained Superior Performance, 1990, 1991; Drug Enforcement Administration Commendations, 1990, 1992, 1993; Attorney General's Director's Award for Superior Performance, 1991; Federal Bureau of Investigation Award and New York City Department of Investigation Award for public corruption investigation and prosecution, 1992; Freedom of Information Hall of Fame, 2001; First Amendment Award, Society of Professional Journalists, 2004; Federal Bureau of Investigation Director's Award, 2006; Book chapters and law review article publications include Seven Weeks: The Making of the USA PATRIOT Act, *The George Washington Law Review*, 2004; FISA's Fruits in Criminal Cases: An Opportunity for Improved Accountability, UCLA Journal of International Law and Foreign Affairs, 2007; Book Chapters include: Real World Problems of Virtual Crime, in Cybercrime: Digital Cops in a Networked Environment, 2007; Foreign Intelligence Surveillance Act: Has the Solution Become the Problem, in Protecting What Matters: Technology, Security, and Liberty Since 9/11, 2006 and articles in the *New York Law Journal, Journal of Internet Law*, the *Vermont Bar Journal*, and *Yale Journal of Law and Technology*; Appointed Commissioner, United States Sentencing Commission, 2004–11; appointed judge, U.S. District Court for the District of Columbia by President Obama on December 27, 2010, took oath of office on January 21, 2011.

JAMES E. BOASBERG, judge; born San Francisco, CA, 1963; son of Emanuel Boasberg III and Sarah Szold Boasberg; graduated St. Albans School, Washington, DC, 1981; B.A., *magna cum laude* in history from Yale College, 1985; M.St. in modern European history from Oxford University, 1986; J.D. from Yale Law School, 1990; law clerk to Judge Dorothy W. Nelson on the U.S. Court of Appeals for the Ninth Circuit, 1990–91; associate, Keker and Van Nest in San Francisco, CA, 1991–94; associate, Kellogg, Huber, Hansen, Todd and Evans in Washington, DC, 1995–96; Assistant United States Attorney for the District of Columbia, 1996–2002; visiting lecturer, George Washington Law School, 2003; Associate Judge, District of Columbia Superior Court, 2002–11; United States District Judge for the District of Columbia, 2011–present; appointed to the U.S. Foreign Intelligence Surveillance Court, May 2014.

AMY BERMAN JACKSON, judge; appointed March of 2011; prior to joining the Court, engaged in private practice in Washington, DC as a member of Trout Cacheris, specializing in complex criminal and civil trials and appeals; earlier, partner at Venable, Baetjer, Howard, and Civiletti; Assistant United States Attorney for the District of Columbia, 1980–86; received Department of Justice Special Achievement Awards for work on murder and sexual assault cases; J.D., cum laude, Harvard Law School, 1979; A.B. cum laude, Harvard College, 1976; law clerk to the Honorable Harrison L. Winter of the United States Court of Appeals for the Fourth Circuit; lectured on corporate criminal investigations and has been a regular teacher at the National Institute of Trial Advocacy, the Georgetown University Law Center CLE Intensive Session in Trial Advocacy Skills, and the Harvard Law School Trial Advocacy workshop; while in private practice, was elected to serve as a DC Bar delegate to the ABA House of Delegates; active in the ABA Litigation Section, the ABA Criminal Justice Section White Collar Crime Committee, and DC Bar and Women's Bar Association committee activities; member of the Parent Steering Committee of the Interdisciplinary Council on Developmental and Learning Disorders; served on the Board of the DC Rape Crisis Center and other educational and community organizations.

RUDOLPH CONTRERAS, judge; appointed to the District Court in March 2012. Prior to joining the District Court, Judge Contreras served from 2006 to 2012 as the Chief of the Civil Division of the United States Attorney's Office of the District of Columbia. In that capacity, he supervised 39 Assistant United States Attorneys who defend and bring civil cases on behalf of the United States. Judge Contreras was awarded his Bachelor of Science degree from Florida State University in 1984 and his Juris Doctor degree, cum laude, from the University of Pennsylvania Law School in 1991, where he was a member of the Order of the Coif and Editor of the University of Pennsylvania Law Review. Following law school, Judge Contreras joined the law firm of Jones, Day, Reavis and Pogue, where he was an Associate in the General Litigation Group. In 1994, Judge Contreras joined the United States Attorney's Office for the District of Columbia as an Assistant United States Attorney in the Civil Division, where he was responsible for a wide array of cases, including employment, Federal Tort Claims Act, Administrative Procedure Act, Bivens and Affirmative Civil Enforcement matters. In 2003, Judge Contreras left the DC Office to become the Chief of the Civil Division for the United States Attorney's Office in Delaware, where he oversaw that civil program and personally handled a wide variety of matters, including environmental and health care fraud cases.

KETANJI BROWN JACKSON, judge; received her commission as a United States District Judge in March 2013. Until December 2014, she also served as a Vice Chair and Commissioner on the United States Sentencing Commission, and she taught a seminar on Sentencing Policy at the George Washington University Law School as an adjunct professor. Prior to her service on the Commission, Judge Jackson was Of Counsel at Morrison and Foerster LLP for three years, with a practice that focused on criminal and civil appellate litigation in both state and federal courts, as well as cases in the Supreme Court of the United States. From 2005 until 2007, prior to joining Morrison and Foerster LLP, Judge Jackson served as an assistant federal public defender in the Appeals Division of the Office of the Federal Public Defender in the District of Columbia. Before that appointment, Judge Jackson worked as an assistant special counsel at the United States Sentencing Commission and as an associate with two law firms, one specializing in white collar criminal defense, the other focusing on the negotiated settlement of mass-tort claims. Judge Jackson also served as a law clerk to three federal judges: Associate Justice Stephen G. Breyer of the Supreme Court of the United States (October Term 1999), Judge Bruce M. Selya of the U.S. Court of Appeals for the First Circuit (1997–1998), and Judge Patti B. Saris of the U.S. District Court for the District of Massachusetts (1996–1997). She received an A.B., magna cum laude, in Government from Harvard-Radcliffe College in 1992, and, in 1996, a J.D., cum laude, from Harvard Law School, where she served as a supervising editor of the Harvard Law Review.

CHRISTOPHER R. COOPER, judge; born Mobile, Alabama, 1966; son of Paulette Reid Cooper and William Madison Cooper; graduated Trinity Preparatory School, Winter Park, Florida, 1984; B.A., summa cum laude, in economics and political science, Yale University,

1988, and member of Phi Beta Kappa; Research Analyst, Strategic Planning Associates, Washington, DC, 1988–90; J.D., with distinction, Stanford Law School, 1993; President, Volume 45, Stanford Law Review, 1992–93; Board Member, East Palo Alto Community Law Project, 1992–93; Law Clerk to then-Chief Judge Abner J. Mikva, United States Court of Appeals for the DC Circuit, 1993–94; United States Department of Justice, Special Assistant to the Deputy Attorney General, Washington, DC, 1994–96; Associate (1996–2000) and Partner (2000), Miller, Cassidy, Larroca and Lewin LLC, Washington, DC; Partner, Baker Botts LLP, Washington, DC (2000–10) and London (2010–12); Partner, Covington and Burling LLP, London (2012–13) and Washington, DC (2013–14); appointed to the United States District Court for the District of Columbia on March 28, 2014.

TANYA S. CHUTKAN, judge; born in Kingston, Jamaica; daughter of Dr. Winston Chutkan and Noelle Chutkan, Esq.; B.A., George Washington University, 1983; J.D., University of Pennsylvania Law School, 1987 (Associate Editor, *Law Review*; Arthur Littleton Legal Writing Fellow); Associate, Hogan and Hartson LLP, 1987–90; Associate, Donovan, Leisure, Rogovin, Huge and Schiller, 1990–91; Staff Attorney and Supervisor, Public Defender Service for the District of Columbia, 1991–2002; Counsel and Partner, Boies, Schiller and Flexner LLP, 2002–14; Steering Committee, Criminal Law and Individual Rights Section of the District of Columbia Bar, 2000–03; member of Visiting Faculty, Harvard Law School Trial Advocacy Workshop; nominated judge, U.S. District Court for the District of Columbia by President Obama; confirmed by the Senate on June 4, 2014; took the oath of office on July 25, 2014.

RANDOLPH D. MOSS, judge, born Springfield, Ohio 1961; son of Dr. Howard A. Moss and Adrienne Moss. A.B., *summa cum laude*, phi beta kappa, philosophy, from Hamilton College in 1983; J.D., Yale Law School, 1986. Law clerk to Judge Pierre Leval, United States District Court for the Southern District of New York, 1986–87. Law clerk to Justice John Paul Stevens, United States Supreme Court, 1988–89. Private practice at Wilmer, Cutler and Pickering, first as associate then as partner, 1989–96. Department of Justice Office of Legal Counsel 1996–2001; Deputy Assistant Attorney General, 1996–98; Acting Assistant Attorney General, 1998–00; Assistant Attorney General, 2000–01. Partner, Wilmer, Cutler, Pickering Hale and Dorr, 2001–14; chair of the firm's Regulatory and Government Affairs Department. Confirmed to the bench November 2014.

AMIT MEHTA, judge; born Patan, India; son of Priyavadan and Ragini Mehta. B.A., *magna cum laude* and Phi Beta Kappa in political science and economics from Georgetown University, 1993; J.D., Order of the Coif, University of Virginia, 1997; Law Clerk to Judge Susan P. Graber, United States Court of Appeals for the Ninth Circuit, 1998–1999; Associate, Counsel and Partner, Zuckerman Spaeder, LLP, 1999–2002, 2007–2014; Staff Attorney, Public Defender Service for the District of Columbia, 2002–2007; Judge, U.S. District Court for the District of Columbia, 2014–present.

SENIOR JUDGES

THOMAS F. HOGAN, senior judge; born in Washington, DC, 1938; son of Adm. Bartholomew W. (MC) (USN) Surgeon Gen., USN, 1956–62, and Grace (Gloninger) Hogan; Georgetown Preparatory School, 1956; A.B., Georgetown University (classical), 1960; master's program, American and English literature, George Washington University, 1960–62; J.D., Georgetown University, 1965–66; Honorary Degree, Doctor of Laws, Georgetown University Law Center, May 1999; St. Thomas More Fellow, Georgetown University Law Center, 1965–66; American Jurisprudence Award: Corporation Law; member, bars of the District of Columbia and Maryland; law clerk to Hon. William B. Jones, U.S. District Court for the District of Columbia, 1966–67; counsel, Federal Commission on Reform of Federal Criminal Laws, 1967–68; private practice of law in the District of Columbia and Maryland, 1968–82; adjunct professor of law, Potomac School of Law, 1977–79; adjunct professor of law, Georgetown University Law Center, 1986–88; public member, officer evaluation board, U.S. Foreign Service, 1973; member: American Bar Association, State Chairman, Maryland Drug Abuse Education Program, Young Lawyers Section (1970–73), District of Columbia Bar Association, Bar Association of the District of Columbia, Maryland State Bar Association, Montgomery County Bar Association, National Institute for Trial Advocacy, Defense Research Institute, The Barristers, The Lawyers Club; chairman, board of directors, Christ Child Institute for Emotionally Ill Children, 1971–74; served on many committees; USDC Executive Committee; Conference Committee on Administration of Federal Magistrates System, 1988–91; chairman, Inter-Circuit Assignment Committee, 1990–present; appointed judge of the U.S. District Court for the District of Columbia by President Reagan on October 4, 1982; chief judge, June 19, 2001; member: Judicial Conference of the United States 2001–present; Executive Committee of the Judicial Conference, July 2001–08, Chair 2005–2008; Edward J. Devitt Distinguished Service to Justice Award, 2011; Director of the Administrative Office of the United States Courts, 2011–2013; member, Foreign Intelligence Surveillance Court, 2009–present, Presiding Judge 2014–present.

ROYCE C. LAMBERTH, senior judge; born in San Antonio, TX, 1943; son of Nell Elizabeth Synder and Larimore S. Lamberth, Sr.; South San Antonio High School, 1961; B.A., University of Texas at Austin, 1966; LL.B., University of Texas School of Law, 1967; permanent president, class of 1967, University of Texas School of Law; U.S. Army (Captain, Judge Advocate General's Corps, 1968–74; Vietnam Service Medal, Air Medal, Bronze Star with Oak Leaf Cluster, Meritorious Service Medal with Oak Leaf Cluster); assistant U.S. attorney, District of Columbia, 1974–87 (chief, civil division, 1978–87); President's Reorganization Project, Federal Legal Representation Study, 1978–79; honorary faculty, Army Judge Advocate General's School, 1976; Attorney General's Special Commendation Award; Attorney General's John Marshall Award, 1982; vice chairman, Armed Services and Veterans Affairs Committee, Section on Administrative Law, American Bar Association, 1979–82, chairman, 1983–84; chairman, Professional Ethics Committee, 1989–91; co-chairman, Committee of Article III Judges, Judiciary Section 1989–present; chairman, Federal Litigation Section, 1986–87; chairman, Federal Rules Committee, 1985–86; deputy chairman, Council of the Federal Lawyer, 1980–83; chairman, Career Service Committee, Federal Bar Association, 1978–80; appointed judge, U.S. District Court for the District of Columbia by President Reagan, November 16, 1987; appointed by Chief Justice Rehnquist to be presiding judge of the United States Foreign Intelligence Surveillance Court, May 1995–2002.

GLADYS KESSLER, senior judge; born in New York, NY, 1938; B.A., Cornell University, 1959; LL.B. Harvard Law School, 1962; member: American Judicature Society (board of directors, 1985–89); National Center for State Courts (board of directors, 1984–87); National Association of Women Judges (president, 1983–84); Women Judges' Fund for Justice, (president, 1980–82); Fellows of the American Bar Foundation; President's Council of Cornell Women; American Law Institute; American Bar Association—committees: Alternative Dispute Resolution, Bioethics and AIDS; Executive Committee, Conference of Federal Trial Judges; private law practice-partner, Roisman, Kessler and Cashdan, 1969–77; associate judge, Superior Court of the District of Columbia, 1977–94; court administrative activities: District of Columbia Courts Joint Committee on Judicial Administration, 1989–94; Domestic Violence Coordinating Council (chairperson, 1993–94); Multi-Door Dispute Resolution Program (supervising judge, 1985–90); family division, D.C. Superior Court (presiding judge, 1981–85); Einshac Institute Board of Directors; U.S. Judicial Conference Committee on Court Administration and Court Management; Frederick B. Abramson Memorial Foundation Board of Directors; Our Place Board of Directors; Vice Chair, District of Columbia Judicial Disabilities and Tenure Commission; appointed judge, U.S. District Court for the District of Columbia by President Clinton, June 16, 1994, and took oath of office, July 18, 1994.

PAUL L. FRIEDMAN, senior judge; born in Buffalo, NY, 1944; son of Cecil A. and Charlotte Wagner Friedman; B.A. (political science), Cornell University, 1965; J.D., *cum laude*, School of Law, State University of New York at Buffalo, 1968; admitted to the bars of the District of Columbia, New York, U.S. Supreme Court, and U.S. Courts of Appeals for the D.C., Federal, Fourth, Fifth, Sixth, Seventh, Ninth and Eleventh Circuits; Law Clerk to Judge Aubrey E. Robinson, Jr., U.S. District Court for the District of Columbia, 1968–69; Law Clerk to Judge Roger Robb, U.S. Court of Appeals for the District of Columbia Circuit, 1969–70; Assistant U.S. Attorney for the District of Columbia, 1970–74, assistant to the Solicitor General of the United States, 1974–76; associate independent counsel, Iran-Contra investigation, 1987–88; private law practice, White and Case (partner, 1979–94; associate, 1976–79); member: American Bar Association, Commission on Multidisciplinary Practice (1998–2000), District of Columbia Bar (president, 1986–87), American Law Institute (1984) and ALI Council, 1998, American Academy of Appellate Lawyers, Bar Association of the District of Columbia, Women's Bar Association of the District of Columbia, Washington Bar Association, Hispanic Bar Association, Assistant United States Attorneys Association of the District of Columbia (president, 1976–77), Civil Justice Reform Act Advisory Group (chair, 1991–94), District of Columbia Judicial Nomination Commission (member, 1990–94; chair, 1992–94), Advisory Committee on Procedures, U.S. Court of Appeals for the D.C. Circuit (1982–88), Grievance Committee; U.S. District Court for the District of Columbia (member, 1981–87; chair, 1983–85); fellow, American College of Trial Lawyers; fellow, American Bar Foundation; board of directors: Frederick B. Abramson Memorial Foundation (president, 1991–94), Washington Area Lawyers for the Arts (1988–92), Washington Legal Clinic for the Homeless (member, 1987–92; vice-president 1988–91), Stuart Stiller Memorial Foundation (1980–94), American Judicature Society (1990–94), District of Columbia Public Defender Service (1989–92); member: Cosmos Club, Lawyers Club of Washington; appointed judge, U.S. District Court for the District of Columbia by President Clinton, June 16, 1994, and took oath of office August 1, 1994; U.S. Judicial Conference Advisory Committee on Federal Criminal Rules.

ELLEN SEGAL HUVELLE, senior judge; born in Boston, MA, 1948; daughter of Robert M. Segal, Esq. and Sharlee Segal; B.A., Wellesley College, 1970; Masters in City Planning, Yale University, 1972; J.D., *magna cum laude*, Boston College Law School, 1975 (Order of the Coif; Articles Editor of the *Law Review*); law clerk to Chief Justice Edward F. Hennessey, Massachusetts Supreme Judicial Court, 1975–76; associate, Williams and Connolly, 1976–84; partner, Williams and Connolly, 1984–90; associate judge, Superior Court of the District of Columbia, 1990–99; appointed judge, U.S. District Court for the District of Columbia by President Clinton in October 1999, and took oath of office on February 25, 2000. Member: American Bar Association, District of Columbia Bar, Women's Bar Association; Fellow of the American Bar Foundation; Master in the Edward Bennett Williams Inn of Court and member of the Inn's Executive Committee; instructor of Trial Advocacy at the University of Virginia Law School; member of Visiting Faculty at Harvard Law School's Trial Advocacy Workshop; Boston College Law School Board of Overseers; seminar instructor at the Peking University School of Transnational Law in Shenzhen, 2010; faculty, CEELI Institute for training Tunisian judges, 2012; appointed by the Chief Justice of the United States to Judicial Conference Committee on Judicial Resources, 2002–09, Judicial Conference Committee on Criminal Law, 2011–present, Judicial Panel on Multidistrict Litigation, 2013–present.

JOHN D. BATES, senior judge; born in Elizabeth, NJ, 1946; son of Richard D. and Sarah (Deacon) Bates; B.A., Wesleyan University, 1968; J.D., University of Maryland School of Law, 1976; U.S. Army (1968–71, 1st Lt., Vietnam Service Medal, Bronze Star); law clerk to Hon. Roszel Thomsen, U.S. District Court for the District of Maryland, 1976–77; Assistant U.S. Attorney, District of Columbia, 1980–97 (Chief, Civil Division, 1987–97); Director's Award for Superior Performance (1983); Attorney General's Special commendation Award (1986); Deputy Independent Counsel, Whitewater Investigation, 1995–97; private practice of law, Miller and Chevalier (partner, 1998–2001), Chair of Government Contracts Litigation Department and member of Executive Committee), Steptoe and Johnson (associate, 1977–80); District of Columbia Circuit Advisory Committee for Procedures, 1989–93; Civil Justice Reform Committee of the U.S. District Court for the District of Columbia, 1996–2001; Treasurer, D.C. Bar, 1992–93; Publications Committee, D.C. Bar (1991–97, Chair 1994–97); D.C. Bar Special Committee on Government Lawyers, 1990–91; D.C. Bar Task Force on Civility in the Profession, 1994–96; D.C. Bar Committee on Examination of Rule 49, 1995–96; Chairman, Litigation Section, Federal Bar Association, 1986–89; Board of Directors, Washington Lawyers Committee for Civil Rights and Urban Affairs, 1999–2001; appointed to the U.S. District Court for the District of Columbia in December, 2001; presiding judge, United States Foreign Intelligence Surveillance Court, 2009–13; Director, Administrative Office of United States Courts, 2013–14; Chairman, Advisory Committee on Federal Rules of Civil Procedure, 2015–present.

OFFICERS OF THE UNITED STATES DISTRICT COURT
FOR THE DISTRICT OF COLUMBIA

Bankruptcy Judge.—S. Martin Teel, Jr.
United States Magistrate Judges: Alan Kay; Deborah A. Robinson; G. Michael Harvey.
Clerk of Court.—Angela Caesar.
Administrative Assistant to the Chief Judge.—Vacant.

UNITED STATES COURT OF INTERNATIONAL TRADE

One Federal Plaza, New York, NY 10278–0001, phone (212) 264–2800

TIMOTHY C. STANCEU, chief judge; born in Canton, OH; A.B., Colgate University, 1973; J.D., Georgetown University Law Center, 1979; appointed to the U.S. Court of International Trade by President George W. Bush and began serving on April 15, 2003; prior to appointment, private practice for 13 years in Washington, DC, with the law firm Hogan and Hartson, L.L.P., during which he represented clients in a variety of matters involving customs and international trade law; Deputy Director, Office of Trade and Tariff Affairs, U.S. Department of the Treasury; where his responsibilities involved the regulatory and enforcement matters of the U.S. Customs Service and other agencies; Special Assistant to the Assistant Secretary of the Office of Enforcement, U.S. Department of the Treasury; Program Analyst and Environmental Protection Specialist, U.S. Environmental Protection Agency, where he concentrated on the development and review of regulations on various environmental subjects.

DELISSA A. RIDGWAY, judge; born in Kirksville, MO, June 28, 1955; B.A. (honors), University of Missouri-Columbia, 1975; graduate work, University of Missouri-Columbia, 1975–76; J.D., Northeastern University School of Law, 1979; Duke University School of Law, LL.M. in Judicial Studies - 2014; Shaw Pittman Potts and Trowbridge (Washington, DC), 1979–94; Chair, Foreign Claims Settlement Commission of the U.S., 1994–98; Adjunct Professor of Law, Cornell Law School, 1999–present; Adjunct Professor of Law/Lecturer, Washington College of Law / The American University, 1992–94; District of Columbia Bar, Secretary, 1991–92; Board of Governors, 1992–98; President, Women's Bar Association, 1992–93; American Bar Association, Standing Committee on Federal Judicial Improvements (2008–11); Co-Chair, Section of Litigation Task Force on Implicit Bias (2010–13); Commission on Women in the Profession, 2002–05; Federal Bar Association, National Council, 1993–2002, 2003–present; Government Relations Committee, 1996–2008, Public Relations Committee Chair, 1998–99; Board of Directors, Federal Bar Building Corporation; Executive Committee, National Conference of Federal Trial Judges, 2004–11; Chair, National Conference of Federal Trial Judges, 2009–10; Board of Directors, American Judicature Society (2010–present); Founding Member of Board, D.C. Conference on Opportunities for Minorities in the Legal Profession, 1992–93; Chair, D.C. Bar Summit on Women in the Legal Profession, 1995–98; Fellow, American Bar Foundation; Member, American Law Institute; Fellow, Federal Bar Foundation; Earl W. Kintner Award of the Federal Bar Association (2000); Woman Lawyer of the Year, Washington, DC (2001); Distinguished Visiting Scholar-in-Residence, University of Missouri-Columbia (2003); sworn in as a judge to the U.S. Court of International Trade in May 1998.

LEO M. GORDON, judge; graduate of Newark Academy in Livingston, NJ; University of North Carolina-Chapel Hill, Phi Beta Kappa, 1973; J.D., Emory University School of Law, 1977; member of the Bars of New Jersey, Georgia and the District of Columbia; Assistant Counsel at the Subcommittee on Monopolies and Commercial Law, Committee on the Judiciary, U.S. House of Representatives, 1977–81; in that capacity, Judge Gordon was the principal attorney responsible for the Customs Courts Act of 1980 that created the U.S. Court of International Trade; for 25 years, Judge Gordon was on the staff at the Court, serving first as Assistant Clerk from 1981–99, and then Clerk of the Court from 1999–2006; appointed to the U.S. Court of International Trade in March 2006.

MARK A. BARNETT, judge; graduated *magna cum laude*, Phi Beta Kappa from Dickinson College; studied at the Dickinson Center for European Studies; J.D., *cum laude* from the University of Michigan Law School; member of the Bars of Pennsylvania and the District of Columbia and admitted to practice before the U.S. Court of International Trade and the U.S. Court of Appeals for the Federal Circuit; practiced in the international trade group at Steptoe and Johnson; joined the Office of Chief Counsel for Import Administration at the U.S. Department of Commerce as a staff attorney, served as a senior counsel, and subsequently served as the Deputy Chief Counsel for Import Administration; member of the U.S. negotiating teams for the U.S.-Morocco Free Trade Agreement, the World Trade Organization's Doha Round Rules Negotiating Group, and the Trans-Pacific Partnership; represented the United States before dispute settlement panels and the Appellate Body of the World Trade Organization and binational panels composed under the North American Free Trade Agreement; detailed to the U.S. House of Representatives, Committee on Ways and Means, Subcommittee on Trade as a Trade Counsel; served two terms as a member of the board of directors of the International Model United Nations Association, Inc., including Vice-Chairman and Chairman; nominated to the U.S. Court of International Trade by President Obama on July 12, 2012, and confirmed by the U.S. Senate on May 23, 2013.

CLAIRE R. KELLY, judge; born in New York, NY. Married to Joseph A DiBartolo. Child: Joseph J. DiBartolo. Attended Sacred Heart Academy, Hempstead, NY; Barnard College, B.A. 1987, *cum laude*; and Brooklyn Law School, J.D., 1993, *magna cum laude*. Professional experience: Coudert Brothers (1993–97) associated; Brooklyn Law School (1997–2013), Legal Writing Instructor, Associate Professor of Law and Professor of Law and Co-Director of the Dennis J. Block Center for the Study of International Business Law. Elected Member of the American Law Institute, 2011; nominated to the U.S. Court of International Trade by President Obama on November 14, 2012, and confirmed by the U.S. Senate on May 23, 2013.

SENIOR JUDGES

GREGORY W. CARMAN, senior judge; born in Farmingdale, Long Island, NY; son of Nassau County District Court Judge Willis B. and Marjorie Sosa Carman; B.A., St. Lawrence University, Canton, NY, 1958; J.D., St. John's University School of Law (honors program), 1961; University of Virginia Law School, JAG (with honors), 1962; admitted to New York Bar, 1961; practiced law with firm of Carman, Callahan and Sabino, Farmingdale, NY; admitted to practice: U.S. Court of Military Appeals, 1962, U.S. District Courts, Eastern and Southern Districts of New York, 1965, Second Circuit Court of Appeals, 1966, Supreme Court of the United States, 1967, U.S. Court of Appeals, District of Columbia, 1982; Councilman Town of Oyster Bay, 1972–80; member, U.S. House of Representatives, 97th Congress; member, Banking, Finance and Urban Affairs Committee and Select Committee on Aging; member, International Trade, Investment, and Monetary Policy Subcommittee; U.S. Congressional Delegate to International I.M.F. Conference; nominated by President Reagan, confirmed and appointed Judge of the U.S. Court of International Trade, March 2, 1983; Acting Chief Judge, 1991; Chief Judge, 1996–2003; Statutory Member, Judicial Conference of United States; member, Executive Committee, Judicial Branch Committee, and Subcommittees on Long Range Planning, Benefits, Civic Education, and Seminars; Captain, U.S. Army, 1958–64; awarded Army Commendation Medal for Meritorious Service, 1964; member, Rotary International, 1964–present; named Paul Harris Fellow of the Rotary Foundation of Rotary International; member, Holland Society, and recipient of its 1999 Gold Medal for Distinguished Achievement in Jurisprudence; member, Federal Bar Association, American Bar Association, Fellow of American Bar Foundation, New York State Bar Association; member, and former Chair, New York State Bar Association's Committee on Courts and the Community, and recipient of its 1996 Special Recognition Award; Doctor of Laws, *honoris causa*, Nova Southeastern University, 1999; Distinguished Jurist in Residence, Touro College Law Center, 2000; Doctor of Laws, *honoris causa*, St. John's University, 2002; Inaugural Lecturer, DiCarlo U.S. Court of International Trade Lecture, John Marshall Law School, 2003; Distinguished Alumni Citation, St. Lawrence University, 2003; Italian Board of Guardians Public Service Award, 2003; director and member, Respect for Law Alliance, Inc.; Recipient of Respect for Law Alliance, 2010, Judiciary Leader Award; Executive Committee member and past president, Theodore Roosevelt American Inn of Court; past president, Protestant Lawyers Association of Long Island; member, Vestry, St. Thomas's Episcopal Church, Farmingdale, NY; married to Nancy Endruschat (deceased); children: Gregory Wright, Jr., John Frederick, James Matthew, and Mira Catherine; married to Judith L. Dennehy.

JANE A. RESTANI, senior judge; born in San Francisco, CA, 1948; parents: Emilia C. and Roy J. Restani; husband: Ira Bloom; B.A., University of California at Berkeley, 1969; J.D., University of California at Davis, 1973; law review staff writer, 1971–72; articles editor, 1972–73; member, Order of the Coif; elected to Phi Kappa Phi Honor Society; admitted to the bar of the Supreme Court of the State of California, 1973; joined the civil division of the Department of Justice under the Attorney General's Honor Program in 1973 as a trial attorney; assistant chief commercial litigation section, civil division, 1976–80; director, commercial litigation branch, civil division, 1980–83; recipient of the John Marshall Award of outstanding legal achievement in 1983; Judicial Improvements Committee (now Committee on Court Administration and Case Management) of the Judicial Conference of the United States, 1987–94; Judicial Conference Advisory Committee on the Federal Rules of Bankruptcy Procedure, and liaison to the Advisory Committee on the Federal Rules of Civil Procedure, 1994–96; member, Judicial Conference of the United States, 2003–10; Executive Committee of the Judicial Conference, 2010; ABA Standing Committee on Customs Laws, 1990–93;

and the Board of Directors, New York State Association of Women Judges, 1992–present; nominated to the United States Court of International Trade on November 2, 1983 by President Reagan; entered upon the duties of that office on November 25, 1983; Chief Judge, 2003–10.

THOMAS J. AQUILINO, JR., senior judge; born in Mount Kisco, NY, December 7, 1939; son of Thomas J. and Virginia B. (Doughty) Aquilino; married to Edith Berndt Aquilino; children: Christopher Thomas, Philip Andrew, Alexander Berndt; attended Cornell University, 1957–59; B.A., Drew University, 1959–60, 1961–62; University of Munich, Germany, 1960–61; Free University of Berlin, Germany, 1965–66; J.D., Rutgers University School of Law, 1966 69; research assistant, Prof. L.F.E. Goldie (Resources for the Future-Ford Foundation), 1967–69; administrator, Northern Region, 1969 Jessup International Law Moot Court Competition; served in the U.S. Army, 1962–65; law clerk, Hon. John M. Cannella, U.S. District Court for the Southern District of New York, 1969–71; attorney with Davis Polk and Wardwell, New York, NY, 1971–85; admitted to practice New York, U.S. Supreme Court, U.S. Court of Appeals for Second and Third Circuits, U.S. Court of International Trade, U.S. Court of Claims, U.S. District Courts for Eastern, Southern and Northern Districts of New York, Interstate Commerce Commission; adjunct professor of law, Benjamin N. Cardozo School of Law, 1984–95; Mem., Drew University Board of Visitors, 1997–present; appointed to the U.S. Court of International Trade by President Reagan on February 22, 1985; confirmed by U.S. Senate, April 3, 1985.

NICHOLAS TSOUCALAS, senior judge; born in New York, NY, August 24, 1926; one of five children of George M. and Maria (Monogenis) Tsoucalas; married to Catherine Aravantinos; two daughters: Stephanie and Georgia; five grandchildren; B.S., Kent State University, 1949; LL.B., New York Law School, 1951; attended New York University Law School; entered U.S. Navy, 1944–46; served in the American and European Theaters of War on board the USS Oden, the USS Monticello and USS Europa; reentered Navy, 1951–52 and served on the carrier, USS Wasp; admitted to New York Bar, 1953; appointed Assistant U.S. Attorney for the Southern District of New York, 1955–59; appointed in 1959 as supervisor of 1960 census for the 17th and 18th Congressional Districts; appointed chairman, Board of Commissioners of Appraisal; appointed judge of Criminal Court of the City of New York, 1968; designated acting Supreme Court Justice, Kings and Queens Counties, 1975–82; resumed service as judge of the Criminal Court of the City of New York until June 1986; former chairman: Committee on Juvenile Delinquency, Federal Bar Association, and the Subcommittee on Public Order and Responsibility of the American Citizenship Committee of the New York County Lawyers' Association; member of the American Bar Association, New York State Bar Association; founder of Eastern Orthodox Lawyers' Association; former president: Greek-American Lawyers' Association, and Board of Directors of Greek Orthodox Church of "Evangelismos", St. John's Theologos Society, and Parthenon Foundation; member, Order of Ahepa, Parthenon Lodge, F.A.M.; appointed judge of the U.S. Court of International Trade by President Reagan on September 9, 1985, and confirmed by U.S. Senate on June 6, 1986; assumed senior status on September 30, 1996.

R. KENTON MUSGRAVE, senior judge; born in Clearwater, FL, September 7, 1927; married May 7, 1949 to former Ruth Shippen Hoppe, of Atlanta, GA; three children: Laura Marie Musgrave (deceased), Ruth Shippen Musgrave, Esq., and Forest Kenton Musgrave; attended Augusta Academy (Virginia); B.A., University of Washington, 1948; editorial staff, Journal of International Law, Emory University; J.D., with distinction, Emory University, 1953; assistant general counsel, Lockheed Aircraft and Lockheed International, 1953–62; vice president and general counsel, Mattel, Inc., 1963–71; director, Ringling Bros. and Barnum and Bailey Combined Shows, Inc., 1968–72; commissioner, BSA (Atlanta), 1952–55; partner, Musgrave, Welbourn and Fertman, 1972–75; assistant general counsel, Pacific Enterprises, 1975–81; vice president, general counsel and secretary, Vivitar Corporation, 1981–85; vice president and director, Santa Barbara Applied Research Corp., 1982–87; trustee, Morris Animal Foundation, 1981–94; director Emeritus, Pet Protection Society, 1981–present; director, Dolphins of Shark Bay (Australia) Foundation, 1985–present; trustee, The Dian Fossey Gorilla Fund, 1987–present; trustee, The Ocean Conservancy, 2000–present; vice president and director, South Bay Social Services Group, 1963–70; director, Palos Verdes Community Arts Association, 1973–79; member, Governor of Florida's Council of 100, 1970–73; director, Orlando Bank and Trust, 1970–73; counsel, League of Women Voters, 1964–66; member, State Bar of Georgia, 1953–present; State Bar of California, 1962–present; Los Angeles County Bar Association, 1962–87 and chairman, Corporate Law Departments Section, 1965–66; admitted to practice before the U.S. Supreme Court, 1962; Supreme Court of Georgia, 1953; California Supreme Court, 1962; U.S. Customs Court, 1967; U.S. Court of International Trade, 1980; nominated to the U.S. Court of International Trade by President Reagan on July 1, 1987; confirmed by the Senate on November 9, and took oath of office on November 13, 1987.

RICHARD W. GOLDBERG, senior judge; born in Fargo, ND, September 23, 1927; married; two children, a daughter and a son; J.D., University of Miami, 1952; served on active duty as an Air Force Judge Advocate, 1953–56; admitted to Washington, DC Bar, Florida Bar and North Dakota Bar; from 1959 to 1983, owned and operated a regional grain processing firm in North Dakota; served as State Senator from North Dakota for eight years; taught military law for the Army and Air Force ROTC at North Dakota State University; was vice-chairman of the board of Minneapolis Grain Exchange; joined the Reagan Administration in 1983 in Washington at the U.S. Department of Agriculture; served as Deputy Under Secretary for International Affairs and Commodity Programs and later as Acting Under Secretary; in 1990 joined the Washington, DC law firm of Anderson, Hibey and Blair; appointed judge of the U.S. Court of International Trade in 1991; assumed senior status in 2001.

DONALD C. POGUE, senior judge; graduated *magna cum laude*, Phi Beta Kappa from Dartmouth College; did graduate work at the University of Essex, England; J.D., Yale Law School and a Masters of Philosophy, Yale University; married 1971; served as judge in Connecticut's Superior Court; appointed to the bench in 1994; served as chairman of Connecticut's Commission on Hospitals and Health Care; practiced law in Hartford for 15 years; lectured on labor law at the University of Connecticut School of Law; assisted in teaching the Harvard Law School's program on negotiations and dispute resolution for lawyers; chaired the Connecticut Bar Association's Labor and Employment Law Section; appointed a judge of the United States Court of International Trade in 1995; Chief Judge, 2010–14; prior to becoming judge, he chaired the Court's Long Range Planning Committee and Budget Committee; he also chaired the Judicial Conference's Committee on the Administrative Office; service by designation in the 2d, 3d, 5th, 9th, 11th and Federal Circuits and in the D.C. and New York Southern district courts. Judge Pogue also serves as a member of the Judicial Conference.

JUDITH M. BARZILAY, senior judge; born in Russell, KS, January 3, 1944; husband, Sal (Doron) Barzilay; children, Ilan and Michael; parents, Arthur and Hilda Morgenstern; B.A., Wichita State University, 1965; M.L.S., Rutgers University School of Library and Information Science, 1971; J.D., Rutgers University School of Law, 1981, Moot Court Board, 1980–81; trial attorney, U.S. Department of Justice (International Trade Field Office), 1983–86; litigation associate, Siegel, Mandell and Davidson, New York, NY, 1986–88; Sony Corporation of America, 1988–98; customs and international trade counsel, 1988–89; vice-president for import and export operations, 1989–96; vice-president for government affairs, 1996–98; executive board of the American Association of Exporters and Importers, 1993–98; appointed by Treasury Secretary Robert Rubin to the Advisory Committee on Commercial Operations of the United States Customs Service, 1995–98; nominated for appointment on January 27, 1998 by President Clinton; sworn in as judge June 3, 1998.

RICHARD K. EATON, senior judge; born in Walton, NY; married to Susan Henshaw Jones; two children: Alice and Elizabeth; attended Walton public schools; B.A., Ithaca College, J.D., Union University Albany Law School, 1974; professional experience: Eaton and Eaton, partner; Mudge Rose Guthrie Alexander and Ferdon, New York, NY, associate and partner; Stroock and Stroock and Lavan, partner; served on the staff of Senator Daniel Patrick Moynihan; confirmed by the United States Senate to the U.S. Court of International Trade on October 22, 1999.

OFFICERS OF THE UNITED STATES COURT OF INTERNATIONAL TRADE

Clerk.—Tina Potuto Kimble (212) 264–2814.

UNITED STATES COURT OF FEDERAL CLAIMS

Lafayette Square, 717 Madison Place, NW., 20439, phone (202) 357–6406

PATRICIA E. CAMPBELL-SMITH, chief judge; born in Baltimore, MD, 1966; B.S.E.E., Duke University, 1987; J.D., Tulane Law School, 1992; admitted to the Bar of Louisiana; judicial extern to Hon. John Minor Wisdom, U.S. Court of Appeals for the Fifth Circuit, 1991; law clerk to Hon. Martin L. C. Feldman, U.S. District Court for Eastern District of Louisiana, 1992–93; associate, Liskow and Lewis, 1993–96, 1997–98; law clerk to Hon. Sarah S. Vance (Chief Judge), U.S. District Court for Eastern District of Louisiana, 1996–97; senior law clerk to Hon. Emily C. Hewitt (Chief Judge), U.S. Court of Federal Claims, 1998–2005; special master, U.S. Court of Federal Claims, 2005–11; chief special master, U.S. Court of Federal Claims, 2011–13; appointed to the U.S. Court of Federal Claims by President Obama on September 19, 2013; appointed chief judge on October 21, 2013.

MARIAN BLANK HORN, judge; born in New York, NY, 1943; daughter of Werner P. and Mady R. Blank; married to Robert Jack Horn; three daughters; attended Fieldston School, New York, NY, Barnard College, Columbia University and Fordham University School of Law; admitted to practice U.S. Supreme Court, 1973, Federal and State courts in New York, 1970, and Washington, DC, 1973; assistant district attorney, Deputy Chief Appeals Bureau, Bronx County, NY, 1969–72; attorney, Arent, Fox, Kintner, Plotkin and Kahn, 1972–73; adjunct professor of law, Washington College of Law, American University, 1973–76; litigation attorney, Federal Energy Administration, 1975–76; senior attorney, Office of General Counsel, Strategic Petroleum Reserve Branch, Department of Energy, 1976–79; deputy assistant general counsel for procurement and financial incentives, Department of Energy, 1979–81; deputy associate solicitor, Division of Surface Mining, Department of the Interior, 1981–83; associate solicitor, Division of General Law, Department of the Interior, 1983–85; principal deputy solicitor and acting solicitor, Department of Interior, 1985–86; adjunct professor of law, George Washington University National Law Center, 1991–present; Woodrow Wilson Visiting Fellow, 1994; assumed duties of judge, U.S. Court of Federal Claims in 1986 and confirmed for a second term in 2003.

LAWRENCE J. BLOCK, judge, born in New York City, March 15, 1951; son of Jerome Block and Eve Silver; B.A., *magna cum laude*, New York University, 1973; J.D., The John Marshall Law School, 1981; law clerk for Hon. Roger J. Miner, United States District Court Judge for Northern District of New York, 1981–83; associate, New York office of Skadden, Arps, Slate, Meagher and Flom, 1983–86; attorney, Commercial Litigation Branch, U.S. Department of Justice, 1986; senior attorney-advisor, Office of Legal Policy and Policy Development, U.S. Department of Justice, 1987–90; adjunct professor, George Mason University School of Law, 1990–91; acting general counsel for legal policy and deputy assistant general counsel for legal policy, U.S. Department of Energy, 1990–94; senior counsel, Senate Judiciary Committee, 1994–02; admitted to the bar of Connecticut; admitted to practice in the U.S. Supreme Court, 1982, the United States District Court for the northern district of New York, 1982, the U.S. Court of Appeals for the Eleventh Circuit, 1985, the United States District Court for the Eastern District of New York, 1985; appointed by President George W. Bush on October 3, 2002, to a 15–year term as judge, U.S. Court of Federal Claims.

SUSAN G. BRADEN, judge, born in Youngstown, OH, November 8, 1948; married to Thomas M. Susman; daughter (Daily); B.A., Case Western Reserve University, 1970; J.D., Case Western Reserve University School of Law, 1973; post graduate study Harvard Law School, Summer, 1979; private practice, 1985–2003 (1997–2003 Baker and McKenzie); Federal Trade Commission: special counsel to Chairman, 1984–85, senior attorney advisor to Commissioner and Acting Chairman, 1980–83; U.S. Department of Justice, Antitrust Division, Senior Trial Attorney, Energy Section, 1978–80; Cleveland Field Office, 1973–78; Special Assistant Attorney General for the State of Alabama, 1990; Consultant to the Administrative Conference of the United States, 1984–85; 2000 co-chair, Lawyers for Bush-Cheney; General Counsel Presidential Debate for Dole-Kemp Campaign, 1996; counsel to RNC Platform, 1996; coordinator for Regulatory Reform and Antitrust Policy, Dole Presidential Campaign, 1995–96;

National Steering Committee, Lawyers for Bush-Quayle, 1992; Assistant General Counsel, Republican National Convention, 1988, 1992, 1996, 2000; elected At-Large Member, D.C. Republican National Committee, 2000–02; member of the American Bar Association (Council Member, Section on Administrative Law and Regulatory Practice, 1996–99), Federal Circuit Bar Association, District of Columbia Bar Association, Computer Law Bar Association; admitted to the Supreme Court of Ohio, 1973, U.S. District Court for the District of Columbia, 1980, U.S. Supreme Court, 1980; U.S. Court of Appeals for the District of Columbia, 1992; U.S. Court of Appeals for the Second Circuit, 1993, U.S. Court of Appeals for the Federal Circuit, 2001; appointed to the U.S. Court of Federal Claims by President George W. Bush on July 14, 2003.

CHARLES F. LETTOW, judge, born in Iowa Falls, IA, 1941; son of Carl F. and Catherine Lettow; B.S.Ch.E., Iowa State University, 1962; LL.B., Stanford University, 1968, Order of the Coif; M.A., Brown University, 2001; Note Editor, Stanford Law Review; married to B. Sue Lettow; children: Renee Burnett, Carl Frederick II, John Stangland, and Paul Vorbeck; served U.S. Army, 1963–65; law clerk to Judge Ben C. Duniway, U.S. Court of Appeals for the Ninth Circuit, 1968–69, and Chief Justice Warren E. Burger, Supreme Court of the United States, 1969–70; counsel, Council on Environmental Quality, Executive Office of the President, 1970–73; associate (1973–76) and partner (1976–2003), Cleary, Gottlieb, Steen and Hamilton, Washington, DC; admitted to practice before the U.S. Supreme Court, the U.S. Courts of Appeals for the D.C., Second, Third, Fourth, Fifth, Sixth, Eighth, Ninth, Tenth, and Federal Circuits, the U.S. District Courts for the District of Columbia, the Northern District of California, and the District of Maryland, and the U.S. Court of Federal Claims; member: American Law Institute, the American Bar Association, the D.C. Bar, the California State Bar, the Iowa State Bar Association, and the Maryland State Bar; nominated by President George W. Bush to the U.S. Court of Federal Claims in 2001 and confirmed and took office in 2003.

MARY ELLEN COSTER WILLIAMS, judge; born in Flushing, NY, April 3, 1953; married with two children; B.A. *summa cum laude* (Greek and Latin) and M.A. (Latin), The Catholic University of America, 1974; J.D. Duke University, 1977; Editorial Board, Duke Law Journal, 1976–77; admitted to the District of Columbia Bar; associate, Fulbright and Jaworski, 1977–79; associate, Schnader, Harrison, Segal and Lewis, 1979–83; Assistant U.S. Attorney, Civil Division, District of Columbia, 1983–87; partner, Janis, Schuelke and Wechsler, 1987–89; administrative judge, General Services Board of Contract Appeals, March 1989–July 2003; secretary, District of Columbia Bar, 1988–89; Fellow, American Bar Foundation, elected 1985; Board of Directors, Bar Association of the District of Columbia, 1985–88; Chairman, Young Lawyers Section, Bar Association of the District of Columbia, 1985–86; Chair, Public Contract Law Section of the American Bar Association, 2002–03; Chair-Elect, Vice-Chair, Secretary, Council, 1995–2002; Delegate, Section of Public Contract Law, ABA House of Delegates, 2003–08 and 2014–present; ABA Board of Governors, 2010–13; Adjunct Professor, Johns Hopkins University, 2006–present; Adjunct Professor, The Catholic University of America Columbus School of Law, 2004–06; appointed to the U.S. Court of Federal Claims on July 21, 2003.

VICTOR JOHN WOLSKI, judge; born in New Brunswick, NJ, November 14, 1962; son of Vito and Eugenia Wolski; B.A., B.S., University of Pennsylvania, 1984; J.D., University of Virginia School of Law, 1991; married to Lisa Wolski; admitted to Supreme Court of the United States, 1995; California Supreme Court, 1992; Washington Supreme Court, 1994; Oregon Supreme Court, 1996; District of Columbia Court of Appeals, 2001; U.S. Court of Appeals for the Ninth Circuit, 1993; U.S. Court of Appeals for the Federal Circuit, 2001; U.S. District Court for the Eastern District of California, 1993; U.S. District Court for the Northern District of California, 1995; U.S. Court of Federal Claims, 2001; U.S. District Court for the District of Columbia, 2002; research assistant, Center for Strategic and International Studies, 1984–85; research associate, Institute for Political Economy, 1985–88; confidential assistant and speechwriter to the Secretary, U.S. Department of Agriculture, 1988; paralegal specialist, Office of the general counsel, U.S. Department of Energy, 1989; law clerk to Judge Vaughn R. Walker, U.S. District Court for the Northern District of California, 1991–92; attorney, Pacific Legal Foundation, 1992–97; general counsel, Sacramento County Republican Central Committee, 1995–97; counsel Senator Connie Mack, Vice-Chairman of the Joint Economic Committee, U.S. Congress, 1997–98; general counsel and chief tax adviser, Joint Economic Committee, U.S. Congress, 1999–2000; associate, Cooper, Carvin and Rosenthal, 2000–01; associate, Cooper and Kirk, 2001–03; associate editor, *Public Contract Law Journal*, 2006–present; appointed by President George W. Bush to the U.S. Court of Federal Claims on July 14, 2003.

THOMAS C. WHEELER, judge; born in Chicago, IL, March 18, 1948; married; two grown children; B.A., Gettysburg College, 1970; J.D., Georgetown University Law School, 1973; private practice in Washington, DC, 1973 2005; associate and partner, Pettit and Martin until 1995; partner, Piper and Marbury (later Piper Marbury Rudnick and Wolfe, and then DLA Piper Rudnick Gray Cary); member of the District of Columbia Bar; American Bar Association's Public Contracts and Litigation Sections; appointed to the U.S. Court of Federal Claims on October 24, 2005.

MARGARET M. SWEENEY, judge; born in Baltimore, MD; B.A. in history, Notre Dame of Maryland, 1977; J.D., Delaware Law School, 1981; Delaware Family Court Master, 1981–83; litigation associate, Fedorko, Gilbert, and Lanctot, Morrisville, PA, 1983–85; law clerk to Hon. Loren A. Smith, Chief Judge of the U.S. Court of Federal Claims, 1985–87; trial attorney in the General Litigation Section of the Environment and Natural Resources Division of the United States Department of Justice, 1987–99; president, U.S. Court of Federal Claims Bar Association, 1999; attorney advisor, United States Department of Justice Office of Intelligence Policy and Review, 1999–2003; special master, U.S. Court of Federal Claims, 2003–05; member of the Bars of the Supreme Court of Pennsylvania and the District of Columbia Court of Appeals; appointed to the U.S. Court of Federal Claims by President George W. Bush on October 24, 2005, and entered duty on December 14, 2005.

ELAINE D. KAPLAN, judge; born in Brooklyn, New York, December 18, 1955; B.A., State University of New York at Binghamton, 1976; J.D., Georgetown University, 1979; Office of the Solicitor General, Department of Labor, 1979–83; Attorney, State and Local Legal Center, 1983–84; Attorney and Deputy General Counsel, National Treasury Employees Union, 1984–98; Special Counsel, Office of Special Counsel, 1998–03; Of Counsel, Bernabei and Katz, 2003–04; Senior Deputy General Counsel, National Treasury Employees Union, 2004–09; General Counsel, U.S. Office of Personnel Management, 2009–13; Acting Director, U.S. Office of Personnel Management, 2013; appointed to the U.S. Court of Federal Claims by President Barack Obama on September 17, 2013.

LYDIA KAY GRIGGSBY, judge; born in Baltimore, MD, January 16, 1968; educated at the Park School, Brooklandville, MD, 1980–86; B.A., University of Pennsylvania, 1990; J.D., Georgetown University Law Center, 1993; member, Bar of Maryland and Bar of the District of Columbia; private practice of law, DLA Piper, 1993–95; Trial Attorney, United States Department of Justice, Civil Division, Commercial Litigation Branch, 1995–98; Assistant United States Attorney, United States Attorney's Office for the District of Columbia, 1998–2004; Counsel, United States Senate Select Committee on Ethics, 2004–06; Privacy Counsel, United States Senate Committee on the Judiciary, 2006–08; Chief Counsel for Privacy and information Policy, United States Senate Committee on the Judiciary 2008–14; appointed by President Obama to the U.S. Court of Federal Claims on December 5, 2014; entered duty on December 15, 2014.

SENIOR JUDGES

JAMES F. MEROW, senior judge; born in Salamanca, NY; educated in the public schools of Little Valley, NY and Alexandria, VA; A.B. (with distinction), George Washington University, 1953; J.D. (with distinction), George Washington University Law School, 1956; member: Phi Beta Kappa, Order of the Coif, Omicron Delta Kappa; married; officer, U.S. Army Judge Advocate General's Corps, 1956–59; trial attorney-branch director, Civil Division, U.S. Department of Justice, 1959–78; trial judge, U.S. Court of Claims, 1978–82; member of Virginia State Bar, District of Columbia Bar, American Bar Association, and Federal Bar Association; judge, U.S. Court of Federal Claims since October 1, 1982, reappointed by President Reagan to a 15-year term commencing August 5, 1983; assumed senior judge status on August 5, 1998.

JOHN PAUL WIESE, senior judge; born in Brooklyn, NY, April 19, 1934; son of Gustav and Margaret Wiese; B.A., *cum laude*, Hobart College, 1962, Phi Beta Kappa; LL.B., University of Virginia School of Law, 1965; married to Alice Mary Donoghue, June, 1961; one son, John Patrick; served U.S. Army, 1957–59; law clerk: U.S. Court of Claims, trial division, 1965–66, and Judge Linton M. Collins, U.S. Court of Claims, appellate division, 1966–67; private practice in District of Columbia, 1967–74 (specializing in government contract litigation); trial judge, U.S. Court of Claims, 1974–82; admitted to the Bar of the District of Columbia, 1966; admitted to practice in the U.S. Supreme Court, the U.S. Court of Appeals for the Federal Circuit, the U.S. Court of Federal Claims; member: District of Columbia Bar Association and American Bar Association; designated in Federal Courts Improvement Act of 1982 as judge, U.S. Court of Federal Claims and reappointed by President Reagan to 15-year term on October 14, 1986.

ERIC G. BRUGGINK, senior judge; born in Kalidjati, Indonesia, September 11, 1949; naturalized U.S. citizen, 1961; married to Melinda Harris Bruggink; sons: John and David; B.A., *cum laude* (sociology), Auburn University, AL, 1971; M.A. (speech), 1972; J.D., University of Alabama, 1975; Hugo Black Scholar and Note and Comments Editor of *Alabama Law Review*; member, Alabama State Bar and District of Columbia Bar; served as law clerk to chief judge Frank H. McFadden, Northern District of Alabama, 1975–76; associate, Hardwick, Hause and Segrest, Dothan, AL, 1976–77; assistant director, Alabama Law Institute, 1977–79; director, Office of Energy and Environmental Law, 1977–79; associate, Steiner, Crum and Baker, Montgomery, AL, 1979–82; Director, Office of Appeals Counsel, Merit Systems Protection Board, 1982–86; appointed to the U.S. Court of Federal Claims on April 15, 1986.

LYNN J. BUSH, senior judge; born in Little Rock, AR, December 30, 1948; daughter of John E. Bush III and Alice (Saville) Bush; one son, Brian Bush Ferguson; B.A., Antioch College, 1970; Thomas J. Watson Fellow; J.D., Georgetown University Law Center, 1976; admitted to the Arkansas Bar in 1976 and to the District of Columbia Bar in 1977; trial attorney, Commercial Litigation Branch, Civil Division, U.S. Department of Justice, 1976–87; senior trial attorney, Naval Facilities Engineering Command, Department of the Navy, 1987–89; counsel, Engineering Field Activity Chesapeake, Naval Facilities Engineering Command, Department of the Navy, 1989–96; administrative judge, U.S. Department of Housing and Urban Development Board of Contract Appeals, 1996–98; nominated by President Clinton to the U.S. Court of Federal Claims, June 22, 1998; and assumed duties of the office on October 26, 1998.

EDWARD J. DAMICH, senior judge; born in Pittsburgh, PA, June 19, 1948; son of John and Josephine (Lovrencic) Damich; A.B., St. Stephen's College, 1970; J.D., Catholic University, 1976; professor of law at Delaware School of Law of Widener University, 1976–84; served as a Law and Economics Fellow at Columbia University School of Law, where he earned his L.L.M. in 1983 and his J.S.D. in 1991; professor of law at George Mason University, 1984–98; appointed by President George H.W. Bush to be a Commissioner of the Copyright Royalty Tribunal, 1992–93; Chief Intellectual Property Counsel for the Senate Judiciary Committee, 1995–98; admitted to the Bar of the District of Columbia; member of the District of Columbia Bar Association, American Bar Association, Supreme Court of the United States, the Federal Circuit and *Association littéraire et artistique internationale*; president of the National Federation of Croatian Americans, 1994–95; appointed by President Clinton as judge, U.S. Court of Federal Claims, October 22, 1998; served as chief judge May 13, 2002–March 11, 2009.

NANCY B. FIRESTONE, senior judge; born in Manchester, NH, October 17, 1951; B.A., Washington University, 1973; J.D., University of Missouri, Kansas City, 1977; one child: attorney, Appellate Section and Environmental Enforcement Section, U.S. Department of Justice, Washington, DC, 1977–84; assistant chief, Policy Legislation and Special Litigation, Environment and Natural Resources Division, Department of Justice, Washington, DC, 1984–85; Deputy Chief, Environmental Enforcement Section, Department of Justice, Washington, DC, 1985–89; associate deputy administrator, Environmental Protection Agency, Washington, DC, 1989–92; judge, Environmental Appeals Board, Environmental Protection Agency, Washington, DC, 1992–95; Deputy Assistant Attorney General, Environment and Natural Resources Division, Department of Justice, Washington, DC, 1995–98; adjunct professor, Georgetown University Law Center, 1985–present; appointed to the U.S. Court of Federal Claims by President Clinton on October 22, 1998.

UNITED STATES TAX COURT

400 Second Street, NW., 20217, phone (202) 521–0700

MICHAEL B. THORNTON, chief judge; born in Mississippi; B.S. in Accounting, *summa cum laude*, University of Southern Mississippi, 1976; M.S. in Accounting, 1997; M.A. in English Literature, University of Tennessee, 1979; J.D. (with distinction), Duke University School of Law, 1982; Order of the Coif, Duke Law Journal Editorial Board; admitted to District of Columbia Bar, 1982; served as Law Clerk to the Honorable Charles Clark, Chief Judge, U.S. Court of Appeals for the Fifth Circuit, 1983–84; practiced law as an Associate Attorney, Sutherland, Asbill and Brennan, Washington, DC, 1982–83 and summer 1981; Miller and Chevalier, Chartered, Washington, DC, 1985–88; served as Tax Counsel, U.S. House Committee on Ways and Means, 1988–93; Chief Minority Tax Counsel, U.S. House Committee on Ways and Means, January 1995; Attorney-Adviser, U.S. Treasury Department, February–April 1995; Deputy Tax Legislative Counsel in the Office of Tax Policy, United States Treasury Department, April 1995–February 1998; recipient of Treasury Secretary's Annual Award, U.S. Department of the Treasury, 1997; Meritorious Service Award, U.S. Department of the Treasury, 1998; appointed by President Clinton as Judge, United States Tax Court, on March 8, 1998, for a term ending March 7, 2013; served as Chief Judge from June 1, 2012, to March 7, 2013; reappointed by President Obama on August 7, 2013, for a term ending August 6, 2028, and at that time resumed the position of Chief Judge.

JOHN O. COLVIN, judge; born in Ohio; A.B., University of Missouri, 1968; J.D., 1971; LL.M., Taxation, Georgetown University Law Center, 1978; admitted to practice law in Missouri (1971) and District of Columbia (1974); Office of the Chief Counsel, U.S. Coast Guard, Washington, DC, 1971–75; served as Tax Counsel, Senator Bob Packwood, 1975–84; Chief Counsel (1985–87), and Chief Minority Counsel (1987–88), U.S. Senate Finance Committee; past Chair, Tax Section, Federal Bar Association and recipient of the FBA Tax Section's Liles Award; Adjunct Professor of Law, Georgetown University Law Center and recipient of Charles Fahy Distinguished Adjunct Professor Award; appointed by President Reagan as Judge, United States Tax Court, on September 1, 1988, for a term ending August 31, 2003; reappointed on August 12, 2004, for a term ending August 11, 2019; served as Chief Judge for two-year terms beginning June 1, 2006, June 1, 2008, and June 1, 2010; served as Chief Judge for an interim period effective March 8, 2013, to August 7, 2013.

JAMES S. HALPERN, judge; born in New York; Hackley School, Terrytown, NY, 1963; D.S., Wharton School, University of Pennsylvania, 1967; J.D., University of Pennsylvania Law School, 1972; LL.M., Taxation, New York University Law School, 1975; Associate Attorney, Mudge, Rose, Guthrie and Alexander, New York City, 1972–74; assistant professor of law, Washington and Lee University, 1975–76; assistant professor of law, St. John's University, New York City, 1976–78; visiting professor, Law School, New York University, 1978–79; associate attorney, Roberts and Holland, New York City, 1979–80; Principal Technical Advisor, Assistant Commissioner (Technical) and Associate Chief Counsel (Technical), Internal Revenue Service, Washington, DC, 1980–83; partner, Baker and Hostetler, Washington, DC, 1983–90; Adjunct Professor, George Washington University Law School, Washington, DC, 1984–present; Colonel, U.S. Army Reserve (retired); appointed by President George H.W. Bush as Judge, United States Tax Court, on July 3, 1990, for a term ending July 2, 2005; reappointed on November 2, 2005, for a term ending November 1, 2020.

MAURICE B. FOLEY, judge; born in Illinois; B.A., Swarthmore College; J.D., Boalt Hall School of Law at the University of California at Berkeley; LL.M., Georgetown University Law Center; attorney for the Legislation and Regulations Division of the Internal Revenue Service, Tax Counsel for the United States Senate Committee on Finance; Deputy Tax Legislative Counsel in the U.S. Treasury's Office of Tax Policy; appointed by President Clinton as Judge, United States Tax Court, on April 9, 1995, for a term ending April 8, 2010; reappointed on November 25, 2011, for a term ending November 24, 2026.

JUAN F. VASQUEZ, judge; born in San Antonio, Texas; attended Fox Tech High School; A.D. (Data Processing), San Antonio Junior College; B.B.A. (Accounting), University of Texas, Austin, 1972; attended State University of New York, Buffalo in 1st year law school, 1975; J.D., University of Houston Law Center, 1977; LL.M., Taxation, New York University Law School of Law, 1978; Certified Public Accountant, Certificate from Texas, 1976; admitted to State Bar of Texas, 1977; admitted to the United States Tax Court, 1978; certified in tax law by Texas Board of Legal Specialization, 1984; admitted to the United States District Court, Southern District of Texas, 1982, Western District of Texas, 1985 and United States Court of Appeals for the Fifth Circuit, 1982; and the Supreme Court of the United States of America, 1996; private practice of tax law, in San Antonio, TX, 1987–April 1995; partner, Leighton, Hood and Vasquez, in San Antonio, TX, 1982–87; Trial Attorney, Office of Chief Counsel, Internal Revenue Service, Houston, TX, 1978–82; accountant, Coopers and Lybrand, Los Angeles, CA, 1972–74; member of American Bar Association, Tax Section; Texas State Bar, Tax Section; Fellow of Texas and San Antonio Bar Foundations; College of State Bar of Texas; National Hispanic Bar Association and Hispanic Bar Association of the District of Columbia; Mexican American Bar Association (MABA) of San Antonio 1982–95; Houston MABA 1978–82; Texas MABA 1986–88; National Association of Hispanic CPA's San Antonio Chapter (founding member) 1983–88; member of Greater Austin Tax Litigation Association 1989–95; served on Austin Internal Revenue Service District Director's Practitioner Liaison Committee, 1990–91 (chairman, 1991); appointed by President Clinton as Judge, United States Tax Court, on May 1, 1995, for a term ending April 30, 2010; reappointed by President Barack Obama on October 13, 2011, for a term ending October 12, 2026.

JOSEPH H. GALE, judge; born in Virginia; A.B., Philosophy, Princeton University, 1976; J.D., University of Virginia School of Law, Dillard Fellow, 1980; practiced law as an Associate Attorney, Dewey Ballantine, Washington, DC, and New York, 1980–83; Dickstein, Shapiro and Morin, Washington, DC, 1983–85; served as Tax Legislative Counsel for Senator Daniel Patrick Moynihan (D–NY), 1985–88; Administrative Assistant and Tax Legislative Counsel, 1989; Chief Counsel, 1990–93; Chief Tax Counsel, Committee on Finance, U.S. Senate, 1993–95; minority Chief Tax Counsel, Senate Finance Committee, January 1995–July 1995; minority Staff Director and Chief Counsel, Senate Finance Committee, July 1995–January 1996; admitted to District of Columbia Bar; member of American Bar Association, Section of Taxation; appointed by President Clinton as Judge, United States Tax Court, February 6, 1996, for a term ending February 5, 2011; reappointed on October 18, 2011, for a term ending October 17, 2026.

L. PAIGE MARVEL, judge; born in Maryland; B.A., *magna cum laude*, College of Notre Dame, 1971; J.D. with honors, University of Maryland School of Law, Baltimore, MD, 1974; Order of the Coif; member, Maryland Law Review and Moot Court Board; Garbis and Schwait, P.A., associate (1974–76) and shareholder (1976–85); shareholder, Garbis, Marvel and Junghans, P.A., 1985–86; shareholder, Melnicove, Kaufman, Weiner, Smouse and Garbis, P.A., 1986–88; partner, Venabel, Baetjer and Howard LLP, 1988–98; member, American Bar Association, Section of Taxation, Vice-Chair, Committee Operations, 1993–95; Council Director 1989–92; Chair, Court Procedure Committee, 1985–87; Maryland State Bar Association, Board of Governors, 1988–90, and 1996–98; Chair, Taxation Section 1982–83; Federal Bar Association, Section of Taxation, Section Council, 1984–90; Fellow, American Bar Foundation; Fellow, Maryland Bar Foundation; fellow and former Regent, American College of Tax Counsel, 1996–98; member, American Law Institute; advisor, ALI *Restatement of Law, Third, The Law Governing Lawyers* 1988–98; University of Maryland Law School Board of Visitors, 1995–2001; Loyola/Notre Dame Library, Inc. Board of Trustees, 1996–2003; Advisory Committee, University of Baltimore Graduate Tax Program, 1986–present; Co-editor, Procedure Department, The Journal of Taxation, 1990–98; member, Commissioner's Review Panel on IRS Integrity, 1989–91; member and Chair, Procedure Subcommittee, Commission to Revise the Annotated Code of Maryland (Tax Provisions), 1981–87; member, Advisory Commission to the Maryland State Department of Economic and Community Development, 1978–81; recipient, President's Medal, College of Notre Dame, 2006; Jules Ritholz award, ABA Tax Section's Civil and Criminal Tax Penalties Comm., 2004; First Annual Tax Excellence Award, Maryland State Bar Association Tax Section, 2002; named one of Maryland's Top 100 Women, 1998; recipient, ABA Tax Section's Distinguished Service Award, 1995; MSBA Distinguished Service Award, 1982–83; listed in *Best Lawyers in America*, 1991–98, *Who's Who in America*, *Who's Who in American Law*, *Who's Who in the East*; author of various articles and book chapters on tax and tax litigation topics; appointed by President Clinton as Judge, United States Tax Court, on April 6, 1998, for a term ending April 5, 2013; reappointed by President Obama on December 3, 2014, for a term ending December 2, 2029.

JOSEPH ROBERT GOEKE, judge; born in Kentucky; B.S., *cum laude*, Xavier University, 1972; J.D., University of Kentucky College of Law, 1975 (Order of the Coif); admitted to Illinois and Kentucky Bar, U.S. District Court for the Northern District of Illinois (Trial Bar), U.S. Court of Federal Claims; Trial Attorney, Chief Counsel's Office, Internal Revenue Service, New Orleans, LA, 1975–80; Senior Trial Attorney, Chief Counsel's Office, Internal Revenue Service, Cincinnati, OH, 1980–85; Special International Trial Attorney, Chief Counsel's Office, Internal Revenue Service, Cincinnati, OH, 1985–88; partner, Law Firm of Mayer, Brown, Rowe and Maw, Chicago, IL, 1988–2003; appointed by President George W. Bush as Judge, United States Tax Court, on April 22, 2003, for a term ending April 21, 2018.

MARK V. HOLMES, judge; born in New York; B.A., Harvard College, 1979; J.D., University of Chicago Law School, 1983; admitted to New York and District of Columbia Bars; U.S. Supreme Court; DC, Second, Fifth and Ninth Circuits; Southern and Eastern Districts of New York, Court of Federal Claims; practiced in New York as an Associate, Cahill Gordon and Reindel, 1983–85; Sullivan and Cromwell, 1987–91; served as clerk to the Hon. Alex Kozinski, Ninth Circuit, 1985–87; and in Washington, DC as Counsel to Commissioners, United States International Trade Commission, 1991–96; Counsel, Miller and Chevalier, 1996–2001; Deputy Assistant Attorney General, Tax Division, 2001–03; member, American Bar Association (Litigation and Tax Sections); appointed by President George W. Bush as Judge, United States Tax Court, on June 30, 2003, for a term ending June 29, 2018.

DAVID GUSTAFSON, judge; born in Greenville, South Carolina; Bob Jones University, B.A. *summa cum laude*, 1978. Duke University School of Law, J.D. with distinction, 1981. Order of the Coif (1981). Executive Editor of the *Duke Law Journal* (1980–81). Admitted to the District of Columbia Bar, 1981. Associate at the law firm of Sutherland, Asbill and Brennan, in Washington, DC, 1981–83. Trial Attorney (1983–89), Assistant Chief (1989–2005), and Chief (2005–08) in the Court of Federal Claims Section of the Tax Division in the U.S. Department of Justice; and Coordinator of Tax Shelter Litigation for the entire Tax Division (2002–06). Tax Division Outstanding Attorney Awards, 1985, 1989, 1997, 2001–05. Federal Bar Association's Younger Attorney Award, 1991. President of the Court of Federal Claims Bar Association (2001). Appointed by President George W. Bush as Judge, United States Tax Court, on July 29, 2008, for a term ending July 29, 2023.

ELIZABETH CREWSON PARIS, judge; born in Oklahoma; B.S., University of Tulsa, 1980; J.D., University of Tulsa College of Law, 1987; LL.M., Taxation, University of Denver College of Law, 1993. Admitted to the Supreme Court of Oklahoma and U.S. District Court for the District of Oklahoma, 1988; U.S. Tax Court, U.S. Court of Federal Claims, U.S. Court of Appeals for the Tenth Circuit, 1993; Supreme Court of Colorado, 1994. Former partner, Brumley Bishop and Paris, 1992; Senior Associate, McKenna and Cueno, 1994; Tax Partner, Reinhart, Boerner, Van Deuren, Norris and Rieselbach, 1998. Tax Counsel to the United States Senate Finance Committee, 2000–08. Member of the American Bar Association, Section of Taxation and Real Property and Probate Sections, formerly served as Vice Chair to both Agriculture and Entity Selection Committees. Member of Colorado and Oklahoma Bar Associations. Recognized as Distinguished Alumnus by the University of Tulsa School of law. Author of numerous tax, estate planning, real property, agriculture articles and chapters. Former adjunct professor, Georgetown University Law Center, LL.M. Taxation Program, and University of Tulsa College of Law. Appointed by President George W. Bush as Judge, United States Tax Court, on July 30, 2008, for a term ending July 29, 2023.

RICHARD T. MORRISON, judge; born in Hutchinson, Kansas; B.A., B.S., University of Kansas, 1989; visiting student at Mansfield College, Oxford University, 1987–88; J.D., University of Chicago Law School, 1993; M.A., University of Chicago, 1994. Clerk to Judge Jerry E. Smith, United States Court of Appeals for the Fifth Circuit, 1993–94. Associate, Baker and McKenzie, Chicago, Illinois, 1994–96. Associate, Mayer Brown and Platt, Chicago, Illinois 1996–2001. Deputy Assistant Attorney General for Review and Appellate Matters, Tax Division, United States Department of Justice, from 2001 to 2008 (except for term as Acting Assistant Attorney General, from July 2007 to January 2008). Appointed by President George W. Bush as Judge, United States Tax Court, on August 28, 2008, for a term ending August 27, 2023.

KATHLEEN KERRIGAN, judge; born in Springfield, Massachusetts; B.S., Boston College 1985; J.D., University of Notre Dame Law School, 1990; admitted to Massachusetts Bar, 1991 and District Columbia Bar, 1992; Legislative Director for Congressman Richard E. Neal, Member of the Ways and Means Committee, 1990 to 1998; associate and partner at Baker and Hostetler LLP, Washington, DC, 1998–2005; tax counsel for Senator John F. Kerry, Member of Senate Finance Committee, 2005–12; appointed by President Barack Obama as Judge, United States, Tax Court, on May 4, 2012, for a term ending on May 3, 2027.

RONALD L. BUCH, judge; born in Flint, Michigan; B.B.A., Northwood Institute, 1987; J.D. with Taxation Concentration, Detroit College of Law, 1993; LL.M. in Taxation, Capital University Law School, 1994; Research Editor of the *Detroit College of Law Review*, 1992–93; Ohio Tax Review Fellow, 1993–94; admitted to the bars of Michigan, inactive (1993), Ohio, inactive (1994), Florida (1994), and the District of Columbia (1995); consultant at KPMG Washington National Tax (1995–97); Attorney-Advisor (1997–2000) and Senior Legal Counsel (2000–01) at the IRS Office of Chief Counsel; associate (2001–05) and partner (2005–09) at McKee Nelson LLP; partner at Bingham McCutchen LLP (2009–13); James E. Markham Attorney of the Year Award, 1999; Chair of the DC Bar Tax Audits and Litigation Committee, 2006–08; Chair of the ABA Tax Section's Administrative Practice Committee, 2008–09; appointed by President Barack H. Obama as Judge, United States Tax Court, on January 14, 2013, for a term ending January 13, 2028.

ALBERT G. LAUBER, judge; born in Bronxville, New York; Yale College (B.A., *summa cum laude*, 1971); Clare College, Cambridge University (M.A., Classics, 1974); Yale Law School (J.D., 1977). Phi Beta Kappa; Woodrow Wilson Fellow; Mellon Fellow; Note Editor, *Yale Law Journal*; Moot Court Prize Argument; Cardozo Prize, Best Moot Court Brief. Law Clerk to Malcolm R. Wilkey, U.S. Court of Appeals for the DC Circuit (1977–78); Law Clerk to Justice Harry A. Blackmun, U.S. Supreme Court (1978–79). Associate Attorney, Caplin and Drysdale, Chtd., Washington, DC (1979–83); Tax Assistant to the Solicitor General, U.S. Department of Justice (1983–86); Deputy Solicitor General, U.S. Department of Justice (1986–87); Partner, Caplin and Drysdale, Chtd., Washington, DC (1988–2005); Visiting Professor and Director, Graduate Tax and Securities Programs, Georgetown University Law Center (2006–13). Professorial Lecturer, George Washington University Law School (1983–84); Lecturer, University of Virginia Law School (1988–90); Adjunct Professor, Georgetown University Law Center (2013–present); Board of Trustees, the Studio Theatre (1993–present); Member, District of Columbia Alcoholic Beverage Control Board (2004–08). Admitted to the Bars of the District of Columbia (1978); U.S. Supreme Court (1983); U.S. Court of Appeals, DC Circuit (1983); U.S. Court of Appeals, Federal Circuit (1994); Connecticut (inactive); Member, American Bar Association, Section of Taxation; appointed by President Barack H. Obama as Judge, United States Tax Court, on January 31, 2013, for a term ending January 30, 2028.

JOSEPH W. NEGA, judge; born in Illinois; DePaul University, B.S.C. in Accounting, 1981; DePaul University School of Law, J.D., 1984; Georgetown University School of Law, M.L.T., 1986. Admitted to the Illinois Bar, 1984. On staff of the Joint Committee on Taxation of the United States Congress: Legislation Attorney, 1985–1989; Legislation Counsel, 1989–2009; and Senior Legislation Counsel, 2009–2013; appointed by President Barack H. Obama as Judge, United States Tax Court, on September 4, 2013, for a term ending September 3, 2028.

CARY DOUGLAS PUGH, judge; born in Virginia; B.A., in Political Science and Russian, *magna cum laude*, Duke University, 1987; M.A., in Russian and East European Studies, Stanford University, 1988; J.D., University of Virginia School of Law, 1994; Order of the Coif, *Virginia Law Review* Executive Editor. Admitted to Virginia State Bar, 1994, District of Columbia Bar, 1995, United States Supreme Court Bar, 1997. Served as Law Clerk to the Honorable Jackson L. Kiser, Chief Judge, U.S. District Court, Western District of Virginia, 1994–1995. Practiced law as an Associate, Vinson and Elkins LLP, Washington, DC, 1995–1999. Served as Minority Tax Counsel and Majority Tax Counsel, Committee on Finance, United States Senate, 1999–2002. Served as Special Counsel to the Chief Counsel, 2002–2005. Recipient of the Chief Counsel's Award 2003. Practiced law as Counsel, Skadden, Arps, Slate, Meagher and Flom LLP, 2005–2014. Member of American Bar Association, Section of Taxation; named John S. Nolan Tax Law Fellow, 2001–2002; served as Chair, Tax Shelter Committee and Government Relations Committee and as Council Director. Fellow, American College of Tax Counsel. Former Adjunct Professor, Georgetown University Law Center, LL.M. Taxation Program; appointed by President Obama as Judge, United States Tax Court, on December 16, 2014, for a term ending December 15, 2029.

TAMARA W. ASHFORD, judge; born in Boston, Massachusetts; B.A., in public policy studies, Duke University (1991); J.D., Vanderbilt University Law School (1994); LL.M., Master of Laws in Taxation, with an honors certificate of specialization in international tax, University of Miami School of Law (1997). Admitted to the Bars of North Carolina; District of Columbia; United States Tax Court; United States Courts of Appeals for the District of Columbia, First, Second, Fourth, Fifth, Sixth, Ninth and Tenth Circuits; United States Supreme Court. Served as Law Clerk to the Honorable John C. Martin, North Carolina Court of Appeals (1994–1996). Practiced law as a Trial Attorney in the Appellate Section, Tax Division, United States Department of Justice (1997–2001). Practiced law as a Senior Associate, Miller and Chevalier, Chartered (2001–04). Served as Assistant to the Commissioner (2004–07) and U.S. Director for the Joint International Tax Shelter Information Centre/Senior Advisor to the Commissioner, Large and Mid-Size Business Division (2007–08) in the Internal Revenue Service. Recipient of the Sheldon S. Cohen National Outstanding Support to the Office of Chief Counsel Award (2006). Practiced law as Counsel, Dewey and LeBoeuf, LLP (2008–11). Recognized for Tax Controversy by the 2010 edition of The Legal 500. Served as Deputy Assistant Attorney General for Appellate and Review (2011–14), Principal Deputy Assistant Attorney General and Acting Deputy Assistant Attorney General for Policy and Planning (2013–14), and Acting Assistant Attorney General (June 2014–December 2014) in the Tax Division, United States Department of Justice. Named a 2012 Person of the Year by Tax Analysts. Appointed by President Obama as Judge, United States Tax Court, on December 19, 2014, for a term ending December 18, 2029.

SENIOR JUDGES

HOWARD A. DAWSON, JR., senior judge; born in Arkansas, 1922; Woodrow Wilson High School, Washington, DC, 1940; B.S. in Commerce, University of North Carolina, 1946; J.D. with honors, George Washington University School of Law, 1949; President, Case Club; Secretary-Treasurer, Student Bar Association; private practice of law, Washington, DC, 1949–50; served with the United States Treasury Department, Internal Revenue Service, as follows: Attorney, Civil Division, Office of Chief Counsel, 1950–53; Civil Advisory Counsel, Atlanta Region, 1953–57; Regional Counsel, Atlanta Region, 1958; Personal Assistant to Chief Counsel, 1958–59, Assistant Chief Counsel (Administration), 1959–62; U.S. Army Finance Corps, 1943–45; two years in European Theater; Captain, Finance Corps, U.S. Army Reserve (Retired); member of District of Columbia Bar (1949), Georgia Bar (1958), American Bar Association (Section of Taxation), Federal Bar Association, Chi Psi, Delta Theta Phi, George Washington University Law Alumni Association; appointed by President Kennedy as Judge, Tax Court of the United States, on August 21, 1962, for a term ending June 1, 1970; reappointed by President Nixon on June 2, 1970, for a term ending June 1, 1985; served as Chief Judge from July 1, 1973 to June 30, 1977, during which time the United States Tax Court's Courthouse was built and dedicated, and served again as Chief Judge from July 1, 1983 to June 1, 1985; retired on June 2, 1985; David Brennan Distinguished Professor of Law, University of Akron Law School, Spring Term, 1986; Professor and Director, Graduate Tax Program, University of Baltimore Law School, 1986–89; Distinguished Visiting Professor of Law, University of San Diego, Winter 1991. Recalled as Senior Judge to perform judicial duties 1990-to-present. In 2009, the Court established the Howard A. Dawson, Jr. Award to honor exemplary service by Tax Court employees. On January 18, 2011, became the longest serving judge in Tax Court history.

HERBERT L. CHABOT, senior judge; born in New York, 1931; Stuyvesant High School, 1948; B.A., *cum laude*, C.C.N.Y., 1952; LL.B., Columbia University, 1957; LL.M. in Taxation, Georgetown University, 1964; served in United States Army, 2 years, and Army Reserves (civil affairs units), for 8 years; served on legal staff, American Jewish Congress, 1957–61; attorney-adviser to Judge Russell E. Train, 1961–65; Congressional Joint Committee on Taxation, 1965–78; elected Delegate, Maryland Constitutional Convention, 1967–68; adjunct professor, National Law Center, George Washington University, 1974–83; member of American Bar Association, Tax Section, and Federal Bar Association; appointed by President Carter as Judge, United States Tax Court, on April 3, 1978, for a term ending April 2, 1993; served as Senior Judge on recall performing judicial duties until reappointed on October 20, 1993, for a term ending October 19, 2008; retired on June 30, 2001, but recalled on July 1, 2001, as Senior Judge to perform judicial duties to the present time.

MARY ANN COHEN, senior judge; born in New Mexico, 1943; attended public schools in Los Angeles, CA; B.S., University of California, at Los Angeles, 1964; J.D., University of Southern California School of Law, 1967; practiced law in Los Angeles, member in law firm of Abbott and Cohen; American Bar Association, Section of Taxation, and Continuing Legal Education activities; received Dana Latham Memorial Award from Los Angeles County Bar Association Taxation Section, 1997; Jules Ritholz Memorial Merit Award from ABA Tax Section Committee on Civil and Criminal Tax Penalties, 1999; Bruce I. Hochman Award from the UCLA Tax Controversy Program, 2007; and Joanne M. Garvey Award from California Bar Taxation Section, 2008; appointed by President Reagan as Judge, United States Tax Court, on September 24, 1982, for a term ending September 23, 1997; served as Chief Judge from June 1, 1996 to September 23, 1997; reappointed on November 7, 1997, for a term ending November 6, 2012, and served again as Chief Judge from November 7, 1997 to May 31, 2000. Assumed senior status on October 1, 2012.

STEPHEN J. SWIFT, senior judge; born in Utah, 1943; Menlo Atherton High School, Atherton, CA, 1961; B.S., Brigham Young University, Political Science, 1967; J.D., George Washington University Law School, 1970. Attorney, U.S. Department of Justice, Tax Division, 1970–74; Assistant U.S. Attorney, Tax Division, U.S. Attorney's Office, San Francisco, CA, 1974–77; Vice President and Senior Tax Counsel, Tax Department, Bank of America N.T. and S.A., San Francisco, CA, 1977–83; adjunct professor, Graduate Tax Programs, Golden Gate University and University of Baltimore. Member of California Bar, District of Columbia Bar, and American Bar Association, Section of Taxation. Appointed by President Reagan as Judge, United States Tax Court, on August 16, 1983, for a term ending August 15, 1998. Served as Senior Judge on recall performing judicial duties until reappointed by President Clinton on December 1, 2000, for a term ending November 30, 2015. Retired on September 7, 2008; recalled to perform judicial duties as Senior Judge from September 8, 2008 to April 7, 2009, from October 1, 2010 to December 31, 2012, and again beginning September 8, 2014 to present time.

JULIAN I. JACOBS, senior judge; born in Maryland, 1937; B.A., University of Maryland, 1958; LL.B., University of Maryland Law School, 1960; LL.M., Taxation, Georgetown Law Center, 1965; admitted to Maryland Bar, 1960; attorney, Internal Revenue Service, Washington, DC, 1961–65, and Buffalo, NY, in Regional Counsel's Office, 1965–67; entered private practice of law in Baltimore, MD, 1967; associate (1972–74) and partner (1974–84) in the Law Firm of Gordon, Feinblatt, Rothman, Hoffberger and Hollander; Chairman, study commission to improve the quality of the Maryland Tax Court, 1978; member, study groups to consider changes in the Maryland tax laws; Commissioner on a commission to reorganize and recodify article of Maryland law dealing with taxation, 1980; Lecturer, tax seminars and professional programs; Chairman, Section of Taxation, Maryland State Bar Association; adjunct professor of Law, Graduate Tax Program, University of Baltimore School of Law, 1991–93; Adjunct Professor of Law, Graduate Tax Program, University of San Diego School of Law, 2001; Adjunct Professor of Law, Graduate Tax Program, University of Denver School of Law, 2001–04; appointed by President Reagan as Judge, United States Tax Court, on March 30, 1984, for a term ending March 29, 1999; recalled on March 30, 1999, as Senior Judge to perform judicial duties from that date to the present.

JOEL GERBER, senior judge; born in Illinois, 1940; B.S., business administration, Roosevelt University, 1962; J.D., DePaul University, 1965; LL.M., Taxation, Boston University Law School, 1968; admitted to the Illinois Bar, 1965; Georgia Bar, 1974; Tennessee Bar, 1978; served with U.S. Treasury Department, Internal Revenue Service, as trial attorney, Boston, MA, 1965–72; senior trial attorney, Atlanta, GA, 1972–76; District Counsel, Nashville, TN, 1976–80; Deputy Chief Counsel, Washington, DC, 1980–84; Acting Chief Counsel, May 1983–March 1984; recipient of a Presidential Meritorious Rank Award, 1983; Secretary of the Treasury's Exceptional Service Award, 1984; Lecturer in Law, Vanderbilt University, 1976–80; appointed by President Reagan as Judge, United States Tax Court, on June 18, 1984, for a term ending June 17, 1999; served as Senior Judge on recall performing judicial duties until reappointed on December 15, 2000, for a term ending December 14, 2015; served as Chief Judge from June 1, 2004, to May 31, 2006; assumed senior status on June 1, 2006.

THOMAS B. WELLS, senior judge; born in Ohio, 1945; B.S., Miami University, Oxford, OH, 1967; J.D., Emory University Law School, Atlanta, GA, 1973; LL.M., Taxation, New York University Law School, New York, 1978; Supply Corps Officer, U.S. Naval Reserve, active duty 1967–70, Morocco and Vietnam, received Joint Service Commendation Medal; admitted to practice law in Georgia; member of law firm of Graham and Wells, P.C.; County Attorney for Toombs County, GA; City Attorney, Vidalia, GA, until 1977; law firm of Hurt, Richardson, Garner, Todd and Cadenhead, Atlanta, until 1981; law firm of Shearer and Wells, P.C. until 1986; member of American Bar Association, Section of Taxation;

State Bar of Georgia, member of Board of Governors; Board of Editors, Georgia State Bar Journal; member, Atlanta Bar Association; Editor of the *Atlanta Lawyer*; active in various tax organizations, such as Atlanta Tax Forum (presently, Honorary Member); Director, Atlanta Estate Planning Council; Director, North Atlanta Tax Council; American College of Tax Counsel, Honorary Fellow; Emory Law Alumni Association's Distinguished Alumnus Award, 2001; Life Member, National Eagle Scout Association, Eagle Scout, 1960; member: Vidalia Kiwanis Club (President); recipient, Distinguished President Award; appointed by President Reagan as Judge, United States Tax Court, on October 13, 1986, for a term ending October 12, 2001; reappointed by President Bush on October 10, 2001, for a term ending October 9, 2016; served as Chief Judge from September 24, 1997 to November 6, 1997, and from June 1, 2000 to May 31, 2004. Assumed senior status on January 1, 2011.

ROBERT PAUL RUWE, senior judge; born in Ohio, 1941; Roger Bacon High School, St. Bernard, OH, 1959; Xavier University, Cincinnati, OH, 1963; J.D., Salmon P. Chase College of Law (graduated first in class), 1970; admitted to Ohio Bar, 1970; Special Agent, Intelligence Division, Internal Revenue Service, 1963–70; joined Office of Chief Counsel, Internal Revenue Service in 1970, and held the following positions: Trial Attorney (Indianapolis), Director, Criminal Tax Division, Deputy Associate Chief Counsel (Litigation), and Director, Tax Litigation Division. Appointed by President Reagan as Judge, United States Tax Court, on November 20, 1987, for a term ending November 19, 2002. Retired on November 20, 2002, but continues to perform judicial duties as Senior Judge on recall.

LAURENCE J. WHALEN, senior judge; born in Pennsylvania, 1944; A.B., Georgetown University, 1967; J.D., Georgetown University Law Center, 1970; LL.M., 1971; admitted to District of Columbia and Oklahoma Bars; Special Assistant to the Assistant Attorney General, Tax Division, Department of Justice, 1971–72; trial attorney, Tax Division, 1971–75; private law practice in Washington, DC, with Hamel and Park (now Hopkins, Sutter, Hamel and Park), 1977–84; also in Oklahoma City, OK, with Crowe and Dunlevy, 1984–87; member of Oklahoma Bar Association, District of Columbia Bar Association, and American Bar Association, appointed by President Reagan as Judge, United States Tax Court, on November 23, 1987, for a term ending November 22, 2002; recalled on November 23, 2002, as Senior Judge to perform judicial duties from that date to the present.

CAROLYN P. CHIECHI, senior judge; born in New Jersey, 1943; B.S. (*magna cum laude*, Class Rank: 1), Georgetown University, 1965; J.D., 1969 (Class Rank: 9); LL.M., Taxation, 1971; Doctor of Laws, Honoris Causa, 2000; practiced with law firm of Sutherland, Asbill and Brennan, Washington, DC and Atlanta, GA (partner, 1976–92; associate, 1971–76); served as attorney-adviser to Judge Leo H. Irwin, United States Tax Court, 1969–71; member, District of Columbia Bar, 1969–present (member, Taxation Section, 1973–99; member, Taxation Section Steering Committee, 1980–82, Chairperson, 1981–82; member, Tax Audits and Litigation Committee, 1986–92, Chairperson, 1987–88); member, American Bar Association, 1969–present (member, Section of Taxation, 1969–present; member, Committee on Court Procedure, 1991–present; member, Litigation Section, 1995–2000; member, Judicial Division, 1997–2000); Federal Bar Association, 1969–present (member, Section of Taxation, 1969–present; member, Judiciary Division, 1992–present); Fellow, American College of Tax Counsel; Fellow, American Bar Foundation; member, Women's Bar Association of the District of Columbia, 1992–present; Board of Governors, Georgetown University Alumni Association, 1994–97, 1997–2000; Board of Regents, Georgetown University, 1988–94, 1995–2001; National Law Alumni Board, Georgetown University, 1986–93; Board of Directors, Stuart Stiller Memorial Foundation, 1986–99; American Judicature Society, 1994–present; one of several recipients of the first Georgetown University Law Alumni Awards (1994); one of several recipients of the first Georgetown University Law Center Alumnae Achievement Awards (1998); admitted to *Who's Who in American Law*, *Who's Who of American Women*, *Who's Who in America*, and *Who's Who in the East*; appointed by President George H.W. Bush as Judge, United States Tax Court, on October 1, 1992, for a term ending September 30, 2007; Retired on September 30, 2007; recalled October 1, 2007, as Senior Judge to perform judicial duties from that date to the present.

DAVID LARO, senior judge; born in Michigan, 1942; Graduate of New York University Law School (LL.M. in Taxation, 1970), the University of Illinois Law School (J.D. 1967) and the University of Michigan (B.A. 1964). Formerly practiced tax law in Flint and Ann Arbor Michigan for 24 years. Regent of the University of Michigan, a member of the State Board of Education in Michigan, and Chairman of the State Tenure Commission in Michigan. Teaches corporate tax and business planning at Georgetown Law School, and the University of San Diego Law School. Co-Author of *Business Valuation and Taxes: Proce-*

dure, *Law and Perspective* (Second edition, 2011), a 500 page text on tax valuation. At the request of the American Bar Association (CEELI), contributed written comments on the Draft Laws of Ukraine and Uzbekistan. As a consultant for Harvard University (Harvard Institute for International Development) and Georgia State University, lectured in Moscow on the subjects of tax reform and litigation. Consultant on Russian Tax Reform under a project through USAID. At the invitation of the Supreme Court of Kazakhstan in 2007, lectured to members of the Kazakhstan Judiciary, and lectured to members of the Russian Judiciary in Moscow in 2007–10. In May 2006, and June 2007, at the invitation of the State Tax Administration and other government officials, lectured in Beijing, China on economic substance. Appointed by President George H.W. Bush as Judge, United States Tax Court, on November 2, 1992, for a term ending November 1, 2007. Retired on November 1, 2007, but continues to perform judicial duties as Senior Judge on recall.

HARRY A. HAINES, senior judge; born in Montana, 1939; B.A., St. Olaf College, 1961; J.D., University of Montana Law School, 1964; LL.M., Taxation, New York University Law School, 1966; admitted to Montana Bar and U.S. District Court, Montana, 1964; practiced law in Missoula, MT, as a partner, Law Firm of Worden, Thane and Haines, 1966–2003; adjunct professor, Law School, University of Montana, 1967–91; appointed by President George W. Bush as Judge, United States Tax Court, on April 22, 2003 for a term ending April 21, 2018. Retired on May 30, 2009, but continues to perform judicial duties as Senior Judge on recall.

ROBERT A. WHERRY, JR., senior judge; born in Virginia, 1944; B.S., and J.D., University of Colorado; LL.M., Taxation, New York University Law School; fellow and former Regent of the American College of Tax Counsel and former chairman of the Taxation Section of the Colorado Bar Association; served as chairman of the Small-Business Tax Committee of the Colorado Association of Commerce and Industry, as president of the Greater Denver Tax Counsel Association, is a past chairman of the Administrative Practice Committee of the American Bar Association Tax Section, a member of the Council, and a member of the Advisory Committee of the American Bar Association Section of Dispute Resolution; listed in *The Best Lawyers in America* (in tax litigation); his articles have appeared in ALI–ABA publications, *The Colorado Lawyer, Tax Notes*, and *State Tax Notes*; former Colorado correspondent for *State Tax Notes* and has spoken at numerous tax institutes, including the University of Denver Tax Institute, Tulane University Tax Institute, and American Bar Association Tax Section programs; was an instructor in Tax Court litigation for the National Institute for Trial Advocacy; appointed by President George W. Bush as Judge, United States Tax Court, on April 23, 2003, for a term ending April 22, 2018. Assumed senior status on April 8, 2014.

SPECIAL TRIAL JUDGES OF THE COURT

Peter J. Panuthos (Chief Special Trial Judge), Robert N. Armen, Jr.; Lewis R. Carluzzo; Daniel A. Guy.

COURT STAFF

Clerk.—Robert R. Di Trolio.
General Counsel.—Douglas W. Snoeyenbos.
Court Administrator.—Fig Ruggieri.
Deputy General Counsel.—Stephanie Servoss.
Case Services Director.—Tina Buckler.
Facilities Management Director.—Joyce Russell Dyck.
Financial Management Director.—Joseph L. Hardy, Jr.
Human Resources Director.—Ellene P. Footer.
Information Systems Director.—Gordon S. Goodrick.
Librarian.—Nancy Ciliberti.
Reporter of Decisions.—Sheila A. Murphy.

UNITED STATES COURT OF APPEALS
FOR THE ARMED FORCES [1]

450 E Street, NW., 20442–0001, phone 761–1448, fax 761–4672

CHARLES E. ERDMANN, chief judge; born in Great Falls, MT; B.A., Montana State University, 1972; J.D., University of Montana Law School, 1975; Air Force Judge Advocate Staff Officers Course, 1981; Air Command and Staff College, 1992; Air War College, 1994; Military Service: U.S. Marine Corps, 1967–70; Air National Guard, 1981–2002 (retired as a Colonel); Assistant Montana Attorney General, 1975–76; Chief Counsel, Montana State Auditor's Office, 1976–78; Chief Staff Attorney, Montana Attorney General's Office, Antitrust Bureau; Bureau Chief, Montana Medicaid Fraud Bureau, 1980–82; General Counsel, Montana School Boards Association, 1982–86; private practice of law, 1986–95; Associate Justice, Montana Supreme Court, 1995–97; Office of High Representative of Bosnia and Herzegovina, Judicial Reform Coordinator, 1998–99; Office of High Representative of Bosnia and Herzegovina, Head of Human Rights and Rule of Law Department, 1999; Chairman and Chief Judge, Bosnian Election Court, 2000–01; Judicial Reform and International Law Consultant, 2001–02; appointed by President George W. Bush to serve on the U.S. Court of Appeals for the Armed Forces on October 9, 2002, commenced service on October 15, 2002.

SCOTT W. STUCKY, judge; born in Hutchinson, KS; B.A. *summa cum laude*, Wichita State University, 1970; J.D., Harvard Law School, 1973; M.A., Trinity University, 1980; LL.M. with highest honors, George Washington University, 1983; Federal Executive Institute, 1988; Harvard Program for Senior Officials in National Security, 1990; National War College, 1993; admitted to bar, Kansas and District of Columbia; U.S. Air Force, judge advocate, 1973–78; U.S. Air Force Reserve, 1982–2003 (retired as colonel), married to Jean Elsie Seibert of Oxon Hill, MD, August 18, 1973; children: Mary-Clare, Joseph; private law practice, Washington, DC, 1978–82; branch chief, U.S. Nuclear Regulatory Commission, 1982–83; legislative counsel and principal legislative counsel, U.S. Air Force, 1983–96; General Counsel, Committee on Armed Services, U.S. Senate, 1996–2001 and 2003–06; Minority Counsel, 2001–03; National Commander-in-Chief, Military Order of the Loyal Legion of the United States, 1993–95; Board of Directors, Adoption Service Information Agency, 1998 2002 and 2004–07; Board of Directors, Omicron Delta Kappa Society, 2006–10; member, Federal Bar Association (Pentagon Chapter), Judge Advocates Association, the District of Columbia Bar; OPM LEGIS Fellow, office of Senator John Warner (R–VA), 1986–87; member and panel chairman, Air Force Board for Correction of Military Records, 1989–96; nominated by President George W. Bush to serve on the U.S. Court of Appeals for the Armed Forces on November 15, 2006; confirmed by the Senate, December 9, 2006; began service on December 20, 2006.

MARGARET A. RYAN, judge; born in Chicago, IL; B.A. *cum laude*, Knox College; J.D. *summa cum laude*, University of Notre Dame Law School; recipient of the William T. Kirby Legal Writing Award and the Colonel William J. Hoynes Award for Outstanding Scholarship; active duty in the U.S. Marine Corps, 1986–99, serving as a communications officer, staff officer, company commander, platoon commander and operations officer in units within the II and III Marine Expeditionary Forces and as a judge advocate in Okinawa, Japan, and Quantico, VA; also served as Aide de Camp to General Charles C. Krulak, the 31st Commandant of the Marine Corps; law clerk to the Honorable J. Michael Luttig, U.S. Court of Appeals for the Fourth Circuit, and law clerk to the Honorable Clarence Thomas, Associate Justice of the Supreme Court of the United States; litigation partner at the law firm of Bartlik Beck Herman Palenchar and Scott LLP and partner in litigation and appellate practices at the law firm Wiley Rein Fielding LLP; nominated by President George W. Bush to serve on the U.S. Court of Appeals for the Armed Forces on November 15, 2006; confirmed by the Senate on December 9, 2006; began service on December 20, 2006.

---

[1] Prior to October 5, 1994, United States Court of Military Appeals.

KEVIN A. OHLSON, judge; born in Sterling, MA; B.A., Washington and Jefferson College, 1982; four-year Army R.O.T.C. scholarship; Phi Beta Kappa; Air Assault training with the 101st Airborne Division at Fort Campbell, Kentucky, 1980; J.D., University of Virginia School of Law, 1985; Airborne training at Fort Benning, GA, 1986; administrative law officer and trial counsel at Fort Bragg, NC, 1986–89; federal prosecutor in Washington, D.C., 1989–97; volunteered to return to active duty and served as a legal advisor to the XVIII Airborne Corps Command Staff during Operation Desert Storm, 1990–91; awarded the Bronze Star; returned to the United States Attorney's Office for the District of Columbia and resumed duties as a federal prosecutor; Chief of Staff to the Deputy Attorney General, 1997–2001; member of the Board of Immigration Appeals, 2001–03; deputy director, and then the director, of the Executive Office for Immigration Review, 2003–09; Chief of Staff and Counselor to the Attorney General of the United States, 2009–2011; chief of the Professional Misconduct Review Unit at the Department of Justice, 2011–13; nominated by the President and confirmed by the Senate to serve on the U.S. Court of Appeals for the Armed Forces; began service on November 1, 2013.

SENIOR JUDGES

WILLIAM HORACE DARDEN, senior judge; born in Union Point, GA; son of William W. and Sara (Newsom) Darden; B.B.A., University of Georgia, 1946; LL.B., University of Georgia, 1948; admitted to bar of Georgia and to practice before the Georgia Supreme Court, 1948; active duty in U.S. Navy from July 1, 1943 to July 3, 1946, when released to inactive duty as lieutenant (jg.); married to Mary Parrish Viccellio of Chatham, VA, December 31, 1949; children: Sara Newsom, Martha Hardy, William H., Jr., Daniel Hobson; secretary to U.S. Senator Richard B. Russell, 1948–51; chief clerk of U.S. Senate Committee on Armed Services, 1951–53; professional staff member and later chief of staff, U.S. Senate Committee on Armed Services, February 1953 to November 1968; received recess appointment as judge of the U.S. Court of Military Appeals from President Johnson on November 5, 1968, to succeed the late Judge Paul J. Kilday; took oath of office on November 13, 1968; nominated by President Johnson for the unexpired part of the term of the late Judge Paul J. Kilday ending May 1, 1976; confirmed by Senate on January 14, 1969; designated Chief Judge by President Nixon on June 23, 1971; resigned December 29, 1973; elected to become Senior Judge on February 11, 1974.

WALTER THOMPSON COX III, senior judge; born in Anderson, SC; son of Walter T. Cox and Mary Johnson Cox; married to Vicki Grubbs of Anderson, SC, February 8, 1963; children: Lisa and Walter; B.S., Clemson University, 1964; J.D., *cum laude*, University of South Carolina School of Law, 1967; graduated Defense Language Institute (German), 1969; graduated basic course, the Judge Advocate General's School, Charlottesville, VA, 1967; studied procurement law at that same school, 1968; active duty, U.S. Army judge advocate general's corps, 1964–72 (1964–67, excess leave to U.S.C. Law School); private law practice, 1973–78; elected resident judge, 10th Judicial Circuit, South Carolina, 1978–84; also served as acting associate justice of South Carolina supreme court, on the judicial council, on the circuit court advisory committee, and as a hearing officer of the judicial standards commission; member: bar of the Supreme Court of the United States; bar of the U.S. Court of Military Appeals; South Carolina Bar Association; Anderson County Bar Association; the American Bar Association; the South Carolina Trial Lawyers Association; the Federal Bar Association; and the Bar Association of the District of Columbia; has served as a member of the House of Delegates of the South Carolina Bar, and the Board of Commissioners on Grievances and Discipline; nominated by President Reagan, as judge of U.S. Court of Military Appeals, June 28, 1984, for a term of 15 years; confirmed by the Senate, July 26, 1984; sworn-in and officially assumed his duties on September 6, 1984; retired on September 30, 1999 and immediately assumed status of Senior Judge on October 1, 1999 and returned to full active service until September 19, 2000.

EUGENE R. SULLIVAN, senior judge; born in St. Louis, MO; son of Raymond V. and Rosemary K. Sullivan; married to Lis U. Johansen of Ribe, Denmark, June 18, 1966; children: Kim A. and Eugene R. II; B.S., U.S. Military Academy, West Point, 1964; J.D., Georgetown Law Center, Washington, DC, 1971; active duty with the U.S. Army, 1964–69; service included duty with the 3rd Armored Division in Germany, and the 4th Infantry Division in Vietnam; R&D assignments with the Army Aviation Systems Command; one year as an instructor at the Army Ranger School, Ft. Benning, GA; decorations include: Bronze Star, Air Medal, Army Commendation Medal, Ranger and Parachutist Badges, Air Force Exceptional Civilian Service Medal; following graduation from law school, clerked with U.S. Court of Appeals (8th Circuit), St. Louis, 1971–72; private law practice, Washington,

DC, 1972–74; assistant special counsel, White House, 1974; trial attorney, U.S. Department of Justice, 1974–82; deputy general counsel, Department of the Air Force, 1982–84; general counsel of the Department of Air Force, 1984–86; Governor of Wake Island, 1984–86; presently serves on the Board of Governors for the West Point Society of the District of Columbia; the American Cancer Society (Montgomery County Chapter); nominated by President Reagan, as judge, U.S. Court of Military Appeals on February 25, 1986, and confirmed by the Senate on May 20, 1986, and assumed his office on May 27, 1986; President George H.W. Bush named him the chief judge of the U.S. Court of Military Appeals, effective October 1, 1990, a position he held for five years; he retired on September 30, 2001 and immediately assumed status of Senior Judge and returned to full active service until Sept. 30, 2002.

SUSAN J. CRAWFORD, senior judge; born in Pittsburgh, PA; daughter of William E. and Joan B. Crawford; married to Roger W. Higgins of Geneva, NY, September 8, 1979; one child, Kelley S. Higgins; B.A., Bucknell University, Pennsylvania, 1969; J.D., *cum laude*, Dean's Award, Arthur McClean Founder's Award, New England School of Law, Boston, MA, 1977; history teacher and coach of women's athletics, Radnor High School, Pennsylvania, 1969–74; associate, Burnett and Eiswert, Oakland, MD, 1977–79; Assistant State's Attorney, Garrett County, Maryland, 1978–80; partner, Burnett, Eiswert and Crawford, 1979–81; instructor, Garrett County Community College, 1979–81; deputy general counsel, 1981–83, and general counsel, Department of the Army, 1983–89; special counsel to Secretary of Defense, 1989; inspector general, Department of Defense, 1989–91; member: bar of the Supreme Court of the United States; bar of the U.S. Court of Military Appeals, Maryland Bar Association, District of Columbia Bar Association, American Bar Association, Federal Bar Association, and the Edward Bennett Williams American Inn of Court; member: board of trustees, 1989–present, and Corporation, 1992–present, of New England School of Law; board of trustees, 1988–present, Bucknell University; nominated by President Bush as judge, U.S. Court of Military Appeals, February 19, 1991, for a term of 15 years; confirmed by the Senate on November 14, 1991, sworn in and officially assumed her duties on November 19, 1991; on October 1, 1999, she became the Chief Judge for a term of five years; retired on September 30, 2006 and assumed the status of Senior Judge on October 1, 2006.

H.F. "SPARKY" GIERKE, senior judge; born in Williston, ND; son of Herman F. Gierke, Jr., and Mary Kelly Gierke; children: Todd, Scott, Craig, and Michelle; B.A., University of North Dakota, 1964; J.D., University of North Dakota, 1966; graduated basic course, the Judge Advocate General's School, Charlottesville, VA, 1967; graduated military judge course, the Judge Advocate General's School, Charlottesville, VA, 1969; active duty, U.S. Army Judge Advocate General's Corps, 1967–71; private practice of law, 1971–83; served as a justice of the North Dakota supreme court from October 1, 1983 until appointment to U.S. Court of Military Appeals; admitted to the North Dakota Bar, 1966; admitted to practice law before all North Dakota Courts, U.S. District Court for the District of North Dakota, U.S. District Court for the Southern District of Georgia, U.S. Court of Military Appeals, and U.S. Supreme Court; served as president of the State Bar Association of North Dakota in 1982–83; served as president of the North Dakota State's Attorneys Association in 1979–80; served on the board of governors of the North Dakota Trial Lawyers Association from 1977–83, served on the board of governors of the North Dakota State Bar Association from 1977–79 and from 1981–84; served as vice chairman and later chairman of the North Dakota Judicial Conference from June 1989 until November 1991; fellow of the American Bar Foundation and the American College of Probate Counsel; member of the American Bar Association, American Judicature Society, Association of Trial Lawyers of America, Blue Key National Honor Fraternity, Kappa Sigma Social Fraternity, University of North Dakota President's Club; in 1984, received the Governor's Award from Governor Allen I. Olson for outstanding service to the State of North Dakota; in 1988 and again in 1991, awarded the North Dakota National Leadership Award of Excellence by Governor George A. Sinner; in 1989, selected as the Man of the Year by the Delta Mu Chapter of the Kappa Sigma Fraternity and as Outstanding Greek Alumnus of the University of North Dakota; also awarded the University of North Dakota Sioux Award (UND's alumni association's highest honor); in 1983–84, served as the first Vietnam era state commander of the North Dakota American Legion; in 1988–89, served as the first Vietnam era national commander of the American Legion; nominated by President George H.W. Bush, October 1, 1991; confirmed by the Senate, November 14, 1991; sworn-in and assumed office on the U.S. Court of Military Appeals, November 20, 1991; on October 1, 2004, he became the Chief Judge until his retirement on September 30, 2006, and assumed the status of Senior Judge on October 1, 2006.

ANDREW S. EFFRON, senior judge; born in Stamford, CT; A.B., Harvard College, 1970; J.D., Harvard Law School, 1975; The Judge Advocate General's School, U.S. Army, 1976,

1983; legislative aide to the late Representative William A. Steiger, 1970–76 (two years full-time, the balance between school semesters); judge advocate, Office of the Staff Judge Advocate, Fort McClellan, Alabama, 1976–77; attorney-adviser, Office of the General Counsel, Department of Defense, 1977–87; Counsel, General Counsel, and Minority Counsel, Committee on Armed Services, U.S. Senate, 1987–96; nominated by President Clinton to serve on the U.S. Court of Appeals for the Armed Forces, June 21, 1996; confirmed by the Senate, July 12, 1996; took office on August 1, 1996; assumed his duties on August 1, 1996. On October 1, 2006, he became Chief Judge for a five year term, and immediately assumed status as Senior Judge on October 1, 2011.

JAMES E. BAKER, senior judge; born in New Haven, CT; education: BA., Yale University, 1982; J.D., Yale Law School, 1990; Attorney, Department of State, 1990–93; Counsel, President's Foreign Intelligence Advisory Board/Intelligence Oversight Board, 1993–94; Deputy Legal Advisor, National Security Council, 1994–97; Special Assistant to the President and Legal Advisor, National Security Council, 1997–2000; military service: U.S. Marine Corps and U.S. Marine Corp Reserve; nominated by President Clinton to serve on the U.S. Court of Appeals for the Armed Forces; began service on September 19, 2000, and became Chief Judge on October 1, 2011; became a Senior Judge on August 1, 2015.

OFFICERS OF THE U.S. COURT OF APPEALS FOR THE ARMED FORCES

Clerk of the Court.—William A. DeCicco.
Chief Deputy Clerk of the Court.—David A. Anderson.
Deputy Clerk for Opinions.—Patricia Mariani.
Court Executive.—Keith Roberts.
Librarian.—Agnes Kiang.

UNITED STATES COURT OF APPEALS
FOR VETERANS CLAIMS

625 Indiana Avenue, NW., Suite 900, 20004, phone (202) 501–5970

LAWRENCE B. HAGEL, chief judge; born in Washington, IN, 1947; B.S., United States Naval Academy, 1969; J.D., University of the Pacific McGeorge School of Law, 1976; LL.M. (Labor Law, with highest honors) The National Law Center, George Washington University, 1983; admitted to the bars of the U.S. Supreme Court, the United States Court of Appeals for the Fourth, Ninth, Tenth, D.C. and Federal Circuits, U.S. Court of Appeals for the Armed Forces, U.S. Court of Appeals for Veterans Claims, Supreme Court of the States of Iowa and California and the District of Columbia; commissioned in the U.S. Marine Corps, second lieutenant, infantry officer 1969–72 service in Vietnam and Puerto Rico; Marine Corps Judge Advocate 1973–90, assignments concentrated in criminal and civil litigation; Deputy General Counsel and General Counsel, Paralyzed Veterans of America, 1990–2003; appointed by President George W. Bush in December 2003, to the U.S. Court of Appeals for Veterans Claims; confirmed by the U.S. Senate to the Court of Appeals on December 9, 2003; sworn in January 2, 2004. He became the Chief Judge on August 7, 2015.

BRUCE E. KASOLD, judge; born in New York, 1951; B.S., United States Military Academy, 1973; J.D., cum laude, University of Florida, 1979; LL.M., Georgetown University, 1982; Honors Graduate, the Judge Advocate General's School Graduate Program, 1984; admitted to the bars of the U.S. Supreme Court, the Florida Supreme Court, the District of Columbia Court of Appeals; member: Florida Bar, District of Columbia Bar, the Federal Bar Association, Order of the Coif; retired from the U.S. Army, Lieutenant Colonel, Air Defense Artillery and Judge Advocate General's Corp, 1994; commercial litigation attorney, Holland and Knight Law Firm, 1994–95; Chief Counsel, U.S. Senate Committee on Rules and Administration, 1995–98; Chief Counsel, Secretary of the Senate and Senate Sergeant at Arms, 1998–2003; appointed by President George W. Bush to the U.S. Court of Appeals for Veterans Claims on December 13, 2003; sworn in December 31, 2003. He became Chief Judge on August 7, 2010 and served in that role until August 6, 2015.

ALAN G. LANCE, SR., judge; born in McComb, OH, April 27, 1949; B.A. in english and history, distinguished military graduate, South Dakota State University, 1971; commissioned U.S. Army, June 1971; graduated University of Toledo School of Law and Law Review, 1973; admitted to the U.S. Supreme Court, U.S. Court of Military Appeals, State of Ohio, State of Idaho; commissioned U.S. Army, Judge Advocate Generals Corps, 1974 and served as Claims Officer, defense counsel, Chief of Defense Counsel, Legal Assistance Officer, Administrative Law Officer and in the absence of a military Judge, military Magistrate for the 172nd Infantry Brigade (Alaska) 1974–77; Army Commendation Medal 1977; served as the Command Judge Advocate, Corpus Christi Army Depot, 1977–78; engaged in private practice of law, Ada County, Idaho, 1978–94; elected to the Idaho House of Representatives, 1990, and served as Majority Caucus chairman, 1992–94; elected as Idaho Attorney General (31st) in 1994 and 1998; Distinguished Alumnus Award, University of Toledo School of Law, 2002; inducted into the Ohio Veterans Hall of Fame, November 2004; nominated as a Judge of the United States Court of Appeals for Veterans Claims by President George W. Bush; confirmed by the U.S. Senate to the Court of Appeals for Veterans Claims, November 2004 and sworn in on December 17, 2004.

ROBERT N. DAVIS, judge; born in Kewanee, IL, September 20, 1953; graduated from Davenport Central High School, Davenport, IA, 1971; B.A., University of Hartford, 1975; J.D. Georgetown University Law Center, 1978; admitted to the bars of the U.S. Supreme Court, the Ninth Circuit Court of Appeals; the State of Virginia; and the State of Iowa; career record 1978–83 appellate attorney with the Commodity Futures Trading Commission; 1983–88 attorney with the United States Department of Education, Business and Administrative Law Division of the Office of General Counsel; 1983 Governmental exchange program with the United States Attorneys office, District of Columbia; Special Assistant United States Attorney; 1988–2001 Professor of Law, University of Mississippi School of Law; 2001–

05 Professor of Law, Stetson University College of Law; Published extensively in the areas of constitutional law, administrative law, national security law and sports law. Founder and Faculty Editor-in-Chief, Journal of National Security Law, arbitrator/mediator with the American Arbitration Association and the United States Postal Service. Gubernatorial appointment to the National Conference of Commissioners on Uniform State Laws 1993–2000. Joined the United States Navy Reserve Intelligence Program in 1988. Presidential recall to active duty in 1999, Bosnia and 2001 for the Global War on Terrorism. Military decorations include Joint Service Commendation Medal, Joint Service Achievement Medal, Navy Achievement Medal, NATO Medal, Armed Forces Expeditionary Medal, Armed Forces Reserve Medal with "M" device, Overseas Service Ribbon, National Defense Ribbon, Joint Meritorious Unit Award, and Global War on Terrorism Medal. Nominated for appointment by President George W. Bush on March 23, 2003; confirmed by the United States Senate on November 21, 2004; commissioned on December 4, 2004 as a Judge, United States Court of Appeals for Veterans Claims.

MARY J. SCHOELEN, judge; born in Rota, Spain; B.A., political science, University of California at Irvine, 1990; J.D., George Washington University Law School, 1993; admitted to the State Bar of California; law clerk for the National Veterans Legal Services Project, 1992–93; legal intern to the U.S. Senate Committee on Veterans' Affairs, 1994; staff attorney for Vietnam Veterans of America's Veterans Benefits Program, 1994–97; Minority Counsel, U.S. Senate Committee on Veterans' Affairs, 1997–2001; Minority General Counsel, March 2001–June 2001; Deputy Staff Director, Benefits Programs/General Counsel, June 2001–03; Minority Deputy Staff Director, Benefits Programs/General Counsel, 2003–04; nominated by President George W. Bush; appointed a Judge of the United States Court of Appeals for Veterans Claims; confirmed by the U.S. Senate to the United States Court of Appeals for Veterans Claims on November 20, 2004; sworn in December 20, 2004.

CORAL WONG–PIETSCH, judge, born in Waterloo, IA, Judge Pietsch has a distinguished career in public service, both in the military and as a civilian. She was commissioned in the U.S. Army Judge Advocate General's Corps and served six years on active duty. Judge Pietsch continued her service in the U.S. Army Reserve and rose to the rank of Brigadier General. She became the first woman to be promoted to the rank of Brigadier General in the U.S. Army Judge Advocate General's Corps and the first woman of Asian ancestry to be promoted to Brigadier General in the Army. Until her appointment to the bench, Judge Pietsch held the position of Senior Attorney and Special Assistant at Headquarters, U.S. Army Pacific located in Honolulu, Hawaii. In this position, she provided and managed legal services in support of the U.S. Army Pacific's mission to train Army Forces for military operations and peacetime engagements aimed at promoting regional stability. As part of the 2007 "surge" in Iraq, Judge Pietsch volunteered as a Department of Defense civilian to deploy to Iraq for a year where she was seconded to the U.S. Department of State to serve as the Deputy Rule of Law Coordinator for the Baghdad Provincial Reconstruction Team. During her deployment to Iraq, Judge Pietsch assisted with numerous civil society projects involving a variety of Rule of Law partners, including the Iraqi Jurist Union, Iraqi Bar Association, law schools, and international rights, women's rights and human rights organizations. She evaluated and sought funding for numerous projects aimed at building capacity within the Iraqi legal community to include the establishment, in close collaboration with the Iraqi Bar Association, of a Legal Aid Clinic at one of Iraq's largest detention facilities. In 2006 Judge Pietsch was appointed by the Governor of Hawaii to the Hawaii Civil Rights Commission where she served for seven years. Shortly after the appointment, the Governor selected Judge Pietsch as its Chair. Earlier in her civilian legal career, Judge Pietsch had been appointed a Deputy Attorney General for the State of Hawaii advising the State Department of Health, State Department of Agriculture, and the State Criminal History Records Division. Judge Pietsch's academic degrees include a bachelor of arts, master of arts, and a juris doctor degree. She was also a Senior Executive Fellow at the Harvard University Kennedy School of Government, is a graduate of the Defense Leadership and Management Program, and a graduate of the Army War College. Her awards and decorations include the Distinguished Service Medal, Legion of Merit, Meritorious Service Medal, Joint Service Commendation Medal, Decoration for Exceptional Civilian Service, the Meritorious Civilian Service Medal, Superior Civilian Performance Medal, and the Global War on Terrorism Medal. She has been the recipient of the Organization of Chinese Americans Pioneer Award, the Hawaii Women Lawyers Attorney of the Year Award, the Honolulu YWCA Achievement in Leadership Award, the Catholic University Alumni Achievement Award, the Federal Executive Board Award for Excellence, the U.S. Army Pacific Community Service Award and recognized for lifetime accomplishments by the Women Veterans Igniting the Spirit of Entrepreneurship. Judge Pietsch is admitted to the bars of the United States Supreme Court, the Ninth Circuit Court of Appeals, U.S. District Court of the District of Hawaii, State Bar of Hawaii, State Bar of Iowa, and the United States Court of Appeals for the Armed Forces;

nominated by President Barack Obama and subsequently appointed a Judge of the U.S. Court of Appeals for Veterans Claims on May 24, 2012 and sworn in June 2012.

MARGARET BARTLEY, judge; born in Pittsburgh, PA, 1959; B.S., *cum laude*, Pennsylvania State University, 1981; J.D., *cum laude*, American University Washington College of Law, 1993; admitted to the bars of the State of Maryland and the United States Court of Appeals for the Federal Circuit; law clerk to now-retired Judge Jonathan R. Steinberg of the United States Court of Appeals for Veterans Claims, 1993–94; staff attorney for National Veterans Legal Services Program, 1994–2005; senior staff attorney for National Veterans Legal Services Program, 2005–12; editor of the NVLSP veterans' law quarterly, *The Veterans Advocate*, 2004–12; Director of Outreach and Education for the Veterans Consortium Pro Bono Program, 2005–12; nominated as a Judge of the United States Court of Appeals for Veterans Claims on June 21, 2011, by President Barack Obama; confirmed by the U.S. Senate May 21, 2012 and sworn in June 28, 2012.

WILLIAM S. GREENBERG, judge, Judge Greenberg was a partner of McCarter and English, LLP. He initially joined the firm as an associate following a judicial clerkship in 1968, then returned as a partner in 1993. The majority of his career has involved litigation in Federal and state courts. Judge Greenberg had been a Certified Civil Trial Attorney by the Supreme Court of New Jersey since 1983. He served as Chairman of the Judicial and Prosecutorial Appointments Committee of the New Jersey State Bar Association, which considers all candidates to be a judge or prosecutor submitted by the Governor of New Jersey. He was President of the Association of Trial Lawyers of America, New Jersey, (The New Jersey Association for Justice) and has served as Trustee of the New Jersey State Bar Association and of the New Jersey State Bar Foundation. He also served as a member of the New Jersey Supreme Court Committee on the Admission of Foreign Attorneys. He established and chaired the New Jersey State Bar Association (public service/pro bono) program of military legal assistance for members of the Reserve Components called to active duty after September 11, 2001. He was a member of the New Jersey Supreme Court Civil Practice Committee. With the approval of the Secretary of Defense, on the recommendation of the White House, Judge Greenberg became Chairman of the Reserve Forces Policy Board in 2009, a Board established by the Secretary of Defense in 1951 and by Act of Congress in 1952. On July 26, 2011, Judge Greenberg was awarded the Secretary of Defense Medal for Outstanding Public Service, the second highest civilian award in the Defense Department, at a public ceremony in the Pentagon, and completed his term in August 2011. In 2006 his *Civil Trial Handbook*, Volume 47 of the *New Jersey Practice Series*, was published by Thomson/West. A special 20th anniversary issue was published in 2009, to commemorate the 1989 publication of its predecessor, *Trial Handbook for New Jersey Lawyers*. A retired Brigadier General, he served as a member of the New Jersey World War II Memorial Commission. In June 2009 he received the highest honor granted by the New Jersey State Bar Foundation, its medal of honor for his work in establishing the military legal assistance program, and especially in his public service representation of soldiers at Walter Reed Army Medical Center during their Physician Disability Hearings. His article in the June 2007 issue of *New Jersey Lawyer Magazine* describes the program in detail. He has served as special litigation counsel to the Adjutants General Association of the United States and was special litigation counsel *pro bono* to the National Guard Association of the United States. Judge Greenberg was a Commissioner of the New Jersey State Commission of Investigation. He also served as Assistant Counsel to the Governor of New Jersey and as Commissioner of the New Jersey State Scholarship Commission. Professor Greenberg served as the first Adjunct Professor of Military Law at the Seton Hall University School of Law. He was chosen the New Jersey Lawyer of the Year for 2009 by the *New Jersey Law Journal*. He received the Distinguished Alumnus Award from the Johns Hopkins University in 2010, and the Rutgers Law School Public Service Award in 2010 for his work in developing and leading the efforts to represent wounded and injured soldiers at Walter Reed. Judge Greenberg is admitted in New Jersey, New York and the District of Columbia. He is a member of the bar of the Supreme Court of the United States, and of the Third, Fourth and Federal Circuits, the Southern District of New York, and the United States Court of Appeals for the Armed Forces. Judge Greenberg is a graduate of the Johns Hopkins University (A.B., 1964) and Rutgers University Law School (J.D., 1967). He is married to the former Betty Kaufmann Wolf of Pittsburgh. They have three children, Katherine of New York, Anthony of Baltimore, and Elizabeth of New York; nominated to the United States Court of Appeals for Veterans Claims by President Barack Obama on November 15, 2012, confirmed by the United States Senate on December 21, 2012, appointed by the President on December 27, 2012, and took the judicial oath on December 28, 2012, for a term of fifteen years.

OFFICERS OF THE U.S. COURT OF APPEALS FOR VETERANS CLAIMS

Clerk of the Court.—Gregory O. Block, 501–5970.
Chief Deputy Clerk Operations Manager.—Anne P. Stygles.
Counsel to the Clerk.—Cary P. Sklar.
Senior Staff Attorney (Central Legal Staff).—Cynthia Brandon-Arnold.
Deputy Executive Officer.—Patrick H. Barnwell.
Librarian.—Allison Fentress.

UNITED STATES JUDICIAL PANEL ON MULTIDISTRICT LITIGATION

Thurgood Marshall Federal Judiciary Building, Room G–255, North Lobby,

One Columbus Circle, NE., 20002, phone (202) 502–2800, fax 502–2888

(National jurisdiction to centralize related cases pending in multiple circuits and districts under 28 U.S.C. §§ 1407 & 2112)

Chairman.—Sarah S. Vance, Chief Judge, U.S. District Court, Eastern District of Louisiana.
Judges:
    Marjorie O. Rendall, U.S. Court of Appeals Judge, Third Circuit.
    Charles R. Breyer, Senior U.S. District Judge, Northern District of California.
    Lewis A. Kaplan, Senior U.S. District Judge, Southern District of New York.
    Ellen Segal Huvelle, U.S. District Judge, District of Columbia.
    R. David Proctor, U.S. District Judge, Northern District of Alabama.
    Catherine D. Perry, Chief Judge, U.S. District Court, Eastern District of Missouri.
Panel Executive.—Thomasenia P. Duncan.
Clerk.—Jeffery N. Lüthi.

ADMINISTRATIVE OFFICE OF THE UNITED STATES COURTS

Thurgood Marshall Federal Judiciary Building
One Columbus Circle, NE., 20544, phone (202) 502–2600

Director.—James C. Duff, 502–3000.
Deputy Director.—Jill C. Sayenga, 502–3015.
Chief of Staff—Gary A. Bowden, 502–1300.
Audit Officer, Office of Audit.—Veleda T. Henderson, 502–1000.
Fair Employment Practices Officer, Office of Fair Employment Practices.—Nancy J. Dunham, 502–3080.
General Counsel, Office of the General Counsel.—Sheryl L. Walter, 502–1100.
Deputy General Counsel.—William E. Meyers, 502–1100.
Ethics Staff.—Sheryl L. Walter, 502–1100.
Chief, Rules Committee Support Staff.—Rebecca Womeldorf, 502–1820.
Judicial Conference Secretariat Officer, Judicial Conference Secretariat.—Katherine Hord Simon, 502–2400.
Public Affairs Officer, Office of Public Affairs.—David A. Sellers, 502–2600.
Legislative Affairs Officer, Office of Legislative Affairs.—Cordia A. Strom, 502–1700.
Deputy Legislative Affairs Officer.—Daniel A. Cunningham, 502–1700.
Associate Director, Department of Administrative Services.—George H. Schafer, 502–2000.
Chief of Staff.—Michael Milby, 502–2000.
Chief, Administrative Systems Office.—Joseph W. Bossi, 502–2200.
Chief Financial Officer, Budget, Accounting and Procurement Office.—Karin O'Leary, 502–2100.
Chief, Financial Liaison and Analysis Staff.—Edward O'Kane, 502–2000.
Judiciary Budget Officer, Budget Division.—James R. Baugher, 502–2100.
Judiciary Procurement Executive, Procurement Division.—Carey M. Fountain, 502–1330.
Chief, Facilities and Security Office.—Melanie F. Gilbert, 502–1200.
Human Resources Officer, Human Resources Office.—Patricia J. Fitzgibbons, 502–1170.
Associate Director, Department of Program Services.— Laura C. Minor, 502–3500.
Chief of Staff.—Michel M. Ishakian, 502–3500.
Chief, Judicial Services Office.—Michele E. Reed, 502–1800.
Chief, Court Services Office.—Mary Louise Mitterhoff, 502–1500.
Chief, Defender Services Office.—Cait T. Clarke, 502–3030.
Chief, Probation and Pretrial Services Office.—Matthew Rowland, 502–1600.
Chief, Case Management Systems Office.—Andrew M. Zaso, 502–2500.
Chief, Judiciary Data and Analysis Office.—Gary Yakimov, 502–1400.
Associate Director, Department of Technology Services.—Joseph R. Peters, Jr., 502–2300.
Chief of Staff.—Terry A. Cain, 502–2300.
Chief, Cloud Technology and Hosting Office.—Robert D. Morse, 502–2730.
Chief, IT Security Office.—Bethany De Lude, 502–2350.
Chief, Systems Deployment and Support Office.—Ronald E. Blankenship, 502–2700.
Chief, Technology Solutions Office.—Farhad K. Safaie, 502–2730.
Chief, Infrastructure Management Office.—Tim Hanlon, 502–2640.
Chief, AO Technology Office.—John C. Chang, 502–2830.

FEDERAL JUDICIAL CENTER
One Columbus Circle, NE., 20002–8003, phone (202) 502–4160

Director.—Judge Jeremy D. Fogel, 502–4160, fax 502–4099.
Deputy Director.—John S. Cooke, 502–4060, fax 502–4099.

Director of:
  Editorial and Information Services Office.—Sylvan A. Sobel, 502–4250, fax 502–4077.
  Education Division.—John S. Cooke (acting), 502–4060, fax 502–4099.
  Federal Judicial History Office.—Clara Altman, 502–4181, fax 502–4099.
  International Judicial Relations Office.—Mira Gur-Arie, 502–4191, fax 502–4099.
  Research Division.—James B. Eaglin, 502–4070, fax 502–4199.
  Information Technology Office.—Esther DeVries, 502–4223, fax 502–4288.

DISTRICT OF COLUMBIA COURTS

H. Carl Moultrie I Courthouse, 500 Indiana Avenue, NW., 20001

phone (202) 879–1010

Executive Officer.—Anne B. Wicks, 879–1700.
  Deputy Executive Officer.—Cheryl R. Bailey, 879–1700; fax 879–4829.
  Director, Governmental and Public Relations.—Leah Gurowitz, 879–1700.

DISTRICT OF COLUMBIA COURT OF APPEALS

430 E Street, NW., 20001

phone (202) 879–1010

Chief Judge.—Eric T. Washington.
  Associate Judges:

Stephen H. Glickman.	Corinne Beckwith.
John R. Fisher.	Catharine F. Easterly.
Anna Blackburne-Rigsby.	Roy W. McLeese.
Phyllis D. Thompson.	

  Senior Judges:

Theodore R. Newman, Jr.	John M. Ferren.
William C. Pryor.	Inez Smith Reid.
James A. Belson.	Warren R. King.
Frank Q. Nebeker.	Michael W. Farrell.
John M. Steadman.	Vanessa Ruiz.
John A. Terry.	

  Clerk.—Julio Castillo, 879–2725.
    Chief Deputy Clerk.—Tracy Nutall, 879–2773.
    Administration Director.—Reginald Turner, 879–2755.
    Admissions Director.—Derek Mitchell, 879–2714.
    Public Office Operations Director.—Terry Lambert, 879–2702.
    Senior Staff Attorney.—Rosanna Mason, 879–2718.

SUPERIOR COURT OF THE DISTRICT OF COLUMBIA

500 Indiana Avenue, NW., 20001

phone (202) 879–1010

Chief Judge.—Lee F. Satterfield.
  Associate Judges:

Jennifer M. Anderson.	Russell F. Canan.
Judith Bartnoff.	Erik P. Christian.
Ronna L. Beck.	Jeanette Clark.
Patricia A. Broderick.	Natalia Combs Greene.
A. Franklin Burgess, Jr.	Laura A. Cordero.
Zoe Bush.	Harold Cushenberry, Jr.
John M. Campbell.	Carol Dalton.

Danya A. Dayson.
Marisa Demeo.
Jennifer A. DiToro.
Herbert B. Dixon, Jr.
Todd E. Edelson.
Anthony Epstein.
Gerald I. Fisher.
Wendell P. Gardner, Jr.
Brian Holeman.
Alfred S. Irving.
Craig Iscoe.
Gregory Jackson.
William M. Jackson.
J. Ramsey Johnson.
Anita Josey-Herring.
Kimberley S. Knowles.
Peter Krauthamer.
Neal E. Kravitz.
Milton C. Lee
Lynn Leibowitz.
José M. López.
Judith N. Macaluso.
John McCabe.

Juliet J. McKenna.
Robert E. Morin.
Thomas J. Motley.
John M. Mott.
Stuart G. Nash.
Michael R. O'Keefe.
Ann O'Regan Keary.
Robert D. Okun.
Florence Y. Pan.
Heidi Pasichow.
Hiram E. Puig-Lugo.
Maribeth Raffinan.
Michael L. Rankin.
Robert I. Richter.
Robert Rigsby.
Maurice Ross.
Michael J. Ryan.
Fern Flanagan Saddler.
Judith Smith.
Frederick H. Weisberg.
Yvonne Williams.
Rhonda Reid Winston.
Melvin R. Wright.

Senior Judges:
Mary Ellen Abrecht.
Geoffrey M. Alprin.
John H. Bayly.
Kaye R. Christian.
Linda Kay Davis.
Frederick D. Dorsey.
Stephanie Duncan-Peters.
Stephen F. Eilperin.
Henry F. Greene.
Brook Hedge.
Rufus G. King III.
Richard A. Levie.
Cheryl M. Long.
Bruce S. Mencher.

Zinora Mitchell-Rankin.
Gregory E. Mize.
Truman A. Morrison III.
Judith E. Retchin.
Nan R. Shuker.
Robert S. Tignor.
Linda D. Turner.
Curtis Von Kann.
Ronald P. Wertheim.
Susan R. Winfield.
Peter H. Wolf,
Patricia A. Wynn.
Joan Zeldon.

Magistrate Judges:
Janet Albert.
Errol Arthur.
Joseph E. Beshouri.
Rainey R. Brandt.
Diane M. Brenneman
Julie Breslow.
Diana Harris Epps.
Tara Fentress.
S. Pamela Gray.
Karen Howze.
Noel Johnson.
Michael J. McCarthy.
Aida Melendez.

Elizabeth Mullin.
Lloyd U. Nolan.
William Nooter.
Adrienne Noti.
Lori Parker.
Renee Raymond.
Gretchen Rohr.
Mary Grace Rook.
Kenia Seoane-Lopez.
Sean Staples.
Frederick J. Sullivan.
Elizabeth Wingo.

Clerk of the Court.—James McGinley, 879–1400.

GOVERNMENT OF THE DISTRICT OF COLUMBIA

John A. Wilson Building, 1350 Pennsylvania Avenue, NW., 20004

phone (202) 724–8000

[All area codes within this section are (202)]

COUNCIL OF THE DISTRICT OF COLUMBIA

Council Chairman (at-Large).—Phil Mendelson, Suite 504, 724–8032.
Chairman Pro Tempore.—Kenyan McDuffie.
Council Members (at-Large):
  Vincent Orange, Sr., Suite 107, 724–8174.
  Anita Bonds, Suite 402, 724–8064.
  David Grosso, Suite 402, 724–8105.
  Elissa Silverman, Suite 408, 724–7772.
Council Members:
  Brianne Nadeau, Ward 1, Suite 105, 724–8181.
  Jack Evans, Ward 2, Suite 106, 724–8058.
  Mary M. Cheh, Ward 3, Suite 108, 724–8062.
  Brandon T. Todd, Ward 4, Suite 105, 724–8052.
  Kenyan McDuffie, Ward 5, Suite 506, 724–8028.
  Charles Allen, Ward 6, Suite 404, 724–8072.
  Yvette M. Alexander, Ward 7, Suite 404, 724–8068.
  LaRuby May, Ward 8, Suite 400, 724–8045.
Council Officers:
  Secretary to the Council.—Nyasha Smith, Suite 5, 724–8080.
  Budget Director.—Jennifer Budoff, Suite 508, 724–8139.
  General Counsel.—Ellen Efros, Suite 4, 724–8026.
  D.C. Auditor.—Kathleen Patterson, 717 14th Street, NW., 727–3600.

EXECUTIVE OFFICE OF THE MAYOR

6th Floor, phone (202) 727–6263, fax 727–6561

Mayor of the District of Columbia.—Hon. Muriel E. Bowser.
Confidential Assistant to the Mayor,—Sward Tondoneh.
Chief of Staff.—John Falcicchio.
Special Assistant to the Chief of Staff.—Vacant, 3rd Floor, 727–2643, fax 727–7743.
Deputy Chief of Staff.—Lindsey Parker.
Deputy Mayor for—
  Education.—Jennifer Niles, Suite 307, 727–3636, fax 727–8198
  Human Services.—Laura Zielinger.
  Planning and Economic Development.—Brian Kenner, Suite 317, 727–6365, fax 727–6703.
  Public Safety and Justice.—Kevin Donahue.
Attorney General.—Karl Racine, 441 4th Street, NW., Suite 1100 South, 727–3400, fax 347–8922.
Inspector General.—Daniel Lucas, 717 14th Street, NW., 5th Floor, 727–2540, fax 727–9846.
General Counsel.—Betsy Cavendish, Suite 300, 727–7681, fax 724–7743.
Secretary of the District of Columbia.—Lauren Vaughn, Suite 419, 727–6306, fax 727–3582.
Director of:
  Budget and Finance.—Matthew Brown, Suite 211, 727–3380, fax 727–5931.
  Communications.—Michael Czin, Suite 311, 727–5011, fax 727–8527.
  Office of Community Relations and Services.—Charon Hines, Suite 327, 442–8150, fax 727–2357.
  Office of Policy and Legislative Affairs.—Maia Estes, Suite 531, 727–6979, fax 727–3765.

OFFICE OF THE CITY ADMINISTRATOR
Suite 513, phone (202) 478–9200, fax (202) 727–9878

City Administrator.—Rashad Young.
Executive Assistant to City Administrator.—Timothy Banner.

COMMISSIONS

Arts and Humanities, 200 I (Eye) Street, SE., Suite 1400, Washington, DC 20003, 724–5613, fax 727–4135, e-mail: lionell.thomas@dc.gov, website: http://dcarts.dc.gov/DC/DCARTS.
Executive Director.—Lisa Richards Toney.
Chairperson.—Judith F. Terra.

Judicial Disabilities and Tenure, 515 5th Street, NW., Building A, Room 246, Washington, DC 20001, 727–1363, fax 727–9718, e-mail: cathaee.hudgins@dc.gov, website: http://cjdt.dc.gov/DC/CJDT.
Executive Director.—Cathaee Hudgins.
Chairperson.—Hon. Gladys Kessler.

Judicial Nominations, 515 5th Street, NW., Suite 235, Washington, DC 20001, 879–0478, fax 879–0755, e-mail: kim.whatley@dc.gov, website: http://jnc.dc.gov/DC/JNC.
Executive Director.—Kim M. Whatley.
Chairperson.—Hon. Emmet G. Sullivan.

Serve DC, Frank D. Reeves Municipal Center, 2000 14th Street, NW., Suite 101, Washington, DC 20009, 727–7200, fax 727–9942, e-mail: jeffrey.richardson@dc.gov, website: http://serve.dc.gov/page/about-serve-dc.
Executive Director.—Kristal Knight.
Chairperson.—Peter Brusoe.

Washington Metropolitan Area Transit, 8701 Georgia Avenue, Suite 808, Silver Spring, MD 20910–3700, (301) 427–0140, fax 588–5262, e-mail: wmorrow@wmatc.gov, website: http://www.wmatc.gov.
Executive Director/General Counsel.—William S. Morrow, Jr.
Chairperson.—Lawrence Brenner.

DEPARTMENTS

Child and Family Services Agency, 400 6th Street, SW., 5th Floor, 20024, 442–6100, fax 727–6505.
Director.—Raymond Davidson.

Consumer and Regulatory Affairs, 941 North Capitol Street, NE., 20002, 442–4400, fax 442–9445.
Director.—Melinda Boling.

Corrections, 1923 Vermont Avenue, NW., Room 207 North, 20001, 673–7316, fax 671–2043.
Director.—Thomas Faust.

Environment, 1200 First Street, NE., 5th Floor, 20002, 535–2600, fax 673–6993.
Director.—Tommy Wells.

Employment Services, 4058 Minnesota Avenue, NE., 20019, 724–7000, fax 673–6993.
Director.—Deborah Carroll.

Fire and Emergency Medical Services, 1923 Vermont Avenue, NW., Suite 201, 20001, 673–3320, fax 462–0807.
Fire Chief.—Gregory Dean.

Health, 899 North Capitol Street, NE., 5th Floor, 20002, 442–5955, fax 442–4795.
Director.—LaQuandra Nesbitt.

Housing and Community Development, 1800 Martin Luther King, Jr. Avenue, SE., 20020, 442–7200, fax 645–6730.
Director.—Polly Donaldson.

Human Services, 64 New York Avenue, NE., 6th Floor, 20002, 671–4200, fax 671–4325.
Director.—Laura Zeilinger.

Insurance, Securities and Banking, 810 1st Street, NE., Suite 701, 20002, 727–8000, fax 535–1196.
Commissioner.—Stephen Taylor.

Behavioral Health, 64 New York Avenue, NE., 4th Floor, 20002, 673–7440, fax 673–3433.
Director.—Dr. Tanya Royster.

Metropolitan Police, 300 Indiana Avenue, NW., 20001, phone 311 or (202) 737–4404 if calling from outside DC, fax 727–9524.
Police Chief.—Cathy L. Lanier.

Motor Vehicles, 301 C Street, NW., 20001, 727–5000, fax 727–4653.
Director.—Lucinda M. Babers.

Parks and Recreation, 3149 16th Street, NW., 20010, 673–7647, fax 673–2087.
Director.—Keith Anderson.

Public Works, 2000 14th Street, NW., 6th Floor, 20009, 673–6833, fax 671–0642.
Director.—Chris Shorter (interim).

Small and Local Business Development, 441 4th Street, NW., Suite 970 North, 20001, 727–3900, fax 724–3786.
Director.—Ana Harvey.

Transportation, 55 M Street, SE., Suite 400, 20003, 673–6813, fax 671–0650.
Director.—Leif Dormsjo.

Youth Rehabilitation Services, 450 H Street, NW., 10th Floor, 20001, 576–8175, fax 727–4434.
Director.—Clinton Lacey.

OFFICES

Administrative Hearings, One Judiciary Square, 441 4th Street, NW., 20001, 442–9091, fax 442–9451.
Chief Judge.—Eugene Adams.

Aging, 441 4th Street, NW., Suite 900 South, 20001, 724–5622, fax 724–4979.
Director.—Brenda Donald (interim).

Asian and Pacific Islander Affairs, 441 4th Street, NW., Suite 721 North, 20001, 727–3120, fax 727–9655.
Executive Director.—David Do.

Attorney General, 441 4th Street, NW., Suite 400 South, 20001, 727–3400, fax 347–8922.
Attorney General.—Karl Racine.

Talent and Appointments, 1350 Pennsylvania Avenue, NW., Suite 600, 20004, 727–1372, fax 727–2359.
Director.—Steven Walker.

Cable Television and Telecommunications, 3007 Tilden Street, NW., Pod P, 20008, 671–0066, fax 332–7020.
Director.—Angie Gates.

Chief Financial Officer, 1350 Pennsylvania Avenue, NW., Suite 203, 20004, 727–2476, fax 727–1643.
Chief Financial Officer.—Jeffrey DeWitt.

Chief Medical Examiner, 1910 Massachusetts Avenue, SE., Building 27, 20003, 698–9000, fax 698–9100.
Chief Medical Examiner.—Dr. Roger Mitchell.

Chief Technology Officer, 441 4th Street, NW., Suite 930 South, 20001, 727–2277, fax 727–6857.
Chief Technology Officer.—Tegene Baharu.

Communications Office, 1350 Pennsylvania Avenue, NW., Suite 310, 20004, 727–5011, fax 727–8527.
Director.—Michael Czin.

Office of Community Affairs, 1350 Pennsylvania Avenue, NW., Suite 327, 20004, 442–8150, fax 727–5931.
Director.—Charon Hines.

Contracting and Procurement, 441 4th Street, NW., Suite 700 South, 20001, 727–0252, fax 727–0245.
Chief Procurement Officer.—George Schutter.

Emergency Management Agency, 2720 Martin Luther King, Jr. Avenue, SE., 20032, 727–6161, fax 715–7288.
Director.—Chris Geldart.

Employee Appeals, 1100 4th Street, SW., Suite 620 East, 20024, 727–0004, fax 727–5631.
Executive Director.—Sheila Barfield, Esq.

Finance and Resource Management, 441 4th Street, NW., Suite 890 North, 20001, 727–0333, fax 727–0659.
Director of Finance Operations.—Mohamed Mohamed.

Human Resources, 441 4th Street, NW., Suite 330 South, 20001, 442–9600, fax 727–6827.
Director.—Ventris Gibson.

Human Rights, 441 4th Street, NW., Suite 570 North, 20001, 727–4559, fax 727–9589.
Director.—Monica Palacio.

Labor Relations and Collective Bargaining, 441 4th Street, NW., Suite 820 North, 20001, 724–4953, fax 727–6887.
Director.—Lionel Sims.

Latino Affairs, 2000 14th Street, NW., 2nd Floor, 20009, 671–2825, fax 673–4557.
Director.—Jackie Reyes-Yanes.

Lesbian, Gay, Bisexual and Transgender Affairs, 1350 Pennsylvania Avenue, NW., Suite 327, 20004, 727–9493, fax 727–5931.
Director.—Sheila Alexander-Reid.

Motion Picture and Television Development, 3007 Tilden Street, NW., 4th Floor, 20008, 727–6608, fax 727–3246.
Director.—Angie Gates.

Office of Planning, 1100 4th Street, SW., Suite E650, 20024, 442–7600, fax 442–7638.
Director.—Eric Shaw.

Policy and Legislative Affairs, 1350 Pennsylvania Avenue, NW., Suite 533, 20004, 727–6979, fax 727–3765.
Director.—Maia Estes.

Department of General Services, 2000 14th Street, NW., 8th Floor, 20009, 724–4400, fax 727–9877.
Director.—Jonathan Kayne.

Risk Management, 441 4th Street, NW., Suite 800 South, 20001, 727–8600, fax 727–8319.
Director.—Jed Ross.

Office of the State Superintendent of Education, 810 First Street, NE., 9th Floor, 20002, 727–6436, fax 727–2019.
Superintendent.—Hanseul Kang.

Unified Communications, 2720 Martin Luther King Jr. Avenue, SE., 20032, 730–0524, fax 730–1425.
Director.—Chris Geldart (interim).

Veterans Affairs, 441 4th Street, NW., Suite 570 South, 20001, 724–5454, fax 727–7117.
Director.—Tammi Lambert (interim).

Victim Services, 441 4th Street, NW., Suite 700, 20004, 727–3934, fax 727–1617.
Director.—Edward Smith.
Zoning, 441 4th Street, NW., Suite 200 South, 20001, 727–6311, fax 727–6072.
Director.—Sara Benjamin Bardin.

INDEPENDENT AGENCIES

Advisory Neighborhood Commissions, 1350 Pennsylvania Avenue, NW., Room 8, 20004, 727–9945, fax 727–0289.
Executive Director.—Gottlieb Simon.

Alcoholic Beverage Regulation Administration, 2000 14th Street, NW., Suite 400 South, 20009, 442–4423, fax 442–9563.
Director.—Fred Moosally.

Board of Elections and Ethics, 441 4th Street, NW., Suite 250 North, 20001, 727–2525, fax 347–2648.
Chairperson of the Board.—Cliff Tatum.

Criminal Justice Coordinating Council, 441 4th Street, NW., Suite 727 North, 20001, 442–9283, fax 724–3691.
Executive Director.—Mannone Butler.

District of Columbia Court of Appeals, 430 E Street, Room 115, 20001, 879–2701, fax 626–8840.
Chief Judge.—Eric T. Washington.

District of Columbia Housing Authority, 1133 North Capitol Street, NE., 20001, 535–1500, fax 535–1740.
Executive Director.—Adrianne Todman.

District of Columbia Public Defender Service, 633 Indiana Avenue, NW., 20001, 628–1200, fax 824–2784.
Director.—Avis Buchanan.

District of Columbia Public Library, 901 G Street, NW., Suite 400, 20001, 727–1101, fax 727–1129.
Director.—Richard Reyes-Gavilan.

District of Columbia Public Schools, 825 North Capitol Street, NW., Suite 9026, 20002, 442–4226, fax 442–5026.
Chancellor.—Kaya Henderson.

District of Columbia Retirement Board, 900 7th Street, NW., 2nd Floor, 20001, 343–3200, fax 566–5000.
Executive Director.—Eric Stanchfield.

District of Columbia Sentencing and Criminal Code Revision Commission, 441 4th Street, NW., Suite 830 South, 20001, 727–8822, fax 727–7929.
Executive Director.—Barbara Tombs-Souvey.

District Lottery and Charitable Games Control Board, 2101 Martin Luther King Jr. Avenue, SE., 20020, 645–8000, fax 645–7914.
Executive Director.—Tracey Cohen.

Housing Finance Agency, 815 Florida Avenue, NW., 20001, 777–1600, fax 986–6705.
Executive Director.—Maria Day Marshall.

Metropolitan Washington Council of Governments, 777 North Capitol Street, NE., 20002, 962–3200, fax 962–3201.
Executive Director.—Dave Robertson.

People's Counsel, 1133 15th Street, NW., Suite 500, 20005, 727–3071, fax 727–1014.
People's Counsel.—Sandra Mattavous-Frye, Esq.

Police Complaints, 1400 I Street, NW., Suite 700, 20005, 727–3838, fax 727–9182.
Executive Director.—Philip K. Eure.

Public Charter School Board, 3333 14th Street, NW., Suite 210, 20010, 328–2660, fax 328–2661.
Executive Director.—Scott Pearson (interim).

Public Employee Relations Board, 1100 4th Street, SW., Suite E630, 20024, 727–1822, fax 727–9116.
Executive Director.—Clarene Phyllis Martin.

Public Service Commission, 1333 H Street, NW., Suite 200 West Tower, 20005, 626–5100, fax 393–1389.
Chairperson.—Betty Ann Kane.

Superior Court of the District of Columbia, H. Carl Moultrie I Courthouse, 500 Indiana Avenue, NW., 20001, 879–1010.
Chief Judge.—Lee F. Satterfield.

Taxicab Commission, 2041 Martin Luther King Jr. Avenue, SE., Suite 204, 20020, 645–6018, fax 889–3604.
Chairperson.—Ernest Chrappah.

Washington Convention Center Authority, 801 Mount Vernon Place, NW., 20001, 249–3012, fax 249–3133.
President and CEO.—Greg O'Dell.

Destination DC, 1212 New York Avenue, NW., Suite 600, 20005, 904–0616 or 249–3012, fax 789–7037.
President and CEO.—Elliot Ferguson.

Water and Sewer Authority, 5000 Overlook Avenue, SW., 20032, 787–2000, fax 787–2210.
Chairman.—William M. Walker.
General Manager.—George S. Hawkins.

Workforce Investment Council, 4058 Minnesota Avenue, NE., 20009, 671–1900, fax 673–6993.
Chairperson.—Vacant.

OTHER

Board of Real Property Assessments and Appeals, 441 4th Street, NW., Suite 430, 20001, 727–6860, fax 727–0392.
Chairperson.—Towanda Paul-Bryant.

Contract Appeals Board, 441 4th Street, NW., Suite N350, 727–6597, fax 727–3993.
Chief Administrative Judge.—Marc D. Loud, Sr.

Justice Grants Administration, 1350 Pennsylvania Avenue, NW., Suite 327A, 20004, 727–6239, fax 727–1617.
Director.—Josh Weber.

Rehabilitation Services Administration, 1125 15th Street, NW., 20005, 730–1700, fax 730–1516.
Administrator.—Vacant.

DISTRICT OF COLUMBIA POST OFFICE LOCATIONS

900 Brentwood Road, NE., 20066–9998, General Information (202) 636–1200

Postmaster.—Gerald A. Roane.

CLASSIFIED STATIONS

Station	Phone	Location / Zip Code
Anacostia	(301) 423–9091/ 9092	3719 Branch Ave., Temple Hills, MD 20748
Ben Franklin	523–2386	1200 Pennsylvania Ave., NW., 20044
B.F. Carriers	636–2289	900 Brentwood Rd., NE., 20004
Benning	523–2391	3937½ Minnesota Ave., NE., 20029
Bolling AFB	767–4419	Bldg. 10, Brookley Ave., 20332
Brightwood	726–8119	6323 Georgia Ave., NW., 20
Brookland	523–2126	3401 12th St., NE., 20017
Calvert	523–2908	2336 Wisconsin Ave., NW., 20007
Cleveland Park	523–2396	3430 Connecticut Ave., NW., 20008
Columbia Heights	523–2192	6510 Chillum Pl., NW., 20010
Congress Heights	523–2112	400 Southern Ave., SE., 20032
Customs House	523–2195	3178 Bladensburg Rd., NE., 20018
Dulles	(703) 471–9497	Dulles International Airport, 20041
Farragut	523–2507	1145 19th St., NW., 20033
Fort Davis	842–4964	3843 Pennsylvania Ave., SE., 20020
Fort McNair	523–2144	300 A St., SW., 20319
Frederick Douglass	842–4959	Alabama Ave., SE., 20020
Friendship	523–2130	4005 Wisconsin Ave., NW., 20016
Georgetown	523–2406	1215 31st St., NW., 20007
Government Mail	523–2138/2139	3300 V Street, NE., 20018–9998
Headsville	357–3029	Smithsonian Institute, 20560
Kalorama	523–2906	2300 18th St., NW., 20009
Lamond Riggs	523–2041	6200 North Capitol St., NW., 20011
LeDroit Park	483–0973	416 Florida Ave., NW., 20001
L'Enfant Plaza	268–4970	458 L'Enfant Plaza, SW., 20026

CLASSIFIED STATIONS—CONTINUED

Station	Phone	Location / Zip Code
Main Office Window	636–2130	Curseen / Morris P&DC, 900 Brentwood Rd., NE., 20066–9998
Martin L. King, Jr.	523–2001	1400 L St., NW., 20043
McPherson	842–1229	1750 Pennsylvania Ave., NW., 20038
Mid City	....	Temporarily Closed
NASA	358–0235	600 Independence Ave., SW., 20546
National Capitol	523–2368	2 Massachusetts Ave., NE., 20002
Naval Research Lab	767–3426	4565 Overlook Ave., 20390
Navy Annex	(703) 920–0815	1668 D Street, 20335
Northeast	388–5216	1563 Maryland Ave., NE., 20002
Northwest	523–2570	5632 Connecticut Ave., NW., 20015
Palisades	842–2291	5136 MacArthur Blvd., NW., 20016
Pavilion Postique	523–2571	1100 Pennsylvania Ave., NW., 20004
Pentagon	(703) 695–6835	Concourse Pentagon (Army-20301 / 20310; Air Force-20330; Navy-20350)
Petworth	523–2681	4211 9th St., NW., 20011
Postal Mus	523–2022	2 Massachusetts Ave., NW., 20002
Randle	584–6807	2341 Pennsylvania Ave., SE., 20023
River Terrace	523–2988	3621 Benning Rd., NE., 20019
Section 2	636–2272 / 2273	Section 2, Curseen / Morris P&DC, 900 Brentwood Rd., NE., 20002–9998
Southeast	523–2174	327 7th St., SE., 20003
Southwest	523–2597	45 L St., SW., 20024
State Department	523–2574	2201 C St., NW., 20520
14th/T Street	232–6301	2000 14th St., NW., 20009
Tech World	523–2019	800 K St., NW., 20001
Temple Heights	523–2563	1921 Florida Ave., NW., 20009
22d Street	523–2411	1255 22nd St., NW., 20037
U.S. Naval	433–2216	940 M St., SE., 20374
V Street	523–2138 / 2139	3300 V St., NE., 20018
Walter Reed	....	6800 Georgia Ave., NW., 20012
Ward Place	523–2109	2121 Ward Pl., NW., 20037
Washington Square	523–3632	1050 Connecticut Ave., NW., 20035
Watergate	965–6278	2512 Virginia Ave., NW., 20037
Woodridge	523–2195	2211 Rhode Island Ave., NE., 20018

INTERNATIONAL ORGANIZATIONS

EUROPEAN SPACE AGENCY (E.S.A.)

**Headquarters: 8–10 Rue Mario Nikis, 75738 Paris Cedex 15, France
phone 011–33–1–5369–7654, fax 011–33–1–5369–7560**

Director General.—Johann-Dietrich Woerner.

Member Countries:

Austria	Hungary	Romania
Belgium	Ireland	Spain
Denmark	Italy	Sweden
Estonia	Luxembourg	Switzerland
Finland	Netherlands	United Kingdom
France	Norway	Czech Republic
Germany	Poland	
Greece	Portugal	

Cooperative Agreement.—Canada.

European Space Operations Center (ESOC), Robert-Bosch-Str. 5, D–64293 Darmstadt, Germany, phone 011–49–6151–900, fax 011–49–6151–90495.

European Space Research and Technology Center (ESTEC), Keplerlaan 1, NL–2201, AZ Noordwijk, ZH, The Netherlands, phone 011–31–71–565–6565, Telex: 844–39098, fax 011–31–71–565–6040.

European Space Research Institute (ESRIN), Via Galileo Galilei, Casella Postale 64, 00044 Frascati, Italy, phone 011–39–6–94–18–01, fax 011–39–6–9418–0280.

European Space Astronomy Centre (ESAC), P.O. Box, E–28691 Villanueva de la Cañada, Madrid, Spain, phone 011–34 91 813 11 00, fax: 011–34 91 813 11 39.

European Astronaut Centre (EAC), Linder Hoehe, 51147 Cologne, Germany, phone 011–49–220360–010, fax 011–49–2203–60–1103.

European Centre for Space Applications and Telecommunications (ECSAT), Atlas Building, Harwell Science & Innovation Campus, Didcot, Oxfordshire, OX11 0QX, United Kingdom, phone 011–44 1235 567900.

European Space Agency Washington Office (EWO), 1201 F Street, NW., Suite 470, Washington, DC 20004.
Head of Office—Micheline Tabache (202) 488–4158, micheline.tabache@esa.int.

INTER-AMERICAN DEFENSE BOARD

2600 16th Street, NW., 20441, phone (202) 939–6041, fax 319–2791

Chairman.—Vice Admiral Gonzalo Rios Polastri, Peru.
Vice Chairman.—General de Brigada Jaime Gonzalez Avalos, Mexico.
Chairman's Chefe de Cabinet.—COLFrançois Laboissonniere, Canada.
Director General.—Brigadier Mayor del Aire Mauricio Ribeiro Gonçalves, Brazil.
Deputy Secretary for Administration.—LTC Enrique Rivera, United States.
Director Conferences.—Coronel Emili Ambrogi, Brazil.

CHIEFS OF DELEGATION

Antigua and Barbuda.—First Secretary Guilliam Joseph.
Argentina.—Gral Brig Juan Rodolfo Brocca.
Barbados. Vacant.
Belize.—Kendall Belisle.

Bolivia.—Vacant.
Brazil.—Mayor General Osmar Lootens Machado.
Canada.—RADM William S. Truelove.
Chile.—GD Guido Montini Gomez.
Colombia.—COL Antonio Maria Beltran Diaz.
Dominican Republic.—GB Julio Ernesto Florian Perez.
El Salvador.—COL Carlos R. Escamilla.
Guatemala.—COL Ronald Ovalle.
Guyana.—COL Kemraj Persaud.
Haiti.—Minister Counselor Charles Leon.
Honduras.—COL Sergio Gomez Perdomo.
Jamaica.—COL Desmond T. Edwards.
Mexico.—GB Victor Hugo Aguirre Serna.
Nicaragua.—LTC Lenin Serrano.
Panama.—Commisionado Manuel S. Moreno Quiroz.
Paraguay.—COL Eulalio Villalba Centurion.
Peru.—General de Brigada Edgardo Zapata Lazo.
Suriname.—AMB Niermala Hindori-Badrising.
Trinidad and Tobago.—COL Darnley Wyke.
United States.—MG Stephen M. Shepro.
Uruguay.—General Carlos H. Loitey Oyharzabal.

INTER-AMERICAN DEFENSE COLLEGE

Director.—RADM Martha Herb.
  Vice Director.—Brigadier del Aire Mauricio Ribeiro Gonçalves.
  Chief of Studies.—CA Francisco Yabar.

INTER-AMERICAN DEVELOPMENT BANK

1300 New York Avenue, NW., 20577, phone (202) 623–1000
http://www.iadb.org

OFFICERS

President.—Luis Alberto Moreno.
  Chief, Office of the President.—Luis Giorgio.
Executive Vice President.—Julie T. Katzman (United States).
Chief Advisor.—Juan Pablo Bonilla.
Director, Office of Evaluation and Oversight.—Cheryl Gray.
Manager of the Research Department and Chief Economist.—Jose Juan Ruiz Gomez.
Executive Auditor.—Jorge Da Silva.
Manager, Office of External Relations—Marcelo Cabrol.
Ombudsperson.—Doris Campos-Infantino.
Secretary.—German Quintana.
Manager, Office of Outreach and Partnerships.—Bernardo Guillamón.
Advisor, Office of Risk Management.—Gustavo De Rosa.
Manager, Office of Strategic Planning and Development Effectiveness.—Verónica Zavala.
Chief, Office of Institutional Integrity.—Maristella Aldana.
Vice-President for Countries.—Alexandre Meira da Rosa.
  Country Manager, Office of:
    Department Andean Group.—Carola Álvarez.
    Department Caribbean Group.—Gerard S. Johnson.
    Department Central America, Mexico, Panama and Dominican Republic.—Gina Montiel.
    Department Haiti.—José Agustin Aguerre.
    Department Southern Cone.—José Luis Lupo.
Vice President for Sectors and Knowledge.—Santiago Levy.
  Manager of:
    Institutions for Development.—Ana María Rodríguez-Ortiz.
    Integration and Trade.—Antoni Estevadeorval.
    Knowledge and Learning.—Federico Basañes.
    Social Sector.—Héctor Salazar a.i.
Vice President for Finance and Administration.—Jaime Sujoy.

Manager of:
Budget and Administrative Services.—Yeshvanth Edwin.
Finance Department.—Gustavo De Rosa.
Human Resources.—Claudia Bock-Valotta.
Information Technology.—Nuria Simo Vila.
Legal Department.—John Scott.
Vice President for Private Sector and Non-Sovereign Guaranteed Operations.—Hans Schul.
Manager of:
Office of Operations, Multilateral Investment Fund.—Fernando Jiménez-Ontiveros (acting).
Opportunities for the Majority Sector.—Luiz Ros.
Structured and Corporate Financing Department. –Hans Schulz.

BOARD OF EXECUTIVE DIRECTORS

Argentina and Haiti.– Andrea Molinari.
Alternate.—Valeria Fernandez Escliar.
Austria, Denmark, Finland, France, Norway, Spain, and Sweden.—Joffrey Roger Celestin.
Alternate.—Maria Rodriguez de la Rua.
Bahamas, Barbados, Guyana, Jamaica, Trinidad and Tobago.—Sherwyn Everade Williams.
Alternate.—Jerry Christopher Butler.
Belgium, China, Germany, Israel, Italy, The Netherlands, and Switzerland.– Leo Kreuz.
Alternate.—Gisella Berardi.
Belize, Costa Rica, El Salvador, Guatemala, Honduras and Nicaragua.—Vacant.
Alternate.– Jose Mauricio Silva.
Bolivia, Paraguay and Uruguay.—Hugo Rafael Caceres Aguero.
Alternate.—Marcelo Bisogno.
Brazil and Suriname.—Ricardo Carneiro.
Alternate. –Frederico Gonzaga Jayme, Jr..
Canada.—James Haley.
Alternate.—Ian Christopher MacDonald.
Chile and Peru.—Tania Lourdes Quispe Mansilla.
Alternate.—Kevin Cowan Logan.
Colombia and Ecuador.—Sergio Diazgranados Guida.
Alternate.—Xavier Santillan.
Croatia, Japan, Korea, Portugal, Slovenia and United Kingdom.—Eimon Ueda.
Alternate.—Hironori Kawauchi.
Dominican Republic and Mexico.—Juan Bosco Marti Ascencio.
Alternate.—Carlos Augusto Pared Vidal.
Panama and Venezuela.—Armando Jose Leon Rojas.
Alternate.—Fernando Ernesto de Leon.
United States of America.– Mark Edward Lopes.

INTER-AMERICAN TROPICAL TUNA COMMISSION
8901 La Jolla, Shores Drive, La Jolla, CA 92037-1508
phone (858) 546-7100, fax (858) 546-7133, http://www.iattc.org

Director.—Guillermo A. Compeán.

Commissioners:

Belize:
Delice Pinkard, Ministry of Finance/Belize High Seas Fisheries Unit, Marina Towers, Suite 204, Newtown Barracks, Belize City, Belize, phone (501) 223 4918, fax (501) 223 5087; e-mail: sr.fishofficer@gmail.com.
Robert Robinson, Ministry of Finance/Belize High Seas Fisheries Unit, Marine Towers, Suite 204, Newtown Barracks, Belize City, Belize, phone (501) 223–4918, fax (501) 223–5048; e-mail: deputydirector.bhsfu@gmail.com
Valerie Lanza, Ministry of Finance/Belize High Seas Fisheries Unit, Marina Towers, Suite 204, Newtown Barracks, Belize City, Belize, phone (501) 223–4918, fax (501) 223–5087; e-mail: director.bhsfu@gmail.com.

Canada:
Larry Teague, British Columbia Tuna Fishermen's Association (BCTFA), Box 372, Shawnigan Lake, British Columbia V0R 2W0, Canada, phone (250) 743–5002; email: bctfa@shaw.ca.

Robert Day, Fisheries and Oceans Canada, 200 Kent Street, Station 8E240, Ottawa, ONT K1A 0E6, Canada, phone (613) 991–6135, fax (613) 993–5995; e-mail: robert.day@dfo-mpo.gc.ca.

China: (Focal Points)

Sun Haiwen, Ministry of Agriculture / Bureau of Fisheries, No. 11 Nongzhanguan Nanli, Beijing 100125, People's Republic of China, phone (86–10) 5919–2928, fax (86–10) 5919–2951; e-mail: fishcngov@126.com.

Zhao Liling, Ministry of Agriculture / Bureau of Fisheries, No. 11 Nongzhanguan Nanli, Beijing, 100125, People's Republic of China, phone (86–10) 5919–2928, fax (86–10) 5919–2951; e-mail: liling.zhao@hotmail.com.

Colombia:

Carlos Alberto Robles Cocuyame, Ministerio de Agricultura y Desarrollo Rural, Avenida Jiménez 7–65, Bogotá, DC 001, Colombia, phone (57–1) 334–1199 ext. 310 (57–1) 283–3977, fax (57–1) 334–1199; e-mail: carlos.robles@minagricultura.gov.co.

Andrea Guerrero, Ministerio de Relaciones Exteriores, Calle 10 No. 5–51 Palacio de San Carlos, Bogotá, DC, Colombia, phone (57–1) 381–4265, fax (57–1) 381–4747; e-mail: Andrea.GuerreroGarcia@cancilleria.gov.co.

Elizabeth Taylor Jay, Ministerio de Ambiente y Desarrollo Sostenible, Calle 35 No. 24–48, Bogota, Colombia, phone (57–1) 288–2132, (57–1) 332–3400; e-mail: etaylor@minambiente.gov.co.

Costa Rica:

Asdrúbal Vásquez, Ministerio de Agricultura y Ganadería, Oriental del TEC, 300 mts. Sur. Oeste, San José, 113–2010, Costa Rica, phone (506) 2234–1498, fax (506) 2253–4321; e-mail: vazqueza1@ice.co.cr.

Antonio Porras, INCOPESCA, Frente a las Instalaciones del Instituto Nacional de Aprendizaje, El Cocal, Puntarenas, 5400, Costa Rica, phone (506) 8712–6772, fax (506) 2630–0636; e-mail: aporras@incopesca.go.cr.

Gustavo Meneses, INCOPESCA, Frente a las Instalaciones del Instituto Nacional de Aprendizaje, El Cocal, Puntarenas 5400, Costa Rica, phone (506) 8726–0876, fax (506) 2630–0636; e-mail: gmeneses@incopesca.go.cr.

Luis Felipe Arauz, Ministerio de Agricultura y Ganadería, Sabana Sur, antiguo Colegio La Salle, San José, Costa Rica, phone (506) 22312344, fax: (506) 22322103 e-mail: despachoministro@mag.go.cr.

Ecuador:

Luis Torres Navarrete, Subsecretaría de Recursos Pesqueros, Ave. 4 y Calle 12, Manta, Ecuador, phone (593–5) 261–1410; e-mail: luis.torres@pesca.gob.ec.

Victor Alcivar, Ministerio de Agricultura Ganadería, Acuacultura y Pesca, Av. 3 y Calle12, Manta, Ecuador, phone (593–5) 261–1410, fax (593–5) 262–7911; e-mail: victor.alcivar@pesca.gob.ec.

Guillermo Morán, Ministerio de Agricultura, Ganadería, Acuacultura y Pesca, Calle 13 entre Ave. 2 y Ave. 3, Manta, Ecuador, phone (593–9) 8488–1516; e-mail: gamv6731@gmail.com.

Pilar Proaño, Ministerio de Agricultura, Ganadería, Acuacultura y Pesca, Calle 13 y 12 Ave. 04, Manta, Ecuador, phone (593–5) 262–7930, e-mail: pproano@magap.gob.ec.

El Salvador:

Gustavo Antonio Portillo, CENDEPESCA, Final 1a. Avenida Norte y Avenida Manuel Gallardo, Santa Tecla, La Libertad, El Salvador, phone (503) 22101–700 fax (503) 2534–9885; e-mail: gustavo.portillo@mag.gob.sv.

Hugo Alexander Flores, Ministerio de Agricultura y Ganadería, Final 1a. Av. Norte y Av. Manuel Gallardo, Santa Tecla, El Salvador, phone (503) 2534–9882; e-mail: hugo.flores@mag.gob.sv.

Manuel Calvo, Calvopesca / Grupo Calvo, Via de Los Poblados No. 1 Edificio B, Planta 5, Madrid, Spain, phone (34–91) 782–3300, fax (34–91) 782–3312; e-mail: mane.calvo@calvo.es.

Ana Marlene Galdamez, CENDEPESCA, Final 1a. Ave. Norte y Ave. Manuel Gallardo, Santa Tecla, La Libertad, El Salvador, phone (503) 2534–9880, fax (503) 2534–9885; e-mail: ana.galdamez@mag.gob.sv.

European Union:

Angela Martini, European Commission, Rue Joseph II, 99, Brussels, 1049, Belgium, phone (32–2) 299–4276, fax (32–2) 299–5570; e-mail: Angela.MARTINI@ec.europa.eu.

Luis Molledo, European Commission, Rue Joseph II, 99, Brussels, 1049, Belgium, phone (32–2) 299–3765, fax (32–2) 299–5570; e-mail: Luis.MOLLEDO@ec.europa.eu.

France:
Christiane Laurent-Monpetit, Ministere de l'Intérieur, de l'Outre-Mer et des Collectivites
T., 27, rue Oudinot, Paris, 75358 F SPO7, France, phone (33–1) 5369–2466, fax
(33–1) 5369–2065; e-mail: christiane.laurent-monpetit@outre-mer.gouv.fr.

Thomas Roche, Ministry of Ecology, Sustainable Development and Energy, Secretariat
d'Etat a la Mer, Tour Voltaire 1 Place DE Degres, Paris, 92055, France, phone
(33–1) 4081–9120; e-mail: thomas.roche@developpement-durable.gouv.fr.

Marie-Sophie Dufau-Richet, Secretariat d'Etat a la Mer, 16 Boulevard Raspail, Paris,
75700, France, phone (33–1) 5363–4153, fax (33–1) 5363–4178; e-mail:
marie.sophie.dufau-richet@pm.gouv.fr.

Michel Sallenave, Haut Commissariat de la République Française en Polynésie, 43 Avenue
Bruat. BP 115, Papeete, 98713, French Polynesia, phone (689) 549–525, fax (689)
434–390; e-mail: affmar@affaires-maritimes.pf.

Guatemala:
Jose Sebastian Marcucci, Ministerio de Agricultura, Ganadería y Alimentación, 7ma.
Avenida 12–90 Zona 13, Guatemala, Guatemala, phone (502) 2413–7035, fax (502)
2413–7036; e-mail: despachovisar@gmail.com.

Alejandro Sánchez, Ministerio de Agricultura, Ganadería y Alimentación, 7a. Ave. 12–
90 zona 13, Guatemala, Guatemala, phone (502) 2413–7000; e-mail:
visarmaga@gmail.com.

Carlos F. Marín, Ministerio de Agricultura, Ganadería y Alimentación, Km. 22 Carretera
al Pacífico, Edif. La Ceiba, 3er. Nivel, Villa Nueva, Guatemala, phone (502) 6640–
9334, fax (502) 6640–9324; e-mail: dipescaguatemala@gmail.com.

Bryslie Siomara Cifuentes Velasco, Ministerio de Agricultura, Ganadería y Alimentación,
Km. 22 Carretera al Pacífico, Edificio La Ceiba, 3er. Nivel, Villa Nueva, Guatemala,
phone (502) 6640–9334, fax (502) 6640–9321; e-mail: brysliec@hotmail.com.

Japan:
Tatsuo Hirayama, Ministry of Foreign Affairs, 2–2–1 Kasumigaseki 2–2–1, Chiyoda-
ku, Tokyo, Japan, phone (81–3) 5501–8338, fax (81–3) 5501–8332; e-mail:
tatsuo.hirayama@mofa.go.jp.

Takashi Koya, Fisheries Agency of Japan, 1–2–1 Kasumigaseki, Chiyoda-ku, Tokyo,
100–8907, Japan, phone (81–3) 3502–8459; e-mail: takashi—koya@nm.maff.go.jp.

Jun Yamashita, Japan Tuna Fisheries Cooperative Association, 2–3–22 Kudankita, Tokyo,
102, Japan, phone (81–3) 5646–2380, fax (81–3) 5646–2651; e-mail:
gyojyo@japantuna.or.jp.

Kiribati: (Contacts, not appointed Commissioners)
Naomi Biribo, Ministry of Fisheries and Marine Resources Development, P.O. Box 64
Bairiki, Tarawa, Kiribati, phone (686) 21099, fax: (686) 21120; e-mail:
naomib@mfmrd.gov.ki.

Aketa Tanga, Ministry of Fisheries and Marine Resources Development, P.O. Box 64
Bairiki, Tarawa, Kiribati, phone (686) 21099, fax: (686) 21120; e-mail:
aketat@mfmrd.gov.ki.

Korea:
Il Jeong Jeong, Ministry of Food, Agriculture, Forestry and Fisheries, 88, Gwanmundo,
Gwacheon-si, Gyeonggi-do, 427–719, Republic of Korea, phone (82–2) 500–2422, fax
(82–2) 503–9174; e-mail: ijeong@korea.kr, icdmomaf@chol.com.

Kim Hongwon, Ministry of Oceans and Fisheries, Government Complex Bldg. #5, room
508, Dasom2-ro, Sejong-City, Sejong, 339–012 Republic of Korea, phone (82–44)
2005368, fax (82–44) 2005379; e-mail: hiro9900@korea.kr.

Jeongseok Park, Ministry of Oceans and Fisheries, Government Complex, Sejong 94,
Damason2-ro, Sejong-City, Republic of Korea, phone (82–2) 500–2426, fax (82–2)
503–9174; e-mail: jspark2@mifaff.go.kr.

Mexico:
Mario Aguilar, Comisión Nacional de Pesca y Acuacultura, Av. Camarón Sábalo
S/N, Mazatlán, Sin 82100, Mexico, phone (52–669) 915–6900, fax (52–669) 915–
6904; e-mail: mario.aguilar@conapesca.gob.mx.

Luis Fleischer, Embassy of Mexico, 1911 Pennsylvania Ave., NW., Washington, DC,
phone (202) 728–1720; e-mail: lfleischer21@hotmail.com.

Michel Dreyfus, Instituto Nacional de la Pesca, Km 97.5 Carretera Tijuana-Ensenada
Ensenada, B.C. 22760, Mexico, phone (52–646) 174–6140, fax (52–646) 174–6135;
e-mail: dreyfus@cicese.mx.

Pablo Arenas, Instituto Nacional de la Pesca, Pitágoras #1320, Piso 8vo. Col. Sta Cruz
Atoyac, Mexico, D.F. 03310 Mexico, phone (52–55) 3781–9501 (52–55) 3871–9502,
fax (52–55) 3626–8421; e-mail: pablo.arenas@inapesca.gob.mx.

Nicaragua:
Armando Segura, Cámara de la Pesca de Nicaragua, Av. 27 de Mayo, Managua, Nicaragua, phone (505) 2266–6704, fax (505) 2222–5818; e-mail: capenic@ibw.com.ni.
Danilo Rosales Pichardo, Instituto Nicaraguense de la Pesca y Acuicultura, Km. 3.5 Carretera Norte, Managua, Nicaragua, phone (505) 2251–0487, fax (505) 2244–2552; e-mail: drosales@inpesca.gob.ni
Julio César Guevara Q, Industrial Atunera de Nicaragua, Balboa Ancón, Panama City, 0843–02264, Panama, phone (507) 6997–5100, fax (507) 204 4651; e-mail: juliocgq@hotmail.com

Panama:
Iván Eduardo Flores, Autoridad de los Recursos Acuáticos de Panamá, Edificio La Riviera, Avenida Justo Arosemena y Calle 46 Bella Vista, diagonal a Estación el Arbol, Panama City, 0819–05850, Panama, phone (507) 511–6074, fax (507) 511–6071; e-mail: iflores@arap.gob.pa.
Raúl Delgado, Autoridad de los Recursos Acuáticos de Panamá Edificio La Riviera, Avenida Justo Arosemena y Calle 46 Bella Vista, diagonal a Estación el Arbol, Panama City, Panama, phone (507) 511–6057, fax (507); e-mail: rdelgado@arap.gob.pa.
María Patricia Díaz, FIPESCA, Clayton #404–A Ancón, Corozal, Panama, phone (507) 511–6013, fax (507) 317–3862; e-mail: mpdiaz@fipesca.com.
Arnulfo Franco, FIPESCA, Corozal, Zona Libre de Proceso, Edif. 319, Panama, phone (507) 317–3644, fax (507) 317–3862; e-mail: arnulfofranco@fipesca.com.

Peru:
Luis R. Arribasplata, Ministerio de Relaciones Exteriores, Jirón Lampa 545, Cercado de Lima, Peru, phone (51–1) 204–3244; e-mail: larribasplata@rree.gob.pe.
Gladys Cárdenas, Instituto del Mar del Perú, Esquina de Gamarra y General Valle s/n Chucuito-Callao Lima, Peru, phone (51–1) 208–8650, fax (51–1) 420–0144; e-mail: gcardenas@imarpe.gob.pe.
José Allemant, Ministerio de Producción, Calle 1 Oeste #066, San Isidro, Lima 27, Peru, phone (51–1) 616–2222; e-mail: jallemant@produce.gob.pe.
Miguel Niquen, Instituto del Mar del Perú, Esquina de Gamarra y General Valle s/n Chucuito-Callao Lima, Peru, phone (51–1) 208–8650; e-mail: mniquen@imarpe.gob.pe.

Chinese Taipei:
Chung-Hai Kwoh, Fisheries Agency, Council of Agriculture, 6F No. 100, Sec. 2 Heping W. Rd Zhongzheng Dist., Taipei, 100, Taiwan, phone (886–2) 3343–6114, fax (886–2) 2332–7366; e-mail: chunghai@ms1.fa.gov.tw.
Hong-Yen Huang, Fisheries Agency, No. 2 Chaozhou St. Zhongzheng Dist., Taipei City, Taiwan, 100, phone (886–7) 823–9828, fax (886–7) 815 8278; e-mail: hangyen@ms1.fa.gov.tw.
Ted Tien-Hsiang Tsai, Fisheries Agency, No. 2, Chaozhou St. Zhongzheng Dist., Taipei City, Taiwan, phone (886–2) 3343–6045, fax (886–2) 3343–6128, e-mail: ted@ms1.fa.gov.tw.

USA:
Donald Hansen, Pacific Fishery Management Council, 34675 Golden Lantern, Dana Point, CA 92629, USA, phone (949) 496–5794; e-mail: don.hansen@noaa.gov.
Edward Weissman, U.S. Commissioner-IATTC, 1857 Spindrift Dr., La Jolla, CA 92037, USA, phone (858) 454 1558; e-mail: eweissman@aol.com.
Barry Thom, NOAA/National Marine Fisheries Service, 1201 NE Lloyd Blvd., Suite 1100, Portland, OR 97232, USA, phone (503) 231–6266, fax (503) 230–5441; e-mail: barry.thom@noaa.gov.
William Fox, U.S. Commissioner-IATTC, P.O. Box 60633, San Diego, CA 92166, USA, phone (202) 495–4397, fax (619) 222–2489; e-mail: bill.fox@wwfus.org.

Vanuatu:
Christophe Emelee, Vanuatu Government, P.O. Box 1640, Port Vila, Vanuatu, phone (678) 774–0219; e-mail: tunafishing@vanuatu.com.vu, c.emelee@yahoo.co.nz.
Dimitri Malvirlani, Vanuatu IATTC Commissioner, Marine Quay, P.O. Box 320, Port-Vila, Vanuatu, phone (678) 23128, fax (678) 22949; e-mail: vma@vanuatu.com.vn.
Laurent Parente, Vanuatu IATTC Commissioner, P.O. Box 1435, Port Vila Vanuatu, phone (447–55) 438–0005; e-mail: laurentparente-vanuatu-imo@hotmail.com.
Roy M. Joy, Embassy of Vanuatu, Avenue de Tervueren 380 Chemin de Ronde, Brussels 1150, Belgium, phone (32–2) 771–7494, fax (32–2) 771–7494; e-mail: rjoy@vanuatuembassy.net, joyroymickey@gmail.com.

Venezuela:
Alvin Delgado Martínez, FUNDATUN–PNOV, Urb. La Floresta Calle B I22, Cumaná, Sucre, 6101, Venezuela, phone (58–293) 433–0431, fax (58–293) 433–0431; e-mail: fundatunpnov@gmail.com.

Tibisay León, Instituto Socialista de la Pesca y Acuacultura, Centro Simón Bolívar, Avenida Lecuna Parque Central, Torre Este, Piso 12 al 14, Caracas, Venezuela, phone (58–212) 461–9225, fax (58–212) 952–0707; e-mail: uii@insopesca.goh ve, orinsopesca@gmail.com.

Nancy Tablante, Instituto Socialista de la Pesca y Acuicultura, Centro Simón Bolívar, Avenida Lecuna Parque Central, Torre Este, Piso 12 al 14, Caracas, Venezuela, phone (58–212) 461–9225, fax (58–212) 953–9972; e-mail: ntablante@hotmail.com, orinsopesca@gmail.com.

INTERNATIONAL BOUNDARY AND WATER COMMISSION,

UNITED STATES AND MEXICO

UNITED STATES SECTION

The Commons, Building C, Suite 100, 4171 North Mesa, El Paso, TX 79902–1441

phone (915) 832–4100, fax 832–4190, http://www.ibwc.gov

Commissioner.—Edward Drusina, 832–4101.
Foreign Affairs Secretary.—Sally Spencer, 832–4105.
Principal Engineers: Jose Nuñez, 832–4749; Carlos Peña, 832–4160.
Human Resources Director.—Fred Graf, 832–4114.
General Counsel / Legal Advisor.—Matt Myers, 832–4728.

MEXICAN SECTION

Avenida Universidad, No. 2180, Zona de El Chamizal, A.P. 1612–D, C.P. 32310,

Ciudad Juarez, Chihuahua, Mexico

P.O. Box 10525, El Paso, TX 79995

phone 011–52–16–13–7311 or 011–52–16–13–7363 (Mexico)

Commissioner.—Roberto F. Salmon Castello.
Foreign Affairs Secretary.—Jose de Jesus Luevano Grano.
Principal Engineers: Gilberto Elizalde Hernandez, L. Antonio Rascon Mendoza.

INTERNATIONAL BOUNDARY COMMISSION, UNITED STATES AND CANADA

UNITED STATES SECTION

2000 L Street, NW., Suite 615, 20036, phone (202) 736–9100

Commissioner.—Kyle Hipsley.
Deputy Commissioner.—John T. Moore.
Administrative Officer.—Tracy Morris.

CANADIAN SECTION

210–88 Booth Street, Ottawa, ON, Canada K1A 0Y7, phone (613) 808–2758

Commissioner.—Peter Sullivan.
Deputy Commissioner.—Daniel Fortin.

INTERNATIONAL COTTON ADVISORY COMMITTEE

Headquarters: 1629 K Street, NW., Suite 702, 20006, secretariat@icac.org
phone (202) 463–6660, fax 463–6950
(Permanent Secretariat of the Organization)

MEMBER COUNTRIES

Argentina	Greece	Sudan
Australia	India	Switzerland
Brazil	Kazakhstan	Tanzania
Burkina Faso	Kenya	Togo
Cameroon	Korea, Republic of	Turkey
Chad	Mali	Uganda
China (Taiwan)	Mozambique	United States
Colombia	Pakistan	Uzbekistan
Côte d'Ivoire	Poland	Zambia
Egypt	Russia	Zimbabwe
France	South Africa	
Germany	Spain	

Executive Director.—José D. Sette.
   Statistician.—Rebecca Pandolp.
   Director of Trade Analysis: Andrei Guitchounts.
   Economist.—Lorena Ruíz.
   Head of Technical Information Section.—M. Rafiq Chaudhry.

INTERNATIONAL JOINT COMMISSION, UNITED STATES AND CANADA

UNITED STATES SECTION
2000 L Street, NW., Suite 615, 20036
phone (202) 736–9000, fax 632–2006, http://www.ijc.org

Chair.—Lana B. Pollack.
   Commissioners: Dereth Glance, Richard Moy.
   Secretary.—Charles A. Lawson.
   Legal Advisor.—Susan Daniel.
   Engineering Advisors: Mark Colosimo, Mark Gabriel.
   Public Information Officer.—Frank Bevacqua.
   Ecologist.—Victor Serveiss.
   GIS Coordinator.—Michael Laitta.
   Policy Advisor.—David Dempsey.
   Senior Advisor.—Shannon Runyon.

CANADIAN SECTION
234 Laurier Avenue West, Ottawa, Ontario Canada K1P 6K6
phone (613) 995–2984, fax 993–5583

Chairman.—Gordon Walker.
   Commissioners: Benoit Bouchard, Richard Morgan.
   Secretary.—Camille Mageau.
   Legal Advisor.—Shane Zurbrigg.
   Public Affairs Advisor.—Bernard Beckhoff.
   Director, Science and Engineering.—Pierre Yves Caux.
   Engineering Advisors: David Fay, Wayne Jenkinson.
   Ecosystem Advisor.—Glenn Benoy.
   Director, Policy and Programs.—Paul Allen.
   Senior Advisor.—Nick Heisler.

GREAT LAKES REGIONAL OFFICE
Eighth Floor, 100 Ouellette Avenue, Windsor, Ontario Canada N9A 6T3
phone (519) 257–6700 (Canada), (313) 226–2170 (U.S.)

Director.—Patricia Morris.

Public Affairs Officer.—Vacant.
Physical Scientists: Antoinette Arvai, Raj Bejankiwar, Jennifer Boehme, Mark Burrows, Matthew Child, Lizhu Wang, John E. Wilson.

INTERNATIONAL LABOR ORGANIZATION
Headquarters: 4, route des Morillons, CH-1211, Geneva 22, Switzerland
phone 41–22–799–6111, http://www.ilo.org
Washington Office, 1808 I Street, NW., Suite 900, 20006
phone (202) 617–3952, fax 617–3960, http://www.ilo.org/washington
Liaison Office with the United Nations
One Dag Hammarskjöld Plaza, 885 Second Avenue, 30th Floor, New York, NY 10017
phone (212) 697–0150, fax 697–5218, http://www.ilo.org/newyork

International Labor Office (Permanent Secretariat of the Organization)
Headquarters Geneva:
  Director-General.—Guy Ryder.
Washington:
  Director.—Nancy Donaldson.
  Deputy Director,—Erick Zeballos.
New York:
  Director.—Jane Stewart.
  Deputy Director.—Vinicius Pinheiro.

INTERNATIONAL MONETARY FUND
700 19th Street, NW., 20431, phone (202) 623–7000
http://www.imf.org

MANAGEMENT AND SENIOR OFFICERS

Managing Director.—Christine Lagarde.
  First Deputy Managing Director.—David Lipton.
  Deputy Managing Director and Chief Administrative Officer.—Carla Grasso.
  Deputy Managing Directors: Mitsuhiro Furusawa, Min Zhu.
  Economic Counselor.—Maurice Obstfeld.
  Financial Counselor.—José Viñals.
  Institute for Capacity Development Director.—Sharmini A. Coorey.
  Legal Department General Counsel.—Sean Hagan.
  Departmental Directors:
    African.—Antoinette Monsio Sayeh.
    Asia and Pacific.—Changyong Rhee.
    Budget and Planning.—Daniel Citrin.
    European.—Poul Mathias Thomsen.
    Communications.—Gerard T. Rice.
    Finance.—Andrew Tweedie.
    Fiscal Affairs.—Vitor Gaspar.
    Human Resources.—Mark Plant.
    Internal Audit and Inspection.—Clare Brady.
    Middle East and Central Asia.—Masood Ahmed.
    Monetary and Capital Markets.—José Viñals.
    Strategy, Policy, and Review.—Siddharth Tiwari.
    Research.—Maurice Obstfeld.
    Secretary.—Jianhai Lin.
    Statistics.—Louis Marc Ducharme.
    Technology and General Services.—Susan Swart (acting).
    Chief Information Officer.—Susan Swart.
    Western Hemisphere.—Alejandro Werner.
  Director, Regional Office for Asia and the Pacific.—Odd Per Brekk.
  Director, Europe Offices.—Jeffrey Franks.
  Director and Special Representative to the United Nations.—Axel Albert Emil Bertuch-Samuels.

Independent Evaluations Office.—Moises J. Schwartz.
Institute for Capacity Development.—Sharmini A. Correy.
Legal and General Counsel.—Sean Hagan.

EXECUTIVE DIRECTORS AND ALTERNATES

Executive Directors:
Fahad Ibrahim A. Alshathri, represents Saudi Arabia.
Herve M. Jodon de Villeroche, represents France.
Audun Groenn, represents Denmark, Estonia, Finland, Iceland, Latvia, Lithuania, Norway, Sweden.
Otaviano Canuto Canuto dos Santos Filho, represents Brazil, Capo Verde, Dominican Republic, Ecuador, Guyana, Haiti, Nicaragua, Panama, Suriname, Timor-Leste, Trinidad and Tobago.
Serge Dupont, represents Antigua and Barbuda, the Bahamas, Barbados, Belize, Canada, Dominica, Grenada, Ireland, Jamaica, St. Kitts and Nevis, St. Lucia, St. Vincent and the Grenadines.
Chilese Mpundu Kapwepwe, represents Angola, Botswana, Burundi, Eritrea, Ethiopia, Gambia, Kenya, Lesotho, Liberia, Malawi, Mozambique, Namibia, Nigeria, Sierra Leone, Somalia, South Africa, South Sudan (Republic of), Swaziland, Tanzania, Uganda, Zambia, Zimbabwe.
Rakesh Mohan, represents Bangladesh, Bhutan, India, Sri Lanka.
Marzunisham Omar, represents Brunei Darussalam, Cambodia, Fiji, Indonesia, Lao People's Democratic Republic, Malaysia, Myanmar, Nepal, Philippines, Singapore, Thailand, Tonga, Vietnam.
Daniel Heller, represents Azerbaijan, Kazakhstan, Kyrgyz Republic, Poland, Serbia, Switzerland, Tajikistan, Turkmenistan.
Fernando Jimenez Latorre, represents Colombia, Costa Rica, El Salvador, Guatemala, Honduras, Mexico, Spain, Venezuela (Republica Bolivariana de).
Ibrahim Canakci, represents Austria, Belarus, Czech Republic, Hungary, Kosovo, Slovak Republic, Slovenia, Turkey.
Ngueto Tiraina Yambaye, represents Benin, Burkina Faso, Cameroon, Central African Republic, Chad, Comoros, Congo (Democratic Republic of), Congo (Republic of), Côte d'Ivoire, Djibouti, Equatorial Guinea, Gabon, Guinea, Guinea-Bissau, Madagascar, Mali, Mauritania, Mauritius, Niger, Rwanda, São Tomé and Principe, Senegal, Togo.
Carlo Cottarelli, represents Albania, Greece, Italy, Malta, Portugal, San Marino.
Mark Sobel, represents United States.
Mikio Kajikawa, represents Japan.
Jafar Mojarrad, represents Afghanistan (Islamic Republic of), Algeria, Ghana, Iran (Islamic Republic of), Morocco, Pakistan, Tunisia.
Sergio Chodos, represents Argentina, Bolivia, Chile, Paraguay, Peru, Uruguay.
Hubert Temmeyer, represents Germany.
Hazem Beblawi Elbeblawi, represents Bahrain, Egypt, Iraq, Jordan, Kuwait, Lebanon, Libya, Maldives, Oman, Qatar, Syrian Arab Republic, United Arab Emirates, Yemen (Republic of).
Aleksei V. Mozhin, represents Russian Federation.
Barry Sterland, represents Australia, Kiribati, Korea, Marshall Islands, Micronesia (Federated States of), Mongolia, New Zealand, Palau, Papua New Guinea, Samoa, Seychelles, Solomon Islands, Tuvalu, Uzbekistan, Vanuatu.
Menno Snel, represents Armenia, Bosnia and Herzegovina, Bulgaria, Croatia, Cyprus, Georgia, Israel, Luxembourg, Macedonia (former Yugoslav Republic of), Moldova, Montenegro Republic, Netherlands, Romania, Ukraine.
Jin Zhongxia, represents China.
Steve Field, represents United Kingdom.

INTERNATIONAL ORGANIZATION FOR MIGRATION

**Geneva Headquarters: 17 Route Des Morillons (P.O. Box 71), CH1211
Geneva 19, Switzerland, phone +41.22.798.61.50
Washington Mission: 1752 N Street, NW., Suite 700
Washington, DC 20036, phone (202) 862–1826
New York Mission: 122 East 42nd Street, 48th Floor
New York, NY 10168–1610, phone (212) 681–7000**

HEADQUARTERS

Director General.—William Lacy Swing (United States).
Deputy Director General.—Laura Thompson (Costa Rica).
Washington Chief of Mission.—Luca Dalloglio (Italy).
New York Chief of Mission.—Vacant.
Permanent Observer to the United Nations.—Ashraf El Nour (South Sudan).

MEMBER STATES

Afghanistan	Ecuador	Mali
Albania	Egypt	Malta
Algeria	El Salvador	Marshall Islands
Angola	Estonia	Mauritania
Antigua and Barbuda	Ethiopia	Mauritius
Argentina	Fiji	Mexico
Armenia	Finland	Micronesia
Australia	France	Moldova (Republic of)
Austria	Gabon	Mongolia
Azerbaijan	Gambia	Montenegro
Bahamas	Georgia	Morocco
Bangladesh	Germany	Mozambique
Belarus	Ghana	Myanmar
Belgium	Greece	Namibia
Belize	Guatemala	Nauru
Benin	Guinea	Netherlands
Bolivia	Guinea-Bissau	Nepal
(Plurinational State of)	Guyana	New Zealand
Bosnia and Herzegovina	Haiti	Nicaragua
Botswana	Holy See	Niger
Brazil	Honduras	Nigeria
Bulgaria	Hungary	Norway
Burkina Faso	Iceland	Pakistan
Burundi	India	Panama
Cambodia	Iran (Islamic Republic of)	Papua New Guinea
Cameroon	Ireland	Paraguay
Canada	Israel	Peru
Cape Verde	Italy	Philippines
Central African Republic	Jamaica	Poland
Chad	Japan	Portugal
Chile	Jordan	Romania
Colombia	Kazakhstan	Rwanda
Comoros	Kenya	Saint Vincent and
Congo	Korea (Republic of)	the Grenadines
Costa Rica	Kyrgyzstan	Samoa
Côte d'Ivoire	Latvia	Senegal
Croatia	Lesotho	Serbia
Cyprus	Liberia	Seychelles
Czech Republic	Libya	Sierra Leone
Democratic Republic of	Lithuania	Slovakia
the Congo	Luxembourg	Slovenia
Denmark	Madagascar	Somalia
Djibouti	Malawi	South Africa
Dominican Republic	Maldives	South Sudan

Spain	Timor-Leste	United Republic of Tanzania
Sri Lanka	Togo	United States of America
Sudan	Trinidad and Tobago	Uruguay
Suriname	Tunisia	Vanuatu
Swaziland	Turkey	Venezuela
Sweden	Turkmenistan	(Bolivarian Republic of)
Switzerland	Uganda	Viet Nam
Tajikistan	Ukraine	Yemen
Thailand	United Kingdom of Great	Zambia
The former Yugoslav	Britain and Northern	Zimbabwe
Republic of Macedonia	Ireland	

OBSERVER STATES (10)

Bahrain	Indonesia	Sao Tome and Principe
Bhutan	Qatar	Saudi Arabia
China	Russian Federation	
Cuba	San Marino	

International Governmental and Non-Governmental Organizations
Organs and Organizations of the United Nations System

United Nations
  Economic and Social Commission for Asia and the Pacific (ESCAP)
  Economic Commission for Africa (ECA)
  Economic Commission for Latin America and the Caribbean (ECLAC)
  Food and Agriculture Organization of the United Nations (FAO)
  International Labour Organization (ILO)
  International Maritime Organization (IMO)
  Office for the Coordination of Humanitarian Affairs (OCHA)
  Office of the United Nations High Commissioner for Human Rights (OHCHR)
  Office of the United Nations High Commissioner for Refugees (UNHCR)
  United Nations Children's Fund (UNICEF)
  United Nations Conference on Trade and Development (UNCTAD)
  United Nations Development Programme (UNDP)
  United Nations Educational, Scientific and Cultural Organization (UNESCO)
  United Nations Entity for Gender Equality and the Empowerment of Women (UN–WOMEN)
  United Nations Environment Programme (UNEP)
  United Nations Human Settlements Programme (UN–HABITAT)
  United Nations Industrial Development Organization (UNIDO)
  United Nations Population Fund (UNFPA)
  United Nations Research Institute for Social Development (UNRISD)
  Universal Postal Union (UPU)

World Bank
  World Food Programme (WFP)
  World Health Organization (WHO)
  World Intellectual Property Organization (WIPO)
  World Meteorological Organization (WMO)
  Intergovernmental organizations and other entities

African Union
  African, Caribbean and Pacific Group of States (ACP Group)
  Asian-African Legal Consultative Organization (AALCO)
  Common Market for Eastern and Southern Africa (COMESA)
  Community of Portuguese Speaking Countries (CPLP)
  Community of Sahel-Saharan States (CEN–SAD)

Council of Europe
  East African Community (EAC)
  Economic Community of Central African States (ECCAS)
  Economic Community of West African States Commission (ECOWAS)

European Union (EU)
  Ibero-American General Secretariat (SEGIB)

Inter-American Development Bank (IADB)
Intergovernmental Authority on Development (IGAD)
International Centre for Migration Policy Development (ICMPD)
International Committee of the Red Cross
International Federation of Red Cross and Red Crescent Societies
Islamic Educational, Scientific and Cultural Organization (ISESCO)
Italian-Latin American Institute

League of Arab States
Organisation internationale de la Francophonie
Organization for Economic Co-operation and Development
Organization of American States
Organization of the Islamic Cooperation
Parliamentary Assembly of the Union for the Mediterranean
Sovereign Order of Malta
Southeast European Cooperative Initiative (SECI) - Regional
Center for Combating Transborder Crime
Southern African Development Community Secretariat (SADC)
Union du Maghreb Arabe (UMA)

Other Organizations With Observer Status

Africa Humanitarian Action
(AHA)
Africa Recruit
African and Black Diaspora
Global Network on HIV
and AIDS (ABDGN)
African Foundation for
Development
American Jewish Joint
Distribution Committee
(JDC) - Center for
International Migration
and Integration (CIMI)
Amnesty International
Assistance pédagogique
internationale (API)
Australian Catholic Migrant
and Refugee Office
(ACMRO)
CARAM Asia
CARE International
Caritas Internationalis
Catholic Relief Services
Center for Migration Studies
of New York (CMS)
Danish Refugee Council
December 18
Episcopal Migration
Ministries
European Youth Forum (YFJ)
Federation of Ethnic
Communities' Councils
of Australia, Inc.
Femmes Africa Solidarité
(FAS)

FOCSIV-Volontari Nel
Mondo (Federation of
Christian Organizations
for International
Volunteer Service)
Food for the Hungry
International
Friends World Committee for
Consultation (FWCC)
Hassan II Foundation for
Moroccans Residing
Abroad
HIAS, Inc.
Human Rights Watch
Internal Displacement
Monitoring Centre
International Catholic
Migration Commission
International Council of
Voluntary Agencies
International Council on
Social Welfare
International Institute of
Humanitarian Law
(IIHL)
International Islamic Relief
Organisation
International Medical Corps
International Organisation of
Employers
International Rescue
Committee
International Social Service
International Trade Union
Confederation (ITUC)
INTERSOS

Islamic Relief
Japan International Friendship
and Welfare Foundation
Jesuit Refugee Service (JRS)
"La Caixa" Foundation
Lutheran World Federation
Migrant Help
Migrants Rights International
(MRI)
NGO Committee on
Migration
Niwano Peace Foundation
Norwegian Refugee Council
Partage avec les enfants du
tiers monde
Paulino Torras Doménech
Foundation
Qatar Charity
Refugee Council of Australia
Refugee Education Trust
(RET)
Sasakawa Peace Foundation
Save the Children
Scalabrini International
Migration Network
(SIMN)
Solidar
Terre des Hommes
International Federation
The Hague Institute for
Global Justice
Tolstoy Foundation, Inc.
United Ukrainian American
Relief Committee
World Council of Churches
World Vision International

DUTY STATIONS 2015

Afghanistan 2
Herat
Kabul

Albania 1
Tirana

Algeria 1
Algiers

Angola 3
Luanda
Maquela d Zombo
Uige

Argentina 1
Buenos Aires

Armenia 2
Gyumri
Yerevan

Australia 6
Brisbane
Canberra
Darwin
Melbourne
Perth
Sydney

Austria 2
Vienna CO
Vienna RO

Azerbaijan 2
Baku
Mingachevir

Bangladesh 3
Chittagong
Dhaka
Sylhet

Belarus 1
Minsk

Belgium 1
Brussels

Benin 1
Cotonou

**Bolivia
(Plurinational State of) 1**
La Paz

Bosnia and Herzegovina 2
Banja Luka
Sarajevo

Botswana 1
Gaborone

Bulgaria 2
Burgas
Sofia

Burkina Faso 1
Ouagadougou

Burundi 3
Bujumbura
Rutana
Ruyigi

Cabo Verde 1
Praia

Cambodia 1
Phnom Penh

Cameroon 1

Yaounde

Canada 1
Ottawa

Central African Republic 3
Bangui
Boda
Kabo

Chad 8
Abeche
Farchana
Faya
Gore
Mao
Moussoro
N'Djamena
Tissi

Chile 1
Santiago

China 2
Beijing
Hong Kong SAR

Colombia 31
Arauca
Armenia
Barranquilla
Bogota
Bucaramanga
Buenaventura
Cali
Cartagena
Cauca Valley
Cucuta
Florencia
Guajira
Ibagué
Manizales
Medellin
Mitu
Mocoa
Monteria
Nariño
Neiva
Pasto
Pereira
Popayan
Quibdo
Santa Marta
Sincelejo
SJ de Guaviare
Tumaco
Tunja
Valledupar
Villavicencio

Congo 1
Brazzaville

Costa Rica 1
San Jose

Côte d'Ivoire 4
Abidjan

Danane
Tabou
Toulepleu

Croatia 1
Zagreb

Cyprus 1
Nicosia

Czech Republic 1
Prague

**Democratic Republic of the
Congo (the) 7**
Bukavu
Bunia
Goma
Kasindi
Kimpese
Kinshasa
Lubumbashi

Denmark 1
Copenhagen

Djibouti 1
Djibouti

Dominican Republic 1
Santo Domingo

Ecuador 1
Quito

Egypt 1
Cairo

El Salvador 1
San Salvador

Estonia 1
Tallinn

Ethiopia 9
Addis Ababa
Assosa
Dollo Addo
Gambella
Jijiga
Moyale
Semera
Shimelba
Shire Endaselas

Finland 1
Helsinki

France 2
Marseille
Paris

Gabon 1
Libreville

Gambia 1
Banjul

Georgia 5

Batumi
Gori
Kutaisi
Tbilisi
Telavi
Germany 2
Berlin
Nuremberg
Ghana 1
Accra

Greece 1
Athens

Guatemala 1
Guatemala City

Guinea 2
Conakry
Nzerekore
Guyana 1
Georgetown

Haiti 3
Gonaives
Ouanaminthe
Port-au-Prince
Honduras 1
Tegucigalpa

Hungary 1
Budapest

India 1
New Delhi

Indonesia 25
Acch Selatan
Acch Timur
Acch Utara
Ambon
Balikpapan
Banda Aceh
Batam
Bener Meriah
Jakarta
Jayapura
Jimbaran
Kupang
Langsa
Lhokseumawe
Makassar
Medan
Menado
Merauke
Pekanbaru
Pontianak
Semarang
Surabaya
Takengon
Tanjung Pinang
Yogyakarta
Iran 1
Teheran

Iraq 6
Al Basrah
Ar Ramadi
Baghdad
Dohuk
Erbil
Sulaymaniah
Ireland 1
Dublin

Italy 2
Rome
Turin

Jamaica 1
Kingston

Japan 1
Tokyo

Jordan 1
Amman

Kazakhstan 2
Almaty
Astana
Kenya 8
Dadaab
Eldoret
Garissa
Kakuma
Lodwar
Marsabit
Nairobi
Wajir
Korea (Republic of) 1
Seoul

Kuwait 1
Kuwait City

Kyrgyzstan 2
Bishkek
Osh
**Lao People's Democratic
   Republic 1**
Vientiane

Latvia 1
Riga

Lebanon 1
Beirut

Lesotho 1
Maseru

Liberia 4
Buchanan
Monrovia
Sinje
Tubmanburg
Libya 2
Benghazi

Tripoli
Lithuania 1
Vilnius

Madagascar 1
Antananarivo

Malawi 1
Lilongwe

Malaysia 1
Kuala Lumpur

Maldives 1
Male

Mali 4
Bamako
Gao
Mopti
Tomboctou
Malta 1
Valletta

Marshall Islands 1
Majuro

Mauritania 1
Nouakchott

Mauritius 1
Port Louis

Mexico 3
Mexico City
Tapachula
Tuxtla
**Micronesia (Federated
   States of) 4**
Chuuk
Kosrae
Pohnpei
Yap
Mongolia 1
Ulaanbaatar

Montenegro 1
Podgorica

Morocco 4
Khouribga
Rabat
Tangier
Tetouan
Mozambique 3
Maputo
Quelimane
Xai-Xai
Myanmar 12
Mon
Ayeyarwady Delt
Bogalay
Hpa-an

Loikaw
Mawlamyinegyun
Myawaddy
Myitkyina
Sittwe
Thaton
Yangon
Ye

Namibia 1
Windhoek

Nepal 4
Chautara
Damak
Gorkha
Kathmandu

Netherlands 3
Schiphol Airp.
The Hague
Zwolle

Nicaragua 1
Managua

Niger 4
Arlit
Diffa
Niamey
Zinder

Nigeria 3
Abuja
Lagos
Yola

Norway 1
Oslo

Pakistan 5
Islamabad
Karachi
Lahore
Mirpur
Peshawar

Panama 1
Panama City

Papua New Guinea 6
Buka
Kimbe
Lae
Manus
Popondetta
Port Moresby

Paraguay 1
Asuncion

Peru 1
Lima

Philippines 8
Cebu
Cotabato City
Guiuan
Manila
Ormoc

Roxas
Tacloban
Zamboanga

Poland 1
Warsaw

Portugal 1
Lisbon

Republic of Moldova 1
Chisinau

Romania 1
Bucharest

Russian Federation 2
Krasnodar
Moscow

Rwanda 1
Kigali

Saudi Arabia 1
Riyadh

Senegal 1
Dakar

Serbia 2
Belgrade
Pristina

Sierra Leone 1
Freetown

Slovakia 2
Bratislava
Kosice

Slovenia 1
Ljubljana

Somalia 4
Bossaso
Garowe
Hargeisa-Somali
Mogadishu

South Africa 1
Pretoria

South Sudan 8
Bentiu
Bor
Juba
Maban
Malakal
Malualkon
Renk
Wau

Spain 1
Madrid

Sri Lanka 6
Ampara
Batticaloa
Colombo

Jaffna
Kilinochchi
Vavuniya

Sudan 8
Abyei
El Fasher
El Fula
Geneina
Kadugli
Kassala
Khartoum
Nyala

Switzerland 5
Altstatten
Basel
Bern
Geneva
Kreuzlingen

Syrian Arab Republic 11
Al Hasakah
Aleppo
Damascus
Deirezzor
Dera'a
Homs
Idleb
Latakia
Quneitra
Sweida
Tartus

Tajikistan 1
Dushanbe

Thailand 10
Bangkok
Chanthaburi
Chiang Mai
Chiang Rai
Mae Hong Son
Mae Sariang
Mae Sot
Phang Nga
Ranong
Songkhla
the former Yugoslav
Republic of Macedonia 1
Skopje

Timor-Leste 1
Dili

Togo 1
Lome

Trinidad and Tobago 1
Port of Spain

Tunisia 2
Tunis
Zarzis

Turkey 3
Ankara
Gaziantep
Istanbul

Turkmenistan 1	United States of America 10	Vanuatu 1
Ashgabad	Chicago	Port Vila
	Guantanamo Bay	Venezuela
Uganda 1	Irvine	
Kampala	Los Angeles	(Bolivarian Republic of) 2
	Miami	Caracas
Ukraine 3	New York	San Cristobal
Kharkiv	New York-JFK	Viet Nam 2
Kiev	Newark	Hanoi
Odessa	SLO New York	Ho Chi Minh City
United Arab Emirates 1	Washington	
Dubai	UNSC resolution	Yemen 3
	1244-administered Kosovo 3	Aden
United Kingdom of Great	Mitrovica	Harad
Britain and Northern	Peje	Sana'a
Ireland 1	Pristina	Zambia 1
London		Lusaka
	Uruguay 1	
United Republic of	Montevideo	
Tanzania 3		Zimbabwe 3
Dar-es-Salaam	Uzbekistan 1	Beitbridge
Kigoma	Tashkent	Harare
Moshi		Mutare

Grand Total 401

INTERNATIONAL PACIFIC HALIBUT COMMISSION
UNITED STATES AND CANADA
Headquarters/Mailing address:
2320 West Commodore Way, Suite 300, Seattle, WA 98199-1287
phone (206) 634-1838, fax 632-2983

American Commissioners:
Dr. Jim Balsiger, National Marine Fisheries Service, P.O. Box 21668, Juneau, AK 99802, (907) 586-7221, fax 586-7249.
Robert Alverson, 4005-20th Avenue West, Room 232, Seattle, WA 98199, (206) 283-7735 Don Lane, P.O. Box 2921, Homer, AK 99603, (907) 399-1295

Canadian Commissioners:
David Boyes, 499 Powerhouse Road, Courtenay, BC, Canada V9N9L1 (250) 388-2188.
Paul Ryall, Suite 200, 401 Burrard Street, Vancouver, BC, Canada V6C3S4 (604) 666-0115.
Ted Assu, 754 Nursery Road, Campbell River, BC, Canada V9H3P4 (250) 287-8868.
Director and Secretary (ex officio).—Dr. Bruce M. Leaman, 2320 West Commodore Way, Suite 300, Seattle, WA 98199-1287.

ORGANIZATION OF AMERICAN STATES
17th Street and Constitution Avenue, NW., 20006
phone (202) 458-3000, fax 458-3967

PERMANENT MISSIONS TO THE OAS

Antigua and Barbuda.—Ambassador Sir Ronald Sanders, Permanent Representative, 3216 New Mexico Avenue, NW., 20016, phone 362-5122/5166/5211, fax 362-5225.
Argentina.—Ambassador Nilda Garre, Permanent Representative, 1816 Corcoran Street, NW., 20009, phone 387-4142/4146/4170, fax 328-1591.
The Bahamas.—Ambassador Elliston Rahming, Permanent Representative, 2220 Massachusetts Avenue, NW., 20008, phone 319-2660 to 2667, fax 319-2668.
Barbados.—Ambassador John E. Beale, Permanent Representative, 2144 Wyoming Avenue, NW., 20008, phone 939-9200/9201/9202, fax 332-7467.
Belize.—Ambassador Patrick Andrews, Permanent Representative, 2535 Massachusetts Avenue, NW., 20008-3098, phone 332-9636, ext. 228, fax 332-6888.

Bolivia.—Ambassador Diego Pary, Permanent Representative, 2728 34th Street, NW., 20008, phone 785–0218 / 0219 / 0224, fax 296–0563.
Brazil.—Ambassador Jose Luis Machaco E Costa, Permanent Representative, 2600 Virginia Avenue, NW., Suite 412, 20037, phone 333–4224 / 4225/4226, fax 333–6610.
Canada.—Ambassador Jennifer Loten, Permanent Representative, 501 Pennsylvania Avenue, NW., 20001, phone 682–1768, Ext. 7724, fax 682–7624.
Chile.—Ambassador Juan Pablo Lira, Permanent Representative, 2000 L Street, NW., Suite 440, 20036, phone 887–5475 / 5476 / 5477, fax 775–0713.
Colombia.—Ambassador Andres Gonzalez Diaz, Permanent Representative, 1609 22nd Street, NW., 20008, phone 332–8003 / 8004, fax 234–9781.
Costa Rica.—Ambassador Pablo Barahona, Permanent Representative, 2112 S Street, NW., Suite 300, 20008, phone 234–9280 / 9281, fax 986–2274.
Dominica.—Ambassador Hubert J. Charles, Permanent Representative, 1001 North 19th Street, Suite 1200., Arlington, VA 22209, phone 571–1370, fax 571–384–7916.
Dominican Republic.—Ambassador Pedro Verges, Permanent Representative, 1715 22nd Street, NW., 20008, phone 332–9142 / 0616 / 0772, fax 232–5038.
Ecuador.—Ambassador Marco Albuja, Permanent Representative, 2600 Virginia Avenue, NW., Suite 212, 20037, phone 234–1494/1692 / 8053, fax 667–3482.
El Salvador.—Ambassador Luis Menendez, Permanent Representative, 2308 California Street, NW., 20008, phone 595–7546 / 7545, fax 232–4806.
Grenada.—Ambassador Angus Friday, Permanent Representative, 1701 New Hampshire Avenue, NW., 20009, phone 265–2561, fax 265–2468.
Guatemala.—Ambassador Jose Maria Argueta, Permanent Representative, 1507 22nd Street, NW., 20037, phone 833–4015 / 4016 / 4017, fax 833–4011.
Guyana.—Ambassador Bayney R. Karran, Permanent Representative, 2490 Tracy Place, NW., 20008, phone 265–6900 / 6901, fax 232–1297.
Haiti.—Ambassador Bocchit Edmond, Permanent Representative, 2311 Massachusetts Avenue, NW., 20008, phone 332–4090 / 4096, fax 518–8742.
Honduras.—Ambassador Leonidas Rosa Bautista, Permanent Representative, 3007 Tilden Street, NW., Suite 4M–400, 20008, phone 244–5430/5653 / 5260, no fax.
Jamaica.—Julia C. Hyatt, Interim Representative, 1520 New Hampshire Avenue, NW., 20036, phone 986–0121 / 0123 / 452–0660, fax 452–9395.
Mexico.—Ambassador Emilio Rabasa Gamboa, Permanent Representative, 2440 Massachusetts Avenue, NW., 20008, phone 332–3663 / 3664 / 3984, fax 234–0602.
Nicaragua.—Ambassador Denis Ronaldo Moncada Colindres, Permanent Representative, 1627 New Hampshire Avenue, NW., 20009, phone 332–1643 / 1644 / 939–6536, fax 745–0710.
Panama.—Ambassador Jorge Miranda, Permanent Representative, 2201 Wisconsin Avenue, NW., Suite C–100, 20007, phone 965–4826 / 4819, fax 965–4836.
Paraguay.—Ambassador Elisa Ruiz Diaz Bareiro, Permanent Representative, 2022 Connecticut Avenue, NW., 20008, phone 232–8020 / 8021 / 8022, fax 244–3005.
Peru.—Ambassador Juan Federico Jimenez Mayor, Permanent Representative, 1901 Pennsylvania Avenue, NW., Suite 402, 20006, phone 232–2281/2282 / 1973, fax 466–3068.
Saint Kitts and Nevis.—Ambassador Dr. Everson Hull, Permanent Representative, 1001 North 19th Street, Suite 1260, Arlington, VA 22209, phone 686–2636/ (571) 527–1360, fax 686–5740.
Saint Lucia.—Ambassador Elizabeth Darius-Clarke, Permanent Representative, 1001 North 19th Street, Suite 1200, Arlington, VA 22209, phone 364–6792/ (571) 527–1375, fax 364–6723/ (571) 384–7930.
Saint Vincent and The Grenadines.— Ambassador La Celia A. Prince, Permanent Representative, 1001 North 19th Street, Suite 1260, Arlington, VA 22209, phone 364–6730, fax 364–6736.
Suriname.—Ambassador Niermala Badrising, Permanent Representative, 3400 International Place, NW., Suite 4L, 20008, phone 629–4402/4401 / 4392, fax 629–4769.
Trinidad and Tobago.—Colin Michael Connelly, Interim Representative, 1708 Massachusetts Avenue, NW., 20036–1903, phone 467–6490, fax 785–3130.
United States of America.—Michael Fitzpatrick, Interim Representative, WHA/USOAS Bureau of Western Hemisphere Affairs, Department of State, Room 5914, 20520–6258, phone 647–9376, fax 647–0911 / 6973.
Uruguay.—Ambassador Hugo Cayrus, Permanent Representative, 1913 I (Eye) Street, NW., 4th Floor, 20006, phone 223–1961, fax 223–1966.
Venezuela.—Ambassador Roy Chaderton Matos, Permanent Representative, 1099 30th Street, NW., Second Floor, 20007, phone 342–5837 / 5838 / 5839 / 5840 / 5841, fax 625–5657.

GENERAL SECRETARIAT

Secretary General.—Luis Almagro, 370–5000.

Chief of Staff to the Secretary General.—Ambassador Jacinth Henry-Martin, 370–0300.
Assistant Secretary General.—Nestor Mendez, 370–0261, fax 458–3011.
Chief of Staff to the Assistant Secretary General.—Ambassador Esteban Lainez, 370 0195.
Executive Secretary for—
  Integral Development.—(Appointment pending) 370–9014.
  Inter-American Commission on Human Rights.—Emilio Alvarez Icaza, 370–9000.
Secretary for—
  Administration and Finance.—Peter Quilter, 370–5401.
  Multidimensional Security.—(Appointment pending) 370–9959.
  Political Affairs.—Francisco Guerrero, 370–9962.
  External Relations.—(Appointment pending) 370–0281.
  Legal Services.—Jean Michel Arrighi, 370–0741.
Director for—
  Summits Secretariat.—(Appointment pending) 370–0281.
  Press and Communications.—Gonzalo Espariz, 370–5437.

ORGANIZATION FOR ECONOMIC CO-OPERATION AND DEVELOPMENT

Headquarters: Paris, France, www.oecd.org

Washington Center, 2001 L Street, NW., Suite 650, 20036, phone (202) 785–6323, fax 785–0350,Washington.contact@oecd.org, www.oecd.org/washington

PARIS HEADQUARTERS

Secretary-General.—Angel Gurría.
Deputy Secretaries-General: William C. Danvers, Stefan Kapferer, Mari Kiviniemi, Rintaro Tamaki.
Chief Economist.—Catherine Mann.

WASHINGTON CENTER

Head of Center.—Carol Guthrie.
Member Countries:

Australia	Hungary	Poland
Austria	Iceland	Portugal
Belgium	Ireland	Slovak Republic
Canada	Israel	Slovenia
Chile	Italy	Spain
Czech Republic	Japan	Sweden
Denmark	Korea	Switzerland
Estonia	Luxembourg	Turkey
Finland	Mexico	United Kingdom
France	Netherlands	United States
Germany	New Zealand	
Greece	Norway	

OECD WASHINGTON CENTER

1776 Eye Street, NW., Suite 450, 20006, phone (202) 785–6323, fax 315–2508

http://www.oecd.org/washington

Head of Center.—Carol Guthrie.

PAN AMERICAN HEALTH ORGANIZATION (PAHO)
REGIONAL OFFICE OF THE WORLD HEALTH ORGANIZATION
525 23rd Street, NW., 20037, phone (202) 974–3000
fax 974–3663

Director.—Dr. Carissa F. Etienne, 974–3408.
Deputy Director.—Dr. Isabella Danel, 974–3178.
Assistant Director.—Dr. Francisco Becerra, 974–3404.
Director of Administration.—Gerald Anderson, 974–3412.

PAHO / WHO FIELD OFFICES
OPS / WHO OFICINAS DE LOS REPRESENTANTES EN LOS PAISES

Barbados and Eastern Caribbean Countries (ECC serves the following countries, territories and departments: Antigua and Barbuda, Barbados, Dominica, Grenada, St. Kitts and Nevis, Saint Lucia, St. Vincent and the Grenadines. Overseas Territories (Anguilla, British Virgin Islands, Montserrat).—Dr. Godfrey Xuereb, Dayralls and Navy Garden Roads, Christ Church, (P.O. Box 508), Bridgetown, Barbados, phone (246) 426–3860 / 435–9263, fax 228–5402, e-mail: ECC@ecc.paho.org, http://www.cpc.paho.org.
Caribbean Program Coordination, CPC.—Eng. Adrianus Vlugman, a.i., Caribbean Program Coordinator, Dayralls and Navy Garden Roads, Christ Church, Bridgetown, Barbados (P.O. Box 508), (French Antilles: Guadaloupe, Martinique, St. Martin and St. Bartholomew, French Guiana), phone (246) 426–3860/ 3865 427–9434, fax 436–9779, e-mail: email@cpc.paho.org, http://www.cpc.paho.org.
PAHO/WHO Representatives:
Argentina.—Dr. Maureen Birmingham, Marcelo T. de Alvear 684, 4o. piso, 1058 Buenos Aires, Argentina, phone (54–11) 4319–4200, fax 4319–4201, e-mail: info@ops.org.ar, http://www.ops.org.ar.
Bahamas (Also serves Turks and Caicos).—Dr. Gerarda Eijkemans, 2nd Floor, Grosvenor Medical Centre, Grosvenor Close, Shirley Street, Nassau, Bahamas, phone (242) 326–7299 / 356–4730, fax 326–7012, e-mail: email@bah.paho.org.
Belize.—Dr. Roberto Escoto, 4792 Coney Drive, Coney Drive Business Plaza, 3rd Floor, (P.O. Box 1834), Belize City, Belize, phone (501–2) 2448–85 / 2339–46, fax 2309–17, e-mail: admin@blz.paho.org, http://www.blz.paho.org.
Bolivia.—Dr. Luis Fernando Leanes, Calle 18 No. 8022, Edificio Parque 18 Piso 2 y 3, Zona Calacoto, La Paz, Bolivia, phone (591–2) 297–9730 / fax 297–1146, e-mail: pwrbol@bol.ops-oms.org, http://www.ops.org.bo.
Brazil.—Dr. Joaquin Molina, Setor de Embaixadas Norte, Lote 19, 70800–400, Brasilia, (Caixa Postal 08–629, 70312–970, Brasilia, D.F., Brasil), phone (55–61) 3251–9455 /9549 /9500, fax 3223–0269, e-mail: email@bra.ops-oms.org, http://www.opas.org.br/.
Chile.—Dra. Paloma Cuchi, Av. Dag Hammarskjold 3269, Vitacura, Santiago, Chile. phone (56–2) 2437–4600 / 4605, fax 207–4717, e-mail: email@chi.ops-oms.org, http:// www.chi.ops-oms.org.
Colombia.—Dr. Gina Watson, Calle 66 No. 11–50, Piso 6 y 7, Edificio Villorio, Bogota, D.C., Colombia, phone (57–1) 314–4141 /254–7050, fax 254–7070, e-mail: ops-col@latino.net.co, http://www.col.ops-oms.org/.
Costa Rica.—Dra. Lilian Reneau-Vernon, Calle 16, Avenida 6 y 8, Distrito Hospital, (Apartado 3745), San Jose, Costa Rica, phone (506) 2521–7045 / 2258–5810, fax 2258–5830, e-mail: email@cor.ops-oms.org, http://www.cor.ops-oms.org.
Cuba.—Dr. Christian Morales, Calle 4 No. 407, entre 17 y 19 Vedado, (Casilla diplomatica 68), La Habana, Cuba C.P. 10400, phone (53–7) 831–8944 / 837–5808, fax 833–2075/ 66–2075, e-mail: pwr@cub.ops-oms.org or cruzmari@cub.ops-oms.org, http:// www.cub.ops-oms.org.
Dominican Republic.—Dr. Alma Morales, Edificio OPS / OMS, y Defensa Civil, Calle Pepillo Salcedo-Recta Final, Plaza de la Salud, Ensanche La Fe, (Apartado Postal 1464), Santo Domingo, Republica Dominicana, phone (809) 562–1519 / 544–3241/542–6177, fax 544–0322, e-mail: email@dor.ops-oms.org, http://www.dor.ops-oms.org.
Ecuador.—Dra. Gina Tambini, Amazonas N. 2889 y Mariana de Jesus, Quito, Ecuador, phone (593–2) 2460–330 / 296 / 215, fax 2460–325, e-mail: email@ecu.ops-oms.org, http:// www.opsecu.org.ec.
El Salvador.—Dr. Carlos Garzón, 73 Avenida Sur No. 135, Colonia Escalón, (Apartado Postal 1072, Sucursal Centro), San Salvador, El Salvador, phone (503) 2511–9500/ 9504/ 9501, fax 2511–9555, e-mail: email@els.ops-oms.org, http://www.ops.org.sv/.
Guatemala.—Dr. Guadalupe Verdejo, Diagonal 6, 10–15 zona 10, Edificio Interamericas, torre norte, cuarto nivel, (Apartado Postal 383), Guatemala, Guatemala, phone (502) 2329–4200 / 2336–7426 / 2336–7425, fax 2334–3804, http://www.ops.org.gt.
Guyana.—Dr. William Adu-Know, Lot 8 Brickdam Staoek, (P.O. Box 10969), Georgetown, Guyana, phone (592) 225–3000 / 227–5159, fax 226–6654 /227–4205, e-mail: email@guy.paho.org.
Haiti.—Dr. Jean Luc Poncelet, No. 295 Avenue John Brown, (Boite Postale 1330), Port-au-Prince, Haiti, phone (509) 2814–3000/ 3001/ 3002/ 3005, fax 2814–3089, e-mail: email@hai.ops-oms.org.
Honduras.—Ing. Ana Solis-Ortega Treasure, Edificio Imperial, 6o.y 7o.piso, Avenida República de Panamá, Frente a la Casa de Naciones Unidas, Tegucigalpa M.D.C., Honduras, phone (504) 2221–6091 / 6098 / 6102, fax 2221–6103, e-mail: pwr@hon.ops-oms.org, http://www.paho-who.hn.

Jamaica (also serves Bermuda and Cayman).—Dr. Noreen Jack, 8 Gibraltar Way, University of the West Indies, Mona Campus, Kingston 7, Jamaica, (P.O. Box 384, Cross Roads, P.O., Kingston 5) phone (876) 970–0016, fax 927–2657, e-mail: email@jam.ops-oms.org.

México.—Dr. Diego Gonzalez, a.i., Horacio No. 1855, 3er. Piso, Of. 305, Colonia Los Morales, Polanco, Del. Miguel Hidalgo, México D.F., 11510, México, phone (52–55) 5980–0880/0871, fax 5395–5681, e-mail: e-mail@mex.ops-oms.org, http://www.mex.ops-oms.org.

Nicaragua.—Dr. Socorro Gross Galiano, Complejo Nacional de Salud, Camino a la Sabana, Apartado Postal 1309, Managua, Nicaragua, phone (505) 2289–4200/4800, fax 2289–4999, e-mail: email@nic.ops-oms.org, http://www.ops.org.ni.

Panamá.—Dr. Federico Hernandez Pimentel, Ministerio de Salud de Panamá, Ancon, Avenida Gorgas, Edificio 261, 2o piso, (Casilla Postal 0843–3441), Panamá, Panamá, phone (507) 262–0030/1996, fax 262 4052, e-mail: email@pan.ops-oms.org, http://opsoms.org.pa.

Paraguay.—Dr. Carlos Castillo Solórzano, Edificio "Faro del Rio" Mcal Lopez 957 Esq. Estados Unidos, (Casilla de Correo 839), Asunción, Paraguay, (Casilla de Correo 839) phone (595–21) 450–495/449–864/ fax 450–498, e-mail: email@par.ops-oms.org, http://www.par.ops-oms.org.

Perú.—Dr. Gustavo Vargas, Los Pinos 251, Urbanización Camacho, La Molina, Lima 12, Perú, phone (51–1) 319–5700/5781, fax 437–8289, e-mail: email@per.opsoms.org, http://www.per.ops.oms.org.

Puerto Rico.—Dr. Raúl Castellanos Bran, P.O. Box 70184, San Juan, Puerto Rico 00936, phone (787) 274–7608, fax 250–6547/767–8341.

Suriname.—Dr. Guillermo Troya, Burenstraat #33, (P.O. Box 1863), Paramaribo, Suriname, phone (597) 471–676/425–355, fax 471–568, e-mail: email@sur.paho.org.

Trinidad and Tobago.—Dr. Bernadette Theodore-Gandi, Sweet Briar Place, First Floor, 10–12 Sweet Briar Road, St. Clair, Trinidad, phone (868) 624–7524/4376/2078/625–4492, fax 624–5643, email: email@trt.paho.org.

Uruguay.—Dr. Eduardo Levcovitz, Ave. Brasil 2697, Aptos. 5, 6 y 8, Esquina Coronel Alegre, Codigo Postal 11300, (Casilla de Correo 1821), Montevideo, Uruguay, phone (598–2) 707–3590/2589, fax 707–3530, e-mail: pwr@uru.ops-oms.org, http://www.ops-oms.org.uy/.

Venezuela (Also serves Netherlands Antilles).—Dra. Celia Riera, Avenida Sexta entre 5a y 6a, Transversal No. 43, Quinta OPS/OMS, Urbanización Altamira, Caracas 1060, Venezuela, (Apartado 6722 - Carmelitas, Caracas 1010, Venezuela) phone (58–212) 206–5022/5000, 265–0403 fax 261–6069, e-mail: email@ven.ops-oms.org, http://www.opsoms.org.ve/.

CENTERS

Caribbean Epidemiology Center (CAREC).—Dr. Beryl Irons, 16–18 Jamaica Boulevard, Federation Park, (P.O. Box 164), Port-of-Spain, Trinidad, phone (1–868) 622–4262, fax 622–2792, e-mail: email@carec.ops-oms.org.

Caribbean Food and Nutrition Institute (CFNI).—Dr. Fitzroy J. Henry, University of the West Indies, (P.O. Box 140–Mona), Kingston 7, Jamaica, phone (1–876), 977–6726/1274, fax 927–2657, e-mail: e-mail@cfni.paho.org.

Latin American and Caribbean Center on Health Sciences Information (BIREME).—Mr. Jacobo Finkelman, a.i., Rua Botucatu 862, Vila Clementino, (Caixa Postal 20381), CEP.04023–901, Sao Paulo, SP, Brasil, phone (55–11) 5576–9800/5572–3226, fax 575–8868/5549–2590, e-mail: email@bireme.ops-oms.org.

Latin American Center for Perinatology and Human Development (CLAP).—Dra. Suzanne Jacob Serruya, Hospital de Clinicas, Piso 16, (Casilla de Correo 627, 11000 Montevideo, Uruguay), 11600 Montevideo, Uruguay, phone (598–2) 487–2929, fax 487–2593, e-mail: postmaster@clap.ops-oms.org.

Pan American Foot-and-Mouth Disease Center (PANAFTOSA).—Dr. Ottorino Cosivi, Governador Leonel de Moura Brizola 7778, (Antiga Avenida Presidente Kennedy), São Bento, Duque de Caxias, 25040–004 Rio de Janeiro, Brasil, (Caixa Postal 589, 11000 Montevideo, Uruguay) phone (55–21) 3661–9000/9005/9002, fax 3661–9001, e-mail: panaftosa@panaftosa.pos-oms.org.

PAHO Foundation.—Mailing address: P.O. Box 27733, Washington, DC 30038–7733/Physical address: 1889 F Street, NW., Suite 313, Washington, DC 20006, phone (202) 974–3416, fax 974–3636.

Regional Program on Bioethics.—Dr. Carla Saenz, Bioethics Regional Advisor, Pan American Health Organization, phone (202) 974–3263, fax: 974–3663.

PAHO HIV Caribbean Office.—112–114 Duke Street, Port-of-Spain, Trinidad W.I., phone (868) 624–0400/623–9417, fax 974–8001.

United States-Mexico Border.—This Center closed in 2013.

PERMANENT JOINT BOARD ON DEFENSE, CANADA-UNITED STATES

CANADIAN SECTION

National Defence Headquarters, MG George R. Pearkes Building, Ottawa, ON Canada K1A OK2, phone (613) 992–4423

Members:
Canadian Co-Chairman.—Hon. Laurie Hawn, P.C., C.D., M.P.
Military Policy.—Cmdre Bob Auchterlonie, Director, of General Plans.
Defence Policy.—Gordon Venner, Assistant Deputy, Minister Policy.
Foreign Affairs.—David Drake, DFATD Director General, Security and Intelligence Bureau.
Canada Strategic Joint Staff.—MGen Charles Lamarre, Director of Staff.
NORAD.—LGen Pierre St-Amand, Deputy Commander NORAD.
Public Safety.—Megan Nichols, Director General, Border Policy and International Affairs.
Military Secretary.—LCol Michael Ward, Directorate of Western Hemisphere Policy.
Political Secretary.—Yasemin Heinbecker, DFADT Directorate of International Defence Relations, (613) 867-1234.

UNITED STATES SECTION

JCS, J–5, Western Hemisphere Directorate, Pentagon, Room 2E773, 20318

phone (703) 695–4955

Members:
U.S. Co-Chair.—Elissa Slotkin, Principal Deputy Assistant Secretary of Defense for International Security Affairs.
Military Policy (Joint Staff).—BG Joseph Whitlock, Deputy Director for Western Hemisphere.
Defense Policy (OSD).—Dr. Rebecca Chavez, Deputy Assistant Secretary of Defense for Western Hemisphere.
State Department.—Karen Choe-Fichte, Deputy Director, Office of Canadian Affairs.
National Security Council.—Denison Offutt, Director of North American Affairs.
USNORTHCOM.—RADM Richard P. Snyder, Director of Strategy, Policy, and Plans.
NORAD.—RADM Richard P. Snyder, Director of Strategy, Policy, and Plans.
DHS.—RDML Joanna Nunan, Military Advisor to the Secretary of DHS.
Military Secretary.—Maj. Francis Marino, Canada Desk Officer on the Joint Staff, 695–4955.
Political Secretary.—Keith Gilges, Political Affairs, Office of Canadian Affairs, 202–647-2228.

SECRETARIAT OF THE PACIFIC COMMUNITY

B.P. D5, 98848 Noumea Cedex, New Caledonia, phone (687) 26.20.00, fax 26.38.18

E-mail: spc@spc.int, http://www.spc.int

Director-General.—Dr. Colin Tukuitonga.
Deputy Director General (Noumea).—Cameron Diver.
Deputy Director General (Suva).—To be appointed.
Director of Public Health Division.—Paula Vivili.
Director of Fisheries, Aquaculture and Marine Ecosystems Division.—Moses Amos.
Director of Land Resources Division.—Inoke Ratukalou.
Director of Economic Development Division.—John Hogan.
Director of the Geoscience Division.—Prof. Michael Petterson.
Director, Social Development Division.—To be appointed.
Director of the Statistics for Development Division.—Dr. Gerald Haberkorn.
Director, Strategic Engagement, Policy and Planning Facility.—Cameron Bowles.
Director of Strategic and Corporate Communications.—Julie Marks.
Director of Human Resources.—Pierre-Henri Suatton.
Director of Finance.—Martin van Weerdenburg.
Director of Climate Change and Environmental Sustainability.—Sylvie Goyet.

U.S. Contact: Bureau of East Asian and Pacific Affairs, Office of Australia, New Zealand and Pacific Island Affairs, Department of State, Washington, DC 20520, phone (202) 736–4741, fax 647–0118

Member Countries and Territories of the SPC:

American Samoa	Northern Mariana Islands
Australia	Palau
Cook Islands	Papua New Guinea
Federated States of Micronesia	Pitcairn Islands
Fiji	Samoa
France	Solomon Islands
French Polynesia	Tokelau
Guam	Tonga
Kiribati	Tuvalu
Marshall Islands	United States
Nauru	Vanuatu
New Caledonia	Wallis and Futuna
Niue	
New Zealand	

SECRETARIAT OF THE PACIFIC REGIONAL ENVIRONMENTAL PROGRAMME
P.O. Box 240, Apia, Samoa, phone (685) 21929, fax (685) 20231
E-mail: sprep@sprep.org, http://www.sprep.org

Director General.—David Sheppard.
Deputy Director.—Kosi Latu.
Director of:
Biodiversity and Ecosystem Management Programme.—Stuart Chape.
Climate Change Programme.—Netatua Pelesikoti.
Environmental Monitoring Governance.—Vacant.
Waste Management and Pollution Control.—David Haynes.

U.S. Contact: Bureau of Oceans and International Environmental and Scientific Affairs, Office of Ocean and Polar Affairs, Department of State, Washington, DC 20520 phone (202) 647–3262

Member Countries and Territories of SPREP:

American Samoa	Northern Mariana Islands
Australia	Palau
Cook Islands	Papua New Guinea
Federated States of Micronesia	Samoa
Fiji	Solomon Islands
France	Tokelau
French Polynesia	Tonga
Guam	Tuvalu
Kiribati	United Kingdom
Marshall Islands	United States
Nauru	Vanuatu
New Caledonia	Wallis and Futuna
New Zealand	
Niue	

UNITED NATIONS

GENERAL ASSEMBLY

The General Assembly is composed of all 193 United Nations Member States.

SECURITY COUNCIL

The Security Council has 15 members. The United Nations Charter designates five States as permanent members, and the General Assembly elects ten other members for two-year terms. The term of office for each non-permanent member of the Council ends on 31 December of the year indicated in parentheses next to its name.

The five permanent members of the Security Council are China, France, Russian Federation, United Kingdom and the United States.

The ten non-permanent members of the Council in 2015 are Chad (2015), Chile (2015), Jordan (2015), Lithuania (2015), Nigeria (2015), Angola (2016), Malaysia (2016), New Zealand (2016), Spain (2016), Venezuela (2016).

ECONOMIC AND SOCIAL COUNCIL

The Economic and Social Council has 54 members, elected for three-year terms by the General Assembly. The term of office for each member expires on 31 December of the year indicated in parentheses next to its name. Voting in the Council is by simple majority; each member has one vote. In 2015, the Council is composed of the following 54 States:

Albania (2015)
Antigua and Barbuda (2016)
Argentina (2017)
Australia (2015)
Austria (2017)
Bangladesh (2016)
Benin (2015)
Bolivia (Plurinational State of) (2015)
Botswana (2016)
Brazil (2017)
Burkina Faso (2017)
China (2016)
Colombia (2015)
Congo (2016)
Croatia (2015)
Democratic Republic of the Congo (2016)
Estonia (2017)
Finland (2016)
France (2017)
Georgia (2016)
Germany (2017)
Ghana (2017)
Greece (2017)
Guatemala (2016)
Haiti (2015)
Honduras (2017)
India (2017)
Italy (2015)

Japan (2017)
Kazakhstan (2016)
Kuwait (2015)
Kyrgyzstan (2015)
Mauritania (2017)
Mauritius (2015)
Nepal (2015)
Pakistan (2017)
Panama (2016)
Portugal (2017)
Republic of Korea (2016)
Russian Federation (2016)
San Marino (2015)
Serbia (2016)
South Africa (2015)
Sudan (2015)
Sweden (2016)
Switzerland (2016)
Togo (2016)
Trinidad and Tobago (2017)
Tunisia (2015)
Turkmenistan (2015)
Uganda (2017)
United Kingdom of Great Britain and
    Northern Ireland (2016)
United States of America (2015)
Zimbabwe (2017)

TRUSTEESHIP COUNCIL

The Trusteeship Council has five members: China, France, Russian Federation, United Kingdom and the United States. With the independence of Palau, the last remaining United Nations trust territory, the Council formally suspended operation on 1 November 1994. By a resolution adopted on that day, the Council amended its rules of procedure to drop the obligation to meet annually and agreed to meet as occasion required—by its decision or the decision of its President, or at the request of a majority of its members or the General Assembly or the Security Council.

INTERNATIONAL COURT OF JUSTICE

The International Court of Justice has 15 members, elected by both the General Assembly and the Security Council. Judges hold nine-year terms. The term of office for each member expires on February of the year indicated in parentheses next to its name. The current composition of the court is as follows:

Julia Sebutinde (Sierra Leone 2021)
Mohamed Bennouna (Morocco 2015)
Abdulqawi Ahmed Yusuf (Somalia 2018)
Hisashi Owada (Japan 2021)

Awn Shawkat Al-Khasawneh (Jordan
    2018)
Xue Hangin (China 2021)
Peter Tomka (Slovakia 2021)

Leonid Skotnikov (Russian Federation
2015)
Bernardo Sepúlveda-Amor (Mexico 2015)
Antônio Augusto Cançado Trindade
(Brazil 2018)
Bruno Simma (Germany 2012)

Ronny Abraham (France 2018)
Kenneth Keith (New Zealand 2015)
Joan E. Donoghue (United States 2015)
Christopher John Greenwood (United
Kingdom 2018)

UNITED NATIONS SECRETARIAT

One United Nations Plaza, New York, NY 10017, (212) 963-1234, http://www.un.org.

Secretary General.—Ban Ki-moon (Republic of Korea).
Deputy Secretary.—Jan Eliasson (Sweden).

EXECUTIVE OFFICE OF THE SECRETARY–GENERAL

Chief of Staff.—Susana Malcorra (Argentina).
Spokesman.—Stéphane Dujarric.

OFFICE OF INTERNAL OVERSIGHT SERVICES

Under-Secretary-General.—Carman Louise Lapointe (Canada).
Assistant Secretary-General.—David Kanja (Kenya).

OFFICE OF LEGAL AFFAIRS

Under-Secretary-General and Legal Counsel.—Miguel de Serpa Soares (Portugal).
Assistant Secretary-General.—Stephen Mathias (United States).

DEPARTMENT OF POLITICAL AFFAIRS

Under-Secretary-General.—Jeffrey Feltman (United States).
Assistant Secretaries-General: Miroslav Jenca (Slovakia), Tayé-Brook Zerihoun (Ethiopia).

DEPARTMENT FOR DISARMAMENT AFFAIRS

Assistant Secretary-General, Acting High Representative for Disarmament Affairs.—Kim Won-soo (Republic of Korea).

DEPARTMENT OF PEACE-KEEPING OPERATIONS

Under-Secretary-General.—Hervé Ladsous (France).
Assistant Secretaries-General: Edmond Mulet (Guatemala), Dimitry Titov (Russia).
Military Adviser.—Lieutenant General Maqsood Ahmed (Pakistan).

DEPARTMENT OF FIELD SUPPORT

Under-Secretary-General.—Atul Khare (India).
Assistant Secretary-General.—Anthony Banbury (United States).

OFFICE FOR THE COORDINATION OF HUMANITARIAN AFFAIRS

Under-Secretary-General, Humanitarian Affairs and Emergency Relief Coordinator.—Stephen O'Brien (United Kingdom).
Assistant Secretary-General / Deputy Emergency Relief Coordinator.—Kyung-wha Kang (Republic of Korea).

DEPARTMENT OF ECONOMIC AND SOCIAL AFFAIRS

Under-Secretary-General.—Wu Hongbo (China).

Assistant Secretary-General, Policy Coordination and Inter-Agency Affairs.—Thomas Gass (Switzerland).
Assistant Secretary-General, Economic Development.—Lenni Montiel (Venezuela).

DEPARTMENT OF GENERAL ASSEMBLY AND CONFERENCE MANAGEMENT

Under-Secretary-General.—Tegegnework Gettu (Ethiopia).
Assistant Secretary-General.—Catherine Pollard (Guyana).

DEPARTMENT OF PUBLIC INFORMATION

Under-Secretary-General.—Cristina Gallach (Spain).

DEPARTMENT OF MANAGEMENT

Under-Secretary-General.—Yukio Takasu (Japan).
Assistant Secretary-General, Controller.—Bettina Tucci Bartsiotas (Uruguay).
Assistant Secretary-General, Human Resources Management.—Carole Wamuyu Wainaina (Kenya).
Assistant Secretary-General, Central Support Services.—Stephen Cutts (United Kingdom).
Assistant Secretary-General, Executive Director of the Capital Master Plan.—Michael Adlerstein (United States).

OFFICE OF THE SPECIAL REPRESENTATIVE OF THE SECRETARY-GENERAL FOR CHILDREN AND ARMED CONFLICT

Under-Secretary-General.—Leila Zerrougui (Algeria).

UNITED NATIONS OFFICE FOR PARTNERSHIPS

Officer-in-Charge and Chief of Operations.—Ann de la Roche.

UNITED NATIONS AT GENEVA (UNOG)

Palais des Nations, 1211 Geneva 10, Switzerland, phone (41–022) 917–1234

Director-General of UNOG.—Michael Moller (Denmark).

UNITED NATIONS AT VIENNA (UNOV)

Vienna International Centre, P.O. Box 500, 1400 Vienna, Austria, phone (43–1) 26060

Director-General.—Yury Fedotov (Russian Federation).

UNITED NATIONS AT NAIROBI (UNON)

P.O. Box 67578, Nairobi, Kenya 00200, phone: +254 20 7621234

Director-General.—Sahle-Work Zewde.

UNITED NATIONS INFORMATION CENTRE

1775 K Street, NW., Suite 400, Washington, DC 20006
phone: (202) 331–8670, fax: (202) 331–9191, email: unicdc@unic.org
http://www.unicwash.org

Director.—Robert Skinner (United States)

REGIONAL ECONOMIC COMMISSIONS

Economic Commission for Africa (ECA), Menelik II Ave., P.O. Box 3001, Addis Ababa Ethiopia, phone 251–11–544 4999, fax 251–11–551–4416.
Executive Secretary.—Carlos Lopes (Guinea-Bissau).

Economic Commission for Europe (ECE) Palais des Nations, 1211 Geneva 10, Switzerland, phone (41–22) 917–1234 (switchboard).
Executive Secretary.—Christian Friis Bach (Denmark).

Economic Commission for Latin America and the Caribbean (ECLAC), Casilla 179–D, Santiago, Chile, Postal code: 7630412, phone (56–2) 2471 2000, 2210 2000, fax (56–2) 208–0252.
Executive Secretary.—Alicia Bárcena (Mexico).

ECLAC Washington Office: 1825 K Street, NW., Washington, DC, Inés Bustillo, Director, phone (202) 596–3713.

Economic and Social Commission for Asia and the Pacific (ESCAP), United Nations Building, Rajadamnern Nok Avenue, Bangkok Thailand, phone (66–2) 288–1234, fax (66–2) 288–1000.
Executive Secretary.—Dr. Shamshad Akhtar (Pakistan).

Economic and Social Commission for Western Asia (ESCWA), P.O. Box 11–8575, Riad El-Solh Square, Beirut, Lebanon, phone 9611–981301, fax 9611–981510.
Executive Secretary.—Rima Khalaf (Jordan).

Regional Commissions, New York Office, (ECE, ESCAP, ECLAC, ECA, ESCWA), phone (212) 963–8088.
Director.—Amr Nour (Egypt).

FUNDS AND PROGRAMS

United Nations High Commissioner for Refugees (UNHCR), Case Postale 2500, CH–1211 Geneve 2 Depot, Switzerland, phone (41–22) 739–8111.
High Commissioner.—António Manuel de Oliveira Gutterres (Portugal)

United Nations High Commissioner for Refugees (UNHCR), Regional Office for the United States and the Caribbean, 1800 Massachusetts Ave., NW., Suite 500, Washington, DC 20036, phone (202) 296–5191.
Regional Representative.—Shelly Pitterman.

United Nations Children's Fund (UNICEF), UNICEF House, 3 United Nations Plaza, New York, NY 10017, phone (212) 326–7000.
Executive Director.—Anthony Lake (United States).

United Nations Conference on Trade and Development (UNCTAD), Palais des Nations, 8–14 Avenue de la Paix, 1211 Geneva 10, Switzerland, phone (41–22) 917–1234.
Secretary General.—Mukhisa Kituyi (Kenya).

International Trade Centre (ITC), Palais des Nations, 1211 Geneva 10, Switzerland, phone (41–22) 730 01 11.

United Nations Development Programme (UNDP), 1 United Nations Plaza, New York, NY 10017, phone (212) 906–5000.
Administrator.—Helen Clark (New Zealand).

United Nations Development Programme (UNDP), Representation Office, 1775 K Street, NW., Suite 420, Washington, DC 20006, phone (202) 331–9130.
Director.—Paul Clayman (United States).

UN Women (United Nations Entity for Gender Equality and the Empowerment of Women), 220 East 42nd Street, New York, NY 10017, phone (646) 781–4400.
Director.—Phumzile Mlambo-Ngcuka (South Africa).

United Nations Volunteers Programme (UNV), Postfach 260 111, D–53153 Bonn, Germany, phone (49–228) 815–2000.
Executive Coordinator.—Richard Dictus (Netherlands).

United Nations Environment Programme (UNEP), United Nations Avenue, Gigiri, P.O. Box 30552, 00100, Nairobi, Kenya, phone (254–20) 762–1234.
Executive Director.—Achim Steiner.

United Nations Environment Programme, Regional Office for North America, 900 17th Street, NW., Suite 506, Washington, DC 20006, phone (202) 785–0465.
Director.—Patricia J. Beneke.

United Nations Human Settlements Programme (UN-HABITAT), United Nations Office at Nairobi, United Nations Avenue, Gigiri, P.O. Box 30030, Nairobi, 00100, Kenya, phone (254–20) 762–1234.
Executive Director.—Joan Clos (Spain).

United Nations Office on Drugs and Crime (UNODC), Vienna International Centre, P.O. Box 500, A–1400 Vienna, Austria, phone (43–1) 26060.
Executive Director.—Yury Fedotov (Russian Federation).

United Nations Population Fund (UNFPA), 605 Third Avenue, New York, NY 10158, phone (212) 297–5000.
Executive Director.—Babatunde Osotimehin (Nigeria).

UNFPA Liaison Office, 2121 K Street, NW., Suite 800–A, Washington, DC 20037, phone (202) 653–1155.
Director.—Sarah Craven (United States).

United Nations Relief and Works Agency for Palestine Refugees in the Near East (UNRWA), Headquarters Amman, Bayader Wadi Seer, P.O. Box 140157, Amman 11814, Jordan, phone (+ 962 6) 580–8100. Headquarters Gaza, P.O. Box 338, IL 78100, Ashqelon, Israel, P.O. Box 371 Gaza City, Palestinian Territory, phone (+ 972 8) 288–7701.
Commissioner-General.—Pierre Krähenbühl (Switzerland).

UNRWA Representative Office, 1889 F Street, NW., 3rd Floor, Washington, DC 20006, phone (202) 974–3528.
Director.—Matthew Reynolds (United States).

World Food Programme (WFP), Via Cesare Giulio Viola 68, Parco dei Medici, 00148 Rome, Italy, phone (39–6) 65131.
Executive Director.—Ertharin Cousin (United States).

WFP U.S. Relations Office, 2121 K Street, NW., Suite 800–A, Washington, DC 20037, phone (202) 653–0010.
Director.—Jon Brause.

OTHER UNITED NATIONS ENTITIES

Office of the United Nations High Commissioner for Human Rights (OHCHR), Palais des Nations, CH–1211 Geneva 10, Switzerland, phone (41–022) 917–9220.
High Commissioner for Human Rights.—Zeid Ra'ad Al Hussein (Jordan).

United Nations Non-Governmental Liaison Office (NGLS), New York Office, United Nations Building DC1, Room 1106, New York, NY 10017, phone (212) 963–3125; Geneva Office, Room A1–50, Palais des Nations, 1211 Geneva 10, Switzerland, phone (41 22) 917–2076.
Officer-in-Charge, New York.—Susan Alzner.
Officer-in-Charge, Geneva.—Hamish Jenkins.

United Nations Office for Project Services (UNOPS), Marmorvej 51, P.O. Box 2695, 2100 Copenhagen, Denmark, phone (45–4) 533–7500.
Executive Director.—Grete Faremo (Norway).

UNOPS Liaison Office, 1775 K Street, NW., Suite 400, Washington, DC, phone (917) 200–8248.
Head of Office.—Felipe Munevar.

United Nations System Chief Executives Board (CEB) for Coordination, Geneva Office, C–553, Palais des Nations, CH–1211 Genève 10, Switzerland, phone (41–22) 917–3276; New York Office, DC2–0610, 2 United Nations Plaza, New York, NY 10017, phone (212) 963–8138.

United Nations System Staff College (UNSSC), Viale Maestri del Lavoro 10, 10127 Torino, Italy, phone (39 011) 653–5911.
Deputy Director and Head of Programmes.—Maria Hutchinson.

United Nations University (UNU), 5–53–70 Jingumae, Shibuya-ku, Tokyo 150–8925, Japan, phone (81–3) 5467–1212.
Rector.—David Malone (Canada).

International Computing Centre (ICC), Palais des Nations, 1211 Geneva 10, Switzerland, phone (41–22) 929–1444.
Director.—Simon Jones.

Joint United Nations Programme on HIV/AIDS (UNAIDS), 20, Avenue Appia, CH–1211 Geneva 27, Switzerland, phone (41–22) 791–3666.
Executive Director.—Peter Piot.

UNAIDS Washington Office, 1889 F Street, NW., 3rd Floor, Washington, DC 20006, phone (202) 223–7611.
Director.—Lisa Carty.

RESEARCH AND TRAINING INSTITUTES

United Nations Institute for Disarmament Research (UNIDIR), Palais des Nations, 1211 Geneva 10, Switzerland, phone (41–22) 917–3186 / 1583.
Director.—Jarmo Sareva (Finland).

United Nations Institute for Training and Research (UNITAR), UNITAR, International Environment House, Chemin des Anémones 11–13, CH–1219 Châtelaine, Geneva-Switzerland, phone (41–22) 917–8400.
Executive Director.—Sally Fegan-Wyles (Ireland).

United Nations International Research and Training Institute for the Advancement of Women (INSTRAW), Part of UN Women as July 2010.

United Nations Interregional Crime and Justice Research Institute (UNICRI), Viale Maestri del Lavoro, 10, 10127 Turin, Italy, phone (39–011) 6537–111.
Director.—Cindy J. Smith (United States).

United Nations Research Institute for Social Development (UNRISD), Palais des Nations, 1211 Geneva 10, Switzerland, phone (41–22) 917–3060.
Director.—Vacant.

SPECIALIZED AGENCIES

Food and Agriculture Organization (FAO), Viale delle Terme di Caracalla, 00153 Rome, Italy, phone (39–6) 57051.
Director-General.—José Graziano da Silva (Brazil).

Food and Agriculture Organization, Liaison Office for North America, Suite 800–B, 2121 K Street, NW., Washington, DC 20037, phone (1–202) 653–2400.
Director.—Ajay Markanday.

International Civil Aviation Organization (ICAO), 999 University Street, Montreal, Quebec H3C 5H7, Canada, phone (1–514) 954–8219.
Secretary-General.— Dr. Fang Liu (China).

International Fund for Agricultural Development (IFAD), Via Paolo di Dono, 44, 00142 Rome, Italy, phone (39–6) 54591.
President.—Kanayo F. Nwanze (Nigeria).

External Affairs Department, IFAD North American Liaison Office, 1775 K Street, NW., Suite 410, Washington, DC 20006, phone (1–202) 331–9099.
Chief.— Deirdre McGrenra.

International Labour Organization (ILO), 4, Routes des Morillons, CH–1211 Geneva 22, Switzerland, phone (41–22) 799–6111.
Director-General.—Guy Ryder (United Kingdom).

ILO Washington Branch Office, 1801 I Street, NW., 9th Floor, Washington, DC 20006, phone (1–202) 617–3952.
Director.—Nancy Donaldson.

International Maritime Organization (IMO), 4 Albert Embankment, London SE1 7SR, United Kingdom, phone (44–20) 7735–7611.
Secretary-General.—Koji Sekimizu (Japan).

International Monetary Fund (IMF), 700 19th Street, NW, Washington, DC 20431, phone (1–202) 623–7000.
Managing Director.—Christine Lagarde (France).

International Telecommunications Union (ITU), Palais des Nations, 1211 Geneva 20, Switzerland, phone (41–22) 730–5111.
Secretary-General.—Houlin Zhao (China).

United Nations Educational, Scientific and Cultural Organization (UNESCO), 7 Place de Fontenoy, 75352 Paris 07 SP, France, phone (33–01) 4568–1000.
Director-General.—Irina Bokova (Bulgaria).

United Nations Industrial Development Organization (UNIDO), Vienna International Centre, Wagramerstr. 5, P.O. Box 300, A–1400 Vienna, Austria, phone (43–1) 26026–0.
Director-General.—Li Yong (China).

Universal Postal Union (UPU), International Bureau, Case Postale 312, 3015 Berne, Switzerland, phone (41–31) 350–3111.
Director-General.—Bishar Abdirahman Hussein (Kenya).

World Bank Group, 1818 H Street, NW., Washington, DC 20433, phone (1–202) 473–1000.
President.—Jim Yong Kim (United States).

World Health Organization (WHO), 20 Avenue Appia, 1211 Geneva 27, Switzerland, phone (41–22) 791–2111.
Director-General.—Margaret Chan (China).

Pan American Health Organization / World Health Organization Regional Office for the Americas (PAHO), 525 23rd Street, NW., Washington, DC 20037, phone (1–202) 974–3000.
Director.—Carissa F. Etienne (Dominica).

World Intellectual Property Organization (WIPO), 34, chemin des Colombettes, CH–1211 Geneva 20, Switzerland, phone (41–22) 338–9111.
Director General.—Francis Gurry (Australia).

World Meteorological Organization (WMO), 7bis, avenue de la Paix, Case Postale 2300, CH–1211 Geneva 2, Switzerland, phone (41–22) 730–8111.
Secretary-General.—Michel Jarraud (France).

RELATED BODY

International Atomic Energy Agency (IAEA), Vienna International Centre, P.O. Box 100 A–1400 Vienna, Austria, phone (431) 2600–0.
Director General.—Yukiya Amano (Japan).

IAEA Washington Office, 1775 K Street, NW., Suite 400, Washington, DC 20006, phone (202) 454–2140.
Respresentative.— Andrew Semmel.

(The IAEA is an independent intergovernmental organization under the aegis of the UN).

SPECIAL AND PERSONAL REPRESENTATIVES AND ENVOYS OF THE
SECRETARY-GENERAL

AFRICA

Africa:
Special Adviser to the Secretary-General on Africa, OSAA.—Maged Abdelaziz (Egypt).
High Representative for the Least Developed Countries, Landlocked Developing Countries and Small Island Developing States, UN–OHRLLS.—Gyan Chandra Acharya (Nepal).

African Union:
Special Representative of the Secretary-General to the African Union, UNOAU.—Haile Menkerios (South Africa).

Burundi:
Special Representative of the Secretary-General for Burundi and Head of the UN Office in Burundi.—Cassam Uteem (Mauritius).
Deputy Head of the United Nations Electoral Observation Mission in Burundi (MENUB).— Issaka Souna (Niger).

Central Africa:
Special Representative of the Secretary-General and Head of UNOCA.—Abdoulaye Bathily (Senegal).

Central African Republic:
Acting Special Representative of the Secretary-General and Head of the United Nations Integrated Peacebuilding Office in the Central African Republic.—Parfait Onanga-Anyanga (Gabon).
Deputy Special Representative of the Secretary-General and Deputy Head of Mission, MINUSCA.—Diane Corner (United Kingdom).
Deputy Special Representative of the Secretary-General in the Central African Republic and UN Resident Coordinator and Resident Representative, BINUCA.—Aurélien Agbenonci (Benin).

Cote d'Ivoire:
Special Representative of the Secretary-General for Cote d'Ivoire and Head of UNOCI.— Aïchatou Mindaoudou Souleymane (Niger).
Deputy Special Representative of the Secretary-General for Cote d'Ivoire, UNOCI.— Simon Munzu (Cameroon).

Deputy Special Representative of the Secretary-General, UN Resident Coordinator, Humanitarian Coordinator and UNDP Resident Representative, UNOCI.—M'Baye Babacar Cisse (Senegal).

Democratic Republic of the Congo:
Special Representative of the Secretary-General for the Democratic Republic of the Congo and Head of MONUSCO.—Martin Kobler (Germany).
Deputy Special Representative of the Secretary-General for the Democratic Republic of the Congo, Rule of Law, MONUSCO.—Abdallah Wafy (Niger).

Equatorial Guinea and Gabon:
Special Adviser to the Secretary-General and Mediator in the border dispute between Equatorial Guinea and Gabon.—Nicolas Michel (Switzerland).

Great Lakes Region:
Special Representative of the Secretary-General for the Great Lakes Region.—Said Djinnit (Algeria).
Special Advisor to the Special Envoy of the Secretary-General to the Great Lakes Region.—Modibo Touré (Mali).

Guinea-Bissau:
Special Representative of the Secretary-General and Head of UNOGBIS.—Miguel Trovoada (São Tomé and Príncipe).
Deputy Special Representative of the Secretary-General (Political) with UNIOGBIS.—Marco Carmignani (Brazil).
Deputy Special Representative of the Secretary-General in Guinea-Bissau, UN Resident Coordinator and UN Development Programme Resident Representative.—Maria Do Valle Ribeiro (Ireland).

Liberia:
Special Representative of the Secretary-General for Liberia and Head of UNMIL.—Farid Zarif (Afghanistan).
Deputy Special Representative for Rule of Law.—Tamrat Samuel (Ghana).
Deputy Special Representative for Recovery and Governance.—Antonio Vigilante (Italy).

Libya:
Special Representative of the Secretary-General and Head of the United Nations Support Mission in Libya.—Bernardino León (Spain).
Deputy Special Representative of the Secretary-General, Resident Coordinator and Humanitarian Coordinator.—Vacant.

Mali:
Special Representative of the Secretary-General and Head of Mission, MINUSMA.— Mongi Hamdi (Tunisia).
Deputy Special Representative of the Secretary-General in MINUSMA.—Koen Davidse (Netherlands).
Deputy Special Representative of the Secretary-General in MINUSMA and UN Resident Coordinator, Humanitarian Coordinator and Resident Representative of UNDP.—Mbaranga Gasarabwe (Rwanda).

Sahel:
Special Envoy of the Secretary-General for the Sahel.—Hiroute Guebre Sellassie (Ethiopia).

Somalia:
Special Representative of the Secretary-General for Somalia and Head of Mission, UNSOM.—Nicholas Kay (United Kingdom).
Deputy Special Representative of the Secretary-General for Somalia.—Raisedon Zenenga (Zimbabwe).
Deputy Special Representative, Resident and Humanitarian Coordinator in Somalia.—Vacant.

Sudan and South Sudan:
Special Envoy of the Secretary-General for Sudan and South Sudan.—Haile Menkerios (South Africa).

South Sudan:
Special Representative of the Secretary-General and Head of UNMISS.—Ellen Margrethe Loj (Denmark).
Deputy Special Representative of the Secretary-General, UNMISS.—Moustapha Soumaré (Mali).
Deputy Special Representative of the Secretary-General, Resident Coordinator, Humanitarian Coordinator and Resident Representative, UNMISS.—Toby Lanzer (United Kingdom).

Sudan / Abyei:
Head of Mission and Force Commander, UNISFA.—Haile Tilahun Gebremariam (Ethiopia).
Sudan / Darfur:
Joint African Union-United National Special Representative for Darfur, Head of UNAMID and Joint Chief Mediator.—Abiodun Oluremi Bashua (Nigeria) (a.i.).
Deputy Joint Special Representative-Pillar One, UNAMID.—Abiodun Oluremi Bashua (Nigeria).
Deputy Joint Special Representative-Pillar Two, UNAMID.—Abdul Kamara (Sierra Leone).
West Africa:
Special Representative of the Secretary-General and Head of UNOWA.—Mohammed Ibn Chambas (Ghana).
Western Sahara:
Special Representative of the Secretary-General for Western Sahara and Head of MINURSO.—Kim Bolduc (Canada).
Personal Envoy of the Secretary-General for Western Sahara.—Christopher Ross (United States).

THE AMERICAS

Guyana / Venezuela:
Personal Representative of the Secretary-General on the Border Controversy between Guyana and Venezuela.—Vacant.
Haiti:
Special Representative of the Secretary-General and Head of Mission, MINUSTAH.—Sandra Honoré (Trinidad and Tobago).
Deputy Special Representative of the Secretary-General, MINUSTAH.—Carl Alexandre (United States).
Deputy Special Representative of the Secretary-General and United Nations Resident Coordinator and Humanitarian Coordinator, MINUSTAH.—Mourad Wahba (Egypt).
Special Adviser to the Secretary-General for Community Based Medicine and Lessons from Haiti.—Paul Farmer (United States).

ASIA AND THE PACIFIC

Afghanistan:
Special Representative of the Secretary-General for Afghanistan and Head of UNAMA.—Nicholas Haysom (South Africa)
Deputy Special Representative of the Secretary-General, UN Resident Coordinator and UN Humanitarian Coordinator for Afghanistan, UNAMA.—Mark Bowden (United Kingdom).
Deputy Special Representative of the Secretary-General (Political) for UNAMA.—Tadamichi Yamamoto (Japan).
Central Asia:
Special Representative of the Secretary-General and Head of the UN Regional Centre for Preventive Diplomacy for Central Asia.—Petko Draganov (Bulgaria).
India-Pakistan:
Chief Military Observer and Head of Mission, UNMOGIP.—Delali Johnson Sakyi (Ghana).
Myanmar:
Special Adviser of the Secretary-General for Myanmar.—Vijay Nambiar (India).
Timor Leste:
Special Adviser of the Secretary-General for Timor-Leste.—Noeleen Heyzer (Singapore).

EUROPE

Cyprus:
Special Representative of the Secretary-General and Head of Mission, UNFICYP.—Lisa Buttenheim (United States).
Special Adviser to the Secretary-General on Cyprus.— Espen Barth Eide (Norway).
Former Yugoslav Republic of Macedonia-Greece:
Personal Envoy of the Secretary-General for the Greece-RYROM talks.—Matthew Nimetz (United States).
Georgia:
Nations Representative.—Antti Turunen (Finland).

Kosovo:
Special Representative of the Secretary-General and Head of Mission, UNMIK.—Farid Zarif (Afghanistan).

MIDDLE EAST

Middle East:
Special Coordinator for the Middle East Peace Process and Personal Representative of the Secretary-General to the Palestine Liberation Organization and the Palestinian Authority.—Nickolay Mladenov (Bulgaria).
Deputy Special Coordinator for the Middle East Peace Process/United Nations Coordinator for Humanitarian Aid and Development Activities in the Occupied Palestinian Territory.—Robert Piper (Australia).
Special Envoy for the Implementation of Security Council Resolution 1559.—Terje Roed-Larsen (Norway).
Head of Mission and Chief of Staff of UNTSO.—Major General Michael Finn (Ireland).

Afghanistan:
Special Representative of the Secretary-General for Afghanistan and Head of UNAMA.—Nicholas Haysom (South Africa).
Deputy Special Representative of the Secretary-General, UN Resident Coordinator and UN Humanitarian Coordinator for Afghanistan, UNAMA.—Mark Bowden (United Kingdom).
Deputy Special Representative of the Secretary-General (Political) for UNAMA.—Tadamichi Yamamoto (Japan).

Iraq (UNAMI):
Special Representative of the Secretary-General for Iraq and Head of Mission, UNAMI.—Ján Kubiš (Slovakia).
Deputy Special Representative of the Secretary-General for Political Affairs, UNAMI.—György Busztin (Hungary).
Deputy Special Representative of the Secretary-General (Development and Humanitarian Support) and Resident Coordinator/Humanitarian Coordinator for Iraq, UNAMI.—Lise Grande (United States).
Special Adviser for Relocation of Camp Hurriya Residents Outside of Iraq.—Jane Holl Lute (United States).

Kuwait:
Humanitarian Envoy of the Secretary-General.—Abdullah al Matouq (Kuwait).

Lebanon:
Special Coordinator of the Secretary-General for Lebanon.—Sigrid Kaag (Netherlands).
Deputy Special Coordinator of the Secretary-General for Lebanon, UN Resident Coordinator and UNDP Resident Representative.—Philippe Lazzarini (Switzerland).
Head of Mission and Force Commander of UNIFIL.—Major General Paolo Serra (Italy).

Libya:
Special Representative of the Secretary-General and Head of Mission, UNSMIL.—Bernardino León (Spain).
Deputy Special Representative and Deputy Head of the United Nations Support Mission in Libya, UNSMIL.—Ali H. Al-Za'tari (Jordan).

Syria:
Special Envoy of the Secretary-General for Syria.—Staffan de Mistura (Italy/Sweden).
Deputy Special Envoy of the Secretary-General for Syria.—Ramzy Ezzeldin Ramzy (Egypt).

Syria Golan Heights:
Head of Mission and Force Commander of the UN Disengagement Observer Force (UNDOF).—Major General Purna Chandra Thapa (Nepal).

Yemen:
Special Adviser to the Secretary-General on Yemen.—Ismail Ould Cheikh Ahmed (Mauritania).

OTHER HIGH LEVEL APPOINTMENTS

Special Adviser to the Secretary-General.—Joseph V. Reed (United States).
Special Adviser to the Secretary-General.—Iqbal Riza (Pakistan).
Special Adviser to the Secretary-General.—Jennifer Welsh (Canada).

Alliance of Civilizations:
High Representative.—Nassir Abdulaziz al-Nasser (Qatar).

Avian and Human Influenza (Bird flu):
Senior United Nations System Coordinator for Avian and Human Influenza.—David Nabarro (United Kingdom).

Children and Armed Conflict:
Special Representative.—Leila Zerrougui (Algeria).

Cities and Climate Change:
Special Envoy.—Michael Bloomberg (United States).

Climate Change:
Special Envoy of the Secretary-General on Climate Change.—John Kufuor (Ghana).
Special Envoy of the Secretary-General on Climate Change.—Mary Robinson (Ireland).
Special Envoy of the Secretary-General on Climate Change.—Jens Stoltenberg (Norway).
Special Adviser to the Secretary-General on Climate Change.—Robert Orr (United States).

Disability and Accessibility:
Special Envoy on Disability and Accessibility.—Lenín Voltaire Moreno (Ecuador).

Disaster Reduction:
Special Representative.—Margareta Wahlström (Sweden).

Disaster Risk Reduction and Water:
Special Envoy.—Han Seung-soo (Republic of Korea).

Ebola Virus Disease:
Special Envoy.—David Nabarro (United Kingdom).

Financing for Development:
Special Adviser.—Phillipe Douste-Blazy (France).

Food Security and Nutrition:
Special Representative.—David Nabarro (United Kingdom).

Global Education:
Special Representative.—Gordon Brown (United Kingdom).

HIV / AIDS in Africa:
Special Envoy.—Speciosa Wandira-Kasibwe (Uganda).

HIV / AIDS in Asia and in the Pacific:
Special Envoy.—Prasada Rao V.R. Jonnalagadda (India).

HIV / AIDS in the Caribbean Region:
Special Envoy.—Edward Green (Gyana).

HIV / AIDS in Eastern Europe and Central Asia:
Special Envoy.—Michel Kazatchkine (France).

Internet Governance Forum:
Chair of the Multi-Stakeholder Advisory Group (MAG).—Jānis Kārkliņs (Latvia).

Malaria and Financing of Health-Related Millennium Development Goals:
Special Envoy.—Ray Chambers (United States).

Migration:
Special Representative.—Peter Sutherland (Ireland).

Millennium Development Goals:
Special Adviser.—Jeffrey D. Sachs (United States).

Prevention of Genocide:
Special Adviser.—Adama Dieng (Senegal).

Post-2015 Development Planning:
Special Adviser.—Amina Mohammed (Nigeria).

Road Safety:
Special Envoy.—Jean Todt (France).

Sexual Violence in Conflict:
Special Representative.—Zainab Hawa Bangura (Sierra Leone).

South-South Cooperation:
Special Envoy.—Yiping Zhou (China).

Sport for Development and Peace:
Special Adviser.—Wilfried Lemke (Germany).

Sustainable Energy for All:
Special Representative.—Kandeh Yumkella (Sierra Leone).

Tuberculosis:
Special Envoy.—Eric Goosby (United States).

Nations International School (UNIS):
Special Representative.—Michael Alderstein (United States).

University for Peace:
Special Representative.—Judy Cheng-Hopkins (Malaysia).
Violence Against Children:
Special Representative.—Marta Santos Pais (Portugal).
Youth:
Envoy.—Ahmad Alhendawi (Jordan).
Youth Refugees and Sport:
Special Envoy.—Jacques Rogge (Belgium)

WORLD BANK GROUP

The World Bank Group comprises five organizations: the International Bank for Reconstruction and Development (IBRD), the International Development Association (IDA), the International Finance Corporation (IFC), the Multilateral Investment Guarantee Agency (MIGA) and the International Centre for the Settlement of Investment Disputes (ICSID).

Headquarters: 1818 H Street, NW., 20433, (202) 473–1000

INTERNATIONAL BANK FOR RECONSTRUCTION AND DEVELOPMENT

President.—Jim Yong Kim.
Managing Director and Chief Operating Officer.—Sri Mulyani.
Managing Director and Chief Financial Officer.—Bertrand Badre.
Chairperson, Inspection Panel.—Gonzalo Castro.
Senior Vice President and General Counsel.—Anne-Marie Leroy.
Senior Vice President, Development Economics, and Chief Economist.—Kaushik Basu.
Senior Vice President, Operations.—Kyle Peters.
Vice President, Human Development Vice Presidency.—Keith Hansen.
Vice President and Chief Information Officer, WBG Information and Technology Solutions.—Stephanie von Friedeburg.
Vice President and Controller.—Bernard Lauwers.
Vice President, Budget, Performance Review and Strategic Planning.—Pedro Alba.
Corporate Secretary and President's Special Envoy.—Mahmoud Mohieldin.
Vice President and Treasurer.—Doris Herrera-Pol (acting).
Vice President of:
   Africa.—Makhtar Diop.
   East Asia and Pacific.—Axel vanTrotsenburg.
   South Asia.—Annette Dixon.
Vice President and Special Envoy.—Rachel Kyte.
Vice President, World Bank Group External and Corporate Relations.—Fiona Douglas (acting).
North American Affairs (External Affairs) Special Representative.—James T. Heimbach.
Europe (External and Corporate Relations) Special Representative.—Stefan Emblad.
UN External Affairs, Special Representative.—Dominique Bichara.
Japan-External and Corporate Relations, Special Representative.—Mika Iwasaki (acting).
Human Resources.—Sean McGrath.
Latin America and the Caribbean.—Jorge Familiar Calderon.
Middle East and North Africa.—Hafez Ghanem.
Vice President of Europe and Central Asia.—Cyril Muller.
Vice President and Network Head, Operations Policy and Country Services.—Hartwig Schafer.
Vice President, Equitable Growth, Finance and Institutions.—Jan Walliser.
Vice President, Sustainable Development Vice Presidency.—Laura Tuck.
Vice President, Development Finance.—Joachim von Amsberg.
Vice President and Bank Group Risk Officer.—Lakshmi Shyam-Sunder.
Vice President, Leadership, Learning and Innovation.—Sanjay Pradhan.
Director-General, Independent Evaluation.—Caroline Heider.
Vice President and Auditor-General.—Hiroshi Naka.
Vice President, Institutional Integrity.—Leonard McCarthy.
Vice President and World Bank Group Chief Ethics Officer.—Leonard McCarthy (acting).

OTHER WORLD BANK OFFICES

London: Millbank Tower, 12th Floor, 21–24 Millbank, London SW1P 4QP.

Geneva: 3, Chemin Louis Dunant, CP 66, CH 1211, Geneva 10, Switzerland.
Paris: 66, Avenue d'Iena, 75116 Paris, France.
Brussels: Avenue Marnix 17, 2nd floor, 1000 Brussels, Belgium.
Tokyo: Fukoku Seimei Building, 10th Floor, 2–2–2 Uchisawai-cho, Chiyoda-Ku, Tokyo 100, Japan.
Sydney: CML Building Level 19–14, Martin Place, Sydney, NSW 2000, Australia.
Berlin: Reichpietschufer 20, 10785 Berlin, Germany.

BOARD OF EXECUTIVE DIRECTORS

Bahrain, Egypt (Arab Republic of), Iraq, Jordan, Kuwait, Lebanon, Libya, Maldives, Oman, Qatar, Syrian Arab Republic, United Arab Emirates, Yemen (Republic of).
   Executive Director.—Merza H. Hasan (Kuwait).
   Alternate.—Karim Wissa (Arab Republic of Egypt).
Saudi Arabia.
   Executive Director.—Khalid Alkhudairy.
   Alternate.—Turki Almutairi.
Austria, Belarus, Belgium, Czech Republic, Hungary, Kazakhstan, Luxembourg, Slovak Republic, Slovenia, Turkey.
   Executive Director.—Franciscus Godts (Belgium).
   Alternate.—Gulsum Yazganarikan (Turkey).
Australia, Cambodia, Kiribati, Korea (Republic of), Marshall Islands, Micronesia (Federated States of), Mongolia, New Zealand, Palau, Papua New Guinea, Samoa, Solomon Islands, Vanuatu.
   Executive Director.—Sung-Soo Eun (Republic of Korea).
   Alternate.—Jason Allford (Australia).
Albania, Greece, Italy, Malta, Portugal, San Marino, Timor-Leste.
   Executive Director.—Patrizio Pagano (Italy).
   Alternate.—Nuno Mota Pinto (Portugal).
United States.
   Executive Director.—Matthew T. McGuire.
   Alternate.—Vacant.
Brazil, Colombia, Dominican Republic, Ecuador, Haiti, Panama, Philippines, Suriname, Trinidad and Tobago.
   Executive Director.—Antonio Henrique Silveira (Brazil).
   Alternate.—Roberto Tan (Philippines).
Germany.
   Executive Director.—Ursula Mueller.
   Alternate.—Wilhelm Rissmann.
Afghanistan, Algeria, Ghana, Iran (Islamic Republic of), Morocco, Pakistan, Tunisia.
   Executive Director.—Nasir Mahmood Khosa (Pakistan).
   Alternate.—Omar Bougara (Algeria).
France.
   Executive Director.—Herve M. Jodon de Villeroche.
   Alternate.—Arnaud Delaunay.
Benin, Burkina Faso, Cameroon, Cape Verde, Central African Republic, Chad, Comoros, Congo (Democratic Republic of), Congo (Republic of), Cote d'Ivoire, Djibouti, Equatorial Guinea, Gabon, Guinea, Guinea-Bissau, Madagascar, Mali, Mauritania, Mauritius, Niger, Rwanda, Sao Tome and Principe, Senegal, Togo.
   Executive Director.—Mohamed Sikieh Kayad (Djibouti).
   Alternate.—Andrew Bouda (Burkina Faso).
Fiji, Indonesia, Lao People's Democratic Republic, Malaysia, Myanmar, Nepal, Singapore, Thailand, Tonga, Vietnam.
   Executive Director.—Rionald Silaban (Indonesia).
   Alternate.—Boonchai Charassangsomboon (Thailand).
Denmark, Estonia, Finland, Iceland, Latvia, Lithuania, Norway, Sweden.
   Executive Director.—Satu-Leena Santala (Finland).
   Alternate.—Sanita Bajare (Latvia).
Russian Federation.
   Executive Director.—Andrey Lushin.
   Alternate.—Eugene Miagkov.
Costa Rica, El Salvador, Guatemala, Honduras, Mexico, Nicaragua, Spain, Venezuela (Republica Bolivariana de).
   Executive Director.—Jose Alejandro Rojas (Venezuela, Rep. Bol. de).
   Alternate.—Beatriz de Guindos Talavera (Spain).
Antigua and Barbuda, Bahamas (The), Barbados, Belize, Canada, Dominica, Grenada, Guyana, Ireland, Jamaica, St. Kitts and Nevis, St. Lucia, St. Vincent and the Grenadines.

Executive Director.—Alister Smith (Canada).
Alternate.—Janet Harris (St. Kitts and Nevis).
Armenia, Bosnia and Herzegovina, Bulgaria, Croatia, Cyprus, Georgia, Israel, Macedonia (former Yugoslav Republic of), Moldova, Netherlands, Romania, Ukraine.
Executive Director.—Frank Heemskerk (Netherlands).
Alternate.—Roman Zhukovskyi (Ukraine)
Japan.
Executive Director.—Masahiro Kan.
Alternate.—Daiho Fujii.
Argentina, Bolivia, Chile, Paraguay, Peru, Uruguay.
Executive Director.—Alejandro Foxley (Chile).
Alternate.—Daniel Kostzer (Argentina).
United Kingdom.
Executive Director.—Gwen Hines.
Alternate.—Clare Roberts.
Angola, Nigeria, South Africa.
Executive Director.—Ana Lourenco (Angola).
Alternate.—Vacant.
Botswana, Burundi, Eritrea, Ethiopia, Gambia (The), Kenya, Lesotho, Liberia, Malawi, Mozambique, Namibia, Seychelles, Sierra Leone, Sudan, Swaziland, Tanzania, Uganda, Zambia, Zimbabwe.
Executive Director.—Louis Rene Peter Larose (Seychelles).
Alternate.—Andrew N. Bvumbe (Zimbabwe).
Bangladesh, Bhutan, India, Sri Lanka.
Executive Director.—Subhash Chandra Garg (India).
Alternate.—Mohammad Tareque (Bangladesh).
Azerbaijan, Serbia and Montenegro, Kyrgyz Republic, Poland, Switzerland, Tajikistan, Turkmenistan, Uzbekistan, Yugoslavia (Fed. Rep. of), Switzerland, Yemen, (Republic of).
Executive Director.—Jorg Frieden (Switzerland).
Alternate.—Wieslaw Szczuka (Poland).
China.
Executive Director.—Shixin Chen.
Alternate.—Jiandi Ye.

INTERNATIONAL DEVELOPMENT ASSOCIATION

[The officers, executive directors, and alternates are the same as those of the International Bank for Reconstruction and Development.]

INTERNATIONAL FINANCE CORPORATION

President.—Jim Yong Kim.
Executive Vice President and Chief Executive Officer.—Jin-Yong Cai.
Vice President and Corporate Secretary.—Mahmoud Mohieldin.
Vice President:
Human Resource.—Sean McGrath.
Risk Management and Portfolio.—Saadia Khairi.
Director-General, Independent Evaluation.—Caroline Heider.
Compliance Advisor/Ombudsman (IFC/MIGA).—Osvaldo Luis Gratacos.
Vice President and General Counsel.—Ethiopis Tafara.
Vice Presidents, Global Client Services: Snezana Stoiljkovic, Dimitris Tsitsiragos.
Vice Presidents, Corporate, Risk and Sustainability: Saran G. Kebet-Koulibaly, James Peter Scriven, Ethiopis Tafara.
Vice President, Treasury and Syndications.—Jingdong Hua.
CEO, IFC Asset Management Company.—Gavin Wilson.
Chief Economist.—Ted Chu.
Director, Corporate Relations.—Bruce Moats.
Chief Information Officer and Director, Corporate Business Technologies.—Stephanie von Friedeburg.
Director, Office of:
Business Planning and Administration.—Bernard Lauwers.
Development Partner Relations.—Anita Bhatia.
Corporate and Portfolio Risk Management: Avi Hofman, Edwin Frank Taverner.
Cross Cutting Advisory Solutions.—Mary Porter Peschka.
Business Climate Cross Cutting Area.—Christian Grossmann.

Transactional Risk Solutions: Khawaja Aftab Ahmed, Morgan J. Landy.
Information and Technology.—Suzannah Herring Carr.
Deputy General Counsels: David N. Harris, Fady M. Zeidan.
East and Southern Africa.—Cheikh O. Seydi.
Environment, Social and Governance.—William Bulmer.
Human Resources.—Davide Bonzano.
Infrastructure and Natural Resources: Sujoy Bose, Bernard Sheahan.
Integrated Risk Management.—Avi Hofman.
Independent Evaluation Group.—Marvin Taylor-Dormond.
Manufacturing, Agribusiness and Services: Alzbeta Klein, Sergio Pimenta.
East Asia and the Pacific.—Vivek Pathak.
East and Southern Africa.—Cheikh O. Seydi.
Europe and Central Asia.—Tomasz Telma.
South Asia.—Mengistu Alemayehu.
Middle East and North Africa.—Mouayed Makhlouf.
Latin America and the Caribbean.—Lizabeth N. Bronder.
Telecom, Media, Tech and Venture Investing.—Atul Mehta.
Special Operations.—Mohamed Gouled.
Treasury Market Operations.—Monish Mahurkar.
Treasury Client Solutions.—Keshav Gaur.
Treasury Quantitative Analysis.—Takehisa Eguchi.
Syndications and Mobilizations.—Georgina E. Baker.
Tokyo.—Noriaki Mizuno.
West and Central Africa.—Vera Songwe.
Western Europe.—Stephanie J. Miller.

MULTILATERAL INVESTMENT GUARANTEE AGENCY

President.—Jim Yong Kim.
Executive Vice President.—Keiko Honda.
Director and General Counsel, Legal Affairs and Claims Group.—Ana-Mita Betancourt.
Compliance Advisor/Ombudsman (IFC/ICC AND MIGA).—Osvaldo Luis Gratacos.
Vice President and Chief Operating Officer.—Karin Finkelston.
Operations Group.—Edith Quintrell.
Director, Economics and Sustainability Group.—Ravi Vish.
Director, Corporate Risk.—Santiago Assalini.
Regional Manager, MIGA Asia Hub.—Muhamet Fall.
Regional Manager, MIGA Europe Hub.—Elena Patel.

FOREIGN DIPLOMATIC OFFICES
IN THE UNITED STATES

AFGHANISTAN

Embassy of Afghanistan
2341 Wyoming Avenue, NW., Washington, DC
20008
phone (202) 483–6410, fax 483–6488
Mr. Ramin Manawi
Counselor (Charge D'Affaires Ad Interim)
Consular Offices:
California, Los Angeles
New York, New York

AFRICAN UNION

Delegation of the African Union Mission
1640 Wisconsin Avenue, NW., Washington, DC
20007
Embassy of the African Union
phone (202) 342–1100, fax 342–1101
Her Excellency Amina Salum Ali
Ambassador (Head of Delegation)

ALBANIA

Embassy of the Republic of Albania
2100 S Street, NW., Washington, DC 20008
phone (202) 223–4942, fax 628–7342
Her Excellency Floreta Faber
Ambassador E. and P.
Consular Offices:
Connecticut, Greenwich
Georgia, Avondale Estates
Louisiana, New Orleans
Massachusetts, Boston
Michigan, West Bloomfield
Missouri, Blue Springs
New York, New York
North Carolina, Southern Pines
Texas, Houston

ALGERIA

Embassy of the Peoples Democratic Republic of
Algeria
2118 Kalorama Road, NW., Washington, DC 20008
phone (202) 265–2800, fax 667–2174
His Excellency Madjid Bougerra
Ambassador E. and P.
Consular Office: New York, New York

ANDORRA

Embassy of Andorra
2 United Nations Plaza, 27th Floor, New York,
NY 10017

phone (212) 750–8064, fax 750–6630
His Excellency Narcis Casal De Fonsdeviela
Ambassador E. and P.
Consular Office: California, La Jolla

ANGOLA

Embassy of the Republic of Angola
2100–2108 16th Street, NW., Washington, DC
20009
phone (202) 785–1156, fax 785–1258
His Excellency Agostinho Tavares da Silva Neto
Ambassador E. and P.
Consular Offices:
California, Los Angeles
New York, New York
Texas, Houston

ANTIGUA AND BARBUDA

Embassy of Antigua and Barbuda
3216 New Mexico Avenue, NW., Washington, DC
20016
phone (202) 362–5122, fax 362–5225
Ms. Joy Dee Samantha Davis
First Secretary (Charge D'Affaires Ad Interim)
Consular Offices:
District of Columbia, Washington
Florida, Miami
New York, New York
Puerto Rico, Guaynabo

ARGENTINA

Embassy of the Argentine Republic
1600 New Hampshire Avenue, NW., Washington,
DC 20009
phone (202) 238–6400, fax 332–3171
Her Excellency Maria Cecilia Nahon
Ambassador E. and P.
Consular Offices:
California, Los Angeles
Florida, Miami
Georgia, Atlanta
Illinois, Chicago
New York, New York
Texas, Houston

ARMENIA

Embassy of the Republic of Armenia
2225 R Street, NW., Washington, DC 20008
phone (202) 319–1976, fax 319–2982
His Excellency Tigran Sargsyan

Ambassador E. and P.
Consular Offices:
  California, Glendale
  District of Columbia, Washington

AUSTRALIA

Embassy of Australia
1601 Massachusetts Avenue, NW., Washington, DC
  20036
phone (202) 797–3000, fax 797–3331
His Excellency Kim Christian Beazley
Ambassador E. and P.
Consular Offices:
  California, San Francisco
  Colorado, Denver
  District of Columbia, Washington
  Hawaii, Honolulu
  Illinois, Chicago
  New York, New York
  Texas, Houston
  Trust Territories of the Pacific Islands:
    Kolonia, Micronesia
    Pago Pago

AUSTRIA

Embassy of Austria
3524 International Court, NW., Washington, DC
  20008–3035
phone (202) 895–6700, fax 895–6773
His Excellency Hans Peter Manz
Ambassador E. and P.
Consular Offices:
  Alaska, Anchorage
  Arizona, Scottsdale
  California:
    Los Angeles
    San Francisco
  Florida:
    Estero
    Hollywood
    Orlando
  Georgia, Atlanta
  Hawaii, Honolulu
  Louisiana, New Orleans
  Massachusetts, Boston
  Michigan, Detroit
  Minnesota, St. Paul
  Missouri:
    Kansas City
    St. Louis
  Nevada, Las Vegas
  New York, New York
  Ohio, Columbus
  Oregon, Portland
  Pennsylvania:
    Philadelphia
    Pittsburgh
  Puerto Rico, San Juan

South Carolina, Cowpens
Texas, Houston
Utah, Salt Lake City
Virgin Islands, St. Thomas
Virginia, Richmond

AZERBAIJAN

Embassy of the Republic of Azerbaijan
2741 34th Street, NW., Washington, DC 20008
phone (202) 337–3500, fax 337–5911
His Excellency Elin Emir Oglu Suleymanov
Ambassador E. and P.
Consular Offices:
  California, Los Angeles
  New Mexico, Santa Fe

BAHAMAS

Embassy of the Commonwealth of The Bahamas
2220 Massachusetts Avenue, NW., Washington, DC
  20008
phone (202) 319–2660, fax 319–2668
His Excelleny Eugene Glenwood Newry
Ambassador E. and P.
Consular Offices:
  District of Columbia, Washington
  Florida, Miami
  Georgia, Atlanta
  New York, New York

BAHRAIN

Embassy of the Kingdom of Bahrain
3502 International Drive, NW., Washington, DC
  20008
phone (202) 342–0741, fax 362–2192
His Excellency Shaikh Abdulla Mohamed Alkhalifa
Ambassador E. and P.
Consular Offices:
  California, San Diego
  New York, New York

BANGLADESH

Embassy of the People's Republic of Bangladesh
3510 International Drive, NW., Washington, DC
  20008
phone (202) 244–0183, fax 244–5366
His Excellency Mohammad Ziauddin
Ambassador E. and P.
Consular Offices:
  California, Los Angeles
  Louisiana, New Orleans
  New York, New York

BARBADOS

Embassy of Barbados
2144 Wyoming Avenue, NW., Washington, DC
  20008
phone (202) 939–9200, fax 332–7467
His Excellency John Ernest Beale
Ambassador E. and P.

Consular Offices:
California:
Los Angeles
San Francisco
Florida, Miami
Georgia, Atlanta
Illinois, Chicago
Kentucky, Louisville
Louisiana, New Orleans
Michigan, Detroit
New York, New York
Oregon, Portland
South Carolina, Charleston
Texas, Sugar Land

BELARUS

Embassy of the Republic of Belarus
1619 New Hampshire Avenue, NW., Washington,
DC 20009
phone (202) 986–1604, fax 986–1805
Mr. Pavel Shidlovsky
Counselor (Charge D'Affaires Ad Interim)
Consular Offices:
District of Columbia, Washington
New York, New York

BELGIUM

Embassy of Belgium
3330 Garfield Street, NW., Washington, DC 20008
phone (202) 333–6900, fax 333–3079
His Excellency Johan Cecilia Verbeke
Ambassador E. and P.
Consular Offices:
Arizona, Phoenix
California:
Los Angeles
San Diego
San Francisco
Colorado, Denver
Connecticut, Greenwich
District of Columbia, Washington
Florida, Miami
Georgia, Atlanta
Hawaii, Honolulu
Illinois:
Chicago
Moline
Kentucky, Louisville
Louisiana, New Orleans
Maryland, Baltimore
Massachusetts, Boston
Michigan, Bloomfield Hills
Minnesota, St. Paul
Missouri, Kansas City
New York, New York
Ohio, Cincinnati
Oregon, Portland

Pennsylvania:
Philadelphia
Pittsburgh
Puerto Rico, San Juan
Texas:
Fort Worth
Houston
San Antonio
Utah, Salt Lake City
Virginia, Virginia Beach
Washington, Seattle
Wisconsin, Milwaukee

BELIZE

Embassy of Belize
2535 Massachusetts Avenue, NW., Washington, DC
20008
phone (202) 332–9636, fax 332–6888
His Excellency Nestor Enrique Mendez
Ambassador E. and P.
Consular Offices:
California:
Los Angeles
San Francisco
District of Columbia, Washington
Florida, Coral Gables
Georgia, Atlanta
Illinois:
Belleville
Des Plaines
Louisiana, New Orleans
Michigan, Detroit
North Carolina, Wilmington
Ohio, Dayton
Texas:
Dallas
Houston
San Antonio

BENIN

Embassy of the Republic of Benin
2124 Kalorama Road, NW., Washington, DC 2008
phone (202) 232–6656, fax (202) 265–1996
His Excellency Omar Arouna
Ambassador E. and P.

BOLIVIA

Embassy of Bolivia
3014 Massachusetts Avenue, NW., Washington, DC
20008
phone (202) 483–4410, fax 328–3712
General Freddy Bersatti Tudela
Minister / Counselor (Charge D'Affaires, Ad
Interim)
Consular Offices:
California, Los Angeles
District of Columbia, Washington
Florida, Miami

New York, New York
Puerto Rico, San Juan

BOSNIA AND HERZEGOVINA

Embassy of Bosnia and Herzegovina
2109 E Street, NW., Washington, DC 20037
phone (202) 337–1500, fax 337–1502
Her Excellency Jadranka Negodic
Ambassador E. and P.
Consular Offices:
Illinois, Chicago

BOTSWANA

Embassy of the Republic of Botswana
1531–1533 New Hampshire Avenue, NW.,
  Washington, DC 20036
phone (202) 244–4990, fax 244–4164
Ms. Emolemo Morake
Minister / Counselor (Charge D'Affaires, Ad
  Interim)
Consular Offices:
California:
  San Francisco
  Santa Monica
Michigan, Southfield
Texas, Houston

BRAZIL

Brazilian Embassy
3006 Massachusetts Avenue, NW., Washington, DC
  20008
phone (202) 238–2700, fax 238–2827
His Excellency Luiz Alberto Figueiredo Machado
Ambassador E. and P.
Consular Offices:
  Arizona, Tempe
  California:
    La Jolla
    Los Angeles
    San Francisco
  Connecticut, Hartford
  District of Columbia, Washington
  Florida, Miami
  Georgia, Atlanta
  Hawaii, Honolulu
  Illinois, Chicago
  Louisiana, New Orleans
  Massachusetts, Boston
  Nevada, Las Vegas
  New York, New York
  Pennsylvania, Philadelphia
  Tennessee, Memphis
  Texas, Houston
  Trust Territories of the Pacific Islands:
    Hong Kong
  Utah, Salt Lake City
  Virginia, Norfolk
  Washington, Seattle

BRUNEI

Embassy of the State of Brunei Darussalam
3520 International Court, NW., Washington, DC
  20008
phone (202) 237–1838, fax 885–0560
Mrs. Dk Nor Hashimah Pg Md Hassan
Minister / Counselor (Charge D'Affaires, Ad
  Interim)

BULGARIA

Embassy of the Republic of Bulgaria
1621 22nd Street, NW., Washington, DC 20008
phone (202) 387–0174, fax 234–7973
Her Excellency Elena B. Poptodorova Petrova
Ambassador E. and P.
Consular Offices:
  California:
    Los Angeles
    Palm Springs
    Sacramento
  District of Columbia, Washington
  Florida, Boca Raton
  Illinois, Chicago
  Maine, Portland
  Massachusetts, Newton
  Nevada, Las Vegas
  New York, New York
  Pennsylvania:
    Media
    West Homestead
  South Carolina, Columbia

BURKINA FASO

Embassy of Burkina Faso
2340 Massachusetts Avenue, NW., Washington, DC
  20008
phone (202) 332–5577, fax 667–1882
Mr. Seydou Sinka
Counselor (Charge D'Affaires, Ad Interim)
Consular Offices:
  California, Los Angeles
  Louisiana, New Orleans

BURMA

Embassy of the Union of Burma
2300 S Street, NW., Washington, DC 20008
phone (202) 332–3344, fax 332–4351
His Excellency Kyaw Myo Htut
Ambassador E. and P.
Consular Office: New York, New York

BURUNDI

Embassy of the Republic of Burundi
2233 Wisconsin Avenue, NW., Suite 408,
  Washington, DC 20007
phone (202) 342–2574, fax 342–2578
His Excellency Ernest Ndabashinze
Ambassador E. and P.
Consular Office: California, Los Angeles

CABO VERDE

Embassy of the Republic of Cabo Verde
3415 Massachusetts Avenue, NW., Washington, DC
20007
phone (202) 965–6820, fax 965–1207
His Excellency Jose Luis Fialho Rocha
Ambassador E. and P.

CAMBODIA

Royal Embassy of Cambodia
4530 16th Street, NW., Washington, DC 20011
phone (202) 726–7742, fax 726–8381
Ms. Pachapor Lam
First Secretary (Charge D'Affaires Ad Interim)
Consular Offices:
California, Long Beach
Massachusetts, Lowell
Pennsylvania, Philadelphia
Washington, Seattle

CAMEROON

Embassy of the Republic of Cameroon
3400 International Drive, NW., Washington, DC
20008
phone (202) 265–8790, fax 387–3826
His Excellency Bienvenu Joseph C. Foe Atangana
Ambassador E. and P.
Consular Offices:
California, San Francisco
Texas, Houston

CANADA

Embassy of Canada
501 Pennsylvania Avenue, NW., Washington, DC
20001
phone (202) 682–1740, fax 682–7726
His Excellency Gary Albert Doer
Ambassador E. and P.
Consular Offices:
California:
Los Angeles
Palo Alto
San Diego
San Francisco
Colorado, Denver
District of Columbia, Washington
Florida, Miami
Georgia, Atlanta
Illinois, Chicago
Louisiana, New Orleans
Iowa, Des Moines
Louisiana, New Orleans
Massachusetts, Boston
Michigan, Detroit
Minnesota, Minneapolis
Montana, Nashua
New Jersey, Princeton
New York, New York

North Dakota, Bismarck
Oregon, Portland
Pennsylvania, Philadelphia
Puerto Rico, San Juan
Texas:
Dallas
Houston
San Antonio
Virginia, Richmond
Washington, Seattle

CAPE VERDE

Embassy of the Republic of Cape Verde
3415 Massachusetts Avenue, NW., Washington, DC
20007
phone (202) 965–6820, fax 965–1207
Her Excellency Maria De Fatima Da Veiga
Ambassador E. and P.
Consular Office: Massachusetts, Boston

CENTRAL AFRICAN REPUBLIC

Embassy of the Central African Republic
2704 Ontario Road, NW., Washington, DC 20009
phone (202) 483–7800, fax 332–9893
His Excellency Stanislas Moussa Kembe
Ambassador E. and P.
Consular Offices:
California, Los Angeles
New York, New York

CHAD

Embassy of the Republic of Chad
2401 Massachusetts Avenue, NW., Washington, DC
20008
phone (202) 652–1312, fax 758–0431
Mr. Hassane Mahamat Nasser
Ambassador E. and P.

CHILE

Embassy of the Republic of Chile
1732–1736 Massachusetts Avenue, NW.,
Washington, DC 20036
phone (202) 785–1746, fax 887–5579
His Excellency Juan Gabriel Valdes Soublette
Ambassador E. and P.
Consular Offices:
Arizona, Phoenix
California:
Los Angeles
San Diego
San Francisco
District of Columbia, Washington
Florida:
Miami
Orlando
Georgia, Atlanta
Hawaii, Honolulu
Illinois, Chicago

Louisiana, New Orleans
Massachusetts, Boston
Michigan, Grosse Pointe Park
Missouri, Kansas City
Nevada, Las Vegas
New York, New York
Pennsylvania, Philadelphia
Puerto Rico, San Juan
South Carolina, Charleston
Texas:
  Dallas
  Houston

CHINA

Embassy of the People's Republic of China
3505 International Place, NW., Washington, DC 20008
phone (202) 495–2000, fax 495–2138
His Excellency Tiankai Cui
Ambassador E. and P.
Consular Offices:
  California:
    Los Angeles
    San Francisco
  Illinois, Chicago
  New York, New York
  Texas, Houston

COLOMBIA

Embassy of the Republic of Colombia
2118 Leroy Place, NW., Washington, DC 20008
phone (202) 387–8338, fax 232–8643
His Excellency Luis Carlos Villegas Echeverri
Ambassador E. and P.
Consular Offices:
  California:
    Beverly Hills
    San Francisco
  District of Columbia, Washington
  Florida:
    Miami
    Orlando
  Georgia, Atlanta
  Illinois, Chicago
  Massachusetts, Boston
  New Jersey, Newark
  New York, New York
  Puerto Rico, San Juan
  Texas, Houston

COMOROS

Embassy of the Union of the Comoros
866 United Nations Plaza, Suite 418, New York, NY 10017
phone (212) 750–1637, fax 750–1657
His Excellency Mohamed Soilihi Soilih
Ambassador E. and P.

Consular Office: Illinois, Chicago

CONGO, DEMOCRATIC REPUBLIC OF THE

Embassy of the Democratic Republic of the Congo
1726 M Street, NW., Suite 601, Washington, DC 20036
phone (202) 234–7690, fax 234–2609
Her Excellency Faida Maramuke Mitifu
Ambassador E. and P.
Consular Office: New York, New York

CONGO, REPUBLIC OF THE

Embassy of the Republic of the Congo
1720 16th Street, NW., Washington, DC 20009
phone (202) 726–5500, fax 726–1860
His Excellency Serge Mombouli
Ambassador E. and P.
Consular Office: Louisiana, New Orleans

COSTA RICA

Embassy of the Republic of Costa Rica
2114 S Street, NW., Washington, DC 20008
phone (202) 234–2945, fax 265–4795
His Excellency Roman Macaya Hayes
Ambassador E. and P.
Consular Offices:
  Arizona, Tucson
  California, Los Angeles
  District of Columbia, Washington
  Florida, Miami
  Georgia, Atlanta
  Illinois, Chicago
  Minnesota, St. Paul
  New York, New York
  Puerto Rico, San Juan
  Texas, Houston

CÔTE D'IVOIRE

Embassy of the Republic of Côte d'Ivoire
2424 Massachusetts Avenue, NW., Washington, DC 20008
phone (202) 797–0300, fax 462–9444
His Excellency Daouda Diabate
Ambassador E. and P.
Consular Offices:
  California, San Francisco
  Connecticut, Stamford
  Florida, Orlando
  Michigan, Detroit
  Texas, Houston

CROATIA

Embassy of the Republic of Croatia
2343 Massachusetts Avenue, NW., Washington, DC 20008
phone (202) 588–5899, fax 588–8936
His Excellency Josip Paro

Ambassador E. and P.
Consular Offices:
  Alaska, Anchorage
  California, Los Angeles
  District of Columbia, Washington
  Illinois, Chicago
  Kansas, Kansas City
  Louisiana, New Orleans
  New York, New York
  Pennsylvania, Pittsburgh
  Texas, Houston
  Washington, Seattle

CUBA

Embassy of Switzerland, Cuban Interests Section
2630 16th Street, NW., Washington, DC 20009
phone (202) 797-8518
Mr. Jose Ramon Cabanas Rodriguez
Counselor (Chief of Interests Section)

CYPRUS

Embassy of the Republic of Cyprus
2211 R Street, NW., Washington, DC 20008
phone (202) 462-5772, fax 483-6710
His Excellency Georgios Chacalli
Ambassador E. and P.
Consular Offices:
  California:
    Los Angeles
    San Francisco
  District of Columbia, Washington
  Georgia, Chamblee
  Illinois, Chicago
  Louisiana, New Orleans
  Michigan, Dearborn
  New York, New York
  North Carolina, Jacksonville
  Oregon, Portland
  Texas, Houston
  Washington, Seattle

CZECH REPUBLIC

Embassy of the Czech Republic
3900 Spring of Freedom Street, NW., Washington,
DC 20008
phone (202) 274-9100, fax 966-8540
His Excellency Petr Gandalovic
Ambassador E. and P.
Consular Offices:
  Alaska, Anchorage
  California:
    Los Angeles
    San Francisco
  Colorado, Boulder
  Florida:
    Ft. Lauderdale
    Orlando
  Georgia, Atlanta

Hawaii, Honolulu
Illinois, Chicago
Louisiana, New Orleans
Massachusetts, Wellesley
Missouri, Kansas City
Montana, Livingston
New York:
  Buffalo
  New York
Oregon, Portland
Pennsylvania:
  Philadelphia
  Pittsburgh
Puerto Rico, San Juan
Texas, Houston
Utah, Salt Lake City
Washington, Seattle

DENMARK

Royal Danish Embassy
3200 Whitehaven Street, NW., Washington, DC
20008
phone (202) 234-4300, fax 328-1470
His Excellency Peter Taksoe Jensen
Ambassador E. and P.
Consular Offices:
  Alabama, Mobile
  Alaska, Anchorage
  Arizona, Scottsdale
  California:
    Los Angeles
    Sacramento
    San Diego
  Colorado, Denver
  Florida:
    Hollywood
    Jacksonville
    Tampa
  Georgia, Macon
  Hawaii, Honolulu
  Illinois, Chicago
  Indiana, Indianapolis
  Iowa, Des Moines
  Kansas, Kansas City
  Louisiana, New Orleans
  Maryland, Baltimore
  Massachusetts, Boston
  Michigan, Detroit
  Minnesota, Minneapolis
  Nebraska, Omaha
  New York, New York
  Ohio, Cleveland
  Oregon, Portland
  Pennsylvania:
    Philadelphia
    Pittsburgh
  Puerto Rico, San Juan
  South Carolina, Charleston

Texas:
  Dallas
  Houston
Utah, Salt Lake City
Virgin Islands, St. Thomas
Virginia, Virginia Beach
Washington, Seattle
Wisconsin, Milwaukee

DJIBOUTI

Embassy of the Republic of Djibouti
1156 15th Street, NW., Suite 515, Washington, DC
  20005
phone (202) 331–0270, fax 331–0302
His Excellency Roble Olhaye
Ambassador E. and P.

DOMINICA

Embassy of the Commonwealth of Dominica
1001 19th Street, N., Suite 1200, Arlington, VA
  22209
phone (571) 527–1370, fax 384–7916
His Excellency Hubert John Charles
Ambassador E. and P.
Consular Offices:
  New York, New York
  Puerto Rico, Guaynabo

DOMINICAN REPUBLIC

Embassy of the Dominican Republic
1715 22nd Street, NW., Washington, DC 20008
phone (202) 332–6280, fax 265–8057
His Excellency Jose Tomas Perez Vazquez
Ambassador E. and P.
Consular Offices:
  California, Glendale
  Florida, Miami
  Illinois, Chicago
  Louisiana, New Orleans
  Massachusetts, Boston
  New York, New York
  Puerto Rico:
    Mayaguez
    San Juan

ECUADOR

Embassy of Ecuador
2535 15th Street, NW., Washington, DC 20009
phone (202) 234–7200, fax 667–3482
His Excellency Francisco Jose Borja Cevallos
Ambassador E. and P.
Consular Offices:
  Arizona, Phoenix
  California:
    Los Angeles
    San Francisco
  Connecticut, New Haven
  District of Columbia, Washington

Florida, Miami
Georgia, Atlanta
Illinois, Chicago
Louisiana, New Orleans
Massachusetts, Boston
Minnesota, Minneapolis
New Jersey, Newark
New York:
  New York
  Woodside
Puerto Rico, San Juan
Texas:
  Dallas
  Houston

EGYPT

Embassy of the Arab Republic of Egypt
3521 International Court, NW., Washington, DC
  20008
phone (202) 895–5400, fax 244–4319
His Excellency Mohamed Mostafa Mohamed
  Tawfik
Ambassador E. and P.
Consular Offices:
  California, Los Angeles
  Illinois, Chicago
  New York, New York
  Texas, Houston

EL SALVADOR

Embassy of the Republic of El Salvador
1400 16th Street, NW., Suite 100, Washington, DC
  20036
phone (202) 265–9671, fax 232–3763
His Excellency Francisco R. Altschul Fuentes
Ambassador E. and P.
Consular Offices:
  Arizona:
    Fountain Hills
    Tucson
  California:
    Chula Vista
    Costa Mesa
    Los Angeles
    Oakland
    San Francisco
    Santa Ana
  District of Columbia, Washington
  Florida, Coral Gables
  Georgia, Woodstock
  Illinois, Chicago
  Nevada, Las Vegas
  New Jersey, Elizabeth
  New York:
    Brentwood
    New York
  Pennsylvania, Philadelphia

Texas:
  Dallas
  Houston
Virginia, Woodbridge
Washington, Seattle

EQUATORIAL GUINEA

Embassy of the Republic of Equatorial Guinea
2020 16th Street, NW., Washington, DC 20009
phone (202) 518–5700, fax 518–5252
His Excellency Miguel Ntutumu Evuna Andeme
Ambassador E. and P.
Consular Office: Texas, Houston

ERITREA

Embassy of the State of Eritrea
1708 New Hampshire Avenue, NW., Washington,
DC 20009
phone (202) 319–1991, fax 319–1304
Mr. Berhane Gebrehiwet Solomon
First Secretary (Charge D'Affaires Ad Interim)
Consular Office: District of Columbia, Washington

ESTONIA

Embassy of the Republic of Estonia
2131 Massachusetts Avenue, NW., Washington, DC
20008
phone (202) 588–0101, fax 588–0108
Her Excellency Eerik Marmei
Ambassador E. and P.
Consular Offices:
  Arizona, Scottsdale
  California:
    Los Angeles
    San Francisco
  Florida:
    Miami
    St. Petersburg
  Georgia, Atlanta
  Illinois, Chicago
  Massachusetts, Boston
  Nebraska, Lincoln
  New Hampshire, Portsmouth
  New York, New York
  North Carolina, Huntersville
  South Carolina, Charleston
  Texas, Houston
  Washington, Seattle

ETHIOPIA

Embassy of the Federal Democratic Republic of
Ethiopia
3506 International Drive, NW., Washington, DC
20008
phone (202) 364–1200, fax 587–0195
His Excellency Girma Birru Geda
Ambassador E. and P.
Consular Offices:

California, Los Angeles
New York, New York
Texas, Houston
Washington, Seattle

EUROPEAN UNION

Delegation of the European Union
2175 K Street, NW., Washington, DC 20037
His Excellency David O. Sullivan
Ambassador (Head of Delegation)

FIJI

Embassy of the Republic of the Fiji
1707 L Street, NW., Suite 200, Washington, DC
20036
phone (202) 466–8320, fax 466–8325
Mr. Akuila Kamanalagi Vuira
First Secretary (Charge D'Affaires Ad Interim)
Consular Offices:
  California:
    El Segundo
    San Francisco
  Oregon, Portland
  Texas, Dallas

FINLAND

Embassy of the Republic of Finland
3301 Massachusetts Avenue, NW., Washington, DC
20008
phone (202) 298–5800, fax 298–6030
Her Excellency Ritva Inkeri Koukku Ronde
Ambassador E. and P.
Consular Offices:
  Alabama, Birmingham
  Alaska, Anchorage
  Arizona, Phoenix
  California:
    Los Angeles
    San Diego
    San Francisco
  Colorado, Highlands Ranch
  Connecticut, Norwich
  Florida:
    Lake Worth
    Miami
  Georgia, Atlanta
  Hawaii, Honolulu
  Illinois, Chicago
  Louisiana, New Orleans
  Maryland, Baltimore
  Massachusetts, Boston
  Michigan:
    Farmington
    Hancock
  Minnesota:
    Minneapolis
    Virginia
  Missouri, Saint Louis

New Jersey, Newark
New York, New York
Pennsylvania, Philadelphia
Puerto Rico, San Juan
Texas:
    Dallas
    Houston
Utah, Salt Lake City
Virginia, Norfolk
Washington, Seattle

FRANCE

Embassy of the French Republic
4101 Reservoir Road, NW., Washington, DC 20007
phone (202) 944–6000, fax 944–6166
His Excellency Gerard Roger Araud
Ambassador E. and P.
Consular Offices:
    Alaska, Anchorage
    Arizona, Phoenix
    Arkansas, Little Rock
    California:
        Los Angeles
        Sacramento
        San Diego
        San Francisco
    Colorado, Denver
    District of Columbia, Washington
    Florida:
        Clearwater
        Jacksonville
        Miami
        Orlando
    Georgia:
        Atlanta
        Savannah
    Guam, Tamuning
    Hawaii, Honolulu
    Idaho, Boise
    Illinois, Chicago
    Indiana, Indianapolis
    Iowa, Indianola
    Kentucky, Louisville
    Louisiana:
        Lafayette
        New Orleans
        Shreveport
    Maine, Portland
    Massachusetts, Boston
    Michigan, Southfield
    Minnesota, Minneapolis
    Mississippi, Hattiesburg
    Missouri, St. Louis
    Montana, Hamilton
    Nebraska, Omaha
    Nevada:
        Las Vegas

Reno
New Jersey, Princeton
New Mexico, Albuquerque
New York:
    Buffalo
    New York
North Carolina:
    Charlotte
    Raleigh
Ohio:
    Cincinnati
    Cleveland
Oklahoma, Oklahoma City
Oregon, Portland
Pennsylvania:
    Philadelphia
    Pittsburgh
Puerto Rico, San Juan
Rhode Island, Providence
South Carolina:
    Greenville
    Mount Pleasant
Tennessee, Nashville
Texas:
    Dallas
    Houston
    San Antonio
Utah, Salt Lake City
Vermont, Burlington
Virginia, Norfolk
Washington, Seattle
Wyoming, Dubois

GABON

Embassy of the Gabonese Republic
2034 20th Street, NW., Washington, DC 20009
phone (202) 797–1000, fax (301) 983–1994
His Excellency Michael Moussa Adamo
Ambassador E. and P.
Consular Office: New York, New York

GAMBIA

Embassy of The Gambia
2233 Wisconsin Avenue, NW., Suite 240,
    Washington, DC 20007
phone (202) 785–1399, fax 785–1430
Mr. Sheikh Omar Faye
Minister / Counselor (Charge D'Affaires Ad Interim)
Consular Office: Florida, Miami

GEORGIA

Embassy of the Republic of Georgia
1824–1826 R Street, NW., Washington, DC 20008
phone (202) 387–2390, fax 387–0864
His Excellency Archil Gegeshidze
Ambassador E. and P.
Consular Offices:

California, Orange
District of Columbia, Washington
New York, New York
South Carolina, Charleston

GERMANY

Embassy of the Federal Republic of Germany
4645 Reservoir Road, NW., Washington, DC
20007
phone (202) 298–4000, fax 298–4249
His Excellency Hans Peter Wittig
Ambassador E. and P.
Consular Offices:
  Alabama, Birmingham
  Alaska, Anchorage
  Arizona, Phoenix
  California:
    Los Angeles
    San Diego
    San Francisco
  Colorado, Denver
  Connecticut, Farmington
  District of Columbia, Washington
  Florida:
    Miami
    Naples
    Orlando
  Georgia:
    Atlanta
    Savannah
  Hawaii, Honolulu
  Illinois, Chicago
  Indiana, Indianapolis
  Iowa, Indianola
  Kansas, Leawood
  Kentucky, Louisville
  Louisiana, New Orleans
  Maine, Portland
  Massachusetts, Boston
  Michigan, Auburn Hills
  Minnesota, Minneapolis
  Mississippi, Jackson
  Missouri, St. Louis
  Nevada, Las Vegas
  New Mexico, Albuquerque
  New York:
    Buffalo
    New York
  North Carolina:
    Charlotte
    Raleigh
  Ohio:
    Cincinnati
    Cleveland
  Oklahoma, Oklahoma City
  Oregon, Portland
  Pennsylvania:

  Philadelphia
  Pittsburgh
  Puerto Rico, San Juan
  South Carolina, Greer
  Tennessee, Nashville
  Texas:
    Dallas
    Houston
    San Antonio
  Trust Territories of the Pacific Islands:
    Manila, Philippines
    Wellington, New Zealand
  Utah, Salt Lake City
  Virginia, Virginia Beach
  Washington, Mercer Island

GHANA

Embassy of Ghana
3512 International Drive, NW., Washington, DC
20008
phone (202) 686–4520, fax 686–4527
His Excellency Joseph Henry Smith
Ambassador E. and P.
Consular Offices:
  New York, New York
  Texas, Houston

GREECE

Embassy of Greece
2217 Massachusetts Avenue, NW., Washington, DC
20008
phone (202) 939–1300, fax 939–1324
His Excellency Christos Panagopoulos
Ambassador E. and P.
Consular Offices:
  California:
    Los Angeles
    San Francisco
  Florida, Tampa
  Georgia, Atlanta
  Illinois, Chicago
  Massachusetts, Boston
  New York, New York
  Texas, Houston

GRENADA

Embassy of Grenada
1701 New Hampshire Avenue, NW., Washington,
DC 20009
phone (202) 265–2561, fax 265–2468
His Excellency Ethelstan Angus Friday
Ambassador E. and P.
Consular Offices: Illinois, Chicago

GUATEMALA

Embassy of Guatemala
2220 R Street, NW., Washington, DC 20008
phone (202) 745–4953, fax 745–1908

His Excellency Julio Ligorria Carballido
Ambassador E. and P.
Consular Offices:
  Alabama, Montgomery
  Arizona, Phoenix
  California:
    Los Angeles
    San Diego
    San Francisco
  Colorado, Denver
  Florida:
    Ft. Lauderdale
    Jupiter
    Miami
  Georgia, Atlanta
  Illinois, Chicago
  Louisiana: Lafayette
  Maryland, Silver Spring
  Massachusetts, Newton
  Missouri, Kansas City
  Nevada, North Las Vegas
  New York, New York
  North Carolina, Charlotte
  Oklahoma, Oklahoma City
  Oregon, Portland
  Puerto Rico, San Juan
  South Carolina, Columbia
  Tennessee, Memphis
  Texas:
    Houston
    San Antonio
  Washington, Seattle
  Wisconsin, Madison

GUINEA

Embassy of the Republic of Guinea
2112 Leroy Place, NW., Washington, DC 20008
phone (202) 986–4300, fax 986–3800
His Excellency Mamady Conde
Ambassador E. and P.
Consular Office: California, Santa Monica

GUYANA

Embassy of Guyana
2490 Tracy Place, NW., Washington, DC 20008
phone (202) 265–6900, fax 232–1297
His Excellency Bayney Ram Karran
Ambassador E. and P.
Consular Offices:
  California, Los Angeles
  Florida, Miami
  New York, New York

HAITI

Embassy of the Republic of Haiti
2311 Massachusetts Avenue, NW., Washington, DC
  20008
phone (202) 332–4090, fax 745–7215

His Excellency Paul Getty Altidor
Ambassador E. and P.
Consular Offices:
  California, San Francisco
  Florida:
    Miami
    Orlando
  Georgia, Atlanta
  Illinois, Chicago
  Louisiana, New Orleans
  Massachusetts, Boston
  New Jersey, Trenton
  New York, New York
  Pennsylvania:
    Philadelphia
    Pottsville
  Texas, Houston

HOLY SEE

Apostolic Nunciature
3339 Massachusetts Avenue, NW., Washington, DC
  20008
phone (202) 333–7121, fax 337–4036
His Excellency Reverend Carlo Maria Vigano
Apostolic Nuncio

HONDURAS

Embassy of Honduras
3007 Tilden Street, NW., Suite 4–M, Washington,
  DC 20008
phone (202) 966–2604, fax 966–9751
His Excellency Jorge Alberto Milla Reyes
Ambassador E. and P.
Consular Offices:
  California:
    Los Angeles
    San Diego
    San Francisco
  Florida:
    Miami
    Tampa
  Georgia, Atlanta
  Hawaii, Honolulu
  Illinois, Chicago
  Louisiana:
    Baton Rouge
    New Orleans
  Maryland, Baltimore
  Missouri, St. Louis
  Nevada, Reno
  New York, New York
  Texas, Houston

HUNGARY

Embassy of Hungary
3910 Shoemaker Street, NW., Washington, DC
  20008
phone (202) 362–6730, fax 966–8135

His Excellency Reka Szemerkenyi
Ambassador E. and P.
Consular Offices:
  California:
    Los Angeles
    Sacramento
    San Francisco
  Colorado, Denver
  Connecticut, Hamden
  District of Columbia, Washington
  Florida:
    Miami
    Sarasota
  Georgia, Morrow
  Hawaii, Honolulu
  Louisiana, Metairie
  Massachusetts, Boston
  Minnnesota, Minneapolis
  Missouri, St. Louis
  New York, New York
  Ohio, Cleveland
  Puerto Rico, Mayaguez
  Texas, Houston
  Utah, Sandy
  Washington, Seattle

ICELAND

Embassy of Iceland
2900 K Street, NW., Suite 509, Washington, DC
20007
phone (202) 265-6653, fax 265-6656
His Excellency Geir Hilmar Haarde
Ambassador E. and P.
Consular Offices:
  Alaska, Anchorage
  Arizona, Phoenix
  California:
    Los Angeles
    San Francisco
  Colorado, Englewood
  Florida:
    Orlando
    Plantation
  Georgia, Atlanta
  Illinois, Chicago
  Kentucky, Louisville
  Louisiana, New Orleans
  Massachusetts, Boston
  Michigan, Detroit
  Minnesota, Minneapolis
  Missouri, Grandview
  New York, New York
  North Dakota, Grand Fork
  Oregon, Portland
  Pennsylvania, Harrisburg
  Puerto Rico, Guaynabo
  South Carolina, Charleston

Texas:
  Dallas
  Houston
Utah, Salt Lake City
Virginia, Norfolk
Washington, Seattle
Wisconsin, Madison

INDIA

Embassy of India
2107 Massachusetts Avenue, NW., Washington, DC
20008
phone (202) 939-7000, fax 483-3972
His Excellency Arun Kumar Singh
Ambassador E. and P.
Consular Offices:
  California, San Francisco
  District of Columbia, Washington
  Georgia, Atlanta
  Illinois, Chicago
  New York, New York
  Texas, Houston

INDONESIA

Embassy of the Republic of Indonesia
2020 Massachusetts Avenue, NW., Washington, DC
20036
phone (202) 775-5200, fax 775-5365
His Excellency Budi Bowoleksono
Ambassador E. and P.
Consular Offices:
  California:
    Los Angeles
    San Francisco
  Illinois, Chicago
  New York, New York
  Texas, Houston

IRAQ

Embassy of the Republic of Iraq
3421 Massachusetts Avenue, NW., Washington, DC
20007
phone (202) 742-1600, fax 462-5066
His Excellency Lukman Abdulraheem A. Al Fally
Ambassador E. and P.
Consular Offices:
  California, Los Angeles
  Michigan, Southfield

IRELAND

Embassy of Ireland
2234 Massachusetts Avenue, NW., Washington, DC
20008
phone (202) 462-3939, fax 232-5993
Her Excellency Anne Anderson
Ambassador E. and P.
Consular Offices:
  California:

Los Angeles
San Francisco
Colorado, Denver
Florida, Orlando
Georgia, Atlanta
Hawaii, Honolulu
Illinois, Chicago
Louisiana, New Orleans
Massachusetts, Boston
Missouri, St. Louis
Nevada, Las Vegas
New York, New York
Pennsylvania, Pittsburgh
Texas, Houston
Washington, Seattle

ISRAEL

Embassy of Israel
3514 International Drive, NW., Washington, DC
20008
phone (202) 364–5500, fax 364–5607
His Excellency Ron Dermer
Ambassador E. and P.
Consular Offices:
California:
Los Angeles
San Francisco
District of Columbia, Washington
Florida, Miami
Georgia, Atlanta
Illinois, Chicago
Massachusetts, Boston
New York, New York
Pennsylvania, Philadelphia
Texas, Houston

ITALY

Embassy of Italy
3000 Whitehaven Street, NW., Washington, DC
20008
phone (202) 612–4400, fax 518–2151
His Excellency Claudio Bisogniero
Ambassador E. and P.
Consular Offices:
Alaska, Anchorage
Arizona, Scottsdale
California:
Fresno
Los Angeles
San Diego
San Francisco
San Jose
Connecticut, Hartford
Florida:
Miami
Orlando
Georgia, Atlanta
Hawaii, Honolulu

Illinois, Chicago
Indiana, Indianapolis
Kansas, Leawood
Louisiana, New Orleans
Maryland, Baltimore
Massachusetts:
Boston
Worcester
Michigan, Detroit
Mississippi, Hattiesburg
Missouri, St. Louis
Nevada, Las Vegas
New Jersey, Newark
New York:
Buffalo
Mineola
Mt. Vernon
New York
Rochester
North Carolina, Charlotte
Ohio, Cleveland
Oregon, Portland
Pennsylvania:
Philadelphia
Pittsburgh
Puerto Rico, San Juan
Rhode Island, Providence
South Carolina, Charleston
Texas, Houston
Utah, Salt Lake City
Washington, Seattle

JAMAICA

Embassy of Jamaica
1520 New Hampshire Avenue, NW., Washington,
DC 20036
phone (202) 452–0660, fax 452–0081
His Excellency Stephen Charles Vasciannie
Ambassador E. and P.
Consular Offices:
California:
Los Angeles
San Francisco
District of Columbia, Washington
Florida, Miami
Georgia, Atlanta
Illinois, Chicago
Massachusetts, Boston
New Hampshire, Concord
New York, New York
Pennsylvania, Philadelphia
Texas, Houston
Virginia, Richmond
Washington, Seattle

JAPAN

Embassy of Japan

2520 Massachusetts Avenue, NW., Washington, DC 20008
phone (202) 238–6700, fax 328–2187
His Excellency Kenichiro Sasae
Ambassador E. and P.
Consular Offices:
  Alaska, Anchorage
  Arizona, Tempe
  California:
    Los Angeles
    San Diego
    San Francisco
  Colorado, Denver
  Connecticut, Simsbury
  District of Columbia, Washington
  Florida:
    Miami
    Orlando
  Georgia, Atlanta
  Guam, Agana
  Hawaii:
    Hilo
    Honolulu
  Idaho, Boise
  Illinois, Chicago
  Indiana, Indianapolis
  Kansas, Prairie Village
  Kentucky, Lexington
  Louisiana, New Orleans
  Massachusetts, Boston
  Michigan, Detroit
  Minnesota, Minneapolis
  Missouri, St. Louis
  Nebraska, Omaha
  Nevada, Las Vegas
  New Mexico, Albuquerque
  New York:
    Buffalo
    New York
  North Carolina, Durham
  Northern Mariana Islands, Mariana Islands
  Ohio, Cincinnati
  Oklahoma, Oklahoma City
  Oregon, Portland
  Pennsylvania, Philadelphia
  Puerto Rico, San Juan
  Tennessee, Nashville
  Texas:
    Dallas
    Houston
  Washington, Seattle

JORDAN

Embassy of the Hashemite Kingdom of Jordan
3504 International Drive, NW., Washington, DC 20008
phone (202) 966–2664, fax 966–3110

Her Excellency Dr. Alia Mohamad Ali Hatough Bouran
Ambassador E. and P.
Consular Offices:
  California, San Francisco
  Illinois, Chicago
  Michigan, Detroit

KAZAKHSTAN

Embassy of the Republic of Kazakhstan
1401 16th Street, NW., Washington, DC 20036
phone (202) 232–5488, fax 232–5845
His Excellency Kairat Umarov
Ambassador E. and P.
Consular Offices:
  California:
    San Francisco
    Santa Monica
  District of Columbia, Washington
  Louisiana, Baton Rouge
  New York, New York
  North Dakota, Fargo

KENYA

Embassy of the Republic of Kenya
2249 R Street, NW., Washington, DC 20008
phone (202) 387–6101, fax 462–3829
His Excellency Robinson Njeru Githae
Ambassador E. and P.
Consular Offices:
  California, Los Angeles
  New York, New York

KIRIBATI

Embassy of the Republic of Kiribati
800 Second Avenue, Suite 400A, New York, NY 10017
phone (212) 867–3310, fax 867–3320
Her Excellency Makurita Baaro
Ambassador E. and P.
Consular Office: Hawaii, Honolulu

KOREA, REPUBLIC OF

Embassy of the Republic of Korea
2450 Massachusetts Avenue, NW., Washington, DC 20008
phone (202) 939–5600, fax 387–0250
His Excellency Ho Young Ahn
Ambassador E. and P.
Consular Offices:
  Alaska, Anchorage
  Arizona, Tucson
  California:
    Los Angeles
    San Francisco
  Colorado, Denver
  Connecticut, Stamford
  District of Columbia, Washington

Florida, Miami
Georgia, Atlanta
Guam, Agana
Hawaii, Honolulu
Illinois, Chicago
Louisiana, New Orleans
Massachusetts, Boston
Michigan, Southfield
Missouri, Saint Louis
Nevada, Reno
New York, New York
Oklahoma, Oklahoma City
Oregon:
  Eugene
  Portland
Pennsylvania, Philadelphia
Puerto Rico, San Juan
Texas:
  Dallas
  Houston
Utah, Salt Lake City
Washington, Seattle

KOSOVO

Embassy of the Republic of Kosovo
2175 K Street, NW., Suite 300, Washington, DC 20037
phone (202) 450–2130, fax 735–0609
His Excellency Akan Ismaili
Ambassador E. and P.
Consular Office: New York, New York

KUWAIT

Embassy of the State of Kuwait
2940 Tilden Street, NW., Washington, DC 20008
phone (202) 966–0702, fax 966–0517
His Excellency Sheikh Salem Abdullah Al-Jaber Al-Sabah
Ambassador E. and P.
Consular Office: California, Los Angeles

KYRGYZSTAN

Embassy of the Kyrgyz Republic
2360 Massachusetts Avenue, NW., Washington, DC 20008
phone (202) 449–9822, fax 386–7550
His Excellency Kadyr Toktogulov
Ambassador E. and P.
Consular Offices:
  District of Columbia, Washington
  New York, New York
  Washington, Maple Valley

LAOS

Embassy of the Lao Peoples Democratic Republic
2222 S Street, NW., Washington, DC 20008
phone (202) 332–6416, fax 332–4923
Mr. Khen Sombandith
Counselor (Charge D'Affaires Ad Interim)

LATVIA

Embassy of Latvia
2306 Massachusetts Avenue, NW., Washington, DC 20008
phone (202) 328–2840, fax 328–2860
His Excellency Andris Razans
Ambassador E. and P.
Consular Offices:
  Alaska, Palmer
  California:
    Mill Valley
    Rancho Santa Margarita
  Florida, Ft. Lauderdale
  Illinois, Chicago
  Massachusetts, Needham
  Michigan, West Bloomfield
  Minnesota, Minneapolis
  New York:
    Buffalo
    Greenwich
    New York
  Ohio, Cincinnati
  Oregon, Salem
  Pennsylvania, Philadelphia
  Rhode Island, North Kingstown
  Texas, Houston
  Washington, Snohomish

LEBANON

Embassy of Lebanon
2560 28th Street, NW., Washington, DC 20008
phone (202) 939–6300, fax 939–6324
His Excellency Antoine Chedid
Ambassador E. and P.
Consular Offices:
  California, Los Angeles
  Massachusetts, Boston
  Michigan, Detroit
  New York, New York
  North Carolina, Raleigh
  Texas, Houston

LESOTHO

Embassy of the Kingdom of Lesotho
2511 Massachusetts Avenue, NW., Washington, DC 20008
phone (202) 797–5533, fax 234–6815
His Excellency Professor Eliachim Molapi Sebatane
Ambassador E. and P.
Consular Offices:
  Louisiana, New Orleans
  Ohio, Dayton
  Texas, Austin

LIBERIA

Embassy of the Republic of Liberia
5201 16th Street, NW., Washington, DC 20011
phone (202) 723–0437, fax 723–0436

His Excellency Jeremiah Congbeh Sulunteh
Ambassador E. and P.
Consular Offices:
District of Columbia, Washington
Florida, Tampa
Georgia, Atlanta

LIBYA

Embassy of Libya
2600 Virginia Avenue, NW., Suite 705, 300, 40,
Washington, DC 20037
phone (202) 944–9601, fax 944–9606
Ms. Wafa M. T. Bughaighis
Minister (Charge D'Affaires Ad Interim)
Ambassador E. and P.
Consular Office: District of Columbia, Washington

LIECHTENSTEIN

Embassy of the Principality of Liechtenstein
2900 K Street, NW., Suite 602B, Washington, DC
20007
phone (202) 331–0590, fax 331–3221
Her Excellency Claudia Fritsche
Minister
Consular Offices:
California, Los Angeles
Georgia, Macon
Illinois, Chicago
Oregon, Portland

LITHUANIA

Embassy of the Republic of Lithuania
2622 16th Street, NW., Washington, DC 20009
phone (202) 234–5860, fax 328–0466
His Excellency Zygimantas Pavilionis
Ambassador E. and P.
Consular Offices:
Alaska, Anchorage
Arizona, Phoenix
California:
Lafayette
Santa Monica
Colorado, Aspen
Florida:
Palm Beach
St. Petersburg
Georgia, Marietta
Illinois, Chicago
Michigan:
Farmington
Lansing
Minnesota, Stillwater
Nevada, Las Vegas
New Hampshire, Manchester
New York:
New York
Webster
Ohio, Cleveland

Oregon, Portland
Pennsylvania, Philadelphia
Texas, Houston
Washington, Seattle

LUXEMBOURG

Embassy of the Grand Duchy of Luxembourg
2200 Massachusetts Avenue, NW., Washington, DC
20008
phone (202) 265–4171, fax 328–8270
His Excellency Jean Louis Wolzfeld
Ambassador E. and P.
Consular Offices:
Arizona, Scottsdale
California:
San Francisco
Woodland Hills
Colorado, Louisville
Florida, Estero
Georgia, Atlanta
Hawaii, Kapolei
Illinois, Elburn
Indiana, Indianapolis
Louisiana, New Orleans
Massachusetts, Boston
Michigan, Auburn Hills
Minnesota, Edina
Missouri, Kansas City
New York, New York
Ohio, Cleveland
Oregon, Portland
Texas, Ft. Worth
Washington, Seattle
Wisconsin, Grafton

MACEDONIA

Embassy of the Republic of Macedonia
2129 Wyoming Avenue, NW., Washington, DC
20008
phone (202) 667–0501, fax 667–2131
His Excellency Vasko Naumovski
Ambassador E. and P.
Consular Offices:
Arizona, Tucson
California:
Ontario
San Diego
Florida:
Hollywood
Naples
Illinois, Chicago
Michigan, Southfield
New Jersey, Clifton
New York, New York
Ohio, Columbus

MADAGASCAR

Embassy of the Republic of Madagascar

2374 Massachusetts Avenue, NW., Washington, DC
20008
phone (202) 265–5525, fax 265–3034
Mrs. Velotiana Rakotoanosy Raobelina
Counselor (Charge D'Affaires Ad Interim)
Consular Offices: New York, New York

MALAWI

Embassy of Malawi
2408 Massachusetts Avenue, NW., Washington, DC
20008
phone (202) 721–0270, fax 721–0288
His Excellency Necton Darlington Mhura
Ambassador E. and P.

MALAYSIA

Embassy of Malaysia
3516 International Court, NW., Washington, DC
20008
phone (202) 572–9700, fax 572–9882
His Excellency Awang Adek Bin Hussin
Ambassador E. and P.
Consular Offices:
  California, Los Angeles
  Hawaii, Honolulu
  New York, New York
  Oregon, Portland

MALDIVES

Embassy of the Republic of Maldives
800 Second Avenue, Suite 400E, New York, NY
10017
phone (212) 599–6195, fax 661–6405
His Excellency Ahmed Sareer
Ambassador E. and P.

MALI

Embassy of the Republic of Mali
2130 R Street, NW., Washington, DC 20008
phone (202) 332–2249, fax 332–6603
His Excellency Tiena Coulibaly
Ambassador E. and P.
Consular Offices:
  California, Cupertino
  Florida, Ft. Lauderdale
  Georgia, Atlanta
  Louisiana, New Orleans

MALTA

Embassy of Malta
2017 Connecticut Avenue, NW., Washington, DC
20008
phone (202) 462–3611, fax 387–5470
Her Excellency Marisa Maria Louise Micallef
Ambassador E. and P.
Consular Offices:
  Arizona, Phoenix
  California:
    Los Angeles

San Francisco
District of Columbia, Washington
Florida, Miami
Georgia, Atlanta
Illinois, Barrington
Louisiana, Metairie
Massachusetts, Bellmont
Michigan:
  Detroit
  Taylor
Minnesota, St. Paul
New York, New York
Pennsylvania, Philadelphia
Tennessee, Kingsport
Texas:
  Dallas
  Houston
Washington, Seattle

MARSHALL ISLANDS

Embassy of the Republic of the Marshall Islands
2433 Massachusetts Avenue, NW., 1st Floor,
Washington, DC 20008
phone (202) 234–5414, fax 232–3236
Mr. Junior Aini
First Secretary (Charge D'Affaires Ad Interim)
Consular Offices:
  Arkansas, Springdale
  Hawaii, Honolulu

MAURITANIA

Embassy of the Islamic Republic of Mauritania
2129 Leroy Place, NW., Washington, DC 20008
phone (202) 232–5700, fax 319–2623
His Excellency Mohamed Lemine El Haycen
Ambassador E. and P.
Consular Office: Pennsylvania, Newtown Square

MAURITIUS

Embassy of the Republic of Mauritius
1709 N Street, NW., Washington, DC 20036
phone (202) 244–1491, fax 966–0983
Mr. Hans Irvin Antish Bhugun
First Secretary (Charge D'Affaires Ad Interim)
Consular Offices:
  California:
    Los Angeles
    San Francisco

MEXICO

Embassy of Mexico
1911 Pennsylvania Avenue, NW., Washington, DC
20006
phone (202) 728–1600, fax 728–1615
Mr. Alejandro Ives Estivill Castro
Minister (Charge D'Affaires Ad Interim)
Consular Offices:
  Alaska, Anchorage

Arizona:
  Douglas
  Nogales
  Phoenix
  Tucson
  Yuma
Arkansas, Little Rock
California:
  Calexico
  Fresno
  Los Angeles
  Oxnard
  Sacramento
  Salinas
  San Bernardino
  San Diego
  San Francisco
  San Jose
  Santa Ana
Colorado, Denver
District of Columbia, Washington
Florida:
  Jacksonville
  Miami
  Orlando
Georgia, Atlanta
Hawaii, Honolulu
Idaho, Boise
Illinois, Chicago
Indiana, Indianapolis
Louisiana, New Orleans
Massachusetts, Boston
Michigan, Detroit
Minnesota, St. Paul
Missouri, Kansas City
Nebraska, Omaha
Nevada, Las Vegas
New Mexico, Albuquerque
New York, New York
North Carolina:
  Charlotte
  Raleigh
Oregon, Portland
Pennsylvania, Philadelphia
Puerto Rico, San Juan
Texas:
  Austin
  Brownsville
  Dallas
  Del Rio
  Eagle Pass
  El Paso
  Houston
  Laredo
  McAllen
  Midland
  San Antonio

Utah, Salt Lake City
Washington, Seattle
Wisconsin, Madison

MICRONESIA

Embassy of the Federated States of Micronesia
1725 N Street, NW., Washington, DC 20036
phone (202) 223–4383, fax 223–4391
His Excellency Asterio R. Takesy
Ambassador E. and P.
Consular Offices:
  Guam, Tamuning
  Hawaii, Honolulu

MOLDOVA

Embassy of the Republic of Moldova
2101 S Street, NW., Washington, DC 20008
phone (202) 667–1130, fax 667–1204
Mr. Veaceslav Pituscan
Minister / Counselor (Charge D'Affaires Ad Interim)
Consular Offices:
  District of Columbia, Washington
  Florida, Miami
  New York, New York
  North Carolina, Hickory

MONACO

Embassy of Monaco
3400 International Drive, NW., Suite 2K–100,
  Washington, DC 20008
Her Excellency Maguy Maccario Doyle
Ambassador E. and P.
Consular Offices:
  California:
    Los Angeles
    San Francisco
  Florida, Miami
  Georgia, Atlanta
  Illinois, Chicago
  Louisiana, New Orleans
  Massachusetts, Boston
  Nevada, Las Vegas
  New York, New York
  Texas, Dallas

MONGOLIA

Embassy of Mongolia
2833 M Street, NW., Washington, DC 20007
phone (202) 333–7117, fax 298–9227
His Excellency Altangerel Bulgaa
Ambassador E. and P.
Consular Offices:
  California, San Francisco
  Colorado, Denver
  District of Columbia, Washington
  Georgia, Atlanta
  Illinois, Chicago
  Montana, Bozeman

New York, New York
South Dakota, Belle Fourche
Texas, Houston

MONTENEGRO

Embassy of the Republic of Montenegro
1610 New Hampshire Avenue, NW., Washington,
DC 20009
phone (202) 234–6108, fax 234–6109
His Excellency Professor Srdan Darmanovic
Ambassador E. and P.
Consular Offices:
Colorado, Denver
New York, New York

MOROCCO

Embassy of the Kingdom of Morocco
1601 21st Street, NW., Washington, DC 20009
phone (202) 462–7980, fax 265–0161
His Excellency Mohammed Rachad Bouhlal
Ambassador E. and P.
Consular Offices:
California, Los Angeles
Colorado, Denver
Hawaii, Honolulu
Illinois, Chicago
Kansas, Kansas City
Kentucky, Louisville
Massachusetts, Cambridge
New York, New York
Texas, Dallas
Utah, Bountiful

MOZAMBIQUE

Embassy of the Republic of Mozambique
1525 New Hampshire Avenue, NW., Washington,
DC 20036
phone (202) 293–7146, fax 835–0245
Her Excellency Amelia Narciso Matos Sumbana
Ambassador E. and P.

NAMIBIA

Embassy of the Republic of Namibia
1605 New Hampshire Avenue, NW., Washington,
DC 20009
phone (202) 986–0540, fax 986–0443
His Excellency Martin Andjaba
Ambassador E. and P.
Consular Offices:
California, San Jose
Florida, Orlando
Georgia, atlanta
Michigan, Detroit
Nevada, Las Vegas
Texas, San Antonio
Virginia, Richmond

NAURU

Embassy of the Republic of Nauru

801 Second Avenue, New York, NY 10017
phone (212) 937–0074, fax 937–0079
Her Excellency Marlene Inemwin Moses
Ambassador E. and P.
Consular Offices:
Guam, Agana

NEPAL

Embassy of Nepal
2131 Leroy Place, NW., Washington, DC 20008
phone (202) 667–4550, fax 667–5534
His Excellency Shankar Prasad Sharma
Ambassador E. and P.
Consular Offices:
California:
Auburn
Los Angeles
San Francisco
Vista
Hawaii, Naalehu
Illinois, Chicago
Maryland, Baltimore
Massachusetts, Boston
New York, New York

NETHERLANDS

Royal Netherlands Embassy
4200 Linnean Avenue, NW., Washington, DC 20008
phone (202) 244–5300, fax 362–3430
His Excellency Rudolf Simon Bekink
Ambassador E. and P.
Consular Offices:
Arizona, Phoenix
California:
Los Angeles
San Francisco
Colorado, Denver
District of Columbia, Washington
Florida:
Jacksonville
Miami
Orlando
Georgia, Atlanta
Hawaii, Honolulu
Illinois, Chicago
Louisiana, New Orleans
Massachusetts, Boston
Michigan:
Grand Rapids
New Baltimore
Minnesota, Minneapolis
Missouri, St. Louis
New York, New York
North Carolina, Raleigh
Oregon, Beaverton
Puerto Rico, Guaynabo
Trust Territories of the Pacific Islands:

Manila, Phillipines
Utah, Salt Lake City
Washington, Bellevue

NEW ZEALAND

Embassy of New Zealand
37 Observatory Circle, NW , Washington, DC 20008
phone (202) 328–4800, fax 667–5227
His Excellency Michael Kenneth Moore
Ambassador E. and P.
Consular Offices:
  California:
    Burlingame
    El Macero
    San Diego
    Santa Monica
  District of Columbia, Washington
  Georgia, Atlanta
  Guam, Tamuning
  Hawaii, Honolulu
  Illinois, Chicago
  New Hampshire, Boston
  New York, New York
  Oregon, Portland
  Texas, Houston
  Trust Territories of the Pacific Islands:
    Pago Pago
  Utah, Salt Lake City
  Vermont, Shelburne
  Washington, Seattle

NICARAGUA

Embassy of the Republic of Nicaragua
1627 New Hampshire Avenue, NW., Washington, DC 20009
phone (202) 939–6570, fax 939–6545
His Excellency Francisco Obadiah Campbell Hooker
Ambassador E. and P.
Consular Offices:
  California:
    Los Angeles
    San Francisco
  District of Columbia, Washington
  Florida, Miami
  Georgia, Atlanta
  Louisiana, Baton Rouge
  Massachusetts, Springfield
  New York, New York
  North Carolina, Charlotte
  Texas, Houston

NIGER

Embassy of the Republic of Niger
2204 R Street, NW., Washington, DC 20008
phone (202) 483–4224, fax 483–3169
His Excellency Hassana Alidou
Ambassador E. and P.

NIGERIA

Embassy of the Federal Republic of Nigeria
3519 International Court, NW., Washington, DC 20008
phone (202) 986–8400, fax 362–6541
His Excellency Adebowale Ibidapo Adefuye
Ambassador E. and P.
Consular Offices:
  Georgia, Atlanta
  New York, New York

NORWAY

Royal Norwegian Embassy
2720 34th Street, NW., Washington, DC 20008
phone (202) 333–6000, fax 459–3990
His Excellency Kaare Reidar Aas
Ambassador E. and P.
Consular Offices:
  Alabama, Mobile
  Alaska, Anchorage
  Arizona, Glendale
  California:
    Los Angeles
    San Diego
    San Francisco
  Colorado, Denver
  Florida:
    Jacksonville
    Miami
    Tampa
  Georgia, Atlanta
  Hawaii, Honolulu
  Illinois, Chicago
  Iowa, Des Moines
  Louisiana, New Orleans
  Massachusetts, Boston
  Michigan, Detroit
  Minnesota, Minneapolis
  Montana, Billings
  Nebraska, Omaha
  New York, New York
  North Dakota, Fargo
  Oklahoma, Tulsa
  Oregon, Portland
  Pennsylvania, Philadelphia
  Puerto Rico:
    Ponce
    San Juan
  South Carolina, Charleston
  South Dakota, Sioux Falls
  Texas:
    Dallas
    Houston
  Utah, Salt Lake City
  Virginia, Norfolk
  Washington, Seattle
  Wisconsin, Madison

OMAN

Embassy of the Sultanate of Oman
2535 Belmont Road, NW., Washington, DC 20008
phone (202) 387–1980, fax 745–4933
Her Excellency Hunaina Sultan Ahmed Al Mughairy
Ambassador E. and P.
Consular Office: Pennsylvania, Pittsburgh

PAKISTAN

Embassy of Pakistan
3517 International Court, NW., Washington, DC
  20008
phone (202) 243–6500, fax 686–1544
His Excellency Jalil Abbas Jilani
Ambassador E. and P.
Consular Office:
  California, Los Angeles
  Connecticut, Rocky Hill
  Illinois, Chicago
  Maine, Portland
  Massachusetts, Boston
  Missouri, St. Louis
  New York, New York
  Pennsylvania, Philadephia
  Texas, Houston

PALAU

Embassy of the Republic of Palau
1701 Pennsylvania Avenue, NW., Suite 300,
  Washington, DC 20036
phone (202) 452–6814, fax 452–6281
His Excellency Hersey Kyota
Ambassador E. and P.
Consular Offices:
  California:
    Carlsbad
    La Canada Flintridge
  Guam, Tamuning
  Illinois, Chicago

PANAMA

Embassy of the Republic of Panama
2862 McGill Terrace, NW., Washington, DC 20007
phone (202) 483–1407, fax 483–8413
His Excellency Emanuel A Gonzalez Revilla Lince
Ambassador E. and P.
Consular Offices:
  Arkansas, Fayetteville
  California, Long Beach
  District of Columbia, Washington
  Florida:
    Miami
    Tampa
  Louisiana, New Orleans
  New York, New York
  Pennsylvania, Philadelphia
  Puerto Rico, San Juan
  Texas:

  Austin
  Houston

PAPUA NEW GUINEA

Embassy of Papua New Guinea
1779 Massachusetts Avenue, NW., Suite 805,
  Washington, DC 20036
phone (202) 745–3680, fax 745–3679
His Excellency Rupa Abraham Mulina
Ambassador E. and P.
Consular Offices:
  California, Los Angeles
  Texas, Houston

PARAGUAY

Embassy of Paraguay
2400 Massachusetts Avenue, NW., Washington, DC
  20008
phone (202) 483–6960, fax 234–4508
His Excellency Igor Alberto Pangrazio Vera
Ambassador E. and P.
Consular Offices:
  California, Los Angeles
  Florida, Miami
  New York, New York
  Texas, Bellaire

PERU

Embassy of Peru
1700 Massachusetts Avenue, NW., Washington, DC
  20036
phone (202) 833–9860, fax 659–8124
His Excellency Luis Miguel Castilla Rubio
Ambassador E. and P.
Consular Offices:
  Arizona, Mesa
  California:
    Los Angeles
    San Francisco
  Colorado, Denver
  Connecticut, Hartford
  District of Columbia, Washington
  Florida:
    Miami
    Tampa
  Georgia, Atlanta
  Illinois, Chicago
  Massachusetts, Boston
  Missouri, St. Louis
  New Jersey, Paterson
  New York, New York
  Oklahoma, Oklahoma City
  Puerto Rico, San Juan
  Texas:
    Dallas
    Houston
  Utah, Salt Lake City
  Washington, Seattle

PHILIPPINES

Embassy of the Republic of the Philippines
1600 Massachusetts Avenue, NW., Washington, DC
20036
phone (202) 467–9300, fax 328–7614
His Excellency Jose Lampa Cuisia, Jr.
Ambassador E. and P.
Consular Offices:
Alaska, Juneau
California:
Los Angeles
San Francisco
District of Columbia, Washington
Georgia, Atlanta
Guam, Tamuning
Hawaii, Honolulu
Illinois, Chicago
Michigan, Livonia
New York, New York
Northern Mariana Islands, Saipan
Oregon, Portland
Texas, Dallas
Trust Territories of the Pacific Islands:
Mariana Islands
Virgin Islands, St. Thomas

POLAND

Embassy of the Republic of Poland
2640 16th Street, NW., Washington, DC 20009
phone (202) 234–3800, fax 588–0565
His Excellency Ryszard Marian Schnepf
Ambassador E. and P.
Consular Offices:
Alaska, Anchorage
Arizona, Phoenix
California:
Belmont
Los Angeles
San Francisco
Colorado, Longmont
District of Columbia, Washington
Georgia, Atlanta
Hawaii, Honolulu
Idaho, Ketchum
Illinois, Chicago
Massachusetts, Boston
Missouri, St. Louis
Nevada, Las Vegas
New York, New York
North Carolina, Raleigh
Ohio, Oxford
Pennsylvania:
Philadephia
Pittsburgh
Puerto Rico, Catano
Tennessee, Knoxville
Texas, Houston

PORTUGAL

Embassy of Portugal
2012 Massachusetts Avenue, NW., Washington, DC
20036
phone (202) 328–8610, fax 462–3726
His Excellency Nuno F. Alves Salvador E Brito
Ambassador E. and P.
Consular Offices:
California:
Los Angeles
San Francisco
Tulare
Connecticut, Waterbury
Florida:
Miami
Orlando
Hawaii, Honolulu
Illinois, Chicago
Louisiana, New Orleans
Massachusetts:
Boston
New Bedford
New Jersey, Newark
New York, New York
North Carolina, Durham
Pennsylvania, Philadelphia
Puerto Rico, San Juan
Rhode Island, Providence
Texas, Houston

QATAR

Embassy of the State of Qatar
2555 M Street, NW., Suite 200, Washington, DC
20037
phone (202) 274–1600, fax 237–0061
His Excellency Mohammed Jaham Al Kuwari
Ambassador E. and P.
Consular Office:
New York, New York
Texas, Houston

ROMANIA

Embassy of Romania
1607 23rd Street, NW., Washington, DC 20008
phone (202) 332–4846, fax 232–4748
His Excellency Iulian Buga
Ambassador E. and P.
Consular Offices:
Arizona, Tempe
California:
Los Angeles
San Francisco
District of Columbia, Washington
Florida:
Cape Coral
Hollywood
Georgia, Atlanta

Illinois, Chicago
Indiana, Indianapolis
Louisiana, New Orleans
Massachusetts, Boston
Michigan, Detroit
Minnesota, Minneapolis
Nevada, Las Vegas
New York, New York
Ohio, Cleveland
Oklahoma, Norman
Oregon, Portland
Pennsylvania, Philadelphia
Texas:
  Dallas
  Houston
Utah, Salt Lake City

RUSSIA

Embassy of the Russian Federation
2650 Wisconsin Avenue, NW., Washington, DC
20007
phone (202) 298–5700, fax (202) 939–8919
His Excellency Sergey Ivanovich Kislyak
Ambassador E. and P.
Consular Offices:
  California:
    Fair Oaks
    San Francisco
  Colorado, Denver
  District of Columbia, Washington
  Florida, Pinellas Park
  Minnesota, Minneapolis
  New York, New York
  Puerto Rico, San Juan
  Texas, Houston
  Utah, Salt Lake City
  Washington, Seattle

RWANDA

Embassy of the Republic of Rwanda
1875 Connecticut Avenue, NW., Suite 540,
  Washington, DC 20009
phone (202) 232–2882, fax 232–4544
Her Excellency Mathilde Mukantabana
Ambassador E. and P.
Consular Offices:
  Illinois, Geneva
  Massachusetts, Boston
  Texas, Houston

SAMOA

Embassy of the Independent State of Samoa
800 2nd Avenue, 4th Floor, New York, NY 10017
phone (212) 599–6196, fax 599–0797
His Excellency Feturi Elisaia
Ambassador E. and P.
Consular Offices:
  American Samoa, Pago Pago

California, Torrance
Florida, Melbourne
Hawaii, Honolulu

SAN MARINO

Embassy of Republic of San Marino
1711 N Street,, NW., Floor 2nd, Washington, DC
20036
phone (202) 223–2418, fax 223–2748
His Excellency Paolo Rondelli
Ambassador E. and P.
Consular Offices:
  District of Columbia, Washington
  Hawaii, Honolulu
  Michigan, Troy
  New York, New York

SAO TOME AND PRINCIPE

Embassy of Sao Tome and Principe
675 Third Avenue, Suite 1807 New York ,NY
10017
phone (212) 651–8116, fax 651–8117
His Excellency C. Azevedo Agostinho Das Neves
Ambassador E. and P.
Consular Offices:
  Georgia, Atlanta
  Illinois, Chicago

SAUDI ARABIA

Embassy of Saudi Arabia
601 New Hampshire Avenue, NW., Washington,
  DC 20037
phone (202) 342–3800, fax (202) 338–6929
His Excellency Adel A M Al Jubeir
Ambassador E. and P.
Consular Offices:
  California, Los Angeles
  District of Columbia, Washington
  Illinois, Chicago
  New York, New York
  Texas, Houston

SENEGAL

Embassy of the Republic of Senegal
2215 M Street, NW., Washington, DC 20037
phone (202) 234–0540, fax 629–2961
His Excellency Babacar Diagne
Ambassador E. and P.
Consular Offices:
  California, Burlingame
  Florida, Miami
  Georgia, Atlanta
  Louisiana:
    Baton Rouge
    New Orleans
  Missouri, Clayton
  New York, New York
  Rhode Island, Providence

SERBIA

Embassy of the Republic of Serbia
2134 Kalorama Road, NW., Washington, DC 20008
phone (202) 332–0333, fax 332–3933
His Excellency Derd Matkovic
Ambassador E. and P.
Consular Offices:
  Colorado, Denver
  Illinois, Chicago
  Louisiana, Metairie
  New York, New York
  Ohio, Cleveland
  Wyoming, Cheyenne

SEYCHELLES

Embassy of the Republic of Seychelles
800 Second Avenue, Suite 400G, New York, NY 10017
Her Excellency Marie Louise Cecile Potter
Ambassador E. and P.
Consular Offices:
  Alaska, Anchorage
  Arizona, Sun City
  New York, New York
  Washington, Seattle

SIERRA LEONE

Embassy of Sierra Leone
1701 19th Street, NW., Washington, DC 20009
phone (202) 939–9261, fax 483–1793
His Excellency Bockari Kortu Stevens
Ambassador E. and P.
Consular Office:
  Florida, Miami
  Georgia, Decatur
  Illinois, Chicago
  Massachusetts, Boston
  Pennsylvania, Philadephia

SINGAPORE

Embassy of the Republic of Singapore
3501 International Place, NW., Washington, DC 20008
phone (202) 537–3100, fax 537–0876
His Excellency Ashok Kumar
Ambassador E. and P.
Consular Offices:
  California, San Francisco
  Florida, Miami
  Illinois, Chicago
  New York, New York

SLOVAK

Embassy of the Slovak Republic
3523 International Court, NW., Washington, DC 20008
phone (202) 237–1054, fax 237–6438
His Excellency Peter Kmec

Ambassador E. and P.
Consular Offices:
  California, San Francisco
  Colorado, Denver
  District of Columbia, Washington
  Florida, Miami
  Illinois, Chicago
  Indiana, Indianapolis
  Massachusetts, Weston
  Michigan, Detroit
  Minnesota, Bloomington
  Missouri, Kansas City
  New York, New York
  Pennsylvania, Pittsburgh
  South Carolina, Columbia
  Texas, Dallas

SLOVENIA

Embassy of the Republic of Slovenia
2410 California Street, NW., Washington, DC 20008
phone (202) 386–6610, fax 386–6633
His Excellency Bozo Cerar
Ambassador E. and P.
Consular Offices:
  California, San Francisco
  Colorado, Denver
  Florida, Miami Beach
  Georgia, Atlanta
  Hawaii, Honolulu
  Illinois, Chicago
  Kansas, Mission Hills
  Michigan, Dearborn
  Minnesota, St. Paul
  New York, New York
  Ohio, Cleveland
  Pennsylvania, Pittsburgh
  Tennessee, Knoxville
  Texas, Houston

SOLOMON ISLANDS

Embassy of the Solomon Islands
800 Second Avenue, Suite 400L, New York, NY 10017
phone (212) 599–6192, fax 661–8925
His Excellency Collin David Beck
Ambassador E. and P.

SOMALIA

Embassy of Somalia
1705 Desales Street, Suite 300, Washington, DC 20036
Mr. Awale Ali Kullane
Minister / Counselor (Charge D'Affaires Ad Interim)

SOUTH AFRICA

Embassy of the Republic of South Africa
3051 Massachusetts Avenue, NW., Washington, DC 20008

phone (202) 232–4400, fax 265–1607
His Excellency Mninwa Johannes Mahlangu
Ambassador E. and P.
Consular Offices:
  California, Los Angeles
  Illinois, Chicago
  Kansas, Kansas City
  Louisiana, New Orleans
  Minnesota, Minneapolis
  New York, New York
  Texas, Dallas
  Wisconsin, Milwaukee

SOUTH SUDAN

Embassy of the Republic of South Sudan
1015 31st Street, NW., Floor 3, Washington, DC
20007
His Excellency Garang Diing Akuong
Ambassador

SPAIN

Embassy of Spain
2375 Pennsylvania Avenue, NW., Washington, DC
20037
phone (202) 452–0100, fax 833–5670
His Excellency Ramon Gil Casares Satrustegui
Ambassador E. and P.
Consular Offices:
  Alabama, Birmingham
  Alaska, Anchorage
  Arizona, Phoenix
  California:
    Los Angeles
    San Diego
    San Francisco
  Colorado, Englewood
  District of Columbia, Washington
  Florida:
    Miami
    Orlando
    Pensacola
    Tampa
  Georgia, Atlanta
  Hawaii, Honolulu
  Idaho, Boise
  Illinois, Chicago
  Louisiana, New Orleans
  Massachusetts, Boston
  Michigan, Ann Arbor
  Missouri:
    Kansas City
    St. Louis
  New Jersey, Newark
  New Mexico:
    Albuquerque
    Santa Fe
  New York, New York
  Oklahoma, Oklahoma City

Puerto Rico, San Juan
Texas:
  Corpus Christi
  Dallas
  El Paso
  Houston
  San Antonio
Utah, Salt Lake City
Washington, Seattle

SRI LANKA

Embassy of the Democratic Socialist Republic of
Sri Lanka
2148 Wyoming Avenue, NW., Washington, DC
20008
phone (202) 483–4025, fax 232–7181
His Excellency Prasad Kariyawasam
Ambassador E. and P.
Consular Offices:
  Arizona, Phoenix
  California, Los Angeles
  Hawaii, Honolulu
  New Hampshire, Boston
  New Mexico, Santa Fe
  New York, New York
  Texas, Houston

ST. KITTS AND NEVIS

Embassy of St. Kitts and Nevis
1001 19th Street, N, Suite 1221, 1229, 1230, 1252,
  1260, 1261, Arlington, VA 22209
Mr. Justin Kareem Hawley
Counselor (Charge D'Affaires Ad Interim)
Consular Offices:
  California, Los Angeles
  Florida, Miami
  New York, New York
  Pennsylvania, Philadelphia
  Puerto Rico, Guaynabo
  Virgin Islands, St. Thomas

ST. LUCIA

Embassy of St. Lucia
1001 19th Street, N, Suite 1233, 1234, 1239, 1254,
  1255, 1256, 1259, Arlington, VA 22209
phone (571) 527–1375, fax (571) 384–7930
Ms. Elizabeth Darius Clarke
Minister/Counselor (Charge D'Affaires Ad Interim)
Consular Offices:
  California, Los Angeles
  Florida, Coral Gables
  New York, New York

ST. VINCENT AND THE GRENADINES

Embassy of St. Vincent and the Grenadines
1001 19th Street, N, Suite 1242, Arlington, VA
22209
phone (202) 364–6730, fax 364–6736

Her Excellency La Celia Prince
Ambassador E. and P.
Consular Offices:
  California, Los Angeles
  Florida, Groveland
  Louisiana, New Orleans
  New York, New York
  Puerto Rico, Guaynabo

SUDAN

Embassy of the Republic of the Sudan
2210 Massachusetts Avenue, NW., Washington, DC
  20008
phone (202) 338–8565, fax 667–2406
Mr. Maowia Osman Khalid Mohammed
Counselor (Deputy Chief of Mission)

SURINAME

Embassy of the Republic of Suriname
4301 Connecticut Avenue, NW., Suite 460,
  Washington, DC 20008
phone (202) 244–7488, fax 244–5878
His Excellency Subhas Chandra Mungra
Ambassador E. and P.
Consular Offices:
  Florida, Miami
  Louisiana, New Orleans

SWAZILAND

Embassy of the Kingdom of Swaziland
1712 New Hampshire Avenue, NW., Washington,
  DC 20009
phone (202) 234–5002, fax 234–8254
His Excellency Reverend Abednego Mandla
  Ntshangase
Ambassador E. and P.

SWEDEN

Embassy of Sweden
2900 K Street, NW., Washington, DC 20007
phone (202) 467–2600, fax 467–2699
His Excellency Bjoern Olof Lyrvall
Ambassador E. and P.
Consular Offices:
  Alaska, Anchorage
  Arizona, Scottsdale
  California:
    San Diego
    San Francisco
  Colorado, Denver
  District of Columbia, Washington
  Florida:
    Ft. Lauderdale
    Tampa
  Georgia, Atlanta
  Hawaii, Honolulu
  Illinois, Chicago

Kansas, Merriam
Louisiana, New Orleans
Massachusetts, Boston
Michigan, Ann Arbor
Minnesota, Minneapolis
Missouri, St. Louis
Nebraska, Omaha
Nevada, Las Vegas
New York:
  Jamestown
  New York
North Carolina, Raleigh
Ohio, Cleveland
Pennsylvania, Ardmore
Puerto Rico, San Juan
Texas:
  Dallas
  Houston
Utah, Salt Lake City
Virgin Islands, St. Thomas
Virginia, Norfolk
Washington, Seattle
Wisconsin, Milwaukee

SWITZERLAND

Embassy of Switzerland
2900 Cathedral Avenue, NW., Washington, DC
  20008
phone (202) 745–7900, fax 387–2564
His Excellency Martin Werner Dahinden
Ambassador E. and P.
Consular Offices:
  Arizona, Scottsdale
  California:
    Los Angeles
    San Francisco
  Colorado, Boulder
  District of Columbia, Washington
  Florida:
    Miami
    Orlando
  Georgia, Atlanta
  Hawaii, Honolulu
  Illinois, Chicago
  Indiana, Indianapolis
  Louisiana, New Orleans
  Massachusetts, Boston
  Michigan, Dearborn
  Minnesota, Minneapolis
  Missouri, Kansas City
  Nevada, Las Vegas
  New York:
    New York
    Williamsville
  North Carolina, Charlotte
  Ohio, Cleveland
  Oklahoma, Edmond

Pennsylvania:
  Philadelphia
  Pittsburgh
Puerto Rico, San Juan
Texas:
  Dallas
  Houston
Trust Territories of the Pacific Islands:
  Pago Pago
Utah, Sandy
Washington, Mercer Island

SYRIA

Embassy of the Syrian Arab Republic
2215 Wyoming Avenue, NW., Washington, DC
  20008
phone (202) 232–6313, fax 234–9548

TAJIKISTAN

Embassy of the Republic of Tajikistan
1005 New Hampshire Avenue, NW., Washington,
  DC 20037
phone (202) 223–6090, fax 223–6091
His Excellency Farhod Salim
Ambassador E. and P.
Consular Office: District of Columbia, Washington

TANZANIA

Embassy of the United Republic of Tanzania
1232 22nd Street, NW., Washington, DC 20037
phone (202) 939–6125, fax 797–7408
Her Excellency Liberata Rutageruka Mulamula
Ambassador E. and P.
Consular Offices:
  California, San Rafael
  Georgia, Atlanta
  Illinois, St. Louis
  Louisiana, New Orleans
  Michigan, Grosse Pointe Farms
  Minnesota, Minneapolis
  New Mexico, Albuquerque
  Pennsylvania, Philadephia

THAILAND

Embassy of Thailand
1024 Wisconsin Avenue, NW., Washington, DC
  20007
phone (202) 944–3600, fax 944–3611
His Excellency Pisan Manawapat
Ambassador E. and P.
Consular Offices:
  Alabama, Montgomery
  California, Los Angeles
  Colorado, Denver
  Florida, Coral Gables
  Georgia, Atlanta
  Hawaii, Honolulu
  Illinois, Chicago

Louisiana, New Orleans
Massachusetts, Boston
New York, New York
Oklahoma, Broken Arrow
Oregon, Portland
Puerto Rico, Hato Rey
Texas:
  Dallas
  Houston
Utah, Salt Lake City

TIMOR LESTE

Embassy of the Democratic Republic of Timor Leste
4201 Connecticut Avenue, NW., Suite 504,
  Washington, DC 20008
phone (202) 966–3202, fax 966–3205
His Excellency Domingos Sarmento Alves
Ambassador E. and P.

TOGO

Embassy of the Republic of Togo
2208 Massachusetts Avenue, NW., Washington, DC
  20008
phone (202) 234–4212, fax 232–3190
His Excellency Edawe Limbiye Kadangha Bariki
Ambassador E. and P.
Consular Offices:
  California, Chatsworth
  Florida, Miami

TONGA

Embassy of the Kingdom of Tonga
250 East 51st Street, New York, NY 10022
phone (917) 369–1025, fax 369–1024
His Excellency Mahe Uliuli Sandhurst Tupouniua
Ambassador E. and P.
Consular Offices:
  California, San Francisco
  Hawaii, Honolulu

TRINIDAD AND TOBAGO

Embassy of the Republic of Trinidad and Tobago
1708 Massachusetts Avenue, NW., Washington, DC
  20036
phone (202) 467–6490, fax 785–3130
His Excellency Dr. Neil Nadesh Parsan
Ambassador E. and P.
Consular Offices:
  Florida, Miami
  New York, New York
  Puerto Rico, San Juan
  Texas, Houston

TUNISIA

Embassy of Tunisia
1515 Massachusetts Avenue, NW., Washington, DC
  20005

phone (202) 862–1850, fax 862–1858
His Excellency Faycal Gouia
Ambassador E. and P.
Consular Offices:
  California, San Francisco
  Florida, Miami
  New York, New York
  Texas, Dallas

TURKEY

Embassy of the Republic of Turkey
2525 Massachusetts Avenue, NW., Washington, DC
  20008
phone (202) 612–6700, fax 612–6744
His Excellency Serdar Kilic
Ambassador E. and P.
Consular Offices:
  California:
    Fair Oaks
    Los Angeles
    Oakland
  Florida, Miami
  Georgia, Atlanta
  Illinois, Chicago
  Maryland, Baltimore
  Massachusetts, Boston
  Michigan, Farmington
  Missouri, Kansas City
  New York, New York
  Texas, Houston
  Washington, Seattle

TURKMENISTAN

Embassy of Turkmenistan
2207 Massachusetts Avenue, NW., Washington, DC
  20008
phone (202) 588–1500, fax 588–0697
His Excellency Meret Bairamovich Orazov
Ambassador E. and P.

TUVALU

Embassy of Tuvalu
800 Second Avenue, Suite 400D, New York, NY
  10017
phone (212) 490–0534
His Excellency Aunese Makoi Simati
Ambassador E. and P.

UGANDA

Embassy of the Republic of Uganda
5911 16th Street, NW., Washington, DC 20011
phone (202) 726–0416, fax 726–1727
Her Excellency Oliver Wonekha
Ambassador E. and P.
Consular Offices:
  California, San Diego

UKRAINE

Embassy of Ukraine
3350 M Street, NW., Washington, DC 20007
phone (202) 349–2920, fax 333–0817
Mr. Yaroslav Brisiuck
Minister / Counselor (Charge D'Affaires Ad Interim)
Consular Offices:
  Alabama, Birmingham
  Arizona, Tucson
  California, San Francisco
  District of Columbia, Washington
  Illinois, Chicago
  Louisiana, New Orleans
  Michigan, Detroit
  New York, New York
  Ohio, Cleveland
  Texas, Houston
  Utah, Salt Lake City

UNITED ARAB EMIRATES

Embassy of the United Arab Emirates
3522 International Court, NW., Washington, DC
  20008
phone (202) 243–2400, fax 243–2432
His Excellency Yousif Mana Saeed Alotaiba
Ambassador E. and P.
Consular Offices:
  California, Beverly Hills

UNITED KINGDOM

British Embassy
3100 Massachusetts Avenue, NW., Washington, DC
  20008
phone (202) 588–6500, fax 588–7870
His Excellency Sir Peter John Westmacott
Ambassador E. and P.
Consular Offices:
  Alaska, Anchorage
  Arizona, Phoenix
  California:
    Los Angeles
    San Francisco
  Colorado, Denver
  District of Columbia, Washington
  Florida:
    Miami
    Orlando
    Tallahassee
  Georgia, Atlanta
  Illinois, Chicago
  Louisiana, New Orleans
  Massachusetts, Boston
  Michigan, Detroit
  Minnesota, Minneapolis
  Nevada, Las Vegas
  New York, New York

North Carolina, Charlotte
Ohio, Cleveland
Oklahoma, Tulsa
Oregon, Portland
Pennsylvania:
  Philadelphia
  Pittsburgh
Puerto Rico, San Juan
Tennessee, Nashville
Texas:
  Dallas
  Houston
  San Antonio
Trust Territories of the Pacific Islands:
  Nuku'alofa, Tonga
Utah, Salt Lake City

URUGUAY

Embassy of Uruguay
1913 I Street, NW., Washington, DC 20006
phone (202) 331–1313, fax 331–8142
His Excellency Juan Carlos Pita Alvariza
Ambassador E. and P.
Consular Offices:
California:
  Los Angeles
  Sacramento
  San Francisco
District of Columbia, Washington
Florida, Miami
Illinois, Chicago
Louisiana, Jefferson
Nevada, Reno
New York, New York
Pennsylvania, Philadephia
Puerto Rico, San Juan
Texas, Houston
Utah, Salt Lake City

UZBEKISTAN

Embassy of the Republic of Uzbekistan
1746 Massachusetts Avenue, NW., Washington, DC 20036
phone (202) 293–6803, fax 293–6804
His Excellency Bakhtiyar Turadjanovich Gulyamov
Ambassador E. and P.
Consular Offices:
District of Columbia, Washington
Georgia, Greensboro
New York, New York
Washington, Seattle
Ukraine
United Arbo Emirates
United Kingdom
Uzbekistan

VENEZUELA

Embassy of the Bolivarian Republic of Venezuela
1099 30th Street, NW., Washington, DC 20007
phone (202) 342–2214, fax 342–6810
Mr. Maximilien Sanchez Arvelaiz
Minister/Counselor (Charge D'Affaires Ad Interim)
Consular Offices:
California, San Francisco
Florida, Miami
Illinois, Chicago
Louisiana, New Orleans
Massachusetts, Boston
New York, New York
Puerto Rico:
  Hato Rey
  San Juan
Texas, Houston

VIETNAM

Embassy of Vietnam
1233 20th Street, NW., Suite 400, Washington, DC 20036
phone (202) 861–0737, fax 861–0917
His Excellency Vinh Quang Pham
Ambassador E. and P.
Consular Offices:
California, San Francisco
New York, New York
Texas, Houston

YEMEN

Embassy of the Republic of Yemen
2319 Wyoming Avenue, NW., Washington, DC 20008
phone (202) 965–4760, fax 337–2017
Mr. Adel Ali Ahmed Alsunaini
Counselor (Charge D'Affaires Ad Interim)
Consular Offices:
California, San Francisco
District of Columbia, Washington
Michigan, Dearborn

ZAMBIA

Embassy of the Republic of Zambia
2419 Massachusetts Avenue, NW., Washington, DC 20008
phone (202) 265–9717, fax 332–0826
His Excellency Palan Mulonda
Ambassador E. and P.

ZIMBABWE

Embassy of Republic of Zimbabwe
1608 New Hampshire Avenue, NW., Washington, DC 20009
phone (202) 332–7100, fax 483–9326

His Excellency Ammon Mutembwa
Ambassador E. and P.

CUBA (Switzerland)
IRAN (Pakistan)
ZIMBABWE

The following is a list of countries with which
diplomatic relations have been severed:

After each country, in parenthesis, is the name
of the country's protecting power in the United
States.

PRESS GALLERIES *

SENATE PRESS GALLERY

The Capitol, Room S–316, phone 224–0241

www.dailypress.senate.gov

Director.—Laura Lytle
  Deputy Director.—Christopher Bois

  Senior Media Relations Coordinators:
    Amy H. Gross
  Media Relations Coordinators:
    Elizabeth B. Crowley
    John E. Mulligan III

Kristyn K. Socknat

Samantha J. Yeider

HOUSE PRESS GALLERY

The Capitol, Room H–315, phone 225–3945

Superintendent.—Annie Tin
  Deputy Superintendent.—Justin J. Supon
    Assistant Superintendents:
    Ric Anderson
    Laura Reed

Molly Cain

STANDING COMMITTEE OF CORRESPONDENTS

Jonathan Salant, NJ Advance Media / Newark Star Ledger, Chariman
Joseph Morton, Omaha World Herald, Secretary
Matthew Daily, Associated Press
Ed O'Keefe, Washington Post
Jim Rowley, Bloomberg

RULES GOVERNING PRESS GALLERIES

1. Administration of the press galleries shall be vested in a Standing Committee of Correspondents elected by accredited members of the Galleries. The Committee shall consist of five persons elected to serve for terms of two years. Provided, however, that at the election in January 1951, the three candidates receiving the highest number of votes shall serve for two years and the remaining two for one year. Thereafter, three members shall be elected in odd-numbered years and two in even-numbered years. Elections shall be held in January. The Committee shall elect its own chairman and secretary. Vacancies on the Committee shall be filled by special election to be called by the Standing Committee.
2. Persons desiring admission to the press galleries of Congress shall make application in accordance with Rule VI of the House of Representatives, subject to the direction and control of the Speaker and Rule 33 of the Senate, which rules shall be interpreted and

---

*Information is based on data furnished and edited by each respective Gallery.

administered by the Standing Committee of Correspondents, subject to the review and an approval by the Senate Committee on Rules and Administration.

3. The Standing Committee of Correspondents shall limit membership in the press galleries to bone fide correspondents of repute in their profession, under such rules as the Standing Committee of Correspondents shall prescribe.

4. An applicant for press credentials through the Daily Press Galleries must establish to the satisfaction of the Standing Committee of Correspondents that he or she is a full-time, paid correspondent who requires on-site access to congressional members and staff. Correspondents must be employed by a news organization:

(a) with General Publication periodicals mailing privileges under U.S. Postal Service rules, and which publishes daily; or

(b) whose principal business is the daily dissemination of original news and opinion of interest to a broad segment of the public, and which has published continuously for 18 months.

The applicant must reside in the Washington, D.C. area, and must not be engaged in any lobbying or paid advocacy, advertising, publicity or promotion work for any individual, political party, corporation, organization, or agency of the U.S. Government, or in prosecuting any claim before Congress or any federal government department, and will not do so while a member of the Daily Press Galleries.

Applicants' publications must be editorially independent of any institution, foundation or interest group that lobbies the federal government, or that is not principally a general news organization.

Failure to provide information to the Standing Committee for this determination, or misrepresenting information, can result in the denial or revocation of credentials.

5. Members of the families of correspondents are not entitled to the privileges of the Galleries.

6. The Standing Committee of Correspondents shall propose no changes in these rules except upon petition in writing signed by not less than 100 accredited members of the galleries. The above rules have been approved by the Committee on Rules and Administration.

PAUL D. RYAN,
Speaker of the House of Representatives.

ROY BLUNT,
Chair, Senate Committee on Rules and Administration.

MEMBERS ENTITLED TO ADMISSION

Abbott, Charles: FERN's Ag Insider by Charles Abbott
Abdul, Shahzad: Agence France-Presse
Ackerman, Andrew: Wall Street Journal / Dow Jones
Ackley, Kate: CQ Roll Call
Adams, Rebecca: CQ Roll Call
Adcock, Beryl: McClatchy Newspapers
Ahmann, Timothy: Thomson Reuters
Ahmed, Akbar Shahid: Huffington Post
Alexander, Charles: Thomson Reuters
Alfaro, Hector: Bloomberg News
Alhendi, Abdulaziz: Saudi Press Agency
Allam, Hannah: McClatchy Newspapers
Allen, William: USA Today
Almohaimeed, Abdullah: Saudi Press Agency
Al-Mubarak, Haita: Saudi Press Agency
Alonso, Hernan Martin: EFE News Services
Alonso, Luis: Associated Press
Alonso-Zaldivar, Ricardo: Associated Press
Alpert, Bruce: New Orleans Times-Picayune
Ampolsk, Sarah: Kyodo News
Amrich, Vladimir: World Business Press
Anderson, Joanna: CQ Roll Call
Anderson, Mark: Wall Street Journal / Dow Jones
Anderson, Nick: Washington Post
Anderson, Stacy: Associated Press
Andrews, Natalie: Wall Street Journal / Dow Jones
Aoki, Mutsumi: Tokyo Chunichi Shimbun
Aoki, Nobuyuki: Sankei Shimbun
Aomoto, Riyo: Kyodo News
Appelbaum, Binyamin: New York Times
Appleby, Julie: Kaiser Health News
Arai, Takuya: Kyodo News
Araki, Yumi: Yomiuri Shimbun
Aratani, Lori: Washington Post
Ardinger, Will: CQ Roll Call
Arkin, James: Real Clear Politics
Armstrong, Joshua: SNL
Arnold, Justin: Yomiuri Shimbun
Ashizuka, Tomoko: Nikkei
Asseo, Laurie: Bloomberg News
Atkins, Kimberly: Boston Herald
Attias, Melissa: CQ Roll Call
Aukofer, Frank: Artists & Writers Syndicate
Awabayashi, Konomi: Kyodo News
Ayuso Determeyer, Sylvia: El Pais
Baker, Peter: New York Times
Baldor, Lolita: Associated Press
Ball, Michael: Argus Media
Ballhaus, Rebecca: Wall Street Journal / Dow Jones

Balz, Daniel: Washington Post
Bandyk, Matt: SNL
Banks, Adelle: Religion News Service
Banks, Alvin: Bloomberg Government
Barakat, Matthew: Associated Press
Barbeta Sanchez, Jordi: La Vanguardia
Barker, Jeffrey: Baltimore Sun
Barnes, Robert: Washington Post
Baron, Martin: Washington Post
Barone, Michael: Washington Examiner
Barrera, Ruben: Notimex Mexican News Agency
Barrett, Barbara: McClatchy Newspapers
Barrett, Devlin: Wall Street Journal / Dow Jones
Barron-Lopez, Laura: Huffington Post
Bartash, Jeffry: MarketWatch
Barthelemy, Laurent: Agence France-Presse
Bartz, Diane: Thomson Reuters
Bassets, Marc: El Pais
Bassett, Laura: Huffington Post
Batthyany, Alexander: Tages Anzeiger
Baumann, David: Merger Market of Financial Times
Baygents, Ronald: Kuwait News Agency
Beary, Brian: Europolitics
Beattie, Jeff: Energy Daily
Beatty, Andrew: Agence France-Presse
Beckel, Michael: Center for Public Integrity
Becker, Amanda: Thomson Reuters
Beckner, Steven: Market News International
Bedard, Paul: Washington Examiner
Beech, Eric: Thomson Reuters
Bell, Alistair: Thomson Reuters
Bell, Jarrett: USA Today
Bello, Marisol: USA Today
Belman, Thomas: Saudi Press Agency
Bendery, Jennifer: Huffington Post
Benjaminson, Wendy: Associated Press
Bennett, Brian: Los Angeles Times
Bennett, John: CQ Roll Call
Benson, Clea: Bloomberg News
Berg, Rebecca: Real Clear Politics
Bergengruen, Vera: McClatchy Newspapers
Berkowitz, Steve: USA Today
Berry, Deborah: Gannett Washington Bureau
Bettelheim, Adriel: CQ Roll Call
Bialecki, Martin: German Press Agency - DPA
Bierman, Noah: Los Angeles Times
Biesecker, Michael: Associated Press
Bifera, Lucas: Argus Media
Bilski, Christina: Nikkei
Birch, Douglas: Center for Public Integrity

MEMBERS ENTITLED TO ADMISSION—Continued

Biskupic, Joan: Thomson Reuters
Bjerga, Alan: Bloomberg News
Blakely, Rhys: Times of London
Bland, Melissa: Thomson Reuters
Bliss, Jeffrey: MLEX US
Bloom, Daniel: CQ Roll Call
Blum, Justin: Bloomberg News
Blumenthal, Mark: Huffington Post
Boak, Josh: Associated Press
Bobic, Igor: Huffington Post
Bocchetti, Mark: MLEX US
Bochinin, Anatoly: Itar-Tass News Agency
Bois, Christopher: Senate Press Gallery (SPG)
Bold, Michael: McClatchy Newspapers
Bondioli, Sara: Huffington Post
Borenstein, Seth: Associated Press
Boshant, Glen: SNL
Bostick, Romaine: Bloomberg News
Bouchard, Mikayla: New York Times
Bowers, Jeremy: New York Times
Boyer, David: Washington Times
Brady, Erik: USA Today
Brandt, Martin: Thomson Reuters
Braun, Stephen: Associated Press
Bravin, Jess: Wall Street Journal / Dow Jones
Brewington, Autumn: Wall Street Journal / Dow Jones
Brodbeck, Scott: LocalNews Now
Brodey, Sam: MinnPost
Brody, Benjamin: Bloomberg News
Brooks, David: La Jornada
Brown, Cory: CQ Roll Call
Brune, Tom: Newsday
Bruneau, Leon: Agence France-Presse
Brush, Silla: Bloomberg News
Bull, Alister: Bloomberg News
Bumiller, Elisabeth: New York Times
Burgues, Miriam: EFE News Services
Burke, Melissa: Detroit News
Burns, Robert: Associated Press
Burr, Thomas: Salt Lake Tribune
Burton, Thomas: Wall Street Journal / Dow Jones
Bykowicz, Julie: Associated Press
Cabo, Melisa: Telam S.E.
Cadei, Emily: Ozy Media
Cahlink, George: CQ Roll Call
Caldwell, Alicia: Associated Press
Camia, Catalina: CQ Roll Call
Capaccio, Anthony: Bloomberg News
Caplan, Abby: Argus Media
Carey, Mary Agnes: Kaiser Health News
Carney, Daniel: USA Today
Carney, Eliza: CQ Roll Call
Carney, Timothy: Washington Examiner
Carr, Christina: CQ Roll Call
Carroll, Lauren: Tampa Bay Times
Carswell, Simon: Irish Times
Carter, Charlene: CQ Roll Call

Carter, John: Market News International
Carter, Katharine: Bloomberg Government
Casey, John: Bond Buyer
Cass, Connie: Associated Press
Cassata, Donna: Associated Press
Casteel, Chris: Oklahoman
Celik, Can: MLEX US
Cepla, Zuzana: World Business Press
Cerbin, Carolyn: USA Today
Chacko, Sarah: CQ Roll Call
Chaddock, Gail: Christian Science Monitor
Chae, Byunggun: Joongang Ilbo
Chaffee, Conrad: Tokyo Chunichi Shimbun
Chambers, Francesca: Daily Mail (UK)
Chamseddine, Jad: CQ Roll Call
Chandra, Shobhana: Bloomberg News
Cheng, Tsung-Shen: Central News Agency
Chiacu, Doina: Thomson Reuters
Chiantaretto, Mariuccia: WolfNews
Chokshi, Niraj: Washington Post
Chon, Gina: Financial Times
Chong, Christina Young: Korea Times
Chowdhry, Aisha: CQ Roll Call
Christensen, Mike: CQ Roll Call
Christian, Rodney: Wall Street Journal / Dow Jones
Chudakov, Anton: Itar-Tass News Agency
Cislo, Conor: Asahi Shimbun
Clark, David: Agence France-Presse
Clark, Lesley: McClatchy Newspapers
Clearfield, Alexander: CQ Roll Call
Clift, Eleanor: Daily Beast
Coats, Christopher: SNL
Cockerham, Sean: McClatchy Newspapers
Codrea, George: CQ Roll Call
Coglianese, Vincent: Daily Caller
Cohen, Ariel: Washington Examiner
Cohen, Kristin: Bloomberg News
Coleman, Michael: Albuquerque Journal
Collins, Brian: American Banker
Collins, Michael: Journal Media Group
Colman, Zachary: Washington Examiner
Condon, Christopher: Bloomberg News
Condon, Jr., George: National Journal
Cook, David: Christian Science Monitor
Cooney, Peter: Thomson Reuters
Cooper, Helene: New York Times
Cooper, Kent: Political Money Line
Cooper, Lauren: Associated Press
Copley, Michael: SNL
Copp, Tara: Washington Examiner
Corasaniti, Nick: New York Times
Cornwell, Susan: Thomson Reuters
Couronne, Ivan: Agence France-Presse
Cowan, Richard: Thomson Reuters
Crabtree, Susan: Washington Examiner
Crampton, Liz: MLEX US
Crane, Marcy: SNL

MEMBERS ENTITLED TO ADMISSION—Continued

Crutsinger, Martin: Associated Press
Cunningham, Geoffrey: Saudi Press Agency
Cunningham, Paige: Washington Examiner
Curry, Thomas: CQ Roll Call
Cusati, Caitlin: Bloomberg Government
da Costa, Mario Navarro: ABIM
Dabbs, Brian: International Trade Today
Dale, Daniel: Toronto Star
Daly, Kyle: SNL
Daly, Matthew: Associated Press
Davenport, Coral: New York Times
Davidson, Joe: Washington Post
Davidson, Julie: LRP Publications
Davidson-Choma, Kate: Wall Street Journal / Dow Jones
Davis, Aaron: Washington Post
Davis, Julie: New York Times
Davis, Robert: Wall Street Journal / Dow Jones
Day, Jim: Energy Daily
de Freytas, Mariko: Kyodo News
DeBonis, Mike: Washington Post
Decamme, Guillaume: Agence France-Presse
DeFrank, Thomas: National Journal
Degen, Colin: CQ Roll Call
DeGeorge, Gail: Bloomberg News
Delane, Andre: Bloomberg News
Delaney, Arthur: Huffington Post
Delgado, Jose: El Nuevo Dia
DelReal-Perez, Jose: Washington Post
Demirjian, Karoun: Washington Post
Desmond, Harold: Thomson Reuters
Dexheimer, Elizabeth: Bloomberg News
DeYoung, Karen: Washington Post
Diaz, Kevin: Houston Chronicle
Dilanian, Ken: Associated Press
Dinan, Stephen: Washington Times
Dlouhy, Jennifer: Hearst Newspapers
Doering, Christopher: Gannett Washington Bureau
Dolan, Christopher: Washington Times
Dolinger, David Allen: Wall Street Journal / Dow Jones
Dong, Mu: Xinhua News Agency
Donnan, Shawn: Financial Times
Donnelly, John: CQ Roll Call
Dorell, Oren: USA Today
Dorning, Mike: Bloomberg News
Doublet, Jean-Louis: Agence France-Presse
Dougherty, Carter: Bloomberg News
Dougherty, Danny: McClatchy Newspapers
Douglas, William: McClatchy Newspapers
Downing, James: Utility Markets Today
Doyle, Michael: McClatchy Newspapers
Drajem, Mark: Bloomberg News
Drawbaugh, Kevin: Thomson Reuters
Drinkard, Jim: Associated Press
Drogin, Robert: Los Angeles Times
Drucker, David: Washington Examiner
Druzin, Heath: Stars and Stripes

Duggan, Loren: Bloomberg Government
Duggan, Paul: Washington Post
Duncan, Ian: Baltimore Sun
Dunham, Will: Thomson Reuters
Dunphy, Harry: Associated Press
Dunsmuir, Lindsay: Thomson Reuters
Earle, Geoff: New York Post
Eaton, Sabrina: Cleveland Plain Dealer
Eckstrom, Kevin: Religion News Service
Edney, Anna: Bloomberg News
Edwards, Julia: Thomson Reuters
Eidelson, Joshua: Bloomberg News
Eilperin, Juliet: Washington Post
Eisler, Peter: USA Today
El Hamti, Maribel: EFE News Services
Elkins, Donald: Associated Press
Ellicott, Val: Gannett Washington Bureau
Elliott, Philip: Associated Press
Ellis, David: CQ Roll Call
Ellis, Kristi: Fairchild Publications
Enders, David: Vice News
Epstein, Edward: Argus Media
Epstein, Jennifer: Bloomberg News
Epstein, Matthew: CQ Roll Call
Erice, Manuel: ABC Newspaper
Evans, Marissa: CQ Roll Call
Fahrenthold, David: Washington Post
Faith, Ryan: Vice News
Faur, Fabienne: Agence France-Presse
Faus Catasus, Joan: El Pais
Feldman, Carole: Associated Press
Feldmann, Linda: Christian Science Monitor
Felker, Edward: CQ Roll Call
Feltman, Peter: CQ Roll Call
Feng, Zhaoyin: World Journal
Ferguson, Ellyn: CQ Roll Call
Fernandez, Alfonso: EFE News Services
Fernandez Pereda, Christina: El Pais
Ferragutcasas, Nuria: Ara
Ferrechio, Susan: Washington Examiner
Ferriss, Susan: Center for Public Integrity
Festa, Elizabeth: SNL
Fields, Gary: Wall Street Journal / Dow Jones
Finkle, Victoria: American Banker
Fireman, Ken: Bloomberg News
Firth, Shannon: MedPage Today
Fiscus, Amy: Los Angeles Times
Fitzgerald, Alison: Center for Public Integrity
Flaherty, Anne: Associated Press
Flaherty, Mary Pat: Washington Post
Flaherty, Michael: Thomson Reuters
Flanders, Gwen: USA Today
Flavelle, Christopher: Bloomberg News
Fleming, Sam: Financial Times
Fordney, Jason: Argus Media
Fortes, Flavia: MLEX US
Fox, Elizabeth: Argus Media

MEMBERS ENTITLED TO ADMISSION—Continued

Fox, Elizabeth: Argus Media
Fram, Alan: Associated Press
Frappolli, Amelia: CQ Roll Call
Fras, Damir: Berliner Zeitung
Freedman, Dan: Hearst Newspapers
Freking, Kevin: Associated Press
Frieden, Joyce: MedPage Today
Fritze, John: Baltimore Sun
Frommer, Frederic: Associated Press
Fuhrig, Frank: German Press Agency - DPA
Fullwood, Adrian: Associated Press
Funahashi, Eiichiro: Kyodo News
Fung, Brian: Washington Post
Fuog, Karin: CQ Roll Call
Furlow, Robert: Associated Press
Galewitz, Phil: Kaiser Health News
Gamboa, Aldo: Agence France-Presse
Gangitano, Alexandra: CQ Roll Call
Gao, Pan: Xinhua News Agency
Gaouette, Nicole: Bloomberg News
Garcia, Maria: Notimex Mexican News Agency
Gardner, Tim: Thomson Reuters
Gates-Davis, Marilyn: CQ Roll Call
Gaudiano Albright, Nicole: Gannett Washington Bureau
Ge, Xiangwen: Xinhua News Agency
Geidner, Chris: Buzzfeed.com
Geier, Peter: Merger Market of Financial Times
Geimann, Stephen: Bloomberg News
Geller, Eric: Daily Dot
Georges, Marc: Scripps Howard News Service
Gettinger, Steve: CQ Roll Call
Gibney, James: Bloomberg News
Gilbert, Jessica: McClatchy Newspapers
Gillespie, Lisa: Kaiser Health News
Gillman, Todd: Dallas Morning News
Gillum, Jack: Associated Press
Gilmour, Jared: Christian Science Monitor
Ginsburg, Steven: Thomson Reuters
Giroux, Gregory: Bloomberg News
Givens, David: Argus Media
Glass, Pamela: Le Mauricien
Glinski, Nina: Bloomberg News
Gnoffo, Anthony: CQ Roll Call
Goers, Stacey: CQ Roll Call
Golden, Rodrek: Thomson Reuters
Goldenberg, Suzanne: Guardian US
Goldmacher, Shane: National Journal
Goldman, Adam: Washington Post
Goldstein, David: McClatchy Newspapers
Goldstein, Steven: MarketWatch
Golle, Vince: Bloomberg News
Gomez, Sergio: El Tiempo
Good, Allison: SNL
Gordon, D. Craig: Bloomberg News
Gordon, Greg: McClatchy Newspapers
Gordon, Marcy: Associated Press
Gordon, Michael: New York Times

Gosselin, Peter: Bloomberg News
Gossman, Jean: LRP Publications
Gourdin, Michael: Bloomberg News
Grant, Annalee: SNL
Gray, Rosie: Buzzfeed.com
Greenwood, Rick: Bloomberg News
Greiling Keane, Angela: Bloomberg News
Gresko, Jessica: Associated Press
Griffith, Stephanie: Agence France-Presse
Grim, Ryan: Huffington Post
Grimaldi, James: Wall Street Journal / Dow Jones
Groppe, Maureen: Gannett Washington Bureau
Grossman, Cathy Lynn: Religion News Service
Guevara, Tomas: El Diario de Hoy
Gugarats, Haik: Argus Media
Guggenheim, Ken: Associated Press
Gulino, Denny: Market News International
Gustin, Georgina: CQ Roll Call
Haas, Brandon: CQ Roll Call
Hager, George: USA Today
Hallerman, Tamar: CQ Roll Call
Halper, Evan: Los Angeles Times
Hamilton, Jesse: Bloomberg News
Hammesfahr, Eric: CQ Roll Call
Hampton, Olivia: Agence France-Presse
Hananel, Sam: Associated Press
Hancock, James: Kaiser Health News
Handley, Paul: Agence France-Presse
Hanson, Clayton: CQ Roll Call
Harder, Amy: Wall Street Journal / Dow Jones
Harris, Bryant: Yomiuri Shimbun
Harris, Gardiner: New York Times
Harris, Hamil: Washington Post
Harrison, David: Wall Street Journal / Dow Jones
Hart, Dan: Bloomberg News
Harte, Julia: Center for Public Integrity
Hartson, Merrill: Associated Press
Hatch, David: Merger Market of Financial Times
He, Yi: Science & Technology Daily
Heath, Brad: USA Today
Heavey, Susan: Thomson Reuters
Hefling, Kimberly: Associated Press
Helderman, Rosalind: Washington Post
Heltman, John: American Banker
Hendel, John: Communications Daily
Henderson, Nell: Wall Street Journal / Dow Jones
Henneberger, Melinda: Bloomberg News
Hennessey, Kathleen: Los Angeles Times
Henriksson, Karin: Svenska Dagbladet
Hernandez, Arelis: Washington Post
Hernandez, Jose: El Universal
Hernandez, Michael: Anatolia News Agency
Herszenhorn, David: New York Times
Higgins, Sean: Washington Examiner
Hinton, Earl: Associated Press
Hoffman, Michael: Military.com
Holan, Angie Drobnic: Tampa Bay Times

MEMBERS ENTITLED TO ADMISSION—Continued

Holland, Jesse: Associated Press
Holland, Steve: Thomson Reuters
Holland, William: SNL
Holly, Christopher: Energy Daily
Holzer, Linda: Gannett Washington Bureau
Hook, Janet: Wall Street Journal / Dow Jones
Hopkins, Cheyenne: Bloomberg News
Horowitz, Jason: New York Times
Horwitz, Jeffrey: Associated Press
Hosaka, Tomoko: Associated Press
Hoskinson, Charles: Washington Examiner
Host, Patrick: Defense Daily
Hotakainen, Rob: McClatchy Newspapers
House, Billy: Bloomberg News
Howell, Kellan: Washington Times
Howell, Thomas: Washington Times
Hoyt, Clark: Bloomberg News
Hsu, Spencer: Washington Post
Hu, Yu Ling: World Journal
Huey-Burns, Caitlin: Real Clear Politics
Hughes, John: Bloomberg News
Hughes, Krista: Thomson Reuters
Hughes, Siobhan: Wall Street Journal / Dow Jones
Hume, Lynn: Bond Buyer
Hunt, Albert: Bloomberg News
Hunt, Terence: Associated Press
Hunter, John: CQ Roll Call
Hurley, Lawrence: Thomson Reuters
Hurst, Steven: Associated Press
Ignatiou, Michail: Ethnos Greece
Ileri, Kasim: Anatolia News Agency
Ilustre, Josefina: Malaya
Imai, Takashi: Yomiuri Shimbun
Insinna, Valerie: Defense Daily
Itkowitz, Colby: Washington Post
Ivanovich, David: Argus Media
Iwaki, Yoshiyuki: Sekai Nippo
Iwamoto, Masako: Nikkei
Jackson, David: USA Today
Jackson, Henry: Associated Press
Jackson, Herbert: Record (Bergen County, NJ)
Jacobson, Louis: Tampa Bay Times
Jakabcin, Anastasia: Bloomberg Government
Jalonick, Mary Clare: Associated Press
Jamieson, Dave: Huffington Post
Jamrisko, Michelle: Bloomberg News
Jan, Tracy: Boston Globe
Jang, Jin: Korea Economic Daily
Jansen, Bart: USA Today
Jenks, Paul: CQ Roll Call
Jha, Lalit: India Press Trust
Jiang, Yujuan: Xinhua News Agency
Jianwu, Guan: Xinhua News Agency
Joachim, David: New York Times
Jogoda, Naomi: Bond Buyer
Johnson, Fawn: National Journal
Johnson, Robert: Thomson Reuters

Johnston, Margaret: German Press Agency - DPA
Johnston, Nicholas: Bloomberg News
Jopson, Barney: Financial Times
Jordan, Bryant: Military.com
Joy, Patricia: CQ Roll Call
Juez-Moreno, Beatriz: German Press Agency - DPA
Junge, Barbara: Der Tagesspiegel
Kamalick, Joseph: ICIS News
Kaminishikawara, Jun: Kyodo News
Kampeas, Ron: Jewish Telegraphic Agency
Kane, Paul: Washington Post
Kano, Hiroyuki: Sankei Shimbun
Karam, Joyce: Al-Hayat
Kastner, Kevin: Market News International
Katz, Ian: Bloomberg News
Kawachi, Motoko: Nikkei
Kawai, Tomoyuki: Nikkei
Kaye, Alexandra: Times of London
Kearns, Jeff: Bloomberg News
Keating, Dan: Washington Post
Keefe, Stephen: Nikkei
Kehoe, John: Austrailian Financial Review
Kellman Blazar, Laurie: Associated Press
Kelly, Chrishopher: Tokyo Chunichi Shimbun
Kelly, Erin: USA Today
Kendall, Brent: Wall Street Journal / Dow Jones
Kennedy, Mark: MLEX US
Kerr, Jennifer: Associated Press
Kertes, Noella: CQ Roll Call
Kessler, Aaron: New York Times
Khatami, Elham: CQ Roll Call
Kiefer, Francine: Christian Science Monitor
Kim, Anne: CQ Roll Call
Kim, Mikyung: Seoul Shinmun Daily
Kim, Sejin: Yonhap News Agency
Kim, Soyoung: Thomson Reuters
Kim, Sung: Chosun Ilbo
King, Neil: Wall Street Journal / Dow Jones
King, Robert: Washington Examiner
Kinoshita, Hideomi: Kyodo News
Kipling, Bogdan: Kipling News Service
Kirsanov, Dmitry: Itar-Tass News Agency
Kitai, Kuniaki: Jiji Press
Kittross, David: LRP Publications
Klapper, Bradley: Associated Press
Klein, Philip: Washington Examiner
Klimas, Jacqueline: Washington Times
Klimasinska, Katarzyna: Bloomberg News
Klimek, Eric: Associated Press
Knight, Chris: Argus Media
Knox, Olivier: Yahoo News
Kobayashi, Kakumi: Kyodo News
Kobayashi, Tetsu: Asahi Shimbun
Koff, Stephen: Cleveland Plain Dealer
Koffler, Keith: White House Dossier
Kohda, Satoru: Jiji Press
Kokumo, Norio: Sankei Shimbun

MEMBERS ENTITLED TO ADMISSION—Continued

Komarow, Steven: CQ Roll Call
Komori, Yoshihisa: Sankei Shimbun
Koring, Paul: Globe and Mail
Korte, Gregory: USA Today
Koss, Geof: CQ Roll Call
Kotake, Hiroyuki: Nikkei
Kovacheva, Iva: Mainichi Shimbun
Kranish, Michael: Boston Globe
Krawzak, Paul: CQ Roll Call
Kreisher, Otto: Freelance
Kubo, Yuichi: Kyodo News
Kucinich, Jacqueline: Daily Beast
Kumar, Anita: McClatchy Newspapers
Kumar, Arun: Indo-Asian News Service
Kumar, Dinesh: Chemical Watch
Kurihara, Kazuhiro: Kyodo News
Kussin-Shoptaw, Samuel: Bloomberg Government
Kwon, Sang Chool: Korea Times
Lachman, Samantha: Huffington Post
Lackey, Katharine: USA Today
Lai, Chao-Ying: United Daily News
Lakashmanan, Indira: Bloomberg News
Lake, Eli: Bloomberg News
Lambert, Lisa: Thomson Reuters
Lambrecht, William: Hearst Newspapers
Lambro, Donald: Universal UClick Syndicate
Landay, Jonathan: McClatchy Newspapers
Landers, James: Dallas Morning News
Landler, Mark: New York Times
Langan, Michael: Agence France-Presse
Lange, Jason: Thomson Reuters
Lanman, Scott: Bloomberg News
Lardner, Richard: Associated Press
Lauter, David: Los Angeles Times
Lawder, David: Thomson Reuters
Lawler, Joseph: Washington Examiner
Layton, Lyndsey: Washington Post
Leal, Lucia: EFE News Services
Leary, Alex: Tampa Bay Times
Lederman, Josh: Associated Press
Lee, Byonghan: Korea Times
Lee, Carol: Wall Street Journal / Dow Jones
Lee, Chang-Yul: Korea Times
Lee, Jea: Munwha Ilbo
Lee, Jeeah: Asahi Shimbun
Lee, Jinmyung: Maeil Business Newspaper
Lee, Jong Kook: Korea Times
Lee, Yongil: McClatchy Newspapers
Lefkow, David: Agence France-Presse
Leinwand Leger, Donna: USA Today
Lemus, Katherina: Thomson Reuters
Leonard, Randall: CQ Roll Call
Lerer, Lisa: Associated Press
Lester, William: Associated Press
Leubsdorf, Ben: Wall Street Journal / Dow Jones
Leubsdorf, Carl: Dallas Morning News
Lever, Robert: Agence France-Presse

Levey, Noam: Los Angeles Times
Levin, Alan: Bloomberg News
Levine, Carrie: Center for Public Integrity
Levine, Sam: Huffington Post
Lewis, Finlay: CQ Roll Call
Lewis, Katherine: Freelance
Lewis, Paul: Guardian US
Liao Han Yuan, Tony: Taiwan Central News Agency
Liebelson, Dana: Huffington Post
Lightman, David: McClatchy Newspapers
Lindeman, Eric: Energy Daily
Linskey, Annie: Boston Globe
Lipari, James: Associated Press
Liptak, Adam: New York Times
Lipton, Eric: New York Times
Litvan, Laura: Bloomberg News
Liu, Jie: Xinhua News Agency
Liu BC, Jie: Xinhua News Agency
Livingston, Rebecca: The Texas Tribune
Lobsenz, George: Energy Daily
Lochhead, Carolyn: San Francisco Chronicle
Locker, Ray: USA Today
Londres, Eduardo: Bloomberg News
Lopez Zamorano, Jose: Notimex Mexican News Agency
Lovelace, Ryan: Washington Examiner
Lowy, Joan: Associated Press
Lu, Jiafei: Xinhua News Agency
Lu, Zhen-Hua: 21st Century Business Herald
Lubold, Gordon: Wall Street Journal / Dow Jones
Lucas, Ryan: CQ Roll Call
Lugones, Paula Mercedes: Clarin
Luo, Xiaoyuan: World Journal
Lustig, Michael: SNL
Luthra, Shefali: Kaiser Health News
Lynch, David: Bloomberg News
Lynch, Ryan: Merger Market of Financial Times
Lynch, Sarah: Thomson Reuters
Lytle, Laura: Senate Press Gallery (SPG)
Lytle, Tamara: Freelance
Maclouf, Malika: Ouest-France
MacPherson, Robert: Agence France-Presse
Magner, Mike: CQ Roll Call
Maher, Aya: Asahi Shimbun
Mak, Tim: Daily Beast
Make, Jonathan: Communications Daily
Maler, Sandra: Thomson Reuters
Malloy, Daniel: Atlanta Journal Constitution
Mandel, Susan: Merger Market of Financial Times
Mannion, James: Agence France-Presse
Markoe, Lauren: Religion News Service
Martin, Jonathan: New York Times
Martosko, David: Daily Mail (UK)
Mascaro, Lisa: Los Angeles Times
Masterson, Lauren: Argus Media
Mathes, Michael: Agence France-Presse
Matsukawa, Yoko: Jiji Press

MEMBERS ENTITLED TO ADMISSION—Continued

Matthews, Mark: Denver Post
Matthews, William: Bloomberg Government
Mauriello, Tracie: Pittsburgh Post-Gazette
Mayeda, Andrew: Bloomberg News
Mazein, Elodie: Agence France-Presse
Mazzo, Michael: Associated Press
McAuliff, Michael: Huffington Post
McCartney, Robert: Washington Post
McConnell, William: Daily Deal
McCrimmon, Ryan: CQ Roll Call
McGarry, Brendan: Military.com
McGill, Brian: Wall Street Journal / Dow Jones
McGrady, Clyde: CQ Roll Call
McGrane, Victoria: Wall Street Journal / Dow Jones
McKendry, Ian: American Banker
McKinnon, John: Wall Street Journal / Dow Jones
McLaughlin, David: Bloomberg News
McLaughlin, Seth: Washington Times
McMahon, Madeline: Bloomberg News
McManus, Doyle: Los Angeles Times
McMorris-Santoro, Evan: Buzzfeed.com
McPherson, Lindsey: CQ Roll Call
McQuillan, Mark: Bloomberg News
Meckler, Laura: Wall Street Journal / Dow Jones
Meehan, Brian: Bloomberg News
Mehall, Craig: CQ Roll Call
Meinert, Peer: German Press Agency - DPA
Mejdrich, Kellie: CQ Roll Call
Melling, Brittany: MLEX US
Memoli, Michael: Los Angeles Times
Meszoly, Robin: Bloomberg News
Meteer, Robert: Bloomberg Government
Meyers, David: CQ Roll Call
Meyers, Jessica: Boston Globe
Michaels, David: Bloomberg News
Michaels, Jim: USA Today
Miedema, Douwe: Thomson Reuters
Milbank, Dana: Washington Post
Milfeld, Becca: Agence France-Presse
Miller, Gregory: Washington Post
Miller, Jonathan: CQ Roll Call
Miller, Kathleen: Bloomberg News
Miller, Richard: Bloomberg News
Miller, S.A.: Washington Times
Millikin, David: Agence France-Presse
Mimms, Sarah: National Journal
Minkoff, Michelle: Associated Press
Mir De Francia, Ricardo: El Periodico
Mizumoto, Tatsuya: Jiji Press
Moday, Todd: Bloomberg News
Mohammed, Arshad: Thomson Reuters
Molotsky, Irvin: Washington Dupont Circle News
Monge, Yolanda: El Pais
Mongilio, Heather: LocalNews Now
Monroe, Sylvester: Washington Post
Montet, Virginie: Agence France-Presse
Montgomery, David: Washington Post

Montgomery, Lori: Washington Post
Morath, Eric: Wall Street Journal / Dow Jones
Morello, Carol: Washington Post
Morgan, David: Thomson Reuters
Morgan, Jon: Bloomberg News
Morton, Joseph: Omaha World-Herald
Mosqueda-Fernandez, Ximena: SNL
Moss, Daniel: Bloomberg News
Mott, Gregory: Bloomberg News
Mracek, Karen: Market News International
Mulligan, John: Senate Press Gallery (SPG)
Murphy, Lauren: SNL
Murray, Brendan: Bloomberg News
Murray, William: Oil Daily
Mutikani, Lucia: Thomson Reuters
Myers, Jim: Freelance
Nadworny, Elissa: Bloomberg News
Nakamura, David: Washington Post
Nasaw, Daniel: Wall Street Journal / Dow Jones
Nather, David: Boston Globe
Nawaguna, Elvina: Market News International
Neergaard, Lauran: Associated Press
Nelson, Colleen: Wall Street Journal / Dow Jones
Nelson, Eliot: Huffington Post
Nerbovig, Ariel: Bloomberg Government
Newhauser, Daniel: National Journal
Nicholas, Peter: Wall Street Journal / Dow Jones
Nishida, Shinichiro: Mainichi Shimbun
Nishigaki, Yuichiro: Jiji Press
Nissenbaum, Dion: Wall Street Journal / Dow Jones
Noble, Andrea: Washington Times
Nocera, Kate: Buzzfeed.com
Noel, Essex: Thomson Reuters
Norman, Jane: CQ Roll Call
Nuckols, Ben: Associated Press
Nutt, Amy: Washington Post
Nutting, Rex: MarketWatch
Nuzzi, Olivia: Daily Beast
Nylen, Leah: MLEX US
O'Brien, Connor: CQ Roll Call
Odion-Esene, Braimoh: Market News International
O'Donnell, Katy: CQ Roll Call
O'Harrow, Robert: Washington Post
Ohlemacher, Stephen: Associated Press
Oikawa, Masaya: Mainichi Shimbun
O'Keefe, Edward: Washington Post
Okudera, Atsushi: Asahi Shimbun
Olchowy, Mark: Associated Press
Oliphant, James: Thomson Reuters
Olivari, Nicholas: Market News International
Olorunnipa, Toluse: Bloomberg News
Olson, Laura: Allentown Morning Call
O'Mara, Stacy: Bloomberg Government
Ordonez, Francisco: McClatchy Newspapers
O'Reilly II, Joseph: Bloomberg News
Orol, Ron: Daily Deal
Oswald, Rachel: CQ Roll Call

MEMBERS ENTITLED TO ADMISSION—Continued

Overly, Steven: Washington Post
Pace, Julie: Associated Press
Page, Paul: Wall Street Journal / Dow Jones
Page, Susan: USA Today
Pagliarulo, Edward: Jiji Press
Paletta, Damian: Wall Street Journal / Dow Jones
Pandi, Nicolas: Jiji Press
Panetta, Alexander: Canadian Press
Pappas, Alex: Daily Caller
Park, Jong: Hankyoreh Daily
Park, Jong Hyun: Segye Times
Park, Kwang Duk: Korea Times
Park, Seyong: Korea Times
Park, Soo Jin: Korea Economic Daily
Parker, Ashley: New York Times
Parnass, Danielle: Bloomberg Government
Peake, Daniel: CQ Roll Call
Pear, Robert: New York Times
Pena, Maria: La Opinion
Pennington, Matthew: Associated Press
Peoples, Steve: Associated Press
Peterson, Kimberly: Argus Media
Peterson, Kristina: Wall Street Journal / Dow Jones
Phelps, Timothy: Los Angeles Times
Phenicie, Carolyn: CQ Roll Call
Phillips, James: Warren Communications News
Phillips, Michael: Wall Street Journal / Dow Jones
Pianin, Eric: Fiscal Times
Pickard-Cambridge, Claire: Argus Media
Picket, Kerry: Daily Caller
Pincus, Walter: Washington Post
Pisani, Silvia: La Nacion
Plocek, Joseph: Market News International
Plungis, Jeff: Bloomberg News
Pollard, Sonya: Bloomberg News
Portlock, Sarah: Wall Street Journal / Dow Jones
Postell, Elliot: Washington Post
Pritchard, David: Asahi Shimbun
Przybyla, Heidi: Bloomberg News
Pugh, Anthony: McClatchy Newspapers
Purce, Melinda: Associated Press
Purdy, Jamisha: CQ Roll Call
Putman, Eileen: Associated Press
Qi, Chen: MLEX US
Quinn, Erin: Center for Public Integrity
Raasch, Charles: St. Louis Post-Dispatch
Radnofsky, Louise: Wall Street Journal / Dow Jones
Rajagopalan, Sethuraman: Pioneer - India
Rajghatta, Chidanand: Times of India
Rappeport, Alan: New York Times
Rascoe, Ayesha: Thomson Reuters
Reber, Paticia: German Press Agency - DPA
Recio, Maria: McClatchy Newspapers
Reever, Paula Marie: Bloomberg Government
Reilly, Ryan: Huffington Post
Renaut, Anne: Agence France-Presse
Ricci, Andrea: Thomson Reuters

Rich, Gillian: Investor's Business Daily
Richardson, Betty: CQ Roll Call
Richey, Warren: Christian Science Monitor
Richter, Nicolas: Sueddeutsche Zeitung
Richter, Paul: Los Angeles Times
Ridel, Kaitlyn: CQ Roll Call
Riechmann-Kepler, Debra: Associated Press
Riley, Michael: Bloomberg News
Riquier, Andrea: Investor's Business Daily
Robb, Gregory: MarketWatch
Roberts, Daniel: Guardian US
Roberts, Gillian: CQ Roll Call
Roberts, Gregory: Baton Rouge Advocate
Robertson, Jordan: Bloomberg News
Robertson, Reiko: Kumamoto Nichinichi Shimbun
Robinson, Eugene: Washington Post
Robinson, James: Los Angeles Times
Robinson, John: Defense Daily
Rogers, Kevin: Washington Times
Rogin, Josh: Bloomberg News
Roh, Hyodong: Yonhap News Agency
Rohner, Mark: Bloomberg News
Roland, Neil: MLEX US
Rose, Matthew: Wall Street Journal / Dow Jones
Rosen, Amy: CQ Roll Call
Rosenberg, Matthew: New York Times
Ross, Andreas: Frankfurter Allgemeine Zeitung
Ross, Sonya: Associated Press
Rotella, Sebastian: Pro Publica
Roth, Bennett: Bloomberg News
Rothstein, Betsy: Daily Caller
Roubein, Rachel: National Journal
Rovner, Julie: Kaiser Health News
Rowland, Christopher: Boston Globe
Rowley, James: Bloomberg News
Rubin, Richard: Bloomberg News
Rucke, Katie: Communications Daily
Rucker, Patrick: Thomson Reuters
Ruf, Renzo: Aargauer Zeitung
Rugaber, Chris: Associated Press
Ruger, Todd: CQ Roll Call
Rund, Jacob: Communications Daily
Rushing, J.T.: Daily Mail (UK)
Ryan, Timothy: Thomson Reuters
Saarikoski, Laura: Helsingin Sanomat
Sadler, Kelly: Washington Times
Sahmkow, Ramon: Agence France-Presse
Saiba, Yasunobu: Tokyo Chunichi Shimbun
Saito, Akira: Yomiuri Shimbun
Salant, Jonathan: NJ Advance Media
Salcedo, Michele: Associated Press
Salmeron, Marvin: Bloomberg News
Sanchez, Raf: London Daily Telegraph
Sanders, Edmund: Los Angeles Times
Sands, Darren: Buzzfeed.com
Sands, David: Washington Times
Sanger, David: New York Times

MEMBERS ENTITLED TO ADMISSION—Continued

Santini, Jean-Louis: Agence France-Presse
Sato, Taketsugu: Asahi Shimbun
Savage, David: Los Angeles Times
Scally, William: William Scally Reports
Schaberg, Caroline: Bloomberg News
Schank, Adam: Bloomberg Government
Scheuble, Kristy: Bloomberg News
Schlisserman, Courtney: Argus Media
Schmidt, Michael: New York Times
Schmidt, Robert: Bloomberg News
Schmitt, Eric: New York Times
Schmitz, Jens: Badische Zeitung
Schneider, Howard: Thomson Reuters
Schneider, Jodi: Bloomberg News
Schoenberg, Tom: Bloomberg News
Schouten, Fredreka: USA Today
Schram, Martin: Tribune News Service
Schroeder, Robert: MarketWatch
Schulberg, Jessica: Huffington Post
Schulte, Fred: Center for Public Integrity
Schultheis, Emily: National Journal
Schultz, Marisa: New York Post
Schwartz, Felicia: Wall Street Journal / Dow Jones
Schwed, Craig: Gannett Washington Bureau
Scott, David: Associated Press
Scott, Heather: Market News International
Scott, Katherine: CQ Roll Call
Scully, Megan: CQ Roll Call
Seibel, Mark: McClatchy Newspapers
Selyukh, Alina: Thomson Reuters
Sementsova, Angelina: Bloomberg Government
Serrano, Richard: Los Angeles Times
Sevastopulo, Demetri: Financial Times
Shaban, Hamza: Buzzfeed.com
Shalal, Andrea: Thomson Reuters
Shanker, Thomas: New York Times
Shastry, Anjali: Washington Times
Shaw, John: Market News International
Shaw, Michael: CQ Roll Call
Shear, Michael: New York Times
Shepardson, David: Detroit News
Sheppard, Kate: Huffington Post
Sherfinski, David: Washington Times
Sherman, Mark: Associated Press
Sherry, Allison: Minneapolis Star Tribune
Shesgreen, Deirdre: Gannett Washington Bureau
Shields, Mark: Creators Syndicate
Shields, Todd: Bloomberg News
Shiffman, John: Thomson Reuters
Shilad, Justin: Smartgrid Today
Shim, In Sung: Yonhap News Agency
Shimada, Minetaka: Akahata
Shimizu, Kenji: Mainichi Shimbun
Shiner, Meredith: Yahoo News
Shirakawa, Yoshikazu: Yomiuri Shimbun
Shishkin, Philip: Wall Street Journal / Dow Jones
Shuppy, Anne: CQ Roll Call

Sichelman, Lew: United Media
Siciliano, John: Washington Examiner
Siddiqui, Sabrina: Guardian US
Siddons, Andrew: New York Times
Simao, Paul: Thomson Reuters
Simendinger, Alexis: Real Clear Politics
Simpson, Ian: Thomson Reuters
Sinderbrand, Rebecca: Washington Post
Singer, Paul: USA Today
Sink, Justin: Bloomberg News
Sisk, Richard: Military.com
Sitov, Andrei: Itar-Tass News Agency
Skiba, Katherine: Chicago Tribune
Slack, Donovan: USA Today
Smialek, Jeanna: Bloomberg News
Smith, Sara: CQ Roll Call
Smith, Sarah: SNL
Smith, Veronica: Agence France-Presse
Snell, Kelsey: Washington Post
Snyder, Jim: Bloomberg News
Sobczyk, Joseph: Bloomberg News
Socknat, Kristyn: Senate Press Gallery (SPG)
Son, Jemin: Kyunghyang Daily News
Sondgeroth, Jessica: Argus Media
Sorcher, Sara: Christian Science Monitor
Spang, Thomas: US-Report (Germany)
Spangler, Todd: Detroit Free Press
Sparshott, Jeffrey: Wall Street Journal / Dow Jones
Spence, Matthew: Times of London
Spencer, Jim: Minneapolis Star Tribune
St. Martin, Victoria: Washington Post
Stanley, Aaron: Financial Times
Stanton, John: Buzzfeed.com
Stapleton, Stephanie: Kaiser Health News
Stebbings, Peter: Agence France-Presse
Stein, Sam: Huffington Post
Steinhauer, Jennifer: New York Times
Stephenson, Emily: Thomson Reuters
Sternberg, William: USA Today
Stewart, Bruce: Sankei Shimbun
Stilwell, Victoria: Bloomberg News
Stohr, Greg: Bloomberg News
Strohm, Chris: Bloomberg News
Strong, Thomas: Associated Press
Stumme, Susan: Agence France-Presse
Sullivan, Andy: Thomson Reuters
Sullivan, Bartholomew: Journal Media Group
Sullivan, Eileen: Associated Press
Sullivan, Gregory: Bloomberg Government
Sullivan, Sean: Washington Post
Sullivan, Sean: SNL
Superville, Darlene: Associated Press
Supon, Justin: House Daily Press Gallery
Sweeney, Jeanne: LRP Publications
Sweet, Lynn: Chicago Sun-Times
Tackett, R. Michael: New York Times
Takei, Toru: Kyodo News

MEMBERS ENTITLED TO ADMISSION—Continued

Talev, Margaret: Bloomberg News
Talley, Ian: Wall Street Journal / Dow Jones
Tamari, Jonathan: Philadelphia Inquirer
Tan, Anjelica: MLEX US
Tanfani, Joseph: Los Angeles Times
Tanis, Tolga: Hurriyet
Tate, Curtis: McClatchy Newspapers
Tatsubo, Mutsumi: Jiji Press
Tau, Byron: Wall Street Journal / Dow Jones
Taylor, Andrew: Associated Press
Taylor, David: Times of London
Taylor, Guy: Washington Times
Taylor, Marisa: McClatchy Newspapers
Teinowitz, Ira: MLEX US
Teitelbaum, Michael: CQ Roll Call
Terkel, Amanda: Huffington Post
Tetreault, Stephan: Stephens Media Group
Theobald, William: Gannett Washington Bureau
Thomas, Ken: Associated Press
Thomas, Richard: Voterama in Congress
Thomma, Steven: McClatchy Newspapers
Thompson, Alexander: New York Times
Thueringer, Tamara: Bloomberg News
Tian, Xueke: Science & Technology Daily
Timiraos, Nick: Wall Street Journal / Dow Jones
Tin, Annie: House Daily Press Gallery
Tiron, Roxana: Bloomberg News
Toiyama, Sakae: Ryukyu Shimpo
Tokito, Mineko: Yomiuri Shimbun
Tomkin, Robert: CQ Roll Call
Torbati, Yeganeh: Thomson Reuters
Tordjman, Jeremy: Agence France-Presse
Toroglu, Bariskan: Anatolia News Agency
Toroglu, Ozkul: Anatolia News Agency
Torres, Carlos: Bloomberg News
Torry, Jack: Columbus Dispatch
Toth, Jacqueline: CQ Roll Call
Tracy, Ryan: Wall Street Journal / Dow Jones
Tracy, Tennile: Wall Street Journal / Dow Jones
Tranfaglia, John: CQ Roll Call
Trevisan, Claudia: O Estado De S. Paulo
Tritten, Travis: Stars and Stripes
Trott, William: Thomson Reuters
Trottman, Melanie: Wall Street Journal / Dow Jones
Troyan, Mary: Gannett Washington Bureau
Trumbull, Mark: Christian Science Monitor
Tsao, Nadia: Liberty Times
Tsao, Stephanie: Argus Media
Tucker, Eric: Associated Press
Tumulty, Brian: Gannett Washington Bureau
Ullerup, Jorgen: Jyllands-Posten
Urano, Eri: Tokyo Chunichi Shimbun
Urban, Peter: Stephens Media Group
Valery, Chantal: Agence France-Presse
Valk, August: Handelsblad
Vanden Brook, Tom: USA Today
Vaughan, Jenny: Agence France-Presse

Velencia, Xhensila: Huffington Post
Vergano, Dan: Buzzfeed.com
Vineys, Kevin: Associated Press
Viser, Matthew: Boston Globe
Viswanatha, Aruna: Wall Street Journal
Vlahou, Toula: CQ Roll Call
Wada, Hiroaki: Mainichi Shimbun
Wagman, Robert: Newspaper Enterprise
Walerius, Randolph: CQ Roll Call
Wallbank, Derek: Bloomberg News
Walsh, Eric: Thomson Reuters
Walsh, Stephen: CQ Roll Call
Walters Custer, Anne: German Press Agency - DPA
Warrick, Joby: Washington Post
Waschinski, Gregor: Agence France-Presse
Wasson, Erik: Bloomberg News
Watkins, Allison: Huffington Post
Watkins, Thomas: Agence France-Presse
Watters, Susan: Fairchild Publications
Weatherhead, Tim: Market News International
Webb, Kayla: Bloomberg Government
Weekes, Jr., Michael: Thomson Reuters
Wehrman, Jessica: Columbus Dispatch
Weigel, David: Washington Post
Weiner, Mark: Syracuse Post-Standard
Weiner, Rachel: Washington Post
Weinstein, Jamie: Daily Caller
Weir, Kytja: Center for Public Integrity
Weisman, Jonathan: New York Times
Weiss, William: CQ Roll Call
Wellisz, Chris: Bloomberg News
Wells, Letitia: McClatchy Newspapers
Werner, Erica: Associated Press
Westwood, Sarah: Washington Examiner
Wetzstein, Cheryl: Washington Times
Weyl, Ben: CQ Roll Call
Whieldon, Esther: SNL
White, Dina: Chicago Tribune
White, Gordon: Washington Telecommunications
   Services
White, Keith: CQ Roll Call
Whiteaker, Chloe: Bloomberg News
Whitelaw, Kevin: CQ Roll Call
Whitesides, John: Thomson Reuters
Whitlock, Craig: Washington Post
Wilber, Del Quentin: Bloomberg News
Wilkins, Emily: CQ Roll Call
Willis, Derek: New York Times
Wilson, Scott: Washington Post
Wilson, Trish: Associated Press
Wingfield, Brian: Bloomberg News
Wire, Sarah: Arkansas Democrat-Gazette
Wise, Lindsay: McClatchy Newspapers
Wiseman, Paul: Associated Press
Witcover, Jules: Tribune Content Agency
Witkin, Gordon: Center for Public Integrity
Witkowski, Nancy: Associated Press
Wolf, Richard: USA Today

MEMBERS ENTITLED TO ADMISSION—Continued

Woo, Yee: CQ Roll Call
Woodruff, Betsy: Daily Beast
Woodward, Bob: Washington Post
Wright, Christopher: CQ Roll Call
Xia, Xiaoyang: Wen Hui Daily
Xian, Wen: China People's Daily
Xiaochun, Lin: Xinhua News Agency
Yamahiro, Tsaneo: Bloomberg News
Yamasaki, Takeshi: Nishi-Nippon Shimbun
Yamawaki, Takeshi: Asahi Shimbun
Yancey, Matthew: Associated Press
Yasue, Kunihiko: Yomiuri Shimbun
Yazawa, Toshiki: Nikkei
Ybarra, Margaret: Washington Times
Yeider, Samantha: Senate Press Gallery (SPG)
Yen, Hope: Associated Press
Yerkey, Gary: Svenska Dagbladet
Yildirim, Gulbin: Anatolia News Agency
Yoder, Eric: Washington Post
Yoder, Tim: CQ Roll Call
York, Byron: Washington Examiner
Yoshino, Naoya: Nikkei

Yoshiura, Hiroto: Kyodo News
Young, Alison: USA Today
Young, Chris: Center for Public Integrity
Young, Donna: Scrip
Young, Jeffrey: Huffington Post
Young, Kerry: CQ Roll Call
Yu, Donghui: China Review News Agency
Yukhananov, Anna: Thomson Reuters
Zajac, Andrew: Bloomberg News
Zanona, Melanie: CQ Roll Call
Zapotosky, Matt: Washington Post
Zargham, Mohammad: Thomson Reuters
Zeller, Shawn: CQ Roll Call
Zeman, Brittany: CQ Roll Call
Zezima, Katherine: Washington Post
Zheng, Qihang: Xinhua News Agency
Zhi, Linfei: Xinhua News Agency
Zitner, Aaron: Wall Street Journal / Dow Jones
Zongker, Brett: Associated Press
Zoroya, Gregg: USA Today
Zoupaniotis, Apostolos: Cyprus News Agency
Zremski, Jerry: Buffalo News

NEWSPAPERS REPRESENTED IN PRESS GALLERIES

House Gallery 225–3945, 225–6722   Senate Gallery 224–0241

21ST CENTURY BUSINESS HERALD—4201 Massachusetts Avenue, Washington, DC 20016: Zhen-Hua Lu.
AARGAUER ZEITUNG—(202) 403–7115: Renzo Ruf.
ABC NEWSPAPER—(202) 617–5882: Manuel Erice.
ABIM—(703) 243–2104; McLean VA 22101: Mario Navarro da Costa.
AGENCE FRANCE-PRESSE—(202) 289–0700; 1500 K Street, NW., Suite 600, Washington, DC 20005: Shahzad Abdul, Laurent Barthelemy, Andrew Beatty, Leon Bruneau, David Clark, Ivan Couronne, Guillaume Decamme, Jean-Louis Doublet, Fabienne Faur, Aldo Gamboa, Stephanie Griffith, Olivia Hampton, Paul Handley, Michael Langan, David Lefkow, Robert Lever, Robert MacPherson, James Mannion, Michael Mathes, Elodie Mazein, Becca Milfeld, David Millikin, Virginie Montet, Anne Renaut, Ramon Sahmkow, Jean-Louis Santini, Veronica Smith, Peter Stebbings, Susan Stumme, Jeremy Tordjman, Chantal Valery, Jenny Vaughan, Gregor Waschinski, Thomas Watkins.
AKAHATA—(202) 393–5238; 978 National Press Building, Washington, DC 20045: Minetaka Shimada.
ALBUQUERQUE JOURNAL—(202) 329–4743; 7777 Jefferson Street, NE., Albuquerque NM 87109: Michael Coleman.
AL-HAYAT—(202) 248–8525; P.O. Box 73522, Washington, DC 20056: Joyce Karam.
ALLENTOWN MORNING CALL—(202) 824–8216; 1090 Vermont Avenue, NW., Suite 1000, Washington, DC 20005: Laura Olson.
AMERICAN BANKER—(571) 403–3837; 4401 Wilson Boulevard, Suite 910, Arlington VA 22209: Brian Collins, Victoria Finkle, John Heltman, Ian McKendry.
ANATOLIA NEWS AGENCY—(202) 662–7435; 529 14th Street, NW., Suite 1131, Washington, DC 20045: Michael Hernandez, Kasim Ileri, Bariskan Toroglu, Ozkul Toroglu, Gulbin Yildirim.
ARA—(914) 954–5521; Washington, DC: Nuria Ferragutcasas.
ARGUS MEDIA—(202) 775–0240; 1012 14th Street, NW., Suite 1500, Washington, DC 20005: Michael Ball, Lucas Bifera, Abby Caplan, Edward Epstein, Jason Fordney, Elizabeth Fox, David Givens, Haik Gugarats, David Ivanovich, Chris Knight, Lauren Masterson, Kimberly Peterson, Claire Pickard-Cambridge, Courtney Schlisserman, Jessica Sondgeroth, Stephanie Tsao.
ARKANSAS DEMOCRAT-GAZETTE—(202) 662–7690; 960-A National Press Building, Washington, DC 20045: Sarah Wire.
ARTISTS & WRITERS SYNDICATE—(703) 820–4232; 582 Brummel Court, NW., Washington, DC 20012: Frank Aukofer.
ASAHI SHIMBUN—(202) 783–1000; 1022 National Press Building, Washington, DC 20045: Conor Cislo, Tetsu Kobayashi, Jeeah Lee, Aya Maher, Atsushi Okudera, David Pritchard, Taketsugu Sato, Takeshi Yamawaki.
ASSOCIATED PRESS—(202) 641–9000; 1100 13th Street, NW., Washington, DC 20005: Luis Alonso, Ricardo Alonso-Zaldivar, Stacy Anderson, Lolita Baldor, Matthew Barakat, Wendy Benjaminson, Michael Biesecker, Josh Boak, Seth Borenstein, Stephen Braun, Robert Burns, Julie Bykowicz, Alicia Caldwell, Connie Cass, Donna Cassata, Lauren Cooper, Martin Crutsinger, Matthew Daly, Ken Dilanian, Jim Drinkard, Harry Dunphy, Donald Elkins, Philip Elliott, Carole Feldman, Anne Flaherty, Alan Fram, Kevin Freking, Frederic Frommer, Adrian Fullwood, Robert Furlow, Jack Gillum, Marcy Gordon, Jessica Gresko, Ken Guggenheim, Sam Hananel, Merrill Hartson, Kimberly Hefling, Earl Hinton, Jesse Holland, Jeffrey Horwitz, Tomoko Hosaka, Terence Hunt, Steven Hurst, Henry Jackson, Mary Clare Jalonick, Laurie Kellman Blazar, Jennifer Kerr, Bradley Klapper, Eric Klimek, Richard Lardner, Josh Lederman, Lisa Lerer, William Lester, James Lipari, Joan Lowy, Michael Mazzo, Michelle Minkoff, Lauran Neergaard, Ben Nuckols, Stephen Ohlemacher, Mark Olchowy, Julie Pace, Matthew Pennington, Steve Peoples, Melinda Purce, Eileen Putman, Debra Riechmann-Kepler, Sonya Ross, Chris Rugaber, Michele Salcedo, David Scott, Mark Sherman, Thomas Strong, Eileen Sullivan, Darlene Superville, Andrew Taylor, Ken Thomas, Eric Tucker, Kevin Vineys, Erica Werner, Trish Wilson, Paul Wiseman, Nancy Witkowski, Matthew Yancey, Hope Yen, Brett Zongker.
ATLANTA JOURNAL CONSTITUTION—(202) 777–7033; 400 North Capitol Street, NW., Suite 750, Washington, DC 20001: Daniel Malloy.
AUSTRAILIAN FINANCIAL REVIEW—(202) 285–9000; 1310 G Street, NW., Suite 750, Washington, DC 20005: John Kehoe.
BADISCHE ZEITUNG—(202) 588–9351; Washington, DC 20009: Jens Schmitz.
BALTIMORE SUN—(410) 979–2052; 1090 Vermont Avenue, NW., Suite 1000, Washington, DC 20005: Jeffrey Barker, Ian Duncan, John Fritze.

NEWSPAPERS REPRESENTED—Continued

BATON ROUGE ADVOCATE—(504) 636–7400; 7290 Bluebonnet Boulevard, Baton Rouge LA 70810: Gregory Roberts.

BERLINER ZEITUNG—(301) 564–0861; Karl-Liebknecht-Strasse 29 D–10178 Berlin Germany: Damir Fras.

BLOOMBERG GOVERNMENT—(202) 654–4399; 1101 K Street, NW., Washington, DC 20005: Alvin Banks, Katharine Carter, Caitlin Cusati, Loren Duggan, Anastasia Jakabcin, Samuel Kussin-Shoptaw, William Matthews, Robert Meteer, Ariel Nerbovig, Stacy O'Mara, Danielle Parnass, Paula Marie Reever, Adam Schank, Angelina Sementsova, Gregory Sullivan, Kayla Webb.

BLOOMBERG NEWS—(202) 654–7300; 1399 New York Avenue, NW., 11th Floor Washington, DC 20005: Hector Alfaro, Laurie Asseo, Clea Benson, Alan Bjerga, Justin Blum, Romaine Bostick, Benjamin Brody, Silla Brush, Alister Bull, Anthony Capaccio, Shobhana Chandra, Kristin Cohen, Christopher Condon, Gail DeGeorge, Andre Delane, Elizabeth Dexheimer, Mike Dorning, Carter Dougherty, Mark Drajem, Anna Edney, Joshua Eidelson, Jennifer Epstein, Ken Fireman, Christopher Flavelle, Nicole Gaouette, Stephen Geimann, James Gibney, Gregory Giroux, Nina Glinski, Vince Golle, D Craig Gordon, Peter Gosselin, Michael Gourdin, Rick Greenwood, Angela Greiling Keane, Jesse Hamilton, Dan Hart, Melinda Henneberger, Cheyenne Hopkins, Billy House, Clark Hoyt, John Hughes, Albert Hunt, Michelle Jamrisko, Nicholas Johnston, Ian Katz, Jeff Kearns, Katarzyna Klimasinska, Indira Lakashmanan, Eli Lake, Scott Lanman, Alan Levin, Laura Litvan, Eduardo Londres, David Lynch, Andrew Mayeda, David McLaughlin, Madeline McMahon, Mark McQuillan, Brian Meehan, Robin Meszoly, David Michaels, Kathleen Miller, Richard Miller, Todd Moday, Jon Morgan, Daniel Moss, Gregory Mott, Brendan Murray, Elissa Nadworny, Toluse Olorunnipa, Joseph O'Reilly II, Jeff Plungis, Sonya Pollard, Heidi Przybyla, Michael Riley, Jordan Robertson, Josh Rogin, Mark Rohner, Bennett Roth, James Rowley, Richard Rubin, Marvin Salmeron, Caroline Schaberg, Kristy Scheuble, Robert Schmidt, Jodi Schneider, Tom Schoenberg, Todd Shields, Justin Sink, Jeanna Smialek, Jim Snyder, Joseph Sobczyk, Victoria Stilwell, Greg Stohr, Chris Strohm, Margaret Talev, Tamara Thueringer, Roxana Tiron, Carlos Torres, Derek Wallbank, Erik Wasson, Chris Wellisz, Chloe Whiteaker, Del Quentin Wilber, Brian Wingfield, Tsaneo Yamahiro, Andrew Zajac.

BOND BUYER—(571) 403–3843; 4401 Wilson Boulevard, Suite 910 Arlington VA 22203: John Casey, Lynn Hume, Naomi Jogoda.

BOSTON GLOBE—(202) 857–5050; 1130 Connecticut Avenue, NW., Suite 725, Washington, DC 20036: Tracy Jan, Michael Kranish, Annie Linskey, Jessica Meyers, David Nather, Christopher Rowland, Matthew Viser.

BOSTON HERALD—(617) 426–3000; 70 Fargo Street, Boston MA 2210: Kimberly Atkins.

BUFFALO NEWS—(202) 234–3188; National Press Building, #841, Washington, DC 20045: Jerry Zremski.

BUZZFEED.COM—1630 Connecticut Avenue, NW., Suite 700, Washington, DC 20009: Chris Geidner, Rosie Gray, Evan Mcmorris-Santoro, Kate Nocera, Darren Sands, Hamza Shaban, John Stanton, Dan Vergano.

CANADIAN PRESS—(202) 641–9734; 1100 13th Street, NW., Washington, DC 20045: Alexander Panetta.

CENTER FOR PUBLIC INTEGRITY—(202) 466–1300; 910 17th Street, NW., 7th Floor Washington, DC 20006: Michael Beckel, Douglas Birch, Susan Ferriss, Alison Fitzgerald, Julia Harte, Carrie Levine, Erin Quinn, Fred Schulte, Kytja Weir, Gordon Witkin, Chris Young.

CENTRAL NEWS AGENCY—1173 National Press Building, Washington, DC 20045: Tsung-Shen Cheng.

CHEMICAL WATCH—(202) 803–5909; 6701 Democracy Boulevard, #300 Bethesda MD 20817-5870: Dinesh Kumar.

CHICAGO SUN-TIMES—(202) 320–6044; 350 North Orleans Street, 10th Floor, Chicago IL 60654: Lynn Sweet.

CHICAGO TRIBUNE—(202) 824–8306; 1090 Vermont Avenue, NW., Suite 1000, Washington, DC 20005: Katherine Skiba, Dina White.

CHINA PEOPLE'S DAILY—(703) 698–1298; 529 14th Street, NW., Suite 450, Washington, DC 20045: Wen Xian.

CHINA REVIEW NEWS AGENCY—(703) 725–0720: Donghui Yu.

CHOSUN ILBO—(703) 865–8310; 1291 National Press Building, Washington, DC 20045: Sung Kim.

Christian Science Monitor—(202) 481–6680; 910 16th Street, NW., Suite 200, Washington, DC 20006: Gail Chaddock, David Cook, Linda Feldmann, Jared Gilmour, Francine Kiefer, Warren Richey, Sara Sorcher, Mark Trumbull.

CLARIN—(202) 476–0920; 988 National Press Building, Washington, DC 20045: Paula Mercedes Lugones.

CLEVELAND PLAIN DEALER—(202) 638–1366; c/o IWMF 1625 K Street, NW., Suite 1275 Washington, DC 20006: Sabrina Eaton.

COLUMBUS DISPATCH—(202) 777–7015; 400 North Capitol Street, Suite 850, Washington, DC 20001: Jack Torry.

Communications Daily—(202) 872–9202; 2115 Ward Court, NW., Washington, DC 20037: John Hendel, Jonathan Make, Katie Rucke, Jacob Rund.

CQ ROLL CALL—(202) 650–6500; 77 K Street, NE., Washington, DC 20002: Kate Ackley, Rebecca Adams, Joanna Anderson, Will Ardinger, Melissa Attias, John Bennett, Adriel Bettelheim, Daniel

NEWSPAPERS REPRESENTED—Continued

Bloom, Cory Brown, George Cahlink, Catalina Camia, Eliza Carney, Christina Carr, Charlene Carter, Sarah Chacko, Jad Chamseddine, Aisha Chowdhry, Mike Christensen, Alexander Clearfield, George Codrea, Thomas Curry, Colin Degen, John Donnelly, David Ellis, Matthew Epstein, Marissa Evans, Edward Felker, Peter Feltman, Ellyn Ferguson, Amelia Frappolli, Karin Fuog, Alexandra Gangitano, Marilyn Gates-Davis, Steve Gettinger, Anthony Gnoffo, Stacey Goers, Georgina Gustin, Brandon Haas, Tamar Hallerman, Eric Hammesfahr, Clayton Hanson, John Hunter, Paul Jenks, Patricia Joy, Noella Kertes, Elham Khatami, Anne Kim, Steven Komarow, Geof Koss, Paul Krawzak, Randall Leonard, Finlay Lewis, Ryan Lucas, Mike Magner, Ryan McCrimmon, Clyde McGrady, Lindsey McPherson, Craig Mehall, Kellie Mejdrich, David Meyers, Jonathan Miller, Jane Norman, Connor O'Brien, Katy O'Donnell, Rachel Oswald, Daniel Peake, Carolyn Phenicie, Jamisha Purdy, Betty Richardson, Kaitlyn Ridel, Gillian Roberts, Amy Rosen, Todd Ruger, Katherine Scott, Megan Scully, Michael Shaw, Anne Shuppy, Sara Smith, Michael Teitelbaum, Robert Tomkin, Jacqueline Toth, John Tranfaglia, Toula Vlahou, Randolph Walerius, Stephen Walsh, William Weiss, Ben Weyl, Keith White, Kevin Whitelaw, Emily Wilkins, Yee Woo, Christopher Wright, Tim Yoder, Kerry Young, Melanie Zanona, Shawn Zeller, Brittany Zeman.

CREATORS SYNDICATE—(202) 662–1255; 5777 West Century Boulevard, Suite 700; Los Angeles CA 90045: Mark Shields.

CYPRUS NEWS AGENCY—(202) 462–5772; 2211 R Street, NW., Washington, DC 20008: Apostolos Zoupaniotis.

DAILY BEAST—(202) 626–2030; 1015 15th Street, NW., Suite 500, Washington, DC 20005: Eleanor Clift, Jacqueline Kucinich, Tim Mak, Olivia Nuzzi, Betsy Woodruff.

DAILY CALLER—(202) 506–2027; 1050 17th Street, Suite 900, Washington, DC 20036: Vincent Coglianese, Alex Pappas, Kerry Picket, Betsy Rothstein, Jamie Weinstein.

DAILY DEAL—(202) 429–2991; 236 Massachusetts Avenue, NE., Washington, DC 20002: William McConnell, Ron Orol.

DAILY DOT—(301) 787–6847; 112 Windsor Road, Suite A391, Austin TX 78703: Eric Geller.

DAILY MAIL (UK)—(646) 885–5105: Francesca Chambers, David Martosko, J.T. Rushing.

DALLAS MORNING NEWS—(202) 661–8421; 1252 National Press Building, 529 14th Street, NW., Washington, DC 20045: Todd Gillman, James Landers, Carl Leubsdorf.

DEFENSE DAILY—(703) 522–6686; 1911 Fort Meyer Drive, Suite 310, Arlington VA 22209: Patrick Host, Valerie Insinna, John Robinson.

DENVER POST—(202) 662–8907; 969 National Press Building, 529 14th Street, NW., Washington, DC 20045: Mark Matthews.

DER TAGESSPIEGEL—Washington, DC 20015: Barbara Junge.

DETROIT FREE PRESS—(703) 854–8942; 1575 Eye Street, NW., Suite 350, Washington, DC 20005: Todd Spangler.

DETROIT NEWS—(202) 662–8736; 969 National Press Building, 529 14th Street, NW., Washington, DC 20045: Melissa Burke, David Shepardson.

EFE NEWS SERVICES—(202) 745–7692; 1220 National Press Building, 529 14th Street, NW., Washingon DC 20045: Hernan Martin Alonso, Miriam Burgues, Maribel El Hamti, Alfonso Fernandez, Lucia Leal.

EL DIARIO DE HOY—(703) 845–4962; 4600 South Four Mile Run Drive, Arlington VA 22204: Tomas Guevara.

EL NUEVO DIA—(202) 662–7360; 960d National Press Building, 529 14th Street, NW., Washington, DC 20045: Jose Delgado.

EL PAIS—(202) 638–1533; 1134 National Press Building, 529 14th Street, NW., Washington, DC 20045: Sylvia Ayuso Determeyer, Marc Bassets, Joan Faus Catasus, Christina Fernandez Pereda, Yolanda Monge.

EL PERIODICO—(202) 679–8656; Washington, DC 20002: Ricardo Mir De Francia.

EL TIEMPO—(202) 607–5929; 5597 Seminary Road, Washington, DC 20041: Sergio Gomez.

EL UNIVERSAL—(202) 662–7190; 1193 National Press Building, 529 14th Street, NW., Washington, DC 20045: Jose Hernandez.

ENERGY DAILY—(703) 236–2405; 110 North Royal Street, Suite 200, Alexandria VA 22314–3240: Jeff Beattie, Jim Day, Christopher Holly, Eric Lindeman, George Lobsenz.

ETHNOS GREECE—(202) 361–7843; 1133 14th Street, NW., Washington, DC 20005: Michail Ignatiou.

EUROPOLITICS—(202) 758–8462; 1403 12th Street, NW., #4, Washington, DC 20005: Brian Beary.

FAIRCHILD PUBLICATIONS—(202) 955–0966; 1730 Rhode Island Avenue, Suite 603, Washington, DC 20036: Kristi Ellis, Susan Watters.

FERN'S AG INSIDER BY CHARLES ABBOTT: Charles Abbott.

FINANCIAL TIMES—(202) (434) 0986; 1023 15th Street, NW., Suite 700, Washington, DC 20005: Gina Chon, Shawn Donnan, Sam Fleming, Barney Jopson, Demetri Sevastopulo, Aaron Stanley.

FISCAL TIMES—(202) 628–3101; 1214 National Press Building, 529 14th Street, NW., Washington, DC 20045: Eric Pianin.

FRANKFURTER ALLGEMEINE ZEITUNG—(202) 248–0980; 2100 Connecticut Avenue, NW., Suite 502, Washington, DC 20016: Andreas Ross.

NEWSPAPERS REPRESENTED—Continued

GANNETT WASHINGTON BUREAU—(202) 854–8900; 1575 Eye Street, NW., Suite 350, Washington, DC 20005: Deborah Berry, Christopher Doering, Val Ellicott, Nicole Gaudiano Albright, Maureen Groppe, Linda Holzer, Craig Schwed, Deirdre Shesgreen, William Theobald, Mary Troyan, Brian Tumulty.

GERMAN PRESS AGENCY-DPA—(202) 662–1220; 1112 National Press Building, 529 14th Street, NW., Washington, DC 20045: Martin Bialecki, Frank Fuhrig, Margaret Johnston, Beatriz Juez-Moreno, Peer Meinert, Paticia Reber, Anne Walters Custer.

GLOBE AND MAIL—(202) 662–7167; 2000 M Street, NW., Suite 330, Washington, DC 20036: Paul Koring.

GUARDIAN US (202) 223–2486; 900 17th Street, NW., Suite 250, Washington, DC 20006: Suzanne Goldenberg, Paul Lewis, Daniel Roberts, Sabrina Siddiqui.

HANDELSBLAD—(202) 957–6115; 2907 Cathedral Avenue, Washington, DC 20008: August Valk.

HANKYOREH DAILY—(703) 989–0723; 821 National Press Building, Washington, DC 20045: Jong Park.

HEARST NEWSPAPERS—(202) 263–6400; 700 12th Street, NW., Suite 1000, Washington, DC 20005: Jennifer Dlouhy, Dan Freedman, William Lambrecht.

HELSINGIN SANOMAT—(301) 907–0080; Vilhonvuorenkatu 11 B, Helsinki Finland 500: Laura Saarikoski.

HOUSTON CHRONICLE—(202) 263–6411; 700 12th Street, NW., Suite 1000, Washington, DC 20005: Kevin Diaz.

HUFFINGTON POST—(202) 567–2634; 1750 Pennsylvania Avenue, NW., #600, Washington, DC 20006: Akbar Shahid Ahmed, Laura Barron-Lopez, Laura Bassett, Jennifer Bendery, Mark Blumenthal, Igor Bobic, Sara Bondioli, Arthur Delaney, Ryan Grim, Dave Jamieson, Samantha Lachman, Sam Levine, Dana Liebelson, Michael McAuliff, Eliot Nelson, Ryan Reilly, Jessica Schulberg, Kate Sheppard, Sam Stein, Amanda Terkel, Xhensila Velencia, Allison Watkins, Jeffrey Young.

HURRIYET—(917) 340–2466; 3700 Massachusetts Avenue, NW., #438 Washington, DC 20016: Tolga Tanis.

ICIS NEWS—(703) 836–3448; 333 North Fairfax Street, Suite 301, Alexandria VA 22314: Joseph Kamalick.

INDIA PRESS TRUST—(301) 881–2963; Rockville MD 20852: Lalit Jha.

INDO-ASIAN NEWS SERVICE—(703) 664–0037; Alexandria VA 22304: Arun Kumar.

INTERNATIONAL TRADE TODAY—(202) 872–9202; 2127 Ward Court, NW., Washington, DC 20037: Brian Dabbs.

INVESTOR'S BUSINESS DAILY—(202) 728–2154; 1001 Connecticut Avenue, Suite 415, Washington, DC 20036: Gillian Rich, Andrea Riquier.

IRISH TIMES—(202) 436–6223: Simon Carswell.

ITAR-TASS NEWS AGENCY—(202) 662–7080; 1004 National Press Building, Washington, DC 20045: Anatoly Bochinin, Anton Chudakov, Dmitry Kirsanov, Andrei Sitov.

JEWISH TELEGRAPHIC AGENCY—(646) 778–5536; 2100 Military Road, Arlington VA 22207: Ron Kampeas.

JIJI PRESS—(202) 783–4330; 550 National Press Building, NW., Washington, DC 20045: Kuniaki Kitai, Satoru Kohda, Yoko Matsukawa, Tatsuya Mizumoto, Yuichiro Nishigaki, Edward Pagliarulo, Nicolas Pandi, Mutsumi Tatsubo.

JOONGANG ILBO—(202) 347–0122; 997 National Press Building, Washington, DC 20045: Byunggun Chae.

JOURNAL MEDIA GROUP—(202) 408–2711; 1100 13th Street, NW., Suite 450, Washington, DC 29995: Michael Collins, Bartholomew Sullivan.

JYLLANDS-POSTEN—1700 Lanier Place, NW., Washington, DC 20009: Jorgen Ullerup.

KAISER HEALTH NEWS—(202) 347–5270; 1330 G Street, NW., Washington, DC 20005: Julie Appleby, Mary Agnes Carey, Phil Galewitz, Lisa Gillespie, James Hancock, Shefali Luthra, Julie Rovner, Stephanie Stapleton.

KIPLING NEWS SERVICE—(202) 686–6388; 12611 Farnell Drive, Silver Spring, MD 20906: Bogdan Kipling.

KOREA ECONOMIC DAILY—(703) 895–0955; 821 National Press Building, 529 14th Street, NW., Washington, DC 20045: Jin Jang, Soo Jin Park.

KOREA TIMES—(703) 941–8002; 7601 Little River Turnpike; Annandale VA 22003: Christina Young Chong, Sang Chool Kwon, Byonghan Lee, Chang-Yul Lee, Jong Kook Lee, Kwang Duk Park, Seyong Park.

KUMAMOTO NICHINICHI SHIMBUN—(301) 299–3775; 10625 Rock Run Drive, Potomac, MD 20854: Reiko Robertson.

KUWAIT NEWS AGENCY—(202) 347–5554; 906 National Press Building, Washington, DC 20045: Ronald Baygents.

KYODO NEWS—(202) 347–5767; 400 National Press Building, 529 14th Street, NW., Washington, DC 20045: Sarah Ampolsk, Riyo Aomoto, Takuya Arai, Konomi Awabayashi, Mariko de Freytas, Eiichiro Funahashi, Jun Kaminishikawara, Hideomi Kinoshita, Kakumi Kobayashi, Yuichi Kubo, Kazuhiro Kurihara, Toru Takei, Hiroto Yoshiura.

KYUNGHYANG DAILY NEWS—(703) 624–3031: Jemin Son.

NEWSPAPERS REPRESENTED—Continued

LA JORNADA—(202) 669–7760; 2708 Fourth Street, NE., Washington, DC 20002: David Brooks.

LA NACION—(202) 744–7737; 1292 National Press Building, Washington, DC 20045: Silvia Pisani.

LA OPINION—(301) 325–4980; 800 4th Street, SW., Washington, DC 20024: Maria Pena.

LA VANGUARDIA—(202) 999–0122; 6812 Algonquin Avenue, Bethesda MD 20817: Jordi Barbeta Sanchez.

LE MAURICIEN—(301) 728–7442; 1084 Pipestem Place, Potomac MD 20854: Pamela Glass.

LIBERTY TIMES—(202) 879–6765; 1294 National Press Building, Washington, DC 20045: Nadia Tsao.

LOCAL NEWS NOW—(703) 348–0583; 1200 18th Street, NW., Washington, DC 20036: Scott Brodbeck, Heather Mongilio.

LONDON DAILY TELEGRAPH—(202) 247–8047; 1310 G Street, NW., Suite 750, Washington, DC 20005: Raf Sanchez.

LOS ANGELES TIMES—(202) 824–8368; 1090 Vermont Avenue, NW., Suite 1000, Washington, DC 20005: Brian Bennett, Noah Bierman, Robert Drogin, Amy Fiscus, Evan Halper, Kathleen Hennessey, David Lauter, Noam Levey, Lisa Mascaro, Doyle McManus, Michael Memoli, Timothy Phelps, Paul Richter, James Robinson, Edmund Sanders, David Savage, Richard Serrano, Joseph Tanfani.

LRP PUBLICATIONS—(703) 350–2198; 1901 North Moore Street, Suite 1106, Arlington VA 22209: Julie Davidson, Jean Gossman, David Kittross, Jeanne Sweeney.

MAEIL BUSINESS NEWSPAPER—909 National Press Building, Washington, DC 20045: Jinmyung Lee.

MAINICHI SHIMBUN—(202) 737–2817; 340 National Press Building, 529 14th Street, NW., Washington, DC 20045: Iva Kovacheva, Shinichiro Nishida, Masaya Oikawa, Kenji Shimizu, Hiroaki Wada.

MALAYA—(703) 715–8879; 10724 Midsummer Drive, Reston, VA 20191: Josefina Ilustre.

MARKET NEWS INTERNATIONAL—(202) 371–2121; 1100 National Press Building, 529 14th Street, NW., Washington, DC 20045: Steven Beckner, John Carter, Denny Gulino, Kevin Kastner, Karen Mracek, Elvina Nawaguna, Braimoh Odion-Esene, Nicholas Olivari, Joseph Plocek, Heather Scott, John Shaw, Tim Weatherhead.

MARKETWATCH—(202) 824–0548; 1025 Connecticut Avenue, NW., Washington, DC 20036: Jeffry Bartash, Steven Goldstein, Rex Nutting, Gregory Robb, Robert Schroeder.

MCCLATCHY NEWSPAPERS—(202) 383–6000; 700 12th Street, NW., Suite 1000, Washington, DC 20005: Beryl Adcock, Hannah Allam, Barbara Barrett, Vera Bergengruen, Michael Bold, Lesley Clark, Sean Cockerham, Danny Dougherty, William Douglas, Michael Doyle, Jessica Gilbert, David Goldstein, Greg Gordon, Rob Hotakainen, Anita Kumar, Jonathan Landay, Yongil Lee, David Lightman, Francisco Ordonez, Anthony Pugh, Maria Recio, Mark Seibel, Curtis Tate, Marisa Taylor, Steven Thomma, Letitia Wells, Lindsay Wise.

MEDPAGE TODAY—13610 Russett Terrace; Rockville MD 20853: Shannon Firth, Joyce Frieden.

MERGER MARKET OF FINANCIAL TIMES—(202) (434) 1075; 1012 14th Street, NW., Suite 915, Washington, DC 20005: David Baumann, Peter Geier, David Hatch, Ryan Lynch, Ryan Lynch, Susan Mandel.

MILITARY.COM—(301) 908–4117; 5505 Connecticut Avenue, NW., Suite 262 Washington, DC 20015: Michael Hoffman, Bryant Jordan, Brendan McGarry, Richard Sisk.

MINNEAPOLIS STAR TRIBUNE—(202) 383–6120; 1090 Vermont Avenue, NW., Suite 1000, Washington, DC 20005: Allison Sherry, Jim Spencer.

MINNPOST—1111 Army Navy Drive, Arlington VA 22202: Sam Brodey.

MLEX US—(202) 909–1238; 1776 I Street, NW., Washington, DC 20006: Jeffrey Bliss, Mark Bocchetti, Can Celik, Liz Crampton, Flavia Fortes, Mark Kennedy, Brittany Melling, Leah Nylen, Chen Qi, Neil Roland, Anjelica Tan, Ira Teinowitz.

MUNWHA ILBO—(202) 270–0148; 1149 National Press Building, Washington, DC 20045: Jea Lee.

NATIONAL JOURNAL—(202) 739–8400; 600 New Hampshire Avenue, NW., Washington, DC 20037: George Condon, Jr., Thomas DeFrank, Shane Goldmacher, Fawn Johnson, Sarah Mimms, Daniel Newhauser, Rachel Roubein, Emily Schultheis.

NEW ORLEANS TIMES-PICAYUNE—(202) 383–7861; 365 Canal Place, Suite 3100, New Orleans, LA 70130: Bruce Alpert.

NEW YORK POST—(202) 393–1787; 1114 National Press Building, Washington, DC 20045: Geoff Earle, Marisa Schultz.

NEW YORK TIMES—(202) 862–0300; 1627 I Street, NW., Suite 700, Washington, DC 20006: Binyamin Appelbaum, Peter Baker, Mikayla Bouchard, Jeremy Bowers, Elisabeth Bumiller, Helene Cooper, Nick Corasaniti, Coral Davenport, Julie Davis, Michael Gordon, Gardiner Harris, David Herszenhorn, Jason Horowitz, David Joachim, Aaron Kessler, Mark Landler, Adam Liptak, Eric Lipton, Jonathan Martin, Ashley Parker, Robert Pear, Alan Rappeport, Matthew Rosenberg, David Sanger, Michael Schmidt, Eric Schmitt, Thomas Shanker, Michael Shear, Andrew Siddons, Jennifer Steinhauer, R. Michael Tackett, Alexander Thompson, Jonathan Weisman, Derek Willis.

NEWSDAY—(202) 408–2715; 1090 Vermont Avenue, NW., Washington, DC 20005: Tom Brune.

NEWSPAPER ENTERPRISE—(301) 320–5559; Bethesda MD 20816: Robert Wagman.

NIKKEI—(202) 393–1388; 815 Connecticut Ave NW, Suite 310, Washington, DC 20006: Tomoko Ashizuka, Christina Bilski, Masako Iwamoto, Motoko Kawachi, Tomoyuki Kawai, Stephen Keefe, Hiroyuki Kotake, Toshiki Yazawa, Naoya Yoshino.

NEWSPAPERS REPRESENTED—Continued

NISHI-NIPPON SHIMBUN—(202) 393-5812; 1012 National Press Building, Washington, DC 20045: Takeshi Yamasaki.

NJ ADVANCE MEDIA—(301) 802-6692; 1101 Connecticut Avenue, Suite 300, Washington, DC 20036: Jonathan Salant.

NOTIMEX MEXICAN NEWS AGENCY—(202) 347-5227; 975 National Press Building, Washington, DC 20045: Ruben Barrera, Maria Garcia, Jose Lopez Zamorano.

O ESTADO DE S. PAULO—(202) 248-0280; 700 13th Street, Suite 555, Washington, DC 20005: Claudia Trevisan.

OIL DAILY—(202) 662-0723; 1411 K Street, NW., Suite 602, Washington, DC 20005: William Murray.

OKLAHOMAN—(202) 459-4921; 1015 15th Street, NW., Suite 500, Washington, DC 20005: Chris Casteel.

OMAHA WORLD-HERALD—(202) 997-9787; 836 National Press Building, Washington, DC 20045: Joseph Morton.

OUEST-FRANCE—Malika Maclouf.

OZY MEDIA—444 Castro Street, Suite 303, Mountain View CA 94041: Emily Cadei.

PHILADELPHIA INQUIRER—(609) 217-8320; 400 North Broad Street; Philadelphia, PA 19130: Jonathan Tamari.

PIONEER-INDIA—(703) 876 6149: Sethuraman Rajagopalan.

PITTSBURGH POST-GAZETTE—(703) 996-9292; 358 North Shore Drive, Pittsburgh, PA 15212. Tracie Mauriello.

POLITICAL MONEY LINE—(202) 237-2500: Kent Cooper.

PRO PUBLICA—(301) 718-4436: Sebastian Rotella.

REAL CLEAR POLITICS—1667 K Street, NW., Suite 1150, Washington, DC 20006: James Arkin, Rebecca Berg, Caitlin Huey-Burns, Alexis Simendinger.

RECORD (BERGEN COUNTY, NJ)—(202) 249-2160; 1 Garret Mountain Plaza, Woodland Park, NJ zero 7424: Herbert Jackson.

RELIGION NEWS SERVICE—(202) 463-8777; 529 14th Street, NW., Suite 425, Washington, DC 20045; Adelle Banks, Kevin Eckstrom, Cathy Lynn Grossman, Lauren Markoe.

RYUKYU SHIMPO—Sakae Toiyama.

SALT LAKE TRIBUNE—(202) 662-8732; 969 National Press Building, Washington, DC 20045: Thomas Burr.

SAN FRANCISCO CHRONICLE—(202) 263-6573; 700 12th Street, NW., Suite 1000, Washington, DC 20005: Carolyn Lochhead.

SANKEI SHIMBUN—(202) 347-2842; 330 National Press Building, Washington, DC 20045: Nobuyuki Aoki, Hiroyuki Kano, Norio Kokumo, Yoshihisa Komori, Bruce Stewart.

SAUDI PRESS AGENCY—(202) 944-3890; 601 New Hampshire Avenue, NW., Washington, DC 20037: Abdulaziz Alhendi, Abdullah Almohaimeed, Haifa Al-Mubarak, Thomas Belman, Geoffrey Cunningham.

SCIENCE & TECHNOLOGY DAILY—(703) 255-1171: Yi He, Xueke Tian.

SCRIP—(301) 216-2433: Donna Young.

SCRIPPS HOWARD NEWS SERVICE—(202) 408-2714; 1100 13th Street, NW., Suite 450, Washington, DC 29995: Marc Georges.

SEGYE TIMES—909 National Press Building, Washington, DC 20045: Jong Hyun Park.

SEKAI NIPPO—(703) 272-8772; 1133 19th Street, NW., 8th Floor, Washington, DC 20036: Yoshiyuki Iwaki

SEOUL SHINMUN DAILY—(202) 393-4061; 905 National Press Building, Washington, DC 20045: Mikyung Kim.

SMARTGRID TODAY—(301) 769-6903: Justin Shilad.

SNL—(434) 977-1600; One SNL Plaza, Charlottesville VA 22902: Joshua Armstrong, Matt Bandyk, Glen Boshant, Christopher Coats, Michael Copley, Marcy Crane, Kyle Daly, Elizabeth Festa, Allison Good, Annalee Grant, William Holland, Michael Lustig, Ximena Mosqueda-Fernandez, Lauren Murphy, Sarah Smith, Sean Sullivan, Esther Whieldon.

ST. LOUIS POST-DISPATCH—(202) 298-6880; 1025 Connecticut Avenue, Suite 1102, Washington, DC 20036: Charles Raasch.

STARS AND STRIPES—(202) 761-0900; 529 14th Street, NW., Suite 350, Washington, DC 20045: Heath Druzin, Travis Tritten.

STEPHENS MEDIA GROUP—(202) 783-1760; 666 11th Street, Suite 535, Washington, DC 20001: Stephan Tetreault, Peter Urban.

SUEDDEUTSCHE ZEITUNG—(301) 469-0650: Nicolas Richter.

SVENSKA DAGBLADET—(202) 362-8253; 3601 Connecticut Avenue, #622, Washington, DC 20008: Karin Henriksson, Gary Yerkey.

SYRACUSE POST-STANDARD—(571) 970-3751; 3900 Fairfax Drive, Suite 1321, Arlington VA 22203: Mark Weiner.

TAGES ANZEIGER—Alexander Batthyany.

TAIWAN CENTRAL NEWS AGENCY—(202) 628-2378; 1173 National Press Building, Washington, DC 20045: Tony Liao Han Yuan.

NEWSPAPERS REPRESENTED—Continued

TAMPA BAY TIMES—(202) 463–0571; 1100 Connecticut Avenue, NW., 4th Floor, Washington, DC 20036: Lauren Carroll, Angie Drobnic Holan, Louis Jacobson, Alex Leary.

TELAM S.E.—(202) 506–3879; 2828 Connecticut Avenue NW., Washington, DC 20008: Melisa Cabo.

THE TEXAS TRIBUNE—Rebecca Livingston.

THOMSON REUTERS—(202) 898–8300; 1333 H Street, Suite 500, Washington, DC 20005: Timothy Ahmann, Charles Alexander, Diane Bartz, Amanda Becker, Eric Beech, Alistair Bell, Joan Biskupic, Melissa Bland, Martin Brandt, Doina Chiacu, Peter Cooney, Susan Cornwell, Richard Cowan, Harold Desmond, Kevin Drawbaugh, Will Dunham, Lindsay Dunsmuir, Julia Edwards, Michael Flaherty, Tim Gardner, Steven Ginsburg, Rodrek Golden, Susan Heavey, Steve Holland, Krista Hughes, Lawrence Hurley, Robert Johnson, Soyoung Kim, Lisa Lambert, Jason Lange, David Lawder, Katherina Lemus, Sarah Lynch, Sandra Maler, Douwe Miedema, Arshad Mohammed, David Morgan, Lucia Mutikani, Essex Noel, James Oliphant, Ayesha Rascoe, Andrea Ricci, Patrick Rucker, Timothy Ryan, Howard Schneider, Alina Selyukh, Andrea Shalal, John Shiffman, Paul Simao, Ian Simpson, Emily Stephenson, Andy Sullivan, Yeganeh Torbati, William Trott, Eric Walsh, Michael Weekes, Jr., John Whitesides, Anna Yukhananov, Mohammad Zargham.

TIMES OF INDIA—(301) 695–9348: Chidanand Rajghatta.

TIMES OF LONDON—(202) 530–9901; 1101 17th Street, NW., Suite 601, Washington, DC 20045: Rhys Blakely, Alexandra Kaye, Matthew Spence, David Taylor.

TOKYO CHUNICHI SHIMBUN—(202) 783–9479; 1012 National Press Building, NW., Washington, DC 20045: Mutsumi Aoki, Conrad Chaffee, Chrishopher Kelly, Yasunobu Saiba, Eri Urano.

TORONTO STAR—(202) 870–0649; 982 National Press Building, Washington, DC 20045: Daniel Dale.

TRIBUNE CONTENT AGENCY—(202) 298–8359: Jules Witcover.

TRIBUNE NEWS SERVICE—(202) 408–1484; 1100 13th Street, NW., Suite 450, Washington, DC 29995: Martin Schram.

UNITED DAILY NEWS—(240) 428–1164; 954 National Press Building, 529 14th Street, NW., Washington, DC 20045: Chao-Ying Lai.

UNITED MEDIA—(301) 494–0430: Lew Sichelman.

UNIVERSAL UCLICK SYNDICATE—(703) 690–8095; 3600 New York Avenue, NE., Washington, DC 20002: Donald Lambro.

USA TODAY—(703) 854–3400; 1575 Eye Street, NW., Suite 350, Washington, DC 20005: William Allen, Jarrett Bell, Marisol Bello, Steve Berkowitz, Erik Brady, Daniel Carney, Carolyn Cerbin, Oren Dorell, Peter Eisler, Gwen Flanders, George Hager, Brad Heath, David Jackson, Bart Jansen, Erin Kelly, Gregory Korte, Katharine Lackey, Donna Leinwand Leger, Ray Locker, Jim Michaels, Susan Page, Fredreka Schouten, Paul Singer, Donovan Slack, William Sternberg, Tom Vanden Brook, Richard Wolf, Alison Young, Gregg Zoroya.

US-REPORT (GERMANY)—(301) 299–5777: Thomas Spang.

UTILITY MARKETS TODAY—(202) 384–4833: James Downing.

VICE NEWS—90 N 11th Street; Brooklyn NY 11249: David Enders, Ryan Faith.

VOTERAMA IN CONGRESS—(202) 332–0857: Richard Thomas.

WALL STREET JOURNAL / DOW JONES—(202) 862–9200; 1025 Connecticut Avenue, NW., Suite 800, Washington, DC 20036: Aruna Viswanatha, Andrew Ackerman, Mark Anderson, Natalie Andrews, Rebecca Ballhaus, Devlin Barrett, Jess Bravin, Autumn Brewington, Thomas Burton, Rodney Christian, Kate Davidson-Choma, Robert Davis, David Allen Dolinger, Gary Fields, James Grimaldi, Amy Harder, Amy Harder, David Harrison, Nell Henderson, Janet Hook, Siobhan Hughes, Brent Kendall, Neil King, Carol Lee, Ben Leubsdorf, Gordon Lubold, Brian McGill, Victoria McGrane, John McKinnon, Laura Meckler, Eric Morath, Daniel Nasaw, Colleen Nelson, Peter Nicholas, Dion Nissenbaum, Paul Page, Damian Paletta, Kristina Peterson, Michael Phillips, Sarah Portlock, Louise Radnofsky, Matthew Rose, Felicia Schwartz, Philip Shishkin, Jeffrey Sparshott, Ian Talley, Byron Tau, Nick Timiraos, Ryan Tracy, Tennile Tracy, Melanie Trottman, Aaron Zitner.

WARREN COMMUNICATIONS NEWS—(202) 872–9202: James Phillips.

WASHINGTON DUPONT CIRCLE NEWS—(202) 328–1121: Irvin Molotsky.

WASHINGTON EXAMINER—(202) 903–2000; 1015 15th Street, NW., Suite 500, Washington, DC 20005: Michael Barone, Paul Bedard, Timothy Carney, Ariel Cohen, Zachary Colman, Tara Copp, Susan Crabtree, Paige Cunningham, David Drucker, Susan Ferrechio, Sean Higgins, Charles Hoskinson, Robert King, Philip Klein, Joseph Lawler, Ryan Lovelace, John Siciliano, Sarah Westwood, Byron York.

WASHINGTON POST—(202) 334–6000; 1150 15th Street, NW., Washington, DC 20071: Nick Anderson, Lori Aratani, Daniel Balz, Robert Barnes, Martin Baron, Niraj Chokshi, Joe Davidson, Aaron Davis, Mike DeBonis, Jose DelReal-Perez, Karoun Demirjian, Karen DeYoung, Paul Duggan, Juliet Eilperin, David Fahrenthold, Mary Pat Flaherty, Brian Fung, Adam Goldman, Hamil Harris, Rosalind Helderman, Arelis Hernandez, Spencer Hsu, Colby Itkowitz, Paul Kane, Dan Keating, Lyndsey Layton, Robert McCartney, Dana Milbank, Gregory Miller, Sylvester Monroe, David Montgomery, Lori Montgomery, Carol Morello, David Nakamura, Amy Nutt, Robert O'Harrow, Edward O'Keefe, Steven Overly, Walter Pincus, Elliot Postell, Eugene Robinson, Rebecca Sinderbrand, Kelsey Snell, Victoria St Martin, Sean Sullivan, Joby Warrick, David Weigel, Rachel Weiner, Craig Whitlock, Scott Wilson, Bob Woodward, Eric Yoder, Matt Zapotosky, Katherine Zezima.

NEWSPAPERS REPRESENTED—Continued

WASHINGTON TELECOMMUNICATIONS SERVICES—(804) 695–4648; 1006 Harrison Circle; Alexandria VA 22304: Gordon White.

WASHINGTON TIMES—(202) 636–3000; 3600 New York Avenue, NE., Washington, DC 20002: David Boyer, Stephen Dinan, Christopher Dolan, Kellan Howell, Thomas Howell, Jacqueline Klimas, Seth McLaughlin, S.A. Miller, Andrea Noble, Kevin Rogers, Kelly Sadler, David Sands, Anjali Shastry, David Sherfinski, Guy Taylor, Cheryl Wetzstein, Margaret Ybarra.

WEN HUI DAILY—(202) 262–6781; 1600 South Eads Street, Suite 1134, North Arlington, VA 22202: Xiaoyang Xia.

WHITE HOUSE DOSSIER—(202) 277–5416: Keith Koffler.

WILLIAM SCALLY REPORTS—(202) 362–2382: William Scally.

WOLFNEWS—(202) 237–1019: Mariuccia Chiantaretto.

WORLD BUSINESS PRESS—(703) 942–8318: Vladimir Amrich, Zuzana Cepla.

WORLD JOURNAL—(202) 751–9023; 954 National Press Building, 529 14th Street, NW., Washington, DC 20045: Zhaoyin Feng, Yu Ling Hu, Xiaoyuan Luo.

XINHUA NEWS AGENCY—(703) 647–1598; 1740 North 14th Street, Arlington VA 22209: Mu Dong, Pan Gao, Xiangwen Ge, Yujuan Jiang, Guan Jianwu, Jie Liu, Jie Liu BC, Jiafei Lu, Lin Xiaochun, Qihang Zheng, Linfei Zhi.

YAHOO NEWS—(202) 669–4950; 1500 K Street, NW., Suite 600, Washington, DC 20005: Olivier Knox, Meredith Shiner.

YOMIURI SHIMBUN—(202) 783–0363; 802 National Press Building, Washington, DC 20045: Yumi Araki, Justin Arnold, Bryant Harris, Takashi Imai, Akira Saito, Yoshikazu Shirakawa, Mineko Tokito, Kunihiko Yasue.

YONHAP NEWS AGENCY—(202) 783–5539; 914 National Press Building, 529 14th Street, NW., Washington, DC 20045: Sejin Kim, Hyodong Roh, In Sung Shim.

PRESS PHOTOGRAPHERS' GALLERY*

The Capitol, Room S–317, 224–6548

www.pressphotographers.senate.gov

Director.—Jeffrey S. Kent.
Deputy Director.—Mark A. Abraham.
Assistant Director.—Tricia Munro.

STANDING COMMITTEE OF PRESS PHOTOGRAPHERS

J. Scott Applewhite, *Chair,* Associated Press
Win McNamee, *Secretary-Treasurer,* Getty Images
Paul Richards, Agence France Presse
Tom Williams, CQ/Roll Call
Stephen Crowley, New York Times
Ronald Sachs, Consolidated News Pictures

RULES GOVERNING PRESS PHOTOGRAPHERS' GALLERY

1. (a) Administration of the Press Photographers' Gallery is vested in a Standing Committee of Press Photographers consisting of six persons elected by accredited members of the Gallery. The Committee shall be composed of one member each from Associated Press Photos; Reuters News Pictures or AFP Photos; magazine media; local newspapers; agency or freelance member; and one at-large member. The at-large member may be, but need not be, selected from media otherwise represented on the Committee; however no organization may have more than one representative on the Committee.

(b) Elections shall be held as early as practicable in each year, and in no case later than March 31. A vacancy in the membership of the Committee occurring prior to the expiration of a term shall be filled by a special election called for that purpose by the Committee.

(c) The Standing Committee of the Press Photographers' Gallery shall propose no change or changes in these rules except upon petition in writing signed by not less than 25 accredited members of the Gallery.

2. Persons desiring admission to the Press Photographers' Gallery of the Senate shall make application in accordance with Rule 33 of the Senate, which rule shall be interpreted and administered by the Standing Committee of Press Photographers subject to the review and approval of the Senate Committee on Rules and Administration.

3. The Standing Committee of Press photographers shall limit membership in the photographers' gallery to bona fide news photographers of repute in their profession and Heads of Photographic Bureaus under such rules as the Standing Committee of Press Photographers shall prescribe.

4. Provided, however, that the Standing Committee of Press Photographers shall admit to the Gallery no person who does not establish to the satisfaction of the Committee all of the following:

(a) That any member is not engaged in paid publicity or promotion work or in prosecuting any claim before Congress or before any department of the Government, and will not become so engaged while a member of the Gallery.

(b) That he or she is not engaged in any lobbying activity and will not become so engaged while a member of the Gallery.

The above rules have been approved by the Committee on Rules and Administration.

PAUL D. RYAN,
Speaker, House of Representatives.

ROY BLUNT,
Chair, Senate Committee on Rules and Administration.

MEMBERS ENTITLED FOR ADMISSION

Ake, David: Associated Press
Alvarez, Miguel: La Prensa Grafica of El Salvador
Andrews, Scott: Canon, USA
Angerer, Drew: Freelance
Antonov, Mladen: Agence France-Presse
Applewhite, J. Scott: Associated Press
Archambault, Charles: Freelance
Arossi, Eddie: Freelance
Ashley, Douglas: Suburban Communications
Augustino, Jocelyn: Freelance
Auth, William: Prensa International
Avci, Erkan: Anadolu Agency
Banks, David: Bloomberg Government
Barouh, Stan: Freelance
Barrett, Stephen: Freelance
Barria, Carlos: Reuters News Pictures
Barrick, Matthew: Freelance
Beiser, H. Darr: USA / Today
Benic, Patrick: United Press International
Berglie, James: Zuma Press
Biddle, Susan: Washington Post
Binks, Porter: Sports Illustrated
Blass, Eileen: USA / Today
Bleier-Schmeets, Karen: Agence France-Presse
Bloom, Richard: National Journal
Boal, John: Freelance
Bongioanni, Carlos: Stars and Stripes
Dotsford, Jabin: Washington Post
Bourg, Jim: Reuters News Pictures
Bowe, Christy: ImageCatcher News
Bowler, Dana: Freelance
Brack, William: Black Star
Brandon, Alex: Associated Press Photos
Brown, Robert: Richmond Times Dispatch
Burke, Lauren: Freelance
Burnett, David: Contact Press Images
Cabrera, Mario: Vision Fotos
Cahallero-Reynolds, Andrew: Agence France-Presse
Calvert, Mary: Freelance
Cameron, Gary: Reuters News Pictures
Campbell, Matt: European Pressphoto Agency
Carioti, Richard: Washington Post
Castoro, Susan: Associated Press Photos
Cedeno, Ken: Freelance
Ceneta, Manuel: Associated Press Photos
Chikwendiu, Jahi: Washington Post
Chung, Andre: Freelance
Clark, Bill: CQ / Roll Call
Cohen, Marshall: Bigmarsh News Photos
Connor, Kristopher: Freelance
Contreras, Oliver: Freelance

Coppage, Gary: Photo Press International
Corum, Samuel: Anadolu Agency
Crowley, Stephen: New York Times
Dan, Bao: Xinhua News Agency
Davidson, Linda: Washington Post
Demczuk, Gabriella: Freelance
Dio, Haiyang: China News Service
Dietsch, Kevin: United Press International
Dougherty, Sean: USA / Today
Douliery, Olivier: Abaca USA
Duarte, Alfredo: El Tiempo Latino
Duggan, James: Freelance
Eile, Evan: USA / Today
Elfers, Stephen: USA / Today
Elswick, Jon: Associated Press Photos
Ernst, Jonathan: Freelance
Falk, Steven: Philadelphia Inquirer
Farrar, Anne: Washington Post
Franko, Jeff: USA / Today
Frey, Katherine: Washington Post
Gail, Carl: Washington Post
Galietta, Wendy: Washington Post
Gamarra, Ruben: EFE News Service
Gandhi, Pareshkumar: Rediff.com / India Abroad
Garcia, Mannie: Freelance
Gilbert, Patrice: Freelance
Glenn, Larry: Freelance
Golden, Melissa: Redux
Golon, MaryAnne: Washington Post
Gripas, Yuri: Freelance
Gromelski, Joseph: Stars and Stripes
Gruber, Jack: USA / Today
Guerrucci, Aude: Polaris Images
Gurbuz, Sait: Freelance
Hambach, Eva: Agence France-Presse
Hamburg, Harry: Freelance
Harnik, Andrew: Associated Press Photos
Harrer, Andrew: Bloomberg
Harrington, John: Black Star
Helber, Stephen: Associated Press Photos
Holt, Victor: Washington Informer
Jennings, Graeme: Washington Examiner
Joachim, Jade-Snow: Washington Post
Jones, Leah: Freelance
Jordan, Kelly: USA / Today
Jorrin, Alexander: Freelance
Joseph, Marvin: Washington Post
Kahn, Greg: Freelance
Kahn, Nikki: Washington Post
Kamm, Nicholas: Agence France-Presse
Kaster, Carolyn: Associated Press Photos

MEMBERS ENTITLED FOR ADMISSION—Continued

Katz, Martin: Chesapeake News Service
Kenasari, Muhammed: Anadolu Agency
Kendall-Ball, Gregory: Freelance
Kennerly, David: Freelance
Key, Michael: Washington Blade
Kim, Hyunsoo: Virginian-Pilot
Kirkpatrick, T.J.: Freelance
Kittner, Sam: Freelance
Kleponis, Chris: Freelance
Kraft, Brooks: Time Magazine
Lamarque, Kevin: Reuters News Pictures
Lamkey, Jr., Rod: Freelance
Lane, Keith: Freelance
Lanham, Yuko: Asahi Shimbun
LaVor, Marty: Freelance
Lawidjaja, Rudy: Freelance
Lessig, Alan: Gannett Government Media
Lewis, Roy: Washington Informer
Lizik, Ronald: Associated Press Photos
Loeb, Saul: Agence France-Presse
Loehrke, Tim: USA/Today
LoScalzo, Jim: European Pressphoto Agency
Lynch, Liz: National Journal
Lynch, Patricia: Freelance
Maddaloni, Chris: Nature
Madrid, Michael: USA/Today
Magana, Jose Luis: Freelance
Mages, Evy: Freelance
Mahaskey, M. Scott: Politico
Malet, Jeff: Freelance
Mallin, Jay: Freelance
Mara, Melina: Washington Post
Markel, Brad: Capri
Marovich, Pete: Freelance
Martin, Jacquelyn: Associated Press Photos
Martinez Monsivais, Pablo: Associated Press
Mathieson, Greg: MAI Photo Agency
McClain, Matt: Washington Post
McDonnell, John: Washington Post
McNamee, Win: Getty Images
Meyer, Cheryl: McClatchy Washington Bureau
Milbrett, Jennifer: Gannett Government Media
Miller, Mark: Washington Post
Miller, Robert: Washington Post
Mills, Douglas: New York Times
Morigi, Paul: Freelance
Morones, Mike: Gannett Government Media
Mount, Bonnie: Washington Post
Naji-Allah, Khalid: Washington Informer
Nash, Gregory: The Hill
Newton, Jonathan: Washington Post
Ngan, Mandel: Agence France-Presse
Nipp, Lisa: Freelance
Nolly Araujo, Angel: Notimex
Nordby, Leslie: Freelance
O'Leary, William: Washington Post
Ommanney, Charles: Washington Post

Owen, Clifford: Freelance
Palu, Louie: Zuma Press
Panagos, Dimitrios: Greek American News
Partlow, Wayne: Associated Press Photos
Patterson, Kathryn: Freelance
Petros, Bill: Freelance
Powers, Carol: Freelance
Powers, Christopher: USA/Today
Premack, Jay: Freelance
Propp, Andrew: Washingtonian
Purcell, Steven: Freelance
Radzinschi, Diego: National Law Journal
Reinhard, Rick: Impact Digitals
Reynolds, Michael: European Pressphoto Agency
Ricardel, Vincent: Freelance
Richards, Paul: Agence France-Presse
Riecken, Astrid: Freelance
Riley, Molly: Freelance
Roberts, Joshua: Freelance
Rolfe, Judy: Freelance
Ryan, Patrick: Freelance
Sachs, Ronald: Consolidated News Pictures
Salisbury, Barbara: Freelance
Samperton, Kyle: Freelance
Sandys, Toni: Washington Post
Saunders, Ray: Washington Post
Savi, Riccardo: Freelance
Schaeffer-Hopkins, Sandra: MAI Photo Agency
Schmalz, Julia: Chronicle of Higher Education
Scott, Andrew: USA/Today
Shelley, Allison: Freelance
Shinkle, John: Politico
Simon, Martin: Corbis
Smialowski, Brendan: Agence France-Presse
Soares, Jared: Freelance
Somodevilla, Kenneth: Getty Images
Sortino, Anna: Daily Caller
Squires, Derek: Tax Analysts'
Susslin, Chet: National Journal
Swall, Lexey: Freelance
Sweets, Fredric: St. Louis American
Sykes, Jack: Professional Pilot Magazine
Szenes, Jason: Freelance
Tatlow, Dermot: Panos Pictures
Theiler, Michael: Freelance
Thew, Shawn: European Pressphoto Agency
Tines, Charles: The Detroit News
Traywick, Catherine: Bloomberg Government
Tripplaar, Kristoffer: Sipa Press
Usher, Chris: Freelance
Varias, Stelios: Reuters News Pictures
Vasquez, Ricardo: Stars and Stripes
Vick, Vanessa: Freelance
Vogel, Leigh: Freelance
Voisard, Amanda: Freelance
Voisin, Sarah: Washington Post
Voss, Stephen: Freelance

MEMBERS ENTITLED FOR ADMISSION—Continued

Vucci, Evan: Associated Press Photos
Walsh, Susan: Associated Press Photos
Watkins, Fred: Freelance
Watson, James: Agence France-Presse
Wells, Jonathan: Sipa Press
Westcott, Jay: Freelance
Wiegold, David: 1105 Media
Williams, Tom: CQ/Roll Call
Williamson, Michael: Washington Post

Wilson, Mark: Getty Images
Wolf, Kevin: Freelance
Wolf, Lloyd: Freelance
Wong, Alex: Getty Images
Woolfolk, Daniel: Gannett
Yim, Heesoon: Hana
Yin, Bogu: Xinhua News Agency
Zhang, Weiran: China News Service

SERVICES REPRESENTED

(Service and telephone number, office address, and name of representative)

1105 MEDIA—8609 Westwood Center Drive, Vienna, VA 22182–2215: Wiegold, David.
ABACA USA—989 6th Avenue, New York City, NY 10018: Douliery, Oliver.
AGENCE FRANCE PRESSE—(202) 414–0521; 1500 K Street, NW., Suite 600, Washington, DC 20005: Mladen, Antonov; Bleir–Schmeets, Karen; Cahellero-Reynolds, Andrew; Hambach, Eva; Kamm, Nicholas; Loeb, Saul; Ngan, Mandel; Richards, Paul; Smialowski,, Brendan; Watson, James.
ANADOLU—1131 National Press Building, Washington, DC 20045: Avic, Erkan; Corum, Samuel; Kensari, Muhammed.
ASAHI SHIMBUN—(202) 783–1000; 1022 National Press Building, 529 14th Street, NW., Washington, DC 20045: Lanham, Yuko.
ASSOCIATED PRESS PHOTOS—(202) 641–9520; 1100 13th Street, NW., Suite 700, Washington, DC 20005: Ake, David; Applewhite, J. Scott; Brandon, James Alex; Castoro, Susan; Ceneta, Manuel B.; Elswick, Ron; Harnik, Andrew; Helber, Stephen; Kaster, Carolyn; Lizik, Ron; Martin, Jacquelyn; Martinez Monsivas, Pablo; Partlow, Wayne; Vucci, Evan; Walsh, Susan.
BIGMARSH NEWS PHOTOS—(202) 364–8332; 5131 52nd Street, NW., Washington, DC 20016: Cohen, Marshall.
BLACK STAR—(703) 547–1176; 7704 Tauxemont Road, Alexandria, VA 22308: Brack, William; Harrington, John.
BLOOMBERG GOVERNMENT—(202) 654–7300; 1399 New York Avenue, Washington, DC 20005: Banks, David; Harrer, Andrew.
CONSOLIDATED NEWS PICTURES—(202) 543–3203; 10305 Leslie Street, Silver Spring, MD 20902–4857: Sachs, Ronald.
CQ/Roll Call—(202) 650–6844; 77 K Street, NE., Washington, DC 20002: Clark, Bill; Williams, Tom.
EFE NEWS SERVICE–7906 Georgia Avenue, Silver Spring, MD 20906: Ruben, Gamara.
EUROPEAN PRESS PHOTO—(202) 347–4694; 529 14th Street, NW., Suite 1122, Washington, DC 20045: Campbell, Matt; LoScalzo, Jim; Reynolds, Michael; Thew, Shawn.
GANNET GOVERNMENT MEDIA—(703) 750–8196; 6993 Commercial Drive, Springfield, VA 22515: Lessig, Alan; Milbrett, Jennifer; Morones, Mike.
GETTY IMAGES—(202) 347–2050; National Press Building, 529 14th Street, NW., Suite 1125, Washington, DC 20045: McNamee, Win; Somodevilla, Kenneth; Wilson, Mark L.; Wong, Alex.
GREEK AMERICAN NEWS AGENCY—(516) 931–2333; 37 Field Avenue, Hicksville, NY 11801: Panagos, Dimitrios.
HANA—(202) 262–4541; 11311 Park Drive, Fairfax, VA 22030: Yim, Heesoon.
IMAGE CATCHER NEWS—4911 Hampden Lane, Bethesda, MD 20815: Bowe, Christy.
IMPACT DIGITALS—(212) 614–8406; 171 Thompson Street, #9, New York, NY 10012: Reinhard, Rick.
LA PRENSA GRAFICA OF EL SALVADOR—(503) 2241–2670; Boulevard Santa Elena, Antiguo Casadian: Alvarez, Miguel Angel.
MAI PHOTO AGENCY—(703) 968–0030; 6601 Ashmere Lane, Centreville, VA 20120: Mathieson, Greg; Schaeffer, Sandra.
MCCLATCHY TRIBUNE—(703) 383–6142; 700 12th Street, NW., Suite 1000, Washington, DC 20005: Meyer, Cheryl.
NATIONAL JOURNAL—(202) 739–8400; 600 New Hampshire Avenue, NW., Washington, DC 20037: Bloom, Richard; Susslin, Chet; Lynch, Liz.
NATIONAL LAW JOURNAL–6516 Gardenwick Road, Baltimore, MD 21209: Radzinschi, Diego.
NOTIMEX—(202) 347–5227; 529 14th Street, NW., Suite 425, Washington, DC 20045–1401: Araju, Angel Nolly.
PANOS—(617) 710–7413; Unit K, Reliance Wharf Hertford Road, London, N15EW, UK: Tatlow, Dermott.
PHILADELPHIA INQUIRER—400 N Broad St., Philadelphia, PA 19130: Falk, Stephen.
POLITICO—(703) 647–7694: 200 Wilson Boulevard, 6th Floor, Alexandria, VA: Mahasky, Scott; Shinkle, John.
PHOTO PRESS INTERNATIONAL—(540) 286–1045; P.O. Box 190, Goldvein, VA 22720: Coppage, Gary.
POLARIS IMAGES–259 West 30th Street, 13th Floor, New York, NY 10001: Guerrucci, Aude.
PROFESSIONAL PILOT MAGAZINE–3014 Colvin Street, Alexandria, VA 22314: Sykes, Jack.
REDIFF.COM/INDIA ABROAD PUB.—(646) 432–6054; 43 West 24th Street, 2nd Floor, New York, NY 10010: Gandhi, Pareshkumar.

SERVICES REPRESENTED—Continued

REUTERS NEWS PICTURES—(202) 898–8333, 1333 H Street, NW., Suite 500, Washington, DC 20005: Bourg, Jim; Cameron, Gary; Lamarque, Kevin; Varias, Stelios.

REDUX—(212) 253–0399; 11 Hanover Square, 26th Floor, New York, NY 10005: Golden, Melissa.

RICHMOND TIMES—(804) 649–6000; 300 East Franklin Street, Richmond, VA 23219: Brown, Robert.

SIPA PRESS—(212) 463–0150; 307 7th Avenue, Suite 807, New York, NY 10001: Triplar, Kristoffer. Wells, Jonathan.

SUBURBAN COMMUNICATIONS CORP.—(248) 568–0006; 872 Dursley Road, Bloomfield Hills, ME 48304: Ashley, Douglas.

THE DETROIT NEWS—(312) 222–2030; 615 West Lafayette Avenue, Photo Department, Detroit, MI 48226: Tines, Charles.

THE HILL—(202) 628–8525; 1625 K Street, Suite 900, Washington, DC 20006: Nash, Greg.

THE NEW YORK TIMES—(202) 862–0300; 1627 Eye Street, NW., Washington, DC 20006: Crowley, Stephen; Mills, Douglas.

STARS AND STRIPES—529 14th St., NW., Suite 350, Washington, DC 20045: Bongioanni, Carlos; Gromelski, Carlos; Vasquez.

THE WASHINGTON INFORMER—(202) 561–4100; 3117 Martin L. King Avenue, SE., Washington, DC 20032: Holt, Victor.

THE WASHINGTON EXAMINER—(202) 903–2000; 1015 15th Street, NW., Suite 500, Washington, DC 20005: Jennings, Graeme.

TIME MAGAZINE—(202) 861–4062; 1130 Connecticut Avenue, Suite 900, Washington, DC 20036: Kraft, Brooks.

THE WASHINGTON POST—(202) 334–7380; 1150 15th Street, NW., Washington, DC 20071: Botsford, Jahin; Biddle, Susan; Carioti, Richard; Chikwendiu, Jahi; Davidson, Linda; Farrar, Anne; Frey, Katherine; Gail, Carl; Galieta, Wendy; Golon, MaryAnne; Joachim, Jade–Snow; Joseph, Marvin; Kahn, Nikki; Mara, Melina; McClain, Matt; McDonnell, John; Miller, Mark; Miller, Robert; Mount, Bonnie; Newton, Jonathan; O'Leary, William, Ommaney, Charles; Sandys, Toni; Saunders, Ray; Voisin, Sarah; Williamson, Michael.

THE YOMIURI SHIMBUN—Room 208, National Press Building, Washington, DC 20045: Konishi, Taro.

UNITED PRESS INTERNATIONAL—(202) 898–8071; 1133 19th Street, Suite 800, Washington, DC 20036: Benic, Patrick T.; Dietsch, Kevin.

USA/TODAY—(703) 854–5216; 7950 Jones Branch Road, McLean, VA 22107: Beiser, H. Darr; Blass, Eileen; Cochran, Mick; Dougherty, Sean; Eile, Evan; Franko, Jeff; Garrett; Madrid, Michael; Jordan, Kelley; Loehrke, Tim; Powers, Chris; Scott, Andrew.

VIRINGIA PILOT—(757) 446–2000; 150 West Brambleton Avenue, Norfolk, VA 23510: Kim, Eugene; Hyunsoo Lee.

VISION PHOTOS–9708 Hale Drive, Clinton, MD 20735: Cabrera, Mario.

WASHINGTONIAN—(202) 296–3600; 1828 L Street, NW., #200, Washington, DC 20036: Propp, Andrew.

XINHUA NEWS AGENCY—(703) 875–0082; 1740N 14th Street, Arlington, VA 22209: Dan Dan Bao; Yim Bogu.

ZUMA PRESS—34189 Pacific Coast Highway, Dana Point, CA 92629: Palu, Louie.

FREELANCE

Freelance-Angerer, Drew, Archambault, Charlon; Augustino, Jocelyn; Barnin, Sian, Barrett, Stephen, Darrick, Matthew; Boal, John; Bowler, Dana; Burke, Lauren; Calvert, Mary; Cedeno, Ken; Chung, Andre; Connor, Kristopher; Contreras, Oliver; Demczuk, Gabriella; Duggan, James; Ernst, Jonathan; Garcia, Mannie; Gilbert, Patrice; Glenn, Larry; Gripas, Yuri; Gurbuz, Sait; Hamburg, Harry; Jones, Leah; Jorrin, Alexander; Kahn; Kendall-Ball, Gregory; Kennerly, David; Kirkpatrick, T.J.; Kittner, Sam; Kleponis, Chris; Lamkey, Jr., Rod; Lane, Keith; LaVor, Marty; Lawidjaja, Rudy; Lynch, Patricia; Magana, Jose Luis; Mages, Evy; Malet, Jeff; Mallin, Jay; Marovich, Pete; Morigi, Paul; Nipp, Lisa; Nordby, Leslie; Owen, Clifford; Patterson, Kathryn; Petros, Bill, Powers; Carol; Premack, Jay; Purcell, Steven; Ricardel, Vincent; Riecken, Astrid; Riley, Molly; Roberts, Joshua; Rolfe, Judy; Ryan, Patrick; Salisbury, Barbara; Samperton, Kyle; Savi, Riccardo; Shelley, Allison; Soares, Jared; Swall, Lexey; Szenes, Jason; Theiler, Michael; Usher, Chris; Vick, Vanessa; Vogel, Leigh; Voisard, Amanda; Voss, Stephen; Watkins, Fred; Westcott, Jay; Wolf, Kevin; Wolf, Lloyd.

WHITE HOUSE NEWS PHOTOGRAPHERS' ASSOCIATION

P.O. Box 7119, Ben Franklin Station, Washington, DC 20044–7119
www.whnpa.org

OFFICERS

Whitney Shefte, WTTG–TV, *President*
Jim Bourg, Reuters, *Vice President*
A.J. Chavar, The New York Time, *Secretary*
Jonathan Elswick, Associated Press, *Treasurer*

EXECUTIVE BOARD

Brendan Smialowski (AFP)
Pablo Martinez Monsivais (Associated Press)
Joshua Roberts (Freelance)
Rodney Batten (NBC News)
Nathan Luna (Hearst TV)
Brad Fulton (CTV)
Nikki Kahn, Contest Chair, Still (Washington Post)
Pege Gilgannon, Contest Co-Chair, Video (WJLA–TV)
Doug Wilkes, Contest Co-Chair, Video (WTTG–TV)
Pierre Kattar, Contest Chair, Multimedia (Freelance)
Kevin Dietsch, Contest Chair, Student (UPI)
Bethany Swain, Contest Co-Chair, Student (University of Maryland)
Pablo Martinez Monsivais, Education Chair (Associated Press)

MEMBERS REPRESENTED

Abdallah, Khalil: CNN
Abraham, Mark: Freelance
Adlerblum, Robin: Freelance
Ake, J. David: Associated Press
Albert, Christopher: CBS News
Alberter, Jr., William: CNN
Allard, Marc: Freelance
Allen, Tom: Washington Post, (Ret.)
Amarai, Kainaz: NPR
Anderson, Kristina: Freelance
Angerer, Drew: Freelance
Applewhite, J. Scott: Associated Press
Apt Johnson, Roslyn: CBS News
Ashley, Douglas: Surburban News Group & ABC TV
Assaf, Christopher: Baltimore Sun
Auth, William: Freelance
Bahler, Barry: Dept. of Homeland Security
Bahruth, William: (Ret.)
Barria, Carlos: Reuters
Barrick, Matthew: Freelance
Batten, Rodney: NBC News
Baysden III, Earl: WTTG–TV

Beiser, H. Darr: USA Today
Bena, John: CNN
Benic, Patrick: UPI
Bennett, Ronald T.: (Ret.)
Berglie, James: Zuma Press
Berkman, Eliezer: Freelance
Biddle, Jr., Michael: Freelance
Biddle, Susan: Freelance
Bing, Bonita: Freelance
Binks, Porter: Freelance
Bivera, Johnny: Freelance
Blair, Adam: ITN
Blaylock, Kenneth: (Ret.)
Bodnar, John: CNN
Bourg, James: Reuters
Bowe, Christy: ImageCatcher News
Bowler, Dana Rene: Freelance
Brack, Dennis: Black Star
Brandon, Alex: Associated Press
Brantley, James R.: Freelance
Brown, Stephen: Freelance
Brown, Randall: NBC News
Brown, Sr., Henry: (Ret.)

MEMBERS REPRESENTED—Continued

Brusk, Steven: CNN
Bryan, Beverly: Freelance
Buell, Hal: AP (Ret.)
Burgess, Robert: Freelance
Burke, Jr., William C.: Page One Photography
Burnett, David: Contact Press Images
Calvert, Mary: Washington Times
Cameron, Gary: Reuters
Cannarozzi, Melissa: Newhouse News Service
Carioti, Ricky: Washington Post
Castoro, Susan: Associated Press
Cedeno, Ken: Freelance
Ceneta, Manuel: Associated Press
Chavar, Anthony: The Washington Post
Chikwendiu, Jahi: Washington Post
Christian, George: CBS News
Chung, Andre: Baltimore Sun
Cirace, Robert: CNN, retired
Clark, Bill: Roll Call
Clarkson, Rich: Rich Clarkson & Associates
Cohen, Marshall H.: Big Marsh News Photos
Colburn, James: Freelance
Cole, Adam: NPR
Collins, Maxine: BBC TV
Conger, Dean: Freelance
Conner, Eric: Fox News Network
Connor, Kristopher: freelance
Contreras, Oliver: Washington Hispanic / ZUMA
   Press
Cook, Dennis: Associated Press, retired
Costello II, Thomas: Asbury Park Press
Curran, Patrick: WTTG–TV
Curtiss, Cathaleen: AOL
Czarnecki, Forrest:
D'Agostino, Matthew: White House Historical
   Association
D'Angelo, Rebecca: Freelance
Daugherty, Bob: Associated Press, retired
Davidson, Linda: Washington Post
Davis, Amy: Baltimore Sun
de la Cruz, Benedict: Washingtonpost.com
Delaney, Danita: The Washington Afro
Demczuk, Gabriella:
Desfor, Max:
Devorah, Carrie: Freelance (Ret.)
DiBartolo, Melissa: Nikon
Dietsch, Kevin: UPI
Doane, Martin: WJLA–TV
Dorwin, Harold: Freelance
Dotschkal, Janna: National Geographic
Douliery, Oliver: Abaca Press
Downing, Larry: Reuters
Drapkin, Arnold: TIME Magazine
Druce, Ian: BBC
Dukehart, Coburn: National Geographic
Dukehart, Jr., Thomas: WUSA–TV, retired
Dunmire, John: WTTG–TV, retired
Eaves, Ed: NBC News

Edmonds, Ron: Associated Press
Edrington, Michael: DMIOC
Elswick, Jonathan: Associated Press
Epstein, Linda: Freelance
Ernst, Jonathan: Freelance
Ewen, McKenna: The Washington Post
Ewing, David: Freelance / NBC News
Falk, Steven: Philadelphia Daily News
Farmer, Sharon: Freelance
Feld, Ric: Associated Press
Feldman, Randy: Viewpoint Communications Inc.
Fielman, Sheldon: NBC News
Fine, Paul: Fine Films
Fine, Holly: Fine Films
Folwell, Frank: Freelance
Fookes, Gary: Freelance (Ret.)
Ford, Nancy: IFPO / American International News
Forrest, James: WRC (Ret.)
Foss, Philip: Freelance
Foster, William: Freelance
Frame, John: WTTG–TV
Fridrich, George: Brighter Images Productions LLC
Fuchs, Christian: Jesuit Refugee Service / USA
Fulton, Bradley: CTV
Gail, C. Mark: Freelance
Gainer, Dennis: USA Today
Garcia, Mannie: Freelance
Geiger, Ken: National Geographic
Geissinger, Michael: Freelance
Gentilo, Richard: Associated Press
Gilgannon, Pege: WJLA
Gmiter, Bernard: ABC News / Freelance (Ret.)
Golden, Melissa: Freelance
Goodman, Jeffrey: NBC / Freelance
Gorman, James: Associated Press
Goyal, Raghubir: Asia Today & India Globe / ATN
   News
Grant, Kelli: Yahoo! News
Greenblatt, William: United Press International
Guerrucci, Aude: Ploaris
Gurbuz, Sait Serkan: Freelance
Haefeli, Brian: Freelance
Hale Thomas, Susan: Freelance
Halstead, Dirck: The Digital Journalist
Hanley-Jette, Patricia: WNET
Harlan, Jeremy: CNN
Harmatz, Ben: Student
Harnik, Andrew: The Associated Press
Harrer, Andrew: Bloomberg
Harrington, John: Freelance
Harrity, Chick: Whimsy Works
Heikes, Darryl: Freelance
Heilemann, Tami: Department of Interior
Hill, Robert: Australian Broadcasting Corp.
Hillian, Vanessa: Washington Post, retired
Hinds, Hugh: WRC / NBC
Hopkins, Brian: WJLA–TV
Horan, Michael: WTTG–TV

MEMBERS REPRESENTED—Continued

Horn, Brad: The Washington Post
Hoyt, Michael: Catholic Standard
Huff, Daniel: Associated Press
Imai, Kesaharu: World Photo Press
Ing, Lance: WTTG–TV
Ingalls, Bill: NASA e Management
Irby, Kenneth: Poynter Institute
Jaeger, Kevin: WJLA–TV
Jennings, Graeme: Washington Examiner
Johnson, Kenneth: ABC–TV
Johnston, Frank: Washington Post
Jones, Nelson: WTTG–TV
Jones, Donnamarie: DCTV
Joseph, Marvin: Washington Post
Judge, Michel: NBC News / Comcast
Kahn, Nikki: Washington Post
Kapustin, Doug: Freelance
Kaster, Carolyn: Associated Press
Kattar, Pierre: Freelance
Katz, Marty: Chesapeake News Service
Kennerly, David Hume: Eagles Roar Inc.
Kent, Jeffrey: Press Photographers' Gallery
Kerchner, Eric: CBS News
Kirkpatrick, TJ: Freelance
Kittner, Sam: Freelance
Kleber, David: (Ret.)
Koppelman, Mitch: Reuters Television
Kozak, Rick: Military Times, (Ret.)
Kraft, Brooks: Time Magazine
Lamarque, Kevin: Reuters
Lambert, H.M.: (Ret.)
Lamkey, Jr., Rod: Freelance
Landy, John: BBC
Larsen, Gregory: Freelance
Lavies, Bianca: Freelance
LaVor, Marty: Freelance
Lawrence, Jeffrey: Freelance
Leaming, Whitney: The Washington Post
Lee, Donald: CBS News
Levine, Lewis: Costal News Service
Levy, Glenn Ann: Freelance
Lizik, Ronald: Associated Press
Lockhart, June: Associate
Loeb, Saul: AFP
LoScalzo, James: EPA
Love, Diane: American University in Bulgaria
Luna, Nathan: CTV (Canadian)
Lynaugh, Mike: Freelance
Lynch, Patricia: Freelance
Lyons, Paul: NET, (Ret.)
MacDonald, Charles: National Geographic Channel
Magana, Jose Luis: Freelance
Mager, Dickon: Sky News
Mallin, Jay: Freelance
Mara, Melina: Washington Post
Markel, Harry: MorePhotos
Marovich, Jr., Peter: Freelance / Corbis

Martin, Ben: ITN
Martin, Gina: National Geographic
Martin, Jacquelin: AP
Martineau, Gerald: Washington Post, (Ret.)
Martinez Monsivais, Pablo: Associated Press
Mason, Thomas: WTTG–TV / retired
Mathieson, Greg: MAI Photo News Agency, Inc.
Mazariegos, Mark: CBS News
Maze, Stephanie: Moonstone Press LLC
Mazer Field, Joni: Freelance
Mazzatenta, O. Louis: Freelance
McCarthy III, Edward: Hudson Valley Black Press / Hudson Valley Press / Hudson Valley News & Entertainment Network
McCarty, Dennis Page: CBS News
McClain, Matthew: Washington Post
McDermott, Richard: NBC Universal
McDonnell, John: Washington Post
McGreevy, Allen: Freelance
McKenna, William: BBC World News America
McKiernan, Scott: Zuma Press
McMichael IV, Samuel: CNN
McNamee, Win: Getty Images
McNamee, Wallace: Freelance
McNay, James: Senior Editor Kobre Guide
McNeeley, Chad: Nikon
Mills, Doug: New York Times
Mock-Bunting, Logan: Freelance
Mole, Robert: NBC, (Ret.)
Moorhead, Jeremy: CNN
Morones, Michael: Military Times
Morris, Larry: Washington Post, (Ret.)
Morris, Peter: CNN
Moulton, Paul: (Ret.)
Mount, Bonnie Jo: Washington Post
Mounts, Ronald: WJLA–TV
Mummert, John: USGA
Murphy, Zoeann: The Washington Post
Murphy, John: Freelance
Murtaugh, Peter: Murtaugh Productions, LLC
Natoli, Sharon: Freelance
Newton, Jonathan: Washington Post
Nguyen, Phi: U.S. House of Representatives
Nighswander, Marcia: Ohio University
Nikpour, Javad: Metropole Photo
Nolan, David: Nolan & Company
Norling, Richard: Freelance
O'Leary, William: Washington Post
O'Molloy, Colm: Freelance / BBC
Osterreicher, Mickey: NPPA
Panzer, Chester: NBC–WRC
Parcell, James: Washington Post, (Ret.)
Partlow, Wayne: Associated Press
Petros, Bill: Freelance
Pinczuk, Samuel: Student
Pinczuk, Murray: Freelance
Polich, John: (Ret.)
Poole, John: NPR

MEMBERS REPRESENTED—Continued

Popper, Andrew: Freelance
Postovit, David: Hearst Television WNB
Potasznik, David: Point of View Production Services Inc.
Powell, Lee: The Washington Post
Powell, Jr., William: NBC/(Ret.)
Powers, Carol: Freelance
Proser, Michael: ABC–News
Rensberger, Scott: Freelance
Reynolds, Michael: European Pressphoto Agency
Ribeiro, Luiz: Freelance
Richards, Paul: AFP
Richardson, Charlotte: Freelance
Riecken, Astrid: Freelance
Riley, Molly: Freelance
Roberts, Joshua: Freelance
Robinson Sr., Clyde: (Ret.)
Rosen, Alexander: CNN
Roth, Jr., Johnie: NBC, (Ret.)
Sachs, Ronald: Consolidated News Photos
Samad, Jewel: AFP
Sandys, Toni: Washington Post
Sardari, Kaveh: Sardari Group, Inc.
Schmick, Paul: Freelance, retired
Schneider, Jack: NBC–TV
Schwartz, Herb: CBS News
Shefte, Whitney: Washingtonpost.com
Shelley, Allison: Freelance
Shepherd, Ray: Defense Media Activity
Sheppard, Kevin: Sky News
Sheras, Michael: Canon USA, Inc.
Shinkle, John: Politico
Shlemon, Christopher: Independent TV News
Sierra, Joann: CNN
Sikes, Laura: Freelance
Silverberg, James: The Intellectual Property Group, PLLC
Silverman, Gabriel: The Washington Post
Sisco, Paul: (Ret.)
Skeans, Jr., Ronald: BBC
Smialowski, Brendan: Freelance
Smith, Patrick: Freelance
Smith, Andrew: CCTV
Smyth, Christopher: Hearst
Sommer, Emilie: Freelance Emilie Inc. Photography
Somodevilla, Kenneth: Getty Images
Stanke, Donald: CCTV America
Stein, Norman: Freelance
Stein III, Arthur: Freelance
Stewart, Jr., Charles: Hudson Valley Press

Stoddard, Mark: Freelance
Suban, Mark: Nikon
Suddeth, Rick: Freelance
Swain, Bethany Anne:
Sweetapple, Daniel: Australian Broadcasting Corp.
Swenson, Gordon: ABC, retired
Swiatkowski, Edward:
Sykes, Jack: American Systems
Tessmer, Joseph: Freelance
Thomas, Margaret: (Ret.)
Tiffen, Steve: The Tiffen Company
Tolbert IV, George Dalton: Freelance/Ret. U.S. Senate
Trippett, Robert: Freelance
Turner, Rob: ITN
Uhl, Kim: CNN
Usher, Chris: Freelance
Valeri, Charlene: National Geographic
Varias, Stelios: Reuters
Vicario, Virginia: ABC News/retired
Vineys, Kevin: Associated Press
Vogel, Leigh: Freelance
Voisin, Sarah: Washington Post
Voss, Stephen: Freelance
Vucci, Evan: Associated Press
Vurnis, Ambrose: NBC News/WRC-TV
Walker, Diana: Freelance
Wallace, Jim: Smithsonian Institution
Walsh, Susan: Associated Press
Ward, Fred: Black Star
Watkins, Duane: Media Links CCTV
Watrud, Donald: WTTG–TV
Watson, James: AFP
Weik, David: ABC Television News (Ret.)
Wescott, William: Freelance
Wiegman, Jr., Dave: NBC (Ret.)
Wilkes, Douglas: WTTG–TV
Williams, Milton: Freelance, (Ret.)
Williams, Thomas: Roll Call Newspaper
Williams, Robert: NBC News
Williams Babic, Indira: Newseum
Williamson, Michael: Washington Post
Wilson, Jim: New York Times Photo
Wilson, Mark: Getty Images
Witte, Joel: CCTV
Wong, Alex: Getty Images
Yarmuth, Floyd: CNN
Zervos, Stratis: Freelance

RADIO AND TELEVISION CORRESPONDENTS' GALLERIES*

SENATE RADIO AND TELEVISION GALLERY

The Capitol, Room S–325, 224–6421

Director: Michael J. Mastrian
Deputy Director: Ellen Eckert
Senior Media Coordinators: Michael Lawrence, Erin Yeatman
Media Coordinators: Charles Moxley, Jason Botelho

HOUSE RADIO AND TELEVISION GALLERY

The Capitol, Room H–320, 225–5214

Director: Olga Ramirez Kornacki
Deputy Director: Andy Elias
Senior Media Logistics Coordinator: Kim Oates
Media Logistics Coordinators: Ryan Dahl, Kinsey Harvey, Anthony Kellaher, Leah Kaplan

EXECUTIVE COMMITTEE OF THE RADIO AND TELEVISION CORRESPONDENTS' GALLERIES

Fred Haberstick, C–SPAN, *Chair*
John Parkinson, ABC, *Vice Chair*
Frank Thorp, NBC, *Treasurer*
Alicia Amling, CBS News
Margaret Chadbourne, FOX News
Lisa Desjardins, PBS NewsHour
Steve Jacobi, CBN News

RULES GOVERNING RADIO AND TELEVISION CORRESPONDENTS' GALLERIES

1. Persons desiring admission to the Radio and Television Galleries of Congress shall make application to the Speaker, as required by Rule 34 of the House of Representatives, as amended, and to the Committee on Rules and Administration of the Senate, as required by Rule 33, as amended, for the regulation of the Senate wing of the Capitol. Applicants shall state in writing the names of all radio stations, television stations, systems, or news-gathering organizations by which they are employed and what other occupation or employment they may have, if any. Applicants shall further declare that they are not engaged in the prosecution of claims or the promotion of legislation pending before Congress, the Departments, or the independent agencies, and that they will not become so employed without resigning from the Galleries. They shall further declare that they are not employed in any legislative or executive department or independent agency of the Government, or by any foreign government or representative thereof; that they are not engaged in any lobbying activities; that

---

*Information is based on data furnished and edited by each respective Gallery.

they do not and will not, directly or indirectly, furnish special information to any organization, individual, or group of individuals for the influencing of prices on any commodity or stock exchange; that they will not do so during the time they retain membership in the Galleries. Holders of visitors' cards who may be allowed temporary admission to the Galleries must conform to all the restrictions of this paragraph.

2. It shall be a prerequisite to membership that the radio station, television station, system, or news-gathering agency which the applicant represents shall certify in writing to the Radio and Television Correspondents' Galleries that the applicant conforms to the foregoing regulations.

3. The applications required by the above rule shall be authenticated in a manner that shall be satisfactory to the Executive Committee of the Radio and Television Correspondents' Galleries who shall see that the occupation of the Galleries is confined to bona fide news gatherers and/or reporters of reputable standing in their business who represent radio stations, television stations, systems, or news-gathering agencies engaged primarily in serving radio stations, television stations, or systems. It shall be the duty of the Executive Committee of the Radio and Television Correspondents' Galleries to report, at its discretion, violation of the privileges of the Galleries to the Speaker or to the Senate Committee on Rules and Administration, and pending action thereon, the offending individual may be suspended.

4. Persons engaged in other occupations, whose chief attention is not given to—or more than one-half of their earned income is not derived from—the gathering or reporting of news for radio stations, television stations, systems, or news-gathering agencies primarily serving radio stations or systems, shall not be entitled to admission to the Radio and Television Galleries. The Radio and Television Correspondents' List in the Congressional Directory shall be a list only of persons whose chief attention is given to or more than one-half of their earned income is derived from the gathering and reporting of news for radio stations, television stations, and systems engaged in the daily dissemination of news, and of representatives of news-gathering agencies engaged in the daily service of news to such radio stations, television stations, or systems.

5. Members of the families of correspondents are not entitled to the privileges of the Galleries.

6. The Radio and Television Galleries shall be under the control of the Executive Committee of the Radio and Television Correspondents' Galleries, subject to the approval and supervision of the Speaker of the House of Representatives and the Senate Committee on Rules and Administration.

Approved.

PAUL D. RYAN,
Speaker, House of Representatives.

ROY BLUNT,
Chair, Senate Committee on Rules and Administration.

MEMBERS ENTITLED TO ADMISSION

Aaron, John: WTOP Radio
Abbey, Francis: WUSA-TV
Abbott, Stacey: National Public Radio
Abdallah, Khalil: CNN
Abdulgawad, Atef: AP-Broadcast
Abdulkareem, Akram: APTVS-American Press &
TV Services
Abdullah, Halimah: NBC News
Abdulrazzaq, Ahmed: Aljazeera Satellite Channel
(Peninsula)
Abe, Takaaki: Nippon TV Network
Abernethy, Bob: Religion & Ethics Newsweekly
Abeshouse, Robert: Aljazeera English
Abtar, Rana: Middle East Broadcasting Networks
(MBN)
Abu Diab, Naser: AP-Broadcast
Abu-Hamdyia, Reema: RTTV America
Abu-Kwaik, Biesan: Aljazeera Satellite Channel
(Peninsula)
Abuelhawa, Daoud: Al Arabiya TV
Aburahma, Eyad: Aljazeera Satellite Channel
(Peninsula)
Accame, Gonzalo: EWTN
Acevedo, Juan: WFDC-TV Univision
Ackerman, Tom: Aljazeera English
Ackland, Matthew: WTTG-Fox Television
Acle, Elizabeth: National Public Radio
Acosta, Jim: CNN
Adams, Angelyn: Al Arabiya TV
Adams, Douglas A.: NBC News
Adams, Karen: WNEW/CBS DC
Adams, Lauren: Lilly Broadcasting
Ade, Erin: RTTV America
Adkinson, Jeff: AP-Broadcast
Adkison, Janet: Rural TV News
Adlerblum, Robin: ABC News
Agredo, Jose: Caracol Television
Ahlquist, Greg: Fox News
Ahmad, Meha: Aljazeera Satellite Channel
(Peninsula)
Ahmed, Ali: Middle East Broadcasting Networks
(MBN)
Ahmed, Lukman: BBC
Ahn, Katherine: Korean Broadcasting Systems
Aich, Atirath: China Central TV Bureau
Aiello, Jr., Augustine "Bud": National Public Radio
Aigner-Treworgy, Adam: CBS News
Akey, Zachary: CBS News
Akhavi, Khodayar: Aljazeera English
Akuffo, Rachelle: China Central TV Bureau
Al-Badry, Rami: CNN

Al Hmoud, Mounira: Canal Plus French TV
Al Huraimi, Nadia: BBC
Al Juboori, Haitham: Aljazeera Satellite Channel
(Peninsula)
Alallak, Firas: Sky News Arabia
Alami, Mohammed: Aljazeera Satellite Channel
(Peninsula)
Alamiri, Yasmeen: Al Arabiya TV
Alarcon, Nefi: CNN
Alarian, Laila: Aljazeera English
Albert, Chris: CBS News
Albert, Mark: CBS News
Alberter, William: CNN
Aldag, Jason: Washingtonpost.com
Alderman, Ashley: Fox News
Alegret, Gustau: RCN-TV (Colombia)
Alemany, Jacqueline: CBS News
Alexander, Clinton: CBS News
Alexander, Kenneth: C-SPAN
Alexander, Peter: NBC News
Alexandre, Lee: Hearst Television Inc.
Alfa, Nadine: Reuters Radio & TV
Alfalahi, Saad: Middle East Broadcasting Networks
(MBN)
Alfarone, Debra: WUSA-TV
Alford, Kelly: Middle East Broadcasting Networks
(MBN)
Aliaga, Julio: China Central TV Bureau
Aliakbar, Nihad: AP-Broadcast
Alinejad, Sina: BBC
Alipour, Damien: Voice of America
Alkadiri, Faisal: ABC News
Alkhirsan, Tima: Aljazeera America
Allard, John: ABC News
Alldredge, Thomas: C-SPAN
Allen, Brian: Voice of America
Allen, Darrell: Voice of America
Allen, Keith: Reuters Radio & TV
Allen, Vadim: Voice of America
Allman, Bryan: NBC News
Alnwick, Melanie: WTTG-Fox Television
Alrawi, Khaldoun: TIMA
Alvey, Jay: WRC-TV/NBC-4
Alwan, Faten: APTVS-American Press & TV
Services
Amirault-Michel, Theresa: C-SPAN
Amling, Alicia: CBS News
Ammerman, Stuart: CBS News
Anastasi, Patrick: CNBC
Andersen, Angela: German TV ARD
Anderson, Charles: WETA

1017

MEMBERS ENTITLED TO ADMISSION—Continued

Anderson, Glenn: McClatchy
Anderson, Glenn Osten: BBC
Anderson, Patrick: Swiss Broadcasting
Anderson, Tetiana: Middle East Broadcasting Networks (MBN)
Andree, Eric: AP–Broadcast
Andress, Jeannie: AP–Broadcast
Andrews, Wyatt: CBS News
Aneiva, Roberto: NBC News
Angelini, Mark: RTTV America
Ankarlo, Kristopher: WNEW / CBS DC
Anthony, Tony: Morningside Partners, LLC
Anyse, Alana: CBS News
Anzur, Matt: Scripps News
Aoyama, Kazuhiro: Nippon TV Network
Applegate, Van: WJLA–TV / Newschannel 8
Arabasadi, Arash: Voice of America
Aragon, Kathy: CNN
Arbogast, Vincent: Fox News
Arena, Bruno: AP–Broadcast
Arenander, Inger: Swedish Broadcasting
Arenas, Andrea: Feature Story News
Arenstein, Howard: CBS News
Arero, Soro: Voice of America
Argyri, Eleni: Hellenic Public TV
Armfield, Robert: Fox News
Armino, Bryan: West Wing Reports
Armstrong, Patricia: NBC News
Armstrong, Thomas: ABC News
Armwood, Adrian: CBS News
Art, Jeremy: C–SPAN
Artesona, Eva: TV3–Televisio De Catalunya
Aryankalavil, Babu: Middle East Broadcasting Networks (MBN)
Ashe, Ari: WTOP Radio
Asher, Julie: TF1–French TV
Asmael, Hussein: TIMA
Atallah, Amjad: Aljazeera English
Atarod, Rahmin: CNN
Atkinson, Emily: CNN
Attawia, Moaz: APTVS–American Press & TV Services
Attkisson, Sharyl: Sinclair Broadcast Group
Atwood, Kylie: CBS News
Augenstein, Neal: WTOP Radio
Augustus, Shannon: C–SPAN
Aulenkamp, Jan: German TV ARD
Auresto, John: AP–Broadcast
Austin, Gail: Hearst Television Inc.
Austin, Jonathan: CTV Canadian TV
Austin, Kenneth: NBC News
Austin, Tiane: CNN
Avila, James: ABC News
Avila Lindo, Martha: RCN–TV (Colombia)
Avner, Philip: AP–Broadcast
Avrutine, Matthew: CNN
Awada, Adam: Fox News
Ayala, Jorge: Notimex

Aylward, Andrew: Australian Broadcasting Corporation
Azais, Jean-Pascal: Swiss Broadcasting
Azar, Kellee: WTTG–Fox Television
Azzam, Heni: Aljazeera Satellite Channel (Peninsula)
Azzizada, Arash: Voice of America
Babb, Carla: Voice of America
Bacon, Joel: C–SPAN
Bacon, Jr., Perry: NBC News
Baghi, Baubak: Aljazeera Satellite Channel (Peninsula)
Bagley, Guy: China Central TV Bureau
Bagnall, Thomas: Voice of America
Bagnato, Barry: CBS News
Bai, Fan: China Central TV Bureau
Baier, Bret: Fox News
Bailey, Wendy: WUSA–TV
Bailor, Michelle: C–SPAN
Baker, Les: Fox News
Baker, Sarah: NBC News
Bakhtiar, Rudi: Reuters Radio & TV
Balcomb, Theo: National Public Radio
Baldacci, Marlena: CNN
Baldwin, Travis Renee: ABC News
Bali, Rahul: WTOP Radio
Balinovic, Daniel: Reuters Radio & TV
Balkhy, Ibrahim: AOL Huffington Post
Ball, Joseph: WJLA–TV / Newschannel 8
Ballou, Jeff: Aljazeera English
Banks, Allyson: WUSA–TV
Banks, Erik: CNN
Banks, James: Eurovision Americas, Inc.
Banks, Josh: Fox News
Banks, Laquasha: Sinclair Broadcast Group
Banks, Mark: ABC News
Banks, Morris: CBS News
Bannigan, Mike: Fox Business Network
Baragona, Steve: Voice of America
Barajas, Joshua: The Newshour with Jim Lehrer
Barber, Ellison: WUSA–TV
Barber, Paul: Agence France Presse (AFP–TV)
Barker, Edward: AP–Broadcast
Barnard, Bob: WTTG–Fox Television
Barnd, Jeff: Sinclair Broadcast Group
Barnes, David: CTV–Community TV of PG County
Barnes, Peter: Fox Business Network
Barnwell, Taurean: NHK
Barondess, Rose: NBC News
Barr, Bryan: Sinclair Broadcast Group
Barreda, Eric: Aljazeera English
Barrett, Calvin: Fox News
Barrett, Ted: CNN
Barriga, Belen: Telesur
Barringer, Reginald: CBS News
Barss, Kyle: Washingtonpost.com
Bartee, Fatima: Aljazeera English
Basch, Michelle: WTOP Radio

Bash, Dana: CNN
Bash, David: WETA
Bashi, Ariel: CNN
Basinger, Stuart: Fox News
Baskerville, Kia: CBS News
Bass, Frank: Aljazeera English
Batson, Katherine: Fox News
Batten, Rodney: NBC News
Battistella, Marilisa: CBS News
Baty, William: Aljazeera English
Baumel, Susan: Voyage Productions
Bautista, Mark: CBN News
Bays, James: Aljazeera English
Baysden III, Earl T.: WTTG–Fox Television
Beahn, James: WTTG–Fox Television
Beal, Robin: Fox News
Beall, Gary: NBC News
Bearne, Adam: Eurovision Americas, Inc.
Becker, Bruce: Fox Business Network
Becker, Chris: Fox News
Becker, Eddie: Free Speech TV (FSTV)
Becker, Farrel: CBS News
Becker, Frank: WJLA–TV / Newschannel 8
Behn, Sharon: Voice of America
Behringer, Charles: Aljazeera Satellite Channel
  (Peninsula)
Beitsch, Rebecca: Stateline.org
Bejarano, Mark: National Public Radio
Belha, Nico: Small House Productions
Bell, Ben: ABC News
Bell, Bradley: WJLA–TV / Newschannel 8
Bella, Timothy: Aljazeera America
Bellis, Michael: ABC News
Belmar, Heidi: Fox News
Bena, John: CNN
Bender, Jason: C–SPAN
Benetato, Michael: NBC News
Benincasa, Robert: National Public Radio
Benitez, Barbara: Aljazeera English
Benjamin, Brian: ABC News
Bennett, Geoffrey: Time Warner Cable
Bennett, Justin: NBC News
Bennett, Mark R.: CBS News
Bennewitz, Alexa: CNN
Bensen, Jackie: WRC–TV / NBC–4
Benson, Miles: KCETLink
Bentouila, Elkheir: Middle East Broadcasting
  Networks (MBN)
Bentz, Leslie: CNN
Berdiel, Daniel: Sirius XM Satellite Radio
Bergal, Jenni: Stateline.org
Bergeman, David: CNN
Berger, Catherine: German TV ZDF
Berger, Judson: Fox News
Berko, Art: Viewpoint Communications
Berkowitz, Jackie: CBS News
Bernal, Richard: CNN
Bernardini, Laura: CNN

Bernstein, Howard: WUSA–TV
Bernstein, Joshua: Aljazeera English
Berryman, Jonathan: CNN
Berset, Kristen: WUSA–TV
Berti, Barbara: Aljazeera America
Betsill, Brett: C–SPAN
Bevington, Ben: BBC
Bevir, Adriana: Feature Story News
Bevir, John: Feature Story News
Beyer, Kevin: Diversified Communications, Inc.
  (DCI)
Beyer, William: WTTG–Fox Television
Bharania, Anoo: Reuters Radio & TV
Bhatia, Varuna: Fox News
Bidar, Musadiq: CBS News
Diet, Clement: TF1 French TV
Bikkers, Remco: NOS Dutch Public Radio & TV
  (VRT)
Bilal, Sadiq: AP–Broadcast
Billing, Christen: Radio Free Asia
Bills, Lindzie: CNN
Binswanger, Joshua: Morningside Partners, LLC
Bintrim, Tim: Voice of America
Bishara, Marwan: Aljazeera English
Bisson, Jean-Francois: Canadian Broadcasting
  Corporation (CBC)
Bjerstrom, Erika: Swedish Broadcasting
Bjorgaas, Tove: Norwegian Broadcasting
Black, Phillip M.: ABC News
Blackman, Jay: NBC News
Blackman, John: NBC News
Blackwill, Sarah: NBC News
Blair, Adam: Independent Television News (ITN)
Blake, Andrew: RTTV America
Blake, Paul: BBC
Blakey, Leona: C–SPAN
Blakley, Kevin: CNN
Blanchette, Shelley: Talk Radio News Service
Blanco, Hugo: AP–Broadcast
Blitzer, Wolf: CNN
Block, Melissa: National Public Radio
Blooston, Victoria: NBC News
Blount, Jeffrey: NBC News
Blum-Dostie, Jacqueline: AP–Broadcast
Boag, Keith: Canadian Broadcasting Corporation
  (CBC)
Boccagno, Julia: CBS News
Bodenhorst, Michael: AP–Broadcast
Bodlander, Gerald: AP–Broadcast
Bodnar, John: CNN
Boerma, Lindsey: CBS News
Boesche, Jan: German Public Radio (ARD)
Bohannon, Garrett: Eurovision Americas, Inc.
Bohannon, Joseph: NBC News
Bohn, Kevin: CNN
Bolden, Warren: Bloomberg Radio & TV
Bond, Larry: Voice of America
Bondy, Kim: Aljazeera America

MEMBERS ENTITLED TO ADMISSION—Continued

Bonewald, Jason: Fox News Radio
Booker, Brakkton: National Public Radio
Boone, Rick: WTTG–Fox Television
Borger, Gloria: CNN
Borja, Jean Paul: RCN–TV (Colombia)
Boser, Kirsten: NBC News
Bost, Mark: WUSA–TV
Boston, Tyrone: CNN
Boswell, Craig: CBS News
Botti, David: BBC
Boughton, Bryan: Fox News
Bourar, Hicham: Middle East Broadcasting
    Networks (MBN)
Bowden, David: Sky News
Bowen, Timothy: WETA
Bowman, Jennifer: Fox News
Bowman, Michael: Voice of America
Bowman, Quinn: The Newshour with Jim Lehrer
Boyd, Wayne: ABC News
Brablec, Radek: National Public Radio
Bradley, Carlotta: AP–Broadcast
Bradner, Eric: CNN
Bragale, Charles: WRC–TV / NBC–4
Brandus, Paul: West Wing Reports
Brannon, Timothy: Voice of America
Bransford, Fletcher: Fox News
Brasch, Darci: WTOP Radio
Brauer, Alexander: WJLA–TV / Newschannel 8
Braun, Joshua: CNN
Bravo, Nestor: WFDC–TV Univision
Brawner, Donald: WETA
Brawner, Greta: C–SPAN
Bream, Shannon: Fox News
Breese, Shiny: Radio Free Asia
Breitenbach, Sarah: Stateline.org
Brennan, Allison: CNN
Brennan, Margaret: CBS News
Brevner, Michael: CNN
Brewster, Shaquille: NBC News
Brice, Andrew: One America
Brickhouse, Ayana: Aljazeera English
Brieger, Annette: German TV ZDF
Bright, Whitney: CBS News
Britch, Ray: CNN
Britton, Jake: Sky News
Brock, Robert: Aljazeera America
Brockell, Gillian: Washingtonpost.com
Brody, Andrew: One America
Brody, David: CBN News
Broleman, Michael: NBC Newschannel
Bronstein, Scott: CNN
Brooks, Kurt: WUSA–TV
Brooks-Grady, Sarah: Time Warner Cable
Broom, William: WUSA–TV
Brower, Brooke: NBC News
Brown, Ashley: WRC–TV / NBC–4
Brown, Beth: WRC–TV / NBC–4
Brown, Donald: C–SPAN

Brown, Kristin: Fox News
Brown, Lauretta: CNSNews.com
Brown, Malcolm: Feature Story News
Brown, Pamela: CNN
Brown, Paul: C–SPAN
Brown, Taylor: BBC
Brown, Tracy: AP–Broadcast
Browning, Robert: C–SPAN
Bruce, Mary: ABC News
Brueggeman, Tia: CNN
Bruer, Wesley: CNN
Brumbaugh, Kathleen: AP–Broadcast
Brumfiel, Geoff: National Public Radio
Bruns, David: AP–Broadcast
Brusk, Steven: CNN
Bryant, Aubrey: WUSA–TV
Bryant, Nicholas: BBC
Brzezinski, Mika: NBC News
Bua, Jon-Christopher: Euronews
Bubaris, Philomena: Aljazeera America
Buchholz, Jenny: Fox News
Buchmann, Arielle: WUSA–TV
Buckhorn, Burke: CNN
Buckley, Daniel: WRC–TV / NBC–4
Buckley, Julia Redpath: National Public Radio
Buckwalter, Sabrina: France 2 Television
Buddenhagen, Kristina: C–SPAN
Buel, Meredith: Voice of America
Buellmann, Rolf: German Public Radio (ARD)
Buesinger, Jennifer: CNN
Bulla, Mark: RTTV America
Bullard, John: ABC News
Bullard, Larry: WRC–TV / NBC–4
Bullard Harmon, Susan: CBS News
Bullock, Peter: Reuters Radio & TV
Bumsted, Robert: AP–Broadcast
Bundock, Susan J.: C–SPAN
Bunyan, Maureen: WJLA–TV / Newschannel 8
Burdick, Leslie: C–SPAN
Burdine, Laura: WUSA–TV
Burgdorf, Louis: NBC News
Burger, Todd: EWTN
Burgess, David: CNN
Burgoyne, Matthew: AP–Broadcast
Burk, Penny: NBC News
Burke, Michael: Voice of America
Burkhard, Betsy: Fox News
Burles, Jason: Canadian Broadcasting Corporation
    (CBC)
Burlij, Terence: CNN
Burman, Blake: Fox Business Network
Burnett, Gordon: Radio Free Asia
Burns, Alison: Cox Broadcasting
Burns, Steven: WMAL Radio
Burton, Matthew: ABC News
Bush, Mia: Voice of America
Butcher, Robert E: National Public Radio

MEMBERS ENTITLED TO ADMISSION—Continued

Butler, James: Diversified Communications, Inc. (DCI)
Butler, Norman: NBC News
Butowsky, Ed: Talk Radio News Service
Buttler, Martina: German Public Radio (ARD)
Butts, Diane: WUSA–TV
Byrnes, Dennis: National Public Radio
Cabague, Joven: Aljazeera English
Cabral, Juan: CNN
Cadigan, Will: CNN
Cahill, Kathy: C–SPAN
Caifa, Karin: CNN
Cakir, Mehmet: Turkish Radio and Television (TRT)
Caldwell, Leigh Ann: NBC News
Caldwell, Traci: CBS News
Calfat, Marcel: Canadian Broadcasting Corporation (CBC)
Callahan, Michael: Bloomberg Radio & TV
Callebs, Sean: China Central TV Bureau
Calo-Christian, Nancy: C–SPAN
Calvert, Kyla: The Newshour with Jim Lehrer
Calvi, Jason: EWTN
Camarda, Tim: Eye-To-Eye Video
Cambron, Andrea: Sirius XM Satellite Radio
Cameron, Carl: Fox News
Camp, Lee: RTTV America
Campbell, Christopher: Aljazeera Satellite Channel (Peninsula)
Campbell, Colin: APTVS–American Press & TV Services
Campbell, Kyla: Cox Broadcasting
Candia, Kirsten: German TV ZDF
Cannon, Catherine: CBS News
Capachi, Casey: CNN
Caperton, Katherine: Sirius XM Satellite Radio
Caplan, Craig: C–SPAN
Capomaccio-Even, Anne-Marie: Radio France Internationale
Capra, Anthony: NBC News
Caravello, David: CBS News
Carbonne, Frederic: Radio France Internationale
Cardoze, Jacques: France 2 Television
Carey, Julie: WRC–TV/NBC–4
Carlson, Brett: Global TV Canada
Carlson, Christopher: ABC News
Carlson, Frank: The Newshour with Jim Lehrer
Carlson, Steve: Fox News
Carlsson, Bjorn: Swedish Broadcasting
Carlsson, Lisa: Swedish Broadcasting
Carmean, Kyle: WTTG–Fox Television
Carney, Keith: FedNet
Carpeaux, Emily: The Newshour with Jim Lehrer
Carpel, Michael: Fox News
Carr, Anthony: Sinclair Broadcast Group
Carr, Evan: WRC–TV/NBC–4
Carr, Martin: WETA
Carrick, Kenneth: C–SPAN

Carroll, Charles: WNEW/CBS DC
Carter, Brianne: WJLA–TV/Newschannel 8
Carter, Dave: WRC–TV/NBC–4
Carter, Jr., Walter: Fox News
Casenco, Anatolie: RTVi/ECHO–TV
Casey, Elizabeth: Aljazeera America
Casey, Sean: WRC–TV/NBC–4
Casey, Susan: RTE–Irish Radio & TV
Cassada, Augusta: One America
Cassano, Joseph: WRC–TV/NBC–4
Castaneda, Diana: RCN–TV (Colombia)
Castellaro, Nick: Aljazeera English
Castiel, Carol: Voice of America
Castro, David: Hispanic Communications Network
Castro, Pablo: Hispanic Communications Network
Catrett, David Keith: CNN
Causey, Mike: Federal News Radio 1500 AM
Cetta, Denise: CBS News
Cevirgen, Celal: Turkish Radio and Television (TRT)
Chadbourn, Margaret: Fox News
Chadwick, Lauren: NBC News
Chaggaris, Steven: CBS News
Chakraborty, Barnini: Fox News
Chalian, David: CNN
Chamberlain, Richard: WJLA–TV/Newschannel 8
Chan, Manila: RTTV America
Chan, Rita: Aljazeera America
Chang, Ailsa: National Public Radio
Chang, Ching-Yi: AP–Broadcast
Chang, Darzen: WETA
Chang, Xiao: Voice of America
Changuris, Zeke: WJLA–TV/Newschannel 8
Chapman, Irwin: Bloomberg Radio & TV
Chapman, Karolina: Aljazeera English
Chapman, Michael: CNSNews.com
Chappell, Jill: CNN
Charles, Dan: National Public Radio
Charters-Bilbassy, Nadia: Al Arabiya TV
Chase, David: Cox Broadcasting
Chattman, Tanya: C–SPAN
Chavar, A.J.: The New York Times On The Web
Chaytor, David: Aljazeera English
Chekuru, Kavitha: Aljazeera English
Chen, Jennifer: Shenzhen Media Group (SZMG)
Chen, Joie: Aljazeera America
Chen, Shen: China Central TV Bureau
Chen, Yi Qiu: Hong Kong Phoenix Satellite Television
Chenevey, Steve: WTTG–Fox Television
Cheng, He: China Central TV Bureau
Cherkaoui, Adil: Aljazeera Satellite Channel (Peninsula)
Cherouny, Robert: Aljazeera English
Chevez, Carlos: National Public Radio
Chichakyan, Gayane: RTTV America
Chick, Jane S.: CBS News
Childs, Lete: NBC News

MEMBERS ENTITLED TO ADMISSION—Continued

Ching, Nike: Voice of America
Chinn Lucie, Surae: WUSA–TV
Chmurak, Elizabeth: CNN
Cho, Diane: WJLA–TV / Newschannel 8
Cho, Eun: Voice of America
Cho, Hans: JTBC
Cho, Michelle: NBC News
Chocarro, Silvia: Radio France Internationale
Choe, Jaywon: The Newshour with Jim Lehrer
Choedron, Trinlae: Voice of America
Chophel, Lobsang: Radio Free Asia
Choto, Raymond: Voice of America
Christian, Christopher: CBN News
Christian, George: CBS News
Chung, E-Ting: CTI–TV (Taiwan)
Chung, Nicole: C–SPAN
Chung, Patrick: NBC News
Chunko, April: WUSA–TV
Cilberti, David: WUSA–TV
Cinque, Vicente: TV Globo International
Claar, Matthew: C–SPAN
Clarenne, Gilles: Agence France Presse (AFP–TV)
Clarenne, Gilles: Eurovision Americas, Inc.
Clark, Grant: Aljazeera America
Clark, James: C–SPAN
Clarke, John: Feature Story News
Clary, Gregory: CNN
Claudet, Marie: Canadian Broadcasting Corporation
   (CBC)
Clemann, William: WUSA–TV
Clemons, Bobby: CNN
Cloherty, Megan: WTOP Radio
Clottey, Peter: Voice of America
Clugston, Gregory: SRN News (Salem)
Cobus, Pete: Voice of America
Cockerham, Richard: Fox News
Cockey, William: WUSA–TV
Cocklin, Anne: ABC News
Cocklin, Stephen: ABC News
Codianni, Ashley: CNN
Cofske, Harvey: Diversified Communications, Inc.
   (DCI)
Cohan, Stacey: CNN
Cohen, Gregory: WUSA–TV
Cohen, Marshall: CBS News
Cohencious, Rebecca: Native American TV (NATV)
Cohencious, Robert: Native American TV (NATV)
Coil, Holley: NBC Newschannel
Colby, Brielle: Fox News
Cole, Bryan: Fox News
Coleau, Manel: WRC–TV / NBC–4
Colella, Anthony: WTTG–Fox Television
Coleman, Steven: AP–Broadcast
Coleman, Thomas: CBS News
Coles, David: The Newshour with Jim Lehrer
Colimore, Eric: Fox News
Coll, Dennis: National Public Radio
Collender, Howard: Mobile Video Services, Ltd.

Collins, Bruce D.: C–SPAN
Collins, Maxine: BBC
Collins, Pat: WRC–TV / NBC–4
Collinson, Stephen: CNN
Colombo-Abdullah, Flavia: AP–Broadcast
Concaugh, Jr., Joseph: Diversified Communications,
   Inc. (DCI)
Condon, Stephanie: CBS News
Conetta, Christine: AOL Huffington Post
Coney, Carol: CBS News
Conlin, Sheila: NBC Newschannel
Conneen, Michael: WJLA–TV / Newschannel 8
Conner, Eric: Fox News
Contreras, Glenda: Telemundo Network
Contreras, Jorge: Univision
Cook, James L.: C–SPAN
Cook, Peter: Bloomberg Radio & TV
Cooke, David M.: Diversified Communications, Inc.
   (DCI)
Cooper, John: CBS News
Cooper, Krystal: WJLA–TV / Newschannel 8
Cooper, Kyle: WTOP Radio
Cooper, Ralph: China Central TV Bureau
Cooper, Rebecca: WJLA–TV / Newschannel 8
Cooper, Jr., Nero: NBC News
Copeland, Natasha: WRC–TV / NBC–4
Corapi, Sarah: The Newshour with Jim Lehrer
Corcoran, Patricia: WTTG–Fox Television
Cordes, Nancy: CBS News
Corke, Kevin: Fox News
Corner, Cleve: C–SPAN
Cornish-Emery, Audie: National Public Radio
Corologos-Medina, Christie: CNN
Correa, Lina: Voice of America
Correa, Pedro: Telemundo Network
Cortes, William: Telesur
Costantini, Bob: Westwood One
Costello, Thomas: NBC News
Costen, Chantal: BET Nightly News
Cote, Tim: NBC News
Coughlan, Victoria: CBS News
Coulter, Pam: CBS News
Counts, Chris: RTTV America
Courson, Paul: Sinclair Broadcast Group
Courtney, Eric: Diversified Communications, Inc.
   (DCI)
Courtney, Sarah: Aljazeera America
Cousins, Bria: CNBC
Cowin, Lauren: Fox News
Cowman, Chris: China Central TV Bureau
Cox, Jerry: This Is America with Dennis Wholey
Cox, Oliver: NBC News
Craca, Thomas: CBS News
Cracchiolo, Marina: CNN
Craig, John: Diversified Communications, Inc.
   (DCI)
Craig, Nathan: C–SPAN
Crane, Stephen: Cronkite News Service

MEMBERS ENTITLED TO ADMISSION—Continued

Crawford, Bob: China Central TV Bureau
Crawford, James: CNN
Crawford, Jan: CBS News
Crawford, Woody: Voice of America
Crawley, Plummer: CNBC
Crews, Mariah: C–SPAN
Cridland, Jeffrey: WUSA–TV
Criswell, Danny: Cox Broadcasting
Crombe, Laura: CBN News
Cronkite, Walter: CBS News
Cross, Katherine: EWTN
Crossling, Robert: WTOP Radio
Crowder, Anja: ABC News
Crowther, Philip: AP–Broadcast
Crum, John: CBS News
Crum, Jonathan: CBS News
Crupi, Nick: Voice of America
Crutchfield, Abigail: CNN
Crutchfield, Curtis: CTV–Community TV of PG County
Cruz, Johnny: Wall Street Journal
Csapo, Jonathan: BBC
Cucchiara, Natalie: NBC News
Cuddy, Matthew: CNBC
Cui, Han: Sinovision
Cui, Lingnan: China Central TV Bureau
Culhane, Patricia: Aljazeera English
Cullen, Michael: National Public Radio
Cullum, Blanquita: Talk Radio News Service
Cullum, James: Talk Radio News Service
Culver, David: WRC–TV / NBC–4
Cumber, Erika: CTV–Community TV of PG County
Cunha, John: CNN
Curran, Patrick: WTTG–Fox Television
Currence, Robert: Voice of America
Currier, Liam: C–SPAN
Curtis, Alexander: C–SPAN
Curtis, Heather: WMAL Radio
Curtis, Jessica: Fox News Radio
Curtis, Jodie: Fox News
Cvetnic, Nicole: McClatchy
Czaplinski, Michael: National Public Radio
Czzowitz, Greg: C–SPAN
D'Andrea, Eugene: Bloomberg Radio & TV
D'Annibale, Thomas: ABC News
Dailey, Kathleen: BBC
Dake, Meredith: CQ / Roll Call
Dakin, Carla: NBC News
Dalton, Benjamin: TV Tokyo
Daly, John: CBS News
Damdul, Dorjee: Radio Free Asia
Danahar, Paul: BBC
Daniels, Pete: C–SPAN
Danilko, Derek: AP–Broadcast
Dann, Caroline: NBC News
Danzig, Abby: Fox News
Dao, Thao: VIETV Network
Dargakis, Minas: Voice of America

Dargham, Alain: Middle East Broadcasting Networks (MBN)
Darling, Addie: EWTN
Daschle, Kelly: AP–Broadcast
Date, Jack: ABC News
Date, Shirish: National Public Radio
Dauchess, Matthew: C–SPAN
Daugherty, Jeffery: Voice of America
David, Ameera: RTTV America
Davie, Bianca: China Central TV Bureau
Davila Castillo, Jaime: CNN
Davis, Clinton: WTTG–Fox Television
Davis, Edward: CNN
Davis, Jennifer: WTTG–Fox Television
Davis, Lynn: WJLA–TV / Newschannel 8
Davis, Mitch: Fox News Radio
Davis, Patrick A.: CNN
Davis, Ray: NBC Newschannel
Davis, Rebecca: National Public Radio
Davis, Susan: National Public Radio
Davis, Tiffani: Aljazeera America
Dawood, Mohamed: APTVS–American Press & TV Services
Dawson, Rob: WNEW / CBS DC
Dawson, Wendy: Fox News
Dayal, Tushar: BBC
De Angioletti, Scott: AP–Broadcast
de Franceschi, Jela: Voice of America
DeGuise, Louis: Canadian Broadcasting Corporation (CBC)
de Saint Hippolyte, Stan: AP–Broadcast
de Saracho, Dinah: Televisa News Network (ECO)
De Schaetzen, Emilie: Eurovision Americas, Inc.
de Vogue, Ariane: CNN
de Vries, Karl: CNN
Deahl, Jess: National Public Radio
Dean, Matthew: Fox News
DeChagas, Bridget: National Public Radio
Decker, Jon: Fox News Radio
DeFeo, Joe: WJLA–TV / Newschannel 8
DeFrank, Debra: Fox News
DeFrank, Joe: Fox News
Degtyarev, Andrey: Voice of America
Dehghanpour, Siamak: Voice of America
Deines, Nicholas: CNN
Del Pino, Javier: Cadena Ser
Del Rosario, Simone: RTTV America
DeLany, Kevin: Westwood One
Deluca, Joan: Voice of America
DeMar, Brian: National Public Radio
DeMarco, Lauren: WTTG–Fox Television
Demaria, Ed: NBC News
Demark, Michael: Fox News
Demas, William: ABC News
DeMilio, Paul: Sirius XM Satellite Radio
Dennert, Mary Pat: Fox News
DePuyt, Bruce: WJLA–TV / Newschannel 8
Dereje, Bethey: CBS News

MEMBERS ENTITLED TO ADMISSION—Continued

Derrien, Mathieu: TF1–French TV
DeRuy, Emily: Univision
Desbois, Laurent: France 2 Television
Desjardins, Lisa: The Newshour with Jim Lehrer
Desvarieux, Jessica: Real News Network
DeVito, Andrea: Fox News
Dezell, Maureen: Washington Bureau News Service
Dhue, Stephanie: CNBC
Diakides, Anastasia: CNN
Diamond, Jeremy: CNN
Diaz, Aixa: Hearst Television Inc.
Diaz, Daniella: CNN
Diaz, Juan Carlos: Small House Productions
Diaz, Robert: CBS News
Diaz Waldman, Ileana: WUSA–TV
Diaz-Briseno, Jose: MundoFox
DiBella, Kate: Fox News
DiCarlo, Patricia: CNN
Dickerson, John: CBS News
Dickerson, Villinda: Aljazeera English
Dickey, Sloan: Wall Street Journal
Diggs, Bridget: C–SPAN
Dill, Danny: C–SPAN
Dillard, Juanita: ABC News
Dillon, John: RealClearPolitics
Ding-Everson, William: TV Asahi
DiPietro, Annamaria: WJLA–TV / Newschannel 8
Disselkamp, Henry: ABC News
Distance, Kenneth: Bloomberg Radio & TV
Divaris, Oliver: German TV ZDF
Dixon, Evan: NBC News
Dixon, Greg: National Public Radio
Dixson, Charles H.: CBS News
Doan, Daniela: ABC News
Doane, Martin C.: WJLA–TV / Newschannel 8
Dobal, Michael: NBC Newschannel
Dockins, Pamela: Voice of America
Doell, Michelle: C–SPAN
Doergeloh, Uwe: German TV ZDF
Doernen, Daniel: German TV ARD
Doherty, Brian: Fox News
Doherty, Peter: ABC News
Dolce, Stephen: CNN
Dolma, Rigdhen: Radio Free Asia
Domen, John: WNEW / CBS DC
Dominick, Katie: CBS News
Donahue, Edward: AP–Broadcast
Donald, William: Eye-To-Eye Video
Donnelly, Kristin: NBC News
Donner, Jason: Fox News
Donovan, Beth: National Public Radio
Donovan, Brian: ABC News
Doocy, Peter: Fox News
Doody, Sean: C–SPAN
Dooley, Erin: ABC News
Dore, Margaret: CBS News
Dorf-Dolce, Heather: German TV ARD

Dorman, Jason: C–SPAN
Dorn, Jason: AP–Broadcast
Dorsey, Steve: CBS News
Dosani, Sanya: Aljazeera America
Doty, Steve: Washington Examiner
Dougherty, Martin: CNN
Dougherty, Paul G.: ABC News
Dourrachad, Mohamed: 50 Frames
Dowdell, Kris: C–SPAN
Doyle, Brian: Talk Radio News Service
Doyle, Geoffrey: Fox News
Drabo, Aboubacar: National Public Radio
Dragsted, Stine: Danish Broadcasting Corporation
Dries, William: CBS News
Druce, Ian: BBC
Du, Yubin: China Central TV Bureau
Duartes, Rolo: WFDC–TV Univision
Dubert, Michelle: NBC News
Duckham, Justin: Talk Radio News Service
Dufresne, Louise: CBS News
Dugan, William: CTV Canadian TV
Duggeli, Peter: Swiss Broadcasting
Dukakis, Alexandra: ABC News
Dukeman, Paige: Fox News
Dumont Baron, Yanik: Canadian Broadcasting
    Corporation (CBC)
Duncan, Victoria: NBC News
Duncombe, Lyndsay: Canadian Broadcasting
    Corporation (CBC)
Dunkin, John: ABC News
Dunlop, William: Eurovision Americas, Inc.
Dunn, Lauren: WRC–TV / NBC–4
Dupree, Jamie: Cox Broadcasting
Durand, Lucho: China Central TV Bureau
Durham, Deborah: Univision
Durkin, Edward: WRC–TV / NBC–4
Dwyer, Devin: ABC News
Dwyer-Shapiro, Lisa: AP–Broadcast
Dyer, Lois: CBS News
Eades, Jr, Paul: C–SPAN
Echevarria, Pedro L.: C–SPAN
Echols, Jerry: Fox News
Eck, Christina: German Press Agency
Eckel, Michael: Voice of America
Eckert, Barton: WTOP Radio
Eckert, Paul: Radio Free Asia
Edem, Ariel: To The Contrary (Persephone
    Productions)
Edmondson, William: Fox News
Edson, Rich: Fox News
Edwards, Brian: CBN News
Edwards, John: NBC News
Edwards, William: Agence France Presse (AFP–
    TV)
Eiras, Arlene: Reuters Radio & TV
Eizeldin, Sam: APTVS–American Press & TV
    Services

MEMBERS ENTITLED TO ADMISSION—Continued

Ejedepang-Koge, Nkwenten: Middle East Broadcasting Networks (MBN)

El-Hamalawy, Mahmoud: Aljazeera Satellite Channel (Peninsula)

El-Komy, Dalia: AP–Broadcast

Elahmed, Mouhamed: Sky News Arabia

Eldridge, James W.: Fox News

Eleazer, Melvin: Voice of America

Elfers, Steve: USA Today

Elgazar, Hosny: AP–Broadcast

Elgin, John: Middle East Broadcasting Networks (MBN)

Elizondo, Gabriel: Aljazeera English

Elker, Jonathan: Washingtonpost.com

Ellard, Nancy: NBC Newschannel

Ellenwood, Gary: C–SPAN

Elliott, Paul: WNEW / CBS DC

Elsetouhi, Mohamed: 50 Frames

Elving, Ronald: National Public Radio

Elvington, Daniel Glenn: ABC News

Emanuel, Mike: Fox News

Engel, Mariam: Aljazeera English

Engel, Seth: C–SPAN

Ensign, Ernie: WJLA–TV / Newschannel 8

Enzmann, Jacqueline: Fuji TV Japan

Epatko, Larisa: The Newshour with Jim Lehrer

Epstein, Steve: Fox News

Erbe, Bonnie: To The Contrary (Persephone Productions)

Erbiti, Katerina: CNN

Ernst, Aaron: Aljazeera America

Ernst, Manuel: German TV ARD

Esfahani, Lara: German TV ZDF

Espinosa, Jose: WFDC–TV Univision

Esquivel, Patricia: C–SPAN

Estes, Diane: The Newshour with Jim Lehrer

Estrada, Rodolfo: AP–Broadcast

Etzlstorfer, Manuel: Austrian Radio & TV (ORF)

Evans, Laura: WTTG–Fox Television

Evans, Sarah: Aljazeera English

Evans, Tyler: Fox News

Ewen, McKenna: Washingtonpost.com

Fabian, Kathleen: Aljazeera English

Fabic, Greg: C–SPAN

Facchinei, Bianca: RTTV America

Faerber, Fritz: AP–Broadcast

Fagen, Joel: Fox News

Fairclough, Owen: China Central TV Bureau

Faison, Alfred: EWTN

Fantacone, John L.: CBS News

Farhi, Arden: CBS News

Farkas, Daniel: Middle East Broadcasting Networks (MBN)

Farkas, Mark: C–SPAN

Farley, Tim: Sirius XM Satellite Radio

Farmer, Christopher: Environment & Energy Publishing, LLC

Farnan, Shane: Talk Radio News Service

Farrell, Kate: BBC

Farzaneh, Sam: BBC

Fastenberg, Dan: Reuters Radio & TV

Fattahi, Kambiz: BBC

Faulders, Katherine: ABC News

Fauqueux-Veit, Hannelore: Austrian Radio & TV (ORF)

Fazio, Rachel: NBC News

Feeney, Joseph: C–SPAN

Fehr, Stephen: Stateline.org

Feist, Sam: CNN

Feldman, Randy: Viewpoint Communications

Felix, Tsitsiki: WFDC–TV Univision

Fell, Jackie: Cox Broadcasting

Fellet, Joao: BBC

Fendley, Gail: Religion & Ethics Newsweekly

Fendrick, Anne-Marie: NHK

Fenghua, Wang: China Central TV Bureau

Fente, Henok: Voice of America

Fenton, Amy: Fox News

Fenwick, Gallagher: AP–Broadcast

Ferder, Bruce: Voice of America

Ferguson, Patrick: Canadian Broadcasting Corporation (CBC)

Feria, Liza: Reuters Radio & TV

Ferrise, Patrick: Sirius XM Satellite Radio

Fertig, Natalie: McClatchy

Fessler, Pam: National Public Radio

Fetzer, Robert: Diversified Communications, Inc. (DCI)

Fiegel, Eric James: CNN

Field, Joan: BBC

Field, Matthew: NHK

Fierro, Juan Martinez: Cope Radio (Spain)

Fifield, Paul: EWTN

Filburn, Sean: RTTV America

Finch, Laura: C–SPAN

Finch, Mark: Fox News

Fingar, Craig: CNN

Finkel, Ben: Viewpoint Communications

Finn, Martin: Fox News

Finnegan, Conor: ABC News

Finney, Richard: Radio Free Asia

Finnigan, Michael: Diversified Communications, Inc. (DCI)

Fischer, Kathryn: RTTV America

Fischer, Tanya: Eurovision Americas, Inc.

Fischoff, Michael: WTTG–Fox Television

Fishel, Justin: ABC News

Fisher, Alan: Aljazeera English

Fisher, Kate: Feature Story News

Fisher, Kristin: Fox News

Fisher, Siobhan: ABC News

Fitzgerald, Megan: WRC–TV / NBC–4

Fitzgerald, Tom: WTTG–Fox Television

Fitzpatrick, Meagan: Canadian Broadcasting Corporation (CBC)

Fitzsimons, Tim: Marketplace Radio

MEMBERS ENTITLED TO ADMISSION—Continued

Flanagan, Danielle: WUSA–TV
Fleeson, Richard: C–SPAN
Fletcher, Lisa: Aljazeera America
Flood, Randy: Native American TV (NATV)
Floquet, Michel: TF1–French TV
Flores, Cesar: BT Video Productions
Flores, Reena: CBS News
Flynn, Robert: Feature Story News
Fodrea, Linda: Fox News
Foellmer, Kristin: German TV ZDF
Fogarty, Kevin: Reuters Radio & TV
Foley, Dennis: WTOP Radio
Foran, Laura: Fox News
Forcier, Vincent: WETA
Ford, Michael: Diversified Communications, Inc.
  (DCI)
Ford, Patrick: CNN
Ford, Sam: WJLA–TV / Newschannel 8
Foreman, Thomas: CNN
Forman, David: NBC News
Fornicola, Jason: Federal News Radio 1500 AM
Forsythe, Jonathan: McClatchy
Forte, Bernard: WRC–TV / NBC–4
Fortner, Amanda: C–SPAN
Forzato, Jamie: WTOP Radio
Foster, Carl: C–SPAN
Foster, Rebecca: Feature Story News
Foster, Scott: NBC News
Foster, Tom: CBS News
Foster Mathewson, Lesli: WUSA–TV
Foty, Tom: CBS News
Foukara, Abderrahim: Aljazeera Satellite Channel
  (Peninsula)
Fouladvand, Hida: Aljazeera English
Fowler, Maria: USA Today
Fox, Darren: Voice of America
Fox, David: ABC News
Fox, Maggie: NBC News
Fox, Matthew: ABC News
Fox, Michael: Aljazeera Satellite Channel
  (Peninsula)
Fox, Peggy: WUSA–TV
Frado, John: CBS News
Frail, Marie: Reuters Radio & TV
Fraley, Jason: WTOP Radio
Frame, John: WTTG–Fox Television
France, Lindsay: RTTV America
Frandino, Nathan: Reuters Radio & TV
Franganillo, Carlos: TVE—Spanish Public
  Television
Frankel, Bruce: TF1–French TV
Frasier, Jordan: NBC News
Frates, Chris: CNN
Frazao, Kristine: Sinclair Broadcast Group
Frazier, Robert: Feature Story News
Frazier, William: C–SPAN
Fredrickson, Drew: NBC News
Freitas, Brad: WNEW / CBS DC

French, Patrick: CBS News
Friar, David: AP–Broadcast
Friedman, Dave: Fox News
Friedman, Mathew: AP–Broadcast
Fritz, Mike: The Newshour with Jim Lehrer
Fritz, Sabrina: German Public Radio (ARD)
Froom, LeRoy: SRN News (Salem)
Fry, James: Voice of America
Fu, Peng: China Central TV Bureau
Fuhr, Michael: WUSA–TV
Fujiue, Mami: NHK
Fulton, Bradley: CTV Canadian TV
Furlow, Tony: CBS News
Furman, Hal E.: CBS News
Fuseya, Hiroto: NHK
Fuss, Brian: CBS News
Futrowsky, David: Voice of America
Gabriel, Oscar: AP–Broadcast
Gaetano, Lawrence: NBC News
Gaffney, Dennis: NBC News
Gaffney, Emily: NBC News
Gaffney, John: NBC News
Galadanchi, Bello: Voice of America
Galdabini, Christian: Fox News
Galey, Travis: CBS News
Gallacher, Andy: Aljazeera English
Gallagher, Bill: C–SPAN
Gallagher, John: C–SPAN
Gallagher, Tim: Sky News
Gallasch, Hillery: German TV ARD
Galowin, Craig: C–SPAN
Gamboa , Angly: WFDC–TV Univision
Gamboa, Suzanne: NBC News
Gandhi, Hetal: Sinclair Broadcast Group
Ganslmeier, Martin: German Public Radio (ARD)
Gao, Qi: China Central TV Bureau
Gao, Sheryl: China Central TV Bureau
Garay, Gavino: Reuters Radio & TV
Garber, Scott: CNN
Garcia, Danelle: CNN
Garcia, Guillermo: Reuters Radio & TV
Garcia, Jon: ABC News
Garcia, July: CBS News
Garcia, Leila: Aljazeera America
Gardella, Richard: NBC News
Garg, Maya: Aljazeera English
Gargagliano, Richard: Native American TV (NATV)
Garifo, Stephen: WUSA–TV
Garland, Eric: The Hill
Garlock, John: C–SPAN
Garner, Dave: WTOP Radio
Garner, Jean: Aljazeera English
Garner, Melodie: CNN
Garraty, Timothy C.: CNN
Garrett, Christopher: CNN
Garrett, Major: CBS News
Garrett-Scott, Amina: CNN

MEMBERS ENTITLED TO ADMISSION—Continued

Garrison, Lynsea: BBC
Garrott, Jennifer: C–SPAN
Gary, Garney: C–SPAN
Gaskin, Keith: NBC News
Gasparello, Linda: White House Chronicle
Gatewood-Gill, Danielle: WUSA–TV
Gatewood-Gill, Danielle: Media General
Gathelier, Julien: Agence France Presse (AFP–TV)
Gato, Pablo: Univision
Gattsek, Bill: Aljazeera English
Gaughan, Timothy: CBS News
Gauthier, Arthur: ABC News
Gaynor, Joshua: CNN
Geewax, Marilyn: National Public Radio
Geffroy, Amelie: TF1–French TV
Gelevska, Irina: Macedonia Radio Television (MRTV)
Gelles, David: CNN
Gembara, Deborah: Reuters Radio & TV
Gentilo, Richard: AP–Broadcast
Gentry, Pamela: Bet Nightly News
Gentry, Robert: TV Asahi
Geoghegan, Tom: BBC
George, Pavithra: Reuters Radio & TV
Georges, Marc: Scripps News
Gerhiser, Gene: National Public Radio
Gerin, Roseanne: Radio Free Asia
Gestoso, Jorge: TeleSUR
Geyelin, Philip: CBS News
Ghandour, Michel: Middle East Broadcasting Networks (MBN)
Ghanem, Pierre: Al Arabiya TV
Ghattas, Kim: BBC
Giaimo, Melissa: CNN
Giammetta, Max: WTTG–Fox Television
Gibson, Jake: Fox News
Gibson, Sheri Lynn: NBC Newschannel
Gibson, Teneille: WRC–TV / NBC–4
Gilchrist, Aaron: WRC–TV / NBC–4
Gile, Charlie: NBC News
Gilgannon, Pege: WJLA–TV / Newschannel 8
Gillam, Katharyn: Agence France Presse (AFP–TV)
Gilliam, Morgan: WJLA–TV / Newschannel 8
Gillis, Gary: Fox News
Ginebra, Nelson: NBC Newschannel
Ginsburg, Benson: CBS News
Giovanni, Nicholas: WUSA–TV
Girard, David: ABC News
Gittlen, Jason: WRC–TV / NBC–4
Giusto, Thomas: ABC News
Glassman, Matt: WRC–TV / NBC–4
Gleitsmann, Verena: Austrian Radio & TV (ORF)
Glennon, John: Fox News
Glick, Jenny: WNEW / CBS DC
Gliha, Lori: Aljazeera America
Glover, Aronica: CBN News
Gobet, Pierre: Swiss Broadcasting
Goddard, Andre: CNN

Godfrey, Autria: WJLA–TV / Newschannel 8
Godinho, Joanna: China Central TV Bureau
Godsick, Andrew L.: NBC Newschannel
Goff, Angie: WRC–TV / NBC–4
Gold, Avra: NBC News
Gold, Emily: NBC News
Gold, Lawrence: AP–Broadcast
Gold, Peter: Fuji TV Japan
Goldberg, Jeff: WJLA–TV / Newschannel 8
Goldman, Jeff Scott: CBS News
Goldman, Julianna: CBS News
Goldrick, Michael: WRC–TV / NBC–4
Gomes, Karina: Aljazeera English
Gomez, Joseph: 24/7 News
Gomez, Serafin: Fox News
Goncalves Perry, Delia: WUSA–TV
Goncalves-de-Oliveira, Alexandra: The Hill
Gong, Sasha: Voice of America
Gongadze, Myroslava: Voice of America
Gonsar, Dhondup: Radio Free Asia
Gonyea, Don: National Public Radio
Gonzalez, Antonio R.: German TV ARD
Gonzalez, Carlos: WTTG–Fox Television
Gonzalez, Erika: WRC–TV / NBC–4
Gonzalez, Fernando: AP–Broadcast
Gonzalez, Irene: RTTV America
Gonzalez, John: WJLA–TV / Newschannel 8
Gonzalez, Liliana: WFDC–TV Univision
Gonzalez, Mario: RCN–TV (Colombia)
Good, Chris: ABC News
Goodall, Sam: CBS News
Goodknight, Charles A: WRC–TV / NBC–4
Goodman, David: CNN
Goodman, Jeffrey: NBC News
Goodrich, Megan: Eurovision Americas, Inc.
Goolsby, Wyatt: EWTN
Gorap, Pema: Voice of America
Gorbutt, Richard: CNN
Gordemer, Barry: National Public Radio
Gordon, Claire: Aljazeera America
Gordon, Herbert: WRC–TV / NBC–4
Gorman, James: AP–Broadcast
Gottlieb, Brian: CBS News
Gould, Robert: C–SPAN
Gould, Robin: WJLA–TV / Newschannel 8
Gracey, Allison: CNN
Gracey, David: CNN
Gracia, Michael: AP–Broadcast
Gradison, Robin: ABC News
Granda, Marco: RCN–TV (Colombia)
Granger, Nicholle: Nippon TV Network
Grasso, Neil: CBS News
Graumann, Eva: German Public Radio (ARD)
Graves, Lindsay: NBC News
Gray, Justin: Cox Broadcasting
Gray, Noah: CNN
Graydon, James: CNN

MEMBERS ENTITLED TO ADMISSION—Continued

Grayson, Gisele: National Public Radio
Green, Clayton: CNN
Green, Jessie J.: WTOP Radio
Green, Miranda: Scripps News
Green, Molette: WRC–TV / NBC–4
Green, Richard: Voice of America
Green, Shannon: USA Today
Greenbaum, Adam: Voice of America
Greenberger, Scott: Stateline.org
Greenblatt, Larry: Viewpoint Communications
Greenblatt, Mark: Scripps News
Greene, James M.: NBC News
Greenfield, Michael: Sky News
Greenfieldboyce, Nell: National Public Radio
Greiner, Nicholas: ABC News
Grether, Nicole: Aljazeera America
Grieder, Samantha: Tokyo Broadcasting System
Griffin, Jennifer: Fox News
Griffin, Kevin: NBC News
Griffitts, William: Mobile Video Services, Ltd.
Griggs, Kendall: WJLA–TV / Newschannel 8
Grigsby, Lee: Eurovision Americas, Inc.
Grip, David: Reuters Radio & TV
Grobe, Stefan: Euronews
Gross, Andrew F.: NBC News
Gross, David: CBS News
Gross, Josh: CBS News
Gross, Jr., Eddie S.: CNN
Grott, John: Talk Radio News Service
Grovum, Jake: Stateline.org
Grow, Erica: WUSA–TV
Grzech, Cherie: Fox News
Guastadisegni, Richard: WJLA–TV / Newschannel 8
Guenburg, Carol: Voice of America
Guerouani, Fayrouz: AP–Broadcast
Guevara, Henry: WFDC–TV Univision
Guez, Bertrand: TF1–French TV
Guidry, Tim: WJLA–TV / Newschannel 8
Guise, Gregory: WUSA–TV
Gulden, Scott: Sirius XM Satellite Radio
Guo, Chun: China Central TV Bureau
Guray, Geoffrey: The Newshour with Jim Lehrer
Gursky, Gregg L.: Fox News
Gustafson, David: Aljazeera America
Gutierrez, Fanny: WFDC–TV Univision
Gutmann, Hanna: Washington Radio And Press Service
Guttman, Nathan: Israel Television And Radio
Guzman, Armando: Azteca America
Guzman, Wilbert: Telemundo Network
Gypson, Katherine: Voice of America
Ha, Gwen: Radio Free Asia
Haake, Garrett: WUSA–TV
Haan, Mike: NBC News
Haberstick, Fred: C–SPAN
Habib, Elias: Al Arabiya TV
Haddad, Tammy: Feature Story News
Hadro, Matt: EWTN

Haefeli, Brian: ABC News
Hager, Mary: CBS News
Hager, Nathaniel: WNEW / CBS DC
Haggerty, Patrick: This Week in Agribusiness
Hahn, Jay: Eurovision Americas, Inc.
Haim, Laura: Canal Plus French TV
Haiqing, Zhu: China Central TV Bureau
Halkett, Kimberly: Aljazeera English
Hall, Alegra: CBN News
Hall, Andrew: One America
Hall, Brett: WNEW / CBS DC
Hall, Kata: Fox News
Hall, Richard: C–SPAN
Hall, Sylvia: Fox Business Network
Haller, Sylvia: NBC News
Haller, Tom: Aljazeera English
Hallman, James: WUSA–TV
Halpern, Jared: Fox News Radio
Halpern, Lacey: Fox News
Halsted, Andy: WFDC–TV Univision
Hamberg, Steven: Viewpoint Communications
Hamby, Peter: CNN
Hamilton, Caleb: FedNet
Hamilton, Christopher: Aljazeera America
Hamilton, James: Aljazeera English
Hamilton, Lawan: Scripps News
Hampton, Brian: CNN
Han, Jiyuan: China Central TV Bureau
Handelsman, Steve: NBC Newschannel
Handly, Jim: WRC–TV / NBC–4
Hanna, Michael: Aljazeera English
Hannah, Daniel: ABC News
Hanner, Mark: WJLA–TV / Newschannel 8
Hanson, Chris: C–SPAN
Hanson, David: NBC News
Harding, Alejandro: Diversified Communications, Inc. (DCI)
Harding, Bill: CBS News
Harkness, Stephen: C–SPAN
Harlan, Jeremy: CNN
Harleston, Robb: C–SPAN
Harmsen, Nicholas: Australian Broadcasting Corporation
Harper, Steven: Aljazeera English
Harrington, Candice: NBC News
Harris, Donna: WJLA–TV / Newschannel 8
Harris, Kasey: C–SPAN
Harris, Leon: WJLA–TV / Newschannel 8
Harris, Richard: National Public Radio
Harris, Roy: Diversified Communications, Inc. (DCI)
Harrison, Byron: CTV—Community TV of PG County
Harrison, Edward: RTTV America
Hartfield, Elizabeth: CNN
Hartman, Brian Robert: ABC News
Hartman, Christopher: NBC News
Harton, Marcus: Voice of America

Hartzenbusch, Lara: Bloomberg Radio & TV
Harvey, Alan: NBC News
Harwood, John: CNBC
Haselton, Brennan: WTOP Radio
Hasenberg, Amy: Fox News
Hash, James: WUSA–TV
Hassel-Schumacher, Bettina: German TV ARD
Hatfield, William: NBC News
Havekost, Amanda: Scripps News
Hawkins, Shonty: WJLA–TV / Newschannel 8
Hawkins, Shonty: WUSA–TV
Haygood, Alicia: TIMA
Haynes, Maurice: C–SPAN
Haynes, Oscar: Voice of America
Hays, Guerin: Aljazeera America
Haywood, Barry: ABC News
He, Alan: CBS News
He, Wenjin: China Central TV Bureau
Headington, Brady: Hearst Television Inc.
Healey, Sean: CBS News
Hecht, Barry: Diversified Communications, Inc. (DCI)
Heckman, Jory: Federal News Radio 1500 AM
Hedges, Thomas: Real News Network
Heffley, William: C–SPAN
Heidarpour, Sarah: NBC News
Heina, Martin: Fox News
Heinbaugh, Jack: WRC–TV / NBC–4
Heiner, Stephen: Middle East Broadcasting Networks (MBN)
Heitz, Dianna: CNN
Hemmer, Bill: Fox News
Henao, Liliana: Telemundo Network
Henderson, Susan: AP–Broadcast
Henderson, Tim: Stateline.org
Hendin, Robert: CBS News
Hendren, John: Aljazeera English
Henning, Daniel: Sirius XM Satellite Radio
Henry, Chas: WNEW / CBS DC
Henry, Ed: Fox News
Henry, Jonelle P.: C–SPAN
Henry, Robert: Sirius XM Satellite Radio
Henry, Shirley: National Public Radio
Herbas, Francis: Fox News
Heritage, Robert: NBC News
Hermelijn, Ryan: NOS Dutch Public Radio & TV (VRT)
Hernandez-Arthur, Simon: CNN
Hernandez-Orellana, Angel: WFDC–TV Univision
Hernon, Louise: NBC News
Herrera, Esequiel: ABC News
Herrera, Ruben: German TV ZDF
Herridge, Catherine: Fox News
Herring, Charles: One America
Hess, Bill: Wmal Radio
Hesse, Alicia: One America
Hesson, Ted: Univision
Hickman, Stacy: Fox News

Higgins, Ricardo: WRC–TV / NBC–4
Hijazin, Paul: Sky News Arabia
Hilk, Matthew: CNN
Hill, Angela: Scripps News
Hill, Ashley: C–SPAN
Hill, Charles: ABC News
Hill, Dallas: C–SPAN
Hill, Joanna: Fox News
Hill, Jonquilyn: Time Warner Cable
Hill, Martin: Fox News
Hill, Robert: Australian Broadcasting Corporation
Hillary, Cecily: Voice of America
Hillyard, Caitlin: C–SPAN
Hillyard, Vaughn: NBC News
Himelein, Scott: Fox News
Hindes, Walter: SRN News (Salem)
Hinds, Hugh: WRC–TV / NBC–4
Hines, Andrea: ABC News
Hinman, Katherine: CNN
Hinson, Elizabeth: CBS News
Hirouchi, Hitoshi: NHK
Hirten, Kevin: Aljazeera English
Ho, King: Radio Free Asia
Hoang, Chan Nhu: Radio Free Asia
Hoar, Adrienne: C–SPAN
Hodge, Darnley: NBC Newschannel
Hoese, Christine: Mobile Video Services, Ltd.
Hoffman, Brian: AP–Broadcast
Hofstedt, Loic: Agence France Presse (AFP–TV)
Hoja, Gulchehra: Radio Free Asia
Holland, John: NBC News
Hollenbeck, Paul: BT Video Productions
Hollingsworth, Barbara: CNSNews.com
Holm, Gro: Norwegian Broadcasting
Holman, Kwame: Medill News Service
Holmes, Horace: WJLA–TV / Newschannel 8
Holmes, Kristen: CNN
Holton, Brett: WJLA–TV / Newschannel 8
Holton, Jennifer: Fox News
Honegger, Arthur: Swiss Broadcasting
Hong, Hyunjin: Korean Broadcasting Systems
Hooper, Molly: The Hill
Hoover, Toni: CBS News
Hopkins, Adrienne Moira: Fox News
Hopkins, Brian: WJLA–TV / Newschannel 8
Hopper, David: BBC
Horacek, Slade: C–SPAN
Horan, Michael: WTTG–Fox Television
Horchler, Andreas: German Public Radio (ARD)
Horie, Tomoko: Nippon TV Network
Hormuth, Thomas: WJLA–TV / Newschannel 8
Horn, Brad: Washingtonpost.com
Horn, Caroline: CBS News
Horn, Charles: Viewpoint Communications
Horne, Latanya: WJLA–TV / Newschannel 8
Horrigan, Derek: CNN
Horsley, Scott: National Public Radio

MEMBERS ENTITLED TO ADMISSION—Continued

Horton, Harry: Independent Television News (ITN)
Hosokawa, Chinatsu: Nippon TV Network
Hotta, Takashi: TV Asahi
House, Amanda: One America
House II, Charles: RTTV America
Hovell, Dean G.: ABC News
Howard, Cory R.: Fox News
Howard, Jim: St. Louis Public Radio
Howard, Kevin: ABC News
Howell, Emily: CNN
Hoye, Matthew: CNN
Hristova, Rozalia: BBC
Hsieh, Yi-Pe: C–SPAN
Hssaini, Nasser: Aljazeera Satellite Channel (Peninsula)
Huang, Zhuo: Hong Kong Phoenix Satellite Television
Hubert, Jason: ABC News
Hubert-Hogg, Aja: China Central TV Bureau
Huchet, Josselin: TF1–French TV
Huether, Andy: National Public Radio
Huff, Dan: AP–Broadcast
Huff, Priscilla: Feature Story News
Hughes, Brittany: CNSNews.com
Hughes, James: NBC News
Hughes, Jillian: CBS News
Hughes, Katherine: C–SPAN
Hume, Brit: Fox News
Humeau, Thierry: Aljazeera English
Hummelsheim, Scott: C–SPAN
Humphreys, Charles: Sinclair Broadcast Group
Hunsicker, Thomas: WUSA–TV
Hunt, Kasie: NBC News
Hunter, Kia: C–SPAN
Hunter, Melanie: CNSNews.com
Hunter, Paul: Canadian Broadcasting Corporation (CBC)
Hunter, Tracy: C–SPAN
Huntsberry, Will: National Public Radio
Hurst, Nate: C–SPAN
Hurst, Whitney: Aljazeera English
Hurt, James: NBC Newschannel
Husain, Zuleqa: Aljazeera English
Hussein, Omar: AP–Broadcast
Hussin, Utami: Voice of America
Hutcherson, Trudy: Aljazeera America
Hutchinson, Heather: WRC–TV / NBC–4
Hydeck, Michael: WUSA–TV
Hyman, Mark: Sinclair Broadcast Group
Hymson, Paige: CNN
Iacone, Amanda: WTOP Radio
Iacone, Brian: NBC News
Iannelli, Nick: WTOP Radio
Iannuzzi, Julie: USA Today
Ibrahim, Mohammed: APTVS–American Press & TV Services
Ibrahim, Yasmeen: CNN
Ibrahim, Zena: TIMA

Ichihara, Mai: TV Asahi
Ide, Charles: WETA
Ifill, Gwen: The Newshour with Jim Lehrer
Ikonomova, Violet: AP–Broadcast
Ing, Lance: WTTG–Fox Television
Ingle, Cynthia: C–SPAN
Inman, Willie: NHK
Inserra, Donna: WJLA–TV / Newschannel 8
Iorio, Katherine: CBS News
Irons, Mark: EWTN
Irwin, Sarah: Reuters Radio & TV
Isella, Elena: Fox News
Isham, Christopher: CBS News
Ishiyama, Kenkichi: NHK
Italiano, Michael: China Central TV Bureau
Ivey, Michael: Voice of America
Jaakson, Uelle-Mall: Austrian Radio & TV (ORF)
Jackson, Clif: Rural TV News
Jackson, George: WJLA–TV / Newschannel 8
Jackson, Jill: CBS News
Jackson, Kai: Sinclair Broadcast Group
Jackson, Katharine: Reuters Radio & TV
Jackson, Roberta: C–SPAN
Jackson, Ryan: ABC News
Jackson, Samuel: WJLA–TV / Newschannel 8
Jacob, Mitchell: WJLA–TV / Newschannel 8
Jacobi, Steve: CBN News
Jacobs, Adia: CNN
Jacobs, Sarah: WNEW / CBS DC
Jafari, Elmira: China Central TV Bureau
Jaffe, Alexandra: CNN
Jaffe, Gary: Voice of America
Jaffe, Michael: WJLA–TV / Newschannel 8
James, Caroline: Sky News
James, Karen: CNBC
James, Thomas: WUSA–TV
Jamison, Dennis: CBS News
Jamshidi, Kaveh: Voice of America
Janney, Oliver: CNN
Janney, Renata: TV Asahi
Janosky, Jesse: WJLA–TV / Newschannel 8
Jansen, Lesa: Fox News
Jansing, Christine: NBC News
Japaridze, Nunu: Fox News
Jarboe, Brian: National Public Radio
Jarrett, Rick: National Public Radio
Jarvis, Julie: NBC Newschannel
Jaskot, Sheila: Hearst Television Inc.
Javers, Eamon: CNBC
Jay, Courtney: CBS News
Jay, Paul: Real News Network
Jazzaa, Ziad: Al Arabiya TV
Jeffcoat, Jan: WUSA–TV
Jefferson, Richard: CBS News
Jeffrey, Terence: CNSNews.com
Jenkins, David: CNN
Jenkins, Gene: CBN News

MEMBERS ENTITLED TO ADMISSION—Continued

Jenkins, Lee: WUSA–TV
Jenkins, William G.: Fox News
Jennings, Alicia: NBC News
Jennings, Jr., Edward B.: ABC News
Jensen, Heidi: ABC News
Jermin, Ede: WRC–TV / NBC–4
Jessen, Peder: Eurovision Americas, Inc.
Jessup, John: CBN News
Jeswani, Geet: CNN
Jette, Patricia: Religion & Ethics Newsweekly
Jewsevskyj, George: Fox News
Jia, Elizabeth: WUSA–TV
Jia, Li: China Central TV Bureau
Jiang, Weijia: CBS News
Jiang, Xin: China Central TV Bureau
Jibai, Wafaa: AP–Broadcast
Jikamshi, Kabir Isa: Deutsche Welle TV
Jimenez, Martin: Fox Business Network
Joehnk, Astrid: German Public Radio (ARD)
Johns, Joseph: CNN
Johnson, Bruce: WUSA–TV
Johnson, Carrie: National Public Radio
Johnson, Fletcher: Aljazeera America
Johnson, Irene: WRC–TV / NBC–4
Johnson, Jennifer: NBC Newschannel
Johnson, Kevin: Cox Broadcasting
Johnson, Kia: Reuters Radio & TV
Johnson, Martha: AP–Broadcast
Johnson, Shanica: CBS News
Johnston, Jeffrey: CBS News
Johnston, Vanessa: Reuters Radio & TV
Joho, Haruka: Fuji TV Japan
Jones, Alvin: FedNet
Jones, Andrew: C–SPAN
Jones, Athena: CNN
Jones, Blake: C SPAN
Jones, Gwyneth: NBC News
Jones, Jay: CNN
Jones, Joe: Independent Television News (ITN)
Jones, Joyce: Bet Nightly News
Jones, Lorna: CBS News
Jones, Lyrone: WRC–TV / NBC–4
Jones, Morris: WJLA–TV / Newschannel 8
Jones, Nelson: WTTG–Fox Television
Jones, Stephen: Fox News
Jones, Susan: CNSNews.com
Jones, Torrance: Fox News
Jones, Victoria: Talk Radio News Service
Jones, Wes: The Hill
Joo, Bora: JTBC
Joost, Nathalie: Fox News
Jordan, Rosiland: Aljazeera English
Joseph, Akilah: Aljazeera English
Joslyn, James: WJLA–TV / Newschannel 8
Joy, Richard: Ventana Productions
Joyal, Mariana: RTTV America
Joyner, Arcelious: Middle East Broadcasting
    Networks (MBN)

Jubar, Muriel: Aljazeera English
Jubilla, Angel: RTTV America
Judd, Donald: CBS News
Judge, Mark: CNSNews.com
Juneja, Girish: Independent Television News (ITN)
Jung, Ahreum: Radio Free Asia
Junk, Heidi: Cox Broadcasting
Just, Sara: The Newshour with Jim Lehrer
Kabbaj, Abdelhakim: TIMA
Kades, Cathy: NBC News
Kalman, Nick: Fox News
Kamat, Anjali: Aljazeera English
Kanani, Bazi: ABC News
Kane, Jason: The Newshour with Jim Lehrer
Kang, Yang Woo: MBC-TV Korea (Munhwa)
Kanicka, Stephen: Fox News
Kanneth, Polson: CNN
Kanneth, Polson: ABC News
Kapadia, Shefali: Federal News Radio 1500 AM
Kaplan, Bill: Metro Teleproductions
Kaplan, Rebecca: CBS News
Karl, Jonathan: ABC News
Kashfi, Monna: China Central TV Bureau
Kashgary, Jilil: Radio Free Asia
Kastens, Katie: ABC News
Kato, Atsushi: NHK
Katz, Craig: CBS News
Katz, Drew: CBS News
Kawamoto, Mitsuo: TV Tokyo
Kawana, Chihiro: Nippon TV Network
Kay, Katty: BBC
Kaye, Matthew: The Berns Bureau, Inc.
Kaye, Stephanie: C–SPAN
Keator, John C.: National Public Radio
Keedy, Matthew: CBN News
Keene, Jeffrey: WUSA–TV
Kehoe, Steve: C SPAN
Keilar, Brianna: CNN
Keith, Tamara: National Public Radio
Kelemen, Michele: National Public Radio
Kellerman, Mike: Xinhua
Kelley, Colleen: Fox News
Kelley, Jon: C–SPAN
Kelley, Pamela: CNN
Kelly, Amita: National Public Radio
Kelly, Cristina: EWTN
Kelly, Terence: NBC News
Kennedy, Robert: C–SPAN
Kennedy, Suzanne: WJLA–TV / Newschannel 8
Kenney, Colleen: China Central TV Bureau
Kent, Peter: NBC News
Kenyon, Linda: SRN News (Salem)
Kerchner, Eric: CBS News
Kerley, David: ABC News
Kern, Barkley: C–SPAN
Kernmayer, Ernst: Austrian Radio & TV (ORF)
Kerr, Roxane: C–SPAN

MEMBERS ENTITLED TO ADMISSION—Continued

Kerr, Ryan: RTTV America
Kerwin, Christopher: WRC–TV / NBC–4
Kerwin, Kristen: WRC–TV / NBC–4
Kessler, Jonathan: CBS News
Kettlewell, Christian: AP–Broadcast
Keyes, Allison: CBS News
Khairy, Khaled: Middle East Broadcasting Networks (MBN)
Khalaf, Lina: Aljazeera Satellite Channel (Peninsula)
Khalid, Barakat: 50 Frames
Khalid, Hind: 50 Frames
Khalid, Zaidoon: 50 Frames
Khan, Mariam: Gray Television
Khan, Muhammed: National Public Radio
Khananayev, Grigory: Fox News
Kharel, Nilu: Sagarmatha Television
Kharel, Ram C.: Sagarmatha Television
Khemlani, Anjalee: RTTV America
Khimm, Suzy: NBC News
Khristenko, Alexander: Russian State TV And Radio (RTR)
Kiang, Kylene: Aljazeera English
Kianpour, Suzanne: BBC
Kidd, Sally F.: Hearst Television Inc.
Kiernan, Ryan: NBC News
Kiesch, Zachary: WRC–TV / NBC–4
Kill, Adrian: Diversified Communications, Inc. (DCI)
Killion, Nikole: Hearst Television Inc.
Killough, Ashley: CNN
Kim, Beomhyun: Yonhap News TV
Kim, Hyunki: JTBC
Kim, Lauren: Yonhap News TV
Kim, SungJin: Korean Broadcasting Systems
Kim, William: Voice of America
Kim, Woo Sik: Seoul Broadcasting System (Sbs)
Kimani, Julia: CBS News
King, John: CNN
King, Kevin: C–SPAN
King, Kevin G.: WUSA–TV
King, Llewellyn: White House Chronicle
King, Nathan: China Central TV Bureau
King Lilleston, Kristi: WTOP Radio
Kirby, Kevin: Fox News
Kirby, Michael: FedNet
Kirkland, Pamela: Washingtonpost.com
Kirkland, Sara: WRC–TV / NBC–4
Kirst, Anna: Austrian Radio & TV (ORF)
Kistner, William: WUSA–TV
Kitchener, Jillian: Reuters Radio & TV
Klayman, Elliot: Eye-To-Eye Video
Kleim, Peter: N-TV German News Channel
Klein, Alexander: N-TV German News Channel
Klein, Kent: Sirius XM Satellite Radio
Klein, Mary: CNN
Klein, Richard: ABC News
Klein, Stacey: NBC News

Kline, Deirdre: Middle East Broadcasting Networks (MBN)
Kline, Jeff: Hispanic Communications Network
Klopp, Felicitas: German TV ARD
Klos, Daniel: CBS News
Knapp, Timothy: Mobile Video Services, Ltd.
Knier, Thomas: Ventana Productions
Knight, Benjamin: Australian Broadcasting Corporation
Knight, Graham: WUSA–TV
Knighton, David: C–SPAN
Knoller, Mark: CBS News
Kodjak, Alison: National Public Radio
Koerber, Ashley: Fox News
Kolinovsky, Sarah: ABC News
Kolpak, Melissa: RTTV America
Konno, Hiroaki: Nippon TV Network
Kono, Torao: NHK
Koolhof, Vanessa M.: WJLA–TV / Newschannel 8
Kopp, Emily: Federal News Radio 1500 AM
Koprowicz, Tatiana: Voice of America
Koran, Laura: CNN
Korff, Jay: WJLA–TV / Newschannel 8
Kornely, Michael: Voice of America
Korte, Cara: CBS News
Kos, Martin: BT Video Productions
Koscielniak, Jessica: McClatchy
Kosinski, Michelle: CNN
Kosnar, Michael: NBC News
Koster, Jesse: Voice of America
Kostrikov, Pavel: Russian State TV And Radio (RTR)
Kotke, Wolfgang: German TV ZDF
Kotuby, Stephanie: The Newshour with Jim Lehrer
Kotuby, Stephanie: Bloomberg Radio & TV
Kovach, Bob: The Newshour with Jim Lehrer
Kozel, Sandy: AP–Broadcast
Krahenbuhl, Raquel: TV Globo International
Kramer, Kent: Radio One
Kreinbihl, Mary: Fox Business Network
Krieger, Hilary: CNN
Krohn, Tina-Jane: Storyhouse Productions
Kroker, Florian: Deutsche Welle TV
Kroll, Donald Eugene: ABC News
Krolowitz, Ben: CNN
Krupin, David: EWTN
Krupnik, Kathryn: Fox News
Ksiazek, Whitney: Fox News
Kube, Courtney: NBC News
Kulman, Betsy: Aljazeera America
Kuo, Frances: China Central TV Bureau
Kupper, Carmen: German TV ZDF
Kurtz, Howard: Fox News
Kurzius, Rachel: Sirius XM Satellite Radio
Kutay, Cumhur: Turkish Radio and Television (TRT)
Kutler, Rebecca: CNN
Kwan, Chi: Shenzhen Media Group (SZMG)

MEMBERS ENTITLED TO ADMISSION—Continued

Labaton, Arnold: Religion & Ethics Newsweekly
Labella, Mike: Aljazeera English
Labott, Elise: CNN
Laboy, Felix: C–SPAN
Lacey, Donna: Fox News
Lafrankie, Susanne: EWTN
Lai, Daniel: Hong Kong Phoenix Satellite Television
Lai, Yunhe: China Central TV Bureau
Lamb, Brian: C–SPAN
Lamb, Debbie: C–SPAN
Lamonica, Ely: Voyage Productions
Lamonica, Gabe: CBS News
Lamonica, Jay: Aljazeera America
Lamp, Kelly: WJLA–TV / Newschannel 8
Landers, Elizabeth: CNN
Landy, Ekaterina: Aljazeera English
Landy, John: BBC
Lane, Christopher: WETA
Lane, Sam: The Newshour with Jim Lehrer
Langkilde, Johannes: Danish Broadcasting Corporation
Lannigan, Katherine: Aljazeera English
Lanningham, Kyle: Swedish Broadcasting
Lanningham, Sarah: Eurovision Americas, Inc.
Lanzendoerfer, Nancy: N24 German TV
Larade, Darren: C–SPAN
Larocca, Justin: Aljazeera America
Larosa, Michael: NBC News
Larotonda, Matt: ABC News
Larsen, Greg: CBS News
Larson, Lauren: Federal News Radio 1500 AM
Laslo, Matt: Laslo Congressional Bureau
Latendresse, Richard: Groupe TVA
Latreille, Christian: Canadian Broadcasting Corporation (CBC)
Latremoliere, France: NBC News
Laughlin, Ara: CTV–Community TV of PG County
Lautenbach, Barbara: German TV ARD
Laville, Molly: C–SPAN
Lawrence, Chris: WRC–TV / NBC–4
Lawrence, John: Ventana Productions
Lawton, Kim: Religion & Ethics Newsweekly
Lazar, Robert: C–SPAN
Lazarev, Anatoly: Channel One Russian TV
Lazernik, Ira: China Central TV Bureau
Leahigh, Pamela: WRC–TV / NBC–4
Leake, Myron: ABC News
Leaming, Whitney: Washingtonpost.com
Lebedeva, Natasha: NBC News
Lecroy, Philip: Fox News
Leddon, Jerome: C–SPAN
Lee, Alex: CNN
Lee, Donald A.: CBS News
Lee, Edward: WETA
Lee, Erik: WUSA–TV
Lee, Jennifer: Hong Kong Phoenix Satellite Television
Lee, Juhan: Korean Broadcasting Systems

Lee, Kangduk: Korean Broadcasting Systems
Lee, MJ: CNN
Lee, Sangbok: JTBC
Lee, Yihua: Voice of America
Legget, Dennis: Aljazeera English
Leidelmeyer, Ronald: WRC–TV / NBC–4
Leiken, Katherine: German TV ZDF
Leimbach, Nicholas: WUSA–TV
Lemes, Jairo: WFDC–TV Univision
Lenghi, Abdulmola: WUSA–TV
Lent, David: German TV ARD
Leong, Dexter: CBS News
Leong, Ming: WJLA–TV / Newschannel 8
Leroy, Jean-Pierre: Voice of America
Leshan, Bruce: WUSA–TV
Lesser, Howard: Washington Radio and Press Service
Lester, Paul: WTTG–Fox Television
Levenson, Michael: Verizon
Levine, Adam: CNN
Levine, Indira: WTTG–Fox Television
Levine, Michael: ABC News
Levitt, Ross: CNN
Levkovich, Denis: Feature Story News
Levy, Adam: CNN
Lewis, Darral: CBS News
Lewis, Edward: Fox News
Lewis, John B.: WJLA–TV / Newschannel 8
Lewis, Kevin: WJLA–TV / Newschannel 8
Lewis, Loretta: Talk Radio News Service
Lewis, Misha: CNN
Lewnes, Lisa: Reuters Radio & TV
Li, Alice: Washingtonpost.com
Li, Meng: China Central TV Bureau
Li, Xiang: AP–Broadcast
Li, Zhujun: China Central TV Bureau
Liao, Nicholas: Religion & Ethics Newsweekly
Liasson, Mara: National Public Radio
Libert, Tara: German TV ARD
Lien, Arthur: NBC News
Lien, Jonathan: CBS News
Liesegang, Albert: Diversified Communications, Inc. (DCI)
Liffiton, Bruce: CBS News
Lilling, Dave: Metro Teleproductions
Lim, Lister: Aljazeera English
Lim, Sang: Mbc–TV Korea (Munhwa)
Limon-Parresol, Alexandra: WTTG–Fox Television
Lin, Chuan: New Tang Dynasty TV
Lin, Hui: China Central TV Bureau
Lin, Joy: Fox News
Linden, Louis: Diversified Communications, Inc. (DCI)
Lindsey, Melvin: ABC News
Lipes, Joshua: Radio Free Asia
Liptak, Kevin: CNN
Lisko, Lisa: WJLA–TV / Newschannel 8
Little, Craig: WTTG–Fox Television

MEMBERS ENTITLED TO ADMISSION—Continued

Littleton, Philip: CNN
Litzinger, Sam: CBS News
Liu, Libo: Voice of America
Liu, Shuai: Xinhua
Liu, Xiyang: China Central TV Bureau
Livelli, Kevin: CBS News
Liversidge, Jade: Independent Television News (ITN)
Lloyd, Brian: C–SPAN
Lloyd, Robert: ABC News
Lobianco, Thomas: CNN
Lodoe, Kalden: Radio Free Asia
Loebach, Joseph W.: NBC News
Loeschke, Paul: C–SPAN
Logan, Lara: CBS News
Logan, Russell: C–SPAN
Logriera, Diana: Voice of America
Loker, Jessica: Fox News
Long, James V.: NBC News
Loomans, Kathryn: AP–Broadcast
Lopez, Juan Carlos: CNN
Lopez Reyes, Edwing: Telemundo Network
Lord, William: WUSA–TV
Lorenz, Brooke: CNN
Lorenzen, Elizabeth: Native American TV (NATV)
Lorenzen, Jacob: Danish Broadcasting Corporation
Lormand, John: SRN News (Salem)
Loughlin, Ryan: Aljazeera America
Love, Alysha: CNN
Lovelace, Anthony: Native American TV (NATV)
Lowman, Wayne: Fox News
Lowther, Jason: Canadian Broadcasting Corporation (CBC)
Lu, Tao: Hong Kong Phoenix Satellite Television
Lucas, David: WJLA–TV / Newschannel 8
Lucchini, Maria Rosa: WFDC–TV Univision
Lucero, Ivette: C–SPAN
Lukas, Jayne: Global TV Canada
Luke, Colette: Reuters Radio & TV
Luna, Nathan: Hearst Television Inc.
Lundin, Lori: WTOP Radio
Lutterbeck, Deborah: Reuters Radio & TV
Luzader, Doug: Fox News
Ly, Sherri: WTTG–Fox Television
Lylo, Natalie: CNN
Lynds, Stacia: Fox News
Lynn, Gary: NBC News
Lyon, Michael: Fox News
Lyons, Kathryn: NBC News
Ma, Jing: China Central TV Bureau
Macaluso, Michelle: Fox News
Macaya, Melissa: CNN
Macchi, Victoria: Voice of America
Macdonald, Neil: Canadian Broadcasting Corporation (CBC)
MacFarlane, Scott: WRC–TV / NBC–4
MacGillivray, Graham: C–SPAN
Macholz, Wolfgang: German TV ZDF

Macias, Mitzi: Voice of America
MacKay, James: WNEW / CBS DC
Mackie, Gerard: Aljazeera English
MacNeil, Lachlan Murdoch: ABC News
MacVicar, Sheila: Aljazeera America
Madigan, Tracey: WJLA–TV / Newschannel 8
Madsen, Marion: NHK
Mager, Dickon: Sky News
Mahboba, Ali: APTVS–American Press & TV Services
Mahdi, Ali: Middle East Broadcasting Networks (MBN)
Maher, Jennifer: ABC News
Majeed, Alicia: NBC News
Makori, Vincent: Voice of America
Malbon, Joy: CTV Canadian TV
Mallin, Alexander: ABC News
Mallonee, Mary Kay: CNN
Malloy, Allison: CNN
Malloy, Brian: Eurovision Americas, Inc.
Malone, James: Voice of America
Maltas, Michael: Fox News
Mamonov, Roman: RTVI / ECHO–TV
Manby, Mary: NBC News
Mandelson, Adam: Eurovision Americas, Inc.
Mann, Jon: WJLA–TV / Newschannel 8
Mansour, Fadi: Aljazeera Satellite Channel (Peninsula)
Manzarpour, Mohammad: Voice of America
Maounis, Nico: AP–Broadcast
Maqbool, Aleem: BBC
Marantz, Michael: WTTG–Fox Television
March, Stephanie: Australian Broadcasting Corporation
Marchione, Mark Anthony: CNN
Marchitto, Tom: National Public Radio
Marcum, James: WJLA–TV / Newschannel 8
Marfil, Jude: Wall Street Journal
Maric, Goran: Aljazeera English
Marion, Marvin: Voice of America
Markarian, Shant: TIMA
Marks, Carole: Talk Radio News Service
Marks, Simon: Feature Story News
Markwell, Lindle: BBC
Marno, Joseph: Aljazeera English
Marques, Antonio: German TV ZDF
Marquez, Maria: Aljazeera English
Marquis, Melissa: National Public Radio
Marrapodi, Eric: CNN
Marriott, Marc: NBC News
Marsh, Rene: CNN
Marshall, Madeline: Wall Street Journal
Marshall, Serena: ABC News
Marshall, Steve: CBS News
Marshall-Genzer, Nancy: Marketplace Radio
Martin, Ben: Independent Television News (ITN)
Martin, David: CBS News
Martin, Greg: NBC News

MEMBERS ENTITLED TO ADMISSION—Continued

Martin, Lori: Fox News
Martin, Michel: National Public Radio
Martin, Wisdom: WTTG–Fox Television
Martin Ewing, Samara: WUSA–TV
Martin, Jr., James: ABC News
Martinez, Carlos: WRC–TV / NBC–4
Martinez, Luis: ABC News
Martinez, Mercedes: Aljazeera English
Martino, Jeff: Canadian Broadcasting Corporation (CBC)
Masecchia, Mark: WTTG–Fox Television
Mason, Julie: Sirius XM Satellite Radio
Mason, Tabetha: Aljazeera English
Masoud, Barin: BBC
Mass, Lilian: WFDC–TV Univision
Massey, Emily: CNN
Massimi, Alice: Fox News
Massoni, Gregory: Sinclair Broadcast Group
Mathis, James: NBC Newschannel
Matkosky, Tim: Cox Broadcasting
Matsuyama, Toshiyuki: Fuji TV Japan
Matthews, Andre: CTV–Community TV of PG County
Matthews, Chris: NBC News
Matthews, Timothy: WJLA–TV / Newschannel 8
Matthews, Valerie: C–SPAN
Mattingly, Phil: Bloomberg Radio & TV
Matza, Max: BBC
Matzka, Jeffrey: SRN News (Salem)
May, Adam: Aljazeera America
Mazariegos, Luis: To The Contrary (Persephone Productions)
Mazariegos, Mark: CBS News
Mazrieva, Eva: Voice of America
Mazyck, Robin: CBN News
Mazza, Mathieu: German TV ZDF
Mazzetti, Margaret: AP–Broadcast
McAleese, Kevin: Feature Story News
McArdle, John: C–SPAN
McCabe, Neil: One America
McCabe, Valerie: Aljazeera America
McCagg, David: NHK
McCalley, Sean: Federal News Radio 1500 AM
McCann, Michael: C–SPAN
McCann, Sean: C–SPAN
McCarren, Andrea: WUSA–TV
McCarthy, Roberto: Telesur
McCarty, D. Jay: CBS News
McCarty, D. Page: CBS News
McCary, Christopher: ABC News
McCash, Douglas: German TV ZDF
McClam, Kevin: Fox News
McClellan, Max: CBS News
McCloskey, George: Fox News
McClure, Tipp: Reuters Radio & TV
McConnell, Dave: WTOP Radio
McConnell, Dugald: CNN
McCrary, Scott: CBS News

McCray, Ronnie: WTTG–Fox Television
McCreesh, Seamus: FedNet
McDevitt, Lauren: Hearst Television Inc.
McDonald, Joel: WUSA–TV
McDonald, William: Talk Radio News Service
McDonough, Constance: Fox News
McDougall, Ian: NBC News
McEachern, Terrance: Fox News
McFarland, Patty: NBC News
McGarrity, Gerard: C–SPAN
McGinnis, Susan: CBS News
McGinty, Derek: WUSA–TV
McGlinchy, Jim: CBS News
McGrath, Megan: WRC–TV / NBC–4
McGreevy, Allen: Aljazeera English / BBC
McGuire, Gitte: Danish Broadcasting Corporation
McGuire, Michael: CBS News
McHenry, Robert: ABC News
McIntosh, Denise: CNN
McIntyre, Colin: Aljazeera English
McIntyre, Jamie: Aljazeera America
McKellogg, Julieann: McClatchy
McKelvey, Tara: BBC
McKelway, Doug: Fox News
McKenna, Duncan: CBS News
McKenna, William: BBC
McKinley, Robert: CBS News
McKinney, Lee: NBC News
McLellan, Daniel: CBS News
McLellan, Jennifer: Sirius XM Satellite Radio
McManamon, Erin T.: Hearst Television Inc.
McManus, Nicole: NBC Newschannel
McMichael IV, Samuel J.: CNN
McMinn, Nan Hee: AP–Broadcast
McMullan, Michael: CNN
McNair, Erik: ABC News
McNary, Kirstin: Fox News Radio
McPike, Erin: CNN
Means, Jeffrey: Voice of America
Mears, Carroll Ann: NBC News
Mebane, Martinez: ABC News
Mecham, John: RTTV America
Meech, James: CNN
Meek, James: ABC News
Mees, John: CTV Canadian TV
Meghani, Sagar: AP–Broadcast
Mei, Yan: China Central TV Bureau
Meier, Kenneth: Verizon
Meier, Lauren: CNN
Meier, Markus: Austrian Radio & TV (ORF)
Melhem, Omar: Al Arabiya TV
Melhem, Richard: Al Arabiya TV
Meluza, Lourdes: Univision
Men, Kimseng: Voice of America
Meraz, Gregorio: Televisa News Network (ECO)
Meredith, Mark: Media General
Merena, Michael: National Public Radio

MEMBERS ENTITLED TO ADMISSION—Continued

Mergener, Tara: CBS News
Merica, Daniel: CNN
Meriwether, Brooks: WUSA–TV
Metcalfe, Rhoda: Canadian Broadcasting
   Corporation (CBC)
Metzger, Justin: C–SPAN
Metzger, Rochelle: CTV–Community TV of PG
   County
Metzler, Rebekah: CNN
Meyer, Alison: CNSNews.com
Meyer, Kellie: Lilly Broadcasting
Meyer, Kerry: Diversified Communications, Inc.
   (DCI)
Michaud, Robert: Aljazeera English
Micklos, Gregg: WJLA–TV / Newschannel 8
Mikell, Jennifer: CNN
Miklaszewski, James: NBC News
Mikols, Glenn: Eurovision Americas, Inc.
Mikutsky, Dave: NBC News
Milam, Greg: Sky News
Milford, Robert H.: Mobile Video Services, Ltd.
Millan, Alejandro: TVE—Spanish Public Television
Millar, Christopher: NBC News
Millar, Lisa: Australian Broadcasting Corporation
Miller, Alex: Gray Television
Miller, Andrew Peter: C–SPAN
Miller, Avery: ABC News
Miller, Charles: German TV ARD
Miller, Emily: WTTG–Fox Television
Miller, Jake: CBS News
Miller, Jason: Federal News Radio 1500 AM
Miller, Joshua: Sinclair Broadcast Group
Miller, Larry: WUSA–TV
Miller, Lawrence: Epa - European Press Agency
Miller, Mitchell: WTOP Radio
Miller, Paul: CNN
Miller, Tim: Middle East Broadcasting Networks
   (MBN)
Mills, Chris: Fox Business Network
Mills, Joe: National Public Radio
Mills, Kate: C–SPAN
Millward, Craig: CNSNews.com
Milton, Pat: CBS News
Minner, Richard: NBC News
Minott, Gloria: WPFW–FM
Mir, Mashaal: Independent Television News (ITN)
Miran, Alec: CNN
Miranda, Alfredo: Estrella TV
Mirsaeedi, Guita: Voice of America
Mishev, Riste: Macedonia Radio Television
   (MRTV)
Mishkin, Jay: WUSA–TV
Mitchell, Andrea: NBC News
Mitchell, Angela: EWTN
Mitchell, Justin: Reuters Radio & TV
Mitnick, Steven: NBC News
Miyake, Yuko: TV Tokyo
Mizell, Shannon: NBC News

Mizukami, Takashi: NHK
Mock, Michael: Aljazeera English
Moe, Alexandra: NBC News
Mogor, John: WUSA–TV
Mohammadi, Nega: Voice of America
Moise, Joseph: WJLA–TV / Newschannel 8
Molinares-Hess, Ione Indira: CNN
Mollenbeck, Andrew: WTOP Radio
Moller, Jeffrey: CNN
Mollet, Melissa: WRC–TV / NBC–4
Monack, David: C–SPAN
Monsalve, Lizeth Juliana: Telemundo Network
Montague, William: Norwegian Broadcasting
Montanaro, Domenico: National Public Radio
Montenegro, Lori: Telemundo Network
Montgomery, Tamara: Fox News
Monthei, Matthew: Aljazeera English
Montoro, Victor: C–SPAN
Mooar, Brian: NBC Newschannel
Moody, Christopher: CNN
Moon, Ho Chul: MBC–TV Korea (Munhwa)
Moore, Camille: Hearst Television Inc.
Moore, Garrette: C–SPAN
Moore, Jacob: CBN News
Moore, Linwood: C–SPAN
Moore, Richard: Voice of America
Moore, Robert: Independent Television News (ITN)
Moore, Stacy: WNEW / CBS DC
Moore, Terrence: 24/7 News
Moore, W. Harrison: Middle East Broadcasting
   Networks (MBN)
Moorer, Willie: Voice of America
Moorhead, Jeremy: CNN
Morada, Ray: NBC News
Morales, Isabel: CNN
Moreno, Jaime: CMI TV (Colombia)
Moreno, Julio: RCN–TV (Colombia)
Morgan, Donald: CBS News
Morgan, Nancy: WETA
Morris, Amy: WNEW / CBS DC
Morris, Brittany: NBC News
Morris, Holly: WTTG–Fox Television
Morris, Kylie: Independent Television News (ITN)
Morris, Michael: CNSNews.com
Morris, Peter: CNN
Morrisette, Roland: Bloomberg Radio & TV
Morrison, Mat: China Central TV Bureau
Morrison, Matthew: BBC
Morrison, Vaughn: AP–Broadcast
Morrissey, John: AP–Broadcast
Morrow, Eric: WUSA–TV
Morse, Richard: Fox News
Mortman, Howard: C–SPAN
Morton, Dan: C–SPAN
Mortreux, Vincent: TF1–French TV
Moseley, Virginia: CNN
Moser, Martin: Kcetlink
Mosley, Matthew: Fuji TV Japan

Moton, Kenneth: ABC News
Moubray, Virginia: China Central TV Bureau
Mounts, Ronald: WJLA–TV / Newschannel 8
Mozaffari, Shaheen: NBC News
Mozgovaya, Natalia: Voice of America
Muhammad, Abdulhafeez: Aljazeera English
Muhammad, Alverda: National Scene News
Muhammad, Askia: National Scene News
Muhammad, Seleena M.: Fox News
Muir, Robert: Reuters Radio & TV
Mulcahy, Bridget: Politico.Com
Mullen, Christopher: WUSA–TV
Mullon, Tiffany: Fox News
Munford, Corey: Radio Free Asia
Munoz, Luis: Middle East Broadcasting Networks (MBN)
Murai, Kiyoshi: Tokyo Broadcasting System
Murakami, Rikako: Nippon TV Network
Murillo, Mike: WTOP Radio
Murphy, John: CBS News
Murphy, Rich: China Central TV Bureau
Murphy, Terry: C–SPAN
Murray, Mark: NBC News
Murray, Matthew: WRC–TV / NBC–4
Murray, Sara: CNN
Murray, Timothy K.: Ventana Productions
Mursa, Alexander: RTTV America
Murtaugh, Peter: BBC
Muscat, Sabine: N24 German TV
Muskat, Steven: NBC Newschannel
Myers, Bryan: Aljazeera America
Myers, Dwayne: WJLA–TV / Newschannel 8
Myrick, Yetta: C–SPAN
Naderi, Dayheem: Aljazeera English
Nado, Jill: Fox News Radio
Naing, Thet: Voice of America
Najarian, Sarkis: Radio Free Asia
Najjar, Ruqaiyah: China Central TV Bureau
Nakano, Junko Tanaka: NHK
Namdar, Asieh: China Central TV Bureau
Nania, Rachel: WTOP Radio
Nannes, Steven: CNN
Narahari, Priya: Eurovision Americas, Inc.
Narayan, Vivek: Scripps News
Narisi, Stephen: N24 German TV
Nash, Todd: To The Contrary (Persephone Productions)
Nasir, Noreen: The Newshour with Jim Lehrer
Nason, Andrew: C–SPAN
Nasser, Mohamed: AP–Broadcast
Nathan, Nancy: CNN
Naylor, Brian: National Public Radio
Naylor, Robert: Voice of America
Neal, Jason: NBC News
Neal, Michelle: NBC News
Neary, Sean: Voice of America
Neely, Brett: Minnesota Public Radio
Negron, Mynellies: WFDC–TV Univision

Neill, Tara: BBC
Nelson, Christopher: National Public Radio
Nelson, Donna: NBC News
Nelson, James: Fox News
Nelson, Joseph: Washington Bureau News Service
Nettles, Meredith: ABC News
Neubauer, Kristin: Reuters Radio & TV
Nevel, Paul "Ja": WETA
Nevins, Elizabeth: NBC News
Newberry, Tom: NBC Newschannel
Newton, Laura: Caracol Television
Nezu, Hirohito: NHK
Nguyen, Anh: Fox News
Nguyen, Giang: China Central TV Bureau
Nguyen, Thao: Voice of America
Nha, Kevin: Korean Broadcasting Systems
Ni, Chia-Hui: TVBS
Nicci, Nicholette: CNN
Niemann, Stefan: German TV ARD
Nikuradze, David: Rustavi 2 Broadcasting Company
Nili, Hadi: BBC
Ninh, Trang (Nicole): C–SPAN
Nishimoto, Momoca: NHK
Nixon, Adam: Middle East Broadcasting Networks (MBN)
Niyongabo, Fidele: Voice of America
Noble, Jeffrey: ABC News
Nobles, Ryan: CNN
Nocciolo, Ernest: CNN
Nolen, John: CBS News
Norins, Jamie: Diversified Communications, Inc. (DCI)
Norling, Richard: ABC News
Norris, Donna: C–SPAN
Norris, James: Middle East Broadcasting Networks (MBN)
Northam, Jackie: National Public Radio
Novosel, James: NBC News
O'Berry, D. Kerry: Fox News
O'Brien, Benen: C–SPAN
O'Brien, David: NBC News
O'Brien, Jane: BBC
O'Connell, Benjamin: C–SPAN
O'Connell, Michael: Federal News Radio 1500 AM
O'Connell, Mike: NBC Newschannel
O'Connell, Rosalie: Voice of America
O'Connor, John: NBC News
O'Connor, Tom: EWTN
O'Donnell, John: RTTV America
O'Donnell, Kelly: NBC News
O'Donnell, Patrick: Eye-To-Eye Video
O'Donoghue, Gary: BBC
O'Gara, Patrick: ABC News
O'Hara, Jessica: Fox News
O'Malley, Ryan: Fox News
O'Molloy, Colm: BBC
O'Neill, Emily: Independent Television News (ITN)
O'Regan, Michael: WRC–TV / NBC–4

MEMBERS ENTITLED TO ADMISSION—Continued

O'Shea, Daniel: ABC News
Oberti, Ralf: Aljazeera English
Oblaender, Carsten: Storyhouse Productions
Och, Andy: Fox News
Odom, Quillie: Fox News
Offermann, Claudia: German TV ZDF
Ogata, Makoto: Tokyo Broadcasting System
Ogrysko, Nicole: Federal News Radio 1500 AM
Oinounou, Mosheh: CBS News
Olabanji, Olajumoke: WJLA–TV / Newschannel 8
Olazagasti, Carlos: Hearst Television Inc.
Olick, Diana: CNBC
Oliger, Brian: WTOP Radio
Ollove, Michael: Stateline.org
Olmsted, Alan: C–SPAN
Olson, Anna: Fox News
Omara, Kamal: AP–Broadcast
Oni, Jesusemen: CTV–Community TV of PG County
Oo, Aung: Voice of America
Oo, Thar: Voice of America
Oo, Thein: Voice of America
Opoku, Stacy: CBN News
Orchard, Mark: Aljazeera America
Orellana, Ernesto: Azteca America
Orenstein, Jayne: Washingtonpost.com
Orgel, Paul: C–SPAN
Ortiz, Fabien: France 2 Television
Oshana, Zaid: Middle East Broadcasting Networks (MBN)
Osinski, Krysia: TIMA
Osman, Abdulaziz: Voice of America
Osman, Jim: Media General
Ouafi, Mohamed: AP–Broadcast
Overby, Peter: National Public Radio
Overzat, Greg: CNN
Owen, Andrea: ABC News
Owens, Dave: WUSA–TV
Ozsancak, Hakan: China Central TV Bureau
Ozug, Matt: National Public Radio
Pacheco, Antonio: WETA
Pacheco-Saenz, Daniel: Caracol Television
Pacuraru, Denis: CBN News
Padial, Maribel: CNN
Padilla-Cirino, Mercy: Hispanic Communications Network
Pagan, Louis: AP–Broadcast
Page, David: CBN News
Page, Steven: CNN
Paggini, Thomas: Swiss Broadcasting
Pal, Meera: WTOP Radio
Palca, Joe: National Public Radio
Palmer, Hope: NBC News
Pande, Aru: Voice of America
Pannell, Ian: BBC
Panov, Alexander: Voice of America
Panzer, Chester: WRC–TV / NBC–4
Paolucci, Chris: West Wing Reports

Papadeas, Tamatha: CBN News
Papinashvili, Aleksandre: Rustavi 2 Broadcasting Company
Papst, Chris: WJLA–TV / Newschannel 8
Paquette, Cherie: Fox News
Parampil, Anya: RTTV America
Park, Bunsoo: MBC-TV Korea (Munhwa)
Park, Edward: Seoul Broadcasting System (SBS)
Park, Jihee: Eurovision Americas, Inc.
Park, Jinkyung: Korean Broadcasting Systems
Park, Jung-Woo: Radio Free Asia
Parker, Andre: CNN
Parker, Beth: WTTG–Fox Television
Parker, Glenn: Canadian Broadcasting Corporation (CBC)
Parker, Marley: CTV Canadian TV
Parker, Robert Geoffrey: CNN
Parkinson, John: ABC News
Parks, Chanlee: Aljazeera English
Parks, Chanlee: Diversified Communications, Inc. (DCI)
Parks, Delbert: Sinclair Broadcast Group
Parks, Maryalice: ABC News
Parks, Melanie: CNN
Parnass, Sarah: Washingtonpost.com
Parsell, Robert: Voice of America
Pathammavong, Kingsavanh: Voice of America
Patience, Keenan: Verizon
Patruznick, Michael: C–SPAN
Patsko, Daniel: ABC News
Pavlov, Nikolai: Reuters Radio & TV
Paxton, Bradford S.: Fox News
Payam, Amir: BBC
Paylor, Eddie: NBC News
Payson-Denney, Wade: CNN
Peace Carr, Renee: WUSA–TV
Peaches, Sandra: CTV–Community TV of PG County
Peacock, Grant: Euronews
Peaks, Gershon: Reuters Radio & TV
Pearson, Hampton: CNBC
Peebles, Daniel: CBS News
Pegues, Jeffrey: CBS News
Pena, Nicolas: Telesur
Pennell, Elizabeth: Morningside Partners, LLC
Pennington, Craig: Aljazeera English
Peppers, Greg: AP–Broadcast
Percha, Julie: Washingtonpost.com
Perez, Bianca: Telesur
Perez, Evan: CNN
Perez, Simone: Aljazeera America
Pergam, Andrew: McClatchy
Pergram, Chad: Fox News
Perkins, Anthony: WTTG–Fox Television
Perkins, Doug: Fox News
Perkins, Vernon: C–SPAN
Perl, Drora: Galei-Tzahal (Israel Army Radio)
Perlmutter-Gumbiner, Elyse: NBC News

MEMBERS ENTITLED TO ADMISSION—Continued

Perlow, Rebecca: CNN
Perrell, Thomas: CNN
Perry, Caitriona: RTE–Irish Radio & TV
Perry, Cal: Voice of America
Perry, Christina: C–SPAN
Perry, Timothy: CBS News
Persinko, Tim: Viewpoint Communications
Persons, Sally Ann: Fox News
Pessin, Don: Reuters Radio & TV
Peterson, Beatrice: Politico.Com
Peterson, Brittany: McClatchy
Peterson II, Robert: CBS News
Petitte, Patti: WRC–TV/NBC–4
Petraitis, Gerald: AP–Broadcast
Petroka, Katelyn: CNN
Pettit, Debra: NBC News
Pexton, Ken: Ventana Productions
Peyton, Michael: CBS News
Pflaum, Nadia: WUSA–TV
Pham, Jacqueline: Fox News
Phan, Thuylan: Viety Network
Phelps, Jordyn: ABC News
Philippe, Jean: Voice of America
Phillips, Steven: Reuters Radio & TV
Piacente Ellen: Morningside Partners, LLC
Pinault, Nicolas: Voice of America
Pinczuk, Murray: Feature Story News
Pinczuk, Murray: NHK
Pineda, Juan: C–SPAN
Ping, Sun: China Central TV Bureau
Pinkston, Randall: Aljazeera America
Pinto, Susanna: EWTN
Pinzon, Wingel: Small House Productions
Piper, Jeff: WRC–TV/NBC–4
Pipkin, Chase: Hearst Television Inc.
Pitocco, Nickolas: C–SPAN
Pitti, Edwin: WFDC–TV Univision
Pizarro, Fernando: Univision
Plante, William: CBS News
Plater, Christopher: WRC–TV/NBC–4
Plater, Roslyn: WJLA–TV/Newschannel 8
Pliszak, Richard: ABC News
Poch, Reasey: Voice of America
Pointinen, Pirkko: Finnish Broadcasting Company
    (YLE)
Pole, Aarti: Global TV Canada
Poley, Michelle: CNN
Policastro, Jacqueline: Gray Television
Pollmann, Mina: TV Tokyo
Polmer, Brendan: CNN
Ponnudurai, Parameswaran: Radio Free Asia
Pontzen, Daniel: German TV ZDF
Poole, John: National Public Radio
Porsella, Claude L.: Radio France Internationale
Porter, Almon: C–SPAN
Porter, Dee: Australian Broadcasting Corporation
Porter, Taylor: C–SPAN
Portnoy, Steve: CBS News

Postovit, David: Hearst Television Inc.
Potts, Charlotte: German TV ARD
Potts, Nina-Maria: Feature Story News
Potts, Tracie: NBC Newschannel
Pourziaiee, Mehrnoosh: BBC
Povich, Elaine: Stateline.org
Powell, Brian William: Radio Free Asia
Powell, Lee: Washingtonpost.com
Prann, Elizabeth: Fox News
Pratapas, Lauren: CNN
Preloh, Anne: C–SPAN
Preston, Mark: CNN
Presutti, Carolyn: Voice of America
Pries, David: C–SPAN
Pronko, Tony: C–SPAN
Proskow, Jackson: Global TV Canada
Pruitt, Claude: Scripps News
Ptacek, Russell: WUSA–TV
Pugliese, Pat: CNBC
Puljic, Ivica: Aljazeera English
Purbaugh, Michael: ABC News
Qi, Xing: Xinhua
Qin, Qi: China Central TV Bureau
Quadrani, Federico: CNN
Quan, Xiangqin: China Central TV Bureau
Quester, Rachel: Scripps News
Quinn, Diana: CBS News
Quinn, John: Voice of America
Quinn, Mary: ABC News
Quinnette, John: NBC News
Quinonez, Omar A.: Aljazeera English
Quiroz, Silvana: WFDC–TV Univision
Rabiee, Mana: Reuters Radio & TV
Rabin, Carrie: CBS News
Rabin, Mark: ABC News
Rabin-Havt, Ari: Sirius XM Satellite Radio
Rad, Ali: Fox News
Raddatz, Martha: ABC News
Rady, Meaghan: NBC News
Raffaele, Robert: Voice of America
Rafferty, Andrew: NBC News
Rafferty, Meghan: CNN
Rager, Bryan: CNBC
Raiford, Roger: Aljazeera English
Raju, Manu: CNN
Rama, Padmananda: AP–Broadcast
Ramadan, Wafik: AP–Broadcast
Ramirez, Edwin: Small House Productions
Ramirez, Luis: Voice of America
Ramirez, Stephanie: WUSA–TV
Ramos, Mario: WFDC–TV Univision
Ramos, Raul: WFDC–TV Univision
Ramos, Stephanie: ABC News
Randev, Sonia: CTV–Community TV of PG County
Randle, James: Voice of America
Raney, Adam: Aljazeera English
Rangel, Hector: WFDC–TV Univision

MEMBERS ENTITLED TO ADMISSION—Continued

Rapalo, Manuel: RTTV America
Rathner, Jeffrey: WETA
Ratliff, Walter: AP–Broadcast
Ratner, Ellen: Talk Radio News Service
Rattansi, Shihab: Aljazeera English
Ratzow, Sandra: German TV ARD
Raullerson, Kevin: EWTN
Raval, Nikhil: C–SPAN
Raviv, Daniel: CBS News
Ray, Alonzo: NBC News
Ray, Douglas: Fox News
Raz, Nicole: Wmal Radio
Rea, Kari: ABC News
Reap, Patrick: Bloomberg Radio & TV
Reber, James: BBC
Reddy, Pallavi: CNN
Reddy, Priya: RTTV America
Reed, Todd: Aljazeera America
Reeve, Richard: WJLA–TV / Newschannel 8
Reeves, Alea: Aljazeera English
Reeves, Austin: WTTG–Fox Television
Reeves, Tralanenia: Sinclair Broadcast Group
Refess, Melanie: NHK
Rehkoph, George: WNEW / CBS DC
Reid, Charles: CBS News
Reid, Paula: CBS News
Reilly, Robert: C–SPAN
Reinsel, Edward: Fox News
Reitz, Kirby: C–SPAN
Remillard, Michele: C–SPAN
Ren, Meixing: AP–Broadcast
Renfro, Owen: Fox News
Renken, David: Fox News
Rensberger, Scott: Cox Broadcasting
Reuter, Cynthia: C–SPAN
Revaz, Philippe: Swiss Broadcasting
Reyes, Elaine: China Central TV Bureau
Reyes, Jeannette: WJLA–TV / Newschannel 8
Reyes, Samantha: CNN
Reyes, Victor: Telemundo Network
Reynolds, Catherine: CBS News
Reynolds, Gioconda: Voice of America
Reynolds, Judy: Religion & Ethics Newsweekly
Reynolds, Robert: Aljazeera English
Reynolds, Talesha: NBC News
Rhee, Sungchul: Seoul Broadcasting System (SBS)
Rhodes, Elizabeth: Fox News
Ribas, Jorge: Washingtonpost.com
Ricalde, Katheryn: Fox News
Ricci, Giuseppe: RTTV America
Rice, John: WJLA–TV / Newschannel 8
Rice, Kelly: China Central TV Bureau
Rice, Lavenia: Bloomberg Radio & TV
Rice, Rodney: Verizon
Richard, Sylvain: Canadian Broadcasting Corporation (CBC)
Richards, Kristen: TIMA

Richardson, Sue: Middle East Broadcasting Networks (MBN)
Richardson, Young: One America
Rickard, Michael: WTTG–Fox Television
Riddle, Casey: CNN
Ridolfi, Sarah: Fox News
Rieger, John: CQ / Roll Call
Riess, Steffanie: German TV ZDF
Riggs, Giaco: NBC News
Rigney, Paul: NBC News
Riha, Anne Marie: Fox News
Riley, Justin: Voice of America
Rios, Delia: C–SPAN
Rios, Paulina: CNN
Rios, Victor: Fox News
Rios-Hernandez, Raul: CNN
Ritchie, Thomas: AP–Broadcast
Rivas-Vazquez, A. Victoria: Telemundo Network
Rivera, Anthony: Laslo Congressional Bureau
Rivera, Denise: Real News Network
Rivera, Matt: NBC News
Riyami, Khadija: Voice of America
Rizvi, Ali: McClatchy
Rizzi, Jared: Sirius XM Satellite Radio
Rizzo, Anthony: WUSA–TV
Rizzo, Jennifer: CNN
Rizzo, John: AP–Broadcast
Rizzolo, Lisa: Fox News
Roane Skehan, Andrea: WUSA–TV
Robbins, Christina: Fox News
Robbins, Diana: German Public Radio (ARD)
Robbins, Francisco: CBS News
Robbins, Michael: Fox News
Robert, Olivier: Eye-To-Eye Video
Roberts, Bryan: WTTG–Fox Television
Roberts, Corinne: ABC News
Roberts, Eugene: ABC News
Roberts, Jean Pierre: Eurovision Americas, Inc.
Roberts, John: Fox News
Roberts, Katherine: WRC–TV / NBC–4
Robertson, Abigail: CBN News
Robertson, Erin: NHK
Robertson, Greg: CNN
Robinson, David: CNN
Robinson, Kelvin: WRC–TV / NBC–4
Robinson, Ralph: Voice of America
Roca, Xavier: Swiss Broadcasting
Rocha, Juan: Ventana Productions
Rocha, Sam: Reuters Radio & TV
Rockell, Kira: Aljazeera English
Rocque, Tiffany: C–SPAN
Rodeffer, Mark: C–SPAN
Rodrigues, Charlitta: CNN
Rodriguez, Eduardo: AP–Broadcast
Rodriguez, Janet: China Central TV Bureau
Rodriguez, Marcela: WFDC–TV Univision
Rodriguez, Martine: C–SPAN
Rodriguez, Valdemar: RCN–TV (Colombia)

MEMBERS ENTITLED TO ADMISSION—Continued

Rodriquez, Eduardo: TIMA
Roeller, Ulf-Jensen: German TV ZDF
Rogers, Rhonda: Fox News
Rohrbaugh, Randy: C–SPAN
Rohrbeck, Douglas: Fox News
Rojas, Simon: Hispanic Communications Network
Rokus, Brian: CNN
Roller, Richard: ABC News
Roof, Peter: NBC Newschannel
Root, Sean: The Hill
Root, Tom: Fox News Radio
Rosario, Eduardo: Eurovision Americas, Inc.
Rosche, Jedd: CNN
Rose, Alicia: NHK
Rose, Art: WTOP Radio
Rose, Francis: Federal News Radio 1500 AM
Rose, Jeff: WJLA–TV / Newschannel 8
Roseboro, Takiha: NBC News
Roseman, Emily: AP–Broadcast
Rosen, Alexander: CNN
Rosen, Ira: CBS News
Rosen, James: Fox News
Rosen, Shari: CNBC
Rosenberg, Gary: ABC News
Rosenberg, Howard: CBS News
Rosero, Rafael: RCN–TV (Colombia)
Ross, Jane: Reuters Radio & TV
Ross Taylor, Allyson: CBS News
Rossetti-Meyer, Misa: Diversified Communications, Inc. (DCI)
Rossoll, Nicole: C–SPAN
Roth, Theodore: ABC News
Roussey, Thomas: WJLA–TV / Newschannel 8
Rowe, Allison: Bloomberg Radio & TV
Rowe, Tom: Reuters Radio & TV
Rowland, Kara: Fox News
Rowls, Megan: WJLA–TV / Newschannel 8
Royce-Bartlett, Lindy: CNN
Roycraft, David: WUSA–TV
Ruck, Ina-Maria: German TV ARD
Rudd, Michael: WJLA–TV / Newschannel 8
Ruderman, Jared: WNEW / CBS DC
Rudman, Kristin: Fox Business Network
Rudnick, Natasha: Washingtonpost.com
Ruff, Jennifer: C–SPAN
Ruffini, Joseph: CBS News
Ruggiero, Diane: CNN
Ruhl, Lisa: Washington Examiner
Rummel, Jordan: NBC News
Rushing, Ian: CBN News
Rushing, Joshua: Aljazeera English
Ruskin, Liz: Alaska Public Radio Network
Russell, Eugene: WTTG–Fox Television
Russell, James: Voice of America
Russert, Luke: NBC News
Ruttenberg, Roee: China Central TV Bureau
Ryan, Kate: WTOP Radio
Rydell, Kate: CBS News

Ryntjes, Daniel: Feature Story News
Rysak, F. David: WTTG–Fox Television
Saada, Nina: Sky News
Sababa, Ghassan: Aljazeera Satellite Channel (Peninsula)
Sacks, Howard: NBC News
Sacks, Sam: RTTV America
Sadighi, Nader: Radio Free Europe
Sadighi, Shahla: Voice of America
Saenz, Katherine: ABC News
Sagalyn, Daniel: The Newshour with Jim Lehrer
Saine-Spang, Cynthia: Voice of America
Sakwa, Jenna: CBS News
Salan, Jennifer: Aljazeera English
Sali, Sanil: Aljazeera English
Salim, Yuni: Voice of America
Salinas, Mary: Voice of America
Saloomey, Kristen: Aljazeera English
Sammon, Bill: Fox News
Sampaio, Frederico: C–SPAN
Samperio, Aurora: Telesur
Sampson, Thomas: AP–Broadcast
Sampy, David: Independent Television News (ITN)
Samuel, Stacey: CNN
Samuels, Stacey: CBS News
Sanchez, George D.: ABC News
Sanchez, Michael: AP–Broadcast
Sanchez, Pablo: Univision
Sanchez, Robert: WNEW / CBS DC
Sanders, Molly: C–SPAN
Sanders-Smith, Sherry: C–SPAN
Sandiford, Michelle: C–SPAN
Sandoval, Polo: CNN
Sands-Sadowitz, Geneva: Univision
Sanfuentes, Antoine: CNN
Sang, Stanley: C–SPAN
Sans, Raquel: TV3–Televisio De Catalunya
Sansone, Amanda: CNN
Sansone, Joseph: CNN
Santa-Rita, Joad: Voice of America
Sanvido, Colleen: NBC News
Sargeant, Nancy: WNEW / CBS DC
Sargent, Mark: WTTG–Fox Television
Sarlin, Benjamin: NBC News
Sarshar, Sahar: China Central TV Bureau
Sarstedt, Jessica: Aljazeera America
Sassenberg, Thomas: Storyhouse Productions
Sasser, Brian: WJLA–TV / Newschannel 8
Satchell, David: WUSA–TV
Sato, Shota: Tokyo Broadcasting System
Satterfield, John: WETA
Saulny, Susan: ABC News
Sauret, Angela: TV3–Televisio De Catalunya
Savage, Craig: Fox News
Savchenko, Yulia: Voice of America
Savoy, Gregory: Reuters Radio & TV
Sawan, Arwa: Middle East Broadcasting Networks (MBN)

MEMBERS ENTITLED TO ADMISSION—Continued

Sawera, Thomas: German TV ARD
Sbalcio, Ian: RTTV America
Scanlan, Bridget: C–SPAN
Scanlan, William: C–SPAN
Scanlon, Jason: Fox News
Schantz, Douglas: CNN
Scharf, Jason: Eurovision Americas, Inc.
Schatz, Rebecca: Washingtonpost.com
Scheimer, Dorey: Cox Broadcasting
Scheiner, Eric: CNSNews.com
Schell, Barbara: Aljazeera English
Scheltens, Elizabeth: Scripps News
Scheuer, John: C–SPAN
Schieffer, Bob: CBS News
Schiff, Brian: Voice of America
Schiffner, Christine: China Central TV Bureau
Schlegel, Barry: ABC News
Schleifer, Teddy: CNN
Schlenker, Aungthu: Radio Free Asia
Schliess, Gero: Deutsche Welle TV
Schloemer, Peter: German TV ZDF
Schneider, Corinne: Aljazeera English
Schneider, Edward: Voice of America
Schneider, Fred: CBS News
Schneider, James: WETA
Schnurr, Samantha: NBC News
Schoenholtz, Howard: ABC News
Schoenmann, Donald: Eye-To-Eye Video
Schonberger, Jennifer: Fox Business Network
Schonder, Gabrielle: CBS News
Schott, Sonia: Radio Valera Venezuela
Schubauer, Katharine: Agence France Presse (AFP–TV)
Schuck, Matthew: One America
Schultze, Franco: WFDC–TV Univision
Schuman, Alex: Media General
Schuster, Henry: CBS News
Schwab, Michael: Politico.Com
Schwandt, Kimberly: Fox News
Schweiger, Ellen: C–SPAN
Schwetje, Lars: Gannett Government Media Corp
Sciacca, Jody: Fox News
Sciutto, James: CNN
Scott, Gurnal: Fox News Radio
Scott, Heather: CBS News
Scott, James: WJLA–TV / Newschannel 8
Scott, Raquel: CNN
Scotto, Michael: Time Warner Cable
Scriabine, Raisa: Kcetlink
Scritchfield, Andrew: NBC News
Scruggs, Wesley: NBC News
Scuiletti, Justin: The Newshour with Jim Lehrer
Scully, Steven: C–SPAN
Seabrook, Andrea: Scripps News
Seabrook, Willliam: WETA
Seaby, Gregory: CNN
Seales, Chance: Media General
Searls, James: WUSA–TV

Sears, Carl: NBC News
Seem, Thomas H.: CBS News
Segears, Leon: EWTN
Segraves, Mark: WRC–TV / NBC–4
Seib, Gerald: Wall Street Journal
Seidman, Joel: NBC News
Seifert, Jan: German TV ZDF
Seipel, Arnie: National Public Radio
Seitz-Wald, Alexander: NBC News
Seium, Michael: Small House Productions
Seldin, Jeff: Voice of America
Semenova, Anna: Russian State TV And Radio (RTR)
Semler, Ashley: BBC
Seo, Ja Ryen: Korean Broadcasting Systems
Serbu, Jared: Federal News Radio 1500 AM
Serdar, Seda: Deutsche Welle TV
Serfaty, Sunlen: CNN
Serhan, Ali: AP–Broadcast
Serna, Adriana: CMI TV (Colombia)
Serper, Noelle: Religion & Ethics Newsweekly
Serrano, Randy: Telemundo Network
Serwer, Adam: NBC News
Sevilla, Maria: NBC News
Shaddick, Lorna: Feature Story News
Shaffir, Gregory: CBS News
Shaffir, Kim: CBS News
Shakhbaz, Samir: RTTV America
Shakhov, Dmytri: Voice of America
Shales, Sarah: WRC–TV / NBC–4
Shalhoup, Joseph: NBC News
Shammo, Hakim: Voice of America
Shannon, Brad: AOL Huffington Post
Shannon, Dennis: CBS News
Shannon, Holly: WJLA–TV / Newschannel 8
Shannon, Michael: ABC News
Sharief, Islam: Aljazeera English
Sharma, Bhupinder: WJLA–TV / Newschannel 8
Sharp, Duncan: Sky News
Shastri, Namgyal: Voice of America
Shaw, Dave: Marketplace Radio
Shaw, Katherine: ABC News
Shaylor, John: CNN
Shear, Margo: WUSA–TV
Sheerin, Jude: Sky News
Shefte, Whitney: Washingtonpost.com
Shelton, Steve: Fox News
Sheppard, Kevin: Sky News
Sheridan, Chris: Aljazeera English
Sherman, Roger: Voice of America
Sherwood, Tom: WRC–TV / NBC–4
Shi, Ying: Voice of America
Shi, Yingshan: Xinhua
Shibaki, Tomokazu: Fuji TV Japan
Shields, Daniel: Fox News Radio
Shields, Michael: Voice of America
Shikaki, Muna: Al Arabiya TV
Shimizu, Jumpei: Nippon TV Network

MEMBERS ENTITLED TO ADMISSION—Continued

Shirley, Matt: China Central TV Bureau
Shlemon, Chris: Independent Television News (ITN)
Shoffner, Harry: NHK
Shon, Robert: WTTG–Fox Television
Shore, Zach: WTOP Radio
Showell, Andre: Bet Nightly News
Shull, Roger: Reuters Radio & TV
Shure, Michael: Aljazeera America
Shutt, Charles: WUSA–TV
Siaden-Pena, Christian: RCN–TV (Colombia)
Sibert, Brandon: NBC News
Sieg, Setareh: Voice of America
Siegel, Benjamin: ABC News
Siegel, David: CNN
Siegel, Robert C.: National Public Radio
Siegfriedt, Anita: Fox News
Sills, Cecil John: NBC Newschannel
Silva, Juan: Mundofox
Silva-Pinto, Daniel: TV Globo International
Silva-Pinto, Lauren: Austrian Radio & TV (ORF)
Silva-Pinto, Luis Fernando: TV Globo International
Silver, Quentin: NBC News
Silverberg, Howard: WUSA–TV
Silverman, Art: National Public Radio
Silverman, Rachel: Feature Story News
Simeone, Ron: NBC News
Simkins, George: Voice of America
Simmons, Sarah: WTTG–Fox Television
Simms, Jeffery: CNN
Simoes, Hugo: Diversified Communications, Inc. (DCI)
Simon, Jeff: CNN
Simon, Matthew: China Central TV Bureau
Simone, Cheryl: WNEW / CBS DC
Simpson, Alvon: ABC News
Simpson, Jennifer: CNN
Sims, Meghan: McClatchy
Sindass, Loriston: WUSA–TV
Sinn, Rebecca: WJLA–TV / Newschannel 8
Sipos, Joseph: Voice of America
Sistrunk, Jocelyn: WJLA–TV / Newschannel 8
Skeans, Ron: BBC
Skeen, Kimberly: Sinclair Broadcast Group
Skeen, Kimberly: CBS News
Skene, Mathieu: Aljazeera English
Skinski, Kathleen: CNN
Skomal, Paul: Eurovision Americas, Inc.
Skopek, Aaron: NBC News
Skov, Oliver: Danish Broadcasting Corporation
Slansky, Heike: German TV ZDF
Slavica, Branka: HRT/Croatian Radio Television
Slen, Peter: C–SPAN
Slie, Charles: NBC News
Sliman, Mostafa: APTVS–American Press & TV Services
Sloan, Steven: CNN
Sloane, Ward C.: CBS News
Slobogin, Kathy: Aljazeera America

Smith, Andrew: China Central TV Bureau
Smith, Anthony: Diversified Communications, Inc. (DCI)
Smith, Christie: NBC Newschannel
Smith, Cynthia: ABC News
Smith, Cynthia: Fox News
Smith, David: Fox News
Smith, Felicia: AP–Broadcast
Smith, James: ABC News
Smith, Jason H.: WTTG–Fox Television
Smith, John: RTTV America
Smith, Lindley: C–SPAN
Smith, Mark: AP–Broadcast
Smith, Max: WTOP Radio
Smith, Michael: WETA
Smith, Paul: EWTN
Smith, Phillip: Aljazeera English
Smith, Randolph: Washingtonpost.com
Smith, William: Cox Broadcasting
Smolkin, Rachel: CNN
Smysom, Osamah: Sky News Arabia
Smyth, Chris: Hearst Television Inc.
Sneed, Kimberly: NBC News
Snell, Cody: RTTV America
So, Linda: Reuters Radio & TV
Sobocinski, Matthew: Politico.Com
Socolovsky, Jerome: Voice of America
Soe, Khin Maung: Radio Free Asia
Soete, Koen: NOS Dutch Public Radio & TV (VRT)
Sok, Pov: Voice of America
Sokolova, Elena: Russian State TV And Radio (RTR)
Solodovnikov, Mikhail: RTTV America
Solorzano, Gilbert: NBC News
Soltermann, Beat: Swiss Broadcasting
Somers, Meredith: Federal News Radio 1500 AM
Sommers, Chloe: CNN
Song, Jiwon: Seoul Broadcasting System (SBS)
Sonnheim, Jon: WRC–TV / NBC–4
Sopel, Jon: BBC
Sorenson, Ben: C–SPAN
Soric, Miodrag: Deutsche Welle TV
Sosa, Joaquin: The Hill
Soucy, Peggy: Eurovision Americas, Inc.
Southee, Haley: C–SPAN
Sozio, George: ABC News
Speck, Alan: C–SPAN
Spector, Teresa: Fox News
Spellman, James: China Central TV Bureau
Spence, Bob: C–SPAN
Spencer, Darcy: WRC–TV / NBC–4
Spencer, Kenneth: National Public Radio
Spencer, Kim: Kcetlink
Sperry, Todd: CNN
Spevak, Joe: WTTG–Fox Television
Spiegler, Theodore: CBS News
Spinelli, Kevin: AP–Broadcast
Spire, Richard: CNN

MEMBERS ENTITLED TO ADMISSION—Continued

Spodak, Cassandra: CNN
Springer, Steven: Voice of America
Spurrier, Sharon: NBC News
St. Jean, Johnny: C–SPAN
St. John, Jonathan: Fox Business Network
Stakelbeck, Erick: CBN News
Stalnaker, Kurt: National Public Radio
Stanke, Donald: China Central TV Bureau
Stansfield, John: One America
Stanton, Jessica: CNN
Starddard, Donna: AP–Broadcast
Starikoff, Gary: C–SPAN
Stark, Lisa: Aljazeera America
Starks, Bill: WUSA–TV
Starling, Alison: WJLA–TV / Newschannel 8
Starling, Nicholas: Gray Television
Starr, Barbara: CNN
Starr, Penny: CNSNews.com
Statler, James: C–SPAN
Staton, Thomas: ABC News
Staudinger, Christian: Austrian Radio & TV (ORF)
Stay, Daniel J.: Fox News
Stead, Scott: CNN
Steck, Charles: Feature Story News
Stefany, Steve: ABC News
Stein, Cari: To The Contrary (Persephone Productions)
Stein, Rob: National Public Radio
Steinberger, Daniel: ABC News
Steinman, Mindy: C–SPAN
Stenval, Henrik: Aljazeera English
Stephens, Mark: WRC–TV / NBC–4
Sterling, Vaughn: CNN
Stevens, Melanie: NBC News
Stevens, Seneca: Fox News
Stevenson, Carrie: CNN
Stevenson, John: CNN
Stewart, Andrew: SRN News (Salem)
Stewart, Kathy: WTOP Radio
Stewart, Robin: Ventana Productions
Stinson, Jeffrey: Stateline.org
Stirewalt, Chris: Fox News
Stix, Gabriel: CBS News
Stoddard, Mark: ABC News
Stoddard, Rick: C–SPAN
Stone, Evie: National Public Radio
Stone, Jessica: China Central TV Bureau
Stone, Shomari: WRC–TV / NBC–4
Storkel, Scott: Voice of America
Storms, Leslie: NBC News
Stout, Matthew: Fox News
Strachan, Jason: CNN
Strand, Paul: CBN News
Strasser, Franz: BBC
Straub, Terry: Diversified Communications, Inc. (DCI)
Streitfeld, Rachel: CNN
Strickland, Kenneth: NBC News

Strickler, Laura: CBS News
Stringer, Ashley: CNBC
Strong, Amber: CBN News
Strothe, Stephen: N24 German TV
Stuard, Christopher: WJLA–TV / Newschannel 8
Stubbs, James: NBC News
Su, Xiaoxiao: China Central TV Bureau
Suarez, Sara: WFDC–TV Univision
Suddeth, James: Fox News
Suddeth, Rick: Fox News
Sughroue, Jon: NBC News
Suiters, Kimberly: WJLA–TV / Newschannel 8
Sullivan, Laura: National Public Radio
Summers, Elizabeth: The Newshour with Jim Lehrer
Summers, Juana: National Public Radio
Summers, Kelly: Fox News
Summers, Patrick: Fox News
Sun, Qingzhao: China Central TV Bureau
Sundel, Stanley: Fox News
Sutherland, Rachel: Fox News Radio
Suto, Ena: TV Asahi
Suzara, Jennifer: Fox News
Svoboda, Sarah: BBC
Svoboda, Sarah: Bloomberg Radio & TV
Swagler, Craig: CBS News
Swain, Bethany: Mobile Video Services, Ltd.
Swain, Susan: C–SPAN
Swain, Todd: Mobile Video Services, Ltd.
Swann, Ben: RTTV America
Swanson, Carl: Voice of America
Sweeney, Robert: WRC–TV / NBC–4
Sweeney, Sam: WJLA–TV / Newschannel 8
Swicord, Jeffrey: Voice of America
Swift, Tim: BBC
Sykes, Ed: Washington Examiner
Sylvester, John: Fox News Radio
Symanski, Mary: C–SPAN
Szeltner, Catherine: EWTN
Szypulski, Tom: Aljazeera English
Tabet, Joseph: Middle East Broadcasting Networks (MBN)
Taguchi, Mai: Nippon TV Network
Taing, Sarada: Radio Free Asia
Taira, So: Tokyo Broadcasting System
Tait, Ted: BBC
Takagane, Yuka: NHK
Talal, Rand: APTVS–American Press & TV Services
Talley, Lauren: Religion & Ethics Newsweekly
Tamary, Gil: Channel 10 Israel
Tamerlani, George: Reuters Radio & TV
Tanaka, Masayoshi: NHK
Tankler, Lauri: Estonian Public Broadcasting
Tanno, Kiyoshi: Nippon TV Network
Tapper, Jake: CNN
Tashi, Lumbum: Radio Free Asia
Tashi, Yeshi: Radio Free Asia
Tate, Simon: Aljazeera English

MEMBERS ENTITLED TO ADMISSION—Continued

Tate, Tiffany: BET Nightly News
Tatum, Laura: CNN
Tavcar, Erik: Reuters Radio & TV
Tawfik, Nada: BBC
Taylor, Audrey: ABC News
Taylor, Christina: C–SPAN
Taylor, Jacqueline: Fox News
Taylor, Jessica: National Public Radio
Taylor, Michael: Aljazeera English
Taylor, Russell: C–SPAN
Taylor, Stephen: Fox News Radio
Tea, Brandon: CBS News
Teboe, Mark: Diversified Communications, Inc.
(DCI)
Teclab, Minia: Voice of America
Teeples, Joseph: C–SPAN
Teicholz, Adam: ABC News
Tejerina, Pilar: Aljazeera English
Temin, Thomas: Federal News Radio 1500 AM
Tenney, Garrett: Fox News
Terpstra, Patrick: Cox Broadcasting
Terrett, John: Aljazeera America
Terry, Janet: WUSA–TV
Tessler, Bart: Westwood One
Tevault, Neil David: National Public Radio
Tha, Kyaw: Voice of America
Thalman, Mark: Ventana Productions
Thein, Kyaw: Voice of America
Theisen, Michael: Voice of America
Thoman, Eric: C–SPAN
Thomas, Amy: ABC News
Thomas, Bert: NBC News
Thomas, Christopher: CTV–Community TV of PG
County
Thomas, Pierre: ABC News
Thomas, Shari: ABC News
Thomas, Shawna: NBC News
Thomas, Will: WTTG–Fox Television
Thomas III, James B.: CNN
Thompson, Cameron: WNEW / CBS DC
Thompson, Joseph: WETA
Thompson, Mallory: CNN
Thompson, Ron: Radio One
Thompson Anderson, Laetitia: WRC–TV / NBC–4
Thorne, C. Patrick: Washington Bureau News
Service
Thornes, Troy: CBS News
Thornton, Ronald: NBC News
Thorp, Frank: NBC News
Thuman, Scott: WJLA–TV / Newschannel 8
Till, Morgan: The Newshour with Jim Lehrer
Tiller, Arthur: C–SPAN
Tillman, Thomas E.: CBS News
Tilman, Brandon: C–SPAN
Tin, San San: Radio Free Asia
Tinaz, Ozlem: Turkish Radio and Television (TRT)
Tisler, Eve: Estonian Public Broadcasting
Tobia, Peter: The Newshour with Jim Lehrer

Tobianski, Sarah: C–SPAN
Todd, Brian: CNN
Todd, Chuck: NBC News
Toksvig, Nick: Aljazeera English
Tolliver, Terri: WTTG–Fox Television
Toman, George: NBC Newschannel
Tomlinson, Lucas: Fox News
Tong, Scott: Marketplace Radio
Torpey, Robert: Fox News
Toso, Nicolas: CNN
Totenberg, Nina: National Public Radio
Touhey, Emmanuel: C–SPAN
Trabandt, Anne: Fox News
Tracey, Bree: Fox News
Trainor, Thomas: Eurovision Americas, Inc.
Tram, Thanh: CNN
Trammell, Michael: WUSA–TV
Tran, Hoa Ai: Radio Free Asia
Trauzzi, Monica: Environment & Energy Publishing,
LLC
Travers, Karen: ABC News
Traynham, Peter C.: CBS News
Trevelyan, Laura: BBC
Triay, Andres: CBS News
Troast, Andrew: CNN
Trosclair, Clayton: Eurovision Americas, Inc.
Truong, Cynthia: Vietv Network
Tschida, Stephen: WJLA–TV / Newschannel 8
Tserenbaljid, Uyanga: German TV ZDF
Tsurumi, Michiko: NHK
Tuan, Shih-Yuan: TVBS
Tucker, Elke: German TV ZDF
Tulachom, Pinitkarn: Voice of America
Tuohey, Kenneth: CNN
Turner, Chris: CNN
Turner, Geoff: CBS News
Turner, Hayley: Fox News
Turner, James: AP–Broadcast
Turner, Robert: Independent Television News (ITN)
Turner, Trish: CBS News
Turner, William: Fox News
Turnham, Stephen: Aljazeera America
Turrell, Elizabeth: CNN
Tuss, Adam: WRC–TV / NBC–4
Tuszynski, Tom: Al Arabiya TV
Tutman, Dan D.: CBS News
Tweed, Robert: CNN
Tyler, Brett: CNN
Tyler, Lamonte: Fox News
Tyler, Thomas: Diversified Communications, Inc.
(DCI)
Tyree, Wade: ABC News
Ubeda, Anna: TVE—Spanish Public Television
Uceda, Claudia: Univision
Uhl, Kim: CNN
Ulbrich-Strothe, Sabine: N24 German TV
Ulery, Brad: Reuters Radio & TV
Uliano, Dick: WTOP Radio

MEMBERS ENTITLED TO ADMISSION—Continued

Ulloa, Melinda: Reuters Radio & TV
Ulloa, Victor: CBS News
Umeh, Maureen: WTTG–Fox Television
Umrani, Anthony R.: CNN
Underwood, Xavier: Sinclair Broadcast Group
Upadhyay, Brajesh: BBC
Uprety, Sharmila: Sagarmatha Television
Upshaw, Justin: CBS News
Ure, Laurie: CNN
Ureta, Juan: NBC News
Uribe, Juvenal: Morningside Partners, LLC
Urquhart, Jonathan: BBC
Usero, Adriana: AOL Huffington Post
Usher, Barbara: BBC
Vaeth-Levin, Ben: Viewpoint Communications
Vaidyanathan, Rajini: BBC
Van Aernum, Sara: WJLA–TV / Newschannel 8
Van Cleave, Kris: CBS News
Van De Mark, Ellen: CNN
Van Der Bellen, Erin: WUSA–TV
Van Der Horst, Arjen: NOS Dutch Public Radio
   & TV (VRT)
Van Susteren, Greta: Fox News
Van Wagtendonk, Anya: The Newshour with Jim
   Lehrer
Vance, Denise: AP–Broadcast
Vanderveen, Lawrence: Mobile Video Services, Ltd.
Vanderveen, Paul: Voice of America
Vargas, Carlos: AP–Broadcast
Vargas, Luke: Talk Radio News Service
Vaselopulos, Peter: Voice of America
Vasiliadis, Joan: WUSA–TV
Vasquez, Jennifer: WRC–TV / NBC–4
Vaughan, Scott: Reuters Radio & TV
Vaughn, Michael: WJLA–TV / Newschannel 8
Ventura, Tyrel: RTTV America
Vera, Jaime: Telesur
Vermaak, Dawid: CNN
Ververs, Vaughn: NBC News
Vesey, Jordan: The Newshour with Jim Lehrer
Vestal, Christine: Stateline.org
Vichi, Thomas: Radio Free Asia
Viczian, Ilona: Aljazeera English
Viers, Dana: ABC News
Viers, Meta: WUSA–TV
Vigil, Marcos: ABC News
Vila, Xavier: Catalunya Radio
Villarreal, Alexandra: Voice of America
Villegas, Catalina: WFDC–TV Univision
Villone Garcia, Patricia: CTV–Community TV of
   PG County
Vincent, Michael: Australian Broadcasting
   Corporation
Vinson, Bryce: Fox News
Viqueira, Mike: Aljazeera America
Virji, Anar: Aljazeera English
Vishnevoy, Dmitry: Channel One Russian TV
Visioli, Todd: Fox News

Visley, Andrew: AP–Broadcast
Vitale, Joseph: Voice of America
Vitorovich, Susan: NBC News
Vittert, Leland: Fox News
Vizcarra, Mario: Univision
Vlahos, Kelley Beaucar: Fox News
Voelzke, Margaret: CNN
Vogel, Phil: Fox News
Vohra, Sweta: Aljazeera English
Volokhonovich, Vera: RTTV America
Von Bonsdorff, Juri: Eurovision Americas, Inc.
Vosti, Andrea: Swiss Broadcasting
Voth, Charles: WETA
Vu, Doanh: Vietv Network
Vu, Tu H.: CNN
Vukmer, David: NBC News
Vurnis, Ambrose: WRC–TV / NBC–4
Waghorn, Dominic: Sky News
Wagner, Paul: WTTG–Fox Television
Waheed, Amina: Aljazeera America
Wait, Kevin: National Public Radio
Waldman, Elliot: Tokyo Broadcasting System
Waldman, Joel: Fox News
Walker, Amanda: Sky News
Walker, Jackie Lyn: ABC News
Walker, James: WJLA–TV / Newschannel 8
Walker, Richard: Deutsche Welle TV
Walker, William: CBS News
Wall, Katharine: NBC News
Wallace, Chris: Fox News
Wallace, Gregory: CNN
Wallace, John L.: Fox News
Wallace, Neil: Fox News
Wallace, Tabetha: RTTV America
Walsh, Deirdre: CNN
Walsh, Mary: CBS News
Walter, Jonathan: Fox News
Walter, Mike: China Central TV Bureau
Walz, Mark: CNN
Wang, Bingru: Hong Kong Phoenix Satellite
   Television
Wang, Cong: Hong Kong Phoenix Satellite
   Television
Wang, Erdan: China Central TV Bureau
Wang, Guan: China Central TV Bureau
Wang, Hui: China Central TV Bureau
Wang, Meng: China Central TV Bureau
Wang, Taofeng: AP–Broadcast
Wang, Wei: China Central TV Bureau
Wang, Xin: China Central TV Bureau
Wang, Yang: New Tang Dynasty TV
Waqfi, Wajd: Aljazeera Satellite Channel
   (Peninsula)
Ward, Derrick: WRC–TV / NBC–4
Ward, Patrick: Fox News
Warfield, R.T.: China Central TV Bureau
Warner, Craig: CBS News
Warner, Jamey: Kcetlink

MEMBERS ENTITLED TO ADMISSION—Continued

Warner, Margaret: The Newshour with Jim Lehrer
Warner, Tarik: WRC–TV / NBC–4
Wasgien, Sonja: German TV ARD
Washburn, Kevin: C–SPAN
Washington, Erick: CBS News
Washington, Ervin: Aljazeera America
Washington, Travis: WJLA–TV / Newschannel 8
Washington-Anderson, Robert: WJLA–TV / Newschannel 8
Wassman, Kathryn: NBC News
Watkins, Duane: China Central TV Bureau
Watrud, Don: WTTG–Fox Television
Watson, Jennifer: WJLA–TV / Newschannel 8
Watts, Andrew: National Public Radio
Weakly, David: NBC News
Webb, Tracey: CNN
Webber, Joseph: Fox News
Weber, Ralph: German Public Radio (ARD)
Webster, Aaron: Fox News
Wegmann, Christopher: Radio One
Wehinger, Amy: Fox News
Wei, Xing: China Central TV Bureau
Wei, Xuejiao: China Central TV Bureau
Weidenbosch, Glenn: China Central TV Bureau
Weinberg, Ali: ABC News
Weinbloom, Hank: Fox News Radio
Weiner, Cydney: NBC News
Weinstein, Richard: C–SPAN
Weinstock, Roy: WRC–TV / NBC–4
Weiss, Alexis: CNN
Weiss, Ellen: Scripps News
Welker, Kristen: NBC News
Weller, George: NBC News
Weller, George: Aljazeera English
Wellford, Rachel: The Newshour with Jim Lehrer
Welna, David: National Public Radio
Welsh, Meghan: Fox News
Werner, Katharina: BBC
West, Caroline: Aljazeera English
West, David: Verizon
West, Jinae: National Public Radio
Westfall, Christopher: RTTV America
Weston, Caitlin: CNN
Wheeler, Blair: WUSA–TV
Wheeler, Brian: Aljazeera English
White, Amanda: CNN
White, Douglas: ABC News
White, Kevin: China Central TV Bureau
White, Mark: CBS News
Whiteman, Caroline: Fox News
Whitley, Walter: Fox News
Whitmire, Sarah: McClatchy
Whitney, Michael: Washington Bureau News Service
Whitson, Ricardo: CBS News
Whittington, Christopher: NBC News
Wholey, Dennis: This Is America with Dennis Wholey

Widmer, Chris: CBS News
Wiersema, Alisa: ABC News
Wiggins, Christopher: NBC Newschannel
Wiggins, Dion: WUSA–TV
Wik, Snorre: German TV ZDF
Wilde, Winston: NBC News
Wilk, Wendy: Hearst Television Inc.
Wilkes, Douglas H.: WTTG–Fox Television
Wilkins, Tracee: WRC–TV / NBC–4
Williams, Abigail: NBC News
Williams, Armstrong: Sinclair Broadcast Group
Williams, Brenna: CNN
Williams, Colleen: Fox News
Williams, David: Fox News
Williams, James: NBC News
Williams, Jeffrey L.: Cox Broadcasting
Williams, John: Fox News
Williams, Kenneth E.: CBS News
Williams, Matt: Independent Television News (ITN)
Williams, Pete: NBC News
Williams, Robert T.: NBC News
Williams, Steven: WTTG–Fox Television
Williams, Tonya: Fox News Radio
Williamson, Christopher: NBC News
Willis, Anne Marie: Fox News
Wilson, Jeffrey: Radio One
Wilson, Kristin: CNN
Wilson, Mark: CBS News
Wilson, Stephanie: WUSA–TV
Wiltz, Teresa: Stateline.org
Winborn, Tracy: CBN News
Windham, Ronald: WJLA–TV / Newschannel 8
Wingfield, Matthew: Federal News Radio 1500 AM
Winston, Natalie: National Public Radio
Winterhalter, Ruthann: C–SPAN
Wintermsmith, Saraya: WNEW / CBS DC
Winters, Ronald: ABC News
Wiseman, Frederick: CNN
Wishon, Jennifer: CBN News
Witkin, Rachel: NBC News
Witte, Joel: China Central TV Bureau
Wittwer, Ruth: Swiss Broadcasting
Woldearegay, Eden: Agence France Presse (AFP–TV)
Wolf, Zachary: CNN
Wolfe, Lisa: Federal News Radio 1500 AM
Wolfson, Paula: WTOP Radio
Wood, Christopher: C–SPAN
Wood, Owen: WETA
Wood, Winston: Voice of America
Woodall, Crystal: CBN News
Woodruff, Judy: The Newshour with Jim Lehrer
Woolbright, Melinda: WRC–TV / NBC–4
Wordock, Colleen: Sinclair Broadcast Group
Workman, Paul: CTV Canadian TV
Worthington, Barry: White House Chronicle
Wortman, Alexander: NHK
Wotring, Melanie: WJLA–TV / Newschannel 8

MEMBERS ENTITLED TO ADMISSION—Continued

Wotshela, Gringo: BBC
Wright, Chris: Euronews
Wright, Dale: WJLA–TV / Newschannel 8
Wright, Dexter: Verizon
Wright, James: Aljazeera English
Wright, Kristin: WRC–TV / NBC–4
Wright, Tammy: Aljazeera English
Wrona, Marcin: TVN Poland
Wu, Hanying: China Central TV Bureau
Wu, Wei: New Tang Dynasty TV
Wyszogrodzki, Marcin: TVN Poland
Xavier, Wilkins: Aljazeera English
Xiao, Hejia: China Central TV Bureau
Xie, Chenguang: China Central TV Bureau
Yack, Angelique: CNN
Yager, Joshua: CBS News
Yaklyvich, Brian: ABC News
Yam, Raymond: Voice of America
Yamada, Keishi: Nippon TV Network
Yamaguchi, Noriyuki: Tokyo Broadcasting System
Yamasaki, Takeshi: NHK
Yamashita, Tatsuya: TV Asahi
Yancy, Shawn: WTTG–Fox Television
Yang, Daniel: The Newshour with Jim Lehrer
Yang, Eun: WRC–TV / NBC–4
Yang, Guofu: Voice of America
Yang, Hee: Radio Free Asia
Yang, Lianhua: American Chinese Television (ACT)
Yang, Stephanie: Hong Kong Phoenix Satellite
    Television
Yang, Sungwon: Radio Free Asia
Yarborough, Rick: WRC–TV / NBC–4
Yarmuth, Floyd: CNN
Yaroshevsky, Alexey: RTTV America
Yates, Mark: Swiss Broadcasting
Yee-Gaffney, Suzanne: AP–Broadcast
Yeshi, Lobsang: Radio Free Asia
Yianopoulos, Karen: Middle East Broadcasting
    Networks (MBN)
Yin, Phillip: China Central TV Bureau
Ying, Francis: Kaiser Health News
Yoder, Alex: Gray Television
Yokoyama, Taka: CNN
Yoon, Robert: CNN
Yorro, Timothy: WNEW / CBS DC
Yoshikawa, Junichi: TV Asahi
Yoshioka, Jumpei: NHK
Young, Jeremy: Aljazeera English
Young, Melissa: ABC News
Young, Robert Latimer: C–SPAN
Young, V. Alan: NBC News
Young Jr., Jerome: CBN News
Younis, Omar: Reuters Radio & TV
Yousef, Dania: Aljazeera English

Yu, Annie: WTTG–Fox Television
Yu, James: Korean Broadcasting Systems
Yu, Ping: New Tang Dynasty TV
Yun, Samean: Radio Free Asia
Yunjin, Li: American Chinese Television (ACT)
Zaatar, Marwan: Middle East Broadcasting
    Networks (MBN)
Zada, Naskah: China Central TV Bureau
Zairi, Said: 50 Frames
Zajko, Robert: Diversified Communications, Inc.
    (DCI)
Zak, Lana: ABC News
Zampa, Peter: Gray Television
Zamperoni, Ingo: German TV ARD
Zang, Guohua: CTI–TV (Taiwan)
Zaru, Deena: CNN
Zatopek, Angela: CBN News
Zayed, Nahedah: Aljazeera English
Zazua, Mayada: APTVS–American Press & TV
    Services
Zderic, Srdjan: Aljazeera English
Zechar, David: ABC News
Zeffler, Markus: BBC
Zeleny, Jeff: CNN
Zeller, Tina: CBS News
Zenke, Masaru: NHK
Zervos, Stratis: Eurovision Americas, Inc.
Zervos, Stratis: ABC News
Zhang, Xiaoyan: Voice of America
Zhang, Xin: China Central TV Bureau
Zhao, Peng: China Central TV Bureau
Zhao, Xiaoyan: China Central TV Bureau
Zhao, Yunjie: China Central TV Bureau
Zheng, Ren: WTOP Radio
Zhodzishsky, Ilya: RTTV America
Zhu, Xiaomeng: China Central TV Bureau
Ziegenbein, Darren: WRC–TV / NBC–4
Ziegler, Julia: Federal News Radio 1500 AM
Zimerman, Ariel: AP–Broadcast
Zimmerman, Douglas: Environment & Energy
    Publishing, LLC
Zmidzinski, Andrew: WJLA–TV / Newschannel 8
Zoldan, Ari: Talk Radio News Service
Zosso, Elizabeth: Middle East Broadcasting
    Networks (MBN)
Zou, Yun: China Central TV Bureau
Zschieschang, Marion: German TV ARD
Zuk, Anne: Canadian Broadcasting Corporation
    (CBC)
Zurcher, Anthony: BBC
Zwart, Wouter: NOS Dutch Public Radio & TV
    (VRT)
Zwillich, Todd: WNYC

NETWORKS, STATIONS, AND SERVICES REPRESENTED

Senate Gallery 224–6421   House Gallery 225–5214

24/7 NEWS—(602) 374–6100; 8403 Colesville Road, #1500, Silver Spring, MD 20910: Joseph Gomez, Terrence Moore.

50 FRAMES—50 F Street, NW., Suite C150, Washington, DC 20001: Mohamed Dourrachad, Mohamed Elsetouhi, Hind Khalid, Zaidoon Khalid, Barakat Khalid, Said Zairi.

ABC NEWS—(202) 222–7700; 1717 DeSales Street, NW., Washington, DC 20036: Faisal Alkadiri, John Allard, James Avila, Ben Bell, Phillip M. Black, Mary Bruce, Christopher Carlson, Anja Crowder, Thomas D'Annibale, Jack Date, Henry Disselkamp, Peter Doherty, Erin Dooley, Alexandra Dukakis, Devin Dwyer, Daniel Glenn Elvington, Katherine Faulders, Conor Finnegan, Justin Fishel, Siobhan Fisher, Jon Garcia, Arthur Gauthier, Thomas Giusto, Chris Good, Robin Gradison, Brian Haefeli, Daniel Hannah, Brian Robert Hartman, Esequiel Herrera, Heidi Jensen, Bazi Kanani, Polson Kanneth, Jonathan Karl, Katie Kastens, David Kerley, Richard Klein, Sarah Kolinovsky, Donald Eugene Kroll, Matt Larotonda, Michael Levine, Lachlan Murdoch MacNeil, Serena Marshall, Luis Martinez, Erik McNair, James Meek, Avery Miller, Kenneth Moton, Meredith Nettles, Patrick O'Gara, Andrea Owen, John Parkinson, MaryAlice Parks, Jordyn Phelps, Richard Pliszak, Mary Quinn, Martha Raddatz, Stephanie Ramos, Kari Rea, Corinne Roberts, Gary Rosenberg, Katherine Saenz, George D. Sanchez, Susan Saulny, Howard Schoenholtz, Benjamin Siegel, Cynthia Smith, James Smith, Steve Stefany, Daniel Steinberger, Audrey Taylor, Adam Teicholz, Amy Thomas, Pierre Thomas, Karen Travers, Dana Viers, Ali Weinberg, Douglas White, Alisa Wiersema, Melissa Young, Lana Zak.

AGENCE FRANCE PRESSE (AFP–TV)—1500 K Street, NW., Washington, DC 20005: Paul Barber, William Edwards, Katharyn Gillam, Loic Hofstedt, Katharine Schubauer, Eden Woldearegay.

AL ARABIYA TV—(202) 355–6614; National Press Building 529 14th Street, NW., Suite 530, Washington, DC 20045: Daoud Abuelhawa, Angelyn Adams, Yasmeen Alamiri, Nadia Charters Bilbassy, Pierre Ghanem, Elias Habib, Ziad Jazzaa, Omar Melhem, Richard Melhem, Muna Shikaki, Tom Tuszynski.

ALASKA PUBLIC RADIO NETWORK—810 East Ninth Avenue, Anchorage, AL 99501: Liz Ruskin.

ALJAZEERA AMERICA—1627 K Street, NW., Washington, DC 20006: Tima AlKhirsan, Timothy Bella, Barbara Berti, Kim Bondy, Robert Brock, Philomena Bubaris, Elizabeth Casey, Joie Chen, Grant Clark, Sarah Courtney, Tiffani Davis, Sanya Dosani, Aaron Ernst, Lisa Fletcher, Leila Garcia, Lori Gliha, Claire Gordon, Nicole Grether, David Gustafson, Christopher Hamilton, Guerin Hays, Trudy Hutcherson, Fletcher Johnson, Betsy Kulman, Jay LaMonica, Justin LaRocca, Ryan Loughlin, Sheila MacVicar, Adam May, Valerie McCabe, Jamie McIntyre, Bryan Myers, Mark Orchard, Simone Perez, Todd Reed, Jessica Sarstedt, Michael Shure, Kathy Slobogin, Lisa Stark, John Terrett, Stephen Turnham, Mike Viqueira, Amina Waheed, Ervin Washington.

ALJAZEERA ENGLISH—1200 New Hampshire Avenue, NW., 2nd Floor, Washington, DC 20036: Robert Abeshouse, Tom Ackerman, Khodayar Akhavi, Laila Alarian, Amjad Atallah, Jeff Ballou, Eric Barreda, Fatima Bartee, Frank Bass, James Bays, Joshua Bornstein, Marwan Dishara, Ayana Brickhouse, Joven Cabague, Nick Castellaro, Karolina Chapman, Kavitha Chekuru, Patricia Culhane, Villinda Dickerson, Gabriel Elizondo, Mariam Engel, Sarah Evans, Kathleen Fabian, Alan Fisher, Hida Fouladvand, Andy Gallacher, Maya Garg, Jean Garner, Bill Gattsek, Karina Gomes, Kimberly Halkett, James Hamilton, Michael Hanna, John Hendren, Kevin Hirten, Whitney Hurst, Zuleqa Husain, Rosiland Jordan, Akilah Joseph, Muriel Jubar, Anjali Kamat, Kylene Kiang, Mike LaBella, Ekaterina Landy, Katherine Lannigan, Dennis Legget, Lister Lim, Gerard Mackie, Goran Maric, Joseph Marno, Maria Marquez, Mercedes Martinez, Tabetha Mason, Colin McIntyre, Robert Michaud, Michael Mock, Matthew Monthei, Craig Pennington, Ivica Puljic, Omar A. Quinonez, Roger Raiford, Shihab Rattansi, Alea Reeves, Robert Reynolds, Kira Rockell, Joshua Rushing, Jennifer Salan, Sanil Sali, Kristen Saloomey, Barbara Schell, Corinne Schneider, Islam Sharief, Chris Sheridan, Mathieu Skene, Phillip Smith, Henrik Stenval, Tom Szypulski, Simon Tate, Michael Taylor, Pilar Tejerina, Nick Toksvig, Anar Virji, Sweta Vohra, Brian Wheeler, Tammy Wright, James Wright, Wilkins Xavier, Jeremy Young, Dania Yousef, Nahedah Zayed, Srdjan Zderic.

ALJAZEERA SATELLITE CHANNEL (PENINSULA)—1200 New Hampshire Avenue, NW., 2nd Floor, Washington, DC 20036: Ahmed Abdulrazzaq, Biesan Abu-Kwaik, Eyad Aburahma, Meha Ahmad, Haitham Al Juboori, Mohammed Alami, Heni Azzam, Baubak Baghi, Charles Behringer, Adil Cherkaoui, Mahmoud El-Hamalawy, Abderrahim Foukara, Michael Fox, Nasser Hssaini, Lina Khalaf, Fadi Mansour, Ghassan Sababa, Wajd Waqfi.

AMERICAN CHINESE TELEVISION (ACT)—(240) 988–4660; 722 Ridgemont Avenue, Rockville, MD 20850: Lianhua Yang, Li Yunjin.

1049

NETWORKS, STATIONS, AND SERVICES REPRESENTED—Continued

AOL HUFFINGTON POST—(202) 624–9300; 1750 Pennsylvania Avenue, NW., Suite 600, Washington, DC 20006: Ibrahim Balkhy, Christine Conetta, Brad Shannon, Adriana Usero.
AP–BROADCAST—(202) 641–9000; 1100 13th Street, NW., Suite 500, Washington, DC 20005: Jeff Adkinson, Nihad Aliakbar, Eric Andree, Jeannie Andress, John Auresto, Philip Avner, Edward Barker, Hugo Blanco, Jacqueline Blum-Dostie, Michael Bodenhorst, Gerald Bodlander, Carlotta Bradley, Tracy Brown, Kathleen Brumbaugh, David Bruns, Robert Bumsted, Matthew Burgoyne, Steven Coleman, Flavia Colombo-Abdullah, Derek Danilko, Kelly Daschle, Edward Donahue, Jason Dorn, Lisa Dwyer-Shapiro, Rodolfo Estrada, Fritz Faerber, David Friar, Mathew Friedman, Oscar Gabriel, Richard Gentilo, Lawrence Gold, Fernando Gonzalez, James Gorman, Michael Gracia, Susan Henderson, Brian Hoffman, Dan Huff, Violet Ikonomova, Christian Kettlewell, Sandy Kozel, Kathryn Loomans, Nico Maounis, Margaret Mazzetti, Nan Hee McMinn, Sagar Meghani, Vaughn Morrison, John Morrissey, Kamal Omara, Louis Pagan, Greg Peppers, Gerald Petraitis, Padmananda Rama, Walter Ratliff, Thomas Ritchie, John Rizzo, Emily Roseman, Michael Sanchez, Felicia Smith, Mark Smith, Kevin Spinelli, Donna Starddard, James Turner, Denise Vance, Carlos Vargas, Andrew Visley, Suzanne Yee-Gaffney.
APTVS–AMERICAN PRESS & TV SERVICES—202 601–2284; 1445 New York Avenue, NW., Suite 500, Washington, DC 20005: Akram Abdulkareem, Moaz Attawia, Colin Campbell, Mohamed Dawood, Sam Eizeldin, Ali Mahboba, Mostafa Sliman, Rand Talal, Mayada Zazua.
AUSTRALIAN BROADCASTING CORPORATION—(202) 466–8575; 2000 M Street, NW., Suite 660, Washington, DC 20036: Andrew Aylward, Nicholas Harmsen, Robert Hill, Benjamin Knight, Stephanie March, Lisa Millar, Dee Porter, Michael Vincent.
AUSTRIAN RADIO & TV (ORF)—1206 Eton Court, NW., Washington, DC 20007: Manuel Etzlstorfer, Hannelore Fauqueux-Veit, Verena Gleitsmann, Uelle-Mall Jaakson, Ernst Kernmayer, Anna Kirst, Markus Meier, Lauren Silva-Pinto, Christian Staudinger.
AZTECA AMERICA—400 North Capitol NW., Suite 361, Washington, DC 20001: Armando Guzman, Ernesto Orellana.
BBC—(202) 223–2050; 2000 M Street, NW., #800, Washington, DC 20009: Lukman Ahmed, Nadia Al Huraimi, Sina Alinejad, Glenn Osten Anderson, Ben Bevington, Paul Blake, David Botti, Taylor Brown, Nicholas Bryant, Maxine Collins, Jonathan Csapo, Kathleen Dailey, Paul Danahar, Tushar Dayal, Ian Druce, Kate Farrell, Sam Farzaneh, Kambiz Fattahi, Joao Fellet, Joan Field, Tom Geoghegan, Kim Ghattas, Rozalia Hristova, Katty Kay, Suzanne Kianpour, John Landy, Aleem Maqbool, Lindle Markwell, Barin Masoud, Tara McKelvey, William McKenna, Matthew Morrison, Tara Neill, Hadi Nili, Gary O'Donoghue, Colm O'Molloy, Ian Pannell, Amir Payam, Mehrnoosh Pourziaiee, James Reber, Ashley Semler, Ron Skeans, Jon Sopel, Franz Strasser, Sarah Svoboda, Tim Swift, Ted Tait, Nada Tawfik, Laura Trevelyan, Brajesh Upadhyay, Jonathan Urquhart, Barbara Usher, Rajini Vaidyanathan, Gringo Wotshela, Anthony Zurcher.
BET NIGHTLY NEWS—(202) 824–6500; 400 North Capitol Street, NW., Suite 361, Washington, DC 20001: Pamela Gentry, Joyce Jones, Andre Showell, Tiffany Tate.
BLOOMBERG RADIO & TV—1399 New York Avenue, NW., 11th Floor, Washington, DC 20005: Michael Callahan, Peter Cook, Kenneth Distance, Lara Hartzenbusch, Phil Mattingly, Roland Morrisette, Patrick Reap, LaVenia Rice, Allison Rowe, Sarah Svoboda.
BT VIDEO PRODUCTIONS—7117 Wolftree Lane, Rockville, MD 20852: Cesar Flores, Paul Hollenbeck, Martin Kos.
C–SPAN—(202) 737–3220; 400 North Capitol Street, NW., #650, Washington, DC 20001: Kenneth Alexander, Thomas Alldredge, Theresa Amirault-Michel, Jeremy Art, Shannon Augustus, Joel Bacon, Michelle Bailor, Jason Bender, Brett Betsill, Leona Blakey, Greta Brawner, Donald Brown, Paul Brown, Robert Browning, Kristina Buddenhagen, Susan J. Bundock, Leslie Burdick, Kathy Cahill, Nancy Calo-Christian, Craig Caplan, Kenneth Carrick, Tanya Chattman, Nicole Chung, Matthew Claar, James Clark, Bruce D. Collins, James L. Cook, Cleve Corner, Nathan Craig, Mariah Crews, Liam Currier, Alexander Curtis, Greg Czzowitz, Pete Daniels, Matthew Dauchess, Bridget Diggs, Danny Dill, Michelle Doell, Sean Doody, Jason Dorman, Kris Dowdell, Paul Eades, Jr, Pedro L. Echevarria, Gary Ellenwood, Seth Engel, Patricia Esquivel, Greg Fabic, Mark Farkas, Joseph Feeney, Laura Finch, Richard Fleeson, Amanda Fortner, Carl Foster, William Frazier, Bill Gallagher, John Gallagher, Craig Galowin, John Garlock, Jennifer Garrott, Garney Gary, Robert Gould, Fred Haberstick, Richard Hall, Chris Hanson, Stephen Harkness, Robb Harleston, Kasey Harris, Maurice Haynes, William Heffley, Jonelle P. Henry, Ashley Hill, Dallas Hill, Caitlin Hillyard, Adrienne Hoar, Slade Horacek, Yi-Pe Hsieh, Katherine Hughes, Scott Hummelsheim, Kia Hunter, Tracy Hunter, Nate Hurst, Cynthia Ingle, Roberta Jackson, Blake Jones, Andrew Jones, Stephanie Kaye, Steve Kehoe, Jon Kelley, Robert Kennedy, Barkley Kern, Roxane Kerr, Kevin King, David Knighton, Felix Laboy, Debbie Lamb, Brian Lamb, Darren Larade, Molly Laville, Robert Lazar, Jerome Leddon, Brian Lloyd, Paul Loeschke, Russell Logan, Ivette Lucero, Graham MacGillivray, Valerie Matthews, John McArdle, Sean McCann, Michael McCann, Gerard McGarrity, Justin Metzger, Andrew Peter Miller, Kate Mills, David Monack, Victor Montoro, Garrette Moore, Linwood Moore, Howard Mortman, Dan Morton, Terry Murphy, Yetta Myrick, Andrew Nason, Trang "Nicole" Ninh, Donna Norris, Benen O'Brien, Benjamin O'Connell, Alan Olmsted, Paul Orgel, Michael Patruznick, Vernon Perkins, Christina Perry, Nickolas Pitocco, Almon Porter,

NETWORKS, STATIONS, AND SERVICES REPRESENTED—Continued

Taylor Porter, Anne Preloh, David Pries, Tony Pronko, Nikhil Raval, Robert Reilly, Kirby Reitz, Michele Remillard, Cynthia Reuter, Delia Rios, Tiffany Rocque, Mark Rodeffer, Martine Rodriguez, Randy Rohrbaugh, Nicole Rossoll, Jennifer Ruff, Frederico Sampaio, Molly Sanders, Sherry Sanders-Smith, Michelle Sandiford, Stanley Sang, Bridget Scanlan, William Scanlan, John Scheuer, Ellen Schweiger, Steven Scully, Peter Slen, Lindley Smith, Ben Sorenson, Haley Southee, Alan Speck, Bob Spence, Johnny Street, Jean, Gary Starikoff, James Statler, Mindy Steinman, Rick Stoddard, Susan Swain, Mary Symanski, Christina Taylor, Russell Taylor, Joseph Teeples, Eric Thoman, Arthur Tiller, Brandon Tilman, Sarah Tobianski, Emmanuel Touhey, Kevin Washburn, Richard Weinstein, Ruthann Winterhalter, Christopher Wood, Robert Latimer Young.

CADENA SER—(202) 596 6969; 4520 Cumberland Avenue, Chevy Chase, MD 20815: Javier del Pino.

CANADIAN BROADCASTING CORPORATION (CBC)—(202) 383–2900; National Press Building 529 14th Street, NW., Suite 500, Washington, DC 20045: Jean-Francois Bisson, Keith Boag, Jason Burles, Marcel Calfat, Marie Claudet, Yanik Dumont Baron, Lyndsay Duncombe, Patrick Ferguson, Meagan Fitzpatrick, Paul Hunter, Christian Latreille, Jason Lowther, Neil MacDonald, Glenn Parker, Sylvain Richard, Anne Zuk.

CANAL PLUS FRENCH TV—(202) 641–9289; 1100 13 Street, NW., Suite 400, Washington, DC 20001: Mounira Al Hmoud, Laura Haim.

CARACOL TELEVISION—(202) 615–3899; 400 North Capitol Street, NW., Suite 361, Washington, DC 20001: Jose Agredo, Laura Newton, Daniel Pacheco-Saenz.

CATALUNYA RADIO—(301) 204–9062; 4608 Cooper Lane, Bethesda, MD 20816: Xavier Vila.

CBN NEWS—(202) 833 2707; 1919 M Street, NW., Street 100, Washington, DC 20036: Mark Bautista, David Brody, Christopher Christian, Laura Crombe, Brian Edwards, Aronica Glover, Alegra Hall, Steve Jacobi, Gene Jenkins, John Jessup, Matthew Keedy, Robin Mazyck, Jacob Moore, Stacy Opoku, Denis Pacuraru, David Page, Tamatha Papadeas, Abigail Robertson, Ian Rushing, Erick Stakelbeck, Paul Strand, Amber Strong, Tracy Winborn, Jennifer Wishon, Crystal Woodall, Jerome Young, Jr., Angela Zatopek.

CBS NEWS—(202) 457–4444; 2020 M Street, NW., Washington, DC 20036: Adam Aigner-Treworgy, Zachary Akey, Jacqueline Alemany, Clinton N. Alexander, Alicia Amling, Stuart Ammerman, Wyatt Andrews, Alana Anyse, Howard Arenstein, Kylie Atwood, Barry Bagnato, Morris Banks, Reginald Barringer, Kia Baskerville, Farrel Becker, Mark R. Bennett, Jackie Berkowitz, Musadiq Bidar, Julia Boccagno, Lindsey Boerma, Craig Boswell, Margaret Brennan, Whitney Bright, Susan Bullard Harmon, Catherine Cannon, Denise Cetta, Steven Chaggaris, Jane S. Chick, George Christian, Marshall Cohen, Stephanie Condon, Carol Coney, John Cooper, Nancy Cordes, Victoria Coughlan, Pam Coulter, Jan Crawford, Walter Cronkite, John Crum, Jonathan Crum, John Daly, Bethey Dereje, Robert Diaz, John Dickerson, Charles H. Dixson, Katie Dominick, Margaret Dore, Louise Dufresne, Lois Dyer, John L. Fantacone, Arden Farhi, Reena Flores, John Frado, Tony Furlow, Hal E. Furman, Brian Fuss, Travis Galey, July Garcia, Major Garrett, Timothy Gaughan, Benson Ginsburg, Julianna Goldman, Jeff Scott Goldman, Brian Gottlieb, Neil Grasso, Josh Gross, David Gross, Mary Hager, Bill Harding, Alan He, Robert Hendin, Elizabeth Hinson, Caroline Horn, Jillian Hughes, Katherine Iorio, Christopher Isham, Jill Jackson, Dennis Jamison, Courtney Jay, Richard Jefferson, Weijia Jiang, Shanica Johnson, Jeffrey Johnston, Lorna Jones, Donald Judd, Rebecca Kaplan, Craig Katz, Eric Kerchner, Jonathan Kessler, Julia Kimani, Daniel Klos, Mark Knoller, Cara Korte, Gabe Lamonica, Donald A. Lee, Jonathan Lien, Sam Litzinger, Kevin Livelli, Lara Logan, Steve Marshall, David Martin, Mark Mazariegos, D. Jay McCarty, D. Page McCarty, Max McClellan, Susan McGinnis, Jim McGlinchy, Michael McGuire, Duncan McKenna, Robert McKinley, Jake Miller, Pat Milton, Donald Morgan, John Nolen, Mosheh Oinounou, Jeffrey Pegues, Timothy Perry, Michael Peyton, William Plante, Steve Portnoy, Diana Quinn, Carrie Rabin, Daniel Raviv, Charles Reid, Paula Reid, Catherine Reynolds, Francisco Robbins, Ira Rosen, Howard Rosenberg, Allyson Ross Taylor, Kate Rydell, Jenna Sakwa, Bob Schieffer, Fred Schneider, Gabrielle Schonder, Henry Schuster, Heather Scott, Thomas H. Seem, Gregory Shaffir, Kim Shaffir, Dennis Shannon, Kimberly Skeen, Ward C. Sloane, Gabriel Stix, Laura Strickler, Craig Swagler, Troy Thornes, Thomas E. Tillman, Peter C. Traynham, Andres P. Triay, Trish Turner, Geoff Turner, Dan D. Tutman, Victor Ulloa, Justin Upshaw, Kris Van Cleave, William Walker, Mary Walsh, Craig Warner, Erick Washington, Mark White, Ricardo Whitson, Kenneth E. Williams, Joshua Yager, Tina Zeller.

CHANNEL 10 ISRAEL—(202) 460–0223; 195 Hardy Place, Rockville, MD 20852: Gil Tamary.

CHANNEL ONE RUSSIAN TV—1100 13th Street, NW., Suite 400, Washington, DC 20005: Anatoly Lazarev, Dmitry Vishnevoy.

CHINA CENTRAL TV BUREAU—(202) 639–4800; 1099 New York Avenue, NW., Washington, DC 20001: Atirath Aich, Rachelle Akuffo, Julio Aliaga, Guy Bagley, Fan Bai, Sean Callebs, Shen Chen, He Cheng, Ralph Cooper, Chris Cowman, Bob Crawford, Lingnan Cui, Bianca Davie, Yubin Du, Lucho Durand, Owen Fairclough, Wang Fenghua, Peng Fu, Qi Gao, Sheryl Gao, Joanna Godinho, Chun Guo, Zhu Haiqing, Jiyuan Han, Wenjin He, Aja Hubert-Hogg, Michael Italiano, Elmira Jafari, Li Jia, Xin Jiang, Monna Kashfi, Colleen Kenney, Nathan King, Frances Kuo, Yunhe Lai, Ira Lazernik, Zhujun Li, Meng Li, Hui Lin, Xiyang Liu, Jing Ma, Yan Mei, Mat Morrison, Virginia Moubray,

NETWORKS, STATIONS, AND SERVICES REPRESENTED—Continued

Rich Murphy, Ruqaiyah Najjar, Asieh Namdar, Giang Nguyen, Hakan Ozsancak, Sun Ping, Qi Qin, Xiangqin Quan, Elaine Reyes, Kelly Rice, Janet Rodriguez, Roee Ruttenberg, Sahar Sarshar, Christine Schiffner, Matt Shirley, Matthew Simon, Andrew Smith, James Spellman, Donald Stanke, Jessica Stone, Xiaoxiao Su, Qingzhao Sun, Mike Walter, Xin Wang, Erdan Wang, Guan Wang, Hui Wang, Meng Wang, Wei Wang, R.T. Warfield, Duane Watkins, Xing Wei, Xuejiao Wei, Glenn Weidenbosch, Kevin White, Joel Witte, Hanying Wu, Hejia Xiao, Chenguang Xie, Phillip Yin, Naskah Zada, Xin Zhang, Yunjie Zhao, Peng Zhao, Xiaoyan Zhao, Xiaomeng Zhu, Yun Zou.

CMI TV (COLOMBIA)—5753 Governor's Pond Circle, Alexandria, VA 22310: Jaime Moreno, Adriana Serna.

CNBC—(202) 776–7405; 400 North Capitol Street, NW., Suite 850, Washington, DC 20001: Patrick Anastasi, Bria Cousins, Plummer Crawley, Matthew Cuddy, Stephanie Dhue, John Harwood, Karen James, Eamon Javers, Diana Olick, Hampton Pearson, Pat Pugliese, Shari Rosen, Ashley Stringer.

CNN—(202) 898–7900; 820 1st Street, NE., Washington, DC 20002: Khalil Abdallah, Jim Acosta, Rami Al-Badry, Nefi Alarcon, William Alberter, Kathy Aragon, Rahmin Atarod, Emily Atkinson, Tiane Austin, Matthew Avrutine, Marlena Baldacci, Erik Banks, Ted Barrett, Dana Bash, Ariel Bashi, John Bena, Alexa Bennewitz, Leslie Bentz, David Bergeman, Richard Bernal, Laura Bernardini, Jonathan Berryman, Lindzie Bills, Kevin Blakley, Wolf Blitzer, John Bodnar, Kevin Bohn, Gloria Borger, Tyrone Boston, Eric Bradner, Joshua Braun, Allison Brennan, Michael Brevner, Ray Britch, Scott Bronstein, Pamela Brown, Tia Brueggeman, Wesley Bruer, Steven Brusk, Burke Buckhorn, Jennifer Buesinger, David Burgess, Terence Burlij, Juan Cabral, Will Cadigan, Karin Caifa, Casey Capachi, David Keith Catrett, David Chalian, Jill Chappell, Elizabeth Chmurak, Gregory Clary, Bobby Clemons, Ashley Codianni, Stephen Collinson, Christie Corologos-Medina, Marina Cracchiolo, James Crawford, Abigail Crutchfield, John Cunha, Jaime Davila Castillo, Edward Davis, Patrick A. Davis, Ariane de Vogue, Karl de Vries, Nicholas Deines, Anastasia Diakides, Jeremy Diamond, Daniella Diaz, Patricia DiCarlo, Stephen Dolce, Martin Dougherty, Katerina Erbiti, Sam Feist, Eric James Fiegel, Craig Fingar, Patrick Ford, Thomas Foreman, Chris Frates, Scott Garber, Danelle Garcia, Melodie Garner, Timothy C. Garraty, Christopher Garrett, Joshua Gaynor, David Gelles, Melissa Giaimo, Andre Goddard, David Goodman, Richard Gorbutt, Allison Gracey, David Gracey, Noah Gray, Noah Gray, James Graydon, Clayton Green, Eddie S. Gross, Jr., Peter Hamby, Brian Hampton, Jeremy Harlan, Elizabeth Hartfield, Dianna Heitz, Simon Hernandez-Arthur, Matthew Hilk, Katherine Hinman, Kristen Holmes, Derek Horrigan, Emily Howell, Matthew Hoye, Paige Hymson, Yasmeen Ibrahim, Adia Jacobs, Alexandra Jaffe, Oliver Janney, David Jenkins, Geet Jeswani, Joseph Johns, Athena Jones, Jay Jones, Polson Kanneth, Brianna Keilar, Pamela Kelley, Ashley Killough, John King, Mary Klein, Laura Koran, Michelle Kosinski, Hilary Krieger, Ben Krolowitz, Rebecca Kutler, Elise Labott, Elizabeth Landers, M.J. Lee, Alex Lee, Adam Levine, Ross Levitt, Adam Levy, Kevin Liptak, Philip Littleton, Thomas LoBianco, Juan Carlos Lopez, Brooke Lorenz, Alysha Love, Natalie Lylo, Melissa Macaya, Mary Kay Mallonee, Allison Malloy, Mark Anthony Marchione, Eric Marrapodi, Rene Marsh, Dugald McConnell, Denise McIntosh, Samuel J. McMichael IV, Michael McMullan, Erin McPike, James Meech, Lauren Meier, Daniel Merica, Rebekah Metzler, Jennifer Mikell, Paul Miller, Alec Miran, Ione Indira Molinares-Hess, Jeffrey Moller, Christopher Moody, Jeremy Moorhead, Isabel Morales, Peter Morris, Virginia Moseley, Sara Murray, Steven Nannes, Nicholette Nicci, Ryan Nobles, Ernest G. Nocciolo, Greg Overzat, Maribel Padial, Steven Page, Robert Geoffrey Parker, Andre Parker, Melanie Parks, Wade Payson-Denney, Evan Perez, Rebecca Perlow, Thomas Perrell, Katelyn Petroka, Michelle Poley, Brendan Polmer, Lauren Pratapas, Mark Preston, Federico Quadrani, Meghan Rafferty, Manu Raju, Pallavi Reddy, Samantha Reyes, Casey Riddle, Raul Rios-Hernandez, Jennifer Rizzo, Greg Robertson, David Robinson, Charlitta Rodrigues, Brian Rokus, Jedd Rosche, Alexander Rosen, Lindy Royce-Bartlett, Diane Ruggiero, Stacey Samuel, Polo Sandoval, Antoine Sanfuentes, Amanda Sansone, Joseph Sansone, Douglas N. Schantz, Teddy Schleifer, James Sciutto, Raquel Scott, Gregory Seaby, Sunlen Serfaty, John Shaylor, David Siegel, Jeffery Simms, Jeff Simon, Jennifer Simpson, Kathleen Skinski, Steven Sloan, Rachel Smolkin, Chloe Sommers, Todd Sperry, Richard Spire, Cassandra Spodak, Jessica Stanton, Barbara Starr, Scott Stead, Vaughn Sterling, John Stevenson, Jason Strachan, Rachel Streitfeld, Jake Tapper, Laura Tatum, James B. Thomas III, Mallory Thompson, Brian Todd, Nicolas Toso, Thanh Tram, Andrew Troast, Kenneth Tuohey, Chris Turner, Elizabeth Turrell, Robert Tweed, Brett Tyler, Kim Uhl, Anthony R. Umrani, Laurie Ure, Ellen Van de Mark, Dawid Vermaak, Margaret Voelzke, Tu H. Vu, Gregory Wallace, Deirdre Walsh, Mark Walz, Tracey Webb, Alexis Weiss, Caitlin Weston, Amanda White, Brenna Williams, Kristin Wilson, Frederick Wiseman, Zachary Wolf, Angelique Yack, Floyd Yarmuth, Taka Yokoyama, Robert Yoon, Deena Zaru, Jeff Zeleny.

CNSNEWS.COM—(571) 267–3500; 325 South Patrick Street, Alexandria, VA 22314: Lauretta Brown, Michael Chapman, Barbara Hollingsworth, Brittany Hughes, Melanie Hunter, Terence Jeffrey, Susan Jones, Mark Judge, Alison Meyer, Craig Millward, Michael Morris, Eric Scheiner, Penny Starr.

COPE RADIO (SPAIN)—4904 Bett Road, NW., Washington, DC 20016: Juan Martinez Fierro.

COX BROADCASTING—(202) 777–7000; 400 North Capitol Street, NW., #750, Washington, DC 20001: Kyla Campbell, David Chase, Jamie Dupree, Jackie Fell, Justin Gray, Kevin Johnson, Heidi Junk, Dorey Scheimer, Patrick Terpstra, Jeffrey L. Williams.

Radio and Television Galleries 1053

NETWORKS, STATIONS, AND SERVICES REPRESENTED—Continued

CQ/ROLL CALL—202–650–6500; 77 K Street, NE., 8th Floor, Washington, DC 20002–4681: Meredith Dake, John Rieger.

CRONKITE NEWS SERVICE—(202) 684–2400; 1834 Connecticut Avenue, NW., Washington, DC 20009: Stephen Crane.

CTI–TV (TAIWAN)—(301) 792–8883; 7 Monona Court, Derwood, MD 20855: E-Ting Chung, Guohua Zang.

CTV CANADIAN TV—(202) 775–0356; 1717 DeSales Street, NW., Suite 354, Washington, DC 20036: Jonathan Austin, William Dugan, Bradley Fulton, Joy Malbon, John Mees, Marley Parker, Paul Workman.

CTV COMMUNITY TV OF PG COUNTY—(202) 383–6061; 9475 Lottsford Road, Largo, MD 20774: David Barnes, Curtis Crutchfield, Ara Laughlin, Rochelle Metzger, Jesusemen Oni, Sandra Peaches, Sonia Randev, Christopher Thomas, Patricia Villone Garcia.

DANISH BROADCASTING CORPORATION—(202) 785–1957; 2000 M Street, NW., Suite 890, Washington, DC 20036: Johannes Langkilde, Jacob Lorenzen, Gitte McGuire, Oliver Skov.

DEUTSCHE WELLE TV—(202) 785–5730; 2000 M Street, NW., Suite 335, Washington, DC 20036: Gero Schliess, Miodrag Soric, Richard Walker.

DIVERSIFIED COMMUNICATIONS, INC. (DCI)—2000 M Street, NW., 3rd Floor, Washington, DC 20036: James Butler, Joseph Concaugh, Jr., David M. Cooke, Robert Fetzer, Adrian Kill, Jamie Norins, Chanlee Parks, Terry Straub, Robert Zajko.

ENVIRONMENT & ENERGY PUBLISHING, LLC—(202) 628–6500; 122 C Street, NW., Suite 722, Washington, DC 20001: Christopher Farmer, Monica Trauzzi, Douglas Zimmerman.

EPA–EUROPEAN PRESS AGENCY—202–347–4694; 1122 National Press Building, Washington, DC 20045: Lawrence Miller.

ESTONIAN PUBLIC BROADCASTING—(202) 910–8644; 400 Massachusetts Avenue, #1210, Washington, DC 20001: Lauri Tankler, Eve Tisler.

EURONEWS—(202) 420–9852.; 1717 DeSales Street, NW., Washington, DC 20036: Stefan Grobe.

EUROVISION AMERICAS, INC.—2000 M Street, NW., Suite 300, Washington, DC 20036: James Banks, Adam Bearne, Garrett Bohannon, Emilie de Schaetzen, William Dunlop, Tanya Fischer, Megan Goodrich, Lee Grigsby, Jay Hahn, Sarah Lanningham, Brian Malloy, Adam Mandelson, Glenn Mikols, Priya Narahari, Jihee Park, Jean Pierre Roberts, Eduardo Rosario, Jason Scharf, Peggy Soucy, Thomas Trainor, Clayton Trosclair, Juri von Bonsdorff.

EWTN—(202) 909–2900; 750 First Street, NE., Suite 1115, Washington, DC 20002: Gonzalo Accame, Todd Burger, Jason Calvi, Addie Darling, Alfred Faison, Paul Fifield, Wyatt Goolsby, Matt Hadro, Mark Irons, Cristina Kelly, Susanne LaFrankie, Angela Mitchell, Susanna Pinto, Leon Segears, Paul Smith, Catherine Szeltner.

EYE–TO–EYE VIDEO—4614 Chevy Chase Boulevard, Chevy Chase, MD 20815: Elliot Klayman, Patrick O'Donnell.

FEATURE STORY NEWS—(202) 296–9012; 1730 Rhode Island Avenue, Suite 405, Washington, DC 20036: Andrea Arenas, Adriana Bevir, John Bevir, Malcolm Brown, John Clarke, Kate Fisher, Robert Flynn, Rebecca Foster, Robert Frazier, Tammy Haddad, Priscilla Huff, Denis Levkovich, Simon Marks, Kevin McAleese, Murray Pinczuk, Nina-Maria Potts, Daniel Ryntjes, Lorna Shaddick, Rachel Silverman, Charles Steck.

FEDERAL NEWS RADIO 1500 AM—3400 Idaho Avenue, NW., Washington, DC 20016: Mike Causey, Jason Fornicola, Jory Heckman, Shefali Kapadia, Emily Kopp, Lauren Larson, Sean McCalley, Jason Miller, Michael O'Connell, Nicole Ogrysko, Francis Rose, Jared Serbu, Meredith Somers, Thomas Temin, Matthew Wingfield, Lisa Wolfe, Julia Ziegler.

FEDNET—50 F Street, NW., Suite 1C, Washington, DC 20001: Keith Carney, Caleb Hamilton, Alvin Jones, Michael Kirby, Seamus McCreesh.

FINNISH BROADCASTING COMPANY (YLE)—2000 M Street, NW., Suite 890, Washington, DC 20036: Pirkko Pointinen.

FOX BUSINESS NETWORK—(202) 684–4000; 400 North Capitol Street, NW., Washington, DC 20001: Mike Bannigan, Peter Barnes, Bruce Becker, Blake Burman, Sylvia Hall, Martin Jimenez, Mary Kreinbihl, Chris Mills, Kristin Rudman, Jennifer Schonberger, Jonathan Street, John.

FOX NEWS—(202) 824–6300; 400 North Capitol Street, NW., Washington, DC 20001: Greg Ahlquist, Ashley Alderman, Vincent Arbogast, Robert Armfield, Adam Awada, Bret Baier, Les Baker, Josh Banks, Calvin Barrett, Stuart Basinger, Katherine Batson, Robin Beal, Chris Becker, Judson Berger, Varuna Bhatia, Bryan Boughton, Jennifer Bowman, Fletcher Bransford, Shannon Bream, Kristin Brown, Jenny Buchholz, Betsy Burkhard, Carl Cameron, Steve Carlson, Michael Carpel, Walter Carter, Jr., Margaret Chadbourn, Barnini Chakraborty, Richard Cockerham, Brielle Colby, Bryan Cole, Eric Colimore, Eric Conner, Kevin Corke, Lauren Cowin, Jodie Curtis, Abby Danzig, Wendy Dawson, Matthew Dean, Debra DeFrank, Joe DeFrank, Michael Demark, Mary Pat Dennert, Andrea DeVito, Kate DiBella, Brian Doherty, Jason Donner, Peter Doocy, Paige Dukeman, Jerry Echols, William Edmondson, Rich Edson, James W. Eldridge, Mike Emanuel, Tyler Evans, Joel Fagen, Amy Fenton, Mark Finch, Martin Finn, Kristin Fisher, Linda Fodrea, Jake Gibson, Gary Gillis, Serafin Gomez, Jennifer Griffin, Cherie Grzech, Gregg L. Gursky, Kata Hall, Lacey Halpern, Amy Hasenberg, Bill Hemmer, Ed

NETWORKS, STATIONS, AND SERVICES REPRESENTED—Continued

Henry, Francis Herbas, Catherine Herridge, Stacy Hickman, Joanna Hill, Martin Hill, Scott Himelein, Jennifer Holton, Adrienne Moira Hopkins, Cory R. Howard, Brit Hume, Elena Isella, Lesa Jansen, Nunu Japaridze, William G. Jenkins, George Jewsevskyj, Torrance Jones, Stephen Jones, Nathalie Joost, Nick Kalman, Stephen Kanicka, Colleen Kelley, Grigory Khananayev, Kevin Kirby, Ashley Koerber, Kathryn Krupnik, Whitney Ksiazek, Howard Kurtz, Donna Lacey, Philip LeCroy, Edward Lewis, Joy Lin, Jessica Loker, Wayne Lowman, Doug Luzader, Stacia Lynds, Michael Lyon, Michelle Macaluso, Michael Maltas, Lori Martin, Kevin McClam, George McCloskey, Constance McDonough, Doug McKelway, Tamara Montgomery, Richard Morse, Seleena M. Muhammad, Tiffany Mullon, James Nelson, Jessica O'Hara, Ryan O'Malley, Quillie Odom, Anna Olson, Cherie Paquette, Bradford S. Paxton, Chad Pergram, Sally Ann Persons, Jacqueline Pham, Elizabeth Prann, Owen Renfro, David Renken, Elizabeth Rhodes, Katheryn Ricalde, Sarah Ridolfi, Anne Marie Riha, Victor Rios, Lisa Rizzolo, Michael Robbins, Christina Robbins, John Roberts, Rhonda Rogers, Douglas Rohrbeck, James Rosen, Kara Rowland, Bill Sammon, Craig Savage, Jason Scanlon, Kimberly Schwandt, Jody Sciacca, Steve Shelton, Anita Siegfriedt, David Smith, Teresa Spector, Daniel J. Stay, Seneca Stevens, Chris Stirewalt, Matthew Stout, Kelly Summers, Patrick Summers, Stanley Sundel, Jennifer Suzara, Garrett Tenney, Lucas Tomlinson, Robert Torpey, Anne Trabandt, Bree Tracey, Hayley Turner, Lamonte Tyler, Greta Van Susteren, Bryce Vinson, Todd Visioli, Leland Vittert, Phil Vogel, Joel Waldman, Neil Wallace, Chris Wallace, John L. Wallace, Jonathan Walter, Patrick Ward, Joseph Webber, Amy Wehinger, Meghan Welsh, Caroline Whiteman, Walter Whitley, Colleen Williams, John Williams, Anne Marie Willis.

FOX NEWS RADIO—(212) 301–5800; 400 North Capitol Street, NW., Washington, DC 20001: Jason Bonewald, Jessica Curtis, Mitch Davis, Jon Decker, Jared Halpern, Kirstin McNary, Jill Nado, Tom Root, Gurnal Scott, Daniel Shields, Rachel Sutherland, John Sylvester, Hank Weinbloom, Tonya Williams.

FRANCE 2 TELEVISION—(202) 833–1818; 2000 M Street, NW., Suite 320, Washington, DC 20036: Sabrina Buckwalter, Jacques Cardoze, Laurent Desbois, Fabien Ortiz.

FREE SPEECH TV (FSTV)—1844 Mintwood Place, NW., Washington, DC 20009: Eddie Becker.

FUJI TV JAPAN—(202) 347–1600; 529 14th Street, NW., Suite 330, Washington, DC 20045: Jacqueline Enzmann, Peter Gold, Haruka Joho, Toshiyuki Matsuyama, Matthew Mosley, Tomokazu Shibaki.

GALEI–TZAHAL (ISRAEL ARMY RADIO)—(301) 520–2503; 112 Shaw Avenue, Silver Spring, MD 20904: Drora Perl.

GANNETT GOVERNMENT MEDIA CORP—(703) 750–7479; 6883 Commercial Drive, Springfield, VA 22159: Lars Schwetje.

GERMAN PRESS AGENCY—(202) 662–1220; 1112 National Press Building, Washington, DC 20045: Christina Eck.

GERMAN PUBLIC RADIO (ARD)—(202) 342–1730; 3132 M Street, NW., Washington, DC 20007: Jan Boesche, Rolf Buellmann, Martina Buttler, Sabrina Fritz, Martin Ganslmeier, Eva Graumann, Andreas Horchler, Astrid Joehnk, Diana Robbins, Ralph Weber.

GERMAN TV ARD—(202) 298–6535; 3132 M Street, NW., Washington, DC 20007: Jan Aulenkamp, Daniel Doernen, Heather Dorf-Dolce, Hillery Gallasch, Antonio R. Gonzalez, Bettina Hassel-Schumacher, Felicitas Klopp, Barbara Lautenbach, Stefan Niemann, Sandra Ratzow, Ina-Maria Ruck, Thomas Sawera, Ingo Zamperoni, Marion Zschieschang.

GERMAN TV ZDF—(202) 333–3909; 1077 31st Street, NW., Washington, DC 20007: Catherine Berger, Annette Brieger, Kirsten Candia, Oliver Divaris, Uwe Doergeloh, Lara Esfahani, Ruben Herrera, Carmen Kupper, Katherine Leiken, Wolfgang Macholz, Claudia Offermann, Daniel Pontzen, Steffanie Riess, Ulf-Jensen Roeller, Peter Schloemer, Jan Seifert, Heike Slansky, Uyanga Tserenbaljid, Elke Tucker.

GLOBAL TV CANADA—(202) 824–6771; 400 North Capitol Street, NW., #850, Washington, DC 20001: Aarti Pole, Jackson Proskow.

GRAY TELEVISION—(202) 910–8644; 400 North Capitol Street, NW., Suite 850, Washington, DC 20001: Mariam Khan, Alex Miller, Jacqueline Policastro, Nicholas Starling, Alex Yoder, Peter Zampa.

GROUPE TVA—(202) 822–4588; 820 1st Street, NE., Washington, DC 20002: Richard Latendresse.

HEARST TELEVISION INC—(202) 457–0220; 1100 13th Street, NW., #425, Washington, DC 20005: Lee Alexandre, Gail Austin, Aixa Diaz, Brady Headington, Sheila Jaskot, Sally F. Kidd, Nikole Killion, Nathan Luna, Lauren McDevitt, Erin T. McManamon, Camille Moore, Carlos Olazagasti, Chase Pipkin, David Postovit, Chris Smyth, Wendy Wilk.

HELLENIC PUBLIC TV—(202) 413–9219; 2742 Thornbrook Court, Odenteon, MD 21113: Eleni Argyri.

HISPANIC COMMUNICATIONS NETWORK—(202) 360–4112; 1126 16th Street, NW., 3rd Floor, Washington, DC 20036: David Castro, Pablo Castro, Jeff Kline, Mercy Padilla-Cirino, Simon Rojas.

HONG KONG PHOENIX SATELLITE TELEVISION—101 Constitution Avenue, NW., #920 East, Washington, DC 20001: Yi Qiu Chen, Zhuo Huang, Daniel Lai, Jennifer Lee, Tao Lu, Bingru Wang.

HRT/CROATIAN RADIO TELEVISION—1230 23rd Street, Washington, DC 20037: Branka Slavica.

INDEPENDENT TELEVISION NEWS (ITN)—400 North Capitol Street, NW., #899, Washington, DC 20008: Adam Blair, Harry Horton, Joe Jones, Girish Juneja, Jade Liversidge, Ben Martin, Mashaal Mir, Robert Moore, Kylie Morris, Emily O'Neill, David Sampy, Chris Shlemon, Robert Turner, Matt Williams.

NETWORKS, STATIONS, AND SERVICES REPRESENTED—Continued

ISRAEL TELEVISION AND RADIO—3412 Woolsey Drive, Chevey Chase, MD 20815: Nathan Guttman.
JTBC—529 14th Street, NW., Suite 997, Washington, DC 20045: Hans Cho, Bora Joo, Hyunki Kim, Sangbok Lee.
KAISER HEALTH NEWS—(202) 654–1466; 1330 G Street, NW., Washington, DC 20005: Francis Ying.
KCETLINK—8715 Persimmon Tree Road, Potomac, MD 20814: Miles Benson, Raisa Scriabine, Kim Spencer.
KOREAN BROADCASTING SYSTEMS—(202) 662–7345; 529 14th Street, NW., Suite 1055, Washington, DC 20045: Katherine Ahn, Hyunjin Hong, SungJin Kim, JuHan Lee, KangDuk Lee, Kevin Nha, Jinkyung Park, Ja Ryen Seo, James Yu.
LASLO CONGRESSIONAL BUREAU—(202) 510–4331; 1705 East West Highway, #519, Silver Spring, MD 20910: Matt Laslo, Anthony Rivera.
LILLY BROADCASTING—(202) 440–3831; 400 North Capitol Street, NW., Washington, DC 22201: Lauren Adams, Kellie Meyer.
MACEDONIA RADIO TELEVISION (MRTV)—(202) 286–5252; 1500 Massachusetts Avenue, NW., Washington, DC 20005: Irina Gelevska, Riste Mishev.
MARKETPLACE RADIO—(202) 263–0204; 1750 K Street, NW., Suite 300, Washington, DC 20006: Tim Fitzsimons, Nancy Marshall-Genzer, Dave Shaw, Scott Tong.
MBC–TV KOREA (MUNHWA)—529 14th Street, NW., #1131, Washington, DC 20045: Yang Woo Kang, Sang Lim, Ho Chul Moon, Bunsoo Park.
MCCLATCHY—(202) 383–6061; 700 12th Street, NW., Suite 1000, Washington, DC 20005: Glenn Anderson, Nicole Cvetnic, Natalie Fertig, Jonathan Forsythe, Jessica Koscielniak, JulieAnn McKellogg, Andrew Pergam, Brittany Peterson, Ali Rizvi, Meghan Sims, Sarah Whitmire.
MEDIA GENERAL—(202) 570–5610; 400 North Capitol Street, NW., Washington, DC 20001: Danielle Gatewood-Gill, Mark Meredith, Jim Osman, Alex Schuman, Chance Seales.
MEDILL NEWS SERVICE—1325 G Street, NW., #730, Washington, DC 20005: Kwame Holman.
METRO TELEPRODUCTIONS—(301) 608–9077; 1400 East West Highway, Suite 628, Silver Spring, MD 20910: Dave Lilling.
MIDDLE EAST BROADCASTING NETWORKS (MBN)—7600–D Boston Boulevard, Springfield, VA 22153: Rana Abtar, Ali Ahmed, Saad Alfalahi, Kelly Alford, Tetiana Anderson, Babu Aryankalavil, Elkheir Bentouila, Hicham Bourar, Alain Dargham, Nkwenten Ejedepang-Koge, John Elgin, Daniel Farkas, Michel Ghandour, Stephen Heiner, Arcelious Joyner, Khaled Khairy, Deirdre Kline, Ali Mahdi, Tim Miller, W. Harrison Moore, Luis Munoz, Adam Nixon, James Norris, Zaid Oshana, Sue Richardson, Arwa Sawan, Joseph Tabet, Karen Yianopoulos, Marwan Zaatar, Elizabeth Zosso.
MINNESOTA PUBLIC RADIO—6631 Eastern Avenue, Takoma Park, MD 20914: Brett Neely.
MOBILE VIDEO SERVICES, LTD.—1620 I Street, NW., #1000, Washington, DC 20006: Howard Collender, William Griffitts, Christine Hoese, Timothy Knapp, Robert H. Milford, Todd Swain, Lawrence VanderVeen.
MORNINGSIDE PARTNERS, LLC—4200 Forbes Road, Suite 200, Lanham, MD 20706: Tony Anthony, Joshua Binswanger, Elizabeth Pennell, Ellen Piacente "fka Portnoy", Juvenal Uribe.
MUNDOFOX—1333 H Street, NW., Suite 8 West, Washington, DC 20005: Jose Diaz-Briseno, Juan Silva.
N–TV GERMAN NEWS CHANNEL—1100 13th Street, NW., Suite 400, Washington, DC 20005: Peter Kleim, Alexander Klein.
N24 GERMAN TV—1620 I Street, NW., Suite 1000, Washington, DC 20006: Stephen Strothe, Sabine Ulbrich-Strothe.
NATIONAL PUBLIC RADIO—(202) 513–2073; 1111 North Capitol Street, NE., Washington, DC 20002: Stacey Abbott, Elizabeth Acle, Augustine Bud-Aiello, Jr., Theo Balcomb, Mark Bejarano, Robert Benincasa, Melissa Block, Brakkton Booker, Radek Brablec, Geoff Brumfiel, Julia Redpath Buckley, Robert E. Butcher, Dennis Byrnes, Ailsa Chang, Dan Charles, Carlos Chevez, Dennis Coll, Audie Cornish-Emery, Michael Cullen, Michael Czaplinski, Shirish Date, Susan Davis, Rebecca Davis, Jess Deahl, Bridget DeChagas, Brian DeMar, Greg Dixon, Beth Donovan, Aboubacar Drabo, Ronald Elving, Pam Fessler, Marilyn Geewax, Gene Gerhiser, Don Gonyea, Barry Gordemer, Gisele Grayson, Neil Greenfieldboyce, Richard Harris, Shirley Henry, Scott Horsley, Andy Huether, Will Huntsberry, Brian Jarboe, Rick Jarrett, Carrie Johnson, John C. Keator, Tamara Keith, Michele Kelemen, Amita Kelly, Muhammed Khan, Alison Kodjak, Mara Liasson, Tom Marchitto, Melissa Marquis, Michel Martin, Michael Merena, Joe Mills, Domenico Montanaro, Brian Naylor, Christopher Nelson, Jackie Northam, Peter Overby, Matt Ozug, Joe Palca, John Poole, Arnie Seipel, Robert C. Siegel, Art Silverman, Kenneth Spencer, Kurt Stalnaker, Rob Stein, Evie Stone, Laura Sullivan, Juana Summers, Jessica Taylor, Neil David Tevault, Nina Totenberg, Kevin Wait, Andrew Watts, David Welna, Jinae West, Natalie Winston.
NATIONAL SCENE NEWS—1718 M Street, NW., #333, Washington, DC 20036: Alverda Muhammad, Askia Muhammad.
NATIVE AMERICAN TV (NATV)—17690 Old Waterford Road, Leesburg, VA, Leesburg, VA 20176: Robert Cohencious, Rebecca Cohencious, Randy Flood, Richard Gargagliano, Elizabeth Lorenzen, Anthony Lovelace.

NETWORKS, STATIONS, AND SERVICES REPRESENTED—Continued

NBC NEWS—(202) 885–4200; 4001 Nebraska Avenue, NW., Washington, DC 20016: Halimah Abdullah, Douglas A. Adams, Peter Alexander, Bryan Allman, Roberto Aneiva, Kenneth Austin, Perry Bacon, Jr., Sarah Baker, Rodney Batten, Gary Beall, Justin Bennett, Jay Blackman, John Blackman, Sarah Blackwill, Victoria Blooston, Jeffrey Blount, Joseph Bohannon, Kirsten Boser, Shaquille Brewster, Brooke Brower, Mika Brzezinski, Louis Burgdorf, Norman Butler, Leigh Ann Caldwell, Anthony Capra, Lauren Chadwick, Lete Childs, Michelle Cho, Patrick Chung, Nero Cooper, Jr., Thomas Costello, Oliver Cox, Natalie Cucchiara, Caroline Dann, Ed Demaria, Evan Dixon, Kristin Donnelly, Michelle Dubert, Victoria Duncan, John Edwards, Rachel Fazio, David Forman, Scott Foster, Maggie Fox, Jordan Frasier, Drew Fredrickson, Lawrence Gaetano, Emily Gaffney, Dennis Gaffney, John Gaffney, Suzanne Gamboa, Richard Gardella, Keith Gaskin, Charlie Gile, Avra Gold, Emily Gold, James M. Greene, Andrew F. Gross, Sylvia Haller, David Hanson, Candice Harrington, Christopher Hartman, Alan Harvey, William Hatfield, Sarah Heidarpour, Robert Heritage, Vaughn Hillyard, John Holland, James Hughes, Kasie Hunt, Brian Iacone, Christine Jansing, Alicia Jennings, Gwyneth Jones, Terence Kelly, Suzy Khimm, Ryan Kiernan, Stacey Klein, Michael Kosnar, Courtney Kube, Michael LaRosa, Natasha Lebedeva, Arthur Lien, Joseph W. Loebach, James V. Long, Gary Lynn, Kathryn Lyons, Mary Manby, Marc Marriott, Greg Martin, Chris Matthews, Lee McKinney, Carroll Ann Mears, James Miklaszewski, Christopher Millar, Richard Minner, Andrea Mitchell, Steven Mitnick, Alexandra Moe, Ray Morada, Brittany Morris, Shaheen Mozaffari, Mark Murray, Jason Neal, Michelle Neal, Donna Nelson, Elizabeth Nevins, David O'Brien, John O'Connor, Kelly O'Donnell, Hope Palmer, Eddie Paylor, Elyse Perlmutter-Gumbiner, Debra Pettit, John Quinnette, Meaghan Rady, Andrew Rafferty, Alonzo Ray, Talesha Reynolds, Paul Rigney, Matt Rivera, Jordan Rummel, Luke Russert, Howard Sacks, Colleen Sanvido, Benjamin Sarlin, Samantha Schnurr, Andrew Scritchfield, Wesley Scruggs, Carl Sears, Joel Seidman, Alexander Seitz-Wald, Adam Serwer, Maria Sevilla, Joseph Shalhoup, Brandon Sibert, Aaron Skopek, Kimberly Sneed, Gilbert Solorzano, Sharon Spurrier, Melanie Stevens, Kenneth Strickland, Jon Sughroue, Shawna Thomas, Ronald Thornton, Frank Thorp, Chuck Todd, Vaughn Ververs, Susan Vitorovich, David Vukmer, Katharine Wall, Kathryn Wassman, David Weakly, Cydney Weiner, Kristen Welker, Christopher Whittington, Winston Wilde, Abigail Williams, Pete Williams, Robert T. Williams, Christopher Williamson, Rachel Witkin, V. Alan Young.

NBC NEWSCHANNEL—(202) 783–2615; 400 North Capitol Street, Suite 850, Washington, DC 20001: Sheila Conlin, Ray Davis, Michael Dobal, Nancy Ellard, Sheri Lynn Gibson, Nelson Ginebra, Andrew L. Godsick, Steve Handelsman, James Hurt, Julie Jarvis, Jennifer Johnson, Nicole McManus, Brian Mooar, Steven Muskat, Tom Newberry, Mike O'Connell, Tracie Potts, Cecil John Sills, Christopher Wiggins.

NEW TANG DYNASTY TV—(202) 449–9480; 8927 Shady Grove Court, Gaithersburg, MD 20877: Chuan Lin, Yang Wang, Wei Wu, Ping Yu.

NHK—(202) 828–5180; 2030 M Street, NW., #706, Washington, DC 20036: Taurean Barnwell, Matthew Field, Mami Fujiue, Hiroto Fuseya, Hitoshi Hirouchi, Willie Inman, Kenkichi Ishiyama, Torao Kono, Marion Madsen, David McCagg, Junko Tanaka Nakano, Hirohito Nezu, Momoca Nishimoto, Erin Robertson, Alicia Rose, Yuka Takagane, Masayoshi Tanaka, Michiko Tsurumi, Alexander Wortman, Takeshi Yamasaki, Jumpei Yoshioka, Masaru Zenke.

NIPPON TV NETWORK—(202) 638–0890; 529 14th Street, NW., #1036, Washington, DC 20045: Takaaki Abe, Kazuhiro Aoyama, Nicholle Granger, Tomoko Horie, Chinatsu Hosokawa, Chihiro Kawana, Hiroaki Konno, Rikako Murakami, Jumpei Shimizu, Mai Taguchi, Kiyoshi Tanno, Keishi Yamada.

NORWEGIAN BROADCASTING—(202) 785–1460; 2000 M Street, NW., #890, Washington, DC 20036: Tove Bjorgaas, Gro Holm.

NOS DUTCH PUBLIC RADIO & TV (VRT)—2000 M Street, NW., #365, Washington, DC 20036: Arjen van der Horst, Wouter Zwart.

NOTIMEX—(202) 255–1819; 975 National Press Building, Washington, DC 20045: Jorge Ayala.

ONE AMERICA—(858) 270–690; 101 Constitution Avenue, NW., Washington, DC 20001: Andrew Brice, Andrew Brody, Augusta Cassada, Andrew Hall, Charles Herring, Alicia Hesse, Amanda House, Neil McCabe, Young Richardson, Matthew Schuck, John Stansfield.

POLITICO.COM—(703) 842–1791; 1100 Wilson Boulevard, Suite 601, Arlington, VA 22209: Bridget Mulcahy, Beatrice Peterson, Michael Schwab, Matthew Sobocinski.

RADIO FRANCE INTERNATIONALE—3700 Massachusetts Avenue, NW., #538, Washington, DC 20016: Anne-Marie Capomaccio-Even, Frederic Carbonne, Claude L. Porsella.

RADIO FREE ASIA—(202) 530–4900; 2025 M Street, NW., #300, Washington, DC 20036: Christen Billing, Shiny Breese, Gordon Burnett, Lobsang Chophel, Dorjee Damdul, Rigdhen Dolma, Paul Eckert, Richard Finney, Roseanne Gerin, Dhondup Gonsar, Gwen Ha, King Ho, Chan Nhu Hoang, Gulchehra Hoja, Ahreum Jung, Jilil Kashgary, Joshua Lipes, Kalden Lodoe, Corey Munford, Sarkis Najarian, Jung-Woo Park, Parameswaran Ponnudurai, Brian William Powell, Aungthu Schlenker, Khin Maung Soe, Sarada Taing, Lumbum Tashi, Yeshi Tashi, San San Tin, Hoa Ai Tran, Thomas Vichi, Hee Yang, Sungwon Yang, Lobsang Yeshi, Samean Yun.

RADIO FREE EUROPE—(202) 457–6900; 1201 Connecticut Avenue, NW., Washington, DC 20036: Nader Sadighi.

NETWORKS, STATIONS, AND SERVICES REPRESENTED—Continued

RADIO ONE—(301) 565–8182; 8515 Georgia Avenue, Silver Spring, MD 20910: Kent Kramer, Ron Thompson, Christopher Wegmann, Jeffrey Wilson.

RADIO VALERA VENEZUELA—529 14th Street, NW., 8th Floor, Washington, DC 20045: Sonia Schott.

RCN–TV (COLOMBIA)—1333 H Street, NW., Washington, DC 20005: Gustau Alegret, Martha Avila Lindo, Jean Paul Borja, Diana Castaneda, Mario Gonzalez, Marco Granda, Julio Moreno, Valdemar Rodriguez, Rafael Rosero, Christian Siaden-Pena.

REAL NEWS NETWORK—(410) 500–5235; 700 12th Street, NW., Suite 1000, Washington, DC 20005: Jessica Desvarieux, Thomas Hedges, Paul Jay, Denise Rivera.

REALCLEARPOLITICS—1667 K Street, NW., Suite 1150, Washington, DC 20006: John Dillon.

RELIGION & ETHICS NEWSWEEKLY—(202) 216–2388; 1819 L Street, NW., Suite 100, Washington, DC 20036: Bob Abernethy, Gail Fendley, Patricia Jette, Arnold Labaton, Kim Lawton, Nicholas Liao, Judy Reynolds, Noelle Serper, Lauren Talley.

REUTERS RADIO & TV—(202) 898 0056; 1333 H Street, NW., 6th Floor, Washington, DC 20005: Nadine Alfa, Keith Allen, Rudi Bakhtiar, Daniel Balinovic, Anoo Bharania, Peter Bullock, Dan Fastenberg, Liza Feria, Kevin Fogarty, Marie Frail, Nathan Frandino, Guillermo Garcia, Deborah Gembara, Pavithra George, Sarah Irwin, Katharine Jackson, Kia Johnson, Jillian Kitchener, Deborah Lutterbeck, Robert Muir, Kristin Neubauer, Gershon Peaks, Don Pessin, Steven Phillips, Mana Rabiee, Sam Rocha, Jane Ross, Tom Rowe, Roger Shull, Linda So, George Tamerlani, Scott Vaughan, Omar Younis.

RTE–IRISH RADIO & TV—(202) 467–5933; 2000 M Street, NW., #315, Washington, DC 20036: Susan Casey, Caitriona Perry.

RTTV AMERICA—(202) 942–7440; 1325 G Street, NW., Suite 250, Washington, DC 20005: Reema Abu-Hamdyia, Erin Ade, Mark Angelini, Andrew Blake, Mark Bulla, Lee Camp, Manila Chan, Gayane Chichakyan, Chris Counts, Ameera David, Simone Del Rosario, Bianca Facchinei, Sean Filburn, Kathryn Fischer, Lindsay France, Irene Gonzalez, Edward Harrison, Edward Harrison, Charles House II, Mariana Joyal, Angel Jubilla, Ryan Kerr, Anjalee Khemlani, Melissa Kolpak, John Mecham, Alexander Mursa, John O'Donnell, Anya Parampil, Manuel Rapalo, Priya Reddy, Giuseppe Ricci, Sam Sacks, Ian Sbalcio, Samir Shakhbaz, John Smith, Cody Snell, Mikhail Solodovnikov, Ben Swann, Tyrel Ventura, Vera Volokhonovich, Tabetha Wallace, Christopher Westfall, Alexey Yaroshevsky, Ilya Zhodzishsky.

RTVI/ECHO–TV—(202) 742–6576; 1001 Pennsylvania Avenue, NW., Suite #6310, Washington, DC 20004: Anatolie Casenco, Roman Mamonov.

RURAL TV NEWS—(202) 554–0514; 611 Pennsylvania Avenue, SE., Suite 397, Washington, DC 20003: Janet Adkison, Clif Jackson.

RUSSIAN STATE TV AND RADIO (RTR)—(202) 262–2595; 2000 N Street, NW., Suite 810, Washington, DC 20007: Alexander Khristenko, Pavel Kostrikov, Anna Semenova, Elena Sokolova.

RUSTAVI 2 BROADCASTING COMPANY—1111 Army Navy Drive Unit 127, Arlington, VA 22202: David Nikuradze, Aleksandre Papinashvili.

SAGARMATHA TELEVISION—(703) 926–9530; 9655 Hawkshead Drive, Lorton, VA 22079: Nilu Kharel, Ram C. Kharel, Sharmila Uprety.

SCRIPPS NEWS—1100 13th Street, NW., Suite 450, Suite 450, Washington, DC 20005: Matt Anzur, Marc Georges, Miranda Green, Mark Greenblatt, Lawan Hamilton, Amanda Havekost, Angela Hill, Vivek Narayan, Claude Pruitt, Rachel Quester, Elizabeth Scheltens, Andrea Seabrook, Ellen Weiss.

SEOUL BROADCASTING SYSTEM (SBS)—(202) 637–9850; 529 14th Street, NW., #979, Washington, DC 20045, Woo Sik Kim, Edward Park, Sungchul Rhee, Jiwon Song.

SHENZHEN MEDIA GROUP (SZMG)—202–815–6463; 1330S Fair Street, Apartment 1101, Arlington, VA 22202: Jennifer Chen, Chi Kwan.

SINCLAIR BROADCAST GROUP—(410) 568–1500; 10706 Beaver Dam Road, Cockeysville, MD 21030: Sharyl Attkisson, Laquasha Banks, Jeff Barnd, Bryan Barr, Kristine Frazao, Hetal Gandhi, Charles Humphreys, Mark Hyman, Kai Jackson, Gregory Massoni, Joshua Miller, Delbert Parks, TraLanenia Reeves, Kimberly Skeen, Colleen Wordock.

SINOVISION—2111 Jefferson Davis Highway, #202N, Arlington, VA 22202: Han Cui.

SIRIUS XM SATELLITE RADIO—(202) 380–4000; 1500 Eckington Place, NE., Washington, DC 20002: Daniel Berdiel, Andrea Cambron, Katherine Caperton, Paul DeMilio, Tim Farley, Patrick Ferrise, Scott Gulden, Daniel Henning, Robert Henry, Rachel Kurzius, Julie Mason, Jennifer McLellan, Ari Rabin-Havt, Jared Rizzi.

SKY NEWS—400 North Capitol Street, NW., #550, Washington, DC 20001: David Bowden, Tim Gallagher, Michael Greenfield, Caroline James, Dickon Mager, Greg Milam, Nina Saada, Duncan Sharp, Jude Sheerin, Kevin Sheppard, Dominic Waghorn, Amanda Walker.

SKY NEWS ARABIA—400 North Capitol, Suite 770, Washington, DC 20001: Mouhamed Elahmed, Paul Hijazin, Osamah Smysom.

SMALL HOUSE PRODUCTIONS—10304 Royal Woods Court, Montgomery Village, MD 20886: Nico Belha, Juan Carlos Diaz, Wingel Pinzon, Edwin Ramirez.

SRN NEWS (SALEM)—(703) 528–6213; 1901 N Moore Street, #201, Arlington, VA 22209: Gregory Clugston, LeRoy Froom, Walter Hindes, Linda Kenyon, John Lormand, Jeffrey Matzka, Andrew Stewart.

NETWORKS, STATIONS, AND SERVICES REPRESENTED—Continued

ST. LOUIS PUBLIC RADIO—(202) 320–9325; 718 McCann Road, Severna Park, MD 21146: Jim Howard.
STATELINE.ORG—202.552.2188; 901 E Street, NW., Suite 700, Washington, DC 20004: Rebecca Beitsch, Jenni Bergal, Sarah Breitenbach, Stephen Fehr, Scott Greenberger, Jake Grovum, Tim Henderson, Michael Ollove, Elaine Povich, Jeffrey Stinson, Christine Vestal, Teresa Wiltz.
STORYHOUSE PRODUCTIONS—2233 Wisconsin Avenue, NW., #420, Washington, DC 20007: Tina-Jane Krohn, Carsten Oblaender, Thomas Sassenberg.
SWEDISH BROADCASTING—(202) 785 1727; 2000 M Street, NW., Suite 890, Washington, DC 20036: Inger Arenander, Erika Bjerstrom, Bjorn Carlsson, Lisa Carlsson, Kyle Lanningham.
SWISS BROADCASTING—(202) 429 9668; 2000 M Street, NW., Suite 370, Washington, DC 20036: Peter Duggeli, Pierre Gobet, Arthur Honegger, Thomas Paggini, Philippe Revaz, Beat Soltermann, Andrea Vosti, Mark Yates.
TALK RADIO NEWS SERVICE—(202) 337–5322; 236 Massachusetts Avenue, NE., Suite 306, Washington, DC 20002: Shelley Blanchette, Ed Butowsky, James Cullum, Blanquita Cullum, Brian Doyle, Justin Duckham, Shane Farnan, John Grott, Victoria Jones, Loretta Lewis, Carole Marks, William McDonald, Ellen Ratner, Luke Vargas, Ari Zoldan.
TELEMUNDO NETWORK—400 North Capitol Street, NW., Suite 850, Washington, DC 20001: Glenda Contreras, Wilbert Guzman, Edwing Lopez Reyes, Lizeth Juliana Monsalve, Lori Montenegro, Victor Reyes, A. Victoria Rivas-Vazquez, Randy Serrano.
TELESUR—(202) 420 5560; 1100 13th Street, NW., Washington, DC 20005: Belen Barriga, William Cortes, Jorge Gestoso, Roberto McCarthy, Nicolas Pena, Bianca Perez, Aurora Samperio, Jaime Vera.
TELEVISA NEWS NETWORK (ECO)—1825 K Street, NW., Suite 710–G, Washington, DC 20006: Gregorio Meraz.
TF1–FRENCH TV—2000 M Street, NW., Suite 870, Washington, DC 20036: Julie Asher, Clement Biet, Mathieu Derrien, Michel Floquet, Bruce Frankel, Amelie Geffroy, Bertrand Guez, Josselin Huchet, Vincent Mortreux.
THE BERNS BUREAU, INC.—SDG 40, Washington, DC 20510: Matthew Kaye.
THE HILL—1625 K Street, NE., Suite 900, Washington, DC 20006: Eric Garland, Alexandra Goncalves-de-Oliveira, Molly Hooper, Wes Jones, Sean Root, Joaquin Sosa.
THE NEW YORK TIMES ON THE WEB—1627 I Street, NW., #1700, Washington, DC 20006: A.J. Chavar.
THE NEWSHOUR WITH JIM LEHRER—3620 S. 27th Street, Arlington, VA 22206: Joshua Barajas, Quinn Bowman, Kyla Calvert, Frank Carlson, Emily Carpeaux, Jaywon Choe, David Coles, Sarah Corapi, Lisa Desjardins, Larisa Epatko, Diane Estes, Mike Fritz, Geoffrey Guray, Gwen Ifill, Sara Just, Jason Kane, Stephanie Kotuby, Bob Kovach, Sam Lane, Noreen Nasir, Daniel Sagalyn, Justin Scuiletti, Elizabeth Summers, Morgan Till, Peter Tobia, Anya van Wagtendonk, Jordan Vesey, Margaret Warner, Rachel Wellford, Judy Woodruff, Daniel Yang.
THIS IS AMERICA WITH DENNIS WHOLEY—1333 H Street, NW., Washington, DC 20005: Jerry Cox, Dennis Wholey.
THIS WEEK IN AGRIBUSINESS—(301) 466–7403; 9915 Hillridge Drive, Kensington, MD 20895: Patrick Haggerty.
TIMA—(202) 304–5110; 1620 I Street, NW., Suite 1000, Washington, DC 20006: Khaldoun Alrawi, Alicia Haygood, Zena Ibrahim, Abdelhakim Kabbaj, Shant Markarian, Krysia Osinski, Kristen Richards, Eduardo Rodriquez.
TIME WARNER CABLE—(202) 783–0565; 400 North Capitol, NW., Suite G–95, Washington, DC 20001: Geoffrey Bennett, Sarah Brooks-Grady, Jonquilyn Hill, Michael Scotto.
TO THE CONTRARY (PERSEPHONE PRODUCTIONS)—1819 L Street, NW., 7th Floor, Washington, DC 20036: Ariel Edem, Bonnie Erbe, Luis Mazariegos, Cari Stein.
TOKYO BROADCASTING SYSTEM—1088 National Press Building, Washington, DC 20045: Samantha Grieder, Kiyoshi Murai, Makoto Ogata, Shota Sato, So Taira, Elliot Waldman, Noriyuki Yamaguchi.
TURKISH RADIO AND TELEVISION (TRT)—(703) 401–6482; 529 14th Street, NW., #1085, Washington, DC 20045: Mehmet Cakir, Celal Cevirgen, Cumhur Kutay, Ozlem Tinaz.
TV ASAHI—529 14th Street, NW., #1280, Washington, DC 20045: William Ding-Everson, Robert Gentry, Takashi Hotta, Mai Ichihara, Renata Janney, Tatsuya Yamashita, Junichi Yoshikawa.
TV GLOBO INTERNATIONAL—(202) 429–2525; 2141 Wisconsin Avenue, NW., Suite L, Washington, DC 20007: Vicente Cinque, Raquel Krahenbuhl, Daniel Silva-Pinto, Luis Fernando Silva-Pinto.
TV TOKYO—1333 H Street, NW., 5th Floor, Washington, DC 20005: Benjamin Dalton, Mitsuo Kawamoto, Yuko Miyake, Mina Pollmann.
TV3–TELEVISIO DE CATALUNYA—(202) 785–0580; 2000 M Street, NW., Suite 830, Washington, DC 20036: Eva Artesona, Raquel Sans, Angela Sauret.
TVBS—2500 Wisconsin Avenue, Washington, DC 20007: Chia-Hui Ni, Shih-Yuan Tuan.
TVE–SPANISH PUBLIC TELEVISION—(202) 785–1813; 2000 M Street, NW., #325, Washington, DC 20036: Carlos Franganillo, Alejandro Millan, Anna Ubeda.
TVN POLAND—7429 Chummley Court, Falls Church, VA 22043: Marcin Wrona, Marcin Wyszogrodzki.

NETWORKS, STATIONS, AND SERVICES REPRESENTED—Continued

UNIVISION—(202) 682–6160; 101 Constitution Avenue, NW., Suite 810E, Washington, DC 20001: Jorge Contreras, Emily DeRuy, Deborah Durham, Pablo Gato, Ted Hesson, Lourdes Meluza, Fernando Pizarro, Pablo Sanchez, Geneva Sands-Sadowitz, Mario Vizcarra.

USA TODAY—7950 Jones Branch Drive, McLean, VA 22107: Steve Elfers, Maria Fowler, Shannon Green, Julie Iannuzzi.

VENTANA PRODUCTIONS—(202) 785–5112; 1819 L Street, NW., Washington, DC 20036: Richard Joy, Thomas Knier, John Lawrence, Timothy K. Murray, Juan Rocha, Robin Stewart, Mark Thalman.

VERIZON: Michael Levenson, Kenneth Meier, Keenan Patience, Rodney Rice, David West, Dexter Wright.

VIETV NETWORK—(215) 883–9738; 1604 Spring Hill Road, Suite 150, Vienna, VA 22182: Thao Dao, ThuyLan Phan, Cynthia Truong, Doanh Vu.

VIEWPOINT COMMUNICATIONS—(301) 565–1650, 8607 2nd Avenue, Suite 402, Silver Spring, MD 20910: Art Berko, Randy Feldman, Ben Finkel, Larry Greenblatt, Steven Hamberg, Charles Horn.

VOICE OF AMERICA—330 Independence Avenue, SW., Washington, DC 20237: Brian Allen, Darrell Allen, Arash Azzizada, Carla Babb, Thomas Bagnall, Steve Baragona, Sharon Behn, Larry Bond, Michael Bowman, Timothy Brannon, Meredith Buel, Michael Burke, Mia Bush, Carol Castiel, Nike Ching, Eun Cho, Trinlae Choedron, Raymond Choto, Peter Clottey, Pete Cobus, Lina Correa, Woody Crawford, Nick Crupi, Robert Currence, Minas Dargakis, Jeffery Daugherty, Jela de Franceschi, Siamak Dehghanpour, Joan Deluca, Pamela Dockins, Michael Eckel, Melvin Eleazer, Henok Fente, Bruce Ferder, Darren Fox, James Fry, David Futrowsky, Bello Galadanchi, Sasha Gong, Myroslava Gongadze, Pema Gorap, Richard Green, Adam Greenbaum, Carol Guenburg, Katherine Gypson, Marcus Harton, Cecily Hillary, Utami Hussin, Michael Ivey, Gary Jaffe, Kaveh Jamshidi, William Kim, Tatiana Koprowicz, Michael Kornely, Jesse Koster, Jean-Pierre Leroy, Libo Liu, Diana Logriera, Victoria Macchi, Mitzi Macias, Vincent Makori, James Malone, Mohammad Manzarpour, Marvin Marion, Eva Mazrieva, Jeffrey Means, Kimseng Men, Guita Mirsaeedi, Negar Mohammadi, Richard Moore, Natalia Mozgovaya, Thet Naing, Robert Naylor, Sean Neary, Thao Nguyen, Fidele Niyongabo, Rosalie O'Connell, Aung Oo, Thar Oo, Thein Oo, Abdulaziz Osman, Aru Pande, Robert Parsell, Cal Perry, Jean Philippe, Nicolas Pinault, Reasey Poch, Carolyn Presutti, John Quinn, Robert Raffaele, Luis Ramirez, James Randle, Gioconda Reynolds, Justin Riley, Khadija Riyami, Ralph Robinson, James Russell, Shahla Sadighi, Cynthia Saine-Spang, Yuni Salim, Mary Salinas, Joad Santa-Rita, Yulia Savchenko, Brian Schiff, Edward Schneider, Jeff Seldin, Namgyal Shastri, Roger Sherman, Michael Shields, Setareh Sieg, George Simkins, Joseph Sipos, Jerome Socolovsky, Pov Sok, Steven Springer, Scott Storkel, Carl Swanson, Jeffrey Swicord, Minia Teclab, Kyaw Tha, Kyaw Thein, Michael Theisen, Pinitkarn Tulachom, Peter Vaselopulos, Alexandra Villarreal, Joseph Vitale, Winston Wood, Raymond Yam, Guofu Yang, Xiaoyan Zhang.

VOYAGE PRODUCTIONS—(202) 276–2848; 565 Pennsylvania Avenue, NW., #302, Washington, DC 20001: Susan Baumel, Ely Lamonica.

WALL STREET JOURNAL—1025 Connecticut Avenue, Washington, DC 20036: Johnny Cruz, Sloan Dickey, Jude Marfil, Madeline Marshall, Gerald Seib.

WASHINGTON BUREAU NEWS SERVICE—7425 Savan Point Way, Columbia, MD 21045: Maureen Dezell, Joseph Nelson, C. Patrick Thorne, Michael Whitney.

WASHINGTON EXAMINER—202–459–4943; 1015 15th Street, NW., Suite 500, Washington, DC 20005: Steve Doty, Lisa Ruhl, Ed Sykes.

WASHINGTON RADIO AND PRESS SERVICE—(301) 229–2576; 6702 Pawtucket Road, Bethesda, MD 20817: Hanna Gutmann, Howard Lesser.

WASHINGTONPOST.COM—1150 15th Street, NW., Washington, DC 20071: Jason Aldag, Kyle Barss, Gillian Brockell, Jonathan Elker, McKenna Ewen, Brad Horn, Pamela Kirkland, Whitney Leaming, Alice Li, Jayne Orenstein, Sarah Parnass, Julie Percha, Lee Powell, Jorge Ribas, Natasha Rudnick, Rebecca Schatz, Whitney Shefte, Randolph Smith.

WEST WING REPORTS—11614 Old Brookville Court, Reston, VA 20194: Bryan Armino, Paul Brandus, Chris Paolucci.

WESTWOOD ONE—202 457–7991; 2020 M Street, NW., Washington, DC 20036: Bob Costantini, Kevin DeLany, Bart Tessler.

WETA—(703) 998–1800; 3939 Campbell Avenue, Arlington, VA 22206: Charles Anderson, David Bash, Timothy Bowen, Donald Brawner, Martin Carr, Darzen Chang, Vincent Forcier, Charles Ide, Christopher Lane, Edward Lee, Nancy Morgan, Paul "Jay" Nevel, Antonio Pacheco, Jeffrey Rathner, John Satterfield, James Schneider, Willliam Seabrook, Michael Smith, Charles Voth, Owen Wood.

WFDC-TV UNIVISION—101 Constitution Avenue, NW., Suite L–100, Washington, DC 20001: Juan Acevedo, Nestor Bravo, Rolo Duartes, Jose Espinosa, Tsitsiki Felix, Angly Gamboa, Liliana Gonzalez, Henry Guevara, Fanny Gutierrez, Andy Halsted, Angel Hernandez-Orellana, Jairo Lemes, Maria Rosa Lucchini, Lilian Mass, Mynellies Negron, Edwin Pitti, Silvana Quiroz, Raul Ramos, Mario Ramos, Hector Rangel, Marcela Rodriguez, Franco Schultze, Sara Suarez, Catalina Villegas.

WHITE HOUSE CHRONICLE—1042 Wisconsin Avenue, NW., Washington, DC 20007: Linda Gasparello, Llewellyn King, Barry Worthington.

WJLA-TV/NEWSCHANNEL 8—(703) 239–9480; 1100 Wilson Boulevard, Arlington, VA 22209: Van Applegate, Joseph Ball, Frank Becker, Bradley Bell, Alexander Brauer, Maureen Bunyan, Brianne

NETWORKS, STATIONS, AND SERVICES REPRESENTED—Continued

Carter, Richard Chamberlain, Zeke Changuris, Diane Cho, Michael Conneen, Krystal Cooper, Rebecca Cooper, Lynn Davis, Joe DeFeo, Bruce DePuyt, AnnaMaria DiPietro, Martin C. Doane, Ernie Ensign, Sam Ford, Pege Gilgannon, Morgan Gilliam, Autria Godfrey, Jeff Goldberg, John Gonzalez, Robin Gould, Kendall Griggs, Richard Guastadisegni, Tim Guidry, Mark Hanner, Leon Harris, Donna Harris, Shonty Hawkins, Horace Holmes, Brett Holton, Brian Hopkins, Thomas Hormuth, LaTanya Horne, Donna Inserra, George Jackson, Samuel Jackson, Mitchell Jacob, Michael Jaffe, Jesse Janosky, Morris Jones, James Joslyn, Suzanne Kennedy, Vanessa M. Koolhof, Jay Korff, Kelly Lamp, Ming Leong, Kevin Lewis, John B. Lewis, Lisa Lisko, David Lucas, Jon Mann, James Marcum, Timothy Matthews, Gregg Micklos, Joseph Moise, Ronald Mounts, Dwayne Myers, Olajumoke Olabanji, Chris Papst, Roslyn Plater, Richard Reeve, Jeannette Reyes, John Rice, Jeff Rose, Thomas Roussey, Megan Rowls, Michael Rudd, Brian Sasser, James Scott, Holly Shannon, Bhupinder Sharma, Rebecca Sinn, Jocelyn Sistrunk, Alison Starling, Christopher Stuard, Kimberly Suiters, Sam Sweeney, Scott Thuman, Stephen Tschida, Sara Van Aernum, Michael Vaughn, James Walker, Travis Washington, Robert Washington-Anderson, Jennifer Watson, Ronald Windham, Melanie Wotring, Dale Wright, Andrew Zmidzinski.

WMAL RADIO—440 Jenifer Street, 4th floor, Washington, DC 20015: Steven Burns, Heather Curtis, Bill Hess, Nicole Raz.

WNEW/CBS DC—(202) 479–0829; 1015 Half Street, SE., Suite 200, Washington, DC 20003: Karen Adams, Kristopher Ankarlo, Charles Carroll, Rob Dawson, John Domen, Paul Elliott, Brad Freitas, Jenny Glick, Nathaniel Hager, Brett Hall, Chas Henry, Sarah Jacobs, James MacKay, Stacy Moore, Amy Morris, George Rehkoph, Jared Ruderman, Robert Sanchez, Nancy Sargeant, Cheryl Simone, Cameron Thompson, Saraya Wintermsmith, Timothy Yorro.

WNYC—1642 C Beekman Place, Washington, DC 20009: Todd Zwillich.

WPFW–FM—2390 Champlain Street, NW., Washington, DC 20009: Gloria Minott.

WRC–TV/NBC–4—Inaugural Credential, 2009, DC 20005: Jay Alvey, Jackie Bensen, Charles Bragale, Beth Brown, Ashley Brown, Daniel Buckley, Larry Bullard, Julie Carey, Dave carter, Sean Casey, Joseph Cassano, Pat Collins, Natasha Copeland, David Culver, Lauren Dunn, Edward Durkin, Megan Fitzgerald, Bernard Forte, Teneille Gibson, Aaron Gilchrist, Jason Gittlen, Matt Glassman, Angie Goff, Michael Goldrick, Erika Gonzalez, Charles A. Goodknight, Herbert Gordon, Molette Green, Jim Handly, Jack Heinbaugh, Ede Jermin, Lyrone Jones, Kristen Kerwin, Christopher Kerwin, Zachary Kiesch, Sara Kirkland, Chris Lawrence, Ronald Leidelmeyer, Scott MacFarlane, Carlos Martinez, Megan mcgrath, Michael O'Regan, Chester Panzer, Patti Petitte, Jeff Piper, Katherine Roberts, Kelvin Robinson, Mark Segraves, sarah shales, Tom Sherwood, Jon Sonnheim, Mark Stephens, Shomari Stone, Laetitia Thompson Anderson, Adam Tuss, Jennifer Vasquez, Roy Weinstock, Tracee wilkins, Melinda Woolbright, Kristin Wright, Eun Yang, Rick Yarborough, Darren Ziegenbein.

WTOP RADIO—3400 Idaho Avenue, NW., Washington, DC 20016: John Aaron, Ari Ashe, Neal Augenstein, Rahul Bali, Michelle Basch, Darci Brasch, Megan Cloherty, Robert Crossling, Dennis Foley, Jamie Forzato, Jason Fraley, Dave Garner, Jessie J. Green, Brennan Haselton, Amanda Iacone, Nick Iannelli, Kristi King Lilleston, Lori Lundin, Dave McConnell, Mitchell Miller, Andrew Mollenbeck, Mike Murillo, Rachel Nania, Brian Oliger, Meera Pal, Art Rose, Kate Ryan, Zach Shore, Max Smith, Dick Uliano, Paula Wolfson, Ren Zheng.

WTTG–FOX TELEVISION—5151 Wisconsin Avenue, NW., Washington, DC 20016: Matthew Ackland, Melanie Alnwick, Kellee Azar, Bob Barnard, Earl T. Baysden III, James Beahn, William Beyer, Rick Boone, Kyle Carmean, Steve Chenevey, Anthony Colella, Patricia Corcoran, Jennifer Davis, Lauren DeMarco, Laura Evans, Michael Fischoff, Tom Fitzgerald, John Frame, Max Giammetta, Michael Horan, Lance Ing, Nelson Jones, Paul Lester, Indira LeVine, Alexandra Limon-Parresol, Craig Little, Sherri Ly, Michael Marantz, Wisdom Martin, Mark Masecchia, Ronnie McCray, Emily Miller, Holly Morris, Beth Parker, Anthony Perkins, Michael Rickard, Bryan Roberts, Eugene Russell, F. David Rysak, Mark Sargent, Robert Shon, Sarah Simmons, Jason H. Smith, Joe Spevak, Will Thomas, Terri Tolliver, Maureen Umeh, Paul Wagner, Don Watrud, Douglas H. Wilkes, Steven Williams, Shawn Yancy, Annie Yu.

WUSA–TV—(202) 895–5588; 4100 Wisconsin Avenue, NW., Washington, DC 20016: Francis Abbey, Debra Alfarone, Wendy Bailey, Allyson Banks, Ellison Barber, Howard Bernstein, Kristen Berset, Mark Bost, Kurt Brooks, William Broom, Aubrey Bryant, Arielle Buchmann, Laura Burdine, Diane Butts, Surae Chinn Lucie, April Chunko, David Cilberti, William Clemann, William Cockey, Gregory Cohen, Jeffrey Cridland, Ileana Diaz Waldman, Danielle Flanagan, Lesli Foster Mathewson, Peggy Fox, Michael Fuhr, Stephen Garifo, Danielle Gatewood-Gill, Nicholas Giovanni, Delia Goncalves Perry, Erica Grow, Gregory Guise, Garrett Haake, James Hallman, James Hash, Shonty Hawkins, Thomas Hunsicker, Michael Hydeck, Thomas James, Jan Jeffcoat, Lee Jenkins, Elizabeth Jia, Bruce Johnson, Jeffrey Keene, Kevin G. King, William Kistner, Graham Knight, Erik Lee, Nicholas Leimbach, Abdulmola Lenghi, Bruce Leshan, William Lord, Samara Martin Ewing, Andrea McCarren, Joel McDonald, Derek McGinty, Brooks Meriwether, Larry Miller, Jay Mishkin, John Mogor, Eric Morrow, Christopher Mullen, Dave Owens, Renee Peace Carr, Nadia Pflaum, Russell Ptacek, Stephanie Ramirez, Anthony Rizzo, Andrea Roane Skehan, David Roycraft, David Satchell, James Searls, Margo Shear,

NETWORKS, STATIONS, AND SERVICES REPRESENTED—Continued

Charles Shutt, Howard Silverberg, Loriston Sindass, Bill Starks, Janet Terry, Michael Trammell, Erin Van der Bellen, Joan Vasiliadis, Meta Viers, Blair Wheeler, Dion Wiggins, Stephanie Wilson.

XINHUA—1740 North 14th Street, Arlington, VA 22209: Mike Kellerman, Shuai Liu, Xing Qi, Yingshan Shi.

YONHAP NEWS TV—529 14th Street, NW., Washington, DC 20045: Lauren Kim, Beomhyun Kim.

FREELANCE

Freelancers: Atef Abdulgawad, Naser Abu Diab, Robin Adlerblum, Firas Alallak, Mark Albert, Chris Albert, Damien Alipour, Vadim Allen, Faten Alwan, Angela Andersen, Patrick Anderson, Arash Arabasadi, Bruno Arena, Soro Arero, Patricia Armstrong, Thomas Armstrong, Adrian Armwood, Eddie Arossi, Hussein Asmael, Jocelyn Augustino, Jean-Pascal Azais, Travis Renee Baldwin, Mark Banks, Rose Barondess, Marilisa Battistella, William Baty, Michael Bellis, Heidi Belmar, Michael Benetato, Barbara Benitez, Brian Benjamin, Kevin Beyer, Remco Bikkers, Sadiq Bilal, Tim Bintrim, John Boal, Warren Bolden, Wayne Boyd, Jake Britton, Michael Broleman, Jon-Christopher Bua, John Bullard, Penny Burk, Alison Burns, Matthew Burton, Andrew Cahallero-Reynolds, Traci Caldwell, Tim Camarda, Christopher Campbell, David Caravello, Brett Carlson, Anthony Carr, Evan Carr, Rita Chan, Ching-Yi Chang, Xiao Chang, Irwin Chapman, David Clayton, Robert Cherouny, Silvia Chocarro, Gilles Clarenne, Gilles Clarenne, Anne Cocklin, Stephen Cocklin, Harvey Cofske, Stacey Cohan, Holley Coil, Manel Coleau, Thomas Coleman, Oliver Contreras, Kyle Cooper, Pedro Correa, Chantal Costen, Tim Cote, Paul Coursney, Eric Courtney, Thomas Craca, John Craig, Danny Criswell, Katherine Cross, Philip Crowther, Erika Cumber, Patrick Curran, Eugene D'Andrea, Carla Dakin, Clinton Davis, Scott De Angioletti, Louis de Guise, Stan de Saint Hippolyte, Dinah De Saracho, Andrey Degtyarev, William Demas, Gabriella Demczuk, Juanita Dillard, Daniela Doan, William Donald, Brian Donovan, Steve Dorsey, Paul G. Dougherty, Geoffrey Doyle, Stine Dragsted, William Dries, James Duggan, John Dunkin, Barton Eckert, Arlene Eiras, Dalia El-Komy, Hosny Elgazar, Steve Epstein, Manuel Ernst, Anne-Marie Fendrick, Gallagher Fenwick, Michael Finnigan, Kristin Foellmer, Laura Foran, Michael Ford, Tom Foster, Tom Foty, David Fox, Matthew Fox, Patrick French, Dave Friedman, Christian Galdabini, Gavino Garay, Amina Garrett-Scott, Lynsea Garrison, Julien Gathelier, Philip Gcyclin, David Girard, John Glennon, Carlos Gonzalez, Sam Goodall, Jeffrey Goodman, Lindsay Graves, Nicholas Greiner, Kevin Griffin, David Grip, Fayrouz Guerouani, Sait Gurbuz, Mike Haan, Tom Haller, Alejandro Harding, Steven Harper, Roy Harris, Byron Harrison, Oscar Haynes, Barry Haywood, Sean Healey, Barry Hecht, Martin Heina, Liliana Henao, Ryan Hermelijn, Louise Hernon, Ricardo Higgins, Charles Hill, Hugh Hinds, Andrea Hines, Darnley Hodge, Toni Hoover, David Hopper, Dean G. Hovell, Kevin Howard, Jason Hubert, Thierry Humeau, Omar Hussein, Heather Hutchinson, Mohammed Ibrahim, Ryan Jackson, Edward B. Jennings, Jr., Peder Jessen, Wafaa Jibai, Kabir Isa Jikamshi, Martha Johnson, Irene Johnson, Vanessa Johnston, Cathy Kades, Bill Kaplan, Atsushi Kato, Drew Katz, Gregory Kendall-Ball, Peter Kent, Allison Keyes, Kent Klein, Wolfgang Kotke, Stephanie Kotuby, Florian Kroker, David Krupin, Nancy Lanzendoerfer, Greg Larsen, France Latremoliere, Pamela Leahigh, Myron Leake, YiHua Lee, David Lent, Dexter Leong, Darral Lewis, Misha Lewis, Lisa Lewnes, Xiang Li, Tara Libert, Albert Liesegang, Bruce Liffiton, Louis Linden, Melvin Lindsey, Robert Lloyd, Jayne Lukas, Colette Luke, Patricia Lynch, Tracey Madigan, Evy Mages, Jennifer Maher, Alicia Majeed, Alexander Mallin, Antonio Marques, James Martin, Jr., Jeff Martino, Emily Massey, Alice Massimi, James Mathis, Tim Matkosky, Andre Matthews, Max Matza, Mathieu Mazza, Christopher McCary, Douglas McCash, Tipp McClure, Scott McCrary, Ian McDougall, Terrance McEachern, Patty McFarland, Allen McGreevy, Allen McGreevy, Robert McHenry, Daniel McLellan, Martinez Mebane, Tara Mergener, Rhoda Metcalfe, Kerry Meyer, Dave Mikutsky, Charles Miller, Alfredo Miranda, Justin Mitchell, Shannon Mizell, Takashi Mizukami, Melissa Mollet, William Montague, Willie Moorer, Martin Moser, Abdulhafeez Muhammad, John Murphy, Matthew Murray, Peter Murtaugh, Sabine Muscat, Dayheem Naderi, Stephen Narisi, Todd Nash, Mohamed Nasser, Nancy Nathan, Anh Nguyen, Lisa Nipp, Jeffrey Noble, Richard Norling, James Novosel, D. Kerry O'Berry, Jane O'Brien, Tom O'Connor, Daniel O'Shea, Ralf Oberti, Andy Och, Mohamed Ouafi, Alexander Panov, Chanlee Parks, Kingsavanh Pathammavong, Daniel Patsko, Kathryn Patterson, Nikolai Pavlov, Grant Peacock, Daniel Peebles, Doug Perkins, Tim Persinko, Robert Peterson II, Ken Pexton, Murray Pinczuk, Juan Pineda, Randall Pinkston, Christopher Plater, Charlotte Potts, Michael Purbaugh, Mark Rabin, Ali Rad, Bryan Rager, Wafik Ramadan, Adam Raney, Kevin Raullerson, Douglas Ray, Austin Reeves, Melanie Refess, Edward Reinsel, Meixing Ren, Scott Rensberger, Giaco Riggs, Paulina Rios, Olivier Robert, Joshua Roberts, Eugene Roberts, Xavier Roca, Eduardo Rodriguez, Richard Roller, Peter Roof, Takiha Roseboro, Misa Rossetti-Meyer, Theodore Roth, Joseph Ruffini, Thomas Sampson, Stacey Samuels, Gregory Savoy, Barry Schlegel, Donald Schoenmann, Michael Seium, Seda Serdar, Ali Serhan, Dmytri Shakhov, Hakim Shammo, Michael Shannon, Katherine Shaw, Ying Shi, Harry Shoffner, Quentin Silver, Ron Simeone, Hugo Simoes, Alvon Simpson, Paul Skomal, Charles Slie, Anthony Smith, Christie Smith, Cynthia Smith, William Smith, Koen Soete, George Sozio, Darcy Spencer, Theodore Spiegler, Thomas Staton, Carrie Stevenson, Kathy Stewart, Mark Stoddard, Leslie Storms, James Stubbs, James Suddeth,

NETWORKS, STATIONS, AND SERVICES REPRESENTED—Continued

Rick Suddeth, Ena Suto, Bethany Swain, Robert Sweeney, Erik Tavcar, Jacqueline Taylor, Stephen Taylor, Brandon Tea, Mark Teboe, Bert Thomas, Shari Thomas, Joseph Thompson, George Toman, William Turner, Thomas Tyler, Wade Tyree, Claudia Uceda, Brad Ulery, Melinda Ulloa, Xavier Underwood, Juan Ureta, Ben Vaeth-Levin, Paul VanderVeen, Ilona Viczian, Marcos Vigil, Kelley Beaucar Vlahos, Amanda Voisard, Ambrose Vurnis, Jackie Lyn Walker, Cong Wang, Taofeng Wang, Derrick Ward, Jamey Warner, Tarik Warner, Sonja Wasgien, Aaron Webster, George Weller, George Weller, Katharina Werner, Caroline West, Chris Widmer, Snorre Wik, Armstrong Williams, David Williams, James Williams, Mark Wilson, Ronald Winters, Ruth Wittwer, Chris Wright, Brian Yaklyvich, Stephanie Yang, David Zechar, Markus Zeffler, Stratis Zervos, Stratis Zervos, Ariel Zimerman.

PERIODICAL PRESS GALLERIES*

HOUSE PERIODICAL PRESS GALLERY

The Capitol, H–304, 225–2941

Director.—Robert M. Zatkowski
Deputy Director.—Gerald Rupert, Jr.
Assistant Directors: Jenn Walters, Ryan Hamel

SENATE PERIODICAL PRESS GALLERY

The Capitol, S–320, 224–0265

Director.—Edward V. Pesce
Deputy Director.—Justin Wilson
Assistant Director.—Shawna Blair

EXECUTIVE COMMITTEE OF CORRESPONDENTS

Heather Rothman, BNA News, *Chairman*
Leo Shane, Sightline Media Group, *Secretary*
Alexander Bolton, The Hill, *Treasurer*
Jay Newton-Small, Time Magazine
Manu Raju, Politico
Jason Dick, Roll Call
Stephen Cooper, Tax Notes

RULES GOVERNING PERIODICAL PRESS GALLERIES

1. Persons eligible for admission to the Periodical Press Galleries must be bona fide resident correspondents of reputable standing, giving their chief attention to the gathering and reporting of news. They shall state in writing the names of their employers and their additional sources of earned income; and they shall declare that, while a member of the Galleries, they will not act as an agent in the prosecution of claims, and will not become engaged or assist, directly or indirectly, in any lobbying, promotion, advertising, or publicity activity intended to influence legislation or any other action of the Congress, nor any matter before any independent agency, or any department or other instrumentality of the Executive Branch; and that they will not act as an agent for, or be employed by the Federal, or any State, local or foreign government or representatives thereof; and that they will not, directly or indirectly, furnish special or "insider" information intended to influence prices or for the purpose of trading on any commodity or stock exchange; and that they will not become employed, directly or indirectly, by any stock exchange, board of trade or other organization or member thereof, or brokerage house or broker engaged in the buying and selling of any security or commodity. Applications shall be submitted to the Executive Committee of the Periodical Correspondents' Association and shall be authenticated in a manner satisfactory to the Executive Committee.

2. Applicants must be employed by periodicals that regularly publish a substantial volume of news material of either general, economic, industrial, technical, cultural, or trade character. The periodical must require such Washington coverage on a continuing basis and must be owned and operated independently of any government, industry, institution, association, or lobbying organization. Applicants must also be employed by a periodical that is published for profit and is supported chiefly by advertising or by subscription, or a periodical meeting the conditions in this paragraph but published by a nonprofit organization that, first, operates independently of any government, industry, or institution and, second, does

---

not engage, directly or indirectly, in any lobbying or other activity intended to influence any matter before Congress or before any independent agency or any department or other instrumentality of the Executive Branch. House organs are not eligible.

3. Members of the families of correspondents are not entitled to the privileges of the Galleries.

4. The Executive Committee may issue temporary credentials permitting the privileges of the Galleries to individuals who meet the rules of eligibility but who may be on short-term assignment or temporarily residing in Washington.

5. Under the authority of Rule 6 of the House of Representatives and of Rule 33 of the Senate, the Periodical Galleries shall be under the control of the Executive Committee, subject to the approval and supervision of the Speaker of the House of Representatives and the Senate Committee on Rules and Administration. It shall be the duty of the Executive Committee, at its discretion, to report violations of the privileges of the Galleries to the Speaker or the Senate Committee on Rules and Administration, and pending action thereon, the offending correspondent may be suspended. The committee shall be elected at the start of each Congress by members of the Periodical Correspondents' Association and shall consist of seven members with no more than one member from any one publishing organization. The committee shall elect its own officers and a majority of the committee may fill vacancies on the committee. The list in the Congressional Directory shall be a list only of members of the Periodical Correspondents' Association.

PAUL D. RYAN,
Speaker, House of Representatives.

ROY BLUNT,
Chair, Senate Committee on Rules and Administration.

MEMBERS ENTITLED TO ADMISSION

Abbott, Ryan M.: Court House News
Abel, Allen J.: Maclean's
Abramson, Julie L.: National Journal
Abse, Nathan: Federal Employees News Digest
Adams, Caralee Johnson: Education Week
Adkins, Lenore T.: BNA News
Adler, Kevin: UCG
Adragna, Anthony G.: BNA News
Aftab, Mirza Z.: BNA News
Al-Faruque, Ferdous: Informa
Albergo, Paul F.: BNA News
Alexis, Alexei: BNA News
Allen, Arthur: Politico
Allen, Jonathan J.: Vox Media
Alston, Tesha L.: RIA
Altman, Alex S.: Time Magazine
Altman, George: Sightline Media Group
Altscher, Judy K.: The Hill
Alvarez, Priscilla N.: National Journal
Ambrosio, Patrick: BNA News
Anselmo, Joseph: Aviation Week
Antoine, LaTrina M.: Afro American Newspapers
Antonides, David Scott: Tax Notes
Aplin, Donald G.: BNA News
Appelbaum, Yonatan A.: Atlantic Monthly
Apter, Melissa Wendy: Washington Jewish Week
Aquino, John T.: BNA News
Arom, Eita: Morning Consult
Ashworth, Jerry: Thompson Information Services
Asker, James R.: Aviation Week
Assam, Cecelia M.: BNA News
Atkins, Pamela S.: BNA News
Atwood, John Hilar: CCH Inc.
August, Melissa A.: Time Magazine
Aulino, Margaret: BNA News
Averitt, Neil Warner: FTC Watch
Ayers, Cameron S.: Thompson Information Services
Ayers, Carl: UCG
Ayers, Judith E.: Weekly Standard
Babb, Lisa E.: Kiplinger Washington Editors
Bade, Rachel M.: Politico
Baine, Trevor: Capitol Forum
Baker, Samuel U.: National Journal
Ball, Molly: Atlantic Monthly
Bancroft, John: Inside Mortgage Finance
Barash, Martina S.: BNA News
Barbagallo, Paul John: BNA News
Bardwell, Brian D.: Tax Notes
Barkoukis, Leah: Townhall
Barnes, Fred W: Weekly Standard

Barnes, James A.: National Journal
Baron, Kevin: Defense One
Barry, Theresa: BNA News
Bartholet, Jeffrey I.: Politico
Basken, Paul A.: Chronicle of Higher Education
Bason, Tamlin H.: BNA News
Basu, Kaustuv: Tax Notes
Basu, Sandra L.: U.S. Medicine
Bater, Jeffrey P.: BNA News
Baumann, Jeannie: BNA News
Beasley, Stephanie M.: BNA News
Beaven, Lara W: Inside Washington Publishers
Becker, Bernard A.: The Hill
Beckwith, Ryan Teague: Time Magazine
Beddingfield, Matthew: BNA News
Beene, Ryan: Crain Communications
Behn, Peter B.: Environment & Energy Publishing
Behsudi, Adam S.: Politico
Beitsch, Rebecca H.M.: Inside Washington
  Publishers
Bellantoni, Christina: Roll Call
Belles, Carina Gayle: Atlantic Information Services
Belz, Emily C.: World Magazine
Ben-Yosef, Andrea L.: BNA News
Bennett, Alison: BNA News
Bennett, Cory L.: The Hill
Bennett, John T.: Sightline Media Group
Bennett, Kate G.: Politico
Benton, Nicholas F.: Falls Church News Press
Berenson, Tessa C.: Time Magazine
Berger, James R.: Washington Trade Daily
Berger, Mary: Washington Trade Daily
Berger, Matthew: BNA News
Berkheiser, Kyra: Thompson Information Services
Berman, Dan: National Journal
Berman, Matt: National Journal
Berman, Russell: Atlantic Monthly
Bernstein, Jeremy: Inside Washington Publishers
Bertuca, Anthony F.: Inside Washington Publishers
Beutler, Brian Alfred: New Republic
Beyoud, Lydia: BNA News
Bidwell, Allie: U. S. News & World Report
Billings, Deborah D.: BNA News
Blad, Evie: Education Week
Bland, Scott: The Hotline
Blank, Peter L.: Kiplinger Washington Editors
Blotner, David A.: Capitol Forum
Blumenstyk, Goldie: Chronicle of Higher Education
Bogardus, Kevin J.: Environment & Energy
  Publishing
Bokermann, Susan E.: BNA News

MEMBERS ENTITLED TO ADMISSION, PERIODICAL PRESS GALLERIES—Continued

Boliek, Brooks: Politico
Bolton, Alexander Bruce: The Hill
Bomster, Mark W.: Education Week
Bonaquist, Maria Koklanaris: Tax Notes
Bordelon, Brendan Joseph: National Review
Bottemiller Evich, Helena: Politico
Boudreau, Catherine: BNA News
Bowman, Bridget M.: Roll Call
Boyd, Aaron T.: Sightline Media Group
Boyles, William R.: Health Market Survey
Bracken, Leonard: BNA News
Bradford, Hazel: Crain Communications
Bradley, Brian G.: Exchange Monitor Publications
Brandolph, David B.: BNA News
Brasher, Philip D.: Agri-Pulse
Braun, Kevin D.: Environment & Energy Publishing
Bravender, Robin L.: Environment & Energy
    Publishing
Breitman, Kendall P.: Politico
Brenneman, Ross: Education Week
Bresnahan, John: Politico
Brevetti, Rossella E.: BNA News
Bridgeford, Lydell C.: BNA News
Brittain, Steven: BNA News
Broder, Jonathan: Newsweek
Brooks, George A.: Inside Mortgage Finance
Brostoff, Tera: BNA News
Brown, Alex: The Hotline
Brown, Dylan: Environment & Energy Publishing
Brown, Jill: Atlantic Information Services
Brownstein, Ronald J.: National Journal
Bruce, R. Christian: BNA News
Bruggeman, Karyn L.: The Hotline
Bruninga, Susan E.: BNA News
Bruno, Michael P.: Aviation Week
Burow, Margaret: Tax Notes
Burroughs IV, Davis C.: Morning Consult
Bush, Daniel: Environment & Energy Publishing
Byers, Alex: Politico
Byrnes, Jesse: The Hill
Cadei, Emily Isabel: Newsweek
Cahn, Emily: Roll Call
Calabresi, Massimo T.: Time Magazine
Caldwell, Christopher: Weekly Standard
Callahan, Madelyn R.: BNA News
Cama, Timothy: The Hill
Camera, Lauren S.: Education Week
Caplan-Bricker, Nora R.: National Journal
Caporal, Jack Ernest: Inside Washington Publishers
Carden, James W: Nation
Carey, William Joseph, Jr.: Aviation International
    News
Carlile, Amy V.: Environment & Energy Publishing
Carlson, Jeffrey E.: CCH Inc.
Carney, Jordain R.: The Hill
Carpenter, Zoe: Nation
Carr, Jennifer: Tax Notes
Carroll, Conn: Townhall

Casabona, Elizabeth: Thompson Information
    Services
Cassidy, William B.: Journal of Commerce
Castelli, Christopher: Inside Washington Publishers
Casuga, Jay-Anne B.: BNA News
Cauterucci, Christina: Washington City Paper
Cavanagh, Sean: Education Week
Cavas, Christopher: Sightline Media Group
Caygle, Heather Nicole: Politico
Cecala, Guy David: Inside Mortgage Finance
Center, Shira R.: Roll Call
Chalfant, Morgan Mary: Red Alert Politics
Chang, Ashley S.: Capitol Forum
Chappell, Carisa D.: Inside Mortgage Finance
Chase, Spencer: Agri-Pulse
Chemnick, Jean M.: Environment & Energy
    Publishing
Cheney, Kyle: Politico
Chibbaro, Jr., Louis M.: Washington Blade
Childers, Andrew J.: BNA News
Chronister, Gregory: Education Week
Cinquegrani, Gayle C.: BNA News
Cirilli, Kevin N.: The Hill
Clark, Andrew: Broadband Census
Clark, Charles S.: Government Executive
Clarke, David: Politico
Clason, Lauren M.: Atlantic Information Services
Clemons, Steven: Atlantic Monthly
Clevenger, Andrew: Sightline Media Group
Coffin, James B.: Public Lands News
Cohen, Janey: BNA News
Cohen, Richard E.: FCW
Cohen, Zachary C.: The Hotline
Cole, Christopher M.: Inside Washington Publishers
Collins, Eliza S.: Politico
Compton, Kimberly Claire: BNA News
Connole, Patrick: Atlantic Information Services
Connolly, Paul C.: BNA News
Conroy, Declan: Food Chemical News
Cook, Jr., Charles E.: Cook Political Report
Cook, Nancy M.: National Journal
Cook, Steven: BNA News
Coomes, Jessica: BNA News
Cooper, Matthew Stanley: Newsweek
Cooper, Perry Elizabeth: BNA News
Cooper, Stephen K.: Tax Notes
Cordaro, Jennifer Rodibaugh: CCH Inc.
Corrin, Amber: Sightline Media Group
Cottle, M. Michelle: National Journal
Coyle, Marcia: National Law Journal
Craver, Martha L.: Kiplinger Washington Editors
Crowley, Michael: Politico
Cullen, David: Heavy Duty Trucking
Cumings, Stephanie M.: BNA News
Curran, John: Telecommunications Reports
Cusack, Robert: The Hill
Dalphonse, Sherri Leslie: Washingtonian
Darcey, Susan W.: Informa

MEMBERS ENTITLED TO ADMISSION, PERIODICAL PRESS GALLERIES—Continued

Dashiell, Steven: UCG
Date, Shirish V.: National Journal
Datlowe, Nicholas A.: BNA News
Davis, Michelle R.: Education Week
Davis, S. Diane: BNA News
Davis, Steve: Atlantic Information Services
Davis, William Robert: Tax Notes
Davison, Laura P.: BNA News
Day, Jeff: BNA News
De Luce, Daniel Richard: Foreign Policy
Debenedetti, Gabriel A.: Politico
Delargy, Christine Anne: Politico
DeLeon, Carrie: Telecommunications Reports
Demko, Paul: Crain Communications
Demko, Paul Jeffrey: Politico
Dennis, Steven T.: Roll Call
DePaul, Jennifer: Tax Notes
Derrick, J. C.: World Magazine
DeRuy, Emily E.: National Journal
Detrow, Scott M.: Environment & Energy
    Publishing
Devaney, Timothy: The Hill
Diamond, Phyllis: BNA News
Dias, Elizabeth J.: Time Magazine
Dick, Jason J.: Roll Call
Dickerson, John F.: Slate
Dickson, Virgil T.: Crain Communications
DiCosmo, Bridget M.: Inside Washington Publishers
Dillon, Jeremy: Exchange Monitor Publications
DiMascio, Jennifer: Aviation Week
DiSciullo, Joseph: Tax Notes
Divis, Dee Ann: Inside GNSS
Dixon, Darius Ajani: Politico
Dixon, Kim: Politico
Dobbs-Allsopp, William C.: Morning Consult
Dobson, Ashley Danielle: Red Alert Politics
Dobson, Will: Slate
Doherty, Daniel P.: Townhall
Dolley, Steven D.: McGraw Hill Financial
Domone, Dana J.: BNA News
Dong, Zhaoxia: Epoch Times
Donlan, Thomas G.: Barron's
Dorrian, Patrick: BNA News
Doubleday, Justin P.: Inside Washington Publishers
Douglas, Genevieve Rose: BNA News
Dovere, Edward-Isaac: Politico
Downey, Kirstin Edith: FTC Watch
Downey, Teddy: Capitol Forum
Doyle, Kenneth P.: BNA News
Doyle, Susan: BNA News
Draper, Robert L.: GQ Magazine
Drennan, Justine Koo: Foreign Policy
Drew, Russell James: Inside Washington Publishers
Drusch, Andrea Michelle: National Journal
Dube, Elliott T.: BNA News
Dube, Lawrence E.: BNA News
Dudley, Julianne E.: Weekly Standard
Duffy, Jennifer: Cook Political Report

Duffy, Michael W.: Time Magazine
Dumain, Emma: Roll Call
Durkin, Erin: Inside Washington Publishers
Dutra, Antonio: BNA News
Eakin, Britain: Court House News
Easley, Cameron: Roll Call
Easley, Jonathan C.: The Hill
Easton, Nina J.: Fortune Magazine
Eckert, Toby L.: Politico
Edney, Hazel Trice: Trice Edney Newswire
Edroso, Roy: UCG
Edwards, Breanna C.: The Root
Edwards, Haley: Time Magazine
Edwards, Jewel W.: BNA News
Ege, Konrad: Freitag
Eggerton, John S.: Broadcasting & Cable
Ehart, William: CEO Update
Ehley, Brianna Megan: Politico
Eisele, Albert: The Hill
Eldridge, David: Roll Call
Elfin, Dana A.: BNA News
Elgatian, Tawny: BNA News
Elliott, Amy S.: Tax Notes
Elliott III, Philip Robert: Time Magazine
Ellis, David: Roll Call
Ellis, Isobel: National Journal
Emma, Caitlin Z.: Politico
Engleman, Eric: Politico
Enoch, Daniel: Agri-Pulse
Ertel, Karen: BNA News
Esquivel, J. Jesus: Proceso
Evans, Megan M.: Roll Call
Everett, John B.: Politico
Everstine, Brian W: Sightline Media Group
Ewing, Philip T.: Politico
Fabian, Jordan H.: The Hill
Faler, Brian D.: Politico
Farmer, Liz: Governing
Feldenkirchen, Markus: Der Spiegel
Ferguson, Andrew: Weekly Standard
Ferguson, Brett: BNA News
Ferris, David: Environment & Energy Publishing
Ferris, Sarah N.: The Hill
Ferullo, Michael: BNA News
Fialka, John J.: Environment & Energy Publishing
Field, Kelly Elizabeth: Chronicle of Higher
    Education
Fischer, Karin: Chronicle of Higher Education
Fischer Martin, Betsy: MORE Magazine
Fischler, Jacob A.: Law360
Fischman, Josh E.: Scientific American
Fitton, Jacqueline: Informa
Fitzpatrick, Jack: The Hotline
Fleming, Matthew G.: Roll Call
Fletcher, Kenneth R.: Exchange Monitor
    Publications
Flood, Brian: BNA News

MEMBERS ENTITLED TO ADMISSION, PERIODICAL PRESS GALLERIES—Continued

Flook, William Clay: Research Institute of America Group
Foran, Clare M.: National Journal
Forbes, Sean I.: BNA News
Ford, Matt S.: Atlantic Monthly
Forman-Cook, Whitney C.: Agri-Pulse
Fortnam, Brett P.: Inside Washington Publishers
Fox, Lauren: National Journal
Francis, Jr., David: Foreign Policy
Francis, Eileen: Informa
Francis, Laura D.: BNA News
Franklin, Mary Beth: Crain Communications
Freda, Diane M.: BNA News
Freebairn, William: McGraw Hill Financial
Freed, Benjamin: Washingtonian
Freeman, Aishia Caryn: BNA News
French, Lauren: Politico
Freund, Lena: Washington Business Information
Friedman, Lisa F.: Environment & Energy Publishing
Frizell, Sam: Time Magazine
Fuller, Matt E.: Roll Call
Gale, Rebecca E.: Roll Call
Galentine, Elizabeth Rome: Employee Benefit Adviser
Gallagher, John A.: Journal of Commerce
Gannon, John: BNA News
Gantz, Rachel: UCG
Garcia, Eric M.: National Journal
Garofalo, Patrick: U.S. News & World Report
Gartrell, Antoinette Nicole: BNA News
Gattoni-Celli, Luca: Tax Notes
Gatz, Nicholas Joseph: Falls Church News Press
Gaynor, Michael: Washingtonian
Gehrke, Jr., Joel S.: National Review
Geisel, Jerry: Crain Communications
Geman, Ben: National Journal
Gentile, Gary: McGraw Hill Financial
Gerstein, Joshua A.: Politico
Gewertz, Catherine: Education Week
Giangreco, Leigh: Inside Washington Publishers
Gibson, Virginia Stella: Newsweek
Gilmer, Ellen M.: Environment & Energy Publishing
Gilpin-Green, Justice L.: Roll Call
Gilston, Meredith L.: Gilston-Kalin Communications
Gilston, Samuel M.: Gilston-Kalin Communications
Gingery, Derrick J.: Informa
Gizzi, John: NewsMax
Glass, Andrew J.: Politico
Glueck, Katie: Politico
Goad, Benjamin: The Hill
Goindi, Geeta: Express India
Gold, Ashley: Politico
Gold, Hadas: Politico
Goldwyn, Brant: CCH Inc.
Gonzalez, Gloria: Crain Communications
Gonzales, Nathan: Rothenberg & Gonzales Political Report

Gonzalez, Sarah S.: Agri-Pulse
Goode, Darren T.: Politico
Goodwine, Velma Denise: Research Institute of America Group
Gould, Joseph M.: Sightline Media Group
Goyal, Raghubir: Asia Today
Graff, Garrett M.: Politico
Graham, David A.: Atlantic Monthly
Grasgreen, Alexandra: Politico
Graves, Lucia E.: National Journal
Gray, William T.: Synopsis
Greene, Michael N.: BNA News
Greenhalgh, Keiron: McGraw Hill Financial
Gregory, Patrick L.: BNA News
Grena Manley, Mary Ann: BNA News
Grieve, Timothy Patrick: National Journal
Griffith, Cara: Tax Notes
Groll, Elias: Foreign Policy
Gross, Grant J.: IDG News Service
Gross, Rachel E.: Slate
Gruber, Amelia M.: Government Executive
Grunewald, Will: Washingtonian
Grunwald, Michael: Politico
Gruss, Michael: Space News
Guida, Victoria T.: Politico
Guillen, Alexander: Politico
Guniganti, Pallavi: Global Competition Review
Gutman, James H.: Atlantic Information Services
Haas, Joseph A.: Informa
Haberkorn, Jennifer A.: Politico
Hagen, Lisa: National Journal
Hagstrom, Jerry: National Journal
Hale, Christian: Roll Call
Halper, Daniel M.: Weekly Standard
Hamilton, Amy L.: Tax Notes
Hamrick, Mark: Bankrate.com
Hancock, Benjamin: Inside Washington Publishers
Haniffa, Aziz: India Abroad
Hansard, Sara E.: BNA News
Hansen, David A.: BNA News
Harball, Elizabeth Erin: Environment & Energy Publishing
Harbrecht, Douglas A.: Kiplinger Washington Editors
Harding, Margaret Elizabeth: Law360
Hardy, Michael L.: Sightline Media Group
Harkins, Gina A.: Sightline Media Group
Harvey, Abby: Exchange Monitor Publications
Haseley, Donna L.: Inside Washington Publishers
Hattem, Julian: The Hill
Hawkings, Jr., David Mark: Roll Call
Hayes, Peter S.: BNA News
Hazzard, Emily Q: Washington City Paper
Hedberg, Lars-Eric: BNA News
Hefling, Kimberly A.: Politico
Hegstad, Maria A.: Inside Washington Publishers
Heikkinen, Niina H.: Environment & Energy Publishing

MEMBERS ENTITLED TO ADMISSION, PERIODICAL PRESS GALLERIES—Continued

Heitin, Liana: Education Week
Helbling, Laura A.: Informa
Helem, Lisa R.: BNA News
Heller, Marc R.: BNA News
Hendrie, Paul J.: BNA News
Hennig, Jutta: Inside Washington Publishers
Henry, Devin Kendrick: The Hill
Herb, Jeremy: Politico
Hess, Hannah C.: Roll Call
Hess, Ryan E.: MII Publications
Hiar, Corbin W.: Environment & Energy Publishing
Higgins, Joshua L.: Inside Washington Publishers
Hill, Keith M.: BNA News
Hill, Richard: BNA News
Hillman, G. Robert: Politico
Hiruo, Elaine: McGraw Hill Financial
Ho, Soyoung: Research Institute of America Group
Hobbs, M. Nielsen: Informa
Hobson, Margaret Kriz: Environment & Energy Publishing
Hodge Seck, Hope: Sightline Media Group
Hoffman, Rebecca E.: BNA News
Hoffman III, William S.: Tax Notes
Hofmann, Mark A.: Crain Communications
Hohmann, James P.: Politico
Holden, Emily H.: Environment & Energy Publishing
Holeman, Cynthia Denise: Tax Notes
Hollers, Logan: BNA News
Holmes, Gwendolyn C.: BNA News
Homan, Timothy Richard: Morning Consult
Hood, David A.: Inside Washington Publishers
Hoover, James C.: Law360
Hoover, Kent: Washington Business Journal
Hopkinson, Jenny A.: Politico
Horowitz, Jay: BNA News
Horwood, Rachel Jane: Economist
Howell, Katie J.: Environment & Energy Publishing
Hudson, Elizabeth Lee: Inside Washington Publishers
Hudson, Jasmin: McGraw Hill Financial
Hudson, John: Foreign Policy
Huffman, Jason A.: Politico
Hughes, Sarah Anne E.: Washington City Paper
Hulac, Benjamin: Environment & Energy Publishing
Hutchins, James Reynolds: Journal of Commerce
Hyland, Kristyn: BNA News
Hyland, Terence M.: BNA News
Iafolla, Robert: BNA News
Ichniowski, Thomas F.: Engineering News-Record
Irfan, Umair: Environment & Energy Publishing
Isenstadt, Alex: Politico
Jackson, Valarie N.: McGraw Hill Financial
Jacobs, Jeremy P.: Environment & Energy Publishing
Jacobson, Todd K.: Exchange Monitor Publications
Jaffe, Harry S.: Washingtonian
Jahner, Kyle R.: Sightline Media Group

Jakes, Lara: Foreign Policy
Jaworski, Thomas: Tax Notes
Jewell, R.J.: BNA News
Jin, Yan: Caijing Magazine
Johnson, Alisa: BNA News
Johnson, Andrew E.: National Review
Johnson, Chris C.: Washington Blade
Johnson, Clarion E.: Capitol Forum
Johnson, David A.: Time Magazine
Johnson, Eliana: National Review
Johnson, Fawn: Morning Consult
Johnson, Katie W.: BNA News
Jones, Caroline E.: Washington City Paper
Jones, George G.: CCH Inc.
Jonson, Nick: McGraw Hill Financial
Joseph, Cameron E.: The Hill
Jost, Kenneth W: CQ Researcher
Jowers, Karen Grigg: Sightline Media Group
Judis, John Barney: National Journal
Judson, Jennifer: Politico
Juliano, Nicholas P.: Environment & Energy Publishing
Just, Richard: National Journal
Kadam, Nitasha: CCH Inc.
Kalish, Brian: Employee Benefit Adviser
Kambhampati, Sandhya: Chronicle of Higher Education
Kamens, Jessie K.: BNA News
Kamisar, Benjamin: The Hill
Kanu, Hassan A.: BNA News
Kaplan, Hugh B.: BNA News
Kapur, Sahil: Talking Points Memo
Karas, Rachel S.: Inside Washington Publishers
Kardish, Christopher: Governing
Karem, Brian J.: Montgomery County Sentinel
Karlin, Sarah: Informa
Karlin, Sarah: Politico
Kashino, Marisa M.: Washingtonian
Kasprzak, Thomas J.: Tax Notes
Katz, Daniel: Aviation Week
Katz, Eric: Government Executive
Kaufman, Bruce S.: BNA News
Kavruck, Deborah A.: Washington Counseletter
Kearns, Kara Ann: Politico
Kelly, Catherine A.: Informa
Kelly, Lauren: Atlantic Information Services
Kelly, Nora E.: National Journal
Kenen, Joanne L.: Politico
Kern, Rebecca M.: BNA News
Khan, Altaf U.: BNA News
Kheel, Rebecca Hillary: The Hill
Khimm, Suzy: New Republic
Kim, Seung Min: Politico
Kime, Patricia N.: Sightline Media Group
King, Pamela: Environment & Energy Publishing
King, Robert P.: Politico
Kirby, Paul: Telecommunications Reports

MEMBERS ENTITLED TO ADMISSION, PERIODICAL PRESS GALLERIES—Continued

Kirkland, Joel G.: Environment & Energy
  Publishing
Klein, Alyson: Education Week
Kliff, Sarah L.: Vox Media
Klingst, Martin E.: Die Zeit
Knowles, Daniel L.: Economist
Knox, Ron: Global Competition Review
Koelemay, Jeffrey D.: BNA News
Koenig, Bryan David: Law360
Konkel, Frank: Government Executive
Koo, Jimmy H.: BNA News
Kopan, Tal: Politico
Korade, Matthew: Politico
Koren, Marina: National Journal
Koss, Geof: Environment & Energy Publishing
Kovach, Kaitlin: Roll Call
Kovski, Alan D.: BNA News
Kramer, Alexis S.: BNA News
Kraushaar, Josh P.: National Journal
Kruse, Michael: Politico
Kubetin, W. Randy: BNA News
Kuckro, Rod: Environment & Energy Publishing
Kukuk, Brad A.: Mine Safety and Health News
Kumar, Vikas: Capitol Forum
Kunzig, Rob L.: Morning Consult
Kurtz, David: Talking Points Memo
Kurtz, Josh: Environment & Energy Publishing
Kushin, Philip H.: BNA News
LaBrecque, Louis C.: BNA News
Lacey, Anthony: Inside Washington Publishers
Laing, Keith: The Hill
Lantigua-Williams, Juleyka: National Journal
Laping, Karen McBeth: McGraw Hill Financial
LaRoss, David: Inside Washington Publishers
Larsen, Kathryn: BNA News
Larson, Cathleen R.: BNA News
Last, Jonathan V.: Weekly Standard
Lavers, Michael K.: Washington Blade
Lawrence, Jill Debra: U. S. News & World Report
Leahy, Colleen C.: Morning Consult
Leatherman, Jacquelyn D.: CCH Inc.
Leber, Rebecca J.: New Republic
Lee, Steve K.: BNA News
Leeuwenburgh, Todd H.: Thompson Information
  Services
Lehmann, Evan W.: Environment & Energy
  Publishing
Leonard, Kimberly L.: U. S. News & World Report
Leone, Daniel M.: Space News
Lerner, Adam B.: Politico
Lesesne, William F.: Research Institute of America
  Group
Lesniewski, Niels P.: Roll Call
Leven, Rachel P.: BNA News
Levin, Joshua: Slate
Levine, Marianne A.: Politico
Levine, Susan K.: Politico
Levinson, Alexis: Roll Call

Levinson, Alexis R.: National Review
Levy, Gabrielle F.: U. S. News & World Report
Liang, John: Inside Washington Publishers
Liberto, Jennifer Rose: Politico
Lillis, Michael: The Hill
Ling, Katherine C.: Environment & Energy
  Publishing
Linger, Jacob Daniel: Court House News
Lippman, Daniel: Politico
Lithwick, Dahlia Hannah: Slate
Littleton, Julia A.: Environment & Energy
  Publishing
Loatman, Michael: BNA News
Lockhart, Giovanna Gray: Glamour Magazine
Logan, Lee: Inside Washington Publishers
Long Rayburn, Karen S.: UCG
Lorenzo, Aaron E.: BNA News
Losey, Stephen: Sightline Media Group
Loughran, Matthew: BNA News
Loviza-Vickery, Amanda L.: Court House News
Lowe, Paul D.: Aviation International News
Lubell, Karina B.: Capitol Forum
Luccioli, Colleen M.: Environment & Energy
  Publishing
Lucero, Kat: Tax Notes
Lucia, William: Government Executive
Lucia, William R.: Inside Washington Publishers
Lunney, Kellie: Government Executive
Lustig, Joe: BNA News
Lynch, Kerry: Aviation International News
Lyngaas, Sean: FCW
Maas, Angela K.: Atlantic Information Services
Macagnone, Michael A.: Law360
MacDonald, Neil A.: Technology
  Commercialization
MacNeal, Caitlin: Talking Points Memo
Macy, Daniel J.: Thompson Information Services
Madara, Matthew: Tax Notes
Madden, Mike R.: Washington City Paper
Mahoney, Brian J.: Politico
Maine, Amanda: CCH Inc.
Mandel, Jennifer A.: Environment & Energy
  Publishing
Mann, Jason: National Journal
Manzo, Kathleen K.: Education Week
Marcos, Cristina: The Hill
Marks, Joseph H.: Politico
Maron, Dina F.: Scientific American
Marshall, Christa L.N.: Environment & Energy
  Publishing
Martel, Catherine A.: Politico
Martin, Betsy Fischer: MORE Magazine
Martinson, Erica L.: Politico
Marx, Claude: FTC Watch
Master, Cyra: Roll Call
Matishak, Martin: The Hill
Maucione, Scott: Inside Washington Publishers
Mauro, Anthony E.: National Law Journal

MEMBERS ENTITLED TO ADMISSION, PERIODICAL PRESS GALLERIES—Continued

Mazmanian, Adam: FCW
Mazumdar, Anandashankar: BNA News
McAllister III, William H.: Amos Press
McBride, Courtney: Inside Washington Publishers
McCabe, David C.: The Hill
McCaffery, Gregory: BNA News
McCarthy, Meghan: Morning Consult
McCaskill, Nolan D.: Politico
McCleskey, Ellen E.: BNA News
McCormack, John M.: Weekly Standard
McCormack, Richard: Manufacturing & Technology News
McCormally, Kevin: Kiplinger Washington Editors
McCracken, Rebecca P.: BNA News
McDonald, Natashka: Hispanic Link News Service
McFarland, Pamela Hunter: Engineering News-Record
McGolrick, Susan J.: BNA News
McGowan, Kevin P.: BNA News
McInerney, Susan M.: BNA News
McKnight, Whitney: Frontline Medical Communications
McLeary, Paul Joseph: Foreign Policy
McMahon, Robert F.: McGraw Hill Financial
McManus, Erin: BNA News
McManus, Lillian F.: Thompson Information Services
McTague, James: Barron's
Meacham, Jane: Thompson Information Services
Medici, Andrew S.: Sightline Media Group
Mehta, Aaron: Sightline Media Group
Mejdini, Fatjona: Politico
Melada, Geoffrey William: Washington Jewish Week
Meredith, Emily: Energy Intelligence
Mershon, Erin: Politico
Meyer, Theodoric: Politico
Milberg, Evan A.: Atlantic Information Services
Miley, John T.: Kiplinger Washington Editors
Milhiser, Ellen: Synopsis
Miller, Zeke J.: Time Magazine
Milligan, Susan E.: U.S. News & World Report
Milone, Tiffany F.: BNA News
Mishory, Jordana L.: Inside Washington Publishers
Mitchell, Charles F.: Inside Washington Publishers
Mitchell, Ellen: Inside Washington Publishers
Mitchell, Corey: Education Week
Mixter, Bronwyn: BNA News
Mokhiber, Russell: Corporate Crime Reporter
Mola, Roger Andrew: Aviation International News
Molnar, Michele: Education Week
Moore, Miles David: Crain Communications
Moore, Andrew (Jack) Jackson: Government Executive
Morales, Cecilio: MII Publications
Moran, Janet: Capitol Forum
Morella, Michael: U.S. News & World Report
Morello, Lauren: Nature

Morring, Jr., Frank: Aviation Week
Morris, Catherine: Diverse: Issues in Higher Education
Morris, David J.: Kiplinger Washington Editors
Morris, Jefferson F.: Aviation Week
Muchmore, Shannon T.: Crain Communications
Mull, Teresa M.: Townhall
Mullins, Luke: Washingtonian
Munoz, Amanda A.: Townhall
Munsil, Leigh: Politico
Murakami, Kery: Law360
Murphy, Joan: Food Chemical News
Mutcherson-Ridley, Joyce: CCH Inc.
Myers, Meghann: Sightline Media Group
Nagele, Lisa A.: BNA News
Nardella, Lauren: Informa
Nartker, Michael: Exchange Monitor Publications
Nasr, Amir Ali: Morning Consult
Nather, David: Politico
Natter, Ari J.: BNA News
Naylor, Sean D.: Foreign Policy
Needham, Vicki: The Hill
Nelson, Rebecca R.: National Journal
Nelson, Steven: U.S. News & World Report
Nesper, Mike: Employee Benefit Adviser
Neuhauser, Alan: U.S. News & World Report
Neumeyer, Ben: Capitol Forum
Newkumet, Christopher J.: McGraw Hill Financial
Newmyer, Tory: Fortune Magazine
Newton-Small, Jay: Time Magazine
Nicholson, Jonathan: BNA News
Noah, Timothy R.: Politico
Noble, Zach: FCW
Norman, Brett: Politico
Norris, Karen: Thompson Information Services
Northey, Hannah M.: Environment & Energy Publishing
O'Brien, Cortney: Townhall
O'Grady, Siobhan Leah: Foreign Policy
O'Neil, Megan: Chronicle of Higher Education
O'Toole, Molly M.: Defense One
O'Toole, Jr., Thomas J.: BNA News
Oberle, Sean F.: Oberle Communications
Obert, Gretchen N.: BNA News
Obey, Douglas: Inside Washington Publishers
Ognanovich, Nancy: BNA News
Oliphant, James: National Journal
Opfer, Christopher R.: BNA News
Orchowski, Margaret S.: Hispanic Outlook
Orr, Elizabeth: Washington Business Information
Orth, Maureen: Vanity Fair
Ostroff, Jim: McGraw Hill Financial
Otto, Nicholas Anthony: Employee Benefit Adviser
Owens, Caitlin N.: National Journal
Pak, Janne Kum Cha C.: USA Journal
Palleschi, Amanda S.: Inside Washington Publishers
Palmer, Anna A.: Politico
Palmer, Doug: Politico

MEMBERS ENTITLED TO ADMISSION, PERIODICAL PRESS GALLERIES—Continued

Palmer, Jonathan Malik: BNA News
Parker, Alexander M.: BNA News
Parker, Stuart H.: Inside Washington Publishers
Parti, Tarini: Politico
Paschal, Mack Arthur: BNA News
Pathe, Simone F.: Roll Call
Patterson, James B.: Kiplinger Washington Editors
Pavgi, Kedar S.: Defense One
Pavlich, Catherine: Townhall
Pawlyk, Oriana: Sightline Media Group
Pazanowski, Bernard J.: BNA News
Pazanowski, Mary Anne: BNA News
Pearson, Sam R.: Environment & Energy Publishing
Peck, Adam N.: New Republic
Pekow, Charles Wayne: American Brewer Media
Penn, Benjamin Surace: BNA News
Perelman, Isabella O.: BNA News
Perera, David: Politico
Perez, Andrew Jason: Newsweek
Perine, Keith: BNA News
Perkins, Derrick Thaddeus: Sightline Media Group
Perks, Ashley J.: The Hill
Peterka, Amanda E.: Environment & Energy
 Publishing
Peters, Katherine M.: Government Executive
Peterson, Denise: Informa
Peterson, Beatrice Elizabeth: Politico
Phillips, Bergrek: Tax Notes
Piemonte, Philip M.: Federal Employees News
 Digest
Pittman, David: Politico
Plank, Kendra Casey: BNA News
Plantz, Kyle J.: The Hill
Plautz, Jason: National Journal
Plotkin, Mark: The Georgetowner
Plunkett, A.J.: UCG
Pluviose, David: Diverse: Issues in Higher
 Education
Polantz, Katelyn J.: National Law Journal
Pollak, Suzanne: Washington Jewish Week
Poltilove, Joshua: UCG
Ponnuru, Ramesh: National Review
Pradhan, Rachana D.: Politico
Prah, Pamela M.: Kiplinger Washington Editors
Prideaux, John: Economist
Prior, Jon: Politico
Prothero, Arianna G.: Education Week
Pulfrey, Christine Mary: BNA News
Purdy, Chase: Politico
Quinones, Manuel: Environment & Energy
 Publishing
Quinton, Sophie A.: National Journal
Raftery, Erin Ashton: Inside Washington Publishers
Railey, Kimberly Grace: National Journal
Rainey, Ryan S.: Inside Washington Publishers
Raju, Manu K.: Politico
Ravindranath, Mohana: Government Executive
Reardon, Sara N.: Nature

Reeves, Dawn: Inside Washington Publishers
Reid, Jonathan T.: Morning Consult
Reilly, Sean: Environment & Energy Publishing
Reishus, Mark: Thompson Information Services
Rennie, David: Economist
Reske, Henry: Tax Notes
Resnick, Brian: National Journal
Ressler, Thomas: Inside Mortgage Finance
Restuccia, Andrew M.: Politico
Reynolds, David E.: Inside Washington Publishers
Reynolds, Maura: Politico
Rhodan, Maya N.: Time Magazine
Ricaurte Knebel, Kristen C.: BNA News
Richardson, Nathaline: BNA News
Richardson, Tyrone: BNA News
Richman, Sheldon B.: BNA News
Richman, Nathan: Tax Notes
Riley, John A.: Metro Weekly
Risen, Thomas J.: U.S. News & World Report
Rizzuto, Pat: BNA News
Robertson, Matthew: Epoch Times
Robillard, Kevin P.: Politico
Robinson, Kimberly S.: BNA News
Robinson, Page: Congressional Digest
Rogers, Alex: National Journal
Rogers, Alex: Time Magazine
Rogers, David E.: Politico
Rogers, Lance: BNA News
Rojas, Warren: Roll Call
Rolfsen, Bruce R.: BNA News
Roller, Emma: National Journal
Romm, Tony: Politico
Rose, Michael F.: BNA News
Rosenberg, Barry: Sightline Media Group
Ross, Brandon J.: BNA News
Rothenberg, Stuart: Rothenberg & Gonzales
 Political Report
Rothman, Heather M.: BNA News
Rotondaro, Vincent J.: National Catholic Reporter
Rousselle, Christine: Townhall
Rubin, Gabe: Morning Consult
Ruoff, Alex: BNA News
Ryan, Laura: National Journal
Ryan, Timothy Joseph: Court House News
Sacks, Mike: National Law Journal
Sadur, Julian Mitsuo: Montgomery County Sentinel
Saenz, Cheryl L.: BNA News
Saiyid, Amena H.: BNA News
Saletan, William: Slate
Salzano, Carlo J.: Waterways Journal
Sama, Anita: CEO Update
Sammon, Richard: Kiplinger Washington Editors
Samuels, Christina: Education Week
Samuelsohn, Darren Sean: Politico
Sanborn, James K.: Sightline Media Group
Sandza, Richard William: Sightline Media Group
Santos, Maria T.: Red Alert Politics
Sasso, Brendan S.: National Journal

MEMBERS ENTITLED TO ADMISSION, PERIODICAL PRESS GALLERIES—Continued

Saunders, Karen J.: BNA News
Savoie, Andy: Aviation Week
Sawchuk, Stephen A.: Education Week
Sawyer, David C.: Tax Notes
Schaffer, Michael: Washingtonian
Scheid, Brian J.: McGraw Hill Financial
Scherer, Michael B.: Time Magazine
Scherman, Bob: Satellite Business News
Schewel, Matthew A.: Inside Washington Publishers
Schlesinger, Robert: U.S. News & World Report
Schneider, Martin A.: Exchange Monitor Publications
Schneider, Elena C.: Politico
Schoeff, Jr., Mark: Crain Communications
Schogol, Jeffrey Duff: Sightline Media Group
Scholtes, Jennifer A.. Politico
Schomisch, Jeffrey: Thompson Information Services
Schor, Elana: Politico
Schreckinger, Benjamin Vose: Politico
Schroeder, Peter C.: The Hill
Schultz, David D.: BNA News
Schwab, Nicole E.: U.S. News & World Report
Schwartz, David H.: BNA News
Scola, Nancy: Politico
Scott, Dean T.: BNA News
Scott, Dylan L.: National Journal
Seligman, Lara: Inside Washington Publishers
Sellers, Steven M.: BNA News
Sermeno, Jose Rodrigo: Kiplinger Washington Editors
Severns, Maggie: Politico
Sfiligoj, Mark L.: Kiplinger Washington Editors
Shabad, Rebecca Danielle: The Hill
Shacat, Jonathon D.: Washington Business Information
Shafer, Jack: Politico
Shah, Nirvi H.: Politico
Shane III, Leo: Sightline Media Group
Shapiro, Dmitriy: Washington Jewish Week
Shapiro, Walter: National Journal
Sharn, Lori: CEO Update
Sharpe, Stephanie: McGraw Hill Financial
Sheets, Scott A.: Tax Notes
Shelton, Michelle: BNA News
Shepard, Steven: Politico
Sheppard, Doug: Tax Notes
Sherman, Jacob S.: Politico
Shinkman, Paul D.: U.S. News & World Report
Shreve, Meg: Tax Notes
Simmons, Quintin: Tax Notes
Simon, Roger M.: Politico
Simon, Vincent Dean: U.S. News & World Report
Sisto, Christine: National Review
Skinner, Liz: Crain Communications
Slattery, Margaret Ann: Politico
Slaughter, David A.: Thompson Information Services
Smelson, Cheryl: BNA News

Smith, Rhonda: BNA News
Smith, Marcia S.: Aviation Week
Smith, Jamil: New Republic
Smith, Abigail K.: Inside Washington Publishers
Sneed, Tierney: U.S. News & World Report
Sneed, Adam T.: Politico
Sneed, Tierney M.: Talking Points Memo
Snell, Kelsey: Politico
Snider, Ann E.: Environment & Energy Publishing
Snow, Nicholas J.: Oil & Gas Journal
Snyder, Katharine: Mine Safety and Health News
Sobczak, Blake H.: Environment & Energy Publishing
Sobieraj, Sandra: People Magazine
Sodergreen, John R.: Scudder Publishing
Soderstrom, Nathan: Capitol Forum
Solomon, Burt: National Journal
Somerville, Glenn: Kiplinger Washington Editors
Sommer, William F.V.: Washington City Paper
Soraghan, Mike: Environment & Energy Publishing
Sorkin, Andrew: Capitol Forum
Spicer, Malcolm E.: Informa
Sprague, John L.: Budget & Program
Sprenger, Sebastian: Inside Washington Publishers
Stahl, Jeremy: Slate
Stam, John H.: BNA News
Stanage, Niall G.: The Hill
Stanton, Lynn E.: Telecommunications Reports
Stark, Holger: Der Spiegel
Starks II, Timothy A.: Politico
Stecker, Tiffany Anne: Environment & Energy Publishing
Stein, Jeffrey H.: Newsweek
Stein, Michelle M.: Inside Washington Publishers
Steinberg, Julie A.: BNA News
Steinke, Scott A.: Informa
Stern, Mark Joseph: Slate
Stern, Nicholas: UCG
Stern, Seth R.: BNA News
Sternberg, Steve: U.S. News & World Report
Stewart, David D.: Tax Notes
Stimson, Leslie P.: NewBay Media
Stoddard, Alexandra B.: The Hill
Stokeld, Frederick William: Tax Notes
Straub, Noelle C.: Environment & Energy Publishing
Strauss, Daniel: Talking Points Memo
Strauss, Daniel L.: Politico
Sturges, Peyton Mackay: BNA News
Sullivan, Peter: The Hill
Superville, Denisa: Education Week
Supiano, Beckie: Chronicle of Higher Education
Sutter, Susan M.: Informa
Sutton, Eileen C.: BNA News
Swan, Jonathan: The Hill
Swann, Deborah: BNA News
Swann, James L.: BNA News
Swarts, Phillip F.: Air Force Times

MEMBERS ENTITLED TO ADMISSION, PERIODICAL PRESS GALLERIES—Continued

Sweeney, Jim: Tax Notes
Swift, James A.: Weekly Standard
Swisher, Larry: BNA News
Szakonyi, Mark D.: Journal of Commerce
Tabirian, Alissa: Exchange Monitor Publications
Tahir, Darius A.: Politico
Tan, Michelle: Sightline Media Group
Tang, Chiachieh: Caixin Media
Taylor, Joy M.: Kiplinger Washington Editors
Taylor, Philip A.: Environment & Energy Publishing
Taylor, Thomas P.: BNA News
Taylor, Vincent E.: UCG
Taylor, Jr., Stuart: National Journal
Teichert, Erica J.: Law360
Temple-West, Patrick C.: Politico
Terzian, Philip: Weekly Standard
Teske, Steven John: BNA News
Thibodeau, Patrick: IDG Communications
Thomas, David J.: Inside Washington Publishers
Thomas, Steff: BNA News
Thompson, Mark J.: Time Magazine
Thompson, Wenoka Wendy: DC Spotlight
  Newspaper
Thrush, Glenn H.: Politico
Tice, James S.: Sightline Media Group
Tilghman, Andrew S.: Sightline Media Group
Tillman, Zoe: National Law Journal
Tomson, Bill: Politico
Toobin, Jeffrey: New Yorker
Toosi, Nahal: Politico
Topaz, Jonathan: Politico
Topor, Eric D.: BNA News
Tosh, Dennis A.: Thompson Information Services
Tricchinelli, Robert: BNA News
Trimarchi, Michael: BNA News
Troop, Donald P.: Chronicle of Higher Education
Trujillo, Frank M.: The Hill
Trygstad, Kyle: Roll Call
Tucker, Patrick M.: Defense One
Tummarello, Kate A.: Politico
Tuutti, Camille A.: Government Executive
Twachtman, Gregory: Frontline Medical
  Communications
Tyler, Eleanor: BNA News
Ujifusa, Andrew: Education Week
Vaidyanathan, Gayathri: Environment & Energy
  Publishing
van den Berg, David: Tax Notes
Vasilogambros, Matt: National Journal
Velarde, Andrew Mims: Tax Notes
Vespa, Matt: Townhall
Viadero, Debra: Education Week
Victor, Kirk: FTC Watch
Viebeck, Elise J.: The Hill
Villacorta, Natalie: Politico
Vinik, Daniel R.: New Republic
Vissiere, Helene: Le Point
Vittorio, Andrea L.: BNA News

Vogel, Kenneth P.: Politico
Volz, Dustin: National Journal
Waddell, Melanie: Investment Advisor Magazine
Waldman, Katy: Slate
Walsh, Kenneth T.: U.S. News & World Report
Walsh, Mark: Education Week
Wang, Herman D.: McGraw Hill Financial
Ware, Patricia Ann: BNA News
Warmbrodt, Zachary: Politico
Warren, Michael R.: Weekly Standard
Wasserman, David N.: Cook Political Report
Waterman, Shaun N.: Politico
Watkins, Steven M.: Sightline Media Group
Watson, Benjamin: Defense One
Weaver, Dustin A.: The Hill
Weber, Maya: McGraw Hill Financial
Weber, Rick: Inside Washington Publishers
Webster, James C.: Agri-Pulse
Wechsler, Jill: Pharmaceutical Executive
Weisgerber, Marcus A.: Defense One
Weixel, Nathaniel L.: BNA News
Welsh, Teresa: U.S. News & World Report
Wheaton, Sarah: Politico
Wheeler, Lydia W: The Hill
Whitaker, Joel: Whitaker Newsletters
White, Molly M.: UCG
Wiener, Aaron M.: Washington City Paper
Wilczek, Yin: BNA News
Wilhelm, Rebecca E.: BNA News
Wilhelm, Colin: Politico
Wilkerson, John Stirling: Inside Washington
  Publishers
Wille, Jacklyn: BNA News
Williams, John: Capitol Forum
Williams, Joseph P.: U.S. News & World Report
Williams, Joseph Paul: Inside Washington
  Publishers
Williams, Katherine B.: The Hill
Williams, Mark A.: BNA News
Williams, Walter J.: CEO Update
Williamson, Michael D.: BNA News
Wilson, Christopher E.: Time Magazine
Wilson, Daniel: Law360
Wilson, Megan R.: The Hill
Wilson, Todd Allen: Inside Washington Publishers
Wilson, Reid H.: Morning Consult
Windsor, Joseph K.: Government Contractor
Winn, Melissa: Employee Benefit Adviser
Wittenberg, Ariel: Environment & Energy
  Publishing
Wogan, J.B.: Governing
Wolfe, Kathryn A.: Politico
Wolverton, Bradley: Chronicle of Higher Education
Wong, Kristina: The Hill
Wong, Scott B.: The Hill
Wood, Graeme C.A.: Atlantic Monthly
Wooten, Casey: BNA News
Wortherly, Kenya: BNA News

MEMBERS ENTITLED TO ADMISSION, PERIODICAL PRESS GALLERIES—Continued

Wright, Austin B.: Politico
Wright, Joseph K.: BNA News
Wright, Jr., James Louis: Afro American
  Newspapers
Wu, Xiuli: Epoch Times
Yachnin, Jennifer: Environment & Energy
  Publishing
Yaksick, Jr., George L.: CCH Inc.
Yamazaki, Kazutami: Washington Watch
Yang, Bettina: Duowei Times
Yauch, Eric S.: Tax Notes
Yehle, Emily J.: Environment & Energy Publishing
Yingling, Jennifer: The Hill

Yochelson, Mindy: BNA News
Yohannan, Suzanne M.: Inside Washington
  Publishers
Yokley, Eli G.: Roll Call
You, Tiandai: Epoch Times
Young, Sam: Tax Notes
Yuill, Barbara: BNA News
Zaneski, Cyril "Cy" T.: Environment & Energy
  Publishing
Zapler, Michael: Politico
Zeefe, Malka: Capitol Forum
Zhang, Yuanan: Caixin Media
Zornick, George: Nation

PERIODICALS REPRESENTED IN PRESS GALLERIES

House Gallery 225–2941, Senate Gallery 224–0265

AFRO AMERICAN NEWSPAPERS—(410) 554–8200; 1917 Benning Road, NE., Washington, DC 20002: LaTrina M. Antoine, James Louis Wright, Jr.

AGRI-PULSE—(573) 873–0800; 110 Waterside Lane, Camdenton, MO 65020: Philip D. Brasher, Spencer Chase, Daniel Enoch, Whitney C. Forman-Cook, Sarah S. Gonzalez, James C. Webster.

AMERICAN BREWER MEDIA—(301) 493–6926; 5225 Pooks Hill Road, #1118N, Bethesda, MD; 20814: Charles Wayne Pekow.

AMOS PRESS—(703) 385–6996; 10121 Ratcliffe Manor Drive, Fairfax, VA 22030: William H. McAllister III.

ASIA TODAY—(202) 271–1100; 27025 McPherson Square Street, Washington, DC 20038: Raghubir Goyal.

ATLANTIC INFORMATION SERVICES—(202) 775–9008; 1100 17th Street, NW., Suite 300, Washington, DC 20036: Carina Gayle Bachman, James M. Clason, Patrick Connole, Steve Davis, James H. Gutman, Lauren Kelly, Angela K. Maas, Evan A. Milberg.

ATLANTIC MONTHLY—(202) 266–7000; 600 New Hampshire Avenue, NW., Washington, DC 20037: Yonatan A. Appelbaum, Molly Ball, Russell Berman, Steven Clemons, Matt S. Ford, David A. Graham, Graeme C.A. Wood.

AVIATION INTERNATIONAL NEWS—(301) 230–4520; 5605 Alderbrook Court, #T6, Rockville, MD; 20851: William Joseph Carey, Jr., Paul D. Lowe, Kerry Lynch, Roger Andrew Mola.

AVIATION WEEK—(202) 383–2300; 1200 G Street, NW., Washington, DC 20005: Joseph Anselmo, James R. Asker, Michael P. Bruno, Jennifer DiMascio, Daniel Katz, Frank Morring, Jr., Jefferson F. Morris, Andy Savoie, Marcia S. Smith.

BANKRATE.COM—(202) 450–4465; National Press Building, Suite 841, Washington, DC 20045: Mark Hamrick.

BARRON'S—(202) 862–6606; 1025 Connecticut Avenue, NW., Suite 800, Washington, DC 20036: Thomas G. Donlan, James McTague.

BNA NEWS—(703) 341–3000; 1801 South Bell Street, Arlington, VA 22202: Lenore T. Adkins, Anthony G. Adragna, Mirza Z. Aftab, Paul F. Albergo, Alexei Alexis, Patrick Ambrosio, Donald G. Aplin, John T. Aquino, Cecelia M. Assam, Pamela S. Atkins, Margaret Aulino, Martina S. Barash, Paul John Barbagallo, Theresa Barry, Tamlin H. Bason, Jeffrey P. Bater, Jeannie Baumann, Stephanie M. Beasley, Matthew Beddingfield, Andrea L. Ben-Yosef, Alison Bennett, Matthew Berger, Lydia Beyoud, Deborah D. Billings, Susan E. Bokermann, Catherine Boudreau, Leonard Bracken, David B. Brandolph, Rossella E. Brevetti, Lydell C. Bridgeford, Steven Brittain, Tera Brostoff, R. Christian Bruce, Susan E. Bruninga, Madelyn R. Callahan, Jay-Anne B. Casuga, Andrew J. Childers, Gayle C. Cinquegrani, Janey Cohen, Kimberly Claire Compton, Paul C. Connolly, Steven Cook, Jessica Coomes, Perry Elizabeth Cooper, Stephanie M. Cumings, Nicholas A. Datlowe, S. Diane Davis, Laura P. Davison, Jeff Day, Phyllis Diamond, Dana J. Domone, Patrick Dorrian, Genevieve Rose Douglas, Kenneth P. Doyle, Susan Doyle, Elliott T. Dube, Lawrence E. Dube, Antonio Dutra, Jewel W. Edwards, Dana A. Elfin, Tawny Elgatian, Karen Ertel, Brett Ferguson, Michael Ferullo, Brian Flood, Sean I. Forbes, Laura D. Francis, Diane M. Freda, Aishia Caryn Freeman, John Gannon, Antoinette Nicole Gartrell, Michael N. Greene, Patrick L. Gregory, Mary Ann, Grena Manley, Sara E. Hansard, David A. Hansen, Peter S. Hayes, Lars-Eric Hedberg, Lisa R. Helem, Marc R. Heller, Paul J. Hendrie, Keith M. Hill, Richard Hill, Rebecca E. Hoffman, Logan Hollers, Gwendolyn C. Holmes, Jay Horowitz, Kristyn Hyland, Terence M. Hyland, Robert Iafolla, R.J. Jewell, Alisa Johnson, Katie W. Johnson, Jessie K. Kamens, Hassan A. Kanu, Hugh B. Kaplan, Bruce S. Kaufman, Rebecca M. Kern, Altaf U. Khan, Jeffrey D. Koelemay, Jimmy H. Koo, Alan D. Kovski, Alexis S. Kramer, W. Randy Kubetin, Philip H. Kushin, Louis C. LaBrecque, Kathryn Larsen, Cathleen R. Larson, Steve K. Lee, Rachel P. Leven, Michael Loatman, Aaron E. Lorenzo, Matthew Loughran, Joe Lustig, Anandashankar Mazumdar, Gregory McCaffery, Ellen E. McCleskey, Rebecca P. McCracken, Susan J. McGolrick, Kevin P. McGowan, Susan M. McInerney, Erin McManus, Tiffany F. Milone, Bronwyn Mixter, Lisa A. Nagele, Ari J. Natter, Jonathan Nicholson, Thomas J. O'Toole, Jr., Gretchen N. Obert, Nancy Ognanovich, Christopher R. Opfer, Jonathan Malik Palmer, Alexander M. Parker, Mack Arthur Arthur Paschal, Bernard J. Pazanowski, Mary Anne Pazanowski, Benjamin Surace Penn, Isabella O. Perelman, Keith Perine, Kendra Casey Plank, Christine Mary Pulfrey, Kristen C. Ricaurte Knebel, Nathaline Richardson, Tyrone Richardson, Sheldon B. Richman, Pat Rizzuto, Kimberly S. Robinson, Lance Rogers, Bruce R. Rolfsen, Michael F. Rose, Brandon J. Ross, Heather M. Rothman, Alex Ruoff, Cheryl L. Saenz, Amena H. Saiyid, Karen J. Saunders, David B. Schultz, David H. Schwartz, Dean T. Scott, Steven M. Sellers, Michelle Shelton, Cheryl Smelson, Rhonda Smith, John H. Stam, Julie A. Steinberg, Seth R. Stern, Peyton Mackay Sturges, Eileen C. Sutton, Deborah Swann, James L. Swann, Larry Swisher, Thomas P. Taylor, Steven John Teske, Steff Thomas, Eric D. Topor, Robert Tricchinelli, Michael Trimarchi, Eleanor Tyler, Andrea L. Vittorio, Patricia Ann Ware, Nathaniel L. Weixel, Yin Wilczek, Rebecca E. Wilhelm, Jacklyn Wille, Mark A. Williams, Michael D. Williamson, Casey Wooten, Kenya Wortherly, Joseph K. Wright, Mindy Yochelson, Barbara Yuill.

BROADBAND CENSUS—(202) 580–8196; 1750 K Street, NW., Suite 1200, Washington, DC 20006: Andrew Clark.

PERIODICALS REPRESENTED IN PRESS GALLERIES—Continued

BROADCASTING & CABLE—(571) 830–6440; 8015 Hatteras Lane, Springfield, VA 22151: John S. Eggerton.

BUDGET & PROGRAM—(202) 328–3860; 1408 Teal Court, Frederick, MD; 21703: John L. Sprague.

CAIJING MAGAZINE—(202) 525–2117; 3133 Connecticut Avenue, NW., 110A, Washington, DC 20008: Yan Jin.

CAIXIN MEDIA—(202) 375–9744; 708 15th Street South, #5; Arlington, VA 22202: Chiachieh Tang, Yuanan Zhang.

CAPITOL FORUM—(202) 601–2300; 1829 M Street, NW., Washington, DC 20036: Trevor Baine, David A. Blotner, Ashley S. Chang, Teddy Downey, Clarion E. Johnson, Vikas Kumar, Karina B. Lubell, Janet Moran, Ben Neumeyer, Nathan Soderstrom, Andrew Sorkin, John Williams, Malka Zeefe.

CCH INC.—(202) 842–7355; 1015 15th Street, NW., 10th Floor, Washington, DC 20005: John Filar Atwood, Jeffrey E. Carlson, Jennifer Rodibaugh Cordaro, Brant Goldwyn, George G. Jones, Nitasha Kadam, Jacquelyn D. Leatherman, AmandaMaine, Joyce Mutcherson-Ridley, George L. Yaksick, Jr.

CEO UPDATE—(202) 721–7656; 1990 M Street, NW., 8th Floor, Washington, DC 20036: William Ehart, Anita Sama, Lori Sharn, Walter J. Williams.

CHRONICLE OF HIGHER EDUCATION—(202) 466–1000; 1255 23rd Street, NW., Suite 700, Washington, DC 20037: Paul A. Basken, Goldie Blumenstyk, Kelly Elizabeth Field, Karin Fischer, Sandhya Kambhampati, Megan O'Neil, Beckie Supiano, Donald P. Troop, Bradley Wolverton.

CONGRESSIONAL DIGEST—(202) 258–2122; 3307 M Street, NW., Suite 301, Washington, DC 20007: Page Robinson.

COOK POLITICAL REPORT—(202) 739–8525; 600 New Hampshire Avenue, NW., Suite 400, Washington, DC 20037: Charles E. Cook, Jr., Jennifer Duffy, David N. Wasserman.

CORPORATE CRIME REPORTER—(202) 737–1680; 1209 National Press Building, Washington, DC 20045: Russell Mokhiber.

COURT HOUSE NEWS—(443)x3–1463; 125 Chester Avenue, Annapolis, MD; 21403: Ryan M. Abbott, Britain Eakin, Jacob Daniel Linger, Amanda L. Loviza-Vickery, Timothy Joseph Ryan.

CQ RESEARCHER—(202) 729–1800; 2600 Virginia Avenue, NW., Suite 600, Washington, DC 20037: Kenneth W. Jost.

CRAIN COMMUNICATIONS—(202) 662–7200; 814 National Press Building, Washington, DC 20045: Ryan Beene, Hazel Bradford, Paul Demko, Virgil T. Dickson, Mary Beth Franklin, Jerry Geisel, Gloria Gonzalez, Mark A. Hofmann, Miles David Moore, Shannon T. Muchmore, Mark Schoeff, Jr., Liz Skinner.

DC SPOTLIGHT NEWSPAPER—(301) 288–7997; P.O. Box 3121, Gaithersburg, MD; 20885: Wenoka Wendy Thompson.

DEFENSE ONE—(202) 739–8501; 600 New Hampshire Avenue, NW., Washington, DC 20037: Kevin Baron, Molly M. O'Toole, Kedar S. Pavgi, Patrick M. Tucker, Benjamin Watson, Marcus A. Weisgerber.

DER SPIEGEL—(202) 347–5222; 1202 National Press Building, Washington, DC 20045: Markus Feldenkirchen, Holger Stark.

DIE ZEIT—(301) 312–8453; 4701 Willard Avenue, #1214, Chevy Chase, MD; 20815: Martin E. Klingst.

DIVERSE: ISSUES IN HIGHER EDUCATION—(703) 385–2981; 10520 Warwick Avenue, Suite B–8; Fairfax, VA 22030: Catherine Morris, David Pluviose.

DUOWEI TIMES—(301) 658–6808; P.O. Box 3353; Gaithersburg, MD 20885: Bettina Yang.

ECONOMIST—(202) 429–0890; 1730 Rhode Island Avenue, NW., Suite 1210, Washington, DC 20036: Rachel Jane Jane Horwood, Daniel L. Knowles, John Prideaux, David Rennie.

EDUCATION WEEK—(301) 280–3100; 6935 Arlington Road, Suite 100, Bethesda, MD; 20814: Caralee Johnson Adams, Evie Blad, Mark W. Bomster, Ross Brenneman, Lauren S. Camera, Sean Cavanagh, Gregory Chronister, Michelle R. Davis, Catherine Gewertz, Liana Heitin, Alyson Klein, Kathleen K. Manzo, Corey Mitchell, Michele Molnar, Arianna G. Prothero, Christina Samuels, Stephen A. Sawchuk, Denisa Superville, Andrew Ujifusa, Debra Viadero, Mark Walsh.

EMPLOYEE BENEFIT ADVISER—(571) 403–3840; 4401 Wilson Boulevard, Suite 910; Arlington, VA 22203: Elizabeth Rome Galentine, Brian Kalish, Mike Nesper Nicholas Anthony Otto, Melissa Winn.

ENERGY INTELLIGENCE—(202) 662–0700; 1411 K Street, NW., Suite 602, Washington, DC 20005: Emily Meredith.

ENGINEERING NEWS-RECORD—(301) 649–3508; 10408 Huntley Avenue, Silver Spring, DC 20902: Thomas F. Ichniowski, Pamela Hunter McFarland.

ENVIRONMENT & ENERGY PUBLISHING—(202) 628–6500; 122 C Street, NW., Suite 722, Washington, DC 20001: Peter B. Behr, Kevin J. Bogardus, Kevin D. Braun, Robin L. Bravender, Dylan Brown, Daniel Bush, Amy V. Carlile, Jean M. Chemnick, Scott M. Detrow, David Ferris, John J. Fialka, Lisa F. Friedman, Ellen M. Gilmer, Elizabeth Erin Harball, Niina H. Heikkinen, Corbin W. Hiar, Margaret Kriz Hobson, Emily H. Holden, Katie J. Howell, Benjamin Hulac, Umair Irfan, Jeremy P. Jacobs, Nicholas P. Juliano, Pamela King, Joel G. Kirkland, Geof Koss, Rod Kuckro, Josh Kurtz, Evan W. Lehmann, Katherine C. Ling, Julia A. Littleton, Colleen M. Luccioli, Jennifer A. Mandel, Christa L.N. Marshall, Hannah M. Northey, Sam R. Pearson, Amanda E. Peterka, Manuel Quinones, Sean Reilly, Ann E. Snider, Blake H. Sobczak, Mike Soraghan, Tiffany Anne Stecker, Noelle C.

PERIODICALS REPRESENTED IN PRESS GALLERIES—Continued

Straub, Philip A. Taylor, Gayathri Vaidyanathan, Ariel Wittenberg, Jennifer Yachnin, Emily J. Yehle, Cyril "Cy" T. Zaneski.
EPOCH TIMES—(301) 515–5422; 7529 Standish Place, Suite 260, Rockville, MD 20855: Zhaoxia Dong, Matthew Robertson, Xiuli Wu, Tiandai You.
EXCHANGE MONITOR PUBLICATIONS—(202) 296–2814; 4301 Connecticut Avenue, NW., Suite 132, Washington, DC 20008: Brian G. Bradley, Jeremy Dillon, Kenneth R. Fletcher, Abby Harvey, Todd K. Jacobson, Michael Nartker, Martin A. Schneider, Alissa Tabirian.
EXPRESS INDIA—(703) 599–6623; 1541 Wellingham Court, Vienna, VA 22182: Geeta Goindi.
FALLS CHURCH NEWS PRESS—(703) 532–3267; 200 Little Falls Street, Suite 508, Falls Church, VA 22046: Nicholas F. Benton, Nicholas Joseph Gatz.
FCW—(703) 876–5100; 8609 Westwood Center Drive, Suite 500M, Vienna, VA 22182: Richard E. Cohen, Sean Lyngaas, Adam Mazmanian, Zach Noble.
FEDERAL EMPLOYEES NEWS DIGEST—(703) 891–8554; 8609 Westwood Center Drive, Suite 500, Vienna, VA 22182: Nathan Abse, Philip M. Piemonte.
FOOD CHEMICAL NEWS—(703) 595–2255; 3 East Cliff Street, Alexandria, VA 22301: Declan Conroy, Joan Murphy.
FOREIGN POLICY—(202) 728–7300; 11 Dupont Circle, NW., Suite 600, Washington, DC 20036: Daniel Richard De Luce, Justine Koo Drennan, David Francis, Jr., Elias Groll, John Hudson, Lara Jakes, Paul Joseph McLeary, Sean D. Naylor, Siobhan Leah O'Grady.
FORTUNE MAGAZINE—(202) 861–4000; 1130 Connecticut Avenue, NW., Suite 900, Washington, DC 20036: Nina J. Easton, Tory Newmyer.
FREITAG—(301) 699–3908; 4506 32nd Street, Mt. Rainier, MD; 20712: Konrad Ege.
FRONTLINE MEDICAL COMMUNICATIONS—(240) 221–4500; 5635 Fishers Lane, Suite 6000, Rockville, MD; 20852: Whitney McKnight, Gregory Twachtman.
FTC WATCH—(703) 684–7171; 1776 I (Eye) Street, NW., Suite 260, Washington, DC 20006: Neil Warner Averitt, Kirstin Edith Downey, Claude Marx, Kirk Victor.
GILSTON-KALIN COMMUNICATIONS—(301) 570–4544; 4816 Sweetbirch Drive, Rockville, MD; 20853: Meredith L. Gilston, Samuel M. Gilston.
GLAMOUR MAGAZINE—(212) 206–4254; 6100 Edgewood Terrace, Alexandria, VA 22307: Giovanna Gray Lockhart.
GLOBAL COMPETITION REVIEW—(202) 706–7031; 2401 Pennsylvania Avenue, NW., Suite 300, Washington, DC 20037: Pallavi Guniganti, Ron Knox.
GOVERNING—(202) 862–8802; 1100 Connecticut Avenue, NW., #1300 Washington, DC 20036: Liz Farmer, Christopher Kardish, J.B. Wogan.
GOVERNMENT CONTRACTOR—(202) 772–8295; 1100 13th Street, NW., Suite 200, Washington, DC 20005: Joseph K. Windsor.
GOVERNMENT EXECUTIVE—(202) 739–8501; 600 New Hampshire Avenue, NW., Washington, DC 20037: Charles S. Clark, Amelia M. Gruber, Eric Katz, Frank Konkel, William Lucia, Kellie Lunney, Andrew "Jack" Jackson Moore, Katherine M. Peters, Mohana Ravindranath, Camille A. Tuutti.
GQ MAGAZINE—(202) 615–5003; 1420 K Street, SE., Washington, DC 20003: Robert L. Draper.
HEALTH MARKET SURVEY—(202) 277–1994; 3767 Oliver Street, NW., Washington, DC 20015: William R. Boyles.
HEAVY DUTY TRUCKING—(703) 683–9935; 320 Mansion Drive, Alexandria, VA 22302: David Cullen.
HISPANIC LINK NEWS SERVICE—(202) 234–0280; 1420 N Street, NW., Washington, DC 20005: Natashka McDonald.
HISPANIC OUTLOOK—(202) 236–5595; 2627 O Street, NW., Washington, DC 20007: Margaret S. Orchowski.
IDG COMMUNICATIONS—(202) 361–2011; 2630 Adams Mill Road, NW., #304, Washington, DC 20009: Patrick Thibodeau.
IDG NEWS SERVICE—(202) 595–9882; 906 Phillip Powers Drive, Laurel, MD; 20707: Grant J. Gross.
INDIA ABROAD—(703) 899–1419; 2747 Centreville Road, Herndon, VA 20171: Aziz Haniffa.
INFORMA—(240) 221–4500; 5635 Fishers Lane, Suite 6000, Rockville, MD; 20851: Ferdous Al-Faruque, Susan W. Darcey, Jacqueline Fitton, Eileen Francis, Derrick J. Gingery, Joseph A. Haas, Laura A. Helbling, M. Nielsen Hobbs, Sarah Karlin, Catherine A. Kelly, Lauren Nardella, Denise Peterson, Malcolm E. Spicer, Scott A. Steinke, Susan M. Sutter.
INSIDE GNSS—(703) 920–9041; 1014 17th Street South, Arlington, VA 22202: Dee Ann Divis.
INSIDE MORTGAGE FINANCE—(301) 951–1240; 7910 Woodmont Avenue, Suite 1000, Bethesda, MD; 20814: John Bancroft, George A. Brooks, Guy David Cecala, Carisa D. Chappell, Thomas Ressler.
INSIDE WASHINGTON PUBLISHERS—(703) 416–8500; 1919 South Eads Street, #201; Arlington, VA 22202: Lara W. Beaven, Rebecca H.M. Beitsch, Jeremy Bernstein, Anthony F. Bertuca, Jack Ernest Caporal, Christopher Castelli, Christopher M. Cole, Bridget M. DiCosmo, Justin P. Doubleday, Russell James Drew, Erin Durkin, Brett P. Fortnam, Leigh Giangreco, Benjamin Hancock, Donna L. Haseley, Maria A. Hegstad, Jutta Hennig, Joshua L. Higgins, David A. Hood, Elizabeth Lee Hudson, Rachel S. Karas, Anthony Lacey, David LaRoss, John Liang, Lee Logan, William R. Lucia, Scott Maucione,

PERIODICALS REPRESENTED IN PRESS GALLERIES—Continued

Courtney McBride, Jordana L. Mishory, Charles F. Mitchell, Ellen Mitchell, Douglas Obey, Amanda S. Palleschi, Stuart H. Parker, Erin Ashton Raftery, Ryan S. Rainey, Dawn Reeves, David E. Reynolds, Matthew A. Schewel, Lara Seligman, Abigail K. Smith, Sebastian Sprenger, Michelle M. Stein, David J. Thomas, Rick Weber, John Stirling Wilkerson, Joseph Paul Williams, Todd Allen Wilson, Suzanne M. Yohannan.

INVESTMENT ADVISOR MAGAZINE—(202) 370–4810; 1301 Connecticut Avenue, NW., Suite 300, Washington, DC 20036: Melanie Waddell.

JOURNAL OF COMMERCE—(202) 499–2285; 700 12th Street, NW., Suite 700, Washington, DC 20005: William B. Cassidy.

JOURNAL OF COMMERCE: 700 12th Street, NW., Suite 700, Washington, DC 20005: John A. Gallagher, James Reynolds Hutchins, Mark D. Szakonyi.

KIPLINGER WASHINGTON EDITORS—(202) 887–6400; 1100 13th Street, NW., Suite 750, Washington, DC 20005: Lisa E. Babb, Peter L. Blank, Martha L. Craver, Douglas A. Harbrecht, Kevin McCormally, John T. Miley, David J. Morris, James B. Patterson, Pamela M. Prah, Richard Sammon, Jose Rodrigo Sermeno, Mark L. Sfiligoj, Glenn Somerville, Joy M. Taylor.

LAW360—(571) 305–2529; 1150 18th Street, NW., Suite 600, Washington, DC 20036: Jacob A. Fischler, Margaret Elizabeth Harding, James C. Hoover, Bryan David Koenig, Michael A. Macagnone, Kery Murakami, Erica J. Teichert, Daniel Wilson.

LE POINT—(202) 244–6656; 3234 McKinley Street, NW., Washington, DC 20015: Helene Vissiere.

MACLEAN'S—(301) 774–6209; 6316 24th Street, N Arlington, VA 22207: Allen J. Abel.

MANUFACTURING & TECHNOLOGY NEWS—(703) 750–2664; P.O. Box 36; Annandale, VA 22003: Richard McCormack.

MCGRAW HILL FINANCIAL—(202) 383–2000; 1200 G Street, NW., Suite 1000, Washington, DC 20005: Steven D. Dolley, William Freebairn, Gary Gentile, Keiron Greenhalgh, Elaine Hiruo, Jasmin Hudson, Valarie N. Jackson, Nick Jonson, Karen McBeth Laping, Robert F. McMahon, Christopher J. Newkumet, Jim Ostroff, Brian J. Scheid, Stephanie Sharpe, Herman D. Wang, Maya Weber.

METRO WEEKLY—(202) 638–6830; 1425 K Street, NW., Suite 350, Washington, DC 20005: John A. Riley.

MII PUBLICATIONS—(202) 495–1879; 1029 Vermont Avenue, NW., Suite 501, Washington, DC 20005: Ryan E. Hess, Cecilio Morales.

MINE SAFETY AND HEALTH NEWS—(703) 217–8270; 5935 4th Street North, Arlington, VA 22203: Brad A. Kuknk, Katharine Snyder.

MONTGOMERY COUNTY SENTINEL—(301) 838–0788; 22 West Jefferson Street; Suite 309, Rockville, MD 20850: Brian J. Karem, Julian Mitsuo Sadur.

MORE MAGAZINE—(202) 716–7443; 6525 Orland Street, Falls Church, VA 22043: Betsy Fischer Martin.

MORNING CONSULT—(202) 436 4394; P.O. Box 15628, Washington, DC 20003: Eita Arom, Davis C. Burroughs IV, William C. Dobbs-Allsopp, Timothy Richard Homan, Fawn Johnson, Rob L. Kunzig, Colleen C. Leahy, Meghan McCarthy, Amir Ali Nasr, Jonathan T. Reid, Gabe Rubin, Reid H. Wilson.

NATION—(202) 546–2239; 110 Maryland Avenue, NE., Suite 308, Washington, DC 20002: James W. Carden, Zoe Carpenter, George Zornick.

NATIONAL CATHOLIC REPORTER—(408) 406–5609; 400 North Capitol Street, NW., Suite G–80, Washington, DC 20001: Vincent J. Rotondaro.

NATIONAL JOURNAL—(202) 739–8400; 600 New Hampshire Avenue, NW., Washington, DC 20037: Julie L. Abramson, Priscilla N. Alvarez, Samuel U. Baker, James A. Barnes, Matt Berman, Dan Berman, Ronald J. Brownstein, Nora R. Caplan-Bricker, Nancy M Cook, M Michelle Cottle, Shmsh V. Date, Emily E. DeRuy, Andrea Michelle Drusch, Isobel Ellis, Clare M. Foran, Lauren Fox, Eric M. Garcia, Ben Geman, Lucia E. Graves, Timothy Patrick Grieve, Lisa Hagen, Jerry Hagstrom, John Barney Judis, Richard Just, Nora E. Kelly, Marina Koren, Josh P. Kraushaar, Juleyka Lantigua-Williams, Jason Mann, Rebecca R. Nelson, James Oliphant, Caitlin N. Owens, Jason Plautz, Sophie A. Quinton, Kimberly Grace Railey, Brian Resnick, Alex Rogers, Emma Roller, Laura Ryan, Brendan S. Sasso, Dylan L. Scott, Walter Shapiro, Burt Solomon, Stuart Taylor, Jr., Matt Vasilogambros, Dustin Volz.

NATIONAL LAW JOURNAL—(202) 457–0686; 1100 G Street, NW., Suite 900, Washington, DC 20005: Marcia Coyle, Anthony E. Mauro, Katelyn J. Polantz, Mike Sacks, Zoe Tillman.

NATIONAL REVIEW—(202) 543–9226; 233 Pennsylvania Avenue, SE., 3rd Floor, Washington, DC 20003: Brendan Joseph Bordelon, Joel S. Gehrke, Jr., Andrew E. Johnson, Eliana Johnson, Alexis R. Levinson, Ramesh Ponnuru, Christine Sisto.

NATURE—(202) 737–2355; 968 National Press Building, Washington, DC 20045: Lauren Morello, Sara N. Reardon.

NEW REPUBLIC—(202) 508–4482; 525 9th Street, NW., Suite 600, Washington, DC 20004: Brian Alfred Beutler, Suzy Khimm, Rebecca J. Leber, Adam N. Peck, Jamil Smith, Daniel R. Vinik.

NEW YORKER—(202) 955–0960; 1730 Rhode Island Avenue, NW., Suite 603, Washington, DC 20036: Jeffrey Toobin.

NEWBAY MEDIA—(703) 852–4600; 5285 Shawnee Road, Suite 100, Alexandria, VA 22312: Leslie P. Stimson.

PERIODICALS REPRESENTED IN PRESS GALLERIES—Continued

NEWSMAX—(202) 465–8730; 1900 K Street, NW., Suite 1120, Washington, DC 20006: John Gizzi.
NEWSWEEK—(202) 626–2000; 1750 Pennsylvania Avenue, NW., Suite 1220, Washington, DC 20006: Jonathan Broder, Emily Isabel Cadei, Matthew Stanley Cooper, Virginia Stella Gibson, Andrew Jason Perez, Jeffrey H. Stein.
OBERLE COMMUNICATIONS—(301) 229–1027; 4907 Bayard Boulevard, Bethesda, MD; 20816: Sean F. Oberle.
OIL & GAS JOURNAL—(703) 533–1552; 7013 Jefferson Avenue, Falls Church, VA 22042: Nicholas J. Snow.
PEOPLE MAGAZINE—(202) 861–4000; 1130 Connecticut Avenue, NW., Suite 900, Washington, DC 20036: Sandra Sobieraj.
PHARMACEUTICAL EXECUTIVE—(301) 656–4634; 7715 Rocton Avenue, Chevy Chase, MD; 20815: Jill Wechsler.
POLITICO—(703) 647–7999; 1100 Wilson Boulevard, 6th Floor, Arlington, VA 22209: Arthur Allen, Rachel M. Bade, Jeffrey I. Bartholet, Adam S. Behsudi, Kate G. Bennett, Brooks Boliek, Helena Bottemiller Evich, Kendall P. Breitman, John Bresnahan, Alex Byers, Heather Nicole Caygle, Kyle Cheney, David Clarke, Eliza S. Collins, Michael Crowley, Gabriel A. Debenedetti, Christine Anne Delargy, Paul Jeffrey Demko, Darius Ajani Dixon, Kim Dixon, Edward-Isaac Dovere, Toby L. Eckert, Brianna Megan Ehley, Caitlin Z. Emma, Eric Engleman, John B. Everett, Philip T. Ewing, Brian D. Faler, Lauren French, Joshua A. Gerstein, Andrew J. Glass, Katie Glueck, Ashley Gold, Hadas Gold, Darren T. Goode, Garrett M. Graff, Alexandra Grasgreen, Michael Grunwald, Victoria T. Guida, Alexander Guillen, Jennifer A. Haberkorn, Kimberly A. Hefling, Jeremy Herb, G. Robert Hillman, James P. Hohmann, Jenny A. Hopkinson, Jason A. Huffman, Alex Isenstadt, Jennifer Judson, Sarah Karlin, Kara Ann Kearns, Joanne L. Kenen, Seung Min Kim, Robert P. King, Tal Kopan, Matthew Korade, Michael Kruse, Adam B. Lerner, Marianne A. Levine, Susan K. Levine, Jennifer Rose Liberto, Daniel Lippman, Brian J. Mahoney, Joseph H. Marks, Catherine A. Martel, Erica L. Martinson, Nolan D. McCaskill, Fatjona Mejdini, Erin Mershon, Theodoric Meyer, Leigh Munsil, David Nather, Timothy R. Noah, Brett Norman, Anna A. Palmer, Doug Palmer, Tarini Parti, David Perera, Beatrice Elizabeth Peterson, David Pittman, Rachana D. Pradhan, Jon Prior, Chase Purdy, Manu K. Raju, Andrew M. Restuccia, Maura Reynolds, Kevin P. Robillard, David E. Rogers, Tony Romm, Darren Sean Samuelsohn, Elena C. Schneider, Jennifer A. Scholtes, Elana Schor, Benjamin Vose Schreckinger, Nancy Scola, Maggie Severns, Jack Shafer, Nirvi H. Shah, Steven Shepard, Jacob S. Sherman, Roger M. Simon, Margaret Ann Slattery, Adam T. Sneed, Kelsey Snell, Timothy A. Starks II, Daniel L. Strauss, Darius A. Tahir, Patrick C. Temple-West, Glenn H. Thrush, Bill Tomson, Nahal Toosi, Jonathan Topaz, Kate A. Tummarello, Natalie Villacorta, Kenneth P. Vogel, Zachary Warmbrodt, Shaun N. Waterman, Sarah Wheaton, Colin Wilhelm, Kathryn A. Wolfe, Austin B. Wright, Michael Zapler.
PROCESO—(202) 737–1538; 529 14th Street, NW., Suite 1117, Washington, DC 20045: J. Jesus Esquivel.
PUBLIC LANDS NEWS—(703) 553–0552; 133 South Buchanan Street, Arlington, VA 22204: James B. Coffin.
RED ALERT POLITICS—(202) 903–2000; 1150 17th Street, NW., Suite 504, Washington, DC 20036: Morgan Mary Chalfant, Ashley Danielle Dobson, Maria T. Santos.
RESEARCH INSTITUTE OF AMERICA GROUP—(202) 842–1240; 1275 K Street, NW., Suite 875, Washington, DC 20005: Tesha L. Alston, William Clay Flook, Velma Denise Goodwine, Soyoung Ho, William F. Lesesne.
ROLL CALL—(202) 650–6000; 77 K Street, NE., 8th Floor, Washington, DC 20002: Christina Bellantoni, Bridget M. Bowman, Emily Cahn, Shira R. Center, Steven T. Dennis, Jason J. Dick, Emma Dumain, Cameron Easley, David Eldridge, David Ellis, Megan M. Evans, Matthew G. Fleming, Matt E. Fuller, Rebecca E. Gale, Justice L. Gilpin-Green, Christian Hale, David Mark Hawkings, Jr., Hannah C. Hess, Kaitlin Kovach, Niels P. Lesniewski, Alexis Levinson, Cyra Master, Simone F. Pathe, Warren Rojas, Kyle Trygstad, Eli G. Yokley.
ROTHENBERG & GONZALES POLITICAL REPORT—(202) 546–2822; 13305 Morning Field Way, Potomac, MD; 20854: Nathan Gonzales, Stuart Rothenberg.
SATELLITE BUSINESS NEWS—(202) 785–0505; 5614 Connecticut Avenue, NW., #300, Washington, DC 20015: Bob Scherman.
SCIENTIFIC AMERICAN—(202) 626–2532; 968 National Press Building, Washington, DC 20045: Josh E. Fischman, Dina F. Maron.
SCUDDER PUBLISHING—(410) 923–0688; 1145 Generals Highway, Crownsville, MD; 21032: John R. Sodergreen.
SIGHTLINE MEDIA GROUP—(703) 750–7400; 6883 Commercial Drive, Springfield, VA 22159: George Altman, John T. Bennett, Aaron T. Boyd, Christopher Cavas, Andrew Clevenger, Amber Corrin, Brian W. Everstine, Joseph M. Gould, Michael L. Hardy, Gina A. Harkins, Hope Hodge Seck, Kyle R. Jahner, Karen Grigg Jowers, Patricia N. Kime, Stephen Losey, Andrew S. Medici, Aaron Mehta, Meghann Myers, Oriana Pawlyk, Derrick Thaddeus Perkins, Barry Rosenberg, James K. Sanborn, Richard William Sandza, Jeffrey Duff Schogol, Leo ShaneIII, Phillip F. Swarts, Michelle Tan, James S. Tice, Andrew S. Tilghman, Steven M. Watkins.

PERIODICALS REPRESENTED IN PRESS GALLERIES—Continued

SLATE—(202) 261-2066; 1350 Connecticut Avenue, Suite 400, Washington, DC 20036: John F. Dickerson, Will Dobson, Rachel E. Gross, Joshua Levin, Dahlia Hannah Lithwick, William Saletan, Jeremy Stahl, Mark Joseph Stern, Katy Waldman.

SPACE NEWS—(571) 356-9532; 1414 Prince Street, Suite 300, Alexandria, VA 22314: Michael Gruss, Daniel M. Leone.

SYNOPSIS—(301) 728-4988; 20312 Aspenwood Lane, Montgomery Village, MD; 20886: William T. Gray, Ellen Milhiser.

TALKING POINTS MEMO—(202) 758-3048; 1615 L Street, NW., Suite 310, Washington, DC 20036: Sahil Kapur, David Kurtz, Caitlin MacNeal, Tierney M. Sneed, Daniel Strauss.

TAX NOTES—(703) 533-4400; 400 South Maple Avenue, Suite 400, Falls Church, VA 22046: David Scott Antonides, Brian D. Bardwell, Kaustuv Basu, Maria Koklanaris Bonaquist, Margaret Burow, Jennifer Carr, Stephen K. Cooper, William Robert Davis, Jennifer DePaul, Joseph DiSciullo, Amy S. Elliott, Luca Gattoni-Celli, Cara Griffith, Amy L. Hamilton, William S. Hoffman III, Cynthia Denise Holeman, Thomas Jaworski, Thomas J. Kasprzak, Kat Lucero, Matthew Madara, Bergrek Phillips, Henry Reske, Nathan Richman, David C. Sawyer, Scott A. Sheets, Doug Sheppard, Meg Shreve, Quintin Simmons, David D. Stewart, Frederick William Stokeld, Jim Sweeney, David van den Berg, Andrew Mims Velarde, Eric S. Yauch, Sam Young.

TECHNOLOGY COMMERCIALIZATION—(703) 522-6648; P.O. Box 100595, Arlington, VA 22210: Neil A. MacDonald.

TELECOMMUNICATIONS REPORTS—(202) 842-8923; 1015 15th Street, NW., 10th Floor, Washington, DC 20005: John Curran, Carrie DeLeon, Paul Kirby, Lynn E. Stanton.

THE GEORGETOWNER—(202) 579-0200; 2801 M Street, NW., Washington, DC 20007: Mark Plotkin.

THE HILL—(202) 628-8500; 1625 K Street, NW., Suite 900, Washington, DC 20006: Judy K. Altscher, Bernard A. Becker, Cory L. Bennett, Alexander Bruce Bolton, Jesse Byrnes, Timothy Cama, Jordain R. Carney, Kevin N. Cirilli, Robert Cusack, Timothy Devaney, Jonathan C. Easley, Albert Eisele, Jordan H. Fabian, Sarah N. Ferris, Benjamin Goad, Julian Hattem, Devin Kendrick Henry, Cameron E. Joseph, Benjamin Kamisar, Rebecca Hillary Kheel, Keith Laing, Michael Lillis, Cristina Marcos, Martin Matishak, David C. McCabe, Vicki Needham, Ashley J. Perks, Kyle J. Plantz, Peter C. Schroeder, Rebecca Danielle Shabad, Niall G. Stanage, Alexandra B. Stoddard, Peter Sullivan, Jonathan Swan, Frank M. Trujillo, Elise J. Viebeck, Dustin A. Weaver, Lydia W. Wheeler, Katherine B. Williams, Megan R. Wilson, Kristina Wong, Scott B. Wong, Jennifer Yingling.

THE HOTLINE—(202) 739-8400; 600 New Hampshire Avenue, NW., Washington, DC 20037: Scott Bland, Alex Brown, Karyn L. Bruggeman, Zachary C. Cohen, Jack Fitzpatrick.

THE ROOT—(202) 261-2075; 95 Morton Street, 4th Floor, New York, NY 10014: Breanna C. Edwards.

THOMPSON INFORMATION SERVICES—(202) 872-4000; 4340 East-West Highway, Suite 300, Bethesda, MD 20814: Jerry Ashworth, Cameron S. Ayers, Kyra Berkheiser, Elizabeth Casabona, Todd H. Leeuwenburgh, Daniel J. Macy, Lillian F. McManus, Jane Meacham, Karen Norris, Mark Reishus, Jeffrey Schomisch, David A. Slaughter, Dennis A. Tosh.

TIME MAGAZINE—(202) 861-4000; 1130 Connecticut Avenue, NW., Suite 900, Washington, DC 20036: Alex S. Altman, Melissa A. August, Ryan Teague Beckwith, Tessa C. Berenson, Massimo T. Calabresi, Elizabeth J. Dias, Michael W. Duffy, Haley Edwards, Philip Robert Elliott III, Sam Frizell, David A. Johnson, Zeke J. Miller, Jay Newton-Small, Maya N. Rhodan, Alex Rogers, Michael B. Scherer, Mark J. Thompson, Christopher E. Wilson.

TOWNHALL—(703) 294-6047, 1901 North Moore Street, Suite 700, Arlington, VA 22209: Leah Barkoukis, Conn Carroll, Daniel P. Doherty, Teresa M. Mull, Amanda A. Munoz, Cortney O'Brien, Catherine Pavlich, Christine Rousselle, Matt Vespa.

TRICE EDNEY NEWSWIRE—(202) 291-9310; 6817 Georgia Avenue, NW., Suite 218, Washington, DC 20012: Hazel Trice Edney.

U.S. MEDICINE—(202) 488-0611; 350 G Street, SW., # N215, Washington, DC 20024: Sandra L. Basu.

U.S. NEWS & WORLD REPORT—(202) 955-2000; 1050 Thomas Jefferson Street, NW., Washington, DC 20007: Allie Bidwell, Patrick Garofalo, Jill Debra Lawrence, Kimberly L. Leonard, Gabrielle F. Levy, Susan E. Milligan, Michael Morella, Steven Nelson, Alan Neuhauser, Thomas J. Risen, Robert Schlesinger, Nicole E. Schwab, Paul D. Shinkman, Vincent Dean Simon, Tierney Sneed, Steve Sternberg, Kenneth T. Walsh, Teresa Welsh, Joseph P. Williams.

UCG—(301) 287-2700; 9737 Washingtonian Boulevard; Suite 200, Gaithersburg, MD 20878: Kevin Adler, Carl Ayers, Steven Dashiell, Roy Edroso, Rachel Gantz, Karen S. Long Rayburn, A.J. Plunkett, Joshua Poltilove, Nicholas Stern, Vincent E. Taylor, Molly M. White.

USA JOURNAL—(202) 714-7330; P.O. Box 714, Washington, DC 20044: Janne Kum Cha C. Pak.

VANITY FAIR—(202) 244-3424; 5146 Klingle Street, NW., Washington, DC 20016: Maureen Orth.

VOX MEDIA—(202) 591-1167; 1201 Connecticut Avenue, NW., Washington, DC 20036: Jonathan J. Allen, Sarah L. Kliff.

WASHINGTON BLADE—(202) 747-2077; 1712 14th Street, NW., Washington, DC 20009: Louis M. Chibbaro, Jr., Chris C. Johnson.

WASHINGTON BLADE: 1712 14th Street, NW., Washington, DC 20009: Michael K. Lavers.

PERIODICALS REPRESENTED IN PRESS GALLERIES—Continued

WASHINGTON BUSINESS INFORMATION—(703) 538–7600; 300 North Washington Street, Suite 200, Falls Church, VA 22046: Lena Freund, Elizabeth Orr, Jonathon D. Shacat.

WASHINGTON BUSINESS JOURNAL—(703) 258–0845; 1555 Wilson Boulevard, Suite 400, Arlington, VA 22204: Kent Hoover.

WASHINGTON CITY PAPER—(202) 332–2100; 1400 I Street, NW., #900, Washington, DC 20005: Christina Cauterucci, Emily Q. Hazzard, Sarah Anne E. Hughes, Caroline E. Jones, Mike R. Madden, William F. Sommer V, Aaron M. Wiener.

WASHINGTON COUNSELETTER—(202) 244–6709; 5712 26th Street, NW., Washington, DC 20015: Deborah A. Kavruck.

WASHINGTON JEWISH WEEK—(301) 230–2222; 11900 Parklawn Drive, Suite 300, Rockville, MD; 20852: Melissa Wendy Apter, Geoffrey William Melada, Suzanne Pollak, Dmitriy Shapiro.

WASHINGTON TRADE DAILY—(301) 946–0817; P.O. Box 1802, Wheaton, MD 20915: James R. Berger, Mary Berger.

WASHINGTON WATCH—(301) 263–9023; 5923 Onondaga Road, Bethesda, MD; 20816: Kazutami Yamazaki.

WASHINGTONIAN—(202) 296–3600; 1828 L Street, NW., Suite 200, Washington, DC 20036: Sherri Leslie Dalphonse, Benjamin Freed, Michael Gaynor, Will Grunewald, Harry S. Jaffe, Marisa M. Kashino, Luke Mullins, Michael Schaffer.

WATERWAYS JOURNAL—(703) 524–2490; 5220 North Carlin Springs Road, Arlington, VA 22203: Carlo J. Salzano.

WEEKLY STANDARD—(202) 293–4900; 1150 17th Street, NW., Suite 505, Washington, DC 20036: Judith E. Ayers, Fred W. Barnes, Christopher Caldwell, Julianne E. Dudley, Andrew Ferguson, Daniel M. Halper, Jonathan V. Last, John M. McCormack, James A. Swift, Philip Terzian, Michael R. Warren.

WHITAKER NEWSLETTERS—(240) 583–0280; P.O. Box 224; Spencerville, MD; 20868: Joel Whitaker.

WORLD MAGAZINE—(202) 744–8987; 310 Laverne Avenue, Alexandria, VA 22305: Emily C. Belz, J.C. Derrick.

CONGRESSIONAL DISTRICT MAPS

ALABAMA—Congressional Districts—(7 Districts)

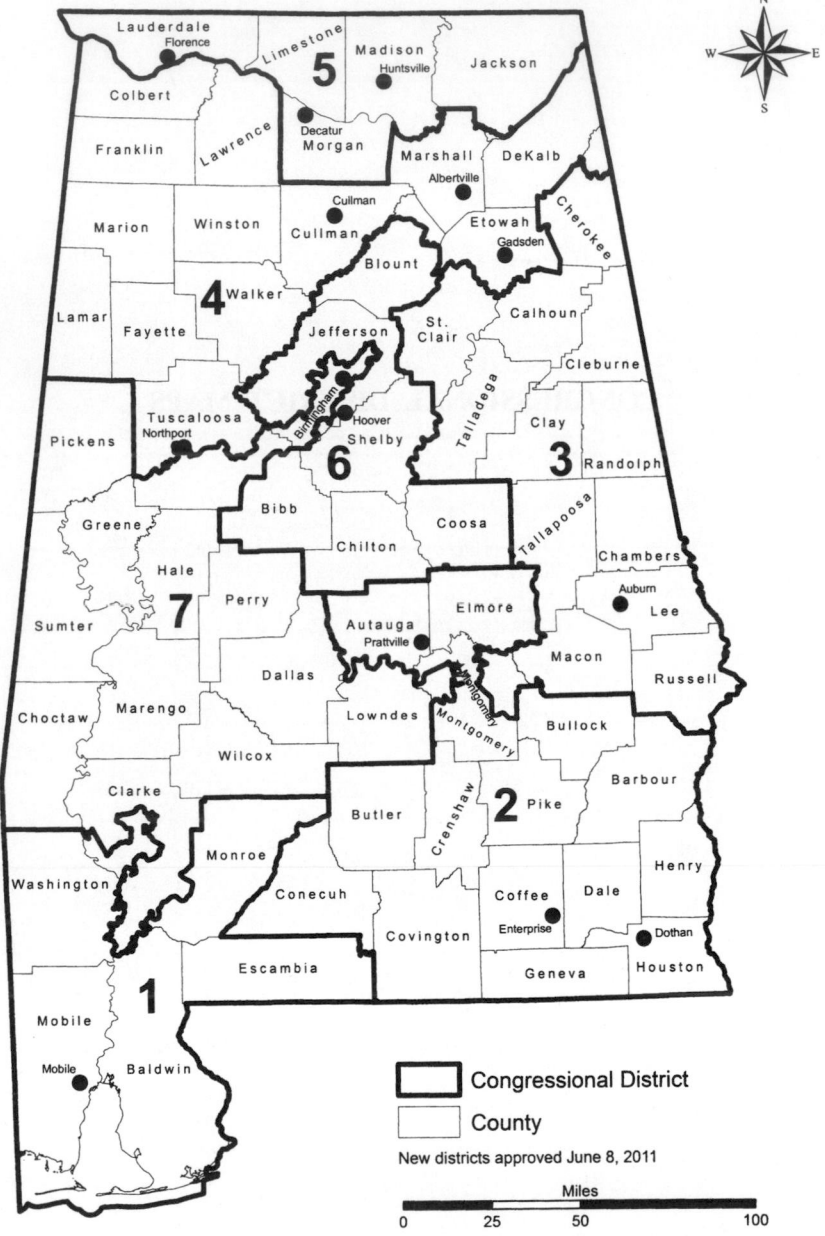

Congressional District

County

New districts approved June 8, 2011

Miles

0   25   50   100

ALASKA—Congressional District—(1 District At Large)

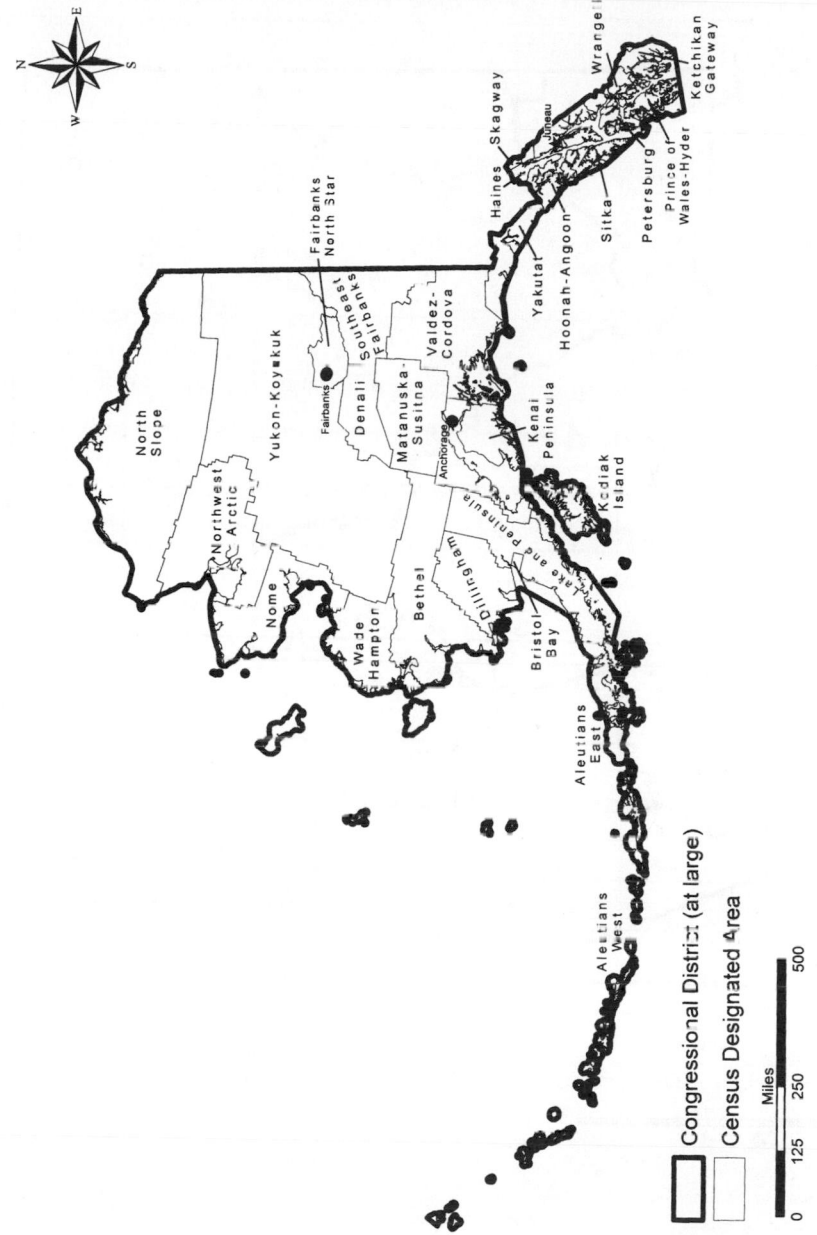

ARIZONA—Congressional Districts—(9 Districts)

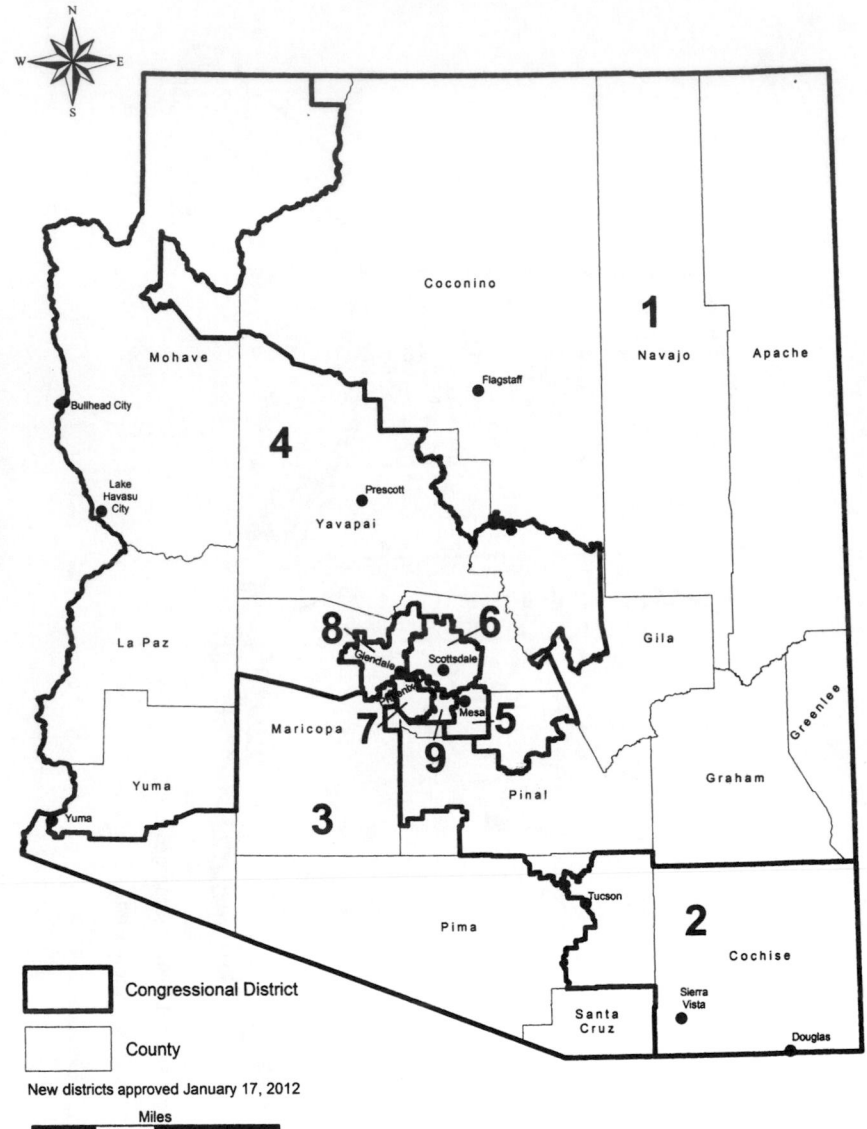

Congressional District

County

New districts approved January 17, 2012

Miles

0   25   50   100

ARKANSAS—Congressional Districts—(4 Districts)

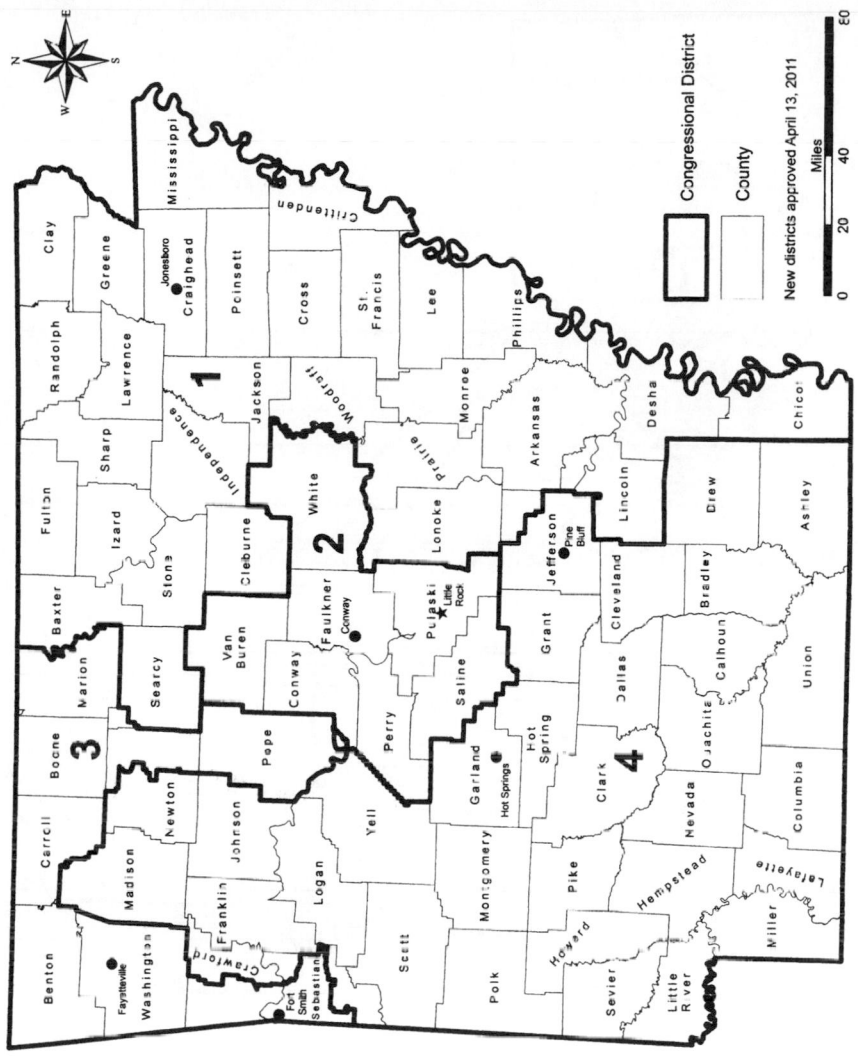

CALIFORNIA—Congressional Districts—(53 Districts)

Congressional District

County

New districts approved August 15, 2011

Miles

0   50   100   200

COLORADO—Congressional Districts—(7 Districts)

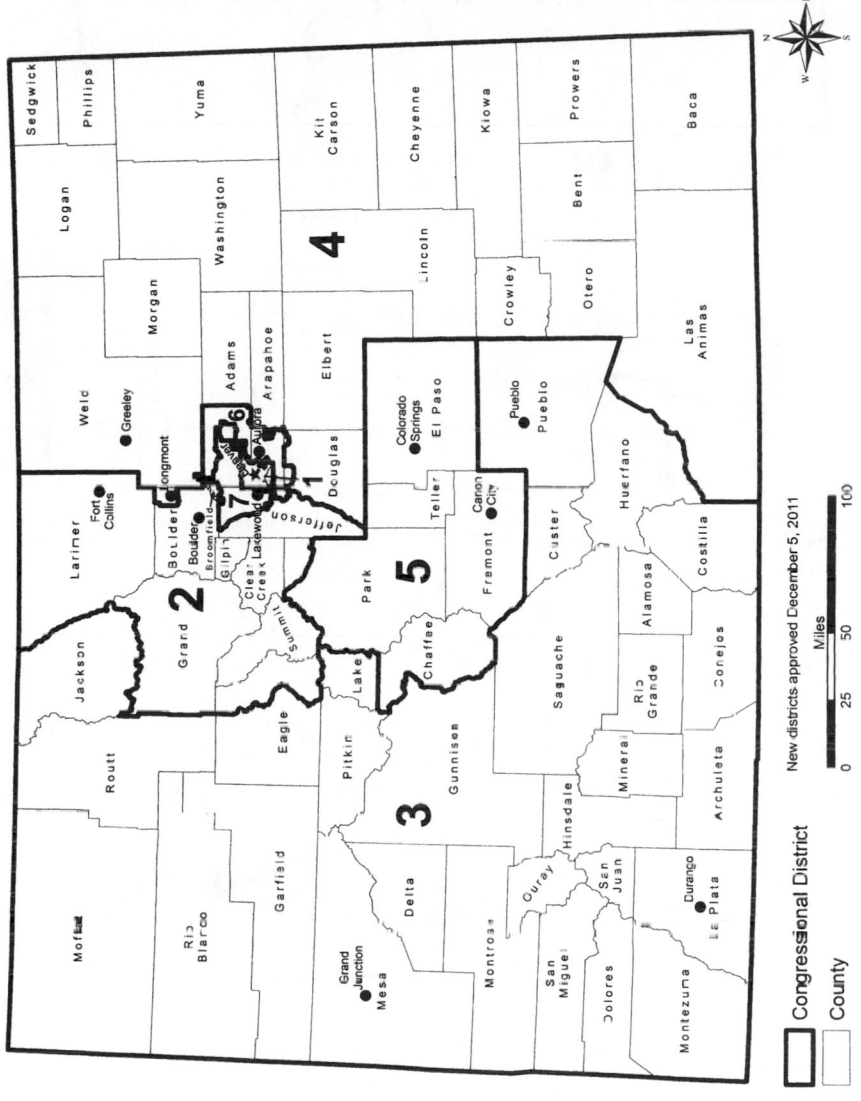

CONNECTICUT—Congressional Districts—(5 Districts)

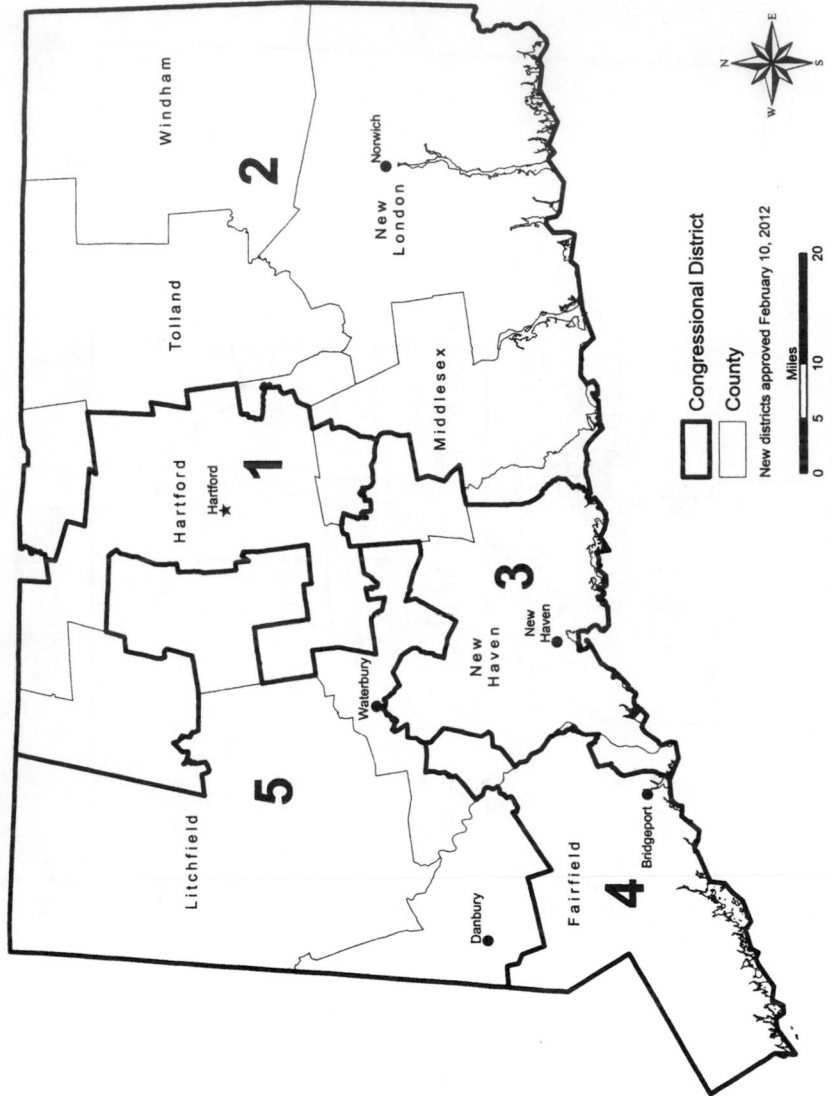

DELAWARE—Congressional District—(1 District At Large)

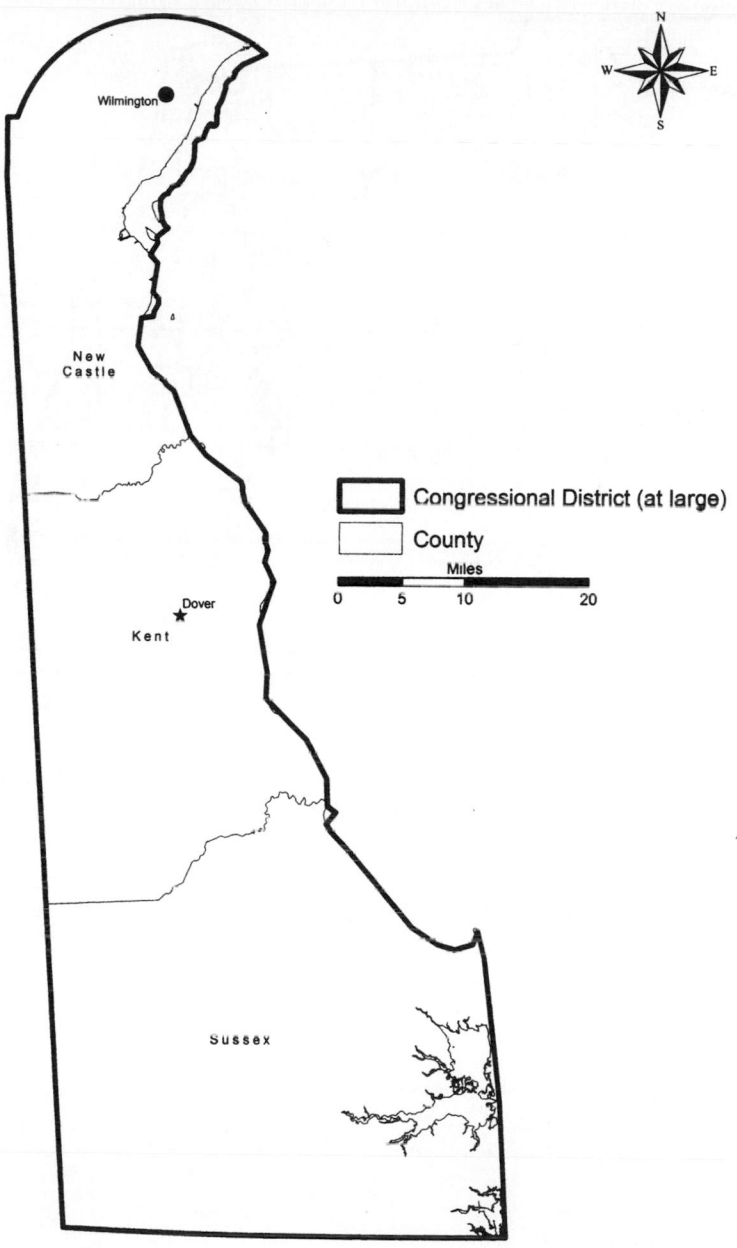

FLORIDA—Congressional Districts—(27 Districts)

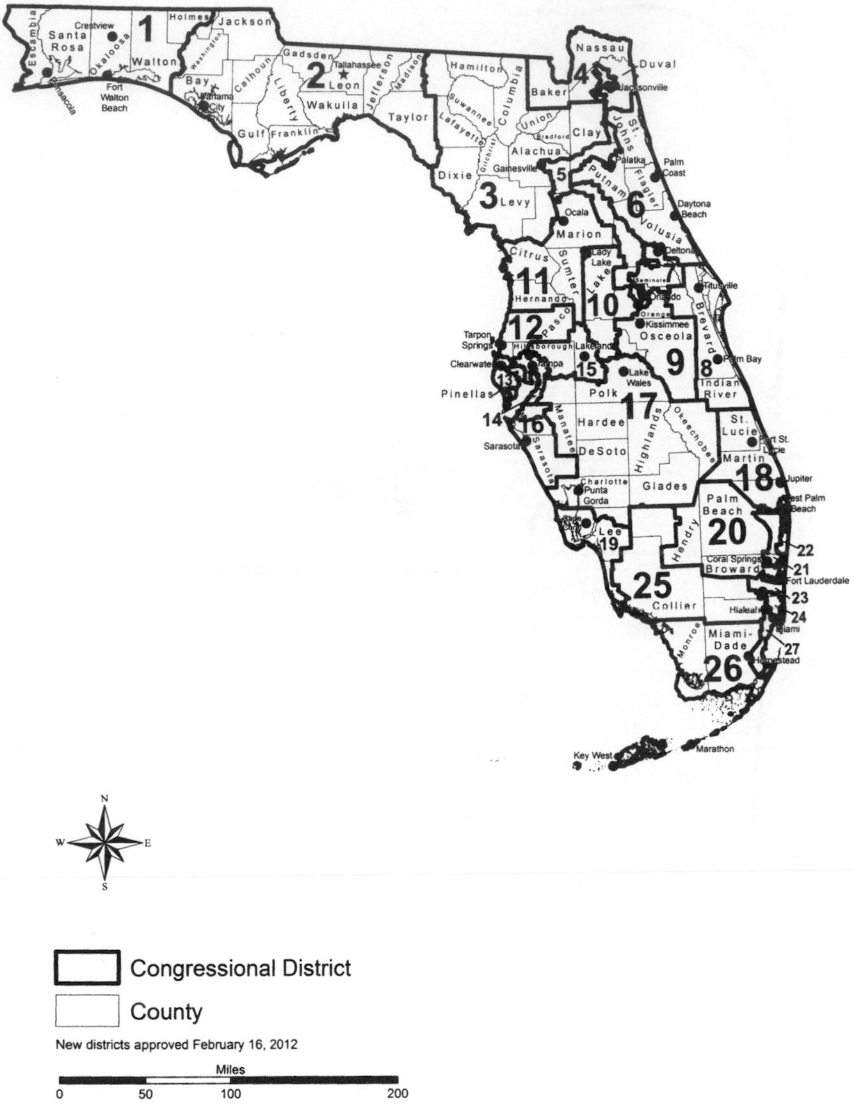

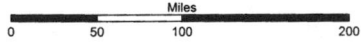

Congressional District

County

New districts approved February 16, 2012

Miles

0   50   100   200

GEORGIA—Congressional Districts—(14 Districts)

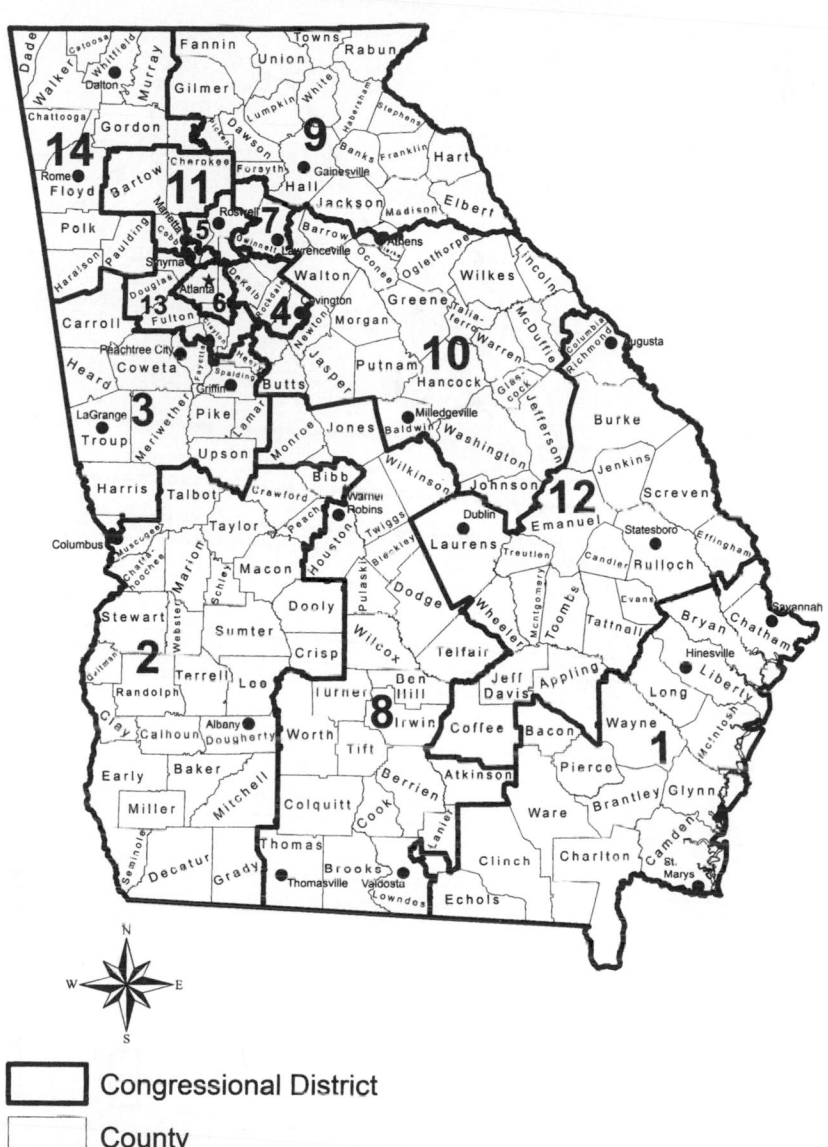

Congressional District

County

New districts approved September 6, 2011

Miles

0   30   60   120

HAWAII—Congressional Districts—(2 Districts)

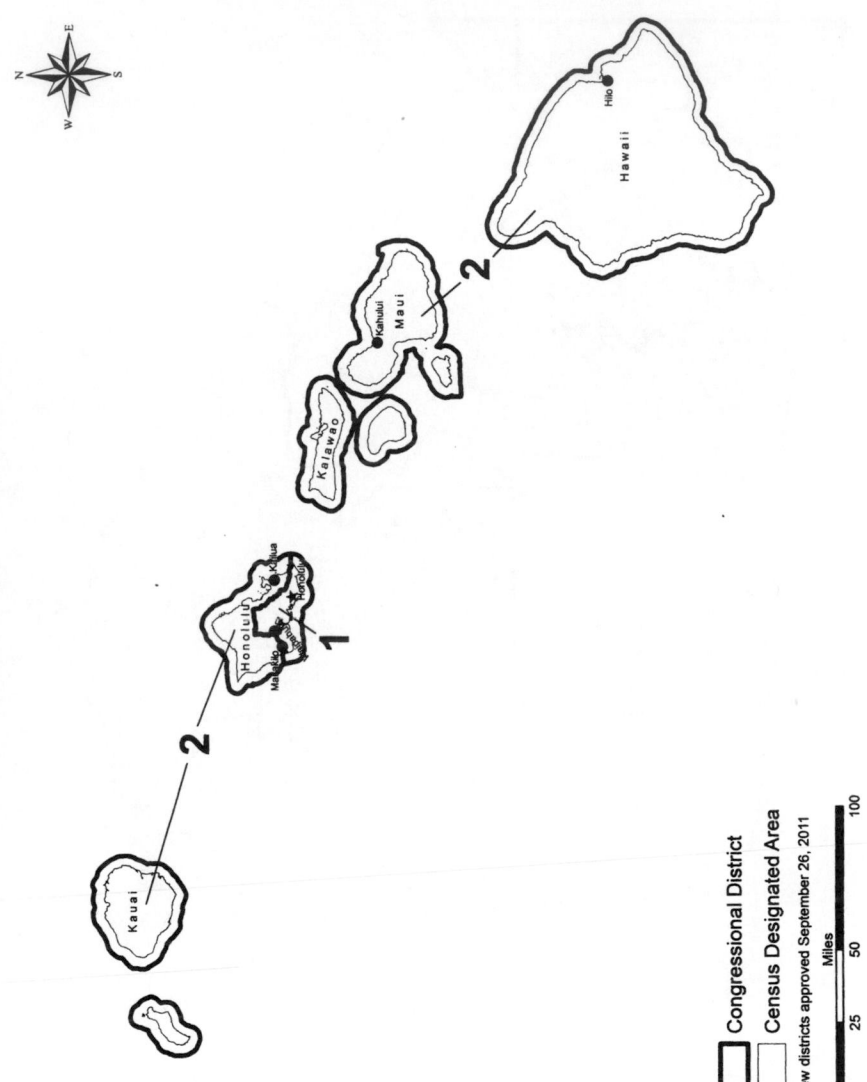

Congressional District

Census Designated Area

New districts approved September 26, 2011

IDAHO—Congressional Districts—(2 Districts)

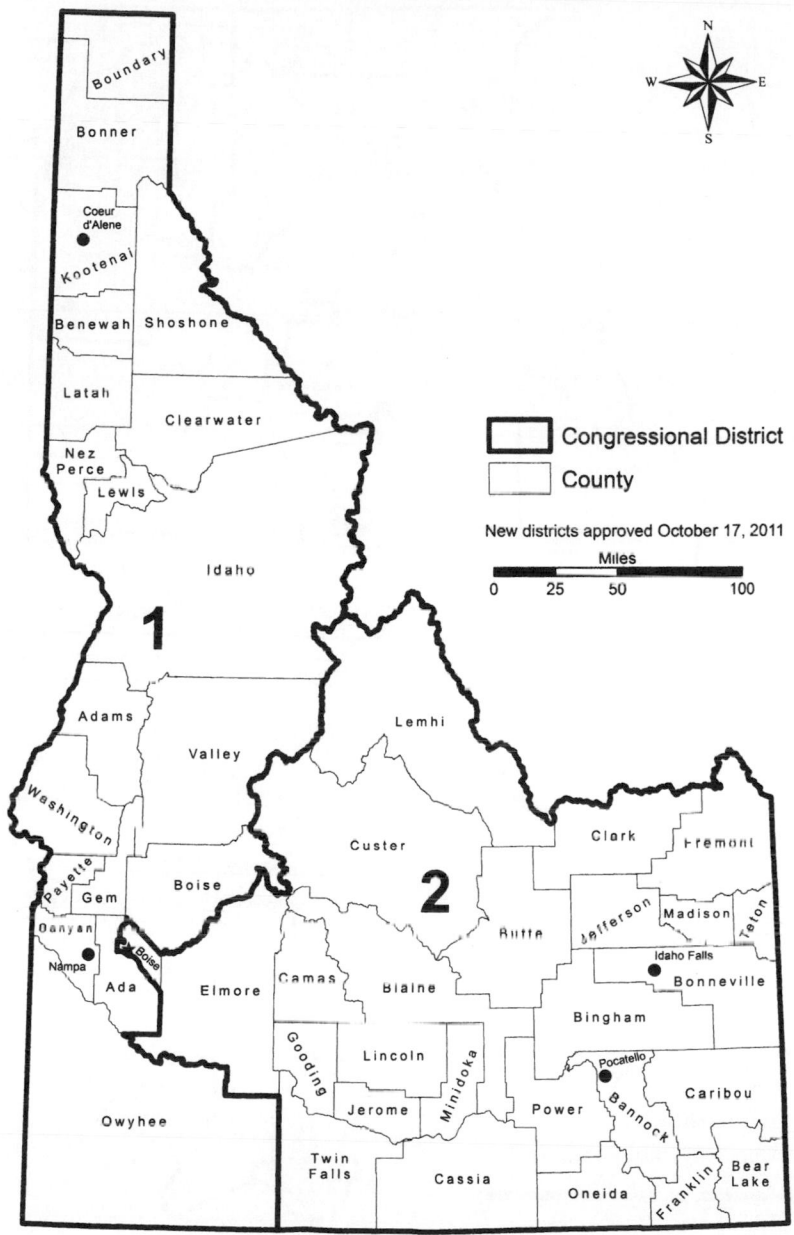

ILLINOIS—Congressional Districts—(18 Districts)

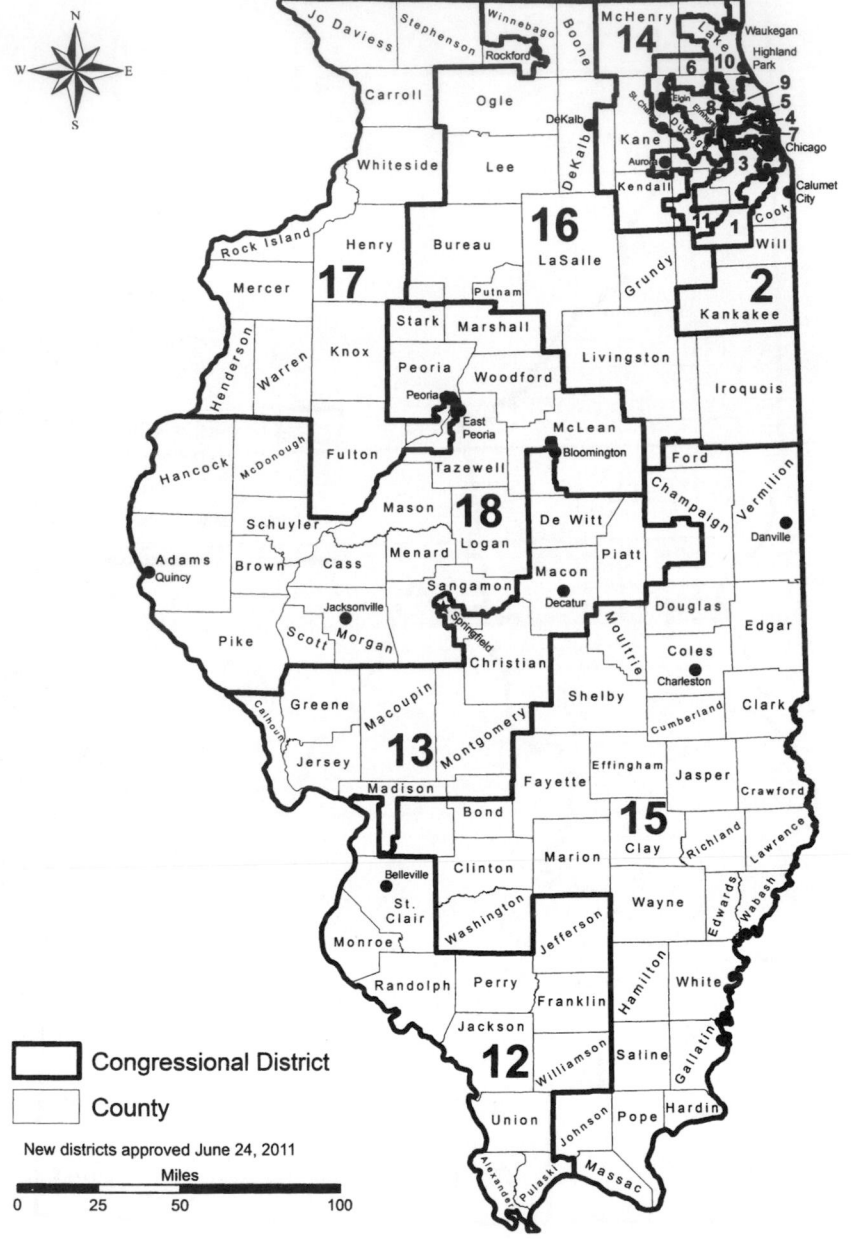

Congressional District

County

New districts approved June 24, 2011

Miles

0   25   50   100

INDIANA—Congressional Districts—(9 Districts)

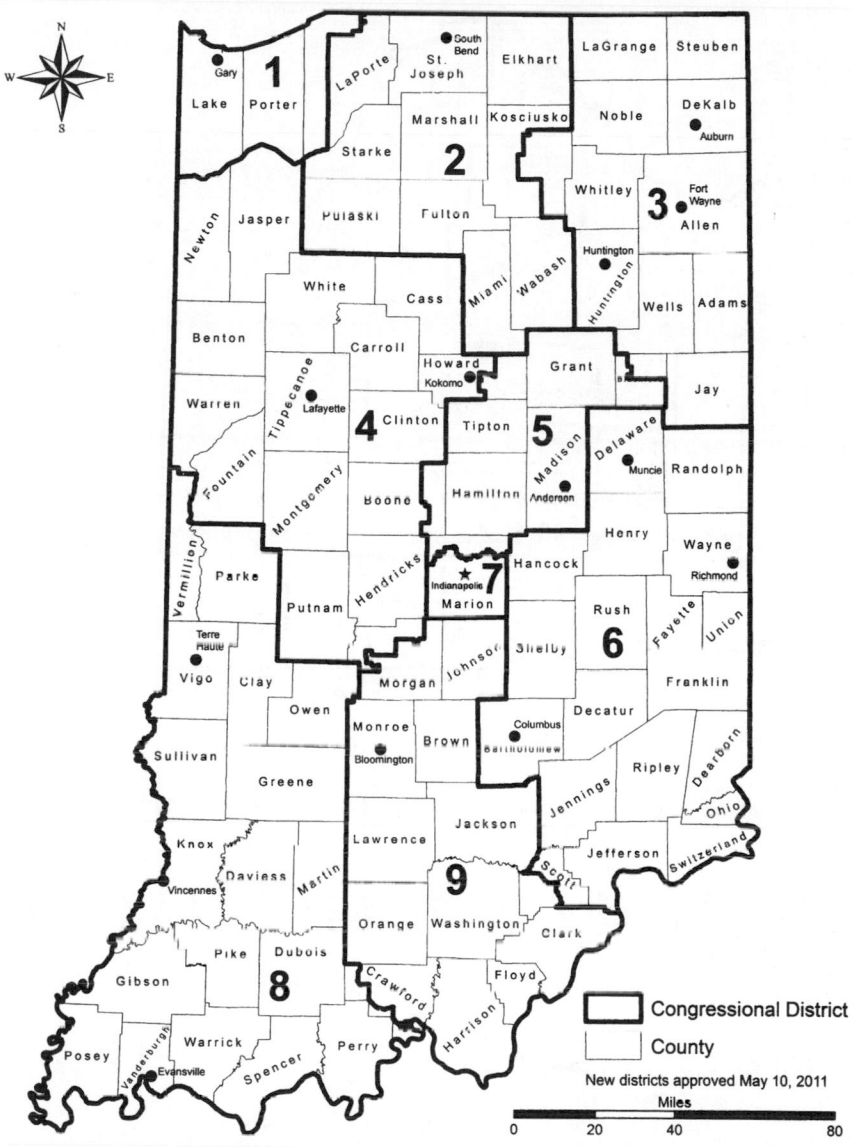

IOWA—Congressional Districts—(4 Districts)

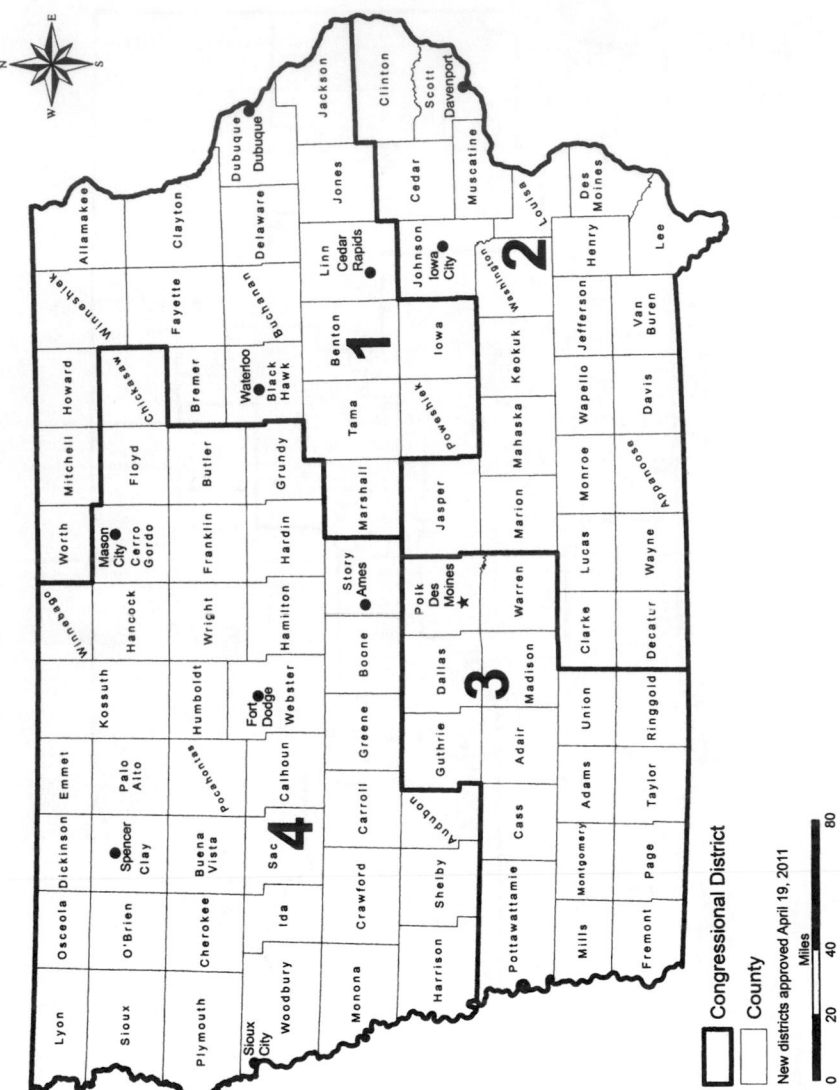

Congressional District

County

New districts approved April 19, 2011

Miles

0   20   40   80

KANSAS—Congressional Districts—(4 Districts)

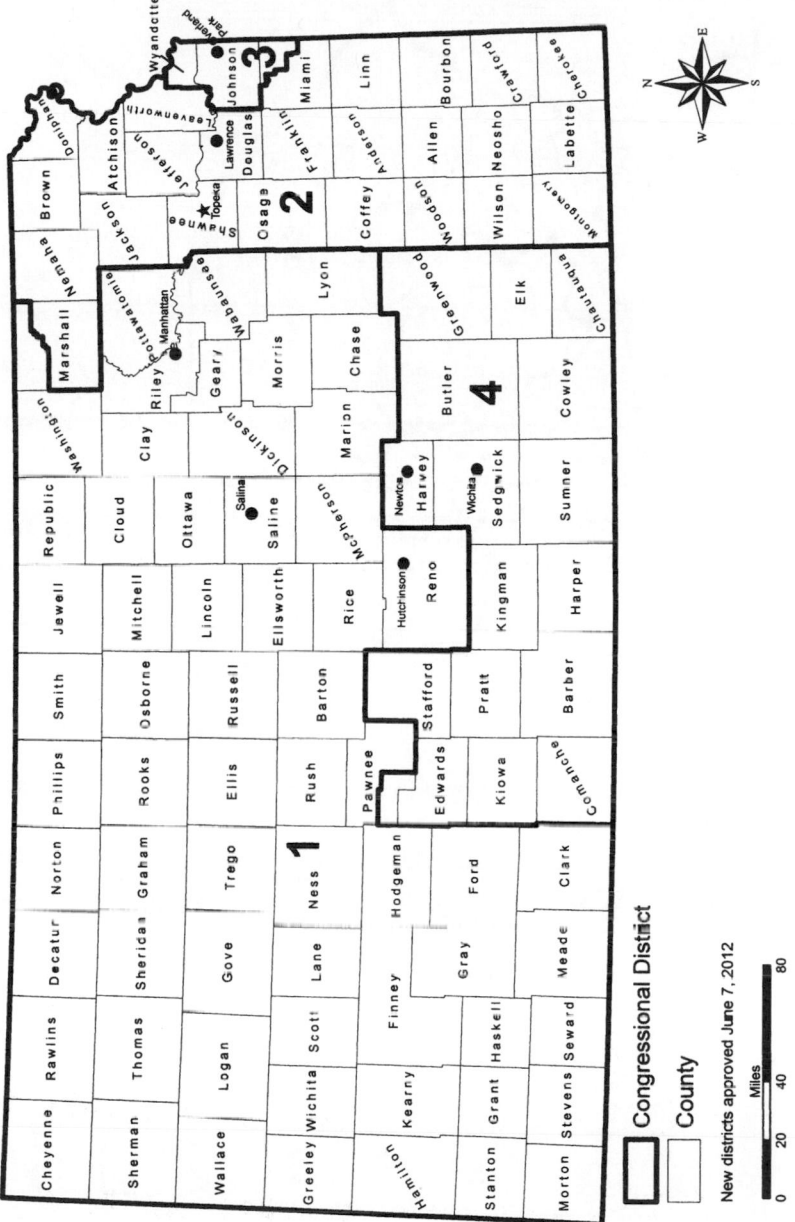

KENTUCKY—Congressional Districts—(6 Districts)

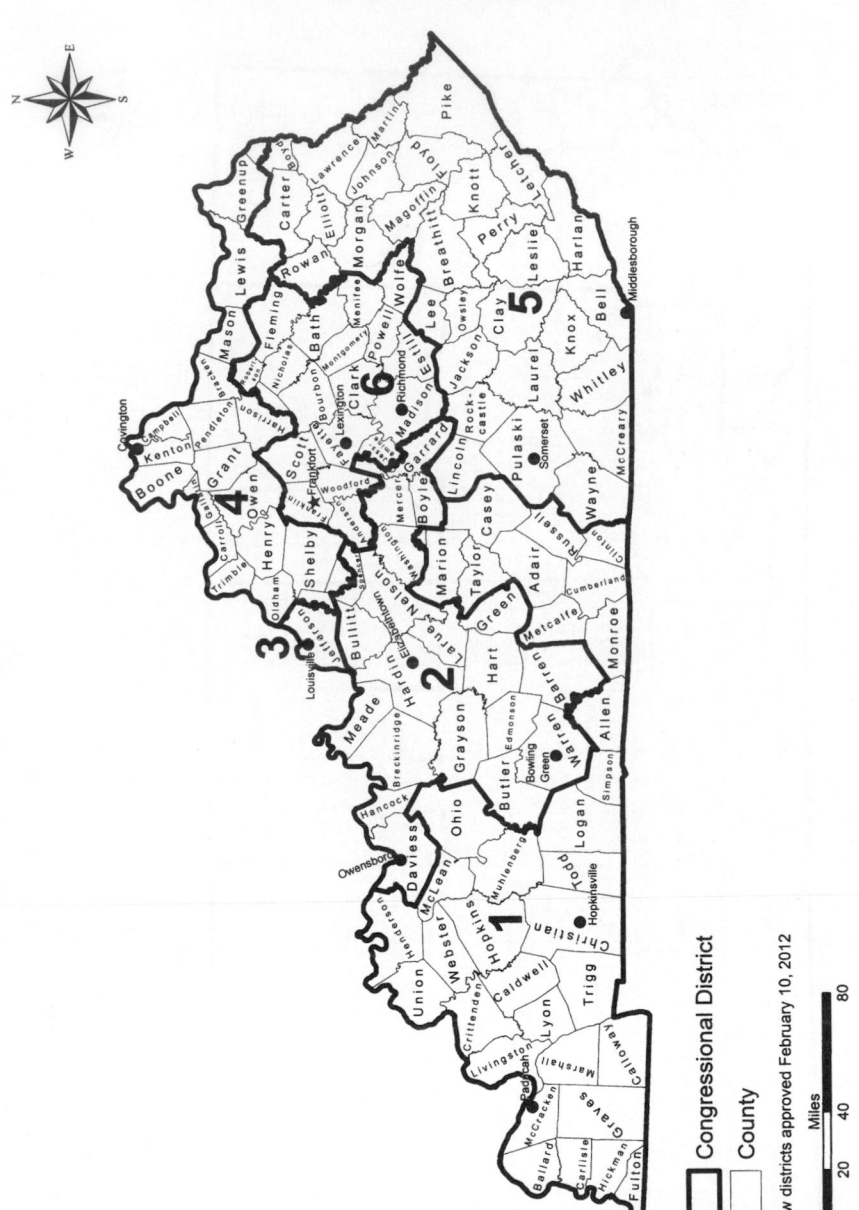

Congressional District

County

New districts approved February 10, 2012

Miles

LOUISIANA—Congressional Districts—(6 Districts)

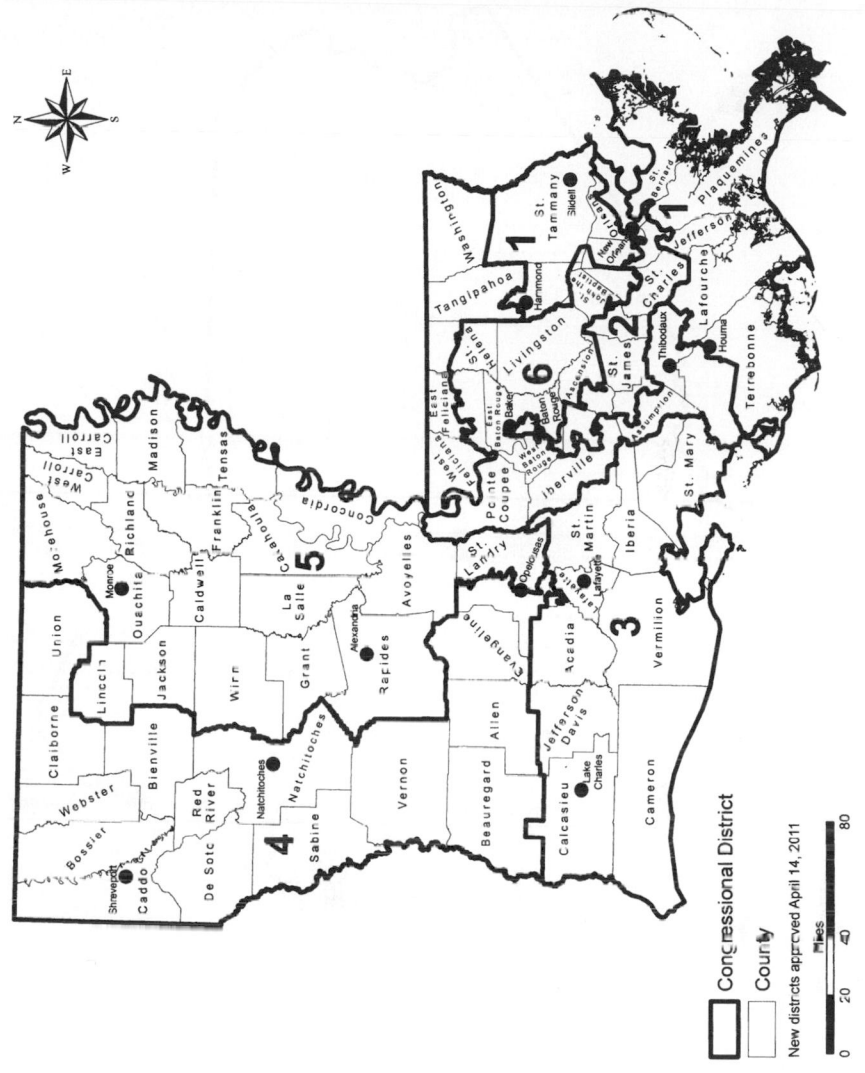

MAINE—Congressional Districts—(2 Districts)

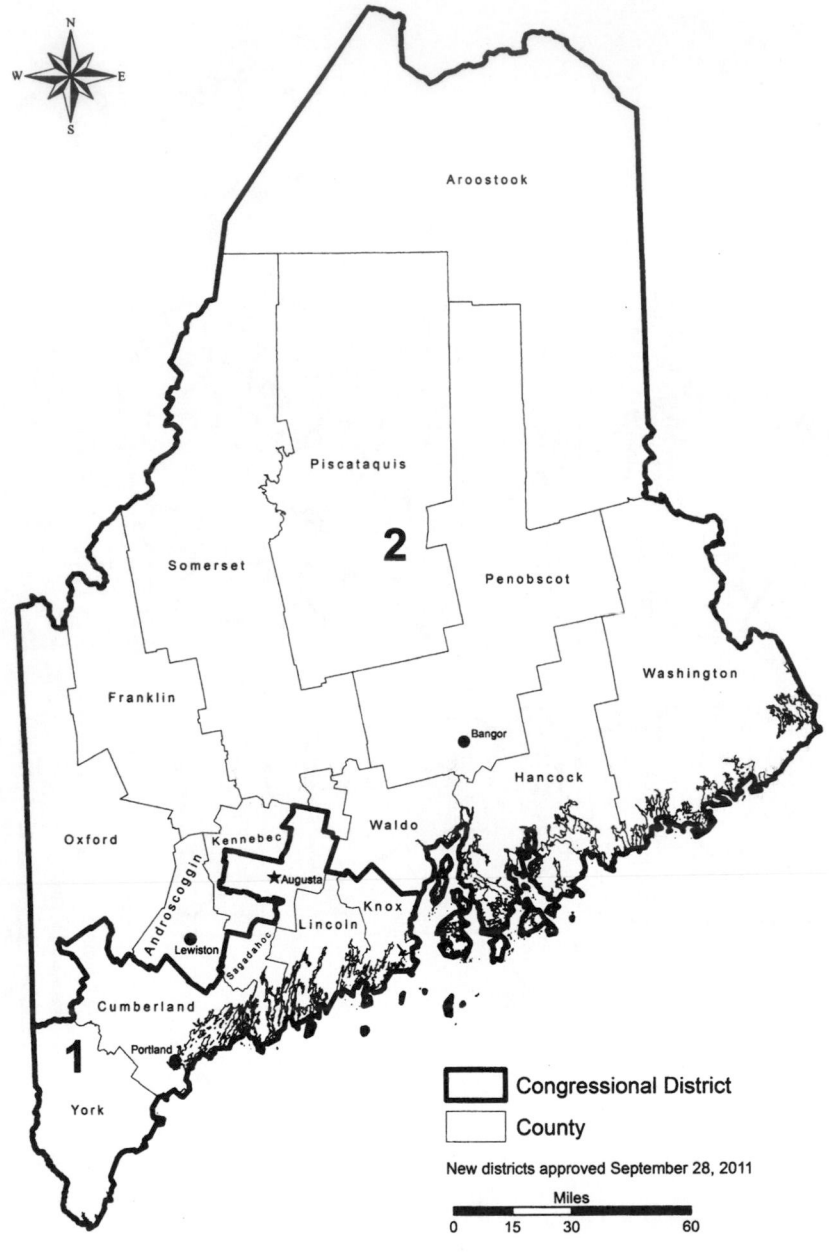

Congressional District

County

New districts approved September 28, 2011

Miles

0   15   30   60

MARYLAND—Congressional Districts—(8 Districts)

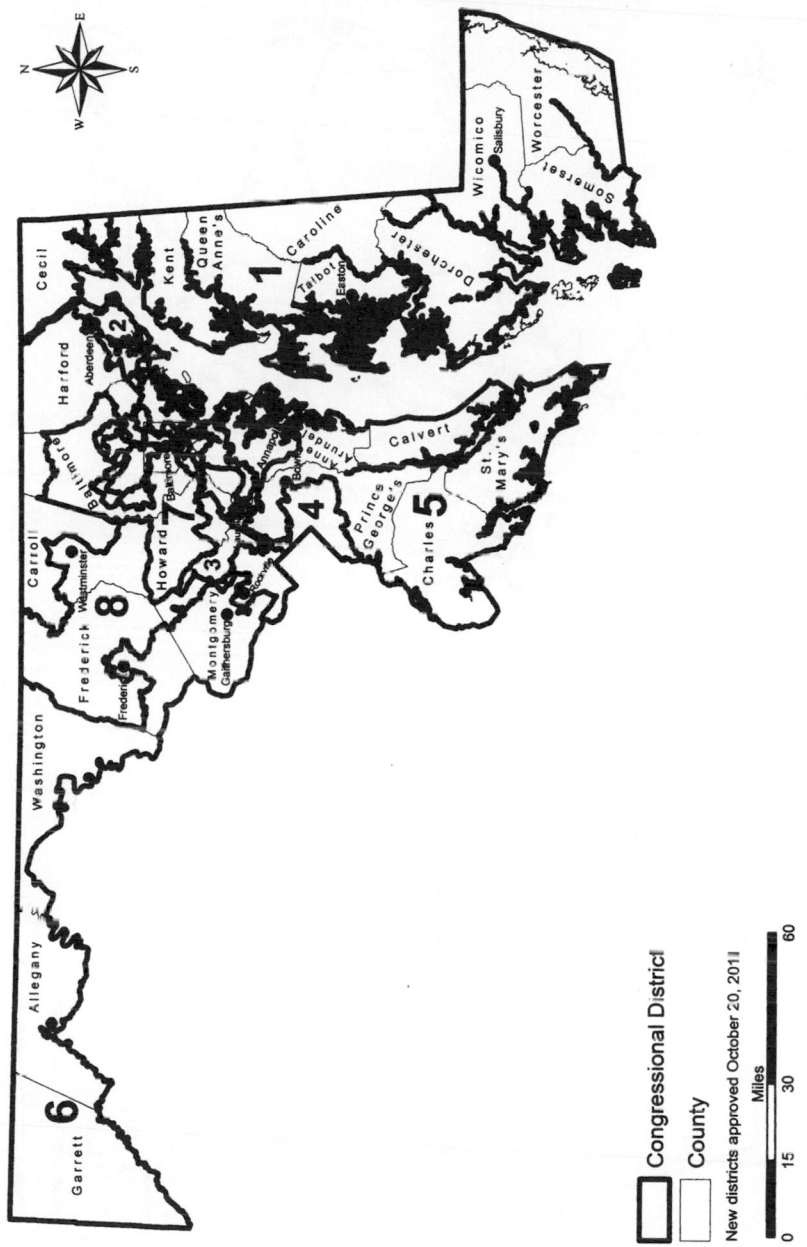

Congressional District

County

New districts approved October 20, 2011

Miles

0   15   30   60

MASSACHUSETTS—Congressional Districts—(9 Districts)

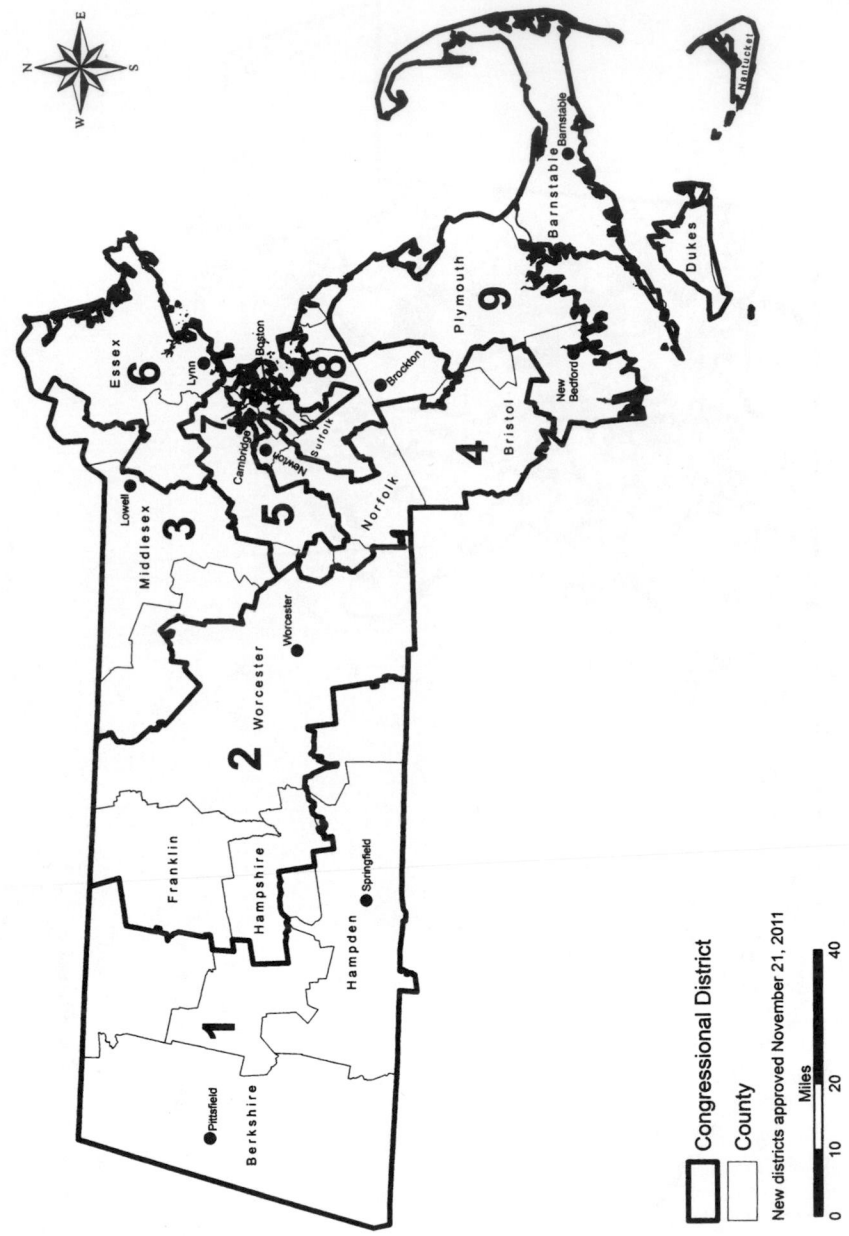

MICHIGAN—Congressional Districts—(14 Districts)

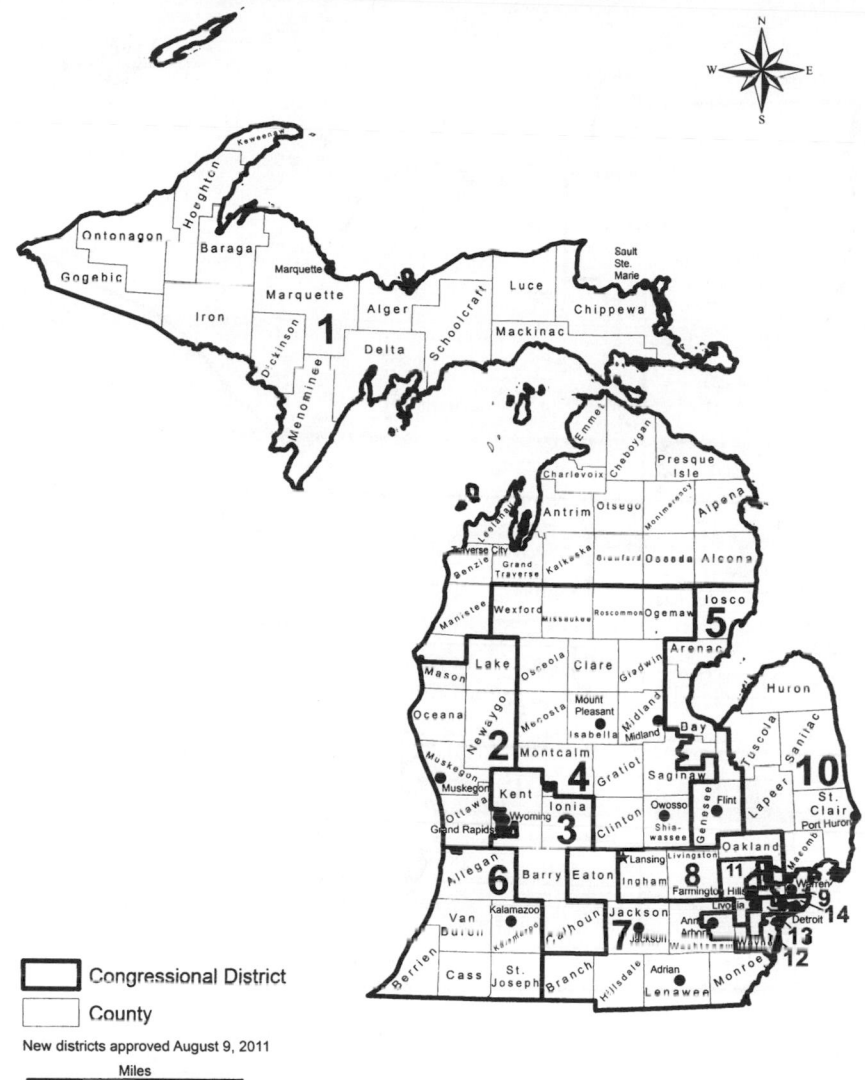

Congressional District

County

New districts approved August 9, 2011

Miles

0   25   50   100

MINNESOTA—Congressional Districts—(8 Districts)

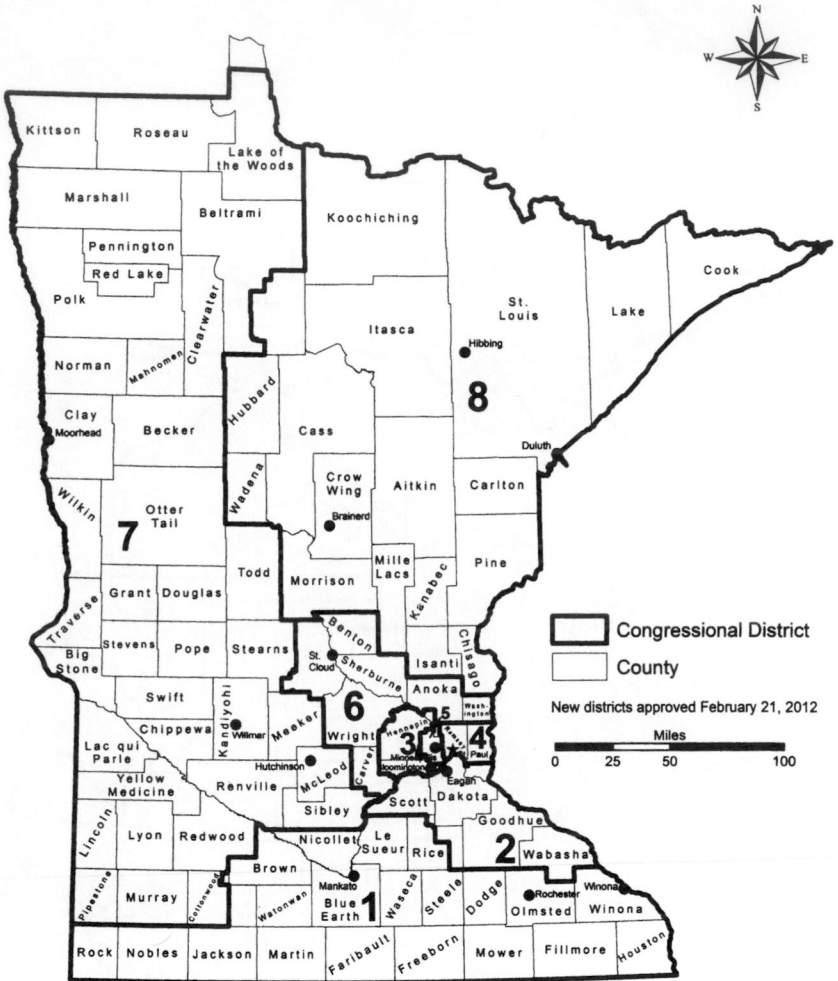

MISSISSIPPI—Congressional Districts—(4 Districts)

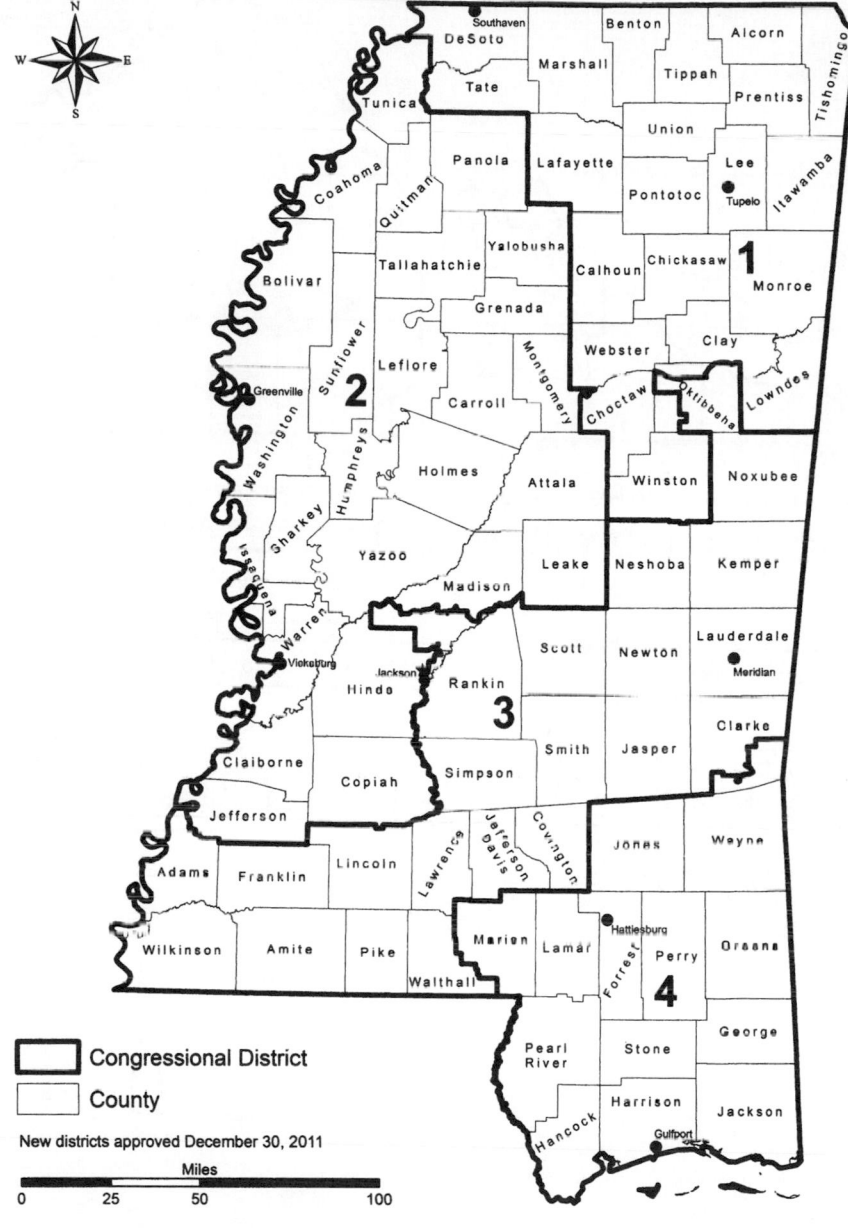

Congressional District

County

New districts approved December 30, 2011

Miles

0   25   50   100

MISSOURI—Congressional Districts—(8 Districts)

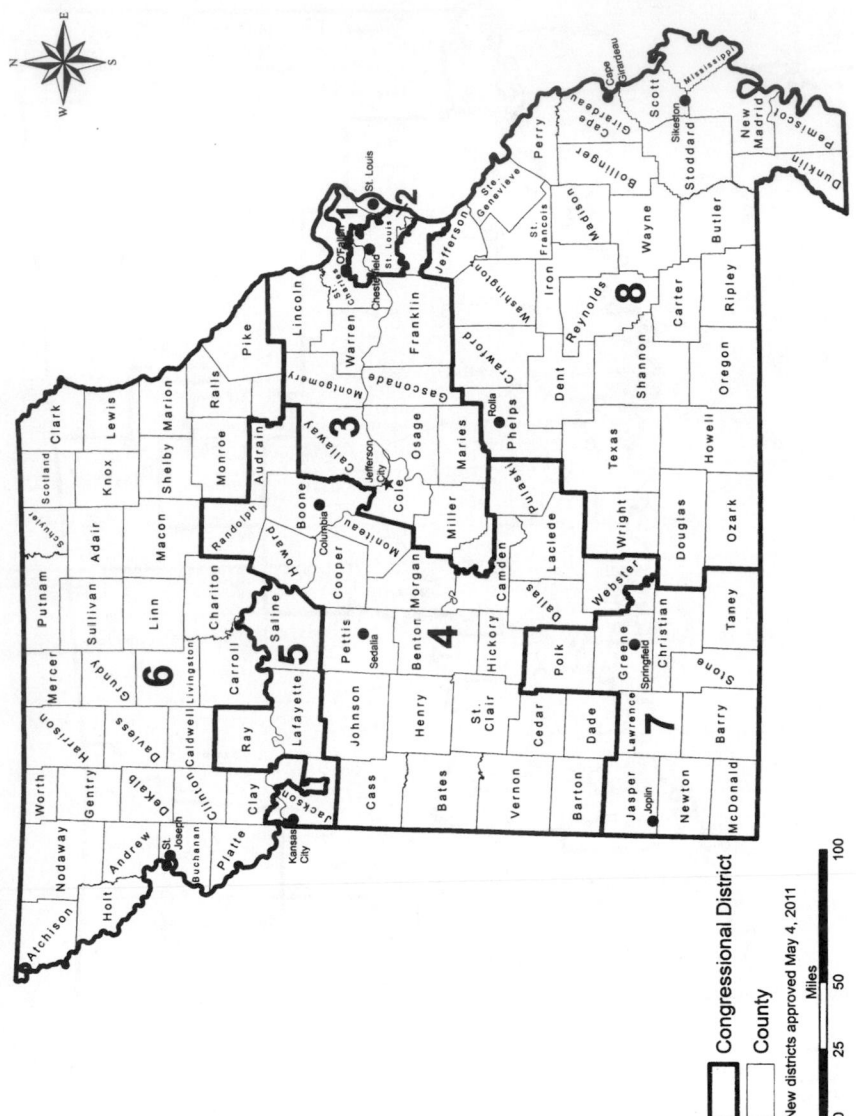

Congressional District

County

New districts approved May 4, 2011

Miles

0   25   50   100

MONTANA—Congressional District—(1 District At Large)

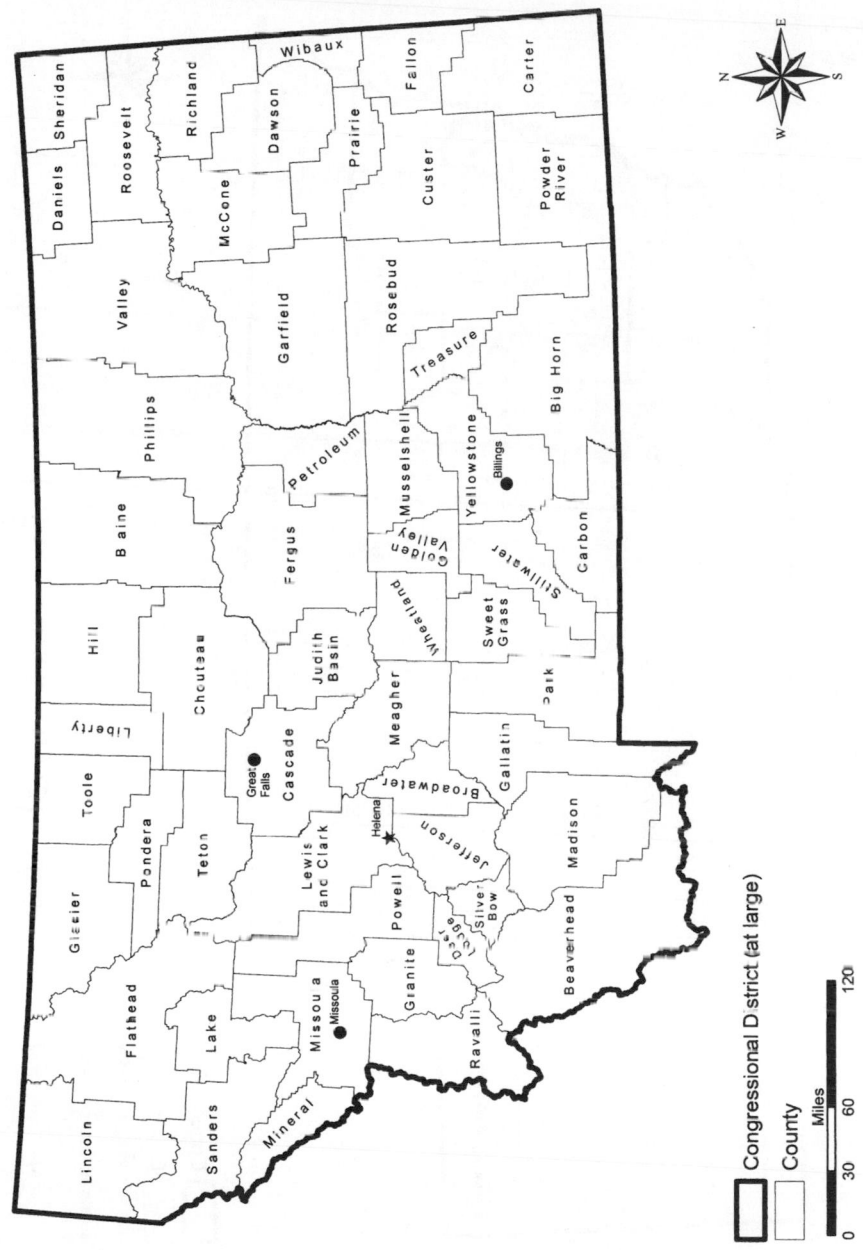

Congressional District (at large)

County

Miles

0 30 60 120

NEBRASKA—Congressional Districts—(3 Districts)

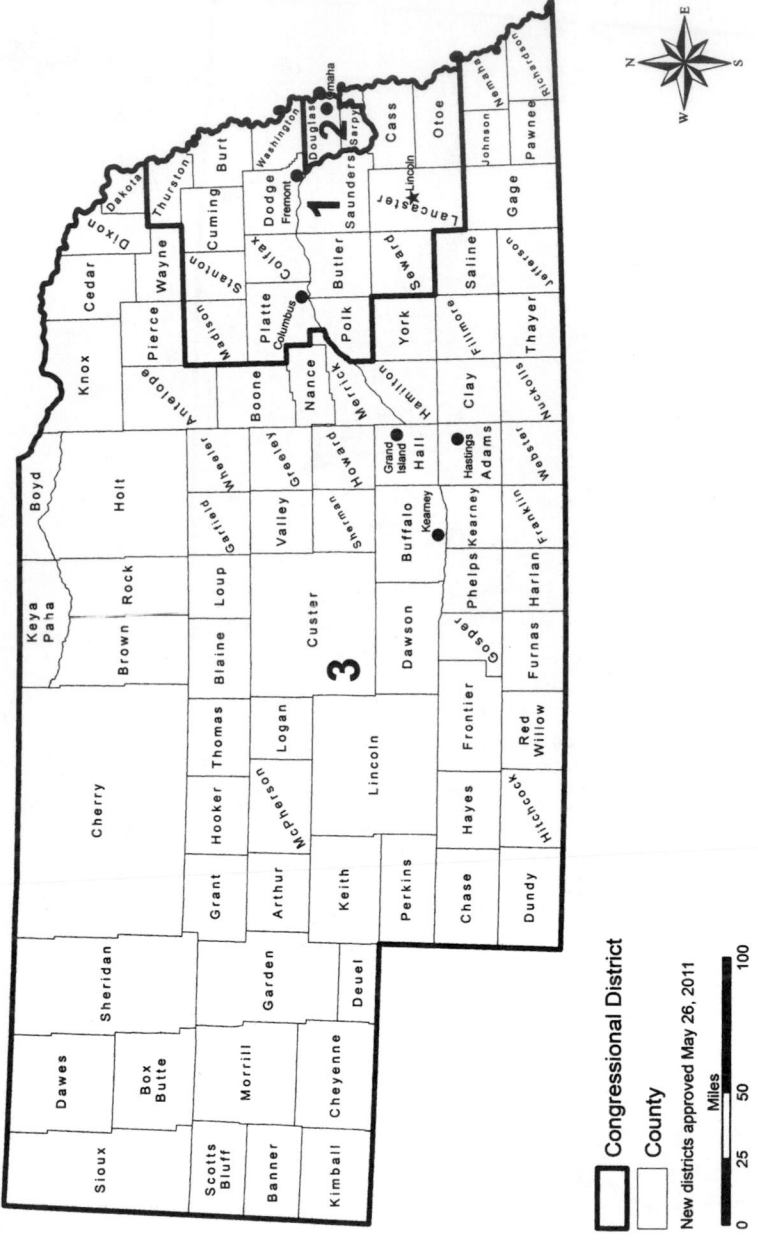

NEVADA—Congressional Districts—(4 Districts)

NEW HAMPSHIRE—Congressional Districts—(2 Districts)

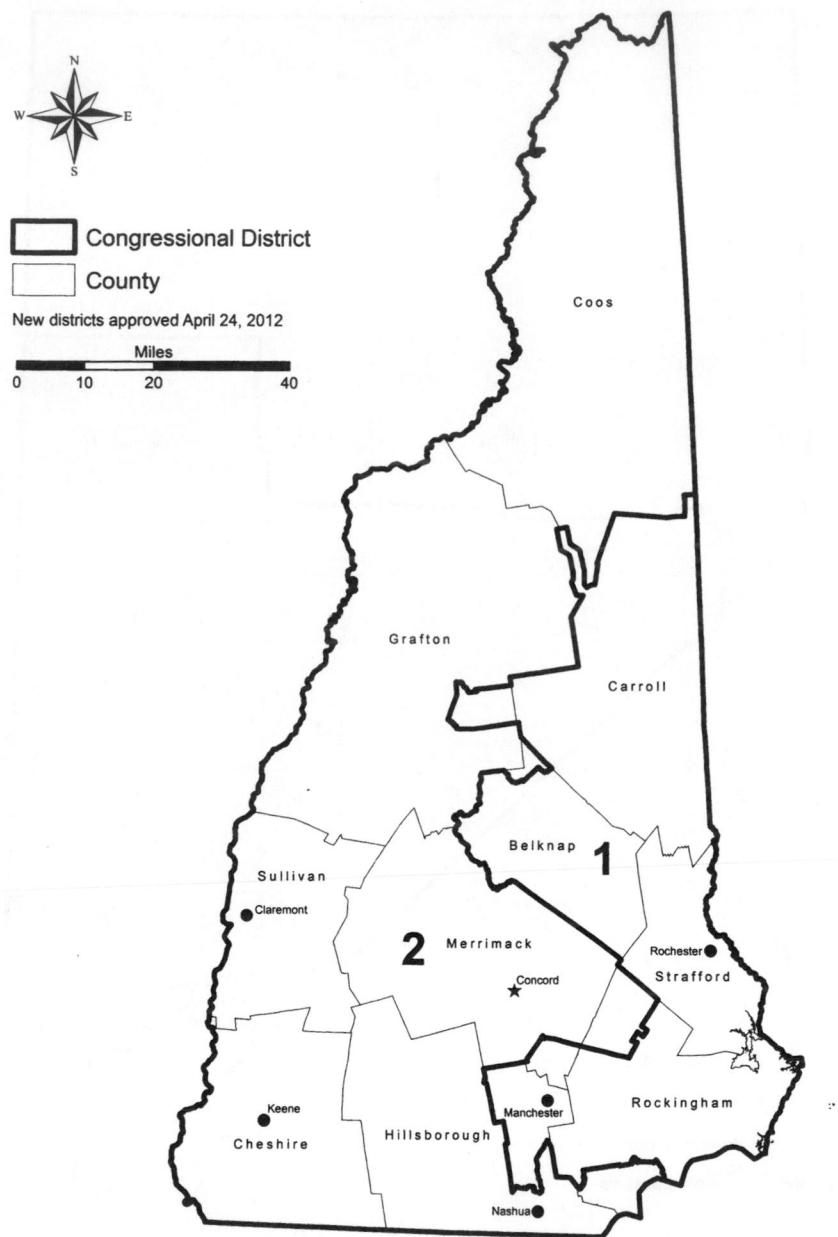

NEW JERSEY—Congressional Districts—(12 Districts)

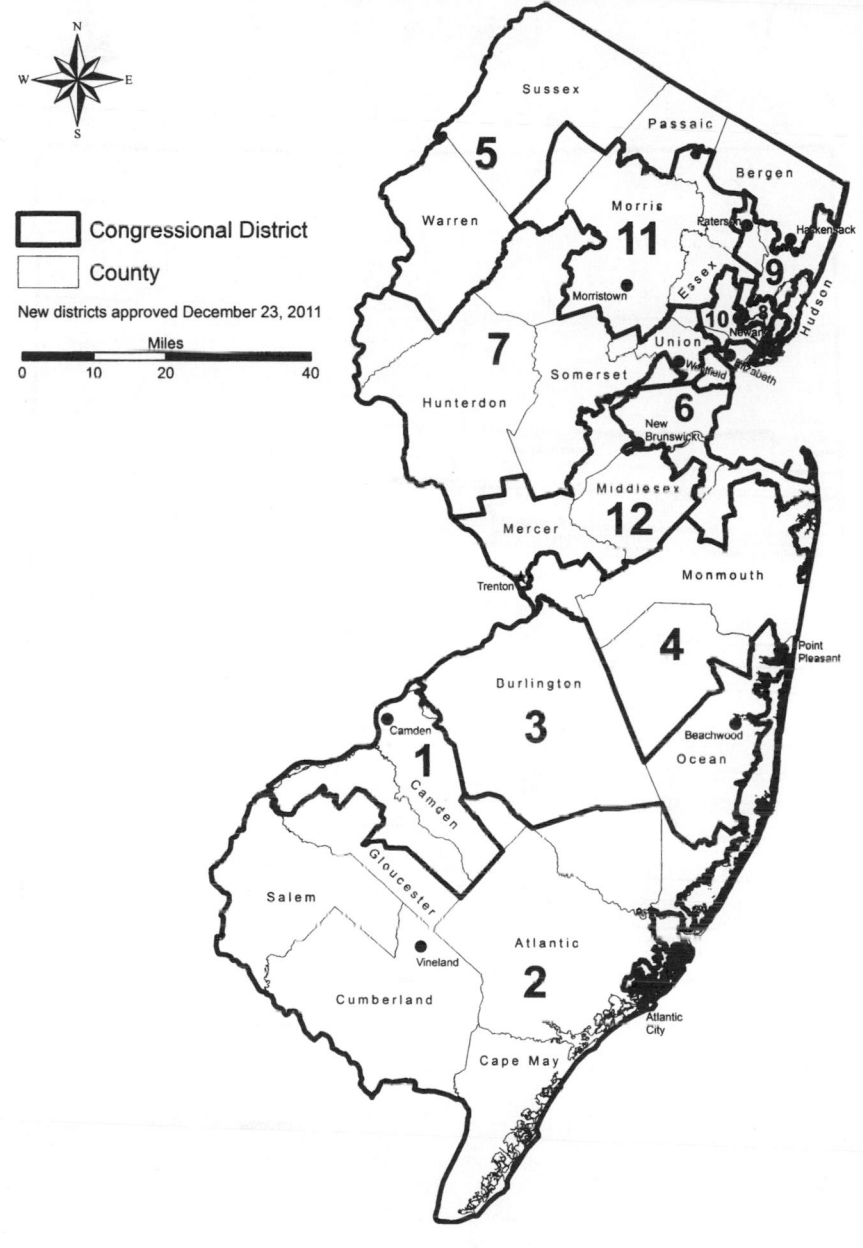

NEW MEXICO—Congressional Districts—(3 Districts)

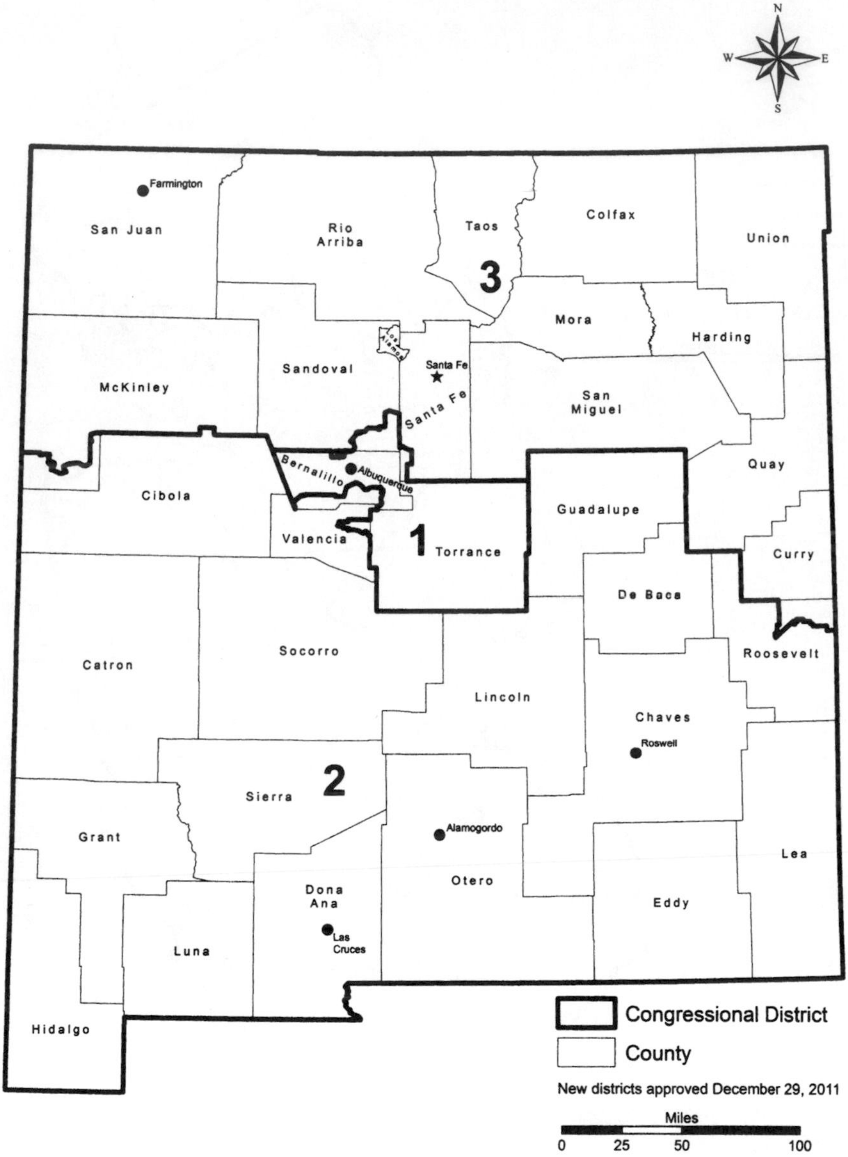

Farmington

San Juan

Rio Arriba

Taos

Colfax

Union

3

Mora

Harding

Sandoval

Santa Fe ★

Santa Fe

San Miguel

McKinley

Cibola

Bernalillo

Albuquerque

Quay

Guadalupe

Valencia

Torrance

1

Curry

De Baca

Socorro

Lincoln

Roosevelt

Catron

Chaves

Roswell

Sierra

2

Alamogordo

Grant

Lea

Dona Ana

Otero

Eddy

Luna

Las Cruces

Hidalgo

☐ Congressional District

☐ County

New districts approved December 29, 2011

Miles

0   25   50   100

NEW YORK—Congressional Districts—(27 Districts)

NORTH CAROLINA—Congressional Districts—(13 Districts)

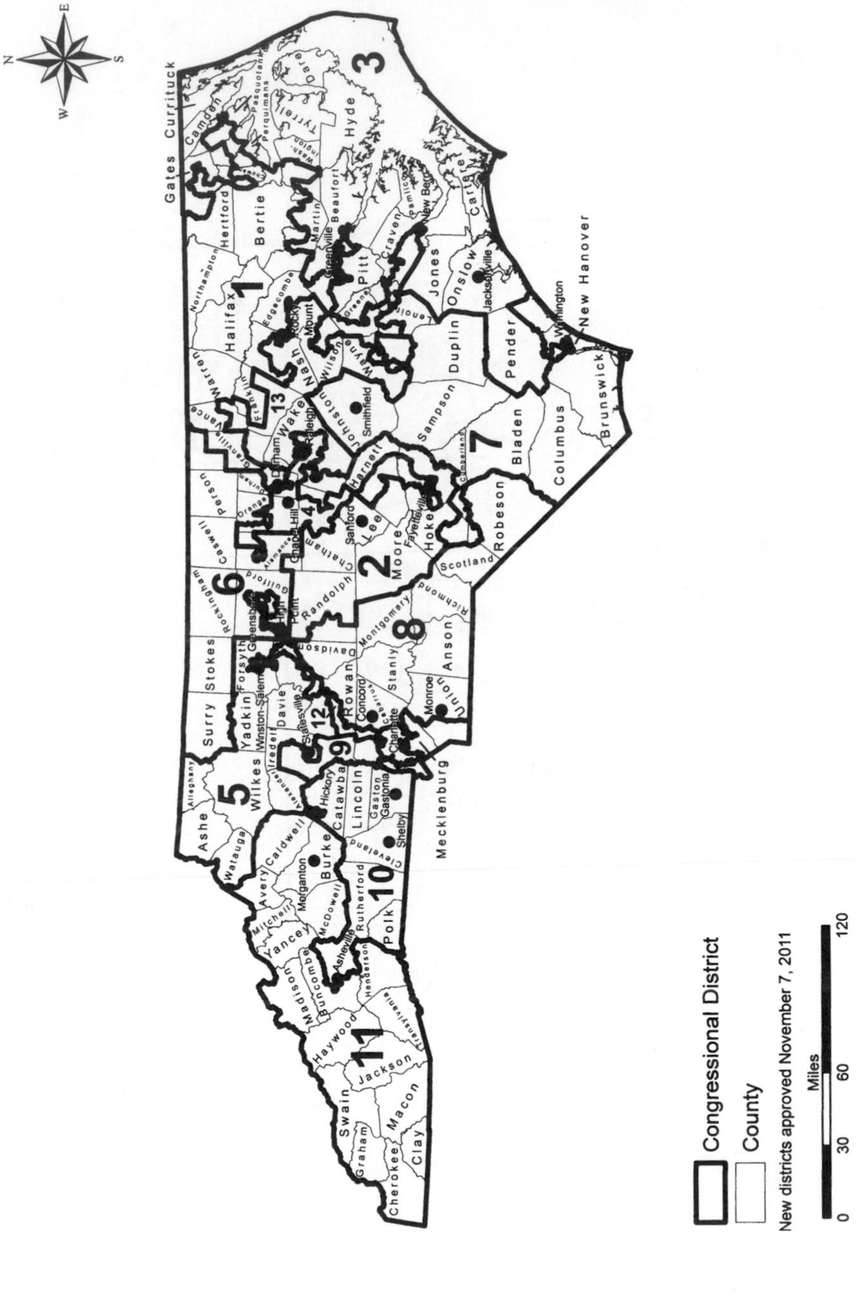

NORTH DAKOTA—Congressional District—(1 District At Large)

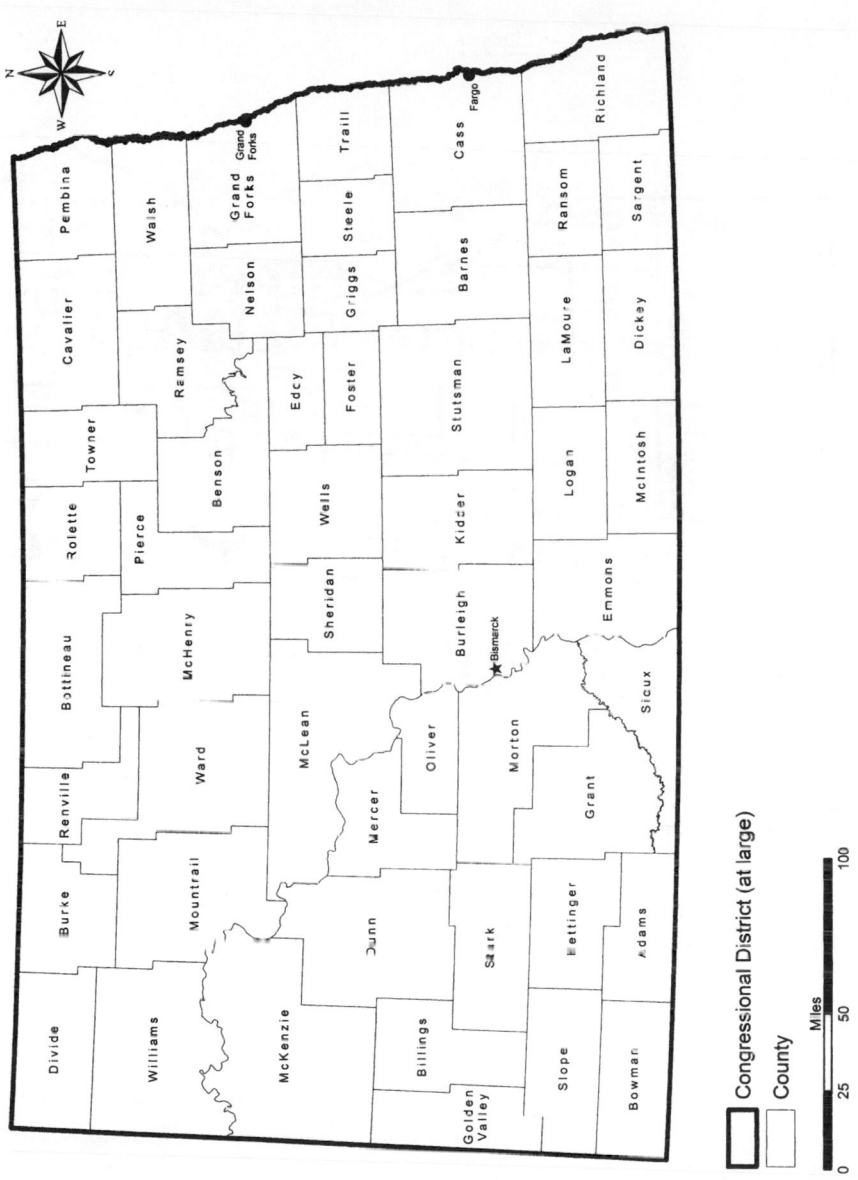

OHIO—Congressional Districts—(16 Districts)

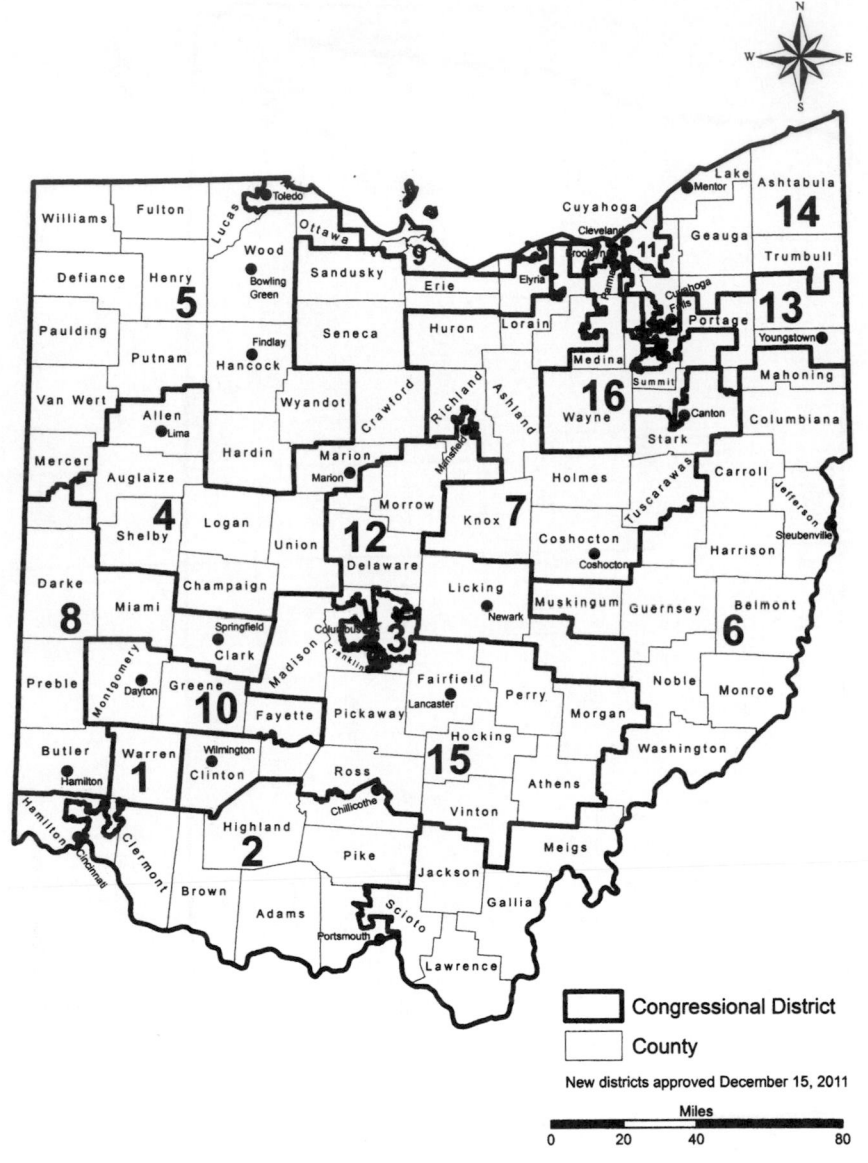

Congressional District

County

New districts approved December 15, 2011

Miles

0   20   40   80

OKLAHOMA—Congressional Districts—(5 Districts)

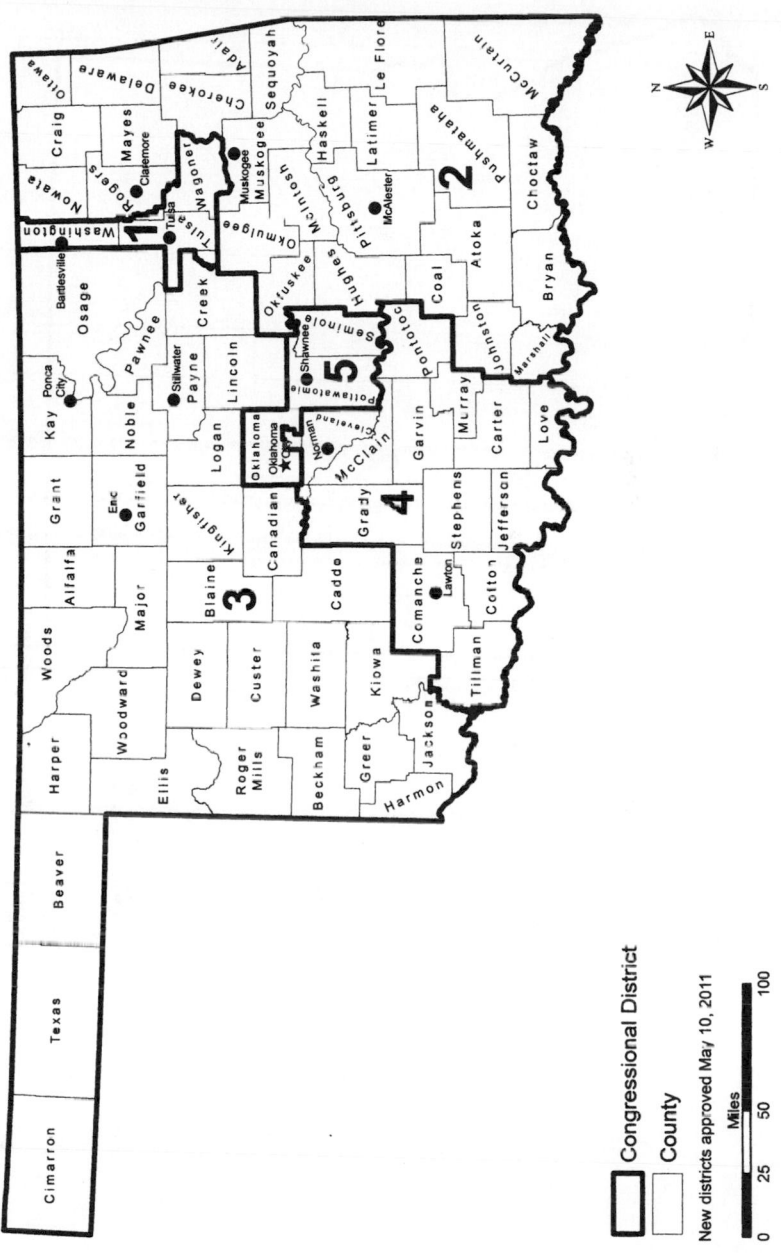

OREGON—Congressional Districts—(5 Districts)

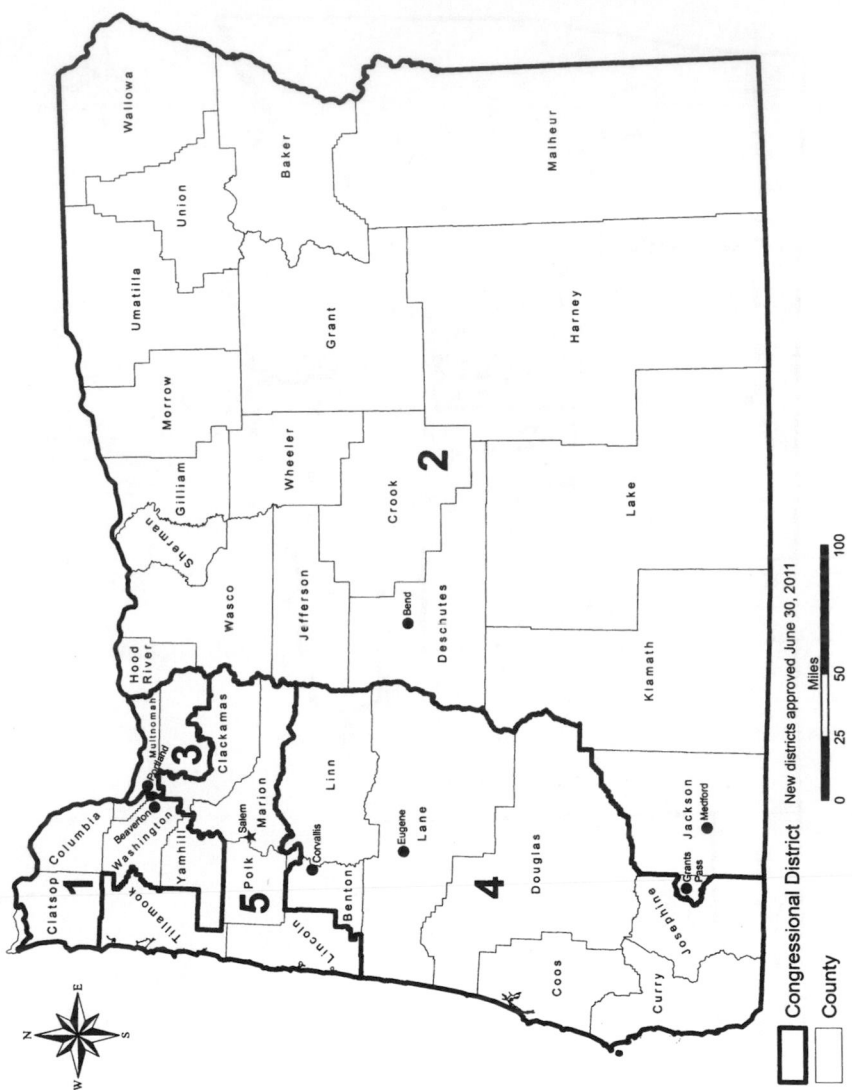

PENNSYLVANIA—Congressional Districts—(18 Districts)

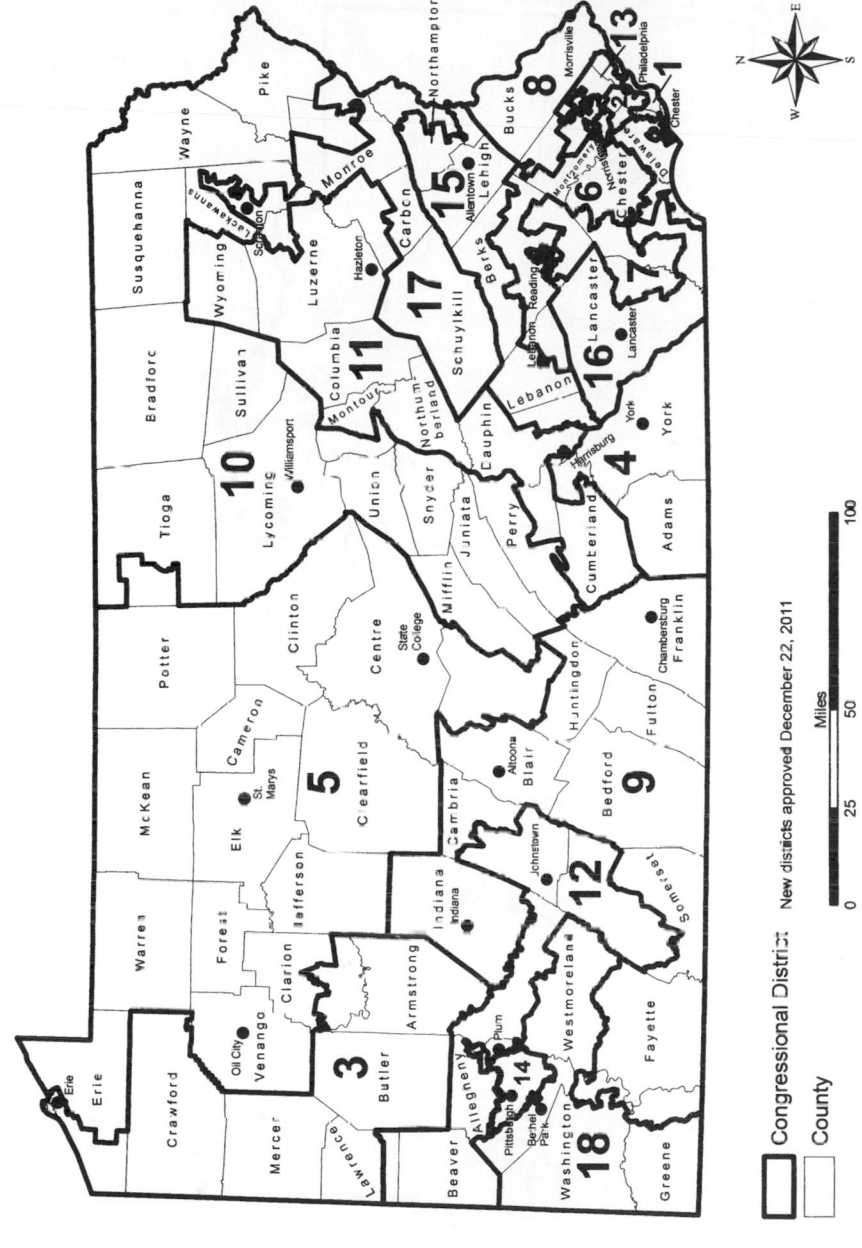

RHODE ISLAND—Congressional Districts—(2 Districts)

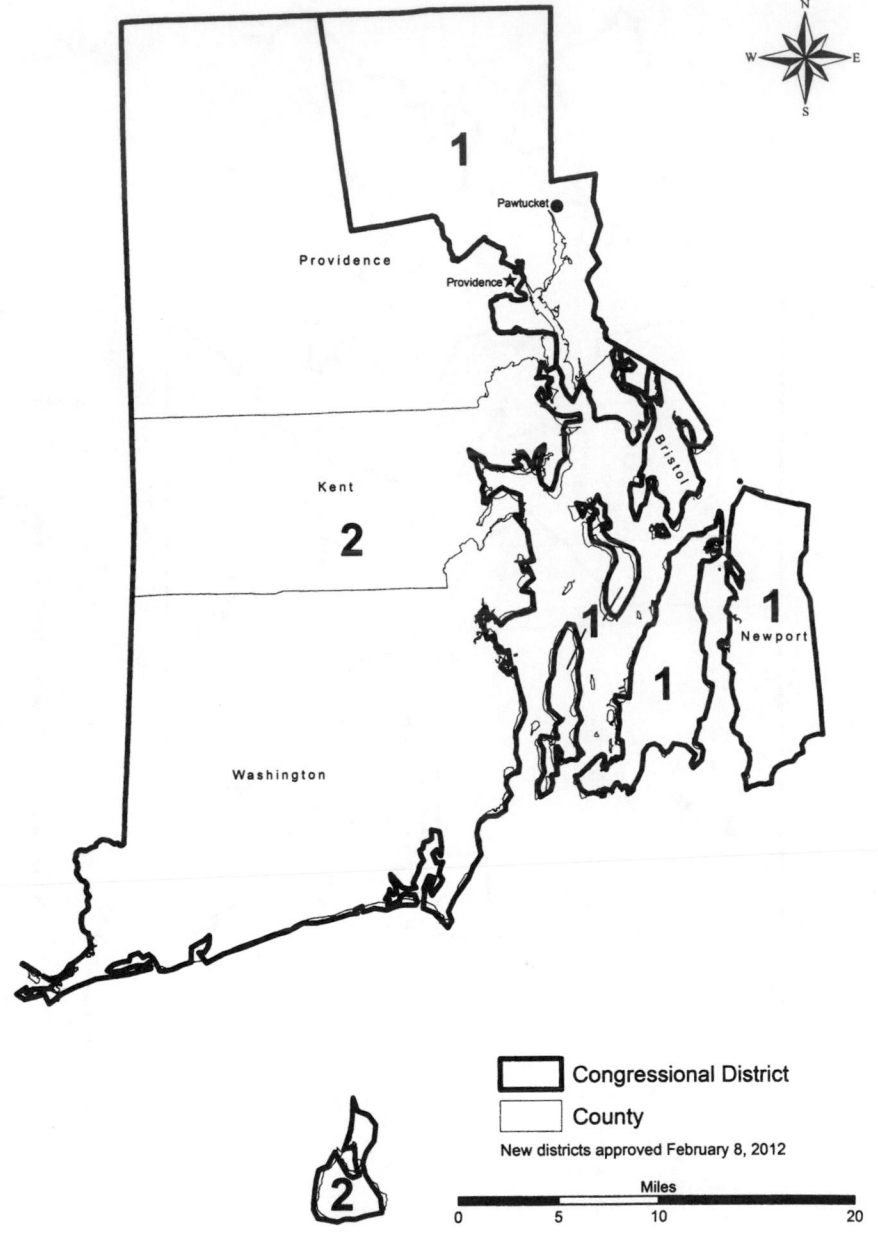

SOUTH CAROLINA—Congressional Districts—(7 Districts)

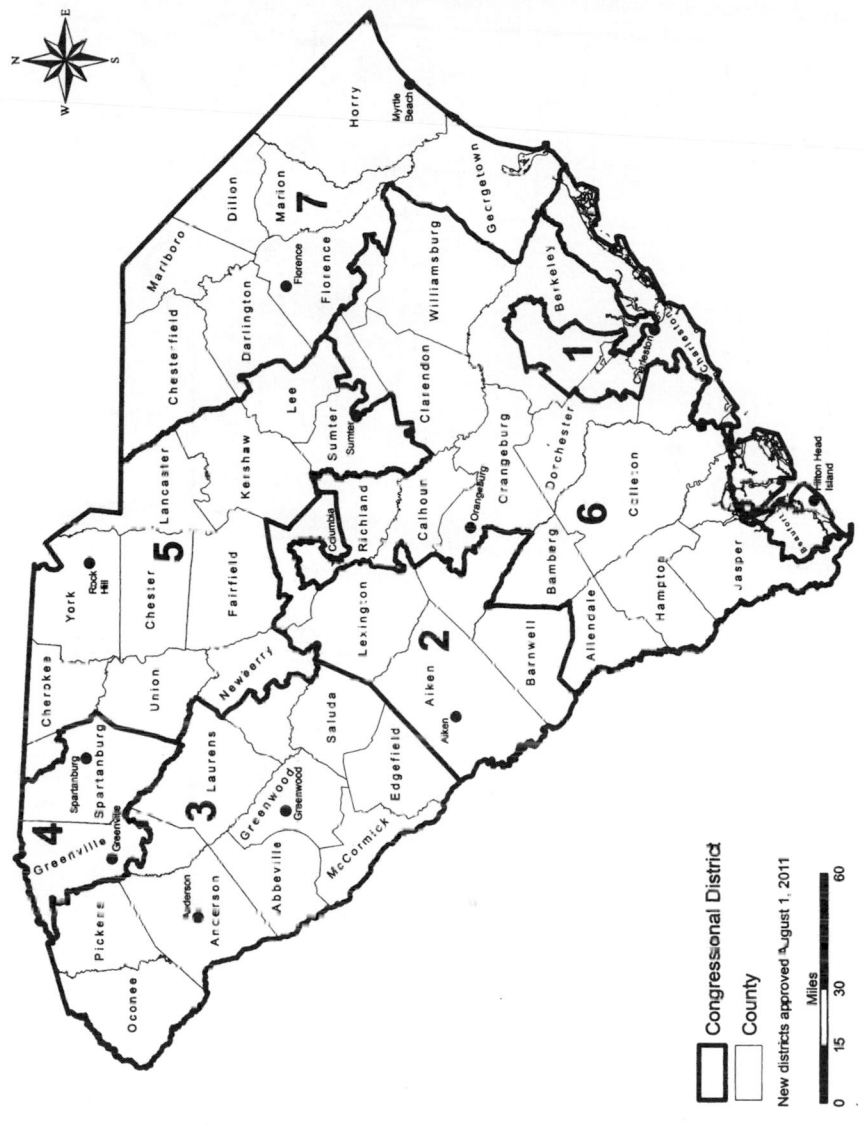

SOUTH DAKOTA—Congressional District—(1 District At Large)

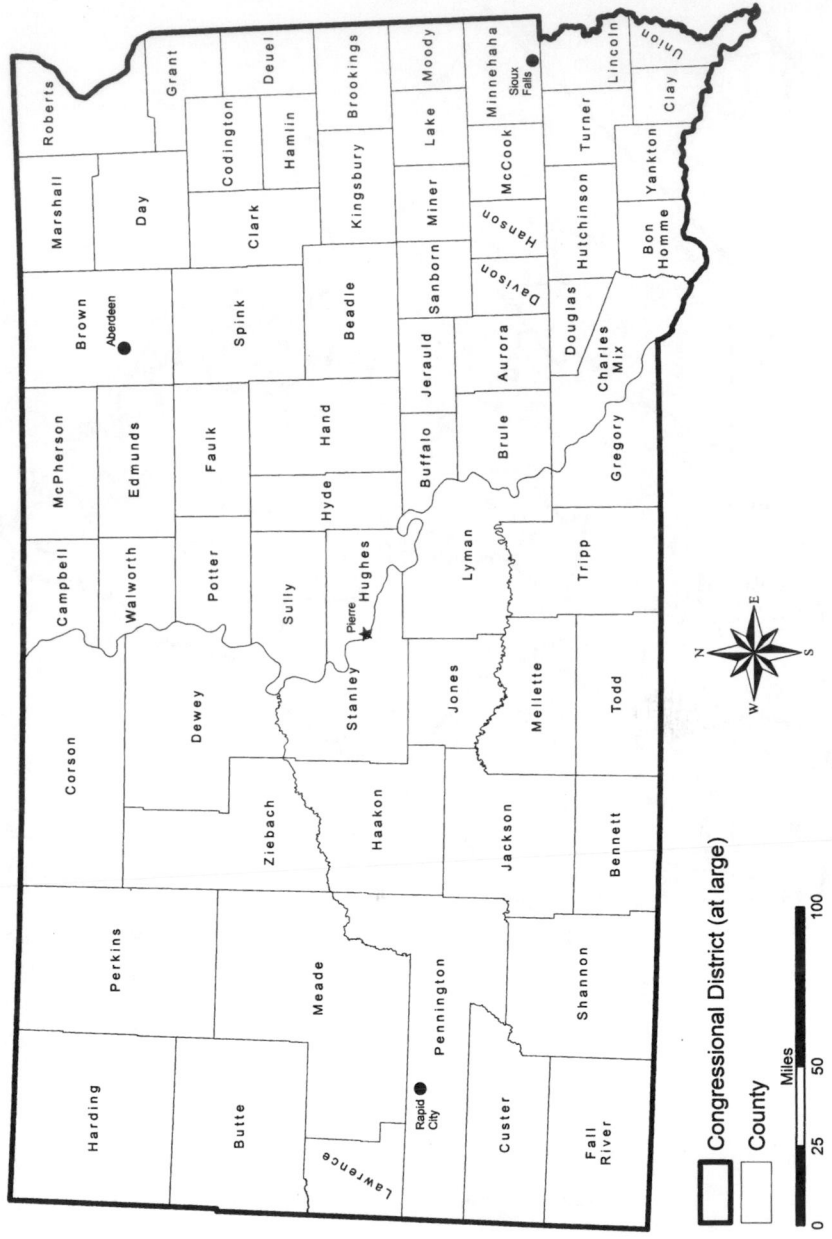

TENNESSEE—Congressional Districts—(9 Districts)

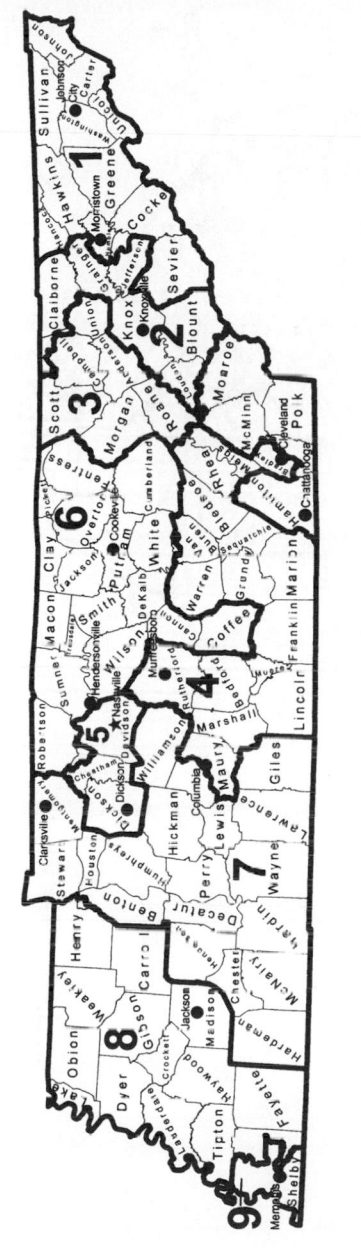

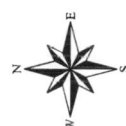

Congressional District

County

New districts approved January 26, 2012

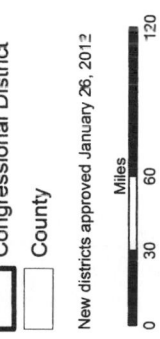

TEXAS—Congressional Districts—(36 Districts)

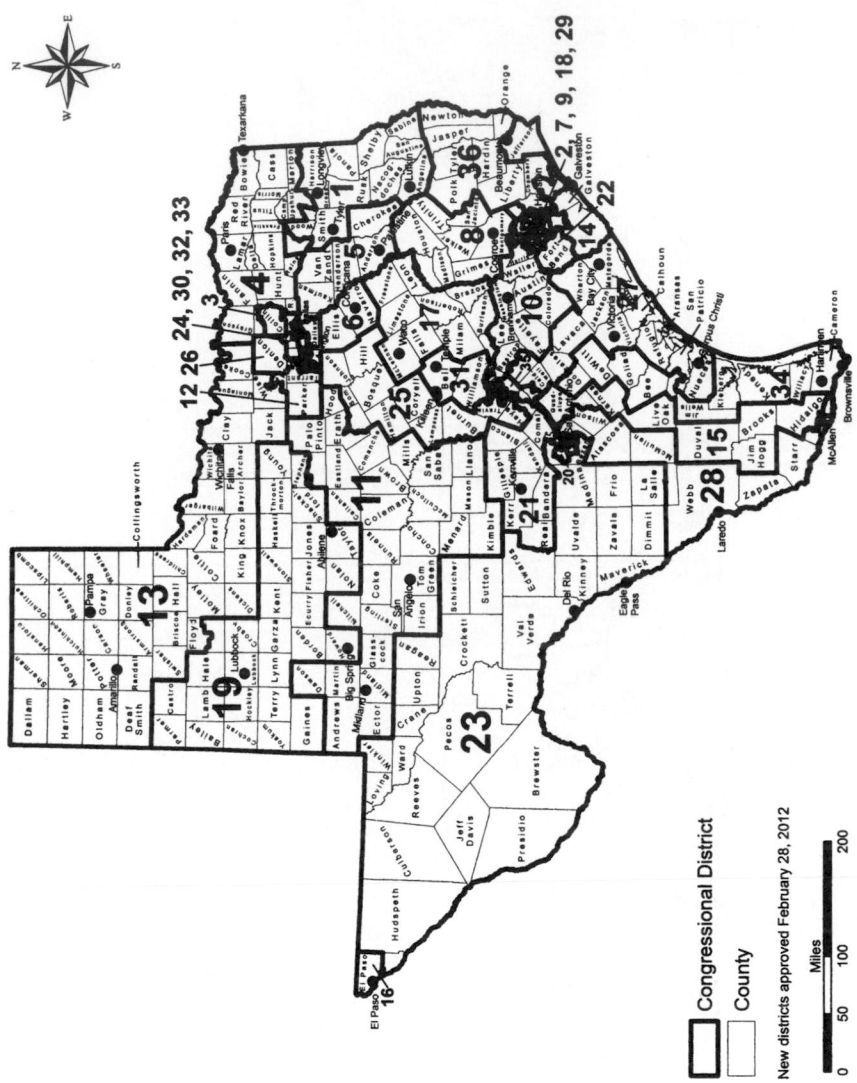

UTAH—Congressional Districts—(4 Districts)

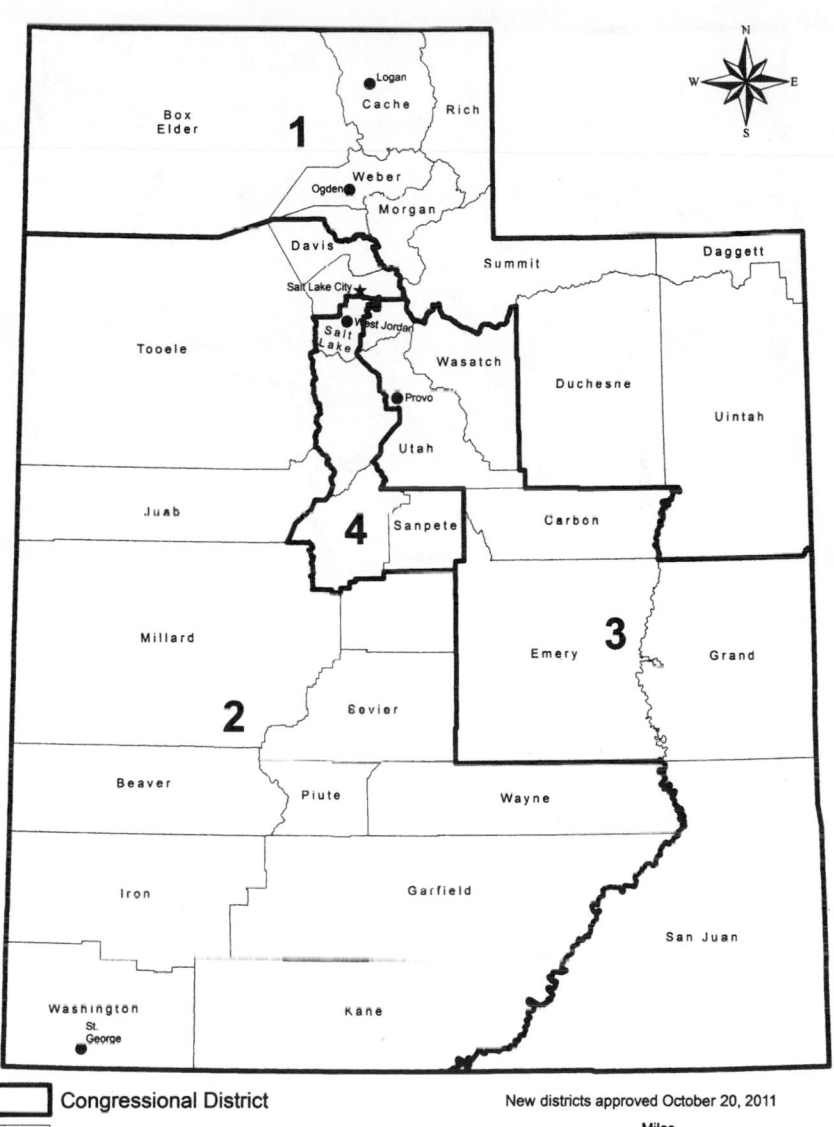

Congressional District

County

New districts approved October 20, 2011

Miles
0   25   50   100

VERMONT—Congressional District—(1 District At Large)

VIRGINIA—Congressional Districts—(11 Districts)

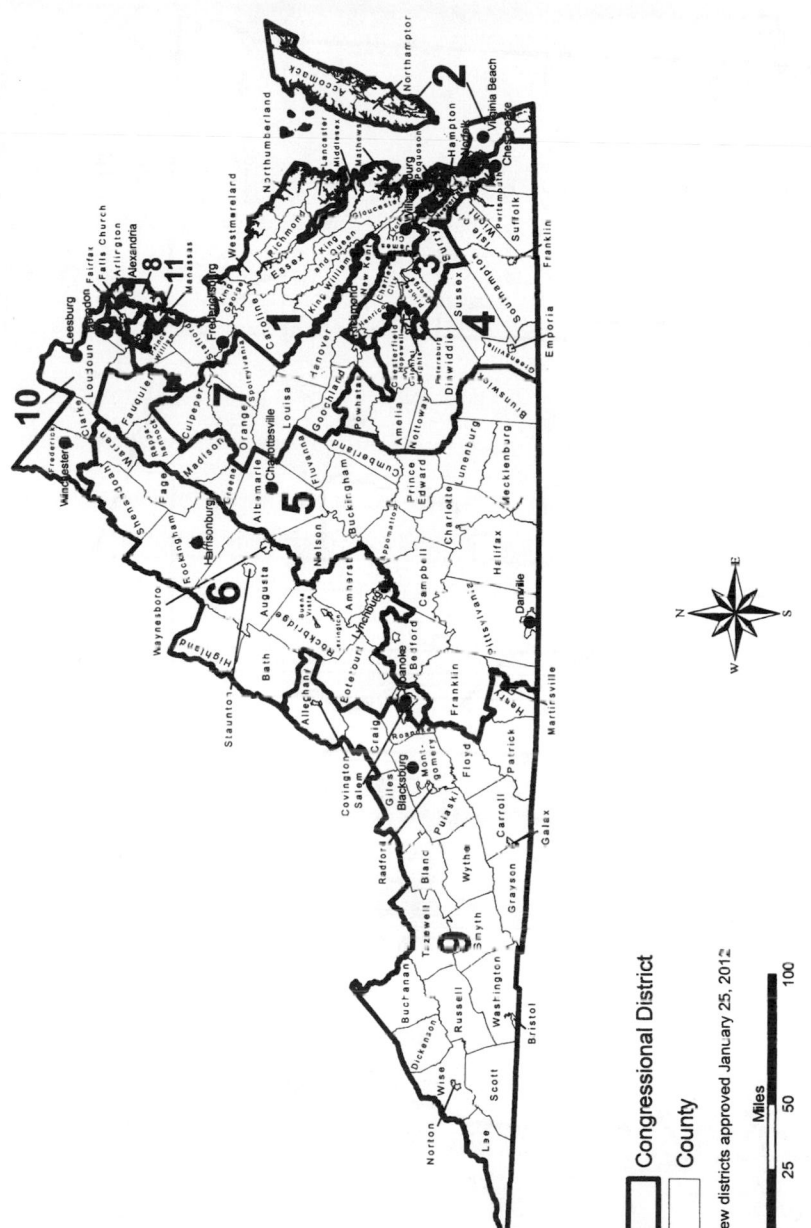

Congressional District

County

New districts approved January 25, 2012

Miles

0   25   50   100

WASHINGTON—Congressional Districts—(10 Districts)

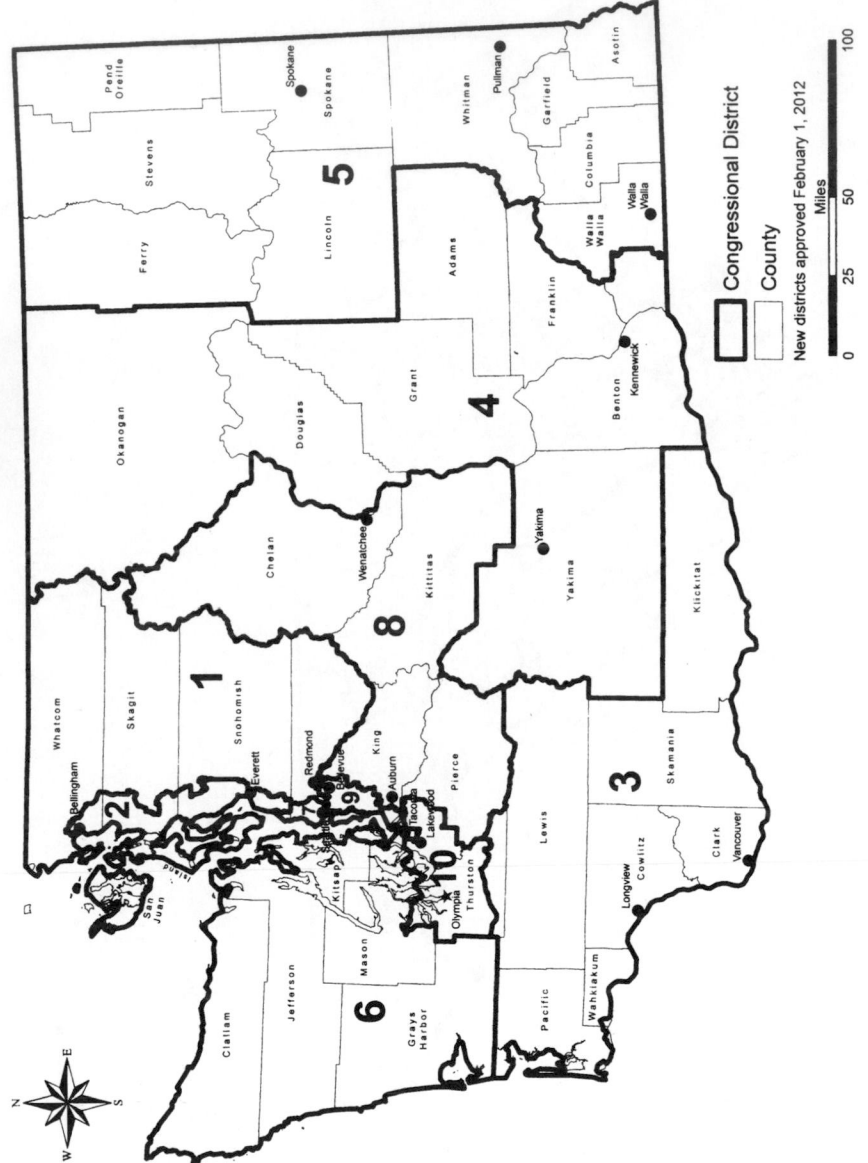

WEST VIRGINIA—Congressional Districts—(3 Districts)

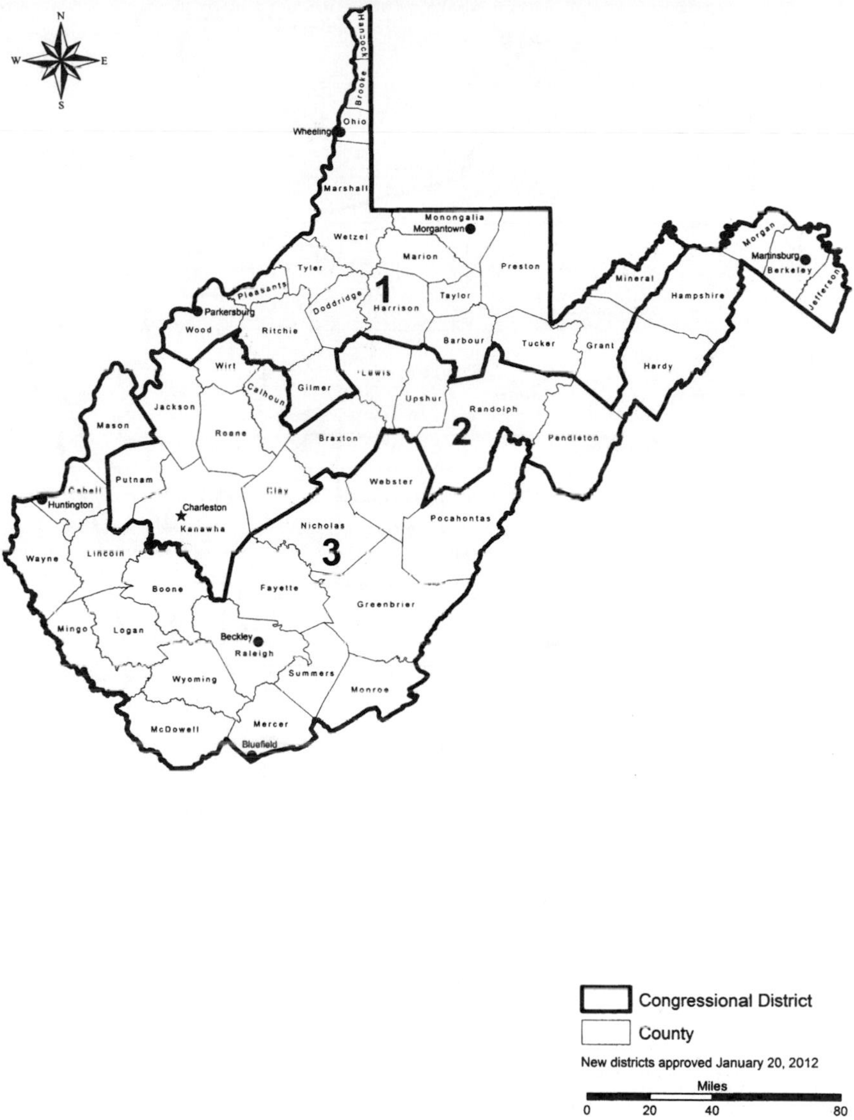

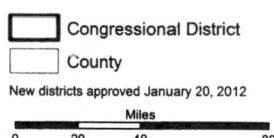

Congressional District
County

New districts approved January 20, 2012

Miles

0   20   40   80

WISCONSIN—Congressional Districts—(8 Districts)

⬜ Congressional District

⬜ County

New districts approved August 9, 2011

Miles

0 ·   25   50   100

WYOMING—Congressional District—(1 District At Large)

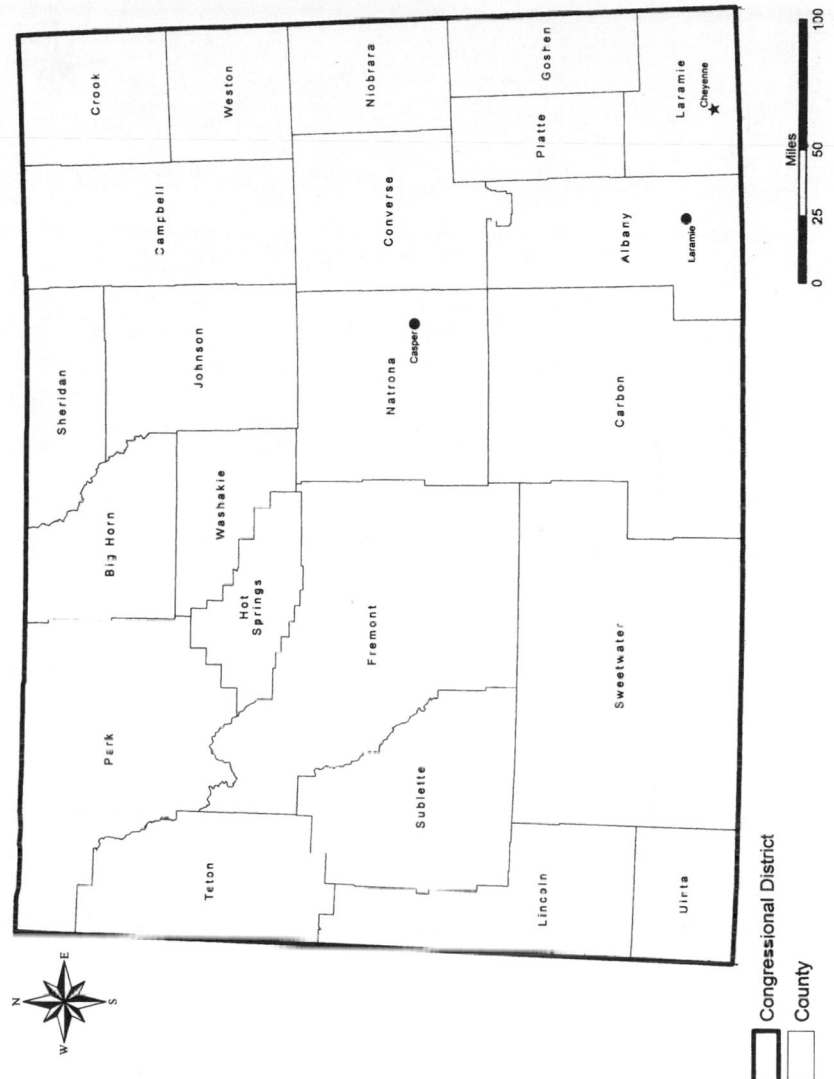

AMERICAN SAMOA—(1 Delegate At Large)

○ Swains Island

Eastern

Manu'a

Western

Rose Island·

| | Islands |

Miles

0   20   40   80

DISTRICT OF COLUMBIA—(1 Delegate At Large)

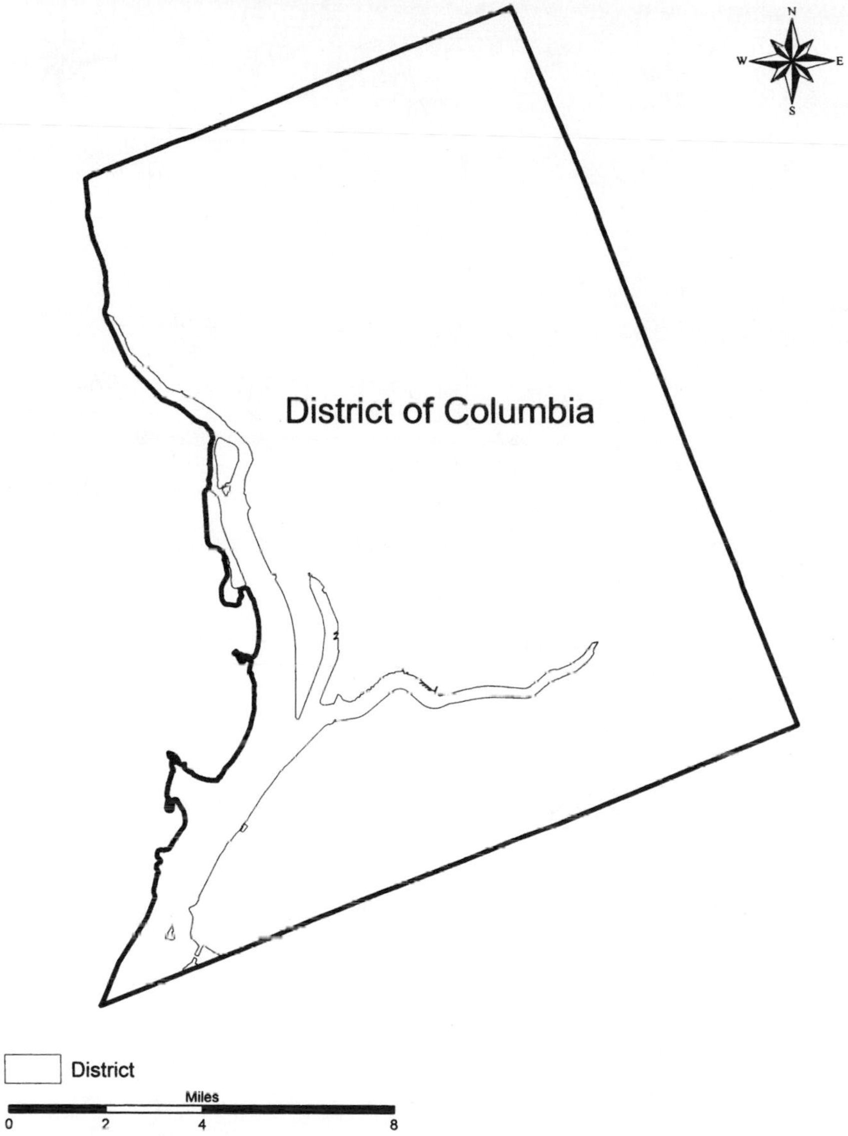

District of Columbia

□ District

Miles

0　　2　　4　　8

GUAM—(1 Delegate At Large)

NORTHERN MARIANA ISLANDS—(1 Delegate At Large)

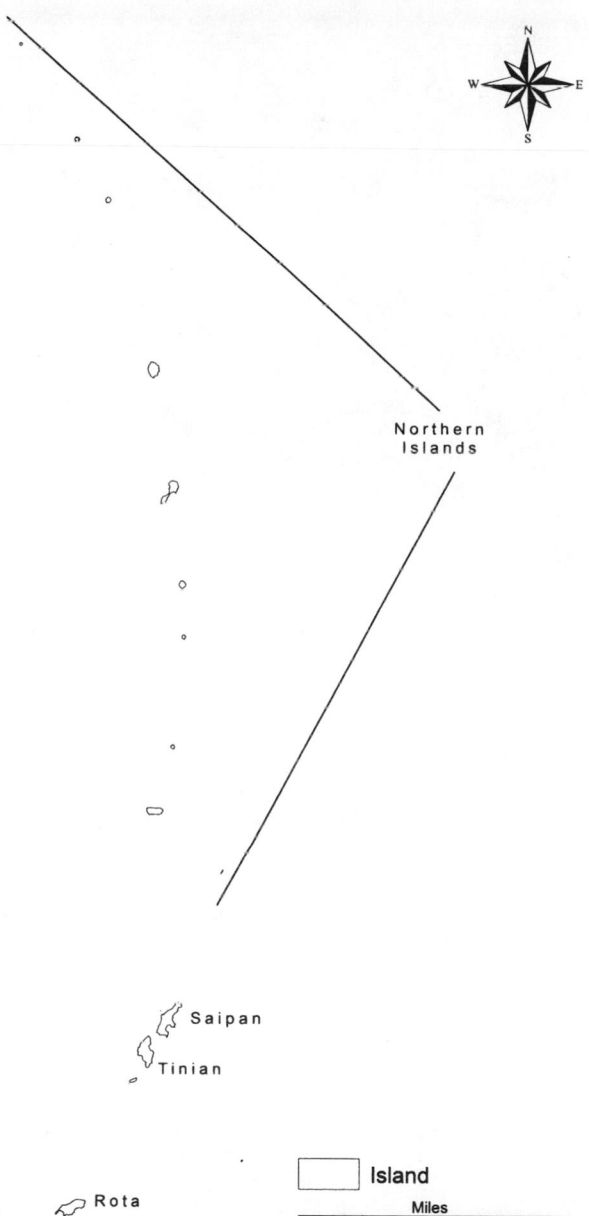

PUERTO RICO—(1 Resident Commissioner At Large)

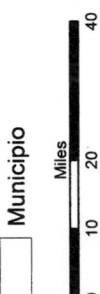

Municipio

Miles

0   10   20   40

THE VIRGIN ISLANDS OF THE UNITED STATES—(1 Delegate At Large)

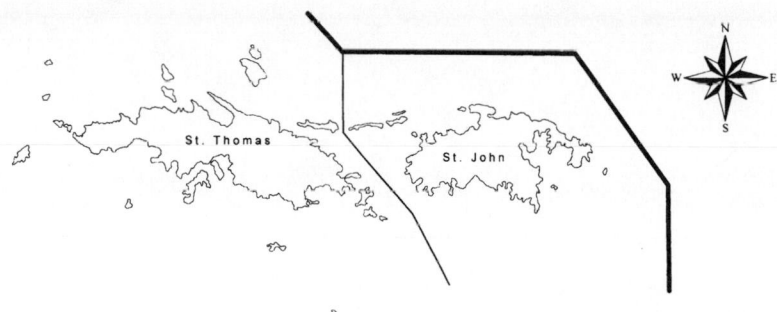

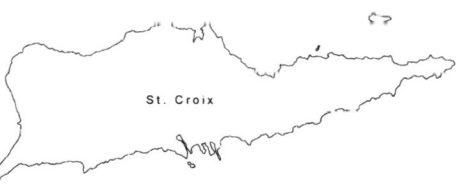

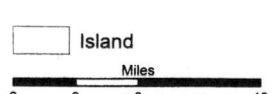

Island

Miles

0   3   6   12

NAME